# CONTEMPORARY
# NOVELISTS

*Contemporary Writers of the English Language*

already published:

*Contemporary Poets*

*Contemporary Novelists*
(including short story writers)

in preparation:

*Contemporary Dramatists*

# CONTEMPORARY
# NOVELISTS

WITH A PREFACE BY
**WALTER ALLEN**

EDITOR
JAMES VINSON, 1921-

ST. JAMES PRESS
LONDON

ST. MARTIN'S PRESS
NEW YORK

COPYRIGHT 1972 BY ST. JAMES PRESS LTD
All rights reserved.   For information, write:
St. James Press Ltd., 1a Montagu Mews North, London W1H 1AJ
or
St. Martin's Press, Inc., 175 Fifth Ave., New York, N.Y. 10010
Printed in Great Britain
ISBN 0 900997 12 5
Library of Congress Catalog Card Number 75–189694
First published in the U.K. and U.S.A. in 1972
Second Printing, 1973

*AFFILIATED PUBLISHERS: Macmillan & Company, Limited, London -
also at Bombay, Calcutta, Madras and Melbourne - The Macmillan Company
of Canada, Limited, Toronto*

# CONTENTS

# PREFACE

The novel, we have been told many times in recent years, is dying: the news, as the appearance of this book shows, doesn't seem to have reached novelists themselves. But I don't recall that the assertion was made until about 1945, and perhaps it ought to be examined. We might at least discover why it is made. Ironically, it seems to have been first propounded at just about the time when the study of novels as a serious form of writing was being taken up in the universities. Today, one sometimes has the impression that little else but novels are studied there. The only ones I remember meeting in prescribed courses when I was an undergraduate studying English at the beginning of the Thirties were Jane Austen's—and, of all things, *The Castle of Otranto*, which must have had something to do with something else. I suppose one might cynically say that the very fact that novels are studied so seriously now in the universities is a sign that the form is dying.

If this were so, there would be nothing intrinsically remarkable about it. Literary forms, or significant variations of them, have disappeared before. For the best part of half a century the verse play was the great glory of English literature. Its death was certainly protracted, but for a hundred years it got steadily weaker until it ended not with a bang but a whimper in the closet poetic drama of the Romantics and the Victorians; and attempts to resurrect it in our time have not been conspicuously successful. Literary forms die or dwindle in importance as a result, I think we can say, of technological changes or of changes in men's interests. The novel itself had its origin in both kinds of change.

One thing it seems to me can be said with some certainty: the novel no longer has the central place in current literature and culture that it had in the nineteenth century. Having made the generalisation with some certainty, I find myself drawing back from it. On second thoughts, I suspect that Tennyson and Ruskin, for instance, were regarded with greater awe, as poets and prophets, than Dickens or George Eliot, who, as novelists, were merely entertainers. But *we* see the novel as central to nineteenth-century literature—it may be for reasons that are much the same as those that lead some people to think the novel is dying.

For one thing, as entertainers the Victorian novelists had virtually no competitors except one another. There were no films, no television, no radio. Dickens, indeed, was almost a Hollywood in himself. If you wanted to be beguiled, taken out of yourself, where could you turn but to the novel? And in the novel, in Dickens, Thackeray, George Eliot, Trollope, you could find a synoptic view of society; English life, depicted on a large enough scale, with enough contrast between social classes to suggest the whole of English life, was spread out in front of you. And there was something else, which is indicated by the historian G. M. Young. Writing on the Victorian age, Young has said: "It was part of the felicity of the fifties to possess a literature which was at once topical, contemporary, and classic; to meet the Immortals in the street and to read them with added zest for the encounter." Among these Immortals, even as young men, were Dickens and Thackeray. But the main emphasis, in my view, has to go on the word "classic"; the role was forced upon the great novelists almost by the situation of the times, which enabled them to identify themselves with their public, to speak for it, to an extent that is impossible for a novelist today. They shared the assumptions about the age common to the age, and when they criticised them they did so in much the same way as their readers were doing. In other words, they were the spokesman of their age, or at least of the most important section of their public, the middle class. But this was not a serious limitation on them, for middle-class values were dominant. The society they wrote for was more homogeneous than ours. Middle-class culture, perhaps even upper middle-class culture was supreme, and seriously to read was to become part of that culture. The notion of cultural splits, the division into highbrow, middle-brow, low-brow, did not exist. And the novelists' identification with their society and their public gave them an authority denied, I suspect, to novelists of our time. Not that the synoptic novelist is unknown today. One thinks of C. P. Snow, whose *Strangers and Brothers* sequence takes in large and diverse areas of experience embracing a whole range of social class from lower-middle to aristocracy. I suspect that Snow's ideal of the novel is the Victorian at the height of its power. But there is a difference, and I think it is fundamental. Snow presents his synoptic, panoramic view of our society through the experiences of his narrator Lewis Eliot, whose life and career bear distinct resemblances to Snow's own. He is pretty obviously a persona for his creator. What Snow gives us, in other words, is one man's view of society. But when Thackeray, Trollope and George Eliot drop into the first person singular we read and accept, I believe, their "I" as "we". We assume an identification with their readers, and for all his idiosyncrasy, we do this with Dickens too. The novelists are not speaking for themselves, but for the consensus of opinion of their age. This is one of the factors that gives their novels a universal quality.

It was such novelists as these that Lionel Trilling had in mind when he wrote his famous passage in *The Liberal Imagination*:

> For our time the most effective agent of the moral imagination
> has been the novel of the last two hundred years. It was never,
> either aesthetically or morally, a perfect form and its faults
> and failures can be quickly enumerated. But its greatness
> and its practical usefulness lie in its unremitting work of
> involving the reader himself in the moral life, inviting him
> to put his own motives under examination, suggesting that

reality is not as his conventional education has led him to see it. It taught us, as no other genre ever did, the extent of human variety and the value of this variety. It was the literary form to which the emotions of understanding and forgiveness were indigenous, as if by the definition of the form itself.

For me, these words of Trilling's constitute the great main justification of the novel. I know, though I had not realized until I read Trilling, that this is where my first interest in the novel began, both as reader and as someone who aspired to be a novelist himself. It is not, of course, the end of my interest in the novel. In our time, however, I feel it is increasingly difficult for the novelist to fulfil Trilling's expectations. Why this is so is indicated by Kingsley Amis's hero in *I Like It Here*, as he contemplates the memorial to Henry Fielding in Lisbon:

> Perhaps it was worth dying in your forties if two hundred years later you were the only non-contemporary novelist who could be read with unaffected and whole-hearted interest, the only one who never had to be apologized for or excused on the grounds of changing taste. And how enviable to live in the world of his novels, where duty was plain, evil arose from malevolence and a starving wayfarer could be invited indoors without hesitation and without fear. Did that make it a simplified world? Perhaps, but that hardly mattered beside the existence of a moral seriousness without the aid of evangelical puffing and blowing.

Well, today duty is not plain, and we can no longer confidently say that evil arises from malevolence. Our faith in our moral judgments has been sapped, principally I suppose by the findings of Freud and his followers. But we also live in a world that presses on us in all its intensity of evil so remorselessly as to seem unassimilable in the novel. The paradigm of the evil is the concentration camps of Nazi Germany; but the evil—at the moment of writing in Vietnam, in Ulster, in East Bengal, and God knows where it will be next year—leaps at us nightly from the television screen. It was something the great Victorians didn't have to take into account, or there was less of it to take into account. Equally, it is something we and our contemporaries must. The difficulty of doing so, perhaps indeed the impossibility, has been stated by George Steiner in *Language and Silence*. That even sixty-five years ago the difficulty could be overcome was shown by Conrad in what now seems his prophetic novel *Nostromo*; and we can see it can be handled in our time from Golding's *Lord of the Flies*, from Graham Greene throughout his career and from Saul Bellow's *Mr. Sammler's Planet*. But novels of this order seem almost special cases.

I am putting forward a number of things that differentiate the contemporary novel from the classic novel, by which in the end rightly or wrongly we tend to judge contemporary work. Briefly, the novel is no longer the main medium of entertainment and instruction. The film tells a story at least as well; and a good part of what, even as late as Lawrence, was taken for granted as belonging to the content of the novel, what may be called the journalistic or documentary and argumentative content, has been taken over by television and the non-fiction book. Best-sellers are no longer, as they were fifty years ago, generally novels. The books that are most widely read and argued about are works of non-fiction, works of reportage, scientific theory and speculation, and controversy. The discussion of current ideas and affairs, the exposures of current abuses, these are now presented to us on television. This is a consequence of technological development, and perhaps nothing can be done about it. But the result is a loss to the novel—and also, I think, to the quality of our response to what is happening everywhere in the world. The world, simply, is too much with us, and too immediately so: we lack the filter of fiction and must suffer instead the immediate brutal impact upon us of events and new ideas. In the past, the writing of a novel was a comparatively leisurely affair. It may still be so. To write a novel takes anything from one year to ten: but now, by the time it is published, and irrespective of the length of time in its writing, it may seem to refer to a world that is irredeemably past.

One consequence of this speeding up of life and the delay between the event and the novelist's assimilation of and reaction towards it is, it seems to me, a distrust of fiction, which is seen almost as a luxury. There is perhaps some evidence of this in the large number of *romans fleuves* which has been so striking a feature of the British novel since the war, sequences like those of Snow, Waugh, Powell, Doris Lessing, Durrell and Olivia Manning. Vastly different from one another though these works are, they have one thing in common: the narrator of each one of them seems to be uncommonly close to his creator, so that there appears in these sequences to be a narration of events akin to those the novelist has himself experienced. It is a short step beyond this to something that, though in many ways comparable to the novel, is not the novel. I am thinking of what has been called the "non-fiction novel," notably Truman Capote's *In Cold Blood* and Norman Mailer's *The Armies of the Night*, a work of reporting of personal experience that only a novelist of great brilliance could have written.

But there is another kind of book, which does not profess in any way to relate to the novel, that all the same seems to cater to the interests of readers who half a century ago would have been reading novels or would have had a comparable experience from reading novels. The books I have in mind are a disparate lot; it includes books like Kate Millet's and Germaine Greer's on Woman's Lib., White's *The Organization Man*, Watson's *The Double Helix*, anthropological and sociological works based on taped interviews, Desmond Morris's *The Naked Ape*, the books of Bruno Bettelheim and the psychological writings of R. D. Laing. All in one way or another are about people. And there are two points here. They are in some sense specialised works the contents of which novelists themselves will generally have no more first-hand knowledge of than the non-specialist reading public. And they also appear to be based on record-ed fact or what looks like it. They appeal, in other words, to a curiosity that in the past the novelist could satisfy but that now he cannot.

These books may be seen as case-histories. They are of the stuff of fiction but *true*; and it may be that we are in a period when readers prefer to read what they think is history rather than the imaginative re-creation of history that is the novel.

It could also be that this interest in history and in what seems to be the scientifically provable is being counterbalanced by an interest in a fiction of what might be called an extreme kind, one that goes beyond the novel and is akin to the romance that we all thought the novel had displaced two and a half centuries ago. It seems significant that for the past four or five years the works of fiction most eagerly devoured by university students in the United States, and I suspect in Britain too, have been the fantasies of Tolkien and the works of Hermann Hesse, works of fiction that lie outside the novel as I conceive it.

What that is will be apparent. For me, though I recognise variants such as the novels of Melville, the novel is a broadly realistic represent-ation of man's life in society which is also a criticism of life and of society. This, as I see it, makes up the mainstream of the English novel from Fielding to Joyce and Lawrence. All the evidence—and it comes from novels themselves—suggests that during the past two or three decades the contemporary novelist has been forced by pressures of circum-stances—technological change, change in men's attitudes towards them-selves and towards the universe, the simple facts of history in our time, and the sheer increase of knowledge in many fields from which as a non-specialist he is barred—to yield much of his former territory to other literary forms and media. Despite himself, he has become more subjective, much less sure of himself. He has lost much of the authority his forbears could take for granted. It seems less possible for the novelist to put forward the mimic world he has invented as a convincing paradigm of the world in which he and his readers live.

There is, I am well aware, a factor that so far I have ignored. Invoking the past, I have referred to the very great novelists of the language. We in this second half of the twentieth century follow in the wake of very great novelists. The years from roughly 1900 to 1940 form one of the peak periods in our literature, in poetry and the novel alike. The great names are obvious enough: in the novel, Conrad, Joyce, Lawrence, Virginia Woolf; Dreiser, Fitzgerald, Hemingway perhaps, Faulkner; and a host of smaller but very significant figures flank them. What impresses us in them today is the scope of their ambitions and their success in realising them. If we have no one to set against them, the same seems to me to be true of the novel throughout the world. But history shows that similar situations have existed before, that an age of intense flowering is often followed by one comparatively barren or in which the growths are smaller. The emergence of a new novelist of the calibre of Conrad or Faulkner could change the literary scene as an earthquake changes a landscape and make nonsense of all my generalisations. Figures of Conrad's and Faulkner's stature can't be produced to order—and it may be worth pointing out that the true greatness of some of the novelists of our century, Conrad among them, was not seen until after their deaths and that their influence, which we now take for granted, was posthumous.

Meanwhile, until that monster the new great novelist arrives, we must put up with what we have. If that sounds churlish, it is not meant to be. Our contemporary novelists are ours, they belong to us, the problems that face them face us their readers too. Their fragmentation reflects ours. But much more can be said than that. If I do not believe that we live in one of the peak periods of the novel, I do emphatically believe that we live in a time distinguished by a bigger concentration of talented men and women only less than the great than has ever been seen before in the history of the novel in English. I have spent almost all my life reading novels (and trying to write them) and I could write down the names of I suspect two score and probably more from Britain and America who have given me pleasure, aesthetic or intellectual, of a keenness that makes it almost impossible for me to think they won't be read at least with interest a century hence. The temptation is to write the names down, but it must be resisted.

No, the novel is not dead or dying, even though its stature may be smaller than a century ago—and that, as I have suggested, the arrival of my monster may change. And there is another reason, besides the prodigality of talent on all sides, which shows no sign of drying up, for believing the novel is not dying. This is the sudden and unexpected appearance of the novel within the past three decades or so in the new countries where English is spoken, the Caribbean islands, India, the countries of Africa. For a congenital reader and student of the novel it has been a moving experience to watch these new literatures come into existence during one's reading lifetime, for they are surely signs of life, not of death. The task of these men and women making these new literatures is, no doubt, different from that of contemporary English and American white novelists, for it is to forge, in Joyce's words, the uncreated conscience of their race. But their novels testify to the variety and diversity of human experience and to the human need to set it down and rejoice in it. It is in the consciousness precisely of that variety and diversity that the novel had its origins; and so long as it remains, so long as men are curious about their fellows and themselves, it seems to me unlikely the novel will die.

WALTER ALLEN

# EDITOR'S NOTE

The selection of writers included in this book is based upon the recommendations of the advisers listed on page xv.

The entry for each writer consists of a biography, a full bibliography, a comment by the writer on his fiction if he chose to make one (more than half of the writers did make a statement), and a signed critical essay on his fiction.

With a few exceptions, only those uncollected short stories specifically referred to, and those critical studies recommended, by the entrant have been listed. British and United States editions of all books have been listed; other editions are listed only if they are the first editions.

We would like to thank the entrants and contributors for their patience and cooperation in helping us compile this book.

# ADVISERS

Walter Allen
Bernard Bergonzi
Earle Birney
Elmer Borklund
Anthony Burgess
D. D. C. Chambers
Leslie Fiedler
Roy Fuller
Albert Guerard
James B. Hall
A. Norman Jeffares
James Korges
John Lehmann

Harry Levin
Harry T. Moore
J. E. Morpurgo
Desmond Pacey
Hal Porter
Anthony Powell
Arthur Ravenscroft
John M. Reilly
Kenneth Rexroth
H. Winston Rhodes
Alan Ross
Barney Rosset
Mark Schorer

# CONTRIBUTORS

Walter Allen
Erica Aronson
Alvin Aubert
Roger Baker
R. G. Baldwin
John Barnes
Alice Bensen
Bernard Bergonzi
Chaim Bermant
Marshall A. Best
William Bittner
William Borden
Elmer Borklund
Frederick Bowers
Anthony Boxill
Malcolm Bradbury
M. E. Bradford
Edgar M. Branch
Laurence Brander
Neville Braybrooke
Dalma H. Brunauer
Herbert C. Burke
Donald Cameron
Frank Campenni
Frederic I. Carpenter
Hayden Carruth
D. D. C. Chambers
Fred Chappell
Paul Seiko Chihara
Anderson Clark
Gloria Cohen
Ruby Cohn
John Colmer
Mary Conroy

Jackson I. Cope
John Cotton
Hallvard Dahlie
David P. Demarest, Jr.
Jeanne Desy
Peter M. Desy
Margaret Dick
R. H. W. Dillard
Dale K. Doepke
Paul A. Doyle
Chester E. Eisinger
Brian Elliott
James A. Emanuel
Elizabeth Evans
Richard J. Fein
John J. Figueroa
Leonard Fleischer
Irving Foote
Roberta J. Forsberg
Reul E. Foster
Warren French
Alan Warren Friedman
Melvin J. Friedman
John Fuegi
Robin Fulton
David Galloway
Norman T. Gates
Addison Gayle, Jr.
R. G. Geering
David J. Geherin
James Gindin
William Goyen
Robert Greacen
Richard Greenleaf

Albert Guerard
Emily Hahn
James B. Hall
John Hall
Robert Daniel Hamner
Maurice Harmon
S. C. Harrex
James A. Hart
Paula L. Hart
Ihab Hassan
Norrie Hearn
David M. Heaton
Leo J. Hertzel
James Hill
Jacqueline Hoefer
Blyden Jackson
Sarah Evelyn Jackson
Louis James
A. Norman Jeffares
Annibel Jenkins
Burton Kendle
Brian Kiernan
H. M. Klein
Marcus Klein
James Korges
Martin L. Kornbluth
Richard Kostelanetz
Leonie Kramer
Ursula Laredo
Margaret Laurence
Anastasia Leech
Robert Liddell
Stanley W. Lindberg
Bernth Lindfors
Jack Lindsay
John Lucas
Robert E. Lynch
David Madden
Hena Maes-Jelinek
Irving Malin
Paul Marx
Roland Mathias
Brian E. Matthews
Frank D. McConnell
John McCormick
Frederick P. W. McDowell
George McElroy
Mary McMurray
Patricia Merivale
Eugene Mirabelli
Naomi Mitchison
John Montague
Gerald Moore
Harry T. Moore
J. E. Morpurgo

Robert K. Morris
Anne Mulkeen
Kay J. Mussell
John M. Muste
Bruce Nesbitt
W. H. New
Leslie Norris
Robert Nye
John P. O'Neill
Bridget O'Toole
Desmond Pacey
Malcolm Page
William Peden
Marian Pehowski
Barbara Perkins
George Perkins
Frank T. Phipps
Hal Porter
David L. Powell
K. R. Prebble
Isabel Quigley
Simon Raven
Arthur Ravenscroft
Ian Reid
J. C. Reid
John M. Reilly
Kenneth Rexroth
H. Winston Rhodes
Lawrence Ries
Louis D. Rubin, Jr.
William M. Ryan
Jack Salzman
Clarence Sandelin
David Sanders
Stewart F. Sanderson
William J. Schafer
Mark Schorer
Alexander Scott
Ian Scott-Kilvert
Cynthia Secor
Alan R. Shucard
Agnes Sibley
Ben Siegel
Fred Silva
Judith Cooke Simmons
Sally Slocum
Curtis C. Smith
Radcliffe Squires
Derek Stanford
Donald E. Stanford
Jane W. Steadman
George Stephenson
Carol Simpson Stern
James R. Stevens
Joan Stevens

Edward Stokes
W. J. Stuckey
Frank Swinnerton
Myron Taylor
Arthur Terry
Roy Thomas
Kent Thompson
Derick S. Thomson
Gillian Tindall
Shirley Toulson
William Trevor
Roland Turner
Ivan Van-Sertima
James Vinson

Thomas A. Vogler
Keith Walker
William Walsh
Harold H. Watts
Christof Wegelin
John A. Weigel
Robert L. Welker
Perry D. Westbrook
Peter R. Weston
Milton White
Thomas F. Wilson
George Woodcock
James Dean Young

# CONTEMPORARY
# NOVELISTS

Ahmad Abbas
Paul Ableman
Peter Abrahams
Dannie Abse
Chinua Achebe
Conrad Aiken
Brian Aldiss
James Aldridge
Nelson Algren
Ahmed Ali
Walter Allen
Eric Ambler
Timothy Aluko
Kingsley Amis
Mulk Raj Anand
Michael Anthony
Ayi Kwei Armah
Sylvia Ashton-Warner
Isaac Asimov
Thea Astley
Louis Auchincloss

Paul Bailey
Elliott Baker
James Baldwin
David Ballantyne
J. G. Ballard
A. L. Barker
Djuna Barnes
Clive Barry
Stan Barstow
John Barth
Donald Barthelme
H. E. Bates
Nina Bawden
David Beaty
Warren Beck
Stephen Becker
Samuel Beckett
Sybille Bedford
Saul Bellow
David Benedictus
John Berger
Thomas Berger
Bhabani Bhattacharya
Earle Birney
Burt Blechman
Fred Bodsworth
Vance Bourjaily
Elizabeth Bowen
John Bowen
Robert O. Bowen

George Bowering
Jane Bowles
Paul Bowles
Martin Boyd
Kay Boyle
Malcolm Bradbury
Ray Bradbury
Melvyn Bragg
John Braine
E. R. Braithwaite
Errol Brathwaite
Richard Brautigan
Paul Brodeur
Christine Brooke-Rose
Jeremy Brooks
Brigid Brophy
Chandler Brossard
George Mackay Brown
Bryher
George Buchanan
Pearl S. Buck
Ernest Buckler
Frederick Buechner
Anthony Burgess
Kenneth Burke
Alan Burns
William Burroughs
A. S. Byatt

James M. Cain
Arthur Calder-Marshall
Erskine Caldwell
Hortense Calisher
Morley Callaghan
W. H. Canaway
Robert Cantwell
Truman Capote
Jan Carew
R. V. Cassill
David Caute
Sid Chaplin
Gerda Charles
Jerome Charyn
John Cheever
Agatha Christie
Richard Church
Kay Cicellis
Eleanor Clark
Walter Van Tilburg Clark
Arthur C. Clarke
Austin C. Clarke
Jon Cleary

Stuart Cloete
Robert M. Coates
Leonard Cohen
Barry Cole
John Collier
Alex Comfort
Richard Condon
Evan S. Connell, Jr.
Cyril Connolly
Robert Conquest
Jack Conroy
Lettice Cooper
William Cooper
Robert Coover
Jack Cope
Peter Cowan
James Gould Cozzens
Ian Cross

Roald Dahl
Edward Dahlberg
O. R. Dathorne
Rhys Davies
Robertson Davies
Dan Davin
Jennifer Dawson
C. Day Lewis
Len Deighton
Nigel Dennis
August Derleth
Anita Desai
G. V. Desani
Peter De Vries
Monica Dickens
J. P. Donleavy
Margaret Drabble
Allen Drury
Maureen Duffy
Maurice Duggan
Daphne du Maurier
Lawrence Durrell
Geoffrey Dutton

William Eastlake
Maurice Edelman
Cyprian Ekwensi
Stanley Elkin
George P. Elliott
Ralph Ellison
David Ely
D. J. Enright
John Espey
Peter Everett

J. G. Farrell

James T. Farrell
Howard Fast
Irvin Faust
Leslie Fiedler
Gabriel Fielding
Shelby Foote
Jesse Hill Ford
John Fowles
Janet Frame
Michael Frayn
Nicholas Freeling
Gillian Freeman
Bruce Jay Friedman
Daniel Fuchs
Edmund Fuller
Roy Fuller

William Gaddis
Ernest J. Gaines
Mavis Gallant
Paul Gallico
Hugh Garner
David Garnett
George Garrett
William Gass
Martha Gellhorn
William Gerhardie
Zulfikar Ghose
Stella Gibbons
Brendan Gill
Penelope Gilliatt
Brian Glanville
John Glassco
Julian Gloag
Rumer Godden
Dave Godfrey
Herbert Gold
Ivan Gold
William Golding
William Goldman
Paul Goodman
Nadine Gordimer
Caroline Gordon
Robert Gover
William Goyen
Winston Graham
Shirley Ann Grau
Robert Graves
Simon Gray
Henry Green
Peter Green
Graham Greene
Alfred Grossman
Albert Guerard
Neil Gunn

A. B. Guthrie, Jr.

William Haggard
Arthur Hailey
Nancy Hale
James B. Hall
Clifford Hanley
Gerald Hanley
James Hanley
Mark Harris
Wilson Harris
Elizabeth Harrower
L. P. Hartley
John Hawkes
Hiram Haydn
Joseph Hayes
Shirley Hazzard
Bessie Head
John Hearne
Robert Heinlein
Joseph Heller
Rayner Heppenstall
A. P. Herbert
Xavier Herbert
James Leo Herlihy
John Hersey
Nigel Heseltine
Granville Hicks
Aidan Higgins
Patricia Highsmith
Noel Hilliard
Chester Himes
Thomas Hinde
Edward Hoagland
Laura Z. Hobson
David Holbrook
John Clellon Holmes
Hugh Hood
Tom Hopkinson
Paul Horgan
Geoffrey Household
Elizabeth Jane Howard
Fred Hoyle
Richard Hughes
William Bradford Huie
William Humphrey
Emyr Humphreys
Evan Hunter
Jim Hunter
Kristin Hunter
Maude Hutchins
R. C. Hutchinson

Hammond Innes
Christopher Isherwood

Charles Israel

Dan Jacobson
C. L. R. James
Storm Jameson
Robin Jenkins
R. Prawer Jhabvala
B. S. Johnson
Josephine Johnson
Pamela Hansford Johnson
Glyn Jones
Gwyn Jones
James Jones
LeRoi Jones
Madison Jones
Mervyn Jones
M. K. Joseph

MacKinlay Kantor
David Karp
William Melvin Kelley
Thomas Keneally
Ken Kesey
Benedict Kiely
John Oliver Killens
Richard Kim
Francis King
Fletcher Knebel
John Knowles
Arthur Koestler
Bernard Kops
Jerzy Kosinski
Uys Krige

Alex La Guma
George Lamming
Jeremy Larner
Margaret Laurence
Mary Lavin
Albert Lebowitz
John LeCarré
Rosamond Lehmann
Lawrence Lerner
Doris Lessing
Ira Levin
Meyer Levin
Norman Levine
Janet Lewis
Robert Liddell
Jack Lindsay
Eric Linklater
Emanuel Litvinoff
Leo Litwak
David Lodge
Earl Lovelace

Robert Lowry
Jack Ludwig
Alison Lurie
Andrew Lytle
David Lytton

Robie Macauley
Ross Macdonald
Colin MacInnes
Helen MacInnes
Compton MacKenzie
Hugh MacLennan
Norman Mailer
Bernard Malamud
Manohar Malgonkar
Frederick Manfred
Jerre Mangione
Don Mankiewicz
Wolf Mankowitz
Leonard Mann
Olivia Manning
Kamala Markandaya
Wallace Markfield
Ngaio Marsh
Bruce Marshall
Paule Marshall
John Masters
Peter Matthiessen
Robin Maugham
William Maxwell
Julian Mayfield
Mary McCarthy
Edward McCourt
John McGahern
Tom McHale
Aubrey Menen
James Michener
O. E. Middleton
Stanley Middleton
Henry Miller
Adrian Mitchell
Joseph Mitchell
Julian Mitchell
W. O. Mitchell
Naomi Mitchison
Nancy Mitford
Nicholas Monsarrat
Brian Moore
Wright Morris
Penelope Mortimer
Nicholas Mosley
Ezekiel Mphahlele
Alice Munro
Iris Murdoch

Vladimir Nabokov
V. S. Naipaul
R. K. Narayan
Robert Nathan
Bill Naughton
Howard Nemerov
Jay Neugeboren
P. H. Newby
Edward Newhouse
J. T. Ngugi
Abioseh Nicol
Christopher Nicole
Anaïs Nin
Hoke Norris
Kathleen Nott
Robert Nye

Joyce Carol Oates
Edna O'Brien
Sean O'Faolain
Liam O'Flaherty
Gil Orlovitz

Kenneth Patchen
Alan Paton
Orlando Patterson
Frances Gray Patton
Bill Pearson
Walker Percy
Kathrin Perutz
Jerzy Peterkiewicz
Harry Mark Petrakis
Ann Petry
William Plomer
Frederik Pohl
Hal Porter
Katherine Anne Porter
Anthony Powell
J. F. Powers
H. F. M. Prescott
Reynolds Price
J. B. Priestley
V. S. Pritchett
Frederic Prokosch
John Pudney
James Purdy
Mario Puzo
Thomas Pynchon

Ann Quin

Thomas Raddall
Ayn Rand
Raja Rao
Frederic Raphael

Simon Raven
Ernest Raymond
John Rechy
Ishmael Reed
Vic Reid
Lynne Reid Banks
Mary Renault
Jean Rhys
Mordecai Richler
Daphne Rooke
Sinclair Ross
Leo Rosten
Henry Roth
Philip Roth
Bernice Rubens

Nayantara Sahgal
Garth St. Omer
J. D. Salinger
Andrew Salkey
William Sansom
Frank Sargeson
William Saroyan
May Sarton
Vernon Scannell
Mark Schorer
Budd Schulberg
J. D. Scott
Paul Scott
Hubert Selby, Jr.
Samuel Selvon
Maurice Shadbolt
Margery Sharp
Irwin Shaw
Robert Shaw
Wilfrid Sheed
Clancy Sigal
Alan Sillitoe
Andrew Sinclair
Jo Sinclair
Isaac Bashevis Singer
Khushwant Singh
David Slavitt
Emma Smith
Iain Crichton Smith
C. P. Snow
Susan Sontag
Terry Southern
Muriel Spark
Elizabeth Spencer
Tom Stacey
Jean Stafford
Christina Stead
Francis Steegmuller
Wallace Stegner

James Stern
Richard G. Stern
J. I. M. Stewart
Monica Stirling
Dal Stivens
Irving Stone
David Storey
Randolph Stow
Michael Straight
Jesse Stuart
William Styron
Hollis Summers
Harvey Swados
Glendon Swarthout
Frank Swinnerton
Julian Symons
Scott Symons

Allen Tate
Elizabeth Taylor
Peter Taylor
Robert Lewis Taylor
Kylie Tennant
Paul Theroux
Gillian Tindall
J. R. R. Tolkien
Rosemary Tonks
Philip Toynbee
Honor Tracy
Robert Traver
William Trevor
Rachel Trickett
Lionel Trilling
Alexander Trocchi
Dalton Trumbo
Niccolò Tucci
Frank Tuohy
George Turner
Amos Tutuola
Anne Tyler

John Updike
Edward Upward
Leon Uris
Fred Urquhart

Laurens van der Post
Mark Van Doren
Gore Vidal
Kurt Vonnegut, Jr.

David Wagoner
John Wain
David Walker
Margaret Walker

Rex Warner
Sylvia Townsend Warner
Robert Penn Warren
Judah Waten
Keith Waterhouse
Auberon Waugh
Jerome Weidman
Eudora Welty
Glenway Wescott
Anthony West
Anthony C. West
Jessamyn West
Morris West
Paul West
Rebecca West
Antonia White
Jon Manchip White
Patrick White
Rudy Wiebe
Thornton Wilder
John A. Williams
Raymond Williams
Tennessee Williams
Wirt Williams

Henry Williamson
Calder Willingham
Angus Wilson
Colin Wilson
Edmund Wilson
Ethel Wilson
Mitchell Wilson
Sloan Wilson
Donald Windham
Adele Wiseman
P. G. Wodehouse
Bernard Wolfe
Douglas Woolf
Herman Wouk
Charles Wright
Philip Wylie

James Yaffe
Richard Yates
Samuel Yellen
Frank Yerby
Marguerite Young
Sol Yurick

**ABBAS, (Khwaja) Ahmad.** Indian. Born in Panipat, 7 June 1914. Educated at Hali Muslim High School; Aligarh Muslim University, B.A. 1933, LL.B. 1935. Married Mujtabai Khatoon in 1942 (deceased, 1958). Reporter and Sub-Editor, 1936–39, and Editor, Sunday Edition, and Columnist, 1939–47, *The Bombay Chronicle*. Since 1947, Contributing Columnist, *Blitz* magazine, Bombay. Leader, Indian Film Delegation, U.S.S.R., 1954. Recipient: *Hindustan Times* prize, 1950; President of India's Gold Medal, for film, 1964; Padma Shree, 1969; Haryana State Robe of Honour, 1969. Address: Philomena Lodge, Church Road, Juhu, Bombay-54, India.

PUBLICATIONS

Novels

    *Tomorrow Is Ours!* Bombay, Popular Book Depot, 1943.
    *Defeat for Death: A Story Without Names.* Baroda, Padmaja, 1944.
    *Blood and Stones.* Bombay, Hind Kitabs, 1947.
    *Inqilab.* Bombay, Jaico, 1955.
    *When Night Falls.* Delhi, Hind Pocket Books, 1968.
    *Mera Naam Joker.* Delhi, Hind Pocket Books, 1970.
    *Maria.* Delhi, Hind Pocket Books, 1971.

Short Stories

    *Rice and Other Stories.* Bombay, Kutub, 1947.
    *Cages of Freedom and Other Stories.* Bombay, Hind Kitabs, 1952.
    *One Thousand Nights on a Bed of Stones and Other Stories.* Bombay, Jaico, 1957.
    *Black Sun and Other Stories.* Bombay, Jaico, 1963.
    *The Most Beautiful Woman in the World.* New Delhi, New Light, 1968.

Uncollected Short Story

    "Sparrows", in *Indian Literature* (London), 1938.

Plays

    *Invitation to Immortality.* Bombay, Padma, 1946.

    Has written screenplays in Hindustani and English; and other plays in Hindustani.

Other

    *Outside India: The Adventures of a Roving Reporter.* Delhi, Hali, 1940.
    *An Indian Looks at America.* Bombay, Thacker, 1943.
    *Report to Gandhiji*, with N. G. Yog. Bombay, Hind Kitabs, 1944.
    *Not All Lies!* Bombay, privately printed, 1945.
    *I Write As I Feel.* Bombay, Hind Kitabs, 1948.
    *Kashmir Fights for Freedom.* Bombay, Kutub, 1948.
    *In the Image of Mao Tse-Tung.* Bombay, Peoples Publishing House, 1953.

*Face to Face with Krushchov.*   Delhi, Rajpal, 1960.
*Till We Reach the Stars: The Story of Yuri Gagarin.*   Bombay, Asia Publishing House, 1961.
*Indira Gandhi: Return of the Red Rose.*   Bombay, Popular Prakashan, 1966.

Ahmad Abbas comments:

Highbrow literary critics in India have sometimes sneeringly labelled my novels and short stories as "mere journalese". Obviously, the fact that most of them are inspired by aspects of the contemporary historical reality, as sometimes chronicled in the press, is sufficient to put them beyond the pale of literary creation. I have no quarrel with the critics. Maybe I am an unredeemed journalist and reporter, masquerading as a writer of fiction. But I have always believed that while the inner life of man undoubtedly is, and should be, the primary concern of literature, this inner personal life impinges upon the life of the community—and of humanity—at every critical turning point of human experience. "No man is an island . . ." said John Donne, and one may add that even if he was, no island is free from the inroads of the sea, as no man is free from the impact of social forces and the life around him.

This inter-action of the individual and society, both in its psychological and social complexity, is of particular interest to me as a writer. It has inspired, provoked, or coloured most of what I have written.

Mirrored in my works are many fragments of our recent history—the war, the religious riots and the killings, the partition, the post-freedom years of disillusionment, of the new hopes engendered, and problems raised, by the industrialization and mechanization of agriculture. But I do hope I have also revealed glimpses of the "inner life" of my contemporaries, the people of a new India, in their moments of tenderness and passion, of frustration and exultation, as they evolve from the passive (but by no means ignoble) fatalism, so characteristic of the Indian peasant rooted in tradition, towards the hopeful dynamism, the remarkable adaptability and the willingness to change, which, paradoxically enough, is also an Indian characteristic.

If there is one thing that I have tried consistently to do in my novels and stories, it is to give the readers a little peep into the hearts and minds, the inner life, of my contemporaries and fellow Indians, to show that their life is being influenced and changed and re-shaped by the historical and social forces that are greater than us and our "destiny".

*         *         *

K. A. Abbas's affinities with the "social conscience" and "national brotherhood" schools of Indian fiction are symbolised by the fact that Mulk Raj Anand wrote an epistolary introduction to *Rice and Other Stories* and that Abbas dedicated *Cages of Freedom* to Anand. Abbas's literary interest in the relationship between the individual and society was probably stimulated by Anand's early novels about the social tragedy of India's untouchable, coolie and peasant poor, who were economically exploited and politically oppressed, victims jointly of British imperialism and Indian vested interests. Abbas in turn has depicted social tragedy, and as such his fiction is conceived as a contribution to Indian humanism. He is essentially a "progressive", "purposeful" writer and sometime propagandist, as he whimsically acknowledges in *Not All Lies!* Although Abbas's literary achievement is only modest and minor, he has centred his attention on important Indian themes.

Mulk Raj Anand has defined the most fundamental of these themes as follows: "the emergence of man from the restraints, inhibitions, codes, conventions and violences of the old society to the status of an individual integrated in a new community of like individuals, so that the development and the expression of human personality should become possible" (*Rice and Other Stories*, p. 9). This "Tradition v. Modernity" crisis is at the centre of Abbas's fiction, particularly his Independence Struggle novels. *Tomorrow Is Ours!* resounds with dated applause for resurgent India's fight for freedom: for "genuine modernism" emerging out of the "ruins of feudalism" and the "tinsel and trash discarded by the West". *Inqilab* (the title is derived from the patriotic battle-cry "Inqilab Zindabad" or Long Live Revolution) competently communicates a sense of what it was like to be committed to the Independence movement during the Twenties and Thirties. *Maria* recalls the endurance and heroism of Goa's struggle against Portuguese colonialism. The Goan heroine is an allegorical soul of India; on her death-bed in 1970, she is destined to re-unite her former Indian comrades who, after their Goan adventure, reverted back into the hostile separatism of communal names and languages and denied their proven common humanity.

In *Inqilab* Abbas explores two themes which are prominent in his writings: the quest for personal identity, and the need for inter-communal brotherhood. Thus Anwar (the dramatic hero of the novel as distinct from Gandhi and Nehru who are its polemical heroes) is Muslim in upbringing but Hindu by birth. The revelation of Anwar's origins results in a traumatic drama of identity, but his discovery of self is also a discovery of India and he is finally integrated into "a strange symbol of unity". Anwar's evolving consciousness and political activities provide a sound basis for Abbas's major comment, which acknowledges the tragedy of sectarian hatred and confusion of aims within the revolutionary movement, but concludes that unity and love can ultimately prevail over division and hate.

That moral integrity is the central value in Abbas's world-view is further exemplified in *When Night Falls* and *Mera Naam Joker*. However, despite the pertinence of the integrity versus corruption theme in *When Night Falls* (a reporter fights for the poor against a diabolical millionaire and refuses to be bought off), the human significance of this theme and of the social evils exposed is vitiated by Abbas's gaudy melodrama, crude characterisation and naive style. This novel reveals Abbas endeavouring to reach a potential cinema audience which relishes gauche sensationalism. *Mera Naam Joker*, by contrast, reveals something of the "inner life" of Indian sensibility. The conceit of the joker's dual personality—the mask of pleasure hiding the man of pain—provides scope for Indian-style expressions of emotion which westerners usually dismiss as sentimental. The sad story of the joker's failure to win the women he loves is presented in terms of Indian existentialism; the joker's destiny is divinely inspired, life is "a huge joke" in the cosmos of the absurd.

Abbas's main limitations as a writer—unsubtlety of form and meaning, transparent contrivances, melodrama, sensationalism—weaken the humane effects he is constantly striving for. Nevertheless, his work often reflects genuinely Indian dispositions of the folk spirit (see his more lyrical short stories), and in *Inqilab* he successfully conveys a reportorial sense of "the contemporary historical reality".

—S. C. Harrex

---

**ABLEMAN, Paul.** British. Born in Leeds, Yorkshire, 13 June 1927; brought up in New York. Attended King's College, London. Military service: 3 years. Married; has one son. Address: Flat 37, Duncan House, Fellows Road, London N.W.3, England.

PUBLICATIONS

Novels

*I Hear Voices.* Paris, Olympia Press, 1958.
*As Near As I Can Get.* London, Spearman, 1962.

*Vac.*   London, Gollancz, 1968.
*The Twilight of the Vilp.*   London, Gollancz, 1969.


Uncollected Short Stories

"The Bay Area", in *Transatlantic Review* (London and New York), Autumn 1967.
"Sir Jacob's Ordeal", in *Men Only* (London), November 1971.


Plays

*Green Julia* (produced Edinburgh, 1965; Washington, D.C., 1968).   London, Methuen,
   1966.
*Tests* (playlets).   London, Methuen, 1966.
*Blue Comedy: Madly in Love, Hawk's Night* (produced London, 1968).   London,
   Methuen, 1968.


Verse

*Bits: Some Prose Poems.*   London, Latimer Press, 1969.


Other

*The Mouth and Oral Sex.*   London, Running Man Press, 1969.


*        *        *


Paul Ableman is a comedian whose favourite joke is the reader. His gadfly gifts first came
to light in a strange novel, *I Hear Voices*, published by the Olympia Press in 1958. This
book is recounted by an imaginary schizophrene, and Philip Toynbee has described it as
presenting "a marvellous entanglement of different levels of reality." The hero is confined
to his room, where he lies in bed, eats his meals, receives the occasional visitor. But by
means of his madness, as Toynbee points out, he becomes a traveller in time and space,
well-equipped to encounter "a wonderful series of dream-like adventures." Ableman has
also written a stage play, *Green Julia*, that had a certain critical success, and he is responsible
for a volume of amusing if somewhat hermetic neo-Dadaist dialogues, *Tests*.
   *As Near As I Can Get* confirmed his special, effervescent, slightly secret talent, but not
until *Vac* did he go some way towards pleasing a wider public. The title of this novel is
exact, fusing the idea of holiday or vacation with that of vacuum. The narrator, Billy
Soodernim, exists somewhere between the two. For twelve years he has been married to
Lucy, warm, sad, accommodating, vulnerable Lucy; he loves Lucy and has looked after
her pretty well, but he never began to promise to be faithful to her, and his flexible notions
of the concept of marriage have now become too much for her. Lucy has taken up with a
nineteen-year-old hashish-smoking Turk, Kemal. The two of them visit Billy when he is in
hospital for a hernia operation, but even this act of bizarre emotional generosity cannot
divert the marriage from the rocks. When the book opens Billy and Lucy are breaking up.
For the rest of the time Billy breaks down.
   There is lifelikeness and immediacy to Ableman's "scene", with its parties and car-rides
and endless bickerings against the flames of the sex war. But there is also a certain whimsical
self-indulgence in his refusal to give imaginative "distance" to his central character. The
joke of Billy's name is not a particularly good joke. By the last pixillated page it has been

made to seem to be at the reader's expense. As a piece of improvisation, though, *Vac* has the virtues of its own recklessness. The prose is highly alert, and often funny, especially about sex, a remark which applies with equal truth to Ableman's other novel *The Twilight of the Vilp*, though the filament-thin slightness of this leaves one in doubt as to whether the author is seriously joking or jokingly serious. Perhaps, in a word, and Joyce's at that, he is *jocoserious*?

*Bits* is a book of experimental prose pieces, all short. In a note, Ableman declares that each "bit" is built round a simple poetic idea, but that this idea has not been explored or embodied in poetic form firstly because he does not think he can write "true" poetry, and secondly because it seems to him that as regards form "the way ahead for literature is a fusion of the chief virtues of prose (breadth, sustained objectivity, naturalness of tone) with those of poetry (syntactical freedom, exactness of expression)." The result is diverting, if rather too determinedly trivial. In a piece such as "A Man Suddenly Remembering" the process of thinking, the movement of the mind, is aptly caught in the quick uncertain sentence constructions, and in "Lichen" and "Strangers" and "The Ghosts of the Mind" something rarer—a moment seized and turned inside-out for its meaning, as in one of Rimbaud's *Illuminations*, or a Sarraute *tropisme*. Although *Bits* is Ableman's most recently published work of fiction the pieces in it were actually written in 1957.

—Robert Nye

---

**ABRAHAMS, Peter.** South African. Born in Johannesburg in 1919. Educated at Church of England mission schools and colleges. Married to Daphne Elizabeth Miller; has three children. Regular contributor to *The Observer*, London, and the *Herald Tribune*, New York and Paris, 1952–64. Editor, *West Indian Economist*, and Controller, *West Indian News*, Jamaica, 1955–64. Address: Red Hills, St. Andrews, Jamaica.

PUBLICATIONS

Novels

*Song of the City*.   London, Crisp, 1945.
*Mine Boy*.   London, Crisp, 1946; New York, Knopf, 1955.
*The Path of Thunder*.   New York, Harper, 1948; London, Faber, 1952.
*Wild Conquest*.   New York, Harper, 1950; London, Faber, 1951.
*A Wreath for Udomo*.   New York, Knopf, and London, Faber, 1956.
*A Night of Their Own*.   New York, Knopf, and London, Faber, 1965.
*This Island Now*.   London, Faber, 1966; New York, Knopf, 1967.

Short Stories

*Dark Testament*.   London, Allen and Unwin, 1942.

Other

*Return to Goli* (reportage).   London, Faber, 1953.

*Tell Freedom: Memories of Africa.*   London, Faber, and New York, Knopf, 1954.
*The World of Mankind*, with others.   New York, Golden Press, 1962.

Editor, with Nadine Gordimer, *South African Writing Today.*   London, Penguin, 1967.

\*   \*   \*

Peter Abrahams left South Africa in 1939, when he was only twenty years old, but the racial and political problems of that troubled land have continued to dominate his imagination. All but one of the seven novels he has written in the past thirty years have been set entirely or in part in South Africa, and the one exception, a recent work entitled *This Island Now*, deals with race and politics in another potentially explosive plural society, an island in the Caribbean with a poverty-striken black majority and an affluent white minority. Abrahams has also written two autobiographical books, *Tell Freedom* and *Return to Goli*, both of which focus on his experiences as a mulatto in South Africa.

Abrahams' early novels were influenced by Marxist ideas so they tend to be concerned more with race and economics than with politics. *Song of the City* and *Mine Boy* tell of the consequences of urbanization and industrialization on the lives of young black workers who move from the country to the city. *Song of the City* takes place at the time of the second world war, *Mine Boy* against the backdrop of booming gold mines in Johannesburg. In both novels nonwhites are mistreated and oppressed by whites.

In his next novel, *The Path of Thunder*, Abrahams turned to the theme of interracial love, exploring its impact on a young Coloured schoolteacher and an Afrikaner girl whose passionate affair ultimately ends in tragedy when the Afrikaner community discovers they are lovers. Two years later Abrahams moved in yet another direction, this time reconstructing the era of the Afrikaner migration or "Great Trek" in *Wild Conquest*, an historical novel in which he made an effort to be fair to all the major ethnic groups in South Africa— Bantu, Boer and Briton.

After these early works, all of which were written in the 1940's, Abrahams' fiction became more political. *A Wreath for Udomo*, published just before Ghana attained its independence, was an attempt to predict what might happen when independent black African nations were confronted with the choice between the financial advantages of collaborating with the white regimes in southern Africa and the moral imperative of opposing them by actively supporting black liberation movements. *A Night of Their Own* carried the revolutionary theme further by detailing the adventures of an African underground agent involved in smuggling funds to an Indian resistance organization in South Africa. And *This Island Now* told of racial tensions and internal power struggles in a small, black-ruled Caribbean island-state. In each successive novel Abrahams moved further and further away from a depiction of South African social realities to the construction of hypothetical situations which afforded greater creative elbow room. Even *A Night of Their Own*, though set in South Africa, had elements of fantasy and wishful thinking in it. Abrahams' increased dependence on his imagination in these later novels may reflect how far out of touch he is with contemporary conditions in his native land.

Abrahams has always written in a simple, direct prose style which wavers between superior reportage and maudlin romanticizing. He is at his best when transcribing newsworthy events which have a basis in fact; his autobiographical and travel writings, for instance, are superb. But he has a regrettable tendency to sentimentalize personal relationships between men and women, especially if they are of different races, as they so often are in his novels. His accounts of miscegenated love are nearly always literary disasters because they are bathed in lachrymose artificiality.

Yet when he writes of exciting happenings such as spontaneous labor strikes, bloody frontier battles, underground resistance campaigns, or the highly-charged political debates at a Pan-African congress, Abrahams can carry the reader along swiftly and persuasively, building up a spell-binding momentum which is broken only when he suddenly veers from the external world of his characters into the internal world of their thoughts and dreams. Abrahams has not yet learned to write a decent interior monologue, and his novels would be more aesthetically satisfying if his heroes and heroines were less inclined to moments of moody introspection. His surface sketches are much more convincing than his psychological probings.

Because Peter Abrahams was one of the first African writers to achieve international recognition, his works received a good deal of patronizing attention at first. European and American critics were all too eager to embrace him as a literary phenomenon—a nonwhite South African who could not only write but could actually write fairly well!—so they wrote glowing reviews of his early novels, emphasizing their strong points and ignoring obvious flaws. Today, in the midst of an African literary awakening, Abrahams tends to be regarded with less enthusiasm, for his novels are recognized as far less interesting and accomplished than those produced in West Africa by such talented artists as Chinua Achebe, Wole Soyinka, and Ayi Kwei Armah. Abrahams has certainly carved a niche for himself in African literary history, but it is a small niche somewhere at the base of the monument, passionately but clumsily hewn.

—Bernth Lindfors

---

**ABSE, Dannie.** British. Born in Cardiff, Glamorgan, Wales, 22 September 1923. Educated at St. Illyd's College, Cardiff; the University of South Wales and Monmouthshire, Cardiff; King's College, London; and Westminster Hospital, London; qualified as a physician, M.R.C.S., L.R.C.P. Served in the Royal Air Force. Married to Joan Mercer; has three children. Recipient: Foyle Award, 1960; Welsh Arts Council award for verse, 1971. Address: 85 Hodford Road, London N.W.11, England.

PUBLICATIONS

Novels

*Ash on a Young Man's Sleeve.* London, Hutchinson, 1954.
*Some Corner of an English Field.* London, Hutchinson, 1956; New York, Criterion Books, 1957.
*O. Jones, O. Jones.* London, Hutchinson, 1970.

Plays

*Fire in Heaven* (produced London, 1948). London, Hutchinson, 1956.
*House of Cowards* (produced London, 1960). Included in *Three Questor Plays*, 1967; *Twelve Great Plays*, New York, Harcourt Brace, 1970.
*The Eccentric.* London, Evans, 1961.
*Gone* (produced London, 1962). Included in *Three Questor Plays*, 1967.
*The Joker* (produced London, 1962).
*Is the House Shut?* (produced London, 1964).

*Three Questor Plays* (*House of Cowards, Gone,* and *In the Cage,* revised version of *Is the House Shut?*).   London, Scorpion Press, 1967.
*The Dogs of Pavlov* (produced London, 1969).

Verse

*After Every Green Thing*.   London, Hutchinson, 1949.
*Walking under Water*.   London, Hutchinson, 1952.
*Tenants of the House*.   London, Hutchinson, 1957; New York, Criterion Books, 1958.
*Poems, Golders Green*.   London, Hutchinson, 1962.
*Dannie Abse: A Selection*.   London, Studio Vista, 1963.
*A Small Desperation*.   London, Hutchinson, 1968.
*Selected Poems*.   London, Hutchinson, and New York, Oxford University Press, 1970.

Other

*Medicine on Trial*.   London, Aldus Books, 1967; New York, Crown, 1969.

Editor, with Howard Sergeant, *Mavericks*.   London, Editions Poetry and Poverty, 1957.
Editor, *European Verse*.   London, Studio Vista, 1964.

*          *          *

Dannie Abse has spoken of clarifying "dangers in the dark" by writing "tiny flashes in the night." Brief and controlled, his novels illuminate deadly pitfalls. But they also put in relief moments of humane concern, projecting these against a darkness at once social and metaphysical.

Abse's skill at threading his narratives on counterpointed leitmotifs makes his novels as "poetic" as they are socially realistic. The leitmotifs are taken from history, literature, even football, but especially from medicine. The symbolic transformation of detail, however, derives from Abse's anxious yet humorous ambivalence toward the antithetical claims of nihilism and social conscience. (In this respect, he has much in common with another physician-novelist, the psychoanalyst Allen Wheelis.) It is always with some image of the dissecting room in mind that Abse's protagonists hunt a tenuous ethical position. Like a war zone, that horrendous place simultaneously negates and compels the search.

*Ash on a Young Man's Sleeve* is an evocation of adolescence, particularly the amusing side of that period. Set in Cardiff between 1930 and 1940, the story delineates, over against the rise of Fascism, the emergence from boyhood of a Welsh Jew. At first remote, the brutality of Nazism descends in bombs upon the young man's very neighbourhood, killing his best friend and eradicating in a split second a precious relationship they had worked out through periods of rivalry and almost laughable bigotry.

The "ash" of the title signifies the early encroachment of death into youthful life. The title itself modifies Eliot's lines from "Little Gidding":

> Ash on an old man's sleeve
> Is all the ash burnt roses leave.
> Dust in the air suspended
> Marks the place where a story ended.

which serve as an epigraph to the novel and contrast throughout with a refrain from Hopkins: "Glory be to God for dappled things." The work concludes with an exquisite passage on the falling of leaves and the end of innocence which seems to connect the novel attitudinally to Hopkins' poem "Spring and Fall."

*Some Corner of an English Field* is set in a post-World War Two R.A.F. station in England and devastates the military by likening it to a new shallowness of spirit. Drinking himself into courage, the central figure, Dr. Henderson, tells his officer colleagues in a farewell speech: "The symbols of our sick internal reality . . . are here externalized in the airship hangars, in the sound of marching feet, in the shocking uniformity of opinion." The symbolic beating scene which ensues brings the insight to a grim fruition. Henderson is placed, however, between this violent dullness and the temptation of following four drifters in their suicidal meanderings. Of this dilemma, so germaine to Abse's work, the narrator says almost imploringly: "Somewhere there was a way between utter acceptance and complete, destructive rebellion."

In the vein of Amis's *Lucky Jim*, *O. Jones, O. Jones* is Abse's most thoroughly comic novel. The "O" stands for Ozymandias, a cognomen the hero grandly hands himself to make up for his own dull "Herbert." As a medical student "Ozy" deals with one devastating event after another. He comes haltingly to something near Shelley's view of Ozymandias. Because, ironically, his character is his fate and life is fortuitous, Oxy's receptivity to experience cancels out his spurious motivation and he seems at last a serious candidate for good works, for labor no longer glimpsed through an adolescent haze.

—D. M. Heaton

---

**ACHEBE, Chinua.** Nigerian. Born in Ogidi, 16 November 1930. Educated at Government College, Umuahia, 1944–47; University College, Ibadan, 1948–53, B.A. (London) 1953. Married Christie Okoli in 1961; has four children. Talks Producer, Lagos, 1954–57, Controller, Enugu, 1958–61, and Director, Lagos, 1961–66, Nigerian Broadcasting Corporation. Chairman, Citadel Books Ltd., Enugu, 1967. Since 1967, Senior Research Fellow, University of Nigeria, Nsukka. Since 1970, Director of Heinemann Educational Books (Nigeria) Ltd., and Nwankwo-Ifejika and Company (Publishers) Ltd., Enugu. Since 1971, Editor of *Okike*, a Nigerian journal of new writing. Member, University of Lagos Council, 1966; Chairman, Society of Nigerian Authors, 1966. Recipient: Margaret Wrong Memorial Prize, 1959; Nigerian National Trophy, 1960; Rockefeller Fellowship, 1960; UNESCO Fellowship, 1963; Jock Campbell Award, *New Statesman*, 1965. Address: Institute of African Studies, University of Nigeria, Nsukka, Nigeria.

PUBLICATIONS

Novels

> *Things Fall Apart.* London, Heinemann, 1958; New York, McDowell Obolensky, 1959.
> *No Longer at Ease.* London, Heinemann, 1960; New York, Obolensky, 1961.
> *Arrow of God.* London, Heinemann, 1964; New York, Day, 1967.
> *A Man of the People.* London, Heinemann, and New York, Day, 1966.

Short Stories

> *The Sacrificial Egg and Other Stories.*   Onitsha, Nigeria, Etudo, 1962.
> *Girls at War.*   London, Heinemann, and New York, Doubleday, 1972.

Verse

> *Beware Soul-Brother and Other Poems.*   Enugu, Nigeria, Nwankwo-Ifejika, 1971; New
> York, Doubleday, 1972.

Other

> *Chike and the River* (juvenile).   London and New York, Cambridge University Press,
> 1966.
> *How the Leopard Got His Claws* (juvenile).   Enugu, Nigeria, Nwankwo-Ifejika, 1972.

Bibliography: in *Africana Library Journal* (New York), Spring 1970.

Critical Studies: *The Novels of Chinua Achebe* by G. D. Killam, London, Heinemann, and New York, Africana Publishing Corporation, 1969; *Chinua Achebe* by Arthur Ravenscroft, London, Longman, 1969; *Chinua Achebe* by David Carroll, New York, Twayne, 1970.

Chinua Achebe comments:

I am a political writer. My politics is concerned with universal human communication across racial and cultural boundaries as a means of fostering respect for all people. Such respect can issue only from understanding. So my primary concern is with clearing the channels of communication in my own neighbourhood by hacking away at the thickets that choke them.

Africa's meeting with Europe must be accounted a terrible disaster in this matter of human understanding and respect. The nature of the meeting precluded any warmth of friendship. First Europe was an enslaver; then a colonizer. In either role she had no need and made little effort to understand or appreciate Africa; indeed she easily convinced herself that there was nothing there to justify the effort. Today our world is still bedevilled by the consequences of that cataclysmic encounter.

I was born into the colonial era, grew up in the heady years of nationalist protest and witnessed Africa's resumption of independence. (It was not, however, the same Africa which originally lost her freedom that now regained it, but a different Africa created in the image of Europe—but that's another story.) So I have seen in my not very long lifetime three major eras in precipitate succession, leaving us somewhat dazed. My response as a writer has been to try to keep pace with these torrential changes. First I had to tell Europe that the arrogance on which she sought to excuse her pillage of Africa, i.e., that Africa was the Primordial Void, was sheer humbug; that Africa had a history, a religion, a civilization. We reconstructed this history and civilization and displayed it to challenge the stereotype and the cliché.  Actually it was not to Europe alone I spoke. I spoke also to that part of ourselves that had come to accept Europe's opinion of us. And I was not alone nor even the first.

But the gauntlet had barely left our hands when a new historic phrase broke on us. Europe conceded independence to us and we promptly began to misuse it, or rather those leaders to whom we entrusted the wielding of our new power and opportunity. So we got mad at them and came out brandishing novels of disenchantment. Actually we had all been duped. No independence was given—it is never given but taken, anyway. Europe had only made a tactical withdrawal on the political front and while we sang our anthem and unfurled our flag she was securing her iron grip in the economic field. And our leaders in whose faces we hurled our disenchantment neither saw nor heard because they were not leaders at all but marionettes.

So the problem remains for Africa, for black people, for all deprived peoples and for the world. And so for the writer, for he is like the puppy in our proverb: that stagnant water in the potsherd is for none other but him. As long as one people sit on another and are deaf to their cry, so long will understanding and peace elude all of us.

*    *    *

For technical inventiveness both in language and novelistic technique, for profound insight into tragic human experience, for satirical sophistication, and for sustained creative energy, Achebe must still be regarded as the Anglophone African novelist of most considerable stature. The success of his first novel, *Things Fall Apart*, has led to some underestimation of the books that followed. Because Obi in *No Longer at Ease* is a grandson of Okonkwo in the first novel, the second has been regarded as not only a sequel but an attempt at essentially the same kind of tragic novel, and there has been disappointment that expectations aroused by *Things Fall Apart* are not fulfilled in *No Longer at Ease*. Because *Arrow of God* deals with the same sort of traditional Igbo society as forms the setting of *Things Fall Apart*, it has been seen as a less concise exercise over the same ground. Because there is a surface opposition between the young Odili and the corrupt political boss, Chief Nanga, in *A Man of the People*, much of the subtle satire and moral judgement in this novel has been missed.

*Things Fall Apart* is rightly praised as a taut, economically written novel that examines the period of the first Igbo contact with white missionaries and colonial officials in terms that are reminiscent of Greek tragedy. The rise of the self-made man, Okonkwo, in such a society, and his ignominious end are often regarded as the peculiar strength of the novel. Yet what happens to Okonkwo is the result of neither blind fate nor inevitable psychological bias. Okonkwo's very warrior-strength comes from his conscious will; he pursues a particular course from deliberate choice, and suppresses all his humaner tendencies so that his natural affections become warped. Other alternatives are open to him, and taken by others equally valiant. His career parallels and illumines the tragedy that overcomes his people; Igbo society is too inflexible to cope with the imperial power. Although Achebe presents traditional African society and his hero Okonkwo with great sympathy, he retains an admirable artistic objectivity about them. He does not allow his desire to show that the pre-colonial African past had a highly developed culture to obscure its weaknesses—precisely those that enabled the missionaries to get a toehold among the Igbos. The point of view is sympathetic, yet delicately balanced, and complex in the means by which it is conveyed. For instance, the most marked linguistic characteristic is Achebe's use of literal English translations of Igbo proverbs. This device not only makes for surface authenticity, but is a means of indicating how Igbo society is simultaneously strengthened and severely limited by its traditional wisdom inherited through gnomic folk sayings. In an oral culture, the spoken word is extraordinarily utilitarian, but also a form of continuing ritual. While the tragedy is the destruction of an admirable, self-contained society by an intrusive culture, the victim is also seen to have serious inadequacies. Achebe's story is not a lament for the past but an analysis of a process of historical change. The blindnesses of those involved on both sides are revealed with a detachment on the novelist's part that is intimately related to his satirical methods in *No Longer at Ease* and *A Man of the People*.

Although *Arrow of God* provides an even richer evocation of traditional culture than *Things Fall Apart* does, it is more than a similar novel on a grander scale. The organic daily life of the Umuaro clan is drawn in great detail, but not simply to anatomize traditional culture. It is necessary for realizing fully the part of the priest Ezeulu in that society, for Ezeulu is the most complex and ambitious study in characterization that Achebe has yet produced, and his tragedy grows out of the conflict within him between the demands of his semi-divine office as priest of the clan's protective deity and his very human desire for personal power. The theme is a man's attitude to the power he already wields, what he does with that power, and the effects of his misuse of it upon himself and his people. In *Arrow of God*, too, Achebe uses Igbo proverbs, but now not merely to suggest the ordinary rituals of traditional life, but also as means of conveying the twilit area between a man's terrestial life and his function as a semi-spirit mediating on his people's behalf with a deity. It is here that Ezeulu loses his way. Achebe directs the intricate drama with great sympathy and human understanding yet maintains an extraordinary detachment, best illustrated by the sardonic last paragraph of the novel, which casts doubt on the people's over-simple interpretation of Ezeulu's downfall.

In *No Longer at Ease* the characteristics of pre-colonial Igbo culture have become hollow mockeries, just as Obi's youthful idealism is seen to be without foundation before the harsh realities of corruption in modern Lagos. What is satirically laid bare is the chaotic, rootless bewilderment of West African city life, again fully reflected in the characters' speech, as they switch from Igbo to pidgin or to English, according to their relationships with other people. The general crisis of culture is particularized—and humanized—in Obi's career, but Achebe's satire underlines the absence of any larger mode for personal integrity to work within.

In *A Man of the People*, Achebe attacks political corruption and thuggery, not by conventional means, but by using Odili as an anti-hero who lucidly analyses the evils around him, while taking a share in them himself. The only clue to Odili's real fictional function lies in the false, pseudo-sophisticated speech that Achebe places in his mouth. The novel is a brilliant creation, a superb satirical farce.

Perhaps Achebe's greatest strength as a novelist is the steady refinement of his control over language as a means of conveying rather than stating moral insights.

—Arthur Ravenscroft

---

**AIKEN, Conrad (Potter).** American. Born in Savannah, Georgia, 5 August 1889. Educated at Harvard University, Cambridge, Massachusetts, A.B. 1912. Married Jessie McDonald in 1912 (divorced, 1929); Clarice Lorenz, 1930 (divorced, 1937); Mary Hoover, 1937; has three children, John, Jane Aiken Hodge, and Joan. Contributing Editor, *The Dial*, New York, 1916–19; American Correspondent of *Athenaeum*, London, 1919–25, *London Mercury*, 1921–22; London Correspondent for *The New Yorker*, as Samuel Jeake Jr., 1933–36. Instructor, Harvard University, 1927–28. Consultant in Poetry, Library of Congress, Washington, D.C., 1950–52. Recipient: Pulitzer Prize for Poetry, 1930; Shelley Memorial Prize, 1930; Guggenheim Fellowship, 1934; Bryher Award, 1952; National Book Award for Poetry, 1954; Bollingen Prize for Poetry, 1956; Academy of American Poets Fellowship, 1957; National Institute of Arts and Letters Gold Medal for Poetry, 1958; Huntington Hartford Foundation Award, 1961; Brandeis University Creative Arts Award, 1966; National Medal for Literature, 1969. Member, American Academy of Arts and Letters, 1957. Address: Forty-One Doors, Stony Brook Road, Brewster, Massachusetts 02631, U.S.A.

PUBLICATIONS

Novels

> *Blue Voyage*.   London, Howe, and New York, Scribner, 1927.
> *Great Circle*.   New York, Scribner, and London, Wishart, 1933.
> *King Coffin*.   New York, Scribner, and London, Dent, 1935.
> *A Heart for the Gods of Mexico*.   London, Secker-Richards Press, 1939.
> *Conversation; or, Pilgrims' Progress*.   New York, Duell, 1940; as *The Conversation*, London, Rodney Phillips and Green, 1948.
> *The Collected Novels of Conrad Aiken*.   New York, Holt Rinehart, 1964.
> *Three Novels*.   London, W. H. Allen, 1965.

Short Stories

> *Bring! Bring! and Other Stories*.   London, Secker, and New York, Boni and Liveright, 1925.
> *Costumes by Eros*.   New York, Scribner, 1928; London, Cape, 1929.
> *Gehenna*.   New York, Random House, 1930; London, John Rodker, 1931.
> *Among the Lost People*.   New York and London, Scribner, 1934.
> *The Short Stories of Conrad Aiken*.   New York, Duell, 1950.
> *The Collected Short Stories of Conrad Aiken*.   Cleveland, World, 1960; London, Heinemann, 1966.

Play

> *Mr. Arcularis* (earlier version entitled *Fear No More*) (produced Provincetown, Massachusetts, 1949).   Cambridge, Massachusetts, Harvard University Press, 1957; London, Oxford University Press, 1958.

Verse

> *Earth Triumphant and Other Tales in Verse*.   New York, Macmillan, 1914.
> *The Jig of Forslin: A Symphony*.   Boston, Four Seas, 1916; London, Secker, 1921.
> *Turns and Movies and Other Tales in Verse*.   Boston, Houghton Mifflin, 1916.
> *Nocturne of Remembered Spring and Other Poems*.   Boston, Four Seas, 1917.
> *The Charnal Rose, Senlin: A Biography, and Other Poems*.   Boston, Four Seas, 1918.
> *The House of Dust: A Symphony*.   Boston, Four Seas, 1920.
> *Punch: The Immortal Liar*.   New York, Knopf, 1921.
> *Priapus and the Pool and Other Poems*.   Cambridge, Massachusetts, Dunster House, 1922.
> *The Pilgrimage of Festus*.   New York, Knopf, 1923.
> (*Poems*).   New York, Simon and Schuster, 1927.
> *Prelude*.   New York, Random House, 1929.
> *Selected Poems*.   New York, Scribner, 1929.
> *John Deth, A Metaphysical Legend, and Other Poems*.   New York and London, Scribner, 1930.
> *Preludes for Memnon*.   New York, Scribner, 1931.
> *The Coming Forth by Day of Osiris Jones*.   New York, Scribner, 1931.
> *Landscape West of Eden*.   London, Dent, 1934: New York, Scribner, 1935.
> *Time in the Rock: Preludes to Definition*.   New York and London, Scribner, 1936.

*And in the Human Heart.*   New York, Duell, and London, Staples Press, 1940.
*Brownstone Eclogues and Other Poems.*   New York, Duell, 1942.
*The Soldier.*   New York, New Directions, 1944; London, Editions Poetry, 1946.
*The Kid.*   New York, Duell, 1947; London, Lehmann, 1948.
*The Divine Pilgrim.*   Athens, University of Georgia Press, 1949.
*Skylight One: Fifteen Poems.*   New York, Oxford University Press, 1950; London, Lehmann, 1951.
*Collected Poems.*   New York, Oxford University Press, 1953.
*A Letter from Li Po and Other Poems.*   New York, Oxford University Press, 1955.
*The Flute Player.*   Privately printed, 1956.
*Sheepfold Hill: 15 Poems.*   New York, Sagamore Press, 1958.
*Selected Poems.*   New York and London, Oxford University Press, 1961.
*The Morning Song of Lord Zero: Poems Old and New.*   New York, Oxford University Press, 1963.
*A Seizure of Limericks.*   New York, Holt Rinehart, 1964; London, W. H. Allen, 1965.
*The Clerk's Journal: An Undergraduate Poem, Together with a Brief Memoir of Dean LeBaron Russell Briggs, T. S. Eliot, and Harvard, in 1911.*   New York, Eakins Press, 1971.
*Collected Poems 1916–1970.*   New York, Oxford University Press, 1971.

Other

*Skepticisms: Notes on Contemporary Poetry.*   New York, Knopf, 1919.
*Ushant: An Essay* (autobiography).   New York and Boston, Duell-Little Brown, 1952; London, W. H. Allen, 1963; illustrated edition, New York, Oxford University Press, 1971.
*A Reviewer's ABC: Collected Criticism from 1916 to the Present.*   Cleveland, World, 1958; London, W. H. Allen, 1959; as *Collected Criticism*, New York, Oxford University Press, 1968.
*Cats and Bats and Things with Wings* (juvenile).   New York, Atheneum, 1965.
*Tom, Sue and the Clock* (juvenile).   New York, Macmillan, and London, Macmillan, 1966.

Manuscript Collection: Harvard University, Cambridge, Massachusetts.

Critical Studies: "Conrad Aiken Issue" of *Wake* (New York), no. 11, 1952; *Conrad Aiken* by Frederick Hoffman, New York, Twayne, 1962; *Conrad Aiken: A Life of His Art* by Jay Martin, Princeton, New Jersey, Princeton University Press, 1962; in *Times Literary Supplement* (London), 19 April 1963; *Conrad Aiken* by Reuel Denney, Minneapolis, University of Minnesota Press, 1964; interview with Robert B. Wilbur in *Paris Review* (Paris and New York), Winter 1968; *Current Biography* (New York), May 1970.

Conrad Aiken comments:

   All my work, in whatever form—short story, poetry, criticism, or novel, and of course the autobiography *Ushant*—has been concerned with one thing: the telling of the truth about man and man's mind, and man's place in the universe, and in the world of mankind. The epigraphs for *Blue Voyage* and *Ushant* are each a half of Coleridge's poem, "Self-Knowledge", and this is no accident, for the protagonist of *Ushant*, D., is Demarest of *Blue Voyage*. *Blue Voyage* is the stocktaking of a writer midway in his career, *Ushant* in his maturity. *Great Circle*—Freud's favorite—is also profoundly autobiographical, even to containing a dialogue chapter which is the interchange between the protagonist and his friend, an analyst. *Conversation*, in a lighter vein, is more of same. The other novel is less immediately personal, but only a little. The short stories necessarily less so, naturally. But of all the fiction it should be noticed that, apart from this preoccupation with the probing of consciousness, there is always an insistence on structure and form. *Great Circle* and *Conversation* are, in effect, symphonies; so is *Ushant* and, with a difference, *Blue Voyage*. Much the same can be said of the stories: I think of them, as indeed I do of the novels, as one would of music, or poetry, or even a kind of mathematics: a statement which is not only true, but elaborately and logically *designed*: the truth finding an aesthetic form.

*     *     *

Although Conrad Aiken published some short stories in undergraduate periodicals when he was a student at Harvard, he abandoned fiction for many years and made his reputation as a poet. He published ten volumes of verse in the years between 1914 and 1925, and it was only then, in 1925, that he began to publish fiction. In the next fifteen years he brought out five novels and forty-one short stories in three volumes. After 1940 he devoted himself again to poetry (which, to be sure, he had never abandoned: the fifteen years of prose publication saw the publication, too, of nine more volumes of verse) and to the writing of his extraordinary autobiographical volume, *Ushant: An Essay*.

A few of Aiken's more striking stories, notably "Silent Snow, Secret Snow" and "Mr. Arcularis," are widely known through their frequent inclusion in anthologies, but the great bulk of this remarkable body of short fiction, at once so various and so centrally coherent, is little known. Similarly, the novels, at least two of which (*Great Circle* and *King Coffin*) are almost certainly major achievements in American fiction, have few readers. A new reader coming to Aiken today would probably be wise to begin with his last substantial prose work, *Ushant*, which is at once a review of the artist's development and its climax.

In this book the author's *persona* is called simply D., and this is the same figure as the hero of the first novel, *Blue Voyage*, named Demarest (*de mare est*?). Aiken's central characters, it should be said, are always representations of himself, not usually in a baldly literal, autobiographical sense, but in the sense that they are committed to the same psychic search that is the essence of Aiken's experience as an artist.

In *Ushant*, D. remembers how, many years before as a young man in London, his fortune was told him:

> You will achieve a few wonderfully happy incidents, you are of the race of the inspired; and at least two or three times you will have the most wonderful of experiences, the blessed experience of coming suddenly upon a veritable gold-mine of consciousness, seemingly inexhaustible, too, and with the words already hermetically stamped on the gold: perhaps out of some such experience you will even achieve one of those "controlled" masterpieces that are both controlled and uncontrolled, and these are the best, the true artesian water of life: moments of abundance and joy, and the memory of power; but no, not the disciplined knowledge that will enable you to perfect, at will, and repeatedly, true works of art. Perhaps yours is the happier way—I don't know. You are a diviner, a dowser, the hazel twig of vision will tremble in your hands. But—the gift will be capricious, will come and go; and in the end I am afraid I see a sort of final bankruptcy for you, an exhaustion of your virtue, even a debauchery of it.

There is much more than this, not all of it entirely happy, but the interesting point is the mature D.'s comment on that prophecy: "The words had been as fascinating as alarming . . . and how devastatingly true they had turned out to be!" In the prophecy, the two most relevant points are the phrase "gold-mine of consciousness" and the brief comment on the best works of art as "both controlled and uncontrolled."

When Aiken was an undergraduate at Harvard, Sigmund Freud visited the United States and gave his famous lectures on psychoanalysis at nearby Clark University. Whether or not there was a direct connection, Aiken became one of the first American writers to find the insights of psychoanalysis of help to him in his own exploration of consciousness, and, as the pursuit of self-awareness became his great and constant theme, it led him, in fact, to anticipate some of the concerns of post-Freudian psychoanalysis, notably, the whole problem of "identity." (When he read *Great Circle*, Freud was so interested that he himself offered to take the author into analysis.) That constant theme, the persistent delving in the "mine of consciousness," whether or not he always struck gold, is sometimes a bit obscured by Aiken's manner, for in his complex imagination there is a prominent strain of rather bemused irony that, when he gives it free rein, produces stories that are essentially comic, even rather light hearted, with a satiric edge that cuts into a human foible or a paradox of personality deftly, delicately, but without the air either of major surgery or of passionate involvement. Yet even in such stories there is usually another strain, a note struck off from the taut strings of the stretched nerves, something sharp, shrill or somber, sinister, or mockingly morbid, an echo out of psychic chaos.

This is the note that characterizes the most splendid of Aiken's fiction, long and short, stories in which he moves from the utterly mundane into the mysterious, into hysteria, horror, hallucination, phobia, compulsion, dream, the dream of death, and, more often than not, back again into the mundane. The sudden penetration into the shadows of consciousness, a veil surprisingly whipped back and dropped again, something beyond our perception abruptly perceived in it, a mythical beast suddenly gazing curiously up at us from the shrubbery at the end of our own well-kept garden: these are the gestures that give us his unique authorial signal.

Just as the structure of his stories characteristically develops in the effort of the material to discover a level of awareness, to assert a reality beyond or below its mundane shape, so their drama characteristically arises within an individual mind as it struggles to break over the edge of its own limitations to strike the very basis of its identity. In at least one story, "Gehenna," this effort is graphically figured. The central character goes to bed after reflections on the imminence in the materials of consciousness of that disorganization of reality that is madness, falls asleep, and dreams of "a small glass aquarium, square, of the sort in which goldfish are kept."

I observe without surprise that there is water in one half of it but not in the other. And in spite of the fact that there is no partition, this water holds itself upright in its own half of the tank, leaving the other half empty. More curious than this, however, is the marine organism which lies at the bottom of the water. It looks, at first glance, like a loaf of bread. But when I lean down to examine it closely, I see that it is alive, that it is sentient, and that it is trying to move. One end of it lies very close to that point at which the water ends and the air begins; and now I realize that the poor thing is trying, and trying desperately, to get into the air. Moreover, I see that this advancing surface is as if sliced off and raw; it is horribly sensitive; and suddenly, appalled, I realize that the whole thing is simply—consciousness. It is trying to escape from the medium out of which it was created. If only it could manage this—! But I know that it never will; it has already reached, with its agonized sentience, as far as it can; it stretches itself forward, with minute and pathetic convulsions, but in vain; and suddenly I am so horrified at the notion of a consciousness that is pure suffering, that I wake up. . . . The clocks are striking two.

It is at this margin, at this edge, where, without barrier, the water of daily human experience stands against the wall of air that is outside it—it is at this margin that Conrad Aiken's fiction is written. Often the fiction itself, like "Gehenna," plunges over the margin into the chaos all around us and within, and it is in this experience that the fiction becomes,.

in a sense, "uncontrolled"; only to return again with new illumination of the self that reasserts aesthetic control.

Aiken's five novels all dramatize and generally sustain the central concern of the short stories, but there is a development, too, in their treatment of the basic theme of self-awareness, of the search for identity, a movement from the merely psychological to the basically ethical.

*Blue Voyage* tells of Demarest's sailing to England, presumably in quest of a girl who, it develops, is on the same ship and already lost to him, but he is in fact in quest of his self. *Great Circle* is another voyage of self-discovery, told in terms of extended recollections of two events separated by a generation. *King Coffin* is written in another mood: the psychotic plan of a gratuitous murder that ends in suicide; but it is no less concerned with self-discovery, even in self-immolation. *A Heart for the Gods of Mexico* is again an account of a journey, and again embodies the quest theme, now more externally developed through details of scene and emphasizing what we have called the ethical. The last novel, *Conversation; or, Pilgrims' Progress*, maintains the theme, as the subtitle suggests, but much extends the social externals, and concludes that the self discovers its identity not in isolation but through its relations with others. The novels have moved from the single interest in the discovery of self to the double interest in the discovery of self and the consequent relinquishment of self-interest in love, an amplitude of sympathy.

—Mark Schorer

---

**ALDISS, Brian (Wilson).** British. Born in East Dereham, Norfolk, 18 August 1925. Served in the Royal Signals in the Far East, 1943–47. Married Margaret Manson in 1965 (second marriage); has four children. Worked in bookselling, Oxford, 1947–56; Literary Editor, Oxford *Mail*, 1958–69; Editor, Penguin Books Science Fiction novels, London, 1961–64; since 1971, Monthly Art Correspondent, *The Guardian*, London. Chairman, Oxford Branch, Conservation Society, 1968–69. Recipient: *Observer* Book Award for Science Fiction, 1956; Hugo Award, 1961; Nebula Award, 1965; Ditmar Award (Australia), 1969. President, British Science Fiction Association, 1960–65. Address: Heath House, Southmoor, near Abingdon, Berkshire, England.

PUBLICATIONS

Novels

*The Brightfount Diaries.* London, Faber, 1955.
*Non-Stop.* London, Faber, 1958; as *Starship*, New York, Criterion Books, 1959.
*Vanguard from Alpha.* New York, Ace, 1959.
*Bow Down to Nul.* New York, Ace, 1960.
*Galaxies like Grains of Sand.* New York, New American Library, 1960.
*Equator.* London, Digit, 1961.
*The Interpreter.* London, Digit, 1961.
*The Male Response.* Boston, Beacon Press, 1961; London, Dobson, 1963.
*The Primal Urge.* New York, Ballantine, 1961; London, Sphere, 1967.
*Hothouse.* London, Faber, 1962; as *The Long Aftermath of Earth*, New York, New American Library, 1962.

*The Dark Light Years*.   London, Faber, and New York, New American Library, 1964.
*Greybeard*.   London, Faber, and New York, Harcourt Brace, 1964.
*Earthworks*.   London, Faber, 1965; New York, Doubleday, 1966.
*An Age*.   London, Faber, 1967; as *Cryptozoic*, New York, Doubleday, 1968.
*Report on Probability A*.   London, Faber, and New York, Doubleday, 1968.
*Barefoot in the Head*.   London, Faber, 1969; New York, Doubleday, 1970.
*The Hand-Reared Boy*.   London, Weidenfeld and Nicolson, and New York, McCall, 1970.
*A Soldier Erect; or, Further Adventures of the Hand-Reared Boy*.   London, Weidenfeld and Nicolson, and New York, Coward McCann, 1971.

Short Stories

*Space, Time and Nathaniel*.   London, Faber, 1957.
*No Time like Tomorrow*.   New York, New American Library, 1959.
*The Canopy of Time*.   London, Faber, 1959.
*The Airs of Earth*.   London, Faber, 1963.
*Starswarm*.   New York, New American Library, 1964.
*Best SF Stories of Brian Aldiss*.   London, Faber, 1965; as *Who Can Replace a Man?*   New York, Harcourt Brace, 1966; revised edition, Faber, 1971.
*The Saliva Tree and Other Strange Growths*.   London, Faber, 1966.
*A Brian Aldiss Omnibus*.   London, Sidgwick and Jackson, 1969.
*Intangibles Inc. and Other Stories*.   London, Faber, 1969.
*Neanderthal Planet*.   New York, Avon, 1970.
*The Moment of Eclipse*.   London, Faber, and New York, Doubleday, 1971.
*Brian Aldiss Omnibus 2*.   London, Sidgwick and Jackson, 1971.

Other

*Cities and Stones: A Traveller's Jugoslavia*.   London, Faber, 1966.
*The Shape of Future Things*.   London, Faber, 1970; New York, Doubleday, 1971.

Editor, *Best Fantasy Stories*.   London, Faber, 1962.
Editor, *Penguin Science Fiction*.   London, Penguin, 1962.
Editor, *More Penguin Science Fiction*.   London, Penguin, 1963.
Editor, *Yet More Penguin Science Fiction*.   London, Penguin, 1964.
Editor, *Introducing SF: A Science Fiction Anthology*.   London, Faber, 1964.
Editor, with Harry Harrison, *Farewell, Fantastic Venus! A History of the Planet Venus in Fact and Fiction*.   London, Macdonald, 1968; as *All About Venus*, New York, Dell, 1968.
Editor, with Harry Harrison, *Best SF: 1967, 1968, 1969,* and *1970*.   New York, Berkley, 1968, Putnam, 1969, 1970, 1971; as *The Year's Best Science Fiction 1, 2, 3,* and *4*.   London, Sphere, 1968, 1969, 1970, 1971.

Bibliography: *Item Forty-Three: Brian A. Aldiss: A Bibliography 1954–1962*, compiled by Margaret Manson, Wisbech, Cambridgeshire, Fantast (Medway), 1963.

Brian Aldiss comments:

Time is the spectre haunting the stage of most of my books: Time in its own right and in one of its nastier disguises, as Change. The characters cope with this as best they can. Sometimes, Time has only a walk-on role, as in *Barefoot in the Head*; sometimes, it even consents to play the fool, as in my current series of sexual-social novels, of which the first two volumes are *The Hand-Reared Boy* and *A Soldier Erect*.

By nature I'm an obsessive writer. Whatever I am writing at present pleases me most, or else I give it up. My science fiction represents a spectrum moving from extreme science-fictional situations in the early novels towards situations merely coloured by the presence of the future; by the time I reached *Report on Probability A* and *Barefoot*, I was writing a fiction that bears only slight resemblance to traditional SF. The Hand-Reared series (which may run to six or more novels) is a logical extension of this process; here the gaze is directed towards the past, but emphasis is still on Change—change, in this case, as it relates to one man's life. The emphasis in the series is on comedy, with sorrow as a light zither accompaniment; in my science fiction, the arrangement has generally been the other way round.

At present, I am working on a history of science fiction, *The Billion Year Spree*, together with the critic Philip Strick. Perhaps this means (though I hope it doesn't) that the science fiction novel and I are parting company. But I shall continue to write short stories with a futurist-surrealist bent, which may still be considered as my natural medium.

\*       \*       \*

The great contribution Brian Aldiss has made to the art of Science Fiction is to help to raise it to the point where it is now accepted, by all but the chronically bigoted, as a literary form worthy of serious consideration. I suspect that this has much to do with the fact that Aldiss has always looked upon himself primarily as a novelist rather than as a writer of S.F., and he has written several novels other than those on Science Fiction themes.

His first full length Science Fiction novel was *Non-Stop* which was based on the almost classic S.F. theme of a giant space-ship adrift in space. As a piece of story telling it is first class, and it displays all the excellences that are to be found in his later work: the ability to establish by carefully selected detail a convincing atmosphere of place and time, and a logical development of situations so that even the most outlandish become acceptable to the reader. In *Hothouse*, for example, Aldiss creates a world dominated by vegetation where we can sense the continual and overwhelming growth, even breathe the vegetable air, and in *Greybeard* the experience of being in post-atomic Oxford is remarkably vivid. But in *Non-Stop*, while the exploration of the ship (once built by giants) by Roy Complain and his companions has parallels with the sense of awe and wonder experienced by the Old English poets when they encountered the ruins of Roman cities, the space ship becomes a microcosm of Earth which, too, can be seen as a giant ship itself endlessly adrift in space, and the exploration develops into a search for destination and purpose.

A quality which informs Brian Aldiss's work, and which should not be overlooked, is his sense of humour. In *Non-Stop* one aspect of this can be seen in his pursuit of the idea that in the future psychology will develop its own theology and superstitions and replace our present religions. It is a plausible thesis and at the same time an amusing one, and often Aldiss's humour helps to save his S.F. novels from the over-seriousness that has engulfed other practitioners in this genre. It has been responsible too for some excellent humorous novels. The logical consequences of the invention and universal use of an "Emotional Register" are used in *The Primal Urge* to create a fantastic and hilarious story.

In recent years Brian Aldiss has striven to extend the boundaries of his art. In *Report on Probability A* he attempted the first S.F. anti-novel, a study in relative phenomena which proved a tour-de-force, and in *Barefoot in the Head* he produced another "first" where groups of poems and "pop-songs" reflect and comment on the preceding prose chapters. In a Europe reeling psychodelically from an attack by an Arab State with Psycho-

Chemical Aerosol Bombs, Chateris, the hero of *Barefoot in the Head*, gradually absorbs the acid-head poison in the atmosphere to find himself a new Messiah. As social and thought patterns disintegrate so does the language, and Aldiss develops a stunning-punning prose reminiscent of the verbal pyrotechnics of Joyce's *Finnegan's Wake*. At the same time he creates a nightmare world reflecting trends observable in the situation already with us.

Though not strictly within a discussion of Brian Aldiss's novels we should not overlook his collections of short stories, for example *Space, Time and Nathaniel* and *The Canopy of Time*, of which he is justly proud. His most recent enterprise was planned as a quartet of novels constituting a fictional autobiography covering the years from the thirties to the sixties, where through the sexual and spiritual development of Horatio Stubbs are examined certain aspects of the poverty of English middle-class life. *The Hand-Reared Boy*, the first novel in the series, begins with Horatio as a boy, his masturbatory fantasies and his first sexual encounters. The direct and extremely realistic style of the first part of this novel may not be to everyone's taste, but it flowers into a most beautifully controlled story of the young Horatio's first and hopeless love for a woman of mature years. The skill here is in presenting such a touching episode in what is basically an extremely humorous novel.

In the second novel, *A Soldier Erect*, we find Horatio still hard at it in the army and serving in India and Burma, where his sexual and social education is broadened. The coarse brutality of wartime soldiering in the Far East is accurately and as brutally portrayed, but redeemed by humour and set in contrast with Horatio's growing awareness of values beyond the more immediately erotic. Brian tells me that he now plans to make the quartet a sextet as he realised, while writing *Soldier Erect*, what a wealth of personal folk-legend he has to draw on. He is now at work on the third novel in the series, *A Rude Awakening*.

—John Cotton

---

**ALDRIDGE, (Harold Edward) James.** Australian. Born in White Hills, Victoria, 10 July 1918. Married Dina Mitchnik in 1942; has two children. Writer, Melbourne *Herald* and *Sun*, 1937–38, and London *Daily Sketch* and *Sunday Dispatch*, 1939; European and Middle East War Correspondent for the Australian Newspaper Service and the North American Newspaper Alliance, 1939–44; Teheran Correspondent, for *Time* and *Life*, 1944. Recipient: Rhys Memorial Prize, 1945; World Peace Council Gold Medal; International Organization of Journalists prize, 1967. Address: 21 Kersley Street, London S.W.11, England.

PUBLICATIONS

Novels

*Signed with Their Honour*.   London, Joseph, and Boston, Little Brown, 1942.
*The Sea Eagle*.   London, Joseph, and Boston, Little Brown, 1944.
*Of Many Men*.   London, Joseph, and Boston, Little Brown, 1946.
*The Diplomat*.   London, Lane, 1949; Boston, Little Brown, 1950.
*The Hunter*.   London, Lane, 1950; Boston, Little Brown, 1951.
*Heroes of the Empty View*.   London, Lane, and New York, Knopf, 1954.
*I Wish He Would Not Die*.   London, Bodley Head, 1957; New York, Doubleday, 1958.
*The Last Exile*.   London, Hamish Hamilton, and New York, Doubleday, 1961.
*A Captive in the Land*.   London, Hamish Hamilton, 1962; New York, Doubleday, 1963.

*The Statesman's Game.*  London, Hamish Hamilton, and New York, Doubleday, 1966.
*My Brother Tom.*  London, Hamish Hamilton, 1966; as *My Brother Tom: A Love Story*, Boston, Little Brown, 1967.

Short Stories

*Gold and Sand.*  London, Bodley Head, 1960.

Uncollected Short Story

"The Unfinished Soldiers", in *Winter's Tales 15.*  London, Macmillan, 1969.

Plays

*The 49th State* (produced London, 1946).

Several scripts for the television series, "Robin Hood".

Other

*Underwater Hunting for Inexperienced Englishmen.*  London, Allen and Unwin, 1955.
*The Flying 19* (juvenile).  London, Hamish Hamilton, 1966.
*Living Egypt,* with Paul Stand.  London, MacGibbon and Kee, and New York, Horizon Press, 1969.
*Cairo: Biography of a City.*  Boston, Little Brown, 1969; London, Macmillan, 1970.

\*       \*       \*

James Aldridge left Australia when quite a young man as a war-correspondent; and this fact has largely determined the material and the angle of approach in his work. He went through the Greek campaign and wrote two books based directly on his experiences in it. Here his method was strongly affected by Hemingway; but the books were saved from being mere imitations by the genuine freshness and truth of his presentation. He was learning how to build a narrative full of stirring events and based on historical developments which he knew at first-hand, and at the same time to link the story with the personal problems and struggles of his protagonists. With his next book, a collection of stories, came a break from the Hemingway influence. What he had gained from his apprenticeship was now integrated in his own method and outlook. The tales showed how well he was able to grasp situations with very diverse settings and convincingly to define aspects of national character in a compact form. Still drawing on his wartime experiences as a correspondent, he wrote *The Diplomat,* an ambitious large-scale work, dealing with both the Soviet Union and the region of the Kurds in northern Mesopotamia. With much skill he explored the devious world of diplomacy in the postwar world, making the issues concrete by their basis in the difficult national question of the Kurds. Aldridge emerged as an important political novelist. He showed himself able to handle complicated political themes without losing touch with the essential human issues. The political aspects were removed from triviality or narrowness by being linked with the painful struggles of the protagonist to understand the world in which he found himself an actor. Thus what gave artistic validity to the work, beyond any particular conclusions reached in the search for truth, was the definition of that search itself.

In *The Hunter* Aldridge next refreshed himself by dropping all large themes and turning to Canada in a work more concerned with immediacies of experience; his theme was the world of the hunter, a direct relationship to nature; and he showed he could conjure up a dimension of sheer physical living. But it was perhaps significant that when he turned from the theme of contemporary history and politics, it was to the sphere of nature he looked, not to everyday life in some specific society. For good and bad his uprooting through the war had made him into a novelist of the large national conflicts of our age. His material has thus been born of his journalism, but in transforming it into fiction he has overcome the journalistic limitations and been able to penetrate to deep human issues. He sees the problems in terms of real people and has never been guilty of inventing puppets to represent national or political positions.

He now turned again to the Near East, in *Heroes of the Empty View, I Wish He Would Not Die*, and *The Last Exile*, not dealing with such a remote issue as that of the Kurds, but taking up the problems of the Arab world, with special reference to Egypt. He has been helped by having many direct connections and sources of information; but despite his sympathy for the Arabs he has not oversimplified issues or made his works into tracts for a particular point of view. The stories clarify things and deepen one's understanding of the human beings entangled in vast conflicts. In his latest works he has again taken up the question of the Soviet Union but with less force and artistic success than in *The Diplomat* or the books on the Near East. It would be hard to point to any contemporary novelist who has dealt more directly with postwar political problems on the international plane with such success, uniting a warm sympathy for the persons he writes about, with, in the last resort, a true artistic detachment.

—Jack Lindsay

---

**ALGREN, Nelson.** American. Born in Detroit, Michigan, 28 March 1909. Educated at the University of Illinois, Urbana, 1927–31. Served in the United States Army Medical Corps, 1942–45. Worked as a migratory worker, carnival shill and as part-owner of a gas station, 1931–35; for the Works Progress Administration (WPA), 1936–40; for the Venereal Disease Program of the Chicago Board of Health, 1941–42. Editor, with Jack Conroy *q.v.*, of *The New Anvil*, Chicago, 1939–41. Recipient: National Institute of Arts and Letters grant, 1947; Newberry Library Fellowship, 1947; National Book Award, 1950. Address: 1958 West Evergreen, Chicago, Illinois 60622, U.S.A.

PUBLICATIONS

Novels

*Somebody in Boots.* New York, Vanguard Press, 1935.
*Never Come Morning.* New York, Harper, 1942.
*The Man with the Golden Arm.* New York, Doubleday, 1949; London, Spearman, 1959.
*A Walk on the Wild Side.* New York, Farrar Straus, 1955.

Short Stories

*The Neon Wilderness.*   New York, Doubleday, 1946; London, Deutsch, 1965.

Uncollected Short Stories

"All Through the Night", in *Playboy* (Chicago), April 1957.
"Father and Son Cigar", in *Playboy* (Chicago), December 1962.
"Moon of the Arfy-Darfy", in *Saturday Evening Post* (New York), 26 September 1964.
"A Ticket on Skoronski", in *Saturday Evening Post* (New York), 5 November 1966.
"Home to Shawneetown", in *Atlantic* (Boston), August 1968.
"Decline and Fall of Dingdong Daddyland", in *Commentary* (New York), September 1969.
"Get All the Money", in *Playboy* (Chicago), June 1970.
"Swan Lake Re-swum", in *Audience* (Cambridge, Massachusetts), 1970.
"Seven Feet Down and Creeping", in *New Orleans Review*, 1970.
"White Mice and Mama-Sans Take It All", in *Rolling Stone* (San Francisco), no. 83, 1971.
"The Last Carousel", in *Playboy* (Chicago), 1972.

Other

*Chicago: City on the Make.*   New York, Doubleday, 1951.
*Who Lost an American? Being a Guide to the Seamier Sides of New York City, Inner London, Paris, Dublin, Barcelona, Seville, Almeria, Istanbul, Crete and Chicago, Illinois.*   New York, Macmillan, 1962.
*Conversations with Nelson Algren*, with H. E. F. Donohue.   New York, Hill and Wang, 1963.
*Notes from a Sea-Diary: Hemingway All the Way.*   New York, Putnam, 1965.

Editor, *Nelson Algren's Own Book of Lonesome Monsters.*   New York, Lancer, 1960.

Manuscript Collection: Ohio State University, Columbus.

Critical Studies: "Nelson Algren: The Iron Sanctuary" by Maxwell Geismar, in *English Journal* (Champaign, Illinois), March 1953; "Nelson Algren" by George Bluestone, in *Western Review* (Denver), Autumn 1957; "Perspectives: Is It Out of Control?" by Ralph J. Gleason, in *Rolling Stone* (San Francisco), 6 August 1970.

*             *             *

Nelson Algren is a tragic writer, in the sense that his main theme is the effort man makes to escape from, while really fulfilling, an implacable fate. "Knew I'd never get to be twenty-one anyhow," says Lefty, at the end of *Never Come Morning*, Algren's first major novel. He is a left-handed pitcher and boxer from a poor Polish neighbourhood in Chicago. His only evening of innocent happiness is when he takes his childhood sweetheart to a carnival. For a moment they rise in the Ferris wheel above "the troubled streets that led to the abandoned beaches, the for-rent signs above overnight hotels and furnished basement rooms, moving trolleys and rising bridges: the cagework city, beneath a coalsmoke sky."
Then the cage of their environment closes them in. With the complicity of her boy friend,

who is ashamed of his love, Steffi is the victim of a gang-shag more authentically horrifying than anything in Faulkner. Although she is made into a prostitute, she endures her fate with mute helplessness, without betraying her betrayer. There is a tenderness in Algren for the waif who, like Steffi or Molly-O in *The Man with the Golden Arm*, endures the unendurable. As even the hood who is taking her to the whorehouse reflects, "a woman had to go to the wars to get mean. They weren't born that way, any of them."

But under the self-protective toughness something in Lefty cannot accept what he has done: while she is being raped in his gang's headquarters, he kills an outsider who joins the queue. This murder follows him for the rest of his short life, and although he achieves a boyhood ambition, and beats the black Honeyboy Tucker, a former state light heavyweight champion, the precinct captain is waiting outside the dressing room of the victor with the manacles.

> And that was what, at heart, he wanted. He wanted it so, because of what he had made of Steffi R. He had snuck off with a bottle in his hand while the one human he loved had been turned into a loveless thing. And there was in his nature, so deep that it had never before been sounded, the conviction that no punishment was too great for such a betrayal.

Two things relieve this relentless vision. There is the realistic detail; as well as the group rape, the prize fight is probably the most brutally professional in American literature, better even than Jack London or Hemingway; there is no attempt to disguise what is happening as man fights man for the spoils. "Tucker came in snorting blindly into his glove, in a crouch to ease his pain. And got his own right in, fast, four inches below the waistband and two feet into the groin. Got it in close up, from the floor, with three full feet of swing behind it."

And then there is the poetry of his style, which is partly based on that exactness, but also on an insistent rhythm; as with Thomas Wolfe, there is a constant melancholy echo of image and phrase. It is as if all his work was one long lament for the betrayed heart: "the only really ugly thing on earth is the death that comes before true death comes." And in each successive work the message becomes clearer, until in *A Walk on the Wild Side* it achieves the simplicity of a blues song.

*The Man with the Golden Arm* gained a false notoriety as one of the first books on drug addiction but as Algren himself has admitted, he was never an expert on drugs, only on human unhappiness. The *milieu* is again that of small time criminals, older and more battered this time, hungry for affection. The friendship, or rather interdependence, of dealer Frankie Machine and the sneak thief called Sparrow is one of the central examples of this—what Sparrow does not know about is the Monkey on his friend's back, the morphine habit which is the only thing that can reconcile him to his loveless marriage. His wife blames him for the accident that has made her an invalid, and sometimes he accepts the blame, but the truth is that she is mainly concerned about losing him and refuses to be healed in order to exploit his guilt.

The death of their love is paralleled by a physical death, the murder of the pusher, Nifty Louie. And again, as in the previous book, this crime prevents the main character from a second chance at love and life; Frankie's affair with Molly-O is doomed, though it suggests how things could be. Instead Frankie commits suicide, his girl friend goes to jail, his wife to an asylum. Only Blind Pig, who has taken over as pusher, and helps the police in a betrayal, can be said to thrive in such a base world.

At first sight, *A Walk on the Wild Side* seems the lightest of Algren's novels. Instead of the night world of Chicago, the sleazy little brothel in *Never Come Morning*, and the police line-up that begins *The Man with the Golden Arm*, we have the picturesque energy of New Orleans in the Thirties, a hustler's paradise. Dove Linkhorn, a poor white from Texas, earns his living as the stud in a peepshow; as with drugs, Algren was hip to pornography long before it became his nation's delight. "Certainly no reasonable God would hold a grudge against a girl for earning her bread by the sweat of the sex with which He had blessed her." Mama's brothel is as colourful as anything in Southern fiction, and the little pimp Finnerty, who knows how to handle her, and her girls, is treated with grim respect. "Of women he asked no favour. They had no more side for a man to be on than so many fishes in the stream."

Like Blind Pig, Finnerty thrives because he cares for no one, and knows exactly what he is doing. But retribution falls on Dove, as though naivete was the worst sin of all in a fallen world. He gets smashed in a barroom brawl, and when we last see him he is a blind wreck, fumbling his way home to his first love. His final message, though, contradicts Finnerty's though we are not told how it is received. "'If God made anything better than a girl,' Dove thought, 'He sure kept it to Himself.'" The whole book is a kind of hymn to women, and a period when "panties of purple and bras of black, silver G strings and dappled halters hung on the clotheslines in a kind of joint-tog jungle still as all Brazil."

Since these three major efforts, Algren has written little, except to exploit his extraordinary charm as a personality in travelogues like *Who Lost an American?* Perhaps he feels his work is done, and one notices the way he husbands his themes, so that his favourite scenes and stories reappear in the patchwork of his novels. So the Lefty of "Bottle of Milk for Mother" becomes the main character of *Never Come Morning*, the little punk of "Poor Man's Pennies" is transformed into Sparrow in *The Man with the Golden Arm*, the powerful legless cripple of that most horrific story, "The Face on the Barroom Floor", meets a different end after he destroys Dove Linkhorn. Algren's vision was formed early, during the depression, but it goes beyond period to a general compassion for man in a world based on exploitation.

—John Montague

---

ALI, Ahmed.  Pakistani.  Born in Delhi, India, 1 July 1910. Educated at Aligarh University; Lucknow University, B.A. 1931, M.A. 1932. Married Bilquees Jehan in 1950; has four children. Lecturer, Lucknow University, 1932–33, 1936–41; Professor, Agra College, 1933–34; Lecturer, Allahabad University, 1934–36; Professor, Presidency College, Calcutta, 1945–47; British Council Visiting Professor, National Central University, Nanking, 1946–48. Representative and Director, BBC, New Delhi, 1941–44. Director of Foreign Publicity, Pakistan Government, Karachi, 1948–49; Counsellor and Chargé d'Affaires, Pakistan Foreign Service, in Karachi, Peking and Rabat, 1950–60. Since 1966, Adviser to Indus Chemical and Alkalis Ltd., Karachi, and since 1971, Chief Adviser to Advertising and Public Relations Agency, Karachi; since 1970, Managing Director of Lomen Fabrics Ltd., Karachi. Editor, *Indian Writing*, London, 1939–41; *Tomorrow*, Bombay, 1941–42; *PEN Miscellany*, Karachi, 1948–50. Proprietor, Akrash Press, in Delhi, 1940–47, and in Karachi since 1963. Address: 21 A. Faran, Hyder Ali Road, Karachi 5, Pakistan.

PUBLICATIONS

Novels

  *Twilight in Delhi*.  London, Hogarth Press, 1941; New York and London, Oxford
    University Press, 1966.
  *Ocean of Night*.  London, Peter Owen, 1964.

Short Stories (in Urdu)

*Angaray.*   Lucknow, privately printed, 1932.
*Sholay.*   Lahore, Maktaba Urdu, 1934.
*Hamari Gali.*   Delhi, Akrash Press, 1940.
*Qaidkhana.*   Delhi, Akrash Press, 1942.
*Maut Se Pahlay.*   Delhi, Akrash Press, 1945.


Uncollected Short Stories

"When the Funeral Was Crossing the Bridge", in *Lucknow University Journal*, 1929.
"A Stormy Night of Rains", in *Humayun* (Lahore), January 1931.
"Our Lane", in *New Writing* (London), 1936.
"Before Death", in *New Directions 15*.   New York, New Directions, 1956.


Plays

*Land of Twilight* (produced Lucknow, 1931).
*Break the Chains* (produced Lucknow, 1932).


Verse

*Flaming Earth: Selected Poems from Indonesia.*   Karachi, Friends of Indonesia, 1949.
*Purple Gold Mountain.*   London, Keep Sake Press, 1960.
*Bulbul and the Rose.*   Karachi, Jamia, 1962.
*Ghalib: Selected Poems.*   Rome, Ismeo, 1969.


Other

*Mr. Eliot's Penny-World of Dreams.*   Lucknow, Lucknow University, 1941.
*Muslim China.*   Karachi, Institute of International Affairs, 1949.
*Problem of Style and Technique in Ghalib.*   Karachi, American Centre, 1969.


Critical Study: "The Novels of Ahmed Ali" by Laurence Brander, in *Journal of Commonwealth Literature* (Leeds, Yorkshire), July 1967.


Ahmed Ali comments:

Starting with poetry and belles lettres as a young student of 16, the writer moved on at 19 to a Credo of tragic unbelief in a sad unreal world in short stories like "When the Funeral Was Crossing the Bridge", side by side with poems filled with the anguish of adolescence. Simultaneously he was discovering the realities of life and the degrading state of the nation, the social milieu in India of the Simon Commission and the Non-Cooperation Movement of the late 20's and early 30's, which finds its first affirmative expression in the short story "A Stormy Night of Rains". This set him on a career of writing fiction, and led him to found, in association with two friends, the Progressive Writers Movement of India in 1932, and the publication the same year of the now historic and then shocking and banned book of short stories in Urdu—*Angaray* (Burning Coals). Four volumes of short stories followed at irregular intervals, and the publication of the short story "Our Lane", a story giving a cross-section of life in a lane in Delhi, his home town, in which the lane itself becomes a living character with its landmarks of shops and trees and cats and people, and all that happens to them therein. Anyone wanting to understand the writer must read this as the most significant introduction to his work and themes and technique, although from the last point of view his story "Before Death" is equally revealing.

His now most highly considered novel, *Twilight in Delhi*, depicts the life of two generations during the first two decades of this century, going back to 1857 and ending with the start of the National Movement in 1921. On the ideological plane the novel presents the decline of feudalism and, as he wrote in the introduction to the 1966 edition of the novel,

> decay of a whole culture, a particular mode of thought and living, now dead and gone already right before our eyes. Seldom is one allowed to see a pageant of History whirl past and partake in it too. Already, since its publication, the Delhi of the novel has changed beyond recognition. For its culture had been nourished and born within the city walls which lie demolished today; and the distinction between the language of the city and the outside world has disappeared in the rattle of many tongues, even as the homogeneity of its life has been engulfed by the tide of democracy. The British had only built a new Delhi outside the city walls. The present rulers have removed the last relic on which the old culture could have taken a stand within the moat-encircled ground. Thus, the prophecy of the book has come true: Seven Delhis had fallen, and the eighth has gone the way of its predecessors yet to be built and demolished again.

*Ocean of Night*, the writer's second novel, deals with life between the Wars and its complex problems, symbolically set against the background of Lucknow, artificial and fleshly, decaying before it was ripe; clash between the feudal and the modern spirit with resultant decay and defeatist violence. The feeling heart, which was still alive in the world of *Twilight in Delhi*, here displays one half of it as atrophied and dead, the other half searching for it and failing in the utter confusion of not knowing what it wants or is looking for. As Laurence Brander has concluded in his essay on the writer:

> It could be a sermon to all Muslims on the besetting sin of pride, while for the rest of us it is an expression of the sense and accord we experience when we stand in the Mosques and tombs of Islam. In the outer world, the Muslim search is for the Friend and for the mystical experience of reconciliation with life.

Summing up, Brander concludes: "These novels give us a most memorable view of the rich and splendid world of the Muslim mind."

In the third novel of the trilogy the writer had planned at the inception of the first—*Of Rats and Diplomats*, still unpublished, alas—the story of man is taken up after the Second World War and the consequent loss of values, the mess that man has made of life. The mind has developed, but the heart has died in the madness of power and greed for self. Only a faint, far echo is heard, and even that in memory of something undefined in a world from which the big idea has fled. Symptomatically, the setting of the novel is unrecognisable, and the story of diplomats centring round a barter deal for cats, is enacted against a background of international suspicion and intrigue, to end on a note of high tragedy and satire.

In his verse the writer had come to believe, as early as the 40's, in the need for a mythology of Poetry which objectifies and universalises emotion, so much so that even such a sharp writer as Han Suyin was led to mistake his poems, dealing with the most intimate personal experiences and current events, for those written by some Chinese poet of long ago.

On the other hand, in his criticism the writer has believed in unravelling the mind of his subject and critically analysing the currents and cross-sections of history and motives, and wedding them to the subject of criticism. His introduction to *Ghalib* is as typical of his method as it is illustrative of his interest in his culture and the poetry of Muslim India. He likes to interpret a civilisation and mode of thought, recapture the taste, as sharp as of a gourmet, of the past—not so much of the past as of the present through its lingering relish which still persists in spite of the changes wrought by Time and the false gods of the West and America who sit enthroned to preside over the destinies of the East through a haze of foreign mist and obfuscated minds lost between two worlds, one dead, the other alien and unknown or largely misunderstood. He is oriental to the core, though by taste and medium of expression an occidental, yet only in a bilingual way.

*        *        *

The Muslim civilization of India is centred in Delhi and Agra and Lucknow. Delhi and Agra provide the great monuments. Delhi and Lucknow provide the language and the poetry. In its decline the poetry is drenched in remembrance of things past and this agony before the British went was mingled with prophecy of their going and hope that the ancient Moghul splendour would be revived. In the event, the memories have become shadows of shades and the exquisitely civilized Muslim exiles live under the protection of the fighting men of the north.

The two novels of Ahmed Ali are the finest celebration we have in novel form of the nostalgia for former glories and that accompanying Muslim belief in the vanity of earthly life. They are expressions of the pain of our human condition and of the agonized sense of the transitory nature of its happiness. They celebrate aspects of Muslim life in two of the great centres of Muslim culture. The Delhi novel came first. In time, it is set in the early decades of the century. From the old house in a by-lane of Old Delhi we go out to see the Great Durbar held by the King-Emperor in 1911, we see Delhi's reactions during the 1914 War, we glimpse the horror of the influenza epidemic in 1919 which decimated the population and we hear of the political unrest which swept across Northern India in 1920. But these things are on the fringe. At the centre is an old Muslim feudal family, generation following generation in gentle, dignified decay. The essential atmosphere of the novel is of the emptiness of the days as life passes by: the want of meaning. It is a special aspect of the despair which saturates the Gangetic Plain—the earth and air stale with the pain of existence, every atom of dust anguished and exhausted after being so many times vegetable, animal and human.

The story outline is simple and sad. Not tragic; it does not attempt that dimension. Two young people fall in love and for a time their union is thwarted—the girl is of a mere Moghul family, Asian from beyond the Himalayas, while the boy is Arabic, straight from the great families. The difficulties are overcome but eventually his love falters and he is unfaithful. The girl pines but before she dies their love is renewed. The value of the novel is in what is embroidered round this simple tale. The father's delight in the great Delhi pastime of pigeon flying, life in the zenana, the ceremonies at the wedding and the descriptions of all the people in the lanes who must play their part. It is a picture of energetic life and brilliant colour, the energy and colour which make life tolerable with its aching background of despair. Then later, the blows of fate, inevitable and cruel. On one side, the Muslim exuberance; on the other, the acceptance of fate: "Who can meddle in the affairs of God?" *Twilight in Delhi* is the most imaginative picture we have of the old Muslim life in Delhi which disappeared when the British went away; it is a fragment of Muslim history written with the pride of deep affection.

The second novel, *Ocean of Night*, was drafted soon afterwards though put aside and published much later. Instead of the colourful vigour of the first novel we have the mood appropriate to Lucknow, where the story is set. Again we have the Muslim celebration, but this time of the Muslim ideas of love and peace and friendship. The action is sordid, taking place in the house of a dissolute Nawab and the house of his mistress, an accomplished dancing girl. Lucknow is famous as a training ground of courtesans and we see the dancing master and the pimps, and the protector being bled of all his possessions. Sordid, the balancing excess to the expression of another excess, the intensity of mystical Islamic thinking. This more interesting theme is presented as the private search of a Muslim intellectual, a lawyer, for the traditional spiritual fulfilment of Islam. The intensity of this emotion is intellectual, a vivid glimpse of the mystical core of Islam. Religions normally reflect man's search for peace and harmony and in his search this Muslim lawyer had a vision in which the inhabitants of his dream tell him that peace is both love and glory, that friendship and love are what matter and the Muslim must subdue his natural pride for he will experience them only in humility. So are we reconciled with God and man. In these two novels a distinguished Urdu poet offers imaginative glimpses of the grace and the glory of Islam as it flourished once on the Gangetic Plain.

—Laurence Brander

---

**ALLEN, Walter (Ernest).**  British.  Born in Birmingham, 23 February 1911. Educated at Birmingham University, B.A. (honours) in English 1932. Married Peggy Yorke Joy in 1944; has four children. Assistant Master, King Edward's Grammar School, Aston, Birmingham, 1934; Visiting Lecturer in English, University of Iowa, Iowa City, 1935; Features Editor, Cater's News Service, Birmingham, 1935–37; Assistant Technical Officer, Wrought Light Alloys Development Association, Birmingham, 1943–45; Margaret Pilcher Visiting Professor of English, Coe College, Cedar Rapids, Iowa, 1955–56; Assistant Literary Editor, 1959–60, and Literary Editor, 1960–61, *New Statesman*, London; Visiting Professor of English, Vassar College, Poughkeepsie, New York, 1963–64, University of Kansas, Lawrence, 1967, and University of Washington, Seattle, 1967. Since 1968, Professor and Chairman of English Studies, New University of Ulster, Coleraine. Berg Professor of English, New York University, 1970–71. Fellow, Royal Society of Literature, 1960. Address: 6 Canonbury Square, London N.1, England; or, The New University of Ulster, Coleraine, Northern Ireland.

PUBLICATIONS

Novels

  *Innocence Is Drowned*.  London, Joseph, 1938.
  *Blind Man's Ditch*.  London, Joseph, 1939.
  *Living Space*.  London, Joseph, 1940.
  *Rogue Elephant*.  London, Joseph, and New York, Morrow, 1946.
  *Dead Man over All*.  London, Joseph, 1950; as *Square Peg*, New York, Morrow, 1951.
  *All in a Lifetime*.  London, Joseph, 1959; as *Threescore and Ten*, New York, Morrow, 1959.

Other

  *The Black Country* (topography).  London, Elek, 1946.
  *Arnold Bennett*.  London, Home and Van Thal, 1948; Denver, Swallow, 1949.
  *Reading a Novel*.  London, Phoenix House, 1948; revised edition, 1956.
  *Joyce Cary*.  London, Longman, 1953; revised edition, 1963, 1971.

*The English Novel: A Short Critical History*.   London, Phoenix House, 1954; New York, Dutton, 1955.

*Six Great Novelists: Defoe, Fielding, Scott, Dickens, Stevenson, Conrad*.   London, Hamish Hamilton, 1955.

*The Novel Today*.   London, Longman, 1955; revised edition, 1960.

*George Eliot*.   New York, Macmillan, 1964; London, Weidenfeld and Nicolson, 1965.

*Tradition and Dream: The English and American Novel from the Twenties to Our Time*. London, Phoenix House, 1964; as *The Modern Novel in Britain and the United States*, New York, Dutton, 1964.

*The British Isles in Colour*.   London, Batsford, and New York, Viking Press, 1965.

*The Urgent West: An Introduction to the Idea of the United States*.   London, Baker, 1969; as *The Urgent West: The American Dream and Modern Man*, New York, Dutton, 1969.

*Transatlantic Crossing: American Visitors to Britain and British Visitors to America in the Nineteenth Century*.   London, Heinemann, and New York, Morrow, 1971.

Editor, *Writers on Writing*.   London, Phoenix House, 1948; New York, Dutton, 1953.

Walter Allen comments:

My first three novels seem now to have been the outcome of a single impulse, or rather a twin impulse. One side of it was to set down the nature of working-class life as I saw it all about me in the Midland city of Birmingham in a time of industrial depression, the rise of fascism and the threat of war. To this extent, these three novels are very much of the late 1930's. The other side of the impulse was formal: I was concerned with economy, with limits, with unity, almost indeed the Unities, believing that the most intense writing came from a narrow but powerful focus. I found myself unable to write fiction during the war and turned to the writing of criticism, and my first postwar novel, *Rogue Elephant*, turned out to be very different from my earlier work, though it had formal elements in common. I set out to write a work almost of classical comedy. At this time and for a long time to come I was caught up with the novel, as reviewer, publisher's reader and as a historian of the form, to the almost total exclusion of other interests, and this, I am sure, had its consequences. One was that I came increasingly to value what might be called the historical aspects of the novel. I was conscious, writing *Dead Man over All*, that I was attempting a number of disparate things. I wanted to show the influence on individuals of history, heredity, family tradition and so on; to say something about what seemed to me the changing nature of industrialism; to describe life in a factory geared to production for war during war (and that itself would be a contribution of a sort to the history of industry and the recent war); and also to depict a man in what I called an impossible position, impossible because willed for him, as it were, by others, by tradition. All the same, in that novel, I largely retained the narrative pattern of my earlier books. I broke away from it in *All in a Lifetime*. Writing that novel, I was conscious that I was trying to do several things simultaneously: to trace the rise of the British Labour Party through a working man in some sort representative, to adumbrate the growth of a city through half a century, to show the rise to political and cultural awareness of the working class. There was also a personal factor that was probably fundamental to these: I wanted to celebrate my father, who became the model in the novel of my "in some sort representative" working man. But I had to satisfy myself that he might have written what I have him write in the novel—it is in fact the novel—and this dictated the narrative technique of the long letter/Defoe-esque pseudo-autobiographical novel. This emerged only after many false starts.

I don't think my novels have appeared to be particularly playful works; but in the writing of them it is the element of play that I have found most pleasurable, the making of a mimic world through the arrangement, both studied and "accidental", of one's characters. I wouldn't, though, have found much point in the play if it hadn't resulted from time to time in what seemed an acceptable paradigm of the real world.

*       *       *

The title of Walter Allen's novel, *Innocence Is Drowned*, comes from Yeats's well-known lines beginning: "Things fall apart; the centre cannot hold" in which the poet goes on to say that:

> The blood-dimmed tide is loosed, and everywhere
> The ceremony of innocence is drowned.

Walter Allen had in mind not only the approach of the Second World War but also the manner in which his characters came to recognise not only the cruelty and indifference of others but also the cruelty and indifference in themselves. The novel can be seen as their attempt to come to terms with reality.

*Innocence Is Drowned*, Mr. Allen's first novel, has presumably his home-town of Birmingham for its setting, although no name is given to the place in the book. He introduces us to a working-class family. It is one in which the father, Dick Gardiner, is conscientious, hard-working, politically committed: a man who made the mistake of setting up as a master toolmaker instead of remaining a secure employee. The novel—like *Dead Man over All* and *Living Space*—covers only a few days in time: Tuesday, Wednesday and Thursday.

The narrative is largely conveyed through the minds of Mr. Gardiner, his wife and three sons, Ralph, Eric and Sydney. One forms a vivid picture of each character and a clear impression of his (or her) relationships both within and outside the family. The actual events are trivial enough—for instance, the detention at school of the youngest boy causes quite a bit of fuss in the family circle—but they are skilfully built up into a convincing re-creation of pre-War life in the Midlands.

*Innocence Is Drowned* marked the emergence of a writer who has made more impact, perhaps, as a literary critic (he has a specialised knowledge of the English novel from its beginnings to the present day) than as a novelist. It shows, too, how Mr. Allen, while not standing aside from the Left-wing current of his time, knew from the start that propaganda and art are ill-assorted bedfellows.

*Rogue Elephant* represents a considerable advance on the earlier novels. The style is more supple and fluent, and contains less pedestrian descriptive writing. Mr. Allen, like all true artists, obviously learned from his first experiments in his craft as well as from the twentieth-century masters about whom he has written so perceptively.

The central character of *Rogue Elephant* is called Henry Ashley, a fat, clever but unintegrated young man who ambles through the novel, a schemer with a soft core in his personality. This is how he looks at himself: "Mr. Henry Ashley . . . saw himself as the enemy, as miching mallecho which means mischief, as the test-tube of cholera bacillus that is broken into the water supply." For a while Ashley wreaks havoc among two girls (they are cousins) in an upper-class household in Devonshire. Ashley lives for and through his writing. A rising young novelist and critic, he copes with life through ideas and word-spinning. He keeps reality at arm's length. Henry Ashley comes across as a real person, not just as a target for satirical rifle-practice.

Walter Allen's most solid achievement in the novel is undisputably *All in a Lifetime*. It came out, in 1959, at a time when regionalism was beginning to be a potent force in post-War English fiction. That same year saw the publication, for instance, of Keith Waterhouse's *Billy Liar* and Alan Sillitoe's *The Loneliness of the Long-Distance Runner*. Brash, ill-mannered young working-class heroes (or, rather, anti-heroes) without religious, political or moral conviction became fashionable. Walter Allen, an older man than writers such as John Braine, Stan Barstow and the others, stood foursquare against the new gospel of revolt for its own sake.

Billy Ashted, the narrator of *All in a Lifetime*, is in his middle seventies. He looks back calmly on his life and the changes he has lived through. He is portrayed as a man with a strong political faith—a kind of substitute, it may be, for religion—a man who tended to look outward rather than into his own ego. Mr. Allen accurately analyses the place held by religion in the Black Country when Billy Ashted was young: the Nonconformist chapel where the preacher was a "great populariser" who "talked of new ideas and movements of ideas in such a way that your curiosity was stimulated to find out about them at first hand." Opposed to the plain services and Christian Socialism of the chapel, there is the High Anglicanism that repels Billy Ashted because it smacks of Popery and aristocracy.

In a comment on the novel Mr. Allen says that Billy Ashted is based on his father who, like Ashted, was "a working silversmith in Birmingham all his life and never earning at any time more than £5 a week from his craft." Nevertheless, Mr. Allen's father "had a very considerable learning in philosophy and, in the opinion of people much better qualified than me to judge, had genuine ability as a philosopher." Billy Ashted's brief migration to to the U.S. was paralleled by Mr. Allen's own father's experience in that country. The author tells us that his father had lived in Philadelphia whereas Billy Ashted goes to New York for the good reason that the novelist is more familiar with the topography of New York.

Mr. Allen has two aims in writing the novel: first, he wanted to write a chronicle novel in which social change would be explored and the rise of the Labour Party outlined; and second, he wished to write about an old man and so project himself "imaginatively into the experience of old age as it faces death". Already he had, in *Rogue Elephant* and *Dead Man over All*, drawn the portraits of very old men: but they were minor characters and he was determined to essay a major portrait. This he has done with great success, taking care to balance the essentially contemplative Billy Ashted with the more active and politically committed George Thompson.

The novel consists of a "letter" Billy Ashted writes to his sister at a time of family crisis: the ostensible reason for it is to discover how to cope with the present difficulty. He feels this can be achieved by dredging up incidents and people from his long life. Thus past and present are intermingled, and the novel takes on a reality and naturalness it might lack had it been written in the third person.

*All in a Lifetime* did not create much of a stir in the literary world when it appeared. Unlike other novels of the time with a strong regional flavour it has not been filmed or adapted for television. What it lacks in newsworthiness it makes up in sincerity and warmth and, not least, in sheer skill. It will probably be more durable than those novels that have a hard, glittering shell but are soft and cold at the centre.

—Robert Greacen

---

**ALUKO, Timothy (Mofolorunso).** Nigerian. Born in Ilesha, 14 June 1918. Educated at Government College, Ibadan, 1933–38; University of London, 1946–50, B.Sc. in Engineering and Diploma in Town Planning 1950; University of Newcastle upon Tyne (UNESCO Fellow), 1968–69; M.Sc. in Engineering 1969. Married Janet Adebisi Fajemisin in 1950; has six children. Engineer, Public Works Department, Lagos, 1943–46; Executive Engineer, Public Works Department, Ibadan and Lagos, 1950–56; Town Engineer, Lagos Town Council, 1956–60; Director and Permanent Secretary, Ministry of Works and Transport, Western Nigeria, 1960–66; Senior Lecturer, University of Ibadan, 1966. Since 1966, Senior Research Fellow in Municipal Engineering at the University of Lagos. Fellow, Institution of Civil Engineers, Institution of Municipal Engineers, and Nigerian Society of Engineers. O.B.E. (Officer, Order of the British Empire), 1963; O.O.N. (Officer, Order of the Niger), 1964. Address: Faculty of Engineering, University of Lagos, Lagos, Nigeria.

PUBLICATIONS

Novels

One Man, One Wife. Lagos, Nigerian Printing and Publishing Company, 1959;
    London, Heinemann, 1960; New York, Humanities Press, 1968.
One Man, One Matchet. London, Heinemann, 1964; Mystic, Connecticut, Verrey,
    1965.
Kinsman and Foreman. London, Heinemann, and New York, Humanities Press, 1966.
Chief the Honourable Minister. London, Heinemann, 1970.
His Worshipful Majesty. London, Heinemann, 1972.


Uncollected Short Story

"The New Engineer", in African New Writing. London, Lutterworth Press, 1947.


Critical Study: section of Long Drums and Cannons by Margaret Laurence, London,
Macmillan, 1968.

*     *     *

Timothy Aluko stands in the second rank of African novelists. Though he was one of
the first Nigerians to write full-length fiction in English, his work lacks the high moral
seriousness and technical resourcefulness that have come to characterize the contemporary
Nigerian novel. His twenty-five year literary career has been marked by slow, steady artistic
progress, but it is doubtful that he will ever write a masterpiece, for his tendencies toward
superficial characterization, loose organization, and stilted expression seem to be very
deeply ingrained. He is a competent but crude craftsman who has never managed to master
the subtler tools of his trade.

Aluko's forte is light satire, and he frequently wrings humour out of situations of cultural,
religious or political conflict. His first novel, One Man, One Wife, which deals with problems
of polygamy and church politics in a newly Christianized African village, pokes fun at
pagan and convert alike. His second, One Man, One Matchet, exposes the machinations of
an unscrupulous politician who takes advantage of the gullibility of his people and challenges the authority of a young African District Officer in order to thrust himself into a
position of power and wealth. Kinsman and Foreman dramatizes the difficulties of a Nigerian
civil engineer who has the misfortune of being assigned to work in his home town, a post
which leaves him easy prey to the financial demands of his relatives and the local Church.
And Chief the Honourable Minister, his most recent work, tells the story of an honest M.P.
who is destroyed by the corruption and dishonesty of his subordinates. In each of these
novels Aluko ridicules the frailties and imperfections of pretentious officials whose energies
are devoted to exploiting their fellows. He delights in revealing the inefficiency of government bureaucracies, the incompetence of the men at the top, and the pettiness and gross
ambition of those at the bottom who are striving to climb upward. He is at his wittiest
when writing civil service satire.

What vitiates the force of Aluko's humour is that he is content with merely laughing at
his world. Since his laughter contains no undertones of anguish or outrage, it rings hollow
and makes no lasting impact on the reader. Aluko is a critic without a troubled conscience,
a tickling gadfly without a sting. It is the superficiality of his social protest, not the occasional clumsiness of his craftsmanship, that identifies him as a second-rate writer. It is hard
to take such a light-hearted comedian seriously.

—Bernth Lindfors

**AMBLER, Eric.**  British.   Born in London, 28 June 1909. Educated at Colfe's Grammar School; London University. Served in the Royal Artillery, 1940–46: Assistant Director of Army Kinematography, 1944–46. Married Louise Crombie in 1939; Joan Harrison, 1958. Engineering apprentice, 1928; advertising copywriter, 1928–37; director of an advertising agency, 1937–38. Recipient: Edgar Allan Poe Award, 1964. Address: Chemin de l'Ile de Salagnon 1, 1815 Clarens, Switzerland.

PUBLICATIONS

Novels

*The Dark Frontier*.   London, Hodder and Stoughton, 1936.
*Uncommon Danger*.   London, Hodder and Stoughton, 1937; as *Background to Danger*, New York, Knopf, 1937.
*Epitaph for a Spy*.   London, Hodder and Stoughton, 1938; New York, Knopf, 1952.
*Cause for Alarm*.   London, Hodder and Stoughton, 1938; New York, Knopf, 1939.
*The Mask of Dimitrios*.   London, Hodder and Stoughton, 1939; as *A Coffin for Dimitrios*, New York, Knopf, 1939.
*Journey into Fear*.   London, Hodder and Stoughton, and New York, Knopf, 1940.
*Skytip*, with Charles Rodda (as Eliot Reed).   New York, Doubleday, 1950.
*Tender to Danger*, with Charles Rodda (as Eliot Reed).   New York, Doubleday, 1951.
*Judgment on Deltchev*.   London, Hodder and Stoughton, and New York, Knopf, 1951.
*The Schirmer Inheritance*.   London, Heinemann, and New York, Knopf, 1953.
*The Maras Affair*, with Charles Rodda (as Eliot Reed).   New York, Doubleday, 1953.
*Charter to Danger*, with Charles Rodda (as Eliot Reed).   London, Collins, 1954.
*The Night-Comers*.   London, Heinemann, 1956; as *State of Siege*, New York, Knopf, 1956.
*Passage of Arms*.   London, Heinemann, 1959; New York, Knopf, 1960.
*The Light of Day*.   London, Heinemann, 1962; New York, Knopf, 1963.
*A Kind of Anger*.   London, Heinemann, and New York, Atheneum, 1964.
*Dirty Story*.   London, Bodley Head, and New York, Atheneum, 1967.
*The Intercom Conspiracy*.   New York, Atheneum, 1969; London, Weidenfeld and Nicolson, 1970.
*The Green Circle Incident*.   London, Weidenfeld and Nicolson, and New York, Atheneum, 1972.

Plays

Screenplays: *The Way Ahead*, 1944; *United States*, 1945; *The October Man*, 1948; *One Woman's Story* (*The Passionate Friends*), 1948; *Highly Dangerous*, 1951; *The Magic Box*, 1952; *Gigolo and Gigolette*, in *Encore*, 1952; *The Card* (*The Promoter*), 1952; *Roughshoot*, 1953; *The Cruel Sea*, 1953; *Lease of Life*, 1955; *The Purple Plain*, 1955; *Yangtse Incident*, 1957; *A Night to Remember*, 1959; *The Wreck of the Mary Deare*, 1960; *Topkapi*, 1964; *Love Hate Love*, 1970.

Other

*The Ability to Kill and Other Pieces*.   London, Bodley Head, 1963.

Editor, *To Catch a Spy: An Anthology of Favourite Spy Stories*.   London, Bodley Head, 1964; New York, Atheneum, 1965.

Manuscript Collection: Boston University.

Critical Studies: "Eric Ambler Issue" of *Hollins Critic* (Virginia), February 1971 (includes Bibliography).

*     *     *

In Graham Greene's view Eric Ambler is Britain's best thriller writer and there are many reasons for supporting this judgment. The most important is Ambler's capacity for telling a story. He wastes no words; his narrative is economical yet evocative; his grasp of detail matches his control of suspense.

His ability to vary the tempo of a story is subtle. He is a master of reconstruction without boredom. This technique is one of the reasons for the success of an early book, *The Mask of Dimitrios*, where his character Latimer, a detective story writer, becomes obsessed with the mysterious life of a man called Dimitrios whose supposed body he sees in a Turkish morgue. He decides to find out something of the man's odd past, and discovers more and more of his intrigues in many countries, his altering identity, his capacity for murder, pimping, political assassination, drug trafficking, and double crossing. Latimer's own search unfolds slowly, then follows his unwilling cooperation with a former associate and victim of Dimitrios. Gradually the narration speeds up until Latimer is confronted by the fact that Dimitrios is alive, and not only alive but deadly dangerous. The reader is involved in Latimer's searching, in the gradual building up of a biography, in the factual details which reveal the ruthless cleverness of this professional crook. The narration gives us a clear picture of Latimer's thoughts and shows him building up theories about Dimitrios as his knowledge of the man's past increases. Not only does the tension of a search which is progressing steadily despite inevitable setbacks keep the reader's attention clearly focussed on the details of the story, but the relationship between Latimer and the mysterious Mr. Peters also heightens the intensity.

In *The Mask of Dimitrios* no sympathy is evoked for the successful, ruthless criminal, nor indeed for Mr. Peters, the unsuccessful one. There is some alteration of viewpoint in some of Ambler's later novels. For instance, in *Dirty Story*, the main character, Arthur Simpson (he first appeared in *The Light of Day*), is described in an Interpol dossier as interpreter, chauffeur, waiter, pornographer and guide. He is also a pimp, and the story begins with his urgent need for a passport. His stormy interview with Her Majesty's Vice-Consul in Athens leaves us no possibility for illusions about the man whose life, according to the Vice-Consul, is nothing but a long dirty story. Driven by lack of money (with which to buy a Panlibhoncan passport) into acting as a casting director of blue films, he eventually becomes a mercenary in Central Africa. He does not cover himself with credit but eventually escapes to Tangier. One of Ambler's particular skills is a capacity to create modern rogue literature. Morally we despise his character, but such is the power of the tense narration that we follow his adventures with an interest which verges between sympathy, as things go hopelessly wrong, and a wry sense of the sheer comedy latent in Arthur Simpson's incongruous, unscrupulous and ridiculous nature.

The whole unscrupulous world of espionage occupies some of Ambler's attention. In *The Intercom Conspiracy* the protagonist is Theodore Carter, editor of *Intercom*, a journal owned by a retired, somewhat crackpot American general of anti-Communist views. When the general dies the journal is bought by a mysterious Arnold Bloch, who supplies material for the journal which offends west and east alike. Various Intelligence agencies become interested in Carter's sources, and eventually, after being, in the space of a few hours, snatched, interrogated under duress, roughed up, threatened, burgled and gassed, he runs. We know that two clever and unscrupulous colonels have got disgruntled with their role in their respective intelligence services; their plot to play off the major powers and cash in on the situation involves Carter as cats-paw—and, of course, Latimer, Ambler's author character, created much earlier, who is busily writing up the story. The inclusion of Latimer, and his disappearance at the beginning of the book, allows Ambler to tell the story at different levels and from different viewpoints. As usual the tension heightens, the pace speeds up, as the reader becomes sufficiently *au fait* with the complex linkage of events. The story is realistic; its portrayal of the cynicism, indeed the theatrically self-conscious seediness and secrecy of the world of military and political intelligence is convincing in its detail. Ambler's characters have sufficient depth and individuality to match this superb handling of plot. Carter, the journalist, is given to drink; his marriage has broken up earlier; and he is "a man of undoubted ability who takes pleasure in misusing it". Again, the central character is no orthodox hero, and must be taken with blemishes and all: and the two colonels realise he will have dangerous moments. This is a calculated risk and he must take his chance. And take it he does in the respectable surroundings of Geneva.

Ambler has two kinds of story, the simple and the complex. In *The Night-Comers* he unfolds a simple story of an English consulting engineer who is unwillingly involved in a military coup d'etat in an island near Indonesia. He is on his way home, staying for a few days in a friend's flat on the top of the local radio station when the revolution begins. His situation is complicated, indeed endangered by the presence of an Eurasian girl with whom he is having a brief affair when the rebels make this their headquarters. The government forces close in on the radio station, and the novel describes the fighting with skilled economy. Tension is built up, the waiting alternates with hope and despair. Again Ambler's realism keeps the story convincing. At one period, when the Englishman realises that one of the insurgents' leaders is a government agent and that his own life and the girl's are in danger, he is compelled to repair a generator so that the rebel general can broadcast his programme to the outside world. This sudden involvement with the mechanical problems of drying out a generator, damaged by water seeping into the power house after a bomb blast, gives the story an authenticity which is compelling. It adds an extra dimension to the simple narrative by, as it were, describing one aspect of the situation of the insurgents in some depth. The effect of the rising on the hapless spectators, the Englishman and the Eurasian girl, gives the story the necessary counterpointing, and again is used to involve the reader's sympathy, to sharpen and hold his attention.

For Ambler's ability to juggle with a complex plot there is *A Kind of Anger* where a newspaper man becomes involved in the search for a missing girl, the mistress of a murdered Iraqi colonel, a Kurdish conspirator. Here there are rival buyers for the colonel's papers, which the girl possesses, and which the newspaperman, lonely, neurotic, suicidal, eventually helps her to sell. Here the mixture of cross purposes is skilfully woven into the tapestry of the story. This is ingeniously done, and the suspense mounts steadily as the various motives are brought together. While Ambler's plots require sex and violence there is no excess of them, and when they do arise there is a touch of inevitability about them which adds to the conviction his narration has already established in the reader's mind. He is indeed a skilled, professional writer of the highest order.

—A. Norman Jeffares

---

**AMIS, Kingsley (William).** British. Born in London, 16 April 1922. Educated at City of London School; St. John's College, Oxford, M.A. Served in the Royal Corps of Signals, 1942–45. Married Hilary Ann Bardwell in 1948 (marriage dissolved, 1965); Elizabeth Jane Howard, *q.v.*, 1965; has three children. Lecturer in English, University College, Swansea, Wales, 1949–61; Fellow in English, Peterhouse, Cambridge, 1961–63. Visiting Fellow in Creative Writing, Princeton University, New Jersey, 1958–59; Visiting Professor, Vanderbilt University, Nashville, Tennessee, 1967. Recipient: Maugham Award, 1955. Address: c/o A. D. Peters, 10 Buckingham Street, London W.C.2, England.

PUBLICATIONS

Novels

> *Lucky Jim.*   London, Gollancz, and New York, Doubleday, 1954.
> *That Uncertain Feeling.*   London, Gollancz, 1955; New York, Harcourt Brace, 1956.
> *I Like It Here.*   London, Gollancz, and New York, Harcourt Brace, 1958.
> *Take a Girl like You.*   London, Gollancz, 1960; New York, Harcourt Brace, 1961.
> *One Fat Englishman.*   London, Gollancz, 1963; New York, Harcourt Brace, 1964.
> *The Egyptologists*, with Robert Conquest.   London, Cape, 1965; New York, Random House, 1966.
> *The Anti-Death League.*   London, Gollancz, and New York, Harcourt Brace, 1966.
> *Colonel Sun: A James Bond Adventure* (as Robert Markham).   London, Cape, and New York, Harper, 1968.
> *I Want It Now.*   London, Cape, 1968; New York, Harcourt Brace, 1969.
> *The Green Man.*   London, Cape, 1969; New York, Harcourt Brace, 1970.
> *Girl, 20.*   London, Cape, 1971.

Short Stories

> *My Enemy's Enemy.*   London, Gollancz, 1962; New York, Harcourt Brace, 1963.
> *Penguin Modern Stories 11*, with others.   London, Penguin, 1972.

Verse

> *Bright November.*   London, Fortune Press, 1947.
> *A Frame of Mind.*   Reading, Berkshire, Reading School of Art, 1953.
> *A Case of Samples: Poems 1946–1956.*   London, Gollancz, 1956; New York, Harcourt Brace, 1957.
> *The Evans Country.*   Oxford, Fantasy Press, 1962.
> *Penguin Modern Poets 2*, with Dom Moraes and Peter Porter.   London, Penguin, 1962.
> *A Look round the Estate: Poems 1957–1967.*   London, Cape, 1967; New York, Harcourt Brace, 1968.

Other

> *Socialism and the Intellectuals.*   London, Fabian Society, 1957.
> *New Maps of Hell: A Survey of Science Fiction.*   New York, Harcourt Brace, 1960; London, Gollancz, 1961.
> *The James Bond Dossier.*   London, Cape, and New York, New American Library, 1965.
> *Lucky Jim's Politics.*   London, Conservative Political Centre, 1968.
> *What Became of Jane Austen?*   London, Cape, 1970.
>
> Editor, with James Michie, *Oxford Poetry 1949.*   Oxford, Blackwell, 1949.
> Editor, with Robert Conquest, *Spectrum: A Science Fiction Anthology.*   London, Gollancz, 1961; New York, Harcourt Brace, 1962. (and later volumes.)
> Editor, *Selected Short Stories of G. K. Chesterton.*   London, Faber, 1972.

Manuscript Collection (verse): State University of New York, Buffalo.

Kingsley Amis comments:

Anything a novelist (or other artist) says about his own work should be regarded with suspicion. It will depend, at least partly, on his mood, the reception of his latest book, whether the one he is working on at the moment is coming well or badly (actually my own always come well, i.e. slowly but—so far—surely). And a novelist is far from being his own best critic, if only because, as Christopher Isherwood once remarked (in effect), no writer is aware of more than about two-thirds of what he is actually doing and saying. Nor should he be.

Well, anyhow: what I think I am doing is writing novels within the main English-language tradition. That is, trying to tell interesting, believable stories about understandable characters in a reasonably straightforward style: no tricks, no experimental foolery. As the tradition indicates, my subject is the relations between people, and I aim at the traditional wide range of effects: humour, pathos, irony, suspense, description, action, introspection. If I had to find a label for my novels, I should call them serio-comedies, though I like to venture now and again into the kind of genre fiction that has always interested me, and have written a straight espionage thriller, a mainstream novel with espionage and science-fiction elements, and a mainstream novel with a large ghost-story interest. One day I may tackle a straight science-fiction novel and a straight detective story.

What I do not think I am doing, despite what some critics have said, is making any kind of statement about "society". As a private citizen I am deeply interested in politics; as a novelist I merely use political material along with domestic, personal, sexual, farcical, social and other material. The novelist must always try to get the reader to believe that his story and characters are very probable. To do this he must get his background right, or right as he sees it, which means he must try to describe his times; but this is not his prime object. That object is to portray human nature as it has always been, the permanent human passions of love, sorrow, ambition, fear, anger, frustration, joy and the rest. No "commitment" for me, except to literature.

                              *        *        *

Kingsley Amis's principal distinction, in all eight of his novels and his other writings, is the rich comic texture of his prose. Full of mimicry, elaborate satire of ordinary experience (like the taste of food or the pains of waking up with a hangover), stock characters tagged by occupation (dentists' mistresses abound), pseudo-logical analyses of experience, and constant references to contemporary social attitudes, Amis's prose is genuinely sharp and funny. Even when, as in some of the later Amis like *The Anti-Death League*, the prose is generally flatter and less referential, stock characters, farcical events, and startling improbabilities keep the tone and the texture comic. In addition, the prose is iconoclastic, always mocking pretentions to culture or tourist-like enthusiasms for foreign lands or attempts by characters to transcend themselves. Amis consistently writes from the persona of the plain Englishman, fooled by neither the old-fashioned nonsense of faith in official or religious verities nor the contemporary nonsense of following various rebellious or international fads. Amis's wit originates in an attitude of assurance in the clarity and rightness of commonsense.

Amis's iconoclasm is, however, only superficial. His novels are all carefully constructed in conventional ways; thematic strands, embodied in different satirically symbolic characters, are gradually drawn together to explode in a climactic scene that involves almost everyone in the novel. These culminating scenes, like the drunken lecture in *Lucky Jim* or the party in *Take a Girl like You*, invariably take place in public, emphasize the resolutions of the novels in terms that are publicly visible and relevant for the whole society. Like the novels of Henry Fielding, for whom Amis has often shown deep admiration, especially in *I Like It Here*, Amis's novels are satirical and rational constructions lampooning deviation, complexity, or eccentricity and praising the essential soundness of the ordinary man in the ordinary society. Novels, from Amis's point of view, resolve mystery, either explicitly in a novel like *The Green Man* or metaphorically, in social and psychological terms, in a novel like *That Uncertain Feeling*. The novels are never open-ended, contain nothing of the thematic corollaries of the open-ended, of introspection, self-doubt, emotional turbulence, indecision, or romanticism.

Despite all that was popularly said in the late fifties about "Angry Young Men," a rebellion which he supposedly led, Amis's social iconoclasm is even less apparent than his literary. Amis, of course, has never claimed to be a rebel and the novels all demonstrate an acceptance and an ultimate defense of the social status quo. Frequently, as in *One Fat Englishman* and *I Want It Now*, Amis begins by satirizing a central character who pretends to be iconoclastic by showing that his iconoclasm is merely modish opportunism. Yet, as the novel develops, in a characteristic switch, Amis shows that the opportunism is very much like everyone else's, is in fact slightly less selfish and self-deluding than that of others. The opportunist is the man who learns to adjust in contemporary society, who earns the rewards of jobs and good women by sensibly squelching deviation or insistence on self and following the axioms audible around him. Often, as in *Lucky Jim*, *Take a Girl like You*, and *I Want It Now*, the central character is helped materially by an aristocrat, a symbolic representative of the pinnacle of society who leans down, like a fairy god-father, to reward the deserving. Genuine social rebels, those who would transform society in terms of a new or resurrected vision, do not exist in Amis's fiction.

Although Amis generally shapes his novels to endorse the value of adjustment, the attitude toward adjustment has altered in the course of his fictional career. Initially, in *Lucky Jim* and *That Uncertain Feeling*, the value of adjustment was debatable, although the process inevitable for a talented young man. *That Uncertain Feeling*, Amis's least certain and least consoling novel, even develops sympathy for the man who is unable to adjust and must retreat to the provincial society he came from. Later, in *I Like It Here* and *Take a Girl like You*, questions about the value of adjustment become more the matter for superficial comedy and the worth of adjustment, like that of learning to order a meal, drive a car, or lose virginity, is taken for granted. In more recent fiction, like *I Want It Now*, adjustment becomes a positive virtue contrasted to the selfish deviations of eccentrics who are eventually exposed. Yet the rightness of the resolution is always stated negatively, casually. At the end of *Lucky Jim*, Jim Dixon, less arid and phony as a teacher than are the other academics (Amis always retains respect for people who do their job well, no matter what the job) is rewarded because "It's not that you've got the qualifications. . . . You haven't got the disqualifications, though, and that's much rarer"; similarly, at the end of *I Want It Now*, the hero and heroine come together acknowledging that, although bad, they are not quite as bad as others and they can help "each other not to be as bad as we would be on our own."

This kind of casual, unpretentious commitment to the way things go publicly works against any sympathetic presentation of depth or intensity in human emotions. Sexual encounters are almost always material for comedy. The potentially emotional love-making is interrupted by mosquitoes or wasps or a pseudo-logical analysis of how to defend different parts of the anatomy. Interest is focused much more on a plain man's version of sexual technique as part of his skill at operating in society than it is on any emotion involved. When, as in later novels like *I Want It Now* and *The Anti-Death League*, Amis tries to depict a love relationship directly, the comedy disappears, the prose becomes flat and banal, and the scene is sentimental. Amis's characteristic virtue, as well as his characteristic limitation, resides in his sense of distance, his capacity for seeing clearly the ludicrous and pretentious in human affairs even at the price of omitting what is most profoundly or intensely human.

For the most part, Amis provides a sparkling and skillfully comic manual of techniques for survival necessary in a confusing and disordered world. For Amis, man, no matter what the various roles he plays or mimics, must be able to accommodate himself to the world that is, and the sensible man recognizes that he needs all the help that he can get from the already established survivors. Occasionally, however, as in *The Anti-Death League*, he attempts to penetrate experience more deeply, to diagram the theme of necessary sur-

vival, with all its ironies, in all its political, occupational, personal, and psychological ramifications. Yet the best of this novel remains its occasional touches of farce and elaborate
verbal humor, the gratuitous death of the chaplain's dog at the end, the unexpected sexual
performance of a dense security officer, and the final demise of L. S. Caton, a rather slimy
editor and lecturer seen momentarily from a distance in a number of Amis's novels. The
critic, in dealing with Amis, runs the risk of deriving coherent and formulated perspectives
toward experience from what may just happen to be the ordinary exploitation of a special
skill.

—James Gindin

ANAND, Mulk Raj. Indian. Born in Peshawar, 12 December 1905. Educated at Khalsa
College, Amritsar, Punjab University, 1921–24, B.A. (honours) 1924; University College,
London, 1926–29; Cambridge University, 1929–30; League of Nations' School of Intellectual Cooperation, Geneva, 1930–32. Married the actress Kathleen Van Gelder in 1939
(divorced, 1948); the dancer Shirin Vajifdar, 1950; has one child. Lecturer, School of
Intellectual Cooperation, Summer 1930; Workers Educational Association, London, intermittently 1932–45; and the Universities of Punjab, of Banares, Varanasi, and of Rajasthan,
Jaipur, 1948–65; Tagore Professor of Literature and Fine Art, University of Punjab, 1963–
66; Visiting Professor, Institute of Advanced Studies, Simla, 1967–68. Since 1946, Editor
of *Marg* magazine, Bombay. Since 1970, President of the Lokayata Trust, for creating a
community and cultural centre in Hauz Khas village, New Delhi. Fine Art Chairman,
Lalit Kala Akademi (National Academy of Art), New Delhi, 1965–70. Recipient: Leverhulme Fellowship, 1940–42; World Peace Council prize, 1952; Padma Bhushan, India,
1968. Address: 25 Cuffe Parade, Bombay 5; or, c/o Lokayata, Hauz Khas, New Delhi; or,
Village Sukhrali, Gurgaon, Haryana, India.

PUBLICATIONS

Novels

*Untouchable.* London, Wishart, 1935.
*Coolie.* London, Lawrence and Wishart, 1936.
*Two Leaves and a Bud.* London, Lawrence and Wishart, 1937.
*The Village.* London, Cape, 1939.
*Lament on the Death of a Master of Arts.* Allahabad, Kitabistan, 1939.
*Across the Black Waters.* London, Cape, 1940.
*The Sword and the Sickle.* London, Cape, 1942.
*The Big Heart.* London, Hutchinson, 1945.
*Seven Summers: The Story of an Indian Childhood.* London, Hutchinson, 1951.
*The Private Life of an Indian Prince.* London, Hutchinson, 1953; revised edition,
    London, Bodley Head, 1970.
*The Road.* Bombay, Kutub, 1962.
*The Old Woman and the Cow.* Bombay, Kutub, 1963.
*Death of a Hero.* Bombay, Kutub, 1964.
*Morning Face.* Bombay, Kutub, 1968.

Short Stories

> *The Lost Child and Other Stories.*  London, J. A. Allen, 1934.
> *The Barber's Trade Union and Other Stories.*  London, Cape, 1944.
> *The Tractor and the Corn Goddess and Other Stories.*  Bombay, Thacker, 1947.
> *Reflections on the Golden Bed.*  Bombay, Current Book House, 1954.
> *The Power of Darkness.*  Bombay, Jaico, 1966.

Other

> *Persian Painting.*  London, Faber, 1930.
> *Curries and Other Indian Dishes.*  London, Harmsworth, 1932.
> *The Golden Breath: Studies in Five Poets of the New India.*  London, Murray, and New York, Dutton, 1933.
> *The Hindu View of Art.*  Bombay, Asia Publishing House, and London, Allen and Unwin, 1933; revised edition, Asia Publishing House, 1957; New York, Asia Publishing House, 1960.
> *Apology for Heroism: An Essay in Search of a Faith.*  London, Drummond, 1934.
> *Letters on India.*  New York, Transatlantic Arts, 1942; London, Routledge, 1943.
> *Indian Fairy Tales: Retold* (juvenile).  Bombay, Kutub, 1946.
> *On Education.*  Bombay, Hind Kitabs, 1947.
> *The Bride's Book of Beauty*, with K. N. Hutheesing.  Bombay, Kutub, 1947.
> *The Story of India* (juvenile).  Bombay, Kutub, 1948.
> *The King Emperor's English; or, The Role of the English Language in the Free India.*  Bombay, Hind Kitabs, 1948.
> *Lines Written to an Indian Air: Essays.*  Bombay, Kutub, 1949.
> *Indian Theatre.*  London, Dobson, 1950; New York, Roy, 1951.
> *The Story of Man* (juvenile).  Delhi, Sikh Publishing House, 1954.
> *More Indian Fairy Tales* (juvenile).  Bombay, Kutub, 1956.
> *Kama Kala: Some Notes on the Philosophical Basis of Hindu Erotic Sculpture.*  London, Skilton, 1958; New York, Lyle Stuart, 1962.
> *India in Colour.*  Bombay, Taraporevala, London, Thames and Hudson, and New York, McGraw Hill, 1959.
> *Homage to Khajuraho*, with Stella Kramrisch.  Bombay, Marg Publications, 1960.
> *Is There a Contemporary Indian Civilisation?*  Bombay and London, Asia Publishing House, 1963; New York, Asia Publishing House, 1964.
> *The Third Eye: A Lecture on Art.*  Patiala, University of Punjab, 1966.
> *The Volcano: Lectures on the Painting of Rabindranath Tagore.*  Baroda, Maharaja Sayajiroa University, 1968.

> Editor, with Iqbal Singh, *Indian Short Stories.*  London, New India, 1947.
> Editor, *Introduction to Indian Art*, by A. K. Coomaraswamy.  Madras, Theosophical Publishing House, and Wheaton, Illinois, Theosophical Press, 1956.

Critical Studies: *The Lotus and the Elephant* by Jack Lindsay, Bombay, Kutub Popular, 1954; "Mulk Raj Anand Issue" of *Contemporary Indian Literature* (New Delhi), 1965; *An Ideal of Man in Anand's Novels* by D. Riemenschneider, Bombay, Kutub Popular, 1969; *Mulk Raj Anand: Man and Novelist* by Margaret Berry, Amsterdam, Beale, 1970.

Mulk Raj Anand comments:

I began to write early—a kind of free verse in the Punjabi and Urdu languages, from the compulsion of the shock of the death of my cousin when she was nine years old. I wrote a letter to God telling him He didn't exist. Later, going through the dark night of another bereavement, when my aunt committed suicide because she was excommunicated for inter-dining with a Muslim woman, I wrote prose. Again, when I fell in love with a young Muslim girl, who was married off by arrangement, I wrote calf love verses. The poet-philosopher, Muhammad Iqbal, introduced me to the problems of the individual through his long poem, "Secrets of the Self". Through him, I also read Nietzsche to confirm my rejection of God. After a short term in jail, my father, who was pro-British, punished my mother for my affiliations with the Gandhi Movement. I went to Europe and studied various philosophical systems and found that these comprehensive philosophies did not answer life's problems. I was beaten up for not black-legging against workers in 1926, in the coal-miner's strike. I joined a Marxist worker's study circle with Trade Unionist Alan Hutt, and met Palme-Dutt, John Strachey, T. S. Eliot, Herbert Read, Bonamy Dobrée, Harold Laski, Leonard Woolf. During that time I fell in love with a young Welsh girl painter, Irene, whose father was a biologist. For her I wrote a long confession about the break-up of my family, the British impact and my later life. Nobody would publish the 2,000 word narrative. So I began to rewrite portions, as allegories, short stories and novels. On a tour with Irene, in Paris, Rome, Vienna, Berlin, Brussels, I discovered Rimbaud, Dante and Joyce. My first attempt at a novel was revised in Gandhi's Sabarmati Ashram in Ahmedabad, but was turned down by 19 publishers in London. The 20th offered to publish it if E. M. Forster wrote a Preface. This the author of *A Passage to India* did.

Since the publication of this first novel, I have written continuously on the human situa-tion in the lives of people of the lower caste, peasants, lumpen and other eccentrics, thrown up during the transition from the ancient orthodox Indian society to the self-conscious modernist secular democracy.

I believe that creating literature is the true medium of humanism as against systematic philosophies, because the wisdom of the heart encourages insights in all kinds of human beings who grow to self-consciousness through the conflicts of desire, will and mood. I am inclined to think that the highest aim of poetry and art is to integrate the individual into inner growth and outer adjustment. The broken bundle of mirrors of the human personality in our time can only become the enchanted mirror if the sensibility is touched in its utmost pain and sheer pleasure and tenderest moments. No rounded answers are possible. Only hunches, insights, and inspirations and the *karuna* that may come from understanding.

The novelist's task is that of an all-comprehending "God", who understands every part of his creation, through pity, compassion, or sympathy—which is the only kind of catharsis possible in art. The word is itself action of the still centre. The struggle to relate the word and the deed in the life of man is part of the process of culture, through which illumination comes to human beings. The world of art is a communication from one individual to another, or to the group through the need to connect. This may ultimately yield the slogan "love one another", if mankind is to survive (against its own inheritance of fear, hatred and con-tempt, now intensified through money-power, or privileges, and large-scale violence) into the 21st century, in any human form.

*       *       *

Mulk Raj Anand's first five novels including some of his best work, *Coolie, Untouchable, Two Leaves and a Bud, The Village,* and *Across the Black Waters,* appeared between 1933 and 1940, although he had already written a considerable amount before this, including a study of Persian paintings and a book on curries! He was one of three writers (R. K. Narayan and Raja Rao were the others) who defined the area in which the Indian novel was to operate. They established its assumptions, they sketched its main themes, drew the first models of its characters, and elaborated its peculiar logic. Each of them used an easy, natural idiom which was unaffected by the opacity of a British inheritance. Their language has been freed of the foggy taste of Britain and transferred to a wholly new setting of brutal heat and brilliant light.

Mulk Raj Anand is passionately concerned with the villages, with the ferocious poverty and the cruelties of caste, with orphans, untouchables and urban labourers. He writes in an angry reformist way, like a less humorous Dickens and a more emotional Wells, of the personal sufferings induced by economics—really economics, one feels, even when he is writing of caste. His sharpest, best organised novel is *Untouchable*, which was very highly thought of by E. M. Forster. It is an interesting combination of hard material, narrow specific theme, and throbbing Shelleyan manner. The action, occupying a single day, is precipitated by a great "catastrophe", an accidental "touching" in the morning. Everything that follows is affected by it, even the innocent and vividly realised hockey match. Of the three solutions hinted at to the problem of the untouchable—Christ, Gandhi, and Main Drainage—it is the last which is most favoured by Anand. He is a committed artist, and what he is committed to is indicated by Bashir's mockery in *Untouchable*: "greater efficiency, better salesmanship, more mass-production, standardisation, dictatorship of the sweepers, Marxian Materialism and all that". "Yes, yes," is the reply, "all that, but no catch-words and cheap phrases, the changes will be organic and not mechanical."

Mulk Raj Anand's semi-Marxist categories, his furious, and one must say well-grounded indignation, and his habit of undue explicitness, together with a deficiency in self-criticism make him a writer whose work has to be severely sieved. Like many writers impelled by social motives, however worthy, whose attitude to life is too patently dominated by theory, he has a habit of preaching at the reader. But when his imagination burns, and the dross of propaganda is consumed, as in *Untouchable*, *Coolie*, and *The Big Heart*, there is no doubt that he is a novelist of considerable power.

Even politics, that is, even politics as cerebral and doctrinal as this, can be humanised by the ingathering and melting capacity of the Indian mind. It is a quality working right through *Coolie* where Anand showed himself one of the first Indian writers to look on the savagely neglected and maltreated poor with an angry lack of resignation. The novel combines an acrid indignation at the condition of the poor together with a Dickensian vivacity in physical registration *and* a delicate sense of the psychology of Munoo, the waif-hero, in particular of the rhythms of his growth from boy to adolescent. Munoo's victim-rôle brings home to one the passive quality of the Asiatic poor in what Anand shows to be a markedly static and hierarchical society, just as the immense tracts, from Simla to Bombay, covered in the boy's forced journeys convey in a way new to Indian fiction the continental vastness and variety of India.

Mulk Raj Anand belongs to the tradition of the nineteenth-century writer—not necessarily just the British tradition for one is aware of a distinctly European set of influences operating on him, particularly French and Russian influences—in his approach to the novel, in his techniques, his weaving together of theme and event, in his sensibility and in his hope for what the novel may publicly achieve. He is particularly of this tradition in point of his fluency. Creation appears to be no agonising struggle for him, communication something he engages in with an unstrained and vivid enthusiasm, and something of the facility of a Russian writer. He is nineteenth-century, too, in his conception of the novel, seeing it as an organisation strongly based on a double foundation of character and circumstance: character which has to be clearly defined and then developed, largely through the causality of the other constitutive force, social circumstances and influences, usually of a harshly oppressive sort. He has, too, a natural disposition towards the picaresque. The trilogy *The Village*, *Across the Black Waters* and *The Sword and the Sickle* takes the peasant boy Lal Singh, from his North Indian village and a life stifled by suffocating layers of custom and religion, into the ferocity of the 1914–18 war and the crass commercialism of Europe, and then back again to India to a new political stance towards life.

The defect which constricts his real creative capacity is the habit of allowing his moral and social purposes to become separate from the particular actuality of the fiction, so that they frequently lead a collateral rather than a unified existence. This is accompanied by a certain passivity on the part of the characters, apt no doubt when they are the victims of circumstances, which they so frequently are, but out of place in those parts of his work where the individual should be more energetically active in the working out of his own nature. The theme of *The Big Heart*, this very Dickensian novel, is stated in a single sentence: "In the centre of Amritsar is Kucha Billimaran, a colony of traditional coppersmiths called thathiars, now uprooted and on the brink of starvation due to the advent of the factory and the consequent loss of their traditional occupation." The contrast of the two worlds is vividly delineated and the theme is a splendid vehicle for Anand's largeness and generosity. It is less impressive in the characterisation of the hero, Ananta, who suffers again from a certain limpness in action. He feels the attractions of the two kinds of life. He is fulfilled in the craft of smoothing the intractable metal, but he is also anguished by the poverty of the half-starved coppersmiths. He combines in his reactions something of the feeling of William Morris and of an angry Trade Union leader. Moreover, there is as much moral prejudice against him from the poor, whom the boy is trying to help, because he is living with a widow, as political opposition from the tyrannical capitalists. In a sense Ananta manifests the kind of inward friction which frays Anand himself as an artist, and which he has managed to assuage only in a handful of his books.

As a writer Mulk Raj Anand lacks the concrete sagacity, the *finesse*, the "appetite for the illustrational"—to use Henry James's phrase—which marks everything that R. K. Narayan writes; nor does he have that sense of the metaphysical nature of man we find in the other distinguished novelist, Raja Rao. But he has a stricken and genuine feeling for the deprived, a grasp of the social structure of his society and an extraordinary fluency of communication. This fluency of communication has something Russian in it, and Russian too (but in an infinitely more attractive sense than the earlier Marxist-dominated way) are two later works, *Morning Face* and *The Private Life of an Indian Prince* (revised, 1970). These two books which are, it appears from Saros Cowasjee's introduction, highly autobiographical, summon up the great name of Dostoevsky in their pouring out of an intensely realised personal grief. They show in addition how the mind which created *Coolie* came to be formed, how the boy Krishna once folded lovingly into the family, becomes coldly detached and alone. The rhythm of this desperate progress is defined with an unusual purity and precision, and so with the same mastery is the collapse of the prince's mind in *Private Life of an Indian Prince*. In both these works, free as they are from undue political scaffolding, there is an extraordinary combination of psychological perception and human agony.

—William Walsh

---

**ANTHONY, Michael.** Trinidadian. Born in Mayaro, 10 February 1932. Educated at Mayaro Roman Catholic School; Junior Technical College, San Fernando, Trinidad. Married Yvette Francesca in 1958; has four children. Lived in England, 1954–68: Journalist, Reuters News Agency, London, 1964–68. Lived in Brazil, 1968–70. Returned to Trinidad, 1970. Since 1970, Assistant Editor, Texaco Trinidad, Pointe-à-Pierre. Address: c/o Publications Department, Texaco Trinidad, Pointe-à-Pierre, Trinidad.

PUBLICATIONS

Novels

The Games Were Coming. London, Deutsch, 1963; Boston, Houghton Mifflin, 1968.
The Year in San Fernando. London, Deutsch, 1965.
Green Days by the River. Boston, Houghton Mifflin, 1967; London, Deutsch, 1968.

Uncollected Short Stories

"Sandra Street", "Enchanted Valley", "Drunkard of the River", "The Precious Corn", "Vern", "The Valley of Cocoa", "Uncle of the Waterfront", "Hibiscus", "Pita of the Deep Sea", "The Interlude", "The Captain of the Fleet", and "The Sapodilla Tree", in *Bim* (Bridgetown, Barbados), 1958–64.
"The Stranger in the Village", in *The Bajan* (Bridgetown, Barbados), April 1961.

Critical Studies: in *London Magazine*, April 1967; "Novels of Childhood" in *The West Indian Novel and Its Background*, by Kenneth Ramchand, London, Faber, 1970.

Michael Anthony comments:

I see myself principally as a story-teller. In other words, I am not aware that I have any message. I think both the past life and the fascination of landscape play a most important part in my work.

My infancy has been very important in my literary development and so far almost everything I have written—certainly my novels—are very autobiographical.

It is strange that I have never had the desire to write about England, although I spent fourteen years there. To some people, judging from my writing alone, I have never been out of Trinidad. And this is true in some sort of way.

I feel a certain deep attachment to Trinidad and I want to write about it in such a way that I will give a faithful picture of life here. But when I am writing a story I am not aware that I want to do anything else but tell the story.

\*       \*       \*

The appearance of Anthony's first novel, *The Games Were Coming*, added a distinctive voice to West Indian fiction. Not only did Anthony, already living in London for nine years, entirely avoid the *Angst* of exile and of intellectual or class alienation which had become so common in that fiction, but he achieved the most difficult of all prose qualities: an impression of lyrical simplicity, freshness and ease. Unlike many of the exile writers of his generation, Anthony was able to avoid a tone of recollection (a tone through which some quality of present separation or anguish is audible); he seemed able to inhabit the mounting excitement of the boy Dolphus in this first novel as completely as he later inhabited the pain and confusion of his other boy-hero, Francis, in *The Year in San Fernando*.

The art which makes possible the limpid flow of his style is evident also in the cunning with which he weaves together the various tensions which culminate in the cycle-race at the end of the first novel, or in the death of Mrs. Chandles at the end of the second. While Leon, the young cycling champion, is training with ever-mounting intensity for his big race, his sweetheart Sylvia is moving through parallel tensions of her own. Her frustration at Leon's long-sustained refusal to make love to her gradually turns to feverish anticipation at the approach of a new lover, then to dread as she learns of her pregnancy by him, and finally to a convergent excitement as she persuades the unwitting Leon, on the eve of the race, to marry her if he wins. Thus the race is finally more decisive for her than for him.

The twelve-year-old Francis, who is suddenly switched from the rural calm of Mayaro to the big town of San Fernando, where he stays for a year as a sort of schoolboy-servant in the Chandles household, is not living with a familiar but heightened excitement like Leon's young brother Dolphus; he lives instead with a new insecurity and uncertainty about adult motives, actions and relationships, far away from his family and the scenes of his boyhood. Only as a suddenly pathetic Mrs. Chandles approaches death and her two violently conflicting sons converge on the death-bed does Francis begin to feel that he has absorbed what he can of this disturbing adult world. He has aged much more than a year as he prepares to return to Mayaro.

*Green Days by the River* offers a slightly older but sadly confused hero, excitedly exploring the experience of loving two different girls at once. Here, for the first time, Anthony introduces some of the racial complexities of Trinidad, for one of the girls is half-Indian, and her father has all the traditional Indian instinct to protect his daughter's virginity right up to the altar. Far away in Port of Spain the boy's own father is dying, while he himself drifts away from the Indian girl he has given every appearance of courting. Her father brutally recalls him to his responsibilities by setting four fierce dogs on him, but this scene is hard to accept in the spirit intended by the author, for it might as easily have resulted in the boy's death as in his marriage.

With these novels, Anthony seems to have exhausted his capacity to re-create with such totality and freshness the Trinidad of his youth. He will need now to become a new kind of novelist. Speaking in 1968 at Canterbury, he said: "I have really reached the crossroads in my career. If I am to go on writing I feel I must return to the scene of my material." But the Trinidad to which he has now returned is a more bitter, tense and divided island than the one he remembered in these novels.

—Gerald Moore

---

**ARMAH, Ayi Kwei.**   Ghanaian.   Born in Takoradi in 1939. Educated at Groton School, Massachusetts; Harvard University, Cambridge, Massachusetts, A.B. in social studies; Columbia University, New York. Translator, *Revolution Africaine* magazine, Algiers; Scriptwriter for Ghana Television; English Teacher, Navrongo School, Ghana, 1966; Editor, *Jeune Afrique* magazine, Paris, 1967–68. Lives in New York City. Address: c/o Houghton Mifflin Company, 2 Park Street, Boston, Massachusetts 02107, U.S.A.

PUBLICATIONS

Novels

The Beautyful Ones Are Not Yet Born.   Boston, Houghton Mifflin, 1968; London, Heinemann, 1969.
Fragments.   Boston, Houghton Mifflin, 1970.

\*       \*       \*

In three years and two books, Ayi Kwei Armah has established himself as modern Africa's most controlled novelist, most accomplished artist in what developed essentially as a Western art form. To aver such a thing is to risk pricklish reactions. Invidious comparisons with Achebe and Ngugi, for one thing, seem inherent in the observation—yet in a strictly *formal* sense these authors rely more heavily on traditional African proverb and fable than Armah does for their books' surface style and effect. They do it well; Armah, simply, uses fable in a different way, employing its structure (the high man brought low, the trickster tricked, etc.), rather than its local images, to serve his depiction of contemporary society. His direct command of political and behaviourist frames of reference marks his approach to his craft and in its way characterizes the analytic and cathartic bluntness of "realistic" fiction at the same time. These talents are by no means "un-African", of course, however severe they are (in Armah's work) with modern Africa; what they enunciate both starkly clarifies a social-system-in-working-disorder and passionately, painfully, combs the chaos observed for the glimpse of the ideals which the nation—the people—once professed.

As the first novel spells out, in an unfulfilled moment of gentle perception inspired by the name on a bus:

## THE BEAUTYFUL ONES
## ARE NOT YET BORN

In the center of the oval was a single flower, solitary, unexplainable, and very beautiful. . . .

[T]he man was unable to shake off the imprint of the painted words. . . . After a while the image itself of the flower in the middle disappeared, to be replaced by a single, melodious note. . . .

But then suddenly all his mind was consumed with thoughts of everything he was going back to—Oyo, the eyes of the children after six o'clock, the office and every day, and above all the never-ending knowledge that his aching emptiness would be all that the remainder of his own life could offer him.

Indeed, for the nameless, ordinary, central character—Everyman in moral conflict with the world that holds him—time is an inexorable but strangely empty authority. His job as a railway employee demands accurate clocking; days succeed domestic days; years age him into routine and financial nonentity while others concurrently thrive on graft and corruption. But time is thus recurrence without development, and when a coup topples the government, only a different brand of the same system seems (in the Man's experience) likely to replace it. The overriding symbol of the novel is human faeces; the central locus is the latrine, through which, eventually, at his wife's insistence, the Man must lead their "friend", the corrupt Minister Koomson, in order to help him escape the new regime. Koomson had used these people before, but the tables are not turned now, even though he has tumbled to such depths; he simply uses them again. Humanity is reduced to waste, ideals are "consumed with thoughts of . . . every day", and cynical utterance evacuates words of all their latent power to mean and to heal.

For Baako, in *Fragments*, despite his own mental upset and confusion, the future is not such an eschatological void, for he can find physically in a Puerto Rican girl a loving kindred spirit, and he comes to appreciate in his blind grandmother Naana the power of his spiritual kin: the meaning of traditional ceremony, the certain sight of faith, and the palpable community with the "living" world of the "dead". Though the basic conflict in the book—between corrupt modern systems and idealistic individuals—remains unchanged from *The Beautyful Ones*, Armah (perhaps influenced by his strongly traditionalist contemporary and compatriot, Ama Ata Aidoo, to whom he dedicates the book) now chafes his cynical observations with an open exploration of the older value system of his culture. In other words, in fragments of perception, Baako (the "been-to" whose immediate family expects instant prestige, money, and "things" from his return to Ghana) discovers that "system" need not deny his spirit the peace that it seeks. Community proves fertile, in fact—"nothing destroys the soul/ like its aloneness"—but it must be a community of creative sensibilities, not of possessive, competitive, ostentatious material display.

Naana intuitively knows that her daughter and grand-daughter "have smothered another human soul in all their heavy dreams of things". But Baako, after trial (that archetypal process of the questing spirit reaching for renewal), must live. His former teacher Ocran observes: "You have to be alone to find out what's in you." Naana, in her blindness, has known just such isolation, and transcended it. If one aches for "the Man's" impotence in the face of moral chaos, one reaches out also for some of Naana's compassionate ordering faith. In a deliberate recurrent *double entendre*, Armah writes that she "holds her peace". It lies within the range of his enormous talent to affirm such a gentleness, to draw such compellingly rounded characters into life, without dispelling the anger that gives his books their immediacy and energy. In Swiftian fashion the sympathy he extends to individuals turns to protest against their institutions—a dilemma which describes the area of tension he takes as his subject. At the last, however, his voice simply utters what his eyes see: a world at once ugly and beautiful that only reflects the mixed ambitions and beliefs of the people within it.

—W. H. New

---

**ASHTON-WARNER, Sylvia (Constance).**   New Zealander.   Born in Stratford, 17 December 1908. Educated at small country schools, including Te Whiti; Wairarapa College, Masterton; Teachers College, Auckland, 1928–29. Married to Keith Dawson Henderson. Taught with her husband at several country schools in New Zealand. Currently Professor of Education, Aspen Community School Teaching Center, Colorado. Address: Aspen Community School, Box 1939, Aspen, Colorado 81611, U.S.A.

PUBLICATIONS

Novels

Spinster.  London, Secker and Warburg, 1958; New York, Simon and Schuster, 1959.
Incense to Idols.  London, Secker and Warburg, and New York, Simon and Schuster, 1960.
Teacher.  London, Secker and Warburg, and New York, Simon and Schuster, 1963.
Bell Call.  New York, Simon and Schuster, 1964; London, Hale, 1971.
Greenstone.  New York, Simon and Schuster, 1966; London, Secker and Warburg, 1967.
Three.  New York, Knopf, 1970; London, Hale, 1971.

Uncollected Short Stories

"No Longer Blinded by Our Eyes" (as Sylvia Henderson), in *New Zealand Listener* (Wellington), 8 October 1948.
"The Least Thing" (as Sylvia), in *Here and Now* (Auckland), April 1956.
"Floor" (as Sylvia), in *Here and Now* (Auckland), June 1956.
"That Boy Again", in *New Zealand Monthly Review* (Christchurch), March 1961.
"Patricia", in *New Zealand Monthly Review* (Christchurch), May 1962.

Other

Myself.  New York, Simon and Schuster, 1967; London, Secker and Warburg, 1968.

Articles derived from her teaching experience published in journals in New Zealand and the United States since 1952.

Verse published in various periodicals.

Critical Study: "Sylvia Ashton-Warner: A Problem of Grounding" by Dennis McEldowney, in *Landfall* (Christchurch), September 1969.

\*     \*     \*

Sylvia Ashton-Warner's novels have the great merit of being unpredictable. She burst upon the rather conventional literary scene in New Zealand in 1958 with a work, *Spinster*, that was less a novel than an educational thriller, rich with identifiable persons and places, pulsing with anti-Establishment exasperations, and flaring with emotional highlights. It erupted into the artistic scene as well as the educational one, for its exhibition of the tormented inner life of the teacher-narrator, Anna Vorontosov, was more riotously outspoken than local readers expected.

Author and protagonist, fact and fiction, are intimately related in all Sylvia Ashton-Warner's books, and it is difficult to decide which is which, even in the two documentaries, *Myself* and *Teacher*. The educational ideals which are the beloved obsession of Anna in *Spinster* had been explored in stories and articles well before 1958. Using her married name, Sylvia Henderson, Sylvia Ashton-Warner appeared in the *New Zealand Listener* in 1948 with the story "No Longer Blinded by Our Eyes". As "Sylvia", she published further material in *Here and Now* (December 1952, August 1953, December 1955) dealing with her experience in teaching Maori children to read. In 1950, the middle-class *Janet and John* readers for infant classes became current in New Zealand schools, and it is in reaction to their unsuitability for her purposes that Sylvia Ashton-Warner formulated her first direct protest. In *National Education* from December 1955 to May 1956 she preached her new doctrine in five articles under the general heading *"Maori Infant Room:* Organic Reading and the Key Vocabulary." At the same time short impressionistic pieces continued to appear, which embodied in semi-fictional form the infant rooms of her imagination (*Here and Now*, April, June 1956). These she reprinted in 1959 as a linked series in *New Zealand Parent and Child*, describing them as trial runs for *Spinster*.

After the appearance of her first novel, for which the novelist used her maiden name Ashton-Warner, subsequent material appeared under this name. Items include "Waiwini", in *Numbers*, October 1959, and stories in the *New Zealand Monthly Review* in 1961 and 1962. She also published verse in *Comment* in 1962 and in the *New Zealand Poetry Yearbook* for 1964. Evidence of her deep involvement with the Maori people is her publication in December 1960 in *Te Ao Hou*, the Maori journal, of a memorial tribute to the much loved leader Dr. Maharaia Winiata, who belonged to the pa near her husband's school not far from Tauranga.

In all her educational work, Sylvia Ashton-Warner has one dominant message, that the most vital of human concerns is communication between "Thee" and "Me", whether verbal or physical, intellectual or emotional, loving or destructive. Response, and response alone, confers life. To quote *Spinster*:

> Communication is so fiery. It's like flames leaping from one to another . . . I suspect some universal power in communication if only I could put my finger on it . . . Freed from orthodoxy, my Little Ones write of nothing else. . . . This something that goes between one and another . . . one vast love affair. What kind of thing is it? Can you touch it? Has it got feet or wheels or wings? Why is it so magic?

And again, "The only meaning of life; communication."

In *Spinster*, the novelist portrays the lonely woman whose deprivation of the "Thee and Me" relationship has sharpened her perception of its value. Anna Vorontosov, gifted at art, music, and self-dramatisation, lives through a school year with the reader beside her as absorbed eavesdropper. The tumbling chaos of her inner and outer lives has imposed upon it a framework of the four seasons, threaded through with lines from the poems of Gerard Manley Hopkins (especially "The Caged Skylark", "To Seem the Stranger", "Thou Art Indeed Just Lord", and "To R.B."). Faced with her prefabricated infant room exploding with brown and white children, this teacher tries to find ways of releasing the currents locked within these little beings. The frozen puritan *pakeha* Dennis must thaw; the irrepressible Maori Seven must be drawn into creating instead of destroying; Hinewaka, of the injured feet, must be healed of her hospital terrors; and anxious little Riti, whose hair is full of "those things", must in spite of them be allowed to cuddle close, because physical contact is the only way to make connection.

Anna Vorontosov's personal life is less credible than her professional one. Elements which recur in later novels—the musical and horticultural fantasies, the suiciding lover, the anguish of soul—these flare and collide in *Spinster*, threatening to overbalance the novel into hysteria. Yet there is more substance in it than in most novels, substance so rich and so original that the terms "good" or "bad" hardly seem relevant.

In *Incense to Idols*, however, hysteria has the upper hand. Germaine, the improbable Paris pianist who has come to rest in a small New Zealand town, maintains an exotic narrative flow swirling over sex, religion, alcohol, poetry and prophecy, with neither pattern nor real significance emerging.

The treatise *Teacher* appeared next. In the book, Sylvia Ashton-Warner records that her ideas had begun to form during her first years of teaching Maori infants, and had crystallised in 1955–56 when, as she writes, "I at last came upon the Key vocabulary", while coping with some fifty children in the prefabricated classroom described in *Spinster*. In the Letter to my American Editor which prefaces *Teacher*, she writes: "I have been trying to get this Creative Teaching Scheme published in my country for seven years. . . . I badly wanted it to come out in my own country in my own lifetime". The Scheme had, in fact, already "come out" in New Zealand, the basis of it being those articles already noted, published in *National Education* and elsewhere. The American publishers, with a huge potential sale, were able to present the Scheme and supply ample illustration on a scale impracticable in a purely local production, and of course there has been some rearrangement and some addition of fresh matter. But *Teacher*, in spite of the author's prefatory complaint, is really just an expanded collection of material already in print in New Zealand.

Its message is even clearer in book form, that the driving human need is for communication between "Thee and Me". Gathered in this way into a related series, the author's lively and stimulating educational ideas have considerable appeal.

*Bell Call*, published in New York in 1964 but not in New Zealand until 1971, is an attempt to ignore the school bell altogether. This novel like *Incense to Idols* has a bizarre narrative mode, shared as it is between a ghost watching earthly events from some undefined stance, and the ghost's living husband, Daniel Francis, ex-schoolmaster and writer. Tarl Prackett, mother of four, believes that teaching is a sinful intrusion upon a child's free growth. Until a child asks for it, education should not be imposed. These beliefs bring her of course into open conflict with the New Zealand law. She therefore spends the book seeking for the "primitive simplicity" of some backblocks retreat where her children can "merge with nature". Playing opposite to Tarl is Angela, Daniel's daughter, with her tidy house and disciplined offspring. The tale is told in strained, posturing, deliberately fanciful language; its basic mystique is that of its quotation from Whitman:

> I know my words are weapons, full of danger, full of death . . .
> For I confront peace, security, and all the settled laws, to unsettle them . . .
> I heed not, and have never heeded, either experience, cautions, majorities, nor ridicule . . .

Perhaps because the romantic anarchy of these sentiments still has the very great attraction of a releasing daydream, *Bell Call* rode high on the best-selling lists at its belated issue in New Zealand.

*Greenstone* unfortunately is as touristic as its title suggests. It is set on the Wanganui River, where the author taught during the years she describes in *Myself*. Her material, however, seems to be not so much derived from this reality as salvaged from some course of reading in early New Zealand potboilers, with their garbled Maori myths, remittance men figures, halfcaste princesses, and other standard items of popular colonial romance. Sylvia Ashton-Warner's thesis, the need for racial harmony and integration, does of course need recurring emphasis, but its cause is hardly likely to be advanced by such luxuriant sentimentality.

In 1967 came *Myself*, which purports to be the diary of the author's life from 1941 to 1945 at Pipiriki School on the Wanganui River. Whether *Myself* is an accurate daily record, or a pepped up selection of one, or a fictitious reconstruction—the same problem arises with the diary section of *Teacher*—the effect is certainly creative rather than documentary. The events in the outer world are actual, Pearl Harbour, the Home Guard, etc, and the places are identifiable, but there is surely fiction in some of the personal matter? In the background of the little bush community's life, there seem to be elements derived from the experience of Sylvia Ashton-Warner's childhood, when she knew the world of small country schools in which her mother taught. (One notes, by the way, that her father's first name was Francis, used in *Bell Call* as a surname.) At one such school, Te Whiti, her mother recalled the stories of the Maori ghosts haunting the cemetery.

In *Myself* Sylvia Ashton-Warner pictures a woman torn between the different roles of "the wife, the mother, the lover, the teacher, and the violent artist." Her husband Keith Dawson Henderson, appears in person and by name, a loyal and father-like figure who stands by to offer stability and refuge. The turbulent fluctuations of the author's feelings in these diverse roles are conveyed in a straightforward and therefore more effective prose than she uses elsewhere. Incidental material as before reminds the reader of *Spinster*; there is sanctuary in the bush hut ("Selah"), or in a garden studio, the suicide of lovers, the longing for European travel, the schoolroom life, the lover, here called not Paul, but Saul, Dr. Saul Mada. There are "pain and music and memory and wine." Much is made of the Maori children's difficulty in pronouncing "Henderson", just as those in *Spinster* stumbled over "Vorontosov."

The theme of *Myself* is the search for wholeness of person, which the writer sees as the only key to a full life for the woman or the teacher. Near the end, she gives herself a good talking to:

> I must preserve my individuality and not be influenced by what others do . . . I
> must not allow myself to be shaped by the crowd or the inner circle, by a husband
> or even a lover; by economic moulds, professional ethics or by the accident of
> dwelling place . . . I must be true to myself.

The major discovery of the book is that harmony within her own personality is essential to creative teaching, to that kind of communication between teacher and child on which, in her view, true learning rests. Three years after she has left the River for the barer East Coast landscape of *Spinster*, Sylvia Ashton-Warner experienced that moment of revelation when the theme of all her subsequent work, "communication", became plain.

> I took the hand of a child. It was soft, pliant; yielding yet electric. Less tentatively
> I began to hold it, then more firmly. Another linked on, in their funny way, then
> another two. They looked up at me in amazed awareness, I down on them in
> incredulous recognition. . . . Some day I'll be a teacher.

However erratic and embarrassing may be the personal revelations of her work and the exotic pranks of her prose, Sylvia Ashton-Warner's writing carries at its heart a core of passionate human concern. It is this which gives her a claim to serious attention.

—Joan Stevens

ASIMOV, Isaac. American. Born in Petrovichi, Russia, 2 January 1920. Came to the United States in 1923; naturalized, 1928. Educated at Columbia University, New York, B.A. 1939, M.A. 1941, Ph.D. 1948. Served in the United States Army. Married Gertrude Blugerman in 1942; has two children. Instructor, 1949–51, Assistant Professor, 1951–55, and since 1955 Associate Professor of Biochemistry, Boston University School of Medicine. Recipient: Edison Foundation National Mass Media Award, 1958; Blakeslee Award for Non-Fiction, 1960; American Chemical Society's James T. Grady Award, 1965; American Association for the Advancement of Science-Westinghouse Science Writing Award, 1967. Address: Oliver Cromwell Hotel, 3-K, 12 West 72nd Street, New York, New York 10023, U.S.A.

PUBLICATIONS

Novels

*Pebble in the Sky*. New York, Doubleday, 1950; London, Sidgwick and Jackson, 1968.
*I, Robot*. New York, Gnome Press, 1950; London, Grayson, 1952.
*The Stars, Like Dust*. New York, Doubleday, 1951.
*Foundation*. New York, Gnome Press, 1951; London, Weidenfeld and Nicolson, 1953.
*Foundations and Empire*. New York, Gnome Press, 1952.
*The Currents of Space*. New York, Doubleday, 1952; London, Boardman, 1955.
*David Starr: Space Ranger* (as Paul French; juvenile). New York, Doubleday, 1952; London, World's Work, 1953.
*Second Foundation*. New York, Gnome Press, 1953.
*Lucky Starr and the Pirates of the Asteroids* (as Paul French; juvenile). New York, Doubleday, 1953; London, World's Work, 1954.
*The Caves of Steel*. New York, Doubleday, and London, Boardman, 1954.
*Lucky Starr and the Oceans of Venus* (as Paul French; juvenile). New York, Doubleday, 1954.
*The End of Eternity*. New York, Doubleday, 1955.
*Lucky Starr and the Big Sun of Mercury* (as Paul French; juvenile). New York, Doubleday, 1956.
*The Naked Sun*. New York, Doubleday, 1957; London, Joseph, 1958.
*Lucky Starr and the Moons of Jupiter* (as Paul French; juvenile). New York, Doubleday, 1957.
*Lucky Starr and the Rings of Saturn* (as Paul French; juvenile). New York, Doubleday, 1958.
*The Rest of the Robots*. New York, Doubleday, 1964; London, Dobson, 1967.
*Fantastic Voyage*. Boston, Houghton Mifflin, and London, Dobson, 1966.
*A Whiff of Death*. New York, Walker, and London, Gollancz, 1968.

Short Stories

*The Martian Way and Other Stories.*   New York, Doubleday, 1955; London, Dobson, 1964.
*Earth Is Room Enough.*   New York, Doubleday, 1957.
*Nine Tomorrows: Tales of the Near Future.*   New York, Doubleday, 1959; London, Dobson, 1963.
*Through a Glass, Clearly.*   London, New English Library, 1967.
*Asimov's Mysteries.*   New York, Doubleday, and London, Rapp and Whiting, 1968.
*Nightfall and Other Stories.*   New York, Doubleday, 1969; London, Rapp and Whiting, 1970.


Other

*Biochemistry and Human Metabolism*, with Burnham Walker and William C. Boyd. Baltimore, Williams and Wilkins, 1952; revised edition, 1954, 1957.
*Chemicals of Life: Enzymes, Vitamins, Hormones.*   New York, Abelard Schuman, 1954; London, Bell, 1956.
*Races and People*, with William C. Boyd.   New York, Abelard Schuman, 1955; London, Abelard Schuman, 1958.
*Chemistry and Human Health*, with Burnham Walker and M. K. Nicholas.   New York, McGraw Hill, 1956.
*Inside the Atom.*   New York, Abelard Schuman, 1956; revised edition, New York and London, Abelard Schuman, 1958, 1961, 1966.
*Building Blocks of the Universe.*   New York, Abelard Schuman, 1957; London, Abelard Schuman, 1958; revised edition, 1961.
*Only a Trillion.*   London, Abelard Schuman, 1957; New York, Abelard Schuman, 1958; as *Marvels of Science*, New York, Collier, 1962.
*The World of Carbon.*   New York and London, Abelard Schuman, 1958; revised edition, New York, Collier, 1962.
*The World of Nitrogen.*   New York and London, Abelard Schuman, 1958; revised edition, New York, Collier, 1962.
*The Clock We Live On.*   New York and London, Abelard Schuman, 1959; revised edition, New York, Collier, 1962; Abelard Schuman, 1965.
*The Living River.*   New York and London, Abelard Schuman, 1959; revised edition, as *The Bloodstream: River of Life*, New York, Collier, 1961.
*The Realm of Numbers.*   Boston, Houghton Mifflin, 1959; London, Gollancz, 1963.
*Words of Science.*   Boston, Houghton Mifflin, 1959.
*Breakthroughs in Science.*   Boston, Houghton Mifflin, 1960.
*The Intelligent Man's Guide to Science.*   New York, Basic Books, 2 vols., 1960; revised edition, 1965; London, Nelson, 1967.
*The Kingdom of the Sun.*   New York and London, Abelard Schuman, 1960; revised edition, New York, Collier, 1962; Abelard Schuman, 1963.
*The Realm of Measure.*   Boston, Houghton Mifflin, 1960.
*Satellites in Outer Space.*   New York, Random House, 1960; revised edition, 1964.
*The Double Planet.*   New York, Abelard Schuman, 1960; London, Abelard Schuman, 1962; revised edition, 1967.
*The Wellsprings of Life.*   London, Abelard Schuman, 1960; New York, Abelard Schuman, 1961.
*The Realm of Algebra.*   Boston, Houghton Mifflin, 1961; London, Gollancz, 1964.
*Words from the Myths.*   Boston, Houghton Mifflin, 1961; London, Faber, 1963.
*Fact and Fancy.*   New York, Doubleday, 1962.
*Life and Energy.*   New York, Doubleday, 1962; London, Dobson, 1963.
*The Search for the Elements.*   New York, Basic Books, 1962.

*Words in Genesis*.   Boston, Houghton Mifflin, 1962.
*Words on the Map*.   Boston, Houghton Mifflin, 1962.
*View from a Height*.   New York, Doubleday, 1963; London, Dobson, 1964.
*The Genetic Code*.   New York, Orion Press, 1963; London, Murray, 1964.
*The Human Body: Its Structure and Operation*.   Boston, Houghton Mifflin, 1963;
London, Nelson, 1965.
*The Kite That Won the Revolution*.   Boston, Houghton Mifflin, 1963.
*Words from the Exodus*.   Boston, Houghton Mifflin, 1963.
*Adding a Dimension: 17 Essays on the History of Science*.   New York, Doubleday,
1964; London, Dobson, 1966.
*The Human Brain: Its Capacities and Functions*.   Boston, Houghton Mifflin, 1964;
as *The Human Brain: Its Capabilities and Functions*, London, Nelson, 1965.
*Quick and Easy Math*.   Boston, Houghton Mifflin, 1964; London, Whiting and
Wheaton, 1967.
*A Short History of Biology*.   Garden City, New York, Natural History Press, 1964;
London, Nelson, 1965.
*Planets for Man*, with Stephen H. Dole.   New York, Random House, 1964.
*Asimov's Biographical Encyclopedia of Science and Technology*.   New York, Double-
day, 1964.
*An Easy Introduction to the Slide Rule*.   Boston, Houghton Mifflin, 1965; London,
Whiting and Wheaton, 1967.
*The Greeks: A Great Adventure*.   Boston, Houghton Mifflin, 1965.
*Of Time and Space and Other Things*.   New York, Doubleday, 1965; London, Dobson,
1967.
*A Short History of Chemistry*.   New York, Doubleday, 1965.
*The Neutrino: Ghost Particle of the Atom*.   New York, Doubleday, and London,
Dobson, 1966.
*The Genetic Effects of Radiation*.   Washington, D.C., Atomic Energy Commission,
1966.
*The Noble Gases*.   New York, Basic Books, 1966.
*The Roman Republic*.   Boston, Houghton Mifflin, 1966.
*Understanding Physics*.   New York, Walker, 3 vols., 1966; London, Allen and Unwin,
1967.
*The Universe: From Flat Earth to Quasar*.   New York, Walker, 1966; London, Allen
Lane, 1967.
*The Roman Empire*.   Boston, Houghton Mifflin, 1967.
*The Moon*.   Chicago, Follett, 1967.
*Is Anyone There?* (essays).   New York, Doubleday, 1967; London, Rapp and Whiting,
1968.
*To the Ends of the Universe*.   New York, Walker, 1967.
*The Egyptians*.   Boston, Houghton Mifflin, 1967.
*Mars*.   Chicago, Follett, 1967.
*From Earth to Heaven: 17 Essays on Science*.   New York, Doubleday, 1967; London,
Dobson, 1968.
*Environments Out There*.   New York and London, Abelard Schuman, 1968.
*Science, Numbers and I: Essays on Science*.   New York, Doubleday, 1968.
*The Near East: 10,000 Years of History*.   Boston, Houghton Mifflin, 1968.
*Asimov's Guide to the Bible:*
   I. *The Old Testament*.   New York, Doubleday, 1968.
   II. *The New Testament*.   New York, Doubleday, 1969.
*The Dark Ages*.   Boston, Houghton Mifflin, 1968.
*Galaxies*.   Chicago, Follett, 1968.
*Stars*.   Chicago, Follett, 1968.
*Words from History*.   Boston, Houghton Mifflin, 1968.
*Photosynthesis*.   New York, Basic Books, 1969.

*Twentieth Century Discovery.* New York, Doubleday, 1969.
*Opus 100.* Boston, Houghton Mifflin, 1969.
*ABC's of Space.* New York, Walker, 1969.
*Great Ideas of Science.* Boston, Houghton Mifflin, 1969.
*The Solar System and Back.* New York, Doubleday, 1970.
*Asimov's Guide to Shakespeare:*
  I. *The Greek, Roman and Italian Plays.* New York, Doubleday, 1970.
  II. *The English Plays.* New York, Doubleday, 1970.
*Constantinople.* Boston, Houghton Mifflin, 1970.
*ABC's of the Ocean.* New York, Walker, 1970.
*Light.* Chicago, Follett, 1970.
*Stars in Their Courses.* New York, Doubleday, 1971.
*What Makes the Sun Shine.* Boston, Little Brown, 1971.
*Isaac Asimov Treasury of Humor.* Boston, Houghton Mifflin, 1971.
*The Sensuous Dirty Old Man* (as Dr. A.). New York, Walker, 1971.

Editor, *The Hugo Winners 1* and *2.* New York, Doubleday, 1962, 1971.
Editor, with Groff Conklin, *Fifty Short Science Fiction Tales.* New York, Collier, 1963.
Editor, *Tomorrow's Children: 18 Tales of Fantasy and Science Fiction.* New York, Doubleday, 1966.
Editor, *Where Do We Go from Here?* New York, Doubleday, 1971.

Bibliography: in *The Magazine of Fantasy and Science Fiction* (New York), October 1966.

Manuscript Collection: Mugar Library, Boston University.

Isaac Asimov comments:

If there is any category of human being for whom his work ought to speak for itself, it is the writer. If people *insist* on hearing from me, there is my book *Opus 100*, in which I tell people far more about me than they probably want to know.

\*    \*    \*

As with almost every other recognised writer of science fiction, Isaac Asimov has a thorough knowledge of the physical sciences which he combines with an acute perception and understanding of human behaviour. In his case this scientific background is more complete than most, however, since Dr. Asimov is an Associate Professor at Boston University, specialising in biochemistry. Of his 110 books to date, less than a quarter have been science fiction, the remainder of this staggering total having been textbooks and a whole series on popular science. He has in fact acquired a simultaneous reputation as one of the world's leading science writers, approached only by Arthur C. Clarke from within the science fiction field for his lucidity in tackling the most abstruse subjects.

Isaac Asimov's first story appeared in 1939, although his writing career began comparatively quietly compared with the immediate impact made by Robert Heinlein, for instance, who made his debut at about the same time. Many of the science fiction magazines published Asimov's stories but he did not attract a great deal of attention until the appearance of "Nightfall" at the end of 1941. This one novelette has been extensively anthologised and many readers claim that it is Asimov's best story, to the author's great irritation. But by this time, at the age of twenty-one, Asimov had already sold the first of what were to become known as his "robot" stories. Eventually he was to produce twenty or so tales based upon his famous "Three Laws of Robotics"—that robots cannot harm human beings—and a selection of these stories were published in the collection *I, Robot* in 1950. Not only have these stories been immensely popular but the "Laws" have come to be used by an ever-growing body of later science fiction writers, and it is accepted that should robots ever actually be built then they will conform to the assumptions laid down by Asimov in 1941.

Shortly after "Nightfall" Asimov commenced his most ambitious work, based originally upon a reading of *Decline and Fall of the Roman Empire*. He extrapolated this into the death and re-birth of a future Galactic civilisation and his name is now permanently linked with the "Foundation" series of stories, published intermittently from 1942–49. They were assembled into three novels in hard covers in the early 1950's.

Both series of stories were noted for their breadth of imagination and intricacy of plotting. In 1950 Asimov added greater human warmth to these two characteristics of his fiction with *Pebble in the Sky*, a charming novel set within the same general background as "Foundation" although not part of the series. *The Currents of Space* was written along similar lines.

Then in 1953 Asimov produced what must be regarded in many ways as his best novel. *The Caves of Steel* is in a class by itself, successfully combining as it does the best features of the "Robotics" stories (the co-protagonist is a robot) with the social extrapolation of "Foundation". The novel is simultaneously a view of the over-populated "hive" cities of the future, a warm story of people coming to terms with the steel caves in which they must live, and a stimulating detective mystery, one of the few to be set within a science fiction framework. Asimov later attempted a sequel to this novel with *The Naked Sun* which was successful in its own way although it lacked much of the depth of vision of the earlier work. Even more deliberately this set a detective puzzle against a background of science fiction, and the author subsequently adopted this theme at shorter length, with the collection *Asimov's Mysteries*.

This, then, is Isaac Asimov, a prolific and imaginative writer (if not lately of very much fiction) with almost a delight in the intricacies of his story-situations. At the same time he has the vital ability to communicate which has ensured that all of his works have a lasting appeal.

—Peter R. Weston

---

**ASTLEY, Thea (Beatrice May).** Australian. Born in Brisbane, Queensland, 25 August 1925. Educated at the University of Queensland, Brisbane, 1943–47, B.A. 1947. Married Edmund John Gregson in 1948; has one child. Taught English in Queensland, 1944–48, and in New South Wales, 1948–67. Since 1968, Senior Tutor in English, Macquarie University, Sydney. Recipient: Commonwealth Literary Fund Fellowship, 1961, 1964; Miles Franklin Award, 1962, 1965; Moomba Award, 1965. Address: Department of English, Macquarie University, North Ryde, Sydney, New South Wales, Australia.

PUBLICATIONS

Novels

*Girl with a Monkey.* Sydney, Angus and Robertson, 1959.

*A Descant for Gossips.*   Sydney, Angus and Robertson, 1960.
*The Well-Dressed Explorer*.   Sydney, Angus and Robertson, 1962.
*The Slow Natives*.   Sydney, Angus and Robertson, 1965; London, Angus and Robertson, 1966; New York, Evans, 1967.
*A Boat Load of Home Folk*.   Sydney and London, Angus and Robertson, 1968.


Uncollected Short Stories

"Cubby", in *Coast to Coast*.   Sydney, Angus and Robertson, 1961.
"The Scenery Never Changes", in *Coast to Coast*.   Sydney, Angus and Robertson, 1963.
"Journey to Olympus", in *Coast to Coast*.   Sydney, Angus and Robertson, 1965.


Other

Editor, *Coast to Coast, 1969–1970*.   Sydney and London, Angus and Robertson, 1971.

Verse published in periodicals and anthologies.


Critical Study: by the author on her own work: "The Idiot Question", in *Southerly* (Sydney), no. 1, 1970.


Thea Astley comments:

My main interest (and has been through my five published and current unpublished novels) is the misfit. Not the spectacular outsider, but the seedy little non-grandiose non-fitter who lives in his own mini-hell. Years ago I was impressed at eighteen or so by *Diary of a Nobody*, delighted by the quality Grossmith gave to the non-achiever and the sympathy which he dealt out. My five published novels have always been, despite the failure of reviewers to see it, a plea for charity—in the Pauline sense, of course—to be accorded to those not ruthless enough or grand enough to be gigantic tragic figures, but which, in their own way, record the same *via crucis*.

*       *       *

Towards the end of Thea Astley's fifth and, to date, most recent novel (*A Boat Load of Home Folk*) a hurricane descends upon Port Lena and rages violently while the problems and personal crises of the various characters draw towards some sort of resolution. The hurricane as a destructive natural phenomenon is slightly unusual in the imaginative world of Thea Astley, but, as symbol, it is not at all unfamiliar. For her characters seem to move perpetually in the artificially calm eye of the universe's innate anarchy: a symbolic storm encloses, yet also by its very existence and threatening nature, divides them. Moving in this constantly endangered pseudo-equilibrium, they brush often the edges of disaster, succumb to it occasionally, make what order they can with the opportunities that offer.
The impending, eager-to-consume anarchy of Miss Astley's world is manifested variously: it can materialise as the chaos of the emotional life, that destroys identity, reduces "to a spineless receptivity" (*Girl with a Monkey*); it may take the form of spiritual annihilation by human viciousness exquisitely applied and cravenly veiled (*A Descant for Gossips*); or act through the confusing yet endlessly fascinating impulses of the uncomprehended self

(*The Well-Dressed Explorer*); or emerge as that fatal disjunction from an intolerable world, experienced by those who, like "the wandering islands" of A. D. Hope's poem, ply "the long isolation of the heart" (*The Slow Natives*). Anarchy of a kind crowds in upon Miss Astley's characters and they have few resources with which to resist it.

Because the action is caught, as it were, in the eye of the symbolic storm, her novels, especially the earlier ones, seem at times highly, even excessively, deliberated: characters move in a real enough world, yet often with fleetingly dream-like deliberateness, islands of intense self-consciousness seeking, in assertive, almost desperate avowals of identity, bastions against encroaching chaos. Thus Elsie, in *Girl with a Monkey*, is "caught static in a complete island of twenty-four hours"—a metaphor which continually reinforces a sense of extreme deliberation in action and thought. When she hears, at Mass "as through walls of water", it is an apt and summary image for the action of the whole book; similarly, Mrs. Crozier is pictured as moving "Almost epileptically . . . pruning as she went the ambient roses. . . ." In *A Descant for Gossips* the tragic relationship between Helen, Moller and Vinny is captured, with momentary statuesqueness at its very inception, as "a dangerous montage", while, at the end of the book, Vinny, coming to her crucial decision, is described as seeing everything with "an amazing clarity . . . the grass stood in millions of separate blades, green and sharp. . . ." This has that quality of the dream that is not blurred and vague but horrifically more real than real. Again, George Brewster, hero of *The Well-Dressed Explorer*, builds his life on fantasy views of himself and dies in a "dream-streaked sleep" in which that life is paraded, insanely truncated, yet paradoxically illuminating and immensely moving. A similar quality is discoverable, though it is admittedly less obvious amidst a growing complexity, in the remaining two books.

This deliberation, even if it is occasionally overdone, is no mere quirk of "style"; it is a quality, a condition, in the characters' lives and an element in the Astley universe. And it is necessary, indeed indispensable, if the people are to affirm identity and a concept of order in face of a chaos of evil, sordidness, deadly triviality and cavernous loneliness.

It is difficult to determine what real weapons her characters have in this essentially rear-guard action against a universe morally and spiritually anarchic. Perhaps love, but that is plagued by infidelity, impediment or possessiveness; perhaps the child's innocence, but in this world, that innocence, followed out, brings Vinny Lalor and Keith Leverson to tragedy or near tragedy; perhaps religion. Thea Astley is certainly preoccupied with Catholic experience and upbringing, with Catholicism as an influence on personality and intellect and with the guilt and neurosis traditionally associated with Catholic sexual morality. But religion is not much comfort in the eye of the storm: it is at best irrelevant, at worst grotesque, as is attested in the Rosary Crusade (*Girl with a Monkey*), in Brewster's conversion, in the agony of Sister Matthew and Father Lingard (*The Slow Natives*) and in Father Lake's corruption (*A Boat Load of Home Folk*). Grotesquerie and corruption become inseparable from Catholicism in Miss Astley's vision, even if she suggests, in a way reminiscent of Greene, a road to sanctity through intimate knowledge of sin. A deeply personal conflict, between religious commitment and revulsion against unhealthy inhibition, inflexibility and sly corruption, seems to be involved; it may even have been resolved in the most recent novel, the excessive sordidness and grotesqueness of which suggest purgation.

In the course of the five novels, a straining for effect and some self-consciously literary moments in early books give way to a relaxed yet dense prose and a freely operating irony and acidulousness. Though *A Boat Load of Home Folk* poses some problems for anyone trying to predict what she will do next—there seems at least the possibility of a quite new departure—Miss Astley is clearly already an established and important talent in contemporary Australian fiction. She will have more to say.

—Brian Matthews

48385

**AUCHINCLOSS, Louis (Stanton).**   American.   Born in Lawrence, New York, 27 September 1917. Educated at Yale University, New Haven, Connecticut, 1935–38; University of Virginia Law School, Charlottesville, LL.B. 1941; admitted to the New York Bar, 1941. Served in the United States Naval Reserve, 1941–45. Married Adele Lawrence in 1957; has three children. Associate Lawyer, Sullivan and Cromwell, New York, 1941–51. Associate, 1954–58, and since 1958 Partner, Hawkins, Delafield and Wood, New York. Since 1966, President of the Museum of the City of New York. Trustee of the Josiah Macy Jr. Foundation, New York; Member of the Administrative Committee of the Dumbarton Oaks Research Library and Collection, Washington, D.C. Member of the National Institute of Arts and Letters. Address: 1111 Park Avenue, New York, New York 10028, U.S.A.

PUBLICATIONS

Novels

   *The Indifferent Children* (as Andrew Lee).   New York, Prentice Hall, 1947.
   *Sybil.*   Boston, Houghton Mifflin, and London, Gollancz, 1952.
   *A Law for the Lion.*   Boston, Houghton Mifflin, 1952; London, Gollancz, 1953.
   *The Great World and Timothy Colt.*   Boston, Houghton Mifflin, 1956; London, Gollancz, 1957.
   *Venus in Sparta.*   Boston, Houghton Mifflin, and London, Gollancz, 1958.
   *Pursuit of the Prodigal.*   Boston, Houghton Mifflin, 1959; London, Gollancz, 1960.
   *The House of Five Talents.*   Boston, Houghton Mifflin, 1960; London, Gollancz, 1961.
   *Portrait in Brownstone.*   Boston, Houghton Mifflin, and London, Gollancz, 1962.
   *The Rector of Justin.*   Boston, Houghton Mifflin, 1964; London, Gollancz, 1965.
   *The Embezzler.*   Boston, Houghton Mifflin, and London, Gollancz, 1966.
   *A World of Profit.*   Boston, Houghton Mifflin, 1968; London, Gollancz, 1969.

Short Stories

   *The Injustice Collectors.*   Boston, Houghton Mifflin, 1950; London, Gollancz, 1951.
   *The Romantic Egoists: A Reflection in Eight Minutes.*   Boston, Houghton Mifflin, and London, Gollancz, 1954.
   *Powers of Attorney.*   Boston, Houghton Mifflin, and London, Gollancz, 1963.
   *Tales of Manhattan.*   Boston, Houghton Mifflin, and London, Gollancz, 1967.
   *Second Chance.*   Boston, Houghton Mifflin, 1970; London, Gollancz, 1971.

Uncollected Short Stories

   "The Adventures of Johnny Flashback", in *Saturday Review* (New York), 22 October 1955.
   "The Trial of Mr. M.", in *Harper's* (New York), October 1956.

Play

   *The Club Bedroom* (produced New York, 1967).

Other

   *Edith Wharton.*   Minneapolis, University of Minnesota Press, 1961.

*Reflections of a Jacobite.*   Boston, Houghton Mifflin, 1961; London, Gollancz, 1962.
*Ellen Glasgow.*   Minneapolis, University of Minnesota Press, 1964.
*Pioneers and Caretakers: A Study of 9 American Women Novelists.*   Minneapolis,
    University of Minnesota Press, 1965; London, Oxford University Press, 1966.
*Motiveless Malignity* (on Shakespeare).   Boston, Houghton Mifflin, 1969; London,
    Gollancz, 1970.
*Henry Adams.*   Minneapolis, University of Minnesota Press, 1971.
*Edith Wharton: A Biography.*   New York, Viking Press, 1971; London, Joseph, 1972.

Editor, *An Edith Wharton Reader.*   New York, Scribner, 1965.


Manuscript Collection: Yale University, New Haven, Connecticut.


Louis Auchincloss comments:

I do not think in general that authors are very illuminating on their own work, but in view of the harshness of recent (1970) reviewers, I should like to quote from a letter of Edith Wharton in my collection. It was written when she was 63, ten years older than I now am, but the mood is relevant. She is speaking of critics who have disliked her last novel:

You will wonder that the priestess of the life of reason should take such things to heart, and I wonder too. I never have minded before, but as my work reaches its close, I feel so sure that it is either nothing or far more than they know. And I wonder, a little desolately, which.

Mrs. Wharton's work was far from its close, and I hope mine may be!

*        *        *

Louis Auchincloss is among the few dedicated novelists of manners at work in contemporary America. He is a successor to Edith Wharton as a chronicler of the New York aristocracy. In this role he necessarily imbues his novels with an elegiac tone as he observes the passing beauties of the city and the fading power of the white Anglo-Saxon Protestants of old family and old money who can no longer sustain their position of dominance in the society or their aristocratic ideals. His principal subject is thus the manners and morals, the money and marriages, the families and houses, the schools and games, the language and arts of the New York aristocracy as he traces its rise, observes its present crisis, and meditates its possible fall and disappearance. The point of vantage from which he often observes the aristocracy is that of the lawyer who serves and frequently belongs to this class.

The idea of good family stands in an uneasy relation to money in Auchincloss's fiction. Auchincloss dramatizes the dilemma of the American aristocracy by showing that it is necessary to possess money to belong to this class but fatal to one's standing within the class to pursue money. People who have connections with those who are still in trade cannot themselves fully qualify as gentlemen, as the opportunistic Mr. Dale in *The Great World and Timothy Colt* shows. On the other hand, Auchincloss is clearly critical of those aristocrats like Bertie Millinder or Percy Prime who do nothing constructive and are engaged simply in the spending of money. Auchincloss recognizes that the family is the most important of aristocratic institutions and that its place in its class is guaranteed by the conservation of its resources. This task of preserving the family wealth falls to the lawyers, and his fiction is rich in the complexities, both moral and financial, of fiduciary responsibility; *Venus in Sparta* is a novel in point. The paradox that Auchincloss reveals but does not seem sufficiently to exploit is that the conservative impulse of the aristocracy, which emphasizes the past, is concerned ultimately with posterity, which of course emphasizes the future.

Auchincloss does, however, fully exploit the conflict between the marriage arranged for the good of the family, often by strong women, and romantic or sexual impulses that are destructive of purely social goals, as *Portrait in Brownstone* illustrates. Sex and love are enemies to the organicism of conservative societies, in which the will of the individual is vested in the whole. Auchincloss observes the workings of this organic notion in the structure of family and marriage as well as in institutions like the school and the club where a consensus judgment about value and behaviour is formulated and handed down. Such institutions preserve a way of life and protect those who live by it from those on the outside who do not. *The Rector of Justin* is the most obvious of Auchincloss's novels to deal with an institution, or with a man as an institution, that performs this function.

Auchincloss's fiction does more than present us with a mere record of the institutions that support the American aristocracy. The dramatic interest in his novels and whatever larger importance may be accorded them lies in his recognition that the entire class is in jeopardy and that individual aristocrats are often failures. Sometimes Auchincloss sees problems arising within the context of aristocracy itself, as when individual will or desire comes in conflict with the organicism; perhaps Reese Parmalee, in *Pursuit of the Prodigal*, makes the most significant rebellion of all Auchincloss's characters, but he is rejecting a decadent aristocracy and not aristocracy itself. Auchincloss is severely critical of the idea of the gentleman when it is corrupted by allegiance to superficial qualities, like Guy Prime's capacity to hold his liquor or to behave with virile cordiality in *The Embezzler*. But the real failures are those aristocrats who suffer, as so many of Auchincloss's male characters do, from a sense of inadequacy and insecurity that leads them to self-destructiveness. They are not strong and tough-fibred, as so many of the women are; they seem too fastidious and over-civilized, and they are failing the idea of society and their class. In this way, and in others, Auchincloss regretfully chronicles the passing of the aristocracy, which cannot sustain its own ideals in the contemporary world; *A World of Profit* is the most explicit recognition of this failure.

Auchincloss has made his record of the New York aristocracy in a style which is clear and simple, occasionally elegant and brilliant, and sometimes self-consciously allusive. He has a gift for comedy of manners, which he has not sufficiently cultivated, and a fine model in Oscar Wilde. Other influences upon him include Edith Wharton, in ways already mentioned; Henry James, from whom he learned the manipulation of point of view and the faculty of endowing things, art objects for example, with meaning; and St. Simon, a memorialist who did for the French court what Auchincloss wishes to do for Knickerbocker New York. Yet among his faults as a novelist, especially evident because of the particular genre he has chosen, is a failure to give the reader a richness of detail; he does well with home furnishings but is far less successful with the details of institutions. Furthermore, he sometimes loses control of his novels and permits action to overwhelm theme. The most serious criticism to be made of his work is that while he does indeed pose moral dilemmas for his characters, he too easily resolves their problems for them. He does not sufficiently convey a sense of the bitter cost of honesty or courage. He has given us, on balance, a full enough record of upper class life in New York, but he has fallen short of the most penetrating and meaningful kinds of social insight that the best of the novelists of manners offer.

—Chester E. Eisinger

---

**BAILEY, Paul.** British. Born in Battersea, London, 16 February 1937. Educated at the Sir Walter St. John's School, London, 1948–53; Central School of Speech and Drama, London, 1953–56. Actor, 1956–63. Currently, Publisher's Reader for Jonathan Cape Ltd., London. Recipient: Maugham Award, 1968; Arts Council Award, 1968; Authors' Club Award, 1970. Address: 32 St. Stephen's Gardens, London W.2, England.

PUBLICATIONS

Novels

At the Jerusalem.   London, Cape, and New York, Atheneum, 1967.
Trespasses.   London, Cape, 1970; New York, Harper, 1971.

Critical Studies: review by Irving Wardle, in *The Observer* (London), 28 May 1967; by Alan Ross, in *London Magazine*, October 1967; by Maggie Ross in *The Listener* (London), 30 April 1970.

Paul Bailey comments:

I write novels for many reasons, some of which I have probably never consciously thought of. I don't like absolute moral judgments, the "placing" of people into types—I'm both delighted and appalled by the mysteriousness of my fellow creatures. I enjoy "being" other people when I write, and the novels I admire most respect the uniqueness of other human beings. I like to think I show my characters respect and that I don't sit in judgment on them. This is what, in my small way, I am striving for—to capture, in a shaped and controlled form, something of the mystery of life. I am writing, too, to expand and stimulate my own mind. I hope I will have the courage to be more ambitious, bolder and braver in my search for the ultimately unknowable, with each book I write.

*          *          *

Bailey's prize-winning first novel, *At the Jerusalem*, shows us a few months of the life of an old woman in the Jerusalem, a home—actually a converted workhouse—for old ladies. Part 1 reports Mrs. Gadny's first days there, Part 2 describes what happened before (her daughter died so that she went to live in the unsympathetic home of her stepson and his wife, a shortlived arrangement) and Part 3 covers the rest of her stay in the home. Mrs. Gadny is a simple woman, an unsubtle mind but a gentle, reserved human being. She hates the smiles which the Matron turns on and off, the jollity of the other residents, sharing a ward with eight others, toilets with no locks, being naked for a doctor. And so she declines: she tears up her photos, sits outside in the rain, writes to a dead friend, is put in a locked bedroom alone, weeps inexplicably, screams during another's 90th birthday party, and so, finally, is taken to a mental hospital.

Some of the background seems conventionally fictional, like Mrs. Capes, whose homosexual ballet-dancer son killed himself. Bailey occasionally seems superior, sneering too patly at the parents of the stepson's wife, who model their home on pictures in American magazines and read "that beautiful man who writes so movingly about our royal family."

*At the Jerusalem* shows convincingly life in an old people's home, and tells the sad story of one particular old woman, giving age from the viewpoint of the old (we are often within the crumbling consciousness of Mrs. Gadny—for instance, as she dimly perceives different coloured tiles in the corridors). More generally, we have to face—in a way that is often painful and frightening—the pathos, vulgarity and indignity of being old, and the way in which the elderly are treated. Bailey's book has none of the amusement or idiosyncrasy of John Arden's *The Happy Haven* or Muriel Spark's *Memento Mori*: he faces us with the truth.

Bailey's second novel, *Trespasses*, is equally concerned with sad people, with a cheerless worldview. But this time he adds technical ingenuity: the book is composed of fragmentary memories, conversations, diary jottings, lyrical intense moments, often two or three to a page, and apparently disconnected. Each has headings: Her, Him, Boy, Us, or, more diversely, Early, Pleas, Before, Peace, Black. There are references to childhood, courting, a funeral, landladies, and more literary—even over-written—play with roses and apple trees. The longest passage, of 24 pages, is a first-person short story of a country girl's life in London, the narrator's mother, and the two other sustained passages are a seriocomic homosexual's story and an account of a youth visiting a lunatic.

As readers, we have to make an effort to understand. We have to make sense of this man's life, separate with him the important people and experiences from the trivial. We have to understand—if we can—why his wife killed herself, bloodily and purposefully, where he is going now, what life—as represented by the homosexual, his father's mother, the talkative landlady and her sexually-wild widowed daughter—is really like. He emerges as a Camberwell newsagent's son, away from his parents during the war years, loved possessively by his mother, bright but unsure of himself, eventually turning unenthusiastically to teaching. At the end of Part 1 he is able to write: "My ghosts are assembled. I trust them to lead me somewhere." Although later he is in a mental hospital, the last entry is more optimistic: "I write down MAN in the hope that I will one day earn the right to use it about myself. My name is Ralph Hicks and I hope I will become a man." So the headings have served not only to guide the reader, but as attempts by Hicks to face and categorise his past.

Bailey, then, writes fluently and observantly, catching moments of conversation as it floats by, structuring his works carefully, and in the later book attempting an experiment in form. Bailey is not just promising; each of these works is fully achieved.

—Malcolm Page

---

**BAKER, Elliott.** American. Born in Buffalo, New York, 15 December 1922. Educated at Indiana University, Bloomington, B.S. 1944. Served in the United States Army. Recipient: Putnam Award, 1964. Address: 52 Park Close, London W.14, England.

PUBLICATIONS

Novels

*A Fine Madness.* New York, Putnam, and London, Joseph, 1964.
*The Penny Wars.* New York, Putnam, 1968; London, Joseph, 1969.
*Pocock and Pitt.* New York, Putnam, 1971.

Play

*The Penny Wars* (produced New York, 1969).

*       *       *

While Elliott Baker's two novels, *A Fine Madness* and *The Penny Wars*, demonstrate a diversity of ideas and themes, both are concerned with moral and psychological growth and with the life of the imagination. Both are comic novels of modern America, and in both an underlying sense of tragedy informs the comedy with serious direction.

*A Fine Madness* documents the triumph of an American Gulley Jimson over the forces of conformity and death-in-life. Samson Shillitoe is a workingclass hero, a Blakean poet driven by powerful artistic and sexual urges. The story is as involuted as Evelyn Waugh's early comedies, and in it Shillitoe is pursued and seized by a group of psychiatric experimenters. He is analyzed, institutionalized and lobotomized but emerges whole, sane and uncastrated, his creative (and procreative) energies unharmed. Baker uses an inside knowledge of modern psychotherapy to create a convincing view of the artist at war with a mechanical world and the mechanized minds of clinical psychology. Shillitoe, like Gulley Jimson or like Blake himself, is obsessed by imagination, driven by forces beyond his control. He is amoral, anti-social, unconcerned with "adjustment" or mental health. Conversely, the psychologists view him only as a specimen, a sample of neurosis or psychosis. But Shillitoe's view triumphs; Samson manages to conceive and produce an epic-sized poem, and his common-law wife (his version of Catherine Blake) conceives his child. Life and creation vanquish death and destruction. Perhaps the best rubric for the novel is an epigram of William Carlos Williams which Samson quotes: "It's difficult to get the news from poetry, but men die miserably every day for lack of what is found there."

In *The Penny Wars* Baker creates a nostalgic view of adolescence on the eve of WW II. Tyler Bishop, another rebel, grows up in 1939 in squalor and confusion of values. An unreconstructed liberal, Tyler worries about the Nazis while America's smugness and isolationism seem overwhelming, worries about his budding sexuality, worries about the world he will inherit; himself a WASP, he stands up for Jews and Negroes, fights bigotry and ignorance—and loses. Tyler champions Dr. Axelrod, a refugee from Hitler's ovens, even though he finds him personally obnoxious; he champions black people even though he is frightened of them. Ultimately his contradictory feelings collide, and he is left alone, groping toward a complete individualism.

These two novels share the theme of the development of imagination and conscience. Tyler Bishop writes letters to the editor, reads war news from Europe and worries, saying, "I just want to get laid and save the world. . . . In that order." Samson Shillitoe has grown up and into himself, into a complete world of the imagination: "Shillitoe had never read one of his own poems aloud to anyone. Once transferred from him to paper and complete they held little interest for him."

In *A Fine Madness* Baker describes the enormous and mysterious personal energies of art in a figure larger than life, a Gargantua-Dionysus. In *The Penny Wars* Baker creates a confused boy driven by conscience and intelligence to defend a dead Jew he had hated against the attacks of Negroes he wants to love. Baker's first novel details the autonomy of artistic imagination, the second shows the development of moral consciousness. Samson Shillitoe exists in a world beyond political and social realities, while Tyler Bishop grows up in chaos which he tries to shape through a utopian vision. The stories are sides of the same coin, and deep inside Shillitoe the cynic-poet abides the ghost of an idealistic boy bitten once too often by a careless and savage world.

—William J. Schafer

---

**BALDWIN, James (Arthur).**   American. Born in New York City, 2 August 1924. Educated at P.S. 139, Harlem, and DeWitt Clinton High School, Bronx, New York. Lived in Paris, 1948–56. Member, Actors Studio, New York, National Advisory Board of CORE (Congress on Racial Equality), and of the National Committee for a Sane Nuclear Policy. Recipient:

Saxton Fellowship, 1945; Rosenwald Fellowship, 1948; Guggenheim Fellowship, 1954; *Partisan Review* Fellowship, 1956; National Institute of Arts and Letters grant, 1956; Ford Fellowship, 1958; National Conference of Christians and Jews Brotherhood Award, 1962; George Polk Award, 1963; Foreign Drama Critics Award, 1964. D.Litt., University of British Columbia, Vancouver, 1964. Member, National Institute of Arts and Letters, 1964. Address: 137 West 71st Street, New York, New York 10023, U.S.A.


PUBLICATIONS


Novels

> *Go Tell It on the Mountain*.   New York, Knopf, 1953.
> *Giovanni's Room*.   New York, Dial Press, 1955; London, Joseph, 1957.
> *Another Country*.   New York, Dial Press, 1962; London, Joseph, 1963.
> *Tell Me How Long the Train's Been Gone*.   New York, Dial Press, and London, Joseph, 1968.


Short Stories

> *Going to Meet the Man*.   New York, Dial Press, and London, Joseph, 1965.


Uncollected Short Story

> "Any Day Now", in *Partisan Review* (New Brunswick, New Jersey), Spring 1960.


Plays

> *The Amen Corner* (produced Washington, D.C., 1955; New York and London, 1965). New York, Dial Press, 1965.
> *Blues for Mister Charley* (produced New York, 1964; London, 1965).   New York, Dial Press, 1964.


Other

> *Notes of a Native Son*.   Boston, Beacon Press, 1955; London, Joseph, 1964.
> *Nobody Knows My Name: More Notes of a Native Son*.   New York, Dial Press, 1961; as *No Name in the Streets*, London, Joseph, 1972.
> *The Fire Next Time*.   New York, Dial Press, and London, Joseph, 1963.
> *Nothing Personal*, with Richard Avedon.   New York, Atheneum, and London, Penguin, 1964.
> *A Rap on Race*, with Margaret Mead.   Philadelphia, Lippincott, and London, Joseph, 1971.


James Baldwin comments:

I have always found it difficult to speak of my own work. I am not altogether certain that I can identify my "subjects" and "themes". The life that I was born into, or the life that I have lived—which are not, necessarily, the same—certainly account, to some degree, for the structure of my mind. I have made a certain conscious effort to avoid sentimentality. I am still making that effort.

\*      \*      \*

James Baldwin, the most eloquently intense and morally insistent essayist in midcentury America, has published four novels and a book of short stories. Some of his fiction, like some of his drama, has stimulated controversy; but there is general agreement that he has done masterful work in both the novel and the short story forms.

*Go Tell It on the Mountain*, Baldwin's first and best novel, centered upon the religious conversion of John Grimes the night of his fourteenth birthday, is divided into three parts. Part I, "The Seventh Day," introduces the Grimes family in Harlem in March 1935. John feels locked in by the repressive, doom-ridden preachments of his father Gabriel, head deacon of the store-front Temple of the Fire Baptized, and is guiltily aware of sex. He hates his father reciprocally, sometimes hates his mother, and will soon hate all white people—whom his father despises—"if God did not change his heart."

Part II, "The Prayers of the Saints," which comprises in flashbacks well over half the novel, provides background for the family dilemma of John. His sixty-year-old Aunt Florence, driven by her fear of death from cancer, recalls in her prayer the following: the slavery-time memories of her and Gabriel's mother, who envisioned a dominant masculine role in Black family life; Florence's departure from the South in 1900 after her white employer "proposed that she become his concubine"; and the marital love between her and caramel-colored Frank—ended after ten years by her disdain for his "common nigger" friends and by her jars of skin-whitener (despite Frank's reminder that "black's a mighty pretty color"). Florence ends her prayer bitterly asking why God "preferred her mother and her brother, the old, black woman, and the low, black man, while she, who had sought only to walk upright, was come to die, alone and in poverty, in a dirty, furnished room?"

Gabriel, in the long section on his prayer, relives highlights of his twenty-first through fortieth years, mainly his affair with Esther and the birth and death at eighteen of their son Royal. This affair, preceded by wild young Gabriel's marriage of repentance to bony, "sexless" Deborah, humanizes him as trapped in contradictory pietistic and lustful urges so delicately balanced within him as to demand rigid, defensive behavior. Significant are young Gabriel's criticism of "big, comfortable, ordained" ministers at the Twenty-Four Elders Revival Meeting; the intimation of the perfect coincidence of death and life at the burial of Esther and later at the news of her son Royal's death; and John's sense of the artistic value of hatred: "He did not *want* to love his father; he wanted to hate him, to cherish that hatred, and give his hatred words one day." Stylistically notable are the poetic prose description of Gabriel's autumn flight after deserting Esther, and the use of sound, silence, and group movement to signal flashbacks.

Elizabeth, in her section, recalls what love has meant to her. Deprived of her sick mother's questionable love by death, and of her disreputable father's evident love by her aunt's prudishness, Elizabeth finds idyllic love when she and Richard go to New York. But Richard commits suicide after humiliation and beating by police. After the birth of their illegitimate son John, she finds redemption in marriage to Gabriel (Deborah having died), who promises to love her son. In this section about love, the antithesis has its role: Richard's quest for knowledge is energized by hatred of whites; and Elizabeth, after Richard's death, "hated it all—the white city, the white world."

Part III, "The Threshing-Floor," engrossingly describes John's conversion on the floor before the altar, the tortured probings and exhilarations of his mind sharpened by guilt and expanded by hope for salvation. At dawn, the smiling boy, facing an unsmiling father, is confident of his future.

Plainly autobiographical, this novel about a boy's anguished choice between church and jail metaphorically opposes the demands of those institutions as the forces that have long constricted but spiritualized Black people. The "saints" of the store-front church are all martyrs, Florence having been undone by normal ambition, Gabriel by duties too spiritual for his normal flesh, and Elizabeth by love. Jailed within body, family, church, and country, they vacillate between varieties of surrender and feel no sinless ecstasy or power other than singing the mysteries of God. The Biblical enchantment of Baldwin's prose rhythm elevates even his scenes of animal love, and the speech of his characters is vividly true to their heritage.

In *Giovanni's Room*, Baldwin's major fictional deviation from the racial theme, he melo-dramatically but profoundly explores love as illuminated and defined by homosexuality. The action, set in Paris and recalled by David on the eve of homosexual Giovanni's execution for murdering his exploiter Guillaume, concerns David's love and responsibility for Giovanni, whom he deserts to return to his fiancée Hella. Giovanni's indictment of David is central: "You are not leaving me for a *woman*. If you were really in love with this little girl, you would not have had to be so cruel to me" and "You want to *kill* [me] in the name of all your lying little moralities." Baldwin emphasizes that love inspires magnanimity and charity and that morality begins in honesty about oneself.

*Another Country* is Baldwin's major attempt to dramatize the racist destruction of inter-racial affections. In Book I, Rufus Scott, the jazz musician who turns his drums and his Southern white girl friend into objects for the dazzling release of his frustrations over racism, dives suicidally off the George Washington Bridge. His white friends, who failed to imagine his despair, live under its shadow as victims of a loveless, divisive New York. His sister Ida uses Vivaldo Moore's love to hasten her vengeance upon the white world. Vivaldo, loving her partly to shorten the distance that his whiteness maintains, pays in pain the dues that Cass Silenski offers less riskily. In Books II and III, Eric Jones, a young Southern actor who in France discovers his reality homosexually with Yves, moves therapeutically among other characters, teaching as existential man sexual liberation from the chaos of life, love, racism, and death. *Another Country*, although weakened by talkiness, occasionally inconsistent diction, and a questionable ending, is morally keyed to a remark by the preacher at Rufus's funeral: "Try to understand . . . . we got to try to be better than the world."

*Tell Me How Long the Train's Been Gone* follows Leo Proudhammer from the age of ten in Harlem through his years as a famous actor. More to be noted than the typical inclusion of heterosexual, homosexual, and interracial lovemaking are young Leo's despairing father and idolized older brother Caleb. Too much black rum and servility before white men destroy Leo's respect for the former; then police and prison guard brutality, followed by conversion to the ministry during his service in World War II, saps the once admirable militance in Caleb. Leo's affections turn to Christopher, who enters his life as his body-guard and who closes the novel telling him "I think you got to agree that we [Black people] need us some guns." Although Leo, like Christopher, considers religion useless in the racial struggle, he demurs at the thought of violence. This latest novel is occasionally powerful —in the summer workshop and police station scenes, for example—but it is Baldwin's least impressive long work.

Of the eight stories in *Going to Meet the Man*, the first three focus upon father-son relation-ships: "The Rockpile" and "The Outing" (both using characters and situations seen in his first novel) and "The Man Child." Three others show people trying to accept their Blackness: "Previous Condition," "Come Out the Wilderness," and the excellent "This Morning, This Evening, So Soon." The other two are also exceptional: "Sonny's Blues," the best story, and "Going to Meet the Man." The former brilliantly probes the failure of sympathy between two brothers, one an addict, and the latter traces the growth of psychopathic race hatred in an impotent deputy sheriff.

Baldwin's fiction, even when it falters, aims high, grappling with problems by which people measure themselves as humans and lovers. Unsparing but hopeful in its societal and racial criticism, urging self-acceptance and love in personal relations, his novels and stories pain and elevate the consciousness of his vast audience.

—James A. Emanuel

**BALLANTYNE, David (Watt).** New Zealander. Born in Auckland, 14 June 1924. Educated at Gisborne High School. Served in the New Zealand Army, 1942–43. Married Vivienne Heise in 1949; has one child. Journalist, *Auckland Star*, 1943–47, *Southern Cross*, Wellington, 1947–48, *Auckland Star*, 1949–54, and *Evening News*, London, 1955–63; Editor, *Finding Out*, London, 1964; Journalist, *Evening Standard*, London, 1965. Since 1966, Feature Writer, *Auckland Star*. Recipient: Hubert Church Memorial Award, 1949; A.T.V. prize, for television drama, 1961; New Zealand Scholarship in Letters, 1968. Address: Editorial Department, Auckland Star, P.O. Box 3697, Auckland, New Zealand.

PUBLICATIONS

Novels

    *The Cunninghams*.  New York, Vanguard Press, 1948; London, Hale, 1963.
    *The Last Pioneer*.  Christchurch, Whitcombe and Tombs, and London, Hale, 1963.
    *A Friend of the Family*.  Christchurch, Whitcombe and Tombs, and London, Hale, 1966.
    *Sydney Bridge Upside Down*.  Christchurch, Whitcombe and Tombs, and London, Hale, 1968.

Short Stories

    *And the Glory*.  Christchurch, Whitcombe and Tombs, and London, Hale, 1963.

Uncollected Short Stories

    "Only a Kid of Course", in *New Zealand Weekly News* (Auckland), 21 January 1942.
    "A Child's Day", in *New Zealand New Writing 2* (Wellington), October 1943.
    "A Couple of Hacks", in *Arena* (Wellington), 1962.

Plays

    Numerous plays produced on New Zealand and British television.

Other

    Editor, *Around the World: Looking at Other Lands* (juvenile).  London, Purnell, 1965; Boston, Ginn, 1966.

Critical Studies: *New Zealand Literature* by E. H. McCormick, London, Oxford University Press, 1959; *Islands of Innocence* by M. H. Holcroft, Wellington, Reed, 1964; *New Zealand Fiction since 1945* by H. Winston Rhodes, Wellington, McIndoe, 1968.

David Ballantyne comments:

I took my earliest themes from what I knew of the ways of life of my fellow-countrymen.

I wanted to write truthfully about their attitudes and their behaviour. I thought of myself as a realist, in the tradition of writers like Zola, Dreiser, Joyce, Hemingway and Farrell. I drew upon my own experiences for my fiction, but tried for a detachment that would allow me to see the humour and warmth in life as well as the anxiety and pain. I thought a lean writing style, free of pretty phrases and philosophical flourishes, best suited to what I had to say. This was my approach in my first novel *The Cunninghams* and in my short stories. In a later novel, *A Friend of the Family*, written after I had lived in London several years, I used satire to suggest how I viewed certain aspects of contemporary life. And in another novel, *Sydney Bridge Upside Down*, I found parody a useful device. Mainly, though, I have told stories. Some more eventful than others.

*        *        *

All David Ballantyne's work could well be subtitled, "Scenes from Provincial Life". He began in the 1940s as a writer of short stories, notably "And the Glory", which appeared in *Landfall* in 1948 and gave the title to a collected volume in 1963. In this story, Larry, a lowgrade shop hand reprimanded by the boss, goes home to the suburbs to take out his temper there. He doesn't understand his own state of mind. Though he has "a comfortable job, a wife, a son, the prospect of a State house, good health", he still asks in puzzlement "what more did anybody want?" The answer that Ballantyne intends is, it seems, "the power and the glory". But Larry's ensuing verbal battle with the Electric Power Board (was the pun necessary?) over an unpaid bill provides him with only a shabby "glory". Like most of Ballantyne's shorter fiction, this story is economical and swift. Two other elements in it are also, however, constant in his later work: the mediocre, lower middle class "ordinary joker" as subject, and the under-played, undramatic, would-be-realistic lingo of the presentation.

Ballantyne's first novel, *The Cunninghams*, which also appeared in 1948, is set in New Zealand's depression decade, the 1930s; at full novel length, Ballantyne's grey preoccupation with social realism needs a lift of style or symbol to give some strength of dramatic impact. *The Cunninghams* has only a painstaking documentary accuracy. The people of this novel —Gilbert the ex-soldier father, Helen the overdriven wife, Gilbert the sensitive, inhibited and hopeless son—are recognisable enough, and so is the New Zealand small town setting. But these dreary empty lives repel the reader by that very boredom which is meant to evoke his pity. This is, of course, the difficulty inherent in all fiction of social analysis—how to create interest out of uninteresting lives.

Ballantyne made another attempt at picturing the stagnation of "provincial life" in his next novel, *The Last Pioneer*. To the small town of Mahuta come Mr. Wyatt and his son, in search of the pioneer dream. The minutiae of life are given with scrupulous fidelity. Booze in the kitchen or the pub, drama at the local movies ("the flagons and the flicks", as it might be put) represent the range of Mahuta's non-utilitarian activities, plus of course a little fun with sex. As a "decent joker" Wyatt should have been accepted, for the term is "the New Zealander's highest tribute" as someone remarks. "I mean, a decent joker is an ordinary joker, and *that's* what we want. But you'll have to remember to stay ordinary." Still giving the author's view, the speaker goes on to analyse: "We treasure our smallness down here, you know . . . . the State will do *everything* for you if you let it . . . . you can be as mediocre as the next person, mediocre and safe."

The pioneer, individual and striving, is therefore "out of fashion", and Wyatt's country paradise in its own way rejects him. But as before, no insights transcend for us the banal boredom of the surface so minutely delineated. Ballantyne adds up nothing; the arithmetic of generalised perception is left entirely to the reader, and with neither "power" nor "glory" offered to him, he finds the going dreary.

*A Friend of the Family* is a livelier book, verging on farce, about a phoney business tycoon and his associates, all in perpetual and pointless motion. The characterisation is shallow and the action slapstick. At the end, the "ordinary joker" who tells the tale gets some of the satisfactions of power from the bizarre revenges which he takes upon his employers, but we hardly know or like the fellow well enough to get much kick out of this.

*Sydney Bridge Upside Down* (an irrelevant catchpenny title) returns to provincial life. Calliope Bay has a store, a school, a wharf, a river, a railway line, the ruins of the abandoned freezing works, and five houses. The adolescent Harry uses the trailing boyish lingo of the half-educated to tell the story of what he saw and did when his little tart of a cousin, Caroline, came for a country holiday. Neither the manner nor the material is new, and it cannot be said that Ballantyne has anything to add to his previous emphasis on the undistinguished, the unpleasant, and the squalid in sub-standard lives. His shock tactics make the book saleable enough, but no significant pattern emerges from the mosaic of surface trivialities.

Ballantyne has however developed an assured and skilful craftsmanship, which should stand him in good stead when he makes his next move.

—Joan Stevens

---

**BALLARD, J(ames) G(raham).**   British.   Born in Shanghai, China, 15 November 1930. Educated at King's College, Cambridge. Served in the Royal Air Force. Married Helen Mary Matthews in 1953 (deceased, 1964); has three children. Address: 36 Charlton Road, Shepperton, Middlesex, England.

PUBLICATIONS

Novels

*The Wind from Nowhere.*   New York, Berkley, 1962.
*The Drowned World.*   New York, Berkley, 1962; London, Gollancz, 1963.
*The Drought.*   London, Cape, 1965.
*The Crystal World.*   London, Cape, and New York, Farrar Straus, 1966.
*The Atrocity Exhibition.*   London, Cape, 1970.
*Crash!*   London, Cape, 1972.

Short Stories

*The Voices of Time and Other Stories.*   New York, Berkley, 1962.
*Billenium and Other Stories.*   New York, Berkley, 1962.
*The 4-Dimensional Nightmare.*   London, Gollancz, 1963.
*Passport to Eternity and Other Stories.*   New York, Berkley, 1963.
*The Terminal Beach.*   London, Gollancz, 1964.
*The Disaster Area.*   London, Cape, 1967.
*The Day of Forever.*   London, Panther, 1968.
*The Overloaded Man.*   London, Panther, 1968.
*Vermilion Sands.*   New York, Berkley, 1971.

J. G. Ballard comments:

I believe that science fiction is the authentic literature of the 20th century, the only fiction to respond imaginatively to the transforming nature of science and technology. I believe that the true domain of science fiction is that zone I have termed inner space, rather than outer space, and that the present, rather than the future, is now the period of greatest moral urgency for the writer. In my own fiction I have tried to achieve these aims.

*     *     *

Ballard's novels and short stories go well beyond the limits that the term "science-fiction" suggests. They reveal a powerful and sensuous imagination which reinforces a serious and universal concern with human despair in the universe of Nature. In its cosmic scale, Ballard's writing makes the reader uncomfortably aware of the slender filament by which man and all his works depend from the general scheme of things. In this respect, it has a distinctly seventeenth-century flavour—of the preoccupation with death we see in Browne, Burton and Donne—which is expressed by Ransome in *The Drought*: "I've always thought of life as a kind of disaster area." The dominant images which linger with the reader are of disease limiting human aspirations and achievements, leprous beauty, deformed genius and cities of Hell presented as sharply as their visual parallels in Delvaux, Dali and Ernst.

Thematically, Ballard's novels are concerned with the delicate natural equipoise upon which our existence depends, the ease with which the balance may be upset and the consequences of the resulting imbalance. In *The Wind from Nowhere* a global wind turns the world into a dry, howling desert in which human relationships are torn apart and dried of feeling; in *The Drowned World* the earth's protective ionosphere is penetrated as a result of solar storms, and the world turned into a vast equatorial swamp in which man returns to the autistic world of the womb. In both these novels, the natural balance which we take for granted has been drastically upset by chance, with disastrous consequences for mankind; *The Drought* turns the screw by having mankind the instrument of his own disaster by polluting the oceans to such an extent that they are suffocated by a thin film of non-degradable substance which prevents the formation of clouds; once again, Ballard closely examines the destructive effect of such a disaster on human personality and relationships.

None of these novels, however, should be thought of as mere environmentalist propaganda; they go well beyond such a literal stage to a wider concern about man's desperate place in the universe. That Ballard's preoccupation is with the grander scheme is shown in *The Crystal World* which provides both explanation and solution to the problem of maintaining equipoise. Into a world of physical and social disease comes "time with the Midas touch" which petrifies and purifies what it meets. As in *The Wind from Nowhere* and *The Drowned World* random chance introduces the change, but this time the effect shows the way to solution. The crystallization effect results from the repeated collisions of anti-particles with particles, each of which subtracts "from the universe another quantum of its total share of time." The ultimate consequence is foreseen as a single atom producing "an infinite number of duplicates of itself" and so filling "the entire universe from which simultaneously all time has expired." So Ballard's explanation for natural disaster is the impossibility of maintaining balance in a cosmos where time, and therefore movement, is dominant; his solution (and this novel is compellingly hopeful) is that life can only be found in an ultimate, total stillness out of time.

What is very striking about Ballard's work is the degree to which it explores those particular zones of the wasteland whose approach routes were mapped by T. S. Eliot. The first three novels probe areas which directly relate to particular preoccupations in the Prufrock poems and *The Waste Land*, while *The Crystal World* has the same concern as the *Four Quartets* in its search for "the still point of a turning world." Such a comparison, made in terms of image and thematic concerns, might be expected to diminish Ballard, but it doesn't; nor should one conclude that Ballard's energy is dependent on Eliot; it is rather that both derive their strength from their underlying concern about man in his universe.

—Frederick Bowers

**BANKS, Lynne Reid.** See **REID BANKS, Lynne.**

---

**BARAKA, Imamu Amiri.** See **JONES, LeRoi.**

---

**BARKER, A(udrey) L(illian).** British. Born in Kent, 13 April 1918. Educated at Primary and Secondary County Schools. Recipient: Atlantic Award, 1946; Maugham Award, 1947; Cheltenham Festival Award, 1962; Arts Council Award, 1970. Fellow, Royal Society of Literature, 1970. Address: c/o Hogarth Press, 40 William IV Street, London W.C.2, England.

PUBLICATIONS

Novels

*Apology for a Hero.*   London, Hogarth Press, and New York, Scribner, 1950.
*A Case Examined.*   London, Hogarth Press, 1965.
*The Middling: Chapters in the Life of Ellie Toms.*   London, Hogarth Press, 1967.
*John Brown's Body.*   London, Hogarth Press, 1969.

Short Stories

*Innocents: Variations on a Theme.*   London, Hogarth Press, 1947; New York, Scribner, 1948.
*Novelette with Other Stories.*   London, Hogarth Press, and New York, Scribner, 1951.
*The Joy-Ride and After.*   London, Hogarth Press, 1963; New York, Scribner, 1964.
*Lost upon the Roundabouts.*   London, Hogarth Press, 1964.
*Penguin Modern Stories 8,* with others.   London, Penguin, 1971.
*Femina Real.*   London, Hogarth Press, 1971.

Other

Play produced on television; stories broadcast on BBC.

* * *

The theme of A. L. Barker's work is the ambivalence of love and the dangers of egoism. She examines those relationships which exist between victor and victim, he who eats and he who is eaten. This material is handled lightly and skilfully; she has the satirist's ability to select detail, placing her characters socially as well as psychologically. Her territory covers childhood, the worlds of the outcast and the ill and the impoverished lives of the lonely. She is close to the English tradition of the comic novel and like Angus Wilson, a major writer in this genre, she often indulges in caricature.

Many of her short stories reveal a fondness for the macabre, introducing elements of horror into seeming calm. Her first collection, *Innocents*, begins with a study of a boy testing his courage in swimming; he becomes involved in a scene of adult violence that is far more dangerous to him than the tree-roots in his river. Innocence in these stories is seen as inexperience, as the blinkered vision of the mad and as the selfishness of the egoist. *Lost upon the Roundabouts* is a further exploration of these ideas and contains two very fine short stories, "Miss Eagle" and "Someone at the Door".

The central characters in A. L. Barker's novels are parasites, dependent on other people for a sense of their own identity. For Ellie in *The Middling* love means "turning another person into a colony of myself". Charles Candy, the central character of *Apology for a Hero*, loves his wife Wynne "because she could give him himself". After Wynne's death he acquires a housekeeper and finds that "when he was with her he felt located." He meets death on a reckless voyage, persuaded that sea-trading will, at last, show him the real Mr. Candy.

The egoist in *A Case Examined* is Rose Antrobus, the chairman of a charity committee with the power to allocate money either to a destitute family or to the church hassock fund. Rose has always insulated herself against suffering. She remembers a childhood friend, Solange, whom she credits with the understanding of despair: Solange provokes violence, she feels, by her own wickedness. This fantasy is shattered by a visit to Paris and a meeting with the real Solange, whose account of Nazi persecution shakes Rose into compassion. A bridge has been made between the worlds of the two women, between the petty and the tragic, and the committee decision is altered accordingly.

A. L. Barker's latest collection of stories, *Femina Real*, is an entertaining set of portraits, nine studies of the female character. In many of the situations an apparent vulnerability hides an underlying strength. A frail woman dominates those around her; adolescence vanquishes middle-age; a ten-year-old cripple turns the tables on the man holding her prisoner. As always, Miss Barker's clear prose style matches the accuracy of her observations. Hers is a talent to be treasured.

—Judith Cooke Simmons

---

**BARNES, Djuna.** American. Born in Cornwall-on-Hudson, New York, 12 June 1892. Studied art at the Pratt Institute and the Art Students' League, New York. Journalist and Illustrator, 1913–31. Full-time Writer since 1931. Has lived in Paris and London. Trustee, New York Committee, Dag Hammarskjold Foundation. Member, National Institute of Arts and Letters. Address: 5 Patchin Place, New York, New York 10011, U.S.A.

PUBLICATIONS

Novels

*Ryder.* New York, Liveright, 1928.
*Nightwood.* London, Faber, 1936; New York, Harcourt Brace, 1937.

Short Stories

> *The Book of Repulsive Women*.  New York, Bruno Chapbooks, 1915.
> *A Book* (includes poems and plays).  New York, Boni and Liveright, 1923; augmented edition, as *A Night among the Horses*, 1929; as *The Spillway*, London, Faber, 1962.

Plays

> *Three for the Earth* (produced Provincetown, Massachusetts, 1919).  Included in *A Book*, 1923.
> *Kurzy from the Sea* (produced Provincetown, Massachusetts, 1919).  Included in *A Book*, 1923.
> *An Irish Triangle* (produced Provincetown, Massachusetts, 1919).  Included in *A Book*, 1923.
> *She Tells Her Daughter*, in *Smart Set* (New York), 1923.
> *The Antiphon*.  New York, Farrar Straus, and London, Faber, 1958.

Other

> *Ladies Almanack*.  Paris, privately printed, 1928.
> *Selected Works*.  New York, Farrar Straus, 1962.

*       *       *

Djuna Barnes was born in 1892, which makes her from five to twelve years younger than the generation of Classic American Modernists—Wallace Stevens, William Carlos Williams, Ezra Pound, T. S. Eliot and the rest. Only Ezra Pound was earlier on the scene. Not only was she precocious and supporting herself as a journalist and illustrator before the First War but she was, as a young girl, a member of the international bohemia of the first quarter of the century, rather than a member of any specific literary set, a very different thing. She was trained as an artist and was considered equally an artist and writer until *Nightwood* established her literary reputation, when she was past forty. These details are important; they account for a remarkable independence as well as for her special sensibility and for her subject matter. This independence was certainly reinforced by her person and personality. She was an exceptionally beautiful woman, unusually intelligent, a great conversationalist, with a drastic, ironic wit, and finally she was the very archetype of the liberated woman. Also, in the days when most American writers read little except their contemporaries, she was deeply and enthusiastically self educated in classic English literature and in French Modernism. Long before such writing became fashionable, she was developing a style compounded of the more complex Elizabethan prose writers and the most alienated French poets of the early Twentieth Century. Although she is usually grouped with the Classic Modernists of between-the-wars, she is really one of the most perfected writers to come out of the totally subversive bohemia of the turn of the century and belongs with Tristan Corbière and Alfred Jarry rather than with Wallace Stevens or even Eliot—who may have assimilated the anti-Symbolists but who certainly did not share their life attitudes.

The comparisons that spring most readily to mind are Kafka and Céline. From her first stories, Djuna Barnes' subjects are the possessed, the haunted, ghosts, and automata wandering in nightmares come true. The action almost always takes place beyond the end of night. So the resemblance is not, as one might think, to Dostoievsky, whose people are deranged but real Russians, but to the best horror or science fiction. Her people seem to have a different blood chemistry, ammonia, perhaps, instead of water. They inhabit a bohemia of their own, alienated from the dominant society, but not the comforting community of Greenwich

Village or the Café du Dome, but a world of the self-alienated. "I am another", said Rimbaud. The personalities have all split and have begun to distintegrate. Even *Ryder*, a big, eventful novel of domesticity, a satire on masculinity written in a style which owes much to the obstreperous, controversial pamphlets of the Elizabethan Thomas Nashe, is, for all its bawdry and babies, saturated with black humor. When she was writing it she used to say, "I am writing the female *Tom Jones*" but the book would certainly have frightened Henry Fielding, that eminently sane and wholesome man.

In the second novel, *Nightwood*, we are in the limbo of the undamned. The characters are all self condemned to unreality. They seek reality, not in salvation, which they are incapable of even knowing, but in damnation—which is closed to them—and so they find only an immense frivolity. No exit.

*Nightwood* achieves more perfectly than any other of her fictions that haunted, obsessed quality, that atmosphere of inescapable nightmare which is her special *métier*. Its influence has been very great. Nathanael West's *Miss Lonelyhearts* and *The Day of the Locust*, Nelson Algren's *A Walk on the Wild Side*, and the work of Edward Dahlberg, are only a few of its many descendants. Henry Miller's *Tropic of Cancer*, *Tropic of Capricorn*, and especially *Black Spring*, owe much to the precedent of Djuna Barnes, but Henry Miller is far too normal and conventional a man to realize her special horrors. Djuna Barnes is very far indeed from being a naive writer. Similarly she has been a great influence on Anaïs Nin, in whose novels a character "Djuna" occurs again and again. Here the influence is essentially that of personal admiration. Djuna Barnes is an exemplar for Anaïs Nin. One feels she may have modeled her life rather than her fiction on her—a woman of powerful will, immense talent, independence, sexually free and very beautiful. In other words Djuna Barnes is at least as influential as a legend as she is as a writer.

T. S. Eliot in introducing *Nightwood* said that it would "appeal primarily to readers of poetry" because it was written with such an acute feeling for language that only people trained on poetry could fully appreciate it. It is true that all of Djuna Barnes' prose stands out from that of her contemporaries, distinguished by her physiological sense of rhythm and a wit that constantly plays with the reverberating meanings and sounds of words. It may be a conscious style, deliberately and painfully worked out—so was Flaubert's, but like Flaubert's, it gives little evidence of labor. It seems to flow spontaneously, one just word after another, with a music that comes from the sinews of a uniquely integrated human being. At the same time it is distinguished by its elegance. It is as though she had never read anything but the greatest literature and was saturated with it. Her verse play, *The Antiphon*, is a perfect transmutation of the style, the subject, the very personal being, of the nightmare world of the tragedies of John Webster and Cyril Tourneur into completely modern terms. The speeches echo *The Duchess of Malfi* but echo it in the mid-Twentieth Century with its own language and its own nightmares.

Djuna Barnes may be considered as a late born voice of the *fin de siècle* literary Decadence but she is also an early born prophet of the black comedy, theatre of cruelty, and literature of total alienation of the later years of the century, the period of decadence and disintegration of Western Civilization itself, the time of permanent Apocalypse. Hers is a moral esthetic, the esthetic of a "theology of crisis"; " '*We have fashioned ourselves against the Day of Judgment.' This remark was made by Dr. Katrina Silverstaff at the oddest moments, seeming without relevance to anything at all, as one might sigh 'Be still.' *" So begins a story "The Doctors".

—Kenneth Rexroth

---

**BARRY, Clive.** Australian. Born in Sydney, New South Wales, in 1922. Served in World War II; prisoner of war. District Education Officer in East Africa since the mid-1950's.

Since 1961, United Nations Representative in the Congo. Address: c/o Faber and Faber Ltd., 3 Queen Square, London W.C.1, England.

PUBLICATIONS

Novels

*The Spear Grinner*.  London, Faber, 1963.
*Crumb Borne*.  London, Faber, 1965.
*Fly Jamskoni*.  London, Faber, 1969.

\*        \*        \*

Clive Barry's first and third novels are comedies animated by the adventures of the same hero; they are, however, unequal achievements. In *The Spear Grinner* Hector Reed, a gruff though well-intentioned Australian, comes as an Administrative Officer to the small imaginary state of Jamskoni in East Africa. His duties are ill-defined but in his one week stay he manages to kill an elephant and just escapes being killed by another; he prevents a whole cargo of hemp from being smuggled to Yemen, takes part in a ludicrous election campaign and avoids being knived by gangsters by blowing up part of his own house. The only real authority in Jamskoni seems to be exercised by the District Commissioner's office boy, an ex-public-school native called the Ostrich after the emblem of his political campaign for the coming elections. He is a pleasant rogue, the "spear grinner" of the title, who in defiance of the proverb "Only a fool laughs at the spear" cultivates a savage grin and thrives on everyone else's inefficiency. The story is told with brilliant gusto. Barry's dry humour, his elliptical style and the detachment with which he frames the most absurd situations, are well suited to his rendering of the anarchy and inverted sense of values that prevail in Jamskoni. Sheer farce alternates with more subtly satirical scenes. In the end, however, the tragic reverse of amusing chaos, which has been played down through most of the novel, is allowed to emerge: Reed's beautiful housekeeper is found killed and horribly mutilated by the gangsters. There is a suggestion throughout the novel that Reed needs Africa as much as Africa needs him. Yet as an uncommitted witness of other people's predicament, it is without remorse that he flies back to the security of a modern suburbia.

In *Fly Jamskoni* Hector Reed comes back to the small newly-independent state as a United Nations Officer. The Ostrich is Minister of Aviation and apparently still runs the show by himself, though he spends most of his time piloting the country's one biplane. Gangsterism has been eradicated by making the head gangster superintendent of police. The one remaining problem for Reed is to stop the camel-herders from smuggling hemp. As his job depends on the continuance of the trade, he befriends the herders and even helps them to smuggle their hemp by aircraft rather than on camels. He has at last learned from the Ostrich the art of compromise. Unlike *The Spear Grinner*, Barry's third novel is hardly more than a succession of loosely connected farcical incidents. His style has lost nothing of its vividness, and he still relies on the paradoxical to raise an occasional laugh. But it is often hard to make head or tail of what is happening, and the reader is more confused than Reed himself about what the latter is doing in Jamskoni.

*Crumb Borne* portrays an altogether different world: the hopeless society created by a hundred starving prisoners-of-war on a freezing plateau in the middle of nowhere. Their microcosm reproduces the hierarchical functions of the ordinary world even to the need for a scapegoat. The outsider is Frugal, whose quiet self-sufficiency and capacity to survive through strict self-discipline are interpreted by his fellow-prisoners as a threat to their own survival. Actually, Frugal alone remains human while the others' meanness increases with

their physical degradation. The cold, matter-of-fact precision with which Barry describes
the isolated camp and the prisoners' permanent near-hysteria further enhances the depressing
character of the underworld he creates.

—Hena Maes-Jelinek

---

**BARSTOW, Stan(ley).** British. Born in Horbury, Yorkshire, 28 June 1928. Educated at
Ossett Grammar School. Married Constance Mary Kershaw in 1951; has two children.
Draftsman and Sales Executive in the engineering industry, 1945–62. Full-time Writer since
1962. Address: Goring House, Goring Park Avenue, Ossett, Yorkshire, England.

PUBLICATIONS

Novels

*A Kind of Loving.* London, Joseph, 1960; New York, Doubleday, 1961.
*Ask Me Tomorrow.* London, Joseph, 1962.
*Joby.* London, Joseph, 1964.
*The Watchers on the Shore.* London, Joseph, 1966; New York, Doubleday, 1967.
*A Raging Calm.* London, Joseph, 1968; as *The Hidden Part*, New York, Coward
McCann, 1969.

Short Stories

*The Desperadoes.* London, Joseph, 1961.
*A Season with Eros.* London, Joseph, 1971.

Plays

*Ask Me Tomorrow*, with Alfred Bradley (produced Sheffield, Yorkshire, 1964).
London, French, 1966.
*A Kind of Loving*, with Alfred Bradley (produced Sheffield, Yorkshire, 1965). London,
Blackie, 1970.
*An Enemy of the People*, adaptation of a play by Henrik Ibsen (produced Harrogate,
Yorkshire, 1969).
*Listen for the Trains, Love* (produced Sheffield, Yorkshire, 1970).
*Stringer's Last Stand*, with Alfred Bradley (produced York, 1971).

Other

Editor, *Through the Green Woods: An Anthology of Contemporary Writing about Youth
and Children.* Leeds, Arnold, 1968.

Stan Barstow comments:

Came to prominence about the same time as several other novelists from North of England working-class backgrounds, viz. John Braine, Alan Sillitoe, David Storey, Keith Waterhouse, and saw with satisfaction, and occasional irritation, the gains made in the opening up of the regions and the "elevation" of the people into fit subjects for fictional portrayal absorbed into the popular cultures of the cinema and TV drama series and comedy shows. Still, living in the provinces and using mainly regional settings, consider myself non-metropolitan oriented. The publication of some of my work in the U.S. and its translation into several European languages reassures me that I have not resisted the neurotic trendiness of much metropolitan culture for the sake of mere provincial narrowness; and the knowledge that some of the finest novels in the language are "regional" leads me to the belief that to hoe one's own row diligently, thus seeking out the universal in the particular, brings more worthwhile satisfactions than the frantic pursuit of a largely phoney jet-age internationalism.

\*      \*      \*

Barstow belongs centrally to that group of northern novelists—Kirkup, Braine, Sillitoe, Waterhouse, Middleton, Storey—who grew to literary prominence in the fifties and sixties by their realistic portrayal of working class life. In this common bond they are literary descendents of Gissing, Wells and Lawrence, but they each demonstrate particular pre-occupations which distinguish them from their predecessors and each from the others; Braine and Sillitoe for example are very much concerned with class divisiveness, whereas Kirkup and Waterhouse explore much more closely the fabric and feel of working class life.

Barstow's novels take social class and the industrial environment much more for granted; this is not to say that such matters are only sketched in, for they are solidly presented, but the overriding preoccupation is with the development of human wisdom and love in an environment which is indifferent or hostile. The three major novels each present a central character making a marked shift in world-view, from self-interest to an awareness of others. More particularly, they present the conflict between an environment which is materially and spiritually narrow and the growth of love, which prevails at last, not to reach sublime heights but to manage a modicum of human happiness. Vic Brown's relationship with Ingrid (*A Kind of Loving*) descends from youthful romance to cynical despair as a result of the harm Ingrid's mother has done to their marriage through her shallow notions of morality and her semi-detached snobbery; only with a struggle does he eventually manage to rebuild their marriage and turn his back on both ecstasy and despair. At the end of the novel Vic accepts life as it is: "And if you say what is life about I'll say it's about life, and that's all. And it's enough because there's plenty of good things in life as well as bad."

The presentation of a workaday human love not only as the best that one can hope for but also as an essential condition of life is repeated in *Joby* and *A Raging Calm*. Young Joby's summer of decline into petty theft and tacky child sex mirrors his father's own drift into a clumsy affair with Joby's rather retarded but nubile cousin Mona; both Joby and his father reach a point where disintegration of the family seems inevitable, but Joby manages to see beyond his own troubles to his father's: "He saw for the first time his father as a person carrying about with him a world of his own . . . .," and he brings his father back into the family. Similarly, Tom Simkins reintegrates the loose ends of his life by taking Norma and her children under his roof.

Barstow sets his theme against the unsympathetic background of Cressley, a West Riding industrial town of terraced houses, ugly factories, garish cinemas and grubby parks. The meanness of the town is shown to breed both narrow morality and generous love; it is up to the individual to choose one or the other, but Barstow points to his choice: Joby persuades his father, "Oh, come on home with me, Dad. It'll be all right. Me mam's waiting for you. You don't care about me Aunt Daisy and them, do you? They don't matter to us, do they?"

Although Barstow makes no technical innovations (he sticks to traditional narrative forms—first person in *A Kind of Loving*, omniscient linked plots in *A Raging Calm* and third person point of view in *Joby*) his novels rise above the ephemeral in their concrete presentation of human character, their solid settings, their natural dialogue and, above all, their forceful and moving expression of what it is to be human.

—Frederick Bowers

---

**BARTH, John (Simmons).** American. Born in Cambridge, Maryland, 27 May 1930. Educated at the Juilliard School of Music, New York; Johns Hopkins University, Baltimore, A.B. 1951, M.A. 1952. Married Anne Strickland in 1951; Shelley Rosenberg in 1970; has three children. Junior Instructor in English, Johns Hopkins University, 1951–53; Instructor to Associate Professor of English, Pennsylvania State University, University Park, 1953–65. Since 1965, Professor of English, State University of New York at Buffalo. Recipient: Brandeis University Creative Arts Award, 1965; Rockefeller grant, 1965; National Institute of Arts and Letters grant, 1966. Litt.D., University of Maryland, College Park, 1969. Address: R.D. 1, Mayville, New York 14757, U.S.A.

PUBLICATIONS

Novels

> *The Floating Opera.* New York, Appleton Century Crofts, 1956; revised edition, New York, Doubleday, 1967; London, Secker and Warburg, 1968.
> *The End of the Road.* New York, Doubleday, 1958; London, Secker and Warburg, 1962; revised edition, Doubleday, 1967.
> *The Sot-Weed Factor.* New York, Doubleday, 1960; London, Secker and Warburg, 1961; revised edition, Doubleday, 1967.
> *Giles Goat-Boy; or, The Revised New Syllabus.* New York, Doubleday, 1966; London, Secker and Warburg, 1967.

Short Stories

> *Lost in the Funhouse: Fiction for Print, Tape, Live Voice.* New York, Doubleday, 1968; London, Secker and Warburg, 1969.

Uncollected Short Stories

> "Test Borings", in *Modern Occasions*. New York, Farrar Straus, 1966.
> "Help", in *Esquire* (New York), September 1969.
> "Perseid", in *University Review* (New York), 1971.

Manuscript Collection: Library of Congress, Washington, D.C.

*       *       *

Though it may seem nowadays brash to speak of the avant-garde—which way is backward?—John Barth clearly belongs to the small number of American authors who carry their experiments to the limits of fiction, the edge of silence. A master of contradictions, an intimate of the void, Barth knows how to turn the crisis of language and form to his own advantage. In a signal essay, "The Literature of Exhaustion," he says of the new writer: "His artistic victory . . . is that he confronts an intellectual dead end and employs it against itself to accomplish new human work." Older writers, such as Borges, Beckett, or Nabokov, strike us as virtuosos of "exhaustion," and others, younger still than Barth—say Thomas Pynchon or Donald Barthelme—carry the tradition forward.

The skeptical temper of Barth, his parodic genius—which collapses sometimes into puerile humor—are evident throughout his fiction. Intuitively, he understands the existential mummery of our time. Instinctively, he finds the given social or phenomenal world arbitrary, faintly ludicrous. "Which snowflake triggers the avalanche?" he asks. Reality is "a nice place to visit"; and in the same interview, he adds: "My argument is with the facts of life not the conditions of it. . . . I'm not very responsible in the Social Problems way, I guess." Increasingly, Barth wants to inhabit the region of "Ultimacy," which lies beyond irony and fancy, in some pure self-delighting realm of the verbal mind. Like many artists before him, he insists on the artifice of art. Yet, like them too, he becomes a moralist by indirection. His characters often suffer from mirror gazing, or from "cosmopsis," an excess of consciousness; what they must learn, slowly, after many painful travesties of the flesh, is that life can justify itself, and love can justify man.

The first two novels have a certain wry energy though their structures still conform to the conventions of fiction. *The Floating Opera* declares Barth's abiding theme: the uninvolved life "lived by the heartbeat," in total absense of intrinsic values, cerebral and null. Todd Andrews, narrator and anti-hero, coldly contemplates suicide. At the end, he reprieves himself as he awakens to the "floating opera," the mind's own show. (In an earlier version, Todd discovers "relative value" in his concern for a child whose mother, wife to his best friend, is also Todd's acknowledged mistress.) The complexity of the story depends less on its sexual imbroglios, to which Barth returns, than on its self-questioning point of view. The narrative conveys the paradox of Todd Andrews, caught between reason and instinct, voice and silence; and it further suggests the paradox of his author who makes art of a nihilistic theme. "Good heavens," Todd cries, "how does one write a novel! I mean, how can anybody stick to the story, if he's at all sensitive to the significance of things?" The feints and asides, the comedy of *The Floating Opera*, provide a clue if not an answer.

The clue, then, is the play of narrative, the story in itself, as *The End of the Road* again shows. Once more, the anti-hero skirmishes with the endless possibilities of existence, achieves immobility. "In a sense," he says, "I am Jacob Horner"; and mindlessly we add, "Who sat in a corner." Jake, child of multiplicities, has run out of motives. He takes two healers, one to instruct him in arbitrary rules, the other in continuous performances. They fail to give necessity to his choices. But life has its own version of necessity. Embroiled in a sexual triangle, with Rennie and Joe Morgan, Jake witnesses the death of his mistress in an ugly abortion. Thus the discrepancy between physical fact and mental option pushes the nihilistic self still closer to the end of the road. Yet Horner saves himself from complete oblivion by attaching himself to his author. "Articulation!" he cries. "There, by Jove, was *my* absolute, if I could be said to have one. . . . To turn experience into speech. . . ."

In subsequent novels, Barth accepts his self-parodic role even more exuberantly, giving us, he says, works that "imitate the form of the Novel, by an author who imitates the role of Author." *The Sot-Weed Factor* is certainly as prodigious in length as it is farcical in metaphysics. The work calls into question all things—the mystery of human personality, the antics of love, the madness of history, the surrealism of nature—in the form of eighteenth-century gothic and picaresque narratives. It is a pastiche of various styles which break into uninhibited verbal play. Barth strains, indeed transcends, the limits of credibility in a plot, full of devious sub-plots, which adapts the mythic attributes of the Hero, enumerated by Lord Raglan, to the subversive themes of American literature, expounded by Leslie Fiedler. Ostensibly, the author wants to recount the story of another author, Ebenezer Cooke, who actually published in 1708 a poem entitled "The Sot-Weed Factor" (early American for tobacco merchant). Yet the sum of history, for both authors, appears "no more than the stuff of metaphors"; therefore, everything is permitted. Characters shift or exchange their realities; and in the shadow play of appearances, Englishman and American, Paleface and Indian, Catholic and Protestant, Hero and Villain, flicker across the screen of language. The language is often bawdy and outrageous, for destiny is shaped by coitus as that book within a book, *The Secret Historie* of John Smith, attempts to prove. Yet, despite itself, this slapstick epic of Colonial Maryland becomes an allegory of radical innocence in quest of a "seamless universe," an allegory, particularly, of the artist at the end of his tether. Cooke's tutor, Burlingame, that strange, self-creating genius of the novel who seems so often to speak for and against Barth, says: "I am a Suitor of Totality, Embracer of Contradictories, Husband to all Creation, the Cosmic Lover!" This, too, is an aspiration of the novelist who makes cosmic jokes instead.

Pushing farrago and indeterminacy still farther, Barth creates in *Giles Goat-Boy* a rather more self-conscious allegory of all the destructive wisdom of the twentieth century. Letters, forewords, and disclaimers enclose the main narrative in equivocal frames; literary and topical references abound in disorder, as if strewn by some berserk computer which, Barth hints, may be the true author of the book. Presumably, one J. B., an academic novelist, puts aside his favorite project concerning the Cosmic Amateur, in order to reconstruct the story of the Grand Tutor, Giles Goat-Boy, part Christ and part Pan. (Barth playing his pseudo-autobiographical games!) Giles struggles from his animal innocence toward the salvation of our race, losing himself often in the tragic labyrinth of human consciousness. Arduously, he moves toward a unitary vision—again the "seamless universe"—a view not of distinctions but of embrace. In the process, Giles jostles Paradox, batters the Unnamable; exhausted, he cries: "I let go, I let all go." Yet he does attain complete being in the arms of his beloved Anastasia, within the bowels of a monstrous computer, WESCAC: "In the darkness, blinding light! The end of the University! Commencement Day!" For in the central and punning metaphor of the novel, the University becomes the universe, and the Revised New Syllabus of the hero invokes a redeemed consciousness. Thereafter, Giles puts himself beyond the malice and enmities of the mind: "For me, Sense and Nonsense lost their meaning on a night twelve years four months ago, in WESCAC's Belly. . . ." The reader, though, is free to balk at the immense panorama of travesty in the novel. However taut or complex beneath, however ingenious, erudite, or funny, the book tends to pall.

The parodic rage of Barth finds new expression in the stories of *Lost in the Fun House*. Living voice, printed work, and magnetic tape conspire to create a kind of aural montage, a conceit of genres. The forms of fiction turn themselves inside out, shed their skin in search of a new life (Barth's public readings from this collection seem virtuoso performances of intermedia). Thus the narrative attempts to swallow itself by the tail in "Anonymiad"; or vanishes into concentric brackets of itself, like a Chinese box, in "Menelaiad"; or comes to rest in the hovering silence of the tale, the teller, and the told, in "Title." "What is there to say at this late date?" a voice in that last piece asks. "Let me think, I'm trying to think. Same old story. OR. Or? Silence." This internal argument of a sound and stillness concludes nothing. The last sentence trails into a blank space: "How in the world will it ever          " The solipsist narrators of Beckett, droning their way to death, come to mind. Fictions float toward further fictions; words drift like galactic dust. All that remains, in *Lost in the Fun House*, is some distant echo of humor, the valance of loss.

Dazed by the spirit of possibility, seeking relief from himself, muttering brilliantly to that end, John Barth finds his ambiguous freedom in the game that language plays with itself. He wants to align himself with the great narrators of open or whimsical experience: the authors of the *Arabian Nights*—"Scheherezade is my avant-gardiste," Barth has said— Boccaccio, Rabelais, Cervantes, Sterne. Yet Barth is of course much closer to Borges and Beckett, authors of silence in postmodern literature. His despair seems lighter than theirs; his fabulations at times more frivolous. He writes about murder, incest, and madness as if they had no resonance but in hollow laughter. Evasive and arch, teeth clenched, he prefers "Not To." In the end, however, Barth pits the imagination against the void as no other American writer can, making art of heroic absurdity.

—Ihab Hassan

**BARTHELME, Donald.** American. Born in Philadelphia, Pennsylvania, 7 April 1931. Served in the United States Army. Married; has one child. Museum Director, Houston, in the mid-1950's. Formerly, Managing Editor, *Location* magazine, New York. Recipient: Guggenheim Fellowship, 1966. Address: c/o The New Yorker, 25 West 43rd Street, New York, New York 10036, U.S.A.

PUBLICATIONS

Novel

   *Snow White.* New York, Atheneum, 1967; London, Cape, 1968.

Short Stories

   *Come Back, Dr. Caligari.* Boston, Little Brown, 1964; London, Eyre and Spottis-
     woode, 1966.
   *Unspeakable Practices, Unnatural Acts.* New York, Farrar Straus, 1968; London,
     Cape, 1969.
   *City Life.* New York, Farrar Straus, and London, Cape, 1971.

\*     \*     \*

Donald Barthelme's writings have been greeted as those of a new and significant talent in American literature. Many of his stories first appeared in the *New Yorker* magazine, including the only book-length work he has published to date, *Snow White*. That story, taking as it did virtually one whole issue of the magazine, was a significant publishing event, an honor virtually unheard of for a young writer.

The title of Barthelme's first collection of stories, *Come Back, Dr. Caligari*, is useful for understanding his work. Barthelme's mode of story-telling seems not so much existential as surrealistic. If the realism and the freedom from conventional moral values characteristic of Hemingway and Dos Passos might be explained as the American reaction to the period after World War One, one might think of Barthelme's fiction as a reaction to the later world of the Cold War and Vietnam. The earlier cynicism proceeded from a realization that the hopes of Wilsonian idealism were a fraud masking the reality of power politics. The reaction of the later generation, revealed in writers like Barthelme, goes far beyond attacks upon hypocritical ideals to a very real doubt that any values exist at all. The world seems peopled entirely by lunatics, and therefore demands lunacy as the only rational response. In this respect the stories resemble the world of German Expressionism and Surrealism in the 1920's—the world out of which came the original film-mythic-figure Caligari. Furthermore films themselves have contributed heavily to Barthelme's work, providing direct content as well as the fundamental myths around which he could organize fictional experience. The "sane" world of early films is especially useful as a comment on our growing inability to make sense from contemporary experience.

"Me and Miss Mandible" from the *Caligari* volume is a good example of early Barthelme. The thirty-five-year-old narrator of the story has been bureaucratically reversed to eleven and inexplicably enrolled in Miss Mandible's elementary classroom. But his biological maturity has not been similarly reversed. The essential comedy of the situation masks a basic Kafka-like grotesqueness. The narrator himself readily accepts the situation:

> A ruined marriage, a ruined adjusting career, a grim interlude in the Army when
> I was almost not a person. This is the sum of my existence to date, a dismal total.
> Small wonder that my reeducation seemed my only hope. It is clear even to me
> that I need reworking in some fundamental way. How efficient is the society that
> provides thus for the salvage of its clinkers.

The statement involves considerable irony. The narrator is hopeful that his reeducation will
"take": "All of the mysteries that perplexed me as an adult have their origins here, and one
by one I am numbering them, exposing their roots." But sexual drives overcome educational
decorum, and the narrator is surprised in the cloakroom with Miss Mandible and summarily expelled. Few other of the early stories are even this hopeful of making sense of
experience. "The Joker's Greatest Triumph" uses the comic strip characters of Batman
and Robin to tell a daft story of crime and pursuit. The basic comic strip situation is provided with just enough modern detail to make it more realistic (Robin is now mature and
attending Andover). The hard facts of Batmobiles and Batplanes play off against the central
unreality of the narrative. Batman and Robin seem ideal denizens of a consumer society
with two cars in every garage, two planes in every hangar—crime fighters nearly suffocating
in the tasteful luxury of their appointments.
  Barthelme's wide range of literary reference coupled with the brevity of most of his stories
make interpretation difficult. "The Indian Uprising," one of the stories in his second collection *Unspeakable Practices, Unnatural Acts*, combines Nineteenth-century notions of cowboys and Indians with later Twentieth-century concerns about urban guerrillas. Set in a city
that seems at once European and American (the streets are named for American military
figures of the Second World War) the very detail of the environment plays off against the
seeming timelessness of the narrative to produce a surreal effect. "Robert Kennedy Saved
from Drowning" strikes one as most immediately indebted to Kafka. The politically symbolic figure is realized through a series of discreet glimpses of his life, some revealing but
many purposefully banal or baffling or both. Reduced simply to "K" the whole effect is
to atomize the senator's life into meaningless fragments. "Game" is a terrifying tale of two
men charged with the control of the ultimate retaliatory weapons. They eye one another
with the greatest suspiciousness, yet both are far gone in childish lunacy. The story becomes
a fable of our cold-war period. A dwarf is the central figure in "The President" as if to make
physically clear the moral and intellectual qualities of the office-holder. In Barthelme's
stories the lunacy of the narrative line is often in sharp contrast with the specificity of the
minor details. Brand name products familiar through advertising are often present, as if to
suggest that that particular fantasy-world is at least as important to us as any other. Products have become for Barthelme the surrealist equivalent of the material environment so
important for Nineteenth-century realists.
  Barthelme returned to films for the inspiration of his longest and most sustained work so
far, *Snow White*. This version owes more to our memories of the Disney film than to those
of the Brothers Grimm. But this is a Snow White for the Surreal Seventies, not for the
Thirties. Snow White now shares a shower and an apartment with the seven dwarfs who have
become quite respectable bourgeois entrepreneurs. Disney's fetching diamond-diggers have
become the manufacturers and merchandisers of oriental baby foods—Baby Bow Yee, Baby
Dow Shew, Baby Dim Sum—even Baby Water Chestnuts and Baby Kimchi. One gathers
the enterprise prospers. The evil step-mother has become a very different kind of witch:

> No man's plenum, Mr. Quistgaard, is impervious to the awl of God's will. Consider
> then your situation *now*. You are sitting there in your house on Neat Street, with
> your fine dog, doubtless, and your handsome wife and tall brown sons, conceivably,
> and who knows with your gun-colored Plymouth Fury in the driveway and
> opinions passing back and forth, about whether the Grange should build a new
> meeting hall or not, whether the children should become Thomists or not, whether
> the pump needs more cup grease or not. A comfortable American scene. *But I,
> Jane Villiers de l'Isle-Adam, am in possession of your telephone number, Mr. Quist-
> gaard.*

Paul, the prince-hero, turns to conventional infantry tactics in his pursuit of Snow White and in the end proves pure frog. The story ends with a bizarre twist on the conventional notion that hero gets heroine. At one point Barthelme interrupts the narrative to present his readers with a questionnaire and to solicit their advice on how the story should proceed. Inserted titles and quotations give a richness of literary reference that plays off nicely against the simplicity of the basic film story.

*City Life*, Barthelme's recent collection, demonstrates a change in his techniques. "Views of My Father Weeping" seems to derive more from Dostoevsky than Kafka. It is again set in a city that seems quite specifically European and yet at once is outside time or place—a literary convention. "At the Tolstoy Museum" demonstrates a technique of linking drawings and text to provide a new effect for fiction that both Barthelme and others would further cultivate. The grotesquely realistic drawings depicting a super-human Tolstoy seem to suggest that the very stature of the artist becomes comic, as if we ought not demand such stature of our writers. "Bone Bubbles" and "Brain Damage" explore new dimensions of meaninglessness and absurdity, the latter again employing surrealistically-detailed line drawings to heighten the effect. "On Angels" provides one of the most effective of Barthelme's openings:

> The death of God left the angels in a strange position. They were overtaken suddenly by a fundamental question. One can attempt to imagine the moment. How did they *look* at the instant the question invaded them, flooding the angelic consciousness, taking hold with terrifying force? The question was, "what are angels?"

"City Life," the story that provided the title of the collection, again attempts to explore the chaotic sensations of modern urban life.

Barthelme's surrealism seems to preclude his working in long narrative forms. Much of his work seems that of a late-Twentieth-century Edgar Allan Poe. Like Poe's fiction, Barthelme's stories produce their effect precisely because they elude satisfactory interpretation. Similarly the stories of both Poe and Barthelme demand "intellection" but defy rationality. And finally, Barthelme's works, like Poe's, seem to spring from a genuine doubt that any solution does in fact exist to the mysteries and miseries of the human condition.

—Myron Taylor

---

**BATES, H(erbert) E(rnest).**   British. Born in Rushden, Northamptonshire, 16 May 1905. Educated at the Grammar School, Kettering. Served in the Royal Air Force, 1941–45. Married Marjorie Helen Cox in 1931; has four children. Prior to 1926 worked as a provincial journalist and clerk. Fellow, Royal Society of Literature, 1950; resigned, 1963. Address: The Granary, Little Chart, Ashford, Kent, England.

PUBLICATIONS

Novels

*The Two Sisters*.  London, Cape, and New York, Viking Press, 1926.
*Catherine Foster*.  London, Cape, and New York, Viking Press, 1929.
*The Hessian Prisoner*.  London, Jackson, 1930.

*Mr. Esmond's Life*.   London, privately printed, 1930.
*Charlotte's Row*.   London, Cape, 1931; New York, Ballou, 1932.
*The Fallow Land*.   London, Cape, 1932; New York, Ballou, 1933.
*The Poacher*.   London, Cape, and New York, Macmillan, 1935.
*A House of Women*.   London, Cape, and New York, Holt, 1936.
*"Spella Ho"*.   London, Cape, and Boston, Little Brown, 1938.
*Fair Stood the Wind for France*.   London, Joseph, and Boston, Little Brown, 1944.
*The Cruise of "The Breadwinner"*.   London, Joseph, 1946; Boston, Little Brown, 1947.
*The Purple Plain*.   London, Joseph, and Boston, Little Brown, 1947.
*The Jacaranda Tree*.   Boston, Little Brown, 1947; London, Joseph, 1949.
*Dear Life*.   Boston, Little Brown, 1949; London, Joseph, 1950.
*The Scarlet Sword*.   London, Joseph, 1950; Boston, Little Brown, 1951.
*Love for Lydia*.   London, Joseph, 1952; Boston, Little Brown, 1953.
*The Feast of July*.   London, Joseph, and Boston, Little Brown, 1954.
*The Sleepless Moon*.   London, Joseph, and Boston, Little Brown, 1956.
*The Darling Buds of May*.   London, Joseph, and Boston, Little Brown, 1958.
*A Breath of Fresh Air*.   London, Joseph, and Boston, Little Brown, 1959.
*When the Green Woods Laugh*.   London, Joseph, 1960; as *Hark, Hark, the Lark!*, Boston, Little Brown, 1961.
*The Day of the Tortoise*.   London, Joseph, 1961.
*A Crown of Wild Myrtle*.   London, Joseph, 1962; New York, Farrar Straus, 1963.
*O! To Be in England*.   London, Joseph, 1963; New York, Farrar Straus, 1964.
*A Moment in Time*.   London, Joseph, and New York, Farrar Straus, 1964.
*The Fabulous Mrs. V*.   London, Joseph, 1964.
*The Wedding Party*.   London, Joseph, 1965.
*The Distant Hours in Summer*.   London, Joseph, 1967.
*The Wild Cherry Tree*.   London, Joseph, 1968.
*A Little of What You Fancy*.   London, Joseph, 1970.

Short Stories

*The Spring Song and In View of the Fact That . . .: Two Stories*.   London, Archer, 1927.
*Day's End and Other Stories*.   London, Cape, and New York, Viking Press, 1928.
*Seven Tales and Alexander*.   London, Scholartis Press, and New York, Viking Press, 1929.
*A Threshing Day*.   London, Foyle, 1931.
*The Story Without an End and The Country Doctor*.   London, White Owl Press, 1932.
*The Black Boxer: Tales*.   London, Cape, 1932; New York, Ballou, 1933.
*Sally Go Round the Moon*.   London, White Owl Press, 1932.
*The House with the Apricot and Two Other Tales*.   London, Golden Cockerel Press, 1933.
*The Woman Who Had Imagination and Other Stories*.   London, Cape, and New York, Macmillan, 1934.
*Thirty Tales*.   London, Cape, 1934.
*The Duet*.   London, Grayson, 1935.
*Cut and Come Again: Fourteen Stories*.   London, Cape, 1935.
*Something Short and Sweet: Stories*.   London, Cape, 1937.
*I Am Not Myself*.   London, Corvinus Press, 1939.
*My Flying Goat: Stories*.   London, Cape, 1939.
*My Uncle Silas: Stories*.   London, Cape, 1939.
*Country Tales: Collected Short Stories*.   London, Cape, 1940.
*The Beauty of the Dead and Other Stories*.   London, Cape, 1940.
*The Bride Comes to Evensford*.   London, Cape, 1943.
*Thirty-one Selected Tales*.   London, Cape, 1947.

*Colonel Julian and Other Stories.* London, Joseph, and Boston, Little Brown, 1951.

*The Nature of Love: Three Short Novels.* London, Joseph, 1953; Boston, Little Brown, 1954.

*The Daffodil Sky.* London, Joseph, 1955; Boston, Little Brown, 1956.

*Death of a Huntsman: Four Short Novels.* London, Joseph, 1957; as *Summer in Salander*, Boston, Little Brown, 1957.

*Sugar for the Horse.* London, Joseph, 1957.

*The Watercress Girl and Other Stories.* London, Joseph, 1959; Boston, Little Brown, 1960.

*An Aspidistra in Babylon: Four Novellas.* London, Joseph, 1960; as *The Grapes of Paradise: Four Short Novels*, Boston, Little Brown, 1960.

*Now Sleeps the Crimson Petal and Other Stories.* London, Joseph, 1961; as *The Enchantress and Other Stories*, Boston, Little Brown, 1961.

*The Golden Oriole: Five Novellas.* London, Joseph, and Boston, Little Brown, 1962.

*Seven by Five: Stories 1926–1961.* London, Joseph, 1963; as *The Best of H. E. Bates*, Boston, Little Brown, 1963.

*The Four Beauties.* London, Joseph, 1968.


Plays

*The Last Bread.* London, Labour Publishing Company, 1926.
*The Day of Glory* (produced London, 1946). London, Joseph, 1945.


Other

*The Tree.* London, E. Lahr, 1930.

*A German Idyll.* London, Golden Cockerel Press, 1932.

*Flowers and Faces.* London, Golden Cockerel Press, 1935.

*Through the Woods: The English Woodland—April to April.* London, Gollancz, and New York, Macmillan, 1936.

*Down the River.* London, Gollancz, and New York, Holt, 1937.

*The Seasons and the Gardener: A Book for Children.* London, Cambridge University Press, 1940; New York, Macmillan, 1941.

*The Modern Short Story: A Critical Survey.* London, Nelson, 1941; Boston, The Writer, 1949.

*In the Heart of the Country.* London, Country Life, 1942.

*The Greatest People in the World and Other Stories*, by Flying Officer X. London, Cape, 1942; as *There's Something in the Air*, New York, Knopf, 1942.

*How Sleep the Brave and Other Stories*, by Flying Officer X. London, Cape, 1943.

*O! More Than Happy Countryman.* London, Country Life, 1943; revised edition, as *The Country Heart* (includes *In the Heart of the Country*), London, Joseph, 1949.

*The Tinkers of Elstow.* London, Bemrose, n.d. (1946?).

*Edward Garnett.* London, Parrish, 1950.

*The Country of White Clover.* London, Joseph, 1952.

*The Face of England.* London, Batsford, 1952.

*Achilles the Donkey* (juvenile). London, Dobson, and New York, Watts, 1963.

*Achilles and Diana* (juvenile). London, Dobson, and New York, Watts, 1963.

*Achilles and the Twins* (juvenile). London, Dobson, 1964; New York, Watts, 1965.

*The White Admiral* (juvenile). London, Dobson, 1968.

*The Vanished World* (autobiography). London, Joseph, 1969.

*The Blossoming World* (autobiography). London, Joseph, 1971.

*A Love of Flowers* (autobiography). London, Joseph, 1971.

Bibliography: in *Ten Contemporaries*, 2nd series, by John Gawsworth, London, Joiner and Steele, 1933.

Manuscript Collections: University of London; University of Texas, Austin; University of California, Berkeley.

*     *     *

The career of H. E. Bates repudiates those literary critics who have lamented the passing from the 20th century scene of the "complete professional writer" in the Dickens-Thackeray-Lawrence-Faulkner sense of the term. Year in and year out, for almost half a century, Bates has averaged over a book a year: twenty-five or thirty novels, approximately the same number of collections of short stories and novellas, a three-volume autobiography, several volumes of essays, plays, juveniles, a critical/historical commentary on the modern short story, and most recently (1971) a garden book. Yet despite this staggering productivity his work from the beginnings has been consistently good. He believes that it is the business of the writer to entertain rather than to instruct, to give pleasure rather than to preach morality; at the same time he is a compassionate observer of the contemporary scene and a dedicated craftsman who has so mastered the art of fiction that his quietly successful stories and novels make the work of many recent writers appear amateurish or pretentious.

Bates began to write "seriously" in his late teens, led to short fiction by a Stephen Crane short story he "discovered" in a remaindered copy of an anthology, *The Windmill* (some years earlier, inspired by an imaginative school teacher, he had felt that writing was to be his destiny). Between and during jobs as a reporter for the Wellington office of the Northampton *Chronicle* and as a clerk in a warehouse he continued to read—Galsworthy, Conrad, Wells, Maugham, Bennett, Willa Cather, Edith Wharton, James Branch Cabell—and write prodigiously: stories, plays, an unsuccessful novel and, finally, *The Two Sisters* which was accepted by Jonathan Cape late in 1925 when Bates was only twenty. The novel was published the following year and "I knew then," he has written in his autobiography, "I was never going to be, ever, come hell or high water, anything but a writer."

And a writer he became, the hard way, by careful study and unremitting and often anguished dedication to his craft, by writing and rewriting and ultimately rejecting that which did not meet his self-imposed high standards. Equally at home in the character sketch, the expanded incident, the fully plotted short story and the traditional novel in all its varied manners and modes, he became, as one of his contemporaries observed some years ago, a "term of comparison." Despite his productivity, virtuosity, and growing popularity, he has remained "rigidly and restlessly self-critical." "The Triple Echo," for example, Bates' most recent (1971) and one of his very best novellas, was produced over a period of twenty-five years, and he has said without bombast or exaggeration that he has "destroyed scores of poems, several plays, many short stories and three novels . . . because the disciplinarian in me thought they were no damned good."

Variety is as characteristic of Bates' fiction as quantity and quality. Though the English Midlands where he was born and raised provide both subject and theme for much of his work, his novels and stories range in setting from an English airbase during World War Two (the narrative sketches of "Flying Officer X") to the Burma of *The Jacaranda Tree* or *The Purple Plain* (the only one of his novels thus far made into a motion picture, although several of his works have been optioned, and the television series featuring the Larkin family has been an outstanding success on the BBC). Similarly his people. Though he is particularly successful with the world of "little" English cottagers, farmers, workers, and shop-keepers, his cast of characters include a colonel retired from the Indian service, a simple countryman and the girl he obtains through a want ad, a fiddle-playing coffin-maker and his mother, a vacationing Englishman and his seaside love affair with a French girl who is being kept by a middle-aged dandy, and a group of middle-to-upper class English nationals and Burmese servants caught up in the maelstrom of war. Ranging in tone from the sombre to the unrelentingly tragic, from the comedy of the early Uncle Silas stories to the un-zippered gusto of the relatively late novels concerning the Larkins, Bates' people and their experiences underscore the validity of their creator's comment: "if I claim nothing else for myself as a writer, I will not deny myself versatility."

Even in his most sombre fiction, H. E. Bates is never a sadist creating his people to belittle or destroy them. To the contrary, sympathetic understanding and compassion are among the author's hallmarks, as characteristic as the lyrical quality of his prose, its visual clarity, its union of simplicity-with-depth, its admirable control. Also particularly notable is Bates' re-creation of place and setting which usually play such determining roles in the lives of his characters. Few fiction writers have more successfully, more completely, captured the essence of a vanishing past with its customs, manners, and mores, and I know no recent author who writes with more affectionate understanding of the English countryside or who creates with equal skill the miracle of flower, field and bird, the swing of the seasons, the effect of place upon the individual; and it comes as no surprise that among Bates' favorite authors are W. H. Hudson and Edward Thomas to whom he has said he owes the enrich-ment of his ability to "put the English countryside down on paper."

H. E. Bates is a complex man and writer: these complexities are perhaps most effectively summed up in the last pages of his autobiography in which he comments on his affinities with Pop Larkin of *The Darling Buds of May* and the other Larkin novels: "passionate Englishman [with] a profound love of Nature, of the sounds and sights of the countryside, of colour, flowers and things sensual; a hatred of pomp, pretension and humbug; a lover of children and family life; an occasional breaker of rules, a flouter of convention."

—William Peden

---

**BAWDEN, Nina.** British. Born in London, 19 January 1925. Educated at Somerville College, Oxford, B.A. 1946, M.A. 1951; Salzburg Seminar in American Studies, 1960. Married H. W. Bawden in 1946; A. S. Kark, 1954; has three children. Since 1969, Justice of the Peace for Surrey. Fellow, Royal Society of Literature, 1970. Address: 30 Hanger Hill, Weybridge, Surrey, England.

PUBLICATIONS

Novels

Who Calls the Tune. London, Collins, 1953; as Eyes of Green, New York, Morrow, 1953.
The Odd Flamingo. London, Collins, 1954.
Change Here for Babylon. London, Collins, 1955.
The Solitary Child. London, Collins, 1956.
Devil by the Sea. London, Collins, and Philadelphia, Lippincott, 1957.
Just Like a Lady. London, Longman, 1960; as Glass Slippers Always Pinch, Phila-delphia, Lippincott, 1960.
In Honour Bound. London, Longman, 1961.
Tortoise by Candlelight. London, Longman, and New York, Harper, 1963.

*Under the Skin.*   London, Longman, and New York, Harper, 1964.
*A Little Love, A Little Learning.*   London, Longman, and New York, Harper, 1966.
*A Woman of My Age.*   London, Longman, and New York, Harper, 1967.
*The Grain of Truth.*   London, Longman, and New York, Harper, 1968.
*The Birds on the Trees.*   London, Longman, 1970; New York, Harper, 1971.


Other

*The Secret Passage* (juvenile).   London, Gollancz, 1963; as *The House of Secrets*,
  Philadelphia, Lippincott, 1964.
*On the Run* (juvenile).   London, Gollancz, 1964; as *Three on the Run*, Philadelphia,
  Lippincott, 1965.
*The White Horse Gang* (juvenile).   London, Gollancz, and Philadelphia, Lippincott,
  1966.
*The Witch's Daughter* (juvenile).   London, Gollancz, and Philadelphia, Lippincott,
  1966.
*A Handful of Thieves* (juvenile).   London, Gollancz, and Philadelphia, Lippincott,
  1967.
*The Runaway Summer* (juvenile).   London, Gollancz, and Philadelphia, Lippincott,
  1969.
*Squib* (juvenile).   London, Gollancz, and Philadelphia, Lippincott, 1971.


Critical Study: essay on the author's children's books in *Signal* (Stroud, Gloucestershire),
4 January 1971.


Nina Bawden comments:

I find it difficult to comment on my adult novels. I suppose one could say that the later
books, from *Just Like a Lady* onwards, are social comedies with modern themes and settings; the characters moral beings, hopefully engaged in living. People try so hard and fail
so often, sometimes sadly, sometimes comically; I try to show how and why and to be
accurate about relationships and motives. I have been called a "crypto-moralist with a
mischievous sense of humour", and I like this description: it is certainly part of what I aim
to be.

This quotation, from the *Christian Science Monitor*, though not the most flattering,
might be useful:

Nina Bawden is a writer of unusual precision who can depict human foibles with
an almost embarrassing accuracy. Yet for all that she centres dead on target, there
is always a note of compassion in her stories. The light thrown on her characters,
clear though it is, is no harsh spotlight. It is a more diffuse beam that allows one
to peer into the shadows and see causes even while it focuses on effects.

\*       \*       \*

In her abundant energy and in her occasional recourse to melodrama, Nina Bawden may
remind one of her contemporary, Iris Murdoch. Such a comparison is misleading, however, for it is soon apparent that the two women move in opposite directions. On the evidence
of thirteen novels between *Who Calls the Tune* and *The Birds on the Trees*, to say nothing
of seven children's books, Miss Bawden's literary debts are not, like Miss Murdoch's, to

continental phenomenology, but to English sources, specifically to Jane Austen and Charles Dickens. Jane Austen and Dickens make an odd mix, but not so odd when it becomes clear that Jane Austen preponderates.

From *Just Like a Lady*, the first of Miss Bawden's novels that is not frankly a thriller, to her most recent, the essential scene is domestic, suburban, and enclosed, even when the ostensible setting, as in *A Woman of My Age*, is Morocco. The style is efficient, witty, and often satirical in the Austen manner. And like Jane Austen's, Miss Bawden's best novels, *Just Like a Lady*, *A Woman of My Age*, and *The Birds on the Trees*, are about the central characters' efforts to achieve honesty to self, to separate the genuine from the hypocritical or convenient motive, even at the risk, always resisted, of upsetting the social balance. The catch is that modern society does not provide the elaborate mechanism of manners available to Jane Austen; therefore the parallel can only be schematic.

Miss Bawden is dickensian in the theme of *Just Like a Lady*, frequently in her conception of minor characters, and at those frequent points in her narratives where manners must give over to melodrama, where manners are either no longer viable or no longer exist. Lucy, of *Just Like a Lady*, has great expectations: an orphan, she is brought up in confining suburban near-squalor by relatives. She refuses conformity for Oxford, a naive marriage to a pompous fool, an affair with a lukewarm lover, and reconciliation of a sort with her foolish husband. Banal in outline, the novel is anything but banal in execution. This English adventure in *bovarysme* carries freshness, conviction, and the power of psychological truth.

The milieu of the later novels is suburban, middle class, and superficially safe. It is not in fact, however. At the bottom of the garden lives abject poverty in an abandoned bus, its hair infested by horrors and disease in its body. The bus people, or the people of the gravel pit, in *Tortoise by Candlelight*, live by their wits, outside the law. They threaten the good middle class by their very existence, and by the charms they hold for middle-class children. The criminal poor are chaos and excitement, qualities on which the children thrive and from which they may perish. As in Dickens, the past, too, often comes to upset the present: Miss Bawden's closets have dickensian rather than phenomenological skeletons in them.

If Miss Bawden is sometimes tedious, it is because of the numerous children, who narrate events, as in *A Little Love, A Little Learning*, or whose coy habits are dwelt on at length, as in *Tortoise by Candlelight*. Or in the many eccentrics whose foibles are merely exhibited, to the detriment of the usually spare narrative. Any tediousness is forgotten, however, in one's realization that with each succeeding novel, a perceptible advance has occurred. The authority of craft and the authority of perception promise further advances. In the meantime, the satiric eye and the admirable energy abound, most welcome in a dry time.

—John McCormick

---

**BEATY, (Arthur) David.** British. Born in Hatton, Ceylon, 28 March 1919. Educated at Kingswood School, Bath, Somerset; Merton College, Oxford, 1938–40, M.A. in history 1940; University College, London, 1964–67. Served as a Squadron Leader in the Royal Air Force, in the United Kingdom and the Middle East, 1940–46: Distinguished Flying Cross and Bar. Married Betty Smith in 1948; has three children. Senior Captain, BOAC (British Overseas Airways Corporation), 1946–53. Instructor, College of Air Training, Hamble, Hampshire, 1963. Principal, Administrative Civil Service, 1966–70. Since 1970, Administrative Secretary, Centre for Educational Development Overseas, London. Companion, Royal Aeronautical Society. Address: Woodside, Hever, Edenbridge, Kent, England.

PUBLICATIONS

Novels

The Takeoff.   London, Werner Laurie, 1948; as The Donnington Legend, New York, Morrow, 1949.
The Heart of the Storm.   London, Secker and Warburg, 1954; as The Four Winds, New York, Morrow, 1955.
The Proving Flight.   London, Secker and Warburg, 1956; New York, Morrow, 1957.
Cone of Silence.   London, Secker and Warburg, and New York, Morrow, 1959.
Call Me Captain (as Paul Stanton).   London, Joseph, 1960; New York, Morrow, 1961.
The Wind off the Sea.   London, Secker and Warburg, and New York, Morrow, 1962.
Village of Stars (as Paul Stanton).   London, Joseph, and New York, Morrow, 1962.
The Siren Song.   London, Secker and Warburg, and New York, Morrow, 1964.
The Gun Garden (as Paul Stanton).   London, Joseph, and New York, Morrow, 1965.
Sword of Honour.   London, Secker and Warburg, 1965; New York, Morrow, 1966.
The Temple Tree.   London, Secker and Warburg, 1971.


Other

Milk and Honey.   London, Joseph, and New York, Morrow, 1964.
The Human Factor in Aircraft Accidents.   London, Secker and Warburg, 1969; New York, Stein and Day, 1970.


Critical Study: The World of David Beaty by Roberta J. Forsberg, New York, Twayne, 1971.


David Beaty comments:

In my view, the main purpose of a novel is to search out and exhibit truth, illuminating at the same time human behaviour. This should be executed in a way that is both informative and interesting. The reader must be absorbed by what he reads in order to turn the page. The motivation behind the characters' actions, the inter-acting of their personalities within the plot are most important. I am interested in "why", not simply in the events themselves. My novels are built up on a plan, almost a blueprint. "Belief" is all important, and the sustaining of belief is one of the most difficult things to do. Without belief, the novel is nothing—though belief is of course still possible within fantasy and fairy stories. I see the plot as a symphony composed of incidents, complete in themselves, all with their own note and colour. An incident is "wrong" when it is out of tune or clashes with the colour of its neighbour. Every novel is an attempt to capture time, to weave something solid out of air. The author knows it is an impossible task—that is why he keeps on trying.

*       *       *

David Beaty, like Saint-Exupery, makes his fiction out of the world of commercial aviation. And like his predecessor, his poetic insight enables him to add the symbolic dimension to the realism of his characterization and action. That realism centres on the contemporary dilemma, the human being trapped more and more by his own technology. The novelist particularizes this theme in The Siren Song by putting a question, "What is going to happen now that a machine can land an aeroplane a thousand times more safely than a human operator?"

The Beaty concern with man vs. machine has qualities which differentiate his work from that of other writers who discuss this same problem. As reference to the biography will indicate, he is a professional with a distinguished career as a pilot. In addition, he is an expert in certain areas of flying. His most recent research was published in 1969 in *The Human Factor in Aircraft Accidents*. This study of the psychological factors affecting pilot performance was so highly regarded by an international airline that the management wished to serialize it in their house organ. The importance of his past work is that it has an essential bearing on his art, on its emotional depth. In short Mr. Beaty draws upon his experience for more than a life-like milieu and professionally performing men and women.

Many facets of his work reveal the ties between his technology and his poetic fiction, but only two of these can be indicated in a short summary essay. The first aspect one can only call fundamental love of the instrument. Like the ship of the sea, the airship is regarded as a living creature. "As always on a runway, he had a sense of having no right to be there; as though this was the property of the machines that came tearing down it, to lift themselves up just before where he was now standing, and launch themselves into their own element." Obviously David Beaty does not belong to the back-to-nature school of critics, those who would denounce what they see as dirty, ugly, caricatures of birds. To airmen like him they are the vital tools for casting off earth's fetters, for seeing a new beauty, and for finding peace of mind and soul. Man and machine, "each dead without the other," must make their lives together, struggle with the elements together. Often the novelist sees the survival of each as equally important.

But man can use this instrument for bringing about his own damnation, even as the path to hell goes down from the gate to paradise. Thus, in the Beaty world of multiple images, the man-machine twinning becomes a warning symbol of ultimate destruction, as well as a sign of the way to a better world on the humanistic level and of joy on the transcendental level. In *The Wind off the Sea* Gavin Gallagher, the Commander of a nuclear rocket base, has gloried in his god-sized power. "Marching along like this he had a sudden feeling of wisdom and elevation. . . . He was a giant. God. And he looked on it, and it was Good. . . . He said . . . let there be Life. And there was Life. . . . Let there be Death. . . . And there was Death. At the turn of a switch. . . . Quick as God." But a combination of factors culminating in the chilling experience of thinking that he has, through his right-left confusion, accidentally released the rocket, brings him to conversion:

> He walked away down the gravel path, out of the rocket site. Overhead the thin cloud cleared, and the sky was luminous with light. . . . He had the distinct impression that he had been suffocating in a million fragmented thoughts, the metabolism of a life-time's mental processes, a dark pit, a deep sea. And that suddenly he had swum upwards towards a chink of light. . . . He leaned against what had once been a blast wall to protect aircraft. He seemed to see every blade of grass, every branch of every tree, every patch of field and hedge and roadway, every iridescent particle of moonlight held in some warm and loving radiance.

—Roberta J. Forsberg

---

**BECK, Warren.** American. Born in Richmond, Indiana. Educated at Earlham College, Richmond, B.A. 1921; Columbia University, New York, M.A. 1926. Served in the United States Army, 1918, 1945. Married Carmen Haberman in 1930 (divorced, 1956); has one son. Professor of English, Lawrence University, Appleton, Wisconsin, 1926–68; since 1968, Professor Emeritus. Visiting Professor, United States Army University, Shrivenham,

England, 1945; Connecticut College, New London, 1946; Bread Loaf Graduate School of English, Middlebury College, Vermont, Summers 1947–55; University of Minnesota, Minneapolis, 1956; University of Colorado, Boulder, Summers 1956–57; has also taught at writers' conferences at the University of Missouri, Columbia; University of Pittsburgh; Notre Dame University, South Bend, Indiana. Recipient: Friends of American Writers Award, 1945; Rockefeller grant, 1948; Ford Fellowship, 1952; Ehrig Foundation Award (for teaching), 1961; American Council of Learned Societies Fellowship, 1963, and grant, 1969. Litt.D., Earlham College, 1955. Address: 207 North Park Avenue, Appleton, Wisconsin 54911, U.S.A.

PUBLICATIONS

Novels

    *Final Score.*  New York, Knopf, 1944; London, Eyre and Spottiswoode, 1945.
    *Pause under the Sky.*  New York, Morrow, and London, Eyre and Spottiswoode, 1947.
    *Into Thin Air.*  New York, Knopf, 1951.

Short Stories

    *The Blue Sash and Other Stories.*  Yellow Springs, Ohio, Antioch Press, 1941.
    *The First Fish and Other Stories.*  Yellow Springs, Ohio, Antioch Press, 1947.
    *The Far Whistle and Other Stories.*  Yellow Springs, Ohio, Antioch Press, 1951.
    *The Rest Is Silence and Other Stories.*  Denver, Swallow, 1963.

Other

    *Huck Finn at Phelps Farm.*  Paris, Archives des Lettres Modernes, 1958.
    *Man in Motion: Faulkner's Trilogy.*  Madison, University of Wisconsin Press, 1961.
    *Joyce's "Dubliners": Substance, Vision, and Art.*  Durham, North Carolina, Duke
      University Press, 1969.

Has published many scholarly and critical essays, including three essays in 1941 on William Faulkner.

Manuscript Collection: Boston University Library.

Warren Beck comments:

Briefly I call myself fictionist, having begun with short stories and having published my first collection before writing my first novel. *Story Magazine*, edited by Burnett and Foley, suggested working in the mode I cared about as reader, the vein of Chekhov and Joyce's *Dubliners*, Katharine Mansfield, Anderson's *Winesburg, Ohio* and some of Maupassant and Hemingway. *Story* was showing a wide experimental practice in this vein by various American and English writers, in the faith that fiction could go beyond tidy plot dependent upon sentimental cliches, and could suggest the fluidity of experience, with its arrivals at relative personal realizations.

I believe fiction's greatest significations are in a synthesis of dramatic and lyric modes, with human consciousness the theatre of the essential action. However, this subjective material should be objectively conveyed in a produced illusion the reader can answer to imaginatively. The writer should not explain, or seek just to beguile, but by implicative presentation to invoke a concerned assent. And I believe there is no drama without reference to values, as conceived of within the social context but by individuals, with relevance to their own on-going lives. In this light every life has its story, and in a seemingly uneventful existence some crucial personal issue may stand out the more clearly, humanely representative.

While my experiences have extended widely, as journalist, advertising man, teacher, traveler, and incidentally in the army and at odd jobs during my college years, I have not written of these worlds in themselves, but draw on them only incidentally, for factual basis and atmosphere. My first novel concerns a football player and a reporter who sees him as a monstrous pawn; my second is of two lovers held apart by World War II and grated upon by that era's homefront crassness; my third is of a melancholy man's recollection of an adulterous love affair. In my short stories there are students, farmers, clergymen, mechanics, professors, boys of several ages and aged men and women, theatre managers, secretaries, neighbors, sons and fathers, husbands and wives, the almost anonymous persons on trains and in public places, but I chose none of these as such, rather for some human guise they made me notice, stirring my intuition of a phase of their real existence. Critics have generously credited me with "a faculty for transmuting rather ordinary situations into something subtly and absorbingly interesting," and with a "soundly oriented range over the sea of human emotion and experience." Whether or not I achieve such ends, my interest, beyond simple realism, is in surges of imagining how it might be for others, and in embodying that. This does not exclude ironies or even open satire: a fictionist may feel that "there but for some good fortune and providence go I," or his devotion to certain values may spur him to an exposing of their violation. However, I have not written fiction to moralize. Neither do I look for the eccentric, bizarre, or sensational; I merely accept what comes within my ken as true to the human situation, whether forbidding or pathetic or endearingly humorous.

Though locales in my fiction are largely Midwestern, that is a mere accident of long residence; for me regionalism is significant only in its detail supporting what can be true beyond regional boundaries. More widely, as citizen of the United States and humanistically concerned university teacher and committed fictionist, I have been increasingly skeptical of this society's trends. No naive perfectionist, I admit life's inescapable elements of darkness, but I feel a more particular melancholy about my own country, in its megalomania that outruns its resources, material and ethical. Distraught by heterogeneousness, tangled in conflicting opportunisms, it lacks, I fear, both a viable sense of tradition and dynamic vision. Ill-educated, ill-informed, often misled, its people do not know their addiction to illusions, nor estimate their actual prospects. Yet I have faith in the right intentions of all sorts of folks, and I have tried to celebrate their cheerful endurance against confusing odds, and their normal yearning toward some personal realization of the good. So in my fiction I often treat ironically the background and minor characters, but most of my protagonists are cast on the angels' side, however tentatively apprehended. Thus in my second novel the full panorama is satirical—the synthesizing impetus came as I walked a street on a warm evening hearing the same radio program through one window after another and sensing the stifling seductions to conformity. But in that novel my two lovers and many others hold out for individual values, and so I was most gratified when the New Yorker termed it "adult and perceptive . . . a vigorous, unsentimental book, deeply imbued with sentiment," for that assented to my theme, the persistence of genuine human feeling amidst distorting forces. The fate of the human heart in the world's harsh impersonality can be tragic yet triumphant; the freedom to be and become is the most subtle, vulnerable, and precious of freedoms; what is written in and to that spirit can be the most useful art.

No conscious regionalist, neither would I promulgate any systematized social consciousness. I write out of an intense interest (critical and I hope compassionate) in individuals, attempting to embody a sense of their natures and realizations in an implicative portrayal that may draw out a reader's empathetic response, confirming a human solidarity.

\*       \*       \*

*Final Score*, Warren Beck's first novel, appeared in 1944. Several characteristics of this study of an American fascist also mark his later works. The form is a sort of double-flashback, a dialogue over highballs between the writer and the central figure's press agent. Their moral ponderings form so substantial a part of the work as to indicate that it is not the story that counts, but what it may show us: what makes a fascist and what can prevent one. This didactic orientation, the outstanding feature of all Beck's work, leads to his use in the novels of broadly social themes rather than considerations of individual existence. The aim is not epiphany, but explanation. As in his other works, the action is unmistakeably set in the midwest, and the narrators themselves are not Jamesian vibrating consciousnesses, but mid-western sensibilities, confused and a little embarrassed about caring. The concern is with typicality; the lessons are to be those within the ordinary man's grasp.

Beck's second novel is again war-influenced, its hero a bombardier on a three-day pass. Like *Final Score*, *Pause under the Sky* has a melodramatic plot undercut by an undramatic presentation. In this case, the filter is the reflection of the main characters on the action. Fully half of the book is taken up with thinking about the corruptions and materialism of popular culture as evidenced in the constant sounding of commercial radio stations. The book begins with these stations being suddenly stilled by a technologically adept Jeremiah, who interrupts the broadcasts to issue warnings of doom. The novel consists of the quest of the hero and his fiancee for this mysterious controller, a quest which is at the same time a search for a solution to the problems of an increasingly vacuous and grasping America.

In 1951, Beck published his last novel, *Into Thin Air*, a novel more personal than his others, which deals with the problems of old age and guilty love. The form this time is meditation; the old man remembers his life as he watches the house next door, symbol of what has meant most to him, being torn down. Again the plot, of adulterous love and sacrificed ambition, is melodramatic in summary, and again the presentation is indirect and undramatic. The characters are types and the action seems to be a function of philosophy rather than experience. This leaning toward allegory is apparent in all the novels, as in a number of the short stories. But here, perhaps more than in the earlier novels, we have a sense of the mid-American social pattern and the internalized ethic. We see too Beck's concern for lost innocence and opportunity, a concern manifested more fully in much of his shorter fiction.

Perhaps Beck has found the short story a more congenial form than the novel. His volumes of short stories outnumber his novels. By and large they are post-meditated moral crises, frequently told in the first person, often with more activity in the characters' minds than in the events. They frequently deal with the concern of a father for the perilous innocence of his child, of some other child-like character, or for his own moral innocence. Their consistent didactic purpose marks their position in the body of Beck's work.

—Jeanne Desy

---

**BECKER, Stephen (David).** American. Born in Mount Vernon, New York, 31 March 1927. Educated at Harvard University, Cambridge, Massachusetts, 1943–47, B.A. 1947; Yenching University, Peking, 1947–48. Served in the United States Marine Corps, 1945. Married Mary Elizabeth Freeburg in 1947; has three children. Instructor, Tsing Hua University, Peking, 1947–48; Teaching Fellow, Brandeis University, Waltham, Massachusetts, 1951–52. Editor, Western Printing Company, New York, 1955–56. Recipient: Paul Harris Fellowship, 1947; Guggenheim Fellowship, 1954. Address: Box 116, Conway, Massachusetts 01341, U.S.A.

PUBLICATIONS

Novels

*The Season of the Stranger.*   New York, Harper, and London, Hamish Hamilton, 1951.
*Shanghai Incident.*   New York, Fawcett, 1955.
*Juice.*   New York, Simon and Schuster, and London, Muller, 1959.
*A Covenant with Death.*   New York, Atheneum, and London, Hamish Hamilton, 1965.
*The Outcasts.*   New York, Atheneum, and London, Hamish Hamilton, 1967.
*When the War Is Over.*   New York, Random House, 1969; London, Hamish Hamilton, 1970.

Uncollected Short Stories

"To Know the Country", in *Harper's* (New York), August 1951.
"The Town Mouse", in *Harper's* (New York), May 1952.
"Monsieur Malfait", in *Harper's* (New York), June 1953.
"A Baptism of Some Importance", in *Story*.   New York, McKay, 1954.
"The New Encyclopaedist", in *Fantasy and Science Fiction* (New York), May and September 1964.

Other

*Comic Art in America: A Social History of the Funnies, the Political Cartoons, Magazine Humor, Sporting Cartoons, and Animated Cartoons.*   New York, Simon and Schuster, 1959.
*Marshall Field III: A Biography.*   New York, Simon and Schuster, 1964.

Translator, *The Colors of the Day*, by Romain Gary.   New York, Simon and Schuster, and London, Joseph, 1953.
Translator, *Mountains in the Desert*, by Louis Carl and Joseph Petot.   New York, Doubleday, and London, Allen and Unwin, 1954.
Translator, *The Sacred Forest*, by Pierre-Dominique Gaisseau.   New York, Knopf, 1954.
Translator, *Faraway*, by André Dhotel.   New York, Simon and Schuster, 1957.
Translator, *Someone Will Die Tonight in the Caribbean*, by René Puissesseau.   New York, Knopf, 1958; London, W. H. Allen, 1959.
Translator, *The Last of the Just*, by André Schwarz-Bart.   New York, Atheneum, and London, Secker and Warburg, 1961.
Translator, *The Town Beyond the Wall*, by Elie Wiesel.   New York, Atheneum, 1964.

*          *          *

Equally distinguished as a translator, a biographer, a commentator on the popular arts and a novelist, Stephen Becker brings to his fiction a breadth of experience with world culture and human behavior which yields moral complexity and psychological verity in his work. Two major themes intertwine through his novels—the problems of justice and the necessity for self-knowledge and self-fulfillment.

Beginning most clearly with *Juice*, Becker concentrates on the moral and social complexities of law and justice, continuing this theme in *A Covenant with Death* and *When the War Is Over*. The problem Becker's protagonists face is to distinguish between the arbitrary and mechanical justice of the law and true human justice. The rigidity and absoluteness of law collide with human values—especially the need for expiation, mercy and compassion. The characters' dilemma is to choose between true justice and simple retribution and to use the mechanism of blind justice to solve difficult moral problems. Against this theme is developed another—an existential concept of the self, men struggling with themselves, with nature and with circumstances to become fully alive and functioning beings. This theme is isolated most clearly in *The Outcasts*, which describes a group of engineers building a bridge deep in a primeval jungle. There they must overcome the indifferent force of nature, their own weaknesses, their fears and prejudices.

In *Juice* the theme of human and mechanical justice arises when the central character, Joseph Harrison, kills a pedestrian in an auto accident. His friends and employer try to use the law and the power of money and position ("juice") to whitewash the occurrence, while Harrison demands an absolute judgment to redeem his error. The tensions between views of law and truth reshape Harrison's whole existence. In *A Covenant with Death*, a young judge is confronted with a difficult decision in a murder case; through detective work, insights into motivation and a complete understanding of the limits of the law, Judge Lewis is able to render a humane verdict and still satisfy the meaning of law. The forces of procrustean and draconian legalism are averted through the judge's efforts, through an intense moral revaluation which ultimately changes the judge's own life. In this novel, humanity triumphs through the action of the law.

The tragedy of the law is exposed in *When the War Is Over*, Becker's most recent and most satisfying novel. It is the story of the last victim of the Civil War, a boy executed as a Confederate guerrilla long after hostilities had ceased. The moral struggle is embodied in Lt. Marius Catto, a young career officer caught between a genuine love of peace and justice and a natural inclination toward the arts of war. He works to prevent General Hooker from wreaking vengeance through law on the boy but fails and is left scarred and embittered by disillusionment. The novel, based on historical fact, is a brilliant reconstruction of the time and place and an intense scrutiny of moral and social values. It convincingly examines the mechanism of military order, social justice and our conflicting views of violence and law. The story uncovers basic contradictions in our organization of legal murder.

Becker's examination of society's structure and limitations and his portrayal of men seeking "grace under pressure" is a significant contribution to contemporary fiction. The existential premises of the works—individuals finding meaning inside the arbitrary bounds of social order—reflect our acceptance of the civilization we have built.

—William J. Schafer

---

**BECKETT, Samuel (Barclay).** Irish. Born in Dublin, 13 April 1906. Educated at Portora Royal School, County Fermanagh; Trinity College, Dublin, B.A. in French and Italian 1927, M.A. 1931. Worked at the Irish Red Cross Hospital, St. Lô, France, 1945–46. Married Suzanne Dechevaux-Dumesnil in 1948. Lecturer in English, Ecole Normale Supérieure, Paris, 1928–30; Lecturer in French, Trinity College, Dublin, 1930–32. Closely associated with James Joyce in Paris in the late 1920's and the 1930's. Settled in Paris in 1938, and has written chiefly in French since 1945; translates his own work into English. Recipient: London *Evening Standard* Drama Award, 1955; Obie Award, for drama, New York, 1958, 1960, 1962, 1964; International Publishers Prize, 1961; Nobel Prize for Literature, 1969. Litt.D., Trinity College, Dublin, 1959. Address: c/o Editions de Minuit, 7 rue Bernard-Palissy, Paris 6, France.

## PUBLICATIONS

### Novels

*Murphy*.   London, Routledge, 1938; New York, Grove Press, 1957.
*Molloy*.   Paris, Editions de Minuit, 1951; translated by the author and Patrick Bowles, Paris, Olympia Press, and New York, Grove Press, 1955; London, John Calder, 1959.
*Malone Meurt*.   Paris, Editions de Minuit, 1951; translated by the author as *Malone Dies*, New York, Grove Press, 1956; London, John Calder, 1958.
*L'Innomable*.   Paris, Editions de Minuit, 1953; translated by the author as *The Unnamable*, New York, Grove Press, 1958; London, John Calder, 1959.
*Watt* (written in English).   Paris, Olympia Press, 1953; New York, Grove Press, 1959; London, John Calder, 1963.
*Comment C'Est*.   Paris, Editions de Minuit, 1961; translated by the author as *How It Is*, New York, Grove Press, and London, John Calder, 1964.
*Mercier et Camier*.   Paris, Editions de Minuit, 1970.

### Short Stories

*More Pricks Than Kicks*.   London, Chatto and Windus, 1934; New York, Grove Press, 1970.
*Nouvelles et Textes pour Rien*.   Paris, Editions de Minuit, 1955; translated by the author as *Stories and Texts for Nothing*, New York, Grove Press, 1967; included in *No's Knife: Selected Shorter Prose, 1945–1966*, London, Calder and Boyars, 1967.

### Plays

*En Attendant Godot*.   Paris, Editions de Minuit, 1952; translated by the author as *Waiting for Godot: A Tragicomedy in Two Acts* (produced London, 1955; New York, 1956), New York, Grove Press, 1954; London, Faber, 1956.
*All That Fall: A Play for Radio* (broadcast BBC, 1957).   London, Faber, 1957; as *All That Fall*, New York, Grove Press, 1957.
*Fin de Partie: Suivi de Acte sans Paroles*.   Paris, Editions de Minuit, 1957; translated by the author as *Endgame: A Play in One Act; Followed by Act Without Words*, London, Faber, and New York, Grove Press, 1958.
*Endgame* (produced New York and London, 1958).   Included in *Endgame*, 1958.
*Act Without Words* (produced Dublin, 1962).   Included in *Endgame*, 1958.
*Krapp's Last Tape* (produced London, 1958).   Included in *Krapp's Last Tape*, 1959.
*Embers* (broadcast BBC, 1959).   Included in *Krapp's Last Tape*, 1959.
*Krapp's Last Tape and Embers*.   London, Faber, 1959; as *Krapp's Last Tape and Other Dramatic Pieces*, New York, Grove Press, 1960.
*Happy Days* (produced New York, 1961; London, 1962).   New York, Grove Press, 1961; London, Faber, 1963.
*Play and Two Short Pieces for Radio* (includes *Words and Music*, *Cascando*).   London, Faber, 1964.
*The Old Tune*, adaptation of a play by Robert Pinget, in *Three Plays*, by Robert Pinget.   New York, Hill and Wang, 1966; as *Plays*, London, Calder and Boyars, 1966.
*Eh Joe and Other Writings* (includes *Act Without Words*, *Film*).   London, Faber, 1967.
*Come and Go: A Dramaticule*.   London, Calder and Boyars, 1967.
*Cascando and Other Short Dramatic Pieces* (includes *Words and Music*, *Eh Joe*, *Play*, *Come and Go*, *Film*).   New York, Grove Press, 1968.

Verse

*Whoroscope*.   Paris, Hours Press, 1930.
*Echo's Bones and Other Precipitates*.   Paris, Europa Press, 1935.
*Poems in English*.   London, John Calder, 1961; New York, Grove Press, 1963.


Other

*Our Exagmination round His Factification for Incamination of Work in Progress*, with
    others (on James Joyce).   Paris, Shakespeare and Company, 1929.
*Proust*.   London, Chatto and Windus, 1931; New York, Grove Press, 1957; with
    *Three Dialogues*, with Georges Duthuit, London, Calder and Boyars, 1965.
*From an Abandoned Work*.   London, Faber, 1958.
*Bram de Velde*, with others.   Paris, G. Fell, 1958; translated by the author and Olive
    Classe, New York, Grove Press, 1960.
*Imagination Morte Imaginez*.   Paris, Editions de Minuit, 1958; translated by the
    author as *Imagination Dead Imagine*, London, Calder and Boyars, 1965.
*Assez*.   Paris, Editions de Minuit, 1966.
*Bing*.   Paris, Editions de Minuit, 1966.
*Tetes-Mortes* (includes *D'Un Ouvrage Abandonné, Assez, Bing, Imagination Morte
    Imaginez*).   Paris, Editions de Minuit, 1967; translated as "Residua," in *No's Knife*,
    1967.
*A Samuel Beckett Reader*.   London, Calder and Boyars, 1967.
*Sans*.   Paris, Editions de Minuit, 1969; translated by the author as *Lessness*, London,
    Calder and Boyars, 1971.
*Le Dépeupleur*.   Paris, Editions de Minuit, 1971.

*      *      *

Poet, critic, playwright, Samuel Beckett considers that his most valid work is fiction.
Beckett's first published short story, "Assumption," appeared in the June 1929 issue of
*Transition*, along with his essay on Joyce's *Work in Progress*. Soon afterwards, influenced
by Joyce, Beckett began his own Work in Progress, a novel entitled *Dream of Fair to Middling
Women*. After typing 214 pages, Beckett abandoned it, though he published two excerpts
in 1932.

More importantly, he salvaged the novel's protagonist, Belacqua Shuah, for a series of
short stories, which were collected in 1934 as *More Pricks Than Kicks*. The exotic name of
the Dublin-based hero is borrowed from Canto IV of Dante's *Purgatorio*, and the figure
recurs in Beckett's work. Dante's Belacqua sits in a fetal position "more indolent than if
sloth were his sister." Like his namesake, Beckett's Belacqua inclines to indolence, but
circumstances and fair to middling women conspire against him, and he leads quite an
active short life. The ten stories carry him through various adventures, especially with
women, past his death and through his burial. Thrice married, Beckett's Belacqua dies on
the operating table of an overdose of anesthetic. His best friend promptly replaces him in
the arms of his widow. The book closes in a cemetery, where the ground keeper quickly
forgets Belacqua's remains. "So it goes in the world." For the way of the world is not a way
of lingering compassion.

At about the time of the 1934 publication of these ten stories that constitute a picaresque
novel, Beckett began the novel *Murphy*, more traditionally plotted. In name and spirit,
Belacqua was a foreigner in his native Dublin; Murphy the Irishman is a literal foreigner in
London, where Beckett was living when he wrote *Murphy*. The omniscient narrator of
*Murphy* informs us early, "All the puppets in this book whinge sooner or later, except
Murphy, who is not a puppet." Like Belacqua, the non-puppet Murphy cherishes indolence,

and like Beckett's Belacqua, Murphy finds that Woman is the main obstacle to the indolent life of the mind. But Belacqua's several women crystallize into Murphy's Celia Kelly, an avatar of the kind-hearted whore.

In *Murphy* the titular hero's mind and body are in conflict over Celia, who has street-walked her way into the affections of the latter. And so powerful is her effect on that latter that she prevails upon indolent Murphy to seek employment so that she need not continue hers. Murphy becomes an attendant at the Magdalen Mental Mercyseat, which he finds so congenial to his temperament that he renounces the outside world, including Celia. While this ironic reversal is taking place, a virtual posse has set out in search of Murphy—from Cork through Dublin to London, where they converge upon a Murphyless Celia. Murphy, having failed to communicate with his favorite patient, Mr. Endon, retires to meditate in his garret. The gasline explodes, burning him to death. Murphy's various hunters find only his charred remains, and they go on with their separate lives. For the way of the world is not the way of lingering compassion.

*Murphy* was not published until 1938, by which time Beckett had moved to Paris, where he still lives. His first French fiction was the translation of *Murphy* into French, undertaken with Alfred Péron and completed before the outbreak of World War II. After fleeing from the Nazis to Free France, while working as an agricultural laborer, Beckett wrote *Watt*, his last English novel. A remarkable book in any language, *Watt* is in part about language, for its titular hero counts on language to explain phenomena. Using his senses, "his most noble faculties," and his mind, "whatever that may be," Watt seeks to make sense of event, thing, and person at Mr. Knott's establishment, where he undertakes service. But senses and mind are incommensurate with Mr. Knott, and Watt leaves Mr. Knott's house, sadder perhaps but no wiser. At a later date, Watt moves and speaks in inversions; he lives in a mansion where he meets Sam who lives in his mansion, and it is Sam who purports to be the recorder of Watt's adventures as narrated by their hero. It is presumably Sam who divides the novel into four numbered parts and an Addendum; the first and fourth parts show us Watt as a stranger among people of the world, whereas the second and third, in very different styles, trace Watt's adventures at Mr. Knott's establishment. Part 2 is the core of Watt's tragedy—his inability to come to terms with the phenomena of Mr. Knott's house. Part 2 of *Watt* also contains the precursor of Beckett's French fiction—a long, alogical, first-person narration.

Although Beckett had written poems in French and had translated *Murphy* into French, it was not until his return to Paris after World War II that he adopted French as his major writing language. The bulk of Beckett's fiction should be classified as *French* fiction. More-over, that is the work that Beckett himself considers most valid. However, Beckett (with an occasional collaborator) has translated his French fiction into English, and it thus occupies some place as English fiction. The following brief account does proportional injustice to the decisive importance of the French fiction.

After trying out his French fictional hand in the translation of *Murphy*, and in four nouvelles (*La Fin*, *L'Expulsé*, *Premier amour*, and *Le Calmant*) and a novel (*Mercier et Camier*), Beckett embarked on the trilogy, usually considered his major work (published separately as *Molloy*, *Malone Dies*, and *The Unnamable*). The three volumes are not a trilogy in the usual sense; they do not develop a plot through time. Nor, like Lawrence Durrell, does Beckett use his volumes to present different views of the same events. Rather, Beckett's volumes are a trilogy through progressive concentration of events and characters, and through heightened intensity of the first-person narration.

*Molloy*, the first book, is divided into two parts; in the first a grotesque old cripple, hat fastened to his buttonhole by a lace, having arrived mysteriously in his mother's room, writes a disconnected tale of his disconnected voyage toward his mother. In the second part, Jacques Moran, a middle-aged Catholic father of an only namesake son, having returned from a mission to seek Molloy, writes a report for his employer Youdi. In *Malone Dies*, the second volume, paralytic Malone, confined to his bed, tries to order the time of his dying by writing an inventory of his possessions, a description of his present state, and stories. In the third volume, *The Unnamable*, the titular protagonist-speaker seeks to penetrate behind fictional and linguistic formulae to himself. His utterances, stripped of Moran's comic perceptions, Molloy's passion, and Malone's purpose, attains an incantatory anguish of meaning made music.

After the trilogy, genre designations are difficult for Beckett's non-dramatic work. His *Texts for Nothing*, spare of event and character, might be called prose poems or thematic monologues; Beckett calls them "texts." His only book-length work is *How It Is*, in which almost abstract characters meet and part, naked in the mud. The grammatical first person dissolves into colloquial, unpunctuated phrases that are grouped in irregular verses. Certain phrases, permuted and combined and recombined with others, constitute the burden of narration. After *How It Is*, Beckett's short prose pieces are dense with repetitive resonance around the void. There is no final summing up for Beckett's work. He continues to write, always seeking Being beneath the superficies of our civilization and our languages; he expresses his search with musical precision of the language he distrusts—French *or* English.

—Ruby Cohn

---

**BEDFORD, Sybille.** British. Born in Charlottenburg, Germany, 16 March 1911. Educated privately. Married Walter Bedford in 1935. Has worked as a Law Reporter: covered the Auschwitz Trial at Frankfurt for the *Observer*, London, and the *Saturday Evening Post*, New York, 1963–65, and the trial of Jack Ruby at Dallas for *Life*, New York, 1964. Since 1968 has been engaged in researching and writing the official biography of Aldous Huxley. Fellow, Royal Society of Literature, 1964. Address: c/o Messrs. Coutts, 440 Strand, London W.C.2, England.

PUBLICATIONS

Novels

A Legacy.   London, Weidenfeld and Nicolson, 1956; New York, Simon and Schuster, 1957.
A Favourite of the Gods.   London, Collins, and New York, Simon and Schuster, 1963.
A Compass Error.   London, Collins, 1968; New York, Knopf, 1969.

Uncollected Short Story

"Compassionata at Hyde Park Corner", in *23 Modern Stories*.   New York, Knopf, 1963.

Other

The Sudden View: A Mexican Journey.   London, Gollancz, 1953; New York, Harper, 1954.
The Best We Can Do: An Account of the Trial of John Bodkin Adams.   London, Collins, 1958; as *The Trial of Dr. Adams*, New York, Simon and Schuster, 1959.

*The Faces of Justice: A Traveller's Report*.   London, Collins, 1961; New York, Simon and Schuster, 1963.

Critical Studies: by Evelyn Waugh, in *The Spectator* (London), 13 April 1956; by V. S. Pritchett, in *New Statesman* (London), 11 January 1963; by P. N. Furbank, in *Encounter* (London), April 1964; by Bernard Levin, in London *Daily Mail*, 12 September 1966; by Constantine Fitzgibbon, in *Irish Times* (Dublin), 19 October 1968.

*                *                *

A first glance at Sybille Bedford's fiction suggests the genre of social history, perhaps the subordinate form of the family novel. Yet, although the accoutrements of history and generation are present, strongest in the first novel and diminishing in the next two, the actual core of interest resides in the individual character as such and the validity of his action.

The first novel, *A Legacy*, might have commented on the unification of Germany through a parallelling of the events of the Felden Scandal or the marriages that occupy much of the action. The novel might also have commented on the degeneration of the twin dynamos of the early modern age, Voltaire and Rousseau, through the description of the two major families of the book: the Merzes, "wealthy" Berlin Jews whose retiring and bourgeois interests belie their originating ancestor's intellectual passions; and the von Feldens, petty South German barons who are vaguely agrarian and on occasion Catholic. However, the ties are too tenuous and the long build-up accorded the families only serves as an interesting forepiece to the corrupt morality and inadequate vitality that are revealed in the marriages of Julius von Felden to Melanie Merz and later to Caroline Trafford, the generous-spirited English woman who suddenly appears more than half way through the novel and serves as the reader's sounding board.

The second novel, *A Favourite of the Gods*, running from the turn of the century into the period between the World Wars in Italy and England, draws less extensively on social and historical matters, although the characters reflect regional stereotypes and there is some mention made of the First World War and of the opposition to Mussolini. Principally, however, the novel contrasts Anna, a sexually ingenuous and probably repressed blue-stocking from New England who marries a Roman prince, with Constanza, her sexually free, liberal-minded, but intellectually poorly-developed daughter.

The third novel, *A Compass Error*, which takes place in Southern France, is the least socio-historical, having only peripheral mention of anti-fascism and the Second World War. An enlargement of an incident in *A Favourite of the Gods*, it details a hybristic error made by Flavia, the daughter of Constanza, and her short-lived English husband. Within the frame of a backward look the middle-aged Flavia recounts her young belief that she could chart out her life, and her subsequent manipulation by the wife of her mother's lover that changed her own as well as her mother's life.

The socio-historical settings of the novels, although never essential to the action, are often fascinating in themselves. Further, they suggest, as a consideration of the characters will show, the possible mastership of Henry James. Besides the indirection of comment, that sometimes maddening characteristic of James, each of the characters who pair off in the novels' action derives from a different country, again typical. In addition each pair exhibits the contrast between fresh, energetic innocence and degenerate, if attractive, worldliness leading to moral insight that James modulated from *The American* to *The Golden Bowl*. Yet, if the characterization is Jamesian, the shifting point of view of the narrator is not. Nor is the large structure of the novels, as evidenced by the overweighted early part of *A Legacy* and the long background that Flavia relates in *A Compass Error*, at the end of which her fictional auditor is quite understandably asleep.

Although top literary honors cannot be accorded Sybille Bedford's fiction, we can recognize her civilized and informed attitude and the skillfully drawn characters, the delightful evocation of place and time, and the witty well-rendered scenes that have won her contemporary acclaim.

—John P. O'Neill

---

**BELLOW, Saul.** American. Born in Lachine, Quebec, Canada, 10 June 1915. Educated at the University of Chicago, 1933–35; Northwestern University, Evanston, Illinois, 1935–37, B.S. (honors) in sociology and anthropology 1937; University of Wisconsin, Madison, 1937. Served in the United States Merchant Marine, 1944–45. Married Anita Goshkin in 1937 (divorced); Alexandra Tschacbasov, 1956 (divorced); Susan Glassman, 1961; has three children. Teacher, Pestalozzi-Froebel Teachers College, Chicago, 1938–42; Member of the Editorial Department, *Encyclopaedia Britannica*, Chicago, 1943–46; Instructor, 1946, and Assistant Professor of English, 1948–49, University of Minnesota, Minneapolis; Visiting Lecturer, New York University, 1950–52; Creative Writing Fellow, Princeton University, New Jersey, 1952–53; Member of the English faculty, Bard College, Annandale-on-Hudson, New York, 1953–54; Associate Professor of English, University of Minnesota, 1954–59; Co-Founding Editor, *The Noble Savage*, Chicago, 1960–62. Visiting Professor of English, University of Puerto Rico, Rio Piedras, 1961. Since 1962, Professor, Committee on Social Thought, University of Chicago. Fellow, Academy for Policy Study, 1966; Fellow, Branford College, Yale University, New Haven, Connecticut. Recipient: National Institute of Arts and Letters grant, 1952; National Book Award, 1954, 1965, 1971; Ford grant, 1959, 1960; Friends of Literature award, 1960; James L. Dow Award, 1964; Prix International de Littérature, France, 1965; Jewish Heritage Award, 1968. D.Litt., Northwestern University, 1962; Bard College, 1963. Member, National Institute of Arts and Letters. Address: Committee on Social Thought, University of Chicago, 1126 East 59th Street, Chicago, Illinois 60637, U.S.A.

PUBLICATIONS

Novels

> *Dangling Man*. New York, Vanguard Press, 1944; London, Weidenfeld and Nicolson, 1960.
> *The Victim*. New York, Vanguard Press, 1945; London, Weidenfeld and Nicolson, 1965.
> *The Adventures of Augie March*. New York, Viking Press, 1953; London, Weidenfeld and Nicolson, 1954.
> *Henderson the Rain King*. New York, Viking Press, and London, Weidenfeld and Nicolson, 1959.
> *Herzog*. New York, Viking Press, 1964; London, Weidenfeld and Nicolson, 1965.
> *Mr. Sammler's Planet*. New York, Viking Press, and London, Weidenfeld and Nicolson, 1970.

Short Stories

> *Seize the Day, with Three Short Stories and a One-Act Play*. New York, Viking Press, 1956; London, Weidenfeld and Nicolson, 1957.

*Mosby's Memoirs and Other Stories.*   New York, Viking Press, 1968; London, Weidenfeld and Nicolson, 1969.

Plays

*The Wrecker*, in *New World Writing 6*.   New York, New American Library, 1954.
*The Last Analysis* (produced New York, 1964; Derby, 1967).   New York, Viking
Press, 1965; London, Weidenfeld and Nicolson, 1966.
*Under the Weather* (includes *Out from Under*, *The Wen*, and *Orange Soufflé*) (produced
Glasgow, 1966; as *The Bellow Plays*, produced London and New York, 1966).
*The Wen* (produced Glasgow, London and New York, 1966).   Published in *Traverse
Plays*, London, Penguin, 1967.
*Orange Soufflé* (produced Glasgow, London and New York, 1966).   Published in
*Traverse Plays*, London, Penguin, 1967.

Other

*Dessins*, by Jess Reichek; text by Saul Bellow and C. Zervos.   Paris, Editions Cahiers
d'Art, 1960.
*Recent American Fiction: A Lecture*.   Washington, D.C., United States Government
Printing Office, 1963.
*Like You're Nobody: The Letters of Louis Gallo to Saul Bellow, 1961–1962, plus Oedipus-
Schmoedipus, The Story That Started It All*.   New York, Dimensions Press, 1966.
*The Future of the Moon*.   New York, Viking Press, 1970.

Editor, *Great Jewish Short Stories*.   New York, Dell, 1963; London, Vallentine
Mitchell, 1971.

Translator, with others, *Gimpel the Fool and Other Stories*, by Isaac Bashevis Singer.
New York, Farrar Straus, 1957; London, Peter Owen, 1958.

*          *          *

Saul Bellow is the most distinguished novelist of the post-war period in America. He is
the most intellectual of American novelists, but one who, paradoxically, relies finally upon
imagination and feeling. He may be the staunchest defender of the idea of the self in American
fiction, but he frequently recognizes claims of brotherhood and love that limit the egoistic
pursuit of the self. His fiction rests upon a conception of becoming or possibility, yet he
recognizes that human initiative in creating and pursuing process is limited by powerful
determinants beyond human control. Bellow is an optimist, despite the prevailing climate
of pessimism and despair. His novels are built on these dichotomies and paradoxes and
written in a language that is almost always vibrant and resourceful.
    The evolution of Bellow's style is a key to the understanding of his fiction. He began, in
*Dangling Man* and *The Victim*, with a tight conception of both language and structure,
using Flaubert as his model. Both books are disciplined and spare; Bellow has said that
he strove for a kind of correctness that would be acceptable to the Anglo-Saxon Protestant
world that seemed to dominate American literature. But by the time he came to write *The
Adventures of Augie March*, he had discovered rhetoric, he had gained confidence as a writer
and as an American, and the WASP hold on literature in the United States had been
weakened. The result is that the language of this novel streams out of Bellow in a fine, free
flow; it is as larky as its protagonist and as various as the many levels of its discourse
demand, ranging in its versatility from the talk of Jewish immigrants to the intercourse of
University of Chicago intellectuals. As the language expanded, so did the book, and *Augie*

is a sprawling, picaresque work in contrast to the carefully contained earlier novels. Succeeding novels show a curbing of rhetorical extravagance, but *Augie* established the essential mode of expression for the fiction Bellow has done since.

Bellow's taste for a vital and even eccentric language is related, first, to his conviction that words are a form of power, and second, to his hope that character can be preserved in contemporary fiction. With respect to the latter, he has made a considerable contribution by assembling in his novels a gallery of ill assorted oddballs, misfits, geniuses, and cranks, like Einhorn in *Augie*, or confidence men, like Dr. Tamkin in *Seize the Day*. More significantly, the idea of character is associated with the survival of the self. Nothing is more important in Bellow's fiction, and Augie March, Henderson, and Tommy Wilhelm, among his protagonists, are all committed to the quest for identity and the salvation of the self. Bellow knows that, beginning in the nineteenth century, many forces, from Darwinism and Marxism to the Nazis and the logical positivists of the twentieth century, have conspired to eliminate the self, and that writers like Joyce and Beckett have joined in this campaign. He believes, as he has said repeatedly in his fiction, that the main business of a man's life is to carry the burden of his personality or "to be the carrier of a load which was his own self," as he puts it in *Seize the Day*. By realizing the self, one asserts his humanity, that is, lays a claim to sharing in human suffering and joy, in the human destiny.

Realization of the self means surrender of the self. Bellow has always recognized this paradox, which he dramatizes nowhere more effectively than in *Henderson the Rain King*. Henderson begins as a man overwhelmed by the demands of his own ego. Neighbors, wives, children—nothing and nobody is permitted to stand in the way of his self gratification as he listens to an inner voice intoning, "I want! I want!" At the end of the book, his African experience has taught him that what he sought all along, without knowing it, was participation in the magnetic chain of humanity, and that what men need is a right relation with the world of nature and with humanity as a whole. The guardianship he assumes of the lion cub and the little boy is an expression of love in both realms of being that signifies Henderson's surrender of the ego in order to realize the self through immersion in the order of nature and in the community of man. Similarly, Tommy Wilhelm in *Seize the Day* finds the consummation of his heart's need in the abandonment of self concern and the substitution of a generalized love for mankind.

*Mr. Sammler's Planet*, Bellow's last novel as of this writing, is far more critical of the idea of the self than any previous work. It is a book that documents Bellow's conviction that the conception of individualism or the self that we took first from Christianity and then from the Enlightenment has degenerated, in our time, into self indulgence and license. But even in the face of this bitter revision of the optimistic history of the West, Bellow is unwilling to abandon in this novel the possibility that good may be found in human beings, and he persists in showing the need to pursue definition in one's life.

This hedged optimism in the face of his own pessimistic conclusions about the nature and fate of man is one of the most difficult situations that Bellow must confront in his fiction. The evidence tells him that man is depraved. Observation shows that men tend to behave, in crisis, like rats in a sack, as H. G. Wells said. Reason crowds him to an acceptance of absurdity as the prime condition of man and the world. But Bellow simply refuses to credit what observation, reason, and ideas thrust before him. He knows that man is less than what the Golden Age promised us, but he refuses to believe that man is nothing. He is something, Bellow says, and saying it he performs an act of faith. He rests his conviction on his feelings, and like the Transcendentalists upon whom he calls so often in his fiction, he resorts to his intuition. *Herzog* is a clear-cut illustration of Bellow's rejection of pessimistic philosophies. Everyone believes that man is a sick animal, says the protagonist of this novel, but he himself refuses to acquiesce in this judgment or to accept such dark interpretations of human experience as are contained in Kierkegaardian despair and absurdity, Spengler's decline of the West, or Eliot's wasteland complex. Herzog is himself a victim in modern America, but he simply refuses to accept his fate. He refuses to accept the empirical evidence. Persisting in his quest for love, he comes at the end to a restoration of sanity and hope for the future.

As Bellow accepts the epistemological implications of feeling, he also accepts or indeed advocates openness to feeling as sentiment. *Dangling Man*, his first novel, contained a rejection of the stiff-lipped Hemingway code which demands the suppression of emotion, and in all subsequent work he tended to expand the role given to emotion. He believes in the power of feeling and thinks that the novel must show a sympathetic devotion to the life of someone else, that the reader, in other words, must be asked to respond with sympathetic feeling to the life of the characters. In this way, Bellow works toward human connection between author and reader, between reader and characters; these are the connections that will lead to understanding. This emphasis upon emotion in Bellow is to be traced, in part, to the influence of Wilhelm Reich, who related the liberation of the emotions to the struggle for life fulfillment, and in part to the influence of Hasidism, the Jewish creed in which the central proposition is that life is holy joy.

The emphasis upon the self, optimism, and feeling must be understood in relation to Bellow's attitude toward death. He believes that one cannot understand life until one comes to terms with death. He treats the theme everywhere in his fiction, but it is enough here to remark it in three of his books. In *Seize the Day*, Tommy Wilhelm is able to come fully into possession of life, to seize the day, only after he confronts death itself and undergoes a symbolic drowning. Death brings him to the recognition of the heart's ultimate need, which is love. Bellow is equally concerned with death in *Henderson the Rain King* but less successful with it. Henderson insists that we hate and fear death, but that there is nothing like it. He means that we all know we must face it and that we learn from facing it, as he learned from facing the lion, the meaning of life. *Mr. Sammler's Planet* is Bellow's most extensive treatment of death. It is an elegiac meditation, first, on the approaching death of Western culture, brought on by a new barbarism represented by those who have surrendered traditional concepts of value. And it is, further, the story of a man who has come back from the dead, as it were, whose authority as a spokesman rests upon his knowledge of death: he had dug what was supposed to be his own grave but had, by chance, crawled out of it; he had seen the Arab dead rotting at Gaza; he had himself killed a man. Throughout the novel he watches his friend and benefactor die. To have known death and given it is to have absorbed the knowledge of the mystery of dying. To have known death is to know the meaning of life and to know what it means to be a human being.

Bellow's achievement is to have imposed upon the contending forces in his fiction—life and death, optimism and despair, reason and feeling, self and brotherhood—an idea of order. Out of the chaos of experience, out of the tensions of conflicting claims, out of the distractions of modern life, Bellow has created a coherent and a compelling vision of human experience. The supreme paradox is that the disorder he perceives everywhere has been preserved and communicated within the order of a framework willed by the artist.

—Chester E. Eisinger

---

**BENEDICTUS, David.** British. Born in London, 16 September 1938. Educated at Eton College; Balliol College, Oxford, B.A. 1959; University of Iowa, Iowa City. Married in 1971. Assistant Trainee, BBC Radio, London, 1963–64; Drama Director, 1964–65, and Story Editor, "Wednesday Play", 1967, for BBC Television; Trainee Director, Thames Television, Bristol, 1969–70; Assistant Director, Royal Shakespeare Company, London, 1970–71. Address: Flat 5, 14 The Paragon, London S.E.3, England.

PUBLICATIONS

Novels

*The Fourth of June.*   London, Blond, 1962; New York, Dutton, 1963.
*You're a Big Boy Now.*   London, Blond, 1963; New York, Dutton, 1964.
*This Animal Is Mischievous.*   London, Blond, and New York, New American Library, 1965.
*Hump; or, Bone by Bone, Alive.*   London, Blond, 1967.
*The Guru and the Golf Club.*   London, Blond, 1969.
*A World of Windows.*   London, Weidenfeld and Nicolson, 1971.

Plays

*The Fourth of June* (produced London, 1964).
*Angels (Over Your Grave) and Geese (Over Mine)* (produced Edinburgh, 1967).
*Dromedary* (produced Newcastle upon Tyne, 1969).
*What a Way to Run a Revolution!* (produced London, 1971).

David Benedictus comments:

Anything a novelist has to say about his novels invalidates the novels—they ought to explain themselves.

Anything anyone else has to say about them is of only peripheral interest. The novel is dying on its feet—critical essays and learned commentaries will revive it less than a little hard-earned cash.

\*      \*      \*

David Benedictus is one of those novelists whose careers have commenced with a great resounding bang. His brilliant satirical send-up of Eton, *The Fourth of June*, was welcomed alike by critics and the public, inviting comparison, as it does, with Evelyn Waugh's first novel *Decline and Fall* (1928) which also took school-life as its main subject.

Sociologically, as well as fictionally, the book is of importance, since it presents those privileged dwellers in Gray's "distant spires [and] antique towers" with the eye of a scholar who was, in one sense, an outsider within this privileged community. David Benedictus had gone as one of a small number of pupils from grammar schools in a new post-war educational experiment to Eton, that kindergarten and finishing school of wealth and class. Himself escaping the fate of the ex-grammar schoolboy in the novel who is savagely beaten into paralysis by his House Captain, he none the less preserved a quizzing distance between himself and his haughty Alma Mater. His irreverent and hilarious censure is expressed in terms of a scandalous drama which stays just this side of fantasy—or so it seems to the non-Etonian reader. Despite which Mr. Benedictus has told us that "the incidents described did not, so far as I know, happen, but I can see no reason, if they did not, why they did not." At the same time he guarded himself against, one supposes, any possible libel by admitting that "things have changed since I was at Eton," but not, he believes, Etonians. "Younger brothers, and soon eldest sons, will carry on the tradition of snobbery and cruelty" unless the efforts to democratise Eton, initiated by Dr. Robert Birley, are successful.

Large as the social significance of this novel clearly is, it is its literary and imaginative virtues which will, almost certainly, preserve it as a pleasure for future generations. Denounced by a certain obtuse reviewer as a farrago of sex, snobbery and sadism, it delights us by its inversion of all expected *comme il faut*. We read, for example, of a bishop who spends his evenings spying on a chaplain's half-dressed daughter; of the Honourable Mrs. Alethea Berwick who pays a chorus girl in fish-net stockings to deflower her seventeen-year-old son; or of her own seduction of the boy's scurfy middle-aged housemaster in order to obtain mercy for her errant offspring. And all this goes conveyed in a style which ripples with metaphor, wit and innuendo. Neither should a residual touch of fascination with the place (despite its cruelties) go unnoticed. Eton, regarded aesthetically, has its potent grace and comeliness, and these have not escaped this otherwise astringent author's notice.

Just as C. P. Snow's novel *The Masters* (1951) incapsulates the life of a Cambridge college, so *The Fourth of June* offers us a satirically heightened quintessence of Eton. The book is clearly its author's *chef d'oeuvre*, but he has written a number of other interesting fictions, marked by a resolve to discover and develop original themes and situations. *The Guru and the Golf Club*, by its mere title, suggests an unlooked-for juxtaposition, while his kinky novel about a voyeur entitled *A World of Windows* seeks to present his abnormal figure in at least a partly-serious and tragic light.

—Derek Stanford

BERGER, John (Peter).   British.   Born in Stoke Newington, London, 5 November 1926. Attended the Central School of Art, and the Chelsea School of Art, London. Served in the Oxford and Bucks. Infantry, 1944–46. Has two children. Address: c/o Weidenfeld and Nicolson, 5 Winsley Street, London W.1, England.

PUBLICATIONS

Novels

>    *A Painter of Our Time*.   London, Secker and Warburg, 1958; New York, Simon and
>        Schuster, 1959.
>    *The Foot of Clive*.   London, Methuen, 1962.
>    *Corker's Freedom*.   London, Methuen, 1964.
>    *G.*   London, Weidenfeld and Nicolson, 1972.

Other

>    *Permanent Red: Essays in Seeing*.   London, Methuen, 1960; as *Towards Reality:
>        Essays in Seeing*, New York, Knopf, 1962.
>    *The Success and Failure of Picasso*.   London, Penguin, 1965; Baltimore, Penguin, 1966.
>    *A Fortunate Man: The Story of a Country Doctor*.   London, Allen Lane, and New
>        York, Holt Rinehart, 1967.
>    *Art and Revolution: Ernst Neizvestny and the Role of the Artist in the U.S.S.R.*   London,
>        Weidenfeld and Nicolson, and New York, Pantheon Books, 1969.
>    *The Moment of Cubism and Other Essays*.   New York, Pantheon Books, 1969; London,
>        Weidenfeld and Nicolson, 1970.
>    *The Look of Things* (essays).   London, Penguin, 1971.

Translator, with Anya Bostock, *Poems on the Theatre*, by Bertolt Brecht.   London, Scorpion Press, 1961.

Translator, with Anya Bostock, *Helene Weigel, Actress*, by Bertolt Brecht.   Leipzig, Veb Edition, 1961.

Translator, with Anya Bostock, *Return to My Native Land*, by Aimé Césaire.   London, Penguin, 1969.


John Berger comments:

I have little to say about what I have written. I hope that my books transcend the categories into which they are generally forced. The critical essay on Picasso is, for instance, written somewhat like a novel. The sociological study of a country doctor is perhaps also a philosophical essay. The novel, *Corker's Freedom*, is partly a film scenario and partly a historical document. Up to date it seems to me that everything I have written has been no more than a preparation for the work of the last five years on *G*.

\*      \*      \*

John Berger does not like one to divide his work up into catagories; but if one is to consider the three novels published between 1959 and 1964 in isolation from his other published work then what immediately stands out is that he is a very skilful entertainer as well as a Marxist and a painter. Those two last attributes do, however, have a strong, if indirect, bearing on the novels. Mr. Berger is far too much of an artist to mix fiction and polemic, but he is concerned with how his characters behave in a social setting, whether the society is confined to the men's ward of a general hospital, as in *The Foot of Clive*, or a sleazy employment agency in Clapham (*Corker's Freedom*). It is how these microcosms of civilisation affect and shape his characters that matters. For although individuals may have strong ideas about how they intend to fashion their lives, the entrenched structures of society, which somehow always seem to be in league with their own habitual weaknesses, always prove too much for them.

As a painter, Mr. Berger brings to his novels a sensual awareness that is not entirely visual. Reviewing *The Foot of Clive* for *The Observer*, Francis Wyndham wrote, "He can make us smell the ward (lemons and sour milk), taste the tea, hear the Light Programme through the earphones, see the sick men's bodies, above all feel the texture of sheets, pyjamas, human skin." He also has an artist's awareness of structures and of the various complimentary levels on which all facets of life operate. For instance in the act of speaking, we have at one level the words that actually emerge, but behind these in the speaker's mind are the words he would like to say, his feelings, his fantasies, and his instinctively accurate, and usually highly disturbing, knowledge about the existential facts of the immediate situation. All these levels come clear in the illustrated lecture on Vienna which Corker, the seedy, aged bachelor from Clapham, gives to a Church social gathering.

To both these attributes must be added Mr. Berger's skill as an entertainer. He can hold his audience's attention by his dexterity in dealing with his subject matter, and with the wit with which he brings to light the absurd juxtapositions of the human situation.

All these qualities are deepened and extended in his most recent novel, *G*. This work is written more in the form of a film script than an orthodox work of fiction, each paragraph (and some of them contain only one short sentence) being sharp and complete in itself, and often setting a precise visual scene. G is the illegitimate son of a wealthy Italian merchant and rather advanced American girl who later develops Fabian leanings. He was born four years after Garibaldi's death, and the initial by which his author calls him refers equally to that, and to his father's name of Giovanni. He was killed in Trieste on the day that Austria declared war on Italy on account of that city. Although G is intrinsically bound up with

the historical events of his time, he is almost a-political himself. In this chronicle, Berger
has set himself the vast task that Tolstoy undertook: that of depicting how each one of us
is history in that we are both monumentally shaped by events and, in small measure, by
the mere act of inhabiting our skins, influence their course.

—Shirley Toulson

* * *

**BERGER, Thomas (Louis).**   American.   Born in Cincinnati, Ohio, 20 July 1924. Educated
at the University of Cincinnati, B.A. 1948; Columbia University, New York, 1950–51.
Served in the United States Army, 1943–46. Married Jeanne Redpath in 1950. Librarian,
Rand School of Social Science, New York, 1948–51; Staff Member, *New York Times Index*,
1951–52; Associate Editor, *Popular Science Monthly*, New York, 1952–54. Recipient: Dial
Fellowship, 1962; Western Heritage Award, 1965; Rosenthal Award, 1965. Address: c/o
Harold Matson Company, 22 East 40th Street, New York, New York 10016, U.S.A.

PUBLICATIONS

Novels

   *Crazy in Berlin*.   New York, Scribner, 1958.
   *Reinhart in Love*.   New York, Scribner, 1962; London, Eyre and Spottiswoode, 1963.
   *Little Big Man*.   New York, Dial Press, 1964; London, Eyre and Spottiswoode, 1965.
   *Killing Time*.   New York, Dial Press, 1967; London, Eyre and Spottiswoode, 1968.
   *Vital Parts*.   New York, Baron, 1970; London, Eyre and Spottiswoode, 1971.

Uncollected Short Stories

   "Professor Hyde", in *Playboy* (Chicago), December 1961.
   "A Monkey of His Own", in *Saturday Evening Post* (New York), 22 May 1965.

Play

   *Other People* (produced Berkshire Theatre Festival, Massachusetts, 1970).

Manuscript Collection: Boston University Library.

Critical Essay: review of *Vital Parts* by Richard Schickel, in *Commentary* (New York),
July 1970.

Thomas Berger comments:

   I write to amuse and conceal myself.

118

*          *          *

In his novels, Thomas Berger exhibits an extraordinary comic sensibility, a satiric talent for wild caricature and a concern for the quality of middle-class life in middle America. His five novels chronicle the decline and fall of the Common Man in twentieth-century America and describe in meticulous detail the absurdities of our civilization.

The Reinhart saga (*Crazy in Berlin*, *Reinhart in Love* and *Vital Parts*) follows Carlo Reinhart from adolescence to middle age, concentrating on his career as a soldier with the occupation forces in Germany, a student on the GI Bill and a failed wageslave and decrepit father in the bewildering America of 1970. A fumbling, uncertain bear of a man, Carlo Reinhart epitomizes the failure of good intentions. A believer in the American Dream as purveyed in magazines, highschool classrooms and advertisements, Carlo is a continual victim of deceit and fraud. Like the Good Soldier Schweik, Carlo takes the world at face value and assumes that appearance is reality; unlike Schweik, Carlo is guileless and incapable of co-operating with hypocrisy, so he is perpetually victimized and disillusioned. The comedy in Berger's satiric vision arises from the gap between Carlo's expectations and his experiences.

In *Crazy in Berlin*, Carlo is swept up in conspiracy, involved with spies and criminals dividing the spoils of the fallen Nazi state. As a good-natured slob and summer soldier, Carlo manages to survive, but he is driven to murder and finally to madness, shattered not by the horrors of war but the lunacy of peace. The novel alternates between bitter satire on the equal corruption of the Americans, the Russians and the vanquished Germans, and sophisticated slapstick comedy similar to Preston Sturges' films. Carlo, as a bewildered but optimistic average man, can only be driven mad by the Hobbesian nightmare of Occupied Germany.

The second novel, *Reinhart in Love*, continues the mock-heroic saga. In it Carlo has returned to the purported normality of peacetime America to continue college on the GI Bill. Again he finds himself perpetually duped, exploited and betrayed by people and circumstances. Carlo is as romantic and idealistic as Orlando himself, and his love is cosmic, all-embracing: "*Reinhart was in love with everything.*" But as his employer tells him, the world is still a Hobbesian jungle, with every man's hand raised against his fellows: ". . . life, real life, is exactly like the fighting, except in the latter you use guns and therefore don't destroy as many people." The novel ends with Carlo married by deception to a shrew, betrayed by his friends, failed even at suicide and bereft of ideals and ambitions. He is ready to move upward and onward in the postwar world.

The latest installment in Reinhart's story is *Vital Parts*, which moves twenty years into Reinhart's life. He is still married to his shrew and father to a fat, mooning daughter and a vicious ne'er-do-well son who attacks Reinhart's whole way of life. He has failed at every capitalistic enterprise he has tried, lost his hair and his youth, gained debts and a paunch. Again in suicidal despair, he becomes involved with a grotesque scheme to develop cryogenics—the road to immortality through technology. He finally becomes the guinea pig in a semi-fraudulent attempt to freeze and revive a human being. As a tormented failure without hope for the future, Carlo ultimately agrees to the plot—he has little to choose between an absurd life, an absurd death and a chance for some sort of immortality.

In *Little Big Man*, Berger also uses mock-heroic satire, this time in retelling the folk mythology of the Old West. A tale of cowboys and Indians told from *both* views, the novel describes the only white survivor of the Battle of Little Big Horn—111-year-old Jack Crabb, who has been a victim of Indian attacks, an Indian, an Indian-fighter, gunfighter, gambler, con man, etc. The novel follows the "half-man, half-alligator" tradition of frontier humor, magnificent hyperbole and lies as big as the Rockies. It is also a finely detailed and convincing picture of prairie life, both with the Cheyenne (the "Human Beings") and with the white settlers. The violence, squalor and monotony of life in raw nature is as intensely realized as the heroics and the farce. Jack Crabb is a frontier Carlo Reinhart, with the same insecurities, the same propensities for confusion and cowardice, the same common humanity. Perhaps the finest aspect of the story comes through the Cheyennes' perceptions of themselves and their reality, as when the chief, Old Lodge Skins, observes:

Whatever you can say about the white man, it must be admitted *you cannot get rid of him*. He is in never-ending supply. There has always been only a limited number of Human Beings, because we are intended to be special and superior. Obviously not everybody can be a Human Being. To make this so, there must be a great many inferior white people. To my mind, this is the function of white men in the world. Therefore we must survive, because without us the world would not make sense.

This insight into ethnocentricity shows the quality of observation which makes *Little Big Man* incisively comic yet serious in effect.

*Killing Time* concerns Joe Detweiler, a murderer who kills to achieve cosmic justice. Through a Dostoevskian logic, he believes that killing a man liberates him from the bondage of an absurd life, that murder is only a matter of stealing time from the victim, since he is already condemned by his finitude. Joe becomes, in the words of his lawyer, "he who accepts nothing on faith, a kind of scientist of the soul." The novel revolves around Joe's absurdist logic, the idea that he has found an absolute justice in crime beyond the rule of courts and laws. While it is still satiric in effect, the novel is less comic than cutting, and the speculations on sanity and justice are thoroughly serious.

Thomas Berger's gift for wit and comedy, the consistency of his satire, make him an important commentator on contemporary America. His are the ironist's traditional targets —greed, stupidity, hypocrisy, the lies of civilization—while his sympathy extends to all the victims of life.

—William J. Schafer

---

**BHATTACHARYA, Bhabani**. Indian. Born in Bhagalpur, 10 November 1906. Educated at Patna University, B.A. (honours) 1927; University of London, 1929–34, B.A. (honours) 1931, Ph.D. 1934. Married Salila Mukerji in 1935; has three children. Press Attaché, Embassy of India, Washington, D.C., 1949–50; Assistant Editor, *Illustrated Weekly of India*, Bombay, 1950–52; Secretary, Tagore Commemorative Society, New Delhi, 1959–60; Consultant, Ministry of Education, New Delhi, 1961–67; Senior Specialist, East-West Center, Honolulu, 1969–70. Since 1970, Visiting Professor, University of Hawaii, Honolulu. Delegate, Harvard International Seminar, Cambridge, Massachusetts, 1959, and Tokyo, 1960. Lectured as a guest of the government in New Zealand, 1962, Australia, 1962, and West Germany, 1963. Recipient: Universities of New Zealand's Prestige Award, 1962; Indian National Academy of Letters Award, 1967; Ford grant, 1968, 1969. Member, Advisory Board, Indian National Academy of Letters. Address: Hono Hale Towers, Apartment A-105, 827 Kahuna Lane, Honolulu, Hawaii 96814, U.S.A.

PUBLICATIONS

Novels

*So Many Hungers!*  Bombay, Hind Kitabs, 1947; London, Gollancz, 1948,
  *Music for Mohini*.  New York, Crown, 1952; London, Angus and Robertson, 1959.

He Who Rides a Tiger.  New York, Crown, 1954; London, Angus and Robertson, 1960.
A Goddess Named Gold.  New York, Crown, 1960.
Shadow from Ladakh.  New Delhi, Hind Pocket Books, and New York, Crown, 1966; London, W. H. Allen, 1967.


Short Stories

Steel Hawk and Other Stories.  New Delhi, Hind Pocket Books, 1968.

Other

Some Memorable Yesterdays.  Patna, Pustak Bhandar, 1940.
Indian Cavalcade.  Bombay, Nalanda, 1944.
Gandhi the Writer.  New Delhi, National Book Trust, 1969.

Translator, The Golden Boat, by Rabindranath Tagore.  London, Allen and Unwin, 1932; New York, Macmillan, 1933.
Translator, Towards Universal Man, by Rabindranath Tagore.  Bombay, London, and New York, Asia Publishing House, 1961.


Manuscript Collection: Boston University Library.


Critical Studies: "Bhabani Bhattacharya: A Profile" by Lila Ray, in Indian Literature (New Delhi), December 1968; Bhabani Bhattacharya by Dorothy Shimer, New York, Twayne, 1972.


Bhabani Bhattacharya comments:

How did I happen to become a novelist? When I was a student in London in the Thirties, I started writing a novel. Halfway through, I thought it was no good and I was not destined to be a creative writer—I was not a student of Literature anyway. I tore up the manuscript. However, I wrote some short sketches for The Spectator. I translated Tagore. Back in India, I found other preoccupations. Early in the Forties I tried to do a novel again. When half-written, it found its way into a heap of unwanted papers.

Then the great famine swept down upon Bengal. The emotional stirrings I felt (more than two million men, women and children died of slow starvation amid a man-made scarcity) were a sheer compulsion to creativity. The result was the novel So Many Hungers! (The story was concerned with all the intensified hungers of the historic years 1942-43—not food alone: the money hunger, the sex hunger, the hunger to achieve India's political freedom.) Again I tucked the manuscript away. But my wife Salila forced me to have faith in my work. Acceptance by a publisher, and success, were quick.

Music for Mohini, He Who Rides a Tiger, and A Goddess Named Gold followed. My latest novel, Shadow from Ladakh, is not a favourite of reviewers, but that is the one I enjoyed most. The men and women in this story held me obsessed all through the writing.

I have no big literary output, as you see. I have not believed in writing for the sake of writing. I seldom planned a story structure. Each story grew in my subconscious mind, as it were. When it had grown enough, I had to give it a physical form. The characters, even when I had decided how they were going to behave, moved by their own volition, often defeating my purpose.

Finally, why did I choose English as my medium of expression? I have loved writing in English. The creative writer must have full freedom to use the language of his choice. If he decides on a foreign tongue, he will have to cross immense technical hurdles, but that is *his* headache. I have enjoyed the challenge of this literary problem—expressing Indian life in the idiom of an alien tongue.

*         *         *

Bhabani Bhattacharya has stated that he regards art as a criticism of life which reviews current values, and that he conceives the novel as an "idiom of compassion" which is designed to have a curative social effect. His own novels conscientiously reflect these views. Their subject-matter and themes derive from modern Indian history and the problems of contemporary Indian society, and they embody programmes of reform as well as stinging social criticism. This approach, initiated in modern Indian fiction in English by the early novels and short stories of Mulk Raj Anand (from 1935–47), is a feature of the majority of Indian post-Independence novels. Bhattacharya's contribution to the contemporary Indian novel demonstrates that, for literate Indians, fiction is a good medium in which to examine such problems as caste, poverty, ignorance, political injustice, communal intolerance and economic inequality. Many Indian novelists, including Bhattacharya, have revealed how these and many other aspects of Indian life relate to the course of modern Indian history, particularly the Independence struggle, Partition, and "free" India's attempt to create a new social order.

Like many other Indians, Bhattacharya celebrated Independence with the publication of a first novel: *So Many Hungers!* This novel is a harrowing account of famine in Bengal (unfortunately ever-relevant) and a passionate indictment of the human culpability involved, particularly of the grasping parasites (mostly upper-class) who exploit the famine to make black-market fortunes. The story is told from the point of view of the starving peasants who migrated to Calcutta where they died in the streets, and is calculated to shock the reader's sense of humanity in scenes such as that which describes a jackal perched on the thigh of a pregnant woman, tearing at her swollen belly while her screams slash the air.

Bhattacharya's second novel, *Music for Mohini*, is the story of an arranged marriage and the adjustment which the modern city girl, Mohini, has to make to fit into the traditional pattern of life in her husband Jayadev's "Big House", presided over by his aristocratic iron-willed mother. The main theme of the novel is the idea of "synthesis", "a profound union of today with yesterday", whereby the conflict between tradition and modernity will be resolved. Synthesis is achieved in practice as well as theory: finally Mohini and her mother-in-law are agreeably reconciled and Jayadev is transformed, through conjugal and moral stimuli, from ascetic intellectual into village reformer. *Shadow from Ladakh*, set against the background of the Indo-Chinese border conflict following China's annexation of Tibet, is also a variation on the theme of synthesis. Through the relationships of the main characters Bhattacharya advocates for present-day India a cultural fusion based on a love-match between Gandhian idealism and a progressive people's technology.

*He Who Rides a Tiger* and *A Goddess Named Gold* are social fables and as such are Bhattacharya's most formally sophisticated works. The former is the story of an untouchable who successfully poses as a Brahmin holy man; the plot of the latter is a variation of fairytale in which the heroine and her fellow villagers believe that her amulet has the magical power to transform copper into gold whenever she performs a true act of kindness. In *He Who Rides a Tiger* the social theme is developed in terms of irony in order to dramatise the iniquities and hypocrisies of the caste system, while in *A Goddess Named Gold* the moral supremacy of communal unity over landlord selfishness is proposed as a model for independent India.

Although Bhattacharya has a tendency to load his novels with mechanical sociology, over-simplified philosophies, and naively symbolic relationships (as in *Shadow from Ladakh*), these defects are compensated for by the sincerity of his compassion and the relevance of his vision.

—S. C. Harrex

---

**BIRNEY, Earle.** Canadian. Born in Calgary, Alberta, 13 May 1904. Educated at the University of British Columbia, Vancouver, B.A. 1926; University of Toronto, M.A. 1927, Ph.D. 1936; University of California, Berkeley, 1927–30; Queen Mary College, London, 1934–35. Served in the Canadian Army, in the reserves 1940–41, and on active duty 1942–45: Major-in-Charge, Personnel Selection, Belgium and Holland, 1944–45. Married Esther Bull in 1940; has one child. Instructor in English, University of Utah, Salt Lake City, 1930–34; Lecturer, later Assistant Professor of English, University of Toronto, 1936–42; Supervisor, European Foreign Language Broadcasts, Radio Canada, Montreal, 1945–46; Professor of Medieval English Literature, 1946–63, and Professor and Chairman of the Department of Creative Writing, 1963–65, University of British Columbia; Writer-in-Residence, University of Toronto, 1965–67, and University of Waterloo, Ontario, 1967–68; Regents Professor in Creative Writing, University of California, Irvine, 1968. Since 1968, free-lance Writer and Lecturer. Literary Editor, *Canadian Forum*, Toronto, 1936–40; Editor, *Canadian Poetry Magazine*, Edmonton, 1946–48; Editor, *Prism International*, Vancouver, 1964–65; Advisory Editor, *New: American and Canadian Poetry*, Trumansburg, New York, 1966–70. Recipient: Governor-General's Medal for Poetry, 1943, 1946; Stephen Leacock Medal, 1950; Borestone Mountain Poetry Award, 1951; Canadian Government Overseas Fellowship, 1953, Service Medal, 1970; Lorne Pierce Medal, 1953; President's Medal, University of Western Ontario, for poetry, 1954; Nuffield Fellowship, 1958; Canada Council Senior Arts Fellowship, 1962, Medal, 1968, Special Fellowship, 1968, and Travel Award, 1971. LL.D., University of Alberta, Edmonton, 1965. Fellow, Royal Society of Canada, 1954. Address: c/o McClelland and Stewart, 25 Hollinger Road, Toronto 16, Ontario, Canada.

PUBLICATIONS

Novels

> *Turvey: A Military Picaresque*. Toronto, McClelland and Stewart, 1949; London and New York, Abelard Schuman, 1959.
> *Down the Long Table*. Toronto, McClelland and Stewart, 1955; London, Abelard Schuman, 1959.

Uncollected Short Stories

> "Bird in the Bush", in *Mademoiselle* (New York), May 1948.
> "Mickey Was a Swell Guy", in *National Home Monthly* (Toronto), November 1948.
> "The Levin Bolt", in *Canadian Life* (Toronto), March-April 1949.
> "The Strange Smile of Thos Turvey", in *Here and Now* (Toronto), June 1949.
> "What's This Agoosto?", in *Standard* (Montreal), 29 July 1950.
> "Enigma in Ebony", in *Maclean's* (Toronto), 15 October 1953.

Play

> *Damnation of Vancouver: A Comedy in Seven Episodes* (radio play, produced CBC, 1952). Included in *Trial of a City*, 1952; revised edition (stage version, produced Seattle, 1957), in *Selected Poems*, 1966.

Verse

> *David.*   Toronto, Ryerson Press, 1942.
> *Now Is Time.*   Toronto, Ryerson Press, 1945.
> *Strait of Anian.*   Toronto, Ryerson Press, 1948.
> *Trial of a City.*   Toronto, Ryerson Press, 1952.
> *Ice Cod Bell or Stone.*   Toronto, McClelland and Stewart, 1962.
> *Near False Creek Mouth.*   Toronto, McClelland and Stewart, 1964.
> *Selected Poems 1940–1966.*   Toronto, McClelland and Stewart, 1966.
> *Memory No Servant.*   Trumansburg, New York, New Books, 1968.
> *Poems of Earle Birney.*   Toronto, McClelland and Stewart, 1969.
> *Pnomes, Jukollages and Other Stunzas.*   Toronto, Gronk Press, 1969.
> *Rag and Bone Shop.*   Toronto, McClelland and Stewart, 1971.

Other

> *The Creative Writer.*   Toronto, CBC Publications, 1966.
> *The Writing and Reading of Poetry.*   Toronto, Holt Rinehart, 1972.

> Editor, *Twentieth Century Canadian Poetry.*   Toronto, Ryerson Press, 1953.
> Editor, *Record of Service in the Second World War.*   Vancouver, University of British Columbia, 1955.
> Editor, with others, *New Voices.*   Vancouver, Dent, 1956.
> Editor, *Selected Poems of Malcolm Lowry.*   San Francisco, City Lights, 1962.
> Editor, with Margerie Lowry, *Lunar Caustic*, by Malcolm Lowry.   New York, Grossman, 1963; London, Cape, 1968.

Bibliography: in *West Coast Review* (Burnaby, British Columbia), October 1970.

Manuscript Collection: University of Toronto Library.

Critical Studies: review of *Turvey* by Malcolm Lowry, in *Thunderbird* (Vancouver), December 1949; "Earle Birney and the Compound Ghost" by Paul West, in *Canadian Literature* (Vancouver), 1962; Introduction by George Woodcock to *Turvey*, Toronto, McClelland and Stewart, 1963.

Earle Birney comments:

My short stories have been extensions of my work as a poet. More relaxed in style than my best-known poem *David*, they are nevertheless equally symbolic in technique, and unified around a two-person relationship and a definitive action.

My novels, on the other hand, are attempts to contain within one fairly complex form, a multitude of experiences none of which seemed to me naturally separable, and much more likely to be effective if handled together. They are to some extent "documentary", aiming at accuracy in dialogue and in reference to the historic frame; but their over-all preoccupations have been with the mores and philosophy of North American society.

*Turvey*, my first novel, was written out of things that happened to me, or stories told to me, during the Second World War. For the last three years of it my job was interviewing soldiers: in Canada, volunteers, draftees, deserters, or men in sick bays or cells; in England, officer candidates, paratroopers, commandos, psychotics in hospital or psychopaths in detention; in Belgium and Holland, officers and soldiers in every arm and service of an Army, wanting to get into action or out of it, to change their job or their wife, to see a psychiatrist or just to make it back home. This kind of job taught me a lot about the bureaucratic complexity of a modern Army, its capacity for muddle and waste, especially of its human material. The job taught me also something about soldiers in general and the young Canadian one in particular. I came out of the army determined to write a novel whose central character would be a soldier both absurd and eccentric (like me) and wild, funny, naive and long-suffering (like the average Canadian soldier—and perhaps civilian). *Turvey* is my attempt. His only literary cousin, of whom I was conscious, was the Good Soldier Schweik, Hašek's dumb wily Czech private caught in the Austro-Hungarian army of World War One.

My second novel, *Down the Long Table*, is laid in the Depressed Thirties, its scene shifting from Salt Lake City to Toronto to Vancouver. Like *Turvey* it is somewhat picaresque in form but the tone is more serious and the theme more involved in confrontations of ideas. It is not an autobiographical novel, but many of the characters are based on my acquaintance with young American and Canadian radicals of the Thirties, leaders of mine strikes, organizers of the unemployed, Trotskyist theoreticians, Stalinist bureaucrats, and some plain workers and workless of forty years ago, who were honest and brave and helpless and doomed.

*     *     *

Earle Birney is best known as one of Canada's finest contemporary poets, and, especially outside Canada, his reputation in this role has tended to obscure his achievements in fiction. He is the author of two novels, *Turvey* and *Down the Long Table*. Both of them, if not autobiographical, deal with times and settings in which the author was deeply and passionately involved: the Canadian army in the Second World War in the case of *Turvey*, and the social despair and political idealism of the Thirties in the case of *Down the Long Table*. Both novels share with Birney's poetry an inclination towards social satire and a preoccupation with colloquial speech patterns; *Down the Long Table* also shares with Birney's later verse an experimental use of the verbal detritus of political propaganda and the mass media in general.

*Turvey* is described accurately by its author as "a military picaresque". It narrates the adventures of a simple, rustic-minded Canadian, Turvey, who is anxious to serve his country in his local regiment, but becomes involved in a bureaucratic hurdle race which leads him into a series of comic predicaments, out of which in the end he emerges—never having seen a German soldier—to hail with joy his return to civilian life. Inevitably, *Turvey* calls to mind *The Good Soldier Schweik*, but there is a slyness in Schweik which Turvey does not possess. Where from the beginning Schweik seems to use the pretence of stupidity as a subversive weapon, Turvey is throughout the naive enthusiast, and it is the army that condemns itself by its bureaucratic unintelligence. The fighting war is always distant; the real war that Birney invites us to follow is the burlesque combat between a mindless collective machine and Turvey's irrepressible individuality. That Turvey emerges undefeated makes this a statement of faith in the victory of man over the inhumanity of mass organization.

*Down the Long Table* is a novel of memory, projected from the silent Fifties into the troubled Thirties. The basic structure is Proustian; Professor Gordon Saunders, a Canadian teaching in the United States, is brought before a committee investigating Communist affiliations. Before him at the long table he sees a face from the past, that of an ex-Communist turned informer, and this provokes the chain of memories which forms the substance of the book. Gordon remembers the fatal interconnection between personal relationships and political actions, weaving into a rope that shifts his sentimental idealism into militancy, takes him in and rapidly out of the Communist party, and culminates in a brief, violent and disillusioning period as the would-be organizer of a Trotskyist movement among the unemployed and skidroad derelicts of Vancouver.

The greatest merit of *Down the Long Table* is the vividness with which the spirit and even the physical feel of the Thirties are re-created. It is when one considers the book as more than an evocative document that its defects become evident. There is an unassimilable implausibility about Professor Saunders sitting at the long table and, in that instant of time which is undoubtedly all the inquisiting senators would allow him, plunging into almost three hundred pages of chronologically sequential recollection, interrupted, not by the impinging voices of the present, but by chapter-dividing extracts from contemporary newspapers, which enhance the documentary verisimilitude, but which in fictional terms are out of pitch with the essentially romantic tone of the rest of the novel, with its dark but poetic vision of what happens to ideals when they must find expression through human beings twisted and battered by existence. *Turvey* has a wholly convincing comic unity; *Down the Long Table* is divided by the conflict between the historical impulse to reconstruct authentically time past, and the fictional impulse to establish a self-consistent imaginary world.

—George Woodcock

**BLAKE, Nicholas.**   See **DAY LEWIS, C.**

**BLECHMAN, Burt.**   American.   Born in Brooklyn, New York, 2 March 1927. Educated at the University of Vermont, Burlington, B.A. 1949 (Phi Beta Kappa). Recipient: Merrill Foundation Award, 1965. Address: 200 Waverly Place, New York, New York 10014, U.S.A.

PUBLICATIONS

Novels

*How Much?*   New York, Obolensky, 1961; London, Eyre and Spottiswoode, 1963.
*The War of Camp Omongo.*   New York, Random House, 1963.
*Stations.*   New York, Random House, 1963; London, Peter Owen, 1966.
*The Octopus Papers.*   New York, Horizon Press, 1965; London, Peter Owen, 1966.
*Maybe.*   New York, Prentice Hall, and London, Peter Owen, 1967.

Critical Studies: article by Alfred Kazin in *The Great Ideas Today*, Chicago, Encyclopedia Britannica, 1962; essay by Jacques Cabau in *L'Express* (Paris), no. 755, December 1965.

Burt Blechman comments:

My characters don't reflect, they act. As in tabloids. My work is straight reportage; headlines are enough; brevity, a necessity.

*     *     *

"For Armageddon is frightening only<br>to those who fear progress." (Maybe)

Though his first books, *How Much?* and *The War of Camp Omongo*, treated the same self-searching adolescents, ineffectual fathers, domineering mothers, and crass value systems as the work of other young Jewish novelists of the period, Burt Blechman focused on the total social picture rather than on a young male protagonist and created mothers whose comic vulgarity paradoxically earns them the compassion with which Blechman views all his characters (Mrs. Halpern's obsessive search for candlesticks in *How Much?* and boast of "Creative Shopping" during her brief appearance in *Omongo*, and Mrs. Levine's matching her quarter-carat ring against the three and two-and-one-half carat competition of the wealthier *Omongo* mothers). Just as these characters flesh out their caricature outlines, Blechman's entire fictional world transcends, without denying, the episodic structure and rapid pacing of the comic strip. *Stations*, which dramatizes the surrealistic world of a Catholic homosexual, was even stronger proof of Blechman's individuality, as were *The Octopus Papers* and *Maybe*, though all three books have stylistic and thematic parallels with his earlier novels.

Dramatizing their compulsions, Blechman's characters frantically fear and court the destruction that threatens either as individual confinement to perpetually shrinking spaces or as universal annihilation. "Little Normy Greenberg, the lousiest kid in the whole camp, paddling for all he was worth . . ." in a desperate attempt to triumph by the camp code he has always despised, achieves the goal he unconsciously sought: "The water was up to his ankles. Faster. Faster. His arms digging, digging, digging. A spade. A shovel. A grave."' (*The War of Camp Omongo*) And the atmosphere of the novel tends to reinforce the belief of Eagle, the Indian caretaker, that his fellow Omongos are plotting the total slaughter of the white men who have usurped their land and who encourage catastrophe by the ritual war games they enact at the boys' camp.

In *How Much?* Jenny Stern's desire for independence in the home of her daughter and son-in-law, the Halperns, predictably traps her in a converted closet: "A drape, so Mama will think there's a window. We can even put a light behind so when she pulls the drape, open sesame, a little electric sun." Next Jenny inhabits the morgue, the cheapest room in Dr. Zatz's nursing home, where she must play dead during an inspector's visit. As the Halperns continually cry the title question in the face of bankruptcy, war, failure, and unresponsive auctioneers, "How much, dear God, how much does it cost to be happy?" they hasten the fate they profess to fear.

Myra Russell of *Maybe*, compulsively wasting money and time ("Maybe the biggest problem in life is how to spend it.") while she calculates her shrinking future by her dwindling investments, ironically resists her son's advice to move into a maisonette that has both a kitchenette and bathroomette, but is too small for a bedroomette. As the enemy's Tyranny Tests, countered by America's Freedom Tests, threaten to explode Myra's world, the newspapers stress the plight of the trapped Cave Girl. The two alternatives converge.

901, the homosexual voyeur of *Stations*, is driven by a conviction of the impending doom embodied in the vice-detective, Dom, to travel the Via Dolorosa of his confining subway "chapels" for what he believes to be the last time. His menacing universe, peopled by Madonna and Mother Superior, and filled with altars and confessionals, depends on a parody of Catholicism that combines elements of Genet with the science fiction-*cum*-paranoia of William Burroughs. Blechman employs a more general biblical parody in *How Much?*

*Maybe*, and in items like Steiner's commandments in *Omongo*: "Thou shalt have no other loyalties before me for I am the Lord Steiner who hath led thee from bondage in the land of thy parents. . . ." Though often brash and crude, Blechman's parody manages to ridicule both modern perversions of religious creeds and the original creeds themselves. Simultaneously, the parody laments a lost pattern of meaning that prevented or at least explained the chaos that perpetually waits to undo the universe. 901's abortive aspirations toward various careers parallel young Bernard Halpern's strivings in *How Much?* (Since Bernard appears in *The Octopus Papers* as B. Halpern, photographer, and in *Maybe* as B. Halpern, caricaturist, he apparently made a choice of a sort. His role as young Fat Stuff Halpern in *Omongo* reinforces the shared world view and tone of the books.)

*The Octopus Papers*, a collage of documents "selected, adapted, compiled, and annotated by Burt Blechman," is a literary hoax in the manner of *Gulliver's Travels* or *The Dunciad*, though the "Author's Apology" claims to be aping the style of Restoration Comedy. The book traces the history of Arsyn, an organization committed to the synthesis and marketing of the arts. Blechman had more tellingly satirized this tendency in *Omongo*, when a business-man attributed the widespread popularity of Van Gogh's "Sunflowers," in copies with simulated brushstrokes (cf. the "little electric sun" of Jenny's closet), to the artist's brilliant advertising ploy of self-mutilation. Moreover, the shadowy characterizations, thin texture, and surprisingly slow pace of *Octopus* make obtrusive Blechman's perpetual punning, as in the name of the trend-setting Newvoes, while this device seems venial amid the gusto and speed of the other books.

Pathetic little Norman Greenberg (*Omongo*), whose often hilarious obscenity helps define his loveless misery, epitomizes the combination of comic horror and pathos that is Blech-man's major achievement. Similarly the humor in Jenny Stern's struggle against the senile amorousness of Mr. Lazar at the nursing home balances the compassionate responses she and her fellow inmates give to the news of their nurse's pregnancy, while they continue their litany of familiar complaints about their own children. What insures Blechman's status as a comic novelist, despite his often horrifying subject-matter, is his complex parody, his word play that exposes an undercutting level of wit, his stylized handling of realistic dialogue, and, ultimately, in Rabbi Yeslin's lament for his failure as a marriage broker, a prose that mocks an absurdity otherwise too painful to endure: "Nowadays, men wanted a special type, the kind you found late at night, alone in a delicatessen, waiting." (*The War of Camp Omongo*)

—Burton Kendle

---

**BODSWORTH, (Charles) Fred(erick).** Canadian. Born in Port Burwell, Ontario, 11 October 1918. Educated at Port Burwell public and high schools. Married Margaret Neville Banner in 1944; has three children. Reporter, *Times-Journal*, St. Thomas, Ontario, 1940–43; Reporter and Editor, *Daily Star* and *Weekly Star*, Toronto, 1943–46; Staff Writer and Editor, *Maclean's Magazine*, Toronto, 1947–55. Since 1955, free-lance Writer. Director, and a Past President (1965–67), Federation of Ontario Naturalists: Leader of worldwide ornithological tours. Recipient: Doubleday Canadian Prize Novel Award, 1967. Address: 294 Beech Avenue, Toronto 260, Ontario, Canada.

PUBLICATIONS

Novels

The Last of the Curlews. Toronto and New York, Dodd Mead, 1955; London, Museum Press, 1956.

*The Strange One*.  Toronto and New York, Dodd Mead, 1959; London, Longman, 1960.
*The Atonement of Ashley Morden*.  Toronto and New York, Dodd Mead, 1964; as *Ashley Morden*, London, Longman, 1965.
*The Sparrow's Fall*.  New York, Doubleday, and London, Longman, 1967.

Other

*The Pacific Coast* (natural history).  Toronto, Natural Science of Canada, 1970.

Critical Studies: Introduction by James Stevens to *The Last of the Curlews*, Toronto, McClelland and Stewart, 1963; essay by Norah Story in *Oxford Companion to Canadian Literature*, Toronto, Oxford University Press, 1967.

Fred Bodsworth comments:

The major part of my work has been novels linking human and animal characters in a fiction format with strong natural history content and wilderness backgrounds. The nature storyteller who uses birds or mammals in fictional situations treads a narrow path if he wishes to be scientifically authentic and portray them as they really are. On the one hand, he has to personalize his animal as well as his human characters or he simply has no dramatic base for his story. Yet if the personalizing of animal characters goes too far and begins turning them into furry or feathered people—the nature writer's sin of anthropomorphism—the result is maudlin nonsense that is neither credible fable nor fiction. I enjoy the challenge of presenting wildlife characters as modern animal behaviour studies are showing them to be —creatures dominated by instinct, but not enslaved by it, beings with intelligence very much subhuman in some areas yet fascinatingly superhuman in others. Out of this blending of human and animal stories comes the theme that I hope is inherent in all my books: that man is an inescapable part of all nature, that its welfare is his welfare, that to survive he cannot continue acting and regarding himself as a spectator looking on from somewhere else.

\*     \*     \*

Fred Bodsworth, writing in imaginative, uncomplicated prose, has used the Canadian Shield of pine-tree laden granite for the setting in his novels. He calls it "a benign land sometimes amiable, even indulgent, but at other times a land of perverse hostility." These sparsely, Indian-populated lands provide a unique characteristic which distinguishes Canada from its gargantuan neighbor to the south. Bodsworth is then readily identifiable as a Canadian novelist.

The strength of his writing is the skillful portrayal of characters who are dependent upon their milieu and to the forces within it. He is able to make his birds and humans unpredictable because of unforeseen but crucial subtleties in the environmental settings. Bodsworth's naturalist and ornithological knowledge fosters such keen insight. Atook, a native hunter in *The Sparrow's Fall*, seems doomed because Christian myth interferes with his hunting prowess. But the will to survive, which resides in all his characters, eventually causes Atook to cast aside his alien beliefs and adjust to his natural surroundings.

*The Last of the Curlews* is his most stimulating and moving novel. Bodsworth reveals the brutal and senseless slaughter of a bird that has not developed a fear of the earth's most irrational creature, man. In sensitive prose, the tiny bird becomes personalized but not human; thus he avoids sham. The theme of this novel has increased in importance since its writing because of the growing awareness of our threatened environment.

While Bodsworth commits the occasional transgression by allowing his creatures to reason, it does not seriously detract from his animal characters.

In *The Strange One*, he adroitly interweaves the mating of an alien Hebridean Barra goose with a native Canada goose and the love of a young biologist for a Cree maiden, who has been socialized in the whiteman's world. Indian-white miscengenation is as old as Canada itself and this theme intertwined with the geese is unusual in Canadian literature. Bodsworth is the first to write about it. The parallel between man and bird in this novel clearly reveals the interrelationship of man with animal when Rory, the scientist, follows what appears to be almost instinctual feelings, disregards social convention and returns to the beautiful Cree, Kanina.

*The Strange One* and *The Atonement of Ashley Morden* involve what may be melo-dramatic relationships between men and birds, but the two themes are drawn together skill-fully, and are quite effectively written. An underlying theme in both these novels, as well as the others, is the complicated, often contradictory behaviour of men contrasted with the logical, conditioned instincts of animals and birds.

In the context of Canadian literature, Bodsworth is one of the leading traditional novelists.

—James R. Stevens

---

**BOURJAILY, Vance (Nye).** American. Born in Cleveland, Ohio, 17 September 1922. Educated at Bowdoin College, Brunswick, Maine, B.A. 1947. Served in the American Field Service, 1942–44, and in the United States Army, 1944–46. Married Bettina Yensen in 1946; has two children. Taught at the Writers Workshop, 1957–58, Associate Professor, 1960–64, 1966–67, 1971–72, University of Iowa, Iowa City. Served on the United States Department of State Mission to South America, 1959. Distinguished Visiting Professor, Oregon State University, Corvallis, Summer 1968. Address: Redbird Farm, Route One, Iowa City, Iowa 52240; or, c/o Russell and Volkening, 551 Fifth Avenue, New York, New York 10017, U.S.A.

PUBLICATIONS

Novels

*The End of My Life.*  New York, Scribner, 1947; London, W. H. Allen, 1963.
*The Hound of Earth.*  New York, Scribner, 1955; London, Spearman, 1956.
*The Violated.*  New York, Dial Press, 1958.
*Confessions of a Spent Youth.*  New York, Dial Press, 1960; London, W. H. Allen, 1961.
*The Man Who Knew Kennedy.*  New York, Dial Press, 1967.
*Brill among the Ruins.*  New York, Dial Press, 1970; London, W. H. Allen, 1971.

Other

*The Girl in the Abstract Bed* (text for cartoons).  New York, Tiber Press, 1954.
*The Unnatural Enemy* (on hunting).  New York, Dial Press, 1963.

Editor, *Discovery 1–6*.  New York, Pocket Books, 1953–55.

Manuscript Collection: Bowdoin College Library, Brunswick, Maine.

Critical Studies: by the author on his work in *Afterwords*, edited by Thomas McCormack, New York, Harper, 1969; in *The Shaken Realist* by John M. Muste, Baton Rouge, Louisiana State University Press, 1970.

*          *          *

Vance Bourjaily occupies a curious place in modern fiction. A serious writer who deals thoughtfully with important themes, he has for the most part been ignored by the critics; a novelist who delineates in interesting ways the vagaries of American life during the past three decades, he has never been a genuine popular success. Bourjaily is, nevertheless, that rarest of phenomena in American fiction, the novelist who develops and improves his craft in successive books. Without attracting attention as an innovator, he has experimented in interesting ways with different methods of handling and presenting his materials, and he has consistently refined a style that is personal without being idiosyncratic.

Bourjaily's fiction has been centered around the experience of his generation, which grew to maturity just before and during World War II. Although only his first book, *The End of My Life*, can properly be called a war novel, the war occupies a pivotal position in each of his first four novels as the most significant event in the development of that generation. The central character of *The End of My Life* is a young man who leaves college to serve as an ambulance driver, first in the Middle East and later in Italy, where he makes a mistake that brings to a head all of the changes which have accompanied his growth to maturity. His responsibility for the death of a girl he hardly knew leads him to reject everything he had been, and at the end of the book he is left alone, without resources and without belief in himself. Too much in the Hemingway tradition, *The End of My Life* is sometimes juvenile, sometimes sentimental, occasionally moving.

Each of the three novels which followed *The End of My Life* has a broader scope. In *The Hound of Earth* action develops around a man who is running from the knowledge that he had participated in the development of the atomic bomb, and who eventually becomes a stock clerk in a San Francisco department store during the Christmas rush. The book is concerned with the problems of man's responsibility to himself and to other people, with the ironies in the cruel behaviour of people in a season supposedly dedicated to love, and with the inexorable workings of fate, manifested here by the government agents who track down the hero. *The Hound of Earth* fails because it does not show any clear link between the selfishness and cruelty of its characters and the forces which made and used the atomic bomb. It is, nevertheless, an interesting book in its creation of atmosphere and in its depiction of character, and it remains one of the few American novels which have made even an attempt to deal with the problems raised by the development and use of atomic weapons.

*The Violated* is probably the most widely admired of Bourjaily's novels. Considerably more complex than his first two books, both in technique and in plot, it delineates the problems of three men and one girl who grow up just before the war and who find the patterns of their lives crystallized by the war. In different ways, each of them seeks for love and each of them violates the people with whom they come in contact, even as they are violated by life. Played off against this group of characters are a number of children, dominated by the daughter of one of the major adult characters. The children seek to impose some kind of order on their own chaotic lives by producing a play, but the adult world frustrates their efforts. The grim lesson of the novel is that no order seems to be possible in the post-war world; the kinds of love which are available offer no real consolation.

*Confessions of a Spent Youth* is probably Bourjaily's most experimental novel to date.

Told by a first-person narrator, it is organized around topics drawn loosely from de Quincey. The narrator's life closely resembles that of the central character of *The End of My Life* (Bourjaily has said that both novels are to some extent autobiographical), but we are told of his experiences before and after the war, and the war-time experience is seen in a different light. In different sections we learn of the narrator's experiences with women, his vicarious flirtation with crime, his introduction to marijuana, his friendships, his attempts to define himself. Again, the theme is the difficulty of finding order and coherence in the modern world, emphasized by the experience of the war, which shows how cheaply life is held in the modern world. If *Confessions of a Spent Youth* is somewhat diffuse, it evokes brilliantly the wonder and fear of growing up before and during the war, and the closing section, depicting the sometimes manic, sometimes horrifying post war world, is marvelously accurate and evocative.

In his two most recent novels, Bourjaily has made two important changes from the patterns of his first four books. For one thing, the war has ceased to figure in a determining way; as his generation has moved away from the war, so has Bourjaily. Perhaps more important, neither *The Man Who Knew Kennedy* nor *Brill among the Ruins* centers upon the college boys, intellectuals, artists who populate the earlier fiction. The narrator of *The Man Who Knew Kennedy* is a businessman, of a type which Bourjaily has said "did their jobs honorably, took care of their families, didn't stop educating themselves about life and maintained some cultural independence." The novel pivots around the death of John F. Kennedy, the way in which that death affected people, and the way in which Kennedy's life somehow symbolized the hopes, frustrations and disasters of a whole generation. It is weakened by Bourjaily's inability to decide whether the center of interest should be the narrator, with his business and marital problems, or his best friend, "the man who knew Kennedy," whose great charm and talent are dissipated by an improbable and demeaning obsession.

*Brill among the Ruins* is much more successful, Bourjaily's most finished work to date. The central character is a small-town mid-western lawyer who finds the world of the late sixties baffling, but who never stops trying to mitigate its worst features and who is always open to the possibilities of new experience. Hunting, amateur archaeology and an affair with a young woman of the new generation mark Brill's life, and help bring him to an understanding of himself and his responsibilities. The novel contains a good deal of information about Latin American archaelogy and some of the most effective descriptions of hunting in our literature, but its most important virtue is its evocation of Brill's commitment to life.

Bourjaily's chief weakness is perhaps his aversion to plot. Except for *The Violated*, his novels lack strong unifying plots, making for diffuseness of effect and a meandering quality that is sometimes charming but often distracting. But his virtues are much more significant. He writes about man's relationship to nature better than any other writer of his generation; whether his characters are hunting, fishing, enjoying the isolation of the Blue Ridge Mountains or sailing a schooner in the Gulf Stream, he evokes the magnificence and mystery of the natural world and its effect on those characters with genuine mastery. He has the ability to create memorable and distinctive characters, and unusual skill in reproducing the ways in which they talk. His novels taken together make a distinctive picture of American life in the last thirty years, less a social document than a sensitive rendition of what it has been like to live through those times.

—John M. Muste

---

**BOWEN, Elizabeth (Dorothea Cole).**  Irish.  Born in Dublin. Educated at Downe House School, Kent. Married Alan Charles Cameron in 1923 (died, 1952). Recipient: Black Memorial Prize, 1970. D.Litt., Trinity College, Dublin, 1948; Oxford University, 1956. Honorary Member, American Academy of Arts and Letters. C.B.E. (Commander, Order of the British Empire), 1948. Companion of Literature, Royal Society of Literature, 1965. Address: Carbery, Church Hill, Hythe, Kent, England.

PUBLICATIONS

Novels

*The Hotel.*   London, Constable, 1927; New York, Dial Press, 1928.
*The Last September.*   London, Constable, and New York, Dial Press, 1929.
*Friends and Relations.*   London, Constable, and New York, Dial Press, 1931.
*To the North.*   London, Gollancz, 1932; New York, Knopf, 1933.
*The House in Paris.*   London, Gollancz, 1935; New York, Knopf, 1936.
*The Death of the Heart.*   London, Gollancz, 1938; New York, Knopf, 1939.
*The Heat of the Day.*   London, Cape, and New York, Knopf, 1949.
*A World of Love.*   London, Cape, and New York, Knopf, 1955.
*The Little Girls.*   London, Cape, and New York, Knopf, 1964.
*Eva Trout; or, Changing Scenes.*   New York, Knopf, 1968; London, Cape, 1969.

Short Stories

*Encounters: Stories.*   London, Sidgwick and Jackson, 1923; New York, Boni and Liveright, 1926.
*Ann Lee's and Other Stories.*   London, Sidgwick and Jackson, and New York, Boni and Liveright, 1926.
*Joining Charles and Other Stories.*   London, Constable, and New York, Dial Press, 1929.
*The Cat Jumps and Other Stories.*   London, Gollancz, 1934.
*Look at All Those Roses: Short Stories.*   London, Gollancz, and New York, Knopf, 1941.
*The Demon Lover and Other Stories.*   London, Cape, 1945; as *Ivy Gripped the Steps and Other Stories*, New York, Knopf, 1946.
*Selected Stories.*   Dublin, Fridberg, 1946.
*Stories.*   New York, Knopf, 1959.
*A Day in the Dark and Other Stories.*   London, Cape, 1965.

Other

*Bowen's Court.*   London, Longman, and New York, Knopf, 1942.
*English Novelists.*   London, Collins, and New York, Hastings House, 1942.
*Seven Winters.*   Dublin, Cuala Press, 1942; as *Seven Winters: Memories of a Dublin Childhood*, London and New York, Longman, 1943.
*Anthony Trollope: A New Judgement.*   New York and London, Oxford University Press, 1946.
*Why Do I Write: An Exchange of Views Between Elizabeth Bowen, Graham Greene and V. S. Pritchett.*   London, Marshall, 1948.
*Collected Impressions.*   London, Longman, and New York, Knopf, 1950.
*The Shelbourne: A Centre of Dublin Life for More Than a Century.*   London, Harrap, 1951; as *The Shelbourne Hotel*, New York, Knopf, 1951.

*A Time in Rome.*   London, Longman, and New York, Knopf, 1960.
*After-Thought: Pieces about Writing.*   London, Longman, 1962; with *Seven Winters*,
   New York, Knopf, 1962.
*The Good Tiger* (juvenile).   New York, Knopf, 1965.

Editor, *The Faber Book of Modern Stories.*   London, Faber, 1937.
Editor, *Stories*, by Katherine Mansfield.   New York, Knopf, 1956; as *34 Short Stories*,
   London, Collins, 1957.

*          *          *

"The outward, apparent tie between writer and subject," Elizabeth Bowen has told her
readers, "is not fortuitous. . . . A man's whole art may be rendered down, by analysis, to
variations upon a single theme." Moreover, critical analysis may discover behind recurring
theme and compulsive variations the driving force which distinguishes the true writer:
"The child, almost any child, is born with the hope that the universe is somehow to be explained: it may be that the writer does not outlive that hope—here and there his eye passes,
from clue to clue. Through subject he offers his explanation." Miss Bowen's long career as a
novelist reveals just such a dominating concern, present from the beginning and repeated
with increasing force: "I was beating myself against human unknowableness; in fact, I
made it my subject—how many times?" Each novel devises its own particular dramatic
set of variations, satiric or tragic, but the theme persists: a sensitive nature, young or inexperienced, hopeful, eager for expansion and response, is repulsed, thwarted, forced to
confront the isolating "unknowableness" of others. This generalization will hold true, at
least, for the novels written between 1927 and 1949; the extraordinary later works make
such reductive statements difficult.

Miss Bowen published her first short stories when she was in her early twenties. Looking
back at these preliminary ventures she explains that for her generation grown-ups were a
hostile ruling class:

> I was, it seemed, at everybody's disposition. . . . As far as I see now, I must have
> been anxious to approximate to my elders, yet to demolish them. . . . Horror of
> being at a disadvantage may have worked itself out in my aptness to take my
> characters at a disadvantage, to snap them (in a camera sense) at a moment when
> weakness, falseness, or affectation could not but be exposed.

The sketches in *Encounters* and *Ann Lee's* are therefore sharp, knowing, but defensively
ungenerous and finally too easy for a writer of such great natural gifts. "What I regret,"
she confesses, "is the playing safe—which betrays itself in these studies of human extremity
and dereliction." Her first novel, *The Hotel*, shows the strain, perhaps inevitable, of attempting to go beyond the limited range of these initial successes.

In *The Hotel* Miss Bowen meets the problem of creating a sustained plot and assembling
characters for something more than passing encounters by placing her action at a resort
hotel on the Italian Riviera. The story, which is hardly a story at all, tends to break down
into a series of loosely connected portraits: vacationers appear and disappear; a sense of
loneliness and misunderstanding is generated by a cast of characters rather than supported
by deeper exploration of one central situation. The older tourists are stuffy, generally well
meaning and uniformly discontent; the young are open, arrogant and tenderly expectant.
And despite the general diffuseness of the novel, the archetypal Elizabeth Bowen heroine
makes a clear appearance: Sydney Warren, a young girl with "an appetite for pain" becomes
attached to an older woman only to be shut out by the woman's uncomprehending selfishness
and devotion to her own son. Sydney drifts into a compensatory engagement with a sympathetic clergyman, then sensibly pulls back. The season comes to an end; the characters disperse, more bruised than enlightened by their encounters.

Early disillusionment, deprivation and loss of innocence dominate the novels of the thirties. In *The Last September* the characters are brought together by their loyalties to an Anglo-Protestant country house in Ireland during the troubles of the early twenties. Once again there is a wealth of material partially developed and an unwillingness to have one line of action work for a clear primary effect. A young English visitor is tempted to fall in love with a pleasant young man who is senselessly killed in a skirmish. The relationship dies as pitifully as the youth, before either has a chance to grow; the fine old house in which the action has unfolded goes up in equally futile revolutionary flames. A third, somewhat more compassionate novel followed in 1931: *Friends and Relations*, the slightest of Miss Bowen's books, follows a tangle of family tensions and affections with the good humor and acute sense of social comedy which is to become increasingly characteristic of her work. *To the North*, however, is a far more somber novel: an appealing young widow is caught up in an aimless affair with a man unable or unwilling to risk love. By now disappointment is a common fate in Miss Bowen's world: "Very few remain ennobled: one has to live as one can—it is a meaner living, gaudy, necessitous, full of immediate pleasures, like the lives of the poor." But here the young woman consciously or unconsciously resists any shabby compromises and literally drives herself and her lover to death, to the "north" of complete annihilation. Thus these early novels define Miss Bowen's persistent theme, and they establish as well a kind of structural pattern which is to govern her fiction through the forties. None of the novels is experimental in any important sense: the point of view is frankly omniscient; the author feels perfectly free to come forward for comment and generalization. The reader is usually introduced to the main action through the agency of a peripheral character; the situation is then held in suspension and explained by a more or less prolonged series of flashbacks; the action resumes and moves towards the now predictable revelations of failure and despair.

*The House in Paris* and *The Death of the Heart* show Miss Bowen at the height of her mature powers. Both novels deal with the inevitable complications which develop between people who cannot help attracting and injuring each other, but the problem is now made doubly painful by the habit of demonstrating how the inadequacies of one generation infect the emotional resources of the next. "Why should we be at the start of our two lives when everything round us is losing its virtue," cries Portia, the young heroine of *The Death of the Heart* who had hoped for more; "how can we grow up when there's nothing left to inherit, when what we must feed on is so stale and corrupt?" And what would I feel, adds a sympathetic elder, but

> Contempt for the pack of us, who muddled our own lives, then stopped [her from living hers.] Boredom, oh such boredom, with a sort of secret society about nothing. . . . Utter lack of desire to know what it was about. Wish that someone outside would blow a whistle and make the whole thing stop. Wish to have my own innings. Contempt for married people, keeping on playing up. Contempt for unmarried people, looking cautious and touchy. Frantic, frantic desire to be handled with feeling, and, at the same time, to be let alone.

*The Heat of the Day* records the brutal anxieties of wartime Londoners with memorable force. The prose itself grows dark, involuted, hesitant, probing negative states of feeling. A middle-aged widow is compelled to recognize that her lover is an enemy agent; his motives are suggested rather than developed, but the effects are clear and corrosive. Despite some striving for a more affirmative ending—the second front opens, life goes on—Miss Bowen remains most convincing as the spokesman of the betrayed and disappointed. Perhaps because they attempt less, the short stories of this period (collected in *The Demon Lover*) are more successful. Certainly no writer has described so vividly, yet in such understated dramatic terms, the unreal world of the civilian trapped by the massive displacements of war: "You used to know what you were from the things you liked, and chose. Now there was not what you liked, and you did not choose."

*A World of Love*, *The Little Girls* and *Eva Trout* are works of a quite different kind. Much less interested now than before in surface realism, Miss Bowen moves closer to myth and parable. "The apparent choices of art," she wrote in 1946, "are nothing but addictions, predispositions: where did they come from, how were they formed? The aesthetic is nothing but a return to images that will allow nothing to take their place; the aesthetic is nothing but an attempt to disguise and glorify the enforced return. . . . If he be a novelist, all his psychology is merely a new parade of the old mythology." Such enforced returns are also the goals of the characters within these novels. In *A World of Love* the myth is that of eros, now seen in terms of Dante and Traherne: love is literally the force which drives the stars. A young girl on the verge of loving pieces together the unhappy past loves of her elders; but it is significant that Miss Bowen now stops short of dramatizing, as she has done so often before, the next round of failures. Instead, the novel ends on an unmistakable note of romance: the radiant girl and the young man whom she has just met "no sooner looked but they loved". In *The Little Girls*, quite possibly the finest and certainly the most complex of Miss Bowen's novels, three aging women are involved in a recovery of their past, of what once seemed most important to them. The quest both fails and succeeds: what was buried long ago is gone, stolen, disintegrated; what has been found in the searching, however, is a degree of honesty, self-awareness and a final sense of human responsibility. *Eva Trout*, the most directly poetic novel Miss Bowen has written, recapitulates symbolically everything she has discovered about the risks of human relationships. Her early emotional life violated and denied, Eva Trout, with her enormous wealth and obsessive need to love and be loved, tries to make the world over in her terms. In the grotesque but wholly moving last scene Eva too succeeds (a young man comes to love her real and her fictive version of herself) and fails (the child whose pitiful life Eva has willed to be her own possession destroys her).

In "Notes on Writing a Novel" (1945) Miss Bowen defines the novel as essentially a "non-poetic statement of a poetic truth". Without the freedom of poetic license and adornment, bound by the reader's demands for verisimilitude, the novelist must make his particular case yield a general human truth. Here as elsewhere Miss Bowen is unequivocally classical: art must be more philosophic than history; the novel "makes towards abstract truth." Far too little read or understood at the moment, Miss Bowen's work demands—and will withstand—the austere judgments of what she calls elsewhere "the old, relentless tradition" of the novel itself.

—Elmer Borklund

---

**BOWEN, John (Griffith).** British. Born in Calcutta, India, 5 November 1924. Educated at Pembroke College, Oxford, 1948–51; St. Antony's College, Oxford (Frere, Exhibitioner in Indian Studies), 1951–53, M.A., 1953; Ohio State University, Columbus, 1952–53. Served as a Captain in the Mahratha Light Infantry, 1943–47. Assistant Editor, *The Sketch* magazine, London, 1953–56; Copywriter, J. Walter Thompson Company, London, 1956–58; Head of the Copy Department, S. T. Garland Advertising, London, 1958–60; Script Consultant, Associated Television, London, 1960–67. Has spent a short period as an actor in repertory. Began to direct drama students at the London Academy of Dramatic Art in 1967, and has directed professional casts in his own plays at the Stables Theatre, Manchester, the Festival Theatre, Pitlochry, Scotland, and the Hampstead Theatre Club, London. Address: Old Lodge Farm, Lower Tysoe, Warwickshire, England.

PUBLICATIONS

Novels

*The Truth Will Not Help Us: Embroidery on an Historical Theme.*  London, Chatto
and Windus, 1956.
*After the Rain.*  London, Faber, 1958; New York, Ballantine, 1959.
*The Centre of the Green.*  London, Faber, 1959; New York, McDowell Obolensky,
1960.
*Storyboard.*  London, Faber, 1960.
*The Birdcage.*  London, Faber, and New York, Harper, 1962.
*A World Elsewhere.*  London, Faber, 1966; New York, Coward McCann, 1967.

Uncollected Short Stories

"Another Death in Venice", in *London Magazine*, June 1964.
"The Wardrobe Mistress", in *London Magazine*, January 1971.

Plays

*The Essay Prize, with A Holiday Abroad and The Candidate: Plays for Television.*
London, Faber, 1962.
*I Love You, Mrs. Patterson* (produced London, 1964).  London, Evans Brothers, 1964.
*After the Rain* (produced London and New York, 1967).  London, Faber, 1967; New
York, Random House, 1968.
*The Fall and Redemption of Man*, an adaptation of Mystery Plays (produced London,
1967; Pitlochry, Scotland, 1969).  London, Faber, 1968.
*Little Boxes* (includes *The Coffee Lace* and *Trevor*) (produced London, 1968; New
York, 1969).  London, Methuen, 1968.
*Trevor*, in *Modern Short Comedies from Broadway and London.*  New York, Random
House, 1969.
*The Disorderly Women* (produced Manchester, 1969; London, 1970).  London,
Methuen, 1969.
*The Waiting Room* (produced London, 1970).  London, French, 1970.
*The Corsican Brothers* (produced London, 1970).  London, Methuen, 1970.

Plays produced on Associated Television and the BBC.

Other

*Pegasus* (juvenile).  London, Faber, 1957; New York, Day, 1958.
*The Mermaid and the Boy* (juvenile).  London, Faber, 1958; New York, Barnes, 1960.
*Garry Halliday and the Disappearing Diamonds*, with Jeremy Bullmore (as Justin Blake;
juvenile).  London, Faber, 1960.
*Garry Halliday and the Ray of Death*, with Jeremy Bullmore (as Justin Blake; juvenile).
London, Faber, 1961.
*Garry Halliday and the Kidnapped Five*, with Jeremy Bullmore (as Justin Blake; juvenile).
London, Faber, 1962.
*Garry Halliday and the Sands of Time*, with Jeremy Bullmore (as Justin Blake; juvenile).
London, Faber, 1963.

*Garry Halliday and the Flying Foxes*, with Jeremy Bullmore (as Justin Blake; juvenile). London, Faber, 1964.

Has written drama criticism for *London Magazine*, and criticism for the *Sunday Times*, *Times Literary Supplement*, and *New Statesman*, London, and for the *New York Times Book Review*.

Manuscript Collections: Mugar Library, Boston University; Temple University Library, Philadelphia.

Critical Studies: *Postwar British Fiction* by James Gindin, Berkeley, University of California Press, 1962; "The Fable Breaks Down" by James Gindin, in *Wisconsin Studies in Contemporary Literature* (Madison), vol. 8, no. 7, 1967; "Bowen on the Little Box" by Hugh Hebert, in *The Guardian* (London), 6 August 1971.

John Bowen comments:

I have always been interested in problems of form. Thus, in my first novel, *The Truth Will Not Help Us*, I wanted to try to tell a story of an historical occurrence of 1705 in Britain in terms of the political atmosphere and activities of the U.S.A. in 1953: in both those years political witch-hunting caused injustice and harm to innocent persons. My second novel, *After the Rain*, began as an attempt to do for science fiction what Michael Innes had done for the detective story: I failed in this attempt because I soon became more interested in the ideas with which I was dealing than in the form, and anyway made many scientific errors. My third novel was straightforwardly naturalistic, but in my fourth, *Storyboard*, I used an advertising agency as a symbol of a statement about public and private life, just as Zola used a department store in *Au Bonheur des Dames*. In my fifth novel, *The Birdcage*, I attempted to use a 19th-century manner—the objective detachment of Trollope, who presents his characters at some distance, displays and comments on them. In my sixth novel, *A World Elsewhere*, the hero, himself a wounded and needed politician, is writing a fiction about Philoctetes, the wounded archer, and until he has found his own reasons for returning to political life in London, cannot conclude his fiction, because he does not see why Philoctetes should allow himself to accompany Odysseus to Troy. The same interest in different problems of form can be seen in my plays—the first Ibsenesque, the second borrowing from Brecht, Pirandello and the Chinese theatre, the third a pair of linked one-actors, designed as two halves of the same coin, the fourth an attempt to rework the myth of *The Bacchae* as Sartre, Giraudoux and Anouilh had used Greek myths, and to blend verse and prose, knockabout comedy, high tragedy and Shavian argument. My most recent full-length play, *The Corsican Brothers* (an expansion of my earlier television play), has songs set within the play to music pirated from 19th-century composers, and I tried to make, from the melodramatic fantasies of Dumas and Dion Boucicault, a kind of Stendhalian statement about a society based on ideas of honour.

In this commentary, I am more confident in writing of form than of theme. One's themes are for the critics to set out neatly on a board: one is not always so clearly conscious of them oneself. There is a concern with archetypical patterns of behaviour (therefore with myth). There is a constant war between reasonable man and instinctive man. There is the pessimistic discovery that Bloomsbury values don't work, but that there seem to be no others worth holding. There is a statement of the need for Ibsen's "Life Lie" even when one knows it to be a lie, and Forster's "Only connect" becomes "Only accept" in my work.

I believe that novels and plays should tell a story, that the story is the mechanism by which one communicates one's view of life, and that no symbolism is worth anything unless it also works as an element in the story, since the final symbol is the story itself.

Inasmuch as the influences on one's style are usually those writers whom one has discovered in one's adolescence and early twenties, I might be said to have been influenced as a novelist by Dickens, Trollope, E. M. Forster, Virginia Woolf, E. Nesbit, P. G. Wodehouse, and Evelyn Waugh—perhaps a little also by Hemingway and Faulkner. As a playwright, I have been influenced by Ibsen, Tchekov, Shaw, Pirandello, Anouilh, Giraudoux, and Noel Coward. Most of these names, I am sure, would be on any lists made by most of my contemporaries.

*       *       *

John Bowen has always been an intelligent and didactic novelist. His first novel, *The Truth Will Not Help Us*, uses a story of English seamen charged with piracy in a Scottish port in 1705 as a metaphor for the political evil of assuming guilt by rumor or association. *A World Elsewhere*, his latest novel, uses the myth of Philoctetes as a parallel to complicated speculation about hypocrisy and engagement in contemporary political life. *The Birdcage* contains a long essay giving an account of the history and development of commercial television; and a defense of advertising as not necessarily more corrupt than any other institution in urban, capitalistic society introduces *Storyboard*. Although Bowen's fictional lessons are invariably complex and thoughtful, the author's presence is always visible arranging, blocking out, and connecting the material. Myth is made pointedly and explicitly relevant; symbols, like the love-birds in *The Birdcage* or the breaking of a bronze chrysanthemum at a funeral in *The Centre of the Green*, sometimes seem attached heavy-handedly and literally. Bowen always acknowledges his own presence in his fiction, especially in his two most recent novels in which the author addresses the reader directly and becomes playful and intelligently skeptical about the complexities that prevent him from making any easy disposition of the characters and issues he has developed. The author is conspicuously articulate and instructive, but he does not attempt to play God; in fact, the danger of human substitutions for a non-existent or unknowable Deity comprises part of the message of *After the Rain* and the skepticism underlying *The Birdcage* and *A World Elsewhere*.

All of Bowen's novels contain sharply memorable and effective scenes: the retired colonel expressing his style and his strength through his garden in *The Centre of the Green*, the nocturnal trip around Soho in which a character is beaten in *The Birdcage*, the picnic on a Greek Island in *A World Elsewhere*. Often the best scenes involve a witty and comic treatment of dramatic conflict between two characters involved in close relationship, like the familial and sexual relationships in *The Centre of the Green* and *Storyboard* or the brilliantly handled quarrel between two contemporary London lovers who have lived together too long that takes place in the Piazza San Marco in *The Birdcage*. Bowen's comedy, however, no matter how strident initially, invariably turns into sympathy for his characters, a recognition that they are unable to be more human or more dignified than they are and that no man manages more. This characteristic switch from satire to sympathy is emblematic of most of Bowen's fiction which works on reversals, on dramatically presented and thematically central violations of expected conclusions. The simple, muscle-flexing athlete, not the expected sensitive intellectual, finally defies and defeats the tyrant who would make himself God in *After the Rain*. Humanity and integrity appear in just those places most easily and generally thought the most corrupt in modern society in *Storyboard*. The family in which all members seem, superficially, most selfish and isolated can understand and respect each other in *The Centre of the Green*. This engagingly perverse positivism is often applied to social or political clichés, as in the forceful and complicated treatment of E. M. Forster's "Only connect" in *The Birdcage* or the ramifications on "politics is the art of the possible" developed in *A World Elsewhere*. Such clichés, in Bowen's fictional world, never honestly express the concerns or dilemmas of the characters who use them so glibly, although they may yet be partially true in ways the characters never intend and can seldom comprehend.

People, in Bowen's novels, generally haven't a very good idea of what they're about, although this is no reason to deny their humanity or their capacity to invoke sympathy.

Bowen has not published a novel since 1966, but has written six plays for the stage and a number for television. Some of the plays, like *The Disorderly Women* and *The Corsican Brothers*, are, beneath the comedy, darker and more tragic versions of experience than are the novels. Yet drama seems, structurally, the appropriate vehicle for the qualities apparent in Bowen's fiction. Drama compresses the use of myth and symbol, the skill at scenes of dramatic confrontation, and the striking reversals of expectation which underline the humane and intelligent lessons.

—James Gindin

---

**BOWEN, Robert O.** American. Born in Bridgeport, Connecticut, 7 May 1920. Educated at the University of Alabama, B.A. 1948, M.A. 1950; University College of North Wales, Bangor, 1952–53. Served in the United States Navy, 1937–45. Married Mildred E. White in 1952; Naomi L. Misumi, 1968; has two children. Instructor, Cornell University, Ithaca, New York, 1953–55; Visiting Lecturer, University of Iowa, Iowa City, 1955–56; Assistant Professor of English, Montana State University, Missoula, 1956–58, and the University of Washington, Seattle, 1958–60; Associate Professor of English, University of Santa Clara, California, 1960–61, University of Dallas, 1961–63, and Alaska Methodist University, Anchorage, 1963–65. Editor, *Dallas Review*, 1962–63; *Alaska Review*, Anchorage, 1963–65; *Fur Rendezvous Magazine*, Anchorage, 1964. Director of Consumer Relations, Anchorage Chamber of Commerce, 1967–70. Since 1970, Proprietor, North Employment Agency, Anchorage. Address: P.O. Box 1862, Anchorage, Alaska 99501, U.S.A.

PUBLICATIONS

Novels

> *The Weight of the Cross*. New York, Knopf, 1951.
> *Bamboo*. New York, Knopf, 1953.
> *Sidestreet*. New York, Knopf, 1954.

Short Stories

> *Marlow the Master and Other Stories*. Northport, Alabama, Colonial Press, 1963.

Play

> *The Christmas Child* (libretto for opera produced Helena, Montana, 1960).

Other

> *The Truth about Communism*. Northport, Alabama, Colonial Press, 1962.

*College Style Manual.*   Northport, Alabama, Colonial Press, 1963.
*An Alaskan Dictionary.*   Spenard, Alaska, Nooshnik Press, 1965.

Editor, *Practical Prose Studies: A Critical Anthology of Contemporary American Prose
   Readings for the College Freshman.*   New York, Knopf, 1956.
Editor, *The New Professors.*   New York, Holt Rinehart, 1960.
Editor, with Robert A. Charles, *Alaska Literary Directory.*   Anchorage, Alaska Metho-
   dist University, 1964.


Manuscript Collection: University of Florida Libraries, Gainesville.


Robert O. Bowen comments:

   The major thing about my work has been that I have been in principle and practice a
conservative, both in politics and religion. As the revolution advanced in the United States,
pressures against conservative intellectuals increased. During the fifteen or more years that
I actually served as a man-of-letters, I had my mail opened, my telephone listened to and
endured numerous other attacks upon my privacy. I was slandered, threatened, submitted
to attempts to bribe and so on. This attack was consistently because my work, both in lectures
and in writing, both fiction and criticism, was conservative. It is my conviction that the
pressures which finally drove me from letters as a profession have driven hundreds of other
writers out of the field. Many of these are personal friends. For several years in the late
1960's, after leaving the academic and professional literary world, I worked as a public
relations man and manager. In 1970 I opened an employment agency, and for the first time
in many years found some peace and freedom in which to work. It is the major pity of our
time that we have suppressed, often in the name of free speech, our most individual intellectuals. This is a fault that history shall not forgive.
   As a literary man I feel much as though I have lived beyond the time of those who spoke
my language and that I now live as a wanderer in a strange world. I do not see how what
we called *literature* in my youth can be rebuilt with what we now find as *values* in our modern
teaching.
   My own fiction has been consistently analogy. However, in a materialistic time, such as
ours, it is consistently read as journalistic reporting. That is, many of my critics have read
it as autobiography and blamed me for its facts. My second novel, *Bamboo*, was carefully
structured with much conscious design to include a development of both language and
concept from as far back as the narratives of the Saxon period in Britain. However, few
could see in this work a truly serious literary effort because the narrative did not deal with
"intellectuals" as such but rather dealt with men who go to sea and to war.


                         *          *          *


   Two central biographical facts inform the most complex, suggestive work: Robert O.
Bowen was born and raised Catholic in an ambiguous, industrial sprawl of a city on the
American seaboard; secondly, as an enlisted man in the pre-World War II Regular Navy,
he was taken captive in the Philippines by the Japanese and for nearly four years was held
at forced labor on the docks in Manila.
   These biographical facts suggest the importance in the work of authority and bureaucracy in a man's life; the nature of loyalty, custom, cruelty, conformity, and rebellion; the
issues of ritual, suffering; of evil and—possibly—the varieties of salvation. In any event,
Bowen obsessively returns to the themes which are at the dark center of so much of the
world's literature.

Bowen's work divides roughly between prose fiction and journeyman editorial work. In addition, he has published some good poetry and penetrating literary criticism. Characteristically the editorial work is at the service of university teaching; in the past fifteen years Bowen has been a teacher, a writer-in-residence at half a dozen institutions of higher education. The novels and one collection of stories are in the line of the imaginative writers who were themselves men-of-action and concerned with tradition, the sea, evil, and survival. Aside from the American writers of the Naturalistic school, Conrad is the most pervasive influence.

Of the novels *Sidestreet* appears slight in comparison with the earlier *Weight of the Cross* and *Bamboo*. Of the two most interesting novels, *Bamboo* deserves more attention than it received on publication or thereafter. The materials concern an American sailor on leave from his destroyer. As was customary at the time, he removed to the beach, "went native". In the end he returns to the discipline, the tradition, the machinery, the structured life of the Navy. The tone of *Bamboo* is consistent; the pace exact; the prose precisely appropriate for the theme. The book brings together naturalistic detail and the generally romantic atmosphere of a sub-tropical idyll.

Bowen's best known novel, *The Weight of the Cross*, dramatizes the career of a "tin-can" sailor in World War II in the Pacific Theatre: from a hospital psychopathic ward at about the time of Pearl Harbor, to episodes of attempted flight, and finally through dock labor and the prison-of-war experience under Japanese administration. Tom Daley is the typical Bowen-hero: a tormented man, with psychological difficulties; a man broken by a past he understands imperfectly, at times given to extreme actions; and yet cunning, observant, respectful of all machinery, sympathetic with the working man, adaptable—and unresolved. Daley suggests, "Someplace I went the wrong way. Maybe something in my blood or in growing up. . . ." Although Daley survives, the agency of his salvation is never dramatized satisfactorily beyond the implication that he is lucky and works hard. The title of the novel is misleading, for it suggests religious accommodation; actually the religious theme is seldom a felt part of the narrative. A partial resolution of Tom Daley's trouble comes from his acceptance of life; acceptance, however, is not precisely a religious matter.

In the prose fiction concerned with World War II, a great many books pursued the mystery of why some men survived and others did not; still other novels failed to go beyond the gory details and explore the larger relationships of one man to his brothers, of Man to God. Being a first novel, *The Weight of the Cross* does not entirely avoid these difficulties. On the other hand, the book remains a precise vision of life in a dishonorable era. The passing of time will not soon take from the reader the vivid, hard-won episodes of death and survival and the limited wisdom which wars bestow on friend, foe, and authors alike.

—James B. Hall

---

**BOWERING, George.** Canadian. Born in Keremeos, British Columbia, 1 December 1938. Educated at Victoria College, British Columbia; University of British Columbia, Vancouver, B.A. 1960, M.A. 1963; University of Western Ontario, London. Served in the Royal Canadian Air Force, 1954–57. Married Angela Luoma in 1962. Has worked for the British Columbia Forest Service and for the Federal Department of Agriculture. Assistant Professor, University of Calgary, Alberta, 1963–66. Writer-in-Residence, 1967–68, and since 1968 Assistant Professor of English, Sir George Williams University, Montreal. Editor, *Imago* magazine, Montreal. Recipient: Canada Council grant, 1968; Governor-General's Award in Poetry, 1969. Address: Department of English, Sir George Williams University, Montreal 107, Quebec, Canada.

Publications

Novel

   *Mirror on the Floor*.   Toronto, McClelland and Stewart, 1967.

Uncollected Short Stories

   "The Elevator", in *Tamarack Review* (Toronto), 1962.
   "The Hayfield", in *Dalhousie Review* (Halifax), 1965.
   "Flycatcher", in *The Fiddlehead* (Fredericton, New Brunswick), 1965.
   "Ricardo and the Flower", in *West Coast Review* (Burnaby, British Columbia), 1968.

Plays

   *A Home for Heroes*, in *Prism International* (Vancouver), 1962.

   Screenplay: *Mirror on the Floor*, 1971.

Verse

   *Sticks and Stones*.   Vancouver, Tishbooks, 1963.
   *Points on the Grid*.   Toronto, Contact Press, 1964.
   *The Man in the Yellow Boots*.   Mexico City, El Corno, 1965.
   *The Silver Wire*.   Kingston, Ontario, Quarry Press, 1966.
   *Baseball*.   Toronto, Coach House Press, 1967.
   *Two Police Poems*.   Vancouver, Talon Books, 1968.
   *Rocky Mountain Foot*.   Toronto, McClelland and Stewart, 1969.
   *The Gangs of Kosmos*.   Toronto, House of Anansi, 1969.
   *George, Vancouver*.   Toronto, Weed/Flower Press, 1970.
   *Sitting in Mexico*.   Montreal, Imago, 1970.
   *Geneve*.   Toronto, Coach House Press, 1971.
   *Selected Poems*.   Toronto, McClelland and Stewart, 1971.

Other

   *Al Purdy*.   Toronto, Copp Clarke, 1970.
   *Autobiology*.   Vancouver, Vancouver Writing Series, 1971.

   Editor, *Vibrations*.   Toronto, Gage, 1970.
   Editor, *The Story So Far*.   Toronto, Coach House Press, 1971.

Manuscript Collection: Queen's University Library, Kingston, Ontario.

George Bowering comments:

My work in fiction shares many of the concerns of my work in verse. It is vocal, not just verbal, and it is my wish that it be read aloud, which I do at public readings, considering it as useful to do that as to read poetry aloud. It is also highly involved with place, the details of place, and that place's effect on the articulation. I try to avoid the kind of metaphor that is made up by the interpreting mind, though I am wide open to the kind of metaphor made by the accidents and coherences of the language itself, i.e., rime, pun, etc. I don't write what people call easily, "poetic prose". But I believe that those non-contiguous ways of thought common to poetry are highly important to fiction, or any prose writing. So my idea of form is not involved with the notion of the reason controlling the materials. I believe that the reason is only one participant in the process of finding the sentence. My preferences in reading fiction are John Hawkes, William Eastlake, Jack Kerouac, Robert Creeley, Fielding Dawson, and Gertrude Stein.

*     *     *

George Bowering is better known as a poet than a novelist, and one of the special pleasures of his sole published novel, *Mirror on the Floor*, is the linguistic vitality he developed over years of writing lyrics. Bowering wrote several unpublished novels before *Mirror on the Floor*, and he has written at least one more since, which lay in the hands of his publisher for three years before being withdrawn and offered elsewhere. His concern for language has subsequently grown, however, in a way which may have led him to abandon fiction altogether.

Like most of Bowering's fiction—he has also written many short stories—*Mirror on the Floor* is recognizably a close copy of Bowering's own world. The protagonist, Bob Small, is a graduate student at the University of British Columbia, as Bowering himself was. He is jailed in a drug raid on one of Vancouver's waterfront dives, and meets Andrea, a disturbed and oddly exotic refugee from a pathological home. The love between them begins in joy but rapidly turns corrosive as Andrea's needs come to test the resilience of Bob's commitment. Repeating a common pattern in Canadian fiction, Bob feels he is failing her, but seems powerless to stop.

After Andrea's father finally escapes her mother by driving his car off a pier, her relation with Bob reaches a crisis. "She held on to my arm. She had never done that before. All I could think of was getting home." Overbalanced at last, Andrea kills her mother and is packed off to an asylum while, in a conclusion tonally very like *A Farewell to Arms*, Bob sits in her apartment, trying to make sense of it all. For the moral burden of the book is Bob's, not Andrea's; it is he who seems burdened with something resembling choice in this "fucking awful" world.

Romantic, violent, taut, *Mirror on the Floor* is very much a young man's book, and a young literary man's, at that. Discernible echoes of Hemingway and Mordecai Richler (upon whom Bowering has written perceptively) jostle one another, and Jack Kerouac sometimes speaks through Andrea's mouth. For all that, it is a deft and accomplished novel.

Recently, Bowering has concerned himself more and more with the nature of language itself, viewing words increasingly as things-in-themselves rather than symbolic descriptions of external reality, and the process has made him impatient of the artifice of conventional fiction. "The way I used to write novels," he has said,

> just doesn't seem to be the sort of thing you should do now if you're terribly serious. There's really no reason to make up the names of characters and disguise everything, and have to answer all those questions: *Well, did you make this up or is this real life?*
>
> The first assumption is that I'm working with language, and the only way the language will be true or real or actual or whatever any of those things is, is if I don't step outside myself and say, *What effect is this language going to have?* The test for me is, *Is that my language?*

Bowering has just written something he calls an *Autobiology*. One suspects it may be a new vehicle for old obsessions all the same—the obsessions of the novelist.

—Donald Cameron

---

**BOWLES, Jane (Sydney).** American. Born in New York City, 22 February 1917. Educated privately in Switzerland. Married Paul Bowles, *q.v.*, in 1938. Has lived in Tangier since 1952. Address: 2117 Tanger Socco, Tangier, Morocco.

PUBLICATIONS

Novel

   *Two Serious Ladies.* New York, Knopf, 1943; London, Peter Owen, 1965.

Short Stories

   *Plain Pleasures.* London, Peter Owen, 1966.

Uncollected Short Stories

   "Andrew", in *Antaeus* (New York), 1971.
   "Emmy Moore's Journal", in *Antaeus* (New York), 1971.

Play

   *In the Summer House* (produced New York, 1953; Dublin, 1969). New York, Random House, 1954.

Verse

   *Song of an Old Woman* (song). New York, Schirmer, 1946.
   *Two Skies* (song). New York, Schirmer, 1946.

Other

   *The Collected Works of Jane Bowles.* New York, Farrar Straus, 1966.

Manuscript Collection: Humanities Research Center, University of Texas, Austin.

\*       \*       \*

One of the first things we notice in reading Jane Bowles' faultless prose fictions is that the relations between objects and people are notably inharmonious. Places to live are strange and inhospitable—a garishly painted hotel, birdcages standing in the halls and dangling from the ceilings, some of them empty; an apartment bulging with enormous armchairs and a dining table that barely clears the side walls; a pension room quite bare except for four very old, crooked, brass beds in a row. Somebody, we might suppose, has gone off and forgot to arrange the furniture.

The landscape is just as cheerless. One can look out at a leafless tree, a rusted car engine, a square with five pharmacies and seven cigar stores; go bathing at a beach strewn with rocks; bake potatoes in an incinerator near a pig-pen; live on an island that smells of the mainland glue factories. But none of this, we discover, seems to matter much. Only occasionally do the characters note the ugliness and the junk; most of the time, they are incapable of attending to a world outside themselves.

Yet, if we feel that the characters have lost a sense of relationship to their surroundings, surely we will not feel that they have given up their intentions to survive. A minor work, the puppet play, *A Quarreling Pair*, makes this psychological drive quite clear. Harriet, the "older," "stronger-looking" puppet, berates her sister, Rhoda, for having "no self-sufficiency." It would be "lovely," she says, "if you were like me." Her own great satisfaction comes from "the mold I was cast in, and neither heaven nor earth is going to make me damage it." Only one danger lurks for Harriet; she would get "some terrible disease and die" if she thought she "did not live in the right." Rhoda's response to her bullying sister is surprisingly affectionate; "Even though you have a small heart," she says, "I wish there were no one but you and me in the world." What she wants from love is self-protection. "Then," she adds, "I would never feel that I had to go among the others."

This alternation between "self-sufficiency" and the voracious dependence expressed in Rhoda's wish, is in all the work; and in each it has a different emotional coloration and consequence. In the novel, *Two Serious Ladies*, Miss Goering and Mrs. Copperfield are as antithetical in their notions of living as the two puppets. Christina Goering is strong, assertive, self-possessed, utterly indifferent to social relationships. As a child, she was "very much disliked by other children"; as an adult, "no better liked than as a child." But popularity is unimportant to her; she is "only interested . . . to attain her own salvation." Freida Copperfield's goals are more domestic. Meek and whiney, "completely dominated . . . by almost anyone," her sole object in life is "to be happy." Her way of doing so is not to seek adventure—she is afraid of everything—but to "nestle down." Instead of testing herself, as does Christina, she finds it "nice not to have to struggle too much for inner peace."

What these very different ladies have in common is a world in which social values, like the landscape, are hardly visible. The comedy of Christina's religious quest is its private and wholly arbitrary character. Salvation is literally her "own little idea." To achieve it, she must invent her own rituals; she must live "in some tawdry place and particularly in some place where I was not born." For that reason she goes to an unheated house on an island, makes little trips to the mainland, becomes Andy's mistress for eight days, and then goes off with the "heavy-set man in the hearse-like car." The strength of her position, if we may echo the stronger-looking puppet, is her self-sufficiency. At the end, she is gloriously sure that she is "nearer to becoming a saint"; as to whether she is "piling sin upon sin," the question, she concludes, is "of considerable interest but of no great importance." Mrs. Copperfield is less lucky. She falls in love with Pacifica, and although theirs would seem to be a genuine love, it ends with Mrs. Copperfield declaring one moment, "I am satisfied and completely content," and the next, frantic that Pacifica may have left her.

In the brilliant short stories, the consequences of this pattern of love and separateness that we have observed range from comedy to horror. In "A Guatamalan Idyll," a lascivious Guatamalan matron, Señora Ramirez, seduces an American textile buyer who extends his buying trip, "perhaps because he had always heard that a vacation in a foreign country was a desirable thing." The idyll, however, is all on the side of the Señora. She is enchanted with her lover, believes that not "heaven itself could be more wonderful." On his side, the merchant is mysteriously excited and, at the same time, miserable that he is doing something that "none of his friends had ever done before him, nor would do after him." Neither ever has the slightest understanding of the other's sense of things.

But often the tone is darker. "Everything Is Nice" takes place in a "blue Moslem town." The color is significant; it suggests not only the look of the town—its thick protective sea wall, the Moslem houses—but the emotional aloofness that exists between people who do not understand each other and who can only say, cakes are "nice," trucks are "nice," "Everything is nice."

In "Camp Cataract," perhaps the most complex of the short stories, the middle-aged sisters, Sadie and Harriet, both long to go out into the "grown-up world." Harriet gets as far as Camp Cataract, and there devises a "brilliant" plan to make "sallies into the outside world almost unnoticed." But Sadie continues to play "the role" of housewife, quite unaware that in attempting to get Harriet back, she will make an "agonizing voyage" not only "into the world" but into the self.

The characteristic dichotomy shows in its most poignant form in the play, *In the Summer House*. There the characters, as they make their claims and counter claims of love, seem almost to look at one another. Gertrude Eastman Cuevas, a beautiful middle-aged woman, gloats over a childhood victory: her father, she says, "pitied" her sister, Ellen, but he was "proud of me. I was his true love." Her daughter, Molly, cries out to her from the summer house, "I love you. I love you. Don't leave me." Vivian Constable, the summer visitor, wishing to usurp Molly's place, taunts, "I'm in your little house . . . Molly." Mrs. Constable, unloved by her own daughter, cries out to Molly, "Don't leave me." In the end, Molly and Gertrude change places. When Molly declares, "I'm going," Gertrude is furiously determined to keep her. "I've lost my daily life, that's all," she cries out.

This ultimate loss—the security of one's daily life—is implicit in Jane Bowles' work from the beginning. In *Two Serious Ladies*, published in 1943, almost a decade before the dark comedies of the absurdists, the losses are serious. But as the limited conditions of Christina's pilgrimage indicate, in social and metaphysical matters, one can get along on very little. Only later do we see how bad things can really get. Even then, Mrs. Bowles' characters are tenacious. Gertrude clutches at her crumbling world, "You can't go," she says, "I won't let you. I can stop you."

—Jacqueline Hoefer

---

**BOWLES, Paul (Frederick).**   American.   Born in New York City, 30 December 1910. Educated at the University of Virginia, Charlottesville, 1928–29; studied music with Aaron Copland in New York and Berlin, 1930–32, and with Virgil Thomson in Paris, 1933–34. Married Jane Auer Bowles, *q.v.*, in 1938. Music Critic, *New York Herald Tribune*, 1942–46. Composer of operas, ballets, music for plays and films. Recipient: Guggenheim Fellowship, 1941; National Institute of Arts and Letters grant, 1950; Rockefeller grant, 1959. Since 1952 has lived in Tangier. Address: 2117 Tanger Socco, Tangier, Morocco.

PUBLICATIONS

Novels

*The Sheltering Sky*.   London, Lehmann, and New York, New Directions, 1949.

*Let It Come Down*.  London, Lehmann, and New York, Random House, 1952.
*The Spider's House*.  New York, Random House, 1955; London, Macdonald, 1957.
*Up Above the World*.  New York, Simon and Schuster, 1966; London, Peter Owen, 1967.

## Short Stories

*The Delicate Prey and Other Stories*.  New York, Random House, 1950.
*A Little Stone: Stories*.  London, Lehmann, 1950.
*The Hours after Noon*.  London, Heinemann, 1959.
*A Hundred Camels in the Courtyard*.  San Francisco, City Lights, 1962.
*The Time of Friendship*.  New York, Holt Rinehart, 1967.
*Pages from Cold Point and Other Stories*.  London, Peter Owen, 1968.

## Uncollected Short Story

"Afternoon with Antaeus", in *Antaeus* (New York), 1970.

## Verse

*Scenes*.  Los Angeles, Black Sparrow Press, 1968.
*The Thicket of Spring*.  Los Angeles, Black Sparrow Press, 1971.

## Other

*Yallah* (travel).  Zurich, Manesse, 1956; New York, McDowell Obolensky, 1957.
*Their Heads Are Green* (travel).  London, Peter Owen, 1963; as *Their Heads Are Green and Their Hands Are Blue*, New York, Random House, 1963.

Translator, *No Exit*, by Jean-Paul Sartre.  New York, French, 1946.
Translator, *The Lost Trail of the Sahara*, by Roger Frison-Roche.  New York, Prentice Hall, 1962.
Translator, *A Life Full of Holes*, by Driss ben Hamed Charhadi.  New York, Grove Press, 1964; London, Weidenfeld and Nicolson, 1965.
Translator, *Love with a Few Hairs*, by Mohammed Mrabet.  London, Peter Owen, 1967; New York, Braziller, 1968.
Translator, *The Lemon*, by Mohammed Mrabet.  London, Peter Owen, 1969; New York, Herder and Herder, 1972.
Translator, *Mhashish*, by Mohammed Mrabet.  San Francisco, City Lights, 1969.

Published Music: *Tornado Blues* (chorus); *Music for a Farce* (chamber music); *Piano Sonatino*; *Huapango 1* and *2*; *Six Preludes for Piano*; *El Indio*; *El Bejuco*; *Sayula*; *La Cuelga*; *Sonata for Two Pianos*; *Night Waltz* (two pianos); Songs: *Heavenly Grass*; *Sugar in the Cane*; *Cabin*; *Rocking Chair*; *Letter to Freddy*; *The Years*; *Of All the Things I Love*; *A Little Closer, Please*; *David*; *In the Woods*; *Song of an Old Woman*; *Night Without Sleep*; *Two Skies*; *Que te falta?*; *Ya Llego*; *Once a Lady Was Here*; *Bluebell Mountain*; *Three*; *On a Quiet Conscience*; *El Carbonero*; *Baby, Baby*.

Operas: *Denmark Vesey*, 1937; *The Wind Remains*, 1941.

Ballets: *Yankee Clipper*, 1937; *Pastorella*, 1941; *Sentimental Colloquy*, 1944; *Blue Roses*, 1957.

Incidental Music, for plays: *Horse Eats Hat*, 1936; *Dr. Faustus*, 1937; *My Heart's in the Highlands*, 1939; *Love's Old Sweet Song*, 1940; *Twelfth Night*, 1940; *Liberty Jones*, 1941; *Watch on the Rhine*, 1941; *South Pacific*, 1943; *Jacobowsky and the Colonels*, 1944; *The Glass Menagerie*, 1945; *Twilight Bar*, 1946; *On Whitman Avenue*, 1946; *The Dancer*, 1946; *Cyrano de Bergerac*, 1946; *Land's End*, 1946; *Summer and Smoke*, 1948; *Edwin Booth*, 1958; *Sweet Bird of Youth*, 1959; *The Milk Train Doesn't Stop Here Anymore*, 1963; for films: *Roots in the Soil*, 1940; *Congo*, 1944.

Recordings: *The Wind Remains*, M.G.M.; *Mexican Dances*, Art of This Century; *Café Sin Nombre*, New Music; *Sonata for Two Pianos*, Columbia; *Night Waltz*, Columbia; *Scènes d'Anabase*, Columbia; *Music for a Farce*, Columbia; *Song for My Sister*, Disc; *They Cannot Stop Death*, Disc; *Night Without Sleep*, Disc; *Sailor's Song*, Disc; *Rain Rots the Wood*, Disc; *Sonata for Flute and Piano*, Art of This Century; *Six Preludes*, Golden Crest; *Huapango 1* and *2*, New Music; *A Picnic Cantata*, Columbia; *El Bejuco* and *El Indio*, Art of This Century; *Blue Mountain Ballads*, Music Library.

Bibliography: Los Angeles, Black Sparrow Press, 1972.

Manuscript Collection: Humanities Research Center, University of Texas, Austin.

Critical Study: "Paul Bowles and the Natural Man" by Oliver Evans, in *Recent American Fiction*, Boston, Houghton Mifflin, 1963.

*       *       *

Since the publication of his first novel, *The Sheltering Sky*, Paul Bowles has provoked sharply partisan feelings in his readers. To some he is a major prophet for our times; to others his work rather luridly exploits the fashionable themes of nihilism, violence, and despair. Few, however, are able to deny the insistent power of his prose—its urgency, clarity, and lyric compactness. Bowles's subtly acute sense of language no doubt owes a major debt to his training as a musician, his work as a translator, and his life-long interest in poetry. The intricate web of language in which his novels are contained often seems the only protection against the horror and despair which threaten to overwhelm his characters.

*The Sheltering Sky* sounded the major theme with which Bowles was to be concerned in all his work: the elemental clash between the primitive and the civilized. Bowles's central characters, Kit and Port Moresby, arrive in North Africa without any clear past, and make their way through a series of grotesque adventures. They are spiritual somnambulists, exiles, ambassadors from the wasteland of the modern world, and their veneer of civilization is slowly stripped away as they confront the primitive realities of the barren Sahara. *The Sheltering Sky* owes a debt, in its precise rendering of the violence and poverty of the Arab world, to the naturalist tradition, but beneath the novel's precisely rendered surface are undercurrents of symbol and insinuation which continually extend the meaning of the work. Like Edgar Allan Poe, the American writer whom he most admires, Bowles is primarily interested in probing the human soul, and to do so he must first strip it naked. That process most often reveals a spiritual emptiness, a sense of the void which links him to European existentialist writers like Sartre, whose *No Exit* Bowles translated in 1946. As Bowles remarks of one of his own characters, ". . . in order to deal with relative values, he had long since come to deny all purpose to the phenomenon of existence—it was more expedient and more comforting."

Some reviewers felt that *The Sheltering Sky* was merely a retelling of the story of spiritually bankrupt expatriates that Hemingway had recorded in *The Sun Also Rises*. In his second novel, *Let It Come Down*, Bowles made it clear that his interest in *nada* went far beyond Hemingway's essentially romantic attitude toward the dispossessed. The atmosphere of this work is even more stark, malevolent, and absurd than that of the first novel. A sober, sheltered clerk in a New York bank gives up his position in order to work in a friend's travel agency in Tangier; there he discovers the business to be a front for currency black-marketeering, and following that revelation he himself becomes involved in smuggling, narcotics traffic, sexual perversion, espionage and murder, ultimately absconding with an Arab companion and a bundle of stolen currency. Despite the obvious sensationalism of plot, Bowles is again concerned with the psychic disintegration and moral decay which overtake so-called civilized man when he confronts the primitive; the theme pervades his major writing as it does that of Joseph Conrad.

The hero (or anti-hero) of *Let It Come Down* seeks some place in the world to cancel out his meaningless existence, to find self by losing it; rejecting all conventional ideas of order, he acts in a chaotic way that creates and invites violence. Violence also overtakes and destroys the central characters of *Up Above the World*, who celebrate their second wedding anniversary with a trip to an obscure plantation republic. As they wander through wild landscapes, their adventures become increasingly feverish, compulsive, and agonized until hallucination and death overtake them.

The world of Paul Bowles's fiction is morally uninhabitable; it closes down on his characters like a hypnotic spell, as it closes down on the reader willing to grant the author's *donnée*: that there is within each of us the capacity for violence, irrational behavior, and madness, and that modern culture proves increasingly ineffective in giving check to those abysses. Nonetheless, Bowles's most memorable characters struggle for some kind of definition and often gamble for meaning with their very souls. Such concerns are equally present in Bowles's poetry, his travel books, and such edited "translations" as *Love with a Few Hairs*, the autobiography of the young Moroccan, Mohammed Mrabet. Many readers will find his vision discomforting, but it has significant parallels in the work of Sartre and Genet, Camus' *L'Etranger*, and the later work of Norman Mailer. Few modern writers have explored so memorably the contrasts between naivete and guile, Puritan restraint and pagan indulgence, Western sophistication and ancient superstition.

Nonetheless, it is difficult to escape the sense that Bowles's agonized vision, his extraordinary range of talent and his richly international experience have never coalesced to produce the single great work on which a major reputation might be established. The hypnotic atmosphere of *The Sheltering Sky* has been equalled in later work, but never surpassed, and while *The Spider's House* and *Up Above the World* demonstrate a refinement of narrative power, they seem finally like somewhat redundant variations on long-established gothic themes.

—David Galloway

---

**BOYD, Martin (à Beckett).** Australian. Born in Lucerne, Switzerland, 10 June 1893. Educated at Trinity Grammar School, Kew, Victoria; St. John's Theological College, Melbourne; trained as an architect. Served as a Lieutenant in The Buffs, 1916; Observer, Royal Flying Corps, 1917; Pilot, Royal Air Force, 1918. Reviewer, *Times Literary Supplement*, London, 1931–40. Painter: one-man shows, Cambridge, 1964, Melbourne, 1967. Recipient: Australian Literary Gold Medal, 1928, 1956. Lived for 27 years in Australia, 34 years in England, and 16 years on the Continent; now resides in Rome. Address: c/o Australia and New Zealand Bank Ltd., 71 Cornhill, London E.C.3, England.

PUBLICATIONS

Novels

   *Love Gods* (as Martin Mills). London, Constable, 1925.
   *Brangane* (as Martin Mills). London, Constable, 1926; as *The Aristocrat: A Memoir*,
     Indianapolis, Bobbs Merrill, 1927.
   *The Montforts* (as Martin Mills). London, Constable, 1928; as *Madeleine Heritage*,
     Indianapolis, Bobbs Merrill, 1928; revised edition, as Martin Boyd, Adelaide, Rigby,
     1963.
   *Scandal of Spring*. London, Dent, 1934.
   *The Lemon Farm*. London, Dent, 1935; New York, Norton, 1936.
   *The Picnic*. London, Dent, and New York, Putnam, 1937.
   *Night of the Party*. London, Dent, 1938.
   *Nuns in Jeopardy*. London, Dent, 1940.
   *Lucinda Brayford*. London, Cresset Press, 1946; New York, Dutton, 1948.
   *Such Pleasure*. London, Cresset Press, 1949; as *Bridget Malwyn*, New York, Dutton,
     1949.
   *The Cardboard Crown*. London, Cresset Press, 1952; New York, Dutton, 1953.
   *A Difficult Young Man*. London, Cresset Press, 1955; New York, Reynal, 1956.
   *Outbreak of Love*. London, Murray, and New York, Reynal, 1957.
   *When Blackbirds Sing*. London, Abelard Schuman, 1962; New York, Abelard
     Schuman, 1963.
   *The Teatime of Love: The Clarification of Miss Stilby*. London, Bles, 1969.

Verse

   *Retrospect*. Melbourne, Champion, 1920.

Other

   *The Painted Princess* (juvenile). London, Constable, 1936.
   *A Single Flame* (autobiography). London, Dent, 1939.
   *Much Else in Italy: A Subjective Travel Book*. London, Macmillan, 1958.
   *Day of My Delight* (autobiography). Melbourne, Lansdowne Press, 1965.
   *Why They Walk Out: An Essay in Seven Parts*. Privately printed, 1970.

Critical Studies: the "Martin Boyd Issue" of *Southerly* (Sydney), vol. 28, no. 2, 1968, which includes an essay by the author on his own work.

Martin Boyd comments:

My intentions [as a novelist] were the outcome of three major preoccupations—poetic religion; my hatred of war and all victimization; my family and the rich legacies of beauty and wisdom from the past. . . .
I come of a family prolific in painters, with the impulse to record what they see. This impulse is not only in the artist. A child will come in and give an excited and voluble account of something it has seen in the street. A true artist must also have this fresh vision. However, I had the same impulse as my parents and brothers, but used words instead of paints. So

when I began to write I was merely following my instincts without any conscious intentions, though my fundamental beliefs coloured the picture, and for those who disagreed with them disfigured it. In addition to painters, I have on my mother's side about five generations of legal forbears, who have bestowed on me a passion for lucid explanation. I cannot endure that people should go away, or "get away", with a false view of a situation. . . .

With *The Montforts* I had [the] conscious intention . . . to record and elucidate the phenomenon of my family. I remember trying to work out the construction of this book in a mathematical design on the floor, which suggests that I intended to create "a work of art". *Scandal of Spring* was the result of my reading in a newspaper of a girl of sixteen's eloping with a boy of just over that age, and of the boy's being sent to prison. My intention was to record the crucifixion of the poetic and vernal beauty of their love. But it also resulted from another preoccupation which I have not mentioned, one with the fact that the moral law and the law of the state, though related, are not identical. I intended to write it with a truthful simplicity which was lacking in my three earlier books. This again suggests that I had an artistic purpose. . . .

*The Cardboard Crown* and the three following Langton novels . . . had the same intention as *The Montforts*, to record and elucidate the phenomenon of my family, and also, as in *Such Pleasure*, to use material that I had wasted as a beginner. Unlike the latter book, it had an incident to start it off. I had returned to Australia in 1948; and . . . I found there my grandmother's diaries of most of her married life, especially of the years in Europe preceding my birth, so glamorous in my childhood's imagination. . . .

The function of the novelist is not that of a newspaper reporter, and a restricted social range is the greatest boon to him, as it gives him intensity of vision and a complete knowledge of his subject matter. It also gives unity to his work. My wide social range has been a handicap to me. Consequently my best novels are those in which I have retreated into the familiar milieu of my own relatives.

*The Times Literary Supplement*, reviewing my first novel, mentioned my "skill in giving the terms and cadences of natural dialogue". The *Observer* reviewer, thirty years later, wrote of *Outbreak of Love* that it had "page after page of enchanting dialogue". I think that the dialogue is the chief technical merit of my work. I can only use this talent when portraying people of a certain standard of education and social assurance.

In recent years there has been a lot written about the function of art, and some critics have implied that I do not understand it. The function of art is to enhance the quality of our lives, and to give us intensity of vision. Whatever degrades us, however brilliant its technical achievement, is bad art. Oscar Wilde's dictum that "there is no such thing as an immoral book" is insidious nonsense. At the deepest level, morals and aesthetics are the same thing, and morals probably emerged from aesthetic revulsions. Italians say of a thing that is morally bad, that it is "ugly".

—from *Southerly* (Sydney), vol. 28, no. 2,
1968, pages 83–90.

*     *     *

Martin Boyd's contribution to contemporary literature in general, and to Australian literature in particular, is valuable, and has much more literary and sociological tonnage than the actual avoirdupois of his published work would seem to suggest it should have. He achieves in his novels what few, almost no other, writers about Australia do achieve: a kind of wonderfully steady and unblurred X-ray of the Australian ethos. He does this, moreover, while limiting his attention largely to a certain class, doing for the "well-bred" or "upper-crust" Australian what D. H. Lawrence does less convincingly for the "common-man" Australian in *Kangaroo*. Boyd has the fortune to have, as many of his characters have, what he calls "a geographical schizophrenia."

The most telling of his novels deal wittily and tranquilly with the ardours, anxieties, tragedies, pettinesses and passions of a many-branched Anglo-Australian family. As its members—happy-go-lucky, restless, civilized, eccentric—shuttle physically between the Old World of England and Europe, and the New World of Victoria (Australia) and Tasmania, they also as-it-were shuttle emotionally between them, viewing situations most Australianly in England, most Englishly in Australia. Since Boyd's novels are parti-biographical, parti-autobiographical, he writes bi-focally: experience, wisdom, and a dry wit give his style a transparency that is fascinating. His characters are as exquisitely recorded as the earliest nineteenth-century photographers recorded their sitters, and the characters' foibles and despairs, machinations and chivalries, engross the reader even more than they patently engross him. Nevertheless, as annalist, Boyd does not lose his head but remains throughout level-browed and clear-eyed, almost lens-eyed: a Montaigne-like fearlessness strikes through the Montaigne-like quietude of his work. Because of his controlled absorption with them, his characters and their milieu cannot but take on a three-dimensional existence. All is charged with a very life-like life. Absorption is, however, not all. Boyd not only knows every nuance of the social behaviour, moral attitudes, ambitions, spiritual blindnesses, and all-too-human quirks of his characters but has the skill adroitly to manage the nuances of vocabulary by which nuance can best be presented. One observes this skill, this art, at work in the novels of such writers as Henry James and Elizabeth Bowen, and Galsworthy in the better-written of the Forsyte books. Boyd, however, eschews the diffusion and elaboration these writers often do not avoid, particularly in their later novels. He has his own unique limpidity: Edith Wharton at her peak comes to mind.

He reveals a clue to an aspect of his method in *A Difficult Young Man*. In dealing with the difficult young man himself, Dominic Langton, a sombre, troubled and haunting character, somewhat Heathcliffean, at one and the same time fierce and sensitive, alarming and touching, Boyd writes, "I can only proceed like the painter Sisley who, when he wished to convey an effect of green, put a dot of blue on his canvas, and then a dot of yellow beside it. From a little way off the green thus appears more lively and luminous. So I must put these dots of contradictory colour next to each other in the hope that Dominic may ultimately appear alive." Dominic ultimately does, very. The method works as perfectly as the author's explanation of it does. Boyd's style, like Sisley's green, *is* luminous—and lively. He conveys his vision of things to the reader in absolutely unambiguous prose; the vision, at nearly all points, is as crystal-clear as the prose.

He stands at the opposite end of the creative field to Patrick White whose characters are manifestly fictional, and must grope readerwards through a maze of misanthropy and decoration. Boyd's pellucid style is its own decoration, generates its own light in which even the slightest gesture or smallest gaffe is immediately and vividly seen to have a proper importance in the course of events. His instinct for selecting the significant from the nugatory rarely falters. His ear for dialogue is sharp, and he has a flair for injecting the succinctly right dose of it in exactly the right place: no wastes of non-essential conversation mar the well-laid-out compactness of his novels. Although these novels, none of them ponderously long, each has a large and mercurial and even quasi-nomadic cast, many and various settings, and a profusion of events, there is no disorder in narration; all is uncluttered. Boyd achieves this sense of spaciousness in a small space by pincering out the essential, and so arranging it, so lighting it, that it stands out stereoscopically. He uses, too, the classic devices. Often the most harrowing crises, cruel let-downs or squalid liaisons are conveyed to us by a version of the Messenger in a Euripidean tragedy, as for example when the tipsy Arthur gossips of Austin and Hetty's far-off but far-reaching adulteries in *The Cardboard Crown*.

On the other hand, a number of poignant or shocking incidents—a child killed, a fiancé left standing at the altar, a beloved house abandoned, a love-affair ended— are delineated dead-pan, briefly, without melodrama, and seemingly with heartless calm but so also is the resultant anguish or guilt or remorse. He spares none of his characters except those whose nature puts them beyond attack; and certainly pays no lip-service to the cult of those many present-day writers who are obsessed by the isolated state, the over-sensitized personality.

If, sometimes, he writes nostalgically, wit tinges what could be saccharine with bittersweetness. If, sometimes, a *snobisme* shows, he classifies it sharply, drawing a line not between aristocrat and working-class but around the middle-class. He sees the world as worldly, a compound of the civilized and the uncivilized, and writes of it in a worldly and civilized way. Never naive, he is nonetheless never uninnocent nor jaded: an alloy of sophistication and innocence is the oil feeding the incandescent flame of his style.

—Hal Porter

**BOYLE, Kay.** American. Born in St. Paul, Minnesota, 19 February 1903. Educated at the Cincinnati Conservatory of Music; Ohio Mechanics Institute, 1917–19. Married Richard Brault in 1923 (divorced); Laurence Vail, 1931 (divorced); Baron Joseph von Franckenstein (died, 1963); has six children. Lived in Europe for 30 years. Foreign Correspondent, *The New Yorker* magazine, 1946–53. Since 1963, Professor of English, San Francisco State College. Lecturer, New School for Social Research, New York, 1962; Fellow, Wesleyan University, Middletown, Connecticut, 1963; Director, New York Writers Conference, Wagner College, New York, 1964; Fellow, Radcliffe Institute for Independent Study, Cambridge, Massachusetts, 1965; Writer-in-Residence, Hollins College, Virginia, 1970–71. Recipient: Guggenheim Fellowship, 1934, 1961; O. Henry Award, 1935, 1941. D.Litt., Columbia College, Chicago, 1971. Member, National Institute of Arts and Letters. Address: c/o A. Watkins Inc., 77 Park Avenue, New York, New York 10016, U.S.A.

PUBLICATIONS

Novels

> *Plagued by the Nightingale.* New York, Smith, and London, Cape, 1931.
> *Year Before Last.* New York, Smith, and London, Faber, 1932.
> *Gentlemen, I Address You Privately.* New York, Smith, 1933; London, Faber, 1934.
> *My Next Bride.* New York, Harcourt Brace, 1934; London, Faber, 1935.
> *Death of a Man.* New York, Harcourt Brace, and London, Faber, 1936.
> *Monday Night.* New York, Harcourt Brace, and London, Faber, 1938.
> *Primer for Combat.* New York, Simon and Schuster, 1942; London, Faber, 1943.
> *Avalanche.* New York, Simon and Schuster, and London, Faber, 1944.
> *A Frenchman Must Die.* New York, Simon and Schuster, and London, Faber, 1946.
> *1939.* New York, Simon and Schuster, and London, Faber, 1948.
> *His Human Majesty.* New York, McGraw Hill, 1949; London, Faber, 1950.
> *The Seagull on the Step.* New York, Knopf, and London, Faber, 1955.
> *Generation Without Farewell.* New York, Knopf, 1960.

Short Stories

> *Short Stories.* Paris, Black Sun Press, 1929.
> *Wedding Day and Other Stories.* New York, Smith, 1930; London, Faber, 1932.
> *The First Lover and Other Stories.* New York, Random House, 1933; London, Faber, 1937.

*The White Horses of Vienna and Other Stories.*  New York, Harcourt Brace, 1936;
   London, Faber, 1937.
*The Crazy Hunter: Three Short Novels.*  New York, Harcourt Brace, 1940; as *The
   Crazy Hunter and Other Stories*, London, Faber, 1940.
*Thirty Stories.*  New York, Simon and Schuster, 1946; London, Faber, 1948.
*The Smoking Mountain: Stories of Post War Germany.*  New York, McGraw Hill,
   1951; London, Faber, 1952.
*Three Short Novels.*  Boston, Beacon Press, 1958.
*Nothing Ever Breaks Except the Heart.*  New York, Doubleday, 1966.


Verse

*A Glad Day.*  New York, New Directions, 1938.
*American Citizen: Naturalized in Leadville, Colorado.*  New York, Simon and Schuster,
   1944.
*Collected Poems.*  New York, Knopf, 1962.
*Testament for My Students.*  New York, Doubleday, 1970.


Other

*The Youngest Camel* (juvenile).  Boston, Little Brown, and London, Faber, 1939;
   revised edition, New York, Harper, 1959; Faber, 1960.
*Breaking the Silence: Why a Mother Tells Her Son about the Nazi Era.*  New York,
   Institute of Human Relations Press-American Jewish Committee, 1962.
*Pinky: The Cat Who Liked to Sleep* (juvenile).  New York, Crowell Collier, 1966.
*Pinky in Persia* (juvenile).  New York, Crowell Collier, 1968.
*Being Geniuses Together*, with Robert McAlmon.  New York, Doubleday, 1968;
   London, Joseph, 1970.
*The Long Walk at San Francisco State and Other Essays.*  New York, Grove Press,
   1970.

Editor, with others, *365 Days*.  New York, Harcourt Brace, and London, Cape, 1936.
Editor, *The Autobiography of Emanuel Carnevali*.  New York, Horizon Press, 1967.
Editor, *Enough of Dying! An Anthology of Peace Writings*.  New York, Dell, 1972.

Translator, *Don Juan*, by Joseph Delteil.  New York, Smith, 1931.
Translator, *Mr. Knife, Miss Fork*, by R. Crevel.  Paris, Black Sun Press, 1931.
Translator, *Devil in the Flesh*, by Raymond Radiguet.  New York, Smith, 1932;
   London, Grey Walls Press, 1949.

Acted as ghost-writer for the books *Relations and Complications: Being the Recollections of H.H. the Dayang Muda of Sarawak*, by Gladys Palmer Brooke, London, Lane,
1929, and *Yellow Dusk*, by Bettina Bedwell, London, Hurst and Blackett, 1937.


Kay Boyle comments:

   Thomas Mann once said that if the writers of Germany through their vision and their
expression of that vision had made richer and more impelling promises than those Hitler
made, it would have been Hitler, and not the writers of Germany, who would have been
forced into exile. It is *always* the intellectuals, however we may shrink from the chilling
sound of that word, and, above all, it is *always* the writers who must bear the full weight of

moral responsibility. Frenchmen will tell you that the decision to speak out is the vocation and life-long peril by which the intellectual must live. I remember the days in Paris when we who were writers, or painters, or composers, wrote pamphlets and distributed them in the streets and cafés. I remember when we signed manifestos and read them aloud on street-corners, following without humility whatsoever in the tradition of Pascal, Voltaire, Chateaubriand, Victor Hugo, Zola, so that the world would know exactly where we stood; for we considered ourselves a portion of the contemporary conscience, and we had no pity on the compromiser or the poor in spirit of our time. But now the pamphlet and the manifesto are practically non-existent in American letters, although here in America they flourished with great vitality in pre-revolutionary times. American intellectuals, indeed, prepared and oriented our revolution: the only revolution in history, one French critic has pointed out, which did not destroy the intellectuals who had prepared it, but which carried them to power. "By tradition," this French critic said,

> the European intellectual has a special character—a vocation beyond the limits of his own profession of writing or science or teaching. He believes himself called to a more universal responsibility than are other men, and that is to keep watch on the world, and to call the plays as he sees them, at whatever risk to himself. The dangers of his position are as real as poverty, exile, prison or death; and— unlike the soldier or the priest—he has no organized body to defend him.

—from *Liberation* (New York), June 1960

\*    \*    \*

What I remember most in my reading of Kay Boyle are specific scenes—the sight of the sea tide building and crashing through the mouth of a river; a young man, sick with tuberculosis, leaning over a basin to vomit blood; a bus-driver arguing recklessly with his passengers while the bus careens along a cliff road; a run-over dog pulling itself forward, as its spilled-out entrails drag and turn white in the dust; Americans and Germans waiting over real fox holes in a German forest, ready to club the young foxes as they come out, and underground, moving through the tunnels, now near, now distant, the sound of the yelping pack and pursuing dog.

Miss Boyle's concern here is to heighten our responses to these events. She asks us not only to respond to the vivid and extreme sensations which they present, but to see them in sharp moral and aesthetic terms, as beautiful or dangerous or agonizingly brutal.

It is this intense kind of involvement that Miss Boyle asks from us generally. She offers very little neutral ground on which we may look at these scenes on our own. The youthful idealists, who play a major role in her novels, will give us, I think, the right emotional cues for appreciating her work. Inexperienced in the ways of the world, their feelings are open and unmitigated; they do not quite believe in evil and yet they are deeply troubled by pain and injustice. Bridget, Victoria John, Mary Farrant, Milly Roberts—young Americans whose destinies are connected with Europe—are such figures. If the fictional situation would seem to echo James, there are major differences in its development, for Kay Boyle's morality is active rather than introspective.

Indeed, whether her heroes be young Americans in Europe or former German soldiers, they express themselves in concrete acts—Mary Farrant makes her way up a rocky cliff to save the dwarf Marrakech; a middle-aged dandy, terrified of horses, enters the stall of a blind horse, and, for his daughter's sake, stays there while it kicks and rears in fright; Jaeger, a German journalist and ex-P.O.W. from the Afrika Corps, crawls over a heap of sliding rubble to give a cigarette to a power shovel driver trapped inside his cab.

What her heroes have in common is the courage to act—it is the only thing people ever remember, one character says. But action is, of course, no guarantee of success. Involved in every human venture, it would seem, are elements that bring about its destruction. Those elements may be physical nature—not malevolent but merely indifferent—stupid accident, or man's incapacity to make a social world that is supportive and helpful.

Thus, in *Plagued by the Nightingale*, the closely-bound world of a French family becomes so destructive that three daughters and a son wait desperately for an escape. Only Charlotte, the fourth daughter, loves her richly domestic life and her place within the family; and only Charlotte is deprived of it by death. In *Year Before Last*, Martin, a young poet, dying of tuberculosis, and Eve, his aunt, are bound together by their dedication to art. Yet the emotion that shapes their lives is Eve's cruel jealousy of Hanah, whom Martin loves and who would shield him from the agonies of poverty and illness. In *My Next Bride*, the artist, Sorrel, uses the common funds of the art colony to buy a magnificent and expensive auto-mobile. In this shallow attempt to escape poverty and ugliness, he betrays the destitute craftsmen who work for him, as well as the artistic creed he has professed to live by.

Miss Boyle's novels have, I think, a potentially tragic feeling. The qualities she projects in her strongest characters—courage to act as a counter to failure, energy rather than hope-less despair—offer this possibility. Very often, it seems wasted, for although Miss Boyle insists upon courageous action, the possible choices she sees in such action are limited. Also, perhaps equally harmful, these choices do not necessarily grow out of the fictional situation; they seem fixed from the beginning. It is for this reason, perhaps, that her characters sometimes take unreal positions—in *Avalanche*, the mountain men are total in their dedica-tion to a good cause, the German agent, total in his dedication to a bad one; in *The Seagull on the Step*, the doctor commits melodramatic villanies, the teacher-reformer, heroic deeds; in *Generation Without Farewell*, the American colonel is brutal and gross, his wife and daughter are gentle and sensitive. Such extreme divisions in realistic novels are unconvincing. In relation to this kind of fictional situation, we are no longer active readers but spectators, waiting for the author to tell us what is right, what is sad and pitiable, what is mean.

There is a problem also, I think, in Miss Boyle's wish to discover in technology and social reform, the elements of high moral adventure. In *Generation Without Farewell*, for example, Jaeger, the German journalist, and his fellow-townsmen drive through the night to pick up an iron lung for Christoph Horn, dying of bulbar polio, and arrive back in time to save Horn's life, if only for a few days. Later, after Horn's death, the director of America House, Honerkamp, erects a huge thermometer in the town square to register donations for an iron lung that, hopefully, the town will now buy for itself. In both instances, we are expected to share the emotions of the major figures, of Jaeger, who sees the journey as "keeping death at bay," and of Honerkamp, who believes that the Germans will learn something about democracy from this community chest effort.

The focus here is on technical solutions—the iron lung for saving a life; the thermometer, for registering a common social effort. Both are stock images that offer very little oppor-tunity for a fresh response. More important, perhaps, they are mechanical and static. Our involvement with them is necessarily limited, for they have no power to draw us into a situation in which our feelings may be deepened and extended. The best we can offer is a set response.

Yet, I am sure that Miss Boyle would never exclude these social possibilities, whatever the literary risks. In an early poem, she uses the phrase "tough taste." It is a good phrase, I think, to describe her conception of what she is doing.

What gives her work strength are not these special interests, but her understanding that our human connections lie finally in our limitations, most of all in our common mortality. From the beginning, she has had this kind of knowledge.

At moments we see it expressed with startling clarity. In her first novel, Charlotte's family is hastily called to her bedside. Those who have waited through the day—Charlotte's young children, her sisters—make their way through the dark, wet fall night, to Charlotte's house, up the great stairs and to her room. There, they wait in silence until the door is opened, and the children walk "calmly into the roar of Charlotte's death." In her most recent novel of post-war Germany, a power shovel in downtown Frankfurt accidentally un-earths an underground air raid shelter and releases a single survivor, entombed there since the war. As the mad, tattered figure runs wildly across the upturned ground, bewildered by his resurrection, any ideals we may hold about nationality, military success, moral justification, diminish into nothingness. Only a sense of our common inhumanity persists.

In the short stories also, Kay Boyle shows us the complicated devastation that human beings can work on one another and on themselves. Among the best are the stories of post-war Germany in *The Smoking Mountain*. The scale is modest—an American army wife shops in a PX supermarket, three boys search out a center for lost children, a group of local actors put on a play at a Weinstube—the right dimension to make us understand such a catastrophe as an individual, day-to-day experience. Likewise, in the brilliant reportorial piece that opens the collection, on the murder trial of a minor Gestapo official, Heinrich Baab, nothing is obscured by the blare of historical significance. Baab, accused of fifty-seven murders, was, as Miss Boyle says, a "small criminal." For those who sometimes have doubts about the relationship between art and the direct observation of experience, these stories should give a clear answer.

—Jacqueline Hoefer

BRADBURY, Malcolm (Stanley). British. Born in Sheffield, Yorkshire, 7 September 1932. Educated at West Bridgford Grammar School; University College of Leicester, B.A. in English 1953; Queen Mary College, London, M.A. in English 1955; Indiana University, Bloomington, 1955–56; University of Manchester, 1956–58, Ph.D. in American Studies 1963. Married Elizabeth Salt in 1959; has two children. Staff Tutor in Literature, Extra-Mural Department, University of Hull, Yorkshire, 1959–61; Lecturer in English, University of Birmingham, 1961–65. Lecturer in English, 1965–67, Senior Lecturer, 1967–69, Reader, 1969–70, and since 1970, Professor of American Studies, University of East Anglia, Norwich. Recipient: British Association for American Studies Junior Fellowship, 1958; American Council of Learned Societies Fellowship, 1965. Visiting Fellow, All Souls College, Oxford, 1969. Member of the Committee of the British Association for American Studies. Address: 14 Heigham Grove, Norwich NOR 14G; or, Lockington House Cottage, Lockington, near Driffield, East Yorkshire, England.

PUBLICATIONS

Novels

   *Eating People Is Wrong*. London, Secker and Warburg, 1959; New York, Knopf, 1960.
   *Stepping Westward*. London, Secker and Warburg, 1965; Boston, Houghton Mifflin, 1966.

Uncollected Short Stories

   "The Adult Education Class", in *Transatlantic Review* (London and New York), Summer 1966.
   "A Very Hospitable Person", in *Ideal Home* (London), February 1969.
   "A Breakdown", in *Transatlantic Review* (London and New York), Winter 1969–70.

Plays

> *Between These Four Walls*, with David Lodge and James Duckett (produced Birmingham, 1963).
> *Slap in the Middle*, with David Lodge, David Turner, and James Duckett (produced Birmingham, 1965).

Plays broadcast on BBC radio.


Verse

> *Two Poets*, with Allan Rodway.   Nottingham, Byron Press, 1966.


Other

> *Phogey! How to Have Class in a Classless Society*.   London, Parrish, 1960.
> *All Dressed Up and Nowhere to Go*.   London, Parrish, 1962.
> *Evelyn Waugh*.   Edinburgh, Oliver and Boyd, 1964.
> *What Is a Novel?*   London, Arnold, 1969.
> *The Social Context of Modern English Literature*.   Oxford, Blackwell, and New York, Schocken Books, 1971.
> *Possibilities: Essays on the State of the Novel*.   London and New York, Oxford University Press, 1972.

> Editor, *E. M. Forster: A Collection of Critical Essays*.   New York, Prentice Hall, 1965.
> Editor, *E. M. Forster's "A Passage to India": A Selection of Critical Essays*.   London, Macmillan, 1970.
> Editor, with Eric Mottram, *U.S.A. and Latin America*, vol. 3 of *The Penguin Companion to Literature*.   London, Allen Lane-Penguin Press, and New York, McGraw Hill, 1971.
> Editor, with David Palmer, *The American Novel and the Nineteen Twenties*.   London, Arnold, 1971.


Manuscript Collection: Nottingham Public Library.


Malcolm Bradbury comments:

Both of my novels (and the third one I am now writing) are set in universities; the first in a "redbrick", the second, in part, on an American campus, and the third in a new university. Such criticism as has discussed my work seems to have treated it as a species of the campus novel; I am uneasy with the designation. The settings are relatively incidental (any intellectual milieu might do as well), and my main concern has been, within a more or less comic framework, to explore problems and dilemmas of liberalism and issues of moral responsibility. My main characters are typically confused but concerned moral agents; their liberalism is less a political than a moral perspective; their aim is decency and goodwill, and the comedy and indeed the potential tragedy or at least pathos arises when the world, in its contingency, refuses to let them, or blurs the moral perspectives they feel they possess.

I regard comedy as a main means of fulfilling my purposes because it seems to me the best way of distilling my sense not only of the moral difficulties and insufficiencies of men, but also of the difficult pressures of the claims of modern history on those who live through it; it allows me a certain modified realism and tolerance, and a dialectical range within myself. Perhaps another way of saying that is to remark that comedy allows me the chance to demonstrate the ironical situation of values which concern me, allows me in a time when the language of value has little force in modern fiction to explore them at all.

Critics today—I say this as one myself—have a strong tendency to prescribe the limits of reality, to say how little there is of it with which the novelist may deal, to lay their stress on the game—like elements of the fictive act; that, as critics, is one of *their* essential modern fictions, and I can see how they come to it while not necessarily finding myself amidst such problems when I set out to write a novel.

The fact remains that my earlier novels do owe a considerable amount to a liberal climate which is now threatened and could perhaps be dying; and though in the two published novels these strains on liberalism were part of my theme I find myself, in my new book, putting it under much more onerous threats. To this extent I do see my kind of writing as under an historical pressure. *Eating People Is Wrong*, which was largely written when I was an undergraduate, and then revised much later, in part sees the world of the academy and the intellect from outside; but it respects it and grants it goodwill, rather than condemning it as many students now do. *Stepping Westward* likewise tries to see that we can be misused by the historicist, political mind whether it be radical or reactionary. If both books end by linking the desire to mediate with inertia or a failure of will, this is not to condemn the centre of tolerance that I try to create in them both, even if that tolerance itself has comic dimensions. As for what I am now doing, I find myself increasingly obsessed with formal problems and, linked with that, a far greater ironic distance from my characters and any worlds I can give them to inhabit.

*       *       *

Malcolm Bradbury is well acquainted with universities both domestic and trans-Atlantic, and he is an astute critic of literature and ideas. This is most evident in his novels *Eating People Is Wrong* and *Stepping Westward*. The first is a satire of British academic life, the second of American.

These works strike far more deeply into the cultures they mock than *Lucky Jim* or even *One Fat Englishman*, although the themes are comparable. Bradbury's heroes philander with more skill than Amis's, and although their affairs do not culminate in the hilarious scene of ridiculousness that seems to be the Amis trademark, they are as much fun spread over a long period of time.

There is a greater variety of characters in *Eating People Is Wrong* than in the American novel, partly because the presence of Commonwealth characters (the title is a statement solemnly enunciated by an African to whom it evidently was a fresh idea) and because evidently Bradbury sees individualism more clearly in the English than in the American characters, all of whom seem cut from the same piece of plastic.

Moreover the plot of *Stepping Westward* is more dramatic and its satire more comprehensive. Benedict Arnold University, where Bradbury's British protagonist is summoned as writer-in-residence, is impossibly in the center of America culturally and geographically, "somewhere near the point where the various wests collide." Save for Walker, the English visitor, a reactionary Central European emigré, and a sophisticated New York girl with whom Walker runs away to Mexico at mid-term, the characters are all caricatures, but remarkably lifelike ones.

Bradbury is able to poke pitying fun at all kinds of American quirks except those of the Deep South by crowding returning Americans into the ship Walker crosses on (including a group of female college bagpipers), and by sending him from New York to California and back. The academic sequence, which takes up only about a third of the book, toward the center, serves to stick the whole thing together, and it is unified and dramatized by a typical piece of American anti-communist paranoia; each teacher must take an oath of loyalty to the United States. Walker, as a British citizen and a stubborn one at that, refuses and creates a hubbub he runs away from.

Bradbury's novels thus far are delightfully entertaining, but they are entertaining about too many things, and perhaps in too many ways. In observation of the oddities of people and places, his wit is keen; and in the creation of situations that approach the absurd he shows outstanding humour. Perhaps those two approaches do not fit together.

On the other hand his style is so lucid and straightforward that the reader does not notice how tightly packed with witty observations it is unless he goes back and closely analyses it. For example, the "Prologue" and "Epilogue" of *Stepping Westward*, both set at Benedict Arnold University, make a comprehensive satire of American higher education, a superb exercise of wit, yet they humourously tie in with the loyalty oath plot through an ironic turn in faculty politics.

In the first, the committee to choose a writer-in-residence, including representatives from Business Administration, Physical Education, and the university administration, are persuaded by an ambitious young associate professor of English to appoint Walker, whom none of them had ever heard of before, including the Head of the English Department. In the central part of the book Walker, entangled but not involved in their maneuverings, serves as a catalyst. In the end the Head is out, the associate professor is made Head, and the funds for a writer-in-residence have been diverted to finance a literary magazine in his charge.

There have been many novels about academic life published since the war, both in Britain and America. From *Lucky Jim* to *The Masters*, and from *Purely Academic* (by Stringfellow Barr) to Carlos Baker's transplantation of Snow's situation to Princeton University—where it actually happened. Bradbury is the only writer, however, to have treated the absurdities and shams of universities on both sides of the Atlantic, and to have done as well as the best with both.

—William Bittner

---

**BRADBURY, Ray (Douglas).** American. Born in Waukegan, Illinois, 22 August 1920. Educated at Los Angeles High School. Married Marguerite Susan McClure in 1947; has four children. Full-time Writer since 1943. President, Science-Fantasy Writers of America, 1951–53. Member of the Board of Directors, Screen Writers Guild of America, 1957–61. Recipient: O. Henry Prize, 1947, 1948; Benjamin Franklin Award, 1954; National Institute of Arts and Letters grant, 1954; Boys' Clubs of America Junior Book Award, 1956; Golden Eagle Award, for screenplay, 1957. Address: 10265 Cheviot Drive, Los Angeles, California 90064, U.S.A.

PUBLICATIONS

Novels

*Fahrenheit 451.* New York, Ballantine, 1953; London, Hart Davis, 1963.
*Something Wicked This Way Comes.* New York, Simon and Schuster, 1962; London, Hart Davis, 1963.
*The Halloween Tree.* New York, Knopf, 1972.

Short Stories

*Dark Carnival.* Sauk City, Wisconsin, Arkham House, 1947; London, Hamish Hamilton, 1948.

*The Martian Chronicles*.   New York, Doubleday, 1950.
*The Illustrated Man*.   New York, Doubleday, 1951; London, Hart Davis, 1952.
*The Golden Apples of the Sun*.   New York, Doubleday, and London, Hart Davis, 1953.
*The October Country*.   New York, Ballantine, 1955; London, Hart Davis, 1956.
*Dandelion Wine*.   New York, Doubleday, and London, Hart Davis, 1957.
*A Medicine for Melancholy*.   New York, Doubleday, 1959; as *The Day It Rained Forever*, London, Hart Davis, 1959.
*The Machineries of Joy: Short Stories*.   New York, Simon and Schuster, and London, Hart Davis, 1964.
*The Vintage Bradbury*.   New York, Random House, 1965.
–*The Autumn People*.   New York, Ballantine, 1965.
*Tomorrow Midnight*.   New York, Ballantine, 1966.
*I Sing the Body Electric!*   New York, Knopf, 1969; London, Hart Davis, 1970.

Plays

*The Meadow*, in *Best One-Act Plays of 1947–48*.   New York, Dodd Mead, 1948.
*The Anthem Sprinters and Other Antics* (produced Los Angeles, 1968).   New York, Dial Press, 1963.
*The World of Ray Bradbury* (produced Los Angeles, 1964; New York, 1965).
*The Wonderful Ice-Cream Suit* (produced Los Angeles, 1965).
*The Day It Rained Forever*.   New York, French, 1966.
*The Pedestrian*.   New York, French, 1966.
*Christus Apollo*, music by Jerry Goldsmith (produced Los Angeles, 1969).
*The Wonderful Ice Cream Suit and Other Plays*.   New York, Bantam, 1972.

Screenplays: *It Came from Outer Space*, 1952; *Moby Dick*, 1954; *Icarus Montgolfier Wright*, 1961; *The Picasso Summer*, 1968.

Verse

*When Elephants Last in the Dooryard Bloomed*.   New York, Knopf, 1972.

Other

*Switch on the Night* (juvenile).   New York, Pantheon Books, and London, Hart Davis, 1955.
*R Is for Rocket* (juvenile).   New York, Doubleday, 1962; London, Hart Davis, 1968.
*S Is for Space* (juvenile).   New York, Doubleday, 1966; London, Hart Davis, 1968.

Editor, *Timeless Stories for Today and Tomorrow*.   New York, Ballantine, 1952.
Editor, *The Circus of Dr. Lao*.   New York, Bantam, 1956.

Bibliography: in *Magazine of Fantasy and Science Fiction* (New York), May 1963.

Critical Studies: interview with the author in *Show* (New York), December 1964; introduction by Gilbert Highet to *The Vintage Bradbury*, 1965; "The Revival of Fantasy" by Russell Kirk, in *Triumph* (Washington, D.C.), May 1968; "Ray Bradbury's *Dandelion Wine*: Themes, Sources, and Style" by Marvin E. Mengeling, in *English Journal* (Champaign, Illinois), October 1971.

*     *     *

Although he has written the novels *Something Wicked This Way Comes* and *Fahrenheit 451*, Ray Bradbury is primarily a writer of short stories. Ever the storyteller, Bradbury aims in each story at producing the horror, the surprise, or the single dominant effect of Poe, one of his principal mentors. Nonetheless, his short story collections—notably *The Martian Chronicles* and *Dandelion Wine*—have an overall meaning which exceeds the meaning of the parts. Although he often seems to write about disparate bits of experience, Bradbury does have an identifiable view of life.

"Here There Be Tygers" (1951; collected in *R Is for Rocket*) contains several of the elements of that view. Astronauts land on a previously unknown planet. One of them fears that there are dangers ("tygers") on the planet, and he wishes to kill whatever is alive and to exploit the remaining dead matter. He fulfills his own prophecy: the planet kills him. There *are* tygers on this pastoral world, but the other astronauts are drawn to them. The planet is not dead but alive, and when the astronauts dare to dream their favorite forbidden dreams into it, they awake to find them true. Bradbury follows Wordsworth, Coleridge, and Keats in believing that the childlike imagination can create a wonderful but also terrifying, and temporary, pleasure dome. All but one of the astronauts leave the strange Eden.

In *The Martian Chronicles*, the Eden is Mars. The ancient, delicate Martian civilization is destroyed by crass, polluting, materialistic American invaders. Bradbury the dystopian never entirely shuts out Bradbury the believer in fresh starts, however. "The Million Year Picnic" (1946) concerns a family which escapes from nuclear war on Earth and uses the psychic energy or imaginative force of the dead Martians to make themselves into "Martians," capable of starting a new and more humane civilization.

*The Illustrated Man* and *Fahrenheit 451* continue the theme of the imagination threatened but ultimately triumphant. In "The Exiles" Poe, Bierce, and other writers of the fantastic and the macabre perish with their creations on Mars. Fahrenheit 451 is the temperature which the firemen of the future generate to burn all books. Both works point ways out, however. In *Fahrenheit 451* a rebel band memorizes books. "The Rocket," last story in *The Illustrated Man*, concerns a junkman who makes a rocket ship out of tin cans, which creates for his children the illusion of going to Mars.

Thus Bradbury believes that the imagination may operate in humble and private places as well as in space, and that it is as important to make familiar things new as to make the new things of the space age familiar. *Dandelion Wine* grafts suggestions of horror and science fiction machines onto "Green Town," Illinois (presumably a version of the Waukegan, Illinois, of Bradbury's childhood). A man who can remember the Civil War past becomes a "time machine" to the boys who listen to his stories. Electric cars, lawnmowers, and trolleys become as mysterious as spaceships. Each day of the summer of 1928 a flask of dandelion wine—a noble thing made from a common plant—is put away for winter use. Bradbury's short stories are flasks of this wine: each day, or each story, is a little different and must be tasted separately. No single flask of wine contains all the wonders and terrors of our kaleidoscopic world.

The stories of *A Medicine for Melancholy* and *The Machineries of Joy* use terror and delight to purge the reader of melancholy. In "The Day It Rained Forever" seventy-one-year-old Miss Hillgood, who has let her life pass by while she attended only to music, arrives at Joe Terle's Desert Hotel, where for years past there has been rain only one day of the year. When she begins to play, her music suddenly ceases to be sterile, and it magically causes a permanent end of the drought. To Bradbury, the unexpected can always happen. Life can always take a new turn precisely when and where you think of giving it up.

Both *The Machineries of Joy* and *I Sing the Body Electric!* contain Mars stories and others in the familiar Bradbury manner. But (particularly in the latter book) Bradbury experiments with replacing fantasy and plot twists with atmosphere, interior emotion, and character development. Too often the resulting stories lack the motivation and the logic which the fantastic never required. But Bradbury is a flexible and resourceful writer, and he may yet make successful use of the techniques of mainstream fiction.

Perhaps Bradbury's greatest value is as a social critic and a commentator on technology. Perceiving the madness of expansionist technology, Bradbury no longer shares the teenage boy's worship of the astronaut corps in "R Is for Rocket" (1943). But his Martians have a more advanced technology than Earth's, in many respects—their cities last, and Earthmen's do not. "Space travel has made children of us all," says the philosopher on the verso of *The Martian Chronicles*. The American astronauts are childish idiots, but space travel also makes possible the childlike wonder of the million-year picnic. In "The End of the Beginning" (*A Medicine for Melancholy*) a man pauses from mowing his lawn to watch his son rocket into the twilight air to make the first space station. Bradbury suggests the unity of all technology: Ezekiel's wheel in the middle of the air, the wheeling space station and lawn-mower, and the wheels in the man's watch. Moreover, life and technology are interrelated. The amoeba's climb from water to land prepared for man's climb from the Earth. It is now a new age, but the man finishes mowing the lawn after watching the rocket launching. Bradbury is not against technology. He simply believes that man must look around and back at the same time that he looks forward. For attending to the needs and the delight of his readers, and for distinguishing as almost no other writer (science fiction or otherwise) has distinguished between American expansionist technology and technology *per se*, Ray Bradbury deserves close attention and the highest praise.

—Curtis C. Smith

---

**BRAGG, Melvyn.** British. Born in Cumberland, 6 November 1939. Educated at Nelson Thomlinson Grammar School, Wigton, Cumberland, 1950–59; Wadham College, Oxford, M.A. (honours) in Modern History 1961. Married Lise Roche (died, 1971); has one child. Producer, BBC Television, London, 1961–67. Since 1969, Member of the Arts Council Literature Panel. Recipient: Writers Guild Award, for screenplay, 1966; Rhys Memorial Prize, 1968; Northern Arts Association Prose Award, 1970; Silver Pen Award, 1970. Fellow, Royal Society of Literature, 1970. Address: 9 Gayton Road, London N.W.3, England.

PUBLICATIONS

Novels

*For Want of a Nail*.   London, Secker and Warburg, and New York, Knopf, 1965.
*The Second Inheritance*.   London, Secker and Warburg, 1966; New York, Knopf, 1967.
*Without a City Wall*.   London, Secker and Warburg, 1968; New York, Knopf, 1969.
*The Hired Man*.   London, Secker and Warburg, and New York, Knopf, 1969.
*A Place in England*.   London, Secker and Warburg, 1970; New York, Knopf, 1971.
*The Nerve*.   London, Secker and Warburg, 1971.
*The Hunt*.   London, Secker and Warburg, 1972.

Plays

Screenplays: *Play Dirty*, 1969; *Isadora*, 1969; *The Music Lovers*, 1971.

Plays and documentaries produced on BBC Television.

Critical Studies: essay by Roger Pybus, in *Stand* (Newcastle upon Tyne), Summer 1970; essay by Kenneth John Achuty, in *Kenyon Review* (Gambier, Ohio), no. 127, 1971.

Melvyn Bragg comments:

The ways in which I came to write are sketched in the last chapters of *A Place in England*: they are made the notions of a fictional self—Douglas Tallentire.

Present ideas on fiction are represented in the novel *The Nerve* and in an essay "Class and the Novel" in *Times Literary Supplement* (London), 15 October 1971.

*       *       *

Melvyn Bragg began with a tragic story of wasted human resources in *For Want of a Nail*. Precisely for "want of a nail," i.e. parental affection and interest, Tom Graham fails to integrate his faculties and remarkable abilities. He is able, finally, to acknowledge his sterility and ignorance; and such awareness may be his first true step forward. Not all aspects of his situation register clearly, but it is one that is poignant and deeply felt. *The Second Inheritance* rises superior to its faltering beginning in which Bragg changes focus frequently to present figures from opposing social classes. The book reaches power when the characters are at last locked in conflict. John Nelson, a farmer of more than average attainments, becomes the lover of the aristocratic Patricia Langley, who is willing to give herself to him physically but not socially. John's first inheritance is his father's farm, his second, the assurance which the conquering of his passion brings.

*Without a City Wall* is one of the most distinguished of recent novels. Theme and structure reinforce each other as Bragg traces, first, the awakening of passion in Richard Godwin, a self-imposed exile from the chaos of London, for Janice Beattie, a Cumberland girl of unusual intelligence and powerful ambition; and then, the challenges that the life of consummated passion entails for both of them. The drama develops principally from Janice whose ambitions and fastidiousness prove stronger than sexual passion or her sense of responsibility to others. Her passion for Richard contracts, while his for her continues to expand. Richard is driven to the brink of self-destruction but recoils in time to force Janice to some kind of modus vivendi between the claims of his passion and the claims of her individuality. The sombre and remorseless quality of Bragg's vision is sustained throughout as is his insight into the complexities of human motivation.

The alternation of intensity and apathy in the passional life is again one subject explored in *The Hired Man*. Covering the years 1898 to 1920 in the life of John and Emily Tallentire, the novel articulates the nuances of emotion which the rustic characters would themselves never be able to define so sharply. Communication between a man and a woman becomes a function of the body; and tragic estrangement develops when perfect physical accord is broken. After Emily's death at forty John is where he was at the beginning, a man for casual hire on the great farms but now with all zest gone. The book ranges less widely than its predecessor; but Bragg's art in it is notably concentrated and authentic, especially in his honest portrayal of the hard lives of agricultural laborers in the early twentieth century.

Less interest accrues to the career of Joseph Tallentire, John's son, in *A Place in England*. Bragg is much less close to Joseph than to John; in fact, the most memorable pages of *A Place in England* feature the now patriarchal John himself. After much struggle Joseph is able to "be his own man" as owner of a public house; but his success is undercut by the disintegration of his marriage, a loss to him for which he cannot account. The chapters devoted to John's son Douglas are facile and unconvincing as he sets forth his ideas on writing fiction about such people as we find in *The Hired Man* and *A Place in England*.

London figures more than Cumberland in *The Nerve* in which Bragg traces, in a first-person narrative, the stages in the mental breakdown of his protagonist, Ted. Power accrues when Ted, the narrator, actualizes some of his experience of physical and mental pain, but the breakdown which is a "breakthrough" is not precisely characterized.

The immediacy of Bragg's Cumberland milieu is, at least superficially, the quality that impresses most in his fiction. As in Thomas Hardy and D. H. Lawrence, milieu is integrally fused, however, with the fortunes and development of the characters. Like Hardy he has in unusual degree insight into human beings who confront the elemental realities of nature. Bragg's eye for detail, his compelling sense of drama, and his supple and luminous prose have all contributed to his reputation as one of the most significant of emerging novelists.

—Frederick P. W. McDowell

---

**BRAINE, John (Gerard).** British. Born in Bradford, Yorkshire, 13 April 1922. Educated at St. Bede's Grammar School, Bradford; Leeds School of Librarianship, A.L.A., 1949. Served in the British Navy, 1942–43. Married Helen Patricia Wood in 1955; has four children. Librarian, Bingley, Yorkshire Public Library, 1940–51; Northumberland County Library, 1954–56; West Riding County Library, 1956–57. Member, BBC North Regional Advisory Council, 1960–64. Address: The Holt, Pyrford Heath, Pyrford, Woking, Surrey, England.

PUBLICATIONS

Novels

*Room at the Top*. London, Eyre and Spottiswoode, and Boston, Houghton Mifflin, 1957.
*The Vodi*. London, Eyre and Spottiswoode, 1959; as *From the Hand of the Hunter*, Boston, Houghton Mifflin, 1960.
*Life at the Top*. London, Eyre and Spottiswoode, and Boston, Houghton Mifflin, 1962.
*The Jealous God*. London, Eyre and Spottiswoode, and Boston, Houghton Mifflin, 1965.
*The Crying Game*. London, Eyre and Spottiswoode, and Boston, Houghton Mifflin, 1968.
*Stay with Me Till Morning*. London, Eyre and Spottiswoode, 1970; as *The View from Tower Hill*, New York, Coward McCann, 1971.

Plays

*The Desert in the Mirror* (produced Bingley, Yorkshire, 1951).

Television Series: *Man at the Top*, for Thames Television, 1970.

Critical Studies: in *The Modern Age*, London, Penguin, revised edition, 1964; *History of English Literature*, by Emile Legouis and Louis Cazamian, London, Dent, 1964; *Twentieth Century Writing*, edited by Kenneth Richardson, London, Newnes, 1969.

John Braine comments:

What I care about the most is telling the truth about human beings and the world they live in. I'm not interested in making moral judgements as a novelist. I'm not interested in making any sort of propaganda. I do have very strong political beliefs and in a sense can't separate them from my religious beliefs. I'll put it this way: I believe in parliamentary democracy, majority rule, the rule of law, and a fixed morality. I would rather die than live under a government which denied me the freedom to write exactly as I want to. It isn't for me to say whether I write well or badly. But this at least I can say: I have never thought of being anything else but a writer and will never be anything else but a writer. And every word I write is a celebration of my love for the created world and everyone and everything within it.

* * *

John Braine burst upon the literary scene in 1957 with *Room at the Top*, an instantaneous success which enrolled him among "the angry young men," writers who protested the discriminations imposed upon those who came from the working class or the lower middle class. Joe Lampton comes from the wrong social class for worldly success to come easily to him. He is cynical of the establishment but determined to exploit it. At this time he does not realize that he may be absorbed by the class whose wealth he intends to share. He has the same restless desire to gain power and the same lack of scruple that motivate Stendhal's Julien Sorel. Against his will he falls in love with Alice Aisgill, an unhappily married middle-aged woman. Out of opportunism he gives her up but feels guilt for her violent death. He marries Susan Brown, his fairy princess, with painful lack of enthusiasm. Braine implies that any society which demands the sacrifice of integrity as the price of success is corrupt. Should not there be room at the top for those who are not unscrupulous?

*The Vodi* is Braine's least significant novel. In it Dick Corvey decides that he must not allow himself to be intimidated by malign supernatural presences (the Vodi); and by an effort of will he throws them off and overcomes, too, the tuberculosis which has plagued him. Neither the character of the Vodi nor the strength of Corvey is rendered with entire credibility.

*Life at the Top*, a sequel to Braine's first book, is equally fine as a novel. Joe Lampton has by now joined the establishment and become a minor administrator in his father-in-law's firm. He finds that life at the top is empty and that affluence entails severe liabilities. Joe, the rebel against the drabness of Dufton (his native town), now realizes that life at the top can be just as drab, certainly more corrupt. He also experiences much personal conflict. He continually clashes with Susan since the ghost of Alice still holds him. Yet he attains equilibrium when he at last has the power to see that marriage and the duty of parents to their children are inescapable responsibilities. Joe reaches beyond torment to triumph when he accepts the child with love whom he discovers is not his own.

*The Jealous God* is a religious novel which traces the ramifications of Catholicism upon personal life. Vincent Dungarvan has for long been poised between life as priest and life in the world. His possessive mother is more anxious than Vincent for him to become a priest. In the upshot the church and Mrs. Dungarvan win out over Vincent's desire to marry a divorcee whose husband had been homosexual. Braine depicts with urgency and strength the conflicts inherent in Vincent, the sensual man of deep religious commitment. And life in the provincial town is rendered with knowledge, finesse, and sympathy.

*The Crying Game* is a kind of "morality play," depicting Frank Batcombe's oscillating attitudes toward the glamor and easy rewards of London, the intense yet transitory quality of its pleasures. The conflicts do not register clearly because Braine fails to keep his characters at a sufficient ironic distance for him to judge them adequately and the values they embody. Like Milton, Braine at times seems to be of the devil's party represented in the book by Adam Keelby and his sleazy values. Braine, however, seems to be as fascinated by the great world of finance and intrigue as he is critical of it. Frank, a journalist, sees in time the corruption which is about to engulf him as a result of Adam's influence. He turns to his "good angel," Theresa, whom he had thought earlier of being the right girl met at the wrong time. *The Crying Game* does capture the texture of decadent urban life, the corruptness of its luxury, the opportunism inherent in its human relationships, especially in the realm of sex. It is most compelling as an exposé of the temptations which Frank must learn to reject.

In *Stay with Me Till Morning* Braine analyzes marital discord for the first time since *Life at the Top*. The protagonists, Robin and Clive Lendrick, have everything: a fine home in a Yorkshire town, economic security, healthy children, mutual affection and understanding. Yet after some twenty years together they feel that something has gone from their relationship if ever it was there. Infidelity, Braine seems to imply, is preferable to spiritual lassitude. He also implies that a relationship has to be more firmly rooted than that of the Lendricks, for it to withstand the pressures of modern life including its very affluence. Clive and Robin are, however, caught in a relationship they do not wish to dissolve: with each other's knowledge, each keeps on with mistress and lover respectively who provide an emotional enlargement which Clive and Robin do not achieve with each other. The difficulties inherent in marriage except for the extraordinarily strong and its general inflexibility are principal themes in this disquieting dissection of modern mores.

Braine has emerged as a writer alternately fascinated and repelled by the present day upper middle class, especially that segment of it which enjoys prosperity but lacks spiritual stamina. He is a master at analyzing the antagonisms of people thrown together in close association in marriage, friendship, and professional life. Some of his characters, satirically treated, never attain awareness; for them sex has none but a perfunctory significance. Others do attain enlightenment, but with much pain, sometimes even with regret. The acknowledgment of the claims of other people upon them coincides with an acknowledgment of their own personal deficiencies. The unregenerate are those whose egotism is impervious to others' influence. As moralist Braine states his position clearly, but as an artist he perhaps gives the people and the milieu which he ostensibly condemns somewhat more than their due. An intense preoccupation with the material aspects of the lives of his opulent characters belies his strictures of their egotism and insensitivity. As a creator of characters who embody the tensions existing between themselves and others and between themselves and social institutions and conventions, he achieves his greatest distinction.

—Frederick P. W. McDowell

---

**BRAITHWAITE, E(dward) R(icardo).** Guyanan. Born in Georgetown, Guyana, 27 June 1912. Educated at Queen's College, Guyana; City College of New York, B.Sc. 1940; Caius College, Cambridge, M.Sc. in Physics 1949; London University Institute of Education. Served in the Royal Air Force, 1941–45. Schoolteacher, London, 1950–57; Welfare Officer, London County Council, 1958–60; Human Rights Officer, World Veterans' Foundation, Paris, 1960–63; Lecturer and Educational Consultant, UNESCO, Paris, 1963–66. Permanent Representative of Guyana to the United Nations, New York, 1967–68; Ambassador of Guyana to Venezuela, 1968–69; now retired from the diplomatic service. Recipient: Anisfield-Wolf Award, 1960. Address: The Parker 40, Apartment 16K, 305 East 40th Street, New York, New York 10017, U.S.A.

PUBLICATIONS

Novel

*Choice of Straws.* London, Bodley Head, 1965; Indianapolis, Bobbs Merrill, 1967.

Other

> *To Sir, With Love* (autobiography).   London, Bodley Head, 1959; New York, Prentice Hall, 1960.
> *Paid Servant* (autobiography).   London, Bodley Head, 1962; New York, McGraw Hill, 1968.
> *A Kind of Homecoming.*   New York, Prentice Hall, 1962; London, Muller, 1963.

*     *     *

E. R. Braithwaite's writings rest on a wide variety of practical experience. A teacher in the East End of London, and later a London County Council Welfare Officer, a Human Rights Officer and Lecturer and Educational Consultant for UNESCO, Guyana's Permanent Representative to the United Nations and its Ambassador to Venezuela—Braithwaite speaks with authority and compassion to and about a multi-racial world.

His three documentaries, *To Sir, With Love, Paid Servant,* and *A Kind of Homecoming,* have a convincing authority. Describing his experiences as a Negro teacher in a working-class district in London, as a welfare officer, and as a visitor to some of the new countries of Africa, he writes with thoughtfulness and serious concern about the world he knows. The freshness and clarity of the details he chooses, and particularly the narrative form of *To Sir, With Love,* prepare the reader for his compelling novel, *Choice of Straws.*

At first sight, the novel seems almost a case study of a working-class young white man from London's East End, Jack Bennett. Having Jack narrate the story is in no sense a gimmick, however; by keeping to what Jack sees and thinks, Braithwaite is able to build up a believable and poignant portrait of a way of life, with all the nagging pressures and built-in assumptions that finally come to neutralize Jack's positive qualities. Braithwaite firmly keeps the emphasis on the fictional portraits, and not on the racial message.

The plot itself hinges on the unintended deaths resulting from a black-bashing expedition by two whites, Jack and his brother Dave. This is where Braithwaite's originality comes out, for where one expects the novel to center on the racial theme, he writes a compelling characterization of the young white man growing into awareness. The awareness does include the society in which he lives—composed of "reasonably" tolerant working-class whites, emotionally hateful whites, and third generation British Negroes—but more importantly the awareness concerns Jack's first thoughtful looks at his family, his dead brother, and himself. Jack and his twin brother Dave had all their lives functioned as a team—at school, with their girlfriends, in their amusements; they even seemed to share their thoughts with no words being spoken. Yet after Dave is killed, Jack discovers that Dave had a side he didn't know—one which composed poetry, which had vague doubts about his life, which questioned the values of his world. This is a stunning discovery for Jack—his entire past seems a falsehood. The old teasing jealousy he feels towards Jack comes to the surface, especially as he remembers that his Mum always asked when they came home, "That you, Dave?", never "That you, boys?" or "That you, Jack?" This new view seems to free Jack of Dave's dominance; he is able to conduct a love affair with a new girlfriend, whereas before he had always been in Dave's shadow (and impotent). And he strikes up a cautious friendship with Michelle, a Negro girl whose brother had been killed at the same time as Dave. Her beauty and intelligence, as well as her color, spark off the domestic conflicts that lead to the climax of the book. Jack's girlfriend, jealous but awed of Michelle, misunderstands the background of Dave's death; his Mum, griefstricken and full of hate for all Negroes, insults Michelle. And Jack, though impulsively trying to assert his maturity and independence, is forced to return home. The last episode shows Mrs. Bennett greeting him, "That you, Jack?", summing up the dominant claims of her narrow values.

But if the book centers on Jack's unsuccessful attempt to break out into a freer world, an important secondary theme focuses on the Negro characters. Here too the theme is freedom. Manufactured tolerance or rational acceptance does not satisfy the two important

Negroes in the book, Michelle and Ron. For Ron, striving for equality leads to false values, a mimicking of white standards and goals. He says, "I'm not interested in equality. . . . I want to be so free that, like you, I don't ever have to give a thought to being equal. I want to work and live with you, agreeing or disagreeing, liking or not liking, without having to qualify any of it by your whiteness or my blackness."

*Choice of Straws* is no masterpiece. Its narrative movement—dominated by short episodes and too-frequent flashbacks—is sluggish and unsophisticated, perhaps partly because of the first-person narrator. Some of the details seem a bit too "representative" to be credible. But there are many convincing details, especially in the tightknit Bennett family. The mute, sinister communications that take place around the kitchen table suggest a kind of "understanding" like that of Tom and Daisy at the end of *The Great Gatsby*. And the overall picture of Jack's world and its effect on him is poignant and true.

—James Vinson

---

**BRATHWAITE, Errol (Freeman).** New Zealander. Born in Clive, Hawkes Bay, 3 April 1924. Educated at Waipukurau District High School, 1929–37; Timaru Boys' High School, 1938–39. Served in the New Zealand Army in the City of Wellington's Own, 1942–43; Royal New Zealand Air Force, 1943–45, 1947–55; Royal New Zealand Signals, 1955–58. Married Alison Irene Whyte in 1948; has two children. Cadet, New Zealand Railways, 1940–42, 1945; Farm Trainee, Rehabilitation Department, King Country, 1946; Copywriter, New Zealand Broadcasting Corporation, Christchurch, 1959–62, and Dobbs-Wiggins-McCann-Erickson, Christchurch, 1962–66. Since 1969, Copywriter, and since 1971, Manager, Carlton Carruthers du Chateau, Christchurch. Recipient: Otago *Daily Times* Centennial Novel Prize, 1961; New Zealand Literary Fund Award, 1962. Address: 12 Fulton Avenue, Fendalton, Christchurch 1, New Zealand.

PUBLICATIONS

Novels

*Fear in the Night.* Christchurch, Caxton Press, 1959.
*An Affair of Men.* Auckland and London, Collins, 1961; New York, St. Martin's Press, 1964.
*Long Way Home.* Christchurch, Caxton Press, 1964.
*The Flying Fish.* Auckland and London, Collins, 1964; San Francisco, Tri-Ocean, 1969.
*The Needle's Eye.* Auckland and London, Collins, 1965; San Francisco, Tri-Ocean, 1969.
*The Evil Day.* Auckland and London, Collins, 1967; San Francisco, Tri-Ocean, 1969.

Uncollected Short Story

"Williams and Christmas", in *New Zealand Weekly News* (Auckland), 1968.

Other

*The Companion Guide to the North Island of New Zealand.* Auckland, Collins, 1970; London, Collins, 1971.
*The Companion Guide to the South Island of New Zealand.* Auckland, Collins, 1971.

Radio play versions of *An Affair of Men*, *Long Way Home*, and *The Needle's Eye* produced by NZBC.

Errol Brathwaite comments:

It is difficult for me to comment on my own work, since I never write with any other end in view than to tell a good story; and, that being so, any situations around which I build up my story must be rich in dramatic possibilities.

I regard life as a constant battle between good and evil, albeit a highly complex warfare, since both sides in any given encounter have within them leanings towards both good and evil. I strive to make my characters positive, though not necessarily strong—never clean-cut good or evil, though tending infinitely more strongly in one direction (usually towards good) than the other. I acknowledge the complexity of the battle by giving my creations multi-faceted characters; and while I comment on life, I try to allow the commentary to grow as a by-product of observations and reportage. I do not deliberately attack attitudes or situations, but merely use them. To do otherwise would be to obtrude, to force myself and my opinions on the reader.

If I want a particular character to be a hero, I make him progress towards an obviously desirable goal somewhat in spite of himself, sometimes fortuitously and always with much stumbling and a modicum of obtuseness. I try to let the reader see the desirable objective, as it were from a height, observing the hero's ground-level side-tracking and stumbling progress. I do this in an attempt to involve the reader, which I regard as being a first principle of good entertainment.

I suppose that this is why war has so often been, if not the subject, then the setting of my novels. It is a pattern, in bold relief, of life itself. It is full of dramatic possibilities. It can face ordinary good/evil man with a rapid series of searing moral and other dilemmas.

I don't expect that I shall always write about war, but I regard conflict as being one of the two major dramatic themes, the other being the "Robinson Crusoe" situation, wherein man overcomes circumstance and bends it to his will.

What else is there to say? I believe that life itself is seldom tidy, and that its conclusion inevitably leaves a number of more or less untidy loose ends flapping around. I realise that in a novel there must be a rather greater degree of contrivance than in life, but I don't care to make my novels too unlifelike.

I suppose, to sum it all up, that I regard myself as an entertainer; a teller, as Kai Lung used to say, of imagined tales. I have, therefore, one source of material, which is human behaviour, and three forms of presentation, which are drama, romance and comedy. Drama and comedy call for high, bold colouring techniques—the dash and splash of bright oils. Romance calls for water-colour treatment, and I don't think that my brushwork is subtle enough. Therefore, I suppose that the highly dramatic will continue to be my chosen form, and that if there is any change, it will be to comedy.

\*          \*          \*

In Errol Brathwaite's novels, the basic formula is that of men in a dangerous war-situation, submitted to physical and mental stress, which strips them down to basic responses and confronts them with moral dilemmas. His work represents an endeavour to add to the war-novel an extra dimension of moral significance and to highlight the complexity of circumstances which are usually treated in terms of mere physical endurance. His strength lies in his keen historical sense, his ability to tell exciting stories, his understanding of the psychology of fighting men (women make very rare appearances in his fiction) and his clean-cut, unfussy style. His weaknesses are seen in his tendency to view his characters at times as human beings, at others as representing abstract qualities, and his slightly mechanical organisation of moments of tension. But he is one of the most readable of New Zealand novelists and at the same time sets his sights high.

His first two novels were *Fear in the Night* and *Long Way Home*. (Despite the publication date of *An Affair of Men*, 1961, it was written after *Long Way Home*.) Both come from the author's own aviation experience. In *Fear in the Night*, the crew of a bomber forced down in Japanese territory are under pressure to repair the plane before they are captured. Brathwaite's technical knowledge and his eye for detail combine with his skill in exploring the minds of his characters under strain to create a convincing situation remarkable for its concentration of effect. *Long Way Home*, which deals with a search and rescue operation in New Zealand's Southern Alps, is similarly organised.

There is a real advance in *An Affair of Men*, which won the *Otago Daily Times* Centennial Novel Competition and has been translated into several languages. This time the suspense story does not so much include moral attitudes as dramatise them. Allied airmen who have crashed on the Pacific island Bougainville are pursued by the Japanese under Captain Itoh. His search is frustrated by a Christian-educated headman, Sedu, who insists on remaining neutral. The clash of wills and ideologies is handled with continual invention and boldness and is resolved in terms of the psychology and background of the antagonists. The drama reflects modern man's dilemma in his choice between two different sets of values, between peace and violence.

Brathwaite's trilogy, *The Flying Fish*, *The Needle's Eye* and *The Evil Day*, follows the experiences of the fictional Major Williams in the Maori Wars of the 1860s and is the most ambitious treatment of this subject so far written. Again, it is not only the details of strategy and battles which engage Brathwaite and the various kinds of military sensibility which he analyses, although these are treated with careful attention to historical fact, but the personal and moral problems posed by war itself. A further theme is the development of mutual understanding, paradoxically, between Maori and European through the wars and the question of where the real blame for the conflict lay. The characterisation is firm and varied and Major Williams is one of the most completely realised characters in New Zealand fiction.

—J. C. Reid

---

**BRAUTIGAN, Richard.** American. Born in Tacoma, Washington, 30 January 1933. Recipient: National Endowment for the Arts grant, 1968. Address: c/o Simon and Schuster Inc., 630 Fifth Avenue, New York, New York 10020, U.S.A.

PUBLICATIONS

Novels

*In Watermelon Sugar*. San Francisco, Four Seasons, 1964; London, Cape, 1970.

*A Confederate General from Big Sur*.   New York, Grove Press, 1965; London, Cape, 1971.
*Trout Fishing in America*.   San Francisco, Four Seasons, 1967; London, Cape, 1970.
*The Abortion: An Historical Romance*.   New York, Simon and Schuster, 1971.

Short Stories

*Revenge of the Lawn*.   New York, Simon and Schuster, 1971.

Verse

*The Return of the Rivers*.   San Francisco, Inferno Press, 1957.
*The Galilee Hitch-Hiker*.   San Francisco, White Rabbit Press, 1958.
*The Octopus Frontier*.   San Francisco, Carp Press, 1960.
*The Pill Versus the Springhill Mine Disaster (Poems 1957–1968)*.   San Francisco, Four Seasons, 1968; London, Cape, 1971.
*Rommel Drives on Deep into Egypt*.   New York, Dell, 1970.

*          *          *

In the first section of *Trout Fishing in America*, Brautigan asks: "Was it Kafka who learned about America by reading the autobiography of Benjamin Franklin . . . Kafka who said, 'I like the Americans because they are healthy and optimistic.'" This is as good a center as any for a brief look at his work. Brautigan has found a way for Americans who don't much like themselves as Americans to fall in love with an old American Adam reborn once more. He draws on those qualities which are likeable to a Kafka, because so exotic and remote: innocence and good intentions, naïve optimism combined with a practical cunning. The narrator-hero of *The Abortion* says, when forced to leave his library at the end of the book: "Vida was right when she said that I would be a hero in Berkeley." The hero in this case, as always with Brautigan, is not a person or character—he is an attitude, a point of view. He embodies good humor, is unaware of or mystified by evil, and survives catastrophes without even knowing they are there. Brautigan's narrator-heroes are hang-loose and love-able Captain Delanos, with the evil in their worlds pushed even further under the carpet. But for the reader, excluded evil becomes even more conspicuous and significant by its absence, like the plot in a plotless novel. Brautigan's version of the "American Dream" leaves out precisely those things writers like Mailer insist on as the basic substance of the dream.

The nameless innocent narrator of *In Watermelon Sugar* is a good example of these Brautigan qualities. He tells us early on that he has a "gentle life," a "comfortable" life, a life "carefully constructed from watermelon sugar and then travelled to the length of our dreams. . . ." The book, too, is made from "watermelon sugar," and things gone into in it are "travelled in watermelon sugar." What "watermelon sugar" is, then, is indefinable even on the allegorical level. It is like "Trout Fishing in America," a phrase which can be any-thing from a person to the name of a book. It is a combination of language and attitude, a sense of form and response which is at once amorphous and particulate, innocent and cunning. When the narrator stops sleeping with Margaret and starts sleeping with Pauline, Margaret eventually hangs herself. Before that, Pauline asks the narrator how Margaret feels, saying that she seems terribly upset. "I don't know how she feels," is his response. The narrator-hero learned this response early, having watched some "tigers" kill and eat his parents when he was nine. After their meal, the tigers comment enthusiastically on how nice the day is, then they apologize: "Please try to understand. We tigers are not evil. This is just a thing we have to do." The narrator says, "All right . . . thanks for helping me with my arithmetic," and the tigers answer: "Think nothing of it." It is precisely this lack of thought, introduced here in a typical Brautigan *double-entendre*, that means any day, even when one's parents have been eaten, can be a "nice day." At the very end, after Margaret hangs herself from the apple tree, there is a traditional funeral to be followed by a dance. No "thought" is necessary, since there is a traditional way of doing things. No empathy with the motives that might drive the inBOIL gang to cut themselves up ("It's a mystery to us") or drive Margaret to hang herself ("I don't know why") can distract the narrator from the contents of the potato salad, which had a lot of carrots in it.

The more one reads this book, the more uneasy one feels. Perhaps the "point" is as profound as that at the end of *The Brothers Karamazov*. We can't understand the problem of death and evil; so mourn and suffer, but then eat pancakes and be happy. Yet here is a book, not really a novel, that does away with the dialectic of mourning and rejoicing altogether. "We take the juice from the watermelons and cook it down until there's nothing left but sugar, and then we work it into the shape of this thing that we have: our lives." This sugary shape, and the virtuoso power of metamorphosis (the sentence is about it and illustrative of it at the same time) are the essence of Brautigan's art. More process than substance, more wit than wisdom—except that he just might be right, after all. One is left with the same ambivalence of attraction and repulsion felt towards the "So it goes" refrain of Vonnegut's *Slaughterhouse Five*; and with the feeling that any response to so understated a form of art risks overstatement.

—Thomas A. Vogler

---

**BRODEUR, Paul (Adrian, Jr.).** American. Born in Boston, Massachusetts, 16 May 1931. Educated at Harvard University, Cambridge, Massachusetts, B.A. 1953. Served in the United States Army Counter Intelligence Corps, 1953–56. Since 1958, Staff Writer for *The New Yorker* magazine, New York. Currently, Lecturer, Columbia University School of Journalism, New York. Address: c/o *The New Yorker*, 25 West 43rd Street, New York, New York 10036. U.S.A.

PUBLICATIONS

Novels

  *The Sick Fox.* Boston, Little Brown, and London, Gollancz, 1963.
  *The Stunt Man.* New York, Atheneum, and London, Bodley Head, 1970.

Short Stories

  *Downstream.* New York, Atheneum, 1972.

Other

  *Asbestos and Enzymes.* New York, Ballantine, 1972.

\*        \*        \*

Paul Brodeur has written only two novels as yet, but *The Sick Fox* and *The Stunt Man* exhibit a degree of craftsmanship not to be found in the works of more prolific novelists. Both have fast moving, exciting plot lines compressed into the action of a few days, and in both cases the virtues of the narrative are enhanced by a wealth of symbolic overtones which elevate them far above the category of mere adventure tales.

*The Sick Fox* concerns the plight of an American intelligence agent assigned to protect an underground nuclear storage site near a picturesque rural German village. Despite his position, he has a streak of anarchism in his character which accounts for his love of the sparsely populated region in which he works and for his fateful decision not to kill a rabid fox he encounters at the very opening of the novel. He does, however, report seeing the fox to local authorities, and he thereby sets in motion a chain of incidents which ends in a bizarre uprising by the villagers and in his own transfer out of the place whose pastoral tranquillity he had inadvertently shattered. As a guardian of nuclear warheads stockpiled in the interests of world peace, the protagonist embodies that essential contradiction and the sense of cosmic malaise it produces. Regardless of his intentions, he manifests the mentality of the conquering despot to the local citizens, and the violent encounter which resolves the plot also seems to have allegorical implications.

*The Stunt Man* is another novel which is open to various levels of perception. An army draftee named Cameron on his way to basic training goes AWOL and wanders into an area where a movie company is in the process of completing a film concerning a fugitive. He witnesses the accidental death of a stunt man and is hired by the film's eccentric director to replace him. Thus fugitive plays fugitive, while the director, who argues that what is seen on film is on a higher plane of reality than what happens in life, adjusts his movie to coincide with the details of Cameron's predicament. As the police close in on him, Cameron sees that he must flee both forms of authority, since his director envisages a dramatic final scene in which the fate of the film's hero, and of the stunt man portraying him, is uncertain. But Cameron's attempted escape does indeed become part of the film, and whether he finally succeeds or is captured is necessarily left unresolved.

The principal weakness in Brodeur's work is in characterization, for the protagonists of both novels seem to have no life outside the plots. With no past to speak of and certainly no future, they live exclusively in the present. The minor characters are extremely vague and lacking in apparent motivation, especially the women who are far too easily won over to the heroes' desires. But Brodeur's deft merging of external plot and symbolic meaning and his highly lucid and allusive prose more than make up for the lack of complete characterization, which is a flaw, after all, rarely avoided in works of allegorical import.

—Robert E. Lynch

---

**BROOKE-ROSE, Christine.** British. Born in Geneva, Switzerland. Educated at Somerville College, Oxford, 1946–49, B.A., M.A.; University College, London, 1950–54, B.A., Ph.D. Married Jerzy Peterkiewicz, *q.v.*, in 1948. Worked as a free-lance literary journalist, London, 1956–68. Since 1969, Maitre de Conférences, University of Paris, Vincennes. Recipient: Society of Authors Travelling Prize, 1965; Black Memorial Prize, 1967; Arts Council Translation Prize, 1969. Address: c/o Michael Joseph Ltd., 52 Bloomsbury Square, London W.C.1, England.

PUBLICATIONS

Novels

The Languages of Love.  London, Secker and Warburg, 1957.
The Sycamore Tree.  London, Secker and Warburg, 1958; New York, Norton, 1959.
The Dear Deceit.  London, Secker and Warburg, 1960; New York, Doubleday, 1961.
The Middlemen: A Satire.  London, Secker and Warburg, 1961.
Out.  London, Joseph, 1964.
Such.  London, Joseph, 1966.
Between.  London, Joseph, 1968.

Short Stories

Go When You See the Green Man Walking.  London, Joseph, 1970.

Other

A Grammar of Metaphor.  London, Secker and Warburg, 1958.
A ZBC of Ezra Pound.  London, Faber, 1971.

Translator, Children of Chaos, by Juan Goytisolo.  London, MacGibbon and Kee,
  1959.
Translator, Fertility and Survival: Population Problems from Malthus to Mao Tse Tung,
  by Alfred Sauvy.  New York, Criterion Books, 1960; London, Chatto and Windus,
  1961.
Translator, In the Labyrinth, by Alain Robbe-Grillet.  London, Calder and Boyars,
  1968.

Christine Brooke-Rose comments:

Let us not fall into the intentional fallacy.

*     *     *

Christine Brooke-Rose is a European intellectual whose supra-national, multi-disciplinary
belles lettres might serve as a model for New Renaissance woman. Brought up in Geneva
and Brussels, she was educated at Oxford, served as a tough practitioner of Fleet Street
literary journalism, and subsequently wound up teaching Romance studies at the French
government's show-piece university of Vincennes. She started her literary career as a poet,
found her verse poor and became adept at turning a brittle, satirical novel, which in turn
she found unsatisfactory and abandoned in favour of the analogical novaglot essays of
Out, Such, Between and Go When You See the Green Man Walking (collected stories of the
previous eight years).
    States of mind and body, the areas between life and death, and the nature of words and
the meanings with which man invests them are her concerns. They are not chance preoccupations. At a time when she was still a poet and an academic, her husband became ill
and almost died. Her reaction to the state of mind induced by strain was to leave off working
on a critical work (A Grammar of Metaphor) and for the first time to write a novel. The
exercise (The Languages of Love—a soufflé based on the goings-on of university philologists)

performed the function of therapy and also pointed Miss Brooke-Rose in the direction of her proper literary concern. A few years later, in 1962, she herself fell ill, and was convinced that she would die. She wrote one sentence a day before falling exhausted on her pillows. During the illness her consciousness seemed to function at a different level. She has described the experience as "a sense of being in touch with something else—death perhaps". As a result of this changed awareness, she was able to realise a new kind of sensibility, which, from that time onwards, she has attempted to explore in her fiction.

Her early novels (*The Languages of Love*, *The Sycamore Tree*, *The Dear Deceit*, and *The Middlemen*) are works whose value she now denies. They were competent enough vignettes of the witty, intelligent circles in which one might expect to discover Miss Iris Murdoch, and their end result was not far removed from the sum of the parts of Miss Murdoch's own elegant connundrums. One could not help feeling that the authoress was an awfully clever gel, insofar as she could manipulate quite adequately the basic framework of the nineteenth-century novel of manners. Only in *The Dear Deceit* did Miss Brooke-Rose display a certain restlessness over the form of her material—she started her story at the end and wrote on to its beginning.

*Out* was the first work of her convert period; it is itself the story of a world which has come close to death, and survives in an utterly changed form. Set in some unspecified Afro-Eurasia, in some future time following a catastrophe which is always referred to, euphemistically, as "the displacement", *Out* treats with a society in which colour prejudice has a logical basis. Any colour—black, brown or yellow—is equated with health, and consequently with power and privilege. The whites, who after "the displacement" turn out to be prone to a widespread and fatal blood disease, are treated with the contempt and indifference which, in terms of an objective Darwinian calculation, they merit. But it is more than a story of Black Power through superior anti-radiation pigmentation. The book is pervaded with a sense of anarchy at the door, and its black notables and sick white trash are together attempting to arrive at some technique for coping with disorder, sickness, and more generally, a changed order of things. The book begins with an observation of two flies copulating, and ends with a burst of fire and the conclusion: "We are merely marking time and time is nothing, nothing. A moment of agony, of burning flesh, an aspect of the human element disintegrating to ash, and you are dead. But that's another story."

The stylistic devices with which Miss Brooke-Rose coped with the socio-sci-fi of *Out* are characteristic of all her later works. In place of a story she substitutes an apparently formless consideration of states of mind, in which the repetition and reorganisation of thoughts occur randomly, as they will in ordinary human consciousness. The language of this statement and restatement is often so determinedly scientific as to fly above the understanding of a lay reader. In *Out* it is the language of bio-chemistry and molecular physics:

> The left foot in its dirty canvas shoe is wholly contained in a benzene ring, the other, a little less dirty, has its big toe on the top dividing line like a carbon atom. If there were a single carbon atom at every angle the result would be graphite . . . with the appropriate enzyme, represented perhaps by the left heel in a ribose molecule to the South East and the whole series linked by two energy-rich phosphate bonds, the energy can be quantitively transferred from one molecule to another so that the backward and forward reactions are thermodynamically equivalent . . .

*Such* is also a science fiction experiment, and again it deals with death, closely escaped. In this case a man dies at the radio telescope, and in the three minutes time span which the book covers various aspects of his lost psyche are examined before he returns to life like Lazarus or the fortunate subject of a heart masseur. He sees people as a radio telescope sees stars; some are already degenerate matter, others are forming new stars. The metaphor is astro-physical; the vocabulary likewise—even in a mock sentimental duologue between our hero and his woman:

—Larry, everyone deserves the attention of definiteness.

—Even if they prefer uncertain principles?

—They only pretend to prefer it. They have to. You used to say that. Someone would come along and find a unified theory that would do away with indeterminate interpretations, you'd say, and revert to causality. I thought perhaps you might.

—I thought so too. In psychic terms at least. But I didn't. In the meantime we do the best we can, some of us preferring to pretend causality exists, and others, others preferring to prefer its absence. But you can never know with absolute certainty that what looks like the same particle, with the same identity . . .

—Yes but for practical purposes you have to, Larry, in the chemistry of people. Otherwise how can you live?

—You can't. Not really. You pretend to. To save appearances.

—Larry, you can't honestly believe that.

*Between* substitutes for a confusion of astro-physical concepts a tumult of semantic hypotheses. Its protagonist is a simultaneous interpreter from French to German, whose thought processes are affected by three languages and three sensibilities while she receives and transmits, often without understanding, the ideas of conference delegates. Miss Brooke-Rose's characteristic telescoping of time and place are further complicated by a kaleidoscopic narrative which may, during the course of a paragraph, arrange consecutive liaisons of Greek, Latin, German, Czech, Spanish and James Joycese. The link might be an international Nabokovian pun, or simply a leap of the imagination. The confusion is intended; that is what words are for:

> The visitor's attention turns immediately to higher things such as the seven-terraced Tower of Babel on the seventh hauteur du ciel way up above the smattering of the mouthpiece in ces capitales que je connais, que je hais, ah, pardonnez-moi cette vilaine jalousie. Je n'ai jamais aime comme ca between the zest of youth and the wisdom of old age through an indefinitely long period called the middle ages . . .

—John Hall

---

**BROOKS, Jeremy.** British. Born in Southampton, Hampshire, 17 December 1926. Educated at Magdalen College, Oxford, 1944–45; Camberwell School of Art, London, 1947–49. Served in the Royal Naval Volunteer Reserve, 1945–47. Married Eleanor Nevile in 1950; has four children. Has worked as "Dogsbody", Scala Theatre, Dartford, Kent, 1949–50; Feature Writer, *Pictorial Press*, London, 1950–52; Literary Agent, Christy and Moore, London, 1952–53; Waiter and Bartender, 1954–56; Publisher's Reader for Robert Hale, Eyre and Spottiswoode, Macmillan, and David Higham, all London, 1956–58; Fiction and General Reviewer, *The Guardian*, London, 1958–60; Play Reader, BBC-TV, London, 1959–60; Drama Critic, *New Statesman*, London, 1960–61; Fiction Critic, *The Sunday Times*, London, 1961–62. Literary Manager, 1962–69, and since 1969 Literary Adviser, Royal Shakespeare Company, Stratford upon Avon and London. Since 1969, London Representative, Five Continents Film Productions. Address: 12 Bartholomew Road, London N.W.5, England.

PUBLICATIONS

Novels

*The Water Carnival*.   London, Eyre and Spottiswoode, 1957.
*Jampot Smith*.   London, Hutchinson, 1960; New York, St. Martin's Press, 1962.
*Henry's War*.   London, Macmillan, 1962; New York, St. Martin's Press, 1963.
*Smith, As Hero*.   London, Eyre and Spottiswoode, 1965.

Uncollected Short Stories

"I'll Fight You", in *Winter's Tales 2*.   London, Macmillan, 1963.
"Christmas with Sir Henry", in *Transatlantic Review* (London and New York), 1964.

Plays

*The Government Inspector*, with Edward O. Marsh, adaptation of a play by Gogol
    (produced London, 1966).   London, Methuen, 1968.
*Enemies*, with Kitty Hunter Blair, adaptation of a play by Gorky (produced London,
    1971).   London, Methuen, 1972.

Screenplays: *Our Mother's House*, 1967; *Work . . . Is a Four Letter Word*, 1968; *The
Shy Photographer*, 1972.

Other

*The Magic Perambulator* (juvenile).   London, Harrap, 1965; New York, Day, 1966.

Has published poetry in magazines and anthologies.

Jeremy Brooks comments:

My most ambitious project in fiction was to have been a carefully designed sequence of
five novels based on the character Bernard Smith, whom I first introduced as an adolescent
schoolboy in *Jampot Smith*. This novel—the only one of mine which I can still read with
pleasure—explored, through the medium of a group of children on the verge of adulthood,
the common predicament of a person who wishes to avoid the responsibilities of emotional
commitment to other people, but finds, however hard he tries to remain uninvolved, that
his very withdrawal is itself a positive act with unforeseeable consequences for others. A
secondary theme was concerned, as novels about adolescents naturally are, with the problem
of finding a workable self-conception from which to operate. This secondary theme was
picked up as the major theme of the next novel, *Smith, As Hero*, in which Smith, now a
junior naval officer, is seen to be engaged in constructing completely fictitious versions of
himself. He is still attempting to remain uninvolved, but by the end of the book has, willy-
nilly, had some raw human emotion thrust into his face, and this time even he cannot pretend that it's nothing to do with him. One may suppose that this incident will rather belatedly
push him over the edge into adulthood. This novel also had a secondary theme, connected
with the idea that we only have our five fallible senses with which to observe the world "out-

side" us, and a fallible brain with which to synthesise their messages into what each one of us calls "reality", and that it is as possible to place too little reliance on these messages as it is to place too much. I intended that this secondary theme should be the major theme of the next novel, and so on through the sequence of five novels, and in the fifth novel, the various themes, unresolved in the individual books, would find a common point of focus.

I would now consider this an over-schematic approach to writing fiction, but it was not this that stopped me from completing the cycle. What happened was that *after* publication of *Smith, As Hero* (the only one of my novels to be popular enough to reach the best-seller lists) I realised just how many corners I had cut while writing it, how many problems had been shelved or hidden instead of solved, how many passages had a "flip" style which had no place in a novel sequence intended, eventually, to deal with weighty matters. (Try to imagine Kingsley Amis's *Lucky Jim* as part of Anthony Powell's *Music of Time* sequence.) What to do? One can't withdraw a published novel; and the chances of getting a re-written version re-published seemed pretty slim. I have been urged to do this, or to go on regardless. But I am no longer the person who conceived and started to write that cycle of novels.

My present work—apart from film scripts—is neither fiction nor autobiography, but a strange, self-critical mixture of both. I hope it will help me break out of the box I wrote myself into.

\*          \*          \*

Brooks has written two very good novels, and two much weaker ones. *Henry's War* successfully blends light touch and serious content, expressed together in a description of a little woman on an Aldermaston March carrying the banner of the Woking Ladies' Sewing Bee while weeping for Hungary. He begins with comedy, with the paradox of a dull little man who writes thrilling stories; the man wants beer and to be left alone, and has a high-minded girl friend he cannot shake off. Soon the "Castillian Emergency" erupts: Britain is involved in some disreputable overseas military exploit, resembling the Suez attack of 1956. Henry and his best friend are recalled to the army, and instead flee to a Welsh hill farm, near their birthplace. On the farm they prepare for sheep-shearing, and Henry finishes a book and thinks about his new girl friend. The pastoral combines with debate over pacifism in the age of the Bomb, as Brooks responds urgently, personally to the concern with nuclear disarmament of the late fifties and early sixties.

More deeply concerned with particular people, more ambitious and penetrating, is *Jampot Smith*, a first-person account of a boy growing up during the war in Llandudno, North Wales. The youth is nicknamed "jampot" because of his supposed ability to attract girls like jam attracts wasps; actually he is unsure and uncertain, but nevertheless finally achieves the love of the charming Kathy. Especially the novel describes Bernard Smith's struggles to understand his feelings, and why other people behave as they do. As the *Times Literary Supplement* reviewer mentions, the book shows so much of the mid-teens, "its loves and inhibitions, its group fantasies and enthusiasms, its intimacies and withdrawals, its advances towards and retreats from maturity, its betrayals and regroupings, its intrusive intuitions and obtrusive gaucheries." Brooks shows with delicacy and total conviction ecstasies, griefs, embarrassments: he knows how important their loves and tragedies are for them. He attends also to the feel of the town: the action goes on in the shadow of the Great Orme and close to the sea, at school and in cafés and dance-halls, rarely at home or with adults. They are influenced by the beauties of the surrounding shores and hills; on one blissfully happy winter's day Smith and Kathy climb a mountain to feed sugar lumps to wild ponies. The war at first is no more than the distant smoke of burning Liverpool, but is an ever-growing uncertainty as the boys reach the age when they will be conscripted. Though the book was highly praised on publication, it is not nearly as well known as it deserves.

The sequel, *Smith, As Hero*, is disappointing. Smith is now a midshipman in the navy in the last weeks of the war, with two objectives, "He must, as quickly as possible, lose his virginity; he must, as quickly as possible, become a hero." Both are slowly achieved. Brooks hints at important themes in his opening—"The dividing-line between innocence and ignorance is seldom charted; often, the two are confused"—but what he actually writes is scrappy and over-familiar. The background, in Malta, Tunisia and onboard ship, is touristy compared with his Llandudno. Most of his ideas and characters are merely touched on and dropped: one or two people from *Jampot Smith* come with news of Kathy; the sheer ignorance of military men about the reasons for their actions is emphasised; in case we think Brooks is Smith, an officer whimsically named J. C. M. Brooks enters. This novel lacks depth, with slick surface jokes about the navy and immaturity.

The remaining novel, *The Water Carnival*, has not the serious side of the other three, but is merely intermittently entertaining. A few months of the frantic, comic life at a Thames-side hotel run primarily as a centre for would-be artists are described, culminating in a carnival. The chief amusement is the gallery of English eccentrics, such as the egoistic, gullible patron of the humanities, the Communist intellectual-turned-farmer, and "the Small-Public-School-fighter-pilot-slangy-jolly-good-fellow-gone-in-for-hotel-management type."

—Malcolm Page

---

**BROPHY, Brigid.** British. Born in London, 12 June 1929. Educated at St. Paul's Girls' School; St. Hugh's College, Oxford (Jubilee Scholarship), 1947–48. Married Michael Levey in 1954; has one child. Collaborated with Maureen Duffy, *q.v.*, in making and exhibiting Prop Art (3-D Construction), London, 1969. Vice-President, National Anti-Vivisection Society of Great Britain, 1970. Recipient: Cheltenham Literary Festival prize for a first novel, 1954; *London Magazine* prize for prose, 1962. Address: Flat 3, 185 Old Brompton Road, London S.W.5, England.

PUBLICATIONS

Novels

*Hackenfeller's Ape.* London, Hart Davis, 1953; New York, Random House, 1954.
*The King of a Rainy Country.* London, Secker and Warburg, 1956; New York, Knopf, 1957.
*Flesh.* London, Secker and Warburg, 1962; Cleveland, World, 1963.
*The Finishing Touch.* London, Secker and Warburg, 1963.
*The Snow Ball.* London, Secker and Warburg, 1964.
*The Snow Ball*, with *The Finishing Touch.* Cleveland, World, 1964.
*In Transit.* London, Macdonald, 1969; New York, Putnam, 1970.

Short Stories

*The Crown Princess and Other Stories.* London, Collins, and New York, Viking Press, 1953.

181

Plays

> *The Burglar* (produced London, 1967).    London, Cape, and New York, Holt Rinehart, 1968.
> *The Waste-Disposal Unit*, in *Best Short Plays of the World Theatre 1958–67*.    New York, Crown, 1968.

Other

> *Black Ship to Hell*.    London, Secker and Warburg, and New York, Harcourt Brace, 1962.
> *Mozart the Dramatist: A New View of Mozart, His Operas and His Age*.    London, Faber, and New York, Harcourt Brace, 1964.
> *Don't Never Forget: Collected Views and Reviews*.    London, Cape, 1966; New York, Holt Rinehart, 1967.
> *Religious Education in State Schools*.    London, Fabian Society, 1967.
> *Fifty Works of English and American Literature We Could Do Without*, with Michael Levey and Charles Osborne.    London, Rapp and Carroll, 1967; New York, Stein and Day, 1968.
> *Black and White: A Portrait of Aubrey Beardsley*.    London, Cape, 1968.
> *Prancing Novelist: A Defence of Fiction in the Form of a Critical Biography in Praise of Ronald Firbank*.    London, Cape, 1972.

*        *        *

In the agreeably self-dramatizing preface to her play *The Burglar*, Brigid Brophy provides a definitive statement of her aims and methods as a critic and novelist. Like Shaw (whom she sees, along with Freud, as one of the "two mainstays of the twentieth century"), Miss Brophy is an evolutionary vitalist, essentially optimistic despite a sharp eye for human failings and hypocrisies. And like Shaw she assumes the existence of a driving Life Force which strives to express itself in ever more competent and complex forms. Sex provides the energy, reason the guide for the continuing evolution of man, for whom "the one consistently natural thing is to try by intelligence and imagination to improve on nature". "I try to live reasonably," she asserts

> but I wouldn't dream of trying to live by reason, for the simple reason that reason offers no reason for staying alive at all, let alone for loving people (including one-self, which is necessary to staying alive) and for trying to create works of art. . . . For motive power, I, like every other living thing, am dependent on instinct, which asserts . . ."I must live"—an assertion there's no proving or disproving. But for *how* we shall live all adult non-moron humans must consult reason.

Art itself is a "function of the life instinct", which by its potent illusions brings us "into accord with reality" (unlike religion, which makes the mistake of taking its illusions as literal truths). The human race is a species "uniquely capable of imagination, rationality and moral choice", and therein lies man's justification and perilous responsibility. For Miss Brophy, like Shaw once more, knows full well that our powers may be misused, that the human race is frighteningly capable of undoing what the Life Force has accomplished thus far. From Freud Miss Brophy takes over the conception of life as a dynamic struggle between Eros, the binding and civilizing force, and Thanatos, the death instinct which seeks to destroy the work of Eros. Thus *Black Ship to Hell* has as its theme "man as a destructive and, more particularly, a self-destructive animal" and is in effect an encyclopedic investigation of the interrelationships of the two opposing principles in war, politics, art and religion.

Miss Brophy sees her work, finally, in the life-affirming tradition of Shaw and Freud: "I too am aiming to reform civilization". The necessary balance between Eros and Thanatos, the integration of work, love and responsibility, gives Miss Brophy the theme of her fiction: in the long run there may be reason to hope for civilization, but in the short run of individual lives there are failures as well as successes, an infinite fund of dramatic possibilities to be exploited.

Miss Brophy's didacticism is apparent at once in her first collection of short stories, *The Crown Princess*, many of which are no more than fictionalized statements of a thesis or problem (the suffocating isolation of the privileged person in "The Crown Princess", the destructive vanity of the actor in "His Wife Survived Him" and so on). But there is one story here, "Fordie", which unmistakably reveals a writer of remarkable power and intelligence. An intricate fable about the differences between the true creator and the self-seeking failure, "Fordie" belongs in the company of Henry James' great series of artist-parables. *Hackenfeller's Ape*, Miss Brophy's first novel, is a disappointingly thin version of one of her persistent concerns, the treatment of animals "whom we have no right to maim, torture or kill". Embedded here, however, is a dialogue between opposing forces which illustrates clearly the truth of Miss Brophy's statement that all of her works are "baroque", that is, they all "proceed by contraposition; and in a reductive analysis the elements contraposited are always Eros and Thanatos". *The King of a Rainy Country*, a much more engaging novel, dramatizes the disordered forms Eros may assume in individual lives—in regressive, homo-erotic relationships and more specifically in doomed, infantile quests for the "perfect moment". In this comic anti-romance the heroine learns at some painful cost that the static ideal is impossible: "you give from one person and take from another—give and take vitality, I mean. Nobody is a reservoir. It's just an exchange. It goes round in an endless cycle." *Flesh* continues to explore this vital give and take, dramatizing with splendid economy and wit the way in which love reclaims a diffident young man. Miss Brophy avoids sentimentality, however, by indicating that in this particular relationship the cost of integration has been high: the young man brought to life by Eros is now an object of both horror and desire for his wife; pain becomes a sinister bond in "a hostile and perhaps perverted situation".

The baroque method of construction is increasingly important in Miss Brophy's later work, "deploying masses in such a way that each, as well as performing its own function, constitutes a funnel down which one gets a sharply unexpected view—ironic, tragic or comic." *The Snow Ball* is architectural with a vengeance: its complexity, Miss Brophy boasts, "defies even my own intellectual analysis". But unfortunately the opposite is true: in this brittle, pretentious reworking of the Don Juan-Donna Anna theme (to which Miss Brophy is addicted, seeing in the myth a paradigm of the human sexual emotions), only the contrived and quite obvious design engages the reader's attention. Man is not only *homo faber* and *homo artifax* for Miss Brophy, but *homo Fabergé* as well, and hence her fascination with Beardsley, Firbank and other aesthetes and dandies. *The Finishing Touch*, besides providing another example of Eros distorted, is an homage to Ronald Firbank, an imitative recreation of the very highest order.

*In Transit* is a radical departure from the quasi-naturalistic style of the earlier books. In "Fordie" the narrator had reflected that "perhaps the personality surrenders some of its philosophic right to be called a personality when the babbling to oneself, which is the mark of human identity, is halted. I would write a book on the subject, if anyone would attend to it." *In Transit* is that book, and a good deal more, anatomizing the layers of individual personality in a wild, punning Joycean flow of rhetoric which defies coherent description. The hero-heroine (we are hurled into a vortex where sexual differences are superficial) is "in transit", literally waiting to board a plane, but psychically in transit as well, pulled and pushed by a host of new energies:

Perhaps our whole century is in transit—a century whose suctions and pressures seek to dislodge you, its inhabitants, from it; a wind tunnel of a century, on whose sides we sit insecure, scarcely able to snatch breath for the vacuum-force gale sucking us towards the sci-fi-futuristensce and the gritty, soiled, brick-dusty industrial-city-Zephyr sand-blasting us back to the Glasweg-Edwardian rose-red soot-gothi-stone-tenements which our own architecture can't/hasn't time-to think up a replacement for . . .

The secondary or simultaneous protagonist of *In Transit* is language itself, which is extended, inverted, parodied and finally blown to bits by the onslaught of modern life. "I am," the psyche insists, but "communication is broken". In a sleight-of-hand finale, however, which is typical of Miss Brophy's invincible optimism, the psyche is reintegrated "for Love of You"—the "You" being (apparently) the expectant interlocutor our consciousness by necessity posits and the eternal "you" of the audience, waiting for the voice of the artist to bring it back into accord with even the most disruptive modern reality.

—Elmer Borklund

---

**BROSSARD, Chandler.** American. Born in Idaho Falls, Idaho, 18 July 1922. Self-educated; left school at 11. Married in 1948; has two children. Reporter, *The Washington Post*, 1940–42; Writer, *The New Yorker*, 1942–43; Senior Editor, *Time* magazine, New York, 1944; Executive Editor, *The American Mercury*, New York, 1950–51; Senior Editor, *Look* magazine, New York, 1956–67. Associate Professor, Old Westbury College, Oyster Bay, Long Island, New York, 1968–70; Visiting Professor, Centre for Contemporary Cultural Studies, University of Birmingham, England, 1970. Address: 251 West 89th Street, New York, New York 10024, U.S.A.

PUBLICATIONS

Novels

> *Who Walk in Darkness*. New York, New Directions, 1952.
> *The Bold Saboteurs*. New York, Farrar Straus, 1953.
> *The Wrong Turn* (as Daniel Harper). New York, Avon, 1954.
> *All Passion Spent*. New York, Popular Library, 1954.
> *The Double View*. New York, Dial Press, 1961.
> *Wake Up. We're Almost There*. New York, Baron, 1971.

Plays

> *Harry the Magician* (produced St. Louis, 1961).
> *Some Dreams Aren't Real* (produced St. Louis, 1962).
> *The Man with Ideas* (produced St. Louis, 1962).

Other

> *The Insane World of Adolf Hitler*. New York, Fawcett, 1967.
> *The Spanish Scene*. New York, Viking Press, 1968.

Editor, *The Scene Before You: A New Approach to American Culture*. New York, Rinehart, 1955.

Manuscript Collection: George Arents Collection, Syracuse University, New York.

Critical Studies: in *The Beat Generation and the Angry Young Men*, edited by Max Gartenberg and Gene Feldman, New York, Citadel Press, 1958; *The Beats*, edited by Seymour Krim, New York, Fawcett, 1960.

Chandler Brossard comments:

I guess my fiction is concerned with those experiences which society forbids or which one lies to oneself about. One might say the reality of the spiritual-cultural underground. This is sometimes expressed in what I could call hallucinatory fiction, which fiction began in my own case with my second novel, *The Bold Saboteurs*. I might add that I am apparently concerned with the demonism of contemporary society: those drives, those reifications that our society creates, clings to and is being destroyed by. Most lately, in my last work of fiction, *Wake Up. We're Almost There*, I see that I have gone into the labyrinths of linguistics, so to speak. Specifically, I think I could make a case for language as Fiction, since all western fiction has been projected by way of a particular language or style structure (as exemplified by, say, Hemingway on one hand, and Henry James on another). My own language fiction attempts to bring out the hidden meanings—phonemes?—which give the manifest language its base of meaning, and give these hidden deep meanings their full manifest play. Plus one other thing: identity. I am challenging, in my fiction, the concept of identity in western society as represented in its fiction. What I'm saying is that I don't really believe in the validity of individual identity. I think we are all flowing in and out of each other at all times. Identity is simply a kind of negotiation individuals make with other individuals to give each other the illusion of separate independence.

\*　　\*　　\*

Chandler Brossard is two different men, one a serious novelist of some talent and the other a hack journalist. If he could keep the two identities separate he would have fewer problems as an artist, but it is his fate to be unable to separate them, or even to tell which is which. Thus his novels are published usually under his own name, but at least once under a pseudonym (*The Wrong Turn*, by "Daniel Harper"), sometimes in quality hard cover editions (*Who Walk in Darkness*, New Directions) and sometimes in cheap paperbacks (*All Passion Spent*, Popular Library), sometimes under one title and sometimes under another (*All Passion Spent*, reprinted as *Episode with Erika*). All contain passages of good writing and passages of sloppy prose and characterization, with the proportions varying considerably from novel to novel.

Similarly, the theme of duality is common within the works. In *The Double View* a man who has been insane makes love to the wife of his best friend, who is now confined to an asylum. In *All Passion Spent* the narrator leaves his prim academic wife in order to share the bed of a girl whom he later discovers to be not only promiscuously heterosexual but bisexual as well. Psychiatrists appear frequently and are given to sexual exploitation of the female patients whose tangled lives they boast of straightening.

Brossard's most recent novel, *Wake Up. We're Almost There*, exhibits these qualities at their worst. Hailed as "Chandler Brossard's masterpiece" on the dust jacket, it runs to a quarter of a million words, and yet, judged by any standard other than weight, *Wake*

*Up* is a dismal failure. It ranges widely—New York to London to Rome to Vietnam to Paris —with the disintegration of Western civilization as its theme. Scenes of photographic accuracy merge with scenes of murky surrealism. The narrative center slips easily from mind to mind and from country to country, but all characters talk the same and all minds operate the same, with sex always as primal and final motivation (taken as an anthology of graphic sexuality the work would be impressive if only all the orgies contained in it were not so similar—except for incidental details of country, race, and physical combinations).

Some of his earlier books are much better. *Who Walk in Darkness* deals with the lower depths of Bohemian life in New York. *The Bold Saboteurs*, hardly a novel at all in any traditional sense, is nevertheless a memorable evocation of a childhood spent in delinquency. It deserves a wider readership than it has thus far obtained. The boy narrator, his brother, and at least one of his companions come sharply to life. Erika, too (from *All Passion Spent*), is disturbingly memorable. Generally in these earlier works the proportion of good prose, accurately captured dialogue, believable characterization, striking description, and meaningful plotting is much higher than it is in later works. Some of these qualities continue to exist in *The Double View*, but that book reads more like the scenario for a novel than a completely realized work—there is little internal evidence to suggest that Brossard spent much time with it. *Wake Up* is certainly the result of time and somewhere within its bulk there may be a novel, but Brossard has not discovered it for us. If we are to give him his due as a writer of fiction we must begin with his earliest works and not be put off by his latest.

—George Perkins

---

**BROWN, George Mackay.** British. Born in Stromness, Orkney, Scotland, 17 October 1921. Educated at Stromness Academy; Newbattle Abbey College; Edinburgh University, M.A. 1960. Recipient: Arts Council Award for Poetry, 1966; Society of Authors Travel Award, 1968; Scottish Arts Council Literature Prize, 1969, and award, for verse, 1971; Katherine Mansfield Menton Short Story Prize, 1971. Address: 3 Mayburn Court, Stromness, Orkney, Scotland.

PUBLICATIONS

Novel

   *Greenvoe*. London, Hogarth Press, 1972.

Short Stories

   *A Calendar of Love*. London, Hogarth Press, 1967; New York, Harcourt Brace, 1968.
   *A Time to Keep*. London, Hogarth Press, 1969; New York, Harcourt Brace, 1970.

Uncollected Short Stories

   "Mister Scarecrow", in *Ghost Book 5*. London, Barrie and Rockliff, 1969.

"The Drowned Rose", in *Ghost Book 6*.   London, Barrie and Jenkins, 1970.
"Sara", in *Ghost Book 7*.   London, Barrie and Jenkins, 1971.

Plays

*Witch* (produced Edinburgh, 1969).   Included in *A Calendar of Love*, 1967.
*A Spell for Green Corn* (produced Edinburgh, 1970).   London, Hogarth Press, 1970.

Verse

*The Storm*.   Orkney, Orkney Press, 1954.
*Loaves and Fishes*.   London, Hogarth Press, 1959.
*The Year of the Whale*.   London, Hogarth Press, 1965.
*The Five Voyages of Arnor*.   Falkland, Fife, K. D. Duval, 1966.
*Twelve Poems*.   Belfast, Festival Publications, 1968.
*Fishermen with Ploughs: A Poem Cycle*.   London, Hogarth Press, 1971.
*New and Selected Poems*.   London, Hogarth Press, 1971.

Other

*An Orkney Tapestry*.   London, Gollancz, 1969.

Manuscript Collections: Scottish National Library, Edinburgh; Edinburgh University.

George Mackay Brown comments:

I find it very difficult to comment on my own work, except in some imaginary context. I have recently finished a short story called "Seal Skin" about a musician. He reads, in Dublin, an old Celtic manuscript, about "the intricate web of creation" that men are mindlessly exploiting and tearing; and he is much moved by it. The last paragraphs are as follows:

> He [Magnus Olafson the musician] thought of the men who have thrown off all restraint and were beginning now to raven in the most secret and delicate and precious places of nature. They were the new priesthood; the world went down on its knees before every tawdry miracle—the phonograph, the motor car, the machine-gun, the wireless—that they held up in triumph. And the spoliation had hardly begun.

> Was this then the task of the artist: to keep in repair the sacred web of creation—that cosmic harmony of God and beast and man and star and plant—in the name of humanity, against those who in the name of humanity are mindlessly and systematically destroying it?

> If so, what had been taken from him was a necessary sacrifice.

*     *     *

Grace, the quality which Edwin Muir found in Mackay Brown's first verse collection, *The Storm*, is also present in his short stories. This quality is extremely difficult to describe, but Mackay Brown appears to have no difficulty whatever in expressing it. In "Celia," where one of the characters complains to the heroine about his loneliness, she replies— "gently," says the author—"Everyone is lonely. We're all prisoners. We must try to find a way to be pardoned." Yet the girl who speaks those words is no plaster saint but an alcoholic drinking with any and every man who will bring her the only anodyne for what she feels to be the agony of existence. These stories are without the slightest trace of sentimentality, but they show the cruelty of life as being everywhere and anytime chastened by a charity of such loveliness as to seem more than mortal. Even in the most terrible of the tales, "Witch," the pitying merciful swiftness of the executioner redeems the legalistic cruelty of the heroine's accusers.

Although Mackay Brown has been a Catholic since 1961, his own charity is much too wide for him to give it literary expression only in sectarian terms. In "The Eye of the Hurricane," where an old sea-captain drinks himself to death in despair, the person through whom grace shines is his poorly-educated maidservant, who rattles a tambourine with the Salvation Army; and in the title story of *A Time to Keep*, the hero (who tells the tale in the first person) remains an atheist throughout, and the charity which people show to one another in extremities is illustrated in wholly humanistic ways—through shared work between neighbours and shared sacrifice between man and woman, a sacrifice which becomes a blessing to them and to the community. For in almost all of these stories there is an underlying sense of communal activity, of the interaction of the comic and the tragic and the humdrum in everyday local affairs which at the same time have much more than simply local relevance. The scene is always in or around Orkney—a fact about which some critics have been unwise enough to complain, as if one were to protest that all the best Gauguins are "limited" to Tahiti—and the writer's intimate knowledge of his native place, past and present, gives him the freedom of all human nature, viewed with an unsentimental sympathy which arises from an inner conviction that while "we are poor people . . . born to hunger and meikle hardship," we are equally all "princes, potentates, heirs and viceroys of a Kingdom."

Although the quality of grace was present in Mackay Brown's work long before he became a Catholic, his religion has added a further dimension to his writing by providing his sympathetic appreciation of his fellow-men with a firm philosophical base. Writing in a style of pointed simplicity, Mackay Brown provides fundamental insights into our common humanity. His stories are not only admirable, they are—in the highest sense—lovable; and yet they are as keen and sharp as the Orkney wind.

—Alexander Scott

---

**BRYHER.** Formerly Annie Winifred Ellerman.   British.   Born in Margate, Kent, 1894. Educated privately and at Queenwood School, Eastbourne, Sussex. Married the writer Robert McAlmon in 1921 (marriage dissolved, 1926); Kenneth Macpherson in 1927 (marriage dissolved, 1947). Published, with Kenneth Macpherson, *Close Up* magazine. Address: Kenwin, Burier, Vaud, Switzerland.

PUBLICATIONS

Novels

*Development*.   London, Constable, and New York, Macmillan, 1920.

*Two Selves*.   Paris, Contact, n.d. [c. 1923]; New York, Chaucer Head, n.d. [c. 1927].
*Civilians*.   Territet, Switzerland, Pool, 1927; London, Pool, 1930.
*The Lighthearted Student*, with Trude Weiss.   London, Pool, 1930.
*The Fourteenth of October*.   New York, Pantheon Books, 1952; London, Collins, 1954.
*The Player's Boy*.   New York, Pantheon Books, 1953; London, Collins, 1957.
*Roman Wall*.   New York, Pantheon Books, 1954; London, Collins, 1955.
*Beowulf*.   New York, Pantheon Books, 1956.
*Gate to the Sea*.   New York, Pantheon Books, 1958; London, Collins, 1959.
*Ruan*.   New York, Pantheon Books, 1960; London, Collins, 1961.
*The Coin of Carthage*.   New York, Harcourt Brace, 1963; London, Collins, 1964.
*Visa for Avalon*.   New York, Harcourt Brace, 1965.
*This January Tale*.   New York, Harcourt Brace, 1966; London, Secker and Warburg,
   1968.
*The Colors of Vaud*.   New York, Harcourt Brace, 1969.


Verse

*Arrow Music*, with others.   London, Bumpus, 1922.


Other

*Amy Lowell: A Critical Appreciation*.   London, Eyre and Spottiswoode, 1918.
*A Picture Geography for Little Children: Asia*.   London, Cape, 1925.
*West* (on the United States).   London, Cape, 1925.
*Film Problems of Soviet Russia*.   London, Pool, 1929.
*Cinema Survey*, with others.   London, Brendin, 1937.
*The Heart to Artemis: A Writer's Memoirs*.   New York, Harcourt Brace, 1962;
   London, Collins, 1963.
*The Days of Mars: A Memoir, 1940–1946*.   New York, Harcourt Brace, 1972.


*      *      *


Anyone interested in the novels of Bryher should read her remarkable autobiography, *The Heart to Artemis*, for in it lies the key to them. There she describes a childhood in which the seeds of all her later interests and achievements were sown. Travel with intelligent parents proved marvellously fruitful, the child gathering her sense of time and place and history through leisurely wanderings around the Mediterranean and the Middle East, acquiring the rudiments, at least, of the extraordinary power that came later to project herself into other worlds, to live in other ages. "Fate was kind and I did few formal lessons in my childhood," she writes, "with the result that my mind developed freely and was ravenous for knowledge. . . . I was reading history from books written not for children but for scholars by the time I was ten, I could chatter in Arabic, I knew some hieroglyphics. More important perhaps than knowledge, I had been near to poverty, fire and death." The heroes of these stimulating early years were Shakespeare, Homer and *The Swiss Family Robinson*; and G. A. Henty, the writer of boys' books, of whom she says: "He taught me history." Other influences were Colette and Dorothy Richardson, and the autobiography is dedicated "to the memory of my master, Stéphane Mallarmé."

These varied influences converged in a woman of remarkable mental powers; and at the same time of an almost mystical power to absorb the alien and the past, to assimilate other cultures than her own. Her novels are set in the past, generally the distant past, and nearly always at a time of dissolution and transition, when old worlds are crumbling and new ones have yet to emerge from the violence. Fear lies at their centre, a sense of doom and yet of defiance; and at the same time, with hindsight which enriches the whole, we know that out of the ruins other worlds were to grow, that the misery and despair would break down into a compost to nourish other civilisations. This empathy that enables her to live through the past rather than merely to recreate it is found in the best of modern historical novelists, whether they write for adults or the young (the distinction has little meaning, today, at a high level of writing): Marguerite Yourcenar, Henry Treece, Rosemary Sutcliffe. In Bryher the sense of other worlds is so strong that one is oneself swept into them, as if through poetry. Edith Sitwell, in an introduction to *The Fourteenth of October*, a story about the Danes invading Yorkshire seen from the point of view of the doomed Saxons, wrote: "The prose rhythms are of great beauty . . . these rhythms vary, they fluctuate, grow hard and terrible as in the battle scenes, or are exquisite and tender."

What is astonishing is Bryher's range, as well as depth, of historical knowledge and feeling. *Roman Wall* is set in a Roman outpost in what is now Switzerland, when German tribes are massing on the far bank of the Rhine, threatening to pour in. *Ruan* is set in 6th-century Britain, in the Celtic parts—Cornwall and the Scillys, Wales and Ireland—a generation after the death of Arthur. *The Coin of Carthage*, which was distantly inspired by G. A. Henty's *The Young Carthaginian*, is about Greek traders in a Greek settlement on the Italian coast, at the time of Hannibal. *Gate to the Sea* is set in the 4th century BC, when Poseidonia had been conquered by the Lucanians after the death of Alexander. And the same sense of doom (in this case of doom accomplished) hangs over *This January Tale*, which is about England after the Conquest, when, Bryher writes, "Art and learning virtually disappeared. A magnificent language was destroyed." Then, characteristically, she links the ages, making a valid modern parallel: "1940 almost followed the pattern of 1066."

The atmospheric intensity of Bryher's novels makes them stay in the mind, become part of one's own experience.

—Isabel Quigley

---

**BUCHANAN, George (Henry Perrott).** British. Born in Kilwaughter, County Antrim, Northern Ireland, 9 January 1904. Educated at Campbell College and Queens University, Belfast. Served in the Royal Air Force Coastal Command, 1940–45. Married Mary Corn in 1938 (marriage dissolved, 1945); Noel Beasley, 1949 (deceased, 1951); the Hon. Janet Margesson, 1952 (deceased, 1968); has two daughters. Book Reviewer for the *Times Literary Supplement*, London, 1928–40; on the editorial staff, *The Times*, London, 1930–35; Columnist and Drama Critic, *News Chronicle*, London, 1935–38. Chairman, Town and Country Development Committee, Northern Ireland, 1949–53. Since 1954, Member of the Executive Council of the European Society of Culture, Venice. Address: 27 Ashley Gardens, London S.W.1, England.

PUBLICATIONS

Novels

*A London Story*. London, Constable, 1935; New York, Dutton, 1936.
*Rose Forbes: The Biography of an Unknown Woman* (part 1). London, Constable, 1937.
*Entanglement*. London, Constable, 1938; New York, Appleton Century, 1939.

*The Soldier and the Girl*.   London, Heinemann, 1940.
*Rose Forbes* (parts 1 and 2).   London, Faber, 1950.
*A Place to Live*.   London, Faber, 1952.
*Naked Reason*.   New York, Holt Rinehart, 1971.

## Plays

*Dance Night* (produced London, 1934).   London, French, 1935.
*A Trip to the Castle* (produced London, 1960).
*Tresper Revolution* (produced London, 1961).
*War Song* (produced London, 1965).

## Verse

*Bodily Responses*.   London, Gaberbocchus, 1958.
*Conversation with Strangers*.   London, Gaberbocchus, 1961.
*Annotations*.   Oxford, Carcanet, 1970.

## Other

*Passage Through the Present: Chiefly Notes from a Journal*.   London, Constable, 1932;
    New York, Dutton, 1933.
*Words for Tonight: A Notebook*.   London, Constable, 1936.
*Green Seacoast* (autobiography).   London, Gaberbocchus, 1959; New York, Red Dust,
    1968.
*Morning Papers* (autobiography).   London, Gaberbocchus, 1965.

George Buchanan comments:

A novel is a poetic work. The French emphasis on *écriture*, the Russian Formalists' on "poetic speech", are converging points of view. Novels must have the same sudden careless quality as poems.

I prefer work that is artificial, am against autobiographical novels. (Better to face the truth in an undisguised autobiography, and try to turn the past into knowledge.) A novel should *au fond* be erotic. Otherwise it is on the side of death. Note the quantity of death novels, openly popularising the idea of murder.

The novel is an event in consciousness. Our aim isn't to copy actuality, but to modify and recreate our sense of it. The novelist is inviting the reader to watch a performance in his own brain. The people of the novel are in me and I am in them, from the beginning. I am making, rather than knowing. Much of the making is outside my understanding. I seek to create groups in an imaginary version of society, but a society which is accepted as being in history. These would include neo-persons, individuated constructs of the author. By thinking in a situation, each would be propelled to new positions. Story would thus emerge, not be imposed beforehand. It would also tend to be non-scenic. The characters will theorise, not dramatise, themselves. We don't necessarily grasp life in terms of scenes, as in film and theatre. It is this other style of dealing with the drift of persons that is left to the novel. Narrative will be more critical than descriptive. The author will write, as Victor Shklovsky said, with *sang froid*. Detachment, not identification, is the first sign of seriousness.

Allow me to retain my own services as narrator. I rarely employ the technique of impersonating one of the characters. If it is feared that by telling the story myself, I destroy the illusion, I ask, "The illusion of what?" I don't wish the reader to feel that he is watching a piece of actuality. He is reading a book which sets out to give an impression of an imaginary event. But sometimes another voice does begin to be heard behind the author's. The work that I do is not only inside me but also apart from me, so that I address myself to it as an attentive associate, and I must be attentive. For a voice seems always about to speak to me out of the words that I myself write. I must be ready to hear.

It may be that our civilisation will depend on the success with which we can make a secondary life, surrounded by imaginary elements. The novel has an important role in this. There may be some value in the notion of treating fiction as an account of the socially possible—not going the length of science fiction but offering limited deviations from familiar functioning. "A large measure of the reader's pleasure comes from participation in an empirical venture. Novels are risks" (Herbert Gold). Perhaps novels will be creating persons on their journey into half-known, half-guessed, half-anticipated areas.

*        *        *

George Buchanan's concern in his novels is with presenting a certain precise, forceful, and utterly convincing kind of reality, with showing the way people really live and think. But this is done, not through a species of naturalistic description, but through a slightly different method. If he presents episodes of London life in all its variety, they are not meant to add up to one strong deterministic point. His poetic precision and honesty won't allow him to make life fall into a pattern so consistent. In fact, his reality is full of dichotomies, confusions, conflicts within characters who often seem contradictory. Yet this does not damage the truth he tries to communicate; paradoxically, it gives it added force. In his earliest book, *Passage Through the Present*, he writes: "These notes were made by a mind endowed with 'negative capability'—content if careful expression should be spent upon stating only irresolution."

His most "plotted" novels, *A Place to Live* and *The Soldier and the Girl*, even though structured around questions—will Sinton Kells give up his small-town backwater for a London life? will Alice give up Colin Gray, her painter husband, for her seemingly glamorous first love, Nigel Troop?—remain faithful to a view of life that realizes that the answers to such questions are never final. Sinton Kells' job as manager of a seaside hotel, and his marriage to a domestic, complacent girl trained to like dusting, predispose him to accept "the myth of the Happy Man". But he has doubts. In the hotel kitchen, the entrails of fowls remind him of the Romans' reliance on visceral influences, and this leads to a contrast between instinct— "inner" promptings—and intellect. His doubts are encouraged by a sophisticated London journalist who calls the "myth of the Happy Man" a "vulgar ideal", and who urges him to try for a more purposeful life. Sinton, though, gives way to the influences of job and wife, and the end of the novel sees him set up in a communal house on the sea with two other couples—though his lack of feeling settled or committed persists.

Alice's problem, in *The Soldier and the Girl*, is somewhat simpler—choosing between Colin and Nigel. All three characters are complex. But the fact that Alice changes from a rather vigorous, simple Irish girl who feels Colin is too cerebral ("all that thought") to a questioning, questing woman, and the fact that Colin changes from an intellectual who uses art to assert and protect his own identity to a person who is aware of the "idiotic mixture" of life with its consequent anguish, make them more suitably matched. Their openness to change validates their individuality, whereas Nigel's military glamor is only the stiff covering of a flabby, sentimental conventionality. Nigel is terrified of life; Colin's maturity allows him to recognize and thus repudiate life's possible terrors.

*The Soldier and the Girl* is on a larger scale than *A Place to Live*, and its obvious links are with the two "London" novels, *A London Story* and *Entanglement*. These books are less conventionally plotted, *A London Story* having an ironic, circular structure, and *Entanglement* covering a one-year period (March 1937-March 1938); *A London Story* could, in fact, be shuffled into *Entanglement* without either losing too much in unity. Since Buchanan is interested in creating an image of social and economic London in as much variety and depth as possible, he centers his attention on commerce and business. Drancers Store, in fact, dominates both books almost as much as the Courts of Chancery dominate *Bleak House*, though with a better-lit sinisterness. Along with the large manufacturing firm of Polle's, Drancers gives a center of social as well as economic power. These are rather bitter books, and both are full of economic and social hypocrisy, manifested in many ways: Lord Flowerfield (the symbol of success and decisiveness in both books) subscribes to a patriotic fund when war threatens, but invests abroad; landlords are "invisible oppressors" acting through agents; factory foremen and dock bosses bully their men. Other establishment figures almost instinctively rely on intellect, "the agreeable continuity of conversation", or "historical perspective" to allow themselves to play a role of authority without honestly reacting to what they see around them. The rich continue their social rituals, from debutante balls to stag hunts, in the midst of poverty, seemingly with an invisible protective shield around both their bodies and their minds. In this London, conventional heroism requires action "in the distance" (i.e., not "here"); all bosses have the secret savor of their power always in their minds; making money, ordering policemen about, not having to consider whether you love your husband—these are the marks of success. For Buchanan, of course, this London is full of evasion, of secret fears and worries underlying the sophisticated and smooth surface. Honest living requires a more flexible, thoughtful response to experience. Even Lord Flowerfield has his moments of doubt (suggesting that Buchanan is not really interested in stereotypes), and the director of Polle's, Charles Manwick, and his wife become prey to real terror as their security is questioned. But the real centers of attention in the books are the young men, Nicholas in *A London Story* and Kevin and Tom in *Entanglement*, who *do* think and attempt to evaluate the world they live in. In a moving moment of *Entanglement*, Kevin and Rona kiss, aware that suffering surrounds them, but responding to the need to live now, not in the past or the future. The general feeling we are left with is that the characters in the books are yet capable of surprising us, that their lives are being lived as we watch, and not that the author has carefully arranged before us a paradigm of life. The concluding sentences of *Entanglement* makes this clear: "Whichever way life goes, the entangled human life remains, shining and dark, unfitted to geometry, with contradiction and paradox. Its essence is always more inventive than any man's imagination that it contains."

This comment can also be applied to perhaps the most startling and convincing of all Buchanan's books, *Rose Forbes*. Rose's life has little pattern. The daughter of a small farmer in Northern Ireland, she marries a childhood sweetheart. He is drowned soon afterwards; and Rose drifts to England, encounters various men who either reinforce her sense of being alive, or cramp her growing need for freedom. Unfortunately, she marries an utterly conventional merchant, and later leaves him for a young idealist, only to realize that the young man is not really interested in her. Part One, published as a complete work, ends with Rose facing this problem, a startling ending to a novel. Not until Part Two was published is her reaction made clear: she becomes a showgirl in London, meets various other men, drifts back to Belfast, and finally marries a schoolmaster and has her first child in her late 30's. Yet, even at the end of the book, the reader doesn't feel that Rose's life is finished. (In fact, she and her husband turn up casually at the end of *A Place to Live*, sharing the big house with Sinton Kells.) Buchanan's refusal to tie his fiction to conventional development makes this novel unusual and appealing; and its mixture of seriousness, precision, and beauty is something the reader gets only in a novel like Henry Green's *Living* (1929).

Buchanan's first novel in 19 years, *Naked Reason*, is a pared-down view of a woman's life from schoolgirl age (in 1952) to maturity (in 1963). One could almost call it a postscript to *Rose Forbes*. Concentrating on Ellie's sexual liberation, the novel is pithy, epigrammatic, and convincing. Her diary entry from the Tao,

> The vulgar are clever, self-assured,
> I alone depressed,
> patient as the sea,
> adrift, seemingly aimless

along with the title of the book itself, sums up her constant concerns. And this latest novel concentrates Buchanan's complexity and clarity into a moving record of life.

—James Vinson

---

**BUCK, Pearl S(ydenstricker).**   American.   Born in Hillsboro, West Virginia, 26 June 1892; daughter of Presbyterian missionaries in China. Educated at boarding school in Shanghai, China, 1907–09; Randolph-Macon College, Lynchburg, Virginia, B.A. 1914; Cornell University, Ithaca, New York, M.A. 1926. Married John Lossing Buck in 1917 (divorced, 1935); Richard J. Walsh, 1935 (died, 1960); has two children and eight adopted children. Taught psychology at Randolph-Macon College, 1914; taught English at the University of Nanking, 1921–31, Southeastern University, Nanking, 1925–27, and Chung Yang University, Nanking, 1928–31. Co-Editor, *Asia* magazine, New York, 1941–46. Founder and Director, East and West Association, 1941–51. Founder, Welcome House, an adoption agency, 1949, and the Pearl S. Buck Foundation, 1964. Member, Board of Directors, Weather Engineering Corporation of America, Manchester, New Hampshire, 1966. Recipient: Pulitzer Prize, 1932; Howells Medal, 1935; Nobel Prize for Literature, 1938; National Conference of Christians and Jews' Brotherhood Award, 1955; President's Commission on Employment of the Physically Handicapped Citation, 1958; Woman's National Book Association's Skinner Award, 1960; ELA Award in Literature, 1969. M.A., Yale University, New Haven, Connecticut, 1933; D.Litt., University of West Virginia, Morgantown, 1940; St. Lawrence University, Canton, New York, 1942; Delaware Valley College, Doylestown, Pennsylvania, 1965; LL.D., Howard University, Washington, D.C., 1942; Muhlenberg College, Allentown, Pennsylvania, 1966; L.H.D., Lincoln University, Pennsylvania, 1953; Woman's Medical College of Philadelphia, 1954; University of Pittsburgh, Pennsylvania, 1960; Bethany College, West Virginia, 1963; Hahnemann Medical College, Philadelphia, 1966; Rutgers University, New Brunswick, New Jersey, 1969; D.Mus., Combs College of Music, Philadelphia, 1962; D.H., West Virginia State College, Institute, 1963. Member, American Academy of Arts and Letters. Address: Route 1, Box 164, Perkasie, Pennsylvania 18944, U.S.A.

PUBLICATIONS

Novels

   *East Wind: West Wind.*   New York, Day, 1930; London, Methuen, 1931.
   *The Good Earth.*   New York, Day, and London, Methuen, 1931.
   *Sons.*   New York, Day, and London, Methuen, 1932.
   *The Mother.*   New York, Day, and London, Methuen, 1934.
   *A House Divided.*   New York, Reynal and Hitchcock, and London, Methuen, 1935.
   *This Proud Heart.*   New York, Reynal and Hitchcock, and London, Methuen, 1938.
   *The Patriot.*   New York, Day, 1939; London, Methuen, 1941.
   *Other Gods: An American Legend.*   New York, Day, and London, Macmillan, 1940.
   *China Sky.*   Philadelphia, Triangle, 1942.
   *Dragon Seed.*   New York, Day, and London, Macmillan, 1942.
   *The Promise.*   New York, Day, 1943; London, Methuen, 1945.

*China Flight.*   Philadelphia, Triangle, 1945.
*The Townsman* (as John Sedges).   New York, Day, 1945; London, Methuen, 1946.
*Portrait of a Marriage.*   New York, Day, 1945; London, Methuen, 1946.
*Pavilion of Women.*   New York, Day, 1946; London, Methuen, 1947.
*The Angry Wife* (as John Sedges).   New York, Day, 1947; London, Methuen, 1948.
*Peony.*   New York, Day, 1948; as *The Bondmaid*, London, Methuen, 1949.
*Kinfolk.*   New York, Day, 1949; London, Methuen, 1950.
*The Long Love* (as John Sedges).   New York, Day, 1949; London, Methuen, 1950.
*God's Men.*   New York, Day, and London, Methuen, 1950.
*The Hidden Flower.*   New York, Day, and London, Methuen, 1952.
*Satan Never Sleeps.*   New York, Pocket Books, 1952.
*Bright Procession* (as John Sedges).   New York, Day, and London, Methuen, 1952.
*Come, My Beloved.*   New York, Day, and London, Methuen, 1953.
*Voices in the House* (as John Sedges).   New York, Day, 1953; London, Methuen, 1954.
*Imperial Woman.*   New York, Day, and London, Methuen, 1956.
*Letter from Peking.*   New York, Day, and London, Methuen, 1957.
*Command the Morning.*   New York, Day, and London, Methuen, 1959.
*The Living Reed.*   New York, Day, and London, Methuen, 1963.
*Death in the Castle.*   New York, Day, 1965; London, Methuen, 1966.
*The Time Is Noon.*   New York, Day, and London, Methuen, 1967.
*The New Year.*   New York, Day, and London, Methuen, 1968.
*The Three Daughters of Madame Liang.*   New York, Day, and London, Methuen, 1969.
*Mandala.*   New York, Day, 1970; London, Methuen, 1971.


## Short Stories

*The First Wife and Other Stories.*   New York, Day, and London, Methuen, 1933.
*Today and Forever: Stories of China.*   New York, Day, and London, Macmillan, 1941.
*Far and Near: Stories of Japan, China and America.*   New York, Day, 1948; as *Far and Near: Stories of East and West*, London, Methuen, 1949.
*Fourteen Stories.*   New York, Day, 1961; as *With a Delicate Air and Other Stories*, London, Methuen, 1962.
*Hearts Come Home and Other Stories.*   New York, Pocket Books, 1962.
*Stories of China.*   New York, Day, 1964.
*The Good Deed and Other Stories of Asia, Past and Present.*   New York, Day, 1969; London, Methuen, 1970.


## Plays

*Flight into China* (produced New York, 1939).
*Sun Yat Sen: A Play, Preceded by a Lecture by Dr. Hu-Shih.*   New York, Universal Distributors, and London, China Campaign Committee, n.d. [1944?].
*The First Wife* (produced New York, 1945).
*A Desert Incident* (produced New York, 1959).
*Christine* (produced New York, 1960).
*The Guide*, adaptation of the novel by N. K. Narayan (produced New York, 1965).


## Other

*The Young Revolutionist* (juvenile).   New York, Day, and London, Methuen, 1932.
*Is There a Case for Foreign Missions?*   New York, Day, 1932; London, Methuen, 1933.

*East and West and the Novel: Sources of the Early Chinese Novel.*   Peking, College of Chinese Studies, 1932.

*The Exile* (biography).   New York, Reynal and Hitchcock, and London, Methuen, 1936.

*Fighting Angel: Portrait of a Soul* (biography).   New York, Reynal and Hitchcock, 1936; London, Methuen, 1937.

*The Chinese Novel.*   New York, Day, and London, Macmillan, 1939.

*Stories for Little Children.*   New York, Day, 1940.

*When Fun Begins* (juvenile).   London, Methuen, 1941.

*Of Men and Women.*   New York, Day, 1941; London, Methuen, 1942.

*American Unity and Asia.*   New York, Day, 1942; as *Asia and Democracy*, London, Methuen, 1943.

*The Chinese Children Next Door* (juvenile).   New York, Day, 1942; London, Methuen, 1943.

*The Water Buffalo Children* (juvenile).   New York, Day, 1943; London, Methuen, 1945.

*What America Means to Me.*   New York, Day, 1943; London, Methuen, 1944.

*The Dragon Fish* (juvenile).   New York, Day, 1944; London, Methuen, 1946.

*Talk about Russia*, with Masha Scott.   New York, Day, 1945.

*Tell the People: Talks with James Yen about the Mass Education Movement.*   New York, Day, 1945.

*Yu Lan: Flying Boy of China* (juvenile).   New York, Day, 1945; London, Methuen, 1947.

*How It Happens: Talk about the German People, 1914–1933*, with Erna von Pustau. New York, Day, 1947.

*The Big Wave* (juvenile).   New York, Day, 1947; London, Methuen, 1956.

*American Argument*, with Eslanda Goode Robeson.   New York, Day, 1949; London, Methuen, 1950.

*One Bright Day* (juvenile).   New York, Day, 1950; as *One Bright Day and Other Stories for Children*, London, Methuen, 1952.

*The Child Who Never Grew.*   New York, Day, 1950; London, Methuen, 1951.

*The Man Who Changed China: The Story of Sun Yat Sen* (juvenile).   New York, Random House, 1953; London, Methuen, 1955.

*My Several Worlds* (autobiography).   New York, Day, 1954; London, Methuen, 1955.

*The Beech Tree* (juvenile).   New York, Day, 1954.

*Johnny Jack and His Beginnings* (juvenile).   New York, Day, 1954; London, Methuen, 1955.

*Christmas Miniature* (juvenile).   New York, Day, 1957; as *The Christmas Mouse*, London, Methuen, 1958.

*Friend to Friend*, with Carlos P. Romulo.   New York, Day, 1958.

*The Delights of Learning.*   Pittsburgh, University of Pittsburgh Press, 1960.

*The Christmas Ghost* (juvenile).   New York, Day, 1960; London, Methuen, 1962.

*A Bridge for Passing* (autobiography).   New York, Day, 1962; London, Methuen, 1963.

*The Joy of Children.*   New York, Day, 1964.

*Welcome Child* (juvenile).   New York, Day, 1964.

*The Gifts They Bring: Our Debts to the Mentally Retarded*, with Gweneth T. Zarfoss. New York, Day, 1965.

*Children for Adoption.*   New York, Random House, 1965.

*The Big Fight* (juvenile).   New York, Day, 1965.

*The People of Japan.*   New York, Simon and Schuster, 1966; London, Hale, 1968.

*For Spacious Skies: Journey in Dialogue*, with Theodore F. Harris.   New York, Day, 1966.

*The Little Fox in the Middle* (juvenile).   New York, Collier, and London, Macmillan, 1966.

*My Mother's House*, with others.   Richwood, West Virginia, Appalachia Press, 1966.

*To My Daughters, With Love.*   New York, Day, 1967.

*Matthew, Mark, Luke, and John* (juvenile).   New York, Day, 1967.
*The People of China*.   London, Hale, 1968.
*The Kennedy Women*.   New York, Cowles-Day, and London, Methuen, 1970.
*China as I See It*, edited by Theodore F. Harris.   New York, Day, 1970; London,
   Methuen, 1971.
*The Story Bible*.   New York, Batholomew, 1971.

Editor, *China in Black and White: An Album of Woodcuts by Contemporary Chinese
   Artists*.   New York, Day, 1945.
Editor, *Fairy Tales of the Orient*.   New York, Simon and Schuster, 1965.

Translator, *All Men Are Brothers*, by Shui Hu Chan.   New York, Day, and London,
   Methuen, 1933.

*          *          *

Pearl Buck's career and reputation blossomed with the publication of *The Good Earth*
in 1931. This epic *roman-fleuve* analyzes Wang Lung, his wife O-lan, and their relatives and
friends with convincing familiarity in a stately and lyrical style which combines the simplicity of the old Chinese sagas with the mellifluousness of the King James version of the
Bible. The depiction of one peasant family's trials, successes, and tragedies gives the book
an embracing universality so that although the setting is somewhat strange and foreign,
there is an immediate identification with common, recognized human experiences. Especially
effective is the objective handling of the material. Life itself seems to be speaking; the
author's presence becomes unobtrusive, almost nonexistent. Several critics have commented
on this approach and about the novel's alleged Naturalism. *The Good Earth*, despite the
objectivity of narration, the documentary treatment, the stress on environment and heredity,
and the emphasis on the lower social classes, is not Naturalistic. Free will operates clearly
and exerts its influence, and the novel's characters, unlike those of Zola, for instance, are
not overwhelmed by social and economic forces they cannot control. Further, a fundamental
meliorism exists which would never be discovered in typical Naturalistic writing. An optimistic feeling pervades Pearl Buck's books. Although problems are clearly described and
herculean difficulties abound, there is a marked stress on the point that good will, dedication,
serious moral purpose, and similar elements can achieve improvement and make man's
lot and the world itself better.
    *Sons* and *A House Divided* are sequels to *The Good Earth*; this grouping forms the *House
of Earth* trilogy. Neither novel, however, achieves artistic effectiveness primarily because
the characterizations are too superficial and externalized. Obvious manipulation distracts,
and several plot improbabilities intrude. Much more important and meaningful is *The
Mother*, which presents the title character in the role of universal mother, suffering and
enduring and rejoicing while caught in a cyclical flow of time. The use of a never-ending
symbolic type participating in almost every experience and feeling which a mother undergoes becomes a sharply defined, moving, and starkly realistic encounter with truth. Unfortunately, the style has been so deliberately muted and simplified that it is unable to support
adequately the weight of the subject matter.
    Two outstanding biographies—*The Exile* and *Fighting Angel*—heighten Pearl Buck's
early career. *The Exile* describes the life of her own mother blighted by an incompatible
husband, religious doubts, and homesickness for the United States. As the wife of a missionary in China, Caroline Stulting performs all marital, moral, and social duties required
of her and engages in numerous humanitarian activities. But her underlying unhappiness
and a torturing series of self-doubts produce dramatic tension and a depth of character
revelation rare in most biographies. *Fighting Angel*, the companion biography about Miss
Buck's father, is even better. Absalom Sydenstricker was an intensely dedicated and scholarly
missionary. No obstacle or hardship deterred him from missionary duty. Since Pearl Buck

disliked her father in several ways, his portrait is painted in harsher and more critical terms. She cannot forgive him for subordinating his family to his religious cause. The two books are also masterful portraits of nineteenth-century individualism and the missionary attributes which permeated an earlier period. Both biographies were significant factors in enabling Pearl Buck to win the 1938 Nobel Prize. The Chairman of the Nobel Committee asserted that these books deserved "classic rank." They substantiated and reënforced the impression given by *The Good Earth* and were particularly widely read in European countries. Mrs. Buck's popularity with readers throughout the world is, among American writers, rivalled only by Mark Twain.

*The Patriot*, a post-Nobel Prize novel, demonstrated a perceptive knowledge of historical and contemporary conditions in both China and Japan and carefully described the onset of war between these countries. It was about this time, however, that Pearl Buck's work began to decline. She now wrote more prolifically for magazines, newspapers—indeed in almost every medium. She became concerned with reaching a larger audience and turned often to non-fiction. She dedicated herself with fervor to numerous humanitarian causes and served on countless charitable and libertarian organizations and committees. Further, she commenced to intrude propaganda into her fiction. For example, the stylistically effective novel *Dragon Seed* loses much artistry because of its preachment against Japanese militarism and its advocacy of China's cause. From this point on, Mrs. Buck's writing is weakened by didactic commentary on a variety of subjects and her open espousal of partisan causes. Even though her heart was always in the right place and she supported the most moral, democratic, and humanitarian principles, she was now a crusader first and a novelist second. Such best selling efforts as *Other Gods*, *Pavilion of Women*, *Kinfolk*, *God's Men*, and *Command the Morning* wrestle impressively with various social and intellectual problems of considerable importance, but the obtrusive hand of the author is more than noticeable. Artistic objectivity and focus have vanished.

In addition, a lack of depth and subtlety in characterization, present even in some of the earlier novels, now increased. In such an ambitious novel as *Imperial Woman*, a fictionalized biography of the Chinese Empress Tzu Hsi who died in 1908, one finds an important theme (Western imperialism) presented with vivid realism, effective suspense, and pageantry both colorful and delightfully kaleidoscopic. Yet this book fails, like most of Mrs. Buck's later work, because the characters do not come completely alive. This is particularly true of Tzu Hsi who is seen externally in her ambition, cruelty, and cleverness, but without the inner workings of her personality revealed. An excessive remoteness exists about her. She is a puppet with practically no dimension.

Mrs. Buck should have retained her authorial objectivity and her careful probing of character (found in *The Good Earth*) which she has discarded in favor of her now obvious propagandistic concerns. Up to the present she continues her career in this later vein. She has come to write too often and too much. A recent novel such as *Death in the Castle* is admittedly a potboiler, but the Pearl Buck of the 1930's would not have produced such a lifeless, inane book. On occasion she still demonstrates flashes of her original talent. Novels like *The Living Reed* and *The Three Daughters of Madame Liang* contain several artistic episodes and some expert handling of narrative interest, yet they are marred by her didactic obsessions and by a too facile conception of characterization. Well-intentioned literary critics persist in hoping that Mrs. Buck will return to the fiction techniques and approach which characterized her literary efforts up to 1940; apparently now this wish will never be realized.

—Paul A. Doyle

**BUCKLER, Ernest.** Canadian. Born in Dalhousie West, Nova Scotia, 19 July 1908. Educated at Dalhousie University, Halifax, Nova Scotia, B.A. 1929; University of Toronto, M.A. in philosophy, 1930. Actuarial employee, Manufacturers Life Insurance Company, Toronto, 1930–35. Sometime Farmer, and Free-lance Writer, since 1936. Columnist, *Saturday Night*, Toronto, 1947–48; Book Reviewer, *New York Times* and *Los Angeles Times*, 1962–66. Recipient: *Maclean's* magazine prize, 1948; President's Medal, University of Western Ontario, 1957, 1958; Canada Council Fellowship, 1960, 1963, 1966. D.Litt., University of New Brunswick, Federiction, 1969; LL.D., Dalhousie University, 1971. Address: R.R. 3, Bridgetown, Nova Scotia, Canada.

PUBLICATIONS

Novels

    *The Mountain and the Valley.* New York, Holt, 1952.
    *The Cruelest Month.* Toronto, McClelland and Stewart, 1963.

Other

    *Ox Bells and Fireflies: A Memoir.* Toronto, McClelland and Stewart, and New York, Knopf, 1968.
    *Window on the Sea*, with Hans Weber (on Nova Scotia). Toronto, McClelland and Stewart, 1972.

    Has written radio plays for the CBC.

Manuscript Collection: University of Toronto Library.

Ernest Buckler comments:

    It is extremely difficult to list the various "themes" of my work—but by far the most recurrent is an attempt to render the texture of life in the Nova Scotian country in all its complexity. Such life, often thought to be crude and simple, is nothing of the kind. It is a microcosm in which every facet of whatever macrocosm one can think of (particularly in cases of the spirit) is illustrated and parabled.

*     *     *

    Though he has written three books and innumerable essays, stories, radio plays and other works, Ernest Buckler's reputation rests especially on one book: his first novel, *The Mountain and the Valley*.
    Set in the time-eroded farmland of Nova Scotia's Annapolis Valley, *The Mountain and the Valley* is one of the most rich, densely-textured and complex of Canadian novels—too much so at times, indeed, shading away into occasional over-elaboration and obscurity. As Claude Bissell has said, it is "a novel written in praise of the family", and it traces the development of David Canaan, an unusually sensitive and intelligent boy who loves language and appears something of an artist *manqué*. The promise David shows, the attentiveness with

which he notices every nuance of mood and shift in interaction, the capacity he reveals to describe these subtleties—none of these qualities receives full play in the country village to which something in him remains deeply committed. David's health, never robust, is seriously weakened by a fall from a barn loft, and when he dies at thirty, he has been for some time a slightly eccentric bachelor living in the family home with only his grandmother.

But to focus on plot in *The Mountain and the Valley* is to miss the point, for the novel's life is in its characters and its language. Buckler has done graduate study in philosophy, and the reflectiveness, the psychological sophistication and the intricate symbolic construction of his work leave an impression which has less to do with art narrowly conceived than with wisdom. The book seems slow—until one realizes that the pace is that of country living, allowing time for observation, contemplation, attention to the phenomena of nature and of man meshed with nature. Despite some obvious weaknesses which spring in part from the nature of Buckler's enterprise, *The Mountain and the Valley* is one of the most rewarding and expressive works of the Canadian imagination.

*The Cruelest Month* was pummelled by the reviewers, as the successor to a brilliant first novel normally is, and it has rarely been read with the kind of care it warrants. To Paul Creed's guest-house in Nova Scotia comes a disparate group, including a novelist, an aged professor of archaeology and his spinster daughter, a well-to-do couple from Greenwich, Connecticut, and a withdrawn former medical student. Each one—Paul included—faces a personal crisis of some sort. The interplay among these private anguishes forms the action of the novel, which concludes as all but Paul and his housekeeper, Letty, drive away through a roaring forest fire.

*The Cruelest Month* has Buckler's usual faults. A compulsion to find an exact verbal equivalent for every shade of experience produces over-writing; some passages are merely coy. But if the reviewers were right to find Buckler's second novel less impressive than his first, they were wrong to dismiss it as briskly as many did. Like all Buckler's work, it is shrewd and craftsmanlike; and Buckler at his worst is more serious and more honest than most Canadian novelists at their best.

With *Ox Bells and Fireflies*, his most recent book, Buckler abandoned the novel form almost entirely. He calls the book "a fictive memoir": an accurate phrase for an attempt to capture the nimbus of life in his native village fifty years ago. Though it lacks the thrust and intensity of a novel, *Ox Bells and Fireflies* is a beautiful book, with passages which read like verse, bits of folk wisdom imbedded in it like raisins in cake, country words and phrases polished and set like gems, and a haunting feeling for the evanescent terror and magnificence of life which has always spoken to Buckler with a unique intensity in the country.

*Ox Bells and Fireflies* presents itself as the distillation of a sensitive man's love for common experience. Though no one but Buckler could have written it, it is curiously impersonal, almost the voice of the land and its rooted people themselves. Buckler maintains that the universal inheres in the local, that his own village contains all man's tragedy and joy. His own work is powerful evidence for that theory.

—Donald Cameron

---

**BUECHNER, (Carl) Frederick.** American. Born in New York City, 11 July 1926. Educated at Princeton University, New Jersey, A.B. 1947; Union Theological Seminary, New York, B.D. 1958; ordained a Minister of the United Presbyterian Church, 1958. Served in the United States Army, 1944–46. Married Judith Friedrike Merck in 1956; has three children. English Master, Lawrenceville School, New Jersey, 1948–53; Instructor in Creative Writing, New York University, summers 1953–54; Head of the Employment

Clinic, East Harlem Protestant Parish, New York, 1954–58; Chairman of the Religion Department, 1958–67, and School Minister, 1960–67, Phillips Exeter Academy, Exeter, New Hampshire. William Belden Noble Lecturer, Harvard University, Cambridge, Massachusetts, 1969. Recipient: O. Henry Prize, 1955; Rosenthal Award, 1959. Address: Pawlet, Vermont 05761, U.S.A.

PUBLICATIONS

Novels

    *A Long Day's Dying.*   New York, Knopf, 1950; London, Chatto and Windus, 1951.
    *The Season's Difference.*   New York, Knopf, and London, Chatto and Windus, 1952.
    *The Return of Ansel Gibbs.*   New York, Knopf, and London, Chatto and Windus, 1958.
    *The Final Beast.*   New York, Atheneum, and London, Chatto and Windus, 1965.
    *The Entrance to Porlock.*   New York, Atheneum, and London, Chatto and Windus, 1970.
    *Lion Country.*   New York, Atheneum, and London, Chatto and Windus, 1971.

Uncollected Short Story

    "The Tiger", in *The New Yorker*, 1955.

Other

    *The Magnificent Defeat* (meditations).   New York, Seabury, 1966; London, Chatto and Windus, 1967.
    *The Hungering Dark* (meditations).   New York, Seabury, 1969.
    *The Alphabet of Grace* (autobiography).   New York, Seabury, 1970.

Manuscript Collection: Princeton University, New Jersey.

Frederick Buechner comments:

    When I started out writing novels, my greatest difficulty was always in finding a plot. Since then I have come to believe that there is only one plot. It has to do with the way life or reality or God—the name is perhaps not so important—seeks to turn us into human beings, to make us whole, to make us Christs, to "save" us—again, call it what you will. In my fiction and non-fiction alike, this is what everything I have written is about.

*        *        *

    The six novels of Frederick Buechner represent a movement from a consideration of psychological textures to an assessment of the religious values that are expressed by those textures. The fact that Mr. Buechner is an ordained Presbyterian clergyman may not strike the reader of the earlier novels—*A Long Day's Dying, The Season's Difference,* and *The Return of Ansel Gibbs*—as particularly relevant to the interpretation of those novels. His early novels, indeed, may impress the casual reader as works that are in the tradition of Henry James, concerned as they are with rather delicate and tenuously resolved relations among cultivated and privileged Americans. The characters in these novels are preoccupied with resolutions of their difficulties, but these resolutions go no farther than clarification of their identities in relation to each other. This clarification is conveyed in a style that was regarded, at the time of the novels' appearance, as oblique and over-worked. The actual course of event in the early novels issues, as indicated, in changes of orientation that can be spoken of as a clearing out of the psychological undergrowth that impedes the discovery of purpose and self-knowledge on the part of the chief characters. The course of the narratives is marked by a taste for ironic comedy—a comedy that records the experience of living in a world that, unlike the world of some older comedy, is bare of generally shared values. The values that are to be detected are values for a particular person and do not have much wider relevance.

It is in the later novels—*The Final Beast*, *The Entrance to Porlock*, and *Lion Country*—that one can see Buechner moving, in an ironic and quite self-protective way, toward concerns that his ordination as a clergyman would suggest. He moves from concern with particular persons in special situations toward more inclusive concerns which announce that the lives of individual characters are oblique annunciations of the general constraint and opportunity which all human beings can, if they are responsive, encounter. The psyche is also a soul—a focus of energy that achieves fulfillment by coming into relation with patterns that religion and mythology testify to. The style of the later work becomes simpler, and Buechner delights in reporting farcical aspects of American experience that found little place in his earlier work. And these farcical elements are organized by invocation of narrative patterns that are widely known. The narrative pattern that underpins *The Entrance to Porlock* is drawn from that item of popular culture, *The Wizard of Oz*; the motley company of this novel repeats and varies the quest that took Dorothy Gale and her companions along the Road of Yellow Bricks. In *Lion Country*, the grotesque menagerie of characters has experiences that are organized by nothing less than the traditional patterns of the Christian religion itself. That religion undergoes parody that on the surface is blasphemous, is offered variation that is ironical rather than confirming, and yet—in the long run—achieves the only kind of validation that is possible at the present time.

Thus, Buechner can be seen as a novelist for whom initial study of the human self has led to an oblique rendering of august forces that, in both popular myth-work like the Oz books and Christian religion, have been associated with self-mastery and self-discovery. Or can be by a novelist animated by inclinations like Buechner's.

—Harold H. Watts

---

**BURGESS, Anthony.** British. Born in Manchester, 25 February 1917. Educated at Manchester University, B.A. 1940. Served in the British Army Education Corps, 1940–46. Married Llewela Isherwood Jones in 1942 (died, 1968); Liliana Macellari, 1968; has one child. Lecturer, Extra-Mural Department, University of Birmingham, 1946–48; Education Officer and Lecturer, Central Advisory Council for Adult Education in the Forces, 1946–48; served in the Ministry of Education, 1948–50; Master, Banbury Grammar School, Oxfordshire, 1950–54; served in the Colonial Service as an Education Officer in Malaya and Brunei, 1954–59. Professor, Columbia University, New York, 1970–71; Visiting Fellow, Princeton University, New Jersey, 1970–71. Since 1972, Literary Adviser, Guthrie Theatre, Minneapolis, Minnesota. Fellow, Royal Society of Literature, 1969. Address: c/o Jonathan Cape, 30 Bedford Square, London W.C.1, England.

PUBLICATIONS

Novels

> Time for a Tiger.  London, Heinemann, 1956.
> The Enemy in the Blanket.  London, Heinemann, 1958.
> Beds in the East.  London, Heinemann, 1959.
> The Right to an Answer.  London, Heinemann, 1960; New York, Norton, 1961.
> The Doctor Is Sick.  London, Heinemann, 1960; New York, Norton, 1966.
> The Worm and the Ring.  London, Heinemann, 1961.
> Devil of a State.  London, Heinemann, 1961; New York, Norton, 1962.
> One Hand Clapping (as Joseph Kell).  London, Davies, 1961; New York, Knopf, 1971.
> A Clockwork Orange.  London, Heinemann, 1962; New York, Norton, 1963.
> The Wanting Seed.  London, Heinemann, 1962; New York, Norton, 1963.
> Honey for the Bears.  London, Heinemann, 1963; New York, Norton, 1964.
> Inside Mr. Enderby (as Joseph Kell).  London, Heinemann, 1963.
> Nothing Like the Sun: A Story of Shakespeare's Love-Life.  London, Heinemann, and New York, Norton, 1964.
> The Eve of Saint Venus.  London, Sidgwick and Jackson, 1964; New York, Norton, 1967.
> The Long Day Wanes (includes Time for a Tiger, The Enemy in the Blanket, and Beds in the East).  New York, Norton, 1965.
> A Vision of Battlements.  London, Sidgwick and Jackson, 1965; New York, Norton, 1966.
> Tremor of Intent.  London, Heinemann, and New York, Norton, 1966.
> Enderby Outside.  London, Heinemann, 1968.
> Enderby (includes Inside Mr. Enderby and Enderby Outside).  New York, Norton, 1968.
> MF.  London, Cape, and New York, Knopf, 1971.

Other

> English Literature: A Survey for Students (as John Burgess Wilson).  London, Longman, 1958.
> The Novel Today.  London, Longman, 1963.
> Language Made Plain.  London, English Universities Press, 1964; New York, Crowell, 1965.
> Here Comes Everybody: An Introduction to James Joyce for the Ordinary Reader.  London, Faber, 1965; as Re Joyce, New York, Norton, 1965.
> The Novel Now: A Student's Guide to Contemporary Fiction.  London, Faber, 1967; as The Novel Now: A Guide to Contemporary Fiction, New York, Norton, 1967; revised edition, Faber, 1971.
> Urgent Copy: Literary Studies.  London, Cape, 1968; New York, Norton, 1969.
> Shakespeare.  London, Cape, 1970; New York, Knopf, 1971.
> Joysprick: An Introduction to the Language of James Joyce.  London, Deutsch, 1972.

> Editor, Coaching Days of England.  London, Elek, 1966.
> Editor, A Journal of the Plague Year, by Daniel Defoe.  London, Penguin, 1966.
> Editor, A Shorter Finnegans Wake, by James Joyce.  London, Faber, 1966; New York, Viking Press, 1967.
> Editor, with Francis Haskell, The Age of the Grand Tour.  New York, Crown, 1967.

> Translator, with Llewela Burgess, The New Aristocrats, by Michel de Saint-Pierre.  London, Gollancz, 1962.

Translator, with Llewela Burgess, *The Olive Trees of Justice*, by Jean Pelegri.   London, Sidgwick and Jackson, 1962.

Translator, *The Man Who Robbed Poor Boxes*, by Jean Servin.   London, Gollancz, 1965.

Translator, *Cyrano de Bergerac*, by Edmond de Rostand.   New York, Knopf, 1971.


Manuscript Collection: Mills Memorial Library, Hamilton, Ontario.


Critical Studies: in *The Red Hot Vacuum* by Theodore Solotaroff, New York, Atheneum, 1970; in *Shakespeare's Lives* by Samuel Schoenbaum, Oxford, Clarendon Press, 1970.


Anthony Burgess comments:

I hesitate to say much about my own work, which I can lay less claim to understanding than a really perceptive professional critic. I was shocked to be told that the name of the hero of *A Vision of Battlements* (R. Ennis) spells sinner backwards—a fact it took me fifteen years to realise. Since then, I have become so used to my unconscious mind dictating not only the themes of my novels but also the names and symbols that I regard myself as a mere hen, non-ovivorous. But the novels are probably all about the same thing—man as a sinner, but not sufficiently a sinner to deserve the calamities that are heaped upon him. I suppose I try to make comic novels about man's tragic lot.

\*       \*       \*

Anthony Burgess' first novel, *A Vision of Battlements*, was written in 1949 but remained unpublished until 1965. As a young man he had been interested in composing music rather than writing books, but he produced *A Vision of Battlements* as an attempt to exorcise the oppressive memory of his war service in Gibraltar. It makes a good starting point for the discussion of his work, as it already displays, if in an undeveloped form, many of the characteristics of his later novels. Its hero, Richard Ennis, a sergeant in an education branch of the British Army in Gibraltar, is a victim of his environment—in this case the military hierarchy —but although he suffers many defeats he fights back resiliently, and wins the occasional tactical victory. He is a lapsed Catholic and the burden of his religious upbringing weighs heavily upon him. Ennis has fairly strong libidinous urges but he is also fastidious in his attitudes to sex, being as much repelled by the flesh as drawn to it; he is at home in squalid surroundings, whilst aspiring to a materially comfortable life. Life presents itself to him as a rapid alternation of comic and melodramatic incidents. Basically *A Vision of Battlements* is a semipicaresque novel that draws heavily on Burgess' memories of wartime Gibraltar. Yet it is characteristic that he complicated his story by underpinning it with the plot of the *Aeneid* ('Ennis'=Aneas) in a manner directly imitative of Joyce's use of the *Odyssey* in *Ulysses*. The influence of Joyce is pervasive, too, in Burgess' endless fascination with language and his love of verbal games, an influence reinforced in his later fiction by that of Nabokov. The other dominant influence is that master of cruel comedy, Evelyn Waugh, particularly his early work.

It was to be several more years before Burgess emerged as a novelist. In the fifties he published his *Malayan Trilogy* (in America called *The Long Day Wanes*) which drew on his experiences as a Colonial Civil Servant in Malaya during the final phase of British rule. Here, too, one finds a sad, comic, victimised hero, and a highly episodic story line. The essential nature of Burgess' fiction has not changed since then, though his particular effects have become increasingly sophisticated. He can reasonably be described as a writer of black comedy, who is preoccupied with certain quasi-religious themes. Burgess himself is what he has called a "renegade Catholic", who comes from an old Lancashire Catholic family and attended a Catholic school in Manchester; in the opening of *Tremor of Intent* he describes the terrifyingly repressive atmosphere of such a school, in what reads like an autobiographical account, and which is reminiscent of Joyce's *Portrait of the Artist*. He has remarked that "The God my religious upbringing forced upon me was a God wholly dedicated to doing me harm. . . . A big vindictive invisibility." If he has abandoned the practice of Catholicism, Burgess has certainly not turned to the agnostic liberal humanism professed by most English-speaking intellectuals. He remains preoccupied in a Jansenist way by the separation between Nature and Grace, and is deeply suspicious of progressive social ideals and movements. This Augustinian pessimism, which is more convinced of the depravity of man than of the likelihood of transcendent goodness, has antecedents in Baudelaire and Graham Greene and T. S. Eliot, and it pervades Burgess' finest novel, *A Clockwork Orange*.

This novel is an anti-utopian fable about the near future, when teenage gangs habitually terrorize the inhabitants of a shabby metropolis. The story is told in the first person by a young criminal, Alex, in a superb piece of impersonatory writing by Burgess. Alex may be morally vicious but he is mentally alert, and through his flow of complicated slang (much of it of Russian origin) one distinguishes a coherent though desperate view of life. Alex is cruel and ruthless, though usually cheerful, given to beating up older citizens and raping girls and destroying books. And if he acts in this way it is not because he has had an unhappy childhood or lives in an under-privileged community, as liberal-minded psychologists might say, but because he has deliberately chosen evil, as an assertion of spiritual freedom in a world of sub-human conformists. Like all Burgess' novels, *A Clockwork Orange* has a largely episodic plot, but it rises to a powerful climax when Alex is subject by the state to a form of psychological conditioning that removes his capacity to engage in criminal acts. Here Burgess touches on a question of great philosophical importance: in what sense is a man who has been *forced* to be good better than a man who deliberately asserts his humanity by choosing evil? *A Clockwork Orange* works brilliantly as a metaphysical thriller. It has thematic affinities with another accomplished novel, *The Right to an Answer*, which Burgess has described as "a study of provincial England, as seen by a man on leave from the East, with special emphasis on the decay of traditional values in an affluent society". It is one of Burgess' funniest books, but it is pervaded by a profound distaste for the contemporary English scene, where the comic elements are held in tension with a sense that England is a flat and dismal place of petty lusts and feeble adulteries, drawing all its values from the mass media. In *The Wanting Seed* Burgess draws another pessimistic vision of the future, this time of a society grappling with overpopulation, where history moves cyclically, a severe Augustinian ideology persisting for a while, then giving place to a relaxed Pelagian one, and so on indefinitely. These three novels of the early sixties are full of wit and inventiveness, and are convincing as novels of ideas.

Burgess' later novels are numerous, for he is an extraordinarily prolific writer. They develop the characteristics of his early fiction, notably the combination of verbal brilliance and loose, episodic structure. Although Burgess is sympathetic to experimental fiction, his own work is basically conventional, despite his taste for Joycean manipulations of language. He has become increasingly more ingenious and has turned to a variety of themes or models. *Nothing Like the Sun* is a novel about Shakespeare, who is treated in a very unromantic way, and where Burgess uses Elizabethan language with great finesse. *Tremor of Intent* is an attempt to use the conventions of the sensational spy-story to write a serious novel, though it is little more than a series of bravura episodes. In *Inside Mr. Enderby* and its sequel *Enderby Outside* (published in America in one volume as *Enderby*), Burgess returns to familiar Joycean ground; its hero, the middle-aged poet, F. X. Enderby, can only compose in the lavatory. He is a lapsed Catholic, who associates the Catholic religion with his frightful stepmother who has frightened him off women for life. Enderby prefers solitary sex, but in the later part of the story he marries, against his will, and gets involved in a series of fast-moving if incredible adventures. Here, as elsewhere, in his fiction, Burgess has devised a convincing and interesting character, but can do nothing with him except thrust him into a rapid episodic narrative. Almost all of Burgess' novels reflect this basic weakness in maintaining and developing a large-scale structure. In one of his most recent books, *MF*, Burgess has, it seems, deliberately made a virtue of this limitation, and has moved decisively away from the tradition of realistic fiction. *MF* draws heavily on the anthropological researches of Claude Levi-Strauss, in a bizarre melange of riddles and incest myths and identical twins and bird symbolism, with a range of puns and word-play spanning many languages. The novel is all cryptic incident, with little attempt at characterization. The odds are that it is more an ingenious and entertaining *jeu d'esprit* than a significant new departure by Burgess. Nevertheless, it amply illustrates his unending inventiveness and capacity to surprise one, qualities which give him a unique place among living British novelists.

—Bernard Bergonzi

---

**BURKE, Kenneth (Duva).** American. Born in Pittsburgh, Pennsylvania, 5 May 1897. Educated at Peabody High School, Pittsburgh; Ohio State University, Columbus, 1916–17; Columbia University, New York, 1917–18. Married Lily Mary Batterham in 1919 (divorced); Elizabeth Batterham, 1933; has five children. Research Worker, Laura Spelman Rockefeller Memorial, New York, 1926–27. Music Critic, *Dial*, New York, 1927–29, and *The Nation*, New York, 1934–35. Editor, Bureau of Social Hygiene, New York, 1928–29. Lecturer, New School for Social Research, New York, 1937; University of Chicago, 1938, 1949–50; Bennington College, Vermont, 1943–61; Princeton University, New Jersey, 1949; Kenyon College, Gambier, Ohio, 1950; Indiana University, Bloomington, 1953, 1958; Drew University, Madison, New Jersey, 1962, 1964; Pennsylvania State University, University Park, 1963; Regents Professor, University of California at Santa Barbara, 1964–65; Lecturer, Central Washington State University, Ellensburg, 1966; Harvard University, Cambridge, Massachusetts, 1967–68; Washington University, St. Louis, 1970–71. Recipient: *Dial* Award, 1928; Guggenheim Fellowship, 1935; National Institute of Arts and Letters grant, 1946; Princeton Institute for Advanced Study Fellowship, 1949; Stanford University Center for Advanced Study in the Behavioral Sciences Fellowship, 1957; Rockefeller grant, 1966; Brandeis University Creative Arts Award, 1967; National Endowment for the Arts Award, 1968. D.Litt., Bennington College, 1966; Rutgers University, New Brunswick, New Jersey; Dartmouth College, Hanover, New Hampshire. Member, American Academy of Arts and Letters; American Academy of Arts and Sciences. Address: R. D. 2, Andover, New Jersey 07821, U.S.A.

PUBLICATIONS

Novel

    *Towards a Better Life: Being a Series of Epistles or Declarations.* New York, Harcourt Brace, 1932; revised edition, Berkeley, University of California Press, and London, Cambridge University Press, 1966.

Short Stories

    *The White Oxen and Other Stories.* New York, Boni, 1924.

*The Complete White Oxen: Collected Shorter Fiction.*   Berkeley, University of California Press, 1968.


Verse

*Book of Moments: Poems 1915–1954.*   Los Altos, California, Hermes, 1955.
*Collected Poems, 1915–1967.*   Berkeley, University of California Press, and London, Cambridge University Press, 1968.


Other

*Counter-Statement.*   New York, Harcourt Brace, 1931; revised edition, Berkeley, University of California Press, and London, Cambridge University Press, 1968.
*Permanence and Change: An Anatomy of Purpose.*   New York, New Republic, 1935; revised edition, Los Altos, California, Hermes, 1954.
*Attitudes Towards History.*   New York, New Republic, 2 vols., 1937; revised edition, Los Altos, California, Hermes, 1959.
*The Philosophy of Literary Forms: Studies in Symbolic Action.*   Baton Rouge, Louisiana State University Press, 1941; revised edition, New York, Random House, 1957; London, Peter Smith, 1959.
*A Grammar of Motives.*   New York, Prentice Hall, 1945; London, Dobson, 1947.
*A Rhetoric of Motives.*   New York, Prentice Hall, 1950; London, Bailey Brothers and Swinfen, 1955.
*The Rhetoric of Religion: Studies in Logology.*   Boston, Beacon Press, 1961.
*Perspective by Incongruity*, edited by Stanley Edgar Hyman.   Bloomington, Indiana University Press, 1964.
*Terms for Order*, edited by Stanley Edgar Hyman.   Bloomington, Indiana University Press, 1964.
*Language as Symbolic Action: Essays on Life, Literature and Method.*   Berkeley, University of California Press, and London, Cambridge University Press, 1966.

Translator, *Death in Venice*, by Thomas Mann.   New York, Knopf, 1925.
Translator, *Genius and Character*, by Emil Ludwig.   New York, Harcourt Brace, 1927; London, Cape, 1930.
Translator, *Saint Paul*, by Emile Baumann.   New York, Harcourt Brace, 1929.


*          *          *


During the "traumatic" months following the stock market crash of 1929 Kenneth Burke tells us ("Preface", *Towards a Better Life*), probably more for heuristic reasons than in the interests of autobiographical accuracy, that he worked diligently at a novel which would open with two men talking within the circumstantial setting of a Greenwich Village "dive". After three failures to carry out the elementary requirements of realistic exposition, he realized the project was misconceived. Rather than a novel that moved centrifugally toward a world of objective details he found that he wished instead to focus exclusive attention on a world constituted out of discourse. Clear in his purpose Burke then, according to the anecdote, reversed the typical process of narrative composition "emphasizing the essayistic rather than the narrative." And the result is the artful display in *Towards a Better Life* of the application of eloquence to the problems of literary form.

Inferentially Burke's novel contains the plot of John Neal's love for Florence, envy and rejection of Anthony whose mistress she becomes, and later dallying with Genevieve. Neal's consciousness, however, is an unusually solitary source of movement, since *Towards*

207

*a Better Life*, which may be contrasted with other modern esthetic experiments, deliberately omits the contingencies that provide context to Joyce's Bloom and the present events with which James' Strether interacts. Moreover, Neal's story is as distant from psychological realism as it is from the conventions of objective realism, since, rather than flowing without deliberate control, his mentality manifests itself on the occasions of his emotional predicaments in the composition of one or another of the rhetorical modes Burke has elsewhere termed the Six Biblical Characteristics: lamentation, rejoicing, beseechment, admonition, sayings, and invective. Each of Neal's rhetorical efforts is conceived with the formal purpose of literature, as they are intended to be epistles to Anthony. The workings of raw emotion, thus, are excluded from the novel, compelling the reader to attend carefully in order to discover the latent meaning only symbolically present in the interior form. That Burke's technique posits a solipsist goes without saying. Neal's rhetoric reveals through its apparent deceits and reversals, its unconcealed contempt and malice, the disintegration of character driven to declamations addressed to projections of himself and finally to silence.

Eight years before *Towards a Better Life* Burke published the collection of short fiction titled *The White Oxen*. Even without his telling us in a useful self-comment, the volume of short fiction reveals a progressive exploration of formal problems. The realism of the title story pervaded by a symbolism revelatory of interior action is followed by a sequence of dramatic monologues dispensing with most of the exigencies of realism. Then, in the final section of the collection the expressively surreal montages are divorced entirely from objective event or stated motive. Anticipating his novel in these latter stories, Burke has made the principle of composition the central dynamics. Art itself becomes the subject of each story, and the process of arrangement, the inferential basis for linking the vignettes and episodes of montage, becomes the meaning.

For many who read his fiction its conjunction with Burke's theory that literary form emerges from the artist's rhetorical management of material to create emotional effects and the desire for them in the minds of his auditors is the mark of its importance. This is not to say, though, that *The White Oxen* and *Towards a Better Life* are documentary illustrations of the esthetics Burke enunciated in the essays he was writing at approximately the same time—the essays collected in *Counter Statement* and *Permanence and Change*. Rather the observation of a unity between notable experimentation in fiction that anticipates the *anti-roman* by at least twenty years and theoretical synthesis, as finely managed in fiction as essay, of the ancient art of persuasion with the insights of modern psychology, amply demonstrates why Kenneth Burke holds an inestimable place in American letters.

—John M. Reilly

---

**BURNS, Alan.** British. Born in London, 29 December 1929. Educated at the Merchant Taylors' School, London; Inns of Court (Middle Temple), London; called to the Bar, 1956. Served in the Royal Army Education Corps, 1949–51. Married Carol Lynn in 1954; has two children. Practised as Barrister, London, 1956–59; Research Assistant, London School of Economics, 1959; Assistant Legal Manager, Beaverbrook Newspapers, London, 1959–62; Lecturer, National County Libraries Summer School, 1970; First Holder, Henfield Fellowship, University of East Anglia, Norwich, 1971. Founded "Writers Reading", with B. S. Johnson, *q.v.*, to encourage and organise prose readings at colleges and universities, 1969. Recipient: Arts Council Maintenance Grant, 1967, 1969, and Bursary, 1969. Address: 26 Ladbroke Gardens, London W.11, England.

PUBLICATIONS

Novels

> Buster, in New Writers One.   London, John Calder, 1961; as Buster, New York, Red
> Dust Books, 1971.
> Europe after the Rain.   London, John Calder, 1965; New York, Day, 1970.
> Celebrations.   London, Calder and Boyars, 1967.
> Babel.   London, Calder and Boyars, 1969; New York, Day, 1970.
> Dreamerica!   London, Calder and Boyars. 1972.

Play

> Palach (produced London, 1970).   London, Penguin Books, 1971.

Critical Studies: two articles by Robert Nye in The Scotsman (Edinburgh), 17 April 1965,
and 7 October 1967; a profile in The Guardian (London), 30 April 1970; an interview in the
Times Educational Supplement (London), 18 September 1970.

Alan Burns comments:

An elite and upper-class residential neighbourhood conceals unexpected stories of sex
orgies and wife-swapping.
The boredom the boredom the boredom the boredom the boredom.
An intensely dramatic account of a love affair between a French politician and a beautiful
empty desperately insecure model.
The boredom the boredom the boredom the continuous unmitigated incapacitating
tedium.
A school-teacher dying of an incurable disease spends her last months in a dilapidated
cabin on the sea coast where she makes a curious friendship with a wandering Indian.
Who publishes who criticises who publicises who sells who buys who reads this pre-
digested pap?
Wild frank and shocking novel celebrates the force and beauty of the naked negro.
Who gives their life's blood for this crap?
Set in Poland during World War II this novel follows the story of four women whose
lives intertwine in the forced intimacy of a German concentration camp.
Red like the egg when it is green.
Ironic savage bitterly funny it is about a long automobile ride from Los Angeles to San
Francisco.
Regarding shock: shock requires a background against which to create shock. Therefore
shock tactics are academic. Thus what we do is not in protest against the past. The avant
garde finds its identity through shock but I find it among the refuse.
Novel about book publishing in which a young whiz kid engages in battle of wits with
older directors bent on his destruction.
No stretching of word power no daring no leap no courage no imaginative muscularity.
Story of human courage and weakness set in wine-growing community of Australia.
In our times there are no longer any ideas; they are as rare as smallpox. But it goes without
saying that there are images caught, and for once well caught, real slaps in the face of any
kind of good sense.
We can learn from the film: to explode time . . . from painting: to achieve simultaneity

. . . from surrealism: to juxtapose fantastically, dive into the unconscious, inhabit the dream . . .

Everything of which I know, but of which I am not at the moment thinking; everything of which I was once conscious but have now forgotten; everything perceived by my senses but not noted by my conscious mind; everything which, involuntarily and without paying attention to it, I feel, think, remember, want, and do; all the future things that are taking shape in me and will sometime come to consciousness; all this is the content of the unconscious.

Storm Jameson! Oh elegance of expression! Oh feeling!

Oh sensitivity! Oh hair-brush! Oh liberal lady!

The shrewd, careful, open-eyed lady laments the mediocrity of her contemporaries, she looks forward to "a novel to help us read our world". She allows that painting, music, poetry, sexual ethics have "exploded". Though she links the explosion with Cezanne, Picasso, Apollinaire, she regrets the distintegration of form and finds it particularly unsuited to the novel. "Inside a violently exploding society" the novel must tamely "evolve".

Miss Jameson fails to see that it is precisely because the novel has in the main stuck fast in its 19th century rut that it gives off that stink of staleness and old age of which she herself is tentatively aware.

It's not "society" (far less "everything") which is disintegrating: it is merely capitalist society: a passing historical phase, no more.

Preserve our Literary Heritage.

The reactionary nature of words themselves: each word dragged down by its load of historical and social associations. Paint and music travel light.

Cubism turned reality inside out, simultaneously presenting the in and the out.

I imply something about the simultaneous reporting of world events where "world time" alters with geography, and about the fluidity of time in the subconscious dream world in which the action of *Babel* takes place.

Throttled by narrative, strait-jacketed by rigid limitations of the perceived world, stunted by psychology, by politics, by morals, by sociology: remember Céline's barbaric energy. Allow the antiquated scientists their territory: go quietly: retreat into your world, the one you know.

The unconscious stores up, gathers into itself, as a slow accumulation, all our experiences. The more poignant, the more deeply does it imprint itself there. There is that "other" as a residue, which we can't account for personally—there in the unconscious as a kind of carry over of non-memory which we inherit with our blood at birth . . . Here is a rich field of content. To be acted on consciously. To be made known, to get the thing there, in the words, which strike meaning from an object . . .

The prevailing culture of any society is the culture of its ruling class. Capitalist culture rewards those concerned to perpetuate the myth of stability. It invests in the narrative line. So: Cultivate indifference to money.

A novel about a middle-aged unmarried school-teacher who centres her entire life around a younger more attractive woman.

If a contemporary best-selling novel had been published 50 years ago the chances are that it would have been well received; the essential form and style would have been entirely acceptable. Of no other art form is this true.

God, the atom, the empire, the family, have all fragmented: why not the novel?

If all else fails: Write-a-novel-about-writing-a-novel.

Exploit the cut-up to make multiple sentences which express two or three (preferably contradictory) meanings simultaneously.

I break the tyranny of syntax by fragmenting the narrative line of the sentence, just as the overall construction of *Babel* fragments the narrative of the novel.

Reality moves too unreally, too swiftly, too fiercely, too illogically, too complicatedly . . . to be trapped.

The magic of unforeseen affinities.

The result is an uncertain mixture of references to a series of events: exactly the kaleidoscopic, dialectical effect I wish to achieve.

Don't end up with another museum: coast close to insanity: risk.

Of what is the young girl afraid when she runs into Matt Jepson's arms in the park at night?

—Originally appeared in *Books and Bookmen* (London), September 1970.

\*    \*    \*

Alan Burns has to date written three novels that deserve the attention of serious readers. The first, *Europe after the Rain*, taking its title from a painting by Max Ernst, established him as a kind of infra-realist. Set in the unspecified future, in a Europe devastated by internecine strife within "the party", it deals with ruined figures in a ruined landscape, purposelessly dedicated to "the work" which is the only thing the party will reward with the food necessary to keep alive. The unnamed narrator alone possesses any genuine purpose. His quest to find and take care of the daughter of the Trotskyite leader of the rebel forces is inspired by something like love, doubtfully implicit in his actions, later developed into a statement of hope which comes as the one redeeming human fact in a world blasted beyond the usual trappings of humanity, but arrived at only after much violence: a woman is flogged, a dog stabbed and its legs dislocated, people fight over corpses for the gold fillings in the teeth, a leg is wrenched off a corpse and eaten by a woman, other women pursue and stone and half-crucify and eventually beat to death the commander of the forces who are in power at the book's beginning. To this nightmarish action Burns applies a style which may be described as burnt-out. His sentences are mostly short, or built up of short phrases resting on commas where one might have expected full-stops, the total effect being clipped, stripped, and abrupt.

*Celebrations* is similarly uncompromising, with six characters and seven funerals. Williams, boss of a factory, has two sons, Michael and Phillip, whom he dominates. A hero to himself, Williams is a most uncertain personality, inconstant in his psychological attributes, extravagant in behaviour which is nevertheless always reported in the same flat and colourless prose. Phillip's death, following an accident which necessitates the amputation of his leg, leaves an even sharper taste of doubt in the reader's mind—for while it throws his father and his brother into grim rivalry for the attention of his widow, Jacqueline, these affairs are chronicled with such irony that they hardly seem to occur. All the time, it appears, we are meant to be reminded of Kierkegaard's dictum, "The thought of death condenses and intensifies life", as Burns piles violence on violence, and funeral on funeral, abbreviating whole lives to a tapestry of gesture.

With *Babel* Burns seems to have reached a dead end, though it confirms him in his rôle as infra-realist, anti-poet, steely perceiver of disconnections, writing as though he looks down on the rest of us from a private spaceship in unwilling orbit. Here he has assembled an ice-cold report on a world in chaos, stitching together clichés from the newspapers, fragments of misunderstood conversation, a babble of jokes and warnings. The cunningly fragmented styles owe too much to Burroughs and Ballard, and the comedy cannot quite conceal something merely self-disgusted in such furious insistence on unmeaning.

—Robert Nye

---

**BURROUGHS, William (Seward).**    American.    Born in St. Louis, Missouri, 5 February 1914. Educated at Los Alamos Ranch School, New Mexico; Harvard University, Cambridge,

Massachusetts, A.B. 1936; studied medicine at the University of Vienna. Served in the United States Army, 1942. Married Jean Vollmer in 1945; has one child. Has worked as a journalist, private detective and bartender; now a full-time writer. Address: c/o Jonathan Cape Ltd., 30 Bedford Square, London W.C.1, England.

PUBLICATIONS

Novels

> *Junk* (as William Lee). New York, Ace, 1953; as *Junkie*, as William Burroughs, Ace, 1964; London, New English Library, 1966.
> *The Naked Lunch*. Paris, Olympia Press, 1959; as *Naked Lunch*, New York, Grove Press, 1962; London, John Calder, 1964.
> *The Soft Machine*. Paris, Olympia Press, 1961; New York, Grove Press, 1966; London, Calder and Boyars, 1968.
> *The Ticket That Exploded*. Paris, Olympia Press, 1962; New York, Grove Press, 1967; London, Calder and Boyars, 1968.
> *Dead Fingers Talk*. Paris, Olympia Press, 1963; London, John Calder, 1964.
> *Nova Express*. New York, Grove Press, 1964; London, Cape, 1966.
> *The Wild Boys*. New York, Grove Press, 1971; London, Calder and Boyars, 1972.

Play

> *The Last Words of Dutch Schultz* (filmscript). London, Cape Goliard, 1970.

Verse

> *The Exterminator*. San Francisco, Auerhahn Press, 1960; Bletchley, Buckinghamshire, McBride and Broadley, 1968.
> *Minutes to Go: Poems*, with others. Paris, Two Cities, 1960; San Francisco, Beach Books, 1968; Bletchley, Buckinghamshire, McBride and Broadley, 1969.
> *Time*. New York, privately printed, 1965.
> *The Third Mind*. New York, Grove Press, 1970.

Other

> *The Yage Letters*, with Allen Ginsberg. San Francisco, City Lights, 1963.
> *APO-33: A Metabolic Regulator: A Report on the Synthesis of the Amorphine Formula*. San Francisco, Beach Books, and Bletchley, Buckinghamshire, McBride and Broadley, 1968.
> *The Job: An Interview with William Burroughs*, by Daniel Odier. New York, Grove Press, and London, Cape, 1970.

*     *     *

Critical opinion regarding the work of William Burroughs takes an unusually wide range, from the encomiums of Norman Mailer ("I think William Burroughs is the only American novelist living today who may conceivably be possessed by genius") and Jack Kerouac

("Burroughs is the greatest satirical writer since Jonathan Swift") to the objections of the English critic David Lodge: "Burroughs has, principally, two claims on the attention of serious readers: as a moralist, and as an innovator. On both counts, it seems to me, he cannot be considered as more than a minor, eccentric figure. Undoubtedly he has a certain literary talent, particularly for comedy and the grotesque, but in both precept and practice he is deeply confused and ultimately unsatisfying." Burroughs himself has not much assisted appreciation of his work by an interview which he gave *The Paris Review* (number 35, Fall 1965) in which he declared his opposition to "the Aristotelian construct" as one of "the great shackles of Western civilisation", nor by the book-length dialogue with Daniel Odier which was published as *The Job*, where he seems determined to talk in headlines, every breath a banner, every sentence a proclamation.

Burroughs' first book, *Junkie*, published in 1953 under the pseudonym of William Lee, is a straightforward account of his addiction to morphine. He has allowed this text to be reprinted under his own name but he does not think highly of it. Some readers, however, regard its brutal account of a man's reduction of himself to so many dope-sick cells as an achievement, a solid piece of reporting. Psychologically it is also of interest in that it contains a measure of reasonably sustained self-analysis, from which it emerges that the designation "Dope fiend" gave Burroughs a similar sense of identity to that which Genet found in being branded "Thief", and that once addicted to narcotics the author's principal pleasure lay in the monotony of relief. The book's austere equation of habit and necessity, and its unromantic description of the greyness of the addict's world commands sympathy: "The kick of junk is that you have to have it. Junkies run on junk-time and junk-metabolism. They are subject to junk-climate. They are warmed and chilled by junk. The kick of junk is living under junk conditions." Written in depressed, unpretentious, staccato prose, *Junkie* reads like a report to society from the morgue.

*The Naked Lunch* also begins as a first person narrative by a drug addict, but this mode soon breaks down as Burroughs separates himself from the confines of linear discourse and moves in the direction of creating what he has called an "image-track"—that is, a sort of hallucinatory continuum where the viewpoint is in a constant state of flux, violent images collide but seldom coalesce, and language itself seems in a state of *articulo mortis*. Such coherence as the text possesses is achieved through a repetition of certain phrases and certain kinds of imagery, mostly of a sensationally homosexual nature. There are passages where the narrative dislocations seem justified by the power of the satirical effect resulting, but the book's melodramatic excesses outweigh these. Mary McCarthy suggested that the latter might be derived from "withdrawal" symptoms, and *The Naked Lunch* thus considered as the nightmare of a morphine addict cut off from his drug. Such a reading has something to commend it, but if the book is then compared with another modern novel in which an attempt is made to construct a work of art upon the inferno of addiction—Malcolm Lowry's *Under the Volcano* (1947), in which the drug is of course alcohol—the clinically limited nature of Burroughs' achievement becomes apparent.

By the time of his next experiments in the novel form—*The Soft Machine* and *The Ticket That Exploded*—Burroughs had learned from a fellow American expatriate, Brion Gysin, a technique which led to what they termed "cut-ups". To make a cut-up demanded a minimum of creative or critical endeavour. One simply took a page with words on it, cut or tore it up, and stuck it together again, preferably with bits from other pages that might be expected to provide baffling or amusing semantic juxtapositions. Gysin himself had already achieved Solomon plus Shakespeare plus Eliot plus St John Perse plus Aldous Huxley plus Grundig— by jumbling up choice extracts from their works on a tape-recorder and publishing the result as a poem called *The Song of Songs*. Burroughs favoured the more popular parts of James Joyce (the end of *The Dead*, for instance), such Shakespeare passages as one might find in an anthology (Prospero on this insubstantial pageant, etc), a gross of images from Rimbaud, a little Kafka, Conrad, Richard Hughes, Graham Greene, and a good deal of science fiction by less literary writers. Desiring originality, he also developed a novel-making process of his own, which he called "fold-in", involving cross-column reading and random word-play. Since it has been claimed that cut-ups were "invented" in 1881, it seems as well to point out that they are essentially just an extension of the cento technique and therefore at least as old as Ausonius or that life of Christ written by the Empress Eudoxia in lines taken from Homer. There is even a precedent for their name in the work of a sixth century grammarian, Vergilius Maro, who wrote a series of fifteen epitomae on the more unusual literary experiments of his contemporaries. Number 13 is devoted to "Ars Scissendi"—the Art of Cutting Up—and is in all important respects a fair description of what Burroughs does today. According to Vergilius Maro, the ultimate here was achieved by one Galbungus, who chopped up a sentence until it began: PPPP. PPP. RRR. RRR. LM. SSS.

There is nothing quite as impenetrable as this in *Nova Express* (1964), but as a folded-in "composite of many writers living and dead" it remains Burroughs' most opaque and difficult text, a series of syntactic manipulations that only infrequently add up to anything as social as a sentence. Of this author's work in general it may be said that he has a savage sense of comedy, and a cleverly educated ear for the casual but haunting phrase ("So pack your ermines, Mary"). There is also a certain compulsive private rhythm in his writing—see the way he keeps returning to the fragments about Lykin, and the Old Doctor you can't call twice, as well as Mary and her ermines, not just in *Nova Express* but in *The Ticket That Exploded* and *Dead Fingers Talk* as well.

—Robert Nye

---

**BYATT, A(ntonia) S(usan).**    British.    Born in Sheffield, Yorkshire, 24 August 1936; sister of Margaret Drabble, *q.v.* Educated at Newnham College, Cambridge, B.A. (honours) in English, 1957; Bryn Mawr College, Pennsylvania (English Speaking Union Fellowship), 1957–58; Somerville College, Oxford, 1958–59. Married I. C. R. Byatt in 1959; Peter J. Duffy, 1969; has three children. Since 1965, Extra-Mural Lecturer, London University. Recipient: Arts Council grant, 1968. Address: 17 Earlsfield Road, London S.W.18, England.

PUBLICATIONS

Novels

> *Shadow of a Sun*.    London, Chatto and Windus, and New York, Harcourt Brace, 1964.
> *The Game*.    London, Chatto and Windus, 1967; New York, Scribner, 1968.

Other

> *Degrees of Freedom: The Novels of Iris Murdoch*.    London, Chatto and Windus, and New York, Barnes and Noble, 1965.
> *Wordsworth and Coleridge in Their Time*.    London, Nelson, 1970.

A. S. Byatt comments:

My fiction is concerned with habits of mind—the nature of the imagination, the ways in which different people take in the world, the uses they make of what they think or see.

*     *     *

The first half of *Shadow of a Sun* takes place in a hot Summer in a beautiful countryside. Henry, a brilliant novelist, "looked like a cross between God, Alfred Lord Tennyson and Blake's Job." He is protected by his devoted wife, who dotes on her conformist son, Jeremy, and is baffled by her awkward adolescent daughter, Anna. Staying with them are a dry academic, Oliver, and his beautiful unhappy wife, Margaret. Slowly, Byatt guides us to mistrust the glib and verbal, who understand too readily, like Oliver, and those who fit in too readily and have never sought themselves, like Jeremy. We are led to understand and sympathize with the people who are out-of-the-ordinary, who do not know themselves, like Henry, Anna and perhaps Margaret. We feel compassionately for Anna—this is what it is like to see oneself as shy, useless, inarticulate, with one's privacy disrupted by the adult world. But the second half is far more commonplace. Anna, dominated by Oliver, goes to Cambridge University, and there to bed with him. Pregnant, she agrees to marry a rich, mother-dominated youth, then—at the very end—runs away from him and back, at least temporarily, to Oliver. Byatt has many styles in this leisurely book, including unashamed "fine writing" and long analytical talks of a kind that surely never took place. She observes people carefully, and has striking, straining passages on Henry as a Blake-Lawrence visionary.

*The Game* studies two sisters in their thirties, Cassandra, a don, and Julia, novelist and wife of a Norwegian do-gooder. Julia has problems with her husband, who brings to their flat homeless slum dwellers, with her next book, and with her lover, a TV producer, while the less attractive sister suffers inroads on her sanity. The pair are linked by Simon, whom they both loved in childhood, now a traveller who talks about reptiles on television, who comes back into their lives after ten years abroad. The outer life is rich: the Oxford women's college, the Quaker earnestness of their upbringing and the snowbound Northumberland house to which they return as their father dies. Their inner life is more significant, the way the past has shaped them and still affects them.

Even this is only a part: there is a deeper level, "a structure of meaning beyond that afforded directly by day-to-day reality" (Malcolm Bradbury, *Encounter*, July 1968). "The Game" of the title is their all-absorbing childhood fantasy, a board game with cards and figures about medieval battles and courtly romance that developed into literary inspiration—literature used to create literature. As adults they continue the Game, Julia manipulating the people around her and Cassandra her fantasy Middle Ages world. During the novel's action they again play each other. The Game and various other references point to the Brontës' life as one of Byatt's guiding principles. More crucial are snakes, so fascinating to Simon and so threatening to Cassandra. Irving Wardle in his *Observer* review briskly summed up the symbol as standing "for Cassandra's reptilian withdrawal, for the survival of primitive impulse, and for the primal curse of humanity as Coleridge defined it, 'ours is the reptile's lot.'" Television is discussed, satirized, and, in Wardle's phrase, used to illustrate "the power of a medium to condition perception."

The novel is formidably—almost suffocatingly—dense and difficult, and as summation I am driven back to Wardle's attempt to grasp it, "a complex moral image as irreducible as a many-faceted precious stone."

—Malcolm Page

---

CAIN, James M(allahan). American. Born in Annapolis, Maryland, 1 July 1892. Educated at Washington College, Chestertown, Maryland, A.B. 1910, A.M. 1917. Served in the United States Army, 1918–19: Editor, *Lorraine Cross*, the official newspaper of the 79th Division, 1919. Married Mary Rebecca Clough in 1920; Elina Sjosted Tyszecka, 1927; Aileen Pringle, 1944; Florence Macbeth Whitwell, 1947. Staff Member, *Baltimore American*,

1917–18; Reporter, *Baltimore Sun*, 1919–23; Professor of Journalism, St. John's College, Baltimore, 1923–24; Editorial Writer, *New York World*, 1924–31. Recipient: Grand Masters Award, Mystery Writers of America, 1970. Address: 6707 44th Avenue, University Park, Hyattsville, Maryland 20782, U.S.A.

PUBLICATIONS

Novels

*The Postman Always Rings Twice*.  New York, Knopf, and London, Cape, 1934.
*Serenade*.  New York, Knopf, 1937; London, Cape, 1938.
*Mildred Pierce*.  New York, Knopf, 1941; London, Hale, 1943.
*Love's Lovely Counterfeit*.  New York, Knopf, 1942.
*Three of a Kind: Career in C Major, The Embezzler, Double Indemnity*.  New York, Knopf, 1943; London, Hale, 1945.
*Past All Dishonor*.  New York, Knopf, 1946.
*The Butterfly*.  New York, Knopf, 1947.
*The Sinful Woman*.  New York, Avon, 1947.
*The Moth*.  New York, Knopf, 1948; London, Hale, 1952.
*Three of Hearts: Love's Lovely Counterfeit, The Butterfly, Past All Dishonour*.  London, Hale, 1949.
*Jealous Woman*.  New York, Avon, 1950; with *The Sinful Woman*, London, Hale, 1955.
*The Root of His Evil*.  New York, Avon, 1951; London, Hale, 1954.
*Galatea*.  New York, Knopf, 1953; London, Hale, 1954.
*Mignon*.  New York, Dial Press, 1962; London, Hale, 1963.
*The Magician's Wife*.  New York, Dial Press, 1965; London, Hale, 1966.

Uncollected Short Stories

"Pastorale", in *American Mercury* (New York), March 1928.
"The Baby in the Icebox", in *American Mercury* (New York), January 1933.
"Dead Man", in *American Mercury* (New York), March 1936.
"The Birthday Party", in *Ladies' Home Journal* (New York), May 1936.
"The Girl in the Story", in *Liberty* (New York), 6 January 1940.

Play

*The Postman Always Rings Twice* (produced New York, 1936).

Other

*Our Government*.  New York, Knopf, and London, Allen and Unwin, 1930.

Editor, *For Men Only: A Collection of Short Stories*.  Cleveland, World, 1944.

\*       \*       \*

James M. Cain is the twenty-minute egg of the hard-boiled school. In the movies and novels of the Thirties, the tough guy, at home and abroad, was one of the most visible American images. Dashiell Hammett in *The Maltese Falcon* (1929) and Raymond Chandler in *The Big Sleep* (1939) departed from the British-style novel of crime detection; their private detectives, Sam Spade and Philip Marlowe, developed "outsider" codes of ethics that enabled them to survive encounters with both criminals and corrupt officials. Cain's *The Postman Always Rings Twice* (1934), B. Traven's *The Treasure of Sierra Madre* (1927–35), and Horace Mc-Coy's *They Shoot Horses, Don't They?* (1935) exemplified a purer tough guy strain that had little to do with detective stories. Few of Cain's novels are concerned with investigators and organized crime; his men and women commit major crimes only once. In the Thirties and Forties, the tough-guy novel made a lasting impact on "serious" American and European fiction; for instance, Albert Camus admitted that *The Postman* was a model for *The Stranger*.

Cain has said that he has always had only one story to tell: a love story.

> I write of the wish that comes true, for some reason a terrifying concept. . . . I think my stories have some quality of the opening of a forbidden box, and that it is that, rather than violence, sex, or any of the things usually cited by way of explanation, that gives them the drive so often noted.

The act of forcing the wish to come true isolates Cain's obsessed lovers from society and places them on what he calls a "love-rack."

If his "heels and harpies" are to consummate and prolong their sexual passion, they must commit a crime. Frank Chambers and Cora in *The Postman* must murder Cora's husband, Nick; Juana in *Serenade* must slaughter Winston Hawes, a homosexual symphony conductor, to ensure the sexual salvation of her lover, Howard Sharp, an opera singer; sex and money are the motive in Walter's and Phyllis's murder of her husband in *Double Indemnity*; when his apparently incestuous lust for his daughter Kady is threatened, Jess Tyler, a West Virginia farmer, shoots Moke Blue. This love-rack and wish-come-true formula is repeated, in various combinations with sex, money, pride, and violence, in Cain's less successful novels as well.

Cain's raw material and his formulas are not, of course, unique. Two things account for his special success: the way he blends major and minor elements, giving richness and dimension to his spare novels; and his use of techniques that transform those elements.

In the Thirties, Cain revealed in his rather cynical magazine essays and satirical dramatic dialogs (collected in *Our Government*) his profound insights into the American character and scene and into the way American dreams degenerate into nightmares. His novels dealing with criminal love, and even his romances, *Career in C Major* and *Galatea*, and his historical works, *Past All Dishonor* and *Mignon*, dramatize these insights obliquely, but effectively. But in his novels of character, *Mildred Pierce* and *The Moth*, set in the depression years, his scrutiny is more direct. Physically and often intellectually aggressive, Cain's audacious American male is an inside-dopester equipped with great know-how in many areas; but self-dramatizing inclinations, a suppressed sentimentality and a misconceived American romanticism and optimism sometimes defeat him. The female is realistic, ruthless, materialistic and sensitive to minor social taboos even while violating major laws. A deadly pair, they are more often destroyed by their own sexual and materialistic overreaching than by the police.

Among other recurring elements in Cain's novels are blasphemy, a sham religious mystique and the supernatural. Having taken refuge in a rural Mexican church during a thunderstorm, Howard Sharp and Juana (in *Serenade*) cook a live iguana in sacramental wine, then make love at the altar. Frank and Cora make love beside the body of their victim; when Cora announces she is pregnant, she and Frank attempt to purify themselves and become reborn in the ocean; an hour later, she is killed. The supernatural figures in the death of the husband in *Galatea* and in the "hoodooed" cotton that causes murder in *Mignon*. Cain also exploits his reader's interest in food and music. Mildred Pierce makes her living baking pies and later running a chain of restaurants; the hero of *The Magician's Wife* is a frozen meat packager; a crash diet in *Galatea* has violent consequences. Although Cain abandoned his youthful

217

desire to become an opera singer (his mother was a superb soprano and his fourth wife, Florence Macbeth, was a famous coloratura), opera singing dominates *Serenade* and *Career in C Major*, and is an intriguing wish-fulfillment factor in most of his other novels; Mildred's cruel daughter Veda is a singer.

Without his style and technique, Cain's rich and fascinating subject matter, energized by imagination and controlled by formula, would lack sustaining power. A few characters and a simple plot with a first-person narrator—this is the magic combination of a Cain "natural," producing a style like the "metal of an automatic," a pace like "a motorcycle," and a sense of immediacy that hypnotizes even the most literate and sophisticated reader into a "suspension of disbelief." The man's compulsion to confess (often after the woman is dead) is the pretext for the first-person narrative; Frank writes his story in his death cell; Jess in a cabin, with Moke's relatives closing in to kill him; Walter on a ship just before he and Phyllis deliver themselves to the sharks.

The first person narration enables Cain to use with skill and special appropriateness technical devices that in lesser works betray the hack and in "serious" novels are refined into moments of the highest achievement. Although the notion of symbolism is distasteful to him, Cain uses very adroitly motifs and patterns that contribute to a sense of unity. And although Cain failed as a playwright and a Hollywood scriptwriter, dialog is a distinctively effective element in all his novels; but it is especially powerful when it is all of a piece with the cold objectivity and immediacy of the arrogant, commanding first person voice; and dialog, performing many functions, contributes to surface action and pace—in which, above all, Cain is a master.

Since Cain's conscious intention is to "cast a spell on the beholder," anything that gets the story well-told is valid. Cain has stated that he developed "the habit of needling a story at the least hint of a breakdown," striving for a "rising coefficient of intensity." He believes that "the worst offense of narrative . . . is tepidity, and in my work, God willing, you will never find it." Not in his best work, but it yawns too often when the author speaks in his own voice: *Love's Lovely Counterfeit, Sinful Woman, The Magician's Wife* (a recasting of the *Postman* formula). Although *Mildred Pierce* is among his best novels, its moments of tedium may be traced to the style produced by Cain's third person narration. But because of a time-space scope too vast and a plot too complex, even the first person narration of *The Moth* and, to a greater degree, *Mignon* suffers deficiency in style.

Cain would never use the term "existential," but as a consequence of his primary intention to tell a story superbly well, he has created an objective, disinterested, often pessimistic view of life that is simultaneously terrifying and starkly beautiful. Chance, bad luck, cruel coincidence and perfect planning gone to smash push his characters over the precipice (not all, some live on happily). But not before they have moved swiftly through some high adventure in which the best that is in them has been thrust fully into play, though often in the most corrupt exploits. In their total commitment to each other, severing all ties to other people, Cain's lovers experience a blazing, self-consuming flash of self-deceptive purity and hideous innocence.

—David Madden

---

**CALDER-MARSHALL, Arthur.** British. Born in Wallington, Surrey, 19 August 1908. Educated at St. Paul's School, 1920–27; Hertford College, Oxford, B.A. 1930. Married Violet Nancy Sales in 1934; has two children. Schoolmaster, Denstone College, Stafford-shire, 1931–33; Scriptwriter, MGM, Hollywood, 1937; served in the Petroleum Warfare Department, 1941, and in the Films Division of the Ministry of Information, London,

1942–45. Fellow, Royal Society of Literature, 1958. Address: c/o Elaine Greene Ltd., 42 Great Russell Street, London W.C.1, England.

PUBLICATIONS

Novels

*Two of a Kind.*   London, Cape, 1932.
*About Levy.*   London, Cape, 1933; New York, Scribner, 1934.
*At Sea.*   London, Cape, and New York, Scribner, 1934.
*Dead Centre.*   London, Cape, 1935.
*Pie in the Sky.*   London, Cape, and New York, Scribner, 1937.
*The Way to Santiago.*   London, Cape, and New York, Reynal and Hitchcock, 1940.
*A Man Reprieved.*   London, Cape, 1949.
*Occasion of Glory.*   London, Cape, 1955.
*The Scarlet Boy.*   London, Hart Davis, 1961; New York, Harper, 1962.

Short Stories

*The Crime Against Cania.*   London, Golden Cockerel Press, 1934.
*A Pink Doll.*   London, Grayson, 1935.
*Date with a Duchess and Other Stories.*   London, Cape, 1937.

Plays

Screenplays: *The World Is Rich*, 1946, and numerous other documentary films.

Other

*Challenge to Schools: A Pamphlet on Public School Education.*   London, Hogarth Press, 1935.
*The Changing Scene.*   London, Chapman and Hall, 1937.
*Glory Dead* (travel).   London, Joseph, 1939.
*The Watershed* (travel).   London, Contact Publications, 1947.
*The Book Front.*   London, Lane, 1947.
*The Magic of My Youth* (autobiography).   London, Hart Davis, 1951.
*No Earthly Command.*   London, Hart Davis, 1957.
*The Man from Devil's Island* (juvenile).   London, Hart Davis, 1958.
*The Fair to Middling* (juvenile).   London, Hart Davis, 1959.
*Havelock Ellis: A Biography.*   London, Hart Davis, 1959; as *The Sage of Sex: Havelock Ellis*, New York, Putnam, 1960.
*Lone Wolf: The Story of Jack London* (juvenile).   London, Methuen, 1961; New York, Sloane, 1962.
*The Enthusiast* (biography).   London, Faber, 1962.
*The Innocent Eye* (biography).   London, W. H. Allen, 1963; New York, Harcourt Brace, 1966.
*Wish You Were Here: The Art of Donald McGill.*   London, Hutchinson, 1966.
*Prepare to Shed Them Now: The Ballads of George R. Sims.*   London, Hutchinson, 1968.

*Lewd, Blasphemous and Obscene* (19th century trials).   London, Hutchinson, 1972.

Editor, *The Bodley Head Jack London*.   London, Bodley Head, 4 vols., 1963–66.

Arthur Calder-Marshall comments:

I regard myself as an author rather than as a novelist, who writes other things on the side. At least for me, my work is a whole, part of an attempt to understand the nature, meaning and purpose of the universe in which we live. The course I have taken has been tortuous, and since I have never written two books about the same subject or with the same object, my work may appear contradictory to others, though to me it is psychologically consistent, and even logically defensible.

The older I grow, the more conscious I become of the enormous amount there is to learn and the impossibility of saying anything that can be regarded as absolutely true. Rather than finding this a cause for pessimism, which I might have when young, I am consoled by the thought that if I can either create or discover something which now or later will give someone pleasure, amusement or food for thought, I can be pardoned the self-indulgence of my greatest delight, putting words on paper.

\*        \*        \*

Arthur Calder-Marshall is an important figure in the world of letters. His work has ranged from a pamphlet on public school education to the four volume Bodley Head edition of Jack London. He is representative of the best characteristics of the professional writer; his work as a writer of fiction is only a part—in fact a rather small part—of his whole list of publications, titles which include biography, criticism, books of travel, and a series of juveniles, as well as the fiction designed for adults. Over a period of thirty years, from 1932 to 1961, he published nine novels and three collections of short stories, using a wide variety of techniques to set out an equally wide variety of themes and characters.

In general, Calder-Marshall presents his characters as exploring their own individual needs and values in the context of the conventional English social structure. In *Two of a Kind* both father and daughter misjudge the people they fall in love with because neither father nor daughter can reconcile passion with idealism. The characters in *About Levy* condemn him not by the establishment of abstract justice but by the way they respond to him and the account of his trial. The young couple in *At Sea* are on their honeymoon, and the lonely and frightening hours they spend together become for them a review of their past life, an attempt to realize themselves as unique, and at the same time to become one as man and wife. Their failure to do any of these things creates within them despair amounting to spiritual death and rebirth as they are rescued.

*Dead Centre, Pie in the Sky* and *A Man Reprieved* are directly concerned with the familiar structure of English society. *Dead Centre* examines the world of the small public school from some sixty different points of view, showing clearly the pettiness, the shoddiness, the inefficiency, indeed downright hypocrisy, of the masters and the utter confusion of their charges. The very slight series of incidents—the homesickness of the younger boys; the death of Jeffers, killed on the "tackling machine"; the terror of George who runs away because he thinks he has got the servant girl pregnant—serve as a frame for a number of memorable characterizations. *Pie in the Sky* includes a cross section of several groups of contrasting English character types. There is the mill owner, Carder Yorke, and his two sons, Bernard, weak and ineffectual, and Fenner, a dabbler in socialism and journalism. All three, Carder and his two sons, share an interest in Wynne Morris, an honest and forthright barmaid. There are the Boltons—mother, father and daughter. They represent the best of the working-folk tradition even though the father has lost his job as the daughter loses her school teaching post. Along with these there are the party leaders and members in the communist party of post-World War I in England. The elaborate scheme of the relationship of these various characters makes up the theme of the novel. At the conclusion whatever their adventures have been the characters all settle into the usual middle-class system of their world. The whole of the novel is presented in a kind of gentle, ironic fashion. *A Man Reprieved*, set in London just after the second World War, is about people with somewhat more education and financial security, but the structure of society is as rigid as that in *Pie in the Sky*. Julius Akens, a journalist returning to London quite disillusioned about war, does manage to become "a man reprieved" from his stuffy middle-class marriage but not without much uncertainty.

Two of the novels are set in Mexico. *The Way to Santiago* takes place just before the beginning of the second World War and is the story of the murder of a journalist and the curious fanaticism of a dedicated German fascist. Lionel Transit, the German, remarks that "journalists are the yeast of life. They leaven the dough of common events into the bread which is news." This quotation, in fact, describes the novel. *Occasion of Glory* is set in an imaginary Mexican tourist resort. It spans the week of Easter and suggests a kind of parallel to the sacrifice and death of Christ in the death of Alberto Rivera, whose story and that of his family is told in a chapter entitled "An Indian Who Might Be Jesus." The suggested modern myth is in no way successful, however, and the symbols are meaningless. In fact the book is so obviously "message"-filled that it is difficult to fit it into a discussion of the other complex, sophisticated novels Calder-Marshall has done.

Perhaps the most notable characteristic of Calder-Marshall as a writer of fiction is his dramatic and skillful use of various techniques to present his material. *Dead Centre*, *About Levy*, and *At Sea* are all three highly unconventional in their use of point of view. *Dead Centre* is divided into sixty-seven sections, each told in first person point of view, thus leaving the reader to draw his own conclusions from a point at "dead centre". Levy never appears in the novel about his trial and conviction for murder. *At Sea* employs a modified stream of consciousness technique to advance the plot as well as set out character and theme.

Arthur Calder-Marshall is distinguished as a writer, not merely as a novelist. His fiction is an important part of his work as a whole, however, especially as it gives the reader, interested in the novel from 1930 onwards in our century, the opportunity to examine a master craftsman at work.

—Annibel Jenkins

---

**CALDWELL, Erskine.** American. Born in Moreland, Georgia, 17 December 1903. Educated at Erskine College, Due West, South Carolina, 1920–21; University of Virginia, Charlottesville, 1922, 1925–26; University of Pennsylvania, Philadelphia, 1924. Married Helen Lannigan in 1925; Margaret Bourke-White, 1939; June Johnson, 1942; Virginia Moffett Fletcher, 1957; has four children. Reporter, *Atlanta Journal*, Georgia, 1925; Foreign Correspondent in Mexico, Spain, Czechoslovakia, Russia, and China, 1938–41. Hollywood Screenwriter, 1933–34, 1942–43. Editor, American Folkways series, 1941–55. Recipient: *Yale Review* award, 1933. Member, National Institute of Arts and Letters. Address: P.O. Box 820, Dunedin, Florida 33528, U.S.A.

## PUBLICATIONS

### Novels

*The Bastard.*   New York, Heron Press, 1930; London, Bodley Head, 1963.
*Poor Fool.*   Chicago, Argus, 1930; London, Bodley Head, 1963.
*Tobacco Road.*   New York, Scribner, 1932; London, Cresset Press, 1933.
*God's Little Acre.*   New York, Viking Press, and London, Secker, 1933.
*The Journeyman.*   New York, Viking Press, 1935; revised edition, New York, Duell,
    and London, Secker, 1938.
*The Sacrilege of Alan Kent.*   Portland, Maine, Falmouth Book House, 1936; London,
    Bodley Head, 1963.
*Trouble in July.*   New York, Duell, and London, Cape, 1940.
*All Night Long: A Novel of Guerilla Warfare in Russia.*   New York, Duell, 1942;
    London, Cassell, 1943.
*Tragic Ground.*   New York, Duell, 1944; London, Grey Walls Press, 1947.
*A House in the Uplands.*   New York, Duell, 1946; London, Grey Walls Press, 1947.
*The Sure Hand of God.*   New York, Duell, 1947; London, Grey Walls Press, 1949.
*This Very Earth.*   New York, Duell, 1948; London, Grey Walls Press, 1949.
*Place Called Estherville.*   New York, Duell, 1949; London, Grey Walls Press, 1951.
*Episode in Palmetto.*   New York, Duell, 1950; London, Grey Walls Press, 1951.
*A Lamp for Nightfall.*   New York, Duell, and London, Grey Walls Press, 1952.
*Love and Money.*   New York, Duell, 1954; London, Heinemann, 1955.
*Gretta.*   Boston, Little Brown, 1955; London, Heinemann, 1956.
*Claudelle Inglish.*   Boston, Little Brown, 1958; London, Heinemann, 1959.
*Jenny by Nature.*   New York, Farrar Straus, and London, Heinemann, 1961.
*Close to Home.*   New York, Farrar Straus, and London, Heinemann, 1962.
*The Last Night of Summer.*   New York, Farrar Straus, and London, Heinemann, 1963.
*Miss Mamma Aimee.*   New York, New American Library, 1967; London, Joseph,
    1968.
*Summertime Island.*   Cleveland, World, 1968; London, Joseph, 1969.
*The Weather Shelter.*   Cleveland, World, 1969; London, Joseph, 1970.
*The Earnshaw Neighborhood.*   Cleveland, World, 1971; London, Joseph, 1972.

### Short Stories

*American Earth.*   New York, Scribner, 1931; London, Secker, 1935.
*Mama's Little Girl.*   Mount Vernon, Maine, privately printed. 1932.
*Message for Genevieve.*   Mount Vernon, Maine, privately printed, 1933.
*We Are the Living: Brief Stories.*   New York, Viking Press, 1933; London, Secker, 1934.
*Kneel to the Rising Sun and Other Stories.*   New York, Viking Press, and London,
    Secker, 1935.
*Southways: Stories.*   New York, Viking Press, 1938; London, Heinemann, 1953.
*Jackpot: The Short Stories of Erskine Caldwell.*   New York, Duell, 1940.
*Georgia Boy.*   New York, Duell, 1943; London, Grey Walls Press, 1947.
*Stories by Erskine Caldwell: 24 Representative Stories.*   New York, Duell, 1944.
*Jackpot: Collected Short Stories.*   London, Grey Walls Press, 1950.
*The Courting of Susie Brown.*   New York, Duell, and London, Grey Walls Press, 1952.
*Complete Stories.*   New York, Duell, 1953.
*Gulf Coast Stories.*   Boston, Little Brown, 1956; London, Heinemann, 1957.
*Certain Women.*   Boston, Little Brown, 1957; London, Heinemann, 1958.
*When You Think of Me.*   Boston, Little Brown, 1959; London, Heinemann, 1960.
*Men and Women: 22 Stories.*   Boston, Little Brown, 1961.

Other

*Tenant Farmer*.   New York, Phalanx Press, 1935.
*Some American People*.   New York, McBride, 1935.
*You Have Seen Their Faces*, with Margaret Bourke-White.   New York, Viking Press, 1937.
*North of the Danube*, with Margaret Bourke-White.   New York, Viking Press, 1939.
*Say! Is This the U.S.A.?*, with Margaret Bourke-White.   New York, Duell, 1941.
*All-Out on the Road to Smolensk*.   New York, Duell, 1942; as *Moscow under Fire: A Wartime Diary, 1941*, London, Hutchinson, 1942.
*Russia at War*, with Margaret Bourke-White.   New York and London, Hutchinson, 1942.
*The Caldwell Caravan: Novels and Stories*.   Cleveland, World, 1946.
*The Humorous Side of Erskine Caldwell*.   New York, Duell, 1951.
*Call It Experience: The Years of Learning How to Write*.   New York, Duell, 1951; London, Hutchinson, 1952.
*Molly Cottontail* (juvenile).   Boston, Little Brown, 1958; London, Heinemann, 1959.
*Around about America*.   New York, Farrar Straus, 1964.
*In Search of Bisco*.   New York, Farrar Straus, 1965.
*The Deer at Our House* (juvenile).   New York, Collier, and London, Collier Macmillan, 1966.
*In the Shadow of the Steeple*.   London, Heinemann, 1967.
*Deep South: Memory and Observation* (includes *In the Shadow of the Steeple*).   New York, Weybright and Talley, 1968.
*Writing in America*.   New York, Phaedra, 1968.


Manuscript Collection: Baker Library, Dartmouth College, Hanover, New Hampshire.


Critical Study: *Erskine Caldwell* by James Korges, Minneapolis, University of Minnesota Press, 1969.

*       *       *

Balzac notoriously claimed that anyone wanting to know trades, manners, or business in the France of his time could learn about them by reading his novels. Erskine Caldwell, good as some of his novels are, is not Balzac's equal; precious few writers are. Yet the social historian as well as the literary critic will in the future turn to Caldwell's novels finding in them a representation of the Southern region of the United States, a representation in its own way unequalled by the other great writers of the region—Flannery O'Connor, William Faulkner, R.P. Warren, Endora Welty, and others. For Caldwell has been observing and writing for longer than any other great writer in the region, his novels taken as a whole coming to produce one of the most fascinating measures of the life and times, attitudes and temperaments of the area. One has only to set the recent *The Weather Shelter* beside the earlier *Trouble in July* to have one of the most graphic and moving indications of the changes taking place in the Southern region of the United States. Indeed, in his autobiography of his public career, *Call It Experience*, Caldwell suggests that his novels form a "cyclorama of the South". To argue for long in this manner, however, would seem to indicate that Caldwell's novels are a mere adjunct to social studies (sometimes called "science"). Caldwell closely observes the social scene, but he is also a literary artist of high quality and the author of some splendid novels.

This brief essay is not the place to consider the wide range of his achievements as a writer—and indeed as editor of the invaluable *American Folkways* series of regional books (1941–

1955). His achievements in reporting and analysis would alone place him in the front rank of contemporary prose writers in the English language. I have written elsewhere (*Erskine Caldwell*, University of Minnesota Press) about Caldwell's tact and his success in the forms of biography and autobiography. In each mode he undertook a very difficult subject. His biographical writing ranges from scaldingly satirical chapters in, especially, his early political, social, and economic commentary, to the tender and affecting memoir of his father, a well-known Presbyterian minister, which is full of sentiment without being sentimental—surely one of the most difficult kinds of writing. In the autobiographical mode, Caldwell undertook to write about the most banned and censored writer of his time, without being vindictive; and at the same time about the most financially successful writer of his time, without being pompous. As in his autobiography he keeps this perilous balance between self-justification and righteous scorn, so in his travel books he is both objective in his reports yet compassionate; and his eye for detail is shrewdly discerning. These qualities which mark his non-fiction are abundantly clear also in his best novels, as is his prose style which remains one of the most outstanding in this period in American literature. Every reader is impressed by the rich evocativeness of Faulkner's style, and the stylistic tension which contributes such force to Flannery O'Connor's great stories; yet not enough readers have noticed and praised the great lucid "plain" style of Erskine Caldwell. Some of his best writing is in his non-fiction, especially the Swiftian commentaries in *Some American People* (including Tenant Farmers) as well as the later and gentler *In Search of Bisco* and *Deep South*. And I will argue again while I have the opportunity for the great text-picture books he brought back into print, as the Agee-Walker *Let Us Now Praise Famous Men*; for the books Caldwell created with Margaret Bourke-White are among the greatest of the genre, especially *You Have Seen Their Faces, North of the Danube*, and *Say! Is This the U.S.A.?* These are masterpieces in an art form too often ignored. It required the happy conjunction of writer and photographer working as one author, not as one illustrating or explaining the work of the other.

When one considers Caldwell's prose fiction, one is confronted with a huge body of work; and as with all prolific writers, literary quality has ebbed and flowed in the novels and stories. Some of the novels are best read as groups or variations on themes. And despite his reputation as a writer of sexy and violent novels, Caldwell is often in the novels concerned with family relations, often tested by ideological or social conflicts. He presents resulting actions often in a comic way, which of course has the unfortunate tendency to make some readers suppose that the actions are therefore not "serious". The novels also disappoint readers who suppose that the "serious" novel must of necessity explore characters psychologically in the manner of Dostoevsky, James or Faulkner, if the novel is to be given critical attention. Yet as Restoration comedy was once dimissed because it was not Shakespearean (and because it is sexy), and Joyce scorned because he did not write real novels as obviously Mr. Galsworthy did, so recently some simplistic notions about "the novel" have tended to lead critics to dismiss Caldwell's work because he does not write like Faulkner or Flannery O'Connor. Faulkner himself annoyed Hemingway no end by remarking his failure to risk much in his novels; and irritated his own admirers by placing himself second in achievement to Thomas Wolfe. Yet Faulkner's much publicised list of the five greatest American novelists of his generation has another surprise, for the currently much patronized Caldwell is on it: Wolfe, Faulkner, Dos Passos, Caldwell, Hemingway. (He was right about Dos Passos, also currently out of critical fashion.)

Though the whole of Caldwell's production—in fiction and non-fiction—will continue to be valuable to the student of Southern society and to the literary historian, the books that will survive as works of literary art are relatively few—as in the case of, say, Scott. Caldwell has in a way chronicled the South; his books if read in chronological succession show not just the author's mellowing into compassionate old age, but a South that slowly changes in mood and attitude. Yet Caldwell also produced three books of fiction that are masterpieces: *Tobacco Road, God's Little Acre*, and *Georgia Boy*. With these novels, twenty or thirty of his best short stories (some of this century's finest) will form a lasting body of prose fiction which, when set beside his considerable achievement in non-fiction, will clearly mark him one of the most important writers of our time.

Perhaps Caldwell's best known work, *Tobacco Road*, almost failed to survive its initial publication. Sales were so small that Caldwell's advance was barely covered. Some time later Jack Kirkland dramatized the story; but the play almost closed after two weeks. By chance, the play survived, to run longer than any previous play; and *Tobacco Road* became a best-seller book, second only to the Bible. These curiosities of publishing history are not in themselves important to literary criticism; though in this case the history of the book is especially ironic, since one of the themes of the novel is human tenacity in the face of rejection and failure. The physical hunger of Jeeter, the sexual appetites of Ellie May and Sister Bessie, the sterile marriage of Pearl and Tom, all are more than a comic presentation of low-life characters on land made sterile by cultivation of tobacco that once made the region's owners rich. The deformed characters (some physically, some mentally or spiritually) wait for God; as Jeeter says: "Him and me has always been fair and square with each other. . . . I don't know nothing else to do, except wait for Him to take notice." And they seem to act out a superior will, suggested more strongly in some of the later books.

*God's Little Acre* is a masterpiece. If, as many critics argue it is less than *Absalom! Absalom!*, then it is less in the way that *Dead Souls* is less than *War and Peace*, or *Volpone* less than *King Lear*; but clearly at this level of literary competence, ranking becomes the parlor game of bored professors. Unfortunately all the censorship and banning gained *God's Little Acre* a reputation for being comic pornography; and some critics have continued to see the book as merely a comic exposé of Southern local color. The book is about southern mentality in about the same way the typist at tea-time section of *The Waste Land* is about unfair labor practices in London. I do not make the comparison lightly; for *God's Little Acre* is a novel about sterility; it is a comic presentation of one of the most ancient moral problems, here stated in low country terms by Ty Ty Walden, the digger after gold: "There was a mean trick played on us somewhere. God put us in the bodies of animals and tried to make us act like people. That was the beginning of trouble." The book itself is structured on contrasts of characters, and on a progression of scenes alternating between farm and town and building to a climax of great technical brilliance.

*Georgia Boy*, on the other hand, is episodic, a series of closely related incidents narrated by a twelve year old boy. It is equalled by only two other works in recent American fiction: Wright Morris' *My Uncle Dudley* and Faulkner's *The Reivers*. The earnestly innocent reports of adult behavior tend to transform what is said and done in the books, so that fictional strategy is itself a criticism of life.

The short stories present a problem by their very number; but a reader attempting to see Caldwell for the various and talented fictionist he is may be helped by this list of some of the best stories: "Country Full of Swedes", "The People *v*. Ake Lathan, Colored", "Candy-Man Beechum", "After-Image", "An Evening in Nuevo Leon", "We Are Looking at You, Agnes", "An Autumn Courtship", "A Swell-looking Girl", and "Meddlesome Jack". There are many other stories as good, or almost as good, in Caldwell's collections; and one suspects that we would have to go back to Maupassant to find his equal in short story writing.

—James Korges

---

**CALISHER, Hortense.** American. Born in New York City, 20 December 1911. Educated at Barnard College, New York, A.B. 1932. Married Curtis Harnack in 1959; has two children by a previous marriage. Adjunct Professor of English, Barnard College, 1956–57; Visiting Professor, University of Iowa, Iowa City, 1957, 1959–60, Stanford University, California, 1958, Sarah Lawrence College, Bronxville, New York, 1962, Brandeis University, Waltham, Massachusetts, 1963–64; Adjunct Professor of English, Columbia University, New York,

1968–70. Clark Lecturer, Scripps College, Claremont, California, 1969. Recipient: Guggenheim Fellowship, 1952, 1955; Department of State American Specialists grant, 1958; National Institute of Arts and Letters grant, 1967; National Endowment for the Arts Award, 1967; Address: c/o Candida Donadio-Robert Lantz Agency, 111 West 57th Street, New York, New York 10019, U.S.A.

PUBLICATIONS

Novels

> *False Entry*.   Boston, Little Brown, and London, Secker and Warburg, 1962.
> *Textures of Life*.   Boston, Little Brown, and London, Secker and Warburg, 1963.
> *Journal from Ellipsia*.   Boston, Little Brown, 1965; London, Secker and Warburg, 1966.
> *The Railway Police and The Last Trolley Ride* (two novellas).   Boston, Little Brown, 1966.
> *The New Yorkers*.   Boston, Little Brown, and London, Cape, 1969.
> *Queenie*.   New York, Arbor House, 1971.

Short Stories

> *In the Absence of Angels: Stories*.   Boston, Little Brown, 1952; London, Heinemann, 1953.
> *Tale for the Mirror: A Novella and Other Stories*.   Boston, Little Brown, and London, Secker and Warburg, 1963.
> *Extreme Magic: A Novella and Other Stories*.   Boston, Little Brown, and London, Secker and Warburg, 1964.

Uncollected Short Stories

> "Gargantua", in *Harper's Bazaar* (New York), October 1964.
> "A Summer Psychosis", in *Harper's Bazaar* (New York), September 1967.

Other

> Has contributed articles to the *New York Times Book Review*, *The Nation* and *The Reporter*, New York, and *The American Scholar*, Washington D.C.

Critical Studies: in *Don't Never Forget* by Brigid Brophy, London, Cape, 1966, and New York, Holt Rinehart, 1967; review of *The New Yorkers* by Cynthia Ozick in *Midstream* (New York), 1969; essay by the author on her own work: "Ego Art: Notes on How I Came to It", in *Works in Progress*, New York, Doubleday, 1971.

Hortense Calisher comments:

> *False Entry* and *The New Yorkers* are connected novels; either may be read first; together

they are a chronicle perhaps peculiarly American, according to some critics, but with European scope, according to others. *Journal from Ellipsia* was perhaps one of the first or the first serious American novel to deal with "verbal" man's displacement in a world of the spatial sciences; because it dealt with the possibility of life on other planets it was classed as "science fiction" both in the USA and in England. The *Dublin Times* understood it; its review does well by it. It also satirizes male-female relationships, by postulating a planet on which things are otherwise. In category, according to some, it is less an ordinary novel than a social satire akin to *Erewhon, Gulliver's Travels, Candide*, etc. *The Railway Police* and *The Last Trolley Ride*—the first is really a long short story of an individual, the second a novella built around an environs, a chorale of persons really, with four main parts, told in the interchanging voice of two men.

I usually find myself alternating a "larger" work with a smaller one, a natural change of pace. *Textures of Life*, for instance, is an intimate novel, of a young marriage, very personal, as *Journal* is not. After the latter, as I said in an interview, I wanted to get back to people. *The New Yorkers* was a conscious return to a "big" novel, done on fairly conventional terms, descriptive, narrative, leisurely, and inclusive, from which the long monologue chapters of the two women are a conscious departure. Its earlier mate, *False Entry*, has been called the only "metaphysical" novel in the America of its period—I'm not sure what that means, except perhaps that the whole, despite such tangible scenes as the Ku Klux Klan and court-room episodes, is carried in the "mind" of one man. It has been called Dickensian, and in its plethora of event I suppose it is; yet the use of memory symbols and of psyche might just as well be French (Proust and Gide)—by intent it does both, or joins both ways of narration. *The New Yorkers* is more tied to its environs in a localized way; part of its subject *is* the environs.

*Queenie* is a satire, a farce on our sexual mores, as seen through the eyes of a "modern" young girl. As it is not yet out at this writing, I shall wait to be told what it is about.

\*     \*     \*

In spite of her zest, intelligence, humor and general readability, Hortense Calisher makes life difficult for critics who like to pigeon-hole authors. She will not stay put in any of their categories. During the years when she was first appearing in print it was easier for them to classify her, simply because writers of short stories are allowed unusual latitude: the tag is enough. Even in this field, however, she exhibits scope and imagination, and is impishly fugitive. Not that she is thoroughly inconsistent. One quality is common to her stories whether they treat of school, loneliness, or the supernatural—love of the English language. Miss Calisher can manage the medium. She uses words carefully, thoughtfully, and in fresh ways, as a graphic artist might use unexpected shapes and colors. If this seems an obvious and un-necessary comment on an American modern, read some of the others and ask yourself to how many the same truth applies.

Most writers with stamina go the other way about their work, first attempting to write enormous novels and later trying short stories—possibly because students of writing are so often told that short stories are harder to produce. (Incidentally, that is a statement I have never accepted.) Though I am Hortense's friend, I do not know if she did begin, tentatively, on a novel which she later dropped. I doubt it, because at the age when most university graduates try such ambitious experiments her energies were diverted. In turn, she took a job in a department store and then was a social worker; she married, had children, published a few stories, taught, and held an editorial post on a girls' magazine. This was all experience, of course, but it hardly contributed to the tranquillity one should have for sustained writing. When, awarded a Guggenheim Fellowship on the strength of her published stories, she was asked what she intended to do as a project, she replied that she wanted to go to England, sit there for a year, and just think.

Her first published novel, *False Entry*, has much of England in it as a result, but there is much else as well. Woven through the story, among the threads that tie together Europe,

New York and the South—this last-named locale providing one of the most haunting episodes I can recall reading anywhere—are accounts of characters we meet again in a much later novel, *The New Yorkers*. It is typical of Hortense Calisher that she should do this unconventional thing, picking up a group of people who were not her main actors in the first book and writing in depth about them in a totally new story which could not in any respect be called a sequel to *False Entry*. I find it absorbing to contrast the two books if only because they are so widely different in treatment. Even in these circumstances Miss Calisher refuses to be typed. Hers is a world of varying climates.

Between these two long novels she has produced other works—collections of short or shorter stories and two novels, *Textures of Life* and *Journal from Ellipsia*. *Textures* has been accepted as her most nearly run-of-the-mill tale, dealing as it does with a young couple and their problems with their child. Described in these words the story sounds commonplace, but it is not. The reader remembers the young people in their New York loft, the little girl struggling with asthma, and somehow it becomes a new story about contemporary crises. At the other end of the scale is *Journal from Ellipsia* in a completely different *genre*, which I find wildly funny. Reviewers had an especially hard time with the *Journal* because, like the author, it is so hard to classify. One critic, in despair, ended by listing it as science fiction. Whatever one calls it, I like it—perhaps more than any of her other books—but I reserve the right to change my mind. Already I find myself wondering. There are many ways to read Hortense Calisher, and she creates many moods in the reader.

Her latest novel, *Queenie*, is another romp, about a girl who grows up among a weirdly out-of-time group of aging demi-mondaines in New York. Cherished, sheltered and totally unprepared for life as it is today, Queenie goes out to grapple with reality in an up-to-the-minute progressive college. I say "reality," but . . . but what is the use of outlining plots? It is what Miss Calisher does with them that counts.

—Emily Hahn

---

**CALLAGHAN, Morley (Edward).** Canadian. Born in Toronto, Ontario, 22 September 1903. Educated at St. Michael's College, University of Toronto, B.A. 1925; Osgoode Hall Law School, LL.B. 1928. Married Loretto Florence Dee in 1929; has two children. Chairman of the radio forum, "Of Things to Come", during World War II. Recipient: Governor-General's Award, 1952; Lorne Pierce Medal, 1960; Medal of Merit, City of Toronto, 1962; Canada Council Medal, 1966; Moslon Award, 1969. LL.D., University of Western Ontario, London, 1965. Address: 20 Dale Avenue, Toronto, Ontario, Canada.

PUBLICATIONS

Novels

*Strange Fugitive.* Toronto, Macmillan, and New York, Scribner, 1928.
*It's Never Over.* Toronto, Macmillan, and New York, Scribner, 1930.
*A Broken Journey.* New York, Scribner, 1932.
*Such Is My Beloved.* Toronto, Macmillan, and New York, Scribner, 1934.
*They Shall Inherit the Earth.* Toronto, Macmillan, and New York, Random House, 1935; London, Chatto and Windus, 1936.

*More Joy in Heaven.*   Toronto, Macmillan, and New York, Random House, 1937.
*Varsity Story.*   Toronto and London, Macmillan, and New York, Macmillan, 1948.
*The Loved and the Lost.*   New York, Macmillan, 1951; London, MacGibbon and Kee,
   1961.
*The Many Colored Coat.*   Toronto, Macmillan, and New York, Coward McCann,
   1960; London, Macmillan, 1963.
*A Passion in Rome.*   Toronto, Macmillan, and New York, Coward McCann, 1961;
   London, Macmillan, 1964.


Short Stories

*Native Argosy.*   Toronto, Macmillan, and New York, Scribner, 1929.
*Now That April's Here.*   Toronto, Macmillan, and New York, Random House, 1936.
*Stories.*   Toronto, Macmillan, 2 vols., 1959, 1967; London, MacGibbon and Kee,
   1963, 1964.


Play

*Turn Again George* (produced New York, 1940).


Other

*No Man's Meat.*   Paris, E. W. Titus, 1931.
*Luke Baldwin's Vow* (juvenile).   Philadelphia, Winston, 1948.
*That Summer in Paris: Memories of Tangled Friendships with Hemingway, Fitzgerald
   and Some Others.*   New York, Coward McCann, 1963; as *That Summer in Paris:
   Memories of Tangled Friendships with Hemingway, Fitzgerald and Others*, London,
   MacGibbon and Kee, 1963.


\*       \*       \*


The capacity which could produce Morley Callaghan's clipped, significant short stories,
studies of the mysteriousness of the ordinary and the bewildering discrepancies of human
fact, is not very evident in the early novels, *Strange Fugitive*, *It's Never Over*, and *A Broken
Journey*, which are muddy in texture and melodramatic in action. It revealed itself first in
*Such Is My Beloved*, a novel of which the whole air and idiom belong to the thirties, the
thirties of the depression, of insecurity, unemployment, malnutrition, meanness.

The separation of two worlds, Christian and bourgeois, is the initiating contrast of the
novel. Father Dowling speaks of it in his sermon in a lofty, generalising way. The novel
shows it becoming biting and personal—"inevitable" in this way—in his own life. For all
his spiritual and social conviction, and in spite of his working class origins, he himself,
because of his education, his status, his looks, his popularity with the parishioners, has a
recognised position in the bourgeoisie. Officially he is on the side of religion against bourgeois
convention; in reality he has at least one foot in both camps. The point at which the antagonism of the two orders becomes incorporated into his own life, the point at which he
starts to be harrowed by the necessity for deciding between them, comes when he meets the
two young prostitutes, Ronnie and Midge.

The economy of naturalness characteristic of Morley Callaghan—which is a reconstruction
of movement rather than a Zolaesque realism of detail—is best realised in this between
Father Dowling and the prostitutes. Its growth, like that of all complex human feeling,
is checked, troubled, backsliding, never wholly smooth or continuous; and yet it moves

229

irresistibly onward, obeying and balancing an inward initiative as well as outer circumstances. At first, it is sympathetic but embarrassed on one side, suspect and then irritated on the other. As the priest begins to understand the economic forces beating on the young women his attention is less firmly concentrated on the rescue from prostitution and more on bringing a spontaneous human response from them.

The contradiction between the donors and the deniers of life is at the heart of *Such Is My Beloved*. It is the conclusion to which the original division between the religious and the bourgeois worlds finally leads. Father Dowling in his efforts to be as richly a donor as he can becomes a scandal to the deniers. The novel makes it quite clear why; and not only clear but convincing. It has nothing to do with any sentimental falsification of the girls or of prostitution.

Poetry and religion have a universalising effect in *Such Is My Beloved*, making it appear to the British reader more accessible and less off-puttingly embedded in alien ground than, say, *More Joy in Heaven*, which wears an aspect—I can only put it like this—of continental parochialism. *More Joy in Heaven* is irremediably indigenous, North-American in a limiting way. It is the story of a paroled criminal's effort to re-enter the society which has first punished and then forgiven him. Behind it stands an ethos of violence and the myth of the heroic gangster. Its setting is the brutal North-American city, ugly and unhistorical and very much "a machine for living", the sense of which is conveyed with confident incisiveness.

The paradox of one's reaction to *More Joy in Heaven* is that while its pure Americanism is so remote (it is, it seems to me, markedly more American than Canadian, unlike *Such Is My Beloved*) its cinematic conception, technique, imagery and characterisation are intimately familiar, part indeed of the history of one's own life. So much so that it is impossible to think about *More Joy in Heaven* without seeing it as a film and without casting its characters from those familiar names: Victor McLaglen, William Bendix, Janet Gaynor, Veronica Lake, Humphrey Bogart, Richard Widmark, Sidney Greenstreet, Franchot Tone, Edwin Arnold, Edward G. Robinson. *More Joy in Heaven* would make—perhaps, for all I know, it has already made—a superb film script.

I have stressed what I take to be the essential limitation in *More Joy in Heaven* but it remains a strong piece of work and an impressive example of its *genre*. It is solid, vigorous, lean and precise, the product of a serious mind. It has more weight than the documented but insubstantial study of a university institution, *Varsity Story*, more bite than the more vaguely organised *A Passion in Rome*. *More Joy in Heaven* is a member of the group of novels which includes *Such Is My Beloved*, *The Many Colored Coat*, and *The Loved and the Lost* to which I turn now. These novels, different in theme and setting, have in common a preoccupation with what I should like to call self-preservation, as long as I may remove from the term any hint of selfishness or over-personal concern. Morley Callaghan is fascinated by what Henry James in the Preface to *What Maisie Knew* called a character's "truth of resistance", the gift or genius that some have for preserving intact the lineaments of their nature. It is a power which has at its heart a certain insistent simplicity: not self confidence but trust in self. In Father Dowling it shows itself as a steady flame of goodness impervious even to the most high-minded opposition, in Kip Caley as the persistent, and finally desperate, trust of an abrasively independent identity. In *The Loved and the Lost* it is the girl Peggy Sanderson who possesses this faculty. It reveals itself in conduct which ignores or evades—rather than defies—the acceptable canons of behaviour in her world. The well-disposed think her capricious, the suspicious perverse. Her strangeness lies in her unpredictability, in her assumption that she is not caught in the same net as everybody else. She is described by his friend Foley to James McAlpine, a University teacher and would-be newspaper columnist, who is our source of awareness during this novel, in a fumbling conversation which tries to define her strangeness, as a blue jay, a bird which flies off at crazy and unpredictable angles.

The substance of the novel is the search for the true nature of the girl's odd, disconcerting individuality. It is conducted against the quietly insinuated but effectively established presence of Montreal. In no other novel of Morley Callaghan is the city context so significantly part of the story and—at least to a British reader—so attractive. Incidentally, unobtrusively and, at every point, relevantly, the dimensions of the city appear.

*The Many Colored Coat* is one of the finest of Morley Callaghan's novels, and the one I take to represent his latest, and most developed work. The medium is in the same mode, quiet, unpretentious, close to speech and movement and with much of the flexibility and versatility of the spoken language. The medium, at once masculine and unpretentious, is in accord with Morley Callaghan's attitude, which is, characteristically, both self-effacing and positive. The theme of *The Many Colored Coat* is that of Joseph, the gifted and beloved young man. The novel rehearses the theme of the fortunes of the fortunate man. The biblical reference comes through, as the novel unfolds, without the least touch of impropriety or tactlessness, and it testifies to the steadiness Callaghan sees in human nature and to his perception of the permanent content of the varying crises it has to face.

The importance attributed in this novel to pride, not in any doctrinal way but by suggestive, concrete pointing, is justified not only by the facts of the case in this novel and the intelligent psychological investigation of them, but by a certain habit of sensibility in Morley Callaghan himself. He has, as Edmund Wilson pointed out in a perceptive and sympathetic essay, *O Canada*, "an intuitive sense of the meaning of Christianity" (p. 20). The human vision of these novels depends on a Christian style of feeling, of a particular tradition of religious sensibility which is present not as dogma or metaphysic but as a mode of perception and reaction.

I speak of Callaghan's Christian response, but, of course, that response and the whole economy of feeling of which it is a part, are sunk deep in the constitution of the novelist. If Callaghan is a Christian novelist, this is the way in which he is one. He is not the spokesman of religion, but the artist who possesses it as part of his personal nervous equipment. This traditional steadiness blends in Callaghan with that acute feeling for contemporary society, which, to a European at least, seems very natural to an artist working in the New World, and the combination makes him a novelist of an impressively serious quality. The contemporary flavour appears everywhere in his work, in themes, situations, characters and procedures. A single notable example of it in *The Many Colored Coat* is his treatment of the life of the streets. The street in a modern industrial society presents itself to him as an image of that society and its experience. His skill in rendering the flow of life through the street, the brutality and ugliness, the glimpses the street provides of other, less tangible experiences, the altercations, the moments of communication, show the street not only as a place but as the analogue of human vitality and representativeness. "That night," he writes of Harry Lane after his fall, in words which are apt to describe the impression all Morley Callaghan's best work makes, "he walked through the streets for hours feeling he was wandering through his own life".

—William Walsh

---

**CALVIN, Henry.**   See **HANLEY, Clifford.**

---

**CANAWAY, W(illiam) H(amilton).**   British.   Born in Altrincham, Cheshire, 12 June 1925. Educated at Altrincham Grammer School; University College, Bangor, Wales, B.A. (honours) 1948, Dip.Ed. 1949, M.A. 1951. Served in the Queen's Royal Regiment and

Intelligence Corps, in Italy and the Middle East, 1943–46. Married to Pamela Mary Burgess; has five children. Lecturer in technical colleges, 1949–62. Lives in Wales. Address: c/o Curtis Brown Ltd., 13 King Street, Covent Garden, London WC2E 8HU, England.

PUBLICATIONS

Novels

*The Ring-Givers*.  London, Joseph, 1958.
*The Seal*.  London, Joseph, 1959.
*Sammy Going South*.  London, Hutchinson, 1961; as *Find the Boy*, New York, Viking Press, 1961.
*The Hunter and the Horns*.  London, Hutchinson, and New York, Harper, 1962.
*My Feet upon a Rock*.  London, Hutchinson, 1963.
*Crows in a Green Tree*.  London, Hutchinson, and New York, Doubleday, 1965.
*The Grey Seas of Jutland*.  London, Hutchinson, 1966.
*The Mules of Borgo San Marco*.  London, Hutchinson, 1967.
*A Moral Obligation*.  London, Hutchinson, 1969.
*A Declaration of Independence*.  London, Hutchinson, 1971.

Plays

*Horse on Fire* (produced Hawkesyard Priory, 1961).
*Roll Me Over* (produced Birmingham, 1971).

Screenplays: *The Ipcress File*, with James Doran, 1965; *Rendezvous in Black*, 1972.

Other

*A Creed of Willow* (on fishing).  London, Joseph, 1957.
*A Snowdon Stream (the Gwyrfai) and How to Fish It*.  London, Putnam, 1958.

\*　　　\*　　　\*

A novelist who writes a best seller early in his career is both lucky and limited; lucky for obvious reasons, limited, to some extent, by its success. For ever after it he tends to be known as "Author of Such-and-such"; however hard he may try to write something different, it dogs him. This happened to W. H. Canaway after he published *Sammy Going South* in 1961, and it was successfully filmed, Penguinised and made famous over the next few years.

There is no "typical" Canaway novel, however, and if he has been typed as an adventure story writer it is mostly the fault or the merit of *Sammy Going South*. Two early novels, *The Seal* and *My Feet upon a Rock*, are set in modern Wales; *The Ring-Givers*, about Beowulf, in the 6th century A.D. Later, the novels seem to fit into familiar slots but never quite do so. *Crows in a Green Tree* is almost domestic rural comedy, but too bleak and bitter to qualify exactly; *The Mules of Borgo San Marco*, fast moving and energetic and full of Latin low life, is almost wartime farce; *The Grey Seas of Jutland* is almost a family saga—English and German cousins whose lives interweave before, then during, the First World War. And in the adventure stories there is almost, though again not quite, a common situation—some quest, chase or trial through danger and difficulty, an ordinary character tested through extraordinary circumstances.

In *Sammy Going South* the ten-year-old hero makes his way down the whole continent of Africa, starting alone and penniless and in danger at Port Said, ending triumphantly in Durban. In *The Hunter and the Horns* a greenhorn schoolmaster finds himself facing the terrors of the desert, the intense loneliness of life among Arabs who despise him, and whom he mistrusts. In *A Moral Obligation* a young officer in the Far East at the end of the war finds himself involved in panicky wanderings through a jungle in which enemies, though he does not know it, have overnight become allies. In each case the hero has to face, not just physical dangers—though these are hair-raising enough, and described with an exactness that makes one really credit them, live through them—but the dangers inherent in himself, in his own outlook, spirit and limitations. In writing of spiritual as well as physical adventure, Canaway becomes much more than a realistic writer of exciting stories.

There is a particular quality about his realism, too, that makes him go beyond "mere" adventure, a quality one might call over-realism, or "going too far": the ability to face what is almost unfaceable, to produce a moment of vivid physical horror that stays in the mind as a kind of photographic flash: the arm in *The Grey Seas of Jutland*, with the woollen sleeve impacted into it by blast; the beggar in *Sammy Going South* when the stones of the camp fire explode in his face; the casual shooting of the hero's knee at close range in *A Moral Obligation* —the sense of his appalling pain, his total panic.

In the same way, realism extends to ordinary life, not just to moments of danger. Even when Canaway writes about children, an uncosy sense of adult evil lies about them, and at his quietest there is a sense of violence, even when it is subdued—violence of feeling, reaction and spirit. His characters are not likeable, on the whole, and this includes his child characters; but one is never sure if he himself dislikes them. This ambiguity is a proof of his ability to lose himself, as narrator, in his characters, to take on their presence, their standards, and not to show his own. The spirit of places, particularly of the country—outdoor life all over the place, from Wales to Vietnam—he catches remarkably well. But where people are concerned he is a chameleon novelist, taking the spirit, as well as the colour, of his characters.

—Isabel Quigley

---

**CANTWELL, Robert (Emmett).**    American.    Born in Little Falls (now Vader), Washington, 31 January 1908. Educated at the University of Washington, Seattle, 1924–25. Served in the 248th Coast Artillery of the Washington State National Guard, 1925–26. Married Mary Elizabeth Chambers in 1931; has three children. Veneer Clipperman, Harbor Plywood Company, Hoquiam, Washington 1925–29; Literary Editor, *New Outlook*, New York, 1931–35; Literary Editor, *Time* magazine, New York, 1935–37; Member of the Editorial Board, *Fortune* magazine, New York, 1937–38; Foreign News and National Affairs Editor, 1939–43, on special assignments, 1943–45, *Time*; Literary Editor, *Newsweek* magazine, New York, 1949–54; Editor, Limited Editions Club, New York, 1956–57. Associate Editor, 1957–64, and since 1961, Senior Editor, *Sports Illustrated* magazine, New York. Address: Sports Illustrated, Time and Life Building, Rockefeller Center, New York, New York 10020, U.S.A.

PUBLICATIONS

Novels

  *Laugh and Lie Down.*   New York, Farrar and Rinehart, 1931.

*The Land of Plenty.*   New York, Farrar and Rinehart, and London, Bell, 1934.

Uncollected Short Stories

"Hanging by My Thumbs", in *New American Caravan.*   New York, Macaulay, 1929.
"Under Every Green Tree", in *The Miscellany* (New York), 1930.
"Babe Foley", in *The Miscellany* (New York), 1930.
"Never Mind", in *American Caravan 4.*   New York, Macaulay, 1931.
"East of the Mountains", in *Pagany: A Native Quarterly* (Boston), 1932.
"The Wreck of the Gravy Train", in *New Republic* (New York), 1932.
"Hills Around Centralia", in *Proletarian Literature in the United States*, edited by Granville Hicks.   New York, International Publishers, 1935.


Other

*Nathaniel Hawthorne: The American Years.*   New York, Rinehart, 1948.
*Famous American Men of Letters.*   New York, Dodd Mead, 1956.
*Alexander Wilson: Naturalist and Pioneer.*   Philadelphia, Lippincott, 1961.
*The Real McCoy: The Life and Times of Norman Selby.*   Princeton, New Jersey, Auerbach, 1971.
*The Hidden Northwest.*   Philadelphia, Lippincott, 1972.

Editor, *The Humorous Side of Erskine Caldwell.*   New York, Duell, 1951.

Translator, *The Charterhouse of Parma*, by Stendhal.   New York, Heritage Press, 1956.


Manuscript Collection: University of Oregon, Eugene.


Critical Studies: in *The Radical Novel in the United States* by Walter Rideout, Cambridge, Massachusetts, Harvard University Press, 1956; *The American Writer and the Great Depression* by Harvey Swados, Indianapolis, Bobbs Merrill, 1966; by Jack Conroy, in *Proletarian Writers of the Thirties*, edited by David Madden, Carbondale, Southern Illinois University Press, 1968.


*        *        *


Although Robert Cantwell continues to write, he has not published any fiction since 1935; indeed, virtually all his stories and novels were published in the brief period from 1929–1935. His work during this time has led to his being identified as a "proletarian novelist," and while the term is not invalid as it applies to Cantwell, it is too restrictive to adequately define the range and quality of his art.

In "Hanging by My Thumbs," for example, which Alfred Kreymborg included in the 1929 *New American Caravan*, Cantwell evinces no concern for those matters which in the ensuing years were to dominate the writings of the literary Left. The story is a first-person account of the failure of love, and Cantwell's interest is in his narrator's inability to accept this failure. (It was to this story that F. Scott Fitzgerald alluded when, on 21 January 1930, he wrote to Maxwell Perkins of Scribners, "In the new *American Caravan* amid much sandwiching of Joyce and Co. is the first work of a 21 year old named *Robert Cantwell.* Mark it well, for my guess is that he's learned a better lesson from Proust than Thornton Wilder did and has a destiny of no mean star.") So, too, in such stories as "Under Every Green Tree" and "Never Mind," Cantwell is not at all concerned with social issues: the awkwardness of a youth in love and the break-up of a marriage are his respective subject matters in these two stories. And even in a story published in *Pagany* as late as 1932, Cantwell wrote about a frightening encounter between two young boys and the father of a retarded child; the sense of terror which dominates the story calls to mind not the proletarian works of the 1930s but a novel such as Harper Lee's *To Kill a Mockingbird*.

All this, however, is not to suggest that Cantwell's fiction is devoid of social involvement. "Babe Foley," for example, which was published in *The Miscellany* just four months after "Under Every Green Tree," is another of Cantwell's stories which deals with the confused sensibility of a young man. But in this story the narrator's intense anxiety is not the result of his love for a woman; rather, it stems from his admiration on the one hand for Babe Foley, the crude "head dogger" of his father's lumber mill, and from his desire, at the same time, to share the world of his fraternity brother, Harold Ainsley, whose very clothing gives him "an almost aristocratic appearance, a careless look suggesting an indifferent and unconscious superiority." Yet even here, where Babe Foley represents "everything in the world that seemed attractive and impossible to achieve," Cantwell's ironic viewpoint prevents the story from becoming a paean to the working class. Similarly, in his first novel, *Laugh and Lie Down*, which was published in 1931, Cantwell uses the mill as the backdrop for his tale. But, again, though he is most sympathetic towards his characters, the novel is dominated by what Horace Gregory once referred to as an original tone of half-ironic terror; it is a story, that is, which is primarily concerned not with the economic conditions of mill workers but with the disillusionment and psychic disassociation of three young people.

There are, in fact, only four works of fiction by Cantwell which clearly may be designated as "proletarian": "The Wreck of the Gravy Train," a brief narrative which appeared in *The New Republic* in 1932; "The Land of Plenty," a powerful story about the pressures of working in a plywood factory, which was included in Edward J. O'Brien's *The Best Stories of 1933*; "Hills Around Centralia," which deals with the Wobblies and the lynching of Wesley Everett; and *The Land of Plenty*, Cantwell's second and last novel. It is for this last work that Cantwell is best known, and rightly so. He had spent most of his childhood in Washington, and for many years had worked in a lumber mill. To varying degrees, most of his fiction makes use of the experience he had as a youth. The factory Cantwell describes in *The Land of Plenty*, however, is entirely fictional, for the plant in which he worked had none of the oppressive qualities of the mill in his novel. Yet the book is permeated with an extraordinary sense of factory life; as Jack Conroy recently wrote of *The Land of Plenty*: "it has . . . no close rival for authenticity and accuracy. For one who has worked in a factory from necessity, as I have, it rings as true as a well-tempered bell and is as fresh and strong as it was more than 30 years ago." The workers who go out on strike in *The Land of Plenty* are brutally defeated, yet Cantwell had clearly achieved his purpose in writing the novel. He had wanted to give the "working class people a sense of their own dignity" (as he quoted one of André Malraux's characters), and in *The Land of Plenty* he did just that. It is without question one of the finest novels to come out of the left-wing movement in the United States.

—Jack Salzman

---

**CAPOTE, Truman.** American. Born in New Orleans, Louisiana, 30 September 1924. Educated at Trinity School and St. John's Academy, New York; Greenwich High School, Connecticut. Has worked in the Art Department of *The New Yorker* magazine, and as a writer for the television show, "Talk of the Town"; now a full-time Writer. Recipient:

O. Henry Award, 1946, 1948, 1951; National Institute of Arts and Letters grant, 1959; Edgar Allan Poe Award, 1966; Emmy Award, for television adaptation, 1967. Member, National Institute of Arts and Letters. Lives in New York City. Address: c/o Random House Inc., 457 Madison Avenue, New York, New York 10022, U.S.A.


PUBLICATIONS

Novels

Other Voices, Other Rooms.   New York, Random House, 1948; London, Heinemann, 1968.
The Grass Harp.   New York, Random House, 1951; London, Heinemann, 1952.


Short Stories

A Tree of Night and Other Stories.   New York, Random House, 1949.
Breakfast at Tiffany's: A Short Novel and 3 Stories.   New York, Random House, 1958; London, Hamish Hamilton, 1959.
A Christmas Memory.   New York, Random House, 1966.


Plays

The Grass Harp (produced New York, 1952).   New York, Random House, 1952.
House of Flowers, with Harold Arlen (produced New York, 1954).   New York, Random House, 1968.
The Thanksgiving Visitor.   New York, Random House, 1968; London, Hamish Hamilton, 1969.

    Screenplays: Beat the Devil, 1953; The Innocents, 1962.


Other

Local Color.   New York, Random House, 1950.
The Muses Are Heard: An Account.   New York, Random House, 1956.
Observations, with Richard Avedon.   New York, Simon and Schuster, and London, Weidenfeld and Nicolson, 1959.
Selected Writings, edited by Mark Schorer.   New York, Modern Library, and London, Hamish Hamilton, 1963.
In Cold Blood: A True Account of a Multiple Murder and Its Consequences.   New York, Random House, and London, Hamish Hamilton, 1966.


Manuscript Collection: Library of Congress, Washington, D.C.


*       *       *


Among postwar American writers, few came to be known so young as Truman Capote; literary glamor of a certain kind came to him early to stay. There is no elegant way to summarize his work. His styles vary too much, though style itself remains a central part of his achievement. Born and raised in the Deep South, his earliest fiction develops some mannerisms of the region. Yet the legacy of Faulkner affects Capote in a peculiar way, less gothic than exotic, less elemental than oneiric. An ethereal sexuality, often homoerotic, suffuses his fiction. Nor does the Southern manner cling to him for long. He says: "I have lived in many places besides the South and I don't like to be called a Southern writer." There is the crackling travelogue, from Ischia to Haiti, of *Local Color*. There is the hilarious account of a trip to Russia, with the cast of *Porgy and Bess*, in *The Muses Are Heard*. There is the New York or Kansas setting of his later novels.

As the locale of Capote's work changes, so do the forms of his fiction open. His preciosity gives way to social curiosity, to laughter; witness the zany film script, *Beat the Devil*. Intelligence inhabits his fantasies. Behind the frills and fashions of his prose, one senses the tenacity of some purpose. It is as if the solitary gaze of Narcissus, watery, vague, could in time sharpen enough to discern contours of reality rising beneath the surface.

Already in the first stories of Capote, collected in *A Tree of Night*, a distinction may be observed between his nocturnal and daylight styles, the nightmares and reveries of Narcissus. A sense of dread attends "the instant of petrified violence," the locked dream, the disintegrating psyche, in such stories as "Miriam," "The Headless Hawk," "A Tree of Night." Symbol and metaphor dredge the unconscious; animism and fable meet. Yet if terror and the preternatural define the nocturnal mode, comedy and social manners characterize the daylight view of "My Side of the Matter," "Jug of Silver," "Children on Their Birthdays." The tone is chatty, admits of first-person anecdotes; the characters engage concrete realities in a small Southern town rather than abstract horrors in a Northern metropolis. For Capote, then, dreams contain the destructive element of the isolated soul but also express the creative element of life; their release is a prerequisite of love.

His first two novels heighten this contrast, though both are still romances, that "neutral territory," Hawthorne once said, "somewhere between the real world and fairy-land, where the Actual and the Imaginary may meet, and each imbue itself with the nature of the other." *Other Voices, Other Rooms* remains a *tour de force* of the dark, mythic sensibility which the Southern formalist critics helped to make fashionable in the Forties and early Fifties. The book enfolds the reader in its poetic language, original and also over-wrought, enfolds him in an inscape of fright and perversion. The action centers on the boy, Joel Knox, whose initiation leads him through many mysteries, to the spectral Cloud Hotel where he is finally confirmed in his identity. The quest for the Other—be he god, father, seducer, or mirror image—ends in a hallucination of self-knowledge, a vision of love, loneliness, and mutability. Set also in the South, *The Grass Harp* deals similarly with the end of boyhood innocence, though its tone is far less eerie than nostalgic. As Collin Fenwick hears the voice of the wind through a field of Indian grass, he recovers a crisis of his youth among elderly women, besieged in a tree-house by the wicked World which, sooner than later, must storm the Heart. Yet song and memory redeem present, adult, realities by releasing the impulses of love.

Here ends the Southern phase of Capote's fiction, his pre-possession for the fantastic, the monstrous, the bizarre. A new kind of whimsy or camp affects his next work, *Breakfast at Tiffany's*, set mainly in New York, which celebrates headlong Holly Golightly. Bitter-sweet in its naïve abandon, current with chic *argot*, the narrative suggests the interest of the times in neo-picaresques, in open forms. Thus the bruised innocence of Holden Caulfield returns in Holly who is more frivolous, but also passionately honest and free. "I'd rather have cancer than a dishonest heart," she cries.

Less than a decade later, Capote once again changes his role. We see him *In Cold Blood* as herald of a new genre, "the non-fiction novel," which recognizes the convergence of fiction and fact in times of outrage, the insane surrealism of daily life. Based upon accounts of grisly Kansas murders of a wealthy farmer and his entire family, the book ends by raising vast questions about American society, the anger and deprivation of men, the workings of justice. Years of research, mounds of tapes and notes, endless interviews are compelled into form. With covert art, Capote selects, organizes, juxtaposes; he draws nets of animal imagery around his characters; he manages to keep the violence controlled. His sympathy for stunted life quickens the work with life of its own. The fierce controversy which greeted the work centered on two issues: the authenticity of the "non-fiction" form as a medium of narrative, and the authenticity of the author in his relation to the two killers, waiting execution on death row.

Capote survives controversy, though he may not thrive on it as Mailer does. He has endurance as well as wit. He projects many images of himself—the aesthete, the terrorist, the humorist, the jet-setter, the social critic—and his mastery of language is clear. Yet, with the possible exception of *In Cold Blood*, he has failed to provide the age with some compelling image of itself. Readers do not turn to him as they do to other writers who, in their inventions, reveal more about the world in which we live. If this is no final criterion of a novelist's measure, it is an increasingly significant one. We do well to remember, though, that Capote has the special gift of surprise; and he is still in mid-career.

—Ihab Hassan

---

**CAREW, Jan (Rynveld).** Guyanan. Born in Agricola, British Guiana, now Guyana, 24 September 1925. Educated at Methodist Primary School, Agricola; Loyola Primary School, New Amsterdam, 1930–34; Berbice High School, 1934–39; Howard University, Washington, D.C., 1945–46; Western Reserve University, Cleveland, 1946–48; Charles University, Prague, 1949–50; the Sorbonne, Paris, 1950–51. Teacher, Berbice High School, 1939; Customs Officer, British Guiana Government Service, 1940–43; Senior Officer, Government of Trinidad Price Control Office, 1943–44; Editor, *De Kim* poetry magazine, Amsterdam, Holland, 1951; Actor, with Laurence Olivier Productions, London and New York, 1952; Editor, *Kensington Post*, London, 1953; Lecturer in Race Relations, London University Extra-Mural Department, 1953–54; Writer and Editor, BBC Overseas Service, London, 1954–57; Latin American Correspondent, *Observer*, London, 1961–63; Director of Culture, and Minister of Culture, Government of Guyana, 1962; Adviser to the Publicity Secretariat, Government of Ghana, and Editor, *The African Review*, 1965–66. Since 1969, Senior Fellow in the Council of Humanities and Lecturer in the Department of Afro-American Studies, Princeton University, New Jersey. Paintings exhibited, London, 1948. Recipient: Canada Arts Council Fellowship, 1969. Address: c/o Department of Afro-American Studies, Princeton University, Princeton, New Jersey 08540, U.S.A.

PUBLICATIONS

Novels

Black Midas. London, Secker and Warburg, 1958; as *Touch of Midas*, New York, Coward McCann, 1958.
*The Wild Coast.* London, Secker and Warburg, 1958.
*The Last Barbarian.* London, Secker and Warburg, 1961.
*Moscow Is Not My Mecca.* London, Secker and Warburg, 1964; as *Green Winter*, New York, Stein and Day, 1965.

Plays

*Miracle in Lime Lane*, with Sylvia Wynter, adaptation of a play by Coventry Taylor (produced Spanish Town, Jamaica, 1962).
*University of Hunger* (produced Georgetown, Guyana, 1966).
*Gentlemen Be Seated* (produced Toronto, 1967).

Plays produced on television and radio in England and Canada.


Other

*The Third Gift* (juvenile).   Boston, Little Brown, 1972.

Verse published in anthologies.

\*          \*          \*

If a theme common to the novels of Jan Carew may be discerned through a study of his work it is the theme of flight from origins and the quest for roots, the legend of men who make a journey in search of a new sense of home or status or image of themselves and lose or discover identity and direction somewhere along that journey.

In his first novel, *Black Midas*, the journey of the orphan-boy Aron away from the oppressive impoverishment of his native village, and his quest for a new ground and status in society, prove abortive. Aron grows into the legendary diamond-king, Ocean Shark, a spectacular myth of a man in the Big City he had dreamed of conquering, but he remains virtually unchanged behind the splendour of the myth, inevitably overreaching himself and losing everything. The tale of Ocean Shark's rise and fall is richly steeped in the folklore of the Guyana forest and the vigour of Carew's portraits of porknockers and prostitutes, the lilting musical ring of much of the dialogue, the colour and robust exuberance of the narrative stamp this first novel with a rugged authenticity and distinction.

The orphan figure, man of obscure or confused origins, appears again in Carew's second novel, *The Wild Coast*. Hector, like the village boy Aron in *Black Midas*, is brought up by guardians. Like Aron too his mother is unknown and his father, though alive, is less of a man than a legend. Here, however, the similarity ends though the need to feel their roots and find a true image of themselves is still the common problem. There is in Hector's blood a battle between his love for the Negro nurse who brings him up and his inheritance as a rich man of white ancestry, between the Christianity too of his home and the pagan beliefs and rituals of the village people. Unlike Aron, Hector is not contemptuous of the environment in which he first takes root. His is a struggle, futile but earnest, to find a truly meaningful place in Tarlogie, to understand and to belong, to see himself as an integral part of the native life of the villagers. Discovery of his real identity and direction, however, underlines the necessity for him to transplant himself into the world beyond and his roots are cut one by one by a combination of events which in their pattern seem like a conspiracy of Providence.

His third novel, *The Last Barbarian*, set in America, is essentially a study of uprooted fragments of West Indian and African life cast up on a street in Harlem. Centre of the canvas of lost men is the Brazilian artist Tiberio whose paintings make him famous but who seeks, in an increasingly bitter and lonely struggle, to create a new image of himself, to escape being trapped in a Negro context of symbol and emerge as an artist in his own right.

His fourth and latest novel, *Moscow Is Not My Mecca*, documents the dilemma of a young black Leningrad student, whose illusions about the Communist world as an answer to the Capitalist West are shattered. This book points prophetically to the future alignment of the "coloured" races in a Third World stance against the "white" super-powers. A prolific writer of plays for radio and television, Carew's latter concern has been to explore the

revolutionary energy and potential massing behind the rage and impotence, the contradictions and futilities of that emergent world.

—Ivan Van-Sertima

---

**CASSILL, R(onald) V(erlin).** American. Born in Cedar Falls, Iowa, 17 May 1919.
Educated at the University of Iowa, Iowa City, B.A. 1940, M.A. 1947; the Sorbonne, Paris,
1952–53. Served in the United States Army, 1942–46. Married Karilyn Kay Adams in 1956;
has three children. Instructor, University of Iowa, 1948–52; Editor, *Western Review*, Iowa
City, Iowa, 1951–52; Lecturer, Columbia University, New York, and the New School for
Social Research, New York, 1957–59, and the University of Iowa, 1960–65; Writer-in-
Residence, Purdue University, Lafayette, Indiana, 1965–66. Since 1966, Associate Professor
of English, and since 1967, President of the Associated Writing Programs, Brown University,
Providence, Rhode Island. Also a painter and lithographer. Recipient: *Atlantic* "Firsts"
prize for a short story, 1947; Rockefeller grant, 1954; Guggenheim grant, 1968. Address:
31 Cabot Street, Providence, Rhode Island, U.S.A.

PUBLICATIONS

Novels

    *The Eagle on the Coin*.   New York, Random House, 1950.
    *Dormitory Women*.   New York, Lion, 1953.
    *The Left Bank of Desire*.   New York, Ace, 1954.
    *A Taste of Sin*.   New York, Ace, 1955.
    *The Hungering Shame*.   New York, Avon, 1956.
    *The Wound of Love*.   New York, Avon, 1956.
    *Naked Morning*.   New York, Avon, 1957.
    *Lustful Summer*.   New York, Avon, 1958.
    *Nurses Quarters*.   New York, Gold Medal, 1958.
    *The Wife Next Door*.   New York, Gold Medal, 1959.
    *Clem Anderson*.   New York, Simon and Schuster, 1961.
    *My Sister's Keeper*.   New York, Avon, 1961.
    *Night School*.   New York, New American Library, 1961.
    *Pretty Leslie*.   New York, Simon and Schuster, 1963; London, Muller, 1964.
    *The President*.   New York, Simon and Schuster, 1964.
    *La Vie Passionée of Rodney Buckthorne: A Tale of the Great American's Last Rally and
        Curious Death*.   New York, Geis, 1968.
    *Doctor Cobb's Game*.   New York, Geis, 1970.

Short Stories

    *15 x 3*, with Herbert Gold and James B. Hall.   New York, New Directions, 1957.
    *The Father and Other Stories*.   New York, Simon and Schuster, 1965.
    *The Happy Marriage and Other Stories*.   West Lafayette, Indiana, Purdue University
        Press, 1967.

Other

*Writing Fiction.*   New York, Pocket Books, 1963.
*In an Iron Time: Statements and Reiterations: Essays.*   West Lafayette, Indiana, Purdue
    University Press, 1967.

Editor, *Intro 1, 2,* and *3.*   New York, Bantam, 1968–70.

Manuscript Collection:   Sugarman Library, Boston University.


R. V. Cassill comments:

My most personal statement is probably to be found in my short stories. If few of them are
reliably autobiographical at least they grew from the observations, moods, exultations and
agonies of early years. If there is a constant pattern in them, it is probably that of a hopeful
being who expects evil and finds worse.

From my first novel onward I have explored the correspondences between the interior
world—of desire and anxiety—and the public world of power—extra-social violences and
politics. In *The Eagle on the Coin* I wrote of the ill-fated attempt of some alienated liberals,
including a compassionate homosexual, to elect a Negro to the schoolboard in a small
mid-western city. In *Doctor Cobb's Game* I used the silhouette of a major British political
scandal as the area within which I composed an elaborate pattern of occult-sexual-political
forces weaving and unweaving. Between these two novels, almost twenty years apart, I have
played with a variety of forms and subject matter, but the focus of concern has probably
been the same, under the surface of appearances. In *Clem Anderson* I took the silhouette of
Dylan Thomas's life and within that composed the story of an American poet's self-destructive triumph. It probably is and always will be my most embattled work, simply because in its
considerable extent it replaces most of the comfortable or profitable clichés about an artist's
life with tougher and more painful diagrams.

But then perhaps my whole productive life has been a swimming against the tide. A
Midwesterner by origin, and no doubt by temperament and experience, I worked through
decades when first the Southern and then the urban-Jewish novel held an almost monopolistic
grip on the tastes and prejudices of American readers. In my extensive reviewing and lecturing I have tried more to examine the clichés, slogans, and rallying cries of the time than to
oppose or espouse them—thus leaving myself without any visible partisan support from any
quarter. To radicals I have appeared a conservative, to conservatives a radical—and to both
a mystification or, I suppose, I would not have been tolerated as long as I have been. As I
grow older I love the commonplace of traditional thought and expression with a growing
fervor, especially as their rarity increases amid the indoctrinating forces that spoil our good
lives.

*          *          *

From the first novel, *The Eagle on the Coin,* and the early stories, R. V. Cassill's art shows
a steady development from the autobiographical and the imitative to the fully dramatic
capabilities of the mature novelist and short story writer. The range of his talent is wide:
from near-pastoral impressions of Mid-Western America, to urban life in Chicago and
New York, to his most technically accomplished work, *Doctor Cobb's Game,* based on the
Profumo scandals in London.

Cassill's most complex work relies on four broad kinds of material: stories and novels about the Mid-West, most notably Iowa as in *Pretty Leslie*; stories and novels concerning academic life, as in "Larchmoor Is Not the World" and *The President*; materials about art and the artist's life (*Clem Anderson*); and finally materials of a less regional nature which may be called the vision of modernity found in the short story "Love? Squalor?" and *Doctor Cobb*. A second, lesser known order of Cassill's work consists of a dozen novels, "paperback originals" so-called because of the contractual circumstances of their first publication. For the most part *The Wound of Love, Dormitory Women,* and others await sophisticated literary evaluation. These shorter, often more spontaneous novels also exploit the same kinds of material. It should be well understood that these categories are intended to be only suggestive; the most ambitious work, for example, displays all these materials.

Beyond the technical accomplishments of any professional novelist, Cassill's most noteworthy literary quality is the "visual" nature of his prose fiction. There is a steady exploitation of color, of the precise, telling, visual detail, a sensitivity to proportion, and to the architectonics of scene. In fact Cassill began his artistic career as a painter, a teacher of art; from time-to-time he still exhibits his work. His fiction shows some of the same qualities as the Impressionists, the Post-Impressionists, and the German Expressionalistic painters.

The literary influences are wide-ranging and interestingly absorbed. In general, these influences are evoked when necessary rather than being held steadily as "models" in any neo-classic sense. Specifically, Cassill values Flaubert, James, Joyce, and especially D. H. Lawrence. Of a different order of specific influence would be *Madam Bovary*, Gissing's *The New Grub Street*, and Benjamin Constant's *Adolphe* (1815). It is interesting that Cassill has written the best extant appreciation of *Adolphe*. Thus Cassill is a highly literary writer, with a broad, useful knowledge of American and European literatures; for many years he has been a teacher of contemporary literature and a writer-in-residence at universities, a professional reviewer, essayist, a discerning cultural commentator and critic.

The governing themes of Cassill's work are less easy to identify. A reoccuring situation is the nature and the resultant fate of a human pair, the destiny of a man or woman in the throes of new love, old love, marriage, or adultery. Closely bound to these concerns are the nature of love and responsibility; the implications of choice, loyalty and liberty. Often there are conflicts generated between rationality and a merely emotional yearning—real or imagined—genuine affection as against the implied necessity of sexual aggression or the ironies of "modern love". At times these relationships are between teacher and pupil, lovers, man and wife; between artist and patron, mistress, or the world "out there".

A fascination with these and other difficult themes places a heavy obligation on the novelist, especially in the matter of plot-structures and the handling of sex scenes. Throughout Cassill's work there is the insistence on the centrality of the sexual aspect of all human relationships. If in real life such concerns are seldom finally resolved, so is it in many novelistic structures which tend to rely on sexual involvements as a central motivation. Often, therefore, a story or novel will begin with a vivid, strong situation which in the end is obscured or vague rather than suggestive or resolved. The reliance on the sexual drive as a compelling motive becomes more insistent in the later work.

Although primarily a novelist, Cassill's most sustained work is often in the short fiction, of which he is a master. The best stories focus on domestic scenes, memories of youth, the pathos of age, the casual, lost relationship, conversations on art, ideas, literature, and the meaning of life itself.

Taken together, the stories, novels, and criticism show a strongly unified sensibility, a dedicated, energetic artist, a man in a modern world imaginatively and at times romantically comprehended, a man whose powerful gifts are his best protection against his own vision of America and of the Mid-West where modernity is rampant and the end is nowhere in sight.

—James B. Hall

**CAUTE, (John) David.** British. Born in Alexandria, Egypt, 16 December 1936. Educated at Wadham College, Oxford, M.A., D.Phil.; Harvard University, Cambridge, Massachusetts (Henry Fellow), 1960–61. Served in the British Army, 1955–56. Fellow, All Souls College, Oxford, 1959–65; Visiting Professor, New York University and Columbia University, New York, 1966–67; Reader in Social and Political Theory, Brunel University, Uxbridge, Middlesex, 1967–70. Recipient: London Authors' Club Award, 1960; Rhys Memorial Prize, 1960. Address: c/o Elaine Greene Ltd., 42 Great Russell Street, London W.C.1, England.

PUBLICATIONS

Novels

*At Fever Pitch.* London, Deutsch, 1959; New York, Pantheon Books, 1961.
*Comrade Jacob.* London, Deutsch, 1961; New York, Pantheon Books, 1962.
*The Decline of the West.* London, Deutsch, and New York, Macmillan, 1966.
*The Occupation.* London, Deutsch, 1971; New York, McGraw Hill, 1972. (With the play *The Demonstration* and the essay *The Illusion*, forms part of *The Confrontation: A Trilogy*.)

Plays

*Songs for an Autumn Rifle* (produced Edinburgh, 1961).
*The Demonstration* (produced Nottingham, 1969; London, 1970). London, Deutsch, 1970. (With the novel *The Occupation* and the essay *The Illusion*, forms part of *The Confrontation: A Trilogy*.)

Other

*Communism and the French Intellectuals, 1914–1960.* London, Deutsch, and New York, Macmillan, 1964.
*The Left in Europe since 1789.* London, Weidenfeld and Nicolson, and New York, McGraw Hill, 1966.
*Fanon.* London, Fontana, and New York, Viking Press, 1970.
*The Illusion.* London, Deutsch, 1971; New York, Harper, 1972. (With the novel *The Occupation* and the play *The Demonstration*, forms part of *The Confrontation: A Trilogy*.)
*The Fellow-Travellers.* London, Weidenfeld and Nicolson, and New York, Macmillan, 1972.

Editor, *Essential Writings*, by Karl Marx. London, MacGibbon and Kee, 1967; New York, Macmillan, 1968.

Critical Studies: reviews in *The Times* (London), 22 July 1971; *The Listener* (London), 22 July 1971; *The Guardian* (London), 22 July 1971; *New Statesman* (London), 23 July 1971; and *The Sunday Telegraph* (London), 25 July 1971.

David Caute comments:

A rather unpleasant American historian once said to me, in the heat of his liquor: "Having just read your last novel, or part of it, I'd advise you to give up writing fiction—if you weren't such a lousy historian." Four years later I'm still searching for a good reply. But the fact is that I enjoy working in both fields, mutually antagonistic as they sometimes seem to be, and the theatre pulls me too, so I'm doomed to remain jack of all trades. The trouble is, a historian absorbs a certain kind of language—analytical, conceptual, categorising, dry—which doesn't help him as a novelist to remember or evoke how individual people look, sound, behave and smell. On the other hand my local historian has furnished my local novelist with some good material, often political, which I don't regret. Perhaps the tension between man's private and public existences is the central "problematic" of my thinking and writing. Nowadays I'm more preoccupied by questions of literary form than I used to be. Another thing: it scarcely used to occur to me that I owed my readers an occasional smile or even laugh, but I'm learning now to open the cage on humour a bit, to let it out, to be unashamedly frivolous if I feel like it. So far the response has been encouraging. The novelist, who is really a "blind performer", one who never sees his audience, needs every bit of encouragement he can get if he is to continue to labour in solitude to reach a couple of thousand readers.

*     *     *

David Caute is a rare breed among contemporary English novelists. Indeed, he is probably unique. For his novels are written out of a deep ideological commitment to Marxism, and they are thus attempts to explore and account for the nature of Imperialism, bourgeois capitalism and Western liberal democracy. To say as much is to indicate how extraordinarily at odds they are with the customary modest scope and intention of the contemporary English novel.

It is a generally accepted, if unwritten, rule for the novelist that he can only write well about what he knows from first-hand experience. The raw material out of which he fashions his art must, that is, be familiar enough to him for him to be able to handle it with confidence and authority. In other words, one wants the "ring of truth" in all that is depicted, one expects authenticity of detail and verification of fact that will allow us as readers to have confidence that the author quite simply knows what he is talking about.

In so far as this is a demand we make of the novel, it is clear that David Caute frequently falls short of meeting it. To look at his first novel is to see this. The handling of the African colonial life in *At Fever Pitch* quite lacks the kind of grasp of the sweaty actual that we find in the work of a master journalist-novelist like Graham Greene, for example, or that is so vividly present in Anthony Burgess's early and brilliant *Malayan Trilogy*. Caute very obviously cannot match their keenness of eye and ear for local colour, for realistic exactness. Yet he would no doubt reply that such veracity is unimportant for him and is finally unimportant to the novel as such. For what essentially matters is not how minutely you can detail all aspects of a way of life, but what deep and penetrative understanding you have of it; and for Caute such understanding can come only through Marxism. His novels are therefore living histories, analyses of societies which try to define their true nature through the historical and economic arguments of Karl Marx.

So far, so good. But then it may be argued, and indeed frequently *is*, that Caute's fictional writing is so much arid didacticism, a dressing-up of Marxist orthodoxy which succeeds only in suffocating the poor life of the novel itself. Caute, the argument runs, attempts to put a covering of skin over the bones of his theory, with the result that his novels can very clearly be seen to be skeletons, lifeless, inert, crucially artificial. None of his novels has suffered more from this criticism than the second one, *The Decline of the West*, and of none, perhaps, is the criticism more just. For as the un-ironic use of Oswald Spengler in the title implies, Caute is out to ram a thesis about capitalism in decay down our throats, and the consequence is that we turn away in irritation.

Yet to say this is not to question the validity of the novel of ideas. Sartre is an obvious and distinguished example of a novelist whose ideology is present in his fiction without constricting it, and what is true of him is true of others. But the difference between Sartre and Caute, at least in his early work, is that Sartre understands that to write a novel of ideas does not require the novelist to be impatient of anything *but* ideas. "No ideas but in things" the great American poet, William Carlos Williams said, and there is heartening evidence that David Caute is beginning to realise as much. Certainly his most recent novel suggests that he has become aware of the problem that George Eliot formulated over a hundred years ago, when she remarked that her prime difficulty was "to make certain ideas incarnate, as if they had revealed themselves to me first in the flesh." On the evidence of David Caute's new work, he, too, has seen the need to provide an ampler covering for the bones of his theory.

—John Lucas

---

**CHAPLIN, Sid(ney).** British. Born in Shildon, Durham, 20 September 1916. Attended the Workers' Educational Association, University of Durham, 1932–46; Fircroft College for Working Men, Birmingham, 1939. Married Irene Rutherford in 1941; has three children. Miner, 1931–50; Branch Secretary, Miners Federation of Great Britain, 1943–45. Writer for various coal industry publications and Public Relations Officer for the Northern Division of the National Coal Board, 1950–71. Member, Northern Region Advisory Council, BBC, 1963–68. Recipient: Atlantic Award, 1946. Address: c/o David Higham, 76 Dean Street, London W.1, England.

PUBLICATIONS

Novels

> *My Fate Cries Out.* London, Phoenix House, and New York, Dent, 1949.
> *The Thin Seam.* London, Phoenix House, and New York, Dent, 1950.
> *The Big Room.* London, Eyre and Spottiswoode, 1960.
> *The Day of the Sardine.* London, Eyre and Spottiswoode, 1961.
> *The Watchers and the Watched.* London, Eyre and Spottiswoode, 1962.
> *Sam in the Morning.* London, Eyre and Spottiswoode, 1965.
> *The Mines of Alabaster.* London, Eyre and Spottiswoode, 1971.

Short Stories

> *The Leaping Lad and Other Stories.* London, Phoenix House, and New York, Dent, 1946; revised edition, London, Longman, 1970.
> *The Thin Seam and Other Stories.* Oxford, Pergamon Press, 1968.

Play

> *Close the Coalhouse Door*, with Alan Plater and Alex Glasgow (produced Newcastle upon Tyne and London, 1968). London, Methuen, 1969.

Other

*The Smell of Sunday Dinner*.   Newcastle upon Tyne, Frank Graham, 1971.

Editor, with A. Wise, *Us Northerners*.   London, Harrap, 1970.

Bibliography: "Sid Chaplin" by George Stephenson, in *Newcastle Life*, January 1969.

Critical Study: "Prodigal Sons" by Michael Standen, in *Stand* (Newcastle upon Tyne), vol. 10, no. 3, 1969.


Sid Chaplin comments:

Beginning with the early mining stories my work has been concerned with man's survival in modern industrial society; a theme first picked up in rural mining life continued in novels of the city. Survival is equated with conscience.

*               *               *

Sid Chaplin's first book of short stories *The Leaping Lad* established him almost immediately as a regional writer of talent and potential. His intimate understanding of the Durham mining community comes out very well in these stories. This book was followed by *My Fate Cries Out*, a historical novel about the Weardale district of the 1740s, that perhaps owes something in inspiration to Stevenson and Meade Faulkener. It certainly conveys a very special feeling the author has for the moorscape of this part of Durham.

It was with his third book, however, *The Thin Seam*, that Sid Chaplin came to maturity as a writer. It is a novella with a coalmine as setting. The chief character, Chris, is a young man raised in a mining village who has aspired to a wider horizon through a working-men's college before deciding to return to the life in the pit he thought he had left for good. He is one of a team, and the story takes us with Matty, Art, Daniel, and Andrews, through the labour and travail of one shift underground. A short space of time, a single setting, a handful of characters, suffice to reveal the inner nature of the hero to the reader. The exploratory nature that is given us of Chris is a masterly one. Moorscape also plays a part in *The Big Room*, a family drama, again revolving round a mine, but with the characterisation deepened and the conflict heightened. The economy of the setting are such that it is not surprising that it was recently (1970) dramatised for the stage.

His work is a gradual progress, a continuing broadening of the regional base, so that each novel develops out of its predecessor. Newcastle and "the big city" were themes that he explored next in *The Watchers and the Watched* and *The Day of the Sardine*. His own experience as always gives the satisfactory solidity of factory and excavation-site locales in these two lively and exciting books. In *Sam in the Morning* he deals with a different aspect of cityscape: the fascination with the monolithic building that houses the corporate enterprise, and the managerial society, cut off from both the workers and the boardroom in their own quest for power. In this novel his North-east hero is placed in a metropolitan setting. He keeps in touch with his regional roots while expanding his scale. It is as though by this stage he can leave the immediate Tyneside scene confident that it is always there to come back to if he needs it.

His latest novel, *The Mines of Alabaster*, continues this expansion. He now moves with ease whatever the setting, be it London, East Anglia, or Italy. His main character, Harry John Brown, has problems which are not those of an expatriate Geordie, but the more universal concerns of any human being in trouble.

Critics are sometimes inclined to put regional writers into a second division. Sid Chaplin confounds the critics by his continuing and changing variety. The regional theme is still there but it is one on which he can now play infinite variations.

—George Stephenson

---

**CHARLES, Gerda.** British. Born in Liverpool. Educated in Liverpool schools. Recipient: Black Memorial Prize, 1964; Arts Council grant, 1970; Whitbread Literary Award, 1971. Address: 22 Cunningham Court, London W.9, England.

PUBLICATIONS

Novels

*The True Voice*. London, Eyre and Spottiswoode, 1959.
*The Crossing Point*. London, Eyre and Spottiswoode, 1960; New York, Knopf, 1961.
*A Slanting Light*. London, Eyre and Spottiswoode, and New York, Knopf, 1963.
*A Logical Girl*. London, Eyre and Spottiswoode, and New York, Knopf, 1967.
*The Destiny Waltz*. London, Eyre and Spottiswoode, 1971.

Uncollected Short Stories

"The Staircase", in *Vanity Fair* (London), April 1956.
"Rosh Hashanah in Five Weeks", in *Pick of Today's Short Stories 11*. London, Putnam, 1960.
"The Czech-Slovakian Chandelier", in *Modern Jewish Stories*. London, Faber, 1963; New York, Prentice Hall, 1964.
"A Mixed Marriage", in *Quest* (London), 1965.
"The Difference", in *Jewish Chronicle* (London), 24 November 1967.

Other

Editor, *Modern Jewish Stories*. London, Faber, 1963; New York, Prentice Hall, 1964.

Critical Studies: "The World of Gerda Charles", in *Jewish Quarterly* (London), Summer 1967; "Facing the Music" by C. P. Snow, in *Financial Times* (London), 15 April 1971; "Revenge Is Sour," in *The Guardian* (London), 27 May 1971; "Gerda Charles: A Visionary Realist", in *Jewish Quarterly* (London), Summer 1971.

Gerda Charles comments:

Though known primarily as an Anglo-Jewish writer, my five novels all deal in general with what I have described (in my third book, *A Slanting Light*) as "the region of everyday hurt". My books are not concerned with extremes—which I believe to be largely unrelated to the real problems of living. They are not concerned with madness but rather with the job of maintaining sanity, dignity and order. They advocate the unfashionable virtues of delicacy, tact and generosity of heart within the context of day-to-day life.

*         *         *

*The True Voice* is an excellent first novel in which Gerda Charles develops a principal theme—the alienation felt by a person of talent when he is unable to articulate his aspirations and to communicate his inner intensities to others. After two disillusioning experiences with men, Lindy Frome finds that her only valid resource is the self, as she attains awareness of "the compassionate irony with which it was necessary to confront life; how flexibility, awareness and forgiveness were all."

With *The Crossing Point* Miss Charles wrote her best book. She asserts through Rabbi Leo Norberg that Judaism is the most viable of religions for human beings since it is at "the crossing point" where opposites such as asceticism and sensuousness, mysticism and secularism, idealism and practicality converge. Boruch Gabriel is imposing as a presence but not as an influence since his conception of religion is literal and monolithic. His daughter, Sara, illustrates the true strength of Judaism as it gives her courage to face her father and her own life of impaired fulfilment. Rabbi Norberg is the novel's intellectual center. Humane and imaginative, he sometimes lacks the courage to act upon his insights. Knowing the best in Sara Gabriel, he chooses, out of a certain perversity and false pride, the second best, a calculating and fourth-rate woman, for wife. The characters, big with life, give the book its stature. They are human beings who also happen to be Jews, as they falter or triumph in achieving their destinies.

*A Slanting Light* is a notable if less arresting book. A psychically immolated American playwright, Bernard Zold, is protagonist. His chief antagonist is a power-hungry mother; his wife is superficial and his child unloving. He is a sufferer rather than a doer, a man of sympathetic imagination rather than of active confidence. For the narrator he is emblematic of "the whole role of the Jew in the historic life of the world's soul" and exemplifies "the suffering, the humane, the pacific, the enduring, the compassionate strands in the composite human nature of society." Zold hardly achieves this archetypal dimension, and Miss Charles' analysis of Zold as artist lacks immediacy and exactitude. But as a novel exploring entangled relationships it has distinction and force.

In *A Logical Girl*, Miss Charles' best book since *The Crossing Point*, Rose Morgan's views of what ought to be are in abrupt contrast with the way things are. In World War II in a seaside town, she develops from naive adolescence to maturity while the town is "invaded" by European and American troops. Her sensitivity allows her to see how selfish, impersonal, and degrading her associates and family often are, while they impress the world as models of virtue and propriety. The elements of deceit, inconsiderateness, and cruelty which all too often determine human relationships, are the reflection in little of the injustices and sadism in the Nazi regime on the continent. Rose learns that human beings do not behave consistently and logically, that impulse is often triumphant over honesty. Miss Charles finely controls her irony as she demonstrates in Rose how the individual who sees the truth is disregarded by most other people in their reverence for the flashy, the meretricious, and the materialistic.

*The Destiny Waltz* is Miss Charles' longest and least satisfactory novel. It concerns the surviving influence of Paul Salomon, a great poet from the 1920's who had been passed over in his lifetime. At the instigation of a television company, Jimmy Marchant, a retired band leader and Paul's closest friend, meets Michele Sandburg, a college teacher in her forties who has written the best life of the poet. They are to help make a documentary film about Salomon's life. Much pathos and intense feeling develop when Jimmy realizes that in Michele he may yet find the happiness that eluded him in his marriage and sexual affairs. Yet Jimmy lacks interest and presence, and his moralizing, while genuine, is frequently labored. Again, Miss Charles fails to make her artist believable; we have, in short, little idea of what Salomon's poetry was like. She does depict with assuredness the studio milieu, wherein prudential motives and the requirements of art are in locked conflict. In sum, Miss Charles has over-extended her materials for the value which accrues to them.

Miss Charles has analyzed with sympathy and comprehension the spiritual misfit in modern life. Her insight into human nature is penetrating; and her eccentrics, as well as her fully developed figures, are authentic. She establishes the outlines of her characters economically by concentrated analysis and persuasive dialogue. As a stylist her prose is always perspicuous and perfectly modulated to convey a sense of Jamesian complexities in character and situation. Her main preoccupation is with the painful incursion of moral knowledge. The process whereby her protagonists determine "how to be" is fraught with anguish, on occasion with muted triumph, always with the ring of truth.

—Frederick P. W. McDowell

---

**CHARYN, Jerome.** American. Born in New York City, 13 May 1937. Educated at Columbia University, New York, B.A. (cum laude) 1959. Former Recreation Leader, New York City Department of Parks. English Teacher, High School of Music and Art and School of Performing Arts, New York, 1962–64; Assistant Professor of English, Stanford University, California, 1965–68. Since 1968, Assistant Professor of English, Herbert Lehman College of the City University of New York. Since 1970, Founding Editor, *The Dutton Review*, New York. Address: c/o Candida Donadio, 111 West 57th Street, New York, New York 10019, U.S.A.

PUBLICATIONS

Novels

*Once Upon a Droshky*. New York, McGraw Hill, 1964.
*On the Darkening Green*. New York, McGraw Hill, 1965.
*Going to Jerusalem*. New York, Viking Press, 1967; London, Cape, 1968.
*American Scrapbook*. New York, Viking Press, 1969.
*Eisenhower, My Eisenhower*. New York, Holt Rinehart, 1971.
*The Tar Baby*. New York, Holt Rinehart, 1972.

Short Stories

*The Man Who Grew Younger*. New York, Harper, 1967.

Uncollected Short Stories

"Faigele the Idiotke", in *Commentary* (New York), March 1963.
"On Second Avenue", in *Commentary* (New York), July 1963.

"God Bless Captain Freddy and Private Ming", in *Mademoiselle* (New York), April 1964.
"Sing, Shaindele, Sing", in *Transatlantic Review* (London and New York), Autumn 1966.
"The Changeling", in *Transatlantic Review* (London and New York), Spring 1968.


Play

Screenplay: *Crayola Detective*, 1971.


Other

Editor, *The Single Voice: An Anthology of Contemporary Fiction.*  New York, Collier, 1969.
Editor, *The Troubled Vision.*  New York, Collier, 1970.


Critical Studies: reviews in *Life* (New York), 6 June 1969; *Newsweek* (New York), 9 June 1969; *Time* (New York), 4 July 1969; *Christian Science Monitor* (Boston), 24 July 1969; *Saturday Review* (New York), 23 August 1969; *Midstream* (New York), October 1969; and *New York Times Book Review*, 28 March 1971; introductions by the author to *The Single Voice*, 1969, and *The Troubled Vision*, 1970.

*       *       *

The scope of Jerome Charyn's work may be limited, but within his special field—the depiction of ghetto life in modern urban society—few writers can match the synthesis of realism and lyricism he achieves in his best works. His characters are civilization's cast-offs, emotional, physical, or intellectual misfits, in whose attempts to understand themselves and their place in the world Charyn finds both comedy and poetry.

Charyn's earliest novels, *Once Upon a Droshky* and *On the Darkening Green*, are set in New York City in the thirties and forties. Each has a first person narrator whose simple, coarse, and yet melodic language accounts for much of the merit in the stories they tell. *Once Upon a Droshky* concerns a group of Yiddish tenants fighting modern society in the form of an eviction notice. Their struggle is doomed from the start, but Charyn avoids depicting their ultimate defeat; instead he ends the story just before their final confrontation with the authorities. The atmosphere is not very different in *On the Darkening Green*. Here the tenements are in the Bronx and the victims not the very old but the very young. The narrator is supposedly Italian, but this book too is filled with stereotypical Jewish types, and the setting eventually shifts to the Blattenburg Home for Wayward Jewish Boys. Although the narrator accepts a position as counsellor at the Home, his natural instincts align him with the boys, and he even joins them in a futile rebellion against their oppressors.

Almost all the stories in *The Man Who Grew Younger* are also narrated by children or teenagers, and it is in this collection that Charyn falls into the trap he narrowly skirted in the earlier novel. Here the romanticizing of the juvenile delinquent, especially in the novella "1944," becomes clearly excessive. Charyn's implicit contention that power over others is corrupting, that the only ones free of corruption are the powerless, leads to the simplistic conclusion that human decency is invariably and exclusively the single possession of the dispossessed.

Charyn's need to break away from his preoccupation with the big city is reflected in *Going to Jerusalem* and *American Scrapbook*. The first begins at the South Brooklyn Military Academy, but the chief characters soon leave Brooklyn for a series of chess exhibitions across the American countryside. The novel is told through the eyes and the mind of an epileptic, and the reader has difficulty deciding whether the bizarre series of misadventures he endures are real or imaginary. The picaresque plot ends, appropriately, on Crazy Day in Yell County, Arkansas, as the narrator's increasing inability to cope with it all leads to an inevitable breakdown. This discomforting picture of America is continued in *American Scrapbook*, a novel about life in the camps set up for Japanese Americans during World War II. The divided loyalties of the inmates, their cultural dislocation, are portrayed through the eyes of various members of the Tanaka family, some of whom work with the American authorities, some of whom join an organization of Japanese terrorists. The most sympathetic characters, however, are those who are repulsed by both forms of oppression but who cannot find an alternative way of life in the camp.

The allegorical mood of *American Scrapbook* is carried over into Charyn's recent novel, *Eisenhower, My Eisenhower*, a surrealistic story about the conflict between the powerful "Anglos" and a mysterious race of beings called "Gypsies" in a city named Bedlam. The narrator is a Gypsie who has succeeded in the Anglo world but who decides at the end to rejoin his own people and fight for their liberation. Thus in *Eisenhower, My Eisenhower* Charyn returns to the urban scene of his earlier works, but with a form and a political interest more representative of the time in which he writes.

—Robert E. Lynch

---

**CHEEVER, John.** American. Born in Quincy, Massachusetts, 27 May 1912. Educated at Thayer Academy. Served in the United States Army in World War II. Married Mary M. Winternitz in 1941; has three children. Taught at Barnard College, New York, 1956–57. Recipient: Guggenheim Fellowship, 1951; Benjamin Franklin Award, 1955; O. Henry Award, 1956, 1964; National Institute of Arts and Letters grant, 1956; National Book Award, 1958; Howells Medal, 1965. Member, National Institute of Arts and Letters. Address: Cedar Lane, Ossining, New York 10562, U.S.A.

PUBLICATIONS

Novels

*The Wapshot Chronicle*. New York, Harper, 1957.
*The Wapshot Scandal*. New York, Harper, and London, Gollancz, 1964.
*Bullet Park*. New York, Knopf, and London, Cape, 1969.

Short Stories

*The Way Some People Live: A Book of Stories*. New York, Random House, 1943.
*The Enormous Radio and Other Stories*. New York, Funk and Wagnalls, and London, Gollancz, 1953.
*Stories*, with others. New York, Farrar Straus, 1956.
*The Housebreaker of Shady Hill and Other Stories*. New York, Harper, 1958; London, Gollancz, 1959.

*Some People, Places and Things That Will Not Appear in My Next Novel.* New York,
    Harper, and London, Gollancz, 1961.
*The Brigadier and the Golf Widow.* New York, Harper, 1964; London, Gollancz,
    1965.

*    *    *

John Cheever has been a consistently successful writer of short stories whose three ventures
into the more ambitious form of the novel have been, with the exception of *The Wapshot
Chronicle*, a failure. He is a shrewd observer of the manners and morals of American middle
class life, especially in the suburbs. He is also, rather unexpectedly, a keen and appreciative
observer of light and shadow, sea foam and cloud; he has a sensuous rapport with the world
of nature. His work reveals a sensibility that has retained a certain naive faith and romantic
glow despite a recognition of man's capacity for error and sin and despite a conviction that
things are growing steadily worse in contemporary society.

The sprightly social comedy that Cheever writes cannot hide, and is not intended to hide,
the fact that Cheever is delivering judgments on his characters as they blunder or claw their
way through life. And he judges them, in their modern folly, by conventional and traditional
standards. If he is amused by the carnal anarchy that he records as the characteristic sexual
pattern of suburban life, he is likely to punish those who engage in it. He records the disintegration of the middle class in America with the accuracy and detachment of the sociologist
but he is in reality concerned and disapproving. When he shows that people cannot maintain
their marriages intact, the thrust of the story clearly indicates Cheever's sense of their inadequacy. When, in a story like "The Cure," a divorced couple comes together again in a
moving moment, Cheever is triumphant in the affirmation of domestic stability and the sanctity of marriage. Like most other social observers, Cheever knows that Americans cannot
cope with love, which he unabashedly if not profoundly celebrates. He does not abjure the
discussion of sex, but he treats the matter with dignity and a rather old-fashioned reticence.
He portrays his sophisticated characters as failures in parenthood who either abuse or neglect
their children; the people in "The Sutton Place Story" see their child only at the cocktail
hour and can know neither the joys nor the sorrows of raising her. Cheever's protagonists,
his modern anti-heroes, are frequently immoral, lecherous, frightened, fraudulent, empty,
and failing human beings.

It is the note of failure that says so much for Cheever's penetration to the realities of
American society. He has seen beneath the glossy surface—he himself makes the distinction
between the appearance and the reality of things—of prosperous America where the imminent possibility of failure lies like lead in the heart of the suburbanite as he lolls at poolside or
plans his bomb shelter. Cheever's people know that they must scramble for success and that
some of them will not reach it. They know they must cling to respectability, and some of them
will fail. Cheever recognizes the dynamic quality of American society, but he takes a dim
view of it because change can mean lack of community or downward mobility. In Cheever's
stories change can be for the worse, and frequently is, because no one has a fixed place or a
fixed identity. The class lines are always shifting. The irony of Cheever's fiction is that
behind the bright surfaces presented by the station wagon and the Georgian home of the
suburbs are the tensions of lives in disorder and the fears of losing one's place.

In a few stories dealing with the international theme, Cheever has been critical of expatriates, whose efforts to adopt another culture constitute another kind of failure. He rejects the international experience out of a view, again old-fashioned and unashamed, that
his own country, flawed as it is, is superior to others. *The Wapshot Chronicle* reveals the nature
of Cheever's engagement with America, which is a nostalgic and romantic attachment to its
past. Successfully skirting sentimentality, Cheever re-creates a dying fishing village in Massachusetts. The quality of life in the past here stands as a rebuke to the shabby present. The
hero of the novel possesses virtues and vitality derived from the past; they are a living criticism
of life in the present. Leander Wapshot loves his sons, he loves the rituals of life, especially

those pertaining to manliness, he loves his native place, and he recognizes a compelling urge to come into a right relation with the world of nature. He rejects modern skepticism and despair. The dignity, compassion, courage, and trust that he brings to the world make him an anachronism. The contrast between the present and Leander and the past to which he belongs is summed up in the loss of his job. He is the skipper of a ferry boat which he loses to his wife, who converts it into New England's only floating gift shoppe. Leander commits suicide by swimming off into the sea.

*The Wapshot Scandal*, which deals with the lives of Leander's sons, is a thesis-ridden novel in which Cheever mounts a predictable attack upon contemporary American life. He laments the failure of community which results in impersonal living arrangements marked by heartlessness and loneliness. He protests against science and technology with the usual humanistic complaint that they can create the weapons to destroy our cities but they cannot tell us anything about lust or pain. He protests against cold plastic and glass airports and supermarkets, against the degradation of language in the television era, against all the forces of modern culture that make us less than human.

*Bullet Park*, which considers familiar Cheever subjects like the suburbs and failure, is so feeble a novel that the less said about it the better. Cheever does not have the intellectual powers and the intensity of imagination to sustain a long fiction. But he does have the courage to assert the validity of the old virtues and the rhetoric to move us to admiration for them. In our dreary time he speaks unblushingly of loving gentle women, of stout-hearted friends, of admiring the world, of the bread and wine of life. He almost persuades us that these goods are still available.

—Chester E. Eisinger

---

**CHRISTIE, Agatha (Mary Clarissa).** British. Born in Torquay, Devon, 15 September 1890. Married Colonel A. Christie in 1914 (divorced, 1928); Sir Max Mallowan, the archaeologist, in 1932; has one child. Served as a volunteer nurse in the First and Second World Wars. Has worked as an assistant to her husband on excavations in Iraq and Syria and on excavations of Assyrian ruins. Recipient: New York Drama Critics Circle Award, 1955. D.Litt., University of Exeter, 1961. Fellow, Royal Society of Literature, 1950. C.B.E. (Commander, Order of the British Empire), 1956; D.B.E. (Dame Commander, Order of the British Empire), 1971. Address: Winterbrook House, Wallingford, Berkshire, England.

PUBLICATIONS

Novels

*The Mysterious Affair at Styles: A Detective Story*. London, Lane, and New York, Dodd Mead, 1920.
*The Secret Adversary*. London, Lane, and New York, Dodd Mead, 1922.
*The Murder on the Links*. London, Lane, and New York, Dodd Mead, 1923.
*The Man in the Brown Suit*. London, Lane, and New York, Dodd Mead, 1924.
*The Secret of Chimneys*. London, Lane, and New York, Dodd Mead, 1925.
*The Murder of Roger Ackroyd*. London, Collins, and New York, Dodd Mead, 1926.
*The Big Four*. London, Collins, and New York, Dodd Mead, 1927.

*The Mystery of the Blue Train.*   London, Collins, and New York, Dodd Mead, 1928.

*The Seven Dials Mystery.*   London, Collins, and New York, Dodd Mead, 1929.

*The Murder at the Vicarage.*   London, Collins, and New York, Dodd Mead, 1930.

*Giants' Bread* (as Mary Westmacott).   London, Collins, and New York, Doubleday, 1930.

*The Sittaford Mystery.*   London, Collins, 1931; as *The Murder at Hazelmoor*, New York, Dodd Mead, 1931.

*Peril at End House.*   London, Collins, and New York, Dodd Mead, 1932.

*Lord Edgware Dies.*   London, Collins, 1933; as *Thirteen at Dinner*, New York, Dodd Mead, 1933.

*Why Didn't They Ask Evans?*   London, Collins, 1934; as *Boomerang Clue*, New York, Dodd Mead, 1935.

*Murder on the Orient Express.*   London, Collins, 1934; as *Murder on the Calais Coach*, New York, Dodd Mead, 1934.

*Murder in Three Acts.*   New York, Dodd Mead, 1934; as *Three Act Tragedy*, London, Collins, 1935.

*Unfinished Portrait* (as Mary Westmacott).   London, Collins, and New York, Doubleday, 1934.

*Death in the Clouds.*   London, Collins, 1935; as *Death in the Air*, New York, Dodd Mead, 1935.

*The A.B.C. Murders: A New Poirot Mystery.*   London, Collins, and New York, Dodd Mead, 1936.

*Cards on the Table.*   London, Collins, and New York, Dodd Mead, 1936.

*Murder in Mesopotamia.*   London, Collins, and New York, Dodd Mead, 1936.

*Death on the Nile.*   London, Collins, 1937; New York, Dodd Mead, 1938.

*Dumb Witness.*   London, Collins, 1937; as *Poirot Loses a Client*, New York, Dodd Mead, 1937.

*Appointment with Death: A Poirot Mystery.*   London, Collins, and New York, Dodd Mead, 1938.

*Hercule Poirot's Christmas.*   London, Collins, 1939; as *Murder for Christmas: A Poirot Story*, New York, Dodd Mead, 1939.

*Murder Is Easy.*   London, Collins, 1939; as *Easy to Kill*, New York, Dodd Mead, 1939.

*Ten Little Niggers.*   London, Collins, 1939; as *And Then There Were None*, New York, Dodd Mead, 1940.

*One, Two, Buckle My Shoe.*   London, Collins, 1940; as *The Patriotic Murders*, New York, Dodd Mead, 1941.

*Sad Cypress.*   London, Collins, and New York, Dodd Mead, 1940.

*Evil under the Sun.*   London, Collins, and New York, Dodd Mead, 1941.

*N or M? The New Mystery.*   London, Collins, and New York, Dodd Mead, 1941.

*The Body in the Library.*   London, Collins, and New York, Dodd Mead, 1942.

*The Moving Finger.*   New York, Dodd Mead, 1942; London, Collins, 1943.

*Five Little Pigs.*   London, Collins, 1942; as *Murder in Retrospect*, New York, Dodd Mead, 1942.

*Death Comes as the End.*   New York, Dodd Mead, 1942; London, Collins, 1945.

*Towards Zero.*   London, Collins, and New York, Dodd Mead, 1944.

*Absent in the Spring* (as Mary Westmacott).   London, Collins, and New York, Farrar and Rinehart, 1944.

*Sparkling Cyanide.*   London, Collins, 1945; as *Remembered Death*, New York, Dodd Mead, 1945.

*The Hollow: A Hercule Poirot Mystery.*   London, Collins, and New York, Dodd Mead, 1946.

*Taken at the Flood.*   London, Collins, 1948; as *There Is a Tide . . .*, New York, Dodd Mead, 1948.

*The Rose and the Yew Tree* (as Mary Westmacott).   London, Heinemann, and New York, Rinehart, 1948.

*Crooked House.*   London, Collins, and New York, Dodd Mead, 1949.

*A Murder Is Announced.*   London, Collins, and New York, Dodd Mead, 1950.

*They Came to Baghdad.*   London, Collins, and New York, Dodd Mead, 1951.

*They Do It with Mirrors.*   London, Collins, 1952; as *Murder with Mirrors*, New York, Dodd Mead, 1952.

*Mrs. McGinty's Dead.*   London, Collins, and New York, Dodd Mead, 1952.

*A Daughter's a Daughter* (as Mary Westmacott).   London, Heinemann, 1952.

*After the Funeral.*   London, Collins, 1953; as *Funerals Are Fatal*, New York, Dodd Mead, 1953.

*A Pocket Full of Rye.*   London, Collins, 1953; New York, Dodd Mead, 1954.

*Destination Unknown.*   London, Collins, 1954; as *So Many Steps to Death*, New York, Dodd Mead, 1955.

*Hickory, Dickory, Dock.*   London, Collins, 1955; as *Hickory, Dickory, Death*, New York, Dodd Mead, 1955.

*Dead Man's Folly.*   London, Collins, and New York, Dodd Mead, 1956.

*The Burden* (as Mary Westmacott).   London, Heinemann, 1956.

*4:50 from Paddington.*   London, Collins, 1957; as *What Mrs. McGillicuddy Saw!* New York, Dodd Mead, 1957.

*Ordeal by Innocence.*   London, Collins, and New York, Dodd Mead, 1958.

*Cat among the Pigeons.*   London, Collins, and New York, Dodd Mead, 1959.

*The Pale Horse.*   London, Collins, 1961; New York, Dodd Mead, 1962.

*The Mirror Crack'd from Side to Side.*   London, Collins, 1962; as *The Mirror Crack'd*, New York, Dodd Mead, 1963.

*The Clocks.*   London, Collins, 1963; New York, Dodd Mead, 1964.

*A Caribbean Mystery.*   London, Collins, 1964; New York, Dodd Mead, 1965.

*At Bertram's Hotel.*   London, Collins, and New York, Dodd Mead, 1965.

*Third Girl.*   London, Collins, 1966; New York, Dodd Mead, 1967.

*Endless Night.*   London, Collins, 1967; New York, Dodd Mead, 1968.

*By the Pricking of My Thumb.*   London, Collins, and New York, Dodd Mead, 1968.

*Passenger to Frankfurt.*   London, Collins, and New York, Dodd Mead, 1970.

*Nemesis.*   London, Collins, and New York, Dodd Mead, 1971.


Short Stories

*Poirot Investigates.*   London, Lane, 1924; New York, Dodd Mead, 1925.

*Partners in Crime.*   London, Collins, and New York, Dodd Mead, 1929.

*The Underdog*, with *Blackman's Wood*, by Phillips Oppenheim.   London, Reader's Library, 1929.

*The Mysterious Mr. Quin.*   London, Collins, and New York, Dodd Mead, 1930.

*The Thirteen Problems.*   London, Collins, 1932; as *The Tuesday Club Murders*, New York, Dodd Mead, 1933.

*The Hound of Death and Other Stories.*   London, Odhams Press, 1933.

*Parker Pyne Investigates.*   London, Collins, 1934; as *Mr. Parker Pyne, Detective*, New York, Dodd Mead, 1934.

*The Listerdale Mystery and Other Stories.*   London, Collins, 1934.

*Murder in the Mews and Other Stories.*   London, Collins, 1937; as *Dead Man's Mirror and Other Stories*, New York, Dodd Mead, 1937.

*The Regatta Mystery and Other Stories.*   New York, Dodd Mead, 1939.

*The Labours of Hercules: Short Stories.*   London, Collins, 1947; as *Labors of Hercules: New Adventures in Crime by Hercule Poirot*, New York, Dodd Mead, 1947.

*Witness for the Prosecution and Other Stories.*   New York, Dodd Mead, 1948.

*Three Blind Mice and Other Stories.*   New York, Dodd Mead, 1950.

*Under Dog and Other Stories.*   New York, Dodd Mead, 1951.

*The Adventures of the Christmas Pudding, and Selection of Entrées.* London, Collins, 1960.
*Double Sin and Other Stories.* New York, Dodd Mead, 1961.
*13 for Luck: A Selection of Mystery Stories for Young Readers.* New York, Dodd Mead, 1961; as *13 for Luck: A Selection of Mystery Stories*, London, Collins, 1966.
*Star over Bethlehem and Other Stories* (as A. C. Mallowan). London, Collins, and New York, Dodd Mead, 1965.
*Surprize! Surprize! A Collection of Mystery Stories with Unexpected Endings.* New York, Dodd Mead, 1965.
*13 Clues for Miss Marple: A Collection of Mystery Stories.* New York, Dodd Mead, 1965.
*The Golden Ball and Other Stories.* New York, Dodd Mead, 1971.

Plays

*Black Coffee* (produced London, 1931). London, Ashley, 1934.
*Love from a Stranger*, with Frank Vosper (produced London, 1936). London, French, 1936.
*Ten Little Niggers* (produced London, 1943). London, French, 1944; as *Ten Little Indians* (produced New York, 1944), New York, French, 1946.
*Appointment with Death* (produced London, 1945). London, French, 1945.
*Murder on the Nile* (produced London and New York, 1946). London, French, 1946.
*The Hollow* (produced London, 1951). London, French, 1952.
*The Mousetrap* (produced London, 1952; New York, 1960). London, French, 1956.
*Witness for the Prosecution* (produced London, 1953; New York, 1954). London and New York, French, 1956.
*The Spider's Web* (produced London, 1954). London, French, 1957.
*Towards Zero*, with Gerald Verner (produced London, 1956). London, French, 1958.
*Verdict* (produced London, 1958). London, French, 1958.
*The Unexpected Guest* (produced London, 1958). London, French, 1958.
*Go Back for Murder* (produced London, 1960). London, French, 1960.
*Rule of Three* (*Afternoon at the Seaside*, *The Patient*, and *The Rats*) (produced London, 1963). London, French, 1963.
*Fiddlers Five* (produced Cambridge, 1971).

Verse

*The Road of Dreams.* London, Bles, 1925.

Other

*Come Tell Me How You Live* (travel). London, Collins, and New York, Dodd Mead, 1946.

*         *         *

Agatha Christie is the most durable, as well as the most celebrated, English writer of the "classic" detective story, that is, the one involving a detective, a tightly-organised crime puzzle, clues indicating the murderer and a surprise solution. Her pre-eminence in the field is the result not only of her steady productivity at a steady level of quality, but also of the craftsmanship which underlies the construction of a splendidly articulated story and of the fertile imagination which has enabled her to create more ingenious plot devices than any other living crime novelist. Nobody in the history of the detective story has hit upon so many ways of concealing the identity of the criminal. *The Murder of Roger Ackroyd* is regarded widely as one of the ten best detective novels ever written; *Death on the Nile* and *Ten Little Niggers* are also candidates for this honour. Nor has Agatha Christie been less successful in baffling theatre audiences, as witness the success of *Witness for the Prosecution* and the record-breaking *The Mousetrap*.

Her two most frequently used detectives are the Belgian, Hercule Poirot and Miss Marple. Poirot, originally a rather over-characterised figure, with his patent-leather shoes, his fierce moustaches, his "little grey cells" and his meagre handful of French phrases, has mellowed over the years into a less flamboyantly-seen personality. Miss Marple, the village spinster, whose solution of mysteries rests upon her ear for gossip and her country-won knowledge of human foibles, has shown less mutation.

Miss Christie's style tends to be undistinguished, if efficient, and her characters tend to be slightly old-fashioned stereotypes. However, she has shown an increasing sureness in handling her genre. Many admirers regard her best period as that from 1925 to about 1940, despite excellent later work. More recently, she has sometimes repeated, in *Endless Night*, for instance, plot devices she has used before; her readers, too, have learned to anticipate her misdirections and to find clear clues in the character-revealing sections which open several of her novels. Yet she still has the capacity to bluff the most self-assured reader.

Apart from their high entertainment value, Miss Christie's novels also offer an interesting insight into the century's social changes. She has tried to mirror the transformation of English society in her lifetime, but at the same time, she is naturally conservative and clings to older values of life and conduct, as shown especially in her somewhat outdated village settings. Although critical of the upper classes of interwar Britain, she resists the blurring of social distinctions and the lessening respects for tradition. Threats to society, rationalised in terms of crime, are eliminated by the detective who, in catching the criminal, restores the old balance of life. Ambivalently, she clings to belief in the possibility of a stable, ordered world, yet she recognises inevitable change and the defects in the older class system. Her novels, in fact, reveal more about the attitudes of her class and shifting social concepts than many of those who read them for their ingenious patterns of plot realise.

—J. C. Reid

---

**CHURCH, Richard (Thomas).** British. Born in London, 26 March 1893. Educated at Dulwich Hamlet School, London, 1905–08. Married Caroline Parfett in 1915; Catherina Schimmer, 1930 (died, 1965); Dorothy Beale, 1967; has four children. Civil Servant, London, 1909–33; Editor, J. M. Dent, publishers, London, 1933–51. Co-Founder, *The Criterion*, London, 1921; regular contributor to *The Spectator* and *New Statesman*, London; for the past forty years contributor of a monthly essay to the "Home Forum Page" of the *Christian Science Monitor*, Boston. Director, English Festival of Spoken Poetry, until it merged with the Arts Council Poetry Panel. Recipient: Femina Vie Heureuse Prize, 1938; *Sunday Times* Gold Medal, 1955; Foyle Poetry Prize, 1957. President, P.E.N., 1958–59, Kent and Sussex Poetry Society, 1962, and the English Association, 1964–65. Fellow, 1950, and Vice-President, 1968, Royal Society of Literature. Fellow, Royal Society of Art, 1970. C.B.E. (Commander, Order of the British Empire), 1957. Address: The Priest's House, Sissinghurst Castle, Cranbrook, Kent, England. *Died 4 March 1972.*

PUBLICATIONS

Novels

*Oliver's Daughter: A Tale.*   London, Dent, 1930.
*High Summer.*   London, Dent, 1931; New York, Smith, 1932.
*The Prodigal Father.*   London, Dent, and New York, Day, 1933.
*The Apple of Concord.*   London, Dent, 1935.
*The Porch.*   London, Dent, 1937.
*The Stronghold.*   London, Dent, 1939.
*The Room Within.*   London, Dent, 1940.
*The Sampler.*   London, Dent, 1942.
*The Dangerous Years.*   London, Heinemann, 1956; New York, Dutton, 1958.
*The Crab-Apple Tree.*   London, Heinemann, 1959.
*Prince Albert.*   London, Heinemann, 1963.
*Little Miss Moffatt.*   London, Heinemann, 1969.

Play

*The Prodigal: A Play in Verse* (produced Canterbury, 1953).   London, Staples Press,
   1953.

Verse

*The Flood of Life and Other Poems.*   London, Fifield, 1917.
*Hurricane and Other Poems.*   London, Selwyn and Blount, 1919.
*Philip and Other Poems.*   Oxford, Blackwell, 1923.
*The Portrait of the Abbot: A Story in Verse.*   London, Benn, 1926; New York, Dial
   Press, n.d.
*The Dream and Other Poems.*   London, Benn, 1927.
*Mood Without Measure.*   London, Faber and Gwyer, 1927.
*Theme with Variations.*   London, Benn, 1928.
*The Glance Backward: New Poems.*   London, Dent, 1930.
*News from the Mountain.*   London, Dent, 1932.
*Twelve Noon.*   London, Dent, 1936.
*The Solitary Man and Other Poems.*   London, Dent, 1941.
*Twentieth Century Psalter.*   London, Dent, 1943.
*The Lamp.*   London, Dent, 1946.
*Collected Poems.*   London, Dent, 1948.
*Selected Lyrical Poems.*   London, Staples Press, 1951.
*The Inheritors: Poems, 1948–1955.*   London, Heinemann, 1957.
*(Poems).*   London, Hulton, 1959.
*North of Rome.*   London, Hutchinson, 1960.
*The Burning Bush: Poems, 1958–1966.*   London, Heinemann, 1967.
*25 Lyrical Poems.*   London, Heinemann, 1967.

Other

*Mary Shelley.*   London, Howe, 1928.
*Calling for a Spade* (essays).   London, Dent, 1939.
*Eight for Immortality* (essays).   London, Dent, 1941.
*Plato's Mistake* (essay).   London, Routledge, 1941.

*A Squirrel Named Rufus* (juvenile).   London, Dent, 1941; Philadelphia, Winston, 1946.
*British Authors: A Twentieth Century Gallery*.   London, Longman, 1943; revised edition, 1948.
*Green Tide*.   London, Country Life, 1945.
*Kent*.   London, Hale, 1948.
*The Cave* (juvenile).   London, Dent, 1950; as *Five Boys in a Cave*, New York, Day, 1951; revised edition, Dent, 1953.
*A Window on a Hill* (essays).   London, Hale, 1951.
*The Growth of the English Novel*.   London, Methuen, 1951; New York, Barnes and Noble, 1961.
*Dog Toby: A Frontier Tale* (juvenile).   London, Hutchinson, 1953; New York, Day, 1958.
*A Portrait of Canterbury*.   London, Hutchinson, 1953; revised edition, 1968.
*Over the Bridge: An Essay in Autobiography*.   London, Heinemann, 1955; as *Over the Bridge: An Autobiography*, New York, Dutton, 1956.
*The Royal Parks of London*.   London, Ministry of Works, 1956.
*Small Moments*.   London, Hutchinson, 1957; New York, Dutton, 1958.
*The Golden Sovereign: A Conclusion to "Over the Bridge"* (autobiography).   London, Heinemann, and New York, Dutton, 1957.
*Down River* (juvenile).   New York, Day, 1957; London, Heinemann, 1958.
*Country Window: A Round of Essays*.   London, Heinemann, 1958.
*The Bells of Rye* (juvenile).   London, Heinemann, 1960; New York, Day, 1961.
*Calm October: Essays*.   London, Heinemann, 1961.
*The Voyage Home* (autobiography).   London, Heinemann, 1964; New York, Day, 1966.
*A Stroll Before Dark: Essays*.   London, Heinemann, 1965.
*A Look at Tradition*.   London, Oxford University Press, 1965.
*London: Flower of Cities All*.   London, Heinemann, and New York, Day, 1966.
*Speaking Aloud*.   London, Heinemann, 1968.
*The White Doe* (juvenile).   London, Heinemann, 1968; New York, Day, 1969.
*A Harvest of Mushrooms*.   London, Heinemann, 1970.
*The Wonder of Words*.   London, Hutchinson, 1970.
*The French Lieutenant: A Ghost Story for Young Readers*.   London, Heinemann, 1971.
*London in Colour*.   London, Batsford, 1971.
*Kent's Contribution*.   Bath, Adams and Dart, 1972.

Editor, *Poems and Prose*, by Algernon C. Swinburne.   London, Dent, and New York, Dutton, 1940.
Editor, with M. M. Bozman, *Poems of Our Time, 1900–1942*.   London, Dent, 1945.
Editor, *John Keats: An Introduction and a Selection*.   London, Phoenix House, 1948.
Editor, *Poems*, by Percy Bysshe Shelley.   London, Cassell, 1949.
Editor, *Poems for Speaking*.   London, Dent, 1950.
Editor, *Out of the Dark: New Poems*, by Phoebe Hesketh.   London, Heinemann, 1954.
Editor, *The Spoken Word: A Selection from Twenty-Five Years of "The Listener"*.   London, Collins, 1955; revised edition, 1960.
Editor, *The Little Kingdom: A Kentish Collection*.   London, Hutchinson, 1964.
Editor, *Essays by Divers Hands*.   London, Oxford University Press, 1965.

Manuscript Collection: University of Texas, Austin.

Critical Studies: in two works by L. A. G. Strong: *Personal Remarks*, London, Peter Nevill, 1953, and *Green Memory*, London, Methuen, 1961.

Richard Church comments:

As a novelist, I have always worked on the belief that poetry and fiction are one art; the presentation of life by means of the image. The novel has taken the place of the long, architectured poem in the twentieth century. Thus the story, in a novel, should symbolise life in a significant way. I have never written a novel merely with a sensational purpose.

\*      \*      \*

If Richard Church's novels seem strange and archaic to us today, it is because he is one of the few novelists still writing who can convince us that people can be consciously motivated by moral absolutes, rather than by the changing pressures of immediate needs. It is not that either he or his characters are unaware of the movements of biological urges or the stirrings of the subconscious. They regard them as something that the forces of reason and godly living must constantly be armed against. This means that their defeat, and they are necessarily defeated, is a dramatic catastrophe tinged with that inevitable doom which shadows the work of Thomas Hardy.

The comparison with Hardy's work hold good in two other respects. Both writers are very English in their sense of place. The Kentish Weald of *The Crab-Apple Tree* (the story of a wanderer's return after seven years at sea) carries the same authenticity as the landscapes of Hardy's Wessex. And like Hardy, Richard Church is concerned with the impact of war on the fortunes of individuals. *The Stronghold* is set during the first world war. The rights and wrongs of the conflict and the course of its battles are of less direct concern than the disruption of patterns of society which the state of being at war brings about. The characters curse it for the misery and loss it brings, while at the same time half welcoming the chance it gives them to look for other solutions to their personal problems.

More dramatically, the world disaster supplies the irrational and uncontrolable power that can overturn a troubled individual's hard won *modus vivendi*. The bright, energetic, outgoing Phyllis Drayton, who for long managed to cover the wounds of a tragic childhood, is turned by disease and loss into a frenetic madwoman giving birth in a cowshed. One of the other characters remarks that Phyllis becomes a sort of incarnation from the middle ages. There is something medieval too about Malcolm Moffatt, the priest of the last novel *Little Miss Moffatt*. Driven by a desperate sense of harsh Calvinistic religion, this Anglican vicar cuts out all human warmth and tolerance from his life, and sets out with grim and inflexible determination to save the soul of his young niece. The tensions that he builds up in the course of this struggle can only be resolved by a physical disaster, though in this case they arise out of his own repressed nature and not out of an international conflagration.

What matters to Richard Church is that moment at which men and women break out of the patterns which they or their professions have imposed on them. He is always very much aware of the world of work, and takes into account how much an individual is moulded by the ethos and demands of his profession whether it be the church, the civil service or medicine. In this too he is perhaps typical of many writers of this time.

—Shirley Toulson

CICELLIS, Kay. Greek. Born in Marseilles, France, 24 September 1926. Educated at Pierce College, Athens. Married N. M. Paleologos in 1957; has two children. Occasional writer and translator for Greek radio and for the BBC; free-lance Translator. Recipient: Ford grant, 1970. Address: 6 Hatzikostas Street, Mavili Square, Athens 602, Greece.

PUBLICATIONS

Novels

*No Name in the Street*.   London, Harvill Press, and New York, Grove Press, 1952.
*Ten Seconds from Now*.   London, Harvill Press, and New York, Grove Press, 1957.

Short Stories

*The Easy Way*.   London, Harvill Press, and New York, Scribner, 1950.
*Death of a Town*.   London, Harvill Press, 1954.
*The Way to Colonos: A Greek Triptych*.   London, Secker and Warburg, and New York,
    Grove Press, 1960.

Uncollected Short Stories

"Funeral Games", in *Encounter* (London), March 1955.
"Orpheus in Hades", in *Atlantic* (Boston), June 1955.
"Arise and Eat", in *London Magazine*, June 1960.
"The Mark", in *Mundus Artium* (Athens, Ohio), Winter 1970.
"The Good Death", in *Quarterly Review of Literature* (Princeton, New Jersey), July
    1971.

Other

Translator, *Their Most Serene Majesties*, by Angel Vlachos.   London, Bodley Head,
    1963.

Critical Study: Introduction by Vita Sackville-West, to *The Easy Way*, 1950.

Kay Cicellis comments:

I find it difficult to give a general statement about my work. Each book I've written posed
an entirely new problem that had to be faced in its own particular way. Writing, I think, is a
"mode of cognition": one tries to find out about things by writing about them—*through* the
process of writing; the knowledge isn't there beforehand. One tries to work some kind of
pattern, of design, out of chaos. And so form often becomes content, subject-matter. One
begins from scratch with each new book. As I grow older, I tend to search for a way of
writing that will let situations produce events in the same inevitable way that clouds produce
rain—a kind of invisible writing. I haven't come anywhere near achieving this yet. I'm not
even sure the novel and the short story are the suitable vehicles for what I want to do. On the
whole I prefer the novella (the long short story) as a form.

I write more about situations than about "people" in the sense of "characters". I am attracted to the schematic aspect of situations, the hidden pattern in them, and the sudden
conflict that highlights the pattern.

For the last ten years, I have been undergoing a loss of faith in the written word, with the
result that I have produced very little, a few stories, two unfinished novels. I find writing a
frightening and painful business, with only occasional moments of joy. I've never felt that

mysterious compulsion to write which many writers speak of. Yet there remains this nagging, rather hopeless curiosity about how things are, how they reveal themselves; and about the subterranean workings of the writing process that bring this about.

*     *     *

Kay Cicellis has worked as a journalist and in radio in Greece and Britain. Both the virtues and the deficiencies of journalism are reflected in her literary output as a writer of fiction. She has clear, sharp powers of observation; the good reporter's gift of seizing on the important facts and stating them objectively; and a command of swift, uncluttered, workmanlike prose. There is another item on the credit side of the balance-sheet: she has also the ability, found in the best reporters, to arouse the reader's emotional response by her selection of facts and details. The objectivity and detachment are apparent only; the *choses vues* are seen with an artist's eye.

But the ledger has also a debit column. Like many journalists who turn to fiction, she lacks staying-power over the longer distances and especially in the management and development of plot and character. Her best work, *Death of a Town*, is a mere hundred pages long: it is in fact a latter-day representative of that now unfashionable literary genre, the long-short story or *conte*.

Born in Marseilles of Greek parents, Miss Cicellis spent her early childhood in France and then in Greece. She is said to have learnt English from her governesses and the books they introduced her to, and she handles the English language literally as to the manner born. She is not the first foreigner to have done so, but in this respect she bears comparison with the best.

Her first published book, *The Easy Way*, was a volume of short stories. These are concerned with what happens to people, and to their relationship with each other, when the normal routine of daily life is suddenly interrupted by unforseen events. For all the author's insights into changes of emotion and attitude, the dissolution of old and the resolution of new patterns, one feels she is not fully in control of her material; but certainly an original if uneven talent was displayed to the public. She followed this minor success with *No Name in the Street*, a novel which broods on the relationship between myth and fact, exemplified in terms of the myths built up about the Resistance in Greece and the protagonist's inability to accept them, until finally he is compelled to construct his own personal myth of alienation. This ambitious novel again falls short of complete success: the reader is left with an impression that symbolism and story have not been thoroughly decocted and distilled.

*Death of a Town* is however a brilliant and concentrated piece of writing. It tells, very simply, of the destruction of a small Ionian city by an earthquake. The sense of the total disruption of the continuities of time, nature, and society is conveyed partly by intense description of the physical events when houses are shattered and dust hangs in the harsh sunlit air, and partly by the economical description of the actions of a varied cast of characters, who are stripped down to the essential core of their personalities. In 1957 Miss Cicellis published *Ten Seconds from Now*, a novel set in a Greek radio station where the unifying eye of the receptionist gives meaning to the fragmented relationships of the staff. Though absorbing, it does not rival *Death of a Town* for tragic emotional intensity.

—Stewart F. Sanderson

---

**CLARK, Eleanor.** American. Born in Los Angeles, California, 6 July 1913; grew up in Roxbury, Connecticut. Educated at Vassar College, Poughkeepsie, New York, B.A. 1934.

Married Robert Penn Warren, *q.v.*, in 1952; has two children. Editorial Staff Member, W. W. Norton and Company, publishers, New York, 1936–39. Worked for the United States Office of Strategic Services, Washington, D.C., 1943–45. Recipient: National Institute of Arts and Letters grant, 1947; Guggenheim Fellowship, 1947, 1949; National Book Award, for non-fiction, 1965. Member, National Institute of Arts and Letters. Address: 2495 Redding Road, Fairfield, Connecticut 06430, U.S.A.

PUBLICATIONS

Novels

> *The Bitter Box.* New York, Doubleday, 1946; London, Joseph, 1947.
> *Baldur's Gate.* New York, Pantheon Books, 1970.

Other

> *Rome and a Villa.* New York, Doubleday, 1952; London, Joseph, 1953.
> *Song of Roland* (juvenile). New York, Random House, 1960; London, Muller, 1963.
> *The Oysters of Locmariaquer.* New York, Pantheon Books, 1964; London, Secker and Warburg, 1965.

> Translator, *Dark Wedding*, by Ramón José Sender. New York, Doubleday, 1943; London, Grey Walls Press, 1947.

Eleanor Clark comments:

I do not feel it is wise or in most cases helpful for writers to analyze their own work. In any case, I find it impossible, except to remark that, concerning impulse, motive and kind of personal involvement, I find no clear line of demarcation between my novels and non-fiction books (*Rome* and *Oysters*). This does not of course refer to essays—a different job altogether.

Can a woman be a good writer (artist) and a good mother? I have no idea. Are the two in conflict? Of course—so is art and everything else. Do I love and value my two children above my books? Certainly. Would I have stopped writing altogether if necessary for the children's happiness? Well, yes, but it would perhaps not have been physically possible—in the sense that one eats when hungry and scratches when itching—and with a little sleight-of-hand it was never quite necessary for too fatally long at a time. However, these facts do relate to *Baldur's Gate* having been written over a period of many years. It was in gestation, with false starts, long before that, but the home-town scene (the usual first novel) was too close. I disposed of it when young in a story, "Hurry, Hurry", found a built-in distance for my first published novel, *The Bitter Box*, and came to the perspective for the original one only years later, possibly through the fact of having children.

\*        \*        \*

Twenty-four years separate Eleanor Clark's first novel and her latest, and in comparison one gives the impression of looking backward and the other of looking forward. *The Bitter Box*, though published in 1946, reflects the leftist social ferment of the thirties. The novel's center is a timid, punctilious bank clerk named Mr. Temple who in his teller's cage serves efficiently, almost worshipfully, the symbol of capitalism until driven by a sense of oppression to search out and embrace another god vaguely defined as "the party," the official organ of which is the *Word*. His ultimate realization that both gods are false and corrupt is accompanied by an awakening to the redemptive influences of suffering and love. By painfully relinquishing the safety of a life of order and obedience he gradually learns to trust and to give of himself in concern for others. This theme of surrender into life, present also in *Baldur's Gate*, fails of effect in *The Bitter Box* largely because of a patronizing, detached point of view which creates a curiously remote and improbable hero whose political activism seems arbitrary rather than necessary and probable.

*Baldur's Gate*, an ambitious work rich in symbol and allusion, deals with a wealth of themes: the preservation of tradition, the search for values, the function of art, commercialism, ecology, among others. Eva Buckingham Hines relates the events in a complex style—disordered chronology, internal monologue, depth analysis—which complements her personal tortuous course out of the often painful and sometimes alluring memories of the past toward acceptance of the present and courage for the future. The memories derive from growing up in Jordan, an old Connecticut town rich in tradition and in the history of human weakness and error. And though she seems to be committed to the future, having married Lucas Hines and borne a son, in reality she is hostage to her past: to the pain and frustration of an indifferent and alcoholic mother, an ineffectual father, a corrupt brother, a once proud family socially disgraced, and to the memory of a love betrayed.

Her futile attempt to renew this early love affair with Jack Pryden and thus redeem the past is the motivating force behind many of the events, but it is the presence of the seventy-year-old sculptor, Baldur Blake (the name suggesting his role as demi-god and mystic) which lifts the novel above this rather trivial love affair. Having himself fought the battle of disillusionment with the heritage of the past, he returns to vision and creativity, like a fertility god in spring, revitalizing the whole community with promise that the future which destroys the past can also generate new beauty and harmony.

In the closing scene as Eva stands in the falling snow viewing the town dump, symbol of waste but also of change, the fundamental law of things, she reflects that his message had been "not to kid ourselves, about what art, home, love, Jordan, anything could ever mean to us again, and yet to keep capable of love, of work, of hope." The dream of a new community fails of realization, but the vision of the gate model Baldur never lived to complete remains, the "intimation of some large serenity always in the act of rising out of torment." The novel captures that torment and the courage to master it, but more frequently in the rhetoric than in the characters and situations. In the final analysis the plot and characters seem not quite the equal of the novel's deep philosophical vision.

—Dale K. Doepke

---

**CLARK, Walter Van Tilburg.** American. Born in East Orland, Maine, 3 August 1909. Educated at the University of Nevada, Reno, B.A. 1931, M.A. 1932; University of Vermont, Burlington, M.A. 1934. Married Barbara Frances Morse in 1933; has two children. Taught in high schools in Cazenovia and Rye, New York, 1936–45; Associate Professor of English, University of Montana, Missoula, 1953–56; Professor of English and Creative Writing, San Francisco State College, 1956–62. Fellow in Fiction, Center for Advanced Studies, Wesleyan University, Middletown, Connecticut, 1960–61. Since 1962, Writer-in-Residence, University of Nevada. Recipient: O. Henry Award, 1945. D.Litt., Colgate University, Hamilton, New York, 1958; University of Nevada, 1969. Address: Department of English, University of Nevada, Reno, Nevada 89507, U.S.A. *Died 11 November 1971.*

PUBLICATIONS

Novels

> The Ox-Bow Incident. New York, Random House, 1940; London, Gollancz, 1941.
> The City of Trembling Leaves. New York, Random House, 1945; as Tim Hazard, London, Kimber, 1951.
> The Track of the Cat. New York, Random House, 1949; London, Gollancz, 1950.

Short Stories

> The Watchful Gods and Other Stories. New York, Random House, 1950.

Verse

> Christmas Comes to Hjalsen, Reno. Reno, Nevada, Reno Publishing House, 1930.
> Ten Women in Gale's House and Shorter Poems. Boston, Christopher Publishing House, 1932.

Other

> Editor, The Journals of Alf Doten. Reno, University of Nevada Press, 1972.

Manuscript Collection: Library of Congress, Washington, D.C.

Critical Study: Walter Van Tilburg Clark by Max Westbrook, New York, Twayne, 1970.

\* \* \*

In his three novels, Walter Van Tilburg Clark has worked with the first-rank novelist's instinct for subject matter and sense of place; usually he sustains the concomitant interest in his characters and their development through the circumstances of plot. What has barred him from the first rank, ultimately, has been the lack of unerring sense of proportion in matching structure, plot, and characterization that makes great novels.

The publication of The Ox-Bow Incident in 1940 brought Clark deserved notoriety for it is, for the most part, an incisive, exciting study of mob violence. Through the skilful manipulation of a variety of characters who debate what to do after the report of a murder reaches the cattle town of Bridger's Wells, and congeal into a posse intent on finding and summarily hanging the culprits, Clark conveys the insight that the tyranny of the mob can only triumph by default. Boredom and the will to do something are forces that cannot easily be stemmed if there is someone present strong and clever enough to use them. The mob seeks the most single-minded leadership available and once such a ruthless, charismatic character as Major Tetley takes charge, even intelligent men are willing to be borne by the event they are making. In Bridger's Wells, there is simply no one, not even the over-articulate storekeeper, Davies, who is sufficiently committed or forceful to do whatever is necessary to stop the leader. It is not surprising that although the novel is set in the American West, in the days of gun law, many readers took The Ox-Bow Incident to be a parable of the rise of the European tyrants in the thirties.

The Ox-Bow Incident suffers from a structural defect: while it is true that the street debate about whether the crowd should act or not does serve to delineate character and theme, it is so over-long that it interferes with the pacing of the novel. There is another, probably more serious, flaw: in an otherwise tautly written work, there are long, inappropriately sententious speeches by various characters, notably Davies, explaining states of mind and points of view. Yet there is no denying Clark's overall success in exploring his theme through a wide range of vivid characters.

Clark's second novel, *The City of Trembling Leaves*, is not a bad novel because its plot is implausible or its characters too contrived. It is poor precisely because the incidents in the rambling chronicle of Timothy Hazard, the sensitive musician who is the protagonist, are banal and the people in his life mostly stock characters. It is not a novel of maturation in the way that, say, *Huckleberry Finn* is, but of romantic adolescence that must surely appeal mainly to romantic adolescents. A tale of emotional development arrested at the stage of a schoolboy infatuation may arouse some sympathy, but little interest. Whatever strength the book has is derived primarily from Clark's use of the West, particularly of the mountains and desert of western Nevada, as a source of spiritual energy, much as Hemingway uses the mountains in *The Sun Also Rises*.

The artistic, as well as popular, success of *The Track of the Cat* demonstrated that *The City of Trembling Leaves* had been an aberrant second novel and that Clark was capable of fulfilling the promise of *The Ox-Bow Incident*. With a sense of gripping immediacy, the novel deals with the hunting of a marauding mountain lion in the premature Sierra winter by each of the three Bridges sons in turn, and simultaneously with the tense relationships among the members of the family who remain at the ranch. The killer cat is both a physical entity and the spiritual *bête noire* of its trackers, who have invested it with supernatural size. The cat becomes, in fact, a symbolic manifestation of the hunters' deficiencies: Arthur, the artist-dreamer, is struck down because he cannot cope with reality and forgets the menacing cat; Curt, the overbearing realist, is killed because he cannot manage the mythic quality the cat assumes, and is driven off a cliff by the fear of it.

Clark plays an indoor drama in counterpoint to the hunt. The mother looms as large at the Bridges ranch as the panther does in the mountains, as she oversees Arthur's burial and attempts to break up the romance between Harold, the youngest son, and his visiting fiancée. Harold is able to move from ranch to mountain to destroy the panther at the end of the novel —and thereby fuse the two subplots—because in his treatment of the mother he has shown that he has in him the necessary balance of dreamer and doer. As Joe Sam, the ancient, mystical Indian ranch hand, who is one of the important unifying elements of the novel, implies, Harold can slay the beast because it is not his own particular black cat.

*The Track of the Cat*, too, has its imperfections: the real and magical cat requires a greater adversary than Clark provides in the person of Curt, whose striving with the cat accounts for the bulk of the novel. The necessary intensity that is suggested in Curt early in the book proves to be mainly bluster; he is not long in the cold wilderness before he abandons the food he needs to survive. The father is a stereotypical drunk, a nuisance to people inside and outside of the book alike. Yet Walter Van Tilburg Clark's narrative power is strong enough, and the portrait of the mother memorable enough, to diminish the effect of the weaknesses and make his audience regret that he has not published another novel in over two decades. It is as if when he caused Harold to return to the Bridges ranch to take charge, Clark's own quest, expressed first through Art Croft, the cowboy narrator of *The Ox-Bow Incident*, then through Timothy Hazard, and finally through the hunters of the black cat, was snowbound in the cold of the Nevada winter.

—Alan R. Shucard

**CLARKE, Arthur C(harles).**  British.  Born in Minehead, Somerset, 16 December 1917. Educated at Huish's Grammar School, Taunton, Somerset, 1927–36; King's College, London, B.Sc. (1st class honours) in physics and mathematics 1948. Flight Lieutenant in the Royal Air Force, 1941–46; served as Radar Instructor, and Technical Officer on the first Ground Controlled Approach radar; originated proposal for use of satellites for communications, 1945. Married Marilyn Mayfield in 1954 (divorced, 1964). Assistant Auditor, Exchequer and Audit Department, London, 1936–41; Assistant Editor, *Physics Abstracts*, London, 1949–50. Since 1954, engaged in underwater exploration and photography of the Great Barrier Reef of Australia and the coast of Ceylon. Has made numerous radio and TV appearances, and has lectured widely in Britain and the United States. Commentator, for CBS-TV, on lunar landing flights of Apollo 11, 12 and 15. Recipient: International Fantasy Award, 1952; UNESCO-Kalinga Prize, 1961; Boys' Clubs of America Junior Book Award, 1961; Stuart Ballantine Medal of the Franklin Institute, 1963; Robert Ball Award of the Aviation Space-Writers' Association, 1965; American Association for the Advancement of Science-Westinghouse Science Writing Award, 1969. Chairman, British Interplanetary Society, 1946–47, 1950–53. Fellow of the Royal Astronomical Society. Address: 47/5 Gregory's Road, Colombo 7, Ceylon; or, 88 Nightingale Road, London N.22, England.

PUBLICATIONS

Novels

*Prelude to Space: A Compelling Realistic Novel of Interplanetary Flight.*  New York, World Editions, 1951; London, Sidgwick and Jackson, 1953.
*The Sands of Mars.*  London, Sidgwick and Jackson, 1951; New York, Gnome Press, 1952.
*Islands in the Sky.*  Philadelphia, Winston, and London, Sidgwick and Jackson, 1952.
*Against the Fall of Night.*  New York, Gnome Press, 1953.
*Childhood's End.*  New York, Ballantine, 1953; London, Sidgwick and Jackson, 1954.
*Earthlight.*  New York, Ballantine, and London, Muller, 1955.
*The City and the Stars.*  New York, Harcourt Brace, and London, Muller, 1956.
*The Deep Range.*  New York, Harcourt Brace, and London, Muller, 1957.
*Across the Sea of Stars* (includes *Childhood's End, Earthlight*, and eighteen short stories). New York, Harcourt Brace, 1959.
*A Fall of Moondust.*  New York, Harcourt Brace, and London, Gollancz, 1961.
*From the Oceans, From the Stars* (includes *The Deep Range, The City and the Stars*, and twenty-four short stories).  New York, Harcourt Brace, 1962.
*Dolphin Island: A Story of the People of the Sea.*  New York, Holt Rinehart, and London, Gollancz, 1963.
*Glide Path.*  New York, Harcourt Brace, 1963; London, Sidgwick and Jackson, 1969.
*Prelude to Mars* (includes *Prelude to Space, The Sands of Mars*, and sixteen short stories).  New York, Harcourt Brace, 1965.
*2001: A Space Odyssey.*  New York, New American Library, and London, Hutchinson, 1968.
*The Lion of Comarre, and Against the Fall of Night.*  New York, Harcourt Brace, 1968; London, Gollancz, 1970.

Short Stories

*Expedition to Earth: Eleven Science-Fiction Stories.*  New York, Ballantine, 1953; London, Sidgwick and Jackson, 1954.

*Reach for Tomorrow.* New York, Ballantine, 1956; London, Gollancz, 1962.
*Tales from the White Hart.* New York, Ballantine, 1957.
*The Other Side of the Sky.* New York, Harcourt Brace, 1958; London, Gollancz, 1961.
*Tales of Ten Worlds.* New York, Harcourt Brace, 1962; London, Gollancz, 1963.
*The Nine Billion Names of God: The Best Short Stories of Arthur C. Clarke.* New York, Harcourt Brace, 1967.
*A Wind from the Sun.* New York, Harcourt Brace, 1972.

Play

Screenplay: *2001: A Space Odyssey*, with Stanley Kubrick, 1968.

Other

*Interplanetary Flight: An Introduction to Astronautics.* London, Temple, 1950; New York, Harper, 1951; revised edition, Temple and Harper, 1960.
*The Exploration of Space.* London, Temple, and New York, Harper, 1951; revised edition, Harper, 1959.
*The Young Traveler in Space.* London, Phoenix House, 1954; as *Going into Space*, New York, Harper, 1954.
*The Exploration of the Moon*, with R. A. Smith. London, Muller, 1954; New York, Harper, 1955.
*The Coast of Coral.* London, Muller, and New York, Harper, 1956.
*The Making of a Moon: The Story of the Earth Satellite Program.* New York, Harper, and London, Muller, 1957; revised edition, Harper, 1958.
*The Reefs of Taprobane: Underwater Adventures Around Ceylon.* London, Muller, and New York, Harper, 1957.
*Voice Across the Sea.* London, Muller, and New York, Harper, 1958.
*Boy Beneath the Sea*, with Mike Wilson. New York, Harper, 1958.
*The Challenge of the Spaceship: Previews of Tomorrow's World.* New York, Harper, 1959; London, Muller, 1960.
*The First Five Fathoms: A Guide to Underwater Adventure*, with Mike Wilson. New York, Harper, 1960.
*The Challenge of the Sea.* New York, Holt Rinehart, and London, Muller, 1960.
*Indian Ocean Adventure*, with Mike Wilson. New York, Harper, 1961; London, Barker, 1962.
*Profiles of the Future: An Inquiry into the Limits of the Possible.* New York, Harper, and London, Gollancz, 1962.
*The Treasure of the Great Reef*, with Mike Wilson. New York, Harper, and London, Barker, 1964.
*Indian Ocean Treasure*, with Mike Wilson. New York, Harper, 1964.
*Man and Space*, with the editors of *Life*. New York, Time, 1964.
*Voices from the Sky: Previews of the Coming Space Age.* New York, Harper, 1965; London, Gollancz, 1966.
*The Promise of Space.* New York, Harper, and London, Hodder and Stoughton, 1968.
*First on the Moon*, with the astronauts. Boston, Little Brown, 1970.
*Report on Planet Three.* New York, Harper, 1972.
*The Lost Worlds of 2001.* New York, New American Library, 1972.
*Beyond Jupiter*, with Chesley Bonestell. Boston, Little Brown, 1972.
*Into Space*, with Robert Silverberg. New York, Harper, 1972.

Editor, *Time Probe: The Science in Science Fiction.* New York, Dial Press, 1966; London, Gollancz, 1967.
Editor, *The Coming of the Space Age: Famous Accounts of Man's Probing of the Universe.* New York, Meredith Press, and London, Gollancz, 1967.

Manuscript Collection: Mugar Library, Boston University.

Critical Study: "Out of the Ego Chamber" by Jeremy Bernstein, in *The New Yorker,* 9 August 1969.

Arthur C. Clarke comments:

I regard myself primarily as an entertainer and my ideals are Maugham, Kipling, Wells. My chief aim is the old s.f. *cliché,* "The search for wonder". However, I am almost equally interested in style and rhythm, having been much influenced by Tennyson, Swinburne, Housman and the Georgian poets.
My main themes are exploration (space, sea, time), the position of Man in the hierarchy of the universe, and the effect of contact with other intelligences. The writer who probably had most influence on me was W. Olaf Stapledon (*Last and First Men*).

*       *       *

Arthur C. Clarke writes adventures of the near and far future, in which men seek knowledge and explore new environments. The most notable aspect of his fiction is the perfect welding of the expository passages, containing accurate but clear scientific explanations of how the adventures will sooner or later become possible, to the narrative passages.
Several of the adventures occur at or near the beginnings of exploration of a new environment. *Prelude to Space* fictionalizes what leads up to the first trip to the moon. *Earthlight* depicts the workings of the lunar colony, and *The Sands of Mars* does the same for that planet. *Islands in the Sky* explores the uses of space stations, and *The Deep Range* and *Dolphin Island* explore the uses of the sea, such as whale farming and cooperation with dolphins.
Three of Clarke's novels are primarily religious and philosophical. *Against the Fall of Night,* completed in 1946 and published in 1953, was rewritten as *The City and the Stars.* Diaspar, a city of the remote future, has (to paraphrase a favorite Clarke generalization) a technology so advanced that it cannot be distinguished from magic. But the city is a womb from which none of its citizens dare to escape until one courageous explorer goes on a quest for knowledge of the past, which opens up for man a new future. In *Childhood's End,* alien "Overlords" stop man's development of space travel until man, remade by his own unsuspected psychic powers, rises to a new level of childhood and moves toward the stars. The quest of David Bowman in *2001: A Space Odyssey* transforms him into Star-Child, who will "think of something" to move man up the ladder of evolution.
Clarke does in his short stories (such as those collected in *Reach for Tomorrow, The Other Side of the Sky, Tales of Ten Worlds,* and *Tales from the White Hart*) what he does elsewhere— plus some things which he does not do elsewhere. "Breaking Strain," for example, is a study of contrasting personalities in crisis; "Hate" is a moral fable; "Transience" is a nearly plotless poem written in prose which compares and contrasts three stages of man's existence.
Although Clarke's style can be wordy and pedestrian at times (as when he overexplains), at other times it is sparse and poetic. His typical mode of narration—focusing all data through a first or second-person persona—generally facilitates his effective presentation of the concrete.

The universe challenges us, Clarke believes, by its inexhaustible beauty, strangeness, and richness. Unless we rise to the challenge by keeping our curiosity and extending our environment, both our art and our science will stagnate. The scientist is as likely to lack the necessary vision and spirit of adventure as the humanist; the romantic maverick is Clarke's protagonist. The eternal renewal of childhood in a never-ending expansion into the unknown is Clarke's theme.

—Curtis C. Smith

CLARKE, Austin C(hesterfield). Barbadian. Born in Barbados, 26 July 1934. Educated at Combermere Boys' School, Barbados; Harrison's College, Barbados; Trinity College, University of Toronto. Married Betty Joyce Reynolds in 1957; has three children. Hoyt Fellow, 1968, and Visiting Lecturer, 1969, 1970, Yale University, New Haven, Connecticut; Fellow, Indiana University School of Letters, Bloomington, 1969; Margaret Bundy Scott Visiting Professor of Literature, Williams College, Williamstown, Massachusetts, 1971; Lecturer, Duke University, Durham, North Carolina, 1971–72. Member, Board of Trustees, Rhode Island School of Design, Providence, 1970. Recipient: Belmont Short Story Award, 1965; President's Medal, University of Western Ontario, 1966; Canada Council Senior Arts Fellowship, 1967, 1970. Address: 432 Brunswick Avenue, Toronto 4, Ontario, Canada.

PUBLICATIONS

Novels

The Survivors of the Crossing. Toronto, McClelland and Stewart, and London, Heinemann, 1964.
Amongst Thistles and Thorns. Toronto, McClelland and Stewart, and London, Heinemann, 1965.
The Meeting Point. Toronto, Macmillan, and London, Heinemann, 1967; Boston, Little Brown, 1972.
A Storm of Fortune. Boston, Little Brown, 1972.

Short Stories

When He Was Free and Young and He Used to Wear Silks. Toronto, House of Anansi, 1971.

Uncollected Short Stories

"I Hanging on Please God", in Bim (Bridgetown, Barbados), 1964.
"Leaving This Island Place", in Bim (Bridgetown, Barbados), 1964.
"An Easter Carol", in Bim (Bridgetown, Barbados), 1965.
"Four Stations in His Circle", in Saturday Night (Toronto), 1965.

"The Woman with the BBC Voice", in *Tamarack Review* (Toronto), 1966.
"The Collector", in *Transatlantic Review* (London and New York), 1968.
"Why Didn't You Use a Plunger", in *Tamarack Review* (Toronto), 1969.
"A Wedding in Toronto", in *Tamarack Review* (Toronto), 1970.
"What Happened?", in *Evergreen Review* (New York), 1970.

Critical Study: "The West Indian Novel in North America: A Study of Austin Clarke" by Lloyd W. Brown, in *Journal of Commonwealth Literature* (Leeds, Yorkshire), July 1970.

Austin C. Clarke comments:

Whenever I am asked to give a statement about my work I find it difficult to do. All I can say in these situations is that I try to write about a group of people, West Indian immigrants (to Canada), whose life interests me because of the remarkable problems of readjustment, and the other problems of ordinary living. The psychological implications of this kind of life are what make my work interesting and I hope relevant to the larger condition of preservation. The themes are usually those of adjustment, as I have said, but this adjustment is artistically rendered in the inter-relationship of the two predominant groups of which I write: the host Jewish-Anglo Saxon group, and the black group (West Indian and expatriate black American).

*        *        *

No brief essay does justice to the stories wrought painstakingly by Austin C. Clarke, the Barbadian writer who has been living and writing in Toronto for most of the time since 1956, with extended periods in the United States as visiting lecturer in Black Studies at such universities as Yale, Indiana, Williams College, and Duke. If the problem of race is a key problem now, then Clarke is a key writer in Canada, if not Canada's one black writer of distinction. But first he is a key writer because he writes impeccably and is fascinating to read, fascinating not the least because what he writes reflects what he calls the "non-vindictive racism" of Black Literature to distinguish it from the "vindictive." Lloyd W. Brown identifies Clarke's major themes as similar to those of most West Indian novelists of the last three decades: "black awareness, national identity, the hateful ambiguities of the West, and the heroic potential of the black peasant." Brown adds that Clarke has "helped to contribute a North American dimension" to these pressing Third World themes; he becomes for Brown "the major West Indian writer" now on this continent.

By his own admission, Clarke takes among his models the interior monologue of Joyce, the childhood fantasies of Dylan Thomas, the gusto of J. P. Donleavy, the earnestness of Saul Bellow, to say nothing of the rightful concerns of such black writers as Samuel Selvon of Trinidad and the Americans Richard Wright and LeRoi Jones. The hallmark of Clarke's writing, however, comes from his ear for the rhythms and nuances of the daily speech of his people. Their dialogue, vigorous, finely tuned, comes to the reader as living speech, spoken in a dramatic verbal music in which rhythm is more important than word. Each person speaks in his own voice, but all share the peculiar words and expletives, and the twofold or threefold speech patterns (dependent on emotional intensity) of their people, earthy, sensuous, commonsensical, their speech sounding in the inner ear, its blend of real voices calling to be read aloud. This achievement of vital human speech, often interior speech, adds breadth and depth to his character building. More than in any other way, he develops character, as he develops action, through spoken dialogue and through interior monologues (past, present, future, daydream, outrage), and through the writing of letters in the character's mind, often letters never put down on paper. This use of letter-writing is notable, since a letter, perhaps beginning *in medias res* or remaining unfinished, may reveal otherwise inaccessible facets of loneliness, anger, frustration, or occasional joy. In all, his stories and novels are finely constructed, economic, dramatically immediate, swift of pace, and charged with human meaning.

In his first novel, *The Survivors of the Crossing*, Barbados is the setting as in his second, the semi-autobiographical *Amongst Thistles and Thorns*. In the first he moves steadily, with little exposition or scene-painting, within the personality of its focal character, the sugar-plantation worker Rufus, removing him for only one short period from the novel's stage. Well on in years, labour and poverty have left him pretty much impotent, while his tragi-comic efforts to rouse his fellows from their apathy (or dealings with the plantation system) by organizing a strike fizzle out into his imprisonment. But he ends in prison not for this strike action, but for robbing an old woman who sells sweet meats at a portable stand in the village. Throughout the second novel, he remains constantly in touch with the personality, the fears, hopes and dreams of the schoolboy, Milton Sobers (Clarke's swift handling here compares interestingly with George Lamming's semi-autobiographical, more leisurely *In the Castle of My Skin*, also set in Barbados). After a gospel-meeting climax which equals the great gospel-meeting episode in James Baldwin's *Go Tell It on the Mountain*, the boy finally gains a degree of self-identity, nurtured partly from the dream of "Harlem New York City America," given him by his outcast father Willy-Willy who had one time gone there and realized himself, but by novel's end has been pathetically drowned. Milton's self-identity, however, serves to alienate him from his mother and her reluctantly-accepted lover, Nathan, who know nothing of his dream and could not care less in their final, if apathetic, grasp for some personal living.

Of his more recent work, Clarke says he is trying to write of "a group of people, West Indian immigrants (to Canada) whose life interests" him because of the difficulties of adjustment they experience in ordinary living as newcomers in a largely white culture. For him, the "psychological implications" involved add searching interest to the perennial matter of human survival. The human scenes rendered gain complexity if not tragedy as he gives strong dramatic life to the kinds of interpersonal difficulty analyzed by Calvin C. Hernton in *Sex and Racism in America*.

In Clarke's third novel, *The Meeting Point*, as in his fourth, *A Storm of Fortune*, the sexual dimension is treated with candour, and with both earnestness and good humour, in a number of diverse relationships, one lesbian, several interracial. In one closing instance, an interracial marriage falls into open tragedy. Related to this essential area of sexuality lies what Brown refers to as "the actual process of black self-identification." In these two Toronto novels, it involves "a painful, and often unresolved, series of conflicts *within* each awakening consciousness." There may be growing black self-confidence, but there may also linger either the old self-hate, or the old apathy, each to varying degrees white-induced. So a pervasive irony comes into sharper focus as the reader moves from the Barbadian to the Toronto novels. Brown puts it well: "The internal conflicts of self-identification are heightened in direct ratio to the intensity of emergent blackness." If the old apathy lingers on, it receives from Clarke what might be called a scornful compassion, given dramatically through action and dialogue, or through monologues of comic self-justifying. If the old self-hate prevails, the person may be driven mad, as Jefferson Theophilus Belle in the prize-winning story, "Four Stations in His Circle." If the internal conflicts persist, he may be driven to suicide, as Henry White in the story, "Give Us This Day: And Forgive Us," which story becomes the closing instance of tragedy in *A Storm of Fortune*. As story or episode, it understates the tragedy of a man driven to question his very being by a dominant, alien culture (even though it once named him "porter of the year," taking his picture with the Prime Minister). But further irony is involved. He has married a Jewish wife. Her devotion to racial justice seems evident, but she is blind to the patronizing harm she does the black man whom she has married against her family's prejudices. Although the pair strive for a genuine relationship, they struggle against a constant threat of hate from both outside and within. All ends with terrible tears.

In both Toronto novels, the central consciousness is a woman's; in *The Meeting Point*, of Bernice Leach, a lonely Barbadian who has left a young son and an elderly mother on the island. She works resentfully in the wealthy Jewish, Burrmann home in Forest Hill, wondering whether to send for the boy's father but waits until it is too late. In *A Storm of Fortune*, the central consciousness is that of Estelle Shepherd, Bernice's half-sister, who comes to Toronto in the first of the novels to visit her, but cannot accept the latter's thwarted, constrained world of the domestic. This leads her almost inevitably into a love-in-hate affair with the complicated Sam Burrmann, Bernice's employer, and ends with her nearly dying after an attempt to abort their child. Estelle's choice, in *A Storm of Fortune*, to keep her child on her own proves a measure of her achievement of self-identity, an achievement for which Bernice so far, in her mixture of smugness and voyeurism, of anger and apathy, lacks the wherewithal.

Thus Clarke writes about, and through his honest commitment to, people who are black and who must attempt to find themselves in a white world, but first he writes about recognizable human beings. In spite of the centrality of the racial theme in his writing, it really comes second to his concern for his characters in and of themselves. This is another of the strengths of his story telling, his devotion to the people whom he creates, or better, who come to a life of their own in his pages. They grow there as they will grow; while they do so, Clarke has a deftness, even in the short story, for moving in and out of their several minds. As we enter more deeply into their minds and emotions, they show themselves as alienated many times over. They were in Barbados; they are even more in Canada, with its ice and snow, its white "wasp" ubiquity.

In the short story, "They Heard a Ringing of Bells," he has the Trinidadian Sagaboy scold a Barbadian girl who has grown reminiscent, even naively ecstatic, by the hymn-playing on the carillon bells above the campus of the University of Toronto, where they are resting on the grass. Sagaboy explodes:

> It ain't no wonders of no blasted God, woman! You have just start to live like you should have been living from the day you born. But instead, you been spending your lifetime down in Barbados, the same way as your forefathers and foremothers been spending it . . . in the kiss-me-arse canefield, and in slavery.

After further explodings about that "topsy-turvy world down there," Sagaboy voices one of Clarke's persistant concerns, when he says:

> Revolution run up inside your head, child, and you start to put two and two together. And you say, be-Christ, it ain't true, pardner, that is not true at all! So what happen next? You pull up stakes and run abroad. You come up here in a more progressive country, but you still going exist in a worser life than what you was accustomed to back home.

Outsiders in Barbados, even more in Canada. Alienated from much in whatever white society they find themselves, they are also alienated from many of their own, either because they are led to be unjust or cruel to their own by their selfish ambitions, or because they are unjustly treated by their own for the same reason. The cruel sacrifice of one's own kind for obsessive selfishness is dramatized in both the Barbadian and Toronto settings.

As yet, Clarke cannot apparently foresee a resolution to the alienations and conflicts of race, with all the tragedy they imply, even if he mutes that dark vision with vitality and a constant play of good humour and exuberance.

—Herbert C. Burke

**CLEARY, Jon (Stephen).**   Australian.   Born in Sydney, 22 November 1917. Educated at Marist Brothers School, Randwick, New South Wales, 1924–32. Served in the Australian Imperial Forces in the Middle East and New Guinea, 1940–45. Married Constantine Lucas in 1946; has two children. Prior to 1939 worked as a commercial traveller, bush worker and commercial artist. Full-time Writer since 1945. Journalist, Government of Australia News and Information Bureau, in London, 1948–49, and in New York, 1949–51. Recipient: Australian Broadcasting Commission Prize, for radio drama, 1944; Second Prize, *Sydney Morning Herald* Novel Contest, 1946; Australian Section Prize, *New York Herald Tribune* World Short Story Contest, 1950. Address: c/o John Farquharson Ltd., 15 Red Lion Square, London W.C.1, England.

PUBLICATIONS

Novels

> *You Can't See round Corners.*   New York, Scribner, 1947; London, Eyre and Spottis-
>     woode, 1948.
> *The Long Shadow.*   London, Werner Laurie, 1949.
> *Just Let Me Be.*   London, Werner Laurie, 1950.
> *The Sundowners.*   New York, Scribner, and London, Werner Laurie, 1952.
> *The Climate of Courage.*   London, Collins, 1954; as *Naked in the Night*, New York,
>     Popular Library, 1955.
> *Justin Bayard.*   London, Collins, and New York, Morrow. 1955.
> *The Green Helmet.*   New York, Morrow, and London, Collins, 1957.
> *Back of Sunset.*   New York, Morrow, and London, Collins, 1959.
> *North from Thursday.*   New York, Morrow, and London, Collins, 1960.
> *The Country of Marriage.*   New York, Morrow, and London, Collins, 1962.
> *Forests of the Night.*   New York, Morrow, and London, Collins, 1963.
> *A Flight of Chariots.*   New York, Morrow, 1963; London, Collins, 1964.
> *The Fall of an Eagle.*   New York, Morrow, 1964; London, Collins, 1965.
> *The Pulse of Danger.*   New York, Morrow, and London, Collins, 1966.
> *The High Commissioner.*   New York, Morrow, and London, Collins, 1966.
> *The Long Pursuit.*   New York, Morrow, and London, Collins, 1967.
> *Season of Doubt.*   New York, Morrow, and London, Collins, 1968.
> *Remember Jack Hoxie.*   New York, Morrow, and London, Collins, 1969.
> *Helga's Web.*   New York, Morrow, and London, Collins, 1970.
> *The Liberators.*   New York, Morrow, 1971; as *Mask of the Andes*, London, Collins,
>     1971.
> *The Ninth Marquess.*   New York, Morrow, 1972; as *Man's Estate*, London, Collins,
>     1972.

Short Stories

> *These Small Glories.*   Sydney, Angus and Robertson, 1945.
> *Pillar of Salt.*   Sydney, Horwitz, 1963.

Plays

> Screenplays: *The Siege of Pinchgut*, with Harry Watt, 1959; *The Green Helmet*, 1961;
> *The Sundowners*, 1961.

Jon Cleary comments:

I write primarily to entertain, but, having stated that, I also write to inform about the world we live in. I have no overall theme, unless it is to affirm my belief that Man can, somehow, overcome the effects of his own disasters. I do my best not to be categorised, mainly because I want to keep fresh my enthusiasm for writing; but I'm afraid critics tend to overlook those books in which I do not write about adventure in exotic places (such as *The Country of Marriage* and *Remember Jack Hoxie*), and I'm resigned now to being classified as an "adventure" writer. I have a principle that I will not write about a place I have not visited—this involves me in a lot of travel and is, I hope, opening me up for a book or two of wider scope in the future. I am, I suppose, an old-fashioned story-teller—but I feel that stories, combining action with character, will always be read. I hope so—the job opportunities for out-of-work novelists in their fifties are not too numerous.

*      *      *

Jon Cleary's conviction that he has been virtually "classified as an 'adventure' writer" despite books like *The Country of Marriage* and *Remember Jack Hoxie* should not come as a surprise. The great bulk of his work does, after all, invite such a classification: his characters confront ill-fortune, the elements, physical dangers and personal ordeals in places as separated and contrasting as Bhutan and the Australian outback, New Guinea and Beirut. Yet it is in those relatively few novels in which neither locale nor the pace and excitement of suspenseful action are paramount that Cleary is at his best.

He has a sensitive understanding of the fractional shifts in mood, the alterations in psychological atmosphere, the delicacy of the thread of communication that characterize—yet also in certain circumstances bedevil—the relationship between man and woman and, more particularly, husband and wife. Equally, he seems intuitively to grasp, and to be able to evoke with tact and controlled inference, that sense of the enduringly passionate undercurrent in successful love relationships: a passion which persists despite tangible and external vicissitudes. These are qualities which make *The Country of Marriage* such an impressive achievement; they also contribute significantly to the impact of *The Sundowners* which, for all its picaresque and unsophisticated sprawl, remains one of Cleary's most engaging successes—a Lawsonian picture of, among other things, a marriage weathering crises which are partly induced by the very nature of the "place", the bush environment.

But the full range of Jon Cleary's work reveals emphatically that action not only suits his pen—he describes scenes of action with enormous zest and tough economy—but also his temperament. He is attracted to movement, suspense, resolution through decisive action. And it is this preoccupation which comes to predominate in his work. *Justin Bayard* is one of several novels in which conflicting forces in Cleary's artistic sensibility become evident: on the one hand there is a concern with marital tension, with the power of love and sexual passion to surmount external difficulties and with the alienating, corrosive effect of the outback upon the personality. On the other hand though, the book is a disguised "country house thriller": the protagonists are virtually marooned in a homestead while evil and ultimately murder work among them. Violent action decides or overwhelms most of the personal dilemmas. *The Climate of Courage*, immediately preceding *Justin Bayard*, is similarly preoccupied with marital success and failure and the growth of love despite daunting obstacles. But again, it is action—a brilliantly narrated episode of the New Guinea campaign—which resolves the human issues, not by allowing them to be worked out, but, as it were, by default.

Action and adventure, flavoured by exotic or dramatic geographical settings, thus emerge as important distinguishing features of Cleary's considerable output. A characteristic Cleary "hero" evolves: a man of action plagued by an inner tentativeness, a fear of decision and responsibility. Paddy Carmody (*The Sundowners*), Vern Radcliffe (*The Climate of Courage*), Justin Bayard, Paul Tancred (*Season of Doubt*), Jack Marquis (*The Pulse of Danger*), Adam Nash (*The Country of Marriage*) are all recognizably in this mould. And in *almost* every case, danger and action provide the crucial test, the decisive resolution.

Despite some falterings—occasional plot flaws, uneasiness at times with non-Australian characters, indebtedness to the suspense/thriller genre—Jon Cleary is undoubtedly a skilful teller especially talented in depicting swift or violent action. In may be, however, that his final reputation will rest most securely upon those novels in which his interest in the subtleties and vagaries of human relationships outweighs or controls the penchant for action.

—Brian Matthews

---

**CLOETE, (Edward Fairly) Stuart (Graham).** South African (born British). Born in Paris, 23 July 1897. Educated at Bilton Grange, Rugby; Lancing College, Sussex. Married Florence Eileen Horsman in 1918 (divorced, 1940); Mildred Elizabeth (Tiny) Ellison, 1941. Served in the King's Own Yorkshire Light Infantry, 1914–17, and in the Coldstream Guards, 1917 until his retirement because of wounds, 1925. Farmer and Rancher in South Africa, 1926–37, 1949–53. Trustee, South African Foundation. Recipient: National Institute of Arts and Letters Fellowship, 1957. Address: Box 164, Hermanus, South Africa.

PUBLICATIONS

Novels

*The Turning Wheels.*  London, Collins, and Boston, Houghton Mifflin, 1937.
*Watch for the Dawn.*  London, Collins, and Boston, Houghton Mifflin, 1939.
*The Hill of Doves.*  Boston, Houghton Mifflin, 1941; London, Collins, 1942.
*Christmas in Matabeleland.*  New York, Doubleday, 1942.
*Congo Song.*  London, Collins, and Boston, Houghton Mifflin, 1943.
*The Curve and the Tusk: A Novel of Change among Elephants and Men.*  Boston, Houghton Mifflin, 1952; London, Collins, 1953.
*Mamba.*  Boston, Houghton Mifflin, 1956; London, Collins, 1957.
*The Mask.*  Boston, Houghton Mifflin, 1957; London, Collins, 1958.
*Gazella.*  London, Collins, and Boston, Houghton Mifflin, 1958.
*The Fiercest Heart.*  Boston, Houghton Mifflin, 1960; London, Collins, 1961.
*Rags of Glory.*  London, Collins, and New York, Doubleday, 1963.
*The Thousand and One Nights of Jean Macaque.*  New York, Simon and Schuster, 1965.
*The Abductors.*  New York, Simon and Schuster, 1966; London, Collins, 1970.
*How Young They Died.*  London, Collins, 1969.

Short Stories

*The Soldiers' Peaches and Other African Stories.*  London, Collins, and Boston, Houghton Mifflin, 1959.
*The Silver Trumpet and Other African Stories.*  London, Collins, 1961.
*The Looking Glass and Other African Stories.*  London, Collins, 1963.
*The Honey Bird and Other African Stories.*  London, Collins, 1964.

*The Writing on the Wall and Other African Stories.* London, Collins, 1967.
*Three White Swans and Other Stories.* London, Collins, 1971.

Uncollected Short Story

"My Friend William", in *Tonkees Adam* (Durban), 1970.

Verse

*The Young Men and the Old.* Boston, Houghton Mifflin, 1941.

Other

*Yesterday Is Dead* (sociology). New York, Smith and Durrell, 1940.
*Against These Three: A Biography of Paul Kruger, Cecil Rhodes, and Lobengula, Last King of the Matabele.* Boston, Houghton Mifflin, 1945; as *African Portraits: A Biography of Paul Kruger, Cecil Rhodes, and Lobengula, Last King of the Matabele*, London, Collins, 1946.
*The Third Way* (sociology). Boston, Houghton Mifflin, 1947.
*The African Giant: The Story of a Journey.* Boston, Houghton Mifflin, 1955; London, Collins, 1956.
*Storm over Africa: A Study of the Mau Mau Rebellion, Its Causes, Effects, and Implications in Africa South of the Sahara.* Cape Town, Culemborg, 1956.
*West with the Sun.* London, Collins, and New York, Doubleday, 1962.
*South Africa: The Land, Its People and Achievements.* Johannesburg, Da Gama, 1969.
*A Victorian Son* (autobiography). London, Collins, 1971.

Manuscript Collection: Boston University Library.

Stuart Cloete comments:

Most of my work deals with Africa south of the Sahara. The non-fiction is reporting and commentary.

In fiction my aim has been to entertain since I see the novelist as primarily a story teller in the old tradition, the tradition of the campfire and the spinner of yarns. My only novel with a theme was *The Abductors*—an effort to arouse people to the fact that a world-wide traffic in women continues to exist. In a world torn apart by hatred and dissension, it seems to me that a novel should provide an escape from the present and transport the reader into other situations, where he can, for a while at least, lose himself and forget his worries.

I am not particularly intellectual or literary. Having left school at 17 and gone straight into the army and war, such education as I have has been through my association with men, women and events, being like every other man a product of what I have seen and lived through. A writer only differs from other people in his sensitivity to such experiences. These sensations filtered through the mind become stories over which the author often enough has very little real control. Minor characters take major and unforeseen parts, as occurred with Elsie in *Rags of Glory*.

Though I am a writer, I should have preferred to be a painter, particularly of horses, women, and flowers. That is to say, of beauty. Again, as in my writing, an escape from the sordid and ugly into what many would call the sentimental and banal. My joys have come from women and animals—horses, dogs, and cats in particular—and this shows in my work.

I was brought up to believe in heroes, to believe in love, in beauty—all very old-fashioned today. I like stories with a beginning, a middle and an end. I believe with Freud that sex, or sublimated sex, is the driving force of life. I find it difficult to believe in any established religion or dogma, or in the existence of a benevolent God, but remain aware of a power that transcends man's comprehension.

In much of what I have written about Africa in *The African Giant* and about world conditions in *Yesterday Is Dead* and *The Third Way*, I have unfortunately been proved right on most counts, though the events I foretold came more swiftly than I expected.

Finally, as a man I am very happy, but as a human being I am in despair, as I see no answer to overpopulation or pollution. These views are, I think, all apparent in my work.

\*        \*        \*

Stuart Cloete is a prolific novelist and an indefatigable story-teller. Most of his novels take place in Africa, which he knows extremely well and to which he is deeply attached. At various stages in his career he wrote historical novels about the Boers of South Africa. Together these novels form a vast epic retracing the country's history from 1815 to the end of the Boer War, chronicled in his most ambitious work *Rags of Glory*. They explain to some extent the complex tensions in contemporary South Africa. Though not blind to their shortcomings, Cloete is very sympathetic to the Boers, their fierce individualism and courage. Stimulated by their fanatical love of independence to withdraw from hardly conquered land or to fight the English, who harassed from the South, meeting with the resistance of Africans who were pressing down from the North, they suffered such hardships individually from one generation to another that hatred was inevitable. Though Africans are seldom present in his novels as individuals, Cloete's view of history is, on the whole, unprejudiced. He presents the wars fought by the Boers as ineluctable clashes of cultures with the Africans on the one hand and the English on the other, in many ways similar to the wars fought by the American pioneers.

Most of Cloete's novels are built on a similar pattern, and the psychology of his characters is fairly simple. The males are led by two ruling motives: love in its different guises and the need to assert their virility through courage or violence; the females are exclusively concerned with the fulfilment of their womanhood. For this reason the characters in the South African novels tend to be stereotyped, all the more so as their virtues and vices are shown to be largely hereditary. Yet they are also memorable because they are flesh and blood people living through extraordinary adventures. Good and evil are seen as relative notions; not justice but blind chance rules the world, and the best human beings can do is to fulfil themselves according to their nature. In this respect, men are not so different from animals as they are willing to acknowledge, while the latter often prove more capable of psychological subtlety than is generally assumed. A masterly illustration of this view is to be found in *The Curve and the Tusk*, a novel about elephant hunting in Mozambique.

A prominent documentary trend supports Cloete's vision of life as an endless cycle of reproduction and destruction in which man's participation is only relative. All life, whether human, animal, vegetable or mineral, is interdependent; everything is part of everything else, and all things merge imperceptibly into each other. Though Cloete shows that civilization cannot be halted, his African novels suggest that, except in cities, the white man has so far made no real impact south of the Sahara. He has destroyed much and attempted to leave his stamp on the African continent, but most of it remains untamed and is perhaps untamable. Cloete's descriptions of the multifaced and mysterious "African giant" are among the best parts of his fiction.

Only a few of Stuart Cloete's novels are purely imaginary. Among his latest works *How Young They Died* is a story of initiation into warfare and love in the First World War, while *The Abductors*, a novel about sex and morals in Victorian England, is based on an actual case of white slavery. Whatever its subject, his fiction is highly readable and no doubt appeals to a large public.

—Hena Maes-Jelinek

---

**COATES, Robert M(yron).** American. Born in New Haven, Connecticut, 6 April 1897. Educated at Yale University, New Haven, B.A. 1919. Served in the United States Navy, 1917–18. Married Elsa Kirpal in 1927 (divorced, 1946); Astrid Peters, 1946; has one child. Art Critic for *The New Yorker* magazine. Member, National Institute of Arts and Letters. Address: R.F.D., Old Chatham, New York, U.S.A.

PUBLICATIONS

Novels

    *The Eater of Darkness.* Paris, Contact Editions, 1926; New York, Macaulay, 1929.
    *Yesterday's Burdens.* New York, Macaulay, 1933.
    *The Bitter Season.* New York, Harcourt Brace, 1946; London, Gollancz, 1949.
    *Wisteria Cottage.* New York, Harcourt Brace, 1948; London, Gollancz, 1949.
    *The Farther Shore.* New York, Harcourt Brace, 1955; as *Darkness of the Day*, London, Gollancz, 1955.

Short Stories

    *All the Year Round: A Book of Stories.* New York, Harcourt Brace, 1943.
    *The Hour after Westerly and Other Stories.* New York, Harcourt Brace, 1957.
    *Accident at the Inn and Other Stories.* New York, Harcourt Brace, and London, Gollancz, 1957.
    *The Man Just Ahead of You.* New York, Sloane, 1964; London, Gollancz, 1965.

Other

    *The Outlaw Years: The History of the Land Pirates of the Natchez Trace.* New York, Macaulay, 1930.
    *The View from Here* (autobiography). New York, Harcourt Brace, 1960.
    *Beyond the Alps: A Summer in the Italian Hill Towns.* New York, Sloane, 1961; London, Gollancz, 1962.
    *South of Rome: A Spring and Summer in Southern Italy and Sicily.* New York, Sloane, 1966.

    Translator, *Discoverer: A New Narrative of the Life and Hazardous Adventures of the Genoese, Christopher Columbus*, by André de Hevesy. New York, Macaulay, 1928; London, Butterworth, 1929.

\*     \*     \*

Through his long career as novelist, short story writer and essayist, as well as art critic for *The New Yorker*, Robert M. Coates is generally assessed as a "civilized" writer. His calm, controlled, urbane works—particularly his stories—peel back the well-tailored surfaces of character to reveal, not the shockingly indecent, but rather decency in dismay at its own inadequacy.

In his 1955 novel, *The Farther Shore*, Coates observes that civilized life provides man with "many layers of protection" so that insanity, which boils up from beneath, has "all the more distance to go and resistance to meet before reaching the surface." Yet in general his works are not studies in the abnormal. (A well-received exception is his psychological thriller, *Wisteria Cottage*, with its series of brutal murders.) Coates more often studies the layered complexity of ordinary, modern, city-dwelling man. New York and its suburbs are his favorite settings.

Sketchy or episodic in plot, Coates' stories are lightly laced together by minute revelations of character. Increment of detail draws stories toward conclusion, as in "The Man Who Vanished" (from *The Hour after Westerly*) where the shy, inadequate, 47-year-old porcelain dealer, Charlie Ballantine, literally fades out of competitive real life and into the fantasy world of youthful memory. Sporadic but increasing invisibility becomes the metaphor for personal nonentity until Charlie completely slips his protective covering of job, marriage and social life—and disappears.

Coates reiterates the predictability of the unpredictable in man again and again, sometimes spelling it out as in the opening of his "A Friendly Game of Cards": "One of the first things you learn—and one of the last things too, though by that time it may be too late—is that there are no hard and fast rules for human conduct. You can't judge by appearances . . ."

In his first full-length work, *The Eater of Darkness*, Coates in 1926 produced what Ford Madox Ford hailed as a Dadaist novel, though more likely it is a burlesque of the standard mystery novel with kaleidoscopic shifts of scene and a scientist-hero who commits twenty murders by radio. His second novel, *Yesterday's Burden*, although convoluted in style, follows a restless young Everyman in New York. His later novels are more conventional in subject and treatment—the emotional plight of an ordinary, non-combatant American in World War II in *The Bitter Season*, and a slowly disenchanted Hungarian-American's loosening grip on life in *The Farther Shore*.

Coates' stories, collected in *All the Year Round, The Hour after Westerly* and *The Man Just Ahead of You* as well as his uncollected stories from *The New Yorker, Esquire* and other magazines, constitute his most enduring works.

He has also written a popular history of the Natchez land pirates, *The Outlaw Years*; and two descriptive travel books on Italy, *Beyond the Alps* and *South of Rome*. His relaxed, autobiographical *The View from Here* describes the gentle personal landscape of his own childhood and youth in America and abroad.

—Marian Pehowski

---

**COHEN, Leonard (Norman).** Canadian. Born in Montreal, Quebec, 21 September 1934. Educated at McGill University, Montreal, B.A. 1955; Columbia University, New York. Composer and Singer: has given concerts in Canada, the United States and Europe. Recipient: McGill University Literary Award, 1956; Canada Council Award, 1960; Quebec Literary Award, 1964. D.L., Dalhousie University, Halifax, Nova Scotia, 1971. Address: c/o Machat and Kronfeld, 1501 Broadway, 30th Floor, New York, New York 10036, U.S.A.

PUBLICATIONS

Novels

> *The Favorite Game.*   New York, Viking Press, and London, Secker and Warburg, 1963.
> *Beautiful Losers.*   New York, Viking Press, and Toronto, McClelland and Stewart, 1966; London, Cape, 1970.

Verse

> *Let Us Compare Mythologies.*   Montreal, McGill Poetry Series, 1956.
> *The Spice-Box of Earth.*   Toronto, McClelland and Stewart, 1961; New York, Viking Press, 1965; London, Cape, 1971.
> *Flowers for Hitler.*   Toronto, McClelland and Stewart, 1964.
> *Parasites of Heaven.*   Toronto, McClelland and Stewart, 1966.
> *Selected Poems, 1956–1968.*   New York, Viking Press, and Toronto, McClelland and Stewart, 1968; London, Cape, 1969.
> *Leonard Cohen's Song Book.*   New York, Collier, 1969.

> Recordings: *The Songs of Leonard Cohen*, Columbia, 1968; *Songs from a Room*, Columbia, 1969; *Songs of Love and Hate*, Columbia, 1971.

\*       \*       \*

Few modern authors have presented critics so clearly as Leonard Cohen does with the problem of how to regard the writer who personifies the Zeitgeist. With astonishing rapidity, in the mid-1960s, Cohen passed from the obscurity of a romantic Canadian poet into the celebrity of an international pop singer who seemed to exemplify the decade's popular culture.

Time will decide how far, when fashion abandons him, Cohen's real qualities will sustain his standing as a writer. What the critic perceives even now is that the factors which made Cohen popular are those he shares with modish culture: conventionalism masquerading as independence; a slightly acrid romanticism merging into a solipsistic sentimentality; an echoing of past movements like the Decadence, Art Nouveau and Dada, which elevated style above substance. The fiction such movements have produced has usually been strained and eccentric. *The Picture of Dorian Gray*, the novels of Huysmans and, later, Raymond Queneau, are examples.

Cohen stands in this company; his novels, *The Favorite Game* and *Beautiful Losers*, are interesting examples of black romance, and though *Beautiful Losers* projects a bizarre kind of splendour, as the novels of poets often do, it is a work of solitary fantasy that stands apart from the main stream of fiction in our time.

A shallowness of feeling, a solipsistic passionlessness masquerading as stylized passion, infects almost all of Cohen's writings. It is linked with the Pygmalion urge that is a dominant theme in his novels, exemplified in F's delusions of godly creativeness in *Beautiful Losers* and in the fantasies of occult power that haunt Breavman throughout *The Favorite Game*. "I want to touch people like a magician," he says to one of his mistresses, "to change them or hurt them, leave my brand, make them beautiful."

To be beautiful, and to be a loser; both desires find their places in the romantic fancy; their juxtaposition in the title of Cohen's second novel is neither accidental nor inappropriate. The solipsist creates beauty within the mind and that is his only real world; he loses because the actual world does not correspond with his visionary world yet impinges on his life. F., the quasi-hero of *Beautiful Losers*, lives in flamboyant style; he is killed, in true decadent tradition, by syphilis.

Cohen's first novel, *The Favorite Game*, tells the development of a rich Montreal Jewish boy into a poet and folk singer; the resemblances to Cohen's life are close enough to justify an assumption that this is the autobiographical novel with which many writers make their first sacrifice to the muse of fiction. *The Favorite Game* is an episodic work, its shuffled time sequences strung along the thread of Breavman's affair with the all-American girl, Shell, most recent of his mistresses; the account of his experience becomes a kind of dialogue with Shell, from whom in the end he parts, as he has parted from her predecessors. His life has been measured off by relationships with girls, yet in none has Breavman been able to evade in passion that observing mind which is the alien participant.

Parallel to these uninvolved liaisons runs the continuing current of Breavman's friendship with Krantz, which survives all the broken love affairs. But the moment of real involvement comes when, working as a staff member in a Jewish summer camp, Breavman encounters the boy Martin, "a divine idiot" with a mathematical mania who spends his time counting grass blades and pine needles, and dies grotesquely when he is crushed by a bulldozer while killing and counting mosquitoes in a marsh.

Martin represents the other pole in Cohen's world to profane love. He is—albeit in disguise—of the company of saints, those exalted and obsessed ones to whom Cohen is always drawn. Destroyed saints appear often in his poems; Martin is one of them. Yet he dies at the peak of joy, rating his days at "98 percent"—and the joyful saint is always present in Cohen's world:

> Something about him so loves the world that he gives himself to the laws of gravity and chance. Far from flying with the angels, he traces with the fidelity of a seismograph needle the state of the solid bloody landscape. His house is dangerous and finite, but he is at home in the world. He can love the shapes of human beings, the fine and twisted shapes of the human heart.
>
> (*Beautiful Losers*)

To the Cohen alive to the call of sainthood as the complement of earthly love, the world takes on dual aspects. Breavman, inexperienced, sees decay everywhere. "The works themselves were corruption, the monuments were made of worms." But in *Beautiful Losers*, when "I" puts the classic decadent point about "the diamonds in the shit," F. replies, "It's all diamond."

It is the unity in duality of the erotic and the spiritual that provides the bridge from *The Favorite Game* to *Beautiful Losers*. But, though there are many ways in which—in details of plot and imagery—the earlier novel anticipates its more ambitious successor, *Beautiful Losers* moves into a quite different category. Young artist novels can only be written once, and Cohen makes his escape in the same direction as Joyce, in the aestheticist reconstruction of life. *Beautiful Losers* is very much a work of artifice, and makes no concession to verisimilitude.

Of the three parts into which this novel is divided, the first contains the erratic musings of the onanist "I". Edith, his wife who has committed bizarre suicide, and F., the megalomaniac lover of them both, move in memory within a pattern which F. describes when he declares, "I was your journey and you were my journey and Edith was our holy star." Whether they have ever existed is not important, since they are absorbed in a timeless dream continuum where they are no more and no less real, no more and no less distant, than the Mohawk saint, Catherine Tekakwitha, three centuries dead, whose monumental holy masochism fascinates both F. and "I". F. becomes an industrialist who uses his unmanned factory for playing games, a member of Parliament quickly discredited, a leader of the Quebec underground, but these achievements are no more substantial than the grandiose fantasies which, one eventually realises, are the products of a brain rotted by the pox.

This becomes evident in the wild inventions of the "Long Letter from F"; in the central episode described in this document, F. and Edith, after packing "I" off on an absurd research assignment, set off for Argentina with a bag of erotic devices, and indulge in a long orgy in which they are ravished in turn by the "Danish vibrator" (a machine that develops and fulfils desires of its own) and finally bathe "three in a tub" with a waiter who provides human soap and turns out to be Hitler in exile.

Book III, an "Epilogue in the Third Person", closes with a description of the last dissolving days of "I", who has learnt to combine F's debauchery and Catherine Tekakwitha's self-mortifications in a regressive tree-house existence; he is saint and sinner, at once himself and F. and Edith, and he disappears in a puff of ambiguity.

*Beautiful Losers* is filled with interesting experiments, some of which belong to poetry rather than fiction; indeed there are passages which are actually concealed verse. But the burlesque element is overdone and the savage sexual comedy quickly palls. As a novel the book has no functioning unity; Cohen lacks the architectonic power with which Céline, for example, transformed similar material into self-consistent and convincing works of fiction.

—George Woodcock

---

**COLE, Barry.** British. Born in Woking, Surrey, 13 November 1936. Served in the Royal Air Force for two years. Married Rita Linihan in 1958; has three children. Worked in the Central Office of Information, London, 1965–70. Northern Arts Fellow in Literature, Universities of Newcastle upon Tyne and Durham, 1970–72. Address: c/o Jonathan Clowes Ltd., 20 New Cavendish Street, London W.1., England.

PUBLICATIONS

Novels

> *A Run Across the Island.* London, Methuen, 1968.
> *Joseph Winter's Patronage.* London, Methuen, 1969.
> *The Search for Rita.* London, Methuen, 1970.
> *The Giver.* London, Methuen, 1971.
> *Doctor Fielder's Common Sense.* London, Methuen, 1972.

Verse

> *Blood Ties.* London, Turret, 1967.
> *Ulysses in the Town of Coloured Glass.* London, Turret, 1968.
> *Moonsearch.* London, Methuen, 1968.
> *The Visitors.* London, Methuen, 1970.
> *Vanessa in the City.* London, Trigram, 1971.

Barry Cole comments:

I have no general statement to make about my novels, but the epigraphs which precede *The Giver* may say more than any collected exegeses:

*And down I set, abruptly I believe; what I had heard all in my head.* (Fielding).

*Aesthetics cannot exist because an artist never solves any problems except those which are entirely of his own creation.* (Jean-Francois Revel).

*The thought of the epistolary diary had long interested and troubled me.* (Nabokov).

*Everyone should read a book; to read two books shows intelligence; to read three is showing off.* (Rita Linihan, 15).

*A poet is the most unpoetical of anything in existence, because he has no identity; he is continually in for, and filling, some other body . . .* (Keats).

*No Costaguanero had ever learned to question the eccentricities of a military force.* (Conrad).

*He spoke in English and pronounced even the name "Boris" as if it were English.* (Turgenev).

*. . . getting the disorder of one's own mind in order . . .* (Yeats).

*Let not the critic ask how Corporal Trim could come by all this . . .* (Sterne).

*The Commissioner gazed at them with suspicion, almost with revulsion. Then he fell to laughing.* (Jorge Luis Borges).

*There is something funny about the human condition, and civilized intelligence makes fun of its own ideas.* (Saul Bellow).

*But Hetty's face had a language that transcended her feelings.* (George Eliot).

*Is it only that? said the willow-wren;*

  *It's that as well, said the stars.* (W. H. Auden).

*Themes and thimes and habit reburns. To flame in you.* (Joyce).

*"Were you drunk?" asked Pleasant.* (Dickens).

\*          \*          \*

Barry Cole has so far produced four novels. These novels have one striking thing in common. They are extremely well-written. It may, of course, be said that to write well is not so much a virtue in a novelist as a necessity. Yet the fact is that the majority of novelists lack Barry Cole's gifts of verbal precision, wit, exact ear for conversation, and his feeling for the elastic possibilities of language, the way it can be stretched and twisted to provide unexpected meanings and insights. No doubt the fact that he is also a very fine poet accounts for much of his virtue as a writer of prose, but this should not be taken to mean that he writes poetic prose. On the contrary: his style is as free as possible from those encrustations of adjective and epithet that identify "fine" writing.

*A Run Across the Island* is a brilliant *tour de force* and for it Mr. Cole invented a form that he has found it possible to use for all his subsequent novels. Although by far the larger part of the novel is seen through the eyes of its hero, Robert Haydon, there is no straightforward narrative or division into chapters. Instead, we move about in time, each remembered detail or incident given a section, small or large, that is juxtaposed against others. By the end of the novel, however, the different incidents have been worked out and together compose one man's life, and it has been so resourcefully done that we have a much more *real* sense of a man's identity than we would have through a straightforward narrative.

The major theme of *A Run Across the Island* is, perhaps, of loneliness, of the difficulties of establishing relationships, of the slippery impermanence of friendship and love. And this theme is also present in the next novel. *Joseph Winter's Patronage* is, however, very different from *A Run Across the Island* in that its characters are almost exclusively old people. Indeed, the novel is mostly set in an Old People's Home, and the novelist manages with great sensitiveness to create the feeling of the Home itself and of its inhabitants. *Joseph Winter's Patronage* is the most touching and warmly sympathetic novel that Barry Cole has so far written.

By contrast, *The Search for Rita* is the most glittering. It is an extremely elegant novel, but the elegance is not one that marks how far its author stands fastidiously aloof from life. It is rather that the mess of life is met by a keen-eyed wit that can be ironic, self-deprecatory, satiric and bawdy by turns. Style means everything in a novel of this kind, and the novelist's style does not let him down.

Barry Cole has been called one of the most promising of our younger novelists. It seems better to adapt a line of Robert Graves and say that already there is nothing promised he has not performed.

—John Lucas

---

**COLLIER, John.** British. Born in London, 3 May 1901. Educated privately. Poetry Editor of *Time and Tide*, London, in the 1920's and 1930's. Scriptwriter in the United States; lived in France. Now lives in London. Address: c/o A. D. Peters and Company, 10 Buckingham Street, London W.C.2, England.

PUBLICATIONS

Novels

> *His Monkey Wife; or, Married to a Chimp.* London, Davies, 1930; New York, Appleton, 1931.
> *Full Circle: A Tale.* New York, Appleton, 1933; as *Tom's A-Cold*, London, Macmillan, 1933.
> *Defy the Foul Fiend; or, The Misadventures of a Heart.* London, Macmillan, and New York, Knopf, 1934.

Short Stories

> *No Traveller Returns.* London, White Owl Press, 1931.
> *Epistle to a Friend.* London, Ulysses Bookshop, 1931.
> *Green Thoughts.* London, Joiner and Steele, 1932.
> *The Devil and All.* London, Nonesuch Press, 1934.
> *Variation on a Theme.* London, Grayson, 1935.
> *Presenting Moonshine: Stories.* London, Macmillan, and New York, Viking Press, 1941.
> *A Touch of Nutmeg and More Unlikely Stories.* New York, Heritage Press, 1943.
> *Fancies and Goodnights.* New York, Doubleday, 1951.
> *Pictures in the Fire.* London, Hart Davis, 1958.

Verse

> *Gemini: Poems.* London, Harmsworth, 1931.

Play

> *Wet Saturday.* New York, One-Act, n.d.

Other

*Just the Other Day: An Informal History of Britain since the War*, with Iain Lang. London, Hamish Hamilton, and New York, Harper, 1932.

Editor, *Scandal and Incredulities*, by John Aubrey. London, Davies, and New York, Appleton, 1931.

Bibliography: in *Ten Contemporaries*, 2nd series, by John Gawsworth, London, Joiner and Steele, 1933.

\*     \*     \*

John Collier is a worker in fantasy and has exercised his talents chiefly in short tales. The tales usually commence with the depiction of a character in an ordinary modern situation: a man in the solitude of a great city or the even more grim solitude of an unsatisfactory marriage or that solitude experienced by a young man who has not yet found his direction in life. But in almost all the tales there is a swerve which transforms the recognizable situation into one that people do not ordinarily experience. There is an encounter with a supernatural messenger, usually diabolic, as in "Halfway to Hell." Or, as in "Green Thoughts", a man, his sister, and a cat are caught up in a growing plant. Or a man is tricked by a servant genie into the bottle from which the genie has been freed ("Bottle Party"). The reader of Collier's stories comes to expect—and justly—that the texture of ordinary experience will quickly become very odd indeed. Even in stories which lack this characteristic element, e.g., "De Mortuis", a husband saddled with an unsuitable wife receives from grotesque chance circumstance instruction on how to dispose of her. Or a man who is enamoured of a young woman in almost unshakeable slumber ("Sleeping Beauty") discovers that his sleeping princess is not the creature he dreamed of—temporarily awakened, she is revealed to be a vulgar shrew—and allows her to sink into sleep again; he makes his living exhibiting her to crowds.

Such stories have plots and materials that easily remind one of current "black humor" by John Hawkes and John Barth. But these younger writers employ their swerves into incoherence to reveal the irrational abyss upon which ordinary experience rests; the result is, for most readers, a horrified questioning of the texture of experience that they have constructed for themselves. In contrast, the fantastic world built piece by piece in John Collier's succession of tales does not call into question the ability of either author or reader to master *his* world. The emotional infatuations and the baseless hopes of the characters Collier creates are plainly not those of Collier himself or of the cultivated readers who make up his audience. Indeed, the Collier characters "ask for" what happens to them. For example, the disaster that overtakes the stupid, stern father of "Thus I Refute Beelzy" (he is carried off by the diabolic creature whose existence he has denied) is right and just; nor is the reader under any impression that the fate of the stupid father might well be his. Instead, the Collier stories only confirm the sensible reader's moral and intellectual well-being. Conventional self-assurance is neither threatened by Collier's fantasy, as it is by the oddities of "black humor", nor confirmed. That self-assurance is simply amused and diverted by strange events which clearly lie outside the confines of sensible, enlightened experience.

Collier's entertaining stories are done with a brevity and and elegance of language which stir admiration. The element of surprise is exploited fully, particularly in the brief conclusions that both disconcert and delight expectation. There is no waste motion in Collier's expeditions into worlds of experience that are of no real concern to well-insulated readers.

—Harold H. Watts

**COMFORT, Alex(ander).** British. Born in London, 10 February 1920. Educated at Highgate School, London; Trinity College, Cambridge, M.B., B.Ch. 1944, M.A. 1945; The London Hospital, D.C.H. 1945; Ph.D. (biochemistry) 1949, D.Sc. (gerontology) 1963; Member of the Royal College of Surgeons; Licentiate of the Royal College of Physicians. Refused military service in World War II. Married Ruth Muriel Harris in 1943; has one child. Editor, *Lyra, New Roads*, and *Poetry Folios*, in the early 1940's. House Physician, The London Hospital, 1944; Resident Medical Officer, Royal Waterloo Hospital, London, 1944–45. Lecturer in Physiology, 1945–51, Honorary Research Associate, Department of Zoology, since 1951, Director of the Medical Research Group on the Biology of Ageing, 1966–70, and Director of Research in Gerontology since 1970, University College, London. President, British Society for Research on Ageing, 1967. Recipient: Ciba Foundation Prize, 1958; Karger Memorial Prize in Gerontology, 1969. Address: University College, Gower Street, London WC1E 6BT, England.

PUBLICATIONS

Novels

   *The Silver River: Being the Diary of a Schoolboy in the South Atlantic.* London, Chapman and Hall, 1937.
   *No Such Liberty.* London, Chapman and Hall, 1941.
   *The Almond Tree: A Legend.* London, Chapman and Hall, 1942.
   *The Powerhouse.* London, Routledge, 1944; New York, Viking Press, 1945.
   *On This Side Nothing.* London, Routledge, 1948; New York, Viking Press, 1949.
   *A Giant's Strength.* London, Routledge, and New York, British Book Service, 1952.
   *Come Out to Play.* London, Eyre and Spottiswoode, 1961.

Short Stories

   *Letters from an Outpost.* London, Routledge, 1947.

Plays

   *Into Egypt: A Miracle Play.* London, Grey Walls Press, 1942.
   *Cities of the Plain: A Democratic Melodrama.* London, Grey Walls Press, 1943.

Play produced on television.

Verse

   *France and Other Poems.* London, Favil Press, 1941.
   *Three New Poets*, with Roy McFadden and Ian Seraillier. London, Grey Walls Press, 1942.
   *A Wreath for the Living.* London, Routledge, 1942.
   *Elegies.* London, Routledge, 1944.
   *The Song of Lazarus.* Barnet, Hertfordshire, Poetry Folios, and New York, Viking Press, 1945.
   *The Signal to Engage.* London, Routledge, 1946.
   *And All But He Departed.* London, Routledge, 1951.

*Haste to the Wedding*. London, Eyre and Spottiswoode, 1962; Chester Springs, Pennsylvania, Dufour, 1964.

Other

*Art and Social Responsibility: Lectures on the Ideology of Romanticism*. London, Grey Walls Press, 1947.
*The Novel and Our Time*. Letchworth, Hertfordshire, Phoenix House, and Denver, Swallow, 1948.
*Barbarism and Sexual Freedom: Six Lectures on the Sociology of Sex from the Standpoint of Anarchism*. London, Freedom Press, 1948.
*First Year Physiological Techniques*. London and New York, Staples Press, 1948.
*The Pattern of the Future*. London, Routledge, and New York, Macmillan, 1949.
*Authority and Delinquency in the Modern State: A Criminological Approach to the Problem of Power*. London, Routledge, 1950.
*Sexual Behaviour in Society*. London, Duckworth, and New York, Viking Press, 1950; revised edition, Duckworth, 1963; as *Sex in Society*, New York, Citadel Press, 1966.
*The Biology of Senescence*. London, Routledge, and New York, Rinehart, 1956; revised edition, Routledge, 1964; as *Aging: The Biology of Senescence*, New York, Holt Rinehart, 1964.
*Darwin and the Naked Lady: Discursive Essays on Biology and Art*. London, Routledge, 1961; New York, Braziller, 1962.
*The Process of Ageing*. London, Weidenfeld and Nicolson, 1965.
*The Nature of Human Nature*. New York, Harper, 1965; as *Nature and Human Nature*, London, Weidenfeld and Nicolson, 1966.
*The Anxiety Makers: Some Curious Preoccupations of the Medical Profession*. London, Nelson, 1967.

Editor, *History of Erotic Art, I*. London, Weidenfeld and Nicolson, and New York, Putnam, 1969.

Translator, with Allan Ross Macdougall, *The Triumph of Death*, by C. F. Ramuz. London, Routledge, 1946.
Translator, *Koka Shastra*. London, Allen and Unwin, 1964; New York, Stein and Day, 1965.

Bibliography: "Alexander Comfort: A Bibliography in Progress" by D. Callaghan, in *West Coast Review* (Burnaby, British Columbia), 1969.

Critical Essays: *The Freedom of Poetry* by Derek Stanford, London, Falcon Press, 1947; two essays by Wayne Burns, "The Scientific Humanism of Alex Comfort", in *The Humanist* (London), November-December 1951, and "Kafka and Alex Comfort", in the *Arizona Quarterly* (Tucson), Summer 1952; "The Anarchism of Alex Comfort" by John Ellerby, "Sex, Kicks and Comfort" by Charles Radcliffe, and "Alex Comfort's Art and Scope" by Harold Drasdo, all in *Anarchy* (London), November 1963; "Alex Comfort as Novelist" by John Doheny in *Limbo* (Vancouver), November 1964.

\*      \*      \*

During the Second World War Alex Comfort established a name for himself as a critic, poet and playwright concerned with expounding an ethic and aesthetic of freedom, a morality of the Good Samaritan, and a policy of "direct action" and "mutual aid". The leading anarcho-pacifist of his own generation in letters, he presented his ideas through his fiction in such novels as *No Such Liberty*, *The Powerhouse* and, later, *On This Side Nothing*. Since his pacifism and anarchism, however, derive from prior attitudes of pessimism and idealism, and since these latter attitudes are fully expressed in his early novel *The Almond Tree*, it is as well to consider this first.

For a certain type of mind, the pathos of life resides in recognizing the unattainable while helplessly committed, for all time, to the finite; and *The Almond Tree* may be regarded as an illustrated thesis upon this theme. Then, too, idealism in this novel is powerfully linked with pessimism, and references to *Ecclesiastes* and Solomon's doctrine of the vanity of all things is made quite explicit. The story (like most of the author's fiction) has a European setting. Pyotr, the patriarch, is very old and dying. Through the death of his son, his grape-farm has passed to his grand-daughter Teresa and her German husband—a fact which Pyotr resents but cannot alter. A family tyrant, though often kindly, Pyotr has constricted and warped the lives of his children who have found it difficult to break away from his parental possessiveness and authority. One by one they make their bid for freedom and independence, all of them in some sense failing. And, along with old Pyotr, all of them regard, or remember, the almond tree as a fixed symbol of beauty, the one constant in their world of flux, a visual—almost metaphysical—absolute. In this novel time and experience are seen as diminishing or destroying factors, giving rise to the pessimism which the characters respectively feel. On the other hand, the almond tree is equated with a feeling of idealism, a transcendental feature acting as a magnet or focus above the currents of mutability in which men's lives pass and flounder. In the vicious circle this novel traces—with its final return to the inevitable—there are certain parallels with Flaubert's great chronicle of emotional vanity *Sentimental Education*. There is, though, one difference in the conclusion of these novels. The defeatism in Flaubert implies a cynicism whereas defeat in Alex Comfort's fiction never quite severs the connection which its characters maintain—through the tree—with the ideal.

Of his anarcho-pacifist novels *The Powerhouse* is the most important. Set in occupied France, it preaches, through the words and actions of four young men, a message of civil disobedience and non-cooperation. "We are," remarks one of the characters, "the enemies of society, and we must learn disobedience. Then we shall probably inherit the earth by default when the maniacs have burnt each other to a cinder"; and again: "The weak do a great deal—every woman who hides a deserter, every clerk who doesn't scrutinize a pass, every worker who bungles a fuse saves somebody's life for a while." Seven years later, another novel *On This Side Nothing* again chose a wartime setting, and argued, in dramatic terms, the uncertain ethics of—in Auden's words—"the necessary murder."

In more recent years, Alex Comfort's libertarianism has operated in the field of sexological writing, and his novel *Come Out to Play* reflects this interest in terms of a satirical fantasy about a biologist Dr. George Goggins deeply learned in the knowledge of human mating habits.

—Derek Stanford

---

**CONDON, Richard (Thomas).** American. Born in New York City, 18 March 1915. Educated in New York public schools. Married Evelyn Hunt in 1938; has two children. Publicist in the American film industry for 21 years; Theatrical Producer, New York, 1951–52. Currently lives in Ireland. Address: c/o Harold Matson, 30 Rockefeller Plaza, New York, New York 10020, U.S.A.; or, c/o A. D. Peters, 10 Buckingham Street, Adelphi, London W.C.2, England.

PUBLICATIONS

Novels

The Oldest Confession.   New York, Appleton Century Crofts, 1958; London, Longman,
    1959.
The Manchurian Candidate.   New York, McGraw Hill, 1959; London, Joseph, 1960.
Some Angry Angel: A Mid-Century Faerie Tale.   New York, McGraw Hill, 1960;
    London, Joseph, 1961.
A Talent for Loving; or, The Great Cowboy Race.   New York, McGraw Hill, 1961;
    London, Joseph, 1963.
An Infinity of Mirrors.   New York, Random House, and London, Heinemann, 1964.
Any God Will Do.   New York, Random House, and London, Heinemann, 1966.
The Ecstasy Business.   New York, Dial Press, and London, Heinemann, 1967.
Mile High.   New York, Dial Press, and London, Heinemann, 1969.
The Vertical Smile.   New York, Dial Press, 1971; London, Weidenfeld and Nicolson,
    1972.

Plays

Men of Distinction (produced New York, 1953).

Screenplays: A Talent for Loving, 1965; The Summer Music, 1969; The Long Loud
Silence, 1970.

Manuscript Collection: Boston University Library.

                              *        *        *

    Mr. Condon brings to his fiction an acute sense of the importance of things, of objects;
great ability with the wheels-within-wheels plot; and a gargantuan love of the grotesque, the
exaggerated, and the absurd. It is natural, then, to talk about him in Hollywood terms, and
not only because—naturally enough—his best-known book, The Manchurian Candidate,
made, with only the most minor tinkering, as good a movie as it had been a book.
    The Manchurian Candidate is the world as screenplay, with somebody else writing every-
body's material. Even before Raymond realizes that he has been scripted by Yen Lo (in a
Manchurian research pavilion that has been put up like nothing so much as a movie set), he
knows that he is playing the sergeant, playing the war hero, and knows that his stepfather
is so much a character of other people's creation that there is no inside to the man at all. In
such a universe it seems correct and credible that Johnny Iselin, a bumbling right-wing caricature, should actually be doing the bidding of the Red Chinese; it even seems right, somehow,
that his wife, the wicked witch of the West, should turn out to be a right-winger using the
left-wingers to use the rightwingers. There are no real politics any more; there are only
script-writers. The sudden intrusion of Mrs. Iselin's use of drugs or her incestuous acts with
her son, or the outrageous melodrama of the conclusion—all things for which more conventional fiction might be justly criticised—fit perfectly into Condon's insane world. It is
difficult to decide whether it is American politics or the Hollywood eyeglass through which
we are forced to view them that takes the most cutting criticism.
    It is in a lesser-known but equally outrageous book, A Talent for Loving, that the satire of
the cinema world-view becomes most overt. The action takes place in Texas and Mexico,
where ranches are bigger than countries and ranch-houses may turn out to be Scottish castles

(just as one may discover London Bridge spanning a dry river); the gamblers gamble more, the barflies drink furniture polish without a quiver, and the people who love cheese can carry on about cheese for days on end. A Rabelaisian affection for things in excess, piled up *ad absurdum*, is married to the frontier American love of exaggeration and run through every cliche of the western film, so that the climactic scene, in which the Indians arrive just in time to save the train from the cavalry (which is charging in its underwear in order not to get its uniforms dirty) becomes one of the most consummately ridiculous scenes in recent fiction.

Like most of Condon's other fiction, the book is saved from sheer silliness by its tremendous gusto, which more often than not recalls the verbal excesses of Davy Crockett or the vitality of *Life on the Mississippi*; this gusto, the plot skill evident in *The Manchurian Candidate*, and the movie-world unreality of Condon's fiction, serve him well in his later books, in which he deals with the movies directly, the world of organized crime, and the spy business—but never, I think, as well as in the two books discussed above.

—Irving F. Foote

**CONNELL, Evan S(helby), Jr.** American. Born in Kansas City, Missouri, 17 August 1924. Educated at Dartmouth College, Hanover, New Hampshire, 1941–43; University of Kansas, Lawrence, 1946–47, A.B. 1947; Stanford University, California, 1947–48; Columbia University, New York, 1948–49. Served in the United States Navy, 1943–45. Editor, *Contact* magazine, Sausalito, California, 1960–65. Recipient: Saxton Fellowship, 1952; Guggenheim Fellowship, 1962; Rockefeller grant, 1967. Address: 2355 Polk Street, San Francisco, California, U.S.A.

PUBLICATIONS

Novels

Mrs. Bridge. New York, Viking Press, 1957; London, Heinemann, 1958.
The Patriot. New York, Viking Press, 1960; London, Heinemann, 1962.
Notes from a Bottle Found on the Beach at Carmel. New York, Viking Press, 1963; London, Heinemann, 1964.
The Diary of a Rapist. New York, Simon and Schuster, 1966; London, Heinemann, 1967.
Mr. Bridge. New York, Knopf, and London, Heinemann, 1969.

Short Stories

The Anatomy Lesson and Other Stories. New York, Viking Press, 1957; London, Heinemann, 1958.
At the Crossroads: Stories. New York, Simon and Schuster, 1965; London, Heinemann, 1966.

Other

Editor, *I Am a Lover*, by Jerry Stoll.    Sausalito, California, Angel Island Publications, 1961.
Editor, *Woman by Three*.    Menlo Park, California, Pacific Coast Publishers, 1969.

Manuscript Collection: Boston University Library.

Critical Study: "After Ground Zero" by Gus Blaisdell, in *New Mexico Quarterly* (Albuquerque), Summer 1966.

*        *        *

Evan S. Connell's *Anatomy Lesson* drew generous praise from reviewers for its mature craftsmanship and wide range of theme and technique. The short stories sounded the dominant motifs which the author's novels would later develop, and made clear his interest in mood and psychology. *Mrs. Bridge*, his first novel, grew directly from one of the earlier stories and remains his most satisfying work of fiction.

The highly episodic story of a midwestern housewife, *Mrs. Bridge* is noteworthy for Connell's masterful handling of tone. His heroine has led a triumphantly correct life, raising three children, supporting her lawyer husband in his career, and making all the correct social gestures, but she must face the last years of her life as a lonely widow. Despite the author's apparently matter-of-fact tone, beneath the surface a fine light of sympathy, wit and wisdom bathes the heroine. Mrs. Bridge is a triumph of ironic characterization, and the attentive reader perceives her as at once comic and pathetic, although she herself never realizes the significance of her plight.

*The Patriot* is a far more ambitious novel than *Mrs. Bridge*, a *Bildungsroman* that follows the life of a young aviation cadet—his military career, his postwar studies as an art student, and his frustrating relationship with a militaristic father. *The Patriot* is a discursive work and unnecessarily long; it is a convincing description of a young man's slow realization of his true emotional needs, but it lacks the unity of vision that informs *Mrs. Bridge*.

The spare and firmly disciplined prose of Connell's second collection of short stories, *At the Crossroads*, looks forward to his brilliant use of language in *The Diary of a Rapist*. The novel takes the form of a diary in which a young government clerk, married to a woman who rejects him, records his emotional needs and his growing sense of desperation, which leads him to seek refuge in hopeless ambitions and petty violence. By slow degrees the shadows of madness gather over his meditations, and a chilling air of probability haunts his disintegration.

*Mr. Bridge*, a companion volume to Connell's first novel, sets down brief fragments of experience from the lives of a typical suburban couple between the two world wars. More than one hundred separate episodes trace the outlines of their social propriety and the spiritual aridity of their lives together. Connell handles the technique so adroitly that his characters emerge with remarkable vividness and clarity. If at times they seem somewhat one-dimensional, the fault lies in themselves, not in their creator. A similar stylistic device is employed in *Notes from a Bottle Found on the Beach at Carmel*, a book based on "fragments of mankind's spiritual and intellectual past," arranged as a loose prose poem containing notes and ancedotes about the constancy of man's search for spiritual and psychic unity.

Connell has repeatedly chronicled the absurdity, the quiet agonies and the vanities of marginal men and women. Occasionally, out of boredom or despair, such characters are drawn into violence, but more often they are doomed to float along on a sea of tedious detail that slowly drowns them. In the hands of a less skillful or a less humane writer, such lives might appear merely comical, but Connell sees the pathos at the heart of their absurdity, and the meticulous prose in which their experiences are rendered raises them above the inconsequence that seems their birthright.

—David Galloway

---

**CONNOLLY, Cyril (Vernon).**   British.   Born in Coventry, 10 September 1903. Educated at Eton College, Buckinghamshire; Balliol College, Oxford (Brackenbury Scholar). Married Dierdre Craig in 1959; has two children. Founding Editor, *Horizon* magazine, London, 1939–50; Literary Editor, *The Observer*, London, 1942–43. Since 1951, Columnist for the *Sunday Times*, London. Chevalier, Legion of Honour. Address: 48 St. John's Road, Eastbourne, Sussex, England.

PUBLICATIONS

Novel

   *The Rock Pool.*   Paris, Obelisk Press, and New York, Scribner, 1936; London, Hamish Hamilton, 1947.

Other

   *Enemies of Promise.*   London, Routledge, 1938; Boston, Little Brown, 1939; revised edition, New York, Macmillan, 1948; Routledge, 1949.
   *The Unquiet Grave: A Word Cycle, by Palinarus.*   London, Hamish Hamilton, 1944; New York, Harper, 1945; revised edition, Hamish Hamilton, 1952.
   *The Condemned Playground: Essays 1927–1944.*   London, Routledge, 1945; New York, Macmillan, 1946.
   *The Missing Diplomats.*   London, Queen Anne Press, 1952.
   *Ideas and Places.*   London, Weidenfeld and Nicolson, and New York, Harper, 1953.
   *Enemies of Promise and Other Essays: An Autobiography of Ideas.*   New York, Doubleday, 1960.
   *Les Pavillons: French Pavilions of the Eighteenth Century*, with Jerome Zerbe.   New York, Macmillan, 1962; London, Hamish Hamilton, 1963.
   *Previous Convictions.*   London, Hamish Hamilton, 1963; New York, Harper, 1964.
   *The Modern Movement: 100 Key Books from England, France and America, 1880–1950.*   London, Deutsch, 1965; New York, Atheneum, 1966.

   Editor, *Horizon Stories.*   London, Faber, 1943; augmented edition, New York, Vanguard Press, 1946.
   Editor, *Great English Short Novels.*   New York, Dial Press, 1953.
   Editor, *The Golden Horizon.*   London, Weidenfeld and Nicolson, 1953; New York, University Books, 1956.

   Translator, *Put Out the Light*, by Vercors.   London, Macmillan, 1944; as *Silence of the Sea*, New York, Macmillan, 1944.

*     *     *

Cyril Connolly, like his American compeers Edmund Wilson and Lionel Trilling, has devoted almost, but not quite all of his energies to literary criticism, and like Wilson in particular has been an influential admirer of the new in literary climates dominated by insular and heavily academic commitments. For several years Connolly edited *Horizon*, the distinguished liberal (though largely nonpolitical) literary magazine which played an important role in bringing new French writers to the attention of post-War English audiences. When *Horizon* ceased publication in 1949 Connolly remarked, in his typically pessimistic and melodramatic way, "'Nothing dreadful is ever done, no bad thing gets any better; you can't be too serious.' This is the message of the Forties from which, alas, there seems no escape, for it is closing time in the gardens of the West and from now on the artist will be judged only by the resonance of his solitude or the quality of his despair." Somewhat earlier he had also confessed "like most critics, I drifted into the profession through a lack of moral stamina . . . I wanted to write a novel . . . but my novel fell so short of the standards my reading had set that I despaired . . . and, despairing, slipped into the habit of writing short-term articles about books." These characteristic strains of pessimism and self-criticism are also apparent in Connolly's one work of fiction, *The Rock Pool*, a short, caustic work more durable, perhaps, than all but the very best of his criticism.

*The Rock Pool* is a deliberately "unpleasant" book, so much so that it had to make its first appearance under the auspices of the Obelisk Press in Paris: no English publisher would take the risk, though the novel is far from lubricous in its description of the raffish community of Trou-sur-Mer. The anti-hero, Naylor, is a weak sensualist, a faintly pathetic moral coward on holiday ("unable to love . . . neither very intelligent nor especially likeable and certainly not successful"), who smugly decides to write about the seedy bohemians and eccentrics of the Riviera rock pool so that he might derive "a pleasant sense of power". But Naylor, far from being a lordly artist-interpreter, is himself no more than a curious specimen of "English pseudo-virginity." With a good deal of savage glee Connolly traces the decline and fall of Naylor, who becomes "just another bum", dissolved by Pernod and a series of humiliating love-affairs. "The lesson he had learnt," Connolly observes, "that all of us are alone, fighting for ourselves in a world that is daily growing more savage, he would necessarily have to acquire somewhere and in some place, but at home he would have learnt it gradually, slowly encrusting himself with the gentlemanly protection of English selfishness." What Naylor learns from the denizens of the rock pool is a kind of stringent naturalism, a belief in the happiness of the moment which is at least more honest than the hypocritical respectability of his culture:

> What was fine in them, their refusal to conform, was their own; what was weak, their instability, hopelessness and predatory friendships, was the result of a system: of the clumsy capitalist world that exalts money-making and poisons leisure, that suppresses talent, starves its artists, and persecutes its sexual dissenters, that denies opportunity, infects charity, and encourages only the vulgarity of competition, the triumphs, the suspicion, the heart-break of the acquisitive life.

At the conclusion of the novel two newly-arrived English tourists see Naylor as a stumbling wreck, but the last line is finely ambiguous: "Just another bum? I wonder." The final "I wonder" faintly suggests that Naylor's fall has in part been a fortunate one. In his elegant collection of aphorisms and reflections, *The Unquiet Grave*, Connolly remarks that what great works of art have in common is "a sense of perfection and a faith in human dignity, combined with a tragic apprehension of the human situation, and its nearness to the Abyss." *The Rock Pool* is a tough, abrasive, comic reflection of these issues, more than able to hold its own in the company of far better known works by Huxley and Waugh.

—Elmer Borklund

**CONQUEST, (George) Robert (Acworth).** British. Born in Great Malvern, Worcester-shire, 15 July 1917. Educated at Winchester College, Hampshire; Magdalen College, Oxford, B.A. 1939; University of Grenoble, France. Served in the Oxfordshire and Buckinghamshire Light Infantry, 1939–46. Married Caroleen Macfarlane in 1964; has two children by a previous marriage. Member of the U.K. Diplomatic Service, 1946–56; Fellow, London School of Economics, 1956–58; Lecturer in English, State University of New York at Buffalo, 1959–60; Literary Editor, *The Spectator*, London, 1962–63; Senior Fellow, Columbia University, New York, 1964–65. Recipient: P.E.N. verse prize, 1945; Festival of Britain verse prize, 1951. O.B.E. (Officer, Order of the British Empire), 1955. Address: 4 York Mansions, Prince of Wales Drive, London S.W.11, England.

PUBLICATIONS

Novels

A World of Difference. London, Ward Lock, 1955; New York, Ballantine, 1964.
The Egyptologists, with Kingsley Amis. London, Cape, 1965; New York, Random House, 1966.

Uncollected Short Stories

"A Long Way to Go", in Analog (New York), 1966.
"The Veteran", in Analog (New York), 1967.
"No Planet Like Home", in Galaxy (New York), 1970.

Verse

Poems. London, Macmillan, and New York, St. Martin's Press, 1955.
Between Mars and Venus. London, Hutchinson, and New York, St. Martin's Press, 1962.
Arias from a Love Opera. London, Macmillan, and New York, Macmillan, 1969.

Other

Common Sense about Russia. London, Gollancz, and New York, Macmillan, 1960.
Courage of Genius: The Pasternak Affair. London, Collins-Harvill, and Philadelphia, Lippincott, 1961.
Power and Policy in the U.S.S.R. London, Macmillan, and New York, St. Martin's Press, 1962.
Russia after Khrushchev. London, Pall Mall Press, and New York, Praeger, 1965.
The Great Terror: Stalin's Purges of the Thirties. London, Macmillan, and New York, Macmillan, 1968.
The Nation Killers: The Soviet Deportation of Nationalities. London, Macmillan, and New York, Macmillan, 1970.

Editor, New Lines I and II. London, Macmillan, 1956, 1963.
Editor, Back to Life (anthology). London, Hutchinson, and New York, St. Martin's Press, 1958.

Editor, with Kingsley Amis, *Spectrum: A Science Fiction Anthology*.  London, Gollancz, 1961; New York, Harcourt Brace, 1962. (And later volumes.)
Editor, *Soviet Studies Series*, 8 vols.   London, Bodley Head, 1968; New York, Praeger, 1969.

\*       \*       \*

In the contemporary literary world, Robert Conquest is best known for editing that small volume of poetry in 1956, *New Lines*. His preface was as influential as the poetry itself in causing the nine poets presented in that volume to be recognized as having common themes and techniques, and to be soon labeled as "The Movement." Of equal interest, if perhaps of less importance, has been the *Spectrum* series of science-fiction stories that he has edited with Kingsley Amis. These activities indicate Conquest's initiative and ingenuity, even if one does not take into consideration his own poetry (three volumes) and his somewhat prolific political and cultural writing on the U.S.S.R. But such credentials are no guarantee of talent for writing fiction; his slight accomplishments as a novelist hardly challenge in significance his achievements noted above.

*A World of Difference* is a science-fiction novel which lacks even the virtues of that genre. There is little in the story to delight the imagination, and those passages which deal with the science of the future read as if they were taken from a scientific handbook rather than coming from the pen of one sensitive to the language. His characters evoke little sympathy until the final chapters, where the slight plot finally becomes evident. The concept behind this novel is its most saving virtue, and it may have succeeded in a more compressed version. The central concern is the preservation of individual liberties in a future age when the government has at its disposal the means to control minds. A group of citizens, called "The Watch-dogs," have set themselves up as the guardians of these liberties. As the government and "The Watch-dogs" move towards a tense confrontation, the latter group ironically proves to be more oppressive than the government in its struggle to protect the citizens' freedoms. The worst atrocity of the rulers is that they have invented a machine that creates art, but the final revelation, that this machine can only imitate or create second class art, conveniently absolves the government. Subtlety and complexity, the only excuses to cast this story in the form of a novel instead of a short story, are also dispensed with. In a novel poorly written and ineptly developed, there is a kind of comic relief in having the spaceships named after "Movement" poets: the Gunn, the Larkin, the Enright, and the Holloway.

*The Egyptologists*, written in collaboration with Kingsley Amis, is a comedy of manners that fails again for not having the substance to sustain its length. The very slight plot revolves upon the point that a group of Englishmen have formed an elite club of Egyptologists, with none of them possessing a minimal knowledge of the subject. The reader is left for approximately one half the book guessing half-heartedly at the nature of their weekly meetings. It is revealed finally that they use their club, with its exotic Isis room, as a means of hiding their sexual affairs from their wives. There is neither good writing, delicate characterization, nor tasteful humor to compensate for the drawn-out tale.

If the talent of Robert Conquest as an editor or poet leads the reader to expect equal accomplishments as a fiction writer, he will be disappointed. These two attempts in the novel form have obviously shown to the author himself the limitations of his talent. Since the publication of *The Egyptologists*, he has limited his infrequent efforts at fiction to the short story.

—Lawrence Ries

**CONROY, Jack (John Wesley Conroy).** American. Born in Moberly, Missouri, 5 December 1899. Attended the University of Missouri, Columbia, 1920–21. Married Gladys Kelly in 1922; has two children. Migratory worker in the 1920's. Editor, *The Rebel Poet*, Moberly, 1931–32; *The Anvil*, Moberly, 1933–37; with Nelson Algren, *q.v., The New Anvil*, Chicago, 1939–41; Literary Editor, Chicago *Defender*, 1946–47; Chicago *Globe*, 1950. Associate Editor, Nelson's Encyclopedia, and Universal World Reference Encyclopedia, Chicago, 1943–47; Senior Editor, New Standard Encyclopedia, Chicago, 1947–66; Director, Standard Information Service, Chicago, 1949–52. Instructor in Creative Writing, Columbia College, Chicago, 1962–66. Recipient: Guggenheim Fellowship, 1935; Society of Midland Authors' Dow Award, 1967; *Literary Times* Award, 1967. Address: 701 Fisk Avenue, Moberly, Missouri 65270. U.S.A.

PUBLICATIONS

Novels

*The Disinherited*. New York, Covici Friede, 1933; London, Lawrence and Wishart, 1936.
*A World to Win*. New York, Covici Friede, 1935.

Other

*The Fast Sooner Hound*, with Arna Bontemps (juvenile). Boston, Houghton Mifflin, 1942.
*They Seek a City: A Study of Negro Migration*, with Arna Bontemps. New York, Doubleday, 1945; revised edition, as *Anyplace But Here*, New York, Hill and Wang, 1966.
*Slappy Hooper: The Wonderful Sign Painter*, with Arna Bontemps (juvenile). Boston, Houghton Mifflin, 1946.
*Sam Patch: The High, Wide and Handsome Jumper*, with Arna Bontemps (juvenile). Boston, Houghton Mifflin, 1951.

Editor, with Edward R. Cheyney, *Unrest 1929*. London, Stockwell, 1929.
Editor, with Edward R. Cheyney, *Unrest 1930*. London, Studies Publications, 1930.
Editor, with Edward R. Cheyney, *Unrest 1931*. New York, Henry Harrison, 1931.
Editor, *Midland Humor: A Harvest of Fun and Folklore*. New York, Wyn, 1947.

Bibliography: "A Preliminary Checklist of the Writings of Jack Conroy" by John Gordon Burke, in *American Book Collector* (Chicago), Summer 1971.

Critical Studies: Introduction by Daniel Aaron to *The Disinherited*, New York, Hill and Wang, 1963; "Versatile Performer" by Hoke Norris, in *Chicago Sun-Times*, 14 April 1963; essays by Warren Beck, in *Chicago Tribune Magazine of Books*, 12 May 1963, and by Erling Larsen, in *Proletarian Writers of the Thirties*, Carbondale, Southern Illinois University Press, 1968; statement by the author on his own work in a radio interview reprinted in the *Chicago Daily News*, 18 May 1963; "Home to Moberly", autobiographical article by the author in *Missouri Library Association Quarterly* (Columbia), March 1968.

Jack Conroy comments:

*The Disinherited* isn't really a novel—as some critics have said. I agree with that. Novel or not, just so it tells the truth. I describe myself as a witness to the times, not as a novelist. And that's what I prefer to be known as. If I succeeded in conveying something of the times, something of the terror and the uncertainty and the actual desperation, then I'm content.

\*       \*       \*

Despite the fact of an extensive and variegated literary career, Jack Conroy's reputation is associated primarily with his first novel, *The Disinherited*. The novel was published in 1933, in a moment when "proletarian literature" was a prominent cause and an occasion for debate. It was obviously autobiographical—indeed, Conroy had written it as an essay in auto-biography originally, only later and by order of his publisher transforming it into fiction. The hero of the novel is the son of a coal miner, and therefore he is of the family of America's "disinherited." He tells the story of his boyhood in a company-owned coal town, and then the story of his young manhood during the first years of the Great Depression, spent pursuing laboring jobs and wandering when there are no jobs. All of his experiences present evidence of a conspiracy against ordinary workers. The coal company places profits above safety; two of his brothers and his father are killed in the mine. Government connives with industry to break strikes, and union leaders are corrupted. The interests of laboring men are defeated by the technique of anti-Communist hysteria. The hero discovers that nonetheless there exists a latent unity among workers. The novel ends with the double event of a group of farmers resisting the eviction of a debtor from his home, and the hero's resolve to become an active agent in the class struggle.

Marxist criticism tended to be virtually scholastic in its discriminations, and it was objected that Conroy's hero had inclinations towards poetry. The novel was, however, almost un-impeachable: it was written by a genuine proletarian, it touched upon all of the proper themes, and it ended in polemic. Conroy's book secured great reputation for its purity. It has re-mained a primary document of the social literature of the 1930's.

That historical judgement has perhaps obscured the fact that the novel—and Conroy's ambitions in general—were much less ideological than they appeared to be. Conroy has himself, in later years, expressed skepticism about the place of ideology in literature. (See his essay "Home to Moberly," 1968.) His novel in fact engaged dramatically materials which were quite unproletarian, and developed themes much more in the tradition of American pastoral. The novel begins and ends with scenes of the Missouri mining town of the hero's boyhood, and in spite of the record of capitalist tyrannies which the hero recounts, the novel presents the town in terms of a pervading loveliness. There are woods nearby, where the young bucks play their accordians and flutes. The youngsters have Indian games, the plot and even the vocabulary of which seem to come from the novels of James Fenimore Cooper. The boy falls in love with a girl who is a farmer's daughter, who has all of the flouncing and charming righteousness of Becky Thatcher in *Tom Sawyer*. The novel dwells on such materials for almost a third of its length. In another large part, as the hero moves from job to job, the novel dwells on the craft that is in industry—the workman's requisite skills in the making of steel, rubber, automobiles, etc. It is these credibilities—the small town, the woods, the sense of individual craft—from which the hero will be disinherited, and the novel is its own social action, rather than a call to social action, by the amount that it vivifies them. By that amount also it testifies to the implication of American "proletarian literature" in a much broader American myth.

—Marcus Klein

**COOPER, Lettice (Ulpha).** British. Born in Eccles, Lancashire, 3 September 1897. Educated at St. Cuthbert's School, Southbourne; Lady Margaret Hall, Oxford. Associate Editor, *Time and Tide*, London, 1939–40. Served in the Public Relations Division, Ministry of Food, London, 1940–45. President, Robert Louis Stevenson Club, 1958. Address: 95 Canfield Gardens, London N.W.6, England.

PUBLICATIONS

Novels

*The Lighted Room.* London, Hodder and Stoughton, 1925.
*The Old Fox.* London, Hodder and Stoughton, 1927.
*Good Venture.* London, Hodder and Stoughton, 1928.
*Likewise the Lion.* London, Hodder and Stoughton, 1929.
*The Ship of Truth.* London, Hodder and Stoughton, and Boston, Little Brown, 1930.
*Private Enterprise.* London, Hodder and Stoughton, 1931.
*Hark to Rover.* London, Hodder and Stoughton, 1933.
*We Have Come to a Country.* London, Gollancz, 1935.
*The New House.* London, Gollancz, and New York, Macmillan, 1936.
*National Provincial.* London, Gollancz, and New York, Macmillan, 1938.
*Black Bethlehem.* London, Gollancz, and New York, Macmillan, 1947.
*Fenny.* London, Gollancz, 1953.
*Three Lives.* London, Gollancz, 1957.
*A Certain Compass.* London, Gollancz, 1960.
*The Double Heart.* London, Gollancz, 1962.
*Late in the Afternoon.* London, Gollancz, 1972.

Other

*Robert Louis Stevenson.* London, Home and Van Thal, 1947; Denver, Swallow, 1948.
*Yorkshire: West Riding.* London, Hale, 1950.
*George Eliot.* London, Longman, 1951; revised edition, 1960, 1964.
*Great Men of Yorkshire* (juvenile). London, Lane, 1955.
*The Young Florence Nightingale* (juvenile). London, Parrish, 1960; New York, Roy, 1961.
*Blackberry's Kitten* (juvenile). Leicester, Brockhampton Press, 1961; New York, Vanguard Press, 1963.
*The Young Victoria* (juvenile). London, Parrish, 1961; New York, Roy, 1962.
*The Bear Who Was Too Big* (juvenile). London, Parrish, 1963; Chicago, Follett, 1966.
*Bob-a-Job* (juvenile). Leicester, Brockhampton Press, 1963.
*James Watt* (juvenile). London, Black, 1963.
*Garibaldi* (juvenile). London, Methuen, 1964; New York, Roy, 1966.
*The Young Edgar Allan Poe* (juvenile). London, Parrish, 1964; New York, Roy, 1965.
*Contadino* (juvenile). London, Cape, 1964.
*The Fugitive King* (juvenile). London, Parrish, 1965.
*The Twig of Cypress* (juvenile). London, Deutsch, 1965; New York, Washburn, 1966.
*We Shall Have Snow* (juvenile). Leicester, Brockhampton Press, 1966.
*A Hand upon the Time: A Life of Charles Dickens* (juvenile). New York, Pantheon Books, 1968; London, Gollancz, 1971.
*The Gun-Powder Treason Plot* (juvenile). London and New York, Abelard Schuman, 1970.
*Robert Louis Stevenson* (juvenile). London, Barker, 1970.

Manuscript Collection: The Public Library, Eccles, Lancashire.


Critical Study: "Lettice at 70" by Francis King, in *Sunday Telegraph* (London), 1967.


Lettice Cooper comments:

I want to write stories about people in depth, using the traditional form, but hoping to show how the unconscious pressures and situations are always there beneath the conscious pattern. I want to indicate both the inner and outer life of my characters, and to "explore the truth of the human situation".

                            *        *        *


Lettice Cooper has been writing novels for many years, and social historians of the future may well study them for their careful reflection of middleclass English life at various stages of this century. The worlds she described in her younger days may have gone, but this does not mean that the novels themselves have dated: technically and psychologically they still stand up well. Their settings are domestic, though their domesticity varies. In *Fenny*, one of the most ambitious and successful, we see some grandish Italian interiors; in *National Provincial*, lower middleclass North Country life; in *The Ship of Truth*, a young clergyman's home, penny-pinching through necessity; in *The New House*, an upper middleclass family, suffocatingly cosy and financially quite secure; in *The Double Heart*, more townish and trendy people; in the last novel, *Late in the Afternoon*, a smartish background in the main characters, very different ones in the others, who include a wandering hippy.

In some of the novels, institutions stand behind the domesticity. In *Three lives*, it is an adult education college; in *We Have Come to a Country*, an "occupational centre for unemployed men" (the time is the mid-thirties). In these cases, the institutions are not just decorative backgrounds, realistically painted flats; we get inside them, learn how they work. Nothing, in Lettice Cooper's novels, is put in without a point or a place in the action, without being properly inserted and made familiar. Miss Cooper is always professional, a writer whose care, and whose respect for her readers, deserve respect.

Two places are of primary importance in her novels—her native Yorkshire, standing rocklike and immoveable, often a symbol of stability in a shifting world, sometimes of narrowness in a wider one (London beckons the young); and the country for which she feels the deep love of the enchanted (though knowlegeable) outsider: Italy, and more specifically Tuscany. Again and again the novels are set in, or have excursions to, one or other of these places. Both, in a sense, seem to represent homecoming.

If the settings of the novels are domestic, the action, as a rule, is unadventurous, in the sense of undramatic—except in terms of feelings and personalities. But this might be said, of course, of the majority of English fiction written by women, from *Middlemarch* downwards, and implies no narrowness of outlook. Miss Cooper has kept fairly firmly within the worlds she knows and undertands, but that they have opened out with the years is clear from her most recent novel, in which, from the standpoint of an elderly woman, she deals sympathetically with the new young, and makes a spendidly unpatronising excursion into a working-class household touched but not radically altered by the new prosperity. From her domestic settings she deals, in fact, with the basic issues and problems: love and indifference, parental selfishness, the young's longing for escape, moral dilemmas, varying standards of behaviour, of loyalty and truth. In what seems a straightforward way she concentrates much into seemingly simple scenes and passages; her strength lying in an intelligent understanding of human nature, in warmth tempered with briskness and humour, and in an intuitive interpretation of events, psychological and spiritual. At its simplest this concentration appears in her children's books, outstandingly good among which is *Bob-a-Job*, a small masterpiece of insight on that attractive menace the predatory wolf-cub, out to help.

—Isabel Quigley

---

**COOPER, William.** Pseudonym for Harry Summerfield Hoff. British. Born in Crewe, Cheshire, 4 August 1910. Educated at Christ's College, Cambridge, M.A. 1933. Served in the Royal Air Force, 1940–45. Married Joyce Barbara Harris in 1950; has two daughters. Schoolmaster, Leicester, 1933–40; Assistant Commissioner, Civil Service Commission, London, 1945–58. Part-time Personnel Consultant, for the United Kingdom Atomic Energy Commission, since 1958, and for the Central Electricity Generating Board, since 1960. Address: 14 Keswick Road, London S.W.15, England.

PUBLICATIONS

Novels

*Trina* (as H. S. Hoff).   London, Heinemann, 1934; as *It Happened in PRK*, New York, Coward McCann, 1934.
*Rhéa* (as H. S. Hoff).   London, Heinemann, 1937.
*Lisa* (as H. S. Hoff).   London, Heinemann, 1937.
*Three Marriages* (as H. S. Hoff).   London, Heinemann, 1946.
*Scenes from Provincial Life*.   London, Cape, 1950.
*Scenes from Metropolitan Life*.   1951. Suppressed by threat of libel.
*The Struggles of Albert Woods*.   London, Cape, 1952; New York, Doubleday, 1953.
*The Ever-Interesting Topic*.   London, Cape, 1953.
*Disquiet and Peace*.   London, Macmillan, 1956; Philadelphia, Lippincott, 1957.
*Young People*.   London, Macmillan, 1958.
*Scenes from Married Life*.   London, Macmillan, 1961.
*Scenes from Life* (includes *Scenes from Provincial Life* and *Scenes from Married Life*).   New York, Scribner, 1961.
*Memoirs of a New Man*.   London, Macmillan, 1966.
*You Want the Right Frame of Reference*.   London, Macmillan, 1971.

Uncollected Short Stories

"Ball of Paper", in *Winter's Tales 1*.   London, Macmillan, 1955.
"A Moral Choice", in *Winter's Tales 4*.   London, Macmillan, 1958.

Plays

*Strawberry Leaves* (produced London, 1951).
*Prince Genji* (produced Oxford, 1958).   London, Evans Brothers, 1959.

Other

C. P. Snow.   London, Longman, 1959; revised edition, 1971.
Shall We Ever Know? The Trial of the Hosein Brothers for the Murder of Mrs. McKay.
London, Hutchinson, 1971.


Manuscript Collection: Humanities Research Center, University of Texas, Austin.


Critical Studies: *Tradition and Dream* by Walter Allen, London, Phoenix House, 1964;
Introduction by Malcolm Bradbury to *Scenes from Provincial Life*, London, Macmillan,
1969.


William Cooper comments:

I don't know that I specially believe in artists making statements about their own work.
An artist's *work* is *his* statement. And that's that. The rest is for other people to say. Perhaps
a writer whose original statement has turned out obscure may feel it useful to present a
second that's more comprehensible—in that case I wonder why he didn't make the second
one first.

Speaking for myself, *Scenes from Provincial Life* seems to me so simple, lucid, attractive
and funny that anyone who finds he can't read it probably ought to ask himself: "Should I be
trying to read books at all? Wouldn't it be better to sit and watch television or something?"
I think about the real world and real people in it. And I stick pretty close to what I've had
some experience of. That's why *Scenes from Metropolitan Life*, which is also simple, lucid,
attractive and funny, was suppressed. *Scenes from Married Life* makes the third of a trilogy.
*Albert Woods* and *Memoirs of a New Man* are about goings-on in the world of science and
technology; *You Have the Right Frame of Reference* in the world of the arts—they have an
added touch of wryness and malice. An unusual marriage is the core of *Young People* and
*Disquiet and Peace*, the former set in the provinces in the '30's, the latter in Edwardian upper-
class London—its small group of admirers think it's a beautiful book. *The Ever-Interesting
Topic* is about what happens when you give a course of lectures on sex to a boarding-school
full of boys: what you'd expect. *Shall We Ever Know?* is a day-by-day account of a most
surprising and mystifying murder trial, a kidnapping for ransom in which no trace whatsoever of the body was ever found, and two men were found guilty of murder.


*        *        *


William Cooper is the pen-name of an author who had already published four novels
under his own name, H. S. Hoff, when in 1950 he emerged with a new literary identity, and
won a new literary reputation, with *Scenes from Provincial Life*—a novel which quickly
became a classic of a new kind of realism and undoubtedly had a significant influence on the
general development of the English novel in the 1950s and since. A delightful, tough-minded
story set among young provincial intellectuals, in a midlands town suspiciously like Leicester,
over the months just before the outbreak of the Second World War, and dealing with their
mores and emotions, *Scenes from Provincial Life* was the forerunner of a sequence of books
which, in the postwar years, were to treat local English life, the familiar and ordinary experience of recognizable people, with a youthful, fresh, exploratory, critical curiosity. There
can be little doubt that the book did help encourage, if not directly influence, a number of
younger writers like John Braine, David Storey, Stanley Middleton and Stan Barstow, some
of whom have directly expressed indebtedness to Cooper's work; and it certainly helped

postwar writers to find a sense of direction. Its force was strengthened by the fact that Cooper —along with C. P. Snow, Pamela Hansford Johnson and some other rather younger writers like Kingsley Amis and John Wain—was deliberately, and in obvious reaction against the Bloomsbury-dominated climate of "cultured" experimentalism, seeking out a form of fiction much more social, detailed, empirical, realistic and humanly substantial in character, concerned with the felt sense of contemporary life. This spirit in writing has been characterized by some critics as middlebrow, and its spirit has been seen as banal, but it retained a humanist vigour and a closeness to familiar life in the practice of serious English writing at a time when, in literary traditions in other countries, deeper signs of strain were obviously being felt. Cooper's book had a general influence on that, the more important because it was not only one of the first, but also one of the best, of the kind.

Cooper has since produced eight more novels, all marked by the same commitment to familiar life and all marked with the same qualities of luminosity and delicacy. One of them, *Disquiet and Peace*, is an historical novel, set in the high society milieu of political and drawing-room life in the Edwardian England when the period of Liberal domination was ending. The rest are all in a sense banal novels—concerned with the world of day-to-day social experience, under the conditions we most of us know. Set in the provinces, the suburbs, or the world of the urban middle-classes, a slice of social experience which Cooper knows and details very well, they represent ordinary things happening to intelligent, sceptical people: they have affairs, get married, breed families, and they work in schools and offices. The stratum in question is usually that of the new men of the pre- and post-war meritocratic world. Most of them are rising toward social and intellectual possession, and part of their realistic pleasure in the world around comes from the fact that it is obviously open to their mobility and talents. In form and content, Cooper's world is not a world of the exceptionable or the unexpected; even *Disquiet and Peace* is a study in depth of marriage, that institution and area of emotional and psychic activity of which Cooper is among the best modern analysts.

But if one of Cooper's striking qualities is his realism, another is his comedy. The life in which he deals may be familiar, but he lights it up with a remarkable sense of human oddity, and of the quirkiness and extremity that exist within his dense and recognizable characters. Ordinariness is set off against outrage, often deriving from the cool, undercutting tone of the narrator himself. Like Muriel, who in *Disquiet and Peace* brings disorder into the world of the book by donning an eyeglass and dropping it into her soup, Cooper, or his surrogate Joe Lunn, enters his fictional world to introduce the oblique vision. Most of the struggles and desires of the characters, desires for social, material or sexual success, become matters for very cool irony. His plots often seem to be about moral conflicts, between liberal and traditional values, but Cooper by the end seems to move lightly away from the conflict, leaving the entire experience ridiculous. Such is the case with *The Ever-Interesting Topic*, dealing with a headmaster who tries to introduce lectures on sex education into his public school. Cooper has always a buoyant, vitalist view of sexuality and a sense of the way it renders most human pretensions ridiculous. Comedy in his books serves to show up ridiculousness and peculiarity, and helps make his realism into a writing of surprise. As a result the books have a sharp revealing clarity which is part of his distinctive style, and which distinguishes his work from that of, say, C. P. Snow—about whom he has written warmly—who writes about a somewhat similar world, and who shares his interest in those in the field of administration and technology, in the struggles of the new men, in the Albert Woods and Joe Lunns of modern society. Comedy too makes his heroes attractive centres of vision. This is especially true of the most successful of all, Joe Lunn, the first-person narrator of both *Scenes from Provincial Life* and *Scenes from Married Life*. Lunn, being both a performer in the action and the artistic observer recalling and shaping it, neatly shows off the writer's balance between sympathy and irony, fact and fiction. In other books, other narrative techniques are used, but the result is usually an adept mixture of sympathetic identification with characters and an ironic distance from them.

As a result, Cooper's novels do possess a distinctive style and vision. Nonetheless, they vary somewhat in quality; and his luminous delicacy, his gift for catching the flavour and quality of the right, revealing scene, for cutting deep into life, is more apparent in some than others. What distinguishes his work at best from other writing superficially like it is a very precise artistic control. It is most evident when he is catching at the flavour of a distinctive ethos and time and catching the behaviour of vital people in it (e.g. as in *Young People*). The comparison with H. G. Wells is not inexact; he has the same gift for conveying hopeful, buoyant contingency, youthful pleasure in life. But there is also at times (as in *Scenes from Provincial Life*) a balance of reminiscence, irony and sentiment so carefully composed as to recall the "artistic" realism of, say, Turgenev. His technique is not always particularly noticeable (except when the narrator, as occasionally happens, intrudes very self-consciously on the action to comment) but it is self-conscious and adept. The result is that his work is not only socially and humanely dense and comically and morally illuminating, but is also shot through with literary perspectives. It is this that has helped to give *Scenes from Provincial Life*—which remains probably his best novel—the status of a small modern classic which it now possesses.

—Malcolm Bradbury

---

**COOVER, Robert.**   American.   Born in Charles City, Iowa, 4 February 1932. Educated at Southern Illinois University, Carbondale, 1949–51; Indiana University, Bloomington, B.A. 1953; University of Chicago, 1958–61, M.A. 1965. Retired Lieutenant in the United States Navy; on active duty, 1953–57. Married Pilar Sans-Mallafré in 1959; has three children. Recipient: Faulkner Award, 1966; Brandeis University Creative Arts Award, 1969. Address: c/o E. P. Dutton and Company, 201 Park Avenue South, New York, New York 10003, U.S.A.

PUBLICATIONS

Novels

   *The Origin of the Brunists.*   New York, Putnam, 1966; London, Barker, 1967.
   *The Universal Baseball Association, Inc., J. Henry Waugh, Prop.*   New York, Random House, 1968; London, Hart Davis, 1970.

Short Stories

   *Pricksongs & Descants.*   New York, Dutton, 1969; London, Cape, 1971.

Uncollected Short Stories

   "Blackdamp", in *Noble Savage* (Chicago), October 1961.
   "The Square-Shooter and the Saint", in *Evergreen Review* (New York), July-August 1962.
   "Dinner with the King of England", in *Evergreen Review* (New York), November-December 1962.
   "D. D., Baby", in *Cavalier* (New York), July 1963.
   "The Duel", in *Evergreen Review* (New York), June 1967.

"The Cat in the Hat for President", in *New American Review 4*.  New York, New American Library, 1968.
"Some Notes about Puff", in *Iowa Review* (Iowa City), Winter 1970.
"The Reunion", in *Iowa Review* (Iowa City), Winter 1971.


Plays

*The Kid*, in *Tri-Quarterly* (Evanston, Illinois), Spring 1970.
*Love Scene*, in *New American Review 12*.  New York, Simon and Schuster, 1971.

Filmed and assembled the documentary *On a Confrontation in Iowa City*, 1969.


Other

Verse published in magazines.


Critical Study: in *Fiction and the Figures of Life* by William Gass, New York, Knopf, 1971.


\*        \*        \*


Robert Coover's vocabulary, the sheer sense of power in the word, is luxurious, and his control over it is manifest in the sure interplay of a number of styles: ballad, colloquial, ritualistic, parodic, apocalyptic. But the interplay is itself controlled by his commitment to the primacy of formal plot, and an ability to control a dizzying display of several plots which, anti-formal in their engagement with one another, are each separately geometric in spare simplicity.

The apparent formalism and the ultimate anti-formalistic result of Coover's methods emerge from three basic themes of which the formal properties are both product and epiphany. These themes are game, number (in the sense suggested by one of Coover's own epigraphs from Valéry which reads: "They set me this problem of the equality of appearance and numbers"), and perpetual, repetitive rituals which can destroy or define the self. Coover himself sums up his credo in asserting that contemporary fiction must use "familiar mythic or historical forms to combat the content of those forms, and to conduct the reader . . . to the real, away from . . . mystery to revelation." It is consistent with this theory that the works are almost always founded upon a prior "mythic or historical" source from which they are then released, and from which the reader is released, in the anti-formal revelation.

The first of Coover's novels, *The Origin of the Brunists*, is already a full expression of these principles of composition. The plot narrates the encounter of Justin Miller, athlete-turned-editor, with the chiliastic afterbirth of an Appalachian coal-mining disaster survived only by a silent and enigmatic Giovanni Bruno around whom is formed a sect which brings into unholy and unstable union fundamentalists and theosophists. The primary analogue is the founding of the Christian religion: there are Marcella, Bruno's virgin sister in white, the apocryphal white bird seen at every crucial juncture, the bleeding heart of Marcella, and countless details of how the original mystic experience is abstracted into a theology. However, the apparent allegory is violently wrenched awry by the anti-Brunist Miller's physical and psychic crucifixion in the last pages. The frustration and dissolution of form are echoed in the use of number. The Brunists are numerologists, looking for the Apocalypse, seeking meaning everywhere in multiples of fourteen (Bruno was the ninety-eighth man to emerge from the mine, etc.). So permeating is this numbers game that the attentive reader must play it, becoming a self-demonstration of the folly of ritualistic mysteries when Miller finally articulates his own breakthrough: "Half-consciously he'd been waiting for 7 or 14, and knew now he'd never hear it." These are but the most important exemplars of multiple ways in which *The Brunists* bears out Coover's theory on the function of fiction and justifies the novel's final statement on the emptiness of forms: "the various Divine Substances took their leave. The only trouble was that by that time the enormity of the support organization and the goal hunger of the participants was such that the absented Divine Substances were never missed. The proceedings, indulging the everlasting lust for perpetuity and stage directions, dragged on happily through the centuries." Something of the consistency which Coover manages within virtuoso variety is suggested when one notices that the language used here is metaphorically enacted, as it were, in the brief play, *Love Scene*, in which a puzzled deity-stage director attempts repeatedly to breathe life into the Adam and Eve puppets who go through the ritual of love without feeling, since the Director is gone, only a disembodied voice from above stage.

The second novel, Coover's finest achievement to date, *The Universal Baseball Association, Inc., J Henry Waugh, Prop.* develops the themes of *The Brunists* with a complexity only adumbrated by the earlier novel and which can only be suggested. J. Henry Waugh, an aging bachelor petty accountant, is a genius at games who has finally centered his life upon a baseball game played with dice and charts. The reality of the world outside his shabby room is subsumed by the reality of the records which compose his paper league. "History. Amazing how we love it. And . . . without numbers or measurements, there probably wouldn't be any history," Henry says. Reality is defined, rationalized, perhaps created by a history which is dice, charts, number in its double manifestation as unpredictability and inevitable order. This is the narrative and ideational framework for a novel which interlaces and discards mythic source upon source: baseball, political history (what Coover has elsewhere called the "civil religion" of America—an emphasis explored in a novella, "The Cat in the Hat for President" and in a "Western" play, *The Kid*), the Old Testament and the New. The resolution is, for all of the rich development, again the simple but earned freeing of reader and protagonist (in this case not J. Henry Waugh but his creature, as the former's Jehovah name implies) from mythic and ritual forms into an individual freedom of play beyond the old game's circumscribed rules.

Coover's most recent book is *Pricksongs & Descants*, a collection of twenty shorter pieces and a theoretical "Prólogo" from which I have already quoted. The variety is a guide to Coover's experimental temperament. There are brief, evocative parables enacted upon a landscape of stark outlines masking a confusion which ultimately irrupts in terror as stark and definite as the scene ("The Leper's Helix", "The Wayfarer", "Scene for 'Winter'"). There are Biblical episodes retold from a de-mythologising point of view ("The Brother" on one whom Noah left behind, and "J's Marriage", and aged Joseph's several times revised accounts of the Immaculate Conception). There are parodies of contemporaries which gradually emerge as remarkably serious adaptations ("Morris in Chains"). But the most accomplished and innovative fictions are those based upon the fairy tale and upon the medium of television. The former ("The Door", "The Magic Poker", "The Gingerbread House") sometimes fold tales in upon one another until Jack becomes the Giant, Red Riding Hood her own grandmother, caught in myths of life become ineluctable rituals of death (a pattern differently treated in "The Leper's Helix" and "In a Train Station"). At other times, the tale is told, then retold, remodelled, not as one whole version replacing another, but as alternating possibilities throughout, as if to offer a vision of the imagination's power to implement Coover's ideal of a contingency which can discard old forms even in their process of becoming. And yet, the story-telling artist-father of Hansel and Gretel hears the black rags of the witch flapping behind the pulsing heart-like ruby door of the gingerbread house, "wishes his poor children well," but knows "there are no reasonable wishes"; the lake is calm but empty, "a frog lies dead, a strange creature lies slain" at the close of "The Magic Poker". Both the technique of continuous revisions of narrative and the sense of no escape are intensified in the television-oriented masterpiece of the collection, "The Babysitter," where screen and reality combine to create one another, and all of the alternative deadly endings are retained in a single climax of absurdity. And there are, of course, pieces structured upon numerological illusion ("The Elevator" and "A Pedestrian Accident") and upon the dangers of gamesmanship ("Panel Game").

In *Pricksongs & Descants* the protagonists seldom escape their mythic destinies. But as the deadliness and frangibility of old and modern aesthetic forms are demonstrated through Coover's ability to rearrange them into new patterns that clarify their sterility, the reader is again given a revelation of the persistent imagination's potential for reforming itself.

—Jackson I. Cope

---

**COPE, Jack.** South African. Born in Mooi River, Natal, 3 June 1913. Educated at Durban High School. Married Lesley de Villiers in 1942 (divorced, 1956); has two children. Reporter, *Natal Mercury*, Durban, 1930–35; Correspondent in London for South African Morning Newspapers, 1936–40; Farmer in Natal, 1941–42; engaged in shark-fishing enterprise, Cape Town, 1943–45; Director, South African Association of the Arts, Cape Town, 1946–48. Free-lance Writer and Reporter since 1949. Founding-Editor, *Contrast* magazine, Cape Town, since 1960. Recipient: South African Arts and Sciences Prose Prize, 1959; British Council travel grant, 1960; Carnegie Travel Fellowship, 1966; South African Festival of the Soil Award, 1970. Address: Sea Girt, Second Beach, Clifton, Cape Town, South Africa.

PUBLICATIONS

Novels

    *The Fair House.* London, MacGibbon and Kee, 1955.
    *The Golden Oriole.* London, Heinemann, 1958.
    *The Road to Ysterberg.* London, Heinemann, 1959.
    *Albino.* London, Heinemann, 1963.
    *The Dawn Comes Twice.* London, Heinemann, 1969.
    *The Rain-Maker.* London, Heinemann, 1971.
    *The Student of Zend.* London, Heinemann, 1972.

Short Stories

    *The Tame Ox.* London, Heinemann, 1966.
    *The Man Who Doubted.* London, Heinemann, 1967.

Verse

    *Lyrics and Diatribes.* Cape Town, Stewart, 1948.
    *Marie: A Satire.* Cape Town, Stewart, 1949.

Other

    *Comrade Bill* (biography). Cape Town, Stewart, 1943.

Editor, with Uys Krige, *The Penguin Book of South African Verse*.   London, Penguin, 1968.

Editor, *Seismograph: New South African Writing in English and Afrikaans*.   Cape Town, Reijger, 1970.

Translator, with William Plomer, *Selected Poems of Ingrid Jonker*.   London, Cape, 1968.


Jack Cope comments:

Raised by a farming family on the South African veld a long way from anywhere, I had made up my mind at about 10 years of age that I was going to be a writer. How to do it was another thing. I am still on that search. It has been said that the art of writing lies in the struggle against the inability to write. I was a third generation from settlers in a practically empty region of Natal; white, English-speaking. Zulus came up from the warm bush country to work on the cold high-veld and they were often the only playmates I and my brothers had. We got to know them, liked them, learnt from them.

In the old stone farmhouse there were thousands of books—sermons, religious tracts and poetry, Victorian novels by "Ouida", Disraeli, Mrs. Gaskell, Wilkie Collins, Mrs. Henry Wood, etc. But there were also Fenimore Cooper, Kingsley, Defoe, Mark Twain, Dickens, Ruskin, Scott, William Morris, Thackeray; there were Shakespeare and all the English poets up to Browning. The Bible was part of one's life, though we were too far away to go to church more than a few times. I knew that I couldn't model myself on any of the writers I read—we had no Redskins, no sea or pirates, no rivers, lakes, forests, no cities, no factories, no art, no stage. Living in a mental desert, what did one specially see and feel, let alone write about? We hunted and had guns and dogs and horses, but it was all so ordinary. At 12 I was sent 100 miles to boarding school in Durban, a seaport which seemed duller, more lonely even than the farm.

Then I left school, refused to enter university and went instead into a newspaper in Durban as an "apprentice". A mistake. I was ten years in journalism and never liked it. Learnt how not to write. One thing the newspaper business did for me—it got me out of South Africa and to London. I worked in Fleet Street. In four years I was almost flattened out into an Englishman. But there's the paradox, the nearer you are, the further you are away from a thing. Anyway I remained African. Language, blood, family, tradition were all on one side; but the break of nearly a century was too long. I belonged to Africa or to nowhere.

Of course I had long since made a mental holocaust of *white* race attitudes as no-one can like somebody born into them. Mad about Shaw and Morris, Russell, Marx, Ibsen, Pound (!), Eliot and O'Casey, I cultivated a polyglot creed, a sort of anarcho-social-communo-nihilist with a strong dash of pacifism. Wrote bad verse with an admiring eye on Yeats, Lawrence or Pound, and my stories limped on crutches of Gorky, Bunin, Hemingway. No nationalism, no dogma, no traditionalism, I thought myself a citizen of that other country, The World. My time—the coming apocalypse.

The war drove me morosely from England home to Natal, to the farm, the loneliness. I tried to start writing consistently, seriously. To my astonishment and disgust I found I just couldn't. The novel I started with a family-historical background went through four re-writes over a period of 12 years—all torn up or burnt. Friends used to put down my type-script in embarrassment. The book was *The Fair House*. The fifth script I sent to London. Back came a cable from a young publisher, James MacGibbon: "Fair House is magnificent." I got very drunk. I'd like to believe it was true. But I know: it was shaky but a beginning. Meanwhile I was suddenly writing short stories that got accepted.

That was the break-out. I stumbled about after that but have made it a point not to get frozen into a "manner" (substitute for style) or be carried away by form. In each story and novel, as in my poems, I wanted all the elements, rhythm, structure, tone, to work separately and together within a different context and to be ruled by it. Each book, I hope, shifts a peg on. Seven novels so far, two books and a lot of uncollected stories—the objective is still to produce one good book by the time I pack in, and then I'll feel there was something in my dream at the age of ten.

Writing in South Africa is not easy. There's a high voltage of tension. There's Censorship, intimidation; one's books get banned. But I don't believe in quitting; you can't see things straight from too great a distance, from exile. I am against writing dirt for sales or for its own sake. Life's full enough of dirt and if it gets into a book the context must give it an absolute necessity. I remain an African, and Africa somehow keeps a certain innocence, a certain newness and strength. It's not a political slogan. Or a garbage dump.

To fight against isolation I've always tried to work back from my own experience and to draw together the younger writers, raise critical standards, demand sound craftsmanship. I make translations from Afrikaans, Zulu, Sotho, Xhosa, and this I feel helps create links in a multi-national society. Writers cannot get a wide enough readership in the developing languages and therefore aim to master English or Afrikaans. To command a new language and learn to write in it is a mammoth task—one can be helped or encouraged, but there are no short cuts. In 1960 I took part in starting a two-language literary quarterly, *Contrast*, and still edit it. The magazine has been a mouthpiece as well as workshop for many promising young poets, fiction writers, dramatists, artists.

South Africa still has a small enough population for writers even living thousands of miles apart to get to know each other. They come from every nationality, race, belief, outlook. Many are banned, exiled. But they form a kind of republic of talent rising above the jargon and propaganda, throwing shadows ahead.

*       *       *

As his novels, and even more his short stores, show, Jack Cope is not only a skilled writer, but one whose range—as regards character, setting and plot—is greater than that of many South African novelists. His work has moved from the historical and purely regional approach of *The Fair House* (based on an armed rising of the Zulu in 1902) and *Albino* (life in rural Natal), through a consideration of general moral issues (*The Road to Ysterberg*), to a fairly optimistic appraisal of the black resistance movement in *The Dawn Comes Twice*. Cope's characters include black politicians and intellectuals (notably in *The Golden Oriole*, which offers a fascinating glimpse into the world of black politics forty years ago); people on the fringes of society, both black and white; and ordinary South Africans of all races and of all classes. Bushmen, *trekboers* (nomadic farmers), "poor whites" and bewildered immigrants have all claimed his sympathetic attention, and he invests these less well-known South African types with a humanity denied them by most previous writers. In two of his novels, *The Road to Ysterberg* and *The Dawn Comes Twice*, a Coloured (i.e., a half-caste) woman is given a central role, and it must be recognised that Cope is one of the very few white South African writers who is able to present such characters simply and credibly as human beings. His characters are always intimately related to their background, and in his detailed evocations of the South African landscape—desert, mountain, sub-tropical farmland, or uncultivated bush—he has produced some of his most impressive writing.

What one may, however, find disturbing in Cope's work, in spite of its undeniable competence and authenticity, is his tendency to romanticise the real and unpleasant issues which dominate contemporary South African life: the inequality and injustice of *apartheid* (racial segregation); the powerlessness of the black majority; the callousness of most whites. As his novels show, Cope is not unaware of these issues; but, by focussing his attention on tribal Africans, by suggesting that underground resistance movements are fairly well-organised, and most of all, by a deliberate and too-often melodramatic manipulation of plot to avoid embarrassing personal confrontations (between, for instance, a white man and a black woman), Cope distinctly blurs the edges of his realism, and presents his readers with an attractive but subtly distorted version of South Africa. The reason for this is not hard to find. Unlike many of his contemporaries, who have in recent years chosen to live abroad, Cope lives and works within a South African context. This means, among other things, that he is subject to the increasingly complex network of censorship legislation which has, under the present government, come to affect not only the literature which may be distributed inside the country, but that which is being produced as well. Cope's own awareness of the effect of this deliberate clamp on imagination is shown in his story, "A Face of Stainless Steel", which offers a poignant glimpse into the mind of a sensitive man who feels himself trapped and bound by a society he knows to be evil, but to which he is committed. The glittering mask of "Steel" (a party disguise) symbolises the emotional sterility which is the inevitable concomitant of such knowledge. In some ways, Cope's choice is an admirable one: he, at least, can and does write from *within* a tortured society: his voice is still a rational one. But, ultimately, the price exacted by this society, from a writer of integrity, may come to seem inordinately high.

—Ursula Laredo

---

**COWAN, Peter.** Australian. Born in Perth, Western Australia, 4 November 1914. Educated at the University of Western Australia, Nedlands, B.A. 1940, Dip.Ed. 1946. Served in the Royal Australian Air Force, 1943–45. Member of the faculty of the University of Western Australia, 1946–50; Senior English Master, Scotch College, Swanbourne, Western Australia, 1950–62. Since 1964, Senior Tutor, English Department, University of Western Australia. Recipient: Commonwealth Literary Fund Fellowship, 1963. Address: c/o English Department, University of Western Australia, Nedlands, Western Australia 6009, Australia.

PUBLICATIONS

Novels

Summer. Sydney and London, Angus and Robertson, 1964.
Seed. Sydney and London, Angus and Robertson, and San Francisco, Tri-Ocean, 1966.

Short Stories

Drift: Stories. Melbourne, Reed and Harris, 1944.
The Unploughed Land: Stories. Sydney, Angus and Robertson, 1959.
The Empty Street: Stories. Sydney and London, Angus and Robertson, and San Francisco, Tri-Ocean, 1965.

Other

Editor, Short Story Landscape: The Modern Short Story. Melbourne, Longman, 1964.

Co-Editor, *Spectrum One* and *Two*.   Melbourne, Longman, 1970; London, Longman, 1971.

Editor, *Today: Contemporary Short Stories*.   Melbourne, Longman, 1971.

Critical Studies: "The Short Stories of Peter Cowan" by John Barnes, in *Meanjin* (Melbourne), 1960; "New Tracks to Travel: The Stories of White, Porter and Cowan" by John Barnes, in *Meanjin* (Melbourne), 1966; essay by Grahame Johnston in *Westerly* (Perth), 1967.

Peter Cowan comments:

Up to the present time writing has been for me as much something I wanted to do to please myself as something aimed solely at publication and any kind of wide audience. Now, I don't think this kind of attitude is any longer possible, and the chances for this kind of fiction have greatly diminished.

My writing may have been concerned as much with place as with people, though I have tried to see people against a landscape, against a physical environment. If isolation is one of the themes that occur frequently, particularly in the short stories, this is perhaps enforced by the Australian landscape itself. I am deeply involved in everything to do with the physical Australia, the land, its shapes and seasons and colors, its trees and flowers, its birds and animals. And its coast and sea.

I have been more interested in the short story than the novel. The technical demands of a short story are high, and seldom met, and through the short story a writer has perhaps a better chance of trapping something of the fragmentary nature of today's living.

*        *        *

Peter Cowan is a quietly introspective writer, and consequently his intensity of vision and his scrupulous craftsmanship can easily be under-rated. Although he has written novels, his talent appears to be most suited to the short story or novella, in which he can focus on a single relationship and explore a single line of feeling. His stories, written in a spare, taut style, have as a recurring theme the relationship of a man and a woman seeking relief from their loneliness in sexual love. Cowan is intent upon an inner reality: his characters are seldom individualized very far, they seem almost anonymous, and the sensuous reality of the external world is only faintly felt. His imagination is compelled by a painful awareness of the feelings of loneliness and alienation that lie beneath the surface of commonplace lives; and in exploring this territory he has become, more than is generally recognized, a significant interpreter of Australian realities, the realities portrayed by an Australian painter like Robert Dickerson (whose painting, *Boy in a Street*, Cowan chose for the dustjacket of his volume, *The Empty Street*).

In Cowan's first collection of stories, *Drift*, the preoccupations of his mature work are merely sketched in. Uneven in quality and stylistically in debt to Hemingway, the book nevertheless has a coherence and a unity of impression unexpected in the work of a young writer. Cowan has known his subject right from the start. Most of these early stories are set in the poor farming country of south-western West Australia before the Second World War, and they centre on the lives of people who are emotionally unfulfilled or unable to express themselves in normal relationships.

Over the next fourteen years Cowan wrote little. In his second collection, *The Unploughed Land*, he reprinted seven of his stories from *Drift*, along with six new stories, which represent a distinct advance in technique. These new stories include the much-anthologized "The Red-backed Spiders", a powerful story of a boy whose resentment at his brutal father leads to the man's death. The title story is an extended treatment of that pre-war country life about which he writes in his first volume. In its evocation of that life it is one of his finest pieces, and it marks the end of the first phase of his development.

From this point onward Cowan has been more prolific and more varied—though compared with most writers he has a small and narrow output. In his third collection, *The Empty Street*, there is a noticeable shift in setting. Cowan now writes of people in suburbia, for whom the country is a refuge. The sense of being caught in an irresistible and disastrous historical process is expressed in a story like "The Tractor", which concerns the efforts of a hermit to stop the clearing of the land. Cowan's sympathies are with those who oppose "progress", but he sees their dilemma truly. "The Empty Street", a novella, is an impressive study of an unhappy middle-aged clerk, whose marriage is now a mere shell, and whose children are strangers to him: desperate to escape the pressures of a life that is meaningless to him, he collapses into schizophrenia and turns murderer. Cowan is especially responsive to the theme of the middle-aged, defeated and desolate in marriage, groping for a way out.

A number of his stories remain uncollected, including "The Rock" (*Meanjin Quarterly* [Melbourne] 4/1965), in which his mastery of the short story is perhaps best seen.

Peter Cowan's two attempts at novels have not been very successful. *Summer* is a short novel, more like two short stories that have been expanded and linked together. A business-man whose marriage has failed takes a job on the wheat bins, and in this lonely setting forms a relationship with the wife of the nearby storekeeper. The violent resolution is not well managed, and the central character tends to be a mouthpiece for Cowan's reflections on the spoiling of the natural environment. Yet there are some fine sequences establishing the relationship of the two lonely people in a solitary landscape.

In *Seed* Cowan set out to portray a group of middle-class families living in Perth. An Australian reader feels the force of his thesis about the boredom and frustration of suburban living, but it remains a thesis and seldom quickens into drama. It is a disappointing work, the result of Cowan's trying to write against the grain of his talent. He is not skilled at creating personalities or at suggesting the social facts of life, but in this rather old-fashioned, realistic novel the emphasis falls on just those aspects of his writing where he is weakest.

The distinction of Peter Cowan's stories rests on his insight into what Yeats once called "the quarrel with ourselves". He writes of a character in *Seed*:

> At such times he knew a strange duality, as if he were at the edge of two kinds of life, one of people, their buildings, of the work he did all day, the other his interest in the places where people did not go and where other forms of life took on an increasing reality, a significance, that at times he found hard to return from, not easily displaced by what others regarded, and would assure him, was the normal world of human beings. It was as if he belonged nowhere. An emptiness, an uncertainty, displaced the simple affirmation of life, creating an ambivalence he supposed people sensed in some of his painting. And which he supposed was why they did not like it.

Substituting "writing" for "painting", we have an interpretation of Peter Cowan more acute than that any critic could hope to offer.

—John Barnes

---

**COZZENS, James Gould.** American. Born in Chicago, Illinois, 19 August 1903. Educated at the Kent School, Connecticut; Harvard University, Cambridge, Massachusetts, 1922–24. Served in the United States Army Air Force, 1942–45: Major. Married Bernice

Baumgarten in 1927. School Teacher, Santa Clara, Cuba, 1925. Associate Editor, *Fortune* magazine, New York, 1938. Recipient: O. Henry Award, 1936; Pulitzer Prize, 1949; Howells Medal, 1960. Litt.D., Harvard University, 1952. Member, National Institute of Arts and Letters. Address: Shadowbrook, Williamstown, Massachusetts 01267, U.S.A.

PUBLICATIONS

Novels

> *Confusion.*  Boston, Brimmer, 1924.
> *Michael Scarlett: A History.*  New York, Boni, 1925.
> *Cock Pit.*  New York, Morrow, 1928.
> *The Son of Perdition.*  New York, Morrow, and London, Longman, 1929.
> *S. S. San Pedro: A Tale of the Sea.*  New York, Harcourt Brace, and London, Longman, 1931.
> *The Last Adam.*  New York, Harcourt Brace, 1933; as *A Cure of Flesh*, London, Longman, 1933.
> *Castaway.*  New York, Random House, and London, Longman, 1934.
> *Men and Brethren.*  New York, Harcourt Brace, and London, Longman, 1936.
> *Ask Me Tomorrow; or, The Pleasant Comedy of Young Fortunatus.*  New York, Harcourt Brace, and London, Longman, 1940.
> *The Just and the Unjust.*  New York, Harcourt Brace, 1942; London, Cape, 1943.
> *Guard of Honor.*  New York, Harcourt Brace, 1948; London, Longman, 1949.
> *By Love Possessed.*  New York, Harcourt Brace, 1957; London, Longman, 1958.
> *Morning Noon and Night.*  New York, Harcourt Brace, and London, Longman, 1968.

Short Stories

> *Children and Others.*  New York, Harcourt Brace, 1964; London, Longman, 1965.

\*     \*     \*

In the Epilogue to *Morning Noon and Night* James Gould Cozzens writes: "My creative effort is hardly one to serve the high end that has been defined as enriching the reader's soul and enlarging his personality . . ." A little later he adds:

> Of necessity the useful truths of this life are trivial; they are helpful hints when met with quandaries of ordinary existence. Any truth that purports to be great by so purporting must make itself an untruth, will have only the stopgap usefulness the earnestly told lie may sometimes have.
>
> (*Morning Noon and Night*, page 404.)

These remarks, in the first instance, represent the comment of the novel's narrator, Henry Worthington, on the tale he has just told; they can also stand as Cozzens' own assessment of the longer series of novels he has written. The general texture of the novels themselves suggests that Cozzens is suspicious of writers who shatter the universe to make it anew on the basis of some dogma, psychological or political or religious. Cozzens' intent is rather to assess the upper-class tradition that has shaped him, to note the dangers that threaten it, and to defend it by strategies of analysis that are rational and sometimes even cold.

The novels, often charged with much narrative interest, tell of the attack on inherited values in the twentieth century; they are usually the values of the well-placed, the well-educated although the early novel, *The Last Adam*, is a kind of exception to this generalization since its doctor-hero offers one the vision of natural man beleaguered and oppressed by conventional society. But the bulk of the fiction, in contrast, centers interest on figures who experience threat to the imperfect, somewhat orderly world which they have inherited. It is the threat of world conflict in *Guard of Honor*, local violence to a small community in *The Just and the Unjust*, and the experience of disruptive passion to the hero himself in *By Love Possessed*.

If there is an archetypal plot in the novels of Cozzens, it is this one. The hero—the focus of awareness, as Henry James would say—is a man who has reached "the middle of the journey". Like Dante in *The Divine Comedy*, the Cozzens hero has accumulated, in the ordinary process of existing, a body of impressions about his share of experience. Then some circumstance threatens the continuation of ordinary life. The reaction of the endangered Cozzens hero is, in many a novel, protective. He usually judges that he has lived a life which, by ordinary humane standards, has been marked by decency and some degree of order. His share in the general human lot has not been a contemptible one; it is a share that falls short of perfection, to be sure, but it is also worth a degree of esteem. Thus, when some sort of disorder enters on the scene, the resolution and intelligence of the chief character set to work. What has been taken too much for granted—the comforts of peace, the sustaining web of justice executed in a community, the relations with wife and children that had seemed permanent but that are not—must or should have continuation. It is a continuation that frequently turns out to be a "diminished thing", in Robert Frost's words. Thus, on the practical level, the Cozzens hero is involved in a salvage operation; the Cozzens hero must learn how to face up to the "quandaries of ordinary existence." He wishes to preserve from a fairly acceptable past what can be preserved. If there are elements that are irretrievable, the Cozzens figure accepts the correction which comes to him from the nature of things: a nature that, out of thoughtlessness and an uninspected optimism, he has not fully understood.

The Cozzens figures are capable of decisions; they are decisions that are never taken until the emergent problem has been carefully studied. For human action must proceed cautiously; for example, the hero of *The Just and the Unjust* draws not only on his own wisdom but on the wisdom which, in a time of stress, he remembers from the sage discourse of his father, a model of calm, rational, and admittedly upper-class insight.

But over and above this kind of thought—thought addressed to a very practical goal—there is in the novels of Cozzens a more generalizing vein of meditation; it is a vein that finally, in *Morning Noon and Night*, overshadows the narrative interest. The novels attempt to assess the meaning and value of life in America at a certain time and place. Cozzens may have begun with the doctor figure of *The Last Adam*, who is an assertion of the rights of the natural and primitive and spontaneous. But in the later novels the meditative capacities of men in crisis move in on this view. What becomes increasingly important is man's power to assess, to weigh pros and cons. This tendency becomes intense in the last two or three novels. Thus, the most recent one—*Morning Noon and Night*—is less a straightforward narrative than a free-moving inspection which a sixty year old man offers to every element of his experience: his impressively successful consulting business, his two marriages, and his daughter's failure to find stability. (A character's actual age is not of much importance; each hero is in fact in the middle of *his* journey.)

From all of Cozzens' effort a kind of consensus among his heroes emerges, a consensus that does not come to a revolutionary illumination but emerges little by little as is perhaps proper for the discovery of "useful truths." Negatively, there is—on the part of Cozzens and his meditative heroes—an aversion to the succession of panaceas, social and personal, that have passed across the field of twentieth century vision. For example and from Cozzens' point of view, the liberal imagination of our time has been in error even though it has the virtue of being more explicit than Cozzens' casual accumulation of "useful truths." These truths, as Cozzens represents them, come not from doctrinaire thinkers but from men like the father in *The Just and the Unjust*—men who give continuation to the styles of the world into which they were born. Such men are revealed as worthy servants of an essential, permanent reality. For they serve a tradition which they have experienced rather than indulge in facile speculation about better worlds to come.

Cozzens' frequent popularity may rest in part on his power to dramatize such impressions as those just mentioned. It rests also on his power to project these impressions into novels that are full of interest; plots move with dignity and order, and characters are recognizable. It must be noted that Cozzens' style becomes complex and involved in his later work, reaching a kind of climax in his study of familial relations disordered by passion, *By Love Possessed*. As already indicated, along with a movement from clarity to complexity goes a diminished attention for events in themselves; what counts for Cozzens in his latest work is the useful meaning that may be drawn from those events.

—Harold H. Watts

---

**CROSS, Ian.** New Zealander. Born in Wanganui in 1925. Educated at Wanganui Technical College. Married to Tui Tunnicliffe; has four sons. Associate Nieman Fellow in Journalism, Harvard University, Cambridge, Massachusetts, 1954–55; Public Relations Officer, New Zealand Police and Justice departments, 1956–58; Robert Burns Fellow, Otago University, Dunedin, 1959. Address: 6 Blackbridge Road, Wellington, New Zealand.

PUBLICATIONS

Novels

*The God Boy*.   New York, Harcourt Brace, 1957; London, Deutsch, 1958.
*The Backward Sex*.   London, Deutsch, 1960.
*After Anzac Day*.   London, Deutsch, 1961.

Uncollected Short Story

"Love Affair", in *Atlantic* (Boston), 1958.

Other

Play produced on television, 1970.

\*       \*       \*

Ian Cross has written three novels of social concern, which explore the tensions in personal relationships, especially those given emphasis by the narrow experience of small communities. *The God Boy* presents this material through the eyes of a thirteen year old boy who has, two years previously, been a participant in a family tragedy which he observed but did not understand, and which has left its mark upon him. Torn between his father and his mother, young Jimmy reacts with violence and obsession, a classic case history. A clever child who has thought of himself as "chosen", he expects God to give him a helping hand, but no aid comes. He therefore sets up his own private "mutiny against God." The book is notable for its skilful handling of a difficult narrative mode, and for its successful evocation of the speech and ways of an average New Zealand boy. Irony thickens the texture. The reader is closely involved with Jimmy, and like the social worker whose concern this kind of situation so often becomes, begins to comprehend the disaster from within, with sympathetic insight.

*The Backward Sex* disappoints by being too similar in both manner and material. Raggleton, the coastal settlement of *The God Boy*, has become Albertville, but is otherwise the same place, with a wider range of wharves, sandhills, lupins, and suburban lives as befits the older teller, this time a boy of 17. The topic is the fumbling sexuality of adolescence, but the theme does not seem serious, and the novel is not far above the level of melodrama.

*After Anzac Day* is wider in both scope and narration. Four people share the telling: The Girl, whose life is going wrong (she is pregnant but unmarried); The Woman, wife of Rankin, ex-soldier and public servant, whose marriage has become a prison with "solitary cells" where the inmates do not even attempt to communicate; The Man, her husband; and The Old Man, her father. These four play out a domestic drama springing from the presence in The Woman's expensive well-oiled home of Jennie, The Girl, to whom her husband has unexpectedly extended a helping hand. Each narrator is given a short turn, which allows Ian Cross to weave four different attitudes and backgrounds into the texture of his fictional world. Clearly, he means to raise wide social, personal, and even historical issues in the New Zealand of 1960. Had he succeeded fully, the elaborate narrative apparatus would have been justified, perhaps. But the problems of John and Margaret Rankin seldom lift above the level of private affairs; the story remains a family drama, without any transfer of significance to the wider issues. *The God Boy*, however, the best of these three novels, is a remarkable little work.

—Joan Stevens

---

**CUNNINGHAM, E. V.** See **FAST, Howard.**

---

**DAHL, Roald.** British. Born in Llandaff, South Wales, 13 September 1916. Educated at Repton School, 1929–32. Served in the Royal Air Force, 1939–45. Married the actress Patricia Neal in 1953; has four children. Member of the Eastern Staff, Shell Company, London, 1933–37, and Shell Company of East Africa, Dar-es-Salaam, 1937–39. Recipient: Edgar Allan Poe Award, 1952, 1954. Address: Gipsy House, Great Missenden, Buckinghamshire, England.

PUBLICATIONS

Novel

*Sometime Never: A Fable for Supermen.* New York, Scribner, 1948; London, Collins, 1949.

Short Stories

> *Over to You: 10 Stories of Flyers and Flying.* New York, Reynal and Hitchcock, 1946; London, Hamish Hamilton, 1947.
> *Someone Like You.* New York, Knopf, 1953; London, Secker and Warburg, 1954; revised edition, London, Joseph, 1961.
> *Kiss, Kiss.* New York, Knopf, and London, Joseph, 1960.
> *Twenty-Nine Kisses.* London, Joseph, 1969.
> *Selected Stories.* New York, Random House, 1970.
> *Penguin Modern Stories 12*, with others. London, Penguin, 1972.

Uncollected Short Stories

> "The Visitor", in *Playboy* (Chicago), April 1965.
> "The Last Act", in *Playboy* (Chicago), January 1966.

Plays

> *The Honeys* (produced New York, 1955).

> Screenplays: *You Only Live Twice,* 1965; *Chitty-Chitty-Bang-Bang,* 1967; *The Night-Digger,* 1970; *The Lightning Bug,* 1971; *Willie Wonka and the Chocolate Factory,* 1971.

Other

> *The Gremlins* (juvenile). New York, Random House, 1943; London, Collins, 1944.
> *James and the Giant Peach* (juvenile). New York, Knopf, 1961; London, Allen and Unwin, 1967.
> *Charlie and the Chocolate Factory* (juvenile). New York, Knopf, 1964; London, Allen and Unwin, 1967.
> *The Magic Finger* (juvenile). New York, Harper, 1966; London, Allen and Unwin, 1968.
> *Fantastic Mr. Fox* (juvenile). New York, Knopf, and London, Allen and Unwin, 1970.

Critical Studies: in *New York Herald-Tribune*, 7 February 1960; *Wilson Library Bulletin* (New York), February 1962; *Saturday Review* (New York), 17 February 1962; *Contemporary Authors*, vol. 1, Detroit, Gale Research Company, 1967.

Roald Dahl comments:

I am primarily a short-story writer. But a good plot is hard to find, and it gets harder all the time. No short-story writer should continue in this field when he has run out of plots, otherwise he finishes up producing indifferent work, as well as "mood-pieces" and essays all labelled "short stories"—which they are not.

I now write books for children. It gives me great pleasure. Sometimes I write screenplays for my wife, who is an actress.

*    *    *

Conventional human responses to bizarre circumstances domesticate Dahl's carefully detailed, grotesque world. This shock of the familiar makes credible the logic of a cautionary tale in a universe that initially seems devoid of guidelines. "An African Story," which only tangentially develops the theme of Dahl's first adult book, *Over to You: Ten Stories of Flyers and Flying*, foreshadows the pattern dominating his later work. A neurotic's sensitivity to unpleasant animal habits causes an elderly Englishman to sacrifice him to a deadly Mamba snake that can, in a characteristic Dahl touch, drink milk from a cow. Though the neurotic is punished rather more severely than he might be at home, the vengeful old man emerges as a champion of the typical English dedication to animals which operates even in the jungle. The snake's contented sip of milk after the killing produces a simultaneous effect of horror and conventional moral righteousness.

Dahl's only adult novel, *Sometime Never: A Fable for Supermen*, which attempts to raise the war horrors and hallucinations of *Over to You* to the mythic level, effectively details some deadpan accounts of the discovery of gremlins, who "scraped platinum off the points and put it carefully into small leather purses which had zip-fasteners on them." However, Dahl's whimsical treatment of these creatures undercuts their lethal activities, which are "a bit too much like death to be funny . . . far too ridiculous to be amusing." And an atomic holocaust, that familiar feature of post-World War II novels, turns the gremlins of the second half of the book into rational thinkers contemptuous of the insanity of human war-making, though Dahl gives them Thurberish names like Snogs, Bogglers, and Hornswogglers. The final irony that equates total disappearance of human beings, an event long awaited by the gremlins, with the vanishing of these creatures themselves, since they are merely projections of the human imagination, does not resolve the contradictory roles of the gremlins and the resulting confusion in tone. Dahl's earlier children's book, *The Gremlins*, wisely maintains a comic atmosphere.

The quintessential pattern of domesticated (often in both senses) horror was firmly established in the stories Dahl collected as *Someone Like You* and *Kiss, Kiss*. Frequently these stories focus on a bet or competition, usually rigged, and the perverse morality of Dahl's universe causes the dishonest victor to lose his status as a gourmet in "Taste," a Chippendale commode in "Parson's Pleasure," his money *and* his life in "Dip in the Pool," and the title of "Champion of the World," among partridge poachers. (Conversely, the juvenile novel *Charlie and the Chocolate Factory* utilizes the contest motif to stress the rewards of virtuous triumph.) Dahl gives verisimilitude to these situations by bombarding the reader with a wealth of detail involving such disciplines as wine lore, period furniture, and partridge trapping. Often, this almost statistical documentation simultaneously reinforces otherwise improbable anecdotes and ridicules self-styled expertise.

The many stories involving mutilation, either real or threatened, also depend on factual data both to mitigate and substantiate the horror. "Skin" seems so knowledgeable about the details of Soutine's life and technique, and so deadpan in its dialogue, that negotiations for the picture Soutine inconveniently painted on the back of an elderly beggar seem at once utterly absurd and frighteningly realistic. Apparently factual data similarly buttress Dahl's treatment of experiments in the monstrous, whether the sinister effects of feeding a sickly baby on "Royal Jelly," or a downtrodden wife's reaction to the survival of her dead husband's brain in "William and Mary." Her practical wifely stance parallels a husband's malevolently commonsense response in "Edward the Conqueror" to his wife's ecstatic discovery that a stray cat houses the soul of Liszt.

Such mismatches occur frequently in Dahl's fiction and are often symbolized by the disproportionate physical dimensions of the partners: the diminutive husband and his "big rather than tall wife" in "My Lady Love, My Dove"; the tiny, repressed clergyman of "Georgy Porgy" and his amorous female parishioners, notably Miss Roach, ". . . a striking person—unusually muscular for a woman, with broad shoulders and powerful arms and a huge calf bulging on each leg." Dahl also stresses physiognomy, especially the mouth, as an index to character. People with "salmon" mouths ("Nunc Dimittis") and "caterpillar" mouths ("Mr. Hoddy") display the appropriate traits, and the gourmet's mouth in "Taste" functions not merely as the key to his character, but as the character itself: ". . . all mouth—

mouth and lips—the full, wet lips of the professional gourmet, the lower lip hanging downward in the center, a pendulous, permanently open taster's lip, shaped open to receive the rim of a glass or a morsel of food. Like a keyhole, I thought, watching it; his mouth is like a large wet keyhole."

The symbolic possibilities of the mouth achieve fullest development in "Georgy Porgy," the title itself suggesting Dahl's gift for playing with the perverse implications of the childlike. The sex education given the protagonist by his progressive mother goes awry when the boy, witnessing the birth of rabbits, sees that the fondling, kissing mouth of the mother rabbit is devouring its offspring. Immediately, the child perceives his own mother's "huge red mouth opening wider and wider until it is just a great big round gaping hole with a black black centre . . ." This regrettable epiphany foreshadows his response years later when Miss Roach attempts to kiss him: "I saw this great mouth of hers coming slowly down on top of me, starting to open, and coming closer and closer, and opening wider and wider . . . I had never in all my life seen anything more terrifying than that mouth. . . ." The clergyman's final insane conviction that he has been swallowed and now inhabits the woman's interior is made credible by his matter-of-fact tone: "It is all a trifle bizarre for a man of conservative tastes like myself. Personally, I prefer oak furniture and parquet flooring. . . ." Though Dahl avoids underlining the ultimate significance of his key symbol, he illuminates it obliquely through the clergyman's wonderfully detailed experiments with the sex drives of rats. In blending the ordinary and the grotesque, in ballasting both with convincing details and, especially, in preserving a delightfully ambivalent attitude toward the reader's credulity, "Georgy Porgy" might serve as the archetype for Dahl's fiction.

—Burton Kendle

---

**DAHLBERG, Edward.** American. Born in Boston, Massachusetts, 22 July 1900. Educated at the University of California, Berkeley; Columbia University, New York, B.S. in philosophy 1925. Served in World War I. Married Winifred Donlea in 1942; Julia Lawlor, 1967; has two children. Taught at Boston University, 1947; New York University, Summer 1950; University of Missouri at Kansas City (Cockefair Professor), 1964–65; Columbia University, 1968. Recipient: Longview Foundation Award, 1961; National Institute of Arts and Letters award, 1961; Rockefeller grant, 1965; Ariadne Foundation award, 1970; Cultural Council Foundation award, 1971. Member, National Institute of Arts and Letters. Address: c/o Walter Arnold, E. P. Dutton, publishers, 201 Park Avenue South, New York, New York 10003, U.S.A.

PUBLICATIONS

Novels

*Bottom Dogs.*   London, Putnam, 1929; New York, Simon and Schuster, 1930.
*From Flushing to Calvary.*   New York, Harcourt Brace, 1932; London, Putnam, 1933.
*Those Who Perish.*   New York, Day, 1934.

Short Stories

*Kentucky Blue Grass Henry Smith.*   Cleveland, White Horse Press, 1932.

Verse

*Cipango's Hinder Door*.   Austin, University of Texas Press, 1965.


Other

*Do These Bones Live*.   New York, Harcourt Brace, 1941; revised edition, as *Can These Bones Live*, New York, New Directions, 1960.
*Sing, O Barren*.   London, Routledge, 1947.
*The Flea of Sodom*.   New York, New Directions, and London, Peter Nevill, 1950.
*The Sorrows of Priapus*.   New York, New Directions, 1957.
*Truth Is More Sacred: A Critical Exchange on Modern Literature*, with Herbert Read.   London, Routledge, and New York, Horizon Press, 1961.
*Alms for Oblivion: Essays*.   Minneapolis, University of Minnesota Press, and London, Oxford University Press, 1964.
*Because I Was Flesh* (autobiography).   New York, New Directions, 1964; London, Methuen, 1965.
*Reasons of the Heart: Maxims*.   New York, Horizon Press, 1965.
*The Edward Dahlberg Reader*.   New York, New Directions, 1967.
*Epitaphs of Our Time: The Letters of Edward Dahlberg*.   New York, Braziller, 1967.
*The Leafless Americans*.   Sausalito, California, Beacham Press, 1967.
*The Carnal Myth: A Search into Classical Sensuality*.   New York, Weybright and Talley, 1968; London, Calder and Boyars, 1970.
*The Confessions of Edward Dahlberg*.   New York, Braziller, 1971.


Bibliography: *A Bibliography of Edward Dahlberg* by Harold Billings, Austin, University of Texas Press, 1971.


Manuscript Collection: University of Texas, Austin.


Critical Studies: Introduction by D. H. Lawrence to *Bottom Dogs*, 1929; Introduction by Sir Herbert Read to *Sing, O Barren*, 1947; Introduction by Paul Carroll to *The Edward Dahlberg Reader*, 1967; *Edward Dahlberg: American Ishmael of Letters*, edited by Harold Billings, Austin, Texas, Roger Beachum, 1968; "Edward Dahlberg Issue" of *Tri-Quarterly* (Evanston, Illinois), Fall 1970.

*       *       *

Edward Dahlberg began as a novelist of social realism but burst that harness in his early thirties and, harkening to the Sirens in the ancient seas of his reading, became the greatest American essayist of the period. Fiction could wait, and for thirty years immersed in a rare-book collection such as institutions boast he delved as he urges all to do if they would ply his trade. Slowly, with infinite labor, essays took form—prophetic, critical, satirical, erudite. Within these types other qualities are found: paragraphs are in turn epigrammatically prosed and lyrically versed. There is also a separate volume of poetry, and who else today writes a whole book of epigrams? The mastery of rhetoric and prosody is everywhere. A classicist, he is by nature clear and precise. If the reader falters, the reason is a want of vocabulary which is no concern of Dahlberg's but simply a matter between the reader and several dictionaries containing Middle English and rare and aureate terms from the Renaissance.

As a gleaner of the whole lexicon as well as a defier of Establishments he has brought much criticism on his head; his attackers most often set up his special diction as the target—words like *hebenon, aconited, brimborion*. But defense is easy; we might say the matter is one of relative literacy. A historical linguist, for example, will have much less difficulty with Dahlberg's words than will someone with no formal training in the language and only a slight reading background. All specialties aside, taking Dahlberg as a universal author, we are challenged by some of the strange forms that flit through his pages, exactly as we are by Burton and Browning and a host of others. Ignorance in a reader can hardly be called a proof of obscurantism.

This seasoning with esoteric words is a feature of the essays and also, but on a lesser scale, of the bulk of his work, including his letters. (When writing to a friend it is natural for him to use the English of a five hundred year old man.) In his narratives—both fiction and autobiography—the vocabulary is closer to vernacular, "appropriate," as D. H. Lawrence said in his introduction to *Bottom Dogs*. The early books, the novels, were spared the charges of pedantry and obscurantism. In fact their only persistent detractor has been the author himself, who to this day discredits *Bottom Dogs* ("dunghill fiction"), *From Flushing to Calvary* ("a heap of pleonasms, misconceived metaphors, outrageous similes, and 'new' conceits"), and *Those Who Perish*, in spite of the hospitality they enjoyed in the thirties.

It is one of Edward Dahlberg's distinctions that he can so subtly combine genres within a single work. Once past his youthful period of story-telling, through the many years of ladening himself with the substance of his masters he developed an essay in which flashes of narrative charge his arguments, and the pure notes of lyric and heroic poetry alter the moods of gloom. Humor also is often present. In the three early novels he had pretty well stuck to uncomplicated story, depending on symbolic characters and actions to transmit his ideas. Years later, spilling over with the lore of a dozen cultures and centuries, he apparently became impatient of "prose fiction" and used the forge of exposition and dialectic.

The nineteen sixties—his sixties too—saw him return to narrative which is dramatic like Chaucer's. He was at work on "my Spanish novella" in 1966, following publication of one of his finest books, the autobiographical *Because I Was Flesh*. He has just released his *Confessions*, which, like *Because I Was Flesh*, provides many novelistic details of characterization and events. *Confessions* is different in one respect which is of great significance: it not only presents a person who is essentially a product of the creative imagination, but, even more important, this persona has a healthy libido problem which prompts shocking but impeccably phrased dialogue on a high comic level.

Dahlberg's ability to write humorously is something to wonder at. The lack of felicity in his life, most of which has been spent in near-penury, would not seem conducive to a mirthful outlook in this septuagenarian who has, nevertheless, explosively proved that his affinities with Aristophanes, Chaucer, Rabelais, Moliere, and Voltaire are not due just to literary securities which they all hold in common but to the very fibers of the men. How is he able to change his mask at this date? The first answer is growth; a new phase is entered, new techniques are tried. Also, the bitch goddess of whom he was first to speak, who spurned him in the book markets for so long, has relented, and his volumes since 1960 have brought him a rain of praise, on one who cried alone in the desert for many a year. Though grief and pain are old fellows to him he remains a mirthful man, one who now finds it possible to show more of himself.

From the early novels, on to *Because I Was Flesh*, and on to *The Confessions*, comedic growth is easy to trace. In each there are the sure flicks of detail and the true dialogue of a great storyteller. *The Confessions*, moreover, bodies forth a gallery of characters quaintly named—Anybody's Miserable Chagrin (the narrator), Dr. However Pointless, Busy Perverse, and others of simple nomenclature who remain abstractions like Langland's (Dahlberg's model): Reason, Logic, Intelligence, Pity, Humility, Alone, Want, Feeling. They are used ironically, as in *Piers Plowman*, and the mood is light, however serious the content.

To him sex is either sacred or comic. Its preludes, after an honored tradition, are ludicrous. But he always stops short of pornographic amplification. For example, in *Confessions* his yearning suitor is like the demanding husbands in Lysistrata, or "hende" and handy Nicholas seizing the Miller's heroine by queynte and haunch-bone. Minutes after meeting his beloved's father the young Dahlberg of *The Confessions* is accused by him of intending to "suck up the breath of my daughter's skirts," and Mary herself is thus addressed: "Daughter, his eyes are sewers gluttonously lapping you up." The bones of politesse are roughly rattled by impropriety and the unexpectedness both of the young suitor's "goat-toothed madness" and the father's graphic remarks. Dahlberg's dialogue, incidentally, blends Elizabethan and Restoration formality and flourish with the worn devices of melodrama.

Underneath he is, naturally, always in earnest. As the Greeks preached moderation, the medievals salvation, the neoclassicists progress, so Dahlberg ceaselessly strives to make men wise. His method alters—in cycles, it seems—for he turned from fiction and its human types and their bodies, mouths, foods, odors, appetites. Giving long service with essays of thought and truth he cerebrally glorified the senses but chose not to use the form of story. The essays rail against greed and pride, injustice, hypocrisy of men and of artists in particular. At the same time, incessantly beseeching us to love, they make a fifth gospel composed by a man who is Swedish and Jewish and not in the formal sense "Christian." In all of his work he sings the beauty of Creation, and marine images are pervasive. (They superabound in *Those Who Perish*.) Now, with *Because I Was Flesh* and *The Confessions* he has triumphantly shown how much he can offer beyond polemics on literary criticism and social ills. The Beat writers found in him an oracle, and the late sixties and early seventies establish him as the only older living writer popular among collegian cultists of some sophistication, among whom the most alert and knowledgeable read his every word.

There is, however, a schism between him and other writers near his age. Strict, sometimes harsh, in his judgements, he has attacked most of the "great" novelists and poets of the first half of this century as well as critics such as Edmund Wilson who help to run the American Establishment. At the beginning he alienated Farrell, Caldwell, Dos Passos and others and, he says, was barred by many publishers. Of real significance is the failure by his contemporaries to include in discussions of current literature the name of one who may be called the giant in their midst. He makes his way without them; the help he has received has come from publishers and editors such as William Jovanovich, Harold Billings, and Jonathan Williams. Most recently American and British book-reviewers have begun to join his court. And about time they did.

—William M. Ryan

---

**DATHORNE, O(scar) R(onald).** British. Born in Georgetown, Guyana, 19 November 1934. Educated at the University of Sheffield, Yorkshire, 1955–58, B.A. 1958, M.A. 1960, Ph.D. 1966; University of London, 1958–59, Cert.Ed. 1959, Dip.Ed. 1967. Married Hildegard Ostermaier in 1959; has two children. Lecturer, Ahmadu Bello University, Zaria, Nigeria, 1959–63, and University of Ibadan, Nigeria, 1963–66; UNESCO Consultant to the Government of Sierra Leone, 1967–68; Professor of English, Njala University College, University of Sierra Leone, Freetown, 1968–69. Since 1970, Professor, Afro-American Studies Department, University of Wisconsin, Madison. Address: 8904 Friedburg bei Augsburg, Luberstrasse 2, Germany.

PUBLICATIONS

Novels

*Dumplings in the Soup*. London, Cassell, 1963.

*The Scholar Man.*   London, Cassell, 1964.

Uncollected Short Stories

"Hodge", in *Nigerian Radio Times* (Ibadan), 1967.
"The Nightwatchman and the Baby Nurse", in *Nigerian Radio Times* (Ibadan), 1967.
"The Wintering of Mr. Kolawole", in *Black Orpheus* (Ibadan), 1967.
"Constable", in *Political Spider*.   London, Heinemann, 1969.

Other

Editor, with others, *Young Commonwealth Poets '65*.   London, Heinemann, 1965.
Editor, *Caribbean Narrative*.   London, Heinemann, 1965.
Editor, *Caribbean Verse*.   London, Heinemann, 1967.
Editor, with Willfried Feuser, *Africa in Prose*.   London, Penguin, 1969.

Verse published in magazines.

Bibliography: in *Bibliography of Neo-African Literature from Africa, America and the Caribbean* by Jahnheinz Jahn, London, Deutsch, and New York, Praeger, 1965.

Critical Studies: "Guyanese Writers" by Wilfred Cartey, in *New World* (Georgetown, Guyana), 1966; *The Islands in Between* by Louis James, London, Oxford University Press, 1968; *The Chosen Tongue* by Gerald Moore, London, Longman, 1969.

O. R. Dathorne comments:

My work has in general utilized situations which seemed near enough for me to handle. Black immigration in England, a black man's quest for identity in Africa have been the starting points for what I hope have been larger involvements of the protagonist's new understanding of the world. Frequently, the "new" contact with reality cannot be resolved on a rational level and this is why in plays and poetry I have moved towards an intentionally "irrational" approach which expresses bewilderment.

I lived for ten years in Africa; they taught me to be wary of novelty, as did the creative urges of young African writers like myself. Only incidentally, I became a "critic" of the new African literature; only incidentally, I was forced to learn about a man's world-view (which I had to understand) before I spoke. Only incidentally this led me back to myself and the large interrogatives concerning my history. Now I am aware of the manifestations of curious parallels in cultural experience and it is this I proclaim.

\*       \*       \*

O. R. Dathorne as a novelist has two characteristics—an eye for comic idiosyncrasy, in particular African and West Indian, and a concern for the predicament of the expatriate. The first is uppermost in *Dumplings in the Soup*. Here John Jiffey Jacket gets a room in a London tenement crowded with immigrant lodgers. They are dominated by Boffo, a genial non-rent-paying confidence man who enlivens the religious devotions of the local Shakers club with strong drinks, and lets his landlord's cellar to a newcomer from Africa for fifty pounds in advance. The book is lively and readable, but the comic exaggeration undermines the more serious undertones, and ultimately, some of the comedy itself.

*The Scholar Man* is a more complex and successful book. Adam Questus, a West Indian, goes in search of Egor, an English-born mulatto who has had such a strong impression on his childhood that Adam looks to him for a meaning for his life. He teaches English at a University in an African state on the brink of independence. In his quest he visits a village where cult-drumming induces a trance in which he glimpses his slave-ancestry: at the same time the cult-whip inflicts a blow that would have been fatal but for the self-sacrifice of a University servant. He finds Egor has vanished, but making love to the mentally deficient girl Egor had run away with, he glimpses the highly ambiguous "reality" he had been seeking.

The search, with its echoes of Conrad's *Heart of Darkness*, is interwoven with satirical comedy about expatriate academic life and the political turmoil of a country exchanging one set of superstitions for another in its own search for identity. Some of the humour is again too forced, but the comedy also touches the wider theme, the absurdities of reality.

—Louis James

---

**DAVIES, Rhys.** British. Born in Rhondda Valley, Wales, 9 November 1903. Educated at Porth County School. Served in the British War Office, 1939–41. Recipient: Welsh Arts Council Prize, 1971. O.B.E. (Officer, Order of the British Empire), 1968. Address: c/o Curtis Brown Ltd., 13 King Street, London W.C.2, England.

PUBLICATIONS

Novels

*The Withered Root.*   London, Holden, 1927; New York, Holt, 1928.
*Rings on Her Fingers.*   London, Shaylor, and New York, Harcourt Brace, 1930.
*Count Your Blessings.*   London, Putnam, 1932; New York, Covici Friede, 1933.
*The Red Hills.*   London, Putnam, 1932; New York, Covici Friede, 1933.
*Honey and Bread.*   London, Putnam, 1935.
*A Time to Laugh.*   London, Heinemann, 1937; New York, Stackpole, 1938.
*Jubilee Blues.*   London, Heinemann, 1938.
*Under the Rose.*   London, Heinemann, 1940.
*Tomorrow to Fresh Woods.*   London, Heinemann, 1941.
*The Black Venus.*   London, Heinemann, 1944; New York, Howell Soskin, 1946.
*The Dark Daughters.*   London, Heinemann, 1947; New York, Doubleday, 1948.
*Marianne.*   London, Heinemann, 1951; New York, Doubleday, 1952.
*The Painted King.*   London, Heinemann, and New York, Doubleday, 1954.
*The Perishable Quality.*   London, Heinemann, 1957.
*Girl Waiting in the Shade.*   London, Heinemann, 1960.
*Nobody Answered the Bell.*   London, Heinemann, and New York, Dodd Mead, 1971.

Short Stories

*The Song of Songs and Other Stories.*   London, Archer, 1927.

*Aaron.*   Privately printed, 1927.
*A Bed of Feathers.*   London, Mandrake Press, 1929.
*Tale.*   London, E. Lahr, 1930.
*The Stars, the World, and the Women.*   London, Joiner and Steele, 1930.
*A Pig in a Poke.*   London, Joiner and Steele, 1931.
*A Woman.*   London, Capell at the Bronze Snail Press, 1931.
*Arfon.*   London, Foyle, 1931.
*Daisy Matthews and 3 Other Tales.*   Waltham St. Lawrence, Berkshire, Golden Cockerel Press, 1932.
*Love Provoked.*   London, Putnam, 1933.
*One of Norah's Early Days.*   London, Grayson, 1935.
*The Things Men Do.*   London, Heinemann, 1936.
*A Finger in Every Pie.*   London, Heinemann, 1942.
*Selected Stories.*   Dublin, Fridberg, 1945.
*The Trip to London.*   London, Heinemann, and New York, Howell Soskin, 1946.
*Boy with a Trumpet.*   London, Heinemann, 1949; as *Boy with a Trumpet and Other Selected Short Stories*, New York, Doubleday, 1951.
*Collected Stories.*   London, Heinemann, 1955.
*The Darling of Her Heart and Other Stories.*   London, Heinemann, 1958.
*The Chosen One and Other Stories.*   London, Heinemann, and New York, Dodd Mead, 1967.

Play

*No Escape*, with Archibald Batty (produced Eastbourne, 1954).   London, Evans, 1955.

Other

*My Wales.*   London, Jarrolds, 1937; New York, Funk and Wagnalls, 1938.
*Sea Urchin: Adventures of Jorgen Jorgensen.*   London, Duckworth, 1940.
*The Story of Wales.*   London, Collins, and New York, Hastings House, 1943.
*Print of a Hare's Foot* (autobiography).   London, Heinemann, and New York, Dodd Mead, 1969.

Bibliography: in *Ten Contemporaries* by John Gawsworth, London, Benn, 1932.

Manuscript Collections: Humanities Research Center, University of Texas, Austin; The Sterling Library, University of London.

Critical Studies: *Rhys Davies: A Critical Sketch* by R. L. Mégroz, London, Foyle, 1932; *The Contemporary Anglo-Welsh Novelists: Jack Jones, Rhys Davies, and Hilda Vaughan* by G. F. Adam, Bern, Francke, 1950.

Rhys Davies comments:

My novels and short stories, for the most part, take Wales for background, but I have tried to avoid depicting the behaviour of Welsh people as natively or peculiarly idiosyncratic, except when they deserve it.

*     *     *

No Anglo-Welsh writer of the twentieth century has been so prolific as Rhys Davies and no writer so uncompromisingly professional. If he has made his name particularly in the field of the short story, it is because his special talent is for the small cast, the confined scene and the few reiterated motifs which together create a microcosm and interpret it. He has little use for a language that has a life of its own: for him it is always the servant of the mood or intention: the almost irrepressible lyricism of a Glyn Jones or the pointed wit of a Gwyn Thomas, tirelessly blowing up and pricking a social balloon held in the observer's hand, are equally foreign to his method. A quotation from Francis Quarles, which came to Neville Braybrooke's mind after reading Rhys Davies, seems particularly apposite: "The heart is a small thing, but desireth great matters; it is not sufficient for a kite's dinner, yet the whole world is not sufficient for it." It may be added that "the whole world" has a way of matching itself in size to the heart. What Rhys Davies does best is the concentration of "great matters" into the vocabulary and consciousness of the ordinary man and woman. They are there without grandiloquence and their colour is native.

Yet it would be false to suggest that the writing of Rhys Davies was from the beginning as it has just been described. He was in his teens when Caradoc Evans's *My People* and the other earthquakers which succeeded it shook a horrified Wales and produced seismic tremors amongst Welsh exiles in London. Chronologically Rhys Davies was Caradoc's most immediate successor: the compass had been set for the Anglo-Welsh short story and most of its practitioners who had work in print by 1937 were affected, in varying degrees, by the notoriety, the blackened lineaments, of Caradoc's Cardiganshire peasants. Rhys Davies did not succeed to Caradoc's hate, but he did succeed to his eccentricity—that is, to the established manner of displaying Welsh eccentricity for the amusement of London. For a writer who had to make his way with nothing in his head and heart but a Welsh upbringing it was almost inevitable that it should be so. Thus we see him usually as the amused onlooker rather than the boy or youth involved: what he made of Tonypandy from the beginning was much less the grim face of unemployment (though there are stories about this) than a parade of social quirks—like his own juvenile corpse-viewing proclivities—and pinpricks suffered by settled and puritan attitudes in the Valleys. Generalization, however, is peculiarly difficult with Rhys Davies: undoubtedly he did take from Caradoc Evans that sense of oppression which the limitation of the human qualities or interests and the life-topics to be annotated can so fully convey: in *Arfon*, for instance, the cruelty of parents, schoolmaster, minister and companions in school may fairly be compared with the unthinking, inevitable cruelty of Caradoc's scrabbling peasants, and "Nightgown", in its picture of shut-in, put-upon woman-hood, makes use of just that inexorable selectivity that Caradoc claimed he learned from listening to the stories of Marie Lloyd. But from the beginning Rhys Davies wrote stories of many kinds: the humour of "The Dilemma of Catherine Fuchsias" is quite different from anything within Cardoc's power. Rhys Davies's particular delight revealed itself not in blackening puritanism so much as confronting it with the erotic, with the anti-social, with the irresponsible, and "crossing" the strands of belief and attitude in such fashion as to show more fully the complexities of Welsh life. One often feels this to be deliberately quizzical: it is Noah Watts, the ministerial student, for instance, who emerges as the most challenging aspirant to the hand of the heiress Olwen Powell in the "courting in bed" *series* depicted in *The Black Venus*; in the short story "The Benefit Concert" it is not solely the deacons of Horeb who score points for sharp management—Jenkin, whose benefit it is, and Madame Sarah Watkins, not to mention the embattled parties to the argument, are all attempting to capitalise on their positions. It is important, perhaps, to note the objectivity of much of this writing, serious as well as humorous: the author's *interest* is unrevealed: while there is plenty of verbal rebellion, there is no possible revolution to be pointed at, no idealism to be singled out for underlining. Unlike the single-eyed propagandist in Gwyn Thomas, inventive as he may be, Rhys Davies is a writer of many eyes, most of them bland, a few penetrating, all non-committal.

But Rhys Davies has not written only about Wales. It may even be said that his absence from Wales for many years has meant recently a certain tiredness in his writing about his native country: the forms in which his stories are cast tend to refer endlessly to the Wales of the teens and twenties which made him and with which he was actively in touch. It is no accident, therefore, that in *The Darling of Her Heart* the best story is set in Provence (France is a country Davies has written penetratingly about in recent decades) and is limited in its scope to a consideration of three people, Ewart, a successful painter undergoing a crisis in his artistic development, Elinor, his tearful and sexually-deserted wife, and Francis, a young student admirer of Ewart's. "Tears, Idle Tears" is not merely a most revealing study of the personality and outlook of an entirely believable painter: it is also conceived in the terms that are Rhys Davies's greatest strength—a limited cast, the development of character and emotion against a precise measurement of time and a minutely observed background. The world, however microcosmic, is powerful and complete. The narrative triumphantly avoids cliché: the author shows his hand neither by a positive intrusion of view nor by a dressing of sentiment.

These are the qualities shown again in his latest novel, *Nobody Answered the Bell*. It is a short book of 150 odd pages, no more than twice the length of "Tears, Idle Tears", its virtues again those of concentration. That this is Rhys Davies's true strength is plain enough: some of his novels at least lose force as they open out and become more talkative: his earlier Welsh novels have dated insofar as they admit a form of verbose romanticism foreign to his later work. *Nobody Answered the Bell* is a study of a Lesbian situation, the "man" a usurper invited in while the "woman" is under stress (after the murder of her stepmother): the household becomes more and more isolated as the claustrophobia increases and the macabre conclusion is of the sort only possible in a situation so severed from life's generality.

Rhys Davies as a writer has the inscrutable quality of Alec Guinness as an actor. His characters live of themselves. His stamina and dedication and consistent quality have rightly been recognised in 1971 by the award of a Welsh Arts Council Prize.

—Roland Mathias

---

**DAVIES, Robertson.** Canadian. Born in Thamesville, Ontario, 28 August 1913. Educated at Upper Canada College; Queen's University, Kingston, Ontario; Balliol College, Oxford, 1936–38, B.Litt. 1938. Married Brenda Mathews in 1940; has three children. Teacher and Actor, Old Vic Theatre School and Repertory Company, London, 1938–40; Literary Editor, *Saturday Night*, Toronto, 1940–42; Editor and Publisher, *Examiner*, Peterborough, Ontario, 1942–63. Since 1960, Professor of English, and since 1962, Master of Massey College, University of Toronto. Formerly, Governor, Stratford, Ontario Shakespeare Festival; Member, Board of Trustees, National Arts Centre. Recipient: Louis Jouvet Prize, Dominion Drama Festival, for directing, 1949; Leacock Medal, 1955; Lorne Pierce Medal, 1961. LL.D., University of Alberta, Edmonton, 1957; Queen's University, Kingston, 1962; D.Litt., McMaster University, Hamilton, Ontario, 1959, University of Windsor, Ontario, 1971; D.C.L., Bishop's University, Lennoxville, Quebec, 1967. Fellow, Royal Society of Canada, 1967. Address: Massey College, 4 Devonshire Place, Toronto 5, Ontario, Canada.

PUBLICATIONS

Novels

*Tempest Tost*. Toronto, Clarke Irwin, 1951; London, Chatto and Windus, and New York, Rinehart, 1952.
*Leaven of Malice*. Toronto, Clarke Irwin, 1954; London, Chatto and Windus, and New York, Scribner, 1955.
*A Mixture of Frailties*. Toronto, Macmillan, London, Weidenfeld and Nicolson, and New York, Scribner, 1958.
*Fifth Business*. Toronto, Macmillan, and New York, Viking Press, 1970; London, Macmillan, 1971.

Plays

*Hope Deferred* (produced Montreal, 1948). Included in *Eros at Breakfast*, 1949.
*Fortune My Foe* (produced Ottawa, 1948). Toronto, Clarke Irwin, 1949.
*Eros at Breakfast* (produced Ottawa, 1948). Included in *Eros at Breakfast*, 1949.
*Overlaid* (produced Ottawa, 1949). Included in *Eros at Breakfast*, 1949.
*Eros at Breakfast and Other Plays*. Toronto, Clarke Irwin, 1949.
*At My Heart's Core* (produced Peterborough, Ontario, 1950). Toronto, Clarke Irwin, 1950.
*King Phoenix* (produced Peterborough, Ontario, 1950).
*A Masque of Aesop* (produced Toronto, 1952). Toronto, Clarke Irwin, 1952.
*A Jig for the Gypsy* (produced Toronto, 1954). Toronto, Clarke Irwin, 1954.
*Hunting Stuart* (produced Toronto, 1955).
*Love and Libel* (produced New York, 1960).
*A Masque of Mr. Punch* (produced Toronto, 1962). Toronto, Oxford University Press, 1963.

Other

*Shakespeare's Boy Actors*. London, Dent, 1939; New York, Russell, 1964.
*Shakespeare for Young Players: A Junior Course*. Toronto, Clarke Irwin, 1942.
*The Diary of Samuel Marchbanks* (essays). Toronto, Clarke Irwin, 1947.
*The Table Talk of Samuel Marchbanks* (essays). Toronto, Clarke Irwin, 1949.
*Renown at Stratford: A Record of the Shakespeare Festival in Canada, 1953*, with Tyrone Guthrie. Toronto, Clarke Irwin, 1953.
*Twice Have the Trumpets Sounded: A Record of the Stratford Shakespearean Festival in Canada, 1954*, with Tyrone Guthrie. Toronto, Clarke Irwin, 1954; London, Blackie, 1955.
*Thrice the Brinded Cat Hath Mew'd: A Record of the Stratford Shakespearean Festival in Canada, 1955*, with Tyrone Guthrie. Toronto, Clarke Irwin, 1955.
*A Voice from the Attic*. New York, Knopf, and Toronto, McClelland and Stewart, 1960.
*The Personal Art: Reading to Good Purpose*. London, Secker and Warburg, 1961.
*Samuel Marchbanks' Almanack*. Toronto, McClelland and Stewart, 1967.
*Stephen Leacock: Feast of Stephen*. Toronto, McClelland and Stewart, 1970.

Manuscript Collection: Massey College, University of Toronto.

Robertson Davies comments:

The theme which lies at the root of all of my novels and several of my plays is the isolation of the human spirit. This sounds somewhat gloomy but I have not attempted to deal with it in a gloomy fashion but rather to demonstrate that what my characters do that might be called really significant is done entirely on their own volition and usually contrary to what is expected of them. This theme, which might be called in C. G. Jung's phrase "The Search for the Self", is worked out in terms of characters, usually young, who are trying to escape from early influences and find their own place in the world, but who are reluctant to do so in a way that will bring pain and disappointment to others, and particularly to people of the previous generation. As I say, this may not look like a theme for comedy but I find it so, and many readers of my books have assured me that they agree.

*       *       *

Much that is best in the attempt to create a Canadian personality in literature has been satirical and self-denigrating. A nation that has as yet produced little that is memorable in lyrical or contemplative poetry has as its prized literary possession a superb anthology of sharp comic verse and among its poets at least one, F.R. Scott, who, though seldom noticed outside Canada, deserves to take his place among the few considerable satirical poets of this century.

Robertson Davies is in some senses the Frank Scott of Canadian prose. Like Scott he is cultivated, irascible, unbending, a relentless persecutor of the bourgeois mentality, the provincialism and the pretentiousness of his countrymen and yet, in the last resort, proudly patriotic and intensely optimistic that his scalpel-pen will remove the ulcers that inhibit the growth of a culture that is both truly Canadian and of international worth. And like so many of the leading Canadian writers—like Scott, MacLennan and A. J. M. Smith—Davies acquired his intellectual and artistic standards in part at least outside Canada. Even more than MacLennan, Scott or Smith, in middle-age he remains quintessentially the product of a British education. He is, again like so many Canadian authors, also an academic but in Davies' case, though his career has been set in Kingston and Toronto, he seems to dance still to tunes that are played at ancient universities and the wit, the stylishness and *hauteur* of his essays and his novels seem to be accompanied by the sound of donnish gossip and the port-decanter sliding across well polished tables.

High-toned critics have attempted to read into Davies' work some grandiose purpose: generally, a parable of the conflict between the lovely and lovable powers of the imagination and the hideous and pervasive forces of materialism. Such purpose it is not difficult to construct from the evidence of Davies' novels, but the effort reduces to pomposity the ingenuity of Davies' comedy. Because it blows him up to the level of universal genius, it tends to make Davies himself appear as one of those Canadian minnows whose whale-pretensions he is so eager to reduce to true scale. Because it aspires to place him in a very small group of grand masters whose achievements are beyond him it blunts the sharp edge of his satire on the hard stone of a *tu quoque*.

Enough to accept that Davies writes brilliantly, with a sense of comedy that is not often found in Canadian novels, and that, despite his superficial conservatism, he is at heart a reformer, his cause limited (but none the worse for that)—the destruction of the provincialism that is the canker of Canadian society.

Davies' fiction is a comparatively small part of his total work. He has written much for the theatre, a literary form in which Canada's achievement is remarkably slight and to which Davies has added little of lasting quality. He has been prolific as critic and essayist, but the prelude and in many ways the preliminary exposition of his novels is in two collections of newspaper columns: *The Diary of Samuel Marchbanks* and *The Table Talk of Samuel Marchbanks*, for in these there first appeared the satirical themes which were to be elaborated and given substance in his Salterton trilogy.

Marchbanks, a character who was unashamedly a Canadian and twentieth century re-incarnation of Samuel Johnson, abused in caustic fury the pettiness of Canadian life, laying about him with such uncompromising brutality that it is a miracle that he was allowed to practise his severe wit in the pages of a Canadian newspaper.

The novels that followed are superficially both more gentle—and certainly far more comic. In them Davies seems to have abandoned the sharpness of Samuel Johnson for the quiet satire of Anthony Trollope and though he hardly troubles to hide the fact that Salterton, the city of his fiction, is in fact Kingston, Ontario, it is not difficult to think of it as Barchester transplanted—and (because Davies sees the outmodishness of so much in Canada) a Barchester not much modernised.

But for all the comedy, in the novels, Davies' knife pierces the skin and gets to work on the very vitals of Canadian existence. Salterton-Kingston is plush with opportunities for a satirist. It has its university, its military college, its industries, its old families rich in little but the battered traditions of the United Empire Loyalists, and its new families rich in dollars and eager for traditions that are not theirs. The middle-class Saltertonians look with eyes full of envy towards the United States and spike their conversation with malice about all things American. Britain has for them a fascination that is equalled only by their insistence that the British are decadent. Salterton seldom looks at itself but Davies looks and sees balloons pretending to be human-beings.

The first of Davies' novels, *Tempest Tost*, is an uproarious travesty of Shakespeare's play in which Prospero, Miranda, Ferdinand, Caliban and Ariel are each given a Salterton and distorted-mirror image. The other novels in the Salterton trilogy, *Leaven of Malice* and *A Mixture of Frailties* have some of the same qualities, and particularly the same skill in plotting romance to satirical purpose. *Leaven of Malice* is less comic than *Tempest-Tost, A Mixture of Frailties* more serious than *Leaven of Malice*. The comedy is spasmodic and where it has been excised its place is taken by melodrama. Davies has come to believe that Canada is close to achieving an integrity of culture. A satirist who has lost his satirical purpose is like the vanishing Fool in *King Lear*. He has gone to bed at noon.

—J. E. Morpurgo

---

**DAVIN, Dan(iel Marcus).**   British.   Born in Invercargill, New Zealand, 1 September 1913. Educated at Marist Brothers' School, Invercargill; Sacred Heart College, Auckland; Otago University, Dunedin, M.A., Dip.M.A. 1936; Balliol College, Oxford (Rhodes Scholar), B.A., M.A. 1945. Served in the Royal Warwickshire Regiment, 1939–40, and in the New Zealand Division, 1940–45; M.B.E. (Member, Order of the British Empire), 1945. Married Winifred Gonley in 1939; has three children. Junior Assistant Secretary, 1946–48, and Assistant Secretary, 1948–69, Clarendon Press, Oxford; since 1970, Deputy Secretary to the Delegates of the Oxford University Press. Fellow of Balliol College, 1965. Address: 103 Southmoor Road, Oxford, England.

PUBLICATIONS

Novels

*Cliffs of Fall.*   London, Nicholson and Watson, 1945.

*For the Rest of Our Lives*.   London, Nicholson and Watson, 1947.
*Roads from Home*.   London, Joseph, 1949.
*The Sullen Bell*.   London, Joseph, 1956.
*No Remittance*.   London, Joseph, 1959.
*Not Here, Not Now*.   London, Hale, 1970.


Short Stories

*The Gorse Blooms Pale*.   London, Nicholson and Watson, 1947.


Other

*Introduction to English Literature*, with John Mulgan.   London, Oxford University Press, 1947; New York, Oxford University Press, 1948.
*Crete*.   Wellington, New Zealand Government War History Department, and London and New York, Oxford University Press, 1953.
*Writing in New Zealand: The New Zealand Novel*, with W. K. Davin.   Wellington, School Publications Board, 1956.
*Katherine Mansfield in Her Letters*.   Wellington, School Publications Board, 1959.

Editor, *New Zealand Short Stories*.   London and Wellington, Oxford University Press, 1953.
Editor, *Katherine Mansfield's Short Stories*.   London and Wellington, Oxford University Press, 1953.
Editor, *English Short Stories of Today: Second Series*.   London, Oxford University Press, 1958.


Critical Studies: in *New Zealand Literature* by Eric McCormick, London, Oxford University Press, 1959; in *Landfall* (Christchurch), September 1970.


Dan Davin comments:

My latest published novel more or less concludes, as far as I can at present project, a sequence of novels that I had in mind as long ago as 1939. The war and the turn my career subsequently took gave the novels I intended to write a different cast and brought in new themes and substance. Thus *Not Here, Not Now*, the last of the sequence, is the one I originally intended to have done first.

My work has suffered and gained from the fact that so large a share of my energies has had to go into an exacting and very responsible job.

My most recently written novel, *Brides of Price*, has only lately been submitted to my publisher for consideration. It makes a new departure (for me) in subject and technique. It may also be the last novel to be written by me.

*          *          *

On the evidence of his short stories and novels, Dan Davin might well echo Katherine Mansfield's nostalgic cry: "New Zealand is in my very bones." Despite his long residence as an expatriate in England, he returns continually to the haunts of his childhood and youth. As a New Zealander who has left his country, an Irish Catholic who has lost both creed and community, as a soldier in the New Zealand Division who cannot retain the comradeship he found in the service, he has kept faith with his memories, relives his estrangement from early allegiances and, with sympathetic if critical understanding, contemplates his fellow-country-men wherever they may be found. By so doing he has discovered a starting-point for much wider human explorations than the search for national identity, a starting-point not an anchorage.

Yet the anchorage is suggested if only because no writer has walked more consistently on his own shadow and in the places where that shadow has appeared. It is tempting, but in-accurate, to describe him as a regional novelist or perhaps as the historian and cartographer of a small enclave of Irish Catholics, farming and labouring within the confines of Southland and sending some of their children northwards as far as the University of Otago. His characters bear such names as Mark Burke, Ned Hogan, Tom O'Dwyer, Frank Fahey, Hugh Egan and Martin Cody; they have an assortment of qualities and fortunes that are not very dissimilar to Davin's. Whether they are in London, North Africa or more commonly in New Zealand, their Southland backgrounds travel with them and are described with loving care and great accuracy; their experiences and conflicts provide material for discussion and meditation; but the shadow of Dan Davin is always present, and his *Roads from Home* turn back towards the homeland that fires his imagination.

Nevertheless, that much of Davin's writing is comprised of incidents, places and people recollected in tranquillity is less important than his possession of the historian's eye for the appropriate detail and the artist's instinct for a workable situation. By remaining true to his memories he is able to give authenticity to his glimpses of provincial life, and by remaining true to himself fits them into a pattern of human change and struggle. His single collection of short stories, *The Gorse Blooms Pale*, contains clear and vivid evidence both of his bio-graphical dependence and of his ability to recreate and select from the local minutiae those features that best serve his purpose, for it is not the scene but the aim of his endeavour that becomes significant. Davin's provincial studies of an earlier Southland have not been under-taken as a simple act of piety to former days, but because he had discovered the fascination that the retracing of steps holds for those who are more than usually conscious of the con-tinuity of life and know that the future is contained in the womb of the past.

It is in *Roads from Home* rather than in his earlier or later novels dedicated to his memories of Southland that the thematic structure rivets attention and indicates some of his major pre-occupations. The plot serves, but no more than serves, the purpose. Davin is concerned with the implications of his title—the roads down which men travel from youth to age, the many roads they might have taken, the changing ways of the world, the old paths followed by established traditions and the new that excite the young and disturb their seniors. Southland has provided him with a microcosm of community life and aspiration, and with provincial material sufficient to reanimate old themes. Family relationships, complicated by a protestant daughter-in-law, unsettled by a son's loss of faith, the slow secularisation of life, the pathos of the clash between generations, the failure of communications between parents and children, husbands and wives, together with the threats of separation and departure, are unified by recurrent imagery associated with the walls that divide human beings and the roads that lead in different directions.

A characteristic feature of Davin's writing, not unconnected with his biography, is his ability to switch from a simple and unaffected language which catches the casual accents and speech habits of New Zealanders to a more complex and literary style. In his use of the interior monologue he combines the inward thoughts with indirect authorial elaboration that be-comes metaphorical and allusive, and is able to suggest wider implications than the bare narrative can supply. This is most apparent in his fictional record of the New Zealand Division in North Africa. Some have been inclined to dismiss *For the Rest of Our Lives* because it attempts, in the author's words, "to combine history and fiction in order to produce the illusions of reality," but fails to give that illusion through defects in its rendering of the fragments of dislocated lives and in the creation of character. It remains, however, an im-pressive novel, not because it achieves aims imposed on the writer from outside, but because its thematic structure serves another function, prescribed by its subject of war for the rest of our lives.

It has been praised for its realistic portrayal of the Desert war, condemned for unnecessary detail of leave periods with women and alcohol in Cairo, but rarely has the true nature of its achievement been acknowledged. War is its theme, not people; and war is impersonal. In their different ways all the characters of the book are conscious of the imminent presence of death, of fear, of the meaninglessness of life. By imagery, related episodes, by description and meditation, the emphasis is placed on the appalling insignificance of the individual in the immensity of time, on his feelings of helplessness and guilt in the midst of heroic exploits and the unbreakable unity of the Division, on the centuries-old martyrdom of man and the frightful continuity of history in pain and suffering. Behind the authentic record and under the guise of fiction it is "the warp and woof of things" that receives most attention, both by the major characters and by the organising skill of the novelist-recorder.

It is this concern with "the warp and woof of things," a concern deeper than that involving the norms usually considered as of over-riding importance in the writing of novels, with which throughout his career Davin has been most affected. It has often led to an indulgence in more discussion and reflection on social, political and philosophic problems than is customary and detracts from the illusion of reality which is usually the aim of a novelist. Nevertheless, it indicates that Davin's propensity to return to the homesteads of Southland and to abandoned household gods is not accountable to nostalgia alone, but rather to his desire to explore all the roads down which men pass as they seek to know and understand "the warp and woof of things."

—H. Winston Rhodes

---

**DAWSON, Jennifer.** British. Educated at Mary Datchelor School, London; St. Anne's College, Oxford, B.A. 1952. Has worked for the Clarendon Press, Oxford, and as a social worker in a mental hospital. Recipient: Black Memorial Prize, 1962. Address: c/o Anthony Blond Ltd., 56 Doughty Street, London W.C.1, England.

PUBLICATIONS

Novels

*The Ha-Ha.* London, Blond, and Boston, Little Brown, 1961.
*Fowler's Snare.* London, Blond, 1963.
*The Cold Country.* London, Blond, 1966.

Short Stories

*Penguin Modern Stories 10*, with others. London, Penguin, 1972.

\*       \*       \*

Novels which explore madness have certain qualities in common. They describe a world which is enclosed, static and ruled by obsessions; they are vivid, fragmented, highly personal documents in which only one character can be fully realised. This intensity is double-edged.

It can exclude, and ultimately bore, the reader or it can provide him with a vision of life which has a relevance beyond the barriers of mental illness. Kafka's metaphors have been readily accepted and understood. Jennifer Dawson's *The Ha-Ha* is one of the few contemporary novels significant enough to deserve the appellation Kafkaesque.

*The Ha-Ha* is set in a mental hospital where the narrator, Jean, is slowly recovering from a breakdown. She has progressed from the ward and the company of the irretrievably mad; she is now allowed her own room and promised a suitable job, an eventual regrading. Even as the nurse explains these steps towards freedom, we see their sad irrelevance. Jean's private world is ready to obtrude at any moment; her existence is precarious, threatened by the anarchy in her own imagination. One of the most moving illustrations of her plight is given in the description of her work as a librarian. She happily catalogues books for an elderly couple in the nearby town but is nonplussed by their casual, friendly conversation. When fine weather is mentioned she remarks "I wonder whether the monkeys would be better at the tops or the bottoms of the trees." Her own company of animals, spotted, sleek, furred and quilled, wait relentlessly for the time when she will step back into their universe.

The inevitable relapse is brought about by her first real relationship, a love affair with another patient. Alastair is critical of doctors and routines; he alarms Jean by telling her the true nature of her illness and she panics when he leaves the hospital. She runs away, is picked up by the police and brought back to face "the black box crashing down around my head." It is at this point that the novel changes direction. Jean remembers Alastair for his anger; she begins to share his indignation, rejects the doctors and escapes for good, feeling that her own identity is worth more than any medical tag of health.

Schizophrenia is a disease that has received much attention from modern writers. It has been used to symbolise the artist's alienation from society and, by extension, presented as the condition of modern man, lost, lonely, unable to communicate. The schizophrenic is sometimes hailed as a prophet, whose view of life is not only as valid as that of his doctors but also morally superior to the standards they uphold. Jennifer Dawson shares this fashionable, essentially romantic, attitude but her writing is without the stridency of propaganda. The parallels with Sylvia Plath's *The Bell Jar* are many and the prose is equally fine. Miss Dawson has written two further explorations of her subject but has not yet matched the sustained brilliance of this first novel.

—Judith Cooke Simmons

---

**DAY LEWIS, C(ecil).** Pseudonym: **Nicholas Blake.** Born in Ballintubber, Ireland, 27 April 1904. Educated at Sherborne School, Dorset; Wadham College, Oxford, M.A. Served as an Editor in the Ministry of Information, London, 1941–46. Married Mary King in 1928 (divorced, 1951); Jill Balcon, 1951; has four children. Taught at Summerfields School, Oxford, 1927–28; Larchfield, Helensburgh, 1928–30; Cheltenham College, 1930–35. Has lectured at Cambridge University (Clark Lecturer, 1946, Sidgwick Lecturer, 1956); the British Academy (Warton Lecturer, 1951); Oxford University (Professor of Poetry, 1951–56); University of Nottingham (Byron Lecturer, 1952); Queen's University, Kingston, Ontario (Chancellor Dunning Lecturer, 1954); Harvard University, Cambridge, Massachusetts (Norton Professor of Poetry, 1964–65); University of Hull (Compton Lecturer, 1968). Since 1954, Director of Chatto and Windus Ltd., publishers, London. Member of the Arts Council of Great Britain, 1962–67. Fellow, 1944, Vice-President, 1958, and Companion of Literature, 1964, Royal Society of Literature; Honorary Member, American Academy of Arts and Letters, 1966; Member, Irish Academy of Letters, 1968. D.Litt., University of

Exeter, 1965; University of Hull, 1969; Litt.D., Trinity College, Dublin, 1968. Honorary Fellow, Wadham College, Oxford, 1968. C.B.E. (Commander, Order of the British Empire), 1950. Poet Laureate, 1968. Address: 6 Crooms Hill, Greenwich, London S.E.10, England.

PUBLICATIONS

Novels

*The Friendly Tree.* London, Cape, 1936; New York, Harper, 1937.
*Starting Point.* London, Cape, 1937; New York, Harper, 1938.
*Child of Misfortune.* London, Cape, 1939.

Novels (as Nicholas Blake)

*A Question of Proof.* London, Collins, and New York, Harper, 1935.
*Thou Shell of Death.* London, Collins, 1936; as *Shell of Death*, New York, Harper, 1936.
*There's Trouble Brewing.* London, Collins, and New York, Harper, 1937.
*The Beast Must Die.* London, Collins, and New York, Harper, 1938.
*The Smiler with the Knife.* London, Collins, and New York, Harper, 1939.
*Malice in Wonderland.* London, Collins, 1940; as *Summer Camp Mystery*, New York, Harper, 1940.
*The Case of the Abominable Snowman.* London, Collins, 1941; as *Corpse in the Snowman*, New York, Harper, 1941.
*Minute for Murder.* London, Collins, 1947; New York, Harper, 1948.
*Head of a Traveller.* London, Collins, and New York, Harper, 1949.
*The Dreadful Hollow.* London, Collins, and New York, Harper, 1953.
*The Whisper in the Gloom.* London, Collins, and New York, Harper, 1954.
*A Tangled Web.* London, Collins, and New York, Harper, 1956.
*End of Chapter.* London, Collins, and New York, Harper, 1957.
*A Penknife in My Heart.* London, Collins, and New York, Harper, 1958.
*The Widow's Cruise.* London, Collins, and New York, Harper, 1959.
*The Worm of Death.* London, Collins, and New York, Harper, 1961.
*The Deadly Joker.* London, Collins, 1963.
*The Sad Variety.* London, Collins, and New York, Harper, 1964.
*The Morning after Death.* London, Collins, and New York, Harper, 1966.
*The Nicholas Blake Omnibus.* London, Collins, 1966.
*The Private Wound.* London, Collins, and New York, Harper, 1968.

Verse

*Beechen Vigil and Other Poems.* London, Fortune Press, 1925.
*Country Comets.* London, Martin Hopkinson, 1928.
*Transitional Poem.* London, Hogarth Press, 1929.
*From Feathers to Iron.* London, Hogarth Press, 1931.
*The Magnetic Mountain.* London, Hogarth Press, 1933.
*Collected Poems, 1929–1933.* London, Hogarth Press, 1935; with *A Hope for Poetry*, New York, Random House, 1935.
*A Time to Dance and Other Poems.* London, Hogarth Press, 1935.
*Noah and the Waters.* London, Hogarth Press, 1936.

*A Time to Dance, Noah and the Waters and Other Poems, with an Essay, Revolution in Writing.* New York, Random House, 1936.
*Overtures to Death and Other Poems.* London, Cape, 1938.
*Poems in Wartime.* London, Cape, 1940.
*Selected Poems.* London, Hogarth Press, 1940.
*Word over All.* London, Cape, 1943; New York, Transatlantic, 1944.
*(Poems).* London, Eyre and Spottiswoode, 1943.
*Short Is the Time: Poems, 1936–1943* (includes *Overtures to Death* and *Word over All*). New York, Oxford University Press, 1945.
*Poems, 1943–1947.* London, Cape, and New York, Oxford University Press, 1948.
*Collected Poems, 1929–1936.* London, Hogarth Press, 1948.
*Selected Poems.* London, Penguin, 1951; revised edition, 1957, 1969.
*An Italian Visit.* London, Cape, and New York, Harper, 1953.
*Collected Poems.* London, Cape-Hogarth Press, 1954.
*Pegasus and Other Poems.* London, Cape, 1957; New York, Harper, 1958.
*The Gate and Other Poems.* London, Cape, 1962.
*Requiem for the Living.* New York, Harper, 1964.
*The Room and Other Poems.* London, Cape, 1965.
*C. Day Lewis: Selections from His Poetry.* London, Chatto and Windus, 1967.
*Selected Poems.* New York, Harper, 1967.
*The Whispering Roots.* London, Cape, 1970.


Other

*Dick Willoughby* (juvenile). Oxford, Blackwell, 1933; New York, Random House, 1938.
*A Hope for Poetry.* Oxford, Blackwell, 1934; with *Collected Poems*, New York, Random House, 1935.
*Revolution in Writing.* London, Hogarth Press, 1935; New York, Random House, 1936.
*We're Not Going to Do Nothing.* London, Left Review, 1936.
*Poetry for You: A Book for Boys and Girls on the Enjoyment of Poetry.* Oxford, Blackwell, 1944; New York, Oxford University Press, 1947.
*The Poetic Image.* London, Cape, and New York, Oxford University Press, 1947.
*Enjoying Poetry: A Reader's Guide.* London, National Book League, 1947.
*The Colloquial Element in English Poetry.* Newcastle upon Tyne, Literary and Philosophical Society, 1947.
*The Otterbury Incident* (juvenile). London, Putnam, 1948; New York, Viking Press, 1949.
*The Poet's Task.* Oxford, Clarendon Press, 1951.
*The Grand Manner.* Nottingham, University of Nottingham, 1952.
*Notable Images of Virtue: Emily Brontë, George Meredith, W. B. Yeats.* Toronto, Ryerson Press, 1954.
*The Poet's Way of Knowledge.* Cambridge, University Press, 1957.
*The Buried Day* (autobiography). London, Chatto and Windus, and New York, Harper, 1960.
*The Lyric Impulse.* Cambridge, Massachusetts, Harvard University Press, and London, Chatto and Windus, 1965.
*Thomas Hardy*, with R. A. Scott-James. London, Longman, 1965.
*A Need for Poetry?* Hull, University of Hull, 1968.

Editor, with W. H. Auden, *Oxford Poetry 1927.* Oxford, Blackwell, 1927.
Editor, with others, *A Writer in Arms*, by Ralph Fox. London, Lawrence and Wishart, 1937.

Editor, *The Mind in Chains: Socialism and the Cultural Revolution.*   London, Muller, 1937.

Editor, *The Echoing Green: An Anthology of Verse.*   Oxford, Blackwell, 3 vols., 1937.

Editor, with Charles Fenby, *Anatomy of Oxford: An Anthology.*   London, Cape, 1938.

Editor, with L. A. G. Strong, *A New Anthology of Modern Verse, 1920–1940.*   London, Methuen, 1941.

Editor, *The Golden Treasury*, by Francis Turner Palgrave.   London, Collins, 1954.

Editor, with John Lehmann, *The Chatto Book of Modern Poetry, 1915–1955.*   London, Chatto and Windus, 1956.

Editor, with others, *New Poems 1957.*   London, Joseph, 1957.

Editor, *A Book of English Lyrics.*   London, Chatto and Windus, 1961; as *English Lyric Poems, 1500–1900*, New York, Appleton Century Crofts, 1961.

Editor, *The Collected Poems of Wilfred Owen.*   London, Chatto and Windus, 1963; New York, New Directions, 1964.

Editor, *The Midnight Skater: Poems for Young Readers*, by Edmund Blunden.   London, Bodley Head, 1968.

Editor, *A Choice of Keats's Verse.*   London, Faber, 1971.

Translator, *The Georgics of Virgil.*   London, Cape, 1940; New York, Oxford University Press, 1947.

Translator, *The Graveyard by the Sea*, by Paul Valéry.   London, Secker and Warburg, 1947.

Translator, *The Aeneid of Virgil.*   London, Hogarth Press, and New York, Oxford University Press, 1952.

Translator, *The Eclogues of Virgil.*   London, Cape, 1963; with *The Georgics*, New York, Doubleday, 1964.

Bibliography: *C. Day Lewis, The Poet Laureate: A Bibliography* by Geoffrey Handley-Taylor and Timothy d'Arch Smith, London and Chicago, St. James Press, 1968.

Manuscript Collections: New York Public Library; State University of New York at Buffalo; British Museum, London; University of Liverpool.

*         *         *

The fiction of Day Lewis breaks neatly into two categories, if one excludes his children's stories. He has, from the mid-thirties to the present, been a prolific writer of mystery novels under the pseudonym, Nicholas Blake; also in the Thirties he began, but quickly abandoned, the writing of novels of social comment.

His detective stories are both literate and sophisticated, as readers of Day Lewis might expect. Nigel Strangeways is not so much the indomitable sleuth as the English gentleman observer who is as likely to utter cynical social commentary as he is to identify the mysterious figure in the carpet. Strangeways seems at times to speak for the author as when, in *The Morning after Death*, he comments on the nature of the mystery story: "[Detective fiction] is not an art form. It's an entertainment. . . . I have no use for those who seek to turn the crime novel into an exercise in morbid psychology. Its chief virtue lies in its consistent flouting of reality: but crime novelists today are trying to write variations on *Crime and Punishment* without possessing a grain of Dostoevsky's talent. They've lost the courage of their own agreeable fantasies, and want to be accepted as serious writers. . . . Still, novels that are all plot—just clever patterns concealing a vacuum—one does get bored with them." Day Lewis has said elsewhere that he uses the detective novel as an outlet for his inner cruelty, as another man might hunt animals. It is significant as well that such writing provided him with the financial independence to pursue the more important task of writing poetry and poetry criticism.

The novels of social comment, all written in the 1930's, remain today as somewhat classic period pieces. The poetry of that decade has almost totally overshadowed the fiction produced by that discontented generation. And Day Lewis possessed the poetic sensitivity and imagination to capture both the idealism and disillusionment of an age. These novels emerge from the consciousness that he describes elsewhere in his poetry:

> We who "flowered" in the Thirties
> Were an odd lot; sceptical yet susceptible,
> Dour though enthusiastic, horizon-addicts
> And future-fans, terribly apt to ask what
> Our all-very-fine sensations were in aid of.
> We did not, you will remember, come to coo.

*Starting Point* narrates the history of four young men from their last term at Oxford during the general strike until 1936. At that time, one commits suicide, another secludes himself in a monastery, the third is a successful chemist, while the fourth leaves to fight in the Spanish Civil War. The characterization and development give an insight into the age that poetry is incapable of expressing. *The Friendly Tree*, the simple love story of an innocent girl and an embittered radical, displays a similar eloquence. Why Day Lewis did not continue to write in this vein after the 1930's is difficult to guess. Perhaps the disillusionment that set in with the outcome of the Spanish Civil War and the beginnings of the Second World War destroyed the passion. On the other hand, the author might have realized that these novels, reminiscent of the social dramas of Forster and Galsworthy, belonged to another age, and that this style would become less and less acceptable as the century progressed. Although these novels have been neglected, without good reason, they can hardly be passed over by anyone attempting to understand the cultural and social mood of the 1930's.

—Lawrence Ries

---

**DEIGHTON, Len.**   British.   Born in London, 18 February 1929. Educated at the Royal College of Art, London. Married to Shirley Thompson. Address: c/o Anton Felton and Partners, Continuum One, 25 Newman Street, London W.1, England.

PUBLICATIONS

Novels

*The Ipcress File.*  London, Hodder and Stoughton, 1962; New York, Simon and Schuster, 1963.
*Horse under Water.*  London, Cape, 1963; New York, Putnam, 1968.
*Funeral in Berlin.*  London, Cape, 1964; New York, Putnam, 1965.
*The Billion Dollar Brain.*  London, Cape, and New York, Putnam, 1966.
*An Expensive Place to Die.*  London, Cape, and New York, Putnam, 1967.
*Only When I Larf.*  London, Joseph, 1968.

*Bomber*.   London, Cape, and New York, Harper, 1970.
*Close-Up*.   London, Cape, 1972.


Short Stories

*Declarations of War*.   London, Cape, 1971.


Other

*Action Cook Book: Len Deighton's Guide to Eating*.   London, Cape, 1965; as *Cookstrip
   Cook Book*, New York, Geis, 1966.
*Où est le Garlic; or, Len Deighton's French Cook Book*.   London, Penguin, 1965.
*Len Deighton's Continental Dossier: A Collection of Cultural, Culinary, Historical,
   Spooky, Grim and Preposterous Fact*, compiled by Victor and Margaret Pettitt.
   London, Joseph, 1968.

Editor, *London Dossier*.   London, Cape, 1967.


*          *          *


In seven novels Len Deighton has made the transition from being an Ian Fleming-with-
literary-graces to being utterly unpredictable. *The Ipcress File, Horse under Water, Funeral
in Berlin, The Billion Dollar Brain*, and *An Expensive Place to Die* are spy stories with the
same character as central figure, although he changes considerably from book to book. The
only unchanging thing about him is that he likes Gauloise cigarettes and works the crossword puzzle in the *New Statesman. Only When I Larf* is a hilarious story about a team of
confidence tricksters; *Bomber* an encyclopedic account of a misdirected bombing raid over
Germany, seen from the point of view of both sides.

In the early spy stories the nearly-nameless main character (he later has several names,
probably none of them his own) is a cheerful dilettante who works out of an office filled with
eccentrics. In the successive books he becomes more and more jaded, tired, and distrustful—
and less adventurous. By the last two of the series he takes hardly any risks, but lets others do
it.

Nevertheless, Deighton's are not only very superior spy stories, sounding of authenticity
down to the appendices that tie his fictional situations in with actual organisations and
events of espionage, but they are sound novels with vivid characters, realistic settings, and
sound motivation. His situations seem real because, no matter how fantastic, there is or has
been something like that somewhere in the world. The "billion dollar brain," for instance, is
a computer used by a private espionage and sabotage organisation; and there actually are
fanatic American millionaries who finance private armies in the United States and (mostly
imaginary except in the mind of the recipient of the funds) underground forces behind the
Iron Curtain.

These stories are entertaining, with quiet humour and discerning observation, but *Only
When I Larf* is a truly funny book. There may be as ingenious con men as Bob, Liz, and Silas,
who take turns in telling the story, chapter to chapter, but they probably do not have as
much fun, and certainly they do not create as much. Beginning with their last successful
swindle, and ending when one cheats the other two, it is ideal for the motion pictures, and it
appears that is how it began.

*Bomber*, however, is as serious as the war it depicts. Deighton used a computer to coordi-
nate the minute-by-minute events in his portrayal of the day before and night of a 700-
bomber R.A.F. raid that accidentally near-demolished a small German town near the Dutch
border that was of hardly any military importance. The multitude of characters are all very

effectively portrayed, some at greater length than others, yet there is no single protagonist. Perhaps the main character is air war itself, and if so it is the villain.

—William Bittner

---

**DENNIS, Nigel (Forbes).** British. Born in Bletchingley, Surrey, 16 January 1912. Educated at Plumtree School, Southern Rhodesia; Oldenwaldschule, Germany. Married Mary-Madeleine Massias; Beatrice Ann Hewart Matthew in 1959; has two children. Secretary, National Board of Review of Motion Pictures, New York, 1935–36; Assistant Editor, and Book Reviewer, *The New Republic*, New York, 1937–38; Staff Book Reviewer, *Time*, New York, 1940–59. Since 1960, Drama Critic, and Joint Editor, 1967–70, *Encounter*, London; since 1961, Staff Book Reviewer, *The Sunday Telegraph*, London. Recipient: Houghton Mifflin-Eyre and Spottiswoode Award, 1950; Heinemann Award, for non-fiction, 1966. Fellow, Royal Society of Literature, 1966. Address: c/o A. M. Heath and Company, 35 Dover Street, London W.1, England.

PUBLICATIONS

Novels

> *Boys and Girls Come Out to Play*. London, Eyre and Spottiswoode, 1949; as *Sea Change*, Boston, Houghton Mifflin, 1949.
> *Cards of Identity*. London, Weidenfeld and Nicolson, and New York, Vanguard Press, 1955.
> *A House in Order*. London, Weidenfeld and Nicolson, and New York, Vanguard Press, 1966.

Plays

> *Cards of Identity* (produced London, 1956). Included in *Two Plays and a Preface*, 1958.
> *The Making of Moo* (produced London, 1957; New York, 1958). Included in *Two Plays and a Preface*, 1958.
> *Two Plays and a Preface* (includes *Cards of Identity* and *The Making of Moo*). London, Weidenfeld and Nicolson, 1958; New York, Vanguard Press, 1959.
> *August for the People* (produced Edinburgh and London, 1961). London, French, 1962.

Verse

> *Exotics: Poems*. London, Weidenfeld and Nicolson, 1970; New York, Vanguard Press, 1971.

Other

> *Dramatic Essays*. London, Weidenfeld and Nicolson, 1962.

*Jonathan Swift: A Short Character.*  New York, Macmillan, 1964; London, Weidenfeld and Nicolson, 1965.
*An Essay on Malta.*  London, Murray, 1972.

\*        \*        \*

Although Nigel Dennis has published only three novels, their quality is high enough to
give him a place as one of the best English novelists of his generation. He lived in America for
many years and in fact the principal characters of his first novel, *Boys and Girls Come Out to
Play*, are all American. It is set in the summer of 1939, on the eve of the Second World War,
and the action takes place partly in America and partly in Poland. A liberal journalist, Max
Divver, goes to Poland to report on the political situation for a progressive magazine, accompanied by Jimmy Morgan, the adolescent son of the rich woman who owns and edits
the magazine. Jimmy is a difficult boy, who is liable to fits, but the visit proves the making of
him, whereas it is the undoing of Max, a forceful but insecure character, who is consumed by
self-loathing. Nigel Dennis develops the relationship between them in a leisurely fashion that
allows for much indulgence in psychological nuance but results in a long book that has rather
a lot of static passages. There is a slightly uneasy contrast between the reflective sections and
the element of adventure that builds up as Max and Jimmy try to escape from Poland just
before the German invasion. The interest is essentially in the characters and the Polish
setting never really seems convincing. The novel leaves no doubt, however, of the quality of
Dennis' writing, shown for instance in the dazzling account of the attempts by a mechanic
to start a large and ancient car (a vehicle which much later comes to play a crucial part in the
plot). It also shows a satirical inclination, and a tendency to allegory or fable in that Max
Divver is clearly meant to embody the insufficiencies of the liberal intellectual at a time of
great historical crisis.

These tendencies were fully developed in Nigel Dennis' next novel, *Cards of Identity*,
which established his reputation and remains one of the most brilliant works of post-war
English fiction. It is about the "problem of identity" which is so much discussed in the modern
world, and the essence of the novel lies in the characters' difficulty in knowing who they are
supposed to be. Yet *Cards of Identity* also indicates the time and place of its composition. The
setting is an English country house where a body called the Identity Club is holding its annual
meeting, at which the members listen to papers describing the case-histories of interesting
identity problems. Much of the detail reflects English life in the late forties and early fifties, a
period of ration-books and identity cards and continuing post-war privations. One of the
case-histories is about an ex-communist turned monk who is writing his memoirs in a
monastery, all of whose inmates have had a similar communist past; it is very entertaining,
but inevitably seems rather dated now. On the other hand, the story of the Co-Wardens of
the Badgeries, and the sad farcical events that took place while ceremoniously leading a
symbolic stuffed badger across London in the funeral procession of the Lord Royal, is still a
valid satire on the more absurd manifestations of English public traditionalism. The case
histories are told with great verve and are full of Dennis' imaginative exuberance. But where
*Cards of Identity* transcends the treatment of individual forms of identity crisis and looks at
the problem of English cultural identity as a whole, is not in the separate case-histories but in
the narrative framework of the novel. The setting of the events is a traditional country-
house of the kind familiar in innumerable English novels. But it has been empty for a long
time, and in order to find staff for it the local representatives of the Identity Club abduct
various of the local inhabitants and by unspecified but infallible means transform them into
typical denizens of the English country house, such as the butler, the cook and the eccentric
gardener. In fact they construct, specially for the Club, a model of the comfortable timeless
milieu of much traditional English fiction, though it proves in the end no more than a house
of cards, and identity-cards at that. In this brilliantly comic and ingenious novel Nigel
Dennis probes at many contemporary problems. The satirical examination of the way in

which the familiar symbols of English cultural identity have been losing their validity is an important part of the meaning of *Cards of Identity*.

Dennis' third novel, *A House in Order*, also dwells on the question of identity, though it is more personal and less culturally specific than its predecessor. The subject is deliberately narrow and intensely treated: during a war between two unnamed powers a prisoner is kept confined in a greenhouse by the soldiers of one side. He cannot be moved as he is an object of contention between two branches of the military establishment, though neither of them is interested in his personal welfare. With enormous patience the man cultivates the small plants he finds in the greenhouse and in the yard outside where he is allowed to exercise; he thereby keeps not only his house but his mind in order, and preserves his sense of self. At the end of the story, when he has been released and returned to his own country and a greenhouse of his own, he even looks back nostalgically to the days of his imprisonment as to some vanished ideal order. The story has of course many obviously allegorical implications about the human condition, but Dennis embodies them in a detailed convincing narrative that never becomes thinly symbolic, and where the humour that distinguished *Cards of Identity* is still noticeable. *A House in Order* is remarkable for the way in which it works as a novel, even while being an evident moral fable.

—Bernard Bergonzi

---

**DERLETH, August (William).** American. Born in Sauk City, Wisconsin, 24 February 1909. Educated at the University of Wisconsin, Madison, B.A. 1930. Married Sandra Winters in 1953 (divorced, 1959); has two children. Editor, Fawcett Publications, Minneapolis, 1930–31; Editor, *The Midwesterner*, Madison, 1931; Lecturer in American Regional Literature, University of Wisconsin, 1940–43. Since 1939, Editor and Owner of Arkham House, Publishers (including the imprints Mycroft and Moran, and Stanton and Lee), Sauk City. Since 1941, Literary Editor and Columnist for the Madison *Capital Times*. Editor, *The Arkham Sampler*, Sauk City, 1948–49, and *Hawk and Whippoorwill*, Sauk City, 1960–63. Since 1967, Editor of *The Arkham Collector*, Sauk City. Recipient: Guggenheim Fellowship, 1938; Midland Authors Golden Anniversary Award for Poetry, 1965; Wisconsin Governor's Award, for service to the creative arts, 1966. Address: Arkham House, Sauk City, Wisconsin 53583, U.S.A. *Died 4 July 1971.*

PUBLICATIONS

Novels

*Murder Stalks the Wakely Family.* New York, Mussey, 1934; as *Death Strikes the Wakely Family*, London, Newnes, 1937.
*The Man on All Fours.* New York, Mussey, 1934; London, Newnes, 1936.
*Sign of Fear.* New York, Mussey, 1935; London, Newnes, 1936.
*Three Who Died.* New York, Loring and Mussey, 1935.
*Still Is the Summer Night.* New York, Scribner, 1937.
*Wind over Wisconsin.* New York, Scribner, 1938.
*Restless Is the River.* New York, Scribner, 1939.
*Bright Journey.* Saulk City, Wisconsin, Arkham House, 1940.

*Sentence Deferred.*   New York, Scribner, 1940; London, Heinemann, 1941.
*The Narracong Riddle.*   New York, Scribner, 1940.
*Evening in Spring.*   New York, Scribner, 1941.
*Sweet Genevieve.*   New York, Scribner, 1942.
*Shadow of Night.*   New York, Scribner, 1943.
*The Seven Who Waited.*   New York, Scribner, 1943.
*Mischief in the Lane.*   New York, Scribner, 1944.
*No Future for Luana.*   New York, Scribner, 1945.
*The Shield of the Valiant.*   New York, Scribner, 1945.
*"In Re: Sherlock Holmes": The Adventures of Solar Pons.*   Sauk City, Wisconsin,
   Mycroft and Moran, 1945.
*Something Near.*   Sauk City, Wisconsin, Arkham House, 1945.
*The Memoirs of Solar Pons.*   Sauk City, Wisconsin, Mycroft and Moran, 1951.
*Three Problems of Solar Pons.*   Sauk City, Wisconsin, Mycroft and Moran, 1952.
*Fell Purpose.*   New York, Arcadia House, 1953.
*Death by Design.*   New York, Arcadia House, 1953.
*The Mask of Cthulhu.*   Sauk City, Wisconsin, Arkham House, 1958.
*The Return of Solar Pons.*   Sauk City, Wisconsin, Mycroft and Moran, 1958.
*The House on the Mound.*   New York, Duell, 1958.
*The Hills Stand Watch.*   New York, Duell, 1960.
*The Reminiscences of Solar Pons.*   Sauk City, Wisconsin, Mycroft and Moran, 1961.
*The Trail of Cthulhu.*   Sauk City, Wisconsin, Arkham House, 1962.
*The Shadow in the Glass.*   New York, Duell, 1963.
*The Casebook of Solar Pons.*   Sauk City, Wisconsin, Mycroft and Moran, 1965.
*The Adventure of the Orient Express.*   New York, Candlelight Press, 1965.
*Praed Street Papers.*   New York, Candlelight Press, 1965.
*A Praed Street Dossier.*   Sauk City, Wisconsin, Arkham House, 1968.
*Wisconsin Murders.*   Sauk City, Wisconsin, Arkham House, 1968.
*The Beast in Holger's Woods.*   New York, Crowell, 1968.
*Mr. Fairlie's Final Journey.*   Sauk City, Wisconsin, Arkham House, 1968.
*The Prince Goes West.*   Des Moines, Iowa, Meredith Press, 1968.
*The Wind Leans West.*   New York, Candlelight Press, 1969.
*The Chronicles of Solar Pons.*   Sauk City, Wisconsin, Mycroft and Moran, 1971.


Short Stories

*Place of Hawks.*   New York, Loring and Mussey, 1935.
*Country Growths.*   Sauk City, Wisconsin, Arkham House, 1940.
*Someone in the Dark.*   Sauk City, Wisconsin, Arkham House, 1941.
*The Lurker at the Threshold,* with H. P. Lovecraft.   Sauk City, Wisconsin, Arkham
   House, 1945; London, Gollancz, 1968.
*Not Long for This World.*   Sauk City, Wisconsin, Arkham House, 1948.
*Sac Prairie People.*   Sauk City, Wisconsin, Stanton and Lee, 1948.
*The Survivor and Others,* with H. P. Lovecraft.   Sauk City, Wisconsin, Arkham House,
   1957.
*Wisconsin in Their Bones.*   New York, Duell, 1961.
*Lonesome Places.*   Sauk City, Wisconsin, Arkham House, 1962.
*Mr. George and Other Odd Persons* (as Stephen Grendon).   Sauk City, Wisconsin,
   Arkham House, 1963.
*The House of Moonlight.*   Iowa City, Prairie Press, 1963.
*Colonel Markesan and Less Pleasant People,* with Mark Schorer.   Sauk City, Wis-
   consin, Arkham House, 1966.
*The Shadow out of Time and Other Tales of Horror,* with H. P. Lovecraft.   London,
   Gollancz, 1968.

Verse

*Hawk on the Wind*.   Philadelphia, Ritten House, 1938.
*Man Track Here*.   Philadelphia, Ritten House, 1939.
*Here on a Darkling Plain*.   Philadelphia, Ritten House, 1940.
*Wind in the Elms*.   Philadelphia, Ritten House, 1941.
*Rind of Earth*.   Prairie City, Illinois, Decker Press, 1942.
*Selected Poems*.   Prairie City, Illinois, Decker Press, 1944.
*And You, Thoreau!*   New York, New Directions, 1944.
*The Edge of Night*.   Prairie City, Illinois, Decker Press, 1945.
*Psyche*.   Iowa City, Prairie Press, 1953.
*Country Poems*.   Iowa City, Prairie Press, 1956.
*West of Morning*.   Francestown, New Hampshire, Golden Quill Press, 1960.
*This Wound*.   Iowa City, Prairie Press, 1962.
*Country Places*.   Iowa City, Prairie Press, 1965.
*The Only Place We Live*.   Iowa City, Prairie Press, 1966.
*By Owl Light*.   Iowa City, Prairie Press, 1967.
*Collected Poems, 1937–1967*.   New York, Candlelight Press, 1967.
*Caitlin*.   Sauk City, Wisconsin, Arkham House, 1969.
*The Landscape of the Heart*.   Iowa City, Prairie Press, 1970.
*Listening to the Wind*.   New York, Candlelight Press, 1971.
*Last Light*.   New York, Candlelight Press, 1971.

Verse Recordings: *Psyche: A Sequence of Love Lyrics*, Cuca Records, 1960; *Sugar Bush by Moonlight and Other Poems of Man and Nature*, Cuca Records, 1962; *Caitlin*, Cuca Records, 1971.

Other

*Consider Your Verdict: Ten Coroner's Cases for You to Solve* (as Tally Mason).   New York, Stackpole, 1937.
*Any Day Now*.   Chicago, Normandie House, 1938.
*Atmosphere of Houses*.   Muscatine, Iowa, Prairie Press, 1939.
*Still Small Voice: The Biography of Zona Gale*.   New York, Appleton Century, 1940.
*Village Year: A Sac Prairie Journal*.   New York, Coward McCann, 1941.
*The Wisconsin: River of a Thousand Isles*.   New York, Farrar and Rinehart, 1942.
*H.P.L.: A Memoir*.   New York, Ben Abramson, 1945.
*Oliver, The Wayward Owl*, with Clare Victor Dwiggins (juvenile).   Sauk City, Wisconsin, Stanton and Lee, 1945.
*Writing Fiction*.   Boston, The Writer, 1946.
*The Habitant of Dusk: A Garland for Cassandra*.   Boston, Walden Press, 1946.
*Village Daybook: A Sac Prairie Journal*.   Chicago, Pelligrini and Cudahy, 1947.
*A Boy's Way: Poems* (juvenile).   Sauk City, Wisconsin, Stanton and Lee, 1947.
*Sauk County: A Centennial History*.   Baraboo, Wisconsin, Sauk County Centennial Committee, 1948.
*It's a Boy's World: Poems* (juvenile).   Sauk City, Wisconsin, Stanton and Lee, 1948.
*The Milwaukee Road: Its First 100 Years*.   New York, Creative Age Press, 1948.
*The Captive Island* (juvenile).   New York, Aladdin, 1952.
*The Country of the Hawk* (juvenile).   New York, Aladdin, 1952.
*Empire of Fur: Trading in the Lake Superior Region* (juvenile).   New York, Aladdin, 1953.
*The Land of Grey Gold: Lead Mining in Wisconsin* (juvenile).   New York, Aladdin, 1954.

*Father Marquette and the Great Rivers* (juvenile).   New York, Farrar Straus, 1955; London, Burns Oates and Washbourne, 1956.

*Land of Sky Blue Water* (juvenile).   New York, Aladdin, 1955.

*St. Ignatius and the Company of Jesus* (juvenile).   New York, Farrar Straus, and London, Burns Oates and Washbourne, 1956.

*Columbus and the New World* (juvenile).   New York, Farrar Straus, and London, Burns Oates and Washbourne, 1957.

*The Moon Tenders* (juvenile).   New York, Duell, 1958.

*The Mill Creek Irregulars: Special Detectives* (juvenile).   New York, Duell, 1959.

*Wilbur, The Trusting Whippoorwill* (juvenile).   Sauk City, Wisconsin, Stanton and Lee, 1959.

*Arkham House: The First Twenty Years—1939-1959.*   Sauk City, Wisconsin, Arkham House, 1959.

*Some Notes on H. P. Lovecraft.*   Sauk City, Wisconsin, Arkham House, 1959.

*The Pinkertons Ride Again* (juvenile).   New York, Duell, 1960.

*The Ghost of Black Hawk Island* (juvenile).   New York, Duell, 1961.

*Walden West* (autobiography).   New York, Duell, 1961.

*Sweet Land of Michigan* (juvenile).   New York, Duell, 1962.

*Concord Rebel: A Life of Henry D. Thoreau.*   Philadelphia, Chilton, 1962.

*The Tent Show Summer* (juvenile).   New York, Duell, 1963.

*Countryman's Journal.*   New York, Duell, 1963.

*The Forest Orphans* (juvenile).   New York, Ernest, 1964.

*The Irregulars Strike Again* (juvenile).   New York, Duell, 1964.

*Wisconsin Country: A Sac Prairie Journal.*   New York, Candlelight Press, 1965.

*The House by the River* (juvenile).   New York, Duell, 1965.

*The Watcher on the Heights* (juvenile).   New York, Duell, 1966.

*A House above Cuzco.*   New York, Candlelight Press, 1967.

*Wisconsin: Consultant: Russell Mosely.*   New York, Coward McCann, 1967.

*Vincennes: Portal to the West.*   New York, Prentice Hall, 1968.

*Walden Pond: Homage to Thoreau.*   Iowa City, Prairie Press, 1968.

*Return to Walden West.*   New York, Candlelight Press, 1970.

*Three Straw Men* (juvenile).   New York, Candlelight Press, 1970.

*Love Letters to Caitlin.*   New York, Candlelight Press, 1971.


Editor, with R. E. Larsson, *Poetry Out of Wisconsin.*   New York, Harrison, 1937.

Editor, with Donald Wandrei, *The Outsider and Others*, by H. P. Lovecraft.   Sauk City, Wisconsin, Arkham House, 1939.

Editor, *Sleep No More: Twenty Masterpieces of Horror for the Connoisseur.*   New York, Farrar and Rinehart, 1944.

Editor, *Who Knocks? Twenty Masterpieces of the Spectral for the Connoisseur.*   New York, Rinehart, 1946.

Editor, *The Night Side: Masterpieces of the Strange and Terrible.*   New York, Rinehart, 1947.

Editor, *The Sleeping and the Dead.*   Chicago, Pelligrini and Cudahy, 1947.

Editor, *Dark of the Moon: Poems of Fantasy and the Macabre.*   Sauk City, Wisconsin, Arkham House, 1947.

Editor, *Strange Ports of Call.*   New York, Pelligrini and Cudahy, 1948.

Editor, *The Other Side of the Moon.*   New York, Pelligrini and Cudahy, 1949; London, Grayson, 1956.

Editor, *Something about Cats and Other Pieces*, by H. P. Lovecraft.   Sauk City, Wisconsin, Arkham House, 1949.

Editor, *Beyond Time and Space.*   New York, Pelligrini and Cudahy, 1950.

Editor, *Far Boundaries: 20 Science-Fiction Stories.*   New York, Pelligrini and Cudahy, 1951.

Editor, *The Outer Reaches: Favorite Science-Fiction Tales Chosen by Their Authors*. New York, Pelligrini and Cudahy, 1951.

Editor, *Beachheads in Space*. New York, Pelligrini and Cudahy, 1952; London, Weidenfeld and Nicolson, 1954.

Editor, *Night's Yawning Peal: A Ghostly Company*. Sauk City, Wisconsin, Arkham House, 1952.

Editor, *Rendezvous in a Landscape*. New York, Fine Editions Press, 1952.

Editor, *Worlds of Tomorrow: Science-Fiction with a Difference*. New York, Pelligrini and Cudahy, 1953; London, Weidenfeld and Nicolson, 1954.

Editor, *Time to Come: Science-Fiction Stories of Tomorrow*. New York, Farrar Straus, 1954.

Editor, *Portals of Tomorrow: The Best Tales of Science Fiction and Other Fantasy*. New York, Rinehart, 1954; London, Cassell, 1956.

Editor, *The Shuttered Room and Other Pieces by H. P. Lovecraft and Divers Hands*. Sauk City, Wisconsin, Arkham House, 1959.

Editor, *Fire and Sleet and Candlelight*. Sauk City, Wisconsin, Arkham House, 1961.

Editor, *Dark Mind, Dark Heart*. Sauk City, Wisconsin, Arkham House, 1962.

Editor, *When Evil Wakes: A New Anthology of the Macabre*. London, Souvenir Press, 1963.

Editor, *The Dunwich Horror and Others: The Best Supernatural Stories by H. P. Lovecraft*. Sauk City, Wisconsin, Arkham House, 1963.

Editor, *Over the Edge*. Sauk City, Wisconsin, Arkham House, 1964; London, Gollancz, 1967.

Editor, *At the Mountains of Madness and Other Novels*, by H. P. Lovecraft. Sauk City, Wisconsin, Arkham House, 1964.

Editor, *Dagon and Other Macabre Tales*, by H. P. Lovecraft. Sauk City, Wisconsin, Arkham House, 1965.

Editor, with Donald Wandrei, *Selected Letters, 1911–1925*, by H. P. Lovecraft. Sauk City, Wisconsin, Arkham House, 1965.

Editor, *Travellers by Night*. Sauk City, Wisconsin, Arkham House, 1967; London, Gollancz, 1968.

Editor, with Donald Wandrei, *Selected Letters, 1925–1929*, by H. P. Lovecraft. Sauk City, Wisconsin, Arkham House, 1968.

Editor, *New Poetry out of Wisconsin*. Sauk City, Wisconsin, Arkham House, 1969.

Editor, *Tales of the Cthulhu Mythos*, by H. P. Lovecraft and others. Sauk City, Wisconsin, Arkham House, 1969.

Editor, *The Horror in the Museum and Other Revisions*, by H. P. Lovecraft. Sauk City, Wisconsin, Arkham House, 1970.

Editor, with Donald Wandrei, *Selected Letters, 1929–1931*, by H. P. Lovecraft. Sauk City, Wisconsin, Arkham House, 1971.

Bibliography: *100 Books by August Derleth*, Sauk City, Wisconsin, Arkham House, 1962.

Manuscript Collection: State Historical Society of Wisconsin Library, Madison.

*       *       *

August Derleth is almost certainly the most prolific of modern American writers and, the author of well over one hundred books, perhaps of American writers in all time. He is also among the most various. Except for the very long poem and the drama, he has probably published in every current literary form, and not once in each but many times. His fiction itself is extremely various, not only in a formal sense—short story, novelette, novel—but also in a generic sense, ranging as it does from the macabre story and the mystery novel to the poetic novelette and the historical chronicle, and, what is more, addressing itself now to an adult, now to a juvenile audience.

He is above all a novelist of place, and the place is his homeplace, which he calls "Sac Prairie" but which is in fact the two little adjoining Wisconsin villages named Sauk City and Prairie du Sac. These little towns on the Wisconsin River are set among marshland, hills, and prairie, and they provide the intimately experienced natural detail of most of Derleth's writing as they also provide the prototypes for many of his characters. Beyond Sac Prairie is the entire state of Wisconsin and its history since early pioneer times. These two settings, the small one within the larger, divide his most important fiction into two sets of novels which he designates as "Sagas"—the Sac Prairie Saga, consisting of eight novels, and the Wisconsin Saga, consisting of five. But the Sac Prairie saga spills over into other works, into at least seven books of short stories, at least six works of miscellaneous or discursive prose, and into a dozen volumes of verse.

The novels in the saga series comprise Derleth's most substantial work. Solidly constructed historical narratives, based on a sure sense of past achievement, evolving growth, and the inevitable currents of change, these novels move through a wide range of effects, from the bucolically comic through the delicately pathetic to the dramatically tragic, and the vast cast of characters similarly ranges from country clowns to fabled heroes. Through all their variety there is one constant element, Derleth's profound feeling for an intimate knowledge of the natural environment, and this feeling works paradoxically in, on the one hand, recreating vividly and with deep affection the particular locality that he has made his own, and, on the other, through the universal rhythms of nature, moving his narratives beyond any special time and place into the timeless and the enduringly human.

Substantial as his achievement in the sagas is, Derleth's own preferences (and those of many of his readers) are for other work. Notable among these in the fiction is his early lyric tale of adolescent love, *Evening in Spring*. But perhaps even more impressive are two books that are not fiction at all even though they give us the very roots of his fiction, books made up of entries from his journals with sharp observation of village life and the natural life around it. He called them *Walden West* and *Return to Walden West*, and it is probable that they are classics of their kind.

—Mark Schorer

---

**DESAI, Anita.** Indian. Born in Mussoorie, 24 June 1937. Educated at Queen Mary's Higher Secondary School, Delhi; Miranda House, Delhi University, B.A. in English literature 1957. Married Ashvin Desai in 1958; has four children. Address: 63 Sector 5, Chandigarh, India.

PUBLICATIONS

Novels

*Cry, The Peacock*. London, Peter Owen, 1963.
*Voices in the City*. London, Peter Owen, 1965.
*Bye-Bye, Blackbird*. Delhi, Hind Pocket Books, 1971.

Uncollected Short Stories

"Circus Cat, Alley Cat", in *Thought* (Delhi), 1957.
"Tea with the Maharani", in *Envoy* (London), 1959.
"Grandmother", in *Writers Workshop* (Calcutta), 1960.
"An Examination", in *Writers Workshop* (Calcutta), 1960.
"To Sell a Picture", in *Writers Workshop* (Calcutta), 1961.
"Mr. Bose's Private Bliss", in *Envoy* (London), 1961.
"Ghost House", in *Quest* (Bombay), 1961.
"Private Tuition by Mr. Bose", in *Indian Literature* (Calcutta), 1970.
"Descent from the Rooftop", in *Illustrated Weekly of India* (Bombay), 1970.

Critical Study: *Indian Writing in English* by Paul Verghese, Bombay, Asia Publishing House, 1970.

Anita Desai comments:

I have been writing, since the age of 7, as instinctively as I breathe. It is a necessity to me: I find it is in the process of writing that I am able to think, to feel, and to realize at the highest pitch. Writing is to me a process of discovering the truth—the truth that is nine-tenths of the iceberg that lies submerged beneath the one-tenth visible portion we call Reality. Writing is my way of plunging to the depths and exploring this underlying truth. All my writing is an effort to discover, to underline and convey the true significance of things. That is why, in my novels, small objects, passing moods and attitudes acquire a large importance. My novels are no reflection of Indian society, politics or character. They are part of my private effort to seize upon the raw material of life—its shapelessness, its meaninglessness, that lack of design that drives one to despair—and to mould it and impose on it a design, a certain composition and order that pleases me as an artist and also as a human being who longs for order.

While writing my novels, I find I use certain images again and again and that, although real, they acquire the significance of symbols. I imagine each writer ends by thus revealing his own mythology, a mythology that symbolizes his private morality and philosophy. One hopes, at the end of one's career, to have made some significant statement on life—not necessarily a water-tight, hard-and-fast set of rules, but preferably an ambiguous, elastic, shifting and kinetic one that remains always capable of further change and growth.

Next to this exploration of the underlying truth and the discovery of a private mythology and philosophy, it is style that interests me most—and by this I mean the conscious labour of uniting language and symbol, word and rhythm. Without it, language would remain a dull and pedestrian vehicle. I search for a style that will bring it to vivid, surging life. Story, action and drama mean little to me except insofar as they emanate directly from the personalities I have chosen to write about, born of their dreams and wills. One must find a way to unite the inner and the outer rhythms, to obtain a certain integrity and to impose order on chaos.

*          *          *

Anita Desai's first two novels both deal with spiritual collapse among upperclass Indians whose traditional religion and manner of life have been undermined by modern ways and concepts. The heroine of the first novel, *Cry, The Peacock*, is the clingingly affectionate daughter of a wealthy, dilettantish North Indian Brahmin under whose protective upbringing she has acquired a hypersensitivity to the beauties of nature, literature, art, and music. After her marriage she retains her aesthetic attachments, but she finds her husband unresponsive to her affection. As a result she lavishes her love on her dog and her flowers. *The Bhagavad-Gita*, which she quotes at length, warns against strong attachments. Nature, art, animals, human beings are illusions, or maya (this unhappy woman's name is, significantly, Maya); and undue dependence on them can result only in unhappiness or disaster. If she at times seems to forget this doctrine so central to her ancestral religion, her husband repeatedly reminds her of it. A busy and successful lawyer, he has himself achieved non-attachment, as his name, Gautama (one of the Buddha's names), suggests.

The story of the married life of this couple is told mainly through Maya's stream of consciousness, which is recorded in a rich, sensuous, sometimes truly poetic prose. Almost completely misunderstood by her husband, who regards her as little more than an attractive household appurtenance, Maya is by education and temperament incapable of finding fulfillment through outside activities. Indeed her situation illustrates many points made by Simone de Beauvoir concerning woman's plight in a man-dominated society. But Maya's problem is more than a socio-cultural one. It is deeply rooted in the spirit, and it is incurable. Her condition deteriorates from one of mild hysteria at the beginning of the book to full-fledged psychosis at the end. In this state she murders her husband.

In her second novel, *Voices in the City*, Mrs. Desai traces the disintegrative effects of residence in Calcutta on the lives and personalities of three talented young people—two sisters and a brother—who come to the metropolis from a Himalayan hill station. The brother, Nirode, becomes bitterly alienated from his family and from society and submerges himself in a life of squalor and dissipation. Monisha, the older of the two sisters, is the victim of an arranged marriage into a crassly bourgeois family. Virtually a slave to her husband and in-laws, she dies, first spiritually, and then physically as a suicide. Amla, the younger sister, starts a career as a commercial artist, but her initial enthusiasm for her work and the city ends in desolate disillusionment.

Calcutta as depicted in the novel is a place of death, in which no ambition or hope can survive. Indeed the very name of the city, according to some, is derived from Kali, the black Goddess of Death, who is worshipped as a major deity in Bengal. Mrs. Desai alludes frequently, though unobtrusively, to Kali, thus adding a religious and mythological element to the novel and deepening the impression of terror evoked by her descriptions of the city. For example, Kali seems to appear as a street-dancer and singer, a woman of grim and foreboding visage, at the time of Monisha's suicide. But Kali, the consort of Siva, has many aspects—one of them that of the Mother Goddess, who after the periodic destructions of the universe creates it anew. At the end, Nirode, in a state of mystical excitement, claims to see in his own mother an embodiment of the Mother Goddess. "See," he exclaims to Amla, "how still and controlled her lips and hands are, because she has at last seized and mastered death, she has become Kali. . . . Kali is the mother of Bengal, she is the mother of us all. Don't you see, Amla, how once she has given birth to us, she must also deal us our deaths?" On this note of desperate acceptance the novel is concluded.

—Perry D. Westbrook

---

**DESANI, G(ovindas) V(ishnoodas).** British. Born in Nairobi, Kenya, 8 July 1909. Correspondent, Reuters and Associated Press, 1935–45; Lecturer for the British Ministry of Information and the Imperial Institute, and BBC broadcaster during World War II. After the war, lived in monasteries in India, Burma, and Japan, for 19 years. Special Contributor, and writer of the weekly column, "Very High and Very Low", *Illustrated Weekly of India*, Bombay, 1960–68. Fulbright-Hays Lecturer, 1968, and since 1969, Professor of Philosophy, University of Texas at Austin. Address: Department of Philosophy, University of Texas, Austin, Texas 78712, U.S.A.

PUBLICATIONS

Novel

All about H. Hatterr.   London, Francis Aldor, 1948; as All about H. Hatterr: A Gesture, New York, Farrar Straus, 1948; revised edition, London, Bodley Head, and Farrar Straus, 1970.

Uncollected Short Stories

"Mephisto's Daughter", in Noble Savage (Chicago), no. 4, 1961.
"With Malice Aforethought", in Noble Savage (Chicago), no. 5, 1962.
"The Second Mrs. Was Wed in a Nightmare", in Transatlantic Review (London and New York), no. 9, 1962.
"The Last Long Letter", in Illustrated Weekly of India (Bombay), 8 January 1967.

Play

Hali.   London, Saturn Press, 1950.

*     *     *

G. V. Desani's published fiction consists of a small number of short stories and one novel, All about H. Hatterr. In addition, he has published a prose poem, in dramatic form, titled Hali, which some critics consider his most significant work. Hali has also been called a "story of passion"; but whatever its classification, it serves as companion piece for Desani's novel. In both works the author is taking the measure of man—in Hali, ideal man, and in All about H. Hatterr, everyman or man as he really is in a far-from-perfect world. Hali is written in the prophetic and exalted style that its subject demands. In it the young hero, Hali, passes through fear, defeat, and sorrow to achieve a selfless, changeless, Christ-like love for all humanity. Discarding deities that he had revered earlier, he now worships only his newly found God of Love, who is "eternally incarnated" in the human form.

H. Hatterr in All about H. Hatterr has accurately been described as "the mathematical opposite of Hali." The same may be said of the styles and the tones of the two works. A Eurasian born in Penang but a resident for long periods in India and England, H. Hatterr is indeed fitted for the role of everyman that Desani intends him to fill. The language employed by H. Hatterr as he narrates his "Autobiographical" is a mixture, wholly unique in literature, of cockney and babu English with liberal infusions of American slang, the argot of criminals, the jargon of the medical and legal professions, and literal translations from Hindi, the whole being sprinkled with quotations and misquotations from Shakespeare and other poets. Desani has aptly been called "a playboy of the English language, a juggler with words." His virtuosity in this respect is one of the chief pleasures and wonders of his novel: e.g., "Only a few days ago . . . I was sitting in my humble belle-vue-no-view, cul-de-sack-the-tenant, a landlady's up-and-do-'em opportunity apartment-joint in India." H. Hatterr's incessant flow of vulgarisms, cynicisms, sarcasms, and malapropisms reflects the vulgarity-cum-naïveté of his character as a twentieth-century everyman. In contrast to Hali's religion of selfless love, H. Hatterr phrases his philosophy as follows: "To be easy and comfortable appears to be the aim of all man: even at the expense of the other feller [sic]." H. Hatterr's application of this simple rule of conduct in seven "life-encounters" supplies the action of the novel. Each of the "encounters" is preceded by a humorous "Instruction," in which an eccentric guru voices some general truth about the human condition, and a "Presumption," which presents H. Hatterr's distortion of this truth. The "encounters" themselves are absurd and fantastic, and from each of them H. Hatterr emerges rather badly battered. But he always bounces back for more. *"Life,"* he avers, "is no one-way pattern. It's *contrasts* all the way. And *contrasts* by Law! . . . I am not fed up with *Life*. . . ." The fact that H. Hatterr enjoys the absurdity of life, at least as he leads it, serves to raise him somewhat above the stature of a mere buffoon and to give the reader the sense that the author's purpose is one of life-affirmation.

In his short fiction, G. V. Desani writes in one or the other of the two contrasting veins of *Hali* and *All about H. Hatterr*. Thus "The Last Long Letter" records the ecstatic visions of a young man, a suicide, who casts his soul back into the opaque void of the universe, where it had been a light, as he has previously cast his jeweled ring into the depths of the sea to symbolize his belief that from time to time spirit illuminates matter but then withdraws, leaving all in chaos and darkness until its next coming. Other stories—*e.g.* "Mephisto's Daughter," "With Malice Aforethought," and "The Second Mrs. Was Wed in a Nightmare"—are fantasies, sometimes with a satiric sting, which further exemplify the talent that made *All about H. Hatterr* one of our century's major contributions to the literature of the absurd.

—Perry D. Westbrook

---

**DE VRIES, Peter.** American. Born in Chicago, 27 February 1910. Educated at Calvin College, Grand Rapids, Michigan, A.B. 1931; Northwestern University, Evanston, Illinois, 1931. Married Katinka Loeser in 1943; has four children. Editor of community newspapers, Chicago, 1931; candy vending machine operator, and radio actor, Chicago, 1931–38; Associate Editor, 1938–42, and Co-Editor, 1942–44, *Poetry* magazine, Chicago. Since 1944, Staff Member of *The New Yorker* magazine. Recipient: National Institute of Arts and Letters grant, 1946. Member, National Institute of Arts and Letters, 1969. Address: 170 Cross Highway, Westport, Connecticut 06880, U.S.A.

PUBLICATIONS

Novels

> *But Who Wakes the Bugler?*  Boston, Houghton Mifflin, 1940.
> *The Handsome Heart.*  New York, Coward McCann, 1943.
> *Angels Can't Do Better.*  New York, Coward McCann, 1944.
> *The Tunnel of Love.*  Boston, Little Brown, 1954; London, Gollancz, 1955.
> *Comfort Me with Apples.*  Boston, Little Brown, and London, Gollancz, 1956.
> *The Mackerel Plaza.*  Boston, Little Brown, and London, Gollancz, 1958.
> *The Tents of Wickedness.*  Boston, Little Brown, and London, Gollancz, 1959.
> *Through the Fields of Clover.*  Boston, Little Brown, and London, Gollancz, 1961.
> *The Blood of the Lamb.*  Boston, Little Brown, and London, Gollancz, 1962.
> *Reuben, Reuben.*  Boston, Little Brown, and London, Gollancz, 1964.
> *Let Me Count the Ways.*  Boston, Little Brown, and London, Gollancz, 1965.
> *The Vale of Laughter.*  Boston, Little Brown, 1967; London, Gollancz, 1968.
> *The Cat's Pajamas and Witch's Milk.*  Boston, Little Brown, 1968.

*Mrs. Wallop.* Boston, Little Brown, and London, Gollancz, 1970.
*Into Your Tent I'll Creep.* Boston, Little Brown, 1971.

Short Stories

*No But I Saw the Movie.* Boston, Little Brown, 1952; London, Gollancz, 1954.

Play

*The Tunnel of Love,* with Joseph Fields (produced New York, 1957). Boston, Little Brown, 1957.

Bibliography: "Peter De Vries—The First Thirty Years: A Bibliography, 1934–1964" by Edwin T. Bowden, in *Studies in Literature and Language* (Austin, Texas), vol. VI, 1965.

Manuscript Collection: Boston University Library.

Critical Studies: *Peter De Vries* by Roderick Jellema, Grand Rapids, Michigan, Eerdmans, 1967; interviews with Roy Newquist in *Counterpoint*, Chicago, Rand McNally, 1964, and with Richard B. Sale in *Studies in the Novel* (Denton, Texas), Fall 1969.

*     *     *

Peter De Vries is a wit who writes humorous, often very funny, moral fables that look like novels but are in reality just vehicles for his comic energies. His sense of play tends to overwhelm his plot, which frequently suffers from discontinuity and misplaced emphasis. His characters generally lack size and complexity; they exist more as De Vries's witty and insouciant mouthpieces than as individualized fictional creations. Not that De Vries is incompetent in plotting a novel: when he puts his mind to it, as *Comfort Me with Apples* illustrates, he contrives an action as satisfyingly complicated as the Cretan maze. And not that he is without imagination in the handling of character. De Vries has great skill with role-playing. When his characters indulge in it, he uses this device with the joy of a writer dedicated to the exploitation of fantasy and self-delusion. In many of the books in which he uses a first person narrator, De Vries himself seems to play a role, ranging, in his virtuoso way, from that of a shrewd Connecticut Yankee to that of a Polish piano mover in Indiana. He has certain technical skills in fiction, then, but he applies them haphazardly to his work. It is not the craft of fiction that is of real interest in his work but the nature of his humor, his religious and moral attitudes, and his social commentary.

De Vries is like a precocious child at play—word play, of course, which seems to flow spontaneously from his pen. His novels are packed with pun and parody, with solecism and epigram, with caricature, and with sheer, delightful idiocy. He is dedicated to nonsense, which he regards as a lowly but tricky art, because the penalty for its failure is silliness. His skills are largely verbal, but he can do situation comedy too, in the zany mode of the Marx Brothers. But of course he goes beyond play to assume the traditional burden of the humorist as critic. As a novelist of manners, his mode is satire. His literary criticism is expressed mostly in parody; *The Tents of Wickedness* is the outstanding example among his books, with its laughing attack on Faulkner's style, on the excessive depravity of Erskine Caldwell's characters and on the excessive guilt of Graham Greene's. De Vries humor also has a dark side. He knows that a joke may be a device for resolving fear. He knows that the "real" world is mad and that it makes men desperate. One of his humorous devices is to permit his characters to escape to fantasy; another, as in the Tom Waltz section of *Let Me Count the Ways*, is to counter the world's madness with the most extravagant and wildest kind of individual action. Like any good humorist, De Vries knows that the vale of laughter is not far from the vale of tears.

The religious and moral problems in his fiction certainly owe much to his Dutch Calvinist background. The general movement of his fiction is from a youthful total rejection of Calvinism to a hard-won agnosticism. The novels are full of guilt, especially with respect to religion and sexual behaviour, as De Vries works to liberate himself from his heritage. It is not always clear whether it is the characters' guilt as they move toward fornication or adultery or the author's, but De Vries is certainly pre-occupied with sex and unsure of the morality that should govern it. One of the characters in *The Mackerel Plaza* says we do not know how to cope with guilt because we have done away with the concept of sin. De Vries seems to want freedom from sin, but he has contempt for atheism, which would abolish the idea. Stein, the atheist in *The Blood of the Lamb*, enjoys the deprivations of faith that are self-inflicted and cannot forgive God for not existing. De Vries also has contempt for liberal Christianity and for its ministers who are ignorant of theology and preach in split-level churches. In *The Blood of the Lamb*, a semi-documentary novel about a father and his daughter who dies of leukemia, De Vries has made his most painful and most incisive statement about agnosticism. The child reveals to the father that human beings have only the human trinity to fall back upon: reason, courage, and grace. And this is the view, tentatively and skeptically entertained, that De Vries seems, in his maturity, to have adopted.

De Vries's social comment, a part of his humor and implicit in his attitude toward religion and morality, deals largely with the middle and upper middle classes in suburbia. He has a keen ear for the linguistic pretentions of this class and a keen eye for its yearning for factitiously "gracious" living. He observes America as an anthropologist or as a witty foreign writer might, and he directs his ridicule and laughter at everything from aptitude tests for corporation personnel to the generation gap, always making fun of the maniacal zeal for sociological research into their own lives that Americans habitually reveal. In *The Vale of Laughter*, the take-off on the Masters-Johnson investigation into sexual behaviour is perhaps the high point of this kind of hi-jinks. The apostles of behaviourism, like the child psychologist or the marriage counsellor, are a constant butt of his humor. He is overwhelmed by the excesses of people who have unlimited opportunities for consumption in an affluent society; they not only have too much of everything but most of what they buy is synthetic. The protest he makes is easily recognizable as that of a traditionalist and humanist who regrets that men and women are foolish, greedy, gullible, lecherous, and essentially incompatible. De Vries is a humorist like so many others who have made laughter out of the failure of human beings to live up to the moral and social standards that the society has set for itself. His difficulty is that he is unsure of these standards himself and full of a sense of his own failings and guilt. Yet it is this condition which enables his reader to identify with him and enables him to speak so persuasively to the reader.

—Chester E. Eisinger

---

**DICKENS, Monica (Enid).** British. Born in London, 10 May 1915. Educated at St. Paul's Girls' School, London. Married Commander Roy Olin Stratton, U.S. Navy, in 1951; has two children. Worked as a maid and cook in private houses; as a factory worker, nurse, and with the Samaritans. Columnist, *Woman's Own*, London, 1946–65. Address: Main Street, Post Office Box 386, North Falmouth, Massachusetts 02556, U.S.A.; or, 2 Gore Street, London S.W.7, England.

PUBLICATIONS

Novels

*Mariana.* London, Joseph, 1940; as *The Moon Was Low*, New York, Harper, 1940.
*The Fancy.* London, Joseph, 1943; as *Edward's Fancy*, New York, Harper, 1944.
*Thursday Afternoons.* London, Joseph, 1945.
*The Happy Prisoner.* London, Joseph, 1946; Philadelphia, Lippincott, 1947.
*Joy and Josephine.* London, Joseph, 1948.
*Flowers on the Grass.* London, Joseph, 1949; New York, McGraw Hill, 1950.
*No More Meadows.* London, Joseph, 1953; as *The Nightingales Are Singing*, Boston, Little Brown, 1953.
*The Winds of Heaven.* London, Joseph, and New York, Coward McCann, 1955.
*The Angel in the Corner.* London, Joseph, 1956; New York, Coward McCann, 1957.
*Man Overboard.* London, Joseph, 1958; New York, Coward McCann, 1959.
*The Heart of London.* London, Joseph, and New York, Coward McCann, 1961.
*Cobbler's Dream.* London, Joseph, and New York, Coward McCann, 1964.
*Kate and Emma.* London, Heinemann, 1964; New York, Coward McCann, 1965.
*The Room Upstairs.* London, Heinemann, and New York, Doubleday, 1966.
*The Landlord's Daughter.* London, Heinemann, and New York, Doubleday, 1968.
*The Listeners.* London, Heinemann, 1970; as *The End of the Line*, New York, Doubleday, 1970.

Other

*One Pair of Hands* (autobiography). London, Joseph, and New York, Harper, 1939.
*One Pair of Feet* (autobiography). London, Joseph, and New York, Harper, 1942.
*My Turn to Make the Tea* (autobiography). London, Joseph, 1951.
*My Fair Lady* (juvenile). New York, Four Winds, 1967.
*The Great Fire* (juvenile). London, Kaye and Ward, 1970.
*The House at World's End* (juvenile). London, Heinemann, 1970; New York, Doubleday, 1971.
*The Great Escape* (juvenile). London, Kaye and Ward, 1971.
*Summer at World's End* (juvenile). London, Heinemann, 1971; New York, Doubleday, 1972.
*Follyfoot* (juvenile). London, Heinemann, 1971.
*World's End in Winter* (juvenile). London, Heinemann, 1972; New York, Doubleday, 1973.
*Dora at Follyfoot* (juvenile). London, Heinemann, 1972.
*Cape Cod.* New York, Viking Press, 1972.

Monica Dickens comments:

My novels are mostly based on my own firsthand experience. Before I was married and had children, I used to actually go and do the jobs or join the communities in which I was interested. Now, not being able to throw up everything for an idea and start a new chapter of life every few years, I work more like a journalist, and research by observing and listening. Perhaps it will be helpful to name the backgrounds which led to each book:

*Mariana.* The first novel everyone writes sooner or later, about one's own childhood and growing up.

*The Fancy.* I worked in a factory that repaired Spitfires during the Battle of Britain.

*Thursday Afternoons.* I was a hospital nurse for most of the war.

*The Happy Prisoner.* I nursed a patient who was adjusting to amputation.

*Joy and Josephine.* I used my own background of Notting Hill and the Portobello Road where I was born and brought up.

*Flowers on the Grass.* I did many of the various jobs that the central character tries (holiday camp, companion to sick boy, teaching, etc.).

*No More Meadows.* I used my own experiences in marrying into the US Navy and joining Washington Service society.

*The Winds of Heaven.* Observation of changing family patterns in which there is no room for the ageing parent.

*Man Overboard.* Observation of forcibly retired Service people.

*The Heart of London.* My own background again, of Notting Hill, plus months of research among the black community, social workers, police, teachers, churches, road construction gangs, midwives.

*Cobbler's Dream.* My own experiences with horses. Plus extensive work with the RSPCA.

*Kate and Emma.* Extensive field work with the NSPCC and juvenile courts.

*The Room Upstairs.* My own family experiences with the problems and terrors of an old lady, and with a nearby house in Massachusetts, USA, bisected by a highway.

*The Listeners.* My own experiences as a Samaritan.

My aim is to entertain, rather than instruct. I want readers to recognize life in my books, either as they know it, or as they are able to understand it, however alien the situation.

Increasingly, as I grow more prolific, my writing is for me the greater part of life. I live fully, surrounded by people and animals, but find more and more reality and interest in the people and worlds I create. Writing is a cop-out. An excuse to live perpetually in fantasy land, where you can create, direct and watch the products of your own head. Very selfish.

\*       \*       \*

Monica Dickens' three autobiographical books belong to a genre popular in the late '30's and '40's: amusing, mildly satiric, loosely-organized personal experiences, usually written by a woman, a shrewd observer of the eccentricities of commonplace people, adroit at illuminating character with sudden flashes of insight, never herself top girl in any group, but always more radical and socially-conscious than most of the people she works or lives among. Thus, the heroine of *One Pair of Hands*, after picaresque adventures as a cook-general for a Dickensian series of employers, ends with her speech delivered at a Household Fair, suggesting improvements in the treatment of servants. With rueful irony she reports audience reaction: "'Words, words, words, and when you think of it, what did all that talk amount to?' 'Don't ask me, dear. I was asleep.'"

This book gave Miss Dickens the episodic structure for later plots as in *Flowers on the Grass* or *Man Overboard*, whose heroes go from job to job, each with a cluster of satirically-sketched personalities. Another favourite, closely-related pattern, the concurrent picaresque, so to speak, is an intercutting from group to group of persons tenuously related by a common character as in *The Heart of London* and *The Listeners*. The incidents of these plots are often conventionally melodramatic, although they seem less stereotypic in her later novels where violence arises from urban slums and is the self-damage of the life-damaged.

Miss Dickens, while prodigal in characterisation, has always been economical in subject matter. Her own experience while training as a nurse has, for example, produced both the autobiographical *One Pair of Feet* and the novel *Thursday Afternoons*, in which Dr. Sheppard, trapped by his own bedside manner, longs for active naval duty in the imminent Second World War. In *Flowers on the Grass* Daniel's rebellious adventures include a hospital episode in which Nurse Saunders recalls Nurse Dickens. Elizabeth of *The Happy Prisoner* is a private nurse who marries her patient; May, the district midwife of *Heart of London*, saves her best friend's premature illegitimate baby; even when it serves no useful plot function, a hospital may be part of a character's background as it is in Christine Cope's (*No More Meadows*).

Likewise Miss Dickens' wartime factory work provided material for *The Fancy* and for a long episode in *Joy and Josephine*, whose heroine prefers making airplanes to dilettante canteen service. Other books draw on Miss Dickens' experience as a reporter and as a Samaritan.

Certain characters also reappear: e.g. the slightly feeble-minded spinster, the married man with an affair, and especially the one-legged or lame man, who may be as engaging as Oliver (*Happy Prisoner*) or as selfish as David (*The Fancy*). In another group of novels these cripples become girls in wheelchairs or crippled boys. Naval officers recur, sometimes as minor as Uncle Tim (*Mariana*), married to "a walking Gieve's", or as crucial as Commander Vinson Gaegler, who inflicts on his English bride the protocol of American admirals' wives (*No More Meadows*). In *Man Overboard*, Commander Ben Francis, R.N., dismissed as redundant in postwar cutbacks, tries to find a civilian career. From this novel on, Miss Dickens has generally turned more explicitly to social or socio-psychological themes: racial tension, schools, urban redevelopment, perversion, alcoholism (*Heart of London*); child-abuse (*Kate and Emma*); old age (*The Winds of Heaven* and *The Room Upstairs*); the feeble-minded, the suicidal, the alone (*The Listeners*). Here she is interested in strange emotional liaisons, often touching but also grotesque. Emma Bullock, daughter of a Children's Court Magistrate, becomes the "blood comrade" of Kate, a mistreated adolescent who in turn beats and chains her own scapegoat child. The vulgarly sinister Dorothy Grue (*Room Upstairs*) adores Roger, a budgerigar, who imitates her voice. Charlotte (*The Landlord's Daughter*) welcomes Peter as a lover although he has killed and dismembered a former love, whose incriminating hank of hair Charlotte hides lest Peter, finding it, have no reason to let her live herself.

In contrast to the earlier overflowing novels, these books are grim. Their minor personages are still likely to be humour characters, but the monomanias or ruling passions lack the ebullient comic inventiveness of Miss Dickens' earlier works, perhaps because the eccentricities of urban poverty, however compassionated, are rarely amiable ones. Still, all her novels show her eye for visual detail, her understanding of absurdities and values, petty satisfactions and hugged-tight rancors, and her assumption that not even the most minor and peripheral characters need lack identity and idiosyncrasy.

—Jane W. Steadman

---

**DONLEAVY, J(ames) P(atrick).** Irish. Born in Brooklyn, New York, 23 April 1926; became an Irish Citizen, 1967. Educated at Trinity College, Dublin. Served in the United States Naval Reserve. Married to Mary Wilson Price; has two children. Recipient: London *Evening Standard* Drama Award, 1960; Brandeis University Creative Arts Award, for drama, 1961. Address: Balsoon House, Bective, Navan, County Meath, Ireland.

PUBLICATIONS

Novels

*The Ginger Man.* Paris, Olympia Press, 1955; London, Spearman, 1956; New York, McDowell Obolensky, 1958; complete edition, London, Corgi, 1963; New York, Seymour Lawrence-Delacorte Press, 1965.

*A Singular Man.*  Boston, Little Brown, 1963; London, Bodley Head, 1964.
*The Saddest Summer of Samuel S.*  New York, Seymour Lawrence-Delacorte Press, 1966; London, Eyre and Spottiswoode, 1967.
*The Beastly Beatitudes of Balthazar B.*  New York, Seymour Lawrence-Delacorte Press, 1968; London, Eyre and Spottiswoode, 1969.
*The Onion Eaters.*  New York, Seymour Lawrence-Delacorte Press, and London, Eyre and Spottiswoode, 1971.

Short Stories

*Meet My Maker the Mad Molecule.*  Boston, Little Brown, 1964; London, Bodley Head, 1965.

Plays

*The Ginger Man* (produced London and Dublin, 1959; New York, 1963).  New York, Random House, 1961; as *What They Did in Dublin, with The Ginger Man: A Play*, London, MacGibbon and Kee, 1962.
*Fairy Tales of New York* (produced London, 1961).  London, Penguin, and New York, Random House, 1961.
*A Singular Man* (produced Cambridge and London, 1964; Westport, Connecticut, 1967).  London, Bodley Head, 1965.
*The Plays of J. P. Donleavy.*  London, Penguin, and New York, Seymour Lawrence-Delacorte Press, 1972.

*       *       *

The late Betty Smith often said she wished she had written her novels in reverse order, since the first one, *A Tree Grows in Brooklyn*, overshadowed everything else she wrote. One suspects that another Brooklyn-born writer wishes for less categorization on the part of readers and critics; for J. P. Donleavy's work still tends to be thought of in two categories: his first published novel *The Ginger Man*, and all the rest.

One does not need to denigrate the success of that first novel to point to the unfairness of the categories and critical judgments. For certainly *The Ginger Man* is a fine, funny, lusty—even obscene for its time—and sad novel of comic genius. If the later books do not roar along with the reckless wit and charm, even, of the first novel, they do attempt a deeper examination of the human condition, in all its comic pathos and lonely absurdity. Donleavy's vision of man in his universe is not happy, after all, despite all the bright remarks of his characters, and the hilarities of his black humor. The fragmentation of Donleavy's prose style, increasing in subtle effects with each novel, is surely no mere trick of style, but the proper medium for rendering the perceptions of his heroic anti-heroes in their gay assertions of life's goodness even in squalor and confusion: "World so lonely. Voices in song. Raised in thanksgiving. Off key I croaked out a note or two. In transit between lands." That is from his most recent novel, *The Onion Eaters*, a book about Clayton Clay Cleaver Clementine, distinguished by his possession of three testicles—true sign that he is rightful heir to Charnal Castle. This book, like the others, is about debts, monetary and emotional: for the pawning and scheming of *The Ginger Man* were more than "comic relief." The recurring incidents in all Donleavy's novels of masturbation, betrayed relationships, homosexual anxieties contribute to the theme of the outsider—the singular man, marked off somehow from a world he tries to live in with freedom and joy.

All these outsiders keep trying to find, in their fragmented stream-of-consciousness narratives, a form of love, permanence, meaning which always eludes them. The beatitudes

357

are beastly, the universities "baleful behind great iron gates," life is a sad summer. Yet *The Onion Eaters* (one might think of it almost as Kafka's *Castle*, had Joseph K. actually got in and discovered the chaos of the place) ends with a passage in its way characteristic of the affirmative, almost mystical strain so often neglected in studies of Donleavy's work:

> Walk now over this little bridge. Where the brook tumbles under. And grey speckled trout speed for cover. . . . Out there far away the rest of the world has gone modern. With whole new jumping generations. And holy hell is the only thing we have up to date here. To make the stars bark. When the west's awake. Over the cliffs and roaring sea. Where the moon hides and weeps at night.

—James Korges

---

**DRABBLE, Margaret.**   British.   Born in Sheffield, Yorkshire, 5 June 1939; sister of A. S. Byatt, *q.v.* Educated at the Mount School, York; Newnham College, Cambridge, B.A. (honours) 1960. Married Clive Swift in 1960; has three children. Recipient: Rhys Memorial Prize, 1966; Black Memorial Prize, 1968. Lives in London. Address: c/o Weidenfeld and Nicolson Ltd., 5 Winsley Street, London W.1, England.

PUBLICATIONS

Novels

A Summer Bird-Cage.   London, Weidenfeld and Nicolson, 1963; New York, Morrow, 1964.
The Garrick Year.   London, Weidenfeld and Nicolson, 1964; New York, Morrow, 1965.
The Millstone.   London, Weidenfeld and Nicolson, 1965; New York, Morrow, 1966.
Jerusalem the Golden.   London, Weidenfeld and Nicolson, and New York, Morrow, 1967.
The Waterfall.   London, Weidenfeld and Nicolson, and New York, Knopf, 1969.
The Needle's Eye.   London, Weidenfeld and Nicolson, 1972.

Short Stories

Penguin Modern Stories 3, with others.   London, Penguin, 1969.

Uncollected Short Stories

"Hassan's Tower", in Winter's Tales 12.   London, Macmillan, 1966.
"The Reunion", in Winter's Tales 14.   London, Macmillan, 1968.
"The Gifts of War", in Winter's Tales 16.   London, Macmillan, 1970.

Plays

    *Bird of Paradise* (produced London, 1969).

    Screenplay: *A Touch of Love*, 1969.

Other

    *Wordsworth*.  London, Evans, 1966.

    Editor, with B. S. Johnson, *London Consequences* (a group novel).  London, Greater
    London Arts Association, 1972.


Margaret Drabble comments:

    My books are I think mainly concerned with privilege and justice. Equality and egali-
tarianism preoccupy me constantly, and not very hopefully. None of my books is about
feminism, because my belief in the necessity for justice for women (which they don't get
at the moment) is so basic that I never think of using it as a subject. It is part of a whole.


                          \*          \*          \*


    Margaret Drabble began novel writing early, after a brilliant undergraduate career at
Cambridge and a short period as an actress. She is a deliberately conventional novelist, who
likes to write what she calls "a good traditional tale" and has no time for avant-garde innovations. Her principal model is George Eliot and she writes in the tradition of English moral
seriousness, of which George Eliot was such a distinguished exponent. The narrators of
her novels, and the other characters in them, are constantly alert for signs of self-deception
in themselves and of insincerity in other people; there is a prevalent atmosphere of sharp
intelligence and of probing into motives. Margaret Drabble can display an agreeably
incisive wit but rather little sense of humour. Her language is always sensitive to moral
nuance, and its flexibility and subtlety are clearly indebted to Henry James.
    Her first novel, *A Summer Bird-Cage*, was characteristically intelligent and witty, a study
of two sisters, one clever and just down from Oxford, the other beautiful and on the point
of marrying a fashionable novelist, and of the tensions between them. For a first novel, it
was immensely accomplished though the moral sharpness often declined into a rather
brittle cynicism. In *The Garrick Year* Margaret Drabble, who had married an actor and
lived for some time in Stratford-on-Avon, wrote entertainingly about actors and worked
off some of her own ambivalent feelings about theatrical life. But more importantly she
began to develop themes which have a genuine newness about them, despite her conservative
attitudes to form and technique. The heroine of *The Garrick Year*, Emma, has two small
children; at a crucial moment in the story she is suddenly distracted from her conversation
with the theatrical producer with whom she is having a remarkably half-hearted affair, and
plunges into a river to rescue one of her children. It is a vivid piece of writing, showing
how a basic maternal instinct suddenly asserts itself through the more trivial sentiments
that lie closer to the surface of Emma's life.
    It is Margaret Drabble's particular contribution to the contemporary novel to have
devised a genuinely new kind of character and predicament. There are, of course, innumerable women novelists who write from a feminine viewpoint, but Margaret Drabble differs
from them in writing about young women who are not merely intelligent, educated, more
or less attractive, and sharply observant. They are also mothers, and their involvement

with their children cuts sharply across their concern with a career, and their desire for emotional freedom. For many novelists the emancipated woman and the mother are two sharply different types; Margaret Drabble has shown that in the modern world the two roles are often combined in the same person. Her finest novel, *The Millstone*, is a lucid and moving exploration of this problem. Her heroine, Rosamund Stacey, is a dedicated scholar completing a Ph.D. thesis on Elizabethan poetry. After a single brief encounter with a young man she has no particularly strong feelings about, she becomes pregnant. She decides to have the baby and to keep it, to the general astonishment of her friends. Margaret Drabble gives a compelling account of the complexities of pregnancy, as they impinge on a young woman who is psychologically quite unprepared for them. In encounters with gynaecologists and midwives at an ante-natal clinic in a poor area of London, Rosamund not only discovers unexpected things about her own physical and psychological make-up, but by meeting the other expectant mothers who attend the clinic she is forced into an awareness of ordinary life and its attendant suffering, from which she had been cut off in the enclosed world of scholarship. After the sharpness and detachment of Margaret Drabble's first two novels there is a remarkable compassion and humanity in *The Millstone*.

Its two successors, *Jerusalem the Golden* and *The Waterfall* are, in comparison, disappointments. As attempts to unfold the consciousness of young women who are deeply in love with more or less unsuitable men they have moments of remarkable psychological insight, but are also embarrassing and unconvincing over long stretches. They illustrate Margaret Drabble's great difficulty in presenting credible male characters, particularly men who are supposed to be full of sexual attractiveness. Margaret Drabble may have reached a certain crisis point in her career. She is a serious novelist with a genuine concern for the situation of women in a world where their role is subject to all kinds of strains and ambiguities. She takes her writing very seriously, and the influence of George Eliot and Henry James has been thoroughly absorbed. But there is another side to her writing, a rather narrow concern with exclusively feminine attitudes and reactions that is in complete contrast to George Eliot's breadth of vision, and which has affinities with the popular fiction in women's magazines. In her last two novels she has moved dangerously close to such fiction.

—Bernard Bergonzi

---

**DRURY, Allen (Stuart).** American. Born in Houston, Texas, 2 September 1918. Educated at Stanford University, California, B.A. 1939. Served in the United States Army, 1942–43. Editor, Tulare, California, *Bee*, 1940–41; Country Editor, Bakersfield *Californian*, 1941–42; Member, United Press Senate Staff, Washington, D.C., 1943–45; National Editor, *Pathfinder* magazine, Washington, D.C., 1947–53; Member, Congressional Staff, *Washington Evening Star*, 1953–54, and *New York Times*, 1954–59. Since 1959, Political Correspondent, *Reader's Digest*, New York. Recipient: Sigma Delta Chi award, for journalism, 1941; Pulitzer Prize, for fiction, 1960. Lit.D., Rollins College, Winter Park, Florida, 1961. Address: c/o DruKill Company, Box 927, Maitland, Florida 32751, U.S.A.

PUBLICATIONS

Novels

*Advise and Consent*.   New York, Doubleday, 1959; London, Collins, 1960.

*A Shade of Difference.*   New York, Doubleday, 1962; London, Joseph, 1963.
*That Summer.*   London, Joseph, 1965; New York, Coward McCann, 1966.
*Capable of Honor.*   New York, Doubleday, 1966; London, Joseph, 1967.
*Preserve and Protect.*   New York, Doubleday, and London, Joseph, 1968.
*The Throne of Saturn.*   New York, Doubleday, and London, Joseph, 1971.


Other

*A Senate Journal, 1943–45.*   New York, McGraw Hill, 1963.
*Three Kids in a Cart: A Visit to Ike and Other Diversions.*   New York, Doubleday, 1965.
*"A Very Strange Society": A Journey to the Heart of South Africa.*   New York, Simon and Schuster, 1967; London, Joseph, 1968.
*Courage and Hesitation: Notes and Photographs of the Nixon Administration.*   New York, Doubleday, 1971; London, Joseph, 1972.


*         *         *


Allen Drury's experiences as a journalist, especially as a political correspondent in Washington, D.C., have left their mark, for better or worse, on his novels and non-fiction. Five of six novels are largely concerned with political battles, attacks by the media on members of the government, and the dangers threatening the American nation; and two of his three non-fiction works contain people and events that have counterparts or parallels in the political novels. Not surprisingly, his Washington novels (in particular *Advise and Consent*) have been read as *romans à clef*. The two works lying outside the District of Columbia arena are *That Summer*, a novel set in an exclusive resort in the Sierras, and *"A Very Strange Society,"* a collection of interviews and impressions drawn from his trip to South Africa that is the most moderate and balanced of his works. Perhaps he is too ready to depreciate the achievements of black African nations, but he acknowledges the complex problems of a multi-racial society.

Of his novels, *Advise and Consent* is the first published and the best. It would undoubtedly benefit from severe pruning, but there is a momentum built upon a melodramatic presentation of events that carries the reader along, even if he is wary of the hysterical undertone of the book. In the detailing of Congressional infighting and the tension of significant debates in the Senate, Drury is at his strongest. Here his years as a member of the United Press Senate Staff are effectively used. He is not so strong, however, when presenting the actions of the president or the left-wingers. As in later books, many characters are stereotypes. Even in this book, a Pulitzer prize winner, he uses a plot that appears contrived (even though it has real life counterparts) and characters that are mere puppets.

Three subsequent novels carry on the story of political struggles and national alarums through outbreaks of "liberal"-inspired violence and presidential assassination. Instead of refining and subtilizing the promising material and fictional technique of *Advise and Consent*, he seems to have been pushed by an increasing fear for the preservation of traditional American values and institutions into composing novels that are more overtly propagandistic statements of his conservative political beliefs than aesthetically pleasing books. Readers who share his deep distrust of liberals and his hatred of Communism may accept his fiction more readily, but they too probably find his prose heavy and his plots excessively sensational. Even characters such as Orrin Knox, who are interestingly depicted in the early novels, begin to pall in the later works. The use of melodramatic incident (often to compensate for feeble characterization) is strikingly exemplified in *Preserve and Protect*, which opens with the death of President Harley M. Hudson in a fiery plane crash and (on the last page) concludes with the assassination before a huge crowd of either the presidential or the vice-presidential nominee—in movie-serial fashion we are not told which one:

No one in the crowd heard anything, no one saw anything. For several moments the full import of the sudden confusion on the platform did not penetrate.

It was so bright and hot and sunny.

It was such a happy day.

They could not quite comprehend, in that bright, hot, sunny, awful instant, the dreadful thing that had occurred so swiftly and so silently before their eyes.

(Eagle edition, p. 447)

Non-American readers are probably irritated by the obtrusive patriotism and the condescension or scorn shown for foreigners. Drury seems unable or unwilling to present foreigners with sympathy or in depth. Too often, he resorts to stereotypes—Lord Claude Maudulayne, the British Ambassador, is something less than a caricature. In addition, by failing to develop credible characters for the ambassadors at the UN and in Washington, he loses the chance to utilize them effectively as a kind of Greek chorus commenting on American tragedies.

Yet even the later books suggest that, with firm guidance, Allen Drury might yet fulfil the promise of *Advise and Consent*. In *Preserve and Protect* he is still able to involve the reader in the machinations preceding a political convention, and in *A Shade of Difference* even a reader who correctly foresees the result may nevertheless be caught in the suspense surrounding a close Senate vote. But to be successful aesthetically, Drury will have to use tauter plots and prose, more credible characters, and a less obtrusively partisan point of view.

—James A. Hart

---

**DUFFY, Maureen.** British. Born in Worthing, Sussex, 21 October 1933. Educated at King's College, University of London, B.A. (honours) 1956. School teacher for five years. Collaborated with Brigid Brophy, *q.v.*, in making and exhibiting Prop Art (3-D Construction), London, 1969. Recipient: City of London Festival Playwright's Prize, 1962; Arts Council Bursary, for drama, 1963, and for literature, 1966. Address: 8 Roland Gardens, London S.W.7, England.

PUBLICATIONS

Novels

*That's How It Was*. London, Hutchinson, 1962.
*The Single Eye*. London, Hutchinson, 1964.
*The Microcosm*. London, Hutchinson, and New York, Simon and Schuster, 1966.
*The Paradox Players*. London, Hutchinson, 1967; New York, Simon and Schuster, 1968.
*Wounds*. London, Hutchinson, and New York, Knopf, 1969.
*Lovechild*. London, Weidenfeld and Nicolson, and New York, Knopf, 1971.

Plays

*The Lay Off* (produced London, 1962).

*The Silk Room* (produced Watford, Hertfordshire, 1966).
*Rites* (produced London, 1969).   London, Methuen, 1969.
*Solo, Olde Thyme* (produced Cambridge, 1970).


Verse

*Lyrics for the Dog Hour: Poems*.   London, Hutchinson, 1968.
*The Venus Touch*.   London, Weidenfeld and Nicolson, 1971.


Other

Translator, *A Blush of Shame*, by Domenico Rea.   London, Barrie and Rockliff, 1963.


*          *          *


Maureen Duffy is a prolific young novelist, poet and playwright whose work has developed rapidly in range and importance. *That's How It Was* won her immediate acclaim for its simplicity and forcefulness. It is a moving account of the relationship between a mother and daughter; their existence is poor. insecure, even brutal but transcended by mutual love. "I grew six inches under the light touch of her hand" explains the narrator. The little girl has an acute sense of social isolation and a fierce loyalty to the one constant figure in her universe; her mother's death is thus cause for more than grief, it brings total despair. The loneliness, restlessness and sexual hunger which spring from the situation are the dominating themes of each subsequent novel.

Realism is the touchstone of Miss Duffy's style; like many other observers of working-class life, she is at her best when she relies on accurate, detailed reportage and at her weakest when tempted by sentiment. *The Paradox Players* is an example of her writing at its most compelling. It describes a man's retreat from society to live for some months in a boat moored on the Thames. The physical realities of cold, snow, rats and flooding occupy him continually and the hardship brings him peace. He is a novelist, suffering from the hazards peculiar to that profession and has some pertinent comments to make about the vulnerability of the writer. "When I saw the reviews I could have cut my throat. You see they're very kind to first novels for some mistaken reason but when the poor bastard follows it up with a second and they see he really means it they tear its guts out." The experience of winter on the river restores his faith in his own ability to survive.

Miss Duffy's observations are acute, her use of dialogue witty and direct; this authenticity is complemented by an interest in the bizarre, the fantastic. Her best known book uses these qualities to great effect in a study of Lesbian society which is both informative and original. *The Microcosm* begins and ends in a club where the central characters meet to dance, dress up and escape from the necessity of "all the week wearing a false face." Their fantasies are played out in front of the juke box; then the narrative follows each woman back into her disguise, her social role. Steve is Miss Stephens, a schoolmistress; Cathy is a bus conductress; Matt works in a garage. Their predicament as individuals, the author suggests, extends beyond the interest of their own minority group. A plea is made for tolerance, understanding and that respect without which the human spirit must perish. "Society isn't a simple organism with one nucleus and a fringe of little feet, it's an infinitely complex structure and if you try to supress any part . . . you diminish, you mutilate the whole." Miss Duffy's recent novels *Wounds* and *Lovechild* reaffirm this belief.

—Judith Cooke Simmons

**DUGGAN, Maurice.** New Zealander. Born in Auckland, New Zealand, 25 November 1922. Attended the University of Auckland. Married Barbara Platts in 1945; has one child. Since 1961, has worked in advertising; with J. English Wright (Advertising) Ltd., Auckland, since 1965. Recipient: Hubert Church Memorial Award, 1957; Esther Glenn Award, 1959; Katherine Mansfield Award, 1959; Robert Burns Fellowship, Otago University, 1960; New Zealand Literary Fund Scholarship, 1966; Freda Buckland Award, 1970. Address: 58 Forrest Hill Road, Takapuna, Auckland 10, New Zealand.

PUBLICATIONS

Short Stories

> *Immanuel's Land: Stories.* Auckland, Pilgrim Press, 1956.
> *New Authors: Short Story 1,* with others. London, Hutchinson, 1961.
> *Summer in the Gravel Pit: Stories.* Auckland, Janet and Blackwood Paul, and London, Gollancz, 1965.
> *O'Leary's Orchard.* Christchurch, Caxton Press, 1970.

Other

> *Falter Tom and the Water Boy* (juvenile). Auckland, Janet and Blackwood Paul, 1957; London, Faber, and New York, Criterion Books, 1958.

Critical Study: "The Short Stories of Maurice Duggan" by Terry Sturm, in *Landfall* (Christchurch), March 1971.

\*          \*          \*

A small output does not preclude a high reputation. When careful craftsmanship is associated with creative vitality and a coherent moral vision, the demand for quantity gives place to a respect for quality, and expectation changes its focus. With only three slim volumes of short stories to his credit, Maurice Duggan has nonetheless received much critical acclaim for his narrative skill, stylistic competence and attention to graphic detail, all of which help to give wider meaning and deeper substance to his brief sorties into the hostile territory of human behaviour.

The title of his first collection, *Immanuel's Land*, together with its epigraph: "a most pleasant mountainous country beautified with woods vineyards fruits of all sorts flowers also with springs and fountains very delectable to behold . . .," invited readers to contrast the New Zealand they thought they knew with the disillusive insights that followed. His second collection, *Summer in the Gravel Pit*, which also included three of his earlier stories, bore a title with similar ironic overtones. Duggan is the chronicler of lost innocence, the recorder of human rancour and misunderstanding, the biographer of the excluded and uncertain. He holds a mirror up to ill-nature and, in so doing, catches a fleeting glimpse of kindness in a corner, pity and pathos in the background but, in the centre, a confusion of dream with reality that frequently provides the groundswell of his theme. Any conclusion reached by the reader, however, receives no evident confirmation from the author, for Duggan is absorbed in a complex series of seemings in order to reveal aspects and not positives of the human predicament.

Many of his stories separate themselves conveniently into undefined groups with related themes, and appearances by the same characters give the impression that they belong to chapters extracted from an unpublished novel. This does not mean that any single story fails to be complete in itself or shows signs of incoherence; rather it indicates that people and situation have been so clearly visualised that their creator knows much more about them than is immediately relevant. Thus the Lenihan series recounts a number of traumatic incidents occurring within a family of Irish-Catholic origin, and one is reminded that elsewhere Duggan has noted "the sad Irish bravura, the drear Irish Catholicism, the Irish syndrome— booze, melancholy and guilt, the pointless, loud pride . . . the intolerance; the low superstition; the peculiar Irish deceit." It is not surprising, therefore, that unlike Dan Davin, another New Zealand writer who continually returns to his Irish-Catholic background, Duggan looks back to childhood without regret and contemplates the progress from innocence to experience with sardonic attention.

Another series is that concerned with the inmates, both Brothers and adolescent boys, of a Catholic Boarding School, where the personalities and attitudes of the adults are counterpointed against those of the youngsters in their charge. What emerges from both these series is an intricate pattern of the illusory hopes of childhood and youth, of dreams that cannot couple with reality, of the inner turmoil caused by feelings of guilt, lust, suspicion, and the sense of injustice and loneliness. Bunyan's "most pleasant mountainous country" located in the antipodes has become a grey suburban desert from which can be drawn few pleasurable memories of growing-up among "woods and vineyards," and little but the rags and tatters of a debased Irish tradition to give artificial warmth and colour to a depressing, if vivid, picture.

If this were all it would not be insignificant, for Duggan's power of evocation is everywhere present, his humane attitudes implied, and his characters, lightly but deftly sketched, emerge as memorable representatives of a blighted world. However, it is by no means all; and as Duggan veered away from these vignettes of unhappy families and desolate schooldays, his themes expanded, his technical control increased and the note of deep compassion underlying and blending with his excursions into the waste land intensified. "Blues for Miss Laverty" belongs to another group of stories in which lonely and dejected women seek a little human warmth to comfort their existence—a little human warmth, that is all; but the discouraging response of a fellow-boarder is "What a hope, lady, what a hope." The hope recedes because those who hunger for affection not only encounter barriers of indifference and misunderstanding, but because they themselves are maimed, their vitality impaired and their capacity for fulfilment destroyed. Once again it is a sad and dispirited world, one in which the advice tendered in another story becomes grimly pertinent: "take it lightly, or you'll find you can't take it at all. Man is altogether Evil." Not quite altogether, for Duggan's brooding compassion for the victims of unloveliness and indecision underwrites his record of human inadequacies.

These inadequacies are not unrelated to man's inability to distinguish between dream and reality, a theme to which Duggan continually returns and on which he plays many variations. In an earlier story comes the counsel: "Do not let yourself be imposed on by reality." Some of the problems of the young narrator of "Along Rideout Road That Summer" stem from his failure to adjust the idea of "a damsel with a dulcimer" to his vision of "the reputedly wild Hohepa girl perched on the gate, feet hooked in the bars, ribbons fluttering from her ukulele." In "O'Leary's Orchard," the same character, grown older and conscious of the deceptive dream and the burden of years, combines romantic illusion with the rueful awareness of actuality and disillusion. Duggan's latest novella, "Riley's Handbook," which takes the shape of a long involved monologue, is prefaced by the Yeatsian "How know the dreamer from the dream? Who dreams damp Riley in the green morning at his maypole dancing? And what does Riley dream?"

This compulsive preoccupation with the phantasmagoria of life determines Duggan's approach to the complexities of human motivation as it likewise impels him to experiment with stylistic devices, the better to reveal both inner conflict and outward expression. The total effect of his longer and more elaborate fictions, from "Chapter" and "Along Rideout Road That Summer" to "O'Leary's Orchard" and "Riley's Handbook" is such that the reader is forced to examine his own conception of reality and explore his own illusions in terms of the imaginative world that Duggan has created.

—H. Winston Rhodes

---

**du MAURIER, Daphne.**   British.   Born in London, 13 May 1907. Educated privately and in Paris. Married Major, later Lieutenant-General Sir Frederick Browning in 1932 (died, 1965); has three children. Fellow, Royal Society of Literature, 1952. D.B.E. (Dame Commander, Order of the British Empire), 1969. Address: Kilmarth, Par, Cornwall, England.

PUBLICATIONS

Novels

> *The Loving Spirit.*   London, Heinemann, and New York, Doubleday, 1931.
> *I'll Never Be Young Again.*   London, Heinemann, and New York, Doubleday, 1932.
> *The Progress of Julius.*   London, Heinemann, and New York, Doubleday, 1933.
> *Gerald: A Portrait.*   London, Gollancz, 1934; New York, Doubleday, 1935.
> *Jamaica Inn.*   London, Gollancz, and New York, Doubleday, 1936.
> *Rebecca.*   London, Gollancz, and New York, Doubleday, 1938.
> *Frenchman's Creek.*   London, Gollancz, 1941; New York, Doubleday, 1942.
> *Hungry Hill.*   London, Gollancz, and New York, Doubleday, 1943.
> *The King's General.*   London, Gollancz, and New York, Doubleday, 1946.
> *The Parasites.*   London, Gollancz, 1949; New York, Doubleday, 1950.
> *My Cousin Rachel.*   London, Gollancz, 1951; New York, Doubleday, 1952.
> *Mary Anne.*   London, Gollancz, and New York, Doubleday, 1954.
> *The Scapegoat.*   London, Gollancz, and New York, Doubleday, 1957.
> *Castle Dor*, with Arthur Quiller-Couch.   London, Dent, and New York, Doubleday, 1962.
> *The Glass Blowers.*   London, Gollancz, and New York, Doubleday, 1963.
> *The Flight of the Falcon.*   London, Gollancz, and New York, Doubleday, 1967.
> *The House on the Strand.*   London, Gollancz, and New York, Doubleday, 1969.

Short Stories

> *Come Wind, Come Weather.*   London, Heinemann, and New York, Doubleday, 1941.
> *The Apple Tree: A Short Novel and Some Stories.*   London, Gollancz, 1952; as *Kiss Me Again, Stranger: A Collection of Eight Stories, Long and Short*, New York, Doubleday, 1953.
> *The Breaking Point: Eight Stories.*   London, Gollancz, 1959; as *The Breaking Point*, New York, Doubleday, 1959.
> *Early Stories.*   London, Todd, 1959.
> *The Treasury of du Maurier Short Stories.*   London, Gollancz, 1960.
> *Not after Midnight.*   London, Gollancz, 1971.

Plays

> Rebecca (produced Manchester and London, 1940; New York, 1945). London, Gollancz, 1940; New York, Dramatists Play Service, 1943.
> The Years Between (produced Manchester, 1944; London, 1945). London, Gollancz, 1945; New York, Doubleday, 1946.
> September Tide (produced Oxford and London, 1948). London, Gollancz, 1949; New York, Doubleday, 1950.

Other

> The du Mauriers. London, Gollancz, and New York, Doubleday, 1937.
> Happy Christmas. London, Todd, and New York, Doubleday, 1940.
> The Infernal World of Branwell Brontë. London, Gollancz, 1960; New York, Doubleday, 1961.
> Vanishing Cornwall. London, Gollancz, and New York, Doubleday, 1967.

> Editor, The Young George du Maurier: A Selection of His Letters, 1860–1867. London, Davies, 1951; New York, Doubleday, 1952.
> Editor, Best Stories, by Phyllis Bottome. London, Faber, 1963.

\*       \*       \*

The novels of Daphne du Maurier continue to fascinate each successive generation of readers. Beginning with *The Loving Spirit* and continuing through three decades with such works as the now classic *Rebecca* and her latest, *The House on the Strand*, she has responded to that universal love of a story well told. Characters skillfully drawn, mystery and suspense, the broad historical sweep of the centuries, plots laced with intrigue and violence, strange and supernatural events, brute force and touching beauty and tenderness, irony and intensity —all combine to create the works that have brought her acclaim as a novelist.

There has, however, been little serious study of her seventeen novels. The critical eye can see the flaws that the captive reader forgives and forgets, anxious as he is for the delight she gives. Many of her works reveal similar plots, with the heaping on of incidents that show her love of the melodramatic. Time and again the reader is drawn into those events that conclude with the bizarre ending and the ironic twist, such as in *Rebecca* and *My Cousin Rachel*. Her first work, *The Loving Spirit*, reveals the germ of her later development. The gothic and romantic qualities find lavish expression. The romanticism at times declines into sentimentality, as in Christopher's references to the simple folk. The brooding Byronic hero is here in the figure of Joseph Coombe and appears with slight alteration in *Jamaica Inn*, *Rebecca* and *The Flight of the Falcon*. One is drawn to these characters but is interested primarily in the events that happen to them. The ceaseless activity of the plot gives little time for development of character, and motivation is often vague and with slight validity. Direct characterization frequently yields to indirect, and little analysis is needed because both motives and feelings are clearly stated for the reader.

Pervading all the novels is a moralist tone, although not didactic. Exotic protagonists struggle against an awesome fate that is irrevocable after the first page. Evil does not triumph, but the forces of evil leave their marks in her imaginary world and often bring torment to noble heroes and heroines. Once again, however, the fascination lies not in the universal insights into such matters as the nature of evil or the essence of humanity but rather in the fast-moving plot full of suspense. The themes that are tantalizingly suggested will not bear the close scrutiny of analysis, for the structure of the whole is too flimsy.

And yet the themes remain to haunt the reader. The cyclic pattern of life recurs too often to enumerate. Life repeats itself, and there is a oneness to existence. The mysterious passing

367

backward and forward in time, occurring in *The Loving Spirit*, suggests that indeed time may be "all-dimensional yesterday, today, tomorrow running concurrently in ceaseless repetition," so aptly suggested by Richard Young in *The House on the Strand*. The allusions to Adam and the tree of knowledge and "Cain's cry of protest against God" reveal the depth of the idea. Although the development may lack fullness, Daphne du Maurier throughout her novels suggests the yearnings of the human heart as one character after another reaches for what is beyond him into areas that test man's intellectual and emotional comprehension. Miss du Maurier's protagonists do not always stand triumphant at their end, but they remain vital and alive. Such figures as Madame Duval in *The Glass Blowers* continue to exist for the reader long after the concluding lines are read.

—Sarah Evelyn Jackson

**DURRELL, Lawrence (George).** British. Born in Julundur, India, 27 February 1912. Educated at the College of St. Joseph, Darjeeling, India; St. Edmund's School, Canterbury. Married three times; has two children. Has held many jobs, including jazz pianist and composer, automobile racer, and real estate agent. Editor, with Henry Miller and Alfred Perles, *The Booster* (later *Delta*), Paris, 1937–39; Columnist, *Egyptian Gazette*, Cairo, 1941; Editor, with Robin Fedden and Bernard Spencer, *Personal Landscape*, Cairo, 1942–45; Special Correspondent in Cyprus for *The Economist*, London, 1953–55; Editor, *Cyprus Review*, Nicosia, 1954–55. Taught at the British Institute, Kalamata, Greece, 1940. Press Service Officer and Public Relations Officer, British Information Office, Cairo, 1941–44, Alexandria, 1944–45, Dodecanese Islands, Greece, 1946–47, Belgrade, 1949–52, and Cyprus in the 1950's. Director of the British Council Institute, Cordoba, Argentina, 1947–48. Recipient: Duff Cooper Memorial Prize, 1957; Prix du Meilleur Livre Etranger, 1959. Fellow, Royal Society of Literature, 1954. Resides in France. Address: c/o National and Grindlay's Bank, 13 St. James's Square, London S.W.1, England.

PUBLICATIONS

Novels

*Pied Piper of Lovers*. London, Cassell, 1935.
*Panic Spring* (as Charles Norden). London, Faber, and New York, Covici Friede, 1937.
*The Black Book: An Agon*. Paris, Obelisk Press, 1938; New York, Dutton, 1960.
*Cefalû*. London, Editions Poetry, 1947; as *The Dark Labyrinth*, New York, Ace, 1958.
*White Eagles over Serbia*. London, Faber, and New York, Criterion Books, 1957.
*The Alexandria Quartet:*
  *Justine*. London, Faber, and New York, Dutton, 1957.
  *Balthazar*. London, Faber, and New York, Dutton, 1958.
  *Mountolive*. London, Faber, 1958; New York, Dutton, 1959.
  *Clea*. London, Faber, and New York, Dutton, 1960.
*Aut Tunc Aut Nunquam:*
  *Tunc*. London, Faber, and New York, Dutton, 1968.
  *Nunquam*. London, Faber, and New York, Dutton, 1970.

Short Stories

> *Esprit de Corps: Sketches from Diplomatic Life.*   London, Faber, 1957; New York, Dutton, 1958.
> *Stiff Upper Lip: Life among the Diplomats.*   London, Faber, 1958; New York, Dutton, 1959.
> *Sauve Qui Peut.*   London, Faber, 1966; New York, Dutton, 1967.

Plays

> *Sappho: A Play in Verse* (produced Hamburg, 1959; Edinburgh, 1961; Evanston, Illinois, 1964).   London, Faber, 1950; New York, Dutton, 1958.
> *Acté* (produced Hamburg, 1961).   London, Faber, and New York, Dutton, 1965.
> *An Irish Faustus: A Morality in Nine Scenes* (produced Sommerhausen, Germany, 1966).   London, Faber, 1963; New York, Dutton, 1964.

> Recording: *Ulysses Come Back: Sketch for a Musical* (story, music and lyrics by Lawrence Durrell), 1971.

Verse

> *Quaint Fragment: Poems Written Between the Ages of Sixteen and Nineteen.*   London, Cecil Press, 1931.
> *Ten Poems.*   London, Caduseus Press, 1932.
> *Bromo Bombastes.*   London, Caduseus Press, 1933.
> *Transition: Poems.*   London, Caduseus Press, 1934.
> *A Private Country.*   London, Faber, 1943.
> *Cities, Plains and People.*   London, Faber, 1946.
> *On Seeming to Presume.*   London, Faber, 1948.
> *Deus Loci.*   Ischia, Italy, Di Mato Vito, 1950.
> *Private Drafts.*   Nicosia, Cyprus, Proodos Press, 1955.
> *The Tree of Idleness and Other Poems.*   London, Faber, 1955.
> *Selected Poems.*   London, Faber, and New York, Grove Press, 1956.
> *Collected Poems.*   London, Faber, and New York, Dutton, 1960; revised edition, 1968.
> *Penguin Modern Poets 1*, with Elizabeth Jennings and R. S. Thomas.   London, Penguin, 1962.
> *Beccafico Le Becfigue* (English, with French translation by F.-J. Temple).   Montpellier, France, La Licorne, 1963.
> *La Descente du Styx* (English, with French translation by F.-J. Temple).   Montpellier, France, La Murène, 1964.
> *Selected Poems 1935–63.*   London, Faber, 1964.
> *The Ikons: New Poems.*   London, Faber, 1966; New York, Dutton, 1967.
> *The Red Limbo Lingo: A Poetry Notebook for 1968–1970.*   London, Faber, 1971.

Other

> *Prospero's Cell: A Guide to the Landscape and Manners of the Island of Corcyra.*   London, Faber, 1945; New York, Dutton, 1960.
> *Key to Modern Poetry.*   London, Peter Nevill, 1952; as *A Key to Modern British Poetry*, Norman, University of Oklahoma Press, 1952.
> *Reflections on a Marine Venus: A Companion to the Landscape of Rhodes.*   London, Faber, 1953; New York, Dutton, 1960.

*Bitter Lemons* (on Cyprus).   London, Faber, 1957; New York, Dutton, 1958.
*Art and Outrage: A Correspondence about Henry Miller Between Alfred Perles and Lawrence Durrell, with an Intermission by Henry Miller.*   London, Putnam, 1959; New York, Dutton, 1960.
*Lawrence Durrell and Henry Miller: A Private Correspondence*, edited by George Wickes.   New York, Dutton, and London, Faber, 1963.
*Spirit of Place: Letters and Essays on Travel*, edited by Alan G. Thomas.   London, Faber, and New York, Dutton, 1969.

Editor, with others, *Personal Landscape: An Anthology of Exile.*   London, Editions Poetry, 1945.
Editor, *A Henry Miller Reader.*   New York, New Directions, 1959; as *The Best of Henry Miller*, London, Heinemann, 1960.
Editor, *New Poems 1963: A P.E.N. Anthology of Contemporary Poetry.*   London, Hutchinson, 1963.

Translator, *Six Poems from the Greek of Sekilanos and Seferic.*   Rhodes, Lawrence Durrell, 1946.
Translator, with others, *The King of Asine and Other Poems*, by George Seferis.   London, Lehmann, 1948.
Translator, *The Curious History of Pope Joan*, by Emmanuel Royidis.   London, Verschoyle, 1954; revised edition, as *Pope Joan: A Personal Biography*, London, Deutsch, 1960; New York, Dutton, 1961.

Bibliography: by Alan G. Thomas, in *Lawrence Durrell: A Study* by G. S. Fraser, London, Faber, 1968.

Critical Studies: *The World of Lawrence Durrell* edited by Harry T. Moore, Carbondale, Southern Illinois University Press, 1962; *Lawrence Durrell and the Alexandria Quartet* by Alan Warren Friedman, Norman, University of Oklahoma Press, 1970.

*         *         *

Lawrence Durrell, prolific since the mid-1930's, suddenly achieved commercial and critical success with *The Alexandria Quartet* in the late 1950's. Protean and eclectic, Durrell yet reveals an evolving consistency of concerns and techniques: a lush and baroque style; a rich patterning of ideas and ideas about ideas; a multidimensional universe and vision transcending temporal barriers; an aesthetic dependent on personal mythos (often eroticism), on felt reality rather than "objective" fact. The sense of deracination and concomitant need to belong are central to Durrell's writing; for like most placeless men, Durrell worships place: his landscapes embody, parallel, even motivate and control the workings of his characters. Thus, their individuality seems often suffused, subordinated, to some *deus loci* —as, on the largest scale, Alexandria dominates the *Quartet*, for in it "Only the city is real." Durrell's writing is pervaded by the evanescent glow of place that functions as central metaphor, as touchstone, for the individual maturing into meaningful human involvement. Further, Durrell's early fiction, poetry, verse plays, and island books all anticipate the *Quartet*'s theme of isolation and the individual's attaining full potential in both art and life only through total, active commitment to the creative process: art for love's sake. Thus, Justine associates work with love; Mountolive's failures in love are correlatives of his hating his work; Darley and Clea become lovers and artists at last. Each successful Durrellean protagonist creates in his own image an internal deity of selfhood, an analogue of the external *deus loci*.

In addition to the *Quartet*, Durrell's major fiction includes *The Black Book* and *Aut Tunc Aut Nunquam*. In both, demonically named protagonists reach beyond defining constrictions towards freedom and creativity. *Black Book*'s Lawrence Lucifer struggles to escape the spiritual sterility embodied by smug, dying England; he finally emerges into creative affirmation symbolized by Greece's warmth, color, and fertility. The book's style, like that of the contemporaneous *Zero* and *Asylum in the Snow*, anticipates the *Quartet*'s, for its rich interweaving of naturalistic and poetic narrations transforms language into something fluid, unstructured, a dual-functioning medium expressing a timeless present embodying all time. In *Aut Tunc Aut Nunquam*—a satire on science fiction, gothic, romantic, and business exposé novels—the master inventor, Felix Charlock, becomes ensnared in the international cartel, Merlin. He sells—and sells out—his work; love consequently becomes horrific, for, in Durrell, to deny the validity of one's work is to negate love. His ultimate task is to fashion an indistinguishable, "living" replica of the beautiful Greek Io: ex-prostitute, world-famous actress, and now dead. But the wholly successful product (able even to copulate) cannot bear the world's reality and climactically "commits suicide."

Virtually all of Durrell's protagonists ultimately flee inhospitable surroundings, and, as his poems suggest, seek meaning and selfhood in landscape and language. The verse plays, all successfully produced, dramatize attempts to make of life a work of art. In *Sappho*, the military leader Pittakos imposes an aesthetic vision through conquest—until, appalled by his "creation," Sappho leads the forces that destroy him. His antithetical twin brother Phaon is what the *Quartet*'s Pursewarden, Durrell's supreme creative embodiment, desires to become: an artist evolved beyond art, one whose life manifests the beauty and certitude lesser poets grope towards in their work. Phaon attains an ultimate quietism, a peace with self and surroundings, Durrell's necessary pre-condition for proper creative functioning. Sappho, like Justine, becomes desolated by success: her existence expresses desire frustrated by fulfillment. *Acté*'s Nero, a fat, hypochondracal homosexual, also proposes an aesthetic pattern for life. Opposed by Fabius, the loyal Roman torn by love, the beautiful Scythian Acté, is allowed to lead her people's rebellion against Roman misrule. Petronius, the play's aesthetician, writes the story to see if art and life can be one. But Acté, now embodying her land as Queen, rejects Fabius's offers of flight and suicide; and, in his defeating and decapitating her, life once again triumphs over art. Petronius, rejecting life even while claiming to affirm it, commits suicide at the end as an aesthetic act.

Durrell's Irish Faustus represents a reversal. Ironically and climactically, he drags a protesting Mephisto into hell's purgative fires to destroy a magic ring that, presumably, contains power to create pattern out of flux. Faustus emerges purged of fear and illusions, defined by quietism that leads him to a hermitage amid the "snowy panorama of mountains and clouds" where life and death are complementary. Nothing, it seems, actually happens —except that, as at the spiritually violent climaxes of almost all the fiction, Durrell's art is transformed and renewed by sudden visionary insight searing away blindness and self-delusion.

The trilogy of non-fiction island books most fully and successfully exploits Durrell's love of place, of landscape corresponding and responding to man's needs and proportions without dominating him. *Prospero's Cell*'s pre-war Corfu, *Marine Venus*'s post-war Rhodes, *Bitter Lemon*'s incipient civil war Cyprus are concomitants of failures in art and love. Yet the permanence and strength of Durrell's Greek pattern undergird and inspirit his island books, transforming them from travel reportage into the unaging realm of vision become art.

The *Quartet*'s multiplicity of mutually qualifying voices all speak with the force of privileged authenticity—especially on the ubiquitous subject of love. For love, without contradiction different for every participant and viewer, offers endless potential for variation. In the *Quartet*, all dichotomies are not harmonized—for that is impossible and undesirable— but brought into organic contact; though irreconcilable, they become mutually sustaining: interpenetrating, fusing and enriching one another. In Durrell, character becomes, in effect, anticharacter: not so much imposing itself upon its surroundings as imposed upon; qualities of traditional heroes (valor, marked individuality, an ego defining itself in action) are lacking or attributed to something beyond individuals—largely to Alexandria. The city, like its human inhabitants elevated to higher power and synthesized into a complex unity, has many sides and many voices. Inevitably, then, solutions compound more mystery than they solve; even death (witness Pursewarden, Scobie, Capodistria) is contingent and tentative. Conventional distinctions—between major and minor characters, main and subplots, protagonist and antagonist—are largely obliterated. Every character is theoretically the independent fountainhead of actions progressively multiplying both in consequence and in the number of people upon whose lives they significantly impinge. For Durrell, what man knows remains elusive, endlessly caught in an incessant stream of becoming, and truth lacks validity unless and until someone responds and interprets it through an aesthetically dynamic imagination. Thus, the *Quartet* is simultaneously promise and fulfillment, culmination and prophecy, a finished work of art and one prematurely made public with scaffolding still lying about, a vast multiple genre bearing the signs of an enduring and proliferating achievement.

Durrell's *Key to Modern British Poetry*, defining the difference between Victorianism and modernism, provides a "key" to Durrell himself. Durrell maintains that notions of human possibility, personality, values, validity, and time were irreversibly altered by Darwin, Einstein, and Freud in the modern world of their creating. Certainty's rock foundation reveals itself as restive sand blown by winds of pluralism, relativity, subjectivity, indeterminacy.

Like impressionist novels in general, the *Quartet* dramatizes a limited narrator who seeks understanding of a circumscribed sequence of events. Yet truth's hard core remains forever elusive, for everything is susceptible of, and receives, contradictory interpretations. In such novels, the more "facts" we learn, the less significant they seem; not despite but because *Mountolive tells* us most, offers the most objective, external reality, it says least about truth itself, the essence of reality captured, if anywhere, in the heart and mind of the interpreter. A 1946 poem, "Eight Aspects of Melissa," anticipates the *Quartet*'s devices—mirrors, prisms, images, lake water—and expresses Durrell's early concern with multifaceted personality, love, landscape, time. Both "Eight Aspects" and the *Quartet* remain open-ended, implying that all aspects examined are equally valuable and that indeterminate additional aspects await the diligent seeker after truth. Neither pretends to exhaust the many questions it raises, for each answer contains both multitudes of new questions and a proliferating chain of "truths."

Durrell's *Quartet* and *Key* reveal him as conscious heir to Ford-Conrad impressionism and Proust-Joyce stream of consciousness, and perhaps most significant of contemporary experimental novelists. Each of the *Quartet*'s books impressionistically renders an overlapping complex of events. In the *Key*, Durrell writes, "Under the terms of [Einstein's indeterminacy principle] a precise knowledge of the outer world becomes an impossibility. This is because we and the outer world (subject and object) constitute a whole. If we are part of a unity we can no longer objectivize it successfully." Thus, Durrell's characters partake of a vast mythical presence; they appear as poetic aspects of a larger whole—simultaneously independent and interdependent: no wonder they view a fragmented reality with visions encompassing realms of meaning broader than narrowly circumscribed facts. For the truth of facts, Alexandria substitutes the Truth of myth and poetry, of art and love.

The open-endedness of the *Quartet* suggests not that all has been arranged but that, past and present having accommodated themselves to each other, the future can begin to begin. Pathways now exist where there had seemed only dead ends. With "Once upon a time . . ." all avenues are open; no visionary world of man's imagination remains artificially precluded. At least for the moment—and therefore for all time, since each moment contains all time—impeding checks are removed; art and life are dynamically possible.

Durrell does not claim mastery of Einsteinian relativity or Freudian psychology, but he recognizes their radical influence upon literature; ranging widely, he has made uniquely his own and his art's all he has read and experienced. Despite his considerable achievement in poetry, drama, and island books, Durrell's most enduring place will likely be in the experimental novel's tradition. For, like this century's supreme novelists—Conrad, Proust, Joyce, Faulkner, Mann—Durrell seeks both to create art of lasting significance and to proclaim new modes of thought, new ways of envisaging a world he too has helped bring into being.

—Alan Warren Friedman

---

**DUTTON, Geoffrey (Piers Henry).** Australian. Born in Anlaby, South Australia, 2 August 1922. Educated at Geelong Grammar School, Victoria, 1932–39; University of Adelaide, 1940–41; Magdalen College, Oxford, 1946–49, B.A. 1949. Served as a Flight Lieutenant in the Royal Australian Air Force, 1941–45. Married Ninette Trott in 1944; has three children. Senior Lecturer in English, University of Adelaide, 1954–62; Visiting Lecturer in Australian Literature, University of Leeds, 1960; Visiting Professor, Kansas State University, Manhattan, 1962. Editor, Penguin Australia, Melbourne, 1961–65. Since 1965, Editorial Director of Sun Books Pty. Ltd., Melbourne. Co-Founder, *Australian Letters*, Adelaide, 1957, and *Australian Book Review*, Kensington Park, 1962. Member of the Australian Council for the Arts, 1968–70. Address: Old Anlaby, Kapunda, South Australia 5373, Australia.

PUBLICATIONS

Novels

    *The Mortal and the Marble*. London, Chapman and Hall, 1950.
    *Andy*. Sydney and London, Collins, 1968.
    *Tamara*. Sydney and London, Collins, 1970.

Verse

    *Nightflight and Sunrise*. Melbourne, Reed and Harris, 1945.
    *Antipodes in Shoes*. Sydney, Edwards and Shaw, 1955.
    *Flowers and Fury*. Melbourne, Cheshire, 1963.
    *On My Island: Poems for Children*. Melbourne, Cheshire, 1967.
    *Poems Soft and Loud*. Melbourne, Cheshire, 1968.
    *Findings and Keepings*. Adelaide, Australian Letters, 1970.

Other

    *A Long Way South* (travel). London, Chapman and Hall, 1953.
    *Africa in Black and White*. London, Chapman and Hall, 1956.
    *States of the Union* (travel). London, Chapman and Hall, 1958.
    *Founder of a City: The Life of William Light*. Melbourne, Cheshire, and London, Chapman and Hall, 1960.
    *Patrick White*. Melbourne, Lansdowne Press, 1961; London, Oxford University Press, 1971.
    *Walt Whitman*. Edinburgh, Oliver and Boyd, 1961.

*Paintings of S. T. Gill.*   Adelaide, Rigby, 1962.
*Russell Drysdale* (art criticism).   London, Thames and Hudson, 1962.
*Tisi and the Yabby* (juvenile).   Sydney and London, Collins, 1965.
*Seal Bay* (juvenile).   Sydney and London, Collins, 1966.
*The Hero as Murderer: The Life of Edward John Eyre, Australian Explorer and Governor
   of Jamaica, 1815–1901.*   Melbourne, Cheshire, and London, Collins, 1967.
*Tisi and the Pageant* (juvenile).   Adelaide, Rigby, 1968.

Editor, *The Literature of Australia.*   Melbourne, Penguin, 1964; Baltimore, Penguin,
   1965.
Editor, *Modern Australian Writing.*   London, Fontana, 1966.
Editor, with Max Harris, *The Vital Decade: 10 Years of Australian Art and Letters.*
   Melbourne, Sun Books, 1968.


Geoffrey Dutton comments:

My three novels, although completely different in characters and in settings, have all
basically dealt with the same theme, that of Australian innocence as against the experience
of "older" countries. In more detail, *The Mortal and the Marble* deals with the impact of
European migrants on Australia after the second world war; *Andy* with the idiocy of war,
especially in a country on whose soil it is never fought; *Tamara* with the impact on an
intelligent but relatively unsophisticated Australian scientist of the complex world of Soviet
Russian poetry.

\*     \*     \*

In a country where the all-round man of letters is even rarer than elsewhere, Geoffrey
Dutton is widely admired for his accomplishments as poet and critic, publisher and biographer, journalist and editor. His three novels are not the basis of this reputation but
part of his work in many literary fields, and although they are entertaining in themselves
they are most interesting in revealing personal and social concerns of their author.

The characteristics of a Dutton novel are a central figure who presents the personal experiences and concerns of the author, secondary characters who point up dramatically
the conflicts within the central character, and a combination of lyrical, frequently allusive
and "literary" writing with bold narrative description. Although they vary widely in their
settings and development, the novels have these structural similarities and are all concerned with the conflicts between Australian and foreign values, between individual freedom
and social restriction, and between the natural and the civilized worlds.

His first novel, *The Mortal and the Marble*, reveals its period by exhibiting what the
Australian critic A. A. Phillips has called the "cultural cringe". With an eye on the overseas
market, it explains local folkways in the obtrusive way that has characterized "colonial
novels" for over a century, and even such hallowed clichés as the incongruity of eating
Christmas pudding in the middle of summer find their place. The theme of the novel is
Mark Vaughan's ambivalence towards two conflicting sets of values—the traditional culture
of the Europe he has never seen and the material comfort and natural beauty of his own
"uncultured" country. And, the reader feels, *The Mortal and the Marble* is itself the author's
attempt to resolve a similar conflict between his own "literary" notions of the novel and
the incongruous, because "unliterary", actuality of his experiences in Australia.

Dutton attempts not only to work out dramatically the concern of the Australian novelist
who feels his "complex fate" but also a more fundamental theme. As well as the encounters
between the Vaughans and such representatives of European culture (and of the post
World War II immigration to Australia) as their Russian friend Alexey and the Germans

Paul, Willi and Professor Klein, there is contrast between personal and social life. The aridity of ordinary suburbia and the frigidity of Melbourne "Society" are both contrasted with the Vaughans' escapes to the bush. When the characters go to an island for a holiday the conflicts between Australian and European values and between the "natural" and the civilized life are explored in almost fable form, and action, rather than dialogue, becomes the vehicle of the theme.

The author is more successful with his description of the young married lovers in the bush than he is with them in "Society", where his concerns become too overtly stated through the dialogue. Dutton has talents for describing action and natural setting (as his *The Hero as Murderer* reveals), and the passages of natural description draw with ease and enthusiasm on the English Romantic poetic tradition, while the most memorable sections of this first novel are accounts of body surfing and an interpolated story of stunt flying.

The resolution of Mark Vaughan's conflict is curious. His European friends, as in much New World writing, prove to be corrupt and degenerate beneath their charm and erudition. Dinkum Aussie values are finally vindicated but Mark also secures his ticket to the Europe he has idealized. The ending does not resolve his conflicts so much as allow him to have the best of both worlds. It is a novelettish ending to a book in which what is happening at the level of the author's own involvement with his characters (especially the impossibly stereotyped Professor Klein, embodiment of European degeneracy) proves more interesting than their involvement with each other.

In Dutton's second novel, *Andy*, nostalgia for the old Australia before the American alliance eroded the national virtues of independence and self-reliance lurks beneath the comic picaresque story of a young R.A.A.F. pilot's conflicts with authority. *Andy* is deliberately freer in form and more comic than the first novel, but again one senses personal experiences and responses to social change are being worked out through fantasies that are indistinguishable from those of the novelette. Andy however is not unequivocally an autobiographical projection. The author's merging with his hero is balanced by his merging with other characters as well—with the virginal and intellectual Ian Almond and with the idealized Tasmanian squire John Lydford.

More thematically than structurally organized, *Andy* is a free-wheeling comedy of the moral education of a pilot during World War II; but it is impossible to say what his moral education consists of because of a complete surrender to fantasy at the end. Like the first novel, *Andy* contains too much to be controlled and directed. It seems, appropriately for its hero, a cavalier enterprise, a deliberately off-handed indulgence in irresponsible *joie-de-vivre* accompanied by a nostalgia for youth and the past with which it is associated.

Dutton's third novel, *Tamara*, is his most satisfactory to date. Like the works of others, e.g. Malamud and Updike, who have visited the U.S.S.R. and attempted to come to grips with their own confused impressions through fiction, it presents the contradictions perceived in contemporary Russian society—warm humanity and cold bureaucracy, technological advance and bad plumbing, a national passion for literature and rigorous political censorship. Such contradictions offer possibilities for both social comedy and serious social concern and Dutton blends the two more successfully in this novel than in its predecessors. He is a fine travel writer and his descriptive powers are seen at their best in the scenes which present Russian, especially Georgian, life.

The story is one of a simple soil scientist from Kangaroo Island who is invited to Russia as Australian delegate to a literary conference and who falls in love with Russia's leading poetess. Through this romantic and not very probable story is expressed a serious concern with the position of the writer in the Soviet Union as a critical point for evaluating the whole direction of post-Stalinist Russia. The presentation of Russian society is vivid and sympathetic and, although it is a romantic comedy, *Tamara* avoids the wish-fulfilment endings of the earlier novels. It is more mature in every sense, revealing a developing confidence, more skilful craftsmanship and, most importantly, greater detachment and wider concern for social issues.

—Brian Kiernan

**EASTLAKE, William (Derry).** American. Born in New York City, 14 July 1917. Attended the Alliance Française, Paris, 1948–50. Served in the United States Army in World War II. Married Martha Simpson in 1943. Writer-in-Residence, Knox College, Galesburg, Illinois, 1967–68; Lecturer, University of New Mexico, Albuquerque, 1968–69; Writer-in-Residence, University of Southern California, Los Angeles, 1969, and University of Arizona, Tucson, 1969–71. Recipient: Ford grant, 1964; Rockefeller grant, 1966. D.Litt., University of Albuquerque, 1970. Address: Las Campanas, Route 2, Box 761A, Tucson, Arizona 85715, U.S.A.

PUBLICATIONS

Novels

> Go in Beauty.  New York, Harper, 1956; London, Secker and Warburg, 1957.
> The Bronc People.  New York, Harcourt Brace, and London, Deutsch, 1958.
> Portrait of an Artist with Twenty-Six Horses.  New York, Simon and Schuster, 1963; London, Joseph, 1965.
> Castle Keep.  New York, Simon and Schuster, 1964; London, Joseph, 1965.
> The Bamboo Bed.  New York, Simon and Schuster, and London, Joseph, 1970.

Uncollected Short Stories

> "Ishimoto's Land", in Essai (Geneva, Switzerland), Summer 1952.
> "Little Joe", in Accent (Urbana, Illinois), Autumn 1954.
> "Two Gentlemen from America", in Hudson Review (New York), Fall 1954.
> "Homecoming", in Quarto (New York), Fall 1954.
> "The Barfly and the Navajo", in Nation (New York), 12 September 1959.
> "There's a Camel in My Cocktail", in Harper's (New York), April 1966.
> "Jack Armstrong in Tangiers", in Evergreen Review (New York), August 1966.
> "The Last Frenchman in Fez", in Evergreen Review (New York), December 1967.
> "Now Lucifer Is Not Dead", in Evergreen Review (New York), November 1968.
> "The Message", in New Mexico Quarterly (Albuquerque), Winter 1968.
> "The Hanging at Prettyfields", in Evergreen Review (New York), February 1969.
> "A Dead Man's Guide to Mallorca", in New Mexico Quarterly (Albuquerque), Winter-Spring 1969.
> "The Dancing Boy", in Evergreen Review (New York), December 1970.

Verse

> A Child's Garden of Verses for the Revolution (verse and essays).  New York, Grove Press, 1971.

Critical Studies: "The Novels of William Eastlake" by Delbert W. Wylder, in New Mexico Quarterly (Albuquerque), 1965; "Of Cowboys, Indians and the Modern West" by Peter M. Kenyon, in Sage Magazine (Las Vegas, Nevada), Winter 1969; William Eastlake by Gerald Haslam, Austin, Texas, Steck Vaughn, 1970.

William Eastlake comments:

As long as we are serving a life sentence on this earth there has got to be something to make the time go easy. The thing to work at is to be the best writer on the earth, or the best magician, for writing is magic, and like all the things that are important you do it all alone. As I expressed it in *The Bronc People:*

> "You can't give anyone anything."
> "You mean I've got to do it alone?"
> "Yes."
> "But the missionary says no man is an island."
> "Well, he is."
> "You think the missionary got that saying from another preacher?"
> "Yes."
> "We've got to go it all alone?"
> "Yes, we do."

My last book, *A Child's Garden of Verses for the Revolution,* is a comment on the end of America and the west, the only part of the earth I really know. But the artist is sentenced and elected as medicine man because he holds out hope. That is his job. That is what he was hired for. My hope is in the youth of the world. The people of the earth turn more and more to the writer, the medicine man, as their tribal leaders fail them. And as our present tribal leaders are unworthy even of the dignity of death, the medicine man, through his novels, fulfills man through artistic re-enactment.

> One upon a time there was time. The land here in the Southwest had evolved slowly and there was time and there were great spaces. Now a man on horseback from atop a bold mesa looked out over the violent spectrum of the Indian Country —into a gaudy infinity where all the colors exploded soundlessly. "There is not much time," he said.

The death of all of us worthy of death is enacted by the Indian medicine man. Death he calls "Something big is happening to me." Any place the writer, the medicine man, the shaman, lives is the center of the earth.

> Below at the post, the exact center and the capital of the world for The People, two Indians crouched at the massive stone root of the petrified-wood house where it made its way into the ground.
> "This crack," the Indian said, tracing it with his brown finger.
> "They can fix it," Rabbit Stockings said.
> "No. And perhaps even The People cannot stop something coming apart and beginning here at the center of the world."

The artist's job is to hold the world together. What the politicians cannot do with reality the artist does with magic, even if the artist is an epileptic Dostoievsky, a failed Melville working in a customs house, a wandering Walt Whitman peddling his *Leaves of Grass* from door to door. The artist finds life everlasting in his magic. William Shakespeare is still very much alive. God is pronounced dead.

*       *       *

At first glance William Eastlake appears to be America's most paradoxical literary artist. Although he was born in New York and grew up in New Jersey and although he traveled widely in Europe after World War II and for some years lived and worked in Los Angeles, he purchased land in an isolated, remote area of New Mexico and there for some years lived the life of the small-spread rancher and literary man. Eastlake thereby became a strongly committed regionalist and one of the most astute observers of present-day American Indian life. Although isolated, Eastlake's concerns were always with national policy, our establishment in Washington and in Vietnam, or the significance of American poverty at home as against American explorations of outer space. On the one hand he appears to seek a kind of peace in a remote area, yet he remains angry at fellow provincials of limited vision, the rednecks and unenlightened army colonels. If Eastlake protests the fate of Mexican, Indian, and Black persons in America, he cannot defend, in the name of a beloved democracy, the violence and the turmoil in our urban centers and on the country roads of out-yonder America. His life-style suggests the pursuit of calm, by association with Nature; yet the work presents a sharp focus on the evils of modernity in an idiom which combines the sardonic and the realistic along with an acceptance of the implied values of both ritual and myth. If these paradoxes are real, then their resolution in Eastlake's work suggests an artist of uncommon personal stability and unusual dedication to his own view of the world. If there is tension implicit in these paradoxical roles, the result is artistic production of a high order.

From the centers of these contradictive conflicts emerge his most significant works. Ostensibly the materials are Indians and tourists; cattlemen and brute geography; the neon market towns and the sagebrush. Beneath this closely observed, naturalistic surface, however, the concern is the modes of right conduct, the moral propositions implicit in actions, the attitudes toward life of the protagonists. Irony, humor, and fantasy are everywhere, and thus the true position of the authorial voice behind the prose fictions is not always easy to discern. In moral considerations a continued reliance on irony is no position at all.

Nevertheless, the pervading irony—and compassion—suggest Eastlake's American literary tradition and major influence. His overt search for materials (the move to New Mexico), his stints as war correspondent in Vietnam, his running commentary on cultural and political policy suggests the tradition of the 19th Century correspondent/writer: Stephen Crane, Jack London, and more recently of Hemingway. Likewise, the concern for a "moral center", for Justice, for the destiny of America and its people suggests Walt Whitman, poet, editor, "correspondent" of an earlier age. Of the direct literary influences, however, Hemingway is the most significant: the terse understatement, the stripped down dialogue, the concept of character, the close focus on the details of war, the sometimes anti-intellectual, anti-bookish, anti-cultural stances strongly suggest the Hemingway of the early novels and the war-correspondent years. Many commonplaces from the criticism of Hemingway, for example, the kind of commentary which identifies the strong romantic element in his work, could be applied as well to Eastlake. If the two men in a great many ways are comparable literary talents, Eastlake's exemplary management of his own talent may prove ultimately the more productive. Eastlake is a model of affirmative experience in the matter of attaining a balance between artistic necessity and humanitarian concern.

Of the novels *The Bronc People* and the short fictions in the same vein attract the most critical attention. Although *Castle Keep* became a successful film and was widely translated, the novel increasingly becomes an example of a book less effective as a whole than the sum of its sometimes brilliant episodes. The Vietnam materials, the journalistic snap shots and quasi-interviews, are repetitive and are less effective together than when they appeared singly in the *Nation*. The poetry of *A Child's Garden of Verses for the Revolution* purports to be "revolutionary" but on balance fails either to move the reader or to offer an effective program beyond the necessity of mutual respect, a change of heart, or other humanistic concerns. While the work varies in quality, the commitment is always firm, and a strong sensibility is apparent everywhere.

If Eastlake's artistic concerns appear now somewhat resolved, this condition is probably a prelude to the continuing search for new materials.

—James B. Hall

**EDELMAN, Maurice.** British. Born in Cardiff, 2 March 1911. Educated at Cardiff High School; Trinity College, Cambridge (Exhibitioner in Modern Languages), B.A. 1932, M.A. 1941. Married Matilda Yager in 1933; has two children. Plastics Researcher in the aircraft industry, 1932–41. War Correspondent in North Africa and France during World War II. Labour Member of Parliament for Coventry West, 1945–50, and since 1950 for Coventry North: Delegate to the Consultative Assembly of the Council of Europe, 1949–51, 1965–70, and Chairman of the Socialist Group of the Western European Union, 1968–70; Leader, Parliamentary Delegation to Hungary, 1965; Colonial Secretary's Special Representative to the Cayman Islands and Turks and Caicos Islands, 1965. Vice-Chairman, British Council, 1951–67. Member, Air League Council, 1966–67. Chevalier, 1954, and Officer, 1960, Legion of Honour. Address: c/o House of Commons, Westminster, London S.W.1, England.

PUBLICATIONS

Novels

A Trial of Love. London, Wingate, 1951.
Who Goes Home. London, Wingate, and Philadelphia, Lippincott, 1953.
A Dream of Treason. London, Wingate, 1954; Philadelphia, Lippincott, 1955.
The Happy Ones. London, Wingate, 1957.
A Call on Kuprin. London, Longman, and Philadelphia, Lippincott, 1959.
The Minister. London, Hamish Hamilton, 1961; as The Minister of State, Philadelphia, Lippincott, 1961.
The Fratricides. London, Hamish Hamilton, and New York, Random House, 1963.
The Prime Minister's Daughter. London, Hamish Hamilton, 1964; New York, Random House, 1965.
Shark Island. London, Hamish Hamilton, and New York, Random House, 1967.
All on a Summer's Night. London, Hamish Hamilton, 1969; New York, Random House, 1970.

Other

G. P. U. Justice. London, Allen and Unwin, 1938.
Production for Victory Not Profit. London, Gollancz, 1941.
How Russia Prepared: The U.S.S.R. Beyond the Urals. London, Penguin, 1942.
France: The Birth of the Fourth Republic. London, Penguin, 1945.
Herbert Morrison. London, Lincolns-Prager, 1948.
Ben-Gurion: A Political Biography. London, Hodder and Stoughton, 1964; as David: The Story of Ben-Gurion, New York, Putnam, 1965.
The Mirror: A Political History. London, Hamish Hamilton, 1966.

Plays produced on television.

\* \* \*

Maurice Edelman has the rare gift of seeing the patterns of history in recent events. This means that his books have the flavour of historical novels, enhanced by the fact that many of them are set in the House of Commons itself. His fictional Members of Parliament represent political types rather than portraits of known statesmen; and it is interesting that, on the whole, it is his Tory back benchers who come over as the most likeable human beings. But although his characters may be translated amalgams of the people he has met in his political life, the actual public events that make up the drama of their lives are taken more or less straight from contemporary affairs.

The public issues that interest him are the final break up of colonialism and the emergence of new independent states (Africa is the issue of *The Minister*; Algeria of *The Fratricides*, and the West Indies of *Shark Island*); the power of the press (the political use of a scandal in *The Prime Minister's Daughter*); and the amalgamation of big businesses (*All on a Summer's Night*). In dealing with all these issues he is sensitive to the almost accidental circumstances which push individuals into aligning themselves with a particular side. His women characters are as significant and powerful as world events in shaping the destinies of his protagonists. He is not interested in women politicians, who make their appearances in his novels only as quickly drawn caricatures (the only characters in his books to do so). What concerns him is the sexual power of women who are always beautiful and intelligent, mostly rich and sometimes neurotic. And he is interested in the compelling and self-destructive sexual needs of these women, just as much as the side effects they have on the careers of the men who desire them. All this happens irrespective of age. Isobel, the forty-two-year-old wife of the rich Jewish industrialist in *All on a Summer's Night*, compulsively flings herself into the arms of the twenty-year-old friend of her son while her husband negotiates the biggest take-over bid of his career. Sylvia Melville (the Prime Minister's daughter) attempts to take her own life and almost ends her beloved father's career on account of an obsessive love for a married, middle-aged American academic.

It is the skilful juxtaposition of the complexities of public issues against the insistent demands of personal needs that make Maurice Edelman's novels both readable and memorable. At the same time he has no illusions about creating great literature; novel writing is a relaxation from the serious business of life and politics. It is as though the reader was privileged to overlook some fascinating and highly original doodles made during a committee meeting, the outcome of which will be decisive for both national and international affairs. Given such an opportunity it is gratuitous to complain of the occasional lapse into melodrama and inconsistency.

—Shirley Toulson

---

**EKWENSI, Cyprian.** Nigerian. Born in Minna, 26 September 1921. Educated at Government College, Ibadan; Achimota College, Ghana; School of Forestry, Ibadan; Higher College, Yaba; Chelsea School of Pharmacy, London University. Married to Eunice Anyiwo; has five children. Lecturer in Biology, Chemistry and English, Igbodi College, Lagos, 1947–49; Lecturer in Pharmacognosy and Pharmaceutics, School of Pharmacy, Lagos, 1949–56; Pharmacist, Nigerian Medical Service, and Head of Features, Nigerian Broadcasting Corporation, 1956–61. Director of Information, Federal Ministry of Information, Lagos, 1961–66, and since 1966 Director of Information Services, Enugu. Chairman, East Central State Library Board, Enugu, 1971. Member, Nigerian Arts Council. Recipient: Dag Hammarskjold International Award, 1968. Address: 50 Ogbete Street, P.O. Box 137, Enugu, Nigeria.

PUBLICATIONS

Novels

*People of the City*. London, Dakers, 1954.
*Jagua Nana*. London, Hutchinson, 1961.
*Burning Grass: A Story of the Fulani of Northern Nigeria*. London, Heinemann, 1962.
*Beautiful Feathers*. London, Hutchinson, 1963.
*Iska*. London, Hutchinson, 1966.

Short Stories

*The Rainmaker and Other Stories*. Lagos, African Universities Press, 1965.
*Lokotown and Other Stories*. London, Heinemann, 1966.

Other

*When Love Whispers* (juvenile). Onitsha, Nigeria, Tabansi Bookshop, 1947.
*Ikolo the Wrestler* (juvenile). London, Nelson, 1947.
*The Leopard's Claw* (juvenile). London, Longman, 1950.
*The Drummer Boy* (juvenile). London, Cambridge University Press, 1960.
*The Passport of Mallam Ilia* (juvenile). London, Cambridge University Press, 1960.
*An African Nights Entertainment: A Tale of Vengeance* (juvenile). Lagos, African Universities Press, and London, Deutsch, 1962.
*Yaba Roundabout Murder* (juvenile). Lagos, Tortoise Series Books, 1962.
*Great Elephant Bird* (juvenile). London, Nelson, 1965.
*Trouble in Form Six* (juvenile). London, Cambridge University Press, 1966.
*The Boa Suitor* (juvenile). London, Nelson, 1966.
*Juju Rock* (juvenile). Lagos, African Universities Press, 1966.

\*     \*     \*

Granted much mawkish sentiment, an eye for the sensational, a technical naïvety that allows abrupt transitions and unlikely coincidences, and a frequently banal use of English, yet Ekwensi cannot be lightly dismissed as a Nigerian writer. His career began in the Onitsha market in Eastern Nigeria, where cheap, sentimental, moralistic stories in English catered for a readership with an English-type primary education obtained in mission schools—and this Onitsha ethos can be detected in all his writings. Yet there are other characteristics also —chiefly a vivid sense of actuality, especially when he places his characters on the streets and in the night clubs and slums of Lagos. Except for *Burning Grass* and stories written for children, Ekwensi's writings convey the heady experience of young Africans from the country being attracted, excited, bemused, usually destroyed by the glitter of city lights. Passing fashions of dress and undress are catalogued, highlife rhythms pulsate in the background, hips wiggle, and bosoms quiver alluringly, but with real understanding Ekwensi evokes the frustration, inner unhappiness, restlessness, and rootlessness of a new urbanized African generation. There is also a muted satirical tone. He attacks political jobbery and public scandal. He invents a Nigerian Ministry of Consolation to epitomize all that is corrupt and inefficient.

All these qualities together suggest that Ekwensi's talent is that of a good journalist rather than a novelist, that he is the chronicler of modern West African urbanization. He clearly disapproves of much that he reports but, like a journalist, is so involved in the reporting that he also becomes excited by the things he would condemn. The banal dialogue of characters in moments of emotional intensity is the banality of the everyday speech of ordinary people—a dedication to the actual precludes any attempt at a literary artefact that would suggest the "real" and yet transcend it. His historical position is clear enough: with *People of the City* he became the first Anglophone African writer who tried to present in fictional terms the human problems that confronted individuals in a time of rapid social and political change in Africa, as the long-established *mores* of village culture came into conflict with westernized city life. *People of the City* held up a series of mirror reflections of themselves to this generation.

Though *Jagua Nana* is still episodic in construction, it gains from being a character-study in depth of a Lagos prostitute desperately trying to find stability before she has worked herself out. The book also probes the thuggery of Nigerian politics in the old Federation. *Beautiful Feathers* is the most successfully satirical of Ekwensi's books, with its wry treatment of politicians and civil servants. Its symbolic big-game hunt, when white observers get away with the quarry while the African delegates to a Conference on African Solidarity squabble among themselves, points to one of Ekwensi's genuine strengths—his sensitiveness to the larger, though sometimes obscured, political issues of the day. Despite its lingering Onitsha qualities, his most recent novel *Iska* warns with prophetic insistence of the dangers of tribal factionalism in Nigeria—on the eve of the Biafran war.

—Arthur Ravenscroft

---

**ELKIN, Stanley (Lawrence).**    American.    Born in New York City, 11 May 1930. Educated at the University of Illinois, Urbana, 1948–60, B.A. 1952, M.A. 1953, Ph.D. 1961. Served in the United States Army, 1957–59. Married Joan Jacobson in 1953; has three children. Since 1960, Member of the English faculty, and since 1968, Professor of English, Washington University, St. Louis. Visiting Lecturer, Smith College, Northampton, Massachusetts, 1964–65; Visiting Professor, University of California at Santa Barbara, Summer 1967, and University of Wisconsin, Milwaukee, Summer 1969. Recipient: Longview Foundation Award, 1962; *Paris Review* prize, 1965; Guggenheim Fellowship, 1966; Rockefeller Fellowship, 1968. Address: Department of English, Washington University, St. Louis, Missouri 63130, U.S.A.

PUBLICATIONS

Novels

> *Boswell.*   New York, Random House, and London, Hamish Hamilton, 1964.
> *A Bad Man.*   New York, Random House, 1967; London, Blond, 1968.
> *The Dick Gibson Show.*   New York, Random House, and London, Weidenfeld and Nicolson, 1971.

Short Stories

> *Criers and Kibitzers, Kibitzers and Criers.*   New York, Random House, 1966; London, Blond, 1968.

*The Making of Ashenden*.   London, Covent Garden Press, 1972.


Uncollected Short Stories

"A Sound of Distant Thunder", in *Epoch* (Ithaca, New York), 1957.
"The Party", in *Views* (Louisville, Kentucky), 1958.
"Fifty Dollars", in *Southwest Review* (Dallas), 1959.


Play

*The Six-Year-Old Man* (filmscript), in *Esquire* (New York), 1969.


Other

Editor, *Stories from the Sixties*.   New York, Doubleday, 1971.


Manuscript Collection: Washington University Library, St. Louis.


Critical Studies: in *Humanism and the Absurd* by Naomi Lebowitz, Evanston, Illinois,
Northwestern University Press, 1971; *City of Words* by Tony Tanner, London, Cape, 1971.


\*        \*        \*


Technically the brilliant qualities of Elkin's fiction are imagery and anecdote or vignette.
Sensuous or pictorial, repellent or ingratiating, the imagery stays in the mind, even randomly recalled—"he watched the mother, squatting on her heels over the (dead) girl,
obscene as someone defecating in the woods". . . ."the peculiar dignity of men seen eating
alone in restaurants on national holidays". . . ."the medallion, like a metal moon, would
catch the light of the electric bulb, and sifting it in its complex corrugated surfaces, throw
off thick rings of bright yellow which seemed to sear themselves into his outstretched,
upraised hands". . . ."liquid douches—you can hear the sea. Rubber goods, the queer
mysterious elastics, supporters, rupture's ribbons and organ's bows". . . ."aphrodisiacs . . .
to float your heart." Elkin's style is often "dense" with imagery—an almost over-richness
that itself becomes part of what the novels are saying.
   The novels build around episodes that are often dramatic entities in themselves, almost
capable of making complete sense in detachment from their contexts. The novels thus
reveal a relish for a shorter dramatic unit that is perhaps not surprising in a writer who
began with and has recurrently returned to the short story form. But more precisely, the
episodic nature of the novels points to a quality of Elkin's imagination that is recognizably
the raconteur's, the joke-teller's delight in entertaining an audience with startling tales,
complete at times to the gagster's punch line. Tall-tale vignettes—Boswell, magically singled
out from his classmates by the world famous psychiatrist Herlitz (M.Pd., Bagdad University), later as pro wrestler meeting the Grim Reaper in the main event; Feldman, of *A Bad
Man*, son of a Jewish salesman, selling his father's body to the highest bidder; and from
*The Dick Gibson Show*, Bernie Perk the pharmacist's campaign to win the love of a Super-
Kotex user, Imperial Japan's wartime pursuit of the dodo bird, plus characters the likes
of the ten-year-old millionaire Henry Harper, Norman the world's last caveman, and the
Credenza family, founders and rulers of Northeast Nebraska. Elkin's anecdotal urge is

perhaps given its freest rein by the structure of *The Dick Gibson Show*, where the radio formats of panel and telephone shows invite a zany set of characters and stories.

It is misleading, however, to imply—with the dust jackets—that Elkin's intentions are primarily comic or satiric. Social satire—directed, when it comes, at the excesses and absurdities of American life—is incidental. The comic effect is central and continuous, but it is typically founded on qualities that, in the last analysis, are not funny at all—the grotesque, the ugly, the deflationary. In fact a fundamental theme of Elkin's fiction is physical waste, mortality. In the fiction's physically premised world, no man can be counted happy in terms beyond what he can momentarily possess or master; since all men are halt and blind, "success" is a temporary assertion or evasion. In this light, comedy is palliative or defensive, a willingness, even a need, to laugh at failure's inevitability. The moralistic bias necessary to satire is anathema to Elkin's more elemental vision (although there is often an intention to shake the illusions of the reader).

All of the novels tend to be dominated, as the titles suggest, by a single character who overshadows all subsidiary roles. Even in *The Dick Gibson Show*, where secondary characters are the centers of the inset stories they narrate, the point holds: relationships between characters who are simultaneously developed and who come to mutual understanding are minimized. The effect is to press Elkin's theme further: man is alone, ego his only certainty. This vision is bodied out as well in the novels' single most brilliant and recurrent rhetorical mode of address—the sales pitch: Lome's selling chunks of clay on the streets of Dallas in *Boswell*, Feldman's and his father's auctioneering in mid-America, Dick Gibson's demo records. The sales pitch is at one level part of the American vulgarity that the novels incorporate as typical idiom; at another it may suggest a Jewish ethos that constitutes a rather unexplicit background to most of Elkin's fiction. But the important point is what the sales pitch suggests about the human ego—its arm's length relation to its fellows, its perpetual effort to enrich itself, but always at a cost, since in selling one both gains and gives and no man can come into full possession. Acquisition and emptiness are the ego's polar possibilities. The novels' imagery, which, in its very profusion, reflects the ego's accumulating expansiveness, pictures the extremes—e.g., Dick Gibson at the knobs of his radio set:

> Then, after the midnight news but before the amen of the sermonette, the station faded irrevocably. He'd learned never to fool with the dial, that it did no good when a signal waned to reclaim it with some careful, surgical twist of a half-dozen kilocycles to the right or left. It was best to wait through the babble and static for the return of the electronic tide. Often it would come, renewed for its hiatus, its cosmic romp and drift, strongly present again.

Despite differences in detail and nuance, Elkin's novels are thus variations on a single theme: given mortality, the ego's need—conventional piosities to the contrary—is the only human motive that demands no justification. Surveying his department store (in which he is "master of all he purveys"), Feldman, a "bad man," sums up: "Nothing, *nothing* could ever excuse a disturbed profit. A lost sale was lost forever, faded irrevocably, something gone out of his life."

—David P. Demarest, Jr.

---

**ELLIOTT, George P(aul).** American. Born in Knightstown, Indiana, 16 June 1918. Educated at the University of California, Berkeley, A.B. 1939, M.A. 1941. Married Mary Emma Jeffress in 1941; has one child. Assistant Professor, St. Mary's College, California,

1947–55, 1962–63, Cornell University, Ithaca, New York, 1955–56, and Barnard College, New York, 1957–60; Lecturer, University of Iowa, Iowa City, 1960–61, and University of California, Berkeley, 1962. Since 1963, Professor of English, Syracuse University, New York. Since 1965, Member of the Corporation of Yaddo. Recipient: Albert Bender grant, 1951; Fund for the Advancement of Education Fellowship, 1953; *Hudson Review* Fellowship, 1956; Guggenheim Fellowship, 1961, 1970; D. H. Lawrence Fellowship, 1962; Ford Fellowship, for theatre, 1965; National Institute of Arts and Letters grant, 1969. Address: Department of English, Syracuse University, Syracuse, New York 13210, U.S.A.

PUBLICATIONS

Novels

   *Parktilden Village.*  Boston, Beacon Press, 1958.
   *David Knudsen.*  New York, Random House, 1962.
   *In the World.*  New York, Viking Press, 1965.
   *Muriel.*  New York, Dutton, 1972.

Short Stories

   *Among the Dangs.*  New York, Holt Rinehart, 1961; London, Secker and Warburg, 1962.
   *An Hour of Last Things and Other Stories.*  New York, Harper, 1968; London, Gollancz, 1969.

Verse

   *Fever and Chills.*  Iowa City, Stone Wall Press, 1961.
   *Fourteen Poems.*  Lanham, Maryland, Goosetree Press, 1964.
   *From the Berkeley Hills.*  New York, Harper, 1969.

Other

   *A Piece of Lettuce: Personal Essays on Books, Beliefs, American Places and Growing Up in a Strange Country.*  New York, Random House, 1964.
   *Conversions: Literature and the Modernist Deviation* (essays).  New York, Dutton, 1971.

   Editor, *Fifteen Modern American Poets.*  New York, Rinehart, 1956; London, Peter Smith, 1963.
   Editor, *Types of Prose Fiction.*  New York, Random House, 1964.

Manuscript Collection: Washington University Library, St. Louis.

Critical Study: "Beyond Nihilism: The Fiction of George P. Elliott" by Blanche H. Gelfant, in *Hollins Critic* (Hollins College, Virginia), vol. 5, no. 5, 1969.

George P. Elliott comments:

His narrative style is intended to keep you at a certain esthetic distance whether the story is ironic or straight, realistic or fantastic, short or novel-length, in verse or in prose. Partly this is to make sure that, if you read the story at all, you must have done some of the work yourself: he freely employs such methods as juxtaposition and reasonable-seeming, mad logic, and he omits a good deal, especially of emotional rhetoric in passages of intensity for the characters. If you do not imagine the story, you will probably quit reading it.

More, he seldom wants you to "lose yourself" in one of his stories, and never for long at a time, because he intends you to think about it too. The sort of literary imagining he values most highly involves not only the senses and the emotions but also the mind. Hence his style is a bit cool, on the intellectual side, seldom sensuous, seldom gorgeous, never opaque. The sentences make narrative sense before they do their other things. Frequently, ambiguity turns a phrase, an odd possibility thickens a paragraph, a satiric patina colors a whole story, but he almost never relies on parody, literary allusion, or special knowledge on the reader's part. For he, a literary traditionalist, wants you to thinking-feel about the matter of the story but not about the author's having done so—and certainly not about how he did it, as a modernist fiction requires. He wants you to be somewhat aware of the verbal surface but even more aware of the people in the story, the pattern of their changing connections, what that pattern and those changes mean.

He aspires to be the kind of storyteller whose books are read for their own sake but whose biography only a cultist of Creativity would be drawn to read because of those books. It is in part to accomplish this end that he keeps the narrative surface lucid and cool, for you will be less inclined to look at the writer if his style performs a mediating, revealing function than if it excites your imagination. He wants you to imagine the characters' world and to be more or less conscious that you are doing so, but he does not want you necessarily to be conscious of how he got you to do it. If the story is in the first person, he wants you to realize that the "I" is a character in the story and not the author of it; if it is in the third person, he intends for the means he uses for controlling and directing your responses to be so unobtrusive that you are not impelled to succumb to him and for his analytic comments to seem so true to the givens on which the story is based that you will not quarrel with him, will not feel him there to be quarreled with. He wants you to feel yourself in the hands of a storyteller who knows what he is doing and who exists in history, but not necessarily in the hands of *this* man who has *this* history of his own. If the story is, as it should be, ordered by the author's vision, you will learn something essential about his self but you need not be concerned with those unmysterious accidents and quirks which are most of what we know of each other in ordinary life. He knows far more about the family next door than about Lady Murasaki; but, in and of itself, the little he knows (and wants ever to know) about her through reading *The Tale of Genji* is infinitely more valuable to him than is the neighboring clutter (about which, all the same, he *could* write a story some day).

But his main rationale for the style—formal-seeming, of a certain polish, rather distancing —is moral. Ultimately, though not proximately, his stories are meant to bring the reader to felt understanding; and, since intense emotion, in fiction as in life, interferes with lucid thought, he intends his characters to have feelings, sentiments, passions which may overwhelm them sometimes but the reader never. The complex relationship among storyteller, characters, and reader are, he believes, intrinsically moral; and without esthetic distance there is not likely to be much moral clarity.

This all sounds neater than it really is, for storytelling entwines esthetics and psychology and ethics inextricably, at least in his experience. Life offers him few higher or more enduring pleasures than making moral-psychological discriminations, especially in the narrative mode. But it does offer at least one.

Occasionally, at moments of intensity which occur only when you have got well into the story, he wants you to disregard literary techniques and philosophical distinctions and ethical judgments and such like for a while and just feel with a character, secure by then that the meaning of the character's behavior will be told you by your very feelings and that the intensity of these feelings will not be in the least diminished by reflection. Whether getting to the state of powerful, no longer critical, yet understanding sympathy with a fictional Other is moral or psychological or esthetic or all three, more this than that, high in this scale but low in that, in fashion or out, he does not much care; it is the thing in the world he most likes doing.

—"Not Me, My Stories", included in *Conversions: Literature and the Modernist Deviation*, 1971.

\*   \*   \*

George P. Elliott's writings comprise numbers of modes and forms, variously including lyric and narrative poetry, lengthy realistic novels virtually in the manner of his nineteenth-century namesake, Swiftian satire in some of his short stories, and a kind of familiar essay which is at once autobiographical and speculative. His subjects and occasions range from reflections on literature and aesthetics to reflections on his own childhood to topical observations, to futuristic fantasies. The work is nonetheless very much of a piece. It is informed continuously by a stubborn faith in divine transcendence. Although Elliott is far from being either a religious apologist or a hierophant in any of the literary modes which he practices, he is basically a Christian writer, whose work in general testifies to a belief in God.

Only a few of his stories deal mainly and directly with Christian materials. In such stories as "The Beatification of BobbySu Wilson" (included in *Among the Dangs*) and "Into the Cone of Cold" (included in *An Hour of Last Things*), a skeptical but dissatisfied secularist is placed in conflict with the representations of the Catholic Church, to the end that his secularism is broken down. Religious realization is more typically, however, a matter of implication or underlying theme. Elliott's more usual terms of conflict are on the one hand rationalism—politics, the physical and behavioral sciences, any merely human system of total explanation—and on the other hand everything that is the opposite of rationalism, including conscience, value, art, and any expression of mysteries, extending from astrology to Jehovah's Witness. His protagonists tend to be men already guilty of modern kinds of intellectual rigidity, devoted to one or another kind of total explanation, who must be chastened. In a term to which Elliott has attached special meaning, they are "mediocre." They accept the thinking of society. Their occasional heroism is something less than the total acceptance of God, an eventuality which they perceive would necessitate the end of their living in the world. But they do achieve decency, the consequence of living in society with the realization that both society and individual humanity are subject to mysteries.

The theme is exemplified in Elliott's most celebrated story, "Among the Dangs." The protagonist, a young anthropologist, visits a primitive tribe by way of furthering his professional career. The events of the story introduce him to, and eventually force him to participate in, the vatical rites of the tribe, to the point where he is almost willing to lose himself forever in the miracle of his prophesying. He escapes that fate, returning to wife and job, but he is bound to its allurement.

Elliott's novels, relying on less spectacular inventions, qualify and complicate the theme. In *Parktilden Village* the protagonist is a young sociologist who must learn what sociology does not recognize, that people are not statistical probabilities. The protagonist in *David Knudsen* is the son of one of the scientists who invented the Hiroshima bomb, and he must rid himself of his inherited but also inherent "radiation sickness," which is to say his deathly scientism. The protagonist of *In the World* presents Elliott's case most comprehensively, perhaps. He is a professor of law become dissatisfied with his profession. He returns to it when he learns that his proper job is discovery of the fundamentals and necessity of man-made law for a humanity to which law is inadequate.

—Marcus Klein

**ELLISON, Ralph (Waldo).** American. Born in Oklahoma City, Oklahoma, 1 March 1914. Educated at Tuskegee Institute, Alabama, 1933–36. Served in the United States Merchant Marine, 1943–45. Married Fanny McConnell in 1946. Worked on the New York Federal Writer's Project. Instructor of Russian and American Literature, Bard College, Annandale-on-Hudson, New York, 1958–61; Alexander White Visiting Professor, University of Chicago, 1961; Visiting Professor of Writing, Rutgers University, New Brunswick, New Jersey, 1962–64; Visiting Fellow in American Studies, Yale University, New Haven, Connecticut, 1966. Since 1970, Albert Schweitzer Professor in the Humanities, New York University. Lecturer, Salzburg Seminar in American Studies, 1954; Whittall Lecturer, Library of Congress, Washington, D.C., 1964; Ewing Lecturer, University of California at Los Angeles, 1964. Chairman, Literary Grants Committee, National Institute of Arts and Letters, 1964–67; Member, National Council of the Arts, 1965–67; Member of the Editorial Board, *American Scholar*, Washington, D.C., 1966–69. Member, Carnegie Commission on Educational Television, 1966–67. Honorary Consultant in American Letters, Library of Congress, Washington, D.C., 1966–72. Currently, Trustee of the John F. Kennedy Center for the Performing Arts, Washington, D.C., the New School for Social Research, New York, Bennington College, Vermont, and the Educational Broadcasting Corporation. Recipient: Rosenwald Fellowship, 1945; National Book Award, 1953; Russwarm Award, of the National Newspaper Publishers Association, 1953; National Academy of Arts and Letters Prix de Rome, 1955, 1956. Ph.D. in Humane Letters, Tuskegee Institute, 1963; Litt.D., Rutgers University, 1966, University of Michigan, Ann Arbor, 1967, and Williams College, Williamstown, Massachusetts, 1970; L.H.D., Grinnell College, Iowa, 1967. Awarded United States Medal of Freedom, 1969. Chevalier de L'Ordre des Artes et Lettres, France, 1970. Member of the American Academy of Arts and Sciences; National Institute of Arts and Letters, 1964. Address: 730 Riverside Drive, New York, New York 10031, U.S.A.

PUBLICATIONS

Novel

*Invisible Man*. New York, Random House, 1952; London, Gollancz, 1953.

Excerpts from novel-in-progress: "The Roof, the Steeple and the People", in *Quarterly Review of Literature* (Princeton, New Jersey), 1960; "And Hickman Arrives", in *The Noble Savage* (Chicago), March 1960; "It Always Breaks Out", in *Partisan Review* (New Brunswick, New Jersey), Spring 1963; "Juneteenth", in *Quarterly Review of Literature*, 1969; "Song of Innocence", in *Iowa Review* (Iowa City), Spring 1970.

Uncollected Short Stories

"Slick Gonna Learn", in *Direction* (Darien, Connecticut), September 1939.
"Afternoon", in *American Writing*. Prairie City, Illinois, James A. Decker, 1940.
"The Birthmark", in *New Masses* (New York), 2 July 1940.
"Mister Toussan", in *New Masses* (New York), 4 November 1941.
"That I Had the Wings", in *Common Ground* (New York), Summer 1943.
"Flying Home", in *Cross Section*. New York, Fischer, 1944.
"In a Strange Country", in *Tomorrow* (New York), July 1944.
"King of the Bingo Game", in *Tomorrow* (New York), November 1944.
"Did You Ever Dream Lucky?", in *New World Writing 5*. New York, New American Library, 1954.
"A Coupla Scalped Indians", in *New World Writing 9*. New York, New American Library, 1956.

"Out of the Hospital and under the Bar", in *Soon, One Morning: New Writing by American Negroes, 1940–1962*.   New York, Knopf, 1963.

Other

*Shadow and Act* (essays).   New York, Random House, 1964; London, Secker and Warburg, 1966.

Bibliographies: by R. S. Lilliard, in *American Book Collector* (Chicago), November 1968; "A Bibliography of Ralph Ellison's Published Writings" by Bernard Benoit and Michel Fabre, in *Studies in Black Literature* (Fredericksburg, Virginia), Autumn 1971.

Critical Studies: *The Negro Novel in America*, revised edition, by Robert A. Bone, New Haven, Connecticut, Yale University Press, 1958; "The Blues as a Literary Theme" by Gene Bluestein, in *Massachusetts Review* (Amherst), Autumn 1967; "Ralph Ellison Issue" of *C.L.A. Journal* (Baltimore), March 1970; an interview in the *Atlantic Monthly* (Boston), December 1970; *Studies in Invisible Man*, edited by Ronald Gottesman, Columbus, Ohio, Merrill, 1971.

*       *       *

From the fact that he has published a single novel and that nearly twenty years ago, Ralph Ellison's reputation as a major American novelist seems phenomenal, but then his novel is a remarkable work. On one level the nameless protagonist of *Invisible Man* is a modern *picaro* moving through the realms of the Southern American black bourgeosie, Northern industrial society, and the radical political movement learning to survive the bewildering contradictions of racial stereotype and reality by converting the instability of personal identity, which he finds to be the normal state of a black person in the white world, into a condition for freedom. His triumph is less than the classical *picaro*'s, for it is conscious knowledge of the absurdity of the situations he has experienced that sustains him after his American progress rather than a tested capacity to determine his fate. In that fact, however, lies both Ellison's commentary on freedom in the modern world and his understanding of a philosophical role for fiction. The self-aware figure of the invisible man is liberated from external sanctions and, in the imagery of Camus, having seen the stage sets collapse knows there is no just authority to support the human inventions of caste. Crouched in his hole in the ground, mentally journeying through time and space while deliberating a responsible plan for living he gathers all of his being into potentiality. Only potentiality, though, because *Invisible Man*, published in 1952, announces the prerequisite mind set for liberation, not the tactics of the struggle.

The philosophical dynamics of Ellison's novel are embodied in its structure. The narrative of absurd experiences bound between a prologue and epilogue makes clear that the events have already happened to the invisible spokesman and are thus contained within his consciousness where he is free to shape them into significance as he wills. Where the realist or naturalist stresses the clarity of perception, saying he will record only what objectively happens in the world, the surrealist Ellison considers his tale to be an epistemological drama in which the active forces are the conceptions of race and society that determine what each character will perceive. Consequently, the stress upon sight in the title of the novel points not only to stereotypes that obscure our social vision but indicates as well the power of imagination to create a habitable reality.

Ellison's modernist esthetics have earned his novel high critical estimation. In 1965 *Book Week*, then a leading American weekly book review, conducted a poll of critics and found them choosing *Invisible Man* as the most distinguished American fiction of the post-war period. While the book undoubtedly merits its critical distinction, the nearly unanimous approval it receives from white critics often carries the implication that Ellison's universal *picaro*—"Who knows," he says, "but that I speak for you"—represents the transcendence of the invariable concerns of black writers. Clearly such sentiment is less an evaluation of Ellison's work than it is a product of the wish that the divisive issue of race could be verbally resolved without disturbing social arrangements or cultural commonplaces. Certainly, from the time of his earliest published writing Ellison has been interested in the universal theme of identity, but he has always conceived the theme in the context of black culture. "Did You Ever Dream Lucky?", which elaborates the story of Mary Rambo, and "Slick Gonna Learn," which tells of an aborted beating of a black workingman, describe experiences typified by their occurrence in the special circumstances of Afro-American life. Several stories ("Afternoon," "That I Had the Wings," "Mister Toussan," "A Coupla Scalped Indians") representing young black boys contending with fear and guilt, learning of sex, and fantasizing retaliation on whites who despise them might be tales of the invisible protagonist in adolescence, while the discovery by a young black aviator in "Flying Home" of his kinship to a black peasant employs race and culture as the basic terms for self discovery. If anything the attention to black life evident in these stories is more marked in *Invisible Man*, where the narrator's consciousness is provided substance by orations and jive sayings, Toms and race men, dreams and behavior from popular black culture.

So, too, does the surreal quality of the narrative manifest black experience. Caste restrictions seem reasonable perhaps to those who enforce them, but for those who experience them they are literally absurd. A society ordered by caste, therefore, can only be described adequately in narrative that departs from the decorum of rationality and insinuates that insanity is perceptive response, or a dream of anxiety a sound analysis.

Growing up in a black culture, and relishing it as he demonstrably does, Ellison found ready-to-hand the premise that would lead to the philosophical position of his invisible man; yet, his application of imagination to the story of the modern *picaro* is, in fact, a major achievement, for he has done nothing less than bring to its culmination a period of Afro-American literary history that had as its motif the sensation described by W. E. B. DuBois in 1903 as a double-consciousness wherein "one ever feels his twoness,—an American, a Negro . . . two warring ideals in one dark body." By liberating his invisible protagonist of the ideals that, like an alien force, had invaded his ego, Ellison has prepared his narrator and those who, through influence, sympathy, or coincidence, will follow him to live with a unitary consciousness of themselves in the world.

—John M. Reilly

---

**ELY, David.** American. Born in Chicago, Illinois, 19 November 1927. Educated at the University of North Carolina, Chapel Hill, 1944–45; Harvard University, Cambridge, Massachusetts, 1947–49, B.A. 1949; St. Antony's College, Oxford (Fulbright Scholar), 1954–55. Served in the United States Navy, 1945–46, and the United States Army, 1950–52. Married Margaret Jenkins in 1954; has four children. Reporter, *St. Louis Post-Dispatch*, 1949–50, 1952–54, 1955–56. Administrative Assistant, Development and Resources Corporation, New York, 1956–59. Address: Costa San Giorgio 47, Florence, Italy.

PUBLICATIONS

Novels

    *Trot*.   New York, Pantheon Books, 1963; London, Secker and Warburg, 1964.
    *Seconds*.   New York, Pantheon Books, 1963; London, Deutsch, 1964.
    *The Tour*.   New York, Delacorte Press, and London, Secker and Warburg, 1967.
    *Poor Devils*.   Boston, Houghton Mifflin, 1970.

Short Stories

    *Time Out*.   New York, Delacorte Press, 1968; London, Secker and Warburg, 1969.

Uncollected Short Stories

    "The Wizard of Light", in *Amazing* (New York), 1961.
    "The Alumni March", in *Cosmopolitan* (New York), 1962.
    "McDaniel's Flood", in *Elks Magazine* (Chicago), 1963.
    "The Captain's Boarhunt", in *Saturday Evening Post* (New York), 1963.
    "The Assault on Mount Rushmore", in *Cavalier* (New York), 1966.
    "The Language Game", in *Playboy* (Chicago), 1970.
    "The Knave of Hearts", in *Ellery Queen's Mystery Magazine* (New York), 1971.
    "The Carnival", in *Antaeus* (New York), 1971.

*    *    *

David Ely's fiction describes the cost and conditions of freedom—what an ordinary man must do to understand himself and his world. His novels are shaped like thrillers; in each a man is driven onto a quest (initially for the wrong motives) which ultimately leads him to himself, to his unconscious mind, his heart. The novels describe with remarkable sensitivity individuals coping with worlds that are alien, inimical and all-powerful. The triumph of the individual spirit in a hostile modern milieu is accompanied by pain and sorrow, loss of innocence and simple comfort, but it brings both self-knowledge and peace.

*Trot*, Ely's first novel, is subtitled "A Novel of Suspense" and predicates the world of all of Ely's fiction: an alien, minatory and hostile environment, in this case the Paris underworld after WW II. An Army CID man, Sergeant Trot, abruptly becomes the victim in a case on which he is assigned. Suspected of corruption and murder, he hides with the criminals he has stalked. The inversion of his world causes him to reassess his concepts of justice and freedom. Finally he is able to reinstate himself by breaking an extortion-murder plot by escaped Nazis. But the significant victory is Trot's own self-revelation.

In *Seconds*, probably Ely's best-known novel, a Babbitt-like man, a cipher known only by the code name "Wilson," abandons his comfortable but aimless upper-middle-class existence when a mysterious corporation offers him a new life, a second chance. He is surgically rehabilitated and supplied a total new identity as a successful artist, but the new freedom proves too painful and challenging. Wilson disintegrates under the stress of his open and unfamiliar world of freedom and nonconformity. "I never had a dream," he says when he returns to the corporation to be erased.

*The Tour* deals with the same theme in a more terrifying form. A parable of American imperialism and military-scientific manipulation of other cultures, it describes a "tour" designed to provide jaded bourgeois travelers with ultimate thrills in a mythical central American banana republic. The tour includes episodes of sex, jungle survival and guerilla fighting, carefully staged for the fuddled gringos. Behind the scenes a test is made on an automated counter-insurgency weapon, a robot tank which wipes out a starveling guerilla band (and its builders) and nearly decimates the tour. The novel develops as an analogue for U.S. involvement in S.E. Asia and for other paramilitary "tours" of policy. It is similar in shape to Peter Matthiessen's important *At Play in the Fields of the Lord.*

Ely's latest work, *Poor Devils,* attacks the sociological concepts of poverty and its alleviation. Another parable, it describes the slow education of a history professor, Aaron Bell, who stumbles onto a Project Nomad, a genocidal agency for a "final solution" to poverty, a technological bureau that fights poverty with coldly mechanical games theory and supertechnology. Bell's education leads him to discover the futility of his life and his career, the absurdity of history and ideals faced with amoral technology. The old man he has pursued, Lindquist, a "picaresque saint," teaches him finally that he must discover (or invent) his values himself. Bell opts out of the system of research and manipulation to become a Whitmanesque wanderer, following the "Lindquist heresy, the preamble written short for men in too big a hurry to read much: *Life, liberty, and the pursuit.*"

Ely's novels are all parables of the New Babbitt redeemed, the affluent and self-satisfied "Executive Man" freed to make real, life-or-death decisions, to direct his life and test the morality of his society. The transformations are costly, painful and sometimes tragic, but they are real and significant actions, leaps of faith which give meaning to the small existences Ely depicts.

—William J. Schafer

---

**ENRIGHT, D(ennis) J(oseph).** British. Born in Leamington, Warwickshire, 11 March 1920. Educated at Leamington College; Downing College, Cambridge, B.A. (honours) in English 1944, M.A. 1946; University of Alexandria, Egypt, D.Litt. 1949. Married Madeleine Harders in 1949; has one child. Lecturer in English, University of Alexandria, 1947–50; Extra-Mural Lecturer, Birmingham University, England, 1950–53; Visiting Professor, Kōnan University, Kobe, Japan, 1953–56; Gastdozent, Free University, West Berlin, 1956–57; British Council Professor of English, Chulalongkorn University, Bangkok, 1957–59; Professor of English, University of Singapore, 1960–70. Temporary Lecturer in English, University of Leeds, Yorkshire, 1970–71. Since 1970, Co-Editor of *Encounter* magazine, London. Since 1971, Editorial Advisor, Chatto and Windus, publishers, London. Fellow, Royal Society of Literature, 1961. Address: c/o *Encounter,* 59 St. Martin's Lane, London W.C.2, England.

PUBLICATIONS

Novels

    *Academic Year.*   London, Secker and Warburg, 1955.
    *Heaven Knows Where.*   London, Secker and Warburg, 1957.
    *Insufficient Poppy.*   London, Chatto and Windus, 1960.
    *Figures of Speech.*   London, Heinemann, 1965.

Verse

*The Laughing Hyena and Other Poems*.   London, Routledge, 1953.
*Bread Rather Than Blossoms*.   London, Secker and Warburg, 1956.
*Some Men Are Brothers*.   London, Chatto and Windus, 1960.
*Addictions*.   London, Chatto and Windus, 1962.
*The Old Adam*.   London, Chatto and Windus, 1965.
*Unlawful Assembly*.   London, Chatto and Windus, and Middletown, Connecticut,
      Wesleyan University Press, 1968.
*Selected Poems*.   London, Chatto and Windus, 1969.
*The Typewriter Revolution and Other Poems*.   New York, Library Press, 1971.
*Daughters of Earth*.   London, Chatto and Windus, 1972.


Other

*A Commentary on Goethe's "Faust"*.   New York, New Directions, 1949.
*The World of Dew: Aspects of Living Japan*.   London, Secker and Warburg, 1955;
      Chester Springs, Pennsylvania, Dufour, 1959.
*Literature for Man's Sake: Critical Essays*.   Tokyo, Kenkyusha, 1955.
*The Apothecary's Shop*.   London, Secker and Warburg, 1957; Chester Springs,
      Pennsylvania, Dufour, 1959.
*Conspirators and Poets*.   London, Chatto and Windus, and Chester Springs, Pennsyl-
      vania, Dufour, 1966.
*Memoirs of a Mendicant Professor*.   London, Chatto and Windus, 1969.
*Shakespeare and the Students*.   London, Chatto and Windus, 1970; New York,
      Schocken Books, 1971.

Editor, *Poetry of the 1950's: An Anthology of New English Verse*.   Tokyo, Kenkyusha,
      1955.
Editor, with Takamichi Ninomiya, *The Poetry of Living Japan*.   London, Murray, and
      New York, Grove Press, 1957.
Editor, with E. de Chickera, *English Critical Texts: 16th Century to 20th Century*.
      London and New York, Oxford University Press, 1962.


Critical Study: in *A Human Idiom* by William Walsh, London, Chatto and Windus, 1965.


D. J. Enright comments:

  The four novels I have published are all really travel books, I am afraid. This is true even
of the second, which is about a sort of Utopia.

                         *         *         *


  D. J. Enright is a writer: not so much of a truism as it might sound when one remembers
the names of a large number of other, contemporary novelists, to whom writing appears
either an unpleasant or untried habit! He is primarily a poet, one of the most significant
and attractive of English poets during the last twenty years; he is also a critic of great acumen
and range. He has appeared in *Scrutiny* and has written on subjects from Shakespeare to
contemporary German playwrights—and there could hardly be a range greater than that.
He is also a novelist whose four novels which appeared between 1955 and 1965, while they

have had considerable critical acclaim, have received less than their due attention from the reading public. All these novels are set abroad, in Alexandria, the imaginary island of Velo, or Bangkok or Japan. No doubt this fits in with the simple biographical fact that Enright has spent a considerable part of his career abroad as a Professor of English Literature in various Far Eastern universities. He undoubtedly knows what he is talking about. But it is also in keeping with his reflective, poetically sensitive and coolly registering mind. He is a writer who believes that "civilization consists in the diminution of human tears", and his response to Far Eastern life contains a quite unsentimental pity for the harsh life of the poor, a cool antagonism for affectation and power whether of academics or politicians, and the small and human virtue of hope, offered by Enright with a characteristic mischief—or flippancy, as some call it.

In the first novel, *Academic Year*, Bacon, Packet and Brett, three teachers of English at the University of Alexandria, embodying the experienced, the ardent and the intolerant in the English character, present a kind of pragmatic English density in opposition to the aspiring and impalpable Egyptian sensibility, both of students and others. The novel is beautifully light in its touch, and it contains scenes, particularly the one on the whole apparatus of examinations in the university, which are the pure milk of gaiety. It may be that there is an inclination to reflect gently on the passage of events and that the action is seen through a slightly misted air, but the spirit, the individuality and the wit are quite extraordinarily rare in modern fiction; and the combination of liberality of spirit with an exquisite capacity for mocking anything grand or spiritually obese, makes *Academic Year* a memorable experience.

*Heaven Knows Where* is Enright's Utopia, which is visited by Packet in response to an advertisement for a teacher of English Literature in the island of Velo. The King of the island is devoted to the *Anatomy of Melancholy* and he accompanies the action with a calculatedly ambiguous commentary upon the disaster which overtakes his rational and delightful society when it is subject to a managerially modern, political take-over. The inhabitants of Velo represent, or are, the quiet, the amused, the merely human, in contrast to the intellectual power maniacs who invade them. The overwhelming military power of the Derthans is subdued or rather folded into an absorbtive embrace, by the Velonians. This pointed parable or analogue of a situation daily to be seen in the newspaper—at least half of it is—confirms in one a sense one has of Enright as a writer with a peculiarly naked sense of actuality. He has in fact the enviably unusual gift of being able to see just what is there for his eyes to see. At the same time as he registers the fact he brings to bear upon it a richly orchestrated feeling for human value in which tenderness and commonsense are particularly notable characteristics.

*Insufficient Poppy* is an effective—it is rather less reflective—an effective, sad novel, closer in mood to Enright's poetry than the lighter *Academic Year* and *Heaven Knows Where*. The sadness which disturbs the even life of three friends in Bangkok, one the manager of a family business dribbling away into nothing, another a teacher of English, and another a weird ex-film star, is not the small sadness we find every day in every breath, but a large and brutal sadness when one of the friends is shot. This calamity shockingly ends the mild pleasures of the trio, conversation, beer, a little opium prudently enjoyed, the odd faithful girl friend. *Insufficient Poppy* is remarkable (as indeed *Academic Year* was in respect of Alexandria) for the tactful indirection by which the life of the place and its people is evoked. There are no set pieces, no *longeurs*, no Scott-like descriptions, but we come to have—no doubt because it is refracted through human beings—the clearest vision of the life and the firmest feeling for its people.

*Figures of Speech*, Enright's last novel, is in my view his best—good as the others are. It is decidedly more active as a story, the characters are more engaging, the fiction altogether more embodied and appealing. There are only three characters in effect, an English Professor, George Lester, Chung Lu a young high-minded Chinese scholar, and Mattie, a crisp girl from Singapore, who displays both the elegance and the forcefulness characteristic of the educated young Chinese woman. The love affair of the two Chinese and the gorgeously comic adventures of George are plaited together with nimble and natural smoothness. There is also a peculiarly abrasive treatment of George's relations with, and betrayal by, the British Council and the Embassy, in which unbridled cautiousness competes with unabashed stupidity to compose a model of the British way of life for foreigners to contemplate. In addition there is a characteristically sharp and understanding account of the Japanese mode of entertaining foreigners which is a marvellous piece of dancing humour and social analysis. It is hard to define the effect of this remarkable book in which an unaffected fastidiousness of spirit is accompanied by the most open and inclusive generosity of response, and in which both are conveyed in an idiom utterly personal and devastatingly witty. It is now six years since Enright published a novel. One must hope that at least a portion of his remarkable creative talent will be engaged in this kind of work again.

Perhaps a particular reason for this desire is that Enright's novels are, in a very special way, *intelligent*. By intelligence I mean the faculty which combines a measure of wisdom with a sense for the concrete occasion, and I stress it because I come more and more to the view that any fool can be clever, but it takes a rare man to be intelligent. This intelligence speaks in all the material of D. J. Enright's fiction, just as it does in the actual writing, which joins a quite athletic strength to sensitivity, and a sardonic vision to great gentleness of response. Enright is professorial alright, a most learned man with several literatures and more countries at his fingertips, but he is also most mischievously comic, the street arab telling the alderman where to get off.

His account of the expatriate life of teachers, their friends, lovers and superiors in Bangkok, Singapore, Japan, is poetically evocative of the places, shrewd in its analysis of them, and at the same time thronged with the common misfortunes of everyone (he quotes in another work Heine's advice to his descendents "to be born with thick skins on their backs"), misfortune which came mostly from acting in an ordinary way in official situations. His protagonist is always the bit of grit in the administrative eye. But while Enright is full of pity for others he is wary about self-pity for himself. And he is always aware of the sanitary necessity of laughter.

So often in official bad books himself, Enright feels intensely for the victims of power, and who of us isn't one of those sometime? In our glum, extreme world we desperately need the gaiety of spirit and the moral feeling shown in these witty, elegant, generous novels.

—William Walsh

---

**ESPEY, John (Jenkins).** American. Born in Shanghai, China, 15 January 1913. Educated at Occidental College, Los Angeles, California, 1931–35, A.B. 1935; Merton College, Oxford (Rhodes Scholar), 1935–38, B.A. 1937, B.Litt. 1939, M.A. 1941. Married Alice Martha Rideout in 1938; has two children. Taught at Occidental College, 1938–48. Since 1948, Member of the English Department, University of California at Los Angeles: Professor of English since 1956. Recipient: Commonwealth Silver Medal, 1945; Guggenheim Fellowship, 1958; California Institute of Creative Arts Fellowship, 1970. Address: Department of English, University of California, 405 Hilgard Avenue, Los Angeles, California 90024, U.S.A.

PUBLICATIONS

Novels

*The Anniversaries.* New York, Harcourt Brace, 1963.
*An Observer.* New York, Harcourt Brace, 1965.

Uncollected Short Stories

"Portrait from Memory", in *Arizona Quarterly* (Tucson), Autumn 1955.
"Bird-Watcher", in *Harper's* (New York), January 1959.
"The Condors", in *Arizona Quarterly* (Tucson), Autumn 1959.


Other

*Minor Heresies* (sketches).   New York, Knopf, 1945; London, Secker and Warburg, 1947.
*Tales Out of School* (sketches).   New York, Knopf, 1947.
*The Other City*.   New York, Knopf. 1950.
*Ezra Pound's "Mauberley": A Study in Composition*.   Berkeley, University of California Press, and London, Faber, 1955.


Manuscript Collection: Occidental College Library, Los Angeles.


Critical Studies: reviews by James Dean Young in *Critique* (Minneapolis), Winter 1964–65, and Spring-Summer 1966.

*          *          *

The stories and novels of John Espey fall into two periods, most of the stories being published during the 1940's and two novels in the 1960's. Between them falls an important scholarly work on Ezra Pound's "Mauberley."

The early volumes, containing some sixty stories, are both typical and problematical. What is typical is the clarity and balance of the prose which describes what it was to be growing up in the China of the 1920's as the son of missionaries. Espey sees himself with characteristic perspective expressed in sharp prose of considerable wit and irony. What is problematical is that we may not have fiction at all. *Minor Heresies* is sometimes classed as autobiography, and even appears in the theology library at one large American university. The extent to which Espey's shaping of his experience causes the categories to change is difficult to determine. We are somewhere between autobiography and fiction; the "Family Circle" comments on the dedication of the first volume indicate that even the members of his own family do not agree on the extent of the mixture of fiction and truth.

The two more recent novels are conceived as part of a series of, perhaps, five novels; the third, as yet unpublished, has been tentatively titled "Winter Return." *The Anniversaries* examines the stratified society of turn-of-the-century Pasadena through a moderately ironic review of nineteenth-century fictional modes. The novel presents scene after scene in different genres with even specific writers as models: the domestic life, drawing-room comedy, the picaresque, the outdoor-hunting novel (Surtee's Jorrocks rather than Dickens' Pickwick), and the Gothic. The use of such genres is firmly based in and actually absorbed by the historical Pasadena, a part of the map of southern California which has become a miniature America in Espey's imagination. In large outline *The Anniversaries* is a romance, suspended between comedy and tragedy; the dominance of the realistic raw-material is dissipated by its ironic presentation. Through the details Espey creates, not the place itself, but the meaning of the place together with the meaning a man is able to see in his life (or discover in his past); the recognition by father and son of the change and the similarity of their lives; and the celebration (as the title suggests) of the past in the present.

In *An Observer*, a somewhat modern counterstatement to the first novel, the young narrator observes himself and others in his late discovery of his Pasadena world. The parody and irony of this novel are established by internal references to a novel which the narrator hopes to write but which sounds very much like *An Observer* itself. Although somewhat tangential to the other novel, the double view is similarly penetrating and revealing in presenting the narrator's self-discovery and his coming to terms with the past.

—James Dean Young

---

**EVERETT, Peter.** British. Born in Hull, Yorkshire, 1 June 1931. Educated at Thorne College; Hull Grammar School. Has worked in a foundry, on a barge, selling electric signs, as a market gardener and labourer, in a wine merchant's, as a toy maker and as a furniture salesman. Recipient: ITV Award, for drama, 1962; Maugham Award, 1965; Arts Council grant, 1970. Address: 9 Laitwood Road, London S.W.12; or, c/o Jonathan Cape Ltd., 30 Bedford Square, London W.C.1, England.

PUBLICATIONS

Novels

  *A Day of Dwarfs.* London, Spearman, 1962.
  *The Instrument.* London, Hutchinson, 1962.
  *Negatives.* London, Cape, 1964; New York, Simon and Schuster, 1965.
  *The Fetch.* London, Cape, 1966; New York, Simon and Schuster, 1967.

Plays

  Screenplays: *Negatives*, 1965; *The Last of the Long-Haired Boys*, 1971.

  Has written plays for radio and television.

Peter Everett comments:

  How much freedom is there? I mean: what is available to us to question? I mean: what are the possible questions still open to us when we've been stitched-up by childhood hang-ups, life's bias, education and tradition? Having tried to sort this out—to hang oneself by one's bookstraps, as it were—how is it possible to ask the question in a form that is the question itself, since I do not seem able to divorce any question I pose from the density of the actuality in which I find it?

  Therefore, to make a form, a shape, with its shift of colours, weathers, shades of meaning, I always start with people in an actual setting: a room, a field, a garden. I move only with what I hear said, what I see, what I smell and taste. Into this, I "edit-in" speculation and ambiguity by juxtaposition, as I live out the uncertainty or certainty of these people in their particular milieu.

  One always fails. Whatever form one arrives at in order to show the "thing" extorts its own payment. Wanting to deal with the nub and quick of things conflicts with a need in me to state the obvious flatly, without simile or metaphor; it still involves me in the blatant rhetoric of form . . . Blatant rhetoric of form? Hamlet's poisoned cups, Claudius' foils and ruses. What the greatest rhetoric does is to contain and permit a moment of impact, the sudden electric shock of reality. The documentary aspect of *Wuthering Heights*, its realism, is haunted by ghosts. Pinter's realistic idiom suffers a sea-change in the final precipitate, just as Kafka's business letter to the world defines the real nature of the company.

No form is inevitable, since it is only a shape articulating many possibilities. At every twist and turn of plot, a fresh aspect can present itself. Character is bias—but to deal truth-fully with the absurdity of being is difficult when one is involved in structure. Characters in fiction must in continuum read Blackpool Blackpool Blackpool, as in a stick of rock when cut at any point—if they don't, if their behaviour patterns shift—they are open to question. At this intersection, certainty of being and new action, the novel is attempted.

It is no longer possible to deal with reality as the traditional novelist dealt with it. Honest as such novels are, often luminous with insight, they reassure as mirrors do; they protect us from our uncertainty. Hence the novel must be concerned with identity; what we become when our lives meet crises which force us to question our norms, attitudes, and fixed attributes.

*        *        *

Peter Everett shares the concern of many 20th-century writers with the destruction of Western man's confident 19th-century image of himself. Everett, in seeing what can be made from the pieces, has been led to explore the conventional frontiers between the sane and the insane and towards a curt, rather disjointed technique that reflects his subject matter and may perhaps be likened to a heap of strangely angled, deeply shadowed still photographs flicked on to the table by an apparently ironic photographer.

In *The Instrument* tormentor and tormented confront each other like cat and mouse in a bare room. Madison, the unfrocked policeman, plans to murder his wife and use as his instrument, Helm, an agonised schizophrenic, who has killed once already and now, released from prison, is struggling vainly to achieve identity as a writer. Madison, deeply involved with Helm from the past, urges him with deadly plausibility that he will find reality not as a writer but as a killer. Helm struggles to escape this deterministic trap but in the end falls into it. In doing so, however, he betrays Madison. The latter, driving into the arms of the police, feels cheated. It is Helm who, by achieving what Madison falsely believes to be his real identity, has found freedom. It is the ruthless, rational Madison who has entered a world of permanent unreality, where the game has become everything.

*The Fetch*, published after but written before *Negatives*, continues Everett's exploration of the private worlds of the sensitive, the lonely, the neurotic, all those shut off from every-day experience by deep-seated emotional disturbance. Bruno, a young cinema projectionist, suspended uneasily between reality and the fantasy world of motion-picture images, inherits the family house on the death of his father. Moving in, he finds himself surrounded by menacing figures: Childers, the gardener-handyman, Jane, his granddaughter, alias Elf, and Uncle Elia. Secluded in his stinking attic, Uncle Elia bombards Bruno with cryptic notes. Gradually he swells, in Bruno's eyes, into a doppelganger or "fetch" of his dead brother, Bruno's father, whose domineering personality has made Bruno the timid, emotion-ally crippled creature that he is. Elf, with whom Bruno falls in love, proves to be not a refuge but a further threat to his stability, encouraging him (as Reingard does Theo in *Negatives*) to don a mask, to act out roles, pushing him further from reality. In the end Bruno achieves release by shooting and wounding Uncle Elia, the symbolic attack he should have made but never did upon his father. But it is too late. Bruno falls back into the world of unreality, of cinema images.

In *Negatives*, Everett's best-known novel, the borders between fantasy and reality become even more blurred. Everett's preoccupation with the search for personal identity becomes stylised into an overt role- and game-playing situation. Written, like *The Fetch*, in the present tense, it is less obsessive in tone, with more feeling for the comic and grotesque. Theo, the antique-dealer, is not, we feel, mad, but inhabiting a contemporary world of super-sanity where personal identity is not a unique inalienable attribute but an ever-changing sequence of masks, do-it-yourself disposable kits, to be used for as long as the mood takes one. Theo and Vivien begin by playing the game of Crippen and/or his wife and mistress, but the arrival of the German photographer Reingard on the scene changes everything. Gradually Reingard asserts a power over Theo, seduces him from his Crippen role to that of Von Richthofen, the First World War air ace, with, in the end, fatal consequences. There are a detachment and irony about this work missing from the earlier novels. Everett's vision has grown sharper and colder. Theo, Vivien and Reingard are all puppets. Artistically the book is an advance, being more fluid and imaginative, but it has lost in compassion and involvement with its characters.

—Keith Walker

---

**FARRELL, J(ames) G(ordon).**   British.   Born in Liverpool, 23 January 1935. Educated at Rossall School; Brasenose College, Oxford, 1956–60, B.A. 1960. Recipient: Harkness Fellowship, for residence in the United States, 1966–68; Arts Council Award, 1970; Faber Memorial Prize, 1971. Address: 16 Egerton Gardens, London S.W.3, England.

PUBLICATIONS

Novels

*A Man from Elsewhere.*   London, Hutchinson, 1963.
*The Lung.*   London, Hutchinson, 1965.
*A Girl in the Head.*   London, Cape, 1967; New York, Harper, 1969.
*Troubles.*   London, Cape, 1970; New York, Knopf. 1971.

Critical Study: "Ireland Agonistes" by Elizabeth Bowen, in *Europa* (London), no. 1, 1971.

J. G. Farrell comments:

About *Troubles*. It is a common misconception that when the historians have finished with a historical incident there remains nothing but a patch of feathers and a pair of feet; in fact, the most important things, for the very reason that they are trivial, are unsuitable for digestion by historians, who are only able to nourish themselves on the signing of treaties, battle strategies, the formation of Shadow Cabinets and so forth. These matters are quite alien to the life most people lead, which consists of catching colds, falling in love, or falling off bicycles. It is this *real* life which is the novelist's concern (though, needless to say, realism is not the only way to represent it). One of the things I have tried to do in *Troubles* is to show people "undergoing" history, to use an expression of Sartre's. The Irish troubles of 1919–1921 were chosen partly because they appeared to be safely lodged in the past; most of the book was written before the current Irish difficulties broke out, giving it an unintended topicality. What I wanted to do was to use this period of the past as a metaphor for today, because I believe that however much the superficial details and customs of life may change over the years, basically life itself does not change very much. Indeed, all literature that survives must depend on this assumption. Another reason why I preferred to use the past is that, as a rule, people have already made up their minds what they think about the present. About the past they are more susceptible to clarity of vision.

\*      \*      \*

In a review of J. G. Farrell's *Troubles*, Stephen Wall observed one of this writer's most distinctive characteristics, his "ability to substantiate the bizarre milieu". Through the eyes of his heroes, isolated, sometimes eccentric figures, we view Mr. Farrell's strange world, while satirical reflections on other people are matched by even more ironic treatment of the hero himself. In style and outlook he has affinities with both Beckett and Nabokov—as with them we can never be unaware that he is an exile—but Farrell's comic style is more closely and richly textured than the former and the view of humanity less chilling than with Nabokov. In *The Lung* the scene is a hospital where Sands, a polio victim, finds himself surrounded by obsessive fellow patients who include an unhappy ex-priest whose sense of failure takes the form of comic blasphemy, and old man Rivers, sitting making baskets, "his mind a complete blank across which a naked woman passed from time to time". The central character of *A Girl in the Head*, Count Boris Slattery, is surrounded for the most part by people of horrifying normality with the result that he himself becomes increasingly strange and isolated. There is a strong sense of the pressure of environment in this book, the suburban fringe of a seaside resort which is presented in vivid detail and becomes a symbol of desperate middle-class cheerfulness.

In *Troubles* J. G. Farrell has found the perfect setting for his particular gifts, the disintegrating world of the Anglo-Irish ascendancy living out its last days in the decaying magnificence of the Majestic Hotel. His hero's melancholy detachment is, in part, a recent legacy from the first world war:

> Although he was sure he had never actually proposed to Angela during the few days of their acquaintance, it was beyond doubt that they were engaged: a certainty fostered by the fact that from the very beginning she had signed her letters "Your loving fiancée, Angela". This had surprised him at first. But with the odour of death drifting into the dug-out in which he scratched out his replies by the light of a candle it would have been trivial and discourteous beyond words to split hairs about such purely social distinctions.

When he arrives in Ireland to claim her in 1919, the Major is forced from an attitude of quizzical bemusement to one of considerable disturbance as the troubles run their course, even though his experience rarely takes him outside the bizarre world of genteel old ladies, cats teeming in the Imperial Bar and huge bulging roots of vegetation which take over the Palm Court. J. G. Farrell has created in the Majestic the perfect symbol for that period of Irish history, and by the completeness of the creation and the entirely convincing observations about the human beings within it, has provided a parable for the present. He is currently working on a novel set in India at the time of the "Mutiny" in which his aim is similar: to cause readers to reflect on the contemporary world, not by writing about them directly, for then people have ready-made political attitudes and preconceptions which act as barriers, but by showing the nature of events in the past and the way people responded to them.

J. G. Farrell has an eccentric and highly sensuous imagination finding expression in a powerful and suggestive use of imagery, much of which takes on the force of symbol. In the best Anglo-Irish literary tradition he is master of language, combining eloquence and humour, but always keeping a firm control over the "beautiful tragic cadences" which so many have found seductive.

—Bridget O'Toole

---

**FARRELL, James T(homas).** American. Born in Chicago, Illinois, 27 February 1904. Educated at DePaul University, Chicago, 1924–25; University of Chicago, 1926–29; New York University, 1941. Married Dorothy Butler in 1931 (divorced); Hortense Alden (divorced, 1955): remarried Dorothy Butler in 1955 (separated, 1958); has one child. Adjunct Professor, St. Peter's College, Jersey City, New Jersey, 1964–65; Writer-in-Residence, Richmond College, Virginia, 1969–70. Recipient: Guggenheim Fellowship, 1936; Book-of-the-Month Club Prize, 1937. D.Litt., Miami University, Oxford, Ohio, 1968. Member, National Institute of Arts and Letters. Address: c/o Doubleday and Company, 277 Park Avenue, New York, New York, 10017, U.S.A.

PUBLICATIONS

Novels

Studs Lonigan: A Trilogy. New York, Vanguard Press, 1935; London, Constable, 1936.
Young Lonigan: A Boyhood in Chicago Streets. New York, Vanguard Press, 1932.
The Young Manhood of Studs Lonigan. New York, Vanguard Press, 1934.
Judgment Day. New York, Vanguard Press, 1935.
Gas-House McGinty. New York, Vanguard Press, 1933; London, United Anglo-American Book Company, 1948; revised edition, New York, Avon, 1950.
Danny O'Neill pentalogy:
A World I Never Made. New York, Vanguard Press, 1936; London, Constable, 1938.
No Star Is Lost. New York, Vanguard Press, 1938; London, Constable, 1939.
Father and Son. New York, Vanguard Press, 1940; as A Father and His Son, London, Routledge, 1943.
My Days of Anger. New York, Vanguard Press, 1943; London, Routledge, 1945.
The Face of Time. New York, Vanguard Press, 1953; London, Spearman and Calder, 1954.
Ellen Rogers. New York, Vanguard Press, 1941; London, Routledge, 1942.
Bernard Carr trilogy:
Bernard Clare. New York, Vanguard Press, 1946; as Barnard Clayre, London, Routledge, 1948; as Bernard Carr, New York, New American Library, 1952.
The Road Between. New York, Vanguard Press, and London, Routledge, 1949.
Yet Other Waters. New York, Vanguard Press, 1952; London, Panther, 1960.
This Man and This Woman. New York, Vanguard Press, 1951.
Boarding House Blues. New York, Paperback Library, 1961; London, Panther, 1962.
A Universe of Time:
The Silence of History. New York, Doubleday, 1963; London, W. H. Allen, 1964.
What Time Collects. New York, Doubleday, 1964; London, W. H. Allen, 1965.

*When Time Was Born*.   New York, The Smith-Horizon Press, 1966.
*Lonely for the Future*.   New York, Doubleday, and London, W. H. Allen, 1966.
*A Brand New Life*.   New York, Doubleday, 1968.
*Judith*.   New York, Doubleday, 1969.
*Invisible Swords*.   New York, Doubleday, 1970.
*New Year's Eve/1929*.   New York, The Smith-Horizon Press, 1967.


Short Stories

*Callico Shoes and Other Stories*.   New York, Vanguard Press, 1934; as *Seventeen and Other Stories*, London, Panther, 1959.
*Guillotine Party and Other Stories*.   New York, Vanguard Press, 1935.
*Can All This Grandeur Perish? and Other Stories*.   New York, Vanguard Press, 1937.
*The Short Stories of James T. Farrell*.   New York, Vanguard Press, 1937; as *Fellow Countrymen: Collected Stories*, London, Constable, 1937.
*Tommy Gallagher's Crusade*.   New York, Vanguard Press, 1939.
*$1000 a Week and Other Stories*.   New York, Vanguard Press, 1942.
*To Whom It May Concern and Other Stories*.   New York, Vanguard Press, 1944.
*When Boyhood Dreams Come True*.   New York, Vanguard Press, 1946.
*More Fellow Countrymen*.   London, Constable, 1946.
*The Life Adventurous and Other Stories*.   New York, Vanguard Press, 1947.
*A Misunderstanding*.   New York, House of Books, 1949.
*An American Dream Girl*.   New York, Vanguard Press, 1950.
*French Girls Are Vicious and Other Stories*.   New York, Vanguard Press, 1955; London, Panther, 1958.
*An Omnibus of Short Stories*.   New York, Vanguard Press, 1956.
*A Dangerous Woman and Other Stories*.   New York, New American Library, 1957; London, Panther, 1959.
*Saturday Night and Other Stories*.   London, Panther, 1958.
*The Girls at the Sphinx*.   London, Panther, 1959.
*Looking 'em Over*.   London, Panther, 1960.
*Side Street and Other Stories*.   New York, Paperback Library, 1961.
*Sound of a City*.   New York, Paperback Library, 1962.
*Childhood Is Not Forever and Other Stories*.   New York, Doubleday, 1969.


Verse

*The Collected Poems of James T. Farrell*.   New York, Fleet, 1965.


Other

*A Note on Literary Criticism*.   New York, Vanguard Press, 1936; London, Constable, 1937.
*The League of Frightened Philistines and Other Papers*.   New York, Vanguard Press, 1945; London, Routledge, 1947.
*The Fate of Writing in America*.   New York, New Directions, 1946; London, Grey Walls Press, 1947.
*Literature and Morality*.   New York, Vanguard Press, 1947.
*My Name Is Fogarty: Private Papers on Public Matters* (as Jonathan Titulescu Fogarty, Esq.).   New York, Vanguard Press, 1950.
*Poet of the People: An Evaluation of James Whitcomb Riley*, with others.   Bloomington, Indiana University Press, 1951.

*Reflections at Fifty and Other Essays.* New York, Vanguard Press, 1954; London, Spearman, 1956.

*My Baseball Diary: A Famed Author Recalls the Wonderful World of Baseball, Yesterday and Today.* New York, A. S. Barnes, 1957.

*It Has Come to Pass* (on Israel). New York, Herzl Press, 1958.

*Dialogue with John Dewey,* with others. New York, Horizon Press, 1959.

*Selected Essays.* New York, McGraw Hill, 1964.

Editor, *Prejudices,* by H. L. Mencken. New York, Knopf, 1958.

Editor, *A Dreiser Reader.* New York, Dell, 1962.

Bibliography: *A Bibliography of James T. Farrell's Writings, 1921–1957* by Edgar M. Branch, Philadelphia, University of Pennsylvania Press, 1959.

Manuscript Collection: University of Pennsylvania, Philadelphia.

\*    \*    \*

Forty years ago James T. Farrell published his first novel, *Young Lonigan.* Presently he has to his credit twenty-three novels, fourteen collections of short stories, and, in all, forty-seven books, with other volumes of fiction in various stages of preparation. This output has established him as a leading practitioner of twentieth century American realism. His subjects and themes are modern, but his methods place his fiction squarely within the great tradition of critical realism.

Farrell has conceived his writing as an evolving but single body of work: a complex sequence encompassing his several cycles of novels and his other fiction. His work, indeed, does form a loosely cohesive whole because it expresses the motivations and tensions that have dominated his personal development while simultaneously it unfolds his story of the making of Americans in typical milieus, from the streets of Chicago to the Italian countryside. As he wrote Van Wyck Brooks, the major concern of his fiction is "the American way of life," the human meaning of modern America, and especially urban America. In realistic and often minute detail his fiction studies representative American destinies. It asks the questions "What happened?" and "How?" and seeks detailed answers. As Farrell develops his characters' lives, often through several novels and tales, he explores self-discovery, growth, socialization, and creativity—as well as their frustration. These are his major themes.

Farrell's best known and, perhaps, his greatest work is *Studs Lonigan,* consisting of *Young Lonigan, The Young Manhood of Studs Lonigan,* and *Judgment Day.* Together with related short stories, this trilogy powerfully evokes the downward thrust of Studs' career over the fifteen years prior to his death at age 29 in 1931. In essence, it portrays the failure of understanding and of the potential for humane growth in Studs, the Irish-Catholic Chicagoan. Farrell shapes that failure into a representative drama of man's self-destruction through Studs' susceptibility to what only seems good, but is not. The trilogy directly communicates, in massive segments of action, the cultural illusions and the isolation that stifle human development. In doing this, it delineates the social evils of urban industrialism. It exposes a middle-class morality that feeds on an illiberal ideal of rugged individualism, and it extends the range of social conflict found in the writings of Upton Sinclair and Theodore Dreiser. Perhaps more than any other American book it intimately reveals adult corruption fully developed in boys. Thus the trilogy lays open early twentieth century American urban life in all its ugliness—social, moral, and personal. Through it we experience not only the failure of modern institutions but also the impotence of love and reason.

The sense of immediacy that *Studs Lonigan* conveys results from Farrell's "objective" method: his re-creation of a sense of what life meant to Studs by unfolding the story largely through Studs' words, thoughts, feelings and actions. Because Farrell permits us to experience through Studs and yet to see him in context, within the dense city environment, we imaginatively participate in both the personal tragedy and the social implications of the drift of Studs' spiritually impoverished life toward an early death.

Farrell's second major cycle is the Danny O'Neill pentalogy: *A World I Never Made, No Star Is Lost, Father and Son, My Days of Anger,* and *The Face of Time.* This work covers the eighteen years up to 1927 in the lives of Danny, the character closest to Farrell, and his family. Studs, in his slavish ignorance, becomes addicted to the trivial and shameful within his restricted Chicago neighborhood. But Danny emerges from a background, not unlike Studs' in some respects, to win a measure of freedom from family and early environment. At the University of Chicago he gains an understanding of self and society, and ultimately he takes first steps toward becoming a writer. Whereas Studs symbolizes the darkness and divisiveness that finally kill, Danny measures the human potential for love and for the creative power of mind and will. The pentalogy is central in Farrell's mind and imagination, and Danny or his surrogates continue to move through Farrell's later fiction.

More nearly than *Studs Lonigan,* the Danny O'Neill books realize Farrell's intention to unfold many American destinies within related social areas. The novels are particularly rich in memorable characterizations of the O'Neills and the O'Flahertys, Danny's relatives on both sides of the family. The over-all story spans a three-generation process in which the laboring immigrant, like Danny's grandfather, is transformed into the intellectual urban American—Danny himself. Although Danny's development is the main thread winding through the five novels, the cycle is not dominated, as *Studs Lonigan* is, by one meager destiny plunging toward doom, but rather mirrors a more open, dynamic society affording many possible alternatives to many people.

By and large, the Danny O'Neil series keeps to the objective method found in *Studs Lonigan*: life is presented as experienced by individuals. But Farrell multiplies the number of his major characters and points of view into a more complex web of experience than that in the earlier cycle. The result is a detailed yet panoramic view of what it meant to be a big-city, Irish-Catholic American of modest income during the first three decades of this century—one reason Farrell is a significant Catholic novelist.

The major dramatic action traced in the stories of Studs and Danny is completed in Farrell's Bernard Carr trilogy (*Bernard Clare, The Road Between,* and *Yet Other Waters*): Studs goes under, Danny discovers his true calling and leaves Chicago, and Bernard, after considerable floundering, succeeds as a writer in New York City during the period from 1927 to 1936. In telling Bernard's story, Farrell shows what happened, spiritually and artistically, to a generation of New York writers and intellectuals, including Communists and fellow travelers of the Thirties. Like Henry James, Dreiser, and Anderson before him, he explores the artist's relation to society. Bernard, in particular, is seen defining himself vis-à-vis his Chicago past, the capitalist economic order, his lovers and wife, and seductive radicalism represented by the American Communist party, which tries to use him for its political ends. Eventually Bernard achieves a rare understanding of others. His actions become increasingly founded upon a democratic social philosophy, a pragmatic trust in experience, a naturalistic metaphysics, and an ethics of self-fulfillment.

Farrell's portrayal of Bernard Carr's world lacks the solidity of Studs' and Danny's worlds. Also the odyssey of Bernard's soul is rather weakly projected through external actions, and most of the other characters of the trilogy come alive only at intervals. Yet despite these weaknesses, Farrell's third cycle rounds out the fable begun in *Young Lonigan* and it extends Farrell's picture of America.

In addition to the series already discussed and to his ongoing work *A Universe of Time,* Farrell has published five individual novels and over two hundred short stories. These works fill in and complicate his imaginative realm, for they interlace with his multivolume cycles in settings, characters, and themes. *Gas-House McGinty,* Farrell's second novel, is a study of men on the job in the dreary Chicago express company where Farrell worked as a young man. It vividly dramatizes the shaping—and scarring—of character through occupation. Both *This Man and This Woman* and *Ellen Rogers* are novels of blighted love in Chicago. The latter, in particular, is a remarkable modern love story, which catches much of the spirit of the 1920's. *Boarding House Blues* and *New Year's Eve/1929* effectively explore Danny O'Neill's Bohemian environment in 1929 and 1930. Each centers around the theme of man's proper use of his brief lifetime. Farrell's short stories spread outward in setting from Chicago to New York, Paris, and Europe at large. They add significant panels to Farrell's broad picture of youth and age, boyish aspiration and adult acceptance, ardent love and tired middle-aged infidelity, family life and the conflict of generations.

Since 1958 Farrell has been engaged primarily in writing *A Universe of Time*, his most ambitious cycle of fiction. When completed, the work should run to approximately thirty volumes, seven of which have been published to date: *The Silence of History*, *What Time Collects*, *When Time Was Born*, *Lonely for the Future*, *A Brand New Life*, *Judith*, and *Invisible Swords*. Farrell has characterized his work in progress as "a relativistic panorama of our times" concerned with "man's creativity and his courageous acceptance of impermanence." The new cycle is based upon a reassessment of his experience. Like much of his earlier work, some of it is built around significant events from his personal past, and it has a central auto-biographical character, Eddie Ryan. But it is designed to yield a more comprehensive view of experience than his past writing affords. This it may well do, but completed volumes suggest that *A Universe of Time* also will reinforce the large patterns of meaning which emerge from the interrelated series on Studs, Danny, and Bernard.

Critics at times have attacked Farrell's naturalistic philosophy. They have pointed out limitations inherent in his objective method of presenting experience, and infelicities of style and structure. Farrell's work is indeed uneven, but its strengths far exceed its weaknesses. Especially in *Studs Lonigan* and the Danny O'Neill cycle Farrell displays an elemental insight, a consuming imagination that greedily transforms experience into a sustained illusion of life, the ability to dramatize great moral and social issues of our times, an unusual power of realistic characterization, and a pronounced architectural skill in constructing massive fictional works derived from firsthand experience.

—Edgar M. Branch

FAST, Howard (Melvin). Pseudonym: E. V. Cunningham. American. Born in New York City, 11 November 1914. Educated at George Washington High School, and the National Academy of Design, New York. Served with the Office of War Information, 1942–43, and the Army Film Project, 1944. Married Bette Cohen in 1937; has two children. War Correspondent in the Far East for *Esquire* and *Coronet* magazines, New York, 1945. Taught at Indiana University, Bloomington, Summer 1947. As a Member of the Joint Anti-Fascist Refugee Committee, was on the Board of Directors of a group which, in association with the Quakers, operated a hospital in Toulouse for sick and war-wounded Spanish Republicans; imprisoned for Contempt of Congress, 1947, for refusing to surrender to the House Committee on Un-American Activities the list of contributors to the hospital's support. After release from prison, because he was unable to find a publisher for his work, founded the Blue Heron Press, New York, 1952, which he liquidated in 1957. Film Writer for Universal, 1958–59, Paramount, 1961, Pennybaker, 1964, and Alfred Hitchcock, 1967. A Founder of the World Peace Movement, and member of the World Peace Council, 1950–55. Currently, Member of The Fellowship for Reconciliation. American Labor Party candidate for Congress for the 23rd District of New York, 1952. Recipient: Bread Loaf Writers Conference Award, 1933; Schomburg Race Relations Award, 1944; Newspaper Guild Award, 1947; Jewish Book Council of America Award, 1948; Stalin International Peace Prize (now Soviet International Peace Prize), 1954; Screenwriters Award, 1960; National Association of Independent Schools Award, 1962. Address: c/o Paul Reynolds Inc., 599 Fifth Avenue, New York, New York 10017, U.S.A.

PUBLICATIONS

Novels

Two Valleys.  New York, Dial Press, 1933; London, Dickson, 1934.
Strange Yesterday.  New York, Dodd Mead, 1934.
Place in the City.  New York, Harcourt Brace, 1937.
Conceived in Liberty: A Novel of Valley Forge.  New York, Simon and Schuster, and London, Joseph, 1939.
The Last Frontier.  New York, Duell, 1941; London, Lane, 1948.
The Unvanquished.  New York, Duell, 1942; London, Lane, 1947.
The Tall Hunter.  New York, Harper, 1942.
Citizen Tom Paine.  New York, Duell, 1943; London, Lane, 1945.
Freedom Road.  New York, Duell, 1944; London, Lane, 1946.
The American: A Middle Western Legend.  New York, Duell, 1946; London, Lane, 1949.
The Children.  New York, Duell, 1947.
Clarkton.  New York, Duell, 1947.
My Glorious Brothers.  Boston, Little Brown, 1948; London, Lane, 1952.
The Proud and the Free.  Boston, Little Brown, 1950; London, Lane, 1952.
Spartacus.  New York, privately printed, 1951; Citadel Press, 1952; London, Lane, 1952.
Fallen Angel (as Walter Erickson).  Boston, Little Brown, 1952.
Silas Timberman.  New York, Blue Heron Press, 1954; London, Lane, 1955.
The Story of Lola Gregg.  New York, Blue Heron Press, 1956; London, Lane, 1957.
Moses, Prince of Egypt.  New York, Crown, 1958; London, Methuen, 1959.
The Winston Affair.  New York, Crown, 1959; London, Methuen, 1960.
The Golden River, in The Howard Fast Reader.  New York, Crown, 1960.
Sylvia (as E. V. Cunningham).  New York, Doubleday, 1960; London, Deutsch, 1962.
April Morning.  New York, Crown, and London, Methuen, 1961.
Power.  New York, Doubleday, 1962; London, Methuen, 1963.
Phyllis (as E. V. Cunningham).  New York, Doubleday, 1962; London, Deutsch, 1963.
Alice (as E. V. Cunningham).  New York, Doubleday, and London, Deutsch, 1963.
Agrippa's Daughter.  New York, Doubleday, 1964; London, Methuen, 1965.
Shirley: An Entertainment (as E. V. Cunningham).  New York, Doubleday, and London, Deutsch, 1964.
Lydia: An Entertainment (as E. V. Cunningham).  New York, Doubleday, 1964; London, Deutsch, 1965.
Penelope: An Entertainment (as E. V. Cunningham).  New York, Doubleday, 1965; London, Deutsch, 1966.
Torquemada.  New York, Doubleday, 1966; London, Methuen, 1967.
Helen (as E. V. Cunningham).  New York, Doubleday, 1966; London, Deutsch, 1967.
Margie (as E. V. Cunningham).  New York, Morrow, 1966; London, Deutsch, 1968.
The Hunter and the Trap.  New York, Dial Press, 1967.
Sally (as E. V. Cunningham).  New York, Morrow, and London, Deutsch, 1967.
Samantha (as E. V. Cunningham).  New York, Morrow, 1967; London, Deutsch, 1969.
Cynthia (as E. V. Cunningham).  New York, Morrow, 1968; London, Deutsch, 1969.

*The Assassin Who Gave Up His Gun* (as E. V. Cunningham).   New York, Morrow, 1969; London, Deutsch, 1970.
*The General Zapped an Angel.*   New York, Morrow, 1970.
*The Crossing.*   New York, Morrow, 1971.


Short Stories

*Patrick Henry and the Frigate's Keel and Other Stories of a Young Nation.*   New York, Duell, 1945.
*Departures and Other Stories.*   Boston, Little Brown, 1949.
*The Last Supper and Other Stories.*   New York, Blue Heron Press, 1955; London, Lane, 1956.
*The Edge of Tomorrow.*   New York, Bantam, 1961.


Plays

*The Hammer* (produced New York, 1950).
*Thirty Pieces of Silver* (produced Melbourne, 1951).   New York, Blue Heron Press, and London, Lane, 1954.
*George Washington and the Water Witch.*   London, Lane, 1956.
*The Crossing* (produced Dallas, 1962).
*The Hill* (screenplay).   New York, Doubleday, 1964.

Screenplays: *Spartacus*, with Dalton Trumbo, 1960; *The Hill*, 1965; *The Hessian*, 1971.


Other

*The Romance of a People.*   New York, Hebrew Publishing Company, 1941.
*Lord Baden-Powell of the Boy Scouts.*   New York, Messner, 1941.
*Haym Solomon, Son of Liberty.*   New York, Messner, 1941.
*The Picture-Book History of the Jews*, with Bette Fast.   New York, Hebrew Publishing Company, 1942.
*Goethals and the Panama Canal.*   New York, Messner, 1942.
*The Incredible Tito.*   New York, Magazine House, 1944.
*Never to Forget: The Story of the Warsaw Ghetto*, with William Gropper.   New York, Book League of the Jewish People Fraternal Order, 1946.
*Tito and His People.*   Winnipeg, Manitoba, Contemporary Publishers, 1948.
*Literature and Reality.*   New York, International Publishers, 1950.
*Peekskill, U.S.A.: A Personal Experience.*   New York, Civil Rights Congress, and London, International Publishing Company, 1951.
*The Passion of Sacco and Vanzetti: A New England Legend.*   New York, Blue Heron Press, 1953; London, Lane, 1954.
*The Naked God: The Writer and the Communist Party.*   New York, Praeger, 1957; London, Bodley Head, 1958.
*The Howard Fast Reader.*   New York, Crown, 1960.
*The Jews: Story of a People.*   New York, Dial Press, 1969.

Editor, *The Selected Works of Tom Paine.*   New York, Modern Library, 1946.
Editor, *Best Short Stories of Theodore Dreiser.*   Cleveland, World, 1947.


Manuscript Collection: University of Pennsylvania Library, Philadelphia.

Howard Fast comments:

From the very beginning of my career as a writer, my outlook has been teleological. Since my first work was published at a very early age—my first novel at the age of eighteen —my philosophical position was naturally uncertain and in formation. Yet the seeds were there, and by the end of my first decade as a writer, I had clearly shaped my point of view. In the light of this, both my historical and modern novels (excepting the entertainments I have written under the name of Cunningham) were conceived as parables and executed as narratives of pace and, hopefully, excitement. I discovered that I had a gift for narrative in the story sense; but I tried never to serve the story, but rather to have it serve my own purpose—a purpose which I attempted in a transcendental sense.

In other words, I was—and am—intrigued by the apparent lunacy of man's experience on earth; but at the same time never accepted a pessimistic conclusion or a mechanical explanation. Thereby, my books were either examinations of moments in history or parables of my own view of history. As a deeply religious person who has always believed that human life is a meaningful part of a meaningful and incredibly wonderful universe, I found myself at every stage in my career a bit out of step with the current literary movement or fashion. I suppose that this could not have been otherwise, and I think I have been the most astounded of any at the vast audiences my work has reached.

Since I also believe that a person's philosophical point of view has little meaning if it is not matched by being and action, I found myself willingly wed to an endless series of unpopular causes, experiences which I feel enriched my writing as much as they depleted other aspects of my life. I might add that the more I have developed the parable as a form of literature, the more convinced I become that truth is better indicated than specified.

All of the above is of course not a critical evaluation of my work; and I feel that a writer is the last person on earth capable of judging his own work as literature with any objectivity. The moment I cease to feel that I am a good writer, I will have to stop writing. And while this may be no loss to literature, it would be a tragic blow to my income.

As for the dozen books I have written under the name of E. V. Cunningham, they are entertainments, for myself primarily and for all others who care to read them. They are also my own small contribution to that wonderful cause of women's liberation. They are all about wise and brave and gallant women, and while they are suspense and mystery stories, they are also parables in their own way.

\*       \*       \*

Howard Fast has written in virtually every genre—novels, plays, poems, filmscripts, critical essays and short stories—and a number of subgenres of fiction, including science fiction, social satire, historical and contemporary novels, spy thrillers and moral allegories. He began publishing novels at the age of eighteen and has kept up a brisk pace of production despite a highly active rôle in leftist politics.

His strongest fictional gifts are a talent for swift, interesting narrative, the vivid portrayal of scenes of action, especially of violence, and an uncluttered style only occasionally marred by sentimental lapses. Although he became identified in the 1940's and '50's as a publicist for the Communist Party line, his novels reveal an intensely emotional and religious nature which eventually clashed with his leftwing allegiances. His ideals and values have reflected a curious compound of slum-culture courage, Judeo-Christian concern for social justice, self-teaching in history, and Cold-War Stalinism. His entire literary career embodies his deepest beliefs, that life has moral significance, that the writer must be socially committed, that literature should take sides.

After two youthful blood-and-thunder romances, Fast found his metier in a series of class-conscious historical novels of the American Revolution. *Conceived in Liberty* exalted the loyalty of the common soldier; *The Unvanquished* celebrated the dogged persistence of

George Washington (despite his aristocracy and wealth, Fast's favorite hero); and *Citizen Tom Paine* exalted that flinty propagandist as the earliest professional revolutionary. Fast then championed anonymous heroes of other races: *The Last Frontier* is a spare but moving account of the heroic flight in 1878 of the Cheyenne Indians to their Powder River home in Wyoming; *Freedom Road* recounts the amazing social experiments of black Southern legislatures in the Reconstruction era. The best-selling of the highly successful novels of the early 40's, *Freedom Road*, shows great power in its scenes of violent conflict but is highly melodramatic and given to simplistic special pleading. By contrast, the poetically evocative *Last Frontier*, perhaps his best novel, enlists profound sympathy through great control and objectivity, and evades the pitfalls of "noble redskin" sentimentality.

In 1946, *The American* detailed the rise and fall of Illinois Governor John Peter Altgeld, who was politically defeated after he pardoned three of the anarchists convicted for allegedly throwing a bomb in Haymarket Square, Chicago, on May 4, 1886. Although Fast's novels had reflected Marxist thought ever since his youthful conversion to socialism, his propagandizing became too obtrusive with *Clarkton* in 1947. This "proletarian strike novel" of life in the Massachusetts textile mills revealed his inability to maintain the necessary distance to interpret contemporary events soundly, and cost him support among critics and readers. He returned in 1948 to the historical novel with *My Glorious Brothers*, a stirring account of the Maccabees and the 30-year Jewish resistance to Greek-Syrian tyranny. This success was duplicated in *Spartacus*, the largely-imagined story of the gladiatorial revolt against Rome in 71 B.C. *Spartacus* was self-published by the author in 1951 after he was blacklisted for Communist activities, and may be the only self-published best-seller in recent publishing history. But, predictably, Fast's other works in the early 1950's were failures in proportion to their nearness to the present day: *The Passion of Sacco and Vanzetti* recounted lyrically but sentimentally the last hours of the doomed Italian anarchists; *Silas Timberman* depicted an academic victim of a McCarthyite witch-hunt; and *The Story of Lola Gregg* described the F.B.I. pursuit and capture of a heroic Communist labor leader. These works of martyred title-heroes, in shackles or on their way to prison, stand as bitter images of their author's own sense of entrapment and isolation (after Fast's release from federal prison in 1950 he was not allowed to leave the country). Not surprisingly, they abound in symbolic Christ-and-Judas figures.

In 1957, Fast startled nearly everyone when he publicly quit the Communist Party and described his tortured apostasy in *The Naked God* that same year. He soon returned to Jewish history as a favored novelistic subject with *Moses, Son of Egypt*, *Agrippa's Daughter*, and *Torquemada*, which also illustrates the dangers of fanatic self-righteousness. He succeeded eloquently twice more with the American Revolution in *April Morning*, which relives 24 hours in the life of 15-year-old Adam Cooper at the Battle of Lexington; and with *The Crossing*, which takes up General Washington's Delaware crossing where *The Unvanquished* had left off. Other historical novels since his apostasy from Communism marked a further re-examination of his earlier themes. *The Winston Affair* deals with the court-martial of an American murderer, homosexual and anti-Semite, and shows how justice wins out in an American military court; while *Power* shows the corruption by power of a John L. Lewis-type of labor leader. These post-Communist reassessments display mature, independent judgment and a new strain of quiet; *Agrippa's Daughter*, for example, rejects the Maccabee-novel's acceptance of "just wars" in favor of the rabbi Hillel's pacifism.

Most readers saw Fast in the 1960's in two new guises, as author of science fiction stories and as writer of Graham Greene-like "entertainments." (Actually, Fast's first short story, published when he was 16, had been science fiction, and in 1952, under the pseudonym Walter Erickson, he had published a spy thriller entitled *The Fallen Angel*.) His later science fiction works include the stories in *Edge of Tomorrow*, *The Hunter and the Trap* and *The General Zapped an Angel*. The dozen or so "entertainments," written under the pseudonym E. V. Cunningham, are each built around such female title characters as *Sylvia*, *Penelope*, *Helen* and *Cynthia*. Both the sci-fi and the thriller books criticize American institutions and values (though usually with a wit and humor lacking in his early works) and all show the deft hand of the professional story-teller at work. Clearly, neither Communism nor the break with Communism crippled his talent, but perhaps politics developed his social vision at the expense of those deeper insights which mark off the major figures of any literature.

—Frank Campenni

---

**FAUST, Irvin.** American. Born in New York City, 11 June 1924. Educated at City College of New York, B.S. 1949; Columbia University, New York, M.A. 1952, D.Ed. 1960. Served in the United States Army, 1943–46. Married Jean Satterthwaite in 1959. Teacher, Manhattanville Junior High School, New York, 1949–53; Guidance Counselor, Lynbrook High School, Long Island, 1956–60. Since 1960, Director of Guidance and Counseling, Garden City High School, Long Island. Taught at Columbia University, Summer 1963. Address: 417 Riverside Drive, New York, New York 10025, U.S.A.

PUBLICATIONS

Novels

   *The Steagle.*  New York, Random House, 1966.
   *The File on Stanley Patton Buchta.*  New York, Random House, 1970.
   *Willy Remembers.*  New York, Arbor House, 1971.

Short Stories

   *Roar Lion Roar and Other Stories.*  New York, Random House, and London, Gollancz, 1965.

Uncollected Short Stories

   "The Dalai Lama of Harlem", in *Sewanee Review* (Tennessee), 1964.
   "The Double Snapper", in *Esquire* (New York), 1965.
   "Operation Buena Vista", in *Paris Review*, 1965.
   "Simon Girty Go Ape", in *Transatlantic Review* (London and New York), 1966.
   "Gary Dis-donc", in *Northwest Review* (Seattle), 1967.

Other

   *Entering Angel's World: A Student-Centered Casebook.* New York, Columbia Teachers College Press, 1963.

Critical Studies: by Richard Kostelanetz in *The New American Arts*, New York, Horizon Press, 1965, in *Tri-Quarterly* (Evanston, Illinois), Winter 1967, and in *On Contemporary Literature*, New York, Avon, 1967; by R. V. Cassill, in *New York Times Book Review*, 29 August 1971.

Irvin Faust comments:

It seems to me that thus far my work has dealt with the displacement and disorganization of Americans in urban life; with their attempt to find adjustments in the glossy attractions of the mass media—movies, radio, t.v., advertising, etc.—and in the image-radiating seductions of our institutions—colleges, sports teams, etc. Very often this "adjustment" is to the "normal" perception a derangement, but perfectly satisfying to my subjects.

Recently my work has moved out to include suburban America and also back in historical directions. My characters to this date have been outside of the white anglo-saxon milieu, but have included Jews, Blacks, Puerto Ricans and the so-called Ethnic Americans.

Both *Roar Lion Roar* and *The Steagle* were published in France (Gallimard) and I feel the reviews were most perceptive, leading me to muse that perhaps, unbeknownst to me, I am quite close to the French literary sensibility.

\*       \*       \*

The name Irvin Faust first appeared in American little magazines in the early sixties above stunning stories that dealt with crazy narrators in New York City; and the accompanying biographical note revealed that Faust, then in his later thirties, had not only received a doctorate in social psychology but he had also authored a book of individual case studies, *Entering Angel's World.* By trade, however, Faust was not a psychologist or even a university professor but a "guidance counselor" at a suburban New York high school, where his major job has been getting the more ambitious students into choice American colleges. His psychology book advocates that the therapist assume "wherever possible, the character and personality" of those with whom he deals, and perhaps the most striking quality of Faust's first collection of stories, *Roar Lion Roar*, is the sheer variety of madnesses apparently *not* the author's own. His narrators include a Puerto Rican boy whose mental existence becomes so entwined with the fate of the Columbia College football team (known as "The Lions") that when they lose to Princeton, he commits suicide; a rather stupid, dreamy fellow who sets out, accompanied by his Sancho, to be the Albert Schweitzer of New York's Central Park; Calvin Coolidge Delaware, a psychopathic egomaniac who regards himself as "The World's Fastest Human"; a fourteen-year-old who takes movies far too seriously and concomitantly suspects he possesses "a magical substance" that makes him immortal; a lonely stockroom boy so pathologically attached to his portable radio that a girl who makes a pass at him must first destroy the radio before she can gain his unobstructed attention. Perhaps the greatest story here, if not one of the masterpieces of recent short fiction, is "Jake Bluffstein and Adolph Hitler", which describes, from the vantage point of an intimate third-person narrator, a mad aging Jew who fondly remembers the time around WWII when Jews found good reason to hate gentiles, who tries to stir anti-gentile sentiment among his neighbors by scribbling late at night the word "JUDE" on the window of his neighborhood butcher, and who comes to believe that all Jews who do not hate gentiles are, like his own rabbi, fundamentally Nazis. In an unforgettable conclusion, Bluffstein imagines himself the messiah of the Jews and then collapses in a psychotic breakdown. The idea of a Jew inventing anti-Semitism, much as the vulgar anti-Semite fabricates imaginary Jews, struck some Jewish-American critics as offensive, needless to say perhaps; and this story was singled out for particularly denunciatory criticism. *Roar Lion Roar* also dealt quite profoundly with various cultural milieus of New York City; and these interests in individual madnesses and urban life would be pursued not only in Faust's subsequent novels, but also in such uncollected stories as the brilliant "Dalai Lama of Harlem", which appeared in *Sewanee Review.*

His first novel, which remains his best, may well be the most perspicacious and sustained portrait of a psychotic breakdown in all novelistic literature. The protagonist of *The Steagle* is Harold Aaron Weissburg, an English professor at a New York City college—ambitious enough to live above his means, yet not particularly devoted to either his work or intellectual pursuits; and the novel relates the fortnight-plus preceding his fall. As in "Jake Bluffstein", which this novel structurally resembles, the theme of incipient breakdown is evident from the fiction's beginning, and the "plot", so to speak, lies in its elaboration to an expected conclusion. However, Weissburg's disintegration is more gradual and various than Bluff-stein's, as well as more sensitively portrayed. Indeed, what is especially impressive is Faust's shrewd and subtle portrayal of a psychotic who, unlike a neurotic (say, Sartre's Roquentin or Mann's Tonio Kroger), is barely aware of his imminent fall; and as a psychotic, Weiss-burg externalizes his fantasies, really believing that he is a movie star named "Bob Hardy" (of the same family as Andy) or a gruff Italian capable of making a stripper fall in love with him. As in "Jake Bluffstein," Faust is also especially adept at rendering with unfailing similitude how an hysterical consciousness distorts the lines between fantasy and reality so that the reader is never fully sure whether certain actions take place in dream or in life; for deeply embedded in Faust's fiction is the psychological truth that the wish can be as significant as the act. Nonetheless, his characterizations are never theoretically mechanical enough to provide "textbook cases", as neither psychological terminology nor conspicuous symbols mar his perceptive descriptions. The deficiencies of *The Steagle* stem from an historical perspective—an increasing preoccupation of Faust's later fiction—that is inade-quately developed, as in the amorphous background is the Cuban Missile Crisis of October, 1962; and certain petty details of characterization—Weissburg seems more of a high school teacher than a college professor—remain unconvincing.

Faust's next project was an historical novel based upon Marinus Willett (1740–1830), a chronic loser who was Mayor of New York City for a year at the beginning of the nineteenth century—he sided with Alexander Hamilton, opposed the development of the steamboat, etc.—but this work has so far remained unfinished. In 1970 appeared *The File on Stanley Patton Buchta* whose protagonist is a fairly sensitive Long-Island WASP who, after serving in Vietnam, decides to become a policeman. Being college-educated and more sophisticated than his colleagues, Buchta is enlisted to become an undercover agent assigned to spy upon both a militant right-wing group and their leftist antagonists. This more "newsy" subject seems to popularize Faust's earlier virtues—the intimate feelings for New York City, the appreciation of ethnic diversity and language, and occasional passages of acute psycho-logical understanding; but just as the plot here is needlessly confused and less credible, so is the style considerably thinner than before. Its successor, *Willy Remembers*, has another Middle-American for its narrator, Willy T. Klienhans, now well into his dotage, whose opening sentences indicate that his recollection is, to say the least, hopelessly scrambled: "Major Bill McKinley was the greatest president I ever lived through. No telling how far he could have gone if Oswald hadn't shot him." This novel is richer in literary excellences than *Stanley Patton Buchta*, and it resembles *The Steagle* in its portrayal of insensitive psychosis. However, though Klienhans, in Faust's portrayal, becomes more imposing than the silly old fool he seems to be at the novel's beginning, he is scarcely as compelling, or resonant, as Weissburg or even Buchta; and the portraiture is extended far too long, sug-gesting perhaps that the material of *Willy Remembers* would have worked better as a short story or a novella. For the while, then, *The Steagle* clearly establishes Faust among the most accomplished psychological novelists today.

—Richard Kostelanetz

---

**FIEDLER, Leslie A(aron).** American. Born in Newark, New Jersey, 8 March 1917. Educated at New York University, B.A. 1938; University of Wisconsin, Madison, M.A. 1939, Ph.D. 1941; Harvard University, Cambridge, Massachusetts (Rockefeller Fellow),

1946–47. Served from Ensign to Lieutenant in the United States Naval Reserve, 1942–46. Married Margaret Ann Shipley in 1939; has six children. Assistant Professor, 1947–48, Associate Professor, 1948–52, Professor of English, 1953–64, and Chairman of the Department of English, 1954–56, Montana State University, Missoula. Since 1965, Professor of English, State University of New York at Buffalo. Fulbright Lecturer, University of Rome, 1951–52, University of Bologna and Ca Foscari University, 1952–53, and University of Athens, 1961–62; Gauss Lecturer, Princeton University, New Jersey, 1956–57; Lecturer, University of Sussex, Brighton, and University of Amsterdam, 1967–68; Visiting Professor, University of Vincennes, Paris, 1970–71. Fellow, Indiana University School of Letters, Bloomington, 1953; Associate Fellow, Calhoun College, Yale University, New Haven, Connecticut, 1969. Advisory Editor, *Ramparts* magazine, New York, 1958–61; Literary Adviser, St. Martin's Press, New York, 1958–61. Recipient: *Furioso* poetry prize, 1951; *Kenyon Review* Fellowship, for non-fiction, 1956; National Institute of Arts and Letters grant, 1957; American Council of Learned Societies grant, 1960, 1961; Guggenheim Fellowship, 1970. Address: 154 Morris Avenue, Buffalo, New York 14214, U.S.A.

PUBLICATIONS

Novels

*The Second Stone: A Love Story.* New York, Stein and Day, 1963; London, Heinemann, 1966.
*Back to China.* New York, Stein and Day, 1965.

Short Stories

*Pull Down Vanity and Other Stories.* Philadelphia, Lippincott, 1962; London, Secker and Warburg, 1963.
*The Last Jew in America.* New York, Stein and Day, 1966.
*Nude Croquet and Other Stories.* New York, Stein and Day, 1969; London, Secker and Warburg, 1970.

Other

*An End to Innocence: Essays on Culture and Politics.* Boston, Beacon Press, 1955.
*The Jew in the American Novel.* New York, Herzl Press, 1959.
*Love and Death in the American Novel.* New York, Criterion Books, 1960; London, Secker and Warburg, 1961; revised edition, New York, Stein and Day, 1966; London, Cape, 1967.
*No! In Thunder: Essays on Myth and Literature.* Boston, Beacon Press, 1960.
*The Riddle of Shakespeare's Sonnets.* New York, Basic Books, 1962.
*Waiting for the End.* New York, Stein and Day, 1964; as *Waiting for the End: The American Literary Scene from Hemingway to Baldwin*, London, Cape, 1965.
*The Return of the Vanishing American.* New York, Stein and Day, and London, Cape, 1968.
*Being Busted.* New York, Stein and Day, and London, Secker and Warburg, 1970.
*Collected Essays.* New York, Stein and Day, 1971.
*The Stranger in Shakespeare.* New York, Stein and Day, 1972.

Editor, *The Art of the Essay.* New York, Crowell, 1958; revised edition, 1969.

Editor, *Selections from "The Leaves of Grass"*, by Walt Whitman.  New York, Dell, 1959.

Editor, with J. Vinocur, *The Continuing Debate: Essays on Education*.  New York, St. Martin's Press, 1965.

Editor, with A. Zager, *O Brave New World*.  New York, Dell, 1967.


Leslie A. Fiedler comments:

My chief interest in the field of fiction has always been the exploration of the comic possibilities inherent in the elusive distinctions between races and generations, as well as between East and West, and Europe and America. I have also been deeply concerned with the difficulties of knowing who is one's father, or is not, for that matter. None of this, however, has seemed to me a proper occasion for tears.

\*          \*          \*

There is no doubt that Leslie A. Fiedler aimed from his professional beginnings to be not just a critic but a genuine all-round man-of-letters, publishing not only controversial essays but also poetry and fiction soon after his literary debut; and he has followed all these muses, as well as a powerful one for public speaking, throughout his career. His fiction is, by common consent, less interesting and less original than his criticism (and his poetry even less substantial); and few critics of conscience have ever honored his imaginative work in print. In his opening critical essays, eventually collected as *An End to Innocence*, Fiedler established a knack for controversial argument, full of far-fetched connections and exaggerated remarks, all expressed in equally provocative prose; few since Mencken have provoked so much outrage. Rejecting the simple sentence along with the simplistic idea, Fiedler concocted a robust style composed of long and convoluted clause-compounded sentences riddled by paradoxes, parentheses and charming self-ironies. However, only the tough-minded intelligence behind this forceful style, rather than the characteristic language, informs his fictions, which nonetheless reflect certain ideas in his criticism (which, in turn, sometimes mentions, if not quotes, his fiction!). The key theoretical text is the brilliant title essay opening his second collection, *No! In Thunder*, where Fiedler argues that the great modern writers have responded to ideals, institutions and even people with uncompromised negation —the Melvillian cry of "No! in Thunder" indicating a complete stripping down that reveals inadequacy, deceit, failure and the impossibility of perfection. "The No! in Thunder is never partisan", Fiedler writes, "it infuriates Our Side as well as Theirs, reveals that all Sides are one, insofar as they are all yea-sayers and hence all liars".

The title of his first collection of stories, *Pull Down Vanity*, announces the characteristic strategy of his fiction, for most of the pieces here are shaped around the uncovering of illusory images presented by a person or group; and in this stripping away of human artifice is unveiled another favorite Fiedler theme of universal culpability. Thus, these stories are structured around actions of exposure and embarrassment—a technique admittedly indebted to Nathanael West's *The Day of the Locust* (1939). Thus, should readers come to believe that one of Fiedler's characters might be honest and good, the rug is pulled out before the story is done, leaving that character too sprawled in the fundamental mud. In "Nude Croquet", first published in *Esquire* in 1957, a busty young thing darkens a party's room and then leads a group of middle-aging "intellectuals" in playing croquet in the buff. Not at all uncomfortable, she flaunts her fresh figure, forcing the others to uncover both their masked bodily defects and, then, their spiritual vanities. One has body hair different in color from that on her head, another a withered leg, a third is flat-chested, while on another level one is insanely jealous, another has never completed his projected and much-announced masterpiece, a third has "sold out" to the commercial theater. When the group's slightly older idol collapses from over-exertion and dies of a heart attack, the girl screams a long blast as the lights go on. "Molly-o", Fiedler writes, "confronted them in the classic pose of nakedness surprised, as if she knew for the first time what it meant to be really nude." Discovering one's nudity is, symbolically, recognizing comparable inadequacies and culpability.

Fiedler's first and best novel takes for its unusual subject the demonic attachment of unrelated twins who, once childhood friends, re-encounter each other over a dozen years. One character speaks of "a comedy of confused identities", and these confusions are not only witty, but also difficult to summarize. The novel's protagonist, Clem Stone, is an unsuccessful writer, while his friend is Mark Stone, an eminent TV intellectual and existentialist rabbi. In the past, Clem was named Mark Stone, and the present Mark's last name was Stein. But as the present Mark changed his surname, Clem, overshadowed by the most successful Mark, became known as Mark the second, or Mark Twain. As the historical author Twain's real identity was Samuel Clemens, Stone takes the first name of Clem. The two Stones have always competed for the same goals, and before the novel is over, Clem seduces Mark's pregnant wife. The novel is similarly erudite in its joking, as in one scene Mark pummels his wife with a rolled-up copy of a magazine entitled *Thou*; and he is described, of course, as unable to stop stuttering "I-I-I-I". Long on such literary gags and arch symbols, *The Second Stone* is also short on credible surface and literary importance.

The protagonist of Fiedler's second novel, *Back to China*, is a college teacher in Montana, whose career in some respects parallels Fiedler's own—a Jew from the East teaching in the West, with a reputation for being the most famous radical on campus, the author of several books, a former wartime Japanese interpreter in the Far East; but whereas Fiedler himself has been a father several times over, Baro Finklestone's main problem is that he and his wife are childless. The reason, as we learn through a series of flashbacks, is that Finklestone's life, as well as the book's plot, turned upon a vasectomy, an irreparable voluntary sterilization, that he underwent in China. His reasons for doing this are never made entirely clear—indeed, the act itself is barely credible—and the novel never quite emerges from a mire of absurdities. Indeed, this slide toward preposterousness, which comes from mixing too much realistic, highly detailed, almost pedantic satire with more wholly symbolic fantasy —a mismating of Sinclair Lewis with Franz Kafka—becomes even more pronounced in the three novellas collected as *The Last Jew in America*; and Fiedler's most recent book of fiction, *Nude Croquet*, adds four slighter stories to those previously collected. A more suggestive step comes in *Being Busted*, an autobiographical memoir devoid of proper names, that successfully elevates to imaginative myth not only Fiedler's 1967 arrest on a marijuana-related charge but also his responses to the life-styles of his children; for Fiedler ranks among the few writers of his post-fifty generation to suffer genuine confrontation and rebirth.

If Fiedler the critic is ambitious and original, as well as appreciative of eccentricity, the novelist is rather conventional in style, structure and subject-matter—his own fiction scarcely acknowledging the innovative literature praised in his criticism; and the impact of his recent rebirth has so far been far more intellectual than artistic. A truth of literature's past apparently unremembered in all this effort is that critics as major as Fiedler have rarely produced consequential fiction, try as much as they otherwise might. With his encompassing theme of deflation, Fiedler's fiction suggests that marriage is insufferable, that adultery is inevitable and just as inevitably disappointing; and his fictions deal as well with ambivalent attitudes toward paternity, to slavish obsessions with seduction's ulterior motives, and the terrors of American professors and intellectuals. This rather limited range is, needless to say perhaps, closer to more prosaic writing than to what Fiedler the critic has defined as the great tradition of American imaginative prose.

—Richard Kostelanetz

**FIELDING, Gabriel.** Pseudonym for Alan Gabriel Barnsley. British. Born in Hexham, Northumberland, 25 March 1916. Educated at The Grange, Eastbourne, Sussex; Llangefri County School, Anglesey, Wales; St. Edward's, Oxford; Trinity College, Dublin, B.A. 1940; St. George's Hospital, London; Member of the Royal College of Surgeons, and Licentiate of the Royal College of Physicians, 1941. Served in the Royal Army Medical Corps, 1942–46. Married Edwina Eleanora Cook in 1943; has five children. General Medical Practitioner, Maidstone, Kent, 1946–66. Author-in-Residence, 1966–67, and since 1967 Professor of English, Washington State University, Pullman. Recipient: St. Thomas More Association Gold Medal, 1963; Smith Literary Award, 1963; National Catholic Book Award, 1964. D.Litt., Gonzaga University, Spokane, Washington, 1967. Address: 1811 Monroe, Pullman, Washington 99163, U.S.A.

PUBLICATIONS

Novels

> *Brotherly Love.* London, Hutchinson, 1954.
> *In the Time of Greenbloom.* London, Hutchinson, 1956; New York, Morrow, 1957.
> *Eight Days.* London, Hutchinson, 1958; New York, Morrow, 1959.
> *Through Streets Broad and Narrow.* London, Hutchinson, and New York, Morrow, 1960.
> *The Birthday King.* London, Hutchinson, 1962; New York, Morrow, 1963.
> *Gentlemen in Their Season.* London, Hutchinson, and New York, Morrow, 1966.

Short Stories

> *Collected Short Stories.* London, Hutchinson, and New York, Morrow, 1971.

Verse

> *The Frog Prince and Other Poems.* Aldington, Kent, Hand and Flower Press, 1952.
> *28 Poems.* Aldington, Kent, Hand and Flower Press, 1955.

Manuscript Collection: McMaster University, Hamilton, Ontario.

Critical Studies: interview in *Counterpoint*, edited by Roy Newquist, Chicago, Rand McNally, 1964; *Gabriel Fielding* by Alfred Borrello, New York, Twayne, 1972.

Gabriel Fielding comments:

I am not a prolific writer, writing only where an obsession leads me. So far I have been led through the intricacies of family life in post-Evangelical northern England, to North Africa where the international drinking set settled for a while, to Germany during the Second World War and to England again where a restless post-war world was unsettling the old guard.

My short stories cover much the same ground: the alchemy of childhood, international and domestic misunderstandings and, again, the impact of the New Morality on the old middle and upper middle classes in England.

*    *    *

Fielding's growing reputation as a major serious novelist rests, in the main, on three of his novels—*In the Time of Greenbloom*, *The Birthday King* and *Gentlemen in Their Season*. Throughout these novels, Fielding explores the theme of individual responsibility which has attracted European writers like Camus, Sartre and Hesse, but which has been largely neglected by English novelists.

The narrative of *Greenbloom*, which forms, with *Brotherly Love* and *Through Streets Broad and Narrow*, a trilogy of the Blaydon family, concerns John Blaydon's growth to adolescence through a period of undeserved blame for the death of his friend Victoria Blount. Fielding presents a world devoted to finding sin in the young and innocent as a means of relieving its own sense of guilt. John only escapes acquiescence in a guilt which the world has persuaded him to own, through the intervention of Horat Greenbloom, an eccentric Jewish undergraduate follower of Wittgenstein and Sartre. Greenbloom's sympathetic interest is that of one scapegoat for another; his therapy, which is explicitly existential, subjective and counter-abstractive, is to make John see that the empty categorizations of adult society lead to personal irresponsibility and consequent feelings of guilt which have to be transferred to the innocent and vulnerable for punishment.

The same theme is further explored in *The Birthday King* which chronicles the rise and fall of Nazi Germany through the history of two Jewish brothers, Alfried and Ruprecht Waitzmann, co-directors of a large industrial group. The brothers are contrasted to present contrary reactions to the mechanistic Hitler society. Ruprecht chooses survival at all costs, running the factories on forced labour for the Nazi regime, betraying Alfried but preserving the family inheritance; Alfried, on the other hand, deliberately and ostentatiously ridicules the system, is imprisoned in concentration camp and tortured to be "cured" of his eccentricity. Together, the brothers present the two faces of Jewishness, survival and sacrifice, and through them Fielding explores the extremes of human response to the absurdity of the world. Of all Fielding's novels, *The Birthday King* comes nearest to the work of Camus in its investigation of individual choice in a society dehumanized and wholly objective. Alfried's response is that of the mystic innocent whose honesty makes him rebel against the "rectitudes, mad superstitions and madder certainties" of romantic Nazism; he consciously and literally makes himself the scapegoat which might liberate others from their guilt. Ruprecht's response, which is that of the opportunist, aggressive, shrewd and lucky, is just as "existential" as Alfried's, but takes the form of an unflamboyant endurance which makes him see Alfried's heroism as a luxury: "What difference does it make that he's in a camp when the whole country's a camp?" So Fielding's theme is no simple contrast between the kind of individual choice made in the face of Nazism; rather it is that the *fact* of choosing is important because we are still free to choose. In this, he echoes Sartre's "We were never more free than under the Nazi occupation. The choice that each of us made of his life and his being was a genuine choice because it was made in the presence of death." Both Ruprecht and Alfried make authentic decisions; they are contrasted with characters like the Kommandent, Baron von Hoffbach, Alexandra von Boehling and Herr Grunwald who sleepwalk through the Hitler-time: "They must have been bored for years without ever knowing it and there must have been thousands like them, practically a whole generation."

Boredom provides the focus of analysis in Fielding's latest novel, *Gentlemen in Their Season*, but here it is the less dramatic though no less deadly boredom of marriage and adultery. The novel is, in many ways, more disturbing than either *Greenbloom* or *The Birthday King*; issues no longer look quite as clear-cut and the setting is too proximate to allow the reader to be uninvolved. The action concerns two middle-aged, middle-class men, Randell Coles and Bernard Presage, whose marriages (to a brisk humanist and devout Catholic, respectively) have entered the dark night of aimless stagnation and dishonest intellectualism which is characterized by "clever" parties, self-conscious devotion to the Third Program, unmotivated religious retreats and rigorous partner criticism. Each of them drift into affairs which have disastrous consequences for an uninvolved third party, Hotchkis, who before finishing his sentence for the manslaughter of his wife's lover, breaks from prison to protect his marriage once more and is killed by the police.

Although the scapegoat figure appears, he is not given the centre of the novel. Fielding instead probes into the lives of the bystanders whose guilt causes, and is atoned by, Hotchkis' death; Coles and Presage are the von Hoffbachs and Grunwalds of the novel, somnambulistic puppets of their wives and of their own abstract preconceptions of marriage which prevent them from acting decisively. Hotchkis' night ends by his triumphant decision to break out of prison and force events by his own action. The dark night of Coles and Presage never ends and they remain hollow drifters, unable even to conduct their extra-marital affairs with pleasure or humanity.

Thus in all his major novels, Fielding presents the admonition that we are all, as humans, involved in the total of human activity; a man's choice is a choice for all men. But if this account might seem to imply that Fielding merely dramatizes a "message", the implication must be dispelled. The didactic conclusions drawn by the reader come not from editorial commentary but from the compelling narrative and evocative imagery which support each other so intimately that the novels transcend their parts to become themselves images of ideas which act on the reader directly, rather than merely persuade by explicit argument and apt illustration. Indeed, the texture of Fielding's novels is akin to that of good dramatic poetry; images cluster and iterate to form a depth of reference which sets up unconscious associations with the reader's conscious awareness of plot and character. The movement of his novels strongly recalls symphonic structure in its series of statements, repetitions, modifications and juxtapositions of action and imagery.

It is on grounds of both thematic force and artistic integrity that one must claim for Fielding a position in the forefront of English novelists.

—Frederick Bowers

---

**FOOTE, Shelby.** American. Born in Greenville, Mississippi, 17 November 1916. Educated at the University of North Carolina, Chapel Hill, 1935–37. Served in the United States Army, 1940–44, and Marine Corps, 1944–45. Married Gwyn Rainer in 1956; has two children. Novelist-in-Residence, University of Virginia, Charlottesville, November 1963; Playwright-in-Residence, Arena Stage, Washington, D.C., 1963–64; Writer-in-Residence, Hollins College, Virginia, 1968. Recipient: Guggenheim Fellowship, 1955, 1956, 1957; Ford Fellowship, 1963; Fletcher Pratt Award, for non-fiction, 1964. Address: 542 East Parkway South, Memphis, Tennessee 38104, U.S.A.

PUBLICATIONS

Novels

*Tournament.*  New York, Dial Press, 1949.
*Follow Me Down.*  New York, Dial Press, 1950; London, Hamish Hamilton, 1951.
*Love in a Dry Season.*  New York, Dial Press, 1951.

*Shiloh.*   New York, Dial Press, 1952.
*Jordan County: A Landscape in Narrative.*   New York, Dial Press, 1954.


Play

*Jordan County: A Landscape in the Round* (produced Washington, D.C., 1964).


Other

*The Civil War: A Narrative:*
  I.   *Fort Sumter to Perryville.*   New York, Random House, 1958.
  II.  *Fredericksburg to Meridian.*   New York, Random House, 1963.
  III. *Red River to Appomattox.*   New York, Random House, 1973.


Bibliography: in *Mississippi Quarterly* (State College), October 1971.


Critical Studies: in *South*, edited by Louis D. Rubin Jr., and R. D. Jacobs, New York, Doubleday, 1961; "Shelby Foote Issue" of *Mississippi Quarterly* (State College), October 1971.


*       *       *


Shelby Foote appears to succeed as a historian, not as a novelist; his multi-volume history *The Civil War: A Narrative* shows his ability to best advantage. However, one should remember that his entrée into the literary world came as a promising novelist. While never creating a masterpiece of American Southern fiction, he did publish five novels in a span of six years (1949–54) which show a serious craftsman at work.

Foote experimented with technique. His first novel, *Tournament*, is a character study—approaching biography—with an objective omniscient point of view. His second novel, *Follow Me Down*, takes a single plot but incorporates a multiple point of view. This method is interesting because it allows eight characters—including protagonist and minor characters—to comment in a limited first person viewpoint on their reactions to a violent murder. Foote's third novel, *Love in A Dry Season*, is a *tour de force* in which the author links two separate stories centered on the subject of money by a character who tries and fails to obtain a place in the financial elite of a small delta town. Foote's fourth novel, *Shiloh*, enters the domain of historical fiction as the author recreates that Civil War battle through the eyes of six soldiers from both camps. Unlike the viewers in *Follow Me Down*, these narrators describe different aspects of the three-day confrontation, and only by adroit maneuvering does the author bring the respective narratives into contact. The battle, therefore, becomes the hero of the novel. Foote's last novel, *Jordan County*, is a collection of seven tales or episodes ranging from 1950 backward to 1797. In each case the locale is Bristol, Jordan County, Mississippi. As his previous novel focused on a single battle, so this chronicles human drama of a fictional area, which becomes the only constant in a world of flux.

With the exception of his historical novel, all of Foote's novels are located in his microcosm, the delta country around Lake Jordan. This fictive locale includes two counties, Issawamba and Jordan, Solitaire Plantation, and the town of Bristol on the Mississippi River. Through a habit of cross reference, Foote links episodes from one novel to another. For instance, the novella "Pillar of Fire" (*Jordan County*) relates the story of Isaac Jameson, founder of Solitaire Plantation and a patriarch of the delta, while *Tournament*, the earliest novel, supplies information about the man, Hugh Bart, who brought Solitaire back from devastation by war and reconstruction.

Foote's use of setting, as well as style, subject matter, themes, and characterization, invites comparison with his geographical neighbor, Faulkner, but Foote's accomplishments suffer thereby. Foote is competent, not great. Normally his style is simple, lean, and direct; it seldom takes on richly suggestive qualities. Most of his themes move in the negative, anti-social direction: violence instead of peace; lust rather than love; avarice, power, and pride instead of self-sacrifice; and loneliness rather than participation in community. At his best Foote deals effectively with dramatic situations and characterizations, for example, the concatenation of episodes in the life of Hugh Bart or Luther Eustis' murder (*Follow Me Down*); however, Harley Drew's career (*Love In A Dry Season*) of lust and avarice seems an exploitation of violence rather than art. In general, Foote chronicles events in the realistic tradition without conveying a larger insight than the particular. Foote's method is a competent beginning beyond which he must go in order to achieve a significant place in Southern literature.

—Anderson Clark

**FORD, Jesse Hill (Jr.).** American. Born in Troy, Alabama, 28 December 1928. Educated at Vanderbilt University, Nashville, Tennessee, B.A. 1951; University of Florida, Gainesville, M.A. 1955; University of Oslo (Fulbright Fellow), 1961. Served in the United States Navy, in the Far East, 1951–53. Married Sally Davis in 1951; has four children. Reporter, *Nashville Tennesseean*, 1950–51; Editorial News Writer, University of Florida, Gainesville, 1953–55; Medical News Writer, Tennessee Medical Association, Nashville, 1955–56; Public Relations Executive, American Medical Association, Chicago, 1956–57. Fellow, Center for Advanced Study, Wesleyan University, Middletown, Connecticut, 1965. Chairman, National Library Week, Tennessee, 1968. Founder, Yellow Rose Productions, Los Angeles, 1969. Trustee, Reelfoot Regional Libraries, Tennessee. Recipient: *Atlantic* "Firsts" Awards, 1959; Guggenheim Fellowship, 1966. D.Litt., Lambuth College, Jackson, Tennessee, 1966. Address: Canterfield Farm, Route 3, Humboldt, Tennessee 38343, U.S.A.

PUBLICATIONS

Novels

    *Mountains of Gilead.* Boston, Little Brown, 1961.
    *The Liberation of Lord Byron Jones.* Boston, Little Brown, 1965; London, Bodley Head, 1966.
    *The Feast of Saint Barnabas.* Boston, Little Brown, 1969.

Short Stories

    *Fishes, Birds and Sons of Men: Stories.* Boston, Little Brown, 1967; London, Bodley Head, 1968.

Plays

The Conversion of Buster Drumwright: The Television and Stage Scripts.  Nashville,
Tennessee, Vanderbilt University Press, 1964.

Screenplay: The Liberation of L. B. Jones, 1969.

*        *        *

One generation removed from the modern Southern Renaissance, Jesse Hill Ford has
begun to establish his legitimate place in that literary heritage. He has shown ability to
treat universal themes embodied in the subjects—people, attitudes, events—of a particular
geographical region, the American South. The greater portion of Ford's work—including
two novels, The Liberation of Lord Byron Jones and Mountains of Gilead, and several short
stories collected in Fishes, Birds and Sons of Men—is set in the author's fictional twentieth-
century microcosm, Somerton, Sligo County, Tennessee. Through the continuity of locale
and the cross reference to particularly prominent families and community events, the
reader of Ford's fiction absorbs one writer's observation of the diversified southern consciousness.

Ford's observation covers an impressive range of themes. For example, the theme of
innocence to experience has several dimensions. Simple childhood reminiscences in "The
Cave" and "The Cow" respectively lead a child to intuit the fact of evil and of death, although
the child can not articulate these experiences. In another short story, "A Strange Sky,"
Ford deals directly with the effects of this progression to experience in the life of his adult
protagonist, Patsy Jo. She examines her past life, especially the seduction and manipulation
by her irresponsible childhood lover, who has continually postponed marriage. Now past
her marriageable prime, Patsy Jo reaches a point of maturity by severing her relationship
as mistress. In the hunting story, "Savage Sound," the same theme is used differently. The
protagonist does not move from innocence to experience; rather, he is responsible for teaching his young whippets to kill rabbits and, thereby, for changing the dogs' loving natures
to that of vicious predators.

Violence as a theme pervades all of Ford's fiction. A catalogue of physical violence includes assault and battery, automobile wrecks, arson, rape, adultery, rusty coat hanger
abortion, castration, cattle-prodding humans, drowning, man-slaughter in self-defense, pre-
meditated murder, and even a bizarre homicide effected by the chomping jaws of a hay
bailing machine. Psychological violence, often a concomitant of the physical, makes
Ford's characters also an emotionally mangled humanity. Both facets of violence show
that in Ford's chaotic world ego-centric modern man chooses to satisfy his own desires at
the expense of his fellowman.

The violence in Ford's fiction is often an adjunct of the revenge theme. His drama, The
Conversion of Buster Drumwright, produced first as a television play and later expanded
for the stage, links murder, a desire for blood revenge, and religion. Ford's plot functions
in such a way as to discredit the impulse toward revenge and sanction the worth, if not the
authenticity, of the Christian message of repentance, forgiveness, and salvation. Mountains
of Gilead, Ford's first novel, artistically uneven, offers a perceptive characterization of a
Southern father caught in the dilemma of avenging his daughter's violated honor while
remembering the unhappy consequences of his own early marital infidelity. That the father
follows the code of revenge, despite his own moral inconsistency, allows the plot to resolve
—after a blood bath, suicide, and time interval—in a melodramatic reunion and marriage
of the estranged youthful lovers.

Another significant theme is racial injustice, prejudice, and discrimination in Ford's
South. The short story "Bitter Bread" recounts the agony and humiliation of a black man
whose wife dies in a hospital corridor because they have no money for admission. Ford
continues this theme of racial injustice in his second novel, The Liberation of Lord Byron

*Jones.* Somerton's respectable black mortician, L. B. Jones, in seeking a divorce from his young, promiscuous wife, precipitates his own violent "liberation," his murder by the white policeman involved in the miscegenous affair. Jones is a believably tragic character as well as a representative of the oppressed southern Negro. Other characters—with varying degrees of success—demonstrate typical attitudes including that of White Citizens' agitator, socially conservative and moderate whites, and simple and militant blacks. Ford takes another viewpoint in the third novel, *The Feast of Saint Barnabas*, by focusing on the forces operating in a southern racial riot. He shows a rich black man manipulating the violent elements in the community for selfish gains. While this novel contains plenty of action, it lacks dimensions of characterization and even psychological suffering which underscore themes of the two earlier impressive works.

As an imaginative craftsman, Ford writes especially well in the short story genre. In this particular genre, in contrast to a drift in his longer works toward the melodramatic or the maudlin, Ford welds dramatic action, effective characterization, and vivid imagery into a thematic unity. His talents in the short story are in the best of Southern Renaissance literary tradition. His narration is simple; his style is clear and direct. In the shorter pieces he handles point of view with strict control, and while *The Liberation* offers a multiple point of view, Ford uses his short story technique of control from section to section. Of primary importance are his vivid eye for details, which often function both literally and symbolically, and his fine ear for dialogue. His sense of humor moves from the rockingly jovial to the grimly ironic, and his best characters possess the complexity and vitality of a gifted artist's imagination.

—Anderson Clark

---

**FOWLES, John.** British. Born in Leigh-on-Sea, Essex, 31 March 1926. Educated at Bedford School; New College, Oxford, B.A. (honours) in French 1950. Served in the Royal Marines. Married Elizabeth Whitton in 1954. Recipient: P.E.N. Silver Pen Award, 1969; Smith Literary Award, 1970. Lives in Lyme Regis, Dorset. Address: c/o Jonathan Cape Ltd., 30 Bedford Square, London W.C.1, England.

PUBLICATIONS

Novels

*The Collector.* London, Cape, and Boston, Little Brown, 1958.
*The Magus.* London, Cape, and Boston, Little Brown, 1966.
*The French Lieutenant's Woman.* London, Cape, and Boston, Little Brown, 1969.

Other

*The Aristos: A Self-Portrait in Ideas.* Boston, Little Brown, 1964; London, Cape, 1965.

*    *    *

John Fowles is a highly manipulative novelist. In all his fiction, situations are carefully contrived, myth and artifice are worked in smoothly to contemporary stories, and the texture is thick with allusions to literature, history, painting, and the decorative arts. Part of the pleasure in reading Fowles's work inheres in appreciating a highly sophisticated detective process, a piecing together of clues and references that carry a thematic meaning. Particularly in *The French Lieutenant's Woman*, the manipulation is so open, so immediately recognizable, full of parodies of old novelistic devices and acknowledgments of deliberate authorial arrangement, that the effect is not to limit or rigidify experience, but, rather, to demonstrate that the novelist is always aware of all the tricks, devices, and correspondences necessary to enable him to convey anything at all meaningful about experience.

The purpose of the manipulation varies somewhat. In *The Collector*, Fowles probes psychologically, attempting to demonstrate what it is in a young man that causes him to want to collect, imprison, and dissect the girl he thinks he loves. *The Magus* extends the dimensions of Fowles's concern, dealing with mystery and magic in a complicated series of elaborate theatricals devised to enchant, enslave, and instruct a young Englishman who has taken a teaching job on a Greek Island. The lines between reality and fabrication, between past and present, and between myth and verifiable history are never certain or clear, for the novelist depicts a world in which we never know how responsible we are for the fantasies others seem to impose upon us. In *The French Lieutenant's Woman*, Fowles uses an apparently Victorian story as the basic narrative of his novel. Yet the reader is constantly led to question what "Victorian" means, to recognize the frequent use of anachronism, parody, research, and quotations from Marx, Darwin, Victorian sociological reports, Tennyson, and Arnold as various means of demonstrating the conditional nature of time and history. Only in acknowledging the perspective of the present, the necessary boundaries in time and space of the creator of the novel, can the author even begin to focus, with any depth or meaning, on the nature of the past. Fowles manipulates numerous literary, historical, and artistic allusions and devices to show what of his story is of the past, what of the present, and what indeterminate. For Fowles, history is always a subject that includes much of the time and perspective of the historian. The novel also has three endings, not simply as a series of tricks, but as a demonstration that three different possible resolutions, each characterizing a different possible perspective itself historically definable toward the events of the novel, could be thoroughly consistent with the issues and characters Fowles has set in motion. The open-ness creates an atmosphere of complexity and relevance, not one of indecision or arid prestidigitation.

*The French Lieutenant's Woman* is also the story of a Victorian enigma, the independent, isolated and passionate woman, enigmatic because she possesses just those qualities her own limited point in time and space is least equipped to understand. The author, with self-deprecation, acknowledges that he may be simply transferring his own inabilities to understand the enigmatic female into the safety of an historically locatable story. Fowles's novels characteristically deal with this theme, with all the rational and manipulative means the male uses to try to understand and control the amorphous and enigmatic female. The male is always limited, his formulations and understandings only partial. And in his frustration, the necessity that he operate in a world where his knowledge is only partial, he acts so as to capture (*The Collector*), desert (*The Magus*), or betray (*The French Lieutenant's Woman*) the female he can only dimly comprehend. Fowles treats this constant theme with growing insight, sympathy, and intelligence, as well as with a fascinating density of sociological, historical, and psychological observation. And the theme itself, metaphorically expandable, always asking how and what man can know of his experience, justifies the manipulation as the mirror of human effort.

—James Gindin

**FRAME, Janet.**   New Zealander.   Born in Dunedin, 28 August 1924. Educated at Oamaru North School; Waitaki Girls' High School; Otago University Teachers Training College, Dunedin. Recipient: Church Memorial Award, 1951, 1954; New Zealand Literary Fund Award, 1960; New Zealand Scholarship in Letters, 1964; Robert Burns Fellowship, Otago University, 1965. Address: c/o Brandt and Brandt, 101 Park Avenue, New York, New York 10017, U.S.A.

PUBLICATIONS

Novels

> *Owls Do Cry.*   Christchurch, Pegasus Press, 1957; New York, Braziller, 1960; London, W. H. Allen, 1961.
> *Faces in the Water.*   Christchurch, Pegasus Press, and New York, Braziller, 1961; London, W. H. Allen, 1962.
> *The Edge of the Alphabet.*   Christchurch, Pegasus Press, New York, Braziller, and London, W. H. Allen, 1962.
> *Scented Gardens for the Blind.*   Christchurch, Pegasus Press, and London, W. H. Allen 1963; New York, Braziller, 1964.
> *The Adaptable Man.*   Christchurch, Pegasus Press, New York, Braziller, and London, W. H. Allen, 1965.
> *A State of Siege.*   New York, Braziller, 1966; London, W. H. Allen, 1967.
> *The Rainbirds.*   London, W. H. Allen, 1968; as *Yellow Flowers in the Antipodean Room*, New York, Braziller, 1969.
> *Intensive Care.*   New York, Braziller, 1970; London, W. H. Allen, 1971.

Short Stories

> *The Lagoon: Stories.*   Christchurch, Pegasus Press, 1951; revised edition, as *The Lagoon and Other Stories*, 1961.
> *The Reservoir: Stories and Sketches, and Snowman, Snowman: Fables and Fantasies.* New York, Braziller, 1963.
> *The Reservoir and Other Stories.*   Christchurch, Pegasus Press, and London, W. H. Allen, 1966.

Verse

> *The Pocket Mirror: Poems.*   New York, Braziller, and London, W. H. Allen, 1967.

Other

> *Mona Minim and the Smell of the Sun* (juvenile).   New York, Braziller, 1969.

*      *      *

"All dreams," Janet Frame writes in her 1970 novel *Intensive Care*, "lead back to the nightmare garden." And all nightmares lead circuitously into truth. In all her novels, the looming threat of disorder, violent and disrupting, persistently attracts those that it frightens, for it proves more fertile, more imaginatively stimulating, more genuine, and more real than the too-familiar world of daily normality. The tension between safety and danger recurs as her characters—voyaging into strange geographies (like the epileptic Toby Withers in *The Edge of the Alphabet*), or madness (like Daphne in *Owls Do Cry*, or Istina Mavet in *Faces in the Water*), or other people's identities (like Ed Glace in *Scented Gardens for the Blind*), or mirrors (like Vic in *The Adaptable Man*), or death (like Godfrey Rainbird in *The Rainbirds*)—discover both the mental debilitation that the safe state, in oxymoronic creativity, engenders, and the disembodying that danger contrives. The opening of *Faces in the Water* demonstrates the author's thematic density and sardonic touch:

> They have said that we owe allegiance to Safety, that he is our Red-Cross God who will provide us with ointment and . . . remove the foreign ideas, the glass beads of fantasy, the bent hair-pins of unreason embedded in our minds. On all the doors which lead to and from the world they have posted warning notices and lists of safety measures to be taken in extreme emergency. . . . Never sleep in the snow. Hide the scissors. Beware of strangers. . . . But for the final day . . . they have no slogan. The streets throng with people who panic, looking to the left and the right, covering the scissors, sucking poison from a wound they cannot find, judging their time from the sun's position in the sky when the sun itself has melted and trickles down the ridges of darkness into the hollows of evaporated seas.

Nightmares and madness, the education in the nature of Apocalypse and survival, become not mere metaphors of sanity, but direct training in the reactivation of the mind's perceiving eyes.

By "shipwrecking" oneself in mad geographies, however (Miss Frame speaks in one novel of "an affliction of dream called Overseas", a brilliant adaptation of a recurrent New Zealand metaphor—as in another she observes that OUT is in man, is what he fears, "like the sea"), one places oneself on "the edge of the alphabet", in possession perhaps of insight, but no longer capable of communicating with the people who stay within regulated boundaries. Malfred Signal, in Janet Frame's weakest novel, *A State of Siege*, for example, leaves her old self to live on an island and to find the perspectives of "the room two inches behind the eyes". What she discovers, when the elements besiege her, is fear, but all she can do then is silently utter the strange new language—

> *O in ambertime*
> *cloudprime*
> *who and done*
> *whone, whone*

—that she clutches, alone, into seacalm and death. Like Ed Glace in *Scented Gardens*, who researches the history of the surname *Strang* and (discovering *Strong*, *Strange*, and *Danger* along the way) wonders if people are merely anagrams, Malfred lives in a mad mirror world of intensely focused perception that anagrammatic Joycean punning—distorting day-to-day language—tries to render. As *Owls Do Cry* had earlier specified, in the shallow suburban character of Chicks, the "safe" world deals in language, too, as a defence against upset, hiding in the familiarity of conventional clichés and tired similes. What the brilliant punning passages of *The Rainbirds* show is what the title poem of *The Pocket Mirror* implies: that convention will not show ordinary men the "bars of darkness" that are optically contained within the "facts of light"; "To undeceive the sight a detached instrument like a mirror is necessary." Or her narratives. But even that vantage point is fraught with deceit. Superstition, like convention, and Platonic forms, like safe order, can all interfere with true interpenetration with "actuality". And to find the live language—the "death-free zone" of Thora Pattern, in *Edge of the Alphabet—as a novelist inevitably dealing with day-to-day words* becomes an increasingly difficult task the stronger the visionary sense of apocalypse and the deeper the commitment to the introspective richness and creative power of the individual mind on its own.

There are passages in Frame that are reminiscent of Doris Lessing—like the apocalyptic scenes of *Scented Gardens* and *Intensive Care*, the one anticipating the atomic destruction of Britain and the birth of a new language, the other observing the destruction of animals in Waipori City (the computerized enactment of the Human Delineation Act which will identify the strong normal law-abiding "humans" and methodically, prophylactically, eliminate the rest), and the ironic intensification of a vegetable human consciousness. In the earlier novel, particularly, the author emphasizes the relationship between the "safety dance of speech" and a kind of Coleridgean death-in-life, and that between winter (the gardenless season) and madness, life-in-death, "Open Day in the factory of the mind". *The Rainbirds*, the writer's gentlest, most comic (however hauntingly, macabrely, relentlessly discommoding) book, takes up the metaphor in its story of a man *pronounced* dead after a car accident. Though Godfrey Rainbird lives, the official pronouncement, the conventional language, the public utterance, takes precedence over the individual spiritual actuality, depriving him of his job, his children, public acceptance, and so on. Indeed, he only becomes acceptable when he has "died" a second time, when his story is sufficiently distanced into legend and into the past to become a tourist attraction. But if you visit the grave in the winter, Janet Frame adds, you must create the summer flowers within yourself. Summer gardens are openly available even to the spiritually blind; winter gardens are not. Her quiet acceptance, however, of that (mad, winter) power to change seasons within the mind expresses her most optimistic regard of humanity.

*Intensive Care* more broodingly evokes the same theme and provokingly points out the difference between the hospitalization of the body and the intensive care required to keep the mind truly alive. When the second world war is long over and the computer mentality takes over after the next impersonal War, all fructifying abnormality seems doomed; Deciding Day will destroy that which is not *named* human. Through the sharp memory of the supposedly dull Milly Galbraith, who is one of the few to appreciate an ancient surviving pear-tree, and the damningly conciliatory (and then expiatory) attitudes of Colin Monk, who goes along with the system, valuing Milly too late to save her, the apocalyptic days of Waipori City are told. Behind them both looms the mythical presence of Colin's twin Sandy, the Reconstructed Man, made of metal and transplanted parts, who is also the Rekinstruckdead Man, a promise of technological finesse and an accompanying sacrifice of man's animal warmth and spiritual being. Milly is exterminated; Sandy is myth; Colin, declared human, breathes:

I was safe. I had won.

I had lost. I began losing the first day, when the news of the Act came to me and I signed the oath of agreement. Why of course, I said, I'll do anything you ask, naturally, it's the only way, the only solution, as I see it, to an impossible situation, as if situations needed solving, I mean, looked at objectively, as it must be seen to be . . .

The skimming words and phrases that need leave no footprints; one might never have been there, but one had spoken; and the black water lay undisturbed beneath the ice; and not a blade of grass quivered or a dead leaf whispered; a race of words had lived and died and left no relic of their civilization.

As it must be seen to be, looked at objectively . . .

The ironies multiply around each other. Language reasserts its fluid focus; the Society for the Prevention of Cruelty to Vegetation plants new pear trees on the Livingstone estate; the computer (not having been programmed for nostalgia) fails to account for the new enthusiasm for old abnormalities; and the Sleep Days cannot erase the time of the fires from the mind of Colin Monk. The mind survives. That her commitment to the spiritual independence of such perception is made so provocative is a tribute to Janet Frame's arresting skill with images. She has an uncanny ability to arouse the diverse sensibilities of shifting moods and to entangle in language the worldless truths of her inner eye.

—W. H. New

---

**FRAYN, Michael.** British. Born in London, 8 September 1933. Educated at Kingston Grammar School, Surrey; Emmanuel College, Cambridge, B.A. 1957. Served in the Royal Artillery and Intelligence Corps, 1952–54. Married Gillian Palmer in 1960; has three children. Reporter, 1957–59, and Columnist, 1959–62, *The Guardian*, Manchester and London; Columnist, *The Observer*, London, 1962–68. Recipient: Maugham Award, 1966; Hawthornden Prize, 1967; National Press Award, 1970. Address: c/o Elaine Greene Ltd., 42 Great Russell Street, London, W.C.1, England.

PUBLICATIONS

Novels

*The Tin Men*. London, Collins, 1965; Boston, Little Brown, 1966.
*The Russian Interpreter*. London, Collins, and New York, Viking Press, 1966.
*Towards the End of the Morning*. London, Collins, 1967; as *Against Entropy*, New York, Viking Press, 1967.
*A Very Private Life*. London, Collins, and New York, Viking Press, 1968.

Plays

*The Two of Us* (produced London, 1970). London, Fontana, 1970.
*The Sandboy* (produced London, 1971).

Has written plays for BBC Television.

Other

*The Day of the Dog* (*Guardian* columns). London, Collins, 1962; New York, Doubleday, 1963.
*The Book of Fub* (*Guardian* columns). London, Collins, 1963; as *Never Put Off to Gomorrah*, New York, Pantheon Books, 1964.
*On the Outskirts* (*Observer* columns). London, Collins, 1964.
*At Bay in Gear Street* (*Observer* columns). London, Fontana, 1967.

Editor, *The Best of Beachcomber*, by J. B. Morton. London, Heinemann, 1963.

*       *       *

Two of Frayn's novels, the first and fourth, are highly original, a satire and a futuristic fantasy; the second and third, on the other hand, are conventional. The second, *The Russian*

*Interpreter*, concerns an English research student in Moscow who serves as interpreter for a mysterious businessman (he seeks ordinary Russians for exchange visits), and the pair become involved with a Russian girl. Though Moscow's streets and weather are described, soon the action is moving swiftly. Books are stolen and sought, somebody is tricking somebody, espionage or smuggling is occurring, and we read on eagerly, awaiting explanations. Even when the student is imprisoned, Frayn focuses on his comic efforts to obtain a towel, and the novel remains a good, cheerful read.

The American title of the third novel points to opposing inertia and conformity; the English one, only a little more relevantly, to the subject of being in the mid-thirties (the hero "had spent his youth as one might spend an inheritance, and he had no idea of what he had bought with it"). Frayn's 37-year-old is a Features Editor, worrying about repairs to his Victorian house with West Indian neighbours in S.W.23 and dreaming of escape, hopefully through appearance on a television panel. The plot is vehicle for comedy about a newspaper office, with a few shrewd observations, as when a girl reflects: "She wasn't a girl at all, in any sense that the fashion magazines would recognize. She was just a young female human being, fit only to be someone's cousin or aunt." Some passages suggest Frayn intends more, a fuller study of his hero's marriage and serious focus on the future of newspapers (a cynical, pushful graduate challenges the office's ways), but these are not pursued.

*The Tin Men*, the first book, is about the William Morris Institute of Automation Research and its eccentric scientists. A thin plot-line turns on a new wing, the arrangements for the Queen to open it, and the TV company that plans to finance it. Most of the fun is about computers: the automating of football results because the Director believes "the main object of organised sports and games is to produce a profusion of statistics," the programmed newspaper, which prints the core of familiar stories such as "I Test New Car" and "Child Told Dress Unsuitable by Teacher," and Delphic I, the Ethical Decision Machine, which expresses its moral processes in units called pauls, calvins and moses. Amid clever jokes, Frayn shows anxiety about the dangerous possibilities of computers and the limitations of the men responsible for them.

*A Very Private Life* begins "Once upon a time there will be a little girl called Uncumber." In her world, "inside people" remain all their lives in windowless houses, supplied by tube and tap and using drugs—Pax, Hilarin and Orgasmin—for every experience. In very brief chapters, Frayn explains how life has grown more private, first physically, then through drugs to cope with anger and uncertainty. Dissatisfied Uncumber meets a man through a wrong number on "holovision" and goes to the other side of the world to visit him. The compelling story is part fairy tale, part fantasy, part morality, so that we ask "Is it plausible?" and "What is the moral?" Frayn's inspiration was contemporary America, where he noticed dark glasses used to hide feelings, and city people buying disused farmhouses to be alone in. He touches on penology, longevity, the treatment of personality, but concentrates on technology making possible a new kind of isolation which excludes uncomfortable realities. And Frayn the moralist never dominates Frayn the story-teller.

—Malcolm Page

---

**FREELING, Nicolas.** British. Born in London in 1927. Served in the British military forces. Married Cornelia Termes in 1954; has five children. Worked as a hotel and restaurant cook, throughout Europe, 1945–60. Full-time Writer since 1960. Recipient: English Crime Writers Award, 1964; Grand Prix de Roman Policier, 1964; Edgar Allan Poe Award, 1967. Address: Grandfontaine, 67-Schirmeck, Bas Rhin, France.

PUBLICATIONS

Novels

    *Love in Amsterdam*.  London, Gollancz, and New York, Harper, 1962.
    *Because of the Cats*.  London, Gollancz, 1963; New York, Harper, 1964.
    *Gun Before Butter*.  London, Gollancz, 1963; as *Question of Loyalty*, New York,
      Harper, 1963.
    *Valparaiso* (as F. R. E. Nicholas).  London, Gollancz, 1964; as Nicolas Freeling,
      New York, Harper, 1965.
    *Double Barrel*.  London, Gollancz, and New York, Harper, 1964.
    *Criminal Conversation*.  London, Gollancz, 1965; New York, Harper, 1966.
    *The King of the Rainy Country*.  London, Gollancz, and New York, Harper, 1966.
    *The Dresden Green*.  London, Gollancz, and New York, Harper, 1966.
    *Strike Out Where Not Applicable*.  London, Gollancz, and New York, Harper, 1967.
    *This Is the Castle*.  London, Gollancz, and New York, Harper, 1968.
    *Tsing-Boum*.  London, Hamish Hamilton, 1969; as *Tsing-Boom!*, New York, Harper,
      1970.
    *Over the High Side*.  London, Hamish Hamilton, 1971; as *The Lovely Ladies*, New
      York, Harper, 1971.


Other

    *Kitchen Book*.  London, Hamish Hamilton, and New York, Harper, 1970.
    *Cook Book*.  London, Hamish Hamilton, and New York, Harper, 1971.


Nicolas Freeling comments:

    I am known as a crime novelist, an expression meaningless unless preceded by the word "commercial", meaning one who writes a series on a similar theme purely for entertainment value and to make a living. This describes my activities accurately enough, but not my ideas, nor my ambitions.

    The advantages of this method—to a writer with a large dependent family, like myself, very great—is that the public for crime novels is large, appreciative, faithful, and generous. For this I am extremely grateful. There is a corresponding large disadvantage: that one is held to and bound by a rigid formula. Any originality or variation in theme is severely discouraged by a sharp drop in sales; this rigidity is the enemy of progress and growth. The writer is expected to concentrate exclusively upon telling an entertaining story, which is indeed the first basic element of the novelist's craft, and to introduce elements of mystery and suspense, melodramatic and largely artificial. The crime novelist who attempts art, his natural function and legitimate ambition, is asking for trouble.

    Few commercial crime novelists make the attempt. Most are content to work in purely mechanical fashion, with no artistic or literary pretension whatever. The result is that they receive no critical attention—indeed they need none, for their public rarely bothers with book reviews and has small interest in literary effort—and have small ambition, being content with a commercial operation and financial success.

    It does not seem to me that the "crime" novelist should have such limited and materialistic ambitions.

    Raymond Chandler agreed. He thought that it should be possible to write a crime "entertainment" which would rejoin the main stream of fiction. It would be about basic human themes and predicaments, of which crime, obviously a phenomenon of much social importance, with increasing impact upon the lives of any and all of us, would be the predominant subject, not necessarily the only subject.

I wish to attempt this ambitious design.

So far I have failed, and am not much ashamed because the ambition is high and the technical problems posed very considerable. Only the best European novelists—Stendhal, Dostoievsky, Conrad are the examples which come first to mind—have succeeded, and then often partially or imperfectly. A real human being, when involved in a traumatic situation such as a crime creates, behaves destructively—towards himself, towards society, and towards I may add the structure and coherence of a novel. This creates pitfalls for the novelist, the most obvious being to fall into mere sociological observation, documentary journalism in the interests of veracity. Also the behaviour of a criminal (a man by definition set at odds with his society) raises wide moral, metaphysical and philosophic problems. To disregard these is to write a play with no third act. Many technically accomplished writers dodge ethical problems of right and wrong on the ground of "tolerance" and because their own ethical, not to say religious beliefs are vague, and often because they are frightened to appear unfashionable.

It has become too fashionable to disregard the craftsmanship of form, shape, and rhythm, on the ground that this is mere artificial mechanical contrivance. Such a notion is both immature and superficial: without form there is no art. The public insists, rightly, that a crime novel shall rebound continually in interest and excitement, and shall culminate, that is to say end in a climax.

I intend to keep trying.

*       *       *

*Love in Amsterdam* began Nicolas Freeling's career as a writer of novels which have an almost startling verisimilitude: their dialogue, setting, and action convey a feeling of exact observation at work. Freeling's Van der Valk is a Dutch detective who is human, individual, unorthodox. He has both compassion and a stern compulsion to solve the puzzles that are presented to him. His thoughts as he proceeds in his investigations are shown clearly to us; we share in his intellectual unravelling of problems of human behaviour; and we believe in the reflections and the actions because the characters are real and the locale so effectively re-created. The flavour of Dutch life, the tempo of Amsterdam, the attitudes of the Dutch emerge convincingly in *Love in Amsterdam*; they are consolidated in *Because of the Cats*, an unfolding of the terrifying ruthlessness displayed by a gang of Dutch teenagers, morally corrupted and warped. This story is set partially in a seaside town of about sixty thousand people, half an hour by train from Amsterdam, "a new town, the pride of Dutch building and planning". Here is where Van der Valk displays his intuition, becomes friendly with the local whore, and understands the parents' relations with their children as he probes into their activities. The tempo of the novel is skilfully varied, and the final speeding up comes with an inevitability which holds the reader's horrified attention. The effect of Freeling's narration is heightened by the sceptical comments, the iconoclastic attitude with which he invests his policeman. Van der Valk's humanity gains by his lack of illusion.

*This Is the Castle* showed a deepening in Freeling's powers of characterization. The story revolves around the Swiss menage of a successful novelist, a neurotic yet likeable man, whose tensions and foibles are seen through his own eyes and his wife's. The relationships between the novelist and his wife (to whom he is God), his secretary-mistress, his Spanish servants, his sons and, above all, his teenage daughter are unfolded with skill and sympathy; the visiting publisher and the American journalist arrive in time for a shooting of a macabre kind. This novel explores the blurred edges between the writer's imagination and the real events of his life: it does much to convey the effort of writing, the nervous strain between books, the dangerous seductiveness of the daydream. It moves away from the genre of *roman policier*.

Freeling's next *roman policier*, *Tsing-Boum*, carries on this deeper interest in human nature. The parallel with Simenon's writing becomes clearer, and indeed Van der Valk mentions Maigret twice in this story of the murder of the wife of a dull Dutch sergeant. She is machine-gunned in her dull municipal flat during a television gangster serial. She leaves behind a daughter whose father is unknown, and as Van der Valk investigates he finds himself puzzling out the connections between this Mevrouw Zomerlust and Dien Bien Phu. This allows Nicolas Freeling to explore the French surrender there and the complex aftermath: a case of cowardice, revenge, blackmail, jealousy, violence. The Dutch police Commissaire, older now (and suffering from wounds incurred in an earlier novel), regards his quarry with sympathy as well as severity, and the pathos of the story is effectively built up, with constant reminders of humanity's frailties as well as moments of bravery.

In *Valparaiso* Freeling develops further his uniting of person and place. Into Porquerolles he brings a second rank Parisian film star. Her coming has an explosive effect upon Raymond, who has drifted around the Mediterranean for years, nourishing a dream of crossing the Atlantic in his boat the *Olivia*. The need to refit the *Olivia* tempts Raymond into crime. The story has a seeming inexorability. The slow lazy tempo of life in Porquerolles gives way to an equally Mediterranean urgency, and the narrative tautens as Raymond becomes more deeply enmeshed in the consequences of what seemed a perfect plan for the quick acquisition of the money which would enable him to act out his dream. In *Valparaiso* Nicolas Freeling again shows his Simenon-like capacity to absorb atmosphere, to assess how far it is created by and how much it affects the human beings whose lives he presents in such concentrated description, such revealing action and inaction.

—A. Norman Jeffares

---

**FREEMAN, Gillian.** British. Born in London, 5 December 1929. Educated at the University of Reading, 1949–51, B.A. (honours) in English literature and philosophy 1951. Married Edward Thorpe in 1955; has two children. Copywiter for C. J. Lytle Ltd., London, 1951–52; Schoolteacher in London, 1952–53; Reporter, *North London Observer*, 1953; Literary Secretary to Louis Golding, 1953–55. Address: c/o Curtis Brown Ltd., 13 King Street, London W.C.2, England.

PUBLICATIONS

Novels

The Liberty Man. London, Longman, 1955.
Fall of Innocence. London, Longman, 1956.
Jack Would Be a Gentleman. London, Longman, 1959.
The Leather Boys (as Eliot George). London, Blond, 1961; New York, Guild Press, 1962.
The Campaign. London, Longman, 1963.
The Leader. London, Blond, 1965; Philadelphia, Lippincott, 1966.
The Alabaster Egg. London, Blond, 1970; New York, Viking Press, 1971.

Uncollected Short Stories

"The Souffle", in *Courier* (London and New York), May 1955.

"Pen Friend", in *Woman's Own* (London), December 1957.
"The Changeling", in *London Magazine*, April 1959.
"The Polka (Come Dance with Me)", in *Woman's Own* (London), December 1962.
"Kicks", in *Axle Quarterly* (London), Summer 1963.
"Dear Fred", in *King* (London), June 1965.
"Venus Unobserved", in *Town* (London), July 1967.


Plays

*Pursuit* (produced London, 1969).

Screenplays: *The Leather Boys*, 1961; *Cold Day in the Park*, 1968; *I Want What I
Want*, 1970.


Other

*The Story of Albert Einstein* (juvenile).   London, Vallentine Mitchell, 1960.
*The Undergrowth of Literature* (sociology).   London, Nelson, 1967; New York,
Delacourt Press, 1969.


Manuscript Collection: University of Reading, Berkshire.


Critical Study: in *Don't Never Forget* by Brigid Brophy, London, Cape, 1966.


Gillian Freeman comments:

I have always been concerned with the problems of the individual seen in relation to society
and the personal pressures brought to bear because of moral, political or social conditions
and the inability to conform. This is reflected in all my work to date, although I have never
set out to propound themes, only to tell stories. After seven novels I am able to make my own
retrospective assessment, and I find recurring ideas and links of which I was unconscious
at the time of writing.
   My first six novels are in some way concerned with the class system in England, either as a
main theme (*The Liberty Man, Jack Would Be a Gentleman*) or as part of the background
(*The Leather Boys*). Although the rigid class patterns began to break up soon after the last
war and have changed and shifted, they still retain subtle delineations that I find absorbing.
In *The Liberty Man* there is the direct class confrontation in the love affaire between the
middle-class school teacher and the cockney sailor. In *Fall of Innocence* I was writing about
the sexual taboos of the middle class attacked by an outsider, a young American girl. This
element, the planting of an alien into a tight social structure, reappears constantly in the
novels—atheist Harry into the Church of England parish in *The Campaign*; the Prossers in
*Jack Would Be a Gentleman* from one class area into an elevated one in the same town; the
cross-visiting of Freda and Derek in *The Liberty Man*; and, strongest of all, Hannah in *The
Alabaster Egg*, transplanted from Munich in the 1930's to post-war London. This is the theme
I want to pursue in my next novel, with a heroine from rural England unable to adapt
completely to life in the United States of America. In *Jack Would Be a Gentleman* the theme
is the sudden acquisition of money without the middle or upper-middle class conditioning
which makes it possible to deal with it. *The Campaign* has the background of a seedy seaside
parish, against which the personal problems of a cross section of individuals (all involved

with a fund-raising campaign) are exacerbated; God and Mammon, the permissive society, the Christian ethics. *The Leather Boys* is the story of two working-class boys who have a homosexual affair; *The Leader* explores fascism in a modern democracy, which, on both sides of the Atlantic, throws up a sufficient number of people who are greedy, ruthless, intolerant, bigoted and perverted enough to gravitate towards the extreme right.

Some of these themes reappear in *The Alabaster Egg*, which I consider my best work to date—fascism, homosexuality, the main characters all victims of the prevailing political scenes. This novel deals with Munich in the 1930's, and, with the device of a fictitious diary, finds parallels between Hitler's Germany and Bismarck's reflecting in two love affairs which end in betrayal. I used real as well as imaginary characters, linking fiction and reality closely. The heroine meets Hitler briefly at a party, for instance, and the diarist is a lover of King Ludwig II.

My choice of Einstein for a children's biography—a highly individual man whose life was spent in trying to eliminate frontiers of prejudice—and the thesis of *The Undergrowth of Literature* (the need for fantasy in the sexually disturbed) illustrate my interest in and compassion for those unable to conform to the accepted social mores. To some extent my film writing has also dealt with social and sexual distress, as did my short play, *Pursuit*.

\*       \*       \*

Gillian Freeman's place among ranking contemporary novelists is secured by her consistent and thorough examination of middle-class England as it emerged from post-war austerity in the mid-1950s through to an affluent and increasingly permissive democracy. Her interest in English class patterns is a constant background and one finds that the behaviour of her main characters is dictated by their social conditioning which affects either a need to rebel from conformity, or their reaction against those who cannot conform. She is concerned also with two particular results of an entrenched social background—the tendency towards fascism, and the need for fantasy whether it is political or sexual. This last theme is explored in some of Miss Freeman's work outside her novels.

*The Liberty Man* was her first novel and revealed a direct class confrontation in the love relationship that develops between a middle-class schoolteacher and a Cockney sailor. It is a simple and direct statement of a theme that is to become more complex. The displacement of a person from his familiar social setting to another is discussed again in *Fall of Innocence* where it is a young American girl who is confronted by the rigidity of the English middle-class. And again in *Jack Would Be a Gentleman* in which a couple, through the sudden acquisition of money, attempt to move into a higher social class in the same town, but lack the upper-middle-class terms of reference that would enable them to handle the situation.

*The Leather Boys* (published in 1961 under the pseudonym Eliot George, but since acknowledged) has a separate importance in Gillian Freeman's work. It implies one of her main themes—social conditioning and this time in the working-class which is explored thoroughly and with remarkable sympathy and understanding of the wilfully rootless, jobless and violent products of a class that is losing its basic pinions of family ties and respect for work. And *The Leather Boys* remains, beyond this, one of the very few novels that reveal the spontaneous emergence of homosexual tendencies—spontaneous in that the central characters find their feelings natural, unprovoked by seduction, example or special pleading. Miss Freeman also scripted the less satisfactory film version.

For her next two novels, Gillian Freeman returned, with a perceptible increase of security, to her earlier field, and in *The Campaign* she handles a cross section of individuals all involved in a fund-raising campaign in a seedy seaside parish—which raises problems of ethics and Christianity and recognises the emergence of what was later to be known as the permissive society. *The Leader* is an impressive and disturbing study in fascism. The peculiar power of this novel lies in Miss Freeman's demonstration that the leader, Vincent Pearman, is cool, calculating and rational whereas those who follow him are blinkered and ultimately destructive, through setting their own, often weird or perverted, needs before the Party's wider interest. In this way *The Leader* has a relevance that extends beyond the boundaries of the novel.

Miss Freeman regards *The Alabaster Egg* as her best work to date. And it is certainly ambitious, much wider in range than any previous work. Again the characters are victims of social and political conditions. Hannah, the central character, is displaced from Munich in the 1930s to post-war London and the novel weaves with considerable skill, pictures of Hitler's Germany and Bismarck's Germany as revealed in a diary kept by a homosexual lover of King Ludwig II. But it is the situation of Hannah in London that remains in the memory—a woman displaced not just politically and geographically, but emotionally:

> The desolation, which I nearly always manage to restrain, swept over me . . . the flat, blank knowledge that the middle of my life had gone without any extension of pleasure or love, that I had reached my fifties without the inward flowering I had expected, that instead there was a chill central core . . .

It is possible to over-intellectualise and thus forget that Gillian Freeman remains essentially a story-teller. She presents us with people, engages our interest and we wish to know what happens to them. Her novels have a serious moral charge certainly, but are enlivened by comedy, by drama and by the accuracy of her ear for dialogue. The prose is simple and direct; there are no purple passages, no striving for an effect.

—Roger Baker

---

**FRIEDMAN, Bruce Jay.** American. Born in New York City, 26 April 1930. Educated at the University of Missouri, Columbia, B. Journalism 1951. Served as a Lieutenant in the United States Army, 1951–53. Married Ginger Howard in 1954; has three children. Editorial Director, Magazine Management Company, publishers, New York, 1953–66. Address: 11 Gateway Drive, Great Neck, Long Island, New York, U.S.A.

PUBLICATIONS

Novels

*Stern.* New York, Simon and Schuster, 1962; London, Deutsch, 1963.
*A Mother's Kisses.* New York, Simon and Schuster, 1964; London, Cape, 1965.
*The Dick.* New York, Knopf, 1970; London, Cape, 1971.

Short Stories

*Far from the City of Class and Other Stories.* New York, Frommer-Posmantier, 1963.
*Black Angels.* New York, Simon and Schuster, 1966; London, Cape, 1967.

Plays

*23 Pat O'Brien Movies* (produced New York, 1966).

*Scuba Duba: A Tense Comedy* (produced New York, 1967).   New York, Simon and
   Schuster, 1968.
*A Mother's Kisses*, music by Richard Adler (produced New Haven, Connecticut, 1968).
*Steambath* (produced New York, 1970).


Other

   Editor, *Black Humor*.   New York, Bantam, 1965.

\*      \*      \*

With his first novel, *Stern*, Bruce Jay Friedman established himself as a wildly comic
chronicler of the agonies of the Jewish neurotic, buffeted and flayed by gentile America. He
has followed, diminishingly, with *A Mother's Kisses* and *The Dick*, along with two short
story collections, *Far from the City of Class* and *Black Angels*. He has also authored several
plays (produced off-Broadway), including *Scuba Duba* and *Steambath*. To each of these
genres, Friedman brings unusual gifts for comic simile, the creation of unpredictable dilemmas and a biting sympathy for his trapped characters. He tends to repeat situations, character
types and even favorite images, and he seems inhibited in developing or climaxing the black
humor of his plots.
   The titular hero of *Stern* is a remarkably successful invention, a tall, fearful man with
"pale, flowing hips," who is obsessed with his own cowardice, with a sense of sexual inadequacy and with a deep suspicion that the gentile world waits to do him in. The plot turns
on a trivial incident when an insensitive neighbor calls Stern's wife a Kike and pushes her to
the ground so that the pantsless woman is exposed. Stern's inability to respond lands him,
ulcered and guilt-ridden, in a bizarre rest-home. But everything happens to Stern no matter
where he is: dogs seize his wrists and lead him on forced walks; his mother takes him in the
shower with her; he vomits on trains; trees suddenly die when he acquires property. What
doesn't happen, he fears will: that he will die of frostbite within yards of his home, that his son
will die and he will be unable to cry convincingly, that each time Stern ogles a woman, a
stranger simultaneously retaliates by raping Stern's distant wife.
   In *A Mother's Kisses*, Friedman creates the ne plus ultra of Jewish Momism: sexy, domineering Meg takes her son Joseph to the only college that will admit him—and then she
refuses to leave. In *The Dick*, Kenneth Sussman, public relations man for the homicide bureau,
changes his name to LePeters, tries, like Stern, to save his wife sexually from aggressive
gentiles. In these novels and in his plays and short stories, Friedman basically replays with
variations the themes of *Stern*: violence, sexuality, racism, identity-crises, abnormal family
relationships, the sense of dread developed by the timidly sensitive in a callous, demanding
society. The fantasizing Stern is a Jewish Mitty in a Salingeresque world where solace is found
by protecting children. Friedman's minor characters in all works are charmingly Dickensian,
except when they are wrenched about to deliver endless punch-lines and sight-gags.
   Perhaps the essence of Friedman's haunted heroes is summed up in Stern's sort-of-Jewish
name which suggests also the conflict between his effeminate softness (symbolized by his
fat, ridiculed posterior) and the toughly masculine demeanor required of American he-men.
Stern's attempts to wear that square-jawed mask are as ineffectual as the vengeous punches
he feels obliged to throw.

—Frank Campenni

**FUCHS, Daniel.** American. Born in New York City, 25 June 1909. Educated at Eastern District High School, Brooklyn; City College of New York. Married in 1932; has two children. Taught elementary school, New York, 1930–37. Since 1937, Scriptwriter, Hollywood. Recipient: Academy Award, for screenplay, 1956; National Institute of Arts and Letters grant, 1962. Address: c/o Alfred A. Knopf, Inc., 201 East 50th Street, New York, New York 10022, U.S.A.

PUBLICATIONS

Novels

Summer in Williamsburg. New York, Vanguard Press, 1934; London, Constable, 1935.
Homage to Blenholt. New York, Vanguard Press, and London, Constable, 1936.
Low Company. New York, Vanguard Press, 1937; as Neptune Beach, London, Constable, 1937.
West of the Rockies. New York, Knopf, and London, Secker and Warburg, 1971.

Short Stories

Stories, with others. New York, Farrar Straus, 1956.

Plays

Screenplays: Love Me Or Leave Me, 1955; Panic in the Streets, 1957; Jeanne Eagels, 1957.

*        *        *

Of the young Jewish novelists who came of age in the 1930s, none depicted ghetto life more effectively than Daniel Fuchs, a Brooklyn schoolteacher who produced three novels in four years. Summer in Williamsburg, appearing when Fuchs was twenty-four, was followed by Homage to Blenholt and Low Company. Each is given over more to private neuroses than public disorders; Fuchs touches rarely on politics—and then only to laugh. Even sex provides less motivation than does the obsessive desire for dignity, success, money.

All three are summer novels. Life then is more exposed, emotions more volatile, uncertainty more evident. Fuchs' hunched little people are not symbols or folk heroes enacting tribal myths; they are clamoring, sweating, lower middle-class Jews who have inched from Ellis Island to Brooklyn across the East River's Williamsburg Bridge. There, locked into stifling little rooms, they are torn between Judaism's high principles and life's low facts. Most are natural losers attaining only anxiety and pain. Summer in Williamsburg catches the cosmic absurdity of their lives. Rejecting a linear narrative for a melange of contrapuntal scenes, Fuchs explores the moral choices confronting a dozen Ripple Street eccentrics during eight sweltering, explosive weeks. He focuses most clearly upon a young would-be writer, Philip Hayman, his family and friends. For Philip, at twenty, the summer is a time of choice and exploration. For several of his neighbors it proves life's end.

Even as a new novelist Fuchs opts for cinematic narrative; to avoid undue literary influence, he derives his structure less from Dos Passos' "Camera Eye" than from actual film-editing techniques. Leaning heavily upon dialogue, gesture, and setting, he bridges his imagistic scenes by a quick dissolve at points of greatest stress. Such mechanical cross-patching has its dangers; a sense of incompletion, fragmentary profiles rather than rounded portraits, characters abandoned with emotions exposed not explained, actions left dangling in mid-gesture. Yet his resolve to look anew at people and events too often glazed by familiarity and sentiment enables Fuchs to infuse *Summer in Williamsburg* with a self-sustaining vitality. It remains a hard, convincing montage of a Brooklyn summer.

*Homage to Blenholt* is an even more mocking commentary on the American dream. Here again, amid the airless redbrick tenements, are self-pitying little people shouting, slamming doors, overflowing kitchen and flat to cover fire-escape, sidewalk, and alley. Gleaning dreams from movie and tabloid, they suffer from barren delusions, bad luck, and crushing conditions. The sad-funny narrative is spun of two hectic days in the lives of three young misfits—Max Balkan, Mendel Munves, and Coblenz—who, striving mightily to enrich their lives, only make them more frantic, comic, and pitiable. Yet each, by accepting without whining his inevitable fate, attains a measure of dignity. In Depression America few can expect much more.

*Homage to Blenholt* evoked charges of cynicism, but Fuchs' cynicism is that of the committed moralist or frustrated idealist who doubts man's ability to control his destiny. Life seems a cosmic burlesque comprised equally of the tragic and comic, sublime and ridiculous. With an eye for every reflex and ambiguity, an ear for every sigh, Fuchs shapes nuance, slang, gesture into telling revelations of character; in the process, he deftly fuses Yiddish-English and Brooklyn patois into a vernacular as idiomatic as Hemingway's, as native as Faulkner's or O'Hara's.

*Low Company* is the most somber and violent of the novels. It is also the best constructed, with plotting tighter, incidents more revealing, and characters more fully realized. Intensifying his caricatures, Fuchs moves from sour humor to greed and brutality, and from Williamsburg to Brooklyn's soggy fringe. Neptune Beach (a composite of Brighton Beach and Coney Island) is a marginal world of squalid beach cottages, sand, weeds, and flimsy boardwalk gaiety. Sun-soaked concessions hide a struggling, embittered world verging always on violence and disaster. Its human flotsam have been cast up on the sands by an inability to cope with city complexities. Maimed, brutalized, rejected, the Neptuners here spend three days messing-up their lives. Most damaged is Shubunka, the ugly, fat brothel operator; a childhood fall had bent both legs, heightened his apelike appearance, and rendered him a lonely grotesque. Intelligent, sensitive, and gentle, he arouses in those about him disgust and suspicion. Yet in the confused reader he evokes not only compassion but guilt for misplaced sympathy. Shubunka at least recognizes his own evil, the peculiar justice of his pathetic fate, and his need for atonement.

Thus Fuchs touches notes long sounded by tragic poets, naturalists, and existentialists: the individual discovers little from experience but to exist and endure. He learns that all prayers are to a God indifferent to individual loss and collapse. Before such cosmic indifference, Fuchs insists, man can rely only on what he can grab, steal or find. He himself neither condemns nor judges.

Time has not changed his ideas. *West of the Rockies*, Fuchs' long-awaited fourth novel, is a vigorous, but formless, distillation of three-decades of accumulated movieland impressions. But despite the California locale, his scurrying hyperactives seem as scarred and self-pitying as their older New York cousins; caught up in the same savage ritual (the need to "make it"), they are propelled by similar anxieties and compulsions. Each is a survivor, with a proved ability to claw a limited victory from any defeat.

To Fannie Case's Palm Springs hotel, in the late 1950s, comes high-strung movie queen Adele Hogue, with three small children, a nervous skin disorder, an imperiled career, and a trail of scandals, broken marriages, and operations. In pursuit is a familiar Hollywood pack: her sinking producer, a torch-carrying ex-racketeer, and assorted talent agents. Among the last is Burt Claris, Fuchs' wry observer and commentator. A no-talent ex-athlete, a loser and "grifter," Burt, clinging desperately to the movie crowd's fringe, is now sexually involved with Adele. Also concerned for the actress is ex-rackets muscle man Harry Case; years back he had deserted his wife Fannie for Adele who, at the last moment, had spurned him.

Fuchs' style is still "cinematic," with characters moving forward, speaking, dissolving. Their talk is the hard, stiff jabs of seasoned winners who suddenly find themselves slipping and, fearing the slide, strike out at those nearest. With Burt watching and waiting, Harry and Adele repeatedly cut and slash at each other; moving back and forth between them is Fannie Case, loving and hating them both. Tough, generous Fannie is the classic Hollywood first wife, the one discarded when the ambitious husband, finally hitting it big, goes after a younger woman. Pugnacious Harry Case, a Catskills-rackets veteran with a strong resemblance to Philip Hayman's gangster uncle, Papravel, still lusts for Adele. But, at story's end, Adele and Burt decide that together they can better confront their harsh, tinsel world.

For all its vivid, quick-paced truths, *West of the Rockies* is not vintage Fuchs. Shorter (166 pp.) than his previous novels, with thoughts and deeds summarized rather than acted out, it seems a condensed version of a much longer work, more screenplay synopsis than novel. It hardly matters—Daniel Fuchs, after all, is writing again.

—Ben Siegel

---

**FULLER, Edmund.** American. Born in 1914. Has taught English at Columbia University, New York; Kent School, Connecticut. Address: c/o Random House, Inc., 201 East 50th Street, New York, New York 10022, U.S.A.

PUBLICATIONS

Novels

*A Star Pointed North.* New York, Harper, 1946.
*Brothers Divided.* Indianapolis, Bobbs Merrill, 1951.
*The Corridor.* New York, Random House, and London, Hodder and Stoughton, 1963.
*Flight.* New York, Random House, 1970.

Other

*A Pageant of the Theatre.* New York, Crowell, 1941; revised edition, 1965.
*John Milton.* New York, Harper, 1944; London, Gollancz, 1969.
*George Bernard Shaw: Critic of Western Morale.* New York, Scribner, 1950.
*Vermont: A History of the Green Mountain State.* Montpelier, Vermont, State Board of Education, 1952.
*Tinkers and Genius: The Story of the Yankee Inventors.* New York, Hastings House, 1955.
*Man in Modern Fiction: Some Minority Opinions on Contemporary American Writing.* New York, Random House, 1958.
*Books with Men Behind Them.* New York, Random House, 1962.
*Successful Calamity: A Writer's Follies on a Vermont Farm.* New York, Random House, 1966; London, Gollancz, 1967.
*Commentary on Charles Williams' "All Hallows Eve".* New York, Seabury, 1967.
*God in the White House: The Faiths of the American Presidents*, with D. E. Green. New York, Crown, 1968.

Editor, *Thesaurus of Quotations*.   New York, Crown, 1941.

Editor, *Thesaurus of Anecdotes*.   New York, Crown, 1942.

Editor, *Thesaurus of Epigrams*.   New York, Crown, 1943.

Editor, *Law in Action: An Anthology of the Law in Literature*.   New York, Crown, 1947.

Editor, with Hiram Haydn, *Thesaurus of Book Digests*.   New York, Crown, 1949; London, Arco, 1956.

Editor, *Journey into the Self: Being the Letters, Papers and Journals of Leo Stein*.   New York, Crown, 1950.

Editor, *Mutiny: Being Accounts of Insurrections, Famous and Infamous, on Land and Sea, from the Days of the Caesars to Modern Times*.   New York, Crown, 1953.

Editor, *The Christian Idea of Education*.   New Haven, Connecticut, Yale University Press, and London, Oxford University Press, 2 vols., 1957, 1962.

Editor, *Bullfinch's Mythology: A Modern Abridgement*.   New York, Dell, 1958.

Editor, (*Selections*), by Mark Twain.   New York, Dell, 1958.

Editor, (*Selections*), by Voltaire.   New York, Dell, 1959.

Editor, *Lives of the Noble Greeks: A Selection*, by Plutarch.   New York, Dell, 1959.

Editor, *Lives of the Noble Romans: A Selection*, by Plutarch.   New York, Dell, 1959.

Editor, with Olga Achterhagen, *Four American Novels*.   New York, Harcourt Brace, 1959.

Editor, with Olga Achterhagen, *Four Novels for Adventure*.   New York, Harcourt Brace, 1960.

Editor, with B. J. Thompson, *Four Novels for Appreciation*.   New York, Harcourt Brace, 1960.

Editor, *Five Stories*, by Honoré de Balzac.   New York, Dell, 1960.

Editor, with O. B. Davis, *Four American Biographies*.   New York, Harcourt Brace, 1961.

Editor, with O. B. Davis, *Three World Classics*.   New York, Harcourt Brace, 1963.

Editor, with B. Jo Kinnick, *Adventures in American Literature*.   New York, Harcourt Brace, 1963.

Editor, *The Showing Forth of Christ: Sermons*, by John Donne.   New York, Harper, 1964.

Editor, with O. B. Davis, *The Idea of Man: An Anthology of Literature*.   New York, Harcourt Brace, 1967.

Editor, *Affirmation of God and Man: Writings for Modern Dialogue*.   New York, Association Press, 1967.

Editor, *Poems*, by Henry Wadsworth Longfellow.   New York, Crowell, 1967.

\*       \*       \*

Edmund Fuller argues that "an analysis of the image or doctrine of man inherent in any work must always be a major element in criticism." From this, two convictions follow: first, that "it simply is not possible to express a doctrine about the nature of man without a religious implication," and second, that "for me it is that image of man that is found in the Judeo-Christian tradition, which still primarily influences our moral and ethical thought, and has not become in any way obsolete." To read Fuller's novels is to watch this critical persuasion seek imaginative shape.

Trying not to stack the deck, he makes his protagonists confront the gratuity of suffering, implying always that only love and charity, however imperfect, can make tolerable the random descents of death and hatred. To this end he always incorporates, in a central role, a woman of very refined intuitions, tenacious in the love of those near to her, traditional by and large, but operatively intelligent rather than demure. And he invents spokesmen for positions antagonistic to his benign Christianity; that is, for relativism in sexual values, for aestheticism, for Marxism and for the nihilism of the drug culture. Yet the deck seems stacked, especially as those who carry the load of thoughtful alternatives to Fuller's *Weltanschauung* are invariably either stereotypes or straw-men. Moreover, his work is recurrently discursive and abstract in situations calling for human dialogue. These tendencies have increased in his last two novels and leave one with the feeling that a polemical rather than just an overly thematic preoccupation is diluting his art.

*A Star Pointed North* is the story of Frederick Douglass and shows skillfully the moral uses of his anger, intelligence and hope of freedom. It is compelling for the thoughtful attention Fuller was giving in 1946 to the wrathful core of the slave's servility.

Set against the Depression, *Brothers Divided* delineates the attempts of a minister's sons to live by their idealism. One son embodies a socially conscious Christianity, the other the communism of America's Depression leftists. The first uses his limited talents in achieving what Fuller sees as a balanced manhood, while the second squanders his art on Marxism and his heroism on the Spanish Civil War. If this work is simplistic in its characterization of theatrical people and its evasion of middle-class vices, it is sensitive to the mysterious power of temperament in shaping ideology.

*The Corridor* traces the ruminations of a man as his wife struggles to live after the natural abortion of what would have been their fourth child. He is enabled to put the banality which has been creeping into his marriage into a new perspective and through the near death of his wife see that "the heart perceiving the real abyss, ceases to fear the gully." The novel pursues a strong bias against clinical abortion. It also takes the loss of the child as the consequence of the couple's failure really to plan it. It closes as they intuit after their Christmas Eve love-making that they have just conceived a child by deliberation. Fuller endorses the "intuition."

The main character of *Flight* pursues his fleeing nephew to Venice and discovers in his quest of the unbalanced boy that he is himself running from the deaths of his wife and son. Once there he finds "grace" and the love of a surrogate family. This novel is certainly a reaction to the attitudes and characterizations which sustain Mann's *Death in Venice*. More than any of Fuller's other novels, this one projects contemporary dilemmas against a vast and artistic Christian past, although a basis for this interest had been briefly laid in *Brothers Divided*.

—D. M. Heaton

**FULLER, Roy (Broadbent).** British. Born in Failsworth, Lancashire, 11 February 1912. Educated at private schools; qualified as a solicitor, 1933. Served in the Royal Navy, 1941–46; Lieutenant, Royal Naval Volunteer Reserve. Married Kathleen Smith in 1936; has one son, the poet John Fuller. Assistant Solicitor, 1938–58, Solicitor, 1958–69, and since 1969 Director, Woolwich Equitable Building Society, London. Chairman of the Legal Advisory Panel, 1958–69, and since 1969 Vice-President, Building Societies Association. Chairman of the Poetry Book Society, London, 1960–68. Professor of Poetry, Oxford University, 1968–73. Recipient: Arts Council Poetry Award, 1959; Duff Cooper Memorial Prize, for poetry, 1968; Queen's Gold Medal for Poetry, 1970. Fellow, Royal Society of Literature, 1958. C.B.E. (Companion, Order of the British Empire), 1969. Address: 37 Langton Way, London S.E.3, England.

Publications

Novels

The Second Curtain.   London, Verschoyle, 1953; New York, Macmillan, 1956.
Fantasy and Fugue.   London, Verschoyle, 1954; New York, Macmillan, 1956.
Image of a Society.   London, Deutsch, 1956; New York, Macmillan, 1958.
The Ruined Boys.   London, Deutsch, 1959; as That Distant Afternoon, New York, Macmillan, 1959.
The Father's Comedy.   London, Deutsch, 1961.
The Perfect Fool.   London, Deutsch, 1963.
My Child, My Sister.   London, Deutsch, 1965.
The Carnal Island.   London, Deutsch, 1970.

Verse

Poems.   London, Fortune Press, 1939.
The Middle of a War.   London, Hogarth Press, 1942.
A Lost Season.   London, Hogarth Press, 1944.
Epitaphs and Occasions.   London, Lehmann, 1949.
Counterparts.   London, Verschoyle, 1954.
Brutus's Orchard.   London, Deutsch, 1957; New York, Macmillan, 1958.
Collected Poems, 1936–1961.   London, Deutsch, and Chester Springs, Pennsylvania, Dufour, 1962.
Buff.   London, Deutsch, and Chester Springs, Pennsylvania, Dufour, 1965.
New Poems.   London, Deutsch, and Chester Springs, Pennsylvania, Dufour, 1968.
Off Course.   London, Turret, 1969.

Other

Savage Gold (juvenile).   London, Lehmann, 1946.
With My Little Eye (juvenile).   London, Lehmann, 1948; New York, Macmillan, 1957.
Catspaw (juvenile).   London, Alan Ross, 1966.
Owls and Artificers: Oxford Lectures on Poetry.   London, Deutsch, and New York, Library Press, 1971.
Seen Grandpa Lately? (juvenile).   London, Deutsch, 1972.

Manuscript Collections (verse): State University of New York, Buffalo; British Museum, London.

*       *       *

Roy Fuller is a leading contemporary British poet. He is also a prolific writer of fiction; his production to date includes eight novels, as well as three book-length tales for children. For many poets the novel is in a double sense a sport: a tour de force in an unaccustomed medium written to pass the time when verse is hard to compose. Fuller has committed himself more seriously to fiction. There is not, in his work, any capricious alternation between verse-writing and prose-writing, and the art of the novel has always held for him a particular fascination. He was, long before he began to publish fiction in the 1950s, an ardent student of

Henry James; he was interested in the contributions which the socially conscious crime novelists of the 1930s had made to the wider techniques of fiction; later he was one of a group of English writers, including also Angus Wilson, Walter Allen and George Woodcock, who critically reinstated William Godwin's great novel, *Caleb Williams*, as the true precursor of the modern novel of pursuit and persecution, with its attendant ambiguities.

All these influences can be found reflected in Fuller's own novels which, like his poetry, proceed by a process of refinement from a concern for man in his relationship to society and its demands, to a preoccupation with the narrowing world of the human being who advances out of youth towards age and death.

If one takes an early Fuller novel, like *The Second Curtain*, the whole Godwinian paradox of the individual and his sense of justice, pitted against a society inevitably inhuman, seems to be re-stated in modern terms. Like Caleb Williams, the solitary writer George Garner finds himself involved in a criminal conspiracy. A friend of his dies mysteriously, and Garner is horrified to discover that the very men who are proposing to establish him as editor of a literary magazine are in fact responsible for his friend's death. Their organization, formed to protect wealthy manufacturers against indiscreet inventors who may render their products obsolete, is to be seen as a microcosm of the unregenerate society we inhabit, and Garner becomes the type of the well-intentioned intellectual, anxious to struggle for what is true, but susceptible to fear if not bribery, and, by a positively Godwinian twist, feeling guilty towards those who are his enemies and whom he knows to be evil.

The equivocal relationship between the individual—particularly the intellectual or the artist—and the collectivity is further developed in Fuller's later novels, one of which is significantly entitled *Image of a Society*; the Building Society whose affairs form the background to the shifting relationships of the characters is in fact a metaphorical substitute for society as a whole, containing all its moral sanctions, all its possibilities for tyranny and injustice. In *The Ruined Boys* the collectivity is a private school on the edge of failure, and the spurious loyalties which the Headmaster tries to induce seem to be merely the emanations of more real loyalties that make tenuous but irresistible demands. A further variation of the social frame occurs in *The Father's Comedy*, where the leading figure, a successful and ambitious civil servant, finds his future in "the Authority" (a mysterious corporation which again is an image of society as a whole) threatened by both the past (his own radical youth) and the present (his son's rebellion against a repressive army). It is only in his late novel, *My Child, My Sister*, that Fuller follows in fiction the move he had made in poetry a decade before, and narrows but at the same time widens his focus to embrace the individual and ageing man grappling with his own nature and by the same token with the generalized horror of the human condition.

Of course, that struggle of the individual with himself and with his human destiny had been present in all the novels, and in a sense the social dimension has acted merely as a frame for the moral core of each book, since what the contest with society shows most clearly is the degree of courage, sensitivity and adaptability in the individual. It is in the solitude of his own weakness that George Garner in *The Second Curtain* has to consider his defeat by the evil forces of the Power Industries Protection Corporation. And if, at the end of *The Father's Comedy*, Harold Colmore feels—after he has revealed all the secrets of his left-wing past in order to secure his son's acquittal in a court martial—that he must return "to show himself to the Authority and to Dorothy, to find out what his character and his career had become", the significance of the novel to the reader lies not in what will happen to Colmore's career in the future, but in the fact that in the present he has been able to ignore such possibilities and to commit what may well be a sacrifice of his planned future out of love for his son.

For it is ultimately in the validity of human relationships that the characters of Fuller's novels are tested, and here it is—rather than in any stylistic shaping—that the effects of his early Jamesian enthusiasms may be detected. For the rigid forms of society are complemented by the fragile links that bind human beings in a web of indestructible gossamer, and perhaps Fuller's best achievement as a novelist lies in the restraint and sureness with which he establishes this network of relationships. The relationships may be ambiguous: an elderly man, like Albert Shore in *My Child, My Sister*, feeling sexually stirred by his wife's daughter by a second marriage; Harold Colmore in *The Father's Comedy* clandestinely meeting a girl in whom his conscript son had been interested; Gerald Bracher in *The Ruined Boys* sensing all at once the epicene charms of a younger boy who plays a female part in a school play. Nothing happens in a physical sense; Fuller's novels are almost completely lacking in the scenes of sexual action that figure in so many contemporary novels, and even scenes of violence are rare, petty and dependent on the imperatives of the plot; there is no gratuitous sensationalism of any kind. But the very scantiness of outward action tends to heighten the inward intensity of the relationships.

Almost always, in such relationships, the attraction-repulsion between the young and the ageing is involved, and, as a corollary, the sense in one partner of the loss of a beauty and an innocence that he is trying to regain. It is not merely a sentimental nostalgia that is involved, for often the young seem hardly worthy of the love directed towards them and the person who directs it is at least partly conscious of this fact; the central feeling is rather—less crudely and directly expressed than by the existentialists—of the inexorable progress of every life towards decay.

The tone of Fuller's novels, like the tone of his poetry, is restrained and undramatic; he recognizes that each man to himself is a failure, and it is the inner voice expressing this recognition that he uses. His world is not without fear; indeed, fear pervades it, but it is expressed most often in such forms as anxiety and apprehension. His heroes are of human dimensions, and the whole landscape is that of a normal world which breeds its own terrors, shames and victories without any need to import disaster or false passion from outside. The consequence is that, while so many novels written out of bogus anger in Britain during the 1950s and early 1960s have become as dated as their years of publication, Fuller's have outlived their time, and if they are too muted to survive in detailed memory, they project, on re-reading, an unblurred freshness of tone and sharpness of outline.

—George Woodcock

---

**GADDIS, William.** American. Born in New York City in 1922. Educated at Harvard University, Cambridge, Massachusetts. Recipient: National Institute of Arts and Letters grant, 1963; National Endowment for the Arts grant, 1966. Address: c/o Lantz-Donadio Literary Agency, 111 West 57th Street, New York, New York 10019, U.S.A.

PUBLICATIONS

Novel

*The Recognitions.* New York, Harcourt Brace, 1955; London, MacGibbon and Kee, 1962.

\*     \*     \*

William Gaddis is known as the author of one novel, *The Recognitions*, first published in America in 1955, then in Britain in 1962. It is a long, complicated, and curious book, which was received with outraged hostility by its early reviewers. Since then, however, it has been "rediscovered" with enthusiasm by a number of readers prepared to spend more time in its demanding company. The latest of these, Tony Tanner, devotes several pages of interesting analysis to it in his recent survey of contemporary American fiction, *City of Words* (1971). Dr Tanner does well to direct attention to such an extraordinary text, especially as *The Recognitions* has been generally ignored or neglected in studies of this kind.

The theme of the novel is forgery. Wyatt, the son of an eccentric clergyman, has a gift for painting, but his attitude towards his art has been infected by his Aunt May, his father's father's sister, "a barren steadfast woman, Calvinistically faithful", whose reaction to the boy Wyatt's first drawing is to suggest that the mere fact of its making proves a lack of love for God. "Our Lord is the only true creator, and only sinful people try to emulate him." Wyatt, grown up with a sense of the criminality of art, is tempted by a devil figure, Recktall Brown, to turn his talents to the forging of paintings as by well-known masters. Around these basic events Gaddis weaves a complex web of plot and talk, anecdote, argument, and learned digression. There is much speculation along lines indicated by the Church Fathers, or in heretical opposition to them; there is a good deal of sour satire at the expense of the false and the derivative in the worlds of painting and writing (with a deadly eye, this author can hit off a whole limbo of pretentiousness and awfulness with a phrase in chaotic cocktail-conversation such as, "Oh, Sappho, he was queer, too, wasn't he?"); there is everywhere abundant evidence of an unusually clear and well-read intelligence in the service of a pro-liferating creative energy. James Joyce, Henry James, and the Gide of *Les Faux-Monnayeurs* (1926), along with James Hogg's *The Private Memoirs and Confessions of a Justified Sinner* (1824), provide sensible points of reference or comparison. What Gide said of the latter is true of *The Recognitions* also:

> That a work so singular and so enlightening, so especially fitted to arouse passionate interest, both in those who are attracted by religious and moral questions, and, for quite other reasons in psychologists and artists and above all in surrealists who are so particularly drawn by the demoniac in every shape—how explain that such a work could have failed to become famous?

Perhaps it is the very profundity of Gaddis's achievement that appalls, for at the heart of this giant book—it is nearly a thousand close-packed pages long—lies a seemingly urgent intuition of the improbable nature of reality, expressing in a dozen different ways the feeling that what we perceive as the "real" world is itself quite possibly counterfeit, and that we there-fore somehow plagiarise ourselves by living. It is a formidable idea, but Gaddis shows he has the technique and the seriousness to meet it.

—Robert Nye

---

**GAINES, Ernest J.** American. Born in Oscar, Louisiana, 15 January 1933. Educated at San Francisco State College, 1955–57, B.A. 1957; Stanford University, California, 1958–59. Served in the United States Army, 1953–55. Writer-in-Residence at Denison University, Granville, Ohio, 1971. Recipient: Wallace Stegner Fellowship, 1958; Joseph Henry Jackson Fund grant, 1959; National Endowment for the Arts grant, 1966. Address: 998 Divisadero Street, San Francisco, California 94115, U.S.A.

PUBLICATIONS

Novels

Catherine Carmier.   New York, Atheneum, 1964; London, Secker and Warburg, 1966.
Of Love and Dust.   New York, Dial Press, 1967; London, Secker and Warburg, 1968.
The Autobiography of Miss Jane Pittman.   New York, Dial Press, 1971.

Short Stories

Bloodline.   New York, Dial Press, 1968.

Uncollected Short Stories

"The Turtles", in Transfer (San Francisco), 1956.
"Boy in the Doublebreasted Suit", in Transfer (San Francisco), 1957.
"My Grandpa and the Haint", in New Mexico Quarterly (Albuquerque), Summer 1966.

Ernest J. Gaines comments:

To this date I have written mainly about Black Americans living in the southern part of the United States. Though the places in my stories and novels are imaginary ones, they are based pretty much on the place where I grew up and the surrounding areas where I worked, went to school and travelled as a child. My characters speak the way the people speak in that area. They do the work that the people do there. Since most of my writing is about rural Louisiana, my characters are closely attached to the land.

I do not know that my writing has a specific theme, but I have heard that a recurring theme in my novels and stories is "an attempt (on the part of my characters) to live with courage and dignity under deprivation." That might be a good description of my work. I hope it is; it is such a beautiful description that any writer should be proud of it. I know that my characters are usually poor, mostly uneducated, and almost always very independent. The conflict in which they usually find themselves is *how to live as a man* in that short period of time.

\*     \*     \*

The fictive world of Ernest J. Gaines, as well as certain technical aspects of his works, might be compared to that of William Faulkner. But useful as such a comparison may be, it should not be pursued to the point of obscuring Gaines' considerable originality, which inheres mainly in the fact that he is Afro-American and very much a spiritual product, if no longer a resident, of the somewhat unique region about which he writes: south Louisiana, culturally distinguishable from the state's Anglo-Saxon north, thus from the nation as a whole, by its French legacy, no small part of which derives from the comparative lack of inhibition on the part of its French settlers and their descendants about sexual alliances with blacks.

Gaines' Afro-American perspective enables him to create, among other notable characters both black and white, a Jane Pittman (The Autobiography of Miss Jane Pittman) whose heroic perseverance we experience, rather than a housekeeping Dilsey (The Sound and the Fury) for whom we have little more than the narrator's somewhat ambiguous and irrelevant assurance that "She endured." In general, Gaines' peculiar point of view generates a more complex social vision than Faulkner's, an advantage Gaines has utilized with increasing dramatic force and artistic promise. The society of which he writes consists of whites, blacks, and creoles, a traditionally more "favored" class ("shade" is perhaps more appropriate) of Afro-American given to fantasies of racial superiority of the kind Frantz Fanon explores in *Black Skin, White Masks*, in terms of Martinican society.

The Gainesian counterparts of the Sartorises and Snopeses (the moribund aristocracy and parvenu "poor white trash" of Faulkner's mythical Mississippi county) are the south Louisiana plantation owners, mostly of French extraction, and the cajuns, of French extraction but of lesser "quality". The cajuns are inheriting and spoiling the land; at the same time they are displacing the creoles and blacks, the former tragically though not irrevocably doomed by a persistent folly, the latter a people of promise, mainly because they have never really betrayed the African side of their Afro-American heritage.

All Gaines' works reflect the inherent socio-economic intricacy of this quadruplex humanity, though we are never allowed to lose sight of its basic element of black and white. In the apprentice first novel *Catherine Carmier*, for instance, we see the sickly proscribed love of Jackson, who is black, and Catherine, daughter of an infernally proud creole farmer, as a perverted issue of the miscegenation that resulted from the white male's sexual exploitation of black people. This mode of victimization assumes metaphoric force in Gaines' works, figuring forth in historical perspective the oppression of black people generally. The fictive plantation world, then, is uniquely microcosmic. It is south Louisiana, the south, the nation as a whole. This aspect is explored, for example, in the title story of *Bloodline*. Copper, a character of mythopoeic proportion, the militant young son of a now deceased white plantation owner and a black woman field hand, stages a heroic return, presumably from his education in school and in the world at large, to claim his heritage: recognition of kinship by an aristocratic white uncle and his rightful share of the land.

—Alvin Aubert

---

**GALLANT, Mavis.**   Canadian.   Born in Montreal, 11 August 1922. Address: 14 rue Jean Ferrandi, Paris VI, France.

PUBLICATIONS

Novels

> *Green Water, Green Sky*.   Boston, Houghton Mifflin, 1959; London, Deutsch, 1960.
> *A Fairly Good Time*.   New York, Random House, and London, Heinemann, 1970.

Short Stories

> *The Other Paris*.   Boston, Houghton Mifflin, 1956; London, Deutsch, 1957.
> *My Heart Is Broken: 8 Stories and a Short Novel*.   New York and Toronto, Random House, 1964; as *An Unmarried Man's Summer*, London, Heinemann, 1965.

Has contributed to *The New Yorker* regularly since 1951.

Other

"Things Overlooked Before", an introductory essay to *The Affair of Gabrielle Russier*. New York, Knopf, 1971.

Mavis Gallant comments:

I was born in Montreal. My father was English, my mother German-Rumanian-Breton. My father died when I was still a small child (an only child) and I spent a great deal of time being shifted about here and there and from school to school. I went to seventeen schools in all, beginning with a prison-like French-Canadian convent at the age of four. These schools, all recalled with horror, were in two provinces and two states, Catholic and Protestant, French and English speaking, co-educational and segregated, and this constant shifting and changing made it virtually impossible for me to obtain any education at all.

I have not had "jobs", but have lived entirely on my writing, except for a few years in my twenties when I worked for a newspaper in Montreal. This paper no longer exists.

I live with writing exactly as an architect lives with design or a doctor with medicine. I knew from the beginning that I was a slow writer and would probably not produce much, and I arranged my life around my work. A girl I knew when we were both fifteen in New York told me recently that I had told her then exactly how and where I would live.

Nothing is as obnoxious to me as a writer talking about himself and his aims and theories. These things should be evident in the work (I am talking about serious writers). I have noticed that what interests people is irrelevant. Whenever I have been interviewed I have been asked if I write on a typewriter, if I work in the morning or the afternoon, and how I first sold a story to *The New Yorker*. My answer to the last of these—that I typed a story and sent it in—never seems satisfactory, yet that is all there was to it.

The beginning is easy; what happens next is much harder.

*         *         *

The characters who move through the fiction of Mavis Gallant are unwilling exiles and victims, born or made. Her first collection of short stories, *The Other Paris*, clearly sets the tone of her work: in a series of impersonal, almost clinical sketches the lonely and displaced struggle against an indifferent or hostile world. A naive American girl, engaged to a dull American in Paris, wonders why her colorless days have no connection with the legendary "other Paris" of light and civility; a pathetic American army wife in Germany faces her stale marriage and a rootless future; a bitter, unforgiving set of brothers and sisters gathers after the funeral of their mother, a dingy Roumanian shopkeeper in Montreal; a cow-like Canadian girl with Shirley Temple curls is repeatedly deceived by seedy fiances; a traveler staying in a Madrid tenement watches a petty bureaucrat trying to justify the new order "to which he has devoted his life and in which he must continue to believe." These anti-romantic glimpses of dislocation and despair are rendered in deliberately hard, dry prose, reminiscent, like their subject matter, of Joyce's *Dubliners*. The narrative manner is flat, unadorned, without any relieving touches of wit—or, it seems, compassion (save for the best of the stories, "Going Ashore", in which a sensitive child is dragged from port to port by a desperate, amoral mother). Although there is an admirable consistency of theme and feeling in these stories, and a high degree of professional skill, there is little here to suggest the brilliance of Miss Gallant's later work and her gradual mastery of longer, more demanding fictional forms.

The title of the next collection, *My Heart Is Broken*, reveals a continuation of the same concerns. Yet there is a good deal more vigor here, and an indication as well that the author, if not her characters, may be taking some pleasure in the sharpness of her perceptions. There is also the first clear suggestion of a problem which is to become of major importance in Miss Gallant's later work: the eccentricity and near-madness to which her losers may be driven by want or isolation. Miss Gallant has an appallingly accurate eye for the desperation of the shabby genteel, the Englishwomen who live at the edge of poverty in unfashionable pensions out of season, and a shrewd eye as well for the vulgarities of those who try to keep up the pretense of well being. And there is at least one completely successful story, "An Unmarried Man's Summer", which manages to combine many of the earlier preoccupations with a degree of wit and energy not present before.

Miss Gallant's first experiment with longer fiction, *Green Water, Green Sky*, despite a vivid central section, suffers from an uncertainty of focus. Three of the four parts of the novella offer peripheral views of the breakdown of a young American wife, raised abroad and now living in Paris. The reasons for her drift into madness are never fully explained, although the blame must in part rest with a vain and foolish mother. "It was your fault," Florence thinks of accusing her mother; "I might have been a person, but you made me a foreigner." The sense of withdrawal deepens; Miss Gallant traces with frightening authority the descent into alienation and disorganization. The framing sections of the story, however, are given over to other points of view which are finally inadequate: a young cousin, the mother herself (briefly), a poseur and sponger (a genuine comic creation who succeeds only in drawing the reader's attention to himself)—these reporters are unable to give the narrative the firmness it requires. Florence remains an intriguing and pathetic puzzle; our questions are unanswered, our sympathies largely unresolved.

A second short novel, "Its Image on the Mirror" (published in *My Heart Is Broken*) is an unqualified success, partly because the point of view is strictly limited to one character—a device which is the source of some ambiguity here as well as consistency. The faintly repressed family hostilities which have appeared in various guises in the earlier work are now given sustained treatment. The narrator, Jean, who has always suffered from a sense of drabness and compromise in contrast to her beautiful younger sister, tries to come to terms with her ambivalent feelings. After years of apparent freedom and romance the spoiled Isobel makes what seems to be an unhappy and confining marriage; looking back, Jean is able to move towards compassion and acceptance. But to what degree is she using the narrative as a kind of revenge for the years she was forced to take second place? Is her sympathy finally untainted by satisfaction? The reader has no means of deciding, precisely because the author makes no comments on Jean's reminiscences. The uncertainty we feel at the end of the work, however, is entirely appropriate: Jean herself is still divided between love, pity and jealousy.

*A Fairly Good Time* is a splendidly complex full-length novel. Again the plot is familiar and simple in outline: a well-off, still young Canadian woman passes over the borders of sanity as her second marriage, to a Parisian journalist, dissolves. The reasons for her collapse, again, are hinted at rather than developed: an eccentric, domineering mother, a happy first marriage cruelly ended by a freak accident, the frustrating sense of isolation in a foreign world of would-be intellectuals and amoral opportunists—all of these play a partial role. This time, however, Miss Gallant operates directly inside the mind of her heroine, and the result is a spectacular tour de force: the writing is disconcertingly vivid, full of the unmediated poetry of near-hallucination, yet nothing is irrelevant or misplaced. Shirley's madness has a kind of honesty about it which attracts the users and manipulators around her. The sane world of her husband's family and the Maurel family, into whose civil wars she is thrust, seems finally to offer much less integrity than her own world of memories and fantasies. At the conclusion there is just a hint that Shirley may be returning to reality, as she learns to moderate her hopes: "if you make up your mind not to be happy," runs the epigraph from Edith Wharton, "there's no reason why you shouldn't have a fairly good time."

There are no ideas in Miss Gallant's work, no set of theses. The strong and willful may or may not succeed; the sensitive will almost certainly pay for their gifts. And if they endure, as Shirley may, or as Jean does in "Its Image on the Mirror", the only wisdom is a kind of expensive stoicism:

We woke from dreams of love remembered, a house recovered and lost, a climate imagined, a journey never made. . . . We would waken thinking the earth must stop now, so that we could be shed from it like snow. I knew, that night, we would not be shed, but would remain, because that is the way it was. We would survive, and waking—because there was no help for it—forget our dreams and return to life.

—Elmer Borklund

---

**GALLICO, Paul (William).**   American.   Born in New York City, 26 July 1897. Educated at De Witt Clinton High School, and Columbia University, New York, B.A. 1921. Married Alva Thoits Taylor in 1921 (divorced, 1934); Elaine St. John, 1935 (divorced, 1936); Pauline Gariboldi, 1939 (divorced, 1954); Baroness Virginia von Falz-Fein, 1963; has two children by his first marriage. Review Secretary, National Board of Motion Picture Review, New York, 1921; Assistant Managing Editor and Columnist, *New York Daily News*, 1922–36; War Correspondent for *Cosmopolitan* magazine, New York, 1944–45. Instructor in Short Story Writing, Columbia University, 1939, 1944. Since 1960, Member of the Advisory Board, *The Writer* magazine, Boston. Lives in Monaco. Address: c/o Harold Ober Associates Inc., 40 East 49th Street, New York, New York 10017, U.S.A.; or, c/o Hughes Massie Ltd., 69 Great Russell Street, London W.C.1, England.

PUBLICATIONS

Novels

*The Adventures of Hiram Holiday.*   New York, Knopf, and London, Joseph, 1939.
*The Secret Front.*   New York, Knopf, 1940.
*The Snow Goose.*   New York, Knopf, and London, Joseph, 1941.
*The Lonely.*   London, Joseph, 1947; New York, Knopf, 1949.
*The Abandoned.*   New York, Knopf, 1950; as *Jennie*, London, Joseph, 1950.
*Trial by Terror.*   New York, Knopf, and London, Joseph, 1952.
*Snowflake.*   London, Joseph, 1952; New York, Doubleday, 1953.
*The Foolish Immortals.*   New York, Doubleday, and London, Joseph, 1953.
*The Love of Seven Dolls.*   New York, Doubleday, and London, Joseph, 1954.
*Ludmila: A Legend of Liechtenstein.*   London, Joseph, 1955; as *Ludmila*, New York, Doubleday, 1959.
*Thomasina: The Cat Who Thought She Was God.*   New York, Doubleday, 1957; as *Thomasina*, London, Joseph, 1957.
*Mrs. 'Arris Goes to Paris.*   New York, Doubleday, 1958; as *Flowers for Mrs. Harris*, London, Joseph, 1958.
*Too Many Ghosts.*   New York, Doubleday, 1959; London, Joseph, 1961.
*Mrs. 'Arris Goes to New York.*   New York, Doubleday, 1960; as *Mrs. Harris Goes to New York*, London, Joseph, 1960.
*Scruffy: A Diversion.*   New York, Doubleday, and London, Joseph, 1962.
*Coronation.*   New York, Doubleday, and London, Heinemann, 1962.
*Love, Let Me Not Hunger.*   New York, Doubleday, and London, Heinemann, 1963.
*The Hand of Mary Constable.*   New York, Doubleday, and London, Heinemann, 1964.
*Mrs. 'Arris Goes to Parliament.*   New York, Doubleday, 1965; as *Mrs. Harris, M.P.*, London, Heinemann, 1965.

449

*The Man Who Was Magic: A Fable of Innocence*. New York, Doubleday, and London, Heinemann, 1966.
*The Poseidon Adventure*. New York, Coward McCann, and London, Heinemann, 1969.
*Matilda*. New York, Coward McCann, and London, Heinemann, 1970.
*The Zoo Gang*. London, Heinemann, 1971.

## Short Stories

*Confessions of a Story Writer*. New York, Knopf, 1946.
*Further Confessions of a Story Writer: Stories Old and New*. New York, Doubleday, 1961.
*Confessions of a Story-Teller*. London, Joseph, 1961.

## Plays

Screenplays: *No Time to Marry*, 1937; *Pride of the Yankees*, 1942; *Joe Smith, American*, 1942; *The Clock*, 1945; *Never Take No for an Answer*, 1951; *Lili*, 1953; *Merry Andrew*, 1957; *Big Operator*, 1959; *Thomasina*, 1960.

## Other

*Farewell to Sport*. New York, Knopf, 1938.
*Golf Is a Friendly Game*. New York, Knopf, 1942.
*Lou Gehrig: Pride of the Yankees*. New York, Grosset, 1942.
*The Small Miracle* (juvenile). London, Joseph, 1951; New York, Doubleday, 1952.
*The Steadfast Man: A Biography of St. Patrick*. New York, Doubleday, 1958; as *The Steadfast Man: A Life of St. Patrick*, London, Joseph, 1958.
*The Hurricane Story* (on World War II). New York, Doubleday, 1960.
*The Day the Guinea Pig Talked* (juvenile). London, Heinemann, 1963; New York, Doubleday, 1964.
*The Day Jean-Pierre Was Pignapped* (juvenile). London, Heinemann, 1964; New York, Doubleday, 1965.
*The Silent Miaow: A Manual for Kittens, Strays and Homeless Cats*. New York, Crown, and London, Heinemann, 1964.
*The Day Jean-Pierre Went Round the World* (juvenile). London, Heinemann, 1965; New York, Doubleday, 1966.
*The Golden People* (biography). New York, Doubleday, 1965.
*The Story of Silent Night*. New York, Crown, and London, Heinemann, 1967.
*The Revealing Eye: Personalities of the 1920's*. New York, Atheneum, 1967.
*Manxmouse* (juvenile). New York, Coward McCann, and London, Heinemann, 1968.
*The Day Jean-Pierre Joined the Circus* (juvenile). London, Heinemann, 1969; New York, Doubleday, 1970.

Paul Gallico comments:

I do not know why but I have a distaste for referring to myself as an "author". Somewhere I find something slightly pompous in the word, and when filling out forms or immigration cards, under "profession" I put "Writer".

I consider myself a "Professional Writer" and would not even enlarge that to "Professional

Novelist", for I am still not sure what a novel really is, and even less certain that many of the books I have written could be genuinely classified as novels.

I prefer to think of myself as a "Professional Story Teller". In my early days, say from 1928 through 1940, I was a short story writer and have written some 120, published in various American magazines of the type characterised as "slick", such as the *Saturday Evening Post*, *Cosmopolitan*, *Colliers*, *Red Book*, etc.

Later I turned from writing short stories to writing longer stories, some of which might fall into the category of the novel but two of the books by which I am perhaps best known, *The Snow Goose* and *The Small Miracle*, were certainly not novels; they were long short stories published in book form.

Yes, I have written many books which could be called novels or could have been in the era in which they were produced; in our modern times less so, for they have a beginning, a middle and an end, and they tell the story of conflict and struggle, sometimes serious and sometimes, as with *Scruffy* and *Matilda*, comic or, as with *The Man Who Was Magic* and *Jennie*, pure fantasy.

No two of my books are ever alike, nor do I wish them to be. I have always had a horror of being typed and this again harks back to my idiosyncrasy of styling myself simply a "Professional Writer". In my opinion, the professional writer should be able to deal in form and style with any idea that comes into his head. Since no two ideas are ever wholly alike, the manner in which they are developed and narrated must also differ. If anything, I feel that style must be subordinated to the story or rather adapted each time to the successful exposition of the plot and the characters.

I simply do not know whether I have any "style", unless it is as straightforward a method as I can devise to tell a story in such a manner as to make it easy for my reader to enjoy it. I have always believed that the simpler a story can be told, the more it will be for the reader. I do not believe in baffling a potential client either with non-plots or incomprehensible prose.

Each time I sit down to write a book I hope it will be something worthwhile, and at the time really believe it may be the best I have ever done. Six months after its appearance I am prepared to admit an area of failure on both counts. But this also is something with which a professional writer learns to live. Everything one does seems like a good idea at the time. But times change.

I couldn't for a moment answer a question as to what I consider my best book or books. I can only say that the books I most enjoyed writing and which provided total escape for me during the periods of composition were *Jennie* (*The Abandoned*), *Mrs. 'Arris Goes to Paris*, *Scruffy*, *Matilda*, *Manxmouse* and *The Man Who Was Magic*. Hardly any of these could be called novels. I remember that when *Scruffy* was published, as a disarming subtitle, I called it "An Entertainment". Perhaps this is how I might like to characterise almost all of my books and hope that my readers will agree.

*       *       *

"One is always seeking the touchstone that will dissolve one's deficiencies as a person and a craftsman. And one is always bumping up against the fact that there is none except hard work, concentration and continued application." These two sentences, from his introduction to *Confessions of a Story-Teller*, serve as a useful indication of the strengths and weaknesses of Paul Gallico's work.

The principal strength arises from his very conscious professionalism: every paragraph he writes, whatever its success or failure on other counts, is well-made. Behind this skill lie not only many years of practice as a fiction writer but also a long and arduous schooling in practical journalism. Hence it is natural that in all of his stories (and, in the present critic's opinion, it is in his stories and novellas that he excels, rather than in the longer works) we can sense the thoroughness of his preparation. If the story involves a sport, a locality, a tradition, a piece of history, then we can count on Gallico not only to do his homework but to select and edit his background material so that it does not encroach on the foreground. And structurally his stories move with the sure-footedness that comes only when the author has achieved full understanding of what he is about. Granted, many of the stories are shaped to a formula, and Gallico will frankly admit that he enjoys writing such stories, but this should not obscure the skill required to write a good formula story.

If we ask, however, to what purpose Gallico devotes his craftsmanship, the answer reveals the price paid for that very success. He himself may claim to no more than the confection of saleable fiction, the entertainment of as many readers as possible, and his popularity attests to his realisation of such a purpose. In certain contexts the matter could be left there, but in the context of a survey which reviews the work of many writers who are both less professional and more original than Gallico is, the qualifications must be stated.

For, despite their well-built structure and their accurately researched backgrounds, a very large number of his works have surprisingly soft centres. In a story like *Ludmila* we find an uneasy blend of the journalist and the sentimentalist: the journalist gives us a crystal-clear setting, the sentimentalist wants us to accept his naive personification of the cow's feelings. In the famous Snow Goose story, the sentimentality indeed works against the alleged subject in hand, and trivialises themes that are potentially important. This tendency is inseparable from his treatment of character, because, although his characters all fulfil carefully plotted functions, their very predetermined nature often prevents their various aspects from fusing into credible wholes—as if he cannot risk allowing them to take over for fear of not fitting the exact parts he has already assigned to them. This control, this concentration on the end in view, has its adverse influence also on the details of language. A well-told tale may be intended to rattle along, but the temptation is to reach for the easiest worn phrase ("exquisite little town," "delectable view," "an icy chill seized her heart," etc.). Since fiction exists by virtue of language, this resort to ready-made language means a sacrifice of memorability.

The price paid is the common (but not inevitable) one of fiction created primarily as a consumable product for a market. Success in this field is not easy and demands considerable gifts, but the fact is that "hard work, concentration and continued application" are often not sufficient to achieve the kind of interest we can gain from many writers who are more prepared to take risks, to work not entirely within but at the edge of their capabilities, or even beyond them.

—Robin Fulton

---

**GARNER, Hugh.** Canadian. Born in Batley, Yorkshire, England, 22 February 1913; emigrated to Canada in 1919. Educated in Toronto public schools; Danforth Technical College Institute, Toronto. Served as a soldier in the Spanish Civil War; served in the Royal Canadian Army, 1939–40, and in the Royal Canadian Navy, as a Chief Petty Officer, 1940–45. Married Marie Alice Gallant in 1941; has two children. Free-lance Journalist, 1949–68: Associate Editor, *Saturday Night*, Toronto, 1952–54, and *Liberty*, Toronto, 1963; Columnist, *Toronto Telegram*, 1966. Recipient: Canada Council Senior Arts Fellowship; Governor-General's Award, 1964. Address: 33 Erskine Avenue, Toronto 12, Ontario, Canada.

PUBLICATIONS

Novels

> *Storm Below*.   Toronto, Collins, 1949.
> *Cabbagetown*.   Toronto, Collins, 1950.
> *Waste No Tears*.   Toronto, News Stand Library, 1950.
> *Present Reckoning*.   Toronto, Collins, 1951.
> *The Silence on the Shore*.   Toronto, McClelland and Stewart, 1962.
> *The Sin Sniper*.   New York, Simon and Schuster, 1970.
> *A Nice Place to Visit*.   Toronto, Ryerson Press, 1970.

Short Stories

> *The Yellow Sweater and Other Stories*.   Toronto, Collins, 1952.
> *Hugh Garner's Best Stories*.   Toronto, Ryerson Press, 1963.
> *Men and Women: Stories*.   Toronto, Ryerson Press, 1966.
> *Violation of the Virgins*.   Toronto, McGraw Hill-Ryerson, 1971.

Other

> *Author, Author!* (essays).   Toronto, Ryerson Press, 1964.

Television plays produced in Canada, Great Britain and Australia.

\*      \*      \*

The novels and stories of Hugh Garner are, for the most part, straightforwardly realistic accounts of ordinary life and often reflect his own life experiences. He was brought up in a depressed area of the city of Toronto and came to maturity during the economic depression of the nineteen-thirties, and these experiences are reflected in his novels *Waste No Tears*, *Cabbagetown* and *The Silence on the Shore*, and in many of the short stories collected in the three volumes *The Yellow Sweater*, *Hugh Garner's Best Stories* and *Men and Women*. His wartime experiences as a member of the Canadian navy in World War II found expression in the novel *Storm Below*, which has been called "the most impressive Canadian novel of World War II".

Garner's fiction is honest and workmanlike rather than polished, clever or subtle. He sets down his observations of the world about him in an accurate and almost painstakingly realistic way, and he has the good reporter's gift of catching the revealing sensuous detail, the typical turn of phrase, the suggestive gesture or characteristic manner of dress. His sympathies for the underdogs of our society—the poor, the unemployed, the immigrant, the North American Indian, the itinerant worker—are always readily apparent, but he has no doctrinaire political or social remedies to preach. His sympathy occasionally comes very close to sentimentality in its directness of expression, but most of the time he relies upon accurately observed details to convey the strong emotion he feels. He has a keen ear for the rhythms of casual speech and a strong sense of place.

Garner is probably at his most skilful in his best short stories, for the short story form encourages him to be more economical in his use of words. Such of his novels as *Storm Below* and *Cabbagetown*, however, are so powerful in their realism as to be unforgettable. His essays, collected in *Author, Author!*, are more self-indulgent, although even there the fierce honesty of Garner's outlook gives strength and resilience to otherwise slight pieces of journalism.

Garner has earned a special niche in Canadian literary history by the way in which he has persevered in the realistic treatment of urban life. He was one of a number of young writers who began to write in this manner during the thirties, but he is the only one to have remained consistently true to social realism and to have eschewed experiments with symbolism, surrealism, or stream of consciousness. The record he has thus provided of the lives of ordinary people in our large cities, and to a lesser extent on farms and more remote areas, will always be of great documentary value, whatever the ultimate verdict may be on Garner's artistry.

—Desmond Pacey

---

**GARNETT, David.** British. Born in Brighton, Sussex, 9 March 1892; son of the writer Edward Garnett and the translator Constance Garnett. Educated at University College School, London, 1906–08; Imperial College of Science and Technology, London, 1910–15, A.R.C.S. 1913, D.I.C. 1915. Conscientious objector in World War I; served as a Flight Lieutenant in the Royal Air Force Volunteer Reserve, 1939–40; Planning Officer and Historian, Political Warfare Executive, 1941–46. Married Ray Marshall in 1921 (died, 1940); Angelica Bell, 1942; has six children. Partner, Birrell and Garnett, booksellers, London, 1920–24; Partner, Nonesuch Press, London, 1923–35. Literary Editor, *New Statesman and Nation*, London, 1932–34. Director, Rupert Hart-Davis Ltd., publishers, London, 1946–52. Recipient: Hawthornden Prize, 1923; Black Memorial Prize, 1923. Fellow of the Imperial College of Science and Technology, 1956. C.B.E. (Commander, Order of the British Empire), 1952. Address: Le Verger de Charry, 46-Montcuq, France.

PUBLICATIONS

Novels

Dope Darling (as Leda Burke). London, Werner Laurie, 1919.
Lady into Fox. London, Chatto and Windus, 1922; New York, Knopf, 1923.
A Man in the Zoo. London, Chatto and Windus, and New York, Knopf, 1924.
The Sailor's Return. London, Chatto and Windus, and New York, Knopf, 1925.
Go She Must! London, Chatto and Windus, and New York, Knopf, 1927.
No Love. London, Chatto and Windus, and New York, Knopf, 1929.
The Grasshoppers Come. London, Chatto and Windus, and New York, Harcourt Brace, 1931.
Pocahontas; or, The Nonpareil of Virginia. London, Chatto and Windus, and New York, Harcourt Brace, 1933.
Beany-Eye. London, Chatto and Windus, and New York, Harcourt Brace, 1935.
Aspects of Love. London, Chatto and Windus, 1955; New York, Harcourt Brace, 1956.
A Shot in the Dark. London, Longman, 1958; Boston, Little Brown, 1959.
A Net for Venus. London, Longman, 1959.
Two by Two: A Story of Survival. London, Longman, and New York, Atheneum, 1963.

*Ulterior Motives.*  London, Longman, 1966; New York, Harcourt Brace, 1967.
*A Clean Slate.*  London, Hamish Hamilton, 1971.
*The Sons of the Falcon.*  London, Macmillan, 1972.


Short Stories

*The Old Dovecote and Other Stories.*  London, Mathews and Marriot, 1928.
*A Terrible Day.*  London, Joiner and Steele, 1932.
*An Old Master and Other Stories.*  Tokyo, Yamaguchi Shoten, 1967.


Other

*A Rabbit in the Air: Notes from a Diary Kept While Learning to Handle an Aeroplane.*
  London, Chatto and Windus, and New York, Harcourt Brace, 1932.
*War in the Air, September 1939–May 1941.*  London, Chatto and Windus, and New
  York, Doubleday, 1941.
*The Golden Echo* (autobiography):
  *The Golden Echo.*  London, Chatto and Windus, 1953; New York, Harcourt Brace,
  1954.
  *Flowers of the Forest.*  London, Chatto and Windus, 1955; New York, Harcourt
  Brace, 1956.
  *The Familiar Faces.*  London, Chatto and Windus, 1962; New York, Harcourt
  Brace, 1963.
*The White-Garnett Letters*, with T. H. White.  London, Cape, and New York, Viking
  Press, 1968.

Editor, with others, *The Week-End Book*.  London, Nonesuch Press, and New York,
  Dial Press, 1924.
Editor, *The Letters of T. E. Lawrence*.  London, Cape, 1938; New York, Doubleday,
  1939.

Editor, *Fourteen Stories*, by Henry James.  London, Hart Davis, 1946.
Editor, *The Novels of Thomas Love Peacock*.  London, Hart Davis, 1948.
Editor, *The Essential T. E. Lawrence*.  London, Cape, and New York, Dutton, 1951.
Editor, *The Selected Letters of T. E. Lawrence*.  London, Cape, 1952.
Editor, *Carrington: Letters and Extracts from Her Diaries*.  London, Cape, 1970.

Translator, *The Kitchen Garden and Its Management*, by Professor Gressent.  London,
  Selwyn and Blount, 1919.
Translator, *A Voyage to the Island of the Articoles*, by André Maurois.  London, Cape,
  and New York, Appleton, 1929.
Translator, *338171 (Lawrence of Arabia)*, by Victoria Ocampo.  London, Gollancz,
  and New York, Dutton, 1963.


Manuscript Collection: University of Texas, Austin.


David Garnett comments:

Owing to my first two books *Lady into Fox* and *A Man in the Zoo* dealing with unusual situations, I was labelled a writer of fantasy—and labels stick. I would however describe myself as a poetic realist. Many books are constructed on the principle of a railway train. An engine supplies the power and any number of trucks are hooked on behind. Other books are like aeroplanes, every part of which has to be subordinated to the whole to enable it to fly. I have tried to construct my books like aeroplanes and not like railway trains. This is because, in literature, I particularly value the form and artistic unity which are essential in a great painting. The object of the novel, as of all works of art, is to enlarge experience: not to convey facts. One learns more about passions from *Wuthering Heights* than from Dr. Kinsey.

I would like my own work to be judged purely as that of a creative artist. On the whole I am satisfied with my work. I regret there is not more of it and that I wasted much energy in other activities as a publisher and a farmer and a journalist.

*     *     *

The qualities which make *The Golden Echo* one of the best literary autobiographies of our time animate David Garnett's fiction as well, accounting for both its virtues and its limitations. The three volumes published thus far are marked by an unusual degree of honesty, tempered with a respect for individuality and a freedom from malice or envy which set Garnett apart from many of his Bloomsbury friends. There are a humane tolerance and civility which control all his work, an attractive unwillingness to punish human nature for its weaknesses; yet this respect for private freedom tends to weaken Garnett's purely creative work: the reader often has the feeling that the author has too much affection for his characters, or too much concern for decent manners, to probe very deeply. Reticence and tact lose some of their value inside fiction, where, as E. M. Forster puts it, our sense of a fully revealed character should provide at least the illusion of "perspicacity and power" and thus suggest a more comprehensible and manageable world.

Garnett's first novel, *Dope Darling*, written purely for the sake of earning some badly needed money, appeared under the pseudonym "Leda Burke". "The heroine," Garnett recalls, "is a drug fiend. I enjoyed putting in every cliché I could remember, deliberately basing my style on that of serials in women's papers". *Lady into Fox*, which quickly established Garnett's reputation, is part fantasy, part fable: a pretty young woman inexplicably turns into a vixen; the action traces her anguished husband's struggle to cope with the change, first catering to the fox's remaining human qualities, then, as these disappear, gradually losing his own humanity. Readers may find here what they wish, perhaps, but Garnett himself encouraged a symbolic interpretation when he observed that the underlying theme is a "reductio ad absurdum of the problem of fidelity in love". The great appeal of *Lady into Fox* lies not, however, in the range of its implications, but rather in the clarity and control of its prose. H. G. Wells found it "as astonishing and as entirely right and consistent as a new creation, a new sort of animal . . . suddenly running about in the world"; Conrad called it "flawless in essence and exposition"; but it was Garnett's literary aunt, Clementia Black, who paid the most accurate tribute, calling attention to that "excellent, plain classic English which nobody, nobody writes nowadays. You make me think of Defoe and Swift and Goldsmith." *A Man in the Zoo* attempts to repeat this first success: a lovesick young man gives himself to the Royal Zoo as a specimen of homo sapiens, but his young lady relents and, after a brief Lawrentian struggle, there is a romantic, happy ending. Garnett comments, a little defensively, that "the character of my hero is too proud and individualistic for him to be understood by readers permeated by the spirit of the age of the common man": but while the zoo scenes themselves are fresh and inventive, the story is finally too fragile to embody the theme—the problem of "fitting the secret and private nature of physical passion into the social structure"—with much force.

The success of these first novels caused Garnett to be regarded as a writer of fantasy, but he has observed "I would describe myself as a poetic realist." And poetic realism is in fact the source of much of what is best in the novels that follow. *The Sailor's Return*, a plain, unadorned but oddly moving story, deals with a seaman's doomed attempts to settle into the life of a small English village with his black wife. Garnett's intensely poetic feeling for a rural England still untouched by industrialism or any kind of sophistication gives the novel a pathos which marks *Go She Must!* as well. This less interesting book suffers, however, from its admitted indebtedness to George Moore (presumably the Moore of *Esther Waters*) and in having as its heroine a "rather boring girl" whose bid for freedom is less touching than her father's retreat into a world of private visions and happiness. *No Love*, Garnett's first attempt to deal directly with modern life, is a much stronger work; and although there is some diffuseness in its depiction of two young men (and the girl who loves them) growing up, the novel is effectively unified by a pervasive tone: "there hangs about the whole story," Garnett has commented, "the indefinable melancholy and hopelessness of life." *The Grasshoppers Come* is a slight work (a brief account of a stranded pilot's struggle against a swarm of locusts), while *Pocahontas*, for all its scrupulous detail, never comes to life. The short, much less ambitious *Beany-Eye*, an anecdotal account of (probably) Richard Garnett's kindness to a poor brute of a laborer, is far more convincing.

Twenty years separate *Beany-Eye* from the next series of novels, beginning with *Aspects of Love*. The world of these later books is a totally different world, governed by different forces and rendered in different terms. The characters in *Aspects of Love*, *A Net for Venus* and *Ulterior Motives* are well to do Englishmen, their families and friends, living abroad and wholly preoccupied with falling in and out of love, initiating the young into the painful joys of romance and trying to recapture their own past moments of happiness. The tone is consistently light and mocking, nothing appears to matter terribly in the long run, people are often silly (but finally more likable and forgivable than otherwise); all that seems to count is an openness to experience. The value of human relationships, or of a life entirely alone, reflects the heroine of *Ulterior Motives*, consists simply of

> offering oneself to experience, with no defenses, no anodyne, no drug of habit, nothing but the naked nerve and the object—whatever the object might be— lover, picture, poem, living animal, or the frosty air of winter and the night sky.

That latin tag which closes *Aspects of Love* sums it up: *Pone merum et talos. Pereat qui crastina curat*—"Set down the wine and the dice and perish the thought of tomorrow". Expertly plotted and impeccably rendered, these books nevertheless suggest nothing so much as superior rewrites of popular romances and films. *Two by Two: A Story of Survival*, an engaging retelling of the Noah story from the point of view of two young stowaways on the ark, makes the reader wish that Garnett would return more often to the quiet fantasy of his early work.

The object of fiction, Garnett writes, is "to enlarge experience", but judged by this standard his own novels offer few major disclosures or opportunities for that "extension of consciousness" which Henry James called the novel's finest gift. Garnett's virtues are most completely expressed in *Lady into Fox*, *No Love*, and especially in his memoirs and his superb presentation of Dora Carrington's letters and journals: his portraits of those figures who have mattered to him are likely to prove more enduring than his attempts to make his fictional characters matter to the reader.

—Elmer Borklund

---

**GARRETT, George (Palmer, Jr.).** American. Born in Orlando, Florida, 11 June 1929. Educated at Princeton University, New Jersey, 1947–53, 1955–56, B.A. 1952, M.A. 1956.

Served in the Field Artillery, United States Army, 1953–55. Married Susan Parrish Jackson in 1952; has three children. Assistant Professor, Wesleyan University, Middletown, Connecticut, 1956–60; Visiting Lecturer, Rice University, Houston, 1961–62; Associate Professor, University of Virginia, Charlottesville, 1962–67; Writer-in-Residence, Princeton University, 1964–65; Professor of English, and Director of the Writing Program and Graduate Study, Hollins College, Virginia, 1967–71. Since 1971, Professor of English and Writer-in-Residence, University of South Carolina, Columbia. United States Poetry Editor, *Transatlantic Review*, Rome (later London) and New York, 1958–71; Contemporary Poetry Series Editor, University of North Carolina Press, Chapel Hill, 1963–68; since 1968, Co-Editor, *Hollins Critic*, Virginia; Contributing Editor, since 1970, *Contempora*, Atlanta, and since 1971, *The Film Journal*, New York. Recipient: *Sewanee Review* Fellowship, in poetry, 1958; American Academy of Arts and Letters Prix de Rome, 1958; Ford grant, in drama, 1960; National Endowment for the Arts grant, 1967. Address: 3600 Chateau Drive, Apartment 216, Columbia, South Carolina 29204, U.S.A.

PUBLICATIONS

Novels

*The Finished Man*.   New York, Scribner, 1959; London, Eyre and Spottiswoode, 1960.
*Which Ones Are the Enemy?*   Boston, Little Brown, 1961; London, W. H. Allen, 1962.
*Do, Lord, Remember Me*.   New York, Doubleday, and London, Chapman and Hall, 1965.
*Death of the Fox*.   New York, Doubleday, 1971.

Short Stories

*King of the Mountain*.   New York, Scribner, 1958; London, Eyre and Spottiswoode, 1959.
*In the Briar Patch*.   Austin, University of Texas Press, 1961.
*Cold Ground Was My Bed Last Night*.   Columbia, University of Missouri Press, 1964.
*A Wreath for Garibaldi*.   London, Hart Davis, 1969.

Plays

*Sir Slob and the Princess: A Play for Children*.   New York, French, 1962.

Screenplays: *The Young Lovers*, 1964; *The Playground*, 1965; *Frankenstein Meets the Space Monster*, 1966.

Verse

*The Reverend Ghost: Poems*.   New York, Scribner, 1957.
*The Sleeping Gypsy and Other Poems*.   Austin, University of Texas Press, 1958.
*Abraham's Knife and Other Poems*.   Chapel Hill, University of North Carolina Press, 1961.
*For a Bitter Season: New and Selected Poems*.   Columbia, University of Missouri Press, 1967.

Other

> Editor, *New Writing from Virginia*.   Charlottesville, Virginia, New Writing Associates, 1963.
> Editor, *The Girl in the Black Raincoat*.   New York, Duell, 1966.
> Editor, with W. R. Robinson, *Man and the Movies*.   Baton Rouge, Louisiana State University Press, 1967.
> Editor, with R. H. W. Dillard and John Moore, *The Sounder Few: Selected Essays from "The Hollins Critic"*.   Athens, University of Georgia Press, 1971.
> Editor, with O. B. Hardison, Jr., and Jane Gelfman, *Film Scripts One* and *Two*.   New York, Appleton Century Crofts, 1971.
> Editor, with William Peden, *New Writing in South Carolina*.   Columbia, University of South Carolina Press, 1971.

Bibliography: in *Seven Princeton Poets*, Princeton, New Jersey, Princeton University Library, 1963.

Manuscript Collections: University of Virginia, Charlottesville; Wesleyan University, Middletown, Connecticut.

Critical Studies: "George Palmer Garrett, Jr." by James B. Meriwether, in *The Princeton University Library Chronicle* (New Jersey), vol. XXV, no. 1, 1963; "Imagining the Individual: George Garrett's *Death of the Fox*" by W. R. Robinson, in *Hollins Critic* (Hollins College, Virginia), August 1971.

George Garrett comments:

I feel I am only just beginning, still learning my craft, trying my hand at as many things, as many ways and means of telling as many stories as I'm able to. I hope that this will always be the case, that somehow I'll avoid the slow horror of repeating myself or the blind rigor of an obsession. I can't look back. I'm not ashamed of the work I've done, but it is done. And I am (I hope) moving ahead, growing and changing. Once I've seen something into print I do not re-read it. I have tried always to write out of experience, but that includes imaginative experience which is quite as "real" to me and for me as any other and, indeed, in no way divorced from the outward and visible which we often (and inaccurately) call reality. I only hope to continue to learn and to grow. And to share experience with my imaginary reader. I use the singular because a book is a direct encounter, a conversation between one writer and one reader. Though I couldn't care less how many, in raw numbers, read my work, I have the greatest respect for that one imaginary reader. I hope to manage to please that reader before I'm done, to give as much delight, or some sense of it, as I have received from reading good books by good writers.

*     *     *

Directness, seriousness, a Chaucerian comic sense which in no way conflicts with that seriousness, imaginative vigor and a rich variety of matter and manner—these qualities mark the fiction of George Garrett. An American, a Southerner, Garrett is in his early forties and has published so far four novels, four books of stories, four books of poems, a respectable body of critical work, and he has had three of his screenplays produced as well. These figures suggest his energy and the scope of his interests, and they offer some indication of the seriousness with which he pursues those interests, for none of that large and varied body of work is the result of hack production. Garrett approaches his world and his work with an Elizabethan forcefulness and range, directly and with all his strength. And the result is a body of literature which demands serious attention and rewards that attention when it is given.

Garrett is a Christian artist—not a pietist, but a writer whose very sense of the living world is infused with an Augustinian Christian understanding. He approaches experience directly in his work; he is a realist and not a fabulist, but, because of his Christian belief, his work is never far from parable, his direct reality always formed by the enigmas of the spirit. His four novels are very different each from each in subject, texture and form: *The Finished Man* is a novel of modern Florida politics; *Which Ones Are the Enemy?* takes place in Trieste during the American occupation following the second world war; *Do, Lord, Remember Me* concerns the shattering visit of an evangelist to a small Southern town; *Death of the Fox* is an account of the events, exterior and interior, of the last two days of Sir Walter Ralegh's life. But they are all products of the same central concerns—a blessing of the dark and fallen world, a knowledge of the power of the imagination to create and sustain values in that fallen world, a faith in the possibility of redemption and salvation even in the very process of the fall into sin and death, and a commitment to the individual moment as the sole window on eternity.

Appropriately, Garrett's major work (and his most recent) is the large novel, *Death of the Fox*, for in it all of his major thematic concerns come together in the person of Ralegh, the soldier, the politician, the sailor and explorer, the scholar, the poet, the sinner, and the morally creative man. In his imaginative union with Ralegh, Garrett fuses present and past into an artistic present which is both truth and lie—the disappointing truth which nevertheless burns ideally in the imagination and dreams of the beholder as in Garrett's earlier short story, "An Evening Performance," and the saving lie of love of his poem, "Fig Leaves," which enables us "to live together."

George Garrett is one of the most interesting writers of his generation, for he has continued to grow and change in his work while so many of his contemporaries have faltered or simply repeated themselves book after book. His importance becomes clearer year by year, for his fiction has maintained its freshness and its vitality even as it has developed and matured.

—R. H. W. Dillard

---

**GASS, William (Howard).** American. Born in Fargo, North Dakota, 30 July 1924. Educated at Kenyon College, Gambier, Ohio, 1942–43, 1946–47, A.B. 1947; Ohio Wesleyan University, Delaware, 1943; Cornell University, Ithaca, New York, 1947–50, Ph.D. 1954. Served as an Ensign in the United States Navy, 1943–46. Married Mary Pat O'Kelly in 1952; Mary Alice Henderson, 1969; has three children. Instructor of Philosophy, College of Wooster, Ohio, 1950–54; Assistant Professor of Philosophy, 1955–58, Associate Professor, 1960–65, and Professor, 1966–69, Purdue University, Lafayette, Indiana. Visiting Lecturer in English and Philosophy, University of Illinois, Urbana, 1958–59. Since 1969, Professor of Philosophy, Washington University, St. Louis. Recipient: Longview Foundation Award, 1959; Rockefeller Fellowship, 1965; Guggenheim Fellowship, 1969. Address: 6304 Westminster, University City, Missouri 63130, U.S.A.

PUBLICATIONS

Novels

> *Omensetter's Luck*.   New York, New American Library, 1966; London, Collins, 1967.
> *Willie Masters' Lonesome Wife* (essay-novella).   New York, Knopf, 1971.

Short Stories

> *In the Heart of the Heart of the Country and Other Stories*.   New York, Harper, 1968;
> London, Cape, 1969.

Uncollected Short Stories

> "The Clairvoyant", in *Location* (New York), no. 2, 1964.
> "The Sugar Crock", in *Art and Literature* (Paris), no. 9, 1966.
> "We Have Not Lived the Right Life", in *New American Review 6*.   New York, New
> American Library, 1969.
> "Why Windows Are Important to Me", in *Tri-Quarterly* (Evanston, Illinois), no. 20,
> 1971.

Other

> *Fiction and the Figures of Life* (essays and reviews).   New York, Knopf, 1971.

Manuscript Collection: Washington University Library, St. Louis.


Critical Studies: "Omensetter's Luck" by Richard Gilman, in *New Republic* (Washington
D.C.), 7 May 1966; "The Stone and the Sermon" by Saun O'Connell, in *Nation* (New
York), 9 May 1966; "Nothing But the Truth" by Richard Howard, in *New Republic* (Washington D.C.), 18 May 1968; interview with Thomas Haas in the *Chicago Daily News*,
1 February 1969.


William Gass comments:

I think of myself as a writer of prose rather than a novelist, critic, or story-teller, and I
am principally interested in the problems of style. My fictions are, by and large, experimental
constructions; that is, I try to make things out of words the way a sculptor might make a
statue out of stone. Readers will therefore find very little in the way of character or story
in my stories. Working in the tradition of the Symbolist poets, I regard the techniques of
fiction (for the contemporary artist) as in no way distinct from the strategies of the long poem.

*     *     *

It is difficult to make a brief assessment of William Gass's contribution to literature, for
his works range from the purely imaginative to the imaginatively critical, are varied in form

461

and style, and are powerfully written, with striking images, startling language, and provocative insights. Gass himself gives testimony to the problem of definition when he calls his latest work an "essay-novella" and stresses that he regards himself as a writer of prose rather than a novelist. Yet even the term prose-writer is hardly adequate when so often his words have poetic qualities. His descriptive introduction of Brackett Omensetter in *Omensetter's Luck* is as expansive and natural as that happy man. No less poetic in power are the condensed and obscene ravings of Reverend Jethro Furber, as he cracks under Omensetter's unwitting presence.

In this first novel and his collected short stories, Gass is working out his own literary theories. He does not believe in the narrative re-creation of life but the naked presentation of life through the revelatory speech of the individual. (This must include both spoken words and unspoken thoughts.) In this way, Furber, in the utterances of his madness, fitfully discloses all there is to know about him: his past history, his impressions of Gilean, Ohio, and his convulsive reaction to Omensetter. So, too, does the narrator of the short story "Mrs. Mean" reveal his despicable parasitic nature, the emptiness of his own life, in his fascinated and detailed accounts of that lady's petty but human cruelties. It seems unlikely that any formulated narrative could portray the realities and obsessions of life so truly.

This body-crawling of Gass's also shows us how we give symbolic complexity to our perceptions. Furber's archetypal black garb is an appropriate and constant source of his knowledge-infested brooding. The black, geometric dead roaches become the object of joyous contemplation of perfect order for the life-entrapped female narrator of "The Order of Insects." Omensetter himself becomes a symbol. His elemental rightness is a source of consternation to his Gilean neighbors. It doesn't fit in with their constructs of life. Man-like they need a name for it, as though that will make it understandable. They call it luck and the application of that term to himself destroys Omensetter, making him just another of society's creatures. Henry Pimber, Omensetter's landlord, kills himself when the big man fails to live up to Pimber's interpretation of the luck. Furber, more educated and complex than Pimber, goes mad grappling with the worldly and philosophical problems caused by Omensetter's presence. The difficulty of presenting the intensity of Furber's inner conflict, in fact, accounts for a noticeable flaw in the novel. His excessively lengthy ramblings break the tension needed in a work so highly textured by the necessary events involving the other townsmen, who are men of action.

For all his characters' determination to reveal themselves, Gass handles their lives artistically. While he dismisses the more regular structures of the narrative form, his stories remain taut with the dramatic battles and tensions of the whole being responding to life experiences. Conflicts do not remain cerebral; they are felt in the groin and externalized in the wrinkles and wounds that confirm our existence.

It would be premature to make any encompassing remark about Mr. Gass's style. His short stories show a continuing experimentation in form to create the most fitting way of presenting the life and experience he is treating. The journal-like observations recorded under their appropriate headings by the jilted writer-narrator of "In the Heart of the Heart of the Country" are in word and form a most appropriate expression of that individual at that particular point in his life.

Mr. Gass must be regarded as a vital and significant literary presence.

—Paula L. Hart

---

**GELLHORN, Martha (Ellis).** American. Born in St. Louis, Missouri, in 1908. Educated at the John Burroughs School, St. Louis; Bryn Mawr College, Pennsylvania. Married the writer Ernest Hemingway in 1940 (divorced, 1946); T. S. Matthews, 1954 (divorced, 1963); has one son. War Correspondent for *Collier's Weekly* of New York in Spain, 1937–38, Finland, 1939, China, 1940–41, England, Italy, France and Germany, 1943–45, and Java, 1946; and for *The Guardian* of London in Vietnam, 1966, and Israel, 1967. Recipient: O. Henry Award, 1958. Lives in London and Kenya. Address: c/o Morgan Guaranty Trust Company, 31 Berkeley Square, London W.1, England.

## PUBLICATIONS

### Novels

*What Mad Pursuit.*  New York, Stokes, 1934.
*The Trouble I've Seen.*  New York, Morrow, 1936; London, Putnam, 1937.
*A Stricken Field.*  New York, Duell, 1940; London, Cape, 1941.
*Liana.*  New York, Scribner, and London, Home and Van Thal, 1944.
*The Wine of Astonishment.*  New York, Scribner, 1948.
*His Own Man.*  New York, Simon and Schuster, 1961.
*The Lowest Trees Have Tops.*  London, Joseph, 1967; New York, Dodd Mead, 1969.

### Short Stories

*The Heart of Another.*  New York, Scribner, 1941; London, Home and Van Thal, 1946.
*The Honeyed Peace: Stories.*  New York, Doubleday, 1953; London, Deutsch, 1954.
*Two by Two.*  New York, Simon and Schuster, and London, Longman, 1958.
*Pretty Tales for Tired People.*  New York, Simon and Schuster, and London, Joseph, 1965.

### Other

*The Face of War.*  New York, Simon and Schuster, and London, Hart Davis, 1959.

\*       \*       \*

Some novelists are born to their craft. Others are made. Among the latter kind are those who, while possessing no striking originality of gift or of vision, have nonetheless an ability to handle prose, to depict scenes and to control narrative flow which make them very similar in kind to the good journalist (and the gifts of novelist and journalist do, after all, cross at a great many points). Martha Gellhorn is one of the better "made" writers. None of her novels can be considered a masterpiece, none has pioneered a new kind of fiction and in none do we experience that all-important shock of recognition that comes when we encounter a genuinely original voice. Yet that said it has to be added that if her novels never surprise they rarely disappoint. At the very least there is about them a cool, controlled craftsmanship that rewards our interest in them.

Martha Gellhorn is without doubt remarkable for the utterly candid manner in which she understands and makes the most of her gifts. She does not try to overreach herself; she knows, none better, what she can and what she cannot do, and she keeps her fiction within the scope of her abilities. As a result she is incapable of falling disastrously flat, as is so often the way with would-be "great" writers who lack her sure self-knowledge. On the other hand, it is no good expecting her to take the kind of dangerous risk which is perhaps necessary for the production of major art. Martha Gellhorn is modest, efficient, clever, and above all she is content to move within limits which she knows she can encompass.

Much of her ability as novelist is bound up with her ability as a journalist, and in this respect it is worth noting that as a journalist she is first-rate. A few years ago, for example, she produced a searingly accurate and moving account of her journey to Vietnam to investigate the effect America's war was having on the unhappy people of that country. And what more than anything else comes across from her reports is her candour, her real feeling for people no matter what the colour of their skins or their political ideologies, and the openness, even perhaps acute vulnerability of her conscience. She did not produce bleeding-heart journalism—and indeed all her writing, fiction especially, is remarkable for the wry toughness of her stance towards life (a kind of controlled stoicism which it would probably be unfair to say she derived from her one-time husband, Ernest Hemingway, but which has striking affinities with his steely self-containment). But for all that, there is in her accounts of life in Vietnam a real tenderness of regard for individuals which shows how easily the novelist and journalist blend into each other. For her fiction is above all good in its controlled but never dispassionate observation of different people caught up in fates which they can neither control nor ignore.

In this respect I would think that *A Stricken Field* and *The Trouble I've Seen* are novels in which Miss Gellhorn's powers of judicious, sympathetic, wry and compassionate observation of human beings are at their best. And although both suffer from what is really a muddied narrative (in neither does she manage to tell the story as well as she might), they succeed admirably in bringing home to us their touching sense of how other people live and suffer privately.

Of all her novels, however, it is *Liana* which seems to me most fully to embody her virtues and which is least marred by her faults. True, there is a suspiciously Hemingway-like handling of the dialogue—Miss Gellhorn is always at her weakest in this area—but for the rest there is a sharpness, a truth of observation in the studies of Liana herself and of Marc that would make the novel worth reading if there were nothing else to commend it. Add to that, however, the keen feeling for atmosphere, emotional as well as environmental, and you have a fine piece of fiction. *Liana* alone assures Martha Gellhorn a respectable place among the order of good if not great novelists.

—John Lucas

---

**GERHARDIE, William (Alexander).** British. Born in St. Petersburg, now Leningrad, Russia, 21 November 1895 of British parents. Educated at St. Annen Schule, and Reformierte Schule, St. Petersburg, 1900–13; Kensington College, London, 1913–16; Worcester College, Oxford, 1920–23, M.A. (honours), B.Litt. Served in the British Army in the Royal Scots Greys in World War I: Assistant Military Attaché in the British Embassy, Petrograd, 1917–18, and served in the British Military Missions to Siberia, 1918–20; demobilised with rank of Captain; served in the Officers' Emergency Reserve, 1940. Editor, "English by Radio", BBC, London, 1942–45. Recipient: Phoenix Award, 1965; Arts Council Bursary, 1966. O.B.E. (Officer, Order of the British Empire), 1920. Address: 19 Rossetti House, 106 Hallam Street, London W.1, England.

PUBLICATIONS

Novels

> *Futility: A Novel on Russian Themes.*  London, Cobden Sanderson, and New York, Duffield, 1922.
> *The Polyglots.*  London, Cobden Sanderson, and New York, Duffield, 1925.
> *Jazz and Jasper: The Story of Adams and Eva.*  London, Duckworth, 1928; as *Eve's Apples: A Story of Jazz and Jasper*, New York, Duffield, 1928; as *My Sinful Earth*, London, Macdonald, 1947; as *Doom*, Macdonald, 1971.
> *Pending Heaven.*  London, Duckworth, and New York, Harper, 1930.
> *The Memoirs of Satan*, with Brian Lunn.  London, Cassell, and New York, Doubleday, 1932.
> *Resurrection.*  London, Cassell, and New York, Harcourt Brace, 1934.
> *The Casanova Fable: A Satirical Revaluation*, with Hugh Kingsmill.  London, Jarrolds, 1934.
> *Of Mortal Love.*  London, Barker, 1936.
> *My Wife's the Least of It.*  London, Faber, 1938.

Short Stories

> *A Bad End.*  London, Benn, 1926.
> *The Vanity Bag.*  London, Benn, 1927.
> *Pretty Creatures.*  London, Benn, and New York, Duffield, 1927.

Plays

> *Perfectly Scandalous; or, The Immorality Lady* (produced London, 1968).  London, Benn, 1927; New York, Duffield, 1928; as *Donna Quixote; or, Perfectly Scandalous*, London, Duckworth, 1929.
> *I Was a King in Babylon* (produced Boston, 1948).
> *Rasputin: The Ironical Tragedy* (produced London, 1960).

Other

> *Anton Chekhov: A Critical Study.*  London, Cobden Sanderson, and New York, Duffield, 1923.
> *Memoirs of a Polyglot* (autobiography).  London, Duckworth, and New York, Knopf, 1931.
> *Meet Yourself As You Really Are: About Three Million Detailed Character Studies Through Self-Analysis*, with Prince Leopold of Loewenstein.  London, Faber, and Philadelphia, Lippincott, 1936; as *Analyze Yourself: How to See Yourself as You Really Are*, adapted by Victor Rosen, Englewood Cliffs, New Jersey, Hawthorn Books, 1955; revised edition, as *Meet Yourself As You Really Are*, New York, Tower Publications, 1972.
> *The Romanoffs: Evocation of the Past as a Mirror for the Present.*  New York, Putnam, 1939; London, Rich and Cowan, 1940.
> *My Literary Credo: An Introduction to the First Collected Uniform Revised Edition of the Works of William Gerhardie.*  London, Macdonald, 1947.

Critical Studies: in *Scholars of the Heart* by S. Gorley Putt, New York, Hillary House, 1963; in *Tradition and Dream* by Walter Allen, London, Phoenix House, 1964; "Gerhardie Lives" by James Parkhill-Rathbone, in *Twentieth Century* (London), 1969; prefaces by Michael Holroyd, to the author's *The Polyglots, Of Mortal Love, Futility*, and *Pending Heaven*, London, Macdonald, 1970, 1971; essays by C. P. Snow and Michael Holroyd, in *American Scholar* (Washington, D.C.), 1970; "Of Mortal Love and Civil War" by the author, in *Encounter* (London), March 1971; interviews with the author, in *Books and Bookmen* (London), June 1971; "Masters Apart" by the author, and "Gerhardie as Musician" by Michael Holroyd, in *Books and Bookmen* (London), August 1971; "In My Obscurity Lies My Salvation" by the author, in *Twentieth Century* (London), 1971.

*       *       *

William Gerhardie was born in 1895 in St. Petersburg (now Leningrad), a city that he has described as one of immense squares, wide bridges and lunatic dreams. His grandfather, on the paternal side, was a Londoner who ran away to Manchester, married a Belgian girl there and had six children; then he swept them all off to Russia, where he set up a cotton spinning-mill on the banks of the Neva. Half a century later, when the Revolution broke out, his children, who were now grown up, were forced to flee for their lives. Amongst them was William Gerhardie's father, who spent his last years in a cheap mountain *pension* in the Tyrol. Shortly before his death when he was in great need of money, he submitted an article to the *Daily Mail* recounting his arrival in Riga and the journey by sleigh, pursued by wolves. It was rejected. His youngest son, William, recalls this in the autobiography, *Memoirs of a Polyglot* that he wrote when he was 35.

In the Gerhardi household in St. Petersburg, William, his elder brother and sisters spoke English with their parents as a matter of duty (their mother was born in Lancashire but had been brought to Russia when she was 3). Yet amongst themselves, they preferred to talk in Russian, French or German. Environment far more than blood has left its mark on Gerhardie's fiction.

His first book *Futility* carries the sub-title "A Novel on Russian Themes". Begun soon after the outbreak of the first World War when Gerhardie was serving as a captain on the staff of the British Military Mission to Siberia, it was finished at Worcester College, Oxford, to which he went in 1920. Thirteen firms turned it down, and in despair the author sent the manuscript to Katherine Mansfield. Within a week she had read it, and by the end of a fortnight found it a publisher. "It is a living book", she wrote. "One can put it down and it goes on breathing." The tale it tells is of an Englishman brought up in Russia and of his unrequited love for Nina, the second of three bewitching daughters. It provides too an unforgettable picture of the 1918–20 Allied Intervention, with peasants shouting but not knowing what the word "revolution" means and thinking it a woman, and of soldiers happily marching to royalist tunes.

*The Polyglots* in part overlaps *Futility*. At the time of the Armistice, a spirited English officer visits the Far East and Russia, where he meets many relatives. Some marvellous comic encounters ensue. Here is one between himself and his uncle, whose daughter he has just seduced:

> "If you were alone . . . I would give you a bit of my mind."
> "Then we should exchange our minds like visiting cards."

Towards the end, there is a deeply moving account of a young girl's burial at sea.

In *Jazz and Jasper*, Frank Septimus Dickin becomes involved with a group of Russian emigrés as a confidant, lover and recorder of their lives. He writes a serial about his adventures with them, which he reads to Lord Ottercove, a newspaper proprietor. But their actions soon outstrip his invention. Ottercove is an affectionate portrait of Lord Beaverbrook, to whom Gerhardie dedicated his collection of stories, *Pretty Creatures*. Arnold

Bennett is also presented in the guise of Vernon Sprott, said to be "the foreman of British fiction". In the final chapters, the plot shoots into the realms of fantasy, and ends with a handful of people left on a mountain whilst the rest of the world has disintegrated. Could this be a return to another Eden? The book's sub-title is "The Story of Adams and Eva".

*Jazz and Jasper* was Gerhardie's last novel to introduce Russian-born characters, though a Chekhovian mood still predominates in the rest of his fiction (his study of *Anton Chekhov* remains required reading at Moscow University). *Pending Heaven* charts the rivalry of two literary lions over women—often each other's women: one of them, Max Fisher, is based on Hugh Kingsmill. The settings range from Soho to the south of France and an oasis in the Sahara. *Resurrection* deals with astral projection—and is founded on the author's own personal experience. *Of Mortal Love* is his masterpiece, and explores the fluctuations of the human heart. Dinah Fry, a young woman whose married life began in Manchester, dreams of a world where men will take her to brilliant London parties and marvel at her beauty. The parties come true, but neither her husband nor her lovers can sustain the quality of affection that she craves. Then, suddenly she is cut down in her prime by diphtheria, and "*mortal* love" is translated into "love *transfigured*". The novel is a mixture of tragedy and comedy and offers a vision of eternity. *My Wife's the Least of It* is about a man's attempt and failure to persuade a number of movie magnates to accept a scenario of his. As a last resort he marries a mad woman with a huge fortune and "degenerates" into being a philanthropist. The world is so insane, he decides, that his wife is the least of it.

In 1970 a revised definitive edition of the works of William Gerhardie, with Prefaces by Michael Holroyd, was launched. In all the volumes a number of deletions, corrections and additions have been made, and *Jazz and Jasper*, renamed temporarily *My Sinful Earth*, now emerges retitled as *Doom*. In the mid-1960s the author added an *e* to his surname, explaining to a reporter on *The Times*: "Dante has an *e*, Shakespeare has an *e*, Racine has an *e*, Blake has an *e*, Goethe has an *e*, and who am I not to have an *e*?" Since the end of the second World War, he has been concentrating on a tetralogy to be called *This Present Breath*, some extracts of which were printed in *The Wind and the Rain Easter Book*. These included a scene in a night club, and another in paradise where the hero and heroine are said to breathe not air but truth. Such an apocalyptic note has sounded before in Gerhardie's fiction, and conforms with his long-held view (which he reiterated again in his seventy-fifth year) that a writer is "a two-way channel, [who must] humbly offer the use of his voice to the life everlasting."

—Neville Braybrooke

---

**GHOSE, Zulfikar.** Pakistani. Born in Sialkot, Pakistan, 13 March 1935. Educated at Keele University, England, B.A. in English and philosophy 1959. Married in 1964. Cricket Correspondent for *The Observer*, London, 1960–65. Teacher in London, 1963–69. Emigrated to the United States in 1969. Since 1969, Lecturer in English at the University of Texas, Austin. Address: Department of English, University of Texas, Austin, Texas 78712, U.S.A.

PUBLICATIONS

Novels

*The Contradictions.* London, Macmillan, 1966.

*The Murder of Aziz Khan.*   London, Macmillan, 1967; New York, Day, 1969.
*The Incredible Brazilian, Book I.*   London, Macmillan, 1972.

Short Stories

*Statement Against Corpses*, with B. S. Johnson.   London, Constable, 1964.

Verse

*The Loss of India.*   London, Routledge, 1964.
*Jets from Orange.*   London, Macmillan, and Chester Springs, Pennsylvania, Dufour, 1967.
*The Violent West.*   London, Macmillan, 1972.

Other

*Confessions of a Native-Alien* (autobiography).   London, Routledge, 1965.

*     *     *

Much of the subsequent direction of Zulfikar Ghose's writing can be glimpsed in the five stories that (with nine of B. S. Johnson's) were published as *Statement Against Corpses*. The title refers in part to the recurrent theme of death—to the impact of death on the living and to the metaphysics that unites thought and action, life and death, success and failure, aspiration and accomplishment, and so on—but also to the specific technical reason for the book: to give to the short story "the same precise attention to language as that given normally only to a poem." Except perhaps in England, such an aim could in 1964 scarcely have seemed novel, and indeed the stories belong generally to that critical limbo called "promising". "The Zoo People" is the glorious exception. Thematically complex, linguistically assured, subtle in its evocation of character, delicate in its responses to landscape, provocative in its approach to time, it probes the mind of the English émigré Emily Minns, as she comes to terms with physical and metaphysical perception in an India alien to her upbringing. Is an animal more beautiful in the wild than in a zoo, she asks—and what happens if, taking a cage away, one discovers "primitive wildness" *instead* of beauty? Her ultimate answer arises from her increased sensitivity to Indian paradoxes and her adaptation of them to her "European Enlightenment" patterns of thought:

> Absolute barrenness was a reality with which she now felt a sympathy. There were rocks and rocks: each, whether a pebble or a boulder, was a complete, homogeneous, self-sufficient mass of matter in itself; each stood or lay in the dust at perfect peace with the universe which did no more to it than round its edges; each was there in its established place, a defiant mass of creation, magnificently aloof, without ancestry and without progeny.

Order, in other words, is within her mind's eye.

*The Contradictions* not only continues the metaphor of barrenness, but also structures itself on East-West logical oppositions. The "assertions" that open the book explore an Englishman's inhibited barriers against India, and India's human fecundity nonetheless. The "contradictions" that close it are set in England and pick up each theme and symbol from the first half of the book—not in order to refute them particularly, but to complete them. The English rationalist philosophers must be blended with India's atemporality;

material welfare must be glimpsed concurrently with the noumenal importance of the colour of silk squares; Sylvia's English miscarriage must encourage her to appreciate what her experience of India did not directly allow: that an "area of nothingness" might possess "an odd attraction, and in this darkness, a disturbing power".

Attached ambivalently to a landscape of heart as well as a landscape of mind, Sylvia spirals towards a point of balance between antitheses. For Ghose himself, as his auto-biography clearly announces, the point of balance is represented by the tenuous hyphen in "native-alien". Pakistan, India, British India, and Britain are all part of his experience, and all necessary to him, in conjunction. In another short story, "Godbert", the antithesis is conveyed by a different metaphor: "Donald . . . looked at horizons whereas John examined the texture of cobblestones." Later in the story, in a similar tense vein, Ghose writes: "One chooses a way of life. Or life imposes its own pattern upon one despite oneself." Such a dilemma lies at the core of Ghose's ambitious and moving novel *The Murder of Aziz Khan*, about a peasant farmer's futile effort to preserve his traditional land from industrial expansion, political roguery, blatant thuggery, and the power of money in other people's hands. What ultimately it focusses on is the nature of freedom, and, as with all of Ghose's work, the external material world and the domain of sense and sensitivity are inextricably inter-twined.

—W. H. New

GIBBONS, Stella (Dorothea). British. Born in London, 5 January 1902. Educated at North London Collegiate School for Girls, and University College, London. Married Allan Bourne Webb in 1933 (died, 1959); has one child. Cable Decoder, British United Press. Feature Writer, *Evening Standard*, London, 1926–28; Drama and Literary Critic, *The Lady*, London, 1928–31. Recipient: Femina Vie Heureuse Prize, 1933. Fellow, Royal Society of Literature, 1950. Address: 19 Oakeshott Avenue, London N.6, England.

PUBLICATIONS

Novels

*Cold Comfort Farm*. London, Longman, 1932; New York, Longman, 1933.
*Bassett*. London and New York, Longman, 1934.
*Enbury Heath*. London and New York, Longman, 1935.
*Miss Linsey and Pa*. London and New York, Longman, 1936.
*Nightingale Wood*. London and New York, Longman, 1938.
*My American: A Romance*. London, Longman, 1939; New York, Scribner, 1940.
*The Rich House*. London and New York, Longman, 1941.
*Ticky*. London and New York, Longman, 1943.
*The Bachelor*. London, Longman, and New York, Dodd Mead, 1944.
*Westwood; or, The Gentle Powers*. London, Longman, 1946; as *The Gentle Powers*, New York, Dodd Mead, 1946.
*The Matchmaker*. London, Longman, 1949.
*The Swiss Summer*. London, Longman, 1951.
*Fort of the Bear*. London, Longman, 1953.

*The Shadow of a Sorcerer.*   London, Hodder and Stoughton, 1955.
*Here Be Dragons.*   London, Hodder and Stoughton, 1956.
*White Sand and Grey Sand.*   London, Hodder and Stoughton, 1958.
*A Pink Front Door.*   London, Hodder and Stoughton, 1959.
*The Weather at Tregulla.*   London, Hodder and Stoughton, 1962.
*The Wolves Were in the Sledge.*   London, Hodder and Stoughton, 1964.
*The Charmers.*   London, Hodder and Stoughton, 1965.
*Starlight.*   London, Hodder and Stoughton, 1967.
*The Snow Woman.*   London, Hodder and Stoughton, 1969.
*The Woods in Winter.*   London, Hodder and Stoughton, 1970.

Short Stories

*Roaring Tower and Other Short Stories.*   London and New York, Longman, 1937.
*Christmas at Cold Comfort Farm and Other Stories.*   London and New York, Longman, 1940.
*Conference at Cold Comfort Farm.*   London, Longman, 1949.
*Beside the Pearly Water.*   London, Peter Nevill, 1954.

Verse

*The Mountain Beast and Other Poems.*   London, Longman, 1930.
*The Priestess and Other Poems.*   London and New York, Longman, 1934.
*The Lowland Venus and Other Poems.*   London and New York, Longman, 1938.
*Collected Poems.*   London, Longman, 1951.

Other

*The Untidy Gnome* (juvenile).   London and New York, Longman, 1935.

Has published numerous sketches in *Punch*, London, and other magazines.

Stella Gibbons comments:

I think of myself as a poet, not a novelist, because I am not deeply interested in human beings, but in ideas and in Nature, and, above all, in the possible existence and nature of God. For what I may call ordinary purposes I think of myself as a moralist and a craftswoman, not as an artist, but I *enjoy* writing. I do not enjoy what may be called the peripheral circumstances attached to being a writer: reputation, literary life, meeting other writers, literary gossip. I love making what is arrogantly called "ordinary people" laugh, and perhaps giving them a happier turn of thought or even some hope. I have a strong distaste for drama and "scenes", which I believe has vitiated my powers as a novelist; my books are really a kind of bitter-sweet fairy story, all of them, though I sometimes flatter myself by calling them poetic realism.
I retired from writing novels in 1970.

*          *          *

Stella Gibbons is a prolific and talented writer whose reputation for wit was immediately established by her first novel *Cold Comfort Farm*. This is one of the funniest examples of parody ever put into novel form; it takes on the pulp romance, the philosophy of D. H. Lawrence, the pessimism of Thomas Hardy and all those who, in praising the primitive and the rural, devalue the rational and the urbane.

*Cold Comfort Farm* was published in 1932. It will never date while there are literary critics of more sensibility than sense and a steady annual output of romantic novels. The heroine, Flora, encounters a Lawrence enthusiast who is writing a book to prove that Branwell Brontë is the real author of *Wuthering Heights*. Branwell's sisters, he confides, "were all drunkards, but Anne was the worst of the lot." Reluctantly, Flora accompanies him on a walk. "The stems reminded Mr Mybug of phallic symbols and the buds made him think of nipples and virgins. Flora used sometimes to ask him the name of a tree, but he never knew." While the source material for this portrait is not known, it seems certain that Miss Gibbons' weekly stint of book reviewing provoked such passages as the following. "Claud, who had served in the Anglo-Nicaraguan war of '46, was at his ease in the comfortable silence in which they sat, and allowed the irony and grief of his natural expression to emerge from beneath the mask of cheerful idiocy with which he usually covered his sallow, charming face."

The story of the Doom family frequently recalls the more pessimistic episodes from the sagas of Hardy's Wessex but, at a guess, it was a novel by Mary Webb which provided the immediate inspiration. This is *Precious Bane*, a rural tale in which murder, suicide and infanticide follow each other in quick succession. Thanks to Flora's good sense, none of these misfortunes come to the inhabitants of Cold Comfort Farm. Seth's sexual obsessions are channelled into a career in Hollywood; Elfine is dissuaded from modelling herself on St. Francis of Assisi and groomed for marriage to the local squire, Dick Hawk-Monitor. Even Aunt Ada Doom who as a child "saw something nasty in the woodshed" is restored to health and flies off to Paris in search of a wicked old age.

Since that triumph, Miss Gibbons has sometimes returned to satire but never with such singleness of purpose; her novels are intelligent explorations of the social themes which have always provided the mainstay of English fiction. She writes about love and marriage, class, money, power and if caricature is still a favourite method of attack, this is usually incidental to her main focus of interest. Her heroines tend to be shy single women with the selfishness that can accompany timidity. They gain self-knowledge and a greater capacity for happiness, often through contact with a group of people from a wider social circle, never without a measure of pain and disillusionment.

Society is as important in these novels as it is in the novels of Jane Austen and for the same reason; both authors believe that the most reliable assessment of character is based on close observation of social behaviour. Miss Gibbons resembles her predecessor in many other ways. She plots her stories skilfully, allowing room for development and surprise; she enjoys putting the cat among the pigeons and confronting one set of social values with another totally opposed to it. She has a good sense of the dramatic. She has chosen one sphere of London life as a natural setting for her comedies of manners: the artistic and literary community centred on the two hills of Hampstead and Highgate. Many of her most successful novels chart this territory and its special charm, although in human terms this is shown to hide an underlying ruthlessness. The houses and streets of the area, on the other hand, provide a continuing source of pleasure. Miss Gibbons may dislike nature worship but her evocations of Hampstead Heath in all its moods reveal her affection for London's largest stretch of countryside.

One of her best novels is *Westwood; or, The Gentle Powers*. This was published in 1946 and contains some fine descriptions of wartime London. "Weeds grew in the City itself; a hawk was seen hovering over the ruins of the Temple, and foxes raided the chicken-roosts in the gardens near Hampstead Heath." It is a dropped ration-book, appropriately enough, which provides the link between the heroine and the glamorous Niland family. Margaret is a young teacher with a great capacity for hero-worship. The ration-book which she finds and returns belongs to Hebe Niland, wife of a famous painter and daughter of a famous playwright. The Nilands exploit Margaret from the first but at the same time they educate her; she loses much of her naivety when she discovers that a distinguished playwright can also be a lecherous old man.

Margaret's story is echoed in a later novel of Hampstead life *Here Be Dragons*, a study of egoism which shows the author at her most perceptive. Again, the heroine enters a charmed circle, is at first dazzled, later disillusioned and ultimately gains from the experience. This time the artists are poor, young and struggling and the heroine, Nell, is a natural mother figure for them, a kind, practical girl, not unlike the Flora of *Cold Comfort Farm*. She is fascinated by the leader of the group, a writer of genuine talent and unscrupulous charm who enjoys manipulating people for his own amusement. Nell is in some danger from his influence but is saved by one brutal act of betrayal. A similar theme is handled in *The Charmers*.

Miss Gibbons has never lost her popularity as a writer of traditional, well-constructed novels. Her success is surely based on the two qualities which most characterise her work: a strong sense of moral values and an equally strong sense of fun.

—Judith Cooke Simmons

---

**GILL, Brendan.** American. Born in Hartford, Connecticut, 4 October 1914. Educated at Yale University, New Haven, Connecticut, A.B. 1936. Married Anne Barnard in 1936; has seven children. Since 1936, regular Contributor to *The New Yorker* magazine: Movie Critic, 1961–67; since 1968, Theatre Critic. President, Municipal Art Society, New York; Vice-President, Victorian Society in America, Philadelphia; Member, Board of Directors, Film Society of Lincoln Center, New York. Recipient: National Institute of Arts and Letters grant, 1951; National Book Award, 1951. Address: c/o The New Yorker, 25 West 43rd Street, New York, New York 10036, U.S.A.

PUBLICATIONS

Novels

*The Trouble of One House.*   New York, Doubleday, 1950; London, Gollancz, 1951.
*The Day the Money Stopped.*   New York, Doubleday, 1957; London, Gollancz, 1958.

Uncollected Short Stories

"Knife", in *The New Yorker*, 16 March 1940.
"Sunflower Kid", in *Saturday Evening Post* (Philadelphia), 30 November 1940.
"King Barney the First", in *Saturday Evening Post* (Philadelphia), 28 December 1940.
"Triumph", in *The New Yorker*, 1 February 1941.
"Adriance Prize", in *Saturday Evening Post* (Philadelphia), 22 February 1941.
"All the Right People", in *Saturday Evening Post* (Philadelphia), 22 March 1941.
"Together", in *Saturday Evening Post* (Philadelphia), 8 August 1941.
"Choice", in *The New Yorker*, 16 August 1941.
"Truth and Consequences", in *The New Yorker*, 6 September 1941.
"Little Rain", in *The New Yorker*, 27 December 1941.

"The Cemetery", in *The New Yorker*, 24 April 1943.
"Interest in Boys", in *The New Yorker*, 21 August 1943.
"Grand Old Man", in *Virginia Quarterly Review* (Charlottesville), October 1943.
"Helpmeet", in *The New Yorker*, 20 November 1943.
"Mother Coakley's Reform", in *The New Yorker*, 8 March 1944.
"Will's Girl", in *Collier's* (New York), 28 October 1944.
"The Guide", in *The New Yorker*, 21 April 1945.
"Too Late to Marry, Too Soon to Die", in *The New Yorker*, 19 May 1945.
"And Holy Ghost", in *The New Yorker*, 2 June 1945.
"Fall from Grace", in *Collier's* (New York), 20 December 1945.
"Fine Start", in *Collier's* (New York), 9 February 1946.
"Remembrance", in *The New Yorker*, 29 October 1960.
"Something You Just Don't Do in a Club", in *The New Yorker*, 29 April 1961.
"The Toast", in *The New Yorker*, 13 January 1962.
"Fat Girl", in *The New Yorker*, 26 September 1970.

Play

*La Belle* (produced Philadelphia, 1962).

Verse

*Death in April and Other Poems.*   Windham, Connecticut, Hawthorne House, 1935.

Other

*Cole: A Book of Cole Porter Lyrics and Memorabilia*, with Robert Kimball.   New York, Holt Rinehart, 1971.

*       *       *

> A fly mounted a curtain in the sun, and
> the fly's shadow mounted the shadow of
> lace, like a dream threading a dream.
> *The Trouble of One House*

Reversing conventional causation, Gill's novels and characteristic short stories dramatize a single present situation that seems to create, rather than derive from, a densely-textured past. Both novels ostensibly focus on immediate problems in upper-middle-class Irish Catholic families—the death of a young mother in *The Trouble of One House*, and the dispute over a father's will in *The Day the Money Stopped*. But the books reveal the past to be as alive and insistent as the present, perhaps more insistent, since in *Money* questions from the past demand solution with an urgency which transcends mere significance for the present, and the dead lawyer father compels greater interest than his son, Charlie Morrow, the protagonist. And in *House*, the nuances of the characters' previous relationships with each other not only explain their responses to Elizabeth's death, but actually seem forced into life for the first time by that death.

However, this creation by the present of a vital new past does not totally overshadow the more conventional themes of the shaping power of the past, and its continual struggle with the present. Dependent on fragile and illusory human memory, the force of the past can nevertheless guide the present, as does the unlabelled photograph that begins and ends

*House.* The last thing the dying Elizabeth sees is this picture of her children, an aid to memory at the moment her memory fades. But the photograph will serve the father as long as his memory functions: "There was no indication of where the picture had been taken, or when, or by whom. A stranger would have been able to make nothing of it. It was just a picture of three children on a beach. But they were his children; he was theirs. From now on, he was theirs forever." Objects and places redolent with meaning from the past also stimulate conflict in the present: the dead Elizabeth's sister and mother-in-law vie for her chair at the dining table in *House*, and Charlie is intimidated by his father's office chair in *Money*. The cemetery glimpsed from this office window has served secretaries as a trysting place for as long as Charlie can remember; this death-life image reinforces the struggle between past and present in his own consciousness. In the story "The Cemetery," a doctor's son confronts the mingled accomplishment and futility of his father's life in a similar office opposite a symbolic cemetery. (Gill's fathers tend to be successful doctors and lawyers, as his mothers tend to die young.)

*Money* is a tour-de-force creating past and present largely through dialogue during Charlie's brief visit to his father's office. (Perhaps this abundant dialogue, concentrated time, and single setting prompted Maxwell Anderson's dramatic adaptation.) However, despite the technical skill of the book, *Money* suffers from Gill's failure to endow Charlie with the charm to which the other characters unvaryingly respond. Though *House* is the better novel, the supporting characters act with a vitality denied Elizabeth, who, like Browning's Pippa, merely stimulates others without herself undergoing much change or awareness. Her sister and undertaker brother-in-law perform with an arresting combination of vulgarity and pathos; Father Degnan and Monsignor Brady are dramatized with a blend of satire and compassion that rivals the best of J. F. Powers; and Elizabeth's daughter awakens to sex on the day of her mother's death in an episode sustaining a complex tone of serious irony. But these brilliant vignettes and characterizations threaten to unbalance the novel, since Elizabeth's character fails to act as a unifying force.

Though *House* is a competent, often moving, work, Gill's major accomplishments are his short stories, which escape the structural problems of the novels. Harry Carter in "Something You Just Don't Do in a Club" is a convincing version of the successful scoundrel, a figure familiar in Gill's fiction, but, like Charlie Morrow in *House*, incapable of sustaining an entire novel. Admittedly, there are some early *Saturday Evening Post* stories, "King Barney the First," "Adriance Prize," and "All the Right People," in which prep school or Yale protagonists manage, through a series of plot contrivances and unmotivated epiphanies, to avoid becoming adult versions of Charlie Morrow. But, contemporary with these works and continuing through the present are a wealth of first-rate *New Yorker* pieces, including Gill's finest, "Triumph," which undercuts, without destroying, an impoverished dowager's distorted reminiscences of an elegant past. The couple in "Helpmeet" provide a grimmer version of the relationship between the undertaker and his wife in *House*; the episode in the novel loses some of its strength to the overall diffuseness of the work, while the story preserves its power intact. "Grand Old Man," the most effective of Gill's clerical stories, dramatizes the same ambivalent struggle between religious innocence and practicality as does *House*. "Interest in Boys" portrays a girl like Elizabeth's daughter, awakening to sexuality and learning that the object of her excitement is a young priest. As in all his best stories, Gill eschews the mere manipulation of plot detail to create surprise and conveys a real insight into both the girl and the nature of priestly commitment. And Gill's most recent story, "Fat Girl", shows him, after a decade of publishing many reviews and regrettably little fiction, still in command of his powers and in pursuit of promising new themes.

—Burton Kendle

**GILLIATT, Penelope.** British. Born in London. Educated at Queen's College, London, 1942–47; Bennington College, Vermont, 1948–49. Married Professor R. W. Gilliatt in 1954 (divorced); the playwright John Osborne (divorced); has one child. Film Critic, 1961–65, 1966–67, and Theatre Critic, 1965–66, *The Observer*, London. Since 1967, Six-months-a-year Film Critic for *The New Yorker*. Recipient: National Society of Film Critics Award, 1971; New York Film Critics Award, 1971; British Film Academy Award, 1972. Address: c/o The New Yorker, 25 West 43rd Street, New York, New York 10036, U.S.A.

PUBLICATIONS

Novels

> *One by One*. London, Secker and Warburg, 1965; New York, Atheneum, 1966.
> *A State of Change*. London, Secker and Warburg, and New York, Random House, 1967.

Short Stories

> *What's It Like Out? and Other Stories*. London, Secker and Warburg, 1968; as *Come Back If It Doesn't Get Better*, New York, Random House, 1969.
> *Penguin Modern Stories 5*, with others. London, Penguin, 1970.

Uncollected Short Stories

> "F.R.A.N.K.", in *The New Yorker*, 1 May 1971.
> "Nobody's Business", in *The New Yorker*, 3 July 1971.
> "Position of the Planets", in *The New Yorker*, 14 August 1971.
> "As We Know from Freud, There Are No Jokes", in *The New Yorker*, 2 October 1971.

Plays

> "Property", in *The New Yorker*, 2 May 1970.
> *Bloody Sunday* (screenplay). New York, Bantam, and London, Corgi, 1971.

> Screenplay: *Sunday Bloody Sunday*, 1971.

> Has written documentaries and adapted own short story for BBC Television.

Critical Study: by Vincent Canby, in *New York Times*, 3 October 1971.

*        *        *

Known widely for her film reviews, first for the *Observer* in London and since 1967 for the *New Yorker*, Penelope Gilliatt has written two novels, some two dozen short stories, film and television scripts, and two plays. All of her work reveals a distinctive style and a highly personal view of the human condition. In fiction, however, she has created a series of characters all fiercely independent, often caught in the confusion of an ambivalent and paradoxical world, but stoutly insisting on their right to make their own choices and to maintain their individuality.

Her first novel, *One by One*, is the story of a young couple, Joe and Polly Talbot, living in London in the midst of a mysterious plague. Joe, a doctor of veterinary medicine, feels that he must help care for the plague victims; as the situation becomes increasingly more frightening, he sends Polly away to his mother's home. While she is there Polly has their first child, returning as soon as possible to London only to find that Joe will not return to her and their baby. The actual progression of the story is the revelation of Joe's gradual loss of the ability to face reality and Polly's increasingly frantic attempts first to understand him and then to save him, but without success. Each episode in her attempt becomes more unreal, more absurd than the one before. In the end Joe, unable to recognize her as his wife, retreats into death as he jumps out the hospital window. Polly occupies a somewhat middle position between Joe's mother's conventional and selfish moral judgments and the logic of service to all mankind Joe represents—a logic finally self-destructive. The parable of the dilemma of the young in an absurd world is rather obvious, though the characterization of Polly and the sharp vignette of Joe's selfish mother lend the situation a nice reality, enough perhaps to evoke a slight—however brief—impression upon the reader of Joe as a tragic figure. Certainly at the end it is clear that whatever his choices—reasonable or unreasonable—he can not escape untouched in an absurd world in which a mysterious plague makes its victims mad before it kills them.

Miss Gilliatt's second novel, *A State of Change*, is more realistic than *One by One*. It does not, however, have a conventional plot as such; rather, it too is a series of episodes held together by their relationship to the protagonist, Kakia Grabowska, a Polish girl who goes to London to live in 1949. She becomes friends with Don Clancy, a television executive, and his friend Harry Clopton, a doctor. They remain friends throughout the novel even though their relationships shift in various ways. After some four years as a close friend of Don's, Kakia begins to live with Harry in spite of the complications of Harry's marriage and his imprisonment for performing an abortion. Their understanding and tolerance of each other, their discussions about contemporary views of society, and their association with a series of prototypes of their sophisticated, modish world are the materials by which Miss Gilliatt exercises her skill for witty dialogue. If the substance of the novel is somewhat brittle, its style is nonetheless brilliant.

Taken together the short stories are far more significant than the two earlier novels. The form of short fiction is especially appropriate to Miss Gilliatt's skill, as within its more precise limitation she may concentrate on characterization and leave the reader to whatever conclusions he may wish to draw about themes she does not fully develop. Indeed, the wild insistence of a bizarre series of characters to be themselves and to exist independently allows characterization to equate theme for the reader. And in story after story there are memorable characters indeed. This is not to say that Miss Gilliatt neglects themes; they appear in bewildering abundance—the destructive role of women; the refusal to change with age; the insistence that, whatever the label, life must have some purpose; the need to continue relationships beyond the point of no return; the nagging question of the nature of reality. One of the most successful mergings of character as theme is in "The Redhead"—Harriet, never doing anything properly or effectively but always with a purpose, proposes finally "to die as well as Nelson . . .; her daughter's friends call her 'mannish' and her own generation 'monstrous'." Another very successful character-theme is in "What's It Like Out?" with Milly Wilberforce, aged eighty-six, who, still passionately in love with her husband, refuses to accept her present state as she concludes to herself, "I have no obligation to get used to it."

Taken as a whole Miss Gilliatt's work is even now of major importance to a discriminating, though perhaps somewhat limited, reading public. Her fiction, while it is only a small portion of the whole of her work, deserves careful consideration from the serious student interested in the recent development of the short story and novel. Her work with films—both as author and critic—may be more generally admired than her work with the novel and short story, but it can be no more permanently valuable.

—Annibel Jenkins

**GLANVILLE, Brian (Lester).**   British.   Born in London, 24 September 1931. Educated at Charterhouse School, Surrey, 1945–49. Married Pamela De Boer in 1959; has four children. Literary Adviser, Bodley Head Ltd., publishers, London, 1958–62. Since 1958, Sportswriter for *The Sunday Times,* London. Recipient: Berlin Film Festival Documentary Award, 1963; British Film Academy Documentary Award, 1967; Thomas Coward Memorial Award, 1969. Address: 160 Holland Park Avenue, London W.11, England.

PUBLICATIONS

Novels

*The Reluctant Dictator*.   London, Werner Laurie, 1952.
*Henry Sows the Wind*.   London, Secker and Warburg, 1954.
*Along the Arno*.   London, Secker and Warburg, 1956; New York, Crowell, 1957.
*The Bankrupts*.   London, Secker and Warburg, and New York, Doubleday, 1958.
*After Rome, Africa*.   London, Secker and Warburg, 1959.
*Diamond*.   London, Secker and Warburg, and New York, Farrar Straus, 1962.
*The Rise of Gerry Logan*.   London, Secker and Warburg, 1963; New York, Delacorte Press, 1965.
*A Second Home*.   London, Secker and Warburg, 1965; New York, Delacorte Press, 1966.
*A Roman Marriage*.   London, Joseph, 1966; New York, Coward McCann, 1967.
*The Artist Type*.   London, Cape, 1967; New York, Coward McCann, 1968.
*The Olympian*.   New York, Coward McCann, and London, Secker and Warburg, 1969.
*A Cry of Crickets*.   London, Secker and Warburg, and New York, Coward McCann, 1970.

Short Stories

*A Bad Streak and Other Stories*.   London, Secker and Warburg, 1961.
*The Director's Wife and Other Stories*.   London, Secker and Warburg, 1963.
*Goalkeepers Are Crazy: A Collection of Football Stories*.   London, Secker and Warburg, 1964.
*The King of Hackney Marshes and Other Stories*.   London, Secker and Warburg, 1965.
*A Betting Man*.   New York, Coward McCann, 1969.
*Penguin Modern Stories 10*, with others.   London, Penguin, 1972.

Other

*Cliff Bastin Remembers,* with Cliff Bastin.   London, Ettrick Press, 1950.
*Soccer Nemesis*.   London, Secker and Warburg, 1955.
*World Cup*, with Jerry Weinstein.   London, Hale, 1958.
*Over the Bar*, by Jack Kelsey, as told to Brian Glanville.   London, Stanley Paul, 1958.
*Soccer Round the Globe*.   London, Abelard Schuman, 1959.
*Know about Football*.   London, Blackie, 1965.
*People in Sport*.   London, Secker and Warburg, 1967.
*Soccer: A Panorama*.   New York, Crown, 1968; London, Eyre and Spottiswoode, 1969.
*Puffin Book of Football*.   London, Penguin, 1970.
*Goalkeepers Are Different* (juvenile).   London, Hamish Hamilton, 1971.

Editor, *The Footballer's Companion*.    London, Eyre and Spottiswoode, 1962.

Critical Study: "Khaki and God the Father" in *A Human Idiom* by William Walsh, London, Chatto and Windus, 1965.

Brian Glanville comments:

There has, I suppose, been some tendency to categorise my work under three headings; that which deals with Italy (*Along the Arno, A Cry of Crickets, A Roman Marriage*), that which deals with Jewish life (*The Bankrupts, Diamond*), and that which deals with professional football (*The Rise of Gerry Logan* and many of the short stories). I think I might accept the categorisation of the two Jewish novels, but it scarcely places *The Olympian*, which uses an athlete as its figure, athletics as its theme, or rather as its metaphor; or *A Second Home*, which is narrated in the first person by a Jewish actress—and has been bracketed with *A Roman Marriage*, itself narrated by a young girl. Again, one can, and does, use similar material for widely different purposes.

A large disenchantment with the conventional novel and its possibilities has, I think, led one gradually away from it, to more experimental methods. Like many novelists of serious intentions, one lives uneasily from one novel to the elusive next, always questioning and trying to establish the validity of the form.

*          *          *

In our post-Marxist, post-Freudian world—post but not ex—it is remarkable to find a writer who is both sensitive to the times and independent enough to abstain from fashionable abstractions. Brian Glanville, by now the author of a considerable *oeuvre*, something like twelve novels and four books of short stories, illustrates the Jamesian conviction that what counts is what is illustrated. Nothing satisfied except the appetite for the illustrational. All his work shows this feeling for exactness, precision, the specific feeling in the actual situation, so that he makes on the reader a two-fold impression: on the one hand, of modesty in the author, and on the other, of the reality of the objective world. Reality, one feels, in these novels is not being bullied or tricked into false positions or sucked up into some symbolising system. No-one—it is really an original note—no-one in his novels represents anyone but himself. A Jew is a Jew, a footballer a footballer, an actress an actress; otherwise they are merely human.

The range of material dealt with in an idiom which is cool and lucid, supple and versatile, is remarkably wide. It includes the world of athletics in *The Olympian*, of professional footballers in his short stories, of the Jewish middle class and of the theatre in *A Second Home*, of the Mediterranean in *A Roman Marriage, A Cry of Crickets*, and *After Rome, Africa* (one of his earliest books but a thriller of such intelligence that it is in the class of Eric Ambler and the early Graham Greene), of writing and business in *The Artist Type*. The writer's acquaintance with these oddly assorted worlds is inward and convincing. It has the casual authority of one who knows them not simply from, but *as* life. The proof of this inwardness is the astonishing mastery of tone, and a most unusual fidelity to the specific idiom of a given society. Each of these societies, the Jewish, the sporting, the artistic, the Mediterranean, gives Brian Glanville a point of access which is not just fashionable, and certainly not seedily trendy, but which opens in a nervously sensitive way on to central strains in the modern consciousness. In *A Roman Marriage*, for example, a withered Anglo-Saxon consciousness blossoms in the intense warmth of Roman ardour; at the same time this healing difference is destroyed by the claustrophobic oppression of the Roman family, exquisitely conveyed by the stuffily over-furnished flat and the menacing, maternal smothering of the husband's mother. In

*The Rise of Gerry Logan* and *The Olympian*, we see the combination of aesthetic and near-religious appeal which the impersonality of sport exercises, while we observe the implacable infection of its discipline and beauty by publicity and personal vanity. In several novels, but particularly in *A Second Home*, Glanville contrives to indicate in an obliquely convincing manner, the gritty character of modern sex, which, instead of fulfilling, acts as an abrasive influence upon the personalities of the participants, destructive because worshipped as an abstraction instead of enjoyed in a context.

The Jewish world, the subject of many short stories and intermittently present in several novels, is, of all, the most fitted to be the vehicle of human communication, since we see in Jews written out explicitly most of the strains harassing us all. The friction in the family, the distance and the tension between the group and the outside world, the existence of a pure and lofty religion only as an attenuated racial memory, the sense of desperation in the individual and of disintegration within the society—these crucial contemporary experiences, carried in no abstract or *a priori* way but as the distillation of observed fact, realistic event, and mirror-like actuality of character, combine to compose a work of considerable and, it seems, as yet generally unrecognised, distinction.

The evidence of this distinction lies in Glanville's extraordinary command of the spoken language, whether in the slightly off-centre, never-exaggerated diction of the Jewish stories, or the limited, muscular palpability of the footballers and runners. This gift is infinitely more than a habit of observation or a trained fidelity of the ear, much more than a retentive memory or a capacity for mimicry. It is a creative skill requiring in the artist a power of discerning the form of the idiom, shaping the phrase, pitching the tone not so much by means of a perfect ear as by an imaginative intuition. It is a question of distributing weight, patiently encouraging the words into a living rhythm. Glanville's control of the spoken word, and the subtlety and delicacy of his dealings with it, indicate a creative and poetic understanding of the artist's primary and most significant instrument, the living language.

A second mark of Glanville's distinction—both intrinsic and relative—is that his work has at its heart a profoundly moral perception. It is the differentiation—not in any abstract form but in the body of the fiction—between motives which are bedded in concrete living and motives which hang in the air. Or it is the distinction between living as ordinary people have to do from day to day out of innumerable, difficult acts, in keeping with the style of their own nature, and living which is an adherence to a social code; and one must not forget that for so many people today this means believing in a clutch of modish, television abstractions. Morality in Glanville's view is the development of one's personal idiom and its continued extension to new spheres of life; good is not what one merely theoretically believes in but what one warms to; bad is not just what one cautiously avoids, but what one instinctively flinches from; and reality is something rougher, harder, altogether more binding than merely intellectual conceptions.

Given what James said about the nature of fiction, this may well be the deepest truth a novelist can tell us.

—William Walsh

---

**GLASSCO, John (Stinson).** Canadian. Born in Montreal, Quebec, 15 December 1909. Educated at Selwyn House School, Montreal; Bishop's College School, Lennoxville, Quebec, 1923–24; Lower Canada College, Montreal, 1924–25; McGill University, Montreal, 1925–28. Married the dancer Elma von Colmar in 1963. Councillor, 1948–52, and Mayor, 1952–54, Village of Foster, Quebec. Founder, 1951, and Honorary Chairman, 1964, Foster Horse Show. Recipient: Quebec Provincial Prize, 1961; Canada Council Senior Arts Fellowship, 1966. Address: Jamaica Farm, Foster, Quebec, Canada.

PUBLICATIONS

Novels

> *Contes en Crinoline* (as Jean de Saint-Luc).   Paris, Gaucher, 1930.
> *Under the Hill* (completion of the unfinished novel by Aubrey Beardsley).   Paris, Olympia Press, 1959; London, New English Library, 1966; New York, Grove Press, 1967.
> *The English Governess* (as Miles Underwood).   Paris, Olympia Press, 1960.
> *Harriet Marwood, Governess* (as Miles Underwood).   New York, Grove Press, 1967.

Uncollected Short Stories

> "Mr. Noad", in *Canadian Forum* (Toronto), March 1953.
> "A Season in Limbo" (as Silas N. Gooch), in *Tamarack Review* (Toronto), Spring 1962.

Verse

> *Conan's Fig*.   Paris, transition, 1928.
> *The Deficit Made Flesh*.   Toronto, McClelland and Stewart, 1958.
> *A Point of Sky*.   Toronto, Oxford University Press, 1964.
> *Squire Hardman* (as George Colman).   Waterloo, Quebec, Pastime Press, 1966.
> *Selected Poems*.   Toronto, Oxford University Press, 1971.

Other

> *Memoirs of Montparnasse*.   Toronto and New York, Oxford University Press, 1970.
>
> Editor, *English Poetry in Quebec* (Proceedings of the Foster Poetry Conference).   Montreal, McGill University Press, 1965.
> Editor, *The Poetry of French Canada in Translation*.   Toronto, Oxford University Press, 1970.
> Editor, *The Temple of Pederasty*, by Ihara Saikaku.   North Hollywood, California, Essex House, 1970.
>
> Translator, *The Journal of Saint-Denys-Garneau*.   Toronto, McClelland and Stewart, 1962.

Manuscript Collection: McGill University Library, Montreal.

John Glassco comments:

I look on myself mainly as a pornographic novelist, and have sought to create serious and artistic works in this genre. My output, beginning with the completion of Beardsley's *Under the Hill*, has been limited, since such writing is more difficult and demanding than is generally realized.

Pure pornography such as mine—that is, pornography not pretending to be something else—receives little critical attention, and indeed none is expected. Morse Peckham, however, in his *Art and Pornography* (1969) was the first to recognize my two pseudonymous "Victorian" novels, *The English Governess* and *Harriet Marwood, Governess*, placing them in the same category as *The Story of O*.

I regard these two "underground" novels, along with the long essay in verse entitled *Squire Hardman* and my portion of *Under the Hill*, as the part of my literary work which is most likely to survive; I rank them much higher than my poetry.

My ideas on pornography as a valid literary genre are set forth at length in the article "The Art of Pornography", which appeared in the final issue of the Canadian quarterly review *Edge* (Edmonton), Summer 1969.

*          *          *

The intimate details of John Glassco's pornographic writing, and its sheer revelry in orgiastic, voyeuristic, flagellant, and other fetishistic behaviour, not only reveal his will to shock middleclass mores (and perhaps exorcise his own relationship with them) but also testify to the force of style and personality that he himself appreciates about Aubrey Beardsley: "his essential and unabashed reliance on the prodigious inner power of his eroticism, his sense of what makes man's private universe revolve". In completing Beardsley's celebrated story of the liaison between Tannhäuser and Venus, *Under the Hill*, he draws on the distinction between public and private sensibilities to trace Tannhäuser's progress: from the fleshy abundance of the Hill of Venus, to the court of the Pope (to discover that Plenary Absolution is a political commodity more than a spiritual one), and back to the court of Venus seeking annihilation (only to discover himself revivified and restored by love, lunch, and laughter). *Amor vincit omnia*, almost in Chaucerian fashion—ironically condemning the corrupt systems of the current day, though in this case not particularly sympathetic towards the virtues of traditional order as a replacement.

It was in the hope of discovering a new way of life that Glassco left Calvinist Canada and went to Paris in the 1920's, rapidly to appear on the edges of the international artistic community there. His autobiographical account of those years, the magnificent *Memoirs of Montparnasse*, supersedes even Hemingway's *A Moveable Feast* and Callaghan's *That Summer in Paris* for its vivid evocation of place and time, its shrewd analysis of literary movements and affiliations, and its deft novelistic characterization of figures like Hemingway, Callaghan, Joyce, Gertrude Stein, and Lord Alfred Douglas. The book, despite its publication date, has all the fresh feckless immediacy of having been written early in the 1930's (as a kind of therapy, a commitment to life, during the author's illness). The acuteness of observation that Glassco had striven for in experimental poetry found here in prose an apposite form.

A sense of discovery is important to Glassco, and what his book adds to its exploration of Paris is a frank and engaging account of his own coming of age. In the tradition of George Moore's *Confessions of a Young Man*, with no apologies for gaucherie, pride, or hedonistic enjoyment, and regret only for missed opportunities and marred hopes, the *Memoirs* tells a relatively familiar twentieth century tale of a naive boy exiling himself from a comfortable home in search of art, to find instead comradeship, penury, a certain alienation, and an uninhibited prodigal willingness to use himself, body and mind, in his striving to be. But in a sense these comprised the "art" he tried to find. If they led to his illness, they led also to his discriminating sense of style, which has expressed itself since in parody, in "Imitation" (in its eighteenth century sense), in the art of translation, and in a continuing appreciation of what he found in Beardsley:

> an attempt to push back the horizons of experience, to find new formulas of atmosphere and feeling . . . in which . . . the measure of the attempt, and the patience and perfection of the technique employed in the attempt, are simply the measure of his greatness.

Something of the same attempt and the same meticulous control over the patterns of language allowed Glassco to produce, in *Memoirs of Montparnasse*, an entertaining and engrossing documentary and one of the finest sustained works in modern Canadian prose.

—W. H. New

---

**GLOAG, Julian.** British. Born in London, 2 July 1930; son of the writer John Gloag. Educated at Rugby School, Warwickshire; Magdalene College, Cambridge. Served in the British Army. Married Danielle Haase-Dubose in 1968; has one child. Fellow, Royal Society of Literature, 1970. Has lived in the United States since 1956. Address: c/o G. Borchardt Inc., 145 East 52nd Street, New York, New York 10022, U.S.A.

PUBLICATIONS

Novels

> *Our Mother's House.* New York, Simon and Schuster, and London, Secker and Warburg, 1963.
> *A Sentence of Life.* New York, Simon and Schuster, and London, Secker and Warburg, 1966.
> *Maundy.* New York, Simon and Schuster, and London, Secker and Warburg, 1969.

Other

> Editor, *The American Nation: A Short History of the United States,* by John Gloag. London, Cassell, 1954.

\*       \*       \*

Julian Gloag's first three novels have shown him to be the possessor of diverse talents: he can use language in an unexpected and lively way, he can bring the reader into close contact with a variety of characters through the precise creation of patterns of speech and thought, he has a wit that shows itself not only in delightful offshoots—"I been livin' in a foolish paradise"—but in the broader manipulation of narrative, for example in the interweaving of separate conversations with humorous and sometimes meaningful effect. He keeps his reader alert and busy, and as a result his books are extremely readable. Whether they are, or will be, anything more, is open at the present to some question.

For all their moment-to-moment pleasures—partly, perhaps, because of them—Mr Gloag's books increasingly lack form and purpose. *Our Mother's House* hung together best, dominated and to some extent shaped by the contrast between the delicate morbidity of its opening chapters, in which a family of children bury their mother's body secretly in the garden, and the subsequent cheerful, only gradually suspicious, homecoming of their long-absent father. The book's main impact is in line with this contrast. We are made to see the children as both peculiar and normal, their father as repellent yet, on his own terms, justified; we ourselves are manoeuvred into an ambiguous position by the tone of the book, which encourages us to sympathise yet establishes us as adult and therefore hostile. This is Mr Gloag's most unified book, though it carries a hint of disintegration in the introduction of an outsider whose function as promoter of narrative and heightener of pathos is at times over-obvious.

*A Sentence of Life* is given external shape and purpose by its association with the traditional form of a murder enquiry and trial, but the important movement of the book is introspective and fluid as the suspect pursues private definitions of guilt and responsibility by remembering and reinterpreting his past. Looked at coolly, the lines of the book don't converge as certainly as its final pages, which use the warmth of selected memories to promote an optimistic conclusion, suggest. The novel's questioning of responsibility and imaginative range are, nevertheless, worth having. Again the reader is not permitted to sympathise or dislike too easily, and moral judgement remains shifting and uncertain.

It is the flight to certainty, together with the failure even to attempt a form, that makes Mr Gloag's most recent novel, for all its verbal brilliance, less good. *Maundy*, a book about the intrusion of the irrational into an apparently ordered life, is unfair to half its characters and lumpy with significance. Though full of goodies—vivid observation, psychological acuity, wit, and sexy sex—the book cannot be taken seriously. Mr Gloag clearly hasn't lost his talents but he urgently needs to find a use for them.

—Mary Conroy

---

**GODDEN, Rumer.** British. Born in Sussex, 10 December 1907. Educated privately and at Moira House, Eastbourne, Sussex. Married Laurence S. Foster in 1934; James Haynes Dixon, 1949; has two children. Address: Lamb House, Rye, Sussex, England.

PUBLICATIONS

Novels

*Chinese Puzzle.* London, Davies, 1936.
*The Lady and the Unicorn.* London, Davies, 1938.
*Black Narcissus.* London, Davies, and Boston, Little Brown, 1939.
*Gypsy, Gypsy.* London, Davies, and Boston, Little Brown, 1940.
*Breakfast with the Nikolides.* London, Davies, and Boston, Little Brown, 1942.
*Rungli-Rungliot (Thus Far and No Further).* London, Davies, 1944; as *Rungli-Rungliot Means in Paharia, Thus Far and No Further*, Boston, Little Brown, 1946.
*Fugue in Time.* London, Joseph, 1945; as *Take Three Tenses: A Fugue in Time*, Boston, Little Brown, 1945.
*The River.* London, Joseph, and Boston, Little Brown, 1946.
*A Candle for St. Jude.* London, Joseph, and New York, Viking Press, 1948.
*A Breath of Air.* London, Joseph, 1950; New York, Viking Press, 1951.
*Kingfishers Catch Fire.* London, Macmillan, and New York, Viking Press, 1953.
*An Episode of Sparrows.* New York, Viking Press, 1955; London, Macmillan, 1956.
*The Greengage Summer.* London, Macmillan, and New York, Viking Press, 1958.
*China Court: The Hours of a Country House.* London, Macmillan, and New York, Viking Press, 1961.

*The Battle of the Villa Fiorita.*  London, Macmillan, and New York, Viking Press, 1963.
*In This House of Brede.*  London, Macmillan, and New York, Viking Press, 1969.

Short Stories

*Mooltiki: Stories and Poems from India.*  London, Macmillan, and New York, Viking Press, 1957.
*Swans and Turtles: Stories.*  London, Macmillan, 1968; as *Gone: A Thread of Stories*, New York, Viking Press, 1968.

Verse

*In Noah's Ark.*  London, Joseph, and New York, Viking Press, 1949.
*St. Jerome and the Lion.*  London, Macmillan, and New York, Viking Press, 1961.

Other

*Bengal Journey: A Story of the Part Played by Women in the Province, 1939–1945.* London, Longman, 1945.
*The Dolls' House* (juvenile).  London, Joseph, 1947; New York, Viking Press, 1948.
*The Mousewife* (juvenile).  London, Macmillan, and New York, Viking Press, 1951.
*Impunity Jane: The Story of a Pocket Doll* (juvenile).  New York, Viking Press, 1954; London, Macmillan, 1955.
*Hans Christian Anderson: A Great Life in Brief.*  London, Hutchinson, and New York, Knopf, 1955.
*The Fairy Doll* (juvenile).  London, Macmillan, and New York, Viking Press, 1956.
*Mouse House* (juvenile).  New York, Viking Press, 1957; London, Macmillan, 1958.
*The Story of Holly and Ivy* (juvenile).  London, Macmillan, and New York, Viking Press, 1958.
*Candy Floss* (juvenile).  London, Macmillan, and New York, Viking Press, 1960.
*Miss Happiness and Miss Flower* (juvenile).  London, Macmillan, and New York, Viking Press, 1961.
*Little Plum* (juvenile).  London, Macmillan, and New York, Viking Press, 1963.
*Home Is the Sailor* (juvenile).  London, Macmillan, and New York, Viking Press, 1964.
*Two under the Indian Sun*, with Jon Godden (autobiography).  London, Macmillan, and New York, Viking Press, 1966.
*The Kitchen Madonna* (juvenile).  London, Macmillan, and New York, Viking Press, 1967.
*Operation Sippacik* (juvenile).  London, Macmillan, and New York, Viking Press, 1969.
*The Raphael Bible.*  London, Macmillan, and New York, Viking Press, 1970.
*Shiva's Pigeons*, with Jon Godden (documentary).  London, Chatto and Windus, and New York, Viking Press, 1971.
*The Tale of the Tales* (on the film *Tales of Beatrix Potter*).  London, Warne, 1971.
*The Old Woman Who Lived in a Vinegar Bottle* (juvenile).  London, Macmillan, and New York, Viking Press, 1972.

Editor, *A Letter to the World: Poems for Young People*, by Emily Dickinson.  London, Bodley Head, 1968.
Editor, *Mrs. Manders' Cook Book*, by Olga Manders.  London, Macmillan, and New York, Viking Press, 1968.

Translator, *Prayers from the Ark* (verse), by Carmen de Gasztold.    London, Macmillan, and New York, Viking Press, 1962.
Translator, *The Creatures' Choir* (verse), by Carmen de Gasztold.    London, Macmillan, 1962; New York, Viking Press, 1965.

Critical Study: by Marshall A. Best, in *Book-of-the-Month Club News* (New York), 1969.

*       *       *

Rumer Godden inherited a love of language from her philologist father. In whatever vein of fiction she writes—and there have been several—her work is informed with a loving sense of the color and shape and rhythm of the words she chooses. It is not surprising that she is also a poet and has published two narratives in verse: *In Noah's Ark* and *St. Jerome and the Lion*.

The traditional novel of individual lives, however, is her natural medium. She thinks as a novelist. When she came to collect some of her short stories *(Gone)*, she chose to string them together as a "thread," with notes to tell how they had arisen from remembered incidents in her own life. In this sense her novels, too, can be seen to reflect her autobiography.

Three themes, which sometimes interweave, have predominated in the novels and stories: the lives of foreigners in an exotic land (she grew up in India and has often returned there); the religious life (paralleling her own conversion to Roman Catholicism); and the secret lives and thoughts of children viewing their elders through their own fresh eyes. From the latter grows a fourth theme, of imaginative and playful fantasy, which is particularly evident in her many books for children but also occurs in such a novel as *A Breath of Air*, her modern version of *The Tempest*.

In evaluating her novels, one is inclined to give most critical weight, in the Indian group, to *Breakfast with the Nikolides*, a poignantly perceptive study of inter-racial relations, and the beautiful short novel, *The River*, about a childhood tragedy in the mysterious aura of Indian tradition (which she helped Jean Renoir to make into an exceptional motion picture). Experimentally, *China Court*, evoking an English household through several generations with its sense of past and present running concurrently, is perhaps the most interesting. She had earlier tried a similar experiment, less successfully, in *Take Three Tenses*, set in wartime London. Among the books with a religious theme, *In This House of Brede* has the peculiar fascination of a special way of life (a contemporary English Catholic nunnery) shown in intimate detail; it is her most ambitious work, and there is added interest, if not significance, in the fact that she completed it in Lamb House at Rye, the long-time home of Henry James where she now lives by invitation of its owners, the British National Trust. Her short *The Kitchen Madonna* combines the religious theme with the theme of childhood.

The public at large has most loved *Black Narcissus*, about an Anglican sisterhood in India, written before her conversion and her first widely-read novel; *An Episode of Sparrows*, a tender story of street-urchins in London; and *The Greengage Summer*, a mystery involving a family of English children on their own in a French hotel. All three became successful motion pictures. In terms of rather ordinary humans, though often in unusual situations, Rumer Godden wins sympathy by dealing thoughtfully and hopefully with some persistent verities.

—Marshall A. Best

**GODFREY, Dave.** Canadian. Born in Winnipeg, Manitoba, 9 August 1938. Educated at Harvard University, Cambridge, Massachusetts, 1957; University of Toronto, 1957–58; University of Iowa, Iowa City, 1958–60, 1963, 1965–66, B.A. 1960, Ph.D. 1966; Stanford University, California, 1960–61, M.A. 1963; University of Chicago, 1965. Married Ellen Swartz in 1963; has three children. Acting Head of the English Department, Adisadel College, Cape Coast, Ghana, 1963–65; Assistant Professor of English, Trinity College, University of Toronto, 1966–71. Co-Founder and President, Anansi Press, Toronto, 1967–69. Since 1969, Co-Founder and Director of New Press, Toronto. Recipient: President's Medal, University of Western Ontario, 1965; Canada Council Award, 1969; Governor-General's Award, 1971. Address: c/o New Press, 56 The Esplanade East, Toronto 1, Ontario, Canada.

PUBLICATIONS

Novel

The New Ancestors.   Toronto, New Press, 1970.

Short Stories

Death Goes Better with Coca-Cola.   Toronto, House of Anansi Press, 1967.

Uncollected Short Stories

"River Two Blind Jacks", in Canadian Short Stories.   Toronto, Oxford University Press, 1968.
"Newfoundland Night", in Canadian Short Stories.   Toronto, Oxford University Press, 1968.
"Gossip, The Birds That Fell, The Birds That Flew", in New Canadian Writing. Toronto, Clarke Irwin, 1968.
"On the River", in New Canadian Writing.   Toronto, Clarke Irwin, 1968.
"Kwane Bird Lady Day", in New Canadian Writing.   Toronto, Clarke Irwin, 1968.

Other

Editor, with Bill McWhinney, Man Deserves Man.   Toronto, Ryerson Press, 1967.
Editor, Gordon to Watkins to You.   Toronto, New Press, 1970.

Critical Studies: "Dave Godfrey" by Dorah Hood, in Oxford Companion to Canadian Literature, Toronto, Oxford University Press, 1967; essays by Margaret Laurence, in Ellipse Magazine (Quebec), Fall 1970, and in The Mysterious East (Fredericton, New Brunswick), December 1970; essay by Phyllis Grosskurth, in Canadian Forum (Toronto), April 1971.

Dave Godfrey comments:

I am most interested in that portion of literature where myth meets social realities; literary dogma concerning the purity of fantasy or of realism does not interest me. The Canadian environment has influenced me greatly although I write mainly about people from cultures other than my own. A good part of my twenties was spent travelling about the U.S. and Africa. I strive for great complexity in my writing because that is how I find life; I do not believe the writer has a duty to simplify or interpret life for his readers; his major tasks are to be as intelligent as possible and to take flights of imagination into bodies, minds and situations other than his own.

\*      \*      \*

Although Dave Godfrey's novel, *The New Ancestors*, is set in West Africa, and most of his short stories are set in Canada, similar themes appear in both. One of his main themes is expressed with precision and irony in the title of his short story collection, *Death Goes Better with Coca-Cola*. The influence of one culture on another, in what can be termed the colonizing process, ends by destroying the original fabric of the taken-over society. In his stories, this theme often appears in relation to American influence in Canada, whereas in the novel it is seen as the destructive effect of the great powers on African countries, even after independence.

Godfrey's writing is in no sense narrowly or exclusively political. His social analyses are always done through individual character portrayals, and his ability to create complex and vivid characters is quite exceptional. Michael Burdener, the maverick Englishman in *The New Ancestors*, his African wife Ama, the brave and misguided drummer Gamaliel who has his life torn away in his attempt to believe in the necessary dream of a new and perfect Africa—all these are splendidly realized, as the novel assumes the narrative voice of one after another.

Godfrey's second recurring theme is the linkage of past and future, the ways in which archetypal patterns appear in human life and mythology. Our ancestors are reborn, with variations, in us. We, too, are in the process of becoming legendary; we are the "new ancestors" of the novel's title. This theme takes Godfrey deeply into the realm of myth, and some of his writing is an attempt to express our vital mythology in contemporary terms. In his finest story, "The Hard-Headed Collector," Godfrey gives shape to Canadian myth in the form of such men as Piet Catogas, André Mineur, Scrop Calla and Looky McLaww, who represent the many races and cultures which make up the country.

In *The New Ancestors*, Lost Coast is an imaginary West African country with a strong resemblance to Nkrumah's Ghana. It is a land of intrigue, suspicion, bribery and brutality, beneath the drums and the laughter. It is also the dark continent of the mind, where the eternal struggles take place between fathers and sons, matriarchs and their children, the living and the dead but ever-present ancestors, man and his gods, that area of the mind in which we are all forever seeking to re-film in fantasy our own pasts.

Radical in content and frequently in form as well, Godfrey's writing is never propagandist. He is involved with the social scene; he is concerned about man's survival on this planet. His writing, at the same time, is very cool and incisive, moving and entertaining. It is to be hoped that his work will soon become available to a wider readership, as he is undoubtedly the most talented young prose writer in Anglophone Canada, and one of the most interesting anywhere.

—Margaret Laurence

---

**GOLD, Herbert.** American. Born in Cleveland, Ohio, 9 March 1924. Educated at Columbia University, New York, B.A. 1946, M.A. 1948; the Sorbonne, Paris (Fulbright

Scholar), 1949–51. Served in the United States Army, 1943–46. Married Edith Zubrin in 1948 (divorced, 1956); Melissa Dilworth, 1968; has five children. Lecturer in Philosophy and Literature, Western Reserve University, Cleveland, 1951–53; Lecturer in English, Wayne State University, Detroit, 1954–56. Visiting Professor, Cornell University, Ithaca, New York, 1958; University of California, Berkeley, 1963; Harvard University, Cambridge, Massachusetts, 1964; Stanford University, California, 1967. Recipient: Inter-American Cultural grant, to Haiti, 1950; *Hudson Review* Fellowship, 1956; Guggenheim Fellowship, 1957; National Institute of Arts and Letters grant, 1958; Longview Foundation Award, 1959; Ford Fellowship, 1960. Address: 1051-A Broadway, San Francisco, California 94133, U.S.A.

## PUBLICATIONS

### Novels

*Birth of a Hero*.   New York, Viking Press, 1951.
*The Prospect Before Us*.   Cleveland, World, 1954.
*The Man Who Was Not with It*.   Boston, Little Brown, 1956; London, Secker and Warburg, 1965.
*The Optimist*.   Boston, Little Brown, 1959.
*Therefore Be Bold*.   New York, Dial Press, 1960; London, Deutsch, 1962.
*Salt*.   New York, Dial Press, 1963; London, Secker and Warburg, 1964.
*The Fathers: A Novel in the Form of a Memoir*.   New York, Random House, and London, Secker and Warburg, 1967.
*The Great American Jackpot*.   New York, Random House, 1970; London, Weidenfeld and Nicolson, 1971.

### Short Stories

*15 x 3*, with R. V. Cassill and James B. Hall.   New York, New Directions, 1957.
*Love and Like*.   New York, Dial Press, 1960; London, Deutsch, 1961.
*The Magic Will: Stories and Essays of a Decade*.   New York, Random House, 1971.

### Other

*The Age of Happy Problems* (essays).   New York, Dial Press, 1962.

Editor, *Fiction of the Fifties: A Decade of American Writing*.   New York, Doubleday, 1959.
Editor, with David L. Stevenson, *Stories of Modern America*.   New York, St. Martin's Press, 1961; revised edition, 1963.
Editor, *First Person Singular: Essays for the Sixties*.   New York, Dial Press, 1963.

Herbert Gold comments:

Subjects: Power, money, sex and love, intention in America.
Themes: The same.
Moral: Coming next time.

\*        \*        \*

Herbert Gold was born in Cleveland, Ohio, on 9 March 1924. He has written about his family background in various short stories, and in a semi-fictional work, *The Fathers*, which was a long-lasting best seller in America. It tells the story of a Jewish immigrant from Russia who began with a pushcart on the streets and after many difficulties became a successful grocer.

Gold's first novel, *Birth of a Hero*, is the story of a middle-aged lawyer undergoing the process of self-discovery. *The Prospect Before Us*, whose central figure is a hotel proprietor, is a pioneer novel among presentations of black-and-white racial encounters. *The Man Who Was Not with It* (in paperback edition called *The Wild Life*) again represented a new reach, this time a story of roving carnivals and the people connected with them, notably the pitchman called Grack, a striking character strikingly presented. Here Herbert Gold vividly and successfully uses the idiom of carnival men and women to relate the events not only concerned with Grack but also with a young man and a girl who emerge as sympathetic characters learning to work out their destiny, to become "with it." This novel is an important contribution to modern American literature, with its presentation of a kind of life which is somewhat special, but full of problems which are national, even universal, narrated in a lively fashion.

*The Optimist* tells of a man torn between the American pressures of opposing forces, adjustment and competition; the book is disappointing in that the conflict is not dramatized with complete success and in that it often presents a rather superficial picture of its material. *Therefore Be Bold* is a lively and attractive picture of adolescent Americans during the depression period of the 1930s. In 1960 Gold also brought out a collection of short stories, *Love and Like*, which contain various material from his novels, past and future.

The novel *Salt* deals with two men and a young woman whose lives are entangled in the vast spiritual labyrinth of New York life, cleverly and interestingly presented. *The Fathers: A Novel in the Form of a Memoir* has been mentioned as a picture of immigration and adjustment to American life; it concerns a man who became highly successful in the grocery business and also several other immigrants from Russia, a book which Gold speaks of as "a novel in which I have used real names and the sense of some real people in order to make a particular bridge between history and the shaping imagination. . . . Like the name 'Gold,' which is an imaginary name, this is 'an imaginary history. And real. And twice imaginary."

Herbert Gold, after residence in New York and several visits to Haiti and Europe, and after various teaching assignments at leading American universities, settled in San Francisco at the beginning of the 1960s. His novel *The Great American Jackpot*, which has one white and one black protagonist, is set in San Francisco and across the bay at Berkeley. The narrative uses abrupt sentences, not hippy except when a few hippy characters speak; it chiefly tells, in the colloquial style he would employ, the story of a disaffected young graduate student in sociology who rather coolly (and somewhat unbelievably) robs a bank, largely for the sense of having something to do; and he has to create a new self after his legal difficulties, which are not presented grimly, but rather satirically. *The Great American Jackpot* is a thinner book than most of Gold's other engagements with fiction, but it does show a further extension of the comic sense as well as a nimbleness of language and a feeling for character (the black sociology professor is particularly effective) which have helped keep Herbert Gold in the ranks of leading present-day American novelists worth watching.

—Harry T. Moore

**GOLD, Ivan.** American. Born in New York City, 12 May 1932. Educated at Columbia University, New York, 1949–53, B.A. 1953; School of Oriental and African Studies, University of London, 1957–59, B.A. (honours) 1959. Served in the United States Army, 1953–55. Married Vera Cochran in 1968. Taught at Columbia University, 1964–67; currently, teaching at Bard College, Annandale-on-Hudson, New York. Recipient: Guggenheim Fellowship, 1963; Ingram-Merrill Fellowship, 1964; Rosenthal Award, 1964; National Endowment for the Arts grant, 1966. Address: Post Office Box 11, Woodstock, New York 12498, U.S.A.

PUBLICATIONS

Novel

    *Sick Friends.* New York, Dutton, 1969; London, Weidenfeld and Nicolson, 1970.

Short Stories

    *Nickel Miseries.* New York, Viking Press, 1963; London, Chatto and Windus, 1964.

Uncollected Short Stories

    "Fragment of a Consummated Courtship", in *Genesis West* (Burlingame, California), Winter-Spring 1964.
    "Pearl Harbor and the Long Ball, in *Cavalier* (New York), September 1966.

Critical Studies: review in *Times Literary Supplement* (London), June 1964; review by Saun O'Connell, in *The Nation* (New York), 29 September 1969.

\*      \*      \*

Ivan Gold has published two books: *Nickel Miseries*, a collection of two novellas and three short stories, and *Sick Friends*, a novel. Gold's work is marked by an acute sensitivity to nuance of language, and by an intensity which almost invariably erupts into violence. His style, particularly in *Nickel Miseries*, is often elliptical, but the apparent surface confusion masks a firm artistic control. The tone of his work is tough and unromantic, as human relationships are generally reduced to brutal and compulsive power struggles. The two novellas in *Nickel Miseries*, "The Nickel Misery of George Washington Carver Brown," and "Taub East," are set on military bases, and focus on a Negro and Jew respectively. In the first tale, Gold chronicles the pathetic story of a black soldier stationed on an Army post in Georgia. Brown, a scapegoat figure for his company, is cruelly persecuted and lured to his death. The gratuitous brutality of his superiors and the flabby passivity of his "friends" are described in a rich idiomatic prose which captures the military ambience. "Taub East," set in Japan, depicts the desperate efforts of a Jewish soldier to secure a *minyan*, a quorum of ten men, in order to hold religious services. Taub, a former rabbinical student, finds that his pious efforts become inextricably meshed with the sexual lives of his fellow soldiers, one of whom agrees to attend services, so he may be able to spy on his Japanese mistress. Japan is also the locale for "Kimiko's Tale," a bittersweet narrative of a prostitute and her military clientele. Here again, relationships between the sexes become exercises in mutual deception.

This story is the tenderest of the collection, the one least permeated with violence and cruelty. In "A Change of Air," first published when the author was still an undergraduate at Columbia University, a nineteen-year-old girl is raped by a gang of thirty-five young men, appropriately named the Werewolves. The story describes the frantic efforts of some members of the group to relive their triumph some years later. Unmotivated violence is the subject of "All You Faceless Voyagers," a Kafkaesque tale of a young American assaulted, for no apparent reason, on a ship off the coast of Spain. The victim's efforts to understand why he has been attacked, and his subsequent entanglement with official bureaucracy are detailed in a manner which reflects his bewilderment.

*Sick Friends*, like the rest of Gold's work, is most successful in rendering a sense of place, and in capturing the nervous intensity of its protagonist. The novel, transparently auto-biographical, focuses on the relationship between Jason Sams, a thirtyish writer, driven by his failure to live up to early promise, and Christa Sarkissian, a sex-obsessed artist who lives with Sams for several months. *Sick Friends* is a kind of confessional novel, filled with details apparently relevant only because of their actual existence. Gold's use of much undigested material in his novel seems a deliberate effort to render his work more life-like; he has sought to eschew the imposed artificiality of the conventional novel. Sams has little use for the writers whom Christa reads—Gunter Grass and Jean Genet—preferring facts to fantasy, reality to fable. While the author's ear for dialogue is still in evidence, the book lacks that sense of irony which would separate narrator from author. Sams does manage to grow in the course of his self-involved narrative, emerging from the prison of his massive ego— partly through the medium of Christa's diary which he secretly reads—to some degree of self-knowledge. *Sick Friends*, then, becomes the ultimate result of Sams'/Gold's liberation. Gold's vision of love as deceptive games combatants play is amply chronicled, and his hero's furious sexual encounters with Christa are presented in clinical fashion, no detail omitted. But sex fails to bring Sams any solace, as his anxieties continue to plague him, visits to his psychotherapist notwithstanding. The end of his affair with Christa is described in an appropriately fragmented manner which reflects the dreary finale of an empty relationship. One's response to *Sick Friends* will depend on a willingness to tolerate its deluded, rather unlikeable narrator, and an ability to immerse oneself in his solipsistic world.

—Leonard Fleischer

---

**GOLDING, William (Gerald).** British. Born in St. Columb Minor, Cornwall, 19 September 1911. Educated at Marlborough Grammar School, Wiltshire; Brasenose College, Oxford, B.A. 1935. Served in the Royal Navy, 1940–45. Married Ann Brookfield in 1939; has two children. Writer, Actor and Producer in small theatre companies, 1934–40, 1945–54. Schoolmaster, Bishop Wordsworth's School, Salisbury, Wiltshire, 1939–40, 1945–61. Visiting Professor, Hollins College, Virginia, 1961–62. Honorary Fellow, Brasenose College, 1966. M.A., Oxford University, 1961; D.Litt., University of Sussex, Brighton, 1970. Fellow, Royal Society of Literature, 1955. C.B.E. (Commander, Order of the British Empire), 1966. Address: Ebble Thatch, Bowerchalke, Wiltshire, England.

PUBLICATIONS

Novels

*Lord of the Flies.* London, Faber, 1954; New York, Coward McCann, 1955.

*The Inheritors.*   London, Faber, 1955; New York, Harcourt Brace, 1962.
*Pincher Martin.*   London, Faber, 1956; as *The Two Deaths of Christopher Martin*, New York, Harcourt Brace, 1957.
*Free Fall.*   London, Faber, and New York, Harcourt Brace, 1960.
*The Spire.*   London, Faber, 1964; New York, Harcourt Brace, 1965.
*The Pyramid.*   London, Faber, and New York, Harcourt Brace, 1967.

Short Stories

*The Scorpion God* (includes "The Scorpion God", "Clonk, Clonk" and "Envoy Extraordinary").   London, Faber, 1971.

Play

*The Brass Butterfly* (produced London, 1958).   London, Faber, 1958.

Verse

*Poems.*   London, Macmillan, 1934; New York, Macmillan, 1935.

Other

*The Hot Gates and Other Occasional Pieces.*   London, Faber, and New York, Harcourt Brace, 1965.

*        *        *

The fame of the English novelist, William Golding, rests on his early novel, *Lord of the Flies.* It is a novel which takes place in the near-future: a future too near to be read about with anything but horrid fascination. As an incident in a world-wide war a company of boys —the oldest only in their early teens—are isolated on a tropical island and must make the best of their painful situation. They have brought with them imprecise insights of what civilization—English civilization, in particular—was. At the outset of their stay, they set up a social organization, complete with a deliberative assembly and an assignment of the duties that will be necessary for survival: fruit-gathering, shelter construction, hunting of boar-meat, and—most important of all—the feeding of a fire that will send up a pillar of smoke and alert passing ships. Eventual rescue is at the outset the raison d'être of all the boys' activity. But gradually the remnants of English civilization fall into disarray. Belief in rescue wanes, and the mass of the exiles falls into savagery and the life of primitive fear. They paint their bodies, propitiate a nameless numen that haunts the island, and can hardly remember the civilization that, in the early stages of their stay, they aspired to return to. Indeed, just before the actual rescue at the end of the novel, they are hunting down the one boy who has the courage and resistance to remember what the rest are determined to forget. They have not, in the phrase of their British rescuer, put up a "good show."

For a good many readers, this novel of Golding's was a haunting portent; it spoke not so much of island survival as of the chancy conditions of all human survival in decades to come. It reminded readers of the quick lapse into savagery that all men might soon experience. It suggested that the web of human culture was gossamer and that the only reality that would remain after wide destruction was the animating and savage will of the nameless "god" of the island.

Thus, Golding's novel was taken by many to be an uncompromising handwriting on a wall. Its texture of compelling excitement and adventure was the Crusoe experience without the comforts that Defoe presented. Human culture—justice, order, "basic decency"—was but a weak reed and would quickly collapse beneath the hands that touched it for support. That Golding's novel was not unique—that there is, in the twentieth century, a considerable tradition of such works as his—can come as a significant afterthought to one's reading of *Lord of the Flies*. Other works as various as Aldous Huxley's *Ape and Essence* and Robert Heinlein's *Stranger in a Strange Land* make some of the points so tellingly offered in Golding's novel. All these novels suggest that modern man is living on borrowed time.

This is the point made by *Lord of the Flies* considered in isolation from the rest of Golding's work. When it is read in conjunction with the later novels, its meaning is qualified if not greatly altered. For the other novels, in terms of subject-matter at least, present us Golding laboring at tasks somewhat unlike those of a tale in which the harrowing experiences of castaway boys are civilization writ small. *The Inheritors* is perhaps as fanciful as *Lord of the Flies*; it too is a flight in time, though the flight is to ages before the beginning of civilization rather than to a period when civilization is on its way out. For *The Inheritors* tells of the last days of a small group of humanoid beings who go down in defeat before another—and superior—group of fire-builders, who, in the last chapter of the novel, are revealed as mankind's not very admirable progenitors; they are the "inheritors" whose violence takes over the cave and the forest that the humanoid group had regarded as their own. *Pincher Martin* is a kind of flight to the immediate present; it concerns the efforts of a seaman to survive on a rocky islet during World War II.

Quite different in subject-matter and tone are two other novels: *Free Fall* and *The Pyramid*. *Free Fall* is the rather soberly told story of a young Englishman's coming to maturity; the young man recalls his lower-class childhood, his education, his first serious love affair, and the testing of his resolution at the hands of a Nazi inquisitor. Throughout, the first person narrator is engaged in an assessment of his responsibility for his action: how was he free, how bound? *The Pyramid* is concerned with a middle-class hero who resembles the narrator of *Free Fall* in that he too—with an accent of irony that is absent from *Free Fall*—is assessing elements in his rather protected youth; he measures the amatory and artistic encounters that have shaped the mature consciousness with which the past is scanned. These two novels belong to a very common genre in English fiction: tales which relate the experiences of mastery and defeat which young men undergo in the course of their entrance into a real social world.

One other novel, *The Spire*, moves in a quite different direction. It is the tale of the efforts of a Medieval priest to crown his cathedral with a four hundred foot spire, an effort that encounters the scepticism of other men and the grim opposition of the law of gravity itself. Yet, despite the opposition of society and nature, the tower is built, at a human cost that is dreadful. Jocelin, the priest-builder of the novel, is subject to divine guidance or obsession, as one will; angels inspire him at his work, and demons seduce him. The temptations of the flesh dog Jocelin at every step of his work, and yet he finally transcends them.

An effort to see an organizing unity in the novels of Golding is not only troubled by the sheer variety of subject-matter presented, as just noted. The style of presentation varies from novel to novel. The style of *Lord of the Flies* is dramatic, spare, relentless; the experience of the lost boys is reported, not analyzed, and comment and interpretation are the province of the reader. Contrastingly, in *The Inheritors, Pincher Martin*, and *The Spire*, the texture of Golding's prose and the accompanying narrative movement are leisurely, involved, and even nebulous and imprecise. One can understand why these variations occur. Golding, in *The Inheritors*, faces the almost impossible task of rendering the humanoid consciousness which, in theory, is almost pre-verbal; the creatures must be represented as experiencing their perils in terms that are images. The leader of the group often says, "I have a picture." So the novel itself is a succession of pictures and physical stimuli; both are presented at a length that is involved and sometimes tedious. Analogous difficulties mark the reproduction of the World War II castaway in *Pincher Martin*. The style of *The Spire* repeats the qualities of diffuseness and tedium, but for different reasons. The priest Jocelin, as he follows the construction of the great central spire of his cathedral, is engrossed in impressions that are not beneath the human, as in *The Inheritors* and perhaps *Pincher Martin*. Jocelin, as well as his recording author, is trying to find expression for impulses that are either satanic or divine. The consequence is, once again, a texture of language that is neither dramatic nor direct; the prose follows the wanderings of the priest up and down his spire with an oppressive abundance that, in this instance, aims at the transcendent. The wavering of the tower in dangerous winds and the interplay of hope and despair in the mind of the priest find their analogues in sentences that approach their target—the subjective life of the priest—but perhaps do not really reach it.

Somewhere between the extremes of expression just cited falls the prose of *Free Fall* and *The Pyramid*, whose recording personae, adults remembering their adolescent experience and understanding it in part, have some chance of mastering what they present. As noted earlier, *Free Fall* is a sober recreation of adolescent hope, whereas *The Pyramid* is a half-serious, half-ironic recreation of the physical and artistic passions that once swept through the mind of Golding's hero.

In the presence of such variety of style and subject, one is at first inclined to judge that Golding is a master of bravura and moves in several directions. Certainly, the relation between Golding's mind and the impressions about life that he is giving shape varies from novel to novel. One cannot see a single and simple line extending from early work to late as one can in the novels of Henry James or Thomas Mann. Instead, Golding is the master of fresh starts. The question that remains is whether these fresh starts express more than an impressive dexterity, sometimes completely successful as in *Lord of the Flies* and sometimes irritatingly short of the mark, as in *The Inheritors* and *The Spire*. Moreover, the implied intellectual perspective shifts from work to work. It is sociological and anthropological in *Lord of the Flies* and *The Inheritors*. It is psychological in the tales of youth remembered (*Free Fall* and *The Pyramid*). And *The Spire* can be read in two ways. It can be seen as a study in morbid religious mania; just as easily, it can be grasped as a sober measuring of the claims of religious inspiration in times like ours that dismiss such inspiration too quickly.

That a significant center or hub exists in the work of Golding—a hub from which the various novels extend like spokes—is suggested by a passage early in *Free Fall*. The hero—or Golding —writes, justifying his meditation on his past:

> I have hung all systems on the wall like a row of useless hats. They do not fit. They come in from outside, they are suggested patterns, some dull and some of great beauty. But I have lived enough of my life to require a pattern that fits over everything I know; and where shall I find that?
>
> *Free Fall*, p. 6.

Slightly later Golding adds: "The mind cannot hold more than so much; but understanding requires a sweep that takes in the whole of remembered time and then can pause." (p. 7) The body of Golding's work suggests that the "hats" are not altogether useless. Each novel represents a "pause" in the presence of "the whole of remembered time." Golding has worn a series of hats, not always consonant with each other but all expressive of certain ranges of human aspiration. One hat—the humanoid one of *The Inheritors*—makes the whole civilized enterprise look like a betrayal of the chance to exist. Another—the hat of *The Spire*— suggests that civilized enterprise always falls short of what is possible for man. And a third hat—the hat assumed by the heroes of *Free Fall* and *The Pyramid*—indicates, if only temporarily, that the gossamer web of civilized life is worth cherishing. It should not be torn asunder as it is by the thoughtless boys of *Lord of the Flies*.

—Harold H. Watts

**GOLDMAN, William.** American. Born in Chicago, Illinois, 12 August 1931. Educated at Oberlin College, Ohio, B.A. 1952; Columbia University, New York, M.A. 1956. Served in the United States Army, 1952–54. Married Ilene Jones in 1961; has two children. Recipient: Academy Award, for screenplay, 1970. Address: 815 Park Avenue, New York, New York 10021, U.S.A.

PUBLICATIONS

Novels

  *The Temple of Gold.* New York, Knopf, 1957.
  *Your Turn to Curtsy, My Turn to Bow.* New York, Doubleday, 1958.
  *Soldier in the Rain.* New York, Atheneum, and London, Eyre and Spottiswoode,
    1960.
  *Boys and Girls Together.* New York, Atheneum, 1964; London, Joseph, 1965.
  *No Way To Treat a Lady* (as Harry Longbaugh). New York, Gold Medal, 1964;
    as William Goldman, New York, Harcourt Brace, 1968.
  *The Thing of It Is . . . .* New York, Harcourt Brace, and London, Joseph, 1967.
  *Father's Day.* New York, Harcourt Brace, and London, Joseph, 1971.

Plays

  *Blood, Sweat and Stanley Poole,* with James Goldman (produced New York, 1961).
  *A Family Affair,* with James Goldman and John Kander (produced New York, 1962).
  *Butch Cassidy and the Sundance Kid* (screenplay). New York, Bantam, and London,
    Corgi, 1969.

  Screenplays: *Harper* (in England, *The Moving Target*), 1966; *Butch Cassidy and the
  Sundance Kid,* 1969.

Other

  *The Season: A Candid Look at Broadway.* New York, Harcourt Brace, 1969.

\*       \*       \*

William Goldman is an extraordinarily talented writer obsessed with the problems of young men whose vivid anticipations cannot be realized in a humdrum world, so that we generally meet them on what an early reviewer of Goldman's work called "a downward spiral," often complicated by homosexual tendencies.

*Temple of Gold,* Goldman's first novel, epitomizes his strengths and weaknesses. This moving story describes the search of the highly emotional, non-intellectual son of a genteel, classical scholar for "the handle" that will enable him to gain control of his life. Ultimately he fails in college and marriage and is responsible for the death of a brilliant but ugly boy who has been his only close friend. After performing a heroic act in the Army, however, he begins to feel that there is no "handle," and he decides to try to take off and make a new life for himself. The exaggerated style of the first-person narration, however, often obscures the boy's basic struggle to escape influences that cannot help him.

Goldman's next two novels are his most successful. *Your Turn to Curtsy, My Turn to Bow* is the powerful tale of a young man whose prowess on the football field leads him to fancy himself a new Messiah. When he fails to convert his former fans into spiritual disciples he quite literally crucifies himself. The novel focuses on another young man who learns from the failed Christ's example that the only way to preserve one's self in a world without well-grounded faith is to go through life following the routine he had been taught at a juvenile dancing school, where the metronome dictated that it was "your turn to curtsy, my turn to bow."

Reviewers missed the point of *Soldier in the Rain*, seeing it only as a farcical tale about a fat, over-privileged top sergeant and a conniving, semi-literate supply sergeant who have achieved security by making a comfortable home for themselves in the Army. As in Goldman's previous novel, however, the focus is not upon these two grotesques, but on an impressionable young soldier who falls under the influence of this pair, but is at last repulsed by them and determines to seek his own destiny rather than settle for easy security.

Goldman's longest novel, *Boys and Girls Together*, is the case history of a group of people who are brought together in New York to produce a play, although the story focuses on the playwright, who after a life-long struggle for identity succumbs to his homosexual tendencies. Most critics have found the long investigation of the pasts of the principal characters talky and tedious.

Two years later Goldman returned to extremely short, terse books with the first installment in an apparently continuing Story of Amos. *The Thing of It Is* . . . is a devastating analysis of a young American's inability to cope with success that picks up Amos McCracken after he has made a fortune from the songs for a Broadway musical and shows the gradual deterioration of his talent and marriage. The inconclusive *Father's Day* resumes the story after Amos's divorce and the failure of a new show and gruesomely depicts his destructive relationships with his daughter and mistress as he retreats constantly further into fantasy. The novel demands a follow-up in which we learn whether it is finally up or out for Amos.

Goldman has also written some very successful film scripts and a devastating analysis of a year on Broadway, *The Season*. His cynicism about the American Dream has made all his work exciting and controversial.

—Warren French

---

**GOODMAN, Paul.** American. Born in New York City, 9 September 1911. Educated at the City College of New York, B.A. 1931; University of Chicago, Ph.D. 1940 (received, 1954). Married twice; has two daughters. Reader for Metro-Goldwyn-Mayer, 1931; Instructor, University of Chicago, 1939–40; Teacher of Latin, physics, history and mathematics, Manumit School of Progressive Education, Pawling, New York, 1942; has also taught at New York University, 1948; Black Mountain College, North Carolina, 1950; Sarah Lawrence College, Bronxville, New York, 1961; Knapp Professor, University of Wisconsin, Madison, 1964; taught at the Experimental College of San Francisco State College, 1966; University of Hawaii, Honolulu, 1969, 1971. Formerly, Editor, *Complex* magazine, New York; Film Editor, *Partisan Review*, New Brunswick New Jersey; Television Critic, *New Republic*, Washington, D.C. Editor, *Liberation* magazine, New York, 1962–70. Recipient: American Council of Learned Societies Fellowship, 1940; Harriet Monroe Prize, *Poetry*, Chicago, 1949; National Institute of Arts and Letters grant, 1953. Fellow, New York Institute for Gestalt Therapy, 1953; Institute for Policy Studies, Washington, D.C., 1965. Address: 402 West 20th Street, New York, New York 10011, U.S.A.

PUBLICATIONS

Novels

   *The Grand Piano; or, The Almanac of Alienation.*   San Francisco, Colt Press, 1942.
   *The State of Nature.*   New York, Vanguard Press, 1946.
   *The Dead of Spring.*   Privately printed, 1950.
   *Parents Day.*   Saugatuck, Connecticut, 5 x 8 Press, 1951.
   *The Empire City.*   Indianapolis, Bobbs Merrill, 1959.
   *Making Do.*   New York, Macmillan, 1963.

Short Stories

   *The Facts of Life.*   New York, Vanguard Press, 1945; London, Editions Poetry, 1946.
   *The Break-up of Our Camp and Other Stories.*   New York, New Directions, 1950.
   *Our Visit to Niagara.*   New York, Horizon Press, 1960.
   *Adam and His Works: Collected Stories.*   New York, Vintage Books, 1968.

Plays

   *Faustina* (produced New York, 1952).   Included in *Three Plays*, 1965.
   *Father* (produced New York, 1953).
   *Three Plays: The Young Disciple, Faustina, Jonah.*   New York, Random House, 1965.
   *Jonah* (produced New York, 1966).   Included in *Three Plays*, 1965.
   *Tragedy and Comedy: 4 Cubist Plays.*   Los Angeles, Black Sparrow Press, 1970.

Verse

   *Stop-light: Five Dance Poems and an Essay on Noh.*   New York, Vinco Publishing
      Company, 1941.
   *Pieces of Three*, with Meyer Liben and Edouard Roditi.   Harrington, New Jersey,
      5 x 8 Press, 1942.
   *Five Young American Poets*, with others.   New York, New Directions, 1945.
   *The Well of Bethlehem.*   New York, privately printed, n.d. (c. 1950).
   *Red Jacket.*   New York, privately printed, 1956.
   *The Lordly Hudson: Collected Poems.*   New York, Macmillan, 1963.
   *Day and Other Poems.*   New York, privately printed, 1965.
   *Hawkweed.*   New York, Random House, 1967.
   *North Percy.*   Los Angeles, Black Sparrow Press, 1968.
   *Homespun of Oatmeal Gray.*   New York, Random House, 1970.

Other

   *Art and Social Nature* (essays).   New York, Vinco Publishing Company, 1946.
   *Kafka's Prayer.*   New York, Vanguard Press, 1947.
   *Communitas: Means of Livelihood and Ways of Life*, with Percival Goodman.   Chicago,
      University of Chicago Press, and London, Cambridge University Press, 1947;
      revised edition, New York, Knopf, 1960.
   *Gestalt Therapy*, with Frederick S. Perls and Ralph Hefferline.   New York, Messner,
      1951.

*The Structure of Literature.* Chicago, University of Chicago Press, and London, Cambridge University Press, 1954.

*Censorship and Pornography on the Stage, and Are Writers Shirking Their Political Duty?* New York, Living Theatre, 1959.

*Growing Up Absurd: Problems of Youth in the Organized Society.* New York, Random House, 1960; London, Gollancz, 1961.

*The Community of Scholars.* New York, Random House, 1962.

*Utopian Essays and Practical Proposals.* New York, Random House, 1962.

*Drawing the Line.* New York, Random House, 1962.

*The Society I Live In Is Mine.* New York, Horizon Press, 1963.

*Compulsory Mis-Education.* New York, Horizon Press, 1964.

*People or Personnel: Decentralizing and the Mixed System.* New York, Random House, 1965.

*Mass Education in Science.* Los Angeles, University of California, 1966.

*Five Years* (pensées). New York, Brussel and Brussel, 1967.

*Like a Conquered Province: The Moral Ambiguity of America.* New York, Random House, 1967.

*The Open Look.* New York, Funk and Wagnalls, 1969.

*New Reformation: Notes of a Neolithic Conservative.* New York, Random House, 1970.

*Speaking and Language.* New York, Random House, 1971.

Editor, *Seeds of Liberation.* New York, Braziller, 1965.

Editor, *Essays in American Colonial History.* New York, Holt Rinehart, 1967.


Paul Goodman comments:

I think *Adam* is my best single volume. It received not a single review. Next is *The Empire City*, which was withdrawn by the publisher.

\*       \*       \*

It is impossible to separate Paul Goodman's fiction from his other works of social criticism. Indeed his fiction often serves the same function as Plato's myths. Paul Goodman has been the most important "man of letters" writing in America for the past two decades. A combination of Emerson and Thoreau with a dash of Hawthorne, Goodman has been a seminal mind in many areas. He has produced major works in literary theory as well as his novels, short stories and poems, and has made major contributions to social theory, community planning, and educational theory and reform. He has combined this with a high degree of political activism. He has been a frequent speaker on the university lecture circuit, and was perhaps the most influential theorist influencing young people during the 60's.

For a number of reasons Goodman had difficulty getting published. An anarchist, Goodman found acceptance on neither the right nor the left. An explicit homosexual—a major theme in his fiction—Goodman's work was considered too radical for an earlier and more squeamish period of literary taste. Goodman's social radicalism was very much a part of his fiction, and both ideas and fiction found considerable resistance. *The Empire City*, his major novel, was long rejected by publishers, and *Growing Up Absurd*, now recognized as a classic of social thought in the 60's, was rejected by nearly 20 publishers before it finally reached the broad audience it deserved.

Goodman's earliest contributions were in the area of town planning (*Communitas*, which he wrote with his architect brother Percival) and literary theory (*The Structure of Literature*, a product of his doctoral work at the University of Chicago). Of *The Empire City* Goodman wrote in terms that would be applicable to all his fiction: "My one literary theme has been the community, as in *Parents Day* or *Break-up*; in *The Empire City* it is the band that acts as if it were the community and as if the others, who don't make sense, didn't exist." The young people of the novel can be seen as the raw material for *Growing Up Absurd*, which was written a decade later. A life-long resident of New York City, Goodman has made that city the major theme of his writings.

Academic critics trained in the devices of close reading would find little to praise in *The Empire City*. The work is sprawling and diffuse. Goodman, a trenchant critic of the academic scene, would not be bothered by such treatment. Written over a number of years, what the book lacks in narrative unity is more than compensated for by the richness of material and the evidence of evolving insight on the part of the author. The early sections of the novel, written during World War II, seem to owe a lot to the continental literary tradition. One is often reminded of *The Magic Mountain* of Thomas Mann. The later chapters, written in the following decade, become far more personal and gain immeasurably by the richness of the developing awareness of social issues on the author's part. Goodman is very much "in" his novels. He has said that the chapters of *The Empire City* "climax too strongly" for a dramatic work and that the book lacks enough motion towards a single climax. He describes the work as a picaresque epic with considerable justice. Horatio, the urban Huckleberry Finn who is the center of the story, is brought to an improbable maturity in the underground world of New York City in a period suffering from the anxieties of World War II and the disintegration of the modern urban capitalist social fabric. A great deal of Greek influence, particularly from Plato, is obvious. The "pastoral romance" of Horatio and Rosalind is one of the cleanest and most innocent of modern love stories. The story takes Horatio from the early 1940's into the Cold War world of the 50's and deals with the adjustments that he and his children must make to morally survive in a world gone mad.

The journal-notebook *Five Years*, published in 1967, makes clear that the novel *Making Do* (1963) was heavily autobiographical. His most sustained and successful long work of fiction, *Making Do* gives a profound insight into the life of the young. The story deals with a middle-aged social theorist (obviously Goodman himself) who tries fairly unsuccessfully to do something about the monumental problems faced by those who wish to morally relate to the modern world. He encounters and falls in love with a young schizophrenic student (Terry) during a conference appearance; the novel is concerned with their love and his attempts to create a world in which Terry can live and function. The theme of the novel is again that of building a community—that of the young and dispossessed, the addicts, the potheads, the queers—in short those whom Goodman would consider the healthy members of an insane world. Viewed against the realities of urban decay and atomic holocaust, the tiny community of love created by the characters has no chance. The homosexual experience on which the novel was built gave Goodman a magnificent metaphor for dealing with the society in which he lives. The Greek element in the love is probably not accidental. Goodman has never admired the more Roman values of military and social grandeur.

Goodman has felt that his homosexuality has given him useful insight into the world around him. In the essay "Memoirs of an Ancient Activist" (1969) he maintained that his homosexuality had made him a "nigger." An outsider in a domestic, bourgeois society dedicated to marriage and affluence, Goodman was able to stress simple and compassionate values:

> As a rule I don't believe in poverty and suffering as means of education, but in my case the hardship and starvation of my inept queer life have usefully simplified my notions of what a good society is. As with any other addict who cannot get an easy fix, they have kept me in close touch with material hunger. So I cannot take the GNP very seriously, nor status and credentials, nor grandiose technological solutions, nor ideological politics, including ideological liberation movements. . . . I have learned to have very modest goals for society and myself, things like clean air and water, green grass, children with bright eyes, not being pushed around, useful work that suits one's abilities, plain tasty food, and occasional satisfactory nookie.

The novels make essentially the same plea for a human world.

Many critics, including Norman Mailer, have criticized the sloppiness of Goodman's style. But Goodman has a lot to say, and ideas are important to him. Fiction is primarily valuable to Goodman as one way of communicating his vision. Through it he is able to show what a society fully aware of human values might be.

—Myron Taylor

---

**GORDIMER, Nadine.** South African. Born in Springs, Transvaal, 20 November 1923. Educated at the Convent School, and the University of the Witwatersrand, Johannesburg. Married G. Gavron in 1949; Reinhold Cassirer, 1954; has two children. Visiting Lecturer, Institute of Contemporary Arts, Washington, D.C., 1961; Harvard University, Cambridge, Massachusetts, 1969; Princeton University, New Jersey, 1969; Northwestern University, Evanston, Illinois, 1969; University of Michigan, Ann Arbor, 1970; Adjunct Professor of Writing, Columbia University, New York, 1971. Recipient: Smith Literary Award, 1961; Thomas Pringle Award, 1969. Address: 7 Frere Road, Parktown West, Johannesburg, South Africa.

PUBLICATIONS

Novels

*The Lying Days.* London, Gollancz, and New York, Simon and Schuster, 1953.
*A World of Strangers.* London, Gollancz, and New York, Simon and Schuster, 1958.
*Occasion for Loving.* London, Gollancz, and New York, Viking Press, 1963.
*The Late Bourgeois World.* London, Gollancz, and New York, Viking Press, 1966.
*A Guest of Honour.* New York, Viking Press, 1970; London, Cape, 1971.

Short Stories

*Face to Face: Short Stories.* Johannesburg, Silver Leaf Books, 1949.
*The Soft Voice of the Serpent and Other Stories.* New York, Simon and Schuster, 1952; London, Gollancz, 1953.
*Six Feet of the Country.* London, Gollancz, and New York, Simon and Schuster, 1956.
*Friday's Footprint and Other Stories.* London, Gollancz, and New York, Viking Press, 1960.
*Not for Publication and Other Stories.* London, Gollancz, and New York, Viking Press, 1965.
*Penguin Modern Stories 4*, with others. London, Penguin, 1970.
*Livingston's Companions.* New York, Viking Press, 1971; London, Cape, 1972.

Other

Editor, with Lionel Abrahams, *South African Writing Today*. London, Penguin, 1967.

Bibliography: *Nadine Gordimer, Novelist and Short Story Writer: A Bibliography of Her Works* by Racilia Jilian Nell, Johannesburg, University of the Witwatersrand, 1964.

Manuscript Collection: University of Texas, Austin.

Critical Study: "The Theme of Isolation in the Short Stories of Nadine Gordimer" by Dorothy E. Ledbetter, Master's Thesis, San Diego State College, 1969.

Nadine Gordimer comments:

Like any other writer, my allegiance is to what Proust called "That book of unknown signs within me no one could help me read by any rule, for its reading consists in an act of creation in which no one can take our place and in which no one can collaborate." He goes on to say —significantly for me—

> And how many turn away from writing it, how many tasks will one not assume to avoid that one! Every event, whether it was the Dreyfus affair or the war, furnished excuses to writers for not deciphering that book; they wanted to assert the triumph of Justice, to recreate the moral unity of the Nation, and they had no time to think of literature. But those were only excuses because either they did not possess or had ceased to possess genius, that is, instinct. For it is instinct which dictates duty and intelligence which offers pretexts for avoiding it. But excuses do not count, the artist must at all times follow his instinct, which makes art the most real thing, the most austere school in life and the last true judgment.

This does not mean to say that I think I should turn my back on "my" Dreyfus affair in South Africa (bannings and detentions without trial) or "my" war (against apartheid), but that their significance should be nothing less than deeply implicit in whatever I write, since it is *there*: part of the substance of life within which my instinct as a writer must struggle. Unlike Sartre, I believe a "writer's morality" is valid, and the temptation to put one's writing at the service of a cause—whether it is fighting the colour-bar or "the momentary renunciation of literature in order to educate the people", etc.—is a betrayal. Similarly, I should turn back upon him his question, "In a country lacking leaders, in Africa, for instance, how could a native educated in Europe refuse to become a professor, even at the price of his literary vocation?" How should he not? As much as increased crops and more schools and universities, Africa needs an articulated consciousness other than that of newspaper headlines and political speeches.

Although none of my books is formally political, the South African situation has conditioned me as a writer to an extent that could not have happened in any other country, through the extraordinary way in which the political situation has moulded the lives of the people around me. Not only obvious confrontations of black and white are affected; whites among themselves are shaped by their peculiar position, just as black people are by theirs. I write about their private selves; often, even in the most private situations, they are what they are because their lives are regulated and their mores formed by the political situation. You see, in South Africa, society *is* the political situation. To paraphrase, one might say (too often), politics is character—in South Africa. I am not a politically-minded person by nature. I don't suppose, if I had lived elsewhere, my writing would have reflected politics much. If at all. As it is, I have come to the abstractions of politics through the flesh and blood of individual behaviour. I didn't know what politics was about until I saw it all *happening* to *people*. If I've been influenced to recognize man as a political animal, in my writing, then that's come about through living in South Africa.

Is this a limitation? How can I say? I honestly don't think I've ever sacrificed the possible revelation of a private contradiction to make a political point. My method is to let the general seep up through the individual, whether or not the theme can be summed up afterwards as "Jealousy", "Racial Conflict" or what-have-you. Despite what I've said above, quite a lot of my writing could have come about absolutely anywhere—the stories in particular; some of the stories are even set in other countries. My private preoccupations remain, running strongly beneath or alongside or interwined with the influence of the political situation. I don't think I should allow myself to blame any limitations on the impingement of politics; in another situation, I should probably have developed other limitations and found other factors to take the blame.

My stories often originate in what might be called the tail-tip of a situation as it is whisked out of sight. A look, a sentence hanging in mid-air (I'm a great unconscious eavesdropper, always have been, on street corners, in restaurants, planes, etc.). A train of associations begins to play out; the story begins to form about the fragment. When stories arise out of actual experiences of my own, there is usually a lapse of months or even years between the happening and the writing, a lapse during which the experience lies dormant, gathering like a magnet those characters, phrases, ideas, ancillary events, that belong with it in mind, and will transform it. Time means nothing in that part of the mind where this takes place; something that happened ten years ago on the other side of the world coexists with something observed yesterday.

—Excerpted by the author from an interview
with Alan Ross in *London Magazine*, May 1965.

\*       \*       \*

Among the handful of novelists who have begun, during recent decades, to create a distinctive South African literary tradition, Nadine Gordimer occupies a prominent place. Her fiction, like that of Alan Paton, Dan Jacobson and Jack Cope, presents and critically explores many areas of contemporary life, and accurately reflects the tensions inherent in South Africa's white-dominated multi-racial society. Where her contemporaries occasionally allow sentiment or humour to blur the edges of their realism, Nadine Gordimer's vision of life in South Africa has grown steadily bleaker over the years, and her condemnation of the society which has chosen the immoral way of *"apartheid"* to maintain its supremacy, has become harsher. " . . . Afraid, alive, afraid, alive . . ." is the refrain heard by the narrator of *The Late Bourgeois World*, as she lies awake at the end of that novel, having failed to make the small gesture which might have helped a former friend, because of the possibly unpleasant consequences for herself. This novel, Nadine Gordimer's bitterest and most despairing book, implies that the price the whites pay for living in South Africa today is a numbing fear which destroys their capacity to feel, and which, in the end, destroys life itself. The world outside South Africa's borders presents a slightly less gloomy picture, and Miss Gordimer's most recent novel, *A Guest of Honour*, even though it ends with a death, shows little trace of the despair which marks her South African novels and short stories.

In her first four novels, and also in most of her early short stories (which generally highlight particular themes later developed and extended in the novels), Miss Gordimer uses Johannesburg, South Africa's "golden city", as her setting. For her, as for a number of other South African writers, Johannesburg is a microcosm of modern South Africa: a place where the very rich and the very poor live and work, almost side by side; where black and white come into daily contact with one another; where sophisticated Europe rubs shoulders with tribal Africa. It is a cosmopolitan city where loneliness can be a matter of being white in a black crowd. The characters who interest her particularly are sensitive, cultivated men and women. Sometimes they are politically conscious; more often, they are simply anxious to enjoy a comfortable life. All of them are engaged in the same kind of quest: a search for satisfactory personal relationships with others, in which differences of class and colour will be forgotten.

The first four novels are a record of the increasing difficulty of this quest, hampered as it necessarily is in South Africa by restrictive legislation which forbids many kinds of contact between people. The novels are also marked by an obviously growing despair. Helen Shaw, the heroine of *The Lying Days*, is reasonably optimistic about life. At the end of the novel she is still young enough not to have been daunted by the signs of violence and unpleasantness she has begun to notice in her society, and she cherishes a belief in what she terms "the phoenix illusion", hope for a future in which she will find a place in South African society, and will be able to help others, while enjoying personal happiness. Toby Hood, the narrator and central character in *A World of Strangers*, is more dubious about his ability to live in Johannesburg. His world seems split in two: a white half and a black one. In spite of his efforts to unite the two fragments, there seems no possibility of introducing the strangers to one another. Generally, the realism of the urban scenes, the childhood scenes in *The Lying Days*, and the township scenes in *A World of Strangers* (both the latter new in South African fiction), seemed to indicate that Miss Gordimer's talent lay pre-eminently in detailed and minutely recorded observation.

*Occasion for Loving* and *The Late Bourgeois World*, however, marked a new departure. Less concerned with observing and recording typical scenes, and concentrating less on representative characters, these two novels explore, in considerable depth and with increasing complexity, the effect which life in a colour-bar society has on individuals who are fundamentally decent and humane. With a depressing and logical clarity, Miss Gordimer appears to suggest that a withering of the heart is inevitable: that neither genuine love nor real passion can survive in a tortured society. *Occasion for Loving*, based on a triangular relationship (a love affair between a white woman and a black man, with an older white woman as observer and sympathiser) is the less successful book, partly because there is altogether too much material which has been unsatisfactorily absorbed into the pattern of the novel. *The Late Bourgeois World* shows a great improvement in style and in construction: not only is Miss Gordimer's tendency to indulge in somewhat flamboyant imagery kept firmly under control, but the structure is taut and economical, the central theme is clear, and everything else is carefully, but not obtrusively, subordinated to it. The theme, demonstrated in the lives of all the characters, is sterility born of fear—the inevitable concomitant of the particular bourgeois way of life described in the novel.

Against this background, *A Guest of Honour* comes as something of a surprise. Despair and disillusion give way, in this novel, to a joyful and unhesitant acceptance of whatever life has to offer; the frustration experienced by characters who feel themselves trapped by custom and law gives way to an active determination to achieve freedom and dignity. The setting is no longer South Africa, but an unnamed country in central Africa, which has just achieved its independence, and is now facing all the problems associated with freedom: neo-colonialism, foreign exploitation, internal dissension, lingering tribalism, bankruptcy, lack of educational resources. James Bray, a middle-aged Englishman, who has spent most of his life in Africa, is invited back by the new president to help in the organisation and establishment of the territory. There is, of course, very little that anyone in Bray's position can do, and he is well aware of this. At the same time, he is determined to do what he can, and not to waste any time in useless regrets for the past. Both in telling Bray's story, and in portraying the complexities—social, political, historical and geographical—of the country, Miss Gordimer has produced her finest work to date. The novel has a breadth and scope which none of the previous books has, the claustrophobic South African scene being replaced by a much wider and more interestingly imagined world. In this novel, too, the coldness which mars some of the earlier work—an apparent inability to sympathise with her characters—is less obtrusive than formerly. *A Guest of Honour* ends on a deliberately ironic note: Bray dies in mysterious circumstances, and his work appears to have been done in vain. But the weight of the whole novel is against the irony: what Bray has done, has all been done in good faith, and in hope. The "phoenix illusion" has risen again in Africa, though its new form may seem strange, and though its promises, as always, are for the future.

—Ursula Laredo

**GORDON, Caroline.** American. Born in Trenton, Kentucky, 6 October 1895. Educated at Bethany College, West Virginia, A.B. 1916. Married Allen Tate, *q.v.*, in 1924 (divorced, 1959); has one child. Reporter, *Chattanooga News*, Tennessee, 1920–24. Lecturer in English, University of North Carolina Woman's College, Greensboro, 1938–39. Since 1946, has lectured in creative writing at the School of General Studies, Columbia University, New York. Visiting Professor of English, University of Washington, Seattle, 1953; Writer-in-Residence, University of Kansas, Lawrence, 1956, and University of California, Davis, 1962–63. Recipient: Guggenheim Fellowship, 1932; O. Henry Award, 1934; National Institute of Arts and Letters grant, 1950; National Endowment for the Arts grant, 1966. D.Litt., Bethany College, 1946; St. Mary's College, Notre Dame, Indiana, 1964. Address: The Red House, Princeton, New Jersey 08540, U.S.A.

PUBLICATIONS

Novels

    *Penhally*. New York, Scribner, 1931.
    *Aleck Maury, Sportsman*. New York, Scribner, 1934; as *The Pastimes of Aleck Maury: The Life of a True Sportsman*, London, Dickson, 1935.
    *None Shall Look Back*. New York, Scribner, 1937; as *None Shall Look Back: A Story of the American Civil War*, London, Constable, 1937.
    *The Garden of Adonis*. New York, Scribner, 1937.
    *Green Centuries*. New York, Scribner, 1941.
    *The Women on the Porch*. New York, Scribner, 1944.
    *The Strange Children*. New York, Scribner, 1951; London, Routledge, 1952.
    *The Malefactors*. New York, Harcourt Brace, 1956.
    *The Glory of Hera*. New York, Doubleday, 1972.

Short Stories

    *The Forest of the South*. New York, Scribner, 1945.
    *Old Red and Other Stories*. New York, Scribner, 1963.

Other

    *How to Read a Novel*. New York, Viking Press, 1957.
    *A Good Soldier: A Key to the Novels of Ford Madox Ford*. Davis, University of California Library, 1963.

    Editor, with Allen Tate, *The House of Fiction: An Anthology of the Short Story, with Commentary*. New York, Scribner, 1950; revised edition, 1960.

Bibliography: by Joan Griscom, in *Critique* (Minneapolis), Winter 1956.

Critical Studies: "The Novel as Christian Comedy" by Ashley Brown, in *Reality and Myth*, edited by William E. Walker and Robert L. Welker, Nashville, Tennessee, Vanderbilt University Press, 1964; "Caroline Gordon Issue" of *Southern Review* (Baton Rouge, Louisiana), Spring 1971.

*        *        *

The subject matter of Caroline Gordon's novels is the American southern experience as it has shaped the lives of herself, her ancestors, and the history of the regions of the South with which she has had personal associations. Her viewpoint is conservative, Catholic, and Agrarian with a preference for rural life, a dislike of the liberalized urban society of the North, an admiration for a stable, aristocratic society based on landed wealth, and a veneration for the heroism and chivalry of the old South.

In *None Shall Look Back* Miss Gordon depicts the decline of a Kentucky family, the Allards, caused in part by the Civil War and in part by the family's internal weaknesses. Woven into the story of the private tragedy of the Allards is the public tragedy of the South, as epitomized in the epic heroic figure of Nathan Bedford Forrest. The brilliant battle scenes, the pathos of the destruction of an admired way of life, and the skill with which public and private events are unified make this novel one of her finest. *Green Centuries* tells the story of the pioneer couple Rion Outlaw and Cassy Dawson of Carolina who settle in Indian country near the Cumberland Gap during the American Revolution. Their frontier life is realistically presented; yet the novel transcends realism and becomes symbolic of the clash between the communal culture of the Indians and the fierce Promethean individualism of the pioneer whites. *Aleck Maury, Sportsman* is the story of a schoolteacher with a life-long compulsive desire to hunt the woods and fish the streams of his native region. His way of life involving ritual, physical skill, and a sacramental view of nature is sympathetically treated; the hunting and fishing scenes are especially fine. *Penhally* presents the decline of the house of Penhally brought down by jealousy and pride and by the destruction of the Civil War. *The Garden of Adonis* pictures the Allards again, this time living in the depression of the thirties in the degrading conditions of decayed Agrarianism—the men, Adonis figures, at the mercy of their irrational and neurotic women. *The Women on the Porch*, set in the early forties, has as its central figure Catherine Chapman who escapes from New York and her husband, Jim, a rootless midwestern intellectual, to the shelter of enervated relatives living in Tennessee, only to find their decadent way of life also unsatisfactory. She is rescued by a repentant husband who regains her love by a non-intellectual act of jealous violence. In *The Strange Children*, the child-like activities of the adult intellectuals are critically observed by the young girl Lucy who represents the innocent spirit and the hope for individual salvation. In *The Malefactors*, Claiborne, a poet who has lost his creativity because of sterile intellectualism, is rehabilitated by Catherine Pollard, a Catholic philanthropist.

There is a development in Miss Gordon's fiction from a concern with the future of society to a concern with the individual who is capable of salvation regardless of his society. Although her religious and social views are implicit in all her work, she is never doctrinaire; her complex characters and their actions never lose the surface realism which brings them to life.

—Donald E. Stanford

---

**GOVER, (John) Robert.** American. Born in Philadelphia, Pennsylvania, 2 November 1929. Educated at the University of Pittsburgh, B.A. 1953. Married Mildred Vitkovich in 1955 (divorced, 1966); Jeanne-Nell Gement, 1968; has one child. Held a variety of jobs, including that of Reporter on various newspapers, in Pennsylvania and Maryland, until 1961. Address: 540 Picacho Lane, Santa Barbara, California 93108, U.S.A.

PUBLICATIONS

Novels

>One Hundred Dollar Misunderstanding. New York, Grove Press, and London, Spearman, 1962.
>The Maniac Responsible. New York, Grove Press, 1963; London, MacGibbon and Kee, 1964.
>Here Goes Kitten. New York, Grove Press, 1964.
>Poorboy at the Party. New York, Simon and Schuster, 1966.
>J. C. Saves. New York, Simon and Schuster, 1968.

Other

>Editor, The Portable Walter, by Walter Lowenfels. New York, International Publishers, 1968.

*     *     *

In the "After Words" to *J. C. Saves* (the last volume of the trilogy begun with *One Hundred Dollar Misunderstanding* and *Here Goes Kitten*), Robert Gover tells us that at the beginning "I had no preconceived idea where these two characters would lead me, their author." Unfortunately, the reader's sharing of that aimlessness is such that he arrives at the last page of the last volume with the sense that the trilogy is completed only because the author has told him so. There is no reason why the characters might not go on in book after book, *ad infinitum*, like the Rover Boys. When J. C. Holland, the white middle-class protagonist, and Kitten, his black prostitute love, achieve their partial understanding at the end of *J. C. Saves*, it is clear that the slightest alteration provided by another time and other circumstances will be enough to set another story in motion. For the fact is that this is formula fiction: shake up the characters, move them to a new starting point, put them in motion, follow the formula, and you have another book.

Yet there is an honesty in Gover, a vision of the life about him, and a quality of writing that raises him above the level of either the pulp pornographer or the slick composer of best sellers. However much he taxes the reader's impatience with shallow characterizations, absurd plot manipulations, gratuitous sex, and moral implications that are occasionally downright silly, he is at times an accomplished satirist. One must only imagine his books in the form of Classic Comics, illustrated by cartoonists for *Mad Magazine*, to be made aware how sure is his touch for the particular grotesque exaggeration that comically, or cruelly, reveals a specific truth. His are not realistic novels, but verbal comic strips, sharing a good many of the virtues and faults of such a paradigm of the genre as Norman Mailer's *An American Dream*.

In large measure he is a moralist—disgusting at times, bitter and angry at others, but always subordinating the matter to the message. And the message is always the same: the Anglo-Saxon American power structure has created a society in which sex and violence are so perversely twisted together that there is no place for honest respect and affection between individuals, classes, or races. Never showing what society might be, he concentrates his attention on the extremes of actuality that he sees as emblematic of the whole. In some respects his most memorable statement is *The Maniac Responsible*, where he parallels the movements of a reporter covering a brutal sex murder with the man's movements while attempting to seduce his teasingly voluptuous neighbor. Finally driven by circumstances (the natural circumstances, the author suggests, of the American way of life) and his own sensitivity, he becomes a suspect in the murder and breaks down into an admission that he, himself, is the maniac responsible (as we all are) for the rape and murder of the girl.

Sex is in the forefront of all of Gover's novels. However, the human failures he depicts are not to be blamed on sex, but rather on the failure of its right use, the tendency to treat the other human being as a means rather than an end. Significantly, in the twisted world of Gover's vision the individual who seems best to know how to use her sex is Kitten, the Negro prostitute. Significantly, too, the Kitten trilogy, *Poorboy at the Party*, and *The Maniac Responsible* all end in rejections of the middle-class societies they have portrayed.

—George Perkins

GOYEN, (Charles) William.   American.   Born in Trinity, Texas, 24 April 1915. Educated at Rice University, Houston, B.A. 1937, M.A. 1939. Served in the United States Navy, 1940–45. Married Doris Roberts in 1963. Critic and Reviewer, *New York Times*, 1950–65. Taught at the New School for Social Research, New York, 1955–60, and Columbia University, New York, 1964–66. Since 1966, Senior Editor, Trade Department, McGraw Hill Book Company, New York. Recipient: Guggenheim Fellowship, 1951, 1954; Ford grant, for theatre, 1963; ASCAP award, for musical compositions, 1965, 1966, 1968, 1969, 1970. Address: 277 West End Avenue, New York, New York 10023, U.S.A.

PUBLICATIONS

Novels

   *The House of Breath*.   New York, Random House, 1950; London, Chatto and Windus, 1951.
   *In a Farther Country*.   New York, Random House, 1955; London, Peter Owen, 1962.
   *The Fair Sister*.   New York, Doubleday, 1962; as *Savata, My Fair Sister*, London, Peter Owen, 1963.

Short Stories

   *Ghost and Flesh: Stories and Tales*.   New York, Random House, 1952.
   *The Faces of Blood Kindred: A Novella and 10 Stories*.   New York, Random House, 1960.
   *The Collected Stories of William Goyen*.   New York, Doubleday, 1972.

Uncollected Short Stories

   "The Figure over the Town", in *Saturday Evening Post* (New York), 27 April 1963.
   "Tenants", in *Der Diebische Steppenwolf: Drei Erzahlungen*. Frankfurt, Insel-Verlag, 1963.
   "The Thief Coyote", in *Southwest Review* (Dallas), Summer 1971.

Plays

*The House of Breath* (produced New York, 1956).
*The Diamond Rattler* (produced Boston, 1960).
*Christy* (produced New York, 1964).

Other

*A Book of Jesus.*   New York, Doubleday, 1972.

Translator, *The Lazy Ones*, by Albert Cossery.   New York, New Directions, and
London, Peter Owen, 1952.

Lyrics for the film, *The Left-Handed Gun*, 1959.

Manuscript Collection: Fondren Library, Rice University, Houston.

Critical Studies: "The House of Breath" by Katherine Anne Porter, in *New York Times
Book Review*, 20 August 1950; "The First Novel of a Young American" by Ernst Robert
Curtius, in *Neue Schweize Rundschau* (Zurich), March 1952; review by Lon Tinkle, in *Dallas
Morning News*, October 1955; essay by Granville Hicks, in *Saturday Review* (New York),
5 October 1963; *The Poetics of Space* by Gaston Bachelard, New York, Orion Press, 1964;
*The Novel of the Future* by Anaïs Nin, New York, Macmillan, 1966; *Les U.S.A. à la récherche
de leur identité* by Pierre Dommergues, Paris, Grasset, 1966; essay by Daniel Stern, in *Re-
Discovery*, New York, Crown, 1971; essay by Clyde Grimm, Jr., in *Studies in South-Western
Literature* (Austin, Texas), 1971; "The Romance of Prophecy: Goyen's *In a Farther Country*"
by Robert Phillips, in *Southwest Review* (Dallas), Summer 1971.

William Goyen comments:

   My birthplace, once a thriving railroad and sawmill town by the Trinity River, is Trinity,
located in the soft woods-and-meadows area of East Texas. My father's family brought him
as a young man to Trinity from Mississippi. They were sawmill people. My mother's family,
native Texans, was made up of carpenters, railroad men (there was a prominent roundhouse
in Trinity), but her father was Postmaster of the town for many years. We lived in Trinity
until I was seven. The world of that town, its countryside, its folk, its speech and superstition
and fable, was stamped into my senses during those first seven years of my life; and I spent
the first twelve years of my writing life reporting it and fabricating it in short fiction. In my
seventh year we moved to Shreveport, Louisiana, lived there a year, thence to Houston. I
was educated, from the third grade, in that city: grammar school, Junior High School, High
School, Rice University. As a child I was quick and scared; serving; secretly unsettled;
imaginative and nervous and sensual. When I reached Sam Houston High School, I thought
surely I would be a composer, actor, dancer, singer, fantastico. My mother and father were
embarrassed by such ambitions. Nevertheless, I found a way to study dancing, music composition, singing, clandestinely. When this was found out by my parents, who were outraged
by the extents of my determination, I did not run away from home to a city. I decided to go
underground at home, and write. No one could know that I was doing that. It was my own.
This was in my sixteenth year, and what I wrote was lyrical, melancholy, yearning, romantic
and sentimental. Above all, it was homesick, and written at home.
   College for me was intolerable. I hated the classes, the courses, the students. I refused to
study Mathematics, and so failed the required Freshman course in Mathematics for three

straight years. I wanted to make up new things, not "study" what had already been made. In my Junior year, the thunderstrike came. I discovered Shakespeare, Chaucer, Milton, Yeats, Joyce, the French Symbolists, Flaubert, Turgenev, Balzac, Melville, Hawthorne. I was at literature, insatiable, for the next three years, reading, and writing under the glow and turmoil of what I was reading. Suddenly—it seemed—I had accomplished the Masters Degree in Comparative Literature (1939). I had been writing plays and stories, and in my Junior and Senior years I took all the prizes in both forms.

Leaving Rice University, I took a teaching position at the University of Houston in its first year. Near the end of that year, I was drafted; it was 1939. I joined the Navy as an enlisted man, worked a year in the local Recruiting Office of Houston, then was sent to Midshipman School in New York City for Officer Training at Columbia University. It was my first exposure to city life and culture, and I was in uniform, preparing to go to sea and war. After three months of indoctrination, I went off to the war, and I served five years in it, mostly on an aircraft carrier in the South Pacific. During the war, I determined to write as a way of life; and at the end of the war, I went to New Mexico (El Prado, above Taos) and began to write from myself. There I met Frieda Lawrence and Dorothy Brett who became the first real influences on my life as artist. I built a little abode house in El Prado on land given to me by Frieda and began my first novel, *The House of Breath*, in that mud house. I worked close to two years on it there, then finished it in London. It was clear to me now: I saw my life as a writing life, a life of giving shape to what happened, of searching for meanings, clarification, Entirety. It was my Way: expression in words. From then on, I managed to write, with little or no money, with growing distinction—which, I have come to see, brings little usable reward—awards, honors, little money. What I wanted was to make splendor. What I saw, felt, knew was real, was bigger than what I could make of it. That made it a lifetime task, I saw that.

I have felt nagged to write for the theatre from time to time, craving theatricality, collaborative fanfare, and show; have written very scarcely for the films and for television. All forms of writing excite me and pain me and labor me; but the printed word, the Book—especially the short narrative form—most challenges and most frees me.

*         *         *

The literary position of the state of Texas has always been dubious in the spectrum of the Southern Literary Renaissance, that remarkable fluorescence of literary genius in 20th century American writing which matches and in some ways surpasses the great 19th century Flowering of New England. Much of the literary production of Texas seems to belong to a category best labeled "South-Western" rather than "Southern", whereas some novels are obviously closer to the fiction of the South and Border States. Whatever the labels, the literary record of Texas is more impressive than is generally assumed, ranging as it does from the celebrated books of folklorist J. Frank Dobie (such as *Apache Gold and Yaqui Silver*, and *Tales of Old Texas*) and George Sessions Perry's famous novel *Hold Autumn in Your Hand* (1941) to the now almost forgotten novels *The Devil Rides Outside* by John Howard Griffin and *Summer in the Water* by David Westheimer, but also including the works of Katherine Anne Porter, William Humphrey, Walter Clemmons and William Goyen. An attempt to "locate" a body of fiction by state or region may, finally, be misleading. When Goyen's first novel, *House of Breath*, appeared in 1950, reviewers tended to see it in terms of William Faulkner and Thomas Wolfe, and in terms of cliches about the "Southern" novel. To those early reviewers, the sickness of image, some eccentricities of syntax (parentheses within parentheses), the occasional violence, the hurt, and other such elements seemed to indicate a novel in the Southern mode; and certainly East Texas where the action takes place is closer in heritage to the Southern border states than to the wild west stereotypes. But, with the passage of time it has become increasingly apparent that Goyen's themes and fictional strategies are closer to those of Virginia Woolf than to Thomas Wolfe or Faulkner or even Anderson's *Winesburg, Ohio*.

Like the work of Flannery O'Connor, John Hawkes, and the later Mailer, Goyen's fiction is deliberately outside the realist traditions. Virginia Woolf in a review of Dorothy Richardson's *Revolving Lights* pointed out that Richardson was concerned "with states of being and not with states of doing". The violent activity in these writers' stories is often the outward sign for psychic states; so that Mailer in *An American Dream* seems finally uninterested in the murder, but rather more interested in the states of being of his characters— something quite different from Dreiser's treatment of the murder in *An American Tragedy*. Whether concerned with religion, sex or politics the works are Romance. Hawthorne, after all, defined the word "Romance" at the beginning of *The House of the Seven Gables*—and despite Hemingway's brave assertion in *Green Hills of Africa* that all American literature comes from Twain's *Huckleberry Finn*, it is apparent that almost all major American novels can, in their theoretical basis, be traced back to Hawthorne's preface to his novel. William Goyen and a few other contemporary American novelists have taken the process a step further with their increasing reliance on a poetic prose to evoke deep psychic states, and their increasing abandonment of traditional realist themes and strategies: these novels are closer to *Cymbeline* and *A Winter's Tale* than to *Tom Jones* or *Bleak House*.

This particular sort of Romance has been distinguished in Ralph Freedman's important study *The Lyrical Novel*. The lyrical novel he defines as "concentration on the inner life and on its distillation in spiritual or aesthetic forms. The passive hero, recreating his perceptions symbolically, dominates the world of images for whose existence he is responsible." Further, "the lyrical novel assumes a unique form which transcends the causal and temporal movement of narrative within the framework of fiction." Though Freedman centers his examination on European writers of "the lyrical novel" (Rilke, Hesse, Woolf, Gide), that examination might be extended to Anais Nin, John Hawkes, Flannery O'Connor, and William Goyen. I have labored this theoretical point because Goyen's work has been constantly overlooked or even dismissed, since its aims and strategies have been overlooked or mistaken by critics and other readers.

*Faces of Blood Kindred*, for example, is a collection of brilliant "lyrical" stories, in Freedman's sense of the word. In many of them nothing much happens in the sense of external "doing". Yet states of being are evoked, or explored. The stories bear down on moments of revelation, when ties of family or kinship are revealed, usually by chance incidents. The consequences of the revelation or discovery seem less important than the moment of perception itself: in a 19th century English novel, a boy might discover who his parents were, and he would automatically fit into a family structure; but in Goyen's work, the old stable family units have broken down, so that kinship tends to be spiritual rather than social, tends to an archetypal relationship beyond the social world.

To many readers, expecting a different sort of fiction, the stories seem vague, seeking to evoke more than they say, something beyond language at which language can only offer hints and guesses. "There are, indeed, things that cannot be put into words. They *make themselves manifest*. They are what is mystical." These words are not Goyen's but Wittengenstein's in his supposedly "positivist" *Tractatus* (6.522).

Like Carson McCullers, whose stories are also often ostensibly violent yet internalized, Goyen is a true extension of the Transcendental strain in American fiction. The wide, scarred, outcast people of the stories are manifestations of spiritual conditions. In his second novel, *In a Farther Country*, the narrator says: "Here, again, was the frail artifice built by the world that dreamt the solid other, the marriage and mixture of dream and circumstance that breeds back daily the pure race. . . ." His novels and stories are collections of voices (compare Wallace Stevens' great line in "The Woman That Had More Babies Than That": "The self is a cloister full of remembered sounds") each trying to tell of some hidden sort of Platonic other-world of forms or ideal states, or the truth of a life.

The stories and tales collected in *Ghost and Flesh* all concern characters whose telling of their lives, as in conversation, lead Goyen to deal with intermediate states, to the struggles between body and soul, ghost and flesh, the frustrated search of each for the other in a total communion that can at best be only momentary. The intermediacy is also temporal; for as in *House of Breath* the narrator recounts stories that do not happen in the present, yet are not entirely in the past: they are part of what the narrator thinks he might blow away (the house, or family, of the book is, after all, the creation of the telling, the boy-man's breath) yet cannot since it all exists like "a fresco on the wall of [his] skull." The permanence of the fleeting moment, in altered lives as in a single man's memory, constitutes one of the recurring themes. Yet reality always seems to lie elsewhere, somewhere toward which the tensions between ghost and flesh may lead. It is strange to hear Mailer apparently so different from Goyen, now saying in *Maidstone* (1971): "You can't say that this is real now, what we're doing. You can't say what we were doing last night is real; the only thing you can say is that the reality exists somewhere in the extraordinary tension between the extremes."

This questioning of reality is one of the central themes in Goyen's books. His most recent novel, *The Fair Sister*, for example, is a shrewd, witty, and revealing study of religious feeling. The first person narrator, Ruby Drew, tells (or seems to tell) about the Light of the World Holiness Church, her fair sister Savata, and Canaan Johnson who tempted and won. The story of two sisters, one dark and one light, gives us the struggle of ugliness (self-concealed) and devotion (self-congratulated), of holiness and sensuality, cast in the diction and rhythms of a revivalism which is finally ambiguous: who can say what is being revived, or what the truth of the situation is? Or, another example from *In a Farther Country*, the setting in Woolworth's to which the central character returns "every day to smell and touch" the things of this world within the other world of New York City. "She seemed unhurried, unenthusiastic. She asked the same question every day, 'Where is the lunch counter?' as though Woolworth's were a vast unchartered country. . . ." When she gains entry to the store at night, she asks, "But where is Woolworth's?" The counters have been covered with dustcloths, so that the store of the nightwatchman is not the same as the store of the salesgirls. The eccentric behaviour of the woman and her apparently simple questions raise issues of appearance and reality which become central in later chapters, as each character in his telling of his life arrives at some moment of communal insight: "Confusion seeks confusion to clarify itself before falling to confusion again." And the novel rises to a visionary denouement.

I have not dealt with Goyen's superb first novel, *House of Breath*, since it has received ample critical commentary already; nor with his classic stories "The White Rooster" and "Letter in the Cedar Chest," well known through anthologies. For it seems to me crucial that we begin to see the work of this fine literary artist not in terms of the southern gothic novel of violence and race, but in larger terms.

—James Korges

---

**GRAHAM, Winston (Mawdesley).** British. Born in Manchester. Married Jean Mary Williamson in 1939; has two children. Chairman, Society of Authors, London, 1967–69. Fellow, Royal Society of Literature, 1968. Address: Abbotswood House, Buxted, Sussex, England.

PUBLICATIONS

Novels

*The House with the Stained-Glass Windows*.   London, Ward Lock, 1934.
*Into the Fog*.   London, Ward Lock, 1935.
*The Riddle of John Rowe*.   London, Ward Lock, 1935.
*Without Motive*.   London, Ward Lock, 1936.

*Dangerous Pawn.*   London, Ward Lock, 1937.

*Giant's Chair.*   London, Ward Lock, 1938.

*Strangers Meeting.*   London, Ward Lock, 1939.

*Keys of Chance.*   London, Ward Lock, 1939.

*No Exit: An Adventure.*   London, Ward Lock, 1940.

*Night Journey.*   London, Ward Lock, 1941; Bodley Head, 1966; New York, Doubleday, 1968.

*My Turn Next.*   London, Ward Lock, 1942.

*The Merciless Ladies.*   London, Ward Lock, 1944.

*The Forgotten Story.*   London, Ward Lock, 1945; Bodley Head, 1964; as *The Wreck of the Grey Cat*, New York, Doubleday, 1958.

*Ross Poldark: A Novel of Cornwall, 1783–1787.*   London, Ward Lock, 1945; Bodley Head, 1960; as *Renegade*, New York, Doubleday, 1951.

*Demelza: A Novel of Cornwall, 1788–1790.*   London, Ward Lock, 1946; New York, Doubleday, 1953; London, Bodley Head, 1960.

*Take My Life.*   London, Ward Lock, 1947; Bodley Head, 1965; New York, Doubleday, 1967.

*Cordelia.*   London, Ward Lock, 1949; New York, Doubleday, 1950; London, Bodley Head, 1963.

*Night Without Stars.*   London, Hodder and Stoughton, and New York, Doubleday, 1950; London, Bodley Head, 1970.

*Jeremy Poldark: A Novel of Cornwall, 1790–1791.*   London, Ward Lock, 1950; Bodley Head, 1961; as *Venture Once More: A Novel of Cornwall, 1790–1791*, New York, Doubleday, 1954.

*Warleggan: A Novel of Cornwall, 1792–1793.*   London, Ward Lock, 1953; Bodley Head, 1961; as *The Last Gamble*, New York, Doubleday, 1955.

*Fortune Is a Woman.*   London, Hodder and Stoughton, and New York, Doubleday, 1953; London, Bodley Head, 1969.

*The Little Walls.*   London, Hodder and Stoughton, and New York, Doubleday, 1955; London, Bodley Head, 1972.

*The Sleeping Partner.*   London, Hodder and Stoughton, and New York, Doubleday, 1956; London, Bodley Head, 1969.

*Greek Fire.*   London, Hodder and Stoughton, 1957; New York, Doubleday, 1958; London, Bodley Head, 1970.

*The Tumbled House.*   London, Hodder and Stoughton, 1959; New York, Doubleday, 1960; London, Bodley Head, 1970.

*Marnie.*   London, Hodder and Stoughton, and New York, Doubleday, 1961; London, Bodley Head, 1969.

*The Grove of Eagles.*   London, Hodder and Stoughton, 1963; New York, Doubleday, 1964; London, Collins, 1970.

*After the Act.*   London, Hodder and Stoughton, 1965; New York, Doubleday, 1966; London, Bodley Head, 1971.

*The Walking Stick.*   London, Collins, and New York, Doubleday, 1967.

*Angell, Pearl and Little God.*   London, Collins, and New York, Doubleday, 1970.


Short Stories

*The Japanese Girl and Other Stories.*   London, Collins, and New York, Doubleday 1971.


Other

*The Spanish Armadas.*   London, Collins, and New York, Doubleday, 1972.

Winston Graham comments:

I look on myself simply as a novelist. I have written—always—what I wanted to write and not what I thought other people might want me to write. Reading for me has always been in the first place a matter of enjoyment—otherwise I don't read—and therefore I would expect other people to read my books for the enjoyment they found in them—or not at all. Profit from reading a novel should always be a by-product. The essence to me of style is simplicity, and while I admit there are depths of thought too complex for easy expression, I would despise myself for using complexity of expression where simplicity will do.

If there has been a certain dichotomy in my work, it is simply due to a dichotomy in my own interests. I am deeply interested in history and deeply interested in the present; and I find a stimulus and a refreshment in turning from one subject and one form to another.

I like books of suspense at whatever level they may be written, whether on that of Jane Austen or of Raymond Chandler; so I think all my books of whatever kind contain some of that element which makes a reader want to turn the page—the "and then and then" of which E. M. Forster speaks. This can be a liability if over-indulged in; but so of course can any other preference or attribute.

Although I have always had more to say in a novel than the telling of a story, the story itself has always been the framework on which the rest has depended for its form and shape. I have never been clever enough—or sufficiently self-concerned—to spend 300 pages dipping experimental buckets into the sludge of my own subconscious. I have always been more interested in other people than in myself—though there has to be something of myself in every character created, or he or she will not come to life. I have always been more interested in people than in events, but it is only through events that I have ever been able to illuminate people.

*       *       *

Of the thirty-odd novels Winston Graham has published over nearly forty years, many of the modern ones are in some way concerned with crime. But they are not, in the usual sense of the term, "crime stories". In them, crime is a kind of catalyst speeding and provoking action, rather than an end in itself or a sufficient reason for the story, as it is in thrillers. It is seen as an aberration in otherwise normal lives, something non-criminal people, generally respectable and middle-class, may slip into or become involved with, gradually, almost imperceptibly, for all kinds of reasons—greed, love, loyalty, even a sudden impulse, but not through a "professional" criminal background. It is not surprising that his novel *Marnie* became one of Hitchcock's most successful films—since Hitchcock too is interested in the way ordinary people may become entangled in the bizarre.

Graham has written two straightforward thrillers, and what Michael Gilbert wrote in choosing *The Little Walls* for his "classics of detection and adventure" series applies to the other novels equally well. It was, he says, "the very best of those adventure stories which introduce what has come to be known in critical jargon as the anti-hero . . . a useful portmanteau expression to describe someone who undertakes the hero's role, without the hero's normal equipment." The characters in all Graham's novels are, in fact, floundering and all-too-human amateurs, realistically placed in a present-day life that includes jobs and domesticity well observed, and with a normal proneness to fear, indiscretion and lack of nerve; caught in the end by their moral attitudes, by those who love them, by grief, conscience, and the realistic eye of their creator, who knows that their amateur status fails to give them the professional's coolness, his moral indifference.

Graham's sinners are nearly all racked by their sins, and he is fascinated both by the "congenital" liars and outsiders (Marnie, or the crook-lover in *The Walking Stick*), who are conditioned by their past yet devotedly loved in the present, and by their victims, or the victims of circumstances, mistakes, impulses, devotions: the narrator of *After the Act*, for instance, who pushes his ailing wife off a balcony, then finds he cannot face the mistress he ostensibly did it for. Graham values suspense; and, for his own fiction, at least, believes in action rather than analysis as the means to bring his characters to life.

His novels can roughly be divided into two, the modern and the historical. To the historical novels he brings the same *kind* of realism that he does to the present day. Through *Cordelia*, the four Poldark novels set in eighteenth-century Cornwall, or *The Forgotten Story*, another tale about ordinary people involved in murder, this time at the turn of the last century, one walks familiarly. Graham has the good historical novelist's ability to suggest, rather than describe, the physical surroundings; above all to avoid gadzookery and picturesqueness. As he can get the feel of an insurance office, a printing works or an auctioneer's, so he can walk into the past, giving the sense and atmosphere of it rather than the physical detail, making one breathe its air.

—Isabel Quigley

---

**GRANGE, Peter.**    See **NICOLE, Christopher.**

---

**GRAU, Shirley Ann.**    American.    Born in New Orleans, Louisiana, 8 July 1929. Educated at Tulane University, New Orleans, B.A. 1950. Married James Kern Feibleman in 1955; has four children. Recipient: Pulitzer Prize, 1965. Resides in Metairie, Louisiana. Address: c/o Brandt and Brandt, 101 Park Avenue, New York, New York 10017, U.S.A.

PUBLICATIONS

Novels

*The Hard Blue Sky*.   New York, Knopf, 1958; London, Heinemann, 1959.
*The House on Coliseum Street*.   New York, Knopf, and London, Heinemann, 1961.
*The Keepers of the House*.   New York, Knopf, and London, Longman, 1964.
*The Condor Passes*.   New York, Knopf, 1971; London, Longman, 1972.

Short Stories

*The Black Prince and Other Stories*.   New York, Knopf, 1955; London, Heinemann, 1956.

*        *        *

Shirley Ann Grau may be described as a Southern writer, whose range is sometimes narrowly regional. She may also, therefore, be described as a local colorist whose observations of custom and character suggest an anthropologist at work in a fictional mode. She is a white author who deals with Blacks and the Black sub-culture, which makes her an anomaly in a period of black militancy. And she is finally a novelist of manners who is sharply aware of the collapse of conventional behaviour patterns in modern life. The pervasive style and mood of her work may be summed up best in the terms tough, cold, and realistic. The toughness and the apparent realism seem to reveal a debt to Hemingway. She is never sentimental, and almost always she maintains sufficient distance from her characters to depict them with an objectivity that is sometimes little short of chilling. At her best she displays a kind of cold power. But she is, in general, a limited writer. She lacks originality, especially in her treatment of Negroes and of the South. More seriously, she lacks the complex vision that enables her both to see around and to penetrate deeply into her subject. She is a competent writer who stands at some distance from the center of the Southern Renaissance.

Her best work to date is *The Keepers of the House*, a novel about a Southern family. The story concerns Will Howland who inherits a great deal of land and acquires more. After the death of his wife, he brings a Negro girl into his house and has by her three children who survive. Late in the book, it is revealed that Will had secretly married the Negro girl. He is portrayed as a good, compassionate man whose miscegenation arose out of love. His white grand-daughter marries a man who enters politics, joins the Klan, runs for governor, and makes anti-Negro speeches. One of Will's children by the Negro woman reveals that his father is related to a racist politician. As a result of the revelation, the latter is ruined and the Howland family estate attacked. The estate endures, and the daughter revenges herself upon the town.

Miss Grau is fully aware that the glamorous past may be a trap, as one of her short stories reveals. But she also knows that family traditions which are rooted in the past may endow life in the present with an illuminating sense of time and a stabilizing sense of place; in these ways the past provides a sense of continuity which enriches life in the present. This novel centers on these conceptions of life, which are characteristically Southern and which mark the work of other contemporary Southern writers as different as Robert Penn Warren and Eudora Welty. The treatment of inter-racial love here, made acceptable by marriage, appears to be an apologia for Southern miscegenation, which is, of course, usually conceived in much harsher terms. The same is true of the manipulation of racial animosities in politics, which in itself is authentic enough in the novel. But in depicting the defeat of the racist, Miss Grau seems to depart from her characteristically objective stance.

That stance she had maintained in *The Hard Blue Sky*, which reveals her talent for local color. The scene is an island in the Gulf of Mexico inhabited by characters of French and Spanish descent. The principal conflict is between them and the inhabitants of another island who are Slavic in descent. A boy from one island marries a girl from another; the marriage precipitates a feud. Added to the violence of men is the violence of nature, displayed when a hurricane sweeps through the Gulf. Miss Grau does not dwell on the quaintness of character or place in her novel, and she does not patronize her characters, although the temptation to do so must have been quite real, since she conceives them as primitives. She looks at them coldly and clearly, dramatizing their attitudes toward life but passing no judgment on their behaviour. These are people who recognize no canons of respectability, who admit of no restraints on their passions, and who recognize no guilt. Their sexual attitudes are thus quite free, sex being simply in the natural order of things, and their tendency toward violence is always close to the surface, since they believe that a good fight is healthy. Their life is hard and the hazards of nature, whether snakes or wind, make it harder.

Her treatment of the characters in this novel is the same, generally speaking, as her treatment of Negroes throughout her fiction. Her composite Negro lives an unstructured life in which he obeys appetite and impulse in a naturally selfish movement toward gratification. His morality is virtually non-existent, but casual if apparent at all. His capacity for violence is like that of the islanders. This Negro does not rise to the level of self-consciousness. Ralph Ellison might say that he is a stereotype, perceived because the white writer suffers from a psychic-social blindness caused by the construction of the inner eye; that is, either Miss Grau is blind or the real Negro is invisible.

Miss Grau's chief contribution to the novel of manners is *The House on Coliseum Street*. Although it is an inferior work, it demonstrates, as some of her short stories have, that she understands the various kinds of moral corruption that mark modern life. She knows that the contemporary world is without values, and she makes divorce and sexual promiscuity the obvious signs, in this novel, of the disintegration of well-to-do society.

—Chester E. Eisinger

---

**GRAVES, Robert (Ranke).** British. Born in London in 1895. Educated at Charterhouse School, Surrey; St. John's College, Oxford, B. Litt. 1926. Served with the Royal Welsh Fusiliers in World War I; was refused admittance into the armed forces in World War II. Married to Nancy Nicholson; to Beryl Pritchard; has seven children. Professor of English, Egyptian University, Cairo, 1926. Settled in Deya, Majorca, in 1929; with the poet Laura Riding established the Seizin Press and *Epilogue* magazine. Left Majorca during the Spanish Civil War; settled in Glampton-Brixton, Devon during World War II; returned to Majorca after the war. Clark Lecturer, Trinity College, Cambridge, 1954; Professor of Poetry, Oxford University, 1961–66; Arthur Dehon Little Memorial Lecturer, Massachusetts Institute of Technology, Cambridge, 1963. Recipient: Bronze Medal for Poetry, Olympic Games, Paris, 1924; Hawthornden Prize, 1935; Black Memorial Prize, 1935; Femina Vie Heureuse-Stock Prize, 1939; Russell Loines Poetry Award, 1958; National Poetry Society of America Gold Medal, 1960; Foyle Poetry Prize, 1960; Arts Council Poetry Award, 1962; Queen's Gold Medal for Poetry, 1968; Gold Medal for Poetry, Cultural Olympics, Mexico City, 1968. M.A., Oxford University, 1961. Honorary Member, American Academy of Arts and Sciences, 1970. Address: c/o A. P. Watt and Son, 26–28 Bedford Row, London W.C.1, England.

PUBLICATIONS

Novels

*The Real David Copperfield*. London, Barker, 1933; as *David Copperfield by Charles Dickens, Condensed by Robert Graves*, edited by Merrill P. Paine, New York, Harcourt Brace, 1934.

*I, Claudius: From the Autobiography of Tiberius Claudius, Emperor of the Romans, Born B.C. 10, Murdered and Deified A.D. 54*. London, Barker, and New York, Smith and Haas, 1934.

*Claudius the God and His Wife Messalina: The Troublesome Reign of Tiberius Claudius Caesar, Emperor of the Romans (Born B.C. 10, Died A.D. 54), As Described by Himself; Also His Murder at the Hands of the Notorious Agrippina (Mother of the Emperor Nero) and His Subsequent Deification, As Described by Others*. London, Barker, 1934; New York, Smith and Haas, 1935.

*"Antigua, Penny, Puce"*. Deya, Majorca, Seizin Press, and London, Constable, 1936; as *The Antigua Stamp*, New York, Random House, 1937.

*Count Belisarius*. London, Cassell, and New York, Random House, 1938.

*Sergeant Lamb of the Ninth*. London, Methuen, 1940; as *Sergeant Lamb's America*, New York, Random House, 1940.

*Proceed, Sergeant Lamb.*  London, Methuen, and New York, Random House, 1941.
*The Story of Marie Powell: Wife to Mr. Milton.*  London, Cassell, 1943; as *Wife to Mr. Milton: The Story of Marie Powell*, New York, Creative Age Press, 1944.
*The Golden Fleece.*  London, Cassell, 1944; as *Hercules, My Shipmate*, New York, Creative Age Press, 1945.
*King Jesus.*  New York, Creative Age Press, and London, Cassell, 1946.
*Watch the North Wind Rise.*  New York, Creative Age Press, 1949; as *Seven Days in Crete*, London, Cassell, 1949.
*The Islands of Unwisdom.*  New York, Doubleday, 1949; as *The Isles of Unwisdom*, London, Cassell, 1950.
*Homer's Daughter.*  London, Cassell, and New York, Doubleday, 1955.

Short Stories

*The Shout.*  London, Elkin Mathews and Marrot, 1929.
*¡ Catacrok! Mostly Stories, Mostly Funny.*  London, Cassell, 1956.
*Collected Short Stories.*  New York, Doubleday, 1964; London, Cassell, 1965.

Play

*John Kemp's Wager: A Ballad Opera.*  Oxford, Blackwell, and New York, T. R. Edwards, 1925.

Verse

*Over the Brazier.*  London, Poetry Bookshop, 1916.
*Goliath and David.*  London, Chiswick Press, 1916.
*Fairies and Fusiliers.*  London, Heinemann, 1917; New York, Knopf, 1918.
*Treasure Box.*  London, Chiswick Press, 1919.
*Country Sentiment.*  London, Secker, and New York, Knopf, 1920.
*The Pier-Glass.*  London, Secker, and New York, Knopf, 1921.
*Whipperginny.*  London, Heinemann, and New York, Knopf, 1923.
*The Feather Bed.*  Richmond, Surrey, Hogarth Press, 1923.
*Mockbeggar Hall.*  London, Hogarth Press, 1924.
*Welchman's Hose.*  London, The Fleuron, 1925.
*(Poems).*  London, Benn, 1925.
*The Marmosite's Miscellany* (as Paul Boyle).  London, Hogarth Press, 1925.
*Poems (1914–1926).*  London, Heinemann, 1927; New York, Doubleday, 1929.
*Poems (1914–1927).*  London, Heinemann, 1927.
*Poems 1929.*  London, Seizin Press, 1929.
*Ten Poems More.*  Paris, Hours Press, 1930.
*Poems 1926–1930.*  London, Heinemann, 1931.
*To Whom Else?*  Deya, Majorca, Seizin Press, 1931.
*Poems 1930–1933.*  London, Barker, 1933.
*Collected Poems.*  London, Cassell, and New York, Random House, 1938.
*No More Ghosts: Selected Poems.*  London, Faber, 1940.
*(Poems).*  London, Eyre and Spottiswoode, 1943.
*Poems 1938–1945.*  London, Cassell, 1945; New York, Creative Age Press, 1946.
*Collected Poems (1914–1947).*  London, Cassell, 1948.
*Poems and Satires 1951.*  London, Cassell, 1951.
*Poems 1953.*  London, Cassell, 1953.
*Collected Poems 1955.*  New York, Doubleday, 1955.

*Poems Selected by Himself.*   London, Penguin, 1957.
*The Poems of Robert Graves.*   New York, Doubleday, 1958.
*Collected Poems 1959.*   London, Cassell, 1959.
*More Poems 1961.*   London, Cassell, 1961.
*Collected Poems.*   New York, Doubleday, 1961.
*New Poems 1962.*   London, Cassell, 1962; as *New Poems*, New York, Doubleday, 1963.
*The More Deserving Cases: Eighteen Old Poems for Reconsideration.*   N.p., Marl-borough College Press, 1962.
*Man Does, Woman Is 1964.*   London, Cassell, and New York, Doubleday, 1964.
*Love Respelt.*   London, Cassell, 1965.
*Collected Poems 1965.*   London, Cassell, 1965.
*Seventeen Poems Missing from Love Respelt.*   Privately printed, 1966.
*Colophon to Love Respelt.*   Privately printed, 1967.
*Poems 1965–1968.*   London, Cassell, 1968; New York, Doubleday, 1969.
*Poems about Love.*   London, Cassell, and New York, Doubleday, 1969.
*Love Respelt Again.*   New York, Doubleday, 1969.
*Beyond Giving: Poems.*   Privately printed, 1969.
*Poems 1968–1970.*   London, Cassell, 1970.


Other

*On English Poetry.*   New York, Knopf, and London, Heinemann, 1922.
*The Meaning of Dreams.*   London, Cecil Palmer, 1924; New York, Greenberg, 1925.
*Poetic Unreason and Other Studies.*   London, Cecil Palmer, 1925.
*My Head! My Head! Being the History of Elisha and the Shumanite Woman; with the History of Moses as Elisha Related It, and Her Questions to Him.*   London, Secker, and New York, Knopf, 1925.
*Contemporary Techniques of Poetry: A Political Analogy.*   London, Hogarth Press, 1925.
*Another Future of Poetry.*   London, Hogarth Press, 1926.
*Impenetrability; or, The Proper Habit of English.*   London, Hogarth Press, 1926.
*The English Ballad: A Short Critical Survey.*   London, Benn, 1927.
*Lars Porsena; or, The Future of Swearing and Improper Language.*   London, Kegan Paul Trench Trubner, and New York, Dutton, 1927.
*A Survey of Modernist Poetry*, with Laura Riding.   London, Heinemann, 1927; New York, Doubleday, 1928.
*Lawrence and the Arabs.*   London, Cape, 1927; as *Lawrence and the Arabian Adventure*, New York, Doubleday, 1928.
*A Pamphlet Against Anthologies*, with Laura Riding.   London, Cape, 1928; as *Against Anthologies*, New York, Doubleday, 1928.
*Mrs. Fisher; or, The Future of Humour.*   London, Kegan Paul Trench Trubner, 1928.
*Goodbye to All That: An Autobiography.*   London, Cape, 1929; New York, Cape and Smith, 1930; revised edition, New York, Doubleday, and London, Cassell, 1957, London, Penguin, 1960.
*No Decency Left*, with Laura Riding (as Barbara Rich).   London, Cape, 1932.
*T. E. Lawrence to His Biographer Robert Graves.*   New York, Doubleday, 1938; London, Faber, 1939.
*The Long Week-end: A Social History of Great Britain 1918–1939*, with Alan Hodge.   London, Faber, 1940; New York, Macmillan, 1941.
*Work in Hand*, with others.   London, Hogarth Press, 1942.
*The Reader over Your Shoulder: A Handbook for Writers of English Prose*, with Alan Hodge.   London, Cape, 1943; New York, Macmillan, 1944.
*The White Goddess: A Historical Grammer of Poetic Myth.*   London, Faber, and New

York, Creative Age Press, 1948; revised edition, Faber, 1952, 1966; New York, Knopf, 1958.

*The Common Asphodel: Collected Essays on Poetry 1922–1949.* London, Hamish Hamilton, 1949.

*Occupation: Writer.* New York, Creative Age Press, 1950; London, Cassell, 1951.

*The Nazarene Gospel Restored*, with Joshua Podro. London, Cassell, 1953; New York, Doubleday, 1954.

*The Crowning Privilege: The Clark Lectures 1954–1955; Also Various Essays on Poetry and Sixteen New Poems.* London, Cassell, 1955; as *The Crowning Privilege: Collected Essays on Poetry*, New York, Doubleday, 1956.

*Adam's Rib and Other Anomalous Elements in the Hebrew Creation Myth: A New View.* N.p., Trianon Press, 1955; New York, Yoseloff, 1958.

*The Greek Myths.* London and Baltimore, Penguin, 2 vols., 1955.

*Jesus in Rome: A Historical Conjecture*, with Joshua Podro. London, Cassell, 1957.

*They Hanged My Saintly Billy.* London, Cassell, 1957; as *They Hanged My Saintly Billy: The Life and Death of Dr. William Palmer*, New York, Doubleday, 1957.

*Steps: Stories, Talks, Essays, Poems, Studies in History.* London, Cassell, 1958.

*5 Pens in Hand.* New York, Doubleday, 1958.

*Food for Centaurs: Stories, Talks, Critical Studies, Poems.* New York, Doubleday, 1960.

*The Penny Fiddle: Poems for Children.* London, Cassell, 1960; New York, Doubleday, 1961.

*Greek Gods and Heroes.* New York, Doubleday, 1960; as *Myths of Ancient Greece*, London, Cassell, 1961.

*Selected Poetry and Prose*, edited by James Reeves. London, Hutchinson, 1961.

*The Siege and Fall of Troy* (juvenile). London, Cassell, 1962; New York, Doubleday, 1963.

*The Big Green Book.* New York, Crowell Collier, 1962.

*Oxford Addresses on Poetry.* London, Cassell, and New York, Doubleday, 1962.

*Hebrew Myths: The Book of Genesis*, with Raphael Patai. New York, Doubleday, and London, Cassell, 1964.

*Ann at Highwood Hall: Poems for Children.* London, Cassell, 1964.

*Majorca Observed.* London, Cassell, and New York, Doubleday, 1965.

*Mammon and the Black Goddess.* London, Cassell, and New York, Doubleday, 1965.

*Two Wise Children* (juvenile). New York, Harlin Quist, 1966; London, W. H. Allen, 1967.

*Poetic Craft and Principle.* London, Cassell, 1967.

*Spiritual Quixote.* London, Oxford University Press, 1967.

*The Poor Boy Who Followed His Star* (juvenile). London, Cassell, 1968; New York, Doubleday, 1969.

*The Crane Bag and Other Disputed Subjects.* London, Cassell, 1969.

*Poems: Abridged for Dolls and Princes* (juvenile). London, Cassell, 1971.


Editor, with Alan Porter and Richard Hughes, *Oxford Poetry 1921*. Oxford, Blackwell, 1921.

Editor, *John Skelton (Laureate), 1460(?)–1529*. London, Benn, 1927.

Editor, *The Less Familiar Nursery Rhymes*. London, Benn, 1927.

Editor, *English and Scottish Ballads*. London, Heinemann, and New York, Macmillan, 1957.

Editor, *The Comedies of Terence*. New York, Doubleday, 1962; London, Cassell, 1963.


Translator, with Laura Riding, *Almost Forgotten Germany*, by Georg Schwarz. Deya, Majorca, Seizin Press, London, Constable, and New York, Random House, 1936.

Translator, *The Transformations of Lucius, Otherwise Known as The Golden Ass*, by Apuleius. London, Penguin, 1950; New York, Farrar Straus, 1951.

Translator, *The Cross and the Sword*, by Manuel de Jesús Galván. Bloomington, Indiana University Press, 1955; London, Gollancz, 1956.

Translator, *The Infant with the Globe*, by Pedro Antonio de Alarcon. N.P., Trianon Press, 1955; New York, Yoseloff, 1958.

Translator, *Winter in Majorca*, by George Sand. London, Cassell, 1956.

Translator, *Pharsalia: Dramatic Episodes of the Civil Wars*, by Lucan. London, Penguin, 1956.

Translator, *The Twelve Caesars*, by Suetonius. London, Penguin, 1957.

Translator, *The Anger of Achilles: Homer's Iliad*. New York, Doubleday, 1959; London, Cassell, 1960.

Translator, with Omar Ali-Shah, *Rubaiyyat of Omar Khayaam*. London, Cassell, 1967.

Bibliography: *A Bibliography of the Works of Robert Graves* by Fred H. Higginson, London, Nicholas Vane, 1966.

Manuscript Collections: Lockwood Memorial Library, State University of New York at Buffalo; New York City Public Library; University of Texas Library, Austin.

*       *       *

The critic who sets out to comment upon Robert Graves the novelist by considering first his work in other literary forms is not taking an unnecessary detour but the high road to understanding. It is not merely that Graves is a most versatile writer—perhaps more versatile than any of his contemporaries—but that his writing of fiction has been notably affected by his literary interests outside the novel and that those interests illuminate the style, the *mores* and the subject-matter of his novels.

Graves has been biographer, autobiographer, translator, critic, mythologist, biblical commentator, essayist, polemicist, and, above all other things, poet, as well as novelist. He has infused many of these roles into his work as a novelist, and in all of them he has shown himself to be flamboyant, original sometimes to the point of eccentricity, and always superbly competent.

If it is possible to forecast the judgement of posterity then it is likely that he will come to be regarded finally and highly as a poet, but it is as a novelist, and particularly as a historical novelist, that he has won and holds affection among the widest range of contemporary readers. Yet the two novels that are, at least in the mundane sense, his most successful, *I, Claudius* and *Claudius the God and His Wife Messalina*, are palpable extensions of his work as a classical scholar though neither of them is in any sense a scholar's novel. Graves seizes upon a central figure—Claudius, the bumbling, near-lunatic nonentity of the history books— and settles the patterns of his career to fit a subtle psychological interpretation that is history only as Graves would have had it. The background to the novels, of brutality, sensuality and superstition in Rome of the first century, is custom-built for Graves' robust skill.

Similarly, his classical and his biblical scholarship establishes an authority for *King Jesus*, but it is an unorthodox, even a perverse authority. His Jesus like his Claudius is a god, just as Belisarius in *Count Belisarius* and Jason in *The Golden Fleece*, being myth-heroes, are close to being gods, but these gods and myth-heroes he drags from their pedestals, not because he despises the gods themselves but because, by revealing the fallibility of generally-accepted mythology, by reducing to the level of everyday human behaviour he hopes to undermine the power of those—the latter-day priests—who have made myth into religion. "The true fiend governs in God's name."

Paradoxically, Graves is seldom interested in the ordinary. His god-heroes are extraordinary mortals and immortals; even while they move and speak in a superficially ordinary way they are larger than life. His few seemingly contemporary novels such as *Antigua, Penny, Puce* are equally unconnected with reality and almost as fantastical as his novels based on history and mythology. Most of his characters are larger than life, as close to caricature as is myth itself, and in this tendency there is a hint of the autobiographer, the self-revealer, at work, for Graves is himself larger than life—and one suspects that he knows it and revels in the knowledge.

Only one novella, *The Shout*, is more patently written in response to personal experience, though it is not difficult to read even into an ostensibly historical novel, *Wife to Mr Milton*, something of the same confessional quality that is obvious in much of Graves' love poetry, and to see in the novel as in the poems the conflict between ardour and squeamishness which appears to have disrupted his own life. *The Shout*, however, despite its supernatural theme, is founded substantially upon Graves' recollections of the effects of shell-shock and is, as it were, a codicil to his autobiography, *Goodbye to All That*, one of the best autobiographies of this century.

To assert that *Count Belisarius, Sergeant Lamb of the Ninth, Proceed, Sergeant Lamb* as well as the many and fine military passages in other novels are also autobiographies may seem ridiculous and certainly involves the critic in anachronism, yet Graves the soldier is intrinsic to Graves the novelist. Like so many of his literary contemporaries Graves suffered from his experiences in the First World War and seems never to have shaken off the nightmare of the trenches. Like many of them—and notably his friends Sassoon and Blunden—he had been a good front-line soldier, with all that implies of staunchness and courage, and he is at his best when he writes of war, sensitive to its horrors but revelling in the ingenuity, bravery and comradeship that it inspires.

Graves is not in the fullest sense an original writer of fiction. He seldom "creates" plots, characters, or situations. His is the genius that uses what was or what might have been, twists it and moulds it to suit his own polemical and narrative purposes. It is no mean genius.

> Assemble first all casual bits and scraps
> That may shake down into a world perhaps.
> Sigh then, or frown, but leave (as in despair)
> Motive and end and moral in the air;
> Nice contradiction between fact and fact
> Will make the whole read human and exact.

> "The Devil's Advice to Story-tellers"

—J. E. Morpurgo

---

**GRAY, Simon.** British.  Born on Hayling Island, Hampshire, 21 October 1936. Educated at Dalhousie University, Halifax, Nova Scotia, Canada, 1954–57, B.A. (honours) in English 1957; Trinity College, Cambridge, 1958–61, B.A. (honours) in English 1961. Married Beryl Mary Kevern in 1965; has two children. Harper-Wood Student, St. John's College, Cambridge, 1961–62; Research Student, Trinity College, Cambridge, 1962–63; Lecturer in English, University of British Columbia, Vancouver, 1963–64; Supervisor in English, Trinity College, Cambridge, 1964–66. Since 1966, Lecturer in English, Queen Mary College, University of London. Since 1964, Editor of *Delta* magazine, Cambridge. Recipient: *Evening Standard* drama award, 1972. Address: 70 Priory Gardens, London N.6, England.

PUBLICATIONS

Novels

> *Colmain*.   London, Faber, 1963.
> *Simple People*.   London, Faber, 1965.
> *Little Portia*.   London, Faber, 1968.
> *A Comeback for Stark* (as Hamish Reade).   London, Faber, 1969.

Uncollected Short Story

> "The Holman Candidate", in *Winter's Tales 12*.   London, Macmillan, 1966.

Plays

> *Wise Child* (produced London, 1967).   London, Faber, 1968.
> *Sleeping Dog* (produced BBC Television, 1967).   London, Faber, 1968.
> *Dutch Uncle* (produced London, 1969).   London, Faber, 1969.
> *The Idiot* (produced London, 1970).   London, Methuen, 1971.
> *Spoiled* (produced London, 1971).   London, Methuen, 1971.
> *Butley* (produced Oxford and London, 1971).   London, Methuen, 1971.

Other

> Editor, with Keith Walker, *Selected English Prose*.   London, Faber, 1967.

Simon Gray comments:

I really can't write anything useful about the themes or subjects of my novels—I'm not sure I know what "themes" are, except that students get asked about them in examinations on Shakespeare. I'm not conscious, when I'm writing, of having a subject—just a few people in a distinct place having, or failing to have, to do with each other. Of course I begin to get a suspicion when I read the proofs, but I never follow it up and have recently taken to asking my wife to look after proofs for me. I expect that if I could bear to read through anything I've published or had performed on the stage, I could come up with a few phrases and what in the critical/academic professions are called insights, but it would only be patter. I'm not in the slightest interested in what I've *done*; it seems to me in recollection to have been done by somebody else for reasons I can't guess at. I feel the same about my plays—my concern for them ceases about two days after the last word is written and certainly long before the first production. The book in the hand and the play on the stage have in common with my present life only a shared name.

\*       \*       \*

Colmain is the capital of the mythical province of New Thumberland, Canada's least progressive province, which actually sounds remarkably like Halifax, Nova Scotia. Readers who know the Canadian maritimes would enjoy the novel most. Gray is satirical about the blacks, Indians and especially the English element in the province. Of the English, "All the attitudes and performances that had merged so inevitably into the harmonious atmosphere of Kensington or Wembley Park or Reigate became, in Colmain's harsher, less-textured atmosphere, almost stark. The afternoon tea-taking and the tricks of speech seemed matters of calculation almost, little but explicit testimonies to a world that had been left but would never be forgotten." Gray jokes about tactlessness: "'And where is Mrs. Weatherby? I hope that she's enjoying it.' Mr. Weatherby positively loomed. 'Mrs. Weatherby is in Holyoke Cemetery,' he said very distinctly. 'I don't know whether she's enjoying it.'"

The date is 1936, and a new, young Lieutenant Governor is learning his job and about Colmain. (In fact, I have no very clear idea of a Lieutenant-Governor's role after finishing the book.) He is faced with Mrs. Tennant who, like Jane Austen's Mrs. Bennett, makes the business of her life getting her daughter married—preferably to the uneasy Lieutenant-Governor. Mrs. Tennant is obsessed with the importance of good breeding: "It *is* a question of breeding and Myra Davis, although she is a Canadian, is very well-bred, with her husband a judge, you know. Everything in the end comes to that. If we discipline ourselves in private then we appear well-bred in public, and people notice it." The parallel to Trollope is closer, with society in Colmain revolving round the Lieutenant-Governor's residence. Gray refers to the problems of newcomers entering society and the crucial importance of receiving invitations, together with a subplot about shady business which the Lieutenant-Governor cannot begin to comprehend. The novel is gently entertaining, with only a touch of astringency toward a society which is so much more decadent and fatuous than it realises.

*Simple People* takes Logan, a young Canadian, who is smug, serious, rich, polite, earnest and moralistic, to Cambridge University as a research student. The book begins with the big subject of the impact of England on Logan: a nice awareness of the exact uses of "Great!" "I guess" and "Is that right?" is shown, and their incongruity in Cambridge. His caricature academics—the translator of Rumanian epics and the student of Shakespeare's dolphin imagery—are amusing. But soon Logan is involved with Joey, a novelist's mistress, and the subject becomes much narrower. Joey is volatile and unpredictable, startling to the upright Nova Scotian with his own clear idea of how boy-meets-girl has to operate. The novelist lives in a picturesque row off Kings Parade, but otherwise the bulk of the novel does not have much to do with Cambridge or a Canadian's discovery of it. A subplot around some tiresome characters, with hints of mystery around Maria Hodges and her activities, is tedious. Gray's special talent here is for awkward conversations, where the presuppositions are different and the unstated nuances mutually confusing. Finally the novel is neither a slapstick view of university life nor a subtle account of England through a foreigner's eyes, but something much more limited, a mild, quite clever, little comedy.

Gray writes entirely of English characters in *Little Portia*, a rambling account of a youth's experiences from early childhood to early twenties: he is named from Shakespeare's Portia by a homosexual teacher. We read briefly of the unsympathetic maiden aunt who brings up the boy and his sister, their governess, the local private school and the public school where he is briefly a footballing success. His years at Cambridge are described at greater length, with informed discriminations between his clever, fashionable friends and the ordinary ones: he begins as a brilliant scholar, then abandons studying in his final weeks. He has an affair with a young Cockney art student and is going to marry her, fastidiously rejects her, falls in love with her memory, then sees her again. At the end he may be free, but it is inconclusive.

Some observation is neat, for instance, of finding "the proper tone" for scholarship exams: "'It would seem,' 'it could be said,' 'it might be argued,' instead of the 'I think,' 'I feel,' 'I believe' which the History Fifth Master had preferred." Gray's account of the Cambridge "Academy" where the hero teaches English to foreigners is amusing satire, and the Christmas party scene there, with the principal as Santa Claus, is funny. But such set-pieces are few, and coherence is lacking: I cannot see how the experiences described shape the young man. The relationship to the sister remains puzzling, and references to Pip and Estella in *Great Expectations* hint at some buried parallel here: the account of this, too, is abandoned incomplete at the end.

Since 1967 Gray's work has been stage and TV plays, and his accomplishment here is greater than his novels, which lack the originality of *Sleeping Dog*, the psychological subtlety of *Spoiled* and the epigrammatic wit of *Butley*.

—Malcolm Page

———————————————

**GREEN, Henry.** Pseudonym for Henry Vincent Yorke. British. Born near Tewkesbury, Gloucestershire, in 1905. Educated at Eton College, Buckinghamshire; Oxford University. Served in the Fire Service, London, 1939–43. Married the Hon. Mary Adelaide Biddulph in 1929; has one child. Managing Director, H. Pontifex and Company, Birmingham. Lives in London. Address: c/o Hogarth Press, 40–42 William IV Street, London W.C.2, England.

PUBLICATIONS

Novels

*Blindness*. London, Dent, and New York, Dutton, 1926.
*Living*. London, Dent, 1929.
*Party Going*. London, Hogarth Press, 1939; New York, Viking Press, 1951.
*Caught*. London, Hogarth Press, 1943; New York, Viking Press, 1950.
*Loving*. London, Hogarth Press, 1945; New York, Viking Press, 1949.
*Back*. London, Hogarth Press, 1946; New York, Viking Press, 1950.
*Concluding*. London, Hogarth Press, 1948; New York, Viking Press, 1951.
*Nothing*. London, Hogarth Press, and New York, Viking Press, 1950.
*Doting*. London, Hogarth Press, and New York, Viking Press, 1952.

Other

*Pack My Bag* (autobiography). London, Hogarth Press, 1940.

\*    \*    \*

Henry Green is as original a novelist as any of his time and, resembling no other, has defied imitation. From novel to novel he has been unpredictable, a restless experimenter in language and subject-matter alike. It is impossible to pick out any one novel as characteristic of his art: more than most novelists, he is the sum-total of his work.

His first novel, written when he was a schoolboy and published when he was 21, is understandably his least considerable work, but it is easy to see, in the light of his work as a whole, how much it anticipates the later Green. Called *Blindness*, the title sums up its theme, the state of being blind. Green's titles can be taken literally as encapsulating the subject-matter of the novels. Thus *Living* is about living, daily living and getting a living; *Party Going* about going to a party; *Caught* about the state of being caught; *Loving* about loving, not, be it noted, about love but about what is implied in the verbal noun; *Back* about the condition of being a soldier back from the wars; and so on. And there is something else in *Blindness* which anticipates the later novels: the imaginative boldness with which the writer tackles his theme, which is one unusual in so young a writer, and his utter objectivity.

But *Blindness*, which attracted little notice, could have prepared no one for the novel that followed three years later, *Living*, an account largely of the lives of foundry-workers in Birmingham. After more than forty years, it remains probably the best English novel of factory life. In the years immediately after its publication it was often seen as what was called at the time a proletarian novel. It was seen, in other words, in terms of the Marxist aesthetic theories that influenced so many of the young writers of the day. In fact, *Living* is entirely free from political or sociological preoccupations. Green's working-class characters accept their condition as being of the natural order of things; they do not protest or whine; they are completely unpolitical. Three elements especially distinguish the novel: an unconventional use of language, a striking symbolism, and what may be called a poetry of incident. These three elements combine to express Green's delighted sense of the novelty of the scene he is rendering; at the time of writing the novel Green, whose real name is Henry Vincent Yorke, was working his way through the factory he described as the son of its managing director, a position he himself was later to occupy. The one discernible influence one feels upon his prose is that of Gertrude Stein, but the prose, for all the distortions of syntax and such devices as the omission of definite articles, is always close to the language of common life. In many ways it appeared at the time a prose parallel to the early poetry of W. H. Auden. As instance of the symbolism may be quoted Green's use of the flights of homing pigeons that dominate the scene of drab streets and public parks with the factory at their centre. As the flights recur, they become more than simple naturalistic descriptions of a common feature of the English urban scene and are symbols of the characters' impulses to escape their environment and their inevitable return to it; and they give the novel a unity beyond its formal structure. As for the poetry of incident, the best single example is the scene in which the young Welsh foundry worker, whose wife has just given birth to his first son, sings out his joy against the factory noises.

All this is to say that Green writes as a poet, as became increasingly evident in Green's next novel, *Party Going*, a novel disconcertingly different from *Living*. Covering a period of a very few hours, the novel describes what happens when a group of very rich young people meet at Victoria Station in order to catch the boat train to go to a party in France. Fog descends, trains cannot run, they are marooned in the upper rooms of the station hotel, the platforms below are thronged ever more densely by frustrated commuters, who while away the time in community singing. That, in a sense, is all, yet *Party Going* is an extraordinarily rich novel. There is again the bird imagery, the gulls flying out to sea above the fog, and the pigeon that falls dead at the feet of the spinster aunt entering the station and that she picks up, washes and carries round in a brown-paper parcel, an incident, unexplained, that disturbs the party-goers and disturbs the reader. *Party Going* is capable of many interpretations, from simple allegory upwards, but its meaning cannot be reduced to any one moral. It is a "gathering web of insinuations," the phrase Green has used to describe the effects he tries to capture in his own prose.

During the second world war Green served as a fireman in London in the Auxiliary Fire Service, and the outcome of his experiences was *Caught*. It is the finest account we have in fiction of the mood of the people in London during the first months of the war—the "phony war"—and of the first air raids on the London docks, which form the climax of the novel. But it is much more than a documentary. At its centre are two men caught in a situation they cannot escape from; one, the middle-class man Richard Roe, the other his working-class superior officer Pye. They are caught not only in the unwelcome proximity forced upon them by war but also in a tragic situation: Roe's five-year-old son was once abducted by Pye's lunatic sister. It is a situation that is resolved only by Pye's suicide and the action that results from the arrival of the German bombers. It is a tragi-comedy of incomprehension and incommunicability.

The action of Green's next novel, *Loving*, also takes place during the war, but the setting is the servants' hall of a castle in neutral Ireland. The castle, like the hotel rooms in *Party Going* and the fire station in *Caught*, is a web of gossip, intrigue, scandal and misunderstanding. As in *Caught*, the novel proceeds from one central incident: the daughter of the owner of the castle is surprised by the housemaid one morning in bed with her lover. Everything follows from this; from then on in it's inevitable that Raunce, the butler, and Edith, the housmaid, will run away together to England.

*Loving* is probably the most closely knit of Green's novels, and in none is the symbolism more pervasive, as is seen in the peacocks and the doves whose presence and display irradiate the whole novel; they are, as Edward Stokes writes in *The Novels of Henry Green*, the best critical study of the novelist we possess, "complex symbols of pride, vanity, beauty, sex, and greed." And the poetry of incident is vividly present throughout the novel, as for example the magical passage in which two young housemaids waltz in the deserted ballroom among the dustcloth-shrouded furniture, with the five great chandeliers above them. Green's presentation of his material is entirely objective. He makes no attempt to enter his characters' minds. Yet, though he is rendered from the outside only, the central character, Raunce, is a splendidly successful creation, who constantly surprises us by revealing new aspects of his being. He is one of the most memorable characters in modern English fiction.

In the novels that follow *Loving* Green has concentrated on the development of certain sides of his talent to the virtual exclusion of others. Thus in *Back* and *Concluding*, which contrasts old age and youth in a setting of the not-too-distant future, everything seems subordinated to the rendering of visual beauty. In *Concluding*, for instance, Green is scarcely concerned at all in presenting a plausible picture of the future in the manner, say, of Huxley or Orwell; there seems to be a complete absence of the satirical impulse. The aim, rather, seems to be to produce in words the effect of a late Monet painting: what we think of as the normal components of a novel, plot, action, character, setting, are as it were dissolved in the play of light and colour.

The word "lush" has been applied to these novels, and it may have been the recognition of this that led Green in his two later novels, *Nothing* and *Doting*, to jettison the visual almost completely and concentrate on dialogue. Both these novels are renderings of upper-class life in London in the decade after the end of the second world war. They are brilliantly entertaining, for Green has always had what one might call a microphone ear for the subtleties and nuances of common speech. Both novels are *tours-de-force* of a most striking order; but Green's reliance in them on a single side of his talent does mean that their thinness is apparent when set side by side with *Living*, *Party Going*, *Caught* and *Loving*.

Green has published nothing since *Doting* appeared in 1952.

—Walter Allen

---

**GREEN, Peter.** British. Born in London, 22 December 1924. Educated at Trinity College, Cambridge, 1947–52, B.A. (honours) in Classics 1950; Craven Scholar and Student, 1950; M.A., Ph.D. 1954. Served in the Royal Air Force Volunteer Reserve, 1943–47: Burma Command, 1944–46. Married Isobel Lalage Pulvertaft in 1951; has three children. Editor, *Cambridge Review*, 1950–51; Director of Studies in Classics, Selwyn College, Cambridge, 1952–53; Fiction Critic, *The Daily Telegraph*, London, 1953–63; Literary Adviser, Bodley Head Ltd., publishers, London, 1957–58; Consultant Editor, Hodder and Stoughton Ltd., publishers, London, 1960–63; Television Critic, *The Listener*, London, 1961–63; Film Critic, *John o'London's*, 1961–63. Selection Committee Member, Book Society, London, 1959–62. Emigrated to Greece in 1963. Since 1966, Professor of Greek History and Literature, College Year in Athens. Visiting Professor of Classics, University of Texas, Austin, 1971–72. Recipient: Heinemann Award, 1958. Fellow, 1956, and Member of the Council, 1958, Royal Society of Literature. Address: 20 Efkalypton Road, Amaroussion, near Athens, Greece.

Publications

Novels

*Achilles His Armour*.  London, Murray, 1955; New York, Doubleday, 1967.
*Cat in Gloves* (as Denis Delaney).  London, Gryphon, 1956.
*The Sword of Pleasure*.  London, Murray, 1957; Cleveland, World, 1958.
*The Laughter of Aphrodite*.  London, Murray, and Cleveland, World, 1965.

Short Stories

*Habeas Corpus*.  London, Hamish Hamilton, and Cleveland, World, 1962.

Other

*The Expanding Eye: A First Journey to the Mediterranean*.  London, Murray, 1953.
*Sir Thomas Browne*.  London, Longman, 1959.
*Kenneth Graham, 1859–1932: A Study of His Life, Work and Times*.  London, Murray, 1959; as *Kenneth Graham: A Biography*, Cleveland, World, 1959.
*Essays in Antiquity*.  London, Murray, and Cleveland, World, 1960.
*John Skelton*.  London, Longman, 1960.
*Look at the Romans* (juvenile).  London, Hamish Hamilton, 1963.
*Alexander the Great*.  London, Weidenfeld and Nicolson, and New York, Praeger, 1970.
*Armada from Athens*.  New York, Doubleday, 1970; London, Hodder and Stoughton, 1971.
*The Year of Salamis, 480–479 B.C.*  London, Weidenfeld and Nicholson, 1970; New York, Praeger, 1971.
*The Shadow of the Parthenon*.  London, Maurice Temple Smith, 1972.

Editor, *Poetry from Cambridge, 1947–1950*.  London, Fortune Press, 1951.
Editor, *Appreciations: Essays*, by Clifton Fadiman.  London, Hodder and Stoughton, 1962.

Translator, *The Fountain at Marlieux*, by Claude Aveline.  London, Dobson, and New York, Roy, 1954.
Translator, *Escape from Montluc*, by André Devigny.  London, Dobson, 1957; as *Man Escaped*, New York, Norton, 1958.
Translator, *Mission Accomplished*, by Mongo Beti.  New York, Macmillan, 1958; as *Mission to Kala*, London, Muller, 1958.
Translator, *Tanguy: The Story of a Child of Our Time*, by Michel del Castillo.  London, Muller, 1958; as *A Child of Our Time*, New York, Knopf, 1958.
Translator, *The Lottery*, by Paul Guimard.  London, Faber, 1958; as *House of Happiness*, Boston, Houghton Mifflin, 1960.
Translator, *The Lion*, by Joseph Kessel.  London, Hart Davis, and New York, Knopf, 1959.
Translator, *Antoine*, by Marie Gisèle Landes.  London, Muller, 1959.
Translator, *Men of Letters*, by Michel de Saint-Pierre.  London, Hutchinson, 1959.
Translator, *The Children of Lilith*, by Guy Piazzini.  London, Hodder and Stoughton, and New York, Dutton, 1960.
Translator, *Journey into the Blue*, by Gusztáv Rab.  London, Sidgwick and Jackson, and New York, Pantheon Books, 1960.

Translator, *A Room in Budapest*, by Gusztáv Rab.   London, Sidgwick and Jackson, 1961.

Translator, *Destiny of Fire*, by Zoe Oldenbourg.   London, Gollancz, and New York, Pantheon Books, 1961.

Translator, *Massacre at Montségur: A History of the Albigensian Crusade*, by Zoe Oldenbourg.   London, Weidenfeld and Nicolson, 1961; New York, Pantheon Books, 1962.

Translator, *The Novice*, by Giovanni Arpino.   London, Hodder and Stoughton, 1961.

Translator, *The Prime of Life*, by Simone de Beauvoir.   Cleveland, World, 1962; London, Deutsch, 1963.

Translator, *Djamila Boupacha: The Story of the Torture of a Young Algerian Girl Which Shocked Liberal French Opinion*, by Simone de Beauvoir and Gisele Halimi.   London, Deutsch, and New York, Macmillan, 1962.

Translator, *The Black Dove*, by Enrico Emanuelli.   London, Macdonald, 1962.

Translator, *Innocence*, by Diane Giguère.   London, Gollancz, 1962.

Translator, *Douchka: The Story of a Dog*, by Colette Andry.   London, Souvenir Press, 1963; as *Behind the Bathtub: The Story of a French Dog*, Boston, Little Brown, 1963.

Translator, *Diamond River*, by Sadio Garavini de Turno.   London, Hamish Hamilton, and New York, Harcourt Brace, 1963.

Translator, *The Life of Jesus*, by Jean Steinmann.   Boston, Little Brown, 1963.

Translator, *Love Without Grace*, by Luciana d'Arad.   London, Muller, 1963.

Translator, *Calvary Street*, by Miklós Bátori.   London, Constable, 1963.

Translator, *Hindu Kush 1959*, by Fosco Maraini.   London, Hamish Hamilton, 1964; as *Where Four Worlds Meet: Hindu Kush*, New York, Harcourt Brace, 1964.

Translator, *Daily Life in Greece at the Time of Pericles*, by Robert Flacelière.   London, Weidenfeld and Nicolson, and New York, Macmillan, 1965.

Translator, *Okapi Fever*, by Philippe Diolé.   London, Souvenir Press, 1965.

Translator, *Cordelia*, by Françoise Mallet-Joris.   London, W. H. Allen, 1965.

Translator, *Mead and Wine: A History of the Bronze Age in Greece*, by Jean Zafiropulo.   London, Sidgwick and Jackson, and New York, Schocken Books, 1966.

Translator, *The Novel Computer*, by Robert Escarpit.   London, Secker and Warburg, 1966.

Translator, *The Flood*, by Jean Le Clézio.   London, Hamish Hamilton, 1966.

Translator, *The Sixteen Satires of Juvenal*.   London, Penguin, 1967.

Translator, *Danton: A Biography*, by Robert Christophe.   London, Barker, and New York, Doubleday, 1967.

Translator, *The Sardinian Smile*, by Petru Dumitriu.   London, Collins, 1968.

Translator, *Roman Imperial Coins*, by Laura Breglia.   London, Thames and Hudson, 1969.

Translator, *Rome: The Centre of Power*, by Ranuccio Bianci Bandenelli.   London, Thames and Hudson, 1970.


Peter Green comments:

My three full-length novels are all set in the ancient world: *Achilles His Armour* describes the life of Alcibiades against the background of the Peloponnesian War, *The Sword of Pleasure* is an attempt to recreate the lost memoirs of the Roman dictator Sulla, while *The Laughter of Aphrodite* is an account of Sappho, the famous lyric poet of Lesbos, told in the first person. All three are based on careful background research, and endeavour to recreate a life, a mood, a society as far as possible in accordance with Ranke's dictum for writing history—*wie es eigentlich gewesen ist*, "as it really happened". All presuppose the axiom that a person's emotional, sexual, and political make-up is inextricably interwoven.

One reason why I chose to write historical novels was that it seemed to me there were aspects of history that could not be adequately dealt with in terms of ordinary historical—or rather historiographical—conventions. I still hold by that belief: at the back of my mind I have plans for several more historical novels, including one about Archilochus, the Hemingway-like soldier-poet of the 7th century B.C. (tentatively entitled *My Singing Captain*), another on the first Sicilian slave-revolt of 135 B.C., and a third on the period of assimilation in Roman Britain, which I would like to call *Ashes under Uricon*. But at present I am having a period of writing "straight" conventional history: my most recently published works include a biography of Alexander, a study of the ill-fated Sicilian Expedition, and a new history of the Graeco-Persian Wars. If I return to fiction in the near future it will be to deal with more strictly modern themes. My one volume of modern short stories, *Habeas Corpus*, attempted the then unfashionable task of describing sexual relationships honestly, with an absolute minimum of wishful thinking or fantasising. No one wanted this message in 1960 (perhaps they still don't), so, as I have to live by my writing, I never repeated the experiment. I have an unfinished novel about Cambridge life which I would like to complete one day; it shows a side of the place that neither Snow nor Leavis (nor indeed Andrew Sinclair) ever quite got around to chronicling.

*     *     *

Peter Green is one of the few contemporary "men of letters". Although copious and various both in his functions and his publications, he is probably at his best when working in the fields of Ancient History and Classical Literature; and of the four works of fiction which he has published under his own name, three are novels set in antiquity.

*Achilles His Armour* is based on the life of the Athenian hero and traitor, Alcibiades. The writing is self-indulgent, prolix and full of clichés; it is also vigorous, fluent and clear. The treatment is "modern", in the sense that motive and action, whether political or personal, are rendered in terms which would be immediately comprehensible by the Man on the Bakerloo Line; but there is no attempt to draw vulgar or pretentious comparisons between Alcibiades' era and our own. The historical background, as known to scholars, is described with loving skill; and where speculation is required, Mr. Green speculates with the same zestful abandon as his hero exhibits (rather too repeatedly) in his romps through battlefield and brothel.

*The Sword of Pleasure* is altogether a more mature performance. Purporting to be the lost memoirs of the Roman dictator, Lucius Cornelius Sulla, it is not quite so alarmingly hectic as the previous novel and far more concise. Mr. Green introduces a new element of articulate melancholy, which at its best embodies much pithy moral comment, and certainly helps to maintain the illusion that we are reading the testament of a worldly and worn out aristocrat. There is some sharp and memorable narrative of events both historical and fictitious; and Mr. Green's characters have now begun to talk to each other instead of reciprocating lectures.

*The Laughter of Aphrodite* is about the poetess Sappho, a far more difficult subject than either Alcibiades or Sulla, if only because next to nothing is known of her. Mr. Green fabricates his own Sappho with the aid of a poetic but perhaps overheated fancy, which he deploys with a canny sense of literary tactics learnt (by this stage in his career) from long experience of reviewing other men's novels. The result is sometimes sentimental, sometimes lurid, but always fascinating and, to me at least, convincing. This is the first of Mr. Green's novels which one closes quite definitely wishing it were longer.

Mr. Green's paramount gift as a novelist is for presenting blow-by-blow accounts of what happens and why with the immediacy of a brilliant if often tasteless on-the-spot reporter. He is also a man for making, and then insisting upon, unpopular but irrefutable common sense judgments about men and affairs: he dearly loves to coin an "unacceptable" or unfashionable truth. The short stories in *Habeas Corpus* contain several such, as applied to sexual activities. The one thing Mr. Green has not learnt over the years is to disguise his relish at the annoyance which he knows these truths will cause. Inside the weighty and respected *littérateur* there is always the jeering fourth-former cocking two-handed snooks.

—Simon Raven

---

**GREENE, Graham.** British. Born in Berkhamsted, Hertfordshire, 2 October 1904. Educated at Berkhamsted School; Balliol College, Oxford. Served in the Foreign Office, London, 1941–44. Married Vivien Dayrell-Browning in 1927; has two children. Staff Member, *The Times*, London, 1926–30; Movie Critic, 1937–40, and Literary Editor, 1940–41, *Spectator*, London. Director, Eyre and Spottiswoode, publishers, London, 1944–48, and The Bodley Head, publishers, London, 1958–68. Recipient: Hawthornden Prize, 1941; Black Memorial Prize, 1949; Shakespeare Prize, Hamburg, 1968. Litt.D., Cambridge University, 1962; D.Litt. Edinburgh University, 1967. Honorary Fellow, Balliol College, 1963. Companion of Honour, 1966. Chevalier of the Legion of Honour, 1969. Address: c/o The Bodley Head, 9 Bow Street, London W.C.2, England.

PUBLICATIONS

Novels

*The Man Within.* London, Heinemann, and New York, Doubleday, 1929.
*The Name of Action.* London, Heinemann, 1930; New York, Doubleday, 1931.
*Rumour at Nightfall.* London, Heinemann, 1931; New York, Doubleday, 1932.
*Stamboul Train: An Entertainment.* London, Heinemann, 1932; as *Orient Express: An Entertainment*, New York, Doubleday, 1933.
*It's a Battlefield.* London, Heinemann, and New York, Doubleday, 1934.
*England Made Me.* London, Heinemann, and New York, Doubleday, 1935.
*A Gun for Sale: An Entertainment.* London, Heinemann, 1936; as *This Gun for Hire: An Entertainment*, New York, Doubleday, 1936.
*Brighton Rock.* London, Heinemann, 1938; as *Brighton Rock: An Entertainment*, New York, Viking Press, 1938.
*The Confidential Agent.* London, Heinemann, and New York, Viking Press, 1939.
*The Power and the Glory.* London, Heinemann, 1940; as *The Labyrinthine Ways*, New York, Viking Press, 1940.
*The Ministry of Fear: An Entertainment.* London, Heinemann, and New York, Viking Press, 1943.
*The Heart of the Matter.* London, Heinemann, and New York, Viking Press, 1948.
*The End of the Affair.* London, Heinemann, and New York, Viking Press, 1951.
*The Third Man: An Entertainment.* New York, Viking Press, 1950.
*The Third Man and The Fallen Idol.* London, Heinemann, 1950.
*Loser Takes All: An Entertainment.* London, Heinemann, 1955; New York, Viking Press, 1957.
*The Quiet American.* London, Heinemann, 1955; New York, Viking Press, 1956.
*Our Man in Havana: An Entertainment.* London, Heinemann, and New York, Viking Press, 1958.
*A Burnt-Out Case.* London, Heinemann, and New York, Viking Press, 1961.

*The Comedians.*   London, Bodley Head, and New York, Viking Press, 1966.
*Travels with My Aunt.*   London, Bodley Head, 1969; New York, Viking Press, 1970.

## Short Stories

*The Basement Room and Other Stories.*   London, Cresset Press, 1935.
*The Bear Fell Free.*   London, Grayson, 1935.
*Twenty-four Stories*, with James Laver and Sylvia Townsend Warner.   London, Cresset Press, 1939.
*Nineteen Stories.*   London, Heinemann, 1947; New York, Viking Press, 1949; augmented edition, as *Twenty-one Stories*, London, Heinemann, 1954.
*A Visit to Morin.*   Privately printed, 1959.
*A Sense of Reality.*   London, Bodley Head, and New York, Viking Press, 1963.
*May We Borrow Your Husband? and Other Comedies of the Sexual Life.*   London, Bodley Head, and New York, Viking Press, 1967.

## Plays

*The Living Room* (produced London, 1953; New York, 1954).   London, Heinemann, 1953; New York, Viking Press, 1954.
*The Potting Shed* (produced New York, 1957; London, 1958).   New York, Viking Press, 1957; London, Heinemann, 1958.
*The Complaisant Lover* (produced London, 1959; New York, 1961).   London, Heinemann, 1959; New York, Viking Press, 1961.
*Carving a Statue* (produced London, 1964; New York, 1968).   London, Bodley Head, 1964.
*The Third Man: A Film*, with Carol Reed.   London, Lorrimer Films, 1969.

Screenplays: *Brighton Rock*, 1946: *The Fallen Idol*, 1949; *The Third Man*, 1950; *Our Man in Havana*, 1960; *The Comedians*, 1967.

## Verse

*Babbling April: Poems.*   Oxford, Blackwell, 1925.

## Other

*Journey Without Maps: A Travel Book.*   London, Heinemann, and New York, Doubleday, 1936.
*The Lawless Roads: A Mexican Journey.*   London, Longman, 1939; as *Another Mexico*, New York, Viking Press, 1939.
*British Dramatists.*   London, Collins, 1942; included in *The Romance of English Literature*, New York, Hastings House, 1944.
*The Little Train* (published anonymously; juvenile).   London, Eyre and Spottiswoode, 1946; New York, Lothrop. 1958.
*Why Do I Write: An Exchange of Views Between Elizabeth Bowen, Graham Greene and V. S. Pritchett.*   London, Marshall, 1948.
*After Two Years.*   Privately printed, 1949.
*For Christmas.*   Privately printed, 1950.
*The Little Fire Engine* (juvenile).   London, Parrish, 1950; as *The Little Red Fire Engine*, New York, Lothrop, 1952.

*The Lost Childhood and Other Essays.* London, Eyre and Spottiswoode, 1951; New York, Viking Press, 1952.
*The Little Horse Bus* (juvenile). London, Parrish, 1952; New York, Lothrop, 1954.
*The Little Steam Roller: A Story of Mystery and Detection* (juvenile). London, Parrish, 1953; New York, Lothrop, 1955.
*Essais Catholiques*, translated by Marcelle Sibon. Paris, Editions de Seuil, 1953.
*In Search of a Character: Two African Journals.* London, Bodley Head, and New York, Viking Press, 1961.
*The Revenge: An Autobiographical Fragment.* Privately printed, 1963.
*Victorian Detective Fiction: A Catalogue of the Collection Made by Dorothy Glover and Graham Greene, Introduced by John Carter.* London, Bodley Head, 1966.
*Collected Essays.* London, Bodley Head, and New York, Viking Press. 1969.
*A Sort of Life* (autobiography). London, Bodley Head, and New York, Simon and Schuster, 1971.

Editor, *The Old School: Essays by Divers Hands.* London, Cape, and New York, Peter Smith, 1934.
Editor, *The Best of Saki.* London, British Publishers Guild, 1950.
Editor, with Hugh Greene, *The Spy's Bedside Book: An Anthology.* London, Hart Davis, 1957.
Editor, *The Bodley Head Ford Madox Ford.* London, Bodley Head, 4 vols., 1962, 1963.


Bibliography: *Graham Greene*, by J. D. Vann, Kent, Ohio, Kent State University Press, 1970.

*       *       *

Graham Greene himself indicates the nature of his achievement as a novelist when he writes, in the preface to the 1971 edition of *The Confidential Agent*, that he began the novel "with a certain vague ambition to create something legendary out of a contemporary thriller". At the centre of all his novels, from the first, *The Man Within*, onwards, is a man on the run—from society or from the police, from himself or his conscience, or from God. He has, in other words, claimed a popular and often largely disregarded fictional genre for the purposes of serious art in order to express a deeply felt and deeply idiosyncratic view of man's condition. The ambition is perhaps not new: Greene has obvious affinities with novelists of action like Stevenson, a kinsman, and Conrad, by whom he has been much influenced; but the achievement can be measured by the comparison with the admirable novels of "serious" thriller-writers like Eric Ambler and Patricia Highsmith. The difference is precisely one of ambition, the imparting to the basic thriller situation of the "something legendary" which makes Greene's novels paradigms of the human condition as he sees it.

Greene is of course a Roman Catholic convert, but the explicitly Catholic novels, *Brighton Rock*, *The Power and the Glory*, *The Heart of the Matter*, *The End of the Affair* and *A Burnt-Out Case* do not differ in essence or in point of view from the secular novels. Indeed, it is clear that for Greene Catholicism is a religion of desperation, and, a natural nonconformist, he is, one feels, as much against the Roman Catholic Establishment as he is against any other Establishment. Nor, in what may be called his religious novels, do the spokesmen for the Church necessarily get the best of the argument. The last words in *A Burnt-Out Case*, the action of which is set in a leper-colony run by monks in the Congo, are those of the atheist doctor, Colin. For there is another aspect of Greene, what has been called the romantic anarchist. The words seem as good as any to denote a passionate sympathy for the poor and oppressed which goes hand in hand with a distrust of authority, of the established, which is seen in his ambiguous attitude towards Communism. Sometimes his Catholicism, or his religious sense, and his romantic anarchism exist in polarity, as in his most famous and probably his finest novel *The Power and the Glory*. Set in a state in Mexico in which the Church is outlawed, the action dramatises the pursuit and in the end the capture by a police lieutenant of the last priest in the state. The policeman, incorruptible, devoted to the moral and material betterment of his fellows, is the representative of secular idealism; the priest, on the face of it a bad priest, the father of a child and able to keep himself going only by resort to the brandy-bottle, is still the representative of the other-worldly, the divine, God, in whose grace, Greene claims in this novel, man's one hope lies. In *The Power and the Glory* God wins; but what is impressive is Greene's fairness: the policeman is presented as a good man: if the priest attains to something like sanctity, the policeman is something like a secular saint.

In this novel Greene seems to have dramatised two sides of his nature. In the much later novel, *The Comedians*, on the other hand, both sides come together. The setting is Haiti under the Duvalier tyranny, and the spokesmen for Greene's values, the Communist Dr. Magiot, writes to the narrator towards the end of the novel:

> Communism, my friend, is more than Marxism, just as Catholicism—remember I was born a Catholic too—is more than the Roman Curia. There is a *mystique* as well as a *politique*. . . . Communists have committed great crimes, but at least they have not stood aside, like an established society, and been indifferent. I would rather have blood on my hands than water like Pilate. . . . I implore you—a knock on the door may not allow me to finish this sentence, so take it as the last request of a dying man —if you have abandoned one faith, do not abandon all faith. There is always an alternative to the faith we lose. Or is it the same faith under another mask?

Greene's abiding view of man is stated in some words of Newman's which he prefixes to his African travel book *The Lawless Roads*: ". . . either there is no Creator, or this living society of men is in a true sense discarded from His presence . . . *if* there be a God, *since* there is a God, the human race is implicated in some terrible aboriginal calamity." Greene's theme, then, is alienation. It is, throughout the world, the great theme of the contemporary novel, and it is obviously one reason for Greene's immense reputation throughout the world; without question, internationally he is the most seriously regarded of living English novelists. But the theme is one thing: equally important is his treatment of it. For he is an international novelist in a quite other sense than that he commands a worldwide readership, as the settings of his novels show: Sweden in *England Made Me*, Mexico in *The Power and the Glory*, West Africa in *The Heart of the Matter*, Vietnam during the war against the French in *The Quiet American*, Cuba on the eve of the Castro revolution in *Our Man in Havana*, the Congo just before the Belgian withdrawal in *A Burnt-Out Case*, Haiti in *The Comedians*. He seems to have an unerring eye for the trouble spots of the world just as they are on the verge of erupting. This means that the novels when first published have an immediate topical interest, and this is an aspect of fiction never to be despised. Greene is a great journalist in his own right, and this is part of his strength as a novelist. But he is not simply the special correspondent as novelist. The violent places of the earth attract him for an especial reason; in them the in-gredients of the normal world are caught in sharper perspective; the violence that lurks just below the surface of the London of *It's a Battlefield*, of the English seaside resort of *Brighton Rock* or of the English Midlands city of *Gun for Sale*, is the overt and accepted condition of life in Haiti. In Greene's fiction it is London, Brighton and Nottingham, with their relative temperateness of life, that are distortious of the norm, not Saigon and Haiti. The effect is one of universalisation: men are the same everywhere: "Why this is hell, nor am I out of it."

But there is something else, without which all would be nothing. This is Greene's art. He is, to begin with, a superb story-teller, perhaps the best alive, in the simple and fundamental sense that he immediately captures the reader's appetite for excitement and sustains it by his use of detail, his manipulation of suspense and his unceasing invention. One recalls the opening sentences of his novels, of *Brighton Rock*, for instance: "Hale knew they meant to murder him before he had been in Brighton three hours." But one might just as well write, "He is, to end with, a superb story-teller", for his stories are the fruits of his great range of technical skills and resources. There are those novelists who can be called learned novelists, as some painters are called painterly. Greene is one of them. He is learned in the works of the masters and he has made what he has learned from them his own. His most obvious masters are Henry James and Conrad, not least in his ambition to make of a novel a self-contained work of art. But he has also learned from the films. It is not for nothing that for some years as a young man he was a film critic and became a distinguished writer of film-scripts. He uses the image and the cutting from image to image very much as the film-director does, in order to give his action pace, diversity, contrast and immediate impact on the reader; witness, as an obvious instance, the first two paragraphs of *The Power and the Glory*. The result is concision, compactness, intensity of focus, and it is something for which Greene has not been given sufficient credit.

All this may be seen in his extraordinarily idiosyncratic prose style, with its use of the unexpected, sometimes bizarre image, a prose that in its imagery is often strikingly like the early poetry of W. H. Auden. He is, it is difficult not to think, at times the prisoner of his own penchant for the bizarre or melodramatic image. Then he seems to be parodying himself, as in *The Heart of the Matter* in which the thoughts of the central character, Scobie, are given us in a manner stylistically too close to the language of the anonymous narrator. Nevertheless, at its best his style is the perfect, i.e., it seems the only possible, medium of expression for his attitude towards and analysis of the human state.

Something else remains to be said. In recent years Greene has shown himself an admirable and original comic writer; in *Our Man in Havana*, the volume of short stories *May We Borrow Your Husband?* and *Travels with My Aunt*. But the comedy still exists in the realm of Greene's abiding preoccupations.

—Walter Allen

---

**GROSSMAN, Alfred.** American. Born in New York City, 14 May 1927. Educated at Haverford College, Pennsylvania, 1944–48, B.A. 1948; Harvard University, Cambridge, Massachusetts, 1948–49, M.A. 1949. Served in the United States Navy, 1945–46. Married Althea Eudora Van Boskirk in 1971. Editor, *East Europe Magazine*, New York, 1954–61. Since 1968, Editor of the *New York Times Almanac*. Address: 54 Riverside Drive, Apartment 14-A, New York, New York 10024, U.S.A.

PUBLICATIONS

Novels

*Acrobat Admits.* New York, Braziller, 1959; London, Heinemann, 1960.
*Many Slippery Errors.* London, Heinemann, 1963; New York, Doubleday, 1964.
*Marie Beginning.* London, Heinemann, 1964; New York, Doubleday, 1965.
*The Do-Gooders.* New York, Doubleday, and London, Heinemann, 1968.

Uncollected Short Stories

"The Big Girls", in *Rogue* (Evanston, Illinois), 1963.
"The Gobbitch Men", in *Amazing Stories* (New York), 1965.

"The Beauty Contest", in *Transatlantic Review* (London and New York), Winter 1966–67.

Manuscript Collection: Mugar Library, Boston University.

*        *        *

At his best, Grossman is his own acrobat: putting on disguises, slipping effortlessly from one style to another (the barracks monologue of Sarge to the poor-white-trash dialect of the yokel in *Acrobat Admits*), parodying and punning in a zany show of life's lunacy; at his worst, he is the acrobat tripped, caught in his own trick, unable to disentangle himself, finally resorting to any device to take him off-stage. When his performance is deft, he writes in the ironic mode, exposing man's emotional and spiritual impoverishment, his desperate attempts to make contact through sex, the failure of these attempts to do anything but that. When he flounders, he denies the contradictions which sustain his irony and turns his satire on man's hapless attempts to give life meaning into an insignificant story of the disintegration of a neurotic personality.

New York is Grossman's circus with a publishing house (*Acrobat Admits*), the United Nations Secretariat (*Many Slippery Errors*), or a shoe manufacturing corporation (*Marie Beginning*) as the arena. The time is the '60's with the radical right and left battling. His theme is that modern, urban life is insupportable—that the only relief from boredom will come from an action. The possibilities for action vary in Grossman's novels, but in no case does Grossman, a comedian of black humor, allow the action to be positive. In *Acrobat Admits* destruction of another is the central action. Kennan attempts self-destruction in both *Marie Beginning* and again in its self-contained sequel, *Do-Gooders*, and Dicherty succeeds in *Many Slippery Errors*. Finally, in Grossman's most recent novel, *The Do-Gooders*, the act that brings the novel to its conclusion is not murder, nor suicide, but the destruction of some part of the System. In Grossman's second novel, Dicherty's dream of blowing-up Con-Ed is only a dream; in *The Do-Gooders* the dream is fulfilled when Marie, Spider and Kennan blow up the connecting link of a twelve-lane expressway. This reliance on a sophomoric solution diminishes Grossman's art: after sensing the nihilistic vision that lies beneath an often hilarious, but always troubling, surface, the audience expects more from him. Perhaps Grossman's next novel will offer it.

In his arena are his characters: men, imperfectly synchronized with their time—intelligent, restive, bored with the banalities of their jobs and marriages, but always insecure and dependent; and women, of two types, either middle-class and insecure, cloaking that insecurity with the conventions of marriage (Cairo Joy in *Acrobat Admits*, Sally in *Many Slippery Errors*, and Sheila in *Marie Beginning*) or working-class and secure (the typists from Brooklyn: taciturn Pia [*Many Slippery Errors*] or candid Marie [*Marie Beginning* and its sequel], refreshingly blunt with a flawless sense of the possibilities of a moment). The plot revolves around the adventures of these men and women and their constant attempts to couple, which are described in a fashion reminiscent of the rituals in the writings of the Marquis de Sade.

Grossman's strengths lie in his comic voice and his ability to caricature. Few of his characters are deeply motivated; even Marie for whom Grossman has a respect and affection which are lacking in his other portraits, falls short of the mark. But a number of his caricatures are excellent. There are Alexander Forbes, the wealthy playboy who locks women in his padded one-room apartment and subjects them to innumerable indignities as he feeds all his sadistic yearnings and his contempt for his sister; and Dicherty, the aged, wandering lecher who garrulously talks of the vanity of human wishes while he provides a clubhouse for the initiation rites of the toreador-pants set in Brooklyn; and Spider, a mafioso-type with a nice sense of retributive justice; and also Cairo Joy, the embodiment of middle-class consciousness.

His style is often facile, but marred by a self-consciousness which makes much of his dialogue inauthentic. The strained imitation of Hamlet's words in the opening chapter of *Acrobat Admits* provides ample evidence of this defect: "The problem: to start clean, where I am unknown. Self-protection, the bubble that I may burst if needs must, the escape gear of ultimate anonymity, shelter from my own grenades. I intend to complicate, I do not intend to brick myself into a cellar wall. George must not be George."

To complicate life in order to penetrate its banalities is the *raison d'être* of all the antics and pursuits in Grossman's novels. Often the complications are outrageous, occasionally they are hilarious, sometimes, as in his all-too-frequent episodes of amorous impertinences varied with exercises in sadism, they are tedious and without point. A dextrous style saves the superficiality of the characters; a weird but limited imagination creates the lively episodes that carry his art; but until more of Grossman's work emerges, it will not be clear whether he can outgrow his forced service to masters as diverse as Joyce, Shakespeare and Max Schulman, exercise a care with dialogue which will eliminate the inconsistent images and figures that so often make his parodies inauthentic, and perfect the vehicle which will simultaneously express his moral outrage and convince his readers of the substance and importance of both his characters and themes.

—Carol Simpson Stern

---

**GUERARD, Albert (Joseph).** American. Born in Houston, Texas, 2 November 1914. Educated at Stanford University, California, B.A. 1934, Ph.D. 1938; Harvard University, Cambridge, Massachusetts, M.A. 1936. Served in the Psychological Warfare Branch of the United States Army, 1943–45. Married Mary Maclin Bocock in 1941; has three children. Instructor in English, Amherst College, Massachusetts, 1935–36; successively Instructor, Assistant Professor, and Associate Professor of English, 1938–54, and Professor of English, 1954–61, Harvard University. Since 1961, Professor of Literature, and since 1969, Chairman of the Committee on Modern Thought and Literature, Stanford University. Recipient: Rockefeller Fellowship, 1946; Fulbright Fellowship, 1950; Guggenheim Fellowship, 1956; Ford Fellowship, 1959; *Paris Review* Fiction Prize, 1963; National Foundation for the Arts grant, 1967. Member, American Academy of Arts and Sciences. Address: 635 Gerona Road, Stanford, California 94305, U.S.A.

PUBLICATIONS

Novels

   *The Past Must Alter*.  London, Longman, 1937; New York, Holt, 1938.
   *The Hunted*.  New York, Knopf, 1944; London, Longman, 1947.
   *Maquisard: A Christmas Tale*.  New York, Knopf, 1945; London, Longman, 1946.
   *Night Journey*.  New York, Knopf, 1950; London, Longman, 1951.
   *The Bystander*.  Boston, Little Brown, 1958; London, Faber, 1959.
   *The Exiles*.  London, Faber, 1962; New York, Macmillan, 1963.

Uncollected Short Stories

"The Incubus", in *Dial* (New York), no. 2, 1960.
"On the Operating Table", in *Denver Quarterly*, Autumn 1966.
"The Journey", in *Partisan Review* (New Brunswick, New Jersey), Winter 1967.

Other

*Robert Bridges: A Study of Traditionalism in Poetry.* Cambridge, Massachusetts, Harvard University Press, and London, Oxford University Press, 1942.
*Joseph Conrad.* New York, New Directions, 1947.
*Thomas Hardy: The Novels and Stories.* Cambridge, Massachusetts, Harvard University Press, 1949; London, Oxford University Press, 1950.
*André Gide.* Cambridge, Massachusetts, Harvard University Press, and London, Oxford University Press, 1951; revised edition, 1969.
*Conrad the Novelist.* Cambridge, Massachusetts, Harvard University Press, 1958; London, Oxford University Press, 1959.

Editor, *Ecrit aux U.S.A.* Paris, Robert Laffont, 1947.
Editor, *Hardy: A Collection of Critical Essays.* New York, Prentice Hall, 1963.
Editor, *Perspective on the Novel*, the Spring 1963 issue of *Daedalus* (Boston).
Co-Editor, *The Personal Voice: A Contemporary Prose Reader.* Philadelphia, Lippincott, 1964.
Editor, *Stories of the Double.* Philadelphia, Lippincott, 1967.

Manuscript Collection: Stanford University Library.

Critical Studies: *The Modern Novel in America* by Frederick Hoffman, Chicago, Regnery, 1951; *The Hero with the Private Parts* by Andrew Lytle, Baton Rouge, Louisiana State University Press, 1966; essays by Albert Guerard on his own work: "The Vanishing Anarchists", in *Sewanee Review* (Tennessee), Summer 1969; "Was Lya de Putti Dead at 22?", in *Tri-Quarterly* (Evanston, Illinois), Autumn 1970; "My Grande Naufrage", in *Southern Review* (Baton Rouge, Louisiana), Winter 1972.

Albert Guerard comments:

My work has been notably affected by wartime experience (political intelligence work in France) and by the pressures and ambiguities of the subsequent cold war. I have tried without success to put the political subject aside; thousands of unpublished pages, many of them angry, testify to inescapable contemporary pressures.

*Maquisard*, written immediately after the 1944 events it describes, is an affectionate record of wartime comradeships among men who had been in the underground. Apologetically subtitled *A Christmas Tale*, it is the slightest of my novels and was the most warmly received. *Night Journey*, my most complex and most substantial novel, is more truthful in its picture of the political and moral devastation caused by American-Soviet rivalries in a world as deceptive, and as self-deceptive, as that of *1984*. It was, on publication, repeatedly compared to Orwell's book. The confession of Paul Haldan (wandering and evasive, with his final crime left undescribed, and indeed undetected by most readers) is that of a liberal "innocent" who can accept neither his mother's sexual betrayals nor his country's systematic abuse of power and liberal ideology, nor its threatened use of germ warfare. Haldan's night journey into temporary regression takes him into the middle European city of his childhood, disputed by the two great powers and betrayed by both. The ambiguities of an undeclared war are internalized by Paul Haldan, and his psycho-sexual anxieties projected onto the screen of public conflict. *The Exiles* (based on a journey to Cuba, Haiti, and Santo Domingo during the turmoil of 1959) explores deception and self-deception in the tragi-comic context of Caribbean propaganda and political intrigue. It dramatizes the conflict of a quixotic Trujillo assassin incorrigibly drawn to the exiled statesman he is supposed to destroy. Manuel Andrada appears to be the most winning of my fictional creations.

In *The Hunted*, an earlier novel and conventionally realistic in technique, psycho-sexual anxieties and monumental vanities reflect public disorders in a small New England college just before World War II. Oedipal conflicts and fantasies, dramatized fairly unconsciously in *The Past Must Alter*, are central to *Night Journey* and to *The Bystander*, another story of romantic love vitiated by immaturity and regression. The technique of *The Bystander* is that of the French *récit*, with the motives either concealed or distorted by the narrator-protagonist. But the story is also of a collision between American "innocence" and European compromise. One of my central aims has been to avoid, while writing fairly complex psychological novels, the deadening burden of explicit and accurate analysis. *The Bystander*—very easy to read, perhaps too easy to read—requires, to be truly understood, the closest attention to hint, to image, to nuance of voice and style.

My fiction-writing has undoubtedly been affected by the work done on my critical books. Conrad is the most obvious of my masters, as Graham Greene remarked. But Hardy and Gide also helped me overcome, to some extent, the realistic documentary impulses of my first three novels.

\*        \*        \*

Of Albert Guerard's six novels, four are primarily of political or social significance—*The Exiles, Night Journey, Maquisard*, and *The Hunted*—and two are psychological studies involving the necessity of recovery and re-evaluation of one's personal past—*The Bystander* and *The Past Must Alter*. A preoccupation with the psychology of divided loyalties and of fear of betrayal is recurrent throughout Guerard's fiction as well as the theme of recovery of the past.

*The Exiles*, which best exemplifies what the author has called subjective or visionary fiction as opposed to journeyman realism, was suggested by the situation in the Dominican Republic (Santa Isabella) under Trujillo (the Protector). Manuel Andrada, Guerard's most fully realized character, agent and loyal supporter of the Protector, is assigned the task of bringing the exile Justo de Villamayor, a great poet, back to his homeland and, failing that, to kill him. The tormented conscience of the agent, divided between loyalty to the Protector and admiration for Villamayor, is rendered with dramatic and visionary intensity. *Night Journey* presents a nightmare Europe of the future, divided between the dictatorship of the East and the so-called Democracy of the West, engaged in endless, indecisive, and undeclared border warfare. Paul Haldan, an idealistic socialist from England, abandons his superior officer, Philip Montalva, to enemy capture because of Montalva's supposed betrayal of the socialist cause. But Montalva's eventual heroic death in a one man machine gun stand reveals his integrity and the difficulty of making moral judgments in a bleak and dehumanized world. The action of *Maquisard* occurs near a French seaside town during World War II where the Ruc Brigade, composed of former Maquis, is attempting to wipe out a pocket of Germans. Interest centers on Jean Ruyader's attempt to return to a normal life of love and a new marriage after the execution of his wife by the Nazis. The toughness and heroism of the Maquis fighting in the depths of a biting French winter are unforgettably portrayed. *The Hunted*, a novel of social criticism, is the story of an imprudent marriage between a self-centered romantically tempered college English teacher and a beautiful waitress with no social background. Their marriage goes to pieces under the pressure of the snobbish and petty faculty of a small New England town. In *The Bystander* Anthony eventually meets and has an affair with his dream girl, Christiane Mondor, but the liaison ends in Anthony's humiliation when he cannot develop his adolescent concept of a grand passion into mature companionship and love. In *The Past Must Alter*, young Jim Simmons witnesses the breakup of the marriage of his gambling journalist father and his passive and conventional mother. As a result of the boy's terror and isolation, a new and presumably successful marriage of the mother is temporarily prevented until the boy, as a result of meeting a beautiful young actress, breaks the Oedipal bond.

Guerard's social and political views are those of a humane liberal. His highly literate and perceptive style, counter-realist and counter-naturalist, is reminiscent of but not imitative of Conrad. His psychological complexity appears to owe much to Gide and Freud.

—Donald E. Stanford

**GUNN, Neil (Miller).** British. Born in Caithness, Scotland, 8 November 1891. Educated at Highland School and privately. Married Jessie Dallas Frew in 1921. Former Civil Servant; resigned, 1937. Recipient: Black Memorial Prize, 1938. LL.D., Edinburgh University. Address: Dalcraig, Kessock, Inverness, Scotland.

PUBLICATIONS

Novels

*The Grey Coast.* London, Cape, and Boston, Little Brown, 1926.
*Morning Tide.* Edinburgh, Porpoise Press, and New York, Harcourt Brace, 1931.
*The Lost Glen.* Edinburgh, Porpoise Press, 1932.
*Sun Circle.* Edinburgh, Porpoise Press, 1933.
*Butcher's Broom.* Edinburgh, Porpoise Press, 1934; as *Highland Night*, New York, Harcourt Brace, 1935.
*Highland River.* Edinburgh, Porpoise Press, and Philadelphia, Lippincott, 1937.
*Wild Geese Overhead.* London, Faber, 1939.
*Second Sight.* London, Faber, 1940.
*The Silver Darlings.* London, Faber, 1941; New York, Stewart, 1945.
*Young Art and Old Hector.* London, Faber, 1942; New York, Stewart, 1944.
*The Serpent.* London, Faber, 1943; as *Man Goes Alone*, New York, Stewart, 1944.
*The Green Isle of the Great Deep.* London, Faber, 1944.
*The Key of the Chest.* London, Faber, 1945; New York, Stewart, 1946.
*The Drinking Well.* London, Faber, 1946; New York, Stewart, 1947.
*The Shadow.* London, Faber, 1948.
*The Silver Bough.* London, Faber, 1948.
*The Lost Chart.* London, Faber, 1949.
*The Well at the World's End.* London, Faber, 1951.
*Blood Hunt.* London, Faber, 1952.
*The Other Landscape.* London, Faber, 1954.

Short Stories

*Hidden Doors.*   Edinburgh, Porpoise Press, 1929.
*The White Hours and Other Stories.*   London, Faber, 1950.


Plays

*Back Home.*   Glasgow, Wilson, 1932.
*The Ancient Fire* (produced by the Scottish National Players, in the 1930's).
*Choosing a Play: A Comedy of Community Drama.*   Edinburgh, Porpoise Press, 1938.
*Old Music.*   London, Nelson, 1939.
*Net Results.*   London, Nelson, 1939.


Other

*Whisky and Scotland: A Practical and Spiritual Survey.*   London, Routledge, 1935.
*Off in a Boat* (travel).   London, Faber, 1938.
*Storm and Precipice and Other Pieces.*   London, Faber, 1942.
*Highland Pack* (travel).   London, Faber, 1949.
*The Atom of Delight* (autobiography).   London, Faber, 1956.


Bibliography: in *The Bibliotheck* (Glasgow), vol. 3, no. 3, 1961.


Critical Study: *The Scottish Tradition in Literature* by Kurt Wittig, Edinburgh, Oliver and Boyd, 1958.

\*      \*      \*

"The boy's eyes opened in wonder"—this, the opening phrase of Gunn's first entirely successful novel, *Morning Tide*, might be applied to all his most significant work. On the face of it, *Morning Tide* concerns a series of significant episodes in the experience of an adolescent growing up in a small fishing community in the remotest Highlands of Scotland. But those episodes constitute an initiation ceremony, in the course of which the boy is shaken awake from the dream of childhood into realisation of the complex responsibilities of the adult condition. For while Gunn writes prose fiction, his attitude to life has much in common with the poet's. The incidents in *Morning Tide*, or *Highland River*, or *Young Art and Old Hector*, or *The Silver Darlings*, far from providing examples of unusual adventure, illustrate and exemplify universal truths, and the principal characters, although they have their own individuality, are presented not as oddities or eccentrics but as living embodiments of essential human qualities. Gunn also possesses the poet's eye for significant sensuous detail, bringing the scene of the action into the forefront of the reader's awareness by means of strikingly original images.

In *Highland River* there are two initiation ceremonies, for while the fifteen chapters on the hero's boyhood demonstrate the process of his introduction to adult responsibility, the last chapter expresses the individual adult's initiation into acceptance of his own solitariness, combined with a conviction of the unity of the whole of life. The adult hero, seeking the source of the river which ran through the glen where he had spent his formative years becomes a kind of Everyman, an experiencing entity alone with earth and water and sky. For his whole pilgrimage is essentially solitary, and it concludes in paradox, when he finds two sources for the river, one "a black hole . . . in ooze" and the other a loch with "shores . . .

of pure ground quartz." The sensuous delicacy and imaginative power of this chapter make it one of Gunn's finest.

Initiation is also a fundamental concern of Gunn's masterpiece, *The Silver Darlings*, which ends with a five-word sentence summing up all that has gone before—"Life had come for him." Yet as well as being a perceptive study of the young hero's apprenticeship to the sea, this novel describing the growth of the fishing industry around the Highland coast in the early nineteenth century is also a kind of epic poem in prose, a revelation of relationships within a community, a picture of men and women of every sort struggling to establish a new way of life, and a presentation of a whole people—the peasant victims of the Highland Clearances—during a particular historical period. The hero, Finn, while sensuously alive in his own time, is also a kind of recreation of the legendary Celtic hero, Finn MacCoul, and the other major characters all rise to the achievement of epic stature at the most significant moments in the action. Gunn shows the defeated creating a new victory, a new triumph, out of almost total loss; and, without the slightest concession to sentimentalism, the warmth of their humanity glows from every page. This is perhaps the greatest of all modern Scottish novels, the sanest as well as the most deeply imaginative, a study of real people involved in actual situations, and yet at the same time a fable which illuminates the inner life of us all.

—Alexander Scott

---

**GUTHRIE, A(lfred) B(ertram), Jr.** American. Born in Bedford, Indiana, 13 January 1901. Educated at the University of Washington, Seattle, 1919–20; University of Montana, Missoula, A.B. 1923. Married Harriet Larson, 1931 (divorced, 1963); Carol B. Luthin, 1969; has two children. Reporter, 1926–29, City Editor and Editorial Writer, 1929–45, and Executive Editor, 1945–47, Lexington, Kentucky *Leader*. Fellow, and Lecturer, Bread Loaf Writers' Conference, Vermont, 1945–47. Professor of Creative Writing, University of Kentucky, Lexington, 1947–52. Recipient: Nieman Fellowship, 1944; Pulitzer Prize, 1950; Boys' Clubs of America Junior Book Award, 1951; National Association of Independent Schools Award, 1961. Litt.D., University of Montana, 1949. Address: Twin Lakes, Chateau, Montana 59422, U.S.A.

PUBLICATIONS

Novels

> *Murders at Moon Dance*.  New York, Dutton, 1943; London, Long,1961.
> *The Big Sky*.  New York, Sloane, and London, Boardman, 1947.
> *The Way West*.  New York, Sloane, 1949; London, Boardman, 1950.
> *These Thousand Hills*.  Boston, Houghton Mifflin, 1956; London, Hutchinson, 1957.
> *The Blue Hen's Chick*.  New York, McGraw Hill, 1965.
> *Anfive*.  Boston, Houghton Mifflin, 1971.

Short Stories

> *The Big It and Other Stories*.  Boston, Houghton Mifflin, 1960.

Uncollected Short Story

"Loco", in *Esquire* (New York), November 1967.

Plays

Screenplays: *Shane*, 1951; *The Kentuckian*, 1953.

Bibliography: in *Western American Literature* (Fort Collins, Colorado), Summer 1969.

Manuscript Collection: University of Kentucky, Lexington.

*       *       *

The attempt to create fiction out of one of the central facts of American experience, the existence of the Frontier, is as old as American history. John Smith added a gloss of romance to his geographical and autobiographical ramblings and cast himself as hero of a book that is as much a western as the novels of Zane Grey. Fenimore Cooper set his mark upon the whole future of American mythology by the selection as prime theme for his novels of the conflict between a sophisticated, sometimes decadent but essentially Christian ethos of European culture transplanted and the unsophisticated, sometimes savage, but often wonderfully primitive morality of the wild forests. But just about the time when American historians began to comprehend the influence that the Frontier had exerted upon the whole cultural history of their nation, the Frontier was officially closed, and from the last decade of the nineteenth century almost until the opening of the Second World War the life of the Frontier was for the American people little more than a folk-memory, and even that folk-memory was rapidly perverted by the crude exploitation of the authors of dime novels, Hollywood "B" films, and, finally, television serials.

In the late 1930s and early '40s a new school of Western authors (Western in both senses of the word) began to emerge, among them two, Walter Van Tilburg Clark and A.B. Guthrie, Jr., outstanding, who put fact back into fiction. Guthrie in particular is a scholarly historian who adds the accuracy of his research to a novelist's power for creating character, to an artist's eye for scenery, and to a Montanan's affection for his home country.

His first novel, *Murders at Moon Dance*, transcends the conventional melodramatic form of the gun-toting Western only insofar as the action explodes with more than ordinary literary force, but his three major novels, *The Big Sky*, *The Way West* and *These Thousand Hills* together form a persuasive, sensitive and substantial history of the spirit of the West, free from the stereotypes of the Western. A fourth novel, dealing with the homesteading period, has just been published.

Some close-written short-stories in the same *genre*, the autobiographical *The Blue Hen's Chick* (which is virtually the fifth volume in the chronological sequence of his novels), a certain workmanlike verse-writing, a great deal of journalism and much writing for the cinema, complete a lengthy bibliography. But it is upon the three novels that for the moment Guthrie's reputation must rest and in that he has added a sensitivity and historical integrity to the quintessentially American themes of the Western, with those three novels as total evidence still Guthrie must be allowed a place of seniority among contemporary American authors.

—J. E. Morpurgo

**HAGGARD, William.**   Pseudonym for Richard Henry Michael Clayton.   British.   Born in Croydon, Surrey, 11 August 1907. Educated at Lancing College, Sussex; Christ Church, Oxford, B.A. 1929. Served in the Indian Army, 1939–45. Married Barbara Myfanwy Sant in 1936; has two children. Served in the Indian Civil Service, 1931–39; formerly, Controller, Enemy Property, British Home Civil Service, retired 1969. M.A., Oxford University, 1947. Address: Yew Tree Cottage, Farnborough Street, Farnborough, Hampshire, England.

PUBLICATIONS

Novels

  *The Slow Burner*.   London, Cassell, and Boston, Little Brown, 1958.
  *The Telemann Touch*.   London, Cassell, and Boston, Little Brown, 1958.
  *Venetian Blind*.   London, Cassell, and New York, Washburn, 1959.
  *Closed Circuit*.   London, Cassell, and New York, Washburn, 1960.
  *The Arena*.   London, Cassell, and New York, Washburn, 1961.
  *The Unquiet Sleep*.   London, Cassell, and New York, Washburn, 1962.
  *The High Wire*.   London, Cassell, and New York, Washburn, 1963.
  *The Antagonists*.   London, Cassell, and New York, Washburn, 1964.
  *The Powder Barrel*.   London, Cassell, and New York, Washburn, 1965.
  *The Hard Sell*.   London, Cassell, 1965; New York, Washburn, 1966.
  *The Power House*.   London, Cassell, and New York, Washburn, 1966.
  *The Conspirators*.   London, Cassell, 1967; New York, Walker, 1968.
  *A Cool Day for Killing*.   London, Cassell, 1968; New York, Walker, 1969.
  *The Doubtful Disciple*.   London, Cassell, 1969.
  *The Hardliners*.   London, Cassell, and New York, Walker, 1970.
  *The Bitter Harvest*.   London, Cassell, 1971.

Other

  *The Little Rug Book*.   London, Cassell, 1972.

Critical Study: article in *The Sunday Times* (London), 12 May 1963.

William Haggard comments:

  I write suspense stories with a political background.

                              *      *      *

  William Haggard builds his stories around Colonel Charles Russell, head of the Security Executive. He is about sixty, an Anglo-Irishman who looks at the English impersonally. His thoughts are put crisply; what he finds contemptible about the establishment isn't

   its power but its inefficiency. The supine respect for precedent, the passion for soldiers in fancy dress. The leathery clubs and the squalid canteens. Industrial big-wigs talking on telly in terms of economics a generation out of date. Pompous trade unionists as startlingly antique. Compromise. Keep it clean. Russell had once told an eminent journalist that he was an old-fashioned radical. The man had blinked then changed the subject. Russell had known he'd been misunderstood.

Russell is a gentleman in a tough job which he handles with some intuition and considerable scrupulosity. He has a touch of Edwardian courtesy, a sense of what is proper and becoming.

And so he is hurled into the chessboard puzzles of modern diplomatic, industrial, political struggles. He uncovers and sometimes covers up again the seamier side of public and private life. He has his unofficial contacts with the other side of the curtain, as in *The Antagonists* where his friendship with the "Confederate Republic", an independent satellite, pays off. Again in *The Powder Barrel* he and the (Russian) General share information where their interests are common. Colonel Russell is an individual who appreciates other individuals and his is an unusual, strong character, though paradoxically enough he tends to achieve his ends by inaction rather than action. He waits for others to commit their treacheries, peccadillos, plain mistakes. In Russell's world there are Ministers of the Crown, efficient in some cases, less so in others; there is a crafty Prime Minister, a brilliant study; there is the worried director of a Merchant Bank struggling with diabetes. The range is wide but it is largely drawn from the establishment. There are women who are powerful—and dangerous, such as Sheila Raden in *A Cool Day for Killing* or Madam, the weak Sheik's sister, in *The Powder Barrel*. There are men who are weak and blackmailable, men who are vicious, men who are idealistic. Some become stock types—Mortimer the loyal subordinate, Professor Waserman the German-Jewish refugee now Chairman of Amalgamated Steel, and Lord Normer, a C. P. Snow-like character, who advises Russell on radar matters. There are the classic traitors, and these are often self-deluding, weak left-wing intellectuals, such as Margaret Palfrey in *The Antagonists*. There are also ruthless industrialists or the selfish and sophisticated engineers of whom Gervase Leat in *Venetian Blind* is a good example.

The complicated nexus between characters is well handled. Haggard enjoys the interplay of his characters; his dialogue can be lively and is at its best when sophisticated men and women are engaged in conversations, the serious import of which is lightly conveyed. Colonel Russell himself can be surprising in his unorthodoxies: he is careful not to overstep what he thinks are the proper limits of his difficult, dangerous post. He emerges as very human indeed.

The dangers are given full treatment. The action is crisp; there is suspense in plenty—the waiting after a decision is taken, then the action described with sufficient detail to be convincing, with sufficient speed to remain exciting. The backgrounds are sketched in with small touches of accuracy; the atmosphere of a gulf sheikdom, a Malayan state under British protection, an Italian aircraft factory, a London pub, a country house are all evoked with equal skill. The pattern of modern life evolves in all its complexity: not least in the relationships between men and women, where Russell often throws a cool, tolerant yet interested eye on intrigues or relationships which affect the action of the characters. In marriages breaking up—the Leggatts' in *The Unquiet Sleep* or the Lowe-Andersons' in *Venetian Blind* are cases in point—Haggard can capture nuances and clashes and the odd mixtures of loyalty and disloyalty with considerable economy. He can show the complexities of racial differences at times as in the Deshmukhs in *The Conspirators*, he Indian, she an Irish nationalist (yet related, way back, to Colonel Russell).

Perhaps Haggard's chief virtue is that he conveys a sense to the reader of being allowed to know it all works, it being the world as seen by an intelligence service chief. It is not the whole world, but a sophisticatedly stylised one, where an occasional comment—on, say, the reduced role played by a modern head of Mission; or on the restricted options open to a politician, or captain of industry, or chief of police, or diplomat—strikes home with a dash of devastating reality which helps to carry forward the strange doings of Colonel Russell, his helpers and the enemies he often respects.

—A. Norman Jeffares

**HAILEY, Arthur.** Canadian. Born in Luton, England, 5 April 1920; moved to Canada in 1947; became a Canadian citizen, 1952. Served as a Pilot, Flight Lieutenant, in the Royal Air Force, 1939–47. Married Sheila Dunlop in 1951; has six children (three from previous marriage). Worked as an office boy and clerk, London, 1934–39. Editor, MacLean Hunter, publishers, Toronto, 1947–53; Sales Promotion Manager, Trailmobile Canada, Toronto, 1953–56. Since 1956, Owner and President of Arthur Hailey Ltd., Toronto. Recipient: Canadian Council of Authors and Artists Award, 1956; Best Canadian TV Playwright Award, 1957, 1958; Doubleday Prize Novel Award, 1962. Address: Lyford Cay, New Providence, Bahamas.

PUBLICATIONS

Novels

> *Flight into Danger*, with John Castle. London, Souvenir Press, 1958; as *Runway Zero Eight*, New York, Doubleday, 1959.
> *The Final Diagnosis*. New York, Doubleday, and London, Joseph-Souvenir Press, 1959.
> *In High Places*. New York, Doubleday, and London, Joseph-Souvenir Press, 1962.
> *Hotel*. New York, Doubleday, and London, Joseph-Souvenir Press, 1965.
> *Airport*. New York, Doubleday, and London, Joseph-Souvenir Press, 1968.
> *Wheels*. New York, Doubleday, 1971; London, Joseph-Souvenir Press, 1972.

Plays

> *Flight into Danger* (produced CBC TV, 1956; BBC TV, 1957). Published in *Four Plays of Our Time*, London, Macmillan, 1960.
> *Close-up on Writing for Television: Collected Plays*. New York, Doubleday, 1960.

> Screenplays: *Zero Hour*, 1957; *Time Lock*, 1958; *The Young Doctors*, 1961; *Hotel*, 1967; *Airport*, 1970.

Critical Studies: an interview with the author by Frank Cameron, in *Writer's Yearbook '67*, Cincinnati, Ohio, F. and W. Publishing Corporation, 1967; "Arthur Hailey: Novelist at Work", in *Manuscripts* (Carbondale, Illinois), vol. XXII, no. 1, 1970; "The Hailey Papers", in *Maclean's* (Toronto), vol. 84, no. 10, 1971.

Arthur Hailey comments:

My novels are the end product of my work and are widely available. Therefore I see no reason to be analytical about them. I leave that to others, preferring, myself, to get on with the next book.

Each novel takes me, usually, three years: a year of continuous research, six months of detailed planning, then a year and a half of steady writing, with many revisions.

My only other comment is that my novels are the work of one who seeks principally to be a storyteller but reflect also, I hope, the excitement of living here and now.

\*          \*          \*

Arthur Hailey has developed and virtually perfected a highly efficient and extremely successful (and profitable) process of novel writing. Whether he is writing about doctors (*The Final Diagnosis*) or airline pilots (*Flight into Danger*), hotels (*Hotel*) or airports (*Airport*), government (*In High Places*) or industry (*Wheels*), he follows the same formula. Each of his novels is filled with enough information about the subject of his exhaustive research to satisfy the most curious reader; there are enough character types to appeal to the widest possible audience; everything is interwoven into a complex web of plots and sub-plots to satisfy every reader's desire for a good, suspenseful story.

Hailey writes documentary fiction, or what has been called "faction," that is, a mixture of the real and the fictitious. After spending a year of research for each novel, Hailey is prepared to give his reader as much factual information as he can work into the novel. Consequently, only his characters and situations are imaginary, and they are sometimes only slightly fictitious.

To speak of any Hailey novel is to speak of every Hailey novel for there is little to distinguish one from the rest except subject matter. Each novel shares the same characteristic strengths and weaknesses. *Airport* is a typical example. The action of the novel is centered at a fictitious Chicago airport during one of the worst blizzards in the city's history. To give his reader an inside look at the operations of a major airport and into the lives of the people responsible for its existence, Hailey devises several plots; an airliner is stuck in the snow, blocking a runway and causing emergency situations in the air; an air-traffic controller is planning suicide; a trans-Atlantic airliner is about to take off with a bomb aboard; a stewardess has discovered she is pregnant; a group of local citizens is demonstrating against the excessive noise of the airport. The novel follows each plot to its conclusion, but not before the reader's intellectual curiosity about airports and his emotional curiosity about the characters are satisfied.

The narrative is slick and fast-moving, the information is interesting, the prose is readable, but the seams in Hailey's fabric too often show through. In order to introduce all his research-ed information into the novel, he is frequently forced to construct irrelevant sub-plots or to break the flow of the narrative for a lecture on such things as the safety records of commercial airlines or the pressures suffered by air-traffic controllers. To manage all his characters, he is forced into a "holding pattern" of his own. The focus of the novel shifts from one character to another as Hailey abandons characters temporarily only to return to them later when their number in the rotation comes up again. Consequently what unity there is in the book is provided only by the subject matter. The characters themselves are paper thin, reduced to simple dimensions; they are so typical that they could be interchanged from one novel to the next with little difficulty.

Hailey's most recent novel, *Wheels*, is much like *Airport* in its intention and its execution. The main difference is its lack of dramatic suspense; there is less drama to be derived from the introduction of a new car, the primary plot device in the novel, than from the naturally more exciting subjects of the earlier novels.

Hailey is a good popular novelist. He has learned what his audience expects and his audience knows what to expect from him; the reciprocal arrangement ought to ensure a continuing place for Hailey's novels on the best seller lists for years to come.

—David J. Geherin

**HALE, Nancy.** American. Born in Boston, Massachusetts, 6 May 1908. Educated at Winsor School, Boston, and the Boston Museum (Art) School. Married Fredson Bowers in 1942; has two children from previous marriages. Assistant Editor, *Vogue*, New York, 1928–32, and *Vanity Fair*, New York, 1932–33; Reporter, *The New York Times*, 1935. Lecturer, Bread Loaf Writers Conference, Vermont, 1957–62; Phi Beta Kappa Visiting Scholar, 1971–72. Recipient: O. Henry Award, 1933; Benjamin Franklin Citation, 1948; Bellaman Award, 1968. Address: Woodburn, Route 8, Charlottesville, Virginia 22901, U.S.A.

PUBLICATIONS

Novels

> *The Young Die Good.* New York, Scribner, 1932.
> *Never Any More.* New York, Scribner, 1934.
> *The Prodigal Women.* New York, Scribner, 1942.
> *The Sign of Jonah.* New York, Scribner, 1950; London, Heinemann, 1952.
> *Dear Beast.* Boston, Little Brown, 1959; London, Macmillan, 1960.
> *Black Summer.* Boston, Little Brown, 1963; London, Gollancz, 1964.
> *Secrets.* New York, Coward McCann, 1971.

Short Stories

> *The Earliest Dreams.* New York, Scribner, 1936; London, Dickson, 1937.
> *Between the Dark and the Daylight.* New York, Scribner, 1943.
> *The Empress's Ring.* New York, Scribner, 1955.
> *Heaven and Hardpan Farm.* New York, Scribner, 1957.
> *The Pattern of Perfection: 13 Stories.* Boston, Little Brown, 1960; London, Macmillan, 1961.

Plays

> *The Best of Everything* (produced Charlottesville, Virginia, 1951).
> *Somewhere She Dances* (produced Charlottesville, Virginia, 1953).

Other

> *A New England Girlhood.* Boston, Little Brown, and London, Gollancz, 1958.
> *The Realities of Fiction: A Book about Writing.* Boston, Little Brown, 1962; London, Macmillan, 1963.
> *The Life in the Studio.* Boston, Little Brown, 1969.

> Editor, *New England Discovery: A Personal View.* New York, Coward McCann, 1963.

> Verse published in magazines.

Manuscript Collection: Smith College Library, Northampton, Massachusetts.

Nancy Hale comments:

I am averse to making statements on my work because I have found by experience that fiction is so protean that today's aim can be tomorrow's anathema. But I may make the comment that in general I have striven to conceal the purpose underlying my work with "the light touch" since nothing seems to me so self-defeating as overt earnestness. Yet I can assure readers of my work that its purpose is earnest, indeed painful.

\*         \*         \*

For almost four decades Nancy Hale has depicted varying aspects of the changing American social scene in terms of what for a more precise label must still be called the American upper and upper-middle class. Her fiction—some dozen novels and collections of short stories—ranges from recollections of family life in Massachusetts where she was born and raised to the pseudo-sophisticated intellectual circles of New York City where she lived relatively early in her career and the Virginia Piedmont which has been her home for many years. From the beginnings Miss Hale (in private life the wife of a University professor) has been a witty and perceptive observer of individual and societal foibles which she recreates with admirably disciplined craftsmanship.

Miss Hale's fiction has evoked widely different opinions, although even her least understanding critics have been impressed by the artistry and technical expertise which have been her hallmarks. And as her career progressed Miss Hale's compassion deepened, or perhaps it was the other way around. In either case, *A New England Girlhood*, published rather beyond the midpoint of her career, is described as *An Affectionate Re-creation of Things Past* (some sixty years after her grandfather, Edward Everett Hale, had published his *A New England Boyhood*). And affectionate it is, without slopping into bathos or sentimentality: in her subsequent work the author's concern with stupidity, grossness, absurdity—and their opposites—is constantly alive, constantly keen, but she has learned, as has been observed, to shed the blood without disfiguring the bodies of her subjects.

Miss Hale's characters fight no great battles to reform society or change the world. Their stories, as is inevitable in the fiction of manners, are extremely personal, involving relations between parents and children, husbands and wives, individuals versus individuals: the growing antagonism between the three teenage girls of *Never Any More* during a summer holiday; the searing problems of their adult counterparts in Miss Hale's best-known and most commercially-successful novel *The Prodigal Women*, a book about the disorders of love and the warfare between men and women which has been aptly described as a depiction of "one kind of Hell . . . the Gulf of Self-tormenters"; the experiences of the group of emotionally disturbed women and their psychiatrist of *Heaven and Hardpan Farm*; the situation stories from what is perhaps her best collection, *The Empress's Ring*, which center around incidents no more dramatic than a mother's experiences with a sick child or a quiet day at the beach.

The theater of Nancy Hale's fiction is relatively limited, but she works within it with skill, precision, and a high awareness. And it is in the field of what she has called "Autobiographical Fiction" that she displays a wizardry uniquely her own, manifested in many stories and novels and in such recent books as *The Life in the Studio*, recollections of her painter mother, or *Secrets*, an autobiographical memoir. In such work Miss Hale has captured—as she comments in *The Realities of Fiction*—"the atmosphere of the past . . . less by remembering than by inventing; less by calling up than by making up. It is as if to capture that atmosphere I have to create it, because in fact it never was on land or sea, least of all in my own childhood."

—William Peden

**HALL, James B(yron).** American. Born in Midland, Ohio, 21 July 1918. Educated at Miami University, Oxford, Ohio, 1938–39; University of Hawaii, Honolulu, 1938–40; University of Iowa, Iowa City, B.A. 1947, M.A. 1948, Ph.D. 1953; Kenyon College, Gambier, Ohio, 1949. Served in the United States Army, 1941–46. Married Elizabeth Cushman in 1946; has five children. Writer-in-Residence, Miami University, 1948–49; Instructor, Cornell University, Ithaca, New York, 1952–53; Writer-in-Residence, University of North Carolina, Greensville, 1954; Assistant Professor, 1954–57, Associate Professor, 1958–60, and Professor of English, 1960–65, University of Oregon, Eugene; Writer-in-Residence, University of British Columbia, Vancouver, Summer 1956; Guest Artist, Pacific Coast Festival of Art, Reed College, Portland, 1958; Writer-in-Residence, University of Colorado, Boulder, 1963; Director of The Writing Center, and Professor of English, University of California at Irvine, 1965–68. Since 1968, Professor of Literature, and Provost of College V, University of California at Santa Cruz. Co-Founding Editor, *Northwest Review*, Eugene, Oregon, 1957–60; Founder and Director, University of Oregon Summer Academy of Contemporary Arts, Eugene, 1959–64. Editorial Consultant, Doubleday and Company, publishers (West Coast staff), 1960; Cultural Specialist, United States Department of State, Washington, 1964. Recipient: Yaddo grant, 1952; Chapelbrook Fellowship, 1967; Institute of Creative Arts Fellowship, 1967; Balch Fiction Prize, 1967. Address: College V, University of California, Santa Cruz, California 95060; or, "Cardiff House", 1100 High Street, Santa Cruz, California 95060, U.S.A.

PUBLICATIONS

Novels

*Not by the Door*. New York, Random House, 1954.
*TNT for Two*. New York, Ace, 1956.
*Racers to the Sun*. New York, Obolensky, 1960; London, Corgi, 1962.
*Mayo Sergeant*. New York, New American Library, 1967.

Short Stories

*15 x 3*, with Herbert Gold and R. V. Cassill. New York, New Directions, 1957.
*Us He Devours*. New York, New Directions, 1964.

Uncollected Short Stories

"In the Time of Demonstration", in *Western Review* (Denver), Spring 1951.
"By the Distaff's Hot Astonishment", in *Western Review* (Denver), Winter 1952.
"Estate and Trespass: A Gothic Story", in *Epoch* (Ithaca, New York), 1954.
"A Session of Summer", in *Western Review* (Denver), Spring 1955.
"The Fall and the Twilight", in *Esquire* (New York), September 1957.
"Up in Her Room", in *Gent* (New York), March 1958.
"The Fish Camp under the Snow", in *Accent* (Urbana, Illinois), Summer 1958.
"But Who Gets the Children", in *Esquire* (New York), June 1960.
"While Going Down the Road", in *North American Review* (Mount Vernon, Iowa), March 1964.
"Letters Never Sent", in *Kenyon Review* (Gambier, Ohio), Spring 1964.
"The Omphagists", in *Carleton Miscellany* (Northfield, Minnesota), Winter 1964.
"God Cares But Waits", in *Virginia Quarterly Review* (Charlottesville), 1968.

"While Going North", in *Virginia Quarterly Review* (Charlottesville), 1968.
"I Like It Better Now", in *Atlantic* (Boston), August 1969.
"The Other Kingdom", in *Carleton Miscellany* (Northfield, Minnesota), 1970.


Other

Editor, with Joseph Langland, *The Short Story*.   New York, Macmillan, 1956.
Editor, *Realm of Fiction: 61 Short Stories*.   New York, McGraw Hill, 1965; revised
    edition, as *Realm of Fiction: 65 Short Stories*, 1970.
Editor, with Barry Ulanov, *Modern Culture and the Arts*.   New York, McGraw Hill,
    1967.

Verse and criticism published in various anthologies and periodicals.


James B. Hall comments:

Although the novels are interesting, the central significance of the work resides largely
in the short stories; the poetry is various, and by intention ancillary to the prose.

The novels, short stories, and poetry are thematically inter-related. The re-occurring motifs
are the effects of competition on individuals in a system of modified capitalism such as
obtains in the United States. Thus acquisitive, frustrated, evasive protagonists re-occur, some
of them mad or nearly so. Extreme conduct in a hostile world is not infrequent; the adjustments which protagonists make vary from callous acceptance or the exploitation of others to
withdrawal, revenge, and self-destruction. In general, the work shows the difficulty of remaining human in a competitive, non-Darwinian world fashioned in large part by a democratic society. Specifically, *Racers to the Sun* traces the "rise" and fall of a motorcycle racer
who builds his own machine; the hero is injured (used up), and then is dropped by those who
exploited his talent for machinery and speed. Likewise, in the typical short stories, "Us He
Devours" and "The Claims Artist", the protagonists are in some ways laudable, but in the
end are victims of their own and of society's demands. A typical poem, "Pay Day Night",
treats the counter-productive nature of experience in another bureaucracy, the Army.

The short stories are experimental, highly compressed, and exploit language poetically
for artistic effect. They are condensed statements that very often extend the possibilities of
the genre. Many of the stories are anthologized; because they are complex they apparently
"teach well" in classrooms.


                              *         *         *


James B. Hall, like Fitzgerald, Lewis, perhaps most of the important American writers
of this century, sees the American dream as a combination of an ethic once moral and humane,
and a goal of success that inevitably corrupts the ethic and so the dream. This is the theme he
began to delineate in 1954 with the publication of *Not by the Door*, and continued to explore
in subsequent novels. Howard Marcham, the protagonist of the first novel, is an Episcopal
clergyman in a middle American town, "an American priest, with no real background of the
spirit." Marcham is not an evil man, Hall is saying; but it is difficult for an American to hear
a higher call over the rustle of money and the clink of cocktail glasses.

*Racers to the Sun* is an absorbing novel that examines the almost sexual mystique of
machinery and speed—particularly of motorcycle racing—in America. The main character,
Harold Hill, is practically raised in an automobile graveyard in Ohio, from where it seems
perfectly natural for him to move into the world of the motorcycle track, the world of a

worshipper of speed and success named "Gunner," who has transformed herself into a trophy for winners. He understands his motorcycle clearly as "a naked force . . . a dance step which would take him from Savile, Ohio, to the salt flats of Bonneville or to Daytona Beach where demi-gods in leather riding breeches flashed through the electric timers to the immortality of record books." It is a strength of the novel that Hall causes his spokesman to recognize the essence of his life and not give way to adolescent bleating about it.

Hall really hit his stride as a novelist in *Mayo Sergeant*. It is clear from the beginning with the appearance of red, white, and blue sails on the sea, that sailing is in some way symbolic of America; sailing vessels and the code the sport imposes (like the hunting code of Hemingway or Faulkner) are a metaphor of the business ethic and morality in America. The graceful old *Indus* is being replaced by the new *Tektra*, even as whatever was human in Industry has yielded to the unfeeling force of Technocracy. Or is the new order in America actually much different, the new businessman less human, or the new real-estate man more rapacious than the old, as Roberte Glouster, the easy-going narrator with ties to California history, likes to suppose? The conclusion can only be left in doubt.

The resemblance of Mayo Sergeant to Fitzgerald's Gatsby is unmistakable. Both, for example, come from obscure origins in the Midwest; both depend in part on an awkward personal attractiveness and win material success. But Gatsby never comes into harmony with the American dream, and it destroys him. Mayo Sergeant, who may seem more contemptible than Gatsby because Hall makes him more familiar than Gatsby, succeeds because the dream has become as venal as he is. Hall has more in common with Fitzgerald than character and theme: in one of the most successful broad comic chapters in American fiction, Hall, with a satiric sense no less acute than Fitzgerald's, illuminates the sanctimonious greed of land developers. If *Mayo Sergeant* falls short of *The Great Gatsby*, it is because Hall does not sustain the satire, and because he scatters the sympathy of the audience among several important characters.

—Alan R. Shucard

---

**HANLEY, Clifford.** Pseudonym: **Henry Calvin.** Born in Glasgow, Scotland, 28 October 1922. Educated at Eastbank School, Glasgow. Conscientious Objector in World War II. Married Anna E. Clark in 1948; has three children. Reporter, Scottish Newspaper Services, Glasgow, 1940–45; Sub-Editor, *Scottish Daily Record*, Glasgow, 1945–57; Feature Writer, *TV Guide*, Glasgow, 1957–58; Columnist, *Glasgow Evening Citizen*, 1958–60. Member, Close Theatre Management Committee, Glasgow, 1965–71; Inland Waterways Council, 1967–71. Vice-President, Scottish P.E.N., since 1966; Member, Scottish Arts Council, since 1967; Scottish Chairman, Writers Guild of Great Britain, since 1968. Address: 36 Munro Road, Glasgow, Scotland.

PUBLICATIONS

Novels (as Clifford Hanley)

*Love from Everybody*. London, Hutchinson, 1959.
*The Taste of Too Much*. London, Hutchinson, 1960.
*Nothing But the Best*. London, Hutchinson, 1964; as *Second Time Round*, Boston, Houghton Mifflin, 1964.

*The Hot Month.*   London, Hutchinson, and Boston, Houghton Mifflin, 1967.
*The Redhaired Bitch.*   London, Hutchinson, and Boston, Houghton Mifflin, 1969.


Novels (as Henry Calvin)

*The System.*   London, Hutchinson, 1962.
*It's Different Abroad.*   London, Hutchinson, and New York, Harper, 1963.
*The Italian Gadget.*   London, Hutchinson, 1966.
*The DNA Business.*   London, Hutchinson, 1967.
*A Nice Friendly Town.*   London, Hutchinson, 1967.
*Miranda Must Die.*   London, Hutchinson, 1968; as *Boka Lives*, New York, Harper, 1969.
*The Chosen Instrument.*   London, Hutchinson, and New York, Harper, 1969.
*The Poison Chasers.*   London, Hutchinson, 1970.


Plays

*The Durable Element* (produced Dundee, Scotland, 1958).
*Saturmacnalia*, music by Ian Gourlay (produced Glasgow, 1965).
*Oh for an Island*, music by Ian Gourlay (produced Glasgow, 1966).
*Dick McWhittie*, music by Ian Gourlay (produced Glasgow, 1967).
*Oh Glorious Jubilee*, music by Ian Gourlay (produced Leeds, Yorkshire, 1970).


Other

*Dancing in the Streets* (autobiography).   London, Hutchinson, 1958.
*A Skinful of Scotch* (travel).   London, Hutchinson, 1965.


Clifford Hanley comments:

*Dancing in the Streets,* my first published book, was written at the suggestion of my publisher, who wanted a book about the city of Glasgow. At the time I thought it a rather pedestrian recital of childhood memories and was taken aback by its critical and commercial success (it is still used as background reading in schools of social studies and urbanology). My first novel, *Love from Everybody*, written previously but published later, was frankly intended as a light entertainment, to make money, and was later filmed as *Don't Bother to Knock*. Having then retired from journalism, I wrote what I considered my first serious work, *The Taste of Too Much*, as a study of "ordinary" adolescence, without crime or adventitious excitement, and it may well be my most successful book in the sense of fully achieving the author's original conception. In the subsequent novels under my own name, I think my intention was to look at some areas of life—a businessman's troubles, the family situation, the agonies of work in the theatre—simply in my own way, without reference to fashionable literary conceptions. I have often been surprised when people found the novels "funny" because their intention was serious; but an author can't help being what he is. I do see the human condition as tragic (since decay and death are the inevitable end), but I don't distinguish between comedy and tragedy. Funerals can be funny too, and life is noble and absurd at the same time. I also insist on distinguishing between seriousness and solemnity, which are opposite rather than similar. On looking back, I realise that the tone of the novels tends to be affirmation rather than despair. This may be a virtue or a fault, or an irrelevance—a novelist should probably leave such judgments to critics and simply get on with what he must do. Maybe they also betray some kind of moral standpoint of which I was unconscious. This was explicit, in fact, in my first professionally produced play, *The Durable Element*, which was a study of the recurrent urge to crucify prophets. It was also deliberate in *The Chosen Instrument*, a pseudonymous Henry Calvin ten years later, in which a contemporary thriller mode was used to do a sort of feasibility study on the New Testament mythology. (The intention was so well disguised that no critic noticed it.)

But I suppose cheerfulness keeps breaking through. I am an entertainer as well as a novelist, and the two may be compatible. My first commandment as a writer is not at all highfalutin. It is Thou Shalt Not Bore. *A Skinful of Scotch* is an irreverent guide to one man's Scotland and was written for fun. So, originally, were the Henry Calvin Thrillers. I enjoy reading thrillers and I adopted the pen-name simply to feel uninhibited. The thriller too is a morality, but the morality is acceptable only if it has character and pace. These are not intellectual mysteries but tales of conflict between good and evil. My later work for the theatre was exclusively devoted to calculated entertainment and I am glad that people were actually entertained. I find now that I see life in more sombre terms, but whether this will show in future novels is hard to tell. It may even be a temporary condition.

*     *     *

Hanley is by far the funniest of the novelists now writing from and about Scotland. Like the character in the song, he "belongs to Glasgow," and from there, after some twenty years in journalism, he produced his fantasticated autobiography, *Dancing in the Streets*, where the facts are often more fantastically comic than the craziest of fictions. A year later his first novel, *Love from Everybody*, a confection concerned—or unconcerned—with the Edinburgh Festival, revealed his command of witty invention, and then with *The Taste of Too Much* he created a novel about adolescence in and around Glasgow which is as true in feeling as it is funny.

His most hilarious work to date is *The Hot Month*, a deliciously devilish presentation of the wildest and most wicked of all Highland holidays. Fully to enjoy this continuously entertaining work, however, the reader must join the author in making an assumption of the highest improbability—that Scotland might enjoy a whole summer month of unbroken sunshine—and anyone unable to contemplate even the remotest possibility of such a miracle may fail to appreciate the finer flights of Hanley's impish fancy. For the reader who can summon up sufficient suspension of disbelief, the dead-pan humour is irresistible. Yet Hanley achieves long and frequent laughter without ever allowing his characterisation to sink to the low level of farce. As a Highland holiday, *The Hot Month* is also a vacation from the puritanical-Presbyterian view that "sex is no joke", and its laughing liberalism is at the opposite pole from the sexlessness of most recent fiction about the Celtic scene. Unlike much of that fiction, again, Hanley deals with the present, and with people like ourselves—and that, in provincialised Scotland, is dynamite.

Equally dynamic, his most recent novel, *The Redhaired Bitch*, is more analytical in its characterisation of the ambiguities of human relationships, either in the Glasgow theatre—the rocky pivot about which most of the action revolves—or anywhere. The problems arising from the production of a musical comedy about hag-ridden Scotland's most celebrated hag, Mary Queen of Scots, have results which are both dramatic in the wider sense and theatrical in the narrower, and Hanley's intimate acquaintance with the Glasgow scene beyond—as well as on—the stage enables him to paint the back-cloth to his story with as much subtlety as presentation of the large cast.

Under the puckish pseudonym of "Henry Calvin," Hanley has also written some highly entertaining who-dun-its, among which one, *The Chosen Instrument*, is a remarkable *tour de force*, the re-telling of the gospel story in the guise of a contemporary thriller. That these entertainments have not reached the heights—or depths—of popularity achieved by some other modern Scottish adventure stories can be attributed only to the fact that their heroes are fallible human beings rather than indestructible supermen.

—Alexander Scott

**HANLEY, Gerald (Anthony).**   British.   Born 17 February 1916. Served with the Royal
Irish Fusiliers for seven years. Lives in Ireland. Address: c/o David Higham Associates,
76 Dean Street, London W.1, England.

PUBLICATIONS

Novels

*Monsoon Victory*.  London, Collins, 1946.
*The Consul at Sunset*.   London, Collins, and New York, Macmillan, 1951.
*The Year of the Lion*.   London, Collins, 1953; New York, Macmillan, 1954.
*Drinkers of Darkness*.   London, Collins, and New York, Macmillan, 1955.
*Without Love*.   London, Collins, and New York, Harper, 1957.
*The Journey Homeward*.   London, Collins, and Cleveland, World, 1961.
*Gilligan's Last Elephant*.   London, Collins, and Cleveland, World, 1962.
*See You in Yasukuni*.   London, Collins, 1969; Cleveland, World, 1970.

Other

*Warriors and Strangers*.   London, Hamish Hamilton, 1971.

*        *        *

The principal themes of Gerald Hanley's novels are the dissolution of the British Empire
and the impact of that dissolution on the relationships of individuals of different races,
creeds and religions. He also explores subsidiary themes to illuminate these main preoccupations—the nature of courage, the wielding of power, and especially the public results
of personal inadequacy on the part of those responsible for exercising power.

Gerald Hanley has lived through these themes and scenes himself and writes of what he
knows; but although this makes him an interesting and distinctive writer he falls short of
outstanding distinction as a novelist. His plots are sometimes rather obviously contrived
in their resolution; the structural balance from chapter to chapter of interior monologue
and dramatic dialogue is often repetitive; and when this lack of diversification is compounded
with a failure to deepen and intensify the psychological development of his characters, the
total effect is a little monotonous. One can see why he remains in the second rank of contemporary novelists, despite the intrinsic interest of his subject-matter and the clarity of his
prose style.

Before the war Gerald Hanley farmed in Kenya, of all the East and Central African colonies
the one in which the divisions between the hierarchy of colonial administrators, British
settlers, missionaries, Levantine and Indian merchants, and the various African tribes were
most strongly contrasted. Wartime Army service took him through the Somaliland campaign,
another formative experience on which his imagination could later draw.

After *Monsoon Victory* he reached a wide public with *The Consul at Sunset*, the best introduction to his work. The novel is set in sunbaked African terrain where there is a tribal dispute
over the use of water-holes. Responsibility for maintaining peace and justice rests with a
handful of white men whose ability to discharge it successfully demands political realism,
understanding of an alien culture, self-confidence and personal integrity. The political officer
dominated by an African mistress and the well-meaning but weak liberal both fail on some
counts, while the disciplined army officers, a Captain risen from the ranks and a Colonel
of the old school, measure up to the situation. But as he stands bare-headed before the Union

Jack at sunset the Colonel is uneasy about the adequacy of his kind in the changes that must lie ahead beyond the coming war.

In *Year of the Lion* again the seeds of racial, social and political conflict are seen to be germinating in African soil, even though British, African and Dutch all unite to fight the lions and herds of zebra that threaten their farms and grazing, while in *Drinkers of Darkness* the slightly odd tensions of the white settlers have been developed into a crazed blindness to political realities as they struggle to assert their prestige. *The Journey Homeward* turns to the politics of a princely state in the Himalayas after partition, and explores further the political failure of leaders whose private lives are tortured, seedy or corrupt. But Africa is Gerald Hanley's proper milieu, revisited in his clear-eyed travel-book *Warriors and Strangers*.

—Stewart F. Sanderson

---

**HANLEY, James.** British. Born in Dublin in 1901. A merchant seaman and free-lance journalist before becoming a novelist. Has lived in Wales since 1931. Address: c/o London Management, 235/241 Regent Street, London W1A 2JT, England.

PUBLICATIONS

Novels

   *Drift*. London, Joiner and Steele, 1930.
   *Boy*. London, Boriswood, 1931; New York, Knopf, 1932.
   *Ebb and Flood*. London, Lane, 1932.
   *Captain Bottell*. London, Boriswood, 1933.
   *Resurrexit Dominus*. Privately printed, 1934.
   *The Furys*:
      *The Furys*. London, Chatto and Windus, and New York, Macmillan, 1935.
      *The Secret Journey*. London, Chatto and Windus, and New York, Macmillan, 1936.
      *Our Time Is Gone*. London, Lane, 1940; with *The Furys* and *The Secret Journey*, New York, Dent, 1949.
      *Winter Song*. London, Phoenix House, and New York, Dent, 1950.
      *An End and a Beginning*. London, Macdonald, and New York, Horizon Press, 1958.
   *Stoker Bush*. London, Chatto and Windus, 1935; New York, Macmillan, 1936.
   *Hollow Sea*. London, Lane, 1938.
   *The Ocean*. London, Faber, and New York, Morrow, 1941.
   *No Directions*. London, Faber, 1943.
   *Sailor's Song*. London, Nicholson and Watson, 1943.
   *What Farrar Saw*. London, Nicholson and Watson, 1946.
   *Emily*. London, Nicholson and Watson, 1948.
   *The House in the Valley* (as Patric Shone). London, Cape, 1951.
   *The Closed Harbour*. London, Macdonald, 1952; New York, Horizon Press, 1953.
   *The Welsh Sonata: Variations on a Theme*. London, Verschoyle, 1954.
   *Levine*. London, Macdonald, and New York, Horizon Press, 1956.
   *Say Nothing*. London, Macdonald, and New York, Horizon Press, 1962.
   *Another World*. London, Deutsch, 1972.

Short Stories

*The German Prisoner.*   Privately printed, n.d.
*A Passion Before Death.*   Privately printed, 1930.
*The Last Voyage.*   London, W. Jackson-Joiner and Steele, 1931.
*Men in Darkness: Five Stories.*   London, Lane, 1931; New York, Knopf, 1932.
*Stoker Haslett.*   London, Joiner and Steele, 1932.
*Aria and Finale.*   London, Boriswood, 1932.
*Quartermaster Clausen.*   London, Arlan, 1934.
*At Bay.*   London, Grayson, 1935.
*Half an Eye: Sea Stories.*   London, Lane, 1937.
*People Are Curious.*   London, Lane, 1938.
*At Bay and Other Stories.*   London, Faber, 1944.
*Crilley and Other Stories.*   London, Nicholson and Watson, 1945.
*Selected Stories.*   Dublin, Fridberg, 1947.
*A Walk in the Wilderness.*   London, Phoenix House, and New York, Dent, 1950.
*Collected Stories.*   London, Macdonald, 1953.


Plays

*Say Nothing* (produced London, 1962; New York, 1965).   Published in *Plays of the Year, 1962–1963*, London, Elek, 1963.
*The Inner Journey* (produced Hamburg, 1967; New York, 1968).   London, Black Raven Press, and New York, Horizon Press, 1965.
*A Stone Flower* (produced, as *Nones*, on BBC radio).   Included in *Plays One*, 1968.
*Plays One* (includes *The Inner Journey* and *A Stone Flower*).   London, Kaye and Ward, 1968.

Several plays produced on BBC radio.


Other

*Broken Water: An Autobiographical Excursion.*   London, Chatto and Windus, 1937.
*Grey Children: A Study in Humbug and Misery.*   London, Methuen, 1937.
*Between the Tides.*   London, Methuen, 1939.
*Don Quixote Drowned* (essays).   London, Macdonald, 1953.
*J. C. Powys: A Man in the Corner.*   Loughton, Essex, Ward, 1969.
*The Face of Winter* (sketch).   Loughton, Essex, Ward, 1969.
*Herman Melville.*   Loughton, Essex, Ward, 1971.

*       *       *

James Hanley is one of the most prolific of contemporary novelists; between 1930 and 1962 he published twenty-two novels, as well as seven volumes of short stories (and four works of non-fiction). But, though praised by leading writers and critics (including W. H. Auden, E. M. Forster, Herbert Read and C. P. Snow) as "one of the most important of living writers", Hanley has been little read, and has received little critical notice.

Hanley's work is undeniably uneven, and the nature of his subject-matter (usually the world of the urban and sea-going proletariat) has probably had little popular appeal. But the main reason for the neglect of his work may be the mistaken assumption that he is a realist, in a period when realism has been generally considered an inferior fictional mode. "Realist", however, is a no more adequate label for Hanley than for Faulkner, whom he resembles in his selective and prevailingly sombre but compassionate vision of human life; in his power to create larger-than-life characters which achieve an almost mythic stature; and in his surrealistic experiments with language, especially in some of the shorter novels, like *Sailor's Song, No Directions* and *The Welsh Sonata*. Even in the longer novels like *The Furys* and *Hollow Sea*, with their masses of realistic detail, Hanley's primary interest is always in what goes on in the minds of his characters, in their private dreams, fantasies, obsessions and nightmare dreads.

Hanley is usually thought of as a novelist of the sea, but in fact only half-a-dozen of his books are sea-novels. His earliest novels were concerned with youths in the slums of Liverpool; his most ambitious project was a five-volume saga of working-class life centred on the Fury family; and much of his best work is concerned with the Second World War and its aftermath in the lives of war-shattered people.

Of the three earliest novels—*Drift, Boy* and *Ebb and Flood*—the second, praised by Faulkner as "a damn fine job", is the most important. An angry and appalling study of outraged, humiliated and victimized adolescence, it is also Hanley's first novel of the sea.

Dennis Fury, a main character in the Fury saga—*The Furys, The Secret Journey, Our Time Is Gone, Winter Song* and *An End and a Beginning*—has also been a seaman for most of his life. But it is his wife, Fanny, who is the most memorable figure in this gargantuan cycle. One of the great characters in contemporary fiction, she is both prosaic and legendary, at once a middle-aged, dowdy, toil-worn, intensely respectable and bigoted housewife, and a creature as vital, passionate and a-moral as a heroine of Celtic myth. Despite faults of diffuseness and melodrama, the first four novels, held together by the dominating central figure of Mrs. Fury, have an impressive sweeping movement, through growing conflict within the family to the climax in the murder of a lustful money-lender, by the son, Peter, a failed priest, then through the fragmentation of the family to the slow knitting together of the surviving parents and their achievement of some degree of tranquillity. The final volume, centred on Peter Fury, released after fifteen years in prison, is one of Hanley's most successful technical experiments in the fusing of past and present; it really belongs with other studies of loneliness, unfulfilment and inability to communicate written in the fifties.

Hanley began as a sea-writer with two volumes of stories, *Men in Darkness* and *Aria and Finale*; the two most memorable stories are, probably, "The Last Voyage" (which has a close resemblance to O'Neill's *S.S. Glencairn* plays) and "Narrative", which contains the seeds of three later novels of war at sea—*Hollow Sea, The Ocean,* and *Sailor's Song*. Compared with these, the two other sea-novels, *Captain Bottell* (in which Hanley seems to have deliberately challenged Conrad) and *Stoker Bush*, are relatively unimportant.

The three novels about sailors, ships and the sea in time of war represent one of the peaks of Hanley's creative achievement. (No doubt Henry Green was thinking mainly of them when he described Hanley as "far and away the best writer of the sea and seafaring men since Conrad".) Though published within five years (1938–43) they are very different in scale, subject and treatment. The formidably long *Hollow Sea*, concerned with the 1914–18 war, depends far more heavily on Hanley's memories of his own experiences than does the *novella The Ocean*, concerned with the 1939–45 war. *Sailor's Song*, by a remarkable feat, brings into the compass of a short novel the two wars at sea, and the quarter-century between. The first two are, in the main, straightforwardly realistic, but *Sailor's Song* is one of Hanley's most experimental novels, in language and technique.

*Hollow Sea*, in the grand simplicity of its conception, is potentially a great novel. The power of Hanley's imaginative treatment makes the story of a single voyage of a troop-ship into a double parable—a parable of the futility, absurdity and waste of war, and a parable of the conflict between ordinary, decent humanity and impersonal, omnipotent authority. But it loses some of its force by being unnecessarily protracted. In *Sailor's Song* the immediate setting, a raft on which four seamen—one the injured and delirious Manion, whose name is almost an anagram of "any man"—drift helplessly after their ship has been torpedoed, serves mainly as a springboard from which, through Manion's confused and chaotic memories, we plunge back into the past. Hanley was aiming not at individual portraiture, but at a representation of the course of England's maritime history over a quarter of a century, as reflected in the lives, and especially the emotions, of a typical sailor and his family. The experiments in prose-poetry are sometimes unsuccessful, but, at worst, the novel in its intensity, its impassioned striving to give memorable expression to a great theme, is a magnificent failure.

The Ocean is one of Hanley's best three or four novels. In outline it is austerely simple— a war-time survival story. It has complete unity of place, the open boat in which the five survivors suffer unnumbered days of hunger, thirst and exposure; in a sense it has unity of time, for the days are almost identical; it has complete unity of action and atmosphere. Man's struggle against nature in the form of the indifferent but ever-threatening sea could hardly be reduced to simpler or starker terms; but especially in the seaman, Curtain (who has been described as "one of the great figures of the English novel"), the novel presents a vision of the human spirit that refuses to be broken—a vision of meanness, selfishness and weakness redeemed by charity, humility and strength.

Hanley's only novel of the war on land, No Directions, has some similarity to The Ocean and in quality ranks with it. The setting is a single Chelsea house, divided into five flats; the time-scheme is restricted to a single evening during the blitz. But it is more like Sailor's Song in its fusion of realism and fantasy; it is a haunting fantasia rather than a story. The reality that Hanley sought to present was itself a nightmare, and his mingling of wild poetry and bleak naturalism conveys the terror, the macabre confusion, and the horrifying grandeur of the blitz with superb effectiveness.

Of Hanley's post-war novels two (apart from An End and a Beginning) are particularly impressive—The Closed Harbour and Levine. They are very different in tone and atmosphere (the sticky heat of Marseilles is as important in The Closed Harbour as the wintry bleakness of northern England in Levine) but they are alike in that their chief characters are war-scarred ex-sailors who are obsessed by the desire to get back to sea. Both the French merchant captain, Eugene Marius, and the Polish ordinary seaman, Felix Levine, are sole survivors of ships sunk during the war, and both are distrusted outcasts—Marius because he is suspected of the murder of his nephew, Levine because he has no provable past or identity. The end for Marius is insanity, for Levine the murder of the English woman who marries him, and stifles him by the devouring possessiveness of her devotion. These two novels embody, in a pure form, Hanley's vision of human beings as solitary, unable to communicate with one another, the victims of obsessions and compulsive drives. But, psychically self-imprisoned as they are, his people lack neither humanity and compassion (Levine, careless of the consequences to himself, returns to the hospital), nor proud grandeur (his wife, questioned about Levine on her death-bed, will answer nothing). Tragic vision, masterful technical control and the sheer distinction of the writing combine to make these two of the finest English works of the fifties.

James Hanley developed strikingly during his career as a novelist, though his Hardyesque vision—bleak but never misanthropic—remained essentially the same. The melodramatic violence of his earlier work was eliminated without any loss of real power; its clumsiness, crudity and turgidity give way to a style spare, strong, disciplined but flexible, evocative and individual. Despite the neglect of his work which eventually drove him to abandon the novel, few of his British contemporaries have equalled his achievement.

—Edward Stokes

* * *

**HARRIS, Mark.** American. Born in Mount Vernon, New York, 19 November 1922. Educated at the University of Denver, B.A. in English 1950, M.A. in English 1951; University of Minnesota, Minneapolis, Ph.D. in American Studies 1956. Served in the United

States Army, 1943–44. Married Josephine Horen in 1946; has three children. Reporter, *Daily Item*, Port Chester, New York, 1944–45, *PM*, Long Island, New York, 1945, and International News Service, St. Louis, 1945–46; Writer for the *Negro Digest* and *Ebony*, Chicago, 1946–51. Taught at San Francisco State College, 1954–68, and Purdue University, Lafayette, Indiana, 1967–70. Since 1970, Teacher at California Institute of the Arts, Valencia. Fulbright Professor, University of Hiroshima, 1957–58; Visiting Professor, Brandeis University, Waltham, Massachusetts, 1963. Member, San Francisco Art Commission, 1961–64; U.S. Delegate, Dartmouth Conference, Kurashiki, Japan, 1964. Recipient: Ford grant, for theatre, 1960; National Institute of Arts and Letters grant, 1961; Guggenheim Fellowship, 1965; National Endowment of the Arts grant, 1966. Address: California Institute of the Arts, Valencia, California 91355, U.S.A.

PUBLICATIONS

Novels

> *Trumpet to the World*.   New York, Reynal and Hitchcock, 1946.
> *City of Discontent: An Interpretive Biography of Vachel Lindsay, Being Also the Story of Springfield, Illinois, USA, and of the Love of the Poet for That City, That State, and That Nation, by Henry W. Wiggen*.   Indianapolis, Bobbs Merrill, 1952.
> *The Southpaw, by Henry W. Wiggen: Punctuation Inserted and Spelling Greatly Improved*.   Indianapolis, Bobbs Merrill, 1953.
> *Bang the Drum Slowly, by Henry W. Wiggen: Certain of His Enthusiasms Restrained*.   New York, Knopf, 1956.
> *A Ticket for a Seamstitch, by Henry W. Wiggen: But Polished for the Printer*.   New York, Knopf, 1957.
> *Something about a Soldier*.   New York, Macmillan, 1957; London, Deutsch, 1958.
> *Wake Up, Stupid*.   New York, Knopf, 1959; London, Deutsch, 1960.
> *The Goy*.   New York, Dial Press, 1970.

Uncollected Short Stories

> "Carmelita's Education for Living", in *Esquire* (New York), October 1957.
> "The Self-Made Brain Surgeon", in *Noble Savage* (Chicago), March 1960.
> "The Iron Fist of Oligarchy", in *Virginia Quarterly Review* (Charlottesville), Winter 1960.
> "At Prayerbook Cross", in *Cimarron* (Stillwater, Oklahoma), December 1968.

Play

> *Friedman & Son* (produced San Francisco, 1962).   New York, Macmillan, 1963.

Other

> *Mark the Glove Boy: or, The Last Days of Richard Nixon* (autobiography).   New York, Macmillan, 1964.
> *Twentyone Twice: A Journal* (autobiography).   Boston, Little Brown, 1966.
> *Public Television: A Program for Action*, with others.   New York, Harper, 1967.

> Editor, *Selected Poems*, by Vachel Lindsay.   New York, Macmillan, 1963.

Mark Harris comments:

I have written eight novels. I think that a constant line travels through them. I didn't know this was happening while it was happening, but I can see it now, looking back after a quarter of a century since my first novel was published.

They are about the writer. That is, if you will, they are about the artist. Which is to say, if you will, they are about the one man against his society and trying to come to terms with his society, and trying to succeed within it without losing his own identity or integrity.

My novels are always very carefully written. Since hard work makes the writing look easy, there exist stupid reviewers and critics who think I (and others) just slam these writings out. My books are all constructed with great care. Nothing is missing from any of them in the way of plot. I forget nothing.

Of course, although I am spiritually at the center of my novels (every novel is mainly about one man), I am disguised as poet or baseball player or professor or historian. I am always a minority person in some sense, either because I am fictionally left-handed or, most recently, Gentile in a Jewish milieu. (My first book was about a black man in a white milieu.) I don't know why this is so. I believe that it is most deeply the result of being a Jew, but it may be attributable to other things I am not fully aware of. Maybe I was just born that way. It is a mystery.

Subject and theme: sometimes these aren't really stated in the works, and people feel disappointed. They want to know what they shouldn't: where does the author stand? In my heart, if not always dogmatically in my books, I stand for human equality and peace and justice.

I also stand for writing well: I don't believe that good ends can come of false or shoddy or hasty means. Books must be beautiful so that the world is put into a mood of beauty. Books mustn't merely *say* but must, on the other hand, *exist* as beauty.

I am opposed to the reduction or paraphrase of works of art. Thus I feel that I may on this page already have written more than I should.

*        *        *

Mark Harris' fiction and autobiography share several themes: the problems of racism and racial justice, the dilemma of violence and pacifism, the price of individualism and the forms of democracy and social justice. His work is dominated by genial comedy, a gently optimistic view of man's possibilities and capacities, and Mark Harris has pursued his own life through this fiction. His journal-autobiographies *Mark the Glove Boy* and *Twenty-one Twice* complement fictionalized self-portraits like pitcher-author Henry Wiggen (*The Southpaw, Bang the Drum Slowly, A Ticket for a Seamstitch*), boxer-novelist-teacher Lee Youngdahl (*Wake Up, Stupid*), soldier-pacifist Jacob Epstein (*Something about a Soldier*) and historian-diarist Westrum (*The Goy*).

Harris' novels depict individuals in pursuit of themselves, discovering through self-analysis, experience and observation who they are and what their lives mean. His first novel, *Trumpet to the World*, follows a black man through self-discovery and self-education to his rejection of war and violence and his attempts to reach the world through writing. He suffers poverty, hatred and violence but also discovers friendship and love. Through determination and courage, he overcomes dehumanizing conditions to become fully alive, a fully functioning man. The baseball trilogy (*The Southpaw, Bang the Drum Slowly, A Ticket for a Seamstitch*) describes the career of Henry W. Wiggen, a young man who succeeds in big-league baseball. In a Lardneresque style, Wiggen writes the journal of his maturity as an athlete and a man. Wiggen grapples with the mysteries of love, the problem of hatred and violence, becomes reconciled with the finality of death. Each story shows Wiggen's growth, mentally and spiritually, and his progress down a road to self-understanding and reconciliation. Overtly a comedy of athletics and folk-hero rambunctiousness, the three books also form a study of pacifism, love and justice.

*Something about a Soldier* turns explicitly to the problems of violence and nonviolence which appear in the earlier novels. In it Jacob Epp (Epstein) discovers the importance of his identity, the meaning of love and loyalty and the relationship between violence and justice. A young, very bright but naive recruit, Jacob rejects the Army and the war (WW II), militantly works for justice and equality for black people and begins to understand love and friendship. He rejects death for life, war for peace, goes AWOL and through meditation in prison comes to self-reconciliation.

In *Wake Up, Stupid*, Harris uses the epistolary form to follow a crisis of insecurity in the life of a man who is successful as an athlete, teacher and writer. Lee Youngdahl, during a lull in artistic creativity, takes up letter-writing to occupy his imagination. Comic crises of his fantasy life involve all his friends and enemies and lead him to a final understanding of his needs and desires, the sources of his imagination.

*The Goy*, Harris' latest novel, continues this theme of self-discovery. In it, Westrum, a midwestern gentile who has married an eastern Jew, pursues his identity through a massive, life-long journal. He comes to understand, through the journal, his relationship with the Jews in his life, his father's virulent anti-semiticism, his own obsession with history, his relationship with his son, his wife and his mistress. The past, through his journal and his study of history, ultimately explains his present.

All of Mark Harris' fiction is comic in conception, and sports and games are at the center of the work, especially the social games which are the substance of comedy of manners. Lee Youngdahl, in *Wake Up, Stupid*, analyzes American literature in a statement epitomizing Harris' own work:

> What is it that thrusts Mark Twain and Sherwood Anderson into one stream, and Henry James into another? . . . It has so much to do with a man's early relationship to the society of boys and games—that miniature of our larger society of men and business, with its codes and rules, its provision for imagination within these rules, with winning, losing, timing, bluffing, feinting, jockeying, with directness of aim and speech and with coming back off the floor again.

Harris' fiction is solidly within this tradition which translates social games into comedy, a comedy which explains our secret lives more clearly than any social or psychological theory.

—William J. Schafer

---

**HARRIS, (Theodore) Wilson.** British. Born in New Amsterdam, British Guiana, 24 March 1921. Educated at Queen's College, Georgetown. Married to Margaret Whitaker. Government Surveyor, in the 1940's, and Senior Surveyor, 1955–58, Government of British Guiana. Visiting Lecturer, State University of New York at Buffalo, 1970; Writer-in-Residence, Scarborough College, University of Toronto, 1970; Commonwealth Fellow in Caribbean Literature, Leeds University, Yorkshire, 1971. Delegate to the National Identity Conference, Brisbane, 1968; to UNESCO Symposium on Caribbean Literature, Cuba, 1968. Recipient: Arts Council grant, 1968, 1970. Address: c/o Faber and Faber Ltd., 3 Queen Square, London W.C.1, England.

Publications

Novels

The Guiana Quartet:
  Palace of the Peacock.  London, Faber, 1960.
  The Far Journey of Oudin.  London, Faber, 1961.
  The Whole Armour.  London, Faber, 1962.
  The Secret Ladder.  London, Faber, 1963.
Heartland.  London, Faber, 1964.
The Eye of the Scarecrow.  London. Faber, 1965.
The Waiting Room.  London, Faber, 1967.
Tumatumari.  London, Faber, 1968.
Ascent to Omai.  London, Faber, 1970.

Short Stories

The Sleepers of Roraima.  London, Faber, 1970.
The Age of the Rainmakers.  London, Faber, 1971.

Verse

Fetish.  Georgetown, British Guiana, privately printed, 1951.
Eternity to Season.  Georgetown, British Guiana, privately printed, 1954.

Other

Tradition and the West Indian Novel.  London and Port of Spain, Trinidad, New
  Beacon Books, 1965.
Tradition, The Writer and Society: Critical Essays.  London and Port of Spain,
  Trinidad, New Beacon Books, 1967.

Manuscript Collections: University of the West Indies, Mona, Kingston, Jamaica; University of Texas, Austin; University of Indiana, Bloomington.

Critical Studies: Introduction by C. L. R. James to Tradition and the West Indian Novel, 1965; The Novel Now by Anthony Burgess, London, Faber, 1967; essay by John Hearne in The Islands in Between, edited by Louis James, London, Oxford University Press, 1968; Introduction by Kenneth Ramchand to the paperback edition of Palace of the Peacock, London, Faber, 1969; Chosen Tongue by Gerald Moore, London, Longman, 1969; review by Robert Nye of Ascent to Omai in The Scotsman (Edinburgh), 1969; "The Myth of El Dorado in the Caribbean Novel" by Hena Maes-Jelinek, in Journal of Commonwealth Literature (Leeds, Yorkshire), June 1971; "The Writer as Alchemist: The Unifying Role of Imagination in Wilson Harris's Novels" by Hena Maes-Jelinek, in Language and Literature (Copenhagen), Autumn 1971; "Ascent to Omai" by Hena Maes-Jelinek, in Literary Half-Yearly (Mysore), January 1972.

Wilson Harris comments:

*Palace of the Peacock* through *The Guiana Quartet* and successive novels up to *The Sleepers of Roraima* and *The Age of the Rainmakers* are related to a symbolic landscape-in-depth—the shock of great rapids, vast forests and savannahs—playing through memory to involve perspectives of imperilled community and creativity reaching back into the Pre-Columbian mists of time.

I believe that the revolution of sensibility in defining community towards which we may now be moving is an extension of the frontiers of the alchemical imagination beyond an *opus contra naturam* into an *opus contra ritual*. This does not mean the jettisoning of ritual (since ritual belongs in the great ambivalent chain of memory; and the past, in a peculiar sense, as an omen of proportions, shrinking or expanding, never dies); but it means the utilisation of ritual as an ironic bias—the utilisation of ritual, not as something in which we situate ourselves absolutely, but as an unravelling of self-deception with self-revelation as we see through the various dogmatic proprietors of the globe within a play of contrasting structures and anti-structures: a profound drama of consciousness invoking or involving contrasting tones is the variable phenomenon of creativity within which we are prone, nevertheless, to idolise logical continuity or structure and commit ourselves to a conservative bias, or to idolise logical continuity or anti-structure and commit ourselves to a revolutionary bias. Thus we are prone to monumentalise our own biases and to indict as well as misconceive creativity. A capacity to digest as well as liberate contrasting figures is essential to the paradox of community and to the life of the imagination.

\*     \*     \*

Wilson Harris's novels grow out of one another like the concentric circles produced by a stone on the surface of a river. This familiar image symbolizes in *Ascent to Omai* a double process of spiritual liberation and growing consciousness. It applies, however, to the author's own works, whose initial and central *Palace of the Peacock* announces the original developments in style and thought which from one novel to another extend the limits of the creative imagination.

The setting of his novels has so far been the impressive landscape of his native Guyana, whose multiracial population stands for the complex make-up of humanity. The *Guiana Quartet* epitomizes the successive historical conquests of Guyana and the victimization of its various racial communities other than its white post-Columbian conquerors. The progress of a skipper and his crew on a dangerous river in the jungle, the harsh life of a poor East Indian in the savannahs, a tragedy of guilt and innocence on the coast, and the scientific measuring of the rise and fall of a river in the heartland, these dramatize man's encounter with the diversified and grandiose South American landscape, itself evocative of a terrible past that still awaits reinterpretation. The originality of Harris's approach lies in revealing beside the conventional version of historical events neglected possibilities of fulfilment for both the conquerors and the conquered of Guyana. He presents the humble and forgotten victims of the conquests and subsequent migrations as mythological personae capable of inciting their conquerors to spiritual rebirth, and thereby emphasizes the mythological and historical significance of humanity's more humble representatives. Though a sense of social justice may urge these conversions, they are not primarily motivated by a social or political ideal but illustrate a need for individual regeneration as a prelude to a new conception of community.

It appears from Harris's characters that humanity is on the whole divided between hunter and hunted, victor and victim, each category remaining self-deceptively confined to its own monolithic role and trying to extend these divisions to nature and society. But Harris denies the genuineness of those categories. He sees in nature and in all forms of human existence an ambivalence of purpose and design that should be given free play. In the *Guiana Quartet*, for instance, omnipresent nature is both perilous and protective. It is also a mirror reflecting man's dual nature, his spiritual states as well as his physical metamorphoses. Moreover, the reciprocity between the fundamental opposites, spirit and matter, finds expression in the reciprocity between man and the landscape, while this very relationship acts as an incentive to the recognition of a similar reciprocity within man's divided self and between different kinds of men. The landscape always acts as a prime mover to consciousness in Wilson Harris's novels, stirring man's imagination and helping him to define himself. In the later novels the action tends to take place mainly in the characters' mind as they re-live their past lives, and nature becomes more and more identified with their mental landscape, so much so that in *Ascent to Omai* the cosmic dimensions of the natural setting blend with the heights and depths of the human psyche.

The creation of reciprocity at all levels of experience is a dynamic process which partakes of the ever-changing fabric of life. Since everything grows out of everything else, nothing ever dies completely. There lies at the heart of every "ruined personality", whether of an individual, a community or a nation—and these are in fact one community of being—a frail charcoal residue of life that can only revive through feeling and compassion. However hackneyed these words might sound, they do not refer here to an easy or sentimental attitude. They are associated with a painful process by which Harris's characters become aware of the residues of life or latent opposites in their existences as a part of themselves with which they must come to terms. Like a volcano, the past can erupt and ironically strike back in chain-like reactions. Hence the importance of history, and of memory as an adjunct to imagination, when the characters re-create their personal and historical past in order to understand it. This immersion in the darkness of their antecedents or of the unknown areas within themselves is a difficult journey towards self-knowledge. In their confrontation with the natural, or their own spiritual, jungle, with the lost Amerindian tribes or the other dispossessed of this world, imagination is the mainspring of the emerging dialogue.

As Harris's thought gains in depth and terseness, it becomes increasingly clear that imagination as the source of man's urge to conceive "resensitized perspectives of community" is the very subject of his exploration. From his early novels, in which the dispossessed of Guyana were in a sense mythicised, to his recent "fables" (*The Sleepers of Roraima, The Age of the Rainmakers*), in which real Amerindian myths and vestiges of legend are reinterpreted, Wilson Harris has not ceased to inquire into the possibilities of the individual creative imagination to provoke in man a reversal of outlook and stimulate him to a sense of responsibility towards himself and others. The Guyanese, and by implication humanity, have reached a turning point in their history, and their future may depend on their understanding of themselves and their environment. Modern man, however, is often blind to the mysterious in life or unwilling to acknowledge it, though he can be stirred by imagination to respond to it. Mystery in Harris's fiction shrouds those evanescent tribes of Amerindians or escaped slaves who are such an essential part of the Guyanese past. But it is also a significant feature of every possible alternative or "opposite" each individual character learns to recognize at the heart of all life.

The unifying medium between all opposites is itself a synthesis in the making of the primitive, and mysterious, poetic imagination with the modern imagination. Harris shows in *Tumatumari*, a summit in his work, that both are in need of regeneration yet can redeem the individual through the creation of harmony between each other and by uniting with the scientific mind. The union of contraries and the growth of the "alchemical imagination" both as an object and an instrument of exploration correspond to the individual's attempt to break through his self-made fortresses and to his coming to consciousness. Throughout Harris's fiction the creation of consciousness, the opening of new windows on the world, is, as it clearly appears in *Ascent to Omai*, analogous to the artist's creative act. Each novel is an awakening of consciousness through the medium of language, a language which, economic and highly selective as it is, attempts to convey the immediacy and intercommunicability of all being. Harris refuses to impose a "false coherency" on the raw material of life. Not their existence in a social order but their spiritual fulfilment gives his characters substance. Their mental landscape extends in space but eludes chronological time. The limit between the concrete and the intangible is hard to perceive. But with each new novel

564

the extraordinary possibilities of aesthetic and spiritual stimulation Harris discovers in the individual's immediate environment are a challenge to the reader to probe with him into man's genius for recovery and change.

—Hena Maes-Jelinek

---

**HARROWER, Elizabeth.** Australian. Born in Sydney, 8 February 1928. Worked for the Australian Broadcasting Commission, Sydney, 1959–60; Reviewer, *Sydney Morning Herald*, 1960; worked for Macmillan and Company Ltd., publishers, Sydney, 1961–67. Recipient: Commonwealth Literary Fund Fellowship, 1968. Address: c/o Macmillan Company of Australia, 107 Moray Street, South Melbourne, Victoria 3205, Australia.

PUBLICATIONS

Novels

> *Down in the City.* London, Cassell, 1957.
> *The Long Prospect.* London, Cassell, 1958.
> *The Catherine Wheel.* London, Cassell, 1960.
> *The Watch Tower.* London and Melbourne, Macmillan, 1966.

Uncollected Short Stories

> "Lance Harper—His Story", in *Australian Letters* (Adelaide), 1961.
> "The Cost of Things", in *Summer's Tales 1.* Sydney, Macmillan, 1964.
> "The Beautiful Climate", in *Modern Australian Writing.* London, Fontana, 1966.
> "English Lesson", in *Australian Writing Today.* London, Penguin, 1968.

Manuscript Collection: Mitchell Library, Public Library of New South Wales, Sydney.

Critical Studies: "The Novels of Elizabeth Harrower" by Max Harris, in *Australian Letters* (Adelaide), December 1961; *Forty-Two Faces* by John Hetherington, Melbourne, Cheshire, 1962; "Elizabeth Harrower's Novels: A Survey" by R. G. Geering, in *Southerly* (Sydney), no. 2, 1970.

\*      \*      \*

An ideal introduction to Elizabeth Harrower's work is the short story, "The Beautiful Climate", since it provides a paradigm of her fictional universe. It is a world in which selfish men manipulate their women and material possessions in a vain attempt to achieve happiness; frustrated by their blind male egotism, they become subject to fits of smouldering violence and frequent relapses into bouts of alcoholism and morbid self-pity. The woman's role is to suffer, to pity, and to provide the innocent seeing eye for the narrative. In "The

Beautiful Climate", the paranoic male is Mr. Shaw, who secretly buys a holiday island, reduces his wife and daughter to domestic slavery there, then sells the place behind their backs. The consciousness that develops from innocent passivity to partial sad wisdom is the daughter's, who reflects her creator in turning from psychology to literature as a guide to truth. The same basic situations and characters recur throughout the novels; and the tormented relationship between father and daughter in this short story might seem to offer a psychological clue to the novelist's preoccupation with male domination.

In *Down in the City*, a very remarkable first novel, Elizabeth Harrower traces the disenchantment that follows when the heroine exchanges the empty security of her wealthy bay-side suburb in Sydney for the puzzling ups and downs of her husband's shady business world. In describing the characteristic claustrophobia of the flat-dwelling city wife, she succeeds wonderfully well in evoking the typical sights and sounds of Sydney and in establishing a connection between climate and states of mind. And the hero, who oscillates between his classy wife and his obliging mistress, reflects the conflicting drives and split personality of many an Australian business man.

What distinguishes Elizabeth Harrower's second novel, *The Long Prospect*, from all her others is that the malevolent main character is a woman not a man. But once again the viewpoint is through an innocent seeing eye; in this case, it is a child's. By the end of the novel, she has plumbed the seedy adult world to its depths. The scene, in which four irredeemably corrupt adults spy on the twelve-year old and her middle-aged friend, transferring their own "atmosphere of stealth" onto the innocent pair, is only one of many pieces of superb psychological drama in this accomplished novel.

While the third novel, *The Catherine Wheel*, laudably attempts to extend the range of the fictional world by having its setting in London bed-sitter-land, it is a somewhat disappointing work that hardly prepares the reader for the splendid fourth novel, *The Watch Tower*. The conspicuous success in *The Watch Tower* lies in the creation of Felix Shaw, the paranoic Australian business man, who climaxes a series of similar portraits and shares the surname of the father in "The Beautiful Climate". But equally subtle is the analysis of pity, through the contrasted characters of Shaw's two victims, who show that pity may enslave as well as ennoble (this a continuous preoccupation in the novels). Shaw's capriciousness, his bursts of petty pique and rage, his resentment at others' success, his dark nihilism, brutal aggression, unrecognised homosexuality and alcoholism, all point to a profound psychic disorder. But it is the novelist's triumph to suggest that this disorder is at least partly the product of a society that worships materialism and masculinity.

In most of her work, Elizabeth Harrower combines sharp observation of individual life with a searching critique of Australian society. Although she lacks the resilient vitality of such English novelists as Margaret Drabble, her vision of a male-dominated society is depressingly authentic. She has been highly praised and compared favourably with Patrick White, but her unflattering, somewhat drab and disenchanted view of Australian life is unlikely to win her the wide local readership her work certainly deserves.

—John Colmer

---

**HARTLEY, L(eslie) P(oles).**   British.   Born in Whittlesey, Cambridgeshire, 30 December 1895. Educated at Harrow School; Balliol College, Oxford, B.A. 1922. Served in World War I, 1916–1918. Fiction Reviewer for the *Spectator*, *Week-end Review*, *Weekly Sketch*, *Time and Tide*, *Observer*, and *Sunday Times*, all in London, since 1923. Clark Lecturer, Trinity College, Cambridge, 1964. Recipient: Black Memorial Prize, 1948; Heinemann Award, 1954. C.B.E. (Commander, Order of the British Empire), 1956. Address: Flat 10, 53 Rutland Gate, London S.W.7, England.

## PUBLICATIONS

### Novels

*Simonetta Perkins*.   London and New York, Putnam, 1925.
*Eustace and Hilda* (a trilogy).   London, Putnam, 1958; Chester Springs, Pennsylvania, Dufour, 1961.
   *The Shrimp and the Anemone*.   London, Putnam, 1944; as *The West Window*, New York, Doubleday, 1945.
   *The Sixth Heaven*.   London, Putnam, 1946; New York, Doubleday, 1947.
   *Eustace and Hilda*.   London, Putnam, 1947.
*The Boat*.   London, Putnam, and New York, Doubleday, 1950.
*My Fellow Devils*.   London, Barrie, 1951.
*The Go-Between*.   London, Hamish Hamilton, 1953; New York, Knopf, 1954.
*A Perfect Woman*.   London, Hamish Hamilton, 1955; New York, Knopf, 1956.
*The Hireling*.   London, Hamish Hamilton, 1957; New York, Rinehart, 1958.
*Facial Justice*.   London, Hamish Hamilton, 1960; New York, Doubleday, 1961.
*The Brickfield*.   London, Hamish Hamilton, 1964.
*The Betrayal*.   London, Hamish Hamilton, 1966.
*Poor Clare*.   London, Hamish Hamilton, 1968.
*The Love-Adept: A Variation on a Theme*.   London, Hamish Hamilton, 1969.
*My Sister's Keeper*.   London, Hamish Hamilton, 1970.
*The Harness Room*.   London, Hamish Hamilton, 1971.

### Short Stories

*Night Fears and Other Stories*.   London, Putnam, 1924.
*Killing Bottle*.   London, Putnam, 1932.
*The Travelling Grave and Other Stories*.   Sauk City, Wisconsin, Arkham House, 1948; London, Barrie, 1951.
*A White Wand and Other Stories*.   London, Hamish Hamilton, 1954.
*Two for the River*.   London, Hamish Hamilton, 1961.
*The Collected Short Stories of L. P. Hartley*.   London, Hamish Hamilton, 1968; New York, Horizon Press, 1969.
*Mrs. Carteret Receives and Other Stories*.   London, Hamish Hamilton, 1971.

### Other

*The Novelist's Responsibility: Lectures and Essays*.   London, Hamish Hamilton, 1967; New York, Hillary House, 1968.

Bibliography: in *L. P. Hartley* by Peter Bien, London, Chatto and Windus, 1963.

Manuscript Collection: British Museum, London.

Critical Studies: *L. P. Hartley* by Paul Bloomfield, London, Longman, 1962, revised edition, 1970; *Tradition and Dream* by Walter Allen, London, Phoenix House, 1964; "The English Novelist and the American Tradition" by Georgio Melchiori, in *Sewanee Review* (Tennessee), 1968.

*     *     *

"To imitate the surface of life, as Trollope did, without trying to interpret it, no longer satisfies serious modern novelists," L. P. Hartley wrote in 1946. And though in each of his best novels (the *Eustace and Hilda* trilogy, *The Boat*, and *The Go-Between*) the subtly-detailed study of a central character emerges from a rich re-creation of a time and place, Hartley's is basically a mystical-moral vision which sees his people and their sometimes petty problems as involved, often unwittingly, in a much more vast, ancient and serious drama of quest and redemption. Not unlike Hawthorne, whom he admires and describes as an "apocalyptic novelist," one in whose fiction "the main, the only issue, is the struggle between the good and the bad," Hartley tends to see and create symbolically, producing work usually closer to romance, satire or parable than to the realistic novel. In his gallery of portraits of sensitive individuals searching for selfhood and salvation in their respective corners of the twentieth century, Hartley has designed a series of metaphors of that century— of modern man groping nearsightedly among the fragments of the past and present, oblivious to the real and powerful spiritual universe whose laws and forces operate all around him.

Hartley's short stories, brought together in *The Collected Short Stories of L. P. Hartley*, are best seen as sketches for, keys to the more complex novels. Here he isolates elements capable of being combined with symbolic force in his larger works: characters representing given moral attitudes, objects and settings carrying emotional or spiritual significances, situations incarnating moral dilemmas, events suggesting the operation of mysterious universal laws. Many are ghost or horror stories embodying the concept that the visible world is surrounded by a greater invisible one of spiritus, connections, consequences; already a favorite theme is man's indifference to this invisible world, especially his tendency to discount the reality and power of evil—and his inevitable comeuppance. In these stories the only force capable of overcoming the prevailing darkness and self-deception is an all-too-occasional flash of self-sacrificing love.

Hartley's *novella Simonetta Perkins*, first and slightest of the longer works which together attempt a moral anatomy of the twentieth century, has been compared with *Daisy Miller*, but is much less realistic, socially and psychologically: much more a playful, tongue-in-cheek parable or romance (in Hawthorne's sense of imaginative construct), embodying a choice between two value-systems. A proper Bostonian girl weary of her Puritan past is attracted by the natural hedonism of her handsome Venetian gondolier. When, having almost yielded, she rejects the Emilio-solution to life as thoroughly as she rejects the Puritan one, Hartley's mid-twenties book seems to be suggesting that neither an outworn moral code nor complete license will do for the twentieth century. He gives no simple answer about what *will* do, except that Lavinia/Simonetta (she has seen herself as split in two by her dilemma) has begun to live from some unified point within herself.

The three books of the *Eustace and Hilda* sequence, appearing almost twenty years later, and constituting some of Hartley's finest work, follow the gently comic tragedy of Eustace, a lovable, imaginative younger brother locked in a life-and-death struggle with his rigidly realistic sister Hilda. *The Shrimp and the Anemone*, with its central image and dilemma of whether the beautiful flower-form should be allowed to consume the tiny crustacean which it needs for sustenance, shows us the mutually-dependent Eustace and Hilda as children in an almost primordial setting of rocks, sand and destructive sea. *The Sixth Heaven* and *Eustace and Hilda* cast them into parallel worlds of pleasure and romance: Eustace escaping from Hilda's moralistic domination to life among wealthy dilettantes in Venice, Hilda abandoning herself to a passionate love affair. Hilda's near-destruction and need of him call Eustace home to the rocks and sand of Anchorstone, and he prods her back into life and selfhood—at the cost of his own always-fragile life.

*Eustace and Hilda* is on one level a sensitive study of a life and death and of the tragedy of people who love but can only exist at one another's expense; on another level it is a picture of the beginnings of this century—its farewell to Victorianism, to absolutes, to God, and its disappointment with aestheticism and shallow humanism. Hartley's all-pervasive symbolism—at first only slightly emphasizing colors, shapes, objects, oddities of language, then gradually building up to a vast structural metaphor of Venice with its sunlight and shadow, land and water, Baroque and Gothic, arches, squares, circles and rainbow colors— gives the book its shimmering beauty and suggests other and deeper meanings for its story. The Eustace-and-Hilda relationship, the shrimp-and-anemone image, we come to realize, are revelations of a terrible principle of contradiction at the heart of things, by which man on this earth seems doomed always to division, frustration and defeat. But beneath the tragic surface, one senses that Eustace's life and death, terrible as they are, point to man's only possible achievement: Eustace the anti-hero has learned what heroes learn—to love and sacrifice.

*The Boat* is Hartley's war novel: World War II as seen from the little English village of Upton-on-Swirrel, whither middle-aged writer Timothy Casson has retired to produce nostalgic vignettes of old England, and where, deprived of his right to go boating on the river, he soon begins a war of his own. Hartley shifts here to a more satiric or mock-romantic form in which types such as Esther the robust English countrywoman, Magda the society aesthete, Tyro the moralist and near-crank, Vera Cross the Communist *femme fatale*, Volumnia Purbright the unconventional Christian and her husband, the Rector (not quite so Christian), populate the scene of tragic misadventures which relieve Timothy of his excessive innocence, his romantic belief in the goodness of nature (including his own), and his tendency to blame the War on everyone else. *The Boat*'s complex fabric analyzes England's, and humanity's, state as of the 1940's, and we suspect Hartley's own sentiments to be akin to zany Mrs. Purbright's when she judges that "we've sold our capital of happiness, our reserves are gone, we must build them afresh," and, more explicitly, "We can inherit the gifts of Christianity, but not hand them on: I mean, the third generation must renew its faith."

In *The Go-Between*, recently filmed by Harold Pinter and Joseph Losey, aging Leo Colston, alone and unhappy at mid-century, searches an old diary of the year 1900 for the key to the sterility of his past fifty years; step by step he relives the summer of his thirteenth year when, visiting a school friend at Brandham Hall in Norfolk, he was used as messenger in an illicit affair between the daughter of the house and a lowborn tenant farmer. We look at the centrally-focussed love story, the passion and pain of its participants and their unthinking cruelty to the uncomprehending child, through the eyes of the innocent, idealizing young Leo of fifty years ago as seen now through the eyes of his soured present self. The double focus, the frame-story covering fifty years in this man's life-span, enable us to look back as he does, with some comprehension not only of the carelessly destructive lovers, but of the beautiful but meaningless way of life which produced them and the century of individualism and war which was its aftermath. *The Go-Between*, with its carefully-defined structure, its evocation of Edwardian country-house life, its touching portrait of a child and of the grown-up world as seen through his myth-creating vision, is often considered Hartley's finest novel.

Most of L. P. Hartley's novels of the 1950's and 1960's describe more or less involuntary, more or less successful, spiritual quests, each by a modern Everyman in a contemporary setting. Abandoning the distancing afforded his earlier (and more successful) romances by a child's-eye-view or a setting in the past, Hartley satirizes present-day manners and mores while maintaining that the perennial myths and archetypes still operate beneath the surface, that modern witches, devils, sibyls and guardian spirits still perform their duties among us, that words, games, *objets d'art*, the sounds and sights of a life-style, reverberate with inner meaning, that the presence of Evil and the need for redemption are still man's central problems. *My Fellow Devils* is a serio-comic parable about a severe female magistrate who marries a movie star and, disillusioned with his corruption, embarks upon a sincere religious search. Only in this book does Hartley explicitly suggest God as possible instigator of and answer to life's questions; in each of the others in this group—which examine, in *A Perfect Woman*, the testing of a suburban marriage, in *The Hireling*, the shifting of class relationships, in *The Brickfield/The Betrayal*, the deficiencies of the welfare state and loneliness of old age, and in *Poor Clare*, the contradictions of the artistic vocation

—the more or less bumbling protagonist, propelled from a light comedy existence into tragedy, becomes, himself, an unanswered call for a transcending or healing meaning to life.

In *Facial Justice* Hartley blends his ultimate satire on present-day inadequacies with a fairy tale embodying his basically Christian philosophy of history. In a future state in which today's egalitarianism, permissiveness and fear of excellence have become law, precluding excessive beauty, intelligence or imagination, an enterprising heroine falls in love with an angel, thereby rediscovering her own soul. After the carnage and apocalypse to which the new state's policies inevitably lead, she and the shining Michael are charged with establishing a new way of life for mankind. Here Hartley makes his long preoccupation with modern man's spiritual vacuum the very stuff of his story: just as his individual protagonists, searching for happiness in cluttered Edwardian houses or sterile modern suburbs have encountered emptiness and frustration and evil and been forced to look within the stuff of tragedy for a non-material answer to existence, so, Hartley seems to suggest, will a de-spiritualized society have to suffer and die in order to be reborn.

L. P. Hartley's books of the 1970's have been less serious in intent and execution. He is best remembered as a novelist whose intense religious and moral concerns led him to experiment with unique combinations of the realistic and the symbolic—in order to suggest the texture of modern life at the same time that he explored and judged it within larger historical and metaphysical patterns. In the total range of his novels he has translated the central myth of man's tragedy and transformation into each decade of the twentieth century and into each stage of human life from childhood to old age; in the best of them he has created works of art.

—Anne Mulkeen

---

**HAWKES, John (Clendennin Burne, Jr.).** American. Born in Stamford, Connecticut, 17 August 1925. Educated at Harvard University, Cambridge, Massachusetts, 1943–49, A.B. 1949. Served with the American Field Service in Italy and Germany, 1944–45. Married Sophie Goode Tazewell in 1947; has four children. Assistant to the Production Manager, Harvard University Press, 1949–55; Visiting Lecturer in English, 1955–56, and Instructor in English, 1956–58, Harvard University. Assistant Professor, 1958–62, Associate Professor, 1962–67, and since 1967, Professor of English, Brown University, Providence, Rhode Island. Special Guest, Aspen Institute for Humanistic Studies, Colorado, 1962; Visiting Lecturer, Stanford University, California, 1966–67; Visiting Distinguished Professor of Creative Writing, City College of the City University of New York, 1971–72. Member, Panel on Educational Innovation, Washington, D.C., 1966–67. Recipient: National Institute of Arts and Letters grant, 1962; Guggenheim Fellowship, 1962; Ford Fellowship, in theatre, 1964; Rockefeller Fellowship, 1966. Address: Department of English, Brown University, Providence, Rhode Island 02912, U.S.A.

PUBLICATIONS

Novels

*The Cannibal.*  New York, New Directions, 1949; London, Spearman, 1962.
*The Beetle Leg*.  New York, New Directions, 1951; London, Chatto and Windus, 1967.

*The Lime Twig.*   New York, New Directions, 1961; London, Spearman, 1962.
*Second Skin.*   New York, New Directions, 1964; London, Chatto and Windus, 1966.
*The Blood Oranges.*   New York, New Directions, and London, Chatto and Windus, 1971.

### Short Stories

*The Goose on the Grave, and The Owl: Two Short Novels.*   New York, New Directions, 1954.
*Lunar Landscapes: Stories and Short Novels 1949–1963.*   New York, New Directions, 1969; London, Chatto and Windus, 1970.

### Plays

*The Innocent Party: 4 Short Plays* (includes *The Wax Museum*, *The Questions*, *The Undertaker*, and *The Innocent Party*).   New York, New Directions, 1966; London, Chatto and Windus, 1967.
*The Wax Museum* (produced Boston, 1966).   Included in *The Innocent Party*, 1966.
*The Questions* (produced Stanford, California, 1966).   Included in *The Innocent Party*, 1966.
*The Undertaker* (produced Boston, 1967).   Included in *The Innocent Party*, 1966.
*The Innocent Party* (produced Boston, 1968).   Included in *The Innocent Party*, 1966.

### Other

Editor, with others, *The Personal Voice: A Contemporary Prose Reader.*   Philadelphia, Lippincott, 1964.
Editor, with others, *The American Literary Anthology 1: The 1st Annual Collection of the Best from the Literary Magazines.*   New York, Farrar Straus, 1968.

Manuscript Collection: Houghton Library, Harvard University, Cambridge, Massachusetts.

Critical Studies: in *The Fabulators* by Robert Scholes, New York, Oxford University Press, 1967; *Studies in "Second Skin"*, edited by John Graham, Columbus, Ohio, Merrill, 1971.

John Hawkes comments:

I think of myself as an experimental writer. But it's unfortunate that the term "experimental" has been used so often by reviewers as a pejorative label intended to dismiss as eccentric or private or excessively difficult the work in question. My own fiction is not merely eccentric or private and is not nearly so difficult as it's been made out to be. I should think that every writer, no matter what kind of fiction writer he may be or may aspire to be, writes in order to create the future. Every fiction of any value has about it something new. At any rate, the function of the true innovator or specifically experimental writer is to keep prose alive and constantly to test in the sharpest possible way the range of our human sympathies and constantly to destroy mere surface morality. . . .
My own concept of "avant-garde" has to do with something constant which we find running through prose fiction from Quevedo, the Spanish picaresque writer, to the present.

This constant is a quality of coldness, detachment, ruthless determination to face up to the enormities of ugliness and potential failure within ourselves and in the world around us, and to bring to this exposure a savage or saving comic spirit and the saving beauties of language. The need is to maintain the truth of the fractured picture; to expose, ridicule, attack, but always to create and to throw into new light our potential for violence and absurdity as well as for graceful action. . . .

My novels are not highly plotted, but certainly they're elaborately structured. I began to write fiction on the assumption that the true enemies of the novel were plot, character, setting, and theme, and having once abandoned these familiar ways of thinking about fiction, totality of vision or structure was really all that remained. And structure—verbal and psychological coherence—is still my largest concern as a writer. Related or correspond-ing event, recurring image and recurring action, these constitute the essential substance or meaningful density of my writing. However, this kind of structure can't be planned in advance but can only be discovered in the writing process itself. The success of the effort depends on the degree and quality of consciousness that can be brought to bear on fully liberated materials of the unconscious. I'm trying to hold in balance poetic and novelistic methods in order to make the novel a more valid and pleasurable experience. . . .

—from "John Hawkes: An Interview",
in *Wisconsin Studies in Contemporary
Literature* (Madison), Summer 1965.

\*          \*          \*

John Hawkes, perhaps the most original American novelist since Faulkner, bears only superficial resemblances to other contemporary innovators. His work is distinctly less philosophical and less parodic than that of Barth, Nabokov, Pynchon, Durrell, Borges. And if he chooses to create fictional worlds, rather than represent ours—fictional worlds in which one man on a motorcycle may occupy a third of Germany, or a Caribbean island wander in space and time—these visionary landscapes yet seem genuine dynamic pro-jections of our real underground lives. Childhood terror, oral fantasies and castration fears, fears of regression and violence, profound sexual disturbances—these (rather than the spatial inventions of science fiction or of Nabokov's *Ada*) are the components of Hawkes's myths and of the "places" he calls Germany or America or England.

Hawkes claims to have recognized at the outset of his career four enemies: plot, character, setting, theme. Haunting chordal insistences and recurring images replace plot; the symbols of nightmare and neurosis and of the preconscious serve for character; a general vision of deterioration and collapse offers a semblance of theme. All these, and the dark halluci-natory landscapes, are redeemed by humor and by what Tony Tanner calls the "com-plicated and wrought fabric of his style". To a degree rare even in contemporary literature ugly materials—violence, suffering, deliberately reversed sympathies, magnified obscenities of landscape or human form—become things of beauty. Are the visions of violence and collapse prompted, as the author has occasionally insisted, by a belief in order and love? These stylized, distanced enormities maintain a very powerful hold on us, even as we enjoy them aesthetically, in part because they are rarely explained. This is the one thing Hawkes has in common with Robbe-Grillet; his world is unexplained. Hawkes's fictional world simply and dynamically, even magically, *is*.

Such originality and uncompromising difficulty long restricted Hawkes to an under-ground audience. *The Cannibal*, written as a Harvard undergraduate, drew some attention because it appeared to be a powerful symbolic commentary on the American occupation of a diseased, deteriorated Germany. The ruined landscape of 1945 is juxtaposed against a Germany of 1914, already doomed; there is a vision of history as fated yet inconsecutive and absurd. But at least a few readers were drawn rather by powerful scenes of grotesque transformation and psychic substitution (as cannibalism for homosexual assault) and by the nervous, exceptionally brilliant phrasing. *The Cannibal* is, for some readers, the masterpiece of American avant-garde fiction.

*The Beetle Leg* is a cooler vision, at times parodic, often comic, of a mythical American west and sexless wasteland in which helpless persons somnambulistically wander. This excellent novel had few readers at first; *The Goose and the Grave* (a volume containing also *The Owl*) was also almost completely ignored. It has been reissued, with several stories added, as *Lunar Landscapes*. These darkly playful short novels are laid in 20th-century Italy and in a fictionized San Marino locked in medieval legend and ritual: "two sides of a single dream," Tony Tanner has remarked, "centering on human violence in a hostile terrain—sudden deaths in still squares." (Tanner's essay in *City of Words* is one of the best brief introductions to Hawkes's work.)

By 1961, with *The Lime Twig*, a number of major writers and critics had discovered Hawkes, and this novel has become a favorite in American college classrooms. Moreover, Hawkes had by now moved to a more conscious understanding of his own materials and methods, and even some distance toward realism and narrative suspense. Parody of the detective novel form is merely the thin surface or pretext, in *The Lime Twig*, for another powerful vision of violence and tormented sexuality, this time laid in a bleakly plausible wartime and post-war England. Freudian substitutions and displacements are clearly evident as such, and are therefore oddly comic (an injection in the place of sexual penetration, or beating by a truncheon as rape). Yet the writing is so powerful that we continue to experience fascination and terror, even as we coolly watch the author's game. Few novels have dramatized so powerfully ultimate threats to identity.

With *Second Skin*, which lost the National Book Award to Saul Bellow's *Herzog* by one vote, Hawkes reached a much larger audience. And now for the first time the concealed affirmations and sympathies of the earlier books come to the surface in a vision of death and disaster (in America and on a north Atlantic island) succeeded by pastoral bliss on a wandering southern island. The narrator has survived the suicide of father, wife, daughter and, escaped from a world of impotence, has become an artificial inseminator of cows. He is also, possibly, the father of the child of the black Catalina Kate, whom he shares with his messboy Sonny. Some of the dark materials of Hawkes's earlier fiction are present, even on that lush tropical island—a monstrous iguana, for instance, clinging to Catalina Kate's back. But the final vision of equanimity is genuine, reinforced by a conversational style of Nabokovian loveliness.

Hawkes has clearly moved from the brilliant groping of a wholly original, half-conscious, at times primitive visionary to the wholly conscious artistry and calculated rhetoric of a novelist who is also a gifted literary critic and professor of English (at Brown University). The writing of several tightly-constructed plays, collected as *The Innocent Party*, may have contributed to Hawkes's development toward a more open and public art. *The Blood Oranges* has only a few scenes of wildly antirealist invention, though it has many moments of original and exquisite writing. Its comic treatment of two couples who have exchanged partners, yet still live together, often seems both to parody Ford's *The Good Soldier* and to satirize the gravity with which middle-class Americans, in the 1960's, contemplated their sexual anxieties. In one respect *The Blood Oranges* is like its predecessors. The Mediterranean world of "Illyria"—recalling *Twelfth Night* as *Second Skin* evoked *The Tempest* —is absolutely plausible, and absolutely Hawkes's own.

—Albert Guerard

---

**HAYDN, Hiram.** American. Born in Cleveland, Ohio, 3 November 1907. Educated at Amherst College, Massachusetts, 1924–28, A.B. 1928; Western Reserve University, Cleveland, 1936–38, M.A. 1938; Columbia University, New York, 1941–42, Ph.D. 1942. Married Rachel Norris in 1935; Mary Tuttle, 1945; has four children. Taught at the Hawken School, Cleveland, 1928–41; Lecturer, Cleveland College, 1938–41; Assistant Professor, then Associate Professor, University of North Carolina Woman's College, Greensboro, 1942–44; Executive Secretary, United Chapters of Phi Beta Kappa, New York, 1944–45; Lecturer, New School for Social Research, New York, 1946–60; Visiting Professor of Communications, 1965–66, and since 1966 Professor of Communications, Annenberg School of Communications, University of Pennsylvania, Philadelphia. Associate Editor, 1945–48, and Editor-in-Chief, 1948–50, Crown Publishers, New York; New York Editor, Bobbs-Merrill Company, 1950–54; Senior Editor, 1955–56, and Editor-in-Chief, 1956–59, Random House, New York; Co-Founder and Director, Atheneum Publishers, New York, 1959–64. Since 1964, Associate to the President, Harcourt Brace Jovanovich, New York. Since 1944, Editor of *The American Scholar*, Washington, D.C. Fellow, Center for Advanced Studies, Wesleyan University, Middletown, Connecticut, 1964–65. Litt.D., Western Reserve University, 1963. Address: 3620 Walnut Street, Philadelphia, Pennsylvania 19104, U.S.A.

PUBLICATIONS

Novels

> *By Nature Free.*  Indianapolis, Bobbs Merrill, 1943.
> *Manhattan Furlough.*  Indianapolis, Bobbs Merrill, 1945.
> *The Time Is Noon.*  New York, Crown, 1948.
> *The Hands of Esau.*  New York, Harper, and London, Longman, 1962.
> *Report from the Red Windmill.*  New York, Harcourt Brace, 1967.

Play

> *Fool's Christmas: A Christmas Play for Boys.*  New York, French, 1937.

Other

> *The Counter Renaissance.*  New York, Scribner, 1950; London, Peter Smith, 1961.

> Editor, with others, *Explorations in Living: A Record of the Democratic Spirit.*  New York, Reynal, 1941.
> Editor, *The Portable Elizabethan Reader.*  New York, Viking Press, 1946.
> Editor, with John Cournos, *A World of Great Stories.*  New York, Crown, 1947.
> Editor, with Edmund Fuller, *Thesaurus of Book Digests.*  New York, Crown, 1949; London, Arco, 1956.
> Editor, with J. C. Nelson, *A Renaissance Treasury.*  New York, Doubleday, 1953.
> Editor, with Katherine Gauss Jackson, *The Papers of Christian Gauss.*  New York, Random House, 1957.
> Editor, with Betsy Saunders, *The American Scholar Reader.*  New York, Atheneum, 1960.

> Series Editor, *The Twentieth Century Library.*  New York, Scribner, 1946–1954.
> Series Editor, *The Makers of the American Tradition.*  Indianapolis, Bobbs Merrill, 1953–1955.

Bibliography: in *Voyages* (Washington, D.C.), Winter 1970.

Manuscript Collection: Library of Congress, Washington, D.C.

Critical Studies: "Hiram Haydn's Other World" by Fred Chappell, in *Voyages* (Washington, D.C.), Winter 1970; "Anaïs Nin on Hiram Haydn's *Report from the Red Windmill*", in *Voyages* (Washington, D.C.), Winter 1970.

Hiram Haydn comments:

The themes that have most interested me and with which I have been most concerned in my fiction have been these: the discrepancy between the ideal and the actuality; the nature of freedom; the agonies of growth; the ambiguities of personality; commitment and mortality; illusion and reality; the meaning of generation.

*      *      *

In each of his novels Hiram Haydn is most urgently concerned with the notions of individual morality and personal freedom. From which concerns he draws these questions: Is a morality of individualism viable or even possible? How is this morality to be reconciled with the idea of personal freedom? Is individual morality affected by religious and scientific truths? How does it stand in relation to the private moralities of others? And always he sets these problems against the larger contexts of the family and the state.

These comprising his dramatic interests, certain qualities of his books would almost seem dictated to him. His protagonists must perforce be of active rather than of passive character, since they must have freedom and opportunity to make and endure moral choices. They must be stationed economically no lower than middle class, for the same reasons.

These two characteristics are true of Philip Blair in *By Nature Free*, of Lathrop Stone in *The Time Is Noon*, of Walton Herrick in *The Hands of Esau*, and even of Martin Martin in *Report from the Red Windmill*. None of these protagonists is an outward failure, and none of them lacks a high interior courage. Yet the careers of these men, as we follow them in the novels, present developments contrary to what we might expect. They do not trip blithely from one financial and amorous triumph to another; their social circumstances hardly change at all, and soon enough we realize that material goals aren't so very important to them.

What is most important to them is the definitions of their selves. At various points in the books each of the protagonists is presented with moral and social crises which he can solve, or fail to solve, only by an honest examination of his personality and an earnest readjustment of private values. All of them are driven inward by circumstance, and all of them emerge once more to do battle with the world; but the real drama of each book is an interior drama.

Martin Martin says of himself, "I have been busy and dead. . . . I have been split in two parts and I have not been able to put myself together and commit myself." The other protagonists could make the same admission, and each of them displays Martin's tendency to identify the other part of the broken self, the "anti-self," with family or genetic heritage. That is, with history. In these books the self is made whole only when the terms set both by history and by the present individual are recognized and met. Martin Martin and Walton Herrick, though they inhabit separate novels, utter identical sentences: "Both your fathers are . . . gone. Be a father to yourself." (*Manhattan Furlough*, Haydn's second novel, is quite apart from his other books. Though it is the most lyrical and charming, it is probably the least important. He has described it as a "love poem.")

The most striking qualities of Haydn's writing are a deep understanding of the pressures of responsibility, a knowledge of the oppressive weight of family ties, an intense sympathy for helpless bewilderment, and a dogged and unrelenting earnestness of feeling and expression.

—Fred Chappell

---

**HAYES, Joseph.** American. Born in Indianapolis, Indiana, 2 August 1918. Educated at Indiana University, Bloomington, 1938–41. Married Marrijane Johnston in 1938; has three children. Assistant Editor, Samuel French, publishers, New York, 1941–43. Since 1954, Partner, Erskine and Hayes, theatrical producers, New York. Chairman, Sarasota, Florida Community Theatre for the Performing Arts. Chairman, Sarasota Chapter, American Civil Liberties Union. Recipient: Sergel Drama Prize, University of Chicago, 1948; Antoinette Perry Award, for drama, 1956; Edgar Allan Poe Award, for screenplay, 1965. D.H.L., Indiana University, 1970. Address: Obtuse Hill, Brookfield Center, Connecticut; or, 1168 Westway Drive, Sarasota, Florida, U.S.A.

PUBLICATIONS

Novels

> *The Desperate Hours.* New York, Random House, and London, Deutsch, 1954.
> *Bon Voyage*, with Marrijane Hayes. New York, Random House, and London, Deutsch, 1957.
> *The Hours after Midnight.* New York, Random House, 1958; London, Deutsch, 1959.
> *Don't Go Away Mad.* New York, Random House, 1962; London, W. H. Allen, 1963.
> *The Third Day.* New York, McGraw Hill, and London, W. H. Allen, 1964.
> *The Deep End.* New York, Viking Press, and London, W. H. Allen, 1967.
> *Like Any Other Fugitive.* New York, Dial Press, 1971; London, Deutsch, 1972.

Plays

> *And Came the Spring,* with Marrijane Hayes. New York, French, 1942.
> *Christmas at Home.* New York, French, 1943.
> *The Thompsons.* New York, French, 1943.
> *The Bridegroom Waits.* New York, French, 1943.
> *Sneak Date* (as Joseph H. Arnold). New York, Peterson, 1944.
> *Come Rain or Shine*, with Marrijane Hayes. New York, French, 1944.
> *Life of the Party*, with Marrijane Hayes. New York, French, 1945.
> *Ask for Me Tomorrow*, with Marrijane Hayes. New York, French, 1946.
> *Where's Laurie* (as Joseph H. Arnold). New York, French, 1946.
> *Come Over to Our House*, with Marrijane Hayes. New York, French, 1946.
> *Home for Christmas.* New York, French, 1946.
> *A Woman's Privilege.* New York, French, 1947.
> *Quiet Summer*, with Marrijane Hayes. New York, French, 1947.
> *Change of Heart*, with Marrijane Hayes. New York, French, 1948.

*Leaf and Bough* (produced New York, 1949).
*Too Many Dates*, with Marrijane Hayes.  New York, French, 1950.
*Curtain Going Up*, with Marrijane Hayes.  New York, French, 1950.
*Turn Back the Clock*, with Marrijane Hayes.  New York, French, 1950.
*June Wedding*, with Marrijane Hayes.  New York, French, 1951.
*Once in Every Family*, with Marrijane Hayes.  New York, French, 1951.
*Penny*, with Marrijane Hayes.  New York, French, 1951.
*Too Young, Too Old*.  Boston, Baker, 1952.
*Mister Peepers*, with Marrijane Hayes.  New York, French, 1952.
*Head in the Clouds*, with Marrijane Hayes.  New York, French, 1952.
*The Desperate Hours* (produced New York and London, 1955).  New York, Random House, 1955.
*Calculated Risk* (produced New York, 1962).  New York, French, 1963.
*Is Anyone Listening?* (produced Tallahassee, Florida, 1970).

Screenplays: *The Desperate Hours*, 1955; *The Young Doctors*, 1962.


Manuscript Collection: Indiana University, Bloomington.


Joseph Hayes comments:

My basic approach, somewhat reflected in all my works, is that the average man comes to realize himself and to recognize who he is and might be only in crisis, and often too late. The crisis forms the plot or framework of my work, whose inner core is this recognition. I cannot help believing that these personal problems reflect the larger ones of a society that also may come to these recognitions too late. Rather than *society*, one might say *mankind*. I have come to wonder whether it is now already too late.

\*      \*      \*

Adam Wyatt in *The Deep End* speaks for all of the protagonists of Joseph Hayes when he says, "Does a man always realize too late what he has—what he is and what he might be?" The serious novels deal with characters who achieve self-knowledge when confronted with the necessity of overcoming potentially catastrophic situations, usually precipitated by neurotic or psychotic characters.

*The Desperate Hours* and *The Hours after Midnight* are similar in range and subject matter. In the former novel, three escaped convicts terrorize a captive family, while in the latter novel a kidnapped girl is held for ransom by a neurotic youth. The ostensible concern with self-knowledge in the novels is frustrated by the limited conception of reality in which the characters move: stereotypical middle-class, Christian moral principles are taken for granted, the characters being either good or evil. The possibility of internal conflict is almost negated. Hayes' concern at this point with the psychology of the neurotic or psychotic character is also limited by the novels' simplistic conception of reality. As neurotics, Glenn Griffin and Nolan Stoddard are simply aberrations from a norm of behavior, products of a clearly discernible set of external circumstances, rather than anything intrinsically irrational in the nature of man.

*The Third Day* presents a more lucid style and a better handling of characterization than the earlier novels. Amnesia forces the protagonist to discover his identity, simultaneously allowing him to evaluate his life from an objective perspective. The novel ends with the potential tragedy averted, but the events of the novel have caused the protagonist to question whether or not God's in his Heaven and all's right with the world. The question of irrationality is stated in the phrase "all we know is that there's a dark underside to the world." The psychopathic character, Edward Albert, with his physical deformity and nihilistic statements, poses a threat to the theistic conception of the world. Nihilism remains only a threat, for the novel ends on the optimistic note that good will triumph. Here the question of nihilism is raised but not pursued.

*The Deep End* focuses directly on nihilism in the confrontation between a psychopathic hippie, Wilby, and a middle-aged lawyer, Adam Wyatt. Forced by Wilby to think about the issue, Wyatt realizes that he has never examined his beliefs, and when he does he is overwhelmed by the non-existence of God. The focus then shifts to the question of identity and value in an atheistical world. Rejecting the irrational behavior of Wilby, Wyatt decides that it is death which makes life intense, and that an insistence on rationality and humanity in the face of oblivion is man's sole dignity.

*Bon Voyage* is the story of a family's adventures on a European vacation. *Don't Go Away Mad* is a humorous novel about Broadway theatre.

—Thomas F. Wilson

---

**HAZZARD, Shirley.** Australian. Born in Sydney, 30 January 1931. Educated at Queenwood School, Sydney. Married Francis Steegmuller, *q.v.,* in 1963. Worked in Combined Services Intelligence, Hong Kong, 1947–48; United Kingdom High Commissioner's Office, Wellington, New Zealand, 1949–50; United Nations Headquarters, New York (General Service Category), 1951–61. Recipient: National Institute of Arts and Letters grant, 1966. Address: 200 East 66th Street, New York, New York 10021, U.S.A.

PUBLICATIONS

Novels

    *The Evening of the Holiday*.   New York, Knopf, and London and Melbourne, Macmillan, 1966.
    *People in Glass Houses: Portraits from Organization Life*.   New York, Knopf, and London and Melbourne, Macmillan, 1967.
    *The Bay of Noon*.   Boston, Little Brown, and London and Melbourne, Macmillan, 1970.

Short Stories

    *Cliffs of Fall and Other Stories*.   New York, Knopf, and London and Melbourne, Macmillan, 1963.

Critical Study: "Patterns and Preoccupations of Love: The Novels of Shirley Hazzard" by John Colmer, in *Meanjin* (Melbourne), December 1970.

\*      \*      \*

Shirley Hazzard was born and spent her early years in Australia, but she is essentially an expatriate cosmopolitan writer, deeply rooted in the European literary tradition, much travelled, acutely sensitive to the spirit of place, with a keen eye for national differences, and an acute ear for the words that express and unconsciously betray human values. So far she has drawn mainly on experiences gained from foreign travel, ten years employment in UNO, and residence in America for the material of her fiction. However, the brilliant short story "Woollahra Road", which holds in poignant juxtaposition a child's eye and an adult's eye view of Australia during the Depression, suggests that there is a store of memories belonging to the first fifteen years of her life that has yet to find fictional expression. And the portrait in *People in Glass Houses* of the Australian UNO official, Mervyn, protected alike from disenchantment and beauty by his "defensive scepticism," establishes her skill in getting under the skin of certain Australian types.

The publication of *Cliffs of Fall*, a collection of short stories that had already appeared in *The New Yorker*, drew enthusiastic and discriminating praise from reviewers in America and Britain. It did not require the photograph of the author holding a copy of *Madame Bovary* on the dust-jacket to establish her admiration for Flaubert and other continental masters: Maupassant, Chekhov and Turgenev, for example. Her insight into the paradoxes of love, her power to render moments of unspoken anguish (as in "The Worst Moment of the Day"), the combination of reticent suggestion and poetic resonance, the extraordinary economy of means in creating character and situation, and the unerring feel for the *mot juste*, all these qualities link her writing to the continental masters. In several of the stories, especially those set in an Italian pensione, the contrast between true and false values and the concern with sudden moments of illumination is reminiscent of E. M. Forster, without in any way being derivative. Of all the stories, the longest, called "A Place in the Country", is the best and foreshadows the author's later work. And the fact that "The Picnic" deals with the same characters suggests that the material might once have been intended for a novel. The central character in each, Nettie, comes to realise that there is balance but no fairness in life and that the claims of humanity are prior to the demands of reason. These two ideas inform and control Shirley Hazzard's fictional universe.

In *The Evening of the Holiday*, the promise of the Italian short stories is fulfilled, but the work is still only a novella rather than a full length novel. For the experience explored, the form is perfect. Each situation is exactly placed; the relationship between the half English half Italian heroine, Sophie, and the Italian architect Tancredi slowly unfolds towards its moments of piercing illumination and sad climax. It is not only Tancredi's married state that stands in the way of happiness; masculine pride and Sophie's reluctance to commit herself play their part. Sophie, like many of Shirley Hazzard's heroines, is an expatriate of the heart, in search of her spiritual home abroad, but forced to look for it within herself. "She did not really know where she most belonged. Even those places to which she felt most drawn were mere approximations of home." In some respects, *The Bay of Noon* is the natural extension and development of that search, but in between come the dazzlingly witty portraits from organization life called *People in Glass Houses*.

The "Portraits", like the short stories in *Cliffs of Fall*, first appeared in *The New Yorker*. Each could be read as a separate study, but because similar characters recur and a single controlling vision illuminates each, they cohere into an amusing but highly serious work of satirical fiction. Two related paradoxes bring the portraits into a single focus. The first is that the attempt to bring new life to the peoples of the undeveloped countries often destroys not only them but the bureaucrats and technologists themselves, who become the maimed and inhuman servants of a great impersonal machine. The second is that language and reason, the two great sources of truth and reality, become translated into the instruments of power, self-deception and unreality. The irony, which in the other works controls and profoundly modifies the poetic vision, bites deeper here, producing an astringent but still deeply compassionate view of life. And the sensitivity to language, the source of the marvellous evocations of person and place in *Cliffs of Fall* and *The Evening of the Holiday*, becomes one of the main weapons in the author's satiric armoury. What gives *People in Glass Houses* its special power is the author's perception that the debasement of language and the dehumanising of man are but different aspects of a single process. Because the cast of characters is representatively cosmopolitan and because even love affairs are moulded by the great administrative machine, no corner of life seems untouched. As in Heller's *Catch-22*, the reader is caught up in an insane world, which he soon comes to recognise as his own.

Although *The Bay of Noon* develops naturally from *The Evening of the Holiday*, it is much more of a Proustian exercise in fiction than the earlier novella. The story is simple, but the pattern of relationships is intricate and subtle. In essence it deals with the experiences of a young girl, Jenny, who is sent to act as a secretary-translator at a NATO base at Naples. In seeking to escape from a triangular affair involving her brother and her brother's wife, she finds herself enmeshed within an intricate web spun by a beautiful Italian novelist and her film producer lover. The novel seems to suggest that one escapes from one pattern of relationships only to recreate a similar pattern elsewhere. It is centrally concerned with two themes: the achievement of happiness and the search for one's true home. Jenny finds momentary happiness in her flat at Naples, where as a convalescent she looks out on the tranquil bay, but the quest remains. At the end of the novel, Jenny, now married to an English solicitor, revisits Italy, the scene of her search for happiness and quest for spiritual home. Whereas once she had expected to find the object of her pilgrimage in people and places, she has come to realize that the pilgrims of the heart must learn to take their inward bearings if they are to know the meanings of the outward journeys. Memory supplies the signposts. But which point home and which point elsewhere? Through its superbly controlled composition, *The Bay of Noon* invites the reader to bring Jenny's remembered images into final focus. For her, as for the reader, the images, so tinted by sadness and irradiated by hope, serve "not to direct, but to solace us; not to fix our positions, but show us how we came." This is a wise and beautiful novel that shows equal understanding of male pride and female need.

In Shirley Hazzard's fiction, as in the mind of one of her fictional characters, "poetry and reason meet without the customary signs of struggle." This accounts for her classic beauty of form. With exquisite delicacy and restraint, she reveals the coexistence of happiness and sorrow in love, the poignancy of misunderstanding and regret, and the consolations of memory. Through the eyes of her very different heroines, all of whom combine intellectual toughness and extreme vulnerability, she presents a world that immediately strikes the reader as both beautiful and true.

—John Colmer

---

**HEAD, Bessie.** South African (but at present stateless). Born in Pietermaritzburg, 6 July 1937. Educated at Umbilo Road High School. Married Harold Head in 1961; has one son. Teacher in primary schools in South Africa and Botswana, for four years; Journalist, Drum Publications, Johannesburg, for two years. Private and unpaid work in agriculture in Botswana. Address: P.O. Box 15, Serowe, Botswana.

PUBLICATIONS

Novels

*When Rain Clouds Gather*.   New York, Simon and Schuster, and London, Gollancz, 1968.

*Maru*.  London, Gollancz, and New York, McCall's, 1971.

Manuscript Collection: Mugar Library, Boston University.

Bessie Head comments:

I call myself—The New African. It is an extremely painful title full of sudden and disastrous changes of fortune and a sort of mental tight-rope walk with an abyss beneath. The abyss seems to be un-African and to belong to my soul. It is an almost violent urge to make gigantic moral abdications for the sake of mankind. What is African in the urge is the process of learning how to make these abdications in the face of human weakness. I do not believe African society caters for the superman. Other societies do and that is why their Gods are clothed in so much mumbo jumbo and hazy mysticism and dubious holiness. (People in India were angered by a biography about Gandhi which stated that he found celibacy extremely difficult. Gandhi was their God and presumably a superman and they did not care to examine *his* abyss, his humanity, though he clearly stated that celibacy was a mistake for him, I think in a letter to Tolstoy.)

Now, in Africa you have to be pretty clear about what you are thinking and feeling. NO ONE is going to set you up as a God. People are too human, too deep in their understanding of human nature. Therefore, my men—Makhaya and Maru—I first create majestic, with vast, straddling personalities and set them on a tightrope of my own abyss. It is always touch and go. There is really no God in Africa or a feeling of assurance that one would make it to the end of the tightrope and find eternal salvation and perfection, like Buddha, Gandhi and Jesus. The devil is equally paramount but his thought processes can be explained just as much as God's can. This means they are equals here and forced to think things over together. These themes are the basis of my preoccupations, the equality of man, the equality of God and the devil in Africa.

*       *       *

The conception of God is not at all the same in Africa as it is in Europe, though this has been hidden by the Missionaries who want everything to be in their terms. Bessie Head has an acute perception of God in the African sense. It comes through all her writing. When the old Motswana who "looked so lordly for all his tattered coat and rough cowhide shoes" says to Makhaya, the refugee hero of *When Rain Clouds Gather*: "God is everywhere about here", he knew and his author knew. Equally, she knows about people and cattle "as close to each other as breathing". Her account of Makhaya and Paulina coming to the cattle post in the Botswana drought, the vultures circling, all the cattle dead, and in the middle Paulina's little son, the cattle guard, dead too, that's something Bessie knows as well as she knows Modimo—God, who was here in Botswana before the Missions. And Bessie also knows happiness, the quick coming of the thunder-fed rain, the slow coming of love, the wide spread of the dry, golden land and the immense sky over it.

The thing is, she knows it because she has seen it and seen it again and has managed to write down exactly what it is. How did she come to write such fluent English with so ready a vocabulary? Well, some people are like that. Will she ever write about the Republic of South Africa, her life in an orphanage where, but for luck (if there is such a thing—she would probably deny it, saying it was something bigger) she would have been shoved out to work as a kitchen girl, but instead got a teacher training? Or will she move into other countries, breaking into and absorbing their secrets?

For all her perceptions of Africa are from the inside; she has never known water meadows or heather or snowy peaks, so she has no wrong comparisons. Botswana, of which she writes, is a country of secrets, but in the great sweeps of sand or bush veldt there is no place to hide, so the secrets are inside people, only to be perceived by those who can understand and guard secrets.

So far she has written two books, *When Rain Clouds Gather* and *Maru*. Both have an understandable love story and a kind of happy ending, though this is less certain in the second book, much of which is also about chieftancy towards which she, like many educated African people, has a somewhat ambivalent attitude. In some ways hers is a simple vision; it seems to Bessie that things could be clear and beautiful and—I think she would say—of God. There is no lack of hope, however painful the present; nothing need be twisted. It's all right for man and woman to fight and rape so long as they also love. This isn't the usual idea of Africa, but it seems likely that Bessie Head, who is so close to it, knows.

—Naomi Mitchison

---

**HEARNE, John.** Jamaican. Born in Montreal, Canada, 4 February 1926. Educated at Edinburgh University, 1947–49, M.A. 1949; London University, 1949–50, T.D. 1950. Served in the Royal Air Force as an Air Gunner, 1943–46. Married Joyce Veitch in 1947; Leeta Hopkinson, 1955; has two children. Teacher in London and Jamaica, 1950–59; Information Officer, Government of Jamaica, 1962; Resident Tutor, Department of Extra-Mural Studies, 1962–67, and since 1968, Head of the Creative Centre, University of the West Indies, Kingston. Visiting Fellow in Commonwealth Literature, University of Leeds, Yorkshire, 1967; O'Connor Professor in Literature, Colgate University, Hamilton, New York, 1969–70. Recipient: Rhys Memorial Prize, 1956; Institute of Jamaica's Silver Musgrave Medal, 1964. Address: c/o Creative Arts Centre, University of the West Indies, Kingston 7, Jamaica.

PUBLICATIONS

Novels

    *Voices under the Window*.   London, Faber, 1955.
    *Stranger at the Gate*.   London, Faber, 1956.
    *The Faces of Love*.   London, Faber, 1957; as *The Eye of the Storm*, Boston, Little Brown, 1958.
    *Autumn Equinox*.   London, Faber, 1959; New York, Vanguard Press, 1961.
    *Land of the Living*.   London, Faber, 1961; New York, Harper, 1962.
    *Fever Grass*, with Morris Cargill (as John Morris).   London, Collins, and New York, Putnam, 1969.
    *The Candywine Development*, with Morris Cargill (as John Morris).   London, Collins, 1970; New York, Stuart, 1971.

Uncollected Short Stories

    "A Village Tragedy", in *Atlantic* (Boston), November 1958.
    "The Wind in the Corner", in *Atlantic* (Boston), May 1960.

"At the Stelling", in *Atlantic* (Boston), November 1960.
"The Lost Country", in *Atlantic* (Boston), September 1961.


Plays

*The Golden Savage* (produced London, 1965).

Plays produced on television in England.


John Hearne comments:

My first concern has been to try to say something about the way we live now that could not be said except by the use of fiction.

When I first started to write I had the feeling that the novel and the short story are the forms that keep the individual most alive in the necessary but increasing synonymity of the industrial and post-industrial world.

Themes, as such, don't interest me much—only a gesture, made by some unsolicited person, that suddenly seizes the imagination and which must be finally explained.

Style and technique are very important, but if the gesture that comes to you when you're not looking for it really needs explanation, then you'll find the style and technique to work it out.

\*       \*       \*


John Hearne is essentially a West Indian novelist; at the same time he lies outside the main stream of the Caribbean novel. Where this has focussed characteristically on the peasant experience, Hearne has explored the predicament of the middle-class intellectual, who can be twice an exile in the largely black developing nations. In *Voices under the Window* it is Mark Lattimer, a "white" Jamaican lawyer, who has devoted himself to the people, but is cut down pointlessly by a marijuana-smoking peasant in a city riot. In *Stranger at the Gate* the hero is Roy McKenzie, again a lawyer who becomes a communist and dies ramming a police car to allow a communist ex-president of a neighbouring island to escape. In *Autumn Equinox* Jim Diver, a young American of Cuban origin, attempts to run a communist paper on a non-communist island.

These novels do not suggest political solutions; indeed the sketchy treatment of political themes only suggests their irrelevance to his real concern, which is with the difficulty and importance of individual relationships, in particular between men and women. This emerges overtly in *The Faces of Love* and his best novel to date *Land of the Living*. In the latter the love theme is related to recognisable Caribbean social issues through the involvement of Mahler, a German Jew lecturing at a Caribbean university, with Joan Culpepper, a middle-class "white", and Brysie, a "black" bar servant with paternal links with a politico-religious cult.

Hearne's third concern is with the physical experience of the Caribbean, showing a gift for description and narrative put to vivid use also in his "James Bond" type thrillers (with Morris Cargill) *Fever Grass* and *The Candywine Development*. They have helped him create a fictional world, Cayuna, an island closely resembling Jamaica. While unlikely to be placed in the small top group of Caribbean novelists, Hearne has made an individual and important contribution to the mapping of the West Indian experience.

—Louis James

583

**HEINLEIN, Robert (Anson).** American. Born in Butler, Missouri, 7 July 1907. Educated at the United States Naval Academy, Annapolis, Maryland, graduated and commissioned Ensign, 1929; University of California, Los Angeles, 1934. Served in the United States Navy, 1929 until retirement because of physical disability, 1934. Married Virginia Gerstenfeld in 1948. Full-time Writer since 1939. Recipient: Hugo Award, 1956, 1960, 1962, 1966; Boys Club of America Award, 1959; Sequoyah Book Award, 1961. Address: c/o Lurton Blassingame, 60 East 42nd Street, New York, New York 10017, U.S.A.

PUBLICATIONS

Novels

*Rocket Ship Galileo.* New York, Scribner, 1947; London, New English Library, 1971.
*Beyond This Horizon.* Reading, Pennsylvania, Fantasy Press, 1948.
*Space Cadet.* New York, Scribner, 1948; London, Gollancz, 1966.
*Red Planet.* New York, Scribner, 1949; London, Gollancz, 1963.
*Sixth Column.* New York, Gnome, 1949.
*The Farmer in the Sky.* New York, Scribner, 1950; London, Gollancz, 1962.
*Waldo and Magic, Inc.* New York, Doubleday, 1950; London, Gollancz, 1966.
*Between Planets.* New York, Scribner, 1951; London, Gollancz, 1968.
*The Puppet Masters.* New York, Doubleday, 1951; London, Museum Press, 1953.
*The Rolling Stones.* New York, Scribner, 1952; as *Space Family Stone*, London, New English Library, 1971.
*Revolt in 2100.* Chicago, Shasta, 1953; London, Gollancz, 1964.
*Starman Jones.* New York, Scribner, 1953; London, Sidgwick and Jackson, 1954.
*The Star Beast.* New York, Scribner, 1954; London, New English Library, 1971.
*Tunnel in the Sky.* New York, Scribner, 1955; London, Gollancz, 1965.
*Double Star.* New York, Doubleday, 1956; London, Joseph, 1958.
*Time for the Stars.* New York, Scribner, 1956; London, Gollancz, 1958.
*Citizen of the Galaxy.* New York, Scribner, 1957; London, Gollancz, 1969.
*The Door into Summer.* New York, Doubleday, 1957; London, Gollancz, 1967.
*Have Space Suit—Will Travel.* New York, Scribner, 1958; London, Gollancz, 1970.
*Methuselah's Children.* New York, Gnome, 1958; London, Gollancz, 1963.
*Starship Troopers.* New York, Putnam, 1959; London, Four Square, 1961.
*Stranger in a Strange Land.* New York, Putnam, 1961; London, New English Library, 1965.
*Glory Road.* New York, Putnam, 1963; London, Four Square, 1965.
*Podkayne of Mars: Her Life and Times.* New York, Putnam, 1963; London, New English Library, 1969.
*Orphans of the Sky.* London, Gollancz, 1963; New York, Putnam, 1964.
*Farnham's Freehold.* New York, Putnam, 1964; London, Dobson, 1965.
*The Moon Is a Harsh Mistress.* New York, Putnam, 1966; London, Dobson, 1967.
*A Robert Heinlein Omnibus.* London, Sidgwick and Jackson, 1966; as *Three by Heinlein*, New York, Doubleday, 1966.
*A Heinlein Triad.* London, Gollancz, 1967.
*I Will Fear No Evil.* New York, Putnam, 1970; London, New English Library, 1971.

Short Stories

*The Man Who Sold the Moon.* Chicago, Shasta, 1950; London, Sidgwick and Jackson, 1953.

*The Green Hills of Earth.*  Chicago, Shasta, 1951; London, Sidgwick and Jackson, 1954.
*Assignment in Eternity.*  Reading, Pennsylvania, Fantasy Press, 1953; London, Museum Press, 1955.
*The Menace from Earth.*  New York, Gnome, 1959; London, Dobson, 1966.
*The Unpleasant Profession of Jonathan Hoag.*  New York, Gnome, 1959; London, Dobson, 1964.
*The Worlds of Robert A. Heinlein.*  New York, Ace, 1966; London, New English Library, 1970.
*The Past Through Tomorrow: Future History Stories.*  New York, Putnam, 1967.

Plays

Screenplays: *Destination Moon*, 1950; *Project Moonbase*, 1953.

Other

*Of Worlds Beyond: The Science of Science Fiction Writing*, with others.  Reading, Pennsylvania, Fantasy Press, 1947; London, Dobson, 1967.
*The Science Fiction Novel*, with others.  Chicago, Advent, 1959.

Editor, *Tomorrow, The Stars: A Science Fiction Anthology*.  New York, Doubleday, 1952.

Manuscript Collection: University of California Library, Santa Cruz.

Critical Studies: chapter 11 of *Seekers of Tomorrow* by Sam Moskowitz, Cleveland, World, 1966; "Master Craftsman of SF" by Peter R. Weston, in *Books and Bookmen* (London), October 1969.

Robert Heinlein comments:

I got into writing because I was unexpectedly disabled and retired from my chosen profession, the Navy. Like many others in precarious health I turned to what I was physically able to do. Writing is, and has been for thirty years, my only profession and my livelihood. But I have never devoted as much as half my time to it: Mrs. Heinlein and I have traveled much of the time—three times around the world and about 80 countries, in long, leisurely trips. (I have a smattering of several languages; she speaks eight—no, she's not a linguist, she's a chemist and engineer—and a Fellow of the British Royal Horticulturist Society; she experiments in plant genetics.) I am a member of many scientific, engineering, and military associations, plus the Authors League of America, but am not very active in them, as we prefer a quiet life and avoid publicity as much as we can. We are country people, living 15 miles from the nearest town, almost 100 miles from a city. My study faces the Pacific Ocean, past a heated pool and through some of my wife's gardens—I don't work very hard when the weather is good; life is too short and too sweet.

My stories have been mostly speculations about the future and what mankind may make of it. I am hopelessly old-fashioned in many of my opinions and this annoys some people. My writing has been strongly affected by Rudyard Kipling, Winston Churchill, H. G. Wells, et al. My interests and hobbies are catholic, ranging from stone masonry, cats, sculpture, ballistics, fiscal theory, figure skating, to figure drawing. I enjoy life and believe that Man will live forever and spread out through the universe.

*     *     *

At any one time there have never been more than a dozen or so writers working at the very core of the science fiction field, a handful of innovators who to greater or lesser extent influence all other practitioners. It is a measure of Robert Heinlein's success that he has been among—if not led—this select band, almost since the publication of his first story in 1939.

"Innovator" is the key word if we wish to measure Heinlein's contributions to science fiction writing. His innovations have been in ideas, in storytelling techniques, but most importantly of all in *attitudes*. In this respect he is responsible more than any other for establishing the methods and traditions of modern science fiction.

To fully understand his achievement we must look at science fiction as it was, an ingrown species of category fiction confined almost entirely to the American pulp magazines. The vitality and literacy of earlier pioneers such as Wells had been lost, and science fiction was, quite simply, fiction *about* science, with the occasional space operatics for good measure.

Heinlein picked up the field and shook it until it rattled. By his example he changed that definition to mean instead "fiction written according to the scientific method", and there is a vast difference between the two. Almost for the first time there began to appear stories in which the Scientific Marvel was a beginning rather than an end in itself.

Once this bridge had been crossed science fiction could take a large stride towards maturity, and others besides Heinlein started to stress characterisation and the treatment of human responses to new situations. In the three years between 1939 and 1942 Heinlein himself wrote 22 stories for the leading magazine, *Astounding*, including most of his "Future History" series and three major novels, *Sixth Column*, *Beyond This Horizon*, and *Methuselah's Children*.

After the Second World War, Heinlein began to write stories which concentrated even more upon human values rather than on science for science's sake. Quite deliberately he was writing to "make the American public think about the future", and the medium he chose was the *Saturday Evening Post*. Stories such as "Columbus Was a Dope" and "It's Great to Be Back" are beautifully written, and the series is available in the collection *The Green Hills of Earth*.

At this time he also commenced his famous "juvenile" series, which was to eventually amount to thirteen novels in thirteen years. Here again the aim was similar; to "educate" the growing generation, and with the exception of two or three titles this series has tremendous appeal to all ages. Several, such as *Have Space Suit—Will Travel* and *Citizen of the Galaxy* were initially published in adult magazines.

During the 1950's Heinlein produced comparatively few short stories and only four adult novels, of which three—*The Puppet Masters*, *Double Star*, and *The Door into Summer*—may prove to be among his most well-rounded work. The fourth, *Starship Troopers*, marked the beginning of Heinlein's final period.

This and the five subsequent long novels (*Stranger in a Strange Land*, *Glory Road*, *Farnham's Freehold*, *The Moon Is a Harsh Mistress*, *I Will Fear No Evil*) have provoked more comment than any of Heinlein's earlier work. In each case the novels have tackled controversial themes, and although they may show some flaws in construction they have displayed great inventiveness and narrative power.

In the final analysis these are the two reasons why Robert Heinlein has dominated the entire field of science fiction for so long. He has combined a storytelling power that is compulsive with a brilliant and disciplined imagination.

—Peter R. Weston

**HELLER, Joseph.**  American.  Born in Brooklyn, New York, 1 May 1923. Educated at New York University, B.A. 1948; Columbia University, New York, M.A. 1949; Oxford University (Fulbright Scholar), 1949–50. Served in the United States Army Air Force in World War II. Married Shirley Held in 1945; has two children. Instructor in English, Pennsylvania State University, University Park, 1950–52. Advertising Writer, *Time* magazine, New York, 1952–56, *Look* magazine, New York, 1956–58; Promotion Manager, *McCall's* magazine, New York, 1958–61. Recipient: National Institute of Arts and Letters grant, 1963. Address: c/o Simon and Schuster, 630 Fifth Avenue, New York, New York 10020, U.S.A.

PUBLICATIONS

Novels

   *Catch-22.*   New York, Simon and Schuster, 1961; London, Cape, 1962.
   *Something Happened.*   New York, Knopf, 1972.

Plays

   *We Bombed in New Haven* (produced New York, 1967; London, 1971).   New York,
      Knopf, 1968; London, Cape, 1969.
   *Catch-22.*   New York, French, 1971.

Critical Study: "The Sanity of *Catch-22*" by Robert Protherough, in *The Human World* (Swansea), May 1971.

*          *          *

   The Chaplain is an Anabaptist; the officers, from General Scheisskopf down through Colonel Korn, Colonel Cathcart, and Major Major are insane; the hero, Yossarian (who is an Assyrian) is convinced, quite properly, that everyone in the war, friend or enemy, is trying to kill him, and he wants only to go home. No matter how many missions he flies as a bombardier, each time the squadron loses another man, the number of missions required for home leave is raised: thirty-two, forty, fifty-four, seventy. On a mission over Avignon (to bomb the bridge), Snowden bleeds to death on Yossarian's flying suit. Yossarian refuses to wear clothes for days thereafter, creating difficulty for the General who promotes him to Captain and wants to pin a medal on him.
   We are in the world of Joseph Heller's *Catch-22*, one that may occasionally resemble the world of Hašek's *Good Soldier Schweik*, of E. E. Cummings' *The Enormous Room*, or of Evelyn Waugh's *Black Mischief*, those other satires on modern warfare. Any resemblances to his forebears are superficial, however; Heller is an original. He succeeds in that most difficult of literary tasks: to write about war encompassingly, yet without plodding, without naturalistic trappings, and with utter conviction. Heller's method is to juxtapose farce with realistic aerial carnage, elegance of style with military obscenity, vacuous military ideology with low cunning. He is vigorous, inventive, and lengthy. The length is functional, for as one reads on, the line between satire and actuality thins to the point of disappearance. The novel, which deals in nightmares, becomes itself a nightmare, and Joseph Heller may loom in the mind like a Jewish Jonathan Swift.
   Doubt may intrude about Heller's classical stature, however. A literary and literate

writer, Heller's manner has seemed to the unwary to be non-literate and no more than scornful. His impact, particularly upon the young in the decade after publication of his novel in 1961, has been profound. His apparent nihilism, comic, horrifying, has set a pattern of behaviour and a pattern in prose fiction. Undergraduates without exception read Heller even though they may read no other writer. His view of World War II appears to many to have been vindicated by American participation in the war in Indo-China. Heller's idiom has penetrated almost all fiction about the Vietnamese war written in America, while so gifted a writer as Thomas McGuane shows Heller's influence in satire about the homeland.

In ten years, Heller's only other substantial work is a failed play, *We Bombed in New Haven*, which looked rather like self-parody. Given the originality and vitality of *Catch-22*, one can only passionately hope that Heller is not a victim of the American mania for success, that the effort to make even more money and a grander film from a potential second novel has not choked off his powers. The gift of prophecy is rare; Heller most certainly had it in *Catch-22*, just as fully as T. S. Eliot had it in *The Waste Land*. The fact that one reaches out for parallels to figures so different as Swift and Eliot is sufficient evidence that Heller's harrowing first novel was more than black humor become fashionable, more than mere sociological insight.

—John McCormick

---

**HEPPENSTALL, Rayner.** British. Born in Huddersfield, Yorkshire, 27 July 1911. Educated locally and at the Collège Sophie-Berthelot, Calais, France, 1928; University of Leeds, Yorkshire, 1929–33, B.A. 1932; University of Strasbourg, France, 1931. Served in the Royal Artillery and the Royal Army Pay Corps, 1940–45. Married Margaret Edwards in 1937; has two children. Schoolmaster, Eastbrook Senior Boys' School, Dagenham, Essex, 1934; Free-lance Writer, 1935–39. Producer, Features and Drama Department, BBC Radio, London, 1945–67. Since 1968, Member of the Executive Committee of International P.E.N., English Centre. Recipient: Arts Council Novel Prize, 1966, and grant, 1969, 1971. Address: 14c Ladbroke Terrace, London W.11, England.

PUBLICATIONS

Novels

*The Blaze of Noon.* London, Secker and Warburg, and Chicago, Alliance Book Company, 1939.
*Saturnine.* London, Secker and Warburg, 1943; revised and extended version, as *The Greater Infortune*, London, Peter Owen, 1960.
*The Lesser Infortune.* London, Cape, 1953.
*The Connecting Door.* London, Barrie and Rockliff, 1962.
*The Woodshed.* London, Barrie and Rockliff, 1962.
*The Shearers.* London, Hamish Hamilton, 1969.

Uncollected Short Story

"The Wild Man of the Woods", in *Penguin New Writing*. London, Penguin, 1944.

Plays

The Fool's Saga, in Three Tales of Hamlet, with Michael Innes.   London, Gollancz,
1950.

Has written and translated plays performed on radio.

Verse

First Poems.   London, Heinemann, 1935.
Sebastian.   London, Dent, 1937.
Blind Men's Flowers Are Green.   London, Secker and Warburg, 1940.
Poems 1933–1945.   London, Secker and Warburg, 1947.

Other

Apology for Dancing (ballet criticism).   London, Faber, 1936.
Léon Bloy.   Cambridge, Bowes, and New Haven, Connecticut, Yale University Press,
1954.
Four Absentees (memoirs).   London, Barrie and Rockliff, 1960.
The Fourfold Tradition (criticism).   London, Barrie and Rockliff, and New York,
New Directions, 1961.
The Intellectual Part (memoirs).   London, Barrie and Rockliff, 1963.
Raymond Roussel.   London, Calder and Boyars, and Berkeley, University of California
Press, 1966.
Portrait of the Artist as a Professional Man (memoirs).   London, Peter Owen, 1969.
A Little Pattern of French Crime.   London, Hamish Hamilton, 1969.
French Crime in the Romantic Age.   London, Hamish Hamilton, 1970.
Bluebeard and After.   London, Peter Owen, 1972.
The Sex War and Others.   London, Peter Owen, 1972.

Editor, Existentialism, by Guido de Ruggiero.   London, Secker and Warburg, 1947;
New York, Social Science Publishers, 1948.
Editor, Imaginary Conversations (radio scripts).   London, Secker and Warburg, 1948.

Translator, Atala and René, by F. R. de Chateaubriand.   London, Oxford University
Press, 1963.
Translator, with Lindy Foord, Impressions of Africa, by Raymond Roussel.   London,
Calder and Boyars, and Berkeley, University of California Press, 1966.
Translator, A Harlot High and Low, by Honoré de Balzac.   London, Penguin, 1970.
Translator, When Justice Falters, by René Floriot.   London, Harrap, 1971.

Critical Studies: "Il Padre del Nouveau Roman" by Giacomo Antonini, in La Fiera Letteraria
(Milan), April 1962; "Rayner Heppenstall and the Nouveau Roman" by Sylvère Monod,
in Imagined Worlds, London, Methuen, 1968.

Rayner Heppenstall comments:

A notion I had when embarking on The Blaze of Noon was that the novel should not
attempt to do anything which the cinema can do better or more easily. That its story should

be inward and lyrical (hence also, I dare say, the blind-man narrator). Until *The Shearers*, this was nevertheless the least autobiographical of my novels. The manner of telling remains, with me, more important than the thing told. I am conscious that the "sincerest" novels are packs of lies, and in general I prefer those which are openly artificial—*e.g.*, detective stories and P. G. Wodehouse. I was at once attracted by the "anti-novels" of Alain Robbe-Grillet, who did boldly what I had been doing timidly, but I am equally attracted by the unplanned, day-by-day intimate truthfulness of Marcel Jouhandeau. *The Connecting Door* and *The Woodshed* lie somewhere between the two. In *The Shearers*, I accepted a challenge: that presented by a French murder trial which seemed unthinkable in England. I therefore transplanted the story to England and tried the case before an imaginary English court of assize. But of course something personal must shine through all artifice, and I know I am really writing about (or expressing) myself. A difficult thing to do: we are all largely fictitious, even to ourselves.

*     *     *

Rayner Heppenstall is a writer of irritable descriptions that nag at the reader's attention. He has published verse and autobiography, but his eccentric gifts seem best suited by the more fluid forms of the novel—always allowing that in the kind of novel favoured by him the sense of flow is largely illusory, its movement all on the surface. His work is fabricated, clever, elaborately underpinned. It is worth noting that he is one of the few English critics who have seen the joke in the jokes of Raymond Roussel (1877–1933), that little master of verbal procedures who wrote stories in order to link up a series of previously chosen words, or to turn certain sentences inside out, ingeniously punning on the pun of existence. Heppenstall is more human and approachable than this French technician—to whom he has devoted an interesting little critical study—but he shares his penchant for teasing admixtures of the bizarre and the banal, delighting in effects that make fiction read like fact and fact like fiction.

This was not so evident in his first novel, *The Blaze of Noon*, told in the first person by a blind man who is a masseur, a celebration of physical love which has the virtues of simplicity and directness. Heppenstall has admitted to one distinct literary influence on this book—that of Henry de Montherlant, the Montherlant of the Pierre Costals sequence and of *Le Paradis à l'Ombre des Epées*. While disclaiming any role as a literary theorist, he has also admitted to having at that stage "a theoretical notion that the cinema had taken over the story-telling functions of the exteriorised novel" which led him to believe that "prose narrative would do well to become more lyrical, more inward". Lyricism and inwardness were pursued in *Saturnine* (revised as *The Greater Infortune*) and in *The Lesser Infortune*, but unassimilated autobiographical elements disfigure these books and it was not until 1962, with the publication of *The Connecting Door* and *The Woodshed*, that Heppenstall's experiments with the form of the novel began to assume the character now associated with him. His prose, still lyrical enough when occasion demanded, had grown leaner. The inwardness had not been lost either, but it now found a more satisfactory expression in narrative complexity rather than mere self-colloquy. At first sight, this was not immediately apparent, especially in the opening sections of *The Woodshed*, where the narrator, Harold Atha, sitting in a third-class railway-carriage crossing Wales after being summoned home from a holiday at a Welsh seaside village by an enigmatic telegram, observes that in a train one's consciousness streams like a cold:

> If I had a secretary sitting opposite with shorthand notebook, or a dictaphone, I could just talk like this. They reckon about ten thousand words to the hour. In a journey of eight hours, you could finish a book. Change the names, and you'd have a stream-of-consciousness novel. A man travelling somewhere for a purpose. What had led up to it, hopes and fears, retrospect and apprehension mingling, things noted

as the landscape slid by. At the end, some kind of pay-off. The fears were groundless, the person was not there or had changed his mind, some accident took place, the person or place no longer existed. Had just died perhaps.

Atha's musings constitute quite a fair description of the first part of *The Woodshed*, and Heppenstall's technique at this point does still resemble a runny-nosed stream of consciousness. Atha's journey back across England to the Yorkshire town in which he spent his youth, and back across the years to the events of that youth, quickly becomes of more significance in his author's handling of it, however, so *critical* is Heppenstall's attitude to the process of consciousness, so shaped by an awareness of that process as something uncertain, incoherently changing, existing at different times in differing degrees, moving at varying speeds on variable levels, occurring as it were in fits and starts and flashes, and kept in check only by man's capacity for remembering. "If consciousness streams, it is backward. Or, rather, it is like the slack tide in an estuary," says Atha, on the last page of the book. Roussel's other disciple, Alain Robbe-Grillet, stands behind some of the experiment in *The Woodshed* and *The Connecting Door*, particularly in the matter of monotonous description of objects, but on the whole these two books revealed Heppenstall as an original and skilful writer, rather more adventurous than most of his contemporaries in pursuit of a way of organising experience around what Henry James once called "just perceptible presences and general looming possibilities".

That pursuit has been continued in *The Shearers*, only here the pace is quickened by a sly sense of humour which extends to the very title—for a Shearer family might well be supposed to have their station somewhere between an Archer and a Dale, and in effect Heppenstall is taking something like a popular long-running radio myth, the idea of the knockabout variousness of the all-embracing family, as his basic point of reference. The piece could well have been subtitled "An everyday story of murdering folk", for at the moment when we meet them the Shearer family, or eight members of it, are on trial for murder. What is more, they stand accused of having murdered their own grandmothers in a manner that might engage the interest of the cruder Sunday newspapers, and their home background, as it emerges from the trial, includes other cherished habits, such as compound interest, that we all like to imagine among our neighbours. The Shearers, it is said, are no ordinary family. This is rubbish. They are as ordinary as the Earwickers.

Heppenstall's trick here is to put his story down as flatly as he can, but as he has an educated ear this is still agreeably bumpy. He contrives to tell us how the Shearer crime appeared in the newspapers, placing it within a natural catalogue of other disasters, and what Harold Wilson thought of it (not much) over a breakfast of HP sauce on toast and marmalade. Everything about this barbarous tribe is rigorously reduced to cliché, although towards the end a little religion seeps in—perhaps for the sake of cliché too? The impression the book leaves is of a fascinating patchwork of credible elements, with a horror at the heart of it. The gap between the judicial view and the mumblings of the Shearers themselves could be construed as pitiful, but pity seems removed from what this author is after.

—Robert Nye

---

**HERBERT, A(lan) P(atrick).** British. Born in Ashtead, Surrey, 24 September 1890. Educated at Winchester School, Hampshire (Exhibitioner); New College, Oxford (Exhibitioner), 1st class degree in jurisprudence 1914; called to the Bar, Inner Temple, London, 1918, but never practised. Served with the Royal Naval Division in Gallipoli and France, 1914–17; Petty Officer, Naval Auxiliary Patrol, 1939–45. Married Gwendolyn Quilter in 1914; has four children. Since 1910, Contributor, and since 1924, Member of the Staff,

*Punch* magazine, London. Formerly, Private Secretary to Sir Leslie Scott. Independent Member of Parliament for Oxford University, 1935 until university seats were abolished, 1950; introduced the Matrimonial Causes Act, 1937. A Thames Conservator, 1940; Trustee, National Maritime Museum, 1947–53. President, English Association, 1950, and Society of Authors, 1967. President, Inland Waterways Association; Chairman, British Copyright Council. D.L., Queen's University, Kingston, Ontario, 1957; D.C.L., Oxford University, 1958. Knighted, 1945. Companion of Honour, 1970. Address: 12 Hammersmith Terrace, London W.6, England. *Died 11 November 1971.*

PUBLICATIONS

Novels

> *The Secret Battle.* London, Methuen, 1919; New York, Knopf, 1920.
> *The House by the River.* London, Methuen, 1920; New York, Knopf, 1921.
> *The Old Flame.* London, Methuen, and New York, Doubleday, 1925.
> *The Trials of Topsy.* London, Unwin, 1928.
> *Topsy, M.P.* London, Benn, 1929; as *Topsy*, New York, Doubleday, 1930.
> *The Water Gipsies.* London, Methuen, and New York, Doubleday, 1930.
> *Holy Deadlock.* London, Methuen, and New York, Doubleday, 1934.
> *Topsy Turvy.* London, Benn, 1947.
> *Number Nine; or, The Mind-Sweepers.* London, Methuen, 1951; New York, Doubleday, 1952.
> *Why Waterloo?* London, Methuen, 1952; New York, Doubleday, 1953.
> *Made for Man.* London, Methuen, and New York, Doubleday, 1958.
> *The Singing Swan: A Yachtsman's Yarn.* London, Methuen, 1968.

Plays

> *Double Demon,* in *Four One-Act Plays,* with others. Oxford, Blackwell, 1923; as *Double Demon and Other One-Act Plays,* New York, Appleton, 1924.
> *The Blue Peter,* music by Armstrong Gibbs (produced London, 1924).
> *King of the Castle,* music by Dennis Arundel (produced Liverpool, 1924).
> *At the Same Time* (produced London, 1925).
> *The White Witch* (produced London, 1926).
> *Riverside Nights: An Entertainment,* with Nigel Playfair (produced London, 1926). London, Unwin, 1926.
> *The Policeman's Serenade,* music by Alfred Reynolds. London, Chappell, 1926.
> *Fat King Melon and Princess Caraway.* London, Humphrey Milford, 1927.
> *Two Gentlemen of Soho* (produced Liverpool, 1927; London, 1928). London, French, 1928.
> *Plain Jane; or, The Wedding Breakfast,* music by Richard Austin (produced Croydon, Surrey, 1927; London, 1928). London, French, 1929.
> *La Vie Parisienne: A Comic Opera,* music by A. Davies Adams, adaptation of a work by Offenbach (produced London, 1929). London, Benn, 1929.
> *Tantivy Towers: A Light Opera,* music by Thomas Dunhill (produced London, 1931). London, Methuen, and New York, Doubleday, 1931.
> *Derby Day: A Comic Opera,* music by Alfred Reynolds (produced London, 1932). London, Methuen, 1931.
> *Helen: A Comic Opera,* music by E. W. Korngold, adaptation of a work by Henri Meilhac and Ludovic Halévy (produced London, 1932). London, Chappell-Methuen, 1932.

*Mother of Pearl*, adaptation of a play by Alfred Grunwald, after Verneuil (produced London, 1933).

*Streamline*, with Ronald Jeans, music by Vivian Ellis (produced London, 1934).

*Perseverance*, music by Vivian Ellis.  London, Chappell, 1934.

*Home and Beauty* (produced London, 1937).

*Paganini*, with Reginald Arkell, adaptation of a play by Paul Knepler and Bela Jenbach (produced London, 1937).

*Big Ben*, music by Vivian Ellis (produced London, 1946).  London, Methuen, 1946.

*Bless the Bride*, music by Vivian Ellis (produced London, 1947).  London, French, 1947.

*Tough at the Top*, music by Vivian Ellis (produced London, 1949).

*Come to the Ball; or, Harlequin*, with Reginald Arkell, adaptation of a work by Johann Strauss.  London, Benn, 1951.

*The Water Gipsies*, music by Vivian Ellis (produced London, 1951).  London, Chappell, 1957.

*Better Dead* (produced Richmond, Surrey, 1962).

## Verse

*Poor Poems and Rotten Rhymes*.  Winchester, Wells, 1910.

*Play Hours with Pegasus*.  Oxford, Blackwell, 1912.

*Half Hours at Helles*.  Oxford, Blackwell, 1916.

*The Bomber Gipsy and Other Poems*.  London, Methuen, 1918; revised edition, 1919.

*The Wherefore and the Why: Some New Rhymes for Old Children*.  London, Methuen, 1921.

*"Tinker, Tailor": A Child's Guide to the Professions*.  London, Methuen, 1922; New York, Doubleday, 1923.

*Laughing Ann and Other Poems*.  London, Unwin, 1925; New York, Doubleday, 1926.

*She-Shanties*.  London, Unwin, 1926; New York, Doubleday, 1927.

*Plain Jane*.  London, Unwin, and New York, Doubleday, 1927.

*Ballads for Broadbrows*.  London, Benn, 1930; New York, Doubleday, 1931.

*A Book of Ballads: Being the Collected Light Verse of A. P. Herbert*.  London, Benn, 1931; revised edition, 1948.

*Siren Song*.  London, Methuen, 1940; New York, Doubleday, 1941.

*Let Us Be Glum*.  London, Methuen, 1941.

*Bring Back the Bells*.  London, Methuen, 1943.

*A. T. I.: There Is No Cause for Alarm*.  London, Ornum Press, 1944.

*"Less Nonsense"*.  London, Methuen, 1944.

*Light the Lights*.  London, Methuen, 1945.

*"Full Enjoyment" and Other Versus*.  London, Methuen, 1952.

*Silver Stream: A Beautiful Tale of Hare and Hound for Young and Old*.  London, Methuen, 1962.

## Other

*Light Articles Only*.  London, Methuen, 1921; as *Little Rays of Sunshine*, New York, Knopf, 1921.

*The Man about Town*.  London, Heinemann, 1923.

*Misleading Cases in the Common Law*.  London, Methuen, 1927; New York, Putnam, 1930.

*Honeybubble and Co*.  London, Methuen, 1928.

*More Misleading Cases*.  London, Methuen, 1930.

*"No Boats on the River"*.  London, Methuen, 1932.

*Still More Misleading Cases.*   London, Methuen, 1933.

*A. P. Herbert,* selected by E. V. Knox.   London, Methuen, 1933.

*Mr. Pewter* (broadcast talks).   London, Methuen, 1934.

*Uncommon Law.*   London, Methuen, 1935; New York, Doubleday, 1936; revised edition, Methuen, 1969.

*What a Word! Being an Account of the Principles and Progress of "The Word War" Conducted in "Punch" to the Great Improvement and Delight of the People, and the Lasting Benefit of the King's English, with Many Ingenious Exercises and Horrible Examples.*   London, Methuen, 1935; New York, Doubleday, 1936.

*Mild and Bitter.*   London, Methuen, 1936; New York, Doubleday, 1937.

*Sip! Swallow!*   London, Methuen, 1937; New York, Doubleday, 1938.

*The Ayes Have It: The Story of the Marriage Bill.*   London, Methuen, 1937; New York, Doubleday, 1938.

*General Cargo.*   London, Methuen, 1939; New York, Doubleday, 1940.

*Let There Be Liberty.*   London, Macmillan, 1940.

*"Well, Anyhow"; or, Little Talks.*   London, Methuen, 1942.

*A Better Sky; or, Name This Star.*   London, Methuen, 1944.

*The War Story of Southend Pier.*   Southend, Essex, Southend-on-Sea Corporation, 1945.

*The Point of Parliament* (juvenile).   London, Methuen, 1946.

*Mr. Gay's London: With Extracts from the Proceedings at the Sessions of the Peace and Oyer and Terminer for the City of London and the County of Middlesex in the Years 1732 and 1733.*   London, Benn, 1948.

*Leave My Old Morale Alone.*   New York, Doubleday, 1948.

*Independent Member* (autobiography).   London, Methuen, 1950; New York, Doubleday, 1951.

*Codd's Last Case and Other Misleading Cases.*   London, Methuen, 1952.

*Pools Pilot; or, Why Not You?*   London, Methuen, 1953.

*The Right to Marry.*   London, Methuen, 1954.

*"No Fine on Fun": The Comical History of the Entertainments Duty.*   London, Methuen, 1957.

*Anything But Action: A Study of the Uses and Abuses of Committees of Inquiry.*   London, Barrie and Rockliff, 1960.

*"Public Lending Rights": Authors, Publishers and Libraries.*   London, Society of Authors, 1960.

*Look Back and Laugh.*   London, Methuen, 1960.

*Libraries: Free for All?*   London, Institute of Economic Affairs, 1962.

*Bardot, M.P.? And Other Modern Misleading Cases.*   London, Methuen, 1964; New York, Doubleday, 1965.

*The Thames.*   London, Weidenfeld and Nicolson, 1966.

*Wigs at Work: Selected Cases.*   London, Penguin, 1966.

*Sundials Old and New; or, Fun with the Sun.*   London, Methuen, 1967.

*In the Dark.*   London, Bodley Head, 1970.

*A.P.H.: His Life and Times* (autobiography).   London, Heinemann, 1970.

Editor, *Watch This Space (Six Years of It): An Anthology of Space (Fact), 4 October 1957–4 October 1963.*   London, Methuen, 1964.

Bibliography: *The First Editions of A. E. Coppard, A. P. Herbert, and Charles Morgan* by Gilbert H. Fabes, London, Myers, 1933.

*     *     *

At a first glance, the most striking characteristic of A. P. Herbert's literary talent is its versatility. He has been poet, novelist, and satirist; the writer of light verse for *Punch* and jovial accounts of life on boats and barges and in pubs; and the ridiculer of anomalies in the Law. Versatility, however, is not the whole story. Herbert is fundamentally a serious critic of any form of injustice, an ardent lover of liberty, and a believer in the values of simplicity and truthfulness.

He is strong on the subject of the Old School Tie, true symbol of loyalty to one's School, one's University, one's Country, and one's Faith. This is because he was educated at Winchester and Oxford, because during the First World War he endured the horrors of infantry fighting in both Gallipoli and France, and because he has found by experience that integrity is the first of social virtues. These experiences have matured a naturally sensitive temperament to which the infliction of pain and disgrace is abhorrent.

His love of boats and the camaraderie of those who frequent the waterways and local inns of England has been constant; while positive legal training (although he never practised at the Bar), coupled with several years as an independent Member of Parliament, have given him great insight into the processes by which men and women are affected, and sometimes ruined, by the incapacity of others to understand finer natures than their own. He sees that, as Pope remarked, "Man's inhumanity to Man makes countless thousands mourn."

Herbert's first novel, *The Secret Battle*, illustrates this point. It shows how the stupidity of conventional soldiers, persuaded by the misrepresentations of a blackguard, leads to the disgrace of a heroic but highly-strung officer who has always distrusted his own courage. The stresses of warfare are brought right into one's heart; and the character of the victim of military regulations is so subtly demonstrated that in reading the book one is deeply stirred by the sense of tragedy.

In contrast, *The Water Gipsies* has the charm of a fairy story. It roves with Dickensian breadth through the lives of watermen and bargees, laughs at the foibles of modern artists, would-be winners of fortunes on the racecourse, and *cliché*-ridden young Socialists obsessed by the Class War. *The Water Gipsies* is not sentimental; nothing, even the dangerous simplicities of the heroine, an ignorant young girl, is falsified. Fancy and mockery are always in close touch with caustic intelligence. The book is delightful.

Later satires, such as the many volumes of *Misleading Cases in the Common Law*, have been still more caustic; and *Holy Deadlock* revealed the author's determination to bring about the revision of our Marriage Laws. It is in such work that the fundamental gravity of Herbert's approach is clearest. He would teach, as well as amuse; and if this gravity constrains his sense of fun it brings him expressly into line with those great British writers of the past whose zeal for righteousness has strongly and beneficially influenced the national thought.

—Frank Swinnerton

---

**HERBERT, (Alfred Francis) Xavier.** Australian. Born in Geraldton, Western Australia, 15 May 1901. Educated at Western Australia state schools; Christian Brothers College, Fremantle; Technical College, Perth; University of Melbourne, Diploma of Pharmacy. Served in the Australian Imperial Forces in the Pacific, 1942–44. Began career as a hospital pharmacist; has also worked as a deep-sea diver, sailor, miner and stock rider. Superintendent of Aborigines, Darwin, 1935–36. Recipient: Australian Literary Society's Gold Medal, 1939. Address: Redlynch, via Cairns, Queensland 4870, Australia.

PUBLICATIONS

Novels

> *Capricornia.*  Sydney, Publicist, 1937; London, Rich and Cowan, 1939; New York, Appleton Century, 1943.
> *Seven Emus.*  Sydney and London, Angus and Robertson, 1959.
> *Soldiers' Women.*  Sydney, Angus and Robertson, 1961; London, Angus and Robertson, 1962.

Short Stories

> *Larger Than Life: Twenty Short Stories.*  Sydney, Angus and Robertson, 1963; London, Angus and Robertson, 1964.

Other

> *Disturbing Element* (autobiography).  Melbourne, Cheshire, and London, Angus and Robertson, 1963.

Xavier Herbert comments:

All the work I've done so far will become irrelevant with publication of my latest and final *Poor Fellow My Country.*  I'm not a professional writer. I mean I've never done it as a means of livelihood, although I have long made a living from it. My aim has been, through my literary work, to discover whatever is possible of the reality of my own existence . . . and self-discovery means discovery of the world. I work all night and all day at it, away in the bush. I don't give a damn what people think about my work . . . never have, never will.

\*          \*          \*

Impelled by his comic vision of the futility of rational life in an apparently anarchic universe, Xavier Herbert has endowed northern Australia with an allegorical significance rare in Australian fiction. *Capricornia,* his major achievement and the finest Australian novel of the 1930s, chronicles settlement during the first three decades of the twentieth century with exuberant satire. Ostensibly a bitterly ironic indictment of racialism among the Aboriginal and mixed communities strung out along the Northern Territory's railway, its sprawling structure embraces and excoriates the pretensions of the émigré whites, the injustice of their law, the hypocrisies of religion, and the paternalism of government. But above all, for the whole Dickensian range of characters who are exiles in their own land, the indifferent environment emerges as a moral analogue for their simultaneous freedom and entrapment; the unpredictably recurrent cycles of Wet and Dry seasons reinforce the violent death, economic collapse and motiveless malignity which conclude each incident of the episodic irony patterning the novel.

In *Seven Emus,* the tale of an anthropologist who attempts to steal a sacred rock carving from a quarter-caste station owner, Herbert expands the role of the mild picaro figure dominating his later short stories. The twenty stories collected as *Larger Than Life* confirm his abilities in capturing Australian idiom and character types, especially the archetypal Australian *pharmakos,* the scapegoat who is both imposter-victim and self-deprecatingly triumphant ironic hero. Now part of an authentic community in the sub-tropics whose mores (more often than not those of the Aboriginals) are violated, Herbert's scapegoats are consistently victims of their sexual impulses: the theme of both his autobiographical fragment *Disturbing Element* and his last novel, *Soldiers' Women*. Herbert's conviction that man's fatal weakness is his inability to deal with his primal fate, sexual desire, together with his eccentric views on the creative necessity for sublimation, permeates *Soldiers' Women*, a compendium of aberrations in a war-time Sydney deprived of its husbands and lovers and flooded with American intruders. The collective moral restraint removed by the disturbing element of war is replaced by the determinism of individual feminine sexuality, turning young teenagers into murderers, middle-class matrons into whores, and aging matriarchs into avenging dieties. Freedom, then, becomes an alternating current between genetic "ripeness" and the serpent's head of the abortionist's curette.

Herbert has claimed that he is necessarily a "Romantic Liar", and although much of his later work seems to imply a perversely individualistic naturalism, his fiction is increasingly coming to be recognised as a substantial challenge to the conventions of realism in Australian fiction. While his reputation as an ironic satirist is securely based on *Capricornia* and several of his short stories, *Soldiers' Women*, for instance, is clearly a psychological complement to *Capricornia*. Moral disaster is inevitable, yet his scapegoats manage to retain their tottering integrity despite themselves.

—Bruce Nesbitt

---

**HERLIHY, James Leo.** American. Born in Detroit, Michigan, 27 February 1927. Educated at Black Mountain College, North Carolina, 1947–48; Pasadena Playhouse, California, 1948–50; Yale University Drama School, New Haven, Connecticut. Served in the United States Navy, 1945–46. Has worked as a professional Actor and Director. Taught playwriting at City College, New York, 1967–68. Address: c/o Jay Garon-Brooks Associates Inc., 415 Central Park West, New York, New York 10025, U.S.A.

PUBLICATIONS

Novels

    *All Fall Down.* New York, Dutton, 1960; London, Faber, 1961.
    *Midnight Cowboy.* New York, Simon and Schuster, 1965; London, Cape, 1966.
    *The Season of the Witch.* New York, Simon and Schuster, and London, W. H. Allen, 1971.

Short Stories

    *The Sleep of Baby Filbertson and Other Stories.* New York, Dutton, and London, Faber, 1959.
    *A Story That Ends with a Scream and Eight Others.* New York, Simon and Schuster, 1967; London, Cape, 1968.

Plays

*Streetlight Sonata* (produced Pasadena, California, 1950).
*Moon in Capricorn* (produced New York, 1953).
*Blue Denim*, with William Noble (produced New York, 1958; Swansea, Wales, 1970). New York, Random House, 1958.
*Crazy October* (produced New York, 1958).
*Stop You're Killing Me* (includes *Terrible Jim Fitch*, *Bad Bad Jo-Jo*, and *Laughs, Etc.*) (produced Boston, 1968; New York, 1969).   New York, Simon and Schuster, 1970.

*       *       *

In the seven bizarre stories which comprise *The Sleep of Baby Filbertson* James Leo Herlihy first made clear his interest in the themes of loneliness, crippled emotions, and physical debility. The themes converge in his work to create a picture of the modern urban world as a purgatory, but a purgatory lightened somewhat by the pathos and respect with which the author presents his twisted characters. Readers of this collection frequently linked Herlihy's name with such gifted contemporaries as Truman Capote, James Purdy, and Flannery O'Connor.

*All Fall Down*, Herlihy's remarkable first novel, widely extended the dimensions of his ironic humor in chronicling the misadventures and the disintegration of a middle-class family. The father, a disillusioned socialist, declines into alcoholism and the mother into helpless inaction. One son has become a vagabond and petty criminal, and the other is a sixteen-year-old drop-out who imagines his older brother a great romantic rebel against bourgeois convention. Clinton, the younger son, eventually frees himself not only from his family but also from the projections of his own imagination, a process recorded in graphic detail in lengthy extracts from his journal. The very commonplace nature of Herlihy's characters lends an air of authenticity to the novel and intensifies the horror of their dilemmas by making them seem so constant and unavoidable.

This sense of horror was more intensely explored in *Midnight Cowboy*, the story of a simple-minded cowboy, Joe Buck, who travels to New York in the hope of making his fortune as a hustler. Instead, he is cast adrift on a sea of grotesques, eventually casting his lot with that of a crippled pickpocket, with whom he creates a community of love and grudging respect against the hostile world outside. When Ratso becomes ill, Joe cares for him, steals for him, and undertakes a quixotic journey to Florida in the hope that his friend may recover. *Midnight Cowboy* is a grim novel in which the author repeatedly exploits his own talent for depicting the grotesque. Nonetheless, because the central characters' needs are so basic and so human, they rise above the fashions of alienation, urban malaise and sexual degeneracy which are often the gratuitous complements of contemporary fiction.

Gloria Random, the heroine of Herlihy's third novel, *The Season of the Witch*, runs away from home with a friend, a homosexual draft-evader. The novel records their adventures in New York City, Gloria's reunion with her father, and her eventual return to her mother. As a study of the geography of the generation gap, the novel oversimplifies and glamorizes the essential cultural schism which that term loosely designates. Nonetheless, *The Season of the Witch* is a memorable exploration of the growth of a sensitive, troubled consciousness as it struggles to find some correlation between revolutionary hope and quotidian realities.

Herlihy is fascinated by society's rejects, by men and women whose lives seem doomed by their emotional needs and their longing, but who struggle to maintain some shred of human dignity in a world which seems remorseless in its devices for destroying the self. Such themes are also explored in Herlihy's plays, where the raucous spirit of black humor is even more pervasive than in the novels.

—David Galloway

**HERSEY, John (Richard).**    American.    Born in Tientsin, China, 17 June 1914. Educated at Hotchkiss School; Yale University, New Haven, Connecticut, B.A. 1936; Clare College, Cambridge (Mellon Fellow), 1936–37. Married Frances Ann Cannon in 1940 (divorced, 1958); Barbara Day Kaufman, 1958; has five children. Secretary to Sinclair Lewis, 1937; Writer and Correspondent, in China, Japan, the South Pacific, the Mediterranean and Russia, for *Time*, New York, 1937–45, *Life*, New York, 1944–46, and *The New Yorker*, 1945–46; Editor and Director of the writers' cooperative magazine *'47*, 1947–48; Fellow of Berkeley College, 1950–65, and Master of Pierson College, 1965–70, Yale University: Member of the Yale University Council Committee on the Humanities, 1951–56, and Member, 1959–64, and Chairman, 1964–69, Yale University Council Committee on Yale College; Writer-in-Residence, American Academy in Rome, 1970–71. Member, Westport, Connecticut School Study Council, 1945–50, Westport Board of Education, 1950–52, and Fairfield, Connecticut Citizens School Study Council, 1952–56; Trustee, Putney School, 1953–56; Member, National Citizens' Commission for the Public Schools, 1954–56; Consultant, Fund for the Advancement of Education, 1954–56; Chairman, Connecticut Committee for the Gifted, 1954–57; Delegate, White House Conference on Education, 1955; Trustee, National Citizens' Council for the Public Schools, 1956–58; Trustee, National Committee for Support of the Public Schools, 1962–68; Member, Weston, Connecticut Board of Education, 1964–65. Since 1960, Member of the Visiting Committee, Harvard Graduate School of Education, Cambridge, Massachusetts. Member, Westport, Connecticut Town Democratic Committee, 1948–52; Chairman, Connecticut Volunteers for Stevenson, 1952; Member, Stevenson Campaign Staff, 1956. Member of the Council, 1946–71, and Vice-President, 1949–55, Authors League of America; Delegate, P.E.N. Congress, Tokyo, 1958. Since 1946, Member of the Council of the Authors Guild. Recipient: Pulitzer Prize, 1945; Anisfield-Wolf Award, 1950; Daroff Memorial Award, 1950; Sidney Hillman Foundation Award, 1950; Howland Medal, Yale University, 1952; Tuition Plan Award, 1961; Sarah Josepha Hale Award, 1963. Member, American Academy of Arts and Letters, 1953. Address: 420 Humphrey Street, New Haven, Connecticut 06511, U.S.A.

## PUBLICATIONS

### Novels

*A Bell for Adano*.   New York, Knopf, 1944; London, Hamish Hamilton, 1965.
*The Wall*.   New York, Knopf, and London, Hamish Hamilton, 1950.
*The Marmot Drive*.   New York, Knopf, and London, Hamish Hamilton, 1953.
*A Single Pebble*.   New York, Knopf, and London, Hamish Hamilton, 1956.
*The War Lover*.   New York, Knopf, and London, Hamish Hamilton, 1958.
*The Child Buyer: A Novel in the Form of Hearings Before the Standing Committee on Education Welfare and Public Morality of a Certain State Senate Investigating the Conspiracy of Mr. Wissey Jones, with Others, to Purchase a Male Child*.   New York, Knopf, 1960; London, Hamish Hamilton, 1961.
*White Lotus*.   New York, Knopf, and London, Hamish Hamilton, 1965.
*Too Far to Walk*.   New York, Knopf, and London, Hamish Hamilton, 1966.
*Under the Eye of the Storm*.   New York, Knopf, and London, Hamish Hamilton, 1967.
*The Conspiracy*.   New York, Knopf, and London, Hamish Hamilton, 1972.

### Other

*Men on Bataan*.   New York, Knopf, 1942.
*Into the Valley: A Skirmish of the Marines*.   New York, Knopf, 1943.

*Hiroshima.*   New York, Knopf, and London, Penguin, 1946.
*Here to Stay: Studies in Human Tenacity.*   London, Hamish Hamilton, 1962; New
   York, Knopf, 1963.
*The Algiers Motel Incident.*   New York, Knopf, and London, Hamish Hamilton, 1968.
*Robert Capa*, with others.   New York, Paragraphic Books, 1969.
*Letter to the Alumni.*   New York, Knopf, 1970.

Critical Study: *John Hersey* by David Sanders, New York, Tawyne, 1967.

Manuscript Collection: Yale University Library, New Haven, Connecticut.

John Hersey comments:

I believe that a writer should be reticent about himself and his work. Ideally he should,
I feel, appear in his books and nowhere else in public. Each of his works entails a double
act of creation: he makes one part of the finished work, but until the reader brings his
imagination and experience to bear on it, the book does not come to life, does not even
*exist* as a book. I do not think that the writer should attempt to influence the second half
of this partnership of makers by stating his intentions, his "meaning". The writing process
is a mysterious one; the writer works within a magic circle—and his intentions, if indeed
he understands them himself, may not have much to do with the effect he produces. If he
is honest and at all able, the work speaks his deepest self, its themes derive from his view
of humanity, its style comes from the cadences and vibrations of his innermost voice. The
work interprets him better than he can interpret the work.

                              *         *         *

John Hersey once described himself as a novelist of contemporary history, and there is
still no better term to suggest the difference between his fiction and his early journalism.
His first novel, *A Bell for Adano*, was simply fictionalized reporting based on incidents in
the Sicilian campaign he had observed as a correspondent for *Time* and *Life*. It became
widely read and won Hersey a Pulitzer Prize on V-E Day because the vivid, facile story spoke
directly to popular assumptions of how the war should be fought and what the world would
be like after the war was over. In 1946 he visited Hiroshima, interviewed survivors of the
first atomic bomb attack, and published the *New Yorker* article which changed him
profoundly.

In *Hiroshima* and later in his greatest novel, *The Wall*, Hersey drew from the victims
themselves the understanding of history that had eluded him as a war correspondent. The
six Hiroshima residents told him how they had lived before the bomb struck, why they
were not killed, and precisely how illness, exhaustion, and personal sorrow had qualified
their survival. He had no comparable opportunity to interview participants in the Warsaw
ghetto uprisings, but this incident in the attempted extermination of European Jewry
obsessed him. He read such documentary evidence as *The Black Book of the Polish Jewry*,
listened to the victims' eyewitness accounts as sight-translated by Polish Jews who had
escaped to America, and created the archive of Noach Levinson. This fictional scholar
records not merely the events that lead through four years to the uprisings, but also every
occurrence that he feels may help to define the culture under attack. The result is an extraordinary achievement: the whole struggle of the ghetto with its historic implications and
without any melodramatic action or a single sentimental cliché.

Hersey's seven novels since *The Wall* resemble each other only in the author's constant attention to major social issues. In each book he attempts some experiment in narrative form as appropriate as Noach Levinson's archive was to *The Wall*. He failed in *The Marmot Drive*, an allegory that may have referred to political repressions in the McCarthy era. *A Single Pebble* is a very short novel which beautifully illuminates the limitations of technology in achieving human happiness. *The War Lover* is about a bomber pilot who loves his work and a bombardier who hates his. *The Child Buyer* is Hersey's ironic attack on an educational system which, he believes, neglects the bright child. A whole town acquiesces in selling ten-year-old Barry Rudd to United Lymphomilloid, a "defense" firm which will turn him into a human computer capable of reaching an I.Q. of 1000. The story is told in the form of hearings before a state senate committee, an awkward device except at such moments as when the child himself agrees to the conspiracy because "life at U Lympho might at least be *interesting*." Hersey's intention in *White Lotus* was disarmingly simple: to make white readers feel what it would be like if they were members of an oppressed race. His method was extremely cumbersome: the first-person narrative of an American girl transported to slavery in China in some indefinite future told retrospectively from the moment in which she has become a leader in a civil-rights movement. Hersey uses the Faust legend in *Too Far to Walk*, a novel of American student unrest. *Under the Eye of the Storm* opposes the behavior of two yachtsmen, a technologist and a humanist, when they struggle to survive at sea.

Of course, many novelists can be called novelists of contemporary history. Hersey differs from Norman Mailer because he has not written the kind of novel in which the protagonist defines the conditions of his time in the process of writing about himself. He differs from Allen Drury or Irving Wallace because he is also a philosophical novelist and his books are not the result of working up material on a succession of topical issues.

—David Sanders

---

**HESELTINE, Nigel.** Irish. Born in London, 3 July 1916, son of the composer Peter Warlock. Educated at Shrewsbury School; London University, B.Sc. in Economics; Trinity College, Dublin, M.A. Farmer in Ireland and Tanganyika, 1938–51; worked for the Food and Agriculture Organization of the United Nations, mainly in Africa, 1951–65; Under-Secretary, National Development and Planning, Zambia, 1965–68. Since 1968, Economic and Financial Adviser to the President of the Republic, Madagascar. Chevalier de l'Ordre National Malagasy. Fellow, Royal Geographical Society, 1958. Address: B.P. 3658, Tananarive, Madagascar.

PUBLICATIONS

Novel

*The Mysterious Pregnancy*.   London, Gollancz, 1953.

Short Stories

*Tales of the Squirearchy*.   Carmarthen, Wales, Druid Press, 1949.

Uncollected Short Stories

"Break Away If You Can," in *Penguin New Writing 28*.   London, Penguin, 1946.
"A Day's Pleasure", in *Penguin New Writing 32*.   London, Penguin 1947.

Other stories published in magazines and anthologies.

Verse

*Violent Rain*.   London, Latin Press, 1938.
*The Four-Walled Dream*.   London, Fortune Press, 1941.

Other

*Scarred Background: A Journey Through Albania*.   London, Dickson, 1938.
*From Libyan Sands to Chad*.   London, Museum Press, 1959.
*Remaking Africa*.   London, Museum Press, 1961.
*Madagascar*.   London, Pall Mall Press, 1971.

Translator, *Selected Poems of Dafydd ap Gwilym*.   Dublin, Cuala Press, 1944.

*       *       *

Among the greatest poets of our time are the diplomats Perse, Seferis, and Neruda, all winners of the Nobel Prize for literature. The tradition of the public or governmental servant who is also a distinguished writer also runs deep in English literature, from Chaucer through Raleigh to Yeats. The work of the Irish writer Nigel Heseltine is best seen in the light of this tradition, for he is a man of letters who is also a man whose wide-ranging achievements in a variety of undertakings mark him as one among a distinguished company of writers who are also, in Yeats' phrase, "smiling public men". He is a distinguished poet and translator; and his books of observation and exposition will remain among the invaluable records of a now vanished era in Albania and Africa. The book on Albania, *Scarred Background*, is not just a travel book, recording a journey through a changing society; it is a mixture of exposition, dialogue, and narrative, presented with the skill only an accomplished poet and story teller could bring to his observations. Likewise, the African book *From Libyan Sands to Chad* may lack the poetry and romance of St. Exupéry's classic *Wind, Sand, and Stars*, and it may not be constructed with the skill of Hemingway's non-fiction novel, *Green Hills of Africa*; but in other ways it must be considered more successful in its rendering of life in the desert of Africa, and the more lush landscape of Chad. While recounting a journey from Libya to Chad, Heseltine with the skill of a superior narrative artist works in insights into economic, social, archaeological, and military conditions, without destroying the narrative line. His concern for the future of Africa is revealed in the very important volume, *Remaking Africa*, in which the more argumentative and expository style still at important times reveals the sharp eye of a poet and the narrative force of a born story teller.

Heseltine's short stories reveal a wide range of technique and theme; but his major accomplishment as a fictionist is his novel, *The Mysterious Pregnancy*—a title taken from Joseph Fox's 18th century novel *Santa Maria; or, The Mysterious Pregnancy*. Heseltine's novel brilliantly combines scenes of witty chat and gossip with long introspective monologues, suspenseful plotting with episodes of almost torturous character analysis. This fine technical achievement of combining an almost thriller-like plot of question and suspense with psychological and philosophical examination of moral problems, marks this novel as outstanding. The two women in Paris seeking abortions of their illegitimate pregnancies allow for examination of responsiblity, self-deception, passion, possession and recrimination—without sentimentality. Heseltine weaves in other plots of theft and criminal action, along with pretenses, facades, hypocrisies, all undercutting, foiling, heightening the central theme of the novel, responsibility for consequences. The best parts of the novel tend to be these close examinations of moral dilemmas, and (as in the short stories) chapters of first-person psychological examination and revelation; whereas the novel is weakest in motivation and resolution. The skill with which time shifts are accomplished, and the brilliance of description and simile, however, compensate for many weaknesses in the book. Although one wishes Heseltine well in his advisory and diplomatic careers, one hopes he will continue his literary career, giving us another novel at least as fascinating in character, theme, and structure as *The Mysterious Pregnancy*.

—James Korges

---

**HICKS, Granville.** American. Born in Exeter, New Hampshire, 9 September 1901. Educated at Harvard University, Cambridge, Massachusetts, A.B. 1923, M.A. 1929. Married Dorothy Dyer in 1925; has one child. Instructor in Biblical Literature, Smith College, Northampton, Massachusetts, 1925–28; Assistant Professor of English, Rensselaer Polytechnic Institute, Troy, New York, 1929–35; Counselor in American Civilization, Harvard University, 1938–39; Instructor in Novel Writing, New School for Social Research, New York, 1955–58. Berg Visiting Professor, New York University, 1959; Visiting Professor, Syracuse University, Syracuse, New York, 1960; McGuffey Visiting Professor, Ohio University, Athens, 1967–68. Literary Adviser, The Macmillan Company, New York, 1930–65; Member, Editorial Staff, *New Masses*, New York, 1934–39; Literary Consultant. *The New Leader*, New York, 1951–58; Contributing Editor, *Saturday Review*, New York, 1958–69. Acting Executive Director, Corporation of Yaddo, Saratoga Springs, New York, 1970–71. Recipient: Guggenheim Fellowship, 1936; Rockefeller Fellowship, 1945. D.H.L., Skidmore College, Saratoga Springs, New York, 1968; Ohio University, Athens, 1969; Litt.D., Siena College, Loudonville, New York, 1971. Address: Box 144, Grafton, New York, U.S.A.

PUBLICATIONS

Novels

*The First to Awaken*, with Richard M. Bennett.   New York, Modern Age, 1940.
*Only One Storm*.   New York, Macmillan, 1942.
*Behold Trouble*.   New York, Macmillan, 1944.
*There Was a Man in Our Town*.   New York, Viking Press, 1952.

Verse

*New Light*, with Stuart B. Hoppin.   Boston, Birchard, 1932.

Other

*Eight Ways of Looking at Christianity*.   New York, Macmillan, 1926.

*The Great Tradition: An Interpretation of American Literature since the Civil War.*
New York, Macmillan, 1933; London, Macmillan, 1934; revised edition, New York,
Macmillan, 1935, Chicago, Quadrangle, 1969.
*One of Us: The Story of John Reed.*   New York, Equinox Press, 1935.
*John Reed: The Making of a Revolutionary*, with John Stuart.   New York, Macmillan,
1936.
*I Like America.*   New York, Modern Age, 1938.
*Figures of Transition: A Study of British Literature at the End of the Nineteenth Century.*
New York, Macmillan, 1940.
*Small Town.*   New York, Macmillan, 1946.
*Where We Came Out.*   New York, Viking Press, and London, Gollancz, 1954.
*Part of the Truth* (autobiography).   New York, Harcourt Brace, 1965.
*Literary Horizons.*   New York, New York University Press, 1970.

Editor, *Proletarian Literature in the United States: An Anthology.*   New York, International Publishers, 1935; London, Lawrence, 1936.
Editor, with Ella Winter, *The Letters of Lincoln Steffens.*   New York, Harcourt Brace,
2 vols., 1938.
Editor, *The Living Novel: A Symposium.*   New York, Macmillan, 1957.

Bibliography: "Granville Hicks: An Annotated Bibliography, February 1927 to June 1967,
with a Supplement to June 1968", by Robert J. Bicker, in *Emporia State Research Studies*
(Kansas), 1968.

Manuscript Collection: Syracuse University Library, New York.

Granville Hicks comments:

   Although I started out as a critic, I always had an urge to write novels. *The First to Awaken*
was not a serious novel, but a kind of utopian game I played with a friend, Richard Bennett,
artist and architect. *Only One Storm* was serious, an attempt to portray realistically the crisis
of America between Munich and Pearl Harbor. It was reasonably successful, but I was
never satisfied with it as a piece of fiction. *Behold Trouble* came closer to what I wanted both
in style and characterization, but 1944 was no year for a novel about a conscientious objector.
*There Was a Man in Our Town* (for which my working title was *The Prickly Pear*) was worked
over many times—too many I came to think. I decided that I couldn't be the kind of novelist
I wanted to be unless I devoted full time to the job, and that I couldn't afford.
   Although I gave up novel-writing, I continued to find the novel an absorbing literary form,
and I wrote often about fiction, especially the work of young writers, in my regular column
in *The New Leader* and *Saturday Review*. (For the latter I wrote a weekly page for eleven
years.) Some of my pieces have been collected in *Literary Horizons*. In *The Living Novel*
I gathered original essays by younger writers.

*        *        *

   Granville Hicks has taken a goodly share of abuse from people who interpret his famous
work *The Great Tradition* as a radical and possibly a Marxist interpretation of American
literature, but in fact that study can best be understood as an explication of the American
writers' continuing awareness of the moral contradictions of an economic and political
system that requires exploitation to produce wealth. During the period of the Popular Front
in America Hicks brand of moral humanism was consistent with left wing political activity,

for then the Communist Party offered its program as "good Americanism," which by anybody's definition should not require massive exploitation.

The startling development of the Soviet-Nazi Pact of 1939 ended Hicks' involvement in left wing politics. While it can easily be maintained that Socialism is basically humanistic, for Hicks the Pact could not possibly be good even for Russian Socialism and it represented for him a repudiation of his good intentions. He had no choice but to assert his independence of the left. Much to his credit he never has felt the need to "rehabilitate" himself by engaging in the polemics of the domestic anti-Communist crusade. Rather, he has gone along independently espousing his views in critical essays and the book reviews he contributed over the years to *The New Leader* and *Saturday Review*.

Perhaps to gain a broader scope of expression (perhaps, too, because one tires of writing always about other people's books) Hicks also has written four novels.

With Richard M. Bennett, whom he acknowledges as contributing a stimulus in discussion as well as drawings for the volume, Hicks made his first published entry into fiction with a utopia entitled *The First to Awaken*. The pattern is that of Bellamy's *Looking Backward*: George Swain having received cyrogenic treatments awakens in 2040 after a century's events have transformed his native town of Braxton into one of the many self-governing regional cooperatives in a world that has arrived at democratic socialism after major wars, civil strife, and periods of technological experimentation. The historical information Swain gains about the development of the new society is far more plausible than the rationalist fantasy of Bellamy. So, too, is Hicks' departure from the Utopian formula to the extent that he describes a society that has not done away with problems but rather has raised them to a new level of human consideration. For all its technological detail, though, the novel reveals its inspiration to be Jeffersonian democracy and its explicit model the traditional democracy of the New England town.

*Only One Storm*, Hicks' most popular and widely reviewed novel, has the same model, and while the setting is contemporary, the style that of realism, and the development of the book includes considerable discussion derived from Hicks' own experience of the possibility of fulfilling moral commitment within the Communist Party, this novel also suggests the awakening of its protagonists to the values of the humane life that can be led in a small New England town.

*Behold Trouble* is the most tightly structured of Hicks' novels, because it attempts to be less panoramic than the others. Also it poses issues differently, as it does on the experience of Pierre Mason, a neurotic young man who flees his assignment to a work camp for conscientious objectors because he believes government agents are persecuting him. Hicks has said (*Part of the Truth*, p. 213) that the story resembles his own to the extent that Mason is betrayed by good intentions into actions that have unforeseen consequences. In the novel he is careful to avoid taking a position for or against his young protagonist, so careful that many reviewers were baffled by the book; yet, his testimony about personal involvement in the moral dilemma and the abundance of detail of the Berkshire community that is its setting demonstrates again Hicks' fundamental belief that the humane life can only be achieved in a face-to-face community.

His final assertion in fiction of this belief, *There Was a Man in Our Town*, cannot really be said to add anything new. Once again it is evident that autobiography is at the core of the story of a retired professor who after originally trying to shape a small town in accordance with theoretical views eventually learns that a town consists of inviolable and somewhat unpredictable people.

None of Hicks' novels is exceptional. Despite his experience with Communism he tells us less about the moral issues of left politics than Dos Passos or Farrell, to name only anti-Communists. And in each of his novels it is hard to separate his humanistic view of social relationships from the anachronistic theme of a return to the village, but perhaps that is because the importance of Hicks' novels after all is not in what they have to tell us about our lives but in what they record of the author's own struggle to live consistently.

—John M. Reilly

**HIGGINS, Aidan.** Irish.   Born in County Kildare, 3 March 1927. Educated at Celbridge Convent; Killashee Preparatory School; Clongowes Wood College. Married Jill Damaris Anders in 1955; has three sons. Worked as a copywriter for Domas Advertising, Dublin, in the early 1950's; as a factory hand, extrusion moulder, and storeman, London, in the mid-1950's; as a puppet-operator for John Wright's Marionettes, in Europe, South Africa and Rhodesia, 1958–60; Script-Writer for Filmlets (advertising films), Johannesburg, 1960–61. Recipient: British Arts Council grants; Black Memorial Prize, 1967; German Academy stipend, Berlin, 1969; Irish Academy of Letters award, 1970. Lives in London. Address: c/o Calder and Boyars, 18 Brewer Street, London W.1, England.

PUBLICATIONS

Novels

   *Langrishe, Go Down*.   London, Calder and Boyars, and New York, Grove Press, 1966.
   *Balcony of Europe*.   London, Calder and Boyars, 1972.

Short Stories

   *Felo de Se*.   London, John Calder, 1960; as *Killachter Meadow*, New York, Grove Press, 1961.

Uncollected Short Stories

   "Sign and Ground", in *Evergreen Review Reader, 1957–1967*.   New York, Grove Press, 1968.
   "Scenes from a Receding Past", in *Dublin Magazine*, Winter 1971.

Other

   *Images of Africa* (diaries).   London, Calder and Boyars, 1971.

Manuscript Collection: University of Victoria, British Columbia.

Critical Studies: by David Holloway, in *The Bookman* (London), December 1965; "Maker's Language" by Vernon Scannell, in *Spectator* (London), 11 February 1966; in *New Leader* (London), 25 September 1967.

                              *        *        *

   Aidan Higgins made the classic debut of an Irish prose writer, a volume of stories. But in sharp contrast to his predecessors of the Thirties. like O'Connor and O'Faolain, he was not a regionalist in either subject-matter or style. Even in those stories which have an Irish background, the pressure of the outside world is always felt; one of the spinster sisters of "Killachter Meadow" has a brief, violent affair with a German student. And in the longest story, "Asylum" (Higgins has no interest in the brisk formula of the short story, and can let his material exfoliate to *nouvelle* length) the country bumpkin, Eddy Brazill, makes his way to London. But perhaps the most typical are the two stories with German backgrounds, especially "Winter Offensive" where another lecher, Herr Willie Bausch, follows "wherever his cupidity led him".

Such buoyant lubricity contrasts with the melancholy self-destructiveness of the other characters. *Langrishe, Go Down*, Higgin's first novel, is a re-working of "Killachter Meadow" into a definitive statement of these early themes. On the one hand you have provincial Ireland, or the part of it represented by the genteel Langrishes, with their country home in Kildare. Faulkner never listened more carefully to every creak of a decaying mansion than Higgins does to Springfield House. On the other hand, you have the pressures of contemporary history as the world lurches towards the second world war.

The link between them is Otto Beck, a German student who takes over the lodge at Springfield, as well as the youngest daughter, Imogen. Their affair is a kind of symbolic rape of all the frail Langrishes represent, but it is also a brief triumph, for at least one of the family discovers physical passion. And behind the lovers stretches the lugubrious beauty of the Irish countryside, a tapestry woven from the thousand details of Higgin's imagistic style. "The fox covert. Acrid smell of the foxes, bitter scattered bones, rabbit and hen bones, fowl. Plover passing overhead. Dempsey's land. Mournful cries."

Two elements go to the making of this style, which is the outstanding feature of Higgins's work so far: an extension of the Joycean technique of juxtaposed epiphanies and a strong visual sense. He writes, as it were, in pictures, held in stereoscopic depth. Exact, but static, the faults of the style are reflected in the exposition: with its leaps of chronology grafted onto an old fashioned narrative, *Langrishe, Go Down* is often baffling, like a marriage between Maria Edgeworth and Robbe-Grillet. But part of its melancholy power undoubtedly springs from such abrupt contrasts between Ireland and the outside world, between passive introversion and energy:

> Naked in the small cottage bedroom, stretching to draw apart the curtains, opening the window before retiring to bed, her person a little pathetic, a young girl's body. An offering to whom? To Eros?

> Otto disentangled the live rabbit from the snare. Applying his heel to the back of its neck, trapping it against the ground, he yanked it violently upwards by the hinglegs, breaking its spinal cord. He held it up. The rabbit jerked once or twice, involuntary muscular spasms, then was still.

At the end of the novel, the Germans have invaded Austria, and Springfield recedes. Since *Langrishe*, Higgins has been at work on a long novel, *Balcony of Europe*, which, as its title suggests, has a more contemporary theme. Hints of the direction in which he is moving may be found in *Images of Africa*, a diary of the four years he spent in the southern part of that continent. "Things seen but not judged" is the declared intention (*Guardian*, 11 October 1971) but it is not hard to hear the drumbeat of menace behind his opening description:

> And in the twilight, clinging high on the wire fence like bats, naked piccaninnies stretch out their hands to the lighted carriage windows that are gliding slowly past, the dining-car passing; themselves the colour of dust, chanting: "Happy . . . happy . . . happy!" Happy Christmas in South Africa.

The emotional climax of the book is Sharpeville, which as in a Greek tragedy, happens off-stage. Carefully, Higgins searches for the image to link this contemporary disaster to his own world.

> A Johannesburg *Star* photograph of the "weapons" used by the African insurgents at Sharpeville. In 40–45 seconds of firing, so many killed, so many wounded, so

much blood. A pile of knobkerries, sticks, stones. Like what? Windfalls in a winter
wood.

—John Montague

---

**HIGHSMITH, (Mary) Patricia.** American. Born in Fort Worth, Texas, 19 January
1921; has lived in New York since 1927. Educated at Barnard College, New York, B.A. 1942.
Recipient: Mystery Writers of America Special Award, 1956, 1963; Grand Prix de Littérature Policière, 1957; Crime Writers Association of England prize, 1964. Address:
Moncourt 77, France.

PUBLICATIONS

Novels

Strangers on a Train.   New York, Harper, 1950; London, Cresset Press, 1951.
The Price of Salt (as Claire Morgan).   New York, Coward McCann, 1952.
The Blunderer.   New York, Coward McCann, 1954; London, Cresset Press, 1956.
The Talented Mr. Ripley.   New York, Coward McCann, 1955; London, Cresset Press,
    1957.
Deep Water.   New York, Harper, 1957; London, Heinemann, 1958.
A Game for the Living.   New York, Harper, 1958; London, Heinemann, 1959.
This Sweet Sickness.   New York, Harper, 1960; London, Heinemann, 1961.
The Cry of the Owl.   New York, Harper, 1962; London, Heinemann, 1963.
The Two Faces of January.   New York, Doubleday, and London, Heinemann, 1964.
The Glass Cell.   New York, Doubleday, 1964; London, Heinemann, 1965.
The Story-Teller.   New York, Doubleday, 1965; as A Suspension of Mercy, London,
    Heinemann, 1965.
Those Who Walk Away.   New York, Doubleday, and London, Heinemann, 1967.
The Tremor of Forgery.   New York, Doubleday, and London, Heinemann, 1969.
Ripley under Ground.   New York, Doubleday, 1970; London, Heinemann, 1971.
A Dog's Ransom.   London, Heinemann, 1972.

Short Stories

The Snail-Watcher and Other Stories.   New York, Doubleday, 1970; as Eleven,
    London, Heinemann, 1970.

Other

Miranda the Panda Is on the Veranda, with Doris Sanders (juvenile).   New York,
    Coward McCann, 1958.
Plotting and Writing Suspense Fiction.   Boston, The Writer, 1966.

Critical Study: essay by Julian Symons, in *London Magazine,* June 1969.

Patricia Highsmith comments:

I am said to write stories of psychological terror and suspense, but as I think all novels are psychological I cannot understand why this quality is so often singled out in my writing. My main characters, or heroes, are often the culprits, the murderers, and so my books have never any element of mystery. On the contrary, my chief goal is clarity, and if possible an explanation of criminal behaviour.

*       *       *

Although Patricia Highsmith's books are usually categorized and reviewed as crime or detective fiction, some reviewers have indicated that she could just as well be considered a fine serious novelist of great subtlety and skill. Her books are books about crime, especially about murder, but they clearly transcend the formula detective novel in that they are, for the most part, penetrating studies into the psychology of crime. There is very little of the formulaic about her books; they offer no catharsis and very little relief to the reader. Instead, they provide a series of successive portraits of people involved in violent crime, showing their actions and reactions in situations of high tension. Miss Highsmith excels in the creation of believable, ordinary characters who, nevertheless, exhibit aspects of criminal psychology as an essential part of their ostensible normality. They are characters slightly out of focus and their involvement in violence, after careful preparation by the author, seems perfectly plausible given that character and that situation. Unlike the formulaic detective writer, Miss Highsmith focusses upon the how and the why, since the criminal is known. She is more interested in the reasons for and the results of the murder and the impact of the violence upon the character than in the formulaic novel's traditional concern for the process of detection and the eventual imposition of an official sanction for the crime.

Reviewing *The Cry of the Owl* in *New Statesman,* Francis Wyndham writes: "Guilt is her theme, and she approaches it through two contrasting heroes. These may be simplified as the guilty man who has justified his guilt and the innocent man who feels himself to be guilty." In some novels, she focusses upon one; in some, on the other. In her first novel, *Strangers on a Train,* which was filmed by Alfred Hitchcock, she uses both figures and explores the symbiosis as they act upon each other. In *The Talented Mr. Ripley,* filmed as *Purple Noon,* her character is an amoral killer drawn into successive deceits and acts of violence as a conseqence of his own nature and his former actions. The fact that Ripley successfully commits two murders, assuming for a time the identity of one of his victims, and escapes to live again in a later novel differentiates this book from the detective formula. In *The Story-Teller,* she depicts the other of her characters, the innocent man who, nevertheless, feels his guilt. This time the character is a writer with a vivid imagination who, as a game, plants clues indicating that he has murdered his wife. When she disappears, the police naturally suspect him and he tries to imagine what it would be like were he really guilty. Eventually, he murders his wife's lover but it cannot be proven. The story, then, revolves around his "guilt" for a murder he has imagined which leads to genuine guilt for a genuine murder whose consequences he escapes.

All of Miss Highsmith's novels are written in a flat, realistic style that implies a certain detached view of the private world she creates; and the very lack of emphasis upon the events of her plots increases the horror of the irrationality and moral ambiguity she depicts. Her books evoke a quiet tension, a persistent apprehension, which is all the more terrifying and suspenseful for its aura of plausibility.

—Kay J. Mussell

**HILLIARD, Noel (Harvey).**   New Zealander.   Born in Napier, Hawke's Bay, 6 February 1929. Educated at Gisborne High School, 1942–45; Victoria University, Wellington, 1946–50; Wellington Teachers College, 1954–55. Married Kiriwai Mete in 1954; has four children. Journalist, *Southern Cross*, Wellington, 1946–50; Teacher, Khandallah School, Wellington, 1955–56, and District High School, Mangakino, 1956–64; Chief Sub-Editor, *New Zealand Listener*, Wellington, 1965–70. Since 1971, Robert Burns Fellow at the University of Otago, Dunedin. Chairman, Mangakino-Pouakani Maori Executive Committee, and Delegate to the Waiariki District Council of Maori Executive Committees, 1962–64. Recipient: Hubert Church Memorial Award, 1960; New Zealand Literary Fund Scholarship, 1963. Address: c/o English Department, University of Otago, Post Office Box 56, Dunedin, New Zealand.

PUBLICATIONS

Novels

> *Maori Girl*.   London, Heinemann, 1960.
> *Power of Joy*.   London, Joseph, and Christchurch, Whitcombe and Tombs, 1965; Chicago, Regnery, 1966.
> *A Night at Green River*.   London, Hale, and Christchurch, Whitcombe and Tombs, 1969.

Short Stories

> *A Piece of Land*.   London, Hale, and Christchurch, Whitcombe and Tombs, 1963.

Other

> *We Live by a Lake* (juvenile).   Auckland, Heinemann, 1972.

Critical Studies: in *The New Zealand Novel 1869–1965* by Joan Stevens, Wellington, Reed, 1966; *New Zealand Fiction since 1945* by H. Winston Rhodes, Dunedin, McIndoe, 1968; "The Maori and Literature 1938–65" by Bill Pearson in *The Maori People in the Nineteen-Sixties*, Auckland, Paul, 1968; *New Zealand Novels* by H. Winston Rhodes, Wellington, Price Milburn, 1969.

Noel Hilliard comments:

My principal area of interest is life in New Zealand today, and particularly how Maori and pakeha view and behave towards each other.

*       *       *

The question of Maori-European relationships in New Zealand has engaged the attention of novelists for well over a century. Few writers have managed to avoid the extremes of stereotyping or sentimentalising over the Maori; fewer have managed to get inside the Maori mind and make tangible in fiction his special temperament and complex cultural responses to the white man's world. Noel Hilliard has been among the handful who have been successful in this. His *Maori Girl* is a painful piece of unsentimental social realism which dramatises the destructive effect of urban life on a Maori girl uprooted from her life in a rural Maori community where she has been sustained by tradition, human warmth and instinctive understanding. The strength and directness of Hilliard's prose form an ideal medium for the story.

To a degree, this novel and the short stories in *A Piece of Land* deal with characters not explored in much depth and the sociological emphasis leads to a certain simplification of the issues involving them. Yet it seems carping to demand more psychological intensity when Hilliard's realistic backgrounds, his sense of place, his plausible and typical situations and his honest compassion stir the reader's sympathies so deeply and make so real the importance of the small, everyday things in life.

*Power of Joy* is of a different order. Here Hilliard turns to a familiar New Zealand fictional subject—the process of growing-up; but he treats it with striking originality and tenderness. A young man comes gradually to understand the innerness of his childhood experience of Nature and people which he accepted as a mere context of being and to relate it to his identity as a person and as an inhabitant of a particular society. Hilliard's realism gives force to the picture of depression days and the strains in a poor family. *Power of Joy* is a delicate and sensitive book, in which the fragmentary treatment of perceptions creates its own poetry.

In *A Night at Green River*, Hilliard returns to the contrast between Maori and European attitudes. Here again the moral pattern is clear, perhaps too clear, in the carefully organised comparison between the spontaneous, natural life of a Maori household in a farming district with the arrogance and frustration of a European one. Maori non-materialistic values are used as a yardstick with which to measure European attitudes towards possessions and people. The major crisis in the novel leads to a reconciliation of viewpoints, and the parable teaches that New Zealand European life needs enrichment from Maori life-styles. Economical and concentrated in plot as in style, the novel is nevertheless very vigorous and often delightfully comic. Perhaps a shade too patterned to make its point subtly, *A Night at Green River* at the same time speaks truthfully and honestly about New Zealand characters, Maori and European, and basic realities of New Zealand life.

—J. C. Reid

---

**HIMES, Chester (Bomar).** American. Born in Jefferson City, Missouri, 29 July 1909. Educated at Ohio State University, Columbus, 1926–28. Married Jean Lucinda Johnson in 1937. Worked with the Works Progress Administration (WPA) Writers Project in Ohio. Served seven years in prison for armed robbery. Recipient: Rosenwald Fellowship, 1944. Address: c/o William Morrow and Company, 105 Madison Avenue, New York, New York 10016, U.S.A.

PUBLICATIONS

Novels

*If He Hollers Let Him Go.* New York, Doubleday, 1945; London, Grey Walls Press, 1947.

*Lonely Crusade.*   New York, Knopf, 1947; London, Grey Walls Press, 1950.
*Cast the First Stone.*   New York, Coward McCann, 1953.
*The Third Generation.*   Cleveland, World, 1954.
*The Primitive.*   New York, New American Library, 1955.
*For Love of Ima Belle.*   New York, Fawcett, 1957.
*The Crazy Kill.*   New York, Berkley, 1959; London, Panther, 1968.
*The Real Cool Killers.*   New York, Berkley, 1959; London, Panther, 1969.
*All Shot Up.*   New York, Avon, 1960; London, Panther, 1969.
*The Big Gold Dream.*   New York, Avon, 1960; London, Panther, 1968.
*Pinktoes.*   Paris, Olympia Press, 1961; New York, Putnam, and London, Barker, 1965.
*Cotton Comes to Harlem.*   New York, Putnam, and London, Muller, 1965.
*The Heat's On.*   New York, Putnam, and London, Muller, 1966.
*Run Man Run.*   New York, Putnam, 1966; London, Muller, 1967.
*Blind Man with a Pistol.*   New York, Morrow, and London, Hodder and Stoughton, 1969.

Other

*The Quality of Hurt* (autobiography).   New York, Doubleday, 1972.

\*        \*        \*

Whether writing about convicts or police detectives, industrial workers or a bourgeois family, Chester Himes' concern throughout his productive career has been to express the dynamic relationship between social environment and individual personality. Taking up his authorial position within the consciousness of oppressed characters, Himes makes what one has learned to think of, too abstractly, as "the race problem" an experience of psychic conflict: Bob Jones in *If He Hollers Let Him Go* exists mentally on the borderline between fierce hatred, fed by a thousand and one indignities he experiences in a wartime industrial plant, and ego collapse; the career of Lee Gordon, confronted by racism within the union in his "lonely crusade" for black workers' rights, is reduced to a moment in which he braves reprisal for a gratuitous act of defiance; the members of the black bourgeois family of *The Third Generation* turn the hostility generated by caste barriers toward themselves; personally based relationships in *The Primitive* are contaminated by socially conditioned fears; and the white prisoner in *Cast the First Stone* finds love impossible among men, like himself, who have been brutalized.

Himes' vision of the psychic conflicts is naturalistic. Rather than plot the growth of his characters' hostilities or fears of reprisal were they to resist discrimination openly, he records the presence of these feelings as given aspects of personality. Psychic conflicts, thus, replicate the primary reality of social caste conflicts, and each character's mental struggle to survive represents the options of accomodation, flight, or resistance which appear in the collective experience of all black Americans.

Shortly after he chose to exile himself from the United States in 1953 Chester Himes began a series of Harlem crime stories, which, with the exception of the most recent—*Blind Man with a Pistol*—have been originally published in French and subsequently translated for American paperback distribution. These nine novels constitute an adaptation of the tough guy detective genre into a cycle that explores the unique experience of the capital of black America. In the cycle white society is evidently the cause of oppressive social conditions but as the detectives, settings, plots and viewpoint are all black, the Harlemites live under less psychic tension than characters in Himes' earlier novels. In effect, they have the room to determine in a limited way their own values and social relations. Himes' police detectives, Coffin Ed Johnson and Grave Digger Jones, who ruthlessly hunt down crooks that deceive the poor but yet tolerate organized vice, therefore, serve as enforcers of Harlem's specialized justice. Willing to bend the white man's law and regarding his abstract categories of morality as irrelevant to the survival of their people, the tough guys express a humanism decidedly black.

Recently critics have begun to acknowledge the presence in Afro-American writing of an intuitive existentialism. Chester Himes' work might well serve as illustration. Consistently naturalistic, his documentation of the experience of oppression repudiates the bad faith of white American culture, while his portrayal of black culture asserts that people can freely choose in a world of absurd social practice to survive with principle.

—John M. Reilly

---

**HINDE, Thomas.** Pseudonym for Sir Thomas Willes Chitty, Baronet. British. Born in Felixstowe, Suffolk, 2 March 1926; succeeded father to the baronetcy, 1955. Educated at Winchester School, Hampshire; University College, Oxford. Served in the Royal Navy, 1944–47. Married Susan Elspeth in 1951; has four children. Worked for Inland Revenue, London, 1951–53; for Shell Petroleum Company, in England, 1953–58, and in Nairobi, Kenya, 1958–60. Granada Arts Fellow, University of York, 1964–65; Visiting Lecturer, University of Illinois, Urbana, 1965–67; Visiting Professor, Boston University, 1969–70. Address: Bow Cottage, West Hoathly, near East Grinstead, Sussex, England.

PUBLICATIONS

Novels

*Mr. Nicholas.* London, MacGibbon and Kee, 1952; New York, Farrar Straus, 1953.
*Happy as Larry.* London, MacGibbon and Kee, 1957; New York, Criterion Books, 1958.
*For the Good of the Company.* London, Hutchinson, 1961.
*A Place Like Home.* London, Hodder and Stoughton, 1962.
*The Cage.* London, Hodder and Stoughton, 1962.
*Ninety Double Martinis.* London, Hodder and Stoughton, 1963.
*The Day the Call Came.* London, Hodder and Stoughton, 1964; New York, Vanguard Press, 1965.
*Games of Chance: The Interviewer and The Investigator.* London, Hodder and Stoughton, 1965; New York, Vanguard Press, 1967.
*The Village.* London, Hodder and Stoughton, 1966.
*High.* London, Hodder and Stoughton, 1968; New York, Walker, 1969.
*Bird.* London, Hodder and Stoughton, 1970.
*Generally a Virgin.* London, Hodder and Stoughton, 1972.

Other

*Spain: A Personal Anthology.* London, Newnes, 1963.

Manuscript Collection: University of Texas, Austin.

Critical Studies: review, in *New York Herald Tribune*, 24 May 1953; *The Angry Decade* by Kenneth Allsop, London, Peter Owen, 1958; reviews, in *The Times Literary Supplement* (London), 26 May 1961, 27 October 1966, 7 November 1968, 11 September 1970; in *The Observer* (London), 7 June 1964; in *The New York Times*, 9 August 1967.

Thomas Hinde comments:

I write novels because I like novels and I like trying to make my own. These aim to be— but unfortunately hardly ever succeed in being—the novels I will like best of all. Just as my taste in novels changes, so the sort of novel I try to write changes. I also believe in the importance of the novel—one of the few places where individual art as opposed to script-conference art can still flourish. I believe that it can and will change and develop, however fully explored it seems at present. I believe that people will go on wanting to read novels. But however much I am convinced by these logical arguments for the vitality, value and survival of the form, the real reason why I go on writing novels remains personal: despite its anxiety and difficulties, I like the process, and, despite disappointments, I still like the result which I aim for.

\*       \*       \*

When, in 1957, American popular journalism first discovered the "Angry Young Men," Thomas Hinde was listed, in articles in *Time* and *Life*, along with Kingsley Amis, John Wain, and John Braine, as one of the principal progenitors of the "Movement." *Happy as Larry*, Hinde's second novel, had just been published and the novel's protagonist was a rather feckless young man who lost menial jobs, was vaguely trying to write, and irresponsibly drifted away from his wife. Yet the designation of "Angry Young Men," over-generalized and inappropriate as it was for all the writers to whom it was applied, was particularly inappropriate for Hinde. Far from "angry" or defiantly rebellious, Hinde's protagonist wanders about apologetically, full of guilt, trying to help a friend recover a lost photograph that might be used for blackmail. His indecision, inhibitions, and constant self-punishment characterize him far more consistently than do any articulate attitudes toward society. In addition, Hinde's point of view in the novel is far from an unqualified endorsement of his protagonist's actions and attitudes. The ending, like the endings of most of Hinde's novels, is left open, without any definitive or summarizable statement. And the kind of judgment frequently assumed in popular accounts of novelists, the clarion call for a new way of life or the castigation of depraved contemporary morality, is entirely absent.

At the same time, however, in other terms, *Happy as Larry* is a novel of the fifties. The protagonist's wandering, his lack of certainty, his allegiance only to close personal friends, his inhibitions and apologies, his insistence on self as a starting point for value, are all characteristic of much of the serious fiction of the decade. London, too, shrouded in rain and gloom, spotted with crowded pubs that provide the only refuge, is also made the grim post-war city. In addition, Hinde uses a frequent symbol in fifties' fiction, the photograph, as central to the plot of his novel. In a world in which identity was regarded as shifting, unreliable, unknowable, only the photograph, the fixed and permanent image, could give identity any meaning, although that meaning, far more often than not, was itself a distortion, an over-simplification, occasion for blackmail. In fact, Hinde's novels most characteristically begin with categories definable in terms of other novels and novelists, with genres to which the reader is accustomed.

His first novel, *Mr. Nicholas*, chronicles the struggles of a young Oxonian, home on holidays, to define himself against his domineering and insensitive father. Another novel,

*For the Good of the Company*, deals with the struggles for definition and power within the business combine, the complex organization that seemed a microcosm to depict human efforts to maintain a sense of rational control. *The Cage* and *A Place Like Home* are Hinde's African novels, *The Cage* a particularly sensitive and effective treatment of a young British colonial girl in Kenya attempting to retain her ties to the world of her parents while simultaneously understanding sympathetically the emerging black society. *The Village* establishes, without sentimentality or nostalgia, the world of the small English village about to be levelled by bulldozers and flooded for a new reservoir. *High* is Hinde's American visit novel, an account of the forty-year-old British writer teaching at an American university, including the familiar device of a novelist character writing a novel which is itself partly reproduced within the novel. In other words, the themes, techniques, concerns, and atmosphere of Hinde's novels are all familiar, all representative of their time and place—the heroine of *The Cage* often sounds like a more restrained Doris Lessing heroine, the protagonist of *High* is well established in a lineage that stretches back to Eric Linklater—yet Hinde is also an individual novelist of great skill with an individual sense of texture and intelligence.

Hinde is frequently at his best in describing the sensitivities of his young characters—their introspections, their naivetés, their commitments to attitudes and to people they cannot entirely understand. The heroine of *The Cage*, unable to untangle the racial antagonisms she does not entirely understand, thinks her young colonial boyfriend will kill the black man he thinks she's been sleeping with, over-dramatizing a conflict she cannot solve. The young budding capitalist in *For the Good of the Company* makes love to the boss's daughter but cannot really fathom all the perplexities of her emotions. He is loyal to the enigma he has partially observed and partially constructed, always wondering how much he has made up himself. A similarly intelligent sensitivity characterizes the love affair in *The Village* between the harassed local doctor and the opportunistic young stockbroker's wife, an affair in which love is created out of mutual desperation. Hinde's sensitivity is applied not only to personal relationships, but to exterior atmospheres as well. Each novel contains many descriptions of weather, rich and subtle evocations of different climates and seasons—equally acute whether in England, America, or Africa—that are shaped carefully to suit the emotions or the problems of the characters. Weather is both the material for physical description and a principal means of controlling the atmosphere of the novel.

Hinde's novels are also full of action, concerned with plot. Yet the plots never reach definitive conclusions, never entirely resolve the issues they present. The protagonist of *Happy as Larry* finally finds the photograph, but may or may not become a solid citizen and create a home for his faithful wife. The young capitalist in *For the Good of the Company* is enmeshed in the system and, at the end, like his boss, is about to live his past over again. But whether or not he will be any wiser is an open question. *The Village* ends with the feeling that the old English village is probably doomed, as much from its own hypocrisies and inadequacies as from an insensitive "urban bureaucracy," but the fight to save the village is not completely finished. Hinde's novels are, in a way, slices of recognizable contemporary life, a life in which people live and react, in which things happen although those things are not irremediably conclusive, and in which judgment is superficial or irrelevant. And these slices, communicated with a rich sense of personal and historical atmosphere, are never distorted by conversion into an object lesson or part of a message. In fact, Hinde, as author, keeps his distance. He can use familiar themes effectively because he treats them from a distance, stands far enough away to demonstrate a compassionate irony or an intelligent sympathy with his fictional world, a world effectively communicated because, like our larger world, it is one not easily reduced to understandable principles or judgments.

—James Gindin

**HOAGLAND, Edward.** American. Born in New York City, 21 December 1932. Educated at Harvard University, Cambridge, Massachusetts, 1950–54, A.B. 1954. Served in the United States Army, 1955–57. Married Amy Ferrara in 1960; Marion Magid, 1968; has one child. Since 1963, Part-time Teacher at Rutgers University, New Brunswick, New Jersey, Sarah Lawrence College, Bronxville, New York, City College of New York, and the New School for Social Research, New York. Recipient: Houghton Mifflin Literary Fellowship, 1956; Longview Foundation Award, 1961; Guggenheim Fellowship, 1964; American Academy of Arts and Letters Travelling Fellowship, 1964; O. Henry Award, 1971. Address: 31 Jane Street, New York, New York 10014, U.S.A.

PUBLICATIONS

Novels

 Cat Man. Boston, Houghton Mifflin, 1956.
 The Circle Home. New York, Crowell, 1960.
 The Peacock's Tail. New York, McGraw Hill, 1965.

Uncollected Short Stories

 "Cowboys", in Noble Savage (Chicago), 1960.
 "The Last Irish Fighter", in Esquire (New York), August 1960.
 "The Colonel's Power", in New American Review 2. New York, New American
   Library, 1967.
 "The Witness", in Paris Review, Summer 1967.
 "Kwan's Coney Island", in New American Review 5. New York, New American
   Library, 1969.
 "A Fable of Mammas", in Transatlantic Review (London and New York), Summer
   1969.
 "The Final Fate of Alligators", in New Yorker, 18 October 1969.

Other

 Notes from the Century Before: A Journal from British Columbia. New York, Random
   House, 1969.
 The Courage of Turtles (essays). New York, Random House, 1971.

                              *        *        *

 So far Edward Hoagland has not achieved through his novels and non-fiction a secure or influential place as an important American writer, even though his circus and boxing novels have been labelled required reading for those interested in these activities, and his prose style is distinctively his own. It is perhaps this distinctiveness that may disappoint readers who expect an author to be a virtuoso. Hoagland enjoys travelling in relatively primitive areas of North America (witness the detailed recording of his journeying in Notes from the Century Before: A Journal from British Columbia) and detailing life in occupations where brawn or physical skills are more important than intellect. His essay, "Big Cats", is a deft description of the cat family; Cat Man is a novel of circus life that contains sordid but not unrealistic detail about the human struggles unseen by the spectators; and *The Circle Home* is a novel full of information about the training of boxers and life among the destitute. In his third but not best novel, *The Peacock's Tail*, he still shows an interest in the lower classes, for the protagonist is a young white man who gradually loses cultural and racial prejudice as he works among the urban poor.

Throughout his works there is a uniformity of prose style. He is fond of an unembellished, staccato prose that at times is reminiscent of Hemingway, yet because his narrators and protagonists are usually lower class men, relatively uneducated and inarticulate, the direct, colloquial, often simple, prose is not inappropriate. (It is significant that in *Notes from the Century Before* he uses similar rhythms.) In its direct, deflationary tone, the beginning of his short story, "The Final Fate of Alligators," is a succinct introduction to most of his main characters: "In such a crowded, busy world the service each man performs is necessarily a small one. Arnie Bush's was no exception" (p. 52). Yet the lack of subtle, intellectual prose does not mean that the author offers no insights. A description of leopards in motion ends, for example, with a deft comment: "Really, leopards are like machines. They move in a sort of perpetual motion. Their faces don't change; they eat the same way, sleep the same way, pace much the same as each other. Their bodies are constructed as ideally as a fish's for moving and doing, for action, and not much room is left for personality" (p. 95). Regrettably, the final cause may aptly be applied to his characters, for many of them are so busy learning survival techniques in an uncaring world that their personalities are never fully developed. We may believe in them, but we are not always interested in them. The lack of interest sometimes results from the brevity of a character's role or the analysis devoted to it. Thus when characters fall back into self-destructive habits such as self-pity or alcoholism, we feel little sympathy. We impatiently dismiss them as born losers.

An accurate and just sense of Hoagland's strengths and weaknesses in prose style, narrative technique, characterization, and thought may be obtained from *The Circle Home*, the story of Denny Kelly, an irresponsible twenty-nine-year-old who has failed and continues to fail as a prize fighter and husband. In prose direct and at times colourful, the author demonstrates a close knowledge of the world of third-rate boxers:

> A lively fight: One-hand found occasion to manoeuver into every foot the ring provided. He'd be close, mining in the belly, and spring back with a lithe light antelope-type movement. Often when his left returned from thrusts his arms dropped by his sides to balance him. Those leaps, narrow body straight upright and turning in the air to face the way he wanted, were the essence of his style . . . (pp. 125–26).

The author seems intent, not upon muckraking, but upon having readers understand the world of boxers and boxing. The reader comes to know Denny through the straight chronological flow of his attempted comeback, and through a series of flashbacks that chronicle his irresponsible and immature behaviour as a husband and father. In re-creating the flow of events Hoagland shows a keen ear for dialogue. The ending of the novel, however, is weak; it fits the title too neatly: Denny, contrite yet once more, phones to inform his wife that he is determined (because of *his* miseries) to return and to be henceforth a good family man. The title, *The Circle Home*, suggests that at last he will be truly home, but because he has failed so often before and has shown no true deep reformation, the reader may prophesy further backsliding. If we are meant to view Denny's future optimistically, the author's compassion for the dwellers in the "lower depths" has led him to a sentimental conclusion.

From his works as a whole. Hoagland appears as a careful writer who, steeped in first-hand knowledge of his material, attempts with some humour and considerable compassion to show us men and women struggling first to survive and then to improve themselves or the world. Because life embraces much that is sordid, he utilizes it in his works; but he is neither a muckraker nor a sensationalist.

—James A. Hart

**HOBSON, Laura Z(ametkin).** American. Born in New York City, 18 June 1900. Educated at Cornell University, Ithaca, New York, B.A. 1921. Married Thayer Hobson in 1930 (divorced, 1935); has two children. Worked as an Advertising Copywriter until 1934, except for one year as a Reporter for the *New York Post*; Promotion Writer, Time Inc., New York, 1934–40; subsequently Copy Chief of all Time Inc. magazine promotion, then Director of Promotion for *Time* magazine; Full-time Writer and Columnist, 1941–56; Consultant to Time Inc., 1956–62. As Columnist, wrote "Trade Winds" in *Saturday Review of Literature*, New York, 1952–53, a column for International News Service, 1953–54, and the book page for *Good Housekeeping*, New York, 1953–56. Since 1960, Consultant to the *Saturday Review*, New York. Since 1947, Member of the National Council, Authors League of America. Address: c/o Simon and Schuster, 630 Fifth Avenue, New York, New York 10020, U.S.A.

PUBLICATIONS

Novels

  *The Trespassers.* New York, Simon and Schuster, 1943; London, Gollancz, 1944.
  *Gentleman's Agreement.* New York, Simon and Schuster, and London, Cassell, 1947.
  *The Other Father.* New York, Simon and Schuster, and London, Cassell, 1950.
  *The Celebrity.* New York, Simon and Schuster, 1951; London, Cresset Press, 1953.
  *First Papers.* New York, Random House, 1964; London, Heinemann, 1965.
  *The Tenth Month.* New York, Simon and Schuster, and London, Heinemann, 1971.

Uncollected Short Story

  "Custody", in *Ladies' Home Journal* (New York), September 1970.

Other

  *A Dog of His Own* (juvenile). New York, Viking Press, and London, Hamish Hamilton, 1941.
  *I'm Going to Have a Baby.* New York, Day, and London, Heinemann, 1967.

Critical Study: essay by the author on her own work, in *Twentieth Century Authors: First Supplement*, New York, Wilson, 1955.

*      *      *

Since 1941, Laura Z. Hobson has published six novels and two books for children, the latter being indifferently received by the critics. Her reputation rests upon her novels, which are, for the most part, competently written thesis fiction. She is best known for her 1947 novel *Gentleman's Agreement* which sold over 2,000,000 copies in the United States and was in third position on the bestseller list that year. It was also filmed, and that version received the Academy Award for best picture of 1947. Mrs. Hobson's other novels have not been so influential or popular, perhaps because they are less sensational in subject matter than *Gentleman's Agreement*, but all of them relate in some way to her interest in the effect that society and social conditions have on the individual.

The plot of *Gentleman's Agreement* details the experiences of a young New York journalist who pretends to be Jewish for several months in order to gain inside information for a series on anti-semitism for his magazine. Mrs. Hobson's target in this novel is not the professional bigot, but those well-meaning people who acquiesce in prejudice not realizing how deeply it exists in daily life. Her protagonist finds anti-semitism in the employment practices of his own liberal magazine and in his fiancée, who had suggested the series in the first place. Although the novel was criticized for its cardboard characters and contrived plot, most critics agreed that it performed a needed service in alerting readers to the existence of widespread prejudice in American life. Writing in *Survey Graphic*, Harry Hansen stated that it would reach more people precisely because it was written as a slick novel. Mrs. Hobson did not minimize the problem with a happy ending, indicating instead that only concerted action by people who understood the problem could lessen prejudice.

Her other novels have also concerned social themes. *The Trespassers*, her first novel, was a well-documented indictment of the United States' failure to help European refugees before the war; critics generally agreed that the novel's plotting was deficient, but praised her intention. Her most recent novel is about the problems of a forty-year-old unwed mother, and others describe the effects of sudden success upon the individual and the anti-liberal and radical sentiment prior to World War I. All of her novels have New York settings.

Although Laura Z. Hobson has only rarely been accounted a skillful writer, most critics have approved of her subject matter and have found ideals of some merit in her writing. Her sincerity and concern are evident in the novels, even though her tendency to use stock characters, convenient endings and overcharged prose may mar them as literature.

—Kay J. Mussell

---

**HOLBROOK, David (Kenneth).** British. Born in Norwich, Norfolk, 9 January 1923. Educated at Colman Road Primary School; City of Norwich School; Downing College, Cambridge (Exhibitioner), 1941–42, 1945–47, M.A. 1946. Served as a Tank Troop Officer, and Explosives and Intelligence Officer, in the East Riding of Yorkshire Yeomanry, 1942–45. Married Margot Holbrook in 1949; has four children. Assistant Editor, *Our Time* magazine, London, 1947–48; Assistant Editor, Bureau of Current Affairs, London, 1948–51; Tutor in Adult Education and School Teacher, 1951–61: Tutor at Bassingbourn Village College, Cambridgeshire, 1954–61; Fellow, King's College, Cambridge, 1961–65; Part-time Lecturer in English, Jesus College, Cambridge, 1968–70; Writer-in-Residence, Dartington Hall, Devon (Elmgrant Trust grant), 1970–72. Attended Dartmouth Seminar on English Syllabus Reform, Hanover, New Hampshire, 1966; British Council Lecturer in Germany, 1969; appointed Compton Lecturer in Poetry, University of Hull, Yorkshire, 1970 (resigned); visited Australia on British Council grant to work with English teachers, 1970. Recipient: Writing Fellowship, King's College, Cambridge, and Cambridge University Press, 1961; Leverhulme Senior Research Fellowship, 1964; Arts Council grant, 1970. Address: Yonder, Lustleigh, Newton Abbot, Devon, England.

PUBLICATIONS

Novel

*Flesh Wounds*. London, Methuen, 1966.

Short Stories

*Lights in the Sky Country*.   London, Putnam, 1962.

Play

*The Quarry*, music by John Joubert (opera for children).   London, Novello, 1967.

Verse

*Imaginings*.   London, Putnam, 1961.
*Against the Cruel Frost*.   London, Putnam, 1963.
*Penguin Modern Poets 4*, with others.   London, Penguin, 1963.
*Object Relations*.   London, Methuen, 1967.
*Old World, New World*.   London, Rapp and Whiting, 1969.

Other

*Children's Games*.   Bedford, Gordon Fraser, 1957.
*English for Maturity*.   London, Cambridge University Press, 1961.
*Llareggub Revisited* (on Dylan Thomas).   London, Bowes and Bowes, 1962.
*The Secret Places: Essays on Imaginative Work in English Teaching and on the Culture of the Child*.   London, Methuen, 1964.
*English for the Rejected*.   London, Cambridge University Press, 1964.
*The Quest for Love*.   London, Methuen, 1964.
*I've Got to Use Words*.   London, Cambridge University Press, 1966.
*The Flowers Shake Themselves Free* (songs set by Wilfred Mellers).   London, Novello, 1966.
*The Exploring Word*.   London, Cambridge University Press, 1967.
*Children's Writing*.   London, Cambridge University Press, 1967.
*Human Hope and the Death Instinct*.   Oxford, Pergamon Press, 1971.
*The Masks of Hate*.   Oxford, Pergamon Press, 1971.
*Sex and Dehumanisation*.   London, Pitman, 1972.
*Dylan Thomas and the Code of Night*.   London, Athlone Press, 1972.
*The Pseudo-Revolution*.   London, Stacey, 1972.
*English in Australia Now*.   London, Cambridge University Press, 1972.

Editor, *Iron Honey Gold* (anthology of verse).   London, Cambridge University Press, 1961.
Editor, *People and Diamonds* (anthology of stories).   London, Cambridge University Press, 1962.
Editor, *Thieves and Angels* (anthology of drama).   London, Cambridge University Press, 1963.
Editor, *Visions of Life* (anthology of prose).   London, Cambridge University Press, 1964.
Editor, with Elizabeth Poston, *The Cambridge Hymnal*.   London, Cambridge University Press, 1967.
Editor, *Plucking the Rushes* (anthology of Chinese poetry).   London, Heinemann, 1968.
Editor, *I've Got to Use Words* (course for less-abled children).   London, Cambridge University Press, 1969.

Critical Study: essay in school edition of *Flesh Wounds*, London, Longman, 1967.

David Holbrook comments:

Since 1961 I have been working hard in the realms of psychoanalytical theory and philosophy, to try to discover a tenable "point of view", by which I could feel confidence—in a human future, and in man's capacity to find meaning in his existence. I felt it was pointless to go on writing in any mode until I had made up my mind about human nature. The fashionable attitudes to man's nature—Freudian, or "naked ape" theories—did not satisfy me. In the end I tried, in *Human Hope and the Death Instinct*, to state what I thought to be believable about man, and how he could create a future for himself.

Alas, all this work has made me more out of tune with my time than ever before, and has made the creative task even more daunting. Because I believe them to be so wrong philosophically, I cannot follow the present-day stream of "realistic" writers, who see man unmasked as "really" brutal, coarse and aggressive. I believe that a great deal of our culture is devoted to "false solutions", and that a great deal of it is slipping back out of genuine symbolism, into perversion and primitive forms of "acting out"—forms of cultural delinquency. Moreover, I believe that anything I now want to say will seem impossibly "old-fashioned"—just as, to the therapist treating the schizophrenic, ordinary life comes to seem "pallid and artificial" beside the world of desperate psychopathological gestures.

At the moment, when I have just handed in a book intended to inspire English teachers in Australia to be more creative, our cultural scene in England seems hopeless—decadent and destructive, and I begin 1971 with a deep feeling of dismay about creativity and its future. However, I intend soon to begin a new novel on the experiences of a young teacher in England, America and Australia, based on my experiences of these countries in 1966 and 1970, and I have just finished revising another called *Nothing Larger Than Life*. I am at work on a new humanities course and I have half a dozen other books under consideration.

*         *         *

David Holbrook is best-known for his work in education, but also has a reputation as poet and literary and social critic. His *Lights in the Sky Country* contains a novel and four short stories, in which he displays a love of the subtle charms of East Anglia, the "sky country," his dislikes in modern industrial society, and a plotting involving quite a lot of violence and sudden death. The three are awkwardly juxtaposed, and dialogue and characterization are sometimes awkward, too. These apprentice works do not prepare the reader for the quality of his novel, *Flesh Wounds*.

This book takes up the life-story of a youth of 19 in Autumn 1942, as he spends his last weeks before conscription in a Cambridge factory. His lower middleclass background, his view of the importance of art, his discovery of love and sex, are sketched in; they are at times touching but a bit commonplace. Called-up, he endures basic training, then quite enjoys learning about tanks with the Royal Armoured Corps at Sandhurst, Battle School in North Wales and more training in the north of Scotland. He shows the army's cruelty and inhumanity, and also its sheer absurdity. His response is sensitive, but often he cannot find anything new to tell us. Strangely, he comes to like many aspects of army life, and the military spirit wins him from his girl friend.

Nearly half the novel, however, is a detailed description of the Normandy invasion of June 1944. Earlier Holbrook seems to be understanding himself, or explaining himself to his wife, but now he has a subject of general interest to report: though still personal, he becomes less analytical. This is what it felt like to take part in this great event, while it was happening. Somewhat artless, he offers no contrived heights and depths, simply the truth with close to total recall, for each field occupied, each singing bird, each ruined village, each burst of enemy gunfire. He expresses his emotions as he hears the Commanders' messages, the appearance of the first British casualties, and a moving moment when, under heavy mortar-fire for the first time, he notices beetles.

After a couple of weeks in the thick of the Normandy fighting, the hero is wounded and sent back to England. The rest of his war is briefly described up to his return to Cambridge as a student, with some kind of re-discovery of human love. But this is perfunctory, little more than a frame for the central account of the horrors—and occasional excitements—of the Normandy experience. The writing is not of the quality of Graves or Blunden on World War I, or Orwell on the Spanish Civil War, but this is as good as anything I know —as fact or disguised fiction—on World War II in Europe.

—Malcolm Page

* * *

**HOLMES, John Clellon.** American. Born in Holyoke, Massachusetts, 12 March 1926. Educated at Columbia University, New York, 1943, 1945–46; New School for Social Research, New York, 1949–50. Served in the Hospital Corps of the United States Navy, 1944–45. Married Shirley Allen in 1953. Lecturer, Yale University, New Haven, Connecticut, 1959; Visiting Lecturer, Writers Workshop, University of Iowa, Iowa City, 1963–64; Writer-in-Residence, University of Arkansas, Fayetteville, 1966; Visiting Professor, Bowling Green State University, Ohio, 1968, and Brown University, Providence, Rhode Island, 1971–72. Recipient: *Playboy* magazine non-fiction award, 1964, 1970. Address: Box 75, Old Saybrook, Connecticut 06475, U.S.A.

PUBLICATIONS

Novels

   *Go*. New York, Scribner, 1952; London, Ace, 1959.
   *The Horn*. New York, Random House, 1958; London, Deutsch, 1959.
   *Get Home Free*. New York, Dutton, 1964; London, Corgi, 1966.

Uncollected Short Stories

   "Tea for Two", in *Neurotica* (St. Louis), Spring 1948.
   "A Length of Chain", in *Nugget* (New York), August 1960.
   "The Next to the Last Time", in *Escapade* (New York), September 1967.

Other

   *Nothing More to Declare* (essays and memoirs). New York, Dutton, 1967; London, Deutsch, 1968.

   Poetry published in many American magazines.

Manuscript Collection: Boston University Library.

Critical Studies: *Radical Innocence* by Ihab Hassan, Princeton, New Jersey, Princeton University Press, 1961; *The Erotic Revolution* by Lawrence Lipton, Los Angeles, Sherbourne Press, 1965; *Voices from the Love Generation* by Leonard Wolf, Boston, Little Brown, 1968.

John Clellon Holmes comments:

I take as my working-rule D. H. Lawrence's statement: "Man is a great venture in consciousness." To me, this venture into new areas of awareness is the underlying theme of most important 20th century work.

The rebel, the outcast, the artist, the young—all those whose extremes of consciousness match their extremes of experience—are my subjects. The single recurring theme of my work so far has been a concern with the origins and effects of contemporary uprootedness—particularly its psychological and spiritual aspects. The search for new continuities to replace those of the family, religious faith and social idealism—continuities in comradeship, passional love, and artistic creation—occurs again and again in my work.

As a novelist, I find myself wedded to the idea that the building of living characters is the first essential for enduring fiction, and so I tend to work outward, from character toward events, instead of vice versa. The power of the novel to illuminate our lives lies precisely in its ability to convince us that others live as intensely as ourselves.

\*     \*     \*

John Clellon Holmes writes novels that one would find easy to praise extravagantly if they were written by a friend. He is an alert and intelligent observer of the public and private life about him. His prose is precise, his images clearly etched and accurate in detail, his novels carefully structured. Whenever he sits down to write he has a subject squarely in front of him, and for the most part he gives every evidence of knowing precisely what he wants to do with it. Yet his novels are good primarily in the sense that they are pedestrian, workmanlike, and completely serious. They are not great. He has not yet broken through to the BIG novel he might one day write.

Much of his later performance is an extension of what was begun in his first novel, *Go*, where he recorded the life style of his friends in the late 1940's in New York, and because two of those friends were Jack Kerouac and Allen Ginsberg (fictionalized as Gene Pasternak and David Stofsky) the novel has acquired an interest for literary historians that it did not have on its initial appearance. Firmly entrenched as a chronicler of his times after the appearance of *Go* and the fine essay "This Is the Beat Generation," he turned to the world of jazz—told from the perspective of its Negro performers—in *The Horn*. Again the interest is not solely novelistic; the reader's affection for such musicians as Lester Young and Billie Holiday adds a dimension not generally present in the fictional characters who serve as their surrogates. Only in *Get Home Free*, where the life of Holmes himself seems more central than it does in the earlier novels, does he begin to create characters who are asked to exist firmly on their own, without the support of the reader's outside knowledge and interest. (This last statement must be qualified by the recognition that when Holmes began *Go* he could not have known of the fame later to be attained by Kerouac and Ginsberg and when he got into the last hundred pages of *The Horn* he did much to lift his horn player out of the world of fact and into the world of fictional reality.)

One thinks in terms of a BIG novel for Holmes primarily because he has tried to force bigness upon each one that he has thus far written. In *Go* he attempted to define a generation. *The Horn* was the history of a music. In *Get Home Free* he spread the action north to Connecticut and south to Louisiana in search of a geographic definition for the rootlessness of Americans making it in Manhattan. An old-fashioned novelist in some ways, he displays an old-fashioned desire to write the Great American Novel. One of his most annoying traits is his habit of assigning SIGNIFICANCE to the actions of his characters, so that it comes as a relief when an individual scratches his nose without the author informing us that the action is a peculiarly American one, with Freudian overtones, dating from Cotton Mather's investigations of the psychology of the invisible world. His structure, too, can be burdensome, as it is in *The Horn*, where he selects an American literary figure to associate, for reasons not usually clear, with each of his characters.

In *Nothing More to Declare* he informs us that he has less desire now than he once had to classify, to generalize. Whether that also means that he has less urge to write novels is not clear; perhaps it means that if he does write them he will allow the meanings to grow from within rather than imposing them from without. If he does that he may yet write a better book than those he has given us to date.

—George Perkins

HOOD, Hugh (John Blagdon).  Canadian.  Born in Toronto, Ontario, 30 April 1928. Educated at the University of Toronto, 1947–55, B.A. 1950, M.A. 1952, Ph.D. 1955. Married Ruth Noreen Mallroy in 1957; has four children. Teaching Fellow, University of Toronto, 1951–55; Associate Professor, St. Joseph College, West Hartford, Connecticut, 1955–61. Since 1961, Professeur titulaire, University of Montreal. Recipient: President's Medal, University of Western Ontario, 1961, 1967; Beta Sigma Phi Sorority Prize, 1965; Canada Council Senior Arts Fellowship, 1971. Address: 4242 Hampton Avenue, Montreal 261, Quebec, Canada.

PUBLICATIONS

Novels

   *White Figure, White Ground*.   New York, Dutton, and Toronto, Ryerson Press, 1964.
   *The Camera Always Lies*.   New York, Harcourt Brace, and Toronto, Longman, 1967.
   *A Game of Touch*.   Toronto, Longman, 1970.
   *You Can't Get There from Here*.   Ottowa, Oberon Press, and London, Dobson, 1972.

Short Stories

   *Flying a Red Kite*.   Toronto, Ryerson Press, 1962.
   *Around the Mountain: Scenes from Montreal Life*.   Toronto, Peter Martin, 1967.
   *The Fruit Man, The Meat Man, and The Manager*.   Ottawa, Oberon Press, and London, Dobson, 1971.

Other

   *Strength Down Centre: The Jean Beliveau Story*.   Toronto, Prentice Hall, 1970.

Critical Studies: "Line and Form" by Dave Godfrey, in *Tamarack Review* (Toronto), Spring 1965; "Grace: The Novels of Hugh Hood" by Dennis Duffy, in *Canadian Literature* (Vancouver), February 1971.

Hugh Hood comments:

An interviewer recently asked me why all my fiction began with an appearance of realism and then almost always merged into a dream or reverie or fantasy. I thought that this was a very astute question, because this is exactly how I design my work. I consider it as both realist and super-realist, somewhat like the movies of Fellini or the paintings of Stanley Spencer or Alex Colville—where a pertinacious imitation of the appearance of social reality turns without much warning into a very curious and private vision. I couldn't answer the interviewer's question "why?" I just know that this is how I do it. I might add that I do not think that the Romantic Movement failed, nor do I think that it is over. It seems to me that I, at least, am still in the middle of it.

\*        \*        \*

Hugh Hood is a Canadian writer whose work defies easy generalization. Perhaps more than any other writer now publishing in Canada, he is aware of the implications of the recurring problem of a "Canadian identity," and yet his concern is seldom obvious and inevitably, it seems, it is tied to both larger and more particular human problems. He is a complicated craftsman, but his work seems easy to read. He experiments with various prose forms, but does so in such a quiet manner that the experiments do not call attention to themselves. He is a tough moralist, but his work seldom features anything like an obviously dramatic moral confrontation. He is a committed Christian, but he is neither easy nor orthodox about his religion. It is not surprising, therefore, that he has puzzled as many critics as he has impressed.

His first novel, *White Figure, White Ground*, received wide critical acclaim (insofar as any novel can receive "wide critical acclaim" in Canada), but little subsequent attention, and is now out of print. Two later novels, *The Camera Always Lies* and *A Game of Touch*, received "mixed reviews." Almost all the critics seem to be agreed, however, that Hood is a master of the short-story form, and his stories have been widely admired and anthologized. Two short story collections have appeared—*Flying a Red Kite* and *Around the Mountain: Scenes from Montreal Life*. The latter, however, is a totality—a coherent, whole book which examines various aspects of Montreal life, and which happens to use the short-story form as a tool.

But it is perhaps the large, coherent dimensions of Hood's work which make it so significant, and the complexity of these dimensions which makes it so challenging.

The coherence of Hood's work results from a thinking which follows a course something like the following: The initial premise is that the universe is, ultimately, chaotic. The protagonist of *White Figure, White Ground* is an artist who travels from his home in Montreal to Nova Scotia not only to seek out the answers to questions about his immediate ancestry, but also to search for answers about the nature of the universe. Among other things, the novel is a study of the relativity of time and space, and it is not surprising that the work of the artist results in abstract evocations of primal light.

But if the universe is chaotic, what is order? Order, Hood seems to imply, is the result of human assertion. Thus the artist of *White Figure, White Ground* says that "man makes landscape." Human reality is the result of human assertion. Human assertion results in identity.

However, Hood does not pretend that such decisions, however necessary, are easy. They are full of pitfalls. In one short story the heroine chooses to be "fashionable," and, in effect, erases herself. In another—which examines the problem of "identity" in a particularly

Canadian context—the English-Canadian heroine tries to become French-Canadian and, again, fails. She turns up later in *A Game of Touch* as nothing more than a sexual object. Choices are necessary, but they are limited. One must take into account facts of life, and facts of ancestry, culture, and history. But it is in this regard that Hood is a particularly Canadian writer, accepting the challenge, in fact, of the older writer, Hugh MacLennan, who has sought to explore the impact of the specifically Canadian context (its two cultures, for example) on the individual.

Nor is it surprising that the moral choice of identity has led Hood to explore the significance and dimensions of religion. He examines "natural" religion and, more specifically Roman Catholicism, and finds that religion is in fact an agreed-upon creation which imposes an order upon the universe. Again it is a dangerous business; mistakes abound. The very necessity of human decision and its effects can lead one into pride—as it does the hockey players in "The Sportive Centre of Saint Vincent de Paul" (*Around the Mountain*). Again, the moral concern of Hood has an earlier example in Canadian literature—that of Morley Callaghan, and again Hood seems to be accepting the challenge quite consciously.

In the final judgement, it is likely that the profound dimensions of Hood's work will establish his reputation, not only in Canadian literature, but in literature in English.

—Kent Thompson

**HOPKINSON, Tom.** British. Born in Manchester, 19 April 1905. Educated at St. Edward's School, Oxford (Classical Scholarship), 1919–23; Pembroke College, Oxford (Classical Scholarship), 1923–27, B.A. 1927; M.A. 1932. Married Antonia White, *q.v.*, in 1930 (marriage dissolved, 1938); Dorothy Vernon Kingsmill, 1953; has three children. Worked as a free-lance journalist and in advertising and publicity, 1927–34; Assistant Editor of *Clarion*, London, 1934, and of *Weekly Illustrated*, London, 1934–38; Co-Founder and Assistant Editor, 1938–40, and Editor, 1940–50, *Picture Post*, London; Editor, *Lilliput*, London, 1941–46; Features Editor, *News Chronicle*, London, 1954–56; Editor-in-Chief, *Drum* magazine, Johannesburg, 1958–61; Director for Africa, International Press Institute, Nairobi, Kenya, 1963–66. Senior Fellow in Press Studies, University of Sussex, Brighton, 1967–69; Visiting Professor of Journalism and Mass Communication, University of Minnesota, Minneapolis, 1968–69. Since 1970, Director of the School of Journalism Studies, University College, Cardiff. C.B.E. (Commander, Order of the British Empire), 1967. Address: 6 Marine Parade, Penarth, Glamorgan CF6 2BE, Wales.

PUBLICATIONS

Novels

    *A Wise Man Foolish.* London, Chapman and Hall, 1930.
    *The Man Below.* London, Hogarth Press, 1937.
    *Mist in the Tagus.* London, Hogarth Press, 1946; Boston, Little Brown, 1947.
    *Down the Long Slide.* London, Hogarth Press, 1949; New York, Morrow, 1950.

Short Stories

*The Transitory Venus*.   London, Horizon, 1948.
*The Lady and the Cut-Throat: Short Stories*.   London, Cape, 1958.

Other

*A Strong Hand at the Helm; Being a Complete and Final Vindication of the Sincerity, Lucidity, Profundity and Penetration of Our Prime Minister, the Right Honourable J. Ramsay Macdonald* (as Vindicator).   London, Gollancz, 1933.
*Fascists at Olympia: A Record of Eye-Witnesses and Victims* (as Vindicator).   London, Gollancz, 1934.
*Photocrimes*, with Mileson Horton (as Thomas Pembroke).   London, Barker, 1936; New York, Hillman Curl, 1937.
*Love's Apprentice: A Handbook for Combatants in the War of the Sexes*.   London, Cape, 1953.
*George Orwell*.   London, Longman, 1953.
*In the Fiery Continent*.   London, Gollancz, 1962; New York, Doubleday, 1964.
*South Africa*, with the editors of *Life*.   New York, Time, 1964.

Editor, *Picture Post 1938–1950*.   London, Allen Lane and Penguin, 1970.


Tom Hopkinson comments:

I have lead a busy life as a journalist, editor, and teacher of journalism, in England, Africa and America. Throughout it I have tried, with only limited success, to keep a thread of imaginative writing going, having always the dream or intention of retiring at some time to concentrate entirely on imaginative and creative work. So far that time has not arrived. I have, however, for the past six years, been at work on a long slow novel in which I am trying to crystallise my experience of life as a whole together with the profound impact made on me by my nine years in Africa.

Apart from imaginative writing I have inevitably been drawn into writing books based on or related to my journalistic work.

\*       \*       \*

Tom Hopkinson's reputation rests chiefly upon a series of remarkable short stories contributed to *Horizon* and *New Writing* between 1936 and 1946 and collected in a volume entitled *The Transitory Venus*.   The subjects of these stories range from love ("The Third Secretary's Story") to madness ("Over the Bridge"), but in almost all recurs the theme of a man pitting himself against nature in order to prove himself. In "Mountain Madness" a little clerk, shod in plimsolls, attempts a formidable peak; in "Above the Snow Line" a lover describes minutely the sensations of recovering consciousness after a skiing accident. Two other stories describe ordeals at sea; one of these, "I Have Been Drowned," gives a remarkable minute by minute account of what it feels like to drown. Indeed the themes of drowning and ordeal at sea are recurrent.

Tom Hopkinson published two novels before the war, of which *The Man Below* was the most successful. It described the culminating ordeal (again by water) in the life of Sinbad Woodward, a man with a lifelong fear of water. Sinbad is the child of middle class parents who send him to boarding school at the age of seven because, in the opinion of his mother, it will knock the nonsense out of him. His ruses to achieve popularity at King Alfred's, without being rich or good at games, are amusingly described. His adventures at Oxford are also given in some detail up to the point where he meets Kenley, a rich and boastful young man who, knowing nothing of sailing, persuades him to join an expedition in a leaking fishing boat to the Isle of Man. Woodward is determined to overcome his fear of water once and for all. The outcome is inevitable. The leaking ship runs into a storm but Woodward finds in himself reserves of strength which save her from going down. After a twenty-four hour struggle the ship makes land, not on the Isle of Man but somewhere along the coast of Ireland.

After the war Hopkinson published two short novels. These were more successful than his pre-war ones, possibly because, in a smaller space, he was able to sustain lifelike characters. *Mist in the Tagus* describes a girl's holiday in Portugal and her relationship with two homosexuals. It gives a vivid picture of the country. *Down the Long Slide* describes the escape of Brusilov, a political undesirable from a police state which might be taken to be Nazi Germany. It is a concise, well-told story and ends with a desperate tramp across a mountain range in the best Hopkinson tradition.

Tom Hopkinson's most recent work of fiction was *The Lady and the Cut-Throat*, a collection of short stories published in 1958. In the title story, a lady faced with a dangerous journey is given a cut-throat to travel with her in place of the knightly guardian she expected. It is explained to her that even a child can outwit the conventionally honourable man since everyone knows how he will behave. The more dangerous the journey, the more cunning and ruthless must be the escort. In a sense this story typifies the underlying attitudes of all the stories in the collection. They centre upon relationships—sometimes of men and women in love, sometimes of men with one another in business or adventure. Exceptions are the two stories of the Far North written after a visit to Lapland.

—Isabel Quigley

HORGAN, Paul. American. Born in Buffalo, New York, 1 August 1903. Educated at Nardin Academy, Buffalo; Albuquerque, New Mexico public schools; New Mexico Military Institute, Roswell, 1920–23. Served in the United States Army as Chief of the Army Information Branch, 1942–46: advanced through grades to Lieutenant Colonel; awarded Legion of Merit; recalled to active duty, 1952. Member of the Production Staff, Eastman Theatre, Rochester, New York, 1923–26; Librarian, 1926–42, and Assistant to the President, 1947–49, New Mexico Military Institute (the Institute library is named for him); Lecturer, Graduate School of Letters, University of Iowa, Iowa City, 1946. Senior Fellow, 1959–61, and Director, 1962–67, Center for Advanced Studies, and Adjunct Professor of English and Author-in-Residence, 1967–71, and since 1971, Professor Emeritus, Wesleyan University, Middletown, Connecticut. Hoyt Fellow, 1965, and since 1967, Associate Fellow, Saybrook College, Yale University, New Haven, Connecticut. President, Roswell Museum, 1946–52; Member of the Board, Roswell Public Library, 1958–62; Chairman of the Board, Santa Fe Opera, New Mexico, 1958–62. President, American Catholic Historical Association, 1960. Member, National Council on the Humanities, 1966–71. Scholar-in-Residence Aspen Institute, Colorado, 1968. Since 1969. Member of the Editorial Board of The Book of the Month Club, New York. Recipient: Harper Prize Novel Award, 1933; Guggenheim Fellowship, 1945, 1958; Pulitzer Prize, for history, 1955; Bancroft Prize, for history, 1955; Catholic Book Club's Campion Award, 1957; Catholic Book Award, 1965, 1969. Litt.D., Wesleyan University, 1956; Southern Methodist University, Dallas, 1957; University of Notre Dame, Indiana, 1958; Boston College, 1958; New Mexico State University, University Park, 1961; College of the Holy Cross, Worcester, Massachusetts, 1962; University of New Mexico, Albuquerque, 1963; Fairfield University, Connecticut, 1964; D'Youville

College, Buffalo, New York, 1965; Pace College, New York, 1968; Loyola College, Baltimore, 1968; Lincoln College, Illinois, 1969; St. Bonaventure University, New York, 1969; La Salle College, Philadelphia, 1971; D.H.L., Canisius College, Buffalo, 1960; Georgetown University, Washington, D.C., 1963. Knight of St. Gregory, 1957. Member, National Institute of Arts and Letters. Address: 77 Pearl Street, Middletown, Connecticut 06457, U.S.A.

PUBLICATIONS

Novels

    *The Fault of Angels.*  New York, Harper, 1933; London, Hamish Hamilton, 1934.
    *No Quarter Given.*  New York, Harper, and London, Constable, 1935.
    *Mountain Standard Time* (trilogy).  New York, Farrar Straus, and London, Macmillan, 1962.
        *Main Line West.*  New York, Harper, 1936; London, Constable, 1937.
        *Far from Cibolla.*  New York, Harper, 1938.
        *The Common Heart.*  New York, Harper, 1942.
    *A Lamp on the Plains.*  New York, Harper, and London, Constable, 1937.
    *The Devil in the Desert: A Legend of Life and Death in the Rio Grande.*  New York, Longman, 1952.
    *The Saintmaker's Christmas Eve.*  New York, Farrar Straus, 1955; London, Macmillan, 1956.
    *Give Me Possession.*  New York, Farrar Straus, 1957; London, Macmillan, 1958.
    *A Distant Trumpet.*  New York, Farrar Straus, and London, Macmillan, 1960.
    *Things as They Are.*  New York, Farrar Straus, 1964; London, Bodley Head, 1965.
    *Everything to Live For.*  New York, Farrar Straus, 1968; London, Bodley Head, 1969.
    *Whitewater.*  New York, Farrar Straus, 1970; London, Bodley Head, 1971.

Short Stories

    *The Return of the Weed.*  New York, Harper, 1936; as *Lingering Walls*, London, Constable, 1936.
    *Figures in a Landscape.*  New York, Harper, 1940.
    *Humble Powers: 3 Novelettes.*  London, Macmillan, 1954; New York, Doubleday, 1956.
    *The Peach Stone: Stories from 4 Decades.*  New York, Farrar Straus, 1967; London, Bodley Head, 1968.

Plays

    *A Tree on the Plains: A Music Play for Americans*, music by Ernest Bacon.  New York, A. L. Williams, 1942.
    *Yours, A. Lincoln* (produced New York, 1942).  Copyright as *Martyrdom in Washington*, New York, A. L. Williams, 1961.
    *One Red Rose for Christmas.*  New York, Longman, 1952.

Other

    *Men of Arms* (juvenile).  Philadelphia, McKay, 1931.

*From the Royal City of the Holy Faith of Saint Francis of Assisi: Being Five Accounts of Life in That Place.*   Santa Fe, New Mexico, Villagra Bookshop, 1936.

*The Habit of Empire.*   Santa Fe, New Mexico, Rydal Press, and New York, Harper, 1938.

*Look at America: The Southwest*, with the editors of *Look*.   Boston, Houghton Mifflin, 1947.

*Great River: The Rio Grande in North American History.*   New York, Rinehart, 2 vols., 1954.

*The Centuries of Santa Fe.*   New York, Dutton, 1956; London, Macmillan, 1957.

*Rome Eternal.*   New York, Farrar Straus, 1957.

*Citizen of New Salem.*   New York, Farrar Straus, 1961; as *Abraham Lincoln: Citizen of New Salem*, London, Macmillan, 1961.

*Toby and the Nightingale* (juvenile).   New York, Farrar Straus, 1962.

*Conquistadors in North American History.*   New York, Farrar Straus, 1963; as *Conquistadors in American History*, London, Macmillan, 1963.

*Peter Hurd: A Portrait Sketch from Life.*   Austin, University of Texas Press, 1965.

*Songs after Lincoln.*   New York, Farrar Straus, 1965.

*Memories of the Future.*   New York, Farrar Straus, and London, Bodley Head, 1966.

*The Heroic Triad: Essays in the Social Energies of Three Southwestern Cultures.*   New York, Holt Rinehart, 1970; London, Heinemann, 1971.

Editor, with M. G. Fulton, *New Mexico's Own Chronicle: Three Races in the Writings of Four Hundred Years.*   Dallas, Banks Upshaw, 1937.

Editor, *Diary and Letters of Josiah Gregg.*   Norman, University of Oklahoma Press, 2 vols., 1941, 1943.

Editor, *Maurice Baring Restored: Selections from His Work.*   New York, Farrar Straus, and London, Heinemann, 1970.

Manuscript Collection: Yale University, New Haven, Connecticut.

Paul Horgan comments:

In my fiction I hope to enclose in a precisely appropriate and thus beautiful form a story which rises from the interaction of characters brought alive through understanding of human life, in settings which are evocative in atmosphere, set forth in language interesting for its own sake as well as for its suitability to the subject matter.

In my non-fiction—history, biography, other forms—I hope to tell the truth of actual events while retelling them in such a manner that the resources of the novelist in presenting scene and character allow the reader a sense of experiencing the past rather than simply hearing about it.

\*      \*      \*

One literary legend has it that as an orphan Paul Horgan was standing on a Buffalo, New York, street corner singing to passerbys; by chance, and attracted by the quality of the song, a wealthy gentleman befriended the waif and among other things later sponsored professional vocal training at a conservatory. Precisely true or not, this legend gives certain insights into Horgan's life and work.

The Horatio Alger implication of Horgan's career is manifest in steady production and wide variety: novels, short stories, plays; opera, biography, cultural reportage, national, regional, and church history. Among other things, he is an acknowledged national authority on A. Lincoln, Beethoven, the conquistadors, the cultures and history of the Great Southwest in America, most notably the regions of the Rio Grande River. Horgan brings to all his work an artistic integrity of a very high order. The style is supple and clean; the attitude towards all materials is broadly humanistic. The history and the cultural reportage are remarkable for the visual quality, scrupulous attention to detail, and the exploitation of symbolic incident or encounter. Horgan's talent is fully dramatic in nature; his responses to materials is symphonic in scale. Industry for its own sake, however, is not implied for the author's concept of work is of an order which in fact tends to enrich the writer's life. Thus Horgan's well-known gift for friendship is another facet of a productive, well-integrated personality of great warmth and charm. These things are even more remarkable when it is understood that Horgan taught himself to write while serving as a librarian in a boy's school in the Southwest; only after a long literary apprenticeship of frustration and isolation was his talent recognized when he won a major American literary prize for his novel *The Fault of Angels*.

Paul Horgan is a deeply committed Catholic and is America's foremost writer of that conviction at the present time. This fact has several literary implications. Although *Rome Eternal* may suggest a thoroughly Catholic point of view, Horgan is much too deeply committed as an artist to become merely a "spokesman" for the Church. Doubtless he would concur with the suggestion that he is an artist who happens to be a Catholic; yet, presumably, he would not seriously imagine writing to greater advantage from any other viewpoint. Actually the weight of his very personal kind of commitment varies a great deal. When handling church-connected subject matter he treats the theme sympathetically, urbanely, and with great delicacy; when writing on materials less specifically Catholic he displays a characteristic optimism, a charity, a softening of certain reoccurring realities of life. In turn this softening of the hard edge of reality is not so much sentiment as it is an awareness of spiritual forces in the world which may be registered as ultimately harmonious. Whether or not these fundamentally optimistic attitudes are to be equated with either the more fortuitous aspects of his own life and/or his spiritual training is a question too complex for brief analysis.

Ultimately, Horgan's literary significance will rest less with a commitment to Catholicism and much more with his stature as a regional writer. America's literature is a regional literature, and Horgan already is the Master of the Great Southwest. In comparison with Faulkner (of the same literary generation) Horgan's clarity, depth, objectivity, and consistency are the greater; on the other hand, Horgan is the less experimental and is less inclined to focus on the more pervasive, sordid, aspects of modernity. Unlike Faulkner, Horgan probably makes more concessions to the genteel audience, the literary passerbys of America. In any event, the comparison as regionalists of the two talents reflects no discredit on either artist.

Now approaching seventy, Horgan continues to be vital and productive. His life itself is a meaningful, artistic statement of what a gifted writer in America may accomplish even though the odds were great beyond calculation.

—James B. Hall

---

**HOUSEHOLD, Geoffrey (Edward West).** British. Born in Bristol, 30 November 1900. Educated at Clifton College, Bristol, 1914–19; Magdalen College, Oxford, 1919–22, 1st class honours in English literature 1922. Served in the Intelligence Corps, 1939–45: awarded Territorial Decoration; mentioned in despatches; demobilised with rank of Lieutenant Colonel. Married Ilona M. J. Zzoldos-Gutman in 1942; has three children. Engaged in commerce abroad, 1922–35. Address: Church Headland, Whitchurch, Aylesbury, Buckinghamshire, England.

PUBLICATIONS

Novels

*The Third Hour.*   London, Chatto and Windus, 1937; Boston, Little Brown, 1938.
*Rogue Male.*   London, Chatto and Windus, and Boston, Little Brown, 1939.
*Arabesque.*   London, Chatto and Windus, and Boston, Little Brown, 1948.
*The High Place.*   London, Joseph, and Boston, Little Brown, 1950.
*A Rough Shoot.*   London, Joseph, and Boston, Little Brown, 1951.
*A Time to Kill.*   Boston, Little Brown, 1951; London, Joseph, 1952.
*Fellow Passenger.*   London, Joseph, and Boston, Little Brown, 1955.
*Watcher in the Shadows.*   London, Joseph, and Boston, Little Brown, 1960.
*Thing to Love.*   London, Joseph, and Boston, Little Brown, 1963.
*Olura.*   London, Joseph, and Boston, Little Brown, 1965.
*The Courtesy of Death.*   London, Joseph, and Boston, Little Brown, 1967.
*Dance of the Dwarfs.*   London, Joseph, and Boston, Little Brown, 1968.
*Doom's Caravan.*   London, Joseph, and Boston, Little Brown, 1971.

Short Stories

*The Salvation of Pisco Gabar and Other Stories.*   London, Chatto and Windus, 1938;
    Boston, Little Brown, 1940.
*Tales of Adventurers.*   London, Joseph, and Boston, Little Brown, 1952.
*The Brides of Solomon and Other Stories.*   London, Joseph, and Boston, Little Brown,
    1958.
*Sabres on the Sand and Other Stories.*   London, Joseph, and Boston, Little Brown,
    1966.

Other

*The Terror of Villadonga* (juvenile).   London, Hutchinson, 1936; revised edition, as
    *The Spanish Cave*, Boston, Little Brown, 1936; London, Chatto and Windus, 1940.
*The Exploits of Xenophon* (juvenile).   New York, Random House, 1955; as *Xenophon's
    Adventure*, London, Bodley Head, 1961.
*Against the Wind* (autobiography).   London, Joseph, and Boston, Little Brown, 1958.
*Prisoner of the Indies* (juvenile).   London, Bodley Head, and Boston, Little Brown,
    1967.


Geoffrey Household comments:

My first concern is with the English I write, simple, evocative and therefore enabling me to produce the required impact on the reader without any obscurity. I cannot estimate its literary worth, but I suggest that if there is any permanent value in my work it is to be found in my short stories.

My novels are all suspense novels and deal with the individual trapped in an unwelcome or thoroughly dangerous environment. Only one is a "spy" story and none is a "crime" story. I am told that they seem to be written on two levels—which may mean that in order to create the illusion of reality I have to examine the political, ethical or religious motives of the characters.

By and large the books fall into two classes. *The Third Hour, Arabesque, The High Place* and *Thing to Love* are fairly straight novels, though certainly depending on action and the development of plot. The rest are unashamed "thrillers" with the possible exception of *Olura*, *Dance of the Dwarfs* and *Doom's Caravan*, which are less conventional in form or subject or both and may be defined as the reader likes.

Pedigree: a good, working strain directly descended from Defoe, with a dash of thorough-bred blood from Stevenson and Conrad.

*       *       *

Geoffrey Household came slowly to prominence as a novelist by way of banking, business and war-time Intelligence Service. His first notable success, *Rogue Male*, was published in 1939. He had already placed a number of short stories in the upper reaches of the magazine market, written radio plays for children, and published one novel and a collection of his stories. With *Rogue Male* his career as a professional author was finally consolidated though the war years were to interrupt his output.

He specialises in what used to be called "thrillers" or "suspense stories"—action stories with a strong narrative line, unexpected turns and checks of plot, and on the whole rather slight attention to the portrayal and development of character. Probably the best-known of his books in this genre, after *Rogue Male*, are *A Rough Shoot*, *Watcher in the Shadows*, and *Sabres on the Sand*. This is John Buchan-Richard Hannay territory, complete with officers and gentlemen, foreign agents and manhunts, sketchily realised and subordinate female characters, tweeds, shot-guns and sporting rifles whose telescopic sights are suddenly put to use on more sinister targets than red deer.

It is easy to register a sneer at some aspects of Buchan's Hannay novels today—the blatant snobbery, the imperialist ethno-centrism, the toadying to the pre-war "establishment" and monarchy; but one can never fault Buchan's sure-footed narrative pace. It is a tribute to Geoffrey Household's excellence that his Buchanesque novels stand comparison with his master's in this last respect and do very much better in the others.

The main themes he explores are courage and endurance on the extreme edge of danger and at the limits of human survival, the discharge of obligation and duty, loyalty, and personal honour. The best of his man-hunts take place in the English West Country, about which he writes with affection and the kind of knowledge which comes only to those who stalk wild life with field-glasses and camera or gun. The rogue male's survival in his hideout in a thicket-choked lane; the hunt through the Cotswolds by the shadowy watcher; the hero's frenzied tunnelings in the Mendips in *The Courtesy of Death* (a novel whose donnée of a cult dedicated to killing is less credible than the author's usual contrivances); and the dirty work in the hedgerows and rabbit-warrens of *A Rough Shoot*, are stamped with authenticity.

There is a change of milieu to South America in *Thing to Love*, which portrays the conflict between technologically-based progress and a romantic attachment to the traditional way of life, but continues to examine the theme of divided loyalty and an officer's personal honour.

Geoffrey Household has also published children's books. *Xenophon's Adventure*, his retelling of the *Anabasis*, maintains a characteristically swift pace; while *Prisoner of the Indies*, also based on a factual account, tells the story of a cabin-boy on a slave-ship who is captured by the Spaniards, tortured by the Inquisition, and consigned to a monastery before finally escaping. Geoffrey Household has also published a volume of autobiography.

—Stewart F. Sanderson

**HOWARD, Elizabeth Jane.** British. Born in London, 26 March 1923. Educated privately; trained as an actress at the London Mask Theatre School and with the Scott Thorndyke Student Repertory; played at Stratford-upon-Avon, and in repertory theatre in Devon. Served as an Air Raid Warden in London during World War II. Married Peter M. Scott in 1941; James Douglas-Henry, 1959; Kingsley Amis, *q.v.*, 1965; has one child from her first marriage. Worked as a model, and in radio and television broadcasting, 1939–46; Secretary, Inland Waterways Association, London, 1947–50; Editor, for Chatto and Windus Ltd., London, 1953–56, and for Weidenfeld and Nicolson Ltd., London, 1957; Book Critic, *Queen* magazine, London, 1957–60. Honorary Artistic Director, Cheltenham Literary Festival, 1962. Recipient: Rhys Memorial Prize, 1951. Address: Lemmons, Hadley Common, Barnet, Hertfordshire, England.

PUBLICATIONS

Novels

*The Beautiful Visit.* London, Cape, and New York, Random House, 1950.
*The Long View.* London, Cape, and New York, Reynal, 1956.
*The Sea Change.* London, Cape, 1959; New York, Harper, 1960.
*After Julius.* London, Cape, and New York, Viking Press, 1965.
*Something in Disguise.* London, Cape, 1969; New York, Viking Press, 1970.
*Odd Girl Out.* London, Cape, and New York, Viking Press, 1972.

Short Stories

*We Are for the Dark: Six Ghost Stories*, with Robert Aickman. London, Cape, 1951.

Uncollected Short Stories

"Portrait of My Grandfathers", in *Encounter* (London), 1956.
"A Dangerous Thing", in *The New Yorker*, 16 November 1963.

Other

*Bettina: A Portrait*, with Arthur Helps. London, Chatto and Windus, and New York, Reynal, 1957.

Elizabeth Jane Howard comments:

I consider myself to be in the straight tradition of English novelists. I do not write about "social issues or values"—I write simply about people, by themselves and in relation to one another. The first aim of a novel should be readability. I do not write (consciously, at least) about people whom I know or have met.

My methods are to be able to write in one sentence what my novel is to be about, to test this idea for several months, and then to invent situations that will fit the theme. I make the people last—to suit the situations. I write only one draught and rarely make any alterations to it. Occasional cutting has sometimes seemed necessary. I write about 300 words a day with luck and when I am free to do so. I do it chiefly because it is the most difficult thing that I have ever tried to do.

I began by writing plays when I was 14. Before that I wrote 400 immensely dull pages (since destroyed) about a horse. I have also written a film script of *The Sea Change* with Peter Yates, but this has not yet been produced. I would very much like to write a good play, and, indeed, come to that, a first rate novel.

I have written various pieces, critical and autobiographical, for *The Times*, *Evening Standard*, *Sunday Times*, *Sunday Telegraph*, *Queen*, *Observer*, *Encounter*, *Good Housekeeping*, *Daily Mail*, and *The New Yorker*.

*     *     *

All Elizabeth Jane Howard's five novels are distinguished by sharp and sensitive perceptions about people—their loves, their guilts, the damage they wittingly or unwittingly do to others. Frequently, the perceptions are worked into satirical set pieces, like the treatment of a group of feckless post-Oxford young people sponging in London in *Something in Disguise*. Sometimes the satire is more gentle and generous in tone, like that of the patriotic major in *After Julius* who combines long, boring speeches about the past with silent sensitivity to the human dramas around him. And Miss Howard's heroines, simple, unpretentious, gentle girls are always treated with a great deal of sympathy, with respect for their quiet intelligence and their capacity to feel genuinely for others. Any tendency toward the mawkish or sentimental is carefully controlled by a prose that often works on sharp and comic juxtapositions of images from ordinary experience. In *The Sea Change*, a young actress tries desperately to impress a playwright by showing a knowledge of his plays, "broadcasting her innocuous opinions like weed killer on a well kept lawn."

The careful control visible in Miss Howard's prose is also apparent in the structure of her novels. Most frequently, as in all of *The Sea Change* and most of *After Julius*, the novel consists of alternate narrations from the point of view of a small number of closely connected characters. Each episode is seen from at least two points of view, started by one character, taken up by the next who then moves the narrative on a little further until a third character takes it up. In *After Julius*, the action of the novel is even confined to a three-day week-end, although most of the characters are engaged in sorting out causal connections of current problems to the heroic death of Julius at Dunkerque twenty years earlier. The past inevitably leads to the present, and it is, for Miss Howard, only by understanding and acknowledging the truth of past actions and attitudes that characters can work out of current dilemmas. *After Julius* resolves the current dilemmas positively: Julius' wife and each of his two daughters are able to understand and use the relevant past. The structural control, in this novel, indicates a kind of moral control, an insistence on a combination of awareness, responsibility, and refusal to hurt others in order to end the painful isolation of contemporary dilemmas.

More tightly controlled than the other novels, *After Julius* depends, to some extent, on a rather striking co-incidence. The older daughter, visiting her mother for the week-end, finds her London lover whom she had thought in Rome arriving, with his wife, for dinner, and the affair explodes in a scene where fireworks are literal as well as symbolic. But the plot dependent on co-incidence fits with a novel in which moral or immoral actions eventually reveal themselves, in which moral judgment insists that characters take publicly visible responsibility for their actions. In Miss Howard's fictional world, action is not fragmented or irrelevant, not the private gesture of an alienated sensibility. Rather, actions have consequences, visible and direct, on the people closest to one.

The moral framework of the other novels is less coherent, less immediately apparent. In *The Sea Change*, both an aging playwright, looking for love and a renewal of youth, and his assistant, looking for the stability of a home he has never had, fall in love with the playwright's talented secretary, an intelligent and unspoiled young girl brought up in an isolated parsonage. But, before the loves can be declared or decided, the young girl returns to the parsonage because her wise and revered father has just been killed in a bicycle accident. For the innocent young girl, from the author's point of view, neither love merits the justice of resolution, although the girl herself is hardly aware of this. And, in a switch to another point of view at the end, the playwright, having lost the possibility of renewed love, and his wife, having lost her only child (both the child and the young secretary have the same first name), can understand and forgive each other in the acknowledgment of mutual pain. But, again, acknowledgment, the assumption of responsibility, must precede the characters' coming together. In Miss Howard's most recent novel the moral resolution is more difficult to follow. In *Something in Disguise*, the structure is less tightly controlled by interlocking narratives, but the plot is fiercely resolved in melodrama. The mother, having remained a war-widow for about twenty years in order to bring up her children, finally marries a retired army officer to whom both her children object. Underneath the officer's blunt, dull, insensitive exterior, the author slowly reveals, is the criminal heart of a man who would gradually poison his wife for her money, as he has poisoned two previous wives. And the daughter, who unpredictably marries a man who is both exciting and considerate, both a successful man of the world and a paragon of simple understanding and virtue, finds the man killed in an auto accident when sent on a senseless fool's errand by one of the inconsiderate. Both melodramatic revelations occur on Christmas Day. Although moral judgment on each of the characters is clear enough, the plot punishes with an intensity that seems, somewhat sensationally, to detract from the earlier emphasis on moral choice.

Miss Howard's fiction is also dense with descriptions and references that convey the social texture of the times. *The Sea Change* contrasts the conventional life in the village parsonage with that of the fifties' playwright conveying a young girl to London, New York, and a Greek Island. *After Julius* is brilliant with settings: the tiny attic office of the editorial staff of an old, respectable publishing firm; the spacious, chintzy Tudor of the mother's house in Sussex; the cheerful chaos of a young doctor and his family's crowded flat. *Something in Disguise* contains a brilliantly terrifying portrait of daily life in the pseudo-Spanish surroundings of the "distinguished" house on a new housing estate. Within these tartly observed and wholly recognizable environments, certain types appear in novel after novel. The apparently dull retired Army officer, either fundamentally sensitive and kindly or fundamentally criminal, represents an older England, an irrelevant survival. The confident man of the world, playwright in *The Sea Change*, doctor in *After Julius*, international business-man in *Something in Disguise*, has not allowed charm, success, or the modern world to distort his basically simple sense of responsibility. The novels, too, all contain a wise father lost. The heroine of *The Sea Change* will need, after her father's death, to face the perplexity that the young girls of the later novels—whose fathers were killed in the war— have always known. Sympathetic and competent mothers are not enough. The heroines, without the guidance of a father's wisdom, need time and experience to find the responsible man, to replace the safety so suddenly lost. And looking for the safety, always precarious in a world of airplanes and emotions and betrayals, requires a great deal of control. Miss Howard's great distinction is that the search for safety is presented with such rare and intelligent discrimination.

—James Gindin

---

**HOYLE, Fred.** British. Born in Bingley, Yorkshire, 24 June 1915. Educated at Bingley Grammar School; Emmanuel College, Cambridge, M.A. 1936 (Mayhew Prizeman, 1936; Smith's Prizeman, 1938; Goldsmith Exhibitioner; Senior Exhibitioner of the Royal Commission for the Exhibition of 1851). Served in the Admiralty, London, during World War II. Married Barbara Clark in 1939; has two children. Since 1939, Research Fellow, St. John's College, Cambridge; at Cambridge University: Lecturer in Mathematics, 1945–58; Plumian Professor of Astronomy and Experimental Philosophy, 1958–67; since 1967, Director of the Institute of Theoretical Astronomy. Visiting Professor of Astrophysics, California Institute of Technology, Pasadena, 1958; Professor of Astronomy, Royal Institution, London, 1969. Member of the Science Research Council of Great Britain since 1968. Recipient: Kalinga Prize, 1967; Royal Astronomical Society's Gold Medal, 1968. Honorary Degrees: University of East Anglia, Norwich, 1967; University of Leeds, Yorkshire, 1969. Fellow of the Royal Society, 1957. Honorary Member, American Academy of Arts and Sciences, 1964; Foreign Associate, National Academy of Sciences, 1969. Vice-President, Royal Society, 1970–71; President, Royal Astronomical Society, 1971. Knighted, 1972. Address: Institute of Theoretical Astronomy, Madingley Road, Cambridge, England.

PUBLICATIONS

Novels

The Black Cloud.   London, Heinemann, and New York, Harper, 1957.
Ossian's Ride.   London, Heinemann, and New York, Harper, 1959.
A for Andromeda: A Novel for Tomorrow, with John Elliot.   London, Souvenir Press, and New York, Harper, 1962.
Fifth Planet, with Geoffrey Hoyle.   London, Heinemann, and New York, Harper, 1963.
Andromeda Breakthrough: A Novel of Tomorrow's Universe, with John Elliot.   London, Souvenir Press, and New York, Harper, 1964.
October the First Is Too Late.   London, Heinemann, and New York, Harper, 1966.
Rockets in Ursa Major, with Geoffrey Hoyle.   London, Heinemann, and New York, Harper, 1969.
Seven Steps to the Sun, with Geoffrey Hoyle.   London, Heinemann, and New York, Harper, 1970.
The Molecule Men: Two Short Novels, with Geoffrey Hoyle.   London, Heinemann, 1971.

Short Stories

Element 79.   New York, New American Library, 1967.

Play

Rockets in Ursa Major (produced London, 1962).

Other

Some Recent Researches in Solar Physics.   London and New York, Cambridge University Press, 1949.
The Nature of the Universe.   London, Heinemann, and New York, Harper, 1950; revised edition, Harper, and Oxford, Blackwell, 1960.
A Decade of Decision.   London, Heinemann, 1953.

*Frontiers of Astronomy.*   London, Heinemann, and New York, Harper, 1955.
*Man and Materialism.*   New York, Harper, 1956; London, Allen and Unwin, 1957.
*Astronomy.*   London, Macdonald, and New York, Doubleday, 1962.
*Of Men and Galaxies.*   Seattle, University of Washington Press, 1964; London, Heinemann, 1965.
*Galaxies, Nuclei, and Quasars.*   New York, Harper, 1965; London, Heinemann, 1966.
*Encounter with the Future.*   New York, Simon and Schuster, 1965.
*Nucleosynthesis in Massive Stars and Supernovae,* with W. A. Fowler.   Chicago, University of Chicago Press, 1965.
*Man in the Universe.*   New York, Columbia University Press, 1966.

\*        \*        \*

Hoyle's science fiction novels pose two problems which make their evaluation difficult. First, because the reader is usually aware of Hoyle's very considerable reputation in "real" science, he may expect either too much or too little from the fiction; at any rate, he is unlikely to be neutral in his expectations. Second, because some of the novels are the products of collaboration, they have features which might not be attributable to Hoyle; one suspects that in the collaboration Hoyle has contributed the major skeletal resource which his collaborator has fleshed out. At any rate, the independent novels are more integrated than the others which display many technical defects at the same time as exploring sound basic ideas. In terms of theme, if not of technique, then, there is a discernible continuity and major preoccupation through all the novels.

Hoyle's fictional themes derive directly from his scientific work towards a theory of our universe. *The Black Cloud, Ossian's Ride* and the Andromeda novels all explore the consequences following from Hoyle's theoretic conclusion that intelligent life must abound in our universe and in other universes; *October the First* investigates both the theories of subjective time and time reversal and of the cyclical movement of human civilization ending in the inevitable extinction of human life. In all his novels, Hoyle makes the point that human civilization is inherently unstable and therefore unable either to benefit much by the influence of higher intelligence outside earth, or to contribute to it. In evolutionary terms, humans are pretty low on the scale.

This lowliness is illustrated in particular in his early novels, which present the Terran reaction to contact with extra-terrestial intelligence. The Black Cloud is treated first as a threat to be repelled, then, when its nature is recognized it is seen as something to be learned from—but no-one is able to tolerate the scale of information it can transmit. In *Ossian's Ride* and the Andromeda books humans are shown to lack the moral stature to benefit by outside education; the skills introduced by aliens under the guise of the Industrial Corporation of Eire are either not appreciated by twentieth century Luddites or are coveted by private commercial organizations for their own gain.

In his last novel, *October the First Is Too Late,* Hoyle explicitly and emphatically amplifies this theme: human evolution is bound to end in human extinction so there is the choice between artificially preventing the normal course of evolution and enjoying a sort of finite state life, and letting the race develop normally, but disastrously, with the remote prospect that it might contribute "to some higher level of attainment". Either choice leads to extinction because "ultimate continuity, in a physical, material respect is impossible".

The gravity of theme, particularly in *The Black Cloud* and *October the First* is quite clear, and Hoyle's note to the reader in the latter novel leaves no doubt that he intends his evolutionary thesis to be taken seriously. Moreover, these novels in particular are technically competent enough not to undermine their thematic gravity, although they do not go much beyond illustration and exposition. Unfortunately, the same cannot be said for *Ossian's Ride* and the collaborated novels, because the generality and seriousness of the theme represented by their plots are undermined by a too-pronounced parochiality and resulting diminution. It does not help a reader to take the notion of Cosmic Intelligences seriously when it is coupled with a naive picture of New-Elizabethan-Age little England whose role is to act as sole repository of science and intelligence in a generally blockheaded world. Whereas *The Black Cloud* and *October the First* convince the reader of their seriousness, the other novels convey comicness in their jingoistic naivety and disparate contrast. Added to this basic defect are others which must surely arise from collaboration—stilted dialogue, paper characterization and wavering tone.

Because of the uneven quality of his novels, Hoyle's general contribution to the science fiction novel cannot be accounted great. However, his first and last novels rise above the rest to present provocative and serious considerations of some of the consequences of one particular theory of the universe.

—Frederick Bowers

---

**HUGHES, Richard (Arthur Warren).** British. Born in Weybridge, Surrey, 19 April 1900. Educated at Charterhouse School, Surrey; Oriel College, Oxford, B.A. 1922. Served in the British Army, 1918; in the Admiralty, London, 1940–45; O.B.E. (Officer, Order of the British Empire), 1946. Married Frances C. R. Bazley in 1932; has five children. Co-Founder, and Director, Portmadoc Players, Wales, 1922–25; Vice-Chairman, Welsh National Theatre, 1924–36; Petty Constable of Langharne, 1936; Filmwriter, Ealing Studios, London 1945–55. Recipient: Femina Vie Heureuse Prize, 1929; Arts Council Award, 1961. D.Litt., University of Wales, Cardiff, 1956. Fellow, Royal Society of Literature, 1962. Honorary Member, American Academy of Arts and Letters (Blashfield Foundation Address, 1969). Address: c/o Chatto and Windus, 40–42 William IV Street, London W.C.2, England.

PUBLICATIONS

Novels

    *A High Wind in Jamaica.*  London, Chatto and Windus, 1929; as *The Innocent Voyage*, New York, Harper, 1929.
    *In Hazard: A Sea Story.*  London, Chatto and Windus, 1938; as *In Hazard*, New York, Harper, 1938.
    *The Human Predicament:*
        I. *The Fox in the Attic.*  London, Chatto and Windus, and New York, Harper, 1961.
        II. *The Wooden Shepherdess.*  London, Chatto and Windus, and New York, Harper, 1972.

Short Stories

    *A Moment of Time.*  London, Chatto and Windus, 1926.

Plays

    *The Sisters' Tragedy* (produced London, 1922).  Oxford, Blackwell, 1922.

*The Sisters' Tragedy and Other Plays* (includes *The Man Born to Be Hanged, A Comedy of Good and Evil*, and *Danger*).   London, Heinemann, 1924; as *A Rabbit and a Leg: Collected Plays*, New York, Knopf, 1924.

*A Comedy of Good and Evil* (produced London, 1924; as *Minnie and Mr. Williams*, produced New York, 1948).   Included in *The Sisters' Tragedy and Other Plays*, 1924.

*Danger* (produced BBC radio, 1924).   Included in *The Sisters' Tragedy and Other Plays*, 1924.

Verse

*Gipsy Night and Other Poems*.   London, Golden Cockerel Press, and Chicago, Ransom, 1922.

*Confessio Juvenis: Collected Poems*.   London, Chatto and Windus, 1925.

Other

*Richard Hughes: An Omnibus* (stories, plays, poems).   New York, Harper, 1931.

*The Spider's Palace and Other Stories* (juvenile).   London, Chatto and Windus, 1931; New York, Harper, 1932.

*Don't Blame Me and Other Stories* (juvenile).   London, Chatto and Windus, and New York, Harper, 1940.

*The Administration of War Production*, with J. D. Scott.   London, Her Majesty's Stationery Office, 1956.

*Gertrude's Child* (juvenile).   New York, Harlin Quist, 1966; London, W. H. Allen, 1967.

Editor, with Robert Graves and Alan Porter, *Oxford Poetry 1921*.   Oxford, Blackwell, 1921.

Editor, *Poems*, by John Skelton.   London, Heinemann, 1924.

Critical Studies: "Nature and Convention in *A High Wind in Jamaica*" by T. J. Henigan, in *Critique* (Minneapolis), vol. 9, no. 1, 1967; introduction by the author to *Richard Hughes: An Omnibus*, 1931, *A High Wind in Jamaica*, New York, Time/Life, 1963, and *In Hazard*, New York, Time/Life, 1966.

\*       \*       \*

Richard Hughes, in a writing career that has extended for close on fifty years, has written three novels, two of which, *A High Wind in Jamaica* and *In Hazard*, are modern classics, while the third, *The Fox in the Attic*, which is in fact only the first part of a work in progress to be called *The Human Predicament*, is the prelude to what promises to be a major work of fiction of our time. These three novels are so distinct from one another that it seems impossible, where Hughes is concerned, to talk of his development as a novelist in any ordinary sense.

*A High Wind in Jamaica* is a wholly original novel, a work as it were without ancestors. It begins with a brilliant description of the lives of some young English children on a plantation in Jamaica in the eighteen-sixties; then the children, on a sea-voyage to England, are kidnapped by pirates. The originality of the novel lies in Hughes's attitude towards the children. They are seen from the outside, but in a very special way, as though they were a species of animal quite unlike man. Indeed, Hughes says that an adult has no more possibility of "intellectual sympathy" with children than he would have with an octopus, for he is faced with a total difference in kind. Hughes behaves, then, rather as though he is writing a natural history of children, and of children placed in as it were experimental conditions. And the pirates are presented only less originally than the children. In some ways they are more at the mercy of the children than the children are of them, for they are the dwindling, degenerate survivors of a once giant race.

At the centre of it all is Emily Bas-Thornton, a child on the verge of girlhood when captured, beset by premonitions of womanhood by the time of her rescue. She is rendered in part in terms of a kind of symbolism from animal life, but she is always totally credible. Hughes's evocations of tropical landscape and sea seem at once magisterial and effortless. Without long quotation it is almost impossible to communicate the quality of the novel. It is as though one is caught up in a sustained hallucination—one critic has used the phrase "domesticated bizarreness"—and on the edge of fantasy. But *A High Wind in Jamaica* is not fantasy. Everything in the novel is too real, in a sense too thoroughly documented, for that. Rather, it is a unique exploration into alien modes of being, the alien modes of being—from the adult point of view—of the human child.

The subject of *In Hazard* must bring to mind Conrad, the Conrad of *Typhoon* in particular, for it is the story of a steamer and of the behaviour of her officers and crew caught in a hurricane where no hurricane should be. The story is a heroic one, but there are no heroics: and the apparent ease and casualness of Hughes's prose, its brisk, matter-of-fact, conversational tone, give the story remarkable freshness and immediacy, a quality heightened by the author's uncanny knowledge of steamships. Nevertheless, the affinity with Conrad is a real one. Hughes, too, is concerned with the effects on men of the stresses of an extraordinary situation and with their responses to them. Perhaps the real subject of the novel is men at work, and its real theme duty and the skill and confidence that come of professional training.

But that is not all, for towards the end of the novel there is a sudden, surprising twist in the action. It is feared that the Chinese crew may mutiny, and one of its members, Ao Ling, is arrested and put in irons. He is a Communist agitator, aboard the ship with forged papers. Hughes tells Ao Ling's story with considerable sympathy, so that it seems that the Chinese sailor may represent an aspect of duty and of dedication to a cause no less honourable than that of Captain Edwardes. In any event, the entrance of Ao Ling into the action enlarges the whole scope of the novel. Whether Hughes consciously intended symbolism or not, it is impossible to read the novel today without seeing in it a metaphor of the downfall of the British Empire or of the threat to the West generally.

*The Fox in the Attic* has to be considered a fragment. That is to say, it is not a self-contained part of a larger whole like one of the volumes of Snow's *Strangers and Brothers* or Powell's *The Music of Time*. *The Human Predicament*, in Hughes's words, is to be a "historical novel of my own times". The action of *The Fox in the Attic* takes place in 1923, the central character being Augustine Penry-Herbert, a young Welsh squire just too young to have fought in the war, haunted by what he has missed and conscious that he belongs to a generation different from any that has gone before. He goes to Germany to discover for himself the "new Germany" of the Weimar Republic. He may perhaps be taken as representative of the liberal Briton. What he finds in Germany, where he stays in the castle of a Bavarian cousin, is certainly nothing like his preconceptions, for the circle in which he moves recapitulates the old Germany of the Kaisers and contains also the seeds of the later Germany of the Nazis. He falls in love with his cousin Mitzi, ignorant that she knows nothing of his love, is almost blind and is destined to be a nun. Ignorance, indeed, is a large part of his being; he knows nothing of the dreams and intrigues that surround him, which are symbolised, perhaps, by the boy Wolff, younger than himself, whose existence he does not suspect but who is hiding in the attics of the castle having fought in the civil wars in the Baltic provinces. Meanwhile, Hitler and Ludendorff mount their *putsch* in Munich and, defeated, Hitler skulks in the Hanfstaengls' country cottage. The historic events described are rendered so vividly that it is almost impossible to believe that Hughes was not there as eye-witness; and almost miraculously, Hughes brings off the feat of making the real personages in the novel, Hitler, Goering, Roehm and the rest, no less convincing as characters than the fictitious ones.

Presumably, the novel will branch out into a sweeping narrative that will culminate in the second world war. All one can say of *The Fox in the Attic* at this point is that it is a most exciting beginning. If the rest of the book is as good we shall have a great novel.

—Walter Allen

---

**HUIE, William Bradford.** American. Born in Hartselle, Alabama, 13 November 1910. Educated at the University of Alabama, A.B. 1930 (Phi Beta Kappa). Served in the United States Navy, 1943–45; Lieutenant. Married Ruth Pucket in 1934. Reporter, *Birmingham Post*, Alabama, 1932–34. Associate Editor, 1942–43, and Editor and Publisher, 1945–52, *American Mercury*, New York. Address: Hartselle, Alabama 35640, U.S.A.

PUBLICATIONS

Novels

  *Mud on the Stars.* New York, Fischer, 1942; London, Hutchinson, 1944.
  *The Revolt of Mamie Stover.* New York, Duell, 1951; London, W. H. Allen, 1953.
  *The Americanization of Emily.* New York, Dutton, 1959; London, W. H. Allen, 1960.
  *Hotel Mamie Stover.* London, W. H. Allen, 1962; New York, Potter, 1963.
  *The Klansman.* New York, Dial Press, 1967; London, W. H. Allen, 1968.
  *In the Hours of the Night.* New York, Delacorte Press, and London, W. H. Allen, 1971.

Short Stories

  *Wolf Whistle and Other Stories.* New York, New American Library, 1959.
  *The Hero of Iwo Jima and Other Stories.* New York, New American Library, 1962.

Other

  *The Fight for Air Power.* New York, Fischer, 1942.
  *Seabee Roads to Victory.* New York, Dutton, 1944.
  *Can Do! The Story of the Seabees.* New York, Dutton, 1944.
  *From Omaha to Okinawa: The Story of the Seabees.* New York, Dutton, 1946.
  *The Case Against the Admirals: Why We Must Have a Unified Command.* New York, Dutton, 1946.
  *The Execution of Private Slovik: The Hitherto Secret Story of the Only American Soldier since 1864 to Be Shot for Desertion.* New York, Duell, 1954.
  *Ruby McCollum: Woman in the Suwanee Jail.* New York, Dutton, 1956; as *The Crime of Ruby McCollum*, London, Jarrolds, 1957.
  *The Hiroshima Pilot.* New York, Putnam, and London, Heinemann, 1964.
  *Three Lives for Mississippi.* New York, Whitney Communication Corporation, and London, Heinemann, 1965.

*He Slew the Dreamer: My Search with James Earl Ray for the Truth about the Murder of Martin Luther King*.  New York, Delacorte Press, and London, W. H. Allen, 1970.

\*       \*       \*

William Bradford Huie is primarily a journalist, and his fiction shows that in two ways—by his being able to turn out a light, popular novel, and by his recourse to fiction to present a situation of controversy which he could not prove well enough to present as fact. His non-fiction, however, can be read as one reads a novel, for his books are always structured well, and the subjects he chooses are dramatic to the point of being shocking. Only once has he failed to build horrendous suspense in a story, and that was when he was let down in his interviews with James Earl Ray, the convicted murderer of Martin Luther King, by Ray's persisting that he had no accomplices.

*The Revolt of Mamie Stover* and *Hotel Mamie Stover* are lusty stories carried by the character of the title figure. *The Americanization of Emily* is a sentimental story of a love affair between an English girl and an American soldier during the war. Although highly popular, these are ephemeral works, and if Huie had written nothing but this kind of thing and his short stories he would not be the important figure that he is in American writing.

Huie soon became interested in lost, forgotten, or obscured causes. He came across the fact that only one American soldier had been executed for desertion during the second World War; and in *The Execution of Private Slovik* he not only presented a thorough and understanding biography and analysis of that pathetic slum boy, who was chosen out of many deserters as an example because he seemed worthless to the reviewing officers, but made the point of view of all such people come clear. Huie's book is essential to the understanding of a book like Nelson Algren's *The Man with the Golden Arm*.

*The Hiroshima Pilot* blasts the myth that the man who dropped the first atom bomb was consumed by conscience over it—he wasn't the pilot who carried the bomb but flew a weather plane. Huie is a native Southerner, and lives in Alabama, so he has written extensively about the injustices of his region, especially toward Blacks. When three young civil rights workers were murdered in Mississippi in 1964, with at least the connivance of the county sheriff, he investigated deeply and produced *Three Lives for Mississippi*.

Unable to tell all he knew, not only about this atrocity, Huie produced a novel, *The Klansman*, that although too melodramatic and journalistic to be considered a fine novel, is certainly more polished than that earlier polemic, *Uncle Tom's Cabin*. His villain is the system, not people. His sheriff, although a racist, is above the average. His hero, a descendant of the old southern aristocracy, and his victim, a Negro girl with a good job in Chicago, back in Mississippi, are too good to be true. Huie *uses* fiction, but he uses it to good effect.

—William Bittner

---

**HUMPHREY, William.** American.  Born in Clarksville, Texas, 18 June 1924. Educated at Southern Methodist University, Dallas; University of Texas, Austin. Married. Recipient: National Institute of Arts and Letters grant, 1962. Resides in Lexington, Virginia. Address: c/o Alfred A. Knopf, 501 Madison Avenue, New York, New York 10022, U.S.A.

PUBLICATIONS

Novels

> *Home from the Hill.*   New York, Knopf, and London, Chatto and Windus, 1958.
> *The Ordways.*   New York, Knopf, and London, Chatto and Windus, 1965.

Short Stories

> *The Last Husband and Other Stories.*   New York, Morrow, and London, Chatto and
> Windus, 1953.
> *A Time and a Place: Stories.*   New York, Knopf, 1968; as *A Time and a Place: Stories
> of the Red River Country*, London, Chatto and Windus, 1969.

Other

> *The Spawning Run: A Fable.*   New York, Knopf, and London, Chatto and Windus,
> 1970.

*     *     *

After publishing a competent but by no means exceptional collection of short stories, William Humphrey reached best seller status with his first novel, *Home from the Hill*, a sprawling family chronicle of violence, promiscuity, and tragedy set in Humphrey's favorite locale—East Texas. In handling the saga of the Hunnicutt clan, Humphrey probes a region where the codes and rituals of the primitive Southwest are still a pervasive factor in behavior and attitude. When these codes conflict with other standards and values, the result can only be disaster—swift, crushing, and complete. Young Theron Hunnicutt suffers from being pulled in various directions by different loyalties and codes. Eventually, he can only retreat to the deep woods and bury himself alive apart from ordinary life. In a place where no male was considered a man unless he was a hunter, there is a primordial involvement with instinct and emotion sometimes resulting in a blood ritual which involves humans as well as animals.

Such tensions point up standards which the hunter ideally seeks—maturity, honor, and courage. But excessively high ideals lead to disillusionment and despair since they force judgments into oversimplified categories—men seen as clear-cut good or bad types. The shadings in between are not taken into account, and one sees a tendency to forget the general weakness of humanity. Humphrey, strongly aware of the shortcomings of this attitude, stresses man's weakness, the need to understand human faults and to forgive them. Even Will Vinson who kidnaps Sam Ordway's young son is not to be judged as a criminal. While at first Sam regards Vinson with hatred, he gradually comes to realize that Vinson's act was dominated by a wholesome attachment for the boy. Understanding and forgiveness develop to render Sam Ordway more mature, balanced and soundly adjusted.

The importance and necessity of self-reliance are other common themes. Sam Ordway comes to realize it is his duty and responsibility—not the sheriff's—to find his lost child. Theron Hunnicutt has the obligation of continuing the initiation, begun by his father, of mastering the forests and becoming an expert hunter and tracker. Tom and Ella Ordway display almost superhuman resiliency on their perilous post-Civil War trek from Tennessee to Texas. Rugged individualism paradoxically involves a close relationship to one's surroundings, which in turn help to link present and past history as another dominant motif. There is a living in the past which brings events and ancestors especially alive in the present. Tradition and tales are kept fresh and although time passes rapidly, few moments are ever lost. They are remembered constantly and form a foundation for character, attitude, and behavior.

Humphrey conveys a vivid sense of place and time. Saturday marketing day in a small Texas town, a political rally, the excitement and fakery of a traveling circus, the stringent conditions of an orphans' home—these and similar scenes of the late nineteenth and early twentieth century West are depicted with marvelous authenticity. It is evident that Humphrey has been heavily influenced by Faulkner. There are the polysyllabic vocabulary and the long convoluted sentences—which at times must be reread to perceive the full meaning— the delving into family history, the frequent shifting of time, the tall tale narration found especially in the Snopes Trilogy.

Humphrey's deficiencies as a writer are easily epitomized. He relies too heavily on description which often becomes ponderous. There are simply too many long-winded paragraphs juxtaposed with relatively little dialogue. While his style occasionally takes on poetic flavor from the picturesqueness of the setting and the language of the folksy dramatis personae, it is too frequently flat, lacking beauty and lyricism. On too many occasions he is just too derivative of Faulkner, without the latter's admitted genius.

—Paul A. Doyle

---

**HUMPHREYS, Emyr (Owen).** British. Born in Prestatyn, Wales, 15 April 1919. Educated at University College of Wales, Aberystwyth, 1937–39; University College of North Wales, Bangor, 1946–47. Served as a Relief Worker in the Middle East and the Mediterranean during World War II. Married Elinor Myfanwy Jones in 1946; has four children. Teacher, Wimbledon Technical College, London, 1948–50; Pwllheli Grammar School, North Wales, 1951–54. Producer, BBC Radio, Cardiff, 1955–58; Drama Producer, BBC Television, 1958–62; Free-lance Writer and Director, 1962–65. Since 1965, First Lecturer in Drama, University College of North Wales, Bangor. Member of the Welsh Arts Council since 1968. Recipient: Maugham Award, 1953; Hawthornden Prize, 1959. Address: Ysgubor Fawr, Marianglas, Anglesey, Wales.

PUBLICATIONS

Novels

*The Little Kingdom.* London, Eyre and Spottiswoode, 1947.
*The Voice of a Stranger.* London, Eyre and Spottiswoode, 1949.
*A Change of Heart.* London, Eyre and Spottiswoode, 1951.
*Hear and Forgive.* London, Gollancz, 1952; New York, Putnam, 1953.
*A Man's Estate.* London, Eyre and Spottiswoode, 1955; New York, McGraw Hill, 1956.
*The Italian Wife.* London, Eyre and Spottiswoode, 1957; New York, McGraw Hill, 1958.
*Y Tri Llais* (in Welsh). Llandybie, Wales, Llyfrau'r Dryw, 1958.
*A Toy Epic.* London, Eyre and Spottiswoode, 1959.
*The Gift.* London, Eyre and Spottiswoode, 1962.
*Outside the House of Baal.* London, Eyre and Spottiswoode, 1965.
*National Winner.* London, Macdonald, 1971.

645

Short Stories

    *Natives.*   London, Secker and Warburg, 1968.

Uncollected Short Stories

    "A Girl in the Ice", in *New Statesman* (London), 1953.
    "The Obstinate Bottle", in *New Statesman* (London), 1953.
    "Mr. Armitage", in *Welsh Short Stories*.   London, Faber, 1959.

Plays

    *King's Daughter*, adaptation of a play by Saunders Lewis (produced London, 1959; as
      *Siwan*, produced on television, 1960).   Published, as *Siwan*, in *Plays of the Year,
      1959–60*, London, Elek, 1960.
    *Roman Dream*, music by Alun Hoddinott.   London, Oxford University Press, 1968.
    *An Apple Tree and a Pig*, music by Alun Hoddinott.   London, Oxford University
      Press, 1969.
    *Dinas*, with W. S. Jones.   Llandybie, Wales, Llyfrau'r Dryw, 1970.

Verse

    *Ancestor Worship: A Cycle of 18 Poems*.   Denbigh, Wales, Gwasg Gee, 1970.

Bibliography: in *A Bibliography of Anglo-Welsh Literature, 1900–1965* by Brynmor Jones,
Swansea, Library Association, 1970.

Critical Studies: in *The Novel 1945–1950* by P. H. Newby, London, Longman, 1951; *Yllenor
a'i Gwymdeithas* by A. Llewelyn Williams, London, BBC Publications, 1966; *The Dragon
Has Two Tongues* by Glyn Jones, London, Dent, 1969.

*     *     *

Emyr Humphreys's first novel, *The Little Kingdom*, lacked nothing in assurance: if one
turns from it to his latest, *National Winner*, the main developments to be discerned are a
greatly increased use of dialogue both to convey character and advance the narrative and
stronger lines of schematisation within the novel's shape. Always there has been solidity, a
three-dimensional picture, a scene peopled objectively (not by the author standing in front
of his various funfair mirrors): in this sense Emyr Humphreys has been and is a conservative
novelist, using the traditional tools, eschewing an all-enveloping stream-of-consciousness,
overt fantasy or satire. What he has to say comes out of society and goes back into it. Part
of the reason for this is that he is a Welsh writer, with a view of the writer's obligation to
the community in which there is small part for a rootless bohemianism. Part of it arises from
a respect for the past, again a Welsh characteristic, which impels him to make a serious attempt
to evaluate the morality both of previous generations and of his own. He has never repudiated Wales in the manner of some earlier Welshmen who wrote in English: nor has he held
its differences and eccentricities up to ridicule. Equally foreign to his approach is a chauvin-
istic blindness. Basically he inherits the searching morality of Nonconformity at its best,
and one of his all-but-unique qualities as a novelist has been his willingness to present *the*

*good man* in guise other than that of the dullard, the victim or the radical intellectual with special insights denied to his fellows. Howell Morris in *A Change of Heart* and J. T. Miles in *Outside the House of Baal*, in their different ways, are examples of this *good man*—not triumphant, more often misrepresented than understood, not infrequently themselves mis-understanding and perhaps at the last, as with Miles, outmoded and bewildered. In the early fifties Emyr Humphreys outlined in a broadcast talk his concept of "the Protestant novel" (of which perhaps the epitome is the bleakly satisfying scene at the end of *Hear and Forgive* where David Flint returns to the unloved and unsuitable wife who has refused to divorce him and to their spoiled brat of a son, Stanley). Since that time the concept, if not abandoned, has suffered some neglect, but Emyr Humphreys's preoccupation with the discovery of a contemporary morality remains.

His search for it entails, in several novels, more than the portraits of individuals or the analysis of a related group. *National Winner*, his latest book, is *A Toy Epic—Outside the House of Baal* too—a generation further on. Origins in place and tradition, family relation-ships, friendship and trust, betrayed in smaller ways at first, are seen swallowed up in the trans-world technological stewpot: brothers are separated, live in different spheres. What they owe to the past or may still gain from it is matter for harrowing debate.

This is a very general preoccupation, but the form of it is peculiarly Welsh. If Emyr Humphreys, in test-boring society at points prescribed, shows a schematic determination which is bound to be less organic than the sometimes muddled relationships of the closely located community (as, say, in *A Man's Estate*), he nevertheless brings to the task a good deal of wit (especially at the expense of the university scene), a fine ear for dialogue, immense readability and an attitude of mind at once alert and purposeful. His novels both entertain and have a depth-echo which compels the reader to take his own soundings.

—Roland Mathias

HUNTER, Evan. Pseudonym: **Ed McBain.** American. Born in New York City, 15 October 1926. Educated at Cooper Union, New York, 1943–44; Hunter College, New York, B.A. 1950 (Phi Beta Kappa). Served in the United States Navy, 1944–46. Married Anita Melnick in 1949; has three children. Recipient: Mystery Writers of America Award, 1957. Address: c/o Scott Meredith Literary Agency, 580 Fifth Avenue, New York, New York 10036, U.S.A.

PUBLICATIONS

Novels

*Find the Feathered Serpent.*   Philadelphia, Winston, 1952.
*Rocket to Luna* (as Richard Marsten).   Philadelphia, Winston, 1953; London, Hutch-inson, 1954.
*Danger: Dinosaurs* (as Richard Marsten).   Philadelphia, Winston, 1953.
*Cut Me In* (as Hunt Collins).   New York, Abelard Schuman, 1954; London, Board-man, 1960.
*The Blackboard Jungle.*   New York, Simon and Schuster, 1954; London, Constable, 1955.

*The Spiked Heel* (as Richard Marsten).   New York, Holt, 1956; London, Constable, 1957.

*Tomorrow's World* (as Hunt Collins).   New York, Bouregy and Curl, 1956.

*Second Ending.*  New York, Simon and Schuster, and London, Constable, 1956.

*Vanishing Ladies* (as Richard Marsten).   New York, Pocket Books, 1957; London, Boardman, 1961.

*Strangers When We Meet.*  New York, Simon and Schuster, and London, Constable, 1958.

*A Matter of Conviction.*  New York, Simon and Schuster, and London, Constable, 1959.

*Mothers and Daughters.*  New York, Simon and Schuster, and London, Constable 1961.

*Buddwing.*  New York, Simon and Schuster, and London, Constable, 1964.

*The Paper Dragon.*  New York, Dial Press, 1966; London, Constable, 1967.

*A Horse's Head.*  New York, Dial Press, 1967; London, Constable, 1968.

*Last Summer.*  New York, Doubleday, 1968; London, Constable, 1969.

*Sons.*  New York, Doubleday, 1969; London, Constable, 1970.

*Nobody Knew They Were There.*  New York, Doubleday, and London, Constable, 1971.

*Every Little Crook and Nanny.*  New York, Doubleday, and London, Constable, 1972.


## Novels (as Ed McBain)

*Cop Hater.*  New York, Pocket Books, 1956; London, Boardman, 1958.

*The Mugger.*  New York, Pocket Books, 1956; London, Boardman, 1959.

*The Pusher.*  New York, Pocket Books, 1956; London, Boardman, 1959.

*The Con Man.*  New York, Pocket Books, 1957; London, Boardman, 1960.

*Killer's Choice.*  New York, Pocket Books, 1958; London, Boardman, 1960.

*Killer's Payoff.*  New York, Pocket Books, 1958; London, Boardman, 1960.

*April Robin Murders*, with Craig Rice.   New York, Random House, 1958; London, Hammond, 1959.

*Lady Killer.*  New York, Pocket Books, 1958; London, Boardman, 1961.

*Killer's Wedge.*  New York, Pocket Books, 1958; London, Boardman, 1961.

*'Til Death.*  New York, Simon and Schuster, 1959; London, Boardman, 1961.

*King's Ransom.*  New York, Simon and Schuster, and London, Boardman, 1959.

*Give the Boys a Great Big Hand.*  New York, Simon and Schuster, 1960; London, Boardman, 1962.

*The Heckler.*  New York, Simon and Schuster, 1960; London, Boardman, 1962.

*See Them Die.*  New York, Simon and Schuster, 1960; London, Boardman, 1963.

*Lady, Lady, I Did It!*  New York, Simon and Schuster, 1961; London, Boardman, 1963.

*Like Love.*  New York, Simon and Schuster, 1962; London, Hamish Hamilton, 1964.

*Ten Plus One.*  New York, Simon and Schuster, 1963; London, Hamish Hamilton, 1964.

*Ax.*  New York, Simon and Schuster, and London, Hamish Hamilton, 1964.

*The Sentries.*  New York, Simon and Schuster, and London, Hamish Hamilton, 1965.

*He Who Hesitates.*  New York, Dial Press, and London, Hamish Hamilton, 1965.

*Doll.*  New York, Dial Press, 1965; London, Hamish Hamilton, 1966.

*Eighty Million Eyes.*  New York, Dial Press, and London, Hamish Hamilton, 1966.

*Fuzz.*  New York, Doubleday, and London, Hamish Hamilton, 1968.

*Shotgun.*  New York, Doubleday, and London, Hamish Hamilton, 1969.

*Jigsaw.*  New York, Doubleday, and London, Hamish Hamilton, 1970.

*Hail, Hail, The Gang's All Here!*  New York, Doubleday, and London, Hamish Hamilton, 1971.
*Sadie When She Died.*  New York, Doubleday, 1972.
*Let's Hear It for the Dead Man.*  New York, Doubleday, 1972.

Short Stories

*The Last Spin.*  New York, Pocket Books, 1956; London, Constable, 1960.
*The Empty Hours* (as Ed McBain).  New York, Simon and Schuster, 1962; London, Boardman, 1963.
*Happy New Year, Herbie.*  New York, Simon and Schuster, 1963; London, Constable, 1965.
*The Beheading and Other Stories.*  London, Constable, 1971.
*The Easter Man: A Play and Six Stories.*  New York, Doubleday, 1972.
*Seven.*  London, Constable, 1972.

Plays

*The Easter Man* (produced Birmingham and London, 1964; as *A Race of Hairy Men*, produced New York, 1965).
*The Conjuror* (produced Ann Arbor, Michigan, 1969).

Screenplays: *Strangers When We Meet*, 1960; *The Birds*, 1962.

Other

*The Remarkable Harry* (juvenile).  London, Abelard Schuman, 1961.
*The Wonderful Button* (juvenile).  New York, Abelard Schuman, 1961; London, Abelard Schuman, 1962.

Manuscript Collection: Boston University Library.

Evan Hunter comments:

The novels I write under my own name are concerned mostly with identity, or at least they have been until the most recent book. (I cannot now predict what will interest or concern me most in the future.) I change my style with each novel, to fit the tone, the mood, and the narrative voice. I have always considered a strong story to be the foundation of any good novel, and I also apply this rule to the mysteries I write under the Ed McBain pseudonym. Unlike my "serious" novels, however, the style here is unvaried. The series characters are essentially the same throughout (although new detectives appear or old ones disappear from time to time, and each new case involves a new criminal or criminals), the setting is the same (the precinct and the city), and the theme is the same—crime and punishment. (I look upon these mysteries, in fact, as one *long* novel about crime and punishment, with each separate book in the series serving as a chapter.) I enjoy writing both types of novels, and consider each equally representative of my work.

*        *        *

The vividness and immediacy of the author's prose, coupled with the timeliness of his subject, drew considerable attention to Evan Hunter's novel, *Blackboard Jungle*. This story of a young teacher confronting the brutal realities of a big city vocational high school was praised for its realism and for opening to fiction an area of public concern that had begun to attract national attention in the United States. *Second Ending* was an even more aggressively topical novel, tracing the effects of drugs on four young New Yorkers. The central character, a young trumpet player who has been addicted for two years, draws the other characters together, and they are all altered in some way by his descent toward death. Some of the novel's episodes, which were termed "sensational" at the time of publication, now no longer seem so unique, and despite the awkwardness with which portions of the novel are narrated, Hunter's power as a storyteller moved his characters unerringly toward the slough of mutual desperation.

In *Strangers When We Meet* Hunter elected to describe a more muted kind of action in which a young architect, happily married and the father of two children, drifts into an affair with a suburban neighbor. Hunter showed a keen eye for the minute details which slowly gather round the illicit relationship, creating a highly realistic impression of a young man unable to cope with conflicting loyalties. Nonetheless, his characters finally seem insignificant —certainly not sufficiently strong to carry the philosophical baggage which the author gives them in an improbable conclusion.

*Matter of Conviction* was a return to the mode of social protest which Hunter had developed so successfully in his two earlier novels. A polemic against the forces in society that make young men into killers, it was too contrived to offer more than passing interest. *Mothers and Daughters*, which chronicles the youth and maturity of four middle-class women—their dreams and their loves—is a more substantial work, despite its occasional melodrama.

Much of Hunter's fiction is over-written: striving for a realistic thickness, it bogs down in minutiae, and while the author writes with a high and consistent degree of professionalism, his vision rarely penetrates beneath the elaborate surfaces which his prose projects. *Last Summer* is a major exception to this adroit verbosity. It is told with an unforgettable simplicity and directness which nonetheless conveys the author's own highly sophisticated point of view. During a summer holiday two teenage boys and a girl explore an Atlantic island, tell each other the "truth," and dominate a shy young girl. Their experiences end in violence which vividly symbolizes the moral degeneracy of their society.

Few contemporary writers can match the versatility and consummate professionalism of Evan Hunter. His work includes a highly successful series of detective novels published under the pseudonym of Ed McBain; a science-fiction novel for children; a comic cops-and-robbers novel, *A Horse's Head*, written with great inventiveness and wit; and a spirited children's book in verse, illustrated by his own sons. *Sons* tells the story of three generations of a Wisconsin family, powerfully challenging some of the basic presumptions of the American Dream; *The Paper Dragon* is a densely plotted, intriguing story of a five-day plagiarism trial; and *Buddwing* plunges its amnesiac hero into the heart of a Washington Square riot, a hold-up and a crap game. *Nobody Knew They Were There* takes a futuristic look at the innate forces of violence that assail man's attempts to achieve world peace. Throughout a varied and highly prolific career, Hunter has produced a body of work distinguished for its sound craftsmanship, although only one of his novels, *Last Summer*, clearly demonstrates the art which such craft should sustain.

—David Galloway

---

**HUNTER, Jim.** British. Born in Stafford, 24 June 1939. Educated at Gonville and Caius College, Cambridge, 1957–60, B.A. 1960, M.A. 1963; Indiana University, Bloomington,

1960–61; University of Bristol, 1961–62, Cert.Ed. 1962. Assistant English Master, Bradford Grammar School, Yorkshire, 1962–66. Since 1966, Senior English Master, Bristol Grammar School. Recipient: Author's Club Award, 1962. Address: 40 Royal York Crescent, Clifton, Bristol BS8 4JU, England.

PUBLICATIONS

Novels

> *The Sun in the Morning*.   London, Faber, 1961.
> *Sally Cray*.   London, Faber, 1963.
> *Earth and Stone*.   London, Faber, 1963; as *A Place of Stone*, New York, Pantheon Books, 1964.
> *The Flame*.   London, Faber, and New York, Pantheon Books, 1966.
> *Walking in the Painted Sunshine*.   London, Faber, 1970.

Short Stories

> *Introduction*, with others.   London, Faber, 1960.

Other

> *The Metaphysical Poets*.   London, Evans, 1965.
> *Gerard Manley Hopkins*.   London, Evans, 1966.
>
> Editor, *Modern Short Stories*.   London, Faber, 1964.
> Editor, *The Modern Novel in English*.   London, Faber, 1966.
> Editor, *Modern Poets*.   London, Faber, 4 vols., 1968.
> Editor, *Henry IV, Part One*, by William Shakespeare.   London, Evans, 1969.

Jim Hunter comments:

Twentieth-century settings and a generally realistic manner, though some would say leaning upon 19th-century association of unspoken emotion with landscape and weather. The people are unsophisticated, mostly young, non-metropolitan: "ordinary" people not too locked in a particular decade. Yet I hope the incidental reportage, e.g. of growing up in Yorkshire and Indiana in the 1950's, or of youth theatre loyalties in the late '60's, will stand examination. *The Flame* seems like an exception—a semi-political novel on a public theme (right-wing reaction in Britain, on which it has proved partly prophetic); but the best people and the most real people in *The Flame* are peripheral, young, vulnerable, inconspicuous. It remains a book in defence of normality against blazing lights and burning martyrs.

There is a tendency for the style of my more recent work to be less and less discursive, more imagistic. I cannot say where this will lead.

*        *        *

In 1962, after the publication of his first novel, *The Sun in the Morning*, Jim Hunter received the Authors' Club Award for the most promising new writer of that year. Since then he has published four additional novels, edited various collections, and published *The Metaphysical Poets* and *Gerard Manley Hopkins*. One of the early reviewers of his work predicted that he would become "one of the great contemporary writers", while another in reply has said "the prediction is a plain impossibility." For the serious student of the novel in the 1960's his work must surely fall somewhere between these two views. All five of the novels—*The Sun in the Morning, Sally Cray, Earth and Stone, The Flame*, and *Walking in the Painted Sunshine* —deal with unsophisticated, mostly ordinary people who face the conflicts inherent in growing up, responding to love with maturity, and facing the inevitable choices in the timeless cycle of birth, life, and death. Though frequently timid in his descriptions of the sexual crises he creates, Hunter writes realistically about the traditional themes he has chosen.

Set in England during the second world war and after, *The Sun in the Morning* is made up of a kaleidoscope of characters, situations, and themes. There is no single protaganist; instead the narrative is focused on two boys, Philip Stevenson and Terry Carter, and two girls, Clare Grenfell and her friend Kathy. They share the usual experiences of school children—loneliness, uncertainty of their own identities, indecisions as to their futures. The varying relationships of these young people, their friends and communities make up the novel. The various misunderstandings that exist between generations, the interweaving of the experiences among the young people themselves, and the selected impressionistic incidents of their growing up are handled competently for such a patchwork of materials, but the book remains just that—a patchwork.

Philip, Terry, and Kathy are also part of the cast of characters in *The Flame*. The two chief characters here are Douglas Cameron and his brother, Martin, who is the younger and more pragmatic of the two and who returns from America with a Negro girl as his wife. Douglas Cameron becomes the leader of an idealistic crusade to reform and revitalize Britain. Again, as in *The Sun in the Morning*, there is the interweaving of character and theme in an attempt to suggest the futility of reestablishing idealism in post-war race-conscious Britain. Cameron and his followers fall victims to Russell Blekiron, a cynical M.P. who exhibits a mixture of white supremacy and neo-fascism.

Both *Sally Cray* and *Earth and Stone* examine the indecision of the young in the context of the family. Sally Cray comes to Indiana with her father, a university professor. She grows up in a typical American setting, but her problems are those of any girl anywhere as she sees her parents divorced, each finding someone else to marry. Sex becomes her greatest dilemma, a dilemma she never solves satisfactorily. This is the least realized of all the five novels. Hunter, as perhaps one might suppose, is better at the realization of the young man than that of the young woman. *Earth and Stone* is a far better study of the family situation than is *Sally Cray*. It is marred, however, by the fact that almost from the beginning the mother is dying of cancer, and therefore, there is no opportunity for the nuances of the shifting family loyalties to be examined.

Hunter's fifth novel, *Walking in the Painted Sunshine*, is a poetic account of the relationship between a young couple and their older friend and teacher. Again, however, the effect is marred by the somewhat awkward introduction of the illness and impending death of the young husband's mother and the too obvious juxtaposition of the cycle of life and death suggested by the child so soon to be born to them and the mother so soon to die.

Hunter's very real excellence in realizing and portraying the people, the sights and sounds of contemporary Britain deserves a better context of narration than he has yet devised. However timeless and universal the great themes of birth, life, love, death, at this point Hunter has not discovered a formula for putting together his craft and his aspiration.

—Annibel Jenkins

**HUNTER, Kristin.** American. Born in Philadelphia, Pennsylvania, 12 September 1931, only daughter of George L. and Mabel L. (Manigault) Eggleston. Educated at the University of Pennsylvania, Philadelphia, 1947–51, B.S. in Education 1951. Married John I. Lattany in 1968. Teacher, Camden, New Jersey public schools, 1951; Copywriter, Lavenson Bureau of Advertising, Philadelphia, 1952–59; Research Assistant, School of Social Work, University of Pennsylvania, 1961–62; Copywriter, Wermen and Schorr, Philadelphia, 1962–63; Information Officer, City of Philadelphia, 1963–64, 1965–66. Free-lance Writer since 1966. Lecturer in Creative Writing, University of Pennsylvania, 1972. Recipient: Fund for the Republic Prize, for television documentary, 1955; Whitney Fellowship, 1959; Sigma Delta Chi Award, for reporting, 1968; National Council on Interracial Books for Children Award, 1968; National Conference of Christians and Jews Brotherhood Award, 1969; Cheshire Cat Award, University of Wisconsin, for children's book, 1971. Address: P.O. Box 8371, Philadelphia, Pennsylvania 19101; or, c/o Harold Matson Company, 22 East 40th Street, New York, New York 10016, U.S.A.

PUBLICATIONS

Novels

    *God Bless the Child.* New York, Scribner, 1964; London, Muller, 1965.
    *The Landlord.* New York. Scribner, 1966; London, Pan, 1970.
    *The Soul Brothers and Sister Lou* (juvenile). New York, Scribner, 1968; London, Macdonald, 1971.

Uncollected Short Stories

    "To Walk in Beauty", in *Sub-Deb Scoop* (Philadelphia), 1953.
    "Supersonic", in *Mandala* (Philadelphia), 1955.
    "There Was a Little Girl", in *Rogue* (New York), 1959.
    "An Interesting Social Study", in *The Best Short Stories by Negro Writers.* Boston, Little Brown, 1967.
    "Debut", in *Negro Digest* (Chicago), June 1968.
    "Honor among Thieves", in *Essence* (New York), April 1971.
    "Two's Enough of a Crowd", "Mom Luby and the Social Worker", "The Scribe", "A Question", "All Around the Mulberry Tree", "Hero's Return", and "The Kite and the Pillow", in *Directions 4* (juvenile). Boston, Houghton Mifflin, 1972.

Plays

    *The Double Edge* (produced Philadelphia, 1965).

    Play produced on television.

Other

    *Boss Cat* (juvenile). New York, Scribner, 1971.
    *The Pool Table War* (juvenile). Boston, Houghton Mifflin, 1972.
    *Uncle Daniel and the Raccoon* (juvenile). Boston, Houghton Mifflin, 1972.

Verse published in various magazines.

Critical Study: review of *The Landlord* in *Saturday Review* (New York), 14 May 1966.

Kristin Hunter comments:

The bulk of my work has dealt—imaginatively, I hope—with relations between the white and black races in America. My early work was "objective", that is, sympathetic to both whites and blacks, and seeing members from a perspective of irony and humor against the wider backdrop of human experience as a whole. Of late (roughly, since 1968), my subjective anger has been emerging, along with my grasp of the real situation in this society.

*          *          *

Central to each of Kristin Hunter's novels is exposure of a contradiction between reality and the assumptions carried by familiar patterns of popular fiction. Her first book, *God Bless the Child*, tells of the enterprising but low-born youngster who, since the origins of middle class fiction, has set out to achieve riches by the application of nerve and wit in defiance of convention. From a grandmother who has devoted her life to serving well-to-do white people, Hunter's heroine, Rosie Fleming, knows the appearance of success and, with a self-directed ambition akin to her mother's, she attempts to secure the material tokens of success by becoming an entrepreneur in the numbers. Yet when she becomes an irritation, not even a threat, to the white men who manage the poor people's version of finance capitalism, the inescapable facts of American social relations destroy Rosie's fragile prosperity and sacrifice her remarkably vital personality to the illusions of individual self-sufficiency.

Despite her portrayal of the relentless power that destroys Rosie, Hunter is not resigned to a sense of human powerlessness. The sympathetic and complex portrayal of three generations of black women in *God Bless the Child* conveys an intensely humanistic conception of character, which in her second novel, *The Landlord*, becomes the basis for an optimistic theme. Formally *The Landlord* is a novel of maturation. An ineffectual white man, Elgar Enders, has determined to "become a man" in the occupation of slumlord. His expectation, supported by our own observation that people will sink to any occasion, is that he will accomplish his growth when he asserts his mastery in dealing with the tenants and the practical maintenance of his building; however, the ensuing conflict, when Elgar attempts to act the way businessmen should and his tenants resist, results in his being disabused of the mythology of white male dominance. In its place he moves toward what Hunter must feel is genuine maturity: admiration for each person's means of coping with life and positive delight in diverse personalities.

The ironic variations Kristin Hunter plays on the conventions of popular fiction show her to be working also, without irony, in a tradition familiar to literary history, for the practice of demonstrating a disparity between life as it is lived and life as it is framed in the culture's legends is an application of one of the earliest motives of realism. *The Soul Brothers and Sister Lou*, Hunter's novel marketed for "younger readers", thus, extends the exposure of illusions to an audience with an abiding interest in fantasies of success. To satisfy the fantasy Sister Lou's story moves from her yearning for a prolongation of the comradeship she has briefly felt when singing with boys from her neighborhood to the establishment of her success as a recording artist. Achieving the forms of success that eluded Rosie, Sister Lou is nonetheless critical of success ideology, because now freed of the debilitating effects of poverty, she has become subject to the equally restrictive conventions of affluence.

The quality of Hunter's craft is sure, but after three novels she has yet to achieve a satisfactory reconciliation of the optimistic humanism embodied in her skillful portraiture to the knowledge of the destructive power of social environment she displays in ironic structure. In time she must face the fact that contemporary realism requires more than exposing illusions to a disillusioned society.

—John M. Reilly

**HUTCHINS, Maude (Phelps McVeigh).** Born in New York City. Educated at St. Margaret's School, Waterbury, Connecticut; Yale University, New Haven, Connecticut, B.F.A. 1926. Married the educator Robert Maynard Hutchins in 1921 (divorced, 1948); has three children. Sculptor: one-man shows in New York, Chicago, St. Louis, Toledo and San Francisco; works exhibited at the New Haven, Connecticut Paint and Clay Club, the Brooklyn Museum, the National Association of Women Painters and Sculptors, and the Chicago World's Fair Show of Modern Art; represented the State of Illinois at the 3rd annual National Exhibition of American Art, American Fine Arts Society Galleries, New York. Address: 1046 Pequot Road, Southport, Connecticut, U.S.A.

PUBLICATIONS

Novels

    *Georgiana.*   New York, New Directions, 1948.
    *A Diary of Love.*   New York, New Directions, 1950; London, Spearman, 1953.
    *My Hero.*   New York, New Directions, and London, Spearman, 1953.
    *The Memoirs of Maisie.*   New York, Appleton Century Crofts, 1955.
    *Victorine.*   Denver, Swallow, and London, Spearman, 1959.
    *Honey on the Moon.*   New York, Morrow, 1964; London, Blond, 1965.
    *Blood on the Doves.*   New York, Morrow, 1965.
    *The Unbelievers Downstairs.*   New York, Morrow, 1967.

Short Stories

    *Love Is a Pie: Stories and Plays.*   New York, New Directions, 1952.
    *The Elevator: Stories.*   New York, Morrow, 1962.

Other

    *Diagrammatics*, with Mortimer J. Adler.   New York, Random House, 1932.

    Verse published in magazines in the 1930's.

*    *    *

The first book of Maude Hutchins, then the handsome aloof wife of the President of the University of Chicago, and a sculptor of repute, was *Diagrammatics*, in which her own line-drawing collocations of female forms were complemented by similarly abstract logical forms, in double-talk, by Mortimer Adler, her husband's Great Books partner. Her foreword expounded artistic abstraction in a witty, figurative style which she trusted would not be intelligible, since if it were her art would be superfluous.

But she soon took up verbal art, first poems, then fiction. Stories and "plays", collected in *Love Is a Pie*, ranged from memoirs of a male amorist to the love-life of a gorilla. Some played irreverently with Christianity: Mary, on Easter Eve, ecstatically recalling her "affair" with the Heavenly Messenger, but glad Jesus is dead; Jesus—the Wandering Jew—as the cranky inmate of an Old People's Home.

Eight slim novels deal mostly with love—hence sex—in adolescent New England girls resembling herself: slender, dark, attractive, sensorily acute, intelligent, great readers and day-dreamers. Parents are lacking or ineffective, but grand-parents are strong-willed gentry, often in financial decay, with large old houses, Irish or Swedish maids, a farm, a pond, Southern connections, resident relatives, and a doctor as intimate friend. The girls are not sexually precocious or promiscuous, but, as Mrs. Hutchins once remarked, sex seems to be what she has to write about. A woman's story, she says, is necessarily a love story, because "a woman knows what comes first", and physical sex (however sublimated or censored) is the basis of "all affection between persons of all sexes." But significant experiences happen in the mind, not the body, and raise emotion-charged questions about free will and passion, or about "innocence"—naive acceptance—and defensive "guilt".

Mrs. Hutchins is not re-telling one story. She perhaps draws discreetly on autobiography, but her job as an artist is, she believes, to "intuit" others' feelings and actions, make a "spare choice" among her materials, then throw them into various perspectives, on various organizing principles. Her style alternates brisk narrative, involuted thought-streams, wicked satire, and the darting imagery of a well-stocked, wildly associative mind (often, a yeasty *id* seems to be bubbling through a Great Books-saturated *ego*), in sentences where a qualification may hang from every joint: "And I, without portfolio, as it were, in secret, I watch and observe and peek through keyholes, you might say, to solve, being curious and alert, a problem."

*Georgiana* is Freudianly organized (first, formative girlhood influences; last, Georgiana, adult, unconsciously searching in successive lovers for her dominating, perfectionist grand-father) and is at times unreadably quirky, except in the mid-section, Georgiana's Colette-ish diary as a lively, amusing school-girl. The more successful *A Diary of Love* is all "journal", but Noel is, even at 13, more educated in sex (which got the book banned in Chicago and burned in England) and she goes off, not to school but to an unforgettable desert sanitarium. *My Hero* ventured, unconvincingly, into non-genteel life—a mechanically-minded boy who grows into a truck-driver. But it has two genuinely comic creations (an entomologist en-thralled by insect sex, and his social-climbing wife), plus Hutchins-eye sketches of Chicago, from strip joints to the University.

Beginning with *Memoirs of Maisie*—the recollections, real and imaginary, of a cente-narian, fusing oddly with current happenings—life frequently appears in mental distorting-mirrors, comic, grim, or surreal. In *Victorine* a pubescent girl, sexually responsive to church services, finally rejects them for chaste love with a half-wit who makes her see visions of a mystic stallion. A bride, in *Honey on the Moon*, goes from sexual initiation to schizophrenia as her adored older mate turns out to be a homosexual and then shoots himself. In a second short-story collection, *The Elevator*, passengers on an elevator "to Japan" all—including the narrator—prove to be stock characters in the romances of a negro novelist, who himself sounds like a white-man's cliché. A woman finds time so accelerated cigarettes burn her fingers before she can puff; a youth murders from respect for the meanings of words. Most of *Blood on the Doves* transpires, Faulknerianly, in the mind of a lunatic mountain boy with ESP who mingles past, present, and visualized future in obsessively recurring patterns as he strangles a girl and castrates himself; his brother engages in rape and in WWI battles in similarly ghastly style. The incredibly but hilariously precocious 8-year old narrator of

*The Unbelievers Downstairs* (who at times believes she is invisible) reports with naïve knowingness on the scrambled sex-lives of her elders.

Critically, Mrs. Hutchins has always fared best abroad, but her American reception has improved as fashions caught up with her frankness and experimental techniques. Despite her intelligence and wide knowledge she correctly calls herself "no scholar, no historian, no thinker"—that is, no systematic philosopher. But each work is shaped by an idea, paradoxical, perverse, or arrestingly insightful. The short pieces are as economically modelled as her sculptures; in a novel, the idea may wear thin, but the development (which always includes amusing minor "humour" characters) is distinctive and usually interesting.

—George McElroy

---

**HUTCHINSON, R(ay) C(oryton).** British. Born in London, 23 January 1907. Educated at Monkton Combe School, Somerset; Oriel College, Oxford, M.A. 1927. Served in the British Army, 1940–45; Major. Married Margaret Owen Jones in 1929; has four children. Assistant Advertising Manager, J. and J. Colman Ltd., Norwich, 1927–35. Recipient: London *Sunday Times* Gold Medal for Fiction, 1939; W. H. Smith Literary Award, 1966. Fellow, Royal Society of Literature, 1962. Address: Dysart, Blechingley, Redhill, Surrey, England.

PUBLICATIONS

Novels

*Thou Hast a Devil: A Fable*. London, Benn, 1930.
*The Answering Glory*. London, Cassell, and New York, Farrar and Rinehart, 1932.
*The Unforgotten Prisoner*. London, Cassell, 1933; New York, Farrar and Rinehart, 1934.
*One Light Burning: A Romantic Story*. London, Cassell, and New York, Farrar and Rinehart, 1935.
*Shining Scabbard*. London, Cassell, and New York, Farrar and Rinehart, 1936.
*Testament*. London, Cassell, and New York, Farrar and Rinehart, 1938.
*The Fire and the Wood: A Love Story*. London, Cassell, and New York, Farrar and Rinehart, 1940.
*Interim*. London, Cassell, and New York, Farrar and Rinehart, 1945.
*Elephant and Castle: A Reconstruction*. London, Cassell, and New York, Rinehart, 1949.
*Recollection of a Journey*. London, Cassell, 1949; as *Journey with Strangers*, New York, Rinehart, 1952.
*The Stepmother*. London, Cassell, and New York, Rinehart, 1952.
*March the Ninth*. London, Bles, and New York, Rinehart, 1957.
*Image of My Father*. London, Bles, 1961; as *The Inheritor*, New York, Harper, 1961.
*A Child Possessed*. London, Bles, and New York, Harper, 1964.
*Johanna at Daybreak*. London, Joseph, and New York, Harper, 1969.
*Origins of Cathleen: A Diversion*. London, Joseph, 1971.

Uncollected Short Stories

"Every Twenty Years", in *The Best British Short Stories of 1928*.   New York, Dodd
   Mead, 1928.
"All in the Day", in *Pick of Today's Short Stories 4*.   London, Putnam, 1953.
"How I Rose to Be an Australian Shoeshine Boy", in *Pick of Today's Short Stories 7*.
   London, Putnam, 1956.
"Anniversary", in *Best Underworld Stories*.   London, Faber, 1969.


Play

*Last Train South* (produced London, 1938).


Other

*Paiforce: The Official Story of the Persia and Iraq Command 1941–1946* (published
   anonymously).   London, His Majesty's Stationery Office, 1948.


Manuscript Collection: University of Texas Library, Austin.


Critical Study: Introduction by Richard Church to *Shining Scabbard*, London, Duckworth,
1968.


R. C. Hutchinson comments:

   The first business of a novelist is to entertain. Generally the most important material he
uses is the outer and inner life of human beings, discovered or guessed by his observation
of other people and of himself. The essence of his craft (as I see it) is to find ways, within
the limitations of prose, of sharing with the reader the excitements which people and experience provoke in his own thoughts and emotions. Because no two readers are alike in,
for example, their vocabulary, this means a very precise and laborious attention to words,
sentences, paragraphs—their meanings and their emotive overtones. Inevitably, such work
involves a constant sense of inadequacy and failure.
   Didactic writing, required of every author under some political regimes, seems to me
foreign to the novelist's art. But, broadly, I think that a story will lack artistic shape if it
does not imply some moral assumptions: this opinion could be illustrated by an examination
of traditional fairy stories, as well as by reference to masters as diverse as Voltaire and
Tolstoy. To the perceptive reader, a novelist's philosophy will, I think, generally reveal
itself, without deliberate exposition, in his characters and their external or internal adventures. My own philosophy is a total acceptance, within my painfully limited understanding, of the Christian doctrine of the Incarnation.


                              *         *         *


   Perhaps there are a score of novelists who stand out as having an acute perception into
the present age, and are able to portray its ailments, dilemmas and tensions. Such writers
as Camus, Graham Greene, and Boris Pasternak come readily to mind in this respect, and
each reader would add his private list of perhaps a dozen others, to whom he is personally

indebted for an enlarged understanding of the world in which we live. Ray Hutchinson ranks in this eminent gallery.

His writings extend from the 'twenties to the present day, covering the whole of our present age—age of "The Decline of the West." He sees it at a penetrating depth, and exposes it faithfully, but, unlike most of his contemporaries, he dares to give an answer, in his own terms, to the deepest problems that confront us.

At a time when the fabric of civilised life is threatened, and at times is actually breaking down, we ask ourselves (if we dare to ask), what can life be like, let us say, in a concentration camp, in a modern war, in a communist revolution, or in a period when the normal processes of law have broken down? Ray Hutchinson has spent his life giving his answer to these questions. In one novel after another he has selected some scene of human misery, a party of Poles taken to Siberia for "slave labour", life in Germany or the Balkans in the aftermath of war, or a wretched English slum during the depression. With complete conviction he has shown how it would be possible to live under such conditions, and to die under them, and yet to retain values of kindness, love, and, above all, human dignity. No modern author can equal him in his description of human suffering: with a fine sensitivity he takes us down to the depths, as in *Recollection of a Journey*, or *Elephant and Castle*, but at every stage his characters remain human. He seems to say, again and again, that in spite of a very evil world in which we live, there is an essential goodness about the ordinary man and woman which is ineradicable.

He would be the first to admit that this is the expression of a firmly held Christian faith, but he is far too accomplished a craftsman ever to fall into the trap of what he calls "didactic writing." He acknowledges that there is a place for such writing, but as a story teller he gives it no place in his craft.

Over the years it has been a constant disappointment to his admirers that he has been undervalued by the reading public, and a matter of considerable gratification when in 1966 he was awarded the W. H. Smith prize for *A Child Possessed*. It confirms the opinion held by some, that a later age will come to regard Ray Hutchinson as the author who has interpreted Europe of the 20th Century with greater perception and accuracy than any other, at the same time conveying the great sense of hope which animates and controls all his writing.

—K. R. Prebble

---

**INNES, (Ralph) Hammond.**  British.  Born in Horsham, Sussex, 15 July 1913. Educated at Cranbrook School. Served in the British Army in the Artillery, 1940–46: Major. Married Dorothy Mary Lang in 1937. Staff Member, *Financial News*, London, 1934–40. Address: Ayres End, Kersey, Suffolk, England.

PUBLICATIONS

Novels

*Doppelganger*.  London, Jenkins, 1937.
*Air Disaster*.  London, Jenkins, 1937.
*Sabotage Broadcast*.  London, Jenkins, 1938.
*All Roads Lead to Friday*.  London, Jenkins, 1939.

*Wreckers Must Breathe*.  London, Collins, 1940; as *Trapped*, New York, Putnam, 1940.
*The Trojan Horse*.  London, Collins, 1940.
*Attack Alarm*.  London, Collins, 1941; New York, Macmillan, 1942.
*Dead and Alive*.  London, Collins, 1946.
*The Killer Mine*.  London, Collins, and New York, Harper, 1947.
*The Lonely Skier*.  London, Collins, 1947; as *Fire in the Snow*, New York, Harper, 1947.
*Maddon's Rock*.  London, Collins, 1948; as *Gale Warning*, New York, Harper, 1948.
*The Blue Ice*.  London, Collins, and New York, Harper, 1948.
*The White South*.  London, Collins, 1949; as *The Survivors*, New York, Harper, 1949.
*The Angry Mountain*.  London, Collins, and New York, Harper, 1950.
*Air Bridge*.  London, Collins, and New York, Knopf, 1951.
*Campbell's Kingdom*.  London, Collins, and New York, Knopf, 1952.
*The Strange Land*.  London, Collins, 1954; as *The Naked Land*, New York, Knopf, 1954.
*The Mary Deare*.  London, Collins, 1956; as *The Wreck of the Mary Deare*, New York, Knopf, 1956.
*The Land God Gave to Cain*.  London, Collins, and New York, Knopf, 1958.
*The Doomed Oasis*.  London, Collins, and New York, Knopf, 1960.
*Atlantic Fury*.  London, Collins, and New York, Knopf, 1962.
*The Strode Venturer*.  London, Collins, and New York, Knopf, 1965.
*Levkas Man*.  London, Collins, and New York, Knopf, 1971.


Other

*Cocos Gold* (as Ralph Hammond; juvenile).  London, Collins, and New York, Harper, 1950.
*Isle of Strangers* (as Ralph Hammond; juvenile).  London, Collins, 1951; as *Island of Peril*, New York, Westminster, 1953.
*Saracen's Gold* (as Ralph Hammond; juvenile).  London, Collins, 1952; as *Cruise of Danger*, New York, Westminster, 1954.
*Black Gold on the Double Diamond* (as Ralph Hammond; juvenile).  London, Collins, 1953.
*Harvest of Journeys* (travel).  London, Collins, and New York, Knopf, 1960.
*Scandinavia*, with the editors of *Life*.  New York, Time, 1963.
*Sea and Islands* (travel).  London, Collins, and New York, Knopf, 1967.
*The Conquistadors* (history).  London, Collins, and New York, Knopf, 1969.
*Hammond Innes Introduces Australia*, edited by Clive Turnbull.  London, Deutsch, 1971.


Editor, *Tales of Old Inns*, by Richard Keverne, revised edition.  London, Collins, 1947.


Hammond Innes comments:

Writing and travelling can be kept in separate compartments of time. But the organisation and preparation for journeys and voyages cannot. And this is a major problem, for I need the familiarity of my own home and the peace of the country in order to write. I need my books and my maps and charts around me. I also need to live with it seven days a week, for I am a painfully slow writer, usually discarding far more than appears in the final work.

I find it very difficult to be certain at what point I became conscious of the role travel was to play in my writing. I think probably after the war. I had cut my writing teeth in the great depression of the early thirties, a particularly insular period that I believe to have been the result of the mud and blood of Flanders. To earn my living, however, I worked as a journalist on a London daily. My starting wage was a now unbelievable 17s. 6d. a week, and at the time I counted myself fortunate to get the job, for most newspapers were firing, not hiring, staff. All through the thirties I had to be content to discover my own country, so that when I finally did go abroad it was at H.M.'s expense—a voyage round the Cape, my destination the Western Desert.

I was 27 when I joined the Services. I felt the best years of my life were being wasted. It was only when I was demobilised, and had taken the plunge and abandoned journalism for full-time writing, that I realised what a wealth of experience I had been soaking up.

As a youngster, my imagination had been fired by geography almost as much as by literature. On my return to England after the war, I was made strongly aware that, whilst I had been absorbing the atmosphere of the old world of the Mediterranean, the vast majority of the British people had been locked up in their island fortress for six long years. I had characters and backgrounds that seemed to interest them. There is always an element of luck in everything, and in writing the luck is to find that what you want to write, and therefore what you write best, is what people happen to want to read.

I wanted to write about far-off places and people. Because of that I determined to plough back as much of my royalties as possible into travel. And looking back now, how glad I am that I did. A writer has no business, no land, no factory that he can call his own. His capital assets are all in his head, and one of the very few things that can't be taxed, expropriated, or in any way filched by others, is personal experience.

This was a conscious decision, the only one I have ever made about my writing. The rest has developed in the normal haphazard way of things. I cannot even say what it is that draws me at a certain period of time to a certain part of the world. The choice would appear to be intuitive. But I can say that, as with the voyages under sail, a lot of preparation is necessary. The research, the books, the maps, the visits to London to seek out the right contacts. This is all necessary, so that when one arrives in the country itself there is a sense of familiarity; by which I mean that the people and their way of life are at least within one's comprehension. And the journey itself needs to be planned—meetings with ministers, industrialists, writers to get the overall picture, and then, with the country's problems clear in mind, a prolonged stay in one area so that one gets to grips with the people themselves.

Returning, one begins a long, slow process of rendering down. The mind is too often overflowing with all that one has absorbed, and the only way I know to rid oneself of this embarrassment of riches is to write a travel piece—hence my two books in search of background. Even then, it may be two or three years before I am ready to start on the novel, for if it is to be real, the story has to grow out of the background. And in the case of remote areas like the Labrador, or Addu Atoll in the Indian Ocean, there is probably only one real story line that will achieve my purpose and show what the country and the people are really like.

It may appear from this that I am a highly organised writer. I wish this were so. It would make my life a lot easier if it were. But at least by building on a background of very personal travel I know what I am trying to achieve. And whether I succeed or not, it is at least a start to have the goal clear in mind.

\*          \*          \*

Reading the novels of Hammond Innes as they appeared, one forms the opinion that they display great versatility. His settings range from Greece to Western Canada and from North Africa to the Labrador. He displays expertise on flying, sailing, mining, skiing, engineering, and now even archaeology. His situations include German espionage in Britain during the last war, the problems of veterans just beyond the law, the toughest kind of free enterprise from the Berlin airlift to the Maldive Islands, and the continual conflict between the crooked and the straight.

Yet re-read one after the other, these books show a remarkable sameness. His heroes seem all the same, but getting older. His heroines are all resourceful, courageous, and ready to lend a hand when the going gets tough. There is almost always a companion to share the hero's burden—and to provide an excuse for dialogue to salt the long introspective explanations that lend authenticity to the tales. The other side—usually self-made business-men—are single-minded and ruthless, and with assistants who are downright evil.

It is possible to divide these works into groups with great ease. *Attack Alarm* and *The Trojan Horse* concern the infiltration of German agents into the defense establishment. *Dead and Alive*, *Killer Mine*, *The Lonely Skier*, *The Blue Ice*, and *The Angry Mountain* deal with various aspects of the aftermath of the war, as does *Maddon's Rock*, although the latter introduces the theme of man against the sea continued in *The Wreck of the Mary Deare*, *Atlantic Fury* and *The Strode Venturer*. *The White South* shifts from this theme to man against the Antarctic. *The Strange Land* and *The Doomed Oasis* pose North African and Arabian problems, *Campbell's Kingdom* and *The Land God Gave to Cain* those of the Canadian frontier. *Air Bridge* stands by itself as does *Levkas Man*. The latter also has no real villain, but a dedicated archaeologist who will go to any lengths to prove his theory about the migration of prehistoric man.

If Innes' books are mere entertainement, they are very good entertainment indeed. The characters and basic situation are introduced deftly and quickly. There is always a series of suspense-creating surprises. The hero is inevitably carried through a physical ordeal, often in competition with the villain. Always at some point all seems lost. The stories end quickly with the resolution of the conflict. Characterisation is stereotyped as it might be in an adventure film, where the type-cast actor plays himself, but the narrative pace alleviates this.

*Levkas Man* may be a new departure for Innes in a literary sense as well as a new area for his erudition. It is more complex, less sensational, and the characters are more finely shaded. Both sides in the conflict are well-intentioned although both are on the wrong side of the law. Hammond Innes' next book should tell the tale.

—William Bittner

**INNES, Michael.   See STEWART, J. I. M.**

**ISHERWOOD, Christopher.** American. Born in High Lane, Cheshire, England, 26 August 1904. Settled in the United States in 1939; became an American citizen, 1946. Educated at Repton School, 1919–22; Corpus Christi College, Cambridge, 1924–25; King's College, London, as a medical student, 1928–29. Private Tutor, and Secretary to André Mangeot and His Music Society String Quartet, London, 1926–27. Taught English in Berlin, 1930–33. Traveled in Europe, 1933–37; in China, with W. H. Auden, 1938; in South America, 1947–48. Worked in films, in England, for Gaumont-British; and since 1939 in Hollywood for M.G.M., Warner Brothers and Twentieth Century Fox. Worked with the American Friends Service Committee, Haverford, Pennsylvania, 1941–42. Resident Student, Vedanta Society of Southern California, Hollywood; Editor, with Swami Prabhavananda, *Vedanta and the West*, Hollywood, 1943–44. Guest Professor of Modern English Literature, Los Angeles State College, and the University of California at Santa Barbara, 1959–62; Regents Professor, University of California at Los Angeles, 1965–66, and University of California at Riverside, 1966–67. Member, National Institute of Arts and Letters, 1949. Address: 145 Adelaide Drive, Santa Monica, California 90402, U.S.A.

PUBLICATIONS

Novels

*All the Conspirators*.   London, Cape, 1928; New York, New Directions, 1958.
*The Memorial: Portrait of a Family*.   London, Leonard and Virginia Woolf, 1932; New York, New Directions, 1946.
*Mr. Norris Changes Trains*.   London, Hogarth Press, 1935; as *The Last of Mr. Norris*, New York, Morrow, 1935.
*Sally Bowles*.   London, Hogarth Press, 1937.
*Goodbye to Berlin*.   London, Hogarth Press, and New York, Random House, 1939.
*Prater Violet*.   New York, Random House, 1945; London, Methuen, 1946.
*The Berlin Stories* (includes *Mr. Norris Changes Trains*, *Sally Bowles*, and *Goodbye to Berlin*).   New York, New Directions, 1946.
*The World in the Evening*.   New York, Random House, and London, Methuen, 1954.
*Down There on a Visit*.   New York, Simon and Schuster, and London, Methuen, 1962.
*A Single Man*.   New York, Simon and Schuster, and London, Methuen, 1964.
*A Meeting by the River*.   New York, Simon and Schuster, and London, Methuen, 1967.

Plays

*The Dog Beneath the Skin; or, Where Is Francis?*, with W. H. Auden.   London, Faber, 1935; New York, Random House, 1936.
*The Ascent of F6*, with W. H. Auden.   London, Faber, 1936; New York, Random House, 1937.
*On the Frontier*, with W. H. Auden.   London, Faber, 1938; New York, Random House, 1939.
*The Adventures of the Black Girl in Her Search for God*, adaptation of the novel by George Bernard Shaw (produced Los Angeles, 1969).

Screenplays: *Diane*, 1955; *The Loved One*, with Terry Southern, 1965; *Dr. Frankenstein*, with Don Bachardy, 1972.

Other

*Lions and Shadows: An Education in the Twenties*.   London, Hogarth Press, 1938; New York, New Directions, 1948.
*Journey to a War*, with W. H. Auden (on China).   New York, Random House, and London, Faber, 1939.

*The Condor and the Cows: A South American Travel Diary*.  New York, Random House, and London, Methuen, 1949.
*An Approach to Vedanta*.  Hollywood, Vedanta Press, 1963.
*Ramakrishna and His Disciples*.  New York, Simon and Schuster, and London, Methuen, 1965.
*Exhumations: Stories, Articles, Verses*.  New York, Simon and Schuster, and London, Methuen, 1966.
*Essentials of Vedanta*.  Hollywood, Vedanta Press, 1969.
*Kathleen and Frank* (autobiographical).  New York, Simon and Schuster, and London, Methuen, 1971.

Editor, *Vedanta and the Western World*.  Hollywood, Marcel Rodd, 1946; London, Allen and Unwin, 1948.
Editor, *Vedanta for Modern Man*.  New York, Harper, 1951; London, Allen and Unwin, 1952.
Editor, *Great English Short Stories*.  New York, Dell, 1957.

Translator, *Intimate Journals*, by Charles Baudelaire.  London, Blackamore Press, and New York, Random House, 1930.
Translator (verse only), *Penny for the Poor*, by Bertolt Brecht.  London, Hale, 1937; New York, Hillman Curl, 1938; as *Threepenny Novel*, New York, Grove Press, 1956.
Translator, with Swami Prabhavananda, *Bhagavad-Gita: The Song of God*.  Hollywood, Marcel Rodd, 1944; London, Phoenix House, 1947.
Translator, with Swami Prabhavananda, *Crest-Jewel of Discrimination*, by Shankara.  Hollywood, Vedanta Press, n.d.
Translator, with Swami Prabhavananda, *How to Know God: The Yoga Aphorisms of Patanjali*.  New York, Harper, and London, Allen and Unwin, 1953.

Bibliography: *Christopher Isherwood: A Bibliography 1923—1967* by Selmer Westby and Clayton M. Brown, Los Angeles, California State College, 1968.

Critical Studies: *Christopher Isherwood* by Carolyn G. Heilbrun, New York, Columbia University Press, 1970; *Christopher Isherwood* by Alan Wilde, New York, Twayne, 1971.

Christopher Isherwood comments:

All my writing is fundamentally autobiographical—that is to say, I write about experiences I myself have had, at first or second hand. (What I mean by "second hand" is that the attempted suicide in *The Memorial*, for example, was actually experienced and described to me by a friend.) In my novels, much of the action and the dialogue is fictitious and many of the characters are composites; but the experience upon which the scenes and characters are founded is my own.

I write because I am trying to study my life in retrospect and find out what it is, what it is made of, what it is all about. The attempt to do this is ultimately frustrating, of course, but nevertheless the most fascinating occupation I can imagine. At present (aged 67) it seems to me that I would prefer to write direct autobiography, as frank as possible, rather than any more fiction.

\*       \*       \*

Near the opening of his finest novel thus far, *Down There on a Visit*, the Christopher Isherwood of 1962 looks back critically at the young Isherwood of 1928. Despite his anxieties and untested arrogance, the young man had his points: "Perhaps his strongest negative emotion is ancestor hatred. He has vowed to disappoint, disgrace and disown his ancestors. If I were sneering at him I should suggest that this is because he fears he will never be able to live up to them; but this would be less than half true. His fury is sincere. He is genuinely a rebel. He knows instinctively that it is only through rebellion that he will ever learn and grow." There are a number of valid ways of describing Christopher Isherwood's achievements over the past forty years, but it is this theme of rebellion and growth which dominates everything he has written. The early novels, *All the Conspirators* and *The Memorial*, the autobiographical *Lions and Shadows*, and to a lesser extent *The Berlin Stories*, record stages of revolt against the false and dying cultures through which Isherwood and his characters move; the problem is that of finding an authentic self which can avoid compromise and resist destruction. The later work, beginning with *Prater Violet*, gradually questions the earlier goal of self-development—so much so that readers may wonder if Isherwood's final spiritual commitments may not prove incompatible with the kind of egoism which is one of the chief sources of creative energy: to question the value of the ego as radically as Isherwood has done in *Down There on a Visit* and *A Meeting by the River* may be a crucial step in the quest for purity, but it may also be fatal to the artistic projections of the ego. Beyond conversion and renunciation—which is the point towards which Isherwood has been propelling his recent heroes—there can be only the silence of meditation and self-discipline. Isherwood's fiction should be seen in this light, then, as an initial series of movements towards selfhood, rendered with extraordinary clarity, followed by a countermovement of spiritual rebellion against egoism.

The conspirators of *All the Conspirators* are the perpetual enemies of youthful freedom and expression—the family, the job, the routine obligations of living, everything which the older generation represents—and the motto of his first hero is, as Isherwood puts it, "My generation—right or wrong." The record of Philip Lindsay's two abortive rebellions against his family and class is the record of a "trivial but furious battle which the combatants fight out passionately and dirtily to a finish, using whatever weapons come to their hands" ("trivial" here rather than tragic because Lindsay is no Stephen Dedalus, but merely a suffocated only son with a vague desire to "paint and write"). Nevertheless, Lindsay's weak campaigns and pathetic defeat are rendered in a series of sharp, economical scenes of remarkable skill for so young a writer; Isherwood, at least, is no Philip Lindsay. *The Memorial*, a far more ambitious novel, fails, despite brilliant passages, because one of Isherwood's central preoccupations is insufficiently dramatized. The novel was conceived as a bitter memorial to the first World War and its casualties among the living. Those who have survived, if not physically wounded, find themselves "living on in a new world, unwanted, among enemies," while the young must grow up under the shadow of an unmet challenge. In *Lions and Shadows* Isherwood remarks that *The Memorial* was to be "about war", which for his generation meant "the test of your courage, of your maturity, of your sexual prowess. Are you really a man? . . . We young writers of the twenties were all suffering, more or less, from a feeling of shame that we hadn't been old enough to take part in the European War." The dislocation of the older generation is sympathetically presented (Isherwood reveals a good deal of sympathy for at least some members of the older generation who would have been categorically dismissed a few years before), but the uneasiness and mild hysteria of the young are dramatically puzzling and finally inexplicable in terms of the novel as we have it, without the helpful gloss of *Lions and Shadows*.

*The Berlin Stories* (1935–39), Isherwood's most directly autobiographical work, is already something of a modern classic, largely because of two superbly realized characters, Sally Bowles and Arthur Norris. The retiring narrator refers to himself, the young novelist barely making ends meet as an English teacher in Berlin during the rise of Hitler, as simply a "camera", recording the troubled scenes around him. But the image is misleading: cameras don't of themselves select and focus, whereas Isherwood in cool, understated terms carefully selects and focuses on those "small" incidents which will reveal and stand for the greater historical upheavals going on around them.

*Prater Violet*, Isherwood's first book after coming to America, looks back to pre-war London—and at the same time introduces, however tentatively, the author's new mistrust of "personality". The narrator describes his growing attachment to a refugee film-maker, a man of great power and charm who is to preside over the next stage of young Isherwood's education. Bergman is a commanding father figure, as well as an archetype of the artist, but in the splendid climax of this short novel something else is at work. Beyond a series of shadowy lovers the narrator senses for a moment, "but how infinitely faint, how distant, like the far high glimpse of a goat track through the mountains between clouds . . . something else"—something other, that is, than passing attractions and involvements of the superficial, narcissistic self:

> the way that leads to safety. To where there is no fear, no loneliness, no need of J., K., L., or M. For a second, I glimpse it. For an instant, it is even quite clear. Then the clouds shut down, and a breath off the glacier, icy with the inhuman coldness of the peaks, touches my cheek. "No," I think, "I could never do it. Rather the fear I know, the loneliness I know. . . . For to take that other way would mean that I would lose myself. I should no longer be a person. I should no longer be Christopher Isherwood. No. No. That's more terrible than having no lover. That I can never face."

*The World in the Evening* is the weakest of Isherwood's novels. Here the central figure (no longer so clearly a projection of Isherwood himself) uses his money, his considerable charm and sensitivity tyrannically, if half-unconsciously, as a means of confirming his ego: he will exist if others can be made to respond. An apparent accident forces him to review his life and admit his manipulation of others, but the ending is inconclusive, perhaps deliberately so. Is there to be any new growth now that the past has been understood? At the end of the novel Stephen claims that he can forgive anything, even himself: "Do you know," he concludes, "I really do forgive myself, from the bottom of my heart." This knowing self-indulgence is, however, only a version of the sin of pride. "We must overcome this terrible desire to luxuriate in our guilt and our scruples," warns Augustus, the Gerald Heard-like teacher in Isherwood's next novel, *Down There on a Visit*: "as long as we're going to indulge in that sort of vanity, well, it's just hopeless." The novel fails, not because Stephen may still be unable to overcome his egoism, but rather because of Isherwood's uncertainty in handling the American scenes and idioms, and because of a quite uncharacteristic idealization and finally sentimentalization of Stephen's saintly wife and his Quaker friends.

*Down There on a Visit* dramatizes four critical stages in the career of Isherwood's narrative self: in "Mr. Lancaster" and "Ambrose" the young observer watches the destructive power of the ego at work in two radically different kinds of characters; in "Waldemar" the young novelist watches Europe plunging into war; and in "Paul" the now older writer watches the perilous spiritual experiments of a magnetic young man with equal capacity for damnation or sainthood. In each of the episodes the narrator himself moves a little closer to participation and commitment: negatively, he leaves the old world and its claims; positively, he reaches towards Paul and his desperate attempts to find release from the prison of selfhood. *A Single Man* is a moving account of an aging man, a survivor of his own past, drifting towards death, recalling the comforts and pains of his past and trying to make some tentative connection with the young. But it is his most recent novel, *A Meeting by the River*, which provides the clearest indication of the path Isherwood has been travelling: here a young Englishman, a searcher in the earlier Isherwood tradition, is preparing to join a Hindu religious order based on the extinction of the individual ego and its attachments to the material world (Isherwood has described the doctrine of renunciation at length in his biography, *Ramakrishna and His Friends*). Oliver's older brother, a splendid instance of a man caught hopelessly in his own vanity, appears to tempt the novitiate but fails, and in the course of failing comes to realize some of his own evasions. Just possibly he too may be preparing for the state of grace.

At the conclusion of *Down There on a Visit* Paul lashes out at the uneasy, observing Isherwood: "You know, you really are a tourist, to your bones. I bet you're always sending postcards with 'down here on a visit' on them. That's the story of your life." This self-criticism has all the power of a shrewd half-truth. Isherwood's career has been spent in the service of sending extraordinary, synoptic postcards from crucial places at crucial times. But more than that, the messages inscribed offer a symbolic account of the quest for self-purification.

—Elmer Borklund

---

**ISRAEL, Charles (Edward).** American. Born in Evansville, Indiana, 15 November 1920. Educated at the University of North Carolina, Chapel Hill, 1937–39; University of Cincinnati, Ohio, B.A. 1942; Hebrew Union College, Los Angeles, B.H.L. 1943. Served in the United States Merchant Marine, 1943–45. Married Verna Margaret Sweezey in 1950. Deputy Chief of Repatriation, then Deputy Chief of the Voluntary Societies Division, United Nations Relief and Rehabilitation Administration (UNRRA) International Refugee Organization, in Munich, Heidelberg and Bad Kissingen, Germany, 1946–50. Radio and Television Playwright, in Hollywood, 1950–53, and since 1953 in Canada. Member of the Executive Board, 1957–59, and of the Board of Directors, 1965–66, Association of Canadian Radio and Television Artists. Recipient: Genoa Prize, for television film, 1964. Address: 196 Crestwood Road, Willowdale, Ontario, Canada.

PUBLICATIONS

Novels

*How Many Angels.* Toronto and London, Macmillan, 1956.
*The Mark.* New York, Simon and Schuster, and London, Macmillan, 1958.
*Rizpah.* New York, Simon and Schuster, and London, Macmillan, 1961.
*Who Was Then the Gentleman?* New York, Simon and Schuster, and London, Macmillan, 1963.
*Shadows on a Wall.* New York, Simon and Schuster, and London, Macmillan, 1965.
*The Hostages.* Toronto, Macmillan, and New York, Simon and Schuster, 1966.

Plays

*The Labyrinth: A Play for Television.* Toronto, Macmillan, and New York, St. Martin's Press, 1969.

500 radio and television plays and documentaries produced in the United States and
Canada.


Other

*The True North: The Story of Captain Joseph Bernier*, with T. C. Fairley.   Toronto
and London, Macmillan, and New York, St. Martin's Press, 1957.
*Five Ships West: The Story of Magellan*.   New York, Macmillan, 1966; London,
Macmillan, 1967.


\*       \*       \*


The novels of Charles Israel reflect a mind with an extraordinarily wide range of knowledge.
So varied are the settings and the subjects of these books that one can find no linking
thematic patterns among them: *Rizpah*, a sprawling biblical romance; *Who Was Then the
Gentleman?*, the story of Wat Tyler and the peasant revolt of 1381; *The Mark*, contemporary
California and the difficulties of a paroled sex offender in adjusting to society; *Shadows
on a Wall*, a complex narrative centering on black-white relationships, disparate ethnic
values, with action in Europe, Africa and the United States; *The Hostages*, the story of a
group of United Nations members' children who are kidnapped in New York and held as
hostages.

Perhaps the most impressive thing about this varied subject matter is Israel's command
of detail. In rendering accurately and convincingly the surface of things, the particular feel
of a place and time through the careful accumulation of facts, Israel is a master. Perhaps
it is a mark of his concern with such detail that, though he has lived in Canada for the past
sixteen years, he has not yet written a novel with a Canadian setting. ". . . I'd love to write
a novel set here, some day. I don't feel I really know enough about the country yet," he
was quoted as saying a few years back.

Israel's novels are so strongly oriented toward the surfaces of reality that frequently
the fictional structure seems a mere facade that falls away to reveal a kind of semi-documentary or perhaps a social worker's case study. Something of this sort happens in *The
Mark* in which the internal conflicts of the central character are never quite convincing;
we are told of his tensions and his fears, but we cannot truly feel them ourselves. We are
led to view him as a kind of specimen or sample to be studied but the study is cold.

The feeling of a case study is equally strong in *The Hostages*; the book is even structured
in a kind of documentary form. Even at his fictional best, as in *Shadows on a Wall* where
Israel almost succeeds in bringing out the contradictions deep within a human personality
and the contradictions and differences within and between two cultures, the visual orientation rules. Perhaps the difficulty in these books is that we are told that the characters are
emotional, tense, impulsive. Indeed they frequently act on feeling or impulse. But we
seldom see far enough into them to understand why they feel the way they do. They are like
strangers observed at a party, people whom we will never get to know, people about whom
we are told scraps of gossip. Adam, the sophisticated black journalist in *Shadows on a Wall*,
is incapable of making love to a white woman. The scene is a village in Africa. "But oh,
Nancy, I can't. Understand, understand, will you please? *I can't!*" We are told that his
impotence stems from experiences a few years before with "those rich tramps who came
to Harlem for kicks." Here, as in many other such situations in Israel's novels, the explanation seems too thin.

Unlike a writer like Robbe-Grillet, Israel cannot move smoothly from the surface to the
interior. But that is a most subtle art, one found only in the best of novelists. Probably
Israel is not of the absolute best, but he is a skilful observer and craftsman, an extraordinarily

facile and knowing writer, whose range and versatility alone are sufficient to merit him rank among contemporary writers.

—Leo J. Hertzel

———————————

**JACOBSON, Dan.** British. Born in Johannesburg, South Africa, 7 March 1929. Educated at the University of the Witwatersrand, Johannesburg, 1946–49, B.A. 1949. Married Margaret Pye in 1954; has four children. Public Relations Assistant, South African Jewish Board of Deputies, Johannesburg, 1951–52; Correspondence Secretary, Mills and Feeds Ltd., Kimberley, South Africa, 1952–54. Fellow in Creative Writing, Stanford University, California, 1956–57; Visiting Professor of English Literature, Syracuse University, New York, 1965–66. Recipient: Rhys Memorial Prize, 1959; Maugham Award, 1964. Address: c/o A. M. Heath and Company, 35 Dover Street, London W.1, England.

PUBLICATIONS

Novels

    *The Trap*. London, Weidenfeld and Nicolson, and New York, Harcourt Brace, 1955.
    *A Dance in the Sun*. London, Weidenfeld and Nicolson, and New York, Harcourt Brace, 1956.
    *The Price of Diamonds*. London, Weidenfeld and Nicolson, and New York, Knopf, 1957.
    *The Evidence of Love*. London, Weidenfeld and Nicolson, and Boston, Little Brown, 1960.
    *The Beginners*. London, Weidenfeld and Nicolson, and New York, Macmillan, 1966.
    *The Rape of Tamar*. London, Weidenfeld and Nicolson, and New York, Macmillan, 1970.

Short Stories

    *A Long Way from London*. London, Weidenfeld and Nicolson, 1958.
    *The Zulu and the Zeide*. Boston, Little Brown, 1959.
    *Beggar My Neighbour*. London, Weidenfeld and Nicolson, 1964.
    *Through the Wilderness*. New York, Macmillan, 1968.
    *Penguin Modern Stories 6*, with others. London, Penguin, 1970.

Other

    *No Further West: California Visited*. London, Weidenfeld and Nicolson, 1959; New York, Macmillan, 1961.
    *Time of Arrival and Other Essays*. London, Weidenfeld and Nicolson, and New York, Macmillan, 1963.

Bibliography: *Dan Jacobson: A Bibliography* by Myra Yudelman, Johannesburg, University of the Witwatersrand, 1967.


Critical Studies: "The Novels of Dan Jacobson" by Renee Winegarten, in *Midstream* (New York), May 1966; "Novelist of South Africa" by Midge Decter, in *The Liberated Woman and Other Essays*, New York, Coward McCann, 1971.

\*       \*       \*

Dan Jacobson's first two novels, *The Trap* and *Dance in the Sun*, marked him as a writer of considerable ability, with an interest in typically South African "problems." Since then, he has developed rapidly to become one of South Africa's best known and most interesting novelists.

The two early novels are both concerned with the tensions inherent in the extremely close, almost familial, relationships between white employer and black employee, which tend to develop in the particular kind of rural community Jacobson describes (both novels are set on farms); both embody what might be described as allegorical statements about the South African situation. Trapped in their own environment, Jacobson implies, the inhabitants of the country are condemned to perform a ritualistic "dance in the sun", which, to the outsider—the "liberal" narrator—appears to be a form of insanity. This vision of South Africa leaves out of account, or, at best, finds irrelevant the group (English-speaking, liberal, white) to which Jacobson himself belongs, and it is not, therefore, surprising that he should have chosen to live and work abroad. At the same time, however, his novels reflect a continuing fascination with South African themes, particularly with problems of identity: problems which are unusually complex for a writer who, like Jacobson, has roots in Europe as well as in Africa.

Two novels, which lie slightly apart from these major concerns, are *The Price of Diamonds* and *Evidence of Love*. Both utilise Jacobson's own early background, and evoke the provincial life of a South African mining town. *The Price of Diamonds* is a fairly successful comedy; *Evidence of Love* an uneasy attempt to portray an interracial love affair—a subject on which more than one South African novelist has come to grief.

Jacobson's two most recent novels, *The Beginners*, and *The Rape of Tamar*, mark a new stage in his development. These are the novels which have earned him wide critical acclaim, and which together with his prize-winning book of stories, *A Long Way from London*, and his recent essays *Time of Arrival*, have firmly established his reputation as a writer of stature. *The Beginners*, the story of three generations of an immigrant Jewish family, is a penetrating, subtle and complex analysis of what it means to be, as one of the central characters expresses it, "a demi-European at the foot of Africa" as well as a "demi-Jew" in the modern world. Ranging over the entire fabric of contemporary South Africa Life, and free from any obvious political or humanitarian bias, *The Beginners* is one of the finest South African novels yet produced, and certainly it is the most substantial. Although it is technically unremarkable—Jacobson effectively uses old-fashioned narrative methods—the novel commands respect for its skilful control of the large number of representative yet individualised characters, its political sensitivity, its moral commitment, and for its refusal to sentimentalise typical South African attitudes. *The Rape of Tamar* is not set in South Africa. It is a biblical reconstruction (Jacobson has acknowledged his debt to, among others, Thomas Mann) of an episode at King David's court, involving a number of his sons and his favourite daughter, Tamar. More sophisticated than anything Jacobson has previously attempted, this novel is both verbally and structurally a remarkable *tour-de-force*. A political allegory on the power-struggle, the novel combines Jacobson's talent for comedy with his overriding moral concern.

Like other contemporary South African novelists, Jacobson has produced some excellent short stories. Most of them probe the guilts and fears of white South Africans, revealing the irrational impulses which govern the lives of a people who feel themselves perpetually threatened by the surrounding, and for the most part completely unknown, black masses. Two stories, which are among the best things he has done, are "The Zulu and the Zeide" and "Beggar My Neighbour", the title story of a recent collection. "The Zulu and the Zeide" ironically counterpoints the hard-headed acquisitiveness of a successful Jewish businessman with the humanity of a "raw" (i.e. tribal) African. Half-deliberately, Harry Grossman delegates his filial obligations to Paulus, his black servant, and the tenderness and understanding of this man finally shame him into a belated and futile recognition of his own callousness. "Beggar My Neighbour", an apparently simple story, nevertheless encapsulates an entire South African way of life. A chance acquaintance between three children, one white and two black, gradually forces an awareness—on the white child as well as on the reader—of the intricate connections which exist between people in a colour-bar society, even when prejudice has all but destroyed any meaningful contact. In these stories, as in all his work, Jacobson's special skills are displayed: detailed observation, economic presentation, and a compassionate but objective analysis of the varieties of human behaviour.

—Ursula Laredo

---

**JAMES, C(yril) L(ionel) R(obert).**   West Indian.   Born in Trinidad, 4 January 1901. Educated at Queen's Royal College, Port of Spain, Trinidad, 1911–18. Married Selma Jones in 1955; has one child by a previous marriage. Journalist and Teacher in the West Indies until 1932, when he moved to England; Press Correspondent, chiefly on cricket, in England, until 1938; went to the United States in 1938, and remained there, lecturing on politics and literature, until 1953; has resided in England since 1953, except for two years in the West Indies, 1958–60, when he worked as Secretary of the West Indian Federal Labour Party. Address: c/o Hutchinson and Company, 178 Great Portland Street, London W.1, England.

PUBLICATIONS

Novel

*Minty Alley.*   London, Secker, 1936.

Other

*The Life of Captain Cipriani.*   Privately printed, 1933; abridged as *The Case for West Indian Self-Government*, London, Hogarth Press, 1933.
*Cricket and I*, with L. N. Constantine.   London, Allan, 1933.
*World Revolution, 1917–1936: The Rise and Fall of the Communist International.* London, Secker, and New York, Pioneer Publications, 1937.
*A History of Negro Revolt.*   London, Fact, 1938.
*The Black Jacobins: Toussaint Louverture and the San Domingo Revolution.*   London, Secker, and New York, Dial Press, 1938; revised edition, New York, Random House, 1963.

*Mariners, Renegades, and Castaways: The Story of Herman Melville and the World We Live In.*  New York, privately printed, 1953.
*Beyond a Boundary.*  London, Hutchinson, 1963.

*          *          *

C. L. R. James shocked the middle class Trinidadian readers of the late twenties and early thirties with short stories that explored the manners and morals of the indigenous population. For while everyone knew of them, this central area of Caribbean experience was kept out of "respectable" literature. Today levels of moral acceptance, not only in Trinidad, have drastically changed, and the work of writers such as V. S. Naipaul and Samuel Selvon in the same area makes part of James' explorations of lower-class Caribbean life colourless. Nevertheless James' qualities of human compassion in an area land-mined with prejudices of class and colour have not been superseded, and will never be irrelevant.

*Minty Alley*, James' only full-length novel, tells how a young office-worker Haynes is forced by poverty to live in the unfamiliar surroundings of a lower class tenement. It is run by a Mrs. Rouse and her man Benoit, who is also carrying on an affair with a powerful and somewhat sinister woman known only as "the nurse". The community is violent and unstable in its relationships, lit with sudden moments of tenderness, and Haynes quickly becomes involved in it, in particular through his liaison with the servant Maisie, Mrs. Rouse's neice. Although at first Haynes appears a "superior" figure by class and education, by the end he can begin to realise that he came as an immature person, and has been mothered into manhood by the little community. Benoit dies, and, although he has deserted Mrs. Rouse for the nurse, Mrs. Rouse loses all desire to run the house, and Haynes leaves as its inhabitants disperse.

James hoped that a second novel would be his major work, but this never appeared. *Minty Alley*, however, assures him a place in Caribbean fiction.

—Louis James

---

**JAMESON, (Margaret) Storm.**  English.  Born in Whitby, Yorkshire, 8 January 1891. Educated at Leeds University, Yorkshire, 1909–12, B.A. (1st class honours) in English language and literature 1912; King's College, London, 1912–13, M.A. 1914. Married Guy Patterson Chapman in 1924 (second marriage); has one child. Formerly: Copywriter for Carlton Agency, advertising firm, London; Editor, *New Commonwealth*, London, 1919–21; English Representative, and later Co-Manager, Alfred A. Knopf, publishers, New York, 1923–28; Reviewer, *New English Weekly*, London, 1934. President, English Centre of P.E.N., 1938–45. D.Litt., Leeds University, 1943. Address: c/o Macmillan and Company, 4 Little Essex Street, London W.C.2, England.

PUBLICATIONS

Novels

*The Pot Boils.*  London, Constable, 1919.
*The Happy Highways.*  London, Heinemann, 1920.
*The Clash.*  London, Heinemann, 1922.
*The Pitiful Wife.*  London, Constable, 1923; New York, Knopf, 1924.

*Three Kingdoms*.   London, Constable, and New York, Knopf, 1926.
*The Triumph of Time: A Trilogy*.   London, Heinemann, 1932.
   *The Lovely Ship*.   London, Heinemann, and New York, Knopf, 1927.
   *The Voyage Home*.   New York, Knopf, 1930; London, Heinemann, 1931.
   *A Richer Dust*.   London, Heinemann, and New York, Knopf, 1932.
*Farewell to Youth*.   London, Heinemann, and New York, Knopf, 1928.
*That Was Yesterday*.   London, Heinemann, and New York, Knopf, 1932.
*The Single Heart*.   London, Benn, 1932.
*A Day Off*.   London, Nicholson and Watson, 1933.
*Women Against Men* (includes *A Day Off*, *The Delicate Monster*, and *The Single Heart*).
   New York, Knopf, 1933.
*Company Parade*.   London, Cassell, and New York, Knopf, 1934.
*Love in Winter*.   London, Cassell, and New York, Knopf, 1935.
*In the Second Year*.   London, Cassell, and New York, Macmillan, 1936.
*Now Turn Back*.   London, Cassell, 1936.
*The Delicate Monster*.   London, Nicholson and Watson, 1937.
*Moon Is Making*.   London, Cassell, 1937; New York, Macmillan, 1938.
*The World Ends* (as William Lamb).   London, Dent, 1937.
*Loving Memory* (as James Hill).   London, Collins, 1937.
*No Victory for the Soldier* (as James Hill).   London, Collins, 1938.
*Here Comes a Candle*.   London, Cassell, 1938; New York, Macmillan, 1939.
*Farewell, Night: Welcome, Day*.   London, Cassell, 1939; as *The Captain's Wife*, New
   York, Macmillan, 1939.
*Europe to Let: The Memoirs of an Obscure Man*.   London, Macmillan, and New
   York, Macmillan, 1940.
*Cousin Honoré*.   London, Cassell, 1940; New York, Macmillan, 1941.
*The Fort*.   London, Cassell, and New York, Macmillan, 1941.
*Then We Shall Hear Singing: A Fantasy in C Major*.   London, Cassell, and New
   York, Macmillan, 1942.
*Cloudless May*.   London, Macmillan, 1943; New York, Macmillan, 1944.
*The Journal of Mary Hervey Russell*.   London, Macmillan, and New York, Macmillan,
   1945.
*The Other Side*.   London, Macmillan, and New York, Macmillan, 1946.
*Before the Crossing*.   London, Macmillan, and New York, Macmillan, 1947.
*The Black Laurel*.   London, Macmillan, and New York, Macmillan, 1948.
*The Moment of Truth*.   London, Macmillan, 1949.
*The Green Man*.   London, Macmillan, 1952; New York, Harper, 1953.
*The Hidden River*.   London, Macmillan, and New York, Harper, 1955.
*The Intruder*.   London, Macmillan, and New York, Macmillan, 1956.
*A Cup of Tea for Mr. Thorgill*.   London, Macmillan, and New York, Harper, 1957.
*A Ulysses Too Many*.   London, Macmillan, 1958; as *One Ulysses Too Many*, New
   York, Harper, 1958.
*Last Score; or, The Private Life of Sir Richard Ormston*.   London, Macmillan, and
   New York, Harper, 1961.
*The Road from the Monument*.   London, Macmillan, and New York, Harper, 1962.
*A Month Soon Goes*.   London, Macmillan, and New York, Harper, 1963.
*The Aristide Case*.   London, Macmillan, 1964; as *The Blind Heart*, New York, Harper,
   1964.
*The Early Life of Stephen Hind*.   London, Macmillan, and New York, Harper, 1966.
*The White Crow*.   London, Macmillan, 1968.


Short Stories

*Days Off: 2 Short Novels and Some Stories*.   London, Macmillan, 1959.

Other

*Modern Drama in Europe.*   London, Collins, 1920.

*The Georgian Novel and Mr. Robinson.*   London, Heinemann, and New York, Morrow, 1929.

*The Decline of Merry England.*   London, Cassell, and Indianapolis, Bobbs Merrill, 1930.

*No Time Like the Present* (autobiography).   London, Cassell, and New York, Knopf, 1933.

*The Soul of Man in the Age of Leisure.*   London, Nott, 1935.

*The Novel in Contemporary Life.*   Boston, The Writer, 1938.

*A Civil Journey.*   London, Cassell, 1939.

*The End of This Year.*   London, Allen and Unwin, 1941.

*The Writer's Situation and Other Essays.*   London, Macmillan, and New York, Macmillan, 1950.

*Morley Roberts: The Last Eminent Victorian.*   London, Unicorn Press, 1961.

*Journey from the North* (autobiography).   London, Collins-Harvill Press, 2 vols., 1969, 1970; New York, Harper, 1971.

*Parthian Words.*   London, Collins-Harvill Press, 1970; New York, Harper, 1971.

Editor, *Challenge to Death.*   London, Constable, 1934; New York, Dutton, 1935.

Editor, *London Calling.*   New York, Harper, 1942.

Translator, *Mont-Oriol*, by Guy de Maupassant. New York, Knopf, 1924.

Translator, *Horla and Other Stories*, by Guy de Maupassant.   New York, Knopf, 1925.

Translator, with Ernest Boyd, *88 Short Stories*, by Guy de Maupassant.   London, Cassell, 1930.

Manuscript Collections: University of Texas, Austin; Wellesley College, Massachusetts; other libraries have single manuscripts.

Storm Jameson comments:

My earliest novels are not worth reading. Nor are all of the later ones. It took me some years to learn how to write. A short list of those novels worth looking at might run: *That Was Yesterday*; *A Day Off*; *Company Parade, Love in Winter, Now Turn Back*—three novels of an unfinished series; *Farewell, Night: Welcome, Day*; *Europe to Let*; *Cousin Honoré*; *Cloudless May*; *The Journal of Mary Hervey Russell*; *Before the Crossing* and *The Black Laurel*—two novels which are really one; *The Green Man*; *The Hidden River*; *A Cup of Tea for Mr. Thorgill*; *The Road from the Monument*; *The White Crow*.

Of more lasting value is my autobiography: *Journey from the North*. It says all that needs to be said about my novels, myself and my life.

My latest and probably last book, *Parthian Words*, contains my declaration of faith as a writer.

Readers of *Journey from the North* will discover that I have written three novels under other names. One of these, *The World Ends*, by William Lamb, is good, I think.

*          *          *

Margaret Storm Jameson was born in Whitby, Yorkshire, into a family of shipbuilders in 1891; and these basic facts are relevant for both her outlook and writing. Three of her novels—*The Lovely Ship, The Voyage Home* and *A Richer Dust*—form a trilogy in which the author chronicles the fortunes of a shipbuilding family and its Victorian matriarch. Some of her later novels have continued the story of Mary Hervey's descendants, and one may suppose that Miss Jameson drew freely on personal contacts and memories, as well as on records, of her own family.

Storm Jameson has told us much—and told it memorably—about her own life in her autobiography, *Journey from the North*, so it is clear that her own life and her family background have provided a great deal of her subject matter. After reading English at Leeds University she did post-graduate research for her M.A. degree at King's College, London, and her thesis appeared in book form as *Modern Drama in Europe*. Already, then, one notes her interest in European literary art and ideas. Despite her consciousness of and pride in her Yorkshire roots, she is the least insular of writers. As President of the English Centre of P.E.N. she revealed herself as an outspoken liberal and anti-Nazi, and a hard-working friend to refugee writers.

"I have every talent of the good businessman", Miss Jameson has said of herself, "shrewdness, persistence, a talent for strategy—except a talent for enjoying business." More pertinent, perhaps, in considering her fiction is her statement that: "My mother was a Congregationalist and what religion I got in my youth was coloured by that stiff, self-regarding faith. It would be no use for me to deny to myself my Nonconformist upbringing." There one finds both her strength and her limitation, for she appears to have retained the Nonconformist "narrow ideas of right and wrong, its distrust of enjoyment." Few writers can have been so honest as to declare bluntly: "I am not what you may call a born writer, and I should have been much happier as an engineer."

Born writer or not, Miss Jameson has proved herself a prolific writer. She has been candid enough to admit that her earliest novels are not very good; and few critics would wish to dispute the author's own judgment. Out of a great mass of fiction only a handful of novels are worth attention. Those that may be singled out for scrutiny and some praise are *Cousin Honoré, The Road from the Monument, The White Crow* and *A Cup of Tea for Mr. Thorgill*.

*Cousin Honoré*, possibly the most satisfying novel Miss Jameson has written, draws the portrait not only of Honoré Burckheim but of the province of Alsace. She brings out splendidly the flavour of an area which is partly French in character and partly German, but yet remains stubbornly itself. Burckheim is the owner of the family ironworks in the village that bears their name but his real interest—almost to the point of obsession—is his vineyards and the fine Alsatian wine they produce. He likes to turn over in his mind the old rhyme:

> Burckheim, Burckheim,
> A little town, a great wine.

The "Nonconformist" Storm Jameson appears to have been fascinated by her own creation: a wily, yet fundamentally sound, old sensualist. The period of time covered runs from 1918 to 1939, and this gives Miss Jameson the opportunity to reveal her love of France and her contempt for the aggressive, boorish aspect of the German national character that found its ultimate expression in Nazi brutality and hysteria. She also flays those Frenchmen whose corruption and inertia led to the defeat of France in 1940.

Burckheim is studied in depth. A self-willed not to say selfish man, a greedy, self-indulgent man, he nevertheless represents much that is good in the French tradition. But it is Berthelin who stands for the true élite of France: intelligent, honourable, responsible. Siguenau, a schemer and liar, stops short of treachery to his country if not to his friends. Eschelmer, the son of Burckheim's illegitimate daughter and a half-German, works as a German agent; he is hysterical in nature, driven by self-pity and vanity, and ends up as a murderer. Reuss, while not pro-German, does not appreciate that saving Alsace from destruction is too narrow an objective when the West is faced with the destruction of its values.

But *Cousin Honoré* does not consist simply of men and ideas. Miss Jameson explores—and with great sensitivity—the feminine world. She brings to life for us Caroline, Burckheim's second wife, who comes from Boston and assesses her husband as being "as naturally honest as a child and completely unmanageable"; the English Blanche Siguenau who "rode, gardened, dried herbs for the different teas"; and eager young Fanny Siguenau who watches her fiancé go off to fight the incorrigible Boche from across the Rhine.

*Cousin Honoré* is an Englishwoman's tribute to French civilisation. It can also be enjoyed for the skilful way in which Miss Jameson builds up her situations and characters. Perceptive, witty, generous, it is vintage Jameson.

A question Storm Jameson often tries to answer is this: are people really, at bottom, what they seem to others or even to themselves? This theme runs through *The Road from the Monument* and *The White Crow*. In the first of these Gregory Mott comes under the microscope. On the surface his life seems happy and assured; but religious faith and the support of friends fail him when he comes face to face with his real self. Reality is also explored in *The White Crow*. Here, the setting runs from 1890 to 1942, so Miss Jameson takes the opportunity not only to probe into her main character but to underline the social changes of that half-century.

*A Cup of Tea for Mr. Thorgill* satirises the self-consciously clever academic world. She lashes the "profound frivolity—frivolity at a deep level, below whatever you like of scholarship, sophistication, wit" that can be found in the inbred society of an Oxford college. She brings to her task delicacy and irony and not a little feminine malice. Yet, as in all her work, she is a committed writer: one to whom the integrity of the human personality and freedom of individual action are of supreme importance. Had she been less prolific, Storm Jameson's reputation on the literary stock exchange would undoubtedly be quoted at a much higher figure than it is today. Her best work assures her a place among the significant English novelists of our time.

—Robert Greacen

---

**JENKINS, (John) Robin.** British. Born in Cambuslang, Lanarkshire, Scotland, 11 September 1912. Educated at Hamilton Academy; Glasgow University, 1931–35, B.A. (honours) in English 1935, M.A. 1936. Married Mary McIntyre Wylie in 1937; has three children. Taught at Dunoon Grammar School; Ghazi College, Kabul, 1957–59; the British Institute, Barcelona, 1959–61; Gaya School, Sabah, 1963–68. Recipient: Frederick Niven Award, 1956. Address: Southview, 55 Mary Street, Dunoon, Argyll, Scotland.

PUBLICATIONS

Novels

    *Go Gaily Sings the Lark.* Glasgow, Maclellan, 1951.
    *Happy for the Child.* London, Lehmann, 1953.
    *The Thistle and the Grail.* London, Macdonald, 1954.
    *The Cone-Gatherers.* London, Macdonald, 1955.
    *Guests of War.* London, Macdonald, 1956.
    *The Missionaries.* London, Macdonald, 1957.

*The Changeling.*   London, Macdonald, 1958.
*Love Is a Fervent Fire.*   London, Macdonald, 1959.
*Some Kind of Grace.*   London, Macdonald, 1960.
*Dust on the Paw.*   London, Macdonald, and New York, Putnam, 1961.
*The Tiger of Gold.*   London, Macdonald, 1962.
*A Love of Innocence.*   London, Cape, 1963.
*The Sardana Dancers.*   London, Cape, 1964.
*A Very Scotch Affair.*   London, Gollancz, 1968.
*The Holy Tree.*   London, Gollancz, 1969.
*The Expatriates.*   London, Gollancz, 1971.

*          *          *

Jenkins achieved an early success with *Happy for the Child*, an evocative re-creation of a Scottish childhood, but later novels on his native scene, although incisively written, suffered from plots which carried too heavy a weight of symbolic interpretation and broke down into melodramatic situations jarring against the nicely-observed backgrounds. It appeared that his leaning towards the strikingly-significant action required a wider stage than the narrow bounds of a provincialised Scotland. This he eventually discovered in Afghanistan, which became the "Nurania" of *Dust on the Paw*.

Here Jenkins presents a country trying to wrench itself up out of medievalism by its own sandalstraps, a society half-fascinated by modernity and half-afraid of it, with intellectuals and administrators uprooted from ancestral traditions which they despise and yet fiercely defend against criticism from the outside world. Whether Jenkins' picture of Afghanistan is wholly accurate, fair, impartial and unbiased can be judged only by those who have lived there, but to the foreign reader it seems entirely convincing—the alpine sunshine, the dust and the dirt, the peasants dignified in their old poverty and the westernised middle-class desperate in their new, the idealism and the corruption, the blind fanaticism and the wary self-seeking, above all the sheer muddle out of which nevertheless some kind of pattern does appear to emerge as the various characters struggle "between two worlds, one dead, the other powerless to be born."

This pattern suggests that the two worlds are in fact one, in which we all share, whatever our creeds or colours. If this is a platitude, the erstwhile dominant minority of Europeans find it hard to accept and even harder to live up to. One of the book's two heroes is the poet Harold Moffat, whose intellectual assent to the idea of racial equality is undermined by a deep-rooted emotional prejudice which compels him to deny motherhood to his Chinese wife. The characterisation of Moffat, whose self-loathing sours into hatred of the men and women around him who challenge those aspects of his personality most distasteful to himself, searches deep but never becomes unsympathetic.

At least equally successful is the characterisation of the other hero, the Afghan Abdul Wahab whose engagement to an Englishwoman sparks off the action of the book. A patriot divided from his own people by his English university education, Wahab lives on a see-saw of ideas and emotions, one eye on his ideals and the other on the main chance—a man with all his qualities, noble and ignoble, forced into play by the precariousness of his situation as a focal point of change in a society undergoing a revolution. The powers of mature insight and imagination revealed in this character-study, and throughout the book as a whole, have created a work which ranks high among British novels on the Asian scene. It remains Jenkins' most impressive creation, although a more recent work, *The Holy Tree*, a bittersweet tragi-comedy of life in colonial Malaya, comes close to its unblinking awareness of the wide differences which divide the races of mankind and its profound appreciation of the fundamental sympathies which unite us all.

—Alexander Scott

**JHABVALA, R(uth) Prawer.**   British.   Born in Cologne, Germany, of Polish parents, 7 May 1927; went to England as a refugee, 1939; became a British citizen in 1948. Educated at Hendon County School, London; University of London, 1945–51, M.A. in English literature 1951. Married C. S. H. Jhabvala in 1951; has three children. Has lived in India since 1951. Address: 1–A Flagstaff Road, Delhi 6, India.

PUBLICATIONS

Novels

> *To Whom She Will.*   London, Allen and Unwin, 1955; as *Amrita*, New York, Norton, 1956.
> *The Nature of Passion.*   London, Allen and Unwin, 1956; New York, Norton, 1957.
> *Esmond in India.*   London, Allen and Unwin, 1957; New York, Norton, 1958.
> *The Householder.*   London, Murray, and New York, Norton, 1960.
> *Get Ready for Battle.*   London, Murray, 1962; New York, Norton, 1963.
> *A Backward Place.*   London, Murray, and New York, Norton, 1965.

Short Stories

> *Like Birds, Like Fishes and Other Stories.*   London, Murray, 1963; New York, Norton, 1964.
> *A Stronger Climate: 9 Stories.*   London, Murray, 1968; New York, Norton, 1969.
> *An Experience of India.*   London, Murray, 1971; New York, Norton, 1972.
> *Penguin Modern Stories 11*, with other.   London, Penguin, 1972.

Plays

> Screenplays: *The Householder*, 1963; *Shakespeare Wallah*, 1965; *The Guru*, 1968; *Bombay Talkie*, 1970.

R. Prawer Jhabvala comments:

The central fact of all my work, as I see it, is that I am a European living permanently in India. I have lived here for most of my adult life and have an Indian family. This makes me not quite an insider but it does not leave me entirely an outsider either. I feel my position to be at a point in space where I have quite a good view of both sides but am myself left stranded in the middle. My work is an attempt to charter this unchartered territory for myself. Sometimes I write about Europeans in India, sometimes about Indians in India, sometimes about both, but always attempting to present India to myself in the hope of giving myself some kind of foothold. My books may appear objective but really I think they are the opposite: for I describe the Indian scene not for its own sake but for mine. This excludes me from all interest in all those Indian problems one is supposed to be interested in (the extent of Westernisation, modernity vs. tradition, etc! etc!). My work can never claim to be a balanced or authoritative view of India but is only one individual European's attempt to compound the puzzling process of living in it.

\*       \*       \*

Although Ruth Prawer Jhabvala is not Indian-born, it is appropriate to consider her work within the context of contemporary fiction in English written by Indians. Her subject is Indian life, and in particular two aspects of it: that of middle-class urban Indians, on the one hand, and of Europeans living in India, on the other. These largely social situations are presented from the unique dual point of view of the outsider within. This point of view, furthermore, is not static nor stereotyped but changing and developing. Thus the reader of Mrs. Jhabvala's fiction finds development within it in terms both of extending social and thematic range and a shift in the author's sense of her relation to India, from a set of Indian identifications to one of immigrant awarenesses.

In *To Whom She Will* and *The Nature of Passion* Mrs. Jhabvala began her literary exploration of India with a narrowly focused study of the vicissitudes of romantic love, depicting privileged young people contending with such entrenched forces as family tradition, arranged marriage and bourgeois materialism. With *Esmond in India* comes a broadening of horizons (though this phrase is misleading in view of Mrs. Jhabvala's habitual concentration of dramatic action within largely domestic and social interior settings); the novel is structured round the raging frustrations of the decadent Esmond (a European culture merchant and self-pitying sadist who hates India), and a series of conflicts between idealistic and materialistic life-styles. Pointed satire exposes the moral cowardice underlying affected idealism and culture snobbery, and poignant irony confirms the human worth of self-effacing renunciation and integrity. These themes and modes of presentation come to mature fruition in *Get Ready for Battle* and *A Backward Place*.

While each of Mrs. Jhabvala's novels contains clear outlines of feminine psychology, especially of power struggles in the joint-family and of modish girl graduates clashing with their conservative elders, *The Householder* offers the most intimate and sustained portrayal of the marriage relationship in its shy early stage. A feature of this novel is that the story of the struggling newly-weds, learning to adjust to each other and cope with economic and in-law problems, is projected mainly from the male angle. *The Householder*, like R. K. Narayan's *The Bachelor of Arts*, reveals with sympathetic irony the temptation of escape from adult responsibilities by premature progression from the second *ashrama* of the householder (from the first, that of the scholar, in Narayan's novel) to the *sanyasi* stage of life.

Mrs. Jhabvala's style, like Narayan's, is deceptively unassuming and direct. For, with the comedy-of-manners emphasis and growing assurance with which she works through irony and satire, Mrs. Jhabvala has devised subtle as well as entertaining ways of sketching the New Delhi social scene; of exposing the sentimentality, snobbery, vanity, pretentiousness and hypocrisy underlying a variety of manners and behaviour; of providing deft insights into such manifestations of affluence as romantic illusion, status aspiration, indolence, male chauvinism and business Machiavellianism; and of exploring such universal themes as the frailty of race relationships, the weakness and vulnerability of expatriate sensibilities, and the clash between virtue and power, desire and disinterestedness, idealism and bourgeois self-indulgence.

Mrs. Jhabvala is one of India's best novelists writing in English at the present time. (For a critical appreciation of her work see the articles by H. Moore Williams in *Twentieth Century Literature* [Los Angeles], vol. 15, no. 2, and *The Journal of Commonwealth Literature* [Leeds, Yorkshire], vol. VI, no. 1.)

—S. C. Harrex

---

**JOHNSON, B(ryan) S(tanley).** British. Born in London, 5 February 1933. Educated at King's College, London, B.A. (honours) in English. Married Virginia Ann Kimpton in

1964; has two children. Since 1964, Poetry Editor, *Transatlantic Review*, London and New York. Directed the films, *You're Human Like the Rest of Them*, 1967, *Up Yours Too, Guillaume Apollinaire*, 1968, and *Paradigm*, 1969, and the plays, *Backwards* and *The Ramp*, Mermaid Theatre, London, 1970. Founded "Writers Reading", with Alan Burns, *q.v.*, to encourage and organize prose readings at colleges and universities, 1969. First Gregynog Arts Fellow, University of Wales, 1970. Recipient: Gregory Award, 1963; Maugham Award, 1967; Grand Prix, Tours and Melbourne International Short Film Festivals, 1968; Grandara Poetry Prize, 1971. Address: 9 Dagmar Terrace, London N.1, England.

PUBLICATIONS

Novels

*Travelling People*.   London, Constable, 1963.
*Albert Angelo*.   London, Constable, 1964.
*Trawl*.   London, Secker and Warburg, 1966.
*The Unfortunates*.   London, Secker and Warburg, 1969.
*House Mother Normal*.   London, Collins, 1971.
*Xtie Malry's Own Double Entry*.   London, Collins, 1972.

Short Stories

*Statement Against Corpses*, with Zulfikar Ghose.   London, Constable, 1964.
*Penguin Modern Stories 7*, with others.   London, Penguin, 1971.

Uncollected Short Stories

"Aren't You Rather Young to Be Writing Your Memoirs?" in *Transatlantic Review* (London and New York), June 1967.
"These Count as Fictions", in *Encounter* (London), February 1968.

Plays

*You're Human Like the Rest of Them* (screenplay), in *New English Dramatists 14*. London, Penguin, 1970.
*B. S. Johnson Versus God* (*Whose Dog Are You?* and *You're Human Like the Rest of Them*) (produced London, 1971).

Plays and documentaries produced on radio and television.

Verse

*Poems*.   London, Constable, and New York, Chilmark Press, 1964.
*Poems Two*.   London, Trigram Press, 1972.

Other

*Street Children*, with Julia Trevelyan Oman.   London, Hodder and Stoughton, 1964.

Editor, *The Evacuees*.  London, Gollancz, 1968.
Editor, with Margaret Drabble, *London Consequences* (a group novel).  London, Greater London Arts Association, 1972.

Critical Studies: "The Novelist at the Crossroads" by David Lodge, in *Critical Quarterly* (London), Summer 1969; *The Situation of the Novel* by Bernard Bergonzi, London, Macmillan, 1970.

B. S. Johnson comments:

Nathalie Sarraute once described literature in terms of a relay race, the baton of innovation being passed from one generation to another. Not only has the vast majority of British novelists dropped the baton, but it has stood still, turned back, or not even realised that there is a race.

In this century the baton first took the form of *Ulysses*: few except Samuel Beckett took it up of the generation following Joyce. *Ulysses* was a revolution, but a revolution which has been largely ignored as far as it indicated the form the novel must take in the future.

James Joyce was the first to see that the cinema was about to take over from the novel the narrative function which had belonged until the early nineteenth century to the long poem: Joyce started the first cinema in Dublin as early as 1909. *Ulysses* does not tell a story, therefore, but is as full a description as he could make it of one day in the lives of two men, and its virtues are those which uniquely belong to the novel and not to mere storytelling.

All this seems obvious to me. So why do the vast majority (it must be over 95 per cent at a reasonable guess) of novelists writing now still tell stories, still write as though *Ulysses* (let alone *The Unnamable*) had never happened?

It baffles me; but it's not my problem. An analogy. Horseriding is a pleasant hobby or pastime for those who are interested: but serious travellers use today's methods—aircraft, cars, trains. No one wants to stop people riding horses if they want to; but equally no one pretends they are serious about travelling, either, and for their own sakes they're not allowed on motorways.

If a writer's chief interest is in telling stories (even remembering that telling stories is telling lies) then the best place to do it is in television, which is technically better equipped and will reach more people than a novel can today: for television has in turn taken over the narrative function from the cinema, and avant-garde film-makers (Godard, Resnais, Antonioni and others) recognise this and no longer tell stories.

The writing of a novel today cannot help but be an act of faith in the form. Of all forms within the medium of the book the novel is the most threatened by other media. And the book as a technological object is itself threatened with obsolescence, for the Japanese now have a miniature television set the size of a telephone handpiece, with cassette programmes on tiny reels of wire: within ten years these will be as common as transistor radios, and the few unique advantages the book still has (portability, privacy, and ease of reference backwards and forwards) will be unique no longer. With other media taking over so much of the area that used to belong to the novel, the serious novelist has been thrown back more and more on to writing about whatever can be found inside himself. This is not necessarily deprivation, for it is what the best novelists have always done, anyway.

I was recently the plaintiff in a libel action, and my counsel felt it necessary to point out to me that the public (of whom a jury would be composed) were automatically hostile to what he called "avant-garde creativity". Fortunately my case was good enough to win without going to court, but it brought home to me yet again how uninformed opinion is always hostile towards the new. This applies to the majority of reviewers, too, of course: their standards are formed by the reading of the literature of the past, and by definition are therefore simply not adequate to deal with anything different. "Experimental" to them is almost always a synonym for "unsuccessful". I object to the word experimental being applied to my own work: certainly I make experiments, but the unsuccessful ones are quietly hidden away and what I choose to publish is in my terms successful—that is, it is the best way I can find of solving particular writing problems. Where I depart from convention it is because the convention has failed, is inadequate for conveying what I have to say. The relevant questions are surely whether the device works or not, whether it achieves what it set out to achieve, and how less good were the alternatives.

—Originally appeared in *Books and Bookmen* (London), September 1970.

\*        \*        \*

The important thing to remember about B. S. Johnson, when considering him as a novelist, is that he is not only also a poet, but he is primarily a poet. Certainly, his third novel *Trawl* can be seen without difficulty as an extended prose-poem. It uses certain poetic techniques: an imaginative balance of form and content, and the counterpointing of present and past emotions and experiences. The hero is a passenger on a trawler fishing in the Barents Sea. "Why do I trawl the delicate mesh of my mind over the snagged and broken floor of my past?" he asks himself, and the actual trawl of the ship on which he sails symbolizes and underlines the trawl he makes of his memories as he lies on his bunk exhausted by seasickness. It is to seek a pattern and meaning in his past, which will make meaningful his life and his future, which is the resolution towards which the novel moves. In so doing Johnson presents the reader with a serious statement of his concern for truth and the human situation.

It is the poet in him which also causes Johnson to approach the novel as an art where technique and form are intimately related to purpose and meaning. In this he is one of our most innovatory novelists, not afraid to experiment and to devise new techniques. This was true from the first where in *Travelling People* the traditional narrative attempts at verisimilitude are discarded for impressionistic techniques of interludes employing narrative, dramatic and stream of consciousness forms where apposite, and even Tristam Shandy-like pages to denote semi-consciousness and death. The same virtuosity of form and use of language is to be found in Johnson's second novel, *Albert Angelo*, the story of an architect forced by economics to be a relief teacher in an educationally deprived area, and how his love for Jenny becomes involved with his vocational failures.

In *The Unfortunates* he abandons the idea of the conventional book altogether. This novel is written in twenty-seven sections which come in a box, so that apart from the first and last sections the remaining twenty-five can be read in any order the reader chooses. A football reporter goes to a Midlands city on a routine assignment. It is a city he once knew well and past memories mingle with present experiences to bring about a crisis. The form is an attempt to escape from the consecutiveness inherent in the narrative form in order to solve the problem of presenting the random workings of the mind. While I am not convinced that the mind is quite as random, if at all, in its workings as Johnson believes, it is some measure of his skill that he carries it off. His latest novel *House Mother Normal*, set in an old people's home, consists of nine interior monologues where the events of a social evening are seen in relation to the memories of each particular narrator. If these techniques appear cinematic, it will be no surprise to learn that B. S. Johnson has made a highly successful film, *You're Human Like the Rest of Them*.

It was Ezra Pound, in one of his quirkier moments, who said that poetry should be at least as well written as prose. One presumes that the opposite would be desirable. Certainly in B. S. Johnson this is so. It is his mastery of a precise and clean cutting prose style that makes him one of the best young writers at work today, and which enables him to carry off his remarkable experiments with such panache.

—John Cotton

**JOHNSON, Josephine (Winslow).**   American.   Born in Kirkwood, Missouri, 20 June 1910. Educated at Washington University, St. Louis. Married Grant G. Cannon in 1942 (deceased); has three children. Taught at the University of Iowa, Iowa City, 1942–45. Recipient: O. Henry Award, 1934, 1935, 1942–45; Pulitzer Prize, 1935; Alumnae Citation, Washington University, 1955; Cincinnati Institute of Fine Arts Award, 1964. D. H. L., Washington University, 1970. Address: 4907 Klatte Road, Cincinnati, Ohio 45244, U.S.A.

PUBLICATIONS

Novels

*Now in November*.   New York, Simon and Schuster, 1934; London, Gollancz, 1935.
*Jordanstown*.   New York, Simon and Schuster, and London, Gollancz, 1937.
*Wildwood*.   New York, Harper, 1946; London, Gollancz, 1947.
*The Dark Traveler*.   New York, Simon and Schuster, 1963.

Short Stories

*Winter Orchard and Other Stories*.   New York, Simon and Schuster, 1935.
*The Sorcerer's Son and Other Stories*.   New York, Simon and Schuster, 1965.

Verse

*Unwilling Gypsy*.   Dallas, Kaleidograph, 1936.
*Year's End*.   New York, Simon and Schuster, 1937.

Other

*Paulina: The Story of an Apple-Butter Jar*.   New York, Simon and Schuster, 1939.
*The Inland Island* (essays).   New York, Simon and Schuster, 1969.

*       *       *

The world of Josephine Johnson's fiction is circumscribed and quiet, but not untroubled and not without echoes of the wider and more troubled outer world. The affairs in her books are affairs of jealousy, rejection, disappointment and frustration, relieved on every page by the beauty of nature and the music of breath and blood. Larger affairs are not so much shut out as reflected and symbolized. "Salamanders and fungus seem more exciting to me than war or politics," she wrote early in her career, "but it is cowardly and impossible to ignore them or try to escape."

She was prodigious enough to receive the Pulitzer Prize for her first novel, *Now in November*, published when she was 24 years old. It came out of a time when the whole of the economy of the United States was in crisis, and when the agricultural economy was still in the throes of an even older crisis. It tells the story of small farmers in Missouri. A pall of doom is made to hang over every turn of every season, culminating in disastrous fire. And the emotional patterns within the family she depicts are far from idyllic. Yet somehow it is more a celebration of rural life than a denunciation. It has more bitterness than anger, more resignation than protest. It is certainly not the masterpiece some eager reviewers proclaimed it. But the significant view it gave of a part of American life was odd at the time and is still almost entirely unique.

*Jordanstown* was an attempt to increase the proportion of anger and protest in her fiction, in step with the movement for the "proletarian novel" of that time. It was by far less successful than her initial effort, and bears the marks of having been nurtured in a publisher's office rather than in an author's heart.

*Wildwood* and *The Dark Traveler* are novels of terror and disturbance in the young, followed by some degree of resolution and hope. Neither has the unity of conception and execution to be found in *Now in November*; indeed, these later books have the exploratory and tentative qualities which are usually found in a novelist's earliest projects. Furthermore, there is a preoccupation with neurosis and phantasm, and an absence of real harshness and deprivation, that deny to these works the steadiness and balance to be found in the earliest book. She shows that only perfect love casteth out fear, but in showing it she somehow makes the flavor of fear stronger than the flavor of love.

Like many American writers who have turned away from fiction to journalism, memoirs and diaries as a means of expression, Josephine Johnson has most recently tried to give her vision through a calendar of rural life. *The Inland Island* is divided into twelve sections for the months of the year, and records not only the naturalist's findings in the field but the philosopher's accompanying thoughts, in a tradition that goes back to Thoreau's *Walden*. The book came at the beginning of the recent American preoccupation with ecology. Here again, her pessimism seems to have outlasted her love of life: ". . . democracy becomes less and less capable to cope as the numbers increase. If we want to save law, we shall have to stop our lawless, fertile sprawl." She has given up, it would seem, any hope that man can order his affairs in such a way as to accommodate more and more human life upon the planet Earth.

—Richard Greenleaf

---

**JOHNSON, Pamela Hansford.** British. Born in London, 29 May 1912. Educated at Clapham County Secondary School, London. Married Gordon Neil Stewart in 1936; C. P. Snow (Lord Snow), *q.v.*, 1950; has three children. Fellow, Center for Advanced Studies, Wesleyan University, Middletown, Connecticut, and Honorary Fellow, Timothy Dwight College, Yale University, New Haven, Connecticut, 1961. Member of the Société Européenne de Culture. Litt.D., Temple University, Philadelphia, 1963; York University, Toronto, 1967. Fellow, Royal Society of Literature, 1951. Address: c/o Macmillan and Company, 4 Little Essex Street, London W.C.2, England.

PUBLICATIONS

Novels

> *This Bed Thy Centre.* London, Chapman and Hall, and New York, Harcourt Brace, 1935.
> *Blessed above Woman.* London, Chapman and Hall, and New York, Harcourt Brace, 1936.
> *Here Today.* London, Chapman and Hall, 1937.
> *World's End.* London, Chapman and Hall, 1937; New York, Carrick and Evans, 1938.

*The Monument*.  London, Chapman and Hall, and New York, Carrick and Evans, 1938.
*Girdle of Venus*.  London, Chapman and Hall, 1939.
*Too Dear for My Possessing*.  London, Collins, and New York, Carrick and Evans, 1940.
*Tidy Death*, with Neil Stewart (as Nap Lombard).  London, Cassell, 1940.
*The Family Pattern*.  London, Collins, 1942.
*Winter Quarters*.  London, Collins, 1943; New York, Macmillan, 1944.
*Murder's a Swine*, with Neil Stewart (as Nap Lombard).  London, Hutchinson, 1943; as *The Grinning Pig*, New York, Simon and Schuster, 1943.
*The Trojan Brothers*.  London, Joseph, 1944; New York, Macmillan, 1945.
*An Avenue of Stone*.  London, Joseph, 1947; New York, Macmillan, 1948.
*A Summer to Decide*.  London, Joseph, 1948.
*The Philistines*.  London, Joseph, 1949.
*Catherine Carter*.  London, Macmillan, and New York, Knopf, 1952.
*An Impossible Marriage*.  London, Macmillan, and New York, Harcourt Brace, 1954.
*The Last Resort*.  London, Macmillan, 1956; as *The Sea and the Wedding*, New York, Harcourt Brace, 1957.
*The Humbler Creation*.  London, Macmillan, 1959; New York, Harcourt Brace, 1960.
*The Unspeakable Skipton*.  London, Macmillan, and New York, Harcourt Brace, 1959.
*An Error of Judgement*.  London, Macmillan, and New York, Harcourt Brace, 1962.
*Night and Silence, Who Is There? An American Comedy*.  London, Macmillan, and New York, Scribner, 1963.
*Cork Street, Next to the Hatter's: A Novel in Bad Taste*.  London, Macmillan, and New York, Scribner, 1965.
*The Survival of the Fittest*.  London, Macmillan, and New York, Scribner, 1968.
*The Honours Board*.  London, Macmillan, 1970.


Plays

*Corinth House* (produced London, 1948).  London, Macmillan, and New York, St. Martin's Press, 1954.
*The Supper Dance*, with C. P. Snow.  London, Evans, 1951.
*Family Party*, with C. P. Snow.  London, Evans, 1951.
*Spare the Rod*, with C. P. Snow.  London, Evans, 1951.
*To Murder Mrs. Mortimer*, with C. P. Snow.  London, Evans, 1951.
*The Pigeon with the Silver Foot*, with C. P. Snow.  London, Evans, 1951.
*Her Best Foot Forward*, with C. P. Snow.  London, Evans, 1951.
*Six Proust Reconstructions*.  London, Macmillan, 1958; as *Proust Recaptured: Six Radio Sketches, Based on the Author's Characters*, Chicago, University of Chicago Press, 1958.
*The Rehearsal*, with Kitty Black, adaptation of a play by Jean Anouilh (produced London, 1961; New York, 1963).  London, Methuen, 1961; New York, Coward McCann, 1962.
*The Public Prosecutor*, with C. P. Snow, adaptation of a play by Georgi Dzhagarov, translated by Marguerite Alexieva (produced London, 1967).  London, Peter Owen, 1969.


Verse

*Symphony for Full Orchestra*.  London, Sunday Referee-Parton Press, 1934.

Other

> *Thomas Wolfe: A Critical Study*.  London, Heinemann, 1947; as *Hungry Gulliver:*
> *An English Critical Appraisal of Thomas Wolfe*, New York, Scribner, 1948.
> *Ivy Compton-Burnett*.  London, Longman, 1953.
> *On Iniquity: Some Personal Reflections Arising out of the Moors Murder Trial*.  London,
> Macmillan, and New York, Scribner, 1967.

Manuscript Collection: University of Texas, Austin.

Critical Study: *Pamela Hansford Johnson* by Isabel Quigley, London, Longman, 1968.

Pamela Hansford Johnson comments:

I am primarily a novelist, though I have written one stage and many radio scripts, and much criticism.

I suppose I might call myself a psychological novelist. I have written two trilogies, *An Avenue of Stone, Too Dear for My Possessing, A Summer to Decide* (no overall title) and the "Dorothy Merlin Comedies", i.e., *The Unspeakable Skipton, Night and Silence, Who Is There?* and *Cork Street, Next to the Hatter's*. My novels vary much in kind and in background.

*      *      *

Pamela Hansford Johnson has been writing novels at a fairly regular rate since 1935; but the real date of her debut as a serious novelist was 1940. The six years before this have a curious literary history. Her first book, a volume of verse called *Symphony for Full Orchestra*, appeared in 1934, when she was twenty-two. Then came the first novel, *This Bed Thy Centre*, a vigorous and promising story about the shabby gentility of some parts of Clapham, the extreme shabbiness of others, and in particular about a local girl who marries a local boy but without at all the expected happy ending. This had a good deal of success, both critical and popular, and seemed, above all, to be full of the vitality that suggested there was much more to be written, a kind of headlong, overflowing talent. But after it came five novels (five in only four years, and fairly long novels at that) which failed to fulfill its promise. All of them were set in the present, two at least gave a vivid impression of contemporary life among people politically involved in it; they are readable, have dated remarkably little, even at this distance, and to the student of Pamela Hansford Johnson's work they are of course interesting. But they marked no advance, said little that the first novel had not said, seemed to be going nowhere in particular. This brought her up to 1940, when, quite suddenly, her gifts seemed to fall into place, her style to take the right direction. *Too Dear for My Possessing* is the first of the "full-grown" novels, the first to speak with a mature voice, to flow confidently, fully and satisfactorily. A standard, though not a tone or a pattern, was set for the novels she was to write over the next thirty years.

She was to write more than fiction: works of criticism, essays and studies of various kinds, a play, and some remarkable radio programmes that have been published in book form. But it is as a novelist that she is chiefly known; as the writer, not of one particular novel, of a single, outstanding best-seller, but of an impressive body of work that must be seen as a whole, though it is anything but monolithic. Each novel goes its own way, seeking a new direction: she hardly ever repeats a method, never sticks to a formula. The novels vary in method, tone, situation, even in style; in social level and atmosphere, even more in social outlook. They have no common pattern, no repetition of effects; each is individual, unpredictable, and the characters, too, their situations and ways of life, are unpredictable and untypical. Her people never behave as fictional characters are expected to, loving the right person at the right moment, for instance, and so tying their lives in satisfactory knots at the end of the story. Almost every novel ends in an open, inconclusive way, with little that is knotted or neat about it, but plenty of possibilities and available futures. They are "social" novels in the sense that they are closely tied to a particular time and place and social milieu, to particular groups of people, ways of life; anyone seeking to know just how life felt in the forties, fifties or sixties should look at them for a view that is both panoramic and detailed. And this external world really counts, pressing on its people and making them responsible to one another. Work, outside interests, friends, background, loyalties, politics, community feelings, all weigh upon the characters, helping to form them and to shape their destinies. Yet, more than this, they are novels of character, in which primary importance is given to individual people rather than to their surroundings; although, as it is one of Pamela Hansford Johnson's main gifts to be able to balance one with the other, to deal with the inner and outer lives simultaneously, one does not divide the two in considering her books, or consider one without the other.

Untypically for a woman, she is able to enter all kinds of social situations as well as all kinds of characters. There is a sense of breadth about her novels, of a vigorous, far-ranging intellect, reflected in the strong, transparent style, informal, functional and unfrilly. She is not confined by the usual limitations of her sex—the trilogy that begins with *Too Dear for My Possessing* and goes on with *An Avenue of Stone* and *A Summer to Decide*, one of her most successful works, has a man for narrator without any sense of strain; and, more generally, she is not confined by what is often, in women writers, a narrowness of feeling as well as of experience, an inability or unwillingness to go outside a subjective, feminine world. She is not, in fact, subjective in the way that most women writers are, even at a high level; does not reveal her own personality, background or opinions; keeps her artistic distance, and uses time and memory as integral parts of the action, so that, in some of the novels at least, one has a sense of double attitudes towards what happens—the attitude of the time, the retrospective judgement.

In 1959, there was an interesting and highly successful turnabout in manner (rather than method); from "straight" novels, the best of which so far were the trilogy, *Catherine Carter*, *An Impossible Marriage* and *The Last Resort*, Pamela Hansford Johnson moved to satire with *The Unspeakable Skipton*, first and best of a group of three comedies (the others were *Night and Silence, Who Is There?* and *Cork Street, Next to the Hatter's*), in which the same characters keep recurring. *The Humbler Creation*, in 1959, went back to the earlier manner, and was her most successful attempt to enter a small community—the (movingly created) world of a London clergyman, vicar of a rundown parish, domestically wretched and confined. *The Survival of the Fittest*, in 1968, was a very long, ambitious novel covering the adult years of a number of interconnected middle-aged characters. *The Honours Board*, in 1970, took another small community, a boys' preparatory school in Sussex. Where and how further novels will go is anyone's guess; this is a novelist who fits no school or formula, whose past cannot be pigeon-holed, whose future cannot be foreseen.

—Isabel Quigley

---

**JONES, Glyn.** Welsh. Born in Merthyr Tydfil, 28 February 1905. Educated at Castle Grammar School, Merthyr Tydfil; St. Paul's College, Cheltenham. Married Phyllis Doreen Jones in 1935. Formerly a schoolmaster in Glamorgan; now retired. Recipient: Welsh Arts Council Prize, for non-fiction, 1968. Address: 158 Manor Way, Whitchurch, Cardiff, Wales.

PUBLICATIONS

Novels

> *The Valley, The City, The Village*.   London, Dent, 1956.
> *The Learning Lark*.   London, Dent, 1960.
> *The Island of Apples*.   London, Dent, and New York, Day, 1965.

Short Stories

> *The Blue Bed*.   London, Cape, and New York, Dutton, 1937.
> *The Water Music*.   London, Routledge, 1944.
> *Selected Short Stories*.   London, Dent, 1971.

Uncollected Short Stories

> "Lias Lewis", in *The Welsh Review* (Cardiff), 1939.
> "The Golden Pony", in *Chance* (London), 1953.
> "Myra Powell", in *Broadcast* (Cardiff), 1965.

Play

> *The Beach at Falesa*, music by Alun Hoddinott.   London, Oxford University Press, 1973.

Verse

> *Poems*.   London, Fortune Press, 1939.
> *The Dream of Jake Hopkins*.   London, Fortune Press, 1954.

Other

> *The Dragon Has Two Tongues* (essays on Anglo-Welsh writers).   London, Dent, 1968.

> Translator, with T. J. Morgan, *The Saga of Llywarch the Old*.   London, Golden Cockerel Press, 1955.

Critical Study: *Glyn Jones* by Leslie Norris, Cardiff, University of Wales Press, 1972.

Glyn Jones comments:

I began my literary life as a poet. In 1934 I first became friendly with Dylan Thomas, who suggested I should write short stories, as he himself was doing then. My first published book was a volume of short stories, *The Blue Bed*. This was written when the great industrial depression was at its most intense in South Wales and the longest story in the book takes this for its subject. South Wales, industrial and agricultural—this is the theme in all the stories in

*The Blue Bed.* Indeed, all my prose, and much of my poetry, is concerned with this region. The novel *The Valley, The City, The Village*, which is partly autobiographical, tries to convey what it was like to grow up in South Wales; *The Learning Lark* deals with learning and teaching in the area; *The Island of Apples* describes childhood and its fantasies in a closely-knit community in the Welsh valleys.

*The Water Music* has stories about both the industrial east of South Wales (Glamorgan) and the agricultural west (Carmarthen, Pembroke, Cardigan). To quote my publisher—I have "carried the medium (i.e., the imaginative short story) to an unexcelled synthesis of realism and fantasy, magic and humour. From the regional contrasts of industrialism and pastoralism, modernity and tradition, he builds up a world of convincing beauty, and expresses himself in a prose style of unusual poetic vitality." I would accept this as a statement of what I have *tried* to do in my short stories. Whether I've done it is of course quite another question.

*       *       *

"While using cheerfully enough the English language, I have never written in it a word about any country other than Wales, or any people other than Welsh people", wrote Glyn Jones in *The Dragon Has Two Tongues*. This deliberate limitation of his material is the only reason I can suggest for any kind of restriction to the general recognition his gifts deserve.

Certainly his stories and novels, although they share a Welsh background, are set in widely separate countries of the mind, pose different problems, and offer to us recognisable human situations. His prose, too, is very much more than the "cheerful use" of the English language. Always exuberant and seemingly spendthrift ("I fancy words", he says in his poem, "Merthyr"), it is also exact, muscular, very energetic. He can range from elegant and mannered writing—and the use of a vocabulary so exotic that it upset some reviewers of his first novel *The Valley, The City, The Village*—to the direct, racy, almost physical style, the true, idiosyncratic speaking voice we find in some of the stories and in the two later novels.

His Wales commonly has two contrasting faces, that of the idyllic land of country happiness opposing the suppurating mining towns where the ugly, comical people are unfailingly kindly. But it also exists as a metaphysical universe, and the young people who are to be found in almost everything Jones writes are given early experience of both Heaven and Hell. To some extent this duality reflects Glyn Jones's own early life; during his impressionable boyhood he lived in the grimy steel and coal town of Merthyr Tydfil, but spent significant periods in Llanstephan, a beautiful Carmarthenshire village.

His identification with the scenes and characters of his imagination is absolutely complete, and it is noticeable that many of this stories and all three of his novels are told in the first person. Many critics, indeed, thought *The Valley, The City, The Village*, largely autobiographical, although this story of a young painter, aware of his vocation but forced by the obstinate love of his grandmother to go to university to train as a preacher, has only tenuous links with Jones's own life. It is the quality of Glyn Jones's visual imagination and the unjudging tolerance that lies behind his observation that make his young artist credible.

For in the end Glyn Jones's love of his people is the illuminating quality of his work. He has created a whole gallery of memorable characters, some of them fully realised, some of whom enter his pages but once. He sees their blemishes, particularly their physical short-comings, as clearly as their virtues, but to him they are loveable because their faults are the faults of human beings. Even in *The Learning Lark*, that picaresque send-up of the state of education in a corrupt mining valley where teachers have to bribe their way to headships, there is no scalding satire. Both bribed and bribers are seen as only too human and the book is full of gargantuan laughter.

The world of childhood and adolescence, that magical period when the real and the imagined are hardly to be distinguished, has been a particularly fertile area of Glyn Jones's concern. *The Water Music*, for example, is a collection of stories about young people: of his three novels only one is set entirely in the world of adults, and even that one has some very realistic schoolboys in it.

*The Island of Apples* is a full-scale exploration of the world of adolescence, seen through the eyes of the boy Dewi. It is a remarkable novel, using a prose which is obviously the boy's voice, yet flexible and powerful enough to describe an enormous range of events and emotions. Its sensitivity, its combination of dreamlike confusion and the clear, unsentimental observation which is the adolescent state of mind, the exitement with which the boy invests the commonplace with the exotic, are perfectly balanced attributes of a work which is as individual and complete as *Le Grand Meaulnes*, that other evocation of vanishing youth.

Perhaps the greatest of Glyn Jones's qualities is that of delight in the created world and the people who inhabit it. If he writes of a small and often shabby corner of that world—the first story in *The Blue Bed* is called "I Was Born in the Ystrad Valley" and it is to Ystrad that he returns for *The Island of Apples*—yet his writing is a celebration, an act of praise. To this end he has shaped his craftsmanship and inspiration, and his achievement is permanent and real.

—Leslie Norris

---

**JONES, Gwyn.** British. Born in Blackwood, Monmouthshire, 24 May 1907. Educated at Tredegar Grammar School; University College, Cardiff, 1924–29, B.A. 1927, M.A. 1929. Married Alice Rees in 1928. Schoolmaster, 1929–35; Lecturer, University College, Cardiff, 1935–40; Professor of English Language and Literature, University College of Wales, Aberystwyth, 1940–65. Since 1965, Professor of English Language and Literature, University College, Cardiff. Editor, *Welsh Review*, Cardiff and Aberystwyth, 1939–48; Director, Penmark Press, Cardiff, 1939–60. President, Viking Society for Northern Research, 1951–52; Chairman, Welsh Arts Council, 1957–67. Knight of the Order of the Falcon, Iceland, 1963. C.B.E. (Commander, Order of the British Empire), 1965. Address: Department of English, University College, Cardiff CF1 1XL, Wales.

PUBLICATIONS

Novels

*Richard Savage.* London, Gollancz, and New York, Viking Press, 1935.
*Times Like These.* London, Gollancz, 1936.
*The Nine Days' Wonder.* London, Gollancz, 1937.
*A Garland of Bays.* London, Gollancz, and New York, Macmillan, 1938.
*The Green Island.* London, Golden Cockerel Press, 1946.
*The Flowers Beneath the Scythe.* London and New York, Dent, 1952.
*The Walk Home.* London, Dent, and New York, Norton, 1963.

Short Stories

*The Buttercup Field.* Cardiff, Penmark Press, 1945.
*The Still Waters and Other Stories.* London, Davies, 1948.
*Shepherd's Hey and Other Stories.* London, Staples Press, 1953.

Other

*A Prospect of Wales.* London, Penguin, 1948.
*Welsh Legends and Folk Tales: Retold.* London and New York, Oxford University Press, 1955.
*Scandinavian Legends and Folk Tales: Retold.* London and New York, Oxford University Press, 1956.
*The Norse Atlantic Saga: Being the Norse Voyages of Discovery and Settlement to Iceland, Greenland, America.* London and New York, Oxford University Press, 1964.
*A History of the Vikings.* London and New York, Oxford University Press, 1968.

Editor, with E. M. Silvanus, *Narrative Poems for Schools.* London, Rivingtons, 3 vols., 1935.
Editor, *Welsh Short Stories.* London, Penguin, 1940.
Editor, with Gweno Lewis, *Letters from India*, by Alun Lewis. Cardiff, Penmark Press, 1946.
Editor, *Salmacis and Hermaphroditus.* London, Golden Cockerel Press, 1951.
Editor, *Circe and Ulysses: The Inner Temple Masque*, by William Browne. London, Golden Cockerel Press, 1954.
Editor, *Welsh Short Stories.* London, Oxford University Press, 1956.
Editor, *Songs and Poems of John Dryden.* London, Golden Cockerel Press, 1957.
Editor, *The Metamorphosis of Publius Ovidius Naso.* London, Golden Cockerel Press, 1958.
Editor, *The Songs and Sonnets of Shakespeare.* London, Golden Cockerel Press, 1960.
Editor, with Islwyn Ffowc Elis, *Twenty-Five Welsh Short Stories.* London, Oxford University Press, 1971.

Translator, *Four Icelandic Sagas.* London, Allen and Unwin, and Princeton, New Jersey, Princeton University Press, 1935.
Translator, *The Vatnsdalers' Saga.* London, Oxford University Press, and Princeton, New Jersey, Princeton University Press, 1944.
Translator, with Thomas Jones, *The Mabinogion.* London, Golden Cockerel Press, 1948; New York, Dutton, 1950.
Translator, *Sir Gawain and the Green Knight.* London, Golden Cockerel Press, 1952.
Translator, *Egil's Saga.* Syracuse, New York, Syracuse University Press, 1960.
Translator, *Eirik the Red and Other Icelandic Sagas.* London, Oxford University Press, 1961.

Bibliography: in *A Bibliography of Anglo-Welsh Literature, 1900–1965* by Brynmor Jones, Swansea, Library Association, 1970.

\*       \*       \*

Gwyn Jones did not begin as an "Anglo-Welsh" writer—that is, as a Welshman writing in English about Wales; his first book was a weighty historical novel, *Richard Savage*, in which he traced the decline of the eighteenth-century poet against a richly-described background peopled with a large number of real and imaginary characters. The same ability to conjure up the very smell of a bygone age is apparent in his *Garland of Bays*, an even longer, picaresque, novel in which the story of Robert Greene is used to link striking pictures of Elizabethan life—in country and city, in university and prison, at home and abroad. In between these considerable undertakings he produced a Manchester novel—*The Nine Days' Wonder*—in which there is an attempt to depict part-time criminals living otherwise ordinary lives, and his first book with a Welsh background—*Times Like These*, a novel of the General Strike of 1926 as it affected life in a South Wales mining valley.

All Gwyn Jones's fiction after 1938 is set in Wales, but he seems to have largely avoided the themes most immediately associated with Anglo-Welsh writers from South Wales. It is true that a part of *The Flowers Beneath the Scythe* recalls pit disasters, unemployment, and poverty in the Welsh valleys between the wars, but the filter is the middle-class guilt-feelings of the hero, and the novel is equally concerned with the horrors of trench warfare, the rise of the dictators, the debate about pacifism, the challenge of the Second World War—in short, it looks retrospectively at some of the major pre-occupations of the period covered. *The Walk Home*, too, reaches out to more general themes; here Gwyn Jones returns to the historical novel, though this time the place is nineteenth-century Wales and the hero the victim not of his own folly and weakness but of Evil incarnate in experienced, ruthless men.

Of the three volumes of short stories *The Buttercup Field* is the most conventionally "Anglo-Welsh" and it sounds notes of comedy and whimsy heard more rarely in the two later collections. The dominant features of the more impressive stories in this and the later volumes are strong story-lines, dramatic—even melodramatic—situations, and that acceptance of the importance and dignity of ordinary people which so often informs serious regional fiction. The characters and settings are Welsh, certainly, but the Welshness is taken for granted as the elemental situations take hold of the author's imagination.

Orthodox in structure, Gwyn Jones's fiction has been notable for the energy of its narrative style, the vividness of its descriptive passages, and the boldness of its characterisation; it has been most successful when the material has been sufficiently distanced in the exercise of an outstanding talent for research, whether historical or cultural. Many readers will find it interesting to note the tensions between the writer's fascination with crime and violence and his tacit acceptance of the most humane standards of his time, between the shrewdness of his even-toned reflections on human nature and a strain of romanticism not always held in check, between occasional self-indulgence and a strong, versatile prose style rooted in detailed observation and firm self-discipline.

—Roy Thomas

---

**JONES, James.** American. Born in Robinson, Illinois, 6 November 1921. Educated at the University of Hawaii, Honolulu, 1942; New York University, 1945. Served in the United States Army, 1939–44: Bronze Star and Purple Heart. Married Gloria Mosolino in 1957; has two children. Recipient: National Book Award, 1952. Address: 10 Quai d'Orléans, Ile St. Louis, Paris 4e, France.

PUBLICATIONS

Novels

    *From Here to Eternity.*   New York, Scribner, 1951; London, Collins, 1952.
    *Some Came Running.*   New York, Scribner, 1957; London, Collins, 1959.
    *The Pistol.*   New York, Scribner, and London, Collins, 1962.
    *The Thin Red Line.*   New York, Scribner, 1962; London, Collins, 1963.
    *Go to the Widow-Maker.*   New York, Delacorte Press, and London, Collins, 1967.
    *The Merry Month of May.*   New York, Delacorte Press, and London, Collins, 1971.

Short Stories

*The Ice-Cream Headache and Other Stories.*   New York, Delacorte Press, 1968.

Critical Studies: essay by Jonathan Aaron, in *Harper's* (New York), February 1971; review of *The Merry Month of May* by Daniel Stern, in *Village Voice* (New York), 25 March 1971.

                         *       *       *

There have been two basic opinions about James Jones' fiction. One holds that no one else writes as candidly about war, military life, and manhood. The other condemns him for writing too long and too crudely. The truth that may lie in the first judgment has obviously sustained him through twenty years in which five novels—some longer, some more artfully designed, some venturing further in ideas and experience—have failed to repeat his first achievement in *From Here to Eternity*.

James Jones was victimized by the sucess of his first novel, the long, powerful, overly in-clusive story of American soldiers' lives in the year before Pearl Harbor. He was termed the "great natural talent" among contemporaries whose talents were presumably more refined. He was compared to Dreiser and Thomas Wolfe. Worse, he was made a celebrity and given the publicity still witheld from such writers as Truman Capote and Norman Mailer. He was peculiarly vulnerable to adverse criticism as six years passed before the appearance of his second novel.

Unfortunately, *Some Came Running* was almost twice as long as *From Here to Eternity*. If reviewers bothered to note anything more about the book, they observed that the characters were as profane and frustrated as the soldiers in *From Here to Eternity* (one man would write about the "Yahoo morality" in Jones' two books), that they struggled against no antagonist as recognizable as the military system, and that the Middle West in which they wallowed was not as colorful or convenient a geographic focus as the island Oahu. Very few people ac-knowledged that Jones was trying to write a more difficult book or that he had become a more complicated person in six more years of learning how to write.

Jones' essential subject is manhood. He is not abstract about it. His characters do not represent any generalized concept of man in an order of creation. He poses no political or social theory; he knows no organization larger than the United States Army as it was on peacetime duty in 1941. Therefore, he wrote easily and convincingly about Private Robert E. Lee Prewitt and Sergeant Milton Warden. They were the "gentleman rankers" of the verse from which the novel takes its title: enlisted *men*. Their manhood could be surely defined in every love affair and brawl, in any incident that threatened the will through which they had accepted their condition as privates and sergeants. Civilian life was, by comparison, a swamp. Jones felt that he was "free of the damned books of romance" when he turned to write *Some Came Running*, but he did not realize, in quoting *Don Quixote*, that he had cast himself into as oppressive a reality as the one Quixote had withstood with his illusions. Loose on a continent of towns melting into shopping centers and over a world of superhighways and jet flights, his men risk becoming slobs. (Interviewers actually ask Jones if Dave Hirsch of *Some Came Running* or Rod Grant of *Go to the Widow-Maker* are slobs, and Jones answers firmly that they are not.) In *From Here to Eternity*, Prewitt supposes that he will gain revenge for the death of a friend if he should kill a stockade guard. He does, but at the moment that his victim knows that he has been killed he stares at his assailant and fails to recognize him. Prewitt, knowing that there has been no revenge, is left with a precise understanding of the limits of manhood in this circumstance. By contrast, Rod Grant, the main character of *Go to the Widow-Maker*, is a famous playwright who must take up such pastimes as deep-sea diving to find the "reality" of his manhood. After spearing a ray at sixty feet down, the climax of intricate mastery of mask, tank and fins, Grant wonders why he has such a "deflated feeling," why, instead of discovering some "greater reality," his quest for manhood has brought only a wild masturbatory fantasy.

In three other novels—*The Pistol, The Thin Red Line*, and *The Merry Month of May*—Jones set aside his compulsion to write down everything that he knew or questioned. *The Pistol* is little more than the effort to write a symbolic short novel. *The Thin Red Line* is an ironic, disciplined war novel, plainly an attempt to show exactly what infantry combat was like in the Pacific. *The Merry Month of May* is a story of the student uprisings in Paris complicated by the carefully measured stories of outsiders. They are well done, but *From Here to Eternity* and his failures are more interesting.

—David Sanders

---

**JONES, (Everett) LeRoi.** Pseudonym: **Imamu Amiri Baraka.** American. Born in Newark, New Jersey, 7 October 1934. Educated at Howard University, Washington, D.C., B.A. 1954. Served in the United States Air Force, 1954–57. Married Hettie Cohen in 1958 (divorced, 1965); Sylvia Robinson, 1966; has two children. Taught at the New School for Social Research, New York, 1963; State University of New York at Buffalo, Summer 1964; Columbia University, New York, 1964, 1966–67. Founder, *Yugen* magazine, and Totem Press, New York, 1958. Editor, with Diane di Prima, *Floating Bear*, New York, 1961–63. Founder and Director, Black Arts Repertory Theatre, Harlem, New York, 1964–66. Currently, Director of Spirit House, a black community theatre in Newark. Recipient: Whitney Fellowship, 1962; Obie Award, for drama, 1964; Guggenheim Fellowship, 1965; International Art Festival Prize, for drama, Dakar, Senegal, 1966; National Endowment for the Arts grant, 1966. Address: Spirit House, 33 Stirling Street, Newark, New Jersey 07102, U.S.A.

PUBLICATIONS

Novel

> *The System of Dante's Hell.*   New York, Grove Press, 1965; London, MacGibbon and Kee, 1966.

Short Stories

> *Tales.*   New York, Grove Press, 1967; London, MacGibbon and Kee, 1969.

Plays

> *A Good Girl Is Hard to Find* (produced Montclair, New Jersey, 1958).
> *The Eighth Ditch* (produced New York, 1962).   Included in *The System of Dante's Hell*, 1965.
> *Dutchman* (produced New York, 1964; London, 1967).   Included in *Dutchman and The Slave*, 1964.
> *The Slave* (produced New York, 1964).   Included in *Dutchman and The Slave*, 1964.
> *Dutchman and The Slave.*   New York, Morrow, 1964; London, Faber, 1965.

*The Baptism* (produced New York, 1964).   Included in *The Baptism and The Toilet*, 1967.

*The Toilet* (produced New York, 1964).   Included in *The Baptism and The Toilet*, 1967.

*Jello* (produced New York, 1965).

*Experimental Death Unit # 1* (produced New York, 1965).   Included in *Four Black Revolutionary Plays*, 1969.

*A Black Mass* (produced New York, 1966).   Included in *Four Black Revolutionary Plays*, 1969.

*The Baptism and The Toilet*.   New York, Grove Press, 1967.

*Arm Yourself or Harm Yourself* (produced Newark, New Jersey, 1967).

*Slave Ship* (produced Newark, New Jersey, 1967; New York, 1969).   Published in *Negro Digest* (Chicago), 1967.

*Home on the Range* (produced Newark, New Jersey, and New York, 1968).   Published in *Drama Review* (New York), Summer 1968.

*Police*, in *Drama Review* (New York), Summer 1968.

*Great Goodness of Life (A Coon Show)* (produced New York, 1969).   Included in *Four Black Revolutionary Plays*, 1969.

*Four Black Revolutionary Plays* (includes *Experimental Death Unit # 1*, *A Black Mass*, *Great Goodness of Life (A Coon Show)*, and *Madheart*).   Indianapolis, Bobbs Merrill, 1969; London, Calder and Boyars, 1971.

Screenplay: *Dutchman*, 1967.

Verse

*Preface to a Twenty Volume Suicide Note*.   New York, Totem Press, 1962.

*The Dead Lecturer*.   New York, Grove Press, 1965.

*Black Art*.   Newark, New Jersey, Jihad Publications, 1966.

*Black Magic: Poetry, 1961–1967*.   Indianapolis, Bobbs Merrill, and London, Mac-Gibbon and Kee, 1969.

Other

*Blues People: Negro Music in America*.   New York, Morrow, 1963; London, Mac-Gibbon and Kee, 1965.

*Home: Social Essays*.   New York, Morrow, 1966; London, MacGibbon and Kee, 1968.

*Raise Race Rays Raze: Essays since 1965* (as Imamu Amiri Baraka).   New York, Random House, 1971.

Editor, *Four Young Lady Poets*.   New York, Corinth, 1962.

Editor, *The Moderns: An Anthology of New Writing in America*.   New York, Corinth, 1963; London, MacGibbon and Kee, 1965.

Editor, with Larry Neal, *Black Fire: An Anthology of Afro-American Writing*.   New York, Morrow, 1968.

\*          \*          \*

LeRoi Jones (Imamu Amiri Baraka), in fictionally expressing his leadership in the 1960's as wayward literary artist in Greenwich Village, as inspirer of authentic Black theatrical work in Harlem and New Jersey, and as promoter of Black cultural nationalism and political activism from his base in "New Ark," published a novel and a collection of short stories.

In his semiautobiographical novel, *The System of Dante's Hell*, Jones is much less concerned with the elaborately symbolic structure of Dante's poem (to which he refers six or seven times) than with its literal subject, "the state of souls after death." But death-in-life is Jones's subject. Like Dante, he explores the soul moving through states of perception; but he envisions no Beatrice, no Empyrean, no final, unified illumination making the Newark ghetto anything more than "Hell in the head," where God "is simply a white man" and where most Black people die "in a bathroom of old age and segregation." Jones's plan, which his final chapter calls movement "from sound and image ('association complexes') into fast narrative," takes form initially as the young narrator's fragmented, introspective memories and revaluations. Sometimes cryptic or almost perversely obscure, they are usually patterned around what he laments as "the breakup of my sensibility," as "indelicate furtive lust" that left him either victim or debaser, and as the peculiar doom of the artist ("I kill everything. . . . I am left only with my small words"). After a series of impregnated girlfriends, "cold sin in the cities" with homosexuals, and an alienating education during which "Eliot, Pound, Cummings, Apollinaire were living across from Kresges," the narrator remains emotionally the boy who would sit silently in his dark closet wearing green glasses, others' beauty and purity reduced to "sad tinny lies" except for his name that "a black catholic girl had written . . . on a trash can. I love you I love you I love you."

"The Eighth Ditch" (a one-act drama of unrestrained homosexuality) and three short stories resuming the experiences of the narrator—all four previously published—make up the second half of the novel. "The Christians," hinting at satire against technology, culminates in a gang fight at a basement party. The anti-middle class sentiment in "The Rape" gives way to surrealistic excess and almost manic tensions during a wild car ride taken by six young men and a syphilitic whore. The best story, "The Heretics," about two light-skinned Air Force men dissipating in Shrevesport, Louisiana, fixes the theme of sexual perversion more intimately in the narrator Roi's guilt complex. In fact, the essential cultural and sexual impasse haunting the protagonist of the novel despite his intellectual and athletic prowess is expressed thus:

> Can you read? Who is T. S. Eliot? So what? A cross. You've got to like girls. Weirdo. Break, Roi, break. Now come back, do it again. Get down, hard. Come up. Keep your legs high, crouch hard when you get the ball. . . . Talk to me. Goddamnit. Say something. You never talk, just sit there, impossible to love. . . . Move. Frightened bastard.

Noteworthy in "The Heretics," besides the narrator's pitiful lovemaking with Peaches, are Jones's new departures in racial themes. For example, a long strip of segregating, white tape sticking to the floor, bar, and counter in the Cotton Club separates interracial "old friends, touching each other, and screaming with laughter." Black people's sensuous dancing, "a rite no one knew, or had use for outside their secret lives," is explained in terms of both "separate flesh" and closed history. And near the end, Roi finds brief but satisfying racial identification and acceptance among Black people as "Peaches' man." His new, real world of "soft black harmonies and color" is given historical dimension by Jones's advice in the final chapter: that Black people "bring back on ourselves, the absolute pain our people must have felt when they came onto this shore," to recover both selfhood and history.

Filled with private references (the chapter "Thieves" entirely so), thematically intense obscenities, and terse prose-poetry nerved with original metaphor, the novel is Jones's revolt against a ghetto-minded society that, in toughly preserving its own hell, kept him unaware "of what death and lust [he] fondled and thot to make beautiful."

*Tales*, including some autobiographical matter in each selection, consists of seven short stories and nine reflective, partly narrative pieces. Most of the latter are variously allegorical ("The Largest Ocean in the World"), anecdotal ("Uncle Tom's Cabin: Alternative Ending"), personal (the tender "New Spirit"), and prophetic of the new Black Consciousness (five near the end of the book, starting with revolutionary idealism in "New-Sense" and ending with "Answers in Progress," in which victorious Black revolutionaries see spaceships land among them, disgorging "them thin cats hopping around us," the blue invaders observing the rounding up of "blanks"—white people—and "gettin cooled out on carrots," their own super-drug.

Of the bona fide short stories, four are important in themselves or as documentation of Jones's evolving ideas. In "The Alternative," an eccentric fumbler for knowledge sees his university buddies as professionals-to-be who will betray the "flame in the valley" of their Black heritage and, instead, "erect a new world, of lies and stocking caps." In "The Death of Horatio Alger," the skinny narrator suffers a double loss: his call for help, shouted to his best friend in front of jeering companions, somehow emerges as an insulting scream of hatred; and by his shameful failure in the resulting fist fight he incurs the lasting scorn of his parents. "Heroes Are Gang Leaders," in showing the author-narrator reluctant to speak up for his hospital ward-mate being brutalized in police action usable in his own fiction, exemplifies "the airless social compromise that keeps us alive past any use to ourselves." The superior "The Screamers," vividly sensory and tense with the exaltations of intimate dancing and "honking" saxophones, is a steadily impassioned expression of unique Black experience. The saxophonists and the Black audience that follows them dancing into the street to block Newark traffic are perfectly described. The former are "ethnic historians, actors, priests of the unconscious" who give elegant form to their race's "hatred and frustration, secrecy and despair." Of the latter, Jones says tellingly: "We screamed and screamed at the clear image of ourselves as we should always be. Ecstatic, completed, involved in a secret communal expression."

In his best fiction, LeRoi Jones/Imamu Amiri Baraka has been both saxophonist and dancer, blowing "enraged sociologies," his racial memory "ground . . . past passion or moved so fast it blurred intelligence."

—James A. Emanuel

---

**JONES, Madison (Percy, Jr.).** American. Born in Nashville, Tennessee, 21 March 1925. Educated at Vanderbilt University, Nashville, A. B. 1949; University of Florida, Gainesville, A.M. 1951. Served in the United States Army in the Corps of Military Police, Korea, 1945–46. Married Shailah McEvilley in 1951; has five children. Farmer in Cheatham County, Tennessee, in the 1940's; Instructor in English, Miami University, Oxford, Ohio, 1953–54, and University of Tennessee, Knoxville, 1955–56. Since 1956, Member of the Faculty, Auburn University, Alabama: Writer-in-Residence since 1967; Professor of English since 1968. Recipient: *Sewanee Review* Fellowship, 1954; Rockefeller Fellowship, 1968; Alabama Library Association Award, 1968. Address: 800 Kuderna Acres, Auburn, Alabama 36830, U.S.A.

PUBLICATIONS

Novels

*The Innocent.* New York, Harcourt Brace, and London, Secker and Warburg, 1957.
*Forest of the Night.* New York, Harcourt Brace, 1960; London, Eyre and Spottiswoode, 1961.
*A Buried Land.* New York, Viking Press, and London, Bodley Head, 1963.

*An Exile*.   New York, Viking Press, 1967; London, Deutsch, 1970.
*A Cry of Absence*.   New York, Crown, 1971; London, Deutsch, 1972.

Uncollected Short Stories

"The Homecoming", in *Perspective* (St. Louis), 1952.
"Dog Days", in *Perspective* (St. Louis), 1952.
"The Fugitive", in *Sewanee Review* (Tennessee), 1953.
"The Cave", in *Perspective* (St. Louis), 1953.
"Home Is Where the Heart Is", in *Arlington Quarterly* (Texas), Spring 1968.
"A Modern Case", in *Delta Review* (Memphis, Tennessee), July-August 1969.

Critical Studies: reviews, by Ovid Pierce, in *New York Times Book Review*, 4 July 1971; by Joseph Cantinella, in *Saturday Review* (New York), 9 July 1971; by Reed Whittemore, in *New Republic* (Washington, D.C.), July 1971.

Madison Jones comments:

Generally, on a more obvious level, my fiction is concerned with the drama of collision between past and present, with emphasis upon the destructive elements involved. More deeply, it deals with the failure, or refusal, of individuals to recognize and submit themselves to inevitable limits of the human condition.

\*       \*       \*

There is a homogeneity of theme which links together into a coherent body the published fiction of Madison Jones. The setting of these books is invariably Jones' native South. But whether their time be late eighteenth century settlement days or the region's more recent past, his unvarying song is abstraction, ideology, and its consequences. *The Innocent*, his first novel, set in rural Tennessee immediately after the coming of modernity, treats of the attempts by a young Southerner, Duncan Welsh, to repent of earlier impiety and re-establish himself upon inherited lands in inherited ways. The enterprise is a failure because of Duncan's deracinated preconception of it. Welsh "sets up a grave in his house." Soon he and his hopes are buried in another.

Jones' newest work, *A Cry of Absence*, again focuses on a fatal archaist, a middle-aged gentlewoman of the 1960's who is anything but innocent. Hester Glenn finds an excuse for her failures as wife, mother and person in a self-protective devotion to the tradition of her family. But when her example proves, in part, responsible for her son's sadistic murder of a Negro agitator, Hester is driven to know herself and, after confession, to pay for her sins with suicide.

A kind of Puritanism distorts Mrs. Glenn. In *The Innocent* the error is a perversion of the Agrarianism of Jones' mentors (Lytle, Davidson). But in his other novels the informing abstractions are not so identifiably Southern. Jones' best, *A Buried Land*, is set in the valley of the Tennessee River during the season of its transformation. Percy Youngblood, the heir of a stern hill farmer (and a central character who could be any young person of our century), embraces all of the nostrums we associate with the futurist dispensation. He attempts to bury the old world (represented by a girl who dies aborting his child) under the waters of the TVA; but its truths (and their symbol) rise to haunt him back into abandoned modes of thought and feeling. In *An Exile* Hank Tawes, a rural sheriff, is unmanned by a belated explosion of passion for a bootlegger's daughter. His error has no date or nationality, but almost acquires the force of ideology once Tawes recognizes that, because he followed an impulse to recover his youth, his "occupation's gone." *Forest of the Night* tests out an assumption almost as generic, the notion that man is inherently good. An interval in the Tennessee "outback" is sufficient to the disabusement of Jonathan Cannon. There is no more telling exposé of the New Eden mythology.

In all of Jones' fiction there operates an allusive envelope embodied in a concrete action and supported by an evocative texture. That action is as spare as it is archetypal; and in every case its objective is to render consciousness. Jones is among the most gifted of contemporary American novelists, a craftsman of tragedy in the great tradition of his art.

—M. E. Bradford

---

**JONES, Mervyn.** British. Born in London, 27 February 1922. Educated at Abbotsholme School; New York University, 1939–41. Served in the British Army, 1942–47. Married Jeanne Urquhart in 1948; has three children. Assistant Editor, 1955–60, and Dramatic Critic, 1958–66, *Tribune*, London; Assistant Editor, *New Statesman*, London, 1966–68. Address: 10 Waterside Place, Princess Road, London N.W.1, England.

PUBLICATIONS

Novels

    *No Time to Be Young*.  London, Cape, 1952.
    *The New Town*.  London, Cape, 1953.
    *The Last Barricade*.  London, Cape, 1953.
    *Helen Blake*.  London, Cape, 1955.
    *On the Last Day*.  London, Cape, 1958.
    *A Set of Wives*.  London, Cape, 1965.
    *John and Mary*.  London, Cape, 1966; New York, Atheneum, 1967.
    *A Survivor*.  London, Cape, and New York, Atheneum, 1968.
    *Joseph*.  London, Cape, and New York, Atheneum, 1970.
    *Mr. Armitage Isn't Back Yet*.  London, Cape, 1971.

Uncollected Short Stories

    "The Foot", in *English Story* (London), 1948.
    "The Bee-Keeper", in *English Story* (London), 1950.

Other

    *Guilty Men, 1957: Suez and Cyprus*, with Michael Foot.  London, Gollancz, and New York, Rinehart, 1957.
    *Potbank* (documentary).  London, Secker and Warburg, 1961.

*Big Two* (documentary).   London, Cape, 1962; as *The Antagonists*, New York, Potter, 1962.

*Two Ears of Corn: Oxfam in Action*.   London, Hodder and Stoughton, 1965; as *In Famine's Shadow: A Private War on Hunger*, Boston, Beacon Press, 1965.


Mervyn Jones comments:

How difficult it is to live: that's the subject of all serious novels, I suppose, and certainly of mine. If writing has a purpose, it is that some readers may find life a little easier or at least may understand the difficulties. My characters (Acarin in *The Last Barricade*; Helen in *Helen Blake*; Miranda in *A Set of Wives*; John, and also Mary; Martin in *A Survivor*) are men and women who are struggling to explain themselves and to be respected. They don't altogether deserve it, for even the good are sometimes absurd and sometimes dishonest; but to know this of oneself is part of the difficulty. Another way of putting it: we want to be together but ultimately each of us is alone. I've tried to work this out most fully in *A Survivor*, which is the book by which I'd prefer to be judged.

I am much concerned with the nobility and the irony of idealism. I believe in both the nobility and the irony (*The Last Barricade*, *On the Last Day*). The point at which idealism turns into the demand for power is where irony becomes tragedy (*Joseph*). I have political convictions but I've never been able to be a political devotee. There is weakness as well as strength in this; the world needs devotees (though not as novelists) yet also needs to beware of them.

Stylistically I've done nothing very new. I think the narrative form of the classical novel still has resources. I've used alternating narration in *John and Mary* and am surprised that more writers don't.

"Tell me your truth and I'll tell you mine" is a good saying. A novelist is a voice for the truth seen and felt by each of his characters, and, through them, for his own. A little journalism and documentary writing teaches one not to have illusions about absolute truth.


\*     \*     \*


Some writers leap to fame and achievement with their first novel, and then face the problem of avoiding an anti-climax with their next. Others climb the ladder slowly but steadily: Mervyn Jones clearly belongs to the latter category. In his early books he showed himself a first-class reporter with a flair for discovering topical subjects and the knack of familiarising himself with an astonishingly wide range of jobs, classes and walks of life. Since then he has developed his gifts as a creator of character while remaining a keen observer of social experiment and a connoisseur of sharply differing life-styles. The breadth of his interests has opened up to him an exceptionally large range of themes, and the diversity of his subject matter is matched by the versatility of his technique. This has enabled him to write books as different as *The New Town* (documentary-style naturalism), *On the Last Day* (politically flavoured prophecy), *Joseph* (a historical novel on Stalin), *John and Mary* (a novel *à deux*) and many more.

His first substantial novel was *The New Town*, a study of a community born in the idealistic atmosphere of the late 1940's. The strength of the book lies in the accuracy of the reporting and in the author's grasp of the forces which are in conflict from the start—the idealism of the general manager, the competing interests of new arrivals and established residents, the rival demands of industry and Whitehall. There followed two novels dominated by political themes, *The Last Barricade*, a sympathetic study of the exiled president of a Central European state, and *On the Last Day*, a disturbingly plausible projection of a third world war, with an émigré British government quartered on reluctant French Canadian hosts in Quebec.

His next novel, *A Set of Wives*, signalled a great advance in terms of characterisation: there is a tragi-comic chronicle of three sisters, all members of the liberal establishment, married respectively to a barrister, a television commentator and a Labour MP. The plot is set during the run-up to the General Election of 1964, and if the tragic denouement seems a shade contrived, the portraits of the three sisters are brilliantly sketched, and the balance between public and private life perfectly held.

*John and Mary* is an entertaining, slightly artificial *tour de force*, told by the two protagonists in alternating narratives. The pair meet at a party, are strongly attracted, and wake up in John's room the next morning, sexual intimates but social and emotional strangers. The rest of the Sunday is spent in a mating ritual of approach and retreat, as each in turn seeks or evades commitment, but by the end of the day they are planning to spend the rest of their lives together.

*Joseph* is a fictional reconstruction of the life of Stalin, an ambitious conception backed by plenty of solid research. Although Mervyn Jones writes from a strongly left wing standpoint, this is by no means a work of idolatry. But it is written in a dead-pan style, the uniformity of which contrasts so sharply with the exuberance and paradox of his normal manner as to leave the impression that his critical intelligence has been lulled, stunned, or suspended. *A Survivor* is the most accomplished but at the same time the most enigmatic of his books to date: it is also arguably the one which has extended him most fully. The "survivor" is a wartime airman who becomes a successful novelist. He survives his closest friend and wartime comrade and marries the girl they have both loved, knowing that his feelings are never fully returned. He survives her, and survives a succession of affairs, in the sense that none of them can replace the love he has lost, unrequited though it was. The pattern of these relationships resembles a perspective of mutually reflecting mirrors: the novelist reveals much about his mistresses and they about him, but always there is a side which is turned away. He remains a man hard to know and a writer who is unable to communicate all that he wishes to tell. *Mr Armitage Isn't Back Yet* is an entertaining and again a highly topical fable. A middle-aged business man, a perfect specimen of the self-made apostle of private enterprise, is amicably kidnapped by a quartet of drop-outs, who spirit him off to a deserted Scottish island and explain that he is the subject of a study-project: they want to discover what makes him tick. Amid the mutual confessions and couplings that follow, Mr Armitage finds his ideals of self-reliance dissolving, and although his hosts do not arrive at any alternative formula for running society, he returns to civilisation a changed man.

Mervyn Jones' fiction occupies a territory where the work of the novelist shades imperceptibly into that of the publicist. He is keenly aware of the mood and climate of the moment, and if some of his work has the ephemerality of good journalism, he has never ceased to develop and he has always had something new to say.

—Ian Scott-Kilvert

---

**JOSEPH, M(ichael) K(ennedy).** New Zealander. Born in Chingford, Essex, England, 9 July 1914. Educated at Auckland University College, B.A. 1933, M.A. 1934; Merton College, Oxford, B.A. 1938, B. Litt. 1939, M.A. 1945. Served in the British Army in the Royal Artillery, 1940–46. Married Mary Julia Antonovich in 1947; has five children. Lecturer in English, 1945–49, and Senior Lecturer, 1950–59, Auckland University College; Associate Professor of English, 1960–69, and since 1970, Professor of English, University of Auckland. Recipient: Hubert Church Prose Award, 1958; Jessie Mackay Poetry Award, 1959. Address: Department of English, University of Auckland, Private Bag, Auckland, New Zealand.

PUBLICATIONS

Novels

*I'll Soldier No More*.   Auckland, Paul's Book Arcade, and London, Gollancz, 1958.
*A Pound of Saffron*.   Auckland, Paul's Book Arcade, and London, Gollancz, 1962.
*The Hole in the Zero*.   Auckland, Paul's Book Arcade, and London, Gollancz, 1967;
    New York, Dutton, 1968.

Verse

*Imaginary Islands*.   Auckland, privately printed, 1950.
*The Living Countries*.   Auckland, Paul's Book Arcade, 1959.

Other

*Byron the Poet*.   London, Gollancz, 1964.

Editor, *Frankenstein*, by Mary W. Shelley.   London, Oxford University Press, 1969.


M. K. Joseph comments:

I can hardly generalise from only three works, written at longish intervals—one war-novel, one campus-novel, one sf. But I think my main interest in the novel is the old-fashioned one of story-telling and character-creation, and, technically, in finding the right way of presenting each particular novel.

*             *             *

M. K. Joseph is one of the most sophisticated artists in New Zealand fiction. He is keenly aware of the problems of form, which he confronts with a wise urbanity, and his subject-matter is more diverse and his range of intellectual interests wider than those of almost all his contemporaries. While he is seriously concerned with exploring man's nature and his destiny, he also delights in the curious and the unexpected. A gentle irony irradiates the play of ideas in his novels. The general impression they leave is of an exercise of "wit" in its several 18th century senses.

This does not mean that the novels are academic or lacking in sensitivity. On the contrary, it is Joseph's human compassion which removes his fiction from the area of literary exercise. His Catholic sense of an extra dimension to reality and a moral sensibility certainly help to condition his characterisation and, at times, the novels reveal a tension between the hypothetical "freedom" of fictional characters and the way in which ideas manoeuvre them. But Joseph's endeavour to understand his fellow-men makes this tension a creative element in his work.

*I'll Soldier No More*, a war novel without anger or hysteria, treats of the lengthy training period in England, the soul-destroying boredom of "the waiting war" and its effects on, in the main, three members of the same unit. As they move into Germany as part of the army of occupation, they react, in one case tragically, to their environment in terms of their character and values. This semi-documentary novel, which contains a splendid picture of Germany in defeat, explores man's capacity to accept and endure, with mature understanding.

In *A Pound of Saffron*, the scene is a New Zealand university and the plot turns on the machinations of an academic Machiavelli whose attempt to manipulate people's lives in pursuit of his own ambition leads to tragedy. Certain elements of melodrama infect the story, and possibly the novel a shade too insistently illustrates a theme. Yet a wide range of New Zealand social attitudes are skilfully exposed, the common-room atmosphere is finely realised and the limitations of conventional academic positivism shrewdly defined.

Joseph's most surprising and original novel is *The Hole in the Zero*. A science-fiction framework provides the entry into a complex pattern of myth and archetype, in which moral and philosophical concepts are deftly and imaginatively handled. Four people in a deep-space rocket journey beyond the end of the universe and plunge into a series of strange planes of reality and non-reality, during which a struggle develops between philosophical man and sensual man. There are calculated echoes here of a variety of writers, from Milton to C. S. Lewis, yet the book has its own fascinating individuality and the characters do not become mere types. The fusion of fantasy and reality convinces and Joseph's poetic skill raises some passages to a high pitch of sensitivity.

—J. C. Reid

---

**KANTOR, MacKinlay.** American. Born in Webster City, Iowa, 4 February 1904. Educated at Webster City High School. Married Florence Irene Layne in 1926; has two children. Reporter, *Daily News*, Webster City, 1921–24; worked in advertising in Chicago, 1925–26; Reporter, *Republican*, Cedar Rapids, Iowa, 1927; Columnist, *Tribune*, Des Moines, Iowa, 1930–31. Scenario Writer, for Paramount Pictures, M.G.M., Twentieth-Century-Fox, and Samuel Goldwyn. War Correspondent, United States and British air forces, 1943, 1950; Technical Consultant, United States Air Force, 1951–53. Honorary Consultant in American Letters, Library of Congress, 1967. Member of the National Council, Boy Scouts of America. Trustee, 1960–68, and since 1968, Honorary Trustee, Lincoln College, Illinois. Recipient: Pulitzer Prize, 1956; National Association of Independent Schools Award, 1956; Medal of Freedom. D.Litt., Grinnell College, Iowa, 1957; Drake University, Des Moines, Iowa, 1958; Lincoln College, Illinois, 1959; Ripon College, Wisconsin, 1961; LL.D., Iowa Wesleyan College, Mount Pleasant, 1961. Fellow of the Society of American Historians, and of the American Society for Psychical Research. Lives in Sarasota, Florida. Address: c/o Doubleday, 277 Park Avenue, New York, New York 10017, U.S.A.

PUBLICATIONS

Novels

    *Diversey*.   New York, Coward McCann, 1928.
    *El Goes South*.   New York, Coward McCann, 1930.
    *The Jaybird*.   New York, Coward McCann, 1932.
    *Long Remember*.   New York, Coward McCann, and London, Selwyn and Blount, 1934.
    *The Voice of Bugle Ann*.   New York, Coward McCann, and London, Selwyn and Blount, 1935.
    *Arouse and Beware*.   New York, Coward McCann, 1936; London, Gollancz, 1937.

*T*e *Romance of Rosy Ridge*.   New York, Coward McCann, 1937.
*The Noise of Their Wings*.   New York, Coward McCann, 1938; London, Hale, 1939.
*Here Lies Holly Springs*.   New York, Coward McCann, 1938.
*Valedictory*.   New York, Coward McCann, 1939.
*Cuba Libre: A Story*.   New York, Coward McCann, 1940.
*Gentle Annie: A Western Novel*.   New York, Coward McCann, 1942; London, Hale, 1951.
*Happy Land*.   New York, Coward McCann, 1943.
*Glory for Me* (in verse).   New York, Coward McCann, 1945.
*Midnight Lace*.   New York, Random House, 1948; London, Falcon Press, 1950.
*Wicked Water: An American Primitive*.   New York, Random House, 1949; London, Falcon Press, 1950.
*The Good Family*.   New York, Coward McCann, 1949.
*One Wild Oat*.   New York, Fawcett, 1950.
*Signal Thirty-Two*.   New York, Random House, 1950.
*Don't Touch Me*.   New York, Random House, 1951; London, W. H. Allen, 1952.
*Warwhoop: Two Short Novels of the Frontier*.   New York, Random House, 1952.
*The Daughter of Bugle Ann*.   New York, Random House, 1953.
*God and My Country*.   Cleveland, World, 1954.
*Andersonville*.   Cleveland, World, 1955; London, W. H. Allen, 1956.
*The Work of St. Francis*.   Cleveland, World, 1958; as *Unseen Witness*, London, W. H. Allen, 1959.
*Spirit Lake*.   Cleveland, World, 1961; London, W. H. Allen, 1962.
*Beauty Beast*.   New York, Putnam, 1968.


Short Stories

*The Boy in the Dark*.   Webster Groves, Missouri, International Mark Twain Society, 1937.
*Author's Choice: 40 Stories*.   New York, Coward McCann, 1944.
*Silent Grow the Guns and Other Tales of the American Civil War*.   New York, New American Library, 1958.
*Again the Bugle*.   New York, American Weekly, 1958.
*It's about Crime*.   New York, New American Library, 1960.
*The Gun-Toter and Other Stories of the Missouri Hills*.   New York, New American Library, 1963.
*Story Teller*.   New York, Doubleday, 1967.


Verse

*Turkey in the Straw: A Book of American Ballads and Primitive Verse*.   New York, Coward McCann, 1935.


Other

*Angleworms on Toast* (juvenile).   New York, Coward McCann, 1942.
*But Look, The Morn: The Story of a Childhood* (reminiscences).   New York, Coward McCann, 1947; London, Falcon Press, 1951.
*Lee and Grant at Appomattox* (juvenile).   New York, Random House, 1950.
*Gettysburg* (juvenile).   New York, Random House, 1952.
*Lobo* (reminiscences).   Cleveland, World, 1957; London, W. H. Allen, 1958.
*If the South Had Won the Civil War*.   New York, Bantam, 1961.

*Mission with LeMay: My Story*, with General Curtis LeMay.   New York, Doubleday, 1965.
*Missouri Bittersweet* (reminiscences).   New York, Doubleday, 1969.
*Hamilton County*.   New York, Macmillan, 1970.

\*       \*       \*

In a professional writing career that spans almost fifty years, MacKinlay Kantor has achieved his greatest critical and popular success with historical novels based on the American past. His fourth novel, *Long Remember*, describes in vivid detail the events of the three day battle of Gettysburg in 1864. This novel even has been credited with initiating the fashion for American historical fiction that dominated popular literature in the 1930's. Almost unanimously, the critics praised Mr. Kantor for applying the minutely documented details of realistic fiction to the historical romance. The Civil War also provided the theme for his most acclaimed novel, *Andersonville*, which won a Pulitzer Prize in 1956. In this mammoth novel about a Confederate prisoner of war camp, Kantor achieves his finest integration of historical background, individual characterizations, and psychological drama. Such a balance was not reached in *Spirit Lake*, a later historical novel, in which the compilation of multitudinous facts overwhelms any character portrayal and impairs the narrative vigor.

In defense of his dependence on historical data, Mr. Kantor says that in *Andersonville* he hoped "to make the Gettysburg battle as contemporaneous, as much a part of the reader's life, as if the wounded were still having their bandages renewed in the hospitals—as if the wheel-ruts of the Whitworth rifles were still creased across the nasturtium beds." Out of such realistic historical fiction, he hopes the reader will learn a lesson from American history.

Second in popularity to his historical fiction are Mr. Kantor's stories and novels that draw on the less remote past of his own boyhood. Born in 1904 in Webster City, a small Iowa town, Kantor frequently uses his memories of that simplified and sturdier way of life to create a nostalgic atmosphere in his writings. In the novelette, *The Voice of Bugle Ann*, he fabricates a folk legend about a Missouri fox-hound so well loved by her master that he commits murder to revenge the dog's death. More directly autobiographical are *God and My Country*, a fictionalization of his youthful experiences in the Boy Scouts and *But Look, The Morn*, a reminiscence of his mother's stamina and courage in raising her small family without a husband. Also included among this collection of nostalgic works is Kantor's most recent publication, *Hamilton County*, which is a collection of photographs and prose that tries to capture the old-fashioned virtues of ten typical American counties.

But Mr. Kantor's career has also encompassed a great variety of writing efforts. In *Turkey in the Straw*, a collection of verses and ballads, he writes in a quasi-primitive style designed to recall the tone as well as the events of the American past. A novel done in verse, *Glory for Me*, formed the basis for an Academy Award winning movie on World War Two veterans, *The Best Years of Our Lives*. Also among his publications are many magazine short stories, children's books, a political biography, and two formula Westerns.

All of Mr. Kantor's writings share a mixture of sentiment and realism. Many readers feel his historical novels are "educational" and, therefore, valuable. His narrative style generally provides rapid and enjoyable reading, but his characters too frequently are only romanticized stereotypes. Like many authors of popular literature, Mr. Kantor provides technically good writing that reassures his readers that traditional American values are still recognized and appreciated.

—Mary McMurray

**KARP, David.** American. Born in New York City, 5 May 1922. Educated at the City College of New York, 1940–42, 1946–48, B.S.Sc. 1948. Served in the United States Army in the South Pacific and Japan, 1943–46. Married Lillian Klass in 1944; has two children. Continuity Director, Radio Station WNYC, New York, 1948–49. Free-lance Writer since 1949. Since 1968, President of Leda Productions Inc., Los Angeles. Member, Executive Board, Writers Guild of America East, 1963–66. Since 1967, Member of the Executive Council, and President of the Television-Radio Branch, 1969–71, Writers Guild of America West, Los Angeles. Member of the Editorial Board of *Television Quarterly*, 1966–71. Recipient: Guggenheim Fellowship, 1956; Ohio State University Award, for drama, 1948, and for television drama, 1958; Mystery Writers of America Award, for television drama, 1959; National Academy of Television Arts and Sciences Award, for television drama, 1965. Address: 1116 Corsica Drive, Pacific Palisades, California 90272; or, c/o Frank Cooper Associates, 9000 Sunset Boulevard, Los Angeles, California 90069, U.S.A.

PUBLICATIONS

Novels

*The Big Feeling.* New York, Lion, 1952.
*The Brotherhood of Velvet.* New York, Lion, 1952.
*Cry, Flesh.* New York, Lion, 1953; as *The Girl on Crown Street*, New York, Banner, 1967.
*Hardman.* New York, Lion, 1953.
*Platoon* (as Adam Singer). New York, Lion, 1953.
*One.* New York, Vanguard Press, 1953; London, Gollancz, 1954.
*The Charka Memorial* (as Wallace Ware). New York, Doubleday, 1954.
*The Day of the Monkey.* New York, Vanguard Press, and London, Gollancz, 1955.
*All Honorable Men.* New York, Knopf, and London, Gollancz, 1956.
*Leave Me Alone.* New York, Knopf, and London, Gollancz, 1957.
*Enter, Sleeping.* New York, Harcourt Brace, 1960; as *The Sleep-Walkers*, London, Gollancz, 1960.
*The Last Believers.* New York, Harcourt Brace, and London, Cape, 1964.

Uncollected Short Stories

"All American", in *Argosy* (New York), October 1950.
"Life of the Party", in *American Magazine* (New York), January 1951.
"Wait for Her Laughter", in *Esquire* (New York), January 1952.
"The Red-Necked Peasant from Dubuque", in *Esquire* (New York), October 1952.
"The Lady with the French Ideas", in *Park East* (New York), February 1953.
"Blood Money", in *Collier's* (New York), 7 August 1953.
"Death Warrant", in *Saturday Evening Post* (Philadelphia), 6 November 1954.

Plays

*Cafe Univers* (produced New York, 1967).

Screenplays: *Sol Madrid*, 1967; *Che!*, 1968; *Tender Loving Care*, 1972.

Has written many plays for radio (1946–60), and for television (1950–70).

Other

    *Vice-President in Charge of Revolution*, with Murray D. Lincoln (biography). New York, McGraw Hill, 1960.

Manuscript Collection: Boston University Library.

David Karp comments:

    If there is such a thing as a moralist novelist I am probably in that class or genre. I am a didactic writer. My first teacher was Upton Sinclair. I devoured all of his works and learned my liberalism from this impassioned teacher. Poverty was given to me by the world into which I was born. I was poor, I was ambitious, I was filled with outrage against injustice and yet I inherited from my mother, I guess, a pragmatism which I have never forgotten. I am, in many ways, the product of the Depression, Judaism, American liberalism and idealism, and Jewish middle class pragmatism and ambition. What kind of an odd bird does that make me? I know it isn't a common species—because I have been shut out of the literary establishment, the avant-garde (which is another kind of establishment) and out of the "mainstream" (what an awful description) of American letters. I have nothing but contempt for most academic critics and the literary games they play. I do not really write short fiction and will not write criticism and do not share the cheap and easy self-hating liberalism which is so fashionable these days. I am isolated by my politics, my tastes, my pragmatism (I think a writer is entitled to earn every bit as much as a movie star) and my belief that clear thinking and clear writing are two beautiful pure fluids which need no adulteration or coloring. I do my work (such as it is) with all the attention and integrity and passion that I can—whatever the work is. I do not disdain writing for television or motion pictures (or radio)—a writer's first responsibility is to survive and to be self-sufficient. I don't think a writer is entitled to be a mendicant on the grounds that his art prevents him from being self-supporting. Nor do I think he should become a freak to exploit his position. A writer has the right to do his work and if it gains acceptance to be modestly grateful and if it is rejected to be immodestly contemptuous but to go on. I will not compromise to be successful, I will not kiss asses to be accepted and I will not give up being a writer because I am ignored. I have written many things—many of them (too many of them) to maintain myself and my family and to maintain my pride in being self-sufficient. I am active in union affairs of a writer's organization because I believe no writer should be exploited by an employer. But I also believe writers should not exploit one another for professional self-aggrandizement. I have too much pride to elbow my way into the public glare. I leave that game to the publicity-seeking wretches whose names I am sure you know so well. Newspaper clippings rot—good work does not.

*    *    *

    The world of David Karp's fiction is one of fairly predictable ironies, most often involving the biter bit, the spider snared in its own web, the bomber hoist with his own petard. Frank Ames, for example, in *The Big Feeling*, is just insane enough to botch up his own insanity plea; and his escape is ruined by the same traits of character that made his robberies successful. Similarly, James Watterson (in *The Brotherhood of Velvet*) and Professor Burden (in *One*) are driven out of jobs, families, and, ultimately, out of personal identity itself by the same conspiracies they have served so well. The ironies are doubled in *Cry, Flesh*, in which Rose Genovese, mercy killer, is herself killed by her lover, Cheval, whose motives are those of compassion and pity; and in which Cheval himself is saved from the consequences of that killing by the same sort of understanding tainted with moral corruption that brought about his own attempt to save Rose from the consequences of *her* killings.

This love of poetic justice, Mr. Karp's deft touches of conventional psychological insight, and his careful attention to the working out of the details of plot—particularly those pertaining to crime—do not, however, distinguish his work from that of half-a-hundred other more or less competent writers of sensational fiction. The qualities which are particularly Karp's are, first, a deep moral sense of the integrity of the individual, and, second, his ability to touch those hideous fantasies that are common to all of us.

At times the individual whom Karp pits against the group is clearly mad, like Frank Ames; at other times he gives us a Rose Genovese, whose madness is a saintly one. But whether the opposition is the police or the *1984*-like organizations of *One* or *The Brotherhood of Velvet*, the individual must lose, the principle of the individual must be vindicated.

Sometimes Karp's fantasies are those common to much police fiction (that of Richard Stark comes to mind)—the perfect bank robbery, for example. More often they are more nightmarish—discovering that the loved one is a killer, killing the loved one. These nightmares are perhaps most successful when they awaken in the reader the latent paranoia of our century—they are after me.

Karp draws these threads together most successfully in *One* (later reissued as *Escape to Nowhere*), which enjoyed some success in the 50s and was favorably compared to *1984*. Its prose is not, of course, as skilful as that of Orwell, but then, almost nobody's is; nor does Karp work out the details of his future society with the same care. But Lark, his chief inquisitor and ex-heretic, is a walking embodiment of the ironies and contradictions with which Karp loves to deal, and his confrontation with Burden, a victim with whom the reader can identify more readily, perhaps more readily than with Orwell's, is loaded with the ultimate moral implications which preoccupy Karp.

*One*'s nightmare is, I think, more nightmarish than Orwell's, because it is less complicated, less gimmicked, and because, finally, the threat of breaking (as in *1984*) is not as horrid as the threat of having one's identity destroyed. Finally, Karp achieves his most successful irony at the end of *One* in the simultaneous triumph and death of Burden.

—Irving F. Foote

---

**KELLEY, William Melvin.** American. Born in New York City in 1937. Educated at Harvard University, Cambridge, Massachusetts. Married to Karen Gibson; has one child. Writer-in-Residence, State University College, Geneseo, New York, Spring 1965. Recipient: Dana Reed Prize, Harvard University, 1960; Rosenthal Foundation Award, 1963; *Transatlantic Review* Award, 1964. Address: c/o Doubleday, 277 Park Avenue, New York, New York 10017, U.S.A.

PUBLICATIONS

Novels

*A Different Drummer.* New York, Doubleday, 1962; London, Hutchinson, 1963.
*A Drop of Patience.* New York, Doubleday, 1965; London, Hutchinson, 1966.
*dem.* New York, Doubleday, 1967.
*Dunsfords Travels Everywheres.* New York, Doubleday, 1970.

Short Stories

  *Dancers on the Shore.*   New York, Doubleday, 1964; London, Hutchinson, 1965.

*     *     *

William Melvin Kelley's novels to date have dealt with inter-racial conflict, but the emphasis has been on the examination of characters, black and white, and the myths with which they delude themselves. His novels pose no "solutions" to the conflict but the solution of self-understanding, and his depiction of the relationships—loving and competitive—between men and women and blacks and whites combines compassion, objectivity, and humor.

His first novel, *A Different Drummer*, set realistically-rendered characters in a fantasy plot. From multiple points of view he displayed the reactions of the whites of a fictional Southern state to the spontaneous, grass-roots emigration of the state's blacks.

A minor incident in *A Different Drummer* concerns Wallace Bedlow, who is waiting for a bus to take him to New York City, where he plans to live with his brother, Carlyle. Bedlow appears only that one time, but he surfaces again in "Cry for Me," probably the best short story in *Dancers on the Shore*, in which he becomes a famous folk singer. In that story the themes of one's public image versus his true self and commercialism versus art are explored.

These themes are developed further in Kelley's second novel, *A Drop of Patience*. The protagonist is a blind, black jazz musician, whose intuitive experimentation is contrasted to the intellectualization of critics, and whose love of music comes into conflict with the com-mercialization of music. More important than these themes, however, is the development of the character himself, who passes through various rites of passage as he learns to deal with sex, love, racism, and fame.

Carlyle Bedlow, who appeared in several of the stories in *Dancers on the Shore*, reappears in *dem*, Kelley's third novel. "Lemme tellya how dem folks live," the novel begins. It goes on to show dem white folks living out their myths of white superiority, masculine prerogative, and soap-opera escapism. They are such victims of the pernicious myths of their culture that they are no longer even a threat to black people.

Kelley has shown himself a skillful craftsman in a variety of styles and approaches. His exploration of character usually develops as the character seeks—or refuses to seek—a unity between the person he feels he is and the personality he or society thinks he should be. In general, his black characters have a firmer grasp on reality and a stronger desire to come to grips with reality than his white characters.

In the development of American literature dealing with racial oppression, his novels represent a significant stage, one in which the focus is not on the plight, or the rebellion, of the black character but on the plight and self-delusion of the white character. The black character is not in the seat of political power, but he is in control of himself, which is more than the white character is. This perspective represents a fictional counterpart to Malcolm X's redefinition of the conflict from that of "the Negro problem" to that of "the white problem."

—William Borden

---

**KENEALLY, Thomas (Michael).**   Australian.   Born in Sydney, 7 October 1935. Educated at St. Patrick's College, Strathfield, New South Wales; studied for the priesthood and studied law. Served in the Australian Citizens Military Forces. Married Judith Martin in 1965; has two children. High School Teacher in Sydney, 1960–64; Lecturer in Drama, University of New England, New South Wales, 1968–70. Recipient: Miles Franklin Award, 1967, 1968; Captain Cook Bi-Centenary Prize, 1970. Address: 5 The Grange, Wimbledon, London S.W.19, England.

PUBLICATIONS

Novels

> *The Place at Whitton.*   Melbourne and London, Cassell, 1964; New York, Walker, 1965.
> *The Fear.*   Melbourne and London, Cassell, 1965.
> *Bring Larks and Heros.*   Melbourne, Cassell, 1967; London, Cassell, and New York, Viking Press, 1968.
> *Three Cheers for the Paraclete.*   Sydney, Angus and Robertson, 1968; London, Angus and Robertson, and New York, Viking Press, 1969.
> *The Survivor.*   Sydney, Angus and Robertson, 1969; London, Angus and Robertson, 1970.
> *A Dutiful Daughter.*   Sydney and London, Angus and Robertson, and New York, Viking Press, 1971.

Thomas Keneally comments:

I would like to be able to disown my first two novels, the second of which was the obligatory account of one's childhood—the book then that all novelists think seriously of writing.

I see my third novel as an attempt to follow out an epic theme in terms of a young soldier's exile to Australia.

The fourth and fifth were attempts at urbane writing in the traditional mode of the English novel: confrontations between characters whose behaviour shows layers of irony and humour, in which all that is epic is rather played down.

For *A Dutiful Daughter*, the best novel I have written (not that I claim that matters much), I have turned to myth and fable, as many a novelist is doing, for the simple reason that other media have moved into the traditional areas of the novel.

*       *       *

Since his first novel, *The Place at Whitton*, Thomas Keneally has been responsible for five other published novels, three or more plays, and at least one abandoned novel about an Australian writer caught up with Sydney peace-marchers and political larrikins. Of this work, Keneally said in 1968, "I don't know which way to turn." In a sense this remark sums up a certain quality pervading much of his published work. The abundance of this, in less than a decade, would appear to make him successful, publisher-esteemed, prize-winning, and what is known on dust-jacket blurbs as "a prolific writer", that is, by and large, the sort of writer of whom the sharp-minded and fastidious reader needs must be wary even though the writer be a Dickens or a Balzac. In Keneally's case wariness is particularly justified. He is a quick-change artist of undoubted skill, presents a wide range of unusual and impressionistically drawn settings occupied by unusual and guilt-riddled people, is generally an alert entertainer, and dabbles earnestly or mischievously with problems of "conscience", the sentimental, limited, and up-to-the-minute conscienceless "conscience" of present-day trouble-makers. The observer finds himself backing towards wariness because he is compelled, in book after book, to be conscious of some lack, some so-to-speak vitamin deficiency, in Keneally's writing. No matter how engaging the felicities they are gap-toothed. Precisely what the lack is is difficult to define. It's not talent, it may be heart; it's not ingenuity, though it could be taste; it's not education, but perhaps percipience or clarity of vision; it's not fact or organized fantasy, both of which he juggles with, yet could be truth.

What adds to the observer's uneasiness, and is disconcerting, is to discover, in each successive novel, that the author has not advanced, is merely making an almost wilfully self-conscious break in yet another direction, is starting to wander off into a different sort of formlessness, to reveal a new brand of sloppiness in technique, to invest in other arrangements of clichés, to blur what seems a highly romanticized realism with a coating of symbolism. Perhaps these are the results of Keneally's never working out a detailed plot before starting to write. Perhaps they are the indirect outcome of a deeply embedded uncertainty, a quasi-fecklessness. Keneally is a Roman Catholic priest *manqué*. This fact would not be worth the recording if the hang-over did not patently, and constantly, infect his work—incertitudes both of vision and technique keep on cropping up.

Since Keneally brazenly confesses to being worried whether "the conventional novel has had it", and to wondering publicly if he should "cast off into a sea of pure fantasy" and "move forward into surrealism", it is scarcely surprising that, despite certain titillating qualities, and an engagement with fashionable (and, therefore not-to-be-trusted) "moral" issues, most of his novels are neither flesh, fowl, nor good red herring. Most, not all: *Three Cheers for the Paraclete*, a brisk and comic chess game of a book, seems more planned. Each move in the game is clear-cut; the prose so well fulfils its purpose that the actors in the comedy take on the semblance of flesh-and-blood creatures howsoever actorish and word-perfect, howsoever adroit with the brilliant riposte and superb exit line.

Usually, however, Keneally is not so deft. Many of his characters are inclined to blur not only at the edges but at the core, are literary hippogriffs neither convincingly human nor assuredly symbolic. Indeed, in his latest novel, *A Dutiful Daughter*, he has cast off into a sea of fantasy (impure rather than pure), and manufactured two symbolic freaks. The dutiful daughter's parents turn, minotaur-like, into half-bull and half-cow, and become victims of their sinister, perverted, part-insane, Joan-of-Arc-haunted monster of a child. Keneally's machinery for dealing with such a grotesque situation is ill-chosen, and handled amateurishly —the product is his most aggressive failure as an artist. Embellishments to the situation (incest, perversion, bestiality, a triple suicide) are dealt with in the coarsely genteel manner which is the one ear-mark of Keneally's style which is otherwise so unjelled that he could be said to have little style at all.

Patrick White's influence is responsible for earlier affectations, for images patently injected, like borrowed penicillin, into the Keneally main-stream. Later admitted influences, Angus Wilson and Evelyn Waugh, are less visible. Waugh is, indeed, quite invisible as an influence, is—surely?—too civilized and exquisitely controlled an artist for the hearty, unsophisticated, texturally coarse, and "conscience"-shackled Keneally to catch. Even Wilson's garrulity has more edge than the present Keneally can use.

Having produced in less than ten years a substantial number of printed pages, Keneally stands today on the danger line most young and fecund writers reach. If it be disturbing that, so far, he has shown few signs of maturity, it may be that it is really too early to expect more. His own stated indecision about what a novel is (or, rather, what a Keneally novel should be) tempts one to hope that a conscious doubting will give way, as such a doubt should, to the assurance an active and gifted writer must have if he seek the immortality Keneally acknowledges he is in pursuit of.

—Hal Porter

**KESEY, Ken (Elton).** American. Born in La Junta, Colorado, 17 September 1935. Educated at the University of Oregon, Eugene, B.A. 1957; Stanford University, California (Woodrow Wilson Fellow), 1958–59. Married Norma Faye Haxby in 1957; has four children. Has worked as a ward attendant in a mental hospital. Since 1964, President of Intrepid Trips Inc., a motion picture company. Recipient: Saxton Memorial Trust Award, 1959. Address: 345 Franklin Street, San Francisco, California, U.S.A.

PUBLICATIONS

Novels

> *One Flew over the Cuckoo's Nest.*   New York, Viking Press, 1962; London, Methuen, 1963.
> *Sometimes a Great Notion.*   New York, Viking Press, 1964; London, Methuen, 1966.

*          *          *

Ken Kesey's critical reputation rests for the time being on his two novels. The first, *One Flew over the Cuckoo's Nest*, was a widely popular success which has been adapted for performance as a play. The second novel, *Sometimes a Great Notion*, has received relatively little attention. Since finishing it, Kesey has announced a shift from "literature" to "life," and has achieved a great deal of public notoriety in the process of making the change. He was public news during the late sixties, forming a band of "Merry Pranksters" (reported on at length in Tom Wolfe's *Electric Kool-Aid Acid Test*) who attempted to live life as a work of comic fiction. Stray pieces of notebooks have been published in the last few years, suggesting that eventually a new work, perhaps a new kind of work, will emerge. Until then, Kesey followers will have to content themselves with *The Last Supplement to the Whole Earth Catalog*. This volume has more of Kesey's writing in it (mostly reviews and articles) than anything published since his second novel.

Both of Kesey's novels are richly north-western and regional in quality, with a strong sense of the impingement of the white man on the Indian's land and way of life. The emphasis is a bit once-sided in *Cuckoo's Nest*, which has for its stream-of-consciousness center and narrator-observer an Indian named Chief, whose father was in fact the last chief of his tribe. The novel could be read as an allegory of how the white man is driven to subjugate and eliminate the Indian because he is a reminder to him of those parts of himself he has lost through a conquest of the will over the passions. More basically, however, the novel reveals the power struggle between man's desire to be free and his fears of the consequence of that freedom. Most of the characters in the mental institution could leave if they wished; but their fear of the outside is more intense than their hatred of the inside. The novel tempts one to allegorical generalities because the institution in which it is set becomes increasingly recognizable as a microcosm of the world we all live in. Recognizable, but comically exaggerated, as are the main characters who represent general qualities and attitudes towards life and humanity. The book captures and reflects the reality of a "Walt-Disney world," as perceived by the "Big Chief" who used to be on our childhood writing tablet covers but is now pretending to be a vegetable in a nut house. What he sees is "Like a cartoon world, where the figures are flat and outlined in black, jerking through some kind of goofy story that might be real funny if it weren't for the cartoon figures being real guys. . . ." The comic-book quality has lent itself nicely to dramatic production, as have the compactness and wild humor of the novel. These qualities also tempt one to allegorize, but at the same time mock the attempt as absurd. For the work is not itself allegorical; it is a report or presentation of the way people see themselves and their world in allegorical or comic-book fashion, yet without being able to laugh at what they see. The reality of the villain, "Big Nurse," is as exaggerated by the characters who fear and hate her as it is by the novelist. The institution, with its equipment and routines, is a focus for sociological and psychological myths and techniques pushed to an illogical but all-too-plausible extreme. The prefrontal lobotomy performed on McMurphy at the end is *any* operation on or treatment of or way of seeing a man, that decides to limit and dehumanize him for his own sake. The Big Nurse is that spirit which loves the "idea" of man so much it can't allow individual men to exist.

*Sometimes a Great Notion* deserves more attention than *Cuckoo's Nest*, and much more than I can give it here. I can indicate its ambition, by pointing out that it is in considerable part an *Absalom, Absalom!* set in Oregon. I pick this example not only to suggest the intense regionalism of the book, but to indicate the intricate complexities of the narrative structure which Kesey has attempted. After the second reading, what at first seem like gratuitous confusions and exploitations of "the miracle of modern narrative technique," begin to emerge as the necessary supports for a novelistic structure which doesn't quite get brought into finished shape. In this novel Kesey has aimed higher than many of his contemporaries, and he has come impressively close to his target.

—Thomas A. Vogler

---

**KIELY, Benedict.** Irish. Born in Dromore, County Tyrone, 15 August 1919. Educated at Christian Brothers' schools, Omagh; National University of Ireland, Dublin. Married Maureen O'Connell in 1944; has four children. Journalist in Dublin, 1939–64. Writer-in-Residence, Hollins College, Virginia, 1964–65; Visiting Professor, University of Oregon, Eugene, 1965–66; Writer-in-Residence, Emory University, Atlanta, Georgia, 1966–68. Since 1970, Visiting Lecturer, University College, Dublin. Member of the Council of the Irish Academy of Letters; Member of the Academic Committee of the American-Irish Foundation. Address: c/o The Irish Times, Westmoreland Street, Dublin, Ireland.

PUBLICATIONS

Novels

*Land Without Stars.* London, Johnson, 1946.
*In a Harbour Green.* London, Cape, 1949; New York, Dutton, 1950.
*Call for a Miracle.* London, Cape, 1950; New York, Dutton, 1951.
*Honey Seems Bitter.* New York, Dutton, 1952; London, Methuen, 1954.
*The Cards of the Gambler: A Folktale.* London, Methuen, 1953.
*There Was an Ancient House.* London, Methuen, 1955.
*The Captain with the Whiskers.* London, Methuen, 1960; New York, Criterion Books, 1961.
*Dogs Enjoy the Morning.* London, Gollancz, 1968.

Short Stories

*A Journey to the Seven Streams: 17 Stories.* London, Methuen, 1963.
*Penguin Modern Stories 5*, with others. London, Penguin, 1970.

Uncollected Short Stories

"Wild Rover No More", in *Northwest Review* (Eugene, Oregon), vol. 8, no. 3, 1952.
"A Bottle of Brown Sherry", in *Kenyon Review* (Gambier, Ohio), Spring 1964.
"A Great God's Angel Standing", in *The New Yorker*, 24 August 1968.
"The Little Wrens and Robins", in *The New Yorker*, 4 April 1970.
"Down Then by Derry", in *Dublin Magazine*, Summer-Autumn 1970.
"God's Own Country", in *Winter's Tales from Ireland*.  Dublin, Gill and Macmillan, 1970.
"The Green Lanes", in *Audience* (Cambridge, Massachusetts), May-June 1971.


Other

*Counties of Contention: A Study of the Origins and Implications of the Partition of Ireland.* Cork, Mercier Press, 1945.
*Poor Scholar: A Study of the Works and Days of William Carleton, 1794–1869.*  London, Sheed and Ward, 1947; New York, Sheed and Ward, 1948.
*Modern Irish Fiction: A Critique.*  Dublin, Golden Eagle Books, 1950.


*         *         *


Benedict Kiely is Irish and a master of nostalgia; and the Irish are probably the most nostalgic of all people. Although the fullest force of his nostalgia is expressed over rural Ireland —probably the County Tyrone where he grew up—his portrayal of Dublin is hardly more realistic. It is not the Dublin of O'Casey or Behan, where poverty is as gray and plentiful as the stones of the houses, but a city of transplanted countrymen. That, although not a complete picture, is an accurate one, for as the Jackeens leave for England or America, people come up from the country to join the civil service or work to acquire pubs. Of the little more than three million Irishmen, over 700,000 live in Dublin.

Kiely's settings range from the rural (*In a Harbour Green* takes place in a small Northern port) to Dublin (*Call for a Miracle*) to both (*Dogs Enjoy the Morning*). His titles seem to be chosen for their picturesque sound rather than to give any indication of what the book is about; for example, the Captain is a minor although vaguely influential figure in *The Captain with the Whiskers*. Lovers of canines might be very much misled to buy *Dogs Enjoy the Morning*.

His style is charming, albeit braided with a gilded strand of blarney. Critics have a great deal of difficulty in deciding what any of his novels is about. In retrospect one remembers episodes of his novels, and those rarely about the principal characters—Captain Conway Chesney lining up his children like recruits in *The Captain with the Whiskers*; the correspondence between the father of Mary Fergus, in *Call for a Miracle*, and the mother of the cripple she loves; and the episode of the foreign sailor lured in a drunken spree to the country in *Dogs Enjoy the Morning*.

The distinctly gracious and often poignant short stories in *A Journey to the Seven Streams* suggest an answer. Kiely is a master of the short story, and the memorable parts of his novels are abortive short stories; the rest is just reeking nostalgia. Moreover, as Padraic Colum has pointed out, his treatment of sex is not to everyone's taste. The women in his books are believable Irish females—as girls secretive giggling challenges to the seducer, as matrons diffidently aware that sex, in the Land of Saints and Scholars, is only more "chisullers."

Still, one cannot write off Benedict Kiely as a last, decadent gasp of the tradition of O'Connor, O'Faolain, O'Flaherty, although he can never be a James Joyce. His major flaw is parochialism, both in subject matter and technique. His words could charm the angels out of heaven, but, save for the short stories written for *The New Yorker*, he has not aimed beyond the narrow horizon of his homeland, and his subject matter has dealt with only the noisy minority in that. After his several years in America, we may find more variety in Benedict Kiely.

—William Bittner

---

**KILLENS, John Oliver.** American. Born in Macon, Georgia, in 1916. Educated at colleges in Atlanta, Jacksonville, Florida, Washington, D.C., and at Columbia University, New York, and New York University. Served in the United States Army in World War II. Married; has two children. Worked for the National Labor Relations Board, Washington, 1936–42, and after 1946. Lives in Brooklyn, New York. Address: c/o Simon and Schuster Inc., 630 Fifth Avenue, New York, New York 10020, U.S.A.

PUBLICATIONS

Novels

*Youngblood.* New York, Dial Press, 1954; London, Bodley Head, 1956.
*And Then We Heard the Thunder.* New York, Knopf, 1962; London, Cape, 1964.
*'Sippi.* New York, Simon and Schuster, 1967.
*Slaves.* New York, Pyramid, 1969.
*The Cotillion; or, One Good Bull Is Half the Herd.* New York, Simon and Schuster, 1971.

Plays

*Lower than the Angels* (produced New York, 1965).

Other

*Black Man's Burden* (essays). New York, Simon and Schuster, 1966.

\*      \*      \*

Born in Macon, Georgia, in 1916, John Oliver Killens grew up in his native town and there received his early schooling. Though he worked for the National Labor Relations Board before and after World War II, his true and permanent interest was writing. By 1954 he was able to witness the publication of *Youngblood*, his first novel. Three other novels, *And Then We Heard Thunder*, *'Sippi*, and *The Cotillion* have followed, with, also, an important book of essays, *Black Man's Burden*, and contributions to the movies and television, notably the script for the film, *Odds Against Tomorrow*. For years now a resident of Brooklyn, with his wife and their two children, Killens has occasionally interrupted his absorption in creative literature to serve as writer-in-residence on various academic campuses. But such interruptions obviously constitute no actual deviation from his devotion to letters. There was a time when Negro writers almost exclusively tended to be of some non-literary vocation first and writers only in their leisure time. Not so with Killens. He has pursued the craft of fiction as his first love and, given his obvious conception of the poet not only as seer but also as obligated, almost surely because of his superior capacities for ascertaining truth, to involve himself personally in attempts at the improvement of society, the very active rôles Killens has played with organizations themselves as active or as "political" as the American Society for African Culture and the Harlem Writers Guild become only additional dimensions of his commitment to the arts.

At the beginning of his career as an author Killens was very clearly an advocate of integration. No message, other than the sheer iniquity of race prejudice, comes so unequivocally out of his novel, *Youngblood*, as the message of the necessity for white and black workers to unite. But, also, a high point in *Youngblood*, an episode in which Negro school children in a Georgia town, under the direction of one of their teachers, convert a concert of Negro spirituals from a submissive gesture to the local whites into a respectful rendering of the meaning of their own past, affirms the theme which now is often represented in the phrase, "black is beautiful." Increasingly, it does seem, it has been the "black is beautiful" theme, even to the extreme of Black Separatism, which has governed Killens in his affirmation of his art, as well as, indeed, in his conduct as a citizen of the world.

—Blyden Jackson

---

**KIM, Richard.** American. Born in Hamhung City, Korea, 13 March 1932; became a United States citizen, 1964. Educated at primary and secondary schools in Korea; Middlebury College, Vermont, 1955–59; Johns Hopkins University, Baltimore, 1959–60, M.A. in writing 1960; University of Iowa, Iowa City, 1960–62, M.F.A. in writing 1962; Harvard University, Cambridge, Massachusetts, 1962–63, M.A. in Far Eastern literature 1963. Served as a First Lieutenant in the Korean Army and Marines, 1950–54. Married Penelope Anne Groll in 1960; has two children. Instructor of English, California State College, Long Beach, 1963–64. Assistant Professor, 1964–68, Associate Professor, 1968–69, and since 1969 Adjunct Associate Professor of English, University of Massachusetts, Amherst; also, Director, University of Massachusetts Imaginative Writers' Workshop, Nantucket, Summers 1967–69. Visiting Writer, Mediterranean Institute, Majorca, 1969. Visiting Professor of English, Syracuse University, New York, 1970–71. Member of the Board of Directors of the American-Korean Foundation, New York. Recipient: Mary Roberts Rinehart Foundation Fellowship, 1961; Ford Foreign Area Fellowship, 1962; Guggenheim Fellowship, 1965. Address: Leverett Road, Shutesbury, Massachusetts 01072, U.S.A.

PUBLICATIONS

Novels

*The Martyred.*   New York, Braziller, and London, Hutchinson, 1964.
*The Innocent.*   Boston, Houghton Mifflin, 1968; London, Hutchinson, 1969.
*Lost Names.*   New York, Praeger, 1970; London, Deutsch, 1971.

*       *       *

Richard Kim's fiction deals with war's effect on private morality. Using an inexperienced first person narrator—an unnamed child in *Lost Names* and a young officer named Lee in *The Martyred* and *The Innocent*—he sensitively delineates questions of bravery, patriotism, humaneness and even the nature of truth as they are clouded by violence and made more complex by despair.

Periods of national crisis in recent Korean history provide a background against which are focused the moral crises of individuals. Love of country, despair over the suffering of its people and pride in their resilience are recurring themes. The forbidding Korean countryside, especially the winter scenery of North Korea, is used to underscore the characters' anguish. At the end of each book, the narrator's education—though incomplete—leads him to hope for Korea's future despite the suffering and death he has seen.

*Lost Names* is a collection of stories dealing with the ordeal of a single family during the last thirteen years of the thirty-six year Japanese occupation. The book is thematically unified by the child's growing awareness that the mere survival of his father is significant heroism. Although the stories vary in weight, the best of them, such as the title story, are taut and powerful. Natural imagery is skillfully used, and the maturation process of a child is well suited to the thematic development.

*The Innocent* treats a compelling question; how much bloodshed can an individual justify by patriotism? The focal character, Colonel Min, is struggling for his soul while leading a *coup d'état*. There is some fine descriptive writing in this book, too, and characters such as Min and Chaplain Koh are strikingly alive, but it does not have the solid power one might wish for. The complexity of the plot detracts from the moral drama, and the large cast of conspirators requires too much sorting out, especially when they are all men designated by military titles and similar monosyllabic Korean names. There is special difficulty with the three characters opposing the coup: General Mah, General Ahn and General Ham.

Kim's best book, *The Martyred*, is uniformly fine. It is tightly plotted, austere in style and moving in subject matter. The tone of passion never approaches bathos; the people are believable and their struggles compelling. Economy of incident and explication heightens the drama. The writing is smooth and strong; necessary information about the movement of armies is worked in unobtrusively and does not detract from the focus on a single moral drama and the half dozen characters intimately concerned with its unfolding. Brutality and helplessness are effectively portrayed without sensational description. *The Martyred* deserves a wide readership.

Though each of these books draws heavily upon the tragic history of Korea, the reader feels that Kim is equipped to deal sensitively with the human condition wherever he finds it. These are not ethnic novels; they simply utilize a compelling historical situation with which the novelist is familiar. Future works by Kim may use different milieux, but one would hope they convey the same awareness of the dramatic, the same moral cogency and keen sense of selectivity he shows in the best passages of these books.

—Barbara M. Perkins

---

**KING, Francis (Henry).** British. Born in Adelboden, Switzerland, 4 March 1923. Educated at Shrewsbury School; Balliol College, Oxford, B.A. 1949, M.A. 1951. Poetry Reviewer, *The Listener*, London, 1945–50; worked for the British Council, 1949–63: Lecturer in Florence, 1949–50, Salonika, 1950–52, and Athens 1953–57; Assistant Representative, Helsinki, 1957–58; Regional Director, Kyoto, 1959–63. Since 1964, Fiction Reviewer, *The Sunday Times*, London. Since 1968, Literary Adviser, Macdonald and Company, publishers, London. Since 1969, Member, Executive Committee, P.E.N., London.

Recipient: Maugham Award, 1952; Katherine Mansfield Short Story Prize, 1965; Arts Council Bursary, 1966. Fellow, Royal Society of Literature, 1952; subsequently resigned; re-elected, 1967. Address: c/o A. M. Heath and Company, 35 Dover Street, London W.1, England.

PUBLICATIONS

Novels

*To the Dark Tower*.   London, Home and Van Thal, 1946.
*Never Again*.   London, Home and Van Thal, 1948.
*An Air That Kills*.   London, Home and Van Thal, 1949.
*The Dividing Stream*.   London, Longman, and New York, Morrow, 1951.
*The Dark Glasses*.   London, Longman, 1954; New York, Pantheon Books, 1956.
*The Firewalkers: A Memoir* (as Frank Cauldwell).   London, Murray, 1956.
*The Widow*.   London, Longman, 1957.
*The Man on the Rock*.   London, Longman, 1957; New York, Pantheon Books, 1958.
*The Custom House*.   London, Longman, 1961; New York, Doubleday, 1962.
*The Last of the Pleasure Gardens*.   London, Longman, 1965.
*The Waves Behind the Boat*.   London, Longman, 1967.
*A Domestic Animal*.   London, Longman, 1970.

Short Stories

*So Hurt and Humiliated and Other Stories*.   London, Longman, 1959.
*The Japanese Umbrella and Other Stories*.   London, Longman, 1964.
*The Brighton Belle and Other Stories*.   London, Longman, 1968.

Verse

*Rod of Incantation*.   London, Longman, 1952.

Other

*Japan*.   London, Thames and Hudson, 1970.

Editor, *Introducing Greece*.   London, Methuen, 1956; revised edition, 1968.

Manuscript Collection: University of Texas, Austin.

Critical Study: essay by the author, "Leaving School", in *Leaving School*, London, Phoenix House, 1957.

Francis King comments:

Except for the period of my schooling and the war, mine has always been an itinerant life.

As a child, I was brought up alternately in India and Switzerland (the country of my birth); subsequently I worked for the British Council in Italy, Greece, Egypt, Finland and Japan. After a maximum of three years in any one house or even any one city, I want to move on. This desire always to set off for another destination is reflected in my novels. Of course, certain themes in them are constant; but I have never wished to be identified with only one type of fiction. Perhaps this has harmed me in popular esteem; the public tends to like its novelists to write the same novel over and over again.

Foreign places have always provided me with imaginative stimulation and the majority of my books have foreign settings. Most English novelists, like the society from which they derive, seem to me to be too much preoccupied with differences of class, which obscure for them differences more profound between human beings. In choosing so often to write about "abroad", I have, perhaps subconsciously, attempted to avoid this class-obsession.

I believe strongly in national character, and a recurrent theme of my books is the way in which people struggle to break out of the patterns of national behaviour in which they have been engaged since birth.

Critics sometimes say that they find my work "depressing" and my readers sometimes ask why I never write about "nice" people or "normal" people—not surprisingly perhaps, since mine is an attitude of profound, if resigned, pessimism about the world. I do not expect people to behave consistently well, and my observation is that few of them do. But I should like to think that the tolerance and compassion that I genuinely feel are also reflected in my writing.

I have always been preoccupied with style and form. I feel that I am most successful in achieving both if the reader is unconscious of any straining for them.

In my early books, written at a period of loneliness in my own life, isolation is a recurrent theme; in my later books I see now that envy and jealousy—to my mind the least attractive of human traits—have taken over.

My biggest and most successful novel was *The Custom House*. The novel that comes nearest to saying what I wanted to say—and that cost me most—was *A Domestic Animal*.

\*      \*      \*

Francis King belongs to that class of writers who, while never meeting with spectacular success, over the years develop an established reputation and have considerably more staying power and real talent than many of the temporarily famous. His literary career began immediately after the Second World War and has gone steadily forward at the rate of about one novel every two or three years plus several volumes of short stories and one of poetry. For much of that time he has been employed by the British Council working in, among other places, Italy, Greece and Japan, but in the last few years he has resigned his Council post to devote himself entirely to writing—a considerable step for someone whose job has patently provided him with much of his best material.

He lived in India and Switzerland as a small boy. His first three books all make some use of the Indian background, though only one of them, *Never Again*, makes direct use of his childhood experience of exile. His first book, *To the Dark Tower*, a promising though uneven work about an obsession and the powerful personality who has inspired it, is a more consciously literary effort. *An Air That Kills*, a novel about a middle aged man's yearning affection for a young boy, is weaker and has dated badly. This is a theme to which Francis King has returned a number of times over the years and has never handled very satisfactorily, perhaps because simple love, whether homosexual or heterosexual, *is* difficult to handle in fiction without lapsing into apparent sentiment. Like many writers, Francis King writes best when there is a certain astringency in his approach to his subject matter and, *unlike* many writers, his best effects are often achieved when he is not apparently writing "close to home" but has had to make an imaginative effort to enter the thoughts of his characters.

Both *The Dividing Stream*, set in Florence, and *The Dark Glasses* which is set on Corfu, have larger casts of characters than the early books, and their involved and dramatic plots are handled with skill and authority. Both treat, in different ways, of relationships between

719

rich foreign visitors and the local working class. Of the two locales, the Grecian one is perhaps slightly better suited to King's talent, possibly because he has a more developed "love-hate relationship" with that ambiguous, half-Eastern country. It subsequently became the background to *The Man on the Rock*, an accomplished and convincing portrait of a parasite, gigolo and ultimate failure, and also to *The Firewalkers*, an engaging account of friendships which for some reason he chose to publish under the pseudonym "Frank Cauldwell". In fact "Frank Cauldwell" appears as a somewhat undeveloped character in his first book, but the relationship between this book and *The Firewalkers* was never explored and it is hard to see why Francis King chose to camouflage his authorship at this point. The book is now restored to the lists of his published work.

His only novel of this period set wholly in England is *The Widow*, an interesting attempt to write from within the mind of a middle aged woman. He returned to this device, and to a London locale, eight years later with his outstanding, best book (so far), *The Last of the Pleasure Gardens*, a poignant, sophisticated and completely convincing picture of a couple with an abnormal child, in which each of the subsidiary characters is a perfectly rounded portrait in its own right. This admirable ability to fill in the detail and to create a plethora of minor personalities is also apparent in his two "Japanese" novels, one written before *The Pleasure Gardens* and one after, *The Custom House* and *The Waves Behind the Boat*. As in a number of Mr King's books, drama and indeed murder make their appearance in these, but the effect is authentic, not melodramatic, and there are scenes of high comedy as well. If there is a weakness in these books, it is a tendency to use the characters' sexual oddities somewhat mechanically to provide a "surprise twist" which does not, in fact, come all that much as a surprise to the reader.

Mr King's latest novel, *A Domestic Animal*, returns to an English setting (like his latest volume of short stories *The Brighton Belle*) and is an altogether slighter work. It seems to lack the humour and perception of his other recent books and to fall into the traps of non-objectivity and misplaced romanticism that disfigure some of his earlier work. However, Francis King has always been an uneven writer and has always had surprises up his sleeve; few of his admirers will be in doubt but that he still has good books in store.

—Gillian Tindall

---

**KNEBEL, Fletcher.** American. Born in Dayton, Ohio, 1 October 1911. Educated at Miami University, Oxford, Ohio, B.A. 1934. Served in the United States Navy in World War II. Married Laura Bergquist in 1965; has two children by a previous marriage. Reporter, *Coatesville Record*, Pennsylvania, 1934, *Chattanooga News*, Tennessee, 1934–35, and *Toledo News-Bee*, Ohio, 1935; Reporter, 1936, and Washington Correspondent, 1937–50, *Cleveland Plain Dealer*; Washington Correspondent, Cowles Publications, Washington, D.C. 1950–64, and writer of the syndicated column, "Potomac Fever", 1951–64. Writer for *Look* magazine, New York, 1950–71. Recipient: Sigma Delta Chi award, for reporting, 1955. D.L., Miami University, 1964; D.LL., Drake University, Des Moines, Iowa, 1968. Address: 208 Edgerstoune Road, Princeton, New Jersey 08540, U.S.A.

PUBLICATIONS

Novels

*Seven Days in May*, with Charles Bailey. New York, Harper, and London, Weidenfeld and Nicolson, 1960.

*Convention*, with Charles Bailey.   New York, Harper, 1962; London, Weidenfeld and
  Nicolson, 1963.
*Night of Camp David*.   New York, Harper, and London, Weidenfeld and Nicolson,
  1965.
*The Zinzin Road*.   New York, Doubleday, 1966; London, W. H. Allen, 1967.
*Vanished*.   New York, Doubleday, and London, W. H. Allen, 1968.
*Trespass*.   New York, Doubleday, and London, W. H. Allen, 1969.
*Exit Nine*.   New York, Doubleday, 1972.


Other

*No High Ground*, with Charles Bailey.   New York, Harper, and London, Weidenfeld
  and Nicolson, 1960.


Critical Study: in *New York Times Book Review*, January 1968.


Fletcher Knebel comments:

My novels are basically suspense stories with a major social or political theme in the background. The first aim is always to tell a good story, but I hope the message comes through.

                          *          *          *

Fletcher Knebel, a former Washington, D.C. journalist, has written six political novels
since 1962, the first two co-authored by Charles W. Bailey, a former colleague. He is recognized as one of the foremost writers of the political suspense thriller in the past decade,
combining his journalistic skill with well-constructed plots to produce popular and entertaining accounts of fictionalized but plausible crises in American politics. Knebel is at his
best in the depiction of behind-the-scenes action, and the vivid immediacy of his plots must
be accounted as a main element of appeal to his audience. His extensive knowledge of the
Washington scene gives him the ability to delineate the surface details of his stories with
verisimilitude, and his journalistic experience has aided him in developing a direct descriptive
prose style. His characters are often vividly drawn, particularly members of the press or
professional politicians, although some reviewers have criticized him for over-dependence
upon stock characters or for caricaturing those characters, such as military or intelligence
chiefs, that he does not like.
    Knebel's plots consistently portray his liberal political views, particularly in his pro-
tagonists' dependence upon rational problem-solving and his antagonists' Machiavellian
disregard for democratic procedures. His books are concerned with such problems as a
projected military takeover of the government, a utopian Presidential plan for peace, mental
illness as a Presidential disability, black terrorism, and the political nomination process.
He is consistently interested in such issues as the acquisition and maintenance of power, the
Presidency as an institution, and conspiracy as a political tool. In his books, both protagonists
and antagonists conspire secretly to accomplish their aims, indicating to the reader that this
is the way goals are reached in American politics.
    The major shortcomings of his novels are inherent in their conception. If Knebel sincerely
believes in the dangers that he warns against and desires to alert his readers to possible pitfalls in the present system, as he has indicated he does, then his choice of the political thriller
as the vehicle for his jeremiads renders those warnings, to some extent, hollow. Because he
relies, somewhat simplistically, upon the rationality and good will of his main characters

to solve the significant and overwhelming problems with which they are faced, he runs the risk of trivializing those problems for the purpose of fictional excitement. Ultimately, it is difficult to see the seriousness of the threats when the books ritually exorcise them in the resolution of the action, reassuring the reader of the essential soundness of his political system. Knebel does well in reporting the events of his stories; he is too competent a journalist to do otherwise. But in his attempts to explore the dilemma of the sensitive man of good will in the face of political apocalypse, he succumbs to the essential optimism of popular fiction, and, in so doing, succeeds in entertaining but fails to develop the ultimate implications of the messages he professes to deliver.

—Kay J. Mussell

---

**KNOWLES, John.** American. Born in Fairmont, West Virginia, 16 September 1926. Educated at Phillips Exeter Academy, New Hampshire; Yale University, New Haven, Connecticut, B.A. 1949. Reporter, *Hartford Courant*, Connecticut, 1950–52; Free-lance Writer, 1952–56; Associate Editor, *Holiday* magazine, New York, 1956–60. Recipient: Rosenthal Foundation Award, 1961; Faulkner Foundation Award, 1961; National Association of Independent Schools Award, 1961. Address: c/o Random House, 201 East 50th Street, New York, New York 10022, U.S.A.

PUBLICATIONS

Novels

*A Separate Peace*. London, Secker and Warburg, 1959; New York, Macmillan, 1960.
*Morning in Antibes*. New York, Macmillan, and London, Secker and Warburg, 1962.
*Indian Summer*. New York, Random House, and London, Secker and Warburg, 1966.
*The Paragon*. New York, Random House, 1971.

Short Stories

*Phineas: 6 Stories*. New York, Random House, 1968.

Other

*Double Vision: American Thoughts Abroad*. New York, Macmillan, and London, Secker and Warburg, 1964.

\* \* \*

John Knowles is, above all, a forceful writer; few readers fail to feel the impelling power of his style, of his action sequences, of his characters, and this alone could account for the almost graph-like rise in popularity which has taken place in the years following the appearance of his first novel—now a classic in its 36th printing—*A Separate Peace*.

Kinetic energy and lean toughness are not only qualities which impress themselves on Mr. Knowles' readers; they are the elementary tools, the survival kit without which there is no chance for survival, with which each of his characters is equipped at the portal of adult life. Weak or vacillating characters need only apply for bit parts in a Knowles novel, for the series of tests which modern man faces in these novels are heroic, and a hero or heroine must meet them. The gross tests are a thing of the past, and a decade of novels shows a subtle world of the challenges of opulence; thus even the characters themselves are not allowed the easy out of a lack of talent or a limited range of comprehension of the choices available or the kinds of life to be led. Myron Stoetzer, the failure who appears in *The Paragon*, both states the problem and shows his function in relation to the strong characters of the novel when he says: "It's just that I might have had another kind of life entirely, more valuable, not leaving so many areas of myself so neglected. Neglect. It's the word I hate most in the English Language."

Mr. Knowles' greatest following is among the young and among those who want to try to understand the post-war generations, for a strong sense of this particular time in history pervades all his fiction. His failures are middle-aged and the centre of interest is that time of life when the essential choices of patterns of behaviour are being made—when promise and potential are about to be tested and must become performance and achievement. Gene and Phineas of *A Separate Peace* are in their last year at an elite boarding school during the war; Cleet Kinsolving in *Indian Summer* (tough as a cleet, and having to discover his kin from the past as well as his kinship with the present) is 23 and has just been discharged into the post-war world from the Air Force; Louis Colfax of *The Paragon* is attempting to channel the energy of many and diverse talents in the seeming calm of university life of the 1950's. The worlds which they all face are anything but simplistic, and each character must make distinct but tortured choices, not so much between right and wrong, but between conflicting kinds of right. Though he is better with and focuses on the male rather than the female, Mr. Knowles allows none of his people easy victories. Rather than Olympic Gold Medals of proved conquest, his characters of superior talent and heroic energy get the chance to continue to compete. We have only the conviction of a certain painfully learned wisdom which may allow them to continue to infuse the reality in which they live with their own unique values and meaning.

This very gifted writer does not hide his talents, and foremost among them is a precise eye and the ability to translate what is seen by it into the medium of descriptive prose. Whether in the above novels, on the Cote d'Azur of *Morning in Antibes*, or in his one travel book about the middle east, *Double Vision: American Thoughts Abroad*, there is the same spareness of style and ability to convey symbolic meaning and literal description with the one stroke of the pen. The second paragraph of *The Paragon* begins:

> Pierson, like all the residential colleges at Yale, had been built to withstand attack. A Bastille psychology had dominated its construction and that of the entire University, girding the campus for obviously imminent assaults by mobs of storming townspeople. Facing the outside world were, at the forefront, the battlements of the Old Campus, frowning intimidatingly down upon the New Haven Green and its three meek churches, inoffensive and cowed. The rear of the campus was blocked by the Gibraltar known as the Payne Whitney Gymnasium, a citadel so formidable that only the most advanced weaponry could have reduced it. In between there were the many residential colleges, designed like the precincts of some long-established and only infrequently attacked permanent military installation. . . .

Throughout all his writing there is a theme which most attracts John Knowles—it could be called wildness in the midst of civilization. The sense of energy, of strength, of choice which pervades his writing bespeaks that "awful ferity with which good men and lovers meet" which Thoreau spoke of, and each of these characters must face the dark side of their moon to emerge into their uniqueness.

—David L. Powell

---

**KOESTLER, Arthur.** British. Born in Budapest, Hungary, 5 September 1905; became a British subject after World War II. Educated at the University of Vienna, 1922–26. Married Dorothy Asher in 1935 (divorced, 1950); Mamaine Paget, 1950 (divorced, 1953); Cynthia Jefferies, 1965. Foreign Correspondent for the Ullstein chain, Berlin, in the Middle East, 1927–29, and in Paris, 1929–30; Foreign Editor, *B.Z. am Mittag*, and Science Editor, *Vossische Zeitung*, Berlin, 1930–32. Member, Graf Zeppelin polar expedition, 1931. Member of the Communist Party, 1932–38. War Correspondent, London *News Chronicle*, in Spain, 1936–37; imprisoned by Nationalists; exchanged through intervention of the British Government. Imprisoned in France, 1939–40; then joined French Foreign Legion, 1940–41, escaped to Britain, and served in the British Pioneer Corps, 1941–42. After discharge, worked for the Ministry of Information, London, and as a night ambulance driver. Special Correspondent in Palestine, for *The Times*, London, 1945, and the *Manchester Guardian* and *New York Herald Tribune*, 1948. Visiting Chubb Fellow, Yale University, New Haven, Connecticut, 1950; Fellow, Center for Advanced Study in the Behavioral Sciences, Stanford University, California, 1964–65. Recipient: Sonning Prize, University of Copenhagen, 1968. LL.D., Queen's University, Kingston, Ontario, 1968. Fellow, Royal Society of Literature, 1957. C.B.E. (Commander, Order of the British Empire), 1972. Address: c/o A. D. Peters, 10 Buckingham Street, London W.C.2, England.

PUBLICATIONS

Novels

    *The Gladiators*, translated by Edith Simon. London, Cape, and New York, Macmillan, 1939.
    *Darkness at Noon*, translated by Daphne Hardy. London, Cape, 1940; New York, Macmillan, 1941.
    *Arrival and Departure*. London, Cape, and New York, Macmillan, 1943.
    *Thieves in the Night: Chronicle of an Experiment*. New York, Macmillan, and London, Macmillan, 1946.
    *The Age of Longing*. London, Collins, and New York, Macmillan, 1951.

Uncollected Short Stories

    "Les Temps Heroiques", in *Occident* (Paris), March 1948.
    "The Episode", in *Encounter* (London), December 1968.
    "The Chimaeras", in *Playboy* (Chicago), March 1969.

Play

*Twilight Bar: An Escapade in Four Acts* (produced Paris and Baltimore, 1946).   London, Cape, and New York, Macmillan, 1945.

Other

*Von Weissen Nachten und Roten Tagen*.   Kharkov, Ukrainian State Publishers for National Minorities, 1933.
*Menschenopfer Unerhort*.   Paris, Carrefour, 1937.
*Spanish Testament* (autobiography).   London, Gollancz, 1937; abridged as *Dialogue with Death*, New York, Macmillan, 1942.
*Scum of the Earth* (autobiography).   London, Cape, and New York, Macmillan, 1941.
*The Yogi and the Commissar and Other Essays*.   London, Cape, and New York, Macmillan, 1945.
*Insight and Outlook: An Inquiry into the Common Foundations of Science, Art, and Social Ethics*.   London, Macmillan, and New York, Macmillan, 1949.
*Promise and Fulfillment: Palestine 1917–1949*.   London, Macmillan, and New York, Macmillan, 1949.
*Arrow in the Blue* (autobiography).   London, Collins-Hamish Hamilton, and New York, Macmillan, 1952.
*The Invisible Writing* (autobiography).   London, Collins-Hamish Hamilton, and New York, Macmillan, 1954.
*The Trail of the Dinosaurs and Other Essays*.   London, Collins, and New York, Macmillan, 1955.
*Reflections on Hanging*.   London, Gollancz, and New York, Macmillan, 1957.
*The Sleepwalkers: A History of Man's Changing Vision of the Universe*.   London, Hutchinson, and New York, Macmillan, 1959; section published as *The Watershed: A Biography of Johannes Kepler*, New York, Doubleday, 1960.
*The Lotus and the Robot*.   London, Hutchinson, 1960; New York, Macmillan, 1961.
*Hanged by the Neck: An Exposure of Capital Punishment in England*, with C. H. Rolph.   London, Penguin, 1961.
*The Act of Creation*.   London, Hutchinson, and New York, Macmillan, 1964.
*The Ghost in the Machine*.   London, Hutchinson, 1967; New York, Macmillan, 1968.
*Drinkers of Infinity: Essays 1955–1967*.   London, Hutchinson, 1968.
*The Case of the Midwife Toad*.   London, Hutchinson, and New York, Macmillan, 1971.
*The Roots of Coincidence*.   London, Hutchinson, and New York, Random House, 1972.

Editor, *Suicide of a Nation: An Enquiry into the State of Britain Today*.   London, Hutchinson, 1963; New York, Macmillan, 1964.
Editor, with J. R. Smythies, *Beyond Reductionism: New Perspectives in the Life Sciences: The Alpbach Symposium*.   London, Hutchinson, 1969; New York, Macmillan, 1970.

Critical Studies: "Arthur Koestler" by Derek Stanford, in *Writers of Today*, London, Sidgwick and Jackson, 1946; "Arthur Koestler: The Russian Myth" by J. B. Coates, in *The Crisis of the Human Person*, London, Longman, 1949; "The Art of Koestler" by V.S. Pritchett, in *Books in General*, London, Chatto and Windus, 1953; *Arthur Koestler* by John Atkins, London, Spearman, 1956; foreword by John H. Durston to *The Watershed*, 1960; *Arthur Koestler: Das literarische Werk* by Peter Alfred Huber, Zurich, Fretz and Wasmuth, 1962; Introduction by V.S. Pritchett to *Darkness at Noon*, New York, Time, 1962; commentary by Harry Browne in *Darkness at Noon*, London, Longman, 1968; Introduction by Goronwy Rees to *Darkness at Noon*, London, Heron Books, 1970.

Arthur Koestler comments:

Out of the twenty-five books that I have published to date—1971—only five are novels; thus I can call myself only one-fifth of a novelist. On the other hand, one of the novels, *Darkness at Noon*, has sold more copies than all my other books put together, which somehow redresses the balance. It also makes some of my friends feel that I am wasting my time by not sticking to fiction. I do not agree with them. From my school-days onward, my interests have been divided, and sometimes rather painfully torn, between the two cultures. Out of my quarrels with the human condition I made my novels; the other books are attempts to analyse that same condition in scientific terms. In my more optimistic moments it seems to me that the two add up to a whole. At any rate, without both media I would feel only half alive.

The five novels have one basic theme in common: whether, or to what extent, and in what circumstances, a noble end justifies the use of ignoble means. Whether, when, how far it is justified to inflict pain on individuals in the higher interests of humanity. At what point the surgeon's lancet turns into the butcher's hatchet. How the love of mankind in the abstract can engender contempt for man in the flesh. How movements for gradual reform go off the boil; how revolutionary movements start like fresh mountain springs and end up as polluted rivers strewn with corpses.

The problem of Ends and Means sounds theoretical, but for my generation of Europeans it has a concrete, bloody meaning. We have lived through 1914–18, the War to end all Wars; listened to the rival promises of the Classless Society and the Thousand Years Reich, and witnessed the holocausts they brought in their wake with relentless logic. Most of my erstwhile friends were sacrificed to that logic in the death factories of Utopia.

*The Gladiators, Darkness at Noon* and *Arrival and Departure* can be read as a trilogy. The first has as its subject the abortive revolt of the Roman Slaves in 73–71 B.C. The slave army, led by Spartacus, defeated one Roman general after another and very nearly conquered the capital, but went to pieces—because its leaders did *not* accept that the end justifies the means and rejected revolutionary terror.

In *Darkness at Noon* we witness the opposite tragedy—reason running amok in the great Russian Purges, where the victims concurred with their executioners that expediency must come before morality, and the revolution must be allowed to devour its own children if it is to triumph in the end. In *Arrival and Departure* the same problem is transferred from the historical plane to that of individual psychology. Its hero, young Peter Slavek, suffers a nervous breakdown and comes out of it with a tentative solution of the dilemma that haunted him—and the author.

If the theme of the trilogy is the ethics of revolution, the theme of *Thieves in the Night* is the ethics of survival—as reflected in the tangled events that preceded the birth of the State of Israel. Lastly, *The Age of Longing*, written at the height of the Cold War, can be read as a kind of parable or warning—a companion piece to *Nineteen Eighty-Four*.

Two of the novels—*Darkness at Noon* and *Thieves in the Night*—had unexpected political repercussions which I have described in *The Invisible Writing* (p. 464, pp. 490 ff.). These two incidents are to me the most satisfactory rewards a writer can hope for.

My first two novels I wrote in German, but collaborated on their English translations. Since 1940 I have written only in English.

\*          \*          \*

As a novelist, Arthur Koestler belongs to that phase of Western culture which reflects the abandonment and destruction of blind faith in Russian Communism that distinguished the nineteen-thirties and forties. Koestler had himself been a member of the Communist Party for seven years—from 1932 to 1938—and like many others (Max Eastman, say, in the U.S. and Douglas Hyde in Britain) in his reversion he was as emphatic and adamant as he had earlier been in his adherence. But whereas Eastman and Hyde were publicists, theorists and commentators, expressing their position in critical terms, Koestler (besides performing these roles also) added through his fictional writing a creative and imaginative wing to this phase of psychological and political withdrawal. Readable as his four main novels remain, it was their topicality at the time of publication which focussed so much attention upon them. As imaginative expositions, in terms of human drama, of this particular moment of history they have a permanent value. Compared with such a political novel as H. G. Wells' *The New Machiavellian*, these fictions of Arthur Koestler are more immediately informed of the facts and forces operating in their field. As a committed long-acquainted member, he was familiar with the behaviour and procedure of the Communist Party. Wells—apart from his meeting with Lord Curzon in a London club—knew little of the structure and hierarchy of the Conservative Party.

But it was not this political inside information solely which made Arthur Koestler the imaginative chronicler of "the dying god" Communism. Fiction, as an art-form, has its own obligations and needs; and the person who would write a good novel must feel a duty to both his subject and his medium. Unlike so many novelists dealing with polemical issues, Arthur Koestler recognised this double observance called for from him. Some of the ideas which he held regarding the function of the modern novel may be found by referring to an article "Les Tentations du Romancier" in *La France Libre* which was later reprinted in his critical book *The Yogi and the Commissar*. In it, he envisages the author as a figure looking at the world from behind a window. The first temptation which visits him—at a time when the scene grows riotous, when truncheons are drawn and stones thrown in the street—is to close the curtains and settle to work by artificial light. This is a return to the ivory tower. The second temptation which the author may feel is an urge to throw the window up, leap upon the sill and there participate in the struggle by exhorting the side whose cause he favours. This is the position of the propagandist. With neither of these roles does Arthur Koestler agree. The author must master the art of mental balance; achieve by discipline a kind of nervous patience. He must learn how to stand before the open window; controlled though not indifferent, sympathetic but not a partisan. A strong-point of intelligence and imagination between two magnetic tensions—such is Arthur Koestler's idea of what the political novel should be; and such, in fact, within reasonable limits, his own works of fiction are.

*The Gladiators* was the book with which Arthur Koestler made his début as a novelist in England. Its subject was the rebellion of Spartacus, known in Roman History as the Slave War. In this book the invoice of hope is matched by a crippling bill of disappointment. At first, the gladiators, slaves and under-dogs are successful in their venture against tyranny and officialdom. Spartacus founds a Sun State and allies himself with powerful enemies of the Empire. But the revolutionary spirit of his followers becomes corrupt and withers, and in the end they are massacred by the cohorts under Crassus who lines the Appian Way to Rome with the crucified bodies of these pioneers of equality. The inward corruption of the revolutionary ideal, in this phase of Roman history, constituted a topical parallel with the corruption of Soviet Communism under Stalin.

This was a theme which Arthur Koestler's most famous novel *Darkness at Noon* was to explore, but another train of thought in the novel which he was subsequently to develop was the conflict between Ends and Means. "He who yearns for the Sun State and the Realm of Goodwill should not use political wiles and sinister facetious tricks," declares one character, to which another—intimating that there is no short cut to Utopia—replies: "The law of detours. None can act outside it. Everyone with a goal in front is forced to its baleful track," a conclusion which the first speaker will not accept. "Many a man," he says," has strutted the road of tyranny, at the outset solely with the purpose of serving his lofty ideals, and in the end the road alone has made him carry on."

*Darkness at Noon* presents us with an old-guard Bolshevik deciding to make a public confession to the Party Torquemadas of political crimes he has never committed. The "crimes" in question constitute not actions but errors (if indeed they be errors) of judgment. The trial, we see, is a trial for heresy—for thinking for oneself, out of prescribed limits. Like Nicolas Berdyaev's book *Origins of Russian Communism*, this novel shows the essentially theological nature of Soviet thinking—its bigotry and crusading ardour, its unreality and ruthless inhumanity.

*Arrival and Departure*, his next published novel, may be regarded as the continuation of the debate between Political Man and Ethical Man which made up the drama of *Darkness at Noon*. Instead of listening to the brief of the political sense (whose canons are necessity and expediency) and the ethical sense (whose canon is conscience), here we witness the tug-of-war between the dictates of psychology (whose canons are pleasure and self-fulfilment) and the plea of the spirit (whose proof and goal are the sense of glory). The questions raised by this story are of the deepest importance. Sonia, the psychologist, suggests that all who oppose society—reformers, rebels, revolutionaries—do so out of a sense of guilt: neurosis. She traces the zeal for violent change in Peter—an ex-martyr in the cause of revolution—to a subconscious desire to expiate, by hard endurance, a sin committed in early childhood. Acceptance, she tells him, is the secret of "the good life." At first, Peter is deeply impressed and prepares to leave Europe to rejoin his hedonistic girl-friend in America. At the last moment, however, he gives up this bright lure of pleasure to return to the dangerous political struggle in his own country. The dictates of the spirit have triumphed.

*Thieves in the Night* again shows Arthur Koestler fixing his attention upon one of those contemporary situations in which a group or party of people are trying to interpret moral concepts in political terms. In it we see the Palestinian Jews (before the foundation of the State of Israel) "trying," as Anthony Burgess puts it, "to build a society in the face of injustice and their own awareness of how suffering may corrupt rather than enoble." Professor Harold Fisch describes it as "probably the best novel in English so far to deal with the new reality," and goes on to consider how well the author—a sympathetic observer—has none the less eschewed Zionist blinkers in describing the complex field of forces. "What Koestler discerns," he writes,

> is a human structure still marked by duality and paradox. He praises the courage of the new fighters and settlers but smiles at what he feels is the absurdity of their brand of religious mysticism and the quixoticism of their practical socialism. Past and present have not (for him) convincingly joined hands: romance and realism have not been made one.

British Communists and their fellow-travellers powerfully attacked Koestler, ostensibly for his political pessimism, but actually for his devastating exposure of Party-line tyranny in the Soviet. They claimed that his "thesis [had] no relevance to the English scene," which might partly be allowed to be true, largely because the machinations of Communism in Britain were comparatively without due effect.

—Derek Stanford

---

**KOPS, Bernard.** British. Born in London, 28 November 1926. Educated in various London elementary schools, to age thirteen. Married Erica Gordon in 1956; has four children. Has worked as a docker, chef, salesman, waiter, lift man and barrow boy. Recipient: Arts Council Bursary, for drama, 1957. Address: Flat 1, 35 Canfield Gardens, London N.W.6, England.

PUBLICATIONS

Novels

*Awake for Mourning*.   London, MacGibbon and Kee, 1958.

*Motorbike*.   London, New English Library, 1962.
*Yes from No-Man's Land*.   London, MacGibbon and Kee, 1965; New York, Coward
   McCann, 1966.
*The Dissent of Dominick Shapiro*.   London, MacGibbon and Kee, 1966; New York,
   Coward McCann, 1967.
*By the Waters of Whitechapel*.   London, Bodley Head, 1969; New York, Norton, 1970.
*The Passionate Past of Gloria Gaye*.   London, Secker and Warburg, and New York,
   Norton, 1971.


Plays

*The Hamlet of Stepney Green* (produced Oxford, 1957; London and New York, 1958).
   London, Evans, 1959.
*Goodbye World* (produced Guildford, Surrey, 1959).
*Change for the Angel* (produced London, 1960).
*The Dream of Peter Mann* (produced Edinburgh, 1960).   London, Penguin, 1960.
*Enter Solly Gold* (produced Wellingborough, Northamptonshire, 1962; London, 1970).
   Included in *Four Plays*, 1964.
*Four Plays* (includes *The Hamlet of Stepney Green*, *Enter Solly Gold*, *Home Sweet
   Honeycomb*, and *The Lemmings*).   London, MacGibbon and Kee, 1964.
*The Boy Who Wouldn't Play Jesus* (juvenile).   London, Cassell, 1965.
*Stray Cats and Empty Bottles* (produced London, 1967).
*David It Is Getting Dark* (produced Rennes, France, 1970).   Paris, Gallimard, 1969.


Plays produced on radio and television.


Verse

*Poems*.   London, Bell and Baker Press, 1955.
*Poems and Songs*.   Lowestoft, Suffolk, Scorpion Press, 1958.
*An Anemone for Antigone*.   Lowestoft, Suffolk, Scorpion Press, 1959.
*Erica, I Want to Read You Something*.   Lowestoft, Suffolk, Scorpion Press, and New
   York, Walker, 1967.
*For the Record*.   London, Secker and Warburg, 1971.


Other

*The World Is a Wedding* (autobiography).   London, MacGibbon and Kee, 1963;
   New York, Coward McCann, 1964.


*          *          *


The novels of Bernard Kops may be taken as studies in the disintegration of those exclusive
closed Jewish communities which were a feature of English society before the Second
World War. It is particularly London Jewish life which Bernard Kops presents: that of the
poor East End or prosperous, quietly ostentatious Golders Green. The tone of his fiction
begins as tragic and elegaic in the novel *Yes from No-Man's Land* and becomes wildly,
sometimes preposterously, comic in *The Dissent of Dominick Shapiro* and *By the Waters
of Whitechapel*.

*Yes from No-Man's Land* is largely a stream-of-consciousness novel. Joe Levene, dying
in Hackney Hospital, recapitulates his past experience of pogrom and persecution in Eastern

Europe and poverty in the East End of London in the Thirties. Thoughts on existence in Israel combine with these recollections to constitute a sort of history of his race in terms of the last two generations. Joe's lamentations are the more pathetic since he knows his son Barry will not follow in his footsteps or beget a child to continue the tradition. Professor Harold Fisch has described this work as "ultimately an elegy for the passing of the Jew and his faith."

The same authority has characterised Bernard Kops' play *The Dream of Peter Mann* as an illustration of the "radical revolt against the Jewish mother [which] has been building up in the mid-twentieth century in Jewish writing on both sides of the Atlantic." The author's portrait of Sonia the mother shows her as bullying and assertive, not from any sadistic tendency but from an over-riding force of otherwise unchannelled affection. The bearing of this work upon Bernard Kops' fiction is readily apparent. He is one of those authors —Philip Roth and Montagu Haltrecht are two others—who have written novels with a central theme of the Jew as drop-out figure. The tone of the most outstanding of these fictions is richly humorous, and the conformity from which the characters seek to release themselves is familial rather than religious.

Whereas it is the mother who is seen as the obstacle in *The Dream of Peter Mann*, it is the father in *The Dissent of Dominick Shapiro* who features the more largely. But both the parents of the young sixteen-year-old Dominick have helped to create confusion in their son not through oppressive authority so much as excessive indulgence. Dominick's revolt, in which he runs away to join what his father terms "a Hippie Kibbutz," is therefore just an aspect of adolescent pyrotechnics and no carefully cogitated protest-gesture at all. It is, in fact partially a satire on hipster social theories (one of Dominick's young protesting friends describing himself as "a Nothingist").

*By the Waters of Whitechapel* is probably Bernard Kops' masterpiece. Aubrey, at thirty-five, is still tied to his mother's apron-strings. He lives mostly in fantasy and when those fantasies impinge, in action, upon the outward world, the comic dimensions of the novel receive an additional inflation. Aubrey's mother keeps a little sweet-shop in a street off the Commercial Road, but Aubrey—all-but-unemployed and living on his mother's charity— dreams of himself as a rich barrister and seeks to make others accept this dream. Aubrey's fantasies of material wealth and power are, of course, the engines of his own drop-out impulses—a further ironical and paradoxical feature in a wonderfully ironical fantasy. Bernard Kops has, deservedly, a reputation as a poet, and the inventive and colourful use of language in *By the Waters of Whitechapel* proves that a transition to prose cannot dampen or diminish the author's fervid verbal imagination.

—Derek Stanford

---

**KOSINSKI, Jerzy (Nikodem).** American. Born in Lodz, Poland, 14 June 1933; emigrated to the United States in 1957; became a United States citizen, 1965. Educated at the University of Lodz, 1950–55, M.A. in history 1953, M.A. in political science 1955; Columbia University, New York, 1958–64; New School for Social Research, New York, 1962–65. Married Mary Hayward Weir in 1962 (deceased, 1968). Aspirant (Associate Professor), Polish Academy of Sciences, Warsaw, 1955–57; Fellow, Center for Advanced Studies, Wesleyan University, Middletown, Connecticut, 1968–69; Senior Fellow, Council for the Humanities, and Visiting Lecturer in English Prose, Princeton University, New Jersey, 1969–70; Professor of English Prose and Criticism, School of Drama, and Resident Fellow, Davenport College, Yale University, New Haven, Connecticut, 1970–72. Member of the Executive Board, American P.E.N. Club. Recipient: Polish Academy of Sciences grant, 1955; Ford Fellowship, 1958; Prix du Meilleur Livre Etranger, France, 1966; Guggenheim Fellowship,

1967; National Book Award, 1969; American Academy of Arts and Letters grant, 1970; John Golden Fellowship in Playwriting, 1970. Address: Suite 9–I, 440 East 79th Street, New York, New York 10021, U.S.A.

PUBLICATIONS

Novels

*The Painted Bird.*   Boston, Houghton Mifflin, 1965; London, W. H. Allen, 1966; revised edition, New York, Modern Library, 1970.
*Steps.*   New York, Random House, 1968; London, Bodley Head, 1969.
*Being There.*   New York, Harcourt Brace, and London, Bodley Head, 1971.

Other

*The Future Is Ours, Comrade* (as Joseph Novak).   New York, Doubleday, 1960; London, Reinhardt, 1961.
*No Third Path* (as Joseph Novak).   New York, Doubleday, 1962.
*Notes of the Author on "The Painted Bird" 1965.*   New York, Scientia Factum, 1965.
*The Art of the Self: Essays à propos "Steps".*   New York, Scientia Factum, 1968.
*The Time of Life: The Time of Art* (essays; in Dutch).   Amsterdam, De Bezige Bij, 1970.

Criticial Studies: "Out of the Fires" by Stanley Kauffmann, in *New Republic* (Washington, D.C.), 26 October 1968; "The Other Side of the Moon" by Irving Howe, in *Harper's* (New York), March 1969; "The Fabrication of a Culture Hero" by John W. Aldridge, in *Saturday Review* (New York), 24 April 1971.

Jerzy Kosinski comments:

As an actor playing Hamlet is neither Hamlet nor merely an actor, but, rather, an actor as Hamlet, so is a fictive event neither an actual event nor totally a created fiction with no base in experience: it is an event as fiction. A symbol is both concrete and abstract. It is neither literal reality nor illusion; it is both illusory and concrete. Naturally, the stimulus that gave birth to it can never be fully known; if it could, there would be no need for the symbol. It can never be defined; it can, at best, be interpreted. . . .

The modern literary use of language is contrapuntal, employed to lay bare the significant area which exists between language and action, and to highlight the gulf between them. [Often] the situation is taken further; in the attempt to recall the primitive, the symbols are sought more pertinently and immediately than through the superficial process of speech and dialogue. In addition, the sense of alienation is heightened by depriving the characters of the ability to communicate freely. Observation is a silent process; without the means of participation, the silent one must observe. Perhaps this silence is also a metaphor for dissociation from the community and from something greater. This feeling of alienation floats on the surface of the work and manifests the author's awareness, perhaps unconscious, of his break with the wholeness of self.

—from *Notes of the Author*, 1965.

There is a kind of grotesque . . . in which symbols rationally unrelated in subject, tone, and emotional content are lured together into a collage which the mind comprehends on a subconscious level. Here, again, the work produces in us responses we cannot normally summon up; the aroused emotions take us by surprise, bringing to the surface truths which lie beneath.

Displacing particular images, shifting them into contexts with which they are not usually associated, makes us aware of another reality in the midst of our commonplace one. Bosch was a master of this kind of grotesque. By placing sexual scenes in settings which require religious ones and *vice versa*, he displayed the exaggerated, the twisted, the strange subconscious links which bind the mind. The result is a dream-like, nightmarish reality which shocks, astonishes, and is easily accessible. In truth, its familiarity and its power to stun are fused. The grotesque is the language of the emotions which silently provokes our actions. Hence the subversive quality of art.

—from *The Art of the Self*, 1968.

\*      \*      \*

*The Painted Bird* and *Steps* are distinguished works by Jerzy Kosinski, who was born in Poland in 1933 but who came to the United States after World War II. Although Europe is the principal locale for his two novels and English is a second language for him, Kosinski writes an appropriately taut English, almost a subdued psychological lyricism on human abuse.

Both novels are committed to the outrageous. The plot of *The Painted Bird* centers around the harsh experiences of a boy six to twelve years of age, who wanders around Eastern Europe (presumably Poland) during the years of World War II. Considered a gypsy or a Jew by the superstitious and malicious peasants who inhabit the villages through which he wanders, the child is subject to or witnesses many forms of human and animal insult and degradation. Kosinski keeps a tight rein on his prose, which at one point depicts the rape of an entire village. Many of the scenes take on a mythic import as the violent images move from their particular shock to harsh and vivid metaphors for the human condition—not the human condition under the aegis of all time, but that condition as it has been felt in this century and particularly during and after World War II.

In its infatuation with nightmare, with victims and with violence, Kosinski's novels, critics have pointed out, show the influence of Kafka and Babel and Céline and Dinesen. His novels also have scenes, particularly those involving the human body, that leave one with the impact of images recalled from movies. Kosinski's writing can also be compared with pictures by Bosch, or Goya, or Francis Bacon. His visual effects are strong and shocking. On the other hand, human speech is kept to a minimum, none appearing at all in *The Painted Bird*, with only a few conversations recorded in the next novel. Kosinski's desire or disinclination to record human conversation can be a way of gauging the ability of his main character to explore his experiences with another person.

In *Steps*, which won the National Book Award in 1969, the narrative element is almost entirely removed. The series of vignettes that constitutes *Steps* does not possess the narrative advantages of *The Painted Bird*. However, the scenes in the second novel do bear upon one another. By the end of *Steps*, it can be assumed that the debauched or seduced woman who then must go on living is Kosinski's image of the muse.

The fiction of Kosinski is testimonial to man's ability to invent, to witness, to experience, and finally to explore human abuse. In that regard it is surely a reflection of 20th century experience. But his novels are something more than testimony to the history that is reduced to personal nightmare. The obsessions with human violation in Kosinski's works are strange hymns to human suffering. To transcend that suffering, or to place it in some meaningful context, would be for Kosinski a final dishonor.

—Richard J. Fein

**KRIGE, Uys.** South African. Born in Swellendam, Cape Province, in 1910. Educated at Stellenbosch University, B.A. in law 1929. Married Lydia Lindeque in 1937; has two children. Lived in France and Spain, 1931–36. Newspaper Correspondent, Cape Town, 1936. War Correspondent in Egypt and Abyssinia during World War II; captured; Prisoner of War in Italy, 1941 until his escape in 1943. Returned to South Africa in 1946. Address: P.O. Box 25, Onrust (C.P.), South Africa.

PUBLICATIONS

Short Stories

> *Die Palmboom* (in Afrikaans). Pretoria, Van Schaik, 1940.
> *The Dream and the Desert.* London, Collins, 1953; Boston, Houghton Mifflin, 1954.
> *Orphan of the Desert.* Cape Town, John Malherbe, 1967.

Plays

> *Magdalena Retief* (in Afrikaans). Cape Town, Unie-Volkspers, 1938; revised edition, 1948.
> *Die Wir Muur* (in Afrikaans). Cape Town, Unie-Volkspers, 1940.
> *Alle Paaie Gaan Na Rome* (in Afrikaans). Cape Town, Unie-Volkspers, 1949.
> *Die Twee Lampe* (in Afrikaans). Johannesburg, Afrikaanse Pers, 1951; translated as *The Two Lamps,* Cape Town, Hollands-Afrikaanse Uitgewers Maatskappy, 1964.
> *Die Sluipskutter* (in Afrikaans). Johannesburg, Afrikaanse Pers, 1951.
> *Die Ryk Weduwee* (in Afrikaans). Johannesburg, Afrikaanse Pers, 1953.
> *Die Goue Kring* (in Afrikaans). Cape Town, Balkema, 1956.
> *The Sniper and Other One-Act Plays.* Cape Town, Hollands-Afrikaanse Uitgewers Maatskappy, 1962.
> *Yerma* (in Afrikaans), adaptation of a play by Lorca. Cape Town, Hollands-Afrikaanse Uitgewers Maatskappy, 1963.

Verse

> *Kentering* (in Afrikaans). Pretoria, Van Schaik, 1935.
> *Rooidag* (in Afrikaans). Pretoria, Van Schaik, 1940.
> *Die Einde van die Pad* (in Afrikaans). Pretoria, Van Schaik, 1947.
> *Hart Sonder Hawe* (in Afrikaans). Cape Town, Unie-Volkspers, 1949.
> *Vir die Luit en die Kitaar* (in Afrikaans). Johannesburg, Afrikaanse Pers, 1950.
> *Ballade van die Groot Begeer* (in Afrikaans). Cape Town, Balkema, 1960.
> *Eluard en die Surrealisme* (in Afrikaans). Cape Town, Hollands-Afrikaanese Uitgewers Maatskappy, 1962.

Other

> *The Way Out: Italian Intermezzo.* London, Collins, and Cape Town, Unie-Volkspers, 1946; revised edition, Cape Town, Maskew Miller, 1955.
> *Sol y Sombra* (in Afrikaans). Pretoria, Unie-Volkspers, 1948; revised edition, Pretoria, Van Schaik, 1955.
> *Ver in die Wereld* (sketches; in Afrikaans). Johannesburg, Afrikaanse Pers, 1951.

*Sout van die Aarde* (sketches; in Afrikaans).  Cape Town, Hollands-Afrikaanse Uitgewers Maatskappy, 1961.

Editor, *Poems of Roy Campbell*.  Cape Town, Maskew Miller, 1960.
Editor, *Olive Schreiner: A Selection*.  Cape Town and London, Oxford University Press, 1968; New York, Oxford University Press, 1969.
Editor, with Jack Cope, *The Penguin Book of South African Verse*.  London, Penguin, 1968.

Critical Study: *Uys Krige* by Christina Van Heyningen and Jacques Berthoud, New York, Twayne, 1966.

\*       \*       \*

Uys Krige is one of the very few white South African writers who have established a literary reputation in both the official languages of the country: English and Afrikaans. Of Afrikaner descent, and brought up in an Afrikaans environment, Krige's first allegiance is, naturally, to Afrikaans; and his contribution to its rapidly growing literature is considerable, comprising poetry, plays and criticism. Characteristic of his work is an obvious delight in exploring the nuances of a relatively new and constantly changing language. His linguistic facility is seen to good advantage in his successful comedy, *Die Ryk Weduwee* (*The Wealthy Widow*), in much of his recent poetry, and in his translations from Spanish, notably Garcia Lorca's play, *Yerma*. He has also successfully translated *Twelfth Night*, adapting Shakespeare's verse patterns into idiomatic and colourful Afrikaans.

Krige's interest in English, consciously developed throughout his writing career, was stimulated by his extensive pre-war travels in Europe, and by his experience during the Second World War, first as a war correspondent in Africa, later as a prisoner of war in Italy. Contact with Europe sharpened his awareness of European civilization, and contact with Englishmen stimulated his desire to write for an English audience. On his return to South Africa in 1946, he began not only to write in English, but to translate some of his own work, in an attempt to bridge the language barrier which, traditionally, separates the white races in South Africa. His work has thus become available to a much wider audience than that reached by most Afrikaans authors, and has opened hitherto largely inaccessible areas of experience to the non-Afrikaans reader. Krige, that is, writes as an Afrikaner, about Afrikaners, and his work is valuable for its patently honest, consistently realistic account of a people who, more often than not, have been portrayed as conscienceless, narrow-minded white supremacists. Krige's Afrikaners are ordinary people, involved in the common human experiences of birth, love and death. He is particularly conscious of Afrikaner traditions, which both link the people with, and separate them from their European ancestors. He is aware, too, of their limitations, as well as justly proud of their achievements. His poetic sensibility enables him to see his characters in a close and living relationship with the peculiar South African landscape, which has always had a strong fascination for him, and which he presents with accuracy and deep feeling, disguising neither its harshness nor its great beauty.

"The Coffin" and "The Dream", both of which appear in *The Dream and the Desert*, demonstrate one side of Krige's awareness. "The Coffin" is a story about a kindly Afrikaner patriarch, living life to the full though always conscious of death, and prepared to meet it, with his coffin standing ready in the loft. "The Dream" is a delightful evocation of a half-rural South African childhood, in which humorous irony controls but does not destroy the deliberately romantic nostalgia for a way of life which is rapidly disappearing. *The Two Lamps* displays another facet of the Afrikaner personality, and of Krige's talent. This play, which has received much critical acclaim in America as well as in South Africa, dramatises, in a typically South Africa version, the conflict between father and sons. It presents an uncompromising study of the Calvinist conscience, which is powerless, finally, to avert overwhelming tragedy. Set against a haunting background of mist, marsh and lush farmland, *The Two Lamps* is possibly Krige's finest achievement.

An important part of Krige's work is not confined exclusively to South Africa. Much of this is criticism, translation (from French and Spanish), and a popular genre in South Africa, travel literature. In addition however, there is some fine war writing, in which Krige's talent for objective reportage is seen to good advantage. *The Way Out* is an account of Krige's escape from an Italian prison camp, but it is more than a simple escape story. The narrative develops into a penetrating psychological study of men under stress, and at the same time celebrates the loyalty and courage of the impoverished Italian partisans who risked their lives to help the escapers. "The Death of the Zulu", also based on his war experiences, is one of the few stories in which Krige attempts to deal with black characters. Although it is very slight, being hardly more than the description of a single incident (one man's death in the desert), the story shows Krige's ability to present all his characters, whatever their race, with genuine sympathy.

Where many South African writers succumb to a self-conscious humanitarianism, understandable in the present political context, but often destructive of literary merit, it is Krige's distinctive achievement to write without any obvious bias: his work thus reflects the reality of the South Africa he knows, and of which he is part. Although this reality is limited (to the extent that it virtually excludes black South Africa, and includes "non-whites" only as servants and inferiors), it is a reality which is a living part of the South African experience, and deserves recognition as such.

—Ursula Laredo

---

**LA GUMA, Alex.** South African. Born in Cape Town, 20 February 1925. Educated at Trafalgar High School, Cape Town; Cape Technical College, Cape Town; London School of Journalism. Married Blanche Valerie in 1954; has two children. Staff Writer, *New Age Weekly*, Cape Town, 1955–62. Active in political movement in South Africa; arrested for treason, 1956, acquitted, 1960; proscribed under Suppression of Communism Act, 1962; under house arrest, Cape Town, 1962–66, and detained in solitary confinement, 1963 and 1966; exiled to Great Britain in 1966, where he now works as a free-lance Journalist. Recipient: Afro-Asian Writers Association Lotus Prize, 1969. Address: 36 Woodland Gardens, London N10 3UA, England.

PUBLICATIONS

Novels

*And a Threefold Cord.* Berlin, Seven Seas, 1964.
*The Stone Country.* Berlin, Seven Seas, 1967.
*In the Fog of the Season's End.* London, Heinemann, 1972.

Short Stories

*A Walk in the Night.* Ibadan, Nigeria, Mbari, 1962.

*Quartet: New Voices from South Africa*, with others.  New York, Crown, 1963;
London, Heinemann, 1965.
*A Walk in the Night and Other Stories*.  London, Heinemann, 1967.

Critical Studies: *The African Image* by Ezekiel Mphahlele, London, Heinemann, 1962;
"Tribute to Alex La Guma" by Ezekiel Mphahlele, in *Sechaba* (London), February 1971.

Alex La Guma comments:

All my works are concerned with the contemporary South African scene, particularly
the experiences of the non-White population.

\*       \*       \*

Alex La Guma is a naturalistic novelist and short story writer who specializes in docu-
menting the misery in which lower-class nonwhites in South Africa are forced to live. Most
of his heroes are men made criminals by their environment. Underdogs, perpetual losers,
victims of circumstance and unjust laws, they nevertheless possess a stubborn courage and
a will to resist the forces that push them to the bottom. They are rebels with a cause.

In La Guma's fiction our sympathies are always with the underdog and the underdog is
always nonwhite. However, not all nonwhites are sympathetically portrayed. Those who
take jobs as prison guards or policeman are considered sell-outs to the white world, and those
who rob and murder their own people are despised. La Guma does not stoop to tell the reader
all this. He sets his characters in motion, stands back, and lets the reader judge them for himself. La Guma's work is so skillfully done that the reader cannot fail to develop the right
attitudes and make the appropriate judgements.

La Guma's style is concrete, vivid, sometimes impressionistic, always documentary.
Often his protest is conveyed entirely through starkly etched pictures of oppression and injustice. A crowded tenement building in a Cape Town ghetto is described in minute detail,
testifying to the degeneracy and moral decay in the society at large. A pleasant-looking stone
prison with thick walls separating overprivileged white prisoners from suffering black
prisoners becomes a metaphor for South Africa. Even the most trifling incident or image in
La Guma's fiction is likely to have symbolic undertones, to be pregnant with social message.
La Guma is probably the most committed of all South Africa's militant nonwhite writers in
exile.

La Guma's graphic social realism resembles the naturalism of American novelists such
as Frank Norris, Theodore Dreiser and James Farrell. The hero is seen as an individual at
the mercy of his environment and passions, a man who doesn't stand much of a chance unless
he is well-adapted or willing to adapt to the particular set of circumstances in which he finds
himself. However, La Guma differs from the American naturalists in his belief that man
should struggle against his bonds, should seek to change his environment rather than adapt
himself to it. He suggests that the South African underdog's only hope for a better future
rests upon his willingness to continue his seemingly futile battle against the forces that
hold him down. La Guma's outlaw heroes may never win but at least they never give up
trying to win. They persist in the belief that man can change his universe and shape his future.
Thus, deep in the heart of La Guma's harsh realism runs a vein of pure romanticism.

—Bernth Lindfors

**LAMMING, George (Eric).**  Barbadian.  Born in Barbados in 1927. Taught school in Trinidad and Venezuela. Host of a book review programme for the West Indian Service of the BBC, London, 1951. Member of the Faculty, University of the West Indies, Kingston, Jamaica, 1968. Recipient: Guggenheim Fellowship, 1954; *Kenyon Review* Fellowship, 1954; Maugham Award, 1957. Lives in London. Address: c/o Longman, 74 Grosvenor Street, London W.1, England.

PUBLICATIONS

Novels

*In the Castle of My Skin.*   London, Joseph, and New York, McGraw Hill, 1953.
*The Emigrants.*   London, Joseph, 1954; New York, McGraw Hill, 1955.
*Of Age and Innocence.*   London, Joseph, 1958.
*Season of Adventure.*   London, Joseph, 1960.
*Water with Berries.*   London, Longman, 1972.

Other

*The Pleasures of Exile.*   London, Joseph, 1960.

Verse published in many anthologies.

\*       \*       \*

The critical reception of George Lamming's first four novels has fallen short of their real merits and originality. It is often said that Lamming demands too much of the reader; it might be truer to say that the reader demands too little of Lamming. West Indian fiction has often been distinguished by a certain energy and rhetorical glow but not, except in the work of Lamming and Wilson Harris, by much complexity of form or texture. Right from his first book, *In the Castle of My Skin*, Lamming made it clear that the real complexity of West Indian experience demanded some adequate response of its writers. He has since elaborated this view in an important essay called "The Negro Writer and His World", where he wrote: "To speak of his [the Negro Writer's] situation is to speak of a general need to find a centre as well as a circumference which embraces some reality whose meaning satisfies his intellect and may prove pleasing to his senses. But a man's life assumes meaning first in relation to other men. . . ."

*In the Castle of My Skin* may at first appear to be an autobiography of childhood, but it soon becomes apparent that the book is also the collective autobiography of a Barbadian village moving through the break-up of the old plantation system dominated by the Great House and into the new age of nationalism, industrial unrest and colonial repression. The four boys who stand at the centre of the book are given a more or less equal importance though it is "George" who ultimately registers the meaning of their disparate experiences as they are driven asunder by education, travel and emerging social distinctions.

The collective quality already evident in this, the most personal of all Lamming's books, is more strongly present in *The Emigrants*. Here the portrait is of one boatload of the black emigrants (the title is significant, for it stresses what they leave as well as what they find) who flocked from the Caribbean to Britain between 1950 and 1962. On the boat the emigrants discover a new identity as "West Indians", only to lose it again as they fly centrifugally apart under the stresses of life in an alien culture.

*The Emigrants* is the saddest of all Lamming's books, because there is almost no focus of hope amid so much disillusionment and despair. By contrast both *Of Age and Innocence* and *Season of Adventure* are powerfully positive books in which what is shed is a set of values adhering to the older generation, those who are unable to match the pace and tendency of the times. *Of Age and Innocence* is set in San Cristobal, a fictional Caribbean island colony rapidly approaching independence. The dominant generation of islanders is unable to break away from its class and racial identities to work together for a new society which will redeem the past of slavery and colonialism, but it is throughout juxtaposed to the generation of its children, who struggle towards that meaning which the nationalist leader Shepherd has glimpsed and then lost again:

> I had always lived in the shadow of a meaning which others had placed on my presence in the world, and I had played no part at all in making that meaning, like a chair which is wholly at the mercy of the idea guiding the hand of the man who builds it. . . . But like the chair, I have played no part at all in making that meaning which others use to define me completely.

Shepherd is destroyed by the forces of the past, but the children look out through the flames of destruction which end the novel towards a future they have already presaged in their games. At the centre of *Season of Adventure* stands another unawakened character, the "big-shot coloured" girl Fola, whose father is a West Indian police officer imbued with all the old ideas of order, dominance and segregation. A visit to a Voduñ ceremony awakens her to the real capacity of her nature for self-discovery and self-renewal. This awakening by ancestral drums is in itself a *cliché* of Caribbean literature, but here it escapes banality by the intensity of Lamming's lyrical style and the bizarre violence of much of the action. *Season of Adventure* is in some ways the finest of his novels, just as *The Emigrants* is certainly the weakest. Yet the hesitancy which overtakes the drums at the end of the novel, in the very moment of their triumph as the expression of popular values, is analogous to the problem of language Lamming faces in projecting a West Indian culture which will be truly united, consistent and free: "But remember the order of the drums . . . for it is the language which every nation needs if its promises and its myths are to become a fact."

After a silence of more than ten years, Lamming has two new novels awaiting publication. Perhaps the drums have now found that new language in which to speak.

—Gerald Moore

---

**LARNER, Jeremy.** American. Born in Olean, New York, 20 March 1937. Educated at Brandeis University, Waltham, Massachusetts, A.B. 1958; University of California, Berkeley, 1958–59. Since 1965, Member of the Editorial Board, *Dissent* magazine, New York. Recipient: Delta Novel Prize, 1964; Aga Khan Prize, *Paris Review*, 1964; National Endowment for the Arts award, 1966. Address: c/o Candida Donadio, 111 West 57th Street, New York, New York 10019, U.S.A.

PUBLICATIONS

Novels

*Drive, He Said.* New York, Dial Press, 1964; London, Blond, 1965.
*The Answer.* New York, Macmillan, 1968.

Uncollected Short Stories

"Oh, The Wonder!", in *Paris Review*, Winter-Spring 1965.
"They Are Taking My Letters", in *Harper's* (New York), October 1968.


Plays

Screenplays: *Drive, He Said*, with Jack Nicholson, 1970; *The Candidate*, 1971.


Other

*The Addict in the Streets*, with Ralph Tefferteller.   New York, Grove Press, 1965; London, Penguin, 1966.
*Nobody Knows: Reflections on the McCarthy Campaign of 1968*.   New York, Macmillan, 1970.


Editor, with Irving Howe, *Poverty: Views from the Left*.   New York, Morrow, 1968.


Manuscript Collection: Boston University Library.


\*          \*          \*


In theme and technique Jeremy Larner's two novels are the hip extensions of Heller's *Catch-22* and West's *A Cool Million*. They are also a composite of *Mad* magazine, black humor, and everything "experimental."

His first novel, *Drive, He Said*, mixes fantasy and dream with reality, psychosis and horror with social satire. In a world where outrageously insane public acts are reported mundanely, the college student hero Herbert Bloom carries on his quest: "All I want is a person, a real person." But he attempts, above all, to find himself in a society dominated by classes, basketball games, professors on the rise, "good" students, "rational" adults, munitions manufacturers, and the bomb: the whole structure of present civilization that makes life absurd and confuses and buries personal identity. Larner is looking for an answer to Creeley's lines in "I Know a Man" (the novel's title is from another line in the same poem): "the darkness sur-/ rounds us, what/ can we do against/ it."

However, Larner never really provides a solution to the problem of identity and sanity in a world that more and more approaches a state of moral Phantasmagoria. Unlike Barth, whose vision of absurdity leads directly to nihilism, his hero still looks to a possible future. At the end of the novel the narrator is not sure if anyone can remain sane in our time: "Perhaps our hero had become deranged, or had been all along. That can happen these days when each man inside himself swears he is sane but from the outside who can tell?" *Maybe* Bloom, still breathing, will save himself: "he would get over it, *yes*. Or else he would never get over it. *Oh he would get over it*. He would get over it. Yes." Yet we aren't convinced. But this is one strength of the novel, that the hero can't find any easy answer; but he hasn't been had, he saves that much. That was Augie March's strength: he resisted, and that seems the most fundamental posture of many characters in modern American fiction.

*The Answer*, Larner's other novel, is, thematically, more focused but is less interesting and convincing as a "quest." The title refers to the Answer Drug, something like LSD, which promises for Alex Randall (another college student) liberation from failed love and the modern mess in general. In the end, the drug culture is severely condemned; it is not the Answer to the fundamental question the novel poses: what does it mean to be alive? One of the chief weaknesses of *The Answer* is that the myth of the questor is used too narrowly.

In *Drive, He Said*, the main character moved in a complex world that was recognizable and substantial; in this novel, the enticement of the drug scene cannot bear the total weight of an alternate way of life, especially since those who've never taken drugs cannot relate to the eighty pages of psychodelic description by Alex Randall.

Yet, this weakness is somewhat redeemed by Larner's rejection (through Randall) of the drug guru, Dr. Magus Tyrtan, on the basis that his solution is too simple, the problems too complex. Larner does anticipate, though, that the drug solution will be adopted by considerable numbers. In the epilogue to the novel (which takes place in 1980), the youth are turned off by their druggie parents. He appears to be saying that the simple answers are, unfortunately, the ones which have the most appeal.

—Peter Desy

---

**LAURENCE, (Jean) Margaret**. Canadian. Born in Neepawa, Manitoba, 18 July 1926. Educated at the University of Manitoba, Winnipeg, B.A. 1947. Married John F. Laurence in 1947 (divorced, 1969); has two children. Has lived in Canada, Somaliland, Ghana and England. Writer-in-Residence, University of Toronto, 1969–70. Recipient: Beta Sigma Phi award, 1960; President's Medal, University of Western Ontario, for short story, 1961, 1962, 1964; Governor-General's Award, 1967; Canada Council Senior Fellowship, 1967. Address: Elm Cottage, Beacon Hill, Penn, Buckinghamshire, England.

PUBLICATIONS

Novels

> *This Side Jordan*. Toronto, McClelland and Stewart, London, Macmillan, and New York, St. Martin's Press, 1960.
> *The Stone Angel*. Toronto, McClelland and Stewart, London, Macmillan, and New York, Knopf, 1964.
> *A Jest of God*. Toronto, McClelland and Stewart, London, Macmillan. and New York, Knopf, 1966.
> *The Fire-Dwellers*. Toronto, McClelland and Stewart, London, Macmillan, and New York, Knopf, 1969.

Short Stories

> *The Tomorrow-Tamer: Stories*. Toronto, McClelland and Stewart, and London, Macmillan, 1963; New York, Knopf, 1964.
> *A Bird in the House*. Toronto, McClelland and Stewart, London, Macmillan, and New York, Knopf, 1970.

Other

> *A Tree for Poverty* (anthology of Somali poetry and folk tales). Nairobi, Kenya, Eagle Press, 1954.

*The Prophet's Camel Bell* (travel).   Toronto, McClelland and Stewart, and London, Macmillan, 1963; as *New Wind in a Dry Land*, New York, Knopf, 1964.

*Long Drums and Cannons: Nigerian Dramatists and Novelists, 1952–66*.   London, Macmillan, 1968; New York, Praeger, 1969.

*Jason's Quest* (juvenile).   Toronto, McClelland and Stewart, London, Macmillan, and New York, Knopf, 1970.

Travel articles in *Holiday* (New York), and *Maclean's* (Toronto).

Bibliography: in *Margaret Laurence* by Clara Thomas, Toronto, McClelland and Stewart, 1969.

Manuscript Collection: McMaster University, Hamilton, Ontario.

Critical Studies: "The Maze of Life" by S. E. Read, in *Canadian Literature* (Vancouver), Winter 1966; "Geographer of Human Identities" by Walter Swayze, in *A.C.U.T.E.* (Ottawa), 1967; *Margaret Laurence* by Clara Thomas, Toronto, McClelland and Stewart, 1969; essays by the author on her own work: "Ten Years' Sentences", in *Canadian Literature* (Vancouver), 1969, and "Sources", in *Mosaic* (Winnipeg), 1970.

\*        \*        \*

Margaret Laurence's first novel, *This Side Jordan*, is set in the Gold Coast, some months before it became Ghana, the first British colony in Africa to gain independence. The novel deals with conflicting pulls of tribal and urban ways, misunderstandings between Europeans and Africans, and between Africans and Africans. Nathaniel Amegbe, a schoolmaster, experiences many of these pressures; he rejects the older pattern of life, yet he constantly feels its influence on him, finally deciding, despite severe setbacks, that his work must be undertaken in the new life of the city. This novel is fundamentally concerned with change; its texture is sufficiently complex to give depth to its picture of rapidly altering Ghananian life. The characters emerge convincingly, and the novel has a pulsating sense of immediacy about it.

Mrs. Laurence's collection of Somali folk tales and poetry, *A Tree for Poverty*, was followed by an account of her life in British Somaliland, *The Prophet's Camel Bell*; and her study of Nigerian literature, *Long Drums and Cannons*, rounds off the picture we form of an author who is sensitive to oral and written literature, but, above all, to human beings.

A rich pattern of African life was exhibited in her early stories, published in book form in *The Tomorrow-Tamer*. In these, too, we see her preoccupation with people rather than background, however successful her portrayal of the contrasts of the African scene. For her characters have humour and pathos, strength and weakness, and a capacity for increasing self knowledge which involves the reader in their fortunes, in their development as human beings. Her further volume, *A Bird in the House*, reinforced the success of *The Tomorrow-Tamer*; Hagar in *The Stone Angel* is a character who reveals herself freely, and continues to hold the reader's attention. In *A Jest of God* Mrs. Laurence developed further a capacity to invest an introspective character's account of her own life with increasing interest as the story develops. In this case it is the sterile life of Rachel Cameron, a spinster schoolteacher of thirty-four living with her mother in a small provincial Canadian town. The story of suddenly awakening and incautious love is unfolded with skill and great sensitivity. The crippling conventionalism of a small community is a suitable background for this study, which is ultimately focussed on Rachel Cameron's escape from this stifling environment into a new and freer life, away from the pain of her past experience. Rachel's relationships with her colleagues, with her friend, and with neighbours, are the punctuation in her story, the pauses for breath in her long monologue with herself.

Mrs. Laurence has a capacity for conveying the intensity of emotion which racks her characters; she chooses detail illuminatingly and economically; and she develops her human sympathies steadily from book to book. The reader is left with a comforting sense of architectonic control at work, however uncontrolled the actions of the characters may seem at some crucial point of story or novel.

—A. Norman Jeffares

LAVIN, Mary. Irish. Born in East Walpole, Massachusetts, 11 June 1912; has lived in Ireland since childhood. Educated at East Walpole schools; Loreto Convent, Dublin; National University of Ireland, Dublin, M.A. (honours) 1938. Married William Walsh in 1942 (deceased, 1954); Michael MacDonald Scott, 1969; has three children. President, P.E.N. (Ireland), 1964–65. Recipient: Black Memorial Prize, 1944; Guggenheim Fellowship, 1959, 1961, 1962; Katherine Mansfield Prize, 1962. D.Litt., National University of Ireland, 1968. President, Irish Academy of Letters, 1971–73. Address: The Abbey Farm, Bective, Navan, County Meath; or, 11 Lad Lane, Dublin, Ireland.

PUBLICATIONS

Novels

>*The House in Clewe Street*. Boston, Little Brown, 1945; London, Joseph, 1946.
>*Mary O'Grady*. Boston, Little Brown, and London, Joseph, 1950.

Short Stories

>*Tales from Bective Bridge*. Boston, Little Brown, 1942; London, Joseph, 1943.
>*The Long Ago and Other Stories*. London, Joseph, 1944.
>*The Becker Wives and Other Stories*. London, Joseph, 1946; as *At Sallygap and Other Stories*, Boston, Little Brown, 1947.
>*A Single Lady and Other Stories*. London, Joseph, 1951.
>*The Patriot Son and Other Stories*. London, Joseph, 1957.
>*A Likely Story*. London, Macmillan, and New York, Macmillan, 1957.
>*Selected Stories*. New York, Macmillan, 1959.
>*The Great Wave and Other Stories*. London, Macmillan, and New York, Macmillan, 1961.
>*The Stories of Mary Lavin*. London, Constable, 2 vols., 1964, 1972.
>*In the Middle of the Fields and Other Stories*. London, Constable, 1967; New York, Macmillan, 1969.
>*Happiness and Other Stories*. London, Constable, 1969; Boston, Houghton Mifflin, 1970.
>*Collected Stories*. Boston, Houghton Mifflin, 1971.
>*A Memory and Other Stories*. London, Constable, 1972.

Other

> The Second Best Children in the World (juvenile). London, Longman, and Boston, Houghton Mifflin, 1972.

Bibliography: by Paul Doyle, in Papers of the Bibliography Society of America (New York), vol. 63, no. 4, 1969.

Manuscript Collection: Southern Illinois University, Carbondale.

Critical Studies: preface to Tales from Bective Bridge, 1942; preface by the author to Selected Stories, 1959; preface by V. S. Pritchett to Collected Stories, 1971.

*    *    *

Mary Lavin has obvious gifts for fiction: she can tell a story, invent characters and give them vivid speech, a life of their own, settings described economically yet evocatively. But she has more also, a capacity for selecting those moments of crisis when the world passes by but time stops still as the meaning of life is suddenly crystalised for some person. She first showed this gift in her short stories which are Chekhovian in scope. Tales from Bective Bridge contained "Love Is for Lovers" where Mathew, an elderly bachelor, is attracted and then repelled by Mrs. Cooligan, a widow. His sudden nausea at the thought of her, of her love of warmth, of her dog, of cushions, of her orange dress, occurs one summer day in her garden. She tips a half dead fly out of her tea: the fly shakes the liquid out of his wings, as though celebrating his release. But the lazy fat dog swallows him. The whole Saturday afternoon's lesson is there, and we are prepared for Mathew's thoughts that evening: he had been trying to go back, to his dreams of a slender girl, a sweet cool fragrant marriage: "But you couldn't go back, ever."

These sudden moments of perception enrich her stories, which also explore the differences between dream and reality. The story "Magenta", for instance, in The Becker Wives builds slowly and remorselessly up to a climax where the girl's quickly invented stories about the supposed actress who employs her, lending her her clothes, are punctured by the small mistake of her being twenty minutes too late for the train back, so that she cannot replace the clothes she has stolen.

There is a remorseless quality about Mary Lavin's fiction which marks her two major novels The House in Clewe Street and Mary O'Grady. In both of these novels she displays an impressive skill in handling different ages in family groupings. The House in Clewe Street explores a boy's growing up under the care of two aunts, and his sudden rebellion and running away with the servant girl. In this story Mary Lavin explores the tyranny given by the possession of both money and ruthless selfconfidence and shows its crippling effect upon Gabriel, the protagonist. The story is, in essence, about the gradual undermining of his innocence. He does not question nor rebel, without the outside stimulus given by his friend Sylvester. The exploration of his school, his growing interest in Onny the servant, his jealousy of her friendships in Dublin are all unfolded with the precision of a surgeon's skill. Yet this is no clinical novel, for we are aware of a compassionate attitude on the part of the authoress towards her characters. They have choice, they even enjoy the after effects of making a wrong choice. They are indeed children to whom Yeat's lines might well apply: "young/We loved each other and were ignorant."

In Mary O'Grady we are given the history of a family living in a Dublin suburb: a devoted husband and wife, their children growing up, and becoming adults, one going to America and eventually returning, one studying to become a priest, the girls finding husbands.

The emotional content is rich and varied, the mother's strength impressive, the children's development into adults charted with convincing knowledge.

If the reader were to concentrate upon one specific aspect of Mary Lavin's story-telling capacity and the subtle human understanding which informs all her fiction it might well be upon that delicate stage where adolescence asserts independence, is critical of parents while half ashamed of being so, yet determined to escape from the round of accustomed family life. In *Mary O'Grady*, for instance, there is the brilliantly evoked evening when the daughters are visited for the first time by the two engineering students who fall in love with them. The shyness, the gaucherie, the gradually developing friendliness of the family are handled with an assurance which not only encourages the reader to accept the narrator's unobtrusive, tactful guidance, but reinforces the sympathetic interest created from the beginning of the novel.

The secret of Mary Lavin's success is, perhaps, to be found in that ability she possesses of taking her readers into her confidence, sharing with them her panoptic survey of those characters whom she regards in a kindly yet detached fashion. She has an awareness of the comedy as well as the tragedy of human life. She relishes its absurdities, weaves them into the tapestry, and keeps her proportions right. Her stories are set in Ireland, but her characters are universal. They may speak with the accents of the Irish countryside or of the city of Dublin, their particular modes of tact or forthrightness may be Irish in emphasis or accent, but these are people who exist anywhere in the world, given the author's ability to see them with insight, and, like Mary Lavin, to portray them with realistic compassion, in their actions and in their self-revealing speech. She believes a writer distills the essence of his thought in a short story, that this kind of writing is only looking closer into the human heart. Her themes are loneliness, despair, escape, paralysis and frustration: her strength comes from the impersonal objectivity with which she depicts unhappy characters. Ultimately she is an enduring writer, because the irony which is the mainstay of her technique is matched by penetrating insight into human thought and its effect on behaviour.

—A. Norman Jeffares

---

**LEBOWITZ, Albert.** American. Born in St. Louis, Missouri, 18 June 1922. Educated at Washington University, St. Louis, A.B. 1945 (Phi Beta Kappa); Harvard Law School, Cambridge, Massachusetts, LL.B. 1948. Served as a Combat Navigator in the United States Army Air Force, in Europe, 1943–45: Air Medal. Married Naomi Gordon in 1953; has two children. Admitted to the Missouri Bar, 1948: Associate, with Frank E. Morris, 1948–55; Partner, Morris, Schneider and Lebowitz, 1955–58, Crowe, Schneider, Shanahan and Lebowitz, 1958–66, Murphy and Roche, 1968–69, and since 1969, Murphy and Schlapprizzi —all in St. Louis. Since 1961, Co-Editor of *Perspective* magazine, St. Louis. Address: 743 Yale Avenue, University City, Missouri 63130, U.S.A.

PUBLICATIONS

Novels

*Laban's Will.*  New York, Random House, and London, Gollancz, 1966.
*The Man Who Wouldn't Say No.*  New York, Random House, 1969.

Manuscript Collection: Washington University Library, St. Louis.

\* \* \*

Literally, Lebowitz's fictional world is much about lawyers and law. Laban, the central character of *Laban's Will*, is a middle-aged lawyer at the top of his game; Halter, of *The Man Who Wouldn't Say No*, is a junior partner deciding what it means to be on the make; David Stein, character in several of the short stories, is a young lawyer. Literally, the recurrent setting is St. Louis, the milieu suburban and Jewish. For those concerned with the literal validity of subject matter, there is the relevant, and unusual, fact that Lebowitz has combined his writing career with a continuing St. Louis law practice.

Literarily, the novels are strong, complex books in which law is only one motif among many. Probably the novels' finest achievement is the presentation of character. Although the main figure in *Laban's Will* is certainly Laban, the dramatic point of view is given to his two daughters, alternating between them chapter by chapter. Such an arrangement suggests more than authorial virtuosity: it points to Lebowitz's generally sympathetic handling of character, to an insistence that people cannot be flattened into blacks and whites. The primary field of dramatic action is the relation of character to character, the weapons of combat often the barbed exchange of intense conversation. Thus, at one level Lebowitz's fiction is witty comedy of manners, maintaining a constant undertone of good humored and satiric laughter wrung from a gallery of lawyers and the people and props of their milieu. But the final point is hardly satiric. In fact, to the extent that satire is founded on an *ex*clusive attitude, Lebowitz's novels question the satiric urge, for they are concerned thematically with the spirit of *in*clusion. Exclusion diminishes the spirit. The problem is how much one can include—even in tolerance for the morally shabby and repugnant—in a coherent, positive sense of self. Death, the ultimate excluder, prompts man to narrow his soul in anguish; the corruption of human affairs causes moral nausea. The final question of the novels is how human sensibility, under these attacks, can avoid a mean defensiveness or an empty cynicism—how it can achieve joyousness.

William Laban, around whom all revolves in *Laban's Will*, exemplifies a joyous acceptance of life. His spirit is summarized at the novel's end in the words of Rabbi Isaacson—"one in whose rejoicing life we have rejoiced"—and in his will, which sets up a yearly award to the person or institution that has done the most to "establish the religious experience of joy." Laban's most characteristic scenes show him presiding over ritualized and costumed family dinners, more often than not Labanized versions of Jewish holy days, or reading before the assembled family the latest version of his will, in which the largest bequest is typically awarded to the child who has last played a vehement practical joke on him. Such comic scenes tend toward the thematic statement that rituals like religion and law are games whose reward is the fun of playing them ingeniously and intensely. In opposition to Laban stand his three children—Rachel and Bernie, who moralistically object to Laban's flippancy, and Leah, who has completely submerged any view of her own. The children are reluctant players, too inhibited to be good sports. Still, Laban *is* difficult to swallow. Most children resent the fact that their father is bigger than life, and Laban is a Rabelaisian figure who always takes center stage whether he means to or not. Moreover, Laban's game, played in the light of his knowledge of a mortal illness, requires intimidating commitments of energy, decision and imagination. The children's experience suggests that religious conviction is gained, not learned. But there is the further tragic sense that even a religion of joy isolates its prophets, especially in their own homes.

*The Man Who Wouldn't Say No* presents a highly successful version of our time's anti-hero. Halter, the main character, is a comic Meursault, a junior partner variant of Lucky Jim set amidst serious issues. He is aware that his job is a yoke or noose, that his being has been drawn and quartered—separated into a mind and body that have no stable relation, divided into home-self and office-self, paralyzed by the disparity between ideal and real. Halter is a modern *picaro*, more acted upon than acting, whose daily trips expose him to the miniature hypocrisies of the office staff, the sanctioned brutalities of his senior partners, the territorial squabbles of the neighborhood association. Surprised innocence threatens to become numbed cynicism as Halter watches his fellow characters reveal what lies behind the masks they wear. Nonetheless, in the end Halter triumphantly decides to resign from the firm, withdraw from public life, and to remarry for love. This ending is more complicated and comic than it sounds, however. Like a Jane Austen protagonist, Halter has happened to choose a wealthy spouse, and he has gradually come to understand that if people are often shockingly different from what one would like to assume they are, they are also as complex, as bewildered by their own many-sidedness, as deserving of sympathy as he. The ending suggests that one may criticize the world but he must also accept it. Halter is left at this elementary stage of Laban's wisdom.

—David P. Demarest, Jr.

---

**LE CARRÉ, John.** Pseudonym for David John Moore Cornwell. British. Born in Poole, Dorset, 19 October 1931. Educated at Sherborne School; Berne University; Lincoln College, Oxford, B.A. in modern languages 1956. Married Alison Ann Veronica Sharp in 1954 (divorced); has three children. Tutor at Eton College, Buckinghamshire, 1956–58. Member of the British Foreign Service, 1960–64: Second Secretary, Bonn, 1960–63; Consul, Hamburg, 1963–64. Recipient: British Crime Novel Award, 1963; Maugham Award, 1964; Edgar Allan Poe Award, 1965. Address: c/o John Farquharson Ltd., 15 Red Lion Square, London W.C.1, England.

PUBLICATIONS

Novels

Call for the Dead. London, Gollancz, 1960; New York, Walker, 1962.
A Murder of Quality. London, Gollancz, 1962; New York, Walker, 1963.
The Spy Who Came In from the Cold. London, Gollancz, and New York, Coward McCann, 1963.
The Looking-Glass War. London, Heinemann, and New York, Coward McCann, 1965.
A Small Town in Germany. London, Heinemann, and New York, Coward McCann, 1968.
The Naive and Sentimental Lover. London, Hodder and Stoughton, and New York, Knopf, 1971.

*      *      *

Though John Le Carré had written two thrillers, Call for the Dead and A Murder of Quality, it was when The Spy Who Came In from the Cold was published that it became obvious that a new talent for writing a different kind of spy story had emerged. John Le Carré caught a new mood of chilling horror in this picture of the beastliness underlying the espionage of the cold war, for this is a novel which shows how man's capacity for inhumanity to man and woman is heightened through the process of espionage. The style matches the material. The moods evoked are of grey despair. The tone is cold, almost clinical. The conversations convince; they have the authentic texture of contemporary speech. And the details of the British, Dutch and German background are painted in with a casual assurance. The story is unfolded, given fresh twists, until the reality of life itself becomes warped. Leamas, the British agent, is created convincingly; he carries out his role of defector only to find that his own people have framed him, in order to frame Fiedler, an East German who has discovered the truth about Mundt, his chief.

This is a world of intellectual skills applied arbitrarily, of brilliance without scruple, of brutality without restraint. The inexorable march of the story continues: its destiny is disaster, the same kind of disaster which opens its account of the effects of treason and betrayal. And yet in the final moment Leamas returns for Liz the English communist party member who befriended him in London, who has been brought to East Germany to testify against him. Before their final moments, before they attempt to cross the Berlin wall he makes his apology to her. To him it seems the world has gone mad. His life and hers, their dignity, are a tiny price to pay. They are, ultimately, the victims of a temporary alliance of expediency. His people save Mundt because they need him, "so that", he says to her, "the great moronic mass that you admire can sleep soundly in their beds at night. They need him for the safety of ordinary crummy people like you and me." He sees the loss of Fiedler's life as part of the small scale war which is being waged, with a wastage of innocent life sometimes, though it is still smaller than other wars. Leamas doesn't believe in anything but he sees people cheated, misled, lives thrown away, "people shot and in prison, whole groups and classes of men written off for nothing". Her party, he remarks, was built on the bodies of ordinary people, and she remembers the German prison wardress describing the prison as one for those who slow down the march, "for those who think they have the right to err".

Le Carré's next book, *The Looking-Glass War*, carries his exploration of the work of intelligence services further. This story opens impressively, with the death of a courier who has gone to Finland to pick up films made by the pilot of a commercial flight apparently off course over Eastern Germany. An unconfirmed report indicates the likelihood of a rocket site there. Then a small intelligence unit is authorized to put an agent into the area. The preparations are described in detail: the recruiting and training of the agent, the ineptitude involved, and the rivalry among the different agencies—and ultimately the schooled indifference with which the older professionals see their scheme fail abysmally. They are already planning the future, disowning the agent whose slow broadcasting on single frequencies on an obsolete radio has doomed him to capture. The story is well told; it explores the stresses and the vanities, the dangerous risks, even delusions, which beset the world of intelligence; it has a curious pathos, accentuated by the naivety and decency of the young man Avery which is opposed in fury by Haldane, who has become a technician: "We sent him because we needed to; we abandon him because we must."

In *A Small Town in Germany* there is an enlarging of scope. Here is a story of the British Embassy in Bonn, from which secret files—and Leo Harting—have vanished. Turner comes from London to investigate. His interrogations of some of the Embassy staff are brilliant. The pattern of thieving, of treachery, of insinuation, of making himself indispensable, of using others, emerges slowly as Turner tries to build up his picture of Leo Harting. The contrasts of personalities as Turner painstakingly pursues his enquiries give this picture depth, and yet the nature of the vanished man remains elusive. The complications of the British negotiations in Brussels where German support is necessary, the student riots and the ugly neo-nazism give the man-hunt an extreme urgency. The attitude of the German authorities, and that of the Head of Chancery surprise Turner. And the events he unravels surprise the reader.

The novel has a continuous tension; the discoveries of the investigator are cumulative; and finally his aggressive desire to hunt out the missing man turns to a sympathetic understanding of just what Harting has been doing. At this point his attitude differs markedly from that of the Head of Chancery. To a certain extent his reactions are parallel to those of Avery in *The Looking-Glass War*. Both are younger men, outside the orthodoxies of their elders, possessed ultimately of more humanity, though they have no capacity to influence the final stages of the story. The difference lies between the character who professes to control the processes of his own mind and the character who believes we are born free, we are not automatons and cannot control the processes of our minds. The novel is, in fact, about the problems of forgetting, and about the problems of idealism, innocence and practical politics; and the incidental picture it gives of the complex working life of an Embassy provides a very suitable background against which political issues can be spotlit.

Le Carré's most recent novel, *The Naive and Sentimental Lover*, lacks the punch and energy of his earlier works. In them the tendency of the characters to be warped, maimed, frustrated men and women mattered little because the action backed by skilful description carried the plot forward at such headlong speed that analysis of character *per se* was less important than the actions taken by the participants. In his latest novel there is a need for a deeper analysis of character, and this does not seem to have been fully achieved, while the story does not move with the same sureness. However, it is likely that Le Carré is experimenting with a new genre, and just as *The Spy Who Came In from the Cold* needed preliminary studies this may herald a development in character depiction similar to his earlier advances in technique and architectonic power in *The Spy Who Came In from the Cold*, which will remain as a chilling exposé of the continuous underground battle of intelligence services.

—A. Norman Jeffares

---

**LEHMANN, Rosamond (Nina).** British. Born in Bourne End, Buckinghamshire, in 1905; sister of the poet and critic John Lehmann and the actress Beatrix Lehmann. Educated at Girton College, Cambridge (Scholar). Married the Honorable Wogen Philipps, later Lord Milford, in 1928 (marriage dissolved); has one son. Past President, English Centre, International P.E.N. International Vice-President, International P.E.N., and Council Member, Society of Authors. Commandeur dans L'Ordre des Arts et Lettres, 1968. Address: 70 Eaton Square, London S.W.1, England.

PUBLICATIONS

Novels

*Dusty Answer*. London, Chatto and Windus, and New York, Holt, 1927.
*A Note in Music*. London, Chatto and Windus, and New York, Holt, 1930.
*Invitation to the Waltz*. London, Chatto and Windus, and New York, Holt, 1932.
*The Weather in the Streets*. London, Collins, and New York, Reynal, 1936.
*The Ballad and the Source*. London, Collins, 1944; New York, Reynal, 1945.
*The Echoing Grove*. London, Collins, and New York, Harcourt Brace, 1953.

Short Stories

*The Gipsy's Baby and Other Stories*. London, Collins, 1946; New York, Reynal, 1947.

Play

    *No More Music*.  London, Collins, 1939.

Other

    *Letter to a Sister*.  London, Hogarth Press, and New York, Harcourt Brace, 1932.
    *A Man Seen Afar*, with W. Tudor Pole.  London, Spearman, 1965.
    *The Swan in the Evening: Fragments of an Inner Life*.  London, Collins, and New York, Harcourt Brace, 1967.

    Editor, with others, *Orion: A Miscellany 1-3*.  London, Nicholson and Watson, 3 vols., 1945–1946.

    Translator, *Genevieve*, by Jacques Lemarchand.  London, Lehmann, 1947.
    Translator, *Children of the Game*, by Jean Cocteau.  London, Harvill Press, 1955; as *The Holy Terrors*, New York, New Directions, 1957.

Manuscript Collection: University of Texas.

*     *     *

    Rosamond Lehmann published her first, outstandingly successful novel, *Dusty Answer*, in 1927, when she herself was in her twenties. It was subsequently, she was to maintain, a source of embarrassment to her, but it established her in the front rank of novelists—something few first novels can genuinely be said to do. There followed *A Note in Music*, probably the least well-known of her works, and then, in the 1930s, *Invitation to the Waltz* and *The Weather in the Streets*. The fourth book is a "sequel" to the third in that it deals with the same characters, but if this suggests a pallid follow-up trading on a popular success that is quite false: in the later book the naive viewpoint of Olivia aged eighteen is exchanged for the experienced, superficially disillusioned but really still vulnerable outlook of Olivia some ten years and a divorce later. The same characters reappear but they are seen differently and play different, quite unexpected and yet convincing roles. The two books taken together form a masterpiece of realistic observation—a kind of ongoing study in depth which few novelists of Miss Lehmann's intensity have attempted and fewer still brought off successfully. It is not clear whether, when she wrote *Invitation to the Waltz*, the author already had the second book in mind but, if not, that is in a way a still greater testimony to the capacity of her characters to go on existing and developing beyond the context of any particular novel.

    In the forties she published *The Ballad and the Source* and an excellent volume of novellas called *The Gipsy's Baby*. Early in the 1950s, still an established literary figure, she wrote *The Echoing Grove*, a complex and fascinating book re-working some of the same themes of adultery and sisterly relationships which *The Weather in the Streets* dealt with, but with a richer and more sophisticated stylistic approach. Here, evidentally, was a writer who was continuing to evolve and of whom much could still be hoped . . . Yet the fact is that, since then, Miss Lehmann has published no more novels. She has also withdrawn almost entirely from the literary scene. As a result, not only are her excellent books unread by the generation that has grown up since *The Echoing Grove* came out, but even her name is unknown to many of them.

    In the late 'sixties she brought out a further book, a kind of memoir and statement of belief centering on her daughter, Sally, who had died tragically some ten years previously, of polio. Since *The Swan in the Evening* is not a novel it is outside the scope of this piece, but it seems far removed in thoughts, attitudes and perceptions from the earlier works, and it is probably fair to say that, whatever the various reasons "why" Miss Lehmann stopped writing novels when apparently in mid-career, outsiders can hardly begin to guess at them.

As a study of a young girl launching herself gauchely upon adult life, *Invitation to the Waltz* remains an excellent book, though it is of course a period piece now—most of the action takes place at a country house ball, and Miss Lehmann's eighteen-year-old is more like a modern fourteen-year-old. By the same token the older Olivia of *The Weather in the Streets* —one of the first heroines in first-class literature to seek a backstreet abortion—seems in spite of her vaunted cynicism and bohemianism, oddly innocent by modern standards. But as an early example of feminine realism, honesty and self-analysis the book remains admirable, a prototype in fact for the many that have followed it. In a rather different way, as a social chronicle of an era and as an example of stream-of-consciousness writing tailored with great artistry to give it point and readability, *The Echoing Grove* remains a book anyone might be proud of and anyone interested in the English novel should read. Yet some readers would say that her best writing of all, lucid, direct, unassuming and genuinely original, is to be found in *The Gipsy's Baby*, particularly in "The Red-haired Miss Daintrys" (a superb evocation of the *otherness* of other families) and in the long story "The Wonderful Holidays" in which Sally, as a school-girl, makes an identifiable appearance.

Of her other books probably the least readable now is *The Ballad and the Source*, which, like *A Note in Music* to a lesser extent, is disfigured by a kind of luxuriance, a giving way to an almost adolescent romanticism which is completely conquered in her later books. As for the first, and most enduringly famous, *Dusty Answer*, it seems, today, an extraordinary piece of work, a joke to others, a farandango of school-girl lesbianism—and yet so much more than that. It contains several themes which were to take root and flourish in subsequent novels: the young girl fascinated by another family and trying to join their life, A who is in love with B who is in love with C, the impossibility of ever recapturing the feeling of an occasion once it is over . . . The relationship of the girl, Judith, with a family near her own age is beautifully done but what makes the novel inacceptable to the modern reader is the relationship between Judith and a college friend, Jennifer. Straightforward, overtly sexual inversion we can accept today, but Judith and Jennifer's extravagently sentimental attachment does not enter into our notions of reality and we do not know how to take it. Possibly another generation, one without our particular inhibitions and standards, will rediscover this book and read it again as it should be read.

—Gillian Tindall

---

**LERNER, Laurence (David).**   British.   Born in Cape Town, South Africa, 12 December 1925. Educated at the University of Cape Town, B.A. 1944, M.A. 1945; Pembroke College, Cambridge, B.A. 1949. Married Natalie Winch in 1948; has four children. Schoolmaster, St. George's Grammar School, Cape Town, 1946–47; Assistant Lecturer, then Lecturer in English, University College of the Gold Coast, Legon, Ghana, 1949–53; Extra-Mural Tutor, then Lecturer in English, Queen's University of Belfast, 1953–62. Lecturer, then Reader, 1962–70, and since 1970, Professor of English, University of Sussex, Brighton. Visiting Professor, Earlham College, Richmond, Indiana, and University of Connecticut, Storrs, 1960–61; University of Illinois, Urbana, 1964; University of Munich, 1968–69. Address: 232 New Church Road, Hove, Sussex BN3 4EB, England.

PUBLICATIONS

Novels

The Englishmen.  London, Hamish Hamilton, 1959.
A Free Man.  London, Chatto and Windus, 1968.

Uncollected Short Stories

"My Father", in Contrast (Cape Town), Spring 1964.
"Customers Are Sometimes Wrong", in Contrast (Cape Town), Autumn 1964.
"My Aunt Alice", in Contrast (Cape Town), Winter 1967.

Verse

Domestic Interior and Other Poems.  London, Hutchinson, 1959.
The Directions of Memory: Poems 1958–1963.  London, Chatto and Windus, 1964.
Selves.  London, Routledge, 1969.

Other

The Truest Poetry.  London, Hamish Hamilton, 1960.
The Truthtellers: Jane Austen, George Eliot, and D. H. Lawrence.  London, Chatto
    and Windus, 1967.
The Uses of Nostalgia: Studies in Pastoral Poetry.  London, Chatto and Windus, 1972.

Editor, Shakespeare's Tragedies: A Selection of Modern Criticism.  London, Penguin,
    1963.
Editor, with John Holmstrom, George Eliot and Her Readers: A Selection of Contempo-
    rary Reviews.  London, Bodley Head, 1966.
Editor, Shakespeare's Comedies: A Selection of Modern Criticism.  London, Penguin,
    1967.
Editor, with John Holmstrom, Thomas Hardy and His Readers: A Selection of Contem-
    porary Reviews.  London, Bodley Head, 1968.

Laurence Lerner comments:

It is not easy for me to make a statement on my work in fiction, since I am only an occasional
novelist: most of my effort has been given to poetry and criticism. I write novels because I
like reading them, and because I'd like to address the public that reads novels but does not
read poetry or criticism—not because I am confident that I have any talent for fiction. The
novelists I most admire are mostly (not all of them) in the great central realistic tradition—
Jane Austen, Stendhal, George Eliot, Tolstoi, Hardy. I love the anti-novel in the 18th century
(Sterne and Diderot) but I can't stand the nouveau roman. I don't believe realism is dead,
or that a documentary element is illegitimate in a novel, though I understand why so many
people think so. I would like to write a novel that has the eccentricity of some modern psychology, that almost seems to take itself seriously. I'm bad at plots, and love unexpected subjects
that enable you to write straight and seem eccentric—that's why I'm better at poems than at
novels.

*      *      *

Though better-known as a poet and critic, Laurence Lerner has published two novels and a number of short stories. *The Englishmen* is a study of racial prejudice in a South African school and its effect on the life of Richard Baxter, a young teacher who is planning to marry and emigrate to England. The "Englishmen" of the title are two new members of staff—Franklin, a bluff but essentially conservative clergyman, and Tracy, a sophisticated and rebellious Cambridge graduate—whose arrival precipitates a series of conflicts which challenge the immature liberalism of the central character. By the end of the novel, Richard has been compelled to take a stand over racial injustice, though in the process he has been rejected by his fiancée, Sara, and has abandoned his plans for leaving South Africa. At both the personal and public levels, the novel is a perceptive account of self-discovery. Though the characters of Franklin and Tracy are a little predictable, the central dilemma is handled with great assurance, and the school setting is skilfully made to reflect the pressures of the surrounding society.

Both Lerner's novels have a considerable documentary interest, especially in their intelligent grasp of social and political issues. In *A Free Man*, the setting is Iceland, and the theme of self-discovery is more explicit than in the earlier book. Peter, the narrator, leaves his job in a travel agency to conduct parties of tourists round Iceland, where for a time he settles with his mistress, Jocelyn. The climax comes when Cartwright, his former boss, joins one of his parties: by a series of twists, Jocelyn falls in love with Cartwright, whom she agrees to marry, but the latter is killed in an accident for which Peter is made to take the blame, and which ultimately costs him his career. The title of the novel is ironical: Peter's wish to become a "free man" serves only to expose his egotism and lack of self-awareness. His routine activities—the problems of a travel guide, the hazards of rock-climbing—are charted with accuracy and insight, and there is a noticeable gain in the quality of the descriptive writing. The main weakness lies in the actual character of the narrator: though some of the less plausible events in the book, like Jocelyn's sudden passion for the hitherto ineffectual Cartwright, can be explained by Peter's lack of concern for others, his prejudices and limited vision are hardly enough to sustain the interest of a whole novel, and the ending seems more of a set-piece than a genuine conclusion.

Lerner has also published three stories: "Customers Are Sometimes Wrong", "My Father" and "My Aunt Alice" (*Contrast*, 1964 and 1967). The first two are shrewdly observed vignettes of South African society and, like *The Englishmen*, should be read in conjunction with the excellent autobiographical piece "Leaving School" (*London Magazine*, April 1964). "My Aunt Alice" is altogether more ambitious: an image of England in the late 1940's, seen through the eyes of a recently-arrived South African girl, written with great penetration and human sympathy.

—Arthur Terry

---

**LESSING, Doris (May).** British. Born in Kermanshah, Persia, 22 October 1919. Married Frank Charles Wisdom in 1939 (divorced, 1943); Gottfried Lessing, 1945 (divorced, 1949); has three children. Lived in Southern Rhodesia, 1924–49; came to England in 1949. Recipient: Maugham Award, 1954. Address: c/o Curtis Brown Ltd., 13 King Street, London W.C.2, England.

PUBLICATIONS

Novels

    *The Grass Is Singing.*   London, Joseph, and New York, Crowell, 1950.
    *Children of Violence:*
      *Martha Quest.*   London, Joseph, 1952.
      *A Proper Marriage.*   London, Joseph, 1954; with *Martha Quest*, New York, Simon
        and Schuster, 1964.
      *A Ripple from the Storm.*   London, Joseph, 1958.
      *Landlocked.*   London, MacGibbon and Kee, 1965; with *A Ripple from the Storm*,
        New York, Simon and Schuster, 1966.
      *The Four-Gated City.*   London, MacGibbon and Kee, and New York, Knopf, 1969.
    *Retreat to Innocence.*   London, Joseph, 1953.
    *The Golden Notebook.*   London, Joseph, and New York, Simon and Schuster, 1962.
    *Briefing for a Descent into Hell.*   London, Cape, and New York, Knopf, 1971.

Short Stories

    *This Was the Old Chief's Country: Stories.*   London, Joseph, 1951; New York,
      Crowell, 1952.
    *Five: Short Novels.*   London, Joseph, 1953.
    *The Habit of Loving.*   London, MacGibbon and Kee, 1957; New York, Crowell, 1958.
    *A Man and Two Women: Stories.*   London, MacGibbon and Kee, and New York,
      Simon and Schuster, 1963.
    *African Stories.*   London, Joseph, 1964; New York, Simon and Schuster, 1965.
    *Nine African Stories.*   London, Longman, 1968.

Plays

    *Each His Own Wilderness* (produced London, 1958).   Included in *New English Dra-*
      *matists*, London, Penguin, 1959.
    *Mr. Dolinger* (produced Oxford, 1958).
    *The Truth about Billy Newton* (produced Salisbury, Wiltshire, 1960).
    *Play with a Tiger* (produced London, 1962; New York, 1964).   London, Joseph, 1962.

Verse

    *Fourteen Poems.*   Lowestoft, Suffolk, Scorpion Press, 1959.

Other

    *Going Home.*   London, Joseph, 1957; New York, Ballantine, 1968.
    *In Pursuit of the English: A Documentary.*   London, Joseph, 1960; as *In Pursuit of the*
      *English*, New York, Simon and Schuster, 1961.
    *Particularly Cats.*   London, Joseph, and New York, Simon and Schuster, 1967.

Bibliography: *Doris Lessing* by C. Ipp, Johannesburg, University of the Witwatersrand
Department of Bibliography, Librarianship and Typography, 1967.

*     *     *

Doris Lessing is unique among women writers today for the scope and variety of her work. Whereas, say, Penelope Mortimer, Muriel Spark or Margaret Drabble are each readily identifiable with one particular style and type of approach, Mrs Lessing is unpredictable and has a far wider range. While their failings are typically those of limited over-absorbtion in a small world, Mrs Lessing's shortcomings result directly from her readiness to try her hand at any subject and to incorporate in her novels ideas which are not necessarily well-digested in their context. Her merits, however, are correspondingly generous and her overall achievements impressive. She seems too flawed a writer quite to deserve the near-adulation which some readers accord her—and yet as soon as one says that one remembers bits of her work which are, indeed, outstanding by any standards. Perhaps, ironically, if she had written less or been slightly more selective in what she has chosen to publish, her stock would be still higher.

Oddly, her first book, *The Grass Is Singing*, a tightly-constructed story of a couple's dissolution set in Rhodesia, has none of the excesses or or long-windedness of her later works nor does it appear to be drawn from her own life. It is in fact peculiarly polished and mature for a first work. It was deservedly successful, as were subsequent novels with an African setting, though, since she left that Continent in 1949 and has been a prescribed immigrant to her homeland since 1957, Africa has gradually faded from her work. Her next big success was *In Pursuit of the English*—not exactly a novel, perhaps, but hardly a straight memoir either, since in it the experiences of her first year in England are selected and presented in such a way that the apparent slice of autobiography becomes a work of art in its own right. The London in which Doris Lessing then found herself, alone with a young child and little money, was a strange, still-postwar land of rations, the black-market and spivs, a vanished era which her book documents with humour and insight, but it was also, to this young woman from another continent, an exotically minature yet threatening world of narrow streets, low skies, tiny, sluggish rivers, unbelievably old buildings and a general Dickensian ugliness. In this book Mrs Lessing displayed fully for the first time her ability to treat commonplace material with that peculiar clarity of perception which is called originality, and which opens the reader's eyes and makes him see, in turn, rather differently.

Other novels followed, mainly concerned with male-female relationships. These, though well-received at the time, do not now seem particularly impressive—no more than any conventional, well-written novels of the 'fifties and early 'sixties—and it seems possible that Mrs Lessing herself did not regard them as anything more than honest pieces of work, since she was concurrently engaged on a longer-term fiction project into which her greatest energies apparently went. This was her "Martha Quest" sequence, ultimately (and with questionable appropriateness) named *Children of Violence*. There are five books in the sequence in all, the last one published in 1969, but this last book is so different from the first in material, scope and outlook that it seems safe to say that when Mrs Lessing embarked on the series she had no idea where it would lead her. It seems likely indeed, that when she wrote *Martha Quest* around 1950 she did not at first envisage there being any sequels, but that these grew later as her own absorption in Martha's preoccupations and search for self (Martha's "quest") developed.

Martha, like her creator, grew up in a southern African land and made an early and brief marriage. The first book is mainly concerned with her attempts to emancipate herself from her background, particularly from her mother, and subsequently (in the second book *A Proper Marriage*) from her husband also. In these two works Mrs Lessing explored certain areas of female experience vividly and in almost obsessional detail years before such exploration became fashionable. The third and fourth books, *A Ripple from the Storm* and *Landlocked*, are less striking. Taken together with the first two they form an impressive record of personal change and growth, but in themselves they seem bogged down and too myopically concerned with political activities which, ultimately, turn out to be not that significant after all—Martha, like her creator, becomes a Communist. A male writer still more famous than Doris Lessing once remarked of these two books that if you were on a long train journey from London to Edinburgh and someone started telling you about the internecine squabbles of Communists in Rhodesia, you would think "How fascinating . . ." as far as Sheffield, but after that a growing sense of unease and ultimate claustrophobic boredom would steal over you. Sharp as this comment may seem, it is not unjustified.

In *Landlocked*, however (which despite its apparent closeness to the preceding one of the series was not written till seven years later) there are traces of a broadening of interest in a wholly unprecedented way. Martha has a transient relationship with someone who seems in some sense "possessed" and Extra-sensory Perception makes its appearance. In that particular context it appears bafflingly out of place, but the theme is picked up again in the last book of the sequence and used there to much greater effect. This book, *The Four-Gated City* is a vast, complex work, heavily flawed yet full of vigour, fresh and interesting ideas and any number of characters. In it the scene shifts at last to England, first to the postwar England of *In Pursuit of the English*, revisited now with an intense and almost apocalyptic vision, and then to the increasingly affluent and (in Mrs Lessing's view) doom-laden England of the 'fifties and 'sixties. Eventually, in its mammoth course, Martha Quest herself, now middle aged, becomes a by-stander, her personal affairs only incidental to the two themes which emerge as major: the impending cataclysm of the world as we know it, and the Extra-sensory powers possessed by the supposedly "mad", who have vital messages for the rest of us if only we will listen to them.

This last idea is not unique to Mrs Lessing, though she is so far the only major novelist to have made use of it. Its chief exponent is the psychiatrist R. D. Laing, whose idea that what we call "schizophrenics" are actually visionaries, kept under by our repressive-conformist society, has been widely publicised not always with much sense or discrimination. Doris Lessing herself seems, in *The Four-Gated City*, to be awarding too much partisan and unqualified acceptance to the Laingian view, and some critics feared when the book came out that this writer had found a vision at the expense of her once-renowned intelligence. Development and change have, however, always been the keynote of this writer's career and they need not have worried. Less than two years later she published another, much shorter and far more controlled novel, *Briefing for a Descent into Hell*. While not one of the Quest sequence, this clever, original and readable tale picks up again the themes of madness, ESP and vision and treats them in a far more sophisticated and indeed ambivalent way. It is left to the reader to make up his mind whether the central character of the book really is a suppressed visionary or just a second-rate telly don with a flair for borrowing other people's fantasies.

One other book by Doris Lessing requires a special mention: *The Golden Notebook*. This has been humorously stigmatised as "a simply enormous book about writer's block", and indeed it is essentially a work for other writers in that it deals, perhaps rather self-indulgently, with the problems of writing or not writing about oneself and whether in fact the "self" that is written about can ever be the real self whatever the writer's intentions. Apart from this, however, the book, in the form of several overlapping notebooks or diaries, is an exhaustive exploration of the problems of women on their own and of relationships between the sexes in general. Just as Mrs Lessing wrote explicitly about childbirth a decade before the present modern-realistic school got going, so *The Golden Notebook* is a fascinating document for students of "Women's Liberation" appearing years before the concept had been formulated by anyone else. Personally I think *The Golden Notebook* hammers away at a number of fundamentally mistaken concepts and is ultimately less perceptive than some of Mrs Lessing's less intense and more incidental works. But there is marvellous material in it, and indeed by producing it as a non-book, an (apparently) amorphous mass of raw material, Mrs Lessing seems to have invited readers to regard it as a quarry full of potentially valuable nuggets rather than as a polished offering. At all events it remains, nearly ten years after its publication, as relevant and interesting a psycho-social document as ever. What themes from this and other works will be developed in future ones, and what new ideas Mrs Lessing will still produce for us, is anyone's guess. She is, in her fifties, one of the most vital, original, gifted and unpredictable of writers.

—Gillian Tindall

**LEVIN, Ira.** American. Born in New York City, 27 August 1929. Educated at Drake University, Des Moines, Iowa, 1946–48; New York University, 1948–50, A.B. 1950. Served in the United States Army in the Signal Corps, 1953–55. Married Gabrielle Aronsohn in 1960 (divorced, 1968); has three children. Recipient: Edgar Allan Poe Award, 1954. Address: c/o Harold Ober Associates, 40 East 49th Street, New York, New York 10017, U.S.A.

PUBLICATIONS

Novels

*A Kiss Before Dying.* New York, Simon and Schuster, 1953; London, Joseph, 1954.
*Rosemary's Baby.* New York, Random House, and London, Joseph, 1967.
*This Perfect Day.* New York, Random House, and London, Joseph, 1970.

Plays

*No Time for Sergeants* (produced New York, 1955; London, 1956). New York, Random House, 1956.
*Interlock* (produced New York, 1958).
*Critic's Choice* (produced New York, 1960; London, 1961). New York, Random House, 1961.
*General Seeger* (produced New York, 1962).
*Drat! The Cat!*, music by Milton Schafer (produced New York, 1965).
*Dr. Cook's Garden* (produced New York, 1967).

\*       \*       \*

The heroine of *Rosemary's Baby* is overwhelmed by the "elaborate . . . evil" of the witches' coven, through whose agency she has unknowingly borne Satan's child, which now lies in a black bassinet with an inverted crucifix for a crib toy. Elaborateness is, indeed, the chief characteristic of evil in Ira Levin's novels. Bud Corliss of *A Kiss Before Dying* makes a neat list of the possible ways of arranging his pregnant girlfriend's death, obtains a "suicide" note by asking her to translate a bit of Spanish for him, and later makes a more elaborate list of her eldest sister's tastes in art, literature, food, etc., in order to attract the sister to him. *This Perfect Day* describes the complex organization of a depressing Utopia in which all human actions are directed ostensibly by a world computer, but really by the unknown subterranean programmers. The extensive routine in which everyone must touch his identification bracelet to scanners before he can do anything, go anywhere, or "claim" any supplies provokes a lovingly-detailed complicated counter-plan from the novel's hero, Chip (or Li RM35M4419, to give him his "nameber").

Procedures, then provide the sustaining interest, even the suspense of Levin's novels, combining neatness and system with grotesque and sinister Satanism, murder, and universal surveillance. Rosemary uses a scrabble set to work out the anagram which proves that her friendly neighbor Roman Castevet is really the devil-worshipping Steven Marcato. The month by month details of Rosemary's pregnancy suspend disbelief in her satanic offspring. In *A Kiss Before Dying*, Dorothy's care in providing herself with "Something old,/Something new,/Something borrowed,/And something blue" later enables her sister Ellen to deduce that Dorothy intended marriage, not suicide. Chip, fighting system with system, twice follows meticulously patterns of behaviour intended to free him from the customary doses of tranquillizer and succeeds the second time. Later he works out a complicated expedition to disable UniComp's memory banks.

In all three novels good and bad characters alike formulate elaborate plans of action which must often be revised on the spur of the crisis, always into equally complex expedients. The pleasure of following Levin's ingenious details is sufficient to make the first two novels, at least, re-readable when their surprise is over.

The forward movement and acceleration of Levin's processes is frequently deliberately interrupted by sudden reversals, single or double, overt or psychological, in which the character, and often the reader, is temporarily disoriented. Rosemary, arriving at the logical conclusion that her husband has joined the witches, "didn't know if she was going mad or going sane. . . ." Ellen's fiance turns out to be her sister's murderer (and Ellen's murderer too). For both these discoveries the reader has been partly prepared, but there are unexpected shocks when Rosemary, thinking herself safe, sees her husband and her witch-obstetrician enter, and when Chip is taken prisoner by the most trustworthy member of his team, only to discover that seeming betrayal is really recruitment by the elite programmers. The effect on the reader of such continual reversals and realignments is a constant uneasiness as to personal safety and moral identity, which produces varying degrees of horror, very successfully in *Rosemary's Baby*, but becoming mechanical in *This Perfect Day*.

In the latter novel, the conventional elements of Levin's subject matter are also most evident. Always skillful rather than innovative, his reversals manipulate shock techniques already apparent in the short stories of Ambrose Bierce and Villiers de l'Isle Adam. Bud's tortured death in a vat of molten copper recalls the archetypal death by blast furnace in H. G. Wells's "The Cone". Although there are significant differences between the society of UniComp and Huxley's Brave New World, Levin's anti-Utopia contains a kind of soma, infinitely-multiplied look-alikes and name-alikes, islands of the "uncivilized" functionally analogous to Huxley's savage reservation, a hero who reads literature from the far past, etc. At the heart of the computer is a conventional mad oriental scientist, rejuvenated by body transference familiar in Edgar Rice Burroughs. In short, Levin has drawn upon the almost inescapable traditional materials of his genres, but he uses them intelligently and individually. Only in *This Perfect Day* do the literary echoes obtrude.

Increasingly, Levin's novels suggest a greater significance than they demonstrate. Looking at the copper smelter, the murderer says seriously, "It makes you realize what a great country this is." Rosemary's subtly evil apartment house is owned by the church next door, and there are seemingly casual references to the Death of God. An ideal universe of "the gentle, the helpful, the loving, the unselfish" is the vision of a power-joyful egoist. These paradoxes, although undeveloped, do extend and intensify the disquieting uncertainty which is Levin's most effective psychological device.

—Jane W. Steadman

---

**LEVIN, Meyer.** American. Born in Chicago, Illinois, 8 October 1905. Educated at the University of Chicago, Ph.B. 1924. Writer-Director of documentary films for the United States Office of War Information, 1942–44. Married Mabel Schamp in 1933 (divorced, 1942); Thereska Szarc Torres, 1948; has four children. Reporter and Writer for the *Chicago Daily News*, 1922–28, and the Jewish Telegraphic Agency, Palestine and New York, 1929–31; opened experimental marionette theatre in Chicago, 1929, and taught puppet-theatre production at the New School for Social Research, New York, 1932; Associate Editor, 1933–38, and Film Critic, 1933–39, *Esquire* magazine, Chicago; Writer in Hollywood, 1939–41; War Correspondent in Europe for the Overseas News Agency and the Jewish Telegraphic Agency, 1944–45. After the war, lived and worked in Palestine and France, writing and making films, until 1952; returned to New York until 1957, and since then has divided his

time between Israel and America. Recipient: Bensonhurst Award, 1966; Daroff Memorial
Award, 1966. Address: Street of the Blue Waves, Herzlia-on-Sea, Israel; or, 62 West 91st
Street, New York, New York 10024, U.S.A.


PUBLICATIONS


Novels

> *Reporter*.   New York, Day, 1929.
> *Frankie and Johnny: A Love Story*.   New York, Day, 1930.
> *Yehuda*.   New York, Ballou, 1931.
> *The New Bridge*.   New York, Covici Friede, and London, Gollancz, 1933.
> *The Old Bunch*.   New York, Viking Press, 1937.
> *Citizens*.   New York, Viking Press, 1940.
> *My Father's House*.   New York, Viking Press, 1947.
> *Compulsion*.   New York, Simon and Schuster, 1956; London, Muller, 1957.
> *Eva*.   New York, Simon and Schuster, and London, Muller, 1959.
> *The Fanatic*.   New York, Simon and Schuster, 1964.
> *The Stronghold*.   New York, Simon and Schuster, and London, W. H. Allen, 1965.
> *Gore and Igor: An Extravaganza*.   New York, Simon and Schuster, and London,
>    W. H. Allen, 1968.
> *The Settlers*.   New York, Simon and Schuster, 1972.


Uncollected Short Story

> "The System Was Doomed", in *Story* (New York), 1936.


Plays

> *Compulsion* (produced New York, 1957; Croydon, Surrey, 1960).   New York, Simon
>    and Schuster, 1959.
> *The Diary of Anne Frank*.   Privately printed, 1967.

> Screenplays: *My Father's House*, 1946; *The Illegals*, 1947; *Bus to Sinai*, 1968; *The
> Falashas*, 1970.


Other

> *The Golden Mountain: Marvellous Tales of Rabbi Israel Baal Shem and of His Great-
>    Grandson Rabbi Nachman, Retold from Hebrew, Yiddish and German Sources*.   New
>    York, Behrman's Jewish Book House, 1932; revised edition, as *Classic Hasidic
>    Tales*, New York, Citadel Press, 1966.
> *If I Forget Thee: A Picture History of Modern Palestine*.   New York, Viking Press, 1947.
> *In Search: An Autobiography*.   New York, Horizon Press, 1950; London, Vallentine
>    Mitchell, 1951.
> *The Story of the Synagogue*, with Tony Kurzband.   New York, Behrman, 1958.
> *The Story of the Jewish Way of Life*, with Tony Kurzband.   New York, Behrman, 1958.
> *God and the Story of Judaism*, with Dorothy Krikpe.   New York, Behrman, 1962.
> *The Story of Israel*.   New York, Putnam, 1966.

*An Israel Haggadah for Passover.*   New York, Abrams, 1970.
*Beginnings in Jewish Philosophy.*   New York, Behrman, 1971.

Editor, and Translator, *Selections from the Buchenwald Kibbutz Diary.*   New York, Zionist Organization, 1946.
Editor, *Diary*, by David S. Kogan.   New York, Beechurst Press, 1955.
Editor, *Golden Egg*, by Arthur D. Goldhaft.   New York, Horizon Press, 1957.
Editor, with Charles Angoff, *The Rise of American Jewish Literature.*   New York, Simon and Schuster, 1970.

Translator, *Tales of My People*, by Sholom Asch.   New York, Putnam, 1948.
Translator, *Dangerous Games*, by Thereska Torres.   New York, Dial Press, 1957; London, W. H. Allen, 1958.
Translator, *Not Yet*, by Thereska Torres.   New York, Crown, 1957; London, W. H. Allen, 1959.
Translator, *The Golden Cage*, by Thereska Torres.   New York, Dial Press, 1959.
Translator, *Women's Barracks*, by Thereska Torres.   London, W. H. Allen, 1960.

Manuscript Collections: Boston University; New York University; Brandeis University, Waltham, Massachusetts; Hebrew University, Jerusalem.

Meyer Levin comments:

Of the American-Jewish authors of my time, many of the most prominent prefer to be viewed as American authors who "write Jewish" because of the happenstance of their background. Though I started with this attitude, I found myself drawn more and more to self-recognition as a Jewish rather than an American author, with deeper roots in Jewish culture, and with the portrayal of the Jewish ethos as the dominant theme in my continuing work.

Thus, my first novel, *Reporter*, was a reaction to the Chicago scene of the Twenties, and my second novel, *Frankie and Johnny*, was an attempt at an urban love story with an American folk quality, in which I erased or transmuted the Jewish quality of my characters. But from the very first, I had been deeply affected by that quality; my earliest serious piece of publication was a sketch of a ghetto group of garment workers listening to a street-corner orator, which appeared in the *Menorah Journal* (predecessor to *Commentary*) while I was at College. Just after graduation, I ended a wander-year in Palestine, and became profoundly affected by the revival of the Jewish spirit among the socialist pioneers. This resulted in many returns to that land, with *Yehuda*, a novel of life in a kibbutz, as the first product.

By chance or by the need to find this material, I stumbled on the folk-lore of Hasidism in this same period, for my American Jewish upbringing had been void of either Zionist or traditional religious orientation. I adapted the Hasidic tales into *The Golden Mountain*, my next book. From then on, I increasingly saw the continuing Jewish consciousness as affected by these sources: life in the dispersion (for me, America); life in the religious tradition (though I was far from orthodox); and life in the Jewish renewal in its source-land.

Three of my novels may be grouped together as impregnated with the American as well as the American-Jewish experience. They are the Chicago novels, *The Old Bunch*, *Citizens*, and *Compulsion*. It is significant that when *The Old Bunch* was completed the publisher who had contracted for it asked me to change the characters to a "melting pot" group and rejected the book when I refused. And though when published by Viking Press it was hailed as a breakthrough in fiction about American Jews, this same publisher then attempted to de-Judaize my next novel, *Citizens*, by asking me to change the Jewish doctor in the steel-strike story to a non-Jew. However, he did not reject the book when I was uncompliant.

The Second World War had begun, and my experience as a correspondent specializing in the death-camps has profoundly affected all that I have written since. I feel that every living Jew bears in his consciousness at every moment the knowledge of the holocaust, the awareness of Israel (even if he is one who is uneasy with it), and the sense of his place as a Jew in the particular society in which he happens to live. This three-stream formation corresponds to the three sources I have discerned for myself as a writer, and virtually all of my post-war novels reflect it—*Eva, The Stronghold, My Father's House, The Fanatic* in particular.

In connection with *The Fanatic* I should explain a career difficulty that has beset me in these post-war years. The novel tells the story of the distortion on Broadway of a manuscript left by a victim of the death camps. It follows quite closely my own sickening history with *The Diary of Anne Frank*, and illuminates an area of politics in literature, even outside the Soviet Union, that is little known.

My dramatization of *The Diary of Anne Frank* was rejected and suppressed through the influence of an acknowledged Stalinist, an American Jewish playwright of high achievement, who persuaded Mr. Frank that it was "unstageworthy" because I was "a novelist and novelists can't write plays". Eventually, another dramatization was produced to world-wide success, but a jury in the New York State Supreme Court found that it was largely derived from my earlier play. The single production of my version, in Israel, was suppressed on the question of rights, but not until the critics had hailed it as "infinitely superior" to the Broadway play, theatrically as well as in literary quality. The crux of the matter was that my play had preserved the full Jewish content, the avowals of faith in Anne Frank's diary, and even the desire of her sister to live in Palestine if she lived. Anti-Zionists who interfered with its production and turned Mr. Frank against me were carrying out the same Stalinist opposition to Jewish writing that was at that very time (1952) resulting in the liquidation of scores of Jewish authors in the Soviet Union. Though since then there have been continuous requests for the presentation of my play, and though Albert Camus, Norman Mailer, Elie Weisel, Bruno Bettelheim, I. B. Singer and many others signed appeals for its production, it is still forbidden. In two decades of battle over this question, I learned that I had indeed even before the *Diary* episode been under anti-Zionist attack, that my novel *My Father's House* had been sabotaged on publication by a Stalinist assigned to do public relations on the book, that my autobiography *In Search* had been turned back under like influence by a publisher who had accepted it, and that negative reviews, particularly on *The Fanatic*, had been planted by literary-political anti-Zionists in important media. Smears, whispering campaigns labelling me a "trouble maker", and literary denigration have proven a great professional handicap. Much of this has spread far beyond the original political sources. Because of it, I believe, there has been no proper evaluation of my work, whatever may be its quality.

*         *         *

Although he has written twelve novels since 1929, it seems now that Meyer Levin's greatest novelistic achievements are to found in only three: *The Old Bunch, Citizens*, and *Compulsion*. The novels written before 1937 are essentially apprentice pieces; those written after 1956 are artistically weak and heavy-handed.

Levin's novels are distinguished by two dominant characteristics: they are generally based upon actual historical events and usually dramatize the Jewish experience in Europe and in America. These characteristics contribute to both Levin's strengths and weaknesses as a novelist. For instead of producing immediacy and human drama, the historical facts frequently overshadow and control the fiction, and the Jewish elements too often are used for propagandistic rather than artistic purposes.

*The Old Bunch* is Levin's first successful novel. In the manner of Dos Passos' *U.S.A.*, Levin freely intermingles fact and fiction in a panoramic depiction of life in the twenties as it is experienced by several young Jewish youths in Chicago. The novel is plotless, depending upon historical events for its action. The characters are stereotyped, distinguished only by the professions they follow. Yet the novel is vivid in its presentation of urban American life in the twenties, culminating in the Depression experience.

*Citizens* also depends upon history, but here Levin molds events into a more unified plot. Based upon the 1937 Memorial Day clash between police and pickets at Republic Steel in Chicago, *Citizens* becomes a vehicle for Levin's criticisms of both capitalism and of Communistic influences in the labor movement. Once again, the characters are flat and uninteresting, puppets or mouthpieces for Levin's ideas. The novel's strength is its presentation of the labor movement in America in the thirties.

His best novel, *Compulsion*, demonstrates Levin's skill in organizing ready-made material, the Leopold-Loeb murder case of 1924, into a fast-moving, dramatic narrative. A minor-scale *Crime and Punishment*, the novel is a compelling study of the human drama, the psychological complexity, and the philosophical implications of the famous murder which shocked America in the twenties.

Levin's later novels, *Eva*, *The Fanatic*, and *The Stronghold*, show his fascination, indeed obsession, with Jewish concerns, a characteristic which can be traced back to *Yehuda*, his first specifically Jewish novel. Although there can be no questioning the seriousness of the themes in these novels—the treatment of the Jews in Nazi Germany—the message frequently overpowers both the characters and the art. This is especially true of *The Fanatic*, which is directly based upon Levin's own unfortunate experiences in attempting to have his dramatization of *The Diary of Anne Frank* produced on Broadway. Because of his need to vindicate himself, the novel suffers from the lack of detachment which contributed greatly to the power of *Compulsion*.

Levin's most recent novel, *Gore and Igor*, traces the international adventures of two peace poets, one Russian, one American. Its comic tone distinguishes this novel from Levin's previous works, yet it too never breaks away from the Jewish material. The climax of the novel is set in Israel during the 1967 war.

Meyer Levin's successes are more those of the talented journalist (a profession he began in 1923) than the creative artist. He is a realistic novelist whose primary skill is producing popular, readable novels based on serious historical themes of the twentieth century. He has all the journalistic qualities of clarity, immediacy, and topicality. But he ultimately lacks both the artist's imaginative insights into the depths of human experience and a sense of the nuances of language. He is in the final analysis a re-creator rather than a creator.

—David J. Geherin

---

**LEVINE, (Albert) Norman.** Canadian. Born in Ottawa, Ontario, 22 October 1924. Educated at McGill University, Montreal, 1946–49, B.A. (1st class honours) in English Language and Literature 1948, M.A. 1949; King's College, London, 1949–50. Served as a Flying Officer in the Royal Canadian Air Force, 1942–45. Married Margaret Payne in 1952; has three children. Employed by the Department of National Defence, Ottawa, 1940–42. Head of the English Department, Barnstaple Boys Grammar School, Devon, 1953–54; Resident Writer, University of New Brunswick, Fredericton, 1965–66. Recipient: Canada Council Fellowship, 1959, and Arts Award, 1969. Has lived in England since 1949. Address: 45 Bedford Road, St. Ives, Cornwall, England.

PUBLICATIONS

Novels

*The Angled Road*. London, Werner Laurie, 1952.
*From a Seaside Town*. London and Toronto, Macmillan, 1970.

Short Stories

> *One Way Ticket*.   London, Secker and Warburg, and Toronto, McClelland and Stewart, 1961.
> *I Don't Want to Know Anyone Too Well: 15 Stories*.   London and Toronto, Macmillan, 1971.

Uncollected Short Stories

> "For Auld Lang Syne", in *Spectator* (London), 28 December 1962.
> "Waiting for the Storm", in *Harper's Bazaar* (New York), September 1963.
> "Boiled Chicken", in *Spectator* (London), 20 December 1963.
> "Nostalgia", in *Across a Crowded Room*.   London, Frewen, 1965.

Verse

> *The Tightrope Walker*.   London, Totem Press, 1950.

Other

> *Canada Made Me*.   London, Putnam, 1958.

> Editor, *Canadian Winter's Tales*.   Toronto and London, Macmillan, 1968.

Manuscript Collection: University of Texas, Austin; York University, Toronto.

Critical Studies: essay by the author on his own work: "The Girl in the Drugstore", in *Canadian Literature* (Vancouver), no. 41, 1969; interview in *Canadian Literature* (Vancouver), no. 45, 1970; profile by Philip Oakes, in the *Sunday Times* (London), 19 July 1970; essay by Alan Heuser in the "Books" section of the *Montreal Star*, 26 September 1970.

Norman Levine comments:

For anyone who wants to know where to begin, I suggest that the start would be *Canada Made Me*, then the short stories, then *From a Seaside Town*.

Writing in the *Atlantic Advocate*, I said: "When you go to a writer's work—it is into his personal world that you enter. What he is doing is paying, in his own way, an elaborate tribute to people and places he has known."

                    *          *          *

Norman Levine is an exigent writer who has so far produced only one small book of poems, two novels, two volumes of short stories, and one travelogue-cum-social commentary, *Canada Made Me*. Although he has lived most of the time since 1949 in England, he remains very much a Canadian writer, and a strong element in all his books is his feelings as an expatriate. His work, as this would suggest, is strongly auto-biographical, and results from a close, almost clinical, observation of his own sensations, of his own sense of identity, and of his personal relationship with his family, his friends, his enemies, and the country—Canada— which made him. He works on a deliberately small canvas, scrupulously avoiding the "larger" issues such as politics and social theory in favour of the smaller but possibly more funda- mental issues of personal life. His work marks an effort at psychological rather than social realism.

He has also sought, with an almost obsessive devotion, a style and structure appropriate to the scope within which he works. His novels and stories are constantly revised and refined to eliminate any verbal excess, any trace of the grandiose, the pretentious or the precious. He seeks always to substitute the denotative for the richly connotative word or phrase, to find the accurate sensory detail rather than the emotive generalization, to break up the long, rhyth- mical sentence into a series of staccato short sentences, some of which are, by deliberate choice, "sentence fragments" according to the rules of formal grammar. His style, thus, often gives the effect of awkwardness or ugliness—but this is the effect he aims for, since he regards it as suitable for the expression of his sceptical, often sombre, vision. Although it is possible to find symbolic suggestiveness in some of the details he records, he seems deliber- ately to discourage such symbol hunting.

The seriousness with which Levine directs himself and his milieu to sceptical examination, however, is often lightened by his humour, which is characteristically subdued but neverthe- less delightful. There exists in Levine, alongside his gift for clinical analysis, a boyish *joie de vivre*, a wry but real zest for experience and a strong sense of the absurd. If the limited nature of his output marks him as a minor writer, he is one of those minor writers who have their own piquant flavour, their own distinctive angle of vision. The most appealing quality in his work is its honesty—like Swift, on his own much more modest scale, he seems always to be saying "things are not as they seem—look!"

—Desmond Pacey

---

LEWIS, Janet. American. Born in Chicago, Illinois, 17 August 1899. Educated at the Lewis Institute, Chicago, A.A. 1918; University of Chicago, Ph.B. 1920. Married the poet and critic Yvor Winters in 1926 (died, 1968); has two children. Passport Bureau Clerk, American Consulate, Paris, 1920; Proofreader, *Redbook* magazine, Chicago, 1921; English Teacher, Lewis Institute, 1921–22. Lecturer, Writers' Workshop, University of Missouri, Columbia, 1952, and University of Denver, 1956; Visiting Lecturer, then Lecturer in English, Stanford University, California, 1960, 1966, 1969, 1970. Recipient: Friends of American Literature award, 1932; Shelley Memorial Award, for poetry, 1948; Guggenheim Fellowship, 1950. Address: 143 West Portola Avenue, Los Altos, California 94022, U.S.A.

PUBLICATIONS

Novels

The Invasion: A Narrative of Events Concerning the Johnston Family of St. Mary's. New York, Harcourt Brace, 1932.
The Wife of Martin Guerre. San Francisco, Colt, 1941; London, Rapp and Whiting, 1967.
Against a Darkening Sky. New York, Doubleday, 1943.

*The Trial of Soren Qvist.*   New York, Doubleday, 1947; London, Gollancz, 1967.
*The Ghost of Monsieur Scarron.*   New York, Doubleday, and London, Gollancz, 1959.

Short Stories

*Goodbye, Son and Other Stories.*   New York, Doubleday, 1946.

Uncollected Short Stories

"At the Swamp", in *The Best Short Stories of 1929.*   New York, Dodd Mead, 1929.
"A Still Small Voice", in *McCall's* (New York), 1946.
"The Breakable Cup", in *Saturday Evening Post* (New York), 27 February 1965.

Play

*The Wife of Martin Guerre*, music by William Bergsma (produced New York, 1956).
   Denver, Swallow, 1958.

Verse

*The Indians in the Woods.*   Bonn, Germany, Monroe Wheeler, 1922.
*The Wheel in Midsummer.*   Lynn, Massachusetts, Lone Gull Press, 1927.
*The Earth-Bound, 1924–44.*   Aurora, New York, Wells College Press, 1946.
*Poems, 1924–1944.*   Denver, Swallow, 1950.

Other

*The Friendly Adventures of Ollie Ostrich* (juvenile).   New York, Doubleday, 1923.
*Keiko's Bubble* (juvenile).   New York, Doubleday, 1961; Tadworth, Surrey, World's
   Work, 1963.
*The U.S. and Canada*, with others.   Green Bay, University of Wisconsin Press, 1970.

Manuscript Collection: Stanford University Library, California.

Critical Studies: essay by Richard F. Goldman, in *Musical Quarterly* (New York), July 1956; "The Historical Novels of Janet Lewis" by Donald Davie, in *Southern Review* (Baton Rouge, Louisiana), January 1966; "Genius Unobserved" by Evan S. Connell, Jr., in *Atlantic* (Boston), December 1969.

Janet Lewis comments:

It is difficult to know what to say about my own work. Most of it needs little if any explanation. In regard to *The Invasion* I can state that I meant to write history as if I were writing fiction. It is in every way, in so far as I could manage, faithful to the facts and the events. When it comes to the three novels based on the famous cases of circumstantial evidence, I can only state again that I intended to write history as if it were fiction. I remained in each case as faithful to the facts as I could, but I was so far from them in time and space that I needed to invent rather freely, in order to clothe the facts with life. In the case of *Martin Guerre* I began with a very brief account of the events, and have learned bit by bit since the day the book was first published more and more about the truth of the matter, so that now, thirty years later, I have at hand the ultimate source for the story, the account by one of the judges, Jean de Coras. My story of Martin Guerre is fiction, but it is very close indeed to the known facts.

*         *         *

Janet Lewis, widow of the poet and critic Yvor Winters, and herself a distinguished poet, is admired as one of the purest stylists in contemporary fiction, and as a novelist who continued to write quietly probing dramas of psycho-moral ambiguity with almost total disregard for the changing fashions of American fiction. She is to be compared in the quiet integrity of her art, with Willa Cather, Caroline Gordon, and her friend Elizabeth Maddox Roberts. Only her modest volume of short stories (*Goodbye, Son*) and the slow-paced, intelligent, at times dreary *Against a Darkening Sky* are contemporary in scene. Her reputation rests instead on her four historical novels, one related to her own part-Indian background, the others laid in remote European times.

*The Invasion* occupies a surprisingly satisfying border region between fiction and history, and contains some of the loveliest prose in modern American literature. Its singular achievement is to present without pretentiousness or strain an Indian culture from within (the Ojibway of the Lake Superior area), and its gradual change and slow obliteration over a century and a half. The family chronicle extends from 1791, when we meet the fourteen year old Woman of the Glade, who marries the trader John Johnston, to the death in 1944 of Anna Maria Johnstone, the Red Leaf. The novel is the work of a poet recording delicate nuances of landscape and mood, and of a scrupulous historian contemplating with equanimity the inevitable outrages of human passion and eroding time. It combines with remarkable success an intimate immersion in scene (a succession of lived moments) and a flow of time that is calm as well as swift. The chronicle's exceptional authenticity is strengthened by the fact that the famous ethnologist, linguist and Indian agent Henry Rowe Schoolcraft is a central figure in the family history.

Three very different historical novels are based on incidents recorded in Phillips' *Famous Cases of Circumstantial Evidence*, an early 19th century work. *The Trial of Soren Qvist*, laid in 17th century Denmark, is the story of a saintly pastor executed for a crime he did not commit. This is a spare and dramatic novel, but meditative too, like everything Janet Lewis has written. *The Ghost of Monsieur Scarron* is the product of years of research, some of it in a part of Paris that has not greatly changed since 1694. It is the minutely realistic story of a bookbinder falsely accused of authoring a libelous pamphlet directed against Louis XIV and Madame de Maintenon. The evocation of the Paris of that time is remarkable.

The best of these novels, one of the greatest short novels in American literature, is *The Wife of Martin Guerre*: a quietly authentic, immaculately written story of a man whose physical "double" (but far more considerate and more loving than the original) returns to claim the wife of a soldier supposed dead in the wars of sixteenth century France. Here as in her other two novels of ambiguous crime and punishment Janet Lewis dramatizes, always calmly, situations exerting extreme pressure on her characters. The marriage of Martin Guerre and Bertrande de Rols, at eleven, is of its time, and so too the execution twenty-one years later. A sentence from Janet Lewis' "Foreword" suggests the human understanding underlying all her work. "The rules of evidence vary from century to century, and the morality which compels many of the actions of men and women varies also, but the capacities of the human soul for suffering and for joy remain very much the same."

—Albert Guerard

**LIDDELL, (John) Robert.** British. Born in Tunbridge Wells, Kent, 13 October 1908. Educated at Haileybury College, Hertford, 1922–27; Corpus Christi College, Oxford, 1927–33 (Passmore Edwards Scholar, 1933), B.A. (1st class honours) 1931, B.Litt. 1933, M.A. 1935. Senior Assistant, Department of Western Manuscripts, Bodleian Library, Oxford, 1933–38. Lecturer, University of Helsinfors, Sweden, 1939, and Farouk I University, Alexandria, 1941–46; Lecturer, 1946–51, and Assistant Professor, 1951–52, Fuad I University, Cairo. Since 1953, British Council Lecturer in Athens. Head of the English Department, Athens University, 1963–68. Fellow, Royal Society of Literature, 1964. Address: c/o Barclays Bank, High Street, Oxford, England.

PUBLICATIONS

Novels

*The Almond Tree.* London, Cape, 1938.
*Kind Relations.* London, Cape, 1939; as *Take This Child*, New York, Greystone Press, 1939.
*The Gantillons.* London, Cape, 1940.
*Unreal City.* London, Cape, 1952.
*The Rivers of Babylon.* London, Cape, 1959.
*An Object for a Walk.* London, Longman, 1966.
*The Deep End.* London, Longman, 1968.
*The Stepsons.* London, Longman, 1969.

Short Stories

*Watering Place.* London, Cape, 1945.
*The Last Enchantments: Short Stories.* London, Cape, 1948; New York, Appleton Century Crofts, 1949.

Other

*A Treatise on the Novel.* London, Cape, 1947; Bloomington, Indiana University Press, 1948.
*Some Principles of Fiction.* London, Cape, 1953; Bloomington, Indiana University Press, 1954.
*Aegean Greece.* London, Cape, 1954.
*The Novels of Ivy Compton-Burnett.* London, Gollancz, 1955.
*Byzantium and Istanbul.* London, Cape, and New York, Macmillan, 1956.
*The Morea* (travel). London, Cape, 1958; Mystic, Connecticut, Verry, 1964.
*The Novels of Jane Austen.* London, Longman, and New York, Barnes and Noble, 1963.
*Mainland Greece.* London, Longman, 1965.

Translator, *Old and New Athens*, by Demetrios Sicilianos. London, Putnam, 1960; Chester Springs, Pennsylvania, Dufour, 1962.

Robert Liddell comments:

I have avoided descriptive writing in my novels, preferring to reserve it for my travel books. My critical books indicate the principles by which I have tried to be guided.

\*       \*       \*

Robert Liddell is an author whose literary parents are both of the same sex, namely, Jane Austen and Ivy Compton-Burnett, on both of whom he has written a critical exposition. This statement, of course, is one of those convenient simplifications, though not without its indicative value. Robert Liddell is a learned authority on fiction, interested in its theory as well as its practice, as his two books on the subject—*A Treatise on the Novel* and *Some Principles of Fiction*—amply demonstrate. Here, it is clear, the great examples of the nine-teenth-century French masters have been carefully examined; yet still it remains that Ivy Compton-Burnett and Jane Austen (the latter largely subsumed in the former) have been the predominant influences. As Mr. Liddell has himself remarked, "the indebtedness of Miss Compton-Burnett to Jane Austen is generously acknowledged." A like generous indebtedness to Ivy Compton-Burnett exists in Robert Liddell's fiction, and in 1947 he declared before her death: "Of all English novelists now writing she is the greatest and the most original artist."

The points of similarity between these writers are enormously evident. As with Ivy Compton-Burnett, Robert Liddell presents us with domestic dramas almost entirely limited to the middle- or upper-middle class—families of professional men or families where money and property, in comfortable measure, are inherited. Though he can write about foreign places—as he has done both in travel-books and fiction (see his novel *Unreal City*)—it is British villages and towns which provide the habitat of most of his characters. He has also a predilection for pre-Second-World-War settings, sometimes specified or sometimes left vague. British society before the Welfare State is what fascinates Mr. Liddell. *Watering Place*, the title of one of his works, suggests the slightly formal old-fashioned world in which his fiction operates. Similarly, *The Last Enchantments* (a reference to Matthew Arnold's famous eulogy of Oxford) deals with that city of cap and gown and its academic outcrop, the suburbs of North Oxford.

Speaking of Ivy Compton-Burnett, Mr. Liddell observed that

> the subject-matter of all her books—tyranny in family-life—is . . . neither unreal nor unimportant . . . it is one of the most important that a novelist can choose. The desire for domination, which in a dictator can plunge the world into misery, can here be studied in a limited sphere. The courage of those who resist dictation, and the different motives which cause people to range themselves on the side of the dictator can be minutely studied.

This tyranny and the resistance to it have been studied by him in his own fiction. The un-married sister Margery in *The Gantillons* is one such petty tyrant and the German step-mother Elsa in *The Stepsons* is another—a crueller and more fearful hounder of the young and innocent than her prototype.

The unveiling of a motive behind its concealing manner is something Mr. Liddell's writing effects which makes us think likewise of Ivy Compton-Burnett or Jane Austen. Margery Gantillon, speaking to a daughter of the late Canon Summerhayes who has taken a job as a governess, shows the claw beneath the velvet glove: "'It's your first place, isn't it?' said Margery pleasantly, but as if she were speaking pleasantly to a housemaid." Another passage between Margery and her niece Peggy, concerning seakale which is one of the ingredients of the dinner, illustrates this laying-bare of sadistic impulse even more succinctly:

> "Is it nice?" asked Peggy.
> "If it wasn't nice, is it likely I should give it you for dinner?" asked Margery.
> It was not at all nice.

Beneath the attic purity of his style, Robert Liddell presents a world in which realities of heart and mind are continually being unravelled from their presuming or pretentious appearances.

—Derek Stanford

**LINDSAY, Jack.** Australian. Born in Melbourne, 20 October 1900, the son of the writer and artist Norman Lindsay. Educated at Brisbane Grammar School; Queensland University, Brisbane, 1918–21, B.A. (1st class honours) in classics 1921. Served in the British Army, 1941–45: in the Royal Corps of Signals, 1941–43, and as a Scriptwriter in the War Office, 1943–45. Married Meta Waterdrinker in 1956; has two children. Editor, with K. Slessor and F. Johnson, *Vision*, Sydney, 1923–24; Editor, with P. R. Stephensen, *London Aphrodite*, 1928–29; Editor, *Poetry and the People*, London, 1938–39; Editor, *Anvil*, London, 1947; Editor, with J. Davenport and R. Swingler, *Arena*, London, 1949–51. Proprietor and Director, Fanfrolico Press, London, 1927–30. Recipient: Australian Literature Society Couch Gold Medal, 1960; Order of Merit, U.S.S.R., 1968. Fellow, Royal Society of Literature, 1945, and the Ancient Monuments Society, 1961. Address: 40 Queen Street, Castle Hedingham, Halstead, Essex, England.

PUBLICATIONS

Novels

> *Cressida's First Lover: A Tale of Ancient Greece.* London, Lane, and New York, Long and Smith, 1932.
> *Rome for Sale.* London, Mathews and Marriot, and New York, Harper, 1934.
> *Caesar Is Dead.* London, Nicholson and Watson, 1934.
> *Last Days with Cleopatra.* London, Nicholson and Watson, 1935.
> *Despoiling Venus.* London, Nicholson and Watson, 1935.
> *Storm at Sea.* London, Golden Cockerel Press, 1935.
> *The Wanderings of Wenamen: 1115–1114 B.C.* London, Nicholson and Watson, 1936.
> *Shadow and Flame* (as Richard Preston). London, Chapman and Hall, 1936.
> *Adam of a New World.* London, Nicholson and Watson, 1937.
> *Sue Verney.* London, Nicholson and Watson, 1937.
> *End of Cornwall* (as Richard Preston). London, Cape, 1937.
> *1649: A Novel of a Year.* London, Methuen, 1938.
> *Brief Light: A Novel of Catullus.* London, Methuen, 1939.
> *Lost Birthright.* London, Methuen, 1939.
> *Guiliano the Magnificent*, adapted from a work by D. Johnson. London, Dakers, 1940.
> *Light in Italy.* London, Gollancz, 1941.
> *Hannibal Takes a Hand.* London, Dakers, 1941.
> *Stormy Violence.* London, Dakers, 1941.
> *We Shall Return: A Novel of Dunkirk and the French Campaign.* London, Dakers, 1942.
> *Beyond Terror: A Novel of the Battle of Crete.* London, Dakers, 1943.
> *The Barricades Are Down: A Tale of the Collapse of a Civilisation.* London, Gollancz, 1945.
> *Hullo Stranger.* London, Dakers, 1945.
> *Time to Live.* London, Dakers, 1946.
> *The Subtle Knot.* London, Dakers, 1948.
> *Men of Forty-Eight.* London, Methuen, 1948.
> *Fires in Smithfield.* London, Lane, 1950.
> *The Passionate Pastoral.* London, Lane, 1951.
> *Betrayed Spring: A Novel of the British Way.* London, Lane, 1953.
> *Rising Tide.* London, Lane, 1953.
> *Moment of Choice.* London, Lane, 1955.
> *A Local Habitation: A Novel of the British Way.* London, Bodley Head, 1957.
> *The Great Oak: A Story of 1549.* London, Bodley Head, 1957.
> *The Revolt of the Sons.* London, Muller, 1960.
> *All on the Never-Never: A Novel of the British Way of Life.* London, Muller, 1961.

*The Way the Ball Bounces.*   London, Muller, 1962.
*Masks and Faces.*   London, Muller, 1963.
*Choice of Times.*   London, Muller, 1964.
*Thunder Underground: A Story of Nero's Rome.*   London, Muller, 1965.

## Short Stories

*Come Home at Last and Other Stories.*   London, Nicholson and Watson, 1936.

## Plays

*Marino Faliero: A Verse-Play.*   London, Fanfrolico Press, 1927.
*Helen Comes of Age: Three Original Plays in Verse.*   London, Fanfrolico Press, 1928.
*Hereward: A Verse Drama.*   London, Fanfrolico Press, 1930.
*The Whole Armour of God* (produced London, 1944).
*Robin of England* (produced London, 1945).
*Face of Coal*, with B. Coombes (produced London, 1946).
*Iphigeneia in Aulis*, adaptation of a play by Euripides (produced London, 1967).
*Hecuba*, adaptation of a play by Euripides (produced London, 1967).
*Electra*, adaptation of a play by Euripides (produced London, 1967).
*Orestes*, adaptation of a play by Euripides (produced London, 1967).
*Nathan the Wise*, adaptation of a play by Lessing (produced London, 1967).

## Verse

*Fauns and Ladies.*   Sydney, J. Kirtley, 1923.
*The Passionate Neatherd.*   London, Fanfrolico Press, 1930.
*Into Action: The Battle of Dieppe: A Poem.*   London, Dakers, 1942.
*Second Front: Poems.*   London, Dakers, 1944.
*Clue of Darkness.*   London, Dakers, 1949.
*Peace Is Our Answer.*   London, Collet, 1950.
*Three Letters to Nikolai Tikhonov.*   London, Fore, 1951.
*Three Elegies.*   Twinstead, Essex, Myriad Press, 1956.

## Other

*William Blake: Creative Will and the Poetic Image.*   London, Fanfrolico Press, 1927; revised edition, 1929.
*Dionysos; or, Nietzsche contra Nietzsche: An Essay in Lyrical Philosophy.*   London, Fanfrolico Press, 1928.
*Runaway* (juvenile).   London, Oxford University Press, 1935.
*Rebels of the Goldfields* (juvenile).   London, Lawrence and Wishart, 1936.
*Mark Antony: His World and His Contemporaries.*   London, Routledge, 1936; New York, Dutton, 1937.
*John Bunyan: Maker of Myths.*   London, Methuen, 1937.
*Anatomy of Spirit: An Enquiry into the Origins of Religious Emotions.*   London, Methuen, 1937.
*To Arms: A Story of Ancient Gaul* (juvenile).   London, Oxford University Press, 1938.
*England My England.*   London, Fore, 1939.
*A Short History of Culture.*   London, Gollancz, 1939; revised edition, London, Studio Books, 1962; New York, Citadel Press, 1964.

*The Dons Sight Devon: A Story of the Defeat of the Invincible Armada* (juvenile). London, Oxford University Press, 1942.
*Perspective in Poetry.* London, Fore, 1944.
*British Achievement in Music and Art.* London, Pilot Press, 1945.
*Song of a Falling World: Culture During the Break-up of the Roman Empire (A.D. 350–600).* London, Dakers, 1948.
*Marxism and Contemporary Science; or, The Fulness of Life.* London, Dobson, 1949.
*A World Ahead: Journal of a Soviet Journey.* London, Fore, 1950.
*Charles Dickens: A Biographical and Critical Study.* London, Dakers, and New York, Philosophical Library, 1950.
*Byzantium into Europe: The Story of Byzantium as the First Europe (362–1204 A.D.) and Its Further Contribution till 1453 A.D.* London, Lane, 1952.
*Rumanian Summer,* with M. Cornforth. London, Lawrence and Wishart, 1953.
*The Lotus and the Elephant.* Bombay, Kutub Popular, 1954.
*Civil War in England: The Cromwellian Revolution.* London, Muller, 1954; New York, Barnes and Noble, 1967.
*George Meredith: His Life and Work.* London, Lane, 1956.
*The Romans Were Here: The Roman Period in Britain and Its Place in Our History.* London, Muller, 1956.
*After the Thirties: The Novel in Britain and Its Future.* London, Lawrence and Wishart, 1956.
*Life Rarely Tells: An Autobiographical Account Ending in the Year 1921 and Situated Mostly in Brisbane, Queensland.* London, Bodley Head, 1958.
*Arthur and His Times: Britain in the Dark Ages.* London, Muller, 1958; New York, Barnes and Noble, 1966.
*Discovery of Britain: A Guide to Archaeology.* London, Merlin Press, 1958.
*1764: The Hurly-Burly of Daily Life Exemplified in One Year of the 18th Century.* London, Muller, 1959.
*The Writing on the Wall: An Account of Pompeii in Its Last Days.* London, Muller, 1960.
*The Roaring Twenties: Literary Life in Sydney, New South Wales, in the Years 1921–26.* London, Bodley Head, 1960.
*The Death of the Hero* (on French art). London, Studio Books, 1960.
*William Morris: Writer.* London, William Morris Society, 1961.
*Our Celtic Heritage.* London, Weidenfeld and Nicolson, 1962.
*Fanfrolico and After* (autobiography). London, Bodley Head, 1962.
*Daily Life in Roman Egypt.* London, Muller, 1963; New York, Barnes and Noble, 1964.
*Nine Days' Wonder: Wat Tyler.* London, Dobson, 1964.
*The Clashing Rocks: A Study of Early Greek Religion and Culture, and the Origins of Drama.* London, Chapman and Hall, 1965.
*Leisure and Pleasure in Roman Egypt.* London, Muller, 1965; New York, Barnes and Noble, 1966.
*Our Anglo-Saxon Heritage.* London, Weidenfeld and Nicolson, 1965.
*J. M. W. Turner: His Life and Work: A Critical Biography.* London, Adams and MacKay, and New York, Graphic Society, 1966.
*Our Roman Heritage.* London, Weidenfeld and Nicolson, 1967.
*Meetings with Poets: Memories of Dylan Thomas, Edith Sitwell, Louis Aragon, Paul Eluard, Tristan Tzara.* London, Muller, 1968.
*Men and Gods on the Roman Nile.* London, Muller, and New York, Barnes and Noble, 1968.
*The Ancient World: Manners and Morals.* London, Weidenfeld and Nicolson, and New York, Putnam, 1968.
*Cézanne: His Life and Art.* London, Adams and MacKay, 1969.
*The Origins of Alchemy in Graeco-Roman Egypt.* London, Muller, 1970.
*Cleopatra.* London, Constable, and New York, Coward McCann, 1971.

*The Origins of Astrology.*  London, Muller, 1971.
*Courbet: His Life and Work.*  Bath, Adams and Dart, and New York, Harper, 1972.

Editor, with Kenneth Slessor, *Poetry in Australia.*  Sydney, Vision Press, 1923.
Editor, *Loving Mad Tom: Bedlamite Verse of the XVI and XVII Centuries.*  London, Fanfrolico Press, 1927.
Editor, with P. Warlock, *Metamorphosis of Aiax,* by John Harrington.  New York, McKee, 1928.
Editor, *Parlement of Pratlers.*  London, Fanfrolico Press, 1928.
Editor (as Peter Meadows), *Delighted Earth,* by Robert Herrick.  London, Fanfrolico Press, 1928.
Editor, *Inspiration.*  London, Fanfrolico Press, 1928.
Editor, *Letters of Philip Stanhop, Second Earl of Chesterfield.*  London, Fanfrolico Press, 1930.
Editor, with Edgell Rickword, *Handbook of Freedom: A Record of English Democracy Through Twelve Centuries.*  London, Lawrence and Wishart, and New York, International Publishers, 1939.
Editor, with others, *New Lyrical Ballads.*  London, Editions Poetry, 1945.
Editor, *Anvil: Life and the Arts: A Miscellany.*  London, Meridian, and New York, Universal Distributors, 1947.
Editor, *New Development Series.*  London, Lane, 1947–48.
Editor, *Herrick: A Selection.*  London, Grey Walls Press, 1948.
Editor, *William Morris: A Selection.*  London, Grey Walls Press, 1948.
Editor, with K. Swingler, *Key Poets.*  London, Fore, 1950.
Editor, *Barefoot,* by Z. Stancu.  London, Fore, 1950.
Editor, *Paintings and Drawings of Leslie Hurry.*  London, Grey Walls Press, 1952.
Editor, *The Sunset Ship: Poems of J. M. W. Turner.*  Lowestoft, Suffolk, Scorpion Press, 1966.
Editor, *The Autobiography of Joseph Priestley.*  Bath, Adams and Dart, 1970.


Translator, *Lysistrata,* by Aristophanes.  Sydney, J. Kirtley, 1925; London, Fanfrolico Press, 1926.
Translator, *Satyricon and Poems,* by Petronius.  London, Fanfrolico Press, 1927; revised edition, Elek, 1960.
Translator, *Homage to Sappho.*  London, Fanfrolico Press, 1928.
Translator, *Complete Poems of Theocritus.*  London, Fanfrolico Press, 1929.
Translator, *Hymns to Aphrodite,* by Homer.  London, Fanfrolico Press, 1929.
Translator, *Women in Parliament,* by Aristophanes.  London, Fanfrolico Press, 1929.
Translator, *The Complete Poetry of Gaius Catullus.*  London, Fanfrolico Press, 1930.
Translator, *Mimes,* by Herondas.  London, Fanfrolico Press, 1930.
Translator, *Sulpicia's Garland: Roman Poems.*  New York, McKee, 1930.
Translator, *Patchwork Quilt: Poems by Ausonius.*  London, Fanfrolico Press, 1930.
Translator, *The Golden Ass,* by Apuleius.  New York, Limited Editions Club, 1931; revised edition, London, Elek, and Bloomington, Indiana University Press, 1960.
Translator, *I Am a Roman.*  London, Mathews and Marriot, 1934.
Translator, *Medieval Latin Poets.*  London, Mathews and Marriot, 1934.
Translator, *Daphnis and Chloe,* by Longus.  London, Daimon Press, 1948.
Translator, with S. Jolly, *Song of Peace,* by V. Nezval.  London, Fore, 1951.
Translator, *Poems of Adam Mickiewicz.*  London, Sylvan Press, and New York, Transatlantic Arts, 1957.
Translator, *Russian Poetry, 1917–1955.*  London, Lane, 1957; Chester Springs, Pennsylvania, Dufour, 1961.
Translator, *Asklepiades in Love.*  Twinstead, Essex, Myriad Press, 1960.
Translator, *Modern Russian Poetry.*  London, Vista, 1960.

Translator, *Cause, Principle, and Unity: 5 Dialogues*, by Giordano Bruno.   London, Daimon Press, 1962; New York, International Publishers, 1964.

Translator, *Ribaldry of Ancient Greece*.   London, Elek, and New York, Ungar, 1965.

Translator, *Ribaldry of Ancient Rome*.   London, Elek, and New York, Ungar, 1965.

Translator, *The Elegy of Haido*, by Teferos Anthias.   London, Anthias Publications, 1966.

Translator, *The Age of Akhenaten*, by Eleonore Bille-de-Mot.   London, Adams and MacKay, 1967; New York, McGraw Hill, 1968.

Translator, *Greece, I Keep My Vigil for You*, by Teferos Anthias.   London, Anthias Publications, 1968.

Critical Study: *Mountain in the Sunlight* by Alick West, London, Lawrence and Wishart, 1958.

Jack Lindsay comments:

I began as a poet and feel that my devotion to poetry has determined my writing career in all its aspects. First as poet and classical scholar I turned to translating Greek and Latin poetry; then as critic seeking to understand the ancient poets I worked at history, needing to grasp their world and find out how far the poems were linked with that world's workings; out of concern for the nature of poetry I turned to philosophy, especially Plato and Nietzsche though also to poet-philosophers like Blake; later the same interests drew me to cultural anthropology and to psychoanalysis. Thus out of various disciplines, which I approached always from the angle of poetry and its nature, I expanded my interests and the range of my work.

A friend and I hand-printed my *Lysistrata* in Sydney, Australia, 1924–25, with illustrations by my father Norman Lindsay. The book was well received and he asked me to come to London to start a fine press, the Fanfrolico (a name devised by my father in *contes drolatiques* he had written for an Abbey of Thelema): we used that name to express the aesthetic we had devised in Australia. The friend handed the press over to me, as he wanted to return to Australia; I was thus involved in much typographical, editing, translating work, and did much literary research at the B.M. Reading Room, as well as writing poetry. When the press ended in 1930 I went to Cornwall in an effort to find a new basis for work, and lived in extreme hardship till 1934 when I managed to synthesise my interests (as outlined above) in the historical novel. I had translated and annotated Catullus, and I now developed a picture of his world in a Roman trilogy.

My method was thus derived wholly from poetry and my quest into its nature as the highest point of human consciousness. It sought to bring together the following elements: (a) the element of sensuous immediacy in experience, the timeless present of the poetic image; (b) the tragic pattern of conflict, breakdown, recognition, triumph as I had learned it from the Greeks, Nietzsche, and Freudian technique, and from my broodings over Shakespeare and Dostoevsky; (c) the related pattern of death-rebirth which was revealed in tribal ritual (especially of the initiation-ceremony) and carried on by the mystery-religions of the ancient world and by Christianity. I then attempted to make a dynamic synthesis of all these elements in an interpretation of the structure of development in history and of the dialectical relation of individual and social whole. I was (and have continued to go on) seeking to grasp in a single conception or image a largescale moment of life, especially a moment of revolutionary change when all the issues come together in full force, and at the same time to realise the situation at a multiple series of levels (personal, social, aesthetic, philosophic, legal, religious etc.).

This has continued to be my method, with varying emphases—though I soon turned to English history as well as to ancient, and then moved on to the contemporary situation.

I have tried to grasp the particular forms of death-rebirth in every period, to grasp both the total movement and the individual refractions. In turn I have expanded this method to deal directly with many periods of history (especially Graeco-Roman Egypt), with problems of anthropology, with the biographies of writers and artists, and so on. I think I can then claim a definite unity in all my work despite its very multifarious nature. The novels have been especially recognized in the Soviet Union, where over a million copies have been sold in translation and *Betrayed Spring* has been printed in its English form as a textbook. Versions have also appeared in Chinese and Mongolian, as well as in German, Polish, Hungarian, Czech, Romanian, Bulgarian. I believe that this wide interest has been because of the fusion I have attempted of a poetic and an historical vision—the way in which my method seeks to grasp the patterns of change in a perspective of all that constitutes the human universal.

*       *       *

Jack Lindsay divides his many novels into two groups: "Historical Novels" and "Contemporary Novels of the British Way". These two groups are closely linked by an overwhelming concern for the socialist ideal in its purist form. What interests this writer primarily is the moment of revolutionary struggle when the forces working for the good life for every human being rise up against the apathy and de-humanisation caused by an out-of-control capitalist system. This moment of change may take place in Rome in 63 B.C., as it does in the early novel *Rome for Sale*, or in the formation of a branch of the Campaign for Nuclear Disarmament in a small midland town, as it does nearly thirty years later in *The Way the Ball Bounces*.

It is no doubt because of this strong political bias that Mr. Lindsay's novels are so widely read in the Soviet Union and the Eastern bloc. But political propaganda and the art of the novelist are two separate activities. One must look beyond the unvarying message, however much one may agree or disagree with it, to discover how these novels take shape and live. The first thing one notices after reading several of them from any period is how strongly they are influenced by Elizabethan drama. These novels are structured as plays, the reader being given a list of the main characters. The plot is almost invariably of a strong and definite nature involving events of life and death; and the action is divided into contrasting scenes, with comic relief supplied in an almost Shakespearean manner in the Roman novels by the most bawdy of the common soldiers and their prostitutes.

As for love, as distinct from lust, that is an emotion that for Mr. Lindsay is very strongly linked with political ideals. Catilina in *Rome for Sale* owes the deep love he has for his wife Orestilla to the knowledge that they are both working for the same cause, the prosperity of the common citizens of Rome. In a much later novel *Revolt of the Sons*, Chris, the youngest of Samuel Todd's five sons, realises his love for his cousin Rebecca at the same time that he becomes convinced of the need to break free of the tyranny of private family capitalism in which he and his brothers are locked. The case of Alan Horton, the young solicitor in *The Way the Ball Bounces*, is somewhat different. A withdrawn young man, he was so emotionally shattered by his experiences in the Korean war that he successfully immured himself against any form of feeling apart from a mild delight in the verbal logic of the law. It takes a short, sincere and slightly desperate affair with a young West Indian girl to batter these defences down.

Mr. Lindsay is above all a very conscious novelist. He does not expect the reader to totally suspend disbelief. So in the historical novels he keeps very closely to the actual recorded events, and in the contemporary novels in imagined settings he often lets the reader observe how the characters are being handled. Francis Musgrave, one of the main characters in *A Local Habitation*, acts as a sort of chorus in *The Revolt of the Sons*. He and his friend Roland have been discussing old Todd, his five sons and the wives of the three older ones. He reports "You might say that family represents our world in miniscule. . . . I said it was a Balzacian theme: the power of money and its ubiquitous tendrils of distortion. He said it was Dostoevskian: the fascination and hatred of authority, the jealous sons surrounding the father-god." In fact, as in so many of these novels, it is both.

—Shirley Toulson

---

**LINKLATER, Eric (Robert Russell).** British. Born in Penarth, South Wales, 8 March 1899. Educated at Aberdeen Grammar School; Aberdeen University, Scotland, M.A. 1925; studied medicine. Served as a Private in the Black Watch, 1917–19; Major in the Royal Engineers, commanding the Royal Engineers Orkney Fortress, 1939–41; Member of Staff, Directorate of Public Relations, War Office, 1941–45; Temporary Lieutenant-Colonel in Korea, 1951; Territorial Decoration. Married Marjorie MacIntyre in 1933; has four children. Assistant Editor, *Times of India*, Bombay, 1925–27; Assistant to the Professor of English Literature, Aberdeen University, 1927–28; Commonwealth Fellow, Cornell University, Ithaca, New York, and the University of California, Berkeley, 1928–30. Rector of Aberdeen University, 1945–48. Deputy Lieutenant of Ross and Cromarty, Scotland, 1968. Recipient: Carnegie Medal, 1945. LL.D., Aberdeen University, 1946. C.B.E. (Commander, Order of the British Empire), 1954. Address: Pitzcalzean House, Easter Ross, Ross-Shire, Scotland.

PUBLICATIONS

Novels

> *White Maa's Saga.* London, Cape, and New York, Peter Smith, 1929.
> *Poet's Pub.* London, Cape, and New York, Farrar and Rinehart, 1930.
> *Juan in America.* London, Cape, and New York, Farrar and Rinehart, 1931.
> *The Men of Ness: The Saga of Thorlief Coalbiter's Son.* London, Cape, 1932; New York, Farrar and Rinehart, 1933.
> *Magnus Merriman.* London, Cape, and New York, Farrar and Rinehart, 1934.
> *The Revolution.* London, White Owl Press, 1934.
> *Ripeness Is All.* London, Cape, and New York, Farrar and Rinehart, 1935.
> *Juan in China.* London, Cape, and New York, Farrar and Rinehart, 1937.
> *The Sailor's Holiday.* London, Cape, 1937; New York, Farrar and Rinehart, 1938.
> *The Impregnable Women.* London, Cape, and New York, Farrar and Rinehart, 1938.
> *Judas.* London, Cape, and New York, Farrar and Rinehart, 1939.
> *Private Angelo.* London, Cape and New York, Macmillan, 1946.
> *A Spell for Old Bones.* London, Cape, 1949; New York, Macmillan, 1950.
> *Mr. Byculla: A Story.* London, Hart Davis, 1950; New York, Harcourt Brace, 1951.
> *Laxdale Hall.* London, Cape, 1951; New York, Harcourt Brace, 1952.
> *The House of Gair.* London, Cape, 1953; New York, Harcourt Brace, 1954.
> *The Faithful Ally.* London, Cape, 1954; as *The Sultan and the Lady*, New York, Harcourt Brace, 1955.
> *The Dark of Summer.* London, Cape, 1956; New York, Harcourt Brace, 1957.
> *Position at Noon.* London, Cape, 1958; as *My Father and I*, New York, Harcourt Brace, 1959.
> *Roll of Honour.* London, Hart Davis, 1961.

*Husband of Delilah.*   London, Macmillan, 1962; New York, Harcourt Brace, 1963.
*A Man over Forty.*   London, Macmillan, and New York, St. Martin's Press, 1963.
*A Terrible Freedom.*   London, Macmillan, 1966.

## Short Stories

*The Crusader's Key.*   London, White Owl Press, 1933; New York, Knopf, 1934.
*God Likes Them Plain: Short Stories.*   London, Cape, 1935.
*Sealskin Trousers and Other Stories.*   London, Hart Davis, 1947.
*A Sociable Plover and Other Stories and Conceits.*   London, Hart Davis, 1957.
*The Stories of Eric Linklater.*   London, Macmillan, 1968; New York, Horizon Press, 1969.

## Plays

*The Devil's in the Soup.*   London, Cape, 1934.
*Crisis in Heaven* (produced Edinburgh, 1944).   London, Macmillan, 1944; New York, Macmillan, 1945.
*Love in Albania* (produced London, 1949).   London, English Theatre Guild, 1950.
*Two Comedies: Love in Albania and To Meet the MacGregors.*   London, Macmillan, and New York, Macmillan, 1950.
*The Mortimer Touch* (produced London, 1952).   London, French, 1952.
*Breakspear in Gascony.*   London, Macmillan, and New York, Macmillan, 1958.

## Verse

*A Dragon Laughed and Other Poems.*   London, Cape, 1930.

## Other

*Ben Johnson and King James: Biography and Portrait.*   London, Cape, and New York, Farrar and Rinehart, 1931.
*Mary, Queen of Scots.*   London, Davies, and New York, Appleton, 1933.
*Robert the Bruce.*   London, Davies, and New York, Farrar and Rinehart, 1934.
*The Lion and the Unicorn; or, What England Has Meant to Scotland.*   London, Routledge, 1935.
*The Cornerstones: A Conversation in Elysium.*   London, Macmillan, and New York, Macmillan, 1941.
*The Defence of Calais.*   London, His Majesty's Stationery Office, 1941.
*The Man on My Back* (autobiography).   London, Macmillan, and New York, Macmillan, 1941.
*The Northern Garrisons: The Defence of Iceland and the Faroe, Orkney and Shetland Islands.*   New York, Garden City Publishing Company, 1941.
*The Raft, and Socrates Asks Why: Two Conversations.*   London, Macmillan, 1942; New York, Macmillan, 1943.
*The Highland Divisions.*   London, His Majesty's Stationery Office, 1942.
*The Great Ship, and Rabelais Replies: Two Conversations.*   London, Macmillan, 1944; New York, Macmillan, 1945.
*The Wind on the Moon* (juvenile).   London, Macmillan, and New York, Macmillan, 1944.
*The Art of Adventure* (essays).   London, Macmillan, 1947.

*The Pirates of the Deep Green Sea* (juvenile).   London, Macmillan, and New York, Macmillan, 1949.
*The Campaign in Italy*.   London, Her Majesty's Stationery Office, 1952.
*Our Men in Korea*.   London, Her Majesty's Stationery Office, 1952.
*A Year of Space: A Chapter of Autobiography*.   London, Macmillan, and New York, Harcourt Brace, 1953.
*The Ultimate Viking* (essays).   London, Macmillan, 1955; New York, Harcourt Brace, 1956.
*Karina with Love* (juvenile).   London, Macmillan, 1958.
*The Merry Muse*.   London, Cape, 1959; New York, Harcourt Brace, 1960.
*Edinburgh*.   London, Newnes, 1960.
*Orkney and Shetland: An Historical, Geographical, Social and Scenic Survey*.   London, Hale, 1965.
*The Prince in the Heather*.   London, Hodder and Stoughton, 1965; New York, Harcourt Brace, 1966.
*The Conquest of England*.   London, Hodder and Stoughton, and New York, Doubleday, 1966.
*The Survival of Scotland: A Review of Scottish History from Roman Times to the Present Day*.   London, Heinemann, 1968; as *The Survival of Scotland: A New History of Scotland from Roman Times to the Present Day*, New York, Doubleday, 1968.
*Scotland*.   London, Thames and Hudson, and New York, Viking Press, 1968.
*The Secret Larder*.   London, Macmillan, 1969.
*The Royal House of Scotland*.   London, Macmillan, 1970.
*Fanfare for a Tin Hat* (autobiography).   London, Macmillan, 1970.
*A Corpse on Clapham Common: A Tale of Sixty Years Ago*.   London, Macmillan, 1971.

Editor, *The Thistle and the Pen: An Anthology of Modern Scottish Writers*.   London, Nelson, 1950.
Editor, *John Moore's England: A Selection from His Writings*.   London, Collins, 1970.

Critical Studies: in *Historical Survey of Scottish Literature* by Agnes Mure Mackenzie, London, Maclehose, 1933; *Scotland*, edited by Henry Meikle, London, Nelson, 1947; *Annals of Scotland* by George Blake, London, British Broadcasting Corporation, 1955; comment by the author on his own work, in *Fanfare for a Tin Hat*, 1970.

\*       \*       \*

In the sombre corridors where literary power is exercised, where reputations are made and broken, the name of Eric Linklater is seldom mentioned even to be derided. For more than forty years he has indulged in many of the sins that cause the priest-pundits of the critical and academic journals to cast a writer for earthly and eternal oblivion. An arrant professional, he has turned a careful hand to biography, history, journalism, children's books, drama, radio and with much that he has done has achieved popularity among readers whose responses do not depend upon the self-elected arbiters of literary taste. He has been prolific, versatile, at times romantic and often deliciously and deliberately comic. Generally well-disposed towards his fellow-men, he has been modest even in his dislikes, writing of them as if he is ready and eager to accept new evidence that will refute his opinions.

Of all Linklater's sins in the eyes of aesthetes, perhaps the most heinous is his identification with a section in British society—Britain's service and ex-servicemen—that is huge but deprived of laureates. Had Linklater chosen to write of soldiers and war in the manner of a Remarque or a Barbusse, driven by its follies and horrors into vicious protest, he might have been accepted as a genius for our times. Linklater does not hold back his distaste for war; it is violent even in the deliberate bathos of *Private Angelo* and in the quiet sentiment of *Roll of Honour*, and inevitable from an author who has seen at too close quarters three wars; but he has no distaste and only ready sympathy, even love, for soldiers, and his sympathy is as quick for generals as for privates. (Another mark against him with those who believe that attacking the authorities is of itself an authoritative form of art.)

It is significant that though Linklater has been a successful novelist since 1929 there is no serious study of his achievement. Admittedly his bibliography is daunting. Not only has he been prolific but his very versatility stands against the possibility of summary. The gusto, disorder and extravagantly picaresque quality of the two Juan books (*Juan in America* and *Juan in China*) have no immediate connection with the Aristophanic comedy of *The Impregnable Women*, the fantasy of *Laxdale Hall* or the uproarious satire of *Magnus Merriman*.

Yet there is a connection that should arouse the interest of the most sophisticated literary scholar. Linklater, as much as any writer of this century and far more than most, is an experimenter, forever groping after the most satisfactory form in which to set his novels. His experiments are not always successful. The disruption of prose by verse (in this case light and generally bawdy) worked well in *Magnus Merriman*, but the poetry in *Roll of Honour* is not sufficiently strong to support the virile prose. The backwards time-sequence of *Position at Noon* makes for some magnificent comedy but becomes laboured as the book moves further into the past. Yet Linklater's most successful experiments are his characters, larger than life, smaller than life, but always drawn from life.

If Linklater's versatility and zest for experiment remove some of his fictions from the conventional classification of the novel-form so does his brimming humanity serve to set him apart from the Scottishness which, at first glance, is palpably his. His characters are most often Scotsmen. He has a pride (that is never conceit) in the achievements, courage and humour of his countrymen, an understanding that again comes close to being pride even in their weaknesses and follies, but for him Scotland is a set of parables that reveal all mankind, and it is not surprising that in the gentlest, most sensitive, most revealing (and most comic) of all his books, *Private Angelo*, his central character is not one of his beloved Scottish soldiers, not even a British soldier, but an "enemy" who is nonetheless all soldiers. Linklater wears his kilt proudly but he carries a standard for all men of all races.

Had Linklater's achievements ended in 1940 with behind him, among other books, *White Maa's Saga*, *Poet's Pub*, the two *Juans*, *Ripeness Is All*, *Magnus Merriman* and *The Impregnable Women*, still he would have deserved much of his contemporaries and of posterity. For those who grew up to the inevitability of a second World War Linklater, a survivor from an earlier and more horrific war, set patterns of gaiety that was unrestrained, and uninhibited even by the certainty that laughter would soon turn sour. But when the second War came still there was Linklater to serve as laureate to the generation that he had reared on laughter.

And twenty-five years after the end of that War still Linklater writes as if he is a young but skilful author bursting with humour, bubbling with experimental zeal, his quick but kindly eyes alert for character.

—J. E. Morpurgo

---

**LITVINOFF, Emanuel.** British. Born in London, 30 June 1915. Served as a Major in the Royal West African Frontier Force, 1940–46. Married Cherry Marshall in 1942 (divorced); has three children. Before World War II, worked in tailoring, cabinet-making, and the fur trade; after the war worked as a journalist and broadcaster, and founded the journal, *Jews in Eastern Europe*, London. Since 1958, Director of the Contemporary Jewish Library, London. Address: 36 Byron Court, Mecklenburgh Square, London W.C.1, England.

PUBLICATIONS

Novels

> The Lost Europeans.   New York, Vanguard Press, 1959; London, Heinemann, 1960.
> The Man Next Door.   London, Hodder and Stoughton, 1968; New York, Norton, 1969.

Short Stories

> Penguin Modern Stories 2, with others.   London, Penguin, 1969.
> Journey Through a Small Planet.   London, Joseph, 1972.

Uncollected Short Stories

> "The God I Failed", in *The Guardian* (London), 1966.
> "Call Me Uncle Solly", in *The Listener* (London), 1967.

Plays

> Plays written for television, 1966–71.

Verse

> Conscripts: A Symphonic Declaration.   London, Favil Press, 1941.
> The Untried Soldier.   London, Routledge, 1942.
> A Crown for Cain.   London, Falcon Press, 1948.

Emanuel Litvinoff comments:

My novel *The Lost Europeans* is haunted by the Holocaust. It describes the morbid psychological obsessions of victim and persecutor in a situation where former German Jews return to Germany after the war and confront their erstwhile neighbours.

*The Man Next Door* is, in a sense, related to this theme. Its central character is a conventional suburban Englishman of the middle-class whose personality begins to disintegrate under the encroachments of middle-age, accompanied by a sense of social and sexual failure. In this process, a mild and commonplace xenophobia turns to rabid hatred of Jews and Negroes of the kind so hideously expressed by the Nazis.

My short stories, set in the milieu of the London Jewish East End, celebrate the idealism, pain, and promise of adolescence.

\*          \*          \*

Emanuel Litvinoff's short stories describe the atmosphere of a close Jewish community in London's East End where he grew up between the wars. The stories contain some poignant and sometimes verbose semi-autobiographical sketches of adolescence:

> "What do you do on week-ends?" I stammered.
> "On Saturday," she whispered, without lifting her head, "I go to the synagogue with my aunt."
> Soft black hair curled on the nape of her slender neck and I was tormented by her narrow, sleepy Russian eyes. I wanted to say something miraculous and un-forgettable, or so sharp, cruel and eloquent it would remain a fresh wound all of her life. But instead I said: "Does your aunt shave on Shabbos?"
> "A View from the Seventh Floor"

In the same story, Litvinoff mentions his early feelings of rootlessness which inform much of his later work: "In those days I had the shadowy premonition that unless my life was shattered to pieces and I could put it together differently, I'd never, never be myself."

As Litvinoff approaches maturity, he becomes increasingly aware of his "ancestry of misfortune". He regards it as mere chance that he was born in Whitechapel. His home could as easily have been in Hitler's Germany or Stalin's Russia. Litvinoff's first novel, *The Lost Europeans*, develops this idea and examines the restless lives of a few World War II survivors.

The novel is set in post-war Berlin, where ex-nazis and communists, hedonistic young Aryans, whores and a few Jews live in awkward peace. Martin Stone, a London accountant, takes time off to visit the city of his childhood and claim the legal restitution of his family's fortune.

The war-blighted Berliners whom Martin meets, involuntarily inflame his smouldering bitterness: There is Hugo Krantz, a fellow Jew, once the witty doyen of Berlin's theatre circles, now a fat businessman in relentless pursuit of sensual pleasures and the friend who betrayed him to the S.S. Hugo arranges accommodation for Martin in the guesthouse of his oldest friend, Frau Goetz. Her gothic hair-do's and bird-like charm cannot conceal the marks of Auschwitz. Every Berliner is a victim. In the parks and pastryshops and honky tonk bars, Martin feels once more "the poisons moving in the bloodstream, the familiar throbbing of the diseased night".

But it is in this city that Martin meets Karin, a docile factory worker from the eastern sector. She too is a victim—raped in childhood by conquering Russian soldiers. In order to offer her his love, Martin must expiate Karin's years of numbness and resolve his own haunting resentments.

Litvinoff's descriptions of the strange personal lives of Hugo and Frau Goetz are especially good, and Hugo's foray into the ambiguous and dangerous world of intelligence agents has all the atmosphere of a first-rate spy thriller. But just as the pace is getting really hot, we are back with the dour, curiously faceless Martin. The impact of each story—Martin's and Hugo's—is reduced rather than enhanced by its entanglement with the other. Nevertheless, *The Lost Europeans* is a very readable and frequently compelling account of the obsessions of German Jews and their former persecutors.

*The Man Next Door*, Litvinoff's only other novel, focuses on Harold Bollam, a man who blossomed early in life. Boarding school, the army and a spell as a store manager in West Africa supported and strengthened his hawkish sentiments on class and race. Back in England he finds life somewhat bewildering:

> The country had gone mad for gimmicks. Young smart alecks were getting in every-where. Long-haired pop-singers bought up the stately homes, public opinion media were in the hands of queers and sensation-mongers who made England look cheap in the eyes of the world. Cheap, indeed, when black college boys became prime ministers of ridiculous "independent" states, dined with the Queen and lectured the British on the what's-what of democracy.

Middle-age does not mellow a man like Bollam; failures and frustrations pile upon him. Relations with his fretful wife Edna are bleak; prospects for promotion at International Utilities dwindle daily; sex is a combat between flesh and despair; his children, away at boarding school, are strangers. When the Winstons (born Weinsteins) move in next door, Bollam's resentments and fears become obsessions. His wife, his colleagues, the Blacks, the Jews, and especially the Jews next door, are all conspiring to degrade and defeat him. Obsession turns to paranoia and Bollam seeks insane revenge. "... as soon as the Winstons arrived he'd guessed it would end badly. They didn't fit. Apart from being Jews, there was something alien and disruptive about them. They were the kind who carried the germ of misfortune wherever they went, like spores of an invisible cancer. ..."

*The Man Next Door* has a certain morbid fascination, but it lacks the authenticity of Litvinoff's first novel. Most of the characters are incredibly stereotyped, and his portrayal of Bollam's grim, neurotic life is often glib. The analogy between Bollam's retrogression and the rise of nazism is obvious but rarely effective.

Litvinoff writes about people whose painful history has left them bitter, tormented and potentially destructive. But he does not have the sheer grasp or the calm incisiveness that characterizes the best writing of this kind.

—Roland Turner

---

**LITWAK, Leo E.** American. Born in Detroit, Michigan, 28 May 1924. Educated at the University of Michigan, Ann Arbor, 1943, 1946; New School for Social Research, New York, 1947; Wayne State University, Detroit, B.A. 1948; Columbia University, New York, 1948–51. Served in the United States Army, 1943–46. Married Mary Katherine Fiske in 1957 (divorced, 1964); has one child. Instructor of Philosophy, Washington University, St. Louis, 1951–60. Since 1961, Professor of English, San Francisco State College. Visiting Lecturer in English, Stanford University, California, 1966. Recipient: Longview Foundation Award, 1958; National Endowment for the Arts award, 1968; Daroff Memorial Prize, 1970; Guggenheim Fellowship, 1970. Address: 1933 Greenwich Street, San Francisco, California 94123, U.S.A.

PUBLICATIONS

Novels

> *To the Hanging Gardens.* Cleveland, World, 1964; London, Deutsch, 1966.
> *Waiting for the News.* New York, Doubleday, 1969; London, MacGibbon and Kee, 1971.

Uncollected Short Stories

> "The Making of a Clerk", in *Midstream* (New York), 1957.
> "All Men Are", in *Partisan Review* (New Brunswick, New Jersey), 1958.
> "Solitary Life of Man", in *Esquire* (New York), 1958.
> "Aid Man", in *Nugget* (New York), 1958.

"In Shock", in *Partisan Review* (New Brunswick, New Jersey), 1968.
"The Cream of Michigan", in *Commentary* (New York), 1969.

Other

  *College Days in Earthquake Country*, with Herbert Wilner.  New York, Random
  House, 1971.

Manuscript Collection: Washington University, St. Louis.

Leo E. Litwak comments:

I probe my experience for illuminating moments. I hang the vision on plot and character.
My inclinations are political and philosophical. My mode is narrative.

*        *        *

Leo E. Litwak's fiction reflects his vision that there is an earthly contest between men
who live by force and men who seek another way. His themes unfold through character
and plot. The main character in Litwak's story "The Making of a Clerk" is a mild and
intellectual Jewish recruit who doesn't have much of a chance in Basic Training. He is
humiliated and terrorized by a brutal hillbilly who is the self-acclaimed chief.

Litwak's strength is the clear delineation of characters and the background that has
molded them. Motivation is clear and the characters are real, complex, with many dimensions.

Set in an academic environment just after World War II, Litwak's first novel, *To the
Hanging Gardens*, relates philosophy professor Al Kraft's tangle of relationships. This associates and acquaintances, struggling for security, grasping for old loves, trying to renew
stale marriages, risking everything for dead dreams, eventually assemble for a climactic
evening in a decadent but elegant nightclub named The Hanging Gardens. But clearly these
gardens are no paradise. In this frantic postwar society, wealth is power and fun is the only
value. Professor Kraft learns that philosophy is not enough; reality awakens him. He sees
that self-seeking brutes have no compassion for the destruction of quiet or weak men.
Bullies may gain the world since no one will fight them. Hitler's horrors have been fought
in a great war, but the battle hasn't been won. Jews are persecuted, Negroes are used,
human dignity is subject to wealth. Perseverance and good luck account for Kraft's meager
success in re-ordering his life, but the victory is inconclusive.

In *Waiting for the News* the struggle is the rise of the labor union in Detroit. Idealistic
Jake Gottlieb fights for and finally wins unionization of the laundry truck drivers in Detroit.
Jake's sons, Ernie and Vic, are caught in the struggle. As they grow up they recognize that
Jake's dangerous fight against the owners includes them too. Jake forces them to swear
revenge if he is harmed, and, after his success at unionizing the drivers, Jake disappears,
evidently in a power struggle within the union. The brawny O'Brien, a fascist force in the
union, is the boys' prime suspect. They must avenge their father. As the Hamlet theme
develops, the paradox becomes clear. Jake had taught them that human beings cannot be
squashed as if they were bugs. But they must become the thing they fight against: they
must squash O'Brien.

Jake's struggle counterpoints the radio news of Hitler's rise to power. The irony that
force must be used to suppress force is thematic, and Jake's family waits for news of Hitler's
dreaded rise as they wait for news of Jake, especially after he is brutally murdered. There
is further irony in that whether the atrocities of Hitler and Nazism are before us or behind us,

the injustices basic to the fascist premises abound in American society. While Jake and his family gasp at Hitler's anti-semitic outrages, they are restricted from living in non-Jewish neighborhoods. The boys are caught between the fantasies of noble heroes like their father and neighborhood thugs, but they come to see the paradox of brutes who want to take over by fear and force and good men who are compelled to use similar methods. Litwak seems to be saying look out or the brutes will take over and if you fight them you become a brute too, but you have no alternative.

—Sally Slocum

---

**LODGE, David.**   British.   Born in London, 28 January 1935. Educated at University College, London, 1952–55. 1957–59, B.A. (1st class honours) in English 1955, M.A. 1959; University of Birmingham, Ph.D. 1967. Served in the Royal Armoured Corps, 1955–57. Married Mary Frances Jacob in 1959; has three children. Assistant, British Council, London, 1959–60. Lecturer in English, 1960–71, and since 1971 Senior Lecturer, University of Birmingham. Visiting Associate Professor, University of California, Berkeley, 1969. Recipient: Harkness Commonwealth Fellowship, 1964. Address: Department of English, University of Birmingham, Birmingham B15 2TT, England.

PUBLICATIONS

Novels

*The Picturegoers.*   London, MacGibbon and Kee, 1960.
*Ginger, You're Barmy.*   London, MacGibbon and Kee, 1962; New York, Doubleday, 1965.
*The British Museum Is Falling Down.*   London, MacGibbon and Kee, 1965; New York, Holt Rinehart, 1967.
*Out of the Shelter.*   London, Macmillan, 1970.

Uncollected Short Story

"The Man Who Wouldn't Get Up", in *Weekend Telegraph* (London), 6 May 1966.

Plays

*Between These Four Walls*, with Malcolm Bradbury and James Duckett (produced Birmingham, 1963).
*Slap in the Middle*, with others (produced Birmingham, 1965).

Other

*Language of Fiction.*   London, Routledge, and New York, Columbia University Press, 1966.

*Graham Greene*.   New York and London, Columbia University Press, 1966.
*The Novelist at the Crossroads and Other Essays*.   London, Routledge, and Ithaca, New York, Cornell University Press, 1971.
*Evelyn Waugh*.   New York and London, Columbia University Press, 1971.

Editor, *Jane Austen's "Emma": A Casebook*.   London, Macmillan, 1968.
Editor, *Emma*, by Jane Austen.   London, Oxford University Press, 1971.
Editor, *Modern Literary Criticism*.   London, Longman, 1972.

Critical Study: an interview with Bernard Bergonzi, in *The Month* (London), February 1970.

David Lodge comments:

My novels belong to a tradition of realistic fiction (especially associated with England) that tries to find an appropriate form for, and a public significance in, what the writer has himself experienced and observed. In my case this experience and observation include such things as: lower-middle-class life in the inner suburbs of South East London; a war-time childhood and a post-war "austerity" adolescence; Catholicism; education and the social and physical mobility it brings; military service, marriage, travel, etc. My first, second and fourth novels are "serious" realistic novels about such themes, the last of them, *Out of the Shelter*, which is a kind of *Bildungsroman*, being, as far as I am concerned, the most inclusive and most fully achieved.

My third novel, *The British Museum Is Falling Down*, was something of a departure in being a comic novel, incorporating elements of farce and a good deal of parody. I plan to write more fiction in the comic mode, as I enjoy the freedom for invention and stylistic effect it affords. On the other hand, I have not (like many contemporary writers) lost faith in traditional realism as a vehicle for serious fiction. The writer I admire above all others, I suppose, is James Joyce, and the combination one finds in his early work of realistic truth-telling and poetic intensity seems to me an aim still worth pursuing.

As an academic critic and teacher of literature with a special interest in prose fiction, I am inevitably self-conscious about matters of narrative technique, and I believe this is a help rather than a hindrance. I certainly think that my criticism of fiction gains from my experience of writing it.

\*       \*       \*

David Lodge combines the writing of fiction with a keen interest in its theory, as is shown in his two books of criticism, *Language of Fiction* and *The Novelist at the Crossroads*. As a critic he is sympathetic to literary experiment and the kind of fiction that probes the problematical relations between art and reality, though as a novelist he still finds the realistic tradition viable and continues to write within it, drawing in large measure on autobiographical material. Of his four novels, only *The British Museum Is Falling Down* is overtly experimental, and that in a broadly comic way.

David Lodge is a Roman Catholic by birth and upbringing. His basic milieu is shabby-genteel Catholic family life in South London, whose nearest literary equivalent lies in the domestic scenes of Joyce's *Portrait of the Artist*. His first novel, *The Picturegoers*, was set against this background, which was treated in a warm and even sentimental manner; he returned to it ten years later in *Out of the Shelter*, where it was regarded with a cool but not contemptuous eye, and with a much greater sense of its narrowness and limitations.

*The Picturegoers* was an ambitious novel, focused on a suburban cinema and showing a broad range of contrasted characters, though it was rather lacking in dramatic movement and interplay. It suggested that despite a speculative interest in the hero's religious struggles, Lodge's basic talent was as a comic novelist. It was followed by *Ginger, You're Barmy*, an obsessively realistic study of army life that was clearly a working-off of unassimilated resentments about the author's military service. *The British Museum Is Falling Down* represented a real development. It was a comic novel on a serious topic, the Roman Catholic ban on contraception. The central character is an anxious Catholic graduate student, married with three children and the nagging possibility that a fourth might be on the way; he spends his days working on a literary thesis at the British Museum, which Lodge presents as an arena for farcical happenings of all kinds. The hero's professional interest in literary style is worked into the fabric of the novel in recurring passages of accomplished parody of distinguished modern novelists.

*Out of the Shelter* is, in all senses, a serious novel, though often showing its author's humorous bias. It is a *Bildungsroman* that traces its hero's childhood in wartime London up to a point in his mid-teens when he spends a holiday with his sister who is a secretary with the American army of occupation in Germany. After the deprivations of English life the boy is overwhelmed by the riches of the American Way of Life: the story, as Lodge tells it, is both an account of individual sensibility, and a representative treatment of a significant Anglo-American cultural encounter. *Out of the Shelter* is a deeply impressive novel; together with the lively and inventive *British Museum Is Falling Down*, it is clear evidence of David Lodge's talent as a novelist. There must, however, be a question about how far he will continue to combine harmoniously his practice as a novelist with his theoretical and analytical interests as a critic.

—Bernard Bergonzi

---

**LOVELACE, Earl.** Trinidadian. Born in Trinidad in 1935. Married. Civil Servant; currently, Agricultural Assistant in Jamaica. Recipient: B. P. Independence Award, 1965. Address: c/o Henry Regnery Co., 114 West Illinois Street, Chicago, Illinois 60610, U.S.A.

PUBLICATIONS

Novels

*While Gods Are Falling*.  London, Collins, 1965; Chicago, Regnery, 1966.
*The Schoolmaster*.  London, Collins, and Chicago, Regnery, 1968.

*     *     *

Whether the setting is rural Trinidad or urban Port of Spain, the focus of Earl Lovelace's novels is on the not so unique socio-economic problems which inevitably accompany the transition of an agrarian people into the complexities of industrialized civilization. In *While Gods Are Falling*, his protagonist Walter Castle, wishes to escape the overcrowding and disorder of the godless city, to return to the less frustrating difficulties of living off the land. As Walter's wife recognizes from the beginning, escape is not the answer. He exhibits an internal deficiency (symptomatic of the malaise affecting all his neighbors) which will not be alleviated by retreat. The solution which finally gives meaning to his life and which appears to be the author's prescription for community improvement is personal involvement.

Utilizing flashbacks, alternated with present action, Lovelace develops a well-rounded plot. His primary weakness is in his overly explicit pronouncements on the social predicament. At times, especially in the early and late chapters, conversations tend to degenerate to shallow examinations of the various sides of an issue. For the most part, however, personalities shine through exposition and interesting human beings with real problems emerge from the prose.

Although the less optimistic second novel also contains a definite "message," it is not as obtrusively didactic and it is a more evenly balanced work. *The Schoolmaster*, even more than *While Gods Are Falling*, brings out Lovelace's Wordsworthian appreciation of simplicity in nature and man. The residents of isolated Kumaca, only vaguely aware of the sacrifices of innocence and peace that they must make, decide to align themselves with the forces of progress and modernization by constructing a local school and a new road to link them more closely with the outside world.

Enlightenment, embodied in the affected, meticulously efficient schoolmaster, comes to the village in spite of the tentative misgivings of Father Vincent and shrewdly detached Consantine Patron's refusal to lend support. These two men along with old Benn, the mule-driving natural philosopher, recognize and regret the approaching extinction of the pastoral way of life. Unfortunately, their pessimism is only too well justified. Quite literally, innocence, in the person of Christiana Dandrade, is raped by the harbinger of knowledge. In a moment of unguarded passion, the schoolmaster sows destruction not only for the girl, but also for the illusion of beneficent progress that has been deceiving the rustics. He pays almost immediately for his transgression with his life, but the general effects of his violation have only begun to tell upon those who trusted and even venerated him. It is an old and versatile theme, yet in this new setting one that retains freshness.

Nostalgia permeates Lovelace's works, and at its best his smoothly flowing style, with passages of graceful repetition and lyrically phrased description, becomes reminiscent of popular narrative tradition. His own editorial voice is sometimes indistinguishable from the idiom of his characters, but if this is a fault, it is a minor one which seldom detracts from the color and feeling of the action that is being portrayed.

—Robert Daniel Hamner

---

**LOWRY, Robert.** American. Born in Cincinnati, Ohio, 28 March 1919. Educated at Withrow High School, Cincinnati; University of Cincinnati, 1937–38. Served in the United States Army Air Force, in Tunisia and Italy, 1942–45. Married four times; has three children. Publisher, The Little Man Press, Cincinnati, 1938–42; Production Manager and Editor, New Directions, publishers, New York, 1945–46; Book Reviewer, *Time* magazine, New York, 1949–50, and the *New York Times*, 1950–56; Staff Writer, *American Mercury*, New York, 1951–53. Address: 3747 Hutton Street, Cincinnati, Ohio 45226, U.S.A.

PUBLICATIONS

Novels

   *Casualty*. New York, New Directions, 1946.

*Find Me in Fire.*   New York, Doubleday, 1948.
*The Big Cage.*   New York, Doubleday, 1949.
*The Violent Wedding.*   New York, Doubleday, 1953; London, Barker, 1954.
*What's Left of April.*   New York, Doubleday, 1956.
*The Prince of Pride Starring.*   Cincinnati, National Genius Books, 1959.
*That Kind of Woman.*   New York, Pyramid, 1959.

Short Stories

*Hutton Street.*   Cincinnati, Little Man Press, 1940.
*The State of the Nation, with 9 Interludes,* with others.   Cincinnati, Little Man Press,
   1940.
*Gup: 3 Adventures.*   Cincinnati, Little Man Press, 1942.
*The Bad Girl Marie.*   Cincinnati, Little Man Press, 1942.
*The Blaze Beyond the Town.*   Bari, Italy, Piccolo Uomo, 1945.
*The Journey Out.*   Bari, Italy, Piccolo Uomo, 1945.
*The Wolf That Fed Us.*   New York, Doubleday, 1949.
*Happy New Year, Kamerades!*   New York, Doubleday, 1954.
*New York Call Girl.*   New York, Doubleday, 1958.
*The Knife.*   Cincinnati, privately printed, 1959.
*Party of Dreamers.*   New York, Fleet, 1962.
*The Last Party: A Memorable Collection of Short Stories.*   New York, Popular Library,
   1965.

Play

*The Violent Wedding,* in *Poet Lore* (Boston), 1961.

Verse

*New Poems.*   Cincinnati, Little Man Press, 1959.

Other

*Pip Pap Po: A Book of Many Things,* with others.   Cincinnati, Little Man Press, 1940.

Manuscript Collections: Boston University; University of Southern California, Los Angeles;
Kent State University, Kent, Ohio.

Robert Lowry comments:

I am a realist in my novels. And a trance realist at that—meaning that I wrote and rewrote
them until I could almost see and hear the events recorded. You will find fantasy only in
my short stories—and most of these fantastic stories have been collected in *Party of Dreamers.*
My first-published novels were war novels. *Casualty* is about Italy in World War II;
and the short novel *The Wolf That Fed Us* is about American-occupied Rome in wartime.
The novel of mine that bridges the war and the peace is *Find Me in Fire,* about an American
soldier and what he finds America is really like when he returns from World War II. *The*

*Violent Wedding* (about a world-champion boxer and an artist in Greenwich Village), *What's Left of April* (about an American fashion model who becomes a movie star), and *The Prince of Pride Starring* (about the nervous breakdown of a magazine editor) are all novels about American careers. So, in its way, is *The Big Cage*, the story of the childhood and adolescence of a literary genius.

And so the pattern my novels follow is the heartbreak of war, the disillusionment of the peace, and the morality of American life after the war. My short stories recreate all areas of American life, from the very rich to the very poor.

*         *         *

A boyhood in Cincinnati, Ohio, service on European battlefields during World War II, and the life of an artist living in Greenwich Village are the major private experiences which Robert Lowry has translated into a series of novels and short stories. While he has never enjoyed wide commercial success, Lowry has remained, often against considerable odds, the consummate professional, and his writing constitutes a continuing *Bildungsroman*—the semi-autobiographical story of his own emergence and development as a writer. Lowry has, at various times, worked as a book reviewer and editor, and some of his work has been published by his own Little Man Press in Cincinnati.

*Casualty*, Lowry's first, short novel, was singled out for special attention by numerous reviewers despite the fact that it was one of a great number of protest novels to follow the Second World War. The novel traces the catastrophic chain of events that follow the hero's broken engagement, and at the same time indicts the culture which forced him to don a uniform. *Casualty* is a bitter novel, but powerfully convincing in its tone, and memorable for the way in which detail accumulates to create a vivid sense of atmosphere and mood.

*Find Me in Fire* records the experiences of a soldier who returns to the small Ohio town where he had grown up and makes an abortive attempt to live his old life there again. Despite the familiarity of the basic material, Lowry was able to suggest that his hero's struggle represented the struggle of all men to gain a sense of belonging, and how their frustration can lead inexorably to violence.

*The Big Cage* is even more explicitly autobiographical than Lowry's first two novels. It follows the life of Dick Black from a Cincinnati childhood to his arrival in New York, armed with the firm ambition to become a writer. Nelson Algren recommended the book for its swift technique and emotional candor, but most reviewers found the hero's adventures rather routine, despite their immediacy. *Violent Wedding* was a more unique conception, the story of a Negro prize fighter and the white girl whom he loved, yet the novel lacked depth of insight in the handling of the central characters.

Lowry early established his reputation as a writer of spare, clean prose that vividly recreated milieu in the best naturalistic tradition. At a time when many writers were directing their attention to the inner workings of personality, he was creating sound, well-disciplined works in the best Hemingway tradition. Fashion in a sense passed Lowry by, but in doing so it overlooked the sardonic humor which often plays just beneath the surface of his writing. It is a quality best realized in his shorter fiction, where the author occasionally feels secure in abandoning his allegiance to naturalism and exercising a sense of the whimsical and the bizarre which also reveals itself in his drawings. "A Roar in the Village" sacrifices no depth of perception or feeling in its elaborate joking, and like most of the stories in *Party of Dreamers* it reveals an aspect of Lowry's talent not immediately visible in his longer fiction.

—David Galloway

**LUDWIG, Jack.** Canadian. Born in Winnipeg, Manitoba, 30 August 1922. Educated at the University of Manitoba, Winnipeg, B.A. 1944; University of California, Los Angeles, Ph.D. 1953. Married Leya Lauer in 1946; has two children. Taught at Williams College, Williamstown, Massachusetts, 1949–53; Bard College, Annandale-on-Hudson, New York, 1953–58; University of Minnesota, Minneapolis, 1958–61. Since 1961, Professor of English, State University of New York at Stony Brook. Co-Founding Editor, *The Noble Savage*, Chicago, 1960–62. Chairman, Humanities Group, International Seminar, Harvard University, Cambridge, Massachusetts, Summers 1963–66. Recipient: Longview Foundation Award, 1960; *Atlantic* "Firsts" Award, 1960; Martha Foley Short Story Award, 1961; O. Henry Award, 1961, 1965; Canada Council Senior Arts Fellowship, 1962, and Fiction Award, 1967. Address: 35 The Serpentine, Roslyn Estates, Long Island, New York 11576, U.S.A.

PUBLICATIONS

Novels

> *Confusions.* New York, New York Graphic Society, and London, Secker and Warburg, 1963.
> *Above Ground.* Boston and Toronto, Little Brown, 1968.

Other

> *Recent American Novelists.* Minneapolis, University of Minnesota Press, 1963.

> Editor, with W. R. Poirier, *Stories British and American.* Boston, Houghton Mifflin, 1963.
> Editor, with Andy Wainright, *Soundings: New Canadian Poets.* Toronto, House of Anansi, 1970.

*             *             *

Let us listen in turn to several of Jack Ludwig's several voices. They carry much provocation.

His editor's voice. A brief excerpt telegraphs meaning, comprehensively. Meaning is packed between the lines. "Poets are truly underground men salvaging underground words. Partisans. The Cold War is language's dark night of the soul. Any gleam is a reminder of sunlight." (*Soundings*, 1970.)

His voice *engagé*. Reading the beat of the times, prophetic, fair.

> So Johnson and Rusk aren't merely blind. They're dumb.
> The country's balance of payments and gold drain fix is a direct result of Vietnam. Cities will be ripped apart. Research will be abandoned. More and more men and money will go into Operation Rathole, dwarfing all others. The bright young men who might save this stupid government will be permanently turned-off by government and political involvements. A stick of grass is better than a cycle of Cathay or an acre of Middlesex ... let's not fool around with fantasy where reality is needed: an America which blows up takes Canada with her—not merely because we is small an' dey is big. What's good in America is what we in Canada have most in common with America. If that goes, all goes. ... So don't identify the U.S.A. with a government or Americans with their temporary leaders. ("Balancing the Books", in *The New Romans*, Edmonton, Hurtig, 1968.)

His voice as literary critic. Seems aware, in Kildare Dobbs' words, of "The tendency towards abstraction, noticeable in all contemporary arts." ("One Is Left with Silence", in *Saturday Night* [Toronto], December 1971.) ". . . the creation of significant action and meaning is a private, almost hermetic art, and not really subject to prescription from even the most friendly of sources." ("Clothes in Search of an Emperor", in *Canadian Literature* [Vancouver], 1960–61.)

Ludwig's narrative voice. Often poetic, often experimental, sometimes compressed, sometimes expansive, sounds the breadth of contemporary North American life, even at times its depths. "Our times have a tonality the novel cannot ignore." (*Recent American Novelists*, 1963.) And he does not. Either in his dialogue or his description (or his narration). Either in his short stories.

> Not once in my whole life, do you hear that, Doctor Morton, never did I do anything I didn't *want* to do. That's why I'm putting myself in your professional hands, Doctor Morton. I've never lost a skirmish. Undefeated Shirley—that's horrible. But still no confidence. Not a smidgeon. I shower twice a day, soak myself in Givenchy and Guerlain because *I belive* people sniff chickenshit on me. I can't get it out of my nostrils—me, the queen of Westmount. . . . ("Shirley", in *Tamarack Review* [Toronto], 1969.)

Or in his novels.

> Forgotten sun poured into the streets. Windswept, buffeted, dustflaked it gusted the avenues, struck fire in dull chrome, speckled glass, rocked on canopies, sprang yellowgreen from window-boxed plants, and potted trees.
> Faces turned upward to be warmed.
> Windows swung wide, scattering sun another window reflected, window to window, towering scaffold of climbing gold. Sun gyrated in mist northward. Black turned color, crosshatchings unearthed, hidden diagonals, brickscorch, wall cracks. For one second the city froze in etching . . . .
> Night town, IBM card, windows punched slits. The Empire State building glowed like a grotesque commericial for spark plugs. (*Above Ground*, 1968.)

Ludwig's personal voice, as in his contribution to Al Purdy's *The New Romans*, can be straightforward. "I'm a Canadian, but I've lived in the U.S.A. among Americans for a long time now. At this moment I'm living in London (should I add, *not* our Canadian London?), and this British-subjected, American-residenced, Canadian-citizened guy. . . ."

His personal voice can be baffling (as are the mephistophelean and rabbinical forces in his first novel, *Confusions*; as is the palimpset symbol in his second novel, *Above Ground*). "So what you have here [in *Confusions*], dear reader, is—I confess—but half a novel, it's an unsettled question if half a novel is better than none. My cleaning lady is the other half. Or your cleaning lady. *Your* newspaper's morgue. Or you." ("On Thermostats, Super-Egos, Theatre Directors, and Cleaning Ladies", in *Tamarack Review* [Toronto], 1967.) What has been compressed into the essay just quoted, despite the tongue-in-cheek, is a neat aesthetic probe of a particular writing experience. What has been compressed into this quotation is perhaps an aesthetic hint about this novel. Abstracting, the essay applies to a good deal of modernist art of the sort which seeks readers (or viewers) who will participate creatively in completing a particular work. This is one of the features that make for the excitement of modernist art and, in this instance, for the excitement of reading *Confusions*. A satire, fast-paced, controlled, chuckle-producing, but serious, it is, as Ludwig says of satire, "a grappling hook thrown up the high wall of the everyday world."

To digress a moment, I should like if possible to sound together all of Ludwig's several voices. Together, they are the voice of a civilized North American; also the voice of a cultured man. His culture, a culture he wears with ease, comes more from the roots of things genuine than from the academy alone. It comes from underground. Ludwig was born into the Jewish community of Winnipeg. He knows it in North America and in its European roots; his own, in Odessa; he knows much of its rich Yiddish and Hasidic backgrounds. In reading him one may think of Mordecai Richler or Philip Roth or I. B. Singer. No comparisons intrude. He is Ludwig; Richler, Roth, Singer are themselves.

To a degree all his writing voices one central, pervasive concern. With his emphasis added, it reads: "... *re-educate yourself, kid, but do it with ebullience.*" (*Recent American Novelists*, 1963.) Was he advising then, in the early '60's, what the early '70's have taken as *the* quest; namely, alternative modes of doing almost everything in everyday life, alternative modes to those which have come to threaten everyday life on almost every hand? The difference would lie with the rarity of ebullience in much of that questing. But in his work it carries the reader joyously, if he be willing. As it does, even in such a short story as "Meersh" (*Tamarack Review* [Toronto], 1961) in which the hero, in that poignant Yiddish mode, is forced daily to sacrifice himself for *un*worthy kin with hardly a murmur of dissent. And as it carries the reader, even when he is telling of his summer spent on the vacant floor of the old Ryan Building in downtown Winnipeg where he wrote *Confusions*.

So in *Confusions*, Ludwig celebrates life and vitality. Even the mock epic hero Joe Galsky (a Roxbury Jew)/Joseph Gillis (a Harvard graduate) does so in his confusions ("confissions"), troubled as he is by trying to follow what his creator refers to as a kind of North American credo, the putting of "Second Things First," second things such as "status-establishing, career-making and image-projecting." Galsky/Gillis will need to admit, "I am confused, therefore I am." One wonders if Ludwig may intend this to mean in part somewhat what Alan Watts means about the wisdom of insecurity in his book of that title. At any rate, Galsky/Gillis refuses to accept mephistophelean aid. He will not seek success as a novelist, if it means creating the kind of book he could not believe in. His closing words echo: "Look on me, ye unmighty, and live a little." (See "Anatomy of Confusion" by Lila Stonehewer, in *Canadian Literature* [Vancouver], 1966–67.) Rabbinical spirit prevails.

In *Above Ground*, Ludwig celebrates life and vitality, more in a lyric than a satiric way, not the least sexual vitality, even though, or perhaps because (is it partly autobiography?), the hero, Joshua, has had to spend almost all his formative years in hospital rooms due to a crippling ailment of the hip-bone. And that sexual vitality appeals.

> I raced the car, feeling her hand, her cheek on my lap. Red blotches, blue spears blinded my eyes as if they were shut a long time, and too suddenly opened. Every movement of her fingers sent a pulse exploding.... My mouth found her, my hands freed her hair, long, in a black lovely wash over her breasts.
>
> "I want your lips, your tits, your cunt, everything, all together, at once, for my cock, my hands, my mouth—"
>
> "If you can do it, do it."
>
> She tasted of heat, toasted sesame, love's spittle; smelled the way she felt, warm and secret and dark, her tongue so soft. A hot wave. My hands turned her legs up, arched high, higher, her breasts swelling, nipples saluting, open, all open with frankness....

It has been suggested (by D. O. Spettique, in *Queen's Quarterly* [Kingston, Ontario], 1968) that the women in Joshua's life may be "death-figures," especially since two of them, his dying mother and an amazing, neurotic mistress, pose "threats to his living integrity." But one wonders. The novel carries such a constant lyricism.

In his extended essay, *Recent American Novelists*, Ludwig writes as though he were already thinking of the form this second of his novels would take. "Serious fiction shows definite signs of turning from Kafkaesque 'Underground Man' to Tolstoian or Conradian 'Above-ground Man,' the hero who breaks out of his real or symbolic, sealed-off rooms to re-enter the world of action and history...." (*The New Romans*, 1968.) At any rate, when his hero Joshua does find himself free of those "symbolic" (at least) "sealed-off rooms," he "re-enters" a world of vital sexual activity which Ludwig celebrates without self-consciousness. (See "Starved in the Hour of Our Hoarding: The Conglomerate as Fiction" by Dave Godfrey, in *Tamarack Review* [Toronto], 1968–69.) Again, in praising Saul Bellow's *The Adventures of*

*Augie March* in *The New Romans*, Ludwig says, "history becomes a dimension of a hero's awareness—if not yet his acts." And he seems to describe the kind of novel *Above Ground* was going to become, one in which the sexual could find honest expression in the hero's awareness. Lastly, *Above Ground* seems to be a novel written in the open form as he had earlier conceived it: ". . . an open form, a way of writing *about* almost anything with almost unlimited scope—i.e., the limits are imposed not by the chosen form of the novel, but rather, as they should be, by the author's own limitations of talent, imagination, and knowledge." Two simple sentences from this same essay seem to define Joshua's growing consciousness. "He lives as an aware Aboveground Man. The man aware knows there is limitless fiction in the fall of a sparrow."

What better way to bring this to a stop than to hear Ludwig speak again: ". . . the novel has broken through, and broken out. Liberated from the tyranny of symbolic smallness it has attempted to become *the* literary form to catch the visible world in all its complexity, clangor, and untriumphant celebration. Our times have a tonality the novel cannot ignore."

Ludwig's is a voice true to his convictions. I like and admire its sound and its sense.

—Herbert C. Burke

---

**LURIE, Alison.** American. Born in Chicago, Illinois, 3 September 1926. Educated at Radcliffe College, Cambridge, Massachusetts, A.B. 1947. Married Jonathan Peale Bishop Jr. in 1948; has three children. Since 1968, Lecturer in English, Cornell University, Ithaca, New York. Recipient: Yaddo Foundation Fellowship, 1963, 1964, 1966; Guggenheim Fellowship, 1965; Rockefeller grant, 1968. Address: c/o Department of English, Cornell University, Ithaca, New York 14850, U.S.A.

PUBLICATIONS

Novels

*Love and Friendship*.   London, Heinemann, and New York, Macmillan, 1962.
*The Nowhere City*.   London, Heinemann, 1965; New York, Coward McCann, 1966.
*Imaginary Friends*.   London, Heinemann, and New York, Coward McCann, 1967.
*Real People*.   New York, Random House, 1969; London, Heinemann, 1970.

Other

*V. R. Lang: A Memoir*.   Munich, privately printed, 1959.

Manuscript Collection: Radcliffe College Library, Cambridge, Massachusetts.

\*       \*       \*

Outstandingly intelligent, Alison Lurie's work has been acclaimed on both sides of the Atlantic, although it is possibly rather *too* intelligent to enjoy a huge popular success. It lacks

791

—and this is much to her credit—the button-holing, narrowly self-obsessed, identify-with-me quality of so much fiction by women, and though two of her four novels treat specifically female dilemmas in an intimate, readable way, the viewpoint is ironic and objective. We are not tempted to suppose that Miss Lurie "is" the breathy, debby New Englander of her first novel, *Love and Friendship*, any more than we believe she "must be" Katharine, the equally New England but suppressed heroine of *The Nowhere City*. And yet the understanding and the eye for detail are those of an involved person, someone who knows about marriage and the trivia of family life and work relationships as well, and who is able to make literary use of these personal insights without simply transferring chunks of personal experience raw onto the page. Only in her latest book, *Real People*, a novella about a woman novelist tussling with herself and others in a literary retreat called Illyria, does Miss Lurie seem to be indulging in that perilously easy author's occupation of writing about what it is like to be a writer.

The story of *Love and Friendship* is the adultery of Emmy, an under-occupied young faculty wife, with a romantically unsuccessful and immoral musician. Eventually she returns to the safety of boring husband and her own monied family traditions. Miss Lurie transforms this hackneyed theme by making our views of the various characters shift subtly as Emmy's own view alters. She performs the same trick, but more startlingly, in *The Nowhere City*, in which the adulterous lover is first presented as odious and then allowed to become gradually attractive to the reader as he does to Katharine. At the same time Katharine herself passes through metamorphoses, from a dreary mutt with sinus trouble to a seducer's victim to a fulfilled woman to a Los Angeles dolly with bleached hair. Meanwhile her husband, another upright young academic, becomes temporarily sucked into Los Angeles life himself. (This book was written before 1965, when it was still credible that academics from the East might find Haight-Ashbury refreshing and appealing.) He finally emerges, chastened but essentially unchanged. He heads East again—reluctantly abandoning Katharine to the city in which she has either lost or found herself, the reader can decide which. Entirely free of moralising, overt or implicit, this book presents a daunting picture of an environment without the dimension of time, where nothing is quite real—but observations in the text to this effect are offered as if in quotes, almost like a parody of the "sensitive" novel.

Alison Lurie's third book, and perhaps her most accomplished, deals with the dotty religious cult of a small town group and with two sociologists who infiltrate in order to observe it. The group call themselves "the Truth Seekers", a phrase which might also be applied to the sociologists. Similarly the "Imaginary Friends" are perhaps not just the Martians of the group's fertile imagination but the sociologists themselves in their role as spies. Eventually one of them loses his detachment (like Katharine in *The Nowhere City*) and comes himself to believe in the supernatural identity the group have projected onto him. Once again, as in previous books, the nature of "personality", or "real life" itself, seems called in question, in a clever, witty and professional piece of work.

—Gillian Tindall

---

**LYTLE, Andrew (Nelson).** American. Born in Murfreesboro, Tennessee, 26 December 1902. Educated at Sewanee Military Academy, Tennessee; Exeter College, Oxford, 1920; Vanderbilt University, Nashville, Tennessee, B.A. 1925; Yale University, New Haven, Connecticut, 1927–29. Married Edna Langdon Barker in 1938 (died, 1963); has three children. Professor of History, Southwestern College, Memphis, Tennessee, 1936; Professor of History, University of the South, Sewanee, Tennessee, and Managing Editor of the *Sewanee Review*, 1942–43; Lecturer, 1946, and Acting Head, 1947, University of Iowa School of Writing, Iowa City; Lecturer in Creative Writing, University of Florida, Gainesville, 1948–61. Lecturer in English, 1961–67, and since 1968 Professor of English, University of the South, Sewanee; also, since 1961, Editor of the *Sewanee Review*. Has lectured at writing workshops and festivals at numerous universities. Recipient: Guggenheim Fellowship, 1940, 1941, 1960; *Kenyon Review* Fellowship, 1956; National Endowment for the Arts grant, 1966. Litt.D., Kenyon College, Gambier, Ohio, 1965; University of Florida, 1970. Address: Department of English, University of the South, Sewanee, Tennessee 37375; or, Log Cabin, Monteagle, Tennessee 37356, U.S.A.

## PUBLICATIONS

### Novels

    *The Long Night.*   Indianapolis, Bobbs Merrill, 1936; London, Eyre and Spottiswoode, 1937.
    *At the Moon's End.*   Indianapolis, Bobbs Merrill, 1941; London, Eyre and Spottiswoode, 1943.
    *A Name for Evil.*   Indianapolis, Bobbs Merrill, 1947.
    *The Velvet Horn.*   New York, McDowell Obolensky, 1957.

### Short Stories

    *A Novel, A Novella and Four Stories.*   New York, McDowell Obolensky, 1958.

### Uncollected Short Story

    "Old Scratch in the Valley", in *Virginia Quarterly* (Charlottesville), 1935.

### Other

    *Bedford Forrest and His Critter Company* (biography).   New York, Minton Balch, 1931; as *Bedford Forrest*, London, Eyre and Spottiswoode, 1938; revised edition, New York, McDowell Obolensky, 1960.
    *The Hero with the Private Parts: Essays* (literary criticism).   Baton Rouge, Louisiana State University Press, 1966.
    *A Wake for the Living: A Memoir.*   New York, Seymour Lawrence-Delacorte Press, 1972.

    Editor, *Craft and Vision: The Best Fiction form "The Sewanee Review".*   New York, Seymour Lawrence-Delacorte Press, 1971.

Bibliography: in *Mississippi Quarterly* (State College), Fall 1970.

Manuscript Collection: Joint University Libraries (Vanderbilt University), Nashville, Tennessee.

Critical Studies: "Andrew Lytle Issue" of *Mississippi Quarterly* (State College), Fall 1970.

Andrew Lytle comments:

My work is best described in the rendition of the fiction I have done and in the critical reading of other books. An artist is not a scientist. He discovers his theme and subject as he writes. When he has dealt totally with either, and brought it all out, he is done for.

\*       \*       \*

The art of Andrew Lytle is clearly within the tradition of Flaubert, James and Joyce. It is the work of a man who has thought carefully about what a novel is supposed to be, a gifted critic, editor and advisor to many younger novelists who have honored his example in their own best production. Lytle's novels are dramatic in the modern sense. They render from within a felt life gathered to some central image or cluster of images, and project that life from the post of observation where resides "the author's seeing eye." The result of this procedure in Lytle's reader is something like a shock, a full and simultaneous engagement of all the faculties in a moment of illumination.

His first novel, *The Long Night*, is a powerful evocation of the character of ante-bellum Southern society. Yet it is not *about* history—except as his times can be said to converge upon Pleasant McIvor, the central character. The plot here is Celtic in overtone and the issue revenge. But the Civil War interrupts the enactment of McIvor honor, reminding Pleasant that it is possible to offend his own dignity by pursuing it privately in a time when the future survival of such values is very much at stake. Pleasant's extravagance is perceived and judged by a younger kinsman who refuses to extend it into later days.

Lytle's *At the Moon's End* (and the related novella "Alchemy") discover form and meaning in the Spanish conquest of Eldorado. Both novel and novella "occur" from the viewpoint of an engaged spectator who, after being overcome by the vital presence of a conquistador, sees in his captain the Promethean pride which dissolved Christendom. In *At the Moon's End* Tovar draws back from the delusion of a worldly beatitude at the behest of De Soto's ghost. The nameless speaker in "Alchemy" retreats from Pizarro after years of reflection on the adventure in Peru. The two conquerors are counters for modernity in being representative of Columbus, their prototype of feudal Spain gone awry.

*A Name for Evil* is Lytle's Tennessee revelation of abstract and self-delusive traditionalism. It is, for an Agrarian, a contributor to the Southern manifesto *I'll Take My Stand*, and devoted champion of the "landed interest," an amazing book. Henry Brent attempts to restore the patriarchy on land cursed by the self-centered severity of his ancestor, Major Brent. As in James' *The Turn of the Screw*, a wicked history prevails over him. Henry hates the Major too much. The "why" of his ruin is revealed ironically in his account of its unfolding. His Eden is too private for an Eve. Wife, unborn child, and therefore the entire enterprise, are the victims.

*The Velvet Horn* is Lytle's masterpiece. Again the scene is the Tennessee of his fathers. The Fall of Man is there re-enacted in the context of another excessive isolation. Years later, Lucius Cree is compelled by ostensible father and by mother and uncle to learn of it. First Captain Cree and then the Cropleighs "pay" for the boy's education. Yet (thanks to them) he comes forth complete from his own loss of innocence to seek a "Paradise within, greater by far." The book is, as Caroline Gordon has written, a "landmark in American fiction."

—M. E. Bradford

**LYTTON, David.** South African. Born in South Africa in 1927. Married; has four children. Emigrated to England in 1949. Actor, 1949–50, and Box Office Manager, 1952–54, Shakespeare Memorial Theatre, Stratford-upon-Avon. School Teacher, 1950–52. Writer and Producer, BBC, 1954–56. Free-lance Writer since 1957. Lives in Stratford-upon-Avon. Address: c/o The Bodley Head, 9 Bow Street, London W.C.2, England.

PUBLICATIONS

Novels

> *The Goddam White Man.* London, MacGibbon and Kee, 1960; New York, Simon and Schuster, 1961.
> *A Place Apart.* London, MacGibbon and Kee, and New York, Simon and Schuster, 1961.
> *The Paradise People.* London, MacGibbon and Kee, and New York, Simon and Schuster, 1962.
> *The Grass Won't Grow Till Spring.* London, Bodley Head, 1964.
> *The Freedom of the Cage.* London, Bodley Head, 1966.

Short Stories

> *A Tale of Love, Alas, and Other Episodes.* London, Bodley Head, 1969.

\*        \*        \*

In his five novels and one volume of short stories, David Lytton has shown himself to be, not only an acute observer of the South African scene, but also a satirist of considerable talent. South African fiction has always tended towards seriousness: writers have been intimately concerned with the very real social and political problems which have grown rather than lessened in the years since Union (1910); and South African novels have reflected this concern. With the exception of *Turbott Wolfe*, William Plomer's satirical novel published in 1924, and Roy Campbell's poetry of the same period, satire—and indeed humour of any kind—has been almost totally absent from the South African literary scene. Lytton, whose tone ranges from the near tragic, through various degrees of satire to compassionate and decidedly humorous irony, may therefore be regarded as something of an innovator. Writing with a detached but imaginative perception, sharpened possibly by his long residence in Britain, away from day to day involvement with the morally corrupting influence of *apartheid* (racial segregation as practised in South Africa), Lytton is able to pinpoint not only the tragedy and nastiness inherent in much contemporary South African life, but also to underline its absurdity. In this respect, his fourth novel, *The Grass Won't Grow Till Spring*, is his best and most savagely funny book. Based on South Africa's notorious "Immorality Law" which forbids miscegenation, the novel delineates the predicament of a white "liberal" caught in a veritable sexual wilderness, from which the only escape, ultimately, is into despair.

Lytton's earlier novels, *The Goddam White Man* and *A Place Apart*, are attempts to deal sympathetically with the experience of black and half-caste South Africans. Like most such attempts by white writers these novels are limited: life seen from the outside only must confine itself to easily observable data. *The Paradise People*, a romanticised account of Boer life, brings Lytton to more familiar ground, though his version of the growth of the Afrikaner personality, and his belief that these people instinctively know that they do not really belong to Africa, is more literary than real. *The Freedom of the Cage* seeks to analyse the mind of a contemporary Afrikaner. The central character is a man who first accepts, and later begins to question, the ideology and way of life which he and his ancestors have helped to create. His growing frustration leads him to attempt a symbolic "assassination" of the Prime Minister (the gun is not loaded), for which he is, inevitably, imprisoned. The "villain" in this novel is an English-speaking liberal and Lytton's sympathies are with the Afrikaner "victim": a neat reversal of the usual South African fictional pattern.

Lytton's most recent book is a collection of short stories, *A Tale of Love, Alas*, which centre on the experiences of a blind white man. Through his contact with a number of representative figures (a humanitarian priest, a Coloured woman, a rural Afrikaner, colonial English ladies), the hero is gradually brought to "see" that there is virtually no place for him in contemporary South Africa. This regretful insight (for his own relationship with his country is also "a tale of love, alas") appears to be Lytton's own view, and is a logical conclusion to his first series of novels.

—Ursula Laredo

MACAULEY, Robie (Mayhew). American. Born in Grand Rapids, Michigan, 31 May 1919. Educated at Kenyon College, Gambier, Ohio, A.B. 1941; University of Iowa, Iowa City, M.F.A. 1950. Served in the United States Army, in the Counter Intelligence Corps, 1942–46. Married Anne Draper in 1948; has one child. Instructor in English, Bard College, Annandale-on-Hudson, New York, 1946–47, and University of Iowa, 1947–50; Assistant Professor, Woman's College of the University of North Carolina, Greensboro, 1950–53. Teacher, Kenyon College, 1953–66, and Editor of the *Kenyon Review*, 1959–66. Since 1966, Fiction Editor of *Playboy* magazine, Chicago. United States State Department Lecturer in Australia, 1962. United States Delegate, International P.E.N. Conference, Tokyo, 1957, Brazil, 1960. Recipient: *Furioso* fiction prize, 1949; Guggenheim Fellowship, 1964; Fulbright Research Fellowship, 1964; O. Henry Award, 1967. Address: 1323 Sandburg Terrace, Chicago, Illinois 60614, U.S.A.

PUBLICATIONS

Novel

*The Disguises of Love.* New York, Random House, 1952; London, Harrap, 1954.

Short Stories

*The End of Pity and Other Stories.* New York, McDowell Obolensky, 1957; London, Harrap, 1958.

Other

*Technique in Fiction*, with George Lanning. New York, Harper, 1964.

Editor, *Gallery of Modern Fiction: Stories from the Kenyon Review*. New York, Salem Press, 1966.

\*     \*     \*

Robie Macauley's prose, like the best poetry, has a startling economy of means and precision of language. Macauley seems to have applied certain poetic theories of his teacher at Kenyon College, John Crowe Ransom, to the demands of fiction. It is not surprising that a writer so attentive to technique should have produced his own poetics of the novel. The book which Robie Macauley wrote with George Lanning, *Technique in Fiction* (appropriately dedicated to Ransom), serves as an addendum to his own practices as a novelist and story writer and asserts his feelings about the importance of craft. The introduction points to the inseparability of the functions of critic and creator, distantly echoing a famous remark of Charles Baudelaire: "The best modern critics of fiction, from the standpoint of technique, and probably the only critics that the beginning writer will find of any specific help, are those who write fiction themselves."

Macauley's *The Disguises of Love* is the enviable product of years spent in close and sympathetic relationship with the best novels from Jane Austen through Joyce. Several reviewers were disturbed at certain things they saw and expressed mild discomfort. Thus Anthony West, writing in *The New Yorker* (December 20, 1952), saw in the novel the "reversal of masculine and feminine roles" which gives it, in the end, "a nonsensical quality." Stanley Edgar Hyman (*Hudson Review*, Autumn, 1953) started with West's argument and proceeded to find "accounts of homosexual relations . . . disguised as accounts of heterosexual relations" in good Proustian fashion. Macauley roundly expressed his disapproval of this reading (in the Winter 1954 *Hudson Review*) by turning Hyman's evidence from the text against him to assure us that he had in no sense tampered with gender.

Indeed, Macauley's temptress Frances (a name which Hyman suggests should more accurately be spelled "Francis") has very little in common with Albertine, Gilberte, Andrée, or Proust's other men-women. In accustomed heterosexual fashion she manages to take to bed with her the straight-laced college professor and paterfamilias Howard Graeme. The novel is shaped by the twists and turns of their love affair. Macauley sets up three "successive centres" (Henry James's expression in his preface to *The Wings of the Dove*) who alternate in the telling of the story; they are: Howard, his wife Helen, and their son Gordon. The eleventh chapter, in contrast to the rest of the novel, offers a babel of voices which open on "the successive windows of other people's interest" (another quotation from the preface to *The Wings of the Dove*). This eleventh chapter seems to have something in common with the "Wandering Rocks" section of Joyce's *Ulysses*.

The accounts by Howard, Helen, and Gordon—often going over the same material from different vantage points—have their own peculiar rhythms. Howard's voice is stuffy and pedantic; Helen's has the unmistakable ring of the soap opera; Gordon's is precocious, mischievous, and ironical. The tellings have in common an unreliability. Howard mistakenly believes Gordon is "in fact pretty much an average boy with all the insensitivity of the average boy . . . ." Helen accepts Howard's pretense that he is writing a book and resists the notion that he is carrying on a love affair. Gordon believes that it is his mother rather than his father who has a lover. The unravelling of the various threads of misunderstanding is performed by outsiders: the succession of gossips in the eleventh chapter; the faculty wives; Professor Llewellen.

*The Disguises of Love*, in a sense, is an academic novel. It has in common with the best examples of the genre, like Kingsley Amis' *Lucky Jim* and Mary McCarthy's *The Groves of Academe*, the uncomfortable feeling that "teaching is the one job where you can hang on for years after you go completely bad" (Howard's words). Macauley knows the precise cadence of academic exchange and reproduces it convincingly at a musical gathering at Professor Llewellen's house and again at a party of the U.F.W.G. (University Faculty Wives' Group), with Helen Graeme acting as one of the hostesses.

Three of the eleven stories in Macauley's *The End of Pity* are also concerned with academics. "The Academic Style" and "The Chevigny Man" are set on college campuses while "A Guide to the Muniment Room" involves a professor in England on "a literary pilgrimage." Stuffiness, phoniness, the narrow devotion to one's "special subject" are exposed in all three. Macauley can only agree with Amis' well-known estimation in *Lucky Jim* of most academic research: ". . . the pseudo-light it threw upon non-problems."

The first four stories in *The End of Pity* have to do with military experiences, removed from the front lines, involving Counter-Intelligence Corps personnel. Macauley mentions in his superb introduction to Ford's *Parade's End* that "some of us went to war ourselves": these stories seem to represent a glance over his left shoulder at the absurdities and ironies of his own World War II encounters. (Military blunders and foibles engaged his attention again in "Debacles Are Big Business," a piece he did for the August 21 and 28, 1971 *New Republic*.)

The remaining four stories have fairly little in common. Two, "The Invaders" and "The Wishbone," end in moments of violence. "Legend of the Two Swimmers" is faintly reminiscent of Katherine Anne Porter's "Old Mortality" with its family secrets and legends. "Windfall" involves the unexpected gesture of another of Macauley's heroes overwhelmed by events; the difference is, however, that Vanderbilt acts with a decisiveness and affirmation which eludes most of the other characters in *The Disguises of Love* and *The End of Pity*.

—Melvin J. Friedman

---

**MACDONALD, Ross.** Pseudonym for Kenneth Millar. American. Born in Los Gatos, California, 13 December 1915. Educated at the University of Western Ontario, London, 1933–38, B.A. 1938; University of Toronto, 1938–39; University of Michigan, Ann Arbor, 1941–44, 1948–49 (Graduate Fellow, 1941–42; Rackham Fellow, 1942–43), M.A. 1942, Ph.D. 1951. Served in the United States Naval Reserve, rising to the rank of Lieutenant Junior Grade, 1944–46. Married Margaret Sturm in 1938; had one child, now deceased. Teacher of English and History, Kitchener-Waterloo Collegiate Institute, Kitchener, Ontario, 1939–41; Teaching Fellow, University of Michigan, 1942–44, 1948–49. Book Reviewer, *San Francisco Chronicle*, 1957–60. National Director, 1960–61, 1964–65, and President, 1965, Mystery Writers of America. Recipient: Mystery Writers of America Scroll, 1962, 1963; Silver Dagger Award, Crime Writers Association, London, 1965. Address: 4420 Via Esperanza, Santa Barbara, California 93110, U.S.A.

PUBLICATIONS

Novels

*The Dark Tunnel* (as Kenneth Millar). New York, Dodd Mead, 1944.
*Trouble Follows Me* (as Kenneth Millar). New York, Dodd Mead, 1946.
*Blue City* (as Kenneth Millar). New York, Knopf, 1947; London, Cassell, 1948.
*The Three Roads* (as Kenneth Millar). New York, Knopf, 1948; London, Cassell, 1949.
*The Moving Target*. New York, Knopf, 1949; London, Cassell, 1950.
*The Drowning Pool*. New York, Knopf, 1950; London, Cassell, 1951.
*The Way Some People Die*. New York, Knopf, 1951; London, Cassell, 1952.

*The Ivory Grin.*   New York, Knopf, 1952; London, Cassell, 1953.
*Meet Me at the Morgue.*   New York, Knopf, 1953; as *Experience with Evil*, London, Cassell, 1954.
*Find a Victim.*   New York, Knopf, 1954; London, Cassell, 1955.
*The Barbarous Coast.*   New York, Knopf, 1956; London, Cassell, 1957.
*The Doomsters.*   New York, Knopf, and London, Cassell, 1958.
*The Galton Case.*   New York, Knopf, 1959; London, Cassell, 1960.
*The Ferguson Affair.*   New York, Knopf, 1960; London, Cassell, 1961.
*The Wycherly Woman.*   New York, Knopf, 1961; London, Collins, 1962.
*The Zebra-Striped Hearse.*   New York, Knopf, 1962; London, Collins, 1963.
*The Chill.*   New York, Knopf, 1964; London, Collins, 1965.
*The Far Side of the Dollar.*   New York, Knopf, 1965; London, Collins, 1966.
*Black Money.*   New York, Knopf, 1966; London, Collins, 1967.
*The Instant Enemy.*   New York, Knopf, 1968; London, Collins, 1969.
*The Goodbye Look.*   New York, Knopf, and London, Collins, 1969.
*The Underground Man.*   New York, Knopf, and London, Collins, 1971.


Short Stories

*The Name Is Archer.*   New York, Bantam, 1955.


Manuscript Collection: University of California at Irvine.


Critical Studies: essay by the author on his own work, "The Writer as Detective Hero", in *Essays Classic and Contemporary*, Philadelphia, Lippincott, 1967; review of *The Underground Man* by Eudora Welty, in the *New York Times Book Review,* 14 February 1971.


Ross Macdonald comments:

Miss Brigid Brophy has alleged against the detective story that it cannot be taken seriously because it fails to risk the author's ego and is therefore mere fantasy. It is true ... that writers since Poe have used detectives like Dupin as a sort of rational strong point from which they can observe and report on a violent no-man's-land. Unfortunately, this violent world is not always fantastic, although it may reflect psychological elements. Miss Brophy's argument disregards the fact that the detective and his story can become means of knowing oneself and saying the unsayable. You can never hit a distant target by aiming at it directly.

In any case I have to plead not guilty to unearned security of the ego. As I write a book, ... my ego is dispersed through several characters, including usually some of the undesirable ones, and I am involved with them to the limit of my imaginative strength. In modern fiction the narrator is not always the protagonist or hero, nor is the protagonist always single. Certainly my narrator Archer is not the main object of my interest, nor the character with whose fate I am most concerned. He is a deliberately narrowed version of the writing self, so narrow that when he turns sideways he almost disappears. Yet his semi-transparent presence places the story at one remove from the author and lets it, as we say (through sweat and tears), write itself.

—Excerpted by the author from his essay, "A Preface to *The Galton Case*", in *Afterwords: Novelists on Their Novels*, New York, Harper, 1969.

*      *.      *

Ross Macdonald is the author of the best-known and most brilliant series of contemporary detective novels, in the hard-boiled tradition pioneered by Dashiell Hammett and Raymond Chandler. Like Hammett's Sam Spade and the Continental Op or Chandler's Phillip Marlowe, Macdonald's hero, Lew Archer, works in Southern California, is dedicated to uncovering truth for its own sake, and views the people around him with tough skepticism; like them also, he narrates his own experiences in a terse, brittle prose. But Archer is less sentimental than Philip Marlowe, less cynical and callous than Sam Spade or the Continental Op, and more human than his antecedents. Macdonald is no mere imitator. He is a much sharper analyst of the social scene than his predecessors, a more refined and consistent stylist, and a writer with a deeper sense of tragic possibility.

Macdonald is an acute observer of the life-styles and folkways of Southern California. The people who employ Lew Archer, and whom he meets in the cases he investigates, form a cross-section of this society, including the rich, the middle-class, the strugglers, and those who cannot find a place within the system. Most of them have, or dream of having, the amenities and luxuries of life in a land of perpetual summer. They believe that they live only for the present, that they are in control of their lives, that they can determine what will happen to them. But all are haunted by the ghosts of the past. Archer, whose own past has made him a man without a private life of his own, functions as the revealer of the past, the man whose investigations force people to confront themselves and their links to the past, to acknowledge that they are captives of long-ago events which have shaped their lives and will shape their futures.

Most of Archer's cases, especially in Macdonald's more recent novels, center around murders or disappearances in the distant past. The search for a lost brother or father or daughter recurs time and again in these books, becoming almost an obsessive theme. Archer, in his search for the lost, almost always uncovers events which people have worked very hard to conceal, revealing relationships and actions which have been buried for years and which have caused the neurotic delusions from which so many of Macdonald's characters suffer. The result, in most of the novels, is long-delayed retribution; occasionally, as in *The Galton Case,* Archer's revelations may make happiness possible for a few characters.

Among the chief virtues of Macdonald's work are his observations of the manners and mores of affluent Americans, his sharp delineation of unusual characters among those who have not made it or whom society has rejected, his objective portrayal of the grimness of urban American life. His prose is lucid and pithy without being overly terse, and his novels are carefully structured. On the other hand, the plots of his novels are sometimes so complicated as to defy the reader's understanding; in *The Instant Enemy*, for example, the long-hidden familial relationships are so incredibly interconnected that the extended revelation at the end is very nearly a parody of other Macdonald novels. The obsession with the lost son or daughter is also a problem, since it has made Macdonald's recent novels follow an easily predictable pattern. Finally, Lew Archer is probably too much a cipher, a man without a life of his own who lives vicariously through the tribulations of his clients. On balance, however, Macdonald's work is an impressive demonstration of the possibilities of the detective novel.

—John M. Muste

---

**MacINNES, Colin.** British. Born in London in 1914; son of the writer Angela Thirkell. Educated in Australia. Served as a Sergeant in the Intelligence Corps in World War II. Address: c/o MacGibbon and Kee Ltd., 3 Upper James Street, Golden Square, London W1R 4BP, England.

PUBLICATIONS

Novels

*To the Victor the Spoils*.  London, MacGibbon and Kee, 1950.
*June in Her Spring*.  London, MacGibbon and Kee, 1952.
*City of Spades*.  London, MacGibbon and Kee, 1957; New York, Macmillan, 1958.
*Absolute Beginners*.  London, MacGibbon and Kee, 1959; New York, Macmillan, 1960.
*Mr. Love and Justice*.  London, MacGibbon and Kee, 1960; New York, Dutton, 1961.
*All Day Saturday*.  London, MacGibbon and Kee, 1966.
*Westward to Laughter*.  London, MacGibbon and Kee, 1969; New York, Farrar Straus, 1970.
*Three Years to Play*.  London, MacGibbon and Kee, and New York, Farrar Straus, 1970.

Other

*England, Half English* (essays).  London, MacGibbon and Kee, 1961; New York, Random House, 1962.
*London: City of My Dreams*.  London, Thames and Hudson, 1962.
*Australia and New Zealand*, with the editors of *Life*.  New York, Time, 1964.
*Sweet Saturday Night*.  London, MacGibbon and Kee, 1967.

*        *        *

Colin MacInnes's eight novels have appeared in three batches: two at the start of the fifties, five years silence followed by the three London novels, six years without any published fiction and then three more 1966–70. The first, *To the Victor the Spoils,* is an autobiographical account of army experiences in Holland and Germany in the closing stages of the war. *June in Her Spring* looks back earlier, to Australia, where he spent his childhood, and is a sheep-station romance of young love frustrated, with a sub-plot of a psychopathic delinquent.

These work are no preparation for the great achievement which followed, the London books. In them MacInnes reports on much-discussed facets of contemporary London life: race relations, youth, and the police. His fascination with understanding his times is shown in the essays collected in *England, Half English,* where his topics include pop music, drinking clubs, and teenage fashions. In one essay there he explains that the actual experiences precede the intent of writing a novel:

A theme, later to be evoked in fiction, has always "moved in on" me and has become, without any deliberate intent, a part of my life almost before I was aware of it, and certainly long before I thought of writing of it. During this period of saturation such apprehension as I have is intuitive, then thoughtful; the factual "documentation" always comes long afterwards.

So he calls these books "poetic evocations of a human situation, with undertones of social criticism."

In the first, *City of Spades* ("spades" are coloured people in England), narration is alternately by an ebullient young Nigerian, Johnny Fortune, who has come to London in search of fortune and adventure, and a well-meaning, naive Colonial Welfare Officer, who follows Johnny as he goes to dubious pubs and clubs, and mixes with hemp-smokers and peddlers, gamblers and ponces. After two experiences with the law, Johnny decides to return to

Africa. The characters have names like Samuel Selvon characters: the activist student Karl Marx Bo, the white homosexual Alfy Bongo, the ponce Billy Whisper; and the Bushman, who says he is a chief, has a speech impediment and sells hemp.

MacInnes shows that African ties are to tribe and family, resulting in a different morality from whites; that coloureds come to Britain seeking the centre of the world, where the action is; that white girls like coloureds for their lovely manners and beautiful way of moving; and that Africans are more assured and self-sufficient than the rootless West Indians. MacInnes appears to prefer the cheerful, amoral, living-in-the-present of his characters to dull, sedate English behaviour. And, though he has no illusions about fighting, drinking and drug addiction, he recommends tolerance.

"Abolute beginners" are teenagers, and MacInnes assumes they are a strange new world, since for the first time they have the money to create their own culture. The story is told in the first person by a boy of eighteen, who describes such different scenes as a smart Chelsea party, a TV studio, a Soho drinking club and a look at the country on a trip up river from Windsor to Marlow. He loves jazz, and we read of a club and a big concert. The date is the late Summer of 1958 and the last episode, detached from the rest, is the race riot in Notting Hill. The youth is shocked to find this occurring in London, and that police and press are concealing how serious it is. Descriptions are exact, as in the contrast between the air terminal and bus station at Victoria:

> There, on one side, were the glamour people setting off for foreign countries, mohair and linen suits, white air lines vanity bags, dark sun spectacles and pages of tickets packed to paradise, every nationality represented, and everyone equal to the sky-dominion of fast air-travel—and there, on the other side, were the peasant masses of the bus terminal shuffling along in their front-parlour-curtain dresses and cut-price tweeds and plastic mackintoshes, all flat feet and fair shares and you-in-your-small-corner-and-I-in-mine.

Because the youth is an individual (he makes big money taking pornographic pictures), he is not wholly convincing as a typical figure, with articulate opinions on everything from politics to television. MacInnes is always there, aware and tender, alive and compassionate.

*Mr. Love and Justice* tells the stories of Frankie Love, the ex-seaman who picks up a Stepney tart and becomes a ponce, and Ted Justice, the plainclothes policeman. Their paths intersect, their roles become blurred and the men are friends in hospital at the end. This novel too contains information about relations between ponces and their girls and ponces and the police, but literary artistry is more marked than in previous works, with the deliberate pairing, and the names prompting us to ask whether this is a fable showing Love may be the more just and Justice the more loving.

Some critics place the novels as no more than painless sociology, with information of a particular date (*Absolute Beginners* especially is dated). The books, however, remain full of energy, of character and of language. MacInnes, in the above-mentioned essay, says "I chose a language for 'coloured people,' or for teenagers, that was almost entirely an invented one; though true, so far as I could make it, to the minds and spirits of the characters I was describing." So, in *Absolute Beginners* for instance, police are always "cowboys," money is always "loot" and anything can be described as "sharp." So the language is English Runyon, and one notes, variously, Cockney, Yiddish, Salinger, underworld terms, and jazz and beatnik idiom. No other writer (critics have invoked Mayhew, Defoe, Hogarth, and Genet to try to convey the flavour) has achieved MacInnes' kind of exuberant, sometimes titillating, fictionalized fact.

*All Day Saturday,* the sixth novel, returns to pre-war Australian sheep-farming country, but with a maturer view than shown in *June in Her Spring.* The men love "their work, their wives, and the odd sheila down at Melbourne for the races, in that order." Saturday is the day for tennis, dancing, drinking and sex—but an urban outsider disrupts the familiar pattern. The prose is lyrical, if inconsistent, and the marriage of practical man and romantic woman is carefully studied. The devotion to sport, a childishness and an unease about loneliness are observed critically, but centrally the tone is of nostalgia for this society where "the cult of *happiness* was paramount: hedonistic, mindless, intent upon the glorious physical instant!"

The last two books are a complete surprise, looking much further back, feats of story-telling which reconstruct the mid-eighteenth century and Elizabethan London. *Westward to Laughter* is a yarn about a Highland youth who goes to sea, travels to the West Indian island of St. Laughter, is unjustly convicted, becomes a slave and runs away, joins a pirate ship and is finally hanged. *Three Years to Play* (which is the working life of a boy actor), the longest of his novels, presents yet another boy in search of fortune in London. He is involved in underworld gangs, acts out a real-life inspiration for *As You Like It* in Epping Forest, and meets Shakespeare and hears of other writers ("Then there is Jonson, baptised Benjamin, but called Ben, that is much sprung into favour these last years"). The language in both is a virtuoso performance. *Westward to Laughter* is pastiche Defoe and Smollett (with an opening echoing Stevenson's *Kidnapped*), while *Three Years* is full of "e'ers" and "perpends"; this is typical: "' I hadn't thought,' said I, 'to find base affairs so patterned on those highest of the State.' 'Well, what is a State but a great stew?' quoth Jenny." As for intention, the earlier book ends with a slave rebellion and the slave trade is the beginning of present-day problems, so moral and political education is half-buried amid the many escapades. But *Three Years* seeks only to immerse us in the authentic 1590's, with priest, puritan, scholar and of course harlot, so that we sense Shakespeare's environment. Like many critics, I would prefer to see MacInnes confront the 1970's.

—Malcolm Page

---

**MacINNES, Helen (Clark).** American. Born in Glasgow, Scotland, 7 October 1907; emigrated to the United States in 1937; naturalized, 1951. Educated at The Hermitage School, Helensburgh; The High School for Girls, Glasgow; Glasgow University, M.A. 1928; University College, London, Diploma in Librarianship 1931. Married the writer Gilbert Highet in 1932; has one son. Special Cataloguer, Ferguson Collection, University of Glasgow, 1928–29; employed by the Dunbartonshire Education Authority to select books for county libraries, 1929–30; acted with the Oxford University Dramatic Society and with the Oxford Experimental Theatre, 1932–37. Recipient: Columba Prize in Literature, Iona College, 1966. Address: 15 Jeffreys Lane, East Hampton, Long Island, New York 11937, U.S.A.

PUBLICATIONS

Novels

*Above Suspicion*.   Boston, Little Brown, and London, Harrap, 1941.
*Assignment in Brittany*.   Boston, Little Brown, and London, Harrap, 1942.
*While Still We Live*.   Boston, Little Brown, 1944; as *The Unconquerable*, London, Harrap, 1944.
*Horizon*.   London, Harrap, 1945; Boston, Little Brown, 1946.
*Friends and Lovers*.   Boston, Little Brown, 1947; London, Harrap, 1948.
*Rest and Be Thankful*.   Boston, Little Brown, and London, Harrap, 1949.

*Neither Five Nor Three*.   New York, Harcourt Brace, and London, Collins, 1951.
*I and My True Love*.   New York, Harcourt Brace, and London, Collins, 1953.
*Pray for a Brave Heart*.   New York, Harcourt Brace, and London, Collins, 1955.
*North from Rome*.   New York, Harcourt Brace, and London, Collins, 1958.
*Decision at Delphi*.   New York, Harcourt Brace, and London, Collins, 1961.
*The Venetian Affair*.   New York, Harcourt Brace, 1963; London, Collins, 1964.
*The Double Image*.   New York, Harcourt Brace, and London, Collins, 1966.
*The Salzburg Connection*.   New York, Harcourt Brace, 1968; London, Collins, 1969.
*Message from Málaga*.   New York, Harcourt Brace, and London, Collins, 1971.


Play

*Home Is the Hunter*.   New York, Harcourt Brace, 1964.


Other

Translator, with Gilbert Highet, *Sexual Life in Ancient Rome*, by Otto Kiefer.   London,
   Routledge, 1934; New York, Dutton, 1935.
Translator, with Gilbert Highet, *Friedrich Engels: A Biography*, by Gustav Mayer.
   London, Chapman and Hall, 1936.


Manuscript Collection: Princeton University Library, New Jersey.


Critical Studies: introduction by the author to her collection of novels, *Assignment: Suspense*,
New York, Harcourt Brace, 1961; essay in *Current Biography* (New York), November 1967;
*The Art of Helen MacInnes* (brochure) by Clifton Fadiman, New York, Harcourt Brace,
1971.


*        *        *


Helen MacInnes (Mrs. Gilbert Highet) has written fifteen novels between 1941 and 1971
and to the reader of adventure-suspense stories her name is familiar. Although the scholar
will not subject such novels to serious critical consideration, the fact remains that many
literate people have read and enjoyed Miss MacInnes's books.

In 1961 three of her earliest novels were re-issued under the title *Assignment: Suspense*
with an introduction answering three questions Miss MacInnes said she had often been
asked about her novels: What is true? How much is invented? Did you yourself experience
any of those situations? She answered that in her novels the physical backgrounds "are as
factual as I can make them"; that the characters and plot are invented; and that it is a
misconception that novelists write only from experiences. The answers are not surprising,
but they do point toward her best characteristics—credible background, convincing suspense,
and likeable characters.

The novels generally fall into three categories: a European setting for adventures concurrent with World War II—*Above Suspicion*, *Assignment in Brittany*, *While Still We Live*,
and *Horizon;* adventures based on World War II secrets that remain dangerous matter
years after the war's end—*Pray for a Brave Heart* and *The Salzburg Connection;* and novels
exposing threats to the West from powerful conspiracies (generally Communist inspired)—
*I and My True Love*, *Neither Five Nor Three*, *North from Rome*, *Decision at Delphi*, *The
Venetian Affair*, and her latest novel, *Message from Málaga*. When Miss MacInnes abandons
these basic patterns, the results are pretty thin, particularly in *Rest and Be Thankful*—a

deplorably bad novel set on a Wyoming cattle ranch—and *Friends and Lovers,* a light, if pleasing, romance. Her one excursion into drama, *Home Is the Hunter,* is a witty and sophisticated comedy of Ulysses's return.

Without question her genre is the adventure-suspense novel and her extensive travels have provided the fine descriptions of Swiss villages, German towns, and winding streets of Athens and Venice where events of intrigue occur. The detail of scenery and custom is an asset; and the presentation of facts reflects careful research and produces tales of espionage and adventure that are exciting and plausible. The situation which works most successfully for her is to place an amateur who usually has a splendid memory—an Oxford Don, an architect-artist, a lawyer, a playwright—into the midst of professional agents and police and to have him perform with great courage and ability. Usually this amateur will be divorced or a bachelor or a widower who meets and wins the ideal woman after rescuing her heroically at the end from the evil forces. Miss MacInnes is not shy of brutal killings, but her protagonists always emerge alive though a little scarred and very weary.

Although Miss MacInnes has said that "a novel is not a thesis, or a sermon, or a political pamphlet," the inveterate reader comes to some purple passages and much political sermonizing which are best read with haste. Sometimes too many sub-plots becloud the main line of action, sometimes Miss MacInnes just takes too long to tell her story, and sometimes the musical and literary allusions are overdone. But these are not fatal flaws. Her special skill of investing a placid setting with convincing terror keeps the reader in the throes of suspense and she has also produced some exceptional characters that the reader can admire— the triangle of Sylvia and Payton Pleydell and Jan Brovic in *I and My True Love,* Richard and Frances Myles in *Above Suspicion* and Bill Mathieson in *The Salzburg Connection.* These characters more than compensate for less convincing ones like the Swiss police agent Keppler in *Pray for a Brave Heart* who listens to the Brahms Fourth Symphony, reads Rilke, and quotes Juvenal.

If serious consideration can be accorded to the western novel, the detective story, and the science fiction novel, then the adventure-suspense story may also deserve attention. One is tempted to label such books as sub-literary and if they are compared with the work of a serious artist like Henry James, the label is justified. But given Miss MacInnes's skill and finesse the result has been adventure-suspense novels of a high order which have pleased many readers, a pleasure reflected in the New York Herald Tribune's book review headlines of *Pray for a Brave Heart* and *Decision at Delphi*—"Don't Skip a Single Page!" and "Suspense Artist at Work." If Miss MacInnes does not deserve the scholar's research, she has won a devoted following of readers.

—Elizabeth Evans

---

**MACKENZIE, Compton.** British. Born in West Hartlepool, County Durham, 17 January 1883; brother of the actress Fay Compton. Educated at St. Paul's School, London; Magdalen College, Oxford, B.A. (honours) in Modern History 1904. Second Lieutenant, 1st Volunteer Battalion, Hertfordshire Regiment, 1900–1902; Lieutenant, 1915, and Captain, 1916, Royal Marines; served in the Dardanelles Expedition, 1915; Military Control Officer, Athens, 1916; Director, Aegean Intelligence Service, 1917 (O.B.E.: Officer, Order of the British Empire, 1919; Chevalier, Legion of Honour); Captain, Home Guard, 1940–44. Married Faith Stone in 1905 (died, 1960); Christina MacSween, 1962 (died, 1963); Lilian MacSween, 1965. Founder, 1923, and Editor, 1923–61, *The Gramophone*, London; Literary Critic, *Daily Mail,* London, 1931–35. Rector, Glasgow University, 1931–34. President, Dickens Fellowship, 1939–46. President, The Croquet Association, 1954–66. President, 1961–64, and since 1964 Patron, The Poetry Society, London. President, Guild of Independent Publishers, 1969. President of the Siamese Cat Club since 1928, of the Wexford Festival since 1951, and of the Songwriters' Guild since 1956; Governor-General of the Royal Stuart Society since 1961. Knight Commander, Royal Order of the Phoenix, Greece, 1966. LL.D., Glasgow University, 1932; St. Francis Xavier University, Antigonish, Nova Scotia, 1961. Fellow, Royal Society of Literature, 1945: Companion of Literature, 1968. Honorary Royal Scottish Academician. Knighted in 1952. Address: 31 Drummond Place, Ediriburgh 3, Scotland.

PUBLICATIONS

Novels

*The Passionate Elopement*.   London, Lane, 1911; New York, Putnam, 1916.

*Carnival*.   London, Secker, and New York, Appleton, 1912.

*Sinister Street*.   London, Secker, 2 vols., 1913, 1914; as *Youth's Encounter* and *Sinister Street*, New York, Appleton, 1913, 1914.

*Guy and Pauline*.   London, Secker, 1915; as *Plashers Mead*, New York, Harper, 1915.

*The Early Life and Adventures of Sylvia Scarlett*.   London, Secker, and New York, Harper, 1918.

*Sylvia and Michael: The Later Adventures of Sylvia Scarlett*.   London, Secker, and New York, Harper, 1919.

*Poor Relations*.   London, Secker, and New York, Harper, 1919.

*The Vanity Girl*.   London, Cassell, and New York, Harper, 1920.

*Rich Relatives*.   London, Secker, and New York, Harper, 1921.

*The Altar Steps*.   London, Cassell, and New York, Doran, 1922.

*The Parson's Progress*.   London, Cassell, 1923; New York, Doran, 1924.

*The Seven Ages of Woman*.   London, Secker, and New York, Stokes, 1923.

*The Old Men of the Sea: A Romance of Adventure in the South Pacific*.   London, Cassell, and New York, Stokes, 1924; revised edition, as *Paradise for Sale*, London, Macdonald, 1963.

*The Heavenly Ladder*.   London, Cassell, and New York, Doran, 1924.

*Coral: A Sequel to "Carnival"*.   London, Cassell, and New York, Doran, 1925.

*Fairy Gold*.   London, Cassell, and New York, Doran, 1926.

*Rogues and Vagabonds*.   London, Cassell, and New York, Doran, 1927.

*Vestal Fire*   London, Cassell, and New York, Doran, 1927.

*Extremes Meet*.   London, Cassell, and New York, Doubleday, 1928.

*Extraordinary Women: Theme and Variations*.   London, Secker, and New York, Macy Masius, 1928.

*The Three Couriers*.   London, Cassell, and New York, Doubleday, 1929.

*April Fools: A Farce of Manners*.   London, Cassell, 1930; as *April Fools: A Comedy of Bad Manners*, New York, Doubleday, 1930.

*Buttercups and Daisies*.   London, Cassell, 1931; as *For Sale*, New York, Doubleday, 1931.

*Our Street*.   London, Cassell, 1931; New York, Doubleday, 1932.

*Water on the Brain*.   London, Cassell, and New York, Doubleday, 1933.

*The Darkening Green*.   London, Cassell, and New York, Doubleday, 1934.

*Figure of Eight*.   London, Cassell, 1936.

*The Four Winds of Love:*

> *The East Wind of Love*.   London, Rich and Cowan, 1937; as *The East Wind*, New York, Dodd Mead, 1937.

> *The South Wind of Love*.   London, Rich and Cowan, and New York, Dodd Mead, 1937.

*The West Wind of Love.* London, Chatto and Windus, and New York, Dodd Mead, 1940.

*West to North.* London, Chatto and Windus, and New York, Dodd Mead, 1941.

*The North Wind of Love.* London, Chatto and Windus, 2 vols., 1944, 1945, as *The North Wind of Love* and *Again to the North*, New York, Dodd Mead, 1945, 1946.

*The Red Tapeworm.* London, Chatto and Windus, 1941.

*The Monarch of the Glen.* London, Chatto and Windus, 1941.

*Keep the Home Guard Turning.* London, Chatto and Windus, 1943.

*Whisky Galore.* London, Chatto and Windus, 1947; as *Tight Little Island*, Boston, Houghton Mifflin, 1950.

*Hunting the Fairies.* London, Chatto and Windus, 1949.

*The Rival Monster.* London, Chatto and Windus, 1952.

*Ben Nevis Goes East.* London, Chatto and Windus, 1954.

*Thin Ice.* London, Chatto and Windus, 1956; New York, Putnam, 1957.

*Rockets Galore.* London, Chatto and Windus, 1957.

*The Lunatic Republic.* London, Chatto and Windus, 1959.

*Mezzotint.* London, Chatto and Windus, 1961.

*The Stolen Soprano.* London, Chatto and Windus, 1965.

*Paper Lives.* London, Chatto and Windus, 1966.


Plays

*The Gentleman in Grey* (produced Edinburgh, 1907).

*Carnival* (produced New York, 1912; as *Columbine*, produced Nottingham, 1922).

*The Lost Cause: A Jacobite Play* (broadcast, 1931). Edinburgh, Oliver and Boyd, 1933.


Verse

*Poems.* Oxford, Blackwell, 1907.

*Kensington Rhymes.* London, Secker, 1912.


Other

*Gramophone Nights*, with Archibald Marshall. London, Heinemann, 1923.

*Santa Claus in Summer* (juvenile). London, Constable, 1924; New York, Stokes, 1925.

*Mabel in Queer Street* (juvenile). Oxford, Blackwell, 1927.

*The Unpleasant Visitors*, with *Posset's Toby Jug* by Mabel Marlowe (juvenile). Oxford, Blackwell, 1928.

*The Adventures of Two Chairs* (juvenile). Oxford, Blackwell, 1929.

*Gallipoli Memories.* London, Cassell, 1929; New York, Doubleday, 1930.

*The Enchanted Blanket* (juvenile). Oxford, Blackwell, 1930.

*Told: Children's Tales and Verses.* Oxford, Blackwell, and New York, Appleton, 1930.

*First Athenian Memories.* London, Cassell, and New York, Doubleday, 1931.

*The Conceited Doll* (juvenile). Oxford, Blackwell, 1931.

*The Fairy in the Window-Box* (juvenile). Oxford, Blackwell, 1932.

*Prince Charlie: De Jure Charles III, King of Scotland, England, France and Ireland.* London, Davies, 1932; New York, Appleton, 1933.

*Unconsidered Trifles.* London, Secker, 1932.

*Greek Memories.* London, Cassell, 1932; withdrawn, and reissued, London, Chatto and Windus, 1939.

*Reaped and Bound: Collected Essays.* London, Secker, 1933.

*Literature in My Time.*  London, Rich and Cowan, 1933; New York, Mussey, 1934.

*The Dining-Room Battle* (juvenile).  Oxford, Blackwell, 1933.

*Prince Charlie and His Ladies.*  London, Cassell, 1934; New York, Knopf, 1935.

*Marathon and Salamis.*  London, Davies, 1934.

*The Enchanted Island* (juvenile).  Oxford, Blackwell, 1934.

*Catholicism and Scotland.*  London, Routledge, 1936.

*The Book of Barra,* with J. L. Campbell.  London, Routledge, 1936.

*The Naughtymobile* (juvenile).  Oxford, Blackwell, 1936.

*Pericles.*  London, Hodder and Stoughton, 1937.

*The Stairs That Kept On Going Down* (juvenile).  Oxford, Blackwell, 1937.

*The Windsor Tapestry: Being a Study of the Life, Heritage and Abdication of H.R.H. the Duke of Windsor, K.G.*  London, Rich and Cowan, and New York, Stokes, 1938.

*A Musical Chair.*  London, Chatto and Windus, 1939.

*Aegean Memories.*  London, Chatto and Windus, 1940.

*Calvary,* with Faith Compton Mackenzie.  London, Lane, 1942.

*Wind of Freedom: The History of the Invasion of Greece by the Axis Powers, 1940–1941.*  London, Chatto and Windus, 1943.

*Mr. Roosevelt.*  London, Harrap, 1943; New York, Dutton, 1944.

*Brockhouse.*  London, J. Brockhouse, 1944.

*Dr Beneš.*  London, Harrap, 1946.

*The Vital Flame.*  London, British Gas Council, 1947.

*All over the Place: Fifty Thousand Miles by Sea, Road and Rail.*  London, Chatto and Windus, 1948.

*Eastern Epic I: An Account of the Part Played by the Indian Army in the Second World War.*  London, Chatto and Windus, 1951.

*The Compton Mackenzie Birthday Book.*  London, Hutchinson, 1951.

*I Took a Journey: A Tour of the National Trust Properties.*  London, Naldritt, 1951.

*The House of Coalport, 1750–1950.*  London, Collins, 1951; New York, Collins, 1952.

*The Queen's House: A History of Buckingham Palace.*  London, Hutchinson, 1953.

*The Savoy of London.*  London, Harrap, 1953; New York, De Graff, 1954.

*Echoes.*  London, Chatto and Windus, 1954.

*Realms of Silver: One Hundred Years of Banking in the East.*  London, Routledge, 1954.

*My Record of Music.*  London, Hutchinson, 1955; New York, Putnam, 1956.

*Sublime Tobacco.*  London, Chatto and Windus, 1957; New York, Macmillan, 1958.

*Cats' Company.*  London, Elek, 1960; New York, Taplinger, 1961.

*Greece in My Life.*  London, Chatto and Windus, 1960.

*Catmint.*  London, Barrie and Rockliff, 1961; New York, Taplinger, 1962.

*On Moral Courage.*  London, Collins, 1962; as *Certain Aspects of Moral Courage,* New York, Doubleday, 1962.

*Look at Cats.*  London, Hamish Hamilton, 1963.

*My Life and Times:*

> *Octave One: 1883–1891.*  London, Chatto and Windus, 1963.
>
> *Octave Two: 1891–1900.*  London, Chatto and Windus, 1963.
>
> *Octave Three: 1900–1907.*  London, Chatto and Windus, 1964.
>
> *Octave Four: 1907–1914.*  London, Chatto and Windus, 1965.
>
> *Octave Five: 1915–1923.*  London, Chatto and Windus, 1966.
>
> *Octave Six: 1923–1930.*  London, Chatto and Windus, 1967.
>
> *Octave Seven: 1930–1938.*  London, Chatto and Windus, 1968.
>
> *Octave Eight: 1939–1946.*  London, Chatto and Windus, 1969.
>
> *Octave Nine: 1946–1952.*  London, Chatto and Windus, 1970.
>
> *Octave Ten: 1953–1963.*  London, Chatto and Windus, 1971.

*Little Cat Lost* (juvenile).  London, Barrie and Rockliff, 1965; New York, Macmillan, 1966.

*The Strongest Man on Earth: Based on the BBC Television Jackanory Programme.*  London, Chatto and Windus, 1968.

*Robert Louis Stevenson.*   London, Morga, 1968; Cranbury, New Jersey, A. S. Barnes, 1969.
*The Secret Island* (juvenile).   London, Kaye and Ward, 1969.
*Butterfly Hill* (juvenile).   London, Kaye and Ward, 1970.
*The Adventures of Jason* (juvenile).   London, Aldus Books, 1971.
*The Adventures of Theseus* (juvenile).   London, Aldus Books, 1971.

Critical Study: *Compton Mackenzie* by Leo Robertson, London, Richards Press, 1955.

Compton Mackenzie comments:

My trouble has always been that as soon as I had written a book I forgot about it and every book of mine which has been republished in hard-back or paper-back was read by me as if it were a new book written by somebody else. I had planned to reread much of my work in my old age but owing to failure of the one eye left to me it is no longer possible. If I had to read even *Sinister Street* again I would not know what the next chapter was going to be about. I have been very lucky in being able to write comic books as well as serious books and to every pot-boiler I have written I have given as much concentration and search for style as to any of my creative work. I have always written against the mood of the moment, which I think has been valuable because it has prevented republication of my earlier books from seeming dated. I had always intended to write plays, but from a theatrical inheritance of 150 years from America and well over 100 years from Great Britain, my plays, however well acted, were never the plays I heard in my own head; so I abandoned play-writing and sat down one afternoon in 1908 to write the ideal performance of my first play—*The Gentleman in Grey*—which, over two years later after being refused by over a dozen publishers, was published in 1911 as *The Passionate Elopement*. When *Sinister Street* came out it was banned by the circulating libraries but they had to surrender to public opinion. Contemporary readers will find it almost incredible that *Sinister Street* was banned, but in 1913 we had hardly emerged from late Victorianism.

\*          \*          \*

Sir Compton Mackenzie published his first novel, *The Passionate Elopement*, more than sixty years ago. It is not one of his best novels, nor even particularly outstanding by the measure of other contemporary novelists. But the circumstances of its composition indicate the personal qualities and gifts which have made its author one of the major writers of the twentieth century.

He had at the time already offered the public a volume of agreeable if derivative verse and had tried his hand in the theatre as both actor and dramatist. In none of these pursuits had he himself been satisfied with the results. In particular his 18th century costume piece *The Gentleman in Grey*, first staged in Edinburgh in 1907, fell far short of his original conception in its presentation in the theatre; and Sir Compton has recorded in his memoirs how he decided to turn the play into a novel so as to present the creatures of his imagination in a form which would not be distorted by the intervention and interpretations of other artists. Thus he wrote his first novel and committed himself to a literary career.

Since then he has published well over a hundred books. These are not by any means all novels. Fictions, history, volumes of biography and autobiography, essays, literary and musical criticism, and children's books have flowed from his pen in a copious stream of literary production, which in recent years has been mainly channelled into ten volumes of memoirs—*My Life and Times: Octaves I-X*—which sweep through a life of impressively rich and varied experience. There are many writers whose lives are of comparatively little interest to anyone but themselves and their immediate circle; but Sir Compton Mackenzie has himself had such a zest for life, such an abundance of energy and vitality, that his achievement as a novelist may too easily seem belittled when viewed in the context of his total activities both as an author and as a man.

Little need be said here about these activities, which range from directing the Aegean Intelligence Service in the First World War to the professional cultivation of daffodil hybrids, and from presiding over the Siamese Cat Club to championing Scottish inshore fishermen. But one should remember that they all represent various ways in which he has exercised the same lively intelligence, critical mind and imaginative sympathies as also go into the making of his novels. One should remember too that in his literary career he has always been more than a novelist, and that he has always aspired to the highest standards of professionalism. He has turned his pen to journalism as well as books, to public issues and controversy as well as fiction. And as a member of a family famous in the annals of the English stage, he has always known that amongst the foremost duties of a professional artist stands that of engaging and holding the interest of his audience. This has sometimes been held against him by critics of narrow sympathies and limited education; but those who know the longer perspectives of the history of the arts need not feel ashamed of joining the vast number of his admirers amongst readers of all ages and of all kinds.

In his book *The Georgian Literary Scene* Frank Swinnerton observed that it should never be forgotten, when considering Compton Mackenzie's work, that the theatre is in his blood. He certainly has a highly developed sense of drama and of the quiddities of human behaviour: to hear him telling a story—and thousands of television viewers have shared this privilege with his personal friends—is to see the characters come to life and act out their dialogue. He has no doubt partly inherited his gift as a mimic, but this is by no means the most important of his assets. Actors are not always very intelligent people; and it is his intellect and critical power that chiefly distinguish Compton Mackenzie and indeed turned him from the stage to literature. This is what controls his power of observation and his ability to penetrate into the essentials of scene, appearance and speech. With these qualities are linked a power of imaginative sympathy which allows him to enter fully into the minds and emotions of a wide variety of people. Henry James perceived this close marriage of intellect and imagination when he declared to his young fellow-author early in his career, "You have the best gift that any writer of novels can have, which is the ability to receive the direct impact of life so that you can return it directly to your readers."

It is hardly surprising, in view of Sir Compton Mackenzie's protean talent, that his novels exhibit a wide range both of subject-matter and of manner. Leaving aside the books for children, of which *Santa Claus in Summer* and *The Stairs That Kept On Going Down* are typical and well-loved examples, most of them do however fall into a number of main groups and sub-groups—the romantic novels from *Carnival* to the *Sylvia Scarlett* sequence, a trilogy of religious novels on the Anglo-Catholic movement in the Church of England, the comic novels with their strains both satirical and farcical, and his most ambitious work of all, *The Four Winds of Love*.

*Carnival* was his first notable success, the romantic story of a young Cockney dancer's life in the variety theatre, a milieu which was explored again in *Coral* and *Figure of Eight*. But his fame was finally established by *Sinister Street*, the tale of a young man's growth from infancy through schooldays and Oxford to his adventures in the London underworld, which is remarkable no less for its vivid, sensitive but firmly controlled evocation of childhood, adolescence, and progress towards emotional maturity, than for its portraiture of various levels of English society at the time. It remains a classic of English literature.

This was followed by *Guy and Pauline*, an idyllic romance of love fore-doomed, and then by *Sylvia Scarlett* which, with *Sylvia and Michael*, and *Vanity Girl*, links together in picturesque adventure some of the large cast of characters already presented in *Sinister Street*.

But Compton Mackenzie was already branching out in another direction with the first of his comedies, *Poor Relations* and its sequel *Rich Relatives*, in which he mined a vein of comic invention whose first lodes may be found in some of the dialogue in *Carnival* and *Sinister Street*, and which was to be exploited in plot as well. Satire and farce were further developed in such novels as *Water on the Brain* and *Keep the Home Guard Turning*, while

*Vestal Fire* and *Extraordinary Women* are sparkling comedies of manners, the latter's tolerant amusement at the antics of some Lesbian ladies contrasting strongly with the spare delicate treatment of the public and private disaster of a homosexual some thirty years later in *Thin Ice*. But returning to the comic novels, probably none has brought so much laughter and joy to his readers as the hilarious series of Highland fantasies which include *The Monarch of the Glen* and *Whisky Galore*.

But his greatest achievement as a novelist is *The Four Winds of Love*, a long and complex work which, partly because its publication was disorganised by the vagaries of war-time publishing, does not seem to have been recognised at large as the outstanding triumph it is.

The novel spans the first forty years of the century and chronicles the life of the central character as he grows from youth to manhood and maturity. In its original conception it was to consist, in the author's own words, of "four love stories and four philosophies of love"; but it encompasses not just affairs of the heart, but also affairs of the mind and of the soul. Emotional, intellectual and spiritual experiences are all explored in the course of the novel's development. So too are the worlds of music, literature, religion, society and politics, while the settings of the action range from Scotland to Italy and from America to Poland and Greece. Its pages teem with ideas. The cast of major and minor characters is enormous, and the novel is crowded from start to finish with lively incident. Yet all this is handled with a sure, deft touch. The craftsmanship and mastery of novelistic technique are superb, and come from a novelist of the greatest capacity in the full maturity of his powers. Of all his work, *The Four Winds of Love* and *Sinister Street* at least are assured of a permanent place in the great tradition of the English novel.

—Stewart F. Sanderson

---

**MacLENNAN, (John) Hugh.** Canadian. Born in Glace Bay, Nova Scotia, 20 March 1907. Educated at Halifax Academy; Dalhousie University, Halifax, B.A. 1928; Oriel College, Oxford (Rhodes Scholar), B.A., M.A. 1932; Princeton University, New Jersey, M.A., Ph.D. 1935. Married Dorothy Duncan in 1936 (died, 1957); Frances Walker, 1959. Since 1935, Classics Master, Lower Canada College, Montreal. Associate Professor, 1951–63, and since 1965 Professor of English, McGill University, Montreal. Recipient: Guggenheim Fellowship, 1943; Governor-General's Award, 1946, 1949, 1960, for non-fiction, 1950, 1955; Lorne Pierce Gold Medal, 1952; Molson Prize, 1966. D.Litt., University of Western Ontario, London, 1952; University of Manitoba, Winnipeg, 1953; Waterloo Lutheran University, Ontario, 1961; LL.D., Dalhousie University, 1955; Bishop's University, Lennoxville, Quebec, 1966; McMaster University, Hamilton, Ontario, 1966; University of Toronto, 1966; University of British Columbia, Vancouver, 1968; St. Mary's University, Halifax, 1968; Mount Alison University, Sackville, New Brunswick, 1969. Fellow, Royal Society of Canada, 1950, and Royal Society of Literature, England, 1955. Companion of the Order of Canada, 1967. Address: 1535 Summerhill Avenue, Montreal 25, Quebec, Canada.

PUBLICATIONS

Novels

    *Barometer Rising*.  Toronto, Collins, and New York, Duell, 1941; London, Harrap, 1942.

*Two Solitudes*. Toronto, Collins, and New York, Duell, 1945; London, Cresset Press, 1946.

*The Precipice*. Toronto, Collins, and New York, Duell, 1948; London, Cresset Press, 1949.

*Each Man's Son*. Toronto, Collins, and Boston, Little Brown, 1951; London, Heinemann, 1952.

*The Watch That Ends the Night*. New York, Scribner, and London, Heinemann, 1959.

*Return of the Sphinx*. New York, Scribner, 1967.

## Other

*Oxyrhynchus: An Economic and Social Study*. Princeton, New Jersey, Princeton University Press, 1935.

*Cross Country*. Toronto, Collins, 1948.

*Thirty and Three* (essays). Toronto, Macmillan, 1954; New York, Macmillan, and London, Macmillan, 1955.

*Scotchman's Return and Other Essays*. Toronto, Macmillan, and New York, Scribner, 1960; as *Scotsman's Return and Other Essays,* London, Macmillan, 1960.

*Seven Rivers of Canada*. Toronto, Macmillan, 1961; as *The Rivers of Canada,* New York, Scribner, 1961.

*The Colour of Canada*. Toronto, McClelland and Stewart, 1967; Boston, Little Brown, 1968.

Editor, *McGill: The Story of a University*. London, Allen and Unwin, 1960.

Manuscript Collection: McGill University Library, Montreal.

Critical Studies: *O Canada* by Edmund Wilson, New York, Farrar Straus, 1965; *Hugh MacLennan* by Peter Buitenhuis, Toronto, Forum House, 1969; *Hugh MacLennan* by George Woodcock, Toronto, Copp Clark, 1969; *Hugh MacLennan* by Alex Lucas, Toronto, McClelland and Stewart, 1970; *Second Image* by Ronald Sutherland, Toronto, New Press, 1971.

Hugh MacLennan comments:

Nearly all of my published non-fiction has been in the form of personal essays. However, I must have published more than sixty pieces over the years dealing with various contemporary situations and problems, many connected with Canada.

As for my novels, after two unpublished books, I discovered that I had as a Canadian a special technical problem. I was writing out of a country at that time unknown even to itself, to say nothing of the rest of the world. All Canadian stereotypes were false. As drama depends upon recognitions, I was forced in my earlier fiction to explore many aspects of the Canadian character and experience in a detail no longer necessary. I always tried to turn this work into as universal a statement as possible, and must to some extent have succeeded because by this time I have been translated into twelve different languages—though not all books were so translated. The most successful translations were in German, but my last novel, *Return of the Sphinx,* seems to have done well in Poland. I have been told that at least one of my books is in Russian but I never saw a copy of it or a confirmation that it is.

*       *       *

Since the First World War Canadian writing—and especially Canadian writing in English —has been in much the same condition as American literature a century earlier. Working in the midst of a people who were discovering for the first time the pangs and delights of nationhood, Canadian authors have too often concerned themselves with the need to give literary expression to the Canadian identity and, frequently, have been so much involved with Canadianism that they have let slip the artist's prime duty: to establish his own literary personality. More even than the Founding Fathers of American literature they have been plagued by external influences, by history, which linked them almost irrevocably to the substantial tradition of London, by geography, which set them virtually inescapably in the suburbs of New York, by language which gave them two giant brothers, and by economics which committed them to a minuscule circulation unless they were prepared to commit the treason of making themselves comprehensible and acceptable in the huge market-places of Britain and the United States.

The analogy between Canada in the fifty years since the end of the First World War and the United States a century earlier is, of course, both incomplete and deceptive, the more so because Canada has produced no unquestionable masters of the order of Melville or Whitman who could transpose national characteristics into the magnificence of universality, nor a Canadian Emerson who could lead rebellion against the courtly and uncourtly muses of the greater literary nations while borrowing the philosophical inheritance that they provided, nor even a Canadian Fenimore Cooper who could create an intrinsically Canadian mythology.

Some Canadian writers, Mazo de la Roche, Thomas Costain, even in a more subtle, less popular and more truly artistic manner, Morley Callaghan, Malcolm Lowry and John Glassco, have on occasion solved the problem of their Canadianism by ignoring it, by writing as if the world is their country. Others of a meaner sort have been persistently parochial and are in consequence acceptable only in the tiny confines of the parish or else, outside it, as folklorish curiosities. Only one Canadian novelist, Hugh MacLennan, has been consistent in his efforts to represent the Canadian character both as something quintessentially idiosyncratic and as a parable to the human condition.

It is no paradox but in itself typical of the Canadian ethos that MacLennan is himself in so many ways an untypical Canadian. For all that he is a fourth generation Nova Scotian, MacLennan is the son of a man who spoke Gaelic or a lilting Highland English and who held to the Calvinist ways of the Scots and to their superstition. His son has inherited the religiosity, something of the fatalism and much of the Scotsman's not unjustified conceit in the pioneering achievements of his race, so that several of his novels—and above all *Each Man's Son* and *Return of the Sphinx*—can be regarded as transatlantic epilogues to the history of Scottish literature, as the records of a pastoral people battered and bewildered by urban society, rather than as the opening chapters of the glorious literary enterprise of an ebullient new nation.

Yet for all his urgent Canadianism and for all his inescapable Scottishness the most obvious influences on MacLennan are cosmopolitan and urbane. True, when he moves outside the Canadian setting, as in parts of *The Precipice* and *Return of the Sphinx*, his novelist's confidence falters, but in everything that he writes, whether fiction or non-fiction, his style is overtly the product of the two great civilised institutions (some would say overcivilised) in which he was educated. His literary manners are set to the precepts of Oxford and Princeton, and fashioned by communities that are centuries and worlds away from the Canada he describes. A classical scholar of repute, his Canadian characters move to patterns that were fashioned long ago by Greek mythology.

To argue that an author's first novel is also his most successful would seem to imply a lack of development, and in one sense this claim for *Barometer Rising* does reduce the stature of all that has come from MacLennan since 1941. Certainly never again has MacLennan achieved an equivalent synthesis of theme and narrative without that constant interruption of didactic exposition which is the prime fault in most of MacLennan's books. But the entire success of *Barometer Rising* is almost an accident; it could hardly be repeated for MacLennan is deliberately both chronicler and creator of parables and there have been few other incidents in Canadian history so significant to Canadian development as the First World War and no one event so open to translation into parable as the Halifax explosion of 1917. The First World War, the foreground and the background of *Barometer Rising,* was the time when Canada discovered its identity, and the explosion is at once a moment from history and an inescapable symbol of the end of the colonial era and the true beginning of nationhood.

Almost all of MacLennan's later work attempts in one form or another a similar fusion of realism and symbolism and always he is concerned not so much with narrative, plot or setting (though with all these elements in the writing of novels, MacLennan is a master) as with laying bare one or the other of the major impulses that lie behind the peculiarly Canadian nature of Canada. In *Two Solitudes,* for example, it is the schism between French and English Canadians. In *The Precipice* and *Each Man's Son* the puritanical sense of guilt that Puritanism has inflicted upon Canadian life, "the belief that man has inherited from Adam a nature so sinful that there is no hope for him and that, furthermore, he lives and dies under the wrath of an arbitrary God who will forgive only a handful of his elect on the Day of Judgment."

Archie MacNeil, the shabby decaying boxer of *Each Man's Son,* is the most complete character in all MacLennan's work and the book as a whole contrives well two seemingly disparate themes, the gentleness of a man who lives by violence, and a threnody for the rural culture of Highlanders condemned by a cynical society to live by coal-mining.

*The Watch That Ends the Night* shows MacLennan as superb craftsman, handling with extraordinary skill a complicated time-sequence and with remarkable vividness the life of English Montreal, but because it is constructed on a grand scale it reveals in broad terms weaknesses which are less palpable in most of the other novels. MacLennan in all his books, but in *The Watch That Ends the Night* (and in *Return of the Sphinx*) more than in the others, is oppressively didactic. He is also an essayist almost more than he is a novelist. His expository asides and his descriptive vignettes though in themselves powerful and often elegant give to the book a stammering indecisiveness in which the hesitations become more compelling and sometimes more substantial than the fiction itself.

With courage beyond that of any other Canadian author, and to-day rare in all literatures, MacLennan writes on a grand scale. *Barometer Rising* and *The Watch That Ends the Night* are not masterpieces of the order of *War and Peace* but MacLennan has attempted to be Canada's Tolstoy and in doing so has disgraced neither himself nor Canada.

—J. E. Morpurgo

---

**MAILER, Norman.** American. Born in Long Branch, New Jersey, 31 January 1923. Educated at Harvard University, Cambridge, Massachusetts, S.B. in Engineering 1943; the Sorbonne, Paris, 1944. Served in the United States Army, 1944–46. Married Beatrice Silverman in 1944 (divorced, 1951); Adele Morales, 1954 (divorced, 1962); Lady Jean Campbell, 1962 (divorced, 1963); Beverly Bentley, 1963; has six children. An Editor of *Dissent,* New York, 1953–63; Columnist, *Esquire* magazine, New York, 1962–63; Co-Founding Editor, *Village Voice,* New York, 1965. Independent Candidate for Mayor of New York City, 1968. Recipient: *Story* magazine prize, 1941; National Institute of Arts and Letters grant, 1960; Pulitzer Prize, for non-fiction, 1969; National Book Award, for non-fiction, 1969. Member, National Institute of Arts and Letters. Lives in Brooklyn. Address: c/o Little Brown and Company, 34 Beacon Street, Boston, Massachusetts 02106, U.S.A.

PUBLICATIONS

### Novels

*The Naked and the Dead.*   New York, Rinehart, 1948; London, Wingate, 1949.
*Barbary Shore.*   New York, Rinehart, 1951; London, Cape, 1952.
*The Deer Park.*   New York, Putnam, 1955; London, Wingate, 1957.
*An American Dream.*   New York, Dial Press, and London, Deutsch, 1965.
*Why Are We in Vietnam?*   New York, Putnam, 1967; London, Weidenfeld and
    Nicolson, 1969.

### Short Stories

*New Short Novels 2*, with others.   New York, Ballantine, 1956.
*Advertisements for Myself* (includes essays and verse).   New York, Putnam, 1959;
    London, Deutsch, 1961.

### Plays

*The Deer Park* (produced in New York, 1967).   New York, Dial Press, 1967.

Films: *Wild Go*, 1967; *Beyond the Law*, 1967; *Maidstone*, 1968.

### Verse

*Deaths for the Ladies and Other Disasters.*   New York, Putnam, and London, Deutsch,
    1962.

### Other

*The White Negro.*   San Francisco, City Lights, 1959.
*The Presidential Papers.*   New York, Putnam, 1963; London, Deutsch, 1964.
*Cannibals and Christians.*   New York, Dial Press, 1966; London, Deutsch, 1967.
*The Bullfight.*   New York, Macmillan, 1967.
*The Armies of the Night: History as a Novel, The Novel as History.*   New York, New
    American Library, and London, Weidenfeld and Nicolson, 1968.
*Miami and the Siege of Chicago: An Informal History of the Republican and Democratic
    Conventions of 1968.*   Cleveland, World, 1969; as *Miami and the Siege of Chicago:
    An Informal History of the American Political Conventions of 1968*, London, Weiden-
    feld and Nicolson, 1969.
*Of a Fire on the Moon.*   Boston, Little Brown, and London, Weidenfeld and Nicolson,
    1970.
*The Prisoner of Sex.*   Boston, Little Brown, and London, Weidenfeld and Nicolson,
    1971.

*      *      *

*Why Are We in Vietnam?* The title of Norman Mailer's recent novel is mocking, accusatory. Why, we might ask, does Mailer point the question at *us* before we ever open the book? In part, surely, to implicate us in the answer. We are asked to understand the story that follows as having something to do with ourselves. Partly, also, to make us see the active social intention of the novel.

But I should like to suggest a third possibility, quite outside Mailer's specific intentions: that the question confronts us with a connection between social catastrophe and personal responsibility present in Mailer from the beginning. If we are to appreciate his development, we must look at Mailer's five novels in order, and in light of this connection.

Mailer's first novel, *The Naked and the Dead*, is about the American invasion of Anopoei, a tiny Pacific island held by the Japanese during World War II. Mailer shows us the war from the vantage point of General Cummings, brilliant commander of the invasion; and of a small reconnaissance platoon, headed by Sergeant Croft. In both instances, power, even of a minor sort, would seem to be incompatible with humanity.

General Cummings counts absolutely on his own superiority. His political notion is that eventually he, and some few like him, will control both man and nature. But he needs an admirer, an "aide" who can appreciate how good he really is. He chooses Hearn, a young, rich, Harvard educated lieutenant. Hearn discovers that to reject the older man's message brings humiliation as well as danger—when Cummings orders him to pick up a cigarette butt, he is astonished by his own submission. He welcomes an opportunity to leave the General's staff and lead Croft's platoon on a special mission.

In the newness of command, Hearn fails to see that he has displaced Croft. The oversight costs him his life. He is killed, tricked by Croft, who is determined to take back the platoon. Croft, it would seem, is Cummings' counterpart in the lower ranks. A tough and cunning fighter, he is respected by the platoon, although they do not much like him.

In the end, Cummings and Croft suffer defeats from both man and nature. Cummings discovers that his brilliant calculations are based on misinformation—the battle is launched and won—accidentally—while he is away from the island. Croft, at the very summit of the mountain he has forced his men to climb, falls into a hornets' nest, and as the men flee, stumbling and running down the slopes they have labored to climb, he realizes that he has lost control.

What hope lies in these defeats? Croft and Cummings survive and keep their power. I suggest that in this first novel, hope lies quite outside the struggle for power, in the men of the platoon who have strong connections with each other and with the life they lived before the war: In Red Valsen, ex-coal miner, dishwasher, bum, who refuses Hearn's offer of a raise in rank, and finally refuses Croft's challenge, because, unlike Hearn, he knows what he is up against. In Goldstein and Ridges, who try to carry their wounded buddy, Wilson, on a crudely-made stretcher, through burning hot meadows, over a muddy jungle trail, and try even to cross a fast-moving river.

In *The Naked and the Dead*, Mailer alludes to ominous political possibilities that might come out of the war. The next novel, *Barbary Shore*, would seem to dramatize those possibilities.

Unlike the panoramic war novel, the scale is small, the physical situation constricted. The narrator, Mikey Lovett, takes a room in a Brooklyn rooming house in order to write a novel. Mikey's biography is almost blank: he has no past, no identity. "Probably," he says, "I was in the war." Even his handsome, youthful face is not his own—"there is nothing I can recognize," he tells us, "not even my age."

When Mikey comes to know his fellow roomers, he discovers that in one sense they are like him—their present has somehow become disconnected from their past. The gaunt, middle-aged McLeod is not merely a mild-mannered department store worker, but a former Communist, once high up in the party. Hollingsworth is not "a simple small-town boy," but a government agent, sent to interrogate McLeod and get from him a "little object" of great importance. Even the voluptuous, red-haired landlady, Beverly Guinevere, has some mystery about her. Guinevere, it turns out, is McLeod's wife.

Mikey Lovett becomes McLeod's friend and confidant, a witness to the interrogation

Hollingsworth conducts; to McLeod's admission of crimes that accomplished nothing; to his desperate attempt to persuade Guinevere to go away with him; and, finally, to his death. But something survives for McLeod. He entrusts Mikey with the "little object," and wishes him well: "may he be alive," his will reads, "to see the rising of the Phoenix."

What Mailer shows here is not merely the failure of a single line of political thought, but the consequences of social disintegration. Something terrible has happened to our normal social connections. We recall Mikey's fantasy of a middle-aged man getting into a taxi, settling back to read the paper and finding suddenly that the taxi is taking the wrong route. But he just sits there, helpless to stop it, unable to believe that it is really happening.

Such derangement, the novel warns us, is terrifying. It leaves us huddled together in dusty, claustrophobic places, in unfamiliar rooms with drawn blinds, our identities missing. And beyond is the threat of Barbary Shore. To the blousy Guinevere, in her chameleon clothes that suggest "everything from breakfast in bed to a formal evening" and her money belt—"I'm prepared," she says proudly—it sounds good. She would like to go there. To McLeod and Mikey Lovett, barbary is a terrifying possibility. Against it, they have only the "little object," the heritage of McLeod's "socialist culture."

In the next book, *The Deer Park*, Mailer writes about a world less mysterious, less real, and—regrettably—less interesting, than that of Guinevere's dusty boarding house.

As in the previous novel, the narrator wants to be a writer. But unlike Mikey Lovett, Sergius O'Shaugnessy is interested in fantasy, not truth. He has been in the war, dropped jellied gasoline on the Japanese; and he would like to forget all that. Desert D'Or, within commuting distance of Hollywood, would seem to be the right place to do so: "everything is in the present tense." It is "all new."

"I was understood," Sergius tells us, "to be an Air Force pilot whose family was wealthy and lived in the East." Actually, he confides, he has no family at all. He is deliberately faking. "There was a real world . . . where orphans burned orphans. It was better," he tells us, "not to think of this. I liked the other world in which almost everybody lived. The imaginary world."

But the imaginary world, Sergius discovers, has real troubles. His friend and mentor, Charles Francis Eitel, Hollywood director, out of a job because of a Congressional investigating committee, is living quietly, trying to write a serious movie script. Eitel and Sergius have complicated love affairs, Eitel with the ex-mistress of a big producer, Sergius with Eitel's ex-wife, Lulu. "The heart of her pleasure," Sergius says, "is to show herself." The outcome is that Eitel tires of being broke and outcast. He reworks his script for commercial film, recants his testimony, gets his job back, and marries. When we hear of him some few years later, he is still married, making commercial films, and having an affair with his ex-wife.

If the old pro fails, there is still hope for Sergius. For Sergius refused a Hollywood offer, got free of the phoney world of Desert D'Or. In the end, he gets a telepathic message from Eitel: "I have lost the final desire of the artist, the desire which tells us that when all else is lost . . . there still remains that world we may create. . . . So, do try Sergius, try for that other world, the real world. . . ."

The real world, Sergius agrees, is where the artist must go. But he would lighten Eitel's message. Pleasure is, after all, as real as pain: "one must," he adds, "look for a good time since a good time is what gives us the strength to try again."

Eitel's message is self-pitying. But Mailer doesn't see this—here or elsewhere in the book. He has Sergius say soberly of Eitel, "It was his speech, and he said it well." A strange view of what would seem to be obviously satiric material, for, of course, he doesn't say it well. Sergius, on the other hand, takes just the right note. But Sergius' comment is merely a fragment. It has little to do with the life of Desert D'Or, a dull, Romance Mag sort of place, where we find out that "he loved her as he had never loved anyone, loved her and knew that the life of such a love was but a minute." In such a place, not only art but interest fails.

In the 60's, Mailer wrote two novels, *An American Dream* and *Why Are We in Vietnam?* Both are about a world—Sergius would call it a real world—in which "orphans burn orphans."

The opening sentences of *An American Dream* tell us about "the years when the gears worked together": "I met Jack Kennedy in November, 1946," Stephen Richards Rojack tells us, "*We were both* war heroes, and both of us had just been elected to Congress." The occasion is a double date. A "fair evening for me," Rojack comments coolly. His girl is Deborah Caughlin Mangaravidi Kelly, the heiress Rojack later marries.

This is the good part of the dream, when everything seems desirable and possible—Rojack and Kennedy, *both*, it would seem, on the same right track. But Rojack's dream goes bad.

When the story actually begins, he is at a party, vomiting over a balcony railing ten stories above the street. The image tells us what Rojack is up to. He has given up politics. For a year now, he has been separating from his wife. Deborah, at first, "a vision of treasure, far-off blood, and fear," has become the "Great Bitch." "I hated her," he tells us, ". . . it seemed as though she were the only achievement I could point to." "I seem to be joining," he says, "with that horde of the mediocre and the mad who listen to popular songs and act upon coincidence."

Rojack's dilemma, it would seem, is that to act otherwise, to choose, is connected with death. At this crucial juncture, it is an active, beckoning reality. Rojack steps across to the "wrong side" of the balcony railing, hears a silvery voice: "Drop," it says. He resists, and slips back. But if not suicide, then murder? for murder, he has told us, "offers the promise of vast relief. It is never unsexual." When Deborah makes obscene sexual taunts, he chokes her to death and pushes her body out the window.

On one level, the book is a detective story—we are anxious to see if Rojack gets away with the murder. On another, it is about Rojack's struggle to stay on the *right side* of the railing.

During the investigation, two things happen—he has a love affair with Cherry, a night club singer; and an interview with his father-in-law, Barney Oswald Kelly. Kelly, who has made a million dollars "two hundred times over," and who knows that Rojack has murdered Deborah, is his real antagonist. The interview ends with Rojack's walking a foot wide parapet 30 stories above the street. He makes it, though Kelly doesn't want him to and, at the very end, tries to poke him off with an umbrella. But Rojack leaps down, hits Kelly across the face with the umbrella, and then "in relief, some relief," hurls it away. So much for Kelly and his old man's weapons. Rojack has outfaced him, dared even to knock him down.

The book ends with his heading out of the country toward Yucatan. But he stops in Vegas to make some money—and to walk out on the desert on a moonlight night and make a phone call to Cherry. Cherry is dead, we know, murdered while Rojack was walking the parapet. But she answers, and Rojack hears what we would all like to hear. "Why, hello, hon," Cherry says, "I thought you'd never call." The next morning he declares himself "something like sane," and goes on.

In the end, then, Rojack has purged himself of money and power. And he has made a connection with death, a gentle and bearable one, it would seem. But the price is high—he is alone and heading *out* of the country.

Mailer has traced, in these four novels, an enormous amount of social damage—first, the catastrophe of the war, the social disintegration that followed, a retreat into the imaginary and unreal, and, finally, at the center of American society, a connection between money and power and death. If we are to believe Rojack's experience, we can only get "some relief," and, finally, we must get out entirely. But we don't get out, of course, and worse things happen. We pick up the extent of the social damage in the fifth novel, *Why Are We in Vietnam?*

The narrator is not a man, trying to understand his experience, but an eighteen-year-old boy, D.J., "Disc Jockey to the world," broadcasting "from Dallas, Big D in Tex," telling us "how to live, how to live. . . ."

The first half of D.J.'s adventure is with Rusty, his father, "the cream of corporation corporateness." Rusty, D.J. tells us, is a "heroic looking figure of a Texan," but when D.J. is high on pot, he sees a different Rusty:

> the smiling Ike grin goes away, and so do all those Henry Cabot Lodge grins, instead there's a thin lippy old hole cut for his mouth—like the first slit on an operation—skin peels back, and in the wound there's teeth. . . . And his nose . . . it looks suddenly like a hand, got a red mean finger at the tip . . . grab your mouth and

twist it off. . . . But it's Rusty's eyes kick off the old concept of dread. . . . You get voids, man, and gleams of yellow fires—the woods is burning somewhere in his grey matter.

Rusty, D.J. assures us, is "the highest grade of ass hole made in America." Therefore, he asks us to see how Rusty "shapes up" on a hunt for grizzly bear, north of the Arctic Circle, Alaska.

The climax of the hunt is when Rusty decides to take D.J. and cut out, look for grizzly on their own. They are "off on a free, father and son," and to D.J.'s astonishment, Rusty sheds "all that paper ass desk shit and glut," and starts talking about wild flowers. They get closer and closer, D.J. "riding on currents of love," when suddenly they come upon bear tracks, huge, the front claws two inches long.

When the grizzly charges, "coming fast as a locomotive barreling on that trail," D.J. fires first, then Rusty from behind. But the bear keeps coming, and D.J. fires again, "not ten yards away, flame of the muzzle meeting flame from the grizzer's red flame ass red mouth." Suddenly, the bear leaves the trail and is gone. They follow, down a steep slope, never sure of what the bear will do. When they find him, sitting in a great pool of blood, D.J. walks toward him, within twenty feet, then closer, and looks into the eyes of the dying animal.

But Rusty has not, we find out, shed "those corporation layers." When they get back to camp and are asked who got the bear, Rusty takes the credit. "Yeah, I guess its mine," he says, and adds for his son who shot the bear from ten yards away and walked close to watch its death—"but one of its sweet legs belongs to D.J." "Final end," says D.J. "of love of one son for one father."

This is not the end of the hunt for D.J. He goes out again, this time with his best friend, Tex Hyde. Their intention is to clean "the pipes," and to do this, they must leave their weapons behind, even their hunting knives. When they see a bear, they watch from a tree.

The bear eats berries, "about two hundred buffalo berries at a pop," blue and red juice running "out of the sides of his black leather mouth." A herd of caribou pass on a ridge, and the grizzly takes off "like a bull locomotive." Except for one calf, the caribou escape. The bear kills her, "slamming his teeth through the big muscles of her back right through to the spine . . . and she breaks like a stick of wood."

Later, as they lie down, side by side, in the Arctic night, they get a message. The Arctic lights begin, "wash and glow colors rippling like a piece of silk," and the boys are "half out of their mind." The lights are telling them *there is something*—"yeah God was here, and He was real and no man was He, but a beast, some beast of a giant jaw and cavernous mouth with a full cave's breath and fangs, and secret call: come to me."

At the end of the hunt, the god whose "secret call" they hear is a murderous beast—all mouth and fangs. They have translated the image that dominates the hunt into a personal message—we recall the bear with the "flame ass red mouth," the bear scooping up berries and "slamming his teeth" into the caribou calf. In their experience, there is no human image which can vie with this kind of power—or terrifying purity of purpose. Humanity is simply "mixed shit." D.J. sees Rusty, we recall, as something hideous—slit mouth, "red mean finger" of a nose, yellow eyes—full of "paper ass desk shit and glut." They have come to purge themselves of this, to clean the "pipes," and when they do, they do not become lovers but "killer brothers." They hear the great beast whispering over and over, "Fulfill my will, go forth and kill."

The hunt, D.J. tells us at the end, really happened two years ago. It is simply in his "consciousness" at this "grope dinner in the Dallas ass manse," given in his honor, because tomorrow he and Tex are "off to see the wizard in Vietnam." So D.J. says goodby—"Disc Jockey to America turning off. Vietnam, hot dam."

In retrospect, these five novels would seem to be set, like stones, in a single developing design. War is a recurring motif—in the first, the dominant action is of men fighting a war; in the next three novels, the central figures remember a war in which they played a part or think they played a part; and, finally, D.J. looks forward to a new war.

In every novel, the central argument is between a man, still unsettled in life, and an older man whose commitments are already decided. In the novels about politics and art, the dialogue is sympathetic—McLeod, we recall, entrusts the future to Mikey, Eitel would like Sergius to be a better artist than he is himself. In the novels about war and money and power, the dialogue is deadly—the hostility between Cummings and Hearn is indirectly responsible for Hearn's death; between Kelly and Rojack, the stakes are equally high; they are both capable of killing each other. But the most dangerous of these masculine competitions is surely between Rusty and his sixteen-year-old son.

The overall movement—if we look at the novels as episodes in a larger development—is a movement in which men are at first brothers, and then, "killer brothers." Social catastrophe is no longer the consequence of a few evil men or large impersonal forces, but of aberrant feelings at the very center of our lives. In *The Naked and the Dead*, the men of Croft's platoon are morally responsive to each other. Cummings and Croft, in their ruthlessness, are the aberrant figures of this world. In *Barbary Shore*, Mikey and Lovett are engulfed in social confusion—yet they continue to resist a world in which "the blind will lead the blind, and the deaf shout warnings to one another until their voices are lost." *The Deer Park* has none of this ominous social potential; it is dangerous in a less important way. Yet, even in the narcissistic world of Desert D'Or, Sergius finds a friend who helps him to see that this "imaginary world" has little connection with anything outside itself.

In *An American Dream*, Rojack is alone, attempting to live, without wife or friend, in a society that is cold, unproductive and unregenerative. The survival tests in such a society reflect precisely these qualities—Rojack's test, we recall, is to walk around the parapet of the Waldorf Towers. Whatever philosophical interpretation we may put upon that walk, from a social point of view, it is a desperate and sterile gesture. In the most recent novel, *Why Are We in Vietnam?* isolation is replaced by active hate. D.J. and Tex, "killer brothers," hear the voice of the beast god, and it leads to "the new life," adventuring with the "wizard in Vietnam."

This "new life," adventuring in Vietnam, is, in fact, where we are now. If we use Mailer's fiction as a gauge, we have got there in a hurry. The first novel in 1948 looks at a different world. It ends, we may recall, when a plodding colonel gets the idea that he might "jazz up" the map reading class by using a pin-up girl picture with a co-ordinate grid system laid over it. "Goddam," the colonel says to himself, "what an idea." Maybe he could write to the War Department Training Aid Section. Maybe every unit in the army would want such an aid. The novel closes with the colonel's yelp of pleasure—"Hot dog." Such mindlessness, Mailer makes clear, is not innocent. But it is surely less terrifying than D.J.'s ruthless parting shot— "Vietnam, hot dam."

Much of modern writing is terse, low-keyed. Beckett, for example, whose emphasis is metaphysical, gives us characters who speak softer and softer and finally settle into silence. Mailer, whose interests are social, would seem to be the obverse side of the coin. As things get worse and worse, Mailer shouts louder and louder, insisting, it seems, that the validity of any claim we make is in our own voice. If we object that D.J.'s adventure is unreal, strident, that it swings far away from real human possibilities, I suggest that the title swings back at us like a boomerang. And there Mailer keeps a corner of human responsibility for us. He asks: why are we in Vietnam? Not they. *We*.

—Jacqueline Hoefer

---

**MALAMUD, Bernard.** American. Born in Brooklyn, New York, 26 April 1914. Educated at Erasmus Hall, New York; City College of New York, 1932–36, B.A. 1936; Columbia University, New York, 1937–38, M.A. 1942. Married Ann de Chiara in 1945; has two children. Teacher, New York high schools, evenings 1940–49; Instructor to Associate Professor of English, Oregon State University, Corvallis, 1949–61. Since 1961, Member of the Division of Language and Literature, Bennington College, Vermont. Visiting Lecturer, Harvard University, Cambridge, Massachusetts, 1966–68. Recipient: *Partisan Review* fellowship, 1956; Rosenthal Award, 1958; Daroff Memorial Award, 1958; Ford Fellowship, 1959, 1960; National Book Award, 1959, 1967; Pulitzer Prize, 1967; O. Henry Award, 1969. Member, National Institute of Arts and Letters, 1964; American Academy of Arts and Sciences, 1967. Address: c/o Russell and Volkening, 551 Fifth Avenue, New York, New York 10017, U.S.A.

PUBLICATIONS

Novels

> *The Natural.*  New York, Harcourt Brace, 1952; London, Eyre and Spottiswoode, 1963.
> *The Assistant.*  New York, Farrar Straus, 1957; London, Eyre and Spottiswoode, 1959.
> *A New Life.*  New York, Farrar Straus, 1961; London, Eyre and Spottiswoode, 1962.
> *The Fixer.*  New York, Farrar Straus, 1966; London, Eyre and Spottiswoode, 1967.
> *Pictures of Fidelman: An Exhibition.*  New York, Farrar Straus, 1969; London, Eyre and Spottiswoode, 1970.
> *The Tenants.*  New York, Farrar Straus, 1971; London, Eyre and Spottiswoode, 1972.

Short Stories

> *The Magic Barrel.*  New York, Farrar Straus, 1958; London, Eyre and Spottiswoode, 1960
> *Idiots First.*  New York, Farrar Straus, 1963; London, Eyre and Spottiswoode, 1964.
> *Penguin Modern Stories 1*, with others.  London, Penguin, 1969.

Uncollected Short Stories

> "Man in the Drawer", in *Atlantic* (Boston), April 1968.
> "My Son the Murderer", in *Esquire* (New York), November 1968.
> "An Exorcism", in *Harper's* (New York), December 1968.
> "God's Wrath", in *Atlantic* (Boston), 1971.

Other

> *A Malamud Reader,* edited by Philip Rahv.  New York, Farrar Straus, 1967.

Bibliography: *Bernard Malamud* by R. N. Kosofsky, Kent, Ohio, Kent State University Press, 1969.

Manuscript Collection: Library of Congress, Washington, D.C.

Critical Studies: *Bernard Malamud* by Sidney Richman, New York, Twayne, 1966; *Bernard Malamud and the Critics*, edited by Leslie and Joyce Field, New York, New York University Press, 1970.

*        *        *

Unquestionably, Bernard Malamud is one of the most important authors of contemporary fiction, though critics still differ in assigning him a precise place in the Jewish school of American novelists. His place is his own. It is obvious that Malamud reclaims the Hebraic tradition to a brash new world. His work implies Yiddish lore, the wry and equivocal quality of the Jewish joke, the cadences of some immemorial speech. His lucid style, spare in pain, rich in sensuous inflections, tenacious as poetry can be, carries Jewish conscience into our midst. Yet it is also clear that both Malamud's style and morality transcend the heritage of Judaism. "Jews," he says, "are absolutely the very *stuff* of drama"; and the purpose of the writer is "to keep civilization from destroying itself." Thus the heroes of Malamud become, no less that the author himself, symbols of struggling humanity, partaking in its ambiguous fate.

The heroes of Malamud, usually common and solitary people, so gracelessly human, conform superficially to the image of the *schlemiel-schlimazel*. Yet they serve to affirm the possibilities of dignity for all; prisoners of circumstance, they still find the means of regeneration. This is Malamud's abiding theme—conversion, moral rebirth—which sustains his humanism in an age full of the various terrors of apocalypse. Suffering makes for laughter as it makes for truth, and the last, acting on the heart, renews the whole man. The density of social facts in Malamud's fiction may, in the minds of some readers, awaken memories of the proletarian novels of the Thirties. But the facts of Malamud are not prescriptive, and his characters translate themselves continually from social scapegoats to mythic redeemers. Thus his vision comprises myth and actuality, the spirit's freedom and the weight of the world; trust and irony are part of his single craft.

Malamud's first novel, *The Natural*, received belated recognition. Obscure in parts and original, it came slowly into focus in the larger pattern of his fiction. The story enmeshes the life of a modern baseball hero, Roy Hobbs, into various legendary patterns. Heavily overlaid with symbols, the work evokes the popular mystique of baseball, the Horatio Alger paradigm of success, Homeric tales, Arthurian quest motifs, and ancient vegetation rites. The snappy slang of sport and the sacred archetypes of tradition come together. The ordeals of the thirty-three year old hero—Christ, Dionysus, the Fisher King stand uneasily behind this "Natural"—are concretely American: money, fame, sex. Yet his failures also project the temptations of contemporary man who acts, on the one hand, without a sense of a sustaining myth, and acts, on the other, without a sense of the limits of myth in history. Hobbs betrays the ideal code of baseball and rejects the love of a true woman; he has no sense, as his would-be murderess says, of "something over and above earthly things." Primary as is Malamud's theme, his method remains open to questions. How integral is the mythic structure to the purpose of the book? How congenial is its grotesque tone to the author himself?

None of these questions occur in reading *The Assistant*. Here Malamud develops the theme of spiritual conversion in flawless form. Set in a milieu of immigrant shopkeepers and minority groups, the novel transforms downbeat city streets into some drab version of pastoral, into a discrete myth of renascence. The heaviness of poverty or ignorance, the alienation of the Jew in a land of Gentiles, the violence of unformed desire, the persistence of hope, qualify the love story of Frank Alpine and Helen Bober. The Bobers toil sixteen hours a day in a grocery store, barely eking out a living; this is their share of the American Dream. But their daughter, Helen, reads in the library and holds out for a better fate. Into their midst comes "the assistant," Frank, to whom pain is familiar though still unintelligible. An Italian among Jews, Frank discovers himself slowly, purgation in humility, regeneration through love and sacrifice. He suffers circumcision, becomes after Passover a Jew. The subtle twists of the plot, the reversals which affect all the characters, create a unique moral and dramatic perspective. How else can experience be evaluated but from different points of view? Thus old Bober, who acts as Frank's silent teacher, seems lacking to his daughter: "He could, with a little more courage, have been more than he was." Yet the rabbi who buries him says: "Yes, Morris Bober was to me a true Jew. . . . He suffered, he endured, but with hope." Without sentimentality, the novel engages the harsh, contradictory stuff of existence. Its luminous metaphors, its clear rhythms, speak beyond irony, beyond inconclusiveness, of human responsibility.

Two collections of stories, *The Magic Barrel* and *Idiots First*, follow. These contain some of the best as well as the poorest fiction of Malamud. The best usually deal with Jewish material— "The Magic Barrel," "Take Pity," "The Mourners," "Idiots First," "The Last Mohican"—the worst, set abroad, have a glossy quality. Written with marvelous economy, the finest stories combine humor with poetry, and probe the same moral center: the aches and indignities of daily life which add, often crazily, to a kind of nobility.

In *A New Life*, Malamud pursues his central theme in a more open form, a kind of Stendhalian academic picaresque. But there is something forced in the book, something second hand in its felt life. This may be due to the faintly sour character of its hero, S. Levin, who leaves New York City streets in search of fuller possibilities in the Far West (Oregon?). The pattern of escape is archetypal, though Levin himself, bearded liberal academic, has a limited capacity for freedom. The novel includes many topical references to politics—the Korean War, McCarthyism, American Democracy—and much social satire. Its turning point comes, however, when Levin discovers his love for Pauline Gilley, the wife of a colleague. This is no great romantic love. It is a love born of some unacknowledged imperative, sustained by irony, a willed commitment. At the end, when Levin leaves with Pauline and all of her adopted children—she is also pregnant by him—he does so toward an uncertain destiny. Clarified by some moral perception of himself, he remains, nonetheless, an encumbered soul.

*The Fixer* suggests a far more frightening and splendid destiny for man. Drawing freely on a historical incident of Jewish persecution—the trial of Mendel Beiliss, accused in Kiev, 1913, of the "ritual murder" of a Christian child—the work distills history into a parable of terror and absurdity resisted, superhumanly, to the last. Yakov Bok, a poor and frail fixer, pits himself against the history of human despotism, the absurdity of existence, to insist on his innocence. Thus he restores to all men not merely justice or dignity but a place, a meaning, in the universe. Bok will settle only for the largest questions. "Who invented my life?" he asks. Tormented in solitary confinement—stripped, chained, stripped again, searched in his intimate parts daily—he struggles with his Czarist tormentors, with his Jewish legacy, with his God. "He's with us till the Cossacks come galloping, then he's elsewhere," Bok bitterly says of God. Unlike his father-in-law, Shmuel, or his adulterous wife, Raisl, unlike Job even, Bok maintains his own way in the face of all. This minimal man gives a new meaning to heroism. Querulous, impotent, quixotic, Bok leaves one prison, his *shtehtl*, to fall into another. But the prison from which he finally emerges is one to which all men are born. With harrowing control, Malamud guides the story of his fixer to an end that is perhaps too abrupt. The language at once sears and sings. The process of continuous genocide which we call history finds in this novel both a challenge and a response.

There are, of course, comic and grotesque touches in *The Fixer*. These become more inept, in *Pictures of Fidelman*. Parts of this work—"The Last Mohican," for instance, or "Still Life"—appeared in earlier collections. The book, however, aspires to some unity through its setting, Italy, its main character, Arthur Fidelman, failed painter, and through its central theme, the relation of art to love and life. Cracked, funny, and often frivolous, the various episodes refract the attempts of Fidelman to justify his existence in the mirror of his art. Only in the last episode, "Glass Blower of Venice," does he remake his world with a deeper sensual knowledge of himself. The work, one feels, adds little to the stature of Malamud.

The figure of the artist becomes more richly symbolic in *The Tenants*, symbolic of the contemporary "occluded self." In a crumbling house, deserted by all except two fanatic writers, Lesser and Spearmint, one a Jew, the other black, a spectral drama of art, sex, and race is played out. Each, locked in his own sense of fate, destroys life around him, painfully destroying himself. The complex hostility of Jew and Black assumes other oppositions between form and energy, art and politics, self-hatreds of various kinds. Malamud nearly evades the stereotypes of his charged subject by reversing some patterns—the Jewish girl,

Irene, and her black friend, Mary, weave the intricacies of love—and by insisting on the artistic identity of his main characters, on their human anguish. Without carrying his themes to a new level of insight, Malamud displays both tact and tensity in the writing of this book, a novel, elliptic style blending narrative and dream. The point of view shifts in the shadowy symbolic space of a tenement waiting for the wreckers' ball, while the various authors write their way to death. Inconclusively, the novel suggests alternate ends of itself. Yet the novel also stands as a prophetic parable of our tenancy in this world, and as a plea "for the invention of choices to outwit tragedy."

On the whole, Malamud is not an experimentalist in fiction. His genius is not expansive, his moral imagination almost too steadfast. Still, in his rigorous art, he gives to the Jew a deep-hued definition in American society. Above all a humanist, affirmative beneath all ambiguities, Malamud aspires to recover justice and decency in the world, recover the human measure of universal things, and to embrace the spirit's renewal.

—Ihab Hassan

---

**MALGONKAR, Manohar (Dattatray).** Indian. Born in Bombay, 12 July 1913. Educated at Karnatak College, Dharwar; Bombay University, B.A. (honours) in English and Sanskrit 1936. Served in the Maratha Light Infantry, rising to the rank of Lieutenant Colonel, 1942–52. Married Manorama Somdutt in 1947; has one child. Professional Big-Game Hunter, 1935–37; Cantonment Executive Officer, Government of India, 1937–42. Owner, Jagalbet Mining Syndicate, 1953–59. Since 1959, self-employed Farmer in Jagalbet. Address: P. O. Jagalbet, Londa, Belgaum District, India.

PUBLICATIONS

Novels

Distant Drum. Bombay, Asia Publishing House, 1960; London and New York, Asia Publishing House, 1961.
Combat of Shadows. London, Hamish Hamilton, 1962.
The Princes. London, Hamish Hamilton, 1963; New York, Viking Press, 1964.
A Bend in the Ganges. London, Hamish Hamilton, 1964; New York, Viking Press, 1965.
The Devil's Wind: Nana Saheb's Story. New York, Viking Press, and London, Hamish Hamilton, 1972.

Uncollected Short Stories

More than 50 stories; the earliest is "The Cheat", in Illustrated Weekly of India (Bombay), 1948; the most recent is "Hush", in Illustrated Weekly of India (Bombay), 1970.

Play

Spy in Amber (screenplay). Delhi, Hind, 1971.

Other

*Kanhoji Angray, Maratha Admiral: An Account of His Life and His Battles with the*
   *English.*  Bombay and London, Asia Publishing House, 1959.
*Puars of Dewas Senior.*  Bombay, Orient Longman, 1963.
*The Chhatrapatis of Kolhapur.*  Bombay, Popular, 1971.

Critical Studies: *An Area of Darkness* by V. S. Naipaul, London, Deutsch, 1964; an essay
by the author on his own work, "Purdah and Caste Marks", in *Times Literary Supplement*
(London), 4 June 1964; *Eating the Indian Air* by John Morris, London, Hamish Hamilton,
1968.

Manohar Malgonkar comments:

Praise can embarrass but it does not call for a rejoinder. Censure often does, so here goes.
Those who disparage my work think that (1) I write with one eye on Hollywood, (2) my
writing is "withdrawn" from the reality of my country's poverty as well as the reality of the
four-letter word, and (3) I inject my values and politics and prejudices into my writings.

Well, I do strive to write the sort of novel I also like to read, full of meat, exciting, well-
constructed, plausible and with a lot of action—in short, to tell a good story. If this is what
Hollywood also likes, good for Hollywood and, I hope, some day for me too. I know one
admits this rather shamefacedly, as one might say "I'm afraid I do chew paan", or "Yes, I
do use a night shirt." At the same time, I often think of myself as belonging to the advance
guard in the swing back of the romantic novel. The pedlars of erotica and drug dreams may
churn out best sellers, but these are not novels; and the interminable ramblings about a day
in the life of somebody or the other are like dissecting the veins in every single leaf of a
cabbage. All this was a phase and it has had too long a run, but you cannot go on playing
with a cabbage forever. The novel will be back, plot, action and all; the signs are already
there.

Withdrawn? I maintain that my novels are close enough to the ground to pass off for
straight history. The withdrawal is seen in my refusal to be trapped in the dirt and misery
of India. The social life of millions of Indians centres around the dustbins of cities. Granted.
But mine doesn't, and for me to write about it would be as insincere as a white man writing
about Harlem life. And this is perhaps related to my other "withdrawal"—the disrelish for
the language of graffiti. For two years during my army service, I was in daily contact with
British and other ranks and can thus claim to have acquired a fairly full vocabulary of raw
words which I can use far more naturally than those who discovered a handful of them since
*Fanny Hill* came out as a paperback. I don't use them for the same reason that I don't have
my characters talking in local accents: they would show up as being utterly false to my style.

But the third point of criticism I accept as a kind of compliment. I believe that it is the
thinking man's business to influence. In a country such as ours, where democracy itself is
threatening to throttle individual freedom, it is the duty of every writer to do so.

\*       \*       \*

Essentially a romantic novelist of action, Malgonkar adds the freshness of an exotic
scene and the novelty of a bi-focal viewpoint to an expert use of tried and true Western
techniques. English is his own first language and his life style is westernized (unlike his
compatriot R. K. Narayan, for example). He had a university education and is a man of
cosmopolitan culture, widely read; but he has lived for the past many years on a remote
estate in the heart of India. He commands a lively and colloquial English, full of vivid
metaphors. He uses dialogue fluently. One thinks of affinities to Conrad on the one hand
and John Masters on the other.

In the earliest of his novels first published in the West, *Combat of Shadows*, he writes of British tea planters in the last years of the British Raj, somewhat in the vein of a disillusioned Kipling; he is able to mock the pukka-sahib Establishment by letting the reader see it through the eyes of its own cynics and outcasts. But it is primarily a story of love and derring-do rather than social comment. *The Princes*, on the other hand, deals with the old Indian aristocracy before the Princely States were absorbed into the new India, and with the painful transition. This has been his most widely-read, most thoughtful, and perhaps most distinguished work. Here E. M. Forster comes to mind.

*A Bend in the Ganges*, though politically objective, echoes recent history in its personal love story set against the cruelty of a great civil disaster—the Indian-Pakistani split of 1947. Two other novels of post-Independence days, still un-published in the West, reflect his involvement with current Indian politics, in which he has participated from a minority position to the right of the dominant Congress Party. One is an adventure story of the Indian take-over of Goa; the other a character study of a land-owning politician in a country district.

Malgonkar's latest novel, *The Devil's Wind*, goes back a century to the so-called "Indian Mutiny," never before presented from the Indian point of view. He narrates it in the person of Nana Saheb, an actual princely leader of the rebellion and a notorious villain in British eyes. Neither a hero nor an anti-hero, he is the kind of ambiguous character that Malgonkar delights in. In being a historical novel, and in its marked change of sympathy toward the British, this is a new departure; but in style and in story-telling qualities, particularly its violence, it has the characteristics of his other best novels.

While Malgonkar's books all have thoughtful overtones, he is first of all the story teller. He enjoys heroic characters fighting the odds and struggling with inner conflicts. He understands how to stretch the reader's willing suspension of disbelief for the sake of a dramatic confrontation. He makes graphic the hunt for a rogue elephant or a tiger; the crude violence of a human massacre; the tragic dislocations of civil war, from the burning of a single house to bombers over a great city. He bridges the nostalgia of India's past with the turbulence of her present.

—Marshall A. Best

---

**MANFRED, Frederick (Feikema).**   Pseudonym (1944–1951): **Feike Feikema.**   American. Born near Doon, Rock Township, Iowa, 6 January 1912. Educated at Western Academy, Hull, Iowa; Calvin College, Grand Rapids, Michigan, 1930–34, B.A. 1934; Nettleton Commercial College, Sioux Falls, South Dakota, 1937; correspondence courses, University of Minnesota, Minneapolis, 1941–42. Married Maryanna Shorba in 1942; has three children. Worked as a filling-station attendant, harvest and factory hand, salesman, etc., 1934–37; Reporter, *Minneapolis Journal*, 1937–39; Interviewer, Minnesota Opinion Poll, St. Paul, 1939–40; patient in a tuberculosis sanitarium, 1940–42; Abstract Writer, *Modern Medicine*, Minneapolis, 1942–43; Reporter, *East Side Argus*, Minneapolis, 1943–44. Writer-in-Residence, Macalester College, St. Paul, Minnesota, 1949–52. Since 1958, Writer-in-Residence, University of South Dakota, Vermillion. Recipient: Rockefeller Fellowship, 1944, 1945; National Institute of Arts and Letters grant, 1945; Field Fellowship, 1948; Andreas Fellowship, 1949, 1952; McKnight Fellowship, 1959; Huntington Hartford Fellowship, 1963, 1964. Address: Blue Mound, Luverne, Minnesota 56156; or, c/o Curtis Brown Ltd., 60 East 56th Street, New York, New York 10022, U.S.A.

PUBLICATIONS

Novels (as Feike Feikema)

*The Golden Bowl.* St. Paul, Minnesota, Webb, 1944; London, Dobson, 1947.
*Boy Almighty.* St. Paul, Minnesota, Itasca Press, 1945; London, Dobson, 1950.
*This Is the Year.* New York, Doubleday, 1947.
*The Chokecherry Tree.* New York, Doubleday, 1948; London, Dobson, 1949; revised edition, Denver, Swallow, 1961.
*World's Wanderer*; revised edition, as *Wanderlust*, Denver, Swallow 1962.
  *The Primitive.* New York, Doubleday, 1949.
  *The Brother.* New York, Doubleday, 1950.
  *The Giant.* New York, Doubleday, 1951.

Novels (as Frederick Manfred)

*Lord Grizzly.* New York, McGraw Hill, 1954; London, Corgi, 1957.
*Morning Red: A Romance.* Denver, Swallow, 1956.
*Riders of Judgment.* New York, Random House, 1957.
*Conquering Horse.* New York, McDowell Obolensky, 1959.
*Scarlet Plume.* New York, Simon and Schuster, 1964.
*The Man Who Looked Like the Prince of Wales.* New York, Simon and Schuster, 1965.
*King of Spades.* New York, Simon and Schuster, 1966.
*Eden Paradise.* New York, Simon and Schuster, 1968.
*Milk of Wolves.* Blue Earth, Minnesota, Piper, 1972.

Short Stories

*Arrow of Love.* Denver, Swallow, 1961.
*Apples of Paradise and Other Stories.* New York, Simon and Schuster, 1968.

Verse

*Winter Count: Poems 1934–1965.* Minneapolis, Thueson, 1966.

Bibliography: *Frederick Manfred: A Bibliography* by George Kellogg, Denver, Swallow, 1965.

Manuscript Collection: University of Minnesota, Minneapolis.

Critical Studies: in "Writing in the West and Midwest Issue" of *Critique* (Minneapolis), Winter 1959; "The Novel in the American West" by John R. Milton, in *South Dakota Review* (Vermillion), Autumn 1964; "Sinclair Lewis-Frederick Manfred Issue" of *South Dakota Review* (Vermillion), Winter 1969–70; in *The Literature of the American West* by J. Golden Taylor, Boston, Houghton Mifflin, 1971.

Frederick Manfred comments:

It has been my dream for many years to be able to finish a long hallway of pictures in fiction dealing with the country I call Siouxland (located in the center of the Upper Midlands, USA) from 1800 and on to the day I die. Not only must the history be fairly accurate, and the description of the flora and fauna fairly precise, and the use of the language of the place and time beautiful, but the delineation of the people by way of characterization living and illuminating. It has long been my thought that a "place" finally selects the people who best reflect it, give it voice, and allow it to make a cultural contribution to the sum of all world culture under the sun. In fact, it is the sun beating on a certain place in a certain time that at last causes that place to flower into literature, the highest expression of intelligence (and not necessarily human intelligence).

It has been my feeling for some time that Middle America is more apt to speak with a clear voice from this continent than are either of the two American seaboards, the East with New York as the center and the West with Los Angeles as the center. The East in New York (and Boston and Washington, etc.) still speaks in part with an alien voice. It is not clear. It is muddy. It is as polluted with foreign sounds as is the air with foreign particles. And the West in Los Angeles (and all other California points) speaks with a most artificial voice, that of Hollywood, of the sudden uncultured rich. Only the Upper Midlands (and in my case, only my Siouxland) has a chance to speak with as clear a separate voice within the whole Western Culture complex as say Madrid for Spain and Paris for France and London for England.

The final test of good fiction rests with how well the characters come through, their reality, their meaning, their stature, their durability, no matter what the situation may be. The characters should be so well done that the reader should not be aware of plot or the unraveling of time in the work. The reader should be lost in the story. The plot should be hidden like a skeleton is in a flying eagle.

If a "place" truly finds voice at last the ultimate sacred force speaks.

And in the USA, Western American literature does this the best.

*       *       *

The author was born Frederick Feikema; later as Feike Feikema he changed his name again (1951) and thereafter is Frederick Feikema Manfred. The final name-taking is apparently of literary impulse, for in the most characteristic early novels the main protagonist is Thurs Manfred Wrâldsoan, an orphan, a wanderer, a reader of Lord Byron. Thus an invented character's name becomes in fact the author's name. This literary anomaly, with its strong implication of continuing self-analysis, indicates that questions of identity indeed are central to a full appreciation of the most significant prose fiction.

For example, *The Primitive*, *The Brother*, and *The Giant* constitute a trilogy wherein the main protagonist embarks on a journey of dual intention: a literary journey from a "Siouxland" college of fundamentalist persuasion to New York City and return. This is a quest for identity, for a viable past, for meaningful human relationships; by parallel, although not always comprehended by Wrâldsoan, himself, there is an inner quest for spiritual enlightenment, psychic resolutions, for means of artistic expression, for adulthood, for wisdom. In *Conquering Horse*, a characteristic later work of considerably higher literary quality, the quest for identity is dramatized in the emergence from adolescence of an American Indian. A comparison and contrast of the supportative institutions shown in the midwestern trilogy in contrast to parallel institutions in an Indian culture is instructive and—incidentally— suggests one measure of Manfred's artistic growth.

The breadth of the subject matter of the novels is greater than the reoccurring thematic concerns might suggest. The early *Golden Bowl* dramatizes the conflict between two generations of midwest "Siouxland" farmers; *Boy Almighty* is the semi-autobiographical tale of a writer's life as a patient in a mid-western tuberculosis sanitarium; *This Is the Year* concerns a wilful Frisian-American farmer; *Morning Red* treats politics and journalism in a small Minnesota town; "Arrow of Love" and *Scarlet Plume* are best described as Romance; *Lord Grizzly* and *Riders of Judgment* exploit materials of the American past, the mountain men, and the cattle wars in Wyoming in the 1890's. The poetry in *Winter Count* is of little technical interest and suffers from a rhetoric which is often inappropriate for the subject matter; the two irregular short story collections command discerning approval. On balance, possibly because of his unswerving commitment to a midwestern, American region "Siouxland" where the literary audience is notoriously few and unfit, Manfred's work remains not much appreciated at the present time.

By no means, however, can it be said that Manfred's work is an example of isolated literary genius. Far from it. The novels are very much a part of a little explored sub-genre of American Literature: those works of "epic" vision, of great vigor and industry by writers who value a direct rendering of their own life-experience; from one point-of-view those writers may be seen in contrast to the more cloistered, the merely "literary" artists who rely on the received virtues of consistency, of well-wrought structure, the "fully dramatic" posture. Aside from the controversial implications of the suggested sub-genre of American literature, Manfred's materials, themes, scope, "giantism", reliance on autobiography—and an inevitable redundancy of effect—suggest a close alignment with the novels of Thomas Wolfe (d. 1938). In the use of dialect, "down-home folks" protagonists, and a stubborn, at times anti-intellectual concern with "Truth", Manfred's work also suggests the tone and the strengths of Sherwood Anderson (d. 1941). In Manfred's intensity of attitude towards materials—though not always in erudition—the work also suggests the novels of Vardis Fisher (d. 1968). All of these writers, including possibly Upton Sinclair, are to be distinguished from the American Naturalistic School. Manfred and the others are more consciously democratic, in the Whitmanesque sense of that word; more empirical in their methods. As a matter of literary principle they remain unreconstructed by continental or British literary conventions. The price paid for this fierce, regional independence is high: critical acclaim comes slowly, if at all; the weakest fictions teeter on the edge of literary disaster. Yet the best novels, by force of authorial energy alone, appear to sweep all merely literary reservations aside.

Presently this sub-genre of American literature is insufficiently explored possibly because it represents an old-fashioned, limited concept of the novel form. Understandably, the present age does not much approve of a reoccurring, implied didacticism, or of authorial voices behind the works which freely elected the novel form and then declined to assume the full obligations of the totally aware literary artist.

Now sixty years of age Manfred continues to live and to work at Blue Mound (Luverne, Minnesota). The literary community of America and Britain deserves a more readily available, artistically arranged collection of his prose fiction. With that impressive panoply of work at hand, the novels may well attain the monumental effect which is everywhere present, for each chapter has the great, good quality of fidelity to a vision stoutly defended.

—James B. Hall

---

**MANGIONE, Jerre (Gerlando).** American. Born in Rochester, New York, 20 March 1909. Educated at Syracuse University, New York, B.A. 1931. Married Patricia Anthony in 1957. Staff Writer, *Time* magazine, New York, 1931; Book Reviewer, *New York Herald Tribune*, 1931–35, and the *New Republic*, New York, 1931–37; Book Editor, Robert M. McBride Company, New York, 1934–37; National Coordinating Editor, Federal Writers' Project, 1937–39; Information Specialist, 1940–42, Special Assistant to the United States Commissioner, 1942–48, and Editor-in-Chief of the *Monthly Review*, 1945–48, Immigration and Naturalization Service of the United States Department of Justice; Advertising and Public Relations Writer for various firms in New York and Philadelphia, 1948–61. Lecturer, 1961–63, Associate Professor, 1963–68, and since 1968, Professor of English and Director of the Writing Program, University of Pennsylvania, Philadelphia. Visiting Lecturer, Bryn Mawr College, Pennsylvania, 1967–68. Chairman, Literary Arts Committee, Philadelphia Art Alliance, 1958–61. Editor-in-Chief, *WFLN Philadelphia Guide*, 1959–61. National President, Friends of Danilo Dolci Inc., New York, 1969–71. Recipient: Guggenheim Fellowship, 1946; Keys to the City of Rochester, 1963; Fulbright Research Fellowship, 1965; Rockfeller grant, 1968; American Philosophical Society grant, 1971. Commendatore, Order of the Star of Italian Solidarity, 1971. Address: 1939 Panama Street, Philadelphia, Pennsylvania 19103, U.S.A.

PUBLICATIONS

Novels

    *Mount Allegro.*   Boston, Houghton Mifflin, 1943.
    *The Ship and the Flame.*   New York, Wyn-Current Books, 1948.
    *Night Search.*   New York, Crown, 1965; as *To Walk the Night*, London, Muller, 1967.

Short Stories

    *Life Sentences for Everybody* (fables).   New York and London, Abelard Schuman, 1966.

Other

    *Reunion in Sicily.*   Boston, Houghton Mifflin, 1950.
    *A Passion for Sicilians: The World Around Danilo Dolci.*   New York, Morrow, 1968.
    *America Is Also Italian.*   New York, Putnam, 1969.
    *The Dream and the Deal: Federal Writers' Project, 1935–1943.*   Boston, Little Brown 1971.

Manuscript Collection: University of Pennsylvania, Philadelphia.

Critical Studies: *Current Biography* (New York), 1943; *The Italian in America* by Lawrence Frank Pisani, New York, Exposition Press, 1957.

Jerre Mangione comments:

    As a writer I am motivated by the need to understand myself and the world around me. This need was first nourished by the circumstance of being born and raised among Sicilian relatives in an urban American environment. That experience, which is the substance of my first book, *Mount Allegro*, accentuated for me the sharp contrast between the philosophical values of the old world and those of the new. It also succeeded in casting me in the role of the outsider who, belonging to neither world, tries to create his own world by the writing of fiction. Two of my novels, *The Ship and the Flame* and *Night Search* (*To Walk the Night* in England) are efforts in that direction, and for that reason may be more truly autobiographical than the three books I have written in the first person, namely *Mount Allegro*, *Reunion in Sicily*, and *A Passion for Sicilians*. Although *Mount Allegro* is somewhat fictional in content, it is a basic part of this trilogy which extends over a span of fifty years and deals largely with my public identity as a Sicilian-American observing the people and places he knows best.

My other books are more simply explained.

*Life Sentences for Everybody* consists of fables dealing with contemporary characters. "Life Sentences" were inspired by the challenge of telling a story within the confines of a single sentence. These are, frankly, exercises in procrastination (I was trying to work on a novel when I wrote the first batch), which gave me more pleasure than I usually derive from the act of writing. At least two critics have written that "Life Sentences" represent a new genre. And that too is pleasurable, for who doesn't enjoy being an innovator?

In recent years I have written two social histories: *America Is Also Italian*, a brief telling of the Italian-American immigrant saga; and *The Dream and the Deal*, an account of the Federal Writers' Project of the thirties. These two histories were written because I was personally involved in both of them and felt that they needed to be told.

*       *       *

Jerre Mangione's prose style is straightforward and lively. Because he often employs a first person narration his work conveys the impression of conversation liberally sprinkled with anecdote and description. Much of it is factual or semi-fictional accounting of the author's experiences. The ordering of this material is subtle and it is only at the end of a book such as *Mount Allegro* or *A Passion for Sicilians* that one sees the cumulative effect of the massing of seemingly unrelated detail.

At the heart of Mangione's prose are the mountains, temples and people of Sicily. He draws from his Sicilian relatives, his acquaintances in all levels of Sicilian society, and his extensive travels on the island a wealth of fascinating detail. On one level the last chapters of *Mount Allegro*, *Reunion in Sicily* and *A Passion of Sicilians* function as travel books to introduce the reader to a land, comparatively untouched by tourism, which has fascinated and lured observers like D. H. Lawrence by its forbidding beauty. The ruined Greek temples of Agrigento, the hilltop castle of Mussomeli built atop a Saracen fortification, the beautiful fishing village of Scopello are tantalizingly described. But the slums of Palermo are not forgotten. Villages with beautiful mountain views but no water, and hovels where ten people live in one room are painted with the same force and clarity.

His presentation of people is no less effective. The transplanted families of the Mount Allegro section of Rochester, New York, who try to keep Sicily alive there with their gregariousness, their intimate brand of Catholicism, their devotion to food and their resignation to *destinu* are presented with warmth and vitality. Their Sicilian counterparts are also sympathetically and clearly drawn, but the author's partisanship is not blind. Danilo Dolci, for instance, who is studied at length in *A Passion for Sicilians*, is presented as a complex man who desires approval but sometimes courts dissension, who attracts and alienates followers. The reader is allowed to sort out for himself the powers and foibles of this pacifist and his programs for economic and social reform.

Mangione displays similar talents in his fiction. In the novel *The Ship and the Flame*, which deals with the development of the will to act in Stiano Argento, a Sicilian refugee from fascism, we are presented with the action as Stiano experiences it and we see his need to act taking shape. He is a passenger, with his wife and daughter, on a Portuguese ship filled with people fleeing several European countries. Although they have been issued entrance visas to Mexico, they find when they arrive there that these visas are not authentic and that Mexican officials will not allow them to land. Goaded to action by the suicide of his friend Josef Renner, the love of Tereza Lenska and the bravery of Peter Sadona, Stiano helps secure permission for most of them to land in the United States. If there are problems with

Mangione's method in this book they are shown in Stiano's frustrated love affair with Tereza. Although reviewers at the time seem to have found it torrid, the effect today is quite the opposite. The limits permissible for sexual description have changed so much in the intervening years that a reader now finds it hard to believe in the force of this passion.

Books like *Mount Allegro* and *A Passion for Sicilians* fare better. In these the material remains interesting even though not current. The process of assimilation in America is a fascinating one and the stories of *Mount Allegro* enliven our understanding of what has happened and is occurring. Social action is a continuing interest to us: Dolci's work goes on and it is important to be shown that imperfect people can accomplish much and a single life can affect the lives of others.

—Barbara M. Perkins

---

**MANKIEWICZ, Don M(artin).**   American.   Born in Berlin, Germany, 20 January 1922. Educated at Columbia University, New York, 1938–42, B.A. 1942; Columbia Law School, 1942. Served in the United States Army, as a Staff Sergeant, 1942–46. Married Ilene Korsen in 1946; has two children. Reporter for *The New Yorker* magazine, 1946–48. Free-lance Writer since 1948. Since 1969, Instructor at the New York University Institute of Film and Television. Democratic-Liberal Candidate, New York State Assembly, 1952; since 1953, Vice-Chairman, Nassau County (Long Island, New York) Democratic Committee; Democratic Town Leader, Oyster Bay, New York, 1960–61; Delegate, New York State Constitutional Convention, 1967. Member, Board of Governors, Television Academy of Arts and Sciences, New York Chapter. Recipient: Harper Novel Prize, 1954. Address: 115 Minnesota Avenue, Long Beach, Long Island, New York 11561, U.S.A.

PUBLICATIONS

Novels

   *See How They Run*.   New York, Knopf, 1951.
   *Trial*.   New York, Harper, and London, Deutsch, 1955.
   *It Only Hurts a Minute*.   New York, Putnam, 1966; London, Deutsch, 1968.

Plays

   Screenplays: *Trial*, 1955; *I Want to Live*, 1958.

   Plays produced on television.

*    *    *

Two of Mankiewicz's three novels (*See How They Run* and *It Only Hurts a Minute*) are set in a world of gambling houses and racetracks. Thus, the people he observes are successful or broken gamblers, jockeys, horsetrainers, touts, houseplayers and racketeers. The uninitiate may often find it difficult to follow the intricate descriptions of the logic, betting procedures and techniques of blackjack, craps, roulette and poker and may ask himself if it is indeed true that "an easy six-four-deuce, or five-ace would lose his don't pass and odd bets," or that "people who bet long shots any other way than to win are the back-bone of the industry." Do such statements reveal the wisdom and judgement of a character or his foolishness? Yet, despite these obstacles the novels hold the reader's interest because they are well paced and deftly plotted and manage to make this world a believable abstraction of our own. Mankiewicz displays the talent and skill of a good journalist but his weakness lies in the narrow range of his perceptions and inadequate development of characters whose personal relationships are superficial, who require no intimacy and minimal passion; who live in a man's world in which women play a minor role, and for whom sexual attraction, not to mention love, is quite unimportant. Thus, Lisa Fortune (*It Only Hurts a Minute*), surrounded by an aura of magic and symbolic of Lew White's irrationality, is unreal and two-dimensional, while Abbe Klein's primary function in *Trial* is to confront David Blake with a history of communist wickedness and offer him a possible alternative of action which, prior to his own discovery, he rejects. Since Mankiewicz is not particularly concerned with the inner life of his characters, his drama can turn on some principle of courage and honor, rather than on the thoughts and feelings that lead to the decisions and choices necessary in a crisis.

*See How They Run* focuses on one race, described from the point of view of three characters who are vitally concerned with its outcome. Both Nick Bragg, the jockey, and Commodore Terhune, the manager of the stable, lack the courage to stand up to the villainous Artie Dooley, who *is* "the organization in New Jersey." Frightened by Artie's veiled threats to his life, Nick follows orders and throws the race but, ironically, is killed in the process, while the Commodore, equally cowardly, must henceforth "take not one beating but an infinite series of them." Only Sam Gleason, the Irish horsetrainer, retains his honor and self respect because, unlike the others, he is the product of a tradition which does not condone corrupt practices on the racetrack and, by implication, in society as a whole, and because his father had instilled in him that professional pride which motivated his "romantic resolution" to get a Derby horse and win the Derby. He alone resists Dooley and returns to Ireland where "a race horse walks the way a race horse was meant to walk, on grass."

Lew White, the reformed gambler in *It Only Hurts a Minute*, accidentally finds a poker chip in his pocket and is tempted to take the champagne flight to Las Vegas. In the process of decision he recalls both the pleasures and pains of the years he had spent in gambling houses and his final degeneration into a broken gambler, "a vegetable who has lost his nerve to gamble." The change to respectability occurred at the end of a Labor Day weekend when, accompanied by the significantly named Lisa Fortune, he won and lost $60,000, as well as the girl. Alone, hungry and completely broke, Lew finally understands, at least intellectually, the cause of his compulsion: without admitting it even to himself, he had believed that "there was such a thing as luck, but that luck was female and a bitch with a wicked sense of humor, who derived satisfaction from tormenting [him]." Stripped of his overt claim to being a "reasoning mechanism," he had felt compelled to prove himself by winning. Within the context of his recent insight and new outlook on life, however, he no longer regards luck or fortune as a magical force but, rather, a quality of winners and he is ready to explore alternative paths of distinguishing himself from the herd.

But the novel is open-ended and we are told that "he is not going to Las Vegas. Not tonight," and that he had not discarded the chip. Although Lew is an intelligent and articulate narrator, he reveals surprisingly little of himself so that we lack evidence to evaluate and trust him. Are we then to conclude that Lew is likely to use the chip in the future, that there is a basic flaw, a weakness in his character or, as he says elsewhere in the novel, that all men are defective and that any improvement is, therefore, bound to be temporary?

David Blake, the young lawyer in *Trial*, decent and politically liberal, is flawed by his naiveté and becomes the unsuspecting tool of the communist party which is eager to exploit for money and propaganda the case of a young Mexican, unjustly accused of rape and murder. Unable to see that his client is worth more dead than alive to the radical Left, he follows the party line, loses the case and suffers the guilt for Angel Chavez's death. For his participation in the trial he is requested to appear before the "Battle Committee" (Committee on Subversion and Disloyalty, headed by Carl Baron Battle) to defend himself from the charge of sedition. Thus, David must now stand trial and prepare his own defense.

Mankiewicz seems to find it difficult to conclude his novels. This is less apparent in *See How They Run* because the story is specifically divided into three parts. Lew White's conversion in *It Only Hurts A Minute* was initiated by Billie, a casual acquaintance, who qualified because she had been a psychology major at Hunter College and, after much lecturing on the philosophy and psychology of gambling, she is able to prod him into an attempt at self-analysis. In *Trial* Mankiewicz introduces, in the last six pages, a *deus ex machina* in the character of Charles White, who resides at "White's House" and is editor of the *Record*, an independent newspaper. White persuades David that publication of his private journal in which he had meticulously recorded his impressions of the Chavez trial would, because it is the unadorned "Truth", vindicate him and force the Committee to drop the charges.

Mankiewicz may wish to close his book prosperously, but the clouds of misfortune lift with a rapidity that defies logic. It is hard to believe that a world composed of cowards, some of whom had pretended to be David's friends but abandoned him in his hour of need, and villains from both sides of the political fence, would suddenly bow and accept the truth. Unless White's advice is meant ironically, and there is no indication that the irony here extends beyond the names, it provides a very naive answer to a complex problem. And, morally, why should David be permitted to go free having caused, however unwittingly, a man's death, while the innocent Angel had to pay with his life? From the point of view of life as a gambling casino, the conflict we are witnessing seems a set-up with the manager backing the wrong man. Perhaps David is simply lucky in that the author shows greater sympathy for him than for his other characters. But, as he tells us in *See How They Run*, "luck is after all only the friendly operation of chance."

—Erica Aronson

---

**MANKOWITZ, Wolf.** British. Born in London, 7 November 1924. Educated at East Ham Grammar School, London; Downing College, Cambridge, M.A. (English tripos) 1946. Married Ann Margaret Seligman in 1944; has four children. Recipient: Society of Authors Award, for poetry, 1946; Venice Film Festival Prize, 1955; Edinburgh Film Festival Prize, 1955; British Film Academy Award, 1955, 1961; Academy Award, 1957; Film Council of America Golden Reel, 1957; *Evening Standard* drama award, 1959. Address: Simmonscourt Castle, Dublin 4, Ireland.

PUBLICATIONS

Novels

*Make Me an Offer.* London, Deutsch, and New York, Dutton, 1952.
*A Kid for Two Farthings.* London, Deutsch, 1953; New York, Dutton, 1954.

*Laugh Till You Cry: An Advertisement.* New York, Dutton, 1955; included in *The Penguin Wolf Mankowitz*, 1967.
*My Old Man's a Dustman.* London, Deutsch, 1956; as *Old Soldiers Never Die*, Boston, Little Brown, 1956.
*Cockatrice.* London, Longman, and New York, Putnam, 1963.
*The Biggest Pig in Barbados: A Fable.* London, Longman, 1965.

Short Stories

*The Mendelman Fire and Other Stories.* London, Deutsch, and Boston, Little Brown, 1957.
*Expresso Bongo: A Wolf Mankowitz Reader.* New York, Yoseloff, 1961.
*The Blue Arabian Nights.* London, Vallentine Mitchell, 1972.

Plays

*The Bespoke Overcoat* (produced London, 1953). London, Evans, 1954.
*The Boychick* (produced London, 1954).
*Five One-Act Plays.* London, Evans, 1955.
*The Mighty Hunter* (produced London, 1956).
*Expresso Bongo*, with Julian More (produced London, 1958). London, Evans, 1960.
*Make Me an Offer* (produced London, 1959).
*It Should Happen to a Dog* (televised, 1961; produced Princeton, New Jersey, 1967). Published in *Religious Drama 3*, Cleveland, Meridian, 1959.
*Belle; or, The Ballad of Doctor Crippen* (produced London, 1961).
*Pickwick* (produced London, 1963).
*Passion Flower Hotel* (produced London, 1965).
*The Samson Riddle* (produced Dublin, 1972). London, Vallentine Mitchell, 1972.

Screenplays: *Make Me an Offer*, 1954; *A Kid for Two Farthings*, 1955; *The Bespoke Overcoat*, 1955; *Trapeze*, 1955; *Expresso Bongo*, 1959; *The Two Faces of Dr. Jekyll*, 1959; *The Long and the Short and the Tall*, 1960; *The Millionairess*, 1960; *The Day the Earth Caught Fire*, 1960; *The Waltz of the Toreadors*, 1961; *Casino Royal*, 1966; *The Twenty-fifth Hour*, 1967; *Assassination Bureau*, 1968; *Bloomfield*, 1970; *Black Beauty*, 1970; *Treasure Island*, 1971; *The Hebrew Lesson*, 1972.

Verse

*XII Poems.* Dublin, Dolmen Press, 1972.

Other

*The Portland Vase and the Wedgwood Copies.* London, Deutsch, 1952.
*Wedgwood.* London, Batsford, and New York, Dutton, 1953.
*ABC of Show Business.* London, Daily Express Book Department, 1956.
*A Concise Encyclopedia of Pottery and Porcelain*, with R. G. Haggar. London, Deutsch, and New York, Hawthorne Books, 1957.
*The Penguin Wolf Mankowitz.* London, Penguin, 1967.

*     *     *

Wolf Mankowitz writes in the tradition of the Yiddish storyteller, holding his audience by a powerful blend of cynicism and sentiment. His narration is simple and direct; his subject matter ranges from life in London's East End to the manipulations of the antique trade and show business. This material gives him a scope for satire which he exploits to the full. He pokes gentle fun at the characters of whom he is fond and tears the others apart. Above all, he cares that people should care, whether for eighteenth century English pottery or for their religion or for the happiness of their children. His villains are those with no emotions to hide.

*Make Me an Offer* is about a man who cares obsessively for Wedgwood and is both lucky and unscrupulous enough to track down the object of his passion, an early copy of a Portland vase. It is a fantasy rooted in the reality of double dealing, bluff and auction rigging. The central character knows all the tricks he needs and has no illusions about his profession; Mankowitz makes him attractive for his humour, his knowledge and his genuine love of beauty. "Who knew better than he that nothing is given, that everything passes, the woods decay. He was the ultimate human being. He resigned himself to making a profit."

The immediate success of this novella, which was made into a prize-winning musical, is paralleled by the acclaim given to *A Kid for Two Farthings*. This is a celebration of the author's Cockney childhood, told with a warmth and pathos that is wholly irresistible. "Life is all dreams—dreams and work," says the tailor Kandinsky to his six year old friend Joe. Joe's dream comes true: he goes to the market to buy a unicorn and finds one, the kid of the title and of the Passover song.

Mankowitz conveys the flavour of Jewish life in ancedote and dialogue; he lets moral values and social attitudes emerge out of business confrontations and family relationships. "The Mendelman Fire" is a particularly fine treatment of paternal love, told by Mr Mendelman's admiring accountant, a man who "could make a company for twelve pounds and liquidate it for five." Many of the stories in this collection are set in Russia and have the charm of folk-tale, a form which, transposed to the West Indies, is used in the author's most recent work, *The Biggest Pig in Barbados*.

Perhaps the most original of the novels is *My Old Man's a Dustman*, a study of survival and friendship at the lowest levels of human experience. It takes place in a Beckett-like landscape of shacks and rubbish-tips but is lightened by Cockney songs and Cockney cheek. *Cockatrice* is a far more bitter book in a far plushier setting. We meet the hero, Daniel Pisarov, in "a Regency bed with swans' heads": like everything else, this belongs to his boss, the film producer whom he is vainly trying to double-cross. Mankowitz takes a grim pleasure in putting Danny through the hoops of ambition and corruption; in the film industry, the story suggests, no dreams are realised, only the nightmares come true.

—Judith Cooke Simmons

---

**MANN, Leonard.** Australian. Born in Melbourne, Victoria, 15 November 1895. Educated at Wesley College, Melbourne; University of Melbourne, LL.B. 1920. Served in the Australian Army, Infantry and Engineers, in France and Flanders, during World War I. Married Florence Eileen Archer in 1926; has two children. President, 1938, 1941, and Honorary Life Member, 1967, Fellowship of Australian Writers, Victoria. Since 1963, Member of the Council, Australian Society of Authors, Sydney. Recipient: Australian Literary Society award, 1932; Crouch Award, for poetry, 1941; Grace Leven Award, for poetry, 1957. Address: Ferncroft, Greenthorpe Road, Olinda, Victoria 3788, Australia.

PUBLICATIONS

Novels

   *Flesh in Armour*.   Melbourne, Robertson and Mullens, 1932.
   *Human Drift*.   Sydney, Angus and Robertson, 1935.
   *A Murder in Sydney*.   London, Cape, and New York, Doubleday, 1937.
   *Mountain Flat*.   London, Cape, 1939.
   *The Go-Getter*.   Sydney, Angus and Robertson, 1942.
   *Andrea Caslin*.   London, Cape, 1959.
   *Venus Half-Caste*.   London, Hodder and Stoughton, 1963.

Verse

   *The Plumed Voice*.   Sydney, Angus and Robertson, 1938.
   *Poems from the Mask*.   Melbourne, Hawthorn Press, 1941.
   *The Delectable Mountains*.   Sydney, Angus and Robertson, 1944.
   *Elegiac and Other Poems*.   Melbourne, Cheshire, 1957.

Critical Studies: "Leonard Mann's *A Murder in Sydney*" by Maurice Vintner, in *Overland* (Melbourne), Winter 1970; essay by the author on his own work: "A Double Life", in *Southerly* (Sydney), 1969.

Leonard Mann comments:

   In the nineteen twenties and thirties Australian writing suddenly grew up, adult in age, vigour and content. It was considerably nationalistic. The Australian people were then become aware of their own individuality. They were already become politically one nation. The experience of the Australian soldiery in the war of 1914–18, in which they had shown themselves second to none, asserted that awareness.
   The new writers were, therefore, much concerned to show the Australian people to themselves, as not only in a different physical environment but as different within a new nation from the British peoples from which they were derived. The British past, including its literature, belongs also to Australia, but its present, from the beginning of this century, became quite rapidly not much more than an influence, for good and ill, so that now it is only a part, though a major one, of influences from the world at large, in literature and in other affairs. In my own case, for instance, the influence of the French writers of the last century, and to some extent of the present, has been much greater than that of British writers.
   Another, not unrelated, opinion of mine is that all discussion, all dialogue, that is, all talk should so far as possible be excluded from the novel except it be part of the *res gestae*. And further, that the novel should not be a forum for the author's self-display, not for smartness, not for instruction, but be rather an incitement and provocation of the reader's own mind, thinking and feeling, within himself. At any rate that has always been my intention: any debate a debate by the reader with himself.

                              *         *         *

   The fiction of Leonard Mann is not remarkable for any great formal accomplishment. It offers little in the way of structural subtlety or stylistic virtuosity. What does command respect in his work is the penetrating honesty with which he scrutinizes some of the most important areas of twentieth-century Australian social experience. His first book, *Flesh in Armour*, records a decisive phase in the country's growth: its participation in the First World War. Concentrating on the activities of men in one platoon of an A.I.F. battalion, Mann shows a sense of community, of distinctive Australianity, developing in this motley group of soldiers. The writing has dull patches and is sometimes even clumsy, but without detracting from the strong impression of authenticity. Then, having observed the emergence of a national spirit, Mann attempted in his next novel to uncover the roots of that spirit in the Victorian goldfields of the 1850s. *Human Drift* is less an examination of personal relationships than an evocation of life in the diggings, and its central narrative event is the celebrated fight at the Eureka Stockade, when about thirty diggers were killed in a dispute with police over mining licences.

*A Murder in Sydney* is a crime story, but of a more complex sort than its title seems to suggest. The reader is in no doubt about who the murderer is, so interest derives not from whodunnit suspense but from the interaction of personalities seen against background patterns of urban life. That is to say, it is essentially a city novel; and indeed Mann was one of the earliest writers to turn his attention to the specific of urbanization. Like that of *A Murder in Sydney*, the action of *The Go-Getter* takes place during the Great Depression, and again a large city provides the conditioning environment—this time Melbourne. By tracing the main character's search for self-respect to the point where he decides to resist involvement in a shady political deal, Mann is able to comment incisively on the values that the modern city lives by. Between these two city novels came *Mountain Flat*, a study of claustrophobic tensions in a small rural community of mixed ethnic character. Particular emphasis falls on the economic rivalry which exists between two farming families and which is complicated by sexual jealousies.

The gap of seventeen years between *The Go-Getter* and *Andrea Caslin* is explained by the fact that a huge novel dealing with the conditions of Australian society during the Second World War was written and rewritten during those years but failed to find a publisher. Its length was a difficulty, but there is also reason to think that publishers found it too outspoken; during the thirties, Mann's political position had moved steadily to the left.

While all his novels show a sure grasp of social realities, they are notable too for their psychological insights. The hypersensitive self-analysis of Frank Jeffreys in *Flesh in Armour*, the moral conflicts experienced by Chris Gibbons in *The Go-Getter*, the varieties of greed among the characters in *Mountain Flat*—all these are memorably represented. But Mann's finest achievement as an analyst of personality is in his conception of the title character in *Andrea Caslin*, a woman who hardens herself emotionally as a defensive measure, and who becomes in consequence impervious to healing influences. *Venus Half-Caste*, his last book, is a compassionate account of a girl adrift between two cultures—her dissolving aboriginal heritage and the society confronting her in modern Melbourne—and of two men who are attracted to her, one white and the other half-caste like herself. There is some treatment of inter-racial friction, but this is not a novel of social protest; as in *Andrea Caslin*, the primary focus is psychological.

—Ian Reid

---

**MANNING, Olivia.** British. Born in Portsmouth, Hampshire. Educated in private schools. Married R. D. Smith in 1939. Press Officer, United States Embassy, Cairo, 1942; Press Assistant, Public Information Office, Jerusalem, 1943–44, and British Council, Jerusalem, 1944–45; Novel Reviewer, *Spectator*, London, 1949–50, and *Sunday Times*, London, 1965–66. Recipient: Tom-Gallon Trust Award, 1949. Address: 36 Abbey Gardens, London N.W.8, England.

PUBLICATIONS

Novels

> *The Wind Changes.* London, Cape, 1937; New York, Knopf, 1938.
> *Artist among the Missing.* London, Heinemann, 1949.
> *School for Love.* London, Heinemann, 1951.
> *A Different Face.* London, Heinemann, 1953; New York, Abelard Schuman, 1957.
> *Doves of Venus.* London, Heinemann, 1955; New York, Abelard Schuman, 1958.
> *The Balkan Trilogy:*
>> *The Great Fortune.* London, Heinemann, 1960; New York, Doubleday, 1961.
>> *The Spoilt City.* London, Heinemann, 1962; New York, Doubleday, 1963.
>> *Friends and Heroes.* London, Heinemann, 1965; New York. Doubleday, 1966.
> *The Play Room.* London, Heinemann, 1969; as *The Camperlea Girls*, New York, Coward McCann, 1969.

Short Stories

> *Growing Up: A Collection of Short Stories.* London, Heinemann, and New York, Doubleday, 1948.
> *A Romantic Hero and Other Stories.* London, Heinemann, 1967.
> *Penguin Modern Stories 12*, with others. London, Penguin, 1972.

Uncollected Short Stories

> "Girls Together", in *Winter's Tales 16.* London, Macmillan, 1970.
> "The Banana House", in *Winter's Tales 17.* London, Macmillan, 1971.

Play

> Screenplay: *The Play Room*, 1970.

Other

> *The Remarkable Expedition: The Story of Stanley's Rescue of Emin Pasha from Equatorial Africa.* London, Heinemann, 1947; as *The Reluctant Rescue*, New York, Doubleday, 1947.
> *The Dreaming Shore* (travel). London, Evans, 1950.
> *My Husband Cartwright.* London, Heinemann, 1956.
> *Extraordinary Cats.* London, Joseph, 1967.

Manuscript Collection: University of Texas, Austin.

Critical Studies: *The Novel Today* by Anthony Burgess, London, Longman, 1963; *Tradition and Dream* by Walter Allen, London, Phoenix House, 1964; "Olivia Manning" by James Parkhill Rathbone, in *Books and Bookmen* (London), August 1971.

Olivia Manning comments:

When I have completed a book, I feel I have said all I can say concerning it. My subject is simply life as I have experienced it and I am happiest when writing of things I have known.

\*       \*       \*

Olivia Manning began as a painter, and, from her first novel, *The Wind Changes*, onwards, what seems a painter's eye for the visible world has enabled her to render particularly well the sensuous surface of relatively exotic places and landscapes. This is particularly apparent in *School for Love*, a novel of Jerusalem in wartime as registered through the consciousness of a sixteen-year-old English boy stranded there by the chances of war. An aspect of her painter's eye is a pure and exact prose style: her sentences give pleasure in themselves. At the same time, her art has sometimes seemed an art of diminishing; her exactness has seemed almost too cruel. This is apparent in *A Different Face*, in which the hero returns to the seaside town of Coldmouth, on the south coast of England, to discover that the money he has invested in a private school there has been lost. Coldmouth is vividly—and chillingly—described, but in the end the place-name seems too appropriate. Miss Manning's world, one began to feel, was essentially the world of the defeated, and somehow it seemed that her very excellence as a novelist went towards imparting this feeling. Her work was lucid, ironic and cold. One admired and applauded the integrity but was daunted by the detachment, which seemed, perhaps, the product of too great a fastidiousness.

But lucidity, irony, detachment and fastidiousness are also the hall-marks of her Balkan Trilogy, *The Great Fortune*, *The Spoilt City* and *Friends and Heroes*, which is certainly one of the outstanding achievements in post-war fiction. The achievement is such as to suggest that in it, for the first time, Miss Manning was tackling a subject commensurate with her talents, and part of her success in it certainly comes from the qualities that had formerly seemed somehow to diminish her characters.

These qualities do, in fact, define the central consciousness through which the events of the trilogy are reflected, that of Harriet Pringle, the newly married wife of Guy Pringle, who is a member of the staff of a cultural organisation uncommonly like the British Council. They travel to Bucharest together, and the first novel of the trilogy, *The Great Fortune*, deals with that city during the first year of the war. The second ends with its occupation by the Germans after the fall of France, and *Friends and Heroes*, dealing with the departure of the Pringles for Greece, ends with their escape from Greece after the fall of Crete to Alexandria. This, then, is a trilogy on recent history, a war novel written from the point of view of an English non-combatant in a country remote from the West and doomed to fall to the Nazis. The action is inevitably complex and the canvas large, and everything depends precisely on the eye of the beholder, Harriet Pringle, lucid, ironical, detached, fastidious, and also newly married to a man she scarcely understands. The obvious comparison is with Christopher Isherwood's stories in *Goodbye to Berlin*. Isherwood is certainly not an influence on Olivia Manning, but there is a similar juxtaposition of historical events and the purely personal. Harriet herself is almost totally unpolitical; she is a stranger in an exotic world. She is at once naive and shrewd, and it is this combination that gives her rendering of the fall of a nation its authority and authenticity. This, we feel, is exactly what it must have been like to be the helpless onlooker of the takeover of a country in time of war. As a recreation of history in fiction these novels are admirable; the novelist is doing her proper job, to show us the workings of historical events in living terms, to bring them to the human level. The place and the time, the sense of doom and the consequent corruption, seem caught perfectly. And the characters, British and Rumanian alike, are drawn with delicacy and strength, etched with a fine clarity that often reduces them to absurdity but never lets us see them as anything but suffering human beings. Though the trilogy does not indulge in sensationalism, the violence is never burked and comes over the more strongly because of Olivia Manning's almost Austenish precision. Nothing is exaggerated, and this, despite the horrors in the near background, the very real dangers which threaten Harriet and her husband and overwhelm some of their friends, makes the whole work a comedy of a very poignant kind. Everything is in the balance; we read the work with the advantage of hindsight. We might, otherwise, have been reading tragedy.

But this is not all. At the centre of the novel, the focal point that makes everything else real, is the relationship between Harriet and her husband Guy, the young man she scarcely knows, and sees in action in a world new to her. Throughout the three novels Harriet is constantly discovering new aspects of him. He is a committed man, secure, as he thinks, in his marriage. As Harriet notes: "Guy's attitude impressed her, though she had no intention of showing it. He had the advantage of an almost supernatural confidence in dealing with people. It seemed never to occur to him they might not do what he wanted. He had, she noted with surprise, authority. . . . Only someone capable of giving so much could demand and receive so much. She felt proud of him."

The quotation illustrates something of Harriet's—and her creator's—objectivity; and also her fairness, for Guy Pringle is not an easy man to be married to. He seems to take Harriet for granted when he is engaged on what may be called his errands of mercy. He is a relentless do-gooder. But the word is wrong. Guy Pringle is much more than that. He is a man of great physical presence, an intellectual from the working class, who appears at times something of a saint, something of a fool. And again it is Harriet's not wholly certain attitude towards him that convinces us of his reality. He convinces us as that most maddening of human beings, the good man, and the good man, as Dostoevsky discovered when writing *The Idiot*, was only convincing when made at least a little ridiculous. Guy Pringle is one of the most fascinating explorations of character in contemporary fiction.

So, in the background, great events: in the foreground a very subtle analysis of the relationship between a man and wife. The juxtaposition is everything. It assures us of the truth of both.

—Walter Allen

---

**MARKANDAYA, Kamala (Purnalya).** Indian. Born in 1924. Educated at Madras University. Married; has one child. Has worked as a journalist. Recipient: National Association of Independent Schools Award (U.S.A.), 1967. Address: c/o John Farquharson Ltd., 15 Red Lion Square, London W.C.1, England.

PUBLICATIONS

Novels

*Nectar in a Sieve.* London, Putnam, 1954; New York, Day, 1955.
*Some Inner Fury.* London, Putnam, 1955; New York, Day, 1956.
*A Silence of Desire.* London, Putnam, and New York, Day, 1960.
*Possession.* Bombay, Jaico, London, Putnam, and New York, Day, 1963.
*A Handful of Rice.* London, Hamish Hamilton, and New York, Day, 1966.
*The Coffer Dams.* London, Hamish Hamilton, and New York, Day, 1969.

\*     \*     \*

Kamala Markandaya is one of the best of contemporary Indian women novelists. Her six novels, written between 1954 and 1969, are remarkable for their range of experience. *Nectar in a Sieve* is set in a village and examines the hard agricultural life of the Indian peasant; *Some Inner Fury*, which includes a highly educated young woman and her English lover who are torn apart by the Quit India campaign of the time, has to do with the quarrel between Western and Indian influences, as they are focussed in a marriage; *A Silence of Desire* deals with the middle class, and *A Handful of Rice* with the city poor; *Possession* moves from the West End of London to a South Indian village, and is centred on the conflict of Eastern spirituality with Western materialism; *The Coffer Dams* is a highly contemporary examination of the activities of a British engineering firm which is invited to build a dam in India. She has not the same intimacy and familiarity with all these areas of life, and she has indeed been criticised by Indian critics for a certain lack of inwardness with the life of the Indian poor. Her particular strength lies in the delicate analysis of the relationships of persons, particularly when these have a more developed consciousness of their problems, and particularly when they are attempting to grope towards some more independent existence. She has, too, the genuine novelist's gift for fixing the exact individuality of the character, even if she is less successful at establishing it in a reasonably convincing social context. She has been most successful and at her best, an impressive best, in dealing with the problems of the educated, middle class, and she has a gift in particular for delineating the self-imposed laceration of the dissatisfied.

Perhaps her most achieved and characteristic work is *A Silence of Desire*. It is a delicate, precise study of husband and wife, although the wife has less actuality than the husband, Dandekar, a nervy, conscientious, petty government clerk. He is rocked off his age-old balance by his wife's strange absences, excuses and lies. It turns out that she has a growth and is attending a Faith Healer. The husband is by no means a westernised person, but he is to some degree secular and modern, and the situation enables the author to reflect on the tensions, the strength and the inadequacies and aspirations of middle class Indian life. The book is gentle in tone but sharp in perception, and the mixture of moods, the friction of faith and reason, the quarrel of old and young, are beautifully pointed. There are conventional, perfunctory patches in the novel, but Kamala Markandaya shows very high skill in unravelling sympathetically but unflinchingly the structure of the protagonist's motives and the bumbling and stumbling progress of his anxieties.

Towards the end of *A Silence of Desire* there occurs a suggestion in an encounter between Sarojini and Dandekar, the husband and wife, of a theme which clearly much engages Kamala Markandaya. The wife reverences the tulasi tree as embodying the divine spirit, whereas the husband understands its purely symbolic function. "... You with your Western notions, your superior talk of ignorance and superstition . . . you don't know what lies beyond reason and you prefer not to find out. To you the tulasi is a plant that grows in earth like the rest—an ordinary common plant. . . ." She is preoccupied with the opposition between a cerebral, Western—and she seems to be suggesting, a narrowly Benthamite habit of mind—and the more inclusive, the more ancient and ritualistic Indian sensibility. This is a theme which works its way in and out of *Possession*, in which the artist Valmiki is discovered and taken over by Lady Caroline Bell, a relationship which appears to offer itself as a tiny image of India's being taken over by Britain. Neither Valmiki nor Lady Caroline is irresistibly convincing. There is a certain put-up, slightly expected, air about them. The novel's merit lies in the clarity and point of the prose, in an unusual metaphorical capacity and in a gift for the nice discrimination of human motives. Kamala Markandaya's failure as yet is to establish a context as impressively real and as sympathetically grasped as her central characters. She is very much more conscious in *A Handful of Rice* of the context, in this case an urban one, which nevertheless still suffers from a lack of solidity. Ravi, on the other hand, the central character, an educated peasant, is seen with the coolest and most accurate eye and realised with a very considerable creative skill. Nor does this novel offer any easy solution or any obvious superiority of one side of a spiritual dilemma over the other. The novel ends flatly and hopelessly but rightly in a way which suggests the achievement by the author of a bleaker and more necessary kind of wisdom.

—William Walsh

---

**MARKFIELD, Wallace (Arthur).**   American.   Born in Brooklyn, New York, 12 August 1926. Educated at Brooklyn College, B.A. 1947; New York University,1948–50. Married Anna May Goodman in 1949; has one child. Film Critic, *New Leader*, New York, 1954–55. Recipient: Guggenheim Fellowship, 1965; National Endowment for the Arts grant, 1966. Lives in New York. Address: c/o Alfred A. Knopf Inc., 201 East 50th Street, New York, New York 10022, U.S.A.

PUBLICATIONS

Novels

*To an Early Grave.*   New York, Simon and Schuster, 1964; London, Cape, 1965.
*Teitlebaum's Window.*   New York, Knopf, 1970; London, Cape, 1971.

Uncollected Short Stories

"Notes on the Working Day", in *Partisan Review* (New Brunswick, New Jersey), 1946.
"The Country of the Crazy Horse", in *Commentary* (New York), March 1958.

\*       \*       \*

Philip Roth has helped enormously, if inadvertently, to make people conscious of Wallace Markfield by referring to him in *Portnoy's Complaint*: "The novelist, what's his name, Markfield, has written in a story somewhere that until he was fourteen he believed 'aggravation' to be a Jewish word." Roth is referring to "The Country of the Crazy Horse," which sets the tone and milieu of New York Jewish life that carries through all of Markfield's work: the story begins in this way, "As the train began the long crawl under the tunnel to Brooklyn. . . ." Markfield's characters travel by subway or Volkswagen as they negotiate the impossible distances separating the boroughs of New York City and encounter the unique kind of aggravation which is part of their Jewish vantage point.

Stanley Edgar Hyman spoke of Markfield's first novel, *To an Early Grave*, as a more modest *Ulysses* and as "Mr. Bloom's Day in Brooklyn." The part of *Ulysses* it most nearly resembles is the sixth episode, "Hades." Joyce's "creaking carriage" has been replaced by a Volkswagen; Paddy Dignam has turned into a young writer named Leslie Braverman; and the four mourners who attend the Dignam funeral, Martin Cunningham, Leopold Bloom, John Power, and Simon Dedalus, give way to the more literary foursome of Morroe Rieff, Holly Levine, Felix Ottensteen, and Barnet Weiner. The Jew, Leopold Bloom, feels uncomfortable and unwanted among his Christian companions during the ride to the cemetery.

Braverman and his mourners are Jews, as are the other characters who figure prominently in *To an Early Grave*. Their conversation on the way to the cemetery reflects the urban chic of New York City, with its literary quarterlies, its literary critical conscience ("And he hissed softly, 'Trilling . . . Leavis . . . Ransom . . . Tate . . . Kazin . . . Chase . . .' and saw them, The Fathers, as though from a vast amphitheater, smiling at him, and he smiled at them"), its intellectual's obsession with popular culture, its carefully placed Yiddishisms.

Wallace Markfield has been fascinated by Joyce since his early story "Notes on the Working Day"; there are nods here toward the Joyce of *Finnegans Wake* ("There goes Everyman, Here Comes Everybody, the H.C.E. of our culture-lag") and toward the Joyce of *Ulysses* ("Leopold Bloom of the garment center" and "Leopold fat-belly Bloom"). When the Volkswagen of *To an Early Grave* arrives at a chapel, Braverman's four friends are treated to an elaborate funeral oration by a rabbi, which seems indeed to be the Jewish equivalent of the terrifying sermons which dominate chapter three of Joyce's *A Portrait of the Artist as a Young Man*. Here is a sample of the rabbi's language: "*That* on the Day of Judgment *in* the Valley of Jehosaphat you'll be called up. *Either* to everlasting life *or* to such a shaming there's no imagining *how* terrible." Markfield manages to turn this into a wonderfully comic scene when the four mourners discover on examining the corpse that they have attended the wrong funeral. The novel ends with the most sympathetic of the four mourners, Morroe Rieff, finally breaking into tears—the only genuine tears shed in all of *To an Early Grave*—but the humorous and satirical effects in character and situation linger on; the comic survives the fleeting attempts at tragedy.

*Teitlebaum's Window* is the Brighton Beach-Coney Island version of the *Bildungsroman*, the Jewish boy, Simon Sloan, coming of age between the Depression years and the beginnings of World War II. *To an Early Grave* takes place during a single day, a Sunday, while *Teitlebaum's Window* covers a ten-year period. Joyce continues to be very much on Markfield's mind in his latest novel, especially in the use of certain impressionistic techniques and symbolic patterns. The narrative proceeds in a vastly complicated way, with traditional storytelling methods giving way frequently to diary notations, letters, classroom notes, and snatches of monologue. Many of the chapters begin with a single convoluted sentence which may go on for several pages: dating the events, reintroducing characters, referring to celebrities in the political, film, and comic book worlds, and quoting the signs in Teitlebaum's store window (for example, "There will always be an England but there will not always be such a low low price on belly lox"). These long sentences act rather like the interchapters in Virginia Woolf's *The Waves*. The references to Teitlebaum's window offer the novel a symbolic design and supply the reader with a useful *point de repère*.

*Teitlebaum's Window* is a vintage American-Jewish novel. Here the mother-son confrontation is quite as convincingly realized as it was in *Portnoy's Complaint*. Markfield's Jewish mother, with her "dropped stomach," gargantuan stutter, constant aggravation, and dislocated syntax, is quite as believable in her own way as Sophie Portnoy.

—Melvin J. Friedman

---

**MARSH, (Edith) Ngaio.** New Zealander. Born in Christchurch, 23 April 1899. Educated at St. Margaret's College, Christchurch, 1910–14; Canterbury University College School of Art, Christchurch, 1915–20. Actress, 1920–23; Theatrical Producer, 1923–27; Interior Decorator, London, 1928–32. Served in a Red Cross Unit in World War II. Theatrical Producer for O'Connor Theatre Management, New Zealand, 1944–52. Honorary Lecturer in Drama, Canterbury University, 1948. D.Litt., University of Canterbury, 1963. O.B.E. (Officer, Order of the British Empire), 1948; D.B.E. (Dame Commander, Order of the British Empire), 1966. Fellow, Royal Society of Arts. Address: 37 Valley Road, Cashmere, Christchurch 2, New Zealand.

PUBLICATIONS

Novels

A Man Lay Dead.   London, Bles, 1934; New York, Sheridan, 1942.
Enter a Murderer.   London, Bles, 1935; New York, Sheridan, 1942.
Death in Ecstasy.   London, Bles, 1936; New York, Sheridan, 1941.
The Nursing Home Mystery, with Henry Jellett.   London, Bles, 1936; New York,
    Sheridan, 1941.
Vintage Murder.   London, Bles, 1937; New York, Sheridan, 1940.
Artists in Crime.   London, Bles, and New York, Furman, 1938.
Death in a White Tie.   London, Bles, and New York, Furman, 1938.
Overture to Death.   London, Collins, and Boston, Little Brown, 1939.
Death at the Bar.   London, Collins, and Boston, Little Brown, 1940.
Death of a Peer.   Boston, Little Brown, 1940; as Surfeit of Lampreys, London, Collins,
    1941.
Death and the Dancing Footman.   London, Collins, and Boston, Little Brown, 1941.
Colour Scheme.   London, Collins, and Boston, Little Brown, 1943.
Died in the Wool.   London, Collins, and Boston, Little Brown, 1945.
The Final Curtain.   London, Collins, and Boston, Little Brown, 1947.
Swing Brother Swing.   London, Collins, 1949; as Wreath for Riviera, Boston, Little
    Brown, 1949.
Opening Night.   London, Collins, 1951; as Night at the Vulcan, Boston, Little Brown,
    1951.
Spinsters in Jeopardy.   Boston, Little Brown, 1953; London, Collins, 1954.
Scales of Justice.   London, Collins, and Boston, Little Brown, 1955.
Death of a Fool.   Boston, Little Brown, 1956; as Off with His Head, London, Collins,
    1957.
Singing in the Shrouds.   Boston, Little Brown, 1958; London, Collins, 1959.
False Scent.   Boston, Little Brown, 1959; London, Collins, 1960.
Hand in Glove.   Boston, Little Brown, and London, Collins, 1962.
Dead Water.   Boston, Little Brown, 1963; London, Collins, 1964.
Killer Dolphin.   Boston, Little Brown, 1966; as Death at the Dolphin, London, Collins,
    1967.
Clutch of Constables.   London, Collins, 1968; Boston, Little Brown, 1969.
When in Rome.   London, Collins, and Boston, Little Brown, 1970.
Tied Up in Tinsel.   London, Collins, 1972.


Manuscript Collection: Boston University Library.


Ngaio Marsh comments:

The earliest books were written in the style of their time—post-Dorothy Sayers—and
had perhaps some affinity with Marjorie Allingham rather than with Agatha Christie. They
have developed, I hope, into stories of crime and its detection in which the emphasis is on
style and character rather than on mechanics. The latest, When in Rome, was reviewed by
The Times as a "novel of place".

I began as a painter, became a professional actress and later a director. I still work as a
director. These activities have strongly influenced my choice of subject-matter and background. Six of the books are about people of the theatre. A portrait painter, Troy Allen,
appears in many of them while Artists in Crime concerns itself with a group of painters.

Most of the stories are set in England. Three have a New Zealand background, one concerns a sea voyage, and *When in Rome* is where you'd expect it to be. I have dramatized, in collaboration, three of the books, but so far, although one was bought by a London management, none has been produced there.

*       *       *

With some exceptions (e.g., *Death and the Dancing Footman, Final Curtain, Clutch of Constables*), Ngaio Marsh's novels centre around her detective, Roderick Alleyn. He combines being a good policeman (like French) with being an extremely cultured (M. A., Oxon.; marriage with painter Agatha Troy) as well as socially privileged gentleman (mother: Lady Alleyn, brother George: an ambassador; compare Wimsey, Campion, Appleby) and *not* being a one-sided eccentric (like Holmes or Poirot), but still a strong personality (not quite a Maigret). There is little intellectual or social snobbery about him; he is thoroughly normal, humane, intelligent, sober, yet not over-serious. Surprisingly, he hardly ages: forty-two around 1937 (*Vintage Murder*) he still performs strenuous activities thirty years later. This static quality (from which his private life is partly exempt) he shares, by and large, with his friends and helpers such as detective-sergeants Bailey and Thomson and the invaluable "Br'er" Fox, doomed to eternal inspectordom for all his progress in French and his ingratiating ways with parlour-maids. All this (as also Alleyn's moderate promotion to superintendent) is of course essential to the performance of *their* particular duties with verisimilitude.

Their creator has likewise adhered to her manner since *A Man Lay Dead,* although she has expanded and refined it. She has kept (with exceptions like *Singing in the Shrouds*) to relatively few environments – New Zealand, London, the English countryside – and social strata—the upper classes generally, artists and actors, with a sprinkling of rustics and low cockneys. She has also kept to the conventions of firm social and cultural scales of value and the feeling of security that goes with them, as well as to her narrative technique and the interweaving of a love story into the main action. Guided by a comparatively unobtrusive third-person narrator we mostly follow the events, while perceiving the thoughts and emotions of other characters, with Alleyn—or, sometimes, Troy. Towards the end, however, we are left through information gaps to do some brainwork ourselves and check it against the inevitable, but nicely varied final elucidation. Unhampered by too much physical action or personal danger threatening the detective (one exception is the finale of *Dead Water*) we can concentrate on the lives—or bizarre deaths—of the characters, follow the brilliantly handled dialogues, and enjoy the clever comments, reflections and often quite demanding descriptions of landscape, buildings, and interiors; enjoy, too, the ludid, expressive language with its striking imagery. The eccentricity lacking in Alleyn is amply provided by many people he deals with (see notably the Lampreys, *Death of a Peer*, and the Ancreds, *Final Curtain*).

The later novels, including *When in Rome,* tend to abandon such families along with the overcrowding of the "cast" and the over-intricacy of plot which although amusing slightly fatigue in some earlier books. The later books also tend to move from the private murder puzzle towards collective crime involving murder as a corollary. But Ngaio Marsh never loses the one quality which informed her fiction from the beginnings: the placing of what perforce is a sensational and melodramatic story in a solid background of human lives, experiences, desires, and failings. There are limits to the genre, but within them she has very evenly achieved a great deal. None of her numerous tableaux of this "rum life" are facilely thrilling. A certain amount of intellectual and emotional engagement is needed to appreciate them fully. There are very few reasons for saying "t'uh"—and very many for saying "good-oh".

—H. M. Klein

**MARSHALL, Bruce.** British. Born in Edinburgh, 24 June 1899. Educated at Edinburgh Academy, 1906–09; Trinity College, Glenalmond, 1909–15; St. Andrews University, 1916–17; Edinburgh University, 1922–25, M.A. 1924, B.Com. 1925; admitted a Member of the Society of Accountants, Edinburgh, 1926. Served in the Royal Irish Fusiliers, 1918–20 (lost a leg in action); served in the Royal Army Pay Corps and Intelligence, 1940–46. Married Mary Pearson Clark in 1928; has one child. Chartered Accountant with Peat, Marwick Mitchell Ltd., Paris, 1926–40. Recipient: Wlodimierz Petrzak Prize, Warsaw, 1959. Lives in Cap d'Antibes, France. Address: c/o Lloyds Bank Ltd., 6 Pall Mall, London S.W.1, England.

PUBLICATIONS

Novels

*This Sorry Scheme.* London, Harrap, 1924; New York, Harcourt Brace, 1925.
*Teacup Terrace.* London, Hurst and Blackett, 1926.
*The Stooping Venus.* London, Hurst and Blackett, and New York, Dutton, 1926.
*The Other Mary.* London, Hurst and Blackett, 1927.
*And There Were Giants.* London, Jarrolds, 1927.
*The Little Friend.* London, Jarrolds, 1928; New York, Macaulay, 1929.
*High Brows: An Extravaganza of Manners—Mostly Bad.* London, Jarrolds, 1929.
*The Rough House: A Possibility.* London, Jarrolds, 1930.
*Children of This Earth.* New York, Macaulay, 1930.
*Father Malachy's Miracle.* London, Heinemann, and New York, Doubleday, 1931; revised edition, London, Constable, 1947.
*Prayer for the Living.* London, Gollancz, and New York, Knopf, 1934.
*The Uncertain Glory.* London, Gollancz, 1935.
*Canon to Right of Them.* London, Gollancz, 1936.
*Luckypenny.* London, Gollancz, 1937; New York, Doubleday, 1938.
*Delilah Upside Down: A Tract with a Thrill.* London, Heinemann, 1941.
*Yellow Tapers for Paris: A Dirge.* London, Constable, 1943; Boston, Houghton Mifflin, 1946.
*All Glorious Within.* London, Constable, 1944; as *The World, The Flesh, and Father Smith*, Boston, Houghton Mifflin, 1945.
*George Brown's Schooldays.* London, Constable, 1946.
*The Red Danube.* London, Constable, 1946; as *Vespers in Vienna*, Boston, Houghton Mifflin, 1947.
*To Every Man a Penny.* Boston, Houghton Mifflin, 1949; as *Every Man a Penny*, London, Constable, 1950.
*The Fair Bride.* London, Constable, and Boston, Houghton Mifflin, 1953.
*Only Fade Away.* London, Constable, and Boston, Houghton Mifflin, 1954.
*Girl in May.* London, Constable, and Boston, Houghton Mifflin, 1956.
*The Bank Audit.* London, Constable, 1958; as *The Accounting*, Boston, Houghton Mifflin, 1958.
*A Thread of Scarlet.* London, Collins, 1959; as *Satan and Cardinal Campbell*, Boston, Houghton Mifflin, 1959.
*The Divided Lady.* London, Collins, and Boston, Houghton Mifflin, 1960.
*A Girl from Lubeck.* London, Collins, and Boston, Houghton Mifflin, 1962.
*The Month of Falling Leaves.* London, Constable, and New York, Doubleday, 1963.
*Father Hilary's Holiday.* London, Constable, and New York, Doubleday, 1965.
*The Bishop.* London, Constable, and New York, Doubleday, 1970.
*The Black Oxen.* London, Constable, 1972.

Short Stories

   *As a Thief in the Night and Other Stories.*   Amersham, Buckinghamshire, Morland,
      and London, Foyle, 1919.


Other

   *The White Rabbit.*   London, Evans, 1952; Boston, Houghton Mifflin, 1953.
   *Thoughts of My Cats.*   London, Constable, and Boston, Houghton Mifflin, 1954.


Bruce Marshall comments:

   I started out by writing very bad religious novels which I prefer to forget. In all my novels
the real drama will be found, I think, in the acceptance or rejection of the dictates of conscience for which the theological and, I think, the most accurate term is grace. It is perhaps
for this reason that my books have been more widely read in Germany and in Italy than
in my own country, because both those countries touched bottom at the end of the war and
were therefore more percipient.
   None of my novels is as good as I should have wished it, but *The Bishop*, my last, is not,
I think, in spite of a Jesuit's sneer in *The Sign*, a badly written book. *Father Malachy's
Miracle*, almost unnoticed in Britain, was very popular in America in 1931 and, in proof of
what I have said above, became a bestseller both in Italy and Germany in 1949 and 1950.


                              *        *        *


   Bruce Marshall is a vastly underestimated author largely because he is a Catholic writer
and as such he is expected to deal in matters of less than compelling interest to most of us.
He is inevitably compared to Graham Greene and found to be pallid by comparison, less
richly rounded, almost superficial. But to the common reader, though Mr. Marshall would
doubtless disagree, his Catholicism might appear to be a red herring and his main talents to
lie not in apologetics but in the realm of high farce. The enormous output of this author
falles into four chronologically indistinct categories. They can be divided into novels dealing
with the individual, with international politics, with farcical situations, and with the church
in the modern world.
   Some of the earlier, simpler novels pursue the development of character to a more successful degree than their later counterparts. The faith of a simple priest is convincingly described
in *All Glorious Within*; *George Brown's Schooldays* explores the feelings of the average man
in time of war, while *Father Malachy's Miracle* makes a specifically Catholic point. Then
Mr. Marshall branches out into international politics. *The Red Danube* is set in Vienna at
the end of the war, while a viewpoint that is neither pro-Falangist, nor pro-Communist
in the Spain of 1938 is put forward in *The Fair Bride*. The international cultural bureaucracy
is satirised in *A Girl from Lubeck*. This group of novels is extremely professional though
the characterisation is becoming shallower and the treatment of the issues involved is on a
fairly simple level. They might be described as lightly dramatised essays on various subjects,
designed for the man in the street.
   The farcical novels are more slick and amusing: improbable situation is piled upon
improbable reunion in *Father Hilary's Holiday* set in a quasi-revolutionary neo-Cuba, and
in *The Divided Lady* Mr. Marshall takes his readers to Catholic headquarters, Rome. The
technique of hustling the cast on and off the stage is excellent in all but the occasional flashback, but as characters they have now become eroded into mere lay figures. Finally, in his
latest works, Mr. Marshall shows a wish to return to an exploration of the individual mind
in, needless to say, a Catholic setting. Ambition within the church is analysed in *A Thread Of*

*Scarlet*, and *The Bishop* deals with the burning contemporary issues of birth control and priestly celibacy. The inclusion of an eloping nun is a disaster as the theme emphasises the lack of flesh and blood with which Mr. Marshall clothes his men and women. Indeed it would be true to say that successful and highly workmanlike as entertainments as some of Mr. Marshall's books are, the success of the majority is, sadly, in inverse proportion to the seriousness of their intent.

—Anastasia Leech

---

**MARSHALL, Paule.** American. Born in Brooklyn, New York, 9 April 1929. Educated at Brooklyn College, B.A. (cum laude) 1953 (Phi Beta Kappa). Married Kenneth E. Marshall in 1950 (divorced, 1963); has one child. Recipient: Guggenheim Fellowship, 1961; Rosenthal Award, 1962; Ford Theatre Award, 1964; National Endowment for the Arts grant, 1966. Lives in New York. Address: c/o Harcourt, Brace and Jovanovich, 757 Third Avenue, New York, New York 10017, U.S.A.

PUBLICATIONS

Novels

> *Brown Girl, Brownstones.* New York, Random House, 1959; London, W. H. Allen, 1960.
> *The Chosen Place, The Timeless People.* New York, Harcourt Brace, 1969; London, Longman, 1970.

Short Stories

> *Soul Clap Hands and Sing.* New York, Atheneum, 1961.

\*      \*      \*

From the beginning of slavery times West Indian character and experience have figured prominently in the popular imagination of North Americans. Servile insurrections in British Guiana, Jamaica, Saint Domingue and the smaller islands played their part inspiring the similar though less successful uprisings of the Carolinas and Virginia. More recently charismatic West Indian nationalists of the likes of Marcus Garvey have carried a vision of black autonomy directly to the masses of blacks whose arrival in the Northern cities provide conditions for a new consciousness. Yet, with the exception of the works of Claude McKay and a few others who contributed to the Harlem Renaissance of the 1920's the self-conscious literature of North America has scarcely remarked the significance of the black West Indies. That is until Paule Marshall, whose powerful imagination has raised to the highest levels of art a sensitive perception of the West Indian place in modern life.

Her major novel, *The Chosen Place. The Timeless People*, records the encounter of an American research development team with the "backward" people inhabiting Bournehills, the wasted corner of an island resembling perhaps Barbados but signifying the entire Caribbean. Out of sympathy for the human predicament she portrays both aliens and natives in terms of the motives of guilt and frustration by which they comprehend their personal lives. The North Americans' desire to be useful and to alleviate their pain by working in Bournehills she considers genuine, because they do. Similarly, Marshall permits the cane workers and native families to reveal themselves through their most immediate feelings. Only with opportunists, those who readily do the work of the neo-colonial system, does she allow a distance that encourages readers to doubt their personal sincerity, but even there the readers' urge to mock can be no greater than the characters' own. As the narrative progresses Merle Kinbona, a woman of Bournehills whose residence in England included schooling in painfully exploitive relationships as well as professional training, assumes a predominance that translates personal drama into general social meaning. A native of the island despite her "modernization", Merle shares the timelessness of the people to whom the experience of slavery and particularly the momentary success of the rebellion of Cuffee Ned remains palpably present. On a level as deep as culture and as unavailable to scientific measurement as the subconscious, they know that technological change is nothing compared to the redemption presaged in Cuffee's rebellion, and in their integrity they will settle for nothing less. Ultimately, the theme of *The Chosen Place, The Timeless People* is political. Not the politics of parliaments, nor even of parties, but the politics that grows from knowledge that the configurations of character and the complex relationships of love or resentment gain their shape from historical cultures.

Thematically less comprehensive than *The Chosen Place, The Timeless People*, Marshall's two earlier works also display the interweaving narrative and organically conceived meaning of her masterpiece.

*Brown Girl, Brownstones* traces the maturation of young Selina Boyce beyond a loving father, whose incapacity for the get-ahead life of New York City issues in romantic dreams of a big-paying job or self-sufficiency on two acres of inherited land home in Barbados, and beyond, as well, the equally deadening illusions of her mother who sacrifices her being to the successful Bajan's goal of property ownership. The heroine's autonomy is welcome, but, through her delightful rendition of Barbados English and folk say, Marshall makes it clear that Selina's necessary sacrifice of community with the transplanted islanders tragically likens her to the mass of other rootless Americans.

In the light of her two novels each of the four stories in *Soul Clap Hands and Sing* may be considered Marshall's portrayal of the ways individual animation so frequently is replaced in modern life by a protective but deadening routine. Whether in "Barbados," "Brooklyn," "British Guiana," or "Brazil" an aged man discovers that in seeking ease he has in fact lost the surety of self-hood, so that, as the volume's Yeatsian epigraph put it, he is "a paltry thing."

Simply put, Paule Marshall's art is remarkable. She manages the often summoned but rarely arriving synthesis of the particular and universal, for in revealing the rich texture of West Indian life within her fiction she also constructs a microcosm of the contemporary struggle to be free at last.

—John M. Reilly

---

**MASTERS, John.** British. Born in India, 26 October 1914. Educated at the Royal Military College, Sandhurst. Married; has two children. Served in the British Army, 1934 until his retirement as Lieutenant Colonel in 1948: commissioned 2nd Lieutenant, Indian Army, 1934; served in the 2nd Battalion, 4th Prince of Wales's Own Gurkha Rifles, 1935;

served on the North West Frontier, 1936–37; Adjutant, 1939; served in Iraq, Syria and Persia, 1941; Brigade Major, 114th Indian Infantry Brigade, 1942, and 111th Indian Infantry Brigade, 1943; Commandant, 3rd Battalion, 1944; served in Burma, 1944–45; General Staff Officer-1, 19th Indian Division, 1945; General Staff Officer-2, Staff College, Camberley, Surrey, 1947: D.S.O. (Companion, Distinguished Service Order), 1944; O.B.E. (Officer, Order of the British Empire), 1945. Address: c/o Michael Joseph Ltd., 52 Bedford Square, London W.C.1, England.

PUBLICATIONS

Novels

> *Nightrunners of Bengal.*  London, Joseph, and New York, Viking Press, 1951.
> *The Deceivers.*  London, Joseph, and New York, Viking Press, 1952.
> *The Lotus and the Wind.*  London, Joseph, and New York, Viking Press, 1953.
> *Bhowani Junction.*  London, Joseph, and New York, Viking Press, 1954.
> *Coromandel!*  London, Joseph, and New York, Viking Press, 1955.
> *Far, Far the Mountain Peak.*  London, Joseph, and New York, Viking Press, 1957.
> *Fandango Rock.*  London, Joseph, and New York, Harper, 1959.
> *The Venus of Konpara.*  London, Joseph, and New York, Harper, 1960.
> *To the Coral Strand.*  London, Joseph, and New York, Harper, 1962.
> *Trial at Monomoy.*  London, Joseph, and New York, Harper, 1964.
> *Fourteen Eighteen.*  London, Joseph, 1965; New York, British Book Centre, 1966.
> *The Breaking Strain.*  London Joseph, and New York, Dial Press, 1967.
> *The Rock.*  London, Joseph, and New York, Putnam, 1970.

Other

> *Compleat Indian Angler.*  London, Country Life, 1938.
> *Bugles and a Tiger: A Personal Adventure.*  London, Joseph, 1956; as *Bugles and a Tiger: A Volume of Autobiography*, New York, Viking Press, 1956.
> *The Road Past Mandalay* (autobiography).  London, Joseph, and New York, Viking Press, 1961.
> *Casanova.*  London, Joseph, and New York, Geis, 1969.
> *Pilgrim Son: A Personal Odyssey.*  London, Joseph, 1971.

*          *          *

While John Masters has received deserved acknowledgement as an accomplished narrator of dramatic and exciting stories, it would seem to me that he has not received his full due as a novelist *per se*. There is much more to Masters than the superb story teller. This may have been overlooked because the stories he tells are adventure stories in the old fashioned sense. Heroes stand alone against physical dangers and desperate odds in *Nightrunners of Bengal* and *The Deceivers*; the hero redeems himself after accusations of cowardice in *The Lotus and the Wind*. But these heroes are much more complex than the usual run of romantic adventurers. They suffer doubts and heart searchings as well as fears and privations; their quest is often as much for identity or relationships as for the enemy or the spy.

When William Savage in *The Deceivers* sets out to track down and disband the Thugs by joining them and entering their mysteries, he becomes aware of spiritual dangers as acute as the more obvious physical ones. The struggle is with the worshippers of Kali and within himself; and while Captain Rodney Savage in *Nightrunners of Bengal* has to overcome every kind of danger and hardship to rescue himself and his son from the perils and horrors ensuing from the Indian mutiny, he has also to rescue himself from the bitterness of heart and mind which these experiences engender in him. In *Far, Far the Mountain Peak*, Peter Savage has to wrestle not only with the almost daemonic urge to prove himself, but with the temptation to take others with him. It is not just a superb story of mountaineering and soldiering, but that of spiritual redemption and of relationships which have parallels with Lawrence's *Women in Love*, and it is at this level Masters' novels ought to be discussed. The peculiar affinity which develops between Robin Savage and his adversaries makes *The Lotus and the Wind* much more than a story about the pursuit of spies in Afghanistan. It is this ability to probe deep into motivation, and to engage our sympathy and interest in the internal struggles of characters not immediately likeable or even admirable, which raises Masters above the level of a mere narrator of adventure stories.

In *Bhowani Junction*, where the narrative is divided between the three main protagonists—Patrick Taylor and Victoria Jones, both Anglo-Indians, and Colonel Savage—a story of sabotage and political intrigue, exciting in itself, serves as a background for their search for identity in a rapidly changing India. It would be difficult to find in fiction a more thoroughly sympathetic understanding of the situation of the Anglo-Indian at that time, which brings us to a consideration of these works as historical novels. The history of the Savage family, as told in this series of novels, is closely interwoven with the history of British India, from the seventeenth century in *Coromandel!* to the time of partition in *Bhowani Junction*. It is an India for which Masters has an immense sympathy and understanding, and of which he has an intimate and often first hand knowledge. When John Raymond described *Nightrunners of Bengal* as the best historical novel about the Indian mutiny, he was not exaggerating, and *The Deceivers* displays a knowledge of Thuggee which can be the result only of thorough scholarship, and an understanding which displays a remarkably imaginative insight. There is considerable skill, too, in the way Masters organizes his material. Indeed, it is this and his remarkable qualities of imaginative understanding that make him a novelist who deserves our serious attention.

—John Cotton

---

**MATTHIESSEN, Peter.** American. Born in New York City, 22 May 1927. Educated at Hotchkiss School, Connecticut; Yale University, New Haven, Connecticut, B.A. 1950; the Sorbonne, Paris, 1948–49. Married Deborah Love in 1963; has four children. Commercial Fisherman, 1954–56. Has made anthropological and natural history expeditions to Alaska, the Canadian Northwest Territories, Peru, New Guinea (Harvard-Peabody Expedition, 1961), Africa and Nicaragua. Founder, 1952, and Editor, *Paris Review*, Paris and New York. Trustee of the New York Zoological Society since 1965. Recipient: *Atlantic* "Firsts" Award, 1951; National Institute of Arts and Letters grant, 1963. Address: Bridge Lane, Sagaponack, Long Island, New York 11962, U.S.A.

PUBLICATIONS

Novels

*Race Rock.* New York, Harper, 1954; London, Secker and Warburg, 1955.

*Partisans.*   New York, Viking Press, 1955; London, Secker and Warburg, 1956.

*Raditzer.*   New York, Viking Press, 1961; London, Heinemann, 1962.

*At Play in the Fields of the Lord.*   New York, Random House, 1965; London, Heinemann, 1966.


Other

*Wildlife in America.*   New York, Viking Press, 1959; London, Deutsch, 1960.

*The Cloud Forest: A Chronicle of the South American Wilderness.*   New York, Viking Press, 1961; London, Deutsch, 1962.

*Under the Mountain Wall: A Chronicle of Two Seasons in the Stone Age.*   New York, Viking Press, 1962; London, Heinemann, 1963.

*The Shorebirds of North America.*   New York, Viking Press, 1967.

*Oomingmak: The Expedition to the Musk Ox Island in the Bering Sea.*   New York, Hastings House, 1967.

*Sal Si Puedes: Cesar Chavez and the New American Revolution.*   New York, Random House, 1970.

*Blue Meridian.*   New York, Random House, 1971.


\*          \*          \*


Peter Matthiessen has a dream of mankind living gracefully in the world, one species of many in an organic relationship. Unlike earlier American authors given to a version of this dream, Matthiessen can have no illusions. He writes with our contemporary knowledge that the "natural man," whose free application of energy to the environment was for earlier Americans to be the means of achieving a paradise, has wrought ecological disaster. Materially that disaster derives from the rapacious application of technology to the subjugation of nature, and Matthiessen's seven works of non-fiction are its historical record reporting the extinction and threatened destruction of animal species, the fateful meetings of representatives of industrial society with people yet to experience even the agricultural revolution, and the desperate resistance of American farm workers to the culminating stage of exploitation. Philosophically, the disastrous consequences of the traditional American dream result from the theoretical separation of society, usually conceived of as oppressive, and the individual, always assumed to be noble; thus, people celebrating individualism but nonetheless required to construct a social system find that their rejection of the claims of fraternity does not foster sturdy independence but merely produces anomie. The counterpart of his historical record of the destruction of the natural environment, Matthiessen's four novels are a representation of this disabled American character.

Writing evocatively of his own generation and social class in *Race Rock*, he links four young Americans in exploring the directions their lives have taken since their adolescence in the same seacoast setting. The shifting viewpoint and intermingling of recollection and present event provide the sense of movement we associate with growth, but it is ironic since there has been no growth. Two of the male characters—George and Sam—are the ineffectual products of middle class culture: uncertain of vocation, implausible in deeds, in short unable to complete the arc between thought and action because they doubt the efficacy of their thought. Providing the apex of a triangle is a woman who, though female and, therefore, less intensively drawn by the romance of achievement, is herself ungratified. Her fulfillment must come through the ineffectual males to one of whom she has been married and with the second of whom she is involved in a love affair. The point of reference for all three is Cady, a man whose natural capacity to act let him bully them in childhood. As adults these four are bound as they were in adolescence into personally destructive relationships. Cady's irresponsible brutishness has merely become more lethal. He still seeks to get what he wants according to a base code of individual force, while George, Sam, and Eve ambivalently resent and admire his dominance. For Matthiessen the behavior of the characters has explanation, but no excuse. Carefully avoiding extenuating circumstances that would lift their personal responsibility, he shows that they have neither the direction nor the will to exist in other than an unjustifiably predatory arrangement.

In *Partisans*, Matthiessen again focuses upon an ineffectual son of the American bourgeoisie. Barney Sand, alienated from family and culture, proceeds on a search for a revolutionary who had befriended him as a child. By means of a descent into Parisian working class life on which Barney is led by a Stalinist Party functionary named Marat, Matthiessen parallels the physical search with an inquiry into the motives for revolutionary action. The Brechtian portrayal of proletarian conditions denies Barney the clarity available to those who think in the abstract. The bestial lives of the poor make sympathy, or even the belief in their natural rectitude, impossible for Barney, and a politics without idealism is beneath his consideration. All that Matthiessen permits Barney to grasp is that revolutionaries have strong convictions for which they will sacrifice everything—the man for whom he searches gives life and reputation. But since there can be no doubt that revolutionary forces are in motion, the failure to comprehend must lie in Barney. Matthiessen seems to be suggesting that so long as thought and action are held to be categorically separate, as they are in Barney's mind, no motive will be sufficient for action and no action entirely justifiable. It is integration of both in practice that makes a revolutionary and comprehension of that fact that is necessary for modern men to make their lives adequately human.

Technically Matthiessen's neatest explication of character occurs in *Raditzer*. The figure who gives his name to the book is a passive-aggressive, physically weak and socially a parasite, yet able to strike through the mask of civilized respectability and mastery to reveal in those he victimizes a deep-seated guilt and bewildering remorse. The kinship Raditzer insists he shares with the respectable Navy men whose tenuous security he undermines conveys, as in *Race Rock*, Matthiessen's perception of the split between thought and action that manifests itself in the indecisiveness of American men. The tight narrative construction enforcing psychological parallels goes beyond the earlier novel, however, making it evident in *Raditzer* through the substance of style that the leading characters of the book amalgamate into a general type.

Successful though he has been in the manner of psychological realism, Matthiessen's developing vision has required that he exceed the form of his first three novels, and in *At Play in the Fields of the Lord* he introduces to fiction the comprehensiveness of philosophical anthropology. Carrying the ineffectual civilized types he has previously described into the jungle of South America, Matthiessen strips away the protective coloration they gain from their native culture; thus, they are as exposed as the jungle Indians to the test of survival. As the narrative increasingly centers upon the grand attempt of a reservation trained North American Indian to reclaim his past by immersing himself in the natural and cultural world of the primitive South American Indians, three levels of meaning emerge. The first concerns the historical conflict between modern technological civilization and the less developed societies whose destruction is only a matter of time. Through imaginative sympathy with both Indians and whites Matthiessen, then, establishes a second theme of the unity of desire to humanize the world. For the Indians this involves a balanced relationship to nature that yet allows a sense of transcendence. For the North Americans sharing the same impulse the desire is domination. Certainly their technology will eventually dominate but for the time being they are alone with only personal resources inadequate to sustain their sanity. Finally, on a third level of meaning he reveals both Indians and whites to be lonely beings who must find salvation through development of community that embraces the total material and social world.

With *At Play in the Fields of the Lord* Peter Matthiessen's fiction and non-fiction become one in purpose. As he writes in *Sal Si Puedes*, "In a damaged human habitat, all problems merge." The good life will be achieved, if at all, only when man and society and nature are equally nurtured and cherished.

—John M. Reilly

**MAUGHAM, Robin** (Robert Cecil Romer Maugham; became 2nd Viscount Maugham of Hartfield, 1958); nephew of the writer Somerset Maugham. British. Born in London, 17 May 1916. Educated at Eton College, Buckinghamshire; Trinity Hall, Cambridge, B.A. Served in the British Army, 1939–44: served in the Inns of Court Regiment, 1939; commissioned Fourth County of London Regiment, 1940; served in the Western Desert, 1941–42 (wounded; mentioned in despatches), and in the Middle East Intelligence Centre, 1943. Barrister, Lincoln's Inn, London, until 1939. Address: Casa Cala Pada, Santa Eulalia, Ibiza, Spain.

PUBLICATIONS

Novels

The 1946 MS. London, War Facts Press, 1943.
The Servant. London, Falcon Press, 1948; New York, Harcourt Brace, 1949.
A Line on Ginger. London, Chapman and Hall, 1949; New York, Harcourt Brace, 1950.
The Rough and the Smooth. London, Chapman and Hall, and New York, Harcourt Brace, 1951.
Behind the Mirror. London, Longman, and New York, Harcourt Brace, 1955.
The Man with Two Shadows. London, Longman, 1958; New York, Harcourt Brace, 1959.
November Reef: A Novel of the South Seas. London, Longman, 1962.
The Green Shade. London, Heinemann, and New York, New American Library, 1966.
The Wrong People (as David Griffin). New York, Paperback Library, 1967; revised edition, as Robin Maugham, London, Heinemann, 1970; New York, McGraw Hill, 1971.
The Second Window. London, Heinemann, and New York, McGraw Hill, 1968.
The Link: A Victorian Mystery. London, Heinemann, and New York, McGraw Hill, 1969.
The Last Encounter. London, W. H. Allen, 1972.

Short Stories

The Black Tent and Other Stories, edited by Peter Burton. London, W. H. Allen, 1972.

Plays

The Rising Heifer (produced Dallas, 1952; High Wycombe, Buckinghamshire, 1955).
The Leopard (produced Worthing, Sussex, 1956).
Mr. Lear (produced Worthing, Sussex, 1956). London, English Theatre Guild, 1963.
The Last Hero (produced London, 1957).
A Lonesome Road, with Philip King (produced London, 1957). London, French, 1959.
Odd Man In, adaptation of a play by Claude Magnier (produced London, 1957). London, French, 1958.
The Servant (produced Worthing, Sussex, 1958). London, French, n.d.
The Hermit, with Philip King (produced Harrogate, Yorkshire, 1959).
It's in the Bag, adaptation of a play by Claude Magnier (produced London, 1960).
The Claimant (produced Worthing, Sussex, 1962; London, 1964).

*Azouk*, with Willis Hall, adaptation of a play by Alexandre Rivemale (produced Newcastle upon Tyne, 1962).
*Enemy!* (produced Guildford, Surrey, and London, 1969).   London, French, 1971.

Screenplays: *The Black Tent*, 1956; *The Man with Two Shadows*, 1960; *November Reef*,
1962; *The Carrier*, 1969; *Willie*, 1969; *The Barrier*, 1971.


Other

*Come to Dust*.   London, Chapman and Hall, 1945.
*Approach to Palestine*.   London, Grey Walls Press, 1947.
*Nomad*.   London, Chapman and Hall, 1947; New York, Viking Press, 1948.
*North African Notebook*.   London, Chapman and Hall, 1948; New York, Harcourt
Brace, 1949.
*Journey to Siwa*.   London, Chapman and Hall, 1950; New York, Harcourt Brace,
1951.
*The Slaves of Timbuktu*.   London, Longman, and New York, Harper, 1961.
*The Joyita Mystery*.   London, Parrish, 1962.
*Somerset and All the Maughams*.   London, Heinemann-Longman, and New York,
New American Library, 1966.
*Escape from the Shadows: An Autobiography*.   London, Hodder and Stoughton, 1972.

Editor, *Convoy Magazine: Stories, Articles, Poems from the Forces, Factories, Mines
and Fields*.   London, Collins, 1945.


Critical Studies: by Feliz Marti-Ibanez in *Ariel*, New York, MD Publications, 1962;
"Literary Lord: A Profile of Lord Robin Maugham", in *MD* (New York), December 1969;
by Nancy Hosegood, in *Ibiza Insight*, 7 September 1971.


\*      \*      \*


Robin Maugham creates marketplaces, often in exotic locales, for sexual transactions of
all varieties. Sexual identity is itself ambiguous and fluctuating: the screenwriter of *Behind
the Mirror* alters the sex of a character's youthful lover from male to female to make a film
plot marketable, and a critic in *The Second Window* accuses the writer hero of having similarly
changed the gender of his lover in an autobiographical novel (the writer, in fact, is later
attracted by a thirteen year old girl who looks like a "page-boy in Florentine painting").
These permutations and combinations might serve as paradigms for Maugham's fiction.
*The 1946 MS*, a political novella, is interesting primarily for prefiguring in General
Pointer the megalomaniac idealist of later works: Ewing, who wants to create a "perfect
human being" in *The Wrong People*, and Clift, who must shanghai the inhabitants of his
utopia in *November Reef*. But Maugham's dominant themes are first developed in *The
Servant*, the shortest and, perhaps, best of his novels. Tony's attraction to his butler, Barrett,
is typical of the interest Maugham's moneyed characters display in members of the working
class, though Barrett is a bit older and more aggressive than his later variants. Barrett
provides Tony primarily with the comfort he desires more than anything else, and though
Tony jokes that Barrett would also supply sex, were it demanded, Barrett seems to offer
only Vera for that purpose (Maugham's heroes are still avowedly heterosexual in the early
novels, though some minor figures are homosexual).
Within its range, *The Servant* effectively dramatizes the mystery of human involvement,
a motif Maugham developed more optimistically in *Line on Ginger*, which traces a young

lawyer's compulsive rescue of a workingclass member of his old regiment from a life of crime. Despite the predictable nature of the hero's encounters with his former colleagues, the book succeeds in conveying both his belief in "comradeship," and the legacy of his army experience, material Maugham utilizes in non-fiction works like *Come to Dust* and *Nomad* and in a number of later novels.

With *The Rough and the Smooth*, Maugham began a series of novels dramatizing the pursuit by older men of often deceitful, sometimes innocent, girls and boys. The scheming Pat foreshadows the similarly conniving, boyishly slim Vicky of *The Green Shade*, and the male prostitute in *The Wrong People*. Reg Barker, Pat's vulgar, elderly protector is the most fully characterized and appealing of a series of child fanciers; Sam Newbolt of *The Second Window*, who rents thirteen year old Linda from her grandmother, is the most sinister. Linda and the adolescent Dan of *The Wrong People* represent the child as victim. Since Maugham consistently describes middle-aged bodies as gross and obscene, his older characters understandably expend a great deal of effort and money in the sexual marketplace and are often subjected to varieties of blackmail (Dr. Stacey in *November Reef*, Martin in *The Second Widow*, and Arnold in *The Wrong People*). The impulse causing some men to pursue the young may be merely Arnold's "fiercely intense passion" or Ewing's perverse pedagogical drive in the same book. But, ultimately, Maugham's older protagonists seek a lost childhood fantasy or companion, a lost aspect of the self, or a lost opportunity for life. Even thrillers like *November Reef* and *The Link*, both suggested by historical incidents, and *The Man with Two Shadows*, touch on the concerns of the more serious novels, *The Link* especially stressing the search for the lost self or double that explains many Maugham characters.

The film version turned *The Servant* into an allegory of a decaying aristocracy whose depraved tastes make them the prey of their social inferiors, but the novel, like all Maugham's, has little social or political resonance. Similarly, the African settings of *Behind the Mirror*, *The Green Shade*, *The Wrong People*, and *The Second Window* convey neither a sensitivity for the nuances of a foreign culture, nor the existential excitement triggered by such terrain in Gide's *The Immoralist* or Bowles' *The Sheltering Sky*. And Maugham displays almost no concern for Africa in transition. Locale seems largely decorative, atmospheric: "the stench and dust of the narrow alleys that reached like tentacles from the centre of the Asian quarter to the water-front of Mombasa" (*The Second Window*).

What threatens to defeat all Maugham's work is a style inadequate to his conceptions. The note of portentous melodrama may be acceptable in adventure stories: "The blow was as abrupt as it was unexpected" (*The Link*), or "I have a full bottle of whiskey and at least five hours before they come for me. I will write down the facts as best I can. That is my only hope" (*The Man With Two Shadows*, and a variant of the opening of *The 1946 MS*). But the attempted frankness of Maugham's full-dress treatments of sex after *Line on Ginger* unfortunately results in depictions of passion in which a "dark torrent was surging out into the light, splashing and frothing against the gates, spurting through the opening in heavy spasms, rushing to mix with the waters in the river below, so that, presently, all his fear and grief had been drained away, and he lay, limp and at peace . . ." (*The Rough and the Smooth*), or of a desire aroused by "movement more sensuous than anything Arnold had ever imagined in his most erotic dreams" (*The Wrong People*). For all the secrecy surrounding the pseudonymous publication of *The Wrong People* in America, the book is remarkably unexplicit in its picture of sex, and sometimes inadvertently comic in the breathless prose that avoids literal details. (But perhaps Maugham was aware that the British Museum forces readers of even the innocuous *Behind the Mirror* to sit in the North Library under the watchful eyes of the staff.)

Maugham's most ambitious book, *The Second Window*, which elaborately develops the pervasive themes of his work, suffers not only from this florid and ultimately prudish style, but also from the unwieldy structuring of a series of flashbacks. Perhaps because it attempts a more straightforward probing of motivation than does *The Servant*, but falters on the verge of frankness, *The Second Window* misses both the subtle treatment of ambiguous human relationships of the earlier book and real sexual honesty. Yet in spite of repetitions, and stylistic and formal weaknesses, Maugham's fiction has for over twenty years kept true to a vision of sexual intrigue and its attendant pain.

—Burton Kendle

---

**MAXWELL, William.** American. Born in Lincoln, Illinois, 16 August 1908. Educated at the University of Illinois, Urbana, B.A. 1930; Harvard University, Cambridge, Massachusetts, M.A. 1931. Married Emily Gilman Noyes in 1945; has two children. Member of the English faculty at the University of Illinois, 1931–33. Since 1936, Member of the Staff of *The New Yorker* magazine. Recipient: Friends of American Writers Award, 1938; National Institute of Arts and Letters grant, 1958. Member, National Institute of Arts and Letters. Address: 544 East 86th Street, New York, New York 10028, U.S.A.

PUBLICATIONS

Novels

    *Bright Center of Heaven.* New York, Harper, 1934.
    *They Came like Swallows.* New York, Harper, and London, Joseph, 1937.
    *The Folded Leaf.* New York, Harper, 1945; London, Faber, 1946.
    *Time Will Darken It.* New York, Harper, 1948; London, Faber, 1949.
    *The Château.* New York, Knopf, 1961.

Short Stories

    *Stories,* with others. New York, Farrar Straus, 1956.
    *The Old Man at the Railroad Crossing and Other Tales.* New York, Knopf, 1966.

Other

    *The Heavenly Tenants.* New York, Harper, 1946.
    *Ancestors.* New York, Knopf, 1971.

\* \* \*

The subjects of William Maxwell's major novels vary, but the sensibility that informs them is a Midwestern one. In both *They Came like Swallows* and *The Folded Leaf*, for example, the novelist is reworking and focusing his recollections of an Illinois boyhood and college experience. The materials he draws on in these novels he thus shares with somewhat older writers like Sinclair Lewis and Sherwood Anderson. But these novelists were involved in labors of repudiation; their work was marked by what has been called the "revolt from the village," by a keen sense that the Midwestern setting was a stultifying one from which the writer, by a satirical and unflattering report, had to separate himself. This accent of mockery and dismissal is absent from Maxwell's novels, which render the texture of Midwestern life in the early decades of this century. It is an accent which is absent from Maxwell's

*Ancestors*, a work of non-fiction which gives an attentive account of the writer's forebears.

In general, then, there is a cherishing of the provincial limitations that other writers have found galling. There is, in most of the novels, a precise if not loving recollection of the diversions and the limited esthetic taste that created upper-class, prosperous sensibility in "downstate" Illinois towns. *They Came like Swallows*, for example, tells of the impact of a mother's death on a decent and conventional Illinois household. *Time Will Darken It* is an account of a protracted visit which Southern relatives pay and the disruption that the visitors bring to what was a moderately happy family. *The Folded Leaf*, which the French critic, Maurice Coindreau, has referred to as the best novel about college experience, tells of the adolescent and college experiences of two young Midwestern men; it leaves them on the threshold of an uneasy maturity, a maturity far short of ideal, but the only maturity that is open to them under Midwestern conditions.

The clearest indications of Maxwell's attitude toward his American materials—and also a clue to his account of an American couple's encounter with alien French culture in *The Château*—appears in *The Folded Leaf*. In this novel about the "coming of age" of two boys, the author draws explicit parallels between their rather casual passage from youth to maturity and the "rites of passage" that anthropologists and students of comparative religion describe in the tradition-oriented societies they analyze. Recovering from a suicide attempt, one of the heroes has left behind him his distorting childhood. The man's childhood "would never rise and defeat him again." For he will be "watched over by tree spirits, guarded by Diana the huntress and the King of the Woods. . . ." The Midwestern analogue to the "rites of passage" is complete.

Though Maxwell does not invoke this sort of parallel in *The Château*, the American tourists of the novel undergo contacts with an enigmatic culture—that of the French—which are a series of challenges that are neither mockingly presented, as in Sinclair Lewis's *Dodsworth*, nor offered as proof of American superiority, as in Booth Tarkington's *The Plutocrat*. Rather is Maxwell's prevailing note that of detached comprehension, the same sort of comprehension that the anthropologist offers the alien culture that he wishes to grasp. The anthropologist does not question the values of his "informants"; he reports those values. Such is also the attitude of Maxwell toward the aspirations of the characters he creates.

—Harold H. Watts

---

**MAYFIELD, Julian.** American. Born in Greer, South Carolina, 6 June 1928. Educated at Lincoln University, Pennsylvania. Served in the United States Army, 1946–47. Married Ana Livia Cordero in 1954; has two children. Writer and Editor in the office of President Kwame Nkrumah, Ghana, 1962–66. Founding Editor, *The African Review*, Accra, 1964–66. Fellow, Society for the Humanities, Cornell University, Ithaca, New York, 1967–68; Lecturer, Schweitzer Program in the Humanities, New York University, 1968–70; W. E. B. DuBois Visiting Fellow, Cornell University, 1970–71. Recipient: Rabinowitz Fellowship, 1967. Address: Chaka Farm, R.F.D. 2, Spencer, New York 14883, U.S.A.

PUBLICATIONS

Novels

*The Hit*. New York, Vanguard Press, 1957; London, Joseph, 1959.

*The Long Night.*   New York, Vanguard Press, 1958; London, Joseph, 1960.
*The Grand Parade.*   New York, Vanguard Press, 1961; London, Joseph, 1962.

Plays

*417*, in *Contemporary Reader* (New York), 1954.

Screenplay: *Uptight*, with Ruby Dee and Jules Dassin, 1968.

Other

Editor, *The World Without the Bomb: The Papers of the Accra Assembly.*   Accra,
Ghana Government Press, 1963.

Bibliography: in *Dark Symphony*, New York, Free Press, and London, Collier Macmillan,
1968.

Manuscript Collection: Schomburg Collection, New York Public Library.

*      *      *

In his ironically titled first novel, *The Hit*, Mayfield guides most of his characters into
impasses in which they realize that "the hit," the lucky break, will not come to fulfill their
hopes. The exception is the most persistent dreamer, Hubert Cooley, the Black superintendent of four Harlem tenements who bets heavily on the numbers to win the money to
go to San Francisco, far from his bothersome wife Gertrude. At the end of the novel, his
son James Lee uselessly informs him about John Lewis, the numbers runner who has fled
without paying Cooley his forty-two hundred dollars: "He never comes, pop. Don't you
see that? John Lewis never really comes." Cooley will not believe that Lewis and Number
417, the hit, are only symbols of the dream deferred.

The widow Sister Clarisse finds that she cannot run away with Cooley, and Gertrude
accepts the apparent fact that she will remain unloved by both husband and son. Her son
James Lee, too, faces hard reality in his girlfriend Essie's prudent decision—the breakup of
her own dream—to end their affair. Weaknesses in character, not just ghetto-narrowed
destiny, propel events, and some are related to racial attitudes. Gertrude's selfishness and
masochism, for example, contrast with her husband's delusion that being white would
eradicate his problems. Generally, people in *The Hit*, trying to escape "the locks and chains
of definitions," become "enmeshed by [their] personal Me" (phrases that begin the book)
and must emerge into an acceptance of life-without-luck.

In *The Long Night*, a numbers hit is again important: sent by his mother to collect her
winnings, ten-year-old Steely spends a long night trying to recover the twenty-seven dollars
stolen from him by gang members. After failing to get the money through honest work,
borrowing, and theft, he gets it from his estranged father, whom he mistakes for a sleeping
drunk whose wallet can be lifted. The novel, the simple story of a boy in simple trouble,
is able in characterization and in descriptions of Harlem and Manhattan seen through
Steely's eyes.

Another ironically named novel, *The Grand Parade*, unfolding complicated machinations by a selfish parade of town officials in fictional Gainesboro, climaxes in Southern-style
violence and death at a newly integrated school. Naturalistic and sometimes humorous in
its panorama of sex, corruption, betrayals, and bombings, this novel of practical politics

has, among its many characters, several that are thematically important. Randy Banks, City Councilman from the Black district, has used politics to escape the powerlessness of his slum origins. Joe Weeks, a skilful behind-the-scenes opportunist and image maker, furnishes Banks's political brains. Their white counterparts are Mayor Douglas Taylor and his mentor, Alex Kochek. The author uses the mayor's ethical ambivalence centrally: to Taylor politics is "the deal forever brewing . . . climbing forever toward a place, any place, from which one could look down"; yet he considers himself an upright liberal who now and then compromises to pass good laws. Alex, his brilliant adviser known as a "crusader for honesty in government," typically reminds him: "There are no great moral issues in American life today. Only political issues and power struggles."

Mayfield uses some stock figures: Ralph Blackburn, the government agent; Patty Speed, the numbers queen; Reverend Mathews, president of the Negro Progress Association; J. D. Carson, the bold, unscrupulous seeker of power; and Hank Dean, the misfit whose racism partakes of hysteria. Two others, however, are more than types. Clarke Bryant, certain that God and history have made him a racist, rationalizes his exploitations with perverse intelligence. Banks's moral brother Lonnie, expelled from the Communist Party for having expressed his independence and belief in the goodness of man in a "dangerous and counter-revolutionary" paper, ends up friendless and alienated from America, where he "can't get a cup of coffee in most restaurants, can't get a job and can only live in certain areas."

In this political novel (a genre that increasingly attracts Black authors), Mayfield has characters turn their cynicism satirically upon themselves; human rights are no more than a clever insertion into a speech; and the mayor is shot dead for his peace-making remarks outside the school inside which children are singing "My Country 'Tis of Thee." A few years after its publication, the author was at work on another novel whose tentative title, *Look Pretty for the People*, has political overtones. In his novel of 1961, then, his best, Mayfield might have found the mode in which he will excel himself.

—James A. Emanuel

---

**McBAIN, Ed.** See **HUNTER, Evan.**

---

**McCARTHY, Mary (Therese).** American. Born in Seattle, Washington, 21 June 1912. Educated at Forest Ridge Convent, Seattle; Annie Wright Seminary, Tacoma, Washington; Vassar College, Poughkeepsie, New York, A.B. 1933 (Phi Beta Kappa). Married Harold Johnsrud in 1933; Edmund Wilson, *q.v.*, 1938; Bowden Broadwater, 1946; James Raymond West, 1961; has one child. Editor, Covici Friede, Publishers, New York, 1936–38; Editor, 1937–38, and Drama Critic, 1937–62, *Partisan Review*, New Brunswick, New Jersey. Instructor, Bard College, Annandale-on-Hudson, New York, 1945–46, and Sarah Lawrence College, Bronxville, New York, 1948. Recipient: Guggenheim Fellowship, 1949, 1959; *Horizon* Prize, 1949; National Institute of Arts and Letters grant, 1957. Member, National Institute of Arts and Letters. Address: 141 rue de Rennes, Paris 6, France.

PUBLICATIONS

Novels

> The Company She Keeps.   New York, Simon and Schuster, 1942; London, Weidenfeld
> and Nicolson, 1957.
> The Oasis.   New York, Random House, 1949; as A Source of Embarrassment, London,
> Heinemann, 1950.
> The Groves of Academe.   New York, Harcourt Brace, 1952; London, Heinemann,
> 1953.
> A Charmed Life.   New York, Harcourt Brace, 1955; London, Weidenfeld and Nicol-
> son, 1956.
> The Group.   New York, Harcourt Brace, and London, Weidenfeld and Nicolson, 1963.
> Birds of America.   New York, Harcourt Brace, and London, Weidenfeld and Nicolson,
> 1971.

Short Stories

> Cast a Cold Eye.   New York, Harcourt Brace, 1950; London, Heinemann, 1952.

Uncollected Short Stories

> "The Company Is Not Responsible", in The New Yorker, 22 April 1944.
> "The Unspoiled Reaction", in Atlantic (Boston), March 1946.
> "The Appalachian Revolution", in The New Yorker, 11 September 1954.
> "The Hounds of Summer", in The New Yorker, 14 September 1963.

Other

> Sights and Spectacles, 1937–56.   New York, Farrar Straus, 1956; as Sights and
> Spectacles: Theatre Chronicles, 1937–58, London, Heinemann, 1959; augmented
> edition, as Mary McCarthy's Theatre Chronicles, 1937–62, New York, Farrar
> Straus, 1963.
> Venice Observed: Comments on Venetian Civilization.   New York, Reynal, and London,
> Zwemmer, 1956.
> Memories of a Catholic Girlhood.   New York, Harcourt Brace, and London, Heine-
> mann, 1957.
> The Stones of Florence.   New York, Harcourt Brace, and London, Heinemann, 1959.
> On the Contrary (essays).   New York, Farrar Straus, 1961; London, Heinemann, 1962.
> Vietnam.   New York, Harcourt Brace, and London, Weidenfeld and Nicolson, 1967.
> Hanoi.   New York, Harcourt Brace, and London, Weidenfeld and Nicolson, 1968.
> The Writing on the Wall (essays).   New York, Harcourt Brace, and London, Weiden-
> feld and Nicolson, 1970.

> Translator, The Iliad; or, The Poem of Force, by Simone Weil.   New York, Politics,
> 1948.
> Translator, On the Iliad, by Rachel Bespaloff.   New York, Pantheon Books, 1948.

Bibliography: Mary McCarthy: A Bibliography by Sherli Goldman, New York, Harcourt
Brace, 1968.

Critical Studies: interview with Elisabeth Niebuhr, in the *Paris Review*, Winter-Spring 1962; "Mary McCarthy", in *A View of My Own* by Elizabeth Hardwick, New York, Noonday Press, 1963; *Mary McCarthy* by Barbara McKenzie, New York, Twayne, 1966; *Mary McCarthy* by Irvin Stock, Minneapolis, University of Minnesota Press, 1968.

\*     \*     \*

Mary McCarthy was born in Seattle, Washington, of Irish and Jewish parentage, on 21 June 1912. In *Memories of a Catholic Girlhood*, she tells how she and her three brothers, one of them (Kevin) to become a stage and television actor, were orphaned by the 1918 influenza epidemic. Mary McCarthy was put into a convent and later into an Episcopalian school, after which she attended Vassar College along with several other distinguished-writers-to-be, including Muriel Rukeyser, Elizabeth Bishop, and Eleanor Clark, who joined forces in publishing an unofficial and anonymous magazine, *Con Spirito*. After her graduation from Vassar in 1933 (Phi Beta Kappa), Mary McCarthy went to New York and began reviewing for the liberal magazines. She attracted considerable and startled attention when, with Margaret Marshall, one of the editors of the *Nation*, she collaborated on a series of articles for that magazine, "Our Critics, Right or Wrong . . . ," which violently attacked the then current reviewing standards of the *New York Times*, the *New York Herald-Tribune*, and the *Saturday Review of Literature*.

Mary McCarthy married Harold Johnsrud, an actor, in 1933. Her second marriage, in 1938, was to the brilliant critic Edmund Wilson, by whom she had a son, Reuel, her only child. During their marriage she and Wilson lived mostly in New England, with a year's residence in the Middle West when he taught at the University of Chicago.

An active anti-Stalinist in left-wing literary circles in the 1930s, Mary McCarthy was a member of the Trotskyite faction and was an important contributor to what was then that group's lively journal, *The Partisan Review*. Like Edmund Wilson and several of their friends, she opposed the Second World War, though as it dragged on she became somewhat sympathetic to the Allied cause. She brought out her first book in 1942, *The Company She Keeps*, which she now calls a novel although it is actually a collection of thinly related stories. They are cutting, like her literary and dramatic criticism, and virtually all of them caricature the various people with whom the rather maladjusted girl in the stories comes into contact. The book was a critical success, and members of literary clans took a lively pleasure in identifying the originals of the male characters in the stories: the critic John Chamberlain has admitted he sat for the "Portrait of the Intellectual as a Yale Man," and Miss McCarthy has acknowledged the truth of this, although she further says that she barely knew him. The title story, admittedly based on experience, seemed to some readers, rightly or wrongly, to be a portrait of the one-time presidential candidate, Wendell L. Willkie.

After the Second World War, Mary McCarthy was a teacher at two small institutions in New York State, Bard College and Sarah Lawrence College. In 1946 she married Bowden Broadwater. Her next book was a volume of short stories, *Cast a Cold Eye*, including *The Oasis*, which had been published in New York in a hardback volume in 1949 (the 1950 London edition was called *A Source of Embarrassment*). *The Oasis*, another story of confused intellectuals, had taken up an entire issue of the English magazine *Horizon*, and in granting her that journal's prize its editor, Cyril Connolly, had said that although Mary McCarthy's writing was distinctively American, she derived "partly from the world of Congreve and Constant, of Elizabeth Bowen or Compton-Burnett or the Cambridge world of Virginia Woolf."

*The Groves of Academe*, a novel reflecting Mary McCarthy's experiences as a teacher, told of the efforts of a supposedly liberal college president trying to get rid of an inconvenient professor. The book attracted special interest because it appeared at the time of Senator Joseph McCarthy's hysterical attempts to find communists in government departments and in English departments. *The Groves of Academe* was all the more wickedly satiric not only because the easily recognisable president was made out to be squashy, but also because the professor under fire was a genuine scoundrel. As if to answer *The Groves of Academe*, the poet Randall Jarrell in 1954 brought out *Pictures from an Institution*, which lampooned a woman writer (as "Gertrude Johnson") who became a teacher and used the college which employed her as a place to spy out characters and situations for use in her stories.

Her novel *A Charmed Life*, again full of portraits taken from life, is notable for its erotic candor, particularly in the episode describing the seduction (half rape) of the remarried heroine by her former husband. By this time readers could see that Mary McCarthy's permanent style was journalistic, with long sentences here and there spiked by just the right adjectives, with frequently effective use of image and symbol.

In 1961, Mary McCarthy married James Raymond West, a member of the diplomatic service. Her next novel, *The Group*—a best seller in the United States and in parts of Europe—was an attempt to escape from autobiography by presenting the lives of eight Vassar girls, undergraduates together in 1933, for seven years after their graduation. But the author, although not obviously a character in the book, could not remain apart from the girls she dealt with, and, although their lives diverge somewhat, they all present various aspects of Mary McCarthy's vision of life, which by this time was dominated by the surface effects of American existence. The book is essentially plotless, and the girls never really develop as characters, but many readers in America and elsewhere overlooked these deficiencies and let themselves enjoy the book's socio-factual backgrounds and its pervasive cleverness.

*Vietnam* and *Hanoi* were traveler's reports embodying Miss McCarthy's dislike, shared by a majority of her fellow countrymen, of the undeclared war in Southeast Asia. She returned to America and Europe in a novel, *Birds of America*, which saw the former falling into ruin because packaged grocery items have replaced fresh foodstuff, and a Paris and a Rome bruised by tourists, most of them American. The concentration on trivialities again reveals Mary McCarthy as a social observer who can make lists of what she thinks is wrong, although they lead to nothing profound. The story is plotless—chiefly focusing on an adolescent boy in two summers spent with his mother on the New England coast and in part of his college study in Paris with a visit to Rome, where he feels the noisy Americans should be made to take qualifying examinations in art before being allowed to clutter up the Sistine Chapel. There is once more much cleverness in this book, and some shrewdly dramatized Parisian street scenes, but once again the plotless novel, peopled by a few caricatures rather than characters, leaves the serious reader essentially dissatisfied. The author, perhaps because she cares for ideas rather than people, has not yet lived up to her early promise as a writer of fiction.

—Harry T. Moore

---

**McCOURT, Edward (Alexander).** Irish. Born in Mullingar, 10 October 1907. Educated at the University of Alberta, Edmonton, 1927–32, B.A. (honors) in English 1932; Oxford University, 1932–35 (Rhodes Scholar), B.A. 1934, M.A. 1947. Married Margaret Mackay in 1938; has one child. English Master, Ridley College, St. Catherines, Ontario, 1935–36, and at Upper Canada College, Toronto, 1936–38; Lecturer, Queen's University, Kingston, Ontario, 1938–39; Professor of English, University of New Brunswick, Fredericton, 1939–44. Since 1944, Professor of English, University of Saskatchewan, Saskatoon. Recipient: Ryerson Award, 1947. Address: Department of English, University of Saskatchewan, Saskatoon, Saskatchewan, Canada.

PUBLICATIONS

Novels

The Flaming Hour.  Toronto, Ryerson Press, 1947.
Music at the Close.  Toronto, Ryerson Press, 1947.
Home Is the Stranger.  Toronto, Macmillan, 1950; London, Macmillan, 1951.
The Wooden Sword.  London, Barker, and Toronto, McClelland and Stewart, 1956.
Walk Through the Valley.  London, Barker, 1958.
Fasting Friar.  Toronto, McClelland and Stewart, 1963; as The Ettinger Affair, London, Macdonald, 1963.

Other

The Canadian West in Fiction.  Toronto, Ryerson Press, 1949.
Buckskin Brigadier: The Story of the Alberta Field Force (juvenile).  Toronto and London, Macmillan, and New York, St. Martin's Press, 1956.
Revolt in the West: The Story of the Riel Rebellion (juvenile).  Toronto and London, Macmillan, and New York, St. Martin's Press, 1958.
The Road Across Canada.  Toronto, Macmillan, New York, St. Martin's Press, and London, Murray, 1965.
Remember Butler: The Story of Sir William Butler.  London, Routledge, and Toronto, McClelland and Stewart, 1967.
Saskatchewan: The Traveller's Canada.  Toronto, Macmillan, and New York, St. Martin's Press, 1968; London, Macmillan, 1969.
The Yukon and the Northwest Territories.  Toronto, Macmillan, 1969; London, Macmillan, 1970.

Critical Study: "The Novels of Edward McCourt" by R. G. Baldwin, in Queen's Quarterly (Kingston, Ontario), Winter 1962.

Edward McCourt comments:

In my novels I have been particularly concerned with two things—the influence of environment on character, and the translation of life into literature. I have dealt almost exclusively with the environment with which I am most familiar—that of the Canadian prairies—and have consistently attempted to illustrate the impact of that environment on both natives and aliens.

*        *        *

For thirty years Edward McCourt has gone about his particular business of unearthing for Canadians some of their lateral roots, especially those nurtured in prairie soil. Occasionally, as in his early novel, Music at the Close, twenty years later in Remember [William] Butler, a fine biography of the nineteenth-century's loquacious soldier-traveller (who wrote best and at greatest length about the Canadian North-West), and in some of his sixty or so short stories, most written by the early fifties, he has been more than his characteristically competent self. But for the most part his publishers, almost all Canadian, have been content to have him work quietly away at what some critics have called the primary task of Canadian writers of recent years, explaining the country to its inhabitants by establishing its "background".

Several of his fifteen articles and occasional pieces, in addition to an adventure novel and two juvenile chronicles bearing on the Riel Rebellion, explore Canadian frontier and pioneer history; others, supplementing a book-length study of Western Canadian fiction, have over the years said perceptive things about letters in Canada. The country itself, in a variety of regional descriptions of one sort or another, has been his primary interest of late. These are all simply other vehicles for his abiding interest in things peculiarly Canadian that finds its chief expression in fiction, above all in the novel. His short stories vary greatly in quality, perhaps with the particular medium (which may simply be a way of saying that certain journals print certain kinds of material); but when he is not writing what he has privately called Tales Traded For Bread—technically skilful but insubstantial, sometimes contrived and journalistic pieces—he typically builds his stories on serious (regional) themes developed more fully in his novels.

In most of his books, McCourt has been concerned with the frustrated romantic who achieves fulfilment only when he stops spinning his life out of his own being and finds objectives in something bound to reality. In three of them he studies the prairie's peculiar influence on its people, especially where, as he says, the "profound psychological experiences of newcomers to a frontier community are concerned." His persistent themes in this regional literature, persistent and recurrent because indigenous, are therefore, not surprisingly, loneliness, exile and assimilation, monotony, conflict between groups of settlers, the mystical significance of labour to the prairie farmer, the possibilities for change in the new West. But to these familiar themes, found in *Music at the Close*, *Home Is the Stranger*, and *Walk Through the Valley*, McCourt has added one of his own which, while growing out of the special nature of the region, goes far beyond the limits of regional literature to probe some of the most critical issues that can confront a man or woman wherever located, issues that turn on the place of dreams and the imagination and romantic aspiration in the world of reality. This element in his work provides a conceptual pattern that comprehends all his novels, including the two which are *not* "regional," *The Wooden Sword*—a near clinical analysis of the breakdown of a schizoid academic—and *Fasting Friar* (in Britain, *The Ettinger Affair*)—a fictional reworking of a widely publicized case of academic intrigue in Canada.

Thus although McCourt's primary concern appears to be with people who are being tested by the prairie environment, intensely sensitive people who are experiencing the ordeal of coming to terms with the land or being crushed by it, his more fundamental subject is the relationship between romance and reality, still more generally, the process of awakening to life, depicted in certain crucial relationships often but not always conditioned by the prairie region. Traditional and conventional in the form he employs, somewhat low-pressure in general effect (though unguardedly sentimental at times), Edward McCourt nevertheless conveys in his pursuit of what might be called applied romanticism a tough-minded seriousness of purpose that gives his novels an additional dimension.

—R. G. Baldwin

---

**McGAHERN, John.**   Irish.   Born in Dublin, 12 November 1934. Educated at St. Patrick's, Dublin; University College, Dublin. Primary School Teacher. Research Fellow, University of Reading, Berkshire, 1968. During 1969, and since 1972, Visiting O'Connor Professor of Literature, Colgate University, Hamilton, New York. Recipient: A. E. Memorial Award, 1962; Macauley Fellowship, 1964; Arts Council Award, 1966, 1968, 1971. Address: c/o Faber and Faber Ltd., 3 Queen Square, London W.C.1, England.

PUBLICATIONS

Novels

  *The Barracks*.  London, Faber, 1963; New York, Macmillan, 1964.
  *The Dark*.  London, Faber, 1965; New York, Macmillan, 1966.

Short Stories

  *Nightlines*.  London, Faber, 1970; Boston, Little Brown, 1971.

Plays

  *Sinclair* (produced London, 1972).

  Has written plays for television.

\*      \*      \*

John McGahern achieved immediate fame with his first novel, *The Barracks*. The opening scene—a kitchen interior with a woman darning in the dying twilight, surrounded by her stepchildren—seemed as comfortable as the first act of an old Abbey play. What was new and startling was the quality of the writing; Irish provincial life had never been transcribed with such exactness before. "It was wonderful to feel the warm rug on the sofa with their hands, the lamplight so soft and yellow on the things of the kitchen, the ash branches crackling and blazing up through the turf on the fire; and the lulls of silence were full of the hissing of the sap that frothed white on their ends." Lovingly recorded, these details are yet presented without any protective sentimentality. Regionalists like Francis MacManus and Michael MacLaverty had evoked the details of Irish country life as part of a pattern, a way of belief, suggesting that unhurriedness was all. But McGahern rips all this away, showing that man, as well as nature, was as "red in tooth and claw" in Ireland as elsewhere: "They all lived on each other and devoured each other as they themselves were devoured, who would devour whom the first was the one question."

So Elizabeth Regan reflects at the end of her life, the end of the book. This brilliant study (especially for a young writer in his mid-twenties) of the mind of a dying woman inevitably recalls *Madame Bovary*, both in its subject-matter and the poetic detail of its style. But if McGahern's work is technically anachronistic there is a dimension of sympathy which is absent in Flaubert. Emma Bovary's death is recorded with clinical distaste; although there is a brief look of peace on her face when she receives the Last Sacraments, she never breaks through to the almost mystical acceptance of Elizabeth Regan: "All real seeing grew into smiling and if it moved to speech it must be praise . . . she had come to life out of mystery and would return, it safely held it as by hands . . . ."

The other main character in *The Barracks* is not a seducer but a police sergeant, more pathetic even than his sick wife in his baffled, male violence. This dominant figure appears again in *The Dark* where the ebb and flow of his struggle with his eldest son provide most of the structure of the book. Now all feminine gentleness has disappeared, and McGahern's keening rage against the emptiness of life takes over. Like the adolescent hero we are soiled and insulted by the ordeal of growing up under the double pressures of poverty and piety. Short chapters and flowing, often punctuationless sentences, leave no escape: we have moved from the calm detail of Flaubert to the involving claustrophobia of a Mauriac. And further, for we are not allowed the grim consolations of Jansenism: it is not evil which rules the world but the hopeless clash of our needs. "It seemed that the whole world must turn over in the night and howl in its boredom. . . ."

There is no alleviation of this vision in his collection of stories, *Nightlines*, but there are some extensions of theme and background. "Summer in Strandhill," "Bomb Box", "Korea", still focus on the narrow world of childhood, with its humiliations and adult enforced boredom. There is, however, a more varied treatment of sex; if McGahern had achieved notoriety in Ireland for the masturbation scenes in *The Dark*, the physical relationship between wife and husband in *The Barracks* was treated with unusual tact. The stories move from the familiar initiation theme of "Coming into His Kingdom", through the youthful frustration of "My Love, My Umbrella", to the analysis of a disintegrating marriage in "Peaches". The latter is set in Spain, but neither travel nor love can finally dissolve childhood patterns of guilt and conflict, and we are left with the crude message of the story about building site labourers in London, "Lungs of Oak and Bellies of Brass": "pork chops, pints of bitter and a good old ride before you sleep, that's fukken ambition." Here as elsewhere, McGahern's stripped style approaches self-parody but his emotional honesty and his ear for dialogue make him a harrowing witness of the void which underlies a good deal of Irish, and perhaps modern, life.

—John Montague

---

**McHALE, Tom.** American. Grew up in Scranton, Pennsylvania. Educated at Jesuit schools; Temple University, Philadelphia, graduated 1963; University of Pennsylvania, Philadelphia; University of Iowa, Iowa City. Since 1971, Writer-in-Residence, Monmouth College, West Long Beach, New Jersey. Address: c/o Viking Press, 625 Madison Avenue, New York, New York 10022, U.S.A.

PUBLICATIONS

Novels

   *Principato.*   New York, Viking Press, 1970; London, Joseph, 1971.
   *Farragan's Retreat.*   New York, Viking Press, and London, Joseph, 1971.

*       *       *

Joseph Heller's *Catch-22* established the popularity of the absurdist novel for the 60's. Among the lesser writers who explored this position in the 70's is Tom McHale, whose two novels are tragi-comic, nihilistic, yet sympathetic to the pains of the protagonists. Both Angelo Principato of *Principato* and Arthur Farragan of *Farragan's Retreat* are destroyed by their growing ability to see through the categories of presumed reality, and by their half optimistic, half mindless decency.

The treatment of these Candides, however, is Rabelaisian. A host of absurdly cruel, crass and improbable incidents contrive to teach them that everything is the opposite of what it seems. The Mother Superior encourages Principato's nun-sister to meet her lover in the convent, and Farragan's frigid, pious, loony wife swings with a supposedly castrated lifeguard. Both protagonists are men who too rapidly begin seeing these impossible realities. However, in *Principato*, we are given a man who is disillusioned as the accidents of life and the manipulations of his father show him the truth behind appearances, while Arthur Farragan's existential sufferings derive, the end reveals, from his own actions.

"The church", Nick tells Principato, "is a frigging cancer. You're either with it all the way like you, or limping along outside within shouting distance like me. But you never really get free of it." McHale himself is not limping, but vigorously running in a ring around the rosary. The Catholic motif is everywhere, the Catholicism of the characters essentially informs their actions, and yet the novels are remote from the Catholic novel of Evelyn Waugh and Graham Greene. These are not crises of soul and self, but pseudo-involvements with the symbols of the matter. Principato's wife lusts unashamedly after her young neighbor while staring at the four-foot tall luminescent statue of the Virgin Mary he has given her. Farragan's sister Anna keeps a rosary wrapped around the pistol she carries, to insure perfect aim on the inevitable day a black rapist attacks her. Flocks of St. Christopher's medals and flocks of avaricious priests suggest the cancerous pervasiveness of the Church.

Nevertheless, it is not the often pointed-up corruptions of the Church, but those of the people which are significant. And in many cases the point is not that the Church has corrupted them, but that it can be used as an excuse for their brutal behaviour. McHale's families are pious, rich, shanty Irish Philadelphians. Mother Corrigan of *Principato* is echoed in "the one, true Mother" Farragan, and her clan's primal devotion to her, a devotion little changed by their discovery that she sent one brother to death in the war, not because she believed in patriotism (like the Church, patriotism is an excuse), but because she had caught him in a homosexual act. These mothers, like the police, "have the key to everything."

McHale's characterizations are brutal, multi-dimensional caricatures; the children of the weak Angelo Principato are so lifeless they literally shun the sun like moles; his crippled brother is both childishly and sexually sadistic. These characters are frequently discovered by the protagonists in scenes which fix into tableaus and which they watch with a hypnotized terror.

There is more tension, more purpose, and a more pointed and controlled irony in *Farragan's Retreat* than in *Principato*. These two novels, which appeared less than a year apart, promise an unusual fertility and demonstrate a growth of novelistic technique and control of theme.

—Jeanne Desy

---

**MENEN, (Salvator) Aubrey (Clarence).** British. Born in London, 22 April 1912. Educated at University College, London, 1930–32. Drama Critic, *The Bookman*, London, 1934; Director, The Experimental Theatre, London, 1935–36; worked for Personalities Press Service, London, 1937–39. Head of the English Drama Department, All-India Radio, 1940–41; Script Editor, Information Films, Government of India, 1943–45; Education Officer, Backward Tribes, Indian Political Department, 1946. Head of the Motion Picture Department, J. Walter Thompson Company, London, 1947–48. Now lives in Rome. Address: c/o Mrs. Lois Wallace, William Morris Agency, 1350 Avenue of the Americas, New York, New York 10019, U.S.A.

PUBLICATIONS

Novels

*The Prevalence of Witches.*   London, Chatto and Windus, 1947; New York, Scribner, 1948.
*The Stumbling Stone.*   London, Chatto and Windus, and New York, Scribner, 1949.
*The Backward Bride: A Sicilian Scherzo.*   London, Chatto and Windus, and New York, Scribner, 1950.
*The Duke of Gallodoro.*   London, Chatto and Windus, and New York, Scribner, 1952.
*Rama Retold.*   London, Chatto and Windus, 1954; as *The Ramayana*, New York, Scribner, 1954.
*The Abode of Love: The Conception, Financing and Daily Routine of an English Harem in the Middle of the Nineteenth Century Described in the Form of a Novel.*   New York, Scribner, 1956; London, Chatto and Windus, 1957.
*The Fig Tree.*   London, Chatto and Windus, and New York, Scribner, 1959.
*SheLa: A Satire.*   New York, Random House, 1962; London, Hamish Hamilton, 1963.
*A Conspiracy of Women.*   New York, Random House, 1965; London, Hamish Hamilton, 1966.

Other

*Dead Man in the Silver Market.*   New York, Scribner, 1954; as *Dead Man in the Silver Market: An Autobiographical Essay on National Prides*, London, Chatto and Windus, 1954.
*Rome for Ourselves.*   New York, McGraw Hill, 1960; as *Rome Revealed*, London, Thames and Hudson, 1960.
*Speaking the Language Like a Native: Aubrey Menen on Italy.*   New York, McGraw Hill, 1962; London, Hamish Hamilton, 1963.
*India.*   New York, McGraw Hill, and London, Thames and Hudson, 1969.
*The Space Within the Heart* (autobiography).   New York, McGraw Hill, and London, Hamish Hamilton, 1970.

Manuscript Collection: Boston University.

\*       \*       \*

Aubrey Menen is perhaps the finest satirist writing in English today, and it is strongly to his credit that he is more concerned with amusing than he is with reforming. Satirists fare better in more simple eras, and the present cynical age has shown little appreciation for satirical writing. Aubrey Menen reminds one of Aldous Huxley or of Norman Douglas, except that he does not possess their mastery of social comedy. Nor is he as viciously humorous as Evelyn Waugh. As he himself has put it, "The message of at least one kind of satirist is that human nature is corrupt, but that this is not necessarily either a disastrous or a melancholy thing." He seems to be especially equipped for his amusing forays upon human foibles by virtue of his parentage of an Indian father and an Irish mother. Nor should it be any surprise that Menen was discovered by H. G. Wells, himself a social satirist who wrote novels of ideas in a sophisticated manner. What has most hurt the critical reputation of Menen is that the novel of ideas has not had a fair reading in the post-Freudian age in which the psychological novel reigns supreme. Menen, without apology, uses the novel as a vehicle for his ideas, and in the process he employs but shallow characterization and sketchy psychological description. At the same time, his works hardly follow the traditional novel form. The essays that appear within the novels are always witty and entertaining, showing little use for false intellectual obscurity. In addition, the dialogue of his characters is invariably lively and sophisticated.

Menen uses a wide-angle lens when he chooses subjects for attack. The Devil in *SheLa* might be speaking for the author in explaining the need to laugh at man's stupidity: "If anyone could recall all the collective idiocies that had taken place in his own lifetime, he would go out of his mind." Menen's most persistent theme is the sickness of modern nationalism, from the absurd posturing of supposedly advanced nations like the United States to the ridiculous pretentions of the new African nations. His special quality is that he is not afraid to attack sacred cows. In *The Backward Bride*, false intellectualism is made the butt of his scorn. In a more wide-ranging attack, *The Abode of Love*, the story of a harem in Victorian England, makes fun of conventional religion, morality, and economics. The author has a rare quality for a satirist, and that is his sympathy with his characters. While he might despise pretentious intellectuals and blundering politicians, he shows warm feeling towards those who are victims of powers larger than themselves. The native Indians in *The Prevalence of Witches* are victims of the British law; the heroine of *The Backward Bride* is under attack for her simple beliefs by exponents of modern intellectualism, from existentialism to psychoanalysis. In *SheLa*, two innocent Dalai Lamas, one male (HeLa) and one female (SheLa), are used as pawns to attain influence in the Far East by the great powers, the United States and Russia. The focus of attack is Western rationalism which is mirrored in the talk of God and his angels. Menen undoubtedly sympathizes with the Devil and Buddha whose intuitive thought and relativism are the antithesis of the rationalism and power he is attacking. Again, Menen might himself be speaking through the Devil to make a comment on his total work: "I have no interest in people who feel themselves wicked. I am fascinated, on the other hand, by people who are sure that they are good. I set them a little trap to prove that they are not . . . . As I always say, think what conceited opinions people would have of themselves if it were not for the Devil."

—Laurence Ries

---

**MICHENER, James A(lbert).** American. Born in New York City, 3 February 1907. Educated at Doylestown High School, Pennsylvania; Swarthmore College, Pennsylvania, A.B. (summa cum laude) 1929 (Phi Beta Kappa); University of Northern Colorado, Greeley, A.M. 1936; University of St. Andrews, Scotland. Served in the United States Navy, rising to the rank of Lieutenant Commander, 1944–45. Married Patti Koon in 1935 (divorced, 1948); Vange Nord, 1948 (divorced, 1955); Mari Yoriko Sabusawa, 1955. Master, Hill School, Pottstown, Pennsylvania, 1929–31, and George School, Newtown, Pennsylvania, 1934–36; Professor, University of Northern Colorado, 1936–40; Visiting Professor, Harvard University, Cambridge, Massachusetts, 1940–41; Associate Editor, The Macmillan Company, New York, 1941–49. Free-Lance Writer since 1949. Member, Advisory Committee on the Arts, United States Department of State, 1957; Chairman, President Kennedy's Food for Peace Program, 1961; Secretary, Pennsylvania Constitution Convention, 1967–68. Since 1971, Member of the United States Advisory Commission on Information, Washington, D.C. Recipient: Pulitzer Prize, 1948; National Association of Independent Schools Award, 1954, 1958; Einstein Award, 1967. D.H.L., Swarthmore College, 1954; LL.D., Temple University, Philadelphia, 1957; Litt.D., Washington University, St. Louis, 1967. Address: P.O. Box 125, Pipersville, Pennsylvania 18947, U.S.A.

PUBLICATIONS

Novels

> The Fires of Spring.   New York, Random House, 1949.
> The Bridges at Toko-Ri.   New York, Random House, and London, Secker and
>   Warburg, 1953.
> Sayonara.   New York, Random House, and London, Secker and Warburg, 1954.
> The Bridge at Andau.   New York, Random House, and London, Secker and Warburg,
>   1957.
> Hawaii.   New York, Random House, 1959; London, Secker and Warburg, 1960.
> Caravans.   New York, Random House, 1963; London, Secker and Warburg, 1964.
> The Source.   New York, Random House, and London, Secker and Warburg, 1965.
> The Drifters.   New York, Random House, and London, Secker and Warburg, 1971.

Short Stories

> Tales of the South Pacific.   New York, Macmillan, and London, Macmillan, 1947.
> Return to Paradise.   New York, Random House, and London, Secker and Warburg,
>   1951.

Other

> The Unit in the Social Sciences, with Harold Long.   Cambridge, Massachusetts,
>   Harvard University Graduate School of Education, 1940.
> The Voice of Asia.   New York, Random House, 1951; London, Secker and Warburg,
>   1952.
> The Floating World (on Japanese art).   New York, Random House, 1954; London,
>   Secker and Warburg, 1955.
> Rascals in Paradise, with A. Grove Day.   New York, Random House, and London,
>   Secker and Warburg, 1957.
> Selected Writings.   New York, Modern Library, 1957.
> Japanese Prints from the Early Masters to the Moderns.   Rutland, Vermont, Tuttle,
>   and London, Paterson, 1959.
> Report of the County Chairman.   New York, Random House, and London, Secker
>   and Warburg, 1961.
> Iberia: Spanish Travels and Reflections.   New York, Random House, and London,
>   Secker and Warburg, 1968.
> The Modern Japanese Print: An Appreciation.   Rutland, Vermont, Tuttle, 1968.
> Presidential Lottery: The Reckless Gamble in Our Electoral System.   New York,
>   Random House, 1969.
> The Quality of Life.   Philadelphia, Lippincott, 1970; London, Secker and Warburg,
>   1971.
> Facing East: A Study of the Art of Jack Levine.   New York, Random House, 1970.
> Kent State.   New York, Random House, and London, Secker and Warburg, 1971.

> Editor, The Future of the Social Sciences: Proposals for an Experimental Social-Studies
>   Curriculum.   New York, National Council for the Social Sciences, 1939.
> Editor, Sketch-Books, by Hokusai.   Rutland, Vermont, Tuttle, 1958.

Bibliography: in James Michener by A. Grove Day, New York, Twayne, 1964.

Manuscript Collection: Library of Congress, Washington, D.C.

James A. Michener comments:

I had the good fortune to arrive on the scene when America was broadening its intellectual horizons to include the entire world. Millions of our men would experience the South Pacific; millions of families would live in Japan or Germany, and countries like Great Britain and Italy became commonplace adventures. Had I written as I did twenty years earlier, I doubt seriously that I would have enjoyed much of a readership. America was not only prepared for what I had to say, but apparently eager to hear it.

Also, I came along when the television set was about to command the attention of the middle American family to the exclusion of almost all else, and I made a conscious decision: "If they look at television long enough, they will grow hungry for the more substantial experience they can get only through books," and it became evident to me that instead of abandoning reading, the people I was aiming at would demand more of it, and would be prepared to accept long and difficult books, would indeed seek them out. In this judgment I was confirmed.

I am sometimes thought of, for these reasons, as an exotic writer. On the contrary, I have worked in an unusually wide spectrum of human experience, from politics to ecology to education to Asian art to the fine arts. I have also worked in these fields, having been an active politician and a connoisseur of the arts. My life has been therefore a vain attempt to keep many interests in balance, and my books have been proof of how one or the other of those interests has run away with me from time to time.

My style has always been deceptively simple, and I have worked assiduously to keep it that way. This requires not only careful writing, but endless rewriting, redrafting, rejection, and final polishing. I find that I work principally in a Latinized vocabulary, in fairly long sentences; revision consists of going back to simpler Anglo-Saxon words and shorter sentences. My ideals have been Henry James, Gustave Flaubert and Ivan Turgenev, whom I have never tried to ape, and William Thackeray, Honoré Balzac, Leo Tolstoy and Samuel Butler, whom I have. My influences have thus been almost exclusively European rather than American, a consequence of my education, and I have always felt this to have been a pity.

*     *     *

James Albert Michener is the author of eight novels, two collections of short stories, fifteen book-length works and over 100 articles. The sheer bulk of his writings and his grasp of widely disparate areas of knowledge awe his reader. Japanese prints, Spanish life, the disturbance at Kent State, the problems of drugs and pollution—all find expression. His intensive research of each topic is minutely shared with his reader. *Hawaii* can survive such detailed treatment as the creation of the Pacific islands, and the novel gains; but in *Caravans* and again in *The Source* the research almost takes over, to the detriment of the plot.

Michener does not fit well into the traditional classifications for writers. A novelist, yes. No one would dispute his claim. But his first, and still his most famous work, *Tales of the South Pacific*, is rather a collection of short stories, vignettes beautifully etched, loosely unified by the story of the invasion of Kuralei. It is this work that reveals most cogently Michener's characteristics. He is the inveterate story teller, not the writer of long novels of intricate design and unity. His long novels suffer from this lack of unity. Whereas in *Tales* he focuses on one or two characters in each of his brief glimpses into life on the Pacific atolls—Tony Fry, Bloody Mary, the Remittance man—in a work such as *The Source* he moves so rapidly from the present to 9834 BC and back again that the reader is lost in the flurry of prehistoric dust and artifacts. The main thread of the novel lacks firm development and the characters suffer in credibility.

This deficiency is particularly noticeable in his women and in his complete omission of children. His women are often stereotypes, the general's wife in *Sayonara* and Brubaker's wife in *The Bridges at Toko-Ri*. The brutal spinster aunt and the grotesque Gonoph in *The Fires of Spring* are the first in a long list of women far removed from normal domestic happiness. In *Tales* many of the native women represent the escape image for his men; they are almost part of the setting. He can delineate women, but those characteristics that ennoble them are such masculine qualities as sacrifice (Hana-ogi in *Sayonara*) or brute strength and determination (Wu Chow's Auntie in *Hawaii*). His women who live do so because they are in essense interchangeable with his men.

It is Michener's men of nobility and decency who crowd the memory of his reader. He writes of that which he admires. Sometimes the hortatory impulses take control, and the novels suffer, with his characters becoming the mouthpieces for his views. But his prose is fluid and rich, beautifully descriptive, precise and clear. There is little that is esoteric, and symbolism is almost non-existent. Nor are there passages that require interpretation beyond the obvious. It is perhaps his desire to present his strong convictions that causes him to use a straightforward, indeed journalistic style at times, as in *The Bridge at Andau*.

As Michener has grown older, his novels have developed in size and in diversity. In the early works he displayed a singleness of purpose and a control over his material that are disturbingly absent from his most recent writings. *Tales*, *The Bridges at Toko-Ri* and *Sayonara* reveal organization and unity. Perhaps it is because they are brief and might well be classified as long short stories. *Caravans*, *The Source*, and *The Drifters* confuse the reader with their crowds of characters, their canvasses that stretch from one horizon to the other, and themes that not even 800 pages can develop adequately. It is as though Michener realizes most vividly that he does not "have an infinite number of works left to write" and he wants to put all that he has into those he writes. He would do well to limit his scope. But one might well respond that *Hawaii* can support the weight of all its material. The prose is vibrant and moving, and the reader is quickly caught up in its life. And it will continue to make the name of Michener "count very heavily."

—Sarah Evelyn Jackson

---

**MIDDLETON, O(sman) E(dward).** New Zealander. Born in Christchurch, 25 March 1925. Educated at New Plymouth Boys High School, 1939–41; Auckland University, 1946, 1948; the Sorbonne, Paris (New Zealand Government Bursary), 1955–56. Served in the Royal New Zealand Air Force, 1944–45. Married Maida Edith Middleton (marriage dissolved); has two children. Recipient: New Zealand Literary Fund Award, 1959, and Scholarship, 1965; Hubert Church Award, 1964; Robert Burns Fellowship, University of Otago, 1970. Address: c/o Department of English, University of Otago, Dunedin, New Zealand.

PUBLICATIONS

Short Stories

*Short Stories.* Wellington, Handcraft Press, 1953.
*The Stone and Other Stories.* Auckland, Pilgrim Press-Paul, 1959.

*A Walk on the Beach.*   London, Joseph, 1964.
*The Loners.*   Wellington, Square & Circle, 1972.


Verse

*Six Poems.*   Wellington, Handcraft Press, 1951.

Other

*From the River to the Tide* (juvenile).   Wellington, School Publications Branch, 1964.


Manuscript Collections: Auckland Public Library; Hocken Library, Dunedin.


Critical Study: *New Zealand Fiction since 1945* by H. Winston Rhodes, Dunedin, McIndoe, 1968.


O. E. Middleton comments:

My published fiction comprises two novellas, several dozen short stories and a work for children. Unpublished material includes two novels and numerous stories.

It is not my wish to explain, analyse or otherwise obscure what I have sought to render in fictional terms. I should feel that I had failed as a writer if my work did not speak for itself.

*       *       *

As a short story writer primarily devoted to the New Zealand scene, O. E. Middleton remains faithful to the tradition of unsophisticated realism. He is less interested in technical innovation than in his wide experience of people and places at home and abroad, less attracted to ironic or symbolic patterns than to the rhythms of the spoken language and the texture of the workaday world. The titles of his best-known collections, *The Stone and Other Stories* and *A Walk on the Beach*, are symptomatic of an unpretentious manner and direct approach to subject-matter that is rarely remote from the commonplace, but is raised to a level of significance by its truth of substance.

Unlike some writers held in greater esteem, he never adopts an authorial position from which he finds it convenient to look down on the antics of his characters with fastidious disapproval or superior sensibility. On the contrary he is always democratically at ease in the scene and among the people he has created. The narrators of "The Corporal's Story" and "The Greaser's Story" are familiar with their occupations and in harmony with their backgrounds.

Middleton populates his fictional world with labourers and seamen, farmers and city-dwellers, Europeans and Maoris, children and adolescents. They are ordinary people, generally unremarkable for subtlety of thought or emotion; and the incidents related are associated with their normal activities during work and leisure. Their understanding is limited and their conversation borders on the banal; but what must be lost in felicity of expression is gained in authenticity and restraint. "A Married Man" concludes tritely with "'Never mind,' she said, smiling and friendly, 'It will come right in the end.'" The narrator of "A Day by Itself" observes "It had been a funny day really, and there were things about it which I still didn't understand." Even when stories are based on episodes derived from the eventful years of the writer's wanderings, both language and character become absorbed into the raw material of life.

Despite the absence of any guide-lines which can be attributed to the author, a moral sensibility is distinctly present in choice of theme, development of action and establishment of character. A particular kind of neo-colonial egalitarian humanism informs every aspect of his writing and is readily detected in what he has called "sorties into the No-man's-land of inter-racial relations." The narrator of "Not for a Seagull" is a young Maori who in his daily life is constantly made aware that good fellowship can mask attitudes of discrimination; but elsewhere, as Middleton reveals more by selection than by overt statement, wider human relations are not devoid of exclusiveness.

Surprisingly enough, however, the didacticism latent in such themes does not often obtrude. Middleton is too honest a craftsman to allow strongly held opinions to falsify his representation of the life he has both experienced and observed. His characters are rarely lonely individuals, but play their parts in the diverse activities of the communities in which they find themselves, with the result that any temptation to over-emphasise private perplexities is checked by the recognition of otherness, and Middleton is able both to explore his chosen terrain and disclose rather than publish his humane attitudes.

—H. Winston Rhodes

---

**MIDDLETON, Stanley.** British. Born in Bulwell, Nottingham, 1 August 1919. Educated at High Pavement School, Nottingham; University College of Nottingham, now Nottingham University, 1938–40, 1946–47, B.A. (London) 1940; M.Ed. (Nottingham) 1952. Served in the Royal Artillery and the Army Education Corps, 1940–46. Married Margaret Shirley Welch in 1951; has two children. Since 1947, English Master, and since 1958, Head of the English Department, High Pavement School, Nottingham. Address: 42 Caledon Road, Sherwood, Nottingham NG5 2NG, England.

PUBLICATIONS

Novels

    *A Short Answer.* London, Hutchinson, 1958.
    *Harris's Requiem.* London, Hutchinson, 1960.
    *A Serious Woman.* London, Hutchinson, 1961.
    *The Just Exchange.* London, Hutchinson, 1962.
    *Two's Company.* London, Hutchinson, 1963.
    *Him They Compelled.* London, Hutchinson, 1964.
    *Terms of Reference.* London, Hutchinson, 1966.
    *The Golden Evening.* London, Hutchinson, 1968.
    *Wages of Virtue.* London, Hutchinson, 1969.
    *Apple of the Eye.* London, Hutchinson, 1970.
    *Brazen Prison.* London, Hutchinson, 1971.
    *Cold Gradations.* London, Hutchinson, 1972.

Play

Play produced on BBC radio, 1972.

Manuscript Collection: Central Library, Nottingham.

Stanley Middleton comments:

I put down a few obvious points about my novels.

They are set mainly in the English midlands with characters drawn from the professional middle-classes (students, teachers, actors, writers, architects), though one will find labourers and factory-workers as well as businessmen of real affluence.

The action usually occupies a short period of some months only (*Wages of Virtue* is an exception), and the plot deals with people in a state of crisis or perplexity caused by illness and death, or a breakdown of personal relationships, or the difficulties of creating a work of art (which may be music, *Harris's Requiem*, or poetry, *Him They Compelled*, or a novel in *Brazen Prison*). At this time of dilemmas, friends or relatives intervene, and thus learn their own inadequacies and, sometimes, strengths. No perfect characters or solutions exist; all is difficult, compromising, but a bonus of success or joy is occasionally found.

My idea is not only to tell an interesting story but to demonstrate the complexity of human character and motive. One must not only describe what has happened to people, or what they are like; one must make the characters live out what they are said to be, and this must include deviations from normality and actions "out of character". I find this most difficult, but when I am charged, sometimes, with "mere reportage", I can see no sense at all in the accusation. My novels are imaginative attempts to write down illuminating actions and talk from the lives of fictional people, and not transcriptions of tape-recordings of real conversations or blow-by-blow commentaries on events which have really taken place. I am sometimes praised for the "realism" of my dialogue, and this makes me wonder if these critics, who may of course be using a "shorthand" dictated by the small space at their disposal, know how different my sort of dialogue is from that of real life.

This preoccupation leads to a choice of different levels of writing. A novel cannot always be intense; both by the shape of my work and my use of language I try constantly to interfere with the reader, to rest him as well as violently assault him. Therefore it is galling when I find critics who apparently subscribe to the notion that contemporary novels are either "well-written" (i.e. in "mandarin") or dashed down without care. Mine are usually dumped by such people in the second category. Shifts on my part from the point-of-view of one character to that of another also seem to pass unnoticed.

I am often asked if my novels are didactic. I wouldn't object to that word since the greatest work of art I know—Bach's *St. Matthew Passion*—could be so described. But unless a novel is complex, memorable, capable of holding a reader and moving him deeply, I've not much time for it.

I can't think these notes very helpful. General exegesis as opposed to critical discussion of precise points in specific books has little attraction for me as a writer. A novel should be its own defence; if it does not speak for itself to a well-equipped reader, call out echoes in him, it's not properly written.

*        *        *

When the novels of Stanley Middleton first appeared he was grouped rather too quickly with the regional, kitchen sink novelists who set the trend in the late fifties. Then possibly because he works and writes in and about Nottingham and realises that the act of copulation is central to human motivation, his critics started to compare him with Lawrence. However it is those who see in his novels some of the qualities of E. M. Forster who are perhaps somewhat nearer the mark, an observation supported by the fact that the novelist in *Brazen Prison* is at work on a book which has some affinities in setting and concern with *A Passage to India*.

But all these allusions really emphasise the difficulties which reviewers have in attempting to describe the individual quality of this novelist, who has the rare and surprising gift of making all his characters at the same time both unlikeable and interesting. His women for the most part are tormented frigid tormentors, while his affluent middle class men are mediocrities in their professions and indecisive shamblers in their personal lives. What he has grasped is that people at the end of their tether do not become heroic and loveable through suffering. An emotional snarl-up makes people selfish, irritable and dull. The skill of the dialogue here is that, although the first two qualities are caught, the third is avoided because the reader is held by the way the remarks of one speaker rasp on those of the other.

This is especially true when the participants in the dialogue try to meet across the gaps of generation, social class and economic status. In *Terms of Reference* the two late-middle-aged couples are perplexed and powerless when confronted by the failure of the marriage between the son of the very wealthy pair and the daughter of the academically respectable ones. Yet although they can do nothing to hold their wayward children together, and are by no means altogether certain that it would be a good thing to do so, all four of them are too fascinated by the situation to leave it alone.

Edward Tenby, the architect hero of *Apple of the Eye*, is not only the sole moderately creative and productive character in the novel, he is also the only viable male. He becomes involved with three neurotic women, all young enough to be his daughters. One of them is of sufficient wealth to be able to indulge her sickness to its limit, while the other two are poor enough to be flattered and astounded at making any contact with a man in his position. In *Brazen Prison*, the ex-grammar schoolboy novelist, Charles Stead, has to cope with the social nuances of relating to his wealthy socialite wife and her friends, while at the same time involving himself with the husband and family of the local girl he'd picked up in the dance halls of his youth.

Because all these people are caught in a crisis point of their lives, they lay aside the masks that make the usual run of social intercourse both possible and dull. They speak completely out of their personality, circumstance and background, right down to the endless and infuriating 'er, umph, er's of Professor Dodds-Walker in *Terms of Reference*. That despite it all these people do somehow get something over to each other is the surprising optimism of these bleak novels.

—Shirley Toulson

---

**MILLER, Henry (Valentine).** American. Born in Yorkville, New York, 26 December 1891. Attended the City College of New York, 1909. Married Beatrice Sylvas Wickens in 1917 (divorced, 1924); June Edith Smith, 1924 (divorced, 1934); Martha Lepska, 1944 (divorced, 1952); Eve McClure, 1953 (divorced); Hoki Tokuda, 1967; has three children. Has held many jobs: with the Atlas Portland Cement Company, New York, 1909; Reporter, Washington, D.C., 1917; with the Bureau of Economic Research, New York, 1919; Employment Manager, Western Union Telegraph Company, New York, 1920–24. Lived in Europe, 1930–39: Proofreader, *Chicago Tribune* Paris edition, 1932; Teacher at the Lycée Carnot, Dijon, 1932; Psychoanalyst, 1936; Editor, with Lawrence Durrell and Alfred Perles, *The Booster* (later named *Delta*), Paris, 1937–38; Continental Editor, *Volontes*, Paris, 1938–39;

European Editor, *Phoenix*, Woodstock, New York, 1938–39. Returned to the United States in 1940; has lived in California since 1942. Also an artist: has exhibited watercolors in New York, 1927, London, 1944, Los Angeles, 1966. Recipient: Formentor Prize Committee Citation, 1961. Member, National Institute of Arts and Letters, 1957. Address: 444 Ocampo Drive, Pacific Palisades, California 90272, U.S.A.

## PUBLICATIONS

### Novels

*Tropic of Cancer*.   Paris, Obelisk Press, 1934; New York, Grove Press, 1961; London, John Calder, 1963.
*Black Spring*.   Paris, Obelisk Press, 1936; New York, Grove Press, 1963; London, John Calder, 1965.
*Tropic of Capricorn*.   Paris, Obelisk Press, 1939; New York, Grove Press, 1961; London, John Calder, 1964.
*The Rosy Crucifixion:*
  *Sexus*.   Paris, Obelisk Press, 2 vols., 1949; New York, Grove Press, 1965; London, Weidenfeld and Nicolson, 1969.
  *Plexus*.   Paris, Olympia Press, 2 vols., 1953; London, Widenfeld and Nicolson, 1963; New York, Grove Press, 1965.
  *Nexus*.   Paris, Olympia Press, 1960; London, Weidenfeld and Nicolson, 1964; New York, Grove Press, 1965.
*Quiet Days in Clichy*.   Paris, Olympia Press, 1956; New York, Grove Press, 1965; London, Calder and Boyars, 1966.

### Plays

*Scenario: A Film with Sound*.   Paris, Obelisk Press, 1937.
*Just Wild about Harry: A Melo-Melo in 7 Scenes* (produced Spoleto, Italy, 1963). New York, New Directions, 1963; London, MacGibbon and Kee, 1964.

### Other

*What Are You Going to Do about Alf?*   Paris, Lecram Servant, 1935; Berkeley. California, Bern Porter, 1944.
*Aller Retour New York*.   Paris, Obelisk Press, 1935; Mohegan Lake, New York, Argus, 1945.
*Money and How It Gets That Way*.   Paris, Booster Publications, 1938; Sausalito, California, Bern Porter, 1946.
*Max and the White Phagocytes*.   Paris, Obelisk Press, 1938.
*The Cosmological Eye*.   New York, New Directions, 1939; London, Editions Poetry, 1945.
*Hamlet*, with Michael Fraenkel.   New York, Carrefour, 2 vols., 1939, 1941; London. Carrefour, 1962.
*The World of Sex*.   Chicago, Argus Bookshop, 1940; revised edition, Paris, Olympia Press, 1957; New York, Grove Press, 1965.
*Wisdom of the Heart*.   New York, New Directions, 1941; London, Editions Poetry, 1947.

*The Colossus of Maroussi; or, The Spirit of Greece.* San Francisco, Colt Press, 1941;
    London, Secker and Warburg, 1942.
*The Angel Is My Watermark.* Fullerton, California, Holve Barrows, 1944.
*Sunday after the War.* New York, New Directions, 1944; London, Editions Poetry,
    1947.
*The Plight of the Creative Artist in the United States of America.* Houlton, Maine,
    Bern Porter, 1944.
*Semblance of a Devoted Past.* Berkeley, California, Bern Porter, 1944; unexpurgated
    edition, with *To Paint Is to Love Again*, New York, Grossman, 1968.
*Echolalia: Reproductions of Water Colors by Henry Miller.* Berkeley, California,
    Bern Porter, 1945.
*Why Abstract?*, with Hilaire Hiler and William Saroyan. New York, New Directions,
    1945; London, Falcon Press, 1948.
*Henry Miller Miscellanea.* San Mateo, California, Bern Porter, 1945.
*The Air-Conditioned Nightmare.* New York, New Directions, 1945; London, Secker
    and Warburg, 1947.
*Obscenity and the Law of Reflection.* Yonkers, New York, Oscar Baradinsky, 1945.
*Maurizius Forever.* San Francisco, Colt Press, 1946.
*Patchen: Man of Anger and Light, with A Letter to God by Kenneth Patchen.* New York,
    Padell, 1947.
*Of, By, and About Henry Miller: A Collection of Pieces by Miller, Herbert Read, and
    Others.* Yonkers, New York, Alicat, 1947.
*Portrait of General Grant.* London, Night and Day, 1947.
*Remember to Remember* (vol. 2 of *The Air-Conditioned Nightmare*). New York,
    New Directions, 1947; London, Grey Walls Press, 1952.
*Varda: The Master Builder.* Berkeley, California, George Leite, 1947.
*The Smile at the Foot of the Ladder.* New York, Duell, 1948.
*The Waters Reglitterized* (includes reproductions of pictures by Henry Miller). San
    Jose, California, John Kidis, 1950.
*The Books in My Life.* New York, New Directions, and London, Peter Owen, 1952.
*Nights of Love and Laughter.* New York, New American Library, 1955.
*A Devil in Paradise: The Story of Conrad Mourand, Born Paris, 7 or 7:15 p.m., January
    17, 1887, Died Paris, 10:30 p.m., August 31, 1954.* New York, New American
    Library, 1956; London, New English Library, 1963.
*Argument about Astrology.* Los Angeles, Manas Publishing Company, 1956.
*The Time of the Assassins: A Study of Rimbaud.* New York, New Directions, and
    London, Spearman, 1956.
*Big Sur and the Oranges of Hieronymus Bosch.* New York, New Directions, 1957;
    London, Heinemann, 1958.
*The Red Notebook.* Highlands, North Carolina, Jonathan Williams, 1959.
*Art and Outrage: A Correspondence about Henry Miller Between Alfred Perles and
    Lawrence Durrell, with an Intermission by Henry Miller.* London, Putnam, 1959;
    New York, Dutton, 1961.
*A Henry Miller Reader*, edited by Lawrence Durrell. New York, New Directions,
    1959; as *The Best of Henry Miller*, London, Heinemann, 1960.
*The Intimate Henry Miller.* New York, New American Library, 1959.
*To Paint Is To Love Again* (includes reproductions of pictures by Henry Miller).
    Alhambra, California, Cambria Books, 1960.
*Stand Still like the Hummingbird.* New York, New Directions, 1962.
*Watercolors, Drawings and His Essay "The Angel Is My Watermark".* New York,
    Abrams, and London, Thames and Hudson, 1962.
*Lawrence Durrell and Henry Miller: A Private Correspondence*, edited by George Wickes.
    New York, Dutton, and London, Faber, 1963.
*Books Tangent to Circle: Reviews.* Walkwick, New Jersey, Bern Porter, 1963.
*Greece.* New York, Viking Press, and London, Thames and Hudson, 1964.

*Henry Miller on Writing*.  New York, New Directions, 1964.
*Letters to Anaïs Nin*.  New York, Putnam, and London, Peter Owen, 1965.
*Selected Prose*.  London, MacGibbon and Kee, 2 vols., 1965.
*Order and Chaos chez Hans Reichel*.  Tucson, Arizona, Loujon Press, 1966.
*Writer and Critic: A Correspondence*, with W. A. Gordon.  Baton Rouge, Louisiana
   State University Press, 1968.
*Collector's Quest: Correspondence, 1947–1965*, with J. R. Child.  Charlottesville,
   University Press of Virginia, 1968.
*Insomnia; or, The Devil at Large*.  Albuquerque, New Mexico, Loujon Press, 1970.
*My Life and Times*, edited by Bradley Smith.  Chicago, Playboy Press, 1971.

Bibliographies: *Henry Miller: A Chronology and Bibliography*, by Bern Porter, Berkeley,
California, Bern Porter, 1945; *Bibliography of Henry Miller*, edited by Thomas H. Moore,
Minneapolis, Henry Miller Literary Society, 1961; *A Bibliography of Henry Miller, 1945–
1961*, by Maxine Renken, Denver, Swallow, 1962.

Manuscript Collections: University of California, Los Angeles; University of Minnesota,
Minneapolis.

\*     \*     \*

From the publication of the *Tropic of Cancer* in 1934 to about 1950 Henry Miller was a major influence in world literature and enjoyed a vast, underground popularity with an audience that stretched from T. S. Eliot and Cyril Connolly to Parisian chambermaids and taxi drivers. As the rigors of censorship died away and his major works have been legally published in cheap editions and have come close to being best sellers, that influence has died away. *Black Spring, Tropic of Cancer* and *Tropic of Capricorn* have ceased to be great liberating forces and have become social-historical documents. In the years around the second world war he had an explosive effect upon the young. His books were eagerly passed from hand to hand in every literate country. By 1970 the youth of the Youth Revolt seldom read him except for classes in the modern novel. People once suffered severe penalties for sending his books through the mail. Today they seem little more pornographic than many a successful moving picture. Anarchism, pacifism, sexual freedom, occultism, oriental philosophy, pop-surrealism, astrology, copulation on demand, had all become commonplaces all over the world, a generation after the first underground publication in Paris of the *Tropics*. Nobody meditating in the lotus posture, under the strobe lights amid the incense, over the marshy profundities of Kahlil Gibran and Herman Hesse, was aware that Henry Miller was responsible for the resurrection of these great thinkers. If ever a writer was a success, Miller was, so much so that he now is in danger of being ignored, like the inventor of the wheel or the safety pin. Arthur Rimbaud spoke to only a handful of intellectuals, D. H. Lawrence to a limited audience of highly literate sophisticates. Henry Miller was the first to reach a mass audience with the gospel of the rejection of the rational, scientific synthesis we call modern civilization.

The important thing about Miller is his dates. He was born in 1891 and came to his majority during the presidency of William Howard Taft, two years after the death of Edward VII. Back in those days people matured in the years after puberty and were adults at twenty one, their personalities formed. Miller is very much a man of *cette belle epoque*. Although he came from a well-to-do, educated family (his father was a merchant tailor with a shop on fashionable Fifth Avenue) in those days in America middle class boys went to work, not to college. Miller is self educated. Also, he had the typical youth of a young white collar worker, living in a furnished room, migrating from job to job in the jungle of the city, a life only marginally distinguished from that of hustlers, scufflers and drifters, the lightweight, white collar underworld. Miller did not need to secede from a rationalist, scientific, humanitarian, Western

Civilization. When he was twenty three it blew up in his face. The lights went out over Europe —and America—not to be relit in Lord Grey's time, or Henry Miller's, or ours. Had Henry Miller been a normal, literary writer, by 1914 he already would have published, and a mold would have begun to form around him. Instead he went on working at unskilled white collar jobs, the last and "best" a messenger personnel manager for the telegraph company, a madhouse he has described hilariously in *Tropic of Capricorn*. In 1924 he quit, to live by writing. He did not; he lived by his wits. Except for some pulp fiction he sold to the magazine *Black Mask*, no one was interested in publishing him. In 1930 he went to Paris where he managed to get a job with the Paris *Chicago Tribune*. The World Economic crisis had shut down; the Lost Generation had gone home and the gaudy days of literary Paris-America were over. Most of those who remain were scufflers, drifters, and hustlers, unpublished writers, unexhibited painters, too poor to go home. A few made a living writing hack pornography for a publisher who specialized in under the counter fiction for the Paris tourist trade. This firm published *Tropic of Cancer* in 1934, *Black Spring* in 1936, *Tropic of Capricorn* in 1939 and discovered to their amazement that they had not only published literature but three classics. Meanwhile New Directions had started to issue Miller's mailable writings in the United States. All during the Second War Miller's voice was one of the few raised in total dissent. Another was Kenneth Patchen, and like Patchen his underground popularity grew apace. By the end of the war he was being suggested seriously for the Nobel Prize. In the years since his reputation has increased in bulk, but his significance was already established.

Miller is a typical self-educated bohemian, a revolté, but from a benign and mellow past, come relatively unspoiled to confront a terrible present and a worse future, as though he had been transported by time machine from the world of H. G. Wells and Havelock Ellis, Emma Goldman and Sadakichi Hartmann, Isadora Duncan, and George Bernard Shaw to a bird's-eye view of Auschwitz, Hiroshima and the Moscow Trials. He has remained a young man in stiff, starched, detachable collar and cuffs arguing about Nietzsche and Dostoievsky with his pals in gaslit hall bedrooms and picking up hot stenographers on the subway and in cheap dance halls. A great deal was once made of Miller's erotic writing. There is nothing unusual about it. It's only a description of the sex life of the working class and the lumpen intelligentsia just slightly hypertrophied and still completely ingenuous. The difference from fact is only quantitative. The effect on literary critics and well bred intellectuals was so explosive because they had never known that such things existed. It's not the sex that's important in the first and best books; it's the frank revelation of the behavior and values of the literate dispossessed, the underemployed of the clerkly caste which is our society's principle kind of overproduction. This is a personal and intellectual surplus which pulls the superstructure of society toward a final crisis just as a surplus of commodities produces economic crises. Modern civilization produces outsiders, the same way it dumps wheat and milk and builds obsolescence into automobiles. Miller speaks for Surplus Man to whom the values, the achievements, and the classics of the dominant civilization are meaningless and absurd. Once there were just a few bohemians in Montparnasse, Soho, and Greenwich Village. Now there are millions and so Miller's books sell millions of copies where once they sold hundreds. More and more the universities become reservations where surplus minds are held out of the productive process and so the young begin where Miller left off, which is why he seems dated to so many of them. It's a leap frog phenomenon. *Huckleberry Finn* is relevant to a young person in the last quarter of the twentieth century, three generations after its publication. Miller has written about everything that ever came into his head and there is no evidence that *Huckleberry Finn* was relevant to him when young. But Miller and Mark Twain write about the same thing—innocent comrades adrift on a dark river on a narrow raft through a world of malevolent and greedy frauds.

What will preserve Miller and make him a minor classic is his style, the style of the common man. He has been compared to the French eighteenth century naive writer Restif de la Bretonne and the resemblances are marked. He is almost as garrulous, almost as sex obsessed, almost as full of misinformation, but he is not really naive. Restif was much more an outsider to the bourgeois society which was rising around him than was the Marquis de Sade, who was only the Capitalist writ large, like a *Daily Worker* cartoon. So too Miller is unassimilable and his style is a careful cultivation of all those elements of communication—the speech of inter-personal relations—which violate the mechanisms of the dominant society. It is not just that the sexual capers of his characters expose the Social Lie. His prose disrupts acceptable speech. It does this so easily by simply being the common talk of his declassed caste. The lumpen intelligentsia talked this way in the days of Villon and the wandering scholars who wrote the songs of the *Carmina Burana*. His writing is spontaneous and uncontrolled on principle, but the control is in the principle, in the intention. If Miller just tells you the time of day he could never be mistaken for Edith Wharton. The *Tropics* established a method of which Saroyan early and Kerouac later were outstanding practitioners, a method which would become dominant in the fiction of the latter half of the century—the *roman fleuve* in a different sense—the pages go by like a river in flood. The overwhelming flow of Proust or Joyce or Gertrude Stein is highly contrived and recognizably so. In Miller and his descendants the author begins by overwhelming himself. This is a method where nothing succeeds but success. Miller can sweep you away; he can also bore you to death; and as the style trickles down to third rate practitioners it has become entirely boring.

In such a method there is no place for ironic self consciousness and retrospection, the essence of profound humor. Miller can be hilariously funny but his humor is the humor of old time burlesque and the working class dirty joke, for instance in one of his best stories—the Hindu in the brothel who misuses the bidet. There is a bitter irony in the greatest humor, however bawdy, which is why the Jewish joke is superior to all other folk humor, but such jokes are over Miller's head. There is no tragedy in his comedy, but then, Aristotle says tragedy is the business of gentlemen and Miller's point is that he is not a gentleman, for gentlemen are members of a military caste who stole land from the peasants. "I am," says Miller over and over again, "not a Kshatriya, but a holy old Untouchable. You can keep your shining sword; I'll keep my night soil."

—Kenneth Rexroth

---

**MITCHELL, Adrian.** British. Born in London, 24 October 1932. Educated at Christ Church, Oxford, 1952–55. Served in the Royal Air Force, 1951–52. Formerly, Journalist, writing for the *Oxford Mail*, and the *Evening Standard, Daily Mail, Woman's Mirror, Sun* and the *Sunday Times*, London; more recently, Contributor to *Peace News* and *Black Dwarf*, London. Granada Fellow in the Arts, University of Lancaster, 1967–69. Recipient: Gregory Award, for poetry, 1961; P.E.N. Translation Award, 1966. Lives in London. Address: c/o Jonathan Cape Ltd., 30 Bedford Square, London W.C.1, England.

PUBLICATIONS

Novels

*If You See Me Comin'*. London, Cape, 1962; New York, Macmillan, 1963.
*The Bodyguard*. London, Cape, 1970; New York, Doubleday, 1971.

Plays

*The Ledge*, music by Richard Rodney Bennett (produced London, 1961).

*Marat/Sade*, adaptation of a play by Peter Weiss (produced London, 1964; New York, 1965).   London, John Calder, 1964; New York, Atheneum, 1965.

*The Magic Flute*, adaptation of a libretto by Emanuel Schikaneder; music by Mozart (produced London, 1966).

*The Criminals*, adaptation of a play by Jose Triana (produced London, 1967; Ann Arbor, Michigan, 1970).

*Tyger*, adaptation of works of William Blake (produced London, 1971).

Verse

(*Poems*).   Oxford, Fantasy Press, 1955.
*Poems*.   London, Cape, 1964.
*Out Loud*.   London, Cape Goliard Press, and New York, Grossman, 1968.
*Ride the Nightmare*.   London, Cape, 1971.

Lyrics for the play *US* (produced London, 1966), and for the film *Tell Me Lies*, 1968.

Other

Editor, with Richard Selig, *Oxford Poetry*.   Oxford, Fantasy Press, 1955.

Adrian Mitchell comments:

I am outraged by the cruelty of man to man and especially by the criminal record of the rich white nations. I write out of this outrage. If I tell of my horror with jokes often, it's in order to make it bearable. Viva Cuba! Viva Fidel!

*          *          *

Adrian Mitchell is best-known as a "committed" poet, his verse serving his fiery Far Left views, but his two novels are not narrowly political. The first, *If You See Me Comin'*, springs in part from his participation in various experiments in the late fifties in putting together jazz and poetry. The book is a first person account of six days in the life of Johnny Crane, a blues singer, in an English provincial town. The days include some singing and eating, a rehearsal and a civic ball, with thoughts alternating with the actual sequence of events. His brother, on the run from gangsters, breaks up his room while Johnny, finding himself, rather to his surprise, falling in love with a girl, moves in with her. Some actions are stranger: he gets into a tiny concealed space in a museum and cuts down the flagpost on top of the town hall at night. Finally a girl is murdered and her fiancé kills himself.

The novel's features include "poetic" touches ("Morning sun has the hand of a woman," "His face was obscure and slick as the numberless plastic stopped clock on the wall beyond his shoulder") and some comedy, often irrelevant; parodies of a children's television show about animals and of the country-house murder play, and the sick park-keeper who waylays you with "I shouldn't be doing this, with my chest, everyone says I shouldn't."

Johnny is the kind of man who buys a car when he has money on Wednesday, travels by train that night, and sells the car on Thursday. We read of his response to music, and the ways he feels when he sings, Mitchell giving the words of several of the songs he likes. Equally important is his intense response to suffering and death: he has buried corpses in the Korean War and is obsessed with an approaching execution, so that half-heartedly he collects signatures on a petition for a reprieve. Johnny seems to be made unbalanced by over-sensitivity to the world's pain and horror. But primarily this is a psychological study. His is a mind close to the end of its tether.

The novel overflows with half-disciplined talent, a little incoherent, imaginative, spiky and unsettling.

The second novel, *The Bodyguard*, is more unusual. The time is the mid 1980's, when Britain has an All-Party government operating a police state, which is ineffective in combatting the Resistance. Facets of eighties life include frequent nudity on Saturday mornings in Ladbroke Grove and black Africans kept in a zoo at New Johannesburg in Surrey, with visitors free to do what they like with them.

Mitchell's subject, however, is Len Rossman, whose tape-recorded life story this is. He is "the best-known bodyguard in the British Isles," uncritically serving several masters. In a rapid and varied sequence of adventures, we find him trapping "subverts" as an undercover agent at Oxford University, and plotting an ingenious mock-killing as a training exercise. Mitchell diverts us, too, with the comic rebel whose only weapon is custard and the nudist bridal party Rossman must guard. On one level, Mitchell seems to enjoy writing of violence, with a little crude sex. But among these diversions, we see Rossman as the violent Fascist: "I have dreamed of an England and a Europe which are both strong and clean," he says. While another bodyguard explains: "In the city you can forget all that neighbour stuff. Nobody has to be friends. You're competing, you're struggling, you're using your eyes and your brain and your body. Nobody's equal, ever, in the city. Any city is just a series of little battlefields. Win or lose. I like that. And I don't want either the city or the country to change. Yes, that's why I hate subverts." Mitchell shows in an original, half-amusing, half-frightening way how sterile a policy of more repression towards crime and dissent is, and where it leads.

—Malcolm Page

---

**MITCHELL, (Charles) Julian.** British. Born in Epping, Essex, 1 May 1935. Educated at Winchester College, Hampshire, 1948–53; Wadham College, Oxford, B.A. 1958; St. Antony's College, Oxford, M.A. 1962. Served as a Midshipman in the Royal Naval Volunteer Reserve, 1953–55. Member of the Arts Council Literature Panel, 1966–69. Recipient: Harkness Fellowship, 1959; Rhys Memorial Prize, 1965; Maugham Award, 1966. Address: 68 Christchurch Street, London S.W.3, England.

PUBLICATIONS

Novels

*Imaginary Toys.* London, Hutchinson, 1961.
*A Disturbing Influence.* London, Hutchinson, 1962.
*As Far As You Can Go.* London, Constable, 1963.
*The White Father.* London, Constable, 1964; New York, Farrar Straus, 1965.
*A Circle of Friends.* London, Constable, 1966; New York, McGraw Hill, 1967.
*The Undiscovered Country.* London, Constable, 1968; New York, Grove Press, 1970.

Short Stories

*Introduction*, with others. London, Faber, 1960.

Play

> *A Heritage and Its History*, adaptation of the novel by Ivy Compton-Burnett (produced
> London, 1965).   London, Evans, 1968.

Other

> Editor, with others, *Light Blue, Dark Blue: An Anthology of Recent Writing from
> Oxford and Cambridge*.   London, Macdonald, 1960.

Julian Mitchell comments:

Writing fiction is extremely difficult, and likely to get more so as time goes on. But there
is no replacement for it as an artistic medium, for all the fools who think so, because it is
only through fiction that we can know what it is like to be someone else.
I do not feel competent to write about my own novels.

*       *       *

Julian Mitchell's books reveal a remarkably talented writer, whose work is consistently
fluent, witty and ingenious. But they do leave a doubt in the mind whether his literary gifts are,
in the last analysis, those of a natural novelist. He began his career precociously early, and
published four novels before he was thirty. The first of them, *Imaginary Toys*, is, like many
other first novels, a partly sentimental, partly satirical recreation of university life. It covers
a small group of young people during a few days in one summer term at Oxford; the story
is of the slightest, but Mitchell uses it as the vehicle for some serious disquisitions on sexual
and social problems. The novel is at its most engaging, though, in its fanciful, essay-like
speculations, which make it a little reminiscent of the early Aldous Huxley. Mitchell is like
Huxley, too, in his acute sense of period; *Imaginary Toys* effectively catches the feel of the
late fifties, though this responsiveness to contemporary atmosphere inevitably made the
book seem dated after a few years. His next novel, *A Disturbing Influence*, was not a particularly exciting development, though it was a smoothly written narrative. It described the impact
on a complacent, even sleepy Berkshire village of a strange, destructive, amoral young man,
the "disturbing influence" of the title. Such types evidently have a particular fascination for
Mitchell, for they tend to recur in his fiction. This book was followed by a more substantial
and interesting work, *As Far As You Can Go*, in which Mitchell drew on some of his own
recent experience to write the kind of novel that was to become increasingly common in
England in the nineteen-sixties—the account of a peripatetic Englishman's adventures in
America. Harold Barlow, the central character, is a typical Mitchell hero—intelligent,
amiable, rather inept—and he conveys a tourist's eye view of life in the hipster sub-culture
of California.
*The White Father*, which won Mitchell the Somerset Maugham Award, was a more
determinedly ambitious novel than its predecessors. The narrative is divided between London
and a remote African territory, and Mitchell shows much of the action through the eyes of
Hugh Shrieve, a district officer in Africa who has come to London to plead for his tribe at a
conference to arrange independence for the territory. Shrieve has been out of England for
years, and he is unprepared for what he finds when he arrives: the frenetic beginnings of the
"Swinging London" cult. Mitchell looks satirically though tolerantly at the world of pop
music, and there is a powerful imaginative touch in his portrayal of the megalomaniac Mr.
Brachs, head of a vast commercial empire catering to the youth cult, who is going steadily
mad in his inaccessible penthouse on top of the London skyscraper that houses all his many

enterprises. *The White Father* is one of Mitchell's best novels, which makes some sharp observations about life in a high-consumption society, as well as telling an entertaining story. The novelist and the essayist are more closely fused than is usual in his fiction. Two years later Mitchell published an extremely thin novel, *A Circle of Friends*, which moves between New York and the English Home Counties, showing how one of his characteristically weak young men gets unhappily entangled with a wealthy Anglo-American family, culminating in a wholly undeserved position as co-respondent in a divorce action.

All these novels present, at varying levels of literary achievement, some recurring characteristics: a tendency to draw fairly directly on personal experience and to use the novel as a vehicle for airing ideas, a taste for likeable but weak central characters, and a generally relaxed and good-humoured tone. In *The Undiscovered Country*, which is Mitchell's most striking contribution to recent English fiction, all these qualities are present in a new combination. Unlike his previous novels, it is a deliberately experimental work, which plays with the conventions of fiction writing, and the relations between art and reality, in the manner of Nabokov or Borges. The first part is, on the face of it, undisguised autobiography, where Mitchell writes in his own person about his friendship with an enigmatically attractive young man, Charles Humphries, who dies at an early age. He leaves behind the fragmentary manuscript of a novel called "The New Satyricon", which Mitchell edits with introduction and commentary, and presents as the second part of *The Undiscovered Country*. Undoubtedly "Humphries" is an alter ego for "Mitchell" (whose full Christian names are Charles Julian Humphrey), though the relation between them remains teasing. *The Undiscovered Country* is a generally entertaining novel, and the second part is full of pleasant literary jokes, where Mitchell engages to the full his essayistic tendencies. It is also a watershed in his development as a novelist, and marks his dissatisfaction with his more conventional earlier novels. Indeed, at the end of part one, before he introduces "The New Satyricon", Mitchell observes, "I think it unlikely that I shall write another book of my own for a long time, with the fact of this one before me. Charles said that all art comes from an inner need. He said that I began to write because I wanted to be a writer, and that was the wrong kind of need."

—Bernard Bergonzi

---

**MITCHELL, Joseph.** American. Born in Robeson County, North Carolina, 27 July 1908. Educated at the University of North Carolina, Chapel Hill, 1925–29. Married Therese Dagny Jacobsen in 1931; has two children. Reporter, *New York Herald Tribune*, 1929–31, and *New York World Telegram*, 1931–38. Since 1938, Staff Writer for *The New Yorker* magazine. Recipient: National Institute of Arts and Letters grant, 1965. Member, National Institute of Arts and Letters, 1970. Address: c/o The New Yorker, 25 West 43rd Street, New York, New York 10036, U.S.A.

PUBLICATIONS

Short Stories

    *McSorley's Wonderful Saloon*. New York, Duell, 1943; London, Porcupine Press, 1946.
    *Old Mr. Flood*. New York, Duell, 1948.

*The Bottom of the Harbor.*   Boston, Little Brown, 1959; London, Chatto and Windus, 1961.
*Joe Gould's Secret.*   New York, Viking Press, 1965.


Other

*My Ears Are Bent* (collection of newspaper articles).   New York, Sheridan House, 1938.


Critical Studies: "The Grammar of Facts" by Malcolm Cowley, in *The New Republic* (New York), 26 July 1943; "The Art of Joseph Mitchell" by Stanley Edgar Hyman, in *The New Leader* (New York), 6 December 1965.


*             *             *


Throughout his works Joseph Mitchell places himself in the tradition of the tall tale in America and reveals why he can say in *McSorley's Wonderful Saloon* to the "Gifted Child" that Mark Twain's *Life on the Mississippi* is the one book he likes above all others. He walks in wonder and records what he sees. All of his central figures emerge as larger-than-life people, yet there is almost always a quality of reflection and tone-setting that makes them believable as well as memorable.

In an author's note to *McSorley's Wonderful Saloon* Mr. Mitchell concludes with, "There are no little people in this book. They are as big as you are, whoever you are." And he then works with a fine eye, ear, and hand to give profile to such "little" people as John McSorley, president of "an organization of gluttons called the Honorable John McSorley Pickle, Beefsteak, Baseball Nine and Chowder Club"; Mazie P. Gordon, owner of, ticket seller, and bouncer at the Venice theater in the Bowery; King Cockeye Johnny Nikanov, a Russian and King of the Gypsies in New York; Lady Olga Jane Bardwell, the freak show bearded lady, with a fourteen-and-a-half-inch beard, mustache, and her fourth husband; and various others. His favorite setting is lower Manhattan, and his stories become urban pastorals, strongest when he focuses with care on his people: Mr. Hugh G. Flood, in *Old Mr. Flood*, and Joe Gould, in *Joe Gould's Secret*, exemplify best Mr. Mitchell's role as profilist-story teller.

Mr. Flood, age 93 to 95, wants to live to be 115, is a "seafoodetarian," and can eat bushels of clams and consume large quantities of whiskey. From the many scenes and wild anecdotes of "Old Mr. Flood," "The Black Clams," and "Mr. Flood's Party" comes a man whom the narrator obviously loves, one who, as Mr. Mitchell says, is not one man but "several old men, who work or hang out in Fulton Fish Market." He's too big to exist, but he is nonetheless there, and the *I* of the story penetrates his moods—from extreme loneliness to convivial joy—with touching sensitivity. One feels that Mr. Flood will indeed live to age 115.

Joe Gould, on the other hand, is, as the author says in a note, "a lost soul." As Professor Sea Gull in *McSorley's Wonderful Saloon*, he is a tall-tale character too—a blithe and emaciated little man who has been a notable in the cafeterias, diners, barrooms and dumps of Greenwich Village for a quarter of a century. A Harvard alumnus, class of 1911, he sometimes brags that he is the last of the bohemians. Of chief interest to Mr. Mitchell is Gould's *An Oral History of Our Time*—a document eleven times as long as the *Bible*, over 9,000,000 words in longhand and still unfinished. As a solitary nocturnal wanderer he talks much of his *Oral History* and at his ability, among other things, to translate Longfellow's "Hiawatha" into sea gull. Here he shouts to a Village waitress: "I'm Joe Gould, the poet; I'm Joe Gould, the historian; I'm Joe Gould, the wild Chippewa Indian dancer; and I'm Joe Gould, the greatest authority in the world on the language of the sea gull."

Joe Gould's secret, however, discovered by Mitchell years later, is that there is no *Oral*

*History*. Gould has not only duped Mitchell and the people but has duped himself. He can recite it but cannot put it down. Mitchell keeps the secret until he writes it down in his story, stepping out of, as he says, "the role I had stepped into the afternoon I discovered that the *Oral History* did not exist."

*My Ears Are Bent* and *The Bottom of the Harbor* show Mr. Mitchell's consistency throughout his career in reporting on but also building on the people and places of his world, from Sloppy Louie's, the old Fulton Ferry Hotel, and the "Baymen" to the rats on the waterfront. When he writes of his home country in rural North Carolina he uses his same profilist's eye and feeling for his "people" to bring to life such characters as Mrs. Copenhagen Calhoun in "I Blame It All on Mama," Uncle Dockery in "Uncle Dockery and the Independent Bull" and Mr. Catfish Giddy in "The Downfall of Fascism in Black Ankle County." Mr. Mitchell is the country boy who went to the city to find his way—and found it in *The New Yorker* where he perfected the urban tall-tale pastoral.

—Frank T. Phipps

---

**MITCHELL, W(illiam) O(rmond).** Canadian. Born in Weyburn, Saskatchewan, 13 March 1914. Educated at the University of Manitoba, Winnipeg, 1932–34; University of Alberta, Edmonton, B.A. 1942. Married Merna Lynne Hirtle in 1942; has three children. Has worked as a seaman, salesman, teacher and high school principal. Writer-in-Residence, University of Calgary, Alberta, 1968–71. Recipient: Maclean's Novel Award, 1953; President's Medal, University of Western Ontario, 1953; Leacock Medal, 1962. Address: 3031 Roxboro Glen Road, Calgary, Alberta, Canada.

PUBLICATIONS

Novels

*Who Has Seen the Wind*.  Boston, Little Brown, 1947; London, Macmillan, 1948.
*The Alien*, serialized in *Maclean's Magazine* (Toronto), 15 September 1953–15 January 1954.
*Jake and the Kid*.  Toronto, Macmillan, 1961.
*The Kite*.  Toronto, Macmillan, 1962.
*The Vanishing Point*.  Toronto, Macmillan, 1972.

Short Story

*The Black Bonspiel of Wullie MacCrimmon*.  Calgary, Alberta, Frontiers Unlimited, 1965.

Uncollected Short Stories

"The Owl and the Bens", in *Atlantic* (Boston), 1946.
"Saint Sammy", in *Atlantic* (Boston), 1946.

Plays

*The Black Bonspiel of Wullie MacCrimmon,* in *Three Worlds of Drama.* Toronto,
Macmillan, 1966.

Plays produced on CBC since 1947.

*       *       *

W. O. Mitchell, generally considered a "regional humourist", perhaps himself encourages
such a reputation. In the guise of the homespun philosopher he finds a traditional folk
identity with which to meet contemporary life and a literary format which matches his
penchant for the humour of understatement, wise saws, tall tales, and home truths. But
this is not to say that he spurns sophistication, progress, or the twentieth century. His
stories constantly ask blunt questions about reality and values, probing "sophistication" to
see if it isn't hypocrisy by a different name, and reducing contemporary problems to domestic
proportions in order to reveal the lineage of human foible which the present has inherited.

Most clearly illustrative of such a technique are the wry stories of Jake and the Kid,
which were written first as dramas and were performed on the Canadian Broadcasting
Corporation as a continuing radio series in the 1940's. Set in the ranching country of the
Alberta foothills which Mitchell knows well, they detail the laconic education in the vagaries
of life which Jake, a hired hand, gives to the young son of his employers—and incidentally,
always ironically, to himself. They seldom directly invoke contentious social issues—indeed,
when Mitchell does contend head-on with such matters as race relations, as in his serialized
novel *The Alien,* the result is more melodramatic than provocative. The incidents of Jake's
world (misadventures of the order of those encountered by a crusty bachelor inveigled into
the duties of babysitting) entertain with a quiet wit, reveal a delight in humanity, but like
most domestic anecdotes become quickly dated in their literary technique, whatever their
insight into human behaviour.

One of Mitchell's most successful uses of anecdote occurs in his novel *The Kite,* when the
centenarian central character, Daddy Sherry, irrepressibly individual (particularly when
officialdom dictates prudence to him), accepts a flooding river as an invitation to a South
Seas cruise and sails his uprooted house matter-of-factly away, at dark of night, across the
American border. The wit is paramount, but incidentally Mitchell manages bemused swipes
at customs regulations and bureaucratic nervousness, and builds up the engagingly exaggerated personalities of his cast. The book as a whole celebrates the virtue of living life fully,
of engaging oneself in the *process* of living, of which the cruise incident is merely a genial
sign.

The developing spiritual affinity between Daddy and a young boy varies the Jake-kid
relationship, and adds a Wordsworthian dimension to Mitchell's world that is more readily
seen in his best book, *Who Has Seen the Wind.* In it, the young Brian O'Connal is broken out
of his innocent childhood oneness with the world (into the imperfect loves and prejudices of
ordinary humanity) by his increasingly adaptive encounters with death and disorder. The
"sleep and forgetting" that marks his growth are accompanied by a developing social conscience, however, revealed ultimately in his "mature" child's commitment to agricultural
science, and counterpointed by the novel's subplots. Their exploration of institutional
hypocrisy, educational rigidity, race prejudice, and religious intemperance tends sometimes
towards the maudlin, but in the characters of Saint Sammy and the Young Ben, "naturals"
whose oneness with the prairie and the wind serves as a kind of true spiritual example to
Brian, Mitchell has created unforgettable animated forces. With Brian's renegade Uncle
Sean, they together fill the "Jake" role to Brian's "kid" and widen rather than reduce the
intensity of the effect Jake was meant to exert. For a generation of radio listeners Jake was
a shrewd observer of daily life; Brian's relationship with the world of the Young Ben appeals
to rather more, for the imaginative experience it represents transcends place and time.

Tracing the loss of a child's self and the gain of a man's, the book probes the many dimensions of reality—raising Berkeleyan dilemmas, countering them with Wordsworthian intuitions—and covering all with the gentle humour of a man in love with life whose acute eyes remind him constantly of the failings of mankind as well as its humane possibilities.

—W. H. New

---

**MITCHISON, Naomi (Margaret).** British. Born in Edinburgh, 1 November 1897. Educated at Dragon School, Oxford; St. Anne's College, Oxford. Served as a volunteer nurse, 1915. Married G. R. Mitchison (who became Lord Mitchison, 1964) in 1916 (died, 1970); has five children. Labour Candidate for Parliament, for the Scottish Universities Constituency, 1935; Member of the Argyll County Council, 1945–66; Member of the Highland Panel, Scotland, 1947–65. Since 1966, Member of the Highland and Island Advisory Council, Scotland. Since 1963, Tribal Adviser, and Mmarona (Mother), to the Bakgatla of Botswana. Recipient: Palmes de l'Académie Française, 1921. Address: Carradale, Campbeltown, Argyll, Scotland.

PUBLICATIONS

Novels

> *The Conquered.* London, Cape, and New York, Harcourt Brace, 1923.
> *Cloud Cuckoo Land.* London, Cape, 1925; New York, Harcourt Brace, 1926.
> *The Corn King and the Spring Queen.* London, Cape, and New York, Harcourt Brace, 1931.
> *The Powers of Light.* London, Cape, and New York, Smith, 1932.
> *Beyond This Limit*, with Wyndham Lewis. London, Cape, 1935.
> *We Have Been Warned.* London, Constable, 1935; New York, Vanguard Press, 1936.
> *The Blood of the Martyrs.* London, Constable, 1939; New York, McGraw Hill, 1948.
> *The Bull Calves.* London, Cape, 1947.
> *The Big House.* London, Faber, 1950.
> *Lobsters on the Agenda.* London, Gollancz, 1952.
> *Travel Light.* London, Faber, 1952.
> *To the Chapel Perilous.* London, Allen and Unwin, 1955.
> *Behold Your King.* London, Muller, 1957.
> *Memoirs of a Spacewoman.* London, Gollancz, 1962.
> *When We Become Men.* London, Collins, 1965.
> *Cleopatra's People.* London, Heinemann, 1972.

Short Stories

> *When the Bough Breaks and Other Stories.* London, Cape, and New York, Harcourt Brace, 1924.
> *Black Sparta: Greek Stories.* London, Cape, and New York, Harcourt Brace, 1928.
> *Barbarian Stories.* London, Cape, and New York, Harcourt Brace, 1929.

*The Delicate Fire: Short Stories and Poems*.   London, Cape, and New York, Harcourt Brace, 1933.
*The Fourth Pig*.   London, Constable, 1936.
*Five Men and a Swan: Short Stories and Poems*.   London, Allen and Unwin, 1958.


Uncollected Short Stories

"After the Accident", in *The Year 2000*.   London, Collier Macmillan, 1970.
"Mithras My Saviour", in *Scottish Short Stories*.   London, Oxford University Press, 1970.
"Mary and Joe", in *Nova 1*.   New York, Dell, 1971.


Plays

*Nix-Nought-Nothing: Four Plays for Children*.   London, Cape, and New York, Harcourt Brace, 1929.
*The Price of Freedom*, with L. E. Gielgud.   London, Cape, 1931.
*An End and a Beginning and Other Plays*.   London, Cape, 1937.
*As It Was in the Beginning*, with L. E. Gielgud.   London, Cape, 1939.
*Spindrift*, with Denis Macintosh (produced Glasgow, 1951).   London, French, 1951.


Verse

*The Laburnum Branch*.   London, Cape, 1926.


Other

*Anna Comnena*.   London, Howe, 1928.
*The Hostages and Other Stories for Boys and Girls*.   London, Cape, 1930; New York, Harcourt Brace, 1931.
*Comments on Birth Control*.   London, Faber, 1930.
*Boys and Girls and Gods*.   London, Watts, 1931.
*The Home and a Changing Civilisation*.   London, Lane, 1934.
*Vienna Diary*.   London, Gollancz, and New York, Smith and Haas, 1935.
*Socrates*, with R. H. S. Crossman.   London, Hogarth Press, 1937; Harrisburg, Pennsylvania, Stackpole, 1938.
*The Moral Basis of Politics*.   London, Constable, 1938.
*Kingdom of Heaven*.   London, Heinemann, 1939.
*Men and Herring*, with Denis Macintosh.   Edinburgh, Serif Books, 1949.
*The Swan's Road* (history).   London, Naldrett Press, 1954.
*Graeme and the Dragon* (juvenile).   London, Faber, 1954.
*The Land the Ravens Found* (juvenile).   London, Collins, 1955.
*Little Boxes* (juvenile).   London, Faber, 1956.
*The Far Harbour* (juvenile).   London, Collins, 1957.
*Other People's Worlds* (travel).   London, Secker and Warburg, 1958.
*Judy and Lakshmi* (juvenile).   London, Collins, 1959.
*The Rib of the Green Umbrella* (juvenile).   London, Collins, 1960.
*The Young Alexander the Great* (juvenile).   London, Parrish, 1960; New York, Roy, 1961.
*Karensgaard: The Story of a Danish Farm* (juvenile).   London, Collins, 1961.
*A Fishing Village on the Clyde*, with G. W. L. Paterson.   London, Oxford University Press, 1961.

*Presenting Other People's Children.*   London, Hamlyn, 1961.
*The Young Alfred the Great* (juvenile).   London, Parrish, 1962; New York, Roy, 1963.
*The Fairy Who Couldn't Tell a Lie* (juvenile).   London, Collins, 1963.
*Alexander the Great* (juvenile).   London, Longman, 1964.
*Henny and Crispies.*   Wellington, New Zealand School Publications, 1964.
*Ketse and the Chief* (juvenile).   London, Nelson, 1965.
*Return to the Fairy Hill* (autobiography and sociology).   London, Heinemann, and
    New York, Day, 1966.
*Friends and Enemies.*   London, Collins, 1966; New York, Day, 1968.
*The Big Surprise* (juvenile).   London, Kaye and Ward, 1967.
*Highland Holiday* (juvenile).   Wellington, New Zealand School Publications, 1967.
*African Heroes.*   London, Bodley Head, 1968; New York, Farrar Straus, 1969.
*Don't Look Back* (juvenile).   London, Kaye and Ward, 1969.
*The Family at Ditlabeng* (juvenile).   London, Collins, 1969; New York, Farrar Straus,
    1970.
*The Africans: A History.*   London, Blond, 1970.
*Sun and Moon* (juvenile).   London, Bodley Head, 1970.

Editor, *An Outline for Boys and Girls and Their Parents.*   London, Gollancz, 1932.
Editor, *Re-Educating Scotland.*   Glasgow, Scoop Books, 1944.
Editor, *What the Human Race Is Up To.*   London, Gollancz, 1962.

Manuscript Collection: University of Texas, Austin.

Naomi Mitchison comments:

I write a number of different kinds of books, as you see. When I began writing this was possible because at that time books were written because the authors had something they wanted to say; today books are a commodity like other commodities. What is important is whether publishers think they can sell them. Most publishers have definite selling plans and if a given book does not fit into this, the author has little chance of getting it published. Today, if one wants to write about something special, one has to try and persuade a publisher that this was something he had already thought of. I like writing children's books because one has to write absolutely straight, without playing any of the stylistic or literary tricks which will take in an adult audience. I like digging out the facts of history and seeing what they will add up to. I like thinking what people do in strange situations, for instance in the past, in Africa or India, or in imaginary but possible situations in science fiction. This may enable one—or other people—to make some contribution towards a happier world.

\*       \*       \*

In Lady Mitchison's historical novels and short stories, with which she established her earliest reputation, an essential theme is conflict of loyalties, whether in Gaul at the time of Caesar's conquest, as in her first novel, *The Conquered,* or among the people of a small Aegean island who are dragged willy-nilly, on one side or another, into the bitter fratricidal battle between Athens and Sparta in the 4th century B.C.—the subject of her ironically-entitled *Cloud Cuckoo Land.* Her major work in this genre is *The Corn King and the Spring Queen,* a study in the relationships between the people of three different societies—an agricultural community in the Crimea where the old fertility religion still remains strong enough to provide the folk with purposive unity; a decadent Greece where religious belief has broken down and the struggle to create a just society is conducted—and fails—on a secular basis; and an imperial Egypt where despotism has led to political apathy, disillusion, cynical hedonism, and a frantic search for religious consolation. At once a presentation of personal breakdown and reintegration, a picture of the stresses between idealism and expediency involved in the rise and fall of a revolutionary movement, and an exploration of the relationship between religious conviction and communal solidarity, between scepticism and the loosening of social cohesion, this novel is unsurpassed in 20th century British historical fiction for range and variety of scene and characterisation, for political awareness, and for religious depth.

On Scottish subjects, Lady Mitchison is at her best in *The Big House*, a children's fairytale which is also a tragi-comedy expressing a profound understanding of the intermingled light and darkness of the human situation, a book where the natural magic of childhood, the terrible charm of the supernatural, the dark power of history, and a vision of life as at once dreadful and sublime, are all woven together. From the fairytale she has gone on to science-fiction fantasy with *Memoirs of a Spacewoman*, where she shows—in three related chapters about a world inhabited by butterflies and their larvae—a deep imaginative comprehension of extra-terrestrial modes of existence, and a compassionate reverence for life, even at its most remote and mysterious, which lift her work out of the category of the merely inventive and fanciful to give it something of the universality of legend. A poet as well as a prose-writer, Lady Mitchison has written a futuristic story about the exploration of space which is itself a myth, a concentrated symbolical expression of generations of experience.

Alongside fantasy, Lady Mitchison has also written "documentary" novels on contemporary social experience, some with a Scottish location and some set in Africa, where she has worked in Botswana. In these, characterisation tends to be subordinated to background detail. Perhaps the finest of her contemporary studies is the title-story of her collection *Five Men and a Swan*, a modern Scottish folk-tale which combines tenderness, brutality, humour, beauty and sheer magic in a parable on the theme of human greed and stupidity. While the detail of this story is exactly in period, the writing has a quality of timelessness before which criticism must needs be silent.

—Alexander Scott

---

**MITFORD, Nancy.** British. Born in London, 28 November 1904; daughter of 2nd Lord Redesdale. Educated privately. Married Hon. Peter Rodd in 1933 (divorced, 1958). Managed a London bookshop during World War II. Has lived in France since 1945. Address: 4 rue d'Artois, 78 Versailles, France.

PUBLICATIONS

Novels

*Highland Fling*. London, Butterworth, 1931.
*Christmas Pudding*. London, Butterworth, 1932.
*Wigs on the Green*. London, Butterworth, 1935.
*Pigeon Pie*. London, Hamish Hamilton, 1940.
*The Pursuit of Love*. London, Hamish Hamilton, 1945; New York, Random House, 1946.

*Love in a Cold Climate.*   London, Hamish Hamilton, and New York, Random House, 1949.
*The Blessing.*   London, Hamish Hamilton, and New York, Random House, 1951.
*Don't Tell Alfred.*   London, Hamish Hamilton, and New York, Harper, 1960.

Play

*The Little Hut*, adaptation of a play by André Roussin (produced London, 1950).   London, Hamish Hamilton, 1951.

Other

*Madame de Pompadour.*   London, Hamish Hamilton, and New York, Harper, 1954; revised edition, 1968.
*Voltaire in Love.*   London, Hamish Hamilton, and New York, Harper, 1957.
*The Water Beetle* (essays).   London, Hamish Hamilton, 1962; New York, Harper, 1963.
*The Sun King: Louis XIV at Versailles.*   London, Hamish Hamilton, and New York, Harper, 1966.
*Frederick the Great.*   London, Hamish Hamilton, 1970; New York, Harper, 1971.

Editor, *The Ladies of Alderley: Being the Letters Between Maria Josepha, Lady Stanley of Alderley, and Her Daughter-in-Law Henrietta Maria Stanley, During the Years 1841–1850.*   London, Chapman and Hall, 1938.
Editor, *Noblesse Oblige: An Enquiry into the Identifiable Characteristics of the English Aristocracy.*   London, Hamish Hamilton, 1956.

Translator, *The Princess of Clèves*, by Mme. de Lafayette.   London, Euphorion Books, 1950; New York, New Directions, 1951.

Nancy Mitford comments:

I write in the hope of amusing the public and making money for myself.

\*      \*      \*

Nancy Mitford is something rare, a relatively light and "unimportant" writer who has managed to incarnate in a few short books a whole way of life. The British upper classes, as viewed by her, have taken on the quality of a popular myth with which everyone is familiar. The nearest comparable world is perhaps that of Evelyn Waugh's satiric novels, such as *Decline and Fall*, but essentially Waugh's view in these is sardonically detached whereas one never doubts Nancy Mitford's own involvement with her characters. Her earliest attempts at fiction were farce but her best known books, though really sophisticated fantasy, manage to give the impression of seriousness at key moments: as in life, whatever the deliberately flippant tone of the gossip, the listener is prepared to believe that these are tales about real people which have their tragic side.

Much of the appeal, for readers of all degrees of sophistication, is the Mitford air of documentary. Her characters speak with the authentic voice and vocabulary of the upper classes between the wars, and exude the cultish, inbred atmosphere of a tiny world in which "everyone" knows "everyone" or at least knows about them. People who themselves have connections with that world, or like to think they do, enjoy the legitimate sense of recognition they feel when reading her books; while others, who in real life never meet a lord or anyone who says "Fanny's loo is utter bliss", enjoy the vicarious acquaintance with such things that the books bring them. Nancy Mitford is known as a snob and stigmatised for devoting space to such social niceties as the "U" and "non-U" business (which terms she is said to have invented). But to call this "snobbish" is to miss the chief appeal of her work—the way in which she manages to suggest flatteringly, by implication, that of course the reader is in on the joke. When reading Mitford we all live in vast country houses and marry lords—or would if the houses weren't so cold and the lords so old and boring, so instead we have dear little houses in Oxford with unworldly but clever dons and buy our shoes in sales and worry about our children just like everyone else. . . .

At one level Miss Mitford's novels *are* realistic: it is this that gives them their strength. She has never made any secret of drawing heavily for material on her own family. Her sisters figure—selectively—as the cousins of Fanny, narrator of three of her novels. Her father appears as the grotesque "General Murgatroyd" in the first, very light book, *Highland Fling*, and subsequently as "Uncle Matthew". probably her most famous creation, with his "dammed sewer" and his indiscriminate loathing of all huns, wops, dagoes, Reds and anyone even faintly literary or artistic. Nancy's younger sister Jessica was eventually to write, in her own autobiography:

> Thus Farve became—almost overnight—more of a character of fiction than of real life. . . . So successful was [Nancy] that even the obituary writer of *The Times*, describing my father shortly after his death in 1958, betrayed a certain confusion as to whether he was writing about the Rt. Hon. David Bertram Ogilvy Freeman-Mitford or "the explosive, forthright Uncle Matthew". . . .

In real life, the Mitford family came under a cloud at one period as Nazi sympathisers, and another sister, Diana, married Oswald Mosley, leader of the British Fascist party. Of these events not a shadow ever reached the gay novels, in which everyone has their heart in the right place no matter what endearing prejudices and obsessions they also have. But other real-life dramas—Diana's divorce from Brian Guinness, Jessica's Communism and her elopement to Spain with Esmond Romilly—became the material of fiction, particularly of the most famous of the novels, *The Pursuit of Love*. This book portrays a family of sisters plus their cousin Fanny growing up at "Alconleigh" (in reality Swinbrook in the Cotswolds) in an atmosphere of Victorian seclusion and hilarious clannishness, and seeking escape at the earliest possible moment through the romantic love on which their minds have been fixed all through adolescence. Louisa—"dear, good, dull Louisa"—marries a Scottish peer and has copious children, thus fulfilling one frequent Mitford-stereotype, since the wives in her novels are always either excessively faithful and fertile or excessively gay and faithless. Fanny marries her Oxford don, and Linda, the heroine of the book, marries a banker, runs away from him to a Communist and then from the Communist to an interlude in Paris in the arms of a Latin duke called Fabrice de Sauveterre. She returns to England pregnant when the war breaks out and dies in childbirth, her lover being killed at the same time in the Resistance. A likely tale, you may say, and full of commonplace romanticism? Possibly. But Miss Mitford's careful judgement succeeds in transforming the material of wish-fulfilment into something more. The top-dressing of humour and even cynicism skilfully persuades us that when simple drama breaks in it must be authentic.

A carbon copy of Sauveterre appears in a later novel, *The Blessing*, less good but clever and funny. The Alconleigh family also appear in *Love in a Cold Climate*, more openly satiric than *The Pursuit of Love* but in some ways Miss Mitford's neatest exposé of the habits and ideas of a generation—now a vanished one. The immediately and necessarily dateable nature of the world she portrays has meant that she has not been able to go on writing about it indefinitely. One more novel incorporating both Fanny's family and the characters of *The Blessing* appeared in 1960 (*Don't Tell Alfred*) but although it is an engaging book her style has degenerated into high farce under the pressures of newer, unassimilated social phenonoma and the whole thing is frankly unbelievable. Evidently Miss Mitford realised this, for she has announced her intention of writing no more fiction and now devotes herself entirely to biography.

—Gillian Tindall

---

**MONSARRAT, Nicholas (John Turney).** British. Born in Liverpool, 22 March 1910. Educated at Winchester College, Hampshire, 1923–28; Trinity College, Cambridge, 1928–31, B.A. (honours) in law 1931. Served in the Royal Navy, as Lieutenant Commander, Atlantic Escort ships, 1940–46 (mentioned in despatches). Married Eileen Rowland in 1939 (divorced, 1952); Philippa Crosby, 1952 (divorced, 1961); Ann Griffiths, 1961; has three children. Worked in a solicitor's office in Nottingham, 1931–33; Broadcaster and Journalist, 1934–39; Borough Councillor, Kensington, London, 1946; Chief of British Information Services, in South Africa, 1946–53, and Canada, 1953–56. Chairman, National War Memorial Health Foundation, South Africa, 1951–53; Member of the Board of Directors, Ottawa Philharmonic Orchestra, 1956; Member, Board of Governors, Stratford (Ontario) Shakespeare Festival, 1956–60. Recipient: Heinemann Prize, 1952; Coronation Medal, 1953. Fellow, Royal Society of Literature, 1952. Lives in Malta. Address: c/o Benson and Campbell Thomson, Clifford's Inn, London E.C.4, England.

PUBLICATIONS

Novels

*Think of Tomorrow.* London, Hurst and Blackett, 1934.
*At First Sight.* London, Hurst and Blackett, 1935.
*The Whipping Boy.* London, Jarrolds, 1937.
*This Is the Schoolroom.* London, Cassell, and New York, Knopf, 1939.
*H. M. Corvette.* London, Cassell, and Philadelphia, Lippincott, 1943.
*East Coast Corvette.* London, Cassell, and Philadelphia, Lippincott, 1943.
*Corvette Command.* London, Cassell, 1944.
*Leave Cancelled.* New York, Knopf, 1945.
*H. M. Frigate.* London, Cassell, 1946.
*Depends What You Mean by Love: Heavy Rescue, Leave Cancelled, H.M.S. Marlborough Will Enter Harbour.* London, Cassell, 1947; New York, Knopf, 1948.
*My Brother Denys.* London, Cassell, 1948; New York, Knopf, 1949.
*The Cruel Sea.* London, Cassell, and New York, Knopf, 1951.
*The Story of Esther Costello.* London, Cassell, and New York, Knopf, 1953.
*Castle Garac.* New York, Knopf, 1955.
*The Tribe That Lost Its Head.* London, Cassell, and New York, Sloane, 1956.
*The Nylon Pirates.* London, Cassell, and New York, Sloane, 1960.
*The White Rajah.* London, Cassell, and New York, Sloane, 1961.
*The Time Before This.* London, Cassell, and New York, Sloane, 1962.
*Smith and Jones.* London, Cassell, and New York, Sloane, 1963.
*A Fair Day's Work.* London, Cassell, and New York, Sloane, 1964.
*The Pillow Fight.* London, Cassell, and New York, Sloane, 1965.

*Something to Hide.*   London, Cassell, and New York, Morrow, 1966.
*Richer Than All His Tribe.*   London, Cassell, 1968; New York, Morrow, 1969.
*The Kappilan of Malta.*   London, Cassell, and New York, Morrow, 1972.


Short Stories

*The Ship That Died of Shame and Other Stories.*   London, Cassell, and New York, Sloane, 1959.


Plays

*The Visitor* (produced London, 1936).

Screenplays: *The Cruel Sea*, 1953; *The Ship That Died of Shame*, 1955; *The Way of a Ship*, 1956; *The Story of Esther Costello*, 1957; *Something to Hide*, 1972.


Other

*To Stratford with Love.*   Toronto, McClelland and Stewart, 1963.
*Life Is a Four-Letter Word* (autobiography):
   *Breaking In.*   London, Cassell, 1966.
   *Breaking Out.*   London, Cassell, 1970.
   *Breaking In, Breaking Out.*   New York, Morrow, 1971.

Editor, *Boy's Book of the Sea.*   London, Cassell, 1954; New York, McGraw Hill, 1955.
Editor, *Boy's Book of the Commonwealth.*   London, Cassell, 1957.


*          *          *


Nicholas Monsarrat purveys a standard product of uniformly good quality, with occasional minor variation in shape and texture to correspond with what he conceives (usually rightly) to be current shifts in the public taste. He is a craftsman with an excellent if hardly original formula: a swift narrative of action, which is punctuated and to some degree affected by instances of moral concern or temperamental disability in one or more of the characters involved. Mr Monsarrat is not much interested in the actual nature or interior working of personal and moral dilemmas (for most of those which he presents are superficial at best) but rather in the delays or dangers which the obtrusion of such dilemmas may cause in urgent situations.

*The Cruel Sea*, the novel which first made him famous, provides a good example of this technique. The book depends for its suspense largely on contrasting certain threats, which are posed to a naval crew by the ocean and their German enemies, with the almost equally injurious threats which arise from the break-downs or follies of their friends. The account given of the practical problems of seafaring in war is minute, authoritative and yet admirably economical. The "human" difficulties which inhibit or complicate action are, in this book at least, convincing, since they are well attested by real-life records and therefore need only to be stated, not created, by the writer. Add to this that Mr Monsarrat's timing is superb, and the result is dramatic fiction of a high order, to which its author has seldom attained in the many novels he has written since.

However, *The Tribe That Lost Its Head* has some exciting passages which depend on a slightly different kind of contrast: that between the complex necessities, which must to a great extent govern the actions of colonial officers, and the self-righteous and ill-informed attitudes of intellectuals who are posturing on the touch-line. This in turn leads us to yet another variant on Mr Monsarrat's basic theme of action-contra-moralization, a variant which he renders in *A Fair Day's Work*. This novel hinges on the exploitation by whingers and wreckers of contemporary political fads ("Social Justice", etc) in order to evade obligation, excuse culpable failure and claim disproportionate reward. The issue is sharply drawn if somewhat over-simplified; and the lesson, neatly turned, is that malcontents masquerading as idealists could sooner or later subvert the free world and bring all its institutions to rubble.

But whereas Mr Monsarrat knew the wartime navy intimately and also had a fair understanding of the doomed colonial administrators of the fifties, his acquaintance with politics is less immediate—or certainly appears to be so from his written work. For the ideological conflicts which he gets up cannot begin to stand comparison with his crises of disrupted action at sea or in the jungle. As I have indicated, the human or ethical doubts which help to bring on these crises are often very thinly sketched, for Mr Monsarrat is not a sympathetic student of moral sensitivity; but he knows that it exists right enough and can be a bloody nuisance, a nuisance, that is, which leads to the shedding of blood.

—Simon Raven

---

**MOORE, Brian.** Canadian. Born in Belfast, Northern Ireland, 25 August 1921; emigrated to Canada in 1948; moved to the United States in 1959. Educated at St. Malachy's College, Belfast. Served with the British Ministry of War Transport, in North Africa, Italy and France, 1943–45. Married Jacqueline Scully in 1951; Jean Denney, 1966; has one child. Served with the United Nations Relief and Rehabilitation Administration (UNRRA) Mission to Poland, 1946–47; Reporter, *Montreal Gazette*, 1948–52. Full-time Writer since 1952. Recipient: Authors Club of Great Britain Award, 1956; Beta Sigma Phi Award, 1956; Quebec Literary Prize, 1958; Guggenheim Fellowship, 1959; Governor-General's Award, 1961; National Institute of Arts and Letters grant, 1961; Canada Council Fellowship, 1962. Lives in California. Address: c/o Curtis Brown, 60 East 56th Street, New York, New York 10022, U.S.A.

PUBLICATIONS

Novels

*Judith Hearne*.   Toronto, Collins, and London, Deutsch, 1955; as *The Lonely Passion of Judith Hearne*, Boston, Little Brown, 1956.
*The Feast of Lupercal*.   Toronto and Boston, Little Brown, 1957; London, Deutsch, 1958.
*The Luck of Ginger Coffey*.   Boston, Little Brown, and London, Deutsch, 1960.
*An Answer from Limbo*.   Toronto and Boston, Little Brown, 1962; London, Deutsch, 1963.
*The Emperor of Ice-Cream*.   New York, Viking Press, 1965; London, Deutsch, 1966.
*I Am Mary Dunne*.   New York, Viking Press, Toronto, McClelland and Stewart, and London, Cape, 1968.
*Fergus*.   New York, Holt Rinehart, and Toronto, McClelland and Stewart, 1970; London, Cape, 1971.
*Catholics*.   New York, Holt Rinehart, and London, Cape, 1972.

Uncollected Short Stories

"Sassenach", in *Atlantic* (Boston), March 1957.
"Lion of the Afternoon", in *Atlantic* (Boston), November 1957.
"The Apartment Hunter", in *Best American Short Stories, 1969*.   New York, Ballantine, 1970.


Plays

Screenplays: *The Luck of Ginger Coffey*, 1963; *Torn Curtain*, 1966; *The Slave*, 1967.


Other

*Canada*, with the editors of *Life*.   New York, Time, 1963.
*The Revolution Script*.   New York, Holt Rinehart, and Toronto, McClelland and Stewart, 1971; London, Cape, 1972.


Bibliography: in *Brian Moore* by Hallvard Dahlie, Toronto, Copp Clark, 1969.


Critical Studies: "The Simple Excellence of Brian Moore" by Christopher Ricks, in *New Statesman* (London), 18 February 1966; "Crisis and Ritual in Brian Moore's Belfast Novels" by John Wilson Foster, in *Eire-Ireland* (St. Paul, Minnesota), Autumn 1968; *Brian Moore* by Hallvard Dahlie, Toronto, Copp Clark, 1969; *Odysseus Ever Returning* by George Woodcock, Toronto, McClelland and Stewart, 1970; "The Novels of Brian Moore" by Michael Paul Gallagher, S. J., in *Studies (Ireland)* (Dublin), Summer 1971; "The Crisis of Identity in the Novels of Brian Moore" by Murry Prosky, in *Eire-Ireland* (St. Paul, Minnesota), Summer 1971.

*        *        *

An Irishman who has lived for prolonged periods of time in Montreal, New York and California, Moore is himself "an outsider", and this may partly account for the authenticity with which he deals in his novels and short stories with those who, for one reason or another, are misfits, aliens, or failures. In his first, and probably still his best, novel, *Judith Hearne*, he has given us a moving portrayal of an alcoholic ageing spinster who pathetically yearns for friendship and love; in *The Feast of Lupercal* the "hero" is a bachelor schoolmaster who similarly yearns for love, attempts to seduce a girl in a most inept and ungallant fashion, and finds himself in disgrace for a deed he failed to commit; in *The Luck of Ginger Coffey* a luckless Irish immigrant in Montreal temporarily loses his wife and his self-respect because he cannot find a job commensurate with his romantic aspirations; the central figures of his later novels are similar in their feelings of inadequacy, their frustrated yearning for love, even though they are far more successful in material terms.

Moore deals with these characters in a manner which unites compassion and irony, sympathy and detachment. He feels a tender concern for their frustrations and failures, but at the same time he makes us aware of the pathetic self-deceptions and shabby hypocrisies of which they are capable. To maintain such a balanced attitude is difficult, but Moore almost always succeeds in the attempt: the style and tone of his works are subtle and complex. Most impressive is the way in which Moore reveals the interior lives of his characters: he has an uncanny gift for "seeing through" them, of laying bare the fragile base of pretensions and compromises on which their lives are built. Thus of Diarmuid Devine, in *The Feast of Lupercal*, he writes:

Standing in the tub, soaping his buttocks, he dropped his chin to stare. *Deo gratias*, he could still see it; he had not put on a pot yet. Unused though it was. But dammit, he chided himself, there is no sense in being morbid, no sense thinking things like that. And it was all bunkum, this business of carrying on your line. Take genius, it did not transmit. For example. . . .

But he could not think of an example, offhand. He stepped out onto the rubber mat, wiped the steamy mirror and put on his spectacles, inspecting his stranger face. His hair was getting just a wee bit thin on top. . . . Oh, well, he was not such a bad-looking cuss; he had seen worse in his day. He bowed to himself and gave his mustaches a military twirl. After all, he was off to a party that very night. There would be lots of girls there, you would imagine.

Such a passage convinces us by its authenticity: such is the way we do measure ourselves, find ourselves wanting, and then reassure ourselves by a process of self-deception or the promise of a forthcoming party. Moore has managed at once to make us aware of our common humanity with Devine, and to make us aware of his faults and foibles: we stand both beside him and above him.

Almost equally convincing is Moore's capacity to describe the external world, and to describe it in such a way as to make it a telling objective correlative of the inner lives of his characters. For example, much of Devine's plight is conveyed by this description of his residence:

He lived midway between the school and the city, in a quiet avenue once prosperous, now failing. Its small front gardens had a naked communal look, occasioned by the wartime removal of their iron railings for use in making tanks. The railings had not been replaced, the avenue had not recovered. Dusty squares of lawn, enclosed by low stone parapets, lay like neglected empty pools in front of the houses. It was an avenue whose first owners had moved to new areas, making way for widows on annuities, salesmen on commission and policemen pensioned off.

All this, however, is to give a misleading impression of prevalent drabness, because it has left out of account the countervailing forces of Moore's fiction. One of these countervailing forces is Moore's humour. He has a richly comic strain which entwines most piquantly with his sense of pathos. His humour runs the gamut from quiet, almost undetectable irony to broad farce bordering on burlesque. Such scenes as that of Devine's attempt at seduction are extremely funny, in the tradition of Irish knockabout farce; on the other hand Moore is a master of subdued and ambiguous irony in the tradition of Swift and Goldsmith.

Another of the countervailing forces is Moore's conviction of the possibility of self-redemption, or at any rate of creative self-acceptance. Although his characters begin by being lost and bewildered, and never triumph in any obvious sense, they do all eventually come to some climactic moment of self-discovery, when they decide to come to terms with themselves and their fate, to commit themselves with courage to the destructive element.

An outsider committed to the exploration of the outsider, Moore is also something of an outsider in the stream of contemporary fiction. Although he obviously owes something to Flaubert and Joyce, he has not indulged in any of the fashionable experiments of our period. There is nothing spectacular about his style or his material: quietly, ironically but sympathetically he chronicles the ordinary lives of ordinary people in a predominantly straightforward, unassuming way. It seems certain that at least some of his characters will be remembered for many decades to come.

—Desmond Pacey

**MORRIS, Wright (Marion).**   American.   Born in Central City, Nebraska, 6 January 1910. Educated at Lakeview High School, Chicago; Crane College, Chicago; Pomona College, Claremont, California, 1930–33. Married Mary Ellen Finfrock in 1934 (divorced, 1961); Josephine Kantor, 1961. Has lectured at Haverford College, Pennsylvania, Sarah Lawrence College, Bronxville, New York, and Swarthmore College, Pennsylvania. Since 1962, Professor of English, San Francisco State College. Recipient: Guggenheim Fellowship, 1942, 1946, 1954; National Book Award, 1957; National Institute of Arts and Letters grant, 1960; Rockefeller grant, 1967. Honorary degrees: Westminster College, Fulton, Missouri, 1968; University of Nebraska, Lincoln, 1968. Member, National Institute of Arts and Letters, 1970. Address: 341 Laurel Way, Mill Valley, California, U.S.A.

PUBLICATIONS

Novels

My Uncle Dudley.   New York, Harcourt Brace, 1942.
The Man Who Was There.   New York, Scribner, 1945.
The World in the Attic.   New York, Scribner, 1949.
Man and Boy.   New York, Knopf, 1951; London, Gollancz, 1952.
The Works of Love.   New York, Knopf, 1952.
The Deep Sleep.   New York, Scribner, 1953; London, Eyre and Spottiswoode, 1954.
The Huge Season.   New York, Viking Press, 1954; London, Secker and Warburg, 1955.
The Field of Vision.   New York, Harcourt Brace, 1956; London, Weidenfeld and Nicolson, 1957.
Love among the Cannibals.   New York, Harcourt Brace, 1957; London, Weidenfeld and Nicolson, 1958.
Ceremony in Lone Tree.   New York, Atheneum, 1960; London, Weidenfeld and Nicolson, 1961.
What a Way to Go.   New York, Atheneum, 1962.
Cause for Wonder.   New York, Atheneum, 1963.
One Day.   New York, Atheneum, 1965.
In Orbit.   New York, New American Library, 1967.
Fire Sermon.   New York, Harper, 1971.
War Games.   Los Angeles, Black Sparrow Press, 1972.

Short Stories

Green Grass, Blue Sky, White House.   Los Angeles, Black Sparrow Press, 1970.

Other

The Inhabitants (photo-text).   New York, Scribner, 1946.
The Home Place (photo-text).   New York, Scribner, 1948.
The Territory Ahead (essays).   New York, Harcourt Brace, 1958; London, Peter Smith, 1964.
A Bill of Rites, A Bill of Wrongs, A Bill of Goods (essays).   New York, New American Library, 1967.
God's Country and My People (photo-text).   New York, Harper, 1968.
Wright Morris: A Reader.   New York, Harper, 1970.

Editor, *The Mississippi River Reader*.   New York, Doubleday, 1962.

Manuscript Collection: University of California at Berkeley.

Critical Studies: *Wright Morris* by David Madden, New York, Twayne, 1964; *Wright Morris* by Leon Howard, Minneapolis, University of Minnesota, 1968.

\*       \*       \*

No other contemporary American novelist has managed to be so persistently unfashionable as Wright Morris. Despite his many books, and despite both occasional public honors and a continuous critical assent to his talents, intelligence, integrity, and seriousness, and even in despite of the fact that scholarly monographs on his work are prepared and published, he has never commanded a general attention. His work has resisted categories and obvious affiliations, while in its uniqueness it has prevented imitation. Morris is now an undeniable literary fact, without ever having been an event.

It is in part strange that this should be the case, because no other contemporary American novelist has been so diligently or sensitively in touch with the manners, voices, and things of American civilization. Morris' knowledge has led him, however, to an effort which prohibits ideological assertion for the reason that it prevents final judgements. His novels and other books resist easy categorization because they are so contained within their own procedure toward discovery, rather than being dedicated to conclusive messages. Narrative line in Morris' fiction is seldom forthright. Thematic development is always subject to new doubts and allurements. The prose is elliptical, allusive, punning, to so great an extent as to seem sometimes incapable of statement. Indeed, language itself seems to be for Morris one more of those mysterious objects produced by the American civilization, which is to be explored for the hint of a revelation rather than be exploited. And the individual novels are not even discrete episodes of realization. Morris borrows freely from himself from book to book, re-using not only characters and events but lengthy passages of narration and reflection. He seems to have been long engaged in thinking through a single work—consisting of fiction, photographs, and an amount of literary and cultural criticism—the end of which is not yet in sight.

He has been so engaged for more than thirty years and through some twenty books. In this time his single subject has been American nativity, and, if he has been influenced by any literary or cultural movement, it is that new nationalism which was being predicated in the 1910's and 1920's by Van Wyck Brooks, Lewis Mumford, Waldo Frank, Sherwood Anderson, the photographer Alfred Stieglitz, and others. Brooks had made a case for what he called the "usable past." More particularly, he had called upon American writers and critics to seek their own—American—literary past in such a way as to discover a cultural coherence, in which they then might participate. The invitation had itself become a part of the past by the time that Morris began to write, but he seems to have been impressed by some of the later nationalists, notably James Agee and Walker Evans. In any event, quite like those artists who participated in Brooks's enterprise, Morris has made his field of endeavor the American folk past and its relationship to the American present. The subject is the continuity of the American character, sought in its typicality and in its everydayness.

Despite the continuousness—indeed, the circularity—of effort proposed to Morris by his subject, the subject has also commanded a distinguishable progress in his thinking. He began with a commitment to discovery of the past, and he repeated that commitment without qualification, though with varying kinds of cunning, in the five books which he published in the 1940's. In the first, *My Uncle Dudley*, he composed a narrative which would ironically recapitulate the American past of the early middle nineteenth century. The time present of the novel is the 1920's. Uncle Dudley and his sidekick, the boy who tells the story, do a stint of vagabondage, which secures its significance because it simulates pioneering. In this day and age, the pursuit of the frontier must go from west to east, from Los Angeles to Chicago, and the pretence of the vagabonds to a covered wagon is an ancient touring car. They are assaulted on all sides by contemporary materialism, timidity, and restrictiveness, but they thereby are able to prove the older ways and virtues. And they succeed in their pretence until, just like Huckleberry Finn before them, they are incarcerated in a small town in Missouri. In the succeeding books in this period, Morris reversed his strategy for recovery of the past. *My Uncle Dudley* accepts a conventional myth of the older America and imposes it upon the present. The next books—a volume of novellas, two photo-texts, and a novel— have protagonists who, from their vantage in the present, come upon suggestive, buried, and ambiguous mementos of the past. As is usually the case in Morris' work, the locus of the past is the rural or small-town midwest. The protagonists of these books find a beckoning but elusive vitalism in occasional survivors from the past, and in such artifacts as peeling Mail Pouch signs on old barns, the fading pages of the old mail order catalogue, or an old and sputtering Model T. The process of apprehension is the area of Morris' concern.

This process seems finally, however, to have borne malign implications for Morris. With *The World in the Attic* he began to explore another realization, to the effect that the past was also potentially imprisoning, and the books thereafter become progressively less retrospective. The protagonists are not at home in the present, which is seen to be a spiritual wateland, but they avoid regressive nostalgia. The intent of the books of the 1950's—novels and one volume of literary criticism—is recovery into the present not of the past but of a native American character, which is seen to be at once conservative, practical, desperate for spiritual liberation, and audacious. Salvation, if there is to be any, is in the occasional gesture on the part of the protagonists which combines past and present, transcending both.

Perhaps in response to a more anarchic climate in American society, in his most recent novels Morris has begun to explore still another realization within his general subject. That audacity which had been proposed as one of the resources of heroism in the American character might well be criminal in this time. In *One Day*, he speculates on the native American character as it emerges in the American boy who killed President Kennedy. The novel *In Orbit* speculates, not quite so harshly, on the nativity of those randomly violent American boys who are to be seen crossing the landscape on their motorcycles, in perpetual flight.

These latter novels, too, fail to make final assertions. Like all of Morris' novels, they are populated by characters who confess themselves to be frustrated and bewildered, thereby providing opportunity for other and continuous reaches of realization.

—Marcus Klein

**MORTIMER, Penelope (Ruth).** British. Born in Rhyl, North Wales, in 1918. Attended London University. Married Charles Dimont in 1937 (divorced, 1949); the playwright John Mortimer, 1949 (divorced, 1971); has six children. Movie Critic, *The Observer*, London, 1967–70. Address: 134 Loudoun Road, London N.W.8, England.

PUBLICATIONS

Novels

*Johanna* (as Penelope Dimont).   London, Secker and Warburg, 1947.

*A Villa in Summer*.   London, Joseph, 1954; New York, Harcourt Brace, 1955.
*The Bright Prison*.   London, Joseph, 1956; New York, Harcourt Brace, 1957.
*Daddy's Gone A-Hunting*.   London, Joseph, 1958; as *Cave of Ice*, New York, Harcourt Brace, 1959.
*Saturday Lunch with the Brownings*.   London, Hutchinson, 1960; New York, McGraw Hill, 1961.
*The Pumpkin Eater*.   London, Hutchinson, 1962; New York, McGraw Hill, 1963.
*My Friend Says It's Bullet-Proof*.   London, Hutchinson, 1967; New York, Random House, 1968.
*The Home*.   London, Hutchinson, 1971; New York, Random House, 1972.


Play

Screenplay: *Bunny Lake Is Missing*, with John Mortimer, 1965.


Other

*With Love and Lizards*, with John Mortimer (travel).   London, Joseph, 1957.


Penelope Mortimer comments:

My father was a C. of E. clergyman and I was brought up in Buckinghamshire, Thornton Heath, and Belper in Derbyshire. For various reasons (my father's changing theories as well as residences) I went to seven schools, ending up at a School for the Daughters of the Clergy (disaster). Did a secretarial course in London at the age of 17, hated it, went to London University, left after a year because my father said he was broke, took a job as secretary to the Publicity Manager of Butlins Holiday Camp, decided after three weeks that marriage was preferable, married, had four children, wrote the odd piece for the *New Statesman* and *Our Time* and spent four years writing *Johanna*, which sank like a stone in 1947.

As well as the 8 books and 2 Mortimer children, I wrote a lot for the *New Yorker*, did fiction reviews for the *Sunday Times*, wrote a Lonely Hearts column under the pseudonym of Ann Temple for the *Daily Mail* (2 ghastly years), and did a considerable amount of other journalism.

The canvas of my fiction is narrow—domestic, mainly concerned with sexual and parental relationships—but I hope makes up in depth what it lacks in breadth. So far, I am almost entirely concerned with individuals' motives (i.e. what "makes them tick") and the development of their personalities from an early age (*Pumpkin Eater* and *The Home* particularly). Rather obviously (though not necessarily) I write through the eyes and ears of a woman. My men, I think, are getting better, and maybe I will someday venture to try to put myself inside a man's head and write from there. I believe that comedy is absolutely essential to tragedy, and I hope my books are almost as funny as they are (I'm told) sad or depressing. I would like to enlarge my scope, but not if it's at the expense of depth. Once my characters are established psychologically—heredity, environment, the lot—they take over their own growth and perform their own actions; I have very little to do with it.

*        *        *

The themes of popular fiction remain what they have always been: sex and marriage, class, money and power. What has changed is the writer's attitude towards this material.

905

A Victorian novel in this genre ended with a wedding; nowadays the plot tends to begin with an unhappy marriage, trace the course of the more or less unhappy affairs and end where it began, in sexual stalemate.

Of the many English novelists who have explored this territory, none has more sheer ability to write than Penelope Mortimer. She catalogues the debris of failure: the repetitive rows, the broken resolutions, the betrayals which would exact revenge had they not paralysed their victim. In each book the central relationship is destructive; only the children survive "sitting in a patient row on the sofa . . . their eyes restless as maggots, expecting us to bring them up." This description from *The Pumpkin Eater* is an example of her writing at its best, candid and original.

*Villa in Summer* is an accomplished study of corruption, a portrait of a couple who cling together out of habit as much as out of love. Emily has drifted so far from her husband that he feels "there were two species: Emily and women." Their marriage is vulnerable enough and easily shaken by a predatory pair of adulterers, teachers from the local progressive school.

Emily is the first in a string of lost innocents, heroines who are aware of the truth but unable to act on it. The central character in *Daddy's Gone A-Hunting* is shut off from potential pleasure, experiencing life in waves of guilt and pain. She cannot use her suffering to change her own situation but is able to protect her daughter against their common enemy, Rex, the unfaithful husband and callous father. Rex is typical of the men in Mrs. Mortimer's fiction, drifting in and out of the story, excluded, pacified, accused. Only occasionally does the implicit violence break through into an open declaration of war. "A man has to be drunk, insane or unbalanced by talent before he'll behave like a woman," comments the heroine of *The Pumpkin Eater*, begging an awful lot of questions.

It is ironic that Penelope Mortimer has been both praised and criticised for her analysis of modern marriage. She keeps a witty and compassionate eye on that institution, it is true, but her observations do not set out to be objective. She is not a satirist, nor does her writing reflect the struggles of that old phenomenon, the new woman. Society is of secondary importance in her novels, which are intense, imaginative explorations of an inner world. It is an enclosed world, dominated by fear, in which physical experiences such as sterilisation and abortion isolate her characters from their fellow beings and are metaphors for a deeper spiritual isolation. Her most recent work shows an intensification of this mood. *My Friend Says It's Bullet-Proof* and *Home* are about women at the edge, held from destruction by an obsessive need to record and understand their own despair.

—Judith Cooke Simmons

---

**MOSLEY, Nicholas (Lord Ravensdale).** British. Born in London, 25 June 1923; eldest son of Sir Oswald Mosley, and heir to his father's baronetcy; became 3rd Baron Ravensdale on the death of his aunt, Baroness Ravensdale, 1966. Educated at Eton College, Buckinghamshire, 1937–42; Balliol College, Oxford, 1946–47. Served as a Captain in the Rifle Brigade, 1942–46; awarded Military Cross, 1944. Married Rosemary Laura Salmond in 1947; has four children. Address: 9 Church Row, London N.W.3, England.

PUBLICATIONS

Novels

*Spaces of the Dark*.  London, Hart Davis, 1951.

*The Rainbearers.*   London, Weidenfeld and Nicolson, 1955.
*Corruption.*   London, Weidenfeld and Nicolson, 1957; Boston, Little Brown, 1958.
*Meeting Place.*   London, Weidenfeld and Nicolson, 1962.
*Accident.*   London, Hodder and Stoughton, 1965; New York, Coward McCann, 1966.
*Assassins.*   London, Hodder and Stoughton, 1966; New York, Coward McCann, 1967.
*Impossible Object.*   London, Hodder and Stoughton, 1968; New York, Coward McCann, 1969.
*Natalie, Natalia.*   London, Hodder and Stoughton, and New York, Coward McCann, 1971.

Other

*African Switchback* (travel).   London, Weidenfeld and Nicolson, 1958.
*The Life of Raymond Raynes.*   London, Faith Press, 1961.
*Experience and Religion: A Lay Essay in Theology.*   London, Hodder and Stoughton, 1965: Philadelphia, United Church Press, 1967.
*The Assassination of Trotsky.*   London, Joseph, 1972.

*        *        *

An approach to the work of Nicholas Mosley might be made by considering the reply made to a question asked by a character in *Accident*: "Why is it that modern novels have to be different, cannot just be stories of characters, action and society?" The reply was: "We know too much about characters, action, and society, . . . we can now write about people *knowing*." Certainly Mr Mosley's first three competent and straightforward novels of the 1950s made it plain that he was thoroughly at home in the genre and could produce a convincing picture of life in the post war period. It is with the fourth novel, *Meeting Place*, that the first hint comes that the author might not be content with the novel as a mere chronological narration of events. In the fragmented and impressionistic story of a social worker and the relationships of varying depths he makes with the people around him, Mr Mosley is clearly making an attempt to expand the limits of what he might require a novel to do.

There is a strong philosophical element in all Mr Mosley's work. The title *Accident* indicates a random event as well as referring to the car crash which resolves the coming together of a particular group of people in academic Oxford. One of the characters says: "We imagine we move according to cause and effect but in reality we are particles with velocity but no location." *Accident* is a successful blend of ideas, impressionistically presented visual lushness, and a delicately explored nexus of relationships around the central character of Anna, the catalyst, about whom as a person we are told nothing. Like *Accident*, *Assassins* is "a good story". The daughter of the British Foreign Secretary is abducted from his country house where he is engaged in delicate negotiations with the leader of a communist country. The relationship of the teenage girl with her youthful kidnapper is an example of the kind of writing at which Mr Mosley excels.

The seventh novel, *Impossible Object*, has been described as like a crossword puzzle, or like a Royal Academy problem picture. The average reader might be tempted not to try to hammer out the solution. In form it is eight short stories which switch from one narrator to another to present a central relationship. Interspersed with the narrative are surrealistic essays which, however elusive in meaning, serve to heighten the total impact. This novel is successful in maintaining a balance between what the author has proved he can do so well, and the extension of the techniques of novel writing which, it has become plain, is now his aim. *Natalie, Natalia* concerns a politician who leaves a maritally complex situation to go to

Africa where he has a nervous breakdown. Although the form is looser than in the previous novel, in it Nicholas Mosley attempts the same thing on a greater scale with less success. It is paradoxical that the diversions from the narrative in *Natalie, Natalia* are less opaque and more of a piece than those in *Impossible Object* and yet in some way they dilute it.

It is tempting to speculate about the direction Mr Mosley's future development as a writer might take. Certainly the later novels have a smoothness of style which aquit him of earlier infelicities which caused a reviewer to describe him as a literary grocer dropping dried peas into a bag until he has half a pound or so of paragraph. The reader may still be snatched from one idea to another but he is no longer jerked from word to word. Mr Mosley as a writer is supremely good when he is exploring the relationship of one person to another: the married couple in *Accident*, the lovers in *Impossible Object*, the young girl and her abducter in *Assassins*. He is an interesting writer and difficult to assess because he is not content just to do what he can do well.

—Anastasia Leech

---

**MPHAHLELE, Ezekiel.** South African. Born in Pretoria, 17 December 1919. Educated at Adams College, Natal, 1939–40; University of South Africa, Pretoria, 1946–49, 1953–54, 1956, B.A. (honours) 1949; M.A. in English 1956; University of Denver, Colorado, 1966–68, Ph.D. in English 1968. Married Rebecca Mphahlele in 1945; has five children. Teacher of English and Afrikaans, Orlando High School, Johannesburg, 1945–52; Fiction Editor, *Drum* magazine, Johannesburg, 1955–57; Lecturer in English Literature, University of Ibadan, Nigeria, 1957–61; Director of African Programmes, International Association for Cultural Freedom, Paris, 1961–63; Director of Chemchemi Creative Centre, Nairobi, Kenya, 1963–65; Lecturer, University College, Nairobi, 1965–66; Visiting Lecturer in English, University of Denver, 1966–68; Senior Lecturer in English, University of Zambia, Lusaka, 1968–70. Since 1970, Associate Professor of English, University of Denver. Address: c/o Department of English, University of Denver, University Park, Denver, Colorado 80210, U.S.A.

PUBLICATIONS

Novel

  *The Wanderers.*  New York, Macmillan, and London, Macmillan, 1972.

Short Stories

  *Man Must Live and Other Stories.*  Cape Town, African Bookman, 1947.
  *The Living and Dead and Other Stories.*  Ibadan, Black Orpheus, 1961.
  *In Corner B and Other Stories.*  Nairobi, East African Publishing House, 1967.

Other

  *Down Second Avenue* (autobiography).  London, Faber, 1959; New York, Doubleday, 1971.

*The African Image* (essays).   London, Faber, 1962; New York, Praeger, 1964.
*Voices in the Whirlwind and Other Essays*.   New York, Hill and Wang, and London, Macmillan, 1972.

Editor, with Ellis Komey, *Modern African Stories*.   London, Faber, 1964.
Editor, *African Writing Today*.   London, Penguin, 1967.

Critical Studies: *Seven African Writers* by Gerald Moore, London, Oxford University Press, 1962; *The Chosen Tongue* by Gerald Moore, London, Longman, 1969; essay by the author on his own work: "The South African Short Story", in *Kenyon Review* (Gambier, Ohio), 1969.

Ezekiel Mphahlele comments:

I began my writing career as a short-story writer during World War II. I wrote for *Drum* magazine in Johannesburg, *Fighting Talk* and *New Age* in Johannesburg, and *Africa South* in Cape Town (the last 3 journals since banned by the South African Government). My earliest stories, i.e., *Man Must Live*, were escapist stuff which came spontaneously. I moved on to vitriolic protest fiction. I left South Africa as an exile in September 1957 to teach in Nigeria where I finished the second half of *Down Second Avenue*, my autobiography. Even in exile my fictional themes have always been South Africa. But *In Corner B*, which I wrote in Paris in 1963, has two stories set in Nigeria: "The Barber of Bariga" and "The Ballad of Oyo". The rest are set in South Africa. I wrote these Nigerian stories and "Mrs. Plum" in Paris. The rest had appeared in Johannesburg journals. "Mrs. Plum" in that volume was my first attempt at the long short-story. I have often thought of fiction as my specific commitment; when I am still composing such a work in my mind, I write critical essays—such as *The African Image* and *Voices in the Whirlwind*. *The Wanderers* has an autobiographical outline but the incidents are fictional. I am planning a novel set in Zambia. I am trying to come to terms with the greater Africa as a setting, but I know the South African in me will accompany me to the grave.

\*       \*       \*

Ezekiel Mphahlele has been one of the most versatile and influential of African authors. As literary critic, autobiographer, journalist, short story writer, novelist, dramatist and poet, he has probably contributed more than any other individual to the growth and development of an African literature in English. Since leaving South Africa fifteen years ago, he has travelled widely, stopping to teach for a year or two in at least five different countries— Nigeria, Kenya, Zambia, France and the United States. He is presently a professor of English and African literature at the University of Denver in Colorado.

In South Africa Mphahlele wrote mainly short stories about life in the urban black ghettos where he had grown up and spent most of his adult years. The events in these stories were based on his personal experiences and reflected a wide variety of responses to the people and places he knew best. There were humorous sketches and satirical vignettes as well as more serious stories about human or social problems. Later, as stringent apartheid legislation made life more difficult for urban blacks, Mphahlele began to write angry protest fiction. By the mid-fifties he felt stifled in his home country and applied for an "exit permit," a document allowing him to leave South Africa on the condition that he never return. The South African government granted his request in 1957 and he has lived in exile ever since.

His first major piece of writing abroad was an autobiography, *Down Second Avenue*, in which he tried to work off the emotional steam and creative energy that had been building up inside him during his last years in South Africa. It is a moving story, told with candour and compassion for his people. In 1962 he published a pioneering work of literary criticism, *The African Image*, part of which had been written in South Africa as an M.A. thesis. He also brought out two collections of his short stories and produced a manual for aspiring fiction writers. His first novel, *The Wanderers*, examined the plight of the black South African intellectual in exile, a depressing tale constructed out of the debris of his own personal life.

In most of his recent writing Mphahlele has been able to arrive at the kind of emotional balance and aesthetic distance from his subject matter that he found impossible to achieve while living in South Africa. The element of protest is still strong in his fiction but it is now under much firmer artistic control. Exile, though a painful and frustrating experience, has made Mphahlele a more accomplished literary craftsman.

—Bernth Lindfors

---

**MUNRO, Alice.** Canadian. Born in Wingham, Ontario, 10 July 1931. Educated in Wingham public schools; and at the University of Western Ontario, London, 1949–51. Married James Armstrong Munro in 1951; has three children. Recipient: Governor-General's Award, 1969. Address: 1648 Rockland, Victoria, British Columbia, Canada.

PUBLICATIONS

Novel

*Lives of Girls and Women.*   Toronto, McGraw Hill, 1971.

Short Stories

*Dance of the Happy Shades.*   Toronto, Ryerson Press, 1968.

*       *       *

Alice Munro has been publishing short stories since the early 1950's in such journals as *The Canadian Forum*, *The Tamarack Review*, *Queen's Quarterly*, and *The Montrealer*. In 1968, fifteen of her stories were collected under the title of *Dance of the Happy Shades*, for which she won the Governor-General's Award for Literature.

Alice Munro concerns herself with the small town or rural world, but she is no mere singer of the pastoral virtues. The world she depicts is on the surface orderly, quiet, and uneventful, but its inhabitants are frequently on the edge of despair, fear, or hysteria, and the reader is constantly aware of an undercurrent of sordidness, perversion, or violence which can at any moment engulf her characters. Mrs. Munro's special talent is reflected in the way she juxtaposes her rural settings and their characters against the threatening encroachments of other worlds which are only dimly perceived or understood. Sometimes, as in "The Shining Houses," it is the spectacle of physical urbanization and its accompanying dehumanizing conformity which poses the threat; but more frequently, as in "Walker Brothers Cowboy" or "The Peace of Utrecht," it is a more subtle and incomprehensible threat which insinuates itself and works upon the emerging awareness of some of the more sensitive characters. In all her stories, Mrs. Munro dramatizes the tension which on the surface appears to be between certainty and uncertainty, but which is really an opposition between the many facets of uncertainty. The past, for example, or a strong code of morality, or progress—qualities which the world at large tends to regard favourably—these forces in Alice Munro's works are as threatening and unsettling as the undefined dimensions against which they are juxtaposed.

Mrs. Munro's depicting of the changes taking place in her rural world is not so much sociological as it is moral: she has captured this world at the point where the more sensitive of its characters (usually the girl-narrator figure) recognizes that a kind of moral chaos rules everything, and that one can find nothing tangible which will give existence either security or meaning. "Things are getting out of hand, anything may happen," the narrator reflects in the title story, and this theme is emphasized throughout the collection. On the most tangible and human level, this tension or emptiness is dramatized in situations which Alice Munro describes as "unconsummated relationships." Sometimes, as in "Walker Brothers Cowboy," "Images," or "Boys and Girls," it is the mother figure who, either through a self-imposed puritan code of self-sacrifice or through intolerance, is denied participation or fulfillment; at other times, as in "Postcard," "Sunday Afternoon," or "A Trip to the Coast," it is the girl-narrator who is forced into a state of isolation or rejection. The fulfilled relationships in Alice Munro are rare, and when they do occur, they are either meaningless and sordid, as in "Thanks for the Ride," or fragile and temporary, as in "Red Dress 1946."

With their emphasis on the grotesque, the irrational, the absurd, and the dead past, and in their frequent evocation of the terrors or meaninglessness of an existential void, the stories in *Dance of the Happy Shades* reflect a vision of the world which is both frightening and convincing. The collection as a whole marks Alice Munro as one of the most significant short story writers in Canada today.

—Hallvard Dahlie

---

**MURDOCH, (Jean) Iris.** British. Born in Dublin, Ireland, 15 July 1919. Educated at Froebel Education Institute, London; Badminton School, Bristol; Somerville College, Oxford, 1938–42, B.A. 1942; Newnham College, Cambridge (Sarah Smithson Student in Philosophy), 1947–48. Married the writer John Bayley in 1956. Assistant Principal in the Treasury, London, 1942–44; Administrative Officer with the United Nations Relief and Rehabilitation Administration (UNRRA), in London, Belgium and Austria, 1944–46. Fellow and University Lecturer in Philosophy, 1948–63, and since 1963 Honorary Fellow, St. Anne's College, Oxford. Lecturer, Royal College of Art, London, 1963–67. Address: Cedar Lodge, Steeple Aston, Oxford, England.

PUBLICATIONS

Novels

*Under the Net.* London, Chatto and Windus, and New York, Viking Press, 1954.
*The Flight from the Enchanter.* London, Chatto and Windus, and New York, Viking Press, 1956.

*The Sandcastle.*   London, Chatto and Windus, and New York, Viking Press, 1957.
*The Bell.*   London, Chatto and Windus, and New York, Viking Press, 1958.
*A Severed Head.*   London, Chatto and Windus, and New York, Viking Press, 1961.
*An Unofficial Rose.*   London, Chatto and Windus, and New York, Viking Press, 1962.
*The Unicorn.*   London, Chatto and Windus, and New York, Viking Press, 1963.
*The Italian Girl.*   London, Chatto and Windus, and New York, Viking Press, 1964.
*The Red and the Green.*   London, Chatto and Windus, and New York, Viking Press, 1965.
*The Time of the Angels.*   London, Chatto and Windus, and New York, Viking Press, 1966.
*The Nice and the Good.*   London, Chatto and Windus, and New York, Viking Press, 1968.
*Bruno's Dream.*   London, Chatto and Windus, and New York, Viking Press, 1969.
*A Fairly Honourable Defeat.*   London, Chatto and Windus, and New York, Viking Press, 1970.
*An Accidental Man.*   London, Chatto and Windus, 1971; New York, Viking Press, 1972.

### Plays

*A Severed Head*, with J. B. Priestley (produced Bristol and London, 1963; New York, 1964).   London, Chatto and Windus, 1964.
*The Italian Girl*, with James Saunders (produced Bristol, 1967; London, 1968).
*The Servants and the Snow* (produced London, 1970).

### Other

*Sartre: Romantic Rationalist.*   London, Bowes, and New Haven, Connecticut, Yale University Press, 1953.
*The Sovereignty of Good.*   London, Routledge, 1971.

Manuscript Collection: University of Iowa, Iowa City.

*     *     *

Most of her readers are aware, often a little uneasily, that Iris Murdoch is a professional philosopher, but remain uncertain as to the exact nature of her philosophic commitments and the degree to which some knowledge of them is essential to an understanding of her densely populated, intricately plotted novels. Critical summaries such as this which approach Miss Murdoch's fiction primarily in terms of her intellectual position have the virtue of orderliness, perhaps, and yet should not imply that the novels demand familiarity with the purely philosophic work. Miss Murdoch herself has stated that the novel should be "an art of image", not merely an instrument of analysis and reflection; and the questions she asks of Sartre's work—has a certain transmutation of ideas taken place, has the philosophy been fused completely with the image constituted by the story—are questions she would presumably agree must be asked of her own efforts. In many instances the answer is a positive one: *Under the Net, The Bell, A Severed Head* and at least a few of the later novels do in fact embody a moving and wholly intelligible view of life. Moreover, it would be a mistake to conclude that the fiction is primarily a simplification of ideas developed elsewhere, for more than once Miss Murdoch has complained of "those exasperating moments in philosophy when one seems to be relentlessly prevented from saying something which one is irresistibly impelled to say". Miss Murdoch's activity as a novelist should be seen in part as an implied criticism of the limits of philosophic discourse: "A moral philosophy", she remarks, "should be inhabited."

At the center of Miss Murdoch's work there is a pessimism which may startle her more casual readers. "We are anxiety-ridden animals", she writes; "Our minds are continually active, fabricating an anxious, usually self-protective, often falsifying *veil* which partially conceals the world. . . . We are largely mechanical creatures, the slaves of relentlessly strong selfish forces the nature of which we scarcely comprehend." Although these crucial qualifications, "largely" and "scarcely", save her thought from the blank determinism and inconsistently romantic nihilism she criticizes in Freud and the existentialists, Miss Murdoch nevertheless accepts the definition of man as an accidental creature briefly adrift in a contingent universe:

> That human life has no external point . . . is a view as difficult to argue as its opposite, and I shall simply assert it. I can see no evidence to suggest that human life is not something self-contained. There are properly many patterns and purposes within life, but there is no general and as it were guaranteed pattern or purpose of the kind for which philosophers and theologians used to search. We are what we seem to be, transient mortal creatures subject to necessity and chance. . . . Our destiny can be examined but it cannot be justified or totally explained. We are simply here.

These denials prepare the way for Miss Murdoch's persistent concern as a philosopher and novelist, the nature of ethical behavior. She is finally a kind of modern non-transcendental Platonist for whom freedom, knowledge and virtue are ultimately one, forming the human goal which art is especially potent to depict.

"The world is aimless, chancy, and huge, and we are blinded by self": true knowledge involves the difficult task of coming to see things as they are, without the consoling fantasies of the "fat relentless ego" which longs for a more commanding place and destiny. Miss Murdoch's tactic in her philosophical essays is to point out the inadequacies of two of the conceptions of man which dominate modern thought. Both the existentialist and the linguistic philosopher, she argues, present a shallow view of human nature, a "simplified and impoverished inner life". For Sartre the individual is the center, but "a solipsistic center", a thin blade of pure will in a world where human relationships become impossible, whereas the world of the Oxford philosophers is "a world in which people play cricket, cook cakes, make simple decisions, remember their childhood and go to the circus; not the world in which they commit sins, fall in love, say prayers or join the Communist Party." What is lacking above all in these influential models of human nature is a genuine conception of love and freedom, beginning with a respect for—rather than a hatred or dismissal of—the contingency and final "pointlessness" of life. For Miss Murdoch freedom is not mere exercise of the will, but rather "the experience of accurate vision . . . a disciplined overcoming of self"; virtue, which pre-supposes objective vision, is concerned with "apprehending that other people exist . . . knowing and understanding and respecting things other than ourselves". Thus goodness means knowledge and so "connects us with reality"; and the chief human virtue, love, is finally the exercise of "the extremely difficult realization that something other than oneself is real", manifesting itself as patient, attentive respect for others as separate beings and not merely objects to be grasped and used. The novel proper is "about people's treatment of each other" and the creation and enjoyment of works of art promote that "unselving" which is the beginning of virtue: "What is learnt here is something about the real quality of human nature, when it is envisaged, in the artist's just and compassionate vision, with a clarity which does not belong to the self-centered rush of ordinary life." Art may delineate the good with a fullness denied to philosophy: "we know that the real lesson to be taught is that the human person is precious and unique; but we seem unable to set it forth except in terms of ideology and abstraction."

If the reader has a grasp of what Miss Murdoch means by contingency, freedom, knowledge and love, the most intricate of her plots and the most puzzling of her characters' motivations become readily intelligible, even predictable. There is an archetypal plot at work in each of the novels in which a character is forced by some event, often violent or irrational in nature, to realize his lack of freedom, his inability to know or to love; he may stop at this insight or he may pass beyond, into that difficult-to-dramatize area in which love can be exercised. The complexities of Miss Murdoch's plots usually spring from her trick of surrounding the central action of discovery with a host of variations, comic or serious, in which other characters learn or fail to learn the same lesson. The formal ancestor of Miss Murdoch's novels turn out to be *Point Counter Point*.

At the opening of the first novel, *Under the Net*, for example, Jake Donaghue "hates contingency" and "hates solitude but is afraid of intimacy". After undergoing a series of brilliantly inventive comic adventures, Jake becomes free, able to work and to accept the reality of others. In her study of Sartre Miss Murdoch repeats Gabriel Marcel's question, why does Sartre "find the contingent overabundance of the world nauseating rather than glorious?" At the end of *Under the Net* Jake is happily marvelling at the inexplicable appearance of a siamese kitten in a brood of tabbies: "I don't know why it is. . . . It's just one of the wonders of the world." No other small incident illustrates so well the particular tone and attractiveness of Miss Murdoch's best work—a kind of joyous but far from complacent acceptance of things as they are and as they must be respected for being.

*The Flight from the Enchanter* dramatizes the interlocking efforts of several characters to cope with the domineering Mischa Fox—or some version of what he stands for, the manipulation of others as objects. The central figure, Rosa, escapes, to return to a life clarified but hardly simplified by the knowledge of what Fox represents. The quasi-hero of *The Sandcastle*, Mor, is tempted to escape from a sour marriage and routine career into a romantic dream of freedom and happiness, only to realize the egotism of his temptation; like Rosa he returns to a prosaic world of tasks and obligations. In these early novels, as in most of those which follow, Miss Murdoch seems to agree completely with Sartre's assertion that the writer "has only one subject—freedom".

*The Bell*, perhaps the finest of the novels, traces the disintegrating relationships between a set of characters who seek in a Benedictine lay community "a retreat from human frailty". They represent "a kind of sick people, whose desire for God makes them unsatisfactory citizens of an ordinary life, but whose strength or temperament fails them to surrender the world completely". Their failures are inevitable, and inevitably involve the failure to love: "Imperfect love must not be condemned and rejected, but made perfect." ("Imperfect love" appears emblematically in many of the novels as incest or homosexuality.) As Miss Murdoch observes elsewhere, "It is an empirical fact about human nature that this attempt [to love] cannot be entirely successful. . . . In the practical world there may only be mourning and the final acceptance of the incomplete." The most one can hope for, as often as not, is "a fairly honourable defeat". *A Severed Head* is a splendid comic version of the quest for liberation and maturity, while *An Unofficial Rose* is a muted, almost Jamesian study of an elderly man's final recognition of the meaning of his past and his deeply equivocal attempt to let his son "live". The symbolism of the earlier novels is restrained; much of the action is now conveyed by scene and dialogue, as is to be the case with most of the later novels.

Between 1963 and 1969 Miss Murdoch published no less than six novels, five of them dark, troubling and often obscure in detail. *The Unicorn* is a gothic "fantasy of the spiritual life"—an instructive parody, perhaps, rather than mere fantasy—in which allegory finally overwhelms plausibility. *The Italian Girl*, the briefest and least consequential of the novels, was followed by the cruelly effective *The Red and the Green*, in which unsuccessful attempts to work out individual freedom are ironically mirrored in the abortive Irish uprising of Easter, 1916. (Something affirmative emerges here, however: the doomed actions of "inconceivably brave men . . . saved from the corruption of time and from those ambiguous second thoughts which dim the brightest face of youth".) *The Time of the Angels* fails almost entirely to fuse image and idea (a much put-upon serving girl, for example, literally stumbles over a copy of Heidegger, the Lucifer behind the evil genius of the book, Carel Fisher). *Bruno's Dream* is, finally, a nightmarish account of a grotesque old man's dying attempts to establish bonds of knowing and loving with the world. Flawed as these novels are in many respects, their complexity and seriousness are a source of genuine power. (And it should be emphasized that brief descriptive statements almost always do Miss Murdoch a gross disservice.)

Fortunately much of the vigor and animating intricacy of the earlier work returns in *The Nice and the Good*, *A Fairly Honourable Defeat* and *An Accidental Man*. There is nothing essentially new in any of these novels: drawn from the world of civil servants and *haute bourgeoisie* whose tone Miss Murdoch has completely mastered, an enormous cast of characters struggle with the ethical problems—of every imaginable sort—which break up the decent, conventional surface of their lives. There are the usual tragic and comic consequences of imperfect love (the range is most vividly conveyed in *A Fairly Honourable Defeat*) and the determined effort of the survivors to make the best of a bad job. Miss Murdoch may be writing too much too quickly; readers new to her work should probably begin (and may wish to remain) with *Under the Net* and *The Bell*; but for those intrigued by Miss Murdoch's moral intensity and endless inventive skill she will almost certainly remain, with Angus Wilson, the most accomplished British novelist to come to maturity since the close of World War II.

—Elmer Borklund

---

**NABOKOV, Vladimir.** Pseudonym: V. Sirin (for Russian works). American. Born in St. Petersburg, now Leningrad, Russia, 12 April 1899; left Russia in 1919, and lived in Berlin, 1922–37, and France, 1937–40; since 1940 has lived in the United States; naturalized citizen, 1945. Educated at Prince Tenishev School, St. Petersburg, 1910–17; Trinity College, Cambridge, B.A. 1922. Married Véra Slonim in 1925; has one son. Instructor in Russian Literature and Creative Writing, Stanford University, California, Summer 1941; Lecturer in Russian, Wellesley College, Massachusetts, 1941–48; Professor of Russian Literature, Cornell University, Ithaca, New York, 1948–59. Research Fellow, Museum of Comparative Zoology, Harvard University, Cambridge, Massachusetts, 1942–48; Visiting Lecturer, Harvard University, Spring 1952. Recipient: Guggenheim Fellowship, 1943, 1953; National Institute of Arts and Letters grant, 1951; Brandeis University Creative Arts Award, 1963; American Academy of Arts and Letters Award of Merit Medal, 1969. Currently resides in Montreux, Switzerland. Address: c/o Weidenfeld and Nicolson, 5 Winsley Street, London W.1, England.

PUBLICATIONS

Novels

    *Mashen'ka*. Berlin, Slovo, 1926; translated by the author and Michael Glenny as *Mary*, New York, McGraw Hill, 1970; London, Weidenfeld and Nicolson, 1971.
    *Korol', Dama, Valet*. Berlin, Slovo, 1928; translated by the author and Dmitri Nabokov as *King, Queen, Knave*, New York, McGraw Hill, and London, Weidenfeld and Nicolson, 1968.

*Zashchita Luzhina* (The Luzhin Defense).  Berlin, Slovo, 1930; translated by the author and Michael Scammell as *The Defense*, New York, Putnam, and London, Weidenfeld and Nicolson, 1964.

*Podvig'* (The Exploit).  Paris, Sovremennïya Zapiski, 1932; translated by the author and Dmitri Nabokov as *Glory*, New York, McGraw Hill, 1971; London, Weidenfeld and Nicolson, 1972.

*Kamera Obskura*.  Paris, Sovremennïya Zapiski, and Berlin, Parabola, 1933; translated by W. Roy as *Camera Obscura*, London, Long, 1937; revised and translated by the author as *Laughter in the Dark*, Indianapolis, Bobbs Merrill, 1938; London, Weidenfeld and Nicolson, 1961.

*Otchayanie*.  Berlin, Petropolis, 1936; translated by the author as *Despair*, London, Long, 1937; revised edition, New York, Putnam, and London, Weidenfeld and Nicolson, 1966.

*Priglashenie na Kazn'*.  Paris, Dom Knigi, 1938; translated by the author and Dmitri Nabokov as *Invitation to a Beheading*, New York, Putnam, 1959; London, Weidenfeld and Nicolson, 1960.

*The Real Life of Sebastian Knight*.  New York, New Directions, 1941; London, Editions Poetry, 1945.

*Bend Sinister*.  New York, Holt, 1947; London, Weidenfeld and Nicolson, 1960.

*Dar*.  New York, Izdatel'stvo Imeni Chekhova, 1952; translated by the author and Michael Scammell as *The Gift*, New York, Putnam, and London, Weidenfeld and Nicolson, 1963.

*Lolita*.  Paris, Olympia Press, 2 Vols., 1955; New York, Putnam, 1958; London, Weidenfeld and Nicolson, 1959.

*Pnin*.  New York, Doubleday, and London, Heinemann, 1957.

*Pale Fire*.  New York, Putnam, and London, Weidenfeld and Nicolson, 1962.

*Ada; or, Ardor: A Family Chronicle*.  New York, McGraw Hill, and London, Weidenfeld and Nicolson, 1969.

## Short Stories

*Vozvrashchenie Chorba* (The Return of Chorb).  Berlin, Slovo, 1930.

*Soglyadatay* (The Spy).  Paris, Russkiya Zapiski, 1938; translated by the author and Dmitri Nabokov as *The Eye*, New York, Phaedra, 1965; London, Weidenfeld and Nicolson, 1966.

*Nine Stories*.  New York, New Directions, 1947.

*Vesna v Fial'te i Drugie Rasskazï* (Spring in Fialta and Other Stories).  New York, Izdatel'stovo Imeni Chekhova, 1956.

*Nabokov's Dozen: A Collection of 13 Stories*.  New York, Doubleday, 1958; London, Heinemann, 1959.

*Nabokov's Quartet*.  New York, Phaedra, 1966; London, Weidenfeld and Nicolson, 1967.

## Plays

*Smertj* (Death), *Deduschka* (Grandfather), *Poljus* (The Pole), *Trajedija gospodina Morna* (The Tragedy of Mr. Morn), and *Tschelowek in SSSR* (The Man from the USSR), published in *Rul* (Berlin), 1923–27.

*Izobreteniye Val'sa*, in *Russkiya Zapiski* (Paris), 1938; translated as *The Waltz Invention* (produced St. Paul, Minnesota, 1968), New York, Phaedra, 1966.

*Sobytiye* (The Event) (produced Paris, 1938).  Published in *Russkiya Zapiski* (Paris), 1938.

Screenplay: *Lolita*, 1960.

Verse

*Gorniy Put'* (The Empyrean Path).   Berlin, Grani, 1923.
*Grozd'* (The Cluster).   Berlin, Gamayun, 1923.
*Stikhotvoreniya, 1920–1951* (Poems).   Paris, Rifma, 1952.
*Poems.*   New York, Doubleday, 1959; London, Weidenfeld and Nicolson, 1961.
*Poems and Problems.*   New York, McGraw Hill, 1971; London, Weidenfeld and Nicolson, 1972.

Other

*Nikolai Gogol.*   New York, New Directions, 1944; London, Editions Poetry, 1947.
*Conclusive Evidence: A Memoir.*   New York, Harper, 1951; as *Speak, Memory: A Memoir*, London, Gollancz, 1952; revised edition, as *Speak, Memory: An Autobiography Revisited*, New York, Putnam, 1966; London, Weidenfeld and Nicolson, 1967.
*Nabokov's Congeries: An Anthology.*   New York, Viking Press, 1968.

Editor and Translator, *Eugene Onegin*, by Aleksandr Pushkin.   New York, Pantheon Books, and London, Routledge, 4 vols., 1964.

Translator, *Nikolka Persik* (Colas Breugnon), by Romain Rolland.   Berlin, Slovo, 1922.
Translator, *Anya v Strane Chudes* (Alice in Wonderland), by Lewis Carroll.   Berlin, Gamayun, 1923.
Translator, *Three Russian Poets: Verse Translations from Pushkin, Lermontov and Tyutchev.*   New York, New Directions, 1945; as *Poems by Pushkin, Lermontov and Tyutchev*, London, Drummond, 1948.
Translator, with Dmitri Nabokov, *A Hero of Our Times*, by Mikhail Lermontov.   New York, Doubleday, and London, Mayflower, 1958.
Translator, *The Song of Igor's Campaign: An Epic of the Twelfth Century.*   New York, Knopf, 1960; London, Weidenfeld and Nicolson, 1961.

Numerous papers on lepidoptera published in scientific journals, since 1920.


Bibliography: *Vladimir Nabokov: Bibliographie des Gesamtwerks* by Dieter E. Zimmer, Hamburg, Rowohlt, 1963; revised edition, 1964.


Critical Studies: *The Art of Vladimir Nabokov: Escape into Aesthetics* by Page Stegner, New York, Dial Press, 1966; *Nabokov: His Life in Art* by Andrew Field, Boston, Little Brown, 1967; *Nabokov: The Man and His Work*, edited by L. S. Dembo, Madison, University of Wisconsin Press, 1967; *Keys to Lolita* by Carl R. Proffer, Bloomington, Indiana University Press, 1968; *For Vladimir Nabokov on His Seventieth Birthday*, edited by Charles Newman and Alfred Appel Jr., Evanston, Illinois, Northwestern University Press, 1970, and London, Weidenfeld and Nicolson, 1971; *The Annotated Lolita*, edited by Alfred Appel Jr., New York, McGraw Hill, 1970, and London, Weidenfeld and Nicolson, 1971; *Vladimir Nabokov* by Julian Moynahan, Minneapolis, University of Minnesota Press, 1971; *Nabokov's Deceptive World* by W. Woodlin Rowe, New York, New York University Press, 1971.

*       *       *

The complete works of Vladimir Nabokov would, if collected, run to thirty or forty volumes; this miniature essay will leave some thirty or thirty-five volumes aside in order to say a little about some representative works originally written in English—*Speak, Memory, Pnin, Lolita, Pale Fire*, the edition of *Eugene Onegin*, and *Ada*—each characterized by that verbal playfulness which, like a watermark, calls attention to the art and to its maker.

*Speak, Memory: An Autobiography Revisited* is a carefully designed work of art in which the author has created Vladimir Nabokov, a character perhaps as real and enduring as the central figures in his best fictions. The autobiography here revisited was originally published in the United States under the title *Conclusive Evidence*, being in the author's eyes conclusive evidence that Nabokov existed. The recollections range from St. Petersburg to St. Nazaire and from 1903 to 1940, with a few excursions, but it is not just another perishable emigre memoir. Art survives, and a well-studied life—as Nabokov noted in his *Eugene Onegin* Commentary—will often reveal an artistically satisfying pattern. Consequently, Nabokov selected his evidence with imperious discretion, assembling and fashioning it to bring out a coherent design. The book is luminous with the growth of perception: the discovery of light and motion, of intellectual clarity and time. From "the awakening of consciousness as a series of spaced flashes, with the intervals between them gradually diminishing until bright blocks of perception are formed," on through the usual gray photographs of Czarist grandparents, through the commonplace anecdotes of blockhead tutors, and over the evening sands of the *plage* at Biarritz where each footprint slowly fills up with sunset water, down to the last sentence at St. Nazaire where the ship's funnel suddenly appears among the jumbled walls and roofs "as something in a scrambled picture," we trace the growth of the protagonist's awareness. But unlike the protagonist of most memoirs, the hero of this one is not a particularly likeable fellow. The narrating Nabokov is a lively, attentive, opinionated and dazzlingly fluent biographer of that other past-tense Nabokov, the one who was born so many years ago into an extraordinarily rich, well-connected, cultured, loving family, and whose privileged youth nurtured such regal pastimes as chess and lepidoptery, not to mention writing. Granted such a subject, Nabokov produced a memoir whose author strikes readers as snobbish, callous, arrogant, and too clever by half. Yet it is precisely this—the combination of an interesting but somewhat exotic and unpleasant persona within a delightfully illuminated design—which gives the work its enduring qualities.

*Pnin* is a short, serio-comic novel about a perpetually displaced Russian emigre, the woefully eccentric professor Timofey Pnin. It is one of Nabokov's most accessible novels— four of its seven chapters appeared originally as short sketches in *The New Yorker*—offering the reader a string of episodes in simple, graceful prose and deceptively limpid structure. Pnin, ideally bald, fitted with tortoise-shell glasses and splendid new teeth, is the heart of this work; he is a thoroughly engaging and rather complex figure. When the novel opens Pnin is teaching Russian at Waindel College, having escaped from a Leninized Russia to Prague, from Prague to Paris, thence to New York City and upstate New York. His absent wife Liza, a powerfully beautiful and self-indulgent versifier, had married him in order to speed her recovery from a bad love affair, then deserted him for the obtuse Dr. Eric Wind, a psychiatrist who understood her "organic ego," then returned to Pnin, seven-months pregnant in order to be his "faithful and lawful wife" until they reached Ellis Island where she once more deserted him for their ship-board companion, Dr. Wind. In the course of the novel Liza returns to Pnin again and informs him that she no longer loves Dr. Wind and is leaving him—she merely wants Pnin to assume some responsibility for Victor, Wind's child, now fourteen years old. Pnin and young Victor, superficially so different, are spiritually attuned to each other, so finely resonant that while they sleep a few steps apart Pnin dreams one of Victor's recurrent drowsy fantasies. Nabokov manipulates the tone of this charming sad novel with great authority: he renders the character of Pnin, his wife and her son, the episodes of academic life and Russian emigre society with sensuous detail, controlling the banal sentiment and pathos of his material with comic rigor and delicate irony. The random-looking surface of this story belies its subtle patterning. Pnin is not simply an exile. His past is so filled with petty humiliation and naked tragedy that he must escape it in order to live; yet the past forever pursues him, luring him with cruel nostalgia, displacing him with yet another intolerable injury. As the novel unfolds it gradually becomes apparent that the presumably omniscient author is actually a figure from Pnin's past—an unreliable story teller who constructs a biography from personal recollections, old letters, hearsay, and stylized academic anecdotes. Perhaps the narrator is indeed that lover who tossed Liza aside, leading her to her therapeutic marriage with Timofey; certainly he is that new professor whose arrival at Waindel College to take over the Special Russian Division ousts Pnin from the novel.

*Lolita* is in some respects Nabokov's finest novel and certainly his most popular work. The story—after a pious Foreword by "John Ray, Jr., Ph.D."—is about Humbert Humbert, a cosmopolitan European professor, thirty-seven years old, who tells of his catastrophic affair with an American school girl, Dolores Haze, age twelve. Though the book is as beautifully patterned as a butterfly, and though it moves to its showdown with the elegance of a romantically plotted chess game, though it has splendid satirical views of the American scene and brilliant parodies of everything from motel signs to high literature, what gives the work its great power is the demonic autobiographer at its black heart: the brilliant, comically wretched, imprisoned Humbert Humbert. Ever since the novel was put between boards and shown publicly (an Olympia Press edition circulated underground before *Pnin* was published) Nabokov's scholarly admirers have pained themselves to minimize the sensuous reality and immediacy of Humbert's insatiable lust for his nymphet, Lolita—as if it were possible to have *Moby-Dick* without the whale. In a gambit reminiscent of well drawn pornography, Humbert marries the widowed Mrs. Haze and studies how to get rid of her and how to seduce Lolita; the fact that it is Lolita who seduces him reveals how insecure his grasp of the game is, and though he keeps Lo an automobile prisoner while they drive from motel to motel across the United States, he is finally thwarted, losing her to the shadowy Clare Quilty, a wholly corrupt man whom he murders at the close. Other dimensions lie beneath the novel's opalescent surface: Humbert's lust is a form of nympholepsy, the desire for an unattainable ideal, and *nymph* refers us to a stage in that lovely metamorphosis which culminates with the mature butterfly, ancient symbol of regeneration and the soul; the unregenerate Quilty, bearing a name which expands into the French phrase *that he take you there*, now appears to be Humbert's dark double, one who must be annihilated when Humbert's lechery becomes transfiguring love.

*Pale Fire*, the novel by Nabokov, comprises a mediocre four-canto poem of 999 lines by John Shade entitled "Pale Fire"; the poem has an aggrandizing Foreword by Charles Kinbote and is followed by Kinbote's digressive Commentary and an Index: all this beneath an epigraph from Boswell's *Life of Samuel Johnson*. The burden of this playful work lies neither in Shade's poem—a banal family chronicle in couplets, touching on death, immortality, art—nor in Kinbote's much longer Commentary with its insinuated tale of Kinbote's escape from glassy Zembla, a distant northern land, but rather in the interplay between the text and its exegesis. Because Kinbote is manifestly unreliable, his bizarre explication of the text draws our attention to the process of ascribing or inferring meaning, the process whereby we arrive at a satisfying design. The exchange between the poem and the Commentary, whether it be reflection or refraction, is dramatized in the relationship between the poet and his editor: in his Foreword the sexually inverted Kinbote tells us that he used to peer through Shade's lighted window in order to observe the poet at work on "Pale Fire," and in his poem Shade speaks of that same window as a dim mirror in which the poet can make out his own ghostly image suspended on the exterior scene. Unlike Nabokov, Shade appears to be a writer who holds a mirror up to life, and his humdrum verse faithfully reflects his humdrum years in the town of New Wye. Kinbote, on the other hand, seems to be a paranoid fabulist and his excessive Commentary resembles something by a demented Nabokov. But though the furnishings in Shade's New Wye are more familiar to us than the exotic stuff of Kinbote's Zembla, the American town is not less fictional than the distant northern land—neither can claim a reality outside the printed word. To study the text and Commentary in an effort to unearth a primary reality, as some critics will persist in doing, is to waste the novel; just as Boswell and Johnson are each other's finest creations, so too are Kinbote and Shade. Nabokov has drawn a sly ligature between the purely verbal world of this moebius novel and the one we inhabit: toward the end of his Commentary Kinbote says that he had suggested that Shade entitle his poem *Solus Rex*— the name of an unfinished work, with certain congruencies to *Pale Fire*, composed by Nabokov in the late thirties. In addition to its incidental amusements *Pale Fire* is in form and detail a rich parody of definitive scholarly annotation, the more pointed because Nabokov's next publication was to be his edition of *Eugene Onegin*.

Aleksandr Pushkin's *Eugene Onegin*, translated from the Russian with a Commentary by Vladimir Nabokov, fills four sky-blue volumes. The work has been widely misread: most critics have focused narrowly on the translation—exquisitely literal—and found in it no comeliness, while those others who have tried the Commentary have been overwhelmed by the massed forces of its erudition and offended by the commentator's autocratic attitude. The translation (Volume 1) is best regarded as a trot, a pony, a desk companion for students working their way through the original, and the photographic reproduction of the 1837 edition (Volume 4) is simply a bibliographic document. But the grand central Commentary (Volumes 2 and 3) is a work of art, a witty drama, royal fun for those familiar enough with the rules and stratagems of scholarship to follow the game as Nabokov maneuvers among earlier critics across the checkered history of the poem.

*Ada; or, Ardor: A Family Chronicle* is Nabokov's most fictive work, an invention staged on Antiterra, an alternative world populated by literary figments. The memoir spans close to one hundred years and tells of the princely philosopher-psychologist Van Veen, and his enduring incestuous love for his cousin, actually his sister, Ada Veen (that ample family tree planted on the novel's preliminary pages is not to be trusted), a charmingly wayward and intelligent woman who marries someone else, but eventually returns to Van as he moves toward the completion of his opus, *The Texture of Time*—a work for which this novel itself may be considered a dramatic metaphor. Nabokov's inventive genius reaches its fullest expression in *Ada* and many of the themes and sly techniques found in his earlier books play at large in this one. Ironically, this culminating novel seems destined to go largely unread, being too baroque for science-fiction and too hard for a fairy tale, too confused at the opening, too abstract at the close, and in spite of the sensuous texture of its middle pages, tediously clever and verbal—only for those with an informed sympathy for his previous works, a deep delight, a marvel.

—Eugene Mirabelli

---

**NAIPAUL, V(idiadhar) S(urajprasad).** British. Born in Trinidad, 17 August 1932; emigrated to England in 1950. Educated at Queen's Royal College, Port of Spain, Trinidad, 1943–48; University College, Oxford, 1950–54, B.A. (honours) in English 1953. Married Patricia Ann Hale in 1955. Editor, "Caribbean Voices", BBC, London, 1954–56; Reviewer, *New Statesman*, London, 1957–61. Travelled in the West Indies and South America, 1960–61, India, 1962–63, Africa, 1966, and the United States and Canada, 1969. Recipient: Rhys Memorial Prize, 1958; Maugham Award, 1961; Phoenix Trust Award, 1962; Hawthornden Prize, 1964; Smith Literary Award, 1968; Arts Council grant, 1969; Booker Prize, 1971. Address: c/o André Deutsch Ltd., 105 Great Russell Street, London W.C.1, England.

PUBLICATIONS

### Novels

*The Mystic Masseur.* London, Deutsch, 1957; New York, Vanguard Press, 1959.
*The Suffrage of Elvira.* London, Deutsch, 1958.
*Miguel Street.* London, Deutsch, 1959; New York, Vanguard Press, 1960.
*A House for Mr. Biswas.* London, Deutsch, 1961; New York, McGraw Hill, 1962.
*Mr. Stone and the Knights Companion.* London, Deutsch, 1963; New York, Macmillan, 1964.
*The Mimic Men.* London, Deutsch, and New York, Macmillan, 1967.
*In a Free State.* London, Deutsch, and New York, Knopf, 1971.

### Short Stories

*A Flag on the Island.* London, Deutsch, 1967; New York, Macmillan, 1968.

### Other

*The Middle Passage: Impressions of Five Societies—British, French and Dutch—in the West Indies and South America.* London, Deutsch, 1962; New York, Macmillan, 1963.
*An Area of Darkness: An Experience of India.* London, Deutsch, 1964; New York, Macmillan, 1965.
*The Loss of El Dorado: A History.* London, Deutsch, 1969; New York, Knopf, 1970.
*The Overcrowded Barracoon: Selected Articles 1958–1972.* London, Deutsch, 1972.

Critical Studies: essay by David Pryce-Jones, in *London Magazine*, May 1967; essay by Karl Miller, in *Kenyon Review* (Gambier, Ohio), November 1967; *A Manifold Voice* by William Walsh, London, Chatto and Windus, 1970; *The West Indian Novel* by Kenneth Ramchand, London, Faber, 1970.

V. S. Naipaul comments:

I feel that any statement I make about my own work would be misleading. The work is there: the reader must see what meaning, if any, the work has for him. All I would like to say is that I consider my non-fiction an integral part of my work.

*       *       *

V. S. Naipaul is the most accomplished novelist yet to emerge from the English-speaking Caribbean. This definition, however, can limit his achievement, which stands in the main stream of the modern English novel. Similarly, although it is impossible to discuss his work without seeing it as a progressive exploration of an awareness based in the Caribbean, his concern is with the universal human predicament.

His work to date falls into three phases. His first-written (though third-published) work is *Miguel Street*. It consists of sketches of life in a lower class area of Trinidad. The focus is that of a child, but although this changes as the boy grows older and more comprehending, Naipaul omitted the story intended to show the boy's own involvement in its frustrated and inherently tragic world. (Reprinted as "The Enemy" in *A Flag on the Island*.) The child's point of view can therefore avoid adult implications: in spite of the plots of the stories—which include a prostitute Laura driving her daughter to commit suicide when in her time she also has an illegitimate child, and Man Man, who wants to be crucified as Christ until the villagers throw too large rocks—the tone is one of delicately balanced humour. This is both its achievement and its limitation.

*The Mystic Masseur* achieves a greater complexity. On one hand there is the narrator who views the story from a changing perspective as he grows up; on the other there is use of the main protagonist's own suppressed autobiography, significantly called "The Years of Guilt". The hero moves from humble beginnings as Pundit Ganesh Ramsummair, an incompetent Trinidad masseur, through assumption of powers as a mystic and writer, to the position of G. Ramsay Muir, Esq., M.B.E., member of the Legislative Council. It is at once a satire on the roots of power that lie in popular superstition and apparent education, and of a figure driven by the forces he himself exploits. Ganesh provides a human centre lacking in *The Suffrage of Elvira*, another satire on popular political power in the Caribbean.

These three novels led George Lamming in *The Pleasures of Exile* (1960) to attack Naipaul's work as "castrated satire", an attempt to take a superior ironic stance avoiding full involvement in the Caribbean predicament. Whatever truth lies behind Lamming's criticism, it is not applicable to *A House for Mr. Biswas*, a major novel spanning three generations of life in Trinidad. There is satire on Caribbean ways of life, from the West Indian social structure to such facets as popular journalism. But the satire itself is mediated through the particular sensibility of the ever-present Mohun Biswas. Biswas, born with an extra finger which shows both his endemic bad luck and the effects of malnutrition, reacts to his world with an artist's fastidious consciousness, although in Trinidad the only outlets he can find for his creative imagination are sign-writing and the reporting of sensational episodes for the Trinidad *Sentinel*. Of Brahmin caste, he is seized in marriage by the merchant family of Tulsis, who are hungry for every bit of status they can get, to bolster up their own immigrant insecurity. Everything in the commercial vulgarity and oppresive clannishness revolts Biswas, who struggles to get free of them, while needing (and taking) the home they offer. Mr. Biswas's quest for a house of his own is an attempt to find both independence and some place that he can imbue with meaning. Surrounding this overt theme is Naipaul's sense of the inherent loneliness of man himself—the darkness both physical and spiritual that Biswas faces when a hurricane blows his house from around him causing him a nervous breakdown. But by the end Biswas has his own precarious house, while the Tulsi family is disintegrating. A tender tragi-comedy, in scope and theme the book approaches epic proportions.

With *Mr. Stone and the Knights Companion*—about a middle class Englishman coming to terms with old age—Naipaul's work begins to look more deliberately outward from the Caribbean. *The Mimic Men* is set largely on the fictional West Indian Island of Isabella, and explores the rise to power of Ralph Kriplesingh, building on fortunes from Coca Cola and real estate. It follows up many of the questions *Elvira* poses about the roots of political power in the Caribbean, brought up to date with the advent of Black Power. One possibility for a meaningful society is offered in Ralph's father who becomes a *sunyasi* (holy man), but the novel questions whether any actions in the contemporary island predicament can have meaning. Partly because he too is a "mimic man", Ralph cannot see any. The novel opens and closes in England, and Ralph's vision comes in a moment of existential desolation at the end.

*In a Free State* is a thematically united trio of stories, set between two factual diary entries of a Middle East tour. They concern an Indian servant in the United States, West Indians in England, and an Englishman in an African state at time of revolution. Action and description are stripped to the nerve, and slight actions, such as an image in a television set, or a blank stare, take on momentous impact. The cutting away of the rich detail that characterised *Miguel Street* to elements of consciousness, here reaches a brilliant stage of development. It is the logical progression of both Naipaul's style and themes.

—Louis James

---

**NARAYAN, R(asipuram) K(rishnaswami).** Indian. Born in Madras in 1907. Educated at Maharaja's College, Mysore, graduated 1930. Recipient: National Prize of the Indian Literary Academy, 1958; Padma Bhushan, India, 1964; National Association of Independent Schools Award (U.S.A.), 1965. Litt.D., University of Leeds, Yorkshire, 1967. Address: 15 Vivekananda Road, Yadavagiri, Mysore 2, India.

PUBLICATIONS

Novels

*Swami and Friends: A Novel of Malgudi.*   London, Hamish Hamilton, 1935.
*The Bachelor of Arts.*   London, Nelson, 1937; with *Swami and Friends*, East Lansing, Michigan State College Press, 1954.
*The Dark Room.*   London, Macmillan, 1938.
*The English Teacher.*   London, Eyre and Spottiswoode, 1945; as *Grateful to Life and Death*, East Lansing, Michigan State College Press, 1953.
*Mr. Sampath.*   London, Eyre and Spottiswoode, 1949; as *The Printer of Malgudi*, East Lansing, Michigan State College Press, 1955.
*The Financial Expert.*   London, Methuen, 1952; East Lansing, Michigan State College Press, 1953.
*Waiting for the Mahatma.*   London, Methuen, and East Lansing, Michigan State College Press, 1955.
*The Guide.*   Madras, Higginbothams, London, Methuen, and New York, Viking Press, 1958.
*The Man-Eater of Malgudi.*   New York, Viking Press, 1961; London, Heinemann, 1962.
*The Vendor of Sweets.*   New York, Viking Press, 1967; as *The Sweet Vendor*, London, Bodley Head, 1967.

Short Stories

*Cyclone and Other Stories.*   Mysore, Indian Thought Publications, n.d.
*Malgudi Days.*   Mysore, Indian Thought Publications, 1943.
*An Astrologer's Day and Other Stories.*   London, Eyre and Spottiswoode, 1947.
*Dodu and Other Stories.*   Mysore, Indian Thought Publications, n.d. (1950?).
*Lawley Road.*   Mysore, Indian Thought Publications, 1956.
*Gods, Demons and Others.*   New York, Viking Press, 1964; London, Heinemann, 1965.
*A Horse and Two Goats.*   London, Bodley Head, 1970.

Other

*Mysore*.   Mysore, Indian Thought Publications, 1944.
*My Dateless Diary* (travel in America).   Mysore, Indian Thought Publications, 1960.

*      *      *

No other twentieth-century novelist besides William Faulkner has so well succeeded in creating through a succession of novels an imagined community that microcosmically reflects the physical, intellectual, and spiritual qualities of a whole culture as has R. K. Narayan in his tales of the South Indian community of Malgudi. His stories have made a naive, highly emotional society half a world away as much a part of a reader's experience as Faulkner's novels have made the mad, decadent world of the red hills of Mississippi.

Narayan took longer than Faulkner to discover his metier, though all the Indian writer's novels have been largely set in Malgudi. With his third novel, *Sartoris* (1929), published when he was 32, Faulkner laid the cornerstone for his Yoknapatawpha saga of pride-doomed families. Narayan published four apprentice works based largely on reminiscences before producing, at the age of 43, *Mr. Sampath*, the first of the five most remarkable studies of flamboyant characters who electrified the sleepy city of Malgudi.

It is unlikely that anyone would have guessed that Narayan's first two novels were the work of a major artist. *Swami and Friends* is a kind of charming Indian *Penrod and Sam*, an episodic account of the adventures of two cricket-playing chums as they start high school. *The Bachelor of Arts* is another episodic account of a young man's graduating from college, experiencing a frustrating love affair, wandering about the country disconsolately, returning home to become agent for a big city newspaper, and finally marrying under family auspices. His third novel, *The Dark Room*, is difficult to locate today, but he describes it as dealing with a Hindu wife who submitted passively to an overbearing husband.

His work changed drastically with *The English Teacher* (American title, *Grateful to Life and Death*), a thinly veiled account of his own marriage and the event that most matured and shaped his character, the early death of his beloved wife possibly from an infection received from a fly settling on her lip in a foul outbuilding. This novel begins like Narayan's earlier ones with episodic sketches of a young preparatory school teacher's relationships with his students, colleagues, and family. After the tragic death of the wife while house-hunting, however, the novel becomes a much deeper and more tightly unified work. Through a medium, the teacher learns of the possibility of communicating with his dead wife and, through the director of a school for very young children that his daughter attends, he becomes excited about such institutions. He decides that he must give up the routines of his comfortable position at Albert Mission College (a preparatory school often mentioned in Narayan's work) and find "a harmonious existence." After he resigns, he returns home to find his wife awaiting him. The reader must decide for himself whether the visitor is an apparition or a phenomenon that transcends rational explanation. The narrator concludes only, "The boundaries of our personalities suddenly dissolved. It was a moment of rare, immutable joy—a moment for which one feels grateful to Life and Death."

With his next novel, Narayan settled upon the kind of characters and narrative patterns that he was to employ in his five remarkable explorations of the fantastic agitations beneath the enervating surface of the life of Malgudi. Near the end of *Mr. Sampath* (*The Printer of Malgudi*), Narayan observes of Srinivas, the principal character, that "he felt he had been involved in a chaos of human relationships and activities."

Nearly all of Narayan's subsequent novels involve characters and readers in such chaos. Srinivas is a rather aimless young man who has finally been driven by his family to choose a profession and who comes to Malgudi in 1938—when war clouds hang over the whole world—to found a newspaper that has "nothing special to note about any war, past or future," but is "only concerned with that war that is always going on—between man's inside and outside." He falls into the hands of a printer, Mr. Sampath, who takes a proprietary interest in the success of the paper, but who is lured from his printing trade into a film-producing venture. Even Srinivas is briefly tempted to abandon his paper and take up script writing. Despite frantic activity and great expenditures, however, the movie-making venture collapses. Only Srinivas emerges unscathed. He finds another printer and returns to publishing his paper, reflecting on one of the men involved in the catastrophe he has witnessed:

> throughout the centuries . . . this group was always there: Ravi with his madness, his well-wishers with their panaceas and their apparatus of cure. Half the madness was his own doing, his lack of self-knowledge, his treachery to his own instincts as an artist, which had made him a battle-ground. Sooner or later he shook off his madness and realized his true identity—though not in one birth, at least in a series of them.

The passage is a key to understanding Narayan's major works and their relationship to Hindu philosophy; for the characters he focuses upon are those who are "mad" as a result of their lack of self-knowledge. Some must await another reincarnation; but some manage to shake off the madness and find their true identities.

One who must wait is the title character of *The Financial Expert*, Margayya, whom we meet sitting under a banyan tree assisting peasants in obtaining loans from a co-operative banking institution. The society's officers resent Margayya's activities, but his business flourishes until his spoiled young son throws into a sewer the book in which all accounts are kept. During a trip to collect a red lotus needed for a penitential ritual, Margayya meets Dr. Pal, a self-styled sociologist, who has written a pornographic manuscript based on the *Kama Sutra*. Margayya recoups his fortune by publishing it under the title *Domestic Harmony*; then, embarrassed by the source of his new wealth, he goes back into a money-lending business that is based on withholding the interest from the first installment on the loan. He becomes so successful that he achieves an honored position in the community and recruits Dr. Pal to attract investors into the business by offering twenty per-cent interest, which he pays out of new deposits. The scheme collapses, however, when the son, who has been gambling with Dr. Pal, demands a share in the business; Margayya assaults Dr. Pal, who in turn discredits the money-lender with his investors. When investors demand their money back, both Margayya and his son are ruined and driven back into dealings with the peasants beneath the banyan tree.

Narayan's next novel, *Waiting for the Mahatma*, is one of his most noble-minded, but least successful. It tells, in the episodic manner of his earlier books, of the misadventures of two young disciples of Mahatma Gandhi during the master's long effort to free his native land. Written after Gandhi's assassination, the book is an admirable tribute, but the fictional characters are too sketchily developed to make it of more than historical interest.

Narayan next turned to the work that has generally been recognized as his most outstanding, *The Guide*, an extremely complicated tale of a confidence man turned saint. In flashbacks, we learn of the rise of Raju from food-seller in the Malgudi railroad station to manager and apparent husband of Rose, who becomes an extremely popular dancer, and his quick fall when he is jailed for forging her signature to a package of jewels. We meet him first, however, when he has installed himself in an abandoned temple after his release from jail and has begun to play the role of spiritual advisor to a peasant community that accepts him as a Mahatma. Gradually he comes to believe in the role he has created, and to relieve a drought he feels compelled to make a fifteen-day fast that he has suggested as an appropriate penance. As a great crowd gathers, he gains "a peculiar strength" from, for the first time in his life, "learning the thrill of full application, outside money and love." Despite grave peril to his health he continues to fast until he feels that the rain is falling in the hills. The ending of this novel like that of *The English Teacher* is ambiguous: does Swami Raju die? do the rains come? Narayan tells us only, "He sagged down"; but he has transcended the madness that once affected him and found a fulfillment denied the printer of Malgudi and the financial expert.

Such fulfillment is denied also Vasu, the fanatical taxidermist of *The Man-Eater of Malgudi*, Narayan's greatest picture of the madness that leads to self-destruction. After successfully flaunting his great strength about the community unchecked through a series of outrageous incidents, he finally devises a plot against Malgudi's beloved temple elephant. The beast seems doomed, but Vasu dies instead; and in one of the most spectacular conclusions to any of Narayan's works, the almost incredible but carefully foreshadowed way in which he destroyed himself is disclosed.

The complementary *The Vendor of Sweets* is Narayan's most mellow portrayal of the man who discovers at last his true identity. Jagan had been freed from patriarchal thralldom when he broke with his orthodox family and went to jail in support of Mahatma Gandhi's program. His experiences, however, are of no help to him in dealing with another of the spoiled, insolent, uncommunicative sons that appear in many of Narayan's works. The son prefers American "get-rich-quick" ideas to the simple, self-sacrificial life recommended by Gandhi, and Jagan indulges the boy's whims by selling sweetmeats that he will not eat himself to the luxury-loving community. When the son begins to get into serious troubles, however, Jagan decides that there is nothing he can do. He abandons his business and retires to a decrepit garden of meditation, explaining to one of the protesting opportunists who has fattened on him, "I am going to watch a Goddess come out of a stone." He has freed himself from the successive bondages to parents, hero, and child and has found a tranquility unique in Narayan's tales.

The major Malgudi novels can thus be read not only individually as remarkable character studies, but as a unit describing the soul's progress—despite setbacks—from fanaticism towards serenity and the transcendence of the grimy chaos of the Malgudi railroad station.

—Warren French

---

**NATHAN, Robert (Gruntal).** American. Born in New York City, 2 January 1894. Educated at Public School 6 and the Collegiate School, New York; Ethical Culture School, Geneva; Phillips Exeter Academy, New Hampshire, 1910–12; Harvard University, Cambridge, Massachusetts, 1912–15. Married Dorothy Michaels in 1915 (divorced, 1922); Nancy Wilson, 1930 (divorced, 1936); Lucy Lee Hall Skelding, 1936 (divorced, 1939); Janet McMillen Bingham, 1940 (divorced); Clara May Blum Burns, 1951 (divorced); Shirley Kneeland, 1955 (divorced); Joan Winnifrith, 1970; has one child. Advertising Solicitor, New York, 1916–18. Lecturer, New York University School of Journalism, 1924–25. Screenwriter, Metro-Goldwyn-Mayer, Hollywood, 1943–49. Composer and Illustrator. President, United States P.E.N., 1940–42; Chancellor, Academy of American Poets. Member, National Institute of Arts and Letters, 1935. Address: 1420 North Doheny Drive, Los Angeles, California 90069, U.S.A.

PUBLICATIONS

Novels

*Peter Kindred.*  New York, Duffield, 1919.
*Autumn.*  New York, McBride, 1921.
*The Puppet Master.*  New York, McBride, 1923.

*Jonah.*   New York, McBride, 1925.

*The Fiddler in Barley.*   New York, McBride, 1926.

*The Woodcutter's House.*   Indianapolis, Bobbs Merrill, 1927; London, Mathews, 1932.

*The Bishop's Wife.*   Indianapolis, Bobbs Merrill, and London, Gollancz, 1928.

*There Is Another Heaven.*   Indianapolis, Bobbs Merrill, 1929.

*The Orchid.*   Indianapolis, Bobbs Merrill, 1931; London, Mathews, 1932.

*One More Spring.*   New York, Knopf, and London, Cassell, 1933.

*Road of Ages.*   New York, Knopf, and London, Constable, 1935.

*The Enchanted Voyage.*   New York, Knopf, 1936; London, Constable, 1937.

*The Barley Fields: A Collection of Five Novels.*   New York, Knopf, 1938; London, Constable, 1939.

*Winter in April.*   New York, Knopf, and London, Constable, 1938.

*Journey of Tapiola.*   New York, Knopf, and London, Constable, 1938.

*Portrait of Jennie.*   New York, Knopf, and London, Heinemann, 1940.

*They Went On Together.*   New York, Knopf, and London, Heinemann, 1941.

*Tapiola's Brave Regiment.*   New York, Knopf, 1941.

*The Sea-Gull Cry.*   New York, Knopf, 1942.

*But Gently Day.*   New York, Knopf, 1943.

*Mr. Whittle and the Morning Star.*   New York, Knopf, and London, Low, 1947.

*Long after Summer.*   New York, Knopf, 1948; London, Low, 1949.

*The River Journey.*   New York, Knopf, 1949.

*The Married Look.*   New York, Knopf, 1950; as *His Wife's Young Face*, London, Staples Press, 1951.

*The Innocent Eye.*   New York, Knopf, 1951.

*Nathan 3* (includes *The Sea-Gull Cry*, *The Innocent Eye*, and *The River Journey*). London, Staples Press, 1952.

*The Train in the Meadow.*   New York, Knopf, 1953.

*Sir Henry.*   New York, Knopf, 1955; London, Barker, 1956.

*The Rancho of the Little Loves.*   New York, Knopf, 1956.

*So Love Returns.*   New York, Knopf, 1958; London, W. H. Allen, 1959.

*The Color of Evening.*   New York, Knopf, and London, W. H. Allen, 1960.

*The Wilderness Stone.*   New York, Knopf, and London, W. H. Allen, 1961.

*A Star in the Wind.*   New York, Knopf, and London, W. H. Allen, 1962.

*The Devil with Love.*   New York, Knopf, and London, W. H. Allen, 1963.

*The Fair.*   New York, Knopf, 1964.

*The Mallot Diaries.*   New York, Knopf, 1965.

*Stonecliffe.*   New York, Knopf, 1967.

*Mia.*   New York, Knopf, 1970.


Plays

*Music at Evening* (produced White Plains, New York, 1937).

*Jezebel's Husband, and The Sleeping Beauty.*   New York, Knopf, 1953.

*Juliet in Mantua.*   New York, Knopf, 1966.


Screenplays: *The White Cliffs of Dover*, 1944; *The Clock*, 1945; *Pagan Love Song*, 1950.


Verse

*Youth Grows Old.*   New York, McBride, 1922.

*The Cedar Box.*   Indianapolis, Bobbs Merrill, 1929.

*Selected Poems.*   New York, Knopf, 1935; London, Constable, 1936.

*A Winter Tale: Sonnets and Poems.*   New York, Knopf, 1940.

*Dunkirk: A Ballad.*   New York, Knopf, 1942.
*Morning in Iowa.*   New York, Knopf, 1944.
*The Darkening Meadows.*   New York, Knopf, 1945.
*The Green Leaf: Collected Poems.*   New York, Knopf, 1950.
*The Married Man.*   New York, Knopf, 1962.

Other

*Journal for Josephine* (memoirs).   New York, Knopf, 1943.
*The Snowflake and the Starfish* (juvenile).   New York, Knopf, 1959.
*The Weans* (archaeology).   New York, Knopf, 1960.
*Tappy* (juvenile).   New York, Knopf, 1968.

Bibliography: *Robert Nathan: A Bibliography* by Dan H. Lawrence, New Haven, Connecticut, Yale University Press, 1960.

Manuscript Collection: Yale University, New Haven, Connecticut.

Critical Studies: in *American Literature* by Russell Blankenship, New York, Holt, 1931; Introduction by Stephen Vincent Benet to *The Barley Fields*, 1938; *Robert Nathan* by Clarence Sandelin, New York, Twayne, 1969.

Robert Nathan comments:

I have tried—as far as I could—to be a comforter in the world . . . not through what I know, but what I don't—and cannot—know. I have tried to suggest the mystery and the magic.

*          *          *

A traditionalist in that good sense which describes most popular writers of merit, Robert Nathan has written more than 52 books of fiction, verse, drama, and gently ironic speculation—not to mention the songs, screenplays, essays and obiter dicta which remain uncollected. He is a member of the American branch of the international P.E.N. of which he is past president, was elected in 1935 to the National Institute of Arts and Letters, and is presently a Chancellor of the Academy of American Poets.

In his work he regularly invokes the piety of Hebrew Prophets, the skepticism of Roman Stoics, the absolute awe of Medieval Mystics, and the consternation of contemporary scientists as evidence of the mystery of our being. He recommends a non-sectarian, private, humble faith in God as the best hope of surviving our modern anomie. In his best early treatment of this theme, *Jonah*, there is a lyric balance of humor, earnestness, and hope. By 1962, when he wrote *Star in the Wind*, the humor and hope had all but disappeared, his plea for love and faith grown urgent.

Yet his humor remains as essential ingredient of all his work. *Sir Henry* is a delightful parody of the White Knight we first met in the pages of Lewis Carroll, and *The Weans* is a mock essay in archeology that provides a startling indictment of contemporary morals and manners by means of ironic perspective. Often as not, his novels include worldly dogs, philosophical horses, communistic ants, capitalistic cockroaches, an insecure fox or narcissistic whale, as actors and sooth-sayers, the distorted but essentially honest projections of our own frail humanity, the humorous versions of the truth we can accept in laughter.

Nathan's forte is the short novel of ironic fantasy, employing a melodic prose, relying upon traditional argument, evoking a mood of sympathy and wonder for the everyday miracle of existence. His most popular story, *Portrait of Jennie*, uses a double time pattern to suggest how "fated" lovers can meet as Kindergarten child and adult man in the winter of 1938, and then suffer a traumatic separation as lovers, both 28 years of age, in the following autumn of 1939. The man lives through one year of experience, in this interval, but the woman lives through more than twenty. And this mixture of ordinary and accelerated time is but one game Nathan plays with our arbitrary notions of reality. He also has stories that depend on suspended time, reversed time, impressionistic time, and expressionistic time. The very mystery of time suggests, indeed, our human limitations in a multiverse beyond comprehension.

Of course his fantasy involves other elements as well, such as the displacement of characters from expected into unexpected circumstances, the substitution of place or circumstance to achieve ironic contrasts—as in *There Is Another Heaven* where a Jew who has converted to Christianity arrives in the Protestant heaven defined in accordance with popular convictions and practice, only to find Jesus is not in residence—and the employment of characters and attitudes in bizarre ways, as when the demons of Hell are obsessed with man's self-destruction because, since they must take on the form of those who succeed him as denizens of Earth, they fear they will all turn into cockroaches.

But it is as a man of feeling that Nathan should be remembered. All of his wit and humor, all of his deft fantasy, all of his pellucid prose are secondary to the central function of his work, which is to evoke the sentiment of love. Most of his stories deal with the passionate awakening of young lovers, but the implications go beyond the physical and psychological gratifications this involves. In Nathan's work the mortal love of man and woman, the enfolding love of man for other men, the sympathy of man for the mystery of God's infinite works, all combine at last in a mystical conviction that love is the access to God. It is quite appropriate, therefore, that the principal character in *Stonecliffe*—who is a fictional representation of Nathan himself—insists that "a wizard does things with the heart," for he thus describes in cryptic fashion how all the verbal skill, the imaginative reversals, the rich traditions, and the brilliant commonsense of this particular author, are made to serve the ultimate goal of generating and sustaining in his readers the joy and hope that comes through every kind of love.

—Clarence Sandelin

---

**NAUGHTON, Bill.** British. Born in Ballyhaunis, County Mayo, Ireland, 12 June 1910; grew up in Lancashire, England. Educated at St. Peter and Paul School, Bolton, Lancashire. Civil Defence Driver in London during World War II. Married to Ernestine Pirolt. Has worked as a lorry driver, weaver and coal-bagger. Address: Craigton, Orrisale Road, Ballasalla, Isle of Man, United Kingdom.

PUBLICATIONS

Novels

*Rafe Granite*. London, Pilot Press, 1947.

*One Small Boy*.   London, MacGibbon and Kee, 1957.
*Alfie*.   London, MacGibbon and Kee, 1966.
*Alfie Darling*.   London, MacGibbon and Kee, 1970.


Short Stories

*Late Night in Watling Street and Other Stories*.   London, MacGibbon and Kee, 1959.
*The Goalkeeper's Revenge*.   London, MacGibbon and Kee, 1961.


Plays

*Alfie* (produced London, 1963).
*All in Good Time* (produced London, 1963; New York, 1965).   London, French, 1964.
*Spring and Port Wine* (produced London, 1965; as *Keep It in the Family*, produced New
    York, 1967).   London, French, 1967.
*He Was Gone When We Got There* (produced London, 1966).
*Lighthearted Intercourse* (produced Liverpool, 1971).


Other

*A Roof over Your Head* (autobiography).   London, Pilot Press, 1945.
*Pony Boy* (juvenile).   London, Harrap, 1966.


                        *         *         *


Bill Naughton's first book, *A Roof over Your Head*, was written while he was working as a Civil Defence driver in London during the War. This book, a blend of fiction and auto-biography, deals with working-class life in Lancashire where Naughton, the son of Irish immigrants, grew up. For background, there is the unplanned industrial jungle of the Twenties and Thirties, the grimy, crumbling factories and the monotonous rows of brick houses that L. S. Lowry has so accurately depicted.

*A Roof over Your Head* is artlessly constructed as a series of short sketches: a naïve yet oddly moving and direct account of what life was like under the shadow of the dole queue. Childhood, elopement, married life, a first baby, efforts to find work, a job as a coalman and, finally, extracts from a War-time diary: these form the subject matter that is narrated unsentimentally and without self-pity. Naughton writes frankly but undepressingly about poverty and hardship, and shows how these were made more endurable by the good-hearted camaraderie of Lancashire's ordinary people.

*Pony Boy* is a novel for boys. In it, two Pony Boys—Corky and Ginger—set out to discover "the world". Here is a rollicking, picaresque tale that indicates how well Naughton remembers what boyhood was like. In the 1940's and 50's Naughton was busy writing short stories for magazines, the best of which were collected in *Late Night on Watling Street*.

In these stories descriptive writing is kept to a minimum and Naughton reveals his gift for dialogue that explains situation and illuminates character. He keeps the narrative on the move like a true storyteller. His title story emphasises the solidarity of lorry-drivers, especially in their dealings with bosses and the police and brings out their sense of right and wrong. They ostracise a man who has committed murder but will not "split" on him: "He might have got one across the law, but he hadn't got one across Watling Street." Of this collection Naughton has said: "This book includes stories I heard people tell and I just 'put together', as they say. . . . I write mostly about the life I have known."

More cross-sections of the life Naughton actually experienced may be found in *The*

*Goalkeeper's Revenge*, a collection of stories mainly about but not written specifically for boys. One of these stories, "Gift of the Gab", tells the reader what can happen when a deaf-and-dumb boy is taught to speak. The result is both prosaic and humorous. The boy returns to his home town and at first seems as silent as ever. But he readily bursts into speech when questioned about food in the "institution": "Cold suet pud! Morning, noon and ruddy night—nothing but cold suet pud!"

*One Small Boy* is a novel in which a family—like Naughton's own—leave the West of Ireland for Lancashire's milltowns. A boy grows up and the author explores his relationship with parents and girls. *Alfie*—and Alf is a recurrent name in Naughton's work—was first a radio play called "Alfie Elkins and His Little Life", then a stage play, a film and a novel. Here, too, one finds the usual understated humour, the eye for detail and the tolerant good humour. Yet *Alfie*, despite its sophisticated finish, lacks the urgency and freshness of *A Roof over Your Head* and the best of the short stories.

—Robert Greacen

---

**NEMEROV, Howard.**   American.   Born in New York City, 1 March 1920. Educated at Fieldston School, New York; Harvard University, Cambridge, Massachusetts, A.B. 1941. Served in the Royal Canadian Air Force and the United States Air Force, rising to the rank of First Lieutenant, 1941–45. Married Margaret Russell in 1944; has three children. Instructor in English, Hamilton College, Clinton, New York, 1946–48; Member of the Literature Faculty, Bennington College, Vermont, 1948–66; Professor of English, Brandeis University, Waltham, Massachusetts, 1966–69. Since 1969, Professor of English, Washington University, St. Louis. Visiting Lecturer, University of Minnesota, Minneapolis, 1958–59; Writer-in-Residence, Hollins College, Virginia, 1962–64; Consultant in Poetry, Library of Congress, Washington, D.C., 1963–64. Associate Editor, *Furioso*, Madison, Connecticut, later Northfield, Minnesota, 1946–51. Recipient: *Kenyon Review* Fellowship in Fiction, 1955; Blumenthal Prize, *Poetry*, Chicago, 1958; *Virginia Quarterly Review* Short Story Award, 1958; Harriet Monroe Memorial Prize, *Poetry*, Chicago, 1959; National Institute of Arts and Letters grant, 1961; Golden Rose Trophy, New England Poetry Club, 1962; Brandeis University Creative Arts Award, 1962; National Endowment for the Arts award, 1966; Theodore Roethke Award, 1968; Guggenheim Fellowship, 1968; St. Botolph's Club Prize for Poetry, 1968; Academy of American Poets Fellowship, 1971; Frank O'Hara Prize, *Poetry*, Chicago, 1971. D. L., Lawrence University, Appleton, Wisconsin, 1964; Tufts University, Medford, Massachusetts, 1969. Fellow, American Academy of Arts and Sciences, 1966. Member, National Institute of Arts and Letters, 1965. Address: Department of English, Washington University, St. Louis, Missouri 63130, U.S.A.

PUBLICATIONS

Novels

*The Melodramatists.*   New York, Random House, 1949.
*Federigo; or, The Power of Love.*   Boston, Little Brown, 1954.
*The Homecoming Game.*   New York, Simon and Schuster, 1957.

Short Stories

*A Commodity of Dreams and Other Stories.*  New York, Simon and Schuster, 1959;
London, Secker and Warburg, 1960.
*Stories, Fables and Other Diversions.*  Brookline, Massachusetts, David R. Godine,
1971.

Verse

*The Image and the Law.*  New York, Holt, 1947.
*Guide to the Ruins.*  New York, Random House, 1950.
*The Salt Garden.*  Boston, Little Brown, 1955.
*Mirrors and Windows.*  Chicago, University of Chicago Press, 1958.
*New and Selected Poems.*  Chicago, University of Chicago Press, 1960.
*The Next Room of the Dream: Poems and Two Plays.*  Chicago, University of Chicago
Press, 1962.
*Five American Poets,* with others.  London, Faber, 1963.
*The Blue Swallows*  Chicago, University of Chicago Press, 1967.
*The Winter Lightning: Selected Poems.*  London, Rapp and Whiting, 1968.
*Gnomes and Occasions: Poems.*  Chicago, University of Chicago Press, 1972.

Other

*Poetry and Fiction: Essays.*  New Brunswick, New Jersey, Rutgers University Press,
1963.
*Journal of the Fictive Life.*  New Brunswick, New Jersey, Rutgers University Press,
1965.
*Reflexions on Poetry and Poetics.*  New Brunswick, New Jersey, Rutgers University
Press, 1972.

Editor, *Poets on Poetry.*  New York, Basic Books, 1965.

Critical Studies: *Howard Nemerov* by Peter Meinke, Minneapolis, University of Minnesota
Press, 1968; *The Critical Reception of Howard Nemerov,* edited by Bowie Duncan, Metuchen,
New Jersey, Scarecrow Press, 1971; *The Shield of Perseus,* by Julia Bartholomay, Gaines-
ville, University of Florida Press, 1972.

*          *          *

In *Journal of the Fictive Life,* which is something like a novel about not being able to write
a novel, Howard Nemerov records this meditation: "Of course! To write a work of fiction is
essentially to tell a story. And to tell a story is to tell a lie, because a lie was a story." It is
the words—*story/lie*—that engage his attention, and appropriately so, for Nemerov principally and most notably is a poet, not a novelist. The novel form, however, has enabled him to
explore, in successive stages of authorship, the doubleness of life and Art, as exemplified
in the imagination that both lives and creates. He has thus written four (if one counts
*Journal of the Fictive Life*) novels, and two volumes of shorter pieces. All involve, in one way
or another, the theme of doubleness. His first novel, *The Melodramatists,* is set in Boston in
the early years of the Second World War, and describes the separate paths toward self-
discovery taken by two sisters. One chooses the Roman Church, and at the end finds it
without use as a method of living in the world itself. The other elects psychoanalysis and

sensuality, and finds these even more unsatisfactory; she manages to kill herself in the process. The approach throughout is satirical; it is almost as if a cosmic skeptic had produced, one year before Eliot, a Beacon Street version of *The Cocktail Party*.

In Nemerov's second novel, *Federigo; or, The Power of Love*, the two personalities of the first novel become one—or, rather, become opposite halves of man and döppelgänger. The interaction of Federigo, the double, with an advertising man, Julian Ghent, turns into not merely a witty satire on sophisticated New Yorkers in search of sexual identity, but a mordant examination of human identity in general, as seen from either side of the looking glass.

The third novel, *The Homecoming Game*, subsequently turned into a play and a motion picture, has an academic setting, and probes into the way that reality intrudes upon intellectual contemplation. The intrusion takes the form of a history professor finding that he is about to give a failing grade to the college's star football player. The "double" is here, too; it turns out that the young athlete has failed *two* courses, and the other is likewise taught by a Jew, not one who is thoroughly middle-class American in upbringing and attitudes like the history professor, but a contentious, not-so-assimilated, idea-ridden firebrand from the big city ghetto. Before all is resolved, raw power and atavistic violence get thoroughly mixed in with the pursuit of truth and goodness, and the history professor, to his chagrin, learns that "it is commonly allowed that you may more easily call the things of this world symbolical than say what they are symbolical of."

Eight years intervened before Nemerov turned to novel-length prose fiction again. *Journal of the Fictive Life*, not only utterly unlike his earlier books but resembling almost no other book ever written, presents the ruthlessly honest progression of the thoughts, dreams, and interpretations of dreams of a man trying to write fiction after eight years of mostly poetry. In a very real sense it isn't "fiction" at all (and it is not put forward as such). For though the authorial persona starts out with a name, Felix Ledger, the "pretense" is abandoned halfway through. Yet as the meditation develops, it turns out to have a plot after all; the author is searching for the explanation of his unwilling renunciation of novel writing, and in the process he also discovers what his father's life and death meant for him, and what the imminent arrival of a new child signifies. The story ends with the birth of a son and the making of a poem. Is it fiction? Yes and no; that is the point. "It is, in effect," the narrator declares at one point, "as though I were covertly writing, not my life, but a novel about a life rather like mine, conforming to certain conventions of psychoanalysis." Thus in *Journal of the Fictive Life* the theme of the double becomes that of the author and his persona, the son and the father, the poet and the story-teller. Whether fiction, memoir, or both, *Journal of the Fictive Life* is a remarkable revelation of the creative process, in which notable intellectual perception is turned upon a gifted imagination.

—Louis D. Rubin, Jr.

---

**NEUGEBOREN, Jay.** American. Born in Brooklyn, New York, 30 May 1938. Educated at Columbia University, New York, B.A. 1959 (Phi Beta Kappa); Indiana University, Bloomington, M.A. 1963. Married Betsy Bendorf in 1964; has one child. Junior Executive Trainee, General Motors Corporation, Indianapolis, 1960. English Teacher, Saddle River Country Day School, New Jersey, 1961–62; High School and Junior High School Teacher, New York City public schools, 1963–66. Preceptor in English, Columbia University, 1964–66; Lecturer, Stanford University, California, 1966–67; Assistant Professor, State University of New York, Old Westbury, 1968–69. Since 1971, Writer-in-Residence, University of Massachusetts, Amherst. Recipient: Bread Loaf Writers Conference Fellowship, 1966. Address: Department of English, University of Massachusetts, Amherst, Massachusetts 01002, U.S.A.

PUBLICATIONS

Novels

> *Big Man.*   Boston, Houghton Mifflin, 1966.
> *Listen Ruben Fontanez.*   Boston, Houghton Mifflin, and London, Gollancz, 1968.

Short Stories

> *Corky's Brother and Other Stories.*   New York, Farrar Straus, 1969; London, Gollancz, 1970.
> *Penguin Modern Stories 3*, with others.   London, Penguin, 1970.

Uncollected Short Stories

> "My Son, The Freedom Rider", in *Colorado Quarterly* (Boulder), Summer 1964.
> "Connorsville, Virginia", in *Transatlantic Review* (London and New York), Winter 1969.

Other

> *Parentheses: An Autobiographical Journey.*   New York, Dutton, 1970.

Critical Studies: statement by Ian Watt, in *Listen Ruben Fontanez*, London, Gollancz, 1968; "Parentheses" by Charles Moran, in *Massachusetts Review* (Amherst), Fall 1970; "From Kerouac to Koch" by Michael Willis, in *Columbia College Today* (New York), Winter-Spring 1971.

Jay Neugeboren comments:

*Big Man* is, in part, about a black All-American basketball player, caught in the point-fixing scandals of the early 1950's. The novel takes place five years after the scandals, when he is working in a car wash. *Listen Ruben Fontanez* is, in part, about a 64-year-old Junior High School teacher (Williamsburgh, Brooklyn), in his last year of teaching, who becomes involved with three boys. The boys (two of them Puerto Rican), who make their living by hustling in New York's subways, come to share the protagonist's one-room West Side apartment. *Corky's Brother* is a collection of 12 stories and one novella. Six of the stories ("the Brooklyn stories") concern a group of boys who grow up in Brooklyn during the mid-fifties. Many of the stories in the collection have sports as a background. Others deal with New York City's blacks and Puerto Ricans, though some have other settings (the midwest, a Long Island mental hospital, etc.).

*     *     *

A deep imaginative compassion would appear to be the motive force behind the writing of the American author Jay Neugeboren. For all those who live precariously on the margins of economic, social or psychological safety he has an immediate, instinctive subtle pity. Nor is there the slightest note of emotional patronage about his attitude. First, the pity which he feels is expressed only objectively in terms of artistic distancing; and secondly, it is constituted of understanding and self-identification.

Thus, whether he is writing, in his novel *Listen Ruben Fontanez*, of poor Puerto Ricans in New York or of the Chassidic Jews (at whose singular dress the gentiles laugh) in that city, he is close to them with a sympathetic sixth sense which excludes any chance of superiority in his role as an observer. His approach and technique are largely the same in his book of thirteen shorter tales, *Corky's Brother and Other Stories*, though the earliest of these pieces dates from 1962, and the volume as a whole does not reveal the consistently sure deftness and balance which distinguish *Listen Ruben Fontanez*. The catalysts (rather than objects) of his compassion here include the tough kids of Brooklyn with their obsessive baseball addiction, a young drop-out delinquent negro, and men who are lonely or isolated not through race or social position but through their individual circumstance. It is age (bringing with it the loss of a wife) which creates the loneliness of the two men—a professor and a janitor—in "Finkel," and it is mental instability, on the part of a teen-ager in an institution, in the desperate but beautifully-controlled sketch "The Pass."

Compassion may have the first and last word in Jay Neugeboren's writing but it is a sentiment totally removed from the sentimental. Indeed, in between this first and last compassion other states of mind enjoy a field-day, the most prominent of which are humour, hopelessness and despair. Jay Neugeboren's second novel, *Listen Ruben Fontanez*, might indeed be described as *King Lear* written in prose by James Thurber with contemporary settings. Next go on to make King Lear himself Jewish, and one may possess a zany formula for this strange, deeply moving work of fiction. Old Harry Myers, a Jewish teacher in New York, seeks to keep his heart in cold storage, feeling that sympathetic involvement would dangerously impair his very existence. Like the two old men in the short story "Finkel," Myers' wife has died, leaving him lost, deprived and lonely. The last of six brothers, Myers has only one old friend of his boyhood left. Teaching his Skid Row kids, he is less than a year from retirement, asking only his pension and tail-end peace from life. Concealed but deep-rooted, however, his humanity has got the better of his fear-ridden nature. Against all counsels of prudence and caution, he acts heroically and is saved from the consequence of his gesture by a group of poor Puerto Rican street arabs whom he once taught.

If the last word in this novel is not "love" at least it is one which points to the promise of a release, for the aged protagonist, from the doubt and withdrawal which have him in their grip. Imagine a Kafka writing of the literally rotting tenements of New York, its polyglot children and over-crowded schools. But this Kafka, with a Kafka-like despair, is possessed of another resonance as well: the gift of laughter. And that is Jay Neugeboren.

—Derek Stanford

---

**NEWBY, P(ercy) H(oward).** British. Born in Crowborough, Sussex, 25 June 1918. Educated at Hanley Castle Grammar School, Worcester; St. Paul's College, Cheltenham, 1936–38. Served in the Royal Army Medical Corps, in France and Egypt, 1939–42. Married Joan Thompson in 1945; has two children. Lecturer in English Language and Literature, Fuad I University, Cairo, 1942–46; Free-lance Writer and Journalist, 1946–49. Joined the BBC, London, 1949: Producer, Talks Department, 1949–58; Controller, Third Programme, 1958–70, Radio 3, 1970–71, and since 1971 Director of Programmes (Radio). Recipient: Atlantic Award, 1946; Maugham Award, 1948; Smith-Mundt Fellowship, 1952; *Yorkshire Post* Award, 1968; Booker Prize, 1969. Address: Upton House, Cokes Lane, Chalfont St. Giles, Buckinghamshire, England.

PUBLICATIONS

Novels

*A Journey to the Interior*.   London, Cape, 1945; New York, Doubleday, 1946.
*Agents and Witnesses*.   London, Cape, and New York, Doubleday, 1947.
*Mariner Dances*.   London, Cape, 1948.
*The Snow Pasture*.   London, Cape, 1949.
*The Young May Moon*.   London, Cape, 1950; New York, Knopf, 1951.
*A Season in England*.   London, Cape, 1951; New York, Knopf, 1952.
*A Step to Silence*.   London, Cape, 1952.
*The Retreat*.   London, Cape, and New York, Knopf, 1953.
*The Picnic at Sakkara*.   London, Cape, and New York, Knopf, 1955.
*Revolution and Roses*.   London, Cape, and New York, Knopf, 1957.
*A Guest and His Going*.   London, Cape, and New York, Knopf, 1959.
*The Barbary Light*.   London, Faber, 1962; Philadelphia, Lippincott, 1964.
*One of the Founders*.   London, Faber, and Philadelphia, Lippincott, 1965.
*Something to Answer For*.   London, Faber, 1968; Philadelphia, Lippincott, 1969.

Short Stories

*Ten Miles from Anywhere and Other Stories*.   London, Cape, 1958.

Other

*The Spirit of Jem* (juvenile).   London, Lehmann, 1947; New York, Dial Press, 1967.
*The Loot Runners* (juvenile).   London, Lehmann, 1949.
*Maria Edgeworth*.   London, Barker, and Denver, Swallow, 1950.
*The Novel 1945–1950*.   London, Longman, 1951.

Editor, *Tales from the Arabian Nights*.   New York, Pocket Books, 1967.

Critical Studies: "Portrait of the Artist as a Jung Man" by Lucia Dickerson, in *Kenyon Review* (Gambier, Ohio), Winter 1959; "A Novelist on His Own", in *Times Literary Supplement* (London), 6 April 1962; *The Fiction of P. H. Newby* by F. X. Mathews, Madison, University of Wisconsin Press, 1964; *Identity in Four of P. H. Newby's Novels* by M. G. St. Leger, unpublished master's thesis, Beirut, The American University, 1969.

P. H. Newby comments:

In common with many English novelists my preoccupations have always been with what seems and what is. Many of my novels have been set in the Middle East but that is only because I spent some years there; it does not mean that I regard myself as particularly knowledgable about that part of the world, only that I used this part of my experience to say what I would otherwise have said out of my English background—that the most interesting problem is the relationship between innocence and knowledge.

*          *          *

The lengthy series of novels by P. H. Newby can, with some justice, be assigned to two categories. There are novels which represent Newby's assessment of the contacts of two cultures; *Revolution and Roses*, *The Picnic at Sakkara*, and *Something to Answer For* are examples of these. And there are novels like *A Season in England*, *The Barbary Light*, and *One of the Founders* which abandon the fascinating game of assessing sharp cultural differences and that instead take up an analysis of a single culture: the texture of middle and lower-class British life. The center of awareness in the novels which specialize in cultural clash is always that of some British traveller or teacher who has been thrust into an alien world, usually Arab but in one instance—*Revolution and Roses*—Greek. The center of awareness in novels that take up a specifically British theme is usually that of a fairly well-educated person who can assess the clash and diversity inherent in a society that, to the careless viewer, is or should be homogeneous.

Both varieties of subject-matter have long been worked on by writers of British fiction. Alien cultural contacts experienced in the course of Britain's bearing "the white man's burden" are the stock-in-trade of writers as various as Kipling, E. M. Forster, and Joyce Cary. And novels which relate the maturing of an English hero in his own environment abound. But it is not just to Newby to suggest that he works in two traditions only loosely related to each other. For he brings to either tradition a variation that is his own. Moreover, this variation appears in almost every novel and effects a unity of tone that pervades the novels despite the variety of subject-matter. That tone is the tone of farce.

It is a tone that separates the novels that represent contact with an alien culture from Forster's *A Passage to India* in which the English characters achieve some kind of understanding of the world they visit. Newby's English visitors begin in incomprehension and end there; at certain moments they may indeed think they grasp the mystery of Arab or Greek temperament, but later turns of event and later deeds of the "natives" indicate that the comprehension of the English visitor rests on an insecure basis or no basis at all.

Newby's tone of farce also separates his novels with an English setting from the "coming of age" category they may seem to belong to. For in novels like *The Barbary Light* the characters only seem to "come of age"; new events and new potentialities within the hero's own nature give the lie to stances that had seemed final. Only in *A Season in England* and *One of the Founders* do the heroes finally transcend the texture of farce and achieve positions that are crypto-Christian. More usually, the heroes of the English novels just move through a succession of attitudes—attitudes that are related to each other only in that they flow in upon the same person. They do not come to compose a character, a fixed personality, a settled body of convictions. The attitudes simply overtake the hero, temporarily overwhelm him, and presently give way to other emotions and impressions thrust upon him by new events or by discovery of new potentialities within himself. The character lives in a society which is far from unified; this being so, how can he arrive at any consistency of gesture and aspiration? He has no more chance to arrive at a consistent view of his own motives than does the English visitor in *The Picnic at Sakkara*. He will fall in and out of love, will alter his purposes from year to year. Just as will the travelling Englishmen impose one revision after another on their impressions about "natives".

If a discrimination can indeed be made between the two groups of novels, it is this one. The farce of *The Picnic at Sakkara* and *Revolution and Roses* is overt and often violent. The farce of the British novels—which on the surface seem to be more serious—is covert. If one defines farce as existence seen under the sign of radical inconsequence, the definition is easily applied to the non-British novels, which despite the acuteness of Newby's notations on foreign customs and sensibilities are rich in the traditional pleasures of farce: the pleasures that come to us from events that are unpredictable and utterly disconcerting. A "native" who has seemed to be a friend, in *The Picnic at Sakkara*, turns into a bitter foe—and yet gives the English visitor a farewell gift. A man spits in an English woman's face (*Revolution and Roses*) and yet later turns up in London as a suitor. The pleasures of such foreign contacts are not much more predictable than entrance into a lion's cage; docility or murderous assault is equally likely. Such experience cannot be expected to yield a steady meaning; in its presence the visitor can brace himself to offer resignation and, at the worst, amused contempt. The safest course, in such farcically operating worlds, is to keep one's distance and expect very little in the way of fixed and dependable certainties.

One might expect a diminution of these farcical inconsequences when the hero of a novel is living in a world that is culturally his own. But this is not so of Newby's novels that represent the English world. The farcical texture of that world is simply more difficult to bear just because it is indeed one's own world. Gestures of kindness that ought to yield happy results beget unforeseen consequences—consequences that disconcert because of the unpredictable choices of other characters and, most painfully, because of changes in one's own wishes. For the British world of Newby is, in large part, that of Kingsley Amis's *Lucky Jim*, where farce is the product of an endemic British hypocrisy and, still worse, of a lack of any fixed values that could support social consensus. Farce experienced at one remove, in a visit to a foreign country, has become, in novels like *One of the Founders* and *The Barbary Light*, farce experienced at the very center of the culture one belongs to and, indeed, at the very center of one's own nature. Both tragedy and comedy, in varying ways, presuppose a society of shared values. Farce, instead, invites one to the fashioning of a detached, self-protective monologue that celebrates, as do the novels of Newby, the lack of consequence and coherence. It is a lack that is easily detached in Egypt or some other foreign country. But it is a lack that just as strongly marks one's own culture and, if sharply inspected, one's own nature. If farce is to be left behind, this must be done by religious gesture (as in *One of the Founders*) which is private and quite incommunicable.

—Harold H. Watts

---

**NEWHOUSE, Edward.** American. Born in Budapest, Hungary, 10 November 1911; emigrated to the United States in 1923. Educated at Townsend Harris Hall Preparatory School, New York, 1926–29. Served in the United States Army Air Force, rising to the rank of Major, 1942–46: Legion of Merit; Conspicuous Service Cross. Married Dorothy DeLay in 1941; has two children. Since 1936 has been affiliated with *The New Yorker* magazine, which has published virtually all of his short fiction. Address: Upper Nyack, New York 10960, U.S.A.

PUBLICATIONS

Novels

> *You Can't Sleep Here.* New York, Macaulay, 1934.
> *This Is Your Day.* New York, Lee Furman, 1937.
> *The Hollow of the Wave.* New York, Sloane, 1949; London, Reinhardt and Evans, 1950.
> *The Temptation of Roger Heriott.* Boston, Houghton Mifflin, 1954; London, Gollancz, 1955.

Short Stories

> *Anything Can Happen.* New York, Harcourt Brace, 1941.
> *The Iron Chain.* New York, Harcourt Brace, 1946.
> *Many Are Called.* New York, Sloane, 1951; London, Gollancz, 1952.

Uncollected Short Stories

"The Ambassador", in *The New Yorker*, 20 April 1957.
"The Bromley Touch", in *The New Yorker*, 18 May 1957.
"Howard and Dinah", in *The New Yorker*, 23 November 1957.
"Lead, Damsel, and I Follow", in *The New Yorker*, 8 March 1958.
"Debut Recital", in *The New Yorker*, 26 April 1958.
"Hungarians", in *The New Yorker*, 27 November 1966.

\*      \*      \*

The hero of Edward Newhouse's third novel, *The Hollow of the Wave*, is a commercial artist who once painted many canvases. The first few pages of the book show this young man, Neil Miller, destroying all his paintings because now he finds them bad. When he is finished, he feels cleansed.

This passage is perhaps the most autobiographical in the work of Edward Newhouse, for, if published books were as easy to incinerate as canvases, he would have destroyed his first two novels. And it would have been a pity.

Following his disillusionment with the Communist Party in 1937, Newhouse no longer saw any merit in his work done under the influence of the dream of the revolution to come. Yet, we who are now removed from the anti-Communist hysteria of the late forties and of the fifties, can once more look at those early books with something approaching the wonder which accompanied their original publication.

*You Can't Sleep Here* was published early in 1934, when the author had barely passed his twenty-second birthday. It was an astonishingly precocious work. The hero, Eugene Marsay, a young reporter of Hungarian background, is struggling with the woes of unemployment during the depression. His problems are the simple ones of where to sleep and what to eat, but they are complicated by an intense pride which forbids him to accept charity or even the love of a rich girl; instead, Gene is driven into more and more conscious identification with the hungry, unemployed masses. His path leads to a shanty colony in Queens, to Party work, and to imprisonment. Throughout, the dialog is crackling with wit, and the action fast-moving. The hero's struggles seem so timely as to give the reader a feeling of *déjà vu*, while his vision of a better America to come is almost surrealistic.

Its sequel, *This Is Your Day*, follows Gene Marsay's career as a Communist organizer. Most of the action takes place in a Pennsylvania farming region. The book's greatest triumph is the characterization of Gene's mother-in-law, a Mrs. Darvas, perhaps the most moving, most authentic portrait of a working woman in American letters. Her figure alone would make the novel worth reading. Newhouse dedicated this book to his own mother.

Twelve years elapsed until the next novel was brought out, but the fictional time of *The Hollow of the Wave* takes up soon after the other left off, on the eve of Dunkirk. Paralleling the author's own development, this book's heroes have moved away from revolutionary ideals into disillusionment with Communism; Party members and fellow travelers are seen largely as shams or dupes. Symbolically, Neil Miller is the illegitimate son of a Communist whom he never knew and who became the victim of a purge. Neil's vague search for this unreal father sets the tone for much of the book. The other hero, Larry Holland, born to great wealth, is skillfully drawn—a man who can bloom only under the special stresses of a challenge called war—in everything else, he is a failure. When the war is over, he is caught "in the hollow of the wave," and asks Neil "savagely," "What are we doing here, you and I?"

His fourth and to date last novel, *The Temptation of Roger Heriott*, comes closest to the classical mold. In a two-week period, Roger Heriott, an executive for a musical scholarship foundation, is faced with a number of circumstances which threaten to upset the equilibrium of his life-style. He may lose his job or he may inherit a sizable sum. The second is the greater threat. In a manner reminiscent of Gene Marsay, Roger Heriott remains true to himself. The global struggle has become a very private one—Gene fought for the masses, against kings and dominions; Roger fights against his temptations, and preserves his integrity. In a style that is always lively and with a structure which is always taut, Newhouse brings his book to a satisfactory conclusion.

On his return from his 20,000 mile freight-hopping jaunt, the twenty-four-year old author sold five stories to *The New Yorker*. That magazine has continued, throughout the years, to be the chief publisher of his short fiction. Three collections of these have appeared so far: *Anything Can Happen*, *The Iron Chain*, and *Many Are Called*.

In the eyes of many critics, Edward Newhouse is primarily a short story writer. His strengths lie in what Richard Harrity has described as "an accurate ear, an infallibility of character, and a discerning eye for telling incident." Lincoln Steffens called him "the first authentic and eloquent literary voice of America's next generation." Struthers Burt, writing in *The Saturday Review of Literature*, said of *The Iron Chain*, "So far as I'm concerned, they are by long odds the best American short stories I have read in a long while. The reading of this volume was an event in my life."

In recent years, his only major work has been a long story, "Hungarians." Full of revealing incidents about himself, his family, and Hungarians in general, it caps his achievement as the foremost American literary voice to have come from a Hungarian background.

—Dalma H. Brunauer

---

**NGUGI, J(ames) T.**   Kenyan.   Born in Limuru in 1938. Educated at Makerere University College, and Editor, *Penpoint* magazine, Kampala. Literary and Political Journalist: Regular Contributor to the *Sunday Nation*, Nairobi. Recipient: East African Literature Bureau award, 1964. Address: c/o William Heinemann Ltd., 15 Queen Street, London W1X 8BE, England.

PUBLICATIONS

Novels

*Weep Not, Child*.   London, Heinemann, 1964.
*The River Between*.   London, Heinemann, 1965.
*A Grain of Wheat*.   London, Heinemann, 1967.

Plays

*The Black Hermit* (produced Nairobi, 1962).   London, Heinemann, 1968.
*This Time Tomorrow* (produced Nairobi, 1964).

\*          \*          \*

J. T. Ngugi was a Gikuyu adolescent in Kenya during the Mau-Mau Rebellion, and the events of those years, and the larger issues of black African dispossession by white European settlers, lie at the centre of all three of his novels and most of his short stories so far published. Historically his chief importance as a novelist is that he was the first Anglophone African writer to give in fiction a Gikuyu view of experience during the bitter colonial war that the British authorities euphemistically called the Mau-Mau Emergency—a healthy corrective to other fictional accounts, such as Ruark's, from a white man's point of view.

Some of the dilemmas that faced African people driven from their ancestral lands by white settlers form the main themes of Ngugi's books, though his attitudes to the larger questions are by no means unambiguous in his first two novels—hence some considerable uncertainty of craftsmanship in his earlier fiction. What emerges very clearly from *The River Between* (the first to be written, but the second published) is a deep sense of African deprivation and its concomitant, the desire to win back their lost heritage. It is expressed in *Weep Not, Child* through Ngotho's religious attachment to the land of his ancestors taken from him by Mr Howlands, and through his older sons' determination to fight for their lands by joining the Mau-Mau. But Ngugi is also aware of another part of the African heritage diminished by white colonialism—the Gikuyu religion and tribal culture; it is this aspect of their disinheritance that figures particularly in *The River Between*.

The river is a symbol of sustenance and new growth, but it also divides the christianized half of the tribe from the adherents of traditional tribal ways at a period between the arrival of colonialism and the beginnings of physical resistance by the Africans. Waiyaki, the hero, is an idealistic youth with visions of messianic grandeur, who dreams of leading his people out of colonial tutelage, peacefully, through acquiring the white man's education. He also dreams of reconciling the two religiously divided villages that face each other across the river; though associated with the traditional ways of the tribe, he falls in love with a daughter of the fanatical Christian African pastor. But Waiyaki's enthusiasm for western education blinds him to the need for political action. In the end he is rejected by his people. Waiyaki is a familiar pre-independence African figure, but what is disquieting about the novel is Ngugi's apparent emotional identification with the character. The hero is romanticized and glamorized; his opponents are presented as jealous, vindictive personal enemies; their different political approach is seen as evil because it prevents a young idealist from becoming a mediator among his people.

Njoroge in *Weep Not, Child* is also a self-centred youth with a mission-school education and messianic ambitions, whose long-term hopes are destroyed when the Mau-Mau Rebellion forces him out of school. Again self-centredness and individualism are not part of any ironic regarding of the hero by the novelist. There are plenty of fine sentiments, and one wonders uncomfortably whether Ngugi has not perhaps endowed both Waiyaki and Njoroge with some nostalgic soulfulness from his own adolescence. Yet *Weep Not, Child* is a better novel; for the first time Ngugi develops some complexity of structure. There are ironic parallels between the African devotion to ancestral lands and the white settler's love of the soil he has acquired. Dispossessed of his English cultural heritage by his experiences in 1914–18, Howlands has suffered surprisingly much in common with Ngotho, and, like Njoroge's youth, his too had been shattered by violent upheaval. The opposed characters are oblivious to their common human suffering, and this ironical treatment is a great advance in Ngugi's technique—though not adequately exploited, and to some extent vitiated by his involvement with his hero. The dwelling on vague youthful fervour and yearning that occurs repeatedly in both novels is a sure sign of a youthful novelist. Yet the promise is there, particularly in the convincing portraits of subsidiary characters who betray the very values they struggle to achieve, or who suffer constant frustration.

By comparison *A Grain of Wheat* is an accomplished novel of mature outlook and much subtler technique. Ostensibly about the Uhuru celebrations of Kenya's independence in 1963, it keeps flashing back to individual sufferings in Mau-Mau days. No single, central hero this time, but four major characters, each of whom was guilty of betraying himself and others when sorely tried in the Rebellion. Mugo, regarded by his people as a Mau-Mau hero, has messianic visions before the Rebellion, but his jealousy of the real leader led him to betray him secretly to the British authorities. At last Ngugi is able to treat a messianic figure with detachment, but also with humane sympathy. Mugo's ambitions were obviously obsessive, but the years of his lonely, withdrawn, conscience-ridden life are movingly conveyed. The other characters who were also guilty of various acts of betrayal during the

941

Rebellion painfully learn, first, the depths of utter disillusion, and then, the harrowing experience of coming to terms with their own fleshly limitations. Mugo's public confession of his own crime brings inner peace to himself, and helps them to face the future with some hope. A great strength of this finely orchestrated novel is Ngugi's skilful use of disrupted time sequence to indicate the close inter-relatedness between the characters' behaviour in the Rebellion and the state of their lives (and of the nation) at Independence. Ngugi's maturity in this novel appears also in his sober attitude both to the struggle for, and the attainment of, Independence. He questions whether the new African politicians have not betrayed the ordinary people who suffered under colonialism. Though *A Grain of Wheat* is a disturbing novel, it proclaims cautious, tempered hope for the regenerative capabilities of ordinary human nature.

—Arthur Ravenscroft

**NICOL, Abioseh.** Pseudonym for Davidson Sylvester Hector Willoughby Nicol. Sierra Leonean. Born in Freetown, 14 September 1924. Educated at Schools in Nigeria and Sierra Leone; Christ's College, Cambridge, 1943–50, B.A. 1946, M.A., M.D., Ph.D. Married Marjorie Esme Johnston in 1950; has three children. Science Master, Prince of Wales School, Freetown, 1941–43; House Physician and Research Assistant, London Hospital Medical College, University of London, 1950–52; University Lecturer, The Medical School, Ibadan, 1952–54; Beit Memorial Fellow, 1954, and Benn Levy University Student, 1956, Cambridge University; Fellow and Supervisor in Natural Sciences and Medicine, Christ's College, Cambridge, 1957–59; Senior Pathologist, Sierra Leone Government, 1958–60; Visiting Lecturer, University of California, Berkeley, and The Mayo Clinic, Rochester, Minnesota, 1958; Principal, Fourah Bay College, 1960–67, and Vice-Chancellor, 1966–68, University of Sierra Leone, Freetown; Aggrey-Fraser-Guggisberg Lecturer, University of Ghana, Accra, 1963; Danforth Lecturer, Association of American Colleges, 1968–70. Ambassador of Sierra Leone to the United Nations, 1968–71. Since 1971, High Commissioner of the Republic of Sierra Leone to the United Kingdom, and Ambassador of Sierra Leone to Denmark, Norway, Sweden and Finland. President, Student Christian Movement, Western Nigeria, 1952–54, and Sierra Leone, 1959; Delegate to the World Health Organization Assembly, 1959–60; Member, West African Council for Medical Research, 1959–62; Chairman, Sierra Leone National Library Board, 1959–65; Member, Commission for the Proposed University of Ghana, 1960; Member, Executive Council, Association of Universities of the British Commonwealth, 1960, 1966; Member, Public Service Commission of Sierra Leone, 1960–68; Chairman, University of East Africa Visiting Committee, 1962; President, Sierra Leone Red Cross Society, 1962–66; Delegate, UNESCO Higher Education Conference, Tananarive, 1963; President, West African Science Association, 1964–66; Chairman, West African Examinations Council, 1964–69; Delegate, Commonwealth Prime Ministers Conference, London, 1965, 1969, 1971. Director, Sierra Leone Selection Trust Ltd., 1961–71, Central Bank of Sierra Leone, 1963–68, and since 1961, Consolidated African Selection Trust Ltd., London. Recipient: Margaret Wrong Prize, 1951; Independence Medal, Sierra Leone, 1961. D.Sc., University of Newcastle upon Tyne, 1964; Kalamazoo College, Michigan, 1964; LL.D., University of Leeds, 1968; D.Litt., Davis-Elkins College, Elkins, West Virginia, 1971. Honorary Fellow, Ghana Academy of Sciences. C.M.G. (Companion, Order of St. Michael and St. George), 1964. Address: High Commissioner of Sierra Leone, 33 Portland Place, London W.1.; or, c/o Oxford and Cambridge Club, Pall Mall, London S.W.1, England.

PUBLICATIONS

Short Stories

   *The Truly Married Woman and Other Stories.*   London, Oxford University Press, 1965.
   *Two African Tales.*   London, Cambridge University Press, 1965.

Other

   *Alienation: An Essay.*   London, MacGibbon and Kee, 1960.
   *Africa: A Subjective View.*   London, Longman, 1964.
   *Africanus Horton: The Dawn of Nationalism in Modern Africa.*   London, Longman,
      1969; as *Black Nationalism in Africa, 1867*, New York, Africana Publishing Corpo-
      ration, 1969.

   Verse published in numerous anthologies.

Bibliography: in *A Bibliography of Sierra Leone, 1925–1969*, edited by G. J. Williams,
New York, Africana Publishing Corporation, 1970.

Critical Studies: in *The African Image* by Ezekiel Mphahlele, London, Faber, 1962; *African-
English Literature* by Anne Tibble, London, Peter Owen, 1965.

Abioseh Nicol comments:

   My short stories and poetry have predominantly an African background although a few
are set in Europe and America. Their characters are drawn from all levels of black and white
society in Africa, and are based on observations gained by me during my work as a teacher,
administrator and doctor, plus the insight gained as a black African patriot engaged in
plans towards our independence. I tried to keep an independent and non-racist outlook.
   My appearance in print owes itself to the encouragement of the late Langston Hughes,
the black American writer, who first included me in his anthology of African verse, and to
Stephen Spender, the English poet, and Irving Kristol, the American writer, both of whom, as
former editors of *Encounter*, gave me the unprecedented encouragement of publishing three
of my short stories within a year in their magazine. My literary criticism was encouraged
and fostered in that excellent weekly *West Africa* by its Editor, David Williams, and by Walter
Allen, former Literary Editor of the *New Statesman and Nation*. Without the advice and
encouragement of these writers, my publications would still have been in manuscript form,
at the bottom of a drawer.
   All this, of course, refers to creative writing. I have written a considerable amount also
on higher education and politics over the past twenty years and have also published in
professional journals the results of research carried out in Europe and Africa on medical
and scientific subjects such as malnutrition, tropical diseases, endocrinology, and biochemistry.

                              *        *        *

Abioseh Nicol, one of Africa's most talented short story writers, belongs to the older generation of living African authors who wrote in the twilight of the colonial era, when Africa was still under the political thumb of Europe. Unlike many of his contemporaries, he did not write militant potest fiction but chose instead to deal with the cultural problems and moral dilemmas of Africans and Europeans who lived in this era "with its emphasis on pensionable jobs in Government service, official decorations, and black and white keeping their distance." Nicol has stated that he started writing

> partly because I wanted to and partly because I found that most of those who wrote about us seldom gave any nobility to their African characters unless they were savages or servants or faced impending destruction. I knew differently. I saw all around me worthy Africans who lived and worked with varying degrees of success, distinction, and happiness. I began to write about them.

Nicol's stories are usually set in the past in a part of Africa under British rule and frequently describe situations in which British colonial administrators and Africans strain against each other and toward each other. Nicol, who admits he owes much to E. M. Forster, Joyce Cary, Graham Greene, and Evelyn Waugh, pictures the mutual misunderstandings, the problems of communication, the gropings toward friendship, the lapses into anger and hostility, the hopes and the fears that characterize the relationships between the colonizers and the colonized, between white and black in Africa. It is a credit to Nicol's sensitivity and literary skill that these stories paint both sides of the racial fence accurately and compassionately.

In other stories Nicol investigates the plight of westernized Africans who still cling to traditional beliefs and customs. Victims of internal culture conflict, these men and women have to struggle to maintain their equilibrium in a changing world. Sometimes their difficulties are resolved in hilarious comedy, sometimes in tender pathos. Nicol's sharp eye for human foibles and tolerance for individual eccentricities make these stories a delight to read. He is an urbane humorist with a talent for gently poking fun at some of Africa's most entertaining absurdities.

—Bernth Lindfors

---

**NICOLE, Christopher (Robin).** Pseudonyms: **Andrew York**; **Peter Grange.** British. Born in Georgetown, Guyana, 7 December 1930. Educated at Harrison College, Barbados; Queen's College, Guyana. Married Jean Barnett in 1951; has four children. Clerk, Royal Bank of Canada, in the West Indies, 1947–56. Settled in Guernsey in 1957. Address: South Grange de Beauvoir, St. Peter Port, Guernsey, Channel Islands.

PUBLICATIONS

Novels

*Off White.*  London, Jarrolds, 1959.
*Shadows in the Jungle.*  London, Jarrolds, 1961.
*Ratoon.*  London, Jarrolds, and New York, St. Martin's Press, 1962.
*Dark Noon.*  London, Jarrolds, 1963.

*Amyot's Cay.*   London, Jarrolds, 1964.

*Blood Amyot.*   London, Jarrolds, 1964.

*The Amyot Crime.*   London, Jarrolds, 1965.

*White Boy.*   London, Hutchinson, 1966.

*The Eliminator* (as Andrew York).   London, Hutchinson, 1966; Philadelphia, Lippincott, 1967.

*King Creole* (as Peter Grange).   London, Jarrolds, 1966.

*The Co-Ordinator* (as Andrew York).   London, Hutchinson, and Philadelphia, Lippincott, 1967.

*The Predator* (as Andrew York).   London, Hutchinson, and Philadelphia, Lippincott, 1968.

*The Self-Lovers.*   London, Hutchinson, 1968.

*The Devil's Emissary* (as Peter Grange).   London, Jarrolds, 1968.

*The Deviator* (as Andrew York).   London, Hutchinson, and Philadelphia, Lippincott, 1969.

*The Doom Fisherman* (as Andrew York).   London, Hutchinson, 1969; as *Operation Destruct*, New York, Holt Rinehart, 1969.

*The Thunder and the Shouting.*   London, Hutchinson, and New York, Doubleday, 1969.

*The Dominator* (as Andrew York).   London, Hutchinson, 1969; New York, Lancer, 1971.

*Manhunt for a General* (as Andrew York).   London, Hutchinson, 1970; as *Operation Manhunt*, New York, Holt Rinehart, 1970.

*The Tumult at the Gate* (as Peter Grange).   London, Jarrolds, 1970.

*The Longest Pleasure.*   London, Hutchinson, 1970.

*The Infiltrator* (as Andrew York).   London, Hutchinson, and New York, Doubleday, 1971.

*Where the Cavern Ends* (as Andrew York).   London, Hutchinson, and New York, Holt Rinehart, 1971.

*The Face of Evil.*   London, Hutchinson, 1971.

*The Expurgator* (as Andrew York).   London, Hutchinson, 1972.

*Appointment in Kiltone* (as Andrew York).   London, Hutchinson, 1972; as *Operation Neptune*, New York, Holt Rinehart, 1972.

Other

*West Indian Cricket.*   London, Phoenix House, 1957.

*The West Indies: Their People and History.*   London, Hutchinson, 1965.

Critical Studies: in *Barbados Daily News* (Bridgetown), 18 April 1964; in *Smith's Trade News* (London), 30 July 1966; interviews, in *Smith's Trade News* (London), 1 April 1967 and 26 September 1970; in *Trinidad Guardian* (Port of Spain), 5 February 1969; review, in Boston *Globe*, 16 October 1969.

Christopher Nicole comments:

Born and largely educated in the West Indies, my first eight novels were concerned with the West Indian scene, five historicals, one thriller, and two "serious" studies of West Indian society, although I should say that the historicals are all serious commentaries on this society, and the Amyot trilogy is a history of the Bahamas from 1704 to 1956, i.e., just as the present Bahamian Government was contesting elections for the first time. During this period I also wrote a history of the area, and a history of West Indian cricket. But in 1964, having been absent from the West Indies for eight years, I felt I had said all that I could, with both up-to-date knowledge and understanding, on this subject, although since then I have written *The Self-Lovers*, a critical satire on small island politics.

In the past seven years my work has become quite diversified. Under the Nicole name I have written three novels, which I regard as serious work: *The Thunder and the Shouting* is a study of Poland during World War Two; *The Longest Pleasure* is a study of the Cold War; and *The Face of Evil* is a study of the *mind* of witchcraft. Under the name of Andrew York I have written a series of thrillers concerning the adventures of Jonas Wilde, my most success-ful line; and under the name of Peter Grange I have written three, so far, historical novels which my publisher describes as "picaresque"; they are in fact farces, parodies of historical novels as such. My most enjoyable line. As Andrew York I have now also written several juvenile spy stories.

*     *     *

When one looks for the first time at the list of Christopher Nicole's novels, one is awed by his productiveness (he has written almost thirty books), and by his versatility (his works include a book on cricket, a history of the West Indies, serious novels, historical romances, secret agent thrillers, and adventure novels for young readers; furthermore, his novels are set in places as different as the West Indies and Russia). But this awe turns to skepticism when one realizes that twenty-five of those books were written in about twelve years. Nothing, one is inclined to feel, done so rapidly can have been done well.

This initial prejudice does Nicole's work a real injustice for there is much that is worth-while in it. His secret agent thrillers, although written to a certain formula, are well enough executed to be exciting and suspenseful. Each is distinct enough to prevent it from being completely predictable. These books share with his other novels his excellence at describing physical action and his ability to make dialogue and setting work together towards a final effect. There is a carefulness of craftsmanship and an economy of style which mark the work of the real professional.

However, if Nicole is to be taken as a serious writer, it is his books set in the West Indies which will qualify him for this title. He has written other works set in parts of the world where he has travelled, Poland for example, but these lack the intimacy of insight that he demonstrates when he is writing about the West Indies and Guyana, where he grew up.

His West Indian novels contain all the elements that make his secret agent books so entertaining. In fact, in retrospect, one can see how his earlier West Indian books prepared him for his later adventure stories. The novels about the West Indies indicate his reliance on physical action, and his fascination with the sensational. *Ratoon*, for instance, deals with a slave rebellion, and *Dark Noon* is set in St Vincent at the time of the eruption of the volcano Soufriere. This willingness to remain on the level of the physical gives a sense of superficiality to all his work, which is only occasionally dispelled when the author's precise descriptions of the society in the West Indies produce interesting social and racial reverberations. Nicole is at his best when, in a novel like *Shadows in the Jungle*, he suggests the character of the jungle and develops the relationship between it and its inhabitants.

Much of Nicole's work reminds one of that of Mittelholzer, the older Guyanese novelist. *Off White* echoes *The Life and Death of Sylvia*, *Shadows in the Jungle* seems to have been influenced by *My Bones and My Flute* and *Shadows Move Among Them*, and Nicole's Amyot trilogy bears obvious resemblances to Mittelholzer's Kaywana trilogy. Because Nicole is white, however, he does contribute a different point of view to West Indian Fiction. There are other West Indian novelists who are white, Phyllis Allfrey, Jean Rhys and Geoffrey Drayton come immediately to mind, but these are so few when compared with the non-whites that a novelist who suggests what it is like to be white in the West Indies can make a distinctly original contribution to West Indian Fiction.

Nicole's contribution is sometimes suggestive, but it is too superficial to fulfill its possi-bilities.

—Anthony Boxill

**NIN, Anaïs.** American. Born in Paris in February 1903; emigrated to the United States in 1914. Self-educated. Married in 1920. Lived in Paris, 1930–40. Has worked as a model, dancer, teacher and lecturer; practiced psycho-analysis under Otto Rank. Address: c/o Gunther Stuhlmann, 65 Irving Place, New York, New York 10003, U.S.A.

PUBLICATIONS

Novels

> *House of Incest.* Paris, Siana, 1936; New York, Gemor Press, 1947.
> *Winter of Artifice.* Paris, Obelisk Press, 1939; as *Winter of Artifice: Three Novelettes*, Denver, Swallow, 1961.
> *This Hunger.* New York, Gemor Press, 1945.
> *Ladders to Fire.* New York, Dutton, 1946; London, Peter Owen, 1963.
> *Children of the Albatross.* New York, Duell, 1947; London, Peter Owen, 1959.
> *Four Chambered Heart.* New York, Duell, 1950; London, Peter Owen, 1959.
> *A Spy in the House of Love.* New York, British Book Centre, 1954; London, Spearman, 1955.
> *Solar Barque.* Denver, Swallow, 1958.
> *Cities of the Interior.* Privately printed, 1959.
> *Seduction of the Minotaur.* Denver, Swallow, and London, Peter Owen, 1961.
> *Collages.* Denver, Swallow, and London, Peter Owen, 1964.

Short Stories

> *Under a Glass Bell.* New York, Gemor Press, 1944; as *Under a Glass Bell and Other Stories*, London, Editions Poetry, 1947; New York, Dutton, 1948.

Other

> *D. H. Lawrence: An Unprofessional Study.* Paris, E. W. Titus, 1932; London, Spearman, 1961; Denver, Swallow, 1964.
> *Realism and Reality.* Yonkers, New York, Alicat, 1946.
> *On Writing.* Hanover, New Hampshire, Daniel Oliver, 1947.
> *The Diary of Anaïs Nin*, edited by Gunther Stuhlman. New York, Harcourt Brace, 4 vols., 1966–1971; as *The Journals of Anaïs Nin*, London, Peter Owen, 4 vols., 1966–1972.
> *The Novel of the Future.* New York, Macmillan, 1968.

Critical Studies: "The Charmed Circle of Anaïs Nin" by Karl Shapiro, in "Book Week", *New York Herald Tribune*, 1 May 1966; *Anaïs Nin* by Oliver Evans, Carbondale, Southern Illinois University Press, 1968; "The Art of Anaïs Nin" by Duane Schneider, in *Southern Review* (Baton Rouge, Louisiana), Spring 1970; essays in the periodical *Under the Sign of Pisces: Anaïs Nin and Her Circle*, edited by Richard R. Centing and Benjamin Franklin V (Columbus, Ohio), since Winter 1970.

*       *       *

947

The daughter of the Spanish composer Joaquín Nin and of a French-Danish mother, Rosa Culmell, Anaïs Nin was born in the Parisian suburb of Neuilly in February 1903. When she was eleven, her father deserted his family (including Anaïs and two brothers) and went to America—and the precocious little girl began her diaries, her dialogues with herself and her impressions of the world around her, profoundly intimate journals whose volumes in publication, four of them so far, have won world acclaim in the 1960s and 70s, and a distinguished literary prize in Germany.

Her mother brought her children to the United States just before the First World War, and in New York took over a rooming house. When the girl was fifteen she set out on her own path, becoming an artist's model and a dancer. Besides her diaries, at first written in French, she wrote *D. H. Lawrence: An Unprofessional Study*, which Edward Titus published in a limited edition in Paris, where Anaïs Nin was then living. This little volume showed what mastery she had attained over her acquired language, for it penetrates farther and with more sensitivity into the heart of Lawrence's way of writing than anyone had as yet (or has even now) done.

A member of Paris literary circles, the friend of Henry Miller, Lawrence Durrell, and other writers and artists, Anaïs Nin lived in a houseboat on the Seine. She turned her writing experience to creativity for the first time with her novel, *House of Incest*, originally published in Paris in 1936 with its now well-known epigraph, "All that I know is contained in this book written without witness, an edifice without dimension, a city hanging in the sky." *House of Incest* is what is often called a prose poem, though it stands above most work of this kind, especially in English; it is in the manner of the French *symbolistes*, but it has its own positive individuality in its dreamlike narrative of a woman's profound involvement with life and love. *Winter of Artifice*, first published in Paris in 1939, consists in later editions of three short novels; it is again a dreamlike book written in a prose that edges toward poetry, the experiences in the book (especially in the story "The Voice") reflecting the author's own, both as patient and healer, in psychoanalysis; she underwent analysis by both René Allendy and Otto Rank, becoming for a while an associate of the latter. But the diary, which both doctors suggested she abandon, remained at the center of her life, and she found that she could not give up this self-involved writing, though in later years her fiction became the most important form of her expressive experience. It is to some extent an outgrowth of the diaries, but it develops into its own remarkably special mode of utterance.

In 1946, a few years after Anaïs Nin had taken up permanent American residence, a trade publishing house issued her *Ladders to Fire*; she had herself previously printed and circulated her earlier fiction in New York (with engravings by her husband as illustrations) after purchasing an old foot-power press and setting her own type. Edmund Wilson, the leading American critic, in 1944 had hailed her short stories, *Under a Glass Bell*, saying in the *New Yorker* that she "is a very good artist, as perhaps none of the literary surrealists is." Anaïs Nin was also encouraged by Dr. Frances Steloff of the Gotham Book Mart, who helped to distribute copies of the volumes which the author had printed herself. With commercial publishers further encouraging her, Anaïs Nin wrote novels which, following *Ladders to Fire*, comprise her Cities of the Interior series, *Children of the Albatross*, *Four Chambered Heart*, *A Spy in the House of Love*, *Solar Barque*, and *Seduction of the Minotaur*. Her succeeding novel, *Collages*, is a thinly connected group of stories ranging in scene from Vienna to Los Angeles, from New York to the French Riviera; this work showed no falling-off in the author's writing power, and was hailed by the *Times Literary Supplement* as "a handful of perfectly told fables."

Across the years Anaïs Nin has kept up her critical writings, generally concerned with avant-garde fiction, as in *The Novel of the Future*, a penetrating study with many examples drawn from the works of significant authors of the present day and the immediate past. But Anaïs Nin's most remarkable work has been not only the production of the *Diaries*, of which the four volumes so far published have been edited by Gunther Stuhlmann, but also of her novels and stories with their superb prose, their deep and intense projection of feminine experience, and their vitally imaginative reaching into unexplored spiritual space.

The petite Anaïs Nin, who is gracious and beautiful, frequently lectures at universities.

An unusual honor came to her when librarians and English teachers in 1970 began publishing a journal devoted to her and her friends: *Under the Sign of Pisces: Anaïs Nin and Her Circle.*

—Harry T. Moore

---

**NORRIS, Hoke.** American. Born in Holly Springs, North Carolina, 8 October 1913. Educated at Wake Forest University, Winston-Salem, North Carolina, 1930–34, A.B. 1934; University of North Carolina, Chapel Hill, 1946; Harvard University, Cambridge, Massachusetts (Nieman Fellow), 1950–51; University of Chicago (Ford Fellow), 1960–61. Served in the United States Army Air Force, in the Southwest Pacific, rising to the rank of Captain, 1942–46. Married Edna Dees in 1941; has one child. Reporter, *Daily Advance*, Elizabeth City, North Carolina, 1934–36, and *News and Observer*, Raleigh, North Carolina, 1936–37; Reporter and Editor, Associated Press, Raleigh and Charlotte, North Carolina, 1937–42, 1946; Public Relations Director, Lost Colony, Manteo, North Carolina, 1946–47; Reporter and Editor, *Journal-Sentinel*, Winston-Salem, 1947–55; Reporter and Literary Editor, *Chicago Sun-Times*, 1955–68; Member, Editorial Board, *Chicago Daily News*, 1968–70. Instructor in Creative Writing, University of Chicago, 1959–60. Since 1970, Public Information Director, Chicago Public Library. Recipient: Friends of Literature and Society of Midland Authors Award, 1970. Address: Chicago Public Library, Randolph Street at Michigan Avenue, Chicago, Illinois, U.S.A.

PUBLICATIONS

Novels

    *All the Kingdoms of Earth.* New York, Simon and Schuster, 1956.
    *It's Not Far But I Don't Know the Way.* Chicago, Swallow, 1969.

Uncollected Short Stories

    "Take Her Up Tenderly", in *Prairie Schooner* (Lincoln, Nebraska), 1949.
    "Miss Smith", in *Decade of Short Stories* (Canoga Park, California), 1949.
    "Weed of Sorrow", in *Prairie Schooner* (Lincoln, Nebraska), Fall 1950.
    "Chain", in *Prairie Schooner* (Lincoln, Nebraska), Fall 1951.
    "They Had to Reach Out", in *Prairie Schooner* (Lincoln, Nebraska), Fall 1952.
    "Mirror on the Wall", in *Prairie Schooner* (Lincoln, Nebraska), Winter 1953.
    "Handyman", in *Prairie Schooner* (Lincoln, Nebraska), Summer 1954.
    "The Saving of Sam Tracy", in *Shenandoah* (Lexington, Virginia), Winter 1959.

    Other stories published in magazines and anthologies.

Other

    Editor, *We Dissent.* New York, St. Martin's Press, 1962.

Hoke Norris comments:

My work has been principally about the South but there's coming a time when I must separate myself from my homeland and write about my adopted country. I've been living in Chicago long enough now to write about it; I began to do so in fact in my second novel, which was divided North and South. The writer of fiction must live in a place a long time before he's able to write about it. He isn't the writer of non-fiction, collecting information and assembling it in understandable form; he has to absorb something of the spirit of a place before he can treat it satisfactorily in fiction. I think I've reached that point, now, with Chicago; my next novel, if all goes well, will be about newspapering in Chicago—not *The Front Page* re-done, but about a group of characters who happen to be newspapermen, in a certain place and time and circumstance, working toward a destiny, of sorts.

*        *        *

Though the rural South figures in both his novels, Hoke Norris achieves two impressively distinct variations on this material: the tensions and nuances of communal black awareness in *All the Kingdoms of Earth*, and the shaping force of past values for a transplanted white southerner in *It's Not Far But I Don't Know the Way*. Both novels focus on ministers' sons who find their fathers' traditions inadequate. But while Matt Prescott, the black *deus ex machina* who resolves the racial trouble at the climax of *Kingdoms*, prefers secular learning and law to his father's religion, David Elliot of *It's Not Far* rejects his father's teachings for the folk-wisdom of an agnostic grandfather. (And another preacher's son, young Moses Apple in the story "The Saving of Sam Tracy," literally runs away from the idea of salvation.) Though *Kingdoms* echoes some of the humor and views of life of Faulkner and Caldwell, the strongest temperamental and thematic affinities of the novel lie not with the work of these southern writers, but with Steinbeck's *The Grapes of Wrath* and *Tortilla Flat*. Transcending such temporal distractions as flood, epidemic, the Depression, and World War II, the pattern of life and death in a community of southern blacks dominates *Kingdoms*. This pattern dwarfs the characters, who, unlike Faulkner's Dilsey, seem merely symbols of the continuity of human life. The omnipresent Biblical epigraphs and parallels italicize this theme of endurance in a context of racial oppression and suggest a reworking by Steinbeck of Virginia Woolf's *The Years*. *It's Not Far* roots Elliot's obsession with death in his youthful fascination with his father's moribund parishioners and dramatizes this obsession through a convenient meeting in Chicago with a former girlfriend dying of cancer. (The death-obsession of an atomic scientist in "Weed of Sorrow" is an earlier variation on this theme.)

*Kingdoms* is the stronger novel, offering an ironic perspective on the tangled intimacy of the blacks with the white Norton family over several generations. Norris' dramatization of Pearl Sykes' ambivalent attitude toward her white seducer and his mother provides the most effective scenes in the book. Unfortunately, the symbolic thrust of *Kingdoms* allows full characterization to no one else, though there are charming bits and pieces, like the Joycean evocation of Teeny's developing consciousness. Norris has some success with folk humor, but even an amusing debate in which rival preachers cite Bible texts to support opposing views on vaccination runs counter to the tone of the novel. And Jack Vestal's cancellation of his wife's funeral because of his precipitous remarriage seems a mere anecdote unrooted in character and lacks the comic vitality of a corresponding situation in Faulkner's *As I Lay Dying*. Norris' comedy seems more subservient to abstract sermonizing about black earthiness than to illumination of character. This consistent sacrifice of character to allegory, both in humorous and serious contexts, is epitomized by the inevitable, but unmotivated, appearance of the white Norton grandchild who joins Matt Prescott at the conclusion of *Kingdoms* to symbolize white-black harmony.

*It's Not Far* possesses very real virtues: a vivid rendering of the physical and psychological details of the heroine's disease, a frightening surrealistic graveyard scene, and a harrowing picture of the public execution of a black man (ignoring the existential pronouncements of the novel, the story "Take Her Up Tenderly" focuses on the social implications of a similar execution). But, as in *Kingdoms*, Norris' constant and obtrusive reminders of the significance of character and incident diminish these virtues. The reference to *Death and Resurrection* on the first page signals the theme with an obviousness inherent in the novel; the grotesquely artificial salesgirl, kin to the expressionistic mannequins of *The Hairy Ape*, provides a too-explicit commentary on the heroine's own mutilations; Elliot pointedly links the execution scene to the death theme. This persistent underlying of a single motif serves not to deepen but to dissipate its intensity. And, as is true to a lesser extent in *Kingdoms*, the formal, often forensic, dialogue and interior monologues heighten the self-consciousness of the book. In general, these weaknesses characteristic of the novel are intensified in the more restricted arena of Norris' short stories.

However, despite stylistic tendencies that prevent a fully novelistic treatment of his themes, Norris' novels communicate an attractive commitment to human life and values, and a sense of the ironies inherent not only in particular human societies, but also in existence itself.

—Burton Kendle

---

**NOTT, Kathleen (Cecilia).** British. Born in London. Educated at Mary Datchelor School, London; King's College, London; Somerville College, Oxford, B.A. (honours) in philosophy, politics and economics. Worked in Army Education and with Air Raid Precautions in World War II. President, Progressive League, London, 1958–60. Since 1960, Editor of International P.E.N.'s Bulletin of Selected Books, London. Since 1966, Vice-President, International P.E.N., British Centre. Recipient: Arts Council Bursary, 1968. Address: 6 Newlands Road, Horsham, Sussex, England.

PUBLICATIONS

Novels

 *Mile End.*  London, Hogarth Press, 1938.
 *The Dry Deluge.*  London, Hogarth Press, 1947.
 *Private Fires.*  London, Heinemann, 1961.
 *An Elderly Retired Man.*  London, Faber, 1963.

Verse

 *Landscapes and Departures.*  London, Editions Poetry, 1947.
 *Poems from the North.*  Ashford, Kent, Hand and Flower Press, 1956.
 *Creatures and Emblems.*  London, Routledge, 1960.

Other

 *The Emperor's Clothes: An Attack on the Dogmatic Orthodoxy of T. S. Eliot, Graham Greene, Dorothy Sayers, C. S. Lewis and Others.*  London, Heinemann, 1954.

*A Clean Well-Lighted Place.*   London, Heinemann, 1960.
*Objections to Humanism,* with others.   London, Hodder and Stoughton, 1963.
*A Soul in the Quad.*   London, Routledge, 1969.
*Philosophy and Human Nature.*   London, Hodder and Stoughton, 1970.

Editor, with others, *New Poems 1957: A P.E.N. Anthology.*   London, Joseph, 1957.


Critical Study: in *Times Literary Supplement* (London), 1963.


Kathleen Nott comments:

I write a novel only when I have a novel to write—which doesn't seem to be oftener than every four to five years. I have always regarded myself as primarily a poet and secondarily a philosophical critic with a strong interest in (and generally a strong objection to) ideologies and ideas which have practical social effects. I do not as a rule make use of general ideas in writing my novels. I still think that poetry is and ought to be the major literary art and that most contemporary novels make an artificial use of thought and language. On the other hand, I hate "symbolic" novels. Thus the future, if any, that I foresee anyway for any novel of mine would be a kind of poetic realism—the language might have universal implications but not in any abstract sense. It would try to be about "real people" or, in other words, to convince through character, but their situations might well be intellectual ones, connected with the concepts and situations which actually influence all our lives.

I am at present preparing a collection of short stories. It seems to me that a short story can be a good half-way house between a poem and a prose novel. It is easier at short length to achieve the concrete-universal kind of language which I regard as the essential one for narrative intended to maintain a poetic apperception.

\*       \*       \*

Kathleen Nott is clearly one of the more interesting and wide-ranging intellectuals writing today, and her work as a philosophic critic is refreshingly iconoclastic and provocative. She does not consider herself primarily a novelist, and her four novels (the latest appearing twenty-five years after the first) represent only one aspect of her life's work. They are not, it should be stressed, major literary achievements; at the same time, however, they cannot be dismissed too lightly, since they do have many intrinsic merits, and since they do capture—at least in part—the world view of a significant observer.

Despite the vast differences between these novels, certain common strengths emerge. All are informed by a gentle sense of irony: seldom so obvious as to appear contrived, never bitter or cynical. And all the novels demonstrate Miss Nott's skill in exploring the motivations that lie behind her characters' acts and integrating these interpretations into the action. These analyses, especially in the later novels, reveal the complete absence of religion or other external moral referents as viable systems. Miss Nott once paraphrased Hume as follows: "If philosophy interferes with life, give up philosophy." If there is any common theme in her novels, it is summed up well here.

Miss Nott's novels also share certain weaknesses, however, which diminish their effectiveness. For the most part her fictional prose lacks the crisp clarity of her best nonfiction, and there are some unresolved technical problems (especially with the point of view in *The Dry Deluge* and *Private Fires*) which detract. Such problems tend to be magnified, since there is relatively little action in her novels except within the realm of ideas. Furthermore, her characters often come alive only with great difficulty; they are carefully distinguished from each other intellectually, but many of them fail to live.

*Mile End,* her first and longest novel, appears in many respects to be Miss Nott's most conscious effort as a novelist and shows (especially in several overwritten passages) some of the weaknesses often common to first novels. But these flaws are easily overlooked when one considers the scope of her endeavor here, i.e., to delineate the portrait of three generations of London Jews torn between the pull of the goyim world and their sense of cultural and religious ties. Although both forces are shown to be potentially life-denying and powerful, the movement by the close of *Mile End* is clearly away from the cultural and religious ideologies and toward what can only be called "Life".

*The Dry Deluge* and *Private Fires* are Miss Nott's weakest works. The former traces the development and failure of a socialistic community with utopian plans, dominated by a strange, but charismatic professor; the latter is inhabited by a rather hodge-podge assortment of grotesque but essentially two-dimensional characters suspended in post-World War II London. In both novels the point of view shifts with annoying frequency, creating fictional worlds that suggest the comedy of the absurd, only to lapse into contrived and traditional endings. Of the two, *The Dry Deluge* is clearly superior, but both fall short of *Mile End* and *An Elderly Retired Man.*

In her most recent novel, however, Miss Nott has once again written a compelling work. In all respects, *An Elderly Retired Man* is her finest production, demonstrating firm authorial control and selectivity. The theme is one of belated self-discovery, as related by the major character, Roden Cluer, a newly retired civil servant. The novel records the complex psychological process by which Cluer tries to penetrate previous doubts and self-delusions, only to see his self-assessment seriously thrown in question by his encounter—apparently for the first time—with real passion in himself. It is not a painless process for Cluer, and his unrecognized limitations in evaluating the personalities of his wife and others force the reader to form his own judgments as to motives and facts, especially those surrounding the ambiguous resolution of his only passionate love affair. *An Elderly Retired Man* is a solid piece of fiction, well worth reading.

—Stanley W. Lindberg

**NYE, Robert.** British. Born in London, 15 March 1939. Educated at state schools, 1944–55. Married Judith Pratt in 1959 (divorced); Aileen Campbell, 1966; has four sons and two daughters. Free-lance Writer. Contributes critical articles and reviews to British periodicals, notably *The Scotsman,* Edinburgh, and *The Times* and *The Guardian,* London. Since 1967, Poetry Editor of *The Scotsman;* since 1971, Poetry Critic of *The Times.* Recipient: Gregory Award, for poetry, 1963; Scottish Arts Council bursary, 1970, and publication award, 1970; James Kennaway Memorial Award, 1970. Lives in Edinburgh. Address: c/o Calder and Boyars Ltd., 18 Brewer Street, London W.1, England.

PUBLICATIONS

Novel

*Doubtfire.* London, Calder and Boyars, 1967; New York, Hill and Wang, 1968.

953

Short Stories

> *Tales I Told My Mother*.   London, Calder and Boyars, and New York, Hill and Wang, 1969.
> *Penguin Modern Stories 6*, with others.   London, Penguin, 1970.

Uncollected Short Stories

> *Lines Review 38* (includes 4 uncollected stories, 8 poems, and a film script) (Edinburgh), 1971.

Plays

> *Sawney Bean*, with William Watson (produced Edinburgh, 1969).   London, Calder and Boyars, 1970.
> *Sisters* (radio play; broadcast 1969).   Published in *Lines Review 33* (Edinburgh), 1970.
> *Fugue* (screenplay), in *Lines Review 38* (Edinburgh), 1971.

Verse

> *Juvenilia 1*.   Lowestoft, Suffolk, Scorpion Press, 1961.
> *Juvenilia 2*.   Lowestoft, Suffolk, Scorpion Press, 1963.
> *Darker Ends*.   London, Calder and Boyars, and New York, Hill and Wang, 1969.

Other

> *Taliesin* (juvenile).   London, Faber, 1966; New York, Hill and Wang, 1967.
> *March Has Horse's Ears* (juvenile).   London, Faber, 1966; New York, Hill and Wang, 1967.
> *Wishing Gold* (juvenile).   London, Macmillan, and New York, Hill and Wang, 1970.
> *Poor Pumpkin* (juvenile).   London, Macmillan, and New York, Hill and Wang, 1971.
> *Cricket* (juvenile).   London, Dent, and Indianapolis, Bobbs Merrill, 1972.

> Editor, *A Choice of Sir Walter Ralegh's Verse*.   London, Faber, 1972.

> Translator, *Beowulf* (juvenile).   London, Faber, and New York, Hill and Wang, 1968.

Manuscript Collections: University of Texas, Austin; Colgate University, Hamilton, New York.

*         *         *

Robert Nye is an author of imagination all compact. This quality is manifest in the many forms of writing he has undertaken—the novel, short stories, tales for children, broadcast and stage drama, and poetry—and in the inventive way in which he handles these genres and the themes he chooses to treat of in them.

Probably the basic fact about this writer is that he is a poet using the medium of prose for his own purpose, bending it flexibly this way and that to a manifold number of ends and effects. He himself has spoken of the new franchise of prose through which the doors of fiction were opened to poetry. "I was," he writes, "a belated realiser of an established fact. Prose—and especially the novel—has in the last fifty years been surreptitiously taking over from poetry the field it once claimed as its own exclusive right.... The novel since Joyce has moved closer and closer to poetry.... Robbe-Grillet destroyed the illusion about the useful device of linear narrative for ever."

Story as consistently progressing narration is certainly absent from his curious novel *Doubtfire*. As Karl M. Abenheimer wrote of it: "The subject-matter ... is adolescence, but we are told of it not in a linear narrative but in episodes of subjective awareness which highlight the essential aspects of adolescence and of one particular adolescent." The novel's point of departure from (or is it into?) reality is Southend-on-Sea; but then—as a reviewer in *The Times* remarked—"the Southend they live in is a country of metaphor, a fabulous kingdom by the sea. It is Arthur's Britain, it is fifteenth century France." It is, also, a contemporary Abbey of Thélème since the spirit, and sometimes the method of that "drunken philosopher", the creator of *Gargantua and Pantagruel*, powerfully inform the work. "Rabelais is the master novelist for me, the master of form as well as of content," Robert Nye once confessed in an interview.

Rabelaisian in the manner of its energy and wide (not infrequently wild) discursiveness, all of this author's writings are. They are often Rabelaisian in the commoner implication as well, scatological fantasy (as that in *Tales I Told My Mother* of a man who rescues himself from a snowdrift by using his member as a sort of snowplough) freely proliferating like the carvings of gargoyles in a mediaeval cathedral. Indeed, the stories in the book just mentioned can best be described as a species of permissive Gothic jokes and robustly sick humour. In another separate shorter fiction "The Same Old Story" (*Penguin Modern Stories 6*) we appear to be in the world of Barchester—a Barchester strangely infiltrated by Freud and somehow come to be holding hands with a marvellous grisly parody of a Border Ballad happening rendered into prose.

Another quality distinguishing Robert Nye is his power of protean adaptation. In *Tales I Told My Mother*, he takes over the material of literary biography (passages from the lives and work of Chatterton, the Brontës and D.G. Rossetti) to create something which partakes of fantasy, parody and criticism. Even in his echoes, Robert Nye is always new.

—Derek Stanford

---

**OATES, Joyce Carol.** American. Born in Lockport, New York, 16 June 1938. Educated at Syracuse University, New York, B.A. 1960 (Phi Beta Kappa); University of Wisconsin, Madison, M.A. in English 1961. Married Raymond Joseph Smith in 1961. Instructor in English, 1961–65, and Assistant Professor of English, 1965–67, University of Detroit. Since 1967, Associate Professor of English, University of Windsor, Ontario. Recipient: National Endowment for the Arts grant, 1966, 1968; Guggenheim Fellowship, 1967; O. Henry Award, 1967, and O. Henry Special Award for Continuing Achievement, 1970; Rosenthal Award, 1968; National Book Award, 1970. Address: c/o Department of English, University of Windsor, Windsor, Ontario, Canada.

PUBLICATIONS

Novels

*With Shuddering Fall.* New York, Vanguard Press, 1964; London, Cape, 1965.

*A Garden of Earthly Delights.* New York, Vanguard Press, 1967; London, Gollancz, 1970.

*Expensive People.* New York, Vanguard Press, 1968; London, Gollancz, 1969.

*Them.* New York, Vanguard Press, 1969; London, Gollancz, 1971.

*Wonderland.* New York, Vanguard Press, 1971; London, Gollancz, 1972.

Short Stories

*By the North Gate.* New York, Vanguard Press, 1963.

*Upon the Sweeping Flood and Other Stories.* New York, Vanguard Press, 1966.

*The Wheel of Love.* New York, Vanguard Press, 1970; London, Gollancz, 1971.

Plays

*The Sweet Enemy* (produced New York, 1965).

*Sunday Dinner* (produced New York, 1970).

Verse

*Anonymous Sins and Other Poems.* Baton Rouge, Louisiana State University Press, 1969.

*Love and Its Derangements.* Baton Rouge, Louisiana State University Press, 1970.

\*         \*         \*

Since 1963 Joyce Carol Oates, publishing five novels, three story collections, two plays, and two volumes of verse, has projected a world of people whose search for love and self frequently distintegrates under shattering oppression or mysterious violence. America 1930–1970, the period from the Depression through the urban riots, shapes the lives of these characters. Miss Oates' characters, style, and narrative recall the Naturalist and Southern Renaissance movements in modern American writing so powerfully that many readers associate her with Steinbeck, Welty, Cather, Faulkner, and Dreiser. These apparent literary antecedents may help to explain the strength and the weakness on Oates' work. By grounding herself so deeply in American naturalism, she extends its contemporary possibilities; however, this may also cause her to create characters and situations which have only literary validity.

Violence dominates the stories of *By the North Gate*, set in Eden County, New York, although they suggest the modern literary South. In the title story, a dog Nell, the final companion of an old farmer, has its throat cut for no reason; the collection also describes an unwed mother and a girl with a weak heart who dies during a picnic roughup. These somewhat passionless stories introduced the well-crafted work of a serious writer. Oates' first novel, *With Shuddering Fall*, charts the feverish relationship between Karen Herz, an impulsive seventeen year old, and Shar, a thirty year old racing car driver, who attacks her father, burns down his father's cabin, nearly rapes her, and then takes her on his doom-ridden racing circuit. After Shar's inevitable fiery death Karen cries out: "An accident—his life was an accident but his death wasn't—he made his death for himself. He was a man!" Then follows a riot, Karen's institutionalization, and finally her reintegration into her family. The novel's impressive intensity, narrative control, and strong sense of place cannot finally overcome the uncertain characterization of Karen Herz, who acts compulsively but unaccountably. The epigraph for *Upon the Sweeping Flood* contains an Edward Taylor line: "... they [the Heavens] shed their excrements upon our lofty heads." The eleven stories tell of murders based on mistakes, a contemplated suicide, and death following abortion induced by a motorcycle ride. Because the general gloom surrounds people who have no alternatives, the stories seem contrived by literary necessity and indicate little advance over Oates' first collection.

*A Garden of Earthly Delights* begins a trilogy of American life from the late Twenties to the late Sixties that includes *Expensive People* and *Them*. Clara Walpole, the heroine of *Garden*, born in an open rain-drenched truck in Arkansas, moves stolidly through a devastating childhood among migrant workers, the dreary adolescence of a shop girl, the hidden years of a rich man's mistress, the grasping maneuvers of a rich man's wife, and finally madness in her fifties. The novel opens powerfully with the fragmented point of view of the child Clara responding to the chaotic world of migratory workers—a kind of floating ghetto. This richly complex texture and drive weaken, however, once Clara flees her family and begins her upward struggle. The dreariness of Clara's life culminates in the now standard Oates melodramatic conclusion, but not before she has encountered Oates' obscure male figures: Lowery, who helps her escape the workers' camp; Revere, who keeps her then marries her; Swan, her weak-willed son who kills his father. Once again Oates' good detail, strong narrative, controlled prose and vision are compromised by murky characters, contrived plot twists, and arbitrary violence.

*Expensive People* replaces the ponderous world of Clara Walpole with the absurd mind of Richard Everett, a whacked-up eighteen year old genius who announces, "I was a child murderer" (of his mother Natshya Romanov, née Nancy, changed to Nadia, then shortened to Nada). Richard's elaborately self-conscious recollection of the matricidal events blends hints of the insane snipers of the Sixties, conventional attacks on Suburbia, and commentary on fiction writing, all in a tone reminiscent of the blackly comedic effects of Nabokov's *Lolita* or Purdy's *Malcolm*. Oates, essentially a humorless writer, lacks the requisite lightness of touch.

*Them*, set in Detroit from the Depression through the 1967 riots, concerns Loretta Wendell, who at sixteen awakens next to her murdered lover; her daughter Maureen, who after being beaten into catatonia by her stepfather seduces a married man away from his family; and her brother Jules, a hopeless drifter who find himself in the "senseless dreamy violence" of the Detroit riots. Oates impressively details the circumscribed Wendell world, echoing the confined circumstances of Clyde Griffiths and Carrie Meeber, but rejects the concept of total environmental control. The epigraph contains the line, " . . . because we are poor/ Shall we be vicious?" Avoiding such explanations, Oates fragments the points of view, discouraging cause and effect analysis and creating serious credibility problems. Jules, for example, a protégé of a mysterious gangster, engages in a not very original erotic relationship with the gangster's niece Nadine, an affair that so lacks explanation it never seems real. Similarly, the Detroit riots, which Oates obviously considers critical to *Them*, her own life, and the American urban experience, suffer from unreality. Although Oates' best novel, *Them* remains uneven because of its fragmentary structure and unclear motivations.

*The Wheel of Love* presents some of Oates' best work and may indicate her real strength. Introduced by Donne's "The Canonization," ("We can dye by it, if not live by love . . ."), the twenty stories explore the catastrophic intricacies of love for women in urban or academic circumstances. Somewhat repressed women meet deranged men; easily impressed adolescent girls submit to insistent older men; little girls spend chaotic Saturdays with divorced fathers; an awed college coed marries a middle-aged professor and assumes the mundane role of his previous wife, a recent suicide. Although the story can still explode into pointless violence ("I Was in Love"), these stories represent psychologically sound explorations of souls suffering on a wheel of love. The collection reflects Oates' inclination to focus on a subject obsessively and to concentrate such incredible energy into a short space that the stories impart a compact, savage thrust, recalling the intensity of *With Shuddering Fall* and the opening sections of *A Garden of Earthly Delights* and *Them*.

*Wonderland* increases the growing suspicion that Miss Oates, a writer of excellent short stories, has yet to write a truly unified novel. Dedicated to "all of us who pursue the phantasmagoria of personality" and divided into three books called "variations on an american hymn," "the finite passing of an infinite passion," and "dreaming america," *Wonderland* proclaims its ambition. Jesse Harte's macabre story spans the years 1938–1971, paralleling America's emergence from the Depression and passage into its riot-torn affluence. In 1938 Jesse's insane father slaughters his whole family except the son; Jesse spends some time with a bitter grandfather and in an orphanage before he is adopted by Dr. Pederson, a brilliant, eccentric, and oppressive physician in Lockport, N.Y. Rejected here also, Jesse Pederson now becomes Jesse Vogel, a brilliant, moody brain surgeon, enters an unsuccessful marriage, conducts a foolish affair, and estranges his daughter Shelley, who runs away with a hippie. Once he locates her in Toronto, Jesse takes her out on a lake in a rowboat which the police find empty the next morning. The near victim of a child-murderer has finally become one himself —the circle of horror has been completed. *Wonderland*'s first two episodes, the murder of Jesse's family and his stay with the Pedersons, equal anything in Oates, but the remainder of the novel fails to convince. Oates apparently wants to create a character who suffers so profoundly that he blocks out the event completely yet behaves in response to it. Jesse's oppressive behavior, particularly toward women, which we understand only because we have read the book's opening, remains so unclear to himself, his family, and his colleagues that the situation becomes absurd. His being a brain surgeon complicates his basic inhumanity —a man without a past cannot really be alive in the present and certainly has no future. Although Jesse Harte-Pederson-Vogel probably parallels modern American man, what we end up with in *Wonderland* is a somber collection of bits and no illuminating coherent whole.

Joyce Carol Oates, not yet thirty-five with ten published volumes to her credit, emerges as one of the most promising American writers. Obsessed by America and its social and psychological problems in the mid-twentieth century, possessing formidable gifts of observation and invention, and locating herself in a rich vein of American literary tradition, Miss Oates will undoubtedly produce major work.

—Fred Silva

---

**O'BRIEN, Edna.** Irish. Born in Tuamgraney, County Clare, 15 December 1932. Attended National School, Scariff; Convent of Mercy, Loughrea; pharmaceutical college in Dublin: Licentiate, Pharmaceutical Society of Ireland; practiced pharmacy briefly. Married Ernest Gebler in 1952 (now separated); has two children. Recipient: Kingsley Amis Award, 1962; *Yorkshire Post* Novel Award, 1971. Address: c/o A. M. Heath, 35 Dover Street, London W.1, England.

PUBLICATIONS

Novels

　　*The Country Girls.*　London, Hutchinson, and New York, Knopf, 1960.
　　*The Lonely Girl.*　London, Cape, and New York, Random House, 1962.
　　*Girls in Their Married Bliss.*　London, Cape, 1964; Boston, Houghton Mifflin, 1968.
　　*August Is a Wicked Month.*　London, Cape, and New York, Simon and Schuster, 1965.
　　*Casualties of Peace.*　London, Cape, 1966; New York, Simon and Schuster, 1967.
　　*A Pagan Place.*　London, Weidenfeld and Nicolson, and New York, Knopf, 1970.

Short Stories

　　*The Love Object.*　London, Cape, 1968; New York, Knopf, 1969.

Plays

*A Nice Bunch of Cheap Flowers* (produced London, 1962).   Included in *Plays of the
   Year 1962–1963*, London, Elek, 1963.
*Zee and Co.* (screenplay).   London, Weidenfeld and Nicholson, 1971.

Screenplays: *The Girl with Green Eyes*, 1964; *Three into Two Won't Go*, 1968; *Zee and Co.*,
1972.

Edna O'Brien comments:

I quote from two critics: William Trevor and John Berger.
*A Pagan Place*: "Constitutes a reconstruction of a childhood experience which so far as I
know, is unique in the English language. In this respect, though otherwise it is different, it
invites comparison with Proust; a book whose genius is memory" (Berger).
*The Love Object*: "Rarely has a woman protested as eloquently as Edna O'Brien. In
sorrow and compassion she keens over the living. More obviously now, despair is her
province" (Trevor).
My aim is to write books that in some way celebrate life and do justice to my emotions as
well as form a connection with the reader, the unknown one.

\*       \*       \*

When John Millington Synge's *Playboy of the Western World* was first produced in the
Abbey Theatre, Dublin, in 1907, there were riots because Synge told too much of the truth.
His detractors fumed because he depicted, so they said, his fellow-countrymen as peasants
whose main characteristic was a compound of gormlessness and cunning. More than half a
century later *The Playboy of the Western World* is the Abbey's proudest classic. Voices are
raised only in admiration when it's staged; and without qualification it's recommended to
Ireland's tourist millions.
   Ireland, new in its national fulfilment and with the sensitivity of a small nation, jealously
guards the voices that speak for it. Synge, Yeats, Joyce, O'Casey, Shaw, are recent figures:
revered they may be now, but the reverence cannot be the same as that accumulated over
centuries by a Shakespeare or a Molière. In Ireland time has hallowed no long and ordered
tradition of literature: there is instead the confusion of two languages, of the imposed
Ascendancy, of a culture shared between London and Dublin and then suddenly seeming
suspect. In spite of the literary flowering at the beginning of this century, and the pride now
found in it, Ireland is still as nervously uncertain in a cultural sense as it was when the crowds
howled down the *Playboy*. The old, with the achievements of a lifetime tucked away, can take
criticism without too much flinching. The adolescent becomes shrill.
   In the new, liberated Republic the voice of Edna O'Brien is not widely heard: her books
are banned. Other Irish writers who have suffered that indignity, like Joyce and Frank
O'Connor, may be read in Ireland now, and sooner or later Edna O'Brien will in the same
way come into her own. But it's significant that Miss O'Brien today persists in giving offence,
because she writes occasionally about sex.
   Contemporary novels and plays tend to treat of sexual matters in much the same tone of
voice as they do any other subject: this in itself is something of a novelty, but one that has
by now lost a lot of its original glamour. What is still new, however, is that, where sex on the
page is concerned, women are making the running: women novelists, once famous for romance
and happy endings, have profitably taken over the male province of exploring the sexual
side of their characters. Edna O'Brien has been at the forefront of that change and has become a best-selling novelist not because she is one of the most talented writers of her gener-

ation but because she writes frankly about women's desire for, and response to, sexual attention. From the horse's mouth she corroborates the suggestions on this subject made by Joyce and O'Connor and many another Irish male, and finds herself plunged into a Celtic darkness for her pains. Irish women, it is almost said, should be above such things.

Yet sex, or the lack of it, is only a single aspect of the obsession that powers Miss O'Brien's fiction. Solitude has always been her subject and it remains so: in *The Country Girls* and *The Lonely Girl*, through the less successful, more sophisticated novels of life in London and holidaying abroad, in the stories of *The Love Object*, in *A Pagan Place*.

The O'Brien girls, from Cathleen and Baba of the early novels to the sharp heroine in the story "Paradise", are lost in a desperation of loneness. They long to belong, to find a land they feel has been promised to them, in which there is the comfort of easy communication, in which men are different from the men they know. Rarely does their dream come true and, though she has lost none of her comic inventiveness, Edna O'Brien increasingly writes now with despair.

In *The Country Girls* Mr. Gentleman isn't at all like the crude boozers of the pitch-and-toss schools of Co. Clare. He's a cultured man, of French descent, an older man who in theory at least seems to offer Cathleen the chance of the escape she prays for. But Mr. Gentleman is married: he fades away as a Prince Charming, as does the gentleman who is *The Love Object*. He, too, isn't so young: "The hair was greying on the outside and he had spread the outer grey ribs across the width of his head. . . . He had what you'd call a very religious smile." But behind the smile lay the treachery of ineffectiveness, and weakness when it came to the point. The nice artistic Englishman in the story called "Irish Revel" is younger, but little better. With more of a dash than Mr. Gentleman, he makes his way out of a shy girl's life—on a motor-bike that was once romantic. Such girls are left to fall into the arms of the Hickeys and O'Tooles at dances in Mrs. Rodgers' Commercial Hotel, or to be filled with gin by Dublin jackeens who know all about seizing what chances distress offers them. Pregnant, one of them returns to the family farmhouse:

> Your father told her to speak up, to give the man's name, occupation, earnings and character. Your mother said not to use the word context in that context. Your father told your mother to keep out of it, that it was business between men, and he and the doctor hefted Emma on to the leather pouffe. . . . Your father said did she want grub.

Again and again, in seeking the roots of Edna O'Brien's talent, one is driven back to the country that has in a sense rejected her, to the pillars of the Church on which modern Ireland rests, to the harsh country background that isn't at all like the tourist posters. She is rebellious, she states herself; she comes of a rebellious country. And yet few other women have been as rebellious there, preferring to wait for the honour of motherhood, settling for the affection of sons when the love of men fails them. In her novels and stories—and the best ones erupt from her Irishness—a husband may take, quite naturally, a pitchfork to his wife, and a handsome priest may leave a girl emotionally crippled by his seduction, and a father may savage a daughter with words. Such women weep, accepting their lot, knowing no other; for Ireland—lost for so long in struggles with invaders, with poverty and with the land—has had too little time for the delicacy of polite society and leisurely relationships.

The novels of Edna O'Brien are haunted by this hard Ireland of the past, which often she uses as a microcosm of the world as it always is. The violence, the toughness, the separation of men and women, the Establishments that breed hypocrisy, the falsehoods that pass for honesty, the stones that remain unturned: all this is grist in a mill that grinds out, with its despair, reality and truth.

—William Trevor

**O'FAOLAIN, Sean.** Irish. Born in Cork, 22 February 1900. Educated at University College, Cork, M.A. 1925; Harvard University, Cambridge, Massachusetts (Commonwealth Fellow, 1926–28; John Harvard Fellow, 1928–29), M.A. 1929. Served in the Irish Republican Army. Married Eileen Gould in 1928; has two children. Lecturer in English, Boston College, 1929, and St. Mary's College, Strawberry Hill, Middlesex, 1929–33. Formerly, Editor of *The Bell*, Dublin. Director, Arts Council of Ireland, 1957–59. Address: Knockaderry, Killiney, County Dublin, Ireland.

PUBLICATIONS

Novels

*A Nest of Simple Folk.* London, Cape, 1933; New York, Viking Press, 1934.
*Bird Alone.* London, Cape, and New York, Viking Press, 1936.
*Come Back to Erin.* London, Cape, and New York, Viking Press, 1940.

Short Stories

*Midsummer Night Madness and Other Stories.* London, Cape, and New York, Smith, 1932.
*There's a Birdie in the Cage.* London, Grayson, 1935.
*A Born Genius.* Detroit, Schuman's, 1936.
*A Purse of Coppers: Short Stories.* London, Cape, 1937; New York, Viking Press, 1938.
*Teresa and Other Stories.* London, Cape, 1947; as *The Man Who Invented Sin and Other Stories*, New York, Devin Adair, 1948.
*The Finest Stories of Sean O'Faolain.* Boston, Little Brown, 1957; as *The Stories of Sean O'Faolain*, London, Hart Davis, 1958.
*I Remember! I Remember!* Boston, Little Brown, 1961; London, Hart Davis, 1962.
*The Heat of the Day: Stories and Tales.* Boston, Little Brown, and London, Hart Davis, 1966.
*The Talking Trees.* Boston, Little Brown, 1970; London, Cape, 1971.

Play

*She Had to Do Something* (produced Dublin, 1937). London, Cape, 1938.

Other

*The Life of Eamon de Valera.* Dublin, Talbot Press, 1933.
*Constance Markievicz; or, The Average Revolutionary.* London, Cape, 1934.
*King of the Beggars: A Life of Daniel O'Connell.* London, Nelson, and New York, Viking Press, 1938.
*An Irish Journey.* London and New York, Longman, 1940.
*The Great O'Neill: A Biography of Hugh O'Neill, Earl of Tyrone, 1550–1616.* New York, Duell, 1942; London, Longman, 1943.
*The Story of Ireland.* London, Longman, and New York, Hastings House, 1943.
*The Irish: A Character Study.* London, Penguin, 1947; New York, Devin Adair, 1949; revised edition, Penguin, 1970.

*The Short Story*.   London, Collins, 1948; New York, Devin Adair, 1951.
*Summer in Italy*.   London, Eyre and Spottiswoode, 1949; New York, Devin Adair, 1950.
*Newman's Way: The Odyssey of John Henry Newman*.   London, Longman, and New York, Devin Adair, 1952.
*South to Sicily*.   London, Collins, 1953; as *Autumn in Italy*, New York, Devin Adair, 1953.
*The Vanishing Hero: Studies of the Hero in the Modern Novel*.   London, Eyre and Spottiswoode, 1956; Boston, Little Brown, 1957.
*Vive Moi!* (autobiography).   Boston, Little Brown, 1964; London, Hart Davis, 1965.

Editor, *Lyrics and Satires from Tom Moore*.   Dublin, Cuala Press, 1929.
Editor, *Autobiography*, by Theobald Wolfe Tone.   New York and London, Nelson, 1937.
Editor, *The Silver Branch: A Collection of the Best Old Irish Lyrics*.   London, Cape, and New York, Viking Press, 1938.
Editor, *Short Stories: A Study in Pleasure*.   Boston, Little Brown, 1961.

Critical Study: *Sean O'Faolain: A Critical Introduction* by Maurice Harmon, Notre Dame, Indiana, University of Notre Dame Press, 1966.

\*          \*          \*

Emerging at a period in Irish history when the passionate man cannot identify with any particular group, Sean O'Faolain remains in fundamental discord with society and has to work out his own destiny by relying on his own intense demand for a rich and varied existence, and for a background appropriate to his imagination's image of life. Each of his three novels contains a central figure who abides at first by the canons of respectability that govern the lower middle class to which he belongs, but rebels in favour of more liberal, less restrictive ways and in search of a more desirable vision of life than is available to him in his own class. That rebellion affects all of his subsequent life, cutting him off from the familiar moral and social patterns of his childhood and early life and propelling him in quest of a more congenial and more satisfying adult existence. It is his fate however to be forever denied a happy solution to his search for fulfillment.

O'Faolain's short stories reflect a similar concern. It is through them that his development as a writer may be most fully seen. Beginning with romantic stories that try to deal objectively with his experience as a revolutionary, he moved on to stories that reveal the emergence of a distinctive, pessimistic point of view. The central issue is the plight of the individual in a stagnant, post-revolutionary society. In his second collection, *A Purse of Coppers*, his characters experience an alienation so complete that it becomes an impasse beyond which there seems to be no accessible line of development. But gradually O'Faolain discovered a less rigid response. Instead of portraying the sensitive, intelligent man, struggling against insurmountable social conditions, he treats, gently and humorously, of the ambivalent man, who is not particularly concerned with social or moral issues. In this figure he wanted to express the contradictory forces in Irish life at a time when the country was emerging into a modern civilisation but was moulded instinctively by forces from the past. In the process of describing the contradictory nature of the modern Irishman, O'Faolain came to appreciate the power and the value of the various influences on thought and behaviour that lie beneath the conscious or rational part of the individual. With his greater respect for the deeper psychological experiences, he began to concentrate on the universal themes of time and change, the impermanence of youth and age, and the accommodations of middle age.

No account of O'Faolain's fiction should ignore his other prose, in particular his historical biographies which also study the relation of the individual to his society. Each attempts to understand how a great figure emerges from his background, to calculate to what degree he personifies his people's needs, and to determine the nature of the heritage he created for subsequent Irishmen. Nor should one ignore his work as editor of *The Bell*, in which he sought to stimulate Irish writers and in which he spoke out clearly in favour of liberal values. His many articles in Irish, English and American journals, his literary criticism, and even his travel books are all part of the picture of a man of letters, and one who was deeply engaged as an intellectual and creative writer with the whole range of Irish life. "There is," he said, "only one admirable form of the imagination—the imagination that is so intense that it creates a new reality, that it makes things happen, whether it be a political thing, or a social thing, or a work of art."

—Maurice Harmon

**O'FLAHERTY, Liam.** Irish. Born in the Aran Islands, County Galway, 28 August 1896. Educated at Rockwell College, Cashel, 1908–12; Blackrock College, 1912–13; University College, Dublin, 1913–14. Recipient: Black Memorial Prize, 1926. Address: c/o A. D. Peters, 10 Buckingham Street, London W.C.2, England.

PUBLICATIONS

Novels

*Thy Neighbour's Wife*. London, Cape, 1923; New York, Boni and Liveright, 1924.
*The Black Soul*. London, Cape, 1924; New York, Boni and Liveright, 1925.
*The Informer*. London, Cape, and New York, Knopf, 1925.
*Mr. Gilhooley*. London, Cape, 1926; New York, Harcourt Brace, 1927.
*The Assassin*. London, Cape, and New York, Harcourt Brace, 1928.
*The House of Gold*. London, Cape, and New York, Harcourt Brace, 1929.
*The Return of the Brute*. London, Mandrake Press, 1929; New York, Harcourt Brace, 1930.
*The Puritan*. London, Cape, 1931; New York, Harcourt Brace, 1932.
*Skerrett*. London, Gollancz, and New York, Long and Smith, 1932.
*The Martyr*. London, Gollancz, and New York, Macmillan, 1933.
*Hollywood Cemetery*. London, Gollancz, 1935.
*Famine*. London, Gollancz, and New York, Random House, 1937.
*Land*. London, Gollancz, and New York, Random House, 1946.
*Insurrection*. London, Gollancz, 1950; Boston, Little Brown, 1951.

Short Stories

*Spring Sowing*. London, Cape, 1923; New York, Knopf, 1926.
*Civil War*. London, Archer, 1925.
*The Terrorist*. London, Archer, 1926.
*The Child of God*. London, Archer, 1926.

*The Tent and Other Stories.*  London, Cape, 1926.
*The Fairy Goose and Two Other Stories.*  London, Faber and Gwyer, and New York, Crosby Gaige, 1927.
*Red Barbara and Other Stories.*  London, Dulau, and New York, Crosby Gaige, 1928.
*The Mountain Tavern and Other Stories.*  London, Cape, and New York, Harcourt Brace, 1929.
*The Ecstasy of Angus.*  London, Joiner and Steele, 1931.
*The Wild Swan and Other Stories.*  London, Joiner and Steele, 1932.
*The Short Stories of Liam O'Flaherty.*  London, Cape, 1937.
*Two Lovely Beasts and Other Stories.*  London, Gollancz, 1948; New York, Devin Adair, 1950.
*Dúil.*  Dublin, Sáirséal and Dill, 1953.
*The Stories of Liam O'Flaherty.*  New York, Devin Adair, 1956.


Play

*Darkness.*  London, Archer, 1926.


Other

*The Life of Tim Healy.*  London, Cape, and New York, Harcourt Brace, 1927.
*A Tourist's Guide to Ireland.*  London, Mandrake Press, 1929.
*Two Years.*  London, Cape, and New York, Harcourt Brace, 1930.
*Joseph Conrad: An Appreciation.*  London, Lahr, 1930.
*I Went to Russia.*  London, Cape, and New York, Harcourt Brace, 1931.
*A Cure for Unemployment.*  London, Lahr, and New York, Julian, 1931.
*Shame the Devil* (autobiography).  London, Grayson, 1934.


Bibliography: in *Ten Contemporaries*, 2nd series, by John Gawsworth, London, Joiner and Steele, 1933.


Critical Study: *The Literary Vision of Liam O'Flaherty* by John Zneimer, Syracuse, New York, Syracuse University Press, 1971.

\*     \*     \*

Most of Liam O'Flaherty's novels follow a recurring pattern. The books' protagonists are usually lonely, melancholy, and tormented individuals who are intensely emotional. The hero will be depressed and disillusioned with life and its apparent meaninglessness; he will utter wild sentiments, aspire to herculean achievement, and find solace rarely. When security is obtained, it is usually through a brief unification with the forces of nature. While often beautiful and inspiring, nature can also be hostile and destructive, and O'Flaherty readily demonstrates the ambivalence which nature holds. *The Black Soul, Thy Neighbour's Wife, The Martyr*, and *Skerrett* best exemplify these aspects in which exuberant Romanticism and a glorification of primitive instincts play a dominant role.

*The Informer* and *Mr. Gilhooley* stand as important achievements. The former book is raised above the rank of a mere effective suspense-thriller by a penetrating analysis of Gypo Nolan as a symbol of suffering humanity caught amid the handicaps of physical strength without intelligence and the sordid pervasiveness of the Dublin slums. *Mr. Gilhooley* is one of the most heartrending and realistic studies ever attempted of a middle-aged man trapped in the despair of loneliness and emptiness.

O'Flaherty's strengths as a novelist especially involve three qualities: 1) he is a gifted storyteller whose dynamic sweep and flow capture reader interest; 2) he presents scenes with a compelling pictorial vividness; 3) he possesses a Dostoyevsky-like talent for digging deeply into the psychological and emotional turmoil experienced by his principal characters. These talents mingle with several weaknesses. Episodes of genius are interspersed with ordinary pedestrian prose. While at times O'Flaherty's lyricism is extremely effective, his style is too often heavy-handed, flat, and merely utilitarian. Further, his philosophizing becomes jejune and unconvincing; and, frequently, he is not intellectually equal to his themes, which in themselves are of vital importance. Melodrama is common since he deals with highly temperamental figures and very emotional situations. At times he lets excessive emotionalism distract him both from narrative verisimilitude and character plausibility. He rarely resists parading his own neurasthenic feelings so that both omniscient author and the characters continually wear their hearts on their sleeves.

*Famine*, O'Flaherty's finest novel, is strikingly unlike his other fiction. In this saga he eschews the melodramatic approach and the emphasis on one protagonist and concentrates on heavily Naturalistic social documentary in which feelings are kept subdued. Even the narrator stands apart from the starvation and death portrayed and allows the individual tragic episodes to speak for themselves. So balanced is O'Flaherty's handling that he presents deficiencies in the people as well as in the governing groups. Thus, this novel has a balanced comprehensiveness and an artistic profundity which his other long narratives lack.

O'Flaherty has received considerable praise for his numerous short stories, which are of two types: 1) vignettes of rural scenes and people; 2) sketches of animal life in its physical aspects, such as a wild goat defending its kid from a dog, or an eel struggling to escape a fisherman's net. Such stories are characterized by an acute awareness of nature's power, grim realism focusing on the tragic aspects of existence, and a perceptive attention to closely observed detail. "Going into Exile," "Red Barbara," and "The Cow's Death" are illustrative of O'Flaherty's most impressive work in the genre of the brief narrative.

—Paul A. Doyle

---

**ORLOVITZ, Gil.** American. Born in Philadelphia, Pennsylvania, 7 June 1918. Married Maralyn Orlovitz in 1954; has three children. Screenplay Writer, Columbia Pictures, Hollywood, and free-lance television screenplay writer, in the 1950's; Softcover Book Editor, Universal Publishing and Distributing Corporation, New York, 1960–69. Address: 924 West End Avenue, New York, New York 10025, U.S.A.

PUBLICATIONS

Novels

*Milkbottle H.* London, Calder and Boyars, 1967; New York, Dell, 1968.
*Ice Never F.* London, Calder and Boyars, 1970.

Short Stories

*The Story of Erica Keith and Other Stories, Poems and a Play.* Berkeley, California, Miscellaneous Man, 1957.

Plays

*Stevie Guy*, in *Quarterly Review of Literature* (Princeton, New Jersey), vol. 6, nos. 1
and 3, 1951.
*Gray*, in *Literary Review* (Rutherford, New Jersey), Winter 1959–60.


Verse

*Concerning Man*.  Pawlet, Vermont, Banyan Press, 1947.
*Keep to Your Belly*.  New York, Louis Brigants-Intro, 1952.
*The Diary of Dr. Eric Zeno*.  San Francisco, Inferno Press, 1953.
*The Diary of Alexander Patience*.  San Francisco, Inferno Press, 1958.
*The Papers of Professor Bold*.  Eureka, California, Hearse Press, 1958.
*Selected Poems*.  San Francisco, Inferno Press, 1960.
*The Art of the Sonnet*.  Nashville, Tennessee, Hillsboro Publications, 1961.
*Couldn't Say, Might Be Love*.  London, Barrie and Rockliff, 1969.


Other

Editor, *Award Avant-Garde Reader*.  New York, Award House, 1965.


Critical Studies: "Paradox Made Manifest" by Robert Nye, in *The Scotsman* (Edinburgh),
8 April 1967; "Literary Exile in Residence" by Hale Chatfield, in *Kenyon Review* (Gambier,
Ohio), 1969.

*     *     *

"If Coleridge were here to evaluate Orlovitz, I am confident he would consign the Dadaists
and surrealists to the realm of fancy—and admit, if not elevate, Orlovitz to the kingdom
of the imagination." Thus the American critic, Hale Chatfield, in the course of a long
*Kenyon Review* essay on the work of one of the most interesting and accomplished of modern
American writers. Unfortunately, in the absence of Coleridge, Gil Orlovitz has not met
with a great deal of understanding. He is an original and difficult writer whose reputation
seems likely to grow slowly.
Orlovitz has published two novels of a promised trilogy: *Milkbottle H* and *Ice Never F*.
Briefly, what he does in these books is to present the phenomena of a single life in a fugal
form that will do least injustice to their complexity. His protagonist is called Lee Emanuel.
Lee lives in Philadelphia where his father Levi, descended from the Chief Rabbi of Lithuania, his Russian mother Rachel, and his compulsive liar of a wife, Rena, mark the limits
of his world. Within those limits all is disconcertingly fluid. The subject matter of the books,
as Chatfield points out, is really *mind*. This work is "about" the mind that makes it—Lee
Emanuel being the merest disguise for Gil Orlovitz—and the mind that reads it. In the
first half of that explanation we have the reason why Orlovitz has for some years been
highly regarded by his fellow writers—he is with Joyce and Beckett in that his work can be
taken as a treatise on the subject of writing (a treatise that teaches through example rather
than through precept). The second half of the explanation is the more interesting, however.
Both *Milkbottle H* and *Ice Never F* read the reader in no uncertain fashion. Here is a writer
who has taken "ordinary" experience and refused to step outside it. With Burroughs or
with Beckett, the common reader is sometimes permitted to feel that the subject matter is
so remote from him that he can rest easy in admiring it. Orlovitz begins at home, and stays
there, reproducing human experience that we can all recognise but insisting on its richness

and strangeness. He is a theologian of the commonplace, a sort of Emily Dickinson of the domestic detail of the twentieth century. (In this connection it is instructive to note that Emily Dickinson is one of the few poets this most stringent of writers admires.)

Orlovitz himself has said that his aim in his books is "to educate a protagonist in the ramifications of the paradoxes of apparently commonplace phenomena". This sounds pretentious, but is in fact precise. His writing teems with life. His very genuine gifts deserve to be better known.

—Robert Nye

---

**PATCHEN, Kenneth.** American. Born in Niles, Ohio, 13 December 1911. Educated at Warren, Ohio High School; the Experimental College, University of Wisconsin, Madison, 1928–29. Married Miriam Oikemus in 1934. Also an artist: one-man show of books, graphics, and paintings, Washington, D.C., 1969. Recipient: Guggenheim Fellowship, 1936; Shelley Memorial Award, 1954; National Endowment for the Arts Distinguished Service Grant, 1967. Address: 2340 Sierra Court, Palo Alto, California 94303, U.S.A. *Died 8 January 1972.*

PUBLICATIONS

Novels

*The Journal of Albion Moonlight.* Privately printed, 1941.
*The Memoirs of a Shy Pornographer: An Amusement.* New York, New Directions, 1945; London, Grey Walls Press, 1948.
*Sleepers Awake.* New York, Padell, 1946.
*See You in the Morning.* New York, Padell, 1948; London, Grey Walls Press, 1949.

Uncollected Short Story

"Bury Them in God", in *New Directions 1939.* New York, New Directions, 1939.

Plays

*Now You See It (Don't Look Now)* (produced New York, 1966).

Play produced on CBS radio, 1942.

Verse

*Before the Brave.* New York, Random House, 1936.
*First Will and Testament.* New York, New Directions, 1939.
*Teeth of the Lion.* New York, New Directions, 1942.
*The Dark Kingdom.* New York, Harriss and Givens, 1942.
*Cloth of the Tempest.* New York, Harper, 1943.

*An Astonished Eye Looks Out of the Air.* Waldport, Oregon, Untide Press, 1945.
*Outlaw of the Lowest Planet.* London, Grey Walls Press, 1946.
*Selected Poems.* New York, New Directions, 1946; revised edition, 1958, 1964.
*Pictures of Life and Death.* New York, Padell, 1947.
*They Keep Riding Down All the Time.* New York, Padell, 1947.
*Panels for the Walls of Heaven.* Berkeley, California, Bern Porter, 1947.
*CCCLXXIV Poems.* New York, Padell, 1948.
*Red Wine and Yellow Hair.* New York, New Directions, 1949.
*To Say If You Love Someone.* Prairie City, Illinois, Decker Press, 1949.
*Fables and Other Little Tales.* Karlsruhe, Germany, Jonathan Williams, 1953.
*The Famous Boating Party and Other Poems in Prose.* New York, New Directions, 1954.
*Orchards, Thrones and Caravans.* San Francisco, Print Workshop, 1955.
*Glory Never Guesses.* Privately printed, 1955.
*Surprise for the Bagpipe Player.* Privately printed, 1956.
*When We Were Here Together.* New York, New Directions, 1957.
*Hurrah for Anything: Poems and Drawings.* Highlands, North Carolina, Jonathan Williams, 1957.
*Poem-scapes.* Highlands, North Carolina, Jonathan Williams, 1958.
*Poems of Humor and Protest.* San Francisco, City Lights, 1960.
*Because It Is: Poems and Drawings.* New York, New Directions, 1960.
*Double Header.* New York, New Directions, 1966.
*Hallelujah Anyway.* New York, New Directions, 1966.
*But Even So.* New York, New Directions, 1968.
*Love and War Poems.* Mickleover, Derby, Whisper and Shout, 1968.
*Selected Poems.* London, Cape, 1968.
*The Collected Poems of Kenneth Patchen.* New York, New Directions, 1968.
*Aflame and Afun of Walking Faces.* New York, New Directions, 1970.
*Wonderings.* New York, New Directions, 1971.
*In Quest of Candlelighters.* New York, New Directions, 1972.

Recordings: *Kenneth Patchen Reads His Poetry with the Chamber Jazz Sextet*, Cadence, 1958; *Kenneth Patchen Reads Poetry with Jazz in Canada*, Folkways, 1959; *Kenneth Patchen Reads His Selected Poems*, Folkways, 1959; *Kenneth Patchen Reads His Love Poems*, Folkways, 1961.

Critical Study: "The Moral Prose of Kenneth Patchen" by Ray Nelson, in *Steppenwolf* (Omaha, Nebraska), Summer 1969.

*       *       *

Kenneth Patchen was the son of a steelworker. He had only one year of college at seventeen—on scholarship—and at Alexander Meiklejohn's Experimental College at the University of Wisconsin at Madison, in its day by far the most radical, "progressive" undergraduate school in the world, a kind of college-level Summerhill. He was forced to drop out due to lack of funds and in the next few years held a variety of proletarian jobs including again work in the steel mills. He was at the university long enough to play a little football and severely injure his spine. His later youth was lived in the early years of the World Economic Crisis which began in 1929. He began to write in the period when European literature was moving from Expressionism and Dadaism to revolutionary Surrealism. This was also the time of the extreme Left turn of the Communist Party and of the expulsion of Trotsky and eventually most of the Old Bolsheviks, right or left, and the suppression of "modernist", "formalist" tendencies in revolutionary art and literature and the establishment of literary conservativism in America, whether of the political Left or Right. All of these facts are of the greatest importance in understanding the work of Patchen. He is the only widely published writer of his generation in the United States who did not abandon the international idiom of twentieth-century writing. He is also the only widely published writer who preserved throughout the long period of reaction the revolutionary hope of the first quarter of the century. It was a hope disappointed and betrayed—that is the point of his writing—but hope it is, still there, refusing to be silent. All through the dark years he enjoyed a tremendous underground reputation, especially amongst young people, and in about 1950 he began to emerge as one of the few important poets of his generation and as one of the founders and old masters of the counter culture. His influence on poets such as Allen Ginsberg has been tremendous, but his great influence was moral. He was a light that refused to go out.

His prose is not as well known as his poetry but it is certainly remarkable. *The Journal of Albion Moonlight* and *Sleepers Awake* are amongst the very best products of early Surrealism, Comfuturism, and related movements, and stand up today better than similar work by Louis Aragon and Philippe Soupault. Like them, Patchen uses the mythology of Pop Art, cheap detective, fantasy, and science fiction, and advertising copy to create a symbolic mirror of a society in the grip of public nightmare. Later science fiction, with its intergalactic civilizations which are all one great truck drivers' barroom and gangster orgy, and the psychotic sadism and rape of the vulgarized, hardboiled detective have since overtaken and surpassed the savage satire of Patchen. Long dramatic prose poems using the same material are amongst his best poetry. *Memoirs of a Shy Pornographer* is a *roman à clef* comparable to Wyndham Lewis' *Apes of God*, a hilarious comedy of the literary world of its time, yet a work of greater value in its own right.

Fighting against almost insuperable odds of sickness, pain, slander, obloquy, Patchen managed to become and remain a world writer and a revolutionary voice demanding that total moral and spiritual change without which the human race is certain to perish.

—Kenneth Rexroth

---

**PATON, Alan (Stewart).** South African. Born in Pietermaritzburg, Natal, 11 January 1903. Educated at Maritzburg College, University of Natal, B.Sc. 1923, B.Ed. 1966. Married Doris Francis in 1928 (died, 1967); Anne Hopkins, 1969; has two children by first marriage. Schoolteacher in Natal, 1925–35; Principal, Diepkloof Reformatory, Johannesburg, 1935–48. Honorary Commissioner, Toc H Southern Africa, Botha's Hill, Natal, 1949–58. President of the Convocation, University of Natal, 1951–55, 1957–59. Founder and President, Liberal Party of South Africa, 1958–68. Since 1969, Honorary President, South African National Union of Students. Recipient: Anisfield-Wolf Award, 1948; Newspaper Guild of New York Award, 1949; *Sunday Times* Award, 1949; Freedom House Award, 1960; Free Academy of Arts Medal, Hamburg, 1960; National Conference of Christians and Jews Brotherhood Award, 1962. L.H.D., Yale University, New Haven, Connecticut, 1954; D.Litt., Kenyon College, Gambier, Ohio, 1962; University of Natal, 1968. Fellow, Royal Society of Literature, 1961. Honorary Member, Free Academy of Arts, Hamburg, 1961. Address: P.O. Box 278, Hillcrest, Natal, South Africa.

PUBLICATIONS

Novels

Cry, The Beloved Country. London, Cape, and New York, Scribner, 1948.
Too Late the Phalarope. London, Cape, and New York, Scribner, 1953.

Short Stories

*Meditation for a Young Boy Confirmed*.  London, National Society-S.P.C.K., 1944.
*Debbie Go Home: Stories*.  London, Cape, 1961; as *Tales from a Troubled Land*, New
    York, Scribner, 1965.


Play

*Sponono*, with Krishna Shah (produced New York, 1964).   New York, Scribner, 1965.


Other

*The Land and the People of South Africa*.  Philadelphia, Lippincott, 1955; as *South
    Africa and Her People*, London, Lutterworth Press, 1955; revised edition, Lippincott,
    1965, Lutterworth Press, 1971.
*South Africa in Transition*.  New York, Scribner, 1956.
*Hope for South Africa*.  London, Pall Mall Press, 1958; New York, Praeger, 1959.
*Hofmeyr*.  Cape Town and London, Oxford University Press, 1964; abridged, as *South
    African Tragedy: The Life and Times of Jan Hofmeyr*, New York, Scribner, 1965.
*The Long View*.  New York, Praeger, and London, Pall Mall Press, 1968.
*Instrument of Thy Peace*.  New York, Seabury, 1968.
*Kontakion for You Departed*.  London, Cape, 1969; as *For You Departed*, New York,
    Scribner, 1969.


Bibliography: in *Alan Paton* by Edward Callan, New York, Twayne, 1968.


\*          \*          \*


Alan Paton's growing concern with enlightened penology and his personal harassment
by compatriots resentful of his unflattering picture of his native South Africa have limited
the production of one of the most gifted and compassionate twentieth-century fiction
writers to two novels and a slender collection of short stories. In *Cry, The Beloved Country*
and *Too Late the Phalarope*, however, Paton succeeds in baring to the world the tragic
effects and deep-rooted causes of his country's repressive racist policies. Paton's writings
are powerful modern renderings of one of the great tragic themes of art through the ages
—the contrast between the beauty of the natural world as man found it and the ugly place
that his greed and narrow-mindedness have made of it.

*Cry, The Beloved Country* begins "There is a lovely road that runs from Ixopo into the
hills. These hills are grass-covered and rolling, and they are lovely beyond any singing of
it." From them, "if there is no mist, you look down on one of the fairest valleys in Africa."
But this affectionate note cannot be sustained, for all is not well in the valley. Paton himself
speaks of the novel as describing "a process of deterioration" and identifies its theme as
the change in the black natives' character as, envious of the white man's world, they leave
their tribal lands and discipline to huddle in the slums of the white man's cities.

The novel follows the Reverend Stephen Kumalo of Ndotsheni, Natal, as he searches in
"the great city," Johannesburg, for his son Absalom. He discovers that the boy—who has
been in a reformatory—has shot and killed during a robbery attempt a white man, Arthur
Jarvis, the son of a wealthy landowner who lives in the hills above Ndotsheni. Ironically,
Arthur Jarvis has been one of the most courageous white fighters for justice for the African
blacks. At the time of his death, he had been working on a paper called "The Truth about
Native Crime."

Although Absalom pleads that he shot in fear and did not intend to kill Jarvis, he is sentenced to be hanged. His father takes home the pregnant girl that the boy marries after he is condemned; but the preacher is unsuccessful in bringing home also his errant sister Gertrude. As a result of Arthur Jarvis's young son's visiting Kumalo's church, the elder Jarvis and the black minister are brought together and measures are taken to rehabilitate the black farming community. Thus Jarvis helps realize his dead son's dream of setting up "another system of order and tradition and convention" to replace the old tribal system that the white man has thoughtlessly destroyed, so that at last out of the evil spawned by fear comes a promise of good for the community.

*Too Late the Phalarope* deals only secondarily with racial problems and focuses primarily on the tragic consequences of the austere, loveless way of life of the Afrikaans-speaking descendants of the Dutch settlers in South Africa. Pieter van Vlaanderen has been a heroic soldier in World War II and is a police lieutenant and rugby player whom both black and white communities hold in almost god-like respect. Yet there is a dark, secret side to the young man that is revealed by the distraught, sympathetic aunt who tells his story.

Although always respectful, Pieter has been alienated from his father since the boy at the age of fourteen was deprived of his stamp collection for failing to be at the top of his class. When at seventeen, he received first-class marks in his Matriculation Examination, the collection was restored, but the boy did not thank the father nor would he ever speak about the stamps again. He has also become alienated from his shy, fearful wife because she cannot respond adequately to his demands for love. A dispute over the identification of a bird called the *phalarope* in a book of South African birds that Pieter gives his father promises to bring the two men into the kind of joyous relationship that they had lost long ago; but the novel's title stresses that the older man's overture comes too late. Pieter has already been driven by his strong passions into an illicit affair with a black woman.

Terror assails Pieter as he begins to receive anonymous messages intimating that his liaison has been observed and as the black girl—out of work—begins to beg for money. Pieter is entrapped by a jealous, self-righteous police sergeant; and the news of his crime results in his father's death, his family's ostracism, and the termination of his sister's engagement. The aunt prophesies that after Pieter is released from jail, he and his family will be obliged to leave the country that he has served with such distinction. *Too Late the Phalarope* is not simply a South African tragedy, however. While Pieter van Vlaanderen is a victim of the fear and ignorance of his fellow countrymen, he symbolizes all those extraordinary men everywhere who demand a more dynamic life than their pusillanimous societies can provide and thus must suffer for their honesty, enlightenment, and irrepressible human desires.

The title of *Tales from a Troubled Land*, Paton's collection of short stories, suggests the contents. Perhaps the most memorable, "The Waste Land," epitomizes Paton's ironic view of the South African situation and relates it—through the use of the title of T. S. Eliot's famous poem—to the condition of twentieth-century man generally. The brief tale tells of a frightened black man killing one of three young robbers who are pursuing him across a junkyard and then discovering when the boy's companions shove his body under the same truck chassis that hides the man that the boy is his own son.

—Warren French

---

**PATTERSON, (Horace) Orlando.** Jamaican. Born in Jamaica, 5 June 1940. Educated at the University of the West Indies, Kingston, 1959–62 (Jamaica Government Exhibition Scholar), B.Sc. in economics 1962; London School of Economics (Commonwealth Scholar), Ph.D. in sociology 1965. Married Nerys Wyn in 1963; has two children. Assistant Lecturer in Sociology, London School of Economics, 1965–67; Consultant and Tutor in Sociology, Hawker Siddeley Dynamics, London, 1966–67; Lecturer in Sociology, University of the West Indies, 1967–70. Associate Professor of Afro-American Studies, 1970–71, and since 1971, Professor of Sociology and Allston Burr Senior Tutor, Harvard University, Cambridge, Massachusetts. Member of the Editorial Board, *New Left Review*, London, 1965–66. Recipient: Dakar Festival of Negro Arts Fiction Prize, 1966. M.A., Harvard University, 1971. Address: Leverett House F112, DeWolf Street, Cambridge, Massachusetts 02138, U.S.A.

PUBLICATIONS

Novels

> *The Children of Sisyphus.*   London, Hutchinson, 1964; Boston, Houghton Mifflin, 1965.
> *An Absence of Ruins.*   London, Hutchinson, 1967.
> *Die the Long Day.*   New York, Morrow, 1972.

Uncollected Short Stories

> "The Very Funny Man: A Tale in Two Moods" and "One for a Penny", in *Stories from the Caribbean.*   London, Elek, 1965.
> "The Alien", in *New Left Review* (London), September-October 1965.
> "Into the Dark", in *Jamaica Journal* (Kingston), vol. 1, no. 2, 1968.

Other

> *The Sociology of Slavery: An Analysis of the Origins, Development, and Structure of Negro Slave Society in Jamaica.*   London, MacGibbon and Kee, 1967; Rutherford, New Jersey, Fairleigh Dickinson University Press, 1968.

> Essays on history and literature published in periodicals.

Manuscript Collection: University of the West Indies, Kingston.

Critical Studies: reviews by Robert Baldick, in *Daily Telegraph* (London), 20 March 1964; in *Times Literary Supplement* (London), 2 April 1964; by Robert Nye in *The Guardian* (London), 25 June 1965 and 7 April 1967.

Orlando Patterson comments:

> My main concern is with the theme of survival on all levels—physical, emotional, moral. Also concerned with related themes of isolation and exile.

*        *        *

Jamaican fiction is marked by its "realistic" examination of the local social scene. Though this reduces neither its technical range nor its emotional potency—the prose tone poems of Roger Mais, the imaginative adventures of Andrew Salkey, and the mythmaking of Vic Reid and Lindsay Barrett offer ready evidence to the contrary—it does mean that its central concern for the sociological exigencies of daily life often overcomes the urge to use words to build worlds rather than to analyze them. Of the contemporary analytic writers, three stand out as particularly shrewd observers/participators: John Hearne, whose austere novels explore the political impact of race and class; Sylvia Wynter, whose Marxist economic observations underlie her interpretation of Jamaican history; and Orlando Patterson, the Harvard sociologist, whose sense of individual potential is informed and guided always by his understanding of class structure and slave heritage.

Patterson's treatise, *The Sociology of Slavery*, an analysis of the patterns of negro slave society in Jamaica, supplies an intelligent background to his novels, considering both the subservient and the resistant responses of the slave population to white society, and the social institutions—sorcery, religion, folk song and story, and so on—that provided some way of contending with life. To Patterson's mind, those responses and institutions continue to exert their effect, and in his novels he has attempted to demonstrate the inhibition that such a history casts over the lives of people today. Freedom in such a world is a watchword and a dream, always urging individuals into open acts of defiance, and always thwarted by the dead weight of the past.

*The Children of Sisyphus* is set in the slum world of Kingston, and traces the attempts that the prostitute Dinah makes to break out of the Dungle, to flee her surroundings and the course of life that circumstance has forced her into, and to find happiness, order, peace. Paralleling her search is the back-to-Africa quest of the Rastafarian movement, seeking its heritage and home in Ethiopia—"the soil . . . so fertile with everything that's joy back home in Zion"—and a different dream of freedom. But just as that dream is denied by deceit within Rastafarian ranks, so inside Dinah's experience is the Dungle that she cannot altogether leave. Drawn back to it and destroyed, she is typical of not only *her* world, but in Patterson's view *the* world. The suicide that closes the novel, the "soul-consuming" mockery of the shanty surroundings and the universal void, and the attempt thus to reach paradise wilfully supply an ironic perspective towards man's lot. The human ritual of striving for order appears as nothing so much as flight from uncertainty—a negative rather than a positive action—and because it is founded in emptiness and need, it lacks the selfpossession that might make it anything but futile. Hence the circle back to the Dungle, like Dinah's, is closed, and absurd. For Alexander Blackman, in *An Absence of Ruins*, the discovery of such a relationship with futility voids his attempts not only to enunciate his identity but also to believe in his possession of one. Walking in London at the end, he recognizes himself only as an absence, the nothingness that a cipher concretely and phenomenally represents: "I cannot say whether I am civilized or savage, standing as I do outside of race, outside of culture, outside of history, outside of any value that could make your question meaningful. I am busy going nowhere, but I must keep up the appearance of going in order to forget that I am not." Thus the dilemma of existentiality—the conflict invoked between intention, desire, history, and circumstance—is taken from Camus and given Caribbean voice. As Patterson realizes, freeing the mind from slavery is a greater task than freeing the body, for it cannot be enacted by law. When the freedom is not even believed to be attainable, however, the absurdity of man's actions becomes their only reality, offering little comfort and no panacea with which to continue acting.

—W. H. New

**PATTON, Frances Gray.**   American.   Born in Raleigh, North Carolina, in 1906. Educated at Trinity College, now Duke University, Durham, North Carolina; University of North Carolina, Chapel Hill. Married Lewis Patton in 1927; has three children. Recipient: Christopher Award, 1955. Lives in Durham, North Carolina. Address: c/o Dodd, Mead and Company, 79 Madison Avenue, New York, New York 10016, U.S.A.

PUBLICATIONS

Novel

    *Good Morning, Miss Dove.*   New York, Dodd Mead, 1954; London, Gollancz, 1955.

Short Stories

    *The Finer Things of Life.*   New York, Dodd Mead, 1951; London, Gollancz, 1952.
    *A Piece of Luck.*   New York, Dodd Mead, 1955; as *A Piece of Luck and Other Stories*, London, Gollancz, 1955.
    *Twenty-Eight Stories.*   New York, Dodd Mead, 1969.

\*     \*     \*

The work of Frances Gray Patton is almost entirely contained in three volumes: two collections of short stories, *The Finer Things of Life* and *A Piece of Luck*, and one novel, *Good Morning, Miss Dove*. A third collection, *Twenty-Eight Stories*, is substantially reprints from the earlier two volumes. All the short stories appeared in various magazines (primarily *The New Yorker*) during the 1940's and 1950's and reflect a nostalgic treatment of Southern mores, a concern for family problems, and the initiation of both children and adults into various phases of life.

Mrs. Patton's stories in *The Finer Things of Life* are not strong in plot or character development. The continuity of the volume lies in each story (often little more than a sketch) illustrating a virtue or attitude which Mrs. Patton regards as golden, indeed as a finer thing of life: the acceptance of her own middle age by the new mother in "An Honored Guest"; a Northern wife's discovery that the Southern manners which irritate her really have their charm in "The Falling Leaves"; or the parents' pride in the adolescent son who momentarily displays a gleam of maturity in "Apricot Pie." The volume also contains a fine story, "The Terrible Miss Dove," an episode from Mrs. Patton's highly successful novel. By far the best story in this volume is "A Nice Name." Here Mrs. Patton turns a group of Southern white matrons gathered for their weekly facial into a Dantean group of grotesques as they explode into hysterical laughter over the news that Josephine's delightful correspondence over the past months has been with a Negro woman. There is a strong note of ridicule over smug white supremacy in this story, but the volume as a whole is slight and lacks a sustained attack. This deficiency keeps the book from being little more than brief adventures of people who discover some of the "finer things of life." The quiet domestic scenes of small triumphs and disasters are Mrs. Patton's tools and in them the reader will find moments of insight and skillful penetration of facades. She presents her characters and their world through shrewd and unillusioned eyes and although the discoveries her characters make are usually defensible, one has seriously to doubt that these discoveries are sufficient to mold character or to force re-assessment. When the downfall of Mrs. Purvis in "The Representative Ham" pivots on her serving grocery store ham at the Wednesday Night Church Supper and the daughter in "First Principles" is taught to "lie like a lady" to avoid losing face among her rich private school friends, sentiment has dissolved into sentimentality.

*A Piece of Luck* contains some excellent writing and Mrs. Patton's adept use of irony is particularly successful in "The Homunculus," "Loving Hands at Home," "The Game," and "A Piece of Luck." A 1955 review of this collection which described the stories as "weather reports of the mind, its subtle changes in temperature, occlusions, and tensions" points to the strength of her writing technique. She is excellent in creating Negro characters, in using bits of conversation that both locate and reveal a character, and in preparing for a quiet climax. The ending of "A Piece of Luck" clearly illustrates Mrs. Patton's skill. Negroes are gathered at Durham's Five Points bus stop because it is free treatment day at Duke University Hospital. A man, one eye bandaged, attempts to get a hand-out from a white woman by recounting all the details of his eye removal. A retired Duke janitor comes forward to squelch the man's story because he knows the white lady at hand. The janitor is soundly defeated when the injured man retorts, "If thine eye offend thee, pluck it out." The story ends with this splendid sentence:

> The recollection of success—of being a hero among your own people at Five Points, of scripture falling trippingly off your tongue to stupefy a citizen of Lincoln Heights, of a brute who could have broken you in his hands, a witch who could have hexed you, comely young women whose husbands would have beaten you if you'd spoken to them, all standing aside to let you get on a Duke Hospital bus —that recollection might be a bauble of great sentimental value.

If Mrs. Patton is remembered outside her Southern region, it will be for her novel, *Good Morning, Miss Dove*. A Book-of-the-Month Club selection, a play, and a successful motion picture, the novel is the story of a stoical spinster teacher of sixth grade geography. Mrs. Patton abandoned conventional chapter divisions and employed a dozen viewpoints to relate Miss Dove's past and present and to present her students as children and adults. One reviewer described the narrative as a kind of fugue which effortlessly wove the past and present to an extraordinary affecting climax. The book has been compared to *Good-bye, Mr. Chips* and *Our Town* and regarded by some as a minor classic.

As a character Miss Dove is successfully portrayed as a self-sufficient woman who takes her role of teacher seriously and considers her geography class a place where moral character is built. Her schoolroom is a microcosm where no child is called by a silly nickname and where Miss Dove's word and opinion are law. If Miss Dove is externally isolated from the main stream of society, if her teaching methods fail to capitulate to fads and progressive whims, if she remains rigid in habit and judgment, she nevertheless perceptively judges her pupils and achieves a rare inner peace and self-confidence. The reader is torn between a rejection of the book as sheer exploitation of sentimentality and frank admiration for Mrs. Patton's skill in the narrative style and the creation of the character Miss Dove.

There are fine moments in Mrs. Patton's fiction, but there is not the serious commitment to the art of fiction or to issues that one sees in other contemporary Southern women writers like Flannery O'Connor and Eudora Welty. Her volumes are too few to invite serious study and her range is narrow even though her method is generally competent. She understands and convincingly portrays the Carolina setting, but the critic who dubbed her "the Jane Austen of North Carolina" surely overstated the case.

—Elizabeth Evans

---

**PEARSON, Bill (W. H. Pearson).** New Zealander. Born in Greymouth, 18 January 1922. Educated at Greymouth Technical High School; Canterbury University College, Christchurch, 1939, 1947–48; University of Otago, Dunedin, 1940–41, B.A., M.A.; King's

College, London, 1949–51, Ph.D. 1952. Served in the New Zealand forces, in Fiji, Egypt, Italy and Japan, 1942–46. Student Teacher, Dunedin Teachers Training College, 1940–41; Teacher, Blackball School, 1942, Oxford District High School, 1949, and in London County Council schools, 1952–53; Lecturer in English, University of Auckland, 1954–66; Senior Research Fellow, Department of Pacific History, Australian National University, Canberra, 1967–69. Since 1970, Associate Professor of English, University of Auckland. Closely associated with Maori students at the University of Auckland, 1956–66, and was Patron of their Club for some of those years; internal rapporteur at several Maori Leadership Conferences, 1959–63; active in peace and nuclear disarmament organisations through the 1950's, and in the campaign for Maori representation in a sports tour to South Africa in 1960. Recipient: *Landfall* Readers' Award, in non-fiction, 1960. Address: Department of English, University of Auckland, Private Bag, Auckland, New Zealand.

PUBLICATIONS

Novel

Coal Flat. Hamilton, Paul's Book Arcade, and London, Angus and Robertson, 1963; revised edition, Auckland, Longmans Paul, 1970.

Uncollected Short Stories

"The Sins of the Fathers", in *Canterbury University College Review* (Christchurch), 1947.
"Indemnity", in *Canterbury Lambs* (Christchurch), 1947; in *New-Story* (Paris), July 1951.
"Social Catharsis", in *Landfall* (Christchurch), December 1947; as "Purge", in *New-Story* (Paris), January 1952.
"At the Leicesters'", in *Canterbury Lambs* (Christchurch), 1948.
"Babes in the Bush", in *New-Story* (Paris), May 1951.

Other

Henry Lawson among Maoris. Canberra, Australian National University Press, and Wellington, Reed, 1968.

Editor, Collected Stories, 1935–1963, by Frank Sargeson. Auckland, Blackwood and Janet Paul, 1964; London, MacGibbon and Kee, 1965.

Has published several essays on New Zealand literature and society, and on Pacific history.

Bill Pearson comments:

Some commentators have seen a correspondence between my aims in *Coal Flat* and my analysis of the motifs of New Zealand behaviour and their implications for the artist which I wrote in 1951, "Fretful Sleepers" (published in *Landfall* [Christchurch], September 1952, and, with corrections, in *Landfall Country*, Christchurch, Caxton Press, 1962).

The commentary on my novel which I think the most perceptive is by Allen Curnow: "*Coal Flat*: The Major Scale, The Fine Excess", in *Comment* (Wellington), October 1963. Other comments have been by Joan Stevens in *The New Zealand Novel 1860–1965*, Wellington, Reed, 1966; H. Winston Rhodes in *New Zealand Fiction since 1945*, Dunedin, McIndoe, 1968, and in *N.Z. Monthly Review* (Christchurch), November 1970; and Frank Sargeson in "Conversation in a Train", in *Landfall* (Christchurch), December 1967.

While it has been said that a traditional structure, with subplots and a wide range of characters, is appropriate to a social novel set in a community whose attitudes and aspirations and social relations were rooted in 19th century Britain, it has sometimes been a matter of objection that I chose a structure and style that appeared to take no cognisance of the developments in the form of the novel since Joyce. Yet I think that those commentators who stress the social realism or what they miscall "sociology" have been thrown off by a distaste for what they mistake for an outmoded technique, appropriate to *New Writing* reportage. The writers in the light of whose practice my aspirations as a writer developed were those that in common with young men of my time I read with sympathy and a deep respect, Lawrence, Joyce, Forster, Faulkner, Hemingway, Koestler; and I had a series of passions for the novels of Virginia Woolf and John Dos Passos and Thomas Hardy. At the time of my novel's first conception in 1946, the novelist who most excited me was Graham Greene. What I hoped to do when I was writing it (mostly in 1952 and 1953) was to devise a traditional structure that would be large enough to comprehend a community and sensitive enough to reflect the crises of feeling and conscience that might come to a man who was out of sympathy with the materialist values of the community. The plot would grow easily from the initial situation and by its own logic would reach a satisfying outcome without recourse to any of the tricks and evasions or improbabilities by which some of the 19th century English novelists reached their answers. I had found, I thought, theoretical justification in Aristotle's conception of the plot as the probable and necessary consequence of certain initial acts and I conceived it as having the shape of the noble symmetrical curve that I saw in the plots of *Troilus and Criseyde* and *Wuthering Heights* and the great 19th century Russian novels. This was not a scale that I pretended my ability or the comparatively pedestrian quality of New Zealand life would allow me to reach. But my concern for probability was necessary as a check against the rhetorical falsification that would be the risk of writing in the awareness of such examples, created from other communities and other times. My hope was to achieve an imaginative authenticity that my countrymen would immediately recognise as true, and which at the same time would be sufficiently clear of the accidents of parochiality to translate into human experience recognisable to readers from other societies. Whether I succeeded in this I cannot tell; but no one but an expatriate knows the pleasure of imaginatively recreating one's country in its detail, without sentimentality. It has often surprised me that some New Zealand commentators have seen sourness and "unappeased resentment" in a work that was written with love.

Since the moral meaning of the novel was to be in the sequence or consequence of events and their outcome, it was this rather than diction or characters or setting that demanded most thought. In its thirteen years between conception and the last version, the novel survived a number of re-thinkings and radical overhauls, by which I think it gained. The last major revision was the discarding of a superficially optimistic ending, in keeping with a broadly Marxist literary theory hardly tenable after the events of 1956.

When I am moved to write fiction again, however, it is likely to be different in treatment.

*     *     *

Bill Pearson, essayist, critic and scholar, has edited Sargeson's *Collected Stories*, written about the impact of Western society on the Polynesian as reflected in literature, investigated in *Henry Lawson among Maoris* a little-known area of the Australian writer's life, and produced a number of short stories together with a long novel, *Coal Flat*. Novels are sometimes written with a thesis. This may be religious or sociological but, whichever it is, the thesis may too easily destroy those qualities we have a right to expect in any attempt to create a life-like representation.

*Coal Flat* contains a thesis but survives as a novel. In "Fretful Sleepers", described as "a sketch of New Zealand behaviour and its implications for the artist," Pearson suggested that "our job is to penetrate the torpor and out of meaningless make a pattern that means something." *Coal Flat*, with its depressing but significant title, became not only a demonstration of the difficulties involved in such an attempt, but also as a novel partially fulfilled the aim that had been proposed for at least some artists.

Without allowing it to turn into satire or degenerate into a sociological survey, Pearson chose a small coal-mining and gold-dredging settlement on the West Coast of New Zealand in order to chart the course of family and community life; and by close attention to natural-istic detail evoked its oppressive narrowness, puritanism and smugness. At one level the reader is introduced to a wide range of provincial characters, including the publican, parson, policeman and visiting politicians, to miners, dredgers and their officials, to schoolteachers and children, to the doctor and priest, all firmly established in their local setting that com-bines natural grandeur with human inadequacy. The shriek of the dredge echoes and re-echoes through the book and acts as an inhuman accompaniment to the bitter animosities, perverted affections and destructive behaviour of the people of Coal Flat. At another and perhaps more significant level these become signs and portents of a wider deterioration in the quality of life, extending well beyond its confines. Nevertheless, Coal Flat is by no means an inferno of lost souls. There are kindness, comradeship and loyalty in abundance; there is not even a complete absence of sweetness and light; there are moments of idyllic charm and many good intentions. It is New Zealand, the world, reduced to Coal Flat.

Because its pitfalls cannot always be avoided, a close adherence to the slightly outmoded method of naturalism is liable to provoke criticism that is seldom without justification. *Coal Flat* is not a faultless novel, but it is a valuable one and especially for New Zealand. By the accumulation of detail relevant to the settlement and its inhabitants, by involving the central character, a young teacher of liberal instincts, in a mesh of conflicting loyalties, Pearson is able to dramatise the struggle between the individual conscience and the collec-tive will, explore personal and family relationships in the broader context of the com-munity and reveal distortions of sexual, parental and social love. *Coal Flat* is neither a blue-print for future novels about New Zealand, nor is it an imitation of earlier novels in the naturalistic mode; but its achievement is such that it becomes an anatomy of social and spiritual decline, an exploration of the impoverishment of life, and a melancholy comment on thwarted but confused idealism unable to make headway against the conventional attitudes and mental lethargy of the majority.

—H. Winston Rhodes

---

**PERCY, Walker.** American. Born in Birmingham, Alabama, 28 May 1916. Educated at the University of North Carolina, Chapel Hill, B.A. 1937; Columbia University, New York, M.D. 1941; Intern, Bellevue Hospital, New York, 1942. Contracted tuberculosis, gave up medicine, and became a full-time Writer, 1943. Married Mary Bernice Townsend in 1946; has two children. Recipient: National Book Award, 1962; National Institute of Arts and Letters grant, 1967. Address: Old Landing Road, Covington, Louisiana, U.S.A.

PUBLICATIONS

Novels

*The Moviegoer.* New York, Knopf, 1961; London, Eyre and Spottiswoode, 1963.
*The Last Gentleman.* New York, Farrar Straus, 1966; London, Eyre and Spottis-
woode, 1967.
*Love in the Ruins: The Adventures of a Bad Catholic at a Time Near the End of the World.*
New York, Farrar Straus, and London, Eyre and Spottiswoode, 1971.

*        *        *

Walker Percy may be said to belong to the "waste land" school of modern literature, for
his view of the contemporary scene resembles that of T. S. Eliot, F. Scott Fitzgerald, and his
fellow Southerner, William Faulkner. Like his predecessors, Percy finds the modern world
in a state of moral confusion; the values of the past no longer work and the majority of men
are spiritually dead, abstracted, and, if sensitive, ingrown and cut off from life outside
themselves. Percy's protagonists to some extent share in this confusion, but they are set apart
from other characters by their extraordinary ability to love. And, while the capacity to love
raises them above the general deadness of the world, it also creates for them a special kind
of problem. Simply stated, the problem is: How can the hero find his way in a world that
regards love as a mechanical act, particularly when the traditional view he has to fall back
upon treats love as a set of grand ideals which has little to do with physical reality? Each
novel, in a sense, is a working out of this dilemma.

The Moviegoer concludes with the protagonist, a lusty thirty year old bachelor, failing in
his latest sexual escapade and marrying a neurotic young woman of his own class, apparently
out of affection, a feeling of kinship, and a sense of *experienced* responsibility. In *The Last
Gentleman* the hero, who suffers from abstraction and the modern malaise of detachment,
cures himself through his personal devotion to a dying youth and, in turn, helps cure a confused and beautiful young woman and her older brother, a cynical, corrupt doctor. *Love in
the Ruins*, which is set in the future ("at a time near the end of the world") deals with the
collapse of modern technology and concludes with the responsible marriage of the protagonist who had tried to save his mad world but, failing at that, had given himself up to whisky
and lust for three beautiful women. Significantly he marries the most responsible and moral
of the three and begins to live a simple, natural, and properly lustful life.

While the philosophical and moral bases of Percy's novels are familiar enough, his rendering of characters and scenes is strikingly fresh, vivid and bitingly satirical. He is a moral and,
ultimately, a religious writer, but he is also a novelist of manners who can delineate with
remarkable skill the contrasts between certain kinds of Northerners, Southerners, and Middle
Westerners. Also, though he confines himself for the most part to the region around New
Orleans, Percy is able to extend the implications of his material by creating characters and
events obviously derived from the national scene, such as the white man who, some time back,
went about the country masquerading as a Negro, and the Johnson-Masters studies in sexual
response. Percy's style, which is sensitive and poetic, elevates material that less subtly treated
might have seemed contrived and even moralistic.

—W. J. Stuckey

**PERUTZ, Kathrin.** American. Born in New York City, 1 July 1939. Educated at Barnard College, New York, B.A. 1960; New York University, M.A. 1966. Married Michael Studdert-Kennedy in 1966; has one child. Lived in London, 1960–64. Address: 16 Avalon Road, Great Neck, Long Island, New York 11021, U.S.A.

PUBLICATIONS

Novels

The Garden. London, Heinemann, and New York, Atheneum, 1962.
A House on the Sound. London, Heinemann, 1964; New York, Coward McCann, 1965.
The Ghosts. London, Heinemann, 1966.
Mother Is a Country: A Popular Fantasy. London, Heinemann, and New York, Harcourt Brace, 1968.

Uncollected Short Story

"An American Success", in Voices. London, Joseph, 1965.

Other

Beyond the Looking Glass: America's Beauty Culture. New York, Morrow, 1970; as Beyond the Looking Glass: Life in the Beauty Culture, London, Hodder and Stoughton, 1970.
Marriage Is Hell: It's Better to Burn Than to Marry. New York, Morrow, 1972; as The Marriage Fallacy: It's Better to Burn Than to Marry, London, Hodder and Stoughton, 1972.

Critical Studies: "K. Perutz", in Don't Never Forget by Brigid Brophy, London, Cape, 1966; "The Truth about Fiction" by George P. Elliott, in Holiday (New York), March 1966.

Kathrin Perutz comments:

The only general theme (or background) of my books is America. Mother Is a Country is a direct parody of certain American dreams (the acquisition of power and the desire to become a commodity); A House on the Sound charts the distance from reality to where rich liberals have their camp. Beyond the Looking Glass, a non-fiction book often fictionalized, examines preoccupation with appearance in America, where people have the hope of seeming what they have not yet become, and where self-knowledge is replaced by concern over minutiae of deception.

My first three novels also concern sub-rosa relationships, the area of self that is undeveloped or suppressed. The Garden presents a love affair between two girls, not Lesbian (both girls are young and boy-crazy), but an essential intensity to contradict fears of not existing. A House on the Sound shows different manifestations of embryonic love—homosexuality, incest, masochism—never acknowledged by the characters. The two main characters of The Ghosts have not reconciled themselves to the sexual roles, male and female, they are supposed to play, and often parody or pervert these roles.

But mainly, each book has been my attempt to learn more of the craft. The first was a simple diary; the second tried, in six hours, to cut through time past and present, more similar to movie techniques than traditional flashbacks. The third book tried to give a sense of development, over the space of a year. The fourth, a satire, was deliberately "surface", a board game played over true but generalized emotions. My fifth book presented problems of journalism, in organization of material, tone, pace and the creation of a personal, but abstracted, narrator.

My last book, *Marriage Is Hell*, is an essay on the institution of marriage as it exists today in the West, particularly in America. It deals with the anachronism of marriage, its false expectations, its imprisonment of personality and distortion of both privacy and personal liberty. The book, which is strongly opinionated, attacks marriage from many perspectives—legal, historical, anthropological, sexual, etc.—and then goes on to suggest reform and finally a turning that will make marriage possible again. I consciously tried to keep the style loose and colloquial, the better to let readers argue with me, and literary experiment is superseded in this book by political, or pragmatic, aims.

*        *        *

Kathrin Perutz has a baroque spider-web sensibility; it is as exquisite as it is tough, and permits her to explore such matters as incest, sadomasochism, homosexuality, suicide, and murder with the delicacy of an appropriate dinner wine. It is the most pervasive force in her four novels and the one that diminishes the importance of whatever flaws may appear in them as a consequence of Miss Perutz's experimentation with form and theme.

The first novel, *The Garden*, is a straightforward first-person narrative of life at a small women's college in Massachusetts. Its treatment of the urge to put aside the burden of virginity becomes tedious, and the book is marked with jejune expressions ("O.K., Pats, shoot") that may be true to dormitory life but are vexatious in a novel. Miss Perutz handles the garden symbolism of the novel well, however; describes a memorably tender, vivacious relationship between Kath and the Blossom, the two principal characters; and, with perfect briskness of pace and lightness of tone, captures the banal essence of a party weekend at an American men's college probably better than any other writer has.

*The Ghosts*, Miss Perutz's third novel, walks the maze of a love affair in which the participants—or combatants—Luke, an excessively cerebral writer, and Judith, an under-cerebral but sensitive hairdresser, are haunted chiefly by Luke's dead father and an assortment of cast-off lovers. The deficiency of the volume is that there is no one with whom an audience would much care to identify. Luke is insatiably clinical toward the involvement, and he and Panda, a deep platonic love of his who befriends Judith, are sometimes mouthpieces discussing their actions and Judith's, and examining one of the immediate themes of the novel, abortion, and, of more general metaphysical interest, the nature of human action. The conception of the characters is acute; their mechanism, however, is too much exposed and not enough is left for the reader to infer. They are often pieces of an essay rather than people in a work of fiction. Judith is too pliable, too much a prop for Luke, until the end, when she takes control of herself and Luke becomes more human. But that occurs too late to place the novel in balance.

*Mother Is a Country*, the last of the four novels, is a satiric fantasy that strikes at the mass-produced, antiseptic, Saran-wrapped materialism in American life. That quality accounts for the death of the three main characters, and the most palpable reaction in the cosmically unfeeling nation is that "a mother eagle in her nest flapped powerful wings and laid another egg." Though the book has been criticized for its superficiality of characterization, it can be argued that since superficial consumerism is primarily what the satire is about, John Scudley (a hero with much of the feeling of a Bellow character, but without the profundity) and the other characters are properly shallow.

It was Miss Perutz's second novel, *A House on the Sound*, that proved her excellence. She paints a dinner party of sham liberals on a small canvas with precise detail, probing through the word, the facial expression, the gesture, the nuance of conversation the variety of characters present and their secret relationships. In this and in her control of time through brief, illuminating flashbacks and staging of the movements of her characters, there is the clear echo—but just the echo—of Virginia Woolf. When the experimentation ends, as far as it ever does, it is to be hoped that Miss Perutz will return to a place like the house on the Sound and give full voice to her sensibility.

—Alan R. Shucard

---

**PETERKIEWICZ, Jerzy.** British. Born in Fabianki, Poland, 29 September 1916; emigrated to England in 1940. Educated at Dlugosz School, Wloclawek; University of Warsaw; University of St. Andrews, Scotland, M.A. 1944; King's College, London, Ph.D. 1947. Married Christine Brooke-Rose, *q.v.*, in 1948. Lecturer, 1950–64, and since 1964, Reader in Polish Language and Literature, School of Slavonic and East European Studies, University of London. Address: c/o Christy and Moore Ltd., 52 Floral Street, London W.C.2, England.

PUBLICATIONS

Novels

> *The Knotted Cord.* London, Heinemann, 1953; New York, Roy, 1954.
> *Loot and Loyalty.* London, Heinemann, 1955.
> *Future to Let.* London, Heinemann, 1958; Philadelphia, Lippincott, 1959.
> *Isolation: A Novel in 5 Acts.* London, Heinemann, 1959; New York, Holt Rinehart, 1960.
> *The Quick and the Dead.* London, Macmillan, 1961.
> *That Angel Burning at My Left Side.* London, Macmillan, 1963.
> *Inner Circle.* London, Macmillan, 1966.
> *Green Flows the Bile.* London, Joseph, 1969.

Play

> *Sami swoi* (in Polish) (produced London, 1949).

Verse

> *Prowincja.* Warsaw, 1936.
> *Wiersze i poematy.* Warsaw, 1938.
> *Poematy londynskie i wiersze przedwojenne* (Collected Poems). Paris, Kultura, 1965.

Other

> *The Other Side of Silence: The Poet at the Limit of Language.* London and New York, Oxford University Press, 1970.

Editor, *Polish Prose and Verse*. London, Athlone Press, 1956.

Editor and Translator, *Antologia liryki angielskiej, 1300–1950*. London, Veritas, 1958.

Editor and Translator, with Burns Singer, *Five Centuries of Polish Poetry, 1450–1950*. London, Secker and Warburg, 1960; Chester Springs, Pennsylvania, Dufour, 1962; revised edition, with Jon Stallworthy, as *Five Centuries of Polish Poetry, 1450–1970*, London and New York, Oxford University Press, 1970.

Critical Studies: essay in the *New Statesman* (London), 10 October 1959; essay in *The Sunday Times Magazine* (London), 10 June 1962; essay by the author on his own work: "Speaking of Writing", in *The Times* (London), 9 January 1964; essay in *Le Monde* (Paris), 28 June 1967; *The Novel Now* by Anthony Burgess, London, Faber, 1968; essay by the author, in *Times Literary Supplement* (London), 30 July 1971.

Jerzy Peterkiewicz comments:

If titles are significant, *Isolation* and *Inner Circle* seem to be my representative novels, both structurally and thematically.

\*         \*         \*

Three of Jerzy Peterkiewicz' last six novels are comic entertainments of a high order of literary craftsmanship; three others show a marked falling-off of standards. His first two novels have little bearing on the later work. The earliest, *The Knotted Cord*, is a genuinely moving account of a peasant boyhood in Poland; its hero has to escape from many things, but particularly from the "cord" of the scratchy brown cassock that his pious mother has thrust him into, and from all that cord represents. The work is a "first novel" of promise, and it is a pity that Peterkiewicz has chosen not to develop or integrate into his later work a mode which might have provided a carbohydrate counterbalance to the sometimes too frothy champagne of the books which follow. The second novel, *Loot and Loyalty*, is a trivial and poorly-constructed historical novel about a seventeenth-century Scots soldier of fortune exiled in Poland, and his connection with the "false Dmitri."

*Future to Let*, the first of the really successful books, is less "mannerist" by far than its successors. It is a very funny roman à clef on the tortured loves, English, plots, and politics of contemporary Polish emigrés, chief among them Julian Atrament ("ink" in Polish), quite unidentifiable, of course, but almost recognizable, whose "escape to freedom" by means of his St. Bernard dog is Peterkiewicz' finest comic turn. *Isolation*, probably his best book, parodies the erotic mystifications of a modern spy story with a skill that even the suggestions of deep meanings about the mutual isolation of sexuality, etc., cannot spoil. The Powell-esque (or Waugh-like) Commander Shrimp (alias Pennyworthing), faded semi-spy and bathetic con-man, is a great comic creation. *That Angel Burning at My Left Side* has some of the virtues of *The Knotted Cord*; it is realism with a light touch, of a boy growing up through the Second World War and post-war refugeehood, looking for father, country and self. The gimmick of the "angels" grows tiresome, but descriptions of place and event and the hero himself are vivid and concrete—until the hero gets to England, and everything, including him, suddenly (and apparently inadvertently on the author's part) becomes less real.

The three unsuccessful works include *The Quick and the Dead*, a spoof ghost-story and fantasy of serio-comic realism, involving among other things the amorous relations of the dead in Limbo, the suffering and repentance of ghosts (a somewhat Golding-like concept), and comic, mindless brutality reminiscent of some of Anthony Burgess. The book is loaded with significance, apparently, but the coy handling of its basic situation makes for heavy reading. Still harder to read, but even more significant, is *Inner Circle*, in which a three-layered story of Surface (the far future), Underground (present-day sub-Firbankian London), and Sky (a version of the Eden story), is held together by repeated "circle" and "underground" image patterns, and by analogous destinies. The themes and point-of-view games again make it seem almost like a collaboration between Golding, Burgess, and Arthur C. Clarke. Peterkiewicz' most recent work, *Green Flows the Bile*, is as tastelessly affected a social satire as its title would suggest. It recounts the last journey together of two "fellow-travellers" (in all senses), the Secretary, a "political gigolo," and his employer, the "senior prophet of the age . . . the travelling peace salesman." The comic travelogue is passable in places, but the political satire is either painfully obvious or intensely private; the two pitfalls that await the topical roman à clef have caught Peterkiewicz this time.

Peterkiewicz' heroes are almost all coyly hollow semi-comic shadow-men, pretending to contain abysses and seeking with morose jocularity for an "identity" to which they are fundamentally indifferent. Their human relationships are sketched with equal shallowness. Even the intrigues are lower Greene-land, territory more powerfully explored by Burgess, though at times Peterkiewicz is clearly aiming for the playful, complex "meanings" of a Chesterton, or a Woolf (*Orlando*), or a Nabokov, or for the light, horrid satire of a Waugh (*Scott-King's Modern Europe*). Stage-metaphors, mirrors, masks, costumes, photographs, cute but pallid versions of Nabokovian artifices, crowd the pages of *Isolation*, in which mock-pornography and reciprocal voyeuristic spyings, slowly building up a posthumous portrait, bring to mind *Lolita* (courteously, or perhaps coincidentally, acknowledged in a parrot of that name) or *The Real Life of Sebastian Knight*. These are samples of tone, not assertions of source; but even the best of Peterkiewicz' work is marred by hearing continually-whispered chords made up of the murmurs of other men's voices, almost as if he were unwilling to hear his own voice. His real talent for language and comedy is almost swamped by his need to be terribly à la mode in these six novels, and it is a pity, for, to paraphrase a comment he makes on one of his own characters, "his anonymous extraterritorial aura predicts at every step a possible eruption of personality."

It may be that, for all the polished virtues and assurance of his better novels, Peterkiewicz will be remembered longest and known most widely for his critical essays and anthologies, and for his book *The Other Side of Silence: The Poet at the Limit of Language*, in which he sensitively discusses some intricacies of modern literature and places Polish literature in their context. One would like, however, to have as well his views on his own Polish contemporaries, who are giving us one of the most flourishing of modern minor literatures. Perhaps in his criticism he has more truly earned the right than he has in his fiction, to the inevitable, and specious, comparison with Conrad, that other Polish man of letters who turned himself, in adult life, and not without success, into an English writer.

—Patricia Merivale

---

**PETRAKIS, Harry Mark.** American. Born in St. Louis, Missouri, 5 June 1923. Educated at the University of Illinois, Urbana, 1940–41. Married Diane Perparos in 1945; has three children. Has worked in steelmills, as a real-estate salesman, truck driver and sales correspondent. Since 1960, Free-lance Writer and Lecturer. Taught at the Indiana University Writers Conference, Bloomington, 1964–65. Recipient: *Atlantic* "Firsts" Award, 1957; Benjamin Franklin Citation, 1957; Friends of American Writers Award, 1964; Friends of Literature Award, 1964. D.H.L., University of Illinois, 1971. Address: 80 East Road, Dune Acres, Chesterton, Indiana 46303, U.S.A.

PUBLICATIONS

Novels

> *Lion at My Heart.*   Boston, Little Brown, and London, Gollancz, 1959.
> *The Odyssey of Kostas Volakis.*   New York, McKay, 1963.
> *A Dream of Kings.*   New York, McKay, 1966; London, Barker, 1967.

Short Stories

> *Pericles on 31st Street.*   Chicago, Quadrangle Books, 1965.
> *The Waves of Night and Other Stories.*   New York, McKay, 1969.

Play

> Screenplay: *A Dream of Kings*, 1969.

Other

> *The Founder's Touch: The Life of Paul Galvin of Motorola.*   New York, McGraw Hill,
>    1965.
> *Stelmark: A Family Recollection* (autobiography).   New York, McKay, 1970.

*     *     *

The fiction of Harry Mark Petrakis brings to the contemporary American scene—usually Chicago—the humor, dignity, vitality, sadness and glory of the Greek culture that emerged from the golden age of Pericles, a heritage to which the modern Greek clings fiercely. It is significant, therefore, that Petrakis began his successful career with the short story "Pericles on 31st Street", published in *Atlantic Monthly* in 1956. And while the "Pericles" in this story is merely a vendor of peanuts and hot dogs at the corner of 31st Street and Dart, far from his homeland, the old Greek brings to his little section of Chicago the fighting spirit of his ancestors: he teaches the almost-defeated tenants of the business block on 31st Street to shake their fists in rebellion against the landlord who unfairly raises their rent; he teaches his new friends to stand up and live like men and to drink the heady wine of Greece instead of the watery beer of America. A Petrakis hero dances to bouzouki music instead of the canned music of the American juke box.

Petrakis, as craftsman-writer, understands the impact of words in establishing mood, and since the mood he is after is the haunting quality of Greece, the list of characters in his fiction reads like an Athenian telephone directory: Akragas, Barbaris, Barbaroulis, Glavas, Javaras, Marlas, Matsoukas, Pappas, Sarantis, Volakis, Zenoitis. To evoke the taste and fragrance of Greece, Petrakis uses food and drink—he places much of his fiction in restaurants and bars—to recreate the aura of a Greek taverna: Calamata olives in brine, kaseri cheese, ouzo, mezithra, Kouloura, white feta cheese, retsina, lamb and green beans . . .

In his writing style, which is primarily poetic-prose, Petrakis evolves a Greek-American mythology reminiscent of classical Greek drama. His fiction is filled with the exiled Greek's high cry for happiness, often expressed through the enjoyment of sexuality and the triumph of procreation; but along with this cry is the chant of an old Greek chorus reminding the hero in Petrakis' fiction that the gods of Olympus still rule through the ancient law of Zeus that only through suffering and sorrow does one achieve wisdom. So it is that in *The Odyssey*

PETRAKIS

CONTEMPORARY NOVELISTS

*of Kostas Volakis*, Kostas resigns himself to a destiny in which he loses children he loves; he must even survive knowing that the one son toward whom he is hostile kills the son Kostas loves most of all. In *A Dream of Kings*, Matsoukas, too, struggles against a destiny that robs him of the young son that he adores.

But beyond the Greek theme of the acceptance of destiny, Petrakis deals with the world of the Greek who emigrates to a new and foreign land he enters with hope but must learn to live in with loneliness and despair. The hero in Petrakis' fiction is often the Greek lost in America, the Greek who longs for the wine-dark Aegean, for the golden marble of the Parthenon under a cloudless blue sky, for the rich soil of Greece—Matsoukas in *A Dream of Kings* keeps in his office several handsful of Cretan earth which he presses into his palms whenever he cries out for his homeland. It is this cry for a return to Greece that underlies the work of Harry Mark Petrakis. And Petrakis gives to his fiction a quality of universality by creating heroes who, through deep sorrow, learn that no one can go home again.

—Milton White

---

**PETRY, Ann (Lane).** American. Born in Old Saybrook, Connecticut, 12 October 1912. Educated at the University of Connecticut, Storrs, 1928–31, Ph.G. 1931; Columbia University, New York, 1943–44. Married George D. Petry in 1938; has one child. Pharmacist in Old Saybrook and Old Lyme, Connecticut, 1931–38. Writer and Reporter, *Amsterdam News*, New York, 1938–41, and *People's Voice*, New York, 1941–44. Secretary, Authors League of America, 1960. Recipient: Houghton Mifflin Literary Fellowship, 1946. Address: c/o Russell and Volkening Inc., 551 Fifth Avenue, New York, New York 10017, U.S.A.

PUBLICATIONS

Novels

*The Street.* Boston, Houghton Mifflin, 1946; London, Joseph, 1947.
*Country Place.* Boston, Houghton Mifflin, 1947; London, Joseph, 1948.
*The Narrows.* Boston, Houghton Mifflin, 1953; London, Gollancz, 1954.

Short Stories

*Miss Muriel and Other Stories.* Boston, Houghton Mifflin, 1971.

Other

*The Drugstore Cat* (juvenile). New York, Crowell, 1949.
*Harriet Tubman: Conductor on the Underground Railroad* (juvenile). New York, Crowell, 1955; as *A Girl Called Moses: The Story of Harriet Tubman*, London, Methuen, 1960.
*Tituba of Salem Village* (juvenile). New York, Crowell, 1964.
*Legends of the Saints* (juvenile). New York, Crowell, 1970.

986

Manuscript Collection: Mugar Library, Boston University.

Ann Petry comments:

I write short stories, novels, books for children and young people. I vary what I write even to the style, but the underlying theme deals with race relations in the U.S.A.

*       *       *

Ann Petry's high-school fiction and later practice whenever free from pharmaceutical chores bore fruit in three novels: *The Street, Country Place*, and *The Narrows. The Drugstore Cat* and *Tituba of Salem Village* are juveniles; but her short stories of the early 1940's in *The Crisis* and *Phylon*, as well as more recent fiction in *Redbook* and *The New Yorker*, merit attention. "On Saturday the Siren Sounds at Noon" began her career: its reception encouraged her to write *The Street*. "Like a Winding Sheet" was chosen for *The Best American Short Stories of 1946*. "Solo on the Drums," appearing in *'47 Magazine of the Year*, has a lyrical anguish that reflects her novels in theme and style.

*The Street* offers more than just another example of environmental determinism overshadowed by its precursor, *Native Son*. True, it opens with "a cold November wind" on 116th Street in Harlem that "did everything it could to discourage the people walking along the street" and closes with "the grime and the garbage and the ugliness" of that street as the defeated, pretty heroine-turned-murderess flees by train. Boots Smith, unscrupulous in avoiding a return to "a life of saying 'yes sir' to every white bastard who had the price of a Pullman ticket," is an older Bigger Thomas, with cash, a luxurious car, and political connections. Authorial digressions that rationalize Lutie Johnson's fears of the street—"an evil father and a vicious mother" to Black children like her Bub—replace Boris Max's sixteen-page courtroom speech that blames a racist environment for Bigger's dilemma. Ann Petry's own life had verified the glum details of *The Street*; but her feminine and racial perceptions of those domestic tragedies that cluster in Black slums gave psychological sharpness to passages still alive with meaning. The Connecticut middle class with its insulting generalizations about Black women, the unemployed Harlem men reduced to loitering and philandering and desertion, the Black man with a resentment of his oppressors "so bad and so deep that I wouldn't lift a finger to help 'em stop Germans or nobody else," the tenement radios blaring to kill the feel of unbearable misery, "carrying pain and a shrinking from pain" —all these are realistic types that advance the author's theme of entrapment and resignation. The sometimes excessive description and the rather contrived final plights of Lutie and Bub are redeemed by a sympathy that humanizes even the maniacally obsessed William Jones and the repulsively scarred Mrs. Hedges.

The ugliness of a small-town New England white environment, personified early by the scandalmongering cab driver "the Weasel," permeates *Country Place*. The conflict sustained between past and present is moral in the frustrations of returning war veteran Johnnie Roane and his faithless wife Glory, and philosophical in the insistence of Mrs. Gramby that her middle-aged son Mearns uphold a gracious tradition beyond his powers and desires. Sensitive to fusions of imagery, metaphor, and symbol, the author has Johnnie struggle past storm-felled trees to reach Ed Barrell's cabin and suffer disillusion in Glory's infidelity. The long storm, like the rain in which Johnnie walks after his first doubts about his wife, is emblematic of the turbulence of climatic changes forced upon the main characters. The thematic absorption of disenchantment into thinner but stronger life is presaged in Johnnie's decision not to strangle his wife and, later, not to kill her lover; it is advanced—through an equally distressing decision by Mrs. Gramby—by his opportunity to become an artist in New York. *Country Place*, marred like *The Street* by seemingly thesis-conjured death at the end, continues Ann Petry's attack against a cash-and-carry society hostile to moral beauty.

987

*The Narrows*, titled after its setting, the Black neighborhood in Monmouth, Connecticut, in 1952, not only has a conscience-gripping theme, but is remarkable for its vivid array of minor characters. Sexually radiant, blues-singing Mamie Powther; the frightful amputee, Cat Jimmie, who speeds on his homemade cart to peer under the dresses of women; Cesar the Writing Man, who records his sonorous prophecies on the sidewalk with colored chalk; and Weak Knees, with his collapsible limbs and innumerable gestures and mutterings ("Get away, Eddie, get away!") at the ghost of his best friend—these and others unforgettably enliven Dumble Street and the foggy dock of the River Wye. The novel is about love and its betrayal. Abbie Crunch lets puritanical snobbishness fatally betray her love for her husband, then lets grief betray her love for their adopted child, Link. Later, Link sacrifices his love for rich, white Camilo Treadway to Black pride, while she gives in to jealousy and racism. And mistakenly jealous little Malcolm Powther, having no manhood himself, betrays that of Link. "All of us," Abbie concludes, "had a hand in [Link's death], we all reacted violently . . . because he was coloured and she was white." Almost every character applies to himself the author's repeated refrain: "I, executioner." *The Narrows* is attuned to the 1970's in other racial themes, and it thoughtfully views the responsibilities that attend power and artistic talent. Flashbacks are excessive, sometimes confusing; but stream-of-consciousness passages are skillfully written, and the leaven of humor appears.

The craftsmanship, social truth, and humanity of Ann Petry's fiction deserve wider recognition. Her basically tragic vision, linked in some ways with themes of Lorraine Hansberry and Ralph Ellison, could culminate, if she produces more, in a distinguished, comprehensive novel.

—James A. Emanuel

---

**PLOMER, William (Charles Franklyn).** British. Born in Pietersburg, Transvaal, South Africa, 10 December 1903. Educated at Spondon House School; Beechmont, Sevenoaks, Kent; Rugby School, Warwickshire; St. John's College, Johannesburg. Served in the Naval Intelligence Division, 1940–45. Lived in Japan in the 1920's. Editor, with Roy Campbell, *Voorslag*, 1928. Fiction Reviewer, *Spectator*, London, 1933–38. Succeeded Edward Garnett as Literary Adviser to Jonathan Cape, publishers, London, 1937. Since 1968, President of the Poetry Society, London, and President of the Kilvert Society, Hereford. Recipient: Queen's Gold Medal for Poetry, 1963. D.Litt., Durham University, 1958. Fellow, Royal Society of Literature, 1951. C.B.E. (Commander, Order of the British Empire), 1968. Address: c/o Jonathan Cape Ltd., 30 Bedford Square, London W.C.1, England.

PUBLICATIONS

Novels

    *Turbott Wolfe*. London, Hogarth Press, and New York, Harcourt Brace, 1926.
    *Sado*. London, Hogarth Press, 1931; as *They Never Came Back*, New York, Coward McCann, 1932.
    *The Case Is Altered*. London, Hogarth Press, and New York, Farrar and Rinehart, 1932.
    *The Invaders*. London, Cape, 1934.
    *Museum Pieces*. London, Cape, 1952; New York, Noonday Press, 1954.

Short Stories

*I Speak of Africa.*  London, Hogarth Press, 1927.
*Paper Houses.*  London, Hogarth Press, and New York, Coward McCann, 1929.
*The Child of Queen Victoria.*  London, Cape, 1933.
*Curious Relations*, with Anthony Butts (as William D'Arfey).  London, Cape, 1945;
   New York, Sloane, 1947.
*Four Countries.*  London, Cape, 1949.


Plays

*Gloriana*, music by Benjamin Britten (produced London, 1953).  London, Boosey
   and Hawkes, 1953.
*Curlew River*, music by Benjamin Britten (produced London, 1964).  London, Faber,
   1964.
*The Burning Fiery Furnace*, music by Benjamin Britten (produced London, 1966).
   London, Faber, 1966.
*The Prodigal Son*, music by Benjamin Britten (produced Aldeburgh, Suffolk, 1968).
   London, Faber, 1968.


Verse

*Notes for Poems.*  London, Hogarth Press, 1927.
*The Family Tree.*  London, Hogarth Press, 1929.
*The Fivefold Screen.*  London, Hogarth Press, 1931; New York, Coward McCann,
   1932.
*Visiting the Caves.*  London, Cape, 1936.
*Selected Poems.*  London, Hogarth Press, 1940.
*The Dorking Thigh.*  London, Cape, 1945.
*A Shot in the Park.*  London, Cape, 1955.
*Borderline Ballads.*  New York, Noonday Press, 1955.
*Collected Poems.*  London, Cape, 1960.
*A Choice of Ballads by William Plomer.*  London, privately printed, 1960.
*Taste and Remember.*  London, Cape, 1966.
*Celebrations.*  London, Cape, 1972.


Other

*Cecil Rhodes.*  London, Davies, and New York, Appleton, 1933.
*Ali the Lion: Ali of Tebeleni, Pasha of Janina, 1741–1822.*  London, Cape, 1936; as
   *The Diamond of Janina: Ali Pasha 1741–1822*, Cape, and New York, Taplinger, 1970.
*Double Lives: An Autobiography.*  London, Cape, 1943; New York, Noonday Press,
   1956.
*At Home: Memoirs.*  London, Cape, and New York, Noonday Press, 1958.
*Conversation with My Younger Self.*  Hill House, Ewelme, Oxford, Simon Nowell-
   Smith, privately circulated, 1963.

Editor, *Japanese Lady in Europe*, by Haruko Ichikawa.  London, Cape, and New
   York, Dutton, 1937.
Editor, *Kilvert's Diary 1870–1879.*  London, Cape, 3 vols., 1938–40; abridged edition,
   Cape, 1944; New York, Macmillan, 1947; revised edition, Cape, and Macmillan,
   3 vols., 1960.

Editor, *Selected Poems of Herman Melville*.   London, Hogarth Press, 1943.
Editor, *New Poems 1961: A P.E.N. Anthology*.   London, Hutchinson, 1961.
Editor, *A Message in Code: The Diary of Richard Rumbold, 1932–1960*.   London,
  Weidenfeld and Nicolson, 1964.

Translator, with Jack Cope, *Selected Poems of Ingrid Jonker*.   London, Cape, 1968.

Bibliography: in *William Plomer* by John R. Doyle, New York, Twayne, 1969.

Critical Studies: "Life in Two Parts", in *Times Literary Supplement* (London), 5 October 1951; *The English Novel* by Walter Allen, London, Phoenix House, 1954; *The Japanese Tradition in British and American Literature* by Earl Miner, Princeton, New Jersey, Princeton University Press, 1958; "Black and White" by Ezekiel Mphahlele, in the *New Statesman* (London), 10 September 1960; "The Novel and the Nation in South Africa" by Nadine Gordimer, in *Times Literary Supplement* (London), 11 August 1961; Introduction by Laurens van der Post to *Turbott Wolfe*, London, Hogarth Press, 1965.

William Plomer comments:

My novels and short stories derived their themes from the period between the two World Wars, when most of them were published. They were largely concerned with involvements or conflicts between persons of different racial or social origins. *Turbott Wolfe* is regarded, for example, as the first novel about South Africa which did not take apartheid for granted. *Paper Houses* (influenced, in the opinion of Arthur Waley, by modern Japanese fiction) gave, through a pair of Western spectacles, a fresh view of Japanese society. And *Curious Relations* and *Museum Pieces* represented survivals from the English propertied upper middle class who were at the end of their flowering.

In the rapidly changing world of the last 25 years I have felt no impulsion to write prose fiction, my responses to human character and behaviour having taken more succinct forms in poetry.

\*       \*       \*

William Plomer has said: "My temperament and talent did not impel me to try and make a living by writing books; they impelled me to write books only when I wished and only of whatever kind I wished." He has remained, then, in the best sense an amateur, like his friend E. M. Forster. His output of fiction—he is also a poet—has been small but is distinguished in content, style and perception alike.

Born in 1903 in Northern Transvaal, South Africa, and sent to England to school at Rugby, Plomer returned to South Africa at the age of sixteen to become first a farmer and than a trader in Zululand. Before returning to England, where he has lived ever since, in his late twenties, he lived two years in Japan. He has also spent considerable time in Greece and Italy. As his autobiography, *At Home*, makes plain, he has always felt himself as something of a stranger in the English scene. As he wrote in his preface to his collection of short stories *Four Countries:*

> . . . it does seem to me that my transplantations have not been uncharacteristic of this age of dislocation, disorientation and exile, this age of the Displaced Person. In their way I think most of these stories reflect the age by isolating some crisis caused by a change in environment or by the sudden and sometimes startling confrontation of different races and classes.

The statement provides a key to Plomer's fiction.

His first novel, *Turbott Wolfe*, was published when he was twenty-three. Plomer's, Laurens van der Post has said, "was the first imagination to allow the black man of Africa to enter into it in his own human right. . . . He was the first to accept him without qualification or reservation as a human being." The importance of this novel, together with his African short stories, in the literary history of South Africa is plain; in it he anticipates a whole later South African literature and can be seen as the forbear of such writers as Nadine Gordimer, Daphne Rooke, Dan Jacobson, Jack Cope and David Lytton.

*Turbott Wolfe*, which is written in the very difficult form of a continuous conversation, is the story of a Young Africa movement, the main principles of which are that South Africa cannot be a white man's country and that the future for the black African can only be through miscegenation. What are now especially memorable are the idyllic pasages on native life. Comparable passages, together with bitterly satirical descriptions of white settlers, occur also in the short stories *I Speak of Africa* and *The Child of Queen Victoria*. Outstanding among them is "Ula Masonda," the story of a young Zulu's life in the mines of Johannesburg. It has been written many times since but never better.

The confrontation of different races is the theme of *Sado*, Plomer's novel about Japan, and of *Paper Houses*, his volume of stories on the same country. The short stories are probably more successful than the novel. There Plomer seems uncertain whether he is primarily writing travel sketches and evoking landscape or telling a story. The former he does with brilliant sensitivity, but the story, that of a relationship between a young Japanese, Sado, and the young Englishman who is his friend, is less satisfying. Sado, with his split mind, his feelings of inferiority, his dreams of suicide, is brilliantly rendered. But Lucas, the young Englishman, is less convincing. All the same, it is the index of Plomer's achievement that the novel one compares it with as a study in relationships between men of different colours and alien cultures is Forster's *A Passage to India*.

Plomer's first "English" novel was *The Case Is Altered*. The setting is a boarding-house in London, but the characters are obviously not merely inhabitants of a boarding-house; they are also the inhabitants of an interregnum between two worlds, one dead, the other waiting to be born. The characters, however, for all the intelligence and power of analysis that go to their making, are faint. And so it is with the characters of Plomer's next novel, *The Invaders*. The invaders are the unemployed, lost and almost without hope, who flocked into London during the depression of the nineteen-thirties, and, beyond them, middle-class drifters who feel themselves unwanted in the society of their time. Theme and scene are magisterially established in the first chapter, which describes the crowds that mill aimlessly and unceasingly round Marble Arch. But the characters are somehow faint compared with the Africans of Plomer's earlier fiction. It is as though Englishmen are less real to Plomer than either Zulus or Afrikaners; and one is conscious that the writing lacks the drive of moral indignation that is so powerful in the African books.

Eighteen years passed before Plomer published his next novel, *Museum Pieces*, which at the time of writing is his last. This is a novel conceived in affection, even love, for the main character, Toby D'Arfey, the last of an old English family, a man of wit and talent who, by his upbringing and traditions, is a museum piece precisely—or a displaced person. For another writer D'Arfey could have been a target for satire; but Plomer persuades us to see him in the end as an heroic figure, larger than the life that has defeated him.

Plomer's achievement has been to describe, with wit and urbanity and, where necessary, with controlled anger, the lives of those who, as a favourite novelist of his, George Gissing, has said, "dwell in a limbo external to society. They refuse the statistic norm." As Plomer himself does. This comes out strikingly in his two volumes of autobiography, *Double Lives* and *At Home*, the best commentaries, by implication at any rate, we yet have on Plomer's fiction.

—Walter Allen

**POHL, Frederik.** American. Born in New York City, 26 November 1919. Self-educated. Served in the United States Air Force, in the United States and Italy, 1943–45. Married Carol Ulf in 1952; has four children. Editor, Popular Publications Inc., New York, 1939–43; Copywriter, Thwing and Altman, New York, 1946; Book Editor and Associate Circulation Manager, Popular Science Publication Company, New York, 1946–49; Literary Agent, New York, 1949–53; Editor, Galaxy Publishing Company, New York, 1960–69. Member, Monmouth County, New Jersey Democratic Party Committee, 1956–66. Since 1966, Member of the Executive Board of the Monmouth County Civil Liberties Union, and of the Board of Directors of the New York City Opera Theatre. Recipient: Edward E. Smith Memorial Award, 1966; Hugo Award, 1966, 1967, 1968. Address: 386 West Front Street Red Bank, New Jersey 07701, U.S.A.

PUBLICATIONS

Novels

*The Space Merchants*, with C. M. Kornbluth. New York, Ballantine, 1953; London, Heinemann, 1955.
*Search the Sky*, with C. M. Kornbluth. New York, Ballantine, 1954; London, Rapp and Whiting, 1968.
*Undersea Quest*, with Jack Williamson. New York, Gnome Press, 1954; London, Dobson, 1966.
*A Town Is Drowning*, with C. M. Kornbluth. New York, Ballantine, 1955.
*Gladiator-at-Law*, with C. M. Kornbluth. New York, Ballantine, 1955; London, Gollancz, 1964.
*Presidential Year*, with C. M. Kornbluth. New York, Ballantine, 1956.
*Undersea Fleet*, with Jack Williamson. New York, Gnome Press, 1956; London, Dobson, 1968.
*Slave Ship*. New York, Ballantine, 1957; London, Dobson, 1961.
*Edge of the City*. New York, Ballantine, 1957.
*The Case Against Tomorrow*. New York, Ballantine, 1957.
*Undersea City*, with Jack Williamson. New York, Gnome Press, 1958.
*Tomorrow Times Seven*. New York, Ballantine, 1959.
*Wolfbane*, with C. M. Kornbluth. New York, Ballantine, 1959; London, Gollancz, 1960.
*Drunkard's Walk*. New York, Galaxy, 1960; expanded version, London, Gollancz, 1961.
*The Man Who Ate the World*. New York, Ballantine, 1960.
*The Wonder Effect*, with C. M. Kornbluth. New York, Ballantine, 1962; London, Gollancz, 1967.
*A Plague of Pythons*. New York, Ballantine, 1963; London, Gollancz, 1966.
*The Abominable Earthman*. New York, Ballantine, 1963.
*The Reefs of Space*, with Jack Williamson. New York, Ballantine, 1964; London, Dobson, 1965.
*Starchild*, with Jack Williamson. New York, Ballantine, 1965; London, Dobson, 1966.
*The Frederik Pohl Omnibus*. London, Gollancz, 1966.
*Digits and Dastards*. London, Dobson, 1968; New York, Ballantine, 1970.
*The Age of Pussyfoot*. New York, Simon and Schuster, 1969; London, Gollancz, 1970.
*Rogue Star*, with Jack Williamson. New York, Ballantine, 1969.

Short Stories

*Alternating Currents.*   New York, Ballantine, 1956.
*Turn Left at Thursday.*   New York, Ballantine, 1961.
*Day Million.*   New York, Ballantine, 1970; London, Gollancz, 1971.

Other

Editor, *Beyond the End of Time.*   New York, Permabooks, 1952.
Editor, *Star Science Fiction Stories.*   New York, Ballantine, 3 vols., 1953–54.
Editor, *Assignment in Tomorrow.*   New York, Garden City Books, 1954.
Editor, *Star Short Novels.*   New York, Ballantine, 1954.
Editor, *Star of Stars.*   New York, Doubleday, 1960.
Editor, *The Expert Dreamers.*   New York, Doubleday, 1962; London, Gollancz, 1963.
Editor, *Time Waits for Winthrop and Other Short Novels.*   New York, Doubleday, 1962.
Editor, *The Seventh Galaxy Reader.*   New York, Doubleday, 1964; London, Gollancz, 1965. (and later volumes)
Editor, *Star Fourteen.*   London, Whiting and Wheaton, 1966.
Editor, *The If Reader of Science Fiction.*   New York, Doubleday, 1966; London, Whiting and Wheaton, 1967. (and later volumes)
Editor, *Nightmare Age.*   New York, Ballantine, 1970.

Manuscript Collection: Syracuse University Library, Syracuse, New York.

Critical Study: in *New Maps of Hell* by Kingsley Amis, New York, Harcourt Brace, 1960, and London, Gollancz, 1961.

Frederik Pohl comments:

My principal work has been in science fiction, and within that field in the special kind of science fiction best described as cautionary literature. Now that the world has been well alerted to such problems as pollution, overpopulation and so on—largely, in the first instance, by science-fiction stories—it is old hat to say that we must look to the long-range consequences of our society and technology. My stories have often touched on such themes long before they were fashionable.

Apart from argument, I have been interested in exploring all the possible range of alternate futures for the human race. Some of the work in which I take most pride—short stories like *Day Million*, novels like *Wolfbane*—are not at all cautionary in the sense that they call attention to dangerous current trends; instead, they attempt to show some of the stranger, but quite possible, directions the human world-line may take.

However, no writer, myself least of all, writes very attractively when he writes according to a coldblooded plan. I don't set out to write either political agitprop or think-tank scenarios; I only attempt to think out the consequences of what seem to me to be interesting developments, to set living characters in such worlds and then to let them live their lives.

*     *     *

Frederik Pohl has distinguished himself both as one of the most prolific writers of science fiction and as one of its most explicit promoters. The two distinctions seem to stem from his firm didactic concern with science fiction as a social early warning system. To write science fiction, he says, "is to try to look ahead to see not only what is likely to fall upon us by way of science and technology, but to see what the side effects and the consequences and the second and third order derivatives of these things will be." (M.L.A. Forum on Science Fiction, December 1968). In a Shavian catalogue of prefaces and postscripts, Pohl repeats and amplifies his fictional purpose "to question everything . . . in the light of what Harlow Shepley calls the 'View from a distant star.'"

The explicit didactic purpose is borne out by his fiction, which historically falls in line with that of Wells, Huxley and Hoyle as a kind of allegorical social satire, earth-bound rather than space-speculative. His major novels are concerned with both the special consequences of particular trends in the twentieth century and the general effects of our current population expansion and waste of natural resources. Thus, *Space Merchants* and *Gladiator-at-Law* are, respectively, biting denunciations of twentieth century commercial advertising and corporation monopoly; unrestricted expansion of advertising agencies and super-corporations permits them to become the new power-blocs of the twenty-first century, perverting the democratic process and lowering the quality of life by pandering to society's greed for immediate physical gratification.

In *Reefs of Space* and *Starchild*, Pohl looks further ahead. The earth is teeming with thirteen billion human beings necessarily organised under an entirely totalitarian, computer-directed Plan of Man which has the sole aim of keeping a balance of resources. Private liberty has vanished because previous centuries have wasted natural resources only to turn the earth into a closed-system in which there still "isn't enough to go round." *The Age of Pussyfoot* takes the same distant view but focuses more closely on the quality of personal life in a society so dependent on computers that it is, in fact, symbiotic with them. Instant formation and immediate self-indulgence are possible, yet no attempt has been made to solve the problems of poverty, war and cultural triviality.

Throughout Pohl's work runs the paradoxical theme that, while we progress technologically, we don't improve the quality of living, we don't remove the inequalities of material possession and we don't improve the prospects of human creativity and fulfilment. The only answer is the choice also expounded by Hoyle: we either stay in an entirely closed, programmed system or we evolve to another level.

Although most of Pohl's novels are written with collaborators, there is no discernible difference in the quality of writing of the collaborated and independent work. What emerges is a profoundly disturbing sense of reality, truth and honesty which is Swiftian in its impact. In Pohl's hands, science fiction is a weapon to be used vigorously in defence of humanity. As a social critic, Pohl must rank high. In addition, however, as his *Undersea* novels indicate, he is a first-rate storyteller who never lets the message wholly take over the medium.

—Frederick Bowers

---

**PORTER, Hal.** Australian. Born in Albert Park, Melbourne, Victoria, 16 February 1911. Educated at Kensington State School, 1917; Bairnsdale State School, Victoria, 1918–21; Bairnsdale High School, 1922–26. Married Olivia Parnham in 1939 (divorced, 1943). Cadet Reporter, *Bairnsdale Advertiser*, 1927. Schoolmaster, Victorian Education Department, 1927–37, 1940; Queen's College, Adelaide, 1941–42; Prince Alfred College, Kent Town, South Australia, 1943–46; Hutchins School, Hobart, Tasmania, 1946–47; Knox Grammar School, Sydney, 1947; Ballarat College, Victoria, 1948–49; Nijimura School, Kure, Japan

(Australian Army Education), 1949–50. Director, National Theatre, Hobart, 1951–53. Chief Librarian of Bairnsdale and Shepparton, 1953–61. Full-time Writer since 1961. Australian Writers Representative, Edinburgh Festival, 1962. Lecturer for the Australian Department of External Affairs, in Japan, 1967. Recipient: Sydney Sesquicentenary Prize, 1938; Commonwealth Literary Fund Fellowship, 1956, 1960, 1964, 1968, and Subsidy, 1957, 1962, 1967; *Sydney Morning Herald* Prize, 1958; Sydney Journalists' Club Prize, 1959, for drama, 1961; *Adelaide Advertiser* Prize, 1964, 1970, for non-fiction, 1968; *Encyclopaedia Britannica* Award, 1967; Captain Cook Bi-Centenary Prize, 1970. Address: Glen Avon, Garvoc, Victoria 3275, Australia.

PUBLICATIONS

Novels

    *A Handful of Pennies.*  Sydney, Angus and Robertson, 1958; London, Angus and Robertson, 1959.
    *The Tilted Cross.*  London, Faber, 1961.
    *The Right Thing.*  Adelaide, Rigby, and London, Hale, 1971.

Short Stories

    *Short Stories.*  Adelaide, Advertiser Press, 1942.
    *A Bachelor's Children.*  Sydney and London, Angus and Robertson, 1962.
    *The Cats of Venice.*  Sydney, Angus and Robertson, 1965.
    *Mr. Butterfry and Other Tales of New Japan.*  Sydney, Angus and Robertson, 1970.
    *Selected Stories.*  Sydney and London, Angus and Robertson, 1971.

Uncollected Short Stories

    "Frieze of Victims", in *Point* (Melbourne) 1937.
    "Revenge", in *Flame* (Melbourne), 1937.
    "Holiday", in *Bulletin* (Sydney), 1937.
    "Hyde's Hell", in *Dit* (Sydney), 1944.
    "Festival", in *Bulletin* (Sydney), 1965.
    "I Wonder Who's Kissing Her Now", in *Summer's Tales 2.*  Sydney, Macmillan, 1965.
    "Melbourne in the Thirties", in *London Magazine*, 1965.
    "Brett", in *Bulletin* (Sydney), 1971.
    "Ellie", in *Bulletin* (Sydney), 1971.
    "Mr Jefferson's Tune", in *Quadrant* (Sydney), 1971.
    "The Sale", in *Southerly* (Sydney), 1971.
    "Home Town", in *The Sun* (Melbourne), 1972.

Plays

    *The Tower* (produced London, 1963).  Melbourne, Penguin, 1963.
    *The Professor* (produced London, 1965).  London, Faber, 1966.
    *Eden House* (produced Melbourne, 1969; as *Home on a Pig's Back*, produced Richmond, Surrey, 1972).  Sydney, Angus and Robertson, 1969.
    *Parker* (produced Ballarat, 1972).  Adelaide, Rigby, 1972.
    *The Water Rises* (produced Melbourne, 1972).  Adelaide, Rigby, 1972

Verse

*The Hexagon.*   Sydney, Angus and Robertson, 1956.
*Elijah's Ravens.*   Sydney, Angus and Robertson, 1968.
*In an Australian Country Graveyard.*   Sydney, Angus and Robertson, 1972.

Other

*The Watcher on the Cast-Iron Balcony* (autobiography).   London, Faber, 1963.
*Australian Stars of Stage and Screen.*   Adelaide, Rigby, 1965.
*The Paper Chase* (autobiography).   Sydney, Angus and Robertson, 1966.
*The Actors: An Image of the New Japan.*   Sydney, Angus and Robertson, 1968.
*A History of Bairnsdale.*   Bairnsdale, Victoria, James Yeates, 1972.

Editor, *Australian Poetry 1957.*   Sydney, Angus and Robertson, 1957.
Editor, *Coast to Coast 1961–1962.*   Sydney, Angus and Robertson, 1963.
Editor, *Australian Short Stories.*   Adelaide, Rigby, 1972.

Bibliography: *A Bibliography of Hal Porter* by Janette Finch, Adelaide, Libraries Board of South Australia, 1966.

Manuscript Collection: Mitchell Library, Sydney.

Critical Studies: "The Craft of Hal Porter" by Peter Ward, in *Australian Letters* (Adelaide), October 1962; "New Tracks to Travel: The Stories of White, Porter, and Cowan" by John Barnes, in *Meanjin* (Melbourne), June 1966; *Profile of Australia* by Craig McGregor, Melbourne, Penguin, 1968; essay by Robert Burns, in *Meanjin* (Melbourne), no. 1, 1969; "Hal Porter's Comic Mode" by Mary Lord, in *Australian Literary Studies* (Hobart), October 1970.

Hal Porter comments:

As many Australian writers are, I am, it seems to me, *indubitably*, unavoidably Australian —in tone, attitude, sentiment, and vocabulary—all this no doubt, because of a passionate wish to record clearly an extraordinary country and (once one is beyond the common factors of human behaviour) its unique enough inhabitants. Not only is my writing Australian: it is regionally so. Despite having dealt with nineteenth-century Van Diemen's Land, with Earl's Court, Venice, Occupied Japan, Milan and so on, I see myself as a regional writer, limited, engrossed, timely, in somewhat the same way as, say, Colette is, as Eudora Welty and V. S. Pritchett are. The bulk of my work, particularly the short stories, is based on characters and landscapes of southernmost Australia, the less distraught, arid and intractable part, the greener, colder, well-combed terrain with its nineteenth-century provincial cities and country towns, its seaside resorts on a littoral touched by Antarctic winds.

Since I lack fictional skill and imagination my subjects are by and large shop-lifted almost directly from Life, most often directly, holus-bolus. I think I deal with these dispassionately but perceive a truth in the remarks of a critic who finds them treated with a "pitiless pity". My main aim for several decades has been to write with many-planed clarity, to achieve an incandescence, a style on the clear glass of which are visible as few of my finger-prints as possible. A perverse aim: style is, after all, the author's finger-prints.

Many of my problems stem from the curious complexities of Australian society, the infinitely subtle class distinctions beneath a facade of egalitarianism, the fine-drawn sensibilities and leeriness underlying the over-all bonhomie, the shrewd ruthlessness below the love-thy-neighbourliness. I face these problems warily but with unabating fascination. Since my fervent and high-falutin desire is for an experience to reach the reader in simon-pure condition, and as though the experience has angelically magnetized to itself the most unimpeachable *mots justes*, the aptest, and therefore most pellucid and author-untainted, sentences, I am frequently disconcerted by reviewers who accuse me of "brilliant" imagination, "glittering" satire, sardonicism, irony, malice, *et tout cela*. Perhaps they read too much between the lines, or perhaps one's writing comes out not so dispassionately as one thinks. I do write my first draft, after all, headlong, in reckless long-hand. The second, and final, draft is laboriously typewritten: at this stage, I burnish and prune, intensify and high-light, and cast about for the more pungent word, the more telling clause, the nuance that helps clarify, the astringent turn of phrase that ousts fuzziness.

All in all, in spite of some strictures, I am optimistic about mankind, consider my writing ultimately compassionate, apolitical, disciplined, and as exact as it can be made within the limits I must inevitably work inside.

\*     \*     \*

Hal Porter began writing fiction in the 1930s. At the time the characteristic mode of Australian fiction was realistic. Writers tended to concentrate upon plain, accurate reporting of aspects of Australian society, with particular emphasis upon rural life and landscape. Though much of Porter's work has value as social history, from the first he emerged as a writer of a very different kind from most of his contemporaries—a self-conscious stylist, mannered, and with an eye for the grotesque, the fantastic and the absurd.

Porter's first novel was *A Handful of Pennies*. It is ostensibly an analysis of the post-war phenomenon Occupation Democracy, made in terms of the experiences of Australian occupation forces in Japan. In fact it is an allegorical satire aimed at War, Peace and Occupation Democracy, the latter being categorised as "Delusion's son . . . the sponsor of no Christ, but of guilds of Pontius Pilates." It is notable for its "pyrotechny of words" rather than for the intrinsic interest of its characters or situations. In his second novel, *The Tilted Cross*, Porter turns to Australian history for his subject. The book is set in 19th century Hobart and its central character is a fictional reconstruction of the convict artist Thomas Griffiths Wainewright. Porter keeps closely to biographical and historical facts, but he presents them in such a way as to emphasise the inescapable cruelty of convict society. He juxtaposes the squalor of convict life and the elegant luxury of the colonial aristocracy, and brings together a set of characters whose meetings and clashes are emblems of the contradictions and hypocrisies of the society they represent. Porter establishes a pattern of interaction between innocence and guilt, but there is some inadequacy in the portrayal of characters and some lack of direction in the authorial reflections and the fragmentary symbolism. He gives a vivid account of the freakish and the deformed, of ugliness, impotence, perversion and brutality, but the very mannered style sometimes conveys the impression that the author is more concerned with verbal effects than substantial meaning.

Porter's *Short Stories* contained, with one exception, stories not previously published, and written, according to the author, between the ages of 18 and 23. With two omissions, these were republished in a revised form, and with the addition of 16 stories from magazines and journals, in *A Bachelor's Children*. Together with *The Cats of Venice* these represent over thirty years of his work in the form. A third collection, *Mr. Butterfry*, contains stories set in Japan, and these show a marked change in Porter's attitude to the country since his first visit after the war. Stories from these three volumes appear in *Selected Stories*.

Porter draws heavily on his own experience as subject matter for the stories, and from them some picture of his youth, his aspirations, the beginning of his career as a writer, his friends and his wanderings can be gained. The gift that is most clearly displayed in his two autobiographical works—a total recall of the past in fine detail—is also to be observed in the stories. He is able to recapture and hold the exact details of a scene whether it be a country town, a city hotel, a house, a restaurant, or even the flavour of a period, and by doing so to confer upon the past a peculiar sense of present reality.

Several main themes recur in the short stories. Childhood and youth, loss of innocence, the relationship between past and present, and unique moments of human experience, receive attention in many stories. These, however, are subjects not peculiar to Porter. It is in his treatment of them that his striking individuality asserts itself. There is never any sense that he is writing to a formula. He experiments freely with the form of the short story and each story represents a quite unique approach to its subject. Variety of subject matter is matched by variety of approach. His style, however, remains consistently mannered and idiosyncratic. Its virtues are sharpness, wit, and pungency; its defects a certain wilful extravagance and verbalising not always essential to or justified by his subject.

The problem in assessing Porter's work is underlined when one considers the two autobiographical works, *The Watcher on the Cast-Iron Balcony* and *The Paper Chase*. They bring Porter's life story up to 1949. Some of the material in these works is also to be found in the short stories, and the difficulty, as so often with Porter, is to determine the boundary between fact and fiction. The autobiographies must properly be regarded also as works of fiction. *The Watcher on the Cast-Iron Balcony*, in particular, is shaped as fiction, and given embellishments of style and incident that are characteristic of Porter's writing. *The Paper Chase*, on the other hand, is less coherent, and contains much lively, though unassimilated, social history of Melbourne in the years from 1929–1949. Porter himself, the subject of the book, remains somewhat elusive, splintered into fragments of experience and other peoples' lives.

Porter's work raises basic questions about the relationship between fact and fiction, and literature and life. These questions are not canvassed in any explicit way, but they arise from his treatment of factual material, and from his determination not to "dehydrate the truth of appearances into the lie of fact". If there is one impression that his fiction as a whole conveys, it is of the fragmented nature of experience. There is an air of temporariness about his characters. They are constantly on the move from place to place, cafe to cafe, party to party. His fictional world is in restless motion. It is inhabited by bizarre, pathetic, vicious, grotesque, and comic characters. It is a world firmly controlled and directed by the author, whose sharp, critical, observant eye catches the smallest details of scene and behaviour. It is essentially a creation of his tireless verbal artistry. At times his work seems to display more artifice than substance, but he brings to Australian fiction a unique verve, wit and polish.

—Leonie Kramer

---

**PORTER, Katherine Anne.** American. Born in Indian Creek, Texas, 15 May 1890. Educated in Louisiana and Texas: at home, aged 3 to 8, in private school, 8 to 12, in Ursuline Convent, 12 to 16. Married Eugene Dove Pressly in 1933 (divorced, 1938); Albert Russel Erskine Jr., 1938 (divorced, 1942). Reporter and Arts Critic, *Rocky Mountain News*, Denver, 1919. Lived in Mexico and Europe. Taught at Olivet College, Michigan, 1940; Lecturer in Writing, Stanford University, California, 1948–49; Guest Lecturer in Literature, University of Chicago, Spring 1951; Visiting Lecturer in Contemporary Poetry, University of Michigan, Ann Arbor, 1953–54; Fulbright Lecturer, University of Liège, Belgium, 1954–55; Writer-in-Residence, University of Virginia, Charlottesville, Fall 1958; Glasgow Professor, Washington and Lee University, Lexington, Virginia, Spring 1959; Lecturer on American Literature for the United States Department of State, in Mexico, 1960, 1964;

Ewing Lecturer, University of California at Los Angeles, 1960; Regents' Lecturer, University of California at Riverside, 1961. Library of Congress Fellow in Regional American Literature, 1944; United States Delegate, International Festival of Arts, Paris, 1952; Member, Commission on Presidential Scholars, 1964. Recipient: Guggenheim Fellowship, 1931, 1938; New York University Libraries Gold Medal, 1940; Ford grant, 1960, 1961; O. Henry Award, 1962; Emerson-Thoreau Bronze Medal, 1962; Pulitzer Prize, 1966; National Book Award, 1966; National Institute of Arts and Letters Gold Medal, 1967. D.Litt., University of North Carolina Woman's College, Greensboro, 1949; Smith College, Northampton, Massachusetts, 1958; Maryville College, St. Louis, 1968; D.H.L., University of Michigan, Ann Arbor, 1954; University of Maryland, College Park, 1966; D.F.A., LaSalle College, Philadelphia, 1962. Vice-President, National Institute of Arts and Letters, 1950–52. Member, American Academy of Arts and Letters, 1967. Address: 6100 Westchester Park Drive, Apartments 1517–1518, College Park, Maryland 20740, U.S.A.

PUBLICATIONS

Novel

*Ship of Fools.* Boston, Little Brown, and London, Secker and Warburg, 1962.

Short Stories

*Flowering Judas.* New York, Harcourt Brace, 1930; augmented edition, as *Flowering Judas and Other Stories*, 1935; London, Cape, 1936.
*Hacienda: A Story of Mexico.* New York, Harrison of Paris, 1934; London, Simkin, 1935.
*Noon Wine.* Detroit, Schuman's, 1937.
*Pale Horse, Pale Rider: Three Short Novels.* New York, Harcourt Brace, 1938; London, Cape, 1939.
*The Leaning Tower and Other Stories.* New York, Harcourt Brace, 1944; London, Cape, 1945.
*The Collected Stories of Katherine Anne Porter.* London, Cape, 1964; New York, Harcourt Brace, 1965; augmented edition, Cape, 1967.

Other

*My Chinese Marriage* (as M. T. F.). New York, Duffield, 1921.
*Outline of Mexican Popular Arts and Crafts.* New York, Young and McCallister, 1922.
*What Price Marriage.* New York, Sears, 1927.
*The Days Before: Collected Essays and Occasional Writings.* New York, Harcourt Brace, 1952; London, Secker and Warburg, 1953; augmented edition, as *The Collected Essays and Occasional Writings of Katherine Anne Porter*, New York, Delacorte Press, 1970.
*A Defence of Circe* (essay). New York, Harcourt Brace, 1955.

Translator, *French Song Book.* Paris, Harrison, New York, Minton Balch, and London, Simpkin, 1933.
Translator, *The Itching Parrot.* by Fernandez de Lizard. New York, Doubleday, 1942.

Bibliography: *A Bibliography of the Works of Katherine Anne Porter* by Louis Waldrup and Shirley Ann Bauer, Metuchen, New Jersey, Scarecrow Press, 1969.

*        *        *

"Love," Katherine Anne Porter tells us, is "purely a creation of the human imagination." It is the "most important example," she says, "of how the imagination continually outruns the creature it inhabits."

Miss Porter has looked closely, and again and again, at the tension between our vision of love and our actual experience of love—in the stories she began publishing in the '20's, the short novels that came later, and in her recent long novel. Whether the vision that engages her characters is maternal, romantic, or a vision of friendship, their instinct is to try to realize its ideal possibilities—or what they imagine those possibilities to be. In Miss Porter's early work, this pursuit is vigorous and intense; in spite of painful losses, the characters survive, prepared, it seems, to continue the struggle. But gradually the disparity between what is imagined possible and what actually happens, becomes more damaging. It points not only to the fate of a single person, but to a larger social failure.

I should like to trace this change, as it is expressed in particular works—in the short stories, "María Concepción," and "He"; in the short novel, *Pale Horse, Pale Rider*; in the long story, "The Leaning Tower"; and, finally, in the one long novel, *Ship of Fools*.

María Concepción, the central figure in the story of that name, is a proud, energetic woman. She has worked hard, saved enough money to be married in the church—not behind it, like most in the village. As the story opens, her husband is at work, and she is on her way to market. She walks carefully in the middle of a dusty road, not stopping to take out the cactus thorns from her feet; her back is straight, her eyes serene, her walk, the "free, natural guarded ease of the primitive woman carrying an unborn child." Slung over her shoulder, their legs tightly roped together, are about a dozen live chickens. She is, we are told, "entirely contented."

But María Concepción's contentment is destroyed, for, quite accidentally, she discovers Juan, her husband, with María Rosa. Her pain at his desertion is ghastly, desiccating, as harmful to her body as to her spirit. Suddenly, we see the dusty road, the thorns endured and unavoidable, as adumbrations of her suffering.

We see also the stern, unbending figure, heedless of the wriggling, swollen-legged chickens. It is this unyielding aspect that prepares us for María Concepción's judgment upon María Rosa—"She is a whore," she declares, "she has no right to live." And when María kills one of the chickens, drawing "her knife across its throat, twisting the head off with the casual firmness she might use with the top of a beet," we know the contained, inhuman certainty that she brings to the destruction of "that sinful girl."

In the end, after Juan returns to her, María Concepción kills María Rosa, and takes María Rosa's newborn son to replace the child she herself lost. "He is mine," she says, as she lifts the squirming bundle at the head of the coffin.

That night, she sits near the doorway of her house; hears the breathing of her sleeping husband; bows her head over the sleeping child, "cradled in the hollow of her crossed legs"; and feels a "strange wakeful happiness."

María Concepción has recovered everything; she is again "entirely contented." For Juan, the story is quite different—her "wakeful happiness" is his "bad luck"; it means for him, as it meant for the fallen Adam, "dull and endless labor." But these feelings are quite outside María Concepción's concern. She disregards them, if she sees them at all, as casually as she disregards the squirming chickens she takes to market.

"María Concepción," Katherine Anne Porter's first published story, is a statement of incredible strength. María Concepción has been robbed of something at the very center of her existence—the dignity and order that marriage bestows upon maternity, and which, in her view, is essential to it. Her revenge has a biological fierceness that I think we must admire, even as we are appalled by its cruelty.

"He" is from Katherine Anne Porter's first collection of stories, *Flowering Judas*. Its central figure, Mrs. Whipple, is, like María Concepción, a family woman with family responsibilities. But she possesses none of María Concepción's confidence. From every point of view, her resources are skimpy.

We are told right off that "Life was very hard for the Whipples . . . hard to feed all the hungry mouths . . . hard to keep the children in flannels. . . ." Poor or not, Mrs. Whipple insists that "Nobody's going to get a chance to look down on us." This show of strength, it seems, is expressed in her feeling for her second son—the "He" of the title, "the simple-minded one" whom she loves, she claims, "better than . . . the other two children put together." She was, the narrator adds, "forever saying so."

For a while, Mrs. Whipple's claims about "Him" are reasonably easy to defend, for "He did grow and He never got hurt." He even does more than his share of the chores. But hard times do not let up for the Whipples, and when He has some sort of fit which he does not get over, they are told that they "better put Him in the County Home for treatment right away."

Long before Mrs. Whipple is faced with sending Him "off among strangers," we see that what she fears, even more than people "saying things all the time," are the things she herself says and does. She mutters, almost without knowing it, that he eats everything. When she sees Him leading the bull, she lets out a scream, although she believes that noise will scare the bull. And when the doctors say that he must be sent away, "all at once" she has a vision of family happiness. The misery and humiliation of her poverty, we realize, has been focused on Him.

When finally she takes Him away, dressing up in her black shirtwaist for she "couldn't stand to go looking like charity," an unexpected thing happens. As they settle down in the neighbor's car, she sees that this great, lolling, sick creature, unnamed except for his sex, is crying. Mrs. Whipple is astonished. He has expressed a personal feeling, an identity. Wrapping her arms about him, she herself begins to cry—"frightfully"—her true feelings released. No longer does she claim to love Him more than all the others, but only "as much as she possibly could." She could not make up to "Him for His life." "Oh, what a mortal pity," she laments, "He was ever born."

What we see in Mrs. Whipple's struggle for social respectability is a deep sense of personal despair. In her view, respectable people are able to feed their families, look prosperous, love their children. The difficulty is that in trying for these things, Mrs. Whipple must deceive not only her neighbors, but herself. For she is really poor, and she does not love him—not in the way she imagines she should.

But His crying touches her deeply and unexpectedly. She admits the love and guilt and resentment that she really feels. She also admits, it seems, that these complicated feelings are rooted in a truly "very hard" life—it is "a mortal pity He was ever born." If she finds relief in self-revelation and tears, she also uncovers a hard and complicated truth, one that she has not been prepared to deal with and that, perhaps, she can no longer look away from.

*Pale Horse, Pale Rider* contains all the rich, personal feeling that Mrs. Whipple's world lacks. It is about "the simple and lovely miracle of being two persons named Adam and Miranda, twenty-four years old each, alive and on earth at the same moment." But the uncomplicated exhilaration of falling in love is shadowed by death—the time is World War I, Adam is a soldier about to be shipped out, and the port town in which Adam and Miranda meet is threatened with an influenza epidemic.

The story begins with Miranda's dreaming—of a strangely familiar house where people are about to awaken, of a "lank greenish stranger . . . hanging about the place, welcomed by my grandfather, my great-aunt, my five times removed cousin, my decrepit hound and my silver kitten." "Why did they take to him, I wonder," says the dreamer. But when she saddles a horse and begins to ride, the stranger rides beside her, "easily, lightly . . . straight and elegant in dark shabby garments that flapped upon his bones; his pale face smiled in an evil trance."

The fear of death, the "lank greenish stranger," dominates Miranda's consciousness. On one side are images of life, inestimably valuable—of Adam, "all olive and tan" looking like "a fine healthy apple." On the other, strangers "cawing back and forth," funeral processions, and soldiers "dying like flies" of a "funny new disease."

Miranda's fear culminates in her illness. She comes down with the flu, feels the strange, unreal sensations of sickness, and, then, the miracle of recovery. But Adam too has got sick, and, during Miranda's month-long struggle, he dies. The loss is so bitter, the memory so real, that she speaks aloud to him— "I love you," she says, "Oh, let me see you once more." Quickly, sharply, she draws back—"Oh, no, that is not the way. . . ." The way, Miranda understands, is not through denial. She must acknowledge Adam's death, somehow learn to live without him.

She will succeed, we may suppose, for there is a perverse strength, quite beyond conscious decision, that will carry her though. It is the "particle of being" that has sustained her in her illness: "that knew itself alone, that relied upon nothing beyond itself for strength; not susceptible to any appeal or inducement, being itself composed entirely of one single motive, the stubborn will to live. . . . Trust me, the hard unwinking angry point of light said. Trust me, I stay." Miranda's life has been made empty by grief, but the "hard, unwinking angry point of light" persists, merciless and unwilling to shut out the "dead cold light of tomorrow" that she fears.

The works I have discussed are about people deeply involved with one another—families and lovers. "The Leaning Tower" is about a young man living among strangers.

Charles Upton, an American hoping to become a painter, goes to Berlin, his first stop in Europe. The time is around 1930. He has gone there because a childhood friend, now dead, had "made it seem the one desirable place to be." "If you don't go to Berlin," Kuno had said, "you miss everything"—the streets are "polished like a table top," the buildings, "all stone and marble." The vision Kuno had given him was of "a great shimmering city of castles towering in the misty sky."

What he actually finds is a bleak, joyless place. The beggars stand in slushy snow, ragged and truly starving. The shops are empty. The hotel keepers behave like robbers. When he tries to return a pair of socks, the shopkeeper breaks into tears. Everywhere need is painful, embarrassing.

But it is not only the look of the city and the suffering of strangers that he comes to find disturbing. He takes a room in a pension, a "monstrosity" with heavy velvet hangings, and becomes friends with the pensioners—Herr Bussen, a philosophy student; Hans, from Heidelberg, recovering from a dueling wound; and Tadeusz, a Pole, studying piano. Much of what happens there is puzzling to Charles—the dueling scar, which others call a "real beauty," is repugnant to him; casual impersonal insults—Platt Deutsch are "stupid beyond hope"—make him uneasy. He is unnerved by the fragile truce that exists among them and often dissolves into irritation and strange nationalistic defenses.

The culmination of his stay is going with his new friends to a cabaret on New Year's Eve. The evening is successful—they talk, argue, dance, lock arms at midnight, go home "lordly drunk." But during the evening, Charles realizes, that they have looked at each other in cold hostility—Germans "will be the last race on earth to be civilized"; Poles "have contributed exactly nothing to world-culture"; Americans are "coldhearted indifferent people." Finally, Hans tells them that in the next war, the German will win. All object—they simply want to teach, play the piano, paint. But Hans insists, fingering his dueling scar, "I know what will happen."

When Charles gets home, he notices that a small plaster replica of the Leaning Tower of Pisa has been put back in his room. When he first came, he had picked up the little Tower, touched it lightly, and to his astonishment, it had "simply crumbled." Now, the landlady has patched it together again. He sees it there—"leaning, suspended, perpetually ready to fall but never falling quite, the venturesome little object, a mistake in the first place. . . ." Suddenly, the little Tower means something to him. In his dizzy, tired state, he is not sure what. But he feels something "perishable but threatening, uneasy, hanging over his head."

What the Tower illuminates, we understand, is Charles Upton's experience of Berlin. We recall the hostility among the students, the mention of war, the easily tipped anger. And we know that what Charles Upton is really seeing there is society "leaning . . . perpetually ready to fall. We know also that he is seeing his own image, for he has felt a deeply personal threat in this alien world. Gradually, his own fate has become linked with its social disintegration. Early New Year's morning, he senses the extent of the danger. As he tries to think, he feels suddenly "an infernal desolation of the spirit, the chill and knowledge of death in him."

In the stories and short novels I have discussed, and generally, I think, in Miss Porter's work, the characters are presented sympathetically. We understand Mrs. Whipple's hostility toward her son; Miranda's bitter loss of love; Charles Upton's fear of easily shattered human connections. We see in Maria, the one figure who overcomes her "bad luck," the force of a mythic figure. Her strength, so centered in herself, is surely connected with the "hard unwinking angry point of light" that Miranda is conscious of in her sickness.

Miss Porter's one long novel, *Ship of Fools*, presents us with a very different point of view. Written slowly, over a period of thirty years, the novel is about a voyage from Veracruz to Bremerhaven, Germany in 1931.

Almost every passenger suffers from serious threats and losses. But what we notice about them is not their suffering. Mrs. Treadwell, taught in her youth that "Life was meant to be pleasant, generous, simple," has found that life is "quite disagreeable." Her refuge is to keep away from the "threat of human nearness, of feeling." She goes to her cabin, speaking and smiling "in the same tone and the same smile" for each person she meets, until finally, in the cabin, she is still smiling "into the garments" she carefully unpacks. Timid Frau Schmitt, in mourning for her husband's death and the ruin of all their plans, goes to Sunday morning Mass, gives herself up to "soft emotions . . . mingled love and prayer"—and glances at her fellow-worshipers, the "repellent" Spaniards. William Freytag, anguished over the social hatred that threatens his beloved Jewish wife, comforts himself: "our children's blood will flow as pure as mine, your tainted stream will be cleansed in their German veins." Herr Löwenthal, tortured by gentile food and gentile company, passes the Catholic Mass and restrains "his impulse to spit until he had passed beyond the line of vision of the worshipers." The Captain, who remembers with pride a cruelly authoritarian childhood, has a fantasy of turning "one of those really elegant portable machine guns on a riotous mob somewhere."

What fixes our attention is the self-centered cruelty we see in these passengers—not the humiliations that may in some way account for their behavior. If we are presented with some few passengers who measure up to human standards, their effect is too slight to change our general response to the voyage.

We recall the concentrated and deeply personal struggles of the shorter works; our close and sympathetic view of what they meant. In *Ship of Fools*, as we have seen, our point of view changes.

The change is related, I suggest, to a radical change in scale—the ship is the world, and its passengers are strangers to each other. In this large impersonal context, the possibility of any kind of human relationship is threatened. Distance and separateness are expressed on every level. Miss Porter looks at the individual characters, as one coming in from the outside, observing what she sees there with the cold, unswerving clarity of a total stranger.

The passengers look at each other as strangers. At the beginning, as they come on board, they seem to say, "So there you are again, I never saw you before in my life." As the voyage gets underway, the distance between them does not noticeably lessen. They join in superficial, often vicious, socializing; but their small, mean private histories remain separate, untouched by the larger world around them. At the end, Jenny, a young American, says: "We all remember we're strangers and don't like each other. . . . God, I'd hate to think I'd ever get even a postcard from anybody on this ship again, as long as I live!" There is little danger—the passengers separate casually, scatter at various ports, some in the middle of the night, without anyone even seeing them leave.

Miss Porter says at the beginning of her book, "I am a passenger on that ship." So are we all, and it is important that we understand the conditions of the voyage. Miss Porter has shown us the dangers. What she leaves out are the possibilities of sympathy. But without these possibilities, I do not have much heart to make the voyage. At the end of her long book, I feel, as Charles Upton felt on New Year's morning, "an infernal desolation of the spirit."

—Jacqueline Hoefer

**POWELL, Anthony (Dymoke).**   British.   Born in London, 21 December 1905. Educated at Eton College, Buckinghamshire; Balliol College, Oxford, M.A. Served in the Welch Regiment, 1939–41, and in the Army Intelligence Corps, 1941–45, rising to the rank of Major: awarded Order of the White Lion, Czechoslovakia; Order of Leopold II, Belgium; Oaken Crown and Croix de Guerre, Luxembourg. Married Lady Violet Pakenham in 1934; has two sons. Worked for Duckworth, publishers, London, 1926–35; Scriptwriter, Warner Brothers of Great Britain, 1936; Literary Editor, *Punch*, London, 1953–58; Reviewer for the *Daily Telegraph*, *Times Literary Supplement*, and other London papers. Trustee, National Portrait Gallery, London, since 1962. Recipient: Black Memorial Prize, 1958. D.Litt., University of Sussex, 1971. C.B.E. (Commander, Order of the British Empire), 1956. Address: The Chantry, near Frome, Somerset, England.

PUBLICATIONS

Novels

   *Afternoon Men.*   London, Duckworth, 1931; New York, Holt, 1932.
   *Venusburg.*   London, Duckworth, 1932; New York, Periscope Holliday, 1952.
   *From a View to a Death.*   London, Duckworth, 1933; as *Mr. Zouch: Superman: From a View to a Death*, New York, Vanguard Press, 1934; as *From a View to a Death*, Boston, Little Brown, 1964.
   *Agents and Patients.*   London, Duckworth, 1936; New York, Periscope Holliday, 1952.
   *What's Become of Waring.*   London, Cassell, 1939; Boston, Little Brown, 1963.
   *A Dance to the Music of Time:*
     *A Question of Upbringing.*   London, Heinemann, and New York, Scribner, 1951.
     *A Buyer's Market.*   London, Heinemann, 1952; New York, Scribner, 1953.
     *The Acceptance World.*   London, Heinemann, 1955; New York, Farrar Straus, 1956.
     *At Lady Molly's.*   London, Heinemann, 1957; Boston, Little Brown, 1958.
     *Casanova's Chinese Restaurant.*   London, Heinemann, and Boston, Little Brown, 1960.
     *The Kindly Ones.*   London, Heinemann, and Boston, Little Brown, 1962.
     *The Valley of Bones.*   London, Heinemann, and Boston, Little Brown, 1964.
     *The Soldier's Art.*   London, Heinemann, and Boston, Little Brown, 1966.
     *The Military Philosophers.*   London, Heinemann, 1968; Boston, Little Brown, 1969.
     *Books Do Furnish a Room.*   London, Heinemann, and Boston, Little Brown, 1971.

Plays

   *The Garden God and The Rest I'll Whistle: The Text of Two Plays.*   London, Heinemann, 1971; Boston, Little Brown, 1972.

Other

   *John Aubrey and His Friends.*   London, Heinemann, 1948; New York, Scribner, 1949; revised edition, New York, Barnes and Noble, 1963; Heinemann, 1964.

   Editor, *Novels of High Society from the Victorian Age.*   London, Pilot Press, 1947.
   Editor, *Brief Lives and Other Selected Writings of John Aubrey.*   London, Cresset Press, and New York, Scribner, 1949.

Critical Studies: *The Novels of Anthony Powell* by Robert K. Morris, Pittsburgh, University of Pittsburgh Press, 1968; *Anthony Powell: A Quintet, Sextet and War* by John Russell, Bloomington, Indiana University Press, 1970; "Anthony Powell Issue" of *Summary* (London), Autumn 1970; "Sisyphus Descending: Mythical Patterns in the Novels of Anthony Powell" by Frederick Karl, in *Mosaic* (Winnipeg, Manitoba), vol. 4, no. 3, 1971.

\* \* \*

Anthony Powell has been writing books for over forty years, though it is only in the last ten that he has emerged as one of a small handful of contemporary British novelists who can reasonably be considered major. His reputation rests almost exclusively on the long work-in-progress, *A Dance to the Music of Time*, a panoramic sequence of extraordinary scope and complexity. A work that has never relinquished its surface brilliance for portraying the insular, private, self-contained, snobbish world of the British upper and middle classes has more latterly become a vast canvas on all English life between the wars and afterwards, and in the profoundest way no less than a comic epic on time, history and change.

Powell's novelistic career falls into two parts with World War II as the convenient dividing line. The five novels written in the thirties are wittily structured and skillfully textured, still of some critical interest, but hinting only imperceptibly at the great achievement to come. *Afternoon Men* is perhaps most representative of the thirties' ethos and Powell's early style. Its atmosphere is charged with the insouciance and paralysis of "the lost generation," and resonates with echoes of Waugh and Huxley, though Waugh's bright young things have become older and tarnished, some even rusty, while Huxley's windy intellectuals and poseurs have declined into frustrated, bored, laconic, loveless drifters. *From a View to a Death* is the best of the pre-war books; retrospectively it is certainly the most important, anticipating in its several character sketches the more fully realized and rounded portraits of eccentrics in *The Music of Time*, and thematically introducing a dualism of human nature that has become peculiarly associated with Powell's artistic vision and with the thrust and core of his sequence: the opposition of the man of will and the man of imagination, the power-hungry and the sensualist.

Powell began *The Music of Time* shortly after the war, projecting it initially as six volumes, then expanding the plan to twelve. In a rare aside on his work, Powell stated in 1961 that the series "is concerned with the inter-relations of individuals, their lives and love affairs, and is intended to illustrate and bring up to date considerations of the way in which the middle and upper classes live in England." This confidence proved something of a false scent to his early critics, who tended to read the series as biography or sociology with fiction as mere overlay; nor (in all fairness to them) were its intricacies and formidable design apparent even after the first trilogy: *A Question of Upbringing*, set at Eton and Oxford during the twenties; *A Buyer's Market*, centered in a party-going ambience similar to that of *Afternoon Men*; and *The Acceptance World*, dealing with various gambits to make it both sexually and professionally in the London of the thirties. Narrated leisurely, coolly, and at times in a way that seems maddeningly pointless by Nicholas Jenkins—the hero-narrator of the entire sequence—the first three volumes interweave his life with the lives of a growing nucleus of acquaintances, introduce almost gratuitously several amiable eccentrics, and turn potentially dramatic confrontations into low-keyed comedy of manners.

Looking back over ten volumes of the series, however, one realizes that Powell, from the beginning, has remained consistent to his title and controlling metaphor, both inspired by the painting of Poussin in which "the seasons, hand in hand and facing outward, tread in rhythm to the notes of the lyre that the winged and naked greybeard plays." Like the Seasons, Powell's dancers step "slowly, methodically, sometimes a trifle awkwardly, in evolutions that take recognisable shape: or [break] into seemingly meaningless gyrations, while partners disappear only to reappear again, once more giving pattern to the spectacle." The world of *The Music of Time*, then, is generated through continuing change, though what Powell does with the notion is unique. By seeing all possible, shifting, interchangeable patterns, but by placing the burden of interpreting them squarely on his narrator, he makes the present the center of the novel, enlarges the most underplayed actions or contracts overblown ones without focusing on their immediate significance, integrates individual steps of the dance into the greater flux, and charts necessarily changing sensibilities against the continuum of human history.

Such is the linear movement *in* time, but there is also the vertical movement of *time*: its qualitative rather than quantitative function, the thing-in-itself that makes one "unable ... to control the steps of the dance." As Nick says in *The Kindly Ones*, "Time can play within its own folds tricks that emphasize the insecurity of those who trust themselves over much to that treacherous concept." The prime mover that does not ostensibly move, does—in a sequence continually reshaping the dance—move, itself become part of a "kaleidoscope, the colours of which are always changing, always the same." Sheer, protean, fluid, spatial, time is the backdrop for posing and transposing character, theme and plot, but also the dominating archetype embracing all of life and art and of those who would partake in them.

A dozen or more archetypal patterns throughout the sequence would confirm it as the work of a mythopoeicist rather than realist. Nevertheless, Powell has created a remarkable gallery of "real" characters: originals like Giles Jenkins, General Conyers, Lady Molly Jeavons, Lord Erridge, tinged with the harmless grotesqueries of human behavior; men of imagination like Edgar Deacon, Hugh Moreland, Captain Rowland Gwatkin, Charles Stringham and Peter Templer, romantic transplants from another age who suffer "the strain of living simultaneously in two different historical periods"; and the men of will, cold, mechanical, disciplined, controlling the times and harmonizing with them, of which Kenneth Widmerpool is the most notorious and vital. He is certainly one of the great contemporary comic villains as well. Son of a liquid manure manufacturer, and fat-boy butt of his school fellows at Eton (*A Question of Upbringing*), Widmerpool ascends with astonishing persistence and phoenix-like regularity to positions of status and power. From a highly competent businessman (*The Acceptance World*), to army colonel (*The Military Philosophers*) and Labour M.P. (*Books Do Furnish a Room*), he has moved uninterruptedly and unfeelingly toward success. Yet though Widmerpool is a super-competent, specious, insensitive, self-aggrandizing and dangerous egomaniac, one cannot dislike him. In the dance he occupies a pivotal position; and being but one more partner in the just and harmonious evolutions of time, he, like the several hundred other characters, is treated comically, not satirically. Powell accepts Widmerpool as a phenomenon of the ethos without attempting to correct the failings of either.

More importantly, perhaps, Widmerpool becomes the perfect foil for Nick Jenkins' emergent decency, dignity and probity. Proper, fashionable, sincere, innocent, self-reliant, Nick is above the average, upper class all-right-guy wanting to fit in and keep from becoming defeated, excessively eccentric, too ostentatiously successful, or too scandalously simple. Nick operates through a comic stoicism that one feels is Powell's as well. He witnesses dissolution about him and charts a course between extremes—measuring the smallest signs or gestures against contemporary standards and holding fast to sensible and humane values. From his shadowy beginnings as narrator and his often obvious role as author-surrogate, he has blossomed into a full-blown hero; for above and beyond other things, he has learned how a student of history and society should confront the uses of the past and of men. It is the Nick of *At Lady Molly's* who finally understands that excess of either power or sensuality may become the principal destroyer of society; the Nick of *Casanova's Chinese Restaurant*, thrust into a world of decaying marriages, infidelity, frustration, failure and suicide, whose faith in morals and ethics is shaken, but not annihilated; and the Nick of the war trilogy (*The Valley of Bones*, *The Soldier's Art*, *The Military Philosophers*) who, above all others, remains human in the face of impersonal and fatal dehumanizing processes. Nick's growth and attitude throughout the sequence—and the added realization that through the artifice of fiction he becomes his own best example—prescribe the totally humanistic, logical and balanced perspective on the not always joyless, but admittedly unpleasant themes of change and decay.

For Nick, like Powell, is a life-affirmer, not life-denier; decay is but one part of change, growth is another. If *The Music of Time* has sustained itself over twenty years, if many of the dancers have danced so far, it is because the actions of becoming—and whether one becomes a Widmerpool or a Jenkins is quite beside the point—are the most concrete ways of presenting abstract theories of time, and the comic writer, persisting in his belief that the "past, just as the present, had to be accepted for what it thought and what it was," their most balanced interpreter. Over these ten volumes, Powell has not only shown awareness of the ways in which the individual changes against the sameness of time, but how (in Nick's words again) "the sequence of inevitable sameness that follows a person through life" plays against time's flux. Powell's genius, it seems, lies in the ability to invert these basic conditions without sacrificing meaning or character; to make the reader realize, by means of the authorial mythic vision and comic control, that both the random movements of life and the patterned movements of the dance can be seen as the perfect movement of art.

—Robert K. Morris

---

**POWERS, J(ames) F(arl).** American. Born in Jacksonville, Illinois, 8 July 1917. Educated at Quincy College Academy, Illinois; Northwestern University, Chicago campus, 1938–40. Married the writer Betty Wahl in 1946; has five children. Editor, Illinois Historical Records Survey, 1938. Taught at St. John's University, Collegeville, Minnesota, 1947; Marquette University, Milwaukee, Wisconsin, 1949–51; University of Michigan, Ann Arbor, 1956–57; Smith College, Northampton, Massachusetts, 1965–66. Recipient: National Institute of Arts and Letters grant, 1948; Guggenheim Fellowship, 1948; Rockefeller Fellowship, 1954, 1957, 1967; National Book Award, 1963. Member, National Institute of Arts and Letters. Address: c/o Doubleday and Company, 277 Park Avenue, New York, New York 10017, U.S.A.

PUBLICATIONS

Novel

  *Morte d'Urban.*  New York, Doubleday, and London, Gollancz, 1962.

Short Stories

  *Prince of Darkness and Other Stories.*  New York, Doubleday, 1947; London, Lehmann, 1948.
  *The Presence of Grace.*  New York, Doubleday, and London, Gollancz, 1956.

*          *          *

When the stories of J. F. Powers first appeared in American literary magazines during the 1940's, they were welcomed by many readers with an enthusiasm perhaps even greater than their own merits would otherwise have generated, for here was a new writer—a northern writer, a mid-western writer—whose stories carried as much creative authority as did the southern writing that had dominated American fiction for three decades. Here were the same structural finesse and verbal sensitivity, but now applied to northern materials. And here was the same concern for ultimate value, now transplanted to a milieu in which some southern critics had contended it could never flourish.

In short, Powers wrote about Chicago and the small towns of Illinois and Wisconsin with skills learned essentially from such writers as Caroline Gordon, Eudora Welty, Robert Penn Warren, and other southern fictionists, and thus brought to his materials a more sensitive fictional approach than that of earlier midwestern writers, such as Sinclair Lewis, James T. Farrell, or Nelson Algren. To put it another way, a native metaphysical story-writer, using the term perhaps somewhat loosely, had appeared in the very home of American naturalism and had taken at least some of naturalism's themes for his own, with results that were stimulating to say the least.

Powers had a remarkable ear for the dialects and idioms of midwestern speech, and could put together pages of dialogue with perfect fluency, realism, and economy. At the same time he could construct stories of great significance from the smallest episodes, using reticence of symbol and event to suggest meaning and feeling. As a stylist, he was plain rather than fancy, with a classical instinct for concision and a lively sense of prose rhythm. In general, his early stories centered on two main areas of experience: social conflict in Chicago, especially between whites and blacks, and the lives of the Roman Catholic clergy in America. Both these themes appeared powerfully in his first book, *Prince of Darkness*.

The first, that of racial conflict and the misery of Negroes in northern American cities, is best developed in the story entitled "He Don't Plant Cotton," which tells about three black jazz musicians, two men and a woman, who are fired from their job in a third-rate Chicago night club after a disagreement with drunken white customers. The story is memorable on several counts. For one, Powers wrote about jazz and its place in Negro sensibility without any of the mawkishness or plain musical stupidity that has characterized most other white and even much black writing on the subject. For another, without resorting to violence of either speech or event, he conveyed the real violence of feeling that dominates the black community's response to its predicament in America, and it is worth noting that this was done a full decade before the beginning of the modern civil rights movement. Nothing since then has surpassed Powers' story in seriousness, integrity, and artistic relevance, though much recent writing has been more turbulent.

The second theme, that of Catholic religious life in America, is perhaps best exemplified in the early story called "Lions, Harts, Leaping Does," in which Powers wrote about an elderly Franciscan friar plagued by intellectual self-doubt and spiritual anxiety. As he approaches his own death, his small shortcomings seem more and more ominous to him, until in a state of demoralization he cannot experience the least impulse toward good without questioning it and reversing his motives. Very subtly Powers contrasts this spiritual finicality with the real crassness and brutishness of modern commercial civilization, showing the true value of spiritual discipline even in its own weakest condition.

These two stories, "Lions, Harts, Leaping Does" and "He Don't Plant Cotton," belong among the best short stories written in America during the years of mid-century.

In Powers' second book, *The Presence of Grace*, the religious theme became dominant, and the mood turned from that of spiritual anguish to something more objective and satirical. Some stories in the collection moved toward whimsy, including several narrated by a rectory cat, but though they won much popularity for Powers when they were first published in *The New Yorker*, in retrospect they seem comparatively insubstantial. Other stories dealt more toughly with subversion in the Church and with the restlessness of modern clerics who are drawn from true priestliness by ideas of status, power, and popular success; and these were the stories which culminated in Powers' third and most important book, the satirical novel entitled *Morte d'Urban*.

Father Urban is a proselytizing priest attached to the (fictional) Clementine Order. Beginning with the purest motives, a desire to bring renewed strength and spiritual influence to his Order, he moves more and more in the direction of a manipulator, a spiritual wheeler-and-dealer, in the most degraded American commercial tradition. In other words, he is progressively subverted by the methods and ideals of the wealthy businessmen whom he parasitizes, and though for a time his efforts, like theirs, succeed remarkably, in the end they lead to catastrophe. The novel is perfectly controlled, perfectly articulated in its elaboration of the levels of religious and lay sensibility. What saves it from being merely an "in" novel for Catholic intellectuals is its clear if indirect exposure of the broad social forces at work behind the dereliction of certain elements in the Church.

*Morte d'Urban* is the best American satire of any kind in recent decades, a good deal better, for instance, than Katherine Anne Porter's *Ship of Fools*, which by comparison is messy, overambitious, and inconclusive. Yet when the two books appeared, both in the same year, *Ship of Fools* won most of the critical attention and popularity. Since then little has been heard from Powers. One hopes that he was not unduly disheartened by the misfortunes attending the publication of *Morte d'Urban*, and that soon new work of his will come before us.

—Hayden Carruth

---

**PRESCOTT, H(ilda) F(rances) M(argaret).** British. Born in Latchford, Cheshire, 22 February 1896. Educated at Wallasey High School, Cheshire; Lady Margaret Hall, Oxford (Jephson Scholar), B.A.; Manchester University, M.A. Jubilee Research Fellow, Royal Holloway College, Surrey, 1958–60. Recipient: Black Memorial Prize, for non-fiction, 1941; Christopher Medal, 1953. D.Litt., Durham University, 1957. Fellow, Royal Society of Literature, 1953. Address: Orchard Piece, Charlbury, Oxfordshire, England.

PUBLICATIONS

Novels

    *The Unhurrying Chase.* London, Constable, and New York, Dodd Mead, 1925.
    *The Lost Fight.* London, Constable, and New York, Dodd Mead, 1928.
    *Son of Dust.* London, Constable, 1932; New York, Macmillan, 1956.
    *Dead and Not Buried.* London, Constable, and New York, Macmillan, 1938.
    *The Man on a Donkey: A Chronicle.* London, Eyre and Spottiswoode, 2 vols., 1952; New York, Macmillan, 1952.

Other

    *Spanish Tudor: "The Life of Bloody Mary."* London, Constable, and New York, Columbia University Press, 1940; revised edition, London, Eyre and Spottiswoode, and New York, Macmillan, 1953.
    *Friar Felix at Large: A Fifteenth-Century Pilgrimage to the Holy Land.* New Haven, Connecticut, Yale University Press, 1950; as *Jerusalem Journey: Pilgrimage to the Holy Land,* London, Eyre and Spottiswoode, 1954.
    *Once to Sinai: The Further Pilgrimage of Friar Felix Fabri.* London, Eyre and Spottiswoode, 1957; New York, Macmillan, 1958.

    Translator, *Flamenca,* by "Bernardet the Troubadour." London, Constable, 1933.

\*          \*          \*

With the exception of *Dead and Not Buried*, an articulate, well observed, but basically conventional thriller, H. F. M. Prescott's fictional work has been in the field of historical romance. She is also a historian and her detailed knowledge of the past, sense of period, and sympathy with religious experience led to the achievement of her most recent novel, *The Man on a Donkey*, published in 1952 and brought out as a Penguin Modern Classic in 1969.

Her earlier historical novels are interesting principally for their relationship to this work. *The Unhurrying Chase*, *The Lost Fight* and *Son of Dust*, all set in early medieval France, are preoccupied with the conflict between man's spiritual and carnal impulses, and wring an agony from this conflict that at times seems self-indulgent. The novels' heroes seem happier in renunciation (whether of God or man) than in fulfilment, and coincidence and motiveless actions are invoked to keep them in this state. The reader's feeling of unease is increased by the books' fascination with physical horror—the gouging out of eyes, leprosy, mortifications of the flesh—and by their failure to communicate at all specifically the religious emotion behind the colourful trappings and harsh commands of medieval Catholicism. The books are to some extent redeemed by their passages of delightful, if occasionally repetitive, natural description, and, above all, by their vivid and knowledgeable evocations of the more worldly aspects of medieval life.

*The Man on a Donkey* is happily conceived to incorporate the strengths of Miss Prescott's earlier books and avoid their weaknesses. The book's central subject is firmly historical—the dissolution of the English monasteries and the northern resistance to change that resulted in the Pilgrimage of Grace—and the conflict between religious and secular loyalties becomes at once concrete and credible. The book is written in chronicle form, and the lives of five variously placed men and women of sixteenth-century England are skilfully interwoven. The chronicle form again promotes objectivity and capitalises on the use of invigorating detail, while its sense of controlled movement through time gives the book sufficient impetus to sustain its considerable length. The variety of characters, only some of whom, most importantly Robert Aske, Grand Captain of the Pilgrimage, are historical, gives the book remarkable breadth, a breadth made solid by the fact that the characters are consistently realised as individuals rather than types.

Because religious feeling is tied on the one hand to historical events and on the other to individual experiences of religion—the relaxed faith of Aske, the worried ambition of a reforming priest—the reader can understand and sympathise with it. An exception is the strain of mystical excitement that threads through the book in the person of Malle, a simple-minded servant-woman who sees visions of Christ and darkness in the dales; this, together with the strained exaltation of the ending, lacks the conviction of the rest of the book. As a vividly detailed and comprehensive re-creation of the life of sixteenth-century England, and as a finely shaped thing in itself, *The Man on a Donkey* must nevertheless be considered an ambitious and largely successful work.

—Mary Conroy

---

**PRICE, (Edward) Reynolds.** American. Born in Macon, North Carolina, 1 February 1933. Educated at Duke University, Durham, North Carolina, 1951–55 (Angier Duke Scholar), A. B. (summa cum laude) 1955 (Phi Beta Kappa); Merton College, Oxford, 1955–58 (Rhodes Scholar), B.Litt. 1958. Since 1958, Member of the English Faculty, Duke

University: Assistant Professor, 1961–68; Associate Professor since 1968. Writer-in-Residence, University of North Carolina, Chapel Hill, 1965; University of Kansas, Lawrence, 1967, 1969; University of North Carolina, Greensboro, 1971; Glasgow Professor, Washington and Lee University, Lexington, Virginia, 1971. Editor, *The Archive*, Durham, 1954–55; Advisory Editor, *Shenandoah*, Trumansburg, New York. Recipient: Faulkner Foundation Prize, 1963; Guggenheim Fellowship, 1964; National Association of Independent Schools Award, 1964; National Endowment for the Arts Fellowship, 1967. Address: 4813 Duke Station, Durham, North Carolina 27706, U.S.A.

PUBLICATIONS

Novels

    *A Long and Happy Life*.   New York, Atheneum, and London, Chatto and Windus, 1962.
    *A Generous Man*.   New York, Atheneum, 1966; London, Chatto and Windus, 1967.
    *Love and Work*.   New York, Atheneum, and London, Chatto and Windus, 1968.

Short Stories

    *The Names and Faces of Heroes*.   New York, Atheneum, and London, Chatto and Windus, 1963.
    *Permanent Errors*.   New York, Atheneum, 1970; London, Chatto and Windus, 1971.

Verse

    *Late Warning: Four Poems*.   New York, Albondocani, 1968.

Critical Studies: "A Conversation with Reynolds Price" by Wallace Kaufman, in *Shenandoah* (Trumansburg, New York), Summer 1966; "The Reynolds Price Who Outgrew the Southern Pastoral" by Theodore Solotaroff, in *Saturday Review* (New York), 26 September 1970.

Reynolds Price comments:

I try—in novels, stories, poems—to understand the ways in which I suspect the world to be bound by secret or ignored but probably comic relations and to set the findings in honest usable order, an order which will make clear and irresistible the demands those relations make of our lives.

—From *Who's Who in America*, vol. 36,
1970–71, Chicago, Marquis, 1970.

\*     \*     \*

Reynolds Price has, in five volumes of fiction, moved from detailed examination of North Carolina rural life to an intense concern with the artist's vision of reality. Beginning with the tragicomic saga of the Mustian family (*A Long and Happy Life*, *A Generous Man*, stories in *The Names and Faces of Heroes*), he has come in *Love and Work* and *Permanent Errors* to wrestle with narrative forms closer to the bone. In the preface to *Permanent Errors*, Price described his work as "the attempt to isolate in a number of lives the central error of act, will, understanding which, once made, has been permanent, incurable, but whose diagnosis and palliation are the hopes of continuance."

This applies to all Price's fiction. *A Long and Happy Life* is the inside story of Rosacoke Mustian, a country girl seeking a conventional life with an unconventional young man, Wesley Beavers. Her error is that she conceives "a long and happy life" only in the clichéd terms of romance, of settled-wedded-bliss tradition. She reviews her life, her family's life, is discontent, becomes pregnant by Wesley and finally comes to see him and herself in larger terms, terms of myth, in a Christmas pageant which shows her the complete (and divine) meanings of motherhood, birth and love.

Myth becomes the vehicle of self-understanding more overtly in *A Generous Man*, which shows the Mustian family several years earlier. It describes an allegorical search for an escaped circus python, a giant serpent named Death, and the discovery of a lost treasure. Milo Mustian describes the stifling forces of convention which circumscribe their lives: "... it's what nine-tenths of the humans born since God said 'Adam!' have thought was a life, planned out for themselves—all my people, my Mama, my Daddy (it was what strangled him), Rosacoke. . . ." Only by transcending the everyday, by seeing human life in larger terms, can the individual escape the slow strangulation of "permanent errors" and find direction and meaning in existence.

Price's fiction has become increasingly abstract and complex as he has moved to a more inward vision. From the first he has used sets of images and metaphors to suggest a mysterious or magical reality beyond his pastoral settings. He has deepened this metaphorical (and psychological) interest in *Love and Work* and *Permanent Errors*, where the protagonists are no longer the eccentric pastoral figures of the Mustian clan but are closer to Price's own viewpoint. Price's fiction has always dealt with confusion of the heart and alienation of the mind, but the more recent work draws its images and symbols more directly from Price's own experience—his family, a visit to Dachau prison camp, the writer's situation. The grotesqueness and unfamiliarity of the legendary Mustian clan are replaced by more familiar and universal facts of contemporary life.

Love and death are polarities in Price's work—how to save life from death, how to prevent life from becoming deathly, stale, void of myth and magic? The theme appears most clearly in *A Generous Man*, when the Mustians set out to find and kill "Death," the great serpent, and when they are finally told, "Death is dead." In the course of this magical hunt, Milo Mustian comes to understand what he must do to save himself from slow death of a clichéd life, Rato Mustian, the wise fool, grapples with Death and escapes its coils through his cunning folly, Rosacoke moves from complete innocence to the dawn of maturity. In his later fiction, Price has moved from symbols of external life to more internalized ones: sleep, dreams, a writer seeking a relationship between love and work, self and others, private life and shared life.

Price's fiction describes the individual's perceptions of himself and of the realities around him, the uses of imagination. His characters travel on a quest for the potency of myth and the ability to transcend a closed vision of everyday reality. They move toward permanent truth through "permanent errors."

—William J. Schafer

**PRIESTLEY, J(ohn) B(oynton).** British. Born in Bradford, Yorkshire, 13 September 1894. Educated at Trinity Hall, Cambridge, M.A. Served with the Duke of Wellington's and Devon regiments, 1914–19. Married the writer Jacquetta Hawkes in 1953. Regular Contributor to the *New Statesman*, London. President, P.E.N., London, 1936–37. Theatrical Manager, and Director of the Mask Theatre, London, 1938–39. Radio Lecturer, on the BBC programme Postcripts, during World War II. United Kingdom Delegate, and Chairman, UNESCO International Theatre Conference, Paris, 1947, and Prague, 1948; Chairman, British Theatre Conference, 1948; President, International Theatre Institute, 1949; Member, National Theatre Board, London, 1966–67. Recipient: Black Memorial Prize, 1930; Ellen Terry Award, 1948. LL.D., St. Andrews University; D.Litt., Birmingham and Bradford universities. Has refused three high official honours. Address: Kissing Tree House, Alveston, Stratford upon Avon, Warwickshire, England.

PUBLICATIONS

Novels

   *Adam in Moonshine*. London, Heinemann, and New York, Harper, 1927.
   *Benighted*. London, Heinemann, 1927; as *The Old Dark House*, New York, Harper, 1928.
   *Farthing Hall*, with Hugh Walpole. London, Macmillan, and New York, Doubleday, 1929.
   *The Good Companions*. London, Heinemann, and New York, Harper, 1929.
   *Angel Pavement*. London, Heinemann, and New York, Harper, 1930.
   *Faraway*. London, Heinemann, and New York, Harper, 1932.
   *I'll Tell You Everything*, with Gerald Bullett. London, Heinemann, and New York, Macmillan, 1933.
   *Wonder Hero*. London, Heinemann, and New York, Harper, 1933.
   *They Walk in the City: The Lovers in the Stone Forest*. London, Heinemann, and New York, Harper, 1936.
   *The Doomsday Men: An Adventure*. London, Heinemann, and New York, Harper, 1938.
   *Let the People Sing*. London, Heinemann, 1939; New York, Harper, 1940.
   *Black-Out in Gretley: A Story of—and for—Wartime*. London, Heinemann, and New York, Harper, 1942.
   *Daylight on Saturday: A Novel about an Aircraft Factory*. London, Heinemann, and New York, Harper, 1943.
   *Three Men in New Suits*. London, Heinemann, and New York, Harper, 1945.
   *Bright Day*. London, Heinemann, and New York, Harper, 1946.
   *Jenny Villiers: A Story of the Theatre*. London, Heinemann, and New York, Harper, 1947.
   *Festival at Farbridge*. London, Heinemann, 1951; as *Festival*, New York, Harper, 1951.
   *The Magicians*. London, Heinemann, and New York, Harper, 1954.
   *Low Notes on a High Level: A Frolic*. London, Heinemann, and New York, Harper, 1954.
   *Saturn over the Water: An Account of His Adventures in London, South America and Australia by Tim Bedford, Painter; Edited, with Some Preliminary and Concluding Remarks, by Henry Sulgrave and Here Presented to the Reading Public*. London, Heinemann, and New York, Doubleday, 1961.
   *The Thirty-First of June: A Tale of True Love, Enterprise and Progress in the Arthurian and ad-Atomic Ages*. London, Heinemann, 1961; New York, Doubleday, 1962.

*The Shapes of Sleep: A Topical Tale.*   London, Heinemann, and New York, Double-day, 1962.
*Sir Michael and Sir George: A Tale of COMSA and DISCUS and the New Elizabethans.* London, Heinemann, 1964; as *Sir Michael and Sir George: A Comedy of the New Elizabethans*, Boston, Little Brown, 1966.
*Lost Empires: Being Richard Herncastle's Account of His Life on the Variety Stage from November 1913 to August 1914, Together with a Prologue and Epilogue.*   London, Heinemann, 1965; Boston, Little Brown, 1966.
*It's an Old Country.*   London, Heinemann, and Boston, Little Brown, 1967.
*The Image Men: Out of Town and London End.*   London, Heinemann, 2 vols., 1968; as *The Image Men*, Boston, Little Brown, 1969.


## Short Stories

*Four-in-Hand* (includes essays).   London, Heinemann, 1934.
*Going Up: Stories and Sketches.*   London, Pan, 1950.
*The Other Place and Other Stories of the Same Sort.*   London, Heinemann, and New York, Harper, 1953.


## Plays

*The Good Companions*, with Edward Knoblock (produced London and New York, 1931).   London, French, 1935.
*Dangerous Corner* (produced London and New York, 1932).   London, Heinemann, and New York, French, 1932.
*The Roundabout* (produced Liverpool, London and New York, 1932).   London, Heinemann, and New York, French, 1933.
*Laburnum Grove: An Immoral Comedy* (produced London, 1933; New York, 1935). London, Heinemann, 1934; New York, French, 1935.
*Eden End* (produced London, 1934; New York, 1935).   London, Heinemann, 1934.
*Cornelius: A Business Affair in Three Transactions* (produced Birmingham and London, 1935).   London, Heinemann, 1935.
*Duet in Floodlight* (produced Liverpool and London, 1935).   London, Heinemann, 1935.
*Three Plays and a Preface* (includes *Dangerous Corner*, *Eden End* and *Cornelius*).   New York, Harper, 1935.
*Bees on the Boatdeck: A Farcical Tragedy* (produced London, 1936).   London, Heinemann, 1936.
*Spring Tide* (as Peter Goldsmith), with George Billam (produced London, 1936). London, Heinemann, and New York, French, 1936.
*Time and the Conways* (produced London, 1937; New York, 1938).   London, Heinemann, 1937; New York, Harper, 1938.
*I Have Been Here Before* (produced London, 1937; New York, 1938).   London, Heinemann, 1937; New York, Harper, 1938.
*People at Sea* (produced London, 1937).   London, Heinemann, 1937.
*Mystery at Greenfingers: A Comedy of Detection* (produced London, 1938).   London, French, 1937; New York, French, 1938.
*When We Are Married: A Yorkshire Farcical Comedy* (produced London, 1938; New York, 1939).   London, Heinemann, 1938; New York, French, 1940.
*Music at Night* (produced Malvern, Worcestershire, 1938).   London, French, 1947.
*Johnson over Jordan* (produced London, 1939).   Published as *Johnson over Jordan: The Play, And All about It (An Essay)*, London, Heinemann, and New York, Harper, 1939.

*Good Night, Children* (produced London, 1942).   Included in *Three Comedies*, 1945.
*Desert Highway* (produced Bristol, 1943; London, 1944).   London, French, 1944.
*They Came to a City* (produced London, 1943).   London, French, 1944.
*How Are They at Home: A Topical Comedy* (produced London, 1944).   Included in
   *Three Comedies*, 1945.
*Four Plays* (includes *Music at Night*, *The Long Mirror*, *They Came to a City*, and
   *Desert Highway*).   New York, Harper, 1944; London, Heinemann, 1945.
*The Long Mirror* (produced London, 1946).   Included in *Four Plays*, 1944.
*Three Comedies* (includes *Good Night, Children*; *The Golden Fleece*; and *How Are
   They at Home*).   London, Heinemann, 1945.
*An Inspector Calls* (produced Moscow, 1945; London, 1946; New York, 1947).   New
   York, Dramatists Play Service, 1945; London, Heinemann, 1947.
*The Rose and Crown.*   London, French, 1947.
*Ever Since Paradise: An Entertainment, Chiefly Referring to Love and Marriage* (pro-
   duced London, 1947).   London and New York, French, 1949.
*The Linden Tree* (produced Sheffield and London, 1947; New York, 1948).   London
   and New York, French, 1948.
*Plays.*   London, Heinemann, 3 vols., 1948–1950; New York, Harper, 3 vols., 1950–52.
*Home Is Tomorrow* (produced London, 1948).   London, Heinemann, 1949.
*The High Toby: A Play for the Toy Theatre* (produced London, 1954).   London,
   Penguin, 1948.
*The Olympians*, music by Arthur Bliss (produced London, 1949).   London, Novello,
   1949.
*Summer Day's Dream* (produced London, 1949).   London, French, 1950.
*Bright Shadows* (produced London, 1950).   London, French, 1950.
*Treasure on Pelican* (televised, 1951).   London, Evans, 1953.
*Dragon's Mouth*, with Jacquetta Hawkes (produced London, 1952; New York, 1955).
   London, Heinemann, 1952.
*Private Rooms: A One Act Comedy in the Viennese Style.*   London, French, 1953.
*Mother's Day.*   London, French, 1953.
*Try It Again* (produced London, 1965).   London, French, 1953.
*A Glass of Bitter.*   London, French, 1954.
*The White Countess*, with Jacquetta Hawkes (produced London, 1954).
*The Scandalous Affair of Mr. Kettle and Mrs. Moon* (produced London, 1955).   London,
   French, 1956.
*Those Our Actors* (produced Glasgow, 1956).
*Take the Fool Away* (produced Vienna, 1956).
*The Glass Cage* (produced Toronto and London, 1957).   London, French, 1958.
*The Thirty-First of June* (produced Toronto and London, 1957).
*The Pavilion of Masks* (produced Bristol, 1963).   London, French, 1958.
*A Severed Head*, with Iris Murdoch (produced Bristol and London, 1963; New York,
   1964).   London, Chatto and Windus, 1964.


Screenplays: *They Came to a City*, 1943; *The Foreman Went to France*, 1944; *Last
Holiday*, 1950; *An Inspector Calls*, 1954.

Plays produced on television.


Verse

*The Chapman of Rhymes* (juvenilia).   London, Alexander Moring, 1918.

Other

*Brief Diversions: Being Tales, Travesties and Epigrams.*  Cambridge, Bowes and Bowes, 1922.

*Papers from Lilliput.*  Cambridge, Bowes and Bowes, 1922.

*I for One.*  London, Lane, 1923; New York, Dodd Mead, 1924.

*Figures in Modern Literature.*  London, Wilson, and New York, Dodd Mead, 1924.

*Fools and Philosophers: A Gallery of Comic Figures from English Literature.*  London, Lane, 1925; as *The English Comic Characters*, New York, Dodd Mead, 1925.

*George Meredith.*  London, Macmillan, and New York, Macmillan, 1926.

*Talking: An Essay.*  London, Heinemann, and New York, Harper, 1926.

*Open House: A Book of Essays.*  London, Heinemann, and New York, Harper, 1927.

*Thomas Love Peacock.*  London, Macmillan, and New York, Macmillan, 1927.

*The English Novel.*  London, Benn, 1927; revised edition, London, Nelson, 1935.

*Too Many People and Other Reflections.*  New York and London, Harper, 1928.

*Apes and Angels: A Book of Essays.*  London, Methuen, 1929.

*The Balconinny and Other Essays.*  London, Methuen, 1929; as *The Balconinny*, New York, Harper, 1931.

*English Humour.*  London, Longman, 1929.

*The Town Major of Miraucourt.*  London, Heinemann, 1930.

*Self-Selected Essays.*  London, Heinemann, and New York, Harper, 1932.

*Albert Goes Through.*  London, Heinemann, and New York, Harper, 1933.

*English Journey: Being a Rambling but Truthful Account of What One Man Saw and Heard and Felt and Thought During a Journey Through England During the Autumn of the Year 1933.*  London, Heinemann-Gollancz, and New York, Harper, 1934.

*Midnight on the Desert: A Chapter of Autobiography.*  London, Heinemann, 1937; as *Midnight on the Desert: Being an Excursion into Autobiography During a Winter in America, 1935–1936*, New York, Harper, 1937.

*Rain upon Gadshill: A Further Chapter of Autobiography.*  London, Heinemann, and New York, Harper, 1939.

*Britain Speaks* (radio talks).  New York, Harper, 1940.

*Postscripts* (radio talks).  London, Heinemann, 1940.

*Out of the People.*  London, Collins, and New York, Harper, 1941.

*Britain at War.*  New York, Harper, 1942.

*British Women Go to War.*  London, Collins, 1943.

*Here Are Your Answers.*  London, Socialist Book Centre, 1944.

*Letter to a Returning Serviceman.*  London, Home and Van Thal, 1945.

*The Secret Dream: An Essay on Britain, America and Russia.*  London, Turnstile Press, 1946.

*Russian Journey.*  London, Writers Group of the Society for Cultural Relations with the USSR, 1946.

*Theatre Outlook.*  London, Nicholson and Watson, 1947.

*The Arts under Socialism: Being a Lecture Given to the Fabian Society, with a Postscript on What the Government Should Do for the Arts Here and Now.*  London, Turnstile Press, 1947.

*Delight.*  London, Heinemann, and New York, Harper, 1949.

*Journey down a Rainbow*, with Jacquetta Hawkes (travel).  London, Cresset Press, and New York, Harper, 1955.

*All about Ourselves and Other Essays.*  London, Heinemann, 1956.

*The Writer in a Changing Society.*  Aldington, Kent, Hand and Flower Press, 1956.

*Thoughts in the Wilderness* (essays).  London, Heinemann, and New York, Harper, 1957.

*The Art of the Dramatist: A Lecture Together with Appendices and Discursive Notes.*  London, Heinemann, 1957; Boston, The Writer, 1958.

*Topside; or, The Future of England: A Dialogue.*  London, Heinemann, 1958.

*The Story of Theatre.*  London, Rathbone, 1959; as *The Wonderful World of the Theatre,* New York, Doubleday, 1959.

*Literature and Western Man.*  London, Heinemann, and New York, Harper, 1960.

*William Hazlitt.*  London, Longman, 1960.

*Charles Dickens: A Pictorial Biography.*  London, Thames and Hudson, 1961; New York, Studio Publications, 1962.

*Margin Released: A Writer's Reminiscences and Reflections.*  London, Heinemann, 1962; New York, Harper, 1963.

*Man and Time.*  London, Aldus Books, and New York, Doubleday, 1964.

*Moments and Other Pieces.*  London, Heinemann, 1966.

*All England Listened: J. B. Priestley's Wartime Broadcasts.*  New York, Chilmark Press, 1968.

*Essays of Five Decades.*  Boston, Little Brown, 1968; London, Heinemann, 1969.

*Trumpets over the Sea: Being a Rambling and Egotistical Account of the London Symphony Orchestra's Engagement at Daytona Beach, Florida, in July-August 1967.*  London, Heinemann, 1968.

*The Prince of Pleasure and His Regency, 1811–1820.*  London, Heinemann, and New York, Harper, 1969.

*The Edwardians.*  London, Heinemann, and New York, Harper, 1970.

*Snoggle* (juvenile).  London, Heinemann, 1971.

*Victoria's Heyday.*  London, Heinemann, 1972.

Editor, *Essayists Past and Present: A Selection of English Essays.*  New York, Dial Press, 1925.

Editor, *Tom Moore's Diary.*  London, Macmillan, 1925.

Editor, *The Book of Bodley Head Verse.*  London, Bodley Head, and New York, Dodd Mead, 1926.

Editor, *Our Nation's Heritage.*  London, Dent, 1939.

Editor, *Scenes of London Life, from Sketches by Boz by Charles Dickens.*  London, Pan, 1947.

Editor, *The Best of Leacock.*  Toronto, McClelland and Stewart, 1957; as *The Bodley Head Leacock,* London, Bodley Head, 1957.

Editor, *The Bodley Head Fitzgerald,* vol. 1.  London, Bodley Head, 1958.

Editor, with O. B. Davis, *Four English Novels.*  New York, Harcourt Brace, 1960.

Editor, with O. B. Davis, *Four English Biographies.*  New York, Harcourt Brace, 1961.

Editor, *Adventures in English Literature.*  New York, Harcourt Brace, 1963.

Editor, *An Everyman Anthology.*  London, Dent, 1966.

Critical Studies: *J. B. Priestley* by Ivor Brown, London, Longman, 1957; *J. B. Priestley: An Informal Study of His Work* by David Hughes, London, Hart Davis, 1958; *The World of J. B. Priestley* edited by D. G. MacRae, London, Heinemann, 1967; *J. B. Priestley: Portrait of an Author* by Susan Cooper, London, Heinemann, 1970.

J. B. Priestley comments:

When I published *The Good Companions* and *Angel Pavement* it was possible for successful novels to have enormous sales in their original clothbound editions. This has encouraged some older readers to imagine that my best work in fiction belongs to this earlier period. In my opinion—and that of many friends and critics—this is wrong. My postwar novels, notably *Bright Day* (my own favourite), *Festival at Farbridge, Lost Empires* and *The Image Men,* are the novels I would choose to represent me. Unlike many contemporary writers, I have always believed that novels (and plays) should be entertaining. But that does not mean—as some silly reviewers, especially in America, seem to think—that my novels are entertainment and nothing else. There is always a great deal of social criticism in them, together with much symbolism, both in the action and the characters. So, for example, my last and longest novel, *The Image Men*, is not simply an elderly novelist being funny but is a sharp satire, very topical, on our ideas of education, our mass media, advertising, business expertise, etc. If at times—as in *Saturn over the Water* or *The Shapes of Sleep*—I desert the novel proper for what is really a tale, that is because I really enjoy telling a story now and again. I always write first to please myself because after all I have to spend most time with the book, so I propose to enjoy doing it. But I have almost always a serious purpose, and this is being recognised by psychologists, sociologists, publishers abroad, and the many foreign students who write to tell me they are preparing theses on my work. Probably, taking me all round, I have written too much, but that is because I have always had a lot of ideas that excited me, so I always went ahead, though I knew it has been unfashionable during the last 40 years to be versatile and prolific.

*      *      *

To consider Priestley's novels separately from the rest of his considerable contribution to letters in the form of criticism, plays, essays and radio scripts, is to see a diminished part of his total achievement; diminished, because the whole of Priestley seems greater than the sum of his parts. He is more of a one-man English institution than mere novelist, essayist or dramatist. Yet, obviously he would never have become a public figure at all without his writing. The apparent paradox of the public literary figure whose work attracts less critical attention than that of many minor writers might be explained by the theory that his work in all the various genres is unified only in its role as subdominant medium for the expression of Priestley's views on just about everything; the individual novels, essays and plays are mere messengers, not intended to be regarded as independent works of literary art.

Certainly, this seems to be the case when one considers his novels, written over a period of forty years among a hectic output of plays, essays and documentary pieces. They are so varied in kind and quality that it is difficult to discern in them any one particularly strong, coherent tendency. One feels that at heart Priestley must be the essayist and broadcaster —egocentric, journalistic and crochety—because his novels demonstrate the caprice and eclecticism of the bellelettrist rather than the singleminded artistry one usually associates with even minor novelists. There is no development over the years, and the whole canon has an accidental, or at least occasional, air about it.

To make a rather crude categorization, one can distinguish three groups of novels. First is that which includes all those with some claim to lasting worth—*Good Companions*, *Angel Pavement*, *Bright Day* and *Lost Empires*. Second is the group of light, almost fairytale, romance-adventures which either present what David Hughes has called "lunges out of routine" on the parts of characters whose lives hitherto have been pretty mundane, or concern the struggle between the human individual and a mechanistic establishment of science, technology and bureaucracy: this group is represented by *Adam in Moonshine*, *Faraway*, *The Doomsday Men*, *The Magicians* and *The Shapes of Sleep*. Third are the topical novels of social concern, either written to a programme of social criticism—*Wonder Hero*, *They Walk in the City*, *Low Notes on a High Level* and *Sir Michael and Sir George*—or for particular occasions, like the war-time novels *Let the People Sing*, *Black-Out in Gretley*, *Daylight on Saturday* and *Three Men in New Suits*.

Novels of the first group present Priestley at his best and most liked. All four novels show a real concern for humanity and the quality of individuals' lives, coupled with a vivid, panoramic picture of England. In two of the novels—*Good Companions* and *Lost Empires* —the setting is the Variety Theatre, and this works well at several levels; thematically, the theatre provides an image which underlies Priestley's major point that people need the right roles in life if they are to be reasonably happy; technically, the theatre provides a natural and credible setting for picaresque adventures over the English provinces and, at the same time, it allows free rein to the spirit of magic, which Priestley is at pains to promote in many of his novels, without straining the reader's credulity. Further the "business" of the stage becomes the "business" of the novel, adding both interest and depth. Although they are separated by thirty-six years in the writing, both novels radiate similar atmospheres of human warmth without declining either to mere sentimentality or to earnest editorialising on how to be happy.

*Angel Pavement* and *Bright Day* are more sombre in theme and tone, but probably represent Priestley's greatest achievements in the novel. His picture of London in *Angel Pavement* has all the realism and evocativeness that Conrad manages in *The Secret Agent*; the shabby cynicism, frightening menace and desperate alienation of the city stay long in the reader's memory. Although the reader cannot warm to the characters as he does to those in *Good Companions* he is made to share with them their helplessness in the impersonal city. A similar feeling of sadness is left by *Bright Day*, despite a tacked-on happy ending. This novel is autobiographic of at least a part of Priestley's life and character, being the first-person account by Gregory Dawson of his successful rise to eminence as a novelist and writer for the movies. The concern is with the artificiality of show-business success and its deadening effect on human relationships and artistic integrity. The sad note it strikes originates in the novel itself, but it is heightened for the reader who recalls that Dawson's final opting for artistic integrity is not necessarily Priestley's.

The romance-adventure novels of the second group are, at best, light reading for journeys, with all the elements of hero identification and wish-fulfilment that one associates with the escapist novel. They function, nevertheless, as exponents of their author's world-view by providing opportunities for much editorial comment. Unfortunately, such comment lacks both impact and subtlety, because it is not artistically supported in the novels themselves. Frequently, the mood and tone set up in the valid terms of setting, characterisation and plot, are undermined by contrived opinionising by the author; for example, in *Faraway*, several hundred pages of well-wrought narrative culminate in an irritable attack on Americanism and the sloppiness of South Sea Islanders, which completely reverses the tone already established. In *The Magicians* and *The Shapes of Sleep*, the author's opinions are so obtrusive that the novels are little more than thin allegories.

The novels of the third group are what they were, presumably, meant to be—journalistic, topical and documentary. They do not function as anything more than transient pieces of writing to convey their author's views—encouragement and optimism in the war-time novels, prejudices and grumbles in the post-war novels. That they were written at all confirms one's suspicion that in Priestley the artist never competes with the public man; like his good companions, he is really a very talented amateur who is not willing to take the final step of commitment that the real artist must take. His writing tends to be careless, quick and easy, as though he were not really interested in it. However, his best four novels will entertain readers for a long time after the public figure that wrote them has been forgotten.

—Frederick Bowers

---

**PRITCHETT, V(ictor) S(awdon).** British. Born in Ipswich, Suffolk, 10 December 1900. Educated at Alleyn's School, Dulwich, London. Married Dorothy Rudge Roberts in 1936; has two children. Worked in the leather trade, London, 1916–20, and in the shellac, glue and photographic trade, Paris, 1920–23. Correspondent in Ireland and Spain for the *Christian Science Monitor*, 1923–26. Since 1926, Free-lance Critic for various London periodicals. Since 1926, Critic for the *New Statesman*, London: Permanent Critic since 1937; Director of the *New Statesman* since 1946. Christian Gauss Lecturer, Princeton University, New Jersey, 1953; Beckman Professor, University of California, Berkeley, 1962; Writer-in-

Residence, Smith College, Northampton, Massachusetts, 1966; Visiting Professor, Brandeis University, Waltham, Massachusetts, 1968; Clark Lecturer, Cambridge University, 1969. President, English P.E.N. Club, 1970. Recipient: Heinemann Award, for non-fiction, 1969. D.Lit., Leeds University, 1972. Fellow, Royal Society of Literature, 1969. Honorary Member, American Academy of Arts and Letters, 1971. C.B.E. (Commander, Order of the British Empire), 1969. Address: 12 Regent's Park Terrace, London N.W.1, England.

PUBLICATIONS

Novels

> *Claire Drummer.*   London, Benn, 1929.
> *Shirley Sanz.*   London, Gollancz, 1932; as *Elopement into Exile*, Boston, Little Brown, 1932.
> *Nothing like Leather.*   London, Chatto and Windus, and New York, Macmillan, 1935.
> *Dead Man Leading.*   London, Chatto and Windus, and New York, Macmillan, 1937.
> *Mr. Beluncle.*   London, Chatto and Windus, and New York, Harcourt Brace, 1951.

Short Stories

> *The Spanish Virgin and Other Stories.*   London, Benn, 1930.
> *You Make Your Own Life.*   London, Chatto and Windus, 1938.
> *It May Never Happen and Other Stories.*   London, Chatto and Windus, 1945; New York, Reynal, 1947.
> *Collected Stories.*   London, Chatto and Windus, 1956.
> *The Sailor, The Sense of Humor, and Other Stories.*   New York, Knopf, 1956.
> *When My Girl Comes Home.*   London, Chatto and Windus, and New York, Knopf, 1961.
> *The Key to My Heart.*   London, Chatto and Windus, 1963; New York, Random House, 1964.
> *Blind Love and Other Stories.*   London, Chatto and Windus, 1969; New York, Random House, 1970.
> *Penguin Modern Stories 9*, with others.   London, Penguin, 1971.

Other

> *Marching Spain.*   London, Benn, 1928.
> *In My Good Books.*   London, Chatto and Windus, 1942.
> *The Living Novel.*   London, Chatto and Windus, 1946; New York, Reynal, 1947; revised edition, New York, Random House, 1964.
> *Why Do I Write: An Exchange of Views Between Elizabeth Bowen, Graham Greene and V. S. Pritchett.*   London, Marshall, 1948.
> *Books in General.*   London, Chatto and Windus, and New York, Harcourt Brace, 1953.
> *The Spanish Temper.*   London, Chatto and Windus, and New York, Knopf, 1955.
> *London Perceived.*   London, Chatto and Windus, and New York, Harcourt Brace, 1962.
> *Foreign Faces.*   London, Chatto and Windus, 1964; as *The Offensive Traveller*, New York, Knopf, 1964.
> *New York Proclaimed.*   London, Chatto and Windus, and New York, Harcourt Brace, 1965.

*The Working Novelist.*   London, Chatto and Windus, 1965.

*Dublin: A Portrait.*   London, Bodley Head, and New York, Harper, 1967.

*A Cab at the Door: Childhood and Youth, 1900–1920.*   London, Chatto and Windus, 1968; as *A Cab at the Door: A Memoir*, New York, Random House, 1968.

*George Meredith and English Comedy.*   London, Chatto and Windus, and New York, Random House, 1970.

*By My Own Hand* (essays).   London, Chatto and Windus, 1971.

*Midnight Oil* (autobiography).   London, Chatto and Windus, 1971.

Editor, *This England.*   London, New Statesman and Nation, 1938.

Editor, *Novels and Stories*, by Robert Louis Stevenson.   London, Pilot Press, 1945; New York, Duell, 1946.

Editor, *Turnstile One: A Literary Miscellany from the New Statesman.*   London, Turnstile Press, 1948.

V. S. Pritchett comments:

My chief interests have been: travel, specially Spanish; short stories, which I value most; literary criticism over the years for the *New Statesman.*

\*       \*       \*

V. S. Pritchett is one of the most richly endowed of living men of letters and has written with equal distinction as literary critic, travel-writer, autobiographer, novelist and short-story-writer. In whatever field he writes the work bears his thumb-print and is marked by his unfailing curiosity about the oddities and vagaries of human nature and by his exceedingly close observation of the human scene, and these are allied to a darting, idiosyncratic prose akin to brilliant talk.

If there is one subject that Pritchett has made his own and that, in one way or another, informs his writings, it is puritanism. He is, so to say, the connoisseur of puritanism in its characteristically English manifestations, which are generally lower middle-class. As he writes in his essay on Gosse's *Father and Son:*

> Extreme puritanism gives purpose, drama and intensity to private life. . . . Outwardly, the extreme puritan appears narrow, crabbed, fanatical, gloomy and dull: but from the inside—what a series of dramatic climaxes his life is, what a fascinating casuistry beguiles him, how he is bemused by the comedies of duplicity, sharpened by the ingenious puzzles of the conscience, and carried away by the eloquence of hypocrisy.

Such a character is described in Matthew Burkle, the central figure in Pritchett's early novel, *Nothing like Leather.* As the title indicates, the novel is set against the background of the leather trade: though it may not be its main interest, Pritchett's fiction is always saturated in the actual.

Burkle is a man who, hating sex, channels his energies to making money. To the extent that one feels Pritchett to be moved in his delineation by intellectual curiosity rather than by sympathy, Burkle is still a more or less conventional representation of the puritan. This is true also of the representation of Harry Johnson in *Dead Man Leading*, an explorer who deserts the scientific expedition he is with in Brazil in order to search for his father, who has disappeared in the interior. The background—the heat, damp and squalour of the Amazon forests—is most brilliantly rendered; and so, too, is the tortured mind of Johnson, who goes up the river "with the speechless fear of a son guiltily approaching his father."

But something appears in *Dead Man Leading* that is not present in the earlier novel. Intermittently, Pritchett displays himself as a comic writer, which is how one now thinks of him, and there is, in these comic passages, a sense of liberation, of ease, a delight in human oddity for its own sake.

In Pritchett's major novel, *Mr. Beluncle*, comedy takes over completely, and comedy here is an aspect of sympathy. And in Pritchett's depiction of Mr. Beluncle there are no reservations in his sympathy; Beluncle is accepted totally. Beluncle, a furniture manufacturer on a small scale, during the course of life has been in turn Congregationalist, Methodist, Plymouth Brother, Baptist, Unitarian, Theosophist, Christian Scientist. All these changes are related in some way to his economic situation. When the novel begins, he is a member of an American sect called The Church of the Last Purification, Toronto, a sect that denies the objective existence of evil.

Beluncle may seem and is indeed a self-deceiver, a liar, a cheat, a hypocrite and a domestic tyrant. But all this is not so important as the fact that he is a man who is as it were lived by a dream, the victim of a compulsive fantasy that rules his life and turns everything and everyone he meets into its accomplices, a fantasy that renders his life and those of his children who must suffer under him always dramatic. He is a character in the tradition and even the mode of Dickens, on whom Pritchett, as literary critic, has written with such intuitive understanding. And the novel is extraordinarily faithful to and revealing of one section, which seems to be permanent, of English lower middle-class life.

Pritchett's novels are intellectually exciting and wonderfully well-written. But they are less satisfying aesthetically. *Mr. Beluncle*, for instance, is curiously static. He is there all the time but does not develop or change in his being. The same could be said of Pecksniff, but Pecksniff, great creation though he is, is, in *Martin Chuzzlewit*, only one character among many. One feels, indeed, that for all his great knowledge of it Pritchett is not wholly at home or comfortable in the novel form. In the short story, on the other hand, he is completely at home, and it is in the short story, for which he seems to have abandoned the novel, that he has done his finest work in fiction.

Settings and characters are much the same as in the novels. Very often the scene is the south-east of England, with London and the City not far away; the characters again from the lower middle-class, clerks and commercial travellers. It is a world closely akin to Wells's in his early novels; the characters might be the children or grand-children of Wells's. One thinks of a story like "Many Are Disappointed", with its four characters, office-workers, on a cycling tour dreaming of beer in an inn and, in the end, settling for tea. At times, too, the matter is much the same, as in "The Saint", which might almost be an episode in *Mr. Beluncle*. The difference, however, is that in his short stories Pritchett's touch is absolutely sure; he is the complete master of the form. There are also, of course, the qualities one takes for granted in him: the swift economical language, racy, colloquial, the Dickensian eye for detail, the unerring instinct for idiosyncrasy that reveals character. There is the sense, too, that the stories are not abstractions; one feels that behind them there is a whole actual observable world which in some mysterious way they sum up in themselves. Pritchett is not a writer easily classified; his stories are his own and like no one else's. They seem very English. But each one of them, like Joyce's in *Dubliners*, is the rendering of what Joyce called an "epiphany", an incident or a sudden glimpse of a happening in which a moment of reality is made manifest. This is indeed the modern story-writer's art, and among contemporary writers no one is a greater master of it than Pritchett.

—Walter Allen

**PROKOSCH, Frederic.** American. Born in Madison, Wisconsin, 17 May 1908. Educated at Haverford College, Pennsylvania, 1922–25, M.A. 1926; Yale University, New Haven, Connecticut, 1930–31, Ph.D. 1933; King's College, Cambridge, 1935–37, M.A. 1937. Instructor in English, Yale University, 1932–34; Printer, of modern poetry, in Bryn Mawr, Pennsylvania, Cambridge, Salzburg, Venice and Lisbon, 1933–40; Cultural Attaché, American Legation, Stockholm, 1943–45; Visiting Lecturer, University of Rome, 1950–51. Squash-Racquets Champion of France, 1933–39, and of Sweden, 1944. Recipient: Guggenheim Fellowship, 1937; Harper Prize, 1937; Harriet Monroe Memorial Prize, *Poetry*, Chicago, 1941; Fulbright Fellowship, 1951. Address: "Ma Trouvaille", Plan de Grasse, Alpes Maritimes, France.

PUBLICATIONS

Novels

The Asiatics. New York, Harper, and London, Chatto and Windus, 1935.
The Seven Who Fled. New York, Harper, and London, Chatto and Windus, 1937.
Night of the Poor. New York, Harper, and London, Chatto and Windus, 1939.
The Skies of Europe. New York, Harper, 1941; London, Chatto and Windus, 1942.
The Conspirators. New York, Harper, and London, Chatto and Windus, 1943.
Age of Thunder. New York, Harper, and London, Chatto and Windus, 1945.
The Idols of the Cave. New York, Doubleday, 1946; London, Chatto and Windus, 1948.
Storm and Echo. New York, Doubleday, 1948; London, Faber, 1949.
Nine Days to Mukalla. New York, Viking Press, and London, Secker and Warburg, 1953.
A Tale for Midnight. Boston, Little Brown, 1955; London, Secker and Warburg, 1956.
A Ballad of Love. New York, Farrar Straus, 1960; London, Secker and Warburg, 1961.
The Seven Sisters. New York, Farrar Straus, 1962; London, Secker and Warburg, 1963.
The Dark Dancer. New York, Farrar Straus, 1964; London, W. H. Allen, 1965.
The Wreck of the Cassandra. New York, Farrar Straus, and London, W. H. Allen, 1966.
The Missolonghi Manuscript. New York, Farrar Straus, and London, W. H. Allen, 1968.
America, My Wilderness. New York, Farrar Straus, and London, W. H. Allen, 1971.

Verse

The Assassins. London, Chatto and Windus, and New York, Harper, 1936.
The Carnival. London, Chatto and Windus, and New York, Harper, 1938.
Death at Sea. New York, Harper, and London, Chatto and Windus, 1940.
Chosen Poems. London, Chatto and Windus, 1944; New York, Doubleday, 1947.

Other

Translator, Some Poems of Hölderlin. New York, New Directions, 1943; London, Grey Walls Press, 1947.
Translator, Love Sonnets of Louise Labé. New York, New Directions, 1947; London, Grey Walls Press, 1948.

Manuscript Collection: University of Texas, Austin.

Critical Study: *Frederic Prokosch* by Radcliffe Squires, New York, Twayne, 1964.

Frederic Prokosch comments:

It has always, it appears, been difficult, almost impossible, for English and American critics to classify or label or categorize my novels. Perhaps because an element of poetry has been infused into their themes, style and structure; or perhaps they fall more naturally into the *genre* of Slavic, German, or even French styles of fiction. My influences, I should say at random, were Grimm, Cervantes, Chekov, Conrad, possibly Thomas Mann among the moderns, even Céline, in the employment of a kind of dream-picaresque form to embody certain basic themes of perpetual search, perpetual flight, multiple identities, ambiguities of destiny, and geographical symbolisms. These themes have permeated my work all the way from *The Asiatics* and *The Seven Who Fled* up through *The Missolonghi Manuscript* and *America, My Wilderness*. Thus, my commentaries on "contemporary crises" have been covert, subtle, indirect. In this aversion to purely naturalistic or overtly sociological observation I find, I suppose, a certain kinship in the work of Borges, Nabokov, I. B. Singer, Hermann Hesse, and certain Japanese writers. I pity those poor critics who might try to disentangle the Gordian knot of my obsessive symbols and images.

\*       \*       \*

When Frederic Prokosch's first novel, *The Asiatics*, appeared in 1935 it immediately became clear that here was an important novelist with unique gifts. The metaphoric style touched the reader as does an intimate dream whose intensity leaves the dreamer lonely for the dream when he wakes. The tolerant, sensuous, yet ultimately mysterious young narrator who wanders through the beautifully detailed landscapes of Asia, encountering characters who are in turn vicious and virtuous, neurotic and heroic, mad and wise, enthralled a large audience. Translated into seventeen languages, the book claimed the attention of André Gide who called *The Asiatics* "an authentic masterpiece"; of Thomas Mann who wrote, "I was unable to tear myself away from this astonishing, picaresque romance, flashing with talent and an audacious, adventurous spirit. I count it among the most brilliant and original achievements of the young literary generation."

Prokosch's second novel, *The Seven Who Fled*, published as the Harper Prize novel in 1937, affirmed these impressions, and high praise continued to greet his work for the next decade. Yet it was praise that tended to dwell with the surfaces rather than the recesses of his talent. In this respect the response of Albert Camus is typical:

> He has invented what might be called the geographical novel, in which he mingles sensuality with irony, lucidity with mystery. He conveys a fatalistic sense of life half-hidden beneath a rich animal energy. He is a master of moods and undertones, a virtuoso in the feeling of place, and he writes in a style of supple elegance.

These words are true enough, but they neither ask nor tell the purposes of "the geographic novel."

While Frederic Prokosch's popularity as a novelist has declined, especially in America, since the end of World War II, his stature as a serious novelist, particularly in Europe, has increased. That stature rests upon stubborn teleological strengths that buttress the protean shimmer of his designs. For no aspect of Prokosch's fiction is merely what at first glance it appears to be. The vagrant drift of such novels as *Storm and Echo* contains a symbolic anthropology. The "naturalistic" or "realistic" qualities of such novels as *The Skies of Europe* contain a symbolic history. The historical aspects of such novels as *A Tale for Midnight* contain a symbolic psychology. The biographical qualities of such novels as *The Dark Dancer* or *The Missolonghi Manuscript* contain a symbolic philosophy of art.

In an anagogic sense, the nomadic novels—*The Asiatics, The Seven Who Fled, Storm and Echo, Nine Days to Mukalla*—contemplate man as an evolving, but not an evolved, being. Africa, vibrant with treachery and violence, chthonian gods and Promethean vision, is seen as the amoral but innocent beginning of man's emergence from the moronic babble of Nature. Asia, tricked by its own shrewdness, staggering under the burden of its exquisite civilization, is seen as decadent denouement. However, this extensive symbology is less important than the intensive symbology. The journey-novels—like the journey-poems of the Romantic poets—employ the fortuitous encounter as a means of fixing the fluctuant portrait of man's psychic being. Landscape, natural hardship—whether in Asia or Africa, Europe or America—act upon the characters as an "X-ray" to reveal what is hidden beneath the surface. The hidden self comes forth, the characters come to terms with it or else are destroyed by their fear of it.

But what does it mean, this coming to terms with the submerged atomies of self? It means at least a little more than the simple integration of personality advocated by Carl Jung, for the purpose of such integration involves for Prokosch a liberal yet austere morality. In the late novel *The Seven Sisters* Prokosch pursues the mythic rehearsals of archetypal themes in the careers of seven daughters. Ultimately one sees that these careers embody the conflicting or unmeshed elements of the hero's personality. Until he understands these elements he feels he is "dangling" in life, and his painting is a vagary of discrete daubs. Until he understands and thus reconciles these elements, he cannot love, though he is tyrannized by love; nor can he "create."

The word "create," as it involves the artist, takes us into the core of Prokosch's work. His villains (as his brief portrait of Hitler in *The Skies of Europe* makes evident) are failed artists. His ruined characters are those who, pursuing, like Rimbaud, a fanatical ideal of art, burn out and fail. But that is only the dark side of the problem. Toward the end of *The Asiatics* the narrator admonishes himself not to be

> strong; don't be alone; don't be proud; it's your only chance ever to understand anything at all. Be fragile, be tender, humiliate yourself, and let the discoloration of dream close in on you. Do that, and oddly enough, you'll remain healthy; you'll be yourself; you'll discover the best way to live in this particular most fruitless and tantalizing of possible worlds. The reality becomes a cruel dream while the dream fades into a tender man-made reality.

That rejection of strength and pride is at base a rejection of the imbalance of idealism; it parallels and equals the theme of awareness and integration of personality. Hence, from the fickle and promiscuous can come, as in *The Dark Dancer*, an eternal praise of love, the Taj Mahal. So also in *The Missolonghi Manuscript* (a novel which contains too many witty anachronisms and discrepancies for the careful reader to suppose its intent is simply a biography of Lord Byron) the Romantic ideal of "eternity" can only be attained by acceptance of decay. A susurrus of paradox articulates the resolution: to abandon idealism in life permits life to become an ideal art.

—Radcliffe Squires

**PUDNEY, John (Sleigh).**   British.   Born in Langley, Buckinghamshire, 19 January 1909. Educated at Gresham's School, Holt, Norfolk. Served in the Royal Air Force, 1940–45. Married Crystal Herbert in 1934 (divorced, 1955); Monica Forbes Curtis, 1955; has three children. Producer and Writer for the BBC, London, 1934–37; Correspondent of the *News Chronicle*, London, 1937–41; Book Critic, *Daily Express*, London, 1947–48; Literary Editor, *News Review*, London, 1948–50. Director of Putnam and Company, publishers, London, 1953–63. Recipient: C. P. Robertson Memorial Trophy, 1965. Address: 4 Macartney House, Chesterfield Walk, Greenwich Park, London SE10 8HJ, England.

PUBLICATIONS

Novels

> *Jacobson's Ladder*.   London, Longman, 1938.
> *Estuary*.   London, Lane, 1948.
> *Shuffley Wanderers*.   London, Lane, 1948.
> *The Accomplice*.   London, Lane, 1950.
> *Hero of a Summer's Day*.   London, Lane, 1951.
> *The Net*.   London, Joseph, 1952.
> *A Ring for Luck*.   London, Joseph, 1953.
> *Trespass in the Sun*.   London, Joseph, 1957.
> *Thin Air*.   London, Joseph, 1961.
> *The Long Time Growing Up*.   London, Dent, 1971.

Short Stories

> *And Lastly the Fireworks: Stories*.   London, Boriswood, 1935.
> *Uncle Arthur and Other Stories*.   London, Longman, 1939.
> *It Breathed Down My Neck*.   London, Lane, 1946; as *Edna's Fruit Hat and Other Stories*, New York, Harper, 1946.
> *The Europeans: Fourteen Tales of the Continent*.   London, Lane, 1948.

Verse

> *Spring Encounter*.   London, Methuen, 1933.
> *Open the Sky: Poems*.   London, Boriswood, 1934; New York, Doubleday, 1935.
> *Dispersal Point and Other Air Poems*.   London, Lane, 1942.
> *Beyond This Disregard: Poems*.   London, Lane, 1943.
> *South of Forty: Poems*.   London, Lane, 1943.
> *Almanack of Hope: Poems*.   London, Lane, 1944.
> *Ten Summers: Poems [1933–1943]*.   London, Lane, 1944.
> *Flight above Cloud*.   New York, Harper, 1944.
> *Selected Poems*.   London, Lane, 1946.
> *Selected Poems*.   London, British Publishers Guild, 1947.
> *Low Life: Verses*.   London, Lane, 1947.
> *Commemorations: Poems*.   London, Lane, 1948.
> *Sixpenny Songs*.   London, Lane, 1953.
> *Collected Poems*.   London, Putnam, 1957.
> *The Trampoline*.   London, Joseph, 1959.
> *Spill Out: Poems and Ballads*.   London, Dent, 1967.

*Spandrels: Poems and Ballads.*   London, Dent, 1969.
*Take This Orange.*   London, Dent, 1971.


Other

*The Green Grass Grew All Round.*   London, Lane, 1942.
*Who Only England Knows: Log of a Wartime Journey of Unintentional Discovery of Fellow-Countrymen.*   London, Lane, 1943.
*World Still There: Impressions of Various Parts of the World in Wartime.*   London, Hollis and Carter, 1945.
*Saturday Adventure* (juvenile).   London, Lane, 1950.
*Sunday Adventure* (juvenile).   London, Lane, 1951.
*Monday Adventure* (juvenile).   London, Evans, 1952.
*His Majesty King George VI: A Study.*   London, Hutchinson, 1952.
*The Thomas Cook Story.*   London, Joseph, 1953.
*Tuesday Adventure* (juvenile).   London, Evans, 1953.
*Wednesday Adventure* (juvenile).   London, Evans, 1954.
*The Smallest Room: A History of Lavatories.*   London, Joseph, 1954; New York, Hastings House, 1955; revised edition, as *The Smallest Room: With an Annexe*, Joseph, 1959. .
*Six Great Aviators* (juvenile).   London, Hamish Hamilton, 1955.
*Thursday Adventure* (juvenile).   London, Evans, 1955.
*Friday Adventure* (juvenile).   London, Evans, 1956.
*The Grandfather Clock* (juvenile).   London, Hamish Hamilton, 1957.
*Crossing the Road* (juvenile).   London, Hamish Hamilton, 1958.
*The Seven Skies: A Study of the British Overseas Airways Corporation and Its Forerunners.*   London, Putnam, 1959.
*Home and Away* (autobiography).   London, Joseph, 1960.
*A Pride of Unicorns: Richard and David Atcherley of the R.A.F.*   London, Oldbourne, 1960.
*Bristol Fashion: Some Accounts of the Earlier Days of British Aviation.*   London, Putnam, 1960.
*Spring Adventure* (juvenile).   London, Evans, 1961.
*Summer Adventure* (juvenile).   London, Evans, 1962.
*The Hartwarp Light Railway* (juvenile).   London, Hamish Hamilton, 1962.
*The Hartwarp Dump* (juvenile).   London, Hamish Hamilton, 1962.
*The Hartwarp Balloon* (juvenile).   London, Hamish Hamilton, 1963.
*The Hartwarp Circus* (juvenile).   London, Hamish Hamilton, 1963.
*Autumn Adventure* (juvenile).   London, Evans, 1964.
*The Camel Fighter.*   London, Hamish Hamilton, 1964
*The Hartwarp Bakehouse* (juvenile).   London, Hamish Hamilton, 1964.
*The Hartwarp Explosion* (juvenile).   London, Hamish Hamilton, 1965.
*Winter Adventure* (juvenile).   London, Evans, 1965.
*Tunnel to the Sky* (juvenile).   London, Hamish Hamilton, 1965.
*The Hartwarp Jets* (juvenile).   London, Hamish Hamilton, 1967.
*The Golden Age of Steam.*   London, Hamish Hamilton, 1967.
*Suez: De Lesseps' Canal.*   London, Dent, 1968.
*A Draught of Contentment.*   London, New English Library, 1971.
*Crossing London's River.*   London, Dent, 1972.


Editor, with Henry Treece, *Air Force Poetry.*   London, Lane, 1944.
Editor, *Pick of Today's Short Stories.*   London, Odhams, Putnam, and Eyre and Spottiswoode, 13 vols., 1949–1963.
Editor, *The Book of Leisure.*   London, Odhams, 1957.

Editor, *The Harp Book of Toasts*.   London, Harp Lager, 1963.

Editor, *The Batsford Colour Book of London*.   London, Batsford, 1965; New Rochelle, New York, Soccer Associates, 1966.

Editor, *Flight and Flying*.   London, Hamish Hamilton, and New York, David White, 1968.

John Pudney comments:

I am not able to make a subjective or objective statement about the writing of fiction in which I have been involved off and on for about forty years. I can only offer a kind of practical footnote which is this.

In writing novels, short stories or tales for children I find I am only getting anywhere when the characters begin to talk to me and to indicate by their very existence what the line of action is likely to be. When the characters have not come to life sufficiently to do this the work is hard going and probably the result will be a failure. As I get older I have come to realize that the writing of fiction demands the kind of relaxation in the author which enables the characters to come alive, and also a good measure of courage—or vanity—on the part of the author to create his own suspension of disbelief.

\*         \*         \*

As a novelist John Pudney's main gift lies in his capacity to tell an intricate, slightly fantastic story with all the balanced complexity of a well-worked poem. He also brings to his novels a quality that has made him such a successful writer for children, and that is an ability to create and people a distinctive community. This is especially true of the Thames Valley people in and beside the river in *Hero of a Summer's Day*. His concern is to create an ambience of story, setting and people in which his main protagonist can develop. To do so he does not shrink from the bizarre, the quasi-mystical, the criminal and the perverted. And because these qualities flourish best in luxury, in a state in which money can cushion people from daily necessities, he chooses to set his stories in a fair degree of opulence.

All these qualities can be seen beautifully at work in his last novel, *The Long Time Growing Up*. It is very faintly allegorical in that it concerns the purchase of a castle in Spain, which eventually goes up in smoke, burnt down by an elegantly poised transvestite who lives in a perpetual state of sharp, cool desperation. But it's not his growing up the novel is about, although the last sentence of the book suggests that his growth may be beginning. Mainly though he is just one of the flamboyant, slightly static characters who impinge on Mervyn Rose, an irresponsible director of a family business, living on an indulged and romantic attachment to his cousin's wife and rapidly degenerating into a middle-aged Peter Pan. The novel, told largely in the first person, is an account of his escape from such a fate.

In this and in his other novels, John Pudney shows that he is able to get right into the skin of his main characters whether they are male or female, young, old or adolescent. He is able, in the description of a single gesture or a slight interchange of remarks, to convey the various conflicting drives which result in the one observable action. Because he is mainly an entertainer and a story-teller, this quality of his novels is far too often neglected.

—Shirley Toulson

**PURDY, James.** American. Born in Ohio, 17 July 1923. Recipient: National Institute of Arts and Letters grant, 1958; Guggenheim Fellowship, 1958, 1962; Ford Fellowship, 1961. Address: 236 Henry Street, Brooklyn, New York 11201, U.S.A.

PUBLICATIONS

Novels

Malcolm. New York, Farrar Straus, 1959; London, Secker and Warburg, 1960.
The Nephew. New York, Farrar Straus, and London, Secker and Warburg, 1961.
Cabot Wright Begins. New York, Farrar Straus, 1964; London, Secker and War-
    burg, 1965.
Eustace Chisholm and the Works. New York, Farrar Straus, 1967; London, Cape,
    1968.
Jeremy's Version: Part One of Sleepers in Moon-Crowned Valleys. New York, Double-
    day, 1970; London, Cape, 1971.
I Am Elijah Thrush. New York, Doubleday, 1972.

Short Stories

Don't Call Me by My Right Name and Other Stories. New York, William Frederick
    Press, 1956.
63: Dream Palace. New York, William Frederick Press, 1956; as 63: Dream Palace:
    A Novella and Nine Stories, London, Gollancz, 1957.
Color of Darkness: 11 Stories and a Novella. New York, New Directions, 1957;
    London, Secker and Warburg, 1961.
Children Is All (stories and plays). New York, New Directions, 1962; London, Secker
    and Warburg, 1963.
An Oyster Is a Wealthy Beast (story and poems). Los Angeles, Black Sparrow Press,
    1967.
Mr. Evening: A Story and Nine Poems. Los Angeles, Black Sparrow Press, 1968.
On the Rebound: A Story and Nine Poems. Los Angeles, Black Sparrow Press, 1970.

Play

Cracks (produced New York, 1963).

Verse

The Running Sun. New York, Paul Waner Press, 1971.

Other

Recordings: 63: Dream Palace, Spoken Arts, 1967; Eventide and Other Stories, Spoken
    Arts, 1968.

Manuscript Collection: Yale University, New Haven, Connecticut.

Critical Studies: Introduction by David Daiches to *Malcolm*, 1959; Introduction by Edith Sitwell to *Colour of Darkness*, London, Secker and Warburg, 1961; *The Not-Right House* by Bettina Schwarzschild, Columbia, University of Missouri Press, 1969.

James Purdy comments:

As I see it, my work is an exploration of the American soul conveyed in a style based on the rhythms and accents of American speech. From the beginning my work has been greeted with a persistent and even passionate hostility on the part of the New York literary establishment which tries to rule America's literary taste—and the world's. My early work was privately printed by friends. Dame Edith Sitwell read these works, and persuaded Victor Gollancz to publish the book in England. Without her help I would never have been published in America and never heard of. The mediocrity of the American literary scene, as is evidenced in the *New York Times* and the creatures of the vast New York establishment, has tried to reduce me to starvation and silence. Yet as a matter of fact I believe my work is the most American of any writer writing today. My subject, as I said, is the exploration of the inside of my characters, or as John Cowper Powys put it, "under the skin." The theme of American culture, American commercial culture, that is, is that man can be adjusted, that loudness and numbers are reality, and that to be "in" is to exist. My work is the furthest from this definition of "reality". All individual thought and feeling have been silenced or "doped" in America today, and to be oneself is tantamount to non-existence. I see no difference between Russia and America; both are hideous failures, both enemies of the soul, both devourers of nature, and undisciplined disciplinarians who wallow in the unnatural. Anything in America is sacred which brings in money, and the consumers can easily be persuaded to move from their old crumbling Puritan ethic to belief in things like sexual deviation and coprophilia, provided and only provided these bring in money and notoriety. The one crime is to be oneself, unless it is a "self" approved and created by the commercial forces. Beneath this vast structure of madness, money, and anaesthetic prostitution, is my own body of work.

I prefer not to give a biography since my biography is in my work, and I do not wish to communicate with anybody but individuals, for whom my work was written in the first place. I began writing completely in the dark, and so continue. Were I in a financial position to do so, I would never publish anything commercially, since the literary establishment can promote only lies, and the critics, newspapers, and public having been fed on poison so long are incapable of reading anything that is not an advertisement for their own destruction. The most applauded writers in America are those who have had no contact with native American speech, but who seem to have been born in a television studio, where words are hourly produced from baking tins. In New York City, where American speech is unknown, a writer such as myself is considered a foreigner. Clarity and idiomatic language are considered in fact mad, while the language of dope addicts and coprophiliacs is now standard "American", approved for use by the dowagers who make best-sellers.

\*     \*     \*

James Purdy is fascinated by the "color of darkness." His stories and novels deal with all-consuming narcissism and they assume, consequently, that "normal" love is, for the most part, cruel and nightmarish.

In *Color of Darkness* he gives us many heroes who are confused, lonely, and freakish. They do not know how to love (or to be loved). They are afraid to commit themselves. We see them sitting in dark rooms or roaming city streets; we hear their silent screams. Fenton Riddleway is so tormented by love for Claire, his dying brother, in "63: Dream Palace," the most impressive story in the collection, that he must kill him. The murder is the culmination of perverse love; it is perfectly in keeping with the "not-rightness" and rot of their dream palace.

In another collection, *Children Is All*, Purdy returns to the conflicts in family relationships. Often his heroes are orphans or bachelors. The narrator of "Daddy Wolf," for example, has seen his wife and child leave him; he turns for solace to the invisible "daddy." He calls him on the "trouble phone"; he rants, confesses, and rambles. But he is, finally, alone— except for the rats which crawl near him. "Goodnight, Sweetheart," like all of the best stories, fuses the realistic (or cliché) dialogue and the fantastic incident. It begins with Pearl Miranda walking "stark naked from her class-room in the George Washington School" to the house of Winston, a former pupil. Both are victims of love (or "rape"); both cannot exist in the wolfish world. Unfortunately, they cannot even live with each other. As the story ends, they "both muttered to themselves in the darkness as if they were separated by different rooms from one another." They pray for help.

Purdy's novels are more varied than his stories. (It is questionable whether they surpass the great achievement of the stories.) The hero of his first novel, *Malcolm*, searches for his father, hoping thereby to affirm his own identity and *name*. But like Fenton Riddleway, he cannot exist as a "person"—he becomes another shadow in the rotten city. He is manipulated by others; he is never understood completely, except as a mere reflection of their selfish demands. Malcolm is, to quote his lusty wife, a "little bit of this and that," and when he dies —has he ever lived?—he apparently vanishes into thin air. *Malcolm* is a wonderfully strange mixture of comedy and pathos, and it alone asserts Purdy's impressive gifts as a novelist. Although it deals with the lack of substance in relationships—between men and women; between men and men; between human beings and the cosmos—it creates its own substantial texture largely as a result of Purdy's mixed, "transformational" style.

*The Nephew* is set in Rainbow Center, a small American town. (It is a change from the "fairy-tale" *Malcolm*.) It delights in clichés, minor scandals, and popular holidays; it is, at least superficially, a realistic picture of the middle Americans. But it presents Boyd and Alma (and Cliff, their missing nephew) in such a deceptive, complex way that "local color" changes subtly to universal darkness. When Alma discovers that she has never known Cliff (despite having lived with him for many years) and, consequently, realizes her own needs and dreams, she is depressed *and* exalted. She grasps the hard truth; she understands that we are all "missing" shadows; we live briefly and secretly. She accepts the significance of memorial days—the novel begins and ends on this holiday—and the "faint delicious perfume" of our lives before the court house clock strikes again. Thus *The Nephew*, like all of Purdy's novels, must be read closely (as Alma reads her nephew's life)—it presents two worlds and demands the recognition that only art can reconcile their differences.

*Cabot Wright Begins* is a savage satire on American life. It attacks the automatic, false, and empty values which make us treat people as *valuable objects*. Cabot Wright becomes a rapist because he can assert his identity only as a vital, pumping being. Later he runs away from the others—Bernie, Zoe, and Princeton—who want to trap and use his exotic past for their narcissistic ends. Cabot Wright begins to laugh and write; he rises from the "deadly monotony of the human continuity" when he lies on the ground, "weeping a little from the pain of his laughter, a thread of drivel coming down from his mouth onto his pointed dimpled chin." Despite the cluttered sermons, this novel is brilliantly effective when it says "HA!" to the boredom of our daily routines. It is Purdy's blackest comedy.

*Eustace Chisholm and the Works* details the various strategies of lovers who refuse to acknowledge their own potentialities. The homosexuality which colored *Malcolm*, *The Nephew*, and "63: Dream Palace" flourishes here. Daniel Haws, for example, cannot accept his love for Amos (except at the end); he flees from it into the Army. There he is "satisfied" by sadistic Captain Stadger in a powerfully detailed execution (or embrace?). These Army scenes are perhaps the most brutal ones in all of Purdy's fiction.

Eustace Chisholm is a writer. He resembles Alma, Cabot Wright, and Bernie of *Cabot Wright Begins* in trying to solve the mysteries of love and will in the community; and like them, he discovers that he cannot get to the heart of the matter. He *abdicates*—unlike Purdy himself—and turns instead to his wife for incredible love. He warms her with "a kind of ravening love," knowing that they will probably "consume" each other in the future. He is saved only momentarily.

*Jeremy's Version* is the first part of a uncompleted trilogy called *Sleepers in Moon-Crowned Valleys*, but it stands alone. Jeremy is an adolescent who writes down the sermons, tales, and histories of Matthew Lacy. He is, therefore, the familiar character we have met before, but unlike the other earlier writers, he is more open, innocent, and *human* than they are. He learns as he listens and transcribes.

Jeremy moves into the past. He becomes so involved with the family conflicts of the nineteenth-century Fergises—he identifies especially with Jethro, another adolescent writer—that at times he becomes a free-floating *spirit*. Thus he forces us to recognize that only by giving oneself to others can we survive and create. He offers hope. His "version" is finally a mellow, full, and sunny account which indicates some new directions for Purdy's forth-coming novels.

—Irving Malin

---

**PUZO, Mario.** American. Born in New York City in 1920. Educated at the New School for Social Research, New York; Columbia University, New York. Married; has children. Administrative Assistant in United States Government offices, in New York and overseas, for 20 years. Lives on Long Island, New York. Address: c/o G. P. Putnam Sons Inc., 200 Madison Avenue, New York, New York 10016, U.S.A.

PUBLICATIONS

Novels

*The Dark Arena.* New York, Random House, 1955; London, Heinemann, 1971.
*The Fortunate Pilgrim.* New York, Atheneum, 1965; London, Heinemann, 1966.
*The Godfather.* New York, Putnam, and London, Heinemann, 1969.

Other

*The Runaway Summer of Davie Shaw* (juvenile). New York, Platt and Munk, 1966.
*The Godfather Papers and Other Confessions.* New York, Putnam, 1972.

\*       \*       \*

Puzo's novelistic work is in the strong, rich vein of American Naturalism; his literary forebearers are Frank Norris, Crane, Dreiser, Lewis, and James T. Farrell. As in Dreiser, Puzo shows how institutions work, and how the individual fares in the often traumatic process; unlike Dreiser, however, Puzo seldom treats the larger social or political issues. By comparison, Puzo's vision is private; his strength is in rendering the inner working of a family, in dramatizing what may constitute loyalty or right conduct in a time of crises especially when the issue concerns either prestige or money.

As with nearly all Naturalistic writers, Puzo's world is the city, the urban jungle. Here persons with power exploit without mercy the defenseless and the weak; a reoccurring motive is brute revenge. Love, loyalty, and fidelity more often than not are made viable by well-managed crime; official sentiment is expressed by ostentatious, professionally managed funerals and weddings. Typically the resolutions of human affairs remain ambivalent.

The materials of the three novels are handled with great authority. In fact, Puzo was born and raised in New York's Lower East Side; his version of tenement life of that time is the most comprehensive and the most fully realized of any living American author. The language is straightforward and without pretensions; always there is a variety of lifelike characters.

Of the three novels (in fifteen years) *The Dark Arena* alone takes place largely outside the U.S. The hero is an American ex-soldier who accepts civilian employment with the military government in occupied Germany. The plot is not complex, and traces two major themes: the German-American accommodation in the early years of peace and the implied emergence of a new Germany. The second theme concerns the hero, Mosca, and his attempts at emotional growth, his tragic disappointments in love and his eventual departure from the betrayals of occupation life. The novel deserves to be better known.

*The Fortunate Pilgrim* is Puzo's best novel to date and traces the "rise" of an Italian peasant girl, a new bride in America, from tenement to the end of the American Dream, a bungalow of her own in Long Island. In addition to a wide variety of scenes from lower class immigrant life and the changing mores of individuals and whole neighborhoods, this novel also presents details—and visions—of syndicate-managed crime. The episodes concerning organized crime are at once detailed and also larger than life-size; thus the episodes have a genuine mythic quality. On balance this novel is among the best two or three books ever written on American city life.

A third novel, *The Godfather*, stems directly from the passages on crime in *The Fortunate Pilgrim*. The main protagonist, Don Corleone, is a rebel-founder of a vastly influential crime syndicate. His values are at once "domestic" (he is a family man) and anti-social (he often kills off the opposition). Thus he is patron, Old Testament God, and terrible enforcer. The larger ethical, public issues are never fully dramatized; likewise, the contradictions within Don Corleone are never satisfactorily resolved. Perhaps this ambivalence accounts for the less subtle, less controlled structure of the most recent novel. In any event, when *The Godfather* appeared it became an immediate best seller and helped revive interest in the two earlier, more interesting novels.

Puzo represents an increasingly rare type of American writer: the journeyman. Between novels, for more than fifteen years, he has supported a family on articles, non-fiction, and journalism. He does not teach. He lives not far from the place he was born: the City. In this and other respects his is a sturdy talent of the kind which each day meets the literary competition of a nation's literary capital.

—James B. Hall

---

**PYNCHON, Thomas.**   American.   Born in Glen Cove, New York, 8 May 1937. Educated at Cornell University, Ithaca, New York, B.A. 1958. Served in the United States Navy. Has worked as an Editorial Writer, Boeing Aircraft Corporation, Seattle, Washington. Recipient: Faulkner Award, 1964; Rosenthal Memorial Award, 1967. Address: c/o J. B. Lippincott Inc., East Washington Square, Philadelphia, Pennsylvania 19105, U.S.A.

PUBLICATIONS

Novels

V. Philadelphia, Lippincott, and London, Cape, 1963.
*The Crying of Lot 49.* Philadelphia, Lippincott, 1966; London, Cape, 1967.

*        *        *

Early in *V*, Pynchon's first novel, a character named Benny Profane is hunting alligators in the sewers of New York. He is hunting them on the city payroll, for a great number of baby alligators, bought as pets for children, have been flushed down toilets all over the city and are now breeding in the drainage tunnels. And as he hunts, Profane remembers the legend of Father Fairing, a Catholic priest who, during the Great Depression, decided that the rats were going to inherit the earth and went to live in the sewers, in order to convert the new chosen race to the one true faith. "At no point," Profane realizes, "in the twenty or so years the legend had been handed on did it occur to anyone to question the old priest's sanity. It is this way with sewer stories. They just are. Truth or falsity don't apply."

It is a passage which says a great deal, not only about the dark and manic world of *V*, but about Pynchon's highly individual comic talent, and about the decade of the sixties in which that talent flourished. Upon his first appearance, Pynchon was grouped by most critics with the other so-called "black humorists" of the decade: with writers like Bruce Jay Friedman, Kurt Vonnegut, and John Barth, whose satirical vision of contemporary America, with roots as diverse as Petronius, Nathanael West, and Lenny Bruce, suggested something like a new "movement" in literature, a turning away from the realistic conventions of fifties fiction (e.g. Saul Bellow, J. D. Salinger), and from the political passivism associated with the Eisenhower era. This grouping had, indeed, some polemical point to it, in establishing the major talent and importance of some of its members. But like most other prematurely named "movements," it tended to obscure the vast differences between the writers involved, and finally to obscure even the structure of the works themselves. *V* has finally made it: reprinted as a Modern Library "Classic," it is taught in Modern Novel surveys across the country as an example of "black humor." But *V*, like *The Crying of Lot 49*, is *not* an example of anything, except of its creator's unique vision. For if the "black humor" of Vonnegut consists of a series of simple, bitter parables about man's terrible need of charity, and that of Barth of an immense, baroque fantasia upon solipsism and nihilism, Pynchon's genius, neither allegorical nor epic, remains that of the teller of "sewer stories": tales of the psychotic underground of the modern imagination, where "truth or falsity don't apply."

The image of the sewer, of the underground labyrinth, the secret network, the hidden "plot," is central to both of Pynchon's novels. But his use of this very common metaphor for modern life (one thinks of Gide, Norman Mailer, and Alain Robbe-Grillet) is a unique one. For Pynchon's labyrinths hold no mystery, and his deep dark secrets are, if anything, overillumined. Their terror, that is, is not the terror of the unknown, but precisely that of the *too well* known, of the twisted underbrush of the modern mind which has become so much our daily bread that we can never hope to see it in the full, unfamiliarized ghastliness of its reality. Another name for sewer stories, then, is perhaps "anti-Gothic romances." For Pynchon gives us an America, a world so inured to the unspeakable that one can, actually, speak about it. And his characters are somnambulists inhabiting ghost stories where their distinctive curse is to be incapacitated for horror itself.

Pynchon, while an undergraduate at Cornell, majored in English literature, but with a heavy helping of courses in modern physics: one of his former teachers still wonderingly remembers his apparently voracious appetite for the complexities of elementary particle theory. And physics, along with the myth of the labyrinth, has proved to be crucial to Pynchon's imagination. For if the modern condition may be imagined as a city honeycombed with secret subterranean passages, mind-boggling in their darkness and extensiveness, it may also be imagined as a cosmic version of that most critical quandary of contemporary physics, the so-called "Uncertainty Principle." This principle, in its baldest form, simply states that the complete description of *any* physical event is impossible—not because of the complexity of the event, but because *consciousness itself*, in attempting to examine the event, also alters the event from its "true" form into an impossible maze of self-reflexiveness. It is difficult, indeed, not to think of this principle when, in *The Crying of Lot 49*, the heroine Oedipa Maas faces the difficulty of ever discovering what, in its entirety, the mysterious "Trystero System" might mean: "Now here was Oedipa, faced with a metaphor of God knew how many parts; more than two, anyway. With coincidences blossoming these days wherever she looked, she had nothing but a sound, a word, Trystero, to hold them together." A word, a sound to resolve a metaphor which, like the "many-body" problem of physics, consists of too many parts and is therefore *intrinsically* insoluble: truth and falsity don't, cannot apply in a world where those fundamentally moral values of the reason have been reduced to the dead level of infinitely extensive "facts."

Both Pynchon's novels to date are concerned, in their different ways, with the great and urgent difficulty of finding a human truth within the manifold, labyrinthine coincidences of the modern experience. In *V*, the labyrinth is the gigantic one of European history since the First World War. Herbert Stencil, seeking the truth about the death of his father in 1919, is led on a crazy quest for the identity of "V," a mysterious female—seductress, hag, secret agent—who appears to have been present at every disaster which has contributed to the making of modern Europe and America. The quest for V leads finally to a kind of terminal despair of history, a sense that the "Plot Which Has No Name," the master diabolical plot of the Twentieth Century, is necessarily unknowable to any of its victims. (Stencil himself, who refers to himself only in the third person, is literally a "stencil," a recording instrument incapable of passing moral judgment on that which he records.) But not before Stencil and the "whole sick crew" of existential bums he gathers around him have explored what is literally an underground history of the age, from Sarajevo through the Great Depression and Naziism to the formation of "Yoyodyne," the massive munitions industry which is Pynchon's chief image of the superindustrialized death factories of modern technology. V herself, though of course ultimately unknowable, appears in one of the book's most apocalyptic moments, the bombing of Malta during World War Two, as a seductress who has been systematically replacing her living organs with pieces of precision machinery: the *femme fatale* become a shuddering *fatalité feminisée*.

But as great, sprawlingly inventive, and wildly funny as *V* is, it seems only a preparation for the acid, classically economic satire of *Lot 49*. For here the central labyrinth of the book is no longer history, but the labyrinth of the mind itself, attempting to put together in meaningful order a culture whose order appears meaningless and meaning-destructive. Oedipa Maas (named after that first self-destructive solver of riddles, Oedipus of Thebes) inherits from her millionaire former lover, not only his wealth, but the mystery of a "Trystero System" which, as she comes increasingly to realize, is itself the key to understanding the loneliness and isolation of modern man. The System, whose ambiguous motto is "W.A.S.T.E.," is *either* a counter-cultural communications network designed to undermine the dehumanization of public technology, *or* the most nefarious and subtle method of the technology itself to compound the isolation of person from person. A conventional suburban housewife, Oedipa has stumbled upon the insanity at the heart of her America, an insanity where everything seems fraught with hidden significance, and where therefore the significance of nothing may be determined. One central "clue" to Trystero Oedipa confronts, in fact, is perhaps the hidden matrix of *Lot 49* itself. She goes to hear a revival of a Jacobean tragedy, *The Courier's Tragedy*, which Pynchon "paraphrases" with a marvelous sense of the grimness and absurdity of the Jacobean period. And *Lot 49* itself is a "courier's tragedy," a tragedy of information theory, in which the "facts" in which our world abounds assert themselves terrifyingly as limits to the human imagination, multiplying without end in a complex structure which leaves room for everything except man himself.

Pynchon has not published a novel since *Lot 49* in 1967: and his vision is a dark enough one to argue against the writing of fiction altogether, But, on the basis of his two major works, his reputation and his real value stand secure, for he is one of the most uncompromising and courageous of the analysts of our psychic debilities. And one whom, perhaps, we sorely need: for if his sewer stories are told in the heart of darkness and the labyrinth, they are told, nonetheless, *against* the darkness, that we might better, by talking aloud, see each other.

—Frank D. McConnell

---

**QUIN, Ann (Marie).** British. Born in Brighton, Sussex, 17 March 1936. Educated at the Convent of the Blessed Sacrament, Brighton. Secretary, Hutchinson and Company, publishers, London, 1958–60, Royal College of Art, London, 1960–63, and Chelsea College of Art, London, 1963–64. Since 1970, Part-time Secretary, Beryl Hope and Brauer, London. Recipient: D. H. Lawrence Fellowship, University of New Mexico, 1964; Harkness Fellowship, 1964–67; Arts Council grant, 1969. Address: 22 Lansdowne Road, London W.11, England.

PUBLICATIONS

Novels

Berg. London, Calder and Boyars, 1964; New York, Scribner, 1966.
Three. London, Calder and Boyars, 1966; New York, Scribner, 1968.
Passages. London, Calder and Boyars, 1966.
Tripticks. London, Calder and Boyars, 1972.

Uncollected Short Stories

"Every Cripple Has His Own Way of Walking", in *Nova* (London), 1965.
"Never Trust a Man Who Bathes with His Finger Nails", in *El Corno Emplumado* (Mexico City), 1968.
"Motherlogue", in *Transatlantic Review* (London and New York), 1969.

*        *        *

Ann Quin writes about persons who are made of glass, and then expects us to be surprised that she can see through them. Her second and on the whole most satisfactory novel, *Three*, for example, concentrates on a married couple, Ruth and Leonard, elaborately finding ways to refuse to blame themselves for the disappearance and presumed suicide of a young woman who has been living with them. The young woman is nowhere named in the text (though early on, in a diary entry of Leonard's, she is referred to as "S")—this is not a trick. For Ruth and Leonard, the girl scarcely existed. She was an extension of themselves, their own married confusion. Each of them hopelessly self-divided, relying on the other for a false sense of identity, they share nothing save their wish to become each other (the sex scenes, descriptive of this morbidity, are bleak and terrifying). Because they see each other as ghosts whose only function is to disappoint, they begin to see the girl only when she disappoints them by suddenly being absent, and then through a mist of their own guilt. They feed on her, absorb her into the ritual of their discontent, trying to make three into two.

The book is exquisitely written, as was Ann Quin's first novel, *Berg*, set in a rather seedy and Graham Greeney Brighton, but otherwise wholly original. On one level, this study of a would-be parricide is the most naturalistic of the three books the author has so far published; in its use of imagistic fragments to evoke the atmosphere of a seaside town in the off-season, however, and in its reduction to caricature of all save the three central figures, it reaches forward to the prose-poem techniques exploited in *Three* and *Passages*. Here, as elsewhere, Miss Quin shows herself to be admirably alive to the elusiveness of what happens between people, and to the possibilities of the English language. Her best writing hoards words as if they were pebbles washed smooth by huge seas of experience.

*Passages*, though, did not add much to her reputation. Again there are three characters —a woman, her lover, her displaced brother. Again there is a sense of strenuous insight into shallowness, and some remarkably sensitive prose to match it. But the book is too rigorously informed by Jane Harrison's *Prolegomena to the Study of Greek Religion* and degenerates into a series of academic exercises in lyricism, often beautiful, but seldom venturing beyond its own verbal excitement.

—Robert Nye

---

**RADDALL, Thomas Head.** Canadian. Born in Hythe, Kent, England, 13 November 1903; emigrated to Canada in 1913. Educated at St. Leonard's School, Hythe; Chebucto School, Halifax, Nova Scotia; Halifax Academy. Wireless Operator, Canadian Merchant Marine, 1918–22; served as a Lieutenant in the 2nd (Reserve) Battalion, West Nova Scotia Regiment, 1942–43. Married Edith Margaret Freeman in 1927; has two children. Accountant in the wood pulp and paper industries in Nova Scotia, 1923–38. Full-time Writer since 1938. Recipient: Governor-General's Award, 1944, for non-fiction, 1949, 1958; Boys' Club of America Junior Book Award, 1951; Lorne Pierce Medal, 1956. LL.D., Dalhousie University, Halifax, 1949; Litt.D., St. Mary's University, Halifax, 1969. Fellow, Royal Society of Canada, 1953. Medal of Service, Order of Canada, 1970. Address: 44 Park Street, Liverpool, Nova Scotia, Canada.

PUBLICATIONS

Novels

His Majesty's Yankees. New York, Doubleday, and Toronto, McClelland and Stewart, 1942; Edinburgh, Blackwood, 1944.

Roger Sudden. New York, Doubleday, and Toronto, McClelland and Stewart, 1945; London, Hurst and Blackett, 1946.

Pride's Fancy. New York, Doubleday, and Toronto, McClelland and Stewart, 1946; London, Hurst and Blackett, 1948.

The Nymph and the Lamp. Boston, Little Brown, and Toronto, McClelland and Stewart, 1950; London, Hutchinson, 1951.

Son of the Hawk. Philadelphia, Winston, 1950.

*Tidefall.*   Boston, Little Brown, and Toronto, McClelland and Stewart, 1953; London, Hutchinson, 1955.

*The Wings of Night.*   New York and Toronto, Doubleday, 1956; London, Macmillan, 1957.

*The Governor's Lady.*   New York and Toronto, Doubleday, 1960; London, Collins, 1961.

*Hangman's Beach.*   New York and Toronto, Doubleday, 1966.

Short Stories

*Pied Piper of Dipper Creek and Other Tales.*   Edinburgh, Blackwood, 1939.

*Tambour and Other Stories.*   Toronto, McClelland and Stewart, 1945.

*The Wedding Gift and Other Stories.*   Toronto, McClelland and Stewart, 1947.

*A Muster of Arms and Other Stories.*   Toronto, McClelland and Stewart, 1954.

*Footsteps on Old Floors: True Tales of Mystery.*   New York and Toronto, Doubleday, 1968.

Other

*West Novas: A History of the West Nova Scotia Regiment.*   Halifax, Book Room, 1948.

*Halifax: Warden of the North.*   Toronto, McClelland and Stewart, 1948; London, Dent, 1950.

*The Path of Destiny: Canada from the British Conquest to Home Rule, 1763–1850.*   New York and Toronto, Doubleday, 1957.

*The Rover: The Story of a Canadian Privateer.*   Toronto and London, Macmillan, 1958; New York, St. Martin's Press, 1959.

Critical Studies: "Thomas H. Raddall: The Man and His Work" by W. J. Hawkins, in *Queen's Quarterly* (Kingston, Ontario), Spring 1968; "Thomas Raddall: The Art of Historical Fiction" by Donald Cameron, in *Dalhousie Review* (Halifax), 1970.

Thomas Head Raddall comments:

As a youth I went to sea in Canadian ships, served in the North Atlantic for three years, and then a year as wireless operator on Sable Island, "The Graveyard of the Atlantic". Subsequently these experiences and observations gave me material for short stories and a novel, *The Nymph and the Lamp.* When I left the sea I took a job as book-keeper for a wood-pulp mill in the Nova Scotia forest. This gave me many interesting years of friendship with mill hands, loggers, river-drivers, hunters, and a band of Micmac Indians. I spent most of my spare time in the woods, exploring the Mersey River and its lakes, on foot and by canoe. On the indoor side I had a deep interest in Canadian, and especially Nova Scotian, history, and my experience of the sea and the forest gave me light on many of the old documents I found in the archives at Halifax and elsewhere. Hence, half a dozen novels, many short stories of colonial times, and three books of plain history.

In all my fiction, whether historical or contemporary, I sought to inform as well as to give intelligent entertainment, and to convey in words and style my own delight in the English language.

\*     \*     \*

Despite a long and distinguished career as a professional novelist, Thomas Raddall is curiously ignored by criticism. In part this neglect may be the result of his conservatism: he is no experimenter in either form or choice of material, he is personally retiring, and he unabashedly seeks a wide audience.

More unusually, he has achieved one. Raddall is deeply Nova Scotian, and though his novels sell well elsewhere and have been translated into several languages, perhaps the most unusual feature of his career has been his relationship with his native province. In Nova Scotia the most astonishing spectrum of people reads Raddall, from cabbies to the Cabinet. Nothing remotely parallel exists elsewhere in English Canada, and it is an inspiring example of the public uses to which the novel may still be put.

All Raddall's novels are set in Nova Scotia. Some of them are contemporary—notably *Tidefall* and *The Nymph and the Lamp*, the story of a strange love affair between a radio operator and a frustrated, lonely typist who comes to live with him amidst the collection of isolated men on thinly-disguised Sable Island. Though it has done well in the bookstores, however, the novel has never found much critical favour.

Raddall points out—quite correctly—that he is not just a historical novelist, but historical fiction has yielded his greatest successes. The historical passion is strong in Raddall, and his work includes a volume of Canadian history, *The Path of Destiny*, as well as perhaps the finest work of local history ever written in Canada, *Halifax: Warden of the North*.

Raddall's historical fiction includes *Roger Sudden*, *Pride's Fancy*, *The Governor's Lady*, and *Hangman's Beach*, as well as numerous short stories, Perhaps the best, however, is Raddall's first novel, *His Majesty's Yankees*, an account of the changing loyalties and fortunes of David Strang, a young Nova Scotian fired with revolutionary zeal during the American War of Independence who finally comes to accept the forces which keep his colony British. The change in David is the change in the mood of Nova Scotia itself, and the understanding he achieves of the reasons for the colony's fate is the objective of the novel.

Such a story demands precisely the gifts Raddall possesses: a strong sense of story and a flair for the description of action, a clear and muscular style, an astute awareness of the interrelation between such private concerns as sex and such public concerns as revolution. The political division separates David from part of his family and from his girl, and throws him into the centre of great events. Though he is not an extraordinary young man, he is intelligent, observant and honest, an easy man for the reader to trust.

In conversation, Raddall describes his books not as novels, but as "tales" or "romances". The terms are not ill-chosen. Northrop Frye suggests that in a romance we know at the beginning how the work will end, and in this sense historical fiction is necessarily romantic. Moreover our interest in the hero is not centred in his uniqueness, but in his typicality; he stands not for an individual ideal or value, but for a communal mode of experience.

The hero's experience, says Lukács, is the necessary prehistory of the present; understanding it, we understand our own condition. At his best, Raddall conveys just such an understanding. Because of Nova Scotia's pivotal position in both the great French-English conflict in North America and the American Revolution, his work is relevant to an audience far beyond his beloved native province.

—Donald Cameron

---

**RAND, Ayn.** American. Born in St. Petersburg, now Leningrad, Russia, 2 February 1905; emigrated to the United States in 1926; naturalized, 1931. Educated at the University of Leningrad: graduated in history 1924. Married Frank O'Connor in 1929. Screenwriter, 1932–34, 1944–49. Editor, *The Objectivist*, New York, 1962–71, and since 1971, *The Ayn*

*Rand Letter*, New York. Visiting Lecturer, Yale University, New Haven, Connecticut, 1960, Princeton University, New Jersey, 1960, Columbia University, New York, 1960, 1962, University of Wisconsin, Madison, 1961, Johns Hopkins University, Baltimore, 1961, Harvard University, Cambridge, Massachusetts, 1962, and Massachusetts Institute of Technology, Cambridge, 1962. D.H.L., Lewis and Clark College, Portland, Oregon, 1963. Address: The Ayn Rand Letter, 201 East 34th Street, New York, New York 10016, U.S.A.

PUBLICATIONS

Novels

*We the Living*.   New York, Macmillan, and London, Cassell, 1936.
*Anthem*.   London, Cassell, 1938; revised edition, Los Angeles, Pamphleteers, 1946.
*The Fountainhead*.   Indianapolis, Bobbs Merrill, 1943; London, Cassell, 1947.
*Atlas Shrugged*.   New York, Random House, 1957.

Plays

*Night of January 16th* (produced, as *Woman on Trial*, Hollywood, 1934; New York, 1935).   New York, Longman, 1936.
*The Unconquered* (produced New York, 1940).

Screenplay: *The Fountainhead*, 1949.

Other

*For the New Intellectual*.   New York, Random House, 1961.
*The Objectivist Ethic*.   New York, Branden Institute, 1961.
*The Virtue of Selfishness: A New Concept of Egoism*.   New York, New American Library, 1965.
*Capitalism: The Unknown Ideal*, with others.   New York, New American Library, 1966.
*Introduction to Objectivist Epistemology*.   New York, The Objectivist, 1967.
*The Romantic Manifesto: A Philosophy of Literature*.   Cleveland, World, 1970.
*The New Left: The Anti-Industrial Revolution*.   New York, New American Library, 1971.

Manuscript Collection: Library of Congress, Washington, D.C.

*       *       *

Ayn Rand has developed a considerable public, both for her novels, especially *The Fountainhead* and *Atlas Shrugged*, and for her periodical publications, *The Objectivist* and *The Ayn Rand Letter*. Her novels are meant to display her philosophical speculations; in other words, she is a novelist of "ideas." To insure that these ideas are not misinterpreted, however, she has also published several collections of essays, many of them gathered from *The Objectivist*, in which the principal premises of the novels are made explicit.

Her philosophical credo is objectivism, a peculiarly narrow and wilful form of Romanticism which holds that man is primarily a rational creature, that his happiness lies in self-fulfilment, that his only responsibility is toward himself ("the virtue of selfishness"), and that those few individuals who practice such a doctrine constitute an elite group whose function is to realize fully the rational element in man's nature. Human weakness has no place in her system, and any sympathetic regard for weakness in others is a demonstration of the philosophical bane of the modern world, altruism, which, under the guise of helping the less fortunate, has systematically eroded the artistic, political, economic and social systems of the twentieth century until we have arrived at the chaos in which we live at present. Altruism is non-productive; it takes from the producers and spreads their creativity among the non-producers until finally there is, as shown in her last novel, *Atlas Shrugged*, nothing left for anybody. Altruism is the philosophy which leads to socialism, the ultimate non-creative form of government; or, still worse, to anarchy, non-government, in which property is wrested from the weaker by the stronger by violence, the ultimate negation of reason. The only free society is capitalistic in which the individual is allowed to fulfil his rational destiny, and Rand's capitalistic Utopia is one in which self-fulfilling creativity, be it in science, art, business, or politics, results ironically in the good life which altruism promises but cannot deliver.

The difficulty with Rand's philosophical analysis, and of her applications of its results both in her fiction and in her treatment of social, artistic, and political ills in her essays, is that she is drastically simplistic. A few examples will suffice. In her series of essays on art, *The Romantic Manifesto*, she gives what surely must be one of the most uninformed definitions of Romanticism one is likely to meet. Without quite knowing it, the Romantics achieved an intellectual revolution by elevating volition (self-determinism, i.e. rationalism) to the place of prime importance in the intellectual realm. Aristotle somehow survives the reduction of previous Western civilization to intellectual limbo, but in her limbo are Plato, and by default, St. Augustine, St. Thomas Aquinas, Dante, and, one presumes, Descartes. The same is true of the arts. Shakespeare must be regarded as a failure because his tragic characters are not self-determined. One grows a bit queasy when Rand finally sets up her pantheon of artists worth regarding: Hugo, Dostoevsky, and, in the field of popular literature, Mickey Spillane and Ian Fleming. One would like to have a little more left to read.

One simply need not take Rand seriously; while her novels will not save the world, neither, we might hope, will they propel us into hers; and if one can struggle through novels as long as Dickens's with no intentional comic relief, one has done something.

—James Hill

---

RAO, Raja. Indian. Born in Hassan, Mysore, 21 November 1909. Educated at Nizam College, Hyderabad (University of Madras), B.A. in English 1929; University of Montpellier, France, 1929–30; the Sorbonne, Paris, 1930–33. Married Camille Mouly in 1931; Katherine Jones, 1965; has one son. Has spent half of his life in France; now lives half the year in India and half in Europe and the United States. Since 1965, Professor of Philosophy, teaching one semester a year, University of Texas, Austin. Recipient: The Prize for Literature, Academy of Indian Literature, 1964; Padma Bhushan, Government of India, 1969. Address: Department of Philosophy, University of Texas, Austin, Texas 78712, U.S.A.

PUBLICATIONS

Novels

*Kanthapura.* London, Allen and Unwin, 1938; New York, New Directions, 1963.
*The Serpent and the Rope.* London, Murray, 1960; New York, Pantheon Books, 1963.
*The Cat and Shakespeare: A Tale of India.* New York, Macmillan, 1965.

Short Stories

  *The Cow of the Barricades and Other Stories.*   London and Bombay, Oxford University
  Press, 1947.

Uncollected Short Stories

  "India: A Story", in *Encounter* (London), no. 2, 1953.
  "The Policeman and the Rose", in *Botteghe Oscure* (Rome), 1958.

Other

  *Whither India*, with Iqbal Singh.   Bombay, Padma, 1948.

  Editor, with Iqbal Singh, *Changing India*.   London, Allen and Unwin, 1939.

Bibliography: in *Raja Rao* by M. S. Naik, New York, Twayne, 1972.

Critical Studies: *Raja Rao: A Critical Study of His Work* by C. D. Narasimhiah, London
and Delhi, Heinemann, 1972; *Raja Rao* by M. S. Naik, New York, Twayne, 1972.

Raja Rao comments:

Starting from the humanitarian and romantic perspective of man in *Kanthapura* and *The Cow of the Barricades*—both deeply influenced by Mahatma Gandhi's philosophy of non-violence—I soon came to the metaphysical novel, *The Serpent and the Rope*, and *The Cat and Shakespeare*, based on the Vedantic conception of illusion and reality. My main interest increasingly is in showing the complexity of the human condition (that is, the reality of man is beyond his person), and in showing the symbolic construct of any human expression. All words are hierarchic symbols, almost mathematical in precision, on and of the unknown.

*         *         *

In addition to a volume of short stories titled *The Cow of the Barricades*, Raja Rao has thus far published three novels—*Kanthapura*, *The Serpent and the Rope*, and *The Cat and Shakespeare*. A South Indian Brahmin, Raja Rao is chiefly concerned with religion and philosophy, not only of India but also of the West, which he has come to know through many years of residence and study in France and, more recently, in the United States. During his youth he was deeply influenced by Mahatma Gandhi; and his first novel, *Kanthapura*, testifies unmistakably to its author's intellectual involvement in the Gandhian drive for national independence—to Raja Rao as much a religious as a political movement.

E. M. Forster considered *Kanthapura* to be the best novel ever written in English by an Indian, and indeed it has great literary strength. Not the least of its merits is the picture it gives of life in one of the innumerable villages that are the repositories of India's ancient but living culture. In vivid detail, Raja Rao describes the daily activities, the religious observances, and the social structure of the community, and he brings to life in his pages a dozen or more unforgettable individual villagers. The novel is political on a superficial level in that it chronicles a revolt against an exploitative plantation manager and the police who support him. But more profoundly it traces the origins of the revolt more to an awakening of the long-dormant Indian soul than to the activities of the Congress party. One of the young men of the village, while away, undergoes a mystical conversion to Satyagraha, and returns to incite his fellow villagers to civil disobedience. He arouses in them not only a sense of social wrong but, more importantly, a religious fervor which proves to be the true source of their strength against their oppressors.

*Kanthapura* is a novel in which the reader's interest is held mainly by its action and characters. *The Serpent and the Rope* and *The Cat and Shakespeare* are unabashedly metaphysical novels in which plot, setting and even characters are of secondary interest. Semiautobiographical, *The Serpent and the Rope* records the disintegration of a marriage, mainly on philosophical grounds, of a very scholarly Indian Brahmin and a French woman professor. The union founders on the incompatibility of the Brahmin's vedantic conviction that "reality is my Self" and the wife's Western belief—even though she has become a Buddhist—that the evidence of our senses is based on an objective reality outside ourselves. "The world is either unreal or real—the serpent or the rope," the Brahmin assures his wife. "There is no in-between-the-two. . . . "

The intellectual demands that Raja Rao, roaming at large through world history and among the religions, philosophies, and literatures of Europe and Asia, makes upon his readers are unequalled in any modern novel since Thomas Mann's *The Magic Mountain*. Though he quotes at length from a bewildering assortment of languages, he provides translations in the case of only one—Sanskrit. The reader is flatteringly assumed to be fluent in Latin, Provençal, Italian, Old French and other tongues.

*The Cat and Shakespeare* is much shorter and lighter in tone, though scarcely less metaphysical. The subject of its probings is the problem of individual destiny, and the solution is conveyed in an odd analogy stated by a government clerk: "Learn the way of the kitten. Then you are saved. Allow the mother cat, sir, to carry you." Critics disagree as to what the mother cat symbolizes. The most likely suggestion, made by Uma Parameswaran, is that the cat is karma, the inevitable results of our actions.

All of Raja Rao's work is notable for seriousness of purpose, profundity of thought, a flair for vivid presentation of detail, and a distinctive and vigorous English prose. He asserts:

> We cannot write like the English. We should not. We cannot write only as Indians. We have grown to look at the large world as part of us. Our method of expression therefore has to be a dialect which will some day prove to be as distinctive and colorful as the Irish or the American. Time alone will justify it.

We might add that Raja Rao's books have gone far to justify it.

—Perry D. Westbrook

---

**RAPHAEL, Frederic (Michael).** American. Born in Chicago, Illinois, 14 August 1931. Educated at Charterhouse, Surrey; St. John's College, Cambridge, 1950–54 (Major Classics Scholar, 1950; Harper Wood Student, 1954), M.A. (honours) 1954. Married Sylvia Betty Glatt in 1955; has three children. Since 1962, Contributor to the *Sunday Times*, London: Fiction Critic, 1962–65. Recipient: British Screen Writers' Award, 1965, 1966, 1967; British Academy Award, 1965; United States Academy Award, 1966. Fellow, Royal Society of Literature, 1964. Address: The Wick, Langham, near Colchester, Essex, England; or, Lagardelle, St. Laurent-la-Vallée 24, France.

Publications

Novels

*Obbligato.* London, Macmillan, 1956.
*The Earlsdon Way.* London, Cassell, 1958.
*The Limits of Love.* London, Cassell, 1960; Philadelphia, Lippincott, 1961.
*A Wild Surmise.* London, Cassell, 1961; Philadelphia, Lippincott, 1962.
*The Graduate Wife.* London, Cassell, 1962.
*The Trouble with England.* London, Cassell, 1962.
*Lindmann.* London, Cassell, 1963; New York, Holt Rinehart, 1964.
*Darling.* New York, New American Library, 1965.
*Orchestra and Beginners.* London, Cape, 1967; New York, Viking Press, 1968.
*Like Men Betrayed.* London, Cape, 1970; New York, Viking Press, 1971.
*Who Were You with Last Night?* London, Cape, 1971.

Uncollected Short Stories

"The Day Franco Came", in *New World Writing 22.* Philadelphia, Lippincott, 1964.
"One Star, Two Crossed Knives and Forks and a View of the Sea", in *Thy Neighbour's Wife.* London, Cassell, 1964.
"Yes, But You Won't Catch Me Going There Again", in *Yale Review* (New Haven, Connecticut), 1964.
"When in Rome", in *Voices.* London, Joseph, 1965.

Plays

*A Man on the Bridge* (produced Hornchurch, Essex, 1961).
*Two for the Road* (screenplay). London, Cape, and New York, Holt Rinehart, 1967.

Screenplays: *Nothing But the Best,* 1964; *Darling,* 1965; *Two for the Road,* 1967; *Far from the Madding Crowd,* 1967; *How About Us?,* 1971; *A Severed Head,* 1971.

Critical Study: "The Varied Universe of Frederic Raphael" by Frederick P. W. McDowell, in *Critique* (Minneapolis), Fall 1965.

Frederic Raphael comments:

Although in many ways I am the most marginal of Jews (I am agnostic in religion and wary of communities), I suppose it is honest to say that I would not be a novelist if it were not for the singular experiences of the Jewish people and for my sense of being, if not a direct participant, at least a witness, of them. My themes, if I have themes, are scarcely Jewish since I lack intimate knowledge of the practices and habits of those who live in so-called Jewish society. When I do come in contact with them I do not necessarily find them congenial. Yet, the Final Solution—its vulgarity no less than its brutality, its greedy malice no less than its murderous factories—lies always at the back of my mind even if I myself, as a child growing up in England, suffered nothing more than its bad breath blowing in my face from across the Channel. It may be an indulgence for anyone who did not have closer experience to claim personal acquaintance with the holocaust; it is equally frivolous to ignore it. It is too convenient a conclusion to dispose of the Jewish experience under the Germans (and the Austrians and the Poles and the Hungarians and the Ukranians and the Russians, and the English and the Americans) as a sort of freakish explosion, a San Francisco earthquake of an event, a once-and-for-all catastrophe after which, in the comforter's cliché, one has to "go on living". And yet, of course, one does.

For me, the novelist is, above all, the historian of conscience. How does the individual conscience—in other words, how do I—go on living in a world which gives the clearest possible testimony of the cruelty and indifference of man? How does one continue to worry about the nuances of personal life, about love, friendship, taste and responsibility when all the signs are that man is essentially rapacious, vindictive and stupid? I have no answers to these questions, nor do I pretend they are in themselves new; they have been asked often enough and yet one does live at a particular time and, despite all the elegant suggestions to the contrary, it seems to me that our time is still linear. Certain things are beyond change, others lie ahead.

The problem is, in a sense, of language. Only in language is it possible to assimilate horrors and yet to achieve something which is both clear and, in a sense, pure. The way in which man remembers meaningfully is by not refusing sense in his language to those things which most profoundly influence or instruct him. This might be an argument for writing either history or philosophy and in a way I tried to do this, but I am not a historian or a philosopher. An obsession with a particular instance of the human character and a desire—no less than a tendency—to show the futility of generalisation in the face of the fatuous and magnanimous individuality of human beings, lead me to examine the world through dramatic and emotional states rather than through a study of documents or the analysis of trends. Beyond and through the tragic comes the comic—the comic which does not explode the tragic but defines it—and this interpenetration is only one example of the sort of ambiguities in which the novelist finds himself at home. These ambiguities reveal themselves in drama and I have always found that, in spite of the attractions of both the theatre and the cinema, the drama can be worked out at its most personal in the most piercing fashion in fiction. Truth may be stranger than fiction but fiction is truer.

How loftily one speaks in such generalising terms as these. The actual impulses which start a book are, of course, less grand. They spring as much from a sense of one's own contradictions as from any perception of human inadequacy or follies. When one begins to speak in the first person it sounds like conceit but it is more often confession, at least at my age. I am conscious above all of being equipped to be a novelist because it is only in a multiplicity of characters that I can reconcile my own ragbag personality. When people speak of a crisis of identity, I remind them that we know very well who we are, where we are having dinner and with whom we are sleeping, yet when I consider myself I am less commonsensical.

I was born in Chicago of a British father and an American mother. Beyond them, my grandparents and great-grandparents branched off across the world like an airline network. I was educated at Charterhouse which, I am told, is a great English Public School, and at Cambridge. I was readily influenced both by the ethos of the English middle class and by the intellectual habits of a classical education. Although I now regret much of what I was told and some of what I learned, I cannot shrug off the influence of these places, nor am I certain that I would wish to do so. The conflict of values reveals itself in fiction in the conflict of characters. I am conscious of being foreign in England and I find myself at home to some extent in many other places, yet I cannot sever myself entirely from the country where I live or from the language in which I write. I am sickened by xenophobia and yet in many ways I fear what lies beyond me. I believe that reason is better than unreason and that intelligence is better than instinct but I have not always been impressed by the decency of those who are most intelligent or by the capacity for affection and love of those who are most reasonable.

Within the nooks and crannies of the great edifices of generalisation and judgement, the innocently guilty and the guiltily innocent scurry about carrying nuts to their families, seeking their pleasures, snapping at their enemies and providing, for those who have eyes to see, the proof of the impossibility of final solutions to the human condition.

\*      \*      \*

Frederic Raphael began with a slight novel, *Obbligato*, a satiric and mock-heroic account of the rise to fame of an improvising pop-singer. Literary merit is abundant, however, in Raphael's second book, *The Earlsdon Way*, a realistic novel about the futility of British suburban life and the ineffectual revolt against its mores undertaken by Edward Keggin and his daughter Karen.

*The Limits of Love* is Raphael's most sustained work. Its protagonist, Paul Riesman, is a Jew divorced by his training and inclinations from his race. Because he will not recognize what is necessity for him, his Jewishness, he becomes a selfish, life-destroying man despite his continuing efforts to achieve identity. But Paul increasingly sees that love is a defeating force if it is limited to the personal sphere and if it rejects the community; and he finds in his mother-in-law, Hannah Adler, stability that he lacks and in her daughter Julia, his wife, flexibility and depth. Raphael not only analyzes Paul's nature brilliantly but sets forth with the sureness of personal knowledge the Jewish milieu which Paul must finally accept.

In *A Wild Surmise* Raphael used a technique of montage to reveal his protagonist, Robert Carn, gradually. Carn hopes to escape British conventions in San Roque and to find genuine value through the spontaneous, impassioned, disinterested self. Ultimately he supplements his introspective endeavors with a commitment to others in his efforts, ostensibly unsuccessful, to save some Indians from being poisoned. The novel is powerful and evocative, especially as it charts the inner processes of Carn's mind and the subtleties of his psychic life.

Raphael's next two novels, *The Trouble with England* and *The Graduate Wife*, are short books, ironically executed, which concentrate upon a moral problem and its significance for the chief characters. *The Trouble with England* develops the moral contrasts between two vacationing couples on the French Riviera; *The Graduate Wife* focuses upon the forward development of a priggish heroine to inner stability. Raphael's most recent novel, *Who Were You with Last Night?*, is another short comic novel. The first-person narrator, Charles Hanson, is extremely amusing as he deflates bourgeois values (sometimes his own), recounts his satisfactions and frustrations with wife and mistress, and analyzes the delicate balance existing between love and hate in intimate relationships.

More substantial, and the peak of Raphael's achievement to date in writing the experimental novel, is *Lindmann*. A British civil servant, James Shepherd, has connived in 1942 in preventing the *SS Broda* from landing in Turkey with its Jewish refugees. Shepherd, to expiate his guilt and to achieve self-definition, assumes the identity of Jacob Lindmann, one of the two survivors from the ship who later died from exposure. A certain chastity gives Shepherd as Lindmann his moral force, since he forgoes any kind of fulfillment for himself; and he is, by his spiritual tenacity, something more than the failure he judges himself to be. Through patience and love he tries to influence others to a course of moderation, toleration, consideration, and affection. The book, by virtue of the conflicts explored and its variety of techniques, attains a massiveness that is new in Raphael's work.

This quality is present in Raphael's two more recent novels, *Orchestra and Beginners* and *Like Men Betrayed*. In the first, Raphael analyzes the ineffectual decency and effete decay which characterized British upper middle-class society just prior to World War II. Linda Strauss, though she suffers from the moral paralysis of the class into which as an American she has married, is sympathetically seen, though she fails her husband at his military enlistment because of her intensely personal reactions to experience. Leonard, in turn, is too impersonal toward Linda. Paradoxically, Linda's passion and Leonard's critical intelligence, her preoccupation with the self and his selfless service to others, are both needed in confronting the complexities of modern life. Raphael's psychological acuity, his concern for the involutions of conduct, his moral seriousness, his imaginative reach, and his technical dexterity are to the fore in this novel as they are in *Like Men Betrayed*.

This novel is about Grecian and, by implication, English politics, and it is remarkable for penetrating the relationships between the individual's psyche and social institutions. Three main points in time contrapuntally organize the book: the Greece of the 1930's under the Marshal's moderate dictatorship; Greece during the Second War when factional jealousies are only less intense than hatred for the Italians and Germans; and postwar Greece when a power struggle develops between the corrupt royalist regime and the Leftist insurgents. Artemis Theodoros defects from the Royalists when government troops fail in World War II to support the leftist General Papavastrou against the Germans. The novel is subtle and complex, as it traces Artemis's endeavors to reach spiritual and political truth. As the novel opens he is fleeing north to the frontier where supposedly his forces will reach asylum. Instead, he learns that they will be betrayed. He remains faithful to his inner standards, however, despite misunderstanding, violence, betrayal, imprisonment, and exile. In Artemis a deplorable waste of genius occurs. Such is the ultimate tragedy of civil war: the leaders of the losing side forego all possibilities of using their lives creatively. Artemis, poet, devoted adherent to the Left, leader of men and independent thinker, attains passive exile. The integrity inherent in such a heroic man, however, is the resource which we will have to learn how to use to insure a revitalized polity, Raphael would seem to be saying. The density, elusiveness, complication, and range of this novel are truly impressive as they are in Raphael's fiction as a whole.

—Frederick P. W. McDowell

RAVEN, Simon (Arthur Noel).   British.   Born in London, 28 December 1927. Educated at Charterhouse, Surrey, 1941–45; King's College, Cambridge, 1948–52, B.A. 1951, M.A. 1955. Served in the British Army, 1946–48 (commissioned in India, 1947), and 1953–57 (Captain, King's Shropshire Light Infantry). Married Susan Mandeville Kilner in 1952 (divorced, 1957); has one child. Address: c/o Blond and Briggs Ltd., 56 Doughty Street, London W.C.2, England.

PUBLICATIONS

Novels

   *The Feathers of Death.*   London, Blond, 1959; New York, Simon and Schuster, 1960.
   *Brother Cain.*   London, Blond, 1959; New York, Simon and Schuster, 1960.
   *Doctors Wear Scarlet.*   London, Blond, 1960; New York, Simon and Schuster, 1961.
   *Close of Play.*   London, Blond, 1962.
   *Alms for Oblivion:*
      *The Rich Pay Late.*   London, Blond, 1964; New York, Putnam, 1965.
      *Friends in Low Places.*   London, Blond, 1965; New York, Putnam, 1966.
      *The Sabre Squadron.*   London, Blond, 1966; New York, Harper, 1967.
      *Fielding Gray.*   London, Blond, 1967.
      *The Judas Boy.*   London, Blond, 1968.
      *Places Where They Sing.*   London, Blond, 1970.
      *Sound the Retreat.*   London, Blond, 1971.
      *Come like Shadows.*   London, Blond and Briggs, 1972.

Plays

*Royal Foundation and Other Plays* (produced on BBC, 1961–65).   London, Blond, 1966.
*The Sconcing Stoup* (broadcast, BBC, 1964).   Published in *New Radio Drama*, London,
BBC, 1966.

Screenplay: *Unman, Wittering, and Zigo*, 1971.

Plays, dramatisations, and series produced on BBC television.

Other

*The English Gentleman: An Essay in Attitudes.*   London, Blond, 1961; as *The Decline
of the English Gentleman*, New York, Simon and Schuster, 1962.
*Boys Will Be Boys and Other Essays.*   London, Blond, 1963.

Editor, *The Best of Gerald Kersh.*   London, Heinemann, 1960.

Critical Study: "The Novels of Simon Raven" by Kerry McSweeney, in *Queen's Quarterly*
(Kingston, Ontario), Spring 1971.

Simon Raven comments:

My theme is the vanity of human wishes.
My object is to make money by presenting this theme in such a way as to interest and
amuse intelligent readers of the upper and upper-middle classes.

*        *        *

Simon Raven is frequently compared to Evelyn Waugh. Yet the truth is that his novels
are nearer to the spirit of P. G. Wodehouse. For all their show of satire of contemporary
social *mores*, and for all their dedicated right-wing snobbishness, the fact is that one can't
take them seriously. As entertainments they repay reading; as serious novels they do not.
Raven would probably not mind this being said. His writing has all the marks of the good
*raconteur*; it seeks to amuse and to hold the attention. All of his novels are remarkable
for the ingenious sexual lives of their principal characters, yet in none are we given the
sweaty detail or the naming of parts. Instead, there is hint, innuendo, suggestion. We are
taken as far as the bedroom door (or more interesting doors) but not beyond. And this is
not the result of prudishness, but of calculated prurience. Again, all the novels have a good
deal of plot, there is much coming and going of characters and the settings are customarily
exotic, the English no less than the foreign (Raven's England tends to be bounded by seedy
public schools, gambling salons, and expensive Mayfair apartments inside whose plush
rooms unspeakable happenings occur). Yet it is impossible to believe in the reality of any
of these places. Nor does it much matter. The pace of the narrative seldom drops below a
steady gallop and we are whisked from place to place, incident to incident, in a manner that
hardly allows us to question the substantiality of it all.
Yet it may perhaps be that Raven aims higher than I have suggested. In the first place
there is his novel *Close of Play*, which seems to touch a darker note than is usual with him.
The hero, Hugo Warren, is a person whose motto "never regret anything" carries him through
a series of outrageous adventures that culminate in the murder of his sexual partner and of

his own murder at the hands of relatives and former friends. And for all the high jinks, *Close of Play* is obviously meant to be a study of amorality, even of evil. Yet it is difficult to be very involved with this, because the novel's farcical elements collide so crudely with the more sombre moments.

Then again, there is the novel sequence, *Alms for Oblivion*, of which seven novels have so far appeared. Of these the best is probably *The Rich Pay Late*, though *The Judas Boy* runs it close. But no matter how amusing the individual novels may be, it is impossible to see the point of the sequence as a whole. It can hardly be said to provide an extended study of its central character, Fielding Gray, for he does not develop from one novel to the next. Simply, different things happen to him. But neither can the sequence be said to build up an important study of the contemporary world (or of England), because the settings are too random for that. It may, of course be that when the sequence is finished—we are promised ten novels in all—much will become clear that is at the moment dark. But it is more likely that *Alms for Oblivion* will be remembered for the merits of the individual novels. Still, we can be sure of one thing—it will entertain.

—John Lucas

---

**RAYMOND, Ernest.** British. Born in Argentieres, France, 31 December 1888. Educated at St. Paul's School, London; Chichester Theological College, Sussex; Durham University, L.Th. 1914; ordained, 1914; resigned orders, 1923. Served in the British Army, in the 10th Manchester Regiment, 1915–17, and in the 9th Worcester Regiment, 1917–19; served in Gallipoli, Egypt, France, Mesopotamia, Persia and Russia. Married Zoe Irene Maude Doucett in 1921 (marriage dissolved); Diana Joan Young, 1941; has three children. Assistant Master at Glengorse School, Eastbourne, Sussex, 1908–11, and at St. Christopher's School, Bath, Somerset, 1911–12. President, The Dickens Fellowship, London, 1971. Recipient: Book Guild Gold Medal, 1936. Knight Officer, Order of Merit of the Italian Republic, 1964. Fellow, Royal Society of Literature, 1947. Address: 22 The Pryors, East Heath Road, London N.W.3, England.

PUBLICATIONS

Novels

Tell England: A Study in a Generation. London, Cassell, and New York, Doran, 1922.
Rossenal. London, Cassell, 1922.
Damascus Gate. London, Cassell, 1923.
Wanderlight. London, Cassell, 1924.
Daphne Bruno. London, Cassell, and New York, Doran, 1926.
The Fulfillment of Daphne Bruno. London, Cassell, and New York, Doran, 1926.
Morris in the Dance. London, Cassell, 1927.
The Old Tree Blossomed. London, Cassell, 1928.
A Family That Was. London, Cassell, 1929; New York, Appleton, 1930.
The Jesting Army. London, Cassell, 1930; New York, Appleton, 1931.
Mary Leith. London, Cassell, 1931; New York, Appleton, 1932.
Once in England (includes A Family That Was, The Jesting Army, and Mary Leith).
   London, Cassell, 1932.

*Newtimber Lane: Being a Writing of Sir Edmund Earlwin of Cowbourne in Sussex.*
   London, Cassell, 1933.
*Child of Norman's End.*   London, Cassell, 1934.
*We the Accused.*   London, Cassell, and New York, Stokes, 1935.
*Don John's Mountain Home.*   London, Cassell, 1936.
*The Marsh.*   London, Cassell, and New York, Stokes, 1937.
*The Miracle of Brean.*   London, Cassell, 1939.
*A Song of the Tide.*   London, Cassell, 1940.
*The Last to Rest.*   London, Cassell, 1941; New York, Kinsey, 1942.
*Was There Love Once.*   London, Cassell, 1942.
*The Corporal of the Guard.*   London, Cassell, 1943.
*For Them That Trespass.*   London, Cassell, 1944.
*The Five Sons of Le Faber.*   London, Gifford, 1946.
*The Kilburn Tale.*   London, Cassell, 1947.
*Gentle Greaves.*   London, Cassell, 1949.
*The Witness of Canon Welcome.*   London, Cassell, 1950.
*A Chorus Ending.*   London, Cassell, 1951.
*The Chalice and the Sword.*   London, Cassell, 1952.
*To the Wood No More.*   London, Cassell, 1952.
*The Nameless Places.*   London, Cassell, 1954.
*The Lord of Wensley.*   London, Cassell, 1956.
*The Old June Weather.*   London, Cassell, 1957.
*The City and the Dream.*   London, Cassell, 1958.
*The Quiet Shore.*   London, Cassell, 1958.
*The Visit of Brother Ives.*   London, Cassell, 1960.
*Mr. Olim.*   London, Cassell, 1961.
*The Chatelaine.*   London, Cassell, 1962.
*One of Our Brethren.*   London, Cassell, 1963.
*Late in the Day.*   London, Cassell, 1964.
*The Tree of Heaven.*   London, Cassell, 1965.
*The Mountain Farm.*   London, Cassell, 1966.
*The Bethany Road.*   London, Cassell, 1967.
*A Georgian Love Story.*   London, Cassell, and New York, McCall, 1971.
*Our Late Member.*   London, Cassell, 1972.


Plays

*The Berg* (produced London, 1929).   London, Benn, 1929.
*The Multabello Road* (produced London, 1932).   London, Cassell, 1933.


Other

*The Shout of the King.*   London, Hodder and Stoughton, 1924.
*Through Literature to Life: An Enthusiasm and an Anthology.*   London, Cassell, 1929.
*In the Steps of St. Francis.*   London, Rich and Cowan, 1938; New York, Putnam, 1939.
*Back to Humanity*, with Patrick Raymond.   London, Cassell, 1945.
*In the Steps of the Brontës.*   London, Rich and Cowan, 1948.
*Two Gentlemen of Rome: The Story of Keats and Shelley.*   London, Cassell, 1952.
*Paris: City of Enchantment.*   London, Newnes, and New York, Macmillan, 1961.
*The Story of My Days: An Autobiography, 1888–1922.*   London, Cassell, 1968.
*Please You, Draw Near: An Autobiography, 1922–1928.*   London, Cassell, 1969.
*Good Morning, Good People: An Autobiography, Past and Present.*   London, Cassell,
   1970.

Editor, *The Autobiography of David.*   London, Gollancz, 1946.

Critical Study: comment by the author on his own work in *Please You, Draw Near*, 1969.

        *        *        *

Since his first novel, *Tell England*, gave him the success and the means to set up as a writer in 1922, Ernest Raymond has been a prolific novelist, producing about fifty books in the fifty years that followed, including several volumes of memoirs as well as fiction. Indeed, as his first volume of autobiography showed, the circumstances of his own life were far stranger than those of most of his own fiction, and the remarkable interest and charm of this book and its companion volume on the later years seem to suggest that the closer he sticks to the facts and spirit of his own experience, even in fiction, the more successful his writing tends to be. Until the publication of his first novel Mr Raymond was, first, a schoolmaster, then an Anglican clergyman, seeing the war in Gallipoli (from which came the second part of *Tell England*) as an army chaplain, then serving as a curate in Brighton until doubts about his religious faith made him leave the ministry.

*Tell England*, half a school story and half a war story, still popular half a century and innumerable reprints after its first appearance, was a period piece that exactly caught a certain mood and outlook at the time: that of a man toughened but not embittered by his experiences in the war. In spite of those front-line experiences and its author's close contact with death, fear and physical pain, it is still the work of a man plainly very young and emotionally ingenuous. Its success has in a sense dominated the rest of Mr Raymond's career as a writer, for no other novel of his came near it in fame, success, sales or staying power, and it is by this immature book that many still judge him.

His novels are in a well-established tradition of English fiction. Mostly they deal with middleclass life, observed realistically, sometimes humorously, sometimes quizzically, occasionally with gloom or even some harshness. Their method is detailed and descriptive, their pace leisurely, as a rule. They excel in conjuring particular places (parts of London, for instance, observed with affectionate closeness) and the atmospheres of particular social circles. Their settings vary a good deal. In *One of Our Brethren*, for instance, the clerical years are drawn on—an archdeacon, much loved and admired by some, is tried for immorality; in *The Bethany Road*, an Anglo-Catholic pilgrimage to the Holy Land is described by a narrator who has lost his faith. In *Mr Olim*, the story of a schoolmaster, Mr Raymond seems to be drawing on his own schoolboy years at St Paul's. In *Late in the Day*, a veteran of the First World War returns to Ypres and examines his own life since. *Child of Norman's End*, a story of middleclass London life at the time of Queen Victoria's Diamond Jubilee, *The Tree of Heaven*, the story of a good man turned murderer, and the self-descriptive *A Georgian Love Story* (pre-1914) are all set in topographically and atmospherically exact parts of London. *The Chatelaine* has a more exotic setting in wartime France under the German occupation, and the situation, piercingly familiar to the author from his own life, is of a mother who fails to acknowledge her illegitimate son and treats him as her nephew. *We the Accused* involved detailed research into crime and punishment, the treatment of criminals and their reaction to it, so that the story of a murderer could be written.

Through many of the novels runs a double theme like that of Mr Raymond's own early years: that of outward ordinariness and inner conflict, of middle-class respectability hiding situations dubious, pitiful and unfaced. Another important theme in them is the search for faith, meaning, fulfilment, a search that, from the time he left the security of his own Christian faith, occupied their author. Above all they show a close knowledge of particular times and milieux, a strong sense of period and atmosphere in an English middle-class that seems stable and recurrent yet has its depths, its secrets, and its dark places.

—Isabel Quigley

**RECHY, John (Francisco).** American. Born in El Paso, Texas, 10 March 1934. Educated at Texas Western College, El Paso, B.A.; New School for Social Research, New York. Served in the United States Army. Recipient: Longview Award, 1961. Lives in El Paso. Address: c/o Grove Press, 80 University Place, New York, New York 10003, U.S.A.

PUBLICATIONS

Novels

City of Night. New York, Grove Press, 1963; London, MacGibbon and Kee, 1964.
Numbers. New York, Grove Press, 1967.
This Day's Death. New York, Grove Press, and London, MacGibbon and Kee, 1970.

\*          \*          \*

John Rechy's world is the heir of Hawthorne's. His characters inhabit a moral universe whose codes are as rigorous as Calvin's and whose cops are the vigilantes of a new unmerciful Salem. The "youngmen" of City of Night and Numbers are the fallen angels of an eternally inaccessible paradise and their lives are characterised by a search for the eros that will at last become agape. That the search is frenetic is scarcely surprising; it has all the desperate urgency that characterises the role of the sensitive American—the anguish of exile within one's own country. And although in City of Night Rechy never quite succeeds in conveying Francis Thompson's added sense of "dreadful", it is plain that the implication is there. New York, from the first page, is a metaphor city, a fairy city—in a sense like the London of Stevenson—where anything might happen. That is not to say that Rechy's urban fantasy has the calibre of Purdy's. It is more limited in its focus. Its world is a moral world turned upside down, where the deus absconditus is Priapus. The quest for that god is a never-ending and insatiable one and one in which the tyrants of the old moral order have all the destructive vindictiveness of Diocletian against the Christians.

Having said all that, one should also say that neither City of Night nor Numbers (in spite of the deliberate "allegorical" pretensions of the former) often rises above what seem to be the masturbatory fantasies of an aging queen—bad Genet. Only with his third and by far his best novel, This Day's Death, does Rechy get beyond the unfortunate dualisms of his earlier novels—a catalogue of well-equipped muscleboys on the one hand and a labored novelistic artifice to contain it on the other. That is not to say that This Day's Death does not suffer from a somewhat contrivedly concealed central event and a time scheme that is sometimes confusing and tedious. Its à la récherche de la virginité perdue, however, is convincing in a way that is true of neither of the earlier novels. Rechy's New Mexico, like Steinbeck's Oklahoma, is a small-town world of poverty and pain, the anguish of growth and the desire to break out. His California is the nightmare inversion of that desire—a world where the law is a monster devouring the innocents who nonetheless have a Genet-like fascination with its devious iniquities. And together these worlds, as commentaries on one another, form a larger moral universe than any Rechy has created before.

One could not claim for Rechy that he had arrived at a position of major importance in the novel, or even the American novel. His major concerns are still too restricted to be in any meaningful sense a comment upon the life of the common reader. But This Day's Death is a hopeful sign of what he may become.

—D. D. C. Chambers

**REED, Ishmael.** Afro-American. Born in Chattanooga, Tennessee, 22 February 1938. Attended the University of Buffalo, New York, for three years. Married to Carla Blank-Reed; has one child by a previous marriage. Guest Lecturer in American Literature, University of California, Berkeley, 1968, 1969; Lecturer, University of Washington, Seattle, 1969. Since 1971, Vice-President (Editorial), Yardbird Publishing Corporation. Address: 6 Bret Harte Way, Berkeley, California 94708, U.S.A.

PUBLICATIONS

Novels

The Free-Lance Pallbearers. New York, Doubleday, 1967; London, MacGibbon and Kee, 1968.
Yellow Back Radio Broke-Down. New York, Doubleday, 1969; London, Allison and Busby, 1971.
Mumbo-Jumbo. New York, Doubleday, 1972.

Verse

Catechism of D Neoamerican HooDoo Chuck. London, Paul Bremser, 1970.
Conjure. Amherst, University of Massachusetts Press, 1972.

Other

Editor, 19 Necromancers from Now. New York, Doubleday, 1970.

Critical Studies: "Robin the Cock & Doopeyduk Doing the Boogaloo in Harry Sam with Rusty Jethroe and Letterhead America . . ." by Lawrence Lipton, in Cavalier (Greenwich, Connecticut), no. 70, 1967; review by Tam Fiofori, in Negro Digest (Chicago), December 1969; "Blood of the Lamb" by Calvin Hernton, in Amistad 1, New York, Knopf, 1970.

\*       \*       \*

"I'm shaking off the old skin," remarks Ellison's protagonist in Invisible Man, "and I'll leave it here in the hole. I'm coming out . . . and I suppose it's damn well time." The question confronting the black novelist after 1952 (publication date of Invisible Man) concerned the nature of the world into which Ellison's protagonist would emerge. For James Baldwin the world was Neo-Wrightian, decadent and devoid of love and hope. For John Williams and the black novelists of the sixties, the nature of the world was apocalyptic—one in which men and races alike rushed towards certain armageddon. For the young novelist Ishmael Reed, however, the world was one of confusion and chaos, manifested by the steady growth of science and technology, and the new found faith in Baconian rationalism which imposed rules and restraints subject to correction only by the pen and wit of the satirist.

Reed is our most important Black satirist, and his lineage may be traced to the satirists of the 1920's—to Rudolph Fisher, George Schuyler and Wallace Thurman. However, his milieu encompasses far more than theirs, his range is far greater. A warrior against rationalism, science and technology, he also inveighs against politics, religion and schism in the ranks of Blacks. Drawing upon the oldest artifacts of black culture—voodoo, hoodoo and black magic—his two novels, *The Free-Lance Pallbearers* and *Yellow Back Radio Broke-Down* are as much assaults upon the folkways and mores of an America gone technologically mad as they are upon American racism.

*The Free-Lance Pallbearers* is the story of Bukka Doopey-Duk, former student, Nazarene Priest Aspirant, hospital attendant and a subject in the kingdom of HARRY SAM: "I live in HARRY SAM. HARRY SAM is something else. A big not-to-be-believed out-of-sight, sometimes referred to as O-BOP-SHE-BANG or KLANG-A-LANG-A-DING-DONG." In reality, Sam, the dictator, and the kingdom are the same, for Sam is "master of *himself*"; that is of the kingdom (HARRY SAM). The quest of the hero, therefore, is to become master of *himself*, to usurp control of the kingdom (HARRY SAM) from Sam and establish the town of DOOPEY-DUK: "... I was going to run the whole kit and kaboodle, me dictator of BUKKA DOOPEY-DUK." Doopey-Duk's assault on the rules (formerly he had been a strict constructionist, resorting always to his Nazarene handbook) symbolizes the forces of intuition or irrationality as opposed to the forces of science and rationalism.

In *Yellow Back Radio Broke-Down*, a similar theme is evidenced in the quixotic quest of The Loop Garoo Kid, a black cowboy, to rescue the town of Yellow Back Radio from cattle rancher Drag Gibson. Aided by Gibson and his cowhands, the children of Yellow Back Radio (anti-rationalists) are chased out of town by the cattle ranchers (rationalists, technocrats). The Loop Garoo Kid, aided by the black forces—hoodoo and voodoo—comes to their rescue.

In both novels, Reed is primarily concerned with the inability of a rational world to communicate through new forms, and the necessity for the black writer to return to the cultural artifacts of the race: "No one," remarks The Kid, "says a novel has to be one thing. It can be anything it wants to be, a vaudeville show, the six o'clock news, the mumblings of wild men saddled by demons."

For Reed, the novel is a manual for black magic, the form as chaotic and unstructured as the wildest St. Agnes' Eve. The Loop Garoo Kid is heaven's "errant son" and Doopey-Duk has had "da hoodoo put on him." Both characters reflect Reed's idea of society and the novel; the absurdity of both lay in the fact that each takes itself seriously in a world in which science and technology have destroyed communication—symbolized by *Yellow Back Radio Broke-Down*—between young and old, black and white and black and black, and thus brought us to the brink of cultural and national annihilation—brought us to a world, that is, in which the Free-Lance Pallbearers, the emissaries of grim death, are the most suitable metaphors.

—Addison Gayle, Jr.

---

**REID, Vic(tor Stafford).** Jamaican. Born in Jamaica, 1 May 1913. Educated in Jamaica. Married; has four children. Reporter, Editor, and Foreign Correspondent, for newspapers; worked in advertising. Currently, Managing Director and Chairman of a printing and publishing company, Kingston, Jamaica. Traveled extensively in the Americas, Africa, Europe, and the Middle East. Recipient: Guggenheim Fellowship, 1959; Canada Council Fellowship; Mexican Writers Fellowship. Address. Box 129, Kingston 10, Jamaica.

PUBLICATIONS

Novels

*New Day*. New York, Knopf, 1949; London, Heinemann, 1950.
*The Leopard*. New York, Viking Press, and London, Heinemann, 1958.

Other

*Sixty-Five* (juvenile).   London, Longman, 1960.
*The Young Warriors* (juvenile).   London, Longman, 1967.

\*          \*          \*

Vic Reid gives the impression of being a "loner", a man of few words. His literary out-put has not been large, but he has been an innovative and unusual novelist.

When *New Day* appeared in 1949, it proved to be innovative in two ways: in its use of a formalised and idealised Jamaican English, and in its concerns—for national growth, for the resumption and expansion of responsible government, for the role of a local family in national growth. *The Leopard*, set as it is in Kikuyu land, does not use a distinctive form of Jamaican speech, but it is structurally more interesting than *New Day*, and its concerns are not as unconnected with West Indian experience as they might seem. In fact, Reid's life as a Jamaican would have prepared him well to work out such a combination of gentleness and violence, in fact a fugue and coda, which could also be a prelude to a "new day" in Africa, and in the world.

*New Day*, using the flashback technique, has structural weaknesses, and from time to time its special formalised Jamaican language does not ring absolutely true. (To give two small examples: "Duppy-ghost," p.109; "congo-pea soup," p. 119.) Was Vic Reid too concerned with the fact that his Jamaican characters had to speak not only to each other, but also to a wider audience?

His historical grasp of the political and power situation in 1865 has been criticised both on ideological and historical grounds. In this connection, it should not be forgotten that Reid was very careful to say in the last paragraph of the "Author's Note" prefaced to the first edition of *New Day*:

> I have not by any means attempted a history of the period from 1865 to 1944. . . .
> What I have attempted is to transfer to paper some of the beauty, kindness, and humor of my people, . . . creating a tale that will offer as true an impression as fiction can of the way by which Jamaica and its people come to today.

There are many remarkable things in *New Day*; one notable section (chapter 9) deals with Pastor Humphrey's sermon on "constituted authority." It starts, "Whenever we go to church . . . Naomi and me sit side-and-side . . . but when the sermon begins we close our knees tight, and then there is good space for crab-race. You know how to play crab-race?" That very Jamaican question sets the aspect of the children's presence at the service, while as Humphrey warms to his theme—"Mouth came down *snap* on authority, long neck shot out, then drew back into his cassock like iguana in stonehole"—the Stoney Gut men are about to create a groaning objection to Paul's test on obedience and the pastor's interpretation of it. The chapter ends with "'Let us pray for rain,' says Pastor Humphrey." But we know that it is blood that will soon be quenching the long drought which had intensified, and symbolised, the disillusion and deterioration in St. Thomas Parish.

Often old John Campbell (as narrator) slips delightfully into the skin of the young boy he had been when "in media res": "Good it is to hear her laugh but when mother says *heh*! like that, all of your manhood is gone. . . . Is funny how your breeches drop off anytime Mother says *heh*!" But the ably-used device of having a sleepless narrator recall his family's role in the dawning of the "new day" has its disadvantages. For one thing, John Campbell has to rush a few sequences to help us suspend, willingly, our disbelief, and it might well be this technical difficulty that tends to exaggerate a falsely Romantic view (even in Campbell's mouth) of the fighting years of Jamaican men.

*The Leopard* is in some ways, particularly in structure, even more noteworthy. The clean juxta-positioning of the few personae, the untransitioned switching from group to group of those concerned and then converging for the final point of the story—and meanwhile the leopard alone understands Kenya "for he avoids the strong and eats the wounded, and the weak is stalking the stalked"—all these build up into an image of sick, hunting and hunted man, not unlike Derek Walcott's in "A Far Cry from Africa":

> The violence of beast on beast is read
> As natural law, but upright man
> Seeks his divinity with inflicting pain.
> (from *In a Green Light*, 1962)

In the end the lieutenant ("robbed me of my first Kike") becomes the leopard, whom he has just deprecatingly, but more truthfully than he realises, called "Brother Leopard," and the fate long since planned for that animal becomes the lieutenant's at the hands of Nebu ("one of the loyal bucks"). As Ramon-Fortune has it, in "The Crow":

> The crows prey on the dead
> But men prey on each other.
> (from *Caribbean Voices*, 1966)

Vic Reid is a flexible and varied writer, with, at times, a fist of mail beneath that gauntlet of silk. An innovator on the West Indian literary scene, he has written, besides the novels mentioned, a variety of short stories and books for young people. His work shows forth his giftedness and care, and underlines our need for more from him.

—John J. Figueroa

---

**REID BANKS, Lynne.** British and Israeli. Born in London, 31 July 1929. Educated at the Royal Academy of Dramatic Art, London. Married Chaim Stephenson in 1965; has three sons. Actress in British repertory companies, 1949–53; Secretary to Wolf Mankowitz, *q.v.*, 1953–54; Interviewer, Reporter and Scriptwriter, Independent Television News, London, 1954–61; Teacher, Kibbutz Yasur School and Na'aman High School, Israel, 1962–71. Address: c/o Mrs. Reid Banks, 114 Castelnau, Barnes, London S.W.13, England.

PUBLICATIONS

Novels

> *The L-Shaped Room.* London, Chatto and Windus, 1960; New York, Simon and Schuster, 1962.
> *An End to Running.* London, Chatto and Windus, 1962; as *House of Hope*, New York, Simon and Schuster, 1962.
> *Children at the Gate.* London, Chatto and Windus, and New York, Simon and Schuster, 1968.
> *The Backward Shadow.* London, Chatto and Windus, and New York, Simon and Schuster, 1970.
> *One More River.* London, Vallentine Mitchell, 1972.

Plays

> *It Never Rains* (televised, BBC, 1954; produced Keighley, Yorkshire, 1954).   London,
>    Deane, 1954.
> *The Killer Dies Twice*.   London, Deane, 1956.
> *All in a Row*.   London, Deane, 1956.
> *The Unborn* (produced London, 1962).
> *Already It's Tomorrow* (televised, 1962).   London, French, 1962.
> *The Gift* (produced London, 1965).

Other plays produced on radio and television.

Lynne Reid Banks comments:

I've never gone in much for analysing my work or my work-processes. As a writer, and as a person, I tend to be lazy and disorganised. If my characters do not "take over" and direct my typing fingers, it is nothing but drudgery for me—I write in order to have written. I find out what I had to say after I have said it. But in any case, "things to say" are not my primary driving-force. I am a story-teller. That to me is what fiction is—it is not a subtle way of communicating one's political, social or any other opinions to a host of faceless readers. Praise, to me, is not "How I agreed with you about such-and-such!" but "How I cared about this or that character. . . ."

Although the great rallying-cry to writers these days is "Truth for Truth's sake", objective truth, the chronicling of reality, is not my metier. If it were, I should not write fiction. Fiction means, to me, a reflection of life so "doctored" that its only relationship to truth is an illusion in the reader's mind. The reader must receive this illusion of reality, of course, or else the one binding commandment of the novel-writer—"Involve thy reader"—is broken; but this is not to say that the story need be "true" in the sense of reflecting ordinary, typical people or events.

Jane Austen is the only novelist I know whose peculiar genius lies in taking perfectly ordinary people through ordinary situations, and transmogrifying them into fascinating fiction. Every other great novelist I can think of has either created exceptional characters or has devised for them abnormal events—often both. Dickens, Tolstoi, the Brontës, Victor Hugo—all were allowed their outrageous coincidences, their larger-than-life heroes, their impossible denouements and neat, incredible resolutions. Nobody in those days queried the fiction-writers' right to write *fiction*, and not fiction parading as fact.

Characters in novels may not go beyond the possible. But they should—the principal ones, anyway—be exceptional people. Jane (*The L-Shaped Room*) did not behave like an ordinary girl. Her reactions and decisions were those of, let us say, one girl in ten, or fifty, or a hundred, in her situation. Perhaps the others would have liked to do what she did; perhaps that explains why the book was widely-read. Her exceptional qualities made her interesting and stimulating. The same with Kofi, the Arab in *Children at the Gate*. Some Israelis complained that he was not a typical Arab. I never thought he was. He was not even a typical human being. I made him rare on purpose. I reject the criticism of those who demand that I point out his living counterpart before they will accept him.

However, themes are another matter. The themes one writes about must be true—not objectively true, but true to one's deepest convictions. My fourth novel, *The Backward Shadow*, was criticised by one American woman for its underlying assumption that women need men and cannot live full lives without them. But I believe this. It is in accordance with my own experience and observation. I doubt if I could write a convincing novel about a happy, single, "liberated" woman, not only because I have never met one but because, rightly or wrongly, deep down I don't believe they exist.

One of my recurring themes is women alone. This theme is drawn from the secret places of my own life. I was not, myself, exceptional in my reaction to singleness, but then I am an ordinary woman. My heroines may either react to loneliness with greater courage, awareness and resourcefulness than I did, or sink to lower depths; but they must be more *extreme*, otherwise I cannot be bothered with them, nor can I see why any reader should.

In short, fiction should grow out of life; but the operative word is "out". It should be an extension, an underlining, a highlighting. Above all, it must involve the reader in a process of identification. My novels are not for everyone. They are only for those who are similar enough to me, to sympathise with the characters I create. To any reader who turns away, in boredom, irritation or revulsion, from my heroines, however real they may seem to him, I owe an apology for failure.

*          *          *

*The L-Shaped Room*, Lynne Reid Banks' filmed and much publicised first novel, is still, if not her best book, the one by which she is most widely known. It was published in 1960, and it is easy by now to forget that it belongs to the literature of protest and outcry of that time—protest against the lot of the unmarried mother, the attitude of the medical profession, the puritanical disapproval of the heroine's father, who shows far less understanding of her situation than two total strangers, the negro jazz musician and the fledgling Jewish writer, who are her neighbours in poverty. The predicament of the unmarried mother has since become a well-worn theme and was handled with a good deal more subtlety in Margaret Drabble's *The Millstone*; it is curious that the two novels describe the child as having been conceived in almost exactly the same fashion, after an encounter so casual and meaningless that the heroine could not bear to disclose its consequences to the father. By comparison with this and with the work of other contemporaries who have specialised in the novel of domestic and personal relationships—Penelope Mortimer, Edna O'Brien, Elizabeth Jane Howard, to name a few—Lynne Reid Banks is a somewhat artless writer in terms both of style and of treatment. Much of the appeal of *The L-Shaped Room* lies in its very rawness and directness, the "look-what-happened-to-me" note which dominates it.

Its successor, *An End to Running*, is a considerably more accomplished piece of work. The heroine is engaged as secretary to a young and pampered Jewish writer who is dominated by his sister: the girl falls in love and runs away with him, and for the first half of the book tells the story in the first person: in the second part the writer becomes the "I", and describes their life in a kibbutz and the ultimate breakdown of their relationship. The technical demands of this device tighten the book's construction and introduce surprise and suspense into the narrative, while the contrasts of personality between the two principal characters are so sharp that their alternating moods of attraction and repulsion are thoroughly convincing. There are also some excellent descriptions of the rigours and the more comic elements of kibbutz life.

*Children at the Gate* introduces a new group of characters, but Israel is once more the setting, and the theme once more concerns the personal problems of a lonely woman. Gerda is a Canadian Jewess in her late thirties, who lives alone in the town of Acre and has come to the end of her tether: her marriage has broken up, she can have no more children, and she has taken to drink. She is persuaded to adopt a pair of Arab orphans and much of the plot describes the agonising experience of settling with them into kibbutz life, gradually winning their confidence and then being separated from them on legal grounds. Here the handling of the narrative reverts to the method of *The L-Shaped Room*: it is a personal account in which Gerda is present on every page, but the story is told with an eloquence and a poignancy which the earlier book does not often attain.

*The Backward Shadow* forms a sequel to *The L-Shaped Room*. Jane Graham has left London and settled with her baby son in the country cottage which she has inherited. The plot is mainly occupied with the problems of bringing up her child and with her relationships with the London friends who periodically descend on her. This is the weakest of the novels to date, since there is not a great deal of new material and the interest of the characters carried over from the earlier book is hardly sufficient to support a sequel.

Lynne Reid Banks relies upon experience rather than invention to a degree which makes it difficult to judge her books (with the exception of *An End To Running*) as fiction. There is no doubt that she possesses a strong impulse to write, but it is reminiscent of the Ancient Mariner's. Unmistakably as she passes from land to land the heart within her burns, and at her best the power of speech is strong, but it varies sharply from one novel to another.

—Ian Scott-Kilvert

---

**RENAULT, Mary.** Pseudonym for Mary Challans. British. Born in London, 4 September 1905. Educated at Clifton High School, Bristol; St. Hugh's College, Oxford, M.A.; Radcliffe Infirmary, Oxford, S.R.N. 1936. Worked as a nurse during World War II. Emigrated to South Africa in 1948. National President, P.E.N. Club of South Africa, 1961. Recipient: National Association of Independent Schools Award (U.S.A.), 1963; Silver Pen Award, 1971. Fellow, Royal Society of Literature, 1959. Address: c/o Longman Group Ltd., 74 Grosvenor Street, London W.1, England.

PUBLICATIONS

Novels

*Purposes of Love.*   London, Longman, 1939; as *Promise of Love*, New York, Morrow, 1940.
*Kind Are His Answers.*   London, Longman, and New York, Morrow, 1940.
*The Friendly Young Ladies.*   London, Longman, 1944; as *Middle Mist*, New York, Morrow, 1945.
*Return to Night.*   London, Longman, and New York, Morrow, 1947.
*North Face.*   London, Longman, and New York, Morrow, 1948.
*The Charioteer.*   London, Longman, 1953; New York, Pantheon Books, 1959.
*The Last of the Wine.*   London, Longman, and New York, Pantheon Books, 1956.
*The King Must Die.*   London, Longman, and New York, Pantheon Books, 1958.
*The Bull from the Sea.*   London, Longman, and New York, Pantheon Books, 1962.
*The Mask of Apollo.*   London, Longman, and New York, Pantheon Books, 1966.
*Fire from Heaven.*   New York, Pantheon Books, and London, Longman, 1970.

Other

*The Lion in the Gateway: Heroic Battles of the Greeks and Persians at Marathon, Salamis, and Thermopylae* (juvenile).   London, Longman, and New York, Harper, 1964.

Critical Studies: by John A. Stone, in the author's *The Charioteer*, Cleveland, World, 1962; "Men Are Only Men" by Landon C. Burns, in *Critique* (Minneapolis) vol. 6, no. 3, 1964; essay by the author, in *Afterwords*, New York, Harper, 1969.

Mary Renault comments:

It has been my aim to respect the facts of history and what I believe, after careful reading, to have been the real beliefs and thought-modes, the life-style of a period. The past is a part of the human environment, and should not be polluted by falsehood. Its people should not be modernised to make an easier read, nor judged by standards irrelevant to their own day, in order to make dishonest propaganda for some modern cause: the "committed" historical novelist is of necessity a committed liar. Even the dead are entitled to justice; and the first requirement of justice is to apply to them their current moral standards, however these may differ from our own. Modernised historical characters are a bore; real ones are profoundly interesting, at least to me. I have never knowingly exploited them, but have tried to see them, as far as I am able, along the sight-lines from which they might have seen themselves.

*       *       *

Mary Renault's forte is the historical novel and her own province in that territory is the ambiance of classical, pre-classical and Hellenistic Greece. This is not to say that her other novels are of no account but, except for *The Charioteer* and *Return to Night*, they are of lesser stature than her historical fiction. *The Friendly Young Ladies* has a kind of nostalgic pre-war charm—the poor girl's Evelyn Waugh—and its apparent dalliance with lesbianism is a link with the motif of homosexuality that bulks so large in her Greek novels and is the central theme of *The Charioteer*. But there is something rather "nurses' romance" and "woman's fiction" about these other "English" novels. The toughness that Miss Renault manages in *The Charioteer* (for all its pathos) is missing except for occasional touches—the withered and life-denying Miss Searle (in *North Face*), for instance, having confronted a love that desperately she has tried not to believe, kneeling to her prayers, "the hard pink sheen of the counterpane between her fingers, receiving indifferently the spreading circles of her tears".

The strength of *The Charioteer* lies both in that it is better written and that it is more thoroughly a criticism of life. The dimension of "reality" present in the fiction is in part a consequence of Miss Renault's treatment of the Second World War—the theatre within which the novel is set. Certainly *The Charioteer* is by no means among the first rank of novels to come out of that war (as a comparison with even Pamela Hansford Johnson's *An Avenue of Stone* would show) but the frenetic and shattered sadness of that world nevertheless haunts the reader and the anguish of the central figures is for that reason the more real. And it needs to be said too that this was, in its time, a brave novel—a novel treating of a theme ("the love that dare not speak its name") that was still, even in the late fifties, a distasteful one to many readers and as a consequence little handled in novels except in a vulgar and sensational way.

It would be nice to think that the sentimentality which was avoided in *The Charioteer* did not appear elsewhere. Unfortunately it is a characteristic flaw of much of the phil-Hellenic fiction. The two lovers who are the central figures of *The Last of the Wine* lack the toughness of their twentieth-century warrior counterparts, and there is something scissors and paste about the Athenian world they inhabit. This Athens of Socrates seems more Jowett's than Pausanias's. It seems the fictional equivalent of the American reconstruction of the West Stoa of the Agora. It may be correct to the last of its proportions and the exactest detail but somehow we do not believe it. It may be verity, but it is not verisimilitude. We suspend our disbelief but somehow, at the end of the novel, we come away feeling we have seen a classical play done by the ladies of Vassar in long white dresses. These are modern people in antique dress—a species of ventriloquism.

The distinction is Coleridge's and it is a useful one here where it is the fancy rather than the imagination that we feel has been at work. The difference is the discrimination between Burlington's Palladianism and Smirke's Greek Revival. In the latter's buildings, there is a scrupulous scholarship, an archaeological passion for detail and a reverence for the free spirit of Athenian democracy, but we are not persuaded by it because Smirke did not feel Greece upon his pulses as Burlington had lived Palladio. And if we compare, for instance, Miss Renault's work with Marguerite Yourcenar's fine novel, *The Memoirs of Hadrian*, something of the same distinction is apparent.

That all this is less true of the Minoan novels—*The King Must Die* and *The Bull from the Sea*—is partly attributable to our greater ignorance of that civilisation and partly (perhaps as a consequence of that) to Miss Renault's imaginative powers of persuasion. That dim mythic culture comes alive and Theseus assumes heroic yet convincing proportions that seem entirely in keeping with the moral, physical and psychological labyrinth that contains him.

It is disappointing then to return, in *The Mask of Apollo*, to the world of Attic reconstruction—Plato's Athens. Like *The Last of the Wine* it smells of the scholarly lamp and seems, in retrospect, to be little more than an attempt to repeat the earlier popular success. But its dual themes of theatre v philosophy and truth v statecraft are little removed from their Platonic sources in *Ion* and *The Republic* and ultimately we do not believe the central character (an actor) capable of comprehending them. So the novel remains entertaining—a charming sixth-formish introduction to the life of the late fifth-century BC—but alas eminently forgettable as a novel.

In *Fire from Heaven*, Miss Renault's latest novel, this is less the case. Although its links, in the figure of Aristotle for instance, with *The Mask of Apollo* are obvious, the scope of its fiction is freer. And this, as with the Minoan novels, is again partly the consequence of our ignorance—in this case of Macedonian civilisation. The mystery that still surrounds Pella, for instance, has no parallel in our knowledge of Attic civilisation. Partly for this reason, partly for the very nature of the romance that surrounds Alexander, the novel succeeds where its predecessor fails. That is not to say that it is a great novel or even a great historical novel, but it is fine and eminently readable and, one hopes, an augury of things to come.

—D. D. C. Chambers

---

**RHYS, Jean.** British. Born in Dominica, West Indies, in 1894; emigrated to England in 1910. Educated at the Royal Academy of Dramatic Art, London. Lived in Paris between the wars. Now lives in Devon. Recipient: Arts Council Bursary, 1967; Smith Literary Award, 1967; Heinemann Award, 1967. Address: c/o André Deutsch Ltd., 105 Great Russell Street, London W.C.1, England.

PUBLICATIONS

Novels

> *Postures.* London, Chatto and Windus, 1928; as *Quartet*, New York, Simon and Schuster, 1929.
> *After Leaving Mr. Mackenzie.* London, Cape, and New York, Knopf, 1931.
> *Voyage in the Dark.* London, Constable, 1934; New York, Morrow, 1935.
> *Good Morning, Midnight.* London, Constable, 1939.
> *Wide Sargasso Sea.* London, Deutsch, and New York, Norton, 1966.

Short Stories

*The Left Bank and Other Stories.*   London, Cape, and New York, Harper, 1927.
*Tigers Are Better-Looking, with a Selection from The Left Bank*.   London, Deutsch, 1968.
*Penguin Modern Stories 1*, with others.   London, Penguin, 1969.

Critical Study: Introduction by Francis Wyndham, to *Wide Sargasso Sea*, 1966.

\*      \*      \*

Jean Rhys was born in 1894 in the Windward Islands. Her father was a Welsh doctor who had settled there, and her mother a Creole—that is, a white West Indian. On the verandah of their home at Roseau stood an enormous brass telescope. Through it, their daughter would spy out the steamers passing to Guadeloupe; always, she noted, the Royal Mail was the shabbiest. Overlooking their garden was the tall house of the Editor of the local paper. Papa Dom, as he was nicknamed, was full of race prejudice. He "hated" the white people, not being white himself, and he "despised" the black ones, not being black: "'Coloured' we West Indians call the intermediate shades, and I used to think that being coloured embittered him." Embitterment is a recurring theme in Jean Rhys's books, whether the cause be the shade of a person's skin, lack of money, or the mere fact of being a woman. All her heroines are born victims.

At the age of 16, she came to England to attend the Royal Academy of Dramatic Art. But her father's death, after one term, put a stop to further training. So, she joined a touring company of *Our Miss Gibbs* and every night fluffed her one line—"Lottie, Lottie, don't be so epigrammatic." Her next venture on the stage was as a chorus girl in *The Count of Luxembourg*. Then at the end of the First World War, she married a Dutch poet and went to live on the Continent, where she met many writers and artists, including Ernest Hemingway and James Joyce. In Paris she also met Ford Madox Ford who not only launched her in his bilingual *Transatlantic Review*, but later contributed a long, enthusiastic introduction to her first book.

The dust-jacket of *The Left Bank* describes its contents as "Studies and Sketches of Present-Day Bohemian Paris"—a description that covers the prevailing mood of most of its twenty-two pieces. The exceptions are the flashbacks of her childhood in Roseau, and the 50-page story with which the collection closes. This is set in Vienna, and in the course of it there occurs an outburst to mark: "If there's one hypocrisy I loathe more than another, it's the fiction of the 'good' woman and the 'bad' one."

Jean Rhys's first novel came out under the title of *Postures* in England, and *Quartet* in America. (The author prefers the latter title—and the 1969 English reprint appears under it.) The epigraph warns: "Beware of Good Samaritans . . ." though, perhaps, "Women Beware of Men" might be more to the point. For Marya Zelli, an English ex-chorus girl, is married to a Pole who can charm the birds off the trees. But his business transactions on the antique market are shady, and it is not long before he is caught out and imprisoned for a year. Whilst he is serving his sentence, she is befriended by H. J. Heidler, a German art-dealer. The idea suggested by Heidler's wife is that they should form a *ménage à trois*. Because Marya's husband has made no proper provision for her, she is hard pressed for money and eventually agrees to the arrangement. Any misgivings that she may entertain are tempered by the fact that she is, in turn, both wildly repulsed and madly attracted by Heidler. When her husband is released, there are misgivings among all the quartet—and she loses both men.

Geographically, Paris provides the setting—though when the afternoons are foggy, and there is a cold sharpness in the air, "It might be London," Marya keeps repeating to herself. The truth is it might be any capital city in Europe in which a woman finds herself adrift without private means and without the temperament to make herself economically independent; or, in which she finds herself lumbered with an unstable husband or lover. In Jean Rhys's next novel, *After Leaving Mr. Mackenzie*, Julia Martin is in a similar predicament. She has just received a letter from the solicitors of her ex-lover, Mr. Mackenzie, saying that her allowance has been stopped. So, she leaves her Left Bank hotel and visits London in the hope of tapping some old boy friends. One chapter heading is: "It Might Have Been Anywhere."

In *Voyage in the Dark*, Anna Morgan has come from the Caribbean to try her luck on the boards. She is just 19 and suffers hideously from the English climate; she equates being white with being cold and sad, whereas being black means being warm and gay. Soon she is seduced by an elderly admirer who lets her down, and she sinks gradually into a life of easy virtue. Whilst on tour in the provinces—it is casually let slip that the year is 1914—she learns from Maudie, who shares the same digs, that in Europe some dogs can be more expensive than people. She elaborates:

> "D'you know what a man said to me the other day? 'It's funny,' he said, 'have you
> ever thought that a girl's clothes cost more than the girl inside them?... You can get
> a very nice girl for five pounds... you can get a very nice girl for nothing if you know
> how to go about it. But you can't get a very nice costume for her for five pounds. To
> say nothing of underclothes, shoes, etcetera and so on....'"

For her next heroine in *Good Morning, Midnight*, Jean Rhys chose a woman in her forties. In her time, Sasha Jansen has acted as a guide for the American Express in Paris, been a vendeuse in a dress shop, and given English lessons at ten francs an hour. When the book opens she is to be found revisiting Paris at the suggestion of a friend who thinks she has been going to pot in London. Her aim is to avoid those cafés and bars that will stir memories of the golden days spent with husbands and lovers but which, like all golden days, faded away. She thinks of the French telegraph wires buzzing throughout the capital with the same message from deserted women everywhere: "Send more money, send more money." She has enough for a Pernod—but not enough for a new pair of gloves. Her own are dreadfully shabby, and shabbiness is always something that women notice (even the Royal Mail's). For it diminishes their self-respect and so makes them nervous to take chances on relationships. "Tomorrow I'll go to the Galeries Lafayette... buy anything cheap. Just the sensation of spending, that's the point. And when I have had a couple of drinks, I shan't know whether it's yesterday, today or tomorrow."

Jean Rhys's women belong to an in-between world. In whatever European capital they find themselves, they are the flotsam floating between the rich and the poor, just as, in the West Indies, the Creole belongs to neither white nor black. For example, Anna Morgan longs to be "pure black" with as much desperation as Sasha Jansen longs to be "financially emancipated." Anna may be only in her teens, but she hears her elders use the term "youth" as though it were a crime, whereas Sasha has reached the stage when she is afraid to be young. And between these two heroines, stand the other two, Marya Zelli and Julia Martin— Marya torn between the demands of love and security, and Julia caught at that critical hour, summed up in the first sentence of her story, as the one "between dog and wolf." To all of them, day-dreams offer an escape-hatch; but once they are asleep, their dreams turn to nightmares, based on the injustices done to lovely, foolish women by cruel, deceiving men. In *Wide Sargasso Sea*, her fifth and most ambitious novel, that injustice is less one-sided.

For many years Jean Rhys was obsessed by the figure of the first Mrs. Rochester, the mad Creole wife in *Jane Eyre* who is locked away in the attic of Thornfield Hall. The figure of the lunatic had always seemed to her—especially in contrast with Mr. Rochester and Jane—a "cardboard" one, and she longed to do something about it. *Wide Sargasso Sea* is no pastiche or sequel to Charlotte Brontë's book, though indirectly it does offer a number of possible explanations for Mr. Rochester's violent outbursts—outbursts whose credibility some 19th century critics had challenged when *Jane Eyre* first came out in 1847.

In Charlotte Brontë's novel, Mr. Rochester in one outburst, when woken out of a deep sleep, shouts at Jane: "What have you done with me, witch, sorceress?" In Jean Rhys's novel, both Mr. Rochester and his bride tell their own stories. She thinks that he has married her for her Creole inheritance and dowry, whereas the truth is that he is the down-trodden younger son who has agreed to this arranged marriage because his over-bearing father has demanded it of him. Both husband and wife are victims of circumstances beyond their control. Nor is it surprising that his love should grow cautious after the novelty of the honeymoon has worn off, or that she in turn should visit a local sorceress in Dominica and ask her to try and regain it for her by means of magic.

Between *Good Morning, Midnight* and *Wide Sargasso Sea*, there was, except for a few short stories, a silence of 27 years. In one of these stories, "Tigers Are Better Looking," now included in a volume of that name, Jean Rhys describes a journalist preparing his weekly column for an Australian newspaper. The floor is littered with discarded starts of the article. "He couldn't get the swing of it. The swing's the thing, as everybody knows—otherwise the cadence of the sentence." On radio when Jean Rhys was questioned about her own work, she admitted that she drafted many times and that writing was "either personal or it was wishful thinking." She went on: "There may be people with vast imaginations, great people. But I am not one of them." She was speaking with the modesty of a perfectionist. Yet she has been proved wrong. Her books and stories show the assured touch of a master, and are among the most original and memorable of our time. The book on which she is now working is an autobiography.

—Neville Braybrooke

---

**RICHLER, Mordecai.** Canadian. Born in Montreal, Quebec, 27 January 1931. Educated at Baron Byng High School, and Sir George Williams University, Montreal. Married Florence Wood in 1959; has five children. Writer-in-Residence, Sir George Williams University, 1968–69, and Carleton University, Ottawa, 1972. Recipient: President's Medal, University of Western Ontario, for non-fiction, 1959; Canada Council Junior Arts Fellowship, 1959, 1960, and Senior Arts Fellowship, 1966; Guggenheim Fellowship, 1961; *Paris Review* prize, 1969; Governor-General's Award, 1969. Address: Hillcrest, Kingston Hill, Surrey, England.

PUBLICATIONS

Novels

  *The Acrobats.* Toronto, Ambassador, London, Deutsch, and New York, Putnam, 1954.
  *Son of a Smaller Hero.* Toronto, Collins, and London, Deutsch, 1955; New York, Paperback Library, 1965.
  *A Choice of Enemies.* Toronto, Collins, and London, Deutsch, 1957.
  *The Apprenticeship of Duddy Kravitz.* London, Deutsch, Toronto, Collins, and Boston, Little Brown, 1959.
  *The Incomparable Atuk.* London, Deutsch, and Toronto, McClelland and Stewart, 1963; as *Stick Your Neck Out*, New York, Simon and Schuster, 1963.

*Cocksure.*   Toronto, McClelland and Stewart, London, Weidenfeld and Nicolson, and New York, Simon and Schuster, 1968.

*St. Urbain's Horseman.*   Toronto, McClelland and Stewart, London, Weidenfeld and Nicolson, and New York, Knopf, 1971.

Short Stories

*The Street: Stories.*   Toronto, McClelland and Stewart, 1969; London, Weidenfeld and Nicolson, 1972.

Plays

Screenplays: *No Love for Johnnie*, 1959; *Life at the Top*, 1965.

Other

*Hunting Tigers under Glass: Essays and Reports.*   London, Weidenfeld and Nicolson, and Toronto, McClelland and Stewart, 1969.

Editor, *Canadian Writing Now.*   London, Penguin, 1970.

Critical Studies: *Mordecai Richler* by George Woodcock, Toronto, McClelland and Stewart, 1970; *Mordecai Richler* by G. David Sheps, Toronto, Ryerson Press, 1970; *Mordecai Richler* by Robert Fulford, Toronto, Coles, 1971.

Mordecai Richler comments:

Why do I write?

Doctors are seldom asked why they practice, shoemakers how come they cobble, or baseball players why they don't drive a coal truck instead, but again and again writers, like housebreakers, are asked why they do it.

Orwell, as might be expected, supplies the most honest answer in his essay, "Why I Write".

"1. Sheer egoism. Desire to seem clever, to be talked about, to be remembered after death, to get your own back on grownups who snubbed you in childhood, etc. etc." To this I would add egoism informed by imagination, style, and a desire to be known, yes, *but only on your own conditions.*

Nobody is more embittered than the neglected writer and, obviously, allowed a certain recognition, I am a happier and more generous man than I would otherwise be. But nothing I have done to win this recognition appalls me, has gone against my nature. I fervently believe that all a writer should send into the marketplace to be judged is his own work; the rest should remain private. I deplore the writer as a personality, however large and undoubted the talent, as is the case with Norman Mailer. I also do not believe in special license for the so-called artistic temperament. After all, basically, my problems, as I grudgingly come within spitting distance of middle age, are the same as anybody else's. Easier maybe. I can bend my anxieties to subversive uses. Making stories of them. When I'm not writing, I'm a husband and a father of five. Worried about pollution. The population explosion. My sons' report cards.

"2. Aesthetic enthusiasm. Perception of beauty in the external world, or, on the other hand, in words and their right arrangement." The agonies involved in creating a novel, the un-satisfying draft that follows unsatisfying draft, the scenes you never get right, are redeemed by those rare and memorable days when, seemingly without reason, everything falls right. Bonus days. Blessed days when, drawing on resources unsuspected, you pluck ideas and prose out of your skull that you never dreamt yourself capable of.

Such, such are the real joys.

Unfortunately, I don't feel that I've ever been able to sustain such flights for a novel's length. So the passages that flow are balanced with those which were forced in the hothouse. Of all the novels I've written, it is *The Apprenticeship of Duddy Kravitz* and *Cocksure* which come closest to my intentions and therefore give me the most pleasure. I should add that I'm still lumbered with characters and ideas, the social concerns I first attempted in *The Acrobats*. Every serious writer has, I think, one theme, many variations to play on it.

Like any serious writer, I want to write one novel that will last, something that will make me remembered after death, and so I'm compelled to keep trying.

"3. Historical impulse. Desire to see things as they are. . . . " No matter how long I con-tinue to live abroad, I do feel forever rooted in Montreal's St. Urbain Street. That was my time, my place, and I have elected myself to get it right.

"4. Political purpose—using the word 'political' in the widest possible sense. Desire to push the world in a certain direction, to alter other people's idea of the kind of society that they should strive after." Not an overlarge consideration in my work, though I would say that any serious writer is a moralist and only incidentally an entertainer.

—from a Weidenfeld and Nicolson
promotional brochure, 1971.

*       *       *

Mordecai Richler exemplifies one of the difficulties Canadian critics have always experienced—that of defining the Canadian novelist. Many of those who find their way into histories of Canadian writing have in fact been passing visitors like Brian Moore and Malcolm Lowry and Paul West. To an extent—to a very great extent in Lowry's case—their fiction has been affected in terms of content and even attitude by their residence in Canada. Yet their "Canadian works" constitute a mere phase in lives whose inspiration has remained mainly elsewhere.

On the other side, following the nomadic pattern of life in a great and loosely populated country, some Canadians have left their country and spent most of their writing lives abroad. Of these, Mordecai Richler is the most important. Richler left Canada in 1951, when he was twenty; since then he has lived in Europe—mainly in England—and has returned to Canada only for relatively brief periods. All his novels, and most of his stories, have been written abroad. And yet, as Richler said in 1957, "All my attitudes are Canadian. I'm a Canadian; there's nothing to be done about it." Not merely are his attitudes Canadian; so are the leading figures in all his novels, whether they are shown in his native Montreal or are presented, as has been increasingly the case in recent years, as unassimilable exiles.

Even as a Canadian writer, Richler is extremely localized in his frame of reference. In this he follows the regional pattern characteristic of Canadian fiction, the pattern that makes Morley Callaghan so peculiarly the novelist of Toronto and Hugh MacLennan an unerring portrayer of the Maritimes but an unconvincing voice of Montreal. Richler, for his part, celebrates a vanished way of life in a part of Montreal that has changed completely since he knew it. It is the old Jewish ghetto, the region centred on St. Urbain Street, where Richler's heroes were born into the expatriate community of Jews who had fled from Eastern Europe under the Tsarist regime and who had brought with them a religion and a way of life which were gradually eroded by the social pressures of a city divided between English and French.

If one can isolate a theme from Richler's novels it is that of the Jew who is powerfully conscious of his people's past, and deeply nostalgic for a childhood spent in the chaotic and colourful background of the ghetto, yet who understands that in the modern world traditional Jewish attitudes have become irrelevant. Yet for Richler, in a way, the Jew is only a type of the individual set against the impersonal forces of the modern world. Three of his novels— *The Acrobats*, *A Choice of Enemies* and *Cocksure*—are based on a deliberate inversion of the pattern of the persecuted Jew. In these the hero (or anti-hero if that seems more fitting) is a Gentile, and Jews reveal in their actions towards him that they too can be persecutors if the circumstances permit. At the end of one of these novels—*Cocksure*—we find a clue which illuminates this central Richlerian preoccupation. When Mortimer Griffin is pursued and about to be destroyed by his enemies, a Jewish intellectual remarks to him: "A Jew is an idea. Today you're my idea of a Jew."

It would be an over-simplification to suggest that embedded in Richler's fiction is the idea that the Jew has an exemplary role in the modern world. It is more accurate to say that Richler believes any writer should draw from his own experience whatever has universal significance, and shape that material into a form of social as well as aesthetic meaning. His own experience has been his childhood on St. Urbain and his expatriate life which echoes that of his grandparents. This has resulted in an alternating pattern between the early background and the land of exile. *The Acrobats*, his first novel, was set in Spain; its young Canadian hero was murdered by a psychopathic ex-Nazi. *Son of a Smaller Hero*, set in Montreal, was Richler's portrait of the artist as a young man—a story of the Montreal ghetto and the trauma of self-liberation from its moral pressures. *A Choice of Enemies*—the hero again a Canadian exile—is set in the world of film producers (expatriate from the radical America of the 1930s) with which Richler's need to earn a living as a script writer had made him familiar. Next followed what may well be Richler's best novel, *The Apprenticeship of Duddy Kravitz*, telling of the ruthless rise to wealth of a poor boy of St. Urbain Street, followed by *The Incomparable Atuk*, a fable in the manner of Voltaire on Canadian cultural pretensions. The England of the exile is again the setting in *Cocksure*, a satirical fantasy filled with monsters and hollow men in the manner of Wyndham Lewis. A collection of sketches and short stories, *The Street*, devoted entirely to the vanished past of the Montreal ghetto, completes the pattern of alternations and prepares the way for Richler's most recent novel, *St. Urbain's Horseman*.

In Richler's work up to the early 1970s *St. Urbain's Horseman* is the key novel, combining satire and nostalgia, and bringing the world of the exile and the world of the ghetto together in their proper and intimate relationship. Jake Hersh, a minor character in *The Apprenticeship of Duddy Kravitz*, and a film man like the victim-heroes of *Cocksure* and *A Choice of Enemies*, has reached the final stage in the classic ordeal of the pursued man; he is on trial on a morals charge, a situation brought about by police inventiveness combined with his own foolishness in associating with a blackmailing misanthrope, Harry Stein. As the trial unfolds its sinister background action, we are shown, in parallel streams of memory, Jake's life in England where a marriage that should be happy is marred by his guilts and fears, and his past life in the dense atmosphere of the Jewish family and the noisy streets of Montreal. The two lives are united by Jake's abiding obsession with his cousin, Joey Hersh, the wandering ne'er-do-well whom Jake fantasizes into an avenger seeking to destroy the destroyers of the Jews. As Jake escapes without honour at his trial, the news arrives that Joey has died as a smuggler in Paraguay. Jake is released from perils and obsessions alike, and for once a Richler novel has an ending of happiness neither unthreatened nor inappropriate.

In retrospect, the three novels by Richler that stand most securely are *Son of a Smaller Hero*, *The Apprenticeship of Duddy Kravitz*, and *St. Urbain's Horseman*, those closest to his intensely lived and remembered childhood and youth. Taken together, they form a triptych representing the difficulty of escaping from the mental chains laid on a young Jew by the rigours of his own tradition and the hostility of other traditions. Central to these novels— and indeed to all Richler's works—is the sexual encounter between Jew and Gentile, always, until the last novel, a situation of imperfectly resolved conflict; it is the steering of Jake's mixed marriage through its rapids to final success that distinguishes *St. Urbain's Horseman* and suggests that this book, which took Richler five years to write, represents a critical summation of his work up to the present. It is unlikely that he can again render with the same directness and freshness as in the past his two special themes of Montreal Jewish childhood and manhood exile, and the fact that he is now contemplating a return to Canada suggests that he is also conscious of the need to re-set the compass of his fictional aims.

If *St. Urbain's Horseman*, indeed, represents a thematic reconciliation, it also represents a reconciliation of the two manners that are in conflict or at least in competition in Richler's earlier writings—the fantastic and the realistic. In the vividly remembered scenes of Montreal life it is realism (not naturalism) that prevails. In the foreign scenes, the tendency is to create grotesque and implausible hollow figures of satiric fantasy, beginning with Kraus, the unlikely Nazi of *The Acrobats*, and reaching an apogee in the Starmaker, the monstrous gangster-tycoon of *Cocksure*. In *St. Urbain's Horseman* the fantasy indeed persists, but it is in Jake's mind only, where Joey the Horseman rides on his unlikely quests, and what the novel mainly explores—with much deeper satiric effect—is the fantastic nature of much that happens in the actual world, particularly if one sees with the eyes of a stranger. For twenty years have not been enough to enable Richler to see England with an inside eye; he is still the exile, the essential Canadian, unable to render except in caricature anything outside that hypnotic circle of locality which creates what Northrop Frye has called "the garrison mentality" among Canadian writers. What his novels suggest is that "the idea of a Jew" is very much like the idea of a Canadian, for Canada is a land of minorities, regions, disguised ghettoes. In that lies Richler's appeal to his countrymen, and the reason why, twenty years away from Montreal, he is never considered as other than a Canadian writer.

—George Woodcock

---

**ROOKE, Daphne (Marie).** British and South African. Born in Boksburg, Transvaal, South Africa, 6 March 1914. Educated at Durban Girls' High School. Married Irvin Rooke in 1937; has one child. Has lived in Australia, 1946–53, and since 1965. Recipient: Afrikaanse Pers Beperk novel prize, 1946. Address: Post Office Bardouroka, New South Wales 2315, Australia.

PUBLICATIONS

Novels

*The Sea Hath Bounds.* Johannesburg, A.P.B. Bookstore, 1946; as *A Grove of Fever Trees*, Boston, Houghton Mifflin, 1950; London, Cape, 1951.
*Mittee.* London, Gollancz, 1951; Boston, Houghton Mifflin, 1952.
*Ratoons.* London, Gollancz, and Boston, Houghton Mifflin, 1953.
*Wizards' Country.* London, Gollancz, and Boston, Houghton Mifflin, 1957.
*Beti.* London, Gollancz, and Boston, Houghton Mifflin, 1959.
*A Lover for Estelle.* London, Gollancz, and Boston, Houghton Mifflin, 1961.
*The Greyling.* London, Gollancz, 1962; New York, Reynal, 1963.
*Diamond Jo.* London, Gollancz, and New York, Reynal, 1965.
*Boy on the Mountain.* London, Gollancz, 1969.

Uncollected Short Stories

"The Deal", in *Woman* (Sydney), 26 June 1950.
"Emily", in *John Bull* (London), 1952.
"The Boundary Dog", in *John Bull* (London), 1957.
"The Friends", in *South African Stories*.  London, Faber, 1960.
"Fikizolo", in *Over the Horizon*.  London, Gollancz, 1960.

Other

*The South African Twins* (juvenile).   London, Cape, 1953; as *Twins in South Africa*, Boston, Houghton Mifflin, 1955.
*The Australian Twins* (juvenile).   London, Cape, 1954; as *Twins in Australia*, Boston, Houghton Mifflin, 1956.
*New Zealand Twins* (juvenile).   London, Cape, 1957.
*Double Ex!* (juvenile).   London, Gollancz, 1971.

Bibliography: *Daphne Rooke: Her Works and Selected Criticism: A Bibliography* by Helen Camburg, Johannesburg, University of Witwatersrand, 1969.

Manuscript Collection: Boston University Library.

Critical Studies: by Orville Prescott, in *New York Times*, 1 March 1950; by Dorothy Canfield Fisher, in *Book-of-the-Month Club News* (New York), January 1952; by Sylvia Stallings, in *New York Herald Tribune*, 20 December 1953; in *Illustrated London News*, 21 December 1957; in *Saturday Review of Literature* (New York), 7 March 1959; in Chicago *Tribune*, 26 February 1961; by Paul Scott, in *Country Life* (London), 24 May 1962.

Daphne Rooke comments:

The places where I have lived have been most important to my writing. My early memories of the Transvaal are reflected in *Mittee*. *Ratoons* has for background the South Coast of Natal where I lived for many years on a sugar plantation. Zululand made a most profound impression on me: I lived there for years as a girl: *A Grove of Fever Trees*, *A Lover for Estelle*, and *Wizards' Country* all have Zululand for background. *Beti* is set in India and East Africa, and *Boy on a Mountain* in New Zealand. All are written in the first person.

There is a pattern of sorts in some of the South African works: the race of the narrator has an important bearing on the story. In *Mittee* the whole story hinges on the fact that the narrator Selina is a Coloured girl; in *Ratoons* the narrator is an English-speaking South African girl who falls in love with an Afrikaner; in *Wizards' Country* the narrator is a Zulu; in *A Lover for Estelle* the narrator is an Afrikaans girl whose life is influenced by a sophisticated Englishwoman. I did not consciously set out to create this pattern; it was pointed out to me after I had written *Wizards' Country*.

All the stories, including those for children, are imaginative works but have a basis in fact. In *Wizards' Country* when writing about superstition I attempted to avoid the supernatural; for example, Benge is a hunchback and masquerades as a magic dwarf (the tokoloshi). In my short story for children, "Fikizolo", the ingredients of a fairytale were actually present in Zululand: the two children were called a prince and princess, there was a real old witch, and Fikizolo himself was like a fabled beast, a cross between a donkey and a zebra!

\*       \*       \*

Recently the common verdict has been that Africa is to be written about by Africans, which has implicitly been taken to mean black male writers. And as often as not to mean black male writers preoccupied with violence and politics. Daphne Rooke, therefore, presents the critic with an interesting and not yet fashionable problem. She is a native born South African, white and female.

Racial identity and conflict do not provide the emotional power of Rooke's work. Her interests and point of view are those of a frontier woman. Set mostly on the South African frontier of the past two centuries, her works share with American fiction that sense of space, violence, and sheer physical vitality that attends the north European appetite for quest and contest. Characteristically, she writes what is commonly called women's fiction, a melodramatic form, the roots of which are firmly in the eighteenth-century English novels of sensibility and of gothic terror and suspense.

Rooke does not probe the past. She does not trouble to explain the present. Her narrators, secure in the present, simply recall their past. Its violence is distanced and the lessons learned do not now seem too pressing. Her narrators are each in some way oppressed, being either crippled, insane, female, or coloured. Yet social customs and institutions seem almost immaterial. Her narrators are alive. They have felt and assimilated their experience. Ideological assessment has not intervened. This is women's fiction in the very fundamental sense that the highly touted male faculties of abstraction and rationality are absent—and more ingenuously so than in the works of males who are spoken of as having a feminine sensibility.

Female culture is rich and complex. And it has been described almost exclusively in the works of women novelists because male historians and anthropologists have either been oblivious to its existence or have not deemed it of adequate importance to record. It has been left for such writers as Rooke to reveal the circumscribed but complex ambitions of women and to show how pregnancy, birth, and the management of the domestic realm are as exciting and heroic as war and politics. The richness of *Grove*, *Ratoons*, and *A Lover for Estelle* derive from her intimate awareness of the South Africa that women have experienced.

There is nothing soft and protected about the life Rooke describes. Her best effects invariably involve danger or the threat of it, as when the farmer's widow and her children try to make a little egg money hatching pythons in an abandoned front bedroom. Such moments have the economy and immediacy of a treasured snapshot. Rooke has not the stature of Doris Lessing or Nadine Gordimer, but her success as a popular writer is justified. In retrospect a Rooke work is more haunting than it ought to be—an effect which depends on the part rather than the whole. When the oppressive density of events and the relentless heightening of plot and situation have faded from mind, there remain solid characters and sharp, arresting vignettes.

—Cynthia Secor

---

**ROSS, Sinclair.** Canadian. Born in Shellbrook, Saskatchewan, 22 January 1908. Served in the Canadian Army, 1942–45. Worked for the Royal Bank of Canada for 43 years: in Winnipeg, 1931–42, and in Montreal, 1946–68; now retired. Lives in Spain. Address: Apartado 5362, Barcelona, Spain.

PUBLICATIONS

Novels

> *As for Me and My House.*   New York, Reynal and Hitchcock, 1941.
> *The Well.*   Toronto, Macmillan, 1958.
> *Whir of Gold.*   Toronto, McClelland and Stewart, 1970.

Short Stories

> *The Lamp at Noon and Other Stories.*   Toronto, McClelland and Stewart, 1968.

Uncollected Short Stories

> "A Day with Pegasus", in *Queen's Quarterly* (Kingston, Ontario), Summer 1938.
> "Jug and Bottle", in *Queen's Quarterly* (Kingston, Ontario), Winter 1949–1950.
> "Saturday Night", in *Queen's Quarterly* (Kingston, Ontario), Autumn 1951.

Critical Studies: Introduction by Roy Daniells to *As for Me and My House*, Toronto, McClelland and Stewart, 1957; "Wolf in the Snow" by Warren Tallman, in *A Choice of Critics*, Toronto, Oxford University Press, 1966; Introduction by Margaret Laurence to *The Lamp at Noon*, 1968; "Sinclair Ross's Ambivalent World" by William H. New, in *Canadian Literature* (Vancouver), Spring 1969; "No Other Way: Sinclair Ross's Stories and Novels" by Sandra Djwa, in *Canadian Literature* (Vancouver), Winter 1971.

Sinclair Ross comments:

The little I have done has been spread over so many years that there is no outstanding or unifying theme. Man and nature, perhaps—especially in *The Lamp at Noon* and to some degree in *As for Me and My House*. *The Well* is a bad novel: an attempt, unsuccessful, to stretch a little the prairie and small town world of which I had been writing. *Whir of Gold* is, I suppose, another break-away attempt—or stretch; better, with some fairly good things in it, but small in range.

*      *      *

Sinclair Ross is primarily a chronicler of life on the Canadian prairies, and his first novel, *As for Me and My House*, seems destined to become established as a classic of prairie realism, along with the novels of Frederick Philip Grove and Margaret Laurence. Even better than his first novel are some of his short stories, such as "The Lamp at Noon", "The Painted Door", and "One's a Heifer". Ross's later novels, *The Well* and *Whir of Gold*, have some traces of the subdued intensity which makes his early work so memorable, but as wholes they are disappointing. Ross's career seems to bear out the theory that Herbert Read advanced re that of Wordsworth: that as his memories of his boyhood faded, his art too lost its strength. Ross lived on the prairies as a boy and young man, but his adult life has been lived mainly in Montreal, and in his later work he was too far removed from the life he once knew to write of it with continuous conviction and accuracy.

It is, then, on the early fiction that Sinclair Ross's reputation is almost certain to rest.

The qualities of this early work are quite remarkable. Perhaps most remarkable of all is Ross's gift for empathy, for full identification of himself with the character he is portraying. For the boys who are the central figures of several of his short stories this is not surprising, since one is able to assume that the hero is Ross himself slightly disguised, and that he is drawing heavily upon the memories of his own boyhood. The feat is more surprising when it is applied to Philip Bentley, the clergyman and amateur artist of *As for Me and My House*, particularly since much of the tension in the novel springs from Philip's relationship with his wife: Ross is a bachelor. But what is really remarkable is that Ross is able to enter with apparently equal facility into the minds of women, as in the powerful story of a prairie dust storm, "The Lamp at Noon", and in the portrayal of Mrs. Bentley in the novel.

The special quality in the human situation which seems to attract Ross as an artist and which he treats with consummate skill is the sense of isolation and of alienation, the feeling of being trapped in a set of circumstances from which there is no apparent escape. Thus Philip Bentley finds himself trapped in a profession for which he no longer feels a vocation, in a small prairie town which seems to have no sympathy for the values he cherishes, and in a marriage which has come to be an irritant rather than an unguent. In "The Lamp at Noon", the prairie farm-wife finds herself trapped in an isolated farmhouse when she would like to be in a city, and the dust storm in which she goes mad and her baby dies becomes a symbol of the inexorable doom which is closing in upon her. Only her husband's fidelity and love stand between her and total defeat.

This use of the prairie climate and landscape both as a realistic setting and as a symbolic obbligato to the human situation is another of Ross's strengths as a writer of fiction. In words which are carefully chosen to achieve the maximum of accuracy in description, he makes vivid to us the reality of the prairie landscape with its vast distances and its overwhelming sky, and the fierce extremes of heat and cold, the long harsh winters and brief, brilliant, but often explosive summers, that mark the climate of that region. Beyond the accuracy of the descriptions, however, lie the powerful atmospheric effects which Ross achieves by relating the fluctuations of the weather to the moods and aspirations of his characters, and the way in which snow-storms and wind-storms are made to seem symbolic of the malevolence of the universe in which man finds himself a victim.

The sombreness of Ross's fiction is to some extent relieved, however, by the positive way in which he records the efforts of his characters to overcome or transcend the forbidding environment in which fate has placed them. The wife in "The Lamp at Noon" is broken, but her husband perseveres until he sees the storm go down; for all the tribulations to which the Bentleys are subjected, it is their human will which finally prevails: the last words of the novel are "I want it so". Philip's art is his means of transcending the environment: by portraying the prairie in all its harsh power he reduces it to form, transforms it by the power of the human imagination, asserts his human will in the face of its vast indifference.

Ross's own art as a novelist and writer of short stories represents a similar triumph of the human imagination. By his unremitting honesty in portraying human beings living in a physical environment which presents the maximum challenge to the instinct for survival he has produced a small but significant volume of work which will endure.

—Desmond Pacey

---

**ROSTEN, Leo (Calvin).** American. Born in Lodz, Poland, 11 April 1908; emigrated to the United States in 1910. Educated at the University of Chicago, Ph.B. 1930 (Phi Beta Kappa), Ph.D. 1937 (Research Assistant, Political Science Department, 1933–35; Fellow, Social Science Research Council, 1934–36); London School of Economics, 1934. Married

Priscilla Ann Mead in 1935 (deceased); Gertrude Zimmerman, 1960; has three children. English Teacher in Chicago, 1930–32. Motion Picture Writer, 1937–38; Special Consultant to the National Defense Commission, 1939–40; Director, Motion Picture Research Project (Carnegie Foundation grant), 1939–41; Chief, Motion Picture Division, Office of Facts and Figures, Washington, D.C., 1941–42; Deputy Director, Office of War Information, Washington, 1942–43; Special Consultant to the United States Secretary of War, 1945 (Colonel, United States Army, 1945); Member, Senior Staff, RAND Corporation, Santa Monica, California, 1947–49; Editorial Adviser to *Look* magazine, New York, 1949–71. Since 1955, Lecturer, Columbia University, New York. Ford Visiting Professor of Political Science, University of California, Berkeley, 1960–61. Consultant to the Commission on National Goals, 1960. Member of the National Board of the Authors League of America, and of the Educational Policies Committee of the National Educational Association. Recipient: Rockefeller grant, 1940; George Polk Memorial Award, 1955; Freedoms Foundation Award, 1955; Professional Achievement Award, University of Chicago, 1969. Address: c/o Doubleday and Co. Inc., 277 Park Avenue, New York, New York 10017, U.S.A.

PUBLICATIONS

Novels

*The Education of Hyman Kaplan* (as Leonard Q. Ross).   New York, Harcourt Brace, and London, Constable, 1937.
*Dateline: Europe* (as Leonard Ross).   New York, Harcourt Brace, 1939; as *Balkan Express*, London, Heinemann, 1939.
*The Dark Corner*.   New York, Century, 1945.
*Sleep, My Love*.   New York, Triangle, 1946.
*The Return of Hyman Kaplan*.   New York, Harper, and London, Gollancz, 1959.
*Captain Newman, M.D.*   London, Gollancz, 1961; New York, Harper, 1962.
*A Most Private Intrigue*.   New York, Atheneum, and London, Gollancz, 1967.

Plays

Screenplays: *The Dark Corner*, 1946; *The Velvet Touch*, 1948; *Sleep, My Love*, 1948; *Where Danger Lies*, 1950; *Double Dynamite*, 1951; *Walk East on Beacon*, 1952; *It's Only Money*, 1962.

Other

*The Washington Correspondents*.   New York, Harcourt Brace, 1937.
*The Strangest Places* (as Leonard Ross).   New York, Harcourt Brace, and London, Constable, 1939.
*Adventure in Washington* (as Leonard Ross).   New York, Harcourt Brace, 1940.
*Hollywood: The Movie Colony, The Movie Makers*.   New York, Harcourt Brace, 1941.
*112 Gripes about the French*.   Washington, D.C., United States War Department, 1944.
*The Story Behind the Painting*.   New York, Doubleday-Cowles, 1962.
*The Many Worlds of Leo Rosten*.   New York, Harper, 1964; as *The Leo Rosten Bedside Book*, London, Gollancz, 1965.
*The Joys of Yiddish*.   New York, McGraw Hill, 1968; London, W. H. Allen, 1970.

*A Trumpet for Reason.*   New York, Doubleday, 1970; London, W. H. Allen, 1971.
*People I Have Loved, Known or Admired.*   New York, McGraw Hill, 1970; London, W. H. Allen, 1971.
*Rome Wasn't Burned in a Day: The Mischief of Language.*   New York, Doubleday, 1972.

Editor, *A Guide to the Religions of America.*   New York, Simon and Schuster, 1955; as *Religions of America*, London, Heinemann, 1957; revised edition, as *Religions in America*, Simon and Schuster, 1963.

Manuscript Collection: Brandeis University, Waltham, Massachusetts.

Leo Rosten comments:

I write as my interests guide and seduce me: see the preface to *The Many Worlds of Leo Rosten.* My work ranges from political analysis to humor, from social comment to art to movie screenplays, from inquiries about science and theology to biographical vignettes of Churchill, Freud, Groucho Marx, Leonardo, Adam Smith—and a juicy assortment of wits, half-wits, sages, psychiatrists and trail-blazers—whether in the manufacture of spaghetti or religious credos to uplift true believers.

*People I Have Loved, Known or Admired* suggests the range of my susceptibilities—and the varieties of techniques to which I resort. I write melodrama for pleasure, as some men play chess or go fishing. The titles of my works indicate the range of the nets I have cast into the sea of my fancies. I see no reason to thwart my curiosity or the gratification of varied intellectual appetites. I find writing an indescribably complex, difficult, frustrating, challenging, exhilarating, unyielding, exciting, depressing and joyous calling, to which I commit the resources of the self. I also enjoy the play and elusiveness of my fantasies.

The only reason for being a professional writer is that you just can't help it.

\*       \*       \*

Leo Rosten earned a permanent place (as Leonard Q. Ross) on the rolls of ethnic-humorists with the publication in 1937 of *The Education of H\*Y\*M\*A\*N K\*A\*P\*L\*A\*N*. The title is a parody of the autobiographical "study in failure" of the patrician Henry Adams; Rosten's collection of his *New Yorker* short-stories chronicles the sharply-contrasting efforts of European immigrants to learn "good English" in night school and thereby succeed in America. The brash hero of these episodes is the determined, cagey and warmly likable Kaplan, who signs his name in red crayon capitals, outlined in blue and punctuated with green stars. Kaplan innocently torments his fuss-pot teacher, Mr. Parkhill, with bold syntax, dazzling malapropisms and creative mispronunciations, whereby the plural of "sandwich" is "delicatessen" and the Chinese premier becomes "Shanghai Jack." In 1959, Rosten offered a revival of the popular Kaplan-Parkhill duels, complete with familiar minor characters, but critics agreed that Rosten was too distant from the early years when he had actually taught garment workers in a Chicago night school.

Although his reputation rests on Kaplan's eager shoulders, Rosten's work has been varied, as suggested by one anthology, *The Many Worlds of L\*E\*O R\*O\*S\*T\*E\*N*. His Ph.D. thesis in sociology at the University of Chicago became *The Washington Correspondents,* followed by a Carnegie Foundation-supported study entitled *Hollywood: The Movie Colony, The Movie Makers.* Both studies are methodologically sound, thorough and readable. Among his potboilers, his best is *A Most Private Intrigue,* an old-fashioned spy thriller which eschews James Bond-like violence, sex and technology in favor of romance, plot twists and breath-holding escapes.

Rosten's best-selling novel, *Captain Newman, M.D.*, illustrates his major strengths and weaknesses. As chief of the mental ward of an Air Force base in wartime, psychiatrist Newman is superhumanly insightful, while the ranking officers are as predictably arrogant as the G.I.'s are cute in their shenanigans. If the comic ethnic stereotypes in the Hyman Kaplan stories seemed embarrassing upon re-issue, Rosten nevertheless repeats them all here: the simple-minded Negro private is lovable and humble, the Italian P.O.W.'s roll their eyes and mutter "Mama Mia," the Jewish Laibowitz schemes shrewdly and parries questions with questions. The author skillfully alternates chapters of situation comedy with melodrama to suggest emotional range, but all sequences are as neatly rounded out as in a television series.

Rosten handles many genres with professional competence and intelligence but clearly prefers a light, superficial touch. *The Joys of Yiddish* displayed Rosten's impressive knowledge of the impact of English and Yiddish upon each other, as well as his familiarity with Jewish humor and history. A recent essay collection, *People I Have Loved, Known or Admired*, offers facile interpretations of public figures but is deeply moving in the author's splendid portrait of his own father. The recent *A Trumpet for Reason* resonantly sounds off on contemporary militancy, but the author seems much more attuned to the status quo than he cares to admit. At his best, Rosten writes smooth, witty prose and wears his layers of learning with grace. At worst, he succumbs to the easy appeal of the stock character or belief and reveals the slick writer's affinity for the heart-warming cliché.

—Frank Campenni

---

**ROTH, Henry.** American. Born in Tysmenica, Austria-Hungary, 8 February 1906. Educated at the City College of New York, B.S. 1928. Married Muriel Parker in 1939; has two children. Worked for the Works Progress Administration (WPA), 1939; Teacher, Roosevelt High School, New York, 1939–41; Precision Metal Grinder, in New York, Providence, Rhode Island, and Boston, 1941–46; Teacher, Montville, Maine, 1947–48; Attendant, Maine State Hospital, 1949–53; Waterfowl Farmer, 1953–62; Tutor, 1956–65. Recipient: National Institute of Arts and Letters grant, 1965; City College of New York's Townsend Harris Medal, 1965; D. H. Lawrence Fellowship, University of New Mexico, 1968. Address: 741 Chavez Road, Albuquerque, New Mexico 87107, U.S.A.

PUBLICATIONS

Novel

   *Call It Sleep.*   New York, Ballou, 1934; London, Joseph, 1963.

Manuscript Collection: Boston University.

Henry Roth comments:

   The writing of the novel, I feel, was too long ago for me to have anything cogent to say about it now, which is not to imply that I ever did have a clear notion of what I was doing.

I recall the ambience and the sensation—the affect—of the writing more than I do the "ideas" connected with it. However, one of these does persist in the memory, a kind of guide or credo: That I had no thesis whatever to advance (that I was aware of), only to convey what it felt to be alive, in my time.

I have a strong suspicion that the reason I wrote no more than I did was that I failed of maturity, lost the will to force the next stage in development at the opportune moment.

*        *        *

Although Henry Roth's only novel, *Call It Sleep*, received favorable reviews and sold tolerably well when it first appeared in 1934, it was known to relatively few readers until its republication in 1960. Its first paperback reprinting in 1964 was a turn in the public reception of the book. *Call It Sleep* is now recognized as one of the finest American novels of this century, perhaps the best novel about childhood ever written by an American, rivalling Dickens' or Dostoevsky's sense of the pathos of childhood.

The popularity of *Call It Sleep* during the sixties can be explained on a number of levels. The interest in Jewish writers and the rediscovery of "ethnic identity," along with increasing curiosity about the life of the Jews in the lower East Side of New York around the turn of the century, are some of the explanations for the book's increasing readership. Also, the concern for urban experience and a renewed interest in the writers of the thirties contribute toward a rediscovery of Roth's novel.

The vitality of the novel can be felt in the fact that it relates to and yet escapes convenient literary and social categories. A product of the thirties, and a reflection of some of that decade's concerns, the book can hardly be categorized as a proletarian novel. A description of a Jewish family in New York City during the years preceding World War I, the book cannot be fixed by the term "Jewish novel." A keen portrayal of the mind of a boy, the book cannot quite be called a psychological novel. Yet all of these elements are vibrantly part of the novel.

*Call It Sleep* begins with the child David Schearl slightly less than two years old and continues to the time he is eight, concentrating on his life in the family and in the streets from his sixth to eighth year. His troubled relationships with his mother and father are keenly portrayed by Roth who describes an oedipal situation with the force of actual life and with no factitious clinical details. The novel resembles D. H. Lawrence's *Sons and Lovers* in its ability to evoke that conflict as a literary and not just a clinical event.

The image of the morose, physically powerful and stern father is counterpointed by the characterization of the sympathetic, loving mother. The child is torn between his affection for his mother (his only security in the novel) and his secret desire to emulate and challenge the powerful and threatening stance of his father.

The scenes both in the apartment and in the street, among the family and among other children, are overwhelming experiences for David. He struggles to gain some kind of foothold by means of which he can withstand the onslaught of both his father and the gangs and friends of the street. The terrors of the family life eventually relate to the terrors and the testing of experience outside the family.

There are three levels of language in the book which Roth sometimes interweaves. First of all there is the language of narration; then there is the Yiddish spoken at home, rendered through an intelligible and confident English, unlike the broken and noisy English of the street, the third level. There is even a fourth level of language in one scene when Roth also brings into play the Hebrew of the Bible during a Hebrew class the boy attends. In that scene (in chapter IV of Book III), Roth intersperses the Biblical-ritual Hebrew of the rabbi-teacher; the angry Yiddish of that teacher as he curses his recalcitrant pupils; the puzzled, exploratory thoughts of David; and the whining, aggressive remarks of the children. It is a passage that shows to good effect Roth's absorption of Joyce and Eliot.

In an effort to match the power of his father, to meet the frustrations of his family life, to escape the puzzlements of street life, and to emulate the rabbi's description of Isaiah and the burning coal that purified his soul and burned away his sins, as well as to recover a vision he once had when staring into the light of the East River, David slips a metal milk ladle into a slot of a third rail from a trolley car line. He causes a blinding flash (the light of salvation and of authority that he longs for). He is also knocked unconscious and causes a temporary power failure in the neighborhood. In an unsuccessful effort to bring together many persons from different backgrounds in response to that power failure, Roth is forced to leave the consciousness of the child for the first time in the book and tries an unsuccessful collage of "proletarian voices" around the unconscious child in his search for light. Roth's poetic prose becomes forced at this point but regains its regular force when the novel returns to the now awakened boy who back home thinks of rest and self-possession before he falls again into sleep.

Henry Roth has not written another novel since *Call It Sleep*. A few stories have appeared over the years as Roth destroyed a second novel, imperfectly started a third and went on to hold a number of jobs, finally becoming a raiser of waterfowl in Maine. Probably the best of those stories are "At Times in Flight" and "The Dun Dakotas" (published in *Commentary*, July 1959 and August 1960, respectively). Both tales reflect Roth's difficulty in returning to writing.

A recent interview in the 1969 (no. 2) issue of *Partisan Review* movingly portrays Roth's situation and difficulties from the time he completed *Call It Sleep* to his new thoughts and ambition to write again following the Israeli-Arab six day war in 1967. Whether or not Roth will be able to write again at the level of *Call It Sleep*, he has accomplished in that novel one of the finest works of imagination by an American novelist in this century.

—Richard J. Fein

---

**ROTH, Philip (Milton).** American. Born in Newark, New Jersey, 19 March 1933. Educated at Newark College, Rutgers University, 1950–51; Bucknell University, Lewisburg, Pennsylvania, 1951–54, A.B. 1954; University of Chicago, 1954–55, M.A. 1955. Served in the United States Army, 1955–56. Instructor in English, University of Chicago, 1956–58. Visiting Writer, University of Iowa, Iowa City, 1960–62; Writer-in-Residence, Princeton University, New Jersey, 1962–64; Visiting Writer, State University of New York at Stony Brook, 1966, 1967, and the University of Pennsylvania, Philadelphia, 1967, 1968, 1970, 1971. Member of the Corporation of Yaddo, Saratoga Springs, New York. Recipient: Aga Khan Prize, *Paris Review*, 1958; Houghton Mifflin Literary Fellowship, 1959; Guggenheim Fellowship, 1959; National Book Award, 1960; Daroff Award, 1960; National Institute of Arts and Letters grant, 1960; O. Henry Award, 1960; Ford grant, for playwriting, 1965; Rockefeller Fellowship, 1966. Member, National Institute of Arts and Letters, 1970. Address: c/o Random House Inc., 201 East 50th Street, New York, New York 10022, U.S.A.

PUBLICATIONS

Novels

*Letting Go*. New York, Random House, and London, Deutsch, 1962.
*When She Was Good*. New York, Random House, and London, Cape, 1967.
*Portnoy's Complaint*. New York, Random House, 1969; London, Cape, 1970.
*Our Gang (Starring Tricky and His Friends)*. New York, Random House, and London, Cape, 1971.

Short Stories

> *Goodbye, Columbus and Five Short Stories*.   Boston, Houghton Mifflin, and London,
>     Deutsch, 1959.
> *Penguin Modern Stories 3*, with others.   London, Penguin, 1969.


Manuscript Collection: Library of Congress, Washington, D.C.


Critical Study: "The Journey of Philip Roth" by Theodore Solotaroff, in *The Red Hot
Vacuum*, New York, Atheneum, 1970.

*      *      *

In the title of one of the best essays on Philip Roth, Alfred Kazin used the word "tough-minded." This quality pervades his novels, stories, and essays. Roth's unsparing portraits of Jews too adept at scheming and compromise have upset rabbis and Jewish organizations like the Anti-Defamation League (see Roth's "Writing About Jews," *Commentary*, December, 1963). His frank acknowledgment of such unmentionables as abortion, masturbation, and sexual calisthenics has alarmed the bluenoses. These irate—usually unliterary—responses have fortunately failed to unsettle him. We can expect them to surface again when the impact of his latest book, *Our Gang (Starring Tricky and His Friends)*, begins to be felt. Roth here takes on a formidable adversary, the Nixon administration: he carries a certain Trick E. Dixon from a press conference, an underground meeting with his "coaches," an address to his "fellow Americans," to an election speech—following his assassination—to his "fellow Fallen" in Hell. Passages from Swift and Orwell appropriately serve as epigraphs for this novel. Roth shares the political anxieties of these satirists as he exposes chicanery in high places.

Until now Roth has seemed most at ease with Jewish characters and settings. His ear is especially sensitive to the verbal rhythm and pulse beat of the second-generation American Jew who has recently abandoned the inner city for the suburbs. The stories in Roth's first book, *Goodbye, Columbus*, are almost all concerned with confrontations between Jews of radically different persuasions and temperaments. Thus Neil Klugman, in the title story, confronts the Jewish society of Short Hills, as represented by Brenda Patimkin and her family, where "fruit grew in their refrigerator and sporting goods dropped from their trees!" Neil's wrong-side-of-the-track Judaism fails to make the proper concessions and adjustments. In "Eli, The Fanatic," the assimilated Jews of another suburban community, Woodenton, employ the lawyer Eli Peck to force a Yeshivah to move elsewhere or at least to "modernize." We see a skillful confrontation between the Talmudic logic of the Yeshivah's headmaster and the more worldly logic of Eli. Eli ends by donning the Hasidic garb of one of the Yeshivah instructors—which suggests to his fellow Jews of Woodenton the return of an earlier nervous breakdown. In "Defender of the Faith" Nathan Marx, a Jewish sergeant, finds his integrity seriously threatened by three Jewish recruits in his training company. The outrageous scheming of one of them finally forces Marx to retaliate despite his misgivings about taking punitive action against a coreligionist. Jew is also pitted against Jew in "The Conversion of the Jews." This time the questioning Jewish schoolboy Ozzie Freedman forces embarrassing ideological concessions from Rabbi Binder and the Jewish establishment when he threatens to jump from the roof of the synagogue. The stories in *Goodbye, Columbus* are brilliantly irreverent.

Roth's heterodoxy continues into his first novel, *Letting Go*. He enlarges the focus here to include not only the idiosyncrasies of the Jewish community but also of university faculties, charlatan abortionists, and ill-suited love relationships. Very little is left out. Gabe Wallach's "I" controls the early parts of the novel; then it recedes into a kind of background first-person and finally turns into a more respectably detached third-person. Wallach is the intruder who keeps moving in and out of delicate situations—always avoiding complete involvement—and so this changing of narrative focus is especially apt. He defines his position early in the novel: "It was beginning to seem that toward those for whom I felt no strong sentiment, I gravitated; where sentiment existed, I ran." Wallach's vantage point in *Letting Go* is rather like that of Peter Leverett in William Styron's *Set This House on Fire*. Leverett, like Wallach, increasingly gets drawn into situations not entirely of his making; his shuttling back and forth between detachment and involvement is mirrored by the increasingly background nature of his first-person narrative role. The novels themselves are similar in their rather cineramic shapes, if dissimilar in their subject matter. Reviewers, incidentally, brought up F. Scott Fitzgerald's name when discussing both books.

Wallach's years as a graduate student at the University of Iowa and as an instructor at the University of Chicago offer a rejection of his eastern seaboard Jewish background (born in New York, educated at Harvard). The first words of the novel are the deathbed letter of Gabe Wallach's mother. This letter, inadvertently tucked between the pages of his copy of James's *Portrait of a Lady*, starts Gabe off on the midwestern pilgrimage which involves the series of precarious relationships with Libby and Paul Herz and with Martha Reganhart. The terribly flawed Herz marriage somehow survives Gabe's "meddling"; in fact, it is strengthened by the adoption of a child and by a spirited assertion of Judaism. Gabe Wallach's love affair with Martha Reganhart fares less well. Gabe speaks of himself in a final letter to Libby as an "indecisive man" who had had but "one decisive moment."

Roth also places his next novel, *When She Was Good*, in the midwest—this time a midwest without Jews. The texture of his writing changes markedly; it seems to flatten out, to become, as Theodore Solotaroff suggests, "a language of scrupulous banality." The midwestern Protestantism which underlies the novel is threatened only by an adolescent flirtation with the Catholic Church by the heroine Lucy Nelson; this is lightly dismissed as "all that Catholic hocus-pocus." Lucy's intolerance and uncomfortable moral provincialism manage to get in the way of her own marriage and that of her parents. She cannot put up with her husband's rather puerile brashness and incompetence or with her father's alcoholism.

Roth's view of Liberty Center, where most of the events occur, seems remarkably accurate, especially for a writer who has spent so much of his time reproducing urban Jewish settings. Just as Roth was able to capture the special quality of the conversation of both first and second generation American Jews in *Goodbye, Columbus* and *Letting Go*, so in *When She Was Good* he manages handsomely with the cliché-ridden language of Main Street. Here is Lucy's friend Ellie, educated at Northwestern University and one of the more sophisticated characters in the novel: "And that's what you miss in Chicago, all the fun aside—that kind of really genuine person, who really cares about people and isn't just a fake and a phony."

*Portnoy's Complaint* is a return, with a vengeance, to Roth's earlier manner. It seems to come out of the best pages of *Goodbye, Columbus* and *Letting Go*. Roth has settled here on all the things he knows how to do best, especially in his creation of the urban Jewish family with the mother at its moral center. *Portnoy's Complaint* is the staccato confession of Alexander Portnoy to his psychiatrist Dr. Spielvogel, in heavily free associative prose. (Except for the quality of the language one might be tempted to draw comparisons with Italo Svevo's *Confessions of Zeno*.)

The novel begins with a section entitled "The Most Unforgettable Character I've Met"; the reference is to Sophie Portnoy who dominates not only the family but also the "confessions" of her son. (She is in part anticipated by Aunt Gladys in "Goodbye, Columbus" and Paul Herz's mother in *Letting Go*.) She characteristically pushes to the background her perpetually constipated and henpecked husband and her pathetically unendowed daughter. The confrontation is between mother and son. The fiercely aggressive, domineering mother seems to win out since it is the son who does the confessing from the analyst's couch. Alex, however, gains some measure of revenge through sieges of masturbation in his youth and through affairs with gentiles (*shiksas*) in his more mature years. He masterfully uncovers chinks in his Jewish mother's armor by taunting her with his conquest of Christian girls and by abusing the family rabbi, but always at the expense of his own too active feelings of guilt. Everything in this novel, it would seem, "can be traced to the bonds obtaining in the mother-child relationship." Jewish mothers, in the past few years, have presented a challenge to some of the best American Jewish novelists, like Wallace Markfield, Bruce Jay Friedman, and Herbert Gold. Probably the most realized and convincing of all is Sophie Portnoy.

*Portnoy's Complaint* has had a resounding impact. Erich Segal tried to pass off his *Love Story* as an anti-*Portnoy's Complaint* in various appearances he made across the United States advertising his book. Kingsley Amis found himself distinctly ill-at-ease with *Portnoy*: "The book is in essence a heavily orchestrated yell of rage, rage that is nonetheless rage for being presented as often excessive and ridiculous, and rage wears one down." *Portnoy's Complaint* is fast becoming a part of American popular culture: Jewish mothers have come out against it in newspaper articles and in television appearances. Among recent American novels, only Styron's *The Confessions of Nat Turner* seems to have caused this kind of stir. Just as Styron's novel begot a polemical volume from the Negro intellectuals, *William Styron's Nat Turner: Ten Black Writers Respond*, so we can imagine Roth's book prompting something between covers with a title like *Philip Roth's "Portnoy's Complaint": Ten Jewish Mothers Respond*.

—Melvin J. Friedman

---

**RUBENS, Bernice.** British. Born in Cardiff, Wales, 26 July 1927. Educated at Cardiff High School for Girls; University College of South Wales and Monmouthshire, Cardiff, 1944–47, B.A. (honours) in English 1947. Married the writer Rudi Nassauer in 1947; has two children. Teacher of English, Handsworth Grammar School for Boys, Birmingham, 1947–49. Since 1950, Documentary Film Writer and Director, for the United Nations and others. Recipient: American Blue Ribbon Award, for film-making, 1968; Booker Prize, 1970. Address: 16 Frognal Gardens, London N.W.3, England.

PUBLICATIONS

Novels

 *Set on Edge.* London, Eyre and Spottiswoode, 1960.
 *Madame Sousatzka.* London, Eyre and Spottiswoode, 1962.
 *Mate in Three.* London, Eyre and Spottiswoode, 1965.
 *The Elected Member.* London, Eyre and Spottiswoode, 1969; as *Chosen People*, New York, Atheneum, 1969.
 *Sunday Best.* London, Eyre and Spottiswoode, 1971.

Bernice Rubens comments:

I am never consciously aware of the actual matter of my work and never think about it unless the question is directly raised. There seems to be a terrible finality about assessing one's own work, because such an assessment might bind you to that evaluation for ever. I am open to the most radical changes in my thinking and outlook. I hope it will be reflected in my work. My first four novels were essentially on Jewish themes in a Jewish environment, for in that environment I felt secure. My fifth novel, *Sunday Best*, was an attempt to challenge myself to step outside that familiarity. I noticed that my radical change of location did not involve as radical a change of style, which seems to remain simple, direct, always empty of what in school is called "descriptive passages", for these frighten me. As to the matter of what I write about, I can only be general. I am concerned with the communication, or non-communication as is more often the case, between people and families. A general enough statement, and in this general sense my books will always be about that theme.

*       *       *

Bernice Rubens has in the main been a chronicler of the frayed edge of middle-class Jewish life. The old sources of insecurity are gone. There is no external threat from the gentile world: the natives are friendly. And money, though not abundant, is sufficient. Nor does one find much mutual hostility. The fraying, in the main, comes from love. People are pained and give pain through the deep regard they have for one another, as can be seen in the conflicts between wife, husband and mistress in *Mate in Three*, or at its ultimate in Miss Ruben's fourth and most accomplished novel, *The Elected Member*.

The story of *The Elected Member* suggests that within every close group, in this case the Jewish family, one member comes forward as a sort of Jesus to atone for the sins of the others, or as a conductor for the tremors which trouble their souls. He is broken by the burden, resorts to drugs, becomes subject to horrifying hallucinations and ends in an asylum, while the group as a whole disintegrates.

Miss Rubens does not try to draw a moral. These, she says, are the underlying realities of our situation; it may help to recognise them. Neither does she apportion blame, though towards the end of the novel Norman, who is in fact the elected member, cries out from the depth of his anguish against God: "Your wrath, Your jealousy, Your expectation, Your omnipotence, Your mercy and pity, Your sheer bloody mindedness." It is a cry which many a member of the Chosen Race may have made in the post-Auschwitz era. Who asked to be chosen? The story of Norman is, to an extent, the story of the Jewish people, except that even the darkest moments of Jewish history have been redeemed by Messianic hope. There is no such optimism in Miss Ruben's work, but on the contrary, a brooding pessimism. What redeems it, however, is the humour, which is black and ghoulish, as in her first novel, *Set on Edge*, and wryly Jewish, arising partly from the situation, partly from the eccentricities of character, as displayed for example in *Madame Sousatzka*. Madam, a teacher of pianoforte, owes something to Gogol in her makeup, something to Lewis Carroll, but in the main, she is Miss Rubens' own, a memorable creation.

With four solid novels behind her one felt that Miss Rubens was established as the mistress of a set genre, so that one could recognise a Rubens character if one met one in the street, but her fifth, and most recent novel, *Sunday Best*, is a complete departure, except that here too the central character has his neurosis (you don't have to be Jewish to be neurotic, but it helps): he is a transvestite, enjoying his aberration quietly and only on a Sunday. One day, however, he dons drag, leaves home and finds himself pursued for his own alleged murder. The flavour is vintage Hitchcock, the invention unflagging, the wit outrageous. It is as a result difficult to classify Miss Rubens as this or that sort of writer. She is too versatile to be cubbyholed.

—Chaim Bermant

**SAHGAL, Nayantara (Pandit).** Indian. Born in Allahabad, 10 May 1927. Educated at Wellesley College, Massachusetts, 1943–47, B.A. in history 1947. Married Gautam Sahgal in 1949 (divorced, 1967); has three children. Since 1965, has regularly contributed articles to various Indian newspapers and magazines. Address: 25-C Sujan Singh Park, New Delhi 3, India.

PUBLICATIONS

Novels

*A Time to Be Happy.* New York, Knopf, and London, Gollancz, 1958.
*This Time of Morning.* New York, Norton, and London, Gollancz, 1965.
*Storm in Chandigarh.* New York, Norton, and London, Chatto and Windus, 1969.
*The Day in Shadow.* New Delhi, Vikas, 1971; New York, Norton, 1972.

Uncollected Short Stories

"The Promising Young Woman", in *Illustrated Weekly of India* (Bombay), January 1959.
"The Golden Afternoon", in *Illustrated Weekly of India* (Bombay), February 1959.

Other

*Prison and Chocolate Cake* (autobiography). New York, Knopf, and London, Gollancz, 1954.
*From Fear Set Free* (autobiography). New York, Norton, and London, Gollancz, 1963.
*History of the Freedom Movement.* New Delhi, National Council of Educational Research and Training, 1970.

Critical Studies: *Bridges of Literature* by M. L. Malhotra, Ajmer, Sunanda Publications, 1971; essay by the author in *Adam* (London), August 1971; *Nayantara Sahgal and the Craft of Fiction* by Suresh Kohli, New Delhi, Vikas, 1972.

\*       \*       \*

Whether one likes it or not it makes a difference to a writer to have been born an aristocrat very much in the upper reaches of society surrounded by beauty, intelligence, and above all a depth of commitment which sent her parents to jail in the Indian independence struggle. As Nayantara Sahgal grew up she saw politics from the inside; Nehru was her uncle, her mother—widowed because her father died from illness brought on in prison—a tough ambassador. This world is implicit in her novels. It is also implicit in her style. Here there is nothing extreme but an educated and skilful use of the English language in which there is never any question of her not being at home, although like a true citizen of the world, she clearly knows other languages and cultures as well. This being so, she looks benevolently on other people's religions so long as they are honest and gentle, but what we would call religious motives scarcely enter in her novels. A Brahmin knows that all words are merely symbols; by themselves they mean nothing and books are made of words. Her characters are not "believers" although they may go through certain rites for social ends. *This Time of Morning* is the world of upper class Indian politics described with the confidence of one who has watched and questioned and seen through the normal pretensions and exaggerations. And of course this is clear from her two delightful volumes of autobiography.

But also it makes a difference being beautiful which she was stunningly as a girl and is still among her daughters. It is a matter of confidence, of never having felt basically instable. Certainly it creates difficulties but not so many as it smoothes out. It would be hard for Nayantara to write about an ugly woman; a character may be elderly or have put on fat, but she knows how to wear a sari to the best advantage.

Nayantara is and isn't a New Delhi woman. Certainly she can write about the top people who wouldn't consider living anywhere else except of course for the hills—or sometimes Europe or America—in the hot weather, and her writing has a certain bite to it. She is in real life an excellent hostess without the shocking lavishness of the wickedly rich whom she sometimes describes, but she and her characters are conscious of the time of India away beyond in place and history and a remoteness of feeling. In one of her books her main character, remembering administrators whose spare time had gone not on ladder climbing but on the arts and even the sciences, thinks "Delhi had downgraded leisure". For there is always an implicit moral judgement in Nayantara's work. What are her moral criteria? Probably honesty and gentleness especially for the men, and she has seen in her own lifetime how the honesty and dedication of the early politicians of independence have been eroded by the vast difficulties of running India and by the temptations, above all the temptation to wait in the hope that difficulties will disappear by themselves. But she wants honest relations between men and women which are always next to impossible and are more obviously bedevilled in India by the general assumption of completely different values for men and women, something which Euro-America is growing out of. So far, her women characters are much involved in this social puzzle tangling their lovelife.

Her background is always anciently civilized Indian, not always completely absorbing or understanding alien aesthetics but with its own standards. Yet there are scenes from another life, for instance in *Storm in Chandigarh*, the hideous childhood of Gyan Singh in the garage among the Sikh drivers. Where will she go next?

—Naomi Mitchison

---

**ST. OMER, Garth.** West Indian. Born in Castries, St. Lucia. Educated at the University of the West Indies, Kingston, Jamaica; degree in French. Lived in France and Ghana before settling in London. Address: c/o Faber and Faber Ltd., 3 Queen Square, London W.C.1, England.

PUBLICATIONS

Novels

*A Room on the Hill*. London, Faber, 1968.
*Shades of Grey*. London, Faber, 1968.
*Nor Any Country*. London, Faber, 1969.
*J, Black Bam and the Masqueraders*. London, Faber, 1972.

Uncollected Short Story

"Syrop", in *Introduction 2*.   London, Faber, 1968.

*          *          *

Garth St. Omer creates in his fiction characters filled with an unrest which they themselves cannot define or explain. It is a *malaise* of the islands which makes them hesitate even before opportunities which are apparently dazzling, which makes them hurt and abandon those they love, or turn aside from courses of action they have embarked on with every sign of conviction. The immediacy of his writing springs from the fact that he is so involved himself with this unrest that he is not yet able to distance or judge his heroes. The passion and the pain of these young island lives are fully conveyed, but it is perhaps this very lack of distance that makes his writing, at present, ideally suited to the novella form. His reputation was first made with "Syrop," and the fact that he followed his first novel with a volume comprising two more novellas demonstrates his addiction to the form. His stories are not fragments of unrealised novels, however, although he is probably not yet ready to write a major novel which will fully relate his heroes to a world they are continually evading.

"Syrop" is a harsh, tragic story of a family blighted by inexplicable misfortune, as well as by the poverty they share with their neighbours. Syrop, the young hero, differs from other St. Omer protagonists in that he doesn't live to carry his anguish and restlessness into adult life. He is smashed by a ship's propellers, diving for pennies on the very day he has been chosen to join the fishing crews, and on the eve of his much-loved brother's return from prison. John Lestrade, in St. Omer's first novel *A Room on the Hill*, is older and tougher, but still haunted by intimate misfortunes and early deaths in his little island circle of relatives, friends and lovers. This book ends with a hard gesture towards departure, for it is increasingly obvious that all who stay in the island are doomed or lost, and Lestrade is determined to survive and transmute grief into action.

Of the two stories in *Shades of Grey* the first, "The Lights on the Hill," is the more tightly organised. It starts at a moment of crisis in the hero's relationship with Thea, the beautiful and original girl whom he has long desired and who now loves him. Neither can explain the nature of this crisis and it can only cause pain to them both, yet Stephenson knows in his being that he must now leave her. The madman's cry from the asylum which punctuates this realisation begins and ends the story. In between these cries (or are they the same?) St. Omer cross-cuts a number of short scenes from the hero's past in Jamaica and in his native St. Lucia. We see him charcoal-burning with his father and his illiterate brother Carl in the mountains, or seeking refuge with his mother in the empty barracks on the Morne after the Castries fire of 1948, or drifting into corruption, trial and dismissal as a petty official in the Civil Service. And we see the other affairs, some furtive and bourgeois, others casual and earthy, which have preceded all the phases of his rich relationship with Thea. Through it all we are conscious of the two lovers sitting on the hillside, smoking and talking in the darkness, numbed by their awareness that some force within him is sweeping them apart:

> "Tell me I'm stupid, that I'm imagining things. That you love me."
>
> "You know I do."
>
> "Tell me," she said, "make me feel that I belong to you."
>
> He did not tell her what he felt about people belonging to one another. He said, "Do I have to? Don't you know it?"
>
> She grabbed his shirt. "Do I know it?"
>
> She was laughing and crying now. "Oh, darling, don't you know you must make me feel it?"
>
> He said nothing. But he was passing his hands over her hair.
>
> "You're really old. Old for nothing. Tell me," she had thrown her head back to look at him in the moonlight, "have you ever had a girl friend?"
>
> Suddenly it was dark. They looked up. A black cloud covered nearly all the sky.

St. Omer's writing is full of sharp, perfectly registered dialogue like this. His narrative and descriptive passages are rendered throughout in short, rather spikey paragraphs and staccato sentences, which carry the same burden of unease as the lives they describe. The effect can occasionally be irritating for the reader who longs for a deeper and more measured breath. Again, it is a style for the novella rather than the novel, but it perfectly fits the peculiar and sustained tension of this story in which jobs, lives and love affairs are all snapped off before fruition; for Stephenson's decisions are as inexplicable as the death of his friend Eddie, struck by lightning in the midst of a football field. Here, for example, is a reminiscence of charcoal burning in the holidays:

> In the evening they returned. They walked over the steep tracks, hard underfoot (he was barefoot too) because of the lack of rain. Around them hills arose from crevices deep as the one they seemed continually to be climbing out of. A shout sounded. Sometimes the blow of an axe. The sounds echoed. Parts of the hill were in shadow. Slowly the cloud moved. The hill was like a cat awakening. . . . Then the sun set. The hills were in shadow and dead trees stood white on them everywhere.

This passage contains several sentences of only three or four words, yet it evokes perfectly the hollow, expectant silence and ringing sounds of evening in the mountains as the tired men walk home.

There is, however, one continual irritation in this fine story, and that is St. Omer's fondness for a sort of pseudo-anonymity in his settings. Thus St. Lucia is referred to throughout as "his island home", Jamaica as "this other, larger island" and Trinidad as "a large island in the south". Since no reader can doubt for a moment that the story is set on the Campus at Mona and in the author's native St. Lucia, these circumlocutions are pointless, unless dictated by the whims of a nervous publisher.

The second story, "Another Place Another Time," adopts a more chronological approach to a short period in the boyhood of its hero, Derek Charles. It lacks the originality and power of the first, but is full of a distinctive pain of its own. This pain stems largely from the sheer unlikeableness of this boy, and from the feeling that, if he is in part autobiographical, the author does not now much like him either. He is priggish, snobbish and jumpy, difficult to reach. He behaves brutally to Berthe, the simple girl whom he seduces and throws over. Yet we see in this society of few and roving males, of unfathered children, abortions, poverty and abandonment, how difficult it is for the growing child to find models by which to climb to maturity. It is as though leaving the island were an indispensable part of growing up, a *rite de passage* from which most of the initiates never return. The story is a cry from the forest of exile, a cry to which St. Omer fits the words of Shakespeare: "How like a winter has my absence been/From thee."

St. Omer is particularly good at rendering the speech of those who, though educated elsewhere, are still very close to the islands and unable to relate their living satisfactorily to any other place. The uncertainty of their position is registered in the groping movement of the sentences with which they seek to explain their lives. In *Nor Any Country* the hero, returning for a brief visit to the island after eight years of study overseas, talks to a young black priest in one of the villages. The priest feels acutely the anomaly of his position, one which has always been associated with an alien, white-skinned and aloof kind of authority. He asks:

> "Perhaps for you, too, I'm suspect?"
> "For whom are you?"
> "Some people here who thought I could have prevented the doctor from having to leave."
> "No. You're not suspect to me. I only know that the Church demands loyalty that is absolute. It does not allow loyalty to it to be shared with anything or anybody else. One can only serve her or leave her."
> The priest laughed.

"It's almost as if you're giving me a lecture."
Peter smiled.
"You know I didn't mean to."
"It was a joke."
Then he added, "I can't leave, of course."
"I don't suppose you can."

The handling of dialogue is less successful where it derives from the *patois* of St. Lucia, a dialect largely of French derivation for which St. Omer tries to find an English dialect equivalent. The shape and rhythm of this dialect are necessarily very different from those of *patois* and the effect, despite an occasional "oui" or "non" at the end of a sentence, is vaguely West Indian rather than specifically St. Lucian. Yet it is hard to think of any more faithful alternative which would not leave most readers struggling. The difficulty of balancing fidelity to his material with the demands of communication is already evident in his first story, "Syrop," where several speeches have the slightly clumsy and outlandish effectiveness of this: "You think it so people hit other people. I am not at you now. I can say what I want, it is my mouth. And I still say you cannot make children."

To Peter Breville in *Nor Any Country*, as to all St. Omer's heroes, the memories of St. Lucia are the sore tooth which mars his enjoyment of more exotic pleasures and experiences. That nagging pain draws him at last to revisit the island in which he has left for eight years a scarcely-known wife, married only because of her pregnancy. Yet the return, which perhaps he hoped would be purgative, leads to a partial acceptance of what he is and has ever been. Phyllis is still there, still young, still open to his love and still able to awaken his lust. Peter's long-standing resentment of her existence is modified by what he sees of other lives forgotten during his absence. His brother Paul, who likewise impregnated a local girl, has become a special kind of island failure because of his refusal to marry her. The girl herself has committed suicide but her neglected son Michael has survived, whereas Peter's marriage has produced the mirror image of twins born and dead in his absence but a neglected wife who survives to challenge his egotism by her presence. At the end of his week-long visit Peter knows that he must take both Phyllis and Michael with him now. By this single gesture he will attempt to redeem the past.

*Nor Any Country* thus ends on a more positive note than any of St. Omer's earlier writing. It stints nothing of the narrow fate attending those who stay in the islands. The failures lie steeped in rum and self-pity, whilst the few successes grow flashy and Americanised in their loud insecurity. Yet, when all this is said, it was the long-postponed return to the island which brought Peter Breville to his late maturity. For the last *rite de passage* is the reunification with one's origins, without which the cycle of exile can never be complete.

—Gerald Moore

---

**SALINGER, J(erome) D(avid).** American. Born in New York City, 1 January 1919. Educated in New York City public schools; at Valley Forge Military Academy, Pennsylvania; New York University; Columbia University, New York. Served as a Staff Sergeant in the 4th Infantry Division of the United States Army, 1942–46. Married Claire Douglas in 1953 (divorced, 1967); has two children. Lives in New Hampshire. Address: c/o Harold Ober Associates, 40 East 49th Street, New York, New York 10017, U.S.A.

PUBLICATIONS

Novel

The Catcher in the Rye.   Boston, Little Brown, and London, Hamish Hamilton, 1951.

Short Stories

Nine Stories.   Boston, Little Brown, 1953; as For Esmé—With Love and Squalor and
   Other Stories, London, Hamish Hamilton, 1953.
Franny, and Zooey.   Boston, Little Brown, 1961; London, Heinemann, 1962.
Raise High the Roof Beam, Carpenters, and Seymour: An Introduction.   Boston, Little
   Brown, and London, Heinemann, 1963.

\*       \*       \*

In terms of subject-matter, the fiction of J. D. Salinger falls into two groups. His most
celebrated work, The Catcher in the Rye, tells of several days in the life of a young man,
Holden Caulfield, after he has left the school from which he has been expelled; he wanders
around New York City in a late-adolescent pursuit of contacts that will have meaning for
him. The novel itself is Holden's meditation on these days some months later when he is
confined to a West Coast clinic. The rest of Salinger's work, with the exception of some of the
stories in Nine Stories, has for its subject elements drawn from the experience of the Glass
family who live in New York. The parents, Les and Bessie, are retired vaudeville dancers;
Les is Jewish in origin, Bessie Catholic—a fact that announces the merging of religious
traditions effected in the lives of their seven children. The children, begotten over a considerable period of time, are seven in number. There are Seymour, a gifted poet; Buddy, a writer;
Walker and Wake, twins—one killed in war, the other finally a priest; Boo Boo, a happily
married daughter; and two much younger children, Franny and Zooey.
   The diverse subject-matters of Salinger's fiction tend, in retrospect, to coalesce. Holden
Caulfield's parents, less loving and concerned than the Glass couple, have also begotten
several children. But in Holden's case, there is only one child—a ten-year-old girl—to whom
Holden can turn in his desperation.
   But it is not just the mirror-image of subject-matter that binds the Caulfield narrative
together with the tales of the Glass family. There are a unity of tone and a prevailing interest
that inform all of Salinger's narratives and that have made them appeal deeply to readers
for two decades. The tone and interest combine to produce a sad, often ironic meditation
on the plight of young persons who are coming to maturity in a society where precise and
guiding values are absent. This recurrent meditation, concealed in wrappings that are
usually grotesque and farcical, has drawn readers to Salinger. His characters move through
a "world they never made"; they address questions to that world and receive, for the most
part, only a "dusty answer." Casual social contacts so nauseate Holden Caulfield, for example,
that he is frequently at the point of vomiting. His quest for love is harassed by the sexual
basis of love, and he is repelled. The only good relation in his life rests on the affection he
feels for his young sister; she is the one light in a wilderness of adult hypocrisy, lust, and
perversion. In contrast, affection takes in a larger area in the Glass family chronicles; mutual
esteem and concern bind the family together and somewhat offset the dreary vision of human
relations in The Catcher in the Rye.
   Perhaps one reason for this contrast is that, in The Catcher in the Rye, the narrative is
presented from the point of view of Holden, a malleable, only half-conscious person. He
moves in many directions, but none leads him toward the goals he aspires to. His teachers
are "phonies"; the one in whom he puts some trust turns out to be a homosexual. His en-

counter with a prostitute gives him nothing, and his relations with girls of his class do not offer him the gift of comprehension. His parents are as deceived as he is about the proper use of the gift of life. As indicated, only his young sister can offer him the love he needs, and she is too immature to counter balance the panorama of insincerity that unfolds before Holden's eyes. So for Holden, all is in suspense—an effect that appealed strongly to Salinger's readers.

But for members of the Glass family, all is not fully in suspense. That gifted group of young people has indeed been badly shaken by the suicide of Seymour, their most gifted sibling. Thus, the central "mystery" which they must come to terms with is not Holden's general panorama of hypocrisy; the death and even more the remembered life of Seymour contain a secret that they are haunted by. The actual death of Seymour is briefly narrated in a story, "A Perfect Day for Bananafish," in *Nine Stories*. Later work, told from various points of view, relates the efforts of members of the Glass family to grasp and apply the eclectic religious truths that the memory of Seymour reminds them of. In none of these tales is there an effort to explain the suicide; this is a fact which the brothers and sisters accept rather than assess. What they do assess, in terms of their own later experience, is the teaching presence of Seymour as they recall it. In the two sections of *Franny and Zooey*, the two youngest members of the family reach out in directions that Seymour, in effect, has already pointed out. In "Franny", the heroine is obsessed by the "Jesus prayer" which she has come across in the memoirs of a Russian monk; she does not know how to pray the prayer and is only aware that, until she does, all her other relations will be without meaning. In "Zooey", her charming brother helps her and himself to come to a grasp of what Seymour's existence had announced: repetition of the Jesus prayer transforms life that is contemptible into a constant act of love and reveals that a "fat lady" is indeed Christ—the "fat lady" and every other human being one encounters. In "Raise High the Roof Beam, Carpenters"—told from the point of view of Buddy, the writing brother—the ridiculous circumstances of Seymour's wedding day are related; Seymour and his fiancée finally elope rather than endure an elaborate and empty wedding ceremony. Finally, in "Seymour: An Introduction"—also told from the point of view of Buddy—all that can be recalled of Seymour is put down. Recalled are his mastery of the allusive oriental haiku and his even more important mastery of the process of extorting the greatest significance from trivial event (e.g., a game of marbles becomes the vehicle of Zen instruction).

It is undoubtedly the merging of Eastern and Western religious wisdom—the solution of the "mystery" of existence—that gives the work of Salinger its particular élan. In pursuit of what might be called the Seymour effect, the other Glasses consume innumerable packs of cigarettes and break out into perspiration when they find themselves in blind alleys. But the alleys occasionally open up, and fleeting vistas of human unity flash before the eyes. One can but hope that Holden Caulfield, in his later years, will meet one of the younger Glasses whose personal destinies swell to the proportions of regulative myth.

—Harold H. Watts

---

**SALKEY, (Felix) Andrew (Alexander).** Jamaican. Born in Colon, Panama, 30 January 1928. Educated at St. George's College, Kingston, Jamaica; Munro College, St. Elizabeth, Jamaica; University of London, B.A. in English 1955. Married Patricia Verden in 1957; has two children. English teacher in a London comprehensive school, 1957–59. Since 1952, regular outside contributor, as interviewer and scriptwriter, BBC External Services (Radio), London. Recipient: Thomas Helmore Poetry Prize, University of London, 1955; Guggenheim Fellowship, 1960; Deutscher Kinderbuchpreis, 1967. Address: Flat 8, Windsor Court, Moscow Road, Queensway, London W.2, England.

PUBLICATIONS

Novels

A Quality of Violence.   London, Hutchinson, 1959.
Escape to an Autumn Pavement.   London, Hutchinson, 1960.
The Late Emancipation of Jerry Stover.   London, Hutchinson, 1968.
The Adventures of Catullus Kelly.   London, Hutchinson, 1969.
Come Home, Malcolm Heartland.   London, Hutchinson, 1972.

Other

Hurricane (juvenile).   London, Oxford University Press, 1964.
Earthquake (juvenile).   London, Oxford University Press, 1965.
Drought (juvenile).   London, Oxford University Press, 1966.
The Shark Hunters (school reader).   London, Nelson, 1966.
Riot (juvenile).   London, Oxford University Press, 1967.
Jonah Simpson (juvenile).   London, Oxford University Press, 1969.
Havana Journal.   London, Penguin, 1971.
Georgetown Journal.   London, New Beacon Books, 1972.

Editor, West Indian Stories.   London, Faber, 1960.
Editor, Stories from the Caribbean.   London, Elek, 1965; as Island Voices, New York, Liveright, 1970.
Editor, Caribbean Section, Young Commonwealth Poets '65.   London, Heinemann, 1965.
Editor, Caribbean Prose.   London, Evans, 1967.
Editor, Breaklight: Caribbean Poetry.   London, Hamish Hamilton, 1971.
Editor, Caribbean Essays.   London, Evans, 1972.
Editor, Writing in Cuba since the Revolution.   London, New Beacon Books, 1972.
Editor, with others, Savacou 3 and 4.   Kingston and London, Caribbean Artists Movement, 1972.

Plays and poetry broadcast on BBC radio.

Critical Study: review by Edward Brathwaite, in Bim (Bridgetown, Barbados), 1959.

*      *      *

Salkey's first novel, A Quality of Violence, is his best, a powerful account of savagery and superstition in a Jamaican village in 1900. Because of drought, the villagers begin to despair of reason, and turn to older, darker ways. A white cock is strangled, two men whip each other ritually till both are dead, and eventually a woman is sacrificed, stoned to death. The obeah cult mixes African and Christian forms, and the prologue indicates wider associations: "The drought brings a touch of madness to the land, a kind of rebellion, and a quality of compelling suicide which Calvary once witnessed. Drought first began on Calvary." Related is the conflict between old ways and new: doctors and police are imposed on this society. The hysteria and fickleness of mobs are shown, and also the oddness of children, and the strange things that are important to them. The writing is effective, jagged and unusual, but above all this is a dramatic novel, full of tension and excitement, so it is never certain what will happen next.

*Escape to an Autumn Pavement* takes a more familiar subject for a Caribbean book: the experiences of Johnnie, an alert West Indian in London. He works as a waiter, and learns about class and prejudice. But there is a marked sexual theme: he is torn between a demanding girl and a homosexual who tempts him. The form is disjointed thoughts passing through Johnnie's mind; such section titles as "Notes in the Present for a Time Past" suggest a sophisticated sense of time. This is Salkey's most literary book, its style the most artificial. Late evening is pictured with a kind of poetic immediacy:

> Oxford Street with its squeaking silences under shutters. Wonderland beacons continue their ogling unashamedly with the traffic lights. Sticky, biscuit-sweet, soggy lovers huddle together in a make-believe which excludes Mom and Pop. Can feel the presence of cash registers along the street. But this is different. The moment is magic. The weightiness is different. It's haunting. Metallic buddha-kind of weightiness. Plump and couchant, in a way. A threat.

Several children's books followed, all set in Jamaica, with a rich sense of atmosphere, for shops, streets, and for the weather too. While description may be central in a book like *Hurricane*, a boy's account of a 1951 disaster, usually Salkey is striving for more. In *Drought* we wonder whether the children's spells or the adults with their rational means have finally brought rain. In *Riot* we are asked to ponder whether the unionists who organize a demonstration which turns violent are heroes, unscrupulous orators or men lacking any clear plan. In the most recent, *Jonah Simpson*, a daydreamer seeks to uncover some mystery, but the mystery remains elusive for the reader.

Pessimism about the role of the West Indian dominates the third and fourth adult novels. *The Late Emancipation of Jerry Stover* has a young man in Jamaica just before independence, and Salkey re-creates the social-political atmosphere of the time. Jerry seeks a purpose, but devotes energy too to girls, drinking cheap rum, and pointless trips in ancient cars into the country. He leaves his job to work full time among the poor members of the Rastafarian sect on the Dunghill, and persuades his friends, a group called the Termites because they ineffectually believe they are boring at the Establishment, to assist this work. But then they are killed in a landslide, all but Jerry and an American girl, an outsider. The moral is explicit: "They had no private philosophy, no binding discipline, no real faith in anything. All they had was their freedom, an emancipation that had come much too late. They had not had the time and the kind of society in which to use it intelligently, to benefit from it, to build on it."

*The Adventures of Catullus Kelly* takes a young, educated Jamaican to London, a man similar to Johnnie and Jerry. The form is rambling—presumably to echo Catullus's crumbling sanity—as his protagonist tries teaching, free-lance broadcasting and working in a coffee bar. He is also involved with innumerable girls, at times in pairs, and once on the plinth of Nelson's Column: "he plinthed; they plinthed, like impious pigeons." The year in London results—arbitrarily, perhaps—in a mental hospital in Jamaica. Salkey sees the man as *used* in white society, as a black or as a sex object, and Catullus cannot interest other blacks in *nègritude*. Catullus's two languages—received English and Caribbean dialect—are both displayed, but despite verbal flourishes, this is Salkey's weakest novel.

—Malcolm Page

---

**SANSOM, William.** English. Born in London, 18 January 1912. Educated at Uppingham School, Rutland, and in Europe. Served in the London Fire Service in World War II. Married Ruth Grundy in 1954; has one son and one stepson. Worked in a bank, and an advertising agency, and as a motion picture scriptwriter. Full-time Writer since 1945. Recipient: Society of Authors Scholarship, 1946, and Bursary, 1947. Fellow, Royal Society of Literature, 1951. Address: c/o Elaine Greene Ltd., 42 Great Russell Street, London WC1B 3PN, England.

PUBLICATIONS

Novels

> *The Body.* London, Hogarth Press, and New York, Harcourt Brace, 1949.
> *The Face of Innocence.* London, Hogarth Press, and New York, Harcourt Brace, 1951.
> *A Bed of Roses.* London, Hogarth Press, and New York, Harcourt Brace, 1954.
> *The Loving Eye.* London, Hogarth Press, 1956; New York, Reynal, 1957.
> *The Cautious Heart.* London, Hogarth Press, and New York, Reynal, 1958.
> *The Last Hours of Sandra Lee.* London, Hogarth Press, 1961; Boston, Little Brown, 1962.
> *Goodbye.* London, Hogarth Press, 1966; New York, New American Library, 1967.
> *Hans Feet in Love.* London, Hogarth Press, 1971.

Short Stories

> *Fireman Flower.* London, Hogarth Press, 1944; New York, Vanguard Press, 1945.
> *Three.* London, Hogarth Press, 1946; New York, Reynal, 1947.
> *South: Aspects and Images from Corsica, Italy and Southern France.* London, Hodder and Stoughton, 1948; New York, Harcourt Brace, 1950.
> *The Equilibriad.* London, Hogarth Press, 1948.
> *Something Terrible, Something Lovely.* London, Hogarth Press, 1948; New York, Reynal, 1954.
> *The Passionate North: Short Stories.* London, Hogarth Press, 1950; New York, Harcourt Brace, 1953.
> *A Touch of the Sun.* London, Hogarth Press, 1952; New York, Reynal, 1958.
> *Lord Love Us.* London, Hogarth Press, 1954.
> *A Contest of Ladies.* London, Hogarth Press, and New York, Reynal, 1956.
> *Among the Dahlias.* London, Hogarth Press, 1957.
> *The Stories of William Sansom.* London, Hogarth Press, and Boston, Little Brown, 1963.
> *The Ulcerated Milkman.* London, Hogarth Press, 1966.
> *The Vertical Ladder and Other Stories.* London, Chatto and Windus, 1969.
> *Penguin Modern Stories 1*, with others. London, Penguin, 1969.

Other

> *Jim Braidy: The Story of Britain's Firemen*, with James Gordon and Stephen Spender. London, Drummond, 1943.
> *Westminster in War.* London, Faber, 1947.
> *Pleasures Strange and Simple* (essays). London, Hogarth Press, 1953.
> *It Was Really Charlie's Castle* (juvenile). London, Hogarth Press, 1953.
> *The Light That Went Out* (juvenile). London, Hogarth Press, 1953.

*The Icicle and the Sun.*  London, Hogarth Press, 1958; New York, Reynal, 1959.
*The Bay of Naples.*  New York, Studio Publications, 1960; London, Batsford, 1962.
*Blue Skies, Brown Studies.*  London, Hogarth Press, and Boston, Little Brown, 1961.
*Away to It All.*  London, Hogarth Press, 1964; New York, New American Library, 1966.
*Grand Tour Today.*  London, Hogarth Press, 1968.
*Christmas.*  London, Weidenfeld and Nicolson, 1968; as *A Book of Christmas*, New York, McGraw Hill, 1968.
*The Birth of a Story.*  London, Chatto and Windus, 1972.
*Marcel Proust and His World.*  London, Thames and Hudson, 1972.

Editor, *Choice: Some New Stories and Prose.*  London, Progress, and New York, Universal Distributors, 1946.
Editor, *The Tell-Tale Heart and Other Stories*, by Edgar Allan Poe.  London, Lehmann, 1948.

Translator, *Chendru: The Boy and the Tiger*, by Astrid Bergman.  London, Collins, and New York, Harcourt Brace,.1960.

Manuscript Collection: Berg Collection, New York Public Library.

William Sansom comments:

*Fiction*: A writer of my sort lives in a state of continual wonder at life. Even if the subject or episode is sordid, or plain humdrum, that amazement is still there. It is the sense of this which I want to convey to others. Much of it is visual, I am a painter *manqué*.
*Travel Books*: To get the sensual essence of a place—the smell, taste, touch of it—the sense of being *there* and nowhere else . . . this is my object. No guidebook stuff.
*Essays, etc.*: Apart from the theme, and information to be commented upon, the object here is to keep to a high and pure prose level—and yet to keep it lively, not dry, fun.

*       *       *

William Sansom is one of the most prolific of contemporary British writers of short stories. He is also one of the best. Indeed, with the exception of Angus Wilson there is no other writer who has done as much as Sansom has to keep the short story alive and well. And although he has also written novels and travel books, it is his art as a short story writer which has given him his deservedly high reputation.

Anyone reading among Sansom's stories quickly comes to recognise one important fact about them, that for all their variety—and Sansom does range considerably in subject matter and approach—they all bear the stamp of their author's especial virtues. In exactness of visual detail, in the quiet wit that underscores the treatment of character (a kind of wry and compassionate concern), in the sharpness of ear for the right conversational nuance, in the care with which people are socially placed, in all these ways and in more, Sansom's short stories proclaim their author. Here, for example, are the opening sentences of his story "Gliding Gulls and Going People" (from *The Passionate North*):

Two girls in high shorts, thin plump thighs redly raw in the blue cold; a blood-filled man in black broadcloth, his big stomach carrying him like a sail along; a queer-eyed girl in a transparent white mackintosh; an old gentleman and an old lady eyeing each other, strangers yet; a young man, curly-haired and hard-fleshed, whose frank grey eyes bristled with sneaking contempt; two wives in soldier-peaked hats, navy and nigger, cheery and cake-loving; a small lean man in blue serge and a woolly checkered cap whose friends and family, at his expense, flowed round him only to exclaim and demand.

If you wanted to know how the average Briton dressed at any particular time in the last thirty years you could do a great deal worse than consult a Sansom short story. For Sansom always tells you. He has an almost obsessive concern with dress. But not for trivial reasons. On the contrary, it is important that we are told how people in a Sansom story dress, because knowing that much gives us important information about them; about their incomes, their social status, the part of the country they come from, their work, and so on. Sansom, that is, belongs to that very obvious and central tradition of English fiction which is concerned with getting people socially into focus so that their lives can be made that much more plausible. And because Sansom is essentially a short-story writer he offers us the details about dress as a kind of short-hand way of letting us know important facts without himself having to spell them out for us. The details about dress in a Sansom short-story are not gratuitous. There is no suggestion that he merely wants us to know how clever and observant he is (though he is, of course, both of these things). The sharply perceptive eye does not work randomly; what it chooses to record is dictated by the writer's sense of responsibility to his audience. There is an amount of information we simply must have if we are to make sense of the characters who are his concern.

This brings us to a crucial point about Sansom. For it would be quite wrong to suggest that he is merely or even primarily an observer of the social scene. Look again at those opening sentences from "Gliding Gulls and Going People" and you see that there are descriptive details which humanise and particularise the people he seems to be impression-istically recording. The "queer-eyed girl", for example; or the young man "whose frank grey eyes bristled with sneaking contempt." Or the old gentleman and lady who eye each other, "strangers yet". Behind each of these details is, it seems to me, an unstated query: either, *why* is he/she like that; or, and what *did* happen to them? In other words, Sansom's description of people reveals a fascination, a curiosity that leads him inevitably to enquire into their lives. And all Sansom's best stories are, in fact, just such enquiries. Again and again he will begin with what appear to be deceptively simple observations of people and place, only for the story to open out into a probing exploration of what goes on beneath the surface. Sansom is fascinated by the extraordinariness of the most ordinary people. The queer-eyed girl *must* have something interesting about her; there *has* to be an interesting reason for that young man's look of sneaking contempt; the little man with the woolly checkered cap will *obviously* have a history worthy of investigation.

It is, of course, difficult to make the ordinary seem interesting. Most writers make it merely dull. Yet hardly ever can one accuse Sansom of dullness. Why not? Well, in the first place, he often uses a traditional but perfectly proper fiction writer's gambit of gradually revealing more and more about the characters about whom he is writing, so that the reader is, as it were, present at the peeling of an onion. Layer after layer is stripped away, the truth gradually emerges. (This is also the tactic employed in what to my mind is his best novel—indeed, I would go so far as to say his only really successful novel, *The Face of Innocence*.)

But Sansom does not rely on this gambit alone. There is dialogue, for example. Very few contemporary writers can match Sansom's acute awareness of how much can be revealed about characters through the dialogue they speak. "The Smile" (from *A Touch of the Sun*) is almost entirely a matter of dialogue. And very brilliant it is too. Two men meet in the Paris Central Post Office, the narrator and a man of "perhaps forty, of good looks greyed and shrunk with worry or ill health or madness." The stranger speaks.

"And you, sir? You've been waiting long?"
"No, not long. My letter hasn't . . ."
"Ah? A letter—from your wife, perhaps?"
"No."

"But you *are* married?"

"What?"

"You, sir, are *married*?"

"Oh . . . no."

His eyes studied me with care. There was a kind of pause in which I felt I had to hold my breath—as though he were testing me with a stethoscope. Then he nodded slowly and said softly:

"Marriage can be a very beautiful thing."

It was plain that the conversation was not to become general. Marriage was on his mind. It was only polite for me to inquire:

"So you, sir, are married?"

"Yes. That is to say—I was. Well, I still am in a manner of speaking. But no, not quite . . ."

And we are, of course, hooked. We want to know about the man, about his marriage, about why he speaks with such pedantic sentimentality ("marriage can be a very beautiful thing"). What we might not notice is the sheer skill and economy of Sansom's method. This is, of course, as it should be. Good writers conceal their art, they don't parade it. And if the stitching shows, then we can justly accuse the writer of botching his work. All the same, it is worth pointing out how neatly and unobtrusively Sansom gets across the narrator's embarrassed irritation with the stranger—it comes out in the brusqueness of his replies—and how he is nonetheless reluctantly caught in the other's toils. It is almost like the Ancient Mariner: the narrator the helpless wedding-guest, the mariner/stranger "has his will." Nor do I offer this analogy in a flippant manner. Sansom more than once uses the trick of the trapped spectator or listener in order to lead us into his story. And always the listener is properly particularised, he isn't merely a transparent device. In "The Smile", for example, the narrator is clearly a man of dry wit ("It was plain that the conversation was not to become general").

But there is a third way in which Sansom makes the ordinary interesting, and this is through the very obvious and communicated concern he has for personal relationships, especially love and failed love. And in this context his stories, without ever sacrificing the wit and intelligence that are such marked features of Sansom's writing, are touching and deeply sympathetic. Sansom is particularly good at rendering the faintly ludicrous pathos of the inarticulate, or of those for whom passion is real but uncomfortable because unusual, because it takes them by surprise or unseats the casualness of their daily lives (a recent and excellent example of this can be found in his story "Down at the Hydro", in *Penguin Modern Stories 1*).

I would not maintain that Sansom is a flawless writer, or that all his stories are equally successful. And I think his gifts do not lend themselves to expansion, so that when he writes a novel one has the feeling that it is really no more than a stretched-out short-story. Certainly his recent novel, *Hans Feet in Love*, is a sad disappointment. Yet there is no doubt that Sansom at his best is one of the most gifted writers we have.

—John Lucas

---

**SARGESON, Frank.** New Zealander. Born in Hamilton, 23 March 1903. Educated at Hamilton High School; University of New Zealand; admitted as Solicitor of the Supreme Court of New Zealand, 1926. Estates Clerk, New Zealand Public Trust, Wellington, 1928–29;

has also worked as a Journalist. Recipient: Centennial Literary Competition prize, 1940; New Zealand Government literary pension, 1947–68; Hubert Church Prize, 1952, 1968; Katherine Mansfield Award, 1965. Address: 14 Esmond Road, Takapuna, Auckland 9, New Zealand.

PUBLICATIONS

Novels

*When the Wind Blows.*   Christchurch, Caxton Press, 1945.
*I Saw in My Dream.*   London, Lehmann, 1949.
*I for One. . . .*   Christchurch, Caxton Press, 1954.
*Memoirs of a Peon.*   London, MacGibbon and Kee, 1965.
*The Hangover.*   London, MacGibbon and Kee, 1967.
*Joy of the Worm.*   London, MacGibbon and Kee, 1969.
*Man of England Now* (includes *A Game of Hide and Seek* and *I for One . . .*).   Christ-
church, Caxton Press, and London, Martin Brian and O'Keeffe, 1972.

Short Stories

*Conversations with My Uncle and Other Sketches.*   Auckland, Unicorn Press, 1936.
*A Man and His Wife.*   Christchurch, Caxton Press, 1940.
*That Summer and Other Stories.*   London, Lehmann, 1946.
*Collected Stories, 1935–1963*, edited by Bill Pearson.   Auckland, Blackwood and Janet
Paul, 1964; London, MacGibbon and Kee, 1965.

Uncollected Short Stories

"Just Trespassing, Thanks", in *Landfall* (Christchurch), June 1964.
"City and Suburban", in *Landfall* (Christchurch), March 1965.
"Beau", in *Mate* (Auckland), June 1965.
"Charity Begins at Home", in *Landfall* (Christchurch), September 1966.
"A Final Cure", in *Landfall* (Christchurch), June 1967.
"An International Occasion", in *Landfall* (Christchurch), December 1969.

Plays

*A Time for Sowing* (produced Auckland, 1961).   Included in *Wrestling with the Angel*,
1964.
*The Cradle and the Egg* (produced Auckland, 1962).   Included in *Wrestling with the
Angel*, 1964.
*Wrestling with the Angel: Two Plays: A Time for Sowing and The Cradle and the Egg.*
Christchurch, Caxton Press, 1964.

Other

*Once Is Enough* (autobiography).   Christchurch, Caxton Press, and London, Martin
Brian and O'Keeffe, 1972.

Editor, *Speaking for Ourselves: A Collection of New Zealand Stories*.   Christchurch, Caxton Press, 1945.

Bibliography: in *Collected Stories, 1935–1963*, 1964.

Manuscript Collection: Alexander Turnbull Library, Wellington.

Critical Studies: essay by the author on his own work, "Up onto the Roof and Down Again", in *Landfall* (Christchurch), December 1950-December 1951; *The Puritan and the Waif: A Symposium of Critical Essays on the Work of Frank Sargeson*, edited by Helen Shaw, Auckland, Hoffmann, 1955; Introduction by Bill Pearson to *Collected Stories, 1935–1963*, 1964; "The Art of Frank Sargeson" by E. A. Horsman, in *Landfall* (Christchurch), 1965; *Frank Sargeson* by H. Winston Rhodes, New York, Twayne, 1969.

Frank Sargeson comments:

Speaking very broadly, I write my fiction out of an itch to impose some sort of order upon the chaos of existence: but more particularly, because as a schoolboy I became much aware that I was a European born in a country very remote from Europe: in the form of fiction I have *had* to say what in my view it means to be a New Zealander.

*          *          *

In a public tribute to Frank Sargeson on the occasion of his fiftieth birthday his fellow-craftsmen in New Zealand described him as "a liberating influence on the literature of this country," and as one who had become "a symbol in his own time." Such expressions of esteem were neither rhetorical flourishes nor casual compliments, but indicated accurately and temperately the nature both of his achievement and his influence. He had become a symbol because from an early age he had dedicated himself to the craft of fiction in a society unwilling to recognise or encourage, much less reward, artistic endeavour. Despite a formidable array of obstacles, he had succeeded in creating an imaginative world that provided an indirect commentary on human relations and attitudes.

His early reputation, endorsed not only in New Zealand but also abroad by such writers as E. M. Forster, William Plomer, John Lehmann and Walter Allen, was established on the basis of little more than a decade of experimental work in the short story; but since the late thirties and early forties he has continued to extend his range and develop his techniques in this genre as well as to produce novels, plays and critical essays which have confirmed his central position in the contemporary scene of New Zealand fiction.

It has been said that Sargeson was forced to create his own tradition. In so far as this is true, for traditions are not brought into being by the efforts of a single person, the implication is that he was the first New Zealander to become thoroughly involved with his medium, seeking both a language and a style appropriate to the New Zealand setting of his stories, and attempting to gauge the quality of New Zealand life on which character and behaviour must depend. His apprenticeship occupied many years, but eventually his achievement was such that a younger writer could recall his belief that "Sargeson's was the only possible kind of short story and his people the only true New Zealanders."

Much of his early work was related to experiences during the years of depression; some of the stories were slight moral fables; but all of them revealed an extraordinary control of the medium chosen. Sargeson's habitual mode was the first person narrative which, because his central characters were usually unable to give adequate expression to their thoughts and emotions, excluded authorial comment and any kind of sophisticated analysis. Yet what was so impressive was the manner in which he could suggest through concise and colloquial language both a pattern of ironies and a pattern of values. He was able to combine an unsentimental view of the human situation with a recognition of its underlying humour and pathos. It is by means of his Teds, Bills, Toms and Freds, the flotsam and jetsam of human society, solitary figures who have either been discarded by or opted out of the conventional community that Sargeson reveals the ambiguities and paradoxes of New Zealand, and not only New Zealand, life.

Sargeson's world has been described as "sad and savage", but such a description neglects the positive values implicit in his ironic treatment of incident and attitude. E. M. Forster chose for special praise his evident belief in "the unsmart, the unregulated and the affectionate," and in so doing directed attention to the anti-puritanism which pervades his work. Although he was not the first writer to subject to a critical examination the characteristic New Zealand ethos, based precariously on an adulterated puritanism, Sargeson has been the most successful in exposing many of its more corrosive aspects. Suburbia becomes one of the main objects of his attack, with its pseudo-respectability and artificial refinement, its concern with prohibitions and appearances, its dubious morality and the emphasis placed on "making good" and "getting on," combined with its callous disregard for the feelings and aspirations of outsiders. The destructiveness of a debased puritanism is opposed to the creative life of the senses, the desire for human fellowship and affection in the absence of high prizes.

In the narratives that followed the publication of *That Summer and Other Stories*, it became apparent that the post-war period and the progress of the affluent society, together with Sargeson's absorption in experimental activity, drew him towards an elaboration of what had become his characteristic mode of expression. There was no sudden change in his technique or theme, and "Old Man's Story" (1940) looks forward to the more complex manner of "The Undertaker's Story" (1954) and "Just Trespassing, Thanks" (1964); but character is more subtly revealed and opportunity found for a more sophisticated approach to his material. The masks he had adopted for the presentation of the semi-articulate were proving too restrictive for a writer with richer resources of language and style.

He was already engaged in the writing of longer fictions. "That Summer" (written 1938–41) had been a more developed exploration of the mental and emotional simplicities of the foot-loose non-conformer; but with the first part of *I Saw in My Dream*, published in 1945 (the completed novel appeared four years later), Sargeson had embarked on his second career as a novelist. *I for One . . .*, a short novel, followed; and both of these were concerned with the inhibiting effects of a puritanical environment. The former was perhaps a more ambitious but less successful attempt to link the outward behaviour of the central character with a stream of sub-conscious thoughts and feelings. Underneath its episodic structure and abrupt transitions there is an intricate pattern of correspondences and symbolic threads providing an unorthodox unity to a narrative concerned with a quest for identity and fulfilment. Many disparate elements contribute to this endeavour to capture a significant aspect of the New Zealand scene—elements as disparate as Bunyan's *Pilgrim's Progress*, Joyce's *Portrait of the Artist as a Young Man* and Mark Twain's *Huckleberry Finn*, for Sargeson's originality is not averse to, rather it is displayed by, a willingness to adapt to his own use whatever seems applicable to the local situation.

In like manner some of his techniques are traditional, even old-fashioned, although they gain fresh vitality from their re-employment to suit different circumstances and achieve different aims. *I for One . . .* is written in the form of a private diary but with such concealed contrivance that without interfering with the natural outpourings of a girl communing with herself the reader is able to understand more clearly than the diarist why she seems to be "one set apart." Sargeson's next novel, *Memoirs of a Peon*, was, at one and the same time, a satirical comedy, a picaresque narrative, an exploration of the quality of life in New Zealand and an exposure of what has been called "the cultural cringe." The masks that Sargeson is able to wear with ease are many and various. This time the narrative is in the hands of a super-annuated New Zealand Casanova "stung by the snake of memory", who glories in his past achievements. The style of narration has completely deserted the bare and laconic utterance of the early short stories, the flavour of the feminine diarist's reveries or the over-wrought youth's distracted ponderings. It is mannered and literary, pedantic and involved. Excluding its array of bizarre characters and hilarious incidents, the full significance of *Memoirs of a Peon* is accessible only to those who become aware that it is an elaborate satire on a series of different levels and that the mannered style, reminiscent of the eighteenth century, is part of the cultural cringe that is being satirised, just as the central character is condemning himself out of his own mouth as well as exposing New Zealand manners through the very complexities in which he is entangled.

Two further novels have recently appeared and at least two more are awaiting publication. *The Hangover* once again indicated that Sargeson has never been a follower of social realism. His plot structure is less concerned with the probabilities of life than with the implications of living and, as in *Memoirs of a Peon*, his characters may be grotesques with an uncanny resemblance to real people. He produces fictions that are imaginative analogues to the reality of human experience. *The Hangover* disconcerted some readers who, because of what seemed to be a rapidly moving and horrifyingly dramatic story, failed to come to terms with the agility of Sargeson's mind and deeper concern with the humanities, "that elongated hangover from Socrates and the Academy." The central character, once more an adolescent youth with a puritan background, becomes mentally and emotionally confused by the world in which he lives. His puritan heritage is at odds with the imperatives of the affluent society based on the qualified technician and the accumulation of gadgets, but equally at odds with the beatnik way of life that rejects the "establishment" of the past as well as that of the present. By means of a series of symbolic threads, literary analogues and parallels with ritual and romance Sargeson transforms a narrative that could have carried only social and psychological implications into an imaginative and philosophical commentary on modern civilisation.

A similar transformation is performed in *Joy of the Worm*. This is a richly comic novel with tragic undertones. The wry comedy is concerned with a domineering clerical father and his son who, despite a critical recognition of the defects of the Reverend's character, becomes almost a walking parody of his father; and the tragedy is one of wives reduced to silence and extinguished as a direct consequence of the rationalising indifference and wordy intellectuality of their egotistical husbands. However, the terms "comedy" and "tragedy" are not easily applicable to any of Sargeson's fictions. In *Joy of the Worm* it is by a controlled and complex use of illusion and reality, by irony, patterned loquacity and suggestion, and above all by language that he gains his effects and achieves significance. The illusion is to be found especially in the way in which event, banal though it may be, is transformed as it passes through the crucible of human speech; and it is the relation between illusion and reality that provides depth and substance to a narrative full of incidental perceptions.

Sargeson's work is still "in progress". It is as much "a liberating influence" as it was forty years ago. Because he has remained an experimental writer, each new departure has proved to be only a starting-point for further development; but his preoccupation with manner or ways of saying has not been at the expense of matter. He is essentially both moralist and penetrating critic. He was described once as "the first wasp with a new and menacing buzz" and although the description is not as apt today he may still be regarded, in Browning's words, as "a recording chief inquisitor" of human behaviour and attitudes.

—H. Winston Rhodes

**SAROYAN, William.**   American.   Born in Fresno, California, 31 August 1908. Educated in Fresno public schools. Served in the United States Army, 1942–45. Married Carol Marcus in 1943 (divorced, 1949); has two children, including the poet Aram Saroyan. Worked as grocery clerk, vineyard worker, post office employee, and office manager of the Postal Telegraph Company, San Francisco. Co-Founder, Conference Press, Los Angeles, 1936. Director, Saroyan Theatre, New York, 1942. Writer-in-Residence, Purdue University, Lafayette, Indiana, 1961. Recipient: New York Drama Critics Circle Award, 1940; Pulitzer Prize, for drama, 1940 (refused). Member, National Institute of Arts and Letters. Address: 2729 West Griffin Way, Fresno, California 93705, U.S.A.

PUBLICATIONS

Novels

> *The Human Comedy.*   New York, Harcourt Brace, and London, Faber, 1943.
> *The Adventures of Wesley Jackson.*   New York, Harcourt Brace, 1946; London, Faber, 1947.
> *The Twin Adventures: The Adventures of William Saroyan: A Diary; The Adventures of Wesley Jackson: A Novel.*   New York, Harcourt Brace, 1950.
> *Rock Wagram.*   New York, Doubleday, 1951; London, Faber, 1952.
> *Tracy's Tiger.*   New York, Doubleday, 1951; London, Faber, 1952.
> *The Laughing Matter.*   New York, Doubleday, 1953; London, Faber, 1954.
> *Mama I Love You.*   Boston, Little Brown, 1956; London, Faber, 1957.
> *Papa You're Crazy.*   Boston, Little Brown, 1957; London, Faber, 1958.
> *Boys and Girls Together.*   New York, Harcourt Brace, and London, Davies, 1963.
> *One Day in the Afternoon of the World.*   New York, Harcourt Brace, 1964; London, Cassell, 1965.

Short Stories

> *The Daring Young Man on the Flying Trapeze and Other Stories.*   New York, Random House, 1934; London, Faber, 1935.
> *Inhale and Exhale.*   New York, Random House, and London, Faber, 1936.
> *Three Times Three.*   Los Angeles, Conference Press, 1936.
> *Little Children.*   New York, Harcourt Brace, and London, Faber, 1937.
> *A Gay and Melancholy Flux: Short Stories.*   London, Faber, 1937.
> *Love, Here Is My Hat.*   New York, Modern Age Books, and London, Faber, 1938.
> *A Native American.*   San Francisco, George Fields, 1938.
> *The Trouble with Tigers.*   New York, Harcourt Brace, 1938; London, Faber, 1939.
> *Peace, It's Wonderful.*   New York, Modern Age Books, 1939; London, Faber, 1940.
> *3 Fragments and a Story.*   Cincinnati, Little Man Press, 1939.
> *My Name Is Aram.*   New York, Harcourt Brace, 1940; London, Faber, 1941.
> *Saroyan's Fables.*   New York, Harcourt Brace, 1941.
> *The Insurance Salesman and Other Stories.*   London, Faber, 1941.
> *Razzle Dazzle.*   New York, Harcourt Brace, 1942; London, Faber, 1945.
> *Dear Baby.*   New York, Harcourt Brace, 1944; London, Faber, 1945.
> *The Saroyan Special: Selected Short Stories.*   New York, Harcourt Brace, 1948.
> *The Fiscal Hoboes.*   New York, Press of Valenti Angelo, 1949.
> *The Assyrian and Other Stories.*   New York, Harcourt Brace, 1950; London, Faber, 1951.
> *The Whole Voyald and Other Stories.*   Boston, Little Brown, 1956; London, Faber, 1957.

*After Thirty Years: The Daring Young Man on the Flying Trapeze* (includes essays). New York, Harcourt Brace, 1964.
*Best Stories of William Saroyan.*  London, Faber, 1964.


Plays

*My Heart's in the Highlands* (produced New York, 1939).  New York, Harcourt Brace, 1939.
*The Time of Your Life* (produced New York, 1939).  New York, Harcourt Brace, 1939; included in *Three Plays*, London, Faber, 1942.
*The Hungerers* (produced New York, 1945).  New York, French, 1939.
*A Special Announcement* (broadcast, 1940).  New York, House of Books, 1940.
*Love's Old Sweet Song* (produced New York, 1940).  Included in *Three Plays*, 1940.
*Three Plays: My Heart's in the Highlands, The Time of Your Life, Love's Old Sweet Song.*  New York, Harcourt Brace, 1940; London, Faber, 1942.
*The Ping Pong Game* (produced New York, 1945).  New York, French, 1940.
*Subway Circus.*  New York, French, 1940.
*Something about a Soldier* (produced in stock, 1940).
*Hero of the World* (produced in stock, 1940).
*Sweeney in the Trees* (produced in stock, 1940).  Included in *Three Plays*, 1941.
*The People with Light Coming Out of Them* (broadcast, 1941).  New York, The Free Company, 1941.
*The Beautiful People* (produced New York, 1941).  Included in *Three Plays*, 1941.
*Three Plays: The Beautiful People, Sweeney in the Trees, and Across the Board on Tomorrow Morning.*  New York, Harcourt Brace, 1941; London, Faber, 1943.
*Across the Board on Tomorrow Morning* (produced New York, 1942).  Included in *Three Plays*, 1941.
*Jim Dandy.*  Cincinnati, Little Man Press, 1941; as *Jim Dandy: Fat Man in a Famine*, New York, Harcourt Brace, 1947; London, Faber, 1948.
*Hello, Out There* (produced Santa Barbara, California, 1941; New York, 1942). New York, French, 1949.
*Talking to You* (produced New York, 1942).
*Get Away Old Man* (produced New York, 1943).  New York, Harcourt Brace, 1944; London, Faber, 1946.
*Don't Go Away Mad* (produced New York, 1949).  Included in *Don't Go Away Mad and Two Other Plays*, 1949.
*Don't Go Away Mad and Two Other Plays: Sam Ego's House; A Decent Birth, A Happy Funeral.*  New York, Harcourt Brace, 1949; London, Faber, 1951.
*The Son* (produced Los Angeles, 1950).
*Opera, Opera* (produced New York, 1955).
*The Slaughter of the Innocents* (produced The Hague, 1957).  New York, French, 1958.
*The Cave Dwellers* (produced New York, 1957).  New York, Putnam, and London, Faber, 1958.
*Ever Been in Love with a Midget* (produced Berlin, 1957).
*Once Around the Block.*  New York, French, 1959.
*Settled out of Court*, with Henry Cecil (produced London, 1960).
*Sam, The Highest Jumper of Them All; or, The London Comedy* (produced London, 1960).  London, Faber, 1961.
*High Time along the Wabash* (produced Lafayette, Indiana, 1961).
*Ah Man*, music by Peter Fricker (produced Aldeburgh, Suffolk, 1962).
*The Dogs; or, The Paris Comedy, and Two Other Plays: Chris Sick, or Happy New Year, Anyway, Making Money, and Nineteen Other Very Short Plays.*  New York, Phaedra, 1969.

Screenplays: *The Good Job*, 1943; *The Human Comedy*, 1943.

Ballet: *The Great American Goof*, 1940.

Plays produced on television.

Other

*The Time of Your Life* (miscellany).   New York, Harcourt Brace, 1939.
*Harlem as Seen by Hirschfield*.   New York, Hyperion Press, 1941.
*Hilltop Russians in San Francisco*.   Palo Alto, California, Stanford University-James Delkin, 1941.
*Why Abstract?*, with Henry Miller and Hilaire Hiler.   New York, New Directions, 1945; London, Falcon Press, 1948.
*The Bicycle Rider in Beverly Hills* (autobiography).   New York, Scribner, 1952; London, Faber, 1953.
*The William Saroyan Reader*.   New York, Braziller, 1958.
*Here Comes, There Goes, You Know Who* (autobiography).   New York, Simon and Schuster, 1961; London, Davies, 1962.
*A Note on Hilaire Hiler*.   New York, Wittenborn, 1962.
*Me* (juvenile).   New York, Crowell Collier, 1963.
*Not Dying* (autobiography).   New York, Harcourt Brace, 1963; London, Cassell, 1966.
*Short Drive, Sweet Chariot* (autobiography).   New York, Phaedra, 1966.
*Look at Us: Let's See: Here We Are: Look Hard: Speak Soft: I See, You See, We All See; Stop, Look, Listen; Beholder's Eye; Don't Look Now But Isn't That You? (us? U.S.?)*.   New York, Cowles, 1967.
*Horsey Gorsey and the Frog* (juvenile).   Eau Claire, Wisconsin, E. M. Hale, 1968.
*I Used to Believe I Had Forever; Now I'm Not So Sure*.   New York, Cowles, 1968.
*Letters from 74 rue Taitbout; or, Don't Go But if You Must Say Hello to Everybody*.   Cleveland, World, 1969; as *Don't Go But If You Must Say Hello to Everybody*, London, Cassell, 1970.
*Days of Life and Death and Escape to the Moon*.   New York, Dial Press, 1970; London, Joseph, 1971.

Editor, *Hairenik, 1934–1939: An Anthology of Short Stories and Poems*.   Boston, Hairenik Association, 1939.

Bibliography: *A Bibliography of William Saroyan, 1934–1964* by David Kherdiam, San Francisco, Roger Beachum, 1965.

\*      \*      \*

Though most acclaimed as a playwright, William Saroyan first attracted attention in his early twenties as a writer of the touching short stories collected under the title, *The Daring Young Man on the Flying Trapeze*. During World War II his cloyingly sentimental *My Name Is Aram* and *The Human Comedy* were gobbled up by readers trying to cling to a Norman-Rockwell-inspired American Dream in a world seemingly gone mad; but Saroyan's effusions since 1945 have attracted steadily declining attention. Saroyan has nothing to say to J. D. Salinger's Holden Caulfield or his Beat, Hippie, and Charles Reichean successors. A wave of nostalgia for the movies and music of the 1930's and 1940's has led to a small-scale revival of Saroyan's best-known works, but he has received serious scholarly attention only in Germany. Yet, as a sociological phenomenon, he deserves such attention more than almost any other fundamentally banal writer.

Saroyan's strengths and weaknesses are epitomized by his early short story, "70,000 Assyrians," which deals with two subjects: the plight of the Assyrians, "a mere seventy thousand of that great people, and all others quiet in death, and all the greatness crumbled and ignored," and the plight of the young writer who refuses to sell out: "I am not trying to compete with the great writers of short stories, men like Sinclair Lewis and Joseph Hergesheimer and Zane Grey, men who really know how to write, how to make up stories that will sell."

This bathos so touched the depression-ridden American public that Saroyan was a success in spite of his disclaimers. His major works received that ultimate accolade of financial success for a writer, a Book-of-the-Month Club selection. *My Name Is Aram* begins "One day back there in the good old days when I was nine and the world was full of every imaginable kind of magnificence, and life was still a delightful and mysterious dream. . . ." Saroyan's most successful dreamer is Homer Macauley (Saroyan doesn't mind placing himself in the epic tradition; Homer's brother is named Ulysses), who in *The Human Comedy* keeps his family afloat through tough years by wheeling messages around for the now defunct Postal Telegraph, while his brother Marcus fights World War II and dies for freedom. (The novel had its origins in a film script. Mickey Rooney ultimately played Homer.) The novel's philosophy is propounded by a Mr. Grogan, who announces while in his cups, "All people are one . . . as you are one. Now, as there is mischief in you along with good, there is mischief and good in *all* people." Hard-hit by a depression that they didn't understand and frustrated by World War II, Americans could absorb vast quantities of such maudlin "philosophizing."

Saroyan's decline began with *The Adventures of Wesley Jackson*, his contribution to the series of episodic accounts of the adventures of American GI's during World War II. Unfortunately, the war ended before the book appeared, so that his combination of an uncritical faith in the virtues of the average soldier with a bitter questioning of the Establishment failed to click. The fatuous tone of the book is apparent from the narrator's hope that "every man who was ever drafted into the Army is still alive, out of the Army, back home, and O.K." The sophistication of the book is indicated by the ugly, weepy narrator's comment that he didn't want to kiss or touch the girl he loved, "because I was in love with her the way children are in love with one another."

Since 1946, most of Saroyan's effusions have been greeted by reviewers as "silly," "confused," and "cute." *Tracy's Tiger*, for example, is an elusive allegory about love conquering all that suggests that for a brief period all crime could stop in New York because a temperamental young man has at last substituted as a love object for an imaginary black panther (which he calls a tiger) a girl that he has rescued from the psychiatric ward at Bellevue Hospital. "They were sitting in the parlor they both hated so much but somehow liked, too, and there wasn't a thing going," *Boys and Girls Together* begins: and one wants to read no further, for it is clear that Saroyan's work reflects Americans' view of themselves rather than transcending it and that in his novels there is indeed not a thing going.

Yet Saroyan deserves his humble due. He has never sold out: else he would surely have confected a Herman-Wouk-like plastic fiction to please the age of the corporation man. His very unswerving loyalty to the principles that he worked out as a kid in Fresno in the 20's remains both his personal strength and his artistic weakness. Like many Americans, he has just refused to grow up. He remains a nine-year old Aram contemplating life as a "delightful and mysterious dream." And instead of thinking, he talks—too much. A thirtieth-anniversary edition of *The Daring Young Man on the Flying Trapeze* evoked a 126-page nostalgia-dripping preface from the original author, churned out in one month.

Most reluctantly the United States has had to become more sophisticated than it had been before in the trying years since World War II. If it has not managed to hold its position in the world, it is because it has not become sophisticated fast enough. At least one reason for its failure is the failure of honest but un-self-critical writers like William Saroyan to change their world view, not to accommodate the market and enhance their private fortunes, but to help their fellow-citizens move ahead and develop a new capacity to deal with developing

problems rather than mooning over the simplicities of "the good old days." Saroyan embodies
the strengths and failures of those who fought World War II as Dos Passos does those who
fought World War I.

—Warren French

---

**SARTON, May.** American. Born in Wondelgem, Belgium, 3 May 1912, daughter of the
historian of science George Sarton; emigrated to the United States in 1916; naturalized,
1924. Educated at the Shady Hill School and The High and Latin School, both in Cambridge,
Massachusetts. Apprentice, then Member, and Director of the Apprentice Group, Eva Le
Gallienne's Civic Repertory Theatre, New York, 1930–33; Founder and Director, Appren-
tice Theatre, New York, and Associated Actors Inc., Hartford, Connecticut, 1933–36.
Taught Creative Writing and Choral Speech, Stuart School, Boston, 1937–40. Documentary
Scriptwriter, Office of War Information, 1944–45. Poet-in-Residence, Southern Illinois
University, Carbondale, Summer 1945; Briggs-Copeland Instructor in Composition,
Harvard University, Cambridge, Massachusetts, 1950–53; Lecturer, Breadloaf Writers'
Conference, Middlebury, Vermont, 1951–52, and Boulder Writers' Conference, Colorado,
1953–54; Phi Beta Kappa Visiting Scholar, 1959–60; Danforth Lecturer, 1960–61; Lecturer
in Creative Writing, Wellesley College, Massachusetts, 1960–63; Poet-in-Residence, Linden-
wood College, St. Charles, Missouri, 1964, 1965; Visiting Lecturer, Agnes Scott College,
Decatur, Georgia, Spring 1972. Recipient: New England Poetry Society Golden Rose, 1945;
Bland Memorial Prize, 1945, and Balch Prize, 1966, *Poetry*, Chicago; Reynolds Prize,
American Poetry Society, 1953; Donnelly Fellowship, Bryn Mawr College, Pennsylvania,
1953; Guggenheim Fellowship, 1954; Poetry Festival Award, Johns Hopkins University,
1961; National Endowment for the Arts grant, 1966. Litt.D., Russell Sage College, Troy,
New York, 1958; New England College, Henniker, New Hampshire, 1971. Fellow, American
Academy of Arts and Sciences. Address: Nelson Village, Munsonville, New Hampshire
03457, U.S.A.

PUBLICATIONS

Novels

    *The Single Hound.* Boston, Houghton Mifflin, and London, Cresset Press, 1938.
    *The Bridge of Years.* New York, Doubleday, 1946.
    *Shadow of a Man.* New York, Rinehart, 1950; London, Cresset Press, 1952.
    *A Shower of Summer Days.* New York, Rinehart, 1952; London, Hutchinson, 1954.
    *Faithful Are the Wounds.* New York, Rinehart, and London, Gollancz, 1955.
    *The Birth of a Grandfather.* New York, Rinehart, 1957; London, Gollancz, 1958.
    *The Small Room.* New York, Norton, 1961; London, Gollancz, 1962.
    *Joanna and Ulysses.* New York, Norton, 1963; London, Murray, 1964.
    *Mrs. Stevens Hears the Mermaids Singing.* New York, Norton, 1965; London,
      Peter Owen, 1966.
    *Miss Pickthorn and Mr. Hare: A Fable.* New York, Norton, 1966; London, Dent,
      1968.
    *The Poet and the Donkey.* New York, Norton, 1969.
    *Kinds of Love.* New York, Norton, 1970.

Play

*Underground River*.   New York, Play Club, 1947.

Verse

*Encounter in April*.   Boston, Houghton Mifflin, 1937.
*Inner Landscape*.   Boston, Houghton Mifflin, 1939; with a selection from *Encounter in April*, London, Cresset Press, 1939.
*The Lion and the Rose*.   New York, Rinehart, 1948.
*The Leaves of the Tree*.   Ithaca, New York, Cornell College Chapbook, 1950.
*The Land of Silence and Other Poems*.   New York, Rinehart, 1953.
*In Time like Air*.   New York, Rinehart, 1957.
*Cloud, Stone, Sun, Vine: Poems, Selected and New*.   New York, Norton, 1961.
*A Private Mythology: New Poems*.   New York, Norton, 1966.
*As Does New Hampshire and Other Poems*.   Peterborough, New Hampshire, Richard R. Smith, 1967.
*A Grain of Mustard Seed*.   New York, Norton, 1971.
*A Durable Fire*.   New York, Norton, 1972.

Other

*The Fur Person: The Story of a Cat*.   New York, Rinehart, 1957; London, Muller, 1958.
*I Knew a Phoenix: Sketches for an Autobiography*.   New York, Rinehart, 1959; London, Peter Owen, 1963.
*Plant Dreaming Deep* (autobiography).   New York, Norton, 1968.

May Sarton comments:

The novelists of the moderate human voice, from Trollope through Tchekov and Forster, are not in fashion, but I like to believe that I am in their line of descent, for what has interested me always is ordinary human relations, the heroism, despair, and rich complex fibre of day to day living among the middle class. European as I am by birth, it was natural that my first four novels should be laid in Europe, Belgium and England—my father was Belgian and my mother English—though the important thing has never been the setting but the intimate relationships explored. Five of the novels are centered in a marriage, from the coming of age through marriage of a young man (*Shadow of a Man*), to a marriage in its middle years (*The Bridge of Years*), to late middle age (*The Birth of a Grandfather*), and old age (*Kinds of Love*). The other major theme of my novels has been how the singular man or woman may find his identity and/or fulfillment through an art of profession. In two cases the protagonist is homosexual, a male professor in *Faithful Are the Wounds*, and a female poet in *Mrs. Stevens Hears the Mermaids Singing*. The former is a relentless exploration of the effect of a suicide (a political suicide) on the protagonist's colleagues at Harvard University. The latter is a study of the woman as artist. And the theme of the value of the single woman to society is touched on again in a novel, *The Small Room*, laid in a woman's college. Finally there is a group of slighter short novels, humorous or poetic accounts of how solitary individuals—a woman painter, a male poet—have dealt with kinds of deprivation and triumphed.

It is my hope that all the novels, the books of poems, and the autobiographical works may come to be seen as a whole, the communication of a vision of life that is unsentimental, humorous, passionate, and, in the end, timeless. We can bear any Hell if we can "break through" to each other and come to understand ourselves.

*     *     *

May Sarton is both poet and novelist. The daughter of George Sarton, the historian of science, and Mabel Elwes, an artist, she was born in Belgium and came to the United States with her parents when she was a child. Her first novels reflect her deep-rooted love of her birthplace and her awareness of living in two worlds. *The Single Hound* is set chiefly in Belgium; *The Bridge of Years* deals with the impact of two world wars on a Belgian family. In *Shadow of a Man* and *A Shower of Summer Days*, Europe is seen as providing both a refuge and a vantage point from which to view tensions and problems in America. A dominant idea in these first four novels is the need for a passionate person to order his own inner chaos and renounce a selfish attachment to another person; only by so doing can he become mature enough to give compassion to a suffering world.

Miss Sarton showed, early in her career, an ability to write various types of novel. *The Bridge of Years* is remarkable for its wide scope and sure handling of many themes and situations. *A Shower of Summer Days*, on the other hand, has only a few characters and scenes but is perhaps the most artistically satisfying of her books; it shows how a house, Dene's Court in Ireland, influences the subtle, complex relationships of four people.

Most of the novels written after 1955 are set in New England, where Miss Sarton now lives. In these, the focus is not so much on detachment as on communion. The passionate individual who appears in the early novels is still in evidence, but now he longs to understand other people and help them. In *Faithful Are the Wounds*, set in the time of the McCarthy investigations of Communism, the suicide of a brilliant Harvard professor is shown as self-sacrifice to which he was driven by people's blindness to the world's need. In contrast to his agonized caring for others, the lives of the other characters seem too small, hedged in by doubts and self-seeking. So also, in *The Birth of a Grandfather*, *The Small Room*, and later novels, the author explores reasons for human failures in communication and shows a deep understanding of human loneliness.

In some of her recent fiction Miss Sarton has experimented with new forms. *Joanna and Ulysses*, *Miss Pickthorn and Mr. Hare*, and *The Poet and the Donkey* are tales or fables with simplified, almost stylized plots and characters. The latter and *Mrs. Stevens Hears the Mermaids Singing* emphasize the function of love in the creative process. Her latest novel, *Kinds of Love* is notable for its richness of theme and characterization; in it she emphasizes again, as in earlier works, the variety and complexity of love.

A chief idea in her work is the need to be oneself. No one should "give up his differences." And the achievement of selfhood is brought about largely through the willingness to feel strongly and to suffer. The need for love, as distinct from passion, is emphasized in all the novels. If the fervent individual learns detachment, greater communion and love are possible.

—Agnes Sibley

---

**SCANNELL, Vernon.** British. Born in Spilsby, Lincolnshire, 23 January 1922. Educated at Queen's Park School, Aylesbury, Buckinghamshire; University of Leeds, Yorkshire, 1946–47. Served in the Gordon Highlanders, 1941–45. Married Josephine Higson in 1954; has five children. Formerly, amateur and professional boxer. Teacher of English, Hazlewood School, Limpsfield, Surrey, 1955–62. Free-lance Writer and Broadcaster since 1962. Recipient: Heinemann Award, for poetry, 1960; Arts Council grant, 1967, 1970. Fellow, Royal Society of Literature, 1960. Address: Folly Cottage, Nether Compton, Sherborne, Dorset, England.

PUBLICATIONS

Novels

> *The Fight*.   London, Peter Nevill, 1953.
> *The Wound and the Scar*.   London, Peter Nevill, 1954.
> *The Face of the Enemy*.   London, Putnam, 1961.
> *The Dividing Night*.   London, Putnam, 1962.
> *The Big Time*.   London, Longman, 1965.

Verse

> *Graves and Resurrections*.   London, Fortune Press, 1948.
> *A Mortal Pitch*.   London, Villiers, 1957.
> *The Masks of Love*.   London, Putnam, 1960.
> *A Sense of Danger*.   London, Putnam, 1962.
> *Walking Wounded*.   London, Eyre and Spottiswoode, 1965.
> *Epithets of War*.   London, Eyre and Spottiswoode, 1969.
> *Mastering the Craft*.   Oxford, Pergamon Press, 1970.
> *Selected Poems*.   London, Allison and Busby, 1971.

Other

> *Edward Thomas*.   London, Longman, 1962.
> *The Dangerous Ones* (juvenile).   Oxford, Pergamon Press, 1970.
> *The Tiger and the Rose: An Autobiography*.   London, Hamish Hamilton, 1971.

> Plays broadcast on BBC radio.

Critical Study: "Enriching the Banal: Vernon Scannell's New Novel" by Christine Brooke-Rose, in *Listener* (London), 5 July 1962.

Vernon Scannell comments:

I consider myself to be, if anything, primarily a poet and have not taken the writing of prose fiction nearly seriously enough, and I am painfully aware that this lack of respect for the medium shows clearly in the work, that is to say in the language itself which often lacks the precision and bite that characterize good imaginative prose. However, it is just possible that someone may find interest in spotting the parallel themes in the poetry and the fiction, the preoccupation—perhaps obsession—with war, physical violence, courage and its lack, ageing and the sense of mortality.

*             *             *

Vernon Scannell is a poet and literary critic as well as a novelist. One senses the qualities of the lyric poet in his prose: the concern for the individual phrase and an unusual sensitiveness to atmosphere. The tone of his novels is essentially quiet and reflective, so that the occasional act of violence makes its point effectively.

*The Face of the Enemy* focuses on the group of ex-Servicemen and their women who frequent a scruffy little drinking club in London called "The Combined 'Ops". These men drink heavily and reminisce about the past; they tend to romanticise the War years when they shared in the camaraderie of Service life. In a sense they are War casualties: people who do not fit into post-War society. One of them, increasingly aware of the futility of his life, commits suicide.

Margaret and David are the central characters. Margaret, still unmarried, was introduced to the club by a drunken friend of her dead brother and David is a new member. They have an affair. David seems to use the excuse of having been brought up as a Catholic to avoid getting a divorce—he has long lost contact with his wife. Then he confesses, in the Club, that he had been court-martialled and found guilty of "cowardice in the face of the enemy". Instead of arousing anger or contempt, David wins the respect of the self-styled heroes for his courage in admitting his "lapse".

A novel that probes more deeply into ambiguity and uncertainty is Scannell's *The Dividing Night*. John Shearman, a publisher, has reached middle-age; he is bored with his work and his wife. He meets and is strongly attracted to another man's wife who turns out to be both willing and passionate. An affair develops, with all its necessary trappings of deceit. Shearman becomes obsessed with his mistress who wants him physically but not emotionally.

*The Dividing Night* has a chorus of raffish characters: John Shearman's drop-out brother and the group of arty failures who are his drinking companions. In the end, Shearman's marriage comes apart. But he has the resilience his brother so obviously lacks and the book ends with a hint that the marriage will be patched up. In this novel we see Scannell's commitment to values in a world where anything goes; and it also reveals his ability in recognising and conveying social nuances.

Vernon Scannell was at one time an amateur boxer and this interest in boxing is reflected in *The Fight* and *The Big Time* as well as in a number of his poems. *The Big Time* tells the story of a bid for the world championship. A brilliant amateur heavyweight turns professional under the influence of an unscrupulous tycoon who wants to create "a perfect fighting machine". But Scannell underlines the fact that no man, not even the most disciplined, can be turned into a machine.

Scannell knows from first-hand the idiom of boxers and those who surround them: managers, promotors, journalists, spectators. He understands the factors—courage, skill, determination—that put a boxer in the "big time" and keep him there. His expertise never bores and his narrative seldom flags. Here, as elsewhere, he reveals his deep concern with human motivation and the irony of fate.

—Robert Greacen

---

**SCHORER, Mark.** American. Born in Sauk City, Wisconsin, 17 May 1908. Educated in Sauk City public schools; at the University of Wisconsin, Madison, 1925–29, 1931–36, A.B. 1929, Ph.D. 1936; Harvard University, Cambridge, Massachusetts, 1929–30, M.A. 1930. Married Ruth Tozier Page in 1936; has two children. Instructor of English, Dartmouth College, Hanover, New Hampshire, 1936–37; Instructor of English, 1937–40, and Briggs-Copeland Faculty Instructor, 1940–45, Harvard University. Associate Professor, 1945–47, and since 1947, Professor of English, University of California, Berkeley: Chairman of the Department of English, 1960–65. Christian Gauss Seminarian, Princeton University, New Jersey, 1949; Visiting Professor, Harvard University, 1952, and University of Tokyo, 1956; Fulbright Professor, University of Pisa, 1952–53, and University of Rome, 1964. Fellow, Indiana University School of Letters, Bloomington, since 1947. Member, Board of Directors, American Council of Learned Societies, New York, since 1965; West Coast Adviser, Executive

Council, Authors' Guild, since 1966. Recipient: Guggenheim Fellowship, 1941, 1942, 1948; Center for Advanced Study in the Behavioral Sciences Fellowship, Stanford, California, 1958–59; Bollingen Fellowship, 1960. D.Litt., University of Wisconsin, 1962. Member, American Academy of Arts and Sciences, 1962. Address: 68 Tamalpais Road, Berkeley, California 94708, U.S.A.

PUBLICATIONS

Novels

> *A House Too Old*.   New York, Reynal, 1935.
> *The Hermit Place*.   New York, Random House, 1941.
> *The Wars of Love*.   New York, McGraw Hill, and London, Eyre and Spottiswoode, 1954.

Short Stories

> *The State of Mind: Thirty-Two Stories*.   Boston, Houghton Mifflin, 1947.
> *The State of Mind: Twenty-Two Stories*.   London, Eyre and Spottiswoode, 1956.
> *Colonel Markesan and Less Pleasant People*, with August Derleth.   Sauk City, Wisconsin, Arkham House, 1966.

Other

> *William Blake: The Politics of Vision*.   New York, Holt, 1946.
> *Sinclair Lewis: An American Life*.   New York, McGraw Hill, 1961; London, Heinemann, 1963.
> *Sinclair Lewis*.   Minneapolis, University of Minnesota Press, 1963.
> *The World We Imagine: Selected Essays*.   New York, Farrar Straus, 1968; London, Chatto and Windus, 1969.
> *D. H. Lawrence*.   New York, Dell, 1968.

> Editor, with others, *Criticism: The Foundations of Modern Literary Judgement*.   New York, Harcourt Brace, 1948; revised edition, 1958.
> Editor, *The Story: A Critical Anthology*.   New York, Prentice Hall, 1950; London, Bailey Brothers and Swinfen, 1955; revised edition, Prentice Hall, 1967.
> Editor, *Society and Self in the Novel*.   New York, Columbia University Press, and London, Oxford University Press, 1956.
> Editor, with others, *Harbrace College Reader*.   New York, Harcourt Brace, 1959; revised edition, 1968.
> Editor, *Modern British Fiction*.   New York, Oxford University Press, 1961.
> Editor, *Sinclair Lewis: A Collection of Critical Essays*.   New York, Prentice Hall, 1962.
> Editor, *Selected Writings*, by Truman Capote.   New York, Modern Library, 1963.
> Editor, with others, *American Literature*.   Boston, Houghton Mifflin, 1965.
> Editor, *Galaxy: Literary Modes and Genres*.   New York, Harcourt Brace, 1967.
> Editor, *The Literature of America: Twentieth Century*.   New York, McGraw Hill, 1970.

Manuscript Collection: Bancroft Library, University of California, Berkeley.

Mark Schorer comments:

After my first novel, which was a lugubrious historical chronicle, the interest of my fiction, long and short, has been in the psychological complexities, chiefly destructive, of human relationships, and in the difficulties of self-recognition. An autobiographical novel on which I have been working for several years takes the latter as its explicit theme, and in conjunction with that, the complexities of self-destruction.

*          *          *

Mark Schorer is better known as a biographer, scholar and literary critic than as a novelist. *William Blake: The Politics of Vision* and the monumental yet highly readable *Sinclair Lewis: An American Life* are major works of wide-ranging, even omnivorous intelligence. The brief biography, *D. H. Lawrence*, shows a sympathetic understanding of a violent and prophetic effort to escape emotional failure. The briefer critical essays and prefaces (*The World We Imagine: Selected Essays*) reveal, rather, a craftsman's dedication to form and control. The famous essay "Technique as Discovery" shows how fictional form discovers and evaluates meaning, meaning that is sometimes unintended.

This concern with lucidity and control characterizes the novels, which deserve a much wider public than they have found. They show, over the years, an increasingly Jamesian intelligence fond of solving problems of technique and point of view. And a Jamesian refusal, too, to take the easier way. *A House Too Old* has a sombreness characteristic of its place (a small mid-western town over a hundred years ago) and of its time of writing—a young man's book, in a period that relished grim rural chronicles. But the gray pictures of narrowness and greed, almost Balzacian at times, are to some extent redeemed by richly-rhythmed prose and by descriptions of lyrical beauty. Schorer was writing, in sometimes excessive detail, about places and people he knew.

The craftsman and psychologist deliberately narrowing his world is much more evident in *The Hermit Place*, where authorial wit, very much in the manner of Elizabeth Bowen, blends with yet controls the fuzzy minds of slothful or disorderly persons. This nuanced study of slackness of spirit and failing relationships has its highly dramatic moments and scenes of flashing dialogue. Yet the true explosions are, as in James, those of inward discovery.

Schorer's central insight—that emotional failure is also moral failure and failure of understanding—finds its most perfect expression in *The Wars of Love*, a novel closely resembling Ford Madox Ford's *The Good Soldier*, and quite worthy to be read beside it. Four people, whom we see first as children, move through a grave and intricate dance of the emotions, always threatening to possess each other and destroy. Paralyzed will, dullness of spirit and of flesh, refined and at times brutal cruelties, a simple failure to respond adequately to life—this picture of desolation is saved, once again, by wit, grace, style, and by wholly exceptional formal elegance. The narrator of *The Wars of Love*, like Ford's, only dimly perceives his own sloth and meanness of spirit, and thus largely fails to understand the experience he observes. He does discover himself at last, though, in an ending that continues to resonate in the reader's mind. The ironic device of the obtuse narrator and self-betraying Jamesian "fool" finds here one of its most flawless executions. Schorer's deliberate narrowness of range yet permits large insights into failures of the specifically modern sensibility. Control makes possible epiphany.

Mark Schorer, whose graceful short stories were collected as *The State of Mind*, is Professor of English at the University of California, and has served as chairman of that very large and distinguished department.

—Albert J. Guerard

**SCHULBERG, Budd (Wilson).** American. Born in New York City, 27 March 1914, son of the Hollywood film pioneer, B. P. Schulberg. Educated at Los Angeles High School, 1928–31; Deerfield Academy, 1931–32; Dartmouth College, Hanover, New Hampshire, 1932–36, A.B. (cum laude) 1936. Served in the United States Navy, rising to the rank of Lieutenant Junior Grade, 1943–46. Married Virginia Ray in 1936 (divorced, 1942); Victoria Anderson, 1943 (divorced, 1964); the actress Geraldine Brooks, 1964; has three children. Screenwriter in Hollywood, 1936–39. In charge of photographic evidence for the Nuremberg Trials; Boxing Editor, *Sports Illustrated*, New York, 1954; has taught writing at Columbia University, New York; Phoenixville Veterans Hospital; University of the Streets, New York. Since 1958, President, Schulberg Productions, New York, and since 1965, President, Douglass House Foundation, Watts, Los Angeles. Member, New York Council, Authors' Guild, 1958–60. Recipient: American Library Association Award, New York Critics Award, Foreign Correspondents Award, Screen Writers Guild Award, and Academy Award, for screenplay, 1954; Christopher Award, 1956; German Film Critics Award, for screenplay, 1958. D.Litt., Dartmouth College, 1960. Address: c/o Ad Schulberg, 300 East 57th Street, New York, New York, U.S.A.

PUBLICATIONS

Novels

> *What Makes Sammy Run?* New York, Random House, and London, Jarrolds, 1941.
> *The Harder They Fall.* New York, Random House, and London, Lane, 1947.
> *The Disenchanted.* New York, Random House, 1950; London, Lane, 1951.
> *Waterfront.* New York, Random House, 1955; London, Lane, 1956.
> *Sanctuary V.* Cleveland, World, 1970; London, W. H. Allen, 1971.

Short Stories

> *Some Faces in the Crowd.* New York, Random House, 1953; London, Lane, 1954.

Uncollected Short Stories

> "Passport to Nowhere", in *Story* (New York), 1940.
> "The Real Viennese Schmalz", in *Esquire* (New York), 1941.
> "The Barracudas", in *Playboy* (Chicago), 1958.
> "A Second Father", in *Playboy* (Chicago), 1961.
> "Say Goodnight to Owl", in *Cosmopolitan* (New York), 1966.

> Other stories published in magazines and anthologies.

Plays

> *A Face in the Crowd: A Play for the Screen.* New York, Random House, 1957.
> *Across the Everglades: A Play for the Screen.* New York, Random House, 1958.
> *The Disenchanted*, with Harvey Breit (produced New York, 1958). New York, Random House, 1959.
> *What Makes Sammy Run?* with Stuart Schulberg, music by Ervin Drake (produced New York, 1964).

Screenplays: *Winter Carnival*, with F. Scott Fitzgerald, 1939: *On the Waterfront*, 1954; *A Face in the Crowd*, 1958; *Wind Across the Everglades*, 1958.

Other

*Loser and Still Champion: Muhammad Ali.*   New York, Doubleday, 1972.
*The Four Seasons of Success.*   New York, Doubleday, 1972.

Editor, *From the Ashes: The Voices of Watts.*   New York, New American Library, 1967.

Manuscript Collection: Princeton University, New Jersey.

Budd Schulberg comments:

I was raised in Hollywood, in the middle of the film capital, and had an early education in the vicissitudes of success and failure. I became convinced, before I was out of high school, that the dynamics of success and failure were of earthquake proportions in America, and that Hollywood was only an exaggerated version of the American success drive. Undoubtedly this influenced my first novel, *What Makes Sammy Run?*, as it did *The Harder They Fall*, *The Disenchanted* and many other things I have tried to write. I believe it is the prime American theme, and in fact I am now in the process of publishing a study of Sinclair Lewis, Scott Fitzgerald, William Saroyan, Nathanael West, Thomas Heggen, and John Steinbeck, all writers I knew well, because I believe that the seasons of success and failure are more violent in America than anywhere else on earth. Witness only Herman Melville and Jack London, to name two of the victims.

I have been influenced by Mark Twain, by Frank Norris, Jack London, Upton Sinclair, John Steinbeck and the social novelists. I believe in art, but I don't believe in art for art's sake: while despising the Soviet official societal writing, I believe in art for people's sake. I believe the novelist should be an artist cum sociologist. I think he should see his characters in social perspective. I think that is one of his obligations. At the same time, I think he also has an obligation to entertain. I think the novel should run on a double track. I am proud of the fact that *Uncle Tom's Cabin* and *The Jungle* and *The Grapes of Wrath* helped to change or at least alarm society. I am proud of the fact that books of mine, *Sammy*, or *On the Waterfront*, caught the public attention but also made it more aware of social sores, the corruption that springs from the original Adam Smith ideal of individuality. I think Ayn Rand tries to apply 18th century ideals to 20th century problems—and I'm not sure they worked that well then. My flags are down: I believe in neither Smith nor Marx, in neither Nixon nor Mao nor the Soviet bureaucrats who persecute my fellow writers. There was a time when I was young when I sang the "International". Who would have guessed that the "International" would result in the two largest countries in the world, both "Socialist", brandishing lethal weapons at each other? As long as we can wonder and remember, speculate and (perhaps vainly) hope, we are not dead. The non- or anti-communist humanist writer of novels may be slightly out of style, but there are miles and decades and many books to go before he sleeps.

\*     \*     \*

Budd Schulberg earned fame with his first and best novel, *What Makes Sammy Run?*, published in 1941 on the author's twenty-seventh birthday. This narrative of an obnoxious office boy's quick rise to head of a major motion picture studio threatened to become the

1111

author's type story for all his novels. *The Harder They Fall* told the pathetic story of the rise of Toro Molina to heavyweight boxing champion, although "El Toro" is actually the victim of an ambitious, unscrupulous fight promoter named Nick Latka. Schulberg's *The Disenchanted* traced the doomed comeback attempt of Manley Halliday, a novelist and culture-hero of the 1920's now reduced to writing movie scenarios when sober. In these three early novels and many of the collected short stories of *Some Faces in the Crowd*, Schulberg is absorbed with the theme of rapid success and the psychic losses of public winners: compromise with self, betrayal by or of others, doubt, guilt, isolation and fear haunt and shame his restless characters.

Schulberg's plots have frequently reflected the author's background as screenwriter and son of a Hollywood producer. Not surprisingly, many of his novels have been produced as movies, but his fourth novel, *Waterfront* was a successful movie first, with the novel version a distinct improvement over the author's own scenario. After a fifteen year lapse, Schulberg recently returned to the novel with *Sanctuary V*, a melodramatic study of a failed revolution and the ruinous effects of sudden power. In this least successful novel, Justo Suarez, the provisional president of what is obviously Cuba, has fled from the corrupted revolutionary Angel Bello to take sanctuary in a corrupt embassy among corrupt or perverted refugees and jailer-hosts.

Not only is Angel Bello clearly Fidel Castro, earlier novels just as recognizably modeled their protagonists on real-life counterparts: the hapless, peasant-fighter Toro Molina is Primo Carnera, while Manley Halliday is Scott Fitzgerald, with whom Schulberg ("Shep" in the book) had once worked on a Dartmouth winter carnival scenario. When Schulberg is not "exposing" Hollywood through memories of real-life counterparts or composites, he utilizes journalistic skill and thorough research for fictional exposés of the fight game (*Harder They Fall*) and the brutal life around New York harbor (*Waterfront*). Like most exposés, the novels exploit the most sensational elements, though Schulberg reveals an un-Hollywoodian preference for the seamy over the sexy. He does commit many other major "Hollywood" faults, employing gimmicks, stereotyped characters, sentimentality and mechanical, reflex responses to life-situations in place of serious ideas or a personal vision.

With *Sammy*, however, even the faults seem appropriate. The snappy repartee and artificial dialogue brilliantly sum up the brittle, superficial world of 1930's Hollywood. The novel's fast pace, the picaresque audacity of the almost likable, conscienceless heel-hero, the predictable ending of the betrayer betrayed (and, implicitly, of the hunter about to be hunted) still add up, after thirty years, to one of the best Hollywood novels ever written. Like many other commercial writers, Schulberg knows that first-person is the easiest way to tell a story; he uses this form often and well, and in *What Makes Sammy Run?* he created a minor classic of this form and the Hollywood sub-genre.

—Frank Campenni

---

**SCOTT, J(ohn) D(ick).** British. Born in Lanarkshire, Scotland, 26 February 1917. Educated at Stewart's College, Edinburgh; Edinburgh University, M.A. (honours) in history. Assistant Principal, Ministry of Aircraft Production, London, 1940–44; attached to the Cabinet Office, London, for work on the official history of World War II, 1944. Married Helen Elizabeth Whittaker in 1941; has two children. Literary Editor, *Spectator*, London, 1953–56. Since 1963, Editor of *Finance and Development*, publication of the World Bank, Washington, D.C. Address: 1517 30th Street N.W., Washington, D.C. 20007, U.S.A.

PUBLICATIONS

Novels

The Cellar.   London, Pilot Press, 1947; as *Buy It for a Song*, New York, Pelligrini and
Cudahy, 1948.
The Margin.   London, Pilot Press, 1949; New York, Knopf, 1950.
The Way to Glory; or, The Last Night of the Holidays.   London, Eyre and Spottiswoode,
and New York, Knopf, 1952.
The End of an Old Song.   London, Eyre and Spottiswoode, 1953; New York, Knopf,
1954.
The Pretty Penny.   London, Eyre and Spottiswoode, 1963; New York, Harcourt
Brace, 1964.

Other

The Administration of War Production, with Richard Hughes.   London, Her Majesty's
Stationery Office, 1956.
Life in Britain.   London, Eyre and Spottiswoode, and New York, Morrow, 1956.
The Siemens Brothers, 1858–1958: An Essay in the History of Industry.   London,
Weidenfeld and Nicolson, 1958.
Vickers: A History.   London, Weidenfeld and Nicolson, 1963; Mystic, Connecticut,
Verry, 1964.

*        *        *

J. D. Scott is one of those novelists who, without possessing strikingly original gifts or
having taken command of a subject that can be called his own, is nonetheless a reliably good
writer. Though he will never write a great novel it is equally certain that he will never write a
bad one. He tends to find his subject-matter among the ordinary goings-on of life and his
work is redeemed from dullness by the neat and accurate observation that he brings to bear
upon his characters and the circumstances of their existence.

There is a notable exception to this rule. *The Pretty Penny* opens in the customary Scott
manner. A city director drives home to his comfortable suburban house and mixes himself
his usual cocktail. His wife appears, comfortable, placid, unimaginative; together they spend
an uneventful evening. It is all very ordinary. But the tale then takes off into a fast-moving
adventure story as the director, fearful of losing his job, finds himself caught up in a complicated and thoroughly shady scheme that entails his going to Africa, becoming involved in
gun-running and also leads to an affair with a girl. The real concern of *The Pretty Penny* is
corruption: moral, sexual, political; and it is clear that the novel owes a considerable debt
to those early adventure-novels of Graham Greene. The debt, indeed, is more than Scott
can repay. For although there are some exciting moments, and although the novelist is far
from unsuccessful in his depiction of the heat and strangeness of Africa, the moral theme is
emptied of meaning by the implausibility, not so much of the central adventure, as of the
relationship with the girl. Rarely can an affair of the passionate and erring heart have
seemed so lacking in passion, so enervate. Scott might, of course, reply that that is exactly
the point. His hero is not meant to be seen as a grand sinner, merely a petty one. But in that
case, one is forced to say, too much of a song and dance is made of his affair. And although
it is clear that a Catholic metaphysic is dictating the novel's events it must still be said that
what makes for good theology can make for bad art.

Scott's other novels are, I think, more uniformly successful than *The Pretty Penny*, and
although it is difficult to pick on any one as exemplifying his gifts at their best, I would say

that *The Way to Glory* is as good a novel as he has so far written (it was published in the early 1950's). It is an honest and searching study of a man's attempt to understand the pattern of his own life, to make sense of his commitments to politics and to people, and though there is nothing in the novel that stands out as remarkable, there is everything to admire in the way Scott makes his main character credible and sympathetic. If there is a weakness it is in the dialogue with which, indeed, Scott seldom seems entirely at ease. He is much better when concentrating on narrative, description, and interior monologue.

—John Lucas

---

**SCOTT, Paul (Mark).** British. Born in London, 25 March 1920. Served in the British and Indian Armies, in the United Kingdom, India and Malaya, 1940–46. Married Nancy E. Avery in 1941; has two children. Company Secretary, Falcon Press and Grey Walls Press, London, 1946–50; Director, David Higham Associates, London, 1950–60. Recipient: Eyre and Spottiswoode Literary Fellowship, 1951; Arts Council grant, 1969. Fellow, Royal Society of Literature, 1963. Address: c/o David Higham Associates, 5–8 Lower John Street, Golden Square, London W1R 4HA, England.

PUBLICATIONS

Novels

*Johnnie Sahib*. London, Eyre and Spottiswoode, 1952.
*The Alien Sky*. London, Eyre and Spottiswoode, 1953; as *Six Days in Marapore*, New York, Doubleday, 1953.
*A Male Child*. London, Eyre and Spottiswoode, 1956; New York, Dutton, 1957.
*The Mark of the Warrior*. London, Eyre and Spottiswoode, and New York, Morrow, 1958.
*The Chinese Love Pavilion*. London, Eyre and Spottiswoode, 1960; as *The Love Pavilion*, New York, Morrow, 1960.
*The Birds of Paradise*. London, Eyre and Spottiswoode, and New York, Morrow, 1962.
*The Bender: Pictures from an Exhibition of Middle Class Portraits*. London, Secker and Warburg, 1963; as *The Bender*, New York, Morrow, 1963.
*The Corrida at San Feliu*. London, Secker and Warburg, and New York, Morrow, 1964.
*The Jewel in the Crown*. London, Heinemann, and New York, Morrow, 1966.
*The Day of the Scorpion*. London, Heinemann, and New York, Morrow, 1968.
*The Towers of Silence*. London, Heinemann, 1971; New York, Morrow, 1972.

Plays

Adaptations of novels produced on television.

Manuscript Collection: Humanities Research Center, University of Texas, Austin.

Critical Study: text of a paper by the author read to the Royal Society of Literature, London, December 1968, included in *Essays by Divers Hands*, London, Oxford University Press, 1970.

\*      \*      \*

Paul Scott is known chiefly for his novels about Anglo-India in the final years of British rule during and after the Second World War. At present he is at work on a series of long, inter-linked, closely documented novels that aim to re-create on a grand scale the political and human clashes between British and Indians during this period. The first of the series, *The Jewel in the Crown*, deals with the events leading up to and the consequences of the rape of a white girl by a group of Indians at a particular time of crisis, 1942, in the country's history. In its successor, *The Day of the Scorpion*, Scott shows through an established Anglo-Indian family how the old balance between ruler and ruled is disrupted by the war and the appearance on the scene of a new type of Englishman. Some characters from the earlier novel appear in the latter. Common to both is the theme of the survival of individuals and families at a time of violent change. Both, especially *The Jewel in the Crown*, are slow-moving, ruminative, rather prolix.

Earlier novels by Scott with a wholly or partly Indian background are *The Alien Sky*, *The Birds of Paradise* and *The Mark of the Warrior*. The first of these foreshadows the more recent panoramic novels in its attempt to recapture the personal relations and tensions of English and Indians at the time of Independence. Gower, the liberal editor and planter, is hated and in the end betrayed by both sides. The British here are unable to adapt, small-time victims of violent change. But the tragedy is too predictable, the overall effect too schematic. More interesting is *The Birds of Paradise*, a more fluidly composed work, cast in the form of autobiography, in which the first-person narrator, Conway, recalls his childhood as the son of a Political Agent in an Indian princely State, his time as a Japanese P.O.W., his marriage to a frigid wife, in an attempt to fit his life into some kind of pattern. The tone is more relaxed than in many of Scott's novels, the imagery more subtle. In *The Mark of the Warrior*, the Indian setting, a jungle training camp, is incidental to the theme of the mystique of the soldier, of the qualities of leadership. Craig, the tormented C.O. of the camp, re-stages a river cros-sing during the Burmese campaign which, under his leadership, had ended in disaster. He is confronted by the cadet Ramsay, who, a born leader, throws Craig's deficiencies into relief. Although the book is full of a subtle understanding of the complex motives that inspire men under the stress of danger, the characters tend to dwindle to mere pawns in Scott's game of chess.

The setting of *The Chinese Love Pavilion*, in some ways Scott's most original novel, is once more the jungle, this time in Malaya. The narrator, Brent, a major in Intelligence, conducts a search in the jungle for a former planter and guerrilla leader called Saxby with whom he was once deeply involved. Saxby, it becomes obvious, is mad—or seeking his personal salvation. An ominous stillness lies over the book and it ends with the inevitable catharsis of violent death. Scott's world here is a hard one where significance attaches to actions and they have to be paid for. There is great compassion but little mercy.

The earlier and later groups of Eastern novels are separated by two novels with a con-temporary European setting. *The Bender* is Scott's one essay in comedy, a grey but witty piece about the shabby-genteel George Spruce, ruined by a too-small inherited income. *The Corrida at San Feliu* explores the past life and present consciousness of Edward Thorn-hill, a middle-aged novelist on holiday in Spain, and in particular his growing jealousy of his wife's apparent adultery with a local youth. The book is noteworthy for its attempt to relate the symbols and metaphors that occur in the writer's work (as evidenced in three short pieces, ostensibly by Thornhill, that make up the first part of the novel) with the episodes and incidents of his past and present life. Yet, in spite of Thornhill's guidance, the thicket of symbols becomes so dense at times that movement virtually comes to a halt. This is a deep, subtle, slow, rather over-contrived book.

The flavour of Scott's work is not easy to convey: there is a dryness to it, a metaphysical

1115

urge that appears at odds with his sensuous evocations of background. At times he can appear overconcerned with whatever aspect of human nature it is that strikes him and can hunt an aperçu to death through paragraph after prosy paragraph. In part this accounts for the slowness with which his novels read, the narrative reduced to a trickle between meta-physical and psychological sandbanks. Yet his technique is often of great interest and complexity, in its use of flashback and multiple time-sequence for example. Running through many of Scott's novels is his concern with the relationship between a man and his work. He himself has said that he sees this as a metaphor for the idea that reality is at its sharpest when men are governed by a philosophy to whose truth and rewards they can dedicate themselves. Similarly, Scott claims that he has written so often about the Indian scene not merely because he finds the particular period of which he writes lively and dramatic but as a metaphor for the world he lives in. Yet, ironically, it may well be that it is a certain deficiency in dramatic sense, together with an inability to create characters that can wholly engage the attention and sympathies of the reader, that have led to Scott's comparative neglect as a writer and obscured the depth and complexity of his understanding of human nature under stress.

—Keith Walker

**SELBY, Hubert, Jr.** American. Born in Brooklyn, New York, 23 July 1928. Educated in New York City public schools, including Peter Stuyvesant High School. Served in the United States Merchant Marine, 1944–46. Married Inez Taylor in 1953; Judith Lumino, 1964; Suzanne Shaw, 1969; has four children. Hospital patient, with tuberculosis, 1946–50; held various jobs, including seaman and insurance clerk, 1950–64. Currently, stockclerk. Address: 635 Westbourne Drive, Hollywood, California 90069, U.S.A.

PUBLICATIONS

Novels

> *Last Exit to Brooklyn.* New York, Grove Press, 1964; London, Calder and Boyars, 1966.
> *The Room.* New York, Grove Press, 1971; London, Calder and Boyars, 1972.

Hubert Selby, Jr., comments:

I write by ear. Music of line important. Want to put reader through emotional experience.

\*       \*       \*

Seldom has an author made the impact that Hubert Selby, Jr., has made with *Last Exit to Brooklyn.* And this acclaim is more substantial than the merely sensational aspects surrounding the British obscenity trial would suggest. To say that Selby's vision is Swiftian is not to set the novel outside its time but to suggest the way in which "obscenity", of the kind that attends Swift's "A Young Nymph Going to Bed", may serve a vision that is anything but merely sensationalistic.

The world of *Last Exit* is in fact a world of no exit—an expressway to nowhere, a perennial tour, Dantean fashion, of a hell that is New York. In this circle of the lost the "straights" are present only on sufferance and *fellatio* is the sacrament of the damned. It is a world beyond anything that Fellini has created—in *La Dolce Vita* or even in *Satyricon*—mechanical, loveless and absurd. Here human relations are rocks whelmed against by the flailing nerve-ends of appetite, and the daytime is always night. The queens—drag and otherwise—go by in a parade as endless and meaningless as the processions of Fellini's $8\frac{1}{2}$. And the visions of brutality and death—the sink of iniquity that we are or may be—are like the horror of death's barge with its Fuseli-like horses that Giulietta Masina sees in one moment of terror in *Juliet of the Spirits*.

The novel is, in a sense, episodic, but its six sections are études whose themes (or *leitmotivs*) and characters are connected. The journey through the novel is neither ascent nor descent but remains within the green light at the centre of the maelstrom where all time *is* eternally present and change is only variety. Selby's technique is not that of the satirist (though his sketches have a fine venom) but the tragic ironist. "Why this is hell, nor am I out of it," says Mephistophilis to Faustus and it might well be the text of any of Selby's central figures. The sense of movement and action is frenetic but the movement is nowhere and the achievement is nothing.

This is a world of monologues and soliloquies in which there is no communication because no one listens to anyone else. And the rhetoric, for whose patterns Selby has a keen ear, is like the rhetoric of Milton's fallen angels—designed to keep out the truth, prevent reality, flatter self-esteem, forestall criticism, anything but allow the recognition of another person. Harry Black of the fifth and longest section, "Strike", is like Satan—himself is hell.

The novel has a sense of entropy about it—things run down or fall apart; the ending is a whimper. The language and the action collapse in a heap of jumbled images as the scenes flash by like strobe lights, with only the occasional glimpse of a familiar couple (still screaming) to remind us that even horror has its consistencies. The old women, the chorus, talk on, but they neither see nor understand. The spectacle they are compelled to witness is too great for them. Their speech is another sound.

Ultimately the great anarch who is the god of this twilight world lets the curtain fall. The machine stops, not because this "Landsend" is the final refuge or the point of embarkation, but because there is nowhere to go. Perhaps, to paraphrase Thackeray on Swift, when we have read Selby we have nothing more of nastiness to learn. But what a great deal we have learned.

—D. D. C. Chambers

---

**SELVON, Samuel (Dickson).** Trinidadian. Born in Trinidad, 20 May 1923. Educated at Naparima College, Trinidad, 1935–39. Served as a wireless operator with the Trinidad Royal Naval Volunteer Reserve, 1940–45. Married Draupadi Persaud in 1947; Althea Nesta Daroux, 1963; has three children. Journalist, *Trinidad Guardian*, 1946–50; Civil Servant, with India High Commissioner, London, 1950–53. Full-time Writer since 1954. Recipient: Guggenheim Fellowship, 1954, 1968; Society of Authors Travelling Scholarship, 1958; Trinidad Government Scholarship, 1962; Arts Council of Great Britain grant, 1967, 1968; Humming Bird Medal, Trinidad, 1969. Address: 36 Woodside Avenue, London S.E.25, England.

PUBLICATIONS

Novels

A Brighter Sun.  London, Wingate, 1952; New York, Viking Press, 1953.
An Island Is a World.  London, Wingate, 1955.
The Lonely Londoners.  London, Wingate, 1956; New York, St. Martin's Press, 1957.
Turn Again, Tiger.  London, MacGibbon and Kee, 1958; New York, St. Martin's Press, 1959.
I Hear Thunder.  London, MacGibbon and Kee, and New York, St. Martin's Press, 1963.
The Housing Lark.  London, MacGibbon and Kee, 1965.
The Plains of Caroni.  London, MacGibbon and Kee, 1969.
Those Who Eat the Cascadura.  London, Davis Poynter, 1972.

Short Stories

Ways of Sunlight.  London, MacGibbon and Kee, and New York, St. Martin's Press, 1958.

\*       \*       \*

The synthesis of oriental, African and European elements in the Caribbean has been recent in the consciousness of the East Indian, who lived for a long time in a kind of cultural cocoon (at least on the plantations), his language, religion and ritual preserved largely intact, his experience contrasting sharply at first with that of the more deracinated African. We see the first portrayal of the East Indian community in an early novel by the Guyanese Edgar Mittelholzer, but it was in A Brighter Sun that an East Indian writer himself, Samuel Selvon, spoke for the first time with quiet intimate authority and simple charm about the life of the East Indian family in the Caribbean.

In this novel Selvon treats of a young Indian couple thrown together in their teens by the traditional marriage behind the veil, who grow to maturity at the time of the last war on a housing settlement a few miles out of Port-of-Spain. It is written with a sensitiveness to the delicate touches of beauty in common things and through a series of commonplace events we see the Indian peasant facing crucial adjustments in the movement of the life of the land to the life of the town. The Chinese grocer, the Portuguese neighbours, the African materfamilias are drawn with an equal clarity and sureness and we get a sense of the effect of this cosmopolitan flux upon the Indian psychological fibre. In Turn Again, Tiger, a sequel to this first novel, Selvon returns to the Indian couple, Tiger and Urmilla, and here we see the dilemma of the man who is only educated enough to be restless about his condition but can find no direction or stage for any significant extension or expression. Tiger, bewildered by the shapeless interior shadow of this restlessness, identifies it with a call to return to the life of the land and so he journeys backwards in an attempt to feel his roots again in the virgin territory of Five Rivers. The movement back to the land culminates in a series of disillusionments and he is forced to return to suburban Barataria but the experience brings him closer to a realisation of the true nature of himself and his predicament and an acceptance of the realities he must face in order to live.

These two novels achieve at times an almost poetic simplicity. Selvon is never intense or profoundly disturbing but his work has the freshness and tone of wide open fields and cool, noiselessly running water. There is humour too, lighter perhaps than in Naipaul's early work, but developing into pure classical farce in his novel The Lonely Londoners. Here Selvon, experimenting with the regional dialect with probably more success than any other

Caribbean writer, gives a picture, both hilarious and pathetic, of the plight of West Indian immigrants in London. Selvon proves himself capable of handling an almost purely African cast and English landscape with the same ease and authenticity as the Indian family unit in Trinidad.

Selvon began as a short-story writer and it is as a short-story writer, perhaps, that he is best admired. In *Ways of Sunlight* one sees clearly that his gift for farce finds its happiest expression in that medium. His stories at best have a pointed finish, a rounded artistry lacking in the episodic fragmentation of the novels. In the shorter form he may be compared to his fellow Trinidadian humorist, V. S. Naipaul, although Selvon's dialogue is closer to the quick of the black proletarian of the cities and the Indian peasants of the sugar plantations.

—Ivan Van-Sertima

---

**SHADBOLT, Maurice (Francis Richard).** New Zealander. Born in Auckland, 4 June 1932. Educated at Te Kuiti High School; Avondale College; Auckland University. Married Barbara Magner (second marriage) in 1971; has five children. Journalist for various New Zealand publications, 1952–54; Documentary Scriptwriter and Director, New Zealand National Film Unit, 1954–57. Since 1957, Full-time Writer and Free-lance Journalist. Lived in London and Spain, 1957–60. Recipient: Hubert Church Memorial Award, 1959; New Zealand State Literary Fellowship, 1960, 1970; Katherine Mansfield Award, 1963, 1967; Robert Burns Fellowship, Otago University, 1963; National Association of Independent Schools Award (U.S.A.), 1966; Freda Buckland Award, 1969. Address: 35 Arapito Road, Titirangi, Auckland 7, New Zealand.

PUBLICATIONS

Novels

 *Among the Cinders.* London, Eyre and Spottiswoode, and New York, Atheneum, 1965.
 *This Summer's Dolphin.* London, Cassell, and New York, Atheneum, 1969.
 *An Ear of the Dragon.* London, Cassell, 1971.
 *Strangers and Journeys.* London, Hodder and Stoughton, 1972.

Short Stories

 *The New Zealanders: A Sequence of Stories.* Christchurch, Whitcombe and Tombs, and London, Gollancz, 1959; New York, Atheneum, 1961.
 *Summer Fires and Winter Country.* London, Eyre and Spottiswoode, 1963; New York, Atheneum, 1966.
 *The Presence of Music: 3 Novellas.* London, Cassell, 1967.

Uncollected Short Story

 "End of Season", in *Landfall* (Christchurch), December 1956.

Other

New Zealand: Gift of the Sea, with Brian Brake.  Christchurch, Whitcombe and
    Tombs, and South Pasadena, California, Hutchins, 1963.
The Shell Guide to New Zealand.   Christchurch, Whitcombe and Tombs, 1968; London,
    Joseph, 1969.
Isles of the South Pacific, with Olaf Ruhen.   Washington, D.C., National Geographic
    Society, 1968.


Maurice Shadbolt comments:

I should like to say only that, as a man of my time and place, I have tried to speak for
my time and place. Or perhaps, as a writer, I have simply tried to make sense of it, in the
course of a journey which allows no satisfying destination; my books might thus be seen
as bottled messages tossed out at points along that journey. I know I might have been otherwise: I am frequently unsure why I write at all. But then I look from my study window out
upon a bruised Eden, my country, and I begin again; there is no escape. My equivocal
feeling for the country in which I happened to be born admits of no easy release in either
a physical or literary sense. So I make, in diverse shapes, in stories and novels, my not always
unhappy best of it. As a New Zealander, resident at the ragged edge of Western civilization,
upon the last land of substance to be claimed by mankind, I often feel my involvement with
the rest of the human race rather peripheral—as if upon a lonely floating raft. Yet fires lit
upon the periphery may still illuminate the central and abiding concerns of man—the fires,
I mean, which everywhere the human spirit ignites, and which serve as forge for the artist.
So I make no apology. I might envy a Russian or an American—a Solzhenitsyn or a Mailer—
his capacity to approach the giant themes of the 20th century. But I would not wish, really,
to be otherwise. For I have tried, beyond the particularities of time and place, to observe
and examine those hungers and thirsts which remain constant in man; those hungers and
thirsts which, in my peripheral position, may sometimes be more evident than elsewhere.


                              *          *          *


The full-time professional writer of fiction is a very rare type in New Zealand. Frank
Sargeson is one example, and the most durable one; Maurice Shadbolt is another. Shadbolt
began in 1959 with a volume of short stories, The New Zealanders, which reveal in embryo
most of the themes of his later work and his several methods of approach. The title of the
book, chosen by the publisher, Shadbolt regards as somewhat pretentious, yet the stories
show a wide variety of New Zealanders of different kinds and in sum present his fellow-
countrymen's awareness of their past and their perplexity at its present. The stories, and
those in the following volume, Summer Fires and Winter Country, were criticised as too
superficial in their portrayal of national and individual traits, as slickly contrived and
over-verbose. At the same time, the national problem of identity and the emotional difficulties of people unsure of themselves and enigmatically motivated, as well as a sense of
aspects of life as it is actually lived in the country, all come across forcefully.
In the longer stories in these books, Shadbolt approached the form of the three novellas
which comprise The Presence of Music. These broaden his field of concern to include some
of the problems of the creative personality in New Zealand and collectively represent an
impressive exploration of the complexities of human relationships. One of Shadbolt's most
notable characteristics apparent in these books is his response to Nature. He shares something of the primitivism and romanticism of New Zealand poets in his sensitivity to the
cleansing effects of the countryside on human beings. This is also shown in his first novel,

*Among the Cinders*, a "growing-up" novel, in which the relationship between the young narrator and his eccentric grandfather is developed, in part among the bushlands.

In *This Summer's Dolphin* a new, more mature urbanity controls the lightly satirical treatment of a group of spiritually displaced characters on a harbour island whose relationships are affected by a catalyst in the form of a friendly dolphin. The symbolic juxtaposition of the joy and gentleness of the dolphin with the selfish and materialistic world effectively provides occasion for wit and irony and also for a broad, if possibly somewhat unintegrated, examination of responsibility in personal relationships.

*An Ear of the Dragon*, Shadbolt's most recent novel, is a fictional account of the life of an Italian writer who died in New Zealand in 1964 and whose stories Shadbolt edited. The central character is a writer who is working over the dead man's papers and consoling his widow. Skilfully constructed in a triple narrative which in turn treats of the Italian, the author and his wife, and the author and the Italian's widow, the novel concerns itself seriously with the essential nature of human and literary achievement and the relationship between them. Whether or not the fictional treatment of recently dead and living people's lives and problems is justified by the quality of the novel has been the subject of considerable discussion.

—J. C. Reid

---

**SHARP, Margery.** British. Born in 1905. Educated at Streatham Hill High School, London; Bedford College, University of London, B.A. (honours) in French. Married Major Geoffrey Castle in 1938. Army Education Lecturer in World War II. Lives in London. Address: c/o Westminster Bank Ltd., St. James's Square, London S.W.1, England.

PUBLICATIONS

Novels

*Rhododendron Pie*. London, Chatto and Windus, and New York, Appleton, 1930.
*Fanfare for Tin Trumpets*. London, Barker, 1932; New York, Putnam, 1933.
*The Nymph and the Nobleman*. London, Barker, 1932.
*The Flowering Thorn*. London, Barker, 1933; New York, Putnam, 1934.
*Sophy Cassmajor*. London, Barker, and New York, Putnam, 1934.
*Four Gardens*. London, Barker, and New York, Putnam, 1935.
*The Nutmeg Tree*. London, Barker, and Boston, Little Brown, 1937.
*Harlequin House*. London, Collins, and Boston, Little Brown, 1939.
*The Stone of Chastity*. London, Collins, and Boston, Little Brown, 1940.
*Three Companion Pieces: Sophy Cassmajor, The Tigress on the Hearth, and The Nymph and the Nobleman*. Boston, Little Brown, 1941; London, Collins, 1955.
*Cluny Brown*. London, Collins, and Boston, Little Brown, 1944.
*Britannia Mews*. London, Collins, and Boston, Little Brown, 1946.
*The Foolish Gentlewoman*. London, Collins, and Boston, Little Brown, 1948.
*Lise Lillywhite*. London, Collins, and Boston, Little Brown, 1951.
*The Gypsy in the Parlour*. London, Collins, and Boston, Little Brown, 1954.
*The Eye of Love*. London, Collins, and Boston, Little Brown, 1957.

*Something Light*.   London, Collins, 1960; Boston, Little Brown, 1961.
*Martha in Paris*.   London, Collins, 1962; Boston, Little Brown, 1963.
*Martha, Eric and George*.   London, Collins, and Boston, Little Brown, 1964.
*The Sun in Scorpio*.   London, Heinemann, and Boston, Little Brown, 1965.
*In Pious Memory*.   Boston, Little Brown, 1967; London, Heinemann, 1968.
*Rosa*.   London, Heinemann, 1969; Boston, Little Brown, 1970.
*The Innocents*.   London, Heinemann, 1971.

Plays

*Meeting at Night* (produced London, 1934).
*Lady in Waiting* (produced New York, 1940).   New York, French, 1941.
*The Foolish Gentlewoman* (produced London, 1949).   London, French, 1950.

Other

*The Rescuers* (juvenile).   London, Collins, and Boston, Little Brown, 1959.
*Melisande* (juvenile).   London, Collins, and Boston, Little Brown, 1960.
*Miss Bianca* (juvenile).   London, Collins, and Boston, Little Brown, 1962.
*Miss Turret* (juvenile).   Boston, Little Brown, 1963; London, Collins, 1964.
*Lost at the Fair* (juvenile).   Boston, Little Brown, 1965; London, Heinemann, 1967.
*Miss Bianca in the Salt Mines* (juvenile).   London, Heinemann, and Boston, Little
    Brown, 1966.
*Miss Bianca in the Orient* (juvenile).   London, Heinemann, 1970.
*Miss Bianca in the Antarctic* (juvenile).   London, Heinemann, 1971.

\*          \*          \*

In the forty years from 1930 to 1970 Margery Sharp has brought out some twenty novels.
The genre for which she is best known is light entertainment involving the incongruity of
unclassifiable or even zany characters operating in the most conventional of settings. These
off-beat characters, however, are basically sound, and the conventional persons are basically
kind; all turns out well, and the satire of social assumptions lacks bitterness. Some of the
books are very slightly plotted, depending for their effect on amusing conversation, while
others lead the reader rapidly along a zigzag path through well-planted, but not unexpected,
surprises.
    The novel which best realizes her comic potentialities is her seventh, *The Nutmeg Tree*.
Julia, a minor vaudeville personage, plump and glowing at 39, is discovered in her usual
plight of warding off bailiffs and looking for financial succor from some male source.
Technically, she is also Mrs. Packett, the daughter-in-law of a conservative county family,
widowed in her teens after a necessary wartime marriage. After a year with the kindly Packetts,
she had fled back to the theatre. Now a letter has arrived from her daughter asking her to
come to the south of France to persuade the older Mrs. Packett to assent to her marriage.
Julia genuinely tries to fill her maternal, ladylike role, but since she is without resources
she must use an adventuress's means. Her off-beat nature is immediately recognized by the
young suitor, and a tug-of-war results, for Julia has seen that his essentially picaresque
tastes, so like her own, would prove disastrous in a union with her prim, idealistic daughter.
The price of the young man's renunciation is Julia's refusal, in turn, of the hand of another
guest, the distinguished, elderly Sir William. Julia accepts the sacrifice, but after a paper-chase
all ends well.
    As an entertainer Miss Sharp aims at readers who bring a literary background—though
this is not essential—and a familiarity with the expected social niceties. These last she

values, seeing their utility in easing life's relationships; but she jettisons meaningless social impositions. Of the heroine of *Cluny Brown*, a plumber's niece, everyone keeps saying, "The trouble with young Cluny is she don't know her place." For tall, loping Cluny, with her unmanageable dark hair and large features that distract the imperceptive from her fine eyes and attentive gaze, is a restless explorer, disconcertingly far from the stereotype of clerk, typist, or servant, and her class has no place for such a girl. Neither has the class of county families, but the author sends her as a parlor-maid to such a family in Devon who are harboring also a refugee Polish professor.

Of her less purely comic novels, *The Flowering Thorn* is an unsentimental account of a young London sophisticate's adoption of a little boy and her gradual acceptance of village life. Miss Sharp has written three historical novels. The synoptic, overly thin, *Britannia Mews* presents the social changes from 1865 to 1945 in a West End mews and the courageous life of a woman who, as a young girl, had naively declassed herself.

—Alice Bensen

---

**SHAW, Irwin.** American. Born in New York City, 27 February 1913. Educated at Brooklyn College, New York, B.A. in English 1934. Served as a private in the United States Army Signal Corps, in North Africa, the Middle East, Britain, France and Germany, and as a Warrant Officer, 1942–45. Married Marian Edwards in 1939 (now divorced); has one child. Radio Writer for American networks, 1934–36; Drama Critic, *New Republic*, New York, 1947–48; taught Creative Writing, New York University, 1947–48. Has lived in Europe since 1951. Recipient: O. Henry Award, 1944, 1945; National Institute of Arts and Letters grant, 1946; *Playboy* Award, 1970. Address: P.O. Box 39, Klosters, Switzerland.

PUBLICATIONS

Novels

*The Young Lions.* New York, Random House, 1948; London, Cape, 1949.
*The Troubled Air.* New York, Random House, 1950; London, Cape, 1951.
*Lucy Crown.* New York, Random House, and London, Cape, 1956.
*Two Weeks in Another Town.* New York, Random House, 1959; London, Cape, 1960.
*Voices of a Summer Day.* New York, Delacorte Press, and London, Weidenfeld and Nicolson, 1965.
*Rich Man, Poor Man.* New York, Delacorte Press, and London, Weidenfeld and Nicolson, 1970.

Short Stories

*Sailor off the Bremen and Other Stories.* New York, Random House, and London, Cape, 1940.
*Welcome to the City and Other Stories.* New York, Random House, 1942.
*Act of Faith and Other Stories.* New York, Random House, 1946.

*Mixed Company: Collected Stories.* New York, Random House, 1950; as *Mixed Company: Selected Short Stories*, London, Cape, 1951.
*In the French Style* (stories and screenplay). New York, MacFadden, 1963.
*Love on a Dark Street and Other Stories.* New York, Delacorte Press, and London, Cape, 1965.
*Retreat and Other Stories.* London, New English Library, 1970.

Uncollected Short Stories

"The Mannichon Solution", in *Playboy* (Chicago), 1965.
"Where All Things Wise and Fair Descend", in *Playboy* (Chicago), 1967.
"Whispers in Bedlam", in *Playboy* (Chicago), 1968.
"God Was Here, But Left Early", in *Esquire* (New York), 1969.
"Small Saturday", in *Playboy* (Chicago), 1971.

Plays

*Bury the Dead* (produced New York, 1936). New York, Random House, 1936.
*Siege* (produced New York, 1937).
*The Gentle People* (produced New York, 1939). New York, Random House, 1939.
*Quiet City* (produced New York, 1939).
*Retreat to Pleasure* (produced New York, 1941).
*Sons and Soldiers* (produced New York, 1943). New York, Random House, 1943.
*The Assassin* (produced London and New York, 1945). New York, Random House, 1945.
*The Survivors*, with Peter Viertel (produced New York, 1948). New York, Dramatists Play Service, 1948.
*Patate*, adaptation of a play by Marcel Achard (produced New York, 1958).
*Children from Their Games* (produced New York, 1963). New York, French, 1963.

Screenplay: *In the French Style*, 1963.

Other

*Report on Israel.* New York, Simon and Schuster, 1950.
*In the Company of Dolphins* (travel). New York, Geis, 1964.

Manuscript Collections: Boston University; Morgan Library, Brooklyn College.

Irwin Shaw comments:

If there is one constant thread that can be shown to be woven through almost all of my work, it is that of violence—political, national, international, racial, neighborly, psychological, doctrinaire. My first play, *Bury the Dead*, was laid in the "second year of the war that is to begin tomorrow night". Another play of mine, *The Gentle People*, demonstrated the necessity of violence for peaceful folk who wished to survive in the world of that time (1939). Many of my short stories, such as "Sailor off the Bremen", "Weep in Years to Come", "Preach on the Dusty Roads", reflect the same concern. And of course my novel *The Young Lions* dealt exhaustively with the war, in America, Africa, Italy, England, France and

Germany. And my latest novel, *Rich Man, Poor Man*, is, among other things, a study of the violent climate of America since the end of World War II, and the struggle of one man to subdue the sick violence in his own soul.

At the same time, my work has been involved with the changing social scene, politics, class distinctions, sexual patterns as they form and dissolve. My attitudes have changed from work to work, but a strong streak of irony, sometimes misunderstood and not caught by the critics, has always been evident.

As for style—I have tried to keep mine flexible enough so that I can work in all mediums, the theatre, the short story, the films, the essay, the novel, and fit myself to the particular material I was working on rather than fit the material to a pre-conceived and unchanging form. My search has been for variety and I am still engaged in it.

                                    *        *        *

Irwin Shaw's fiction, both the widely known short stories and the novels, always displays a quality of moral earnestness, a genuine attempt to explore political, sociological, and historical issues in contemporary America. His first novel, *The Young Lions*, uses the alternating points of view of a cosmopolitan liberal intellectual, a naive American Jew, and a German soldier to examine the moral dilemmas involved in World War II. *The Troubled Air* deals with witch-hunting in the broadcast industry in 1950, building to the betrayal of the humane and decent man by the absolute and extreme positions of both the right, who would remove anyone tainted with proximity to Communism from the public air-waves, and the violent left, loyal only to its own dishonest rhetoric. *Lucy Crown*, more narrow sociologically than the other novels, chronicles the failure of a marriage and its effect, for almost twenty years, on the only child. *Rich Man, Poor Man*, following a family through three generations, questions the standard American assumptions that money, physical attractiveness, and material comfort can bring the characters satisfaction or happiness.

Shaw tends to sacrifice the credibility of his characters and situations to the thorough and fair-minded presentation of the sociological ideas and categories they represent. Particularly in *The Young Lions* and *The Troubled Air*, characters shade too easily into abstractions and the moral earnestness of the novels seems somewhat heavy and relentless. Even in *Lucy Crown*, the most dramatically effective and least stereotyped of the novels, characters often talk as if they believe literally in the values they are to represent. In all the novels, Shaw frequently switches the reader's expectation, builds up a situation in one way that he then reverses in order to show the complexity of the idea. Just as the central character, central both morally and politically, in *The Troubled Air* seems to have all the strands of his associations under control, seems with decency and sanity to have mastered the situation, he is assaulted from both the left and the right and his whole world collapses. Similarly, in *Rich Man, Poor Man*, it is the character who had originally been presented as violent and destructive, rather than his apparently humane and industrious brother, who is able to give of himself and to recognize that money and status are not very helpful means of solving the problems of family and relationship that all men face. Such switches, such directly antithetical contrivances, give the novels a blocky kind of structure, a sense of clumsy and massive maneuver designed too schematically to demonstrate a theme.

Despite the allegiance to theme and the heaviness of the artifice, Shaw's novels all contain particular scenes that combine sharp commentary and sensitive observation. *The Troubled Air* depicts an intransigent black man who defends himself in hostile white society by putting on an attitude of shuffling simplicity, a characterization easy to understand in the 1970s but remarkable and original in a novel published in 1951. *Rich Man, Poor Man* presents an effective characterization of the man tightened into his remote concept of his own goodness. *Lucy Crown*, unjustly the least well-known of Shaw's novels, ends with a long and brilliant reconciliation scene between mother and son, a scene that is dramatic, moving, almost entirely convincing and without any sociologically thematic function. The same novel also contains a sharply and sympathetically observed scene of New York bars and restaurants crowded with soldiers on leave during World War II. The most effective parts of Shaw's novels often reveal the talents of the short-story writer, the capacity to present, with intelligence, sensitivity, and a kind of forceful honesty, a single scene, atmosphere, character, or relationship. Shaw's directness and dramatic force are often blurred in the larger and more comprehensive structure of the novel.

—James Gindin

---

**SHAW, Robert (Archibald).** British. Born in Westhoughton, Lancashire, 9 August 1927. Educated at the Truro School, Cornwall; the Royal Academy of Dramatic Art, London. Married Jennifer Bourke in 1952 (divorced); the actress Mary Ure, 1963; has seven children. Stage and Film Actor. Member of the Shakespeare Memorial Theatre Company, Stratford upon Avon, 1949, 1950, and 1953: appeared as Angus in *Macbeth*, Jupiter in *Cymbeline* and Suffolk in *Henry VIII*, 1949; Messenger in *Julius Caesar*, Conrade in *Much Ado about Nothing* and Burgundy in *King Lear*, 1950; Edmund in *King Lear*, Dolabella in *Anthony and Cleopatra*, Tranio in *The Taming of the Shrew* and Gratiano in *The Merchant of Venice*, 1953. Has appeared on the London stage as Rosencrantz in *Hamlet*, 1951; Cassio in *Othello* and Lysander in *A Midsummer Night's Dream*, with the Old Vic Company, 1951; George Lamb in *Caro William*, 1952; Topman in *Tiger at the Gates*, 1955; Lazlo Rimini in *Off the Mainland*, 1956; Blackmouth in *Live like Pigs*, 1958; Lazlo Rajk in *Shadow of Heroes*, 1958; Sergeant Mitchem in *The Long and the Short and the Tall*, 1959; Sewell in *One More River*, 1959; Watson in *A Lodging for the Bride*, 1960; and De Flores in *The Changeling*, 1961; has appeared on the New York stage as Aston in *The Caretaker*, 1961; Mobius in *The Physicists*, 1964; the title role in the musical *Elmer Gantry*, 1970; and Deeley in *Old Times*, 1971. Film appearances include: *The Dambusters*, 1955; *Sea Fury*, 1959; *The Valiant*, 1961; *Tomorrow at Ten*, 1962; *From Russia with Love*, 1963; *The Caretaker*, 1963; *The Luck of Ginger Coffey*, 1964; *The Battle of the Bulge*, 1965; *A Man for All Seasons*, 1966; *Custer of the West*, 1967; *The Birthday Party*, 1968; *Battle of Britain*, 1969; *Royal Hunt of the Sun*, 1969; *Figures in a Landscape*, 1970; *A Town Called Bastard*, 1971; *Labyrinth*, 1971; *Young Winston*, 1971. Recipient: Hawthornden Prize, 1962. Address: c/o Richard Hatton Ltd., 17a Curzon Street, London W.1, England.

PUBLICATIONS

Novels

    *The Hiding Place.* London, Chatto and Windus, and Cleveland, World, 1959.
    *The Sun Doctor.* London, Chatto and Windus, and New York, Harcourt Brace, 1961.
    *The Cure of Souls:*
       I. *The Flag.* London, Chatto and Windus, and New York, Harcourt Brace, 1965.
    *The Man in the Glass Booth.* London, Chatto and Windus, and New York, Harcourt Brace, 1967.
    *A Card from Morocco.* London, Chatto and Windus, and New York, Harcourt Brace, 1969.

Plays

*Off the Mainland* (produced London, 1956).
*The Man in the Glass Booth* (produced London, 1967; New York, 1968).   London,
    Chatto and Windus, 1967; New York, Grove Press, 1968.
*Cato Street* (produced London, 1971).   London, Chatto and Windus, 1972.

Screenplay: *Figures in a Landscape*, 1970.

Plays produced on television.

*     *     *

Actor, playwright, director, script-writer, novelist. One is tempted to feel that a jack of
so many trades must be master of none. Yet Robert Shaw is a highly accomplished and
original novelist, with a rare feeling for words and for people. His characters are customarily
placed in extreme situations, not however in order to provide a sensational adventure-story
(though Shaw is very good at maintaining a narrative form), but so that the novelist can
examine what happens to the human mind in a state of duress, how it reacts when it is faced
with the fact of its own terrifying isolation or when it is brought to understand the difficulties
and treacheries of human relationships.

As one would perhaps expect of an actor, Shaw is very good with dialogue. His brief and
intense *The Man in the Glass Booth* was successfully converted into a play. Yet it would be
quite wrong to assume that Shaw's study of an Eichmann-like Nazi depended on dialogue
alone. Much of the novel's tautness, its feeling of almost suffocating terror and claustrophobia, stems from the exact detail of place, of interiors, of the palpable feeling of the
environment in which Goldman lives and moves and has his being.

The feeling for place is undoubtedly most important and most brilliantly caught in that
very remarkable novel, *The Sun Doctor*. The descriptions of the Angolan swamp and of
the natives themselves are probably as good as anything that has been managed in a novel
of its sort since *The Power and the Glory*. Less successful is the novel's metaphysic, its use
of irony to underpin the central character, Dr. Benjamin Halliday's, sense of the purpose-
lessness of his existence. There is a willed intensity about *The Sun Doctor*, as though Shaw
is determined to wrest the maximum significance from his characters' lives, and while one
can legitimately admire the ambition and energy that have led him to tackle so large a theme,
one is also forced to reflect that the search for significance is responsible for some decidedly
pretentious writing. It is almost as if Conrad, Greene and Patrick White had come together
to parody their own worst excesses. This may seem a harsh judgment on a novel which has
so many virtues, but I think Mr. Shaw deserves to be judged by the highest standards,
and although by such standards *The Sun Doctor* cannot be said totally to succeed, one must
add that there are few contemporary novels which can match its power.

About *The Flag* there need be fewer reservations. This novel is not only successful in the
ways that one would expect—its recreation of the feel of a slum-parish and of bucolic Suffolk
—it also succeeds in making credible the candour and intelligence of its main protagonist,
John Calvin, and of his Christian Socialism and suffering. *The Flag* is a very alert novel
in its probing of corruption, its dark and troubled sense that revolutionary ideals may be
in excess of human possibilities, that, in Yeats' words, it is the worst who are full of passionate
intensity. To say that *The Flag* is very much a novel for our time is not to say that in any
cheap sense it is a fashionable novel, merely that Robert Shaw is one of the most sensitive
and intelligent writers that we have.

—John Lucas

**SHEED, Wilfrid (John Joseph).** American. Born in London, England, 27 December 1930; emigrated to the United States in 1940. Educated at Lincoln College, Oxford, B.A. 1954, M.A. 1957. Married Maria Bullitt Darlington in 1957; has three children. Film Critic, 1957–61, and Associate Editor, 1959–66, *Jubilee* magazine, New York; Drama Critic and Book Editor, *Commonweal* magazine, New York, 1964–67; Film Critic, *Esquire* magazine, New York, 1967–69. Visiting Lecturer in Creative Arts, Princeton University, New Jersey, 1970–71. Since 1971, Columnist for the *New York Times Book Review*. Address: c/o Lantz-Donadio, 111 West 57th Street, New York, New York 10019, U.S.A.

PUBLICATIONS

Novels

A Middle Class Education.   Boston, Houghton Mifflin, 1960; London, Cassell, 1961.
The Hack.   New York, Macmillan, and London, Cassell, 1963.
Square's Progress.   New York, Farrar Straus, and London, Cassell, 1965.
Office Politics.   New York, Farrar Straus, 1966; London, Cassell, 1967.
Max Jamison.   New York, Farrar Straus, 1970; as The Critic, London, Weidenfeld and Nicolson, 1970.

Short Stories

The Blacking Factory, and Pennsylvania Gothic: A Short Novel and a Long Story. New York, Farrar Straus, 1968; London, Weidenfeld and Nicolson, 1969.

Other

Joseph.   New York, Sheed and Ward, 1958.
The Morning After (essays).   New York, Farrar Straus, 1971.

Editor, *G. K. Chesterton's Essays and Poems*.   London, Penguin, 1958.

*       *       *

Wilfrid Sheed's essays on films, drama, literature, sports, and areas of Roman Catholicism, display a mordant wit, revealing detail, and a strong moral sense. Sheed sees accurately what's going on and crackles in telling about it.

As a fiction writer Sheed capitalizes on his essayist talent to populate an absurd world with characters engaged in Twentieth Century man's chief endeavor—search for a self in an increasingly valueless world. To do this Sheed examines the soul-shriveling English public school and university system from which John Chote, a glib, shallow Oxfordian receives a scholarship to flounder around America (*A Middle Class Education*); the fatuous, self-deceiving popular Roman Catholic press which encourages Bert Flax to produce sentimental pieces for a very lowbrow parish periodical (*The Hack*); the vacuity of suburbia, the small town, Greenwich Village, and European Hippie-set playgrounds in which Fred and Alison Cope look for meaning once they have carelessly separated (*Square's Progress*); the quirky introversion of a tiny liberal journal which experiences internecine disorder when its editor suffers a heart attack (*Office Politics*); the ego-tripping atmosphere of the Broadway reviewing scene in which a powerful drama critic skirts the edge of madness (*Max Jamison*).

Sheed's style attracts the reader immediately. The accuracy of the detail creates a lively, contemporary ambiance. The increasingly supple prose reproduces the nuances of modern speech and generally scorches what it aims at. After a shaky and overlong first novel, Sheed turned to a more balanced structure. This has led sometimes to a disquieting sense of unnecessary authorial control, as in *Square's Progress* where Sheed switches the point of view between Fred Cope and his wife Alison almost metronomically. This combined with the satirist's penchant for type-casting fosters an air of contrivance and a willed conclusion. *Max Jamison* staggers because Sheed inexplicably shifts from a marvelous tour through Jamison's mind to the views of his wife and son. This appears to be Sheed's main problem as a novelist. *Office Politics*, his best novel and a contender for the 1966 National Book Award, illustrates his mastery. Here Sheed deftly dissects his social and intellectual targets, and again tosses the point of view among a number of characters, but the shifts have causes and effects in the narrative and the characters suggest complex and compassionate insight, particularly the central figures, Gilbert Twining and George Wren. The resolutions reflect less Sheed's dicta and more the characters' desires.

Sheed's seriousness as a craftsman reflects his world view. In his chaotic world men in crisis ask: "What am I to do about my marriage, my work, my Self?" Max Jamison recognizes that the examined existence offers no easy out: "'Why?' is a question that no man in his right mind asks himself, unless he has an answer rigged." Yet Sheed's characters embark on quests for which he offers only the mature acceptance of what a man truly is and not what an enlarged ego thinks he should be. As George Wren discovers in *Office Politics*: "It doesn't matter who edited the damn thing [*The Outsider*], it always comes out the same." With increasing verbal skill and structural control Wilfrid Sheed continues to offer variations of a modern satirist's warning: Ego, all is Ego.

—Fred Silva

---

**SIGAL, Clancy.** American. Born in Chicago, Illinois, 6 September 1926. Educated at the University of California, Los Angeles, B.A. in English 1950. Served in the United States Army Infantry, rising to the rank of Staff Sergeant, 1944–46. Assistant to the Wage Co-ordinator, United Auto Workers, Detroit, 1946–47. Story Analyst, Columbia Pictures, Hollywood, 1952–54; Agent, Jaffe Agency, Los Angeles, 1954–56. Member, Citizens Committee to Defend American Freedoms, Los Angeles, 1953–56; Group 68, Americans in Britain Against the Indo-China War. Has lived in England since 1957. Recipient: Houghton Mifflin Literary Fellowship, 1962. Address: c/o Jonathan Cape, 30 Bedford Square, London W.C.1, England.

PUBLICATIONS

Novels

*Weekend in Dinlock*. Boston, Houghton Mifflin, and London, Secker and Warburg, 1960.
*Going Away: A Report, A Memoir*. Boston, Houghton Mifflin, 1962; London, Cape, 1963.

*      *      *

Two documentary novels, *Weekend in Dinlock* and *Going Away*, have given Clancy Sigal a large reputation. These novels, imaginative fusions of autobiography, social history and fiction, convey a strong sense of time and place, a powerful feeling of reality.

*Going Away* (Sigal's first novel, though revised and published after *Weekend in Dinlock*) is subtitled "A Report, A Memoir." It is a compendium of significant social and political observations, an "American Studies" novel answering the question, *"What's it like in America these days?"* The time is 1956, the opening days of the Hungarian Revolt, and the autobiographical narrator drives from Los Angeles to New York with the manuscript of a confessional novel, experiencing a nervous breakdown as he passes through America and reviews his past. It is an "on-the-road" novel, a pursuit of lost time, a gathering of the narrator's experiences and a diagnosis of America's spiritual and political malaise: ". . . for years, possibly since adolescence, I have dryly and studiously examined the indications of my own life as a clue to the country at large, as though reading a psychic thermometer."

The narrator is half-Irish, half-Jewish, a radical ex-union-organizer, an ex-Hollywood-agent, an ex-soldier in Occupied Germany; by age 29 he has led half a dozen full, complex lives and reached the end of his road in America. He realizes he must leave America in order to find it. He visits old friends and enemies, sees them in despair and collapse, so he flees his dead past encapsulated in an America of brutalizing forces—billboards, highways, movies, the blank, alienating face of capitalist culture.

Once in England, where he finished *Going Away*, Sigal also wrote a much smaller but beautifully articulated study of Yorkshire mines and miners, *Weekend in Dinlock*. A documentary study of a composite mining village in the midlands, the book compares favorably with George Orwell's classic *The Road to Wigan Pier*. It chronicles the miner's life in the nationalized mines and draws almost the same conclusion Orwell made a generation earlier —that mining is an atrocity, a deadening, dehumanizing torment on which all industrial civilization rests. The novel is also the story of Davie, a Lawrence-like young man who is both a gifted painter and a miner, caught between the need to paint, to escape Dinlock, and the powerful *machismo* ethic of the miners which demands that he stay on the job and prove himself at the coal face. Finally, the narrator leaves Davie wrestling with his irresolvable conflict, still trapped by Dinlock.

This brilliant small study is a logical extension of *Going Away*. The narrator has fled America and found in England's coal country yet another world of dehumanizing technology and alienated individuals. The wide-open feeling of crossing America (the loneliness of the land itself) is replaced by the paranoid claustrophobia of the mine shaft and the paranoid closed society of the provincial village. Both novels chronicle the pressures of modern life on the individual, both reflect Sigal's own history: "I was a member, in good standing, of the Double Feature Generation: nothing new was startling to me." Sigal, in *Going Away*, gives an intense, confessional view of the 1950's in the backwash of McCarthyism, the collapse of the old left, and draws conclusions about his own sense of self: "I see no salvation in personal relationships, in political action, or in any job I might undertake in society. Everything in me cries out that we are meaningless pieces of paste; everything in me hopes this is not the end of the story." Clancy Sigal, in two novels, has depicted America's basic contemporary dilemmas and has asked the questions we must answer to survive.

—William J. Schafer

**SILLITOE, Alan.** British. Born in Nottingham, 4 March 1928. Educated in various Nottingham schools up to the age of 14. Served as a radio operator in the Royal Air Force, 1946–49. Married the poet Ruth Fainlight in 1959; has two children. Travelled in France, Italy and Spain, 1952–58. Since 1970, Literary Adviser to W. H. Allen and Company, publishers, London. Recipient: Authors Club prize, 1958; Hawthornden Prize, 1960. Address: c/o W. H. Allen and Company, 43 Essex Street, London W.C.2, England.

PUBLICATIONS

Novels

Saturday Night and Sunday Morning. London, W. H. Allen, and New York, Knopf, 1958.
The General. London, W. H. Allen, and New York, Knopf, 1960.
Key to the Door. London, Macmillan, and New York, Knopf, 1961.
The Death of William Posters. London, Macmillan, and New York, Knopf, 1965.
A Tree on Fire. London, Macmillan, and New York, Knopf, 1967.
A Start in Life. London, W. H. Allen, 1970; New York, Scribner, 1971.
Travels in Nihilon. London, W. H. Allen, 1971; New York, Scribner, 1972.
Raw Material. London, W. H. Allen, 1972.

Short Stories

The Loneliness of the Long Distance Runner. London, W. H. Allen, and New York, Knopf, 1959.
The Ragman's Daughter. London, W. H. Allen, and New York, Knopf, 1963.
Guzman Go Home. London, Macmillan, and New York, Doubleday, 1968.

Uncollected Short Stories

"Before Snow Comes", in Winter's Tales 14. London, Macmillan, 1968.
"Mimic", in Encounter (London), January 1969.

Plays

All Citizens Are Soldiers, with Ruth Fainlight, adaptation of a play by Lope de Vega (produced Stratford upon Avon, 1967).
This Foreign Field (produced London, 1970).

Screenplays: Saturday Night and Sunday Morning, 1960; The Loneliness of the Long Distance Runner, 1961; The Ragman's Daughter, 1970.

Verse

Without Beer or Bread. London, Outposts Publications, 1957.
The Rats and Other Poems. London, W. H. Allen, 1960.
A Falling Out of Love and Other Poems. London, W. H. Allen, 1964.
Shaman and Other Poems. London, Turret, 1968.

*Love in the Environs of Voronezh and Other Poems.* London, Macmillan, and New York, Doubleday, 1968.

Other

*The Road to Volgograd* (travel). London, W. H. Allen, and New York, Knopf, 1964.
*The City Adventures of Marmalade Jim* (juvenile). London, Macmillan, 1967.


Alan Sillitoe comments:

I write as it comes, without subject or theme, with love and patience, and nothing else.

\*     \*     \*

As Alan Sillitoe's fiction has developed beyond the self-contained and brilliantly presented world of *Saturday Night and Sunday Morning*, the point of view has changed from that of Arthur Seaton, the energetic, unsentimental and superficially self-satisfied protagonist of the first novel, to that of his older brother, Brian, the central figure of *Key to the Door*. Arthur, always aware of the luck involved in the contrast between his current well-paid job at the capstan lathe and his father's life on the dole before World War II, is relatively content so long as he can find a plentiful supply of beer and women. And the depiction of his unsentimental yet perceptive intransigence is forceful. Yet Brian is more the intellectual, more the man who questions and feels strongly, who, like Frank Dawley, the Midlands working-man in *The Death of William Posters* and *A Tree on Fire*, searches for a more complete life he cannot easily find. Brian, in *Key to the Door*, is given more background, more development from childhood, than Arthur was, seen in incidents like that in which he saves pennies to buy a copy of *The Count of Monte Cristo*, his impoverished parents furious that he would waste his hard-scrounged money on a book. And he is portrayed, as a school-boy, reacting strongly and personally to a Shakespeare play, although not in the way his schoolmaster would approve. Part of the difference is also apparent in the treatment of politics. From Arthur's point of view, all political systems are fraudulent rhetoric to cheat the working-man, although he has some sympathy with the Communists because, in England in the fifties, they were so universally despised or ignored. Brian, however, is interested in Communism as an idea, a possible transformation of the society of privilege. When conscripted after the war and sent to Malaya, Brian considers helping a Communist revolution against the establishment he now unwittingly represents. Frank Dawley, running guns to the FLN in Algeria, aids the Communists directly by ideological choice.

Although these presentations of the working-class intellectual developing against strong pressures of class and society are more vulnerable, more likely to slide into sentimentality or rhetorical rant than is Arthur Seaton's tightly controlled perspective, they are also deeper both intellectually and emotionally. Sillitoe always has been interested in ideas, evident even in his second novel, *The General*, in which the symbols of music and mathematics are developed to contrast contradictory attitudes toward experience. In the fiction from *Key to the Door* onward, the ideas become part of a structure integrated into the descriptions of everyday experience, the intellectual becomes part of the perspective. Sillitoe traces the careers of Brian's parents: his mother's childhood as the daughter of a rural blacksmith, his father as the craftsman who slowly decays in an economy that allows him no independent existence (reminding us that, for craftsmen in the north, the slump existed continuously between the two World Wars), the origins of the constant emotional violence and alternations between love and hatred in the parents' lives. Particular scenes of background, like the description of Goose Fair in *Saturday Night and Sunday Morning*, are still done with striking force and clarity in later novels. Especially memorable in *Key to the Door* are a description of the grubby and exciting Saturday night lights and music hall in Nottingham in the twenties and an account of a somewhat baffled and questioning Brian in the warm family kitchen of the girl he eventually has to marry. Sillitoe's prose, too, retains its violent energy, its hard and explosive quality, even in depicting the more complicated growth of the sensitive intellectual from the depression-ridden industrial slums.

In all Sillitoe's fiction, the world is seen as a jungle. Yet the nature of the jungle changes. In the early fiction, like *Saturday Night and Sunday Morning* and "The Loneliness of the Long Distance Runner," society and the exterior world are jungles in which the protagonist, himself neutral, must survive through a combination of luck and shrewd skill. But, from *Key to the Door* on, the exterior jungle is mirrored in the jungle of questions, uncertainties, and false starts within the protagonist himself. Brian Seaton, always more introspective than his brother, Arthur, recognizes all the similarities between jungles in Nottingham, Malaya, and his own soul, tormented by choices between lands, politics, and women. A sense of the brutality of experience is also developed far beyond Arthur's rather cheerful acceptance of a Saturday-night punch-up or a violent blow against institutional authority. For Brian, brutality is deeply ingrained in his origins: he had watched his father, whenever depressed by endless days on the inadequate dole or by lack of cigarets, slug his mother; he had seen his blacksmith grandfather clobber a dog or a child for no apparent reason. And, when he hits his wife in a moment of emotional turmoil, Brian recognizes the same bru-tality in himself. *Key to the Door*, however, shows his capacity to overcome his own sense of brutality. In Malaya, he is able to forego killing a presumed enemy and Sillitoe connects this episode with Brian's learning of his grandfather's death in the character's recognition that violence can be overcome and is not the "key to the door."

The development of the theme of violence is carried further in *The Death of William Posters*. William Posters is the image of the working-class man, defiant, persecuted, who is always hounded by society but never finally caught, never defeated. He can manage only his survival, and he uses violence against others in his own class and himself. Yet Posters is part of the old world, and, in the novel, as Frank Dawley moves out of England and his background, he exorcises the image of Posters, leaving it moribund in Nottingham. Dawley can learn, although not easily, to direct his sense of violence outward, to stop assaulting himself and those close to him and to choose appropriate targets. He can, therefore, join a political or ideological struggle to free Algeria from colonial control as, in the author's point of view, a more focused, intelligent, and worthy outlet for man's brutality.

In his more recent fiction, Sillitoe has also treated a much wider segment of English society. *Saturday Night and Sunday Morning* depicted only the working-class world, an entity, vital in itself, surrounded by a powerful and deadening, but dimly apprehended, establish-ment. *The Death of William Posters* attempts depictions of middle-class characters as well, giving Frank Dawley two middle-class mistresses and a proletarian artist friend of his from Lincolnshire, a posh art-gallery manager. The middle-class characters, however, are not conveyed very effectively. The two mistresses seem identical, superficially placid and com-petent but deeply unfulfilled by their conventional marriages, apparently just waiting for authentic passion, represented by the working-man, to arrive. The art-gallery manager is a cliché of fat, arty sexlessness, competent at business and knowing about art, but unable to form any kind of personal relationship. The husbands of Frank's two mistresses are presented with even less sympathy and complexity, for both represent hollow, educated middle-class men, taking their wives for granted although unable to achieve or realize any sort of life without them. Both are characteristically unable to deal with the violent impulses within themselves, one denying that violence exists, the other so calm superficially that he cracks entirely when Frank runs off with his wife, trying to kill both of them but succeeding only in killing himself. The man unaccustomed to violence can only destroy or be destroyed by it. These portraits, in particular, seem more the demonstration of a social abstraction than the result of observation. Sillitoe also occasionally demonstrates an unexorcised William Posterishness by becoming snide and silly, as he does when one of Frank's mistresses thinks about men from the north: "cloth-capped, hardworking, generous, and bruto, or that was the impression she got from reading a book (or was it books?) called *Hurry on Jim* by Kingsley Wain that started by someone with eighteen pints and fifteen whiskies in him falling downstairs on his way to the top." The reference to Sillitoe's own *Saturday Night and Sunday Morning* is neither subtle nor funny enough to save the remark from becoming just the arid put-down. Frank Dawley is the only one of Sillitoe's heroes about whom the author seems to be defensive, presents defiantly as always skillful, strong, thoughtful and sensitive without being emasculated by sensitivity.

Sillitoe has always felt that the majority of whatever class is unintelligent and unresponsive. He frequently, in much of his fiction, refers to them as "rats." In his long poem called "The Rats," "rats" refer specifically to all the agents of organized religious, political, or industrial society, a category that includes most people. Yet, increasingly in the later fiction, he concentrates his attention on the non-rat, the special person, the man, like Brian Seaton or Frank Dawley, who attempts to challenge experience, to achieve something more than might have been expected. The special person is devoted to work, and *The Death of William Posters* and *A Tree on Fire* contain numerous essays underlining the importance of hard and meaningful work to give dignity to man. The middle-classes and most of the lower-class, especially in England, are diminished by a society that rewards futile, parasitic or soul-destroying work. And the special person, the hero who cares about himself and his work, burns with energy, has roots in a more meaningful past, is, imagistically, "a tree on fire."

Sillitoe's ultimate faith in English society has also changed. Arthur Seaton could remain in the factory, needing only an occasional day in the country, fishing, to retain his sense of dignity. Even his more sensitive brother, Brian, having discovered himself in Malaya, could return to Nottingham. But Frank Dawley needs to get away permanently, leaving the Midlands, Lincolnshire, and London for Spain and Algeria. England is the land of William Posters, completely deadening for the special man on fire. An idyllic retreat on Majorca is also no solution for Frank Dawley. He needs to test his heroism, his specialness, in vital and political connection within the modern world.

Sillitoe's fiction seems to follow that of D. H. Lawrence, sometimes in terms of common themes and attitudes, sometimes in apparent imitation (*The Death of William Posters* particularly resembles *Aaron's Rod*). The similarity is far deeper than a common origin in the working-classes in and near Nottingham. Rather, in the powerful depiction of working-class life, in the need to recognize violence and brutality in human experience, in the incipient romanticism and the essays about work, in the constantly restless thoughtfulness, in the need to get away from England (a need only slowly and hesitantly seen), and even in the occasional densities and lack of sympathy, Sillitoe's fiction genuinely echoes Lawrence's.

—James Gindin

---

**SINCLAIR, Andrew (Annandale).** British. Born in Oxford, 21 January 1935. Educated at Eton College, Buckinghamshire (King's Scholar), 1948–53; Trinity College, Cambridge, 1955–58, B.A. (double 1st) in history 1958, Ph.D. in American history 1962. Served as an Ensign in the Coldstream Guards, 1953–55. Married Marianne Alexandre in 1960 (now divorced); has one child. Harkness Fellow, Harvard University, Cambridge, Massachusetts, and Columbia University, New York, 1959–61; Fellow and Director of Historical Studies, Churchill College, Cambridge, 1961–63; Fellow, American Council of Learned Societies, 1963–64; Lecturer in American History, University College, London, 1965–67. Since 1967, Managing Director, Lorrimer Publishing Ltd., London; since 1969, Film Director and Screenwriter for Timon Films, London. Wrote and directed the films *The Breaking of Bumbo*, 1970, *Under Milk Wood*, 1971, and *Byron's Evil*, 1972. Recipient: Maugham Award, 1967. Address: 47 Dean Street, London W.1, England.

PUBLICATIONS

Novels

*The Breaking of Bumbo.* London, Faber, and New York, Simon and Schuster, 1959.
*My Friend Judas.* London, Faber, and New York, Simon and Schuster, 1959.
*The Project.* London, Faber, and New York, Simon and Schuster, 1960.
*The Hallelujah Bum.* London, Faber, 1963; as *The Paradise Bum*, New York, Atheneum, 1963.
*The Raker.* London, Cape, and New York, Atheneum, 1964.
*Gog.* London, Weidenfeld and Nicolson, and New York, Macmillan, 1967.
*Magog.* London, Weidenfeld and Nicolson, and New York, Harper, 1972.

Uncollected Short Stories

"To Kill a Loris", in *Texas Quarterly* (Austin), Autumn 1961.
"A Head for Monsieur Dimanche", in *Atlantic* (Boston), September 1962.
"Twin", in *The Best of Granta*. London, Secker and Warburg, 1967.

Plays

*My Friend Judas* (produced London, 1959).
*Adventures in the Skin Trade*, adaptation of a work by Dylan Thomas (produced London, 1966; Washington, D.C., 1969). London, Dent, 1967; New York, New Directions, 1968.

Screenplays: *The Breaking of Bumbo*, 1970; *Under Milk Wood*, 1971; *Byron's Evil*, 1972.

Other

*Prohibition: The Era of Excess.* London, Faber, and Boston, Little Brown, 1962.
*The Available Man: The Life Behind the Masks of Warren Gamaliel Harding.* New York, Macmillan, 1965.
*The Better Half: The Emancipation of the American Woman.* New York, Harper, 1965; London, Cape, 1966.
*A Concise History of the United States.* London, Thames and Hudson, and New York, Studio Publications, 1967.
*The Last of the Best: The Aristocracy of Europe in the 20th Century.* London, Weidenfeld and Nicolson, 1969.
*Guevara.* London, Fontana, and New York, Viking Press, 1970.

Translator, *Selections from the Greek Anthology*. London, Weidenfeld and Nicolson, 1967; New York, Macmillan, 1968.
Translator, *Bolivian Diary: Ernesto "Che" Guevara*. London, Lorrimer, 1968.
Translator, with Marianne Alexandre, *La Grande Illusion*, by C. Spaak (scenario). London, Lorrimer, 1968.

Critical Study: in *Intellectuals Today* by T. R. Fyvels, London, Chatto and Windus, 1968.

Andrew Sinclair comments:

One of my great influences, Joyce Cary, wrote that anyone who wished to be a novelist had also to be a historian and a philosopher first. As I had always wanted to try and write one good novel and make one good film before I croaked, I started with the history and political philosophy. I published my early efforts at novels instead of leaving them in drawers. Exposure helps writers as well as strippers. At the same time, history developed my style, allowed me to travel, and paid the rent. I didn't really know how to write a novel until I had published four of them, then found my themes and my style—the thin surface of life over death, the need to act to pass the time of day in Venezuela although action may be useless, the boredom and falsity of motives, the death-struggle between sisters and brothers, an obsession with mythology as the only root to keep a man hoping in this mean mechanized world. And by good fortune, I also fell into movies and independence, serving only a small apprenticeship until I could direct a classic, *Under Milk Wood*, blessing my Scots-Irish stars and Lucifer's luck.

\*         \*         \*

From the beginning Andrew Sinclair established himself as a writer of extraordinary fluency and copiousness, whether in fiction or in American social history. His early novels were light-hearted attempts to capture significant moments in the life of the nineteen-fifties: the misadventures of a young National Service officer in the Brigade of Guards, in *The Breaking of Bumbo*, or life in Cambridge when traditional academic forms were coming apart at the seams, in *My Friend Judas*. Sinclair's awareness of social nuance and his ready ear for changing forms of speech made him an effective observer, though at the cost of making these novels soon seem dated. *The Project* was a deliberate attempt to move to new ground—the moral fable and apocalyptic science fiction—but the result was wooden and contrived. In *The Hallelujah Bum* Sinclair returned to Ben Birt, the cheerfully icono-clastic hero of *My Friend Judas*, and thrust him into a thin but fast-moving narrative about driving across the United States in a stolen car. The book was partly a loving evocation of American landscape, and partly an example of a new fictional genre that emerged in the nineteen-sixties, which showed the impact of America on a visiting Englishman.

Sinclair's next novel, *The Raker*, was a fresh endeavour to get away from the fictional recreation of personal experience, though it was still a projection of personal obsession, in this case what Sinclair has described as a preoccupation with death. *The Raker* is, if anything, too nakedly allegorical, with a strong flavour of Gothic fantasy about it. But it brings together the separate vision of the novelist and the historian, and it is most powerful in its superimposition of the plague-ridden London of the seventeenth century on the modern metropolis. The preoccupation with history and myth in *The Raker* was fully worked out in *Gog*, which is Sinclair's one outstanding contribution so far to contemporary fiction, compared with which he dismisses his previous five novels as no more than "experi-ments in style". "Gog" is a legendary giant of British mythology, personified in the novel by an enormous naked man washed up on the Scottish coast in the summer of 1945. The book is essentially a long picaresque account of his walk to London to claim his inheritance as a representative of the British people. On the way he has many fantastic adventures, some comic, some cruel, but all reflecting Sinclair's extraordinary imaginative exuberance. The journey takes him to many sacred places, such as York Minster, Glastonbury and Stonehenge, and on one level the story is an exploration of the multi-layered past of England, almost like the excavation of an archaeological site. The richness of content is matched by a great variety of formal device: *Gog* draws on the techniques of the comic strip and the cinema, as well as those of the novel. Indeed, since the publication of *Gog* Sinclair has become more and more involved with the cinema, even to the extent of interrupting his career as a writer. At least, the promised sequels to *Gog* have not so far (1971) appeared.

—Bernard Bergonzi

---

**SINCLAIR, Jo.** Pseudonym for Ruth Seid. American. Born in Brooklyn, New York, 1 July 1913. Educated at John Hay High School, Cleveland; attended night classes in playwriting, Western Reserve University, Cleveland. Has worked in a factory, in advertising, as a ghost-writer and trade magazine writer; and for the Works Progress Administration (WPA). Assistant Director, Publicity and Promotion, American Red Cross, Cleveland, 1942–46. Free-lance Writer since 1946. Recipient: Harper Prize, 1946; Daroff Memorial Award, 1956; National Conference of Christians and Jews' Brotherhood Award, 1956; Fund for the Republic Prize, 1956; Wolpaw Playwriting Grant, 1969. Address: 2389 Queenston Road, Cleveland Heights, Ohio 44118, U.S.A.

PUBLICATIONS

Novels

    *Wasteland.* New York, Harper, 1946; London, Macmillan, 1948.
    *Sing at My Wake.* New York, McGraw Hill, 1951.
    *The Changelings.* New York, McGraw Hill, 1955.
    *Anna Teller.* New York, McKay, 1960; London, W. H. Allen, 1961.

Uncollected Short Stories

    "Children at Play", in *Theme and Variation in the Short Story*. New York, Cordon, 1938.
    "Red Necktie", in *America in Literature*. New York, Crofts, 1944.
    "I Was on Relief", in *Social Insight Through Short Stories*. New York, Harper, 1946.
    "The Brothers", in *Cross Section*. New York, Fischer, 1947.

Play

    *The Long Moment* (produced Cleveland, 1951; New York, 1952).

Jo Sinclair comments:

I write because I have to; it's the only meaning I have discovered for my life. Writing is extremely hard for me, and yet nothing else draws me as a profession. I am particularly interested in the psychological aspects of man, woman, and child; in the impact of race and religion on people; and the enormous influence of love and hope on anybody and everybody.

I'd add this: Writer, get yourself a trade, profession, or job—and write, if you must, week ends and holidays. It's no fun to earn little or no money—even on what you consider in your heart a good book. The writer, at least in the United States, needs either a weekly salary or a patron of the arts!

*        *        *

It's not easy to remember when even enlightened people were fearful of consulting a psychiatrist lest they be considered insane or immoral. Now that seeing a "shrink" is almost as casual as going to a dentist, most of the novels which aided and abetted the shift in public opinion toward psychotherapy seem dated. The struggle to survive as reflected in contemporary fiction subsumes without fanfare psychic conflicts that were once daringly controversial.

Jo Sinclair's early fame and fortune were functions of her talent, tenacity, and timing. Back in 1946, alienated by fear and shyness from sources of help, we were ready for *Wasteland*, Jo Sinclair's first and still best-known novel. Winner of the Harper Prize, as well as enthusiastic critical notices, *Wasteland* gained its author a permanent place in that sometimes fickle sun which shines on successful novelists. It is good to be able to report that Jo Sinclair survived the dangerous aspects of these events. The three novels which followed at intervals of approximately five years were spaced far enough apart clearly to imply the kind of deliberation and concern which results in much revising. Unlike the first work, however, they never caught the same public fancy that boomed *Wasteland*.

From the first flash success in 1946 through *Sing at My Wake*, *The Changelings*, and *Anna Teller*, Jo Sinclair's writing certainly did not deteriorate, but readers' interests moved faster toward more violent resolutions than her reasonable humanity allowed for. Jo Sinclair continued to exhort human beings not to be afraid, urging them to scrutinize their wastelands and to cultivate them if possible. She unflinchingly insisted on noting ghetto-problems long before aggressive defenses of minorities had become fashionable. In a real sense she pioneered the so-called Jewish novel, breaking ground for the more sophisticated—but not necessarily more honest—works of Bellow, Malamud, and Roth. Furthermore, Miss Sinclair was virtually the first to focus on the inner conflict in minority identification as amenable to treatment.

Jake, the protagonist of *Wasteland*, was a weakling. He was uncertain of what it meant to be a Jew, anxious and under-potentiated as a man. Supported by his sister's enthusiasm for psychotherapy he finally agreed to consult her psychiatrist. The account of his therapy includes backflashes and relevant digressions, emphasizing particularly the role played in his life by his sister, Debbie. Jake's progress toward understanding is simply and clearly delineated, and the novel possesses a classical unity that Miss Sinclair's later works perforce lack—as her objectives became more complex. Jake's therapy-trip, piloted by a good and wise doctor, was a bold adventure into an unknown which has only since then been charted —*ad nauseam*.

Jo Sinclair's second novel grew out of the author's concern with another kind of alienation. An insecure woman, trying to adjust to an inadequate marriage, finally settled for the mature love of a son she had helped liberate. The problem is personal, but it takes on meaning in the context of Miss Sinclair's championing of all outsiders. If *Wasteland* is a better novel, it is only because the problem is there limited by the structure implicit in the therapeutic process.

*The Changelings* is packed with desperate young people—Jews, blacks, and deviants— each of whom feels as if he were "left in a place secretly, instead of the person who's supposed to be there." The one we care most about is an outrageous tomboy, resembling Debbie in the first novel, whose experiments with sex, race relations, and other existential realities, anticipate contemporary liberation movements.

Finally, in her fourth novel Miss Sinclair engaged a big subject in the life-story of a seventy-four year old woman, who, after fighting in the Hungarian uprisings, fled to America, putative land of freedom. At once bewildered by those aspects of freedom that seemed to her childish, extravagant, and insincere, she eventually, like all Jo Sinclair's protagonists, helped others to transcend the sterility of their wastelands and the bigotries of their ghettoes.

—John A. Weigel

---

**SINGER, Isaac Bashevis.** American. Born in Radzymin, Poland, 14 July 1904; emigrated to the United States in 1935; naturalized, 1943. Educated at Tachkemoni Rabbinical Seminary, Warsaw, 1920–22. Married Alma Haimann in 1940; has one child. Proof Reader and Translator, *Literarishe Bleter*, Warsaw, 1923–33. Since 1935, Journalist for the *Jewish Daily Forward*, New York. Recipient: Louis Lamed Prize, 1950, 1956; National Institute of Arts and Letters grant, 1959; Daroff Memorial Award, 1963; two National Endowment for the Arts grants, 1966; Brandeis University Creative Arts Award, 1969; National Book Award, for children's literature, 1970. D.H.L., Hebrew Union College, Los Angeles, 1963. Member, National Institute of Arts and Letters, 1965; American Academy of Arts and Sciences, 1969; Jewish Academy of Arts and Sciences; Polish Institute of Arts and Sciences. Address: 209 West 86th Street, New York, New York 10024, U.S.A.

PUBLICATIONS

Novels

> *The Family Moskat*, translated by A. H. Gross. New York, Knopf, 1950; London, Secker and Warburg, 1966.
> *Satan in Goray*, translated by Jacob Sloan. New York, Farrar Straus, 1955; London, Peter Owen, 1958.
> *The Magician of Lublin*, translated by Elaine Gottlieb and Joseph Singer. New York, Farrar Straus, 1960; London, Secker and Warburg, 1961.
> *The Slave*, translated by the author and Cecil Hemley. New York, Farrar Straus, 1962; London, Secker and Warburg, 1963.
> *The Manor*, translated by Elaine Gottlieb and Joseph Singer. New York, Farrar Straus, 1967; London, Secker and Warburg, 1968.
> *The Estate*, translated by Joseph Singer, Elaine Gottlieb, and Elizabeth Shub. New York, Farrar Straus, and London, Cape, 1970.
> *Enemies: A Love Story*, translated by Alizah Shevrin and Elizabeth Shub. New York, Farrar Straus, 1972.

Short Stories

> *Gimpel the Fool and Other Stories*, translated by Saul Bellow and others. New York, Farrar Straus, 1957; London, Peter Owen, 1958.
> *The Spinoza of Market Street and Other Stories*, translated by Elaine Gottlieb and others. New York, Farrar Straus, 1961; London, Secker and Warburg, 1962.
> *Short Friday and Other Stories*. New York, Farrar Straus, 1964; London, Secker and Warburg, 1967.

*Selected Short Stories.*   New York, Modern Library, 1966.
*The Séance and Other Stories.*   New York, Farrar Straus, 1968; London, Cape, 1970.
*A Friend of Kafka and Other Stories.*   New York, Farrar Straus, 1970; London, Cape, 1972.

Other

*In My Father's Court* (autobiography), translated by Channah Kleinerman-Goldstein and others.   New York, Farrar Straus, 1966; London, Secker and Warburg, 1967.
*Zlateh the Goat and Other Stories* (juvenile), translated by the author and Elizabeth Shub.   New York, Harper, 1966; London, Secker and Warburg, 1967.
*Mazel and Schlimazel; or, The Milk of a Lioness* (juvenile), translated by the author and Elizabeth Shub.   New York, Harper, 1966.
*The Fearsome Inn* (juvenile), translated by the author and Elizabeth Shub.   New York, Scribner, 1967; London, Collins, 1970.
*When Schlemiel Went to Warsaw and Other Stories* (juvenile), translated by the author and Elizabeth Shub.   New York, Farrar Straus, 1968.
*A Day of Pleasure: Stories of a Boy Growing Up in Warsaw* (juvenile), translated by the author and Elizabeth Shub.   New York, Farrar Straus, 1969.
*Elijah the Slave* (juvenile), translated by the author and Elizabeth Shub.   New York, Farrar Straus, 1970.
*Joseph and Koza; or, The Sacrifice to the Votuda* (juvenile), translated by the author and Elizabeth Shub.   New York, Farrar Straus, 1970.
*Alone in the Wild Forest* (juvenile), translated by the author and Elizabeth Shub.   New York, Farrar Straus, 1971.
*The Topsy-Turvy Emperor of China* (juvenile), translated by the author and Elizabeth Shub.   New York, Harper, 1971.

Editor, with Elaine Gottlieb, *Prism 2*.   New York, Twayne, 1965.

Translator, *Pan*, by Knut Hamsen.   Warsaw, Wilno, 1928.
Translator, *All Quiet on the Western Front*, by Erich Maria Remarque.   Warsaw, Wilno, 1930.
Translator, *The Magic Mountain*, by Thomas Mann.   Warsaw, Wilno, 4 vols., 1930.
Translator, *The Road Back*, by Erich Maria Remarque.   Warsaw, Wilno, 1930.
Translator, *From Moscow to Jerusalem*, by Leon S. Glaser.   New York, privately printed, 1938.

Bibliography: in *Bulletin of Bibliography* (Boston), January-March 1969.

Critical Studies: *Isaac Bashevis Singer and the Eternal Past* by Irving Buchen, New York, New York University Press, 1968; *The Achievement of Isaac Bashevis Singer*, edited by Marcia Allentuck, Carbondale, Southern Illinois University Press, 1969; *Critical Views of Isaac Bashevis Singer*, edited by Irving Malin, New York, New York University Press, 1969; *Isaac Bashevis Singer* by Ben Siegel, Minneapolis, University of Minnesota Press, 1969.

Isaac Bashevis Singer comments:

I believe in story telling and dislike commentary by the author. The events must speak for themselves. A fiction writer who tries to explain his story from a psychological or sociological point of view destroys his chances to endure. I expressed this idea with the words:

Events never become stale; commentary is stale from the very beginning. Commentary has almost destroyed the literature of our present century.

*        *        *

In the early years of the twentieth century Yiddish literature was amongst the most active in the world and in the forefront of the development of the modern sensibility. The Jewish ghettos of New York and Warsaw were literary capitals, although few Gentiles knew it. Isaac Bashevis Singer migrated from Warsaw to New York in 1935 after the great days of the Yiddish literary community were over. He is the last major Yiddish writer but possibly he is the greatest (modern Jews almost all write in Hebrew). Yiddish literature was not provincial; on the contrary it was most cosmopolitan, but it was relatively uninfluenced by the modernist tradition of alienation and revolution of the sensibility that began with Baudelaire. Singer is the exception. He writes in the face of the full blast of the contemporary apocalypse and with a mastery of all the refinements of the twentieth century international style. His stories can be compared at different levels to Bernanos' *Sous le soleil de Satan*, to Céline, to Beckett, even to Artaud. Yet he is singularly independent of specific stylistic influence. His sources lie in the tangled language of the Zohar, the Bible of the Kabbalists, and in the unearthly *Märchen* of the tales of the Hasidic saints.

Martin Buber made the mystic anecdotes of the Hassids popular throughout the civilized world, but his was a sanitized Hasidism, a mystical Judaism that could be assimilated by the assimilated, the Jewish communities of Dahlem and Schlactensee, the fashionable suburbs of Berlin. Singer's Hasidism is inextricably rooted in the *shtetel*, the muddy Jewish villages of Poland and the Warsaw ghetto. There's none of Buber's benignity and enlightenment. There is alienation—from Western civilization, but only incidentally—more fundamentally, from a cultural tradition that goes back through the first Hebrews to be lost in the earliest records of pagan Canaan—alienated but still bound, with nothing left but the witchcraft, the pain, and the blood of brotherhood.

Singer's special vision is revealed most explicitly in his short stories and the novel *Satan in Goray*, but it is there, equally powerful but more implicit in his special handling of the traditional German and Yiddish family epic, *The Family Moskat*, *The Manor* and *The Estate*. In a sense the very subject of these novels is assimilation, but it is a haunted and doomed assimilation, not primarily because we are always aware that the "final solution" of assimilation is the extermination camp, but because the final conclusion is, in the words of James Baldwin, "Who needs to be integrated into a burning house?" In a story based on a Chinese folk tale, the narrator goes to a highly civilized cocktail party in New York and, after he comes away, discovers that the people were all ghosts. It's not just that the rich (Western) cultured Jewish communities of America are haunted by the smoke of the gas ovens. Singer has scarcely ever mentioned them. It's that life itself is haunted. The Goyim are all ghosts, too. We all live in the shadowy frivolous world of a spiritualistic seance. An appreciable number of Singer's stories are about senility and the diseases, loneliness and hopelessness of the discarded old. They have an almost autobiographical veracity but they were written when Singer was not all that old. The point is that somewhere at the heart of reality something is running down. The crystal lattice on which everything is constructed is powdering away. Moral action is irreversible and inconvertible and Carnot's Third Law is operative in the spiritual realm as well as in thermodynamics. This is an ultimately comic vision of the world, ultimate to the point where comedy merges with tragedy into bitter compassion.

So Isaac Bashevis Singer is a writer of philosophic fictions. All too much writing of that sort is amorphous, rhetorical and full of talk by both the author and his characters. Singer is extraordinarily precise and objective. The sensory reality of the Polish village, Warsaw bohemia, New York literary circles, or Florida hotel comes alive with the sharpest imagistic impact. His narrative is continuously dramatic, yet people seem to talk only when they have to, and Singer never talks about them. Of all Yiddish novelists he is probably the least influenced by the standard German novelists, whether Jacob Wasserman or Thomas Mann with their discursiveness, or by Dostoievsky's shameless intimacies. His people suffer the same tortures and nightmares as Dostoievsky's but he writes of them as cleanly as Turgeniev. Singer is probably the most specifically erotic of the major Yiddish writers, but of course by late twentieth century standards that's not very erotic. Sex seems to saturate his characters like a low-grade fever, to emerge in moments of desperation as a substitute for hope. The writer most like him in this regard is Georges Simenon. "Pity and terror," said Aristotle, taking as his model Sophocles, "are the elements of tragedy" —"and eroticism," added Euripides, and so say both Simenon and Singer. People make love in Singer's fictions as they might on a life raft, or as they might hanging all night in ropes on the north face of the Eiger in a storm. Once in a while there is total intimacy, the complete self revelation of love, but at last Carnot's Third Law takes over. Passion cools, but love runs down too. What is left is compassion and comradeship. This of course is what the two bums say at the end of *Waiting for Godot* or what Simenon's Inspector Maigret says as the killers and the dead of the Paris underworld or the bourgeois upper world go by him. So the "modernism" of Isaac Bashevis Singer is far more than a stylistic idiom learned from Stendhal and Baudelaire, James Joyce, German Expressionism, French Surrealism or Russian Futurism. It is the final modernism of the sensibility and the intellect confronted with the long drawn out apocalypse of the twentieth century. He reminds us that it was the Jews who invented apocalyptic writing. Apocalypse, say the theologians, is disappointed prophecy. Singer turns that statement from the business of archangels, beasts with seven heads and chariots of fire to the commonplace relationships of ordinary people.

—Kenneth Rexroth

---

**SINGH, Khushwant.** Indian. Born in Hadali, India, now Pakistan, 2 February 1915. Educated at the Modern School, Delhi; St. Stephens College, Delhi; Government College, Lahore, B.A. 1934; King's College, London, LL.B. 1938; called to the Bar, Inner Temple, London, 1938. Married Kaval Malik in 1939; has two children. Practising Lawyer, High Court, Lahore, 1939–47; Press Attaché, Indian Foreign Service, in London and Ottawa, 1947–51; Member of the Communications Staff, UNESCO, Paris, 1954–56; Editor, *Yejna*, an Indian government publication, New Delhi, 1956–58. Visiting Lecturer, Oxford University, 1964; University of Rochester, New York, 1965; Princeton University, New Jersey, 1967; University of Hawaii, Honolulu, 1967; Swarthmore College, Pennsylvania, 1969. Since 1969, Editor of *The Illustrated Weekly of India*, Bombay. Address: The Illustrated Weekly of India, Dr. Dadabhoy Naoroji Road, Bombay 1, India.

PUBLICATIONS

Novels

> *Train to Pakistan.*  New York, Grove Press, 1955; London, Chatto and Windus, 1956; as *Mano Majra*, Grove Press, 1956.
> *I Shall Not Hear the Nightingale.*  New York, Grove Press, and London, John Calder, 1959.

Short Stories

*The Mark of Vishnu and Other Stories.*  London, Saturn Press, 1950.
*The Voice of God and Other Stories.*  Bombay, Jaico, n.d.; reprinted, 1971.
*A Bride for the Sahib and Other Stories.*  Delhi, Orient Paperbacks, n.d.
*Black Jasmine.*  Bombay, Jaico, 1971.


Other

*The Sikhs.*  London, Allen and Unwin, 1952; New York, Macmillan, 1953.
*A Note on G. V. Desani's "All about Hatterr" and "Hali",* with Peter Russell.  London
    and Amsterdam, Karrell Szeben, 1952.
*Jupji: The Sikh Morning Prayer.*  London, Probsthaein, 1959.
*The Sikhs Today: Their Religion, History, Culture, Customs, and Way of Life.*  Bombay,
    Orient Longman, 1959; revised edition, 1964.
*Fall of the Kingdom of the Punjab.*  Bombay, Orient Longman, 1962.
*A History of the Sikhs, 1469–1964.*  Princeton, New Jersey, Princeton University Press,
    and London, Oxford University Press, 2 vols., 1963, 1966.
*Ranjit Singh: Maharajah of the Punjab, 1780–1839.*  London, Allen and Unwin, 1963.
*Shri Ram: A Biography,* with Arun Joshi.  London, Allen and Unwin, 1963; New York,
    Asia Publishing House, 1968.
*Ghadar, 1919: India's First Armed Revolution,* with Satinda Singh.  New Delhi, R and
    K Publishing House, 1966.
*Homage to Guru Gobind Singh,* with Suneet Veer Singh.  Bombay, Jaico, 1966.
*Hymns of Nanak the Guru.*  Bombay, Orient Longman, 1969.

Editor, *Sunset of the Sikh Empire,* by Dr. Sita Ram Kohli.  Bombay, Orient Longman,
    1967.
Editor, *Sacred Writings of the Sikhs.*  London, Allen and Unwin, n.d.

Translator, with M. A. Husain, *Umrao Jan Ada: Courtesan of Lucknow,* by Mohammed
    Ruswa.  Bombay, Orient Longman, 1961.
Translator, *The Skeleton,* by Amrita Pritam.  Bombay, Jaico, 1964.
Translator, *Land of the Five Rivers,* by Jaya Thadani.  Bombay, Jaico, 1965.
Translator, *I Take This Woman,* by Rajinder Singh Bedi.  Bombay, Jaico, n.d.

*          *          *

Although a prolific and distinguished Sikh historian and editor, Khushwant Singh's
reputation as a fiction writer rests solely upon *Mano Majra* (also published in the United
States under the title *Train to Pakistan*), a harrowing tale of events along the borders of the
newly divided nations of India and Pakistan in the summer of 1947.

The atrocities that accompanied the division of these nations had an enormously depressing
effect on a world that had just fought a long, bitter war to defeat practitioners of genocide.
The somewhat artificial division of the subcontinent (the boundaries remain in dispute)
had been strictly along religious lines: Pakistan was to be a nation of Moslems; India, of
Hindus, Sikhs, and what Singh calls "pseudo-Christians." There were, however, colonies
of non-coreligionists left within each nation. Rather than settle down to peaceful coexistence
or permit a passive exchange of populations, partisans on both sides set out on a violent
campaign of annihilating the communities that were trapped on their ancestral lands beyond
friendly borders.

*Mano Majra* is laid against a background of this ruthless and senseless mass destruction.
This powerful novel derives its title from a squalid border town, where a rail line crosses
from India into Pakistan. At first this mixed community of Sikhs and Moslems is undis-

turbed by the violence that is breaking out elsewhere on the frontier, but inevitably it, too, is caught up in the mass hysteria as ominous "ghost trains" of slain Sikhs begin to arrive in town from across the border. Agitation for reprisals follows when the Moslems of the town are at last rounded up and fanatics urge the Sikhs of the community to kill their former neighbors as the train carrying them to Pakistan passes through town.

Singh's story contrasts the ineffectualness of the educated and ruling classes with the power of the violent and irrational peasants. Early in the story the town's only educated citizen, a Hindu money-lender, is gruesomely murdered by a band of Dacoity (professional bandits). Juggut Singh, a passionate Sikh farmer with a bad record, is suspected of the crime—though he played no part in it—and imprisoned; at the same time, an educated young former Sikh, Iqbal, comes to the community to agitate for a radical cause and is also imprisoned on suspicion of being a Moslem League agent. While these two are off the scene, the unlighted trains with their cargoes of dead begin to roll into town, and the agitation for reprisals begins. Both the young radical and a government commissioner, Hukum Chand, are unable to prevent the vicious plot against the fleeing Moslems from being carried out, and collapse emotionally; but in an extraordinary gesture of self-sacrifice, Juggut Singh—who had been in love with a Moslem girl—foils the plotters and allows the train to roll over his body "on to Pakistan."

Singh's terse fable suggests a profound disillusionment with the power of law, reason, and intellect in the face of elemental human passions. The philosophy that sparked his tale seems to be expressed through the thoughts of Iqbal, the young radical, as he realizes his helplessness and drifts off into a drugged sleep the night of the climactic incident of the train's passing: "If you look at things as they are . . . there does not seem to be a code either of man or of God on which one can pattern one's conduct. . . . In such circumstances what can you do but cultivate an utter indifference to all values? Nothing matters."

The same disillusioned tone characterizes Singh's second novel, *I Shall Not Hear the Nightingale*, but the rather wooden tale is almost overwhelmed by heavy-handed ironies. The action occurs about five years before that of the earlier novel, at a time when the British are expressing a willingness to get out of India once the Axis nations have been defeated in World War II. Sher Singh, the ambitious but lazy son of a Sikh senior magistrate, cannot decide between two worlds, "the one of security provided by his father . . . and the other full of applause that would come to him as the heroic leader of a band of terrorists." His dabblings in terrorism—actually abetted by a cynical young British civil servant—end in the pointless killing of a village leader, who has also been a political spy. Sher is suspected of the murder and imprisoned, but on the advice of his mother (when his father will not speak to him) he refuses to betray his companions. The British release him for lack of evidence, and he is honored as a kind of local hero—seemingly his political future is assured. His father is even honored by the British.

The novel takes a much dimmer view of the human capacity for compassion and self-sacrifice than *Mano Majra* (at one point Sher Singh reflects that "for him loyalties were not as important as the ability to get away with the impression of having them"), so that the novel ends not with the kind of thrilling gesture that its predecessor did, but with the obsequious magistrate, Sher Singh's father, sitting in the Britisher's garden observing, "As a famous English poet has said, 'All's well that ends well.'" The title of the book comes from Sher Singh's reply to his mother when she asks, "What will you get if the English leave this country?" He replies lyrically, "Spring will come to our barren land once more . . . once more the nightingales will sing." Khushwant Singh evidently thinks not, if the land is to fall into such self-serving hands as Sher Singh's.

His ironic short stories resemble Angus Wilson's and express a similar disillusionment about man's rationality. Singh is a brilliant, sardonic observer of a world undergoing convulsive changes; and his novels provide a unique insight into one of the major political catastrophes of this century. His difficulties in fusing his editorial comments with the action in his stories, however, cause his novels to remain principally dramatized essays.

—Warren French

**SLAVITT, David (Rytman).** Pseudonym: **Henry Sutton.** American. Born in White Plains, New York, 23 March 1935. Educated at Phillips Academy, Andover, Massachusetts, graduated 1952; Yale University, New Haven, Connecticut, 1952–56, B.A. (magna cum laude) 1956; Columbia University, New York, M.A. 1957. Married Lynn Neyer in 1956; has three children. Instructor, Georgia Institute of Technology, Atlanta, 1957–58; Associate Editor, *Newsweek* magazine, New York, 1958–65. Address: 11401 South West 87th Avenue, Miami, Florida 33156, U.S.A.

PUBLICATIONS

Novels

> *Rochelle; or, Virtue Rewarded.* London, Chapman and Hall, 1966; New York, Delacorte Press, 1967.
> *The Exhibitionist* (as Henry Sutton). New York, Geis, 1967; London, Geis, 1968.
> *Feel Free.* New York, Delacorte Press, 1968; London, Hodder and Stoughton, 1969.
> *The Voyager* (as Henry Sutton). New York, Geis, and London, Hodder and Stoughton, 1969.
> *Vector* (as Henry Sutton). New York, Geis, 1970; London, Hodder and Stoughton, 1971.
> *Anagrams.* London, Hodder and Stoughton, 1970; New York, Doubleday, 1971.

Verse

> *Suits for the Dead.* New York, Scribner, 1961.
> *The Carnivore.* Chapel Hill, University of North Carolina Press, 1965.
> *Day Sailing and Other Poems.* Chapel Hill, University of North Carolina Press, 1969.

Other

> Translator, *The Eclogues of Virgil.* New York, Doubleday, 1971.

Manuscript Collection: Beinecke Rare Book Library, Yale University, New Haven, Connecticut.

David Slavitt comments:

I distrust general statements, particularly those of writers about their own work. It's rather like the operation of a child's top—if the machine were to pause to explain itself, it would fall down. And my particular career makes general comment even more difficult than it might otherwise be. Any one of my books is for a partial audience and would (and I expect does) bore or repel those who are the natural members of the other parts. While this mostly pleases me, it does make general remarks difficult—they'd be likely to bore or repel everyone at once. And inasmuch as I make my living at this game—and from these audiences—that wouldn't be a very good thing to do.

\*     \*     \*

A highly energetic and productive writer, David Slavitt has published three volumes of verse, a translation of Virgil's *Eclogues*, three novels under his own name, and three widely advertised and financially successful novels under the pseudonym of Henry Sutton. The novels written under his own name are comic treatments of frequent contemporary literary themes, the parody of the Jewish family novel in *Rochelle; or, Virtue Rewarded*, or the satire on the college literary festival that invites outside poets and novelists in *Anagrams*. In these novels, the structures and the plots are vehicles for stringing together a very clever and often funny high-level patter, like that of a sophisticated stand-up comic. Often the lines have a pointed contemporary relevance ("The 'fella' was Governor Rockefeller's word, which means, so far as I can tell, 'peasant.'"); frequently, the patter has a mock eloquence that both parades and parodies Slavitt's knowledge and education. Beneath the comedy, Slavitt's narrators rest in a kind of smug Philistinism, a pride in having seen through the pretense and shallowness of others, an attitude which is never countered or modified by any deeper or more questioning perspective in the novels. Yet the comedy itself, literate, graceful, and well-timed, is sufficient to sustain interest in the novels.

The Henry Sutton novels, written without verbal comedy or pyrotechnics in a flat and banal prose, follow the details of well-known public careers: *The Exhibitionist* provides a fictional account of the lives of Hollywood's most famous father and daughter film stars; *The Voyeur* parallels the career of America's most public anti-Puritan and most commercially successful entrepreneur of clubs and bars selling food and drink in an atmosphere of vicarious sexual stimulation. These novels, in which characters show no change and all behaviour is given a single pop-psychological cause, follow a simple formula: sexual encounter every so many pages, what would commonly be regarded as sexual perversion making up every other sexual encounter, interspersed reflections moralizing about this glamorously sinful life at predictable intervals.

The interest that the Henry Sutton fiction generates is one dependent on gossip columns, movie magazines, or the kind of salacious comment about widely-known public figures that characterizes rather uninventive bar-room conversations. One has heard that so-and-so, the sex symbol, is really a Lesbian or that this famous actor seduced then betrayed his first altruistic drama coach, and then waits in the Sutton fiction for the rumor to be confirmed. It always is, and in exactly the reductive terms common to the gossip column or gossip interchange, unadorned by any humor, insight, or recognition that the author might be dealing with a stereotyped version of a semi-public legend. The Slavitt fiction is similarly reductive, for the differences between the fiction under his own name and that written under the pseudonym are differences of sophistication, wit, degree of invention, not differences in basic attitude toward experience. In both kinds of novel, all complexity and humanity are carefully omitted.

The Henry Sutton fiction adds to the formula explicit moralistic comment that invariably underlines the high price of success or the depravity of the famous of the loss of private self-respect in the public figure. All these banal reflections are purveyed in fictional terms appropriate to conventional fictional versions of the wholesome boy and girl next door. Less obviously, and never crudely demonstrated in the careers of well-known public figures, the David Slavitt fiction re-inforces the same kind of conventionally reductive morality, parades the precepts that fame or achievement or intelligence exacts too high a price and that the notorious or noteworthy or special are inevitably damned. Such fiction, carefully pitched to audiences at superficially different levels under the guise of different authorship, can titillate either audience while simultaneously confirming its simplistic prejudices.

—James Gindin

**SMITH, Emma.** British. Born in Newquay, Cornwall, 21 August 1923. Married R. L. Stewart-Jones in 1951 (died, 1957); has two children. Recipient: Atlantic Award, 1947; Rhys Memorial Prize, 1949; Black Memorial Prize, 1950. Address: c/o Peter Janson-Smith Ltd., 42 Great Russell Street, London W.C.1, England.

PUBLICATIONS

Novels

> *Maidens' Trip*. London, Putnam, 1948.
> *The Far Cry*. London, MacGibbon and Kee, 1949; New York, Random House, 1950.

Uncollected Short Stories

> "The Turning-Point", in *Winter's Tales for Children 1*. London, Macmillan, and New York, St. Martin's Press, 1965.
> "The Boat", in *Miscellany Two*. London, Oxford University Press, 1965.

Other

> *Emily: The Story of a Traveller* (juvenile). London, Nelson, 1959; as *Emily: The Traveling Guinea Pig*, New York, McDowell Obolensky, 1959.
> *Emily's Voyage* (juvenile). London, Macmillan, and New York, Harcourt Brace, 1962.
> *Out of Hand* (juvenile). London, Macmillan, 1963; New York, Harcourt Brace, 1964.
> *No Way of Telling* (juvenile). London, Bodley Head, and New York, Atheneum, 1972.

Emma Smith comments:

What one writes for children is quite as important as what one writes for adults, and I'm not at all sure it isn't more important; because what children read can colour their feelings, and affect their behaviour, for the rest of their lives. If they are sufficiently impressed, what they read is absorbed into themselves and becomes part of their own experience to an extent that can't be so after they've grown up. Consequently, everything I write for children is really full of secret messages and exhortations and warnings of what I think the whole of life, which lies ahead waiting for them, is all about, and what I think they're going to need in the way of equipment.

\*       \*       \*

Emma Smith has published two novels and several books designed for the young. In all her work there is a precise creation of character, a sensitive response to setting, and a careful attention to detail.

Her first book, *Maidens' Trip*, set in England during the second World War, is the story of three girls, Emma, Charity, and Nanette, who, during the manpower shortage, become "boaters" and guide their motorboat *Venus* and its "butty" *Adrane* over the network of locks and canals running through the heartland of the English countryside. Their adventures, observations and problems make up the substance of the story as, without formal plot or characterizations, Miss Smith manages to create a forward-moving, frequently suspenseful narrative. The adventures become misadventures as, awkwardly at first, and later with more skill, the girls make the trip for supplies from London to Birmingham and back again. There are the physical hardships of rain and cold, blistered hands and aching backs; the hazards of machinery broken down, accidents with other boats, mud that sticks and locks that refuse to open. Charity is the housewife; Nanette, the coquette; Emma, the steady "professional" who directs the whole operation. The reality of the constant rain and cold with the contrasted coziness of the little cabin on the *Venus*, the ubiquitous steaming cups of tea, the hearty flavor of the cooking stew, and the sights and sounds of the loading docks form a background for the most memorable feature of the book—the characterization of the girls and their realization of the world of the "boaters", a world completely apart from that of a great nation at war. Even the brief appearance of a young soldier on leave is no more than a vague reminder of the danger and death in the world beyond. The other notable feature of the book is Miss Smith's understanding of the three young girls forced by circumstances to deal with people and situations totally foreign to them. Each is a real person; not one of the three a stereotype of the adolescent. Each, however, at the same time is realized as young and immature.

Miss Smith's second book, *The Far Cry*, is even more distinguished than *Maidens' Trip*. It is the story of an eccentric schoolmaster, Mr. Digby, who flees with his fourteen year old daughter, Teresa, to India and the sanctuary of his elder daughter, Ruth, to escape his estranged second wife, Teresa's mother. Their departure and trip across the ocean make up the first two sections of the book; the trip across India by train, the third. The fourth section is Ruth's as the reader discovers that she and her husband Edwin have not succeeded in resolving all the differences of their marriage. The last section is a kind of summary for Teresa when, confronted by the sudden horror of her father's death from a heart attack and Ruth's accidental death in Calcutta, she is obliged to become more mature than seems possible for her to be. Even at the end she "had yet to learn that the relationships of people are never established, are ever mutable. . . ." All the principal characters are skillfully drawn: Mr. Digby, a failure as husband, father, and schoolmaster; Ruth, an exotic beauty without confidence in herself or her role as wife; Teresa, sensitive and perceptive, escaping from the repression of her unimaginative Aunt May; and Edwin, the young English tea planter who understands India and his tea workers far more than he does his beautiful wife Ruth.

The journey from England to India, the introduction of India itself, and the daily life of the tea plantation make up the chronology of the story. There is hardly a plot in the conventional definition of the term since there is little doubt from the beginning that Teresa and her father will escape her American mother. The real focus of the novel is on Teresa and her varying responses to the people she meets and the constantly shifting scenery she observes. Miss Smith is especially good in realizing the detail of setting—the crowded life on ship board; the arresting picture of camels and their drivers at Port Suez, a kind of point in time for Teresa; the arrival at Bombay and the acquisition of their bearer, Sam; the long uncertain train trip in dirty cramped quarters; the English way of life Ruth has created in the midst of a tea plantation. The book is as full of the multitude of details as is reality itself, but each so skillfully chosen that it seems precisely right for the observation of the character to whom it is assigned. *The Far Cry* is a beautifully sensitive novel of time, place, and character.

The books for the younger audience show the same nice attention to detail and careful delineation of character found in the earlier novels. *Out of Hand* is an account of a family of children on vacation who in fact far from getting "out of hand" protect their elderly hostess from her well meaning but unfeeling relatives. The traveling guinea-pig Emily is yet another of Miss Smith's memorable characters. She has made more than one exciting and perilous voyage, first in *Emily: The Story of a Traveller* and then in *Emily's Voyage*.

If Miss Smith has so far chosen a rather limited range, her virtue is that she has done well what she set out to do, and her work shows an unusual sensitivity to people and a real artist's eye for detail.

—Annibel Jenkins

---

**SMITH, Iain Crichton.** British. Born on the Isle of Lewis, Outer Hebrides, Scotland, 1 January 1928. Educated at the University of Aberdeen, M.A. (honours) in English 1950. Served as a Sergeant in the British Army Education Corps, 1950–52. Secondary School Teacher, Clydebank, 1952–55. Since 1955, Teacher of English, Oban High School. Recipient: Arts Council grant, 1968, for poetry, 1968, 1969, 1971; BBC Award, for television play, 1970; Book Council Award, 1970; Silver Pen Award, for poetry, 1971. Address: 42 Combie Street, Oban, Argyll, Scotland.

PUBLICATIONS

Novels

   *Consider the Lilies.* London, Gollancz, 1968; as *The Alien Light*, Boston, Houghton Mifflin, 1969.
   *The Last Summer.* London, Gollancz, 1969.
   *My Last Duchess.* London, Gollancz, 1971.

Short Stories

   *Burn is Aran* (includes verse; in Gaelic). Glasgow, Gairm Publications, 1960.
   *An Dubh is an Gorm* (in Gaelic). Aberdeen, Aberdeen University, 1963.
   *Maighsirean is Ministearan* (in Gaelic). Inverness, Club Leabhar, 1970.
   *Survival Without Errors and Other Stories.* London, Gollancz, 1970.

Plays

   *An Coileach* (in Gaelic; produced Glasgow, 1966). Glasgow, An Comunn Gaidhealach, 1966.
   *A' Chuirt* (in Gaelic; produced Glasgow, 1966). Glasgow, An Comunn Gaidhealach, 1966.

Verse

   *The Long River.* Edinburgh, M. Macdonald, 1955.
   *New Poets 1959*, with others. London, Eyre and Spottiswoode, 1959.
   *Deer on the High Hills.* Edinburgh, Giles Gordon, 1960.
   *Thistles and Roses.* London, Eyre and Spottiswoode, 1961.
   *The Law and the Grace.* London, Eyre and Spottiswoode, 1965.

*Biobuill is Sanasan Reice* (in Gaelic).   Glasgow, Gairm Publications, 1965.
*At Helensburgh.*   Belfast, Festival Publications, 1968.
*From Bourgeois Land.*   London, Gollancz, 1970.
*Selected Poems.*   London, Gollancz, 1970.
*Penguin Modern Poets 22*, with others.   London, Penguin, 1972.
*Love Poems and Elegies.*   London, Gollancz, 1972.


Other

*Iain Am Measg nan Reultan* (in Gaelic; juvenile).   Glasgow, Gairm Publications, 1970.

Translator, *Ben Dorain*, by Duncan Ban Macintyre.   Preston, Lancashire, Akros Publications, 1969.
Translator, *Poems to Eimhir*, by Sorley Maclean.   London, Gollancz, and Newcastle upon Tyne, Northern House Publications, 1971.


Bibliography: in *Lines Review* (Edinburgh), no. 29, 1969.


Critical Study: interview in *Scottish International* (Edinburgh), 1971.


Iain Crichton Smith comments:

There is no real connection between my first two novels; one is about old age, the other about youth. However, I would like to write novels which have imagistic content, like poetry, but not "poetic" novels. I like them if possible to be generated from some kind of image or "given" imaginative fact.


\*          \*          \*


With three novels and a collection of short stories, in English, and three collections of short stories in Gaelic, Iain Crichton Smith's persona and stature as a prose-writer begin to define themselves. There is a great deal of interaction between the different parts of his *oeuvre* (prose, poetry and plays; English and Gaelic), and one senses that the vital growth-points are in the poetry and the short story, with some evidence of Gaelic being his better medium for the short story.

An autobiographical shadow hangs over much of his prose work. His creative imagination does not win free of it for long, and is sometimes hesitant in this freedom. As a result Mrs. Scott is the only closely-observed character in *Consider the Lilies*, and the others—Big Betty or Donald Macleod for example—often leave a sense of uneasiness when they speak, as though their words and their minds did not mesh. *The Last Summer* is more frankly autobiographical, a re-creation of schooldays, with Malcolm, the narrator, having the greatest psychological depth and credibility. The subsidiary characters here, however, are more closely observed than those in *Consider the Lilies*. Both these novels are mainly memorable, in fact, for the skilfully-built-up mood and atmosphere.

*My Last Duchess* is strongly autobiographical also, at times uncritically so. Mark Simmons comes from a crofting background but seems as divorced from it as his name. The long detailed discussion of Hamlet's character, in the flashback scene in a "northern city's" cafe, is there because it looms large in the author's mind rather than in Mark Simmons'. There are many other autobiographical passages, some of them fitting well into the plot, and perhaps it is mainly in the attempts to disguise the autobiographical mainspring of the novel that dislocations occur.

This book gives the impression of being based partly on material which had a separate existence. The first chapter, with its central theme of a disillusioning visit to a once-famous novelist, is a variant of Smith's Gaelic story "Am Bard", and it includes also some pretentious verbiage, as in the passage about the "Fortinbrases of our civilizations" (p. 16). The rest of Part I, set in the main in the northern University town, has a tangential relation to the theme of Part II, and it may be that earlier material has been modified slightly to fit into a new plot. Part II is much more successful, in that it is written with great pace, and is not marred by false images or gaucheries. There is a fairly steady increase of tension, as we see Lorna maturing and Mark disintegrating, and each character showing a high degree of self-observation. This developing situation is very sensitively handled, and the succession of short chapters is well designed to plot the changing irrational course of events, and their inevitable conclusion, leading to the statement in Part III: ". . . after all this was where he must have wanted to be, in the coldness of truth."

Part II of *My Last Duchess* is Iain Crichton Smith's most sustained achievement in prose to date, and suggests a talent which is still strongly developing. It may be, however, that his talent for writing short stories is stronger still. *Survival Without Error and Other Stories* is an uneven collection in some ways, but it has four or five stories of high quality, in which a strong sense of plot and a beautiful economy of style are brought together in a memorable way. "Survival Without Error" and "Je t'aime" and "Joseph" stand out in a collection that has much subtlety and delicacy. If we consider the variety of this collection, and add to it the still greater variety of his work in Gaelic, there is strong evidence that it is on the scale of the short story that he can best organise his insights, and best minimise the disadvantage (for a novelist) of an intense but limited range of interests.

—Derick S. Thomson

---

**SNOW, C(harles) P(ercy)**; Baron Snow of Leicester. British. Born in Leicester, 15 October 1905. Educated at Alderman Newton's School, Leicester; University College, Leicester, B.Sc. 1927, M.C. 1928; Christ's College, Cambridge, Ph.D. 1930. Married Pamela Hansford Johnson, *q.v.*, in 1950; has one child. Fellow, 1930–50, and Tutor, 1935–45, Christ's College, Cambridge. Editor, *Discovery*, Cambridge, 1938–40. Technical Director, Ministry of Labour, London, 1940–44 (C.B.E. [Commander, Order of the British Empire], 1943); Civil Service Commissioner, 1945–60. Director, English Electric Company, London, 1947–64. Parliamentary Secretary, Ministry of Technology, 1964–66. President, Library Association, 1961. Director, Educational Film Centre, London, 1961–64. Rede Lecturer, Cambridge University, 1959; Godkin Lecturer, Harvard University, Cambridge, Massachusetts, 1960; Regents Professor, University of California, Berkeley, 1960; Rector, St. Andrews University, Scotland, 1961–64. Recipient: Black Memorial Prize, 1955. Interim Fellow, Silliman University, Philippines; Fellow, Yale University, New Haven, Connecticut; Extraordinary Fellow, Churchill College, Cambridge; Honorary Fellow, Christ's College, Cambridge. LL.D., University of Leicester, 1959; University of Liverpool, 1960; St. Andrews University, 1962; Polytechnic Institute of Brooklyn, New York, 1962; University of Bridgeport, Connecticut, 1966; University of York, 1967; D.Litt., Dartmouth College, Hanover, New Hampshire, 1960; Bard College, Annandale-on-Hudson, New York, 1962; Temple University, Philadelphia, 1963; Syracuse University, New York, 1963; University of Pittsburgh, 1964; D.H.L., Kenyon College, Gambier, Ohio, 1961; Washington University,

St. Louis, 1963; University of Michigan, Ann Arbor, 1963; D.Phil.Sc., Rostov State University, East Germany, 1963; D.Sc., Pennsylvania Military College, Chester, 1966. Fellow, Royal Society of Literature, 1951. Honorary Member, American Academy of Arts and Letters. Knighted, 1957; Life Peer, 1964. Address: 85 Eaton Terrace, London S.W.1, England.

PUBLICATIONS

Novels

*Death under Sail.* London, Heinemann, and New York, Doubleday, 1932; revised edition, Heinemann, 1959.
*New Lives for Old* (published anonymously). London, Gollancz, 1933.
*The Search.* London, Gollancz, 1934; Indianapolis, Bobbs Merrill, 1935; revised edition, London, Macmillan, 1958; New York, Scribner, 1959.
*Strangers and Brothers:*
　*Strangers and Brothers.* London, Faber, 1940; New York, Macmillan, 1958.
　*The Light and the Dark.* London, Faber, 1947; New York, Macmillan, 1948.
　*Time of Hope.* London, Faber, 1949; New York, Macmillan, 1950.
　*The Masters.* London, Macmillan, and New York, Macmillan, 1951.
　*The New Men.* London, Macmillan, and New York, Scribner, 1954.
　*Homecomings.* London, Macmillan, 1956; as *Homecoming*, New York, Scribner, 1956.
　*The Conscience of the Rich.* London, Macmillan, and New York, Scribner, 1958.
　*The Affair.* London, Macmillan, and New York, Scribner, 1960.
　*Corridors of Power.* London, Macmillan, and New York, Scribner, 1964.
　*The Sleep of Reason.* London, Macmillan, 1968; New York, Scribner, 1969.
　*Last Things.* London, Macmillan, and New York, Scribner, 1970.
*The Malcontents.* London, Macmillan, and New York, Scribner, 1972.

Plays

*The View over the Park* (produced London, 1950).
*The Supper Dance*, with Pamela Hansford Johnson. London, Evans, 1951.
*Family Party*, with Pamela Hansford Johnson. London, Evans, 1951.
*Spare the Rod*, with Pamela Hansford Johnson. London, Evans, 1951.
*To Murder Mrs. Mortimer*, with Pamela Hansford Johnson. London, Evans, 1951.
*The Pigeon with the Silver Foot*, with Pamela Hansford Johnson. London, Evans, 1951.
*Her Best Foot Forward*, with Pamela Hansford Johnson. London, Evans, 1951.
*The Public Prosecutor*, with Pamela Hansford Johnson, adaptation of a play by Georgi Dzhagarov, translated by Marguerite Alexieva (produced London, 1967). London, Peter Owen, 1969.

Other

*Richard Aldington: An Appreciation.* London, Heinemann, 1938.
*Writers and Readers of the Soviet Union.* Watford, Hertfordshire, Farleigh Press, 1943.
*The Two Cultures and the Scientific Revolution.* London, Macmillan, and New York, Cambridge University Press, 1959; revised edition, as *Two Cultures and a Second Look*, London and New York, Cambridge University Press, 1964.

*Science and Government.*   Cambridge, Massachusetts, Harvard University Press, and London, Oxford University Press, 1961.

*A Postscript to Science and Government.* Cambridge, Massachusetts, Harvard University Press, and London, Oxford University Press, 1962.

*Magnanimity.* St. Andrews, Scotland, University of St. Andrews Students Representative Council, 1962.

*C. P. Snow: A Spectrum: Science, Criticism, Fiction.*   New York, Scribner, 1963.

*Variety of Men.*   London, Macmillan, and New York, Scribner, 1967.

*The State of Siege.*   New York, Scribner, 1969; Oxford, Oxfam, 1970.

*Public Affairs.*   London, Macmillan, and New York, Scribner, 1971.

Editor, with Pamela Hansford Johnson, *Winter's Tales 7.*   London, Macmillan, 1961; as *Stories from Modern Russia*, New York, St. Martin's Press, 1962.


Bibliography: by Bernard Stone, in *The World of C. P. Snow* by Robert Greacen, Lowestoft, Suffolk, Scorpion Press, 1962.

*     *     *

C. P. Snow's *Strangers and Brothers*, a series of eleven novels on the life, career and experiences of the narrator, Lewis Eliot, has been among the most widely read internationally and the most widely discussed works of English fiction of the past half-century. Snow himself was born of the lower middle-class in Leicester in 1905, went to grammar school there, proceeded by scholarship to Cambridge, became a research student, fellow and tutor of Christ's College, a civil servant during the second world war as administrator of scientific personnel at the Ministry of Labour and then after the war a Civil Service Commissioner. He was knighted for his services to the state and in 1964, with the return to power of Harold Wilson, was made a life peer and until 1966 was a member of the Labour Government as Parliamentary Under-Secretary at the Ministry of Technology. His public life, then, has lain outside literature, and in this he resembles many novelists past and present. But with others the public life has little to do with the fiction they wrote; little light is thrown on the novels of Peacock by the knowledge that he was a clerk in the East India Company and not much more on Trollope's by the knowledge that he was employed for many years in the Post Office. With Snow, it seems different: there is an obvious relationship between his career and the matter of his novels, so much so that it is difficult not to wonder at times whether the fact that he was writing his novel sequence did not dictate some of the details of his career.

He has told us himself that he knew his "vocation as a novelist" before he was twenty, but he was trained as a scientist, and an early novel, *The Search*, is a story about a young research scientist. It is very plainly the work of the author of *Strangers and Brothers*; like it, it is written in the first person, and its value lies very largely in the insight it offers into what it is like to be a scientist. In fact, it is the unusual combination in Snow of novelist and man involved in "science-and-government" that has captured the public imagination and given him a place in English life occupied by no other novelist since H. G. Wells and Arnold Bennett. The first volume of *Strangers and Brothers*, itself called by that title, appeared in 1940; the eleventh and last, *Last Things*, in 1970. The work as a whole maintains a remarkable consistency. "The inner design" of the work, according to Snow himself, consists of "a resonance between what Lewis Eliot sees and what he feels," and it may be said that the greater his emotional involvement the greater and more satisfying the resonance. Eliot himself is a man from the lower middle-class of the English Midlands who has made his own way in the world, become a barrister and fellow and law tutor of a Cambridge college and, then during the war, moved into higher ranks of the Civil Service and seen the makings of great decisions—the decision, for instance, to make an atomic bomb, the subject of the novel *The New Men*—at first hand. Though Eliot is not Snow, plainly his career pretty closely parallels his creator's.

The result is an impressive work in which Snow appears, in Ford Madox Ford's phrase, as the "historian of his own times". One has the sense that the experience and findings of a lifetime are being embodied in a fiction uncommonly near to the actual. Snow's is very much a masculine world. He knows men particularly well in their traditionally masculine attributes, men as they are in the company of other men and in competition with other men. It is too crude to suggest, as is sometimes done, that his theme is power. What he knows all about is ambition and the conflicts between ambition on the one hand and the conscience or the stresses of the private life on the other. It is largely because of this that he has so often been compared with Trollope. Reading Snow, one often recalls Archdeacon Grantley in *Barchester Towers* torn between filial grief and the desire to succeed his dying father as bishop.

But there is, of course, another reason for the common comparison with Trollope, though in this instance Trollope is being used simply as a convenient label for the Victorian novel as a whole. Snow is writing in reaction against the subjective novel of Joyce and Virginia Woolf; he is attempting to revive the vast panoramic canvas of Victorian fiction. Even so, it seems likely that he was much less directly influenced by the Victorians than by Proust.

Snow's gifts are seen at their most characteristic and probably at their finest in the novel *The Masters*. The scene is a Cambridge college, the master is dying, and a new master must be elected by the fellows from one of them. What Snow brings out brilliantly is the complexity of the motives that sway the contenders and their supporters, and what he is writing is nothing less than a novel about the nature and practise of politics. The Cambridge senior common room is the world in little. Much of the authority of the novel comes from what might be called Snow's moral agnosticism. He—or rather Lewis Eliot—observes, reports, analyses, comments, but makes no moral judgment; he knows that motives are inextricably mixed. The result is an impression of massive fairness. And perhaps the findings of the sequence as a whole are summed in its title: men are at once strangers to one another and brothers. The paradox seems to be at the heart of the sequence.

This means that Snow's concern is anything but wholly with public faces. Frank Kermode, in his essay on Snow, has said that Snow "is never much interested in, probably doubts the existence of," what D. H. Lawrence called "the last naked him." This may well be true; but it does not mean that "the naked him" has no place in Snow's work. What fascinates him is the juxtaposition of "the naked him" and the public face; he never writes better or more convincingly than when he is dealing with the incommunicable private agony behind the public face. The best example of this is probably to be found in *Homecomings*, which, more than many of the novels in the sequence, is Lewis Eliot's personal story. It relates the break-up of his first marriage and the happiness he finds in his second; what is most surely and most movingly conveyed is the muteness and incommunicability of adult suffering, the suffering a man may carry within him behind the façade of a successful public life.

Kermode, in the essay from which I have quoted, finds "Snow, for all his gifts of pathos, is, like most scientists, a meliorist at least." Yes; but not in every sense, as the title *The Sleep of Reason* shows; and one remembers that Thomas Hardy called himself a meliorist. In *The Light and the Dark*, Snow writes:

> I believe that some parts of our endowment are too heavy to shift. The essence of our nature lay within us, untouchable by our own bonds or any other's, by any chance of things or persons, from the cradle to the grave. But what it drove us to in action, the actual events of our lives—these were affected by a million things, by sheer chance, by the interaction of others, by the choice of our own will.

Snow's view of man is, in fact, a sombre one. In his world the race does not necessarily go to the swiftest or the most brilliant. "Some parts of our endowment are too heavy to shift," and Snow is fascinated by those whose initial promise or whose goodness is frustrated by those parts of their endowment that are too heavy to shift, an intractability or recalcitrance at the depth of their being. One recalls George Passant, in *Strangers and Brothers*, *Homecomings*, and *The Sleep of Reason*, and Roy Calvert in *The Light and the Dark*, characters that are destroyed by a flaw within.

Snow's prose is the plainest possible; it is as though a puritan streak in him forces him to eschew grace, poetry or elegance. But it is a serviceable prose, and there are times when the very honesty and directness of expression produce a powerful eloquence; and even if the prose seems unsubtle it does not prevent Snow from making subtle analyses of character and motive. Lewis Eliot has often been found pompous and even pretentious, and he may be these things, for he is a figure in what is called the Establishment. The fact remains that his pompousness and pretentiousness are much more than compensated for by his human qualities, his love of his brother, his love of his son, in *Last Things*, his gift for friendship, his sense of responsibility. Throughout the *Strangers and Brothers* sequence there run a largeness of mind and a humility in the face of the variety and vagaries of human nature. The impulse is always to see and to understand rather than to judge, and what finally impresses is the balance Snow holds between the private and the public aspects of his characters.

—Walter Allen

---

**SONTAG, Susan**. American. Born in New York City, 16 January 1933. Educated at the University of California, Berkeley, 1948–49; University of Chicago, 1949–51, B.A. 1951; Harvard University, Cambridge, Massachusetts, 1954–57, M.A. 1955; St. Anne's College, Oxford, 1957. Married in 1950 (divorced, 1957); has one child. Instructor in English, University of Connecticut, Storrs, 1953–54; Teaching Fellow in Philosophy, Harvard University, 1955–57; Editor, *Commentary*, New York, 1959; Lecturer in Philosophy, City College of New York, and Sarah Lawrence College, Bronxville, New York, 1959–60; Instructor, Department of Religion, Columbia University, New York, 1960–64; Writer-in-Residence, Rutgers University, New Brunswick, New Jersey, 1964–65. Directed the films *Duet for Cannibals*, 1969, and *Brother Karl*, 1971. Recipient: American Association of University Women Fellowship, 1957; Rockefeller Fellowship, 1965; Guggenheim Fellowship, 1966. Address: c/o Farrar, Straus and Giroux, 19 Union Square West, New York, New York 10003, U.S.A.

PUBLICATIONS

Novels

    *The Benefactor*. New York, Farrar Straus, 1963; London, Eyre and Spottiswoode, 1964.
    *Death Kit*. New York, Farrar Straus, 1967; London, Secker and Warburg, 1968.

Uncollected Short Stories

    "The Will and the Way", in *Partisan Review* (New Brunswick, New Jersey), Summer 1963.
    "Man with a Pain", in *Harper's* (New York), April 1964.

Plays

    *Duet for Cannibals* (screenplay). New York, Farrar Straus, 1970.

Screenplays: *Duet for Cannibals*, 1969; *Brother Karl*, 1971.


Other

*Against Interpretation* (essays).   New York, Farrar Straus, 1966; London, Eyre and
    Spottiswoode, 1967.
*Trip to Hanoi.*   New York, Farrar Straus, 1969.
*Styles of Radical Will* (essays).   New York, Farrar Straus, 1969.


\*      \*      \*


Traditionally readers have approached works of fiction as verbal structures which reveal
and generally make statements about a pre-existing "real" subject. The writer may represent
his subject directly, "imitating" in accordance with conventional understandings about the
probable behavior of the human and the natural order; or he may render his subject indirectly by presenting a metaphor which stands for and usually implies a generalization
about that same reality. Thus traditional criticism was designed to judge the verisimilitude
of fiction and to provide a way of understanding metaphor, allegory and parable as symbolic
statements. It is impossible, however, to discuss the fiction of Susan Sontag in critical terms
derived from this essentially naturalistic tradition, just as Miss Sontag herself has attempted
to construct a new critical approach to do justice to those works of *avant-garde* artists whose
rendering of the modern world she finds significant.

The tough, polemical essays collected in *Against Interpretation* and *Styles of Radical Will*
are more impressive than Miss Sontag's fiction thus far, which too often seems contrived
to illustrate a doctrine. For Miss Sontag, the final "most liberating value of art" is "transparency", which means experiencing "the luminousness of the thing in itself, of things being
what they are." Interpretation, which seeks to replace the work with something else—
usually historical, ethical or psychological paraphrase—is essentially "revenge which the
intellect takes upon art." To interpret is "to impoverish, to deplete." Miss Sontag's chief
interest as a critic is the work of artists (especially film makers) whose work is misunderstood
because it resists "being reduced to a story". Thus Miss Sontag observes that in his film
*Persona* Bergman presents not a story, but "something that is, in one sense, cruder, and, in
another, more abstract: a body of material, a subject. The function of the subject or material
may be as much its opacity, its multiplicity, as the ease with which it yields itself to being
incarnated by a determinate plot or action." Deliberately frustrating any conventional
attempt to determine "what happens", the new novels and films are able, she maintains, to
involve the audience "more directly in other matters, for instance in the very processes of
seeing and knowing. . . . The material presented can then be treated as a thematic resource,
from which different (and perhaps concurrent) narrative structures can be derived as variations." The artist intends his work to remain "partly encoded": the truly modern consciousness challenges the supremacy of naturalism and univocal symbolism.

While vestiges of naturalistic situations remain in Miss Sontag's fiction (her story "The
Will and the Way", for example, seems to be an allegory concerning the image of women in
modern life), "interpretation" is by definition more or less irrelevant. *The Benefactor* is in
its general outline a dream novel; its "thematic resource" is the problem of attaining selfhood and genuine freedom. Just as Miss Sontag sees Montaigne's essays as "dispassionate,
varied explorations of the innumerable ways of being a self", the hero of *The Benefactor*
uses his dreams as a means of achieving freedom. "It seemed to me," Hippolyte concludes,
that "all my life had been converging on the state of mind . . . in which I would finally be
reconciled to myself—myself as I really am, the self of my dreams. That reconciliation is
what I take to be freedom." The device which keeps the reader from treating the novel as
paraphrasable allegory is the deliberate ambiguity of the narrative frame: we are left to
decide whether the narrative is an account of what happened or an account which is at least

in part the construction of a mad Hippolyte whose dreams are symbolic transformations, in the usual Freudian sense, of "what happened". Miss Sontag owes a good deal to Sartre and Camus, but even more to the *auteurs* of *Last Year at Marienbad* and *L'Avventura*. *Death Kit* has as its concern the failure of a man who has no true self: "Diddy, not really alive, had a life. Not really the same. Some people are their lives. Others, like Diddy, merely inhabit their lives." Diddy commits a murder, or thinks he commits a murder: there is no way of determining this, but what matters is how Diddy handles the possibility that he is a murderer, and how he tries to appropriate the self of a blind girl whom he selflessly "loves". Out of the materials of his life Diddy assembles his death; out of his failure the reader may assemble an understanding of vanity, inauthenticity and death. Wholly successful or not, *The Benefactor* and *Death Kit* are haunting works, effective to the degree to which the reader can accept Miss Sontag's powerful arguments elsewhere about the exhaustion of the naturalistic tradition. As the American critic E. D. Hirsch puts it, "Knowledge of ambiguity is not necessarily ambiguous knowledge."

—Elmer Borklund

---

**SOUTHERN, Terry.** American. Born in Alvarado, Texas, 1 May 1924. Educated at Southern Methodist University, Dallas, Texas; University of Chicago; Northwestern University, Evanston, Illinois, B.A. 1948; the Sorbonne, Paris, 1948–50. Served in the United States Army, 1943–45. Married Carol Kaufman in 1956; has one child, Nile. Recipient: British Screen Writers Award, 1964. Address: R. F. D., East Canaan, Connecticut, U.S.A.

PUBLICATIONS

Novels

Flash and Filigree. London, Deutsch, and New York, Coward McCann, 1958.
Candy, with Mason Hoffenberg (as Maxwell Kenton). Paris, Olympia Press, 1958; as Terry Southern and Mason Hoffenberg, New York, Putnam, 1964; London, Geis, 1968.
The Magic Christian. London, Deutsch, 1959; New York, Random House, 1960.
Blue Movie. Cleveland, World, 1970.

Short Stories

Red-Dirt Marijuana and Other Tastes. New York, New American Library, 1967; London, Cape, 1971.

Plays

Screenplays: Candy Kisses, with David Burnett, 1955; Dr. Strangelove, with Stanley Kubrick, 1964; The Loved One, with Christopher Isherwood, 1965; The Cincinnati Kid, with Ring Lardner, Jr., 1966; Barbarella, 1967; Easy Rider, 1968; End of the Road, 1969; Electric Child, 1970.

Other

*The Journal of "The Loved One": The Production Log of a Motion Picture.*   New York,
    Random House, 1965.

Editor, with others, *Writers in Revolt.*   New York, Frederick Fell, 1963.

*     *     *

Southern has baffled American reviewers and annoyed critics since the appearance in
1958 of *Flash and Filigree*, which had been well received in England. This novel and subsequent efforts have variously been labeled "pointless," "pornographic," and "sick" for
their thematic content or apparent lack of it. The form of Southern's fiction similarly defies
easy classification: part put-on, part satire, part parody, with occasional stretches of
"straight," well-written prose. Plotting is rarely conventional: *Flash and Filigree* is really
two completely separate plots, while *The Magic Christian* and *Candy* are disjointedly
picaresque. His recent *Blue Movie* is straightforwardly told, but conventional style and plotting seem strange indeed when used to chronicle (in living detail) the filming, and subsequent
seizure by a Vatican Army, of a Hollywood-produced stag movie.

The main plot in *Flash and Filigree* centers on a dermatologist-sports car buff named Dr.
Frederick Eichner, who is haunted by a prank-playing transvestite named Felix Treevly.
Eichner kills his weird nemesis and is tried for murder and acquitted. Dr. Eichner is too aloofly
repulsive to sustain interest, but the heroine of the sub-plot, Nurse Babs of Eichner's clinic,
is just "darling," Southern's satirical tip-off word about the pretty, puerile, American Dream
Girl he loves to parody. Objects of satire also include television shows ("What's My Disease?"), the medical profession, law courts, the drug scene, the American mania for gadgetry
and technical data and the crazy-culture of California. But the best scene is the seduction in
a taxicab of "darling" Babs the button-nosed beauty.

*Candy* (co-authored with Mason Hoffenberg) was originally published pseudonymously
in Paris in 1958, then published in America in 1964, by which time its shocking pornography
had lost some sting. The titular heroine, a female, saccharine Candide, is reminiscent also of
De Sade's Justine, Harold Gray's Little Orphan Annie and Southern's own Nurse Babs.
The book may be read equally as a satire on cherished American institutions and current
delusions, or as a geography of pornography; in Southern's mind the two areas obviously
blend, perhaps in their common language of cant and cliche. Candy encounters faddists
and fakes in the stronghold of western culture: in academia, the mad bi-sexual Professor
Mephisto: in science, the mother-ridden Irving Krankheit, author of *Masturbation Now!*:
in religion, Guru Grindle, who convinces Candy of matter's unreality even as he enjoys her
body. The most successful scene evolves as a psychotic, witless hunchback—whom sentimental Candy re-names Derek—copulates with the heroine ("he needs me") while he struggles to keep his half-mind on his real goal—money.

Whatever social targets the earlier works neglected, *The Magic Christian* shoots for. Guy
Grand, a rich practical joker, spends ten million a year "making it hot for them": he builds
superlong autos that jam up intersections; publishes a newspaper cluttered with foreign
language phrases; enters a cannibalistic panther in a dog show; and goes on safari with a
75 mm. howitzer. He also inserts short pornographic scenes into film classics; in *The Best
Years of Our Lives*, the war hero's hook-hands grapple under his sweetheart's skirt. Guy also
opens grocery stores with preposterously low prices—then closes them the same night, to
re-locate in mysterious places.

In 1967, Southern's collected short stories, published as *Red-Dirt Marijuana and Other
Tastes*, revealed greater range and sympathy than suspected. Southern writes well of boys
and men, of poor southern whites, of razor fights between Negro brothers, of an American
in Paris who is "too hip," and of a surrealistic auto trip through Mexico. The writing is
uneven and Southern's questionable taste prevails, but style and mood in the successful

stories are superbly lyrical. The recent *Blue Movie* explores sexual boundaries never visited by Candy, but boredom is defeated only by Southern's fine ear for trade talk and some brilliantly awful Hollywood types. Southern is familiar with movie argot and technique, having written scenarios for *Dr. Strangelove, The Loved One* and *Barbarella.* In his movies, he has employed the same shock therapy by indecency and dehumanization which dominates his novelistic black-comedies.

—Frank Campenni

SPARK, Muriel (Sarah).   British.   Born in Edinburgh.  Educated at James Gillespie's School for Girls, Edinburgh. Married S. O. Spark in 1938 (divorced); has one child. Worked in the Political Intelligence Department of the British Foreign Office during World War II. General Secretary of the Poetry Society, and Editor of the *Poetry Review*, London, 1947–49. Recipient: *The Observer* Story Prize, 1951; Italia prize, for radio drama, 1962; Black Memorial Prize, 1966. LL.D., University of Strathclyde, Glasgow, 1971. O.B.E. (Officer, Order of the British Empire), 1967. Lives in Rome. Address: c/o Macmillan and Company, 4 Little Essex Street, London W.C.2, England.

PUBLICATIONS

Novels

*The Comforters.*  London, Macmillan, and Philadelphia, Lippincott, 1957.
*Robinson.*  London, Macmillan, and Philadelphia, Lippincott, 1958.
*Memento Mori.*  London, Macmillan, and Philadelphia, Lippincott, 1959.
*The Ballad of Peckham Rye.*  London, Macmillan, and Philadelphia, Lippincott, 1960.
*The Bachelors.*  London, Macmillan, 1960; Philadelphia, Lippincott, 1961.
*The Prime of Miss Jean Brodie.*  London, Macmillan, 1961; Philadelphia, Lippincott, 1962.
*The Girls of Slender Means.*  London, Macmillan, and New York, Knopf, 1963.
*The Mandelbaum Gate.*  London, Macmillan, and New York, Knopf, 1965.
*The Public Image.*  London, Macmillan, and New York, Knopf, 1968.
*The Driver's Seat.*  London, Macmillan, and New York, Knopf, 1970.
*Not to Disturb.*  London, Macmillan, 1971; New York, Knopf, 1972.

Short Stories

*The Go-Away Bird and Other Stories.*  London, Macmillan, 1958; Philadelphia, Lippincott, 1960.
*Voices at Play* (includes radio plays).  London, Macmillan, 1961.
*Collected Stories I.*  London, Macmillan, 1967; New York, Knopf, 1968.

Plays

*The Interview*, in *Transatlantic Review* (London and New York), Summer 1960.
*Doctors of Philosophy* (produced London, 1962).  London, Macmillan, 1963.

Verse

*The Fanfarlo*.  Aldington, Kent, Hand and Flower Press, 1952.
*Collected Poems I*.  London, Macmillan, 1967.


Other

*Child of Light: A Reassessment of Mary Shelley*.  London, Tower Bridge Publications, 1951.
*Emily Brontë: Her Life and Work*, with Derek Stanford.  London, Peter Owen, 1953.
*John Masefield*.  London, Peter Nevill, 1953.
*The Very Fine Clock* (juvenile).  New York, Knopf, 1958; London, Macmillan, 1969.

Editor, with Derek Stanford, *Tribute to Wordsworth*.  London, Wingate, 1950.
Editor, *A Selection of Poems*, by Emily Brontë.  London, Grey Walls Press, 1952.
Editor, with Derek Stanford, *My Best Mary: The Letters of Mary Shelley*.  London, Wingate, 1953.
Editor, *The Brontë Letters*.  London, Peter Nevill, 1954.
Editor, with Derek Stanford, *Letters of John Henry Newman*.  London, Peter Owen, 1957.


Critical Study: *Muriel Spark* by Karl Malkoff, New York, Columbia University Press, 1968.

\*       \*       \*

Muriel Spark as a novelist is as much *sui generis* as any writer with a highly-developed literary sense, and a great gift for mimicry, might be expected to be. Secreted in the modish patter of her prose there lie the echoes—as residue or tribute—of her love of earlier stylists: John Henry Newman, Max Beerbohm, Marcel Proust. These "sapphires in the mud," however—to quote T. S. Eliot a little out of context—diminish as the stream of her novels progresses, the "literary" element becoming less and less and a deft handling of the vernacular more and more her chosen means of expression. In so far, though, as Muriel Spark's fiction can be associated with any existing literary tendency it belongs to one of two recent traditions in modern English Catholic fiction. On the one hand, we have the novels of Graham Greene where sympathy, compassion and emotional identification characterize the feeling-tone of the writing. On the other hand, the novels of Evelyn Waugh, distinguished by their satirical approach and a sense of cold intellectual distancing between the author and his characters. To the first tradition belongs such a novelist as Mrs. Spark's near-coeval Gabriel Fielding. To the second, Muriel Spark herself. Like Evelyn Waugh, she may be defined as a novelist who does not suffer fools gladly, though the exposure of their foolishness affords her an evident delight. A novelist not over-burdened with feelings of pity or charity, she conceals sharp claws beneath a velvet glove. With a strong sense of righteousness, utterly unallied to the "pi" and largely disguised by a sustained show of wit, she is both prosecutor and executioner—a Torquemada figure, secure in judgment, often unrecognised as such by the readers on account of her fantasy and modish ridicule.

Muriel Spark's fictional career began when she won the *Observer* short story competition in the Christmas of 1951. Her winning entry was entitled "The Seraph and the Zambesi," a religious satire on the commercial festivity of Christmas. Mrs. Spark was fond of quoting Cardinal Newman's diction that a Christian view of the universe was essentially a poetic one. Both before and after her submission to the Roman Faith, she wrote verse, and her fiction is studded with sudden isolated poetic vistas. Sometimes—as in her short story "Daisy Overend"—the passing beam has little more than atmospheric brilliance and nostalgic suggestion about it:

I am seldom in the West End of London, But sometimes I have to hurry across the Piccadilly end of Albemarle Street where the buses crash past like giant orgulous parakeets, more thunderous and more hectic than the Household Cavalry. The shops are on my left and the Green Park lies on my right under the broad countenance of drowsy summer. It is then that, in my mind's eye, Daisy Overend gads again, diminutive, charming, vicious, and tarted up to the nines.

At other times, as in the concluding sentence to *The Ballad of Peckham Rye*, the *epiphany* (to employ James Joyce's term) is more meaningful, the point being that, for the author, there literally is "another world than this"—namely, the spiritual and eternal one:

It was a sunny day for November, and, as he drove swiftly past the Rye, he saw the children playing there and the women coming home from work with their shopping-bags, the Rye for an instant looked like a cloud of green and gold, the people seeming to ride upon it, as you might say there was another world than this.

But more than a poetic view of life, religion—for Muriel Spark—seems to imply a satirical attitude: a sense of things seen *sub species aeternitatis* and therefore found grievously, flagrantly wanting. As Caroline Rose remarks in *The Comforters*, when her boy-friend accuses her of being bad-tempered after attendance at Mass, "It makes the flesh despair."

In an interview Muriel Spark once stated that things seemed to fall into place on her becoming a Catholic. This statement probably applies more to her as a person than as an artist. All the characteristic and conspicuous qualities of her style, structure and imagination were certainly formed before her reception into the Roman Church. It would, however, be correct to say that it was a Christian vision of things (she was an Anglican before becoming a Roman). To her, as a novelist, might be applied those words wherewith she described Sandy Stranger, the schoolgirl who was to become a nun in *The Prime of Miss Jean Brodie*: "Her mind was as full of . . . religion as a night sky is full of things visible and invisible." It is the kind of mind to which the angelical and demonic orders are a strict reality. Ronald Bridges, the epileptic in *The Bachelors*, reflects, "It is all demonology and to do with the creatures of the air," and this—with all the qualifications called for by an orthodox theology —might be accepted as the author's own position.

Religious as the texture of this author's mind substantially is, it would be a mistake to consider Muriel Spark as the writer of a partisan or ideological fiction. She sees herself, one may conjecture, as defending the basic truth of her Faith but not, by any means, as the champion of the whole Catholic ethos, collectively speaking. Very soon after her reception, in fact, many details and statements in her first novel, *The Comforters*, as well as two of her short stories—"The Black Madonna" and "Come Along, Marjorie" (from her collection *The Go-Away Bird*)—though totally without heretical content, gave offence to certain of her co-religionists. Justice demands one should also remark that Mrs. Spark's relentless adherence to what, for many, is an abstraction, and her dismissal of the claims of ordinary loyalty or humanity in the light of this higher good, makes for a distasteful element in her work to those readers who are of a humanistic or humanitarian persuasion. Sandy Stranger's betrayal of her old teacher in *The Prime of Miss Jean Brodie* and the hounding of George by the ghost of Needle in "The Portobello Road" are examples of this anti-humane aspect of Mrs. Spark's writing. The point is that hers is a lonely vision—something of a paradox in a writer as outwardly popular as she undoubtedly is. One may query just how many of the thousand readers diverted by her understand what she is really saying.

A small number of critics might conceivably agree that Muriel Spark's masterpieces are to be found among her shorter fictions, and certainly a few of the tales which have Africa as their background—"The Go-Away Bird," "Bang-bang You're Dead", "The Curtain Blown by the Breeze," and "The Pawnbroker's Wife"—must count among her finest achievements. None the less, it is with her novels that she has won a resounding success in the eyes of the general public. In all, they show an impressive range of theme and subject, though their mood, feeling-tone and technique do not perhaps stretch to a corresponding gamut.

Her first novel, *The Comforters*, is a rather spooky tale about a group of odd people with bohemian affiliations. C. P. Snow, who read the typescript and recommended the book to its publisher, described Muriel Spark as "a novelist with one leg off the ground." This is a phrase which might be employed as an epigraph to all her work. Realism and the reality principle obtain short shrift at her hands, fantasy and/or spiritual truth being the beacon by which this author steers. The title of *The Comforters* is taken from the Book of Job. All the friends of its heroine Caroline Rose are Job's comforters: the advice they offer does not apply. The human soul is ultimately alone.

Her second novel, *Robinson*, preserves both the fantasy and the socio-moral satire. It derives its name from Defoe's famous story about the man on the desert island. This time, however, there are others along with January Marlow, the only woman. Looked at in one light, the novel is an adventure story with strong religious undertones. Looked at in another, it is an allegory about youth, romance and illusion, and age, experience and truth. The third novel, *Memento Mori*, is about characters who are all over seventy or eighty years of age. In one sense, it might be described as a geriatric mystery story. It stresses, in the words of the Penny Catechism, the four last things to be remembered: "Death, Judgment, Hell and Heaven." *The Ballad of Peckham Rye* is a fantasy on South-Bank living as engaged in by the working-class young. *The Bachelors* switches to Kensington, Chelsea and Hampstead for its habitat. It is "U" or educated in tone and concerns a spiritualist forger. Next comes *The Prime of Miss Jean Brodie*, a brilliant parable of psychological Calvinism, followed by *The Girls of Slender Means*, which may perhaps be described as a period extravaganza. *The Mandelbaum Gate*—her longest, most ambitious, and least successful work of fiction—was the fruit of a visit by this Jewish-born author to Israel. *The Public Image* deals with the family, colleagues and camp-followers of a famous film-star living in Rome. *The Driver's Seat* is a brilliant sick study of a woman without a love-life who wills a young sex-maniac recently out on parole to kill her.

To enumerate Muriel Spark's credits, she is, first and foremost, a great mistress of dialogue with a fine gift for mimicry. Secondly, come her powers as a satirist, since with her to understand all is not to forgive all, but rather to possess fuller evidence in support of a totally damning judgment. Thirdly—and hardest to locate precisely—is her own vision of things, turning any reality into something rich and strange. Her fiction—glittering, stylish and formal—suggests the following images: a puppet-theatre, a dolls' ballroom, a balletic opera of marionettes controlled by the conjuror's and ventriloquist's arts.

—Derek Stanford

---

**SPENCER, Elizabeth.** American. Born in Carrollton, Mississippi, 19 July 1921. Educated at Belhaven College, Jackson, Mississippi, 1938–42, A.B. 1942; Vanderbilt University, Nashville, Tennessee, 1942–43, M.A. 1943. Married John Rusher in 1956. Instructor, Northwest Mississippi Junior College, Senatobia, 1943–44, and Ward-Belmont College, Nashville, 1944–45; Reporter, *The Nashville Tennessean*, 1945–46; Instructor, 1948–49, and Instructor in Creative Writing, 1949–51, 1952–53, University of Mississippi, Oxford. Donnelly Fellow, Bryn Mawr College, Pennsylvania, 1962; Creative Writing Fellow, University of North Carolina, Chapel Hill, 1969. Recipient: Women's Democratic Committee Award, 1949; National Institute of Arts and Letters grant, 1952; Guggenheim Fellowship, 1953; Rosenthal Award, 1957; *Kenyon Review* Fellowship, 1957; McGraw Hill Fiction Award, 1960; Bellamann Award, 1968. D.L., Southwestern University, Memphis, Tennessee, 1968. Address: 2300 St. Mathieu, Apartment 610, Montreal, Quebec, Canada.

PUBLICATIONS

Novels

> *Fire in the Morning.*   New York, Dodd Mead, 1948.
> *This Crooked Way.*   New York, Dodd Mead, 1952; London, Gollancz, 1953.
> *The Voice at the Back Door.*   New York, McGraw Hill, 1956; London, Gollancz, 1957.
> *The Light in the Piazza.*   New York, McGraw Hill, 1960; London, Heinemann, 1961.
> *Knights and Dragons.*   New York, McGraw Hill, 1965; London, Heinemann, 1966.
> *No Place for an Angel.*   New York, McGraw Hill, 1967; London, Weidenfeld and Nicolson, 1968.

Short Stories

> *Ship Island and Other Stories.*   New York, McGraw Hill, 1968; London, Weidenfeld and Nicolson, 1969.

Uncollected Short Stories

> "Pilgrimage", in *Virginia Quarterly Review* (Charlottesville), June 1950.
> "Eclipse", in *The New Yorker*, 12 June 1958.
> "Moon Rocket", in *McCall's* (New York), October 1960.
> "Beautiful Day for the Wedding", in *Redbook* (New York), September 1962.
> "Adult Holiday", in *The New Yorker*, 12 June 1965.
> "Pincian Gate", in *The New Yorker*, 16 April 1966.
> "Absence", in *The New Yorker*, 10 September 1966.
> "Those Bufords", in *McCall's* (New York), January 1967.
> "Bad Cold", in *The New Yorker*, 27 May 1967.
> "On the Gulf", in *Delta Review* (Greenville, Mississippi), February 1968.
> "Sharon", in *The New Yorker*, 9 May 1970.
> "The Finder", in *The New Yorker*, 23 January 1971.
> "Presents", in *Shenandoah* (Lexington, Virginia), Winter 1971.

Bibliography: in *A Bibliographical Guide to the Study of Southern Literature* by Louis D. Rubin, Jr., Baton Rouge, Louisiana State University Press, 1969.

Manuscript Collection: University of Kentucky Libraries, Lexington.

Critical Study: *Elizabeth Spencer* by Hilton Anderson, New York, Twayne, 1972.

Elizabeth Spencer comments:

I began writing down stories as soon as I learned how to write; that is, at about age six; before that, I made them up anyway and told them to anybody who was handy and would listen. Being a rural Southerner, a Mississippian, had a lot to do with it, I have been told, with this impulse and with the peculiar mystique, importance, which attached itself naturally

1163

thereto and enhanced it. We had been brought up on stories, those about local people, living and dead, and Bible narratives, believed also to be literally true, so that other stories read aloud—the Greek myths, for instance—while indicated as "just" stories, were only one slight remove from the "real" stories of the local scene and the Bible. So it was with history, for local event spilled into the history of the textbooks: my grandfather could remember the close of the Civil War, and my elder brother's nurse had been a slave. The whole world, then, was either entirely in the nature of stories or partook so deeply of stories as to be at every point inseparable from them. Even the novels we came later to read were mainly English nineteenth century works which dealt with a culture similar to our own—we learned with no surprise that we had sprung from it.

Though I left the South in 1953, I still see the world and its primal motions as story, since story charts in time the heart's assertions and gives central place to the great human relationships. My first three novels, written or projected before I left the South, deal with people in that society who must as the true measure of themselves either alter it or come to terms with it. Years I spent in Italy and more recently in Canada, have made me see the world in other than this fixed geography. The challenge to wring its stories from it became to me more difficult at the same time that it became more urgent that I and other writers should do so. A story may not be the only wrench one can hurl into the giant machine that seems bent on devouring us all, but it is one of them. A story which has been tooled, shaped, and slicked up is neither real nor true—we know its nature and its straw insides. Only the real creature can satisfy, the one that is touchy and alive, dangerous to fool with. The search for such as these goes on with me continually, and I think for all real writers as well.

*        *        *

A native Mississippian, Elizabeth Spencer has perhaps remained too much under the shadow of William Faulkner to receive the recognition she deserves for her extraordinarily cool and perceptive treatment of the sensitive upper-middle-class of her native state, who have been trapped between arrogant and decadent planter aristocrats and politically ambitious bigoted "rednecks." Her first three novels and early stories communicate the tensions generated by a culture's devoting its energies to maintaining an anachronistic system rooted in racial oppression.

Her first novel, *Fire in the Morning*, which takes its title from Djuna Barnes' *Nightwood* and a small Mississippi town's recollections of Yankee soldiers burning down a farmhouse during the Civil War, is a subtle but powerful tale of the paralyzing effects of the evils bred by greed on the small community. The Gerrard family moved into Tarsus in the wake of the havoc wrought by the Civil War and made themselves leading citizens through perjury and blackmail. These efforts lead ultimately, however, only to the destruction of almost everyone involved, except one Gerrard son and a former schoolmate, son of one of the principal victims of the Gerrards, who manage to bury the past and achieve a reconciliation, despite both of their wives' having suffered greatly from the elder Gerrard's machinations. *This Crooked Way* is a less complex and more cynical tale about another opportunist who comes down from the hills to become a Delta planter. Amos has always dreamed of seeing a ladder of angels, but all he has succeeded in doing is wrecking the lives of most of those around him, especially his gently-bred wife, who is driven at last to shoot one of Amos's proteges who has seduced her daughter.

Miss Spencer's most powerful work is *The Voice at the Back Door*, the complicated story of the sacrifices that a well-educated and inherently decent young lawyer must make to win political preferment in Mississippi. It contrasts Duncan Harper, a truculently honest former athlete and idol of the community, who sacrifices a comfortable career in order to protect a Negro from the ignorant community, with Kerney Woolbright, who lies about his knowledge of the situation in order to assure a political victory.

After this chilling revelation of the corruption of the competent and persecution of the decent, Miss Spencer abandoned the Mississippi scene for Italy. Her first two novels of

Americans abroad tell of women who escape to victory. *Light in the Piazza* is a short, intense account of an American woman's scheme to marry her mentally retarded daughter to an attractive young Italian, despite her husband's qualms and the counter-machinations of the Italian's father to make as much money as possible out of the match. *Knights and Dragons* tells the story of an American woman who has fled to Rome after the collapse of her marriage and finds at last that human love demands too much of the individual to be worth the effort and frees herself—like Federico Fellini's Juliet of the Spirits—to become "a companion to cloud and sky."

In her first truly "international novel," *No Place for an Angel*, Miss Spencer returns to her early cool, controlled vision of those who are overwhelmed by life. The story concerns the intricate inter-relationships in Italy, New York, and Dallas of two married couples, their sprawling families, and a young American sculptor, who dreams like Amos Dudley of angels. At one point one wife says of her husband, "Jerry had to be great and he almost made it." The novel is a mature, unsentimental account of almost making it. When the husband in one of the few enduring marriages depicted says to his wife, "In spite of all I can do, life keeps turning into a vacuum," he articulates what all the characters have experienced; but beneath this frustrating surface, the author allows us glimpses of the children of these families who may find greater happiness because they want less.

—Warren French

---

**STACEY, Tom.** British. Born in Bletchingley, Surrey, 11 January 1930. Educated at Wellesley House, 1938–42; Eton College, Buckinghamshire, 1943–48; Worcester College, Oxford, 1950–51. Served as a 2nd Lieutenant in the Scots Guards, in Malaya, 1948–50. Married Caroline Clay in 1952; has five children. Staff Writer, *Picture Post*, London and the Far East, 1952–54; African Correspondent, *Daily Express*, London, 1954–55; Canada and Latin America Reporter, *Montreal Star*, 1955–56; Foreign Correspondent, in the Middle East, 1956–57, American Columnist, 1957, and Diplomatic and Roving Correspondent, 1957–60, *Daily Express*; Chief Roving Correspondent, *Sunday Times*, London, 1960–65; Columnist, *Evening Standard*, London, 1965–67. Since 1967, Editor-in-Chief, *Correspondents World Wide*, London; since 1969, Editor-in-Chief, *Chambers' Encyclopaedia Yearbook*, London, and Managing Director, Tom Stacey Ltd. (publishers), London. Member, Exploratory-Anthropological Expeditions, to Finland, 1951, and to Africa, 1954, 1963, 1968. Conservative Party Parliamentary Candidate, 1964, 1966. Recipient: Rhys Memorial Prize, for non-fiction, 1954; Granada Newspaper Award, 1961. Address: Tom Stacey Ltd., 28–29 Maiden Lane, London W.C.2, England.

PUBLICATIONS

Novel

*The Brothers M.* London, Secker and Warburg, 1960; New York, Pantheon Books, 1961.

Other

*The Hostile Sun: A Malayan Journey.*   London, Duckworth, 1953.
*Summons to Ruwenzori.*   London, Secker and Warburg, 1963.
*Immigration and Enoch Powell.*   London, Stacey, 1970.

Editor, *Today's World.*   London, Collins, 1969.
Editor, *Here Come the Tories.*   London, Stacey, 1970.

Critical Studies: essays in the *New York Times Book Review*, 30 April 1961, and in *Time* (New York), 12 May 1961.

Tom Stacey comments:

*The Brothers M* is an attempt to juxtapose the civilised view of life with the savage, and to extract certain basic truths about the human condition with which it is the chief function of literature to concern itself. As in my next major novel, *The River Expedition*, its material is drawn from my own experience in remote regions among primitive people. As one who has had regular access to the columns of newspapers and magazines, I have come to prefer to make use of fiction, a particularly intimate medium, as rarely as possible, and only when I am satisfied that what I have to say cannot be better said in another form.

\*     \*     \*

Although known primarily as a journalist and latterly as a publisher, Tom Stacey attracted considerable critical attention with his novel, *The Brothers M*, when it was first published in 1960. In the political circumstances of the time, with the first waves of African nationalism in the European colonies beginning to be felt, the novel's theme of the clash between civilised and primitive cultures, as personified by two young Oxford graduates, the Canadian McNair and the Ugandan Musaka, had great topical relevance. Daudi Musaka, the prototype of the advanced Europeanised African, gradually succumbs during the course of a disastrous expedition to the remote mountainous Ruwenzori region of his native land in McNair's company, to the pull of his tribal origins, and—from a European point of view—reverts to a fearful and obscurantist animism that leads him first to hate and later to abandon McNair to his death in a mountain hut. Stacey's insight into the African mind and his ability to project with force and sympathy the spiritual and psychological basis of so-called primitive tribal culture lift the novel far above the level of documentary realism, convincing though it is on this level. McNair's personal cosmology, centring on the individual's personal liberation through full self-consciousness, is shown to be merely a pattern imposed on an unconsciously accepted materialism. McNair, tormented by the loss of Daudi's friendship as the journey progresses, comes to understand something of this. But it is the African who is the focus of Stacey's sympathies. At a time before the anthropological view of primitive cultures had become widely accepted, *The Brothers M* may be regarded as foreshadowing the move away from purely Western-based systems of values that was to mark the coming decade. The novel is long and at times relapses into a rather stiffly self-conscious poeticism that recalls the T. E. Lawrence of the *Seven Pillars* and is at odds with the keenly observed detail of the East African locale.

—Keith Walker

**STAFFORD, Jean.** American. Born in Covina, California, 1 July 1915. Educated at the University of Colorado, Boulder, B.A. 1936, M.A. 1936; Heidelberg University, 1936–37. Married the poet Robert Lowell in 1940 (divorced, 1948); Oliver Jensen, 1950 (divorced, 1953); the writer A. J. Liebling, 1959 (died, 1963). Instructor, Stephens College, Columbia, Missouri, 1937–38; Secretary, *Southern Review*, Baton Rouge, Louisiana, 1940–41; Lecturer, Queens College, Flushing, New York, Spring 1945; Fellow, Center for Advanced Studies, Wesleyan University, Middletown, Connecticut, 1964–65; Adjunct Professor, Columbia University, New York, 1967–69. Recipient: *Mademoiselle*'s Merit Award, 1944; National Institute of Arts and Letters grant, 1945; Guggenheim Fellowship, 1945, 1948; National Press Club Award, 1948; O. Henry Award, 1955; Ingram-Merrill grant, 1969; Chapelbrook grant, 1969; Pulitzer Prize, 1970. Member, National Institute of Arts and Letters, 1970. Address: c/o The New Yorker, 25 West 43rd Street, New York, New York 10036, U.S.A.

PUBLICATIONS

Novels

> *Boston Adventure*. New York, Harcourt Brace, 1944; London, Faber, 1946.
> *The Mountain Lion*. New York, Harcourt Brace, 1947; London, Faber, 1948.
> *The Catherine Wheel*. New York, Harcourt Brace, and London, Eyre and Spottis-woode, 1952.

Short Stories

> *Children Are Bored on Sunday*. New York, Harcourt Brace, 1953; London, Gollancz, 1954.
> *New Short Novels*, with others. New York, Ballantine, 1954; London, Gollancz, 1959.
> *Stories*, with others. New York, Farrar Straus, 1956.
> *Bad Characters*. New York, Farrar Straus, 1964; London, Chatto and Windus, 1965.
> *Collected Stories*. New York, Farrar Straus, 1969; London, Chatto and Windus, 1970.

Other

> *Elephi: The Cat with the High I. Q.* (juvenile). New York, Farrar Straus, 1962.
> *The Lion and the Carpenter and Other Tales from the Arabian Nights Retold* (juvenile). New York, Macmillan, and London, Macmillan, 1962.
> *A Mother in History*. New York, Farrar Straus, and London, Chatto and Windus, 1966.

*          *          *

The publication of her *Collected Stories* in 1969 confirmed Jean Stafford's considerable reputation as a writer of short fiction. At her frequent best she has few peers—indeed very little significant competition. She is, however, an artist who resists simple classification: her concerns are diverse and it is impossible to speak of any "development" in her fiction, since the early stories display the same cool authority and certainty of tone which characterize her recent work. But the temptation to see her fiction as essentially feminine has its attractions (she has never, for example, selected an adult male for a central character or entrusted one with a commanding point of view), particularly if one is willing to speculate that women writers are less likely than men to invent within a framework of ideas and more likely to compose close to the surface and feeling of the individual moment of experience. Thus in one of her finest stories, "Children Are Bored on Sunday", Miss Stafford examines the uneasiness of a sensitive young woman, a transplant into the world of professional New York intellectuals of a now-vanished *Partisan Review* era: "Neither staunchly primitive nor confidently *au courant*, she rarely knew where she was . . . her identity was always mistaken." Emma is rooted in the concrete sensory experiences of her country past and continues to believe that:

> the apple Eve had eaten had tasted exactly like those she had eaten when she was a child visiting her Great-Uncle Graham's farm, and that Newton's observation was no news despite all the hue and cry. Half the apples she had eaten had fallen out of the tree, whose branches she had shaken for this very purpose, and the Apple Experience included both the descent of it and the consumption of it, and Eve and Newton and Emma understood one another perfectly in this particular of reality.

Wandering through the Metropolitan Museum she meets a battered acquaintance from the intellectual camp who may be capable of sympathy—who certainly needs sympathy—and yearns for a moment of contact, however brief or artificially sustained. Yet if it could take place, she wonders, "would it be possible to prevent him from marring it all by talking of secondary matter? That is, of art and neurosis, art and politics, art and science, art and religion?" Abstractions are suspect; ideas may be the refuge and armor of the competent male, while it is the powerful gift to render the "particular of reality", without descending into mindless realism, which makes Miss Stafford's work memorable.

The *Collected Stories* (unfortunately not complete: at least one splendid story, "A Reasonable Facsimile", is missing) are arranged according to their primary settings (Colorado, Boston and New York, and the Europe of American expatriates or travelers). Each of these settings, however, is firmly associated with a particular time of life—and it is this sense of what time rather than place does to people which unifies Miss Stafford's work. At the core of her fiction is the vulnerable, self-conscious child, sometimes literally unwanted, frequently orphaned, always an outcast from the world of more fortunate children and the alien world of adults. Seen years later from an adult point of view, the child's dismay can be a source of comedy ("The Healthiest Girl in Town", "Bad Characters"), but there is nothing funny for the child at the moment of suffering. The children may be trapped, perhaps hopelessly so ("A Summer Day", "Cops and Robbers"); the lucky ones may make a late escape or at least dream of one ("The Liberation", "The Tea of the Stouthearted Ladies"), yet young adulthood and departure to new places seldom bring release. Or if they do, the stories tend to turn into unconvincing wish-fulfillment fantasies ("The Mountain Day", "Caveat Emptor"). More often than not there is only retreat into bitter or bewildered solitude. Old age, rarely represented, means final despair and protective eccentricity.

*The Mountain Lion*, one of the finest of modern short novels, and much of Miss Stafford's astonishingly accomplished first novel, *Boston Adventure*, are concerned with the passage from childhood to adolescence. In *The Mountain Lion* Ralph and his sister Molly, two gawky, precocious children out of place in the genteel world of their mother, spend their summers in the full, natural world of their uncle's ranch. Despite a sexual awakening he cannot fully cope with, Ralph moves towards wholeness and maturity, while his preternaturally clever sister withers into self-contempt and is destroyed in a sudden burst of violence which is often an element of Miss Stafford's work. Sophie Marburg, the central figure of *Boston Adventure*, is the unwanted child of a poor immigrant family who dreams of being adopted by a rich Bostonian spinster. Her wish is granted, but the new world of Boston society proves to be as restricting and loveless as that of her childhood. Sophie is taken up simply because she may be of use to the vain and fearful Miss Pride; and as she assumes a place in the coldly glittering arena of ritual observances, she comes to feel "stormed by a claustrophobia so violent that every element of the scene . . . assumed the proportions of destroying force: there was no reason for this gathering, no reason for this elaborate amity amongst people whose civilization had pruned down their impulses to a set of manners which imperfectly concealed a dead indifference." In the end Sophie has merely exchanged one form of servitude for another. *Boston Adventure* is perhaps too abundant, too prolonged and detailed, but the characters are so fully drawn and their ways of life so precisely fixed that it hardly seems to matter.

*The Catherine Wheel* is, by comparison, something of a failure, unconvincing and contrived in its general effect. The style is densely poetic, mannered and untypically symbolic; the two centers of interest are never really brought into intelligible relationship with each other. A young boy is tortured by the fear that his childish wish for vengeance will be answered; his maiden aunt, who lives in an impossibly idealized realm of rarified taste and perfect scruples, is grotesquely destroyed by those scruples—or perhaps simply by a malignant fate, portentously confirming the epigraph from Eliot's *Murder in the Cathedral*: "Man's life is a cheat and a disappointment; / All things are unreal." Miss Stafford has published relatively little in recent years, but the few stories she has given her readers, such as the superb "The Philosophy Lesson" of 1968, are clearly the work of a faultless observer and accomplished craftsman.

—Elmer Borklund

---

**STEAD, Christina (Ellen).** Australian. Born in Rockdale, Sydney, 17 July 1902. Educated at Sydney University Teachers' College, graduated 1922. Married William James Blake in 1952 (died, 1968). Demonstrator, Sydney University Teachers' College, in Sydney schools, 1922–24; Secretary in Sydney, 1925–28. Moved to Europe in 1928 and worked as a clerk in offices in London, 1928–29, and in Paris, 1930–35. Moved to the United States in 1935: Senior Writer, MGM, Hollywood, 1943; Instructor, Workshop in the Novel, New York University, 1943–44. Now lives in Surrey, England. Recipient: Aga Khan Prize, *Paris Review*, 1966; Arts Council of Great Britain grant, 1967; Australian National University Fellowship in the Creative Arts, 1969. Address: c/o Laurence Pollinger, 18 Maddox Street, London W.1, England.

PUBLICATIONS

Novels

> *Seven Poor Men of Sydney*. London, Davies, 1934; New York, Appleton, 1935.
> *The Beauties and Furies*. London, Davies, and New York, Appleton, 1936.
> *House of All Nations*. London, Davies, and New York, Simon and Schuster, 1938.
> *The Man Who Loved Children*. New York, Simon and Schuster, 1940; London, Davies, 1941.
> *For Love Alone*. New York, Harcourt Brace, 1944; London, Davies, 1945.
> *Letty Fox: Her Luck*. New York, Harcourt Brace, 1946; London, Davies, 1947.
> *A Little Tea, A Little Chat*. New York, Harcourt Brace, 1948.
> *The People with the Dogs*. Boston, Little Brown, 1952.
> *Dark Places of the Heart*. New York, Holt Rinehart, 1966; as *Cotters' England*. London, Secker and Warburg, 1967.

Short Stories

*The Salzburg Tales.*   London, Davies, and New York, Appleton, 1934.
*The Puzzleheaded Girl: 4 Novellas.*   New York, Holt Rinehart, 1967; London, Secker and Warburg, 1968.


Uncollected Short Stories

"A Household", in *Southerly* (Sydney), 1962.
"U.N.O. 1945", in *Southerly* (Sydney), 1962.
"The Woman in the Bed", in *Meanjin* (Melbourne), 1968.
"The Milk Run", in *The New Yorker*, 1971.
"An Iced Cake with Cherries", in *Meanjin* (Melbourne), 1971.
"Street Idyll", in *The Sun* (Melbourne), 1971.
"The Azhdanov Tailors", in *Commentary* (New York), 1971.


Other

Editor, with William J. Blake, *Modern Women in Love*.   New York, Dryden Press, 1945.
Editor, *Great Stories of the South Sea Islands*.   London, Muller, 1956.

Translator, *Colour of Asia*, by Fernand Gigon.   London, Muller, 1955.
Translator, *The Candid Killer*, by Jean Giltène.   London, Muller, 1956.
Translator, *In Balloon and Bathyscaphe*, by August Piccard.   London, Cassell, 1956.


Critical Studies: in the "Christina Stead Issue" of *Southerly* (Sydney), 1962; *Christina Stead* by R. G. Geering, New York, Twayne, 1969.


Christina Stead comments:

I have been interested in depicting scenes in which I myself have taken part either as actor or spectator: and in this sense, my books and stories may be called scenes from contemporary life.

*        *        *

For two or three decades critics and literary historians have sometimes wondered how to fit Christina Stead into their Australian scheme of things. The greater part of her life has been spent abroad and her work, naturally enough, reflects life in the many parts of the world in which she has lived. She has, now and again, drawn directly on the experiences of her early years, but not in any self-consciously Australian way. The Sydney of her first novel, though vividly recreated as an actual locale, might, for the purposes of her story, have been any other poverty-stricken city of the modern world in which people were struggling to make something of their obscure lives. The first half of *For Love Alone* is set in Australia too, but this account of a young woman's desperate search for love takes the heroine, Teresa, to England, where a different destiny from the one she expects awaits her. People are more important than places and, although the places in Christina Stead's fiction are established with that attention to detail and atmosphere which helps us to understand the lives the characters lead, the people are her basic concern. Christina Stead is, to put it simply, a writer absorbed in the individual experience, not an Australian novelist in the more obvious sense of the term, and the measure of her achievement is the readiness with which the sympathetic reader may enter the different worlds she creates in her books.

Though set in the depression years of the late 1920's *Seven Poor Men of Sydney* is a poetic, impressionist rather than a naturalistic, sociological novel. Significantly, the characters who interest the author most are Michael Baguenault and his half-sister Catherine, both tormented, oversensitive people doomed by the very intensity of their relationship and their ill-focused strivings to frustration and defeat. *House of All Nations*, written in a quite different manner, published only four years later and the longest of all Christina Stead's novels, is a scathing account of the world of international high finance as seen in the operation of European private banks and stock exchanges of the 1930's, an account presented with an encyclopaedic wealth of detail that gives to its descriptions of the most fantastic money-making exploits a ring of conviction. But even here, despite the massive documentation, the novelist's basic concern is the force of individual obsession which, under the lure of the absolute, gold, drives such misguided geniuses as the banker Jules Bertillon and the merchant Henri Léon along their crazy paths.

It is, likewise, this sense of the destructive power of human obsessions that gives to *The Man Who Loved Children* and *For Love Alone* much of their dramatic impact. The ironically titled *The Man Who Loved Children*, Christina Stead's finest novel and a book that deserves a place among the masterpieces of twentieth century fiction, depicts with a rare blend of subtlety and intensity the disastrous effects of a jocular, liberal-minded but naif scientist upon the life of his family. Sam Pollit believes the world can be saved by science and humanitarian socialism but his idealism and generosity are corrupted at their source by an incurable egoism and self-righteousness. This book traces with unsparing honesty and profound insight, which extend the artist's sympathy to all those drawn into the family conflict, the bitter, murderous feuding between Sam and his redoubtable antagonist, his wife Henny, through to its tragic and its liberating end. The self-absorption of the eldest child, the adolescent Louisa, the embryonic artist, enables her to survive and win through to the promise of freedom. In a somewhat similar manner the tenacious Teresa, obsessed by the idea of love which will free her from the simpering obscenities of suburbia, and having undergone torments in her devotion to the arrogant, cold-hearted Jonathan Crow, survives her disenchantment and steps finally across the threshold into a world that promises fulfilment for her as both woman and artist. The devastating portraits of male egoism, Sam Pollit and Crow, make the struggles depicted in these two books terrifying real.

The next three novels are, like *The Man Who Loved Children*, American in setting but fall below the high level of that book. *Letty Fox* and *A Little Tea, A Little Chat* provide, among other things, a sardonic commentary on the sexual mores and the materialism of twentieth century America; *The People with the Dogs* is an affectionate recreation of life in one of its backwaters, a country estate inhabited by descendants of nineteenth century Russian liberals, the cultured and eccentric Massines, who live at a stage removed from the brashness of the modern world. Christina Stead's sensitivity to the social and political scene is found too in the last of her published novels, *Cotters' England*, with its telling evocation of seedy Islington of the early 1950's and of the damp, dismal industrial north. The centre of the book once again (and more emphatically than ever) is character. In her presentation of the lesbian, leftist Nellie Cook (born a Cotter of a Tyneside working class family) a tyrannical, intense, self-indulgent, loquacious harpy, Christina Stead has created another of her memorably menacing characters. The remarkable gifts for the fantastic and the grotesque which made *The Salzburg Tales* such a richly entertaining work contribute in *Cotters' England* towards the deeper exploration and realization of character. In the book's central scenes Christina Stead succeeds in fusing the commonplace and the bizarre into a single, compelling poetic vision.

Apart from a few separately published short stories and an early novel of student life in Paris, *The Beauties and Furies* (a curious and unsuccessful blend of reality and fantasy), the only other fiction yet to be mentioned is the late work, *The Puzzleheaded Girl*, a volume of four novellas. Two of these are incisive studies of addle-pated American girls at home and abroad in the post-war years; the third "The Right-angled Creek", subtitled "A Sort of Ghost Story", is a highly successful essay in eerie atmospherics. The title story is quite different again in its slanted and indirect evocation of the strangely elusive Honor Lawrence, a wraith-like figure who seems doomed to wander lost and innocent in the world.

*Cotters' England* and *The Puzzleheaded Girl* are further proofs of the richness, variety, and originality of Christina Stead's art.

—R. G. Geering

---

**STEEGMULLER, Francis.** American. Born in New Haven, Connecticut, 3 July 1906. Educated at Dartmouth College, Hanover, New Hampshire, 1923–24; Columbia University, New York, 1924–28, B.A. 1927, M.A. 1928 (Phi Beta Kappa). Married Beatrice Stein in 1935 (died, 1961); Shirley Hazzard, *q.v.*, in 1963. Recipient: Red Badge Mystery Prize, 1940; National Institute of Arts and Letters award, 1958; National Book Award, for non-fiction, 1971. Chevalier, Legion of Honor, 1957. Member, National Institute of Arts and Letters, 1966. Address: 200 East 66th Street, New York, New York 10021, U.S.A.

PUBLICATIONS

Novels

    *Java-Java* (as Byron Steel). New York, Knopf, 1928.
    *The Musicale.* New York, Cape and Smith, and London, Cape, 1930.
    *A Matter of Iodine* (as David Keith). New York, Dodd Mead, and London, Cassell, 1940.
    *A Matter of Accent* (as David Keith). New York, Dodd Mead, 1943.
    *States of Grace.* New York, Reynal, 1946; London, Collins, 1947.
    *Blue Harpsichord* (as David Keith). New York, Dodd Mead, 1949; London, Collins, 1950.
    *The Christening Party.* New York, Farrar Straus, 1960; London, Hart Davis, 1961.

Short Stories

    *French Follies and Other Follies.* New York, Reynal, 1946.
    *Stories and True Stories.* Boston, Little Brown, and London, Macmillan, 1972.

Other

    *O Rare Ben Jonson.* New York, Knopf, 1928.
    *Sir Francis Bacon: The First Modern Mind.* New York, Doubleday, 1930.
    *America on Relief,* with Marie Dresden Lane. New York, Harcourt Brace, 1938.
    *Flaubert and Madame Bovary: A Double Portrait.* New York, Viking Press, and London, Hale, 1939; revised edition, London, Collins, 1947, Macmillan, 1968; New York, Farrar Straus, 1950, 1968.

*Maupassant: A Lion in the Path.* New York, Random House, 1949; as *Maupassant*, London, Collins, 1950.

*The Two Lives of James Jackson Jarves.* New Haven, Connecticut, Yale University Press, 1951.

*The Grand Mademoiselle.* London, Hamish Hamilton, 1955; New York, Farrar Straus, 1956.

*Apollinaire: Poet among the Painters.* New York, Farrar Straus, 1963; London, Hart Davis, 1964.

*Cocteau: A Biography.* Boston, Little Brown, and London, Macmillan, 1970.

Editor and Translator, *The Selected Letters of Gustave Flaubert.* New York, Farrar Straus, and London, Hamish Hamilton, 1954.

Editor and Translator, with Norbert Guterman, *Selected Essays*, by C. A. Sainte-Beuve. New York, Doubleday, 1963; London, Methuen, 1965.

Editor, *Alcools*, by Guillaume Apollinaire. New York, Doubleday, 1964.

Editor, *November*, by Gustave Flaubert. London, Joseph, 1966; New York, Serendipity Press, 1967.

Translator, *Impressionists and Symbolists*, by Lionello Venturi. New York, Scribner, 1950.

Translator, *Madame Bovary*, by Gustave Flaubert. New York, Modern Library, 1961.

Translator, *Le Hibou et la Poussiquette*, by Edward Lear. Boston, Little Brown, and London, Hart Davis, 1961.

Translator, with Norbert Guterman, *Papillot, Cliquot, et Dodo*, by Eugene Field. New York, Ariel Books, 1964; London, Collins, 1965.

Translator, *Intimate Journal, 1840–1841*, by Gustave Flaubert. New York, Doubleday, and London, W. H. Allen, 1967.

*       *       *

Francis Steegmuller's considerable work in non-fiction is helpful to our understanding of his main preoccupations in his fictional creations. His biographies range from ones of Ben Jonson and Sir Francis Bacon to a whole series of works on major French figures of the seventeenth. nineteenth. and early twentieth centuries, culminating in his superb recent portrait of Cocteau. In almost all of his non-fiction (excluding *America on Relief*), his consistent concern is with an international and almost timeless world, which hovers somewhere between the concern with facts of the nineteenth-century realists and historical novelists and the slightly mad world of Cocteau and Apollinaire. One incident may serve to illustrate the peculiar ambivalence of a supposedly factual world view in which fact consistently competes with fiction. In his biography of Henri IV's granddaughter, *The Grand Mademoiselle*, Steegmuller makes much of the highly improbable but amply verified fact that the urn containing the poorly embalmed entrails of Mademoiselle actually exploded in the midst of her funeral. The explosion of this important historical personage and its spattering of the royal mourners is precisely the kind of madly funny but macabre finale which Steegmuller so often creates in his best known fiction.

In *The Musicale* (his first fictional work published under his own name), he still reins in his tendency to have the detailed factual and psychological world issue into a tangle of improbabilities. This portrait of Madison, Wisconsin, in the 1920's is perhaps his very best work. Under the pseudonym, David Keith, Steegmuller then moves away from the psychological portrait of *The Musicale* (1930), with its clear echoes of *To the Lighthouse* (published in 1927). The detective stories, *A Matter of Iodine* and *A Matter of Accent*, are technically proficient but decidedly minor. Much the same can be said for *States of Grace* and *Blue Harpsichord*. Set in an Egyptian convent (run by a thwarted female who sees herself as surrogate for her brother, an American bishop), *States of Grace* enables Steegmuller to present an international gallery of extraordinary but basically mediocre types. Its slight plot is trumped, however, by the even slighter plot of *Blue Harpsichord*. With a deliberate and total lack of the probable (worthy of a Dickens, a Dumas, or the Dadaists), Steegmuller presents an "extravaganza of human personality." The pseudo-detective story culminates in a totally improbable and coincidental meeting in a New York bar of almost every major character in the novel. Steegmuller's most recent novel, *The Christening Party*, returns, however, to the kind of fictional techniques he had used with conspicuous success in *The Musicale*. Told from the viewpoint of a seven year old, *The Christening Party*, a finely honed psychological portrait, ends, however, in a paroxysm of improbability as a long lost and incredibly wealthy and ancient uncle of the boy uses a crowbar to fight a duel on a funeral mound being excavated at that moment by a mad and amateur British excavator with the improbable name of Kitcat.

The final picture which emerges from all his fiction is summarized perhaps in the twice repeated word in the title of his 1946 collection of short stories, *French Follies and Other Follies*. The world which Steegmuller draws is one in which virtually all human endeavor is best seen under the rubric of the rich French word *folie*, with its simultaneous echoes of life seen both lightly and most darkly. The detailed world of the nineteenth-century realists explodes in Steegmuller's fiction into the madly frivolous improbabilities of the Futurists, Cubists, and Dadaists who also earn the unbounded admiration of this uneven but important contemporary novelist.

—John Fuegi

---

**STEGNER, Wallace (Earle).** American. Born in Lake Mills, Iowa, 18 February 1909. Educated at the University of Utah, Salt Lake City, A.B. 1930; University of Iowa, Iowa City, A.M. 1932, Ph.D. 1935; University of California, Berkeley, 1932–33. Married Mary Stuart Page in 1934; has one child. Instructor, Augustana College, Rock Island, Illinois, 1933–34, the University of Utah, 1934–37, and the University of Wisconsin, Madison, 1937–39; Faculty Instructor, Harvard University, Cambridge, Massachusetts, 1939–45. Professor of English, 1945–69, and Jackson Eli Reynolds Professor of Humanities, 1969–71, Stanford University, California. American Academy of Arts and Letters Writer-in-Residence, 1960; Phi Beta Kappa Visiting Scholar, 1960. West Coast Editor, Houghton Mifflin Company, publishers, Boston, 1945–53. Assistant to the United States Secretary of the Interior, Washington, D.C., 1961. Member, 1962–66, and Chairman, 1965–66, National Parks Advisory Board, Washington, D.C. Editor-in-Chief, *American West* magazine, Palo Alto, California, 1966–68. Recipient: Little Brown Prize, 1937; O. Henry Award, 1942, 1950, 1954; Houghton Mifflin Life-in-America Award, 1945; Anisfield-Wolf Award, 1945; Guggenheim Fellowship, 1949–51, 1959; Rockefeller Fellowship, 1950; Wenner-Gren grant, 1953; Center for Advanced Studies in the Behavioral Sciences Fellowship, 1955; National Endowment for the Humanities Senior Fellowship, 1972. Doctor of Letters, University of Utah, 1968; D.F.A., University of California, 1969. Member, National Institute of Arts and Letters, and American Academy of Arts and Sciences. Address: 13456 South Fork Lane, Los Altos Hills, California 94022, U.S.A.

PUBLICATIONS

Novels

*Remembering Laughter*.   Boston, Little Brown, and London, Heinemann, 1937.

*The Potter's House*.   Muscatine, Iowa, Prairie Press, 1938.
*On a Darkling Plain*.   New York, Harcourt Brace, 1940.
*Fire and Ice*.   New York, Duell, 1941.
*The Big Rock Candy Mountain*.   New York, Duell, 1943; London, Hammond
    Hammond, 1950.
*Second Growth*.   Boston, Houghton Mifflin, 1947; London, Hammond Hammond,
    1948.
*The Preacher and the Slave*.   Boston, Houghton Mifflin, 1950; London, Hammond
    Hammond, 1951; as *Joe Hill: A Biographical Novel*, New York, Doubleday, 1969.
*A Shooting Star*.   New York, Viking Press, and London, Heinemann, 1961.
*All the Little Live Things*.   New York, Viking Press, 1967; London, Heinemann, 1968.
*Angle of Repose*.   New York, Doubleday, and London, Heinemann, 1971.

Short Stories

*The Women on the Wall*.   Boston, Houghton Mifflin, 1948; London, Hammond
    Hammond, 1952.
*The City of the Living*.   Boston, Houghton Mifflin, 1956; London, Hammond Ham-
    mond, 1957.
*New Short Novels 2*, with others.   New York, Ballantine, 1956.

Uncollected Short Stories

"He Who Spits at the Sky", in *Esquire* (New York), March 1958.
"Something Spurious from the Mindanao Deep", in *Harper's* (New York), August
    1958.
"The Wolfer", in *Harper's* (New York), October 1959.

Other

*Mormon Country*.   New York, Duell, 1941.
*One Nation*, with the editors of *Look*.   Boston, Houghton Mifflin, 1945.
*Look at America: The Central Northwest*.   Boston, Houghton Mifflin, 1947.
*The Writer in America*.   South Pasadena, California, Perkins and Hutchins, 1953.
*Beyond the Hundredth Meridian: John Wesley Powell and the Second Opening of the
    West*.   Boston, Houghton Mifflin, 1954.
*Wolf Willow: A History, A Story, and A Memory of the Last Plains Frontier*.   New
    York, Viking Press, 1962; London, Heinemann, 1963.
*The Gathering of Zion: The Story of the Mormon Trail*.   New York, McGraw Hill,
    1964; London, Eyre and Spottiswoode, 1966.
*The Sound of Mountain Water* (essays).   New York, Doubleday, 1969.

Editor, with others, *An Exposition Workshop*.   Boston, Little Brown, 1939.
Editor, with others, *Readings for Citizens at War*.   New York, Harper, 1941.
Editor, with Richard Scowcroft, *Stanford Short Stories, 1946*.   Stanford, California,
    Stanford University Press, 1947. (and later volumes)
Editor, with others, *The Writer's Art*.   Boston, Heath, 1950.
Editor, *This Is Dinosaur: The Echo Park Country and Its Magic Rivers*.   New York,
    Knopf, 1955.
Editor, *The Exploration of the Colorado River of the West*, by J. W. Powell.   Chicago,
    University of Chicago Press, 1957.
Editor, with Mary Stegner, *Great American Short Stories*.   New York, Dell, 1957.

Editor, *Selected American Prose: The Realistic Movement*.   New York, Rinehart, 1958; London, Peter Owen, 1963.

Editor, *The Adventures of Huckleberry Finn*, by Mark Twain.   New York, Dell, 1960.

Editor, *The Outcasts of Poker Flat*, by Bret Harte.   New York, New American Library, 1961.

Editor, *Report on the Lands of the Arid Region of the United States*, by J. W. Powell. Cambridge, Massachusetts, Harvard University Press, and London, Oxford University Press, 1962.

Editor, with others, *Modern Composition*.   New York, Holt Rinehart, 4 vols., 1964.

Editor, *The American Novel: From Cooper to Faulkner*.   New York, Basic Books, 1965.

Editor, *The Big Sky*, by A. B. Guthrie, Jr.   Boston, Houghton Mifflin, 1965.

Editor, with others, *Twenty Years of Stanford Short Stories*.   Stanford, California, Stanford University Press, 1966.

Editor, *Twice-Told Tales*, by Nathaniel Hawthorne.   New York, Heritage Press, 1967.


Manuscript Collections: University of Iowa, Iowa City; Stanford University, California.


Critical Study: *Wallace Stegner* by Robert Canzoneri, New York, Twayne, 1971.


Wallace Stegner comments:

My subjects and themes are mainly out of the American West, in which I grew up. Because I grew up without history, in a place where human occupation had left fewer traces than the passage of buffalo and antelope herds, I early acquired the desire to find some history in which I myself belonged, and some tradition within which I might have a self-respecting part. For that reason, I suppose, I have never been a rebel against tradition in general, however much I may have resisted specific and rigid aspects of it. I have written fiction whose impulse was at least as much social as psychological. I do not think any individual, in fiction or in life, is defined except within the group life that formed him. Even *The Big Rock Candy Mountain*, which deals with a wandering, asteroid-like family on the western frontiers, is a search for a place and a stability. Even *Angle of Repose*, which likewise deals with a pioneering family of a kind, is a study in continuity.

                         *        *        *

Wallace Stegner is a writer whose sizable body of work includes not only novels and volumes of short stories but also historical works such as *Mormon Country, Beyond the Hundredth Meridian*, and *The Gathering of Zion: The Story of the Mormon Trail*. These latter works indicate a mind and a temperament which are profoundly stirred by elements in the American past. It is a past that has great usefulness to a writer who, in many of his works of fiction, tries to see that past as a permanent element in present American experience. This past has its beginnings in Eastern, "cultivated" experience and extends westward, in time and space, across plains and mountains, until it reaches the rich promises and frustrating ambiguities of modern California.

In his novels Stegner singles out various stages of this westward movement and attempts to assess the partial meanings that each stage offers an attentive novelist who brings to his reading of chosen subject-matter insights which he shares with social historians. Stegner's subject-matter is marked by a richness and complexity that are not easily reduced to simple patterns. Yet a kind of constant can be isolated as cropping up again and again as the novels move from New England experience of the present in *Second Growth* to various Western times and places. *On a Darkling Plain* tells of the experiment in isolation made by a young veteran of World War I in Western Canada; the young man, rather significantly in relation to Stegner's later work, feels a need to detach himself from a modern world that has distorted human promise. *The Big Rock Candy Mountain* has for its subject the wanderings of a family in Western lands: lands that offer the group a mixture of promise and defeat. In *The Preacher and the Slave* Stegner offers a fictionized account of the IWW movement of the first decades of this century. Two later novels—*A Shooting Star* and *All the Little Live Things*—move to the California of the present; they measure the sad realization of the promise inherent in the great westward movement. It is a promise badly betrayed in the experience of the neurotic heroine of *A Shooting Star*; it is a promise that is in part realized by the ability of the retired academic in *All the Little Live Things* to be a stern judge of the course that American civilization is taking. The retired academic reappears—in essence if not in fact—as the historian-hero of *Angle of Repose*, a man who is confined to a wheel-chair and passes his time writing a work, part-history, part-fiction, that recreates the Western experience of his grandmother. This woman's life was marked by a kind of promise; she regarded her Western life as an exile from the East and was yet determined to extract meaning from an experience that was frustrating and provincial.

These examples give one some idea of what one will encounter in the novels of Stegner. The subject-matter is, within the limits indicated, various. But the style and the writer's attention to his material create an effect of considerable unity in the entire body of work. The style is sober and expresses the desire of the author to reproduce the persons and the settings of their experience as, supposedly, they actually existed. The novels plainly rest at many points on careful research, as Stegner notes in prefatory remarks to *Second Growth*:

> The making of fiction entails the creation of places and persons with all the seeming of reality, and these places and persons, no matter how a writer tries to invent them, must be made up piece-meal from sublimations of his own experience and his own acquaintance. There is no other material out of which fiction can be made.

This is an observation that is supplemented—but not contradicted by—the "Foreword" to the IWW novel, *The Preacher and the Slave*, where Stegner defends the novelist's right to reshape what has come to him not from direct experience but from research. This is a set of remarks that express and justify the boldness with which the historian-novelist of *Angle of Repose* handles and supplements the letters, articles, and drawings out of which he reconstructs his grandmother's Western life. If there is indeed a "seeming of reality" in Stegner's fiction, it is a reality constructed by a prose that is exhaustive and faithful; there are not turns of language that, as in much modern fiction, mock the reality that the author has created only to put in question.

This style is, of course, an expression of the unfolding assessment of experience in Stegner's novels. It is an assessment that moves toward precision and some bitterness in the most recent novels. But the main outlines of this assessment are already apparent in an early work like *On a Darkling Plain*. When desperate laughter sweeps a roomful of persons suffering from influenza, Stegner indicates that there are two ways to view miserable humanity. The world may indeed be the work of a "malevolent torturer"—a reference to a dark power that is the nearest Stegner comes to theological reference, for he is the most non-theological of novelists. This "torturer" may indeed have peopled the earth with "cannibal apes." Yet Stegner qualifies this vision. "At its worst the world had that face, but at its best, in its stricken hours, one saw the reserves of nobility and endurance and high-hearted courage that kept the race alive." Stegner's hero "knew, as he had always known since Ypres, that in the comradeship of ruin there was a tempering of the spirit; the resiliency of humanity under the whip was justification for all its meannesses."

In his reading of human behavior Stegner tends to separate the "cannibal apes" from those who display "reserves of nobility and endurance and high-hearted courage." In contrast to the resilient in *On a Darkling Plain* is a low-minded, lecherous Cockney who introduces the influenza virus to his betters. *Second Growth* offers us a New England Eden—or comparative Eden—corrupted by the presence of a Lesbian. Stegner's dichotomy becomes intense in *All the Little Live Things* and *Angle of Repose*. Both novels, as noted, are told from the point of view of a meditative, scholarly, and elderly man who is able to remember and reconstruct the hopes of earlier generations. Against these hopes, both men put the current reality. It is a reality in which the privileged have lost the sense that privilege imposes obligations. It is a reality in which the underprivileged have detached themselves from the "comradeship of ruin" and seek the instant salvation that drugs and "meditation" offer. The grandmother of *Angle of Repose* accepted the "comradeship of ruin"; those who have come after her try to evade it. So doing, they turn their backs on the sort of experience that Stegner finds in the Western past. It is this keen sense of wilful modern betrayal, wilful evasion of the harsh conditions under which all men exist, that accounts for the bitter and prophetic ire that now marks Stegner's work.

—Harold H. Watts

---

**STERN, James (Andrew).** British. Born in Kilcairne, County Meath, Ireland, 26 December 1904. Educated at Eton College, Buckinghamshire; Royal Military College, Sandhurst. Married Tania Kurella in 1935. Farmer in Rhodesia, 1925–26; Bank Clerk in London and Germany, 1927–29. Assistant Editor, *London Mercury*, 1929–31. Free-lance Journalist, in much of Europe; lived for 16 years in the United States. Recipient: National Institute of Arts and Letters grant, 1949; British Arts Council award, 1966. Fellow, Royal Society of Literature, 1953. Address: Hatch Manor, Tisbury, Wiltshire, England.

PUBLICATIONS

Short Stories

> *The Heartless Land.*   London, Macmillan, and New York, Macmillan, 1932.
> *Something Wrong.*   London, Secker, 1938.
> *The Man Who Was Loved.*   New York, Harcourt Brace, 1951; London, Secker and Warburg, 1952.
> *The Stories of James Stern.*   London, Secker and Warburg, 1968; New York, Harcourt Brace, 1969.

Uncollected Short Stories

> "The Dunce", in *London Mercury*, July 1931.
> "Strangers Defeated", in *London Mercury*, August 1933.
> "The Man from Montparnasse", in *Penguin Parade 1*.   London, Penguin, 1937.
> "The Thief", in *New Statesman and Nation* (London), 14 September 1940.
> "The Young Lady", in *Penguin Parade 7*.   London, Penguin, 1940.
> "The Ebbing Tide", in *Penguin New Writing*.   London, Penguin, 1942.
> "The Pauper's Grave", in *Harper's Bazaar* (New York), 1946.
> "A Day at the Races", in *Dublin Magazine*, Winter 1970–71.

Other

   *The Hidden Damage* (autobiographical account of pre- and post-Hitler Germany). New York, Harcourt Brace, 1947.

   Editor, *Grimm's Fairy Tales*.   New York, Pantheon Books, 1944; London, Routledge, 1948.

   Translator (as Andrew St. James), *Brazil: Land of the Future*, by Stefan Zweig.   New York, Viking Press, 1941.
   Translator (as Andrew St. James), *Amerigo Vespucci*, by Stefan Zweig.   New York, Viking Press, 1942.
   Translator, *The Rise and Fall of the House of Ullstein*, by Herman Ullstein.   New York, Simon and Schuster, 1943; London, Nicholson and Watson, 1944.
   Translator, with E. B. Ashton (as Andrew St. James), *The Twins of Nuremberg*, by Hermann Kesten.   New York, Fischer, 1946.
   Translator, *Spark of Life*, by Erich Maria Remarque.   New York, Appleton Century Crofts, and London, Hutchinson, 1952.
   Translator, with Tania Stern, *Selected Prose*, by Hugo von Hofmannsthal.   New York, Pantheon Books, and London, Routledge, 1952.
   Translator, with Tania Stern, *Letters to Milena*, by Franz Kafka.   London, Secker and Warburg, 1953; New York, Schocken Books, 1954.
   Translator, *A Woman in Berlin* (anonymous).   New York, Harcourt Brace, and London, Secker and Warburg, 1954.
   Translator, with Robert Pick, *Casanova's Memoirs*.   New York, Harper, 1955.
   Translator, *The Foreign Minister*, by Leo Lania.   Boston, Houghton Mifflin, and London, Davies, 1956.
   Translator, with Tania Stern and W. H. Auden, *The Caucasian Chalk Circle*, by Bertolt Brecht.   London, Methuen, 1960.
   Translator, with Tania Stern, *Description of a Struggle and Other Stories*, by Franz Kafka.   New York, Schocken Books, and London, Secker and Warburg, 1960.
   Translator, with Elisabeth Duckworth, *Letters to Felice Bauer*, by Franz Kafka.   New York, Schocken Books, and London, Secker and Warburg, 1972.


Critical Study: essay by William Plomer, in *London Magazine*, April 1968.


James Stern comments:

   The main comment I feel like making about my fiction is that it is *short*. The difference between a short story writer and a novelist is similar to that between a sprinter and a miler. Unfortunately the short story form has never been popular in England. As a result the writer of stories is frowned upon by publishers. Unless he will consent to write a novel. And this, I believe, is one reason why book-stores and libraries abound in mediocre novels.

*     *     *

   The settings of James Stern's stories are as varied as the parts of the world in which he has travelled and lived for over six decades. The Irish stories reflect the memories of his youth; those laid in South Africa (most of which were collected in his first volume, *The Heartless Land*) his life there as a farmer; there are stories from his years in France, Germany and the United States; there are even several laid in the South Pacific.

His best work, however, is more concerned with a special time of life than a particular place. Certainly his stories of boyhood ("Our Father," "The Beginning and the End," "Under the Beech Tree," and "The Broken Leg," for instance) must be ranked high. Most of these ("The Broken Leg" is an exception) are narrated in the first person. Whether or not, therefore, they represent artistically arranged versions of events in the author's life, these stories have the mark of truth. One knows, in "The Beginning and the End," that this is exactly how a ten year old boy would react to the news of the death of his first "love."

The early South African stories have a special flavor quite their own—possibly because to most readers, even in this jet age, Africa is still the "mysterious continent." And, indeed, Mr. Stern catches something of the primeval force of that land in stories such as "The Cloud." Long before the racial problems of South Africa became matters of world interest, his stories were dealing with them. In fact, "The Force," a story from the 1932 collection, anticipates Alan Paton's use of the theme of miscegenation in *Too Late the Phalarope*

Several good uncollected stories, e.g. "The Dunce" (which must be one of the earliest) and "The Thief," deal with boyhood. But it is a story with an African background, "Strangers Defeated," that one most regrets not finding in any of Mr. Stern's collections. This is the story of a spirited horse and its owner, neither of whom is accepted by the natives until their spirits are broken: the horse's by sickness and the master's by his inability to deal with the stubbornness of his workers. Seeing what happens to the horse and his owner, we are able to better understand a land and its people.

And, indeed, this is what makes James Stern the fine writer that he is. It is not simply that the incidents on which his stories are based are interesting, as they surely must be for success, or that his settings give us a sense of place, or even that his characters are real and, in today's cant term, "psychologically sound." It is, rather, the fact that, in his best stories, because of what his characters do and say as they act out their little dramas in whatever setting Mr. Stern has chosen for them, we, as readers, are able to catch a momentary vision of the truth that shimmers under the surface of life. And if a storyteller can help us to do this, he has done much.

—Norman T. Gates

---

**STERN, Richard G(ustave).** American. Born in New York City, 25 February 1928. Educated at the University of North Carolina, Chapel Hill, B.A. 1947 (Phi Beta Kappa); Harvard University, Cambridge, Massachusetts, M.A. 1949; University of Iowa, Iowa City, Ph.D. 1954. Served as an Educational Adviser, United States Army, 1951–52. Married Gay Clark in 1950; has four children. Lektor, University of Heidelberg, 1950–51; Instructor, Connecticut College, New London, 1951–52. Since 1955, Member of the Faculty, and since 1965, Professor of English, University of Chicago. Visiting Lecturer, University of Venice, 1962–63; University of California at Santa Barbara, 1964; State University of New York at Buffalo, 1966; Harvard University, 1969; University of Nice, 1970. Recipient: Longwood Fellowship, 1960; Friends of Literature Award, 1963; Rockefeller Fellowship, 1965; National Institute of Arts and Letters grant, 1968; National Endowment for the Arts grant, 1969. Address: Department of English, University of Chicago, 1050 East 59th Street, Chicago, Illinois 60637, U.S.A.

PUBLICATIONS

Novels

*Golk*.   New York, Criterion Books, and London, MacGibbon and Kee, 1960.
*Europe; or, Up and Down with Schreiber and Baggish*.   New York, McGraw Hill, 1961;
    as *Europe; or, Up and Down with Baggish and Schreiber*, London, MacGibbon and
    Kee, 1962.
*In Any Case*.   New York, McGraw Hill, and London, MacGibbon and Kee, 1963.
*Stitch*.   New York, Harper, 1965; London, Hodder and Stoughton, 1967.

Short Stories

*Teeth, Dying, and Other Matters, and The Gamesman's Island: A Play*.   New York,
    Harper, and London, MacGibbon and Kee, 1964.
*1968: A Short Novel, An Urban Idyll, Five Stories and Two Trade Notes*.   New York,
    Holt Rinehart, 1970; London, Gollancz, 1971.

Other

*One Person and Another* (essays).   New York, Dutton, 1972.

Editor, *Honey and Wax: Pleasures and Powers of Narrative: An Anthology*.   Chicago,
    University of Chicago Press, 1966.

Manuscript Collection: Regenstein Library, University of Chicago.

Critical Studies: by Marcus Klein, in *Reporter* (Washington, D.C.), 1966; review by Hugh
Kenner, in *Chicago Review*, Summer 1966; an interview with Robert Raeder, in *Chicago
Review*, Summer 1966.

*     *     *

In a time when serious American fiction has tended towards extreme personal assertion
and extravagance of manner, Richard G. Stern has been composing a body of work which is
notable for its detailed craftsmanship, its intricacy, and its reticences. His novels and stories
are neither lyrically confessional nor abstractly experimental. They are processes quite in the
mode of an older tradition, in which character and event discover theme. The process, in
Stern's application, discourages such practices as the foregrounding of language, the
intrusion of prior theories and ideologies, and the appearance of authorial manipulation,
while at the same time—unlike, for instance, the *nouveau roman* in its French or American
versions—it actively seeks moral realizations. In one and another incidental observation
within his fiction, Stern has rejected both the idea of the novel as "a roller coaster of distress
and sympathy, love and desire," and the idea of the novel as a deliberate attack on formal
expectations (*Europe*, p. 151); he has addressed qualification to the view that a story is fully
autonomous (see the sketch called "Introductory" in *1968*), but he has also rejected the idea
of the author as solipsist (see "Story-Making" in *1968*). His own fiction accepts no extremities
of technique and form. Its characteristic tone as well as its strategy of development is created
by ironic modulations.

The tone and the technique are, moreover, exact functions of Stern's characteristic subject. The broad theme is the adjustment of private lives with public events. Typically, Stern's protagonist has been a passive, sensitive fellow, who is a little too old for adventuring, or a little too fat, or a little too fine-grained, but nonetheless possessing romantic inclinations. His latent disposition is tested when public event of one sort and another seeks him out. He is now forced to regard his own actions and the actions of others as moral events. And, typically, this protagonist has found himself engaged in a drama of betrayals, which have the effect of chastening his new ambitions as a public man. The end is his rather baffled, rather weary abandonment of adventure. Between the beginning and the end, his motives are subjected to more and more contingencies. He has been lured from his innocent privacy into life, defined as public action which by its nature is dangerous and ambiguous. At the end he has sacrificed the self-protectedness with which he began, and he has also failed to discover a tenable ground of general participation in life. His modest success is that he has become potentially moral.

Stern's first novel, *Golk*, is somewhat more spare and blatant in its actions than the fictions which follow, but it is otherwise exemplary. The hero is a thirty-seven-year-old boy, Herbert Hondorp, who lives alone with his widowed father in New York City. As he has done for most of the days of his life, he now spends his days wandering in and near Central Park, until on an occasion, abruptly, he is snared into public view and public occupation. The agent is a television program—"Golk"—which is created, precisely, by making public revelation of privacy. Ordinary, unwary people are caught by the television camera in pre-arranged, embarrassing situations. Stern's hero discovers that he likes not only the being caught, as do most of the Golk victims, but he also likes the catching. He takes a job with the television program, and not fortuitously at the same time he secures his first romance. Within this new situation there are moral implications, of course, but both "Golk" and Hondorp's romance are tentative and jesting. The novel then proceeds to raise the stakes of involvement: the program is transformed by its ambitious director into a device for political exposé, and Hondorp's romance becomes a marriage. This newer situation, then, beckons and perhaps necessitates treacheries, which make it morally imperative that public involvement be terminated. Hondorp betrays the director of the program, in order to save the program—so he believes—from the fury of the political powers, and he thereby reduces it to vapidity. In a consequent narrative movement, his wife leaves him. Hondorp goes home at the end, "all trace of his ambition, and all desire for change gone absolutely and forever."

In his subsequent fictions, Stern has avoided such metaphorical ingenuity as the television program in *Golk*, and the lure to public action has been carefully limited to a matter of background or accident but the area of his concern has remained constant. In *Europe; or, Up and Down with Schreiber and Baggish*, the two protagonists are by happenstance American civil employees in post-war occupied Germany. The pattern of their adventuring—despite the comic suggestion in the title of the novel—allows nothing implausible, and there are no sudden reversals. Realization is to be achieved, rather, through implied contrasts and comparisons. Schreiber is an aging sensitive gentleman who tries for intimate understanding of the ancient, bitter, guilty, and conquered people. Baggish is a shrewd young opportunist, who exploits the populace. Baggish succeeds, and Schreiber fails. *In Any Case* is the story of another aging American in post-war Europe, who in this instance is innocent for the reason that he has never sufficiently risked anything, his affections included. His testing comes when he is told that his son, dead in the war, was a traitor. In a belated and ironic act of love, he tries to prove that his son was really innocent, and he discovers that treachery is a vital ingredient of all social living. Although his son was indeed not guilty in the way supposed, everyone is a double agent.

His acceptance of that discovery provides the hero with the possibility of a modest participation in other people's lives. In his more recent fictions, Stern has apparently wanted to make that possibility more emphatic, by bringing historical and aesthetic confirmations to it. *Stitch* is in large part a *roman à clef* about one of the great modern traitors, Ezra Pound. The would-be disciple in the novel receives from the aged master, Stitch, lessons in the fusion of personality with civilization, and the consequence of expression in art. The background of the novel is Venice, which, from the muck of its history, raises its beauties. In the short novel *Veni, Vidi . . . Wendt* (included in *1968*), the protagonist is a composer who is writing an opera about modern love. The opera will extend backwards to include great love affairs of the past, which are founded on adulteries. The composer himself, meanwhile, realizes both his composition and his domestic love for wife and children only after experiments in romantic duplicity.

The endings of Stern's fictions record an acquiescence at the most, and always something less than the assertion of a principle. The kind of realization that is in the novels makes it necessary that they be probationary and open-ended. They are by that, as well as by their detailed, persistent, and moderate account of human motives, in the great tradition of moral realism.

—Marcus Klein

---

**STEWART, J(ohn) I(nnes) M(ackintosh).** Pseudonym: **Michael Innes.** British. Born in Edinburgh, 30 September 1906. Educated at Edinburgh Academy; Oriel College, Oxford, B.A. (1st class) in English 1928: awarded Matthew Arnold Memorial Prize, 1929; Bishop Fraser's Scholar, 1930. Married Margaret Hardwick in 1932; has five children. Lecturer in English, University of Leeds, Yorkshire, 1930–35; Jury Professor of English, University of Adelaide, South Australia, 1935–45; Lecturer, Queen's University, Belfast, 1946–48. Since 1949, Student (i.e., Fellow) of Christ Church, Oxford, and since 1969, Reader in English Literature, Oxford University. Walker Ames Professor, University of Washington, Seattle, 1961. D.Litt., University of New Brunswick, Fredericton, 1962. Address: Fawler Copse, Kingston Lisle, Wantage, Berkshire, England.

PUBLICATIONS

Novels (as J. I. M. Stewart)

*Mark Lambert's Supper*. London, Gollancz, 1954.
*The Guardians*. London, Gollancz, 1955; New York, Norton, 1957.
*A Use of Riches*. London, Gollancz, and New York, Norton, 1957.
*The Man Who Won the Pools*. London, Gollancz, and New York, Norton, 1961.
*The Last Tresilians*. London, Gollancz, and New York, Norton, 1963.
*An Acre of Grass*. London, Gollancz, and New York, Norton, 1965.
*The Aylwins*. London, Gollancz, and New York, Norton, 1966.
*Vanderlyn's Kingdom*. London, Gollancz, and New York, Norton 1967.
*Avery's Mission*. London, Gollancz, and New York, Norton, 1971.
*A Palace of Art*. London, Gollancz, and New York, Norton, 1972.

Novels (as Michael Innes)

*Death at the President's Lodging*. London, Gollancz, 1936; as *Seven Suspects*, New York, Dodd Mead, 1937.
*Hamlet, Revenge!* London, Gollancz, and New York, Dodd Mead, 1937.

*Lament for a Maker*.  London, Gollancz, and New York, Dodd Mead, 1938.
*Stop Press*.  London, Gollancz, 1939; as *The Spider Strikes*, New York, Dodd Mead, 1939.
*The Secret Vanguard*.  London, Gollancz, 1940; New York, Dodd Mead, 1941.
*There Came Both Mist and Snow*.  London, Gollancz, 1940; as *A Comedy of Terrors*, New York, Dodd Mead, 1940.
*Appleby on Ararat*.  London, Gollancz, and New York, Dodd Mead, 1941.
*The Daffodil Affair*.  London, Gollancz, and New York, Dodd Mead, 1942.
*The Weight of the Evidence*.  London, Gollancz, 1943; New York, Dodd Mead, 1944.
*Appleby's End*.  London, Gollancz, and New York, Dodd Mead, 1945.
*From London Far*.  London, Gollancz, 1946; as *Unsuspected Chasm*, New York, Dodd Mead, 1946.
*What Happened at Hazelwood*.  London, Gollancz, 1946; New York, Dodd Mead, 1947.
*Night of Errors*.  London, Gollancz, 1947; New York, Dodd Mead, 1948.
*The Journeying Boy*.  London, Gollancz, 1949; as *The Case of the Journeying Boy*, New York, Dodd Mead, 1949.
*Operation Pax*.  London, Gollancz, 1951; as *Paper Thunderbolt*, New York, Dodd Mead, 1951.
*Private View*.  London, Gollancz, 1952; as *One Man Show*, New York, Dodd Mead, 1952.
*Christmas at Candleshoe*.  London, Gollancz, and New York, Dodd Mead, 1953.
*The Man from the Sea*.  London, Gollancz, and New York, Dodd Mead, 1955.
*Old Hall, New Hall*.  London, Gollancz, 1956; as *A Question of Queens*, New York, Dodd Mead, 1956.
*Appleby Plays Chicken*.  London, Gollancz, 1957; as *Death on a Quiet Day*, New York, Dodd Mead, 1957.
*The Long Farewell*.  London, Gollancz, and New York, Dodd Mead, 1958.
*Hare Sitting Up*.  London, Gollancz, and New York, Dodd Mead, 1959.
*The New Sonia Wayward*.  London, Gollancz, 1960; as *The Case of Sonia Wayward*, New York, Dodd Mead, 1960.
*Silence Observed*.  London, Gollancz, and New York, Dodd Mead, 1961.
*A Connoisseur's Case*.  London, Gollancz, 1962; as *The Crabtree Affair*, New York, Dodd Mead, 1962.
*Money from Holme*.  London, Gollancz, 1964; New York, Dodd Mead, 1965.
*The Bloody Wood*.  London, Gollancz, and New York, Dodd Mead, 1966.
*A Change of Heir*.  London, Gollancz, and New York, Dodd Mead, 1966.
*Death by Water*.  London, Gollancz, and New York, Dodd Mead, 1968.
*Appleby at Allington*.  London, Gollancz, and New York, Dodd Mead, 1968.
*A Family Affair*.  London, Gollancz, 1969; as *Picture of Guilt*, New York, Dodd Mead, 1969.
*Death at the Chase*.  London, Gollancz, and New York, Dodd Mead, 1970.
*An Awkward Lie*.  London, Gollancz, and New York, Dodd Mead, 1971.
*The Open House*.  London, Gollancz, and New York, Dodd Mead, 1972.


Short Stories (as J. I. M. Stewart)

*The Man Who Wrote Detective Stories and Other Stories*.  London, Gollancz, and New York, Norton, 1959.
*Cucumber Sandwiches*.  London, Gollancz, and New York, Norton, 1969.

Short Stories (as Michael Innes)

*Three Tales of Hamlet*, with Rayner Heppenstall.  London, Gollancz, 1950.

*Appleby Talking: Twenty-Three Detective Stories.* London, Gollancz, 1954; as *Dead Man's Shoes*, New York, Dodd Mead, 1954.
*Appleby Talks Again: Eighteen Detective Stories.* London, Gollancz, 1956; New York, Dodd Mead, 1957.

Other (as J. I. M. Stewart)

*Educating the Emotions.* Adelaide, New Education Fellowship, 1944.
*Character and Motive in Shakespeare: Some Recent Appraisals Examined.* London and New York, Longman, 1949.
*Eight Modern Writers.* London and New York, Oxford University Press, 1963.
*Rudyard Kipling.* London, Gollancz, and New York, Dodd Mead, 1966.
*Joseph Conrad.* London, Longman, and New York, Dodd Mead, 1968.
*Thomas Hardy.* London, Longman, and New York, Dodd Mead, 1971.

Editor, *Montaigne's Essays: John Florio's Translation.* London, Nonesuch Press, and New York, Random House, 1931.

\*       \*       \*

Michael Innes is remarkable for his wide range, which extends from intricate closed-group murder cases (e.g., *The Weight of the Evidence, The Long Farewell, The Bloody Wood*) to fights against large-scale criminal operators (e.g., *From London Far*) and organised madness representing a global menace (e.g., *Hare Sitting Up*). His investigators are also diversified. John Appleby, the gentleman turned policeman and rising from plain inspector to knighted commissioner, now living in active retirement at his sculpturing wife's small manor, is the main detective figure. At times, however, he is replaced by the formidable Inspector Cadover (as in *What Happened at Hazelwood*), and some books manage without a detective altogether: psychological studies like *The New Sonia Wayward* or the puzzling *Money from Holme*. The narrative techniques vary as well. A detached third-person narrator dominates, sometimes more obtrusively than desirable; but some stories are told by personally involved, highly self-conscious and unreliable figures like Arthur Ferryman (*There Came Both Mist and Snow*).

Basic characteristics of the novels are: the academic, professional and aristocratic milieu, leading to an inexhaustible interest in, and knowledge of, literature and the arts in most characters—this not only forms a large element of the content but is also frequently used functionally for the plot (as in *The Secret Vanguard*); the distribution of suspense and surprise throughout the stories, but sometimes concentrated in long, gripping accounts of flight and pursuit (most remarkably in *The Journeying Boy, Operation Pax,* and *The Man from the Sea*); a definite strain of the fantastic, indeed the fairy tale (very strong in *The Daffodil Affair* and *Appleby's End*); finally, the aspect of wild comedy, manifesting itself in innumerable verbal jokes, in university-prank interludes, in a stock character like Hildebert Braunkopf with his "voonderable voorlt of art" as well as entire stories (*A Change of Heir*). The latest novels, especially *A Family Affair*, suggest a certain fatigue, but still provide good and intelligent entertainment. Innes may yet surprise us, except that he is unlikely to venture into the remorseless, bleak, and insecure world of modern English crime fiction where integrity no longer is a univeral trait of policemen, where Keats, Piero and Raeburn are irrelevant.

For a considerable time now the author has also produced novels under his real name J. I. M. Stewart. The complex web of connections between the "non-serious" and the "serious" works is a fascinating subject. If his crime stories are often tied up with *objets d'art*, the majority of his serious novels concentrate on the creative process, the artist and his relation to other people. The most obvious link between the two kinds of fiction is the quest for posthumous works of writers or painters—developing a theme from Henry James ("The Aspern Papers"; cf. *Mark Lambert's Supper, The Guardians, An Acre of Grass*). This writer also provides technical inspiration (James' "reflectors"—most patently in *The Aylwins* and *Vanderlyn's Kingdom*). In addition, there is a touch of the regional novel, and a surprising number of studies of old age. The comic and dramatic are equally present, handled with the same skill and tact as in the detective and adventure books. But whereas the refined world of the Oxford don adds a brilliant, strange and poignantly comic lustre to the world of crime, it does not always successfully stand up on its own. In the annals of crime fiction Innes will always loom large. In those of the modern English novel Stewart has so far secured a definite, if confined niche—perhaps mainly on account of *A Use of Riches* and *The Last Tresilians*.

—H. M. Klein

---

**STIRLING, Monica.** British. Born in 1916, daughter of the actor-manager Edward Stirling. Grew up in France. War Correspondent in France, for *Atlantic Monthly*, 1944. Recipient: Metro-Goldwyn award, 1946. Address: c/o Harcourt, Brace and Jovanovich, 757 Third Avenue, New York, New York 10017, U.S.A.

PUBLICATIONS

Novels

*Lovers Aren't Company*.   London, Gollancz, and Boston, Little Brown, 1949.
*Dress Rehearsal*.   London, Gollancz, 1951; New York, Simon and Schuster, 1952.
*Ladies with a Unicorn*.   London, Gollancz, 1953; New York, Simon and Schuster, 1954.
*Boy in Blue*.   London, Gollancz, and New York, Coward McCann, 1955.
*Some Darling Folly*.   London, Gollancz, and New York, Coward McCann, 1956.
*Sigh for a Strange Land*.   London, Gollancz, 1958; Boston, Little Brown, 1959.
*A Sniper in the Heart*.   London, Gollancz, 1960.
*The Summer of a Dormouse*.   London, Collins, and New York, Harcourt Brace, 1967.

Short Stories

*Adventurers Please Abstain: Short Stories*.   London, Gollancz, 1952.
*Journeys We Shall Never Make: Short Stories*.   London, Gollancz, 1957.

Other

*The Little Ballet Dancer* (juvenile).   New York, Lothrop, 1952.
*The Fine and the Wicked: The Life and Times of Ouida*.   London, Gollancz, 1957; New York, Coward McCann, 1958.
*A Pride of Lions: A Portrait of Napoleon's Mother*.   London, Collins, 1961; as *Madame Letizia: A Portrait of Napoleon's Mother*, New York, Harper, 1961.
*The Wild Swan: The Life and Times of Hans Christian Andersen*.   London, Collins, and New York, Harcourt Brace, 1965.
*The Cat from Nowhere* (juvenile).   New York, Harcourt Brace, 1969.

\*          \*          \*

Monica Stirling has written some eight novels, two volumes of short stories, and several biographies and juveniles; all her work is pleasant and entertaining, designed for the general reader. From her own knowledge of Europe just after the war and her close association with the theatre Miss Stirling has, in one novel after another, created situations and characters reflecting her background.

Her first novel, *Lovers Aren't Company*, set in Rome in 1944, tells the story of an American woman of Italian descent who returns to find her sister dead and her niece totally confused. A decade later in *Sigh for a Strange Land* there is another such situation of a girl with an Italian background who becomes much involved with the sorrows and upheavals of refugees fleeing East Europe. In both *Ladies with a Unicorn* and *Boy in Blue* there are characters whose families have been wiped out in the war. In the former, the protagonist, Françoise Jonbert, has lost her husband; in the latter, Laurent, a charming young composer, has lost mother, father, and twin brother in the deliberate destruction by the Germans of a small village in the south of France. In spite of the suggested tragedies the materials are handled in such a way that the reader is never disturbed as in smooth descriptive prose Miss Stirling tells about the events.

In general the most attractive features of the novels are the various settings; the books could very well serve as travelogues. Miss Stirling is obviously thoroughly familiar with Italy, France, and England. The sights and sounds, the way of life, especially the sensuous opulence of the rich and successful in France and Italy, are all a part of her work. In some of the novels these features are successful; in others, they are merely decorative, and, indeed, sometimes they serve to make serious themes trivial and heavy-handed.

*Dress Rehearsal* and *Some Darling Folly* are the two most successful of the novels. *Dress Rehearsal* is hardly a novel in the usual terms; it is, in fact, a series of engaging episodes, strongly autobiographical, of the boarding-school days in England of the daughter of a successful actor. The contrast of the warm family life of the past with the rather chilly properness of an English school is nicely done. *Some Darling Folly* is also about the world of the theatre. In this novel the traditional triangle is handled competently and wittily. It is the story of a French actor, Remy, who, intrigued by the artlessness of a lawyer's wife, is somewhat disconcerted to discover that his "interest" is quite able to discard him without tears and return to her husband.

Miss Stirling's work for juveniles shows her charm and her smooth skill as a writer. *The Little Ballet Dancer* is an account of a little French girl who wanted to become a ballet dancer. *The Summer of a Dormouse* shows a skillful blend of sympathy and charm. It is the story of a young girl's recovery from a mental illness, reflecting perhaps Miss Stirling's biographical study of Hans Christian Andersen.

All of Miss Stirling's work shows the hand of a competent, charming and witty person; unfortunately this charm and wit are seldom a part of her characters, and the themes, while thoroughly admirable, are handled in an obvious and trite fashion. Someone has called her work "quality feminine fiction." If one may designate fiction as "feminine" and thereafter qualify it with any possible meaning of "quality", then perhaps this is a proper label.

—Annibel Jenkins

---

**STIVENS, Dal(las George).**    Australian.    Born in Blayney, New South Wales, 31 December 1911. Educated at Barker College, Hornsby, Sydney, 1927–28. Served in the Australian Army Education Service, 1943–44. Married Winifred Vera Wright in 1945; has two children.

Served in the Australian Department of Information, 1944–50: Press Officer, Australia House, London, 1949–50. Foundation President, 1963–64, Vice President, 1964–66, and President, 1967–72, Australian Society of Authors. Member, New South Wales Advisory Committee, Australian Broadcasting Commission, 1968–72. Chairman, Literary Committee, Captain Cook Bicentenary Celebrations, 1969–70. Recipient: Commonwealth Literary Fund Fellowship, 1951, 1962, 1970; Miles Franklin Award, 1970. Address: 5 Middle Harbour Road, Lindfield, New South Wales 2070, Australia.

PUBLICATIONS

Novels

*Jimmy Brockett: Portrait of a Notable Australian.*   London, Britannicus Liber, 1951.
*The Wide Arch.*   London, Angus and Robertson, 1958.
*Three Persons Make a Tiger.*   Melbourne, Cheshire, 1968.
*A Horse of Air.*   Sydney and London, Angus and Robertson, 1970.

Short Stories

*The Tramp and Other Stories.*   London, Macmillan, 1936.
*The Courtship of Uncle Henry: Short Stories.*   Melbourne, Reed and Harris, 1946.
*The Gambling Ghost and Other Stories.*   London, Angus and Robertson, 1953.
*Ironbark Bill.*   London, Angus and Robertson, 1955.
*The Scholarly Mouse and Other Tales.*   London, Angus and Robertson, 1957.
*Selected Stories, 1936–1968.*   London, Angus and Robertson, 1970.

Other

*A Guide to Book Contracts,* with Barbara Jefferis.   Sydney, Australian Society of Authors, 1957.

Editor, *Coast to Coast: Australian Stories 1957–1958.*   Sydney, Angus and Robertson, 1959.

Critical Studies: "The Author in Search of Himself: Some Notes on Dal Stivens" by Brian Elliott, in *Australian Quarterly* (Sydney), March 1962; Introduction by H. P. Heseltine to *Selected Stories, 1936–1968*, 1970.

Dal Stivens comments:

It is difficult to comment on your own work, particularly when it extends over 35 years. During that time your interest in various aspects of life, etc. has changed. But my underlying interest has been in the tension between illusion and reality, art and life. The most recently published novel, *A Horse of Air*, exemplifies this preoccupation. What is the truth? Is it not relative? Importantly, a novel or a short story isn't a transcript of life. It's an art object just as a painting is—or used to be.

\*          \*          \*

One remembers Dal Stivens as a small man with a bright eye under a jaunty hat, with quick movements and a more or less staccato speech. He is best known for *Jimmy Brockett*, a novel with a kind of jinx. First published in 1951, it has been variously reprinted and eventually reached a paperbook issue, yet the Australian public has consistently failed to acknowledge the brilliance of its image therein reflected. The colour and character of life in Australia have been changing so rapidly and so radically in the years since war shattered the complacency of the Pacific, that a temporary neglect of satire so local is hardly remarkable. Jimmy Brockett is a character in the Falstaffian mould, conceived in terms of a richly coarse humour, an enormity of a man both mentally and physically, in whom speaks the spirit of post-colonial Australian aggressiveness and enterprise, crude, pragmatic, singleminded and utterly philistine—and yet not without a heart, capable of tenderness in a bull-like and domineering way, and especially a conqueror of (and no less a martyr to) women. A comparison might be made with *Babbitt*; but Stivens's satire is, in the Australian way, warmer and more tolerant of human failings. The setting of the novel is Sydney and the banner it carries is for the common man—that is, the uncommon common man, the nobody of genius. Jimmy in dying crowns his career of sad triumphs with a direction which sums up his attitude to the hypocritical world: "I have asked the undertaker to put me on my face in my coffin so that anyone who doesn't like my will can kiss my arse."

*The Wide Arch* abandons serious portraiture and naturalism and attempts a sophisticated murder-mystery form, using as its main intellectual ingredient a scheme of *Hamlet* parallels in a Sydney setting. The book retains its interest rather as a literary experiment than as a narrative of suspense. Experiment still dominates *Three Persons Make a Tiger*, alleged to be an adaptation of a Chinese work but really a free variation on a Chinese theme with so high a degree of fantasy that its Australian satirical content tends to evaporate. It is at its best witty and clever but its successes are fragmentary. The most recent novel, *A Horse of Air*, recovers ground and is agreeably readable besides making an imaginative use of the Australian "mythical" values implicit in the journals of the explorer Giles, whose excursion into the Rawlinson Ranges provides Stivens with a "quest" theme (a search for a rare "night parrot"). However in general his novels since *Jimmy Brockett* all strive too transparently to keep up with the trends.

Similarly in the short stories the pattern is one of decline. The best of all his work appears in *The Tramp* and *The Courtship of Uncle Henry*: stories and sketches of an imaginative truth and insight rare in Australian writing and not inferior to the best of Henry Lawson. In later stories (*The Gambling Ghost, Ironbark Bill* and *The Scholarly Mouse*) he pushed spontaneous invention in the direction of a folksy style which undercut natural inspiration, with the result that, although witty and amusing at best, he lost touch with his own basic originality. He remains, however, an undervalued Australian writer who may some day yet receive the benefit of an upward reassessment.

—Brian Elliott

---

**STONE, Irving.** American. Born in San Francisco, California, 14 July 1903. Educated at Lowell High School, San Francisco; Manual Arts High School, Los Angeles; University of California, Berkeley, A.B. 1923; University of Southern California, Los Angeles, M.A. 1924; University of California, Berkeley, as Ph.D. candidate, 1924–26. Married Jean Factor in 1934; has two children. Teaching Fellow in Economics, University of Southern California, 1923–24, and University of California, Berkeley, 1924–26. Visiting Lecturer in Creative Writing, University of Indiana, Bloomington, 1948, and University of Washington, Seattle, 1961; Lecturer on the writing of biography and the biographical novel, University of Southern

California, 1966; Lecturer, California State Colleges, 1966. Art Critic, *Los Angeles Mirror-News*, 1959–60. United States Department of State Cultural Exchange Specialist, in the Soviet Union, Poland and Yugoslavia, 1962. President, California Writers Guild, 1960–61; California Chairman, National Library Week, 1962; Founder, Academy of American Poets, 1962; Founder, California State Colleges Committee for the Arts, 1967; Trustee, Douglass House Foundation, Watts, Los Angeles, 1967–68; President, Dante Alighieri Society, Los Angeles, 1968–69. Since 1955, Founder and President, Fellows for Schweitzer, Southern California; since 1963, Vice-President, Eugene V. Debs Foundation, Terre Haute, Indiana, and Member, Advisory Board, University of California Institute for the Creative Arts; since 1969, President, Affiliates of the Department of English, University of California, Los Angeles. Recipient: Christopher Award, 1957. D.L., University of Southern California, 1965; D.Litt., Coe College, Cedar Rapids, Iowa, 1967; LL.D., University of California, Berkeley, 1968. Commendatore (Knight Commander), Republic of Italy, 1962. Lives in Beverly Hills, California. Address: c/o Doubleday and Company, 501 Franklin Avenue, Garden City, New York 11530, U.S.A.

PUBLICATIONS

Novels

   *Pageant of Youth*.   New York, King, 1933.
   *Lust for Life*.   New York, Longman, 1934; London, Lane, 1935.
   *Sailor on Horseback*.   Boston, Houghton Mifflin, and London, Collins, 1938.
   *False Witness*.   New York, Doubleday, 1940.
   *Immortal Wife*.   New York, Doubleday, 1944; London, Falcon Press, 1950.
   *Adversary in the House*.   New York, Doubleday, and London, Falcon Press, 1947.
   *The Passionate Journey*.   New York, Doubleday, 1949; London, Falcon Press, 1950.
   *The President's Lady*.   New York, Doubleday, 1951; London, Lane, 1952.
   *Love Is Eternal*.   New York, Doubleday, 1954; London, Collins, 1955.
   *The Agony and the Ecstasy*.   New York, Doubleday, and London, Collins, 1961.
   *Those Who Love*.   New York, Doubleday, 1965; London, Cassell, 1967.
   *The Passions of the Mind*.   New York, Doubleday, and London, Cassell, 1971.

Other

   *Clarence Darrow for the Defense*.   New York, Doubleday, 1941; as *Darrow for the Defence*, London, Lane, 1950.
   *They Also Ran: The Story of the Men Who Were Defeated for the Presidency*.   New York, Doubleday, 1943.
   *Earl Warren*.   New York, Prentice Hall, 1948.
   *We Speak for Ourselves: Self Portrait of America*, with Richard Kennedy.   New York, Doubleday, 1950.
   *Men to Match My Mountains: The Opening of the Far West, 1840–1900*.   New York, Doubleday, 1956; London, Cassell, 1967.
   *The Biographical Novel: Three Views of the Novel*.   Washington, D.C., Library of Congress, 1957.
   *The Irving Stone Reader*.   New York, Doubleday, 1963.
   *The Story of Michelangelo's Pietà*.   New York, Doubleday, 1964.
   *The Great Adventure of Michelangelo*.   New York, Doubleday, 1965.
   *There Was Light: Autobiography of a University, Berkeley, 1868–1968*.   Berkeley, University of California Press, 1970.

Editor, *Dear Theo: The Autobiography of Vincent van Gogh.* Boston, Houghton Mifflin, and London, Constable, 1937.

Editor, with Allen Nivens, *Lincoln: A Contemporary Portrait.* New York, Doubleday, 1962.

Editor, with Jean Stone, *I, Michelangelo, Sculptor: An Autobiography Through Letters.* New York, Doubleday, 1962; London, Collins, 1963.

\*     \*     \*

The historian in Irving Stone has cohabited with the artist through a dozen or so novels now, and although the public sanctions the arrangement by purchasing and reading the offspring books, the union is neither literarily nor historically holy. The novels that come of it suffer congenital defects; for all their broad appeal, there are problems with historical novels that are inescapable. Stone is an astute novelist, insofar as he recognizes a compelling story and can control the reader's attention for the most part, and he is a willing historian who researches his material copiously. But in the novels, the historian tends to inhibit the inventive imagination, embalming the dialogue and losing the plot for long periods in thickets of detail, while the artist always opens the history to a doubt that the most impressive bibliographical lists cannot still. This is, of course, true of all historical novelists, to an extent, but, paradoxically, the generic difficulty is more acute in the case of more serious ones, such as Stone, than in the case of slighter ones, such as Frank G. Slaughter, whose concern is entertainment and not authenticity, and whose works may be consumed like popcorn.

The point may be illustrated by any of Stone's novels. *Love Is Eternal,* for example, which treats the relationship between Mary Todd and Abraham Lincoln to the time of Lincoln's assassination, demonstrates Stone's characteristic use of the most minute details to evoke a sense of historical place. But while the setting and circumstances in which the main characters play are without doubt essentially correct, there remains the question of whether or not the conception of the characters is accurate as well. Stone is unconvincing in his attempt to restore the reputation of Mary Todd Lincoln, who has been excoriated by history. He may be right in his judgment of her, or his vindication of her may be simply an act of sentimental gallantry. There is no way to be certain; if the novel is an unfounded interpretation of her, Stone has misrepresented, and if there is historical evidence for his view, she would have been far better served by a documented history.

Stone is apparently aware, consciously or unconsciously, of the dilemma created by writing fiction that purports to echo fact, for, as in *Passionate Journey,* a fictional biography of the American painter John Noble, he is usually better when his characters act and react with each other according to the scenario provided by historical fact than when he seeks to interpret motivation. Perhaps the use of detail to the point of tediousness is an attempt to bring the problem that is imposed by the *genre* under control—an attempt to overwhelm it. *Those Who Love,* for instance, a treatment of the life and times of John and Abigail Adams, is not only lumbered with wooden dialogue, but overburdened with historical minutiae. The Michelangelo study, *The Agony and the Ecstasy,* as if to counter the effect of a great deal of love interest that smacks of modern interpolation, contains endless description of stone cutting and of anatomy, in a way that is reminiscent of Melville's whaling chapters but is less easily justifiable.

But the biographical novel does exist, of course, and Stone is undeniably one of its ablest practitioners. The history he spoon-feeds is far more palatable and interesting than popcorn, and it is no wonder that an enormous public should devour it.

—Alan R. Shucard

**STOREY, David (Malcolm).** British. Born in Wakefield, Yorkshire, 13 July 1933. Educated at Queen Elizabeth Grammar School, Wakefield; Slade School of Fine Art, London. Married Barbara Rudd Hamilton in 1956; has four children. Played professionally for the Leeds Rugby League Club, 1952–56. Recipient: Macmillan Award, 1960; Rhys Memorial Award, 1961; Maugham Award, 1963; *Evening Standard* Drama Award, 1967, 1970, 1971; Variety Club of Great Britain Writer of the Year Award, 1971. Address: 2 Lyndhurst Gardens, London N.W.3, England.

PUBLICATIONS

Novels

*This Sporting Life*. London, Longman, and New York, Macmillan, 1960.
*Flight into Camden*. London, Longman, and New York, Macmillan, 1961.
*Radcliffe*. London, Longman, 1963; New York, Coward McCann, 1964.
*A Temporary Life*. London, Longman, 1972.

Plays

*The Restoration of Arnold Middleton* (produced Edinburgh and London, 1967). London, Cape, 1967.
*In Celebration* (produced London, 1969). London, Cape, 1969.
*The Contractor* (produced London, 1970). London, Cape, 1970; New York, Random House, 1971.
*Home* (produced London, 1970; New York, 1971). London, Cape, 1970; New York, Random House, 1971.
*The Changing Room* (produced London, 1971). London, Cape, 1972.

Screenplay: *This Sporting Life*, 1963.

\*      \*      \*

David Storey's fiction was originally organized around a concept. In his first novel, *This Sporting Life*, he attempted to show the world of the body, the atmosphere of physicality, in this story of a young man from the lower-middle classes who tries to work his way to money and dignity by playing professional rugby. His second novel, *Flight into Camden*, is the novel depicting soul, the description of the hard spiritual independence of a miner's daughter who defies family to live with her married lover in London. *Radcliffe*, the third and most ambitious novel, portraying the troubled and violent relationship between Leonard Radcliffe, the sensitive descendant of impoverished gentility and aestheticism, and Victor Tolson, the powerful representative of the working classes, demonstrates the incompatibility of body and soul. In all the religious discussions and images in the novel, as well as in the epigraph from Yeats's "Vacillation VII," this irreconcilability between body and soul in human nature is regarded as original sin. Although *Radcliffe* was published in 1963, a projected fourth novel, in which body and soul were to be reconciled, has not yet appeared.

As is most apparent in *Radcliffe*, the conflict between body and soul is mirrored in the conflict between the working classes and the remnants of the aristocracy in northern English society. Beaumont, the place where Leonard's family lives, his father as caretaker and restorer, represents an aesthetically and historically valuable past that cannot survive in current industrial society without special and privileged attention. Similarly, Leonard himself needs the vital and sexual connection to Tolson's physicality in order to feel "whole." Combining the religious, social, and personal dimensions of the controversy between body and soul in one novel is difficult, and, although Storey keeps his metaphors consistent and presents the problems with a fierce emotional intensity, he pushes his characters to the point where the intense, narrow focus and the representational quality can only explode into melodrama. Leonard kills Tolson and soon dies himself; another central character, a buffoon who also wanted Tolson, kills his family and himself. The melodrama seems to simplify the issues of class and religion presented, yet the power of the presentation itself, the intensity, invites the melodrama.

The dominant metaphysical and ideological idea seems to limit some of Storey's fiction without adding anything unique or original. On the other hand, the fiction has considerable power, especially in dramatic scenes that come to life apart from their function as demonstrations of an idea. Characters in revolt from their working-class origins, like Arthur Machin in *This Sporting Life* and Margaret Thorpe and her brother in *Flight into Camden*, are seen with a strong sympathy and complexity, described as partially entering a new world alien to their backgrounds and partially tied to the values and attitudes of their parents. Relationships between parents and children, the unique combinations of love and hatred bred in tidy, self-contained working-class kitchens, are particularly well done. The children, especially Margaret Thorpe and her brother, have been educated because of their parents' effort and self-sacrifice, yet the process of education has moved them further from their parents, produced a difficult combination of independence, stubborn freedom, and guilt. For the parents, educating children had seemed the passport to the good life, to money, freedom, and release from the grinding physicality of survival in the pits, and the parents are baffled when the children feel that education has complicated their lives and severed them from something central and physical in human experience. The children, too, are characterized by a kind of defensive intensity, an inability to release themselves into the flux of contemporary classless experience, as they still carry with them a sense of the working-man's bitter intransigence, his refusal to give up the self which is the only thing he has in the difficult conditions under which he lives.

In combining an interest in metaphysical ideas with a presentation of all the complexities and problems of working-class life, particularly problems between generations in a changing society, Storey's fiction resembles somewhat that of the early D. H. Lawrence. In addition, Storey's best scenes, like the family arguments in *Flight into Camden* or the almost-silent resentments between Arthur Machin and his mistress in *This Sporting Life*, radiate a sense of emotional revelation and intensity similar to scenes in *Sons and Lovers*, *The Rainbow*, and *Women in Love*. Storey's floral imagery, his way of describing and anatomizing flowers and trees, especially in *Radcliffe*, is not unlike Lawrence's. Yet Lawrence's metaphysical ideas, his ruminations on body and soul, his speculations about sex and society, although tied less neatly and metaphorically into his novelistic structure, were more unusual, more capacious, shocking, and stimulating, than Storey's seem to be. Storey's commitment to his ideas is genuine, but the sense of commitment, the emotion of discovery, and the complicated influence of ideas on behavior and relationships are depicted more strongly and deeply than are the ideas themselves.

In the late 1960s, Storey turned toward drama, writing a number of highly praised and effective plays. The situations in the plays are often familiar to readers of the novels. *In Celebration* reveals the highly-charged familial emotions involved when three grown and educated sons return to celebrate their parents' fortieth wedding anniversary in the mining village where they grew up. The parents are reminiscent of the Thorpes in *Flight into Camden*. *The Contractor* divides attention between the workmen setting up a large tent for a wedding and the family of the tenting company's owner, also the father of the bride. Again, family and class issues dominate the play. A similar group of workmen setting up tents was detailed in *Radcliffe*, although the dramatic version is more comic; even the name of the company's owner—Ewbank—is the same. *The Restoration of Arnold Middleton* deals with a schoolmaster's marriage and emotional health, the central character, Arnie, in his dependence and his attitudes towards pupils, not unlike Margaret's lover in *Flight into Camden*. Characterized by forceful, hard, often sardonic dialogue, each of the plays reveals the emotional depth and intensity of a fairly commonplace situation and expresses the same kind of sympathy for a limited and locked experience that is powerfully apparent in the novels.

—James Gindin

---

**STOW, (Julian) Randolph.** Australian. Born in Geraldton, Western Australia, 28 November 1935. Educated at Guildford Grammar School, Western Australia; University of Western Australia, Nedlands, B.A. 1956. Formerly, Anthropological Assistant, working in Northwest Australia and Papua and New Guinea. Taught at the University of Adelaide, 1957; Lecturer in English Literature, University of Leeds, Yorkshire, 1962, and University of Western Australia, 1963; Lecturer in English and Commonwealth Literature, University of Leeds, 1968–69. Recipient: Australian Literature Society Gold Medal, 1957, 1958; Miles Franklin Award, 1958; Commonwealth Fund's Harkness Travelling Fellowship, 1964–66; Britannica-Australia Award, 1966. Address: c/o Curtis Brown Ltd., 13 King Street, London W.C.2, England.

PUBLICATIONS

Novels

*A Haunted Land.*  London, Macdonald, 1956; New York, Macmillan, 1957.
*The Bystander.*  London, Macdonald, 1957.
*To the Islands.*  London, Macdonald, 1958; Boston, Little Brown, 1959.
*Tourmaline.*  London, Macdonald, 1963.
*The Merry-Go-Round in the Sea.*  London, Macdonald, 1965; New York, Morrow, 1966.

Verse

*Act One: Poems.*  London, Macdonald, 1957.
*Outrider: Poems 1956–1962.*  London, Macdonald, 1962.
*A Counterfeit Silence: Selected Poems.*  Sydney and London, Angus and Robertson, 1969.

Other

*Midnite: The Story of a Wild Colonial Boy* (juvenile).  Melbourne, Cheshire, and London, Macdonald, 1967; New York, Prentice Hall, 1968.

Editor, *Australian Poetry 1964.*  Sydney, Angus and Robertson, 1964.

Bibliography: *Randolph Stow: A Bibliography*, Adelaide, Libraries Board of South Australia, 1968.

Critical Studies: by the author on his own work: "Raw Material", in *Westerly* (Nedlands, Western Australia), 1961; "The Quest for Permanence" by Geoffrey Dutton, in *Journal of Commonwealth Literature* (Leeds, Yorkshire), September 1965; "Outsider Looking In" by W. H. New, in *Critique* (Minneapolis), vol. 9, no. 1, 1967; "Waste Places, Dry Souls" by Jennifer Wightman, in *Meanjin* (Melbourne), June 1969; "Voyager from Eden" by Brandon Conron, in *Ariel (Canada)* (Calgary, Alberta), October 1970; *The Merry-Go-Round in the Sea* by Edriss Noall, Sydney, Scoutline Publications, 1971.

*     *     *

Most Australian critics think of *The Merry-Go-Round in the Sea* as Randolph Stow's finest work so far; most others give that honour to *Tourmaline*—which indicates not only the greater local "realism" of *Merry-Go-Round* (and perhaps a mimetic bias in Australian critical tradition) but also the international appeal of the symbolic landscape which elsewhere Stow has made of his native land. *Merry-Go-Round*, the most autobiographical of Stow's novels, by no means eschews symbolic pattern, but it emerges more directly from Australian national sensibilities. The isolating impact that World War II had on the country, for example, can be appreciated not only in this book but also in works by George Turner, George Johnston, and others; what Stow's novel does is link the theme up with the older traditions of convict settlement and South Pacific paradise. (Stow is careful to debunk the easy myths which see convict and bushranger mateyness as the *sole* generative character trait *throughout* Australia; his comic children's book *Midnite*, about the triumphant adventures of a naive bushranger and his gang—a cockatoo and a cat—delightfully overturns assorted local archetypes. Yet with linguistic playfulness it celebrates the spirit of the country as well, which serves as a reminder of the ambivalent blend of prison and paradise which has always provoked the Australian imagination.) For Rick Maplestead, in *Merry-Go-Round*, imprisoned in Changi and then freed only to discover his bonds to history, family, mates, and mediocrity, there is no escape but flight. But as he and his young cousin Rob Coram (whose offshore vision gives the book its title), know, glimpses of paradise are illusory and attempts to inhabit them fraught with disappointment.

By focussing ultimately on the quests of the mind, the book recapitulates many of Stow's earlier themes. His first books, full of mad characters and melodramatic incidents, are the Gothic attempts of a young novelist to record his knowledge of power and passion, of the relationship between man and landscape and the impact of belief on action. Not till these sensibilities were controlled by Stow's anthropological and historical commitments did they exert a powerful literary effect. *To the Islands* reduced the reliance on incident and traced instead the wanderings of a man through the desert of his belief, in search of the afterworld islands of aboriginal dream order. His soul, he discovers, "is a strange country"—which seems at first to be no advance on what he began by knowing. Increasingly, however, that very state of suspended apprehension becomes the world that Stow tries to explore. *Tourmaline*, about a wasteland of that name, which welcomes a stranger as a water-diviner (who begins to clothe himself in such a role), only to be desolated and turn to another authority when he fails, provides an even more archetypal canvas. Consciously symbolic and heavily mannered in style, the book tries to evoke the world of symbol, the fleeting perceptions that symbols try to convey, rather than the realities of everyday event. The reiteration on the part of Law, the narrator, that to describe a heritage as "bitter" is "not to condemn it", urges readers also to consider what it is that he does not say: what it is that he cannot say. As Stow's long, unfinished poem "The Testament of Tourmaline" indicates, *Tourmaline*'s imagery is drawn from Jungian commentary and the mysteries of the Tao. To fathom in that manner the deep intuitive communications of silence, the mind can probe itself beyond the conscious rationale. For the novelist, any glimpse of wordless understanding presents a problem of technique, however, and captivates him in a strange paradise of another kind.

—W. H. New

**STRAIGHT, Michael (Whitney).** American. Born in Southampton, Long Island, New York, 1 September 1916. Educated at the London School of Economics; Cambridge University, M.A. Served in the United States Army Air Force, 1943–45. Married Belinda Crompton in 1939; has five children. Economist, Department of State, Washington, D.C., 1937–38; Ghost-Writer, Department of the Interior, Washington, 1938–41. Contributing Editor, 1941–43, Publisher, 1946–48, and Editor, 1948–56, *New Republic*, Washington, D.C. Secretary, Emergency Committee of Atomic Scientists, 1946–47; National Chairman, American Veterans Committee, 1950–52; President, William C. Whitney Foundation. Since 1969, Deputy Chairman, National Endowment for the Arts. Address: c/o Alfred A. Knopf, 501 Madison Avenue, New York, New York 10022, U.S.A.

PUBLICATIONS

Novels

> *Carrington: A Novel of the West.* New York, Knopf, 1960; London, Cape, 1961.
> *A Very Small Remnant.* New York, Knopf, and London, Cape, 1963.

Other

> *Make This the Last War: The Future of the United States.* New York, Harcourt Brace, and London, Allen and Unwin, 1943.
> *Trial by Television* (on the Army-McCarthy hearings). Boston, Beacon Press, 1954.
> *Three West*, with others (interviews with John R. Milton). Vermillion, South Dakota, Dakota Press, 1970.

*          *          *

Michael Straight writes about the American West, but he is not a writer of westerns, a genre characterized by improbable romance imposed upon a realistic setting. Straight is interested in the West of Indians, settlers, and soldiers as a setting for actions revealing significant truths about human behavior and human destiny.

*Carrington* records the events leading to the massacre on 21 December 1866 in northern Wyoming of an army unit by a force of Sioux warriors. The second novel, *A Very Small Remnant*, relates the incidents surrounding the notorious massacre by U.S. soldiers of peaceful Cheyennes encamped on Sand Creek (southern Colorado), 29 November 1864. Straight imposes a rigorous discipline on his naturally melodramatic material, a discipline, as he explains in an interview published in *Three West*, based on careful research. His departures from history he justifies in Aristotelian terms as an imaginative reaching for universal poetic truths located in action and character.

Colonel Henry Carrington, as Straight conceives him, is a tragic figure—a man of superior intellect and moral integrity, pious and cultured, dedicated to peaceful coexistence with the Indians. But he is also a man too sensitive to human failing ever to succeed through ruthless courage and blind certainty. Carrington pities and pity is self-indulgent in war. Despised by his own troops for his apparent passivism and indecisive in moments demanding firmness, Carrington is undermined by his junior officers, particularly Captain Fetterman, and by his own self-doubt. Fetterman's foolhardy disobedience of Carrington's commands and his consequent death along with all his men symbolize the timeless conflict between men of action and men of caution, between men who see too little and those who see too much.

An atmosphere of inflexible destiny (Straight's acknowledged indebtedness to the Greek tragic mode) conveyed by the swift and relentless narrative movement and by the dramatic rendering of suspicion and hostility on the part of Indian and white leaves the reader despairing of any outcome short of annihilation. In fact Straight makes it too easy to pity and side with the underdog. The passing of the race is by now a cliché theme evoking stereotyped responses, and Straight's partisanship of the Indians and their white defenders threatens to reduce the conflict to an allegory of good vs. evil.

This is especially true in *A Very Small Remnant* where the Indians, already despised and humiliated, are made the pawns of ambitious men. The simple, low-keyed narrative by Major Edward Wynkoop tells how, after reluctantly coming to believe the Cheyennes trustworthy, he tries to honor his own pledge of peace only to find that the settlers, the politicians, the army leaders, and, in a shadowy but compelling way, the national temper demand a bloody Indian defeat. Although Straight takes heart that "a very small remnant" of courageous citizens successfully opposed the popular will by discrediting the ambitious perpetrator of the massacre, the reader is likely to remember the weathered bones of Indians, unburied months after the event. The novels may be read as lessons in personal courage, but they are, even more, lessons in the inefficacy of human effort to shape the course of history to moral ends.

—Dale K. Doepke

---

**STUART, Jesse (Hilton).** American. Born near Riverton, Kentucky, 8 August 1907. Educated at Lincoln Memorial University, Harrogate, Tennessee, A.B. 1929; Vanderbilt University, Nashville, Tennessee, 1931–32; Peabody College, Nashville. Served in the United States Naval Reserve, rising to the rank of Lieutenant Junior Grade, 1943–46. Married Naomi Deane Norris in 1939; has one child. Has worked as a farmer, newspaper editor, and schoolteacher; Superintendent, Greenup, Kentucky City Schools, 1941–43. Taught at the University of Nevada, Reno, Summer 1958, and the American University, Cairo, 1960–61; United States Department of State Lecturer in Egypt, Iran, Greece, Lebanon, Pakistan, the Philippines, Formosa and Korea, 1962–63; Writer-in-Residence, Eastern Kentucky University, Richmond, 1965–66. American Representative, Asian Writers Conference, 1962. Recipient: Davis Poetry Prize, 1934; Guggenheim Fellowship, 1937; National Institute of Arts and Letters grant, 1941; Thomas Jefferson Southern Award, 1944; National Education Association Award, 1949; Berea College Centennial Award, 1955; Academy of American Poets Award, 1961. D.Litt., University of Kentucky, Lexington, 1944; Marietta College, Ohio, 1952; Morris Harvey College, Charleston, West Virginia, 1959; Marshall University, Huntington, West Virginia, 1962; Northern Michigan University, Marquette, 1964; Eastern Kentucky University, 1964; D.H.L., Lincoln Memorial University, 1950; LL.D., Baylor University, Waco, Texas, 1954; Doctor of Pedagogy, Murray State University, Kentucky, 1968. Address: W-Hollow, Greenup, Kentucky 41144, U.S.A.

PUBLICATIONS

Novels

> *Trees of Heaven.* New York, Dutton, 1940.
> *Taps for Private Tussie.* New York, Dutton, 1943; as *He'll be Coming Down the Mountain*, London, Dobson, 1947.

*Mongrel Mettle: The Autobiography of a Dog.*   New York, Books Inc.-Dutton, 1944.
*Foretaste of Glory.*   New York, Dutton, 1946.
*Hie to the Hunter.*   New York, Whittlesey House, 1950.
*The Good Spirit of Laurel Ridge.*   New York, McGraw Hill, 1953.
*Daughter of the Legend.*   New York, McGraw Hill, 1965.
*Mr. Gallion's School.*   New York, McGraw Hill, 1967.
*Old Ben.*   New York, McGraw Hill, 1970.

Short Stories

*Head o' W-Hollow.*   New York, Dutton, 1936.
*Tim: A Story.*   Cincinnati, Little Man Press, 1939.
*Men of the Mountains.*   New York, Dutton, 1941.
*Tales from the Plum Grove Hills.*   New York, Dutton, 1946.
*Clearing in the Sky and Other Stories.*   New York, McGraw Hill, 1950.
*Plowshare in Heaven: Stories.*   New York, McGraw Hill, 1958.
*Save Every Lamb.*   New York, McGraw Hill, 1964.
*A Jesse Stuart Harvest.*   New York, Dell, 1965.
*Come, Gentle Spring.*   New York, McGraw Hill, 1969.

Verse

*Harvest of Youth.*   Howe, Oklahoma, Scroll Press, 1930.
*Man with a Bull-Tongue Plow.*   New York, Dutton, 1934; revised edition, 1959.
*Album of Destiny.*   New York, Dutton, 1944.
*Kentucky Is My Land.*   New York, Dutton, 1952.
*Hold April: New Poems.*   New York, McGraw Hill, 1962.
*My Land Has a Voice.*   New York, McGraw Hill, 1966.

Other

*Beyond Dark Hills: A Personal Story.*   New York, Dutton, and London, Hutchinson, 1938.
*The Thread That Runs So True* (autobiography).   New York, Scribner, 1949.
*The Beatinest Boy* (juvenile).   New York, Whittlesey House, 1953.
*A Penny's Worth of Character* (juvenile).   New York, Whittlesey House, 1954.
*Red Mule* (juvenile).   New York, Whittlesey House, 1955.
*The Year of My Rebirth* (autobiography).   New York, McGraw Hill, 1956; London, Gollancz, 1958.
*God's Oddling: The Story of Mike Stuart, My Father.*   New York, McGraw Hill, 1960.
*The Rightful Owner* (juvenile).   New York, Whittlesey House, 1960.
*Huey the Engineer* (juvenile).   St. Helena, California, J. E. Beard, 1960.
*Andy Finds a Way* (juvenile).   New York, Whittlesey House, 1961.
*A Jesse Stuart Reader.*   New York, McGraw Hill, 1963.
*A Ride with Huey the Engineer* (juvenile).   New York, McGraw Hill, 1966.
*To Teach, To Love.*   Cleveland, World, 1970.

Editor, with others, *Outlooks Through Literature.*   Chicago, Scott Foresman, 1964.
Editor, with A. K. Ridout, *Short Stories for Discussion.*   New York, Scribner, 1965.

Manuscript Collection: Murray State University, Kentucky.

*        *        *

When the definitive history of modern American fiction is written, Jesse Stuart's name may well be near the top of the list. For Stuart, in the timeless vignettes of his fiction, has done what every great writer longs to do. He has created a *place* and wedged it everlastingly in the imagination of America. His fiction has given a voice to the far and lost lands of the Appalachians, a voice which calls us ever and delightedly into the outdoor world. The reader of any volume of Stuart's fiction opens the book and feels immediately the fine mist of nature blowing into his face. Stuart began as a short story writer and gradually worked into the novel. At the present time he is the author of over 400 short stories, published in a very wide variety of periodicals and books.

What is the "world" of his short stories? It is the mountain milieu he knew as a child, a milieu where family loyalty was as strong as religion and led to some spectacular feuds. It was a world where the people lived a hard life, laboring long over the meager soil for scanty returns. There were relaxations in the mountains, such as the burning pleasure of mountain moonshine, protracted religious meetings at Plum Grove church, basket dinners, public hangings, and the sporadic and joyous fights of the young bucks. Fox hunting gave a long nighttime delight to the males of all ages. Guns were a major source of pleasure to the men.

The essence of Stuart's method of fictional narration is its oral character. He uses the famous "talk style" that came into American fiction from the folk tale and the humorous tales of the old South West (J. J. Hooper and George Harris). He begins *in medias res* and tumbles the reader rapidly forward on a rising rush of events. His short stories are frequently told by a first person narrator, usually a mountain boy of eastern Kentucky. His early short stories are rich with mountain dialect. We read words like "casouse", "fittified", "fornenst", "slonchways". Stuart now seems to be our only living writer who can use this dialect unself-consciously. His short stories are marked also by their rich use of figurative language, their exuberant lyricism, tremendous gusto, abandon and brimming joyous humor. Stuart is quite capable of the tall tale ("Sylvania Is Dead") and of a kind of surrealistic or Black Bile humor, in which we get the projection of the comic into the horrible as in the story "Word and the Flesh." There is also a deep tenderness in Stuart, a great pity and love for people. This tenderness appears in his poignant little story, "Thanksgiving Hunter."

All of the above characteristics appear also in his novels. Like Thomas Wolfe, Stuart thinks of himself as a *writing man* and sees no great distinction between fiction and autobiography. He slides easily from one to another. The central fact about Stuart as a novelist is that he has created a spacious, complex imaginative world by projecting the actual one of W-Hollow onto an imaginative plane. His novels are in many ways prolongations of his short stories into a more spacious aesthetic scope. *Taps for Private Tussie* and *Hie to the Hunter* were both begun as short stories, became too long, and were recast and expanded to novel length. Stuart never outlines a novel except for a few notes which may be sketched out on an envelope. He has some image, some hunch, some node of interest in his own mind which is the real subject matter of the novel. His characters begin to come alive and dance their attitudes around this node of interest, shaping a fable which may mean something quite contrary to Stuart's original intent.

Stuart is, in a manner of speaking, the Grandma Moses of the novel. That is, he is a kind of "primitive" also. He uses strong, stark scenes, clearly and sharply delineated. He also has a certain affinity with Dickens. Like Dickens he characterizes obviously and bluntly, using name-typing, and some characterizing mannerism or gesture. Like Dickens his style is dramatic, kinetic, bustling with dialogue and action. Instead of *telling*, he *shows*; he loves the present tense. His style, though, is far simpler than that of Dickens. Stuart cannot be categorized as a realist or as a romantic. There is realism enough in his work, in the dialect, the customs of W-Hollow, in the living characters of his work, yet there is a romantic streak running through his novels, a kind of romantic primitivism in his treatment of nature and in his idealization of Grandpa Tussie in the latter stages of the novel *Taps for Private Tussie*. The romantic motif of the child as seer occurs frequently in his work as does his romantic idealization of the simple people of this world. If he has to be labelled, we can call him a regionalist, who mingles the modes of romanticism and realism in his work.

Consider his novels. His first novel, *Trees of Heaven*, relates the story of patriarch Anse Bushman, who loves the land and wants to own more of it. It is the story of Anse's son Tarvin falling in love with Subrinea Tussie, the beautiful daughter of Boliver Tussie, head of a family of poor white squatters. Anse actually dominates the book and bestrides the entire world of *Trees of Heaven*, as he comes tumultuously alive, striding in his nightshirt through a spring night of rain and lightning to feel the wakening life of the earth beneath his bare feet.

Next, in 1943, came Stuart's best selling novel, *Taps for Private Tussie*, which has sold by now over two million copies. It is the story of a family of mountain poor whites who collect $10,000 life insurance on their soldier-son Private Tussie who has presumably been killed in World War II. The Tussies live joyously for a while in a wild, comic, free-loading spend-thrift spree in the best house in the nearby county seat. Once again the novel is dominated by a single character, Grandpa Tussie. There is a strong element of Huckleberry Finn in the narrator, Sid Tussie, the supposed grandson of Grandpa Tussie. Humor is endemic to the entire novel which carries various nuances of meaning. On one level it is a boisterous ballad of lolling reliefers and inherited indolence. On another level the novel is a sad-comic pastorale of a family caught in the turbulence of acute social change and not realizing the why of all the turbulence. Stuart, though, is an artist, not a polemicist. He does not inveigh against the welfare state. He laughs with Press Tussie who says, "I'm a-living just the way I like to live."

Stuart's next novel, *Foretaste of Glory*, is an episodic *Grand Hotel*-type of novel, which wheels about a central event, the sudden and apocalyptic appearance of the aurora borealis in a little mountain town. In a series of 36 chapters Stuart dramatizes the effect of the "*Lights!*" on the sensibilities of the simple mountain people. Fearing the Second Coming of Christ is at hand, they throng to the courthouse square and confess their most secret sins to their great discomfiture the following morning. The mode is comic, exuberant, joyous. Life throngs through the novel like a great painting by Brueghel the Elder. (It reminds one of such Brueghel paintings as *Peasant Wedding* or *Peasant Dance*.)

In addition to these major novels, Stuart has published several minor ones, such as *Mongrel Mettle*, a novelette about a mongrel dog which has certain overtones relating to America as a melting pot. Then the novel *Hie to the Hunter*, a story in a Tom Sawyer vein of a city boy who goes to a mountain farm during the course of three months and learns through his pal, "Sparkie," the beauty and vigor and honesty of mountain life. Later Stuart published the novel *The Good Spirit of Laurel Ridge*, notable for the characterization of "Op" Akers, a kind of poor man's Henry David Thoreau. The novel is full of Stuart's knowledge of the world of nature, ginseng and nature's hidden world. In 1965 he published *Daughter of the Legend*, a tragic love story dealing with a mysterious people in this country known as Melungeons. It is a romantic novel but does not have the power of *Taps* or *Trees of Heaven*. In 1967 he published *Mr. Gallion's School*, an episodic novel recounting the efforts of a 49-year-old cardiac writer, an ex-teacher, to put a failing high school back on its feet. This story is very close to Stuart's autobiographical work *The Thread That Runs So True*, but does not have the lyric freshness that the young teacher displayed in his earlier work.

In his fiction, Stuart is an affirmer, a yea sayer. Like Thoreau he shows that life close to the bone is hard, but the taste is sweet. Equally important in the appeal of Stuart's work is the glimpse he gives us of the old, free, pastoral world of our fathers. Yet Stuart is not a conscious propagandist for the good old days. He has refused to propagandize and slant his material. He is primarily a *maker*, a *poet*; he depicts things exactly and lets the universal shine through. In this sense he is a true artist. He digs into W-Hollow but says "yes" all along the way; "yes" in spite of sickness, injustice, and death. But he does not preach; he lets his world speak for itself. He has avoided literary cliques and coteries; he has fought alone. His real and lasting reputation is still ahead of him.

—Reul E. Foster

**STYRON, William.** American. Born in Newport News, Virginia, 11 June 1925. Educated at Christchurch School, Virginia; Duke University, Durham, North Carolina, 1943–44, 1946–47, A.B. 1947. Served in the United States Marine Corps, rising to the rank of 1st Lieutenant, 1943–45, 1951. Married Rose Burgunder in 1953; has four children. Associate Editor, McGraw Hill, publishers, New York, 1947. Since 1964, Fellow of Silliman College, Yale University, New Haven, Connecticut. Since 1952, Advisory Editor, *Paris Review*, Paris and New York; since 1970, Member of the Editorial Board, *The American Scholar*, Washington, D.C. Recipient: American Academy of Arts and Letters Prix de Rome, 1952; Pulitzer Prize, 1968; Howells Medal, 1970. D.H., Wilberforce University, Ohio; Litt.D., Duke University, 1968; New School for Social Research, New York; Tufts University, Medford, Massachusetts. Member, National Institute of Arts and Letters, and American Academy of Arts and Sciences. Address: R.F.D., Roxbury, Connecticut 06783, U.S.A.

PUBLICATIONS

Novels

Lie Down in Darkness. Indianapolis, Bobbs Merrill, 1951; London, Hamish Hamilton, 1952.
The Long March. New York, Random House, 1956; London, Mayflower, 1961.
Set This House on Fire. New York, Random House, 1960; London, Hamish Hamilton, 1961.
The Confessions of Nat Turner. New York, Random House, 1967; London, Cape, 1968.

Other

Editor, Best Short Stories from "The Paris Review". New York, Dutton, 1959.

Bibliography: in *William Styron's "The Confessions of Nat Turner"*, a critical handbook edited by Melvin J. Friedman and Irving Malin, Belmont, California, Wadsworth, 1970.

Manuscript Collections: Library of Congress, Washington, D.C.; Duke University, Durham, North Carolina.

Critical Studies: *William Styron* by Robert H. Fossum, Grand Rapids, Michigan, Eerdmans, 1968; *William Styron* by Cooper R. Mackin, Austin, Texas, Steck Vaughn, 1969.

*       *       *

Of the American novelists who have come onto the literary scene since the end of the Second World War, William Styron would seem to have worked most directly in the traditional ways of story-telling. As a writer from the American South, he was heir to a mode of fiction writing most notably developed by William Faulkner and practiced to striking effect by such fellow Southerners as Robert Penn Warren, Thomas Wolfe, Eudora Welty, and Katherine Anne Porter. It involved—as the mode of Hemingway did not involve—a reliance upon the resources of a sounding rhetoric rather than upon understatement, a dependence

1201

upon the old religious universals ("love and honor and pity and pride and compassion and sacrifice," as Faulkner once termed them) rather than a suspicion of all such external moral formulations, and a profound belief in the reality of the past as importantly affecting present behavior—an "historical sense," as contrasted with the dismissal of history as irrelevant and meaningless. Styron's role, imposed by his cast of thought and his attitude toward language and human nature, has been to carry this mode into a new day and a new circumstance.

His first novel, *Lie Down in Darkness*, was strongly indebted to the example of Faulkner; Styron began it, he said, after reading Faulkner night and day for several weeks. Yet though Styron portrayed a young Southern woman, Peyton Loftis, as she battled for love and sanity in a dreary family situation, doomed to defeat by her father's weak, self-pitying ineffectuality and her mother's hypocrisy and sadistic jealousy, and though the setting was a tidewater Virginia city among an effete upper class society, what resulted was not finally Faulknerian. At bottom the causes of Styron's tragedy were familial, not dynastic; the deficiencies of Milton and Helen Loftis were not importantly those of decadent aristocracy whose concept of honor and pride has become empty posturing and self-indulgence, as they would have been for a writer such as Faulkner, but rather personal and psychological. When Peyton flees Virginia for New York City, there is little sense of her plight as representing isolation from the order and definition of a time and place that are no longer available. Instead, hers was a break for freedom, and the failure to make good the break is the result of the crippling conflict within her mind and heart imposed by the example of her parents, and which symbolizes the hatreds engendered by a society that does not know how to love. The suicide of Peyton Loftis represents a plunge into the moral abyss of a self-destructive modern world. Styron, in other words, wrote out of a tradition that taught him to measure his people and their society against the traditional values, and to see the absence of those values in their lives as tragic; but he did not depict that absence as a falling away from a more honorable, more ordered Southern historical past.

The success of *Lie Down in Darkness* was considerable, perhaps in part because a novel that could depict the modern situation as tragic, rather than merely pathetic, and could thus make use of the High Style of language to chronicle it, was all too rare. Styron followed it with *The Long March*, a novella set in a Marine Corps camp during the Korean War period (Styron himself was briefly recalled to active duty in 1951). Depicting the irrationality of war and the military mentality, it demonstrates the dignity, and also the absurdity, of an individual's effort to achieve nobility amid chaos.

Eight years elapsed before Styron's second full-length novel, *Set This House on Fire*. The story of a Southern-born artist, Cass Kinsolving, who is unable to paint, and is married and living in Europe, it involved a man in spiritual bondage, undergoing a terrifying stay in the lower depths before winning his way back to sanity and creativity. In Paris, Rome, and the Italian town of Sambucco, Cass Kinsolving lives in an alcoholic daze, tortured by his inability to create, wandering about, drinking, pitying himself, doing everything except confronting his talent. The struggle is on existential terms. Kinsolving has sought to find a form for his art outside of himself, looking to the society and the people surrounding him for what could only be located within himself: the remorseless requirement of discovering how to love and be loved, and so to create. Only in violence and tragedy can he win his way through to self-respect and the capacity to function effectively in the world.

*Set This House on Fire* encountered a generally hostile critical reception, to some extent because it was sprawling and untidy, occasionally overwritten, and therefore so very different from his well-made first novel. It seemed, too, even further removed than *Lie Down in Darkness* from the customary Southern milieu: not only were there no decaying families, no faithful black retainers, no blood-guilt, and no oversexed Southern matrons, but we are told very little about the protagonist's past, either familial or personal, that might explain how he got the way he was. Yet there *was* a past; but Styron gives it to a friend of Kinsolving's, Peter Leverett, who tells the story. The fact is that Leverett's failure to find definition in his Southern origins is what really accounts for Kinsolving's present-day plight. Styron apparently could not avoid grounding his tragedy in history one way or the other. And after

Kinsolving has fought his way back to personal responsibility and creativity, he leaves Europe and returns to the South. There is thus a kind of circular movement involved in the first two novels. Peyton Loftis finds the Southern community impossible to live within and love within, and she goes to New York. Cass Kinsolving, equally at loose ends, goes abroad and conducts his struggle for identity and definition there, and then comes home to the South. He has had in effect to ratify the individual and social worth of his attitudes and values away from the place and the institutions of their origins, and make them his own, not something merely bequeathed automatically to him.

If so, it is not surprising that Styron's next and most controversial novel, *The Confessions of Nat Turner*, once again is set in the South—in Southside Virginia, no more than an hour's automobile drive from Port Warwick where Peyton Loftis grew up and Newport News, Virginia, where Styron was born and raised—and that it concerns itself squarely with the Southern past, as exemplified in the presence and the role of the black man. For though *The Confessions of Nat Turner* is based upon a famous slave insurrection that took place in 1831, its implications involve race and racism, integration and separatism, and the use of violent means in order to achieve political and social ends. Styron's strategy, for what he termed his "meditation upon history," was to tell his story from the viewpoint of the slave leader Nat Turner, of whose actual life almost nothing is known. Rather than restrict his protagonist's language, however, to that which a plantation slave in the early Nineteenth Century might be expected to have used, Styron decided that the range and complexity of such a man's mind could not be adequately represented in any such primitive fashion, and he cast Nat Turner's reflections in the rich, allusive, polysyllabic mode of the early Victorian novel. Styron was thus able to have his slave leader utilize the resources of a sounding rhetoric in order to look beyond his immediate circumstance into the moral and ethical implications of his actions. And while in so doing Styron was making use of the traditional language mode of the Southern novel, and was drawing on the same attitude towards external ethical values as such Southern novelists as Faulkner and Warren had done before him, he was interpreting the actual history of the South and of slavery from a perspective that no other Southern novelist, not even Faulkner, had managed.

The initial critical verdict on *The Confessions of Nat Turner* was highly favorable, with such critics as Alfred Kazin, Philip Rahv, C. Vann Woodward and others declaring it an impressive contribution both to contemporary American fiction and to the knowledge of slavery. Almost immediately, however, the book became embroiled in a controversy, not so much literary as sociological, which made both novel and novelist into a *cause célèbre*. For in presuming, as a white man, to portray the consciousness of a black revolutionist of a century-and-a-half ago, Styron came into collision with the impetus of the black separatist movement. His novel appeared at a time when the black American was straining as never before to assert his identity and his independence of white paternalism, and the result was that numerous black critics, together with some white sympathizers, began heaping abuse on Styron for his alleged racism, his alleged unwarranted liberties with historical "fact," and his alleged projection of "white liberal neuroses" onto a revolutionary black leader's personality. A host of reviews and essays and even a book appeared in denunciation of Styron. Other critics rose to the rebuttal, and historians joined in to certify the authenticity of Styron's historical portrayal. The outcome has been a voluminous literature of controversy that may well interest future social historians almost as much as the Nat Turner insurrection itself.

As the acrimony of the immediate controversy dies down, however, it appears likely that Styron's *Confessions* will be recognized for the impressive work of literary artistry that it is, and his black protagonist seen as a masterfully created hero, of tremendous human complexity and genuinely tragic dignity.

—Louis D. Rubin, Jr.

**SUMMERS, Hollis (Spurgeon, Jr.).** American. Born in Eminence, Kentucky, 21 June 1916. Educated at Georgetown College, Kentucky, A.B. 1937; Bread Loaf School of English, Middlebury College, Vermont, M.A. 1943; University of Iowa, Iowa City, Ph.D. 1949. Married Laura Vimont Clarke in 1943; has two children. Taught at Holmes High School, Covington, Kentucky, 1937–44; Professor of English, Georgetown College, 1945–49, and the University of Kentucky, Lexington, 1949–59. Since 1959, Distinguished Professor of English, Ohio University, Athens. Adviser, Ford Foundation Conference on Writers in America, 1958; Lecturer, Arts Program, Association of American Colleges, 1958–63; Danforth Lecturer, 1963–66. Recipient: Fund for the Advancement of Education grant, 1951; *Saturday Review* Poetry Award, 1957; Colleges of Arts and Sciences Award, 1958. LL.D., Georgetown College, 1965. Address: 181 North Congress Street, Athens, Ohio 45701, U.S.A.

PUBLICATIONS

Novels

> *City Limit.* Boston, Houghton Mifflin, 1948.
> *Brighten the Corner.* New York, Doubleday, 1952.
> *Teach You a Lesson*, with James Rourke (as Jim Hollis). New York, Harper, 1955; London, Foulsham, 1956.
> *The Weather of February.* New York, Harper, 1957.
> *The Day after Sunday.* New York, Harper, 1968.

Uncollected Short Stories

> "How They Chose the Dead", in *New World Writing 3*. New York, New American Library, 1953.
> "Love", in *Quarterly Review of Literature* (Princeton, New Jersey), vol. 8, no. 2, 1953.
> "The Terrible Death of Mr. Vimont", in *Accent* (Urbana, Illinois), Autumn 1954.
> "Black and White and Gray", in *New Voices 2*. New York, Hendricks House, 1955.
> "Mister Joseph Botts", in *Paris Review*, Spring 1955.
> "The Prayer Meeting", in *Sewanee Review* (Tennessee), Winter 1956.
> "Wizz, Zoom, Whitely, Whatever, and Bang", in *Chicago Review*, Winter 1956.
> "The Professor's New Overalls", in *Arizona Quarterly* (Tucson), Spring 1956.
> "Concerning, I Suppose, My Father", in *Perspective* (St. Louis), Autumn-Winter 1956.
> "Cafe Nore", in *Epoch* (Ithaca, New York), Fall 1957.
> "Dolly", in *Colorado Quarterly* (Boulder), Spring 1958.
> "The Vireo's Nest", in *Prairie Schooner* (Lincoln, Nebraska), Summer 1960.
> "If You Don't Go Out the Way You Came In", in *Colorado Quarterly* (Boulder), Summer 1960.
> "The Man from Cord's", in *Fresco* (Detroit), vol. 1, no. 1, 1960.
> "Fortunato", in *San Francisco Review*, September 1962.
> "The Woman Who Loved Everybody", in *Epoch* (Ithaca, New York), Winter 1963.
> "The Cardboard Screen", in *American Scene: New Voices*. New York, Lyle Stuart, 1963.
> "The Penitent", in *Red Clay Reader 5*. Charlotte, North Carolina, Red Clay Reader, 1968.
> "The Third Ocean", in *Hudson Review* (New York), Summer 1969.

Verse

The Walks near Athens.   New York, Harper, 1959.
Someone Else: Sixteen Poems about Other Children.   Philadelphia, Lippincott, 1962.
Seven Occasions.   New Brunswick, New Jersey, Rutgers University Press, 1965.
The Peddler and Other Domestic Matters.   New Brunswick, New Jersey, Rutgers University Press, 1967.
Sit Opposite Each Other.   New Brunswick, New Jersey, Rutgers University Press, 1970.

Editor, Kentucky Story: A Collection of Short Stories.   Lexington, University of Kentucky Press, 1954.
Editor, with Edgar Whan, Literature: An Introduction.   New York, McGraw Hill, 1960.
Editor, Discussions of the Short Story.   Boston, Heath, 1963.

Hollis Summers comments:

All we are trying to do, I suppose, is to tell it true.
A piece of writing, be it poem or novel, endeavors to draw a ring around experience. The experience and the drawing are of equal importance. The how and the what, the method and the matter are separable only for the luxury of discussion. The what of a piece of writing endures because of the how.

*         *         *

"We live enough on the edge of violence," sighs a Kentucky Baptist minister's wife in Brighten the Corner. She speaks for all Hollis Summers' characters. Their preoccupation with the will of God seems never really to tranquilize them. Although Summers is probably better known as a poet, he has managed in his novels to capture the unique and disturbing mixture of superficial charm and whimsy with a barely disguised underlying bigotry and wrath that characterizes his native Bluegrass region of Kentucky—a land of horse-farms, bourbon, and fundamentalist religion—that has always dominated his vision though he has ironically had to relocate in neighbouring Ohio to be honored as a Distinguished Professor.

Summers' characters chatter so pleasantly that one only gradually realizes that they are often saying frightening things. His first novel, City Limit, seems an idyllic account of two high-school students' blossoming love for each other until one realizes that they are being scourged prematurely into marriage by repressed and repressive elders. Brighten the Corner presents, principally from the viewpoint of two small sons, the life of a Baptist preacher's family at his first church in a Kentucky town. The book might be just another of the many superficial, episodic accounts of growing up in America if it were not for the tensions, often growing to hatred, that flash out from the retired minister who tries to continue to dominate the church, a popular travelling evangelist who hates children, and the younger son, who often unintentionally turns the spiritual life into a parody. In The Weather of February, a forty-year-old woman who has come a long way from the parsonages where she grew up reflects on the husbands and lovers that she has known and articulates the principle that governs a culture notorious for its propensity for feuding, "You don't start all over in Lexington, Kentucky." Everything—as in these memoirs—must be recalled; everything must be reckoned with.

It took another decade for Summers to distill his recollections of this culture into The Day after Sunday, which begins with the hopelessly mixed-up only son of a couple that has ceased being intimate visiting the bedroom of a love-starved spinster nearly his mother's age and making her pregnant. The novel is built around three dreadful Mondays in the family's history: the central voice is that of the middle-aged father, who is seeking to establish some human contact that will steer him away from alcoholism. He cannot find it through his wife, a Bluegrass Madame Bovary, who unmans three generations of "her men"—father, husband, son. The novel's power arises from Summers' making readers see that the heart-shattering irony of this painful work is that these people could live rewarding lives if they could only develop the courage to be honest and generous with each other. But this they cannot do; they can only sink deeper into their own despair and drag a broadening circle of others down with them.

Then one realizes that all Summers' novels inspire a similar vision. His power lies not in what he tells us, but in what he makes us see. Perhaps—like the younger son in *Brighten the Corner*—he can remain bright and artful in dealing with frightening subject matter—in short stories as well as novels—because he remains hopeful that he can awaken readers before they are driven to the same extremes as his characters. He has not escaped the "revivalism" that dominates his region and often his books; but he has achieved through art the reconciliation with life that eludes those obsessed with Judgment rather than understanding.

—Warren French

SUTTON, Henry.   See SLAVITT, David.

SWADOS, Harvey.   American.   Born in Buffalo, New York, 28 October 1920. Educated at the University of Michigan, Ann Arbor, B.A. 1940. Served as a Radio Officer in the United States Merchant Marine, 1942–45. Married Bette Beller in 1946; has three children. Member of the Literature Faculty, Sarah Lawrence College, Bronxville, New York, 1958–60, 1962–70. Visiting Lecturer, University of Iowa, Iowa City, 1956–57; Visiting Professor, San Francisco State College, 1960–61, and Columbia University, New York, 1965–67. Since 1970, Professor, University of Massachusetts, Amherst. Recipient: *Hudson Review* Fellowship, 1957; Sidney Hillman Award, 1958; Guggenheim Fellowship, 1960; National Institute of Arts and Letters grant, 1965; National Endowment for the Arts grant, 1968. Address: Department of English, Bartlett Hall, University of Massachusetts, Amherst, Massachusetts 01002, U.S.A.

Publications

Novels

*Out Went the Candle.*   New York, Viking Press, 1955.
*False Coin.*   Boston, Little Brown, 1959.
*The Will.*   Cleveland, World, 1963; London, Hart Davis, 1965.
*Standing Fast.*   New York, Doubleday, 1970.

Short Stories

*On the Line*.   Boston, Little Brown, 1957; London, Davies, 1958.
*Nights in the Gardens of Brooklyn*.   Boston, Little Brown, 1961; London, Hart Davis
1962.
*A Story for Teddy—And Others*.   New York, Simon and Schuster, 1965; London,
Hart Davis, 1966.

Other

*A Radical's America* (essays).   Boston, Little Brown, 1962.
*A Radical at Large: American Essays*.   London, Hart Davis, 1968.
*Standing Up for the People: The Life and Work of Estes Kefauver*.   New York, Dutton,
1972.

Editor, *Years of Conscience: The Muckrakers: An Anthology of Reform Journalism*.
Cleveland, Meridian, and London, Peter Smith, 1962.
Editor, *The American Writer and the Great Depression*.   Indianapolis, Bobbs Merrill,
1966.

Critical Studies: "Harvey Swados" by Pierre Brodin, in *Présences Contemporains: Ecrivains Américains d'Aujourd'hui*, Paris, Nouvelles Editions Debresse, 1964; "Harvey Swados: Private Stories and Public Function" by Charles Shapiro, in *Contemporary American Novelists*, Carbondale, Southern Illinois University Press, 1966; "Standing Fast" by Paul Cowan, in *Village Voice* (New York), 22 October 1970.

Harvey Swados comments:

While I have been publishing both fiction and non-fiction since I was a teenager in the nineteen thirties, and while I am far from disowning my first novel, *Out Went the Candle*, which seems to me both substantial and authentic, I do believe that in retrospect the main line of my development as a writer dates from *On the Line*. The experience behind those interrelated stories came to me with the force of a revelation. It reawakened in me a latent radicalism and a dormant sympathy for the underdog; it set me to examining—and writing essays about—the lives of the various groups of forgotten Americans; and it culminated after many years of work in *Standing Fast*, the lengthy novel that I see as a kind of summation of these various concerns. Nearly all of my subsidiary activities in recent years—journalistic, essayistic, traveling and teaching—have contributed to that culmination, in my view. I cannot predict what the years ahead will hold in the matter of creative work, but I do feel quite certain that I will undertake nothing unless I feel some inner assurance of a thematic significance and substantiality beyond mere story-telling for its own sake.

*       *       *

*Standing Fast* is by far the most important of Swados' four novels. It is a panoramic novel that focuses on the lives of a group of young socialists who come together in Buffalo, New York, in the late 30's. While the focus for the most part remains on these people and follows them through their twenties and thirties and into middle age, the novel also deals with their parents and with a third generation, their children. During World War II and for 18 years following it, the scene frequently shifts from Buffalo, to the South Pacific, to Israel, to

California, to Alabama, to Long Island, to Washington, D.C., as the group's commitment to the capital-labor issue is swept over by the tide of history and new concerns are forced upon them.

Swados has great respect for almost all the characters in this large cast, the talented, irrepressible Norm and the stoical, dedicated Vera, enthusiastic, hard-working Sy and Bernice, the union leader Bill and his lawyer wife Margaret, the blacks Big Boy and Hamilton Wright, and Joe Link, the All-American boy turned devout socialist. They all stood ready to commit their lives to the building of socialism. But between the 30's and the 60's far-reaching changes took place in American life. Depression and poverty gave way to a prosperity that unexpectedly continued on undiminished well into the post-war years; America became the affluent society. Socialism as a scheme for redistributing wealth and ending poverty became irrelevant. But the appeal of socialism is on more than economic grounds, and for a while Joe Link remains determined to help bring on the revolution. His gallant commitment to the old ideals, however, almost leads to the ruin of himself and his family. Norm, also blessed with great leadership ability, realizes immediately after the war that the Marxist model is no longer applicable. But even if it were, Norm has learned that "you can't persuade people to do what you think they ought to simply because it's moral or logical. . . . People are going to react from a whole series of motives—most of which have no relation to logic." Norm closes his Marx, and becomes one of the breed of journalists Marx despised, a liberal reformist. Similarly, preserving the Jewish remnant and leading the Negro civil rights movement for Sy and for Ham Wright assume higher priorities than socialism.

Swados' achievement in *Standing Fast* recalls the work of the great English novelist of a century ago, George Eliot. Eliot and Swados both see the broad picture. They place the lives of their characters in the context of their times and show the impact made by powerful social forces. And like Eliot, Swados follows the lives of his people with sympathetic understanding. Swados, however, does suffer lapses occasionally. *Standing Fast* is weakest in those sections in which characters such as Fred Vogel/Byrd, the socialist professor who has become a TV quizmaster, and Harry Sturm, the party functionary who has used his devious ingenuity to become a millionaire, are revealed as simply cowardly and self-seeking. Swados does not like these men who have been too ready to abandon their pre-war ideals, and so as they pursue their new careers Swados exposes them with broad, ruthless strokes, thereby denying them their humanity and their credibility as characters.

This is a flaw that plagues Swados' second novel, *False Coin*, in which the super-rich who patronize the arts feel the sting of his contempt. In *False Coin*, Ben Warder is constantly being tempted; only by mustering great strength is he able to come through his ordeal at a foundation-sponsored artists' colony with his ideals intact. Ben foreshadows Swados' wonderful portrait of the isolated but incorruptible painter of *Standing Fast*, Vito Brigante. On the other hand, there are no caricatures in the first novel that showed so much promise, *Out Went the Candle*. Its cast is limited, and Herman Felton, the self-made business success, is rendered with all of Swados' sensitivity. *The Will*, the novel that precedes *Standing Fast*, is on a larger scale, but its studies of three very different brothers contending with each other over an inheritance are all done subtly and compassionately.

—Paul Marx

---

**SWARTHOUT, Glendon (Fred).** American. Born in Pinckney, Michigan, 8 April 1918. Educated at the University of Michigan, Ann Arbor, 1935–39, A.B. 1939, A.M. 1946; Michigan State University, East Lansing, 1952–55, Ph.D. 1955. Served in the United States Army Infantry, rising to the rank of Sergeant, 1943–45. Married Kathryn Blair Vaughn in

1940; has one child. Teaching Fellow, University of Michigan, 1946–48; Instructor, University of Maryland, College Park, 1948–51; Associate Professor of English, Michigan State University, 1951–59; Lecturer in English, Arizona State University, Tempe, 1959–62. Recipient: Theatre Guild Award, in playwriting, 1947; Hopwood Award, 1948; O. Henry Award, 1960. Address: 5045 Tamanar Way, Scottsdale, Arizona 85253, U.S.A.

PUBLICATIONS

Novels

> Willow Run.   New York, Crowell, 1943.
> They Came to Cordura.   New York, Random House, and London, Heinemann, 1958.
> Where the Boys Are.   New York, Random House, and London, Heinemann, 1960.
> Welcome to Thebes.   New York, Random House, and London, Heinemann, 1962.
> The Cadillac Cowboys.   New York, Random House, 1964.
> The Eagle and the Iron Cross.   New York, New American Library, and London, Heinemann, 1966.
> Loveland.   New York, Doubleday, 1968.
> Bless the Beasts and Children.   New York, Doubleday, and London, Secker and Warburg, 1970.
> The Tin Lizzie Troop.   New York, Doubleday, 1972.

Uncollected Short Stories

> "A Horse for Mrs. Custer", in New World Writing 5.   New York, New American Library, 1954.
> "Ixion", in New World Writing 13.   New York, New American Library, 1958.
> "A Glass of Blessings", in Esquire (New York), January 1959.
> "Going to See George", in Esquire (New York), August 1965.

Other

> The Ghost and the Magic Saber, with Kathryn Swarthout (juvenile).   New York, Random House, 1963.
> Whichaway, with Kathryn Swarthout (juvenile).   New York, Random House, 1966; London, Heinemann, 1967.
> The Button Boat, with Kathryn Swarthout (juvenile).   New York, Doubleday, 1969; London, Heinemann, 1971.
> TV Thompson, with Kathryn Swarthout (juvenile).   New York, Doubleday, 1972.

*          *          *

Of the novels Glendon Swarthout has published from 1943 to the present, all are eminently readable; two—They Came to Cordura and Bless the Beasts and Children—are outstanding. Whether set in a World War II bomber plant in Michigan, or in a present-day boy's camp in Arizona, each reflects the author's intense involvement with the persons and places he writes of.

Willow Run, a novel about blue-collar workers in a World War II defense plant, is some-what heavy on win-the-war speeches and lacks story and character development. And while the book is rhapsodic on the details of building airplanes and a bit obvious in the symbolism, it does give us a glimpse into the mind of the factory worker under stress.

Some fifteen years later, Swarthout published his finest novel: *They Came to Cordura*. The tantalizing glance into the factory worker's psyche is explored with a probe—this time using the peace-time soldier as the object. Preparing for World War I, the country needed heroes. The time is 1916, and the place, the Mexican border, where the punitive forces of the U.S. Cavalry are trying to rout the rebels of Villa. Five men are chosen to receive the Congressional Medal of Honor, and it is Major Thorn's duty to keep them alive to receive it. The story concerns their six-day journey to Cordura, during which the men are revealed to be pathetic, corrupt, hypocritical, cowardly, and degenerate. It is a remarkable book for its creation of tension and its probing into the motives which make men behave courageously and selflessly on the battlefield. A gripping novel in every respect, it demonstrates Swarthout's power as a writer of major dimensions.

*Where the Boys Are*, a commercial success, is the story of the annual student spring trek to Florida. Although there is some attempt to inject a serious note into the proceedings by pointing out the possible tragic consequences of sexual indiscretions, it is largely a novel about youth with an appeal to youth—somewhat dated in the light of the freedoms demanded by youth in the decade since its publication.

After the huge commercial and critical success of *They Came to Cordura*, Swarthout and his family moved to southern Arizona. It is here that *The Cadillac Cowboys* is set. This work satirically depicts the pitfalls an Easterner faces in fitting into the not-so-wild West. Basically farcical, this novel nevertheless has elements of sentiment, poignancy, adventure, and nostalgia. Its main appeal, however, is its wild and often outrageous humor, bordering frequently on slapstick.

The same southern Arizona scene provides the background for *The Eagle and the Iron Cross*. The place is a prisoner-of-war camp; the time, 1945; the protagonists, two young German soldiers. They escape and ultimately find refuge with a bedraggled tribe of Indians. Despite the Indians' help, the soldiers meet violent death. Swarthout does not mask his bitterness in this novel: it is a tale of intolerance, misplaced faith, and wanton brutality. There are no winners and no heroes. The young Germans retain their dignity, even in death; the Indians retain theirs and endure life. Our villains are the American super patriots who, under the guise of retaliation, practice atrocities equal to those of the Nazis. It is not a pretty story.

Returning to his native Michigan, Swarthout in *Loveland* depicts the growing-up adventures of a young musician struggling with both adolescence and the depression of the '30's. This story is told with warmth and humor, and captures the frantic era of a waning opulent society and a dying way of life. Heavily larded with the slang and idiom of the '30's, the humor is occasionally strained; essentially though the lighter side of the era is handled tastefully and knowingly. Swarthout has been through this, we feel, and writes lovingly about those innocent days.

Swarthout's recent novel, *Bless the Beasts and Children*, brings the reader back to Arizona. Six sensitive boys from a summer camp witness a buffalo kill. Misfits and castoffs all their lives, their obsession leads them to free the remaining animals. Their nocturnal adventures and ultimate victory are interspersed with delicately handled flashbacks which probe to the core of each boy's personality problem. In the course of the adventure, there is humor, courage, suspense, and tragedy. A book *about* children, it is not necessarily only *for* children.

—Martin L. Kornbluth

**SWINNERTON, Frank (Arthur).** British. Born in Wood Green, Middlesex, 12 August 1884. Married Mary Dorothy Bennett in 1924; has two children. Office Boy, Hay Nisbet and Company, London, 1899–1900; Reception Clerk, and subsequently Confidential Clerk to Hugh Dent, J. M. Dent and Company, publishers, London, 1901–1907; Proof Reader, and subsequently Editor, Chatto and Windus, publishers, London, 1907–1926. Drama Critic, *Truth* and *The Nation*, London, 1919–21; Literary Critic, *The Evening News*, London, 1929–32; Novel Critic, *The Observer*, London, 1937–43; "John O'London" for *John O'London's Weekly*, London, 1949–54. President, Royal Literary Fund, 1962–66. Address: Old Tokefield, Cranleigh, Surrey, England.

PUBLICATIONS

Novels

> *The Merry Heart: A Gentle Melodrama.* London, Chatto and Windus, 1909; New York, Doubleday, 1929.
> *The Young Idea: A Comedy of Environment.* London, Chatto and Windus, 1910.
> *The Casement: A Diversion.* London, Chatto and Windus, 1911; New York, Doran, 1927.
> *The Happy Family.* London, Methuen, and New York, Doran, 1912.
> *On the Staircase.* London, Methuen, and New York, Doran, 1914.
> *The Chaste Wife.* London, Secker, 1916; New York, Doran, 1917.
> *Nocturne.* London, Secker, and New York, Doran, 1917.
> *Shops and Houses.* London, Methuen, and New York, Doran, 1918.
> *September.* London, Methuen, and New York, Doran, 1919.
> *Coquette.* London, Methuen, and New York, Doran, 1921.
> *The Three Lovers.* London, Methuen, and New York, Doran, 1922.
> *Young Felix.* London, Hutchinson, and New York, Doran, 1923.
> *The Elder Sister.* London, Hutchinson, and New York, Doran, 1925.
> *Summer Storm.* London, Hutchinson, and New York, Doran, 1926.
> *A Brood of Ducklings.* London, Hutchinson, and New York, Doran, 1928.
> *Sketch of a Sinner.* London, Hutchinson, and New York, Doubleday, 1929.
> *The Georgian House: A Tale in Four Parts.* London, Hutchinson, and New York, Doubleday, 1932.
> *Elizabeth.* London, Hutchinson, and New York, Doubleday, 1934.
> *Harvest Comedy.* London, Hutchinson, 1937; New York, Doubleday, 1938.
> *The Two Wives.* London, Hutchinson, 1939; New York, Doubleday, 1940.
> *The Fortunate Lady.* London, Hutchinson, and New York, Doubleday, 1941.
> *Thankless Child.* London, Hutchinson, and New York, Doubleday, 1942.
> *A Woman in Sunshine.* London, Hutchinson, 1944; New York, Doubleday, 1945.
> *English Maiden: Parable of a Happy Life.* London, Hutchinson, 1946.
> *The Cats and Rosemary.* New York, Knopf, 1948; London, Hamish Hamilton, 1950.
> *Faithful Company: A Winter's Tale.* London, Hutchinson, and New York, Doubleday, 1948.
> *The Doctor's Wife Comes to Stay.* London, Hutchinson, 1949; New York, Doubleday, 1950.
> *A Flower for Catherine.* London, Hutchinson, 1950; New York, Doubleday, 1951.
> *Mister Jim Probity.* London, Hutchinson, 1952; as *An Affair of Love*, New York, Doubleday, 1953.
> *A Month in Gordon Square.* London, Hutchinson, 1953; New York, Doubleday, 1954.
> *The Sumner Intrigue.* London, Hutchinson, and New York, Doubleday, 1955.
> *The Woman from Sicily.* London, Hutchinson, and New York, Doubleday, 1957.

*A Tigress in Prothero.*  London, Hutchinson, 1959; as *Tigress in the Village*, New York, Doubleday, 1959.

*The Grace Divorce.*  London, Hutchinson, and New York, Doubleday, 1960.

*Death of a Highbrow.*  London, Hutchinson, 1961; New York, Doubleday, 1962.

*Quadrille.*  London, Hutchinson, and New York, Doubleday, 1965.

*Sanctuary.*  London, Hutchinson, 1966; New York, Doubleday, 1967.

*The Bright Lights.*  London, Hutchinson, and New York, Doubleday, 1968.

*On the Shady Side.*  London, Hutchinson, 1970; New York, Doubleday, 1971.

*Nor All Thy Tears.*  London, Hutchinson, and New York, Doubleday, 1972.


Other

*George Gissing: A Critical Study.*  London, Secker, 1912; New York, Kennerley, 1913.

*Robert Louis Stevenson: A Critical Study.*  London, Secker, 1914; New York, Kennerley, 1915.

*Tokefield Papers.*  London, Secker, and New York, Doran, 1927; augmented edition, as *Tokefield Papers, Old and New*, London, Hamish Hamilton, and New York, Doubleday, 1949.

*A London Bookman.*  London, Secker, 1928.

*Authors and the Book Trade.*  London, Howe, and New York, Knopf, 1932.

*The Georgian Scene: A Literary Panorama.*  New York, Farrar and Rinehart, 1934; as *The Georgian Literary Scene*, London, Heinemann, 1935; revised edition, London, Hutchinson, 1938, 1950, 1969; New York, Farrar Straus, 1951; New York, Greenwood Press, 1971.

*Swinnerton: An Autobiography.*  New York, Doubleday, 1936; London, Hutchinson, 1937.

*The Reviewing and Criticism of Books.*  London, Dent, 1939; New York, Oxford University Press, 1940.

*The Bookman's London.*  London, Wingate, 1951; New York, Doubleday, 1952.

*Londoner's Post: Letters to Gog and Magog.*  London, Hutchinson, 1952.

*Authors I Never Met.*  London, Muller, 1956; Los Angeles, Spencer, 1963.

*Background with Chorus: A Footnote to Changes in English Literary Fashion Between 1901 and 1917.*  London, Hutchinson, 1956; New York, Farrar Straus, 1957.

*Figures in the Foreground: Literary Reminiscences, 1917–1940.*  London, Hutchinson, 1963; New York, Doubleday, 1964.

*A Galaxy of Fathers.*  London, Hutchinson, and New York, Doubleday, 1966.

*Reflections from a Village.*  London, Hutchinson, and New York, Doubleday, 1969.

Editor, *Anthology of Modern Fiction.*  London, Nelson, 1937.

Editor, *Literary Taste,* by Arnold Bennett.  London, Cape, 1937.

Editor, *Conversations of James Northcote*, by William Hazlitt.  London, Muller, 1949.


Manuscript Collection: University of Arkansas, Fayetteville.


Frank Swinnerton comments:

I have always written dramatic studies of character, at first set in the London suburbs as known to me, but increasingly in other environments. My aim has been to do in the novel what the Elizabethan playwrights did in their works. My two fundamental assumptions are that "character is Fate" and that "in life there are neither rewards nor punishments; there are consequences." Given the characters, I have built dramatic stories around them. My first model was Louisa May Alcott; my second Henry James; but of course I have chiefly been "inspired" by my own experience of life and my own observant temperament. I have never drawn people known to me; but have invented individuals (using experience solely as reference). This invention comes naturally; and the technique I use is to show the characters as it were stereoscopically, through the eyes of other persons. My grandfathers were both what are called "Master Craftsmen"; and while not claiming to be a master I do regard myself as, first of all, a craftsman. That is, I love my work, regardless of reward.

As critic, I write "by the light of Nature", being more interested in men and women than in their opinions or in aesthetic theory.

*     *     *

One hardly expects a novelist who is alive in the 1970's to be the contemporary of such giants as Conrad, James, Lawrence, or Forster. Yet the truth is that Frank Swinnerton's first novel, *The Merry Heart*, appeared in 1909, two years before Lawrence's *The White Peacock*, Conrad's *Under Western Eyes*, and James's *The Outcry*, and a year before Forster's *Howard's End*. It is important to be aware of this, not for any matter of mere whimsicality, but because we need to recognise that Frank Swinnerton's "masters" could hardly be those tremendous innovators whose presence, sometimes shadowy, sometimes strong, we find behind such contemporary and senior novelists as Graham Greene, with his strong debt to Conrad, and Angus Wilson, who has always been ready to admit the influence of Forster on his writing.

If we are to begin to understand the nature and scope of Frank Swinnerton's fiction, then, we need to be alive to the fact that he began writing during the period of the sudden and vast upthrust of the modern novel, that many of the novelists who helped shape the course of twentieth century fiction were his acquaintances, and that he was able to write about them with easy familiarity in his critical guide to *The Georgian Literary Scene*.

*The Georgian Literary Scene* is a useful work of reference, because of its author's encyclopaedic knowledge of the literature of the period about which he writes. It is a good deal more than useful in its shrewd summaries of the novelists of that era (Swinnerton is less sure on the poets). And, perhaps most important of all, it helps us to understand a good deal about Swinnerton as a novelist himself. For example, at the end of his generous and perceptive pages on Lawrence, Swinnerton remarks that in a hundred years Lawrence will in all probability still be on the literary map, "while I, and those like me, will have sunk without trace from every record of the Georgian era." Two things deserve our attention here. One, that Swinnerton's engaging modesty is in no sense false; he rightly thinks of himself as a minor novelist (though it needs to be said that there are good and bad minor novelists, and that Swinnerton is, so it seems to me, emphatically to be considered a good minor novelist). Two, Swinnerton identifies himself with the Georgian period, and this is very proper. For his fiction *is* essentially Georgian. But what is meant by calling Frank Swinnerton a Georgian novelist?

In the first place, we may note that Swinnerton, who was born in 1884, enjoys that sense of eager—one might almost say fervent—secularism that is so marked a feature of the novelists of the opening decades of the Twentieth Century. Like Forster, Swinnerton believes in the holiness of carnal love, and in his autobiography, *Swinnerton*, he himself has said that he considers himself lucky to have escaped the sense of sin. Thus, when his novels deal with love, and they frequently do, they deal with it in what it seems fair to call a Georgian manner. That is to say, they express neither the sense of guilt or heavy conventionality of the Victorian novel, nor the metaphysical brooding of a Lawrence. For Swinnerton, love is or ought to be simply enjoyable, and anything that impedes or prevents it from being so is for that very reason to be condemned. Putting it another way, we might remark that in dealing with intense personal relationships Swinnerton shows himself to be a true disciple of Meredith and a true contemporary of Forster.

Yet in another context Swinnerton is very unlike Forster. Indeed, although with his customary modesty and truthfulness Swinnerton calls Forster "the most intelligent of all the novelists of the 1880–1900 generation" what he has to say of Forster in *The Georgian Literary Scene* makes clear that Swinnerton finds a good deal to regret about Forster's fictional ways. In particular, he dislikes Forster's "fantasticality", which he sees as an evasion of realism and a refusal to let the life of the novel take over from his insistent moral themes. All of Forster's novels, Swinnerton says, have a quality of "radiant intelligence" but they also have two major faults. First, they are customarily deficient in emotion, in that Forster rarely shows any great involvement with his characters except in so far as they are figures in his moral theorems. Second, Forster is hampered because of his very limited knowledge of English life. Thus it is absurd, Swinnerton says, for Forster to pretend that Leonard Bast, the uneducated clerk of *Howard's End*, would have responded as Forster claims he did to the courtesy of a Cambridge student. "My knowledge of clerks is very extensive," Swinnerton drily remarks, "and I have never met one who would be overwhelmed by decent behaviour on the part of an undergraduate, or one to whom such decent behaviour would seem less than his due."

Now this two-pronged criticism of Forster is instructive, not just because it directs us to faults which Forster certainly has, but because it makes clear that Swinnerton as a novelist himself is very much in the camp of realism. Perhaps we should not be surprised at this. For after all, the year of Swinnerton's *The Casement* (1911) was also the year in which Arnold Bennett published *Hilda Lessways*, the second of his *Clayhanger* trilogy. The following year, Swinnerton published *The Happy Family*, which seems to me one of his best pieces of sustained fiction in its unflurried and deliberately low-pitched observation of life and in its occasional sharp wit and the ready sympathy which the author displays with and for his characters. And in the same year he published *George Gissing: A Critical Study*. The fact is that Swinnerton has many points of similarity with both Gissing and Bennett, those champions of the realist novel (his *Shops and Houses*, 1918, is very akin to the kinds of study that one finds in so much of Bennett's writing, as for example, *Riceyman Steps*). And it is worth noting that Swinnerton writes with rare affection of Bennett in *The Georgian Literary Scene*.

Of all Swinnerton's many novels, *Harvest Comedy* is the one that perhaps most amply testifies to his gifts. It is extremely well-written, it is neatly but unobtrusively plotted, it has the realist's typical fascination with the contours of unremarkable yet unique lives (in this case the lives of three men), and it shows Swinnerton's unemphatic liberal moral position to its best advantage. That position is best summed up, perhaps, by the hero of *A Woman in Sunshine*, when he tells his wife that "You're infected by the pessimism of the children. You, and they, have gone away from simplicity. You're now trying to intellectualise the heart, which can't be done." The words are almost Forsterian, and very obviously they reflect "Georgian" concerns and attitudes. But in his best work Swinnerton finds his own ways of giving both concerns and attitudes a proper fictional life.

—John Lucas

---

**SYMONS, Julian (Gustave).**   British.   Born in London, 30 May 1912. Educated in various state schools. Married to Kathleen Clark; has two children. Has worked as a shorthand typist, secretary for an engineering company, and an advertising copywriter. Editor, *Twentieth Century Verse*, London, 1937–39. Free-lance Writer since 1947. Reviewer, *Manchester Evening News*, 1947–56. Since 1958, Fiction Reviewer for the *Sunday Times*, London. Chairman, Crime Writers Association, 1958–59. Chairman, Committee of Management, Society of Authors, 1969–71. Recipient: British Crime Writers Association Award, 1957, 1966; Edgar Allan Poe Award, 1961, 1966. Address: 37 Albert Bridge Road, London S.W.11, England.

PUBLICATIONS

### Novels

*The Immaterial Murder Case*.   London, Gollancz, 1945; New York, Macmillan, 1957.
*A Man Called Jones*.   London, Gollancz, 1947.
*Bland Beginning*.   London, Gollancz, and New York, Harper, 1949.
*The 31st of February*.   London, Gollancz, and New York, Harper, 1950.
*The Broken Penny*.   London, Gollancz, 1952; New York, Harper, 1953.
*The Narrowing Circle*.   London, Gollancz, and New York, Harper, 1954.
*The Paper Chase*.   London, Collins, 1956; as *Rogue's Fortune*, New York, Harper, 1956.
*The Colour of Murder*.   London, Collins, and New York, Harper, 1957.
*The Gigantic Shadow*.   London, Collins, 1958; as *Pipe Dream*, New York, Harper, 1958.
*The Progress of a Crime*.   London, Collins, and New York, Harper, 1960.
*The Killing of Francie Lake*.   London, Collins, 1962; as *The Plain Man*, New York, Harper, 1962.
*The End of Solomon Grundy*.   London, Collins, and New York, Harper, 1964.
*The Belting Inheritance*.   London, Collins, and New York, Harper, 1965.
*The Man Who Killed Himself*.   London, Collins, and New York, Harper, 1967.
*The Man Whose Dreams Came True*.   London, Collins, and New York, Harper, 1969.
*The Man Who Lost His Wife*.   London, Collins, and New York, Harper, 1971.
*The Players and the Game*.   London, Collins, and New York, Harper, 1972.

### Short Stories

*Murder, Murder*.   London, Fontana, 1961.
*Francis Quarles Investigates*.   London, Panther, 1965.

### Verse

*Confusions about X*.   London, Fortune Press, 1938.
*The Second Man*.   London, Routledge, 1944.

### Other

*A. J. A. Symons: His Life and Speculations*.   London, Eyre and Spottiswoode, 1950.
*Charles Dickens*.   London, Barker, 1951.
*Thomas Carlyle: The Life and Ideas of a Prophet*.   London, Gollancz, and New York, Oxford University Press, 1952.
*Horatio Bottomley*.   London, Cresset Press, 1955.
*The General Strike: A Historical Portrait*.   London, Cresset Press, 1957; Chester Springs, Pennsylvania, Dufour, 1963.
*The Thirties: A Dream Revolved*.   London, Cresset Press, 1960; Chester Springs, Pennsylvania, Dufour, 1963.
*A Reasonable Doubt: Some Criminal Cases Re-examined*.   London, Cresset Press, 1960.
*The Detective Story in Britain*.   London, Longman, 1962.
*Buller's Campaign*.   London, Cresset Press, 1963.
*England's Pride: The Story of the Gordon Relief Expedition*.   London, Hamish Hamilton, 1965.

*Crime and Detection: An Illustrated History from 1840.*   London, Studio Vista, 1966;
    as *A Pictorial History of Crime*, New York, Crown, 1966.
*Critical Occasions.*   London, Hamish Hamilton, 1966.
*Bloody Murder.*   London, Faber, 1972; as *Mortal Consequences*, New York, Harper,
    1972.
*Between the Wars.*   London, Batsford, 1972.
*Notes from Another Country.*   London, Alan Ross, 1972.

Editor, *Anthology of War Poetry.*   London, Penguin, 1942.
Editor, *Selected Writings of Samuel Johnson.*   London, Grey Walls Press, 1949.
Editor, *Selected Works, Reminiscences and Letters*, by Thomas Carlyle.   London,
    Hart Davis, 1956; Cambridge, Massachusetts, Harvard University Press, 1957.
Editor, *Essays and Biographies*, by A. J. A. Symons.   London, Cassell, 1969.

Several plays produced on television.


Manuscript Collection: University of Texas, Austin.


Critical Study: in *Auden and After* by Francis Scarfe, London, Routledge, 1942.


Julian Symons comments:

I think the reason—well, one reason apart from money—for writing crime stories may be
of interest. The quotation comes from the introduction to my Omnibus volume (Collins,
1967):

> Why put such ideas (as those in my books) into the form of crime stories, rather than
> "straight" novels? The thing that absorbs me most in our age is the violence behind
> respectable faces, the civil servant planning how to kill Jews most efficiently, the judge
> speaking with passion about the need for capital punishment, the quiet obedient boy
> who kills for fun. These are extreme cases, but if you want to show the violence that
> lives behind the bland faces most of us present to the world, what better vehicle can
> you have than the crime novel?

\*          \*          \*


Julian Symons, a poet of the Thirties and later a distinguished literary critic (with books
to his credit on Dickens and Carlyle) and social historian (author of *The Thirties* and *The
General Strike*), took to writing crime novels as a sideline to his main literary interests, almost
as a game, but during the years fiction has become one of the main currents of his life as a
writer and a vehicle for his criticism of the world he lives in. He has become one of the few
serious critics of the crime novel as well as one of its most prolific practitioners.

In his novels (such as *The Narrowing Circle, The Colour of Murder, The Progress of a
Crime, The 31st of February, The Immaterial Murder Case, The Broken Penny*) Symons has
used the necessary structure of the thriller—the presence and explanation of a crime or an
apparent crime—for many more purposes than those exploited by the writer of the ordinary
neatly contrived detective story which depends on the solution of a complex puzzle. Symons's
plots are often, by comparison, loose and even obvious, and his denouements are sometimes
deliberately anti-climactic; there is a distinctly ironic element in his attitude towards such
matters. What he injects into his deliberately disjointed version of the classic crime plot is
the kind of content that comes from his own wider interests. He is concerned with the decay

of a society, with cultural pretences, with politics as a corrupting element, with the manners of a world he has made his own: the Bohemian borderland where failed artists and hack writers, advertisement men and broadcasters, and their lesser hangers-on, come together to create a setting whose very alienation from moral stability tends to encourage the emergence of crime. It is a setting where the murderer and the victim seem to attract each other, a world of hollow men which suggests that as a novelist Symons has learnt lessons from Wyndham Lewis.

But it is not merely the landscape of a rotting society that is created. Within it there is likely to be enacted a pursuit in which the ambiguous guilts of unjustly accused men play their part. These novels, indeed, are often psychologically quite complex, and it is such inner drama that in the end is more important than the solution of the crime, or even the crime itself.

Indeed, in *The 31st of February* for example, there is no crime at all, and a man is grimly hunted to insanity, by a detective with a megalomaniac sense of being the agent of divine justice, for a death that was after all not a murder. This novel illustrates the ambiguity of Symons's attitude towards the policeman as a fictional type. Even when the police turn out in the end to be on the side of right, they are still menacing and unpredictable figures, and upon them Symons seems to focus the criticism of society that permeates his novels, and especially the dilemma of self-defeating authority and its semblances of justice which are hollow because they lack the core of justice.

—George Woodcock

SYMONS, Scott. Canadian. Born in Toronto, Ontario, 13 July 1933. Educated at Trinity College School, Port Hope, Ontario; Trinity College, University of Toronto, B.A. in modern history 1955; King's College, Cambridge, M.A. in English literature; the Sorbonne, Paris, Diplome d'Etudes Superieures. Married; has one child. Editorial Writer and Reporter, *Toronto Telegram*, *Quebec Chronicle Telegram*, *Montreal Presse*, and *Montreal Nouveau Journal*. Since 1962, has worked as Curator, Sigmund Samuel Canadiana Collection, and the Canadiana Gallery, Royal Ontario Museum, Toronto, Assistant Professor of Fine Art, University of Toronto, and Consultant, Smithsonian Institution, Washington, D.C. Taught a post-graduate course in Contemporary Art at the University of Pennsylvania, Philadelphia. Recipient: Beta Sigma Phi Award, 1968. Lives in Newfoundland. Address: c/o McClelland and Stewart Ltd., 25 Hollinger Road, Toronto 16, Ontario, Canada.

PUBLICATIONS

Novels

Place D'Armes.  Toronto, McClelland and Stewart, 1967.
Civic Square.  Toronto, McClelland and Stewart, 1969.

Other

Heritage: A Romantic Look at Early Canadian Furniture.  Toronto, McClelland and Stewart, 1971.

Manuscript Collection: Trinity College, University of Toronto.

Scott Symons comments:

> *Place D'Armes* is at once a first novel,
> a meticulously tangled diary,
> an insanely indiscreet autobiography,
> an existential Canadian allegory,
> a book of illicit imagination that is pure fact,
> an implacable manifesto.

                              *        *        *

As a "Para-Canadian, released from any allegiance to the Canadian State but obsessively devoted to the Canadian Nation", Scott Symons presents his novels as acts of faith in the inner logic of Canada. The country's Blandebeestes, Protestant architects of a new Canadian identity, have castrated Canadians by cutting them off from their land, love, heritage, and life; *Place D'Armes* is "an adventure in the senses" intended to reaffirm the sensibilities of the homosentient man, and to challenge the benignant Canadian Death "whose first trait is the social, sexual, moral security, passivity of smugness". "Decarnated", disembodied, detached from his roots as a Tory Radical, Hugh Anderson flees Ontario for Montreal, where he becomes a "demissionary" seeking to be touched by his French-Canadian friends, Roman Catholicism, antique furniture, even the buildings surrounding Old Montreal's Place D'Armes. His notes, Combat Journal (of the Holy War between reality and himself) and Novel gradually merge into an ontological discovery of the Real Presence of joy, of Body and Blood rather than the Bilingualism and Biculturalism of governmental Royal Commission. Anderson's numerous homosexual encounters are thus individual attempts at fusing the stability of English Canadians ("Cubed-Roots") and French Canadian carnality, just as in his growing madness, his heightened sensibility, he finds himself penetrated, "insited" by the Place itself.

*Civic Square* represents the other half of Symon's rhetorical diptych, an epistle to Ontario's Canadacult and the new orthodoxy of perverted Canadian nationalism which drove him to Montreal. His Civic Square is the "Torontoman", the prototype of the Canadian Cube ("An American-Square-in-Committee-of-the-Whole"), and the devil in Symons' seasonal liturgy. "Each season is a Man, a Landscape, a Religious Denomination, a form of Church Architecture, a Mode of Perception and of knowledge . . . and a Political Creed"; the letters to "Dear Reader" comprising the novel are semi-autobiographical and scatalogical accounts of winter, the Great Canadian Heresy's urban-Liberal-Methodism/Presbyterianism, and of spring, rural-Conservative Anglicanadianism: a dialectical "Sensibility Sequence". Childhood memories, his private school, motor-racing and motor-cycling, heterosexual love, high tea with his parents in a fashionable Toronto suburb, metaphorical bird-watching at his small farm, all are data to dispute the reduction of Canadians to "mere Professional Canajuns first—dead on our feet".

Symons' fragmented prose, incorrigible punning and private mythology—accessible principally to readers familiar with Canadian literature and politics during the 1960s— reflect the tangled complexity of his central preoccupation: recapturing the delicately accretive emotional content linking him to his past and his environment. Both *Place D'Armes* and *Civic Square* are dedicated to demonstrating that "you cannot tamper with the inner logic of a people without destroying that people", even if the people themselves are only slowly coming to recognise that they are lamentably willing participants in their own destruction.

—Bruce Nesbitt

**TATE, Allen.** American. Born in Winchester, Kentucky, 19 November 1899. Educated at Georgetown Preparatory School, Washington, D.C.; Vanderbilt University, Nashville, Tennessee, B.A. 1922. Married Caroline Gordon, *q.v.*, in 1924; Isabella Stewart Gardner, 1959; Helen Heinz, 1967; has three children. Member of the Fugitive Group of Poets: Co-Founding Editor, *The Fugitive*, Nashville, 1922–25. Editor, *Sewanee Review*, Tennessee, 1944–46; Editor, Belles Lettres series, Henry Holt and Company, New York, 1946–48. Lecturer in English, Southwestern College, Memphis, Tennessee, 1934–36; Professor of English, The Woman's College, Greensboro, North Carolina, 1938–39; Poet-in-Residence, Princeton University, New Jersey, 1939–42; Lecturer in the Humanities, New York University, 1947–51. Since 1951, Professor of English, University of Minnesota, Minneapolis: Regent's Professor, 1966; Professor Emeritus, 1968. Visiting Professor in the Humanities, University of Chicago, 1949; Fulbright Lecturer, Oxford University, 1953, University of Rome, 1953–54, and Oxford and Leeds universities, 1958–59; Department of State Lecturer at the universities of Liège and Louvain, 1954, Delhi and Bombay, 1956, the Sorbonne, Paris, 1956, Nottingham, 1956, and Urbino and Florence, 1961; Visiting Professor of English, University of North Carolina, Greensboro, 1966, and Vanderbilt University, 1967. Phi Beta Kappa Orator, University of Virginia, Charlottesville, 1936, and University of Minnesota, 1952; Phi Beta Kappa Poet, William and Mary College, Williamsburg, Virginia, 1948, and Columbia University, New York, 1950; Member, Phi Beta Kappa Senate, 1951–53. Since 1948, Fellow, and since 1956, Senior Fellow, Kenyon School of English (now School of Letters, Indiana University, Bloomington). Consultant in Poetry, Library of Congress, Washington, D.C., 1943–44. President, National Institute of Arts and Letters, 1968. Since 1964, Member, Board of Chancellors, Academy of American Poets. Recipient: Guggenheim Fellowship, 1928, 1929; National Institute of Arts and Letters grant, 1948; Bollingen Prize, for poetry, 1957; Brandeis University Creative Arts Award, 1960; Gold Medal of the Dante Society, Florence, 1962; Academy of American Poets Fellowship, 1963. Litt.D., University of Louisville, Kentucky, 1948; Coe College, Cedar Rapids, Iowa, 1955; Colgate University, Hamilton, New York, 1956; University of Kentucky, Lexington, 1960; Carleton College, Northfield, Minnesota, 1963; University of the South, Sewanee, Tennessee, 1970; M.A., Oxford University, 1958. Member, American Academy of Arts and Letters. Address: Running Knob Hollow Road, Sewanee, Tennessee 37375, U.S.A.

PUBLICATIONS

Novel

The Fathers. New York, Putnam, 1938; London, Eyre and Spottiswoode, 1939; revised edition, Denver, Swallow, and Eyre and Spottiswoode, 1960.

Uncollected Short Stories

"The Immortal Woman", in *Hound and Horn* (New York), July-September 1933.
"The Migration", in *Yale Review* (New Haven, Connecticut), Autumn 1934.

Play

The Governess, with Anne Goodwin Winslow (produced Minneapolis, 1962).

Verse

*The Golden Mean and Other Poems,* with Ridley Wills.   Privately printed, 1923.
*Mr. Pope and Other Poems.*   New York, Minton Balch, 1928.
*Ode to the Confederate Dead: Being the Revised and Final Version of a Poem Previously Published on Several Occasions: To Which Are Added Message from Abroad and The Cross.*   New York, Minton Balch, 1930.
*Poems: 1928–1931.*   New York, Scribner, 1932.
*The Mediterranean and Other Poems.*   New York, Alcestis Press, 1936.
*Selected Poems.*   New York and London, Scribner, 1937.
*The Winter Sea: A Book of Poems.*   Cummington, Massachusetts, Cummington Press, 1944.
*Poems, 1920–1945: A Selection.*   London, Eyre and Spottiswoode, 1947.
*Poems, 1922–1947.*   New York, Scribner, 1948.
*Two Conceits for the Eye to Sing, If Possible.*   Cummington, Massachusetts, Cummington Press, 1950.
*Poems.*   New York, Scribner, 1960.
*The Swimmers and Other Selected Poems.*   London, Oxford University Press, 1970; New York, Scribner, 1971.


Other

*Stonewall Jackson: The Good Soldier: A Narrative.*   New York, Minton Balch, 1928; London, Cassell, 1930.
*Jefferson Davis: His Rise and Fall: A Biographical Narrative.*   New York, Minton Balch, 1929.
*Reactionary Essays on Poetry and Ideas.*   New York and London, Scribner, 1936.
*Reason in Madness: Critical Essays.*   New York, Putnam, 1941.
*Invitation to Learning,* with Huntington Cairns and Mark Van Doren.   New York, Random House, 1941.
*Sixty American Poets, 1896–1944: A Preliminary Checklist.*   Washington, D.C., Library of Congress, 1945.
*On the Limits of Poetry: Selected Essays, 1928–1948.*   New York, Swallow Press-Morrow, 1948.
*The Hovering Fly and Other Essays.*   Cummington, Massachusetts, Cummington Press, 1949.
*The Forlorn Demon: Didactic and Critical Essays.*   Chicago, Regnery, 1953.
*The Man of Letters in the Modern World: Selected Essays, 1928–1955.*   Cleveland, Meridian, and London, Thames and Hudson, 1955.
*Collected Essays.*   Denver, Swallow, 1959.
*Essays of Four Decades.*   Chicago, Swallow Press, 1969; London, Oxford University Press, 1970.

Editor, with others, *Fugitives: An Anthology of Verse.*   New York, Harcourt Brace, 1928.
Editor, with Herbert Agar, *Who Owns America? A New Declaration of Independence.*   Boston, Houghton Mifflin, 1936.
Editor, with A. Theodore Johnson, *America Through the Essay: An Anthology for English Courses.*   New York, Oxford University Press, 1938.
Editor, *The Language of Poetry.*   Princeton, New Jersey, Princeton University Press, and London, Oxford University Press, 1942.
Editor, *Princeton Verse Between Two Wars: An Anthology.*   Princeton, New Jersey, Princeton University Press, and London, Oxford University Press, 1942.

Editor, with John Peale Bishop, *American Harvest: Twenty Years of Creative Writing in the United States*. New York, Fischer, 1942.

Editor, *Recent American Poetry and Poetic Criticism: A Selected List of References*. Washington, D.C., Library of Congress, 1943.

Editor, *A Southern Vanguard* (the John Peale Bishop memorial anthology). New York, Prentice Hall, 1947.

Editor, *The Collected Poems of John Peale Bishop*. New York, Scribner, 1948.

Editor, with Caroline Gordon, *The House of Fiction: An Anthology of the Short Story*. New York, Scribner, 1950; revised edition, 1960.

Editor, with Lord David Cecil, *Modern Verse in English, 1900–1950*. London, Eyre and Spottiswoode, and New York, Macmillan, 1958.

Editor, with others, *The Arts of Reading*. New York, Crowell, 1960.

Editor, *Selected Poems of John Peale Bishop*. London, Chatto and Windus, 1960.

Editor, with Robert Penn Warren, *Selected Poems by Denis Devlin*. New York, Holt Rinehart, 1963.

Editor, *T. S. Eliot: The Man and His Work*. New York, Delacorte Press, 1966; London, Chatto and Windus, 1967.

Editor, *The Complete Poems and Selected Criticism of Edgar Allan Poe*. New York, New American Library, 1968.

Translator, *The Vigil of Venus*. Cummington, Massachusetts, Cummington Press, 1943.

Bibliographies: "Allen Tate: A Checklist" by Willard Thorp, in *Princeton University Library Bulletin* (New Jersey), April 1942; reprinted, with "Allen Tate: A Checklist Continued" by James Korges, in *Critique* (Minneapolis), vol. 10, no. 2, 1968.

Critical Studies: Introduction by Arthur Mizener, to *The Fathers*, 1960; *The Last Alternatives* by R. K. Meiners, Denver, Swallow, 1962; *Tradition and Dream* by Walter Allen, London, Phoenix House, 1964; *Allen Tate: A Literary Biography* by Radcliffe Squires, Indianapolis, Bobbs Merrill, 1971.

\*       \*       \*

Allen Tate has published only one novel and two short stories; yet his fiction is as distinguished as his poetry and criticism. His subject, like that of Faulkner and some other Southern writers, is the destruction of the old South. In fictional technique he belongs to the school of Henry James and James Joyce, being essentially a dramatic writer who allows his stories to speak through technique rather than explicit statement.

Anyone familiar with Tate's essays will recognize the main issues of his fiction: The pre-Civil War world, whatever the weaknesses of certain individuals, had the advantage of being based on an economic system that made possible the continuity of a stable society. The key to that order was the cultivation of the land by men who lived on it and loved it apart from what it would bring financially. The destruction of this stable society was brought on by a combination of circumstances: the repeal of the laws of entail that had kept large properties intact, slavery—which raised barriers between landowners and the land—the accumulation in towns of monied individuals still in control of rural properties but cut off from the land and the culture the land nourished, and, finally, the Civil War, which accelerated the destruction of the old South.

The central issue of his novel, *The Fathers*, arises from the contrast between Major Lewis Buchan, the last father of the Buchan family, and his son-in-law George Posey. One critic has said that Major Buchan was a man with serious failings, which is true, but Buchan's failings were more the result of circumstances and of social upheaval than faults of character. For he was the product of an aristocratic agrarian society; his sensibility was, thus, cultural rather than individual; his tragedy was to live during a time when that culture was breaking down and men like George Posey were becoming dominant. Posey was a man of talent and integrity but, having grown up in the city in an eccentric family, he was an individualist with little to guide him in his relationships with others except his own random emotions. It was, in large part, Posey's inability to act in a culturally responsible way that helped bring about the destruction of Major Buchan and the Buchan dynasty.

Ostensibly the story "The Migration" is a loosely constructed chronicle about the settling of the frontier in North Carolina and, later, in West Tennessee. Actually, it is a subtle elegy on the destruction of a Southern agrarian society. "The Immortal Woman," set in Georgetown in modern times, might be called an ironic elegy on the disintegration of an old Southern house. The "immortal" woman of the story is an ancient lady in black who returns periodically to stare at the ruined house that once belonged to her family and which now stands empty in a neighborhood of outsiders and strangers. Both of Tate's stories take on additional significance when read in light of the more complex and more fully realized novel.

—W. J. Stuckey

---

**TAYLOR, Elizabeth.** British. Born in Reading, Berkshire, 3 July 1912. Educated at the Abbey School, Reading. Married John William Kendall Taylor in 1936; has two children. Address: Grove's Barn, Penn, Buckinghamshire, England.

PUBLICATIONS

Novels

At Mrs. Lippincote's. London, Davies, 1945; New York, Knopf, 1946.
Palladian. London, Davies, 1946; New York, Knopf, 1947.
A View of the Harbour. London, Davies, and New York, Knopf, 1947.
A Wreath of Roses. London, Davies, and New York, Knopf, 1949.
A Game of Hide-and-Seek. London, Davies, and New York, Knopf, 1951.
The Sleeping Beauty. London, Davies, and New York, Viking Press, 1953.
Angel. London, Davies, and New York, Viking Press, 1957.
In a Summer Season. London, Davies, and New York, Viking Press, 1961.
The Soul of Kindness. London, Chatto and Windus, and New York, Viking Press, 1964.
The Wedding Group. London, Chatto and Windus, and New York, Viking Press, 1968.
Mrs. Palfrey at the Claremont. London, Chatto and Windus, and New York, Viking Press, 1971.

Short Stories

Hester Lilly and Other Stories. London, Davies, 1954; as Hester Lilly: Twelve Short Stories, New York, Viking Press, 1954.

*The Blush and Other Stories.*   London, Davies, 1958; New York, Viking Press, 1959.
*A Dedicated Man and Other Stories.*   London, Chatto and Windus, and New York, Viking Press, 1965.
*Penguin Modern Stories 6*, with others.   London, Penguin, 1970.
*The Devastating Boys.*   London, Chatto and Windus, and New York, Viking Press, 1972.

Other

*Mossy Trotter* (juvenile).   London, Chatto and Windus, and New York, Harcourt Brace, 1967.

Critical Studies: "The Sensibility Angle" by Michael Toulson, in *Isis* (Oxford), 28 January 1959; "The Novels of Elizabeth Taylor" by Robert Liddell, in *Review of English Literature* (London), April 1960.

Elizabeth Taylor comments:

I think that loneliness is a theme running through many of my novels and short stories, the different ways in which individuals can be isolated from others—by poverty, old age, eccentricity, living in a foreign country—even by having committed murder, as in *A Wreath of Roses* (there are several kinds of loneliness in that novel).

My characters are not from life, and I like especially to stretch my imagination about them, and write of many different kinds of people—of all ages, in different social circumstances, against varied backgrounds. Situations I have sometimes taken from life, as a jumping-off point; but imagining myself into another world, using the eyes of the people I am creating, is what my writing has chiefly been about. I write in scenes, rather than in narrative, which I find boring. I am pleased if the *look* of a page is interesting, broken by paragraphs or dialogue, not just one dense slab of print.

\*     \*     \*

Elizabeth Taylor, an exquisite writer, has now been publishing novels and short stories for more than twenty-five years and is widely read on both sides of the Atlantic; nevertheless she has not yet had the critical appreciation that she deserves. Her work is quiet; her world is very nearly limited to the families of well-to-do commuters living in the elegiac setting of the Thames valley; her tone is polite and serene, never shrill or ill-tempered. She has been writing through this changing quarter of a century and reflecting the changes, but without nostalgia for things past or any strain to get ahead of the future. She is free both from symbolism and from a philosophy; she never sets out to prove anything, and perhaps has nothing that she would care to prove. Her standards are simply those of a very fine and delicate moral sense. Some of her minor characters may belong to minorities: they are Catholic, Communist, vegetarian, homosexual or ex-suffragettes. They live quite comfortably in her fictional world where minorities are easily tolerated. This world—though a world in which love and death occur—is a world entirely free from the filth and violence that were lately so marked a feature of the novel. There is nothing for those critics who do not really care for the novel to take hold of, nothing, in short, but what Jane Austen sought in fiction: "work in which the most thorough knowledge of human nature, the happiest delineation of its varieties, the liveliest effusions of wit and humour are conveyed to the world in the best chosen language."

The language is discreet, un-self-advertising; no doubt a quick or careless reader (and she has many such) will fail to appreciate the exactly chosen word, the delicately placed adverb, or the admirable rhythm of a paragraph. Among the delineations of human nature, she particularly excels in her rendering of the deliberate or unconscious deceiver. The self-deceiver is nearly always set against characters who see her (for it is usually a woman) not as she sees herself; but their vision also needs correcting, and the resulting pattern is subtle, intricate and ironic.

Angel, in the book that bears her name, is a violent, self-hypnotised novelist of the Ouida class. More restrained (and perhaps more interesting) self-deceivers are the possessive mother, Midge, in *The Wedding Group*, or the irresponsible Flora in the book called after her *The Soul of Kindness*. Those who deliberately deceive win our sympathy (apart from the "wanted man" in *A Wreath of Roses*). The dedicated man, in the story that is called after him, who passes himself and a fellow servant off as man and wife out of pure devotion to hotel service, claims our admiration. And in the latest novel Mrs. Palfrey, by an innocent deception, passes off a strange young man on her fellow hotel guests as the grandson who has shamed her by never coming to visit her.

Mrs. Taylor is a pictorial artist, and particularly satisfactory are her portraits of painters, Frances, in *A Wreath of Roses*, who could paint a girl "as only God . . . could ever possibly have seen her"; or Liz Corbett in *The Soul of Kindness*, a "creatively orderly person" who has reassembled "into delicate and intricate patterns" the confused rubbish on the floor of her messy room. In her works it is often the images that stay with us the longest. The cat, for instance: "the shallow arc between the tips of his ears, his baleful stare, and his hunched-up body blown feathery by the wind, gave him the look of a barn-owl." And we remember the weather in the background, the miraculous summer of *In a Summer Season*, or the phlegmy fog, or the rain falling down the window like gin.

It is because she sees things so sharply that Mrs. Taylor has made the beautiful love story of Harriet and Vesey in *A Game of Hide-and-Seek* so real. They meet in a tea-shop as horrible in its way as the inn-parlour of *Great Expectations*, and I do not know that anyone in English fiction since Pip has been more in love than they. Those critics who "like things to happen" have been disappointed in Harriet and Vesey because they never make love; they overlook the fact that it is the nature of their passion to be thwarted, and that the passion that is satisfied is apt to be very uninteresting to the reader. It is the "double sorrow" of Troilus that we care about—his anxiety to possess Cressida and his pain at losing her; while he is with her we are not much interested.

Food is particularly real in these books, especially when it is nasty, like the uneatable Chelsea bun bravely unrolled by Vesey, the objective correlative of his illicit and hopeless love. This, and other solidities, are deliberately overlooked by those who try to make out that Mrs. Taylor is a delicate, feminine writer who escapes from the world in which we have to live. A woman writer she is, as she ought to be. Her women characters are various and robust; one has only to think of the three sharply distinguished women in *A Wreath of Roses*, the alarming "sales ladies" in *A Game of Hide-and-Seek*, and of Mrs. Palfrey, so bravely facing old age and loneliness in the latest novel. The male characters are generally seen through women's eyes (as in Jane Austen) but are wisely and ironically seen.

Mrs. Palfrey, in the sad residential hotel where "they are not allowed to die", may move tears. But this author is also a great mover of laughter: "the liveliest effusions of wit and humour" are also hers. These are best, perhaps, to be found in the perfect phrase, or the sly riposte, but she has also a gruesome humour that recalls that of Sir John Betjeman or Osbert Lancaster. From researches in the pubs of the Thames Valley she has brought to us a collection of "sick" jokes and of "astonishingly horrid" language that are marvellously funny to the contemporary reader, and may be a treasure to the future ethnologist.

There is also a time-honoured source of fun of which she makes use: the illiterate or semi-literate. "I know it is wrong to make fun of simple people", writes one of her characters, but of course it is not wrong to make fun of anyone on earth, so long as one does not hurt them. Those who are too priggish to be amused by her lower classes, must pay the price of their priggishness. Mrs. Secretan (just quoted) was justly amused by her housekeeper, who invented love-letters to herself (one began "my enchantress"). There are also splendid "cleaning-ladies" (anglicè—charwomen), and the cook who has been round the world, and is full of advice learned from "what we did in India".

The great motive power, I believe, behind this author's work is love. Not the love that is a four-letter word, nor yet anything so theoretical as Christian charity, but most certainly a great virtue. This virtue, in combination with a fine sensibility and intelligence, has produced work which has appealed to thousands; if it cannot also win the admiration of the hundreds of the more sophisticated, so much the worse for them.

—Robert Liddell

---

**TAYLOR, Peter (Hillsman).** American. Born in Trenton, Tennessee, 8 January 1919. Educated at Vanderbilt University, Nashville, Tennessee, 1936–37; Southwestern College, Memphis, Tennessee, 1937–38; Kenyon College, Gambier, Ohio, 1938–40, A.B. 1940. Served in the United States Army, 1941–45. Married Eleanor Lilly Ross in 1940; has two children. Taught at the University of North Carolina, Chapel Hill, 1946–67. Since 1967, Professor of English, University of Virginia, Charlottesville. Visiting Lecturer, Indiana University, Bloomington, 1949; University of Chicago, 1951; Kenyon College, 1952–57; Seminar in American Studies, Oxford University, 1955; Ohio State University, Columbus, 1957–63; Harvard University, Cambridge, Massachusetts, 1964. Recipient: Guggenheim Fellowship, 1950; National Institute of Arts and Letters grant, 1952; Fulbright Fellowship, to France, 1955; O. Henry Award, 1959; Ford Fellowship, 1960. Member, National Institute of Arts and Letters, 1969. Address: Department of English, Wilson Hall, University of Virginia, Charlottesville, Virginia 22901, U.S.A.

PUBLICATIONS

Novel

A Woman of Means. New York, Harcourt Brace, and London, Routledge, 1950.

Short Stories

A Long Fourth and Other Stories. New York, Harcourt Brace, 1948; London, Routledge, 1949.
The Widows of Thornton. New York, Harcourt Brace, 1954.
Happy Families Are All Alike: A Collection of Stories. New York, McDowell Obolensky, 1959; London, Macmillan, 1960.
Miss Leonora When Last Seen and 15 Other Stories. New York, Obolensky, 1963.
The Collected Stories of Peter Taylor. New York, Farrar Straus, 1969.

Plays

Tennessee Day in St. Louis. New York, Random House, 1957.
A Stand in the Mountains (produced Barter Theatre, 1971). Published in Kenyon Review (Gambier, Ohio), 1965.

*        *        *

Peter Taylor is part of the literary phenomena called the Southern Renaissance. In particular, his art springs from the same Middle Tennessee source that fed the New Criticism, Fugitive-Agrarianism of Ransom, Tate, Warren, Davidson, Lytle, and others. In common with his lustrous peers, Peter Taylor delights in irony; he has superbly mastered his chosen art form; he has an acute consciousness of time, the presentness of the past, change, and the problem of identity; he is intensely aware of man's inevitable involvement in the subtleties and complexities of evil. Also like his peers, he has a keen sense of being deeply rooted to a place and its traditional values, but he is unique in being more intensely a Tennessean than any of his fellows and in choosing to express life's tensions entirely through the polite manners of Tennessee's gentle class. Tennessee becomes the very *modus operandi* of all his fiction, providing him with a set of manners from which to read and reveal character, with a literal setting and atmosphere for his actors, and with a staple symbol for ordering time, change, and chaos into meaning. Tennessee is the metaphor at the center of his universe.

Tennessee is time, and time is the central theme of all Peter Taylor's works from "A Long Fourth" to "Tennessee Day in St. Louis," from "Venus, Cupid, Folly and Time" to "Miss Leonora When Last Seen." Time is change measured from a fixed point in space, in character, or in social function. Time is also chance and chaos operating in a given place. Time is the erratic element against which man posits his will and control. Yet time is half man-made, a created part from which the whole is known, an artificial arrestment within movement, an artful ordering before new chaos. Whatever else time is, it is always betrayal.

Basic to Peter Taylor's theme is the concept of role playing as the mark of man's personal as well as mankind's collective identity (civilization). *Theatre mundi* concepts are as much in evidence in Taylor's novel as in his dramas and short stories where typically the tensions are drawn between acceptance or rejection of a role, between fidelity to or betrayal of a role, between knowledge or ignorance of role and its relation to ultimate reality.

Roles are half the chancy doings and undoings of time; half the work of man. Within the circumference of chance are the roles one is offered, but the choice of role and the skill with which it is played are man's doing, outside but in time. A role can not be developed except through conventions, traditions, defined rules, arbitrary assigning of values, and the practice of manners. Man develops the role, ascribes to it values relative to some conception of the whole, learns its conventions, and plays it with whatever skill he may possess. Thus manners are the measure of man and their change is the measure of time. Peter Taylor is mainly interested in the manners of those controlled, gentle, doomed people who play roles with the skill and conviction of artists who believe life imitates art.

For these people, identity is the role one plays. In a static society the roles are most clearly understood, the art of playing is most thoroughly appreciated, and the manners that express the role are the most subtly polished. Life in such societies can fully imitate art and maintain the illusion that art is reality. Life becomes ceremonies, rituals, traditions, manners, a clearly defined function relative to the whole. (The whole, for Peter Taylor, is represented by the Southern family and all its extensive connections.) Like his great mentor Henry James, Taylor gives us brilliant portraits of such ladies and gentlemen who knowingly find and maintain their identity through conformation of self to the artful playing of a role. Literary descendents of James' Isabel Archer are Helen Ruth, "A Wife of Nashville," the other wives in "A Long Fourth," "Cookie," *Tennessee Day in St. Louis*, and "Death of a Kinsman," the uncle in "The Other Times," the bachelor brother in "Heads of Houses," the young boy searching for his role in "Promise of Rain," and the old couple in "Venus, Cupid, Folly and Time," the only grotesques in all of Peter Taylor's work. But the maintenance of identity is no easy matter, because Tennessee is no longer a relatively static society and art is illusion and time the final reality. Reality is change and chance, forever making obsolete old roles and giving opportunity for new ones. The old role is betrayed for the new, or if one clings faithfully to the old role, it is betrayed by time making it irrelevant to the whole—functionless, useless, a curiosity from the past, unappreciated and misunderstood by the very society which originally created it. Thus, either way, time, for men, is betrayal, inevitable immersion in evil and knowledge, inescapable like original sin.

Such is man's doom in Peter Taylor's world: betray or be betrayed. Only those flexible enough—one suspects that Peter Taylor would say also those who are opportunists and disloyal enough—are the fittest for survival. But the civilized voice, the gentle voice, can not fail to mourn properly the nearly extinct American swan who sings most beautifully near death. Thus Peter Taylor, as cold-eyed and realistic as he is, can not fail to mourn the art that time betrays and makes known most clearly its beauty just before its extinction. Peter Taylor's most successful stories are concerned with gentle people who, having accepted and played a role with utmost skill, find their role is no longer wanted or understood and thus have no place to be themselves without self betrayal, yet they cling bravely and faithfully to the values of their identity and salvage what little they can from time's chaos. Such a one is Miss Leonora in "Miss Leonora When Last Seen" who is forced by "progress" into an orbit of no place and no time, assuming the outward, but for her meaningless, appearance modernism prescribes—rootless, chic, dyed and painted—but held inevitably to a point in place and time to which she can never return. Another is Munsie in "What You Hear from 'Em?" Her role as one of the elect once unified public and private life. As black mother of a white family, as staunch preserver of the true wealth of human love and respect for the individual, as responsible citizen, she was a lady. She knew her role well and played it with utmost art that neglected no ceremony, no care, no ritual, no understood manner until time betrayed her private concrete life into a hopeless abstraction and her public life into a comic and degraded caricature of her race.

As artist, particularly as short story writer, Peter Taylor too has accepted his role and played it with utmost skill. He apparently conceives of his role as that of awakener to the ironic beauty of illusion and the awful chaos of reality. He is also the recorder of change within the constancy of change, and, like his characters, practices such art that would freeze time for a moment so we may be more keenly aware of what is passing and about to pass. He would give order to change itself so we may see it in all its universality and individuality, its concreteness and abstraction, its manner and meaning, its surface and interior. Part of his role, too, is as elegist, most clearly seen in his skillful modulation of voices, always intelligent, always a little ironic, never so clever as those James employs, but infinitely more gentle and sad, speaking just at the point before full awareness of losses calls for utmost control. Full awareness and utmost control are left for Taylor and the reader.

—Robert L. Welker

---

**TAYLOR, Robert Lewis.** American. Born in Carbondale, Illinois, 24 September 1912. Educated at Southern Illinois University, Carbondale, 1929; University of Illinois, Urbana, 1930–33, B.A. 1933. Served in the United States Navy, rising to the rank of Lieutenant Commander, 1942–46. Married Judith Martin in 1945; has two children. Reporter, Carbondale, 1934; Correspondent in the South Seas for *American Boy* magazine, 1935; Reporter, *St. Louis Post-Dispatch*, 1936–39; Profile Writer, *The New Yorker*, 1939–48. Recipient: Sigma Delta Chi Award, for reporting, 1939; Pulitzer Prize, 1959. Address: Spectacle Mountain Road, Kent, Connecticut 06757, U.S.A.

PUBLICATIONS

Novels

*Adrift in a Boneyard.*  New York, Doubleday, 1947.

*Professor Fodorski: A Politico-Sporting Romance.* New York, Doubleday, 1950.
*The Bright Sands.* New York, Doubleday, and London, Deutsch, 1954.
*The Travels of Jaimie McPheeters.* New York, Doubleday, 1958; London, Macdonald, 1959.
*A Journey to Matecumbe.* New York, McGraw Hill, and London, Hutchinson, 1961.
*Two Roads to Guadalupé.* New York, Doubleday, 1964; London, Deutsch, 1965.

Other

*Doctor, Lawyer, Merchant, Chief.* New York, Doubleday, 1948.
*W. C. Fields: His Follies and Fortunes.* New York, Doubleday, 1949; London, Cassell, 1950.
*The Running Pianist.* New York, Doubleday, 1950.
*Winston Churchill: An Informal Study in Greatness.* New York, Doubleday, 1952.
*Center Ring: The People of the Circus.* New York, Doubleday, 1956.
*Vessel of Wrath: The Life and Times of Carry Nation.* New York, New American Library, 1966.

\*       \*       \*

Six of Robert Lewis Taylor's twelve books are biographical in nature. Some are collections of profiles, many originally contributions to *The New Yorker*, others full-length biographies. The flavour and style of his later fiction bear a strong resemblance to his biographical writing, even to the point of seeming derived from it. The subjects of his life studies are striking personalities, such as Winston Churchill and Carry Nation, who had lives full of rich, dramatic incident. These two aspects, carried along by an easy, lively style, provide the total reading experience, for though the works reveal the dramatic nature of life, they offer little interpretation. His fiction often shows a reliance upon sensational incident. This is shown most clearly in *Adrift in a Boneyard*, where he projects a world-wide catastrophe; but in later books he is fond of the striking situation, such as the placing of Professor Fodorski, a refugee engineer, in a football-crazy Southern town (*Professor Fodorski*) or the depiction of a bizarre Cape Cod summer in *The Bright Sands*.

It is with *The Travels of Jaimie McPheeters*, however, that he finds the appropriate vehicle for his talents and apparent preferences. This travel tale relates the adventures of Jaimie, about 13 at the novel's beginning, and his incorrigibly adventuresome father, Dr. Sardius McPheeters, as they flee Kentucky creditors to solve their financial worries in the California gold fields. The episodic plot is filled with stock but colourful heroes of the trail and frontier who become involved in every kind of dramatic situation that has become the staple for westerns and adventure stories. The innocent Jaimie is little more than a puppet manipulated by Taylor to provide facile humour or introduce new plot developments. Despite these drawbacks, the book justly deserves the Pulitzer Prize it was awarded. Its success rests on the author's ability to relate incidents in bold detail, both horrible and humorous, relying heavily on rich, fast-paced dialogue. The author's extensive research is effectively used to give information and views regarding people of the period, such as the Mormon founders of Salt Lake City. Yet all is unobtrusively worked into Jaimie's adventures. As in many good westerns, tension is supplied, in the absence of plot, by the repeated appearance and disappearance of two villains who keep adding to the score they will have to settle with the protagonists before the story's conclusion. The most entertaining stroke of the author is his manner of narration. Jaimie relates a good share of the story and happily lets his companions do the talking while he records. Interspersed throughout his narration are the journal entries of his physician father and the latter's letters to his wife en route. After being introduced to the stern, practical Mrs. McPheeters in Chapter One, the reader must enjoy envisioning her never-recorded responses to the doctor's ever-optimistic but often grizzly detailed accounts of trail happenings—this after assuring her at the outset that the trip would hold nothing in the way of real danger.

Unfortunately, Taylor has not duplicated the success of his prize-winning fiction with the same adventure-travel formula in *A Journey to Matecumbe* and *Two Roads to Guadalupé*. For example, Davie Burnie, the juvenile narrator of *A Journey to Matecumbe*, is an unconvincing Huck Finn who reveals himself too often in unlikely style for a boy reared by fussy aunts on a Kentucky plantation: "As for me, I'm not sure the rifle cocking story wasn't the best after all; it's more romantical." This time the hero escapes the Ku Klux Klan with his Uncle Jim, heading down the Mississippi and farther south to Key West, where Uncle Jim hopes to find buried treasure with the aid of a map obtained in the Mexican War. Here the characters are too closely patterned after those in *The Travels of Jaimie McPheeters*. Even the narrative device is weakly imitative, with the quack Dr. Snodgrass for some reason writing the letters to Davie's aunts to inform them of their relatives' adventures. The action is stalled while Davie inserts information regarding the unusual names of black children, Indian customs and so on. Neither does fourteen-year-old Sam's adventures in the Mexican War recorded in *Two Roads to Guadalupé* reveal new heights of the author's creativity. Taylor's fictional reputation must rest, for now, on *The Travels of Jaimie McPheeters*. It offers no stirring themes but abounds in fast-paced, vivid action, period information, and deft narration—these are Robert Lewis Taylor's contribution to fiction.

—Paula L. Hart

---

**TENNANT, Kylie.** Australian. Born in Manly, New South Wales, 12 March 1912. Educated at Brighton College, Manly; University of Sydney, 1931. Married Lewis C. Rodd in 1932; has two children. Journalist, Publisher's Reader, Literary Adviser and Editor, 1959–69. Full-time Writer, 1935–59, and since 1969. Life Patron, Fellowship of Australian Writers; Member, Commonwealth Literary Fund Advisory Board, since 1961. Recipient: S. H. Prior Memorial Prize, 1935, 1941; Australian Literary Society Gold Medal, 1941; Commonwealth Jubilee Stage Prize, 1951. Address: 5 Garrick Avenue, Hunter's Hill, New South Wales 2110, Australia.

PUBLICATIONS

Novels

*Tiburon*.   Sydney, Endeavour Press, 1935.
*Foveaux*.   London, Gollancz, 1939.
*The Battlers*.   London, Gollancz, and New York, Macmillan, 1941.
*Ride on Stranger*.   Sydney, Angus and Robertson, New York, Macmillan, and London, Gollancz, 1943.
*Time Enough Later*.   New York, Macmillan, 1943; London, Macmillan, 1945.
*Lost Haven*.   New York, Macmillan, 1945; London, Macmillan, 1947.
*The Joyful Condemned*.   New York, St. Martin's Press, and London, Macmillan, 1953; complete version, as *Tell Morning This*, Sydney and London, Angus and Robertson, 1967.
*The Honey Flow*.   London, Macmillan, and New York, St. Martin's Press, 1956.

Short Stories

*Ma Jones and the Little White Cannibals.*   London, Macmillan, 1967.

Plays

*Tether a Dragon.*   Sydney, Associated General Publications, 1952.
*John o' the Forest and Other Plays* (juvenile).   London, Macmillan, 1952.
*The Bells of the City and Other Plays* (juvenile).   London, Macmillan, 1955.
*The Bushrangers' Christmas Eve and Other Plays* (juvenile).   Melbourne, Macmillan,
   1959.

Other

*Australia: Her Story: Notes on a Nation.*   London, Macmillan, and New York, St.
   Martin's Press, 1953; revised edition, London, Pan, 1964, 1971.
*Long John Silver: The Story of the Film.*   Sydney, Associated General Publications,
   1953; London, Robertson and Mullens, 1954.
*The Development of the Australian Novel.*   Canberra, Commonwealth Literary Fund,
   1958.
*All the Proud Tribesmen* (juvenile).   London, Macmillan, 1959; New York, St. Martin's
   Press, 1960.
*Speak You So Gently* (travel).   London, Gollancz, 1959.
*Trail Blazers of the Air.*   Melbourne, Macmillan, 1965; London, Macmillan, and New
   York, St. Martin's Press, 1966.
*The Australian Essay*, with L. C. Rodd.   Melbourne, Cheshire, 1968.
*Evatt: Politics and Justice* (biography).   Sydney and London, Angus and Robertson,
   1970.
*The Man on the Headland* (biography).   Sydney, Angus and Robertson, 1971; London,
   Angus and Robertson, 1972.

Editor, *Great Stories of Australia 1–7.*   London, Macmillan, and New York, St.
   Martin's Press, 1963–66.
Editor, *Summer's Tales 1* and *2.*   London, Macmillan, and New York, St. Martin's
   Press, 1964, 1965.

Bibliography: in *The Novels of Kylie Tennant* by Margaret Dick, Adelaide, Rigby, 1966.

Manuscript Collection: Australian National Library, Canberra.

Critical Studies: reviews by Frank Swinnerton, in *The Observer* (London), 5 January 1941;
by Richard Church, in *John O'London's*, 10 January 1941; by M.C.R., in *Washington* (D.C.)
*Star*, 10 August 1941; by Ralph Thomson, in *New York Times*, 11 August 1941; by Edwin
Muir, in *The Listener* (London), 25 March 1943; in *An Introduction to Australian Fiction*
by Colin Roderick, Sydney, Angus and Robertson, 1950; "The Novels of Kylie Tennant"
by Dorothy Auchterlonie, in *Meanjin* (Melbourne), no. 4, 1953; "The Tragi-Comedies of
Kylie Tennant" by T. Inglis Moore, in *Southerly* (Sydney), no. 1, 1957; *The Novels of Kylie
Tennant* by Margaret Dick, Adelaide, Rigby, 1966; in *Social Patterns in Australian Literature*
by T. Inglis Moore, Sydney, Angus and Robertson, 1971.

*     *     *

Kylie Tennant is an outstanding figure in the Australian literary scene. Versatile, original, with a strong creative flow, she has produced plays, history, biography, poetry, travel and criticism, but primarily she is a novelist.

Her range is wide, her view of existence complex. High-spirited, humorous, with a pervading sense of the comic cross-purposes of the way life is lived, she combines a delighted appreciation of human idiosyncrasy with an open-eyed acceptance of man's innate destructiveness; affirms the value of life in the face of an ironic perception of the basic futility of the human predicament; uses the imagination of a poet to praise the prosaic and celebrate the commonplace.

When her first book, *Tiburon*, appeared she was hailed in some quarters as a social realist and it is true that there is an element of social challenge in all her work: politics, bureaucracy, education, law, are derided with a good humour that did not in her early days as a writer save her from a considerable backlash of indignation. Yet her sense of the intractability of human nature prevents her from supposing that a change in society would eradicate human perversity. Kylie Tennant, in fact, refuses to be pigeon-holed.

Certain themes recur—the instinctive against the civilised, the value of the outcast and the reject, the country against the city. The country has always been a refuge for her. Her spirits rise to the sights and sounds and smells of the bush, and her evocations of the Australian landscape in *The Battlers*, *Lost Haven* and *The Honey Flow* are unsurpassed. Yet her feeling for the time she lives in insists that for good or ill our age is centred in cities. A line joining the one with the other is the axis on which her writing turns, preserving an almost perfect balance between the two.

*Foveaux*, *Ride on Stranger*, *Tell Morning This*, together create a sense of Sydney that reflects the corruption of city life, the raffishness, crime, struggle and despair that underlie the fine edifices of law and respectable custom. Only the gay comedy, *Time Enough Later*, adds a wholesome, softer note to the grim and grimy city symphony.

Each of Kylie Tennant's books is an exploration of an aspect of reality—a search for meaning and significance in life; yet her approach is pragmatic, her immediate attention directed outwards: her imagination needs firm roots in the actual. Before beginning a novel, she spends long periods immersed in the kind of life she means to represent—travelling for months with the unemployed along the long roads of Australia before writing *The Battlers*, living in a slum in Surry Hills before *Foveaux*, working on boat-building before *Lost Haven*, even contriving to be sent to gaol before *Tell Morning This*.

Her implication in many different ways of life gives her books a generously varied texture, but the effect is far from documentary. Each is a living world, seen in a tragi-comic perspective that is this writer's peculiar stamp: her mode is comedy, but her strength lies in the breadth of her vision and in her ability to handle a dynamic and complex system of relationships with vitality and freedom.

It is good to know that after a long break she is now at work on a new novel.

—Margaret Dick

---

**THEROUX, Paul.** American. Born in Medford, Massachusetts, 10 April 1941. Educated at Medford High School; University of Massachusetts, Amherst, B.A. in English. Married Anne Castle in 1967; has two children. Lecturer, Soche Hill College, Limbe, Malawi, 1963–65; Makerere University, Kampala, Uganda, 1965–68; University of Singapore, 1968–71. Address: c/o Diana Crawfurd Ltd., 5 King Street, London, W.C.2, England.

PUBLICATIONS

Novels

*Waldo*.   Boston, Houghton Mifflin, 1967; London, Bodley Head, 1968.
*Fong and the Indians*.   Boston, Houghton Mifflin, 1968.
*Girls at Play*.   Boston, Houghton Mifflin, and London, Bodley Head, 1969.
*Murder at Mount Holly*.   London, Alan Ross, 1969.
*Jungle Lovers*.   Boston, Houghton Mifflin, and London, Bodley Head, 1971.


Uncollected Short Stories

"Two in the Bush", in *Atlantic* (Boston), March 1968.
"A Real Russian Ikon", in *Commentary* (New York), December 1969.
"Sinning with Annie", in *Harper's Bazaar* (New York), April 1970.
"The Prison Diary of Jack Faust", in *Playboy* (Chicago), September 1970.


Other

Verse published in periodicals.


Paul Theroux comments:

Although three of my novels have equatorial settings, I do not consider myself an "exotic" novelist. Necessity—earning a living—has forced me to live in little countries; I would be happier if I could live in England or America. Then, I am sure, the settings of my novels would change.

I am not sure whether my novels have "themes"; the subjects are the main characters and their dilemmas, if any.

\*       \*       \*

Paul Theroux, a young American writer, has written five novels. His first, *Waldo*, set in the United States, shares a certain similarity of tone with the later ones. It is marred, however, by its self-conscious flashiness and by its much too overtly symbolic settings.

It is in Africa that Theroux finds a setting which complements his outrageous sense of humour, and which permits him to exercise his unusual inventiveness. Theroux has taught in Malawi and Uganda and he has observed the life and scenery of these countries very shrewdly. Although his novels remind one of Evelyn Waugh's African novels, it is clear that Theroux knows more about Africa than Waugh ever did. There is the same close attention to detail, often unpleasant detail, that one finds in Waugh, but there is more feeling in Theroux' novels for Africa and its predicament in having to cope with the generosity thrust upon it by the World Powers. This is especially evident in his most mature work so far, his latest novel, *Jungle Lovers*.

It would be false, however, to suggest that Theroux is interested in Africa for its own sake. Africa is chosen as a setting for his novels so that he can isolate his American characters and exaggerate their traits and mannerisms by contrasting them with people quite unlike them. It is the place where the Romantic idealism of America clashes with reality; where a Peace Corps volunteer's innocent liberalism leads to her rape and suicide; where revolutionary dreams and plans to insure African lives end in disillusionment.

The English characters in the novels fare better than the Americans. They are less susceptible to depression and disillusionment because of their cynicism, which Theroux suggests is a product of their history and experience in the colonies. Beaglehole and Bailey, though ridiculous in their own way, possess much greater resilience than Mullet and Marais.

In contrast to the loquaciousness of the English and the Americans, the Africans seem silent and obtuse. But there is no doubt that there is a bond between the African and his landscape. He at least makes no attempt to see it as exotic. The reality of having to survive in a tough and demanding environment moulds his personality to that of his surroundings in such a way that the white characters all seem intruders.

Working with these three basic types, the American, the English, and the African, Theroux manages to create several interesting and original individual characters. The structure of his novels depends on the conflict between these characters. He has an almost Conradian ability to exploit the landscape of Africa to emphasize the tension in his novels. In *Girls at Play*, the school in the centre of Africa, isolated as it is, functions in much the same way as the outpost in "An Outpost of Progress".

Theroux uses Africa in his fiction as a testing ground for the Non-African. This has been done frequently before by such distinguished writers as Haggard, Conrad, Waugh, Hemingway, Cary and Greene. That he manages to bring freshness to an area already so thoroughly exploited is an indication of his success.

—Anthony Boxill

---

**TINDALL, Gillian (Elizabeth).** British. Born in London, in 1938. Educated at Lady Margaret Hall, Oxford, M.A. (honours) in English literature. Married to Richard Lansdown; has one child. Regular contributor to *The Guardian*, *New Statesman* and *New Society*, all in London. Recipient: Mary Elgin Prize, 1970. Address: 27 Leighton Road, London N.W.5, England.

PUBLICATIONS

Novels

> *No Name in the Street*. London, Cassell, 1959; as *When We Had Other Names*, New York, Morrow, 1960.
> *The Water and the Sound*. London, Cassell, and New York, Morrow, 1961.
> *The Edge of the Paper*. London, Cassell, 1963.
> *The Youngest*. London, Secker and Warburg, 1966; New York, Walker, 1967.
> *Someone Else*. London, Hodder and Stoughton, and New York, Walker, 1969.
> *Fly Away Home*. London, Hodder and Stoughton, and New York, Walker, 1971.

Uncollected Short Story

> "Fiona", in *Winter's Tales 16*. London, Macmillan, 1970.

Other

*The Israeli Twins* (juvenile).    London, Cape, and Mystic, Connecticut, Verry, 1963.
*A Handbook on Witchcraft*.    London, Barker, 1965; New York, Atheneum, 1966.


Gillian Tindall comments:

I really do not have many coherent views on my own work, except that it seems to be
getting better as time goes by, but that I do not imagine I shall go on writing novels for ever.

*            *            *

The women in Gillian Tindall's books have made a trade: in exchange for the insulation
and pre-packaged lives that men present to them—and which they unthinkingly take—
women give away the chance for a recognizable self. And they hardly notice this lack of
independent personality, so smoothly and innocuously does daily life flow, until a violent
event—a husband killed in a car crash (*Someone Else*); a deformed baby murdered by the
mother (*The Youngest*); the Six-Day Israeli War (*Fly Away Home*)—precipitates a search for
the self deferred. "But this fragmentation would not have happened . . . if I had an inner
personality . . . a self to fight against things and actions" (*Fly Away Home*). The nature of
the quest involves an exploration of relationships, backward to mother, father and sister,
and forward to husband and children.

Briefly, as an uncommitted young girl in Paris in the first two novels, the Tindall woman
explores non-familial relationships with a personality that is almost a stereotype of youthful
*sang-froid*. Her self-centeredness allows her to experience her first love affair, a painful miscarriage, the discovery of her French lover's homosexuality (*No Name in the Street*) and a
presumed incestuous relationship (*The Water and the Sound*) with resiliency, courage and
resourcefulness. But no sooner does she marry and beget children, as she does in the later
books, than her spirit and enterprise dissipate.

By the first of the Grown-Woman novels, *The Edge of the Paper*, the wife, Meg, is completely powerless. She has married Roy King, a sadist, whose name symbolizes his place in
the family matrix. At first he seems the perfect dream father-figure to Meg: rich, attractive,
in command. But soon he is revealed as the ultimate destroyer, a man "who can only feel
secure by beating someone else down." King is a psychotic, but he is only the extreme of a
husband like Loic in *Someone Else* whose death reveals to his wife, Joanna, her own absorption into the strong personality of her husband. "Years ago she had transferred to Loic all
the trust she had once placed in parent or diety." During her marriage her own responses
atrophy and when Loic is killed she confronts the tragedy like a child, allowing other men
to shield and protect her from bereavement.

This is the point to which the principal character always comes: a potentially dynamic,
often creative woman finds herself living out a pattern others have set for her. Tindall
structures the novels so that fairly early in the book one dramatic event tears the orderly
pattern and out of necessity the woman begins her self-discovery. This movement results in
a series of insights which the heroine interprets for herself and for the reader: "I began to
realize again . . . how utterly real and inescapable the ties of blood and kin are, of race and
class, in spite of the relative unimportance they may have in day-to-day life." The novels'
undramatic style is often juxtaposed against strangely melodramatic plot devices such as
abortion, incest, homosexuality, murder, car accidents and infanticide.

But the author's strength is insight into people and their *milieu*. With the cold eye of her
youthful protagonist, Tindall sees through the falsity of the Paris Bohemianism of the
Sixties and the contrived artiness of London's TV-advertising-literary life. (Her dissection
of fashionable child-raising in *Someone Else* is particularly sharp and fresh.) *Fly Away Home*

catches the essential mores, pretensions and fears of bourgeois French Jews. (She writes about Jews often, with a curious mixture of admiration and revulsion.) *The Youngest* highlights the demolition and renovation of London, which intimates a shifting class structure and the rapid change of the times. Amidst these unstable settings Tindall's woman tries to find a solid center within.

—Gloria Cohen

---

**TOLKIEN, J(ohn) R(onald) R(euel).** British. Born in Bloemfontein, South Africa, 3 January 1892; emigrated to England in 1896. Educated at King Edward VI School, Birmingham; Exeter College, Oxford, B.A. 1915, M.A. 1919. Served with the Lancashire Fusiliers, 1915–18. Married Edith Mary Bratt in 1916; has four children. Worked as an Assistant on the Oxford English Dictionary, 1918–20. Reader in English, 1920–23, and Professor of the English Language, 1924–25, University of Leeds, Yorkshire. At Oxford University: Rawlinson and Bosworth Professor of Anglo-Saxon, 1925–45; Fellow, Pembroke College, 1926–45; Leverhulme Research Fellow, 1934–36; Merton Professor of English Language and Literature, 1945–59; now Emeritus Fellow, Merton College, and Honorary Fellow, Exeter College. Andrew Lang Lecturer, St. Andrews University, 1939; W. P. Ker Lecturer, University of Glasgow, 1953. Recipient: *New York Herald Tribune* Children's Book Award, 1938; International Fantasy Award, 1957. D.Litt., University College, Dublin, 1954; University of Nottingham, 1970; Dr. en Phil. et Lettres, Liège, 1954. Fellow, Royal Society of Literature, 1957: awarded Benson Medal, 1966. C.B.E. (Commander, Order of the British Empire), 1972. Address: c/o George Allen and Unwin Ltd., 40 Museum Street, London WC1A 1LU, England.

PUBLICATIONS

Novels

   *The Hobbit; or, There and Back Again.*   London, Allen and Unwin, 1937; Boston, Houghton Mifflin, 1938.
   *Farmer Giles of Ham.*   London, Allen and Unwin, 1949; Boston, Houghton Mifflin, 1950.
   *The Lord of the Rings:*
      *The Fellowship of the Ring.*   London, Allen and Unwin, and Boston, Houghton Mifflin, 1954; revised edition, Allen and Unwin, 1966, Houghton Mifflin, 1967.
      *The Two Towers.*   London, Allen and Unwin, and Boston, Houghton Mifflin, 1955; revised edition, Allen and Unwin, 1966, Houghton Mifflin, 1967.
      *The Return of the Ring.*   London, Allen and Unwin, and Boston, Houghton Mifflin, 1956; revised edition, Allen and Unwin, 1966, Houghton Mifflin, 1967.
   *Smith of Wootton Manor.*   London, Allen and Unwin, and Boston, Houghton Mifflin, 1967.

Verse

   *Songs for the Philologists*, with others.   London, privately printed, 1936.

*The Adventures of Tom Bombadil and Other Verses from the Red Book*. London,
Allen and Unwin, 1962; Boston, Houghton Mifflin, 1963.
*The Road Goes Ever On*, music by Donald Swann.  Boston, Houghton Mifflin, 1967;
London, Allen and Unwin, 1968.


Other

*A Middle English Vocabulary*.  London and New York, Oxford University Press, 1922.
*Chaucer as a Philologist*.  London, Philological Society, 1934.
*Beowulf: The Monsters and the Critics*.  London, Oxford University Press, 1937.
*Tree and Leaf*.  London, Allen and Unwin, 1964; Boston Houghton Mifflin, 1965.
*The Tolkien Reader*.  New York, Ballantine, 1966.

Editor, with E. V. Gordon, *Sir Gawain and the Green Knight*.  London and New York,
Oxford University Press, 1925.
Editor, *Ancrene Wisse*.  London, Oxford University Press, 1962; New York, Oxford
University Press, 1963.

*     *     *

"Support Your Local Hobbit" and "Gandalf for President" buttons can be found today
beside "Make Love, Not War" ones, and maps of Middle Earth hang beside posters of
*Easy Rider*. For J. R. R. Tolkien, elderly Oxford Anglo-Saxon specialist, has since the
mid-sixties been a campus cult, in such strange company as Hermann Hesse and Kurt
Vonnegut. His first work of fiction, *The Hobbit*, appeared in the thirties; the massive *Lord
of the Rings* trilogy nearly twenty years later.

Tolkien's Middle Earth variously includes dangerous rivers, impassable mountain ranges,
pleasant forests and frightening ones, the sinister state of Mordor, pastoral ease in Lorien,
awesome halls built long ago by dwarves, and an undemanding life at Bag End in The Shire.
Its history has had three long Ages, each a falling-off from the previous one, and we read of
the final years of the Third Age, to be followed by ours, the Dominion of Men. Middle
Earth is peopled by dwarves, men, elves, ents, trolls, orcs and hobbits, the latter between
two and four feet high, with long curly hair on their feet, lovers of "peace and quiet and good
tilled earth."

In the first book, Bilbo Baggins, a hobbit, acquires an evil magic ring sought by Sauron,
the Dark Lord of Mordor, which would give him absolute power. In the trilogy, Frodo
inherits the ring and, counselled by the wizard Gandalf, makes the perilous journey to the
Crack of Doom in Mordor, the only place where the ring can be destroyed. Two of the six
sections follow the fortunes of other members of the Fellowship of the Ring, fighting the
wicked in Rohan and then for Gondor against Sauron, leading to the restoration of Gondor's
true king. But the end is not unqualified success: Frodo has wounds from which he will never
fully recover and dwarves and elves will decline because their lesser rings have lost their
power. Finally Frodo and some other hobbits and elves set sail for the Uttermost West:
"And the ship went out into the High Sea and passed on into the West, until at last on a
night of rain Frodo smelled a sweet fragrance on the air and heard the sound of singing
that came over the water."

Admirers of *Lord of the Rings* include W. H. Auden, who responded to the Quest theme,
Richard Hughes, who compared it with Spenser and asserted "for width of imagination it
almost beggars parallel," and C. S. Lewis: "If Ariosto rivalled it in invention (in fact he
does not) he would still lack its heroic seriousness. No imaginary world has been projected
which is at once so multifarious and so true . . . . Here are beauties which pierce like swords
or burn like cold iron; here is a book that will break your heart." Tolkien in fact has attempted
the first post-Renaissance romance, and may especially appeal to readers who do not know
the older ones.

Edmund Wilson dissented briefly but firmly, finding "an overgrown fairy story, a philological curiosity," sapped by "an impotence of imagination," appealing only to adults who never outgrow an "appetite for juvenile trash" (*The Bit Between My Teeth*, 1965). Catharine Stimpson's Columbia Essay (No. 41, 1969) adds a Women's Lib. attack, finding the writer "blandly, traditionally masculine," his women "the most hackneyed of stereotypes." She finds "dialogue, plot and symbols are terribly simplistic," and concludes it is "a comic-strip . . . almost as colorful and easy as *Captain Marvel*."

Douglass Parker began the scholarship when he found parallels between the *Ring*-trilogy and *Beowulf*, and pointed out that Orc is in Blake, Gandalf in Old Norse, and that "ent" means "giant" in Old English ("Hwaet We Holbytla," *Hudson Review*, 9, 1956–57). Bruce Beatie noted myths: "The basis of Frodo's journey . . . is clearly in its outlines the myth of the Dying God, the Seasonal Myth" ("The Tolkien Phenomenon," *Journal of Popular Culture*, 3, 1970). So now, as Michael Wood sums up, we have learned of such sources as "lines from heroic lays, a horn from Roland, an interesting case of resurrection from *The Golden Bough*, and a swan from an expensive staging of *Lohengrin*" ("Tolkien's Fictions," *New Society*, 27 March 1969).

But primarily of course Tolkien is a great storyteller, taking the reader, directly and with complete conviction, into a strange world. He makes us care about his odd, non-human creatures, as in the early risky journey to Rivendell avoiding the Black Riders and worrying with Frodo about Gandalf's unexplained absence. The plot advances briskly, though the length obliges one to dwell weeks in Middle Earth. The book is mind-expanding, setting up associations of Good and Evil, of fairies and pioneering settlers, of Bunyan and Malory and Atlantis. We are told only a small part of an enormous, almost endless, whole.

Tolkien himself gives a few clues to his intents. His long essay "On Fairy-Stories" praises tales which take us out of our own time, stimulate flights of imagination, show "the potency of the words and the wonder of things," and establish communication between humans and trees, birds and flowers. In a publisher's statement he wrote: "The invention of languages is the foundation. The 'stories' were made rather to provide a world for the languages than the reverse. I should have preferred to write in 'Elvish.'" Though he may be half-joking, he has many allusions that only a philologist can perceive. More important, however, is his awareness of the literatures of several languages, such as *Sir Gawain and the Green Knight*, which he edited; he wants to make these old forms alive for the present.

Tolkien writes that he dislikes allegory and prefers history, "true or feigned, with its varied applicability to the thought and experience of readers" (Foreword to the revised edition). So we find a scholarly pose: the book has appendices about history, languages and genealogy, and claims to be based on surviving records, particularly the Red Book of Westmarch, begun by Bilbo and Frodo. Robert Sklar suggests comparison with historians like Gibbon and Parkman, who are like Tolkien "artists and builders of worlds" ("Tolkien and Hesse," *Nation*, 8 May 1967).

Another facet is Tolkien the "Oxford Christian," close friend of Lewis and Charles Williams, both eager to write Christian allegory. The reader may be tempted to interpret the hobbits as doing God's work, or Sauron as Hitler, or the ring as nuclear weapons likely to destroy attacker as well as attacked, or the hobbits' love of good food as a reaction to rationing in wartime Britain. Such associations are usually trivial or false. More generally, Wood proposes that the ring "represents the lure of the modern world itself, which must stain all those who try to change it or use it." Tolkien does indeed express a conservative dislike of the present and a nostalgia for a pre-industrial green and pleasant England. So the book shows the end of an age, and the reactions of races and individuals to this, with the prospect that the succeeding age will be another decline.

The trilogy has a far more positive side, which may well account for its appeal. Frodo accepts his mission and rejects "the way that seems easier." He acts and dares, suffering and risking his life, and fulfils his impossible dream. Further, his choice *matters*: that he does what he believes right affects future events. *Lord of the Rings* is thus many-faceted: fairy story and history, magical and realistic, pessimistic about society yet hopeful about individuals, escapist fantasy-romance and aware of human truths.

Tolkien's three other stories are inevitably slight beside the trilogy, but he has been working for many years on *The Silmarillion*, a prose and verse epic about the quest of the potent jewel, the silmaril, and the overthrow of Morgoth, events that took place 6,500 years before those of the *Ring*-trilogy.

—Malcolm Page

---

**TONKS, Rosemary (D. Boswell).**   British.   Born in London. Married. Has lived in West Africa and Pakistan. Poetry Reviewer, BBC European Service. Address: 46 Downshire Hill, London N.W.3, England.

PUBLICATIONS

Novels

> *Opium Fogs*.  London, Putnam, 1963.
> *Emir*.  London, Adam Books, 1963.
> *The Bloater*.  London, Bodley Head, 1968.
> *Businessmen as Lovers*.  London, Bodley Head, 1969; as *Love among the Operators*, Boston, Gambit, 1970.
> *The Way Out of Berkeley Square*.  London, Bodley Head, 1970; Boston, Gambit, 1971.
> *The Halt During the Chase*.  London, Bodley Head, 1972.

Uncollected Short Stories

> "The Vanilla Bull", in *Accent* (London), 1970.
> "My Lamborghini Is Nervous", in *Queen* (London), 1970.
> "The Pick-Up; or, Ercole D'Oro", in *Encounter* (London), 1972.

Verse

> *Notes on Cafés and Bedrooms*.  London, Putman, 1963.
> *Iliad of Broken Sentences*.  London, Bodley Head, 1967.

Other

> *On Wooden Wings: The Adventures of Webster* (juvenile).  London, Murray, 1948.
> *The Wild Sea Goose* (juvenile).  London, Murray, 1951.

Rosemary Tonks comments:

I write down my vision of the inner and the outer worlds. It changes as I change. It's humorous.

*Emir* is the best prose work I have written.

*     *     *

Rosemary Tonks became a novelist some years after she had begun publishing her poetry. Like the poems her novels tend to be rather odd, almost hallucinatory journeys round the inside of one woman's skull. They are written in a style which veers between the brilliant and the absurd and one is oppressed by the feeling that it would clearly be impertinent to enquire what exactly is going on in them. This is not to say that they lack a subject—the usual one is a woman's eye view of the world—but it is to say that one may have a good deal of trouble discriminating between what goes on in the outer world and what is merely the inner world of the narrator's or heroine's imagination. Nor is this necessarily a criticism. It is more a description of the way the novels *are*. Yet the reader is bound to consider the possibility that Rosemary Tonks is not really at home with the novels and that these longish prose exercises are poems in disguise or interior monologues looking for a form of their own.

*Opium Fogs* allows Miss Tonks's particular gifts a fine flowering. The novel is set in an area of wintry London (Hampstead? Blackheath?) and concerns the tensions that exist among a group of intellectuals and writers, most of them no doubt based on actual figures of the London literary scene. Indeed, the novel has all the feeling of being a *roman à clef* and it has a slightly defiant "secretive" air about it, as though it is really intended for those "in the know." Not that this matters very much. For there is a fine acid wit about some of the descriptions, and a free-flowing element of fantasy that prompt one's admiration of Miss Tonks's ingenuity. What perhaps does go wrong with the novel is that one doesn't know quite how to take it because, one suspects, Miss Tonks herself didn't quite know what to do with it. It is neither satire nor fantasy, but then it is not really a happy blend of both. It does, of course, suggest comparison with the late and marvellous Stevie Smith. But whereas with Stevie Smith one is first amused and then convinced by the sure touch of her fantastic imagination, one tends to withhold comparable assent from Miss Tonks. There is a good deal that is willed about her language, and unlike Stevie Smith at her best there are bad lapses from the successful control of tone that is so essential if writing of her sort is to succeed.

*The Bloater* is perhaps the most achieved of her novels, because it is the one where a genuine concern with her subject subdues the conscious mannerisms of her style to the point where they become a genuine contribution to the novel's meaning; and *The Bloater* also has a greater depth of feeling for the girl character(s) who carry the novel's narrative.

—John Lucas

---

**TOYNBEE, (Theodore) Philip.**    British.    Born in Oxford, 25 June 1916; son of the historian Arnold Toynbee. Educated at Rugby School, Warwickshire, 1930–34; Christ Church, Oxford, 1935–38. Served in the Intelligence Corps, 1940–42, the Ministry of Economic Warfare, 1942–45, and at S.H.A.E.F. in France and Belgium, 1944–45. Married Anne Barbara Denise Powell in 1939 (divorced, 1950); Frances Genevieve Smith, 1950; has five children. Editor, *Birmingham Town Crier*, 1938–39; Literary Editor, Contact Publications, London, 1945–46. Since 1950, Member of the Editorial Staff, *The Observer*, London. Address: The Barn House, Brockweir, near Chepstow, Monmouthshire, England.

PUBLICATIONS

Novels

*The Savage Days.*   London, Hamish Hamilton, 1937.
*A School in Private.*   London, Putnam, 1941.

*The Barricades.*   London, Putnam, 1943; New York, Doubleday, 1944.

*Tea with Mrs. Goodman.*   London, Horizon, 1947; as *Prothalamium: A Cycle of the Holy Grail*, New York, Doubleday, 1947.

*The Garden to the Sea.*   London, MacGibbon and Kee, 1953; New York, Doubleday, 1954.

The Pantaloon series (in verse):

*Pantaloon; or, The Valediction.*   London, Chatto and Windus, and New York, Harper, 1961.

*Two Brothers: The Fifth Day of the Valediction of Pantaloon.*   London, Chatto and Windus, 1964; New York, Harper, 1965.

*A Learned City: The Sixth Day of the Valediction of Pantaloon.*   London, Chatto and Windus, 1966.

*Views from a Lake: The Seventh Day of the Valediction of Pantaloon.*   London, Chatto and Windus, 1968.

*Thanatos: A Modern Symposium*, with Maurice Richardson.   London Gollancz, 1963.

Other

*Friends Apart: A Memoir of Esmond Romilly and Jasper Ridley in the Thirties.*   London, MacGibbon and Kee, 1954.

*Comparing Notes: A Dialogue Across a Generation*, with Arnold Toynbee.   London, Weidenfeld and Nicolson, 1963.

Editor, *Fearful Choice: A Debate on Nuclear Policy*.   London, Gollancz, 1958; Detroit, Wayne State University Press, 1959.

Editor, *Underdogs: 18 Victims of Society.*   London, Weidenfeld and Nicolson, 1961; as *Underdogs: Anguish and Anxiety: 18 Men and Women Write Their Own Case-Histories*, New York, Horizon Press, 1962.

Translator, *Kérillis on the Causes of the War*, by Henri de Kérillis and Raymond Cartier. London, Putnam, 1939.


Philip Toynbee comments:

What I am trying to do in *Pantaloon*—no doubt over-ambitiously—is to write something like a modern equivalent of *Don Quixote, The Prelude, Faust*, and *A la Récherche du Temps Perdu*, all in one. That's to say a tragi-comic epic whose hero is representative, but not in the least typical, of the years 1914–1950. Above all I want to stand at a distance from my own hero, and by means of this device give a fair hearing and showing to all the important ideas and human types of the age, without explicitly endorsing any of them. It is part of the old struggle, in fact, to escape from romanticism and return to a classical outlook and method. My chosen medium is verse—in a great many different forms.

*      *      *

Philip Toynbee's four long poems—*Pantaloon, Two Brothers, A Learned City*, and *Views from a Lake*—perhaps fall outside a discussion of Toynbee's fiction. But there are some remarks on imaginative writing in the introduction to *Two Brothers* that cast light on the variety one encounters in Toynbee's prose fiction. Toynbee is justifying unusual elements in the "method" used in his poetry. But his remarks invite application of them to his prose fiction:

Any honest attempt to adopt a new literary method springs in the first place from a sense that "life escapes" when methods are used which have become too familiar and unconsidered. It would be frivolous to try out a new method simply for the sake of novelty, or even for some solely and complacently aesthetic reason. The pleasures of novelty and of a new aesthetic satisfaction may be added as a bonus, but the proper motive for trying to write in a new way is an urgent desire to represent the writer's experience of life more fully and more realistically than any existing method would allow.

It is plain to the reader of Toynbee's fiction that "more realistically" is a phrase that has had varied implications for the writer over the course of his career. In early work like *The Savage Days* a kind of surface realism combines with conventional narrative form to re-produce the *Bildungsroman* experience of a young Englishman. The older Toynbee remarks of such work: "In life as it is being lived, as it is reconstructed in a *Bildungsroman*, each new moment is burdened with the growing weight of all previous experience" (*Two Brothers*, p. 14). But the later Toynbee, it will appear, was concerned to get beneath "the growing weight of all previous experience" and arrive at the core of reality.

Another early novel still some distance from the core as Toynbee came to conceive it is *The Barricades*. In method, *The Barricades* is an anthology of the narrative techniques already well-explored by writers from Henry James onwards. Thus, there is limitation to the awareness of one person and *his* sense of reality—a sense supposedly not identical with that of the novelist himself. Though middle-aged, the hero, Rawlins, is sent through a set of experiences that educate him; his perceptions of his own character *and* the texture of the society where he lives are changed and perhaps refined. This goes forward by means of Rawlins' distant contact with the Spanish Civil War of the thirties. An introspective and rather petulant man, he studies his friends—who constitute a fairly wide spectrum of political and intellectual attitudes—and he sees a protegé of his go off to the conflict in Spain. There is an effort to suggest that Rawlins has learned a valuable lesson from his wanderings: there are "barricades" not only in Spain but also between one generation and another. The novel ends with Rawlins as a solitary person, content to endure the "barricades" that hem him in.

The tone and technique remind one of Aldous Huxley and other not particularly experi-mental writers of the time. Whoever Toynbee's early masters were, their influence wanes in the three other prose works that can be looked at here. In pursuit of writing "more realistically" Toynbee turns from renderings of experience that make the pretence of re-creating actually lived experience, as in *The Barricades* and elsewhere. Instead, and with some boldness, "reality" is fragmented and rearranged in various ways. The persona, which may or may not be the author's own "mask", is discarded in a work like *Tea with Mrs. Goodman*. Instead, there is—thanks to a device which is quite original—a succession of masks. Several persons attend a tea-party at Mrs. Goodman's; the party lasts an hour or less. Each visitor's awareness of the time-period is offered so that events repeat each other as the reader follows the course of one consciousness and then another. But there is no attempt at the psychological realism with which Toynbee reproduced the experience of the hero of *The Barricades*; there are, instead, only poetic and allusive equivalents—in Toynbee's close-wrought sentences—of what "actually" went through the minds of the characters at the tea-party. The result is a very free-moving ballet of sensibility with Toynbee freed of any obligation to take sides, read a moral lesson, or construct a "well-made" narrative. The only "conclusions" of *Tea with Mrs. Goodman* are that all human contacts are inconclusive, fraught with poetry and stupidity, and had best be allowed to run through the fingers like grains of sand. In fact, *Tea with Mrs. Goodman* moves toward the condition of dialogue—but dialogue that is poetic and allusive rather than dramatic and moving.

Two other works, exclusive of the four long poems mentioned at the outset, also allow one to observe Toynbee moving, it can be said, from one realism to another. *The Garden to the Sea* does not, like *Tea with Mrs. Goodman*, offer the reader the presence of several sensibilities, at odds with each other and incommunicative. The dialogue in *The Garden to the Sea* is no longer the compressed equivalent of dialogue among several persons. Rather are the conversations within one "self" named Adam. The "complete" Adam talks with elements of his nature—elements innocent or hopeful or deeply corrupt; and these elements converse with each other. One of the results of the method is a static contemplation of the difficulties that complicate "Adam's" awareness rather than resolve them.

Indeed, resolution of difficulties is no object of curiosity in the later portion of Toynbee's writing career, as it perhaps was in a novel like *The Barricades*. (Toynbee remarks that "the poetic vision is essentially a static and not a moving one" [*Two Brothers*, p. 14].) Thus, in *Thanatos*—written with Maurice Richardson—the ironic depiction of human views on death records ironic, ambiguous conflict among speakers—speakers who define but do not cancel each other. The long, spirited interchange is as full of gay mental life as are similar passages in Peacock or Aldous Huxley. As in *Tea with Mrs. Goodman* one can suspect where merit is and where nonsense. Mr. Christie, a Christian, comes off badly, and Erlebnis, a Jungian, is allowed to talk at convincing length. The book, like those that are entirely Toynbee's, speaks of an era when truths are not known but are just endlessly debated.

Consider the endings of Toynbee's later work. For convenience's sake he writes finis—but not a conclusive finis like that at the end of *The Barricades*. Perhaps the only telling ending to any sort of dialogue in our time is the descent of actual missiles directed at England by a foreign power; at least, this is the ironic conclusion that Toynbee and his collaborator provide for the circling and otherwise endless conversations of *Thanatos*. It is a conclusion that, like so much else in the work of Toynbee, is as cold as ice and likely to tear the bare hand that brushes it inadvisedly.

—Harold H. Watts

---

**TRACY, Honor (Lilbush Wingfield).** British. Born in Bury St. Edmunds, Suffolk, 19 October 1913. Educated at the Grove School, Highgate, London, 1925–29. Specialist, Political Warfare (Japan), in London, 1942–45. Assistant Editor, *The Bell*, Dublin, 1946; Paris, Eastern Europe and Japan Correspondent, *The Observer*, London, 1947–48; Dublin Correspondent, *The Sunday Times*, London, 1950. Address: Four Chimneys, Achill Sound, County Mayo, Ireland.

PUBLICATIONS

Novels

*The Deserters*   London, Methuen, 1954.
*The Straight and Narrow Path*.   London, Methuen, 1956; New York, Random House, 1957.
*The Prospects Are Pleasing*.   London, Methuen, and New York, Random House, 1958.
*A Number of Things*.   London, Methuen, and New York, Random House, 1960.
*A Season of Mists*.   London, Methuen, and New York, Random House, 1961.
*The First Day of Friday*.   London, Methuen, and New York, Random House, 1963.
*Men at Work*.   London, Methuen, and New York, Random House, 1966.
*The Beauty of the World*.   London, Methuen, 1967; as *Settled in Chambers*, New York, Random House, 1967.

The Butterflies of the Province.   London, Methuen, and New York, Random House, 1970.

The Quiet End of Evening.   London, Methuen, and New York, Random House, 1972.


Other

Kakemono: A Sketch Book of Post-War Japan.   London, Methuen, 1950; New York, Coward McCann, 1951.

Mind You, I've Said Nothing: Forays in the Irish Republic.   London, Methuen, 1953; Boston, Little Brown, 1955.

Silk Hats and No Breakfast: Notes on a Spanish Journey.   London, Methuen, 1957; New York, Random House, 1958.

Spanish Leaves.   London, Methuen, and New York, Random House, 1964.


Honor Tracy comments:

I haven't thought about my work in a general way. Roughly, if something interests, pleases or amuses me I imagine it may do the same for other people and I try to pass it on. Also, I have an orderly mind, and writing is a sort of tidying up and clarifying of life.

*          *          *

Toward the end of *A Number of Things* appears a passage that casts light not only on this novel of Honor Tracy's. With necessary modifications it offers illumination that extends its light to most of the other novels of this writer—work intensely comic and, in its own way, intensely sensible. The hero of this novel, a young man named Henry Lamb, has had great success with his first novel; on the basis of this novel, he wins the appointment of roving correspondent for a new liberal publication entitled *Torch*. He is sent to a Caribbean island, to report on the flowering of new black political consciousness; his reports are expected to gratify the liberal prejudices of the magazine he serves. But Henry finds only nonsense rather than wisdom in the island he visits. After a series of farcical adventures, reports of which are deeply disturbing to his enlightened editor, he is deported under humiliating circumstances. He is finally allowed to pay a shore visit to the island of Madeira. He suddenly feels a sense of relief after the exotic nightmare of his Caribbean weeks. Henry's impression of deliverance takes this form:

> I am in Europe! he thought. He had, suddenly, a quite vivid new sense of Europe, not as a place for holidays where the people behaved like foreigners, but of something wonderfully precious, that he had had to go all the way to the mindless tropics to discover, something as old as the hills and young as the flowers in the women's baskets.

Something—Europe—that Henry had been too ready to discard is kindly restored to him, and Henry is beatifically grateful—grateful even for the prospect of once more having back a job for which he once had had contempt.

Henry Lamb's experience is one that is often retraced in the novels of Honor Tracy. Her books are a celebration of the nonsense in which human beings allow themselves to be immersed and, by indirection at least, a celebration of the sense—dull, tedious, but as reliable as anything human can be—which exists as a criticism of nonsense. But if Honor

Tracy is a kind of moralist, she is one who tips her hand very delicately; the bulk of her fictional texture is indeed a reproduction of the follies that seduce persons from the relatively dull life of sense and rationality. Thus, the observer—if not the hero—of *The Straight and Narrow Path* is a dispassionate anthropologist who has come from labors in the Congo for a rest in an Irish village. To his English eyes—English rather than more generally "European" in this novel—the religious customs of the Irish village are no less strange than the primitivism he has been observing in Africa. The visitor observes and reports for the London press the behavior of nuns jumping over fires and assimilates the spectacle to ancient fertility rites practiced the world over. Unwittingly, he has affronted Catholic self-respect, becomes involved in a law-suit, and escapes the consequences of his imprudence only when a simple-minded Irish boy offers the distraction of an apparition of the Virgin. At the end of the novel, the visitor observes a pious procession that includes the only sensible Irishman he has met. Miss Tracy's comment on her hero's discomfiture points up his confusion. "What he had just seen had bereft him of power to think. . . . Now he saw that the joke was far more complex and ramified than he had supposed, and that it was on him." The hero has been, throughout the novel, an apostle of prudent common sense in a world that is determined to lose itself in the superstition, puritanism and deference to authority that are—as Miss Tracy usually sees it—the mark of Irishry.

The common note of all Miss Tracy's work, it should be plain, is to shoot folly where it flies. She is the tart enemy of all simplifying twentieth century expectations, and her powers of invention, as she pursues this task, are considerable. In addition to the themes already inspected—which come to the glorification of the wisdom of simple folk, whether in Ireland or the Caribbean—other modern expectations receive lethal arrows from Miss Tracy. The cult of self-realization receives its just due in *A Season of Mists* and *The Butterflies of the Province*; satirical plotting and the juxtaposition of a raree-show of odd persons demonstrate that there are limits to the pursuit of pleasure and self-esteem. The delusions of the literary life receive their lashings in *Men at Work*; the book tells of the misfortunes of a successful novelist whose vanity and lack of personal scruple make him a sitting target for the syco-phants that gather around him. *Settled in Chambers* brings to the English legal profession the same stringent regard that, in *Men at Work*, strips away the pleasing outer integuments of the literary career. There is, in all the novels, a kind of center—a kind of "Europe"—which amounts to a pervasive and yet unobstrusive judgment on the fretful ignorance of human limits that is the self-indulgence of the characters who move through the fiction.

In all the novels there is an electric vitality; the novels never run down. When a particular source of amusement has reached a point of diminishing returns, Miss Tracy wheels in upon the scene new characters and events which have less to do with a strict all-over design than with the need to keep a tale alive. Thus, in *The Prospects Are Pleasing*—another tale with an Irish setting—the central plot concerns the efforts of feckless Irish youth to steal from the English a painting that "morally" should hang in an Irish gallery. When the profits of ex-hibiting Irish chauvinism ebb, Miss Tracy introduces a new character—a batty noblewoman, member of the Anglo-Irish establishment. Her presence, only faintly related to the theft central to the novel, sets Miss Tracy's selected oddities to twitching again, along with the scandals inevitable in a parish fête. For Miss Tracy's charity does not extend itself to collective human activity—parish fêtes or government house receptions—any more than it does to the motley crew who frequent these meetings. One might say that her novels are designed to be read with a glass of sherry in the hand, preferably in the company of persons as basically sensible as the ideal reader of Miss Tracy's work.

—Harold H. Watts

**TRAVER, Robert.** Pseudonym for John Donaldson Voelker. American. Born in Ishpeming, Michigan, 29 June 1903. Educated at Northern Michigan College, Marquette, 1922–24; University of Michigan, Ann Arbor, LL.B. 1928; admitted to the Michigan State Bar, 1928. Married Grace Taylor in 1930; has three children. Prosecuting Attorney, Marquette County, Michigan, 1935–50; Justice, Michigan Supreme Court, 1957–60. Full-time Writer since 1960. Weekly Columnist, *Detroit News*, 1967–69. LL.D., Northern Michigan College, 1958. Address: Deer Lake Road, Ishpeming, Michigan 49849, U.S.A.

PUBLICATIONS

Novels

   *Anatomy of a Murder.*   New York, St. Martin's Press, and London, Faber, 1958.
   *Hornstein's Boy.*   New York, St. Martin's Press, and London, Faber, 1962.
   *Laughing Whitefish.*   New York, McGraw Hill, 1965; London, W. H. Allen, 1967.

Other

   *Troubleshooter: The Story of a Northwoods Prosecutor.*   New York, Viking Press, 1943.
   *Danny and the Boys: Being Some Legends of Hungry Hollow.*   Cleveland, World, 1951.
   *Small Town D.A.*   New York, Dutton, 1954; London, Faber, 1959.
   *Trout Madness: Being a Dissertation on the Symptoms and Pathology of This Incurable
      Disease by One of Its Victims.*   New York, St. Martin's Press, 1960.
   *Anatomy of a Fisherman.*   New York, McGraw Hill, 1964.
   *The Jealous Mistress.*   Boston, Little Brown, and London, W. H. Allen, 1968.

Robert Traver comments:

   Critically my fiction has for the most part remained resolutely ignored, though I hear rumors that several law schools are lately assigning my *Anatomy* novel as outside reading in their courses on criminal law—which, upon reflection, may only mean that I should have stuck to the law.
   A writer judging his own work is like a deceived husband: he is frequently the last person to appreciate the true state of affairs. With this small caveat I would venture to guess that I am a vestigial remnant of that virtually obsolete breed in the world of modern fiction: a story teller who likes in his yarns for things to turn out fine and dandy.

                              *          *          *

   The most obvious limitation of Robert Traver is that he can write but one novel, and this he has done three times over in *Anatomy of a Murder*, *Hornstein's Boy*, and *Laughing White-fish*. Except for a variation of plot, the three novels share the same characters (with different names), the same setting, and the same rhetorical devices. This accounts for the tepid response to the last two novels after *Anatomy of a Murder* was first received with some enthusiasm. But Paul Biegler, Walt Dressler, and Willy Poe, all sensitive, liberal lawyers, blend into the same protagonist. Their easygoing, back-slapping Midwestern ways become tiresome, and their overlong speeches defending the American judicial and political systems sound like folksy essays rather than the crisp prose of an accomplished novelist. This is not to condemn

1245

Traver for his use of material familiar to him. The most positive aspect of his work is that he possesses a firm knowledge of his subject matter. As a former District Attorney and Michigan Supreme Court Justice, he has the experience to provide his audience with a close look at the intriguing processes of the United States judicial system. Also his love of the country of the Upper Peninsula of Northern Michigan is evident throughout his novels, and if he could write well enough to be taken seriously, he might excel as a local colorist.

But it is in the writing that the author must be judged, and it is here that Traver fails most gravely. He is unfortunately insistent on using the first person for his narrative style. As already noted, the similarity of the narrators renders their stories barely distinguishable in tone. In addition, the easy-going nature of these characters prevents their stories from progressing at an interesting pace. Instead, the home-spun philosophy of the trout-fishing lawyer rambles into long-winded speeches, self-conscious literary allusions, and a great number of puns. As for propaganda, it seems to be the Supreme Court Justice rather than the District Attorney who speaks through the protagonists, for Traver says over and over that although there are many shortcomings in the legal and political system of a democracy, the machinery is workable. His stock villain is the lawyer or newspaper reporter who bends the law or abuses his freedom to his own selfish advantage. On the other hand, the protagonist always has at his side a most selfless character whose only fault is that he sometimes offends middle-class values. Stereotyped characters like these are more frequently found in the Victorian novel than in mid-twentieth century American fiction. And indeed, Traver does seem somewhat outmoded as a novelist, for his most glaring failure in characterization is his inability to understand his characters in any but the most superficial way. He fails to enter into the more subtle aspects of psychological or social problems, while at the same time intimating to his reader that he is interested in such elements. He is a novelist who emphatically separates the "good guys" from the "bad guys." This proves especially embarrassing in *Hornstein's Boy* where, in an attempt at ecumenism, the "good guys" are a WASP, a Jew, and a Negro. It is no surprise that Traver's most recent novel, *Laughing Whitefish*, takes place in 1873, a year that is more in accord with the kind of novel he writes.

—Lawrence Ries

---

**TREVOR, William.** Pseudonym for William Trevor Cox. Irish. Born in Mitchelstown, County Cork, 24 May 1928. Educated at St. Columba's College, Dublin, 1942–46; Trinity College, Dublin, B.A. 1950. Married Jane Ryan in 1952; has two children. History Teacher, Armagh, Northern Ireland, 1951–53; Art Teacher, Rugby, England, 1953–55. Sculptor, in Somerset, 1955–60. Advertising Copywriter, London, 1960–64. Recipient: *Transatlantic Review* prize, 1964; Hawthornden Prize, 1965. Member, Irish Academy of Letters. Address: Stentwood House, Dunkeswell, near Honiton, Devon, England.

PUBLICATIONS

Novels

    *A Standard of Behaviour*.   London, Hutchinson, 1958.
    *The Old Boys*.   London, Bodley Head, and New York, Viking Press, 1964.
    *The Boarding House*.   London, Bodley Head, and New York, Viking Press, 1965.

*The Love Department.*   London, Bodley Head, 1966; New York, Viking Press, 1967.
*Mrs. Eckdorf in O'Neill's Hotel.*   London, Bodley Head, 1969; New York, Viking Press, 1970.
*Miss Gomez and the Brethren.*   London, Bodley Head, 1971.

Short Stories

*The Day We Got Drunk on Cake and Other Stories.*   London, Bodley Head, 1967; New York, Viking Press, 1968.
*Penguin Modern Stories 8,* with others.   London, Penguin, 1971.
*The Ballroom of Romance.*   London, Bodley Head, 1972.

Uncollected Short Stories

"The Last Lunch of the Season", in *Transatlantic Review* (London and New York), Autumn 1965.
"The 47th Saturday", in *The Girl on the Bus and Other Stories.*   London, Pan, 1966.
"A Happy Family", in *Antioch Review* (Yellow Springs, Ohio), Spring 1967.
"The Mark-2 Wife", in *Winter's Tales 14.*   London, Macmillan, 1968.
"An Evening with John Joe Dempsey", in *London Magazine*, November 1969.
"Access to the Children", in *Nova* (London), January 1971.

Plays

*The Old Boys* (produced London, 1971).   London, Davis Poynter, 1972.
*Going Home* (produced London, 1972).

*       *       *

Though he had written some fiction in the Fifties, William Trevor's real career as a novelist seemed to spring full-blown, a decade later and in his own late thirties, from his years in an advertising agency. His expert phrasing, his skill with dialogue, his sense of the quirks of human nature may have been fostered there, adapted to the sweet uses of advertisement. But there was no visible foreshadowing of the rich inventiveness, the immensely effective observation of telling detail, the sardonic view of life, the already mature skill with comic character and ironic situation, that flowered in the first of his better-known novels. *The Old Boys* clearly marked an original new talent. The connecting link among his main characters, all ageing British males, was a class reunion—a device that Franz Werfel, among others, had used successfully before him; but he made it his own with his satiric insights into individuals and their pretensions and evasions. This justly, if surprisingly, won him the Hawthornden Prize.

Another novel in much the same vein, *The Boarding House*, launched him on a full-time writing career. This time his characters were a mixed group of shabby-genteel boarders, mostly oldsters or eccentrics, in league against one another for succession to the management—and in league with each other against Death. His exposure of the fatuousness, futility, and low cunning of most of the types he wrote about in these two novels gives them an added dimension: the comedy, often close to travesty, has a Voltairean undertone.

*The Love Department* is less cynical, more pure fun: its exaggeratedly comic plot has many hilarious incidents, and it is about younger people. The "love department" of a women's magazine employs an innocent provincial to track down a real Lothario, one Septimus Tuam, who has been playing havoc with the hearts of maids and matrons among its correspondents.

The pursuit, on a borrowed bicycle through the highways and byways of Greater London, would be an adroit and playful farce, à la P. G. Wodehouse, were it not for Trevor's gift of serious irony.

Trevor's two latest novels return to the group framework—odd characters living in run-down urban hostels. The locales are a by-passed street in old Dublin and a wasteland of London given over to the developers. The people, too, have noticeable likenesses. He does their aberrations and hangups superbly, as before, and with an increased compassion. But he develops a more complicated plot, with more suspense, binding them all more closely; and he attempts a deeper philosophical note by telling their stories around an outsider introduced as a touchstone or activator. In *Mrs. Eckdorf in O'Neill's Hotel* the activator is a visiting photographer who proves to be a madwoman. In *Miss Gomez and the Brethren* this role is given to a Jamaican girl, a former prostitute, with a religious obsession. Faith can work its wonders even when based on delusions. This device, in both cases, makes the novels seem more contrived and less credible. The principal character's madness or obsession, being at the author's whim, permits him to manipulate the action too easily. But he does it with great skill; and the latter part of *Miss Gomez* consists of a breathless hunt for a missing person and a grim confrontation between The Law and the hapless individual that are not only excellent as suspense but a *tour de force* of irony.

—Marshall A. Best

---

**TRICKETT, (Mabel) Rachel.** British. Born in Lathom, Lancashire, 20 December 1923. Educated at the High School for Girls, Wigan, Lancashire; Lady Margaret Hall, Oxford, 1942–45, B.A. (1st class honours) in English language and literature 1945, M.A. 1949. Assistant to the Curator, Manchester City Art Galleries, 1945–46; Lecturer in English, University College of Hull, Yorkshire, 1946–54. Since 1954, Fellow and Tutor, St. Hugh's College, Oxford, and Lecturer, Oxford University. Visiting Lecturer, 1962–63, and Visiting Drew Professor, 1971, Smith College, Northampton, Massachusetts; Lecturer, Bread Loaf School of English, Middlebury College, Vermont, 1967, 1969. Recipient: Commonwealth Fund Fellowship, 1949; Rhys Memorial Prize, 1953. Address: St. Hugh's College, Oxford, England.

PUBLICATIONS

Novels

    *The Return Home.* London, Constable, 1952.
    *The Course of Love.* London, Constable, 1954.
    *Point of Honour.* London, Constable, 1958.
    *A Changing Place.* London, Constable, 1962.
    *The Elders.* London, Constable, 1966.
    *A Visit to Timon.* London, Constable, 1969.

Uncollected Short Story

    "The Schoolmasters", in *Cornhill* (London), 1963.

Plays

>   *Antigone*, music by John Joubert (broadcast by the BBC, 1954).   London, Novello, 1954.
>   *Silas Marner*, music by John Joubert (produced Cape Town and London, 1960). London, Novello, 1960.

Other

>   *The Honest Muse: A Study in Augustan Verse*.   London and New York, Oxford University Press, 1967.

Rachel Trickett comments:

I have always been particularly interested in my novels in the relationships between people, and between people and their environment. Place plays an important part in all my books. I have also grown increasingly interested in the essential solitude and uniqueness of my characters. This is not the same as the popular idea of alienation or isolation; it is rather the individual differentiating principle which identifies character and is most obviously exhibited in love where so often those who love each other are, consciously or not, learning to recognise their differences, their separateness. The passing of time has become an important element in my novels from *A Changing Place* to *A Visit to Timon*. My works are often retrospective in tone and mood as I am particularly interested in the way in which the imagination plays over the past and relates it to the present.

*          *          *

In one of Rachel Trickett's novels, *The Elders*, a character is asked, "And what is your contribution to the war effort?" to which she replies quite simply, "Literature". The ironic implications of this exchange are best understood in the context of the novel, but we see here one of the rare moments in this writer's work where the relation between the inner and outer worlds is given direct critical presentation. Her chosen territory appears to be the private world of personal relationships, often among highly cultivated people. Nevertheless her presentation of it is such that her work reflects very clearly the changing public world of her time. A tough searching out of the responses of individual sensibilities to private experience, given in language of unfailing clarity, inevitably leads to an accurate recording of how the inner world is affected by the outer. In *A Changing Place*, a working-class hero's attachment to a girl from the upper-middle class follows a course in which private emotions are seen as subtly bound up with the wider social circumstances of pre-war hardship, the war, and the disorientating effects of the war on people's private lives. A more recent novel, *A Visit to Timon*, shows a different reaction to experience on the part of a man whose retreat from public life is complicated by his relationship with a friend who works in television. Similarly, Miss Trickett's ability to evoke a sense of place and of time passing is partly a matter of vividly realised landscape and a rare gift for the delineation of nostalgia, but also rests in a strong sense of the community, a recognition of the relations and tensions in a social structure. This may range in different novels from the non-conformist community of a small town in Yorkshire, to the life of industrial quarry workers in Lancashire, and again to the quite different structures of life in Oxford University.

A common theme is the confrontation between worlds, the invasion of one set of values by another. Often the clash is between spontaneity of feeling and the more sophisticated attitude to experience cultivated by certain artistic, literary and academic circles. In *The*

*Return Home*, the simple and passionate young innocent, Christiana, becomes the victim of more sophisticated beings, but in *The Elders* there is a comic reversal of this theme when the return from abroad of a spontaneous, romantic poet disturbs the existing pattern of relationships in an academic community and causes a reassessment of values by both old and young alike. These confrontations, too, are subject to the processes of Time, and one of Rachel Trickett's gifts as a moralist is the careful account she takes of change and the complexity of the moral life in relation to it. Do civilised rituals of friendship really preserve love, or do they cause it to become atrophied, or do they perhaps simply come to disguise a lack of true commitment? In her work, this is a question that becomes increasingly important. It would be difficult to show by quotation the way in which she uses small acts, remarks and gestures to build gradually a strong sense of the distinctive atmosphere peculiar to a relationship; but this extract from *A Changing Place*, in which she describes the refusal to envisage love, shows another important gift, the ability to describe emotional states with both elegance and accuracy:

> Love of the kind Sarah no longer envisaged is rare after all, because it is so seldom wanted. It seems dangerous in the dependence it creates, and some would rather have less than be threatened with the demand for this surrender. As they grow older the urge to protect themselves from it grows stronger and appears disguised as a sort of wisdom and settled maturity that can afford to smile at excesses of the heart and the imagination. But it is not emotion as such they fear; it is commitment, the loss of any part of themselves. The desire to conserve what remains of the self becomes so strong with age that it grows harder to believe that only he who loses his life shall save it. Superficially we become more generous with time and with new acquaintances and new responsibilities, all those things which have a touch of virtue in them and so often cover up for the lack of any real surrender of the self. It is like a religion that consists entirely of thinking and doing, of theological arguments and pious duties and refuses to take into account feeling, because it is dangerous.

—Bridget O'Toole

---

**TRILLING, Lionel.** American. Born in New York City, 4 July 1905. Educated at Columbia University, New York, B.A. 1925, M.A. 1926, Ph.D. 1938. Married the writer Diana Rubin in 1929; has one child. Instructor in English, University of Wisconsin, Madison, 1926–27, and Hunter College, New York, 1927–32; Instructor, 1932–39, Assistant Professor, 1939–45, Associate Professor, 1945–48, and since 1948, Professor of English, Columbia University: Woodberry Professor of Literature and Criticism, 1965–70. George Eastman Visiting Professor, Oxford University, 1964–65; Norton Visiting Professor of Poetry, Harvard University, Cambridge, Massachusetts, 1969–70. Founder, with John Crowe Ransom and F. O. Matthiessen, and Senior Fellow, Kenyon School of Letters, Kenyon College, Gambier, Ohio, now the Indiana University School of Letters, Bloomington. Recipient: Brandeis University Creative Arts Award, 1968. D.Litt., Trinity College, Hartford, Connecticut, 1955; Harvard University, 1962; Case-Western Reserve University, Cleveland, 1968; L.H.D., Northwestern University, Evanston, Illinois, 1963. Member, National Institute of Arts and Letters, 1951; American Academy of Arts and Sciences, 1952. Address: Hamilton Hall, Columbia University, New York, New York 10027, U.S.A.

Publications

Novel

> *The Middle of the Journey*.  New York, Viking Press, 1947; London, Secker and
> Warburg, 1948.

Uncollected Short Stories

> "Of This Time, Of That Place", in *Partisan Review* (New Brunswick, New Jersey),
> January-February 1943.
> "The Other Margaret", in *Partisan Review* (New Brunswick, New Jersey), Fall 1945.

Other

> *Matthew Arnold*.  New York, Norton, and London, Allen and Unwin, 1939; revised
> edition, New York, Columbia University Press, 1949.
> *E. M. Forster*.  New York, New Directions, 1943; as *E. M. Forster: A Study*, London,
> Hogarth Press, 1944; revised edition, New Directions, 1965, Hogarth Press, 1967.
> *The Liberal Imagination: Essays on Literature and Society*.  New York, Viking Press,
> 1950; London, Secker and Warburg, 1951.
> *The Opposing Self: Nine Essays in Criticism*.  New York, Viking Press, and London,
> Secker and Warburg, 1955.
> *Freud and the Crisis of Our Culture*.  Boston, Beacon Press, 1956.
> *A Gathering of Fugitives*.  Boston, Beacon Press, 1956; London, Secker and Warburg,
> 1957.
> *Beyond Culture: Essays on Literature and Learning*.  New York, Viking Press, 1965;
> London, Secker and Warburg, 1966.

> Editor, *The Portable Matthew Arnold*.  New York, Viking Press, 1949; as *The Essential
> Matthew Arnold*, London, Chatto and Windus, 1969.
> Editor, *Selected Letters of John Keats*.  New York, Farrar Straus, 1951.
> Editor, *Selected Short Stories of John O'Hara*.  New York, Modern Library, 1956.
> Editor, with Steven Marcus, *The Life and Works of Sigmund Freud*, by Ernest Jones.
> New York, Basic Books, and London, Hogarth Press, 1961.
> Editor, *The Experience of Literature: A Reader with Commentaries*.  New York,
> Holt Rinehart, 1967.
> Editor, *Literary Criticism: An Introductory Reader*.  New York, Holt Rinehart, 1970.

*     *     *

Though Lionel Trilling is best known as a literary critic, his short stories and his one novel,
*The Middle of the Journey*, have won him a lasting reputation as a writer of fiction. Like
Matthew Arnold, about whom he has written a book-length study, he is a critic not only of
literature but also of society and ideas. To him a literature is a manifestation of a culture;
it can be meaningfully studied only within its cultural context.

It is not surprising, then, that Trilling attempts in his fiction to convey a sense of the spiritual
and intellectual dilemma of modern man. This purpose is discernible in his two most highly
esteemed short stories, "Of This Time, Of That Place" and "The Other Margaret." It becomes
the guiding principle of *The Middle of the Journey*, which is a study of the predicament of
"the liberal imagination," to use Trilling's phrase, in the middle decades of the twentieth

century. Involved as he has been in the intellectual life of New York City, Trilling has written his novel with the authority of first-hand experience and observation. The central character, John Laskell, is convalescing from a near-fatal illness, in which the Freudian death-wish has exerted a strong pull. Trilling, it must be said, has been a lifelong student of psychoanalysis and thus not one to discount the destructive and anticultural impulses of the id. Laskell, on a journey to the Connecticut Hills, where he hopes to regain his health, suffers a severe attack of angst while waiting at a village railroad station. Throughout the novel, indeed, he struggles to shake off an obsessive awareness of death and to re-involve himself in life. On a biological level he accomplishes this through a fleeting affair with a local village woman, Emily Caldwell, but intellectually his re-acceptance of life is more difficult. Formerly he had been a "liberal" with Marxist sympathies. But now he is appalled by this same position as exhibited in the deterministic views of a young university professor and his wife, the Crooms, who are his closest friends. To them, human beings, while perfectible, are not responsible either for their characters or for their actions but are little more than puppets dancing on the strings of social forces. Laskell, returned from the gates of death, will not accept this degrading view of humanity. He finds equally unacceptable the views of Gifford Maxim, a defected communist who has recently adopted a rigidly orthodox Christian stance: man is totally responsible for all his deeds, deserves eternal punishment if he breaks the moral law, and, in the event that he does transgress, has only God's mercy as a possible refuge.

The Middle of the Journey has rightly been called a "dialectical novel." Caught between his friends' contradictory philosophies, Laskell gropes for a viewpoint with which he can agree. Matters come to a head when Duck Caldwell, the drunkard husband of Laskell's mistress, strikes and unintentionally kills his young daughter. Is Duck responsible for his action or is the society which made him what he is responsible? The Crooms and Maxim take opposing stands on the matter. Under the emotional stress of the moment, Laskell is forced to take a position of his own. He concludes that Duck is neither wholly guilty nor wholly innocent. The individual will is neither entirely free nor entirely conditioned by social and other influences. He rejects his friends' absolutes for what Trilling calls ideas "in modulation."

While The Middle of the Journey is not devoid of action and presents a gallery of convincingly alive characters, it is unabashedly a novel of ideas. A reader unacquainted with the more important intellectual currents of our century, or simply not interested in them, will find the novel hard going. Those who enjoy an interplay of ideas will find it fascinating and stimulating.

—Perry D. Westbrook

* * *

**TROCCHI, Alexander.** British. Born in Glasgow, 30 July 1925. Educated at the University of Glasgow, 1942–43, 1946–50, M.A. 1950. Served in the Royal Navy, 1943–46. Married Lyn Hicks in 1956; has one child. Painter and Sculptor: Visiting Lecturer in Sculpture, St. Martin's School of Art, London. Editor, Merlin magazine, Paris, and Paris Quarterly, 1952–55; The Moving Times, London. Address: c/o Calder and Boyars Ltd., 18 Brewer Street, London W.1, England.

PUBLICATIONS

Novels

The Carnal Days of Helen Seferis. Paris, Olympia Press, 1954; revised edition, North Hollywood, Brandon House, 1967.

*Helen and Desire*.  Paris, Olympia Press, 1954; revised edition, North Hollywood, Brandon House, 1967.
*Young Adam*.  Paris, Olympia Press, 1955; revised edition, London, Heineman, 1961.
*School for Sin*.  Paris, Olympia Press, 1955; revised edition, as *School for Wives*, North Hollywood, Brandon House, 1967.
*White Thighs*.  Paris, Olympia Press, 1955; revised edition, North Hollywood, Brandon House, 1967.
*The Fifth Volume of Frank Harris's My Life and Loves: An Irreverent Treatment*.  Paris, Olympia Press, 1958; London, New English Library, 1966.
*Cain's Book*.  New York, Grove Press, 1960; London, John Calder, 1963.
*The Outsiders* (includes *Young Adam* and short stories).  New York, New American Library, 1961.
*Thongs*.  North Hollywood, Brandon House, 1967.
*Sappho of Lesbos*.  London, Tandem, 1971.


Short Stories

*Four Stories*, in *New Writers 3*.  London, Calder and Boyars, 1965.


Verse

*Man for Leisure*.  London, Calder and Boyars, 1971.


Other

*Drugs of the Mind*.  London, Aldus Books, 1970.

Editor, with others, *Writers in Revolt: An Anthology*.  New York, Frederick Fell, 1963.

Translator, *I, Jan Cremer*, by Jan Cremer.  London, Calder and Boyars, 1965.
Translator, *The Girl on the Motorcycle*, by André Pieyre de Mandiargues.  London, Calder and Boyars, 1966.
Translator, *The Centenarian*, by Rene de Obadia.  London, Calder and Boyars, 1970.

*          *          *

Alexander Trocchi arrived in Paris in the early '50's; there, from Spring 1952 to 1955, he edited (with Richard Seaver and Austryn Wainhouse), the well-known expatriate avant-garde review *Merlin*. It published a number of pieces by Samuel Beckett, Christopher Logue, Patrick Bowles, Ronald Bottrall and others of real distinction. During that same period, Trocchi became, according to Maurice Girodias, a "stalwart" of the Olympia Press (which probably also published *Thongs*, *Sappho*, and other specimens of "robust and funny parodies of pornography" under his pseudonym of Frances Lengel, in the Traveller's Companion series). All Trocchi's works were banned by the French authorities, but most appear to be back in print by now in England or America. As the new editions are often described as "revised," and the English version of *Young Adam* has been somewhat re-written for reasons both of style and decorum, the purist will naturally seek out the earlier editions.
In the late '50's Trocchi is said to have collaborated with Asgar Jorn in the International Situationist movement, the journal of which dealt with visual arts ("pop" emphasis), environment and culture. After leaving Paris, Trocchi lived for some time on a scow on the

Hudson River, where he wrote *Cain's Book* (sections of which appeared in the *Evergreen Review* and elsewhere), his one book to have achieved, as yet, any literary prominence. In the mid-'60's he was to be found in London, active in the "sigma" project, his manifesto for which appeared in *New Saltire* and was reprinted in *City Lights Journal 2* (1964). It was a "Revolutionary Proposal" to bring art into life, leisure and popular culture, by means of "spontaneous universities" and cultural centers, and by making art available everywhere, from hoardings to matchboxes. In June, 1965, he was a co-organizer and master of ceremonies for the famous Albert Hall poetry reading, where Ferlinghetti, Ginsberg, and many others did indeed bring the New Poetry to an audience of thousands. Trocchi seems to have been in or near most "counter-culture" movements for twenty years; his collaborators, editors, and literary acquaintances would almost make up a directory to the underground.

Trocchi's pornography is lively, or, as Girodias puts it, "tingling with sex and fun." (See the *Olympia Reader* for some sketches of Trocchi and two samples of his work.) Girodias gives in his introduction a hilarious and circumstantial account of how Trocchi came to write, by Girodias' computation, four-fifths of *The Fifth Volume of Frank Harris* . . . in ten days, leaving "the odd twenty per cent of real Harris . . . rejuvenated and revitalized." Indeed it is not easy to tell which is Trocchi and which Harris. (The Grove Press edition of the five volumes gives essentially the same text for Volume Five, with no attribution to Trocchi.) *Young Adam* (new edition) and *Cain's Book* are, in different ways, rather dreary. The former is an ordinary story of adultery and accidental murder (on a Scottish scow, this time), remarkable only for a very faint resemblance to Camus' *L'Etranger* (and anticipation of *La Chute*) in the detached, joyless, pleasure-seeking of its hero, his accidental and meaningless violence, and his narcotic semi-awareness of responsibility. *Cain's Book* is even less focussed and plotted than *Young Adam*; indeed it reads as if written in a drug haze. There is a simplistic adoption of the conventions of artifice: "the book I am writing is the book you are reading," and some solipsist, inconclusive brooding about awareness. But the book is essentially a blurred and unimaginative offshoot of the Henry Miller tradition of torrential pseudo-autobiography, and is really a rather dry little brook. There is some sex, but most of the characters' time and energy go into a lethargic search for the next "fix" and a morose description of the "fix" when found. Trocchi only summons up real energy to castigate the present drug laws or to give occasional flashback to his hero's Scottish youth. "Vol. 2" (excerpted in the *Evergreen Review*, V:19) augurs better; it has some sprightly, horrid satire in the Burroughs manner. The short stories have some good writing of a more conventional type, but, all in all, Trocchi remains more interesting as an important figure on a certain literary scene than for anything he seems yet to have written.

—Patricia Merivale

---

**TRUMBO, Dalton.** American. Born in Montrose, Colorado, 9 December 1905. Educated at the University of Colorado, Boulder, 1924–25; University of California, Los Angeles, 1925–27; University of Southern California, Los Angeles, 1927–29. War Correspondent, United States Army Air Force, in World War II. Married Cleo Beth Fincher in 1938; has three children. Screenwriter since 1936. Managing Editor, *The Hollywood Spectator*; Founding Editor, *The Screenwriter*, Los Angeles, 1945. National Chairman, Writers for Roosevelt, 1944; Director, Writers Guild of America, 1945. Recipient: National Booksellers Award, 1939; Academy Award, for screenplay, 1957. Address: 8710 St. Ives Drive, Los Angeles, California 90069, U.S.A.

PUBLICATIONS

Novels

*Eclipse.*   London, L. Dickson and Thompson, 1935.
*Washington Jitters.*   New York, Knopf, 1936.
*Johnny Got His Gun.*   Philadelphia, Lippincott, 1939.
*The Remarkable Andrew: Being the Chronicle of a Literal Man.*   Philadelphia, Lippin-
    cott, 1941; as *The Remarkable Andrew: The Chronicle of a Literal Man*, London,
    Lane, 1941.

Plays

*The Biggest Thief in Town* (produced New York, 1949; London, 1951).   New York,
    Dramatists Play Service, 1949; London, English Theatre Guild, 1952.

Screenplays: *Jealousy*, 1934; *Love Begins at Twenty*, with Tom Reed, 1936; *Road
Gang*, 1936; *The Story of Isadora Bernstein*, 1936; *Devil's Playground*, 1937; *Fugitives
for a Night*, 1938; *A Man to Remember*, 1938; *Sorority House*, 1939; *Career*, 1939;
*Five Came Back*, with Nathanael West and Jerry Cady, 1939; *The Flying Irishman*, with
Ernest Pagano, 1939; *Heaven with a Barbed Wire Fence*, 1939; *Kitty Foyle*, 1940; *Half
a Sinner*, 1940; *We Who Are Young*, 1940; *A Bill of Divorcement*, 1940; *Curtain Call*,
1940; *You Belong to Me*, 1941; *The Remarkable Andrew*, 1942; *Tender Comrade*, 1943;
*A Guy Named Joe*, 1943; *Thirty Seconds over Tokyo*, 1944; *Our Vines Have Tender
Grapes*, 1945; *The Brave One* (as Richard Rich), 1957; *Spartacus*, with Howard Fast,
1960; *Exodus*, 1960; *Lonely Are the Brave*, 1962; *The Sandpiper*, 1965; *Hawaii*, 1966;
*The Fixer*, 1970; *Johnny Got His Gun*, 1970; *The Horseman*, 1971.

Other

*Harry Bridges.*   New York, League of American Writers, 1941.
*An Appeal to the People.*   Los Angeles, privately printed, 1942.
*The Time of the Toad: A Study of Inquisition in America, by One of the Ten.*   Hollywood,
    Hollywood Ten, n.d. (1948?).
*The Devil in the Book.*   Los Angeles, Emergency Defense Committee, 1956.
*Additional Dialogue: Letters of Dalton Trumbo*, edited by Helen Manfull.   New York,
    M. Evans, 1970.

\*       \*       \*

Both in the sense that it is addressed to a wide audience and in the fact that the wide
audience has been eager to receive it, Dalton Trumbo's writing is markedly the work of a
deliberate popular artist. Assessment of his writing, therefore, must be made in terms of
popular art, and since most of his work has been devoted to films—more than thirty of them—
the necessities of that medium may give us our first insight into Trumbo's imagination. After
all, what makes a good screenplay? To begin with there must be an immediately engaging
situation, one that lends itself to representation in overtly active narrative. Any conflicts
in the story have to be clearly delineated, and, to achieve that, the characters must tend to be
types. It is a commonplace observation, of course, that the stories which make the best
screenplays are rarely the work of "major novelists," those authors whose writing depends
upon the complex effects deriving from subtle verbal constructions. Significant as it is in

modern art to continue refining verbal forms so that they function more and more as self-contained constructions, the imagination required for such activity is elite, while the imagination of the effective popular artist, on the screen or elsewhere, is devoted to an art that is immediately referential and extends the awareness of the audience to objects in the world around them.

Between 1935 and 1941 Trumbo published four novels, each of which reveals the capacity for popular invention that today he employs exclusively in the medium of film. *Eclipse* portrays the rapidly passing type of the self-made businessman pitting his good sense and innate virtue against the social hypocrisy of provincial culture. Through a series of farcical circumstances in *Washington Jitters* a sign painter mistaken for the newly appointed co-ordinator of a New Deal bureau becomes the most powerful man in the national capital. Again there is satire of hypocrisy resulting from the passing of American frontier types in *The Remarkable Andrew* when a small town clerk calls upon his ancestor Andrew Jackson to prepare for him a legal defense against the politicians who try to frame him with charges of responsibility for an embezzlement he himself uncovered. Then, in what is probably the most effective anti-war statement in American literature, *Johnny Got His Gun*, Trumbo relates the attempt of a soldier who has lost his limbs and the power of all his physical senses, except touch, to communicate his convictions about the Great World War to those already preparing for the next one.

A tone of ridicule is strong in the novels which deal extensively with American politics. The Congressional figures and bureaucrats in *Washington Jitters* speak and behave as charlatans worse than useless in comparison to the simple but sensible sign painter Henry Hogg, while in *The Remarkable Andrew* President Jackson's bewilderment and outrage at the policies of those governing America in 1941 are intended to suggest that contemporary politicians are more than wrong—they have lost their reason. On the other hand, *Eclipse* and *Johnny Got His Gun* by providing more substantial protagonists give more weight to Trumbo's view of positive American types. When the Great Depression destroys John Abbott and his fortune in *Eclipse* it is a matter for regret, since it is not he but the over-extended capitalist system that has brought on the crash. Within the local economy Abbott is practical and honest, realistic but generous. In short, he has the virtues that have become facade in George F. Babbitt. Likewise, the mutilated soldier in *Johnny Got His Gun* displays justifiable rage and ironically clear vision when he resolves to help other average men fight the masters of society who are their real enemies. Whether the tone of ridicule is primary or secondary, however, all four novels function as satires in which Trumbo posits a norm of rationality, or rather common sense, which induces contempt for those who act as if they had some higher intelligence.

Trumbo readily admits to a sympathy for Marxism and has paid his dues for that. The basic ideology of his fiction, though, is populism. At times populist attitudes and progressive politics may be allied, and surely Trumbo thought they were when he wrote his satiric novels, but even when populism is ignored as it is in the great welfare societies, the cause of the little man, who with his good sense knows that the apparatus of the State and the rhetoric of self-important bigness function to repress him, is an enduring one. With the self-evident task of the popular artist being to speak to people's subjective perception of their lives, Dalton Trumbo's novels reveal the source of his effectiveness to be an imaginative apprehension of the *real* politics of millions.

—John M. Reilly

**TUCCI, Niccolò.** American. Born in Lugano, Switzerland, 1 May 1908; emigrated to the United States for political reasons in 1938; naturalized in 1953. Educated in Florence, Italy, Dr. in law and political sciences, 1933. Began to write in German, but not published in book form owing to his opposition to the Nazi Party; writes in Italian and English. Polemicist and Correspondent, *Politics Magazine*, New York, 1943–46; Co-Founder (1954), and Columnist ("The Press of Freedom"), *Village Voice*, New York; writer for *The New Yorker* (since 1946), *New Republic, Nation, Commonweal, Harper's, Atlantic, Encounter,* and, in Italian, *Corriere della Sera, Illustrazione Italiana, Tempo Presente, Il Mondo, Espresso.* Writer-in-Residence, Columbia University, New York, 1965–66. Recipient: Viareggio Prize, 1956; Ford grant, 1959; Bagutta Prize, 1969. Address: 25 East 67th Street, New York, New York 10021, U.S.A.

PUBLICATIONS

Novels

*Il Segreto.* Milan, Garzanti, 1956.
*Those of the Lost Continent* (in Italian: *Gli Atlantidi*):
  *Before My Time.* New York, Simon and Schuster, 1962; London, Cape, 1963.
  *Unfinished Funeral.* New York, Simon and Schuster, 1964; London, Cape, 1965.
  *Gli Atlantidi.* Milan, Garzanti, 1968.
  *Il Muro del Suo Pianto.* Milan, Garzanti, 1972.
  *Love and Death.* New York, Knopf, 1973.
  *Guenther.* Milan, Garzanti, 1973.

Play

*Posterity for Sale* (written 1939–40; produced New York, 1967).

Other

*How To Get Away Without Murder* (essays). New York, Knopf, 1973.

Niccolò Tucci comments:

Other Biographical Information: Slightly enlarged prostate but no enlarged horizons to match; liver, intestines, heart (touch wood) normal; bloodcount normal, pressure 80; defecation twice daily when I don't read the papers; no TV no radio; alcohol consumption only when good wines available, never more than one glass daily now that I am old; hiatus hernia; two sets of glasses: one to tell characters on page, one across the street; weight normal, no signs of weightlessness; no traces of taxable income; sex-count and telephone unlisted.

The reason I have never allowed anyone to translate me from one of my two present languages into the other is that I consider myself alive, and these two languages are the two parts of me into which my experiences were split, so that my daily effort is to weld them together again. Perhaps I am another Humpty-Dumpty who sees himself as a new Lazarus. I don't know but I see no great danger of self-delusion in this: Lazarus was not a great man and certainly not a writer, he was a poor guinea-pig, and we have never been told how he climbed back into life after his place was taken by his Absence. I only know that no one in the world is worth his absence, and *as a writer*, I feel this very intensely, for I associate with words more than with people. I still don't know how to write a good thank-you letter in English, French, or German, even in my native Italian, but the *word-population* of all these languages is still at my orders for nonsense, fairy tales, plays, stories, polemical articles and even love letters, in spite of my venerable age. In fact I find it hard to limit myself to English and Italian, and none of the king's jet-planes and supermen, let alone his horses and men, could put me together again as well as I do every time I jump back into Italian or into English from that terrible wall. In the process of doing this almost daily repair-work I have learned a great deal about languages, and I know how to avoid the Temptations of the Writing Devil, namely hot-water and wind in the place of blood and soul to fill your characters with. It is an interesting life, but it dooms me to poverty as long as it lasts, because I can't let any-one bury me under *his* words while I am away from one of my two homes. But then this arrangement has its advantages too: the temptations of Success are far more sinister than those of habit, laziness or fatigue, in fact they are the *real* tools of the Devil. Which doesn't mean that I despise success; on the contrary, I have never known anyone with greater ambitions than mine. I don't want to be known: I want ANONIMITY *à la* Shakespeare, so that people really won't know whether I was myself or someone else by my name. And so I live to posthumize myself. Anyone willing to send in his contribution and help me pay for my rent, my telephone bill, my London tailor and my Fall & Resurrection, will not receive a thank-you letter, but a story, a *personal* story or even a novel from the grateful undersigned Niccolò Tucci. P.S. Maximum contributions accepted ONE DOLLAR.

*           *           *

The privileged deserve their literary investigators, as much as do the disadvantaged. Niccolò Tucci has devoted generous attention to an interesting minority group, the continental aristocracy and their heirs. Time and democracy have reduced their numbers and influence, but their fascination remains, less because of what they are than what they represent: the confluence of wealth, education, tradition, power and social *élan* evidenced in a life style where eccentricity and self-will are not fatal flaws but the identifying stripes of their breed.

Like jet travel or new money, the clash of conflicting moral or social values is not Tucci's ostensible concern. Yet it is there, under the Tucci characters' public show of conservatism and propriety. A young Spanish woman in *Unfinished Funeral*, the author's second novel in English, is reminded that she is "a girl of 26" and that her honor may have to be avenged, not because she may or may not have been compromised by an elderly gentleman met on a train, but because all will assume she has been. "The defense of your honor is my business, not yours," her brother insists. To liberate woman is to deprive man of his protector image, and, always, appearances count. Yet paradoxically, the strongest characters in Tucci's English novels are women—not the equals of men, but their proven superiors in the art of tyranny.

Tucci's reputation as a short story writer (his works have appeared in *Encounter*, *Vogue*, *The New Yorker* and *Esquire*) was already established before his first English novel, *Before My Time*, appeared in 1962. The long novel, in part an autobiographical nod to the author's own Russian-Italian parentage, is not merely dominated, but overwhelmed, by the idiosyncratic widow, Mamachen. A rich Russian matriarch at the turn of the century, she plays czarina to the large, elegant and slavish family entourage she pilots from Italy to Switzerland to France to Germany—and to despair at times. Yet there is no family revolution, least of all by the daughter, Mary, who verges on treason by falling in love with a humble Italian doctor, and then in turn makes him a family thrall. The possible rebels are really defectors, the daughter Ludmilla and the son Pierre, who find lives of their own elsewhere. Mamachen's eventual death, with tragicomic dividing of the spoils by her heirs, changes nothing, but merely hands on the matriarchal torch to Mary. Aristocracy persists, Tucci suggests, because its leaders are equal to those they succeed. And why not? They have been hand-picked and rigorously trained.

*Unfinished Funeral* is another investigation of tyranny, this time very compressed in length and told in symbols (largely Freudian) so obvious that they themselves invite questions. Ermelinda, the widowed Duchess of Combon de Triton, is "the acrobat of pain" who has survived 36 major operations and innumerable heart attacks, having found that physical crises are the handles by which she can grasp and hold power. Her funeral cortege is always on call, yet she never dies—and so her son, Bernandrasse, and daughter, Eloise, never really live. The book states and restates a proposition rather than treating a question; hence those who seek ready answers are doomed to disappointment.

In all of Tucci's work the style is witty, clever, polished—appropriate to the worldly figures he illuminates but never dissects.

—Marian Pehowski

---

**TUOHY, Frank.** British. Born in Uckfield, Sussex, 2 May 1925. Educated at Stowe School, Buckinghamshire; King's College, Cambridge, 1943–46, B.A. (1st class honours) 1946. Lecturer, Turku University, Finland, 1947–48; Professor of English Language and Literature, University of Sao Paulo, Brazil, 1950–56; Contract Professor, Jagiellonian University, Krakow, Poland, 1958–60; Visiting Professor, Waseda University, Tokyo, 1964–67; Visiting Professor and Writer-in-Residence, Purdue University, Lafayette, Indiana, 1970–71. Recipient: Katherine Mansfield Prize, 1960; Society of Authors Travelling Fellowship, 1963; Black Memorial Prize, 1965; Faber Memorial Prize, 1965. Fellow, Royal Society of Literature, 1965. Address: c/o Macmillan and Company, Little Essex Street, London W.C.2, England.

PUBLICATIONS

Novels

    *The Animal Game.* London, Macmillan, and New York, Scribner, 1957.
    *The Warm Nights of January.* London, Macmillan, 1960.
    *The Ice Saints.* London, Macmillan, and New York, Scribner, 1964.

Short Stories

    *The Admiral and the Nuns and Other Stories.* London, Macmillan, and New York, Scribner, 1962.
    *Fingers in the Door.* London, Macmillan, and New York, Scribner, 1970.

Other

    *Portugal.* London, Thames and Hudson, 1969; New York, Viking Press, 1970.

Frank Tuohy comments:

Most of what I write seems to start off with the interaction between two cultures, modes of behaviour, ways of living, etc. Sometimes this confrontation is between a foreigner and an alien environment, sometimes between groups in that environment itself. For me, the sense of displacement, loss, anxiety which happens to people derives from the world outside them, in their relationships with that world. If I thought of it as starting inside, as being a part of the Self, I probably would not write at all.

*　　　*　　　*

The novels and short stories of Frank Tuohy are marked by a strong sense of social reality. They are set in various places—England, Brazil, Poland—and give one a vivid sense of the physical place: the climate, landscape, local customs. Against the backdrop of special place, the drama of the characters' lives unfolds. In the short stories, interest focuses usually on intense personal encounters in which the protagonist is made to face some unpleasant decision or harsh truth about himself or people close to him. These stories, sharply etched and intensely though quietly dramatic, have no apparent underlying theme. It is the revelation itself, the exquisitely rendered but "painful bite down on the rotten tooth of fact," to borrow a phrase from Tuohy, that one is meant to savor.

In his novels and longer stories there is the same sharp awareness of external reality and savoring of unpleasant fact, but there is also clearly a discernible moral structure. The writer's sympathies are with those who suffer and respond, who are capable of loyalty and self-abnegation. His dislike is for characters who, protected by money, indulge their appetites at the expense of those socially or culturally inferior or morally more sensitive.

The protagonist of Tuohy's first novel, *The Animal Game*, is Robin Morris, a young Englishman working in Sao Paulo, who encounters the beautiful corrupt daughter of a Brazilian aristocrat. Morris is attracted to this woman but is saved at the end of the novel from a relationship which, one sees, would have been sterile, self-indulgent, and ultimately destructive. Tuohy's moral sense is even more fully involved in his second novel about Brazil, *The Warm Nights of January*, which also deals with self-indulgence and sexual corruption. *The Ice Saints*, his third novel, takes place in Poland, some time after the Stalinist "thaw." Here the protagonist, an attractive, pleasant but inexperienced and pampered young English woman visits her married sister and Polish brother-in-law with the idea of rescuing their son from what she regards as a grim and depressing existence, and taking him back to England to live. Although we are at first allowed to identify with the young woman's point of view (the horrors of Polish life are vividly presented), we are made to see, finally, the moral superiority of the Polish brother-in-law whose human qualities outweigh his lack of polish and urbanity.

Tuohy's stories and novels are written in a style that is compressed and economical yet remarkably evocative. One has the immediate sense of a physical world vividly and objectively presented and yet one also feels, but unobtrusively, the authorial presence choosing and arranging for judgmental effect.

—W. J. Stuckey

**TURNER, George (Reginald).**   Australian.   Born in Melbourne, Victoria, 8 October 1916. Educated in Victoria state schools; at University High School, Melbourne. Served in the Australian Imperial Forces, 1939–45. Employment Officer, Commonwealth Employment Service, Melbourne, 1945–49, and Wangaratta, Victoria, 1949–50; Textile Technician, Buck Mills, Wangaratta, 1951–64; Senior Employment Officer, Volkswagen Ltd., Melbourne, 1964–67. Since 1970, Beer Transferrer, Carlton and United Breweries, Melbourne. Recipient: Miles Franklin Award, 1962; Commonwealth Literary Fund award, 1968. Address: 4 Robertson Avenue, St. Kilda, Victoria 3182, Australia.

PUBLICATIONS

Novels

> *Young Man of Talent*.   London, Cassell, 1959; as *Scobie*, New York, Simon and Schuster, 1959.
> *A Stranger and Afraid*.   London, Cassell, 1961.
> *The Cupboard under the Stairs*.   London, Cassell, 1962.
> *A Waste of Shame*.   Melbourne and London, Cassell, 1965.
> *The Lame Dog Man*.   Melbourne, Cassell, 1967; London, Cassell, 1968.

George Turner comments:

I make few specific statements in my novels, and don't consider it my business to do so since the themes are usually such as bedevil the experts as much as they do the man in the street—insanity, alcoholism, the urge to meddle, the habit of making moral judgments and so on. I try to examine these themes under reasonably familiar circumstances, with no more of the exotic than is to be found in an average life, in the hope that some useful insight or recognition will emerge. The intention is that the reader will be able to identify with the problem as well as the characters.

To eliminate personal point of view as much as possible, I do not plan a novel in detail in advance of writing it. I select my general theme on no better ground than that I find it interesting and challenging, conceive a few characters who could reasonably become involved in such a matter and set them in motion. Since plot is very literally character in action, something useful usually emerges in 20 or 30 thousand words, and I know in which direction I am going.

Only at this point do I begin to shape the work as a whole (and it generally means scrapping everything so far written) but rarely have more than a generalised idea of what the climax and resolution will be. These must be decided by the interactions of the characters; authorial manipulation is restricted to the minimum necessary to give shape and balance to the work.

One personally useful by-product of this method is that I find that such concentration on a problem for many months often changes my original points of view about it, and the outcome is commonly rather far from what I had in mind during the shaping phase.

I am sufficiently old-fashioned to prefer a story with a beginning, a development and a resolution (though not to the point of tying up every loose end in sight) but sufficiently of my time to avoid moral or ethical attitudes. Those of my characters who display them are apt to come to grief as the theme tests and retests them.

For this reason I have been termed "existentialist", which is probably true, and have also been said to have no moral or ethical views at all, which is not. I merely condemn rigidity of attitude and I suppose that in the final summation that is what my novels so far have been about.

\*       \*       \*

George Turner's well-tailored stories of social pressure and private malaise read like nothing so much as Victorian narrative histories overlaid by 1930's "realism". On the surface the problems his characters face are bluntly modern: the hell of total war, political chicanery, alcoholism, mental instability, and broken homes. But underneath these, as the last volume of the Treelake saga (*The Lame Dog Man*) indicates most clearly, there murmurs an Arnoldian unease about the loss of order and the course of time; about Jimmy Carlyon (the social worker central to that book, *A Stranger and Afraid*, and *The Cupboard under the Stairs*), Turner writes: "Change . . . had not so much touched Treelake as ridden roughshod through it. . . . His regret was personal. The severance from the past was inevitable, but the interregnum was violent and unsightly." Carlyon, of course, is in the public service, a cog in the System, attached to an order, but we soon learn that his job is his anodyne (for his troubled childhood) just as alcohol is Joe Bryen's, in the rather weaker novel *A Waste of Shame*. Half-consciously Jimmy knows this: "He made a virtue of . . . playing the observer who sees most of the game, but occasionally surprises a sense of incompletion in himself, of a shade of difference, of being an imitation smart enough to deceive the real." But for Turner that half-awareness is if anything more dangerous than ignorance, for it fosters dreams of power or self-possession that tempt individuals to overstep their limitations and sacrifice others for their own ends.

Turner's first and in many ways best—most self-contained—novel, examines just such a proposition. Set in New Guinea during World War II, it probes the motivations of three Australian soldiers: Scobie, who is thrust to position when his superior is killed and who discovers his taste for command; Payne, the rebel, who becomes Scobie's psychological slave too easily for Scobie's good; and Tolley, the new commander, who operates by rule instead of through human judgment. All three are inversions of each other and all inevitably come into a conflict that destroys them. What survives, to continue, is the army—not that Turner is praising military power particularly, but that in his novel it represents the community interdependence that he later explores in the town of Treelake. His world is one in which individuality is encouraged but in which every individual action has manifold ramifications in the intermarried, interlocked, intertwined town relationships. His approach to structuring a novel, therefore, is somewhat that of a chess player's: moves are plotted several plays ahead, and characters occupy a series of ratiocinative positions as they shift from ploy to ploy and struggle out of one innuendo into another.

Much of the movement of Turner's books depends on dialogue; much of its tone derives from the austere but sardonic balance of his sentences. On behaviour, for example, he writes: "You learned discipline and called it self-control, deprecation and called it modesty; you learned to take delight in the welfare of others—until the interest was not returned and the delight faded and the inturned motive was revealed." That assertion (tone and all) contains the basic Treelake theme. Carlyon ultimately knows that he will distribute compensation money to Johnson, a malingerer who does not deserve it; he also recognizes his mother's façade; but he accepts such deceit:

Why, he thought, I really like the old fake. She plays a hard game, but she plays it with zest, and she plays it for the game's sake. Do that, and you can take your reverses for what they are worth, which is precious little. And life is the pleasure you take in the game.

It seemed very profound and perceptive. It would do for a working basis, a working philosophy.

It seems perhaps more like an exchange of solipsisms. The humanity it reveals is brittle at best, always at the mercy of the social structure. Its range is narrow, and its deepest and most idealistic aspirations appear no more than the adaptations of personal ambition to the *status quo*.

—W. H. New

**TUTUOLA, Amos.** Nigerian. Born in Abeokuta, June 1920. Educated at the Anglican Central School, Abeokuta. Served as a blacksmith in the Royal Air Force, in Lagos, 1943–46. Married Victoria Tutuola in 1947; has two children. Since 1956, Stores Officer, Nigerian Broadcasting Company, Ibadan. Founder, Mbari Club of Nigerian Writers. Address: c/o Nigerian Broadcasting Company, Broadcasting House, Ibadan, Nigeria.

PUBLICATIONS

Novels

The Palm-Wine Drinkard and His Dead Palm-Wine Tapster in the Dead's Town. London, Faber, 1952; New York, Grove Press, 1953.
My Life in the Bush of Ghosts. London, Faber, and New York, Grove Press, 1954.
Simbi and the Satyr of the Dark Jungle. London, Faber, 1955.
The Brave African Huntress. London, Faber, and New York, Grove Press, 1958.
The Feather Woman of the Jungle. London, Faber, 1962.
Abaiyi and His Inherited Poverty. London, Faber, 1967.

Bibliography: in *Amos Tutuola* by Harold R. Collins, New York, Twayne, 1969.

\*       \*       \*

Amos Tutuola's six books follow the same basic narrative pattern. A hero (or heroine) with supernatural powers or access to supernatural assistance sets out on a journey in quest of something important and suffers incredible hardships before successfully accomplishing his mission. He ventures into unearthly realms, performs arduous tasks, fights with fearsome monsters, endures cruel tortures, and narrowly escapes death. Sometimes he is accompanied by a relative or by loyal companions; sometimes he wanders alone. But he always survives his ordeals, attains his objective, and usually emerges from his nightmarish experiences a wiser, wealthier man. The cycle of his adventures—involving a Departure, Initiation, and Return—resembles that found in myths and folktales the world over.

Tutuola's first and most famous book, *The Palm-Wine Drinkard and His Dead Palm-Wine Tapster in the Dead's Town*, which describes a hero's descent into an African underworld in search of a dead companion, was greatly influenced by oral tradition. Tutuola made use of common Yoruba tales and motifs, stringing them together like a fireside raconteur. As a consequence, the book's neat cyclical narrative pattern rests on a very loosely coordinated inner structure. The hero is involved in one adventure after another but these adventures are not well integrated. Like boxcars on a freight train, they are independent units joined with a minimum of apparatus and set in a seemingly random and interchangeable order. There is no foreshadowing of events, no dramatic irony, no evidence of any kind that the sequence of events was carefully thought out. Tutuola appears to be improvising as he goes along and employing the techniques and materials of oral narrative art in his improvisations. This is true of his other writings too.

Recent research has shown that none of Tutuola's works is entirely innocent of literary influence either. He clearly owes his greatest debt to D. O. Fagunwa, who began to publish folkloric "novels" in Yoruba in 1938. In his earliest fiction Tutuola tried to imitate Fagunwa's method of weaving a number of old stories into an elastic narrative pattern that could be stretched into a book. Both Fagunwa and Tutuola appear to have been stimulated by John Bunyan's *The Pilgrim's Progress* and *The Arabian Nights*, which were widely used in Nigerian elementary schools. Later Tutuola turned to other foreign sources of inspiration; Edith

Hamilton's *Mythology* may have been responsible for the nymphs, satyrs, myrmidons and phoenixes which started to infiltrate his African jungles. Goblins, imps and gnomes also turned up regularly. Tutuola, like a great syncretic sponge, easily absorbed these alien creatures into his exotic imaginative universe.

This is not to say, of course, that all his writing is derivative or that it lacks originality or accomplishment. In descriptive ability and sheer visionary power Tutuola far surpasses most of his contemporaries. His fertile imagination, never fettered by reason or common sense, constantly begets the surprising, the unorthodox, the incongruous, the bizarre. Events are recounted with a hallucinatory energy that swiftly transports the reader into realms of fantasy. Characters are painted in the most vivid and memorable colors. Whatever Tutuola borrows from oral or literary tradition he immediately makes his own, enlarging it with details of his own invention. He is a master storyteller.

Tutuola's most conspicuous idiosyncrasy as a writer, and perhaps his most controversial, is his style, which Dylan Thomas once termed "naive English." Because he grew up speaking Yoruba and had only six years of formal schooling, Tutuola tends to make spectacular grammatical and spelling blunders on every page he writes. Some critics hold that this fractured idiom is one of his greatest assets for it adds extra tang to the primitive flavor of his works; his language is just as weird and unpredictable as the adventures he describes. Others argue that it is an unfortunate liability for it quickly tires the average reader who is not conditioned to jumping unfamiliar linguistic hurdles. It is unlikely that this critical debate will have any appreciable effect on Tutuola's writing, for he is not a conscious stylist experimenting with language. He is simply trying to do the best he can in a foreign tongue he has not adequately mastered.

The initial reaction to Tutuola's first books was mixed. Readers in Europe and America were enthusiastic for they had never seen anything quite like them before, and they were convinced that Tutuola was a marvellous "original," a diamond in the rough with rich and dazzling creative powers. Reviewers hailed him as an uncouth genius unspoiled by civilization, a mute, inglorious Milton who had suddenly found his voice, albeit a curiously cracked one. Many educated Nigerians, however, were extremely angry that such an unschooled author should receive so much praise and publicity abroad, for they recognized his borrowings, disapproved of his bad grammar, and suspected he was being lionized by condescending racists who had a clear political motive for choosing to continue to regard Africans as backward and childlike primitives. Since Nigeria was struggling to free itself from colonial rule at the time, Tutuola was more than merely an embarrassment; he was a disgrace, a setback, a national calamity. Later, after Nigeria had achieved its independence, Tutuola was no longer an explosive literary or political issue, and his works began to receive more intelligent critical attention. Today his reputation is secure both at home and abroad, for he has come to be accepted as a unique phenomenon in world literature, a writer who bridges two narrative traditions and two cultures by translating oral art into literary art.

—Bernth Lindfors

**TYLER, Anne.**   American.   Born in Minneapolis, Minnesota, 25 October 1941. Educated at Duke University, Durham, North Carolina, 1958–61, B.A. 1961; Columbia University, New York, 1961–62. Married Taghi Modarressi in 1963; has two children. Address: 222 Tunbridge Road, Baltimore, Maryland 21212, U.S.A.

PUBLICATIONS

Novels

> *If Morning Ever Comes.*   New York, Knopf, 1964; London, Chatto and Windus, 1965.
> *The Tin Can Tree.*   New York, Knopf, 1965; London, Macmillan, 1966.
> *A Slipping Down Life.*   New York, Knopf, 1970.

Uncollected Short Stories

> "I Play Kings", in *Seventeen* (New York), August 1963.
> "Street of Bugles", in *Saturday Evening Post* (New York), 30 November 1963.
> "Nobody Answers the Door", in *Antioch Review* (Yellow Springs, Ohio), Fall 1964.
> "I'm Not Going to Ask You Again", in *Harper's* (New York), September 1965.
> "Everything But Roses", in *Reporter* (New York), 23 September 1965.
> "As the Earth Gets Old", in *The New Yorker*, 29 October 1966.
> "Feather Behind the Rock", in *The New Yorker*, 12 August 1967.
> "Flaw in the Crust of the Earth", in *Reporter* (New York), 2 November 1967.
> "Common Courtesies", in *McCall's* (New York), June 1968.

*          *          *

Although she has only reached the age of thirty, Anne Tyler has published three highly successful novels and received wide critical acclaim. She writes principally of life in Southern small towns and is basically concerned with the themes of loneliness and human isolation and the difficulties people have both in understanding and in communicating with one another. When Ben Joe Hawkes, the protagonist of *If Morning Ever Comes*, returns for a visit to his home town of Sandhill, North Carolina, he ponders the gap which separates him from his family, although they are as friendly and as affectionate to him as their natures will allow. There is family unity at the same moment that there is family disunity. Ben Joe can reach his mother and sisters only half-heartedly, for within them and within himself mysterious factors in the human heart lure and yet resist complete harmony and under-standing. Ben Joe comes to realize that this condition is life itself; he will never fully understand his wife or even his own children when they are eventually born. Parts of every human being and of life itself are forever closed to understanding. Such parts are sadly "unreachable."

This melancholy presentation of existence is related with a painfully sensitive awareness of the tragedy of things as they are. In *The Tin Can Tree* the parents of a six year old girl become exceedingly distraught over the child's accidental death. The mother, in particular, attempts to shut out any further life and light. But her only son suffers so intensely from her neglect that she finally comprehends that life even with its heartbreak and lack of fulfillment is all one has; and, as a consequence, the best should be made of it. Half-fulfilled relation-ships are better than no relationships at all. The ideal or even the semi-ideal cannot be reached in this life, and no matter how unhappy or disappointing life may be, it is life and not death. People are exalted most of all in Miss Tyler's philosophy when they love other mortals although they consciously know that death awaits both themselves and the ones they love. And a further burden is added because the tin can tree is always rattling, never allowing anyone to forget the dead.

Individuals must arrive at deliberate choices on the relative scales of possibility and degree of bittersweetness. For example, one has a choice of imperfect love or no love at all. Anne Tyler's protagonists generally prefer the former, or at least settle for what their consciousness informs them will be the most appropriate degree for them—although outsiders and even close friends continually insist that their selection is both incomprehensible and foolish. A "belonging to" someone else becomes necessary while life starts slipping away from everyone.

Miss Tyler's principal themes are conveyed in crisp, delicate prose which often pleasantly startles because of the preciseness of word choice and the depth of insight. She writes simple descriptive passages and much fresh, brief Hemingway-like dialogue. Her future as a writer of fiction will be closely watched to observe if she can avoid occasional character improbability, a tendency to thematic repetitiveness, and a somewhat limited range of subject matter.

—Paul A. Doyle

---

**UPDIKE, John (Hoyer).** American. Born in Shillington, Pennsylvania, 18 March 1932. Educated in Shillington public schools; at Harvard University, Cambridge, Massachusetts, A.B. (summa cum laude) 1954; Ruskin School of Drawing and Fine Arts, Oxford, 1954–55. Married Mary Pennington in 1953; has four children. Staff Reporter, *The New Yorker*, 1955–57. Recipient: Guggenheim Fellowship, 1959; Rosenthal Award, 1960; National Association of Independent Schools Award, 1963; National Book Award, 1964; O. Henry Award, 1966. Member, National Institute of Arts and Letters. Address: 26 East Street, Ipswich, Massachusetts 01938, U.S.A.

PUBLICATIONS

Novels

*The Poorhouse Fair*. New York, Knopf, and London, Gollancz, 1959.
*Rabbit, Run*. New York, Knopf, 1960; London, Deutsch, 1961.
*The Centaur*. New York, Knopf, and London, Deutsch, 1963.
*Of the Farm*. New York, Knopf, 1965.
*Couples*. New York, Knopf, and London, Deutsch, 1968.
*Rabbit Redux*. New York, Knopf, 1971; London, Deutsch, 1972.

Short Stories

*The Same Door*. New York, Knopf, 1959; London, Deutsch, 1962.
*Pigeon Feathers*. New York, Knopf, and London, Deutsch, 1962.
*The Music School*. New York, Knopf, 1966.
*Penguin Modern Stories 2*, with others. London, Penguin, 1969.
*Bech: A Book*. New York, Knopf, and London, Deutsch, 1970.

Verse

*The Carpentered Hen and Other Tame Creatures*. New York, Harper, 1958; as *Hoping for a Hoopoe*, London, Gollancz, 1959.
*Telephone Poles*. New York, Knopf, and London, Deutsch, 1963.
*Midpoint and Other Poems*. New York, Knopf, and London, Deutsch, 1969.
*Seventy Poems*. London, Penguin, 1972.

Other

    *The Magic Flute* (juvenile).   New York, Knopf, 1962.
    *The Ring*.  New York, Knopf, 1964.
    *Assorted Prose*.  New York, Knopf, and London, Deutsch, 1965.
    *A Child's Calendar*.  New York, Knopf, 1966.
    *Bottom's Dream: Adapted from William Shakespeare's "A Midsummer Night's Dream"*.
    New York, Knopf, 1969.

    Editor, *Pens and Needles*, by David Levine.  Boston, Gambit, 1970.

Critical Studies: interviews with the author in *Life* (New York), 4 November 1966, and in
*Paris Review*, Winter 1968.

*    *    *

   John Updike's fictional domains have local habitation and name: Olinger, Pennsylvania,
Tarbox, Massachusetts, and a few experimental claims staked in New York City. But
regional peculiarities are, though beautifully described and transcribed, topographical
details. The heart of Updike country is the psychic map of conflict between the shapelessness
and plodding futility of the quotidian where only sex and death are absolute, and a sense of
potentiality, a search for nothing less improbable than a discernible pattern in existence. To
varying degrees, Updike's characters are aware of the tension: his most inarticulate protagonist, Rabbit Angstrom, explains his quest: "There's something out there that wants me
to find it." Updike's craftsmanship employs the reader even more acutely than the characters
in recognising and evaluating the conflict. A boy in "Pigeon Feathers" is reassured because
"the God who had lavished such craft upon these worthless birds would not destroy his
whole creation by refusing to let David live forever." Updike as creator forces the reader to
a similar act of faith: no one invests all the talent, the clean articulations and chiselled images
on a seemingly ordinary person and situation without intending something of large significance. Each novel is supported by recognisable sub-surface patterns: Greek mythology,
Biblical story, folk ritual, symbolic elaborations of imagery. The structural possibilities of
these patterns and parallels, and a hint of the tensions they generate, are suggested in T. S.
Eliot's credo in the 1923 apologia for *Ulysses*: the use of myth "is simply a way of controlling,
of ordering, of giving a shape and a significance to the immense panorama of futility and
anarchy which is contemporary history." It is at this level that Updike's intuition of structural
possibilities seems to have settled.
   The metaphoric microcosm in *The Poorhouse Fair*, the first novel, displays in good measure
the "anarchy and futility which is contemporary history." Futility and the proximity of
death thicken the atmosphere surrounding the old people who have as their last home a
poorhouse administered by a bureaucrat who professes humanism, but denies the humanity
of the inmates: "When would they all die and let the human day dawn?" The prefect Conner
and the oldest inmate Hook are representatives of the new and old order—each with its
antithetical and impossible myths. Conner's myth is utopian and futuristic: a world with
"No pain and above all no *waste*." Hook firmly believes in historical continuity and Christianity. Where the two sets of myths collide, the moral victory is Hook's, though in fact,
Conner's order has, as Hook knows, triumphed: "This last decade [the novel is set in the
1970s] . . . has witnessed the end of the world, if the people would but wake to it." In a
grimly ironic parody of the martyring of St. Stephen, the inmates stone their prefect. Attempted anarchy is crushed, not through the harsh reprisals Conner threatens, but through
the total unawareness of anyone outside the poorhouse walls that the event ever happened.
The fair goes on as planned—but it is a fossil ritual which will die with the old people:
"Heart had gone out of these people; health was the principal thing about the faces of the

Americans that came crowding through the broken wall to the poorhouse fair." Apocalypse colors every aspect of the novel; as visual metaphor, it is witnessed by the drugged and dying patients in the hospital wing: ". . . a sublime creature had plunged to death. The titanic yellow furrow . . . was rounded like a comet head nearest the horizon, where the color was most intense, the color of an unnatural element, transuranic, created atom by atom in the scientist's laboratory, at inestimable expense." The myths of martyrdom have become universal in proportion to their impersonality.

"The great urgencies of sex and death," as Updike calls them, provide the fields of force in *Rabbit, Run*. Rabbit Angstrom is terrified by death and anything which reminds him of it. He is compelled by sex, for him a transcendence of death as well as the only real satisfaction provided by a banal existence. His dreary job consists in demonstrating a kitchen gadget called the MagiPeel Peeler, his wife is "only going one way, towards deeper wrinkles and skimpier hair," and terrifies him with her sloppiness and alcoholism. Rabbit's reliance on his sexuality is linked with the adolescent athleticism which made him a high-school basket-ball star and remains the moment of success suspended perpetually in memory. Whenever circumstances threaten his belief that "there is an unseen world" in which perfection is possible, Rabbit runs. Each flight, seeming to reaffirm his freedom to search, narrows the area for maneuver, and hastens the next in the series of betrayals and flights. Rabbit's initial flight is a quest of sorts and possesses a certain legitimacy: the obstacles placed in his path are symbolic encounters with many of the trials set for earlier quests: e.g., Baltimore-Washington is Cerberus, Rabbit must avoid "false intersections with siren voices." Even the extended metaphor of nets set to trap Rabbit (Beatrix Potter's *Peter Rabbit* is the surface source) has a noble lineage and echoes the nets set to trap Orestes in the *Oresteia*. But the dramatic background orchestration is ironic, and in the closing pages the irony is emphasized by a heavily imagistic burden of death laid over the uncertain outcome of the narrative.

*The Centaur*, as the title suggests, allows myth to thicken into vehicle as well as tenor. The myth of Chiron the centaur may diminish or amplify the reality of George Caldwell the highschool teacher, but its main function is to demonstrate the paradox of man: "His top half felt all afloat in a starry firmament of ideals and young voices singing; the rest of his self was heavily sunk in a swamp where it must, eventually, drown." The presence and possibility of death permeate the consciousness of Caldwell and his son Peter (Prometheus) during the three days described in the novel; however, Peter, looking back on this time, feels "We moved somehow, on a firm stage, resonant with metaphor." Love (or sex), the second great urgency "that make[s] unreality . . . so real," is also predictably, if variously, represented, from the overtures and escapades of Vera Hubble (Venus), the gym teacher, to the experi-mental forays of Peter with Penny Fogelman (Pandora), a fellow student. Initially sex and death become hopelessly tangled in Peter's consciousness—but the two sort themselves out in several ways as he learns the life-giving potential of love from Penny and the life-giving potential of self-sacrifice from his father. But art, "this potential fixing of a few passing seconds," is now offered as the true antidote to flux: Peter, from the age of five, had realized "that things do, if not die, certainly change, wiggle, slide, retreat. . . ." More than the x-rays which dispel Caldwell's fear of cancer, more than the sacrificial offering of Caldwell to his students and family, it is art, "the prism . . . made of the tale," which makes *The Centaur* paeon to a father, as well as to man as myth, the only ideal, ultimately, in Updike's own search for pattern.

If *The Centaur* demonstrates the possibilities of art as affirmation and possible salvation, *Of the Farm* qualifies and to some extent undermines the assertion. The action takes place during a weekend in which an advertising man and his second wife visit the farm still owned by his dying mother. Once again, death and sexuality are the prime foci, explored through conversations among the three as they pace each other's boundaries as well as those of the farm, and the meditations of the failed-poet-ad-man, Joey Robinson. The most explicit and detailed mythology belongs to Joey's mother, and her "saga of the farm": even Joey feels "captive within my mother's sense of truth," in which his father, grandmother and ex-wife are among the ghosts allowed to walk. Her idea of love is Platonic—man and woman once were united but split by a jealous God, and "the farm nobody farms" is a sanctuary "where people can come . . . and let their corners rub off, and try to be round again." Death is "a defect she had overlooked in purchasing these acres, a negligible flaw grown huge." Joey had never found the farm a "people sanctuary," and early on made his escape to New York. Instead of a farm, he sees his wife Peggy as his "demesne seized from the world," and, with the exception of one grand sexual metaphor, Joey is unable "to see both her and the farm at once." Though he has many dreams and fantasies about death during his stay, though he feels his mother is trying to "sink" into him the "hook of her death," Joey ends by running both from his mother's farm and death. Peggy's mythology is compounded of amateur psychology and self-justification: Joey's mother had taken the farm as "giant lover" emasculating both husband and son. Peggy sees herself as the agent allowing Joey to enter manhood for the first time. If, as Joey suggests, "truth is constantly being formed from the solidification of illusions," none of these private versions of reality is an absolute, but each has the "minimal truth of existing in at least one mind." Joey and his wife exist also as man and woman sundered by the jealous gods, and their relationship is made resonant with echoes of paradisiacal loss. The two levels of myth working together suggest that, though man yearns for permanence, for a "past apparently unrevised," the best he can do is to create his own patterns to account for, to add significance to, the circumstances of his own life. The creative mythology of *The Centaur* has been surrendered to the privacy of the neurotic imagination—as Joey's failure to be a poet promises from the beginning.

Man's deep need for myth is given its fullest statement in *Couples*, which represents, in microcosmic Tarbox, most of the atmosphere of the '60's. There is an interregnum in all spheres—moral, political, religious—which leaves the characters, ten couples, in a vacuum they must some way fill. "Duty and work yielded as ideals to truth and fun": elaborate rituals evolve, from word games to adultery, complete with tacit rules, taboos and conventions. The town dentist, a failed-doctor and spiritual master of the revels, is the "king of chaos" Freddy Thorne, who sees himself presiding over death and decay in his job and in his rôle as priest. When John Kennedy is shot, Freddy is clearly titillated at this confirmation of chaos. This cynicism and frequent diabolism are somewhat counterbalanced by his sense of the couples "suspended in one of those dark ages that visits mankind between millennia, between the death and the rebirth of the gods when there is nothing to steer by but sex, stoicism and the stars." He believes that they have formed a "church of each other"—"a magic circle of heads to keep the night out." Within the same ritualistic pattern but exerting a contrary force, asserting a contrary belief, is Piet Hanema, carpenter, philanderer, Christian and scapegoat. For Piet, "there was, behind the screen of couples and houses and days, a Calvinist God Who lifts us up and casts us down in utter freedom, without recourse to our prayers or consultation with our wills." Piet, however, is also a pagan life force: as his wife observes, he "spends all his energy defying death." Just as Freddy is confirmed in his sense of chaos by Kennedy's death, Piet is confirmed in his sense of divine order when his own marriage (to Angela/Angel) crumbles, though at the expense of feeling "damned eternally" as a result. As if to further prove God's displeasure, or "as if a conflict in God's heart had been bared," the Congregational church, Piet's church, burns down during a violent rainstorm in which he himself expects to be struck down by lightning. However, Piet, whose imagistic associations include Adam, Lot, the fertility deities and others, departs from twentieth-century Sodom to start a new life in the spring, season of renewal and rebirth, far from the "post-pill paradise" that is Tarbox. Paradoxically, man survives in spite of and because of the myths and rituals which explore and explain his rôle as "the sexiest of the animals and the only one that foresees death."

—Jackson I. Cope

**UPWARD, Edward (Falaise).** British. Born in Romford, Essex, 9 September 1903. Educated at Repton School, 1917–21; Corpus Christi College, Cambridge, 1922–24. M.A. 1924. Married to Hilda Maude Percival; has two children. Schoolmaster, 1928–62. Member, Editorial Board, *The Ploughshare*. Address: c/o William Heinemann Ltd., 15–16 Queen Street, London W.1, England.

PUBLICATIONS

Novels

    *Journey to the Border*.   London, Hogarth Press, 1938.
    *In the Thirties*.   London, Heinemann, 1962.
    *The Rotten Elements*.   London, Heinemann, 1969.

Short Stories

    *The Railway Accident and Other Stories*.   London, Heinemann, 1969.

Verse

    *Buddha*.   London, Cambridge University Press, 1924.

Critical Study: Introduction by W. H. Sellers to *The Railway Accident and Other Stories*, 1969.

*     *     *

Edward Upward as a young writer in the 1930s achieved a great reputation, was indeed something of a legend, among a number of writers of his own age and younger. Christopher Isherwood has told in *Lions and Shadows* how he and Upward (called Chalmers in Isherwood's book) at Cambridge invented a fantasy world they called Mortmere which paralleled and parodied the world about them. Mortmere seems to have been at once sinister and comic, partly surrealist and partly Gothic. That it had affinities with Auden's early poetry, influenced as it was by Freud, seems clear, and something of it seems to emerge in the plays Isherwood wrote in collaboration with Auden, notably *The Dog Beneath the Skin*. Upward, however, overtly pursued the vein of fantasy in his fiction, but, even then politically committed, in the cause of Marxism. The central character of *Journey to the Border* is a middle-class young man employed as a tutor in the house of a rich man; he is constantly struggling against the implications and ignominies of his position but is unable to resolve them. He is persuaded against his will to accompany his employer to a race-meeting. On the way, and while there, he experiences a series of hallucinations that mount in intensity and are the counterparts of the debate going on in his mind. By the end of the novel he is forced to realise that the only solution to this problem, the only way to reality, is for him to identify himself with the working-class struggle.

When the novel was first published, reviewers read the influence of Kafka into it. This is not much apparent now, if it ever existed. Upward's novel is much less complex than Kafka's, and what begins as a work of symbolism peters out in simple allegory. Nevertheless, the voltage of imaginative excitement generated is high, and the dreamlike quality of the work is admirably sustained. It remains a brilliant experimental novel of a very unusual kind.

Upward published nothing for twenty-five years, and then in 1962 there appeared *In the Thirties* and in 1969 *The Rotten Elements*. These are related novels based, it is impossible not to think, on the author's own life. *In the Thirties* describes the stages by which a young middle-class man comes to Communism. In a sense, the theme is that of *Journey to the Border*, but the treatment is entirely different. Fantasy has been replaced by literal realism, which is also the vein in which *The Rotten Elements* is written. Here, the hero of the earlier novel, a school teacher now married, finds himself compelled in the years immediately after the war to leave the Communist Party, not because he has lost his political faith but because for him and his wife the British Communist Party, under the influence of Moscow, has deviated from Marxism-Leninism. These two novels lack the literary interest of *Journey to the Border* but they have an anguish of their own and a documentary quality which suggests that, though they may not be read in the future for their artistic value, they will be essential reading for scholars concerned with the role of the Communist Party in Britain in the thirties and the forties.

—Walter Allen

**URIS, Leon (Marcus).**   American.   Born in Baltimore, Maryland, 3 August 1924. Educated in Baltimore city schools. Served in the United States Marine Corps, 1942–45. Married Betty Beck in 1945 (divorced, 1965); Margery Edwards, 1968 (died, 1969); Jill Peabody, 1970; has three children. Newspaper Driver for the *San Francisco Call-Bulletin* in the late 1940's. Full-time Writer since 1950. Recipient: Daroff Memorial Award, 1959; National Institute of Arts and Letters grant, 1959. Lives in Aspen, Colorado. Address: c/o Doubleday and Company Inc., 277 Park Avenue, New York, New York 10017, U.S.A.

PUBLICATIONS

Novels

*Battle Cry*.   New York, Putnam, and London, Wingate, 1953.
*The Angry Hills*.   New York, Random House, 1955; London, Wingate, 1956.
*Exodus*.   New York, Doubleday, 1958; London, Wingate, 1959.
*Mila 18*.   New York, Doubleday, and London, Heinemann, 1961.
*Armageddon: A Novel of Berlin*.   New York, Doubleday, and London, Kimber, 1964.
*Topaz*.   New York, McGraw Hill, 1967; London, Kimber, 1968.
*Q.B. VII*.   New York, Doubleday, 1970; London, Kimber 1971.

Plays

*Ari*, music by Walt Smith (produced New York, 1971).

Screenplays: *Battle Cry*, 1955; *Gunfight at the OK Corral*, 1957.

Other

*Exodus Revisited.*  New York, Doubleday, 1960; as *In the Steps of Exodus*, London, Heinemann, 1962.
*The Third Temple*, with *Strike Zion*, by William Stevenson.  New York, Bantam, 1967.

\*        \*        \*

Critics were willing to be charitable to Leon Uris's popular first novel, *Battle Cry*, when it appeared in 1953. While it is a war novel not as psychologically complex as Wouk's *The Caine Mutiny*, nor as deeply probing into the nature of man and war as Mailer's *The Naked and the Dead* or Jones's *From Here to Eternity*, it is a good, straightforward, blood-and-guts adventure of the U.S. Marine Corps in which dialogue and action are matched well to characters. Though Uris's treatment by professional critics has generally been much harsher for the five novels that have been published since, their disparagement of his work is, in an important sense, not entirely fair. There is no reason to suppose that the present is different from earlier periods in literary history when there has been a popular, ephemeral literature as distinct from a smaller body of serious and lasting literature with limited public appeal. Uris makes no pretense of contributing to an enduring *corpus* of American literature. He bulls his way forward on the sheer strength of his narrative ability, which was acknowledged at the beginning of his career, and though he may stumble over literary matters of characterisation, of plot detail, of dialogue, of theme, his handling of the story line unfailingly carries him through, and the book-buying public acclaims him over the grumbling of critics.

Yet the faults are real and cannot be overlooked; they are in evidence in all of the novels. *The Angry Hills*, a romantic war adventure of Greek resistance to the Nazi occupation, contains obtrusively contrived circumstances. The invention of the love subplot of *Exodus*, between the Zionist hero, Ari Ben Canaan, and the gentile nurse, Kitty Fremont, often seems gratuitous, and its execution pre-Cinemascope. *Armageddon*, like *Exodus* and Uris's other works, has its plot in large measure constructed by history, in this case Russian-American relations in Berlin after World War II, and especially the American airlift. And, like *Exodus*, it is plagued by a love affair that seems, at times, to be arbitrarily appended to the progression of historical events. It suffers, too, from a weakness of dialogue that is not unusual in Uris, and from the trite response of the main character, an American occupation officer, to the German and Russian nations in turn. *Mila 18* does an injustice to the Jews of the Warsaw ghetto, whose resolute defiance of the Nazis it chronicles, by transforming them into a series of stock characters. Here as elsewhere in his novels, Uris seems to be best when he is recounting the history he has researched and at his worst when he requires one of the obviously indispensable attributes of the novelist—the power to weave the plot line into a smooth integument of all the elements of fiction.

Yet there is the brute force of the narrative in all of the novels that compels the reader through to the finish despite all imperfections, even through the too-lengthy trial and concentration camp horrors of his latest novel, *Q.B. VII*. And, though it would be wrong to assume that Uris has begun to compose deathless prose at this late date, in pitting the American novelist Abraham Cady against the former camp inmate Adam Kelno, he demonstrates an ability now to create characters of interest and depth.

—Alan R. Shucard

**URQUHART, Fred.** British. Born in Edinburgh, 12 July 1912. Educated at village schools in Scotland; Stranraer High School, Wigtownshire; Broughton Secondary School, Edinburgh. Worked in an Edinburgh bookshop, 1927–34. Reader for a London literary agency, 1947–51, and for MGM, 1951–54; London Scout for Walt Disney Productions, 1959–60. Since 1951, Reader for Cassell and Company, London, and, since 1967, for J. M. Dent and Sons, London. Recipient: Tom-Gallon Trust Award, 1951; Arts Council grant, 1966. Address: Spring Garden Cottage, Fairwarp, Uckfield, Sussex, England.

PUBLICATIONS

Novels

> *Time Will Knit.* London, Duckworth, 1938.
> *The Ferret Was Abraham's Daughter.* London, Methuen, 1949.
> *Jezebel's Dust.* London, Methuen, 1951.

Short Stories

> *I Fell for a Sailor and Other Stories.* London, Duckworth, 1940.
> *The Clouds Are Big with Mercy.* Glasgow, Maclellan, 1946.
> *Selected Stories.* Dublin and London, Fridberg, 1946.
> *The Last G.I. Bride Wore Tartan: A Novella and Some Short Stories.* Edinburgh, Serif Books, 1948.
> *The Year of the Short Corn and Other Stories.* London, Methuen, 1949.
> *The Last Sister and Other Stories.* London, Methuen, 1950.
> *The Laundry Girl and the Pole: Selected Stories.* London, Arco, 1955.
> *Collected Stories:*
>    I. *The Dying Stallion and Other Stories.* London, Hart Davis, 1967.
>    II. *The Ploughing Match and Other Stories.* London, Hart Davis, 1968.

Other

> *Scotland in Colour.* London, Batsford, and New York, Studio Publications, 1961.
>
> Editor, with John Maurice Lindsay, *No Scottish Twilight: New Scottish Stories.* Glasgow, Maclellan, 1947.
> Editor, *W. S. C.: A Cartoon Biography* (on Winston Churchill). London, Cassell, 1955.
> Editor, *Great True War Adventures.* London, Arco, 1956; New York, Arco, 1957.
> Editor, *Scottish Short Stories.* London, Faber, 1957.
> Editor, *Men at War: The Best War Stories of All Time.* London, Arco, 1957.
> Editor, *Great True Escape Stories.* London, Arco, 1958.
> Editor, *The Cassell Miscellany (1848–1958).* London, Cassell, 1958.

Manuscript Collections: National Library of Scotland, Edinburgh; University of Texas Library, Austin.

Critical Studies: review by Janet Adam Smith, in *New York Times Book Review,* 31 July 1938; essay by Alexander Reid, in *Scotland's Magazine* (Edinburgh), February 1958; review by Iain Crichton Smith in *The Spectator* (London), 24 May 1968.

Fred Urquhart comments:

I never talk about my work, and I hate writing about it. When someone asks, "And what are you writing now?" I find it difficult to answer. I can't tell them; I find it impossible to explain that I'm writing perhaps three separate things and that, so far, I haven't put a word to paper for any of them. When I'm writing a story I don't want anybody to see it or know about it until it is completely finished and it satisfies me. It's not that I'm a secretive person; actually, I'm rather garrulous. It's just that I hate talking about my work. Apart from that, I'm a slow worker, and I never know when a story will be finished. I have written some stories in a couple of days; others have taken me months. A few were started, abandoned, restarted and part written, and then finally finished after a period of several years. I'm writing a novel just now, but I don't want to say anything about it.

I write mainly about the working class people of Scotland: the people I was brought up among. Sometimes I write about the suburban types of Edinburgh, where I was born and where I lived in my teens and early twenties. Sometimes I write about the farm folk of the Mearns and Aberdeenshire, where I spent several impressionable years. I write a lot about women. Almost all my stories are built around a "heroine". A television interviewer in a programme in which I appeared said that they were mostly neurotic, bitchy women. I suppose he was right. But I don't consider whether they are bitchy or neurotic when I'm writing about them; I just put them down on paper as I've observed them or as I imagine they must feel in certain situations. I hope I write about them with sympathy. I try to. Although I've lived in England for 26 years—nearly half of my lifetime—I don't often write about English characters. I find it harder to understand and to get under the skin of the English country people I've lived among for over 20 years than I do to imagine and reconstruct the lives of the Scottish peasants I knew in my childhood and youth.

When he reviewed my novella *The Last G. I. Bride Wore Tartan*, John Pudney, the poet, wrote: "His specialties are good dialogue and bad women." Another poet, Edwin Muir, writing about my first novel, *Time Will Knit*, said: "The way in which he tumbles out indiscriminately the undignified, the tragic, the comic, the pathetic, the hard-boiled, shows that he has an original imaginative view of life." And in a letter to me, Whit Burnett, editor of *Story*, who printed a number of my early stories in the U.S.A., wrote: "I think they are the best stories I have seen come out of Scotland in many years. They are human, warm and funny, with a deep sense of the oddities and frailties of humankind. I like them all, and you can tell anybody I say so."

\*          \*          \*

Fred Urquhart is a wonderful listener. He gets the exact lilt of Clydeside or the Mearns or Leith or Scots dialect modified by the army or navy. He seems to be fascinated by the corruption of language: how Glasgow speech adds an embroidering diminutive "ie"— flashie, steamie—but is itself a corrupted English from what was the Clyde ditch into which the fleeing Gaelic speakers piled themselves hoping for a puckle siller and a wee housie or roomie to live and love in. Those are his backgrounds. But his tongue or maybe his pen is as skilled as his deeply interested ear. He gets it all down often with a minimal plot but with such liveliness and such involvement of characters that the story line hardly matters. Indeed there are times when he has a good old heart-throb ending but he usually gets away with it because of the way it is told.

These writings of his are too artful and delicate to be in fact the kind of stories which have been told into the unsympathetic ear of a tape recorder. Thus always another human but invisible listener may be asking the odd question that stirs the story up and this invisible other is infinitely aware of the fine points of dialogue and the hidden feelings of the characters, which only appear between the lines, making tensions which are never underlined. Oddly enough Urquhart is best with his women characters, his schoolmistresses and farmers' wives or daughters; his Glasgow lassies on the make or his dirty old wifies. He really gets into the skin of the "Last G.I. Bride". Why? Maybe he finds the toughness of the average male Scot a bit of a bore—as so many women also find it! But he is sensitive to other second class citizens, for instance the Italian prisoners working on a Lowland farm in one of his World War II stories.

He is not a quick writer. Perhaps that is why his novels are really longer short stories. On the whole he spends little time on the background unless it is farm detail, and here he is often away back to the days of splendid Clydesdale mares and comparatively unhygienic byres and dairies. Most comes through conversation or the fleeting thoughts which are near to speech. He is also very much interested in what other writers are doing, especially in Scotland. He must often have been sorely tempted to do a bit of quick slick writing for the "popular" family magazines; perhaps "The Year of the Short Corn" is partly autobiographical. But he believes that writers have a certain duty to tell the truth, even when it is displeasing to the audience they would most like—their own folk. This audience of course is what all writers want but few if any get, because of the corruption of the chosen hearers. It is hard luck to have to wait till you are dead before you are appreciated. One hopes this won't have to happen to Fred Urquhart.

—Naomi Mitchison

---

**van der POST, Laurens (Jan).** South African. Born in Philippolis, 13 December 1906. Educated at Grey College, Bloemfontein. Served in the British Army, in the Western Desert and the Far East, in World War II: Prisoner of War, in Java, 1943–45; Military Attaché to the British Minister, Batavia, 1945–47; C.B.E. (Commander, Order of the British Empire, military division), 1947. Married Marjorie Wendt in 1929 (divorced, 1947); the writer Ingaret Giffard, 1949; has two children. Farmer in the Orange Free State, South Africa, 1948–65. Explorer; has made several missions to Africa for the Colonial Development Corporation and the British Government, including a mission to Kalahari, 1952. Recipient: Anisfield-Wolf Award, 1951; National Association of Independent Schools Award (U.S.A.), 1959; South African Central News Agency Prize, 1963, 1967; *Yorkshire Post* prize, 1967. D.Litt., University of Natal, Pietermaritzburg, 1965. Fellow, Royal Society of Literature, 1955. Address: 27 Chelsea Towers, Chelsea Manor Gardens, London S.W.3; or, Turn-Stones, Aldeburgh, Suffolk, England.

PUBLICATIONS

Novels

In a Province. London, Hogarth Press, 1934; New York, Coward McCann, 1935.
The Face Beside the Fire. London, Hogarth Press, and New York, Morrow, 1953.
Flamingo Feather. London, Hogarth Press, and New York, Morrow, 1955.
A Bar of Shadow. New York, Morrow, 1956.
The Seed and the Sower (includes A Bar of Shadow and The Sword and the Doll). London, Hogarth Press, and New York, Morrow, 1963.
The Hunter and the Whale: A Tale of Africa. London, Hogarth Press, and New York, Morrow, 1967.

Other

> *Venture to the Interior.*  New York, Morrow, 1951; London, Hogarth Press, 1952.
> *The Dark Eye in Africa.*  London, Hogarth Press, and New York, Morrow, 1955.
> *The Lost World of the Kalahari.*  London, Hogarth Press, and New York, Morrow, 1958.
> *The Heart of the Hunter.*  London, Hogarth Press, and New York, Morrow, 1961.
> *Journey into Russia.*  London, Hogarth Press, 1964; as *A View of All the Russias*, New York, Morrow, 1964.
> *A Portrait of All the Russias.*  London, Hogarth Press, and New York, Morrow, 1967.
> *A Portrait of Japan.*  London, Hogarth Press, and New York, Morrow, 1968.
> *The Night of the New Moon: August 6, 1945 . . . Hiroshima.*  London, Hogarth Press, 1970.

Film: *The Lost World of the Kalahari*, 1956.

Critical Study: *Laurens van der Post* by Frederic I. Carpenter, New York, Twayne, 1969.

*     *     *

All the novels of Laurens van der Post have dealt, at least in part, with the life and problems of his native South Africa. All draw upon the author's actual life, which his more famous books of non-fiction (such as *Venture to the Interior*) have described autobiographically. All are distinguished by vivid descriptions of the natural scene, and by psychological depth. But each has been written from a different point of view, and has used a different technique.

*In a Province* is narrated in the first person by a young, white South African whose black friend runs afoul of the law. Both become involved with a communist agitator, and are finally killed by a posse of self-appointed commandos. The novel is realistic in technique, and is distinguished both by its wealth of incidents involving race relations, and by its balance between the theme of racial injustice on the one hand, and communist exploitation on the other. Although the author has opposed apartheid all his life, he has equally opposed communist subversion.

Nineteen years elapsed between the author's first and second novels—years including his move to England and his distinguished service in World War II, ending with his capture and imprisonment by the Japanese. *The Face Beside the Fire* deals with the problems of an expatriate South African artist in London. Narrated by a life-long friend of the hero, the novel covers a period of many years, and moves from Africa to England and back. Its many episodes find unity in the psychological theme of alienation. Its technique is that of the psychological novel pioneered by Thomas Mann.

*Flamingo Feather* is a fast-paced tale of mystery and adventure set in war-time South Africa. Narrated in the first person by a young anthropologist, the plot concerns a communist attempt to subvert a native tribe in the interior. The action includes a vividly narrated trek through tropical jungles. A mystery-melodrama, the novel is distinguished both by its fast action and its vivid description of the wild country of Africa.

*The Seed and the Sower* consists of three "novellas" describing guerilla warfare in Africa and Asia, but focusing on the life of the prisoner-of-war. The first novella, *A Bar of Shadow* (published separately in 1956), centers upon the narrator's attempt to understand his Japanese captors. The second (and longest) returns to South Africa to narrate the early experiences of another officer, and ends with his capture and execution by the Japanese. The third narrates a brief wartime romance. All focus upon the author's experiences as prisoner-of-war, which also shadow much of his autobiographical writing.

*The Hunter and the Whale*, subtitled *A Tale of Africa*, is narrated by a seventeen-year-old boy who serves as lookout on a whaling ship working out of Durban. The novel is richer and more complex than the others, and combines realistic with symbolic techniques. Its unusual subject matter and unusual techniques both suggest comparison with Melville's *Moby Dick*, and help to explain both the fascination and the occasional difficulty of the novel.

At present Mr. van der Post has completed the first of a projected two-volume novel, narrated by a teen-age boy, and set in the back country of Southern Africa in which the author himself grew up.

—Frederic I. Carpenter

---

**VAN DOREN, Mark.**   American.   Born in Hope, Illinois, 13 June 1894. Educated in Urbana, Illinois public schools; at the University of Illinois, Urbana, A.B. 1914, A.M. 1915; Columbia University, New York, Ph.D. 1920. Married to the writer Dorothy Graffe; has two children. Member of the English Faculty, Columbia University, 1920–59: Professor of English, 1942–59. Lecturer, St John's College, Annapolis, Maryland, 1937–57. Literary Editor, 1924–28, and Film Critic, 1935–38, *The Nation*, New York. Visiting Professor of English, Harvard University, Cambridge, Massachusetts, 1963. Recipient: Pulitzer Prize, for verse, 1940; Hale Award, 1960; New England Poetry Society Golden Rose, 1960; Huntington Hartford Creative Award, 1962; Emerson-Thoreau Award, 1964; Academy of American Poets Fellowship, 1967. Litt.D., Bowdoin College, Brunswick, Maine, 1944; University of Illinois, 1958; Columbia University, 1960; Knox College, Galesburg, Illinois, 1966; Harvard University, 1966; Jewish Theological Seminary of America, New York, 1970; L.H.D., Adelphi College, Garden City, New York, 1957; Mount Mary College, Milwaukee, Wisconsin, 1965; M.D., Connecticut State Medical Society, 1966. Member, American Academy of Arts and Letters. Address: Falls Village, Connecticut 06031, U.S.A.

PUBLICATIONS

Novels

   *The Transients.*   New York, Morrow, and London, Heinemann, 1935.
   *Windless Cabins.*   New York, Holt, 1940.
   *Tilda.*   New York, Holt, 1943.

Short Stories

   *The Short Stories of Mark Van Doren.*   New York, Abelard Press, 1950.
   *The Witch of Ramoth and Other Tales.*   York, Pennsylvania, Maple Press, 1950.
   *Nobody Say a Word and Other Stories.*   New York, Holt, 1953.
   *Home with Hazel.*   New York, Harcourt Brace, 1957.
   *Collected Stories.*   New York, Hill and Wang, 3 vols., 1962–1968.

Plays

   *The Last Days of Lincoln* (produced Tallahassee, Florida, 1961).   New York, Hill and
      Wang, 1959.

*Never, Never Ask His Name* (produced Tallahassee, Florida, 1965). Included in *Three Plays*, 1966.

*Three Plays* (includes *Never, Never Ask His Name*; *A Little Night Music*; *The Weekend That Was*). New York, Hill and Wang, 1966.

Verse

*Spring Thunder and Other Poems.* New York, Thomas Seltzer, 1924.
*7 P.M. and Other Poems.* New York, Boni, 1926.
*Now the Sky and Other Poems.* New York, Boni, 1928.
*Jonathan Gentry.* New York, Boni, 1931.
*A Winter Diary and Other Poems.* New York, Macmillan, 1935.
*The Last Look and Other Poems.* New York, Holt, 1937.
*Collected Poems, 1922–1938.* New York, Holt, 1939.
*The Mayfield Deer.* New York, Holt, 1941.
*Our Lady Peace and Other War Poems.* New York, New Directions, 1942.
*The Seven Sleepers and Other Poems.* New York, Holt, 1944.
*The Country Year: Poems.* New York, Sloane, 1946.
*The Careless Clock: Poems about Children in the Family.* New York, Sloane, 1947.
*New Poems.* New York, Sloane, 1948.
*Humanity Unlimited: Twelve Sonnets.* Williamsburg, Virginia, College of William and Mary, 1950.
*In That Far Land.* Iowa City, Iowa, Prairie Press, 1951.
*Mortal Summer.* Iowa City, Iowa, Prairie Press, 1953.
*Spring Birth and Other Poems.* New York, Holt, 1953.
*Selected Poems.* New York, Holt, 1954.
*Morning Worship.* New York, Harcourt Brace, 1960.
*Collected and New Poems, 1924–1963.* New York, Hill and Wang, 1963.
*The Narrative Poems.* New York, Hill and Wang, 1964.
*100 Poems.* New York, Hill and Wang, 1967.
*That Shining Place: New Poems.* New York, Hill and Wang, 1969.

Other

*Henry David Thoreau.* Boston, Houghton Mifflin, 1916.
*The Poetry of John Dryden.* New York, Harcourt Brace, 1920; revised edition, Cambridge, Minority Press, 1931; as *John Dryden: A Study of His Poetry*, New York, Holt, 1946; Bloomington, Indiana University Press, 1960.
*American and British Literature since 1890*, with Carl Van Doren. New York, Century, 1925; revised edition, Appleton Century, 1939.
*Edwin Arlington Robinson.* New York, Literary Guild of America, 1927.
*Dick and Tom: Tales of Two Ponies* (juvenile). New York, Macmillan, 1931.
*Dick and Tom in Town* (juvenile). New York, Macmillan, 1932.
*Shakespeare.* New York, Holt, 1939; London, Allen and Unwin, 1941.
*Studies in Metaphysical Poetry*, with Theodore Spencer. New York, Columbia University Press, 1939.
*The Transparent Tree* (juvenile). New York, Holt, 1940.
*Invitation to Learning*, with Huntington Cairns and Allen Tate. New York, Random House, 1941.
*The New Invitation to Learning.* New York, Random House, 1942.
*The Private Reader: Selected Articles and Reviews.* New York, Holt, 1942.
*Liberal Education.* New York, Holt, 1943.
*The Noble Voice: A Study of Ten Great Poems.* New York, Holt, 1946.

*Nathaniel Hawthorne*.   New York, Sloane, 1949; London, Methuen, 1950.
*Introduction to Poetry*.   New York, Sloane, 1951.
*Don Quixote's Profession*.   New York, Columbia University Press, 1958.
*The Autobiography of Mark Van Doren*.   New York, Harcourt Brace, 1958.
*The Happy Critic and Other Essays*.   New York, Hill and Wang, 1961; Edinburgh,
    Oliver and Boyd, 1962.
*The Dialogues of Archibald MacLeish and Mark Van Doren*.   New York, Dutton, 1964.

Editor, *Samuel Sewell's Diary*.   New York, Macy Masius, 1927.
Editor, *A History of the Life and Death, Virtues and Exploits of General George Washing-*
    *ton*, by Mason Locke Weems.   New York, Macy Masius, 1927.
Editor, *An Anthology of World Poetry*.   New York, Boni, 1928; London, Cassell,
    1929; revised edition, New York, Reynal and Hitchcock, 1936; Harcourt Brace, 1950.
Editor, *The Travels of William Bartram*.   New York, Macy Masius, 1928.
Editor, *Nick of the Woods; or, The Jibbenainosay: A Tale of Kentucky*, by Robert
    Montgomery Bird.   New York, Macy Masius, 1928.
Editor, *A Journey to the Land of Eden and Other Papers*, by William Byrd.   New York,
    Macy Masius, 1928.
Editor, *An Autobiography of America*.   New York, Boni, 1929.
Editor, *Correspondence of Aaron Burr and His Daughter Theodosia*.   New York,
    Covici Friede, 1929.
Editor, with Garibaldi M. Lapolla, *A Junior Anthology of World Poetry*.   New York,
    Boni, 1929.
Editor, *The Life of Sir William Phips*, by Cotton Mather.   New York, Covici Friede,
    1929.
Editor, with Garibaldi M. Lapolla, *The World's Best Poems*.   New York, Boni, 1932.
Editor, *American Poets, 1630–1930*.   Boston, Little Brown, 1932.
Editor, *The Oxford Book of American Prose*.   London and New York, Oxford
    University Press, 1932.
Editor, with John W. Cunliffe and Karl Young, *Century Readings in English Literature*,
    5th edition.   New York, Appleton Century, 1940.
Editor, *A Listener's Guide to Invitation to Learning, 1940–41, 1941–42*.   New York,
    Columbia Broadcasting System, 2 vols., 1940, 1942.
Editor, *The Night of the Summer Solstice and Other Stories of the Russian War*.   New
    York, Holt, 1943.
Editor, *Walt Whitman*.   New York, Viking Press, 1945.
Editor, *The Portable Emerson*.   New York, Viking Press, 1946.
Editor, *Selected Poetry*, by William Wordsworth.   New York, Modern Library, 1950.
Editor, with others, *Riverside Poetry: 48 New Poems by 27 Poets*.   New York, Twayne,
    1956.

Manuscript Collection: "Mark Van Doren Papers", Rare Books and Manuscripts, Columbia
University, New York.

                              *         *         *

For Mark Van Doren the practice of literature means nothing less than a transcendental
perfection of life. An artist might make the world better, he has explained ("The Artist and
the Changing World" 1951) by thinking "deeply and feelingly . . . about the courage it now
takes to be the sort of individual whose dignity matters more than wars and revolutions,
more than welfare and the sovereignties of states." The power thus to transcend history is,
however, given to no one. "It has to be created in the mind . . . amid the total darkness of
other men's refusal to make the attempt at all." True to his own precept, the creation of an

Idealistic reality has been Van Doren's purpose in a dozen works of criticism and auto-biography, over one thousand lyric and narrative poems, three novels, and more than 125 short stories.

Already an accomplished poet and critic, the role in which he continues to be best known, Van Doren turned to fiction in 1934–35 and wrote in rapid succession his first two novels, *The Transients* and *Windless Cabins*. The first of these is a parable relating the visit of two creatures from a realm of perfect spirit to the mortal world. John Bole and Margaret Shade, whose names reflect their distinct yet complimentary qualities, spend a summer month moving separately and then together through New England town and countryside. They become involved briefly in love affairs with mortals and also share a brief idyll together. The intimate relationships must deliberately be broken, though, for John and Margaret are images of perfection, eternally separate from the world; their function is to stimulate the imagination alone.

The plot of a mystery tale provides form for *Windless Cabins*. Through misunderstanding of intentions a young man kills a guest at a motel, buries the body, and successfully conceals the crime from the police. The fact that the murderer is never declared guilty by the law apparently accounts for a five year delay between the writing and publication of the novel, but Van Doren makes clear the young man is punished for his deed—in his own mind, which becomes the primary setting of mystery. In time the guilt-ridden man admits his lover to a share in the ponderous secret. As they marry and leave home the Idealistic premise moves to conclusion. They are to seek forgiveness in themselves. The social world is irrelevant.

*Tilda*, Van Doren's third novel, moves even further into the interior of character. Struc-tured as a romance the dramatic movement is through memory which must be mastered so that the male protagonist may regain sanity. As in his preceding novels, Van Doren's premise issues in a tale of a couple isolated from society through engagement in a secret and personal mission. It is Idealism privatized.

In a burst of productivity beginning in 1946 and lasting nearly a decade Van Doren com-posed the short stories he has issued in four volumes and recently edited for a three volume collection. As is to be expected in the writing of a man whose life has been devoted to the study and teaching of literature a number of the stories have literary sources. Some are retellings of incidents from Classical literature, a few are based on Hawthorne's notebooks, and others are excursions into the mystery tale. Regardless of source—and most derive from the author's imagination working on observation—the tales are all distinctively embodi-ments of Van Doren's Idealism. Framed to lead into memory or structured by plot to focus upon intimate thoughts and feelings, each of the stories puts events into the setting of the mind: secret love and guilt, daydreams becoming emotionally determining, and the past infusing the present. The reality of social or material relationships is largely absent from the stories, as it is from the novels. When it does intrude it brings violence or pain from which the characters retreat, if they survive, in order to resolve confusion by reassertion of mental images.

In this fiction Van Doren imagines a curious aristocracy. Devoted to their feelings the characters seek a monotonous stability (monotony, as in "A Winter Diary," is an honorific term for Van Doren) in a solitude free of material and social necessity. It is an aristocracy because only a few may share it, but it is curious because it neither aspires to nor is capable of action. Expressed in the address on "The Artist and the Changing World" the philosophy of such an aristocracy has the conventional attraction of the statements so commonly offered as rationale for the Liberal Arts. Clothed in the detail of fiction, however, where it must represent life, an Idealism that denies any history but a personal one and any society at all can only be considered at best escapism, at worst delusion.

—John M. Reilly

**VIDAL, Gore.** American. Born in West Point, New York, 3 October 1925. Educated at Phillips Exeter Academy, New Hampshire. Served in the United States Army, 1943–46. Full-time Writer since 1944. Member, Advisory Board, *Partisan Review*, New Brunswick, New Jersey, 1960–71. Democratic-Liberal Candidate for Congress, 1960. Member, President's Advisory Committee on the Arts, 1961–63. Co-Chairman, The New Party, 1968–71. Address: Casa Willi, Klosters, Switzerland.

PUBLICATIONS

Novels

*Williwaw.* New York, Dutton, 1946; London, Heinemann, 1970.
*In a Yellow Wood.* New York, Dutton, 1947.
*The City and the Pillar.* New York, Dutton, 1948; London, Lehmann, 1949; revised edition, Dutton, 1965; London, Heinemann, 1966.
*The Season of Comfort.* New York, Dutton, 1949.
*A Search for the King: A Twelfth Century Legend.* New York, Dutton, 1950.
*Dark Green, Bright Red.* New York, Dutton, and London, Lehmann, 1950.
*The Judgment of Paris.* New York, Dutton, 1952; London, Heinemann, 1953.
*Messiah.* New York, Dutton, 1954; London, Heinemann, 1955; revised edition, Boston, Little Brown, 1965.
*Three: Williwaw, A Thirsty Evil, Julian the Apostate.* New York, New American Library, 1962.
*Julian.* Boston, Little Brown, and London, Heinemann, 1964.
*Washington, D.C.* Boston, Little Brown, and London, Heinemann, 1967.
*Myra Breckinridge.* Boston, Little Brown, and London, Blond, 1968.
*Two Sisters: A Novel in the Form of a Memoir.* Boston, Little Brown, and London, Heinemann, 1970.

Novels (as Edgar Box)

*Death in the Fifth Position.* New York, Dutton, 1952; London, Heinemann, 1954.
*Death Before Bedtime.* New York, Dutton, 1953; London, Heinemann, 1954.
*Death Likes It Hot.* New York, Dutton, 1954; London, Heinemann, 1955.

Short Stories

*A Thirsty Evil: 7 Short Stories.* New York, Zero Press, 1956; London, Heinemann, 1958.

Plays

*Visit to a Small Planet and Other Television Plays.* Boston, Little Brown, 1957.
*Visit to a Small Planet* (stage version; produced New York, 1957). Boston, Little Brown, 1957.
*The Best Man: A Play of Politics* (produced New York, 1960). Boston, Little Brown, 1960.
*Romulus: A New Comedy* (produced New York, 1962). New York, Dramatists Play Service, 1962.

*Three Plays* (includes *Visit to a Small Planet, The Best Man, On the March to the Sea*). London, Heinemann, 1962.
*Romulus: The Broadway Adaptation, and The Original Romulus the Great by Friedrich Durrenmatt, translated by Gerhard Nellhaus*.   New York, Grove Press, 1966.
*Weekend* (produced New York, 1968).   New York, Dramatists Play Service, 1968.
*An Evening with Richard Nixon* (produced New York, 1972).   New York, Random House, 1972.

Screenplays: *The Catered Affair*, 1956; *I Accuse*, 1958; *The Scapegoat*, 1958; *Suddenly Last Summer*, with Tennessee Williams, 1959; *The Best Man*, 1964; *Last of the Mobile Hot-Shots*, 1970.

Other

*Rocking the Boat* (essays).   Boston, Little Brown, 1962; London, Heinemann, 1963.
*Reflections upon a Sinking Ship* (essays).   Boston, Little Brown, and London, Heinemann, 1969.

Critical Study: *Gore Vidal* by Ray Lewis White, New York, Twayne, 1968.

*     *     *

At first glance the sheer number and range of Gore Vidal's books would seem to discourage any useful generalizations. In his mid-forties, with seventeen works of fiction to his credit (three are pseudonymous and another three have been repudiated: nevertheless they exist), Vidal is the author, as he puts it, of "what is probably in plain bulk the largest oeuvre of any contemporary American writer." The diversity of his fiction, from a massive "autobiography" of the Emperor Julian to reports on the American sexual underground, is more apparent, however, than real; for throughout the novels there is a persistent concern with naturalism—and its ethical and political consequences—as the only sensible guide to living. The early novels move towards this position; the later novels, as well as Vidal's vigorous critical essays, are essentially polemical defenses of naturalism against contending points of view.

For this position, which forms one of the dominant strains of western thinking from the pre-Socratics through Santayana, man is a finite, mortal, purely natural creature, living precariously and unsponsored in an accidental universe. Whatever meaning he finds and whatever values he cherishes can be derived only from a capacity to learn from his experiences in a world indifferent to his fate. But while it follows that reason will play a vital role in planning those adjustments necessary for living, the emotions and life of the body are no less real or natural. "Men are wise," reflects the hero of *The Judgment of Paris*, "when they love nature more than dogma"; the self is merely a "temporary arrangement of matter". The fullest statement of Vidal's naturalism, however, occurs in his most recent novel, *Two Sisters*:

listening to Dwight MacDonald talk on and on, entirely happy in his pursuit of thought, I said, "Don't you realize, Dwight, you have nothing to say, only to add?" He stopped short; said he found this a most impressive statement. . . . Yet what I said of him I really meant to say of myself, of us all. For what is there to *say*, finally, except that pain is bad and pleasure good, death nothing? To these obvious texts, one can only add one's life which is so little, particularly if words are one's only means of telling what was, what is, and what ought to be.

The ethical corollary of Vidal's naturalism is a kind of urbane utilitarianism, or calculating hedonism, in which the diverse needs of natural man are satisfied to the fullest extent compatible with social order. The enemies of naturalism are the doctrines which repress these needs (hence Vidal's continuing fascination with Julian the Apostate as a figure who attempted to forestall the triumph of Christianity and its life-denying mandates), as well as the equally natural drive for power and domination over others, in sex or politics. "There is no virtue in any of us," complains the protagonist of *Washington, D.C.*, "we are savages"; we all play a game whose nature is, simply, "war. . . . A conquers B who conquers C who conquers A. Each in his own way [struggles] for precedence and to deny this essential predatoriness [is] sentimental; to accommodate it wrong; to change it impossible." The narrator of *Two Sisters* concludes, "We come and we go and the time between is all we have. I am stoic, and I can be nothing else."

If this were all, however, Vidal's novels would be a good deal less lively than in fact they are, for despite his misgivings about the future of the race, he cannot help admiring human resourcefulness: as the central figure of *Messiah* puts it, our "conception of the inconsequence of human activity . . . is ever in conflict with a profound love of those essential powers that result in human action, a paradox certainly, a dual vision which restrains me from easy judgments." This "dual vision" is the source of Vidal's strength as a writer, even in those early novels which by any reasonable standards must seem fumbling and unpromising.

*Williwaw* is a "war novel" only in the sense that even this first novel defines men's lives as a battle against nature—and the vanity of their fellowmen. The three novels which follow deal in one way or another with the youthful search for freedom and satisfaction. Rather surprisingly the hero of *In a Yellow Wood* decides to "accept the pattern" of conventional behavior, after a thinly dramatized encounter with romantic love and unconventional sex (dismissed here as mere "self-indulgence" rather than genuine freedom). In *The Season of Comfort*—in which Vidal experiments uneasily with something beyond the "national manner of the time . . . colorless, careful prose, deliberately confined to the surface of things" —the protagonist successfully breaks his ties to his mother and moves tentatively towards love and a career as an artist. *The City and the Pillar*, which caused something of a scandal by its earnest (and by current standards completely unsensational) revelations of homosexual life in America, has as its theme not sexual deviation so much as the more general problem of the "romantic fallacy", the fatal desire to recapture a past moment whose perfection was a naive illusion. (*The City and the Pillar* has far more in common with *The Great Gatsby* than with Genet.) Vidal has repudiated *In a Yellow Wood* and *The Season of Comfort*, as well as *A Search for the King* (a pale imitation of medieval romance), quite aware that he had not yet found his "own true voice and pitch".

*Dark Green, Bright Red* is a routine adventure story with a pleasantly ironic twist at the end, but in *The Judgment of Paris* Vidal's apprenticeship comes to an end. The theme is the familiar one—here a young man chooses love rather than political opportunity or "wisdom" —yet the writing is sharp and genuinely witty, revealing for the first time Vidal's great gifts as a comic caricaturist. *Messiah* is a philosophic fantasy, a parable in which the narrator struggles against the perverted naturalism of a powerful religious leader (the theme is repeated in the ambitious *Julian*, which despite its impressive moments finally sinks under the burden of its historical authenticity). *Washington, D.C.*, a panoramic account of power politics shrewdly contrived to have something for everyone, is, nevertheless, wholly engrossing. Vidal finds his "true voice", however, in *Myra Breckinridge*, a scabrous, brilliantly comic survey of American youth and sexuality and satiric dramatization of the familiar sex-as-domination motif. *Two Sisters* is a stylish exploration of vanity and, once again, the un-recapturability of the past, taking irresistible pot-shots along the way at everything and everyone Vidal dislikes, from Nabokov to the Bouvier sisters. Despite all the evidence that man is on a collision course with disaster, the final word for Vidal is an open-ended "Yet—": "Is there any word in English," he asks, "quite so useful, so hopeful, so truly pregnant as yet?" Given proper guidance it is still possible, he concludes, "that human freedom might be sustained, even increased".

—Elmer Borklund

**VONNEGUT, Kurt, Jr.** American. Born in Indianapolis, Indiana, 11 November 1922. Educated at Cornell University, Ithaca, New York, 1940–42; University of Chicago, 1945–47. Served in the United States Army Infantry, 1942–45; awarded Purple Heart. Married Jane Marie Cox in 1945; has three children. Police Reporter, Chicago City News Bureau, 1946; worked in public relations for the General Electric Company, Schenectady, New York, 1947–50. Free-lance Writer since 1950. Since 1965, Teacher, Hopefield School, Sandwich, Massachusetts. Visiting Lecturer, Writers Workshop, University of Iowa, Iowa City, 1965–67; Harvard University, Cambridge, Massachusetts, 1970–71. Recipient: Guggenheim Fellowship, 1967; National Institute of Arts and Letters grant, 1970. Address: Scudder's Lane, West Barnstable, Massachusetts 02668, U.S.A.

PUBLICATIONS

Novels

> *Player Piano.* New York, Scribner, 1952; London, Macmillan, 1953.
> *The Sirens of Titan.* New York, Fawcett, 1959; London, Gollancz, 1962.
> *Mother Night.* New York, Fawcett, 1961; London, Cape, 1968.
> *Cat's Cradle.* New York, Holt Rinehart, and London, Gollancz, 1963.
> *God Bless You, Mr. Rosewater; or, Pearls Before Swine.* New York, Holt Rinehart, and London, Cape, 1965.
> *Slaughterhouse-Five; or, The Children's Crusade: A Duty-Dance with Death, by Kurt Vonnegut, Jr., A Fourth-Generation German-American Now Living in Easy Circumstances on Cape Cod [and Smoking Too Much] Who, as an American Infantry Scout Hors de Combat, as a Prisoner of War, Witnessed the Fire-Bombing of Dresden, Germany, the Florence of the Elbe, a Long Time Ago, and Survived to Tell the Tale: This Is a Novel Somewhat in the Telegraphic Schizophrenic Manner of Tales of the Planet Tralfamadore, Where the Flying Saucers Come From.* New York, Delacorte Press, 1969; London, Cape, 1970.

Short Stories

> *Canary in a Cathouse.* New York, Fawcett, 1961.
> *Welcome to the Monkey House: A Collection of Short Works.* New York, Delacorte Press, 1968.

Plays

> *Very First Christmas Morning,* in *Better Homes and Gardens* (Des Moines, Iowa), December 1962.
> *Fortitude,* in *Playboy* (Chicago), September 1968.
> *Happy Birthday, Wanda June* (produced New York, 1970).

*        *        *

During the decade of the 1960's Kurt Vonnegut, Jr., emerged as one of the most influential and provocative writers of fiction in America. His following is particularly strong among college and university students, who find in him stunningly effective statements of their own disillusionments and fears. His writing, indeed, constitutes an unintermittent protest against certain horrors of our century—the unending sequence of disastrous wars, the plunging decline in the livability of the environment, and the dehumanization of the individual in a society dominated by science and technology. Such protest is by no means new or unique in American and European literature. The peculiar force of Vonnegut's voice among so many others may be traced to its complete contemporaneity. Fantasy (usually of the science variety), black humor, a keen sense of the absurd are the ingredients of his novels and stories.

Vonnegut has described himself as "a total pessimist." And indeed his six novels and most of his other writing offer little except wry laughter to counteract despair. This is certainly true of his first novel, *Player Piano*. The time of the novel is the not-too-distant future and the place is a one-industry city, Ilium, New York, which serves as the setting for much of Vonnegut's fiction and which resembles Schenectady, New York, where Vonnegut worked in public relations for General Electric. In the novel not only the local industry but those of the entire nation have been completely mechanized. Machines supplant human workers, because machines make fewer errors. All national policy is determined by huge computers located in Mammoth Cave. A small elite of scientists—chosen on the basis of intelligence tests administered in high school—are in charge of all production. The masses, who are provided with all material necessities and comforts, including an impressive array of gadgetry, serve either in the military or in work battalions assigned to road repair and the like. Acutely aware of their dehumanization and worthlessness except as mere consumers of the huge output of the machines, the common people revolt under the leadership of a preacher and several renegade scientists. Though the revolt in Ilium, at least, is successful and many of the objectionable machines are destroyed, Vonnegut denies his readers any sense of satisfaction. In tune with his "total" pessimism he records that the rebels destroy not only obnoxious machinery but also the useful and necessary technological devices such as sewer disposal plants. What is more, they soon begin to tinker with the unneeded machines with a view to making them operative again. In the face of such inveterate stupidity the leaders suicidally surrender to the government forces.

An obvious question arises: Why should Vonnegut or his readers concern themselves with the dehumanization of apparent morons? What, indeed, is there to be dehumanized? An answer is not readily forthcoming, but apparently Vonnegut considers that there is some value in attempting to save the human race from its own stupidity. In each of his novels there is at least one person who is aware of human folly, including his own, and thus is living proof that intellectual blindness is not universal. More frequently than not, moreover, these discerning individuals are reformers, as in *Player Piano*, who make self-sacrificing efforts to improve the lot of their fellow men. This is the case with Vonnegut's second novel, *The Sirens of Titan*, which in plot is a rather conventional example of science fiction with an interplanetary setting. The reforming character in this book has been rendered immortal, omniscient, and virtually omnipotent by having been entrapped in a "chrono-synclastic-infundibulum." Thus endowed, he sets about uniting all nations of the world in the bonds of brotherhood by staging an abortive attack against the earth by Martians. The latter are earthlings abducted to Mars and converted to automatons by the insertion into their skulls of radio antennae through which orders are transmitted from a central directorate. These unfortunates are thus subjected to a ruthless dehumanization and exploitation, but to a worth-while end. The scheme is successful; the earth becomes united after the defeat of the Martian attack and the unity is cemented by the establishment of a new religion, the Church of God the Utterly Indifferent. This happy outcome is somewhat clouded, however, by the revelation that the entire history of humanity has been determined by the trivial needs of the inhabitants of the planet Tralfamadore in one of the more remote galaxies.

Vonnegut's forth and fifth novels, *Cat's Cradle* and *God Bless You, Mr. Rosewater*, also focus upon the efforts of altruistic individuals to alleviate human misery. *Cat's Cradle* is notable for its presentation of an entirely new religion. Bokononism (named for its founder), much of the doctrine of which is written in Calypso verse. According to Bokonon, religion *should* be an opiate; its function is to deceive and, by deceiving, make people happier. It teaches that God directs human destinies and that mankind is sacred, and it promotes an ethic of love, which believers manifest by pressing the soles of their feet against those of fellow believers. Bokononism was founded and flourished on a Caribbean island oppressed by a Duvalier-type dictator. It flourished because it was outlawed; for, according to *Cat's Cradle* at least, a religion functions most vigorously when opposed to the existing social order. There can be no doubt that Bokononism brought relief to the wretched islanders, the final horror of whose existence was that of being congealed, along with the rest of the world, by ice-nine, a discovery of an Ilium scientist.

*God Bless You, Mr. Rosewater* recounts the efforts of an enormously wealthy philanthropist to alleviate human misery through the more or less random disbursement of the Rosewater Foundation's almost limitless funds. Like Bokonon's his purpose is to make existence more endurable for the masses. But he is less successful than Bokonon, for even with the millions of dollars at his command he is able barely to scratch the surface of the world's wretchedness. He is taken advantage of by those whom he tries to help, and his friends and relatives consider him a lunatic. Yet he makes the effort and, despite his undoubted eccentricity, does achieve a degree of personal saintliness.

Two remaining novels, *Mother Night* and *Slaughterhouse-Five*, both of which focus upon World War II, contain no such reformers or philanthropists as do the other novels discussed. In these two the protagonists are never really in a position to be altruistic, even if they wished to be. In *Mother Night*, Howard W. Campbell, Jr., serves schizophrenically as the Nazis' chief English-language radio propagandist at the same time that he is one of the allies' most effective spies. Years after the war he finds himself in an Israeli prison awaiting trial along with Adolph Eichmann. Here he commits suicide, even though a bizarre turn of events has ensured his acquittal. Thoughtful readers will probably conclude that Campbell achieves real stature in his self-destruction, for he has realized that by playing his fantastic dual roles he has betrayed beyond recovery his own humanity—a realization achieved by few Vonnegut characters in analogous situations.

*Slaughterhouse-Five*, Vonnegut's most recent and perhaps most powerful novel, presents two characters who can see beneath the surface to the tragic realities of human history but make no attempt to bring about change. These are the author himself, who is a frequent commentator, and the protagonist, Billy Pilgrim. The central event in the novel is the destruction of Dresden by bombs and fire storm—a catastrophe that Vonnegut himself witnessed as a prisoner of war. Billy Pilgrim's liberating insights are the outgrowth of his being freed from the prison of time and, as a result, seeing the past, present, and future as one and coexistent. One consequent realization is that death is an illusion. Though his periods of release from time occur on earth, their significance is explained to him by the inhabitants of the distant planet Tralfamadore, to which he is transported on a Tralfamadorian spaceship. Though Billy finds no way to improve the tragically absurd condition of man, he does arrive at an understanding of it and a resultant deepening of compassion.

In addition to his six novels Vonnegut has written several plays and many sketches and short stories. His first collection of short pieces was *Canary in a Cathouse*; all but one of the selections in this volume appeared, along with many more, in *Welcome to the Monkey House*. In style, theme, and mood the short fiction closely resembles the novels. Notable stories are the title piece of his second collection and "Adam," "Tomorrow and Tomorrow and Tomorrow," and "EPICAC." These and others are fine examples of Vonnegut's skill and originality in combining black humor, a sense of the absurd, and the devices of science-fantasy to produce unforgettable commentaries on our times and the future that awaits us.

—Perry D. Westbrook

**WAGONER, David (Russell).**   American.   Born in Massillon, Ohio, 5 June 1926. Educated at Pennsylvania State University, University Park, B.A. 1947; Indiana University, Bloomington, M.A. 1949. Served in the United States Navy, 1944–46. Married Patricia Parrott in 1961. Instructor, De Pauw University, Greencastle, Indiana, 1949–50, and Pennsylvania State University, 1950–54. Associate Professor, 1954–66, and since 1966, Professor of English, University of Washington, Seattle. Since 1966, Editor, *Poetry Northwest*, Seattle. Elliston Lecturer, University of Cincinnati, 1968. Recipient: Guggenheim Fellowship, 1956; Ford Fellowship, 1964; National Institute of Arts and Letters grant, 1967; Morton Dauwen Zabel Prize, *Poetry*, Chicago, 1967; National Endowment for the Arts grant, for editing, 1969. Address: 1075 Summit Avenue East, Seattle, Washington 98102, U.S.A.

PUBLICATIONS

Novels

>   *The Man in the Middle*.   New York, Harcourt Brace, 1954; London, Gollancz, 1955.
>   *Money, Money, Money*.   New York, Harcourt Brace, 1955.
>   *Rock*.   New York, Viking Press, 1958.
>   *The Escape Artist*.   New York, Farrar Straus, and London, Gollancz, 1965.
>   *Baby, Come On Inside*.   New York, Farrar Straus, 1968.
>   *Where Is My Wandering Boy Tonight?*   New York, Farrar Straus, 1970.

Verse

>   *Dry Sun, Dry Wind*.   Bloomington, Indiana University Press, 1953.
>   *A Place to Stand*.   Bloomington, Indiana University Press, 1958.
>   *The Nesting Ground*.   Bloomington, Indiana University Press, 1963.
>   *Staying Alive*.   Bloomington, Indiana University Press, 1966.
>   *New and Selected Poems*.   Bloomington, Indiana University Press, 1969.
>   *Working Against Time*.   London, Rapp and Whiting, 1970.
>   *Riverbed*.   Bloomington, Indiana University Press, 1972.

Other

>   Editor, *Straw for the Wind: From the Notebooks of Theodore Roethke, 1943–1963*.   New York, Doubleday, 1972.

Manuscript Collection: Rare Book Room, Washington University Library, St. Louis.

Critical Studies: "David Wagoner's Fiction: In the Mills of Satan" by William J. Schafer, in *Critique* (Minneapolis), Vol. 9, No. 1, 1965; "It Dawns on Us That We Must Come Apart", in Richard Howard's *Alone with America*, New York, Atheneum, 1969; "The Poetry of David Wagoner" by Robert Boyers, in *Kenyon Review* (Gambier, Ohio), no. 1, 1970.

David Wagoner comments:

It is almost impossible for me to comment coherently on my own fiction, except to say that I began writing poetry first and received early encouragement as a writer of fiction from

Edward J. Nichols at Penn State and Peter Taylor at Indiana University, and later from Malcolm Cowley at Viking Press and Catharine Carver who was then at Harcourt Brace. I seem to have a penchant for what might be called serious farce, but whether farce can stand the serious strains I put on it, I must leave to others to say. I also recognize my tendency to write what I believe critics call "initiation" novels. I tend to dramatize or write in scenes rather than to be discursive. One clear theme would seem to be the would-be innocent protagonist vs. the corrupt city, perhaps a result of my having grown up between Chicago and Gary, Indiana, where the most sophisticated and effective forms of pollution were first perfected.

*       *       *

In six novels over fifteen years, David Wagoner has pursued the themes of innocence and corruption, of the connections between past, present and future, of the individual trapped in a violent society. The novels depict individuals corrupted by modern urban life, protagonists essentially innocent and helpless damaged by the pressures of family life and further maimed by society. Wagoner skilfully uses Dickensian comedy and drama to create a tragic myth of man stripped and abandoned by his parents and his fellows yet struggling to survive and to remain intact.

The Man in the Middle and Money, Money, Money describe helpless, childlike adults caught up in criminal machinations. The Escape Artist and Where Is My Wandering Boy Tonight? treat the same theme from the viewpoint of juvenile protagonists. Each novel involves criminals and corrupt politicians who pursue and persecute an innocent victim. There is a strong element of picaresque comedy in this drama of innocence adapting to a wicked world. The last three novels also develop a complex sexual theme revolving around an Oedipal relationship—a child confronted and fascinated by a destructive mother figure. Each of the protagonists must overcome this infantile sexual bondage before he is free to live wholly, just as each must learn the depth of the world's wickedness before he can shed his infantile social innocence.

In Rock and Baby, Come On Inside, Wagoner deals with the destructiveness of family life and the crippling effects of the past. Both stories concentrate on the conflict between leaving home and returning home: "You can't go home again" vs. "You must go home again." In each novel, the protagonist tries to recapture his past, to find a home place, but ends in confusion and further exile.

A recurrent pattern in Wagoner's novels is that of pursuit and flight, a nightmarish sense of implacable evil, and a recurrent scene is a metaphorical return to the womb, to primordial shelter. Charlie Bell in The Man in the Middle spends a night in a railway coin locker. Willy Grier is left in a garbage can in Money, Money, Money. Danny Masters in The Escape Artist hides out in a Goodwill Industries collection box and a US mailbox. The pattern of flight and hiding, a fragile individual pursued by a terrifying nemesis, occurs in a comic context—cynical wit and slapstick farce—for the dreamlike or mythic dimension of Wagoner's novels derives from their mixed tone. The stories encompass suspense, adventure, comedy, pathos and a strong sense of the social and political life of midwestern cities.

Wagoner's tragicomedies of violence achieve effects somewhat like François Truffaut's Shoot the Piano Player. The mixture of naivete, tough-guy dialogue, violence, thriller action and insight into complex states of mind creates a fantasy world as an accurate analogue for contemporary urban life. Danny Masters, in The Escape Artist, muses on violence and trickery and how to escape them:

> Danny felt his own life shut inside him, keeping as quiet as it could, shying away. Nobody should be able to break anybody open like a nut and clean out the insides, but some people did it, and he would never let them come close. That was why getting away was important, getting out, getting loose, because they had to make you sit still long enough so they could crack you open, otherwise it spoiled their

aim. They were no good with moving targets, no good if you weren't where they thought you were. They knew a lot of tricks, and that was why you had to keep ahead of them, and then if you got a big enough lead, you could afford to let them know who you were, taunting them from a distance yet always ready to change shape to fool them.

Wagoner's novels reflect society's torments and traps and also explore the paths to freedom— self-understanding, imagination and the uses of experience. While they detail corruption and destruction, they also reflect innocence and virtue. The possibilities in this world are tragic and comic, and the inevitable price of survival is loss of innocence.

—William J. Schafer

---

**WAIN, John (Barrington).** British. Born in Stoke-on-Trent, Staffordshire, 14 March 1925. Educated at The High School, Newcastle-under-Lyme, Staffordshire; St. John's College, Oxford, B.A. 1946; Fereday Fellow, 1946–49; M.A. 1950. Married Marianne Urmstrom in 1947 (marriage dissolved, 1956); Eirian James, 1960; has three children. Lecturer in English, University of Reading, Berkshire, 1947–55. Full-time Writer since 1955. Director, Poetry Book Society Festival, "Poetry at the Mermaid", London, 1961. Churchill Visiting Professor, University of Bristol, 1967; Visiting Professor, Centre Universitaire Experimental, Vincennes, France, 1969; First Holder, Fellowship in Creative Arts, Brasenose College, Oxford, 1971–72. Recipient: Maugham Award, 1958. Fellow, Royal Society of Literature, 1960; resigned, 1961. Lives in Oxford. Address: c/o Macmillan and Company Ltd., 4 Little Essex Street, London W.C.2, England.

PUBLICATIONS

Novels

> *Hurry on Down.* London, Secker and Warburg, 1953; as *Born in Captivity*, New York, Knopf, 1954.
> *Living in the Present.* London, Secker and Warburg, 1955; New York, Putnam, 1960.
> *The Contenders.* London, Macmillan, and New York, St. Martin's Press, 1958.
> *A Travelling Woman.* London, Macmillan, and New York, St. Martin's Press, 1959.
> *Strike the Father Dead.* London, Macmillan, and New York, St. Martin's Press, 1962.
> *The Young Visitors.* London, Macmillan, and New York, Viking Press, 1965.
> *The Smaller Sky.* London, Macmillan, 1967.
> *A Winter in the Hills.* London, Macmillan, 1970.

Short Stories

> *Nuncle and Other Stories.* London, Macmillan, 1960; New York, St. Martin's Press, 1961.
> *Death of the Hind Legs and Other Stories.* London, Macmillan, and New York, Viking Press, 1966.
> *The Life Guard.* London, Macmillan, 1971.

Verse

*Mixed Feelings*.   Reading, Berkshire, Reading University School of Art, 1951.
*A Word Carved on a Sill*.   London, Routledge, and New York, St. Martin's Press, 1956.
*Weep Before God: Poems*.   London, Macmillan, and New York, St. Martin's Press,
   1961.
*Wildtrack: A Poem*.   London, Macmillan, and New York, Viking Press, 1965.
*Letters to Five Artists*.   London, Macmillan, 1969; New York, Viking Press, 1970.
*The Shape of Feng*.   London, Covent Garden Press, 1972.


Other

*Preliminary Essays*.   London, Macmillan, and New York, St. Martin's Press, 1957.
*Gerard Manley Hopkins: An Idiom of Desperation*.   London, Oxford University Press,
   and Folcroft, Pennsylvania, Folcroft, 1959.
*Sprightly Running: Part of an Autobiography*.   London, Macmillan, 1962; New York,
   St. Martin's Press, 1963.
*Essays on Literature and Ideas*.   London, Macmillan, and New York, St. Martin's
   Press, 1963.
*The Living World of Shakespeare: A Playgoer's Guide*.   London, Macmillan, and New
   York, St. Martin's Press, 1964.
*Arnold Bennett*.   New York, Columbia University Press, 1967.
*A House for the Truth* (critical essays).   London, Macmillan, 1972.

Editor, *Contemporary Reviews of Romantic Poetry*.   London, Harrap, and New York,
   Barnes and Noble, 1953.
Editor, *Interpretations: Essays on Twelve English Poems*.   London, Routledge, 1955;
   New York, Hillary House, 1957.
Editor, *International Literary Annual*.   London, Calder and Boyars, and New York,
   Criterion Books, 2 vols., 1959, 1960.
Editor, *Fanny Burney's Diary*.   London, Folio Society, 1960.
Editor, *Anthology of Modern Poetry*.   London, Hutchinson, 1963.
Editor, *Selected Shorter Poems of Thomas Hardy*.   London, Macmillan, and New
   York, St. Martin's Press, 1966.
Editor, *The Dynasts*, by Thomas Hardy. , London, Macmillan, and New York,
   St. Martin's Press, 1966.
Editor, *Selected Shorter Stories of Thomas Hardy*.   London, Macmillan, and New
   York, St. Martin's Press, 1966.
Editor, *Shakespeare: Macbeth: A Casebook*.   London, Macmillan, 1968.
Editor, *Shakespeare: Othello: A Casebook*.   London, Macmillan, 1971.


Critical Studies: "John Wain et le Magie de l'Individu" by Françoise Barriere, in *Le Monde*
(Paris), 8 August 1970; "John Wain: Revolte et Neutralité" by Pierre Yvard, in *Etudes
Anglaises* (Paris), October 1970; essay by the author on his own work: "The New Puri-
tanism, The New Academism, The New . . .", in *A House for the Truth*, 1972.


*         *         *


   When, in the middle 1950s, John Wain's fiction first became well-known, he was widely
regarded as a humorist and iconoclast. *Hurry on Down*, a mock-picaresque, became, in
many journalistic accounts, a symbol for the irreverent rootlessness of the younger generation,
making fun of any established social designation. Yet, beneath the irreverence, beneath the

fabric of imagery that invariably reduced an emotion or a high-flown idea to the ordinary or the simply mechanical, images like "his heart lurched over and over in his breast like a cricket ball lobbed along a dry, bumpy pitch," Wain's perspective was that of the man of orthodox common-sense, the defender of a basic human dignity against the absurd pretenses visible in the modern world. Wain's concerns were always moral in fairly standard English terms. Even the figure of despair, the central character of *Living in the Present*, about to commit suicide, decides that he cannot kill himself unless he also rids the world of the most loathsome and immoral creature he knows. Characteristically and appropriately, he chooses a snide, class-conscious Neo-Fascist.

Initially, Wain's central perspective of plain English common-sense and lack of pretense sometimes seemed insular. In his attempts to lampoon the follies of English class-consciousness (the stages of the journey in *Hurry on Down* are magnifications of the various outposts of the English class-system), Wain often attached images of the Continent or of cosmopolitanism to the particular English class-elaboration he was momentarily deriding. The central character of *The Contenders*, whose point of view Wain generally endorses despite some gentle satire, is the rumpled, unheroic, but basically sound and humane provincial who is contrasted to his boyhood friends who reach out for worldly success and lock themselves into inhumane competition. The competitive artist, at one point, even requires a return to his provincial origins in order to regain himself and his talent. Despite a continuing interest in localism, Wain's attitude is far less provincial in his more recent fiction. The Scots nationalist poet, made so false and foolish in *Living in the Present*, becomes the Welsh bard in *A Winter in the Hills*, a character true to himself and his past, almost heroic, and sympathetically connected with Bretons, Canadians, all who would preserve their local humanity in opposition to the contemporary corporate world. Unlike Kingsley Amis, the more militant anti-tourist as well as the smoother and more finished satirist with whose fiction Wain's was often linked in the middle and late fifties, Wain has become less the defender of the English status-quo as his career has progressed, become more seriously, deeply, and intelligently the critic of contemporary English society.

Much of Wain's early comedy was an exaggeration of the uncomfortable, the assaults of badly behaved children, the pains inflicted by sleeping on worn-out bed-springs, the gastronomic rumblings produced by bad food. Beneath this comedy is a sense of the difficulty of survival, of the effort and consciousness necessary to preserve oneself in an intrusive and demanding world. The worst of characters is always the bully, the worst of societies the totalitarian. The comedy of discomfort continues in Wain's most recent fiction, as in a scene in *A Winter in the Hills* in which the central character, abandoned on a mountain by a girl he has unsuccessfully contrived to seduce, is reduced to misery by a long walk in the pouring rain. In this novel, however, the character is more responsible for his own discomfort, is not simply a victim. In addition, in the later fiction, the theme of the preservation of human dignity is deepened and applied to wider areas of individual and social experience. In *The Smaller Sky*, Wain shows his sympathy with the gentle eccentric who seeks only to still the furies in his own brain by living in Paddington station and who is, therefore, persecuted by all the forces of contemporary society that must isolate, reform, or capitalize on the deviant. In *A Winter in the Hills*, the author values both independent bus owner/drivers and poets who can survive by not manipulating or bullying others, who can preserve themselves, even for a short time, in a world where many exist by mutual manipulation. Wain's defenses of the individual's dignity have become deeper, more central to the contemporary world, less vitiated by sentimentality or self-pity.

Wain's central characters have also become more active and, psychologically, more aware of themselves. In his first three novels, the central characters are passive, men who receive the rewards of the prize job or the prize woman because they accidentally or inexplicably don't attempt to bully or manipulate others. Later characters are more complex, recognize the strains of different elements of humanity within themselves, understand darker sides of experience that are not presented melodramatically. The young man in *Strike the Father Dead* experiences consciously all the complicated and ambivalent stresses of revolt from his father. The central character in *A Winter in the Hills* acknowledges the complexities of his guilt at having been the only member of his family to survive World War II and realizes how and why his guilt has helped propel him into a more active engagement with contemporary life. At times, Wain's humor dwells excessively on simplicities: the melodramatic aspects of the discomforts in *Living in the Present*, the repetitiously callow treatments of the psychological in *A Travelling Woman*, the exterior and political simplicities in *The Young Visitors*. Yet more frequently, Wain focuses on man in relationship with others, recognizes, from *A Travelling Woman* on, that human dignity is a quality that must be preserved not only in the defensive terms of the self, but also in active relationships with others. Women change from rewards or "instruments" to people with pasts, convictions, and experiences; children change from abrasive nuisances to people who need understanding and protection; morality grows beyond the mechanics of survival.

Wain's fiction demonstrates a consistent interest in structure. The reader often feels as if the author has begun by asking a general question on the order of "What would it be like to resolve rationally to commit suicide?" or "How and why would a man live entirely within the confines of a large railroad station?"—questions like those one feels central to Arnold Bennett's novels—and has then explored possible ramifications of the question, shaping the elements in the novel to fit. Sometimes, the material in the novel overwhelms the question and the structure collapses under the weight the author places upon it. At other times, however, the structure compresses and unifies the novel, as in *The Smaller Sky* in which the novel builds to an imagistic conjunction of sky, space, and railroad station that effectively depicts the position of a moral and isolated man within the contemporary universe. The reader feels, in Wain's fiction, the struggle for shape, the use of a conscious and intelligent seriousness by a man of letters (Wain is also a distinguished poet and literary critic) to give form to his searching observations and perceptions about ordinary contemporary experience.

—James Gindin

---

**WALKER, David (Harry).** Canadian. Born in Dundee, Scotland, 9 February 1911. Educated at Shrewsbury School, Shropshire, 1924–29; Royal Military College, Sandhurst, Surrey, 1929–30. Married Willa Magee in 1939; has four children. Served in the British Army, in the Black Watch, 1931–47: served in India, 1932–36, and in the Sudan, 1936–38; Aide-de-Camp to the Governor-General of Canada, 1938–39; Prisoner-of-War in France, 1940–45; Instructor at the Staff College, Camberley, Surrey, 1945–46; Comptroller to the Viceroy of India, 1946–47; retired as Major, 1947; M.B.E. (Member, Order of the British Empire), 1946. Full-time Writer since 1947. Member of the Canada Council, 1957–61. Canadian Commissioner, since 1965, and since 1970, Chairman, Roosevelt Campobello International Park Commission. Recipient: Governor-General's Award, 1953, 1954. D.Litt., University of New Brunswick, Fredericton, 1955. Fellow, Royal Society of Literature, 1950. Address: Strathcroix, St. Andrews, New Brunswick, Canada.

PUBLICATIONS

Novels

*The Storm and the Silence*.   Boston, Houghton Mifflin, 1949; London, Cape, 1950.
*Geordie*.   Boston, Houghton Mifflin, and London, Collins, 1950.

*The Pillar*.   Boston, Houghton Mifflin, and London, Collins, 1952.
*Digby*.   London, Collins, and Boston, Houghton Mifflin, 1953.
*Harry Black*.   London, Collins, and Boston, Houghton Mifflin, 1954.
*Where the High Winds Blow*.   London, Collins, and Boston, Houghton Mifflin, 1960.
*Winter of Madness*.   London, Collins, and Boston, Houghton Mifflin, 1964.
*Mallabec*.   London, Collins, and Boston, Houghton Mifflin, 1965.
*Come Back, Geordie*.   London, Collins, and Boston, Houghton Mifflin, 1966.
*Devil's Plunge*.   London, Collins, 1968; as *CAB—Intersec*, Boston, Houghton Mifflin, 1968.
*The Lord's Pink Ocean*.   London, Collins, and Boston, Houghton Mifflin, 1972.

Short Stories

*Storms of Our Journey and Other Stories*.   Boston, Houghton Mifflin, 1962; London, Collins, 1963.

Other

*Sandy Was a Soldier's Boy* (for young people).   London, Collins, and Boston, Houghton Mifflin, 1957.
*Dragon Hill* (for young people).   Boston, Houghton Mifflin, 1962; London, Collins, 1963.
*Pirate Rock* (for young people).   London, Collins, and Boston, Houghton Mifflin, 1969.
*Big Ben* (for young people).   London, Collins, and Boston, Houghton Mifflin, 1970.

David Walker comments:

My novels have been set in Scotland, Germany, India and Canada, countries where I have lived myself.

They have been varied in genre: "Straight" novels—*The Storm and the Silence*; *The Pillar*; *Harry Black*; *Where the High Winds Blow*; *Mallabec*; Fable or fantasy—*Geordie*; *Come Back, Geordie*; *Sandy Was a Soldier's Boy*; Extravagance or diversion—*Digby*; *Winter of Madness*; *Devils Plunge* (*CAB—Intersec*).

The short stories and the young people's books vary a good deal too. The mood dictates style. One thing common to them all, I suppose, is action, which suits me.

The changes of type have simply happened, perhaps partly because I have never found one kind of novel that I would want always to stay with; partly because something different can be something new and alive.

\*       \*       \*

The novels that have established David Walker's reputation are the kind that inspire critical descriptions like the one excerpted on a subsequent bookjacket: "about good, honest people. . . . no unpleasantness—nothing sordid, nothing evil. No desperate situations—no shocking or heart-rending incidents. I enjoyed it. . . ." All of which means that, in books like *Sandy Was a Soldier's Boy* and *Geordie*, the author has willingly spun together, with all the skill of a confectioner making candy floss, the conventional heroics, sentiments, virtues, and aspirations of the middleclass readership he has intended to entertain. The books are sometimes sentimental—which is their way of allowing the intended reader to identify himself in what for him would be utopian circumstances—yet witty, too, which allows the reader at the same time to distance the events from himself and so take an imaginative adventure away from the world he really does live in. The world of the bestseller is a curiously charmed one, not without passion for all its conventionality, fervently optimistic at heart, adventurous in the terms of childhood romance if not in those of the mature intellect, and so always capable of reminding humanity of the ideals of love and happiness to which it pays lipservice.

The trouble is, as David Walker's "serious", "realistic" novels admit, the "decent" world of love and happiness often reveals an obverse face, forcing readers to see that their Arcadian middleclass contentment might just depend for its existence on someone else serving but not enjoying it. To identify with *that* world is less self-congratulatory, for though it does not deny the need to make ethical decisions, it clouds with the ambivalence of dubiety the arenas in which decisions must be made. This is not to say that Walker's serious protagonists are hesitant men; too much of the aura of the Charmed Adventurer carries over from *Geordie* for that to occur. And forthrightness is, in any event, the talent through which the thrilling secrets of a fantasy like *Winter of Madness* or the violent injustices of the war stories like *The Storm and the Silence*, *The Pillar*, and *Harry Black* are surmounted. Increasingly, however, the Calvinist virtues that Walker's society approves of—work, fear, knowledge, and election—are balanced by the vices it recognizes that it causes in the process of applying the virtues: a delight in destruction in the name of competition, a false pride, and a narrow prejudice. Too much of John Buchan lives in Walker's world for happy resolutions not to be possible, but too much of Robert Louis Stevenson's lives also for the brooding of the spirit to be wholly overlooked.

A novel like *The Pillar*, with its half dozen self-centred prisoners of war looking for escape from themselves as much as from any foreign foe, thus probes the nature of personal identity in such a pressing society as much as it relates a conventional narrative. Harry Black comes to recognize "his old friend, . . . his young friend, . . . his true love" only after being alienated, in India, from the limitations of his native culture, and after discovering the meaning of his ethical position in the expansive continental inclusiveness of Indian belief. And Simon Skafe, in Walker's most ambitious book, *Where the High Winds Blow*, single-mindedly sacrificing family and friends to his financial exploitation of the vast Canadian Arctic and his belief in his catalytic necessity to his society, must learn that virility and warlike power over people are not synonymous. He must learn also to appreciate his rebellious, sensitive son's less arbitrary, more artistically provocative insights into the relationship between culture and identity. Above all he must learn to appreciate the Arctic itself, symbol of the ambivalent power of life—"the white depth of sky and sea, immutable and infinite"—and to fashion for himself an individual way to live that sacrifices none of his inimitable energy, does not weaken him, but embraces mortal humanity and so blends with knowledge and power the perspectives of sympathy. In many ways all of Walker's books are variations of that blend—different distillations of gruff belligerence and dour foreboding, muscular ethics and intuitive sensitivities, heart and heartstring, brawn and brain. With genuine wit, flashes of vigorous dialogue, and occasional rhetorical eloquence, he has managed at times to fashion such qualities into human situations instead of puppet shows, and at those times, however briefly, to vivify fictional lives.

—W. H. New

---

**WALKER, Margaret (Abigail).**   American.   Born in Birmingham, Alabama, 7 July 1915. Educated at Northwestern University, Evanston, Illinois, B.A. 1935; University of Iowa, Iowa City, M.A. 1940, Ph.D. 1965; Yale University, New Haven, Connecticut (Ford Fellow),

1954. Married Firnist James Alexander in 1943; has four children. Professor of English, West Virginia State College, Institute, 1942–43, and Livingston College, Salisbury, North Carolina, 1945–46. Since 1949, Professor of English, and since 1968, Director of the Institute for the Study of the History, Life and Culture of Black Peoples, Jackson State College, Mississippi. Recipient: Yale Series of Younger Poets Award, 1942; Rosenthal Fellowship, 1944; Houghton Mifflin Literary Fellowship, 1966. Address: 2205 Guynes Street, Jackson, Mississippi 39213, U.S.A.

PUBLICATIONS

Novels

    *Come Down from Yonder Mountain.*   Toronto, Longman, 1962.
    *Jubilee.*   Boston, Houghton Mifflin, 1965.

Verse

    *For My People.*   New Haven, Connecticut, Yale University Press, 1942.
    *Ballad of the Free.*   Detroit, Broadside Press, 1966.

*         *         *

Authenticating her facts by extensive research, Margaret Walker enlarged the experiences of her great-grandmother during and after slavery into the epic novel *Jubilee*. The heroine, Vyry, is two years old when she enters the story at the childbed death of her twenty-nine-year-old mother, who has borne fifteen slave children in rural Georgia for her master, John Dutton. The fifty-eight chapters are divided into three sections subtitled "The Ante-Bellum Years," "The Civil War Years," and "Reconstruction and Reaction."

The first section, beginning in 1837, introduces ten major characters, half of whom are removed by tragedy before the middle of the novel. The cook, Aunt Sally, irritably singing "mad-mood" songs, is sold. John Dutton, "yelling and cursing in the night," is dispatched by gangrene; and his "nigra"-hating wife, Big Missy Salina, dies ignominiously of a stroke. Young West Pointer Johnny Dutton and his pacifist brother-in-law, Kevin MacDougall, exit heroically but pitifully as war casulties. Old Brother Zeke, the slave preacher who secretly works for the Underground Railroad, succumbs later while a Union Army spy. Three other characters embody vigorous criticism of slavery and war: Lillian, Vyry's gentle white sister, who goes insane after the death of her Kevin and an assault by one of Sheridan's "bummers"; Ed Grimes, the brutal overseer, who lives to exploit his betters; and Randall Ware, proud blacksmith and freeman from birth, whose love for his wife Vyry "just got caught in the times" during his war service.

Of sections II and III, the former, replete with historical and military details, closely reflects the author's research. It introduces Innis Brown, who slowly convinces Vyry to end her seven-year wait for her husband. The title of the Reconstruction section, "Forty Years in the Wilderness," suits the ruinous adventures of Vyry, Innis, and the children building homes in Alabama. Flooded out, exploited in sharecropping, profoundly stricken when burned out by the Ku Klux Klan, Vyry becomes almost pathologically averse to building again. But by innate acts of humanity and racial dignity in Greenville, she inspires whites to help build the family's final home. An amicable understanding ensues between Innis and Randall Ware, who pays a visit with ideas like W.E.B. DuBois's, and with money to educate the children.

The author's Dedication could have addressed her novel "to all the members of my race [not just 'family'] with all my love." The ancestry of almost every Black reader contains its own Vyry, thus revered in Chapter 57:

> She was only a living sign and mark of all the best that any human being could hope to become. In her obvious capacity for love, redemptive and forgiving love, she was alive and standing on the highest peaks of her time and human personality. Peasant and slave, unlettered and untutored, she was nevertheless the best true example of the motherhood of her race, an ever present assurance that nothing could destroy a people whose sons had come from her loins.

Vyry's actions, always credible, deserve that praise.

*Jubilee* is rich with history. Numerous details of slaves' medical and culinary arts, clothing, shelter, and marriages are given. Their legally enforced illiteracy, the planned destruction of their normal affections for one another, their physical oppressions (ranging from the Black Codes to savage plantation punishments and Confederate murders at Andersonville) are depicted. Over a dozen episodes and circumstances reveal the slaves' aggressive feelings: repressed hatreds, aid to abolitionists, revolts, and escapes after 1861 (including all forty-six Dutton field slaves) to take up either guns or tools for the Union Army. Matters transcending their focus in the slavocracy come to the fore: political events, the birth of the Confederacy, the specie crisis, 1863 analyzed as a turning point in the war, the Freedmen's Bureau, and the maneuvered return of White Home Rule.

The author aims at a realistically balanced treatment. The "good whites" are represented by Lillian and Kevin, Doc, the Shackelfords, and nameless abolitionists—Lillian centralizing the tragedy of war and the psychopathy constantly threatening decent slaveholders. Vicious Grimes has no Black counterpart, and the slaveholders perform no noble deeds like Jim's bringing Johnny home to die. Regional balance is implicit in use of the New York draft riots and the indefensible destructiveness of Union soldiers after the end of the fighting.

*Jubilee* is history explicit in the prototypal experience of one slave woman, issuing contemporaneously in what Innis Brown saw as "a wisdom and a touching humility," and ultimately in what the author's speech in 1968 at the National Urban League Conference in New Orleans expresses as follows: "We are still a [Black] people of spirit and soul. We are still fighting in the midst of white American Racism for the overwhelming truth of the primacy of human personality and the spiritual destiny of all mankind."

—James A. Emanuel

---

**WARNER, Rex (Ernest).** British. Born in Birmingham, 9 March 1905. Educated at St. George's School, Harpenden, Hertfordshire; Wadham College, Oxford, B.A. in classics and English literature 1928. Served in the Home Guard, London, 1942–45. Married Frances Chamier Grove in 1929; Barbara, Lady Rothschild, 1949; remarried Frances Chamier Grove, 1966; has four children. Schoolmaster in Egypt and England, 1928–45; worked for the Control Commission in Berlin, 1945; Director, British Institute, Athens, 1945–47. Tallman Professor, Bowdoin College, Brunswick, Maine, 1962–63. Since 1963, Professor of English University of Connecticut, Storrs. Recipient: Black Memorial Prize, 1961. Commander, Royal Order of the Phoenix, Greece, 1963. D.Litt., Rider College, Trenton, New Jersey, 1968. Honorary Member, New England Classical Association. Address: Horse Barn Hill Lane, Storrs, Connecticut 06268, U.S.A.

PUBLICATIONS

Novels

*The Wild Goose Chase.*   London, Boriswood, 1937; New York, Knopf, 1938.
*The Professor.*   London, Boriswood, 1938; New York, Knopf, 1939.
*The Aerodrome.*   London, Lane, 1941; Philadelphia, Lippincott, 1947.
*Why Was I Killed? A Dramatic Dialogue.*   London, Lane, 1943; Philadelphia, Lippin-
    cott, 1944.
*Men of Stones: A Melodrama.*   London, Lane, 1949; Philadelphia, Lippincott, 1950.
*Escapade: A Tale of Average.*   London, Lane, 1953.
*The Young Caesar.*   London, Collins, and Boston, Little Brown, 1958.
*Imperial Caesar.*   London, Collins, and Boston, Little Brown, 1960.
*Pericles the Athenian.*   London, Collins, and Boston, Little Brown, 1963.
*The Converts.*   London, Bodley Head, and Boston, Little Brown, 1967.

Verse

*Poems.*   London, Boriswood, 1937; New York, Knopf, 1938; revised edition, as *Poems
    and Contradictions*, London, Lane, 1945.

Other

*The Kite.*   Oxford, Blackwell, 1936; revised edition, London, Hamish Hamilton,
    1963.
*The English Public Schools.*   London, Collins, 1945.
*The Cult of Power: Essays.*   London, Lane, 1946; Philadelphia, Lippincott, 1947.
*John Milton.*   London, Max Parrish, and New York, Chanticleer Press, 1950.
*Views of Attica and Its Surroundings.*   London, Lehmann, 1950.
*E. M. Forster.*   London, Longman, 1950.
*Men and Gods.*   London, MacGibbon and Kee, 1950; New York, Farrar Straus, 1951.
*Ashes to Ashes: A Post-Mortem on the 1950–51 Tests*, with Lyle Blair.   London,
    MacGibbon and Kee, 1951.
*Greeks and Trojans.*   London, MacGibbon and Kee, 1951.
*Eternal Greece*, with M. Hurlimann.   London, MacGibbon and Kee, 1951; New York,
    Viking Press, 1953.
*Athens.*   London, Thames and Hudson, 1956; New York, Studio Publications, 1957.
*Athens at War: Retold from The History of the Peloponnesian War of Thucydides.*
    London, Bodley Head, 1970; New York, Dutton, 1971.

Editor, with others, *New Poems 1954: A P.E.N. Anthology.*   London, Joseph, 1954.

Translator, *The Medea of Euripides.*   London, Lane, 1944; New York, Chanticleer
    Press, 1949.
Translator, *Prometheus Bound*, by Aeschylus.   London, Lane, 1947; New York,
    Chanticleer Press, 1949.
Translator, *The Persian Expedition*, by Xenophon.   London, Penguin, 1949.
Translator, *Hippolytus*, by Euripides.   London, Lane, and New York, Chanticleer
    Press, 1950.
Translator, *Helen*, by Euripides.   London, Lane, 1951.
Translator, *The Peloponnesian War*, by Thucydides.   London, Penguin, 1954.
Translator, *Fall of the Roman Empire*, by Plutarch.   London, Penguin, 1958.

Translator, *Poems of George Seferis*.   London, Bodley Head, 1960.
Translator, *War Commentaries of Caesar*.   New York, New American Library, 1960.
Translator, *Confessions of St. Augustine*.   New York, New American Library, 1963.
Translator, with Th. D. Frangopoulos, *On the Greek Style: Essays in Poetry and Hellenism*, by George Seferis.   Boston, Little Brown, 1966.
Translator, *History of My Times*, by Xenophon.   London, Penguin, 1967.
Translator, *Moral Essays*, by Plutarch.   London, Penguin, 1971.


Bibliography: in *The Achievement of Rex Warner*, edited by A. L. McLeod, Sydney, Wentworth Press, 1965.


Manuscript Collection: University of Connecticut, Storrs.


Rex Warner comments:

Most of my novels have been in some sense "political"; they have attempted to deal with contemporary problems of power, responsibility, and motivation. But they have not been "realistic". In the early novels, there is always an element of fantasy, but the later historical novels have still been dealing with the same general subjects.

\*        \*        \*

By date of birth (1905), by education, and by accomplishment Rex Warner belongs to that unusual British generation which includes Auden, Isherwood, MacNeice, Aldous Huxley, Spender, Day Lewis, and Empson. That Warner has not been accorded the fame of many of those writers is an accident of publicity, not an indication of inferior merit. In a less cluttered time than ours, one has no question that Warner's stature would have been perceived from the outset and broadcast.

A classical scholar who has translated Aeschylus, Euripides, Thucydides, Xenophon, Caesar, and Plutarch, Warner began his career as a poet with *Poems*; it is our loss that he did not continue as poet. His first novel, *The Wild Goose Chase*, is unusual in English in that it displays the profound influence of the Czech writer, Franz Kafka. Although Auden and Isherwood in their early work indicated that they had read Kafka and some of the German expressionists, Warner's reaction to Kafka is without parallel in British writing unless one goes back to Carlyle's reaction to Goethe and Schiller. Warner's Kafkaesque work was not mere imitation, but an example of an original mind and temperament permeated and released by a profound influence.

Traditionally the English novelist has been concerned almost exclusively with social reality. In *The Wild Goose Chase* Warner writes expressionist allegory, a form quite foreign to the British mind and taste in prose fiction. Warner's unnamed country with its legendary frontier over which men pass at their peril comes directly from Kafka, while the three brothers and their quest for the wild goose, a symbol of man's political and spiritual hope, derive from myth and *Märchen*. Warner differs significantly from Kafka, however, in that Warner can write with humor as well as in Kafka's vein of the grotesque. At the same time Warner's themes are political and ethical, where Kafka's are suffocatingly psychological. *The Wild Goose Chase*, a near masterpiece, is flawed by the conclusion, in which the always tentative construction of reality dissolves into total expressionism, a theatrical resolution that does not in truth resolve the problems so scrupulously posed earlier on.

*The Aerodrome*, by contrast, written in 1941 during the war, is virtually unflawed. Kafka's influence is still discernible, but now it is totally assimilated and subordinated to a voice that is Warner's unchallenged own. The events of *The Aerodrome* simply relate the effects upon the villagers of the location of a flying field near their village. The villagers are exploited by the ruthlessness of the commanding Air Vice-Marshal, as in turn they are inevitably corrupted. Still writing in a nether region between the Kafkaesque and the realistic, Warner dramatizes the truism that war corrupts all whom it touches, while he does not fall into the expressionistic excesses of his first novel. Warner dominates any tendency to mannerism by intellectual control, and by his adaptation of a plot reminiscent of Greek myth and drama. Narrative economy and Greek directness allow him to write of subjects that in other hands often seem banal: love, hope, suffering, faith, endurance. The narrator's final words typify the qualities of the whole: "'That the world may be clean.' I remembered my father's words. Clean indeed it was and most intricate, fiercer than tigers, wonderful and infinitely forgiving." *The Aerodrome* finally is a novel of ideas presented directly and dramatically. With his conviction of the pathos in the discrepancy between goodness and simplicity, and the necessary corruption of war, Warner achieves tragedy. No better novel appeared in English in the period between 1930 and 1970.

Warner's three novels, *The Professor*, *Why Was I Killed?*, and *Men of Stones* form a second category in his work. They resemble *The Aerodrome* in theme in that they are political and ethical, but their range is narrower, and each novel is more fully determined by style and intellectual control than by imagination and inventiveness. They are lesser only in contrast to Warner's finest work however; in no sense are they negligible.

By the late 1950's, Warner launched into his third period as novelist in those narratives based upon historical themes. In *The Young Caesar*, *Imperial Caesar*, or *Pericles the Athenian*, one may see the classical scholar and translator as opposed to the young Warner who invented his own sources. Warner's historical novels, that is, are valuable for their insights into classical Athens and Rome, but as works of the imagination they are inferior to his early work. Either the historical novelist is bound by his materials, or if he distorts or ignores them, he offends as frivolous. Warner's historical scholarship is impeccable, but his tendency to the expository, present throughout his career, dominates in his third phase. The historical novels emphasize other qualities apparent from the outset in Warner's work: the fact that he possesses an historical view of reality, and that his first allegiance is to rationality. That alone may account for his relative lack of popularity, for as the twentieth century grows older, it becomes anti-historical and anti-rational.

Given Warner's range and special kind of intelligence (and here his essays, *The Cult of Power*, must not be ignored), given his splendid style, the clear product of his work in classics in its elaborateness, its clarity, and its suppleness, one must believe that as long as men honor rationality even slightly, Warner will be read. Certainly *The Aerodrome* must survive, and if later generations sort out our contemporary clutter, Rex Warner will be assured his proper place.

—John McCormick

**WARNER, Sylvia Townsend.** British. Born in Harrow, Middlesex, 6 December 1893. Privately educated. Member of the Editorial Committee of *Tudor Church Music* (Oxford University Press). Contributor to *The New Yorker* since 1935. Fellow, Royal Society of Literature, 1967; Honorary Member, American Academy of Arts and Letters, 1972. Address: c/o Chatto and Windus Ltd., 40 William IV Street, London W.C.2, England.

## Publications

### Novels

*Lolly Willowes; or, The Loving Huntsman.*   London, Chatto and Windus, and New York, Viking Press, 1926.
*Mr. Fortune's Maggot.*   London, Chatto and Windus, and New York, Viking Press, 1927.
*The True Heart.*   London, Chatto and Windus, and New York, Viking Press, 1929.
*Summer Will Show.*   London, Chatto and Windus, and New York, Viking Press, 1936.
*After the Death of Don Juan.*   London, Chatto and Windus, 1938; New York, Viking Press, 1939.
*The Corner That Held Them.*   London, Chatto and Windus, and New York, Viking Press, 1948.
*The Flint Anchor.*   London, Chatto and Windus, and New York, Viking Press, 1954.

### Short Stories

*Some World Far from Ours, and Stay, Corydon, Thou Swain.*   London, Mathews, 1929.
*Elinor Barley.*   London, Cresset Press, and Chicago, Argus, 1930.
*Moral Ending and Other Stories.*   London, Joiner and Steele, 1931.
*The Salutation.*   London, Chatto and Windus, and New York, Viking Press, 1932.
*More Joy in Heaven and Other Stories.*   London, Cresset Press, 1935.
*Twenty-four Stories*, with Graham Greene and James Laver.   London, Cresset Press, 1939.
*The Cat's Cradle Book.*   New York, Viking Press, 1940; London, Chatto and Windus, 1960.
*A Garland of Straw and Other Stories.*   London, Chatto and Windus, 1943; as *A Garland of Straw: Twenty-Eight Stories*, New York, Viking Press, 1943.
*The Museum of Cheats: Stories.*   London, Chatto and Windus, and New York, Viking Press, 1947.
*Winter in the Air and Other Stories.*   London, Chatto and Windus, 1955; New York, Viking Press, 1956
*A Spirit Rises: Short Stories.*   London, Chatto and Windus, and New York, Viking Press, 1962.
*A Stranger with a Bag and Other Stories.*   London, Chatto and Windus, 1966; as *Swans on an Autumn River: Stories,* New York, Viking Press, 1966.
*The Innocent and the Guilty.*   London, Chatto and Windus, 1971.

### Verse

*The Espalier.*   London, Chatto and Windus, and New York, Viking Press, 1925.
*Time Importuned.*   London, Chatto and Windus, and New York, Viking Press, 1928.
*Opus 7: A Poem.*   London, Chatto and Windus, and New York, Viking Press, 1931.
*Whether a Dove or Seagull: Poems*, with Valentine Ackland.   New York, Viking Press, 1933; London, Chatto and Windus, 1934.
*Boxwood*, with Reynolds Stone.   London, Chatto and Windus-Cape, 1960.

### Other

*The Portrait of a Tortoise: Extracted from the Journals and Letters of Gilbert White.* London, Chatto and Windus, 1946.

*Somerset*.   London, Elek, 1949.
*Jane Austen*.   London, Longman, 1951.
*T. H. White: A Biography*.   London, Cape, 1967; New York, Viking Press, 1968.

Editor, *The Week-end Dickens*.   London, Maclehouse, 1932.

Translator, *By Way of Saint-Beuve*, by Marcel Proust,   London, Chatto and Windus,
   1958; as *On Art and Literature, 1896–1917*, New York, Dell, 1964.
Translator, *A Place of Shipwreck*, by Jean René Huguenin.   London, Chatto and
   Windus, 1963.


                                    *       *       *


Sylvia Townsend Warner began life as a poet; in her later years she has come to be known
best for her adroit and sensitive short stories. She has not published a novel since 1954; in
fact her latest major work was not fiction but a biography of a novelist—T. H. White. Yet
it is on the seven novels of her middle years that her enduring reputation is likely to rest.
From the fantasy of the first one, *Lolly Willowes*, to the sober realism of *The Flint Anchor*,
her last, there has been an interesting progression. While all are touched with the poet's
imagination and the insights of a quizzical and independent mind, the trend away from
playfulness toward a more solid confrontation with the world's realities is noticeable.

Through two of its three parts, "fantasy" is a misnomer for *Lolly Willowes*. It is a gently
realistic story, touched with irony, of a spinster living at the mercy of her circle of loving
relations in London's domestic exurbia during the first quarter of this century. A sentence
early in the book gives an unmistakable literary clue: "There is nothing more endangering
to a young woman's normal inclination towards young men than an intimacy with a man
twice her own age." We are clearly confronted with Jane Austen: characters, setting, tone
of voice proclaim a Janeite. But the likeness goes only so far. In Part Three the gentle Aunt
Lolly escapes to live alone in a village in the Chiltern hills, where strange doings soon become
evident. The story passes so naturally into the occult that one goes along with it unquestion-
ingly. The scene in which a kitten becomes the agent for Lolly's metamorphosis into a
witch is one of those magical moments of revelation that Joyce called "Epiphanies". The
book's subtitle is "The Loving Huntsman". Lolly's encounters and dialogue with the
Prince of Darkness are more than fantasy: they make his historic cult plausible in psychological terms.

*Mr. Fortune's Maggot* is pure enchantment. Timothy Fortune, ex-bank clerk, has spent
ten years as a South Seas missionary when the maggot impels him to go on "a sort of pious
escapade"—assignment to a small island where a white man is a rarity. His three-year
encounter with the innocents of that carefree paradise produces only one convert, the youth
Lueli, who loves him. But it produces in Mr. Fortune a change of heart that is shattering.
Beautifully imagined, told with the driest of wise humour, touching and droll by turns, it
elaborates the theme that "we can never love anything without messing it about". The
moment when Mr. Fortune carves a new idol for Lueli, to replace the one he had made him
destroy, is another epiphany. The latent homosexuality of the tie between the missionary
and the boy is cheerfully taken for granted, ahead of its literary time, as it was to be taken
again, to more serious purpose, in *The Flint Anchor*. To suggest *South Wind* as an analogue
for *Mr. Fortune's Maggot* has only the slightest relevance. For many readers it will remain
Miss Townsend Warner's best-loved work.

The next three novels were all in a sense exploratory. They opened new ground, even if
they fell short of a new revelation; and they gained in seriousness with only a little loss of
sheer delight. The most ambitious of these three is the middle one, *Summer Will Show*.
Sophia Willoughby, discontent with a life of county gentility, goes to Paris in search of
personal freedom and incidentally of her errant husband. She finds instead an affinity with
his Polish mistress—who carries her to the barricades in the 1848 Revolution. A somewhat

equivocal attitude toward her spoiled heroine, or call it a failure to make her intentions clear, may account for a sense of implausibility. But if taken as a kind of political fantasy, the book is interesting as evidence of an increased social involvement on the part of this author, too often regarded as unworldly. Of the other two novels of this period, *The True Heart* also looked back into the past century, this time for a glimpse of how a little country cat, from Essex, might look at the Queen in London; and *After the Death of Don Juan* applied fantasy to create a sardonic sequel to the Don Juan legend in a vividly imagined Spanish scene. These, too, carried between the lines a strong element of social criticism.

Nine years were to pass, in which she was clearly gathering her forces, before the appearance of Miss Townsend Warner's masterwork, *The Corner That Held Them*. She has acknowledged that she prefers it to anything else she has written, and feels it the most entirely her own work. There is no fantasy here; only a devoted and unsentimentalized reconstruction of a scene and a way of life, authenticated by the conviction it carries.

The scene is northeast Norfolk, with its moorlands, water meadows, causeways, and little rivers running to the sea; the way of life is that of the Benedictine priory of Oby and of the nearby manor and its peasantry, in Catholic England of the Fourteenth Century. It was the time of the Black Death and later of John Ball's Peasants' Revolt. Against this background, and touched by these events even in its own cloistered corner, the daily life of Oby goes on. Nuns come and go, the good with the bad, each with her personal story; their abbesses round out the cycles of the years; they work at their gilded altar-cloths; struggle for their dream of a new bell tower, see it realized only to be destroyed "by the judgment of God", and struggle on. Their resident priest, with his ambiguous past, supplies a dramatic role; their visitors, and their missions outside, bring news of passing events. As the story, never static, moves forward over half a century, the sense of change wrought by time is beautifully conveyed. Oby's financial difficulties increase in the midst of the Church's enormous wealth and power; its patronage declines; its troubles with the hierarchy multiply; respect for the rule diminishes in the restlessness of the times. One sees in this microcosm a phase of the ongoing revolution—a phase that was not to be completed in England for nearly two hundred years.

Yet readers today, without the author's recent comment, might not be aware that the book was written from a particularized point of view: "It developed from a conversation about the Marxist approach to history, in the course of which it occurred to me that the Marxist approach had never got its teeth into the religious life—a sitting target for it." This adds a dimension to the reading, without changing its other literary values: it is a moving, frequently dramatic, always discerning view of a group of living individuals in a recognizable scene six centuries ago. It is written without any of the trappings of romance: motives, emotions, even speech, which eschews antiquarianism and quaint dialect, seem wholly of today. Comparison with a novel written 20 years later about an English nunnery functioning 600 years later than Oby—Rumer Godden's *In This House of Brede*—is illuminating in its parallels as well as in the difference of ends to which such strikingly similar material can be put.

*The Flint Anchor* rounds off the progression imposingly, if not with quite so much warmth and conviction as before. "Round about 1800," says Miss Townsend Warner, "my great-great-grandfather, John Warner, married a Miss Townsend. They had a son, and soon after his birth the young bride went back to her father's house. Nothing more is known of John Warner, because his memory was obliterated under the statement that he was a wicked young man who must never be spoken of." That mystery was the germ of the novel. In the book as it developed, however, it became only one climactic episode which activates a larger theme: the deadening weight of possessions, class, and conformity upon the free spirit of man. Essentially, the story is more concerned with the young bride's father—once a fancy-free young man in a seaport town (again in Norfolk), who is forced to become a stern paterfamilias and member of the Establishment. Rich with its assorted characters, the book has ample wit and high spirits and "period" charm along with its tragedy; but the total effect is sombre like the flint of its emblematic anchor.

Miss Townsend Warner writes always in a style of subtle distinction and preciseness. It is often musical, like her poetry, and music plays a role in most of her books. It is surely of significance that she had an early love affair with musicology, and shared the editing of the standard ten-volume work on Tudor church music.

—Marshall A. Best

---

**WARREN, Robert Penn.** American. Born in Guthrie, Kentucky, 24 April 1905. Educated at Guthrie High School; Vanderbilt University, Nashville, Tennessee, B.A. (summa cum laude) 1925; University of California, Berkeley, M.A. 1927; Yale University, New Haven, Connecticut, 1927–28; Oxford University (Rhodes Scholar), B.Litt. 1930. Married Emma Brescia in 1930 (divorced, 1950); Eleanor Clark, *q.v.*, 1952; has two children. Assistant Professor, Southwestern College, Memphis, Tennessee, 1930–31, and Vanderbilt University, 1931–34; Assistant and Associate Professor, Lousiana State University, Baton Rouge, 1934–42; Professor of English, University of Minnesota, Minneapolis, 1942–50. Professor of Playwriting. 1950–56, and since 1962, Professor of English, Yale University. Member of the Fugutive Group of poets: Co-Founding Editor, *The Fugitive*, Nashville, 1922–25. Founding Editor, *Southern Review*, Baton Rouge, Louisiana, 1935–42. Consultant in Poetry, Library of Congress, Washington, D.C., 1944–45. Recipient: Caroline Sinkler Award, 1936, 1937, 1938; Levinson Prize, *Poetry*, Chicago, 1936; Houghton Mifflin Literary Fellowship, 1939; Guggenheim Fellowship, 1939, 1947; Shelley Memorial Award, 1943; Pulitzer Prize, for fiction, 1947, for poetry, 1958; Robert Meltzer Award, Screen Writers Guild, 1949; Union League Civic and Arts Foundation Prize, *Poetry*, Chicago, 1953; Sidney Hillman Prize, 1957; Edna St. Vincent Millay Memorial Prize, 1958; National Book Award, for poetry, 1958; Van Doren Award, *New York Herald-Tribune*, 1965; Bollingen Prize, for poetry, 1967; National Endowment for the Arts grant, 1968; Henry A. Bellaman Prize, 1970; Van Wyck Brooks Award, for poetry, 1970; National Medal for Literature, 1970. D.Litt., University of Louisville, Kentucky, 1949; Kenyon College, Gambier, Ohio, 1952; University of Kentucky, Lexington, 1955; Colby College, Waterville, Maine, 1956; Swarthmore College, Pennsylvania, 1958; Yale University, 1959; Fairfield University, Connecticut, 1969; Wesleyan University, Middletown, Connecticut, 1970; LL.D., Bridgeport University, Connecticut, 1965. Member, American Academy of Arts and Letters. Address: 2495 Redding Road, Fairfield, Connecticut 06430, U.S.A.

PUBLICATIONS

Novels

> *Night Rider*. Boston, Houghton Mifflin, 1939; London, Eyre and Spottiswoode, 1940.
> *At Heaven's Gate*. New York, Harcourt Brace, and London, Eyre and Spottiswoode, 1943.
> *All the King's Men*. New York, Harcourt Brace, 1946; London, Eyre and Spottiswoode, 1948.
> *World Enough and Time: A Romantic Novel*. New York, Random House, 1950; London, Eyre and Spottiswoode, 1951.
> *Band of Angels*. New York, Random House, 1955; London, Eyre and Spottiswoode, 1956.

*The Cave.*  New York, Random House, and London, Eyre and Spottiswoode, 1959.
*Wilderness: A Tale of the Civil War.*  New York, Random House, 1961; London, Eyre and Spottiswoode, 1962.
*Flood: A Romance of Our Times.*  New York, Random House, and London, Collins, 1964.
*Meet Me in the Green Glen.*  New York, Random House, 1971.

## Short Stories

*Blackberry Winter.*  Cummington, Massachusetts, Cummington Press, 1946.
*The Circus in the Attic and Other Stories.*  New York, Harcourt Brace, 1947; London, Eyre and Spottiswoode, 1952.

## Plays

*Proud Flesh* (in verse, produced Minneapolis, 1947; revised [prose] version, produced New York, 1948).
*All the King's Men* (produced New York, 1959).  New York, Random House, 1960.

## Verse

*Thirty-Six Poems.*  New York, Alcestis Press, 1935.
*Eleven Poems on the Same Theme.*  New York, New Directions, 1942.
*Selected Poems, 1923–1943.*  New York, Harcourt Brace, 1944; London, Fortune Press, 1951.
*Brother to Dragons: A Tale in Verse and Voices.*  New York, Random House, 1953; London, Eyre and Spottiswoode, 1954.
*Promises: Poems, 1954–1956.*  New York, Random House, 1957; London, Eyre and Spottiswoode, 1959.
*You, Emperors and Others: Poems, 1957–1960.*  New York, Random House, 1960.
*Selected Poems: New and Old, 1923–1966.*  New York, Random House, 1966.
*Incarnations: Poems, 1966–1968.*  New York, Random House, 1968; London, W. H. Allen, 1970.
*Audubon: A Vision.*  New York, Random House, 1969.

## Other

*John Brown: The Making of a Martyr.*  New York, Payson and Clark, 1929.
*I'll Take My Stand: The South and the Agrarian Tradition*, with others.  New York, Harper, 1930.
*Understanding Poetry: An Anthology for College Students*, with Cleanth Brooks.  New York, Holt, 1938; revised edition, 1950, 1960.
*Understanding Fiction*, with Cleanth Brooks.  New York, Crofts, 1943; revised edition, Appleton Century Crofts, 1959.
*A Poem of Pure Imagination: An Experiment in Reading*, in *The Rime of the Ancient Mariner*, by Samuel Taylor Coleridge.  New York, Reynal and Hitchcock, 1946.
*Modern Rhetoric: With Readings*, with Cleanth Brooks.  New York, Harcourt Brace, 1949; revised edition, 1958.
*Fundamentals of Good Writing: A Handbook of Modern Rhetoric*, with Cleanth Brooks.  New York, Harcourt Brace, 1950; London, Dobson, 1952; revised edition, Dobson, 1956.

*Segregation: The Inner Conflict in the South*.  New York, Random House, 1956;
   London, Eyre and Spottiswoode, 1957.
*Remember the Alamo!*  New York, Random House, 1958.
*Selected Essays*.  New York, Random House, 1958; London, Eyre and Spottiswoode,
   1964.
*The Gods of Mount Olympus*.  New York, Random House, 1959; London, Muller,
   1962.
*The Legacy of the Civil War: Meditations on the Centennial*.  New York, Random
   House, 1961.
*Who Speaks for the Negro?*  New York, Random House, 1965.
*Homage to John Dreiser*.  New York, Random House, 1971.

Editor, with Cleanth Brooks and J. T. Purser, *An Approach to Literature: A Collection
   of Prose and Verse with Analyses and Discussions*.  Baton Rouge, Louisiana State
   University Press, 1936; revised edition, New York, Crofts, 1939, Appleton Century
   Crofts, 1952.
Editor, *A Southern Harvest: Short Stories by Southern Writers*.  Boston, Houghton
   Mifflin, 1937.
Editor, with Cleanth Brooks, *Anthology of Stories from the Southern Review*.  Baton
   Rouge, Louisiana State University Press, 1953.
Editor, with Albert Erskine, *Short Story Masterpieces*.  New York, Dell, 1954.
Editor, with Albert Erskine, *Six Centuries of Great Poetry*.  New York, Dell, 1955.
Editor, with Albert Erskine, *A New Southern Harvest*.  New York, Bantam, 1957.
Editor, with Allen Tate, *Selected Poems by Denis Devlin*.  New York, Holt Rinehart,
   1963.
Editor, *Faulkner: A Collection of Critical Essays*.  New York, Prentice Hall, 1967.
Editor, *Selected Poems of Herman Melville*.  New York, Random House, 1971.
Editor, *Selected Poems of John Greenleaf Whittier*.  New York, Random House, 1971.

Bibliography: *Robert Penn Warren* by M. N. Huff, New York, David Lewis, 1968.

Manuscript Collection: Beinecke Library, Yale University, New Haven, Connecticut.

Critical Studies: *Modern Poetry and the Tradition* by Cleanth Brooks, Chapel Hill, Uni-
versity of North Carolina Press, 1939; *Robert Penn Warren* by Klaus Poenicke, Heidelberg,
1959; *The Fugitive Group* by Louise Cowan, Baton Rouge, Louisiana State University
Press, 1959; *Fugitives' Return*, edited by Rob Roy Purdy, Nashville, Tennessee, Vanderbilt
University Press, 1959; *Robert Penn Warren: The Dark and Bloody Ground* by Leonard
Casper, Seattle, University of Washington Press, 1960; *The Faraway Country* by Louis
Rubin, Seattle, University of Washington Press, 1963; *The Hidden God* by Cleanth Brooks,
New Haven, Connecticut, Yale University Press, 1963; *Robert Penn Warren*, edited by John
Longley, New York, New York University Press, 1964; *Robert Penn Warren* by Charles
H. Bohner, New York, Twayne, 1964; *The Burden of Time* by John L. Stewart, Princeton,
New Jersey, Princeton University Press, 1965; *A Colder Fire* by Victor Strandberg, Lexing-
ton, University of Kentucky Press, 1965.

*       *       *

Robert Penn Warren may well be America's most distinguished man of letters now at work.
He has produced nine novels, a collection of short stories, several volumes of poetry, at
least one play, and many essays on literary, sociological, and moral subjects, and he was one
of the founding editors of *The Southern Review*, the leading literary journal of the 1930's
in the United States. In each of these genres he has done distinguished work. Though

younger than some of the others, he was one of the original New Critics and largely responsible for the dissemination of their ideas to generations of students and teachers in the colleges and universities of the United States through a series of textbooks (e.g. *Understanding Fiction*) which he produced in collaboration with Cleanth Brooks and others. Since Faulkner's death Warren has certainly been the most influential novelist from the southern states. Although he studied at the University of California, at Yale, and as a Rhodes Scholar at Oxford, and has lived away from the South for many years, his work bears the marks of his origins. But his Southern credentials are not pure. He was born in Kentucky, a state which remained loyal to the Union, and received his early schooling in Tennessee, one of the last states to secede as well as one of the first to be reunited with the North. In a word, Warren is a border southerner, and his fiction reflects the division implicit in the term. His subject matter is strongly regional but his treatment of it objective and analytical.

A more particular influence, which did much to shape the pattern of Warren's system of values, was exerted by the Fugitives, a group of poets including Allen Tate, John Crowe Ransom, Andrew Lytle, named after the journal in which they published their poetry at Vanderbilt University in Nashville, Tennessee, from 1922 to 1925. "In a very important way," Warren has said, "that group was my education." It taught him that poetry was a vital activity, related to ideas and to life. Later, as he recalled, it taught him more specifically "how literature can be related to place and history." The famous Scopes Trial of 1925, testing a Tennessee law against the teaching of evolutionary theories in public schools, had polarized the cultural contrast between North and South. In a collection of essays entitled *I'll Take My Stand*, Warren and his friends defended the Southern point of view—Southern agrarianism against the encroachment of Northern Industrialism, the contemplative life of the soul against materialism and its servants, science and rationalism. Some of their general principles continued to color Warren's thought and are reflected in his fiction. But he greatly revised his early view of the race problem. His contribution to *I'll Take My Stand* had been a defence of segregation. He had written the essay as a young man abroad, at the very time when he began writing fiction. And the way he later described that moment says a great deal about the impulse behind his fiction. He recalled the discomfort, the sense of evasion he experienced in writing the essay and, on the other hand, the free feeling, the "holiday sense" of writing his first novelette, "Prime Leaf." In the essay he had been "trying to prove something," in the narrative "to find out something, see something, feel something." When he had returned home he had soon realized that his views of segregation had changed: "it wasn't being outside the South that made me change my mind," he recalled later. "It was coming back home." And trying to write fiction—this, too, had made him change his mind, for in writing fiction "you can't allow yourself as much evasion as in trying to write essays." What Warren's backward glance projects with great clarity is the process of scrupulous exploration always behind his fiction and often dramatized by it—this and the light derived from going away and coming back, from contemplating native scenes with a mind schooled by distance. What it suggests is the rigorous discipline, conceptual and formal, which writing fiction is for him and which makes him the superb technician he is.

Warren has always been a reader of history, and his fiction reflects this interest. But he does not write historical novels. Although he has confessed to a romantic interest in the objects of American history, the focus of his novels is not on trappings but on issues. Much of his fiction starts from history. What he looks for in stories are actual events which have caught the public eye because, as he has said, they project "issues in purer form than they come to one ordinarily." Thus *Night Rider* deals with the Kentucky tobacco wars of 1909; *At Heaven's Gate* incorporates the case of a political murder which took place in Nashville in the 1920's; the Willie Stark of *All the King's Men* owes a great deal to the Louisiana politician Huey Long who was assassinated in 1935; *World Enough and Time* closely follows the so-called Kentucky Tragedy, a celebrated murder case of 1825 as well as certain political controversies of the period; *Band of Angels* and *Wilderness* reflect events of the Civil War; *The Cave* starts from a much publicized accident of the 1920's. In its historicity Warren's fiction has something in common with the fiction of Dos Passos; but whereas Dos Passos focussed primarily on the political issues of his own times, contemporaneity is less important to Warren and his focus is moral and philosophical. Indeed, as he wrote in his essay on Conrad's *Nostromo*, Warren finds his own definition of the philosophical novelist as

> one for whom the documentation of the world is constantly striving to rise to the level of generalization about values, . . . for whom images always fall into a dialectical configuration, for whom the urgency of experience, no matter how vividly and strongly experience may enchant, is the urgency to know the meaning of experience. This is not to say that the philosophical novelist is schematic and deductive. It is to say quite the contrary, that he is willing to go naked into the pit, again and again, to make the same old struggle for his truth.

The transformation of fact into symbol is of course what distinguishes fiction or, in Aristotle's sense, poetry from history. And the general emphasis on moral values distinguishes Warren from Dos Passos, who remains closer to history and its accidents, as a comparison of *All the King's Men* with *Number One*, Dos Passos' version of the Huey Long story, would demonstrate. In Warren the truth struggled for is larger than in Dos Passos; it embraces a wider spectrum of human experience; and it produces characters more fully developed, more seen in the round.

The struggle for truth in Warren's fiction also produces form and style. His first book, a historical study entitled *John Brown: The Making of a Martyr*, already exemplifying the transformation of history into something else, gave him the type of his central figure—the idealist corrupted by his dieal. He is exemplified in novel after novel: by Percy Munn, the hollow man of *Night Rider*, by Slim Sarrett of *At Heaven's Gate*, by Willie Stark of *All the King's Men*, by Jeremiah Beaumont of *World Enough and Time*, by Adam Rosenzweig, the Bavarian Jew of *Wilderness*, who comes to America to fight for freedom on the Union side and stumbles into the "crime of monstrous inhumanity." But if the imaginative exploration of historical fact in *John Brown* rendered moral knowledge, in the novels that process is not only reproduced; it is made into a structural principle. It leads to Warren's characteristic experimentation with narrators and commentators, with the juxtaposition of past and present, and with the ironic parallels between main plots and illustrative parables (e.g. the story of Cass Mastern in *All the King's Men*). The very action of some of the novels consists in the exploration of the meaning of the events in which the narrators have participated. Frequently the narrator-protagonists are in quest of their own identities. Some are more perceptive than others; but whether we share their gradual illumination (as in *All the King's Men* and *Flood*) or learn by being made aware of their benightedness and confusion (as in *Night Rider* and *World Enough and Time*), the process always leads to the recognition of values, of moral wisdom. Warren always directs us to set our sights beyond historical fact on poetic truth.

One is tempted to say that the truth Warren aims at is none other than the eternal verities of the human heart Faulkner regarded as the novelist's great charge. The two writers have much in common. They are united in their awareness of history, in their devotion to the South, even if not to the same corner of it. They are united also in their experimentation with narrative structure, voice, and point of view. But unlike the protagonists of Faulkner's most successful novels, Warren's often serve as raisonneurs. As a result the skeleton of abstraction is in Warren more visible through the skin and flesh of fact. And yet the escape from naturalism into a kind of humanism is in Warren very much the same as in Faulkner. Indeed, what Warren said of his fellow Southerner applies to himself: although he, too, portrays his region and its history in vivid detail, he, too, claims our particular attention for "the world he creates out of the materials of the world he presents." He too uses "history" as parable and as raw material for the creation of another, less changeable realm.

—Christof Wegelin

**WATEN, Judah (Leon).**   Australian.   Born in Odessa, Russia, 29 July 1911. Educated at Christian Brothers College, Perth; University High School, Melbourne. Married Hyrell McKinnon Ross in 1945; has one daughter. Former Public Servant: worked for the Australian Postal and Taxation departments. Member of the Committee, Fellowship of Australian Writers, since 1950. Since 1966, Reviewer for *The Age*, Melbourne, and, since 1970 for the *Sydney Morning Herald*. Recipient: *Sydney Morning Herald* Short Story Prize, 1947; Commonwealth Literary Fellowship, 1952, 1970; Melbourne Moomba Festival Award, 1965. Address: 1 Byron Street, Box Hill, Melbourne, Victoria 3128, Australia.

PUBLICATION

Novels

> *The Unbending*.   Sydney, Australasian Book Society, 1954.
> *Shares in Murder*.   Sydney, Australasian Book Society, 1957.
> *Time of Conflict*.   Sydney, Australasian Book Society, 1961.
> *Distant Land*.   Melbourne, Cheshire, and London, Angus and Robertson, 1964.
> *Season of Youth*.   Melbourne, Cheshire, 1966.
> *So Far No Further*.   Melbourne, Wren, 1971.

Short Stories

> *Alien Son*.   Sydney, Angus and Robertson, 1952; London, Angus and Robertson, and New York, Anglobooks, 1953.

Uncollected Short Stories

> "Read Politics, Son", in *Australia Writes: An Anthology*.   Canberra, Cheshire, 1956.
> "His Only Love", in *Coast to Coast 1961*.   Sydney, Angus and Robertson, 1961.
> "Three Generations", in *Caravan*.   London and New York, Yoseloff, 1961.
> "The Knife", in *Two Ways Meet: Stories by Migrants*.   Melbourne, Cheshire, 1963.
> "Love and Rebellion", in *Australian Pavements*.   Melbourne, Lansdowne Press, 1964.

Other

> *From Odessa to Odessa: The Journey of an Australian Writer*.   Melbourne, Cheshire, 1969.
> *The Dour Decade: The 1930's*.   Melbourne, Cheshire, 1971.

> Editor, with Victor G. O'Connor, *Twenty Great Australian Stories*.   Melbourne, Dolphin, 1946.

> Translator, *Between Sky and Sea*, by Herz Bergner.   Melbourne, Dolphin, 1946.

Critical Study: "Three Realists in Search of Reality" by David Martin, in *On Native Grounds*, Sydney, Angus and Robertson, 1968.

Judah Waten comments:

I think I am one of the first novelists and short story writers in Australia to write about foreign migrants, from the inside of a foreign community as well as being a member of the wider Australian community and having grown up in Australia.

My first published book, *Alien Son*, a collection of short stories about migrant life in a small town with the same main characters, was considered an original contribution to Australian literature and also, in the words of the critic of the *Sydney Morning Herald* in 1952, "a study of the problems of migrants, problems that may touch tens of thousands of New Australians today and also the Old Australians who meet them".

A considerable part of my work is about Jewish immigrants struggling to adapt them-selves to Australia.

I should like to think that the *Times Literary Supplement* was right, on September 21, 1962, when it said that I was "a sensitive and humane novelist" and that I had made "an alien group part of Australian writing".

The *TLS* also suggested that behind my concepts of the novel and the short story "lies not the Anglo-American tradition followed by most Australian writers but the traditions of the French and Russian novelists, particularly that of Gogol, of Chekhov, and of Tolstoy". The *TLS* added that I had the sort of command of English that comes from learning it early in life and using it most of the time as my principal language.

A new novel, *So Far No Further*, deals with Jewish and Italian post-war migrants who become prosperous and send their children to the university.

\*         \*         \*

Judah Waten's fiction is usually related to two developments in Australian writing after the Second World War: the conscious effort of "social realist" writers to continue what they saw as the local tradition of proletarian "protest" literature, and the emergence of fiction concerned with the experience of European migrants in their new country. Waten's novels are too varied, however, to be fully covered by these labels.

He first established his reputation as a writer of short stories, especially with the *Alien Son* cycle organized around the theme of the conflicts experienced by European Jewish migrants and their children who are growing up in a strange new culture. In his novels, Waten's experience as a short story writer is apparent from the way he structures his narratives in a series of short scenes, a number of which could be extracted as self-contained episodes.

The first novel, *The Unbending*, retains the best qualities of the *Alien Son* stories—a gently humorous understanding of his migrants' problems and a delicacy in the presentation of the younger generation's cultural conflicts—and combines these with a compelling narrative pace. It opens with the dandified Russian Jew Solomon Kochansky arriving in Australia and settling, against his expectations, into a country town as a hawker. The dashing of Kochansky's high hopes, the education of his son Moses, the impact of the First World War and the conflicts between a conservative society and the International Workers of the World over conscription are the personal and political themes Waten integrates skilfully. The historic conflict over conscription is interesting in itself and it allows him to suggest a significance that goes beyond this small community.

*Shares in Murder* adapts the conventions of the detective thriller for its own purposes. Based on an actual murder case, it explores Melbourne's underworld with a convincing sense of careful documentation lying behind the relationship it discloses between organized crime and respectability. By turning the conventions he adopts on their heads, Waten implies that in a society as corrupt as contemporary Melbourne crime does pay.

*Time of Conflict* again presents historic events, but on a more extended scale and in a more overtly political way than in *The Unbending*. The early struggles of Nick Anderson to make his way in the world with the boxing skills he acquires in reform school, his travels, and his involvement with strikers during the depression are narrated compellingly. But the last third of the novel, concerned with Communist Party politics during the Second World War, strains both structure and characterization because it lacks the integration of dramatic life and significant theme found earlier in this novel, or in *The Unbending* as a whole.

*Distant Land* returns to the migrant theme with the story of another Russian Jewish couple who come to Australia at the beginning of the First World War and settle in a country town. The early scenes of Russian life and of the Kupelschmidts' struggles to prosper in their new land are absorbing and frequently humorous. Towards its end, however, the novel becomes something of a saga of the generations and, as with *Time of Conflict*, the sweep of events (personal rather than political in this case) tends to become external to the chief character.

*Season of Youth* has as its rogue hero a working class lad who wants to become a writer and moves against a varied social background as he pursues his ambition—and the ladies who help educate him.

Contemporary life and the conflicts felt by the children of immigrants are the subjects of *So Far No Further*. Waten overcomes the tendency of *Time of Conflict* and *Distant Land* to fall off towards the end by setting this novel in the present and working back in time to contrast the earlier experiences of the Italian and Polish Jewish parents with those of their children in the present. He uses his technique of working in short dramatic episodes very effectively here to present a broad social spectrum within the framework of the romance between two students; one, who has become involved in radical student politics, is the daughter of a Jewish businessman, the other is the more conservative son of an Italian fruiterer. Any political implication in this novel about contemporary politics seems untendentious—change and conflict are seen as an unavoidable part of life—and the novel remains optimistically open-ended.

—Brian Kiernan

---

**WATERHOUSE, Keith (Spencer).**   British. Born in Leeds, Yorkshire, 6 February 1929. Educated at Osmondthorpe Council School, Leeds. Married Joan Foster in 1950; has three children. Free-lance Journalist and Writer, in Leeds and London, since 1950. Currently, Columnist, *Daily Mirror*, London. Governor, Leeds Theatre Trust. Address: 32 Shaftesbury Avenue, London W.1., England.

PUBLICATIONS

Novels

*There Is a Happy Land*.  London, Joseph, 1957.
*Billy Liar*.  London, Joseph, 1959; New York, Norton, 1960.
*Jubb*.  London, Joseph, 1963; New York, Putnam, 1964.
*The Bucket Shop*.  London, Joseph, 1968; as *Everything Must Go*, New York, Putnam, 1969.

Plays

*Billy Liar*, with Willis Hall (produced London, 1960; Los Angeles, 1963).  London, Joseph, 1960; New York, Norton, 1961.
*Celebration*, with Willis Hall (produced London, 1961).  London, Joseph, 1961.

*England, Our England*, with Willis Hall (produced London, 1962).   London, Evans, 1964.

*Squat Betty* (produced London, 1962).

*The Sponge Room*, with Willis Hall (produced Nottingham and London, 1962).

*All Things Bright and Beautiful*, with Willis Hall (produced London, 1962).   London, Joseph, 1963.

*They Called the Bastard Stephen*, with Willis Hall (produced Bristol, 1964).

*Say Who You Are*, with Willis Hall (produced London, 1965; as *Help Stamp Out Marriage*, produced New York, 1966).   London, Evans, 1967.

*Joey, Joey*, with Willis Hall (produced London, 1966).

*Who's Who*, with Willis Hall (produced Coventry, 1971).

Screenplays, with Willis Hall: *Whistle Down the Wind*, 1961; *A Kind of Loving*, 1962; *Billy Liar*, 1963; *West Eleven*, 1963; *Man in the Middle*, 1964.

Other

*The Cafe Royal: Ninety Years of Bohemia*, with Guy Deghy.   London, Hutchinson, 1955.

*How to Avoid Matrimony*, with Guy Deghy.   London, Muller, 1957.

*Britain's Voice Abroad*, with Paul Cave.   London, Daily Mirror Newspapers, 1957.

*The Joneses: How to Keep Up with Them*, with Guy Deghy (as Lee Gibb).   London, Muller, 1959.

*The Higher Jones*, with Guy Deghy (as Lee Gibb).   London, Muller, 1961.

Editor, *The Future of Television*.   London, Daily Mirror Newspapers, 1958.

Editor, with Willis Hall, *Writers' Theatre*.   London, Heinemann, 1967.

\*         \*         \*

All Keith Waterhouse's fiction is distinguished by a sharp comic sense, a verbal facility that makes almost every line in the first half of the novels funny. The prose is full of discordant images, incongruities that create a consistent interest and amusement. For example, in *Billy Liar*, a character who is one of the two owners of the funeral establishment where Billy works, a man who keeps a copy of Evelyn Waugh's *The Loved One* on his desk in order to get new ideas and who looks forward to the day when all coffins will be made of Fiberglas, is introduced: "He was, for a start, only about twenty-five years old, although grown old with quick experience, like forced rhubarb." Clichés are turned around, all the verbal and grammatical incongruities of a single phrase are explored, and descriptions of towns and houses and people are given in sharp, contemporary images.

Waterhouse's comedy is not, however, entirely a matter of verbal texture. The plots all begin with a kind of adolescent humor. Billy, in *Billy Liar*, invents highly improbable stories, publicizing them fully and inconsistently, weaving a net of fantastic lies that is bound to be discovered by parents, bosses, and the three girl-friends to whom he is simultaneously engaged. He is also a leader in his fantasy land of Ambrosia. He is full of elaborate and comic compulsions: he feels that if he can suck a mint without breaking it or if he walks in certain complex patterns he will manage to escape the consequences of his stories. The perspective of Waterhouse's first novel, *There Is a Happy Land*, is made even more child-like, the novel beginning from the point of view of a young boy on a lower middle-class housing estate who plays at being blind or drunk or maimed, who mimics all his elders (all Waterhouse's central characters are excellent mimics), and who delights in calling out cheeky statements that annoy or embarrass adults. The central character of *Jubb* is neither a child nor an adolescent, but he, too, is full of grandiose schemes that others always see through, constantly mimics and challenges others' accepted pieties, and lives almost wholly in his disordered imagination. Waterhouse's principal characters assault an adult world that pretends it's stable. The humor, inventive, systematic, and iconoclastic, is a highly imaginative extension of the adolescent prank of using the telephone to invent roles and berate or annoy people.

Underneath the texture of mimicry and iconoclasm, Waterhouse develops more serious themes and concerns. In each novel, the verbal and comic fireworks seem to subside as the more serious concern, one usually revealed gradually, comes to dominate the novel. *There Is a Happy Land* begins with the larky and innocent escapades and quarrels of the young boy on the brink of adolescence. He is not quite able to understand the sexuality and perversion around him. The novel changes tone as the boy recognizes that far more sinister actions, ending in the murder of a young girl, take place in picture-windowed houses and abandoned quarries. Just beneath the sparkling and iconoclastic attitude of the prankster is a sense of evil, violence, and emptiness, as if only juvenility wards off, for a short time, the horror of experience. *Jubb* is the portrait of a psychotic, a man whose sexual impotence leads him to become a peeping Tom, a pyromaniac, and a murderer. At first, Jubb, a rent-collector and youth-club leader in a planned "New Town," is treated comically as a man with incessant sexual fantasies and an obsession about organizing a camera club. But Waterhouse gradually reveals the psychosis behind the fantasies and the madness behind the compulsions, showing that Jubb has been responsible for the deaths of his parents and his aunt. As the humor seems to fade from the novel, the revelations become more predictable, more staged, more melodramatic. Without the humor, Waterhouse's novel is less an insightful and profound psychological treatment of character than a melodramatic revelation of a perverse and horrible humanity.

*Billy Liar* is lighter and more sociological than Waterhouse's other novels. Much of the comedy, satire directed against romanticizing an old, rugged Yorkshire tradition, against the new world of coffee bars and record shops, against the winner of the Miss Stradhoughton contest who delivers "whole sentences ready-packed in disposable tinfoil wrapper," is full of sociological reference, characterizing the northern English city of the fifties. Yet the novel does not cohere as any kind of social commentary or statement. Billy himself, at the end of the novel, when all his stories and futile schemes have been discovered, cannot break away from home and take the train to London, cannot make the gesture that would consolidate any kind of statement about his life, cannot commit himself to Liz, the girl who can share his fantasies and who is regarded by the author as the most admirable of the three. Rather, Billy remains the adolescent, the young man who can mimic, scoff, and invent, but who is unable to create any life for himself not dependent on his rather limited and stifling environment. The implication at the end of the novel is that Billy must still grow up, still find himself. Liz also represents no panacea, for she is seen as aimless, directionless, hoping for some meaning she cannot find. In addition, from Waterhouse's point of view, old Councilor Duxbury, initially satirized as the stereotype of the old, rugged Yorkshire tradition, is seen as wise, gentle, and able to see through Billy without delivering a pompous lecture. Despite all the mimicry, the novel leaves a sense that iconoclasm goes only so far, that adolescent rebellion, understandable as it may be, is simply the prelude to a more mature acceptance of society as it is. In *There Is a Happy Land* and *Jubb*, the comedy only thinly covers a sense of the horror and emptiness of experience; in *Billy Liar*, the comedy only thinly covers a sense of the unchangeability of experience, rests on a kind of sentimental social conservatism. In all Waterhouse's fiction, the comedy seems superficial, a guise, a safety valve, rather than a means of exploring a deeply thought or deeply felt version of experience.

Yet this thin covering is a sparkling, often brilliant, one. Waterhouse, in conjunction with Willis Hall, has also written plays characterized by the same witty dialogue and sharp comic observation. Always an excellent mimic, often cogent and terse, Waterhouse has created a comic prose and a sense of the logic of systematic fantasy which, although limited, can be strikingly effective and enjoyable.

—James Gindin

**WAUGH, Auberon (Alexander).** British. Born in Dulverton, Somerset, 11 November 1939; son of the novelist Evelyn Waugh. Educated at Downside School, Somerset; Christ Church, Oxford (Exhibition in English). Served to 2nd Lieutenant in the Royal Horse Guards (The Blues), 1957–58; wounded in Cyprus, 1957; retired on pension, 1958. Married Teresa Onslow in 1961; has four children. Reporter, *Daily Telegraph*, London, 1960–63; Special Writer, International Publishing Corporation, London, 1963–67; Columnist, *News of the World* and *The Sun*, 1969–70, and *The Times*, London, 1970. Chief Political Correspondent, 1967–70 (visited Biafra, 1968), and since 1970, Chief Fiction Reviewer, *The Spectator*, London. Since 1970, Political Correspondent, *Private Eye*, London. Address: Combe Florey House, Taunton, Somerset, England; or, La Pesegado, 11 Montmaur, Aude, France.

PUBLICATIONS

Novels

> *The Foxglove Saga.* London, Chapman and Hall, 1960; New York, Simon and Schuster, 1961.
> *Path of Dalliance.* London, Chapman and Hall, 1963; New York, Simon and Schuster, 1964.
> *Who Are the Violets Now?* London, Chapman and Hall, 1965; New York, Simon and Schuster, 1966.
> *Consider the Lilies.* London, Joseph, and Boston, Little Brown, 1968.
> *A Bed of Flowers; or, As You Like it.* London, Joseph, 1972.

Other

> *Biafra: Britain's Shame*, with Suzanne Croupe. London, Joseph, 1969.

Critical Study: by John Davenport, in *Observer* (London), October 1960.

Auberon Waugh comments:

*The Foxglove Saga*, a first novel, dealt satirically with life in a monastic school and in the British army, using a complicated and baroque plot as a vehicle for this satire against Church and State which became a best seller in two continents.

*Path of Dalliance* satirized various political, artistic and philosophical excesses at Oxford University from the point of view of an innocent, sexually incompetent undergraduate.

*Who Are the Violets Now?* told the sad story of a hack writer for women's magazines, whose self respect was greater than his talent, but whose warm heart led him to work for various suspect organizations.

*Consider the Lilies* is a novel about the plight of Anglican clergymen today, with nothing whatever to do and time to kill, as fewer and fewer people attend their churches. It is not noticeably oecumenical in tone.

Mr. Waugh is a Roman Catholic. His political commentary in London's satirical journal *Private Eye* is one of the established hazards of English political life. His other claim to fame as a journalist is that an article by him which appeared in the London *Times* of March 14th, 1970, caused a riot in Pakistan during which the British Council Library in Rawalpindi was burned to the ground.

His latest novel, *A Bed of Flowers*, concerns itself with the political and moral implications of "dropping out", urging that politically and morally it is preferable to drop out of the modern world than to stay in and try to improve it.

\*       \*       \*

Packed away in Fowler's *Modern English Usage* is a useful, mock-Aristotelian outline for a poetics of the comic: the aim of humor, Fowler proposes, is discovery (of human inadequacies, presumably), the province is human nature and the method observation. More specifically, satire aims, by accentuation, at the amendment of manners and morals, while invective seeks to discredit misconduct by direct statement. The novels of Auberon Waugh suggest an unfortunate subcategory, close to invective but having as their aim something one can only call juvenile *Schadenfreude* of a particularly nasty sort. Waugh's first three novels, at any rate, are little more than sophomoric outbursts against some obvious disgraces of modern life, peppered with "daring" naughty little black jokes about cancer, old age and the church. What is distressing is not Waugh's choice of targets but the utter banality of his perceptions. In *The Foxglove Saga*, which Waugh describes as a "satire against Church and State", readers are informed that schoolboys are messy and foolish, the priesthood sometimes vain and mad, the upper classes cruelly selfish and hypocritical and the working class doltishly ignorant and vulgar. From *Path of Dalliance* we learn that Oxford undergraduates are faddish, foolish and cowardly (and dons eccentric) and that the middle class, while perhaps not so stupid as the workers, has its own appalling vulgarities. There are further startling revelations in *Who Are the Violets Now?*: slick women's magazines are mindlessly dishonest and the semi-educated young especially apt to be taken in by liberal action groups run by mendacious bigots. But the disclosures go no further; they barely touch an obvious surface, giving Waugh the penetration of, say, a moderately literate British Al Capp. Waugh is unable or unwilling to create characters and settles for crude caricatures; his plots are jerked forward by little bursts of simultaneous and paralleling actions, a technique obviously derived from Aldous Huxley's early comic-panoramic novels and perfected by the author's father, Evelyn Waugh. Unfortunately Auberon Waugh has none of Huxley's intellectual seriousness and nothing of his father's brilliant malice and moral indignation. "Compassion", asserts the narrator of *Consider the Lilies*, "is the base currency of second-rate minds, a substitute for thought." Possibly so; but for the would-be satirist simple minded contempt is equally ineffectual: there is nothing to discover in these novels but the obvious, no creative observation and no discernible motive other than self-indulgent peevishness.

*Consider the Lilies* is quite another matter. Here, for whatever motives, Waugh has an object for sustained contempt and something approaching genuine rage: he describes the novel as being "about the plight of the Anglican clergymen today, with nothing whatever to do and time to kill, as fewer and fewer people attend their churches". The central character and narrator, Trumpeter, is a genuine comic creation, a weary La Rochefoucauld the reader can detest with great pleasure; the plot, until the very end, is worked out with far more skill than Waugh had displayed in his first novels. *Consider the Lilies* is a special book, its range obviously limited, but within the terms it sets up it is a complex and almost wholly successful satire.

—Elmer Borklund

**WEIDMAN, Jerome.** American. Born in New York City, 4 April 1913. Educated at the City College of New York, 1930–33; Washington Square College, New York, 1933–34; New York University Law School, 1934–37. Served with the United States Office of War Information, 1942–45. Married Elizabeth Ann Payne in 1943; has two children. Full-time Writer since 1929. President, Authors League of America, since 1968. Recipient: Pulitzer Prize, for drama, 1960; New York Drama Critics Circle Award, 1960; Antoinette Perry Award, for drama, 1960. Address: 1035 Fifth Avenue, New York, New York 10028, U.S.A.

PUBLICATIONS

Novels

> *I Can Get It for You Wholesale.* New York, Simon and Schuster, 1937; London, Heinemann, 1938.
> *What's in It for Me?* New York, Simon and Schuster, 1938; London, Heinemann, 1939.
> *I'll Never Go There Anymore.* New York, Simon and Schuster, 1941; London, Heinemann, 1942.
> *The Lights Around the Shore.* New York, Simon and Schuster, 1943; London, Hale, 1948.
> *Too Early to Tell.* New York, Reynal, 1946.
> *The Price Is Right.* New York, Harcourt Brace, 1949; London, Hammond Hammond, 1950.
> *The Hand of the Hunter.* New York, Harcourt Brace, 1951; London, Cape, 1952.
> *The Third Angel.* New York, Doubleday, 1953; London, Cape, 1954.
> *Give Me Your Love.* New York, Eton, 1954.
> *Your Daughter, Iris.* New York, Doubleday, 1955; London, Cape, 1956.
> *The Enemy Camp.* New York, Random House, 1958; London, Heinemann, 1959.
> *Before You Go.* New York, Random House, 1960; London, Heinemann, 1961.
> *The Sound of Bow Bells.* New York, Random House, 1962; London, Heinemann, 1963.
> *Word of Mouth.* New York, Random House, 1964; London, Bodley Head, 1965.
> *Other People's Money.* New York, Random House, and London, Bodley Head, 1967.
> *The Center of the Action.* New York, Random House, 1969; London, Bodley Head, 1970.
> *Fourth Street East.* New York, Random House, and London, Bodley Head, 1971.

Short Stories

> *The Horse That Could Whistle "Dixie" and Other Stories.* New York, Simon and Schuster, 1939; London, Heinemann, 1941.
> *The Captain's Tiger.* New York, Reynal, 1949.
> *A Dime a Throw.* New York, Doubleday, 1957.
> *My Father Sits in the Dark and Other Selected Stories.* New York, Random House, 1961; London, Heinemann, 1963.
> *Where the Sun Never Sets and Other Stories.* London, Heinemann, 1964.
> *The Death of Dickie Draper and Nine Other Stories.* New York, Random House, 1965.

Plays

> *Fiorello!,* with George Abbott, music by Jerry Bock (produced New York, 1959). New York, Random House, 1960.

*Tenderloin*, with George Abbott (produced New York, 1960).   New York, Random House, 1961.

*I Can Get It for You Wholesale* (produced New York, 1962).   New York, Random House, 1962.

*Cool Off!*, music by Howard Blackman (produced Philadelphia, 1964).

*Pousse Café*, music by Duke Ellington (produced New York, 1966).

*Ivory Tower*, with James Yaffe (produced Ann Arbor, Michigan, 1968).   New York, Dramatists Play Service, 1969.

*The Mother Lover* (produced New York, 1969).

*Asterisk: A Comedy of Terrors* (produced New York, 1970).


Other

*Letter of Credit* (travel).   New York, Simon and Schuster, 1940.

*Back Talk* (essays).   New York, Random House, 1963.

Editor, *A Somerset Maugham Sampler*.   New York, Garden City Books, 1943.

Editor, *Traveler's Cheque*.   New York, Doubleday, 1954.

Editor, with others, *The First College Bowl Question Book*.   New York, Random House, 1961.


*          *          *


In *Other People's Money* Jerome Weidman's protagonist muses as follows: "The trouble with a man who took a small piece of information and instead of conveying it in one lump broke it into bits . . . was that even a slow-witted listener was bound to put the pieces together more rapidly than the man who had broken them apart." This gives the key to Weidman's fictional method as it has developed over three decades of prolific writing. Indeed, it is difficult to see how he could have written these words without being conscious of their ironic application to himself as a story-teller.

Weidman seems to have admired the fat, rich products of such masters as Balzac and Dickens, and somewhat to have emulated such writers, but never to have had their panoramic vision of society as an organism. His postponed and prolonged revelations are of diminishing rather than increasing complexity and universality; the reader either guesses what is coming or feels let down when it comes.

Weidman's preoccupations from the beginning of his career in 1937 have been two: business and Jewishness. *I Can Get It for You Wholesale*, his first novel, is a fast-moving and highly-detailed examination of the ladies' garment industry in New York. It produced something of a sensation because of its realism and cheerful cynicism. In subsequent works of fiction he has explored other forms of industry, commerce and finance. Concurrently he has explored the shape and substance of Jewish metropolitan life, at many different levels of poverty and wealth, ignorance and sophistication.

But however extensively Weidman as a writer has concerned himself with the workings of capitalism in the United States, and with the status of Jews in American life, it cannot be said that he has ever tried to draw up an indictment of capitalism, or a condemnation of racism. He is skilled at showing how large a part deception and meretriciousness play in the conduct of business, and he seems to take an artist's delight in depicting the gory details when dog eats dog. He is skilled in showing the many disguises and essential viciousness of anti-Semitism, and he can be really profound as he traces the inner contortions of Jews of various types as they "live with" pervading prejudice. But it is never his purpose to suggest that any kind of common action could make life harder for deceivers and cheaters, or increase man's stock of honesty and genuineness. Nor does he ever express any real pride in Jewishness as a tradition or a religion, or any firm hope that the strength to be drawn therefrom might be applied to defeat the Philistine and deliver God's people into freedom, milk and honey.

A conversational exchange in *The Sound of Bow Bells* seems to sum up Weidman's whole moral, political and religious attitude:

> "When I first rented this office . . . , for fifteen cents they [the operators of a nearby small restaurant] gave you a sandwich you could hardly lift. Now . . . not only have the sandwiches gone up to fifty-five cents, but they're now about as big as a silver dollar, and . . . they're cutting the tuna fish by mixing it with diced white bread. . . . Some world we live in, eh, Sam?"
>
> "Oh, it's not so bad," Sam said. "I imagine somebody was complaining about the size of the tuna fish sandwiches outside the tent of Henry V at Agincourt."

—Richard Greenleaf

---

**WELTY, Eudora.** American. Born in Jackson, Mississippi, 13 April 1909. Educated at Mississippi State College for Women, Columbus, 1926–27; University of Wisconsin, Madison, B.A. 1929; Columbia University School of Advertising, New York, 1930–31. Since 1958, Honorary Consultant in American Letters, Library of Congress, Washington, D.C. Recipient: Guggenheim Fellowship, 1942, 1968; National Institute of Arts and Letters grant, 1944; Howells Medal, 1955; Brandeis University Creative Arts Award, 1965. D.Litt., Denison University, Granville, Ohio, 1971. Member, American Academy of Arts and Letters, 1971. Address: 1119 Pinehurst Street, Jackson, Mississippi, U.S.A.

PUBLICATIONS

Novels

*The Robber Bridegroom.*   New York, Doubleday, 1942; London, Lane, 1944.
*Delta Wedding.*   New York, Harcourt Brace, 1946; London, Lane, 1947.
*The Ponder Heart.*   New York, Harcourt Brace, and London, Hamish Hamilton, 1954.
*Losing Battles.*   New York, Random House, 1970.

Short Stories

*A Curtain of Green.*   New York, Doubleday, 1941.
*The Wide Net and Other Stories.*   New York, Harcourt Brace, 1943; London, Lane, 1945.
*The Golden Apples.*   New York, Harcourt Brace, 1949; London, Lane, 1950.
*Selected Stories.*   New York, Modern Library, 1954.
*The Bride of the Innisfallen and Other Stories.*   New York, Harcourt Brace, and London, Hamish Hamilton, 1955.
*Thirteen Stories.*   New York, Harcourt Brace, 1965.

Other

*Music from Spain.*   Greenville, Mississippi, Levee Press, 1948.
*Short Stories.*   New York, Harcourt Brace, 1949.
*Place in Fiction.*   New York, House of Books, 1957.
*Three Papers on Fiction.*   Northampton, Massachusetts, Smith College, 1962.
*The Shoe Bird* (juvenile).   New York, Harcourt Brace, 1964.

*          *          *

The most notable quality of Eudora Welty's fiction has been described very felicitously by Robert Penn Warren. "Eudora Welty's vision of—her feeling for—the world is multiple. She never, even when she nods, sinks into what Blake called 'the single vision and Newton's sleep.'" Each of Miss Welty's four novels develops around the theme of multiplicity. A person is not the fixed quality that he at first may appear to be. The behavior of members of any sub-culture is not as predictable as members of adjoining sub-cultures delude themselves into believing.

In Miss Welty's first novel, which is set in frontier Mississippi in the first years of the nineteenth century and which follows the outlines of a Grimm fairy tale, the robber bridegroom, contrary to expectations, is portrayed as a complex, multi-faceted character: bandit and rapist, respectable businessman, tender lover. Thus, Jamie Lockhart in one role is hired by the philosophical planter, Clement Musgrove, to apprehend the attacker of the planter's daughter, Jamie Lockhart in another role. It is not long, however, before Clement begins to penetrate the complexities of reality, and expresses the wish to meet the rapist of his daughter, for since the rape Rosamund's penchant for lying has disappeared. When Clement learns that Rosamund has become Jamie's wife, he declares that he would kill Jamie "if being a bandit were his breadth and scope." But through his own and his family's experiences, Clement has come to realize that "all things are double" and that "this should keep us from taking liberties . . . and acting too quickly to finish things off." And at the end of this brief novel, we have the omniscient narrator saying about Jamie, who with the greatest ease has been able to switch from bandit to merchant, that "he was a hero and had always been one, only with the power to look both ways and to see a thing from all sides."

While *Delta Wedding* is markedly different from *The Robber Bridegroom* in tone, in style, and in the richness of the narrative, the Mississippi aristocratic family that is focused on could be the descendants of Clement Musgrove one hundred years later. Twice the length of the first novel, *Delta Wedding* on the surface dwells in great detail on the activities of the Fairchilds during the week before the wedding of the family beauty Dabney to the plantation overseer Troy Flavin. But what Miss Welty is really interested in are the sensibilities of the numerous members of the immediate and the extended family who come to the plantation for the wedding. One of the important criteria for judging the different characters is how they feel about receiving the overseer into the family. Again, Miss Welty has used an omniscient narrator, and so events and people are seen from different points of view. Dabney's choice of the overseer seems to be a drastic mistake when it is thought about by her father, by an influential aunt, and by her elder sister, Shelley. However, when he is seen and listened to by her mother, Troy's basic goodness and fitness for Dabney become apparent. It becomes clear that objections to Troy are based on nothing more than the fact that his ancestry is undistinguished and that he was born poor. He is delighted with the quilt that his old mother, living alone in the hill country of the northeastern corner of the state, has sent him, and one is led to conclude that, in spite of everything else, a man of his humility and capacity for genuine affection will make a good husband for Dabney, a girl who while not especially perceptive is free of the snobbishness that afflicts other members of the family.

At the same time that the preparations for Dabney's marriage are going forward, the marriage of Dabney's uncle George endures a crisis. It is what some members of the family would have predicted, for in choosing Robbie Reid, who tended the counter in the general store in town, George married "beneath" him. While George's geniality and considerateness have made him a favorite with every member of the family, he is a man whom others find difficult to understand. He seems to love everyone equally, and thus to those, like his wife, who believe they are deserving of a larger portion of his love, he seems almost indifferent. When George risks his life to save the life of a retarded niece, Robbie is so piqued that she is driven to leave George. Robbie, however, in a display of humility that the Fairchild family can hardly believe, returns to George at the plantation two days before Dabney's wedding.

George is a type of man who fascinates Miss Welty. He is goodness personified but seems to be deficient in feeling. The separation of George and Robbie causes Ellen Fairchild, who is married to George's older brother, Battle, to do a great deal of thinking about George. To Ellen, Dabney's mother, George "was the one person . . . who did not have it in him to make of any act a facile thing or to make a travesty out of human beings. . . . Only George left the world she knew as pure . . . as he found it; still real, still bad, still fleeting and hopelessly alluring to her." But Ellen is somewhat naive in her chastizing of Robbie: "George loves a great many people, just about everybody in the Delta. . . . Don't you know that is the mark of a fine man. . . ." As Ellen continues to think about him, she is forced to admit to herself that he is "far from kin to her, scarcely tolerant of her understanding, never dependent on hers or anyone's, or on compassion. . . ." George is both infinitely complex and infinitely simple but at the same time very finite. Ellen is not moved to do anything that would upset the pattern of her life, but her thinking about George produces feelings of love, and she realizes that "she loved what was pure at its heart better than what was understood, or even misjudged, or afterwards forgiven. This was the dearest thing." Earlier, she had concluded that marrying into the Fairchild family had led her to realize "how deep were the complexities of the everyday, of the family, what caves were in the mountains, what blocked chambers, and what crystal rivers that had not yet seen light."

While it is clear that the values and temperament of Ellen Fairchild are the ones Miss Welty most respects, one of the problems with *Delta Wedding* is that the cast is large and there are numerous voices and viewpoints, including those of nine-year-olds. In *The Ponder Heart*, Miss Welty has moved to the other extreme, and has her story told through only one voice. Edna Earle, proprietress of the Hotel Beulah in Clay, Mississippi, tells the story of her Uncle Daniel to a guest at the hotel who is not given the opportunity to speak a single word.

The mystery of Uncle Daniel Ponder is similar to that of George Fairchild. Uncle Daniel is constantly giving his money and possessions away to strangers. But he neglects to bestow any of his bounty upon his seventeen-year-old wife, Bonnie Dee Peacock, whom he became enamored of as she clerked in the local five and ten. Unlike George, Uncle Daniel is very distressed when his wife leaves him. When Edna Earle has heard Daniel's refrain "Where has Bonnie Dee gone?" innumerable times, she hits upon an idea for getting Bonnie Dee back. She places an advertisement in the form of a poem in a newspaper. The poem, a good imitation folk ballad beginning with the lines "O listen to me, Bonnie Dee Ponder,/Come back to Clay, or husband will wonder," includes this important bit of information: "Retroactive allowance will be given." Bonnie Dee returns, "and *things* began to pour into that house —you'd think there wouldn't be room." Miss Welty then seems to pronounce judgment by having Bonnie Dee die during a lightning storm of heart failure.

The totally unexpected twist in plot is one of Miss Welty's favorite narrative devices. The twist here is that the Peacock family press charges of murder against Daniel. Thematically, the purpose of the trial that then takes place is to expose the Peacocks, a farming clan mired in ignorance and poverty.

> We saw them come in. . . . Old Lady Peacock wagged in first, big as a house, in new bedroom slippers this time, with pompoms on the toes. She had all of them behind her—girls going down stairsteps looking funnier and funnier in Bonnie Dee's parceled-out clothes, and boys all ages and sizes and the grown ones with wives and children, and Old Man Peacock bringing up the rear. . . . He had a face as red as a Tom turkey and not one tooth to his name, but he had on some new pants. I noticed the tag still poking out the seam when he creaked in at the door.

The whole family settles on the courthouse steps for lunch, and afterwards the remains of the lunch are left there. Perhaps the worst quality of people like the Peacocks is their utter lack of imagination. "Poor Bonnie Dee: I never believed she had one whit of human curiosity. I never, in all the time she was married to Uncle Daniel, heard her say 'What next?'"

Ridicule of the Peacocks for their country ways is too easy. Even they are worthy of compassion. Thus on the final page of the novel, Miss Welty has Edna Earle say of Bonnie Dee: "And you know, Bonnie Dee Peacock, ordinary as she was and trial as she was to put up with—she's the kind of person you do miss. I don't know why—deliver me from giving you the *reason*. You could look and find her like anywhere. Though I'm sure Bonnie Dee and Uncle Daniel were as happy together as most married people."

*Losing Battles* is Miss Welty's most ambitious work. Into it she has attempted to cram a full lifetime's observations of and reactions to the people of her native region. She has a great deal to say, and, wisely, has wished to avoid the novelist's pitfall of direct statement. She uses the dramatic method. But, unfortunately, she has not avoided the pitfalls of that method. At least 95 per cent of the novel consists of dialogue, and that much dialogue, spoken in dialect by many different voices that frequently seem undifferentiated, is very wearing when it is the means of giving exposition, of pointing out local curiosities, of telling funny stories, of showing characters' penchants for trivia, and of making significant thematic statements, especially since at first the latter seem to be just as insignificant as the rest. Rejecting the single voice of *The Ponder Heart* and the omniscient narrator of *The Robber Bridegroom*, Miss Welty in her fourth novel has chosen a story-telling technique that is both tedious and confusing.

This long novel covers a period of only a day and a half. Again we have a large family gathered together; the occasion is the annual reunion and the celebration of the ninetieth birthday of Granny, who has recently become a great, great grandmother. We have a family that could be the Peacocks of the earlier novel. But now we do not see them through the unsympathetic eyes of a town lady. We are with them in their home territory, for the most part at the farm home of Granny's youngest grandchild, Beulah Beecham Renfro, who is herself a grandmother. One of the several mysteries in this novel has to do with the circumstances under which Beulah's parents met their deaths together and left Beulah and six older children orphaned: "What errand was they both so beat on when they hitched and cut loose from the house so early and drove out of sight of Grandpa and Granny, children and all, that morning?" one voice asks. "Something between man and wife is the only answer and it's what no other soul would have no way of knowing," another voice answered. From *The Robber Bridegroom* on, each marriage that Miss Welty has dealt with has had its unique dynamics and tended to elude definition.

Granny, with her daughter and son-in-law dead, "just tied on her apron, dusted off her cradle, and started in all over again with another set of children." It was this heroic response that has brought Granny the unusual devotion of her grandchildren and that made their presence at the birthday reunion each summer so important to each of them.

For Jack Renfro, Beulah's nineteen-year-old son, this reunion at his own home is extremely difficult to get to. On the eve of the reunion he is across the state in the penitentiary, serving a two-year sentence for an act that any judge having first-hand familiarity with Jack's character would realize had to be more charitable than criminal. So that he may honor Granny by his presence, Jack makes a successful escape—one day before he would have been released on parole. This is typical of Jack's selflessness and devotion to others. It is also typical of the devil-may-care aspect of his character, and in terms of temperament makes him the descendant of George Fairchild and Uncle Daniel. All of his family recognize Jack's unique and prodigious virtue. But outsiders do not, including the school teacher who devoted her life to trying to bring knowledge and enlightenment to this family and to the other poverty-stricken, struggling families in these hills.

Miss Julia Mortimer, the teacher, in the end emerges as one of the most admirable characters in the novel, but she could not find much to admire in Jack. For Jack's scholastic average is only 75. And when Jack learns that Miss Mortimer told the girl he wanted to marry that she would be making a terrible mistake to marry him, Jack loses his respect for her.

This is but one segment of the complex network of judgments, misjudgments, and rejudgments that Miss Welty builds in this novel.

Throughout her four novels, Miss Welty is keenly aware of ambiguity and ambivalence, of irony, of how perspective affects judgment, of the imperfect knowledge of the knowledgeable. This awareness and concern place her in the mainstream of modern literature despite the sound and look of regionalism that her novels have. However, in contrast to her success with the short story Miss Welty has not yet found the optimum narrative technique in the novel for conveying her experience of life and people with maximum impact.

—Paul Marx

---

**WESCOTT, Glenway.** American. Born in Kewaskum, Wisconsin, 11 April 1901. Educated at the University of Chicago, 1917–19. Full-time Writer since 1921. Recipient: Harper Prize, 1927. D.Litt., Rutgers University, New Brunswick, New Jersey, 1963. President, National Institute of Arts and Letters, 1959–62; Member, American Academy of Arts and Letters. Address: Hay-Meadows, Rosemont, New Jersey, U.S.A.

PUBLICATIONS

Novels

*The Apple of the Eye.* New York, Dial Press, 1924.
*The Grandmothers: A Family Portrait.* New York, Harper, 1927.
*The Pilgrim Hawk: A Love Story.* New York, Harper, 1940; London, Hamish Hamilton, 1946.
*Apartment in Athens.* New York, Harper, 1945; as *Household in Athens*, London, Hamish Hamilton, 1945.

Short Stories

*... Like a Lover.* Macon, France, Monroe Wheeler, 1926.
*Good-bye, Wisconsin.* New York, Harper, 1928; London, Cape, 1929.
*The Babe's Bed.* Paris, Harrison, New York, Minton Balch, and London, Simkin, 1930.

Verse

*The Bitterns: A Book of Twelve Poems.* Evanston, Illinois, Monroe Wheeler, 1920.
*Natives of Rock: XX Poems, 1921–1922.* New York, Francisco Bianco, 1936.

Other

*Elizabeth Madox Roberts: A Personal Note.* New York, Viking Press, 1930.
*Fear and Trembling* (essays). New York, Harper, 1932.

*A Calendar of Saints for Unbelievers.*   New York, Minton Balch, and London, Simkin, 1932.

*12 Fables of Aesop, Newly Narrated.*   New York, Museum of Modern Art, 1954.

*Images of Truth: Remembrances and Criticism.*   New York, Harper, 1962; London, Hamish Hamilton, 1963.

Editor, *The Maugham Reader.*   New York, Doubleday, 1950.

Editor, *Short Novels of Colette.*   New York, Dial Press, 1951.

*          *          *

Glenway Wescott's literary reputation has been overshadowed by the reputation of his fellow Upper Midwestern writers, most of them like him expatriates during the famous Twenties: Ernest Hemingway and John Dos Passos from Illinois; Scott Fitzgerald and Sinclair Lewis from Minnesota (along with the presently neglected Kay Boyle); and Idaho's own Ezra Pound. He has written comparatively little, but that little often comes close to an almost lapidary perfection of sentence, paragraph, and scene. Like other "minor" writers, Wescott tends to be forgotten by a public overwhelmed by publishers' announcements of yet more "major" novels and novelists; when the inflated press-releases are consigned to their place as part of the history of advertising rather than as part of literary judgment, however, Glenway Wescott will take his place as one of the finest literary artists in this period's prose for—if nothing else—his novel *The Pilgrim Hawk*, a work which like Joyce's "The Dead," Ford's *The Good Soldier*, and Porter's *Noon Wine*, comes as close to perfection as literary art is liable to allow. Wescott gained an early reputation for technical skill; but we mistake Wescott if we assume his sole virtue is technique.

In *Images of Truth* Wescott collected admirable and admiring essays on Katherine Anne Porter, Maugham, Colette, Dinesen, Mann and Wilder. Wescott shares certain qualities with these writers: attention to the construction of a story, and concern for philosophical problems as they can be bodied forth in prose fiction. It is not now fashionable to suggest that the sensual Colette and the philosophical Mann were closer in spirit and aim than we had suspected; nor is Wescott interested in pressing such comparative evaluations; but his selection of writers indicates both his stated sympathy for the aims and means of these diverse talents and his unstated understanding of the deeper literary and philosophical interests which unite Wilder and Dinesen.

Some of the most powerful of this century's literature in English has been given to the creation of an exile or an expatriate from his home country, his remembrance or his search for a usable past: James Joyce's *Ulysses* or Allen Tate's *The Mediterranean*, for example. In Wescott's ironically titled *Good-bye, Wisconsin* the narrator of the title story sees Midwesterners as forever marked by the accidents of birth, "a sort of vagrant chosen people like the Jews." Wescott, Hemingway, and Fitzgerald in the Paris of the Twenties were among those wandering Midwesterners, discovering in Europe what it means to be an American. Wescott's narrator in this and other stories wants to escape from Wisconsin, its provincialism and puritanism—in some ways fiercer even than that of 19th century New England. This attempt to escape can be traced back at least as far as *Rose of Dutcher's Coolly* (1895) by Hamlin Garland, another Wisconsin novelist. In Garland's novel, a girl tries to escape from the grim drudgery and soul-killing narrowness of life on a Wisconsin farm by going to Chicago to take up a literary life.

Wescott's characters also try to escape, and sometimes into a literary life, or into death, or exile in France. In his first book, *The Apple of the Eye*, Wescott tells three stories; in one the stunted natural growth of the marsh-land setting frames and parallels the stunting of human feelings, emotions, ideals of a woman who must live in that setting; in the second the girl can find escape only through suicide in the marsh, whereas her seducer goes on about the pagan sensuousness of ancient Greeks; and in the third the conflict between stunted marshy landscape and the seduction of the past as made viable in language takes place within a boy. It is the best of the stories. The theme is, like most themes in fiction, a philosophical commonplace: the problem of moderation, a quality Wescott in his essays insists is a good thing in itself.

In so far as Buffon was correct in his "Discours de Réception," that "Le style est l'homme même," we might adduce one example, without being charged with the heresy of biographical criticism. Although a member of that celebrated expatriate generation, Wescott seems to stand to one side of the Fitzgerald, Crane, Hemingway, Stein group, as illustrated by an incident recorded by Malcolm Cowley in *Exile's Return*. At one of those famous editorial sessions of *Broom*, one of the most important of the "little magazines" in the twenties, Crane was explosively arguing with Josephson, Burke was telling a story about a dog, and everybody was drinking, when suddenly Wescott rose from the editorial table, saying as he departed: "How can you people expect to accomplish anything when you can't even preserve ordinary parlor decorum?" It is decorum, moderation, the perilous balance of life which are the themes of Wescott's fiction. As in the contrast of hard-drinking German immigrants in the Midwest with Alwyn Tower's grandparents' teetotal puritanism, deviation to either side (decorum can be breeched as much by haughtiness as by rowdiness) brings distortion to human character; and it brings tragedy.

In *The Apple of the Eye* the boy is confronted with the conflict of family duty (as embodied in the disagreeable orthodoxy of his pioneering aunt) and a sort of pagan exuberance in natural beauty (as suggested by a friend's teaching). Such conflicts run through Wescott's fiction. Yet once the central character of most of the fiction, Alwyn Tower, has got free of the homeplace, he finds that his freedom is compromised by memory: he must find his proper relationship to the past if he is to live successfully in the present. So Alwyn Tower sits in his hotel room in the South of France, having told Wisconsin "goodbye", only to remember his past, a process which enabled Wescott to create one of the finest novels in modern American fiction, *The Grandmothers*.

In an essay in *Images of Truth*, Wescott tells of having been impressed by the passage in the *Odyssey* where the shades are called up so that Odysseus can obtain information he needs to find his way home. This is, of course, the "germ" of *The Grandmothers*; for near Nice, Wescott heard and subsequently made Alwyn Tower hear, some drunken American sailors begin to sing "show me the way to go home", raising the question of where home is and how we truly arrive at the place—and know it, as Eliot says, for the first time. Alwyn Tower in a European hotel turns to a picture album; the visual images trigger his imaginative reconstruction of lives, his forebearers from about 1840 down to his own parents: it is a family portrait tenderly and nostalgically created in all its frustration and tragedy; yet it is also a study of history and of what the past means, of the present and of how we come to know ourselves. Such a long look to the past is central to Wescott's works. In *The Pilgrim Hawk*, Wescott's masterpiece, Alwyn Tower in America looks back at a day in France; and in *Apartment in Athens* the very sight of the Acropolis from a window in the apartment's kitchen suggests the dimension of history in which a parable of freedom is played out in the 20th century.

*The Pilgrim Hawk*, subtitled "a love story," is a great short novel in which a few people visit each other and a whole world of relationships is obliquely revealed. Wescott achieves in this novel a most difficult thing: a style which in its precision seems to be no style at all, and a technique so fused to theme and purpose that the story seems merely to tell itself. His is the art which conceals art. And he has used the first person narrator not just to tell a story, but in one sense to force upon the reader an examination of the very concept of perception— of how one perceives the world and then comes to knowledge, if at all. Wescott has made a tale of great complexity out of the simplest materials: one setting, a house and garden in France; a single afternoon in the 1920's, looked back on twenty years later; a plot consisting of triangular relationships of a small cast of characters—Alwyn Tower, the visiting American writer; his friend Alexandra Henry, owner of the house; two servants, Eva and Jean; and the Cullens, a wealthy roaming Irish couple who bring Ricketts, their chauffeur, and the pilgrim hawk. The action is quite limited. The Cullens arrive, displaying their rich eccentricity as well as their habit of preying on each other and the world; the hawk by contrast is for the most part hooded and quiet. Cullen gets drunk, tries to free the hawk which is recaptured; the narrator discovers the servants and chauffeur in a jealous quarrel in the kitchen; the Cullens leave. Shorly thereafter the Cullens return briefly, Mrs. Cullen with a revolver she carries for her protection, and took from her husband; the revolver is thrown in the lake; again the Cullens leave, and the narrator and his hostess chat briefly about the day's incidents.

Two triangles are at once apparent: the Cullens and the hawk, a triangle which reveals love in its possessive, jealous, even violent aspects, ranging from repressed to domineering, lyrical to savage; and the servants with the chauffeur, a triangle which parallels some of the perverse but vital attachments and needs which constitute involvements of the main triangles. The servant Eva flirts with the chauffeur Ricketts; yet she later explains that her husband Jean needs to be made jealous so that he can express his love, a love otherwise the captive of his reticence. Freedom, then, is dependence, and captivity in love is liberty.

The third triangle is less dramatic, being entirely overlooked by some readers; yet it is central to the examination, in fictional terms, of the conflicts between appetite and control. In revealing Cullen's hatred, the narrator also reveals himself, his own self-interest and captivity. For as a writer he has missed life, as bound to his art as the hooded hawk on Mrs. Cullen's arm. One must finally wonder why the narrator elects to recall this one day when he was the guest of Alexandra Henry who later became his sister-in-law. The reader is not *told* about the conflict of love and art; instead he receives it, as a powerful undercurrent in the story of an Irish couple and a hawk, which is also a story about love and art, freedom and captivity.

*Apartment in Athens* undertakes to present the emotions and psychology of conqueror and conquered; yet it is also an extension of the theme of freedom and captivity, now presented in terms of ideology rather than of love. The fictional approach is direct, rather than oblique as in *The Pilgrim Hawk*, so that the war-time "message" is not obscured by subtle rendering; yet that very "message" has obscured for many readers the other themes of the novel.

A German officer is housed in an apartment in the Athens home of a Greek intellectual who tries to "adjust" to this intrusion of a victor; as the two men try to understand each other, we have a paradigm of part of human experience. When the Greek expresses sympathy for the German whose wife is dead, he is imprisoned and executed for "subversive" remarks— a dark and bitter end, if we read the book as something more than a war-time tract. The long letter smuggled out of jail is for the success of the novel unfortunate, for the blatant intrusion of propaganda unbalances the book, which is really about masks of submission, the reality of masks when deception becomes the reality; about the complex accommodations life requires.

In some of the early stories and in *The Pilgrim Hawk*, the narrator is an alien American in France; in *Apartment in Athens* the alien in Greece is a German enemy. This, together with other shifts in narrative style as well as the announced war-time propagandistic aim of the book, has tended to obscure the relationship of the novel to Wescott's other fictions and concerns: the nature of freedom, the types of captivity of which man is capable (whether by a marsh in *The Apple of the Eye* or an invader in *Apartment in Athens*), the ambiguous relationship of a man to his home place (Alwyn Tower says in *Good-bye, Wisconsin* that he has no land, only a family). One hopes that in the not too distant future, Wescott's prose fiction will again be in print so that it can take its place as one of the truly distinguished achievements in twentieth century literature in English.

—James Korges

**WEST, Anthony (Panther).**  British.  Born in Hunstanton, Norfolk, 4 August 1914; son of the writers H. G. Wells and Rebecca West, *q.v.* Educated at Stowe School, Buckingham-shire. Married Lily Dulany Emmet in 1952; has two children. Dairy Farmer, 1937–43; worked on the Far Eastern Desk, 1943–45, and in the Japanese Service, 1945–47, BBC, London. Since 1950, Staff Writer, *The New Yorker*. Recipient: Houghton Mifflin Literary Fellowship, 1950. Address: c/o The New Yorker, 25 West 43rd Street, New York, New York 10036, U.S.A.

PUBLICATIONS

Novels

On a Dark Night.  London, Eyre and Spottiswoode, 1949; as *The Vintage*, Boston, Houghton Mifflin, 1950.
Another Kind.  London, Eyre and Spottiswoode, 1951; Boston, Houghton Mifflin, 1952.
Heritage.  New York, Random House, 1955.
The Trend Is Up.  New York, Random House, 1960; London, Hamish Hamilton, 1961.
David Rees, Among Others.  New York, Random House, and London, Hamish Hamilton, 1970.

Other

Gloucester.  London, Faber, 1939.
D. H. Lawrence.  London, Barker, 1951; revised edition, 1966.
The Crusades.  New York, Random House, 1954; as *All about the Crusades*, London, W. H. Allen, 1967.
Principles and Persuasions: Literary Essays.  New York, Harcourt Brace, 1957; London, Eyre and Spottiswoode, 1958.
Elizabethan England.  New York, Odyssey Press, and London, Hamlyn, 1965.

Editor, *The Galsworthy Reader*.  New York, Scribner, 1968.

\*       \*       \*

Anthony West is a journalist and critic as well as the author of several novels. *The Vintage*, *Another Kind*, and *The Trend Is Up* are concerned with the moral malaise of twentieth-century man and its effect on his personal, political, and economic life. A different sort of novel is his third, *Heritage*; this and the collection of sequential stories *David Rees, Among Others* deal fictionally with problems similar to his own as a child and young man, the son of famous, brilliant parents who were not married. Both books treat the theme with courage and good humor; *Heritage*, as the young hero gets older and at last meets his father, becomes at times extremely funny. Irrepressible Max Town is an exuberant interpretation of H. G. Wells. The fictional mother—West uses the somewhat trite figure of a great actress—is less successful, and certainly bears little resemblance to Dame Rebecca West. It is Max Town's collisions with—and occasional surprising nostalgia for—conventionality that make the book live. In *David Rees, Among Others*, where the mother appears in the guise of a concert pianist, the study of her problems becomes more interesting. Both books afford subtle insights into the mind of a child and growing boy.

*The Vintage*, published just after the war crimes trials, is a fantasia of the afterlife as John

Wallis, who has just shot out his brains, quests for meaning in company with a German general whom he had helped hang. After reviewing many incidents in his past and rejecting an eternity of pleasure, he sees that there is "nothing vile in manhood" and that in avoiding moral responsibility he had chosen to "walk step by step away" from the goodness of life towards his eventual suicide. This theme of self-disgust is continued in his next novel, *Another Kind*, in which personal malaise, augmented by and contributing to economic sickness, brings contemporary England to a fascination with failure and a suicidal revolution. A defeated architect, Walter Jackson, attempts to put meaning in his life by an affair with a strong blonde courtesan, a former farm-girl, Anne. But his self-loathing taints everything he touches. West had just written a study of D. H. Lawrence, and in the first part of this novel the passages analyzing Walter's evasions and sudden repugnances betray Lawrentian models. Revolution comes and offers a heyday to black-marketeers (among them Walter), wastrels, and sadists. From this vineyard of wrath Anne effects a desperate escape and manages to get back to an old farm-mill to bear the child that Walter (now dead) had insisted that she abort.

*The Trend Is Up*, published after ten years of residence in the United States, ends on no note of hope: Gavin Hatfield, a quite decent New Englander who elected wealth and its power as his goal, is alone in his house in his Florida empire asking "Tell me, tell me what I did wrong!" This long book, lacking the sparkle of *Heritage* and the analysis of the first part of *Another Kind*, and needing concentration, is nevertheless a successful study of an economic boom and the dulling or distorting of the minds and emotions involved. It offers a wide screen of characters; though some tend to remain too allegorical, and Gavin's "northern" wife never comes to life, many are well grasped. Concerned with actualities, and building to a notable ironic climax, it is in some ways West's most powerful novel.

—Alice Bensen

---

**WEST, Anthony C.** Irish. Born in County Down, Northern Ireland, 1 July 1910. Served as an Air Observer and Navigator Bomber in the Pathfinder Force, Royal Air Force, in World War II. Married Olive Mary Burr in 1940; has eleven children. Recipient: Atlantic Award, 1946. Address: Bryn Goleu, Llanberis, Caernarvonshire, Wales.

PUBLICATIONS

Novels

The Native Moment. New York, Obolensky, 1959; London, MacGibbon and Kee, 1961.
Rebel to Judgement. New York, Obolensky, 1962.
The Ferret Fancier. London, MacGibbon and Kee, 1962; New York, Simon and Schuster, 1963.
As Towns with Fire. London, MacGibbon and Kee, 1968; New York, Knopf, 1970.

Short Stories

River's End and Other Stories. New York, McDowell Obolensky, 1957; London, MacGibbon and Kee, 1959.

Anthony C. West comments:

I have a creative and an a-political interest in the human condition, wherever and however it may be found, with the incorrigible hope for social harmony and world tolerance.

*          *          *

The fiction of Anthony C. West is filled with poignant beauty and great tenderness, yet it is not just lyric. The main characters of his novels are all very much attuned to nature, yet *in* the world if not entirely *of* it. He handles scenes of childhood well, yet his children grow up. *As Towns with Fire*, his latest novel, creates a focus, almost a culmination, for *The Native Moment* and *The Ferret Fancier*.

*As Towns with Fire* is the portrait of a man and a war. Beginning New Year's Eve, 1939, it traces the experiences of Christopher MacMannan, an Irishman who has settled in London to train himself as a writer, to the day of his discharge from the R.A.F. after the war has ended. During this time he has done odd jobs and worked with the A.R.P., married, had two children, gone to Belfast where he suffered employment, unemployment, and air raids, joined the Air Force, and flown many missions as observer in Mosquitoes.

There is almost too much in this book, but all of it is good. The war scenes are vivid and suspenseful. There is a charming lyric episode when MacMannan camps out in the hills of Northern Ireland. There is mystery in that, although a long flashback traces his childhood in detail, his history stops when he leaves school; however, references throughout the story imply that between then and the beginning of the story proper, he had travelled widely and saved enough money for a free year in London, at the same time maturing without losing the sensitivity he had as a child. He refuses to submit his poetry for publication until it reaches some form of perfection known only to him. There is some sort of symbolism in his efforts to protect little ducks from the cruelty of thoughtless children.

A similar affinity with nature is in *The Native Moment*, an account of the day Simon Green goes to Dublin with a live eel in a pail; because London sales have dropped off, he is seeking an Irish market for the eels that abound in the northern lakes. He gets drunk, sleeps with a prostitute, is disappointed in a meeting with an old friend, and resolves to marry a girl made pregnant by her uncle. Yet so long as he can keep the eel alive, changing its water regularly he survives his crises. *The Ferret Fancier* is a pastoral in which the same kind of sensitive character is given a ferret as a pet when a child.

West has been compared with Joyce and Beckett, and if one does not seek word play or the broadly comic, it is possible to see the comparison. But in his feeling for nature, for the persons and places of the Irish countryside, he adds another ingredient. For all of their accomplishments this century, Irish writers have tended to be parochially Irish, or write mainly of urban settings or rural settings, but rarely both. West has broken through this barrier.

—William Bittner

WEST, Jessamyn. American. Born in Indiana, in 1907. Educated at Whittier College, California, A.B.; University of California, Berkeley. Married to H. M. McPherson. Taught at Bread Loaf Writers Conference, Vermont; Indiana University, Bloomington; University of Notre Dame, Indiana; University of Utah, Salt Lake City; University of Washington, Seattle; Stanford University, California. Recipient: Thormod Monsen Award, 1958.

Honorary Degrees: Whittier College; Mills College, Oakland, California; Swarthmore College, Pennsylvania; Indiana University; Western College for Women. Lives in California. Address: c/o Harcourt, Brace and Jovanovich, 750 Third Avenue, New York, New York 10017, U.S.A.

PUBLICATIONS

Novels

>   *The Friendly Persuasion.* New York, Harcourt Brace, 1945; London, Hodder and Stoughton, 1946.
>   *The Witch Diggers.* New York, Harcourt Brace, 1951; London, Heinemann, 1952.
>   *Cress Delahanty.* New York, Harcourt Brace, 1953; London, Hodder and Stoughton, 1954.
>   *Love Is Not What You Think.* New York, Harcourt Brace, 1959; as *A Woman's Love*, London, Hodder and Stoughton, 1960.
>   *South of the Angels.* New York, Harcourt Brace, 1960; London, Hodder and Stoughton, 1961.
>   *A Matter of Time.* New York, Harcourt Brace, 1966; London, Macmillan, 1967.
>   *Leafy Rivers.* New York, Harcourt Brace, 1967; London, Macmillan, 1968.
>   *Except for Me and Thee: A Companion to The Friendly Persuasion.* New York, Harcourt Brace, and London, Macmillan, 1969.
>   *Crimson Ramblers of the World, Farewell.* New York, Harcourt Brace, 1970; London, Macmillan, 1971.

Short Stories

>   *Love, Death, and the Ladies' Drill Team.* New York, Harcourt Brace, 1955; as *Learn to Say Goodbye*, London, Hodder and Stoughton, 1957.

Plays

>   *A Mirror for the Sky*, music by Raoul Pene du Bois. New York, Harcourt Brace, 1948.

>   Screenplays: *Friendly Persuasion*, 1956; *The Big Country*, 1958; *Stolen Hours*, 1963.

Other

>   *To See the Dream.* New York, Harcourt Brace, 1957; London, Hodder and Stoughton, 1958.

>   Editor, *A Quaker Reader*. New York, Viking Press, 1962.

\*       \*       \*

Jessamyn West is best known as the author of *The Friendly Persuasion*, a collection of related short stories made into an immensely successful motion picture in 1956. Millions then saw the qualities which had impressed readers of her fiction since 1945. (In *To See the*

*Dream*, Miss West described her contribution to William Wyler's film, a far closer collaboration than most novelists have enjoyed in Hollywood.) The film showed very faithfully that people like the Indiana Quakers, Jess and Eliza Birdwell, who lead good and abundant lives are still open to the full complexity of human experience. It also transferred some of her hard craftsmanship to the screen: the measure of surprise in her carefully constructed plots and the poetry which heightens her language.

She has written about two communities, her Quaker ancestors who settled in the Ohio River Valley in the early nineteenth century and her own generation of Californians who developed the tracts which eventually became the suburbs of Los Angeles. One cleared a wilderness and the other sowed in a desert. Instead of the grim, nostalgic novels of pioneer life one might expect from this heritage, most of Miss West's fiction—even her novels—is made up of stories and sketches. A horse race, a broken vase, an adultery, an imminent death, and a family Christmas must all be gathered into lives meaningful enough to permit such a character as the Quaker nurseryman, Jess Birdwell, to admit to his wife that their frontier world has changed "except for me and thee."

Miss West is one of those fortunate writers whose style was fully matured by the time she published her first book, *The Friendly Persuasion*. She had talent enough to suggest the great wonder with which Jess Birdwell approached everything that happened to him. She was capable of showing the force that an artifact or a human being could have upon that wonder and how it could lead the man to wisdom. She knew how to write about such people without being patronizing, to show how, for example, Jess's love of music was irrepressible and yet, because he was a Quaker married to a Quaker preacher, how it could actually be repressed. Quite as convincingly as Carson McCullers developed a totally opposed theme, Miss West has argued that the heart finds as well as hunts and that it is not impossible for two people ever to be completely together or to choose to be by themselves.

In *South of the Angels* she tried to be similarly perceptive about forty people of all ages from childhood to dying old age who were caught in the settlement of a Southern California tract. But the brief year in which they waited for water to be brought to their dry acres allowed the writer little opportunity to develop more than their transience and frustration. This is enough, however, to establish this neglected book as a superior regional novel. Miss West and Raymond Chandler virtually comprehend all of Southern California regionalism from the turn of the century to World War II—all that has been ignored by the Hollywood novelists—she with the orange groves and the "ranches" and he with "metropolitan L.A."

*Cress Delahanty* and *Leafy Rivers* are wise, humorous books about young women, one entering adolescence and the other giving birth to her first child. *Love, Death, and the Ladies' Drill Team* is the collection of her best short stories; one of the stories, "The Mysteries of Life in an Orderly Manner," is an even more informative statement of her craft than her essay, "The Slave Cast Out." *A Matter of Time* is probably her best novel and, at first reading, her least characteristic work. It is the story of two sisters reunited by the impending death of one of them and committed to a plan in which the older sister will help the younger one take her own life rather than be killed by her cancer. As they wait for the right moment to execute their plan, the older sister remembers everything in their lives that led up to it. Her memories are a little grimmer and less poetically spoken than most incidents in Miss West's earlier fiction, but their sum is, finally, the same abundance and wonder. Miss West chose a statement by Camus as an epigraph for this novel, and it may be the most fitting commentary on all of her writing: "I shall tell of nothing but my love of life. But I shall tell of it in my own way."

—David Sanders

**WEST, Morris (Langlo).** Australian. Born in Melbourne, Victoria, 26 April 1916. Educated at St. Mary's College, St. Hilda, Victoria; University of Melbourne, B.A. 1937. Served as a Lieutenant in the Australian Imperial Forces Corps of Signals, in the South Pacific, 1939–43. Married Joyce Lawford in 1952; has four children. For several years member of the Christian Brothers Order, and taught English, French and European History in New South Wales and Tasmania, 1933 until he left the order before taking final vows, 1939. Secretary to William Morris Hughes, former Prime Minister of Australia, 1934. Publicity Manager, Radio Station 3 DB, Melbourne, 1944–45; Founder, later Managing Director, Australian Radio Productions Pty. Ltd., Melbourne, 1945–54. Since 1954 has worked privately as a film and dramatic writer for the Shell Company and the Australian Broadcasting Network, and as a free-lance commentator and feature writer. Lived in England, 1956–58. Recipient: National Conference of Christians and Jews' Brotherhood Award, 1960; Black Memorial Prize, 1960; Heinemann Award, 1960. D.Litt., University of California, Santa Clara, 1968. Fellow, Royal Society of Literature, 1960. Fellow, World Academy of Arts and Sciences, 1964. Address: c/o Paul R. Reynolds, 599 Fifth Avenue, New York, New York 10017, U.S.A.

PUBLICATIONS

Novels

Moon in My Pocket (as Julian Morris). Sydney, Australasian Publishing Company, 1945.
Gallows on the Sand. Sydney, Angus and Robertson, 1956; London, Angus and Robertson, 1958.
Kundu. Sydney and London, Angus and Robertson, and New York, Dell, 1956.
The Big Story. London, Heinemann, 1957; as The Crooked Road, New York, Morrow, 1957.
The Second Victory. London, Heinemann, 1958; as Backlash, New York, Morrow, 1958.
McCreary Moves In (as Michael East). London, Heinemann, 1958.
The Devil's Advocate. London, Heinemann, and New York, Morrow, 1959.
The Naked Country (as Michael East). London, Heinemann, 1960; New York, Dell, 1961.
Daughter of Silence. London, Heinemann, and New York, Morrow, 1961.
The Shoes of the Fisherman. London, Heinemann, and New York, Morrow, 1963.
The Ambassador. London, Heinemann, and New York, Morrow, 1965.
The Tower of Babel. London, Heinemann, and New York, Morrow, 1968.
Summer of the Red Wolf. London, Heinemann, 1971.

Plays

Daughter of Silence (produced New York, 1961). New York, Morrow, 1962.
The Heretic (produced London, 1970). New York, Morrow, 1969; London, Heinemann, 1970.

Other

Children of the Sun. London, Heinemann, 1957; as Children of the Shadows: The True Story of the Street Urchins of Naples, New York, Doubleday, 1957.

*Scandal in the Assembly: The Matrimonial Laws and Tribunals of the Roman Catholic Church*, with Robert Francis.   London, Heinemann, 1970.

*          *          *

The novels of Morris West bear the imprints of his varied background as religious novitiate, teacher, intelligence officer, political aide, publicist and radio serializer. His autobiographical first novel (by "Julian Morris"), *Moon in My Pocket*, was about a disillusioned young religious, and West has never since abandoned this theme of the quest for moral identity and God's blessing. Two potboilers, *Gallows on the Sand* and *Kundu*, are significant only for providing the funds that allowed West to take up residence in Naples. There he wrote *Children of the Sun*, an outraged and compassionate study of southern Italy's street urchins which gained him attention and signalled his literary commitment to Christian responsibility. When he returned for financial reasons to publicity writing and to the novel of adventure, this deeper strain of moral concern had clearly, permanently been infused into his work.

*The Big Story*, though hastily written as a melodrama of murder and intrigue in Sorrento, suggests the "entertainments" of Graham Greene in its neat balance of swift, violent plot and lonely, existential ponderings. Thus, the American journalist Richard Ashley risks his life to publish "the truth" about the corrupt Duke of Orgagna, only to find that "the truth" exposes everyone's sin and corruption, including his own. When Ashley has miraculously triumphed, his newspaper kills the big story because the publisher has just been appointed U.S. Ambassador to Italy. West in this novel raises another favorite theme, the difficulty of moral choice when individually righteous behavior threatens great social harm in a larger context (Ashley's published "truth" will adversely affect an upcoming election) or, conversely, when personally immoral behavior, such as betrayal or assassination, will result in significant social benefit.

There were three more potboilers between 1958 and 1960, *The Second Victory* (*Backlash* in the U.S.) and, under the pseudonym of Michael East, *McCreary Moves In* and *The Naked Country*. But it was *The Devil's Advocate*, West's seventh book in four years, that lofted him to the heights of bestsellerdom, Book-of-the-Month-Club selection, Reader's Digest condensation and high-priced sale of movie rights. This success, repeated with *Shoes of the Fisherman*, along with the common subject matter of theological and institutional practices inside the Catholic church, has contributed to the undervaluation of West's writings as "theological thrillers" and Biblical bestsellers. West's occasional tendencies to overwrite and to repeat purplish pet phrases ("he felt a chill as though a goose had walked over his grave") lend support to disdainful reviewers, but he is, nevertheless, a talented and well-informed novelist who deals with profound themes and significant events.

In *The Devil's Advocate*, Monsignor Blaise Meredith, who expects to die of cancer within months, agrees to investigate the life and alleged miracles of Giacomo Nerone, an army deserter and father of an illegitimate son but nevertheless a candidate for sainthood. The dramatis personae struggle with their inner contradictions and ironies: Nerone's mistress, Nina, "the village whore," is an illiterate woman of intuitive wisdom and queenly bearing; the Countess de Sanctis is a nymphomaniac in sufficient despair either to commit suicide or to find God; Nicholas Black, artist-homosexual, on the verge of seducing Nerone's bastard son, finds redemption by hanging himself on the Judas tree; and, finally, the detached, scholarly Monsignor Meredith, who has misspent his priestly life because he has never loved anyone, develops a full heart under sentence of death and nearly qualifies for sainthood himself. Throughout the novel, the craggy landscape itself, the Calabrian towns of Gemello Minore and Gemello Maggiore, the cross, the office of "Devil's Advocate" and many characters and incidents take on a brooding symbolism and the rich suggestiveness of allegory. West's other best-known religious novel, *Shoes of the Fisherman*, though not as well-written, conveys the agony and loneliness of a contemporary non-Italian Pope, Kiril I, who tries to serve as keeper of the keys even as he would throw open the windows of the embattled fortress of the modern church. Matching Kiril's loneliness and courage is Father Telemond, a Jesuit scholar-scientist undoubtedly modeled on Teilhard de Chardin and more plausible and attractive as a character. West's Pope Kiril, as a combination of John XXIII and Haroun al Raschid, challenges credulity; his secret missions and personal diplomacy to avert World War III defy it. This novel, like *Daughter of Silence* before it and *The Ambassador* after it, is a *roman à clef* with a journalist-scholar's accurate and complete detailing of places and procedures.

Recently, in *The Ambassador* and *The Tower of Babel*, West has ventured into the political novel with a degree of success. Although West gathered his data for *The Ambassador* in 1963, it offers a remarkably thorough, prescient description of the conditions and problems of American involvement in Vietnam. Told through the eyes of our newly arrived ambassador, the novel-documentary offers no heroes or villains but traces the inevitable failure, moral and political, personal and national, of the well-intentioned ambassador and the government he represents. *The Tower of Babel*, dealing with Middle East intrigue and crisis just prior to the Six Days War, diffuses its focus through the lives and point-of-view of five or six involved characters, but the author's basic approach and judgments are similar: in a complex violent world of conflicting needs and large blind forces, man needs compassion, love and God; with these, personal catastrophe may come but it cannot destroy the dignity, meaning or justice of life.

—Frank Campenni

---

**WEST, Paul.** British. Born in Eckington, Derbyshire, 23 February 1930. Educated at the University of Birmingham, B.A. (1st class honours) 1950; Oxford University, 1950–52; Columbia University, New York, M.A. 1953. Served in the Royal Air Force, rising to the rank of Flight Lieutenant, 1954–57. Married Paula Radcliffe in 1960; has one child. Assistant Professor, then Associate Professor of English, Memorial University of Newfoundland, St. John's, 1957–62. Associate Professor, 1962–68, and since 1968 Professor of English and Comparative Literature, and Senior Fellow, Institute for the Arts and Humanistic Studies, Pennsylvania State University, University Park. Visiting Professor of Comparative Literature, University of Wisconsin, Madison, 1965–66; Crashaw Professor of Literature, Colgate University, Hamilton, New York, Fall 1972. Contributor to the *New Statesman*, London, 1954–62. Since 1962, regular contributor to the *New York Times Book Review*; *Book World*, Washington, D.C., and Chicago; and the *Chicago Sun-Times*. Recipient: Canada Council Senior Fellowship, 1960; Guggenheim Fellowship, 1962. Address: 117 Burrowes Building, Pennsylvania State University, University Park, Pennsylvania 16802, U.S.A.

PUBLICATIONS

Novels

  *A Quality of Mercy.*   London, Chatto and Windus, 1961.
  *Tenement of Clay.*   London, Hutchinson, 1964.
  *Alley Jaggers.*   London, Hutchinson, and New York, Harper, 1966.
  *I'm Expecting to Live Quite Soon.*   New York, Harper, 1970; London, Gollancz, 1971.
  *Caliban's Filibuster.*   New York, Doubleday, 1971.
  *Bela Lugosi's White Christmas.*   London, Gollancz, and New York, Harper, 1972.
  *Colonel Mint.*   New York, Dutton, and London, Calder and Boyars, 1972.

Short Stories

   *Penguin Modern Stories 8*, with others.   London, Penguin, 1971.

Uncollected Short Stories

   "How to Marry a Hummingbird", in *Modern Occasions*.   New York, Farrar Straus,
      1966.
   "The Season of the Single Women", in *New American Review 11*.   New York, Simon
      and Schuster, 1971.
   "The Man Who Ate the Zeitgeist", in *London Magazine*, April–May, 1971.

Verse

   *The Snow Leopard*.   London, Hutchinson, 1964; New York, Harcourt Brace, 1965.

Other

   *The Fossils of Piety: Literary Humanism in Decline*.   New York, Vantage Press, 1959.
   *The Growth of the Novel*.   Toronto, Canadian Broadcasting Corporation, 1959.
   *Byron and the Spoiler's Art*.   London, Chatto and Windus, 1960; New York, St.
      Martin's Press, 1961.
   *The Modern Novel*.   London, Hutchinson, 1963; New York, Hillary House, 1965.
   *I, Said the Sparrow* (autobiography).   London, Hutchinson, 1964.
   *The Wine of Absurdity* (essays).   University Park, Pennsylvania State University Press,
      1966.
   *Words for a Deaf Daughter*.   London, Gollancz, 1969; New York, Harper, 1970.

   Editor, *Byron: A Collection of Critical Essays*.   New York, Prentice Hall, 1963.


Manuscript Collection: Pattee Library, Pennsylvania State University, University Park.


Critical Studies: essay by John W. Aldridge, in *Kenyon Review* (Gambier, Ohio), September
1966; essay by Martin Seymour-Smith in *New Literary History* (Charlottesville, Virginia),
Spring 1970; essay by the author, "The Writer's Situation II", in *New American Review 10*,
New York, New American Library, 1970; interview with George Plimpton, a postscript to
*Caliban's Filibuster*, 1971; review by Frederick Busch, in *New York Times Book Review*, 20
June 1971.


Paul West comments:

   Looking back, I see myself as a late starter who, between thirty and forty, in a sustained
and intensive spell of application, set down half a lifetime's pondering and moved from a
restless contentment with criticism and fairly orthodox fiction to an almost Fellini-like
point of view.
   Imagination, as I see it, is an alembic in limbo: it invents, and what it invents has to be
added to the sum of Creation—even though nothing imagination invents is wholly its own.
In other words, I think the realistic novel has served its turn (for Western society as well as

for me), should be put out to grass with an O.B.E. and a White House Medal. Fiction has to reclaim some of its ancient privileges, which writers like Lucian and Nashe and Rabelais and Grimmelshausen exploited to the full. I think that only the plasticity of a free-ranging imagination can do justice to late-twentieth-century man who, as incomplete as man ever was, keeps on arming himself with increasing amounts of data which, as ever, mean nothing at all.

My own fiction I have come to see as—I want it to be—a kind of linear mosaic, which is what my second novel, *Tenement of Clay*, was in a rudimentary form and which my two most recent ones—*Caliban's Filibuster* and *Colonel Mint*—are in a much more advanced and demanding way. Actually, since both vocabulary and syntax are themselves fictive I don't regard my autobiographical writing as essentially different from my fiction: they're both part of the mosaic I invent.

What matters to me most of all is to write, and live, without preconceptions, which is something any handicapped child (such as Mandy, my deaf daughter, for whom I wrote a book that was enormously successful) can teach us. Elasticity, diversity, openness, these are the things that matter to me most. Whatever I'm writing evinces the interplay between it and my life at the moment of writing, and the result is prose which, as well as being narrative and argumentative and somewhat pyrotechnical, is also symptomatic. Hence *Bloy: Your Own Coin-Operated Super-Nova*, the novel or "text" I'm working on right now, is a synthesis in which I appear in my own persona among the characters; they are me, I am them, but I am also an untransposed me as well.

\*      \*      \*

Paul West is something of a literary all-rounder. A critic—he has written a widely-respected study of Byron's poetry—he is also a poet, an autobiographer and a novelist. It is of course in this last capacity that he is best known, and this is mostly due to the Alley Jaggers sequence of novels (there are now three of them). With the creation of Alley, indeed, Paul West deservedly won his reputation as a highly original novelist.

But it would be unfair to think of West only as the novelist of Alley Jaggers. In fact he had already published two novels before Alley made his first appearance, in 1966. It is fair to say, however, that all West's novels contain the virtues that are best exploited through the Jaggers books. They are remarkable for a quick-firing imagination, a zany, bawdy and farcical humour, and an almost dizzying inventiveness with language. What they lack—and the Jaggers novels are no exceptions to this rule—is any really precise or deep enquiry into human psychology or any steady look at social realities.

On the face of it this may seem an odd charge to bring against West. Surely Alley Jaggers himself is exactly a psychological study, and surely his social background is given us in detail? Well, it is true that West sees his anti-hero as more than mere fictional high-jinks, and also true that he wants us to regard Alley's apparent lunacy as a highly original way of trying to construct a world in which to live (so that the disasters that come to him are a direct result of his barking his shins against the dailiness of an ordinary mundane world that won't give him the freedom he needs to live in *his* world). Yet, although this is West's plan, I do not believe that he succeeds in putting it persuasively into operation. And I think that the novels in the sequence become steadily more attenuated in their inventiveness, so that the most recent, *Bela Lugosi's White Christmas*, is the most fantastic—in every sense of that word.

Yet to say that the Jaggers novels fail on some terms is by no means to regard them as failures. For although we may not be persuaded that Alley is a psychologically interesting case, and although we may find West's treatment of the Midlands oddly unrealistic (the details—and there are plenty of them—have the feeling of being wrongly stuck together, and one wants to protest that Midlands pubs and parks and dance-halls simply aren't as West presents them), there remains much in the novels to enjoy. In the first place, there is a good deal of effectively rumbustious knock-about comedy in the tradition of Fielding and Smollett.

Then there is the frequent neatness and point of the dialogue, its unexpected wit and drive. And above all there is West's seemingly inexhaustible inventiveness for situation and language. The medium for this inventiveness is, of course, Alley, but it is impossible not to feel that it is the author rather than his leading character whose free-wheeling imagination we admire and relish. Putting it rather differently, we might say that while we do not much care about Alley himself, we do care that West should go on writing about him.

—John Lucas

**WEST, Rebecca.** Pseudonym for Cicily Fairfield Andrews. British. Born in London, 25 December 1892. Educated at George Watson's Ladies College, Edinburgh. Married Henry Maxwell Andrews in 1930 (died, 1968); has one child, Anthony West, *q.v.* Reviewer and Political Writer, *Freewoman*, London, 1911, and *Clarion*, London, 1912. Talks Supervisor, BBC, London, during World War II. Member, Order of St. Sava, 1937; Chevalier, Legion of Honour, 1957. Fellow, 1947, Benson Medallist, 1967, and Companion of Literature, 1968, Royal Society of Literature. D.Litt., New York University. Member, American Academy of Arts and Letters. C.B.E. (Commander, Order of the British Empire), 1949; D.B.E. (Dame Commander, Order of the British Empire), 1959. Address: Ibstone House, Ibstone, near High Wycombe, Buckinghamshire, England.

PUBLICATIONS

Novels

   *The Return of a Soldier.* London, Nisbet, and New York, Century, 1918.
   *The Judge.* London, Hutchinson, and New York, Doran, 1922.
   *Harriet Hume: A London Fantasy.* London, Hutchinson, and New York, Doubleday, 1929.
   *The Thinking Reed.* London, Hutchinson, and New York, Viking Press, 1936.
   *The Fountain Overflows.* New York, Viking Press, 1956; London, Macmillan, 1957.
   *The Birds Fall Down.* London, Macmillan, and New York, Viking Press, 1966.

Short Stories

   *The Harsh Voice: Four Short Novels.* London, Cape, and New York, Doubleday, 1935.

Verse

   *Elegy: An In Memoriam Tribute to D. H. Lawrence.* London, Simpkin Marshall, and New York, Phoenix Book Shop, 1930.

Other

*Henry James.* London, Nesbit, and New York, Holt, 1916.
*The Strange Necessity: Essays and Reviews.* London, Cape, and New York, Doubleday, 1928.
*Lions and Lambs*, with Low (as Lynx). London, Cape, 1928; New York, Harcourt Brace, 1929.
*D. H. Lawrence: An Elegy.* London, Secker, 1930.
*Arnold Bennett Himself.* New York, Day, 1931.
*Ending in Earnest: A Literary Log.* New York, Doubleday, 1931.
*St. Augustine.* London, Davies, and New York, Appleton, 1933.
*A Letter to a Grandfather.* London, Hogarth Press, 1933.
*The Modern "Rake's Progress"*, with Low. London, Hutchinson, 1934.
*Black Lamb and Grey Falcon: The Record of a Journey Through Yugoslavia.* London, Macmillan, 2 vols., 1937; as *Black Lamb and Grey Falcon: A Journey Through Yugoslavia*, New York, Viking Press, 2 vols., 1941.
*Rebecca's Cookbook.* Washington, D.C., privately printed, 1942.
*The Meaning of Treason.* New York, Viking Press, 1947; London, Macmillan, 1949; revised edition, London, Penguin, 1965; as *The New Meaning of Treason*, Viking Press, 1964.
*A Train of Powder* (essays). London, Macmillan, and New York, Viking Press, 1955.
*The Court and the Castle: Some Treatments of a Recurrent Theme.* New Haven, Connecticut, Yale University Press, 1957; as *The Court and the Castle: A Study of the Interactions of Political and Religious Ideas in Imaginative Literature*, London, Macmillan, 1958.
*The Vassall Affair.* London, Sunday Telegraph, 1963.

Editor, *Carl Sandburg: Selected Poems.* London, Cape, and New York, Harcourt Brace, 1926.

Critical Studies: "Very little written in English for the last fifty years is helpful (except that Lionel Trilling is always sound), and who am I to hope I am an exception?"

Rebecca West comments:

I have always written in order to discover the truth for my own use, on the one hand, and on the other hand to earn money for myself and my family, and in this department of my work I hope I have honoured the truth I had already discovered. I have like most women written only a quarter of what I might have written, owing to my family responsibilities. I dislike heartily the literary philosophy and practice of my time, which I think has lagged behind in the past and has little relevance to the present, and it distresses me that so much contemporary work is dominated by the ideas (particularly the political and religious ideas) of the late eighteenth or nineteenth century, and those misunderstood. I wish some novelist would arise who would write about the majority of people, who are as unhappy as the characters in modern fiction, but in ways never there referred to.

\*       \*       \*

The "authentic" work of art, Rebecca West asserts in *The Court and the Castle*, is that which the artist creates by "analyzing an experience and synthesizing the results . . . into a form, which excites an appetite for further experience." For an understanding of all this, however, one has to turn to an earlier study, *The Strange Necessity*, in which Miss West argues that the genuine work is essentially an analogue of cortical activity. Pavlov states that "the nervous system possesses on the one hand a definite analyzing mechanism, by means of which it selects out of the whole complexity of the environment those units which are of significance, and, on the other hand, a synthesizing mechanism by means of which individual units can be integrated into an excitatory complex." To this Miss West responds, "but can it really be of the cortex he is speaking? For there never was a better statement of the duplex function that must be fulfilled by any work of art." In *The Strange Necessity* (the necessity being man's basic need to create and experience works of art) she develops a thoroughly behavioristic theory of the value of art in many respects similar to that of I. A. Richards. The artist's sensitive response to experience, his recognition of its component parts, and his synthesis, rendered in aesthetic (that is, organic) form allow the audience to become "much more completely the masters of reality". The artist is engaged in the same struggle to understand complex situations and states of feeling which all men face, and if we are capable of genuine response to his synthesis, our own capacity to cope with reality is strengthened. "Never, I perceive, am I a more healthy, sane, non-neurotic animal than when I let art dictate my reactions," Miss West concludes; the authentic work permits a "new and satisfactory equilibrium for my will to live and my will to die".

*The Court and the Castle* extends the argument, insisting that artistic analysis and synthesis must have a bearing on "the question which concerns us most deeply of all: whether the universe is good or bad," but in this later work the simple psychologism of *The Strange Necessity* is subsumed by a frankly theological conception of the inherent corruption of the human will. Great works of fiction give

> impressive testimony against a heresy which [was] revived by the Renaissance and was steadily to gain adherents till it triumphed in the nineteenth century: against Pelagianism. It was an array of evidence against the theory that man is equally free to choose between good and evil, and that should he choose good, his own natural ability will enable him to reach moral perfection, and that our race could be changed and made innocent without search for a higher authority and submission to it.

Thus for Miss West much of the "liberal" romantic tradition is heretical: "the truth that has to be embraced by the man who desires to be saved is cruel, unreasonable, and incomprehensible"—incomprehensible, that is, in purely human terms. Miss West concludes with an eloquent endorsement of Kafka's aphorism, "The German word *Sein* has two meanings: it means to exist, and it means to belong to Him." The tendency of literature, when it "rises above a certain level, is to involve itself with statecraft and with religion: to exist and to belong to Him".

This ability to perceive complex experience accurately, to analyse it correctly, to synthesize a form suitable for its expression, and finally to reveal man's weaknesses and the possibility of grace—these are the qualities which Miss West makes into critical requirements; and it is not surprising, perhaps, that judged by these ultimate standards her own work is never wholly successful. There can be no doubt about Miss West's powerful capacity to observe the world around her or her passion to do so (with George Orwell she is one of the most distinguished political journalists of our time), nor about the sincerity of her convictions concerning the tragic consequences of human action ("Man is a political animal," observes one of the characters in *The Fountain Overflows*, "but seeing what the animal is, what may politics become?"). The difficulty is, rather, her inability to synthesize a truly satisfactory artistic form, that "perfect equilibrium" in which "there is no character which is not displayed in the right extent of space with the right degree of emphasis . . . there is no part which rebels against the whole, there is the peace of unity." And perhaps most important, Miss West has thus far seemed unwilling to dramatize her essentially theological commitments.

*The Return of a Soldier* is an immature work, a sentimental romance distinguished only by some reliance on the Freudian conception of memory and repression which was soon to become a cliche of popular fiction and drama. *The Judge* is a much more ambitious novel, badly thrown off balance by a divided center of interest. In the first third of the book Miss West is fitfully successful in rendering the perceptions of a naive young Scottish girl, a suffragette determined to wrest more from life than her poverty and sex permit. She marries a young man dominated by his mother, who then becomes the true protagonist of the work, a complex, suffering woman portrayed with a power and immediacy equal to Lawrence at his early best. The ending, however, degenerates into crude melodrama. *Harriet Hume* offers sad proof that Miss West has little talent for fantasy or the comic. This heavy-handed parable about artistic sensitivity and political drive is spoiled by ponderousness, while the next novel, *The Thinking Reed*, is equally spoiled by untypical commercial slickness and some badly dated chic. Again there is an unsuccessful attempt to synthesize the basic elements of the story, in this case a young woman's marital ups and downs and Miss West's rather superficial criticism of the sterility and waste of the world her heroine inhabits.

*The Fountail Overflows*, however, is an extraordinarily moving and real account of a dozen or so years in the life of an Edwardian family. The narrative tone is now completely consistent and assured; the portraits of the Aubreys' brilliant, erratic father and pathetic but finally heroic mother are achievements of the first order. Yet it is difficult not to regard this novel as something of an anachronism. In 1927 Miss West admitted "I have got to live in a world where a large number of people are to varying degrees conditioned by a knowledge of *Ulysses*"; but the world of *The Fountain Overflows* is the world of Dickens, unconditioned by anything later than Bennett or Galsworthy. It is entertainment of remarkable innocence for these times, but wholly satisfying within the terms it sets up. In her latest novel, *The Birds Fall Down*, Miss West once more seems unable to fuse her political acuity and technical control. Based on an actual incident in which a young girl unwittingly plays a part in frustrating a plot against her exiled Tsarist grandfather (in turn frustrating an attempt on the Tsar's life and thereby providing indirect aid for Lenin's rise to power), the novel remains a collection of splendid fragments. The information necessary for grasping the maddeningly tangled intrigue poses insuperable structural problems.

There is so much intelligence at work in Miss West's fiction and in her unjustly neglected criticism that it may seem ungrateful to ask for more. But what one misses, finally, is a creative power equal to the high argument of *The Court and the Castle*.

—Elmer Borklund

---

**WHITE, Antonia.** British. Born in London, 31 March 1899. Educated at the Convent of the Sacred Heart, Roehampton, London, 1908–14; St. Paul's Girls' School, London, 1914–16; Academy of Dramatic Art, London, 1919–20. Married Tom Hopkinson, *q.v.*, in 1930 (marriage dissolved, 1938); has two children. Actress, 1920–21. Copywriter, W. S. Crawford Ltd., London, 1924–31; Assistant Editor, *Life and Letters*, London, 1928–29; Free-lance Journalist, 1931–34; Theatre Critic, *Time and Tide*, London, 1934; Copywriter, J. Walter Thompson, London, 1934–35; Teacher and Writer, London Theatre Studio, 1935–36; Fashion Editor, *Daily Mirror*, London, 1935–37, and *Sunday Pictorial*, London, 1937–39; Writer, BBC, London, 1940–43. Served in the Political Intelligence Department, French Section, Foreign Office, London, 1943–45. Visiting Lecturer, St. Mary's College, Notre Dame, Indiana, 1959. Recipient: Clairouin Prize, for translation, 1950; Arts Council grant, 1967, 1969. Fellow, Royal Society of Literature, 1957. Address: 42 Courtfield Gardens, London S.W.5, England.

PUBLICATIONS

### Novels

*Frost in May*.   London, Harmsworth, 1933; New York, Viking Press, 1934.
*The Lost Traveller*.   London, Eyre and Spottiswoode, and New York, Viking Press,
   1950.
*The Sugar House*.   London, Eyre and Spottiswoode, 1952.
*Beyond the Glass*.   London, Eyre and Spottiswoode, 1954; Chicago, Regnery, 1955.

### Short Stories

*Strangers* (includes verse).   London, Harvill Press, 1954.

### Uncollected Short Story

"Surprise Visit", in *Art and Literature* (Paris), 1965.

### Play

*Three in a Room*.   London, French, 1947.

### Other

*Minka and Curdy* (juvenile).   London, Harvill Press, 1957.
*The Hound and the Falcon: The Story of a Re-Conversion to the Catholic Faith*.   London,
   Longman, 1965.
*Living with Minka and Curdy* (juvenile).   London, Harvill Press, 1970.

Translator, *A Woman's Life*, by Guy de Maupassant.   London, Hamish Hamilton,
   and New York, Pantheon Books, 1949.
Translator, *Reflections on Life*, by Alexis Carrel.   London, Hamish Hamilton, 1952;
   New York, Hawthorn, 1953.
Translator, *Pathway to Heaven*, by Henry Bordeaux.   London, Gollancz, 1952; New
   York, Pelligrini and Cudahy, 1953.
Translator, *The Cat*, by Colette.   London, Secker and Warburg, 1953.
Translator, *Sea of Troubles*, by Marguerite Duras.   London, Methuen, 1953.
Translator, *A German Officer*, by Serge Groussard.   London, Hamish Hamilton, and
   New York, Putnam, 1955.
Translator, *The Wind Bloweth Where It Listeth*, by Paul-André Lesort.   London,
   Collins, 1955; New York, Dutton, 1956.
Translator, *Claudine at School*, by Colette.   London, Secker and Warburg, 1956;
   New York, Farrar Straus, 1957.
Translator, *I Am Fifteen and I Do Not Want to Die*, by Christine Arnothy.   London,
   Collins, 1956.
Translator, *Those Who Wait*, by Christine Arnothy.   London, Collins, 1957.
Translator, *The Branding Iron*, by Paul-André Lesort.   London, Collins, 1958.
Translator, *It Is Not So Easy to Live*, by Christine Arnothy.   London, Collins, 1958;
   New York, Dutton, 1960.

Translator, *The Stories of Colette*.   London, Secker and Warburg, 1958; New York, Farrar Straus, 1959.

Translator, *Claudine in Paris*, by Colette.   London, Secker and Warburg, and New York, Farrar Straus, 1958.

Translator, *Thou Shalt Love*, by Jean-Marc Montguerre.   London, Methuen, 1958.

Translator, *The Swing*, by Fanny Rouget.   London, Bodley Head, 1958.

Translator, *The Charlatan*, by Christine Arnothy.   London, Collins, and New York, Dutton, 1959.

Translator, *Children in Love*, by Claire France.   London, Eyre and Spottiswoode, 1959.

Translator, *Tortoises*, by Loys Masson.   London, Chatto and Windus, 1959.

Translator, *I Will Not Serve*, by Evelyn Mahyère.   New York, Dutton, 1960.

Translator, *Claudine Married*, by Colette.   London, Secker and Warburg, and New York, Farrar Straus, 1960.

Translator, *Till the Shadow Passes*, by Julie Storm.   London, Collins, 1960.

Translator, *The Serpent's Bite*, by Christine Arnothy.   London, Collins, 1961.

Translator, *Claudine and Annie*, by Colette.   London, Secker and Warburg, 1962.

Translator, *The Whale's Tooth*, by Loys Masson.   London, Chatto and Windus, 1963; as *Advocate of the Isle*, New York, Knopf, 1963.

Translator, *The Trial of Charles de Gaulle*, by Alfred Fabre-Luce.   London, Methuen, and New York, Praeger, 1963.

Translator, *The Shackle*, by Colette.   London, Secker and Warburg, 1964.

Translator, *The Captive Cardinal*, by Christine Arnothy.   London, Collins, and New York, Doubleday, 1964.

Translator, *The Innocent Libertine*, by Colette.   London, Secker and Warburg, 1968.

Translator, *The Candle*, by Therese de Sainte Phalle.   London, Harrap, 1968.

Translator, *Memoirs of the Chevalier d'Eon*.   London, Blond, 1970.

Verse published in magazines.

Critical Study: "Reputations: Antonia White" by Samuel Hynes, in *Times Literary Supplement* (London), 3 July 1969.

Antonia White comments:

My novels, I fear, are anything but "contemporary" since they deal only with a period between 1908 and 1922. Much of the material in them, though not all, is based on my own experience, especially as a child at a convent school and as an inmate, for a period in my early twenties, of a lunatic asylum. The first, *Frost in May*, which I began when I was sixteen but did not finish till I was over 30 deals only with the predicament of a child who did not become a Catholic till she was 7—the automatic result of her parents being "converted"—in the bewildering atmosphere of an ultra-strict convent school of the old pre-World War I type.

The other three, written many years later, form a trilogy which, though preferably read in sequence, were each composed to be complete in themselves. The canvas is much wider than that of *Frost in May*, for though the young "anti-heroine" Clara is the central figure, only in the second, *The Sugar House*, are the events seen entirely through her eyes. In *The Lost Traveller* and *Beyond the Glass* they are seen partly through the eyes of her parents, and the relations of her parents to each other as well as their very different relations to their only child, and hers to them, form a complex web of conflicts and misinterpretations, sometimes ludicrous, sometimes tragic, which prevent any real communication between them except at rare and unexpected moments. The peculiar intensity of Clara's relations with her father (of whose implications he is half aware) are the underlying cause of the disastrous marriage to an impotent man and her subsequent disintegration into madness at a point when she had a prospect of achieving happiness. She recovers, only to find that her father, genuinely believing her to be incurable, has destroyed this prospect. However, she manages to resist the temptation to escape back into the world of illusion and braces herself to face the real one again.

*     *     *

Antonia White was born in 1899 in London, and has lived to see her first novel, *Frost in May* (1933), come to be regarded as a classic. She wrote it in 6 weeks and much of it is autobiographical. In it, Nanda Grey, the only daughter of a father recently converted to Catholicism, is sent to be educated at the Convent of the Five Wounds, Lippington. The year is 1908 and she is 9. Her family are lower middle-class, but she is an imaginative child and quick to adapt. In no time she begins talking about her parents' "butler". Nor does this spring from a desire to show off, but simply from an agonising wish to be like everyone else around her. Then there are the girls to compete with from grand Catholic European families such as Léonie de Wesseldorf whose name, in the ears of the community, has something of the ring of Medici or Gonzaga. Nanda's affection and admiration for Léonie grow daily, and one term threatened with "are you my best friend or not?" she reluctantly lends Léonie a novel she has begun writing when she had measles and was confined to the isolation wing. Her aim as the author has been to make her characters as wicked as possible in order that their conversions may seem the more spectacular. Unfortunately Léonie loses the manuscript and the nuns discover it. Even more unfortunately for Nanda, she has only written the first half of her story—and she is asked to leave. *Frost in May* presents an authentic picture of the life lived in many English convent public schools during the first forty years of this century. Everything is caught to perfection—the smell of beeswax in the corridors, the excitement of the cardinal's visit, and the constant fear that Protestants will get hold of the wrong end of the stick. There are as well some marvellous tell-tale touches: the girl who has a copy of *Candide* bound as a missal, and the retreat-giver who observes that Our Lady had no vote and did not want one.

At the time that Antonia White wrote this novel she was a lapsed Catholic and was to remain so for several years more. In a series of letters she brought out under the title of *The Hound and the Falcon*, she tells of her reconversion to the Catholic Faith during the Second World War. One of the main reasons for her alienation was the Church's attitude towards sex. In her trilogy, which began with *The Lost Traveller*, she touches upon this problem in particular.

Clara Batchelor, like Nanda Grey, is sent to a convent public school. Her father, once a young atheist, is now a convert. Her mother is frail and suffers from poor health: three unsuccessful pregnancies and a bad recent miscarriage have taken their toll. She tells her daughter: "... isn't it terrible that men can inflict such torment on us in the name of love? ... And the Catholic Church backs them up. Of course it's run by men." It is not surprising therefore that Clara's relations with the opposite sex remain often inconclusive and that when she marries into a grand Catholic family in the early 1920s, she has the vaguest notion of what marriage can and *should* be. In *The Sugar House*, one suspects her husband's inability to consummate their union and his escape into drink may not entirely be his fault. Like her, he wants to hide from reality, and their "sugar house" in Chelsea soon becomes a prison from which they both want to run away. In *Beyond the Glass*, the civil and religious machinery is set in motion for an annulment. Yet would a decree of nullity, ponders Clara, "mean that it was she herself who was null and void?" More and more bewildered by life, she gradually slides into a state of madness and has to be put into an asylum. Eventually she recovers, returns to her father's house in West Kensington, and the book ends with her clutching a rosary. Throughout the trilogy, there are references to old Catholic observances that are no longer in force such as fish on Friday and fasting from midnight before going to Holy Communion. Then there is the pressing question it leaves—Would it be right for someone with Clara's history to marry later and have children? Certainly her father and the priests

of his day would never have countenanced her using contraceptives. But now, over half a
century later, there are many Catholics with clear consciences who would. The truth is that
time has turned the trilogy into something of a period piece about Catholicism.

Antonia White has also translated a number of novels from the French including several by
Colette, written two children's books about her two cats, and published a volume of short
stories and poems called *Strangers*.

—Neville Braybrooke

---

**WHITE, Jon Manchip.** British. Born in Cardiff, Wales, 22 June 1924. Educated at St.
Catherine's College, Cambridge, 1942–43, 1946–50 (Open Exhibitioner in English Literature),
M.A. (honours) in English literature, prehistoric archaeology, and oriental languages
(Egyptology), and University Diploma in anthropology 1950. Served in the Royal Navy
and Welsh Guards in World War II. Married Valerie Leighton in 1946; has two children.
Story Editor, BBC, London, 1950–51; Senior Executive Officer, Foreign Service, 1952–56.
Free-lance Writer, including four years as a contract screenwriter for the Samuel Bronston
Company in Paris and Madrid, 1956–67. Since 1967, Associate Professor of English, Univer-
sity of Texas at El Paso. Address: c/o Curtis Brown Ltd., 60 East 56th Street, New York,
New York 10022, U.S.A.; or, c/o Harvey Unna Ltd., 14 Beaumont Mews, Marylebone High
Street, London W.1, England.

PUBLICATIONS

Novels

*Mask of Dust*. London, Hodder and Stoughton, 1953, as *The Last Race*, New York,
Mill-Morrow, 1953.
*Build Us a Dam*. London, Hodder and Stoughton, 1954.
*The Girl from Indiana*. London, Hodder and Stoughton, 1955.
*No Home But Heaven*. London, Hodder and Stoughton, 1956.
*The Mercenaries*. London, John Long, 1958.
*Hour of the Rat*. London, Hutchinson, 1962.
*The Rose in the Brandy Glass*. London, Eyre and Spottiswoode, 1965.
*Nightclimber*. London, Chatto and Windus, and New York, Morrow, 1968.
*The Game of Troy*. London, Chatto and Windus, and New York, McKay, 1971.

Verse

*Dragon*. London, Fortune Press, 1943.
*Salamander*. London, Fortune Press, 1943.
*The Rout of San Romano*. Aldington, Kent, Hand and Flower Press, 1952.
*The Mountain Lion*. London, Chatto and Windus, 1971.

Other

*Ancient Egypt.* London, Wingate, and New York, Crowell, 1952; revised edition, London, Allen and Unwin, and New York, Dover, 1970.

*Anthropology.* London, English Universities Press, 1954; New York, Philosophical Library, 1955.

*Marshal of France: The Life and Times of Maurice, Conte de Saxe.* London, Hamish Hamilton, and Chicago, Rand McNally, 1962.

*Everyday Life in Ancient Egypt.* London, Batsford, 1963; New York, Putnam, 1964.

*Diego Velazquez: Painter and Courtier.* London, Hamish Hamilton, and Chicago, Rand McNally, 1969.

*The Land God Made in Anger: Reflections on a Journey Through South West Africa.* London, Allen and Unwin, and Chicago, Rand McNally, 1969.

*Cortés and the Downfall of the Aztec Empire.* London, Hamish Hamilton, and New York, St. Martin's Press, 1971.

Editor, *Life in Ancient Egypt,* by Adolf Erman. New York, Dover, 1971.

Editor, *The Tomb of Tutankhamen,* by Howard Carter. New York, Dover, 1971.

Editor, *Manners and Customs of the Modern Egyptians,* by E. W. Lane. New York, Dover, 1972.

Translator, *The Glory of Egypt,* by Samivel. New York and London, Thames and Hudson, 1955.

Jon Manchip White comments:

The last quarter of a century has been a difficult time for the British novelist. Conrad once said that he wrote for "the post-captain on leave taking his ease on the lawn in the shade of the cedar tree". The cedars have been cut down; the post-captains have departed. The solid, educated, extensive, cultured, book-buying professional class with its knowledge of and interest in the great world to whom the British novelist once addressed himself has vanished. The novelist is now uncertain of the nature and character of his reader.

The shrinkage in readership has been accompanied by a shrinkage in the area of subject-matter. The current greyness and timidity of British life has meant that to be acceptable to British critics a novel must exploit only a narrow segment of human affairs. Where Conrad and Kipling wrote about East and West, about the ocean and engine-rooms, the British novelists now in fashion chronicle the mournful couplings of secondary-school teachers in Sidcup. The British no longer approve of nor enjoy contemplating the world at large, and do not want their novelists to remind them of it. The hostility towards the Common Market is only one token of modern British provincialism and fear of the larger theme.

Since they celebrate the qualities of energy and ambition, novels of my kind are not popular in Britain. My leading characters, in non-fiction as well as fiction, are architects, engineers, soldiers, racing-drivers, artists, adventurers—men who struggle to realize some significant aim in the face of sickness, formidable obstacles and flaws in their own nature. These dynamic personages are not likely to recommend themselves to a generation of readers who have been brought up, in MacNeice's words, to "sit on their arse for forty years and hang their hat on a pension".

For four decades the middle-ground of British political and cultural life has been given over to socialists and crypto-socialists. In literature this means the purveyors of what Leslie Fiedler has called the Sentimental Liberal Protest Novel, the novel in which "all the political content has been converted to sentiment". In a debilitated society, they still rule the roost. However, I am delighted to note, from where I write in Texas, that there are signs that some members at least of the next generation are rebelling against such an unexciting and inglorious creed, based as it is on the fear and dislike of any sort of individual difference and distinction, or often more simply on vulgar material envy. When British life has regained some of its native vigour and breadth, the characters and situations that novelists like me like to write about will be more in fashion.

I try to give my work, whether in prose or verse, a firm outline: maximum force with minimum means, as the hard-edge painters put it. I think that *The Rose in the Brandy Glass* was perhaps my last and best novel in the "traditional" style of British fiction, used by such writers as Joyce Cary, Graham Greene, F. L. Green, L. P. Hartley, C. S. Forester, Alfred Duggan, Emyr Humphreys, J. D. Scott, and J. M. Scott. Since then I have been trying to impart a new texture to my work. While trying to preserve its sense of structure and discipline, I have been attempting to introduce an atmosphere of fantasy and mystery. I have in mind the Welsh classic, *The Mabinogion*, or in recent years Rex Warner in England or Julien Gracq or Julien Green in France. Perhaps this stems in part from my Celtic background, and in part from a recent absorption in the psychological literature of dreams and insanity and in the paintings of Chirico, Ernst, Masson and Tanguy—paintings where the dream-image is sharp and bright yet functions in a strange dramatic landscape. I have never seen the point of committing myself to a novel unless the *donnée* has first struck me as being quite fresh and striking (oh, those novels about the anxious fornications of readers of the *New Statesman* in Sidcup). Above all things, I try to do my reader the service of treating him to something reasonably original. So it may be that for some time to come the activities of my architects and engineers will tend to be played out against increasingly bizarre backgrounds, and will be more experimental and even more "anti-novelistic" in character.

Or perhaps what I have really been aiming at, right from the very beginning, has not been "the novel" at all, but what Northrop Frye in his *Anatomy of Criticism* calls "the romance". Or to put it another way, perhaps all along I have been drawn towards what Edwin Muir in *The Structure of the Novel* calls "the dramatic novel", not what he calls "the novel of character". And perhaps this temperamental tendency will deepen in the years ahead.

\*        \*        \*

Jon Manchip White is first and foremost a novelist of adventure, a narrator of extraordinary events which take place in exotic settings and extend the human frame to the limit. He is a swift and adroit raconteur, not strong on characterisation, but capable of giving his plots an almost vertical take-off: thereafter the impetus is what matters, and the reader finds himself borne up on a steeply rising parabola of excitement. The typical pattern of his novels is that of a race, an escape, an inquisition, a test of endurance, skill or moral fibre. His heroes come through, but they are stretched up to and sometimes beyond the breaking-point: such is the toll of their exploits upon nerve and spirit. He has a weakness for those who are some way past their prime, and there is more of a touch of Hemingway in his fascination with physical ordeals and his mastery of the details of training and technique, of the weaponry and equipment of his soldiers and sportsmen.

Most of these elements are present in his first novel, *Mask of Dust*, which is still one of his best, a story of the world of the international motor Grand Prix. It is set in northern Italy, where the crowds hail this spectacular and lethal sport as the modern equivalent of charioteering. The central figure is a British champion, who in 1940 became a fighter pilot, and who after the war returns to racing, although arguably already "over the hill". Can he crown his career with one final international triumph, or has he stayed too long in the game—and what is the effect of this gamble on his young and beautiful wife? On this occasion White pursues an unashamedly romantic solution, and the novel reveals yet another characteristic which many of his heroes share: like Sherlock Holmes they indulge in unexpected intellectual or aesthetic relaxations. The British member of the driving team relieves his tensions by playing Debussy's *Arabesque*, "his fingers laid like strips of steel over the soft ivory"; the Italian plays chess; the Czech savours the odes of Horace in the original.

White's fiction has always been preoccupied with the rewards and penalties of individualism, and three later books are concerned with men on the run from society. The theme of *No Home But Heaven* is the natural and temperamental clash between the gipsy and the modern welfare state: *The Mercenaries* is an escape drama set in Argentina after the fall of Peron, where an ex-minister and his mistress struggle desperately to evade arrest by the revolutionaries and to find refuge in Paraguay: *Hour of the Rat* deals with the trial of a British civil servant, who kills a member of a Japanese delegation—his former persecutor at a prisoner of war camp—thus taking it upon himself, as he sees it, to avenge his war-time comrades. The one exception to these tales of action is *The Rose in the Brandy Glass*, yet here too the story involves an act of will as demanding as any mere demonstration of physical prowess: the plot hinges on the quixotic refusal of the hero, a retired cavalry colonel, against the wishes of all those nearest to him to put his name to an inaccurate statement in order to share out an inheritance. This is the author's most ambitious attempt to write a novel whose mainspring is social and psychological conflict rather than adventure, but the effort exposes his limitations in the field of characterisation.

White is an experienced writer of screenplays and more recently a strain of phantasmagoria has appeared in his writing, which suggests a cinematic influence on his technique: actuality and dream are juxtaposed, so that minute and sharply focussed details are contrasted with a background of delirium. Thus in *The Game of Troy* the plot is based on the legend of the Minotaur. The central character, a brilliant Daedalus-like architect, is commissioned by a Texas millionaire, with whose wife he has fallen in love, to design a modern labyrinth, complete with elaborate lighting and airconditioning systems. Awakening half-drugged underground, he finds himself being hunted by the murderous husband along the winding corridors and dead-ends of this nightmarish maze. But his most successful achievement in this genre is undoubtedly *Nightclimber*. The hero is an art-historian who is possessed by the craving, much in vogue in pre-war Cambridge, to climb high and dangerous buildings, and his obsession is diabolically exploited by a millionaire collector in search of a mysterious treasure in Greece. In the image of the nightclimber White has hit upon a symbol for the force which drives his heroes and inspires the type of adventure which he excels in chronicling. They are constantly impelled to push their luck, to take something more than a calculated risk, and much of the savour of the adventure lies in the possibility of being swept beyond the point of no return.

—Ian Scott-Kilvert

---

**WHITE, Patrick (Victor Martindale).** Australian. Born in London, England, 28 May 1912. Educated at schools in Australia, 1919–25; Cheltenham College, Gloucestershire, 1925–29; King's College, Cambridge, 1932–35, B.A. 1935. Served in the Royal Air Force as an Intelligence Officer, in the Middle East, 1940–45. Returned to Australia after the war. Recipient: Australian Literary Society Gold Medal, 1956; Miles Franklin Award, 1958, 1962; Smith Literary Award, 1959; National Conference of Christians and Jews' Brotherhood Award, 1962. Address: 20 Martin Road, Centennial Park, Sydney, New South Wales 2021, Australia.

PUBLICATIONS

Novels

*Happy Valley.* London, Harrap, 1939; New York, Viking Press, 1940.
*The Living and the Dead.* London, Routledge, and New York, Viking Press, 1941.

*The Aunt's Story.*  London, Routledge, and New York, Viking Press, 1948.
*The Tree of Man.*  New York, Viking Press, 1955; London, Eyre and Spottiswoode, 1956.
*Voss.*  New York, Viking Press, and London, Eyre and Spottiswoode, 1957.
*Riders in the Chariot.*  New York, Viking Press, and London, Eyre and Spottiswoode, 1961.
*The Solid Mandala.*  New York, Viking Press, and London, Eyre and Spottiswoode, 1966.
*The Vivisector.*  New York, Viking Press, and London, Cape, 1970.

Short Stories

*The Burnt Ones.*  New York, Viking Press, and London, Eyre and Spottiswoode, 1964.

Plays

*The Ham Funeral* (produced Adelaide, 1961).  Included in *Four Plays*, 1965.
*The Season at Sarsaparilla* (produced Adelaide, 1962).  Included in *Four Plays*, 1965.
*Night on Bald Mountain* (produced Adelaide, 1964).  Included in *Four Plays*, 1965.
*A Cheery Soul* (produced Adelaide, 1964).  Included in *Four Plays*, 1965.
*Four Plays* (includes *The Ham Funeral, The Season at Sarsaparilla, Night on Bald Mountain,* and *A Cheery Soul*).  London, Eyre and Spottiswoode, 1965; New York, Viking Press, 1966.

Verse

*The Ploughman and Other Poems.*  Sydney, Beacon Press, 1935.

Bibliography: *A Bibliography of Patrick White* by Janette Finch, Adelaide, Libraries Board of South Australia, 1966.

\*       \*       \*

One indication of the effect Patrick White's work has on the reader in Australia is to be found in the fact that reputable and ordinarily level-headed reviewers there incline to behave as though literary criticism had no decorous laws or respected guide-lines. They either frankly jettison attic temperance, and resort to unabashed adulation, or equally frankly become panicky, and fiercely vilify his novels. One eminent academic scourged his writing as "pretentious and illiterate verbal sludge", and found many to agree with him. Few critics and readers in Australia (and elsewhere?) remain respectably cool. Not surprising: the author himself rejects *le juste milieu.* White does not write of the common-or-garden, happy-go-lucky Australia of contented families, well-heeled provincial cities, of beaches, sky-scrapers, bistros, drive-ins, tennis tournaments, football matches, of the patent, the usual, the ordinary. His quasi-plotless novels are *grandezza*, edificial, epically long, too monolithic to be viewed tepidly. His manner of writing and the apparatus embedded in it compel readers utterly to give themselves up—or not at all. The hypnotizable are hypnotized, and thoroughly. Why? Perhaps one reason, which would repel the more uncompromising reader, is the queerity of White's Australia which can be summed up by a character in his third novel, *The Aunt's Story*, a world in which "Only chairs and tables are sane." For the portrayal of this kind of world White's style is the *sine qua non*.

It is ultimately a limited world, enclosed as Bedlam, in which even the humblest of maid-servants, adolescent hirelings or working-class extras can think in Job-like sonorities or give tongue as grandiloquently as an Ezekiel: White does lack an idiomatic ear. It is a world of obsessed visionaries, Mary Webb simpletons, filthy suburban saints, full-blown mystics trapped in an air-lock, eccentrics bursting at the seams with symbol, of mad and demi-mad solitaries, experience-unhinged foreigners, self-victimized escapees from convention and normality, all in their own ways trudging the quicksands between virginity and lust, reality and delusion, ambition and auto-cannibalism, savagery and sacrifice, God and godlessness. It is a world normal only to the sufficiently abnormal: its floor is the ceiling of the charnel house; whiffs of the Dark Ages lard its air.

In reading through from the first works to the latest it is impossible not to be conscious of White's abiding mannerisms and chronic affectations, his blatant nuances, waspish *apartés*, and repetitive images. At the same time it is impossible to be unaware of the plastic nature of his style which alters in tone and grain, in edginess and vulgarity, in vivacity and obliquity, from work to work as well as within the one work. This chameleonic skill is not always the result of mere maturity, although the charge of experience can be sensed and weighed. White has always been able to adapt his ectoplasmic style to the deed in hand, to re-dye and make-over, to be remarkably protean. This ability has its extraordinary side. His painstaking method of putting together razor-bright sentences, glassy clauses, vitreous jig-saw slices of paradox and poetry, the fastidious gluing on of sharp-edged fragments, could hardly be expected to produce a design not static and brittle as a chandelier. The result is elsewhere. There are, even beneath the most glazed *longueurs*, startling flashes, alert shadows, movement. There is life of a sort in the way that there is life of a sort in a mosaic of little mirrors sewn on a dark and suffocating blanket which is being agitated, bulged upwards, sucked inwards, tormented by the antics of the Form (or Forms) beneath it. One thing at a time is not the rule. This multi-view aspect of White's style—surface glitter and surface shadows stirring partly only because of the activity underneath, and partly otherwise (sometimes contrariwise) because of the lights beating down very poetically or most brutally from outside—can be mesmerizing to those who find lucidity tiresome. To others it can only mean confusion, can mislead and irritate: what are the Forms really doing now? which nasty shape will that Form next take?

Matters not how the Forms are disguised. Matters not which nineteenth-century or twentieth-century victim, black-fellow or white spinster, German explorer or Greek farm-hand, pervert or do-gooder, writhes and gesticulates. What is really convulsing the dark fabric and its encrusting dazzle is a mediaeval Dance of Death, and over all flickers a luridity as from some Satanic mill, a half-light striking up from some Hieronymus Bosch Under-world. Perhaps this is somehow how White sees what he sees. Perhaps he must thus make his puppets posture and utter, thus express what he wants to about life and death. *Wants* to, because, in spite of an uneasy feeling that he writes without temerity, unguarded and un-bridled, hurtling ahead in a trance, exhilarated beyond control, there is his published admission that he rewrites and burnishes, spending years on a novel, agonizing and *mot-juste*-ing with all the finickiness of, say, a Colette or a Flaubert. If so, he would seem to possess the very special skill of making the art that conceals art not quite conceal it. He appears, by and large, to find repugnant those he has created, and to throw humanity less to the forces of Time and Circumstance than into a bottomless pit of his own digging.

Despite its clear-cut disdains, its saw-toothed humour and malicious wit, the over-all texture of his prose is too nerve-ridden and agile, too marbled and grumous, at one and the same time too coarsely coarse and too slyly evasive, to permit either a major influence or a particular adultery of influences to be spotted. There could be none. There could be many. Here and there within the thousands of pages of sedulous work one seems to catch half-glimpses and quarter-glimpses of such an impossibly possible horde of influences that defeat in decision must be admitted: Dorothy Richardson, May Sinclair, Mary Webb, Hardy, D. H. Lawrence, Dostoiëvski, Joyce, Steinbeck, Firbank, Harold Nicholson,

Lawrence Durrell, Tennessee Williams. These might well, at times, fleetingly enter the reader's mind, and yet never have entered White's: he is his own writer, and could well be his own characters for each has unholy resemblances to the others.

One thing unusual about the writing of an author of White's reputation is its anaesthetic quality. This is apart from its undoubted hypnotic quality. Is it the author's indifference to his actors and their fates, an indifference indifferently concealed, which helps anaesthetize? Cruelty, immorality, obsession, anguish, approaching madness, all are talked away, not compassionately or sharply as in life, but tangentially, in an off-hand key, and often in the peculiar Aussie/stage-Cockney/literary turns of phrase most of his lower-class or *déclassé* mouth-pieces make free with when not inspired by simplicity or ecstasy to make exalted annunciations in a richer Shakespearian or Ecclesiastesian mode. Talked away, or written away, shock becomes all edges and no centre, and White's calendar of odious events— beheading, crucifiction, pederasty, suicide, incest, dog-eats-man, and so on—can be scanned with no more than the slightest tremor of distaste. White's attitude (*la morgue littéraire?*) to the event is the narcotic. We are worked upon to feel less than we should, to pass by on the other side. Is this the author's message, or merely a suave and weary comment on his own hand-picked prey? The question is put because, in spite of his attempts to outplumb profundity, White's purpose remains enigmatic. Although perilously involved with his characters' wilful doings (and most of his characters are wilful), he looms most, and mysteriously, on the outskirts of their curdled imaginations, a sky-line silhouette, blurred and ambiguous, yet immovably always there, creator and destroyer in one. This is as it must be: he is an imaginative writer, an anti-realist. No one lives who could sue him for libel. His landscapes would not show on a camera film. His suburb, Sarsaparilla, is a ghetto marked on no municipal map but its own.

Imagination is not insincerity. White's sincerity is all-pervading, and sometimes enervating. In one novel only, *The Tree of Man*, a much-lauded and cyclopean work, his first public success, is a kind of insincerity to be suspected, a well-sustained one. For all its meticulously recorded detail, energetic supporting cast, and its humour (some of his best), the novel rings true only in the folksy way—rural Humanity playing at Narcissus. Stan and Amy Parker, whose history the novel recounts, are left transfixed, like the exaggeratedly statuesque proletarians of a Soviet poster of the 1930s, in the posed attitudes of MAN and WOMAN; an uncomfortably sentimental and suspect stance familiar to readers of Steinbeck and Sheila Kaye Smith.

Whether White's striking technique and profligate talent, and the now-fashionable outrageous events and personages presented by it, will burn on revealingly for posterity, or burn out smokily under its strange eye, is not today foretellable.

At the moment he is a Goliath of a writer too modishly condign and conspicuous to underdefend or overpraise.

—Hal Porter

---

**WIEBE, Rudy.** Canadian. Born in Fairholme, Saskatchewan, 4 October 1934. Educated at the University of Alberta, Edmonton, 1953–56, 1958–60 (International Nickel Graduate Fellow, 1958–59; Queen Elizabeth Graduate Fellow, 1959–60), B.A. 1956, M.A. 1960; University of Tubingen, Germany (Rotary Fellow), 1957–58; University of Manitoba, Winnipeg, 1961; University of Iowa, Iowa City, 1964. Married Tena F. Isaak in 1958; has three children. Research Officer, Glenbow Foundation, Calgary, 1956; Foreign Service Officer, Ottawa, 1960; High School Teacher, Selkirk, Manitoba, 1961; Editor, The Mennonite Brethren *Herald*, Winnipeg, 1962–63; Assistant Professor of English, Goshen College,

Indiana, 1963–67. Since 1967, Member of the Faculty, University of Alberta: currently, Associate Professor of English. Recipient: Canada Council Arts Scholarship, 1964. Address: 11438 75th Avenue, Edmonton, Alberta, Canada.

PUBLICATIONS

Novels

Peace Shall Destroy Many.   Toronto, McClelland and Stewart, 1962; Grand Rapids, Michigan, Eerdmans, 1964.
First and Vital Candle.   Toronto, McClelland and Stewart, and Grand Rapids, Michigan, Eerdmans, 1966.
The Blue Mountains of China.   Toronto, McClelland and Stewart, and Grand Rapids, Michigan, Eerdmans, 1970.

Uncollected Short Stories

"Scrap Book", in Liberty (Toronto), September 1956.
"The Power", in New Voices.   Toronto, Dent, 1956.
"Tudor King", in Christian Living (Scottdale, Pennsylvania), December 1964.
"My Life: That's As It Was", in Canadian Mennonite (Altona, Manitoba), July 1967.
"Millstone for the Sun's Day", in Tamarack Review (Toronto), Summer 1967.
"All on Their Knees", in The Mennonite (Newton, Kansas), December 1968.
"Did Jesus Ever Laugh?", in Fiddlehead (Fredericton, New Brunswick), Spring 1970.
"Oolulik", in The Story-Makers.   Toronto, Macmillan, 1970.
"Bluecoats on the Sacred Hill of the Wild Peas", in The Star Spangled Beaver.   Toronto, Peter Martin, 1971.
"Where Is the Voice Coming from?", in Fourteen Stories High.   Ottawa, Oberon Press, 1971.
"The Fish Caught in the Battle River", in White Pelican (Edmonton), Fall 1971.
"Son of McDougall" (broadcast CBC International Network, 1972).

Other

Editor, The Story-Makers: A Collection of Modern Short Stories.   Toronto, Macmillan, 1970.
Editor, Stories from Western Canada.   Toronto, Macmillan, 1972.

Critical Studies: reviews in Canadian Literature (Vancouver), Winter 1963 and Fall 1966; in Fiddlehead (Fredericton, New Brunswick), Winter 1971; in Saturday Night (Toronto), April 1971; in The Banner (Grand Rapids, Michigan), April 1971; in Christian Living (Scottdale, Pennsylvania), July 1971.

Rudy Wiebe comments:

I believe that the worlds of fiction—story—should provide pleasure of as many kinds as possible to the reader; I believe fiction must be precisely, peculiarly rooted in a particular place, in particular people; I believe writing fiction is as serious, as responsible an activity as I can ever perform. Therefore in my fiction I try to explore the world that I know: the land and people of western Canada; from my particular world view: a radical Jesus-oriented Christianity.

\* \* \*

Central to all of Rudy Wiebe's writings is the Mennonite faith in which he was reared, and central to that is the "extremely individualistic approach to religion" (as he puts it in the foreword to his first novel) which motivates the actions and attitudes of all his characters. His novels, fundamentally and forthrightly Christian (neither tub-thumping nor ritualistic), probe the nature of faith. Deliberately didactic, they investigate the lives of ordinary people with ordinary abilities but passionate minds, to show the virtue of individual action, the power of commitment, and the sterility of material competitiveness and moral apathy. Sometimes the Christian parables intrude awkwardly, artificially, "unfictionalized", into the narrative line and symbolic tapestry, as in *First and Vital Candle* or in the end of *The Blue Mountains of China*, but when the blend is right, Wiebe's indirect style closes in on the intricate balance between intellect and feeling.

The first novel is the simplest in form, taking its title from *Daniel*: "he shall magnify himself in his heart, and by peace shall destroy many: But he shall be broken without hand." The ironic contrast implicit in the book, between Hitler's militant arrogance and the prairie Mennonite Deacon Block's pacifist arrogance, serves to highlight their similarities. The Deacon, certain to himself, is aware only of rules and traditions; always when young members of the community enquire as to the *nature* of the traditions they are told to uphold, routine orders rather than illuminating answers await them. The Deacon destroys his own family by such narrowness. For the central character too, young Thom Wiens—striving to sharpen his mind, answer his conscience, weigh military service in an attractive cause against admirable but paradoxically "enforced" pacifism—the Deacon's negation is no answer either. But the prospect of abandoning his faith seems equally barren. Only the private relation with God and with man—lonely, terrifying, challenging, necessary—can arouse in him any promise of the true internal peace that governments cannot legislate nor other individuals rule.

*The Blue Mountains of China*, Wiebe's most ambitious and most recent book, explores in a flawed but compelling fashion exactly those traditions and histories that Thom sought to discover. Taking up again a theme from the earlier book's foreword, it traces the great Mennonite quest for paradise: "like ancient Israel, they were a religious nation without a country." In the minds of different generations recalling fragmentarily their own history and intuiting dimly their significance in the story of the community as a whole, the 100-year trek from Russia to China to Canada to Paraguay comes to life. But the novel is more than genealogy—more than *Exodus*. By positing the ambivalence of paradise, it tries to explore the impact of an ideal upon the communal mind of a people. From adolescent quarrels early in the book (over the innocence or sinfulness of sexuality), through dissatisfaction with Russian communes, Chinese deserts, Canadian commercialism, South American violence, and arid intellectual pretentiousness, routes to earthly paradises are one after the other quietly closed. Yet all the time *the people* is crossing borders, often in flight, undercover, at night, in the wilderness, or in another language (so that no-one can pinpoint the moment of crossing) and with each change there arises the possibility of metaphysical insight. The title mountains divide the Chinese winds, creating a "contrast between fertile Manchuria and arid Mongolia". As Wiebe metamorphoses them into the Canadian Rockies, they become an ambivalent marker of contemporary Canadian/Mennonite/individual choices, too, hinting that peace (in Vietnam or in the private spirit) is only possible when men surrender their will to control other men and turn to contemplating seriously their own moves and motives instead. Increasingly, for Wiebe's Canada, this means reflecting on the popular prejudices against the native Indians and acting to alter such attitudes. Above all it means acquiring faith in the basic humanity of men and pursuing one's way to the future that humane action can foster.

—W. H. New

**WILDER, Thornton (Niven).** American. Born in Madison, Wisconsin, 17 April 1897. Educated at Oberlin College, Ohio, 1915–17; Yale University, New Haven, Connecticut, A.B. 1920; American Academy in Rome, 1920–21; Princeton University, New Jersey, A.M. 1926. Served in the United States Coast Artillery Corps, 1918–19; in United States Army Air Intelligence, rising to the rank of Lieutenant-Colonel, 1942–45; honorary M.B.E. (Member, Order of the British Empire), 1945. Teacher, 1921–28, and House Master, 1927–28, Lawrenceville School, New Jersey. Full-time Writer since 1928. Lecturer in Comparative Literature, University of Chicago, 1930–36; Visiting Professor, University of Hawaii, Honolulu, 1935; Charles Eliot Norton Professor of Poetry, Harvard University, Cambridge, Massachusetts, 1950–51. Actor in his own plays. United States Delegate: Institut de Cooperation Intellectuelle, Paris, 1937; with John Dos Passos, International P.E.N. Club Congress, England, 1941; UNESCO Conference of the Arts, Venice, 1952. Recipient: Pulitzer Prize, for fiction, 1928, for drama, 1938, 1943; National Institute of Arts and Letters Gold Medal, 1952; Friedenpreis des Deutschen Buchhandels, 1957; Austrian Ehrenmedaille, 1959; Goethe-Plakette, 1959; Brandeis University Creative Arts Award, for drama, 1959; Edward MacDowell Medal, 1960; Presidential Medal of Freedom, 1963; National Book Committee's National Medal for Literature, 1965; Century Association Art Medal; National Book Award, 1968. D.Litt., New York University, 1930; Yale University, 1947; Kenyon College, Gambier, Ohio, 1948; Wooster College, Ohio, 1950; Northeastern University, Boston, 1951; Oberlin College, 1952; University of New Hampshire, Durham, 1953; Goethe University, Frankfurt, 1957; University of Zurich, 1961; LL.D., Harvard University, 1951. Member, Order of Merit, Peru; Order of Merit, Bonn, 1957; Honorary Member, Bavarian Academy of Fine Arts; Mainz Academy of Science and Literature; Chevalier, Legion of Honor, 1951. Member, American Academy of Arts and Letters. Address: 50 Deepwood Drive, Hamden, Connecticut 06517, U.S.A.

PUBLICATIONS

Novels

The Cabala. New York, Boni, and London, Longman, 1926.
The Bridge of San Luis Rey. New York, Boni, and London, Longman, 1927.
The Woman of Andros. New York, Boni, and London, Longman, 1930.
Heaven's My Destination. London, Longman, 1934; New York, Harper, 1935.
The Ides of March. New York, Harper, and London, Longman, 1948.
The Eighth Day. New York, Harper, and London, Longman, 1967.

Plays

The Trumpet Shall Sound (produced New York, 1927).
The Angel That Troubled the Water and Other Plays (includes sixteen "Three-Minute Plays"). New York, Coward McCann, and London, Longman, 1928.

*The Long Christmas Dinner and Other Plays in One Act* (includes *The Happy Journey to Trenton and Camden, Love and How to Cure It, Queens of France, Such Things Only Happen in Books,* and *Pullman Car Hiawatha*). New York and New Haven, Connecticut, Coward McCann-Yale University Press, 1931; as *The Long Christmas Dinner and Other Plays,* London, Longman, 1931.

*The Long Christmas Dinner* (produced New Haven, Connecticut, 1931; Liverpool, 1932). Included in *The Long Christmas Dinner,* 1931; with music by Paul Hindemith (produced Mannheim, Germany, 1961; New York, 1963); libretto published, Mainz and New York, B. Schotts Sohne, 1961.

*The Happy Journey to Trenton and Camden* (produced New Haven, Connecticut, 1931). Included in *The Long Christmas Dinner,* 1931; revised edition, as *The Happy Journey,* New York, French, 1934; London, French, 1947.

*Such Things Only Happen in Books* (produced New Haven, Connecticut, 1931). Included in *The Long Christmas Dinner,* 1931.

*Love and How to Cure It* (produced New Haven, Connecticut, 1931; Liverpool, 1932). Included in *The Long Christmas Dinner,* 1931.

*Queens of France* (produced Chicago, 1932). Included in *The Long Christmas Dinner,* 1931.

*Pullman Car Hiawatha* (produced New York, 1962). Included in *The Long Christmas Dinner,* 1931.

*Lucrece,* adaptation of a play by André Obey (produced New York, 1932). Boston, Houghton Mifflin, and London, Longman, 1933.

*A Doll's House,* adaptation of a play by Henrik Ibsen (produced Central City, Colorado, 1937).

*The Merchant of Yonkers,* adaptation of a play by Johan Nostroy, based on *A Well-Spent Day* by John Oxenford (produced Boston and New York, 1938; London, 1951). New York and London, Harper, 1939; revised version, as *The Matchmaker* (produced Edinburgh, 1954; Philadelphia and New York, 1955), New York, Harper, 1955; London, French, 1957.

*Our Town* (produced Princeton, New Jersey, and New York, 1938; London, 1946). New York, Coward McCann, 1938; London, Longman, 1956.

*The Skin of Our Teeth* (produced New Haven, Connecticut, and New York, 1942; London, 1945). New York and London, Harper, 1942.

*Our Century.* New York, Century Association, 1947.

*The Victors,* adaptation of a play by Jean-Paul Sartre (produced New York, 1949).

*A Life in the Sun* (produced Edinburgh, 1955); as *The Alcestiad,* with music by L. Talma (produced Frankfurt, Germany, 1962).

*The Drunken Sisters.* New York, French, 1957.

*Bernice* (produced Berlin, 1957).

*The Wreck of the 5:25* (produced Berlin, 1957).

*Plays for Bleecker Street* (includes *Infancy, Childhood,* and *Someone from Assisi*) (produced New York, 1962).

*Infancy and Childhood* (produced London, 1972). New York, French, 2 vols., 1960, 1961.

Screenplays: *Our Town,* 1940; *Shadow of a Doubt,* 1943.


Other

*The Intent of the Artist,* with others. Princeton, New Jersey, Princeton University Press, 1941.

*       *       *

When Thornton Wilder was twenty-three years old he spent a year in residence at the American Academy in Rome and at this time he began work on his first novel, *The Cabala*. When that novel was published, it caused no great critical stir, but it was evident to discerning readers that a talent of high originality had been announced in this tableau-like presentation of the sophisticated self-involvement of a closed circle of decadent international figures in Rome, and that that talent had a signature quite its own. Its most evident qualities were the wit and urbanity of mind and the elegance of its prose. Then there was the classic, chiselled control of narrative, together with the ambience of a Virgilian idyll, far removed from the chaos and the tawdriness of the world of modern commerce even while the reality of that world was acknowledged. The classic overtones were heightened by the fact that each of these characters seemed to be a contemporary embodiment of one of the ancient Roman gods, all grown old, overwhelmed by Christianity and modern life. Into this classic frame was woven the favorite (as it would prove), highly romantic, indeed Proustian theme of the sad hopelessness of obsessive love. If *The Cabala* had a novelistic weakness it lay in its episodic character and in the fact that its three stories were really separate, not quite fused into unity by the total atmosphere. But that Wilder was highly gifted was perfectly clear.

In his next novel, *The Bridge of San Luis Rey*, a great popular success, that gift was not only widely acknowledged but, more important, consolidated. This novel moves back in time to the early eighteenth century and in place to Lima, Peru (where Wilder had never been). His recreation of a place that he had never seen is as impressive as a related quality, already evident in *The Cabala*—his skill in the delineation of characters of varying national temperament. In this story, five people are abruptly plunged to their death when an osier-woven bridge collapses. Why, the novel asks, these five? Was it the will of God? Was it sheer accident? Was it somehow self-decreed? The novel explores the life of each of these five characters and their personal relationships, and it transcends the fault of *The Cabala* not only by a skillful interweaving of those lives before the catastrophe and in their common fate, but more particularly by the question that that common fate illuminates. The novel gives no final answer to the problem of the three possibilities, even though it implies that the three, in some complex and unanalyzable geometry, are all involved. It does, however, ask a further question, and that has again to do with the nature of love, love as dedication, as obsession, as selflessness, and the novel ends with as much of an answer as the novelist can give: "There is a land of the living and a land of the dead and the bridge is love, the only survival, the only meaning."

*The Woman of Andros*, a tragic interpretation of Terence's *Andria*, is set in ancient times, shortly before the birth of Christ. The Woman is a beautiful hetaera, Chrysis, brilliant and learned in Athenian philosophy, and to her house, with other young bachelors, comes Pamphilus, for whom she holds an unexpressed love. Pamphilus, in turn, falls in love with Chrysis' young sister, Glycerium, whom he is determined to marry although the social situation would forbid that, and who is presently to bear his child. Chrysis dies and in the end Glycerium dies in childbirth, but the moral uneasiness that seems to have troubled this Platonist world before Christ, with the birth of Christ impending, seems to be resolved in the end when Pamphilus concludes that there is a meaning, however inscrutable, in his life and in the lost lives he has known, and he contemplates the serene stars over "the land soon to be called Holy." The death of the young mother and child marks the end of the pagan world as another mother and child are promised.

Wilder evidenced in these three novels a highly delicate gift of symbolism that summaries such as the one above abuse, but it should be evident that his great departure from contemporary fictional modes was in his rejection of the compulsive compilations of naturalism and the literal-minded social concerns of most naturalistic fiction. The result was that, with the publication of *The Woman of Andros*, he became the subject of literary abuse and the center of a literary controversy such as seldom raged in the United States. In the *New Republic* in 1930, the then well-known communist critic, Michael Gold, published a "Marxist" denunciation of Wilder's aesthetic remoteness from the affairs of real life. He charged that his work created "a museum, not a world," and demanded to know whether Wilder was "a Greek or is he an American?" It is ironical that Wilder, always aloof from literary as from real politics, was to be involved in a similar controversy in 1942, when the authors of *A Skeleton Key to Finnegans Wake* accused him of having plagiarized from Joyce's last book in his play, *The Skin of Our Teeth*. While Wilder had for long been interested in Joyce and while Joyce's book almost certainly gave him certain suggestions for his play, the charge was absurd and irresponsible. Wilder emerged from both controversies unruffled and unharmed.

Still, in his next novel, *Heaven's My Destination*, he seemed almost to be turning the tables on Michael Gold. Not only is this novel set in America in the years of the Great Depression but in the very heart of the Sinclair Lewis country, the middle west, and peopled by characters who might almost have stepped out of a Sinclair Lewis novel. And yet, in spite of all the apparent resemblance in the closely observed details of physical scene—the tawdry boarding houses, cheap hotels, crummy smoking cars, "greasy spoon" diners—and in the exactly reported midwestern vernacular—in spite of all this, the resemblance is at best superficial.

George Brush, the young hero of *Heaven's My Destination*, a textbook salesman, is also, as has been suggested by a number of critics, a kind of Quixotic saint, and the point of the book, as demonstrated by George Brush's experience, is that the world can tolerate anything except absolute goodness. George is good to the point of being simple-minded, and his utterly unselfish and utterly unself-important determination to do good to others inevitably gets him into trouble, sometimes into outrageously comic trouble, and inevitably outrages those whom he would assist. Yet he is never more than momentarily discouraged. His faith in the goodness of the world is as unshakeable as is his personal goodness. But the man who would literally apply Christian principles to his own conduct is also, in the world as it is, a clown and a bore. One of Wilder's remarkable achievements in this novel is that, while showing his hero to be precisely these things, he also wins the reader's sympathy and affection for him, even as, in the end, after what would be shattering disappointments to anyone else, his saintliness persists. And what persists as well, over the tawdry scene and the farcical action, is Wilder's elegance of novelistic form and essential seriousness of purpose. This may well be his greatest achievement in fiction.

Between *Heaven's My Destination* and his next novel, following on many shorter dramatic experiments, came Wilder's two great successes in the theater—*Our Town*, that gently nostalgic recreation of village life in New England, and *The Skin of Our Teeth*, the boldly experimental and endlessly inventive dramatic hymn to human endurance—both plays that, more than three decades later, retain all of their original force and are almost certainly permanent items in the American theatrical repertoire.

The remaining two novels are perhaps a slight falling off in imaginative weight even while they retain the now expected command of form and the always inventive narrative sense. *The Ides of March* is a novel about the life of Julius Caesar revealed through documents, the life of a great public man, just and thoughtful, always courteous, kind, tolerant, responsible and self-responsible but without self-importance. He is indeed, in a sense, without *self*. He has known passion but perhaps not very profoundly; he has loved a few people but he does not really need love. He is in many ways a grand figure but his grandeur lacks a spiritual dimension, and the novel, fascinating as it is as a literary performance, suffers accordingly.

Wilder's last novel, the recent *The Eighth Day*, returns him to the American scene in the early years of this century. It is a chronicle of two families in Coaltown, Illinois, families whose lives intertwine in complex ways and center in the solution of a mystery. This mystery raises large questions that pertain to problems of environment and heredity, destiny and chance. As with *The Bridge of San Luis Rey*, the novelist gives no final answers to these questions, but again, his meditative intelligence illuminates the questions and, as with so much of his fiction, enables the reader to conclude this skillful telling with a strong sense that he is wiser than he was when he began it.

—Mark Schorer

**WILLIAMS, John A(lfred).**   American.   Born in Jackson, Mississippi, 5 December 1925. Educated at Central High School, Syracuse, New York; Syracuse University, A.B. 1950. Served in the United States Navy, 1943–46. Married Carolyn Clopton; Lorrain Isaac; has three children. Has worked for publishers, in an advertising agency, and for the American Committee on Africa, New York. Recipient: National Institute of Arts and Letters grant, 1962; Syracuse University Outstanding Achievement Award, 1970. Lives in New York. Address: c/o Doubleday and Company, 277 Park Avenue, New York, New York 10022, U.S.A.

PUBLICATIONS

Novels

    *The Angry Ones.*   New York, Ace, 1960.
    *Night Song.*   New York, Farrar Straus, 1961; London, Collins, 1962.
    *Sissie.*   New York, Farrar Straus, 1963; as *Journey out of Anger*, London, Eyre and
       Spottiswoode, 1965.
    *The Man Who Cried I Am.*   Boston, Little Brown, 1967; London, Eyre and Spottis-
       woode, 1968.
    *Sons of Darkness, Sons of Light.*   Boston, Little Brown, 1969.
    *The Ordeal of Abraham Blackman, The Negro Soldier.*   New York, Doubleday, 1971.

Other

    *Africa: Her History, Lands and People.*   New York, Cooper Square, 1962.
    *This Is My Country, Too.*   New York, New American Library, 1965.
    *The Most Native of Sons* (biography of Richard Wright).   New York, Doubleday,
       1970.
    *The King God Didn't Save.*   New York, Coward McCann, 1970; London, Eyre and
       Spottiswoode, 1971.

    Editor, *Beyond the Angry Black*.   New York, Cooper Square, 1967.
    Editor, *Amistad I* and *II*.   New York, Knopf, 1970, 1971.

John A. Williams comments:

    I think art has always been political and has served political ends more graciously than those of the muses. I consider myself to be a political novelist and writer to the extent that I am always aware of the social insufficiencies which are a result of political manipulation. The greatest art has always been social-political, and in that sense I could be considered striving along traditional paths.

*     *     *

    Serious critical reaction against Richard Wright's *Native Son* was less concerned with the validity of Bigger Thomas as a representative of twenty million black Americans than it was with Bigger's lack of racial, cultural and group consciousness. The idea of the rootless, raceless, existential black with ties to neither his group nor the nation, was one which the

1355

black writers in the post-*Native Son* world would have to correct. Despite the similarity between Bigger and the characters of his own earlier novels, no writer has done more to demolish the idea upon which Wright's characterization of his protagonist rested than John A. Williams.

*The Angry Ones* takes us back to Bigger Thomas. In Steve Hill we have a character engaged in his own private warfare against American racism, one who feels that the conflicts which he undergoes—discrimination in terms of jobs and housing—are personal and can be resolved only by a personal commitment to his role as an artist. The theme of the embattled artist, alone, fighting American racism for the sake of self survival, is also the theme of *Night Song*. Richie Stokes (Charlie Yardbird Parker), jazz musician, his identity with his race symbolized in the music that he plays, nevertheless wages a private war against a world of booze, broads and music.

Not until *Sissie* does Williams present a protagonist, conscious of his racial identity, who is united with the race by the color of his skin. During a tenure in the army, Ralph Joplin, playwright, is attacked by a white soldier. Seeking revenge, Ralph arrives at the realization that: "He's frightened. I'm not one black man, I'm all of them. All their strength and hatred and fury—it's in me."

*The Man Who Cried I Am* and *Sons of Darkness, Sons of Light* evidence the progression of Williams' protagonists from men preoccupied with self to men preoccupied with the problems of the race as a whole, from men alone to men united by group experiences. The progression is due in part to the growth of Williams as a novelist, to his mastery of technique —refining the form of the novel so that it becomes a social and historical vehicle as well as a literary one—and in part to the heightened perception of many black Americans in post-Newark America.

This heightened perception—racism in the American society is an eternal given—accounts for the rise of black nationalism so eloquently symbolized in the character Minister Q (Malcolm X) in *The Man Who Cried I Am*. It also accounts for the conversion of many of the black middle class, symbolized by Eugene Browning in *Sons of Darkness, Sons of Light*: ". . . One morning I woke up and the enormity of what's been done to me was resting like a ball of deadly lead in my stomach, but it had got down; it went down, and I couldn't pretend anymore that it had meaning for me. Not only for me but for all the Negroes out there."

The theme of integration (the lack of it is the major theme of *Native Son*) gives way to the theme of black unity; the search for identity ends in the discovery of a racial and cultural past. No longer rootless nor ahistorical, the black protagonists of Williams later novels are cognizant of group cohesiveness, and of their role as racial warriors: "I'm the way I am, the kind of writer I am," Harry Ames (Richard Wright) remarks to Max Reddick in *The Man Who Cried I Am*, "because I'm a black man; therefore, we're in rebellion; we've got to be. We have no other function as valid as that one."

—Addison Gayle, Jr.

---

**WILLIAMS, Raymond (Henry).** British. Born in Llanfihangel Crucorney, Wales, 31 August 1921. Educated at Abergavenny Grammar School, 1932–39; Trinity College, Cambridge, 1939–41, 1945–46, M.A. 1946, Litt.D. 1969. Served as a Captain in the Anti-Tank Regiment, Guards Armoured Division, 1941–45. Married Joy Dalling in 1942; has three children. Editor, *Politics and Letters*, 1946–47. Staff Tutor in Literature, Oxford University Delegacy for Extra-Mural Studies, 1946–61. Since 1961, Fellow of Jesus College, Cambridge, and since 1967, Reader in Drama, Cambridge University. General Editor, New Thinkers Library, 1962. Reviewer for *The Guardian*, London. Member of the Welsh Academy. Address: Jesus College, Cambridge, England.

PUBLICATIONS

Novels

> *Border Country*.   London, Chatto and Windus, 1960; New York, Horizon Press, 1962.
> *Second Generation*.   London, Chatto and Windus, 1964; New York, Horizon Press, 1965.
> *The Volunteers*.   London, Chatto and Windus, 1972.

Uncollected Short Stories

> "Sack Labourer", in *English Story 1*.   London, Collins, 1941.
> "A Fine Room to Be Ill in", in *English Story 7*.   London, Collins, 1947.

Plays

> *Koba*, in *Modern Tragedy*.   London, Chatto and Windus, 1966.
> *A Letter from the Country* (televised, 1966).   Published in *Stand* (Newcastle upon Tyne), 1971.
> *Public Inquiry* (televised, 1967).   Published in *Stand* (Newcastle upon Tyne), 1968.

Other

> *Reading and Criticism*.   London, Muller, 1950.
> *Drama from Ibsen to Eliot*.   London, Chatto and Windus, 1952; New York, Oxford University Press, 1953; revised edition, as *Drama from Ibsen to Brecht*, Chatto and Windus, 1968, Oxford University Press, 1969.
> *Drama in Performance*.   London, Muller, 1954; Chester Springs, Pennsylvania, Dufour, 1961; revised edition, 1968.
> *Preface to Film*, with Michael Orrom.   London, Dobson, 1954.
> *Culture and Society, 1780–1950*.   London, Chatto and Windus, and New York, Columbia University Press, 1958.
> *The Long Revolution*.   London, Chatto and Windus, and New York, Columbia University Press, 1961.
> *Communications*.   London, Penguin, 1962; revised edition, London, Chatto and Windus, 1966; New York, Barnes and Noble, 1967.
> *Modern Tragedy*.   London, Chatto and Windus, and Stanford, California, Stanford University Press, 1966.
> *The English Novel from Dickens to Lawrence*.   London, Chatto and Windus, 1970.
> *Orwell*.   London, Fontana, 1971.

> Editor, *Two Prakit Versions of the Manipati-Carita*.   London, Luzac, 1959.
> Editor, *May Day Manifesto*.   London, Penguin, 1968.
> Editor, *Pelican Book of English Prose: From 1780 to the Present Day*.   London, Penguin, 1970.

Critical Studies: essay by Dennis Potter, in *New Left Review* (London), 1961; essay by Graham Martin, in *Views* (London), 1965; "The Novel, Truth and Community" by James R. Bennett, in *D. H. Lawrence Review* (Fayetteville, Arkansas), 1970–71.

Raymond Williams comments:

When I came out of the army in 1945 I began writing the novel which was eventually published as *Border Country*. It went through some seven rewritings. It has been described as autobiographical, but this is in many ways misleading. For example, the central character, Harry Price, is a railway signalman, as was my father, but I found I could not get the book right until I had invented another character, his friend and opposite Morgan Rosser, who is in many ways as close to my own father as the character usually taken as based on him. In its final version, the novel had moved far enough from anything that can ordinarily be called autobiography for it to have to be seen in quite other ways. The chapter on the General Strike in *Border Country* has nothing autobiographical in it, yet it is the chapter of my novel-writing that I am most satisfied with.

During that period of writing and rewriting I completed two other novels, *A Map of Treason* and *The Grasshoppers*, which are still in the desk drawer. During the early sixties I wrote my second published novel, *Second Generation*, which seems to be preferred to *Border Country* only in Eastern Europe, though I think it is exactly what I wanted to write as the working-class experience—personal and social rather than political—of the sixties. Since then I have been working on two novels, *The Brothers* and *The Volunteers*. The latter, set in Europe in the 1990's, will probably be the first published. The former, which is closer to *Border Country*, should be completed during the next two years.

I find novel-writing very important and rewarding, and I have given much more time to it than my list of publications might suggest. But I revise and rework a great deal, and shall be satisfied if by the time I have finished I have five or six novels which I can feel are really my own. The fact that I also write social criticism has led to a simple formula in which my novels are seen as by-products, but the two kinds of writing have always been equally important to me, and in fact the novel-writing came first and will, I think, go on longer. Some of the themes of the novels overlap with the social criticism, but I only write in novel form what I am sure could not be written in essays and analysis. As to method, although I found *Border Country* difficult to write, I think the form and language of memory and the past are more accessible to contemporary novelists than a form and language of the true present, as attempted in *Second Generation*. *The Volunteers*, set in the future, has required much more extended technical experiment; this is the main reason why it has taken so long to write.

\*       \*       \*

Raymond Williams has a well deserved reputation for his critical works such as *Culture and Society*, but has also ventured an unperformed play, included in the English edition of his *Modern Tragedy*, two good television plays (published in *Stand*) and two novels.

*Border Country* describes how a young university lecturer leaves his London home to return to the Welsh border village where he grew up, to visit his sick father. Back in his childhood environment, he finds himself on a border between his past and his present, between different classes, ambitions and generations. Most of the novel consists of memories evoked by the visit, through which he tries to understand his father, the rural way of life, and the experiences that have made him what he is. Obviously this is intensely personal for Williams, a book he had to write. Personal recollections—the death of his grandfather, fears that he had lost a pound note—mingle with a wealth of detail about the village, like the Eisteddfod and the excitement of catching a swarm of bees.

Matthew explores his deep relationship with his father, who "lived direct, never by any other standard at all." Through his father and friends, the relationship between work and life is examined: the signalbox routine has provided a meaningful core, a necessary job, close to home. Because work matters, the outside world has a big impact with the 1926 General Strike and its moral problems, vividly conveyed. A lifelong friend has taken a different course and become a successful minor capitalist, while Matthew fears his job and life do not connect.

Further, Matthew feels the Border community has a strength missing in his own more mobile society, and looks at it reverently. As a local tells him, "Here it's got to be in the open, because in the end there's no hiding things, and none of us is going away. . . . It isn't your kind of settlement, that any day might break up." The Eisteddfod adjudicator has come annually for years, remembering everyone, and Matthew "knew how much this ceremony of memory and identification meant to the silent and apparently unresponsive listeners." But lorries are turning the village into "a name you pass through, houses along a road." Ideas about old-time organic country life that we may have thought sentimental gain a new reality from Williams' picture.

He presents truthfully the experience of child growing away from parent, leaving village for suburb, which can appeal directly to those who share it and explain much to those who do not. The novel is leisurely, dignified, always serious.

*Second Generation* is more ambitious and more uneven. Two brothers, who have come in the 1930's from Wales to work in a car factory in a university town, live side by side, Harold, an active unionist, and Gwyn, politically apathetic. Harold's wife, frustrated intellectually, has an affair with a lecturer she meets through the Labour Party. Their son is a graduate student studying "community" theoretically and doubting the value of his work, wondering also whether to marry a girl he has known a long time. Finally, declining an American offer, he decides to work in the factory to make "a new kind of enquiry, with ourselves involved in it."

Williams, explained Irving Howe in the *New Republic*, is showing "both the continuities and differences between the old England of 'classical' capitalism and the new England of the welfare state." So it has less personal feeling than *Border Country* and is more of a document —and sometimes very good on this level, especially in conveying what a strike and threat of redundancy are like. What Williams thinks is often prominent at the expense of what he knows. As fiction, too, *Second Generation* is weaker than the earlier book, with over-solemnity, clumsiness and prolonged wordy dialogues more frequent and conspicuous.

—Malcolm Page

---

WILLIAMS, Tennessee (Thomas Lanier Williams). American. Born in Columbus, Mississippi, 26 March 1911. Educated at the University of Missouri, Columbia, 1930–32; Washington University, St. Louis, 1936–37; University of Iowa, Iowa City, 1938, A.B. 1938. Clerical Worker and Manual Laborer, International Shoe Company, St. Louis, 1934–36; held various jobs, including waiter and elevator operator, New Orleans, 1939; teletype operator, Jacksonville, Florida, 1940; worked at odd jobs, New York, 1942, and as a Screenwriter for MGM, 1943. Full-time Writer since 1944. Recipient: Rockefeller Fellowship, 1940; National Institute of Arts and Letters grant, 1944, and Gold Medal, 1969; Pulitzer Prize, for drama, 1948, 1955; New York Drama Critics Circle Award, 1945, 1948, 1955, 1962; Brandeis University Creative Arts Award, 1964. Member, National Institute of Arts and Letters. Lives in Key West, Florida and New York. Address: c/o Audrey Wood, International Famous Agency, 1301 Avenue of the Americas, New York, New York 10019, U.S.A.

PUBLICATIONS

Novel

The Roman Spring of Mrs. Stone.   New York, New Directions, and London, Lehmann, 1950.

Short Stories

*One Arm and Other Stories.* New York, New Directions, 1948.
*Hard Candy: A Book of Stories.* New York, New Directions, 1954.
*Three Players of a Summer Game and Other Stories.* London, Secker and Warburg, 1960.
*Grand.* New York, House of Books, 1964.
*The Knightly Quest: A Novella and Four Short Stories.* New York, New Directions, 1967; augmented edition, as *The Knightly Quest: A Novella and Twelve Short Stories,* London, Secker and Warburg, 1968.

Plays

*Cairo! Shanghai! Bombay!* (produced Memphis, 1936).
*The Magic Tower* (produced St. Louis, 1936).
*Headlines* (produced St. Louis, 1936).
*Candles in the Sun* (produced St. Louis, 1936).
*Fugitive Kind* (produced St. Louis, 1937).
*Spring Song* (produced Iowa City, Iowa, 1938).
*The Long Goodbye* (produced New York, 1940). Included in *27 Wagons Full of Cotton,* 1946.
*Battle of Angels* (produced Boston, 1940). Murray, Utah, Pharos-New Directions, 1945; revised version, as *Orpheus Descending* (produced New York, 1957; London, 1959), published as *Orpheus Descending, with Battle of Angels,* New York, New Directions, 1958; as *Orpheus Descending,* London, Secker and Warburg, 1958.
*At Liberty,* in *American Scenes,* edited by William Kozlenko. New York, Day, 1941.
*Stairs to the Roof* (produced Pasadena, California, 1944).
*You Touched Me,* with Donald Windham (produced Cleveland, 1944; New York, 1945). New York, French, 1947.
*The Glass Menagerie* (produced Cleveland and New York, 1944; London, 1956). New York, Random House, 1945; London, Lehmann, 1948.
*27 Wagons Full of Cotton and Other One-Act Plays* (includes *The Purification, The Lady of Larkspur Lotion, The Last of My Solid Gold Watches, Portrait of a Madonna, Auto-da-Fé, Lord Byron's Love Letter, The Strangest Kind of Romance, The Long Goodbye, Hello from Bertha,* and *This Property Is Condemned*). New York, New Directions, 1946; London, Grey Walls Press, 1947; augmented edition (includes *Talk to Me Like the Rain and Let Me Listen* and *Something Unspoken*), New Directions, 1953.
*This Property Is Condemned* (produced New York, 1946; London, 1953). Included in *27 Wagons Full of Cotton,* 1946.
*Portrait of a Madonna* (produced Los Angeles, 1946; New York, 1959). Included in *27 Wagons Full of Cotton,* 1946.
*The Last of My Solid Gold Watches* (produced Los Angeles, 1946). Included in *27 Wagons Full of Cotton,* 1946.
*Lord Byron's Love Letter,* in *27 Wagons Full of Cotton,* 1946; revised version, with music by Raffaello de Banfield (produced London, 1964); libretto published, Milan and New York, Riccordi, 1955.
*27 Wagons Full of Cotton* (produced New York, 1955). Included in *27 Wagons Full of Cotton,* 1946.
*The Purification* (produced Cambridge, England, 1955; New York, 1959). Included in *27 Wagons Full of Cotton,* 1946.
*Hello from Bertha* (produced Bromley, Kent, 1961). Included in *27 Wagons Full of Cotton,* 1946.
*Auto-da-Fé* (produced Bromley, Kent, 1961). Included in *27 Wagons Full of Cotton,* 1946.

*The Lady of Larkspur Lotion* (produced London, 1968).   Included in *27 Wagons Full of Cotton*, 1946.

*The Strangest Kind of Romance* (produced London, 1969).   Included in *27 Wagons Full of Cotton*, 1946.

*Mooney's Kid Don't Cry* (produced Los Angeles, 1946; London, 1971).   Included in *American Blues*, 1948

*A Streetcar Named Desire* (produced New York, 1947; London, 1949).   New York, New Directions, 1947; London, Lehmann, 1949.

*Summer and Smoke* (produced Dallas, 1947; New York, 1948; London, 1952).   New York, New Directions, 1948; London, Lehmann, 1952; revised version, as *The Eccentricities of a Nightingale* (produced Nyack, New York, 1964), published as *The Eccentricities of a Nightingale, and Summer and Smoke*, New York, New Directions, 1965; revised version, as *Summer and Smoke*, with music by Lee Hoiby (produced St. Paul, Minnesota, 1971).

*American Blues: Five Short Plays* (includes *Mooney's Kid Don't Cry, The Dark Room, The Case of the Crushed Petunias, The Long Stay Cut Short; or, The Unsatisfactory Supper*, and *Ten Blocks on the Camino Real*).   New York, Dramatists Play Service, 1948.

*Ten Blocks on the Camino Real*, in *American Blues*, 1948; revised version, as *Camino Real* (produced New York, 1953; London, 1957), New York, New Directions, 1953; London, Secker and Warburg, 1956.

*The Dark Room* (produced London, 1966).   Included in *American Blues*, 1948.

*The Case of the Crushed Petunias* (produced Glasgow, 1968).   Included in *American Blues*, 1948.

*The Long Stay Cut Short; or, The Unsatisfactory Supper* (produced London, 1971).   Included in *American Blues*, 1948.

*The Rose Tattoo* (produced New York, 1951; London, 1959).   New York, New Directions, 1951; London, Secker and Warburg, 1955.

*I Rise in Flame, Cried the Phoenix: A Play about D. H. Lawrence* (produced New York, 1953; London, 1971).   New York, New Directions, 1951.

*Talk to Me Like the Rain and Let Me Listen* (produced Westport, Connecticut, 1958).   Included in *27 Wagons Full of Cotton*, 1953.

*Something Unspoken* (produced New York and London, 1958).   Included in *27 Wagons Full of Cotton*, 1953.

*Cat on a Hot Tin Roof* (produced New York, 1955; London, 1958).   New York, New Directions, 1955; London, Secker and Warburg, 1956.

*Three Players of a Summer Game* (produced Westport, Connecticut, 1955).

*Sweet Bird of Youth* (produced Coral Gables, Florida, 1956; New York, 1959; Watford, Hertfordshire, 1968).   New York, New Directions, 1959; London, Secker and Warburg, 1961.

*Baby Doll: The Script for the Film, Incorporating the Two One-Act Plays Which Suggested It: 27 Wagons Full of Cotton and The Long Stay Cut Short; or, The Unsatisfactory Supper*.   New York, New Directions, 1956; as *Baby Doll: The Script for the Film*, London, Secker and Warburg, 1957.

*Garden District: Something Unspoken, Suddenly Last Summer* (produced New York and London, 1958).   New York, New Directions, 1958; London, Secker and Warburg, 1959.

*The Fugitive Kind: Original Play Title: Orpheus Descending* (screenplay).   New York, New American Library, 1958.

*A Perfect Analysis Given by a Parrot*.   New York, Dramatists Play Service, 1958.

*The Enemy: Time*, in *Theatre* (New York), March 1959.

*The Night of the Iguana* (produced Spoleto, Italy, 1959; revised version, produced New York, 1961; London, 1965).   New York, New Directions, 1962; London, Secker and Warburg, 1963.

*Period of Adjustment: High Point over a Cavern: A Serious Comedy* (produced Miami,

1959; New York, 1960; London, 1962).   New York, New Directions, 1960; London, Secker and Warburg, 1961.

*To Heaven in a Golden Coach* (produced Bromley, Kent, 1961).

*The Milk Train Doesn't Stop Here Anymore* (produced Spoleto, Italy, 1962; revised versions, produced New York, 1962; Abington, West Virginia, 1963; New York, 1964; London, 1968).   New York, New Directions, and London, Secker and Warburg, 1964.

*Slapstick Tragedy* (*The Mutilated* and *The Gnadiges Fräulein*) (produced New York, 1966).   New York, Dramatists Play Service, 2 vols., 1967.

*Kingdom of Earth*, in *Esquire* (New York), February 1967; revised version, as *Kingdom of Earth: The Seven Descents of Myrtle* (produced New York, 1968), New York, New Directions, 1968.

*The Two Character Play* (produced London, 1967; revised version, produced London, 1969).   New York, New Directions, 1969; revised version, as *Out Cry* (produced Chicago, 1971).

*In the Bar of a Tokyo Hotel* (produced New York, 1969; London, 1971).   New York, Dramatists Play Service, 1969.

*I Can't Imagine Tomorrow* (televised, 1970).   Included in *Dragon Country*, 1970.

*Dragon Country: A Book of Plays* (includes *In the Bar of a Tokyo Hotel*, *I Rise in Flame, Cried the Phoenix*, *The Mutilated*, *I Can't Imagine Tomorrow*, *Confessional*, *The Frosted Glass Coffin*, *The Gnadiges Fräulein*, and *A Perfect Analysis Given by a Parrot*).   New York, New Directions, 1970.

*Small Craft Warnings* (produced New York, 1972).

Screenplays: *Senso*, 1949; *The Glass Menagerie*, with Peter Berneis, 1950; *A Streetcar Named Desire*, 1951; *The Rose Tattoo*, with Hal Kanter, 1955; *Baby Doll*, 1956; *Suddenly Last Summer*, with Gore Vidal, 1959; *The Fugitive Kind*, with Meade Roberts, 1960; *Boom*, 1968.

Verse

*Five Young American Poets*, with others.   New York, New Directions, 1944.
*In the Winter of Cities: Poems*.   New York, New Directions, 1956.

*        *        *

> . . . when you attempt to set those details down in a tale, some measure of obscurity or indirection is called for to provide the same, or even approximate, softening effect that existence in time gives to those gross elements in the life itself.
>
> "Hard Candy"

Tennessee Williams' fiction is a series of euphemisms for situations actually less shocking than these disguises imply. Sometimes the language merely dresses up a physical fact: Mrs. Stone's domination by "the moon of pause." More often, the commonplace becomes mythic: "Desire and the Black Masseur" (*One Arm*), perhaps Williams' best-known story, turns a Turkish bath into an arena for religious passion and the masochistic Anthony Burns into an actual eucharist, while a Lenten crowd of disarrayed celebrants underlines the symbolism. The masturbation scene of "One Arm" transforms a mutilated hustler who "looked like a broken statue of Apollo" into a Christ holding a literal eternity in the palm of his hand: "Too late, the resurrection." His tardy recognition of the divinity of his sex echoes Lawrence's phallic Christ in "The Man Who Died" crying "I have risen." This perpetual immanence of the transcendent and richness of allusion are predictable in a dramatist whose *Orpheus Descending* shows the poet-hero destroyed just before Easter.

Thus, Williams' fiction, especially *One Arm* and *The Roman Spring of Mrs. Stone*, aims high and occasionally justifies its aspirations in an allegorical tale like "The Poet," which traces the last days of a pied piper for sexually awakening adolescents, a more cosmic version of Sebastian in the play *Suddenly Last Summer*. The arresting opening sentence—"The poet distilled his own liquor and had become so accomplished in this art that he could produce a fermented drink from almost any kind of organic matter"—works so well as a metaphor for the poet's craft that the more literal second sentence is momentarily shocking, though the story manages to sustain both levels: "He carried it in a flask . . ." Supported by only skeletal symbolic details, this work is the best of Williams' poet stories like "The Angel in the Alcove" and "The Important Thing" and dramatizes the dying artist's triumphant, if transient, power to incorporate death into his vision, an important theme in Williams.

Williams' later dramatization of some of his stories perhaps justifies their minimal dialogue and tendency toward summarized action, and suggests that they were either sketches for future plays or exercises in which the developing dramatist sought his real talent. Occasionally the stories have virtues that do not translate to drama: "Portrait of a Girl in Glass," when transformed to *The Glass Menagerie*, loses the wonderful detail of Laura's constant rereading of *Freckles*, the key index to her character. The stories also reveal the complex genesis of later plays: the name and some characteristics of Oliver Winemiller in "One Arm" apparently fuse with those of Alma Tutwiler in "The Yellow Bird" and undergo yet further changes in *The Eccentricities of a Nightingale* and *Summer and Smoke*.

Like his stories, Williams' novel, *The Roman Spring of Mrs. Stone*, also suffers from inadequate dramatization. The narrative's negative summary of the heroine's character and motivations does not mesh with what seems a normal post-menopausal awakening to sexuality and to the charms of a young Roman gigolo and does not validate the charge of an angry friend that Mrs. Stone is a female "Tiberius." Despite these flaws, however, the book is sufficiently engrossing to generate disturbing questions. How can Mrs. Stone be simultaneously a predatory monster constantly equated to a voracious bird of prey and an obvious victim of both her susceptibility and the centuries of Roman duplicity objectified in the Contessa who supplies young men to wealthy foreigners? (Even James' Daisy Miller faced nothing so formidable.) The book lacks the irony necessary to resolve these contradictory views of Mrs. Stone. Is the beautiful ubiquitous young man who reveals his intentions by urinating in public merely another stage in Mrs. Stone's "corruption" or an angel of death, as some hints suggest? (In the latter role, he seems to fuse with the wandering poet Jimmy Dobyne—"anybody" spelled backwards?—who unsuccessfully tries to comfort/dupe an even older American lady in "Man Bring This Up Road" and, ultimately, becomes a poet/Christ/death-angel in the various versions of the play *The Milk Train Doesn't Stop Here Anymore*.) Whether Mrs. Stone merits laughter or compassion, she commands enough attention to make these questions pertinent.

Less ambitious in conception than these earlier works are those collected as *Hard Candy*. The title story and "The Mysteries of the Joy Rio" employ the same gallery of a decaying movie theater as a setting for furtive homosexual encounters. Freed of the mythic parallels of "One Arm," these pieces proceed straightforwardly, despite apologetic comments on sex and a style occasionally as furtive as the characters. "Mysteries," in particular, creates a moving picture of the last act of an enduring homosexual union, reminiscent of McCullers' *The Heart Is a Lonely Hunter*, and develops a favorite Williams theme of love as the force mitigating the pain of death. "The Vine" and "Two on a Party" skillfully depict symbiotic relationships that salvage would-be losers, a married couple in "Vine," and a homosexual and an aging playgirl in "Party." The sensual landlady of "The Mattress by the Tomato Patch" is convincing without becoming an archetypal earth-mother, as she would in the earlier stories.

This more relaxed mood carries over into *The Knightly Quest*, especially in "Grand," a deftly understated reminiscence of a grandmother's long life and painful death. "Mama's

Old Stucco House" continues the symbiosis of "Vine" and "Party," in uniting a homo-sexual southern artist and his young Negro maid. While "The Kingdom of Earth," which became the play *The Seven Descents of Myrtle*, overdoes a broadly comic treatment of sex, the narrator, Chicken, is an amusing version of Williams' heterosexual boor, almost a parody of Stanley Kowalski, like Billy Spangler in the title novella, "The Knightly Quest." However, despite Billy's presence, "Quest," a paranoid vision of a conformist, incipiently fascistic America, remains unfocused, though there are some funny moments, and the improbable happy ending is almost a send-up of the entire piece. Ironically, it is the imperceptive husband in "Vine" who articulates this growing freedom from pretension and apology in Williams' later fiction: "No wonder people who lived those obscenely solitary lives did things while sober that *you* only did when drunk. . . ."

—Burton Kendle

---

**WILLIAMS, Wirt (Alfred, Jr.).** American. Born in Goodman, Mississippi, 21 August 1921. Educated at Delta College, Cleveland, Mississippi, 1937–40, B.A. in English and American literature 1940; Louisiana State University, Baton Rouge, 1940–41, M.A. in journalism 1941; University of Iowa City, 1950–53, Ph.D. in English and American literature 1953. Served in the United States Navy, 1942–46: Gunnery Officer and Assistant Gunnery Officer, *U.S.S. Decatur*, 1942–44; Executive Officer and Navigator, 1944–45, and Commanding Officer, 1945–46, *U.S.S. LSM 437*; since 1954, Lieutenant-Commander, United States Naval Reserve. Married Ann Meredith in 1954; has one child. Correspondent, Associated Press, Cleveland, Mississippi, 1938–40; News Editor, 1941–42, and capitol correspondent, 1946, *Shreveport Times*, Louisiana; Reporter, Special Writer and City Editor, *New Orleans Item*, 1946–49. Assistant Professor, 1953–57, Associate Professor, 1957–60, and since 1960, Professor of English, California State College at Los Angeles. Guest Literary Editor, *Los Angeles Times*, 1960–61, 1968. Recipient: ABC Award, for reporting, 1949; Huntington Hartford Fellowship, 1958. Address: 7100 Hillside, Los Angeles, California 90046, U.S.A.

PUBLICATIONS

Novels

    *The Enemy.*   Boston, Houghton Mifflin, 1951; London, Corgi, 1967.
    *Love in a Windy Space.*   New York, Reynal, 1957.
    *Ada Dallas.*   New York, McGraw Hill, 1959; London, Muller, 1960.
    *A Passage of Hawks.*   New York, McGraw Hill, 1963; London, Muller, 1964.
    *The Trojans.*   Boston, Little Brown, 1966; London, Barrie and Rockliff, 1967.
    *The Far Side.*   New York, Horizon Press, 1972.

Uncollected Short Story

    "The Unbeaten", in *Statement* (Los Angeles), Winter 1953.

Other

Translator, *The Blue Angel*, by Heinrich Mann.   New York, New American Library, 1959.


Manuscript Collection: Boston University.


Critical Studies: essay-reviews by Robert Kirsch, in the *Los Angeles Times*, 8 October 1959, and 17 December 1966; *The Recent Political Novel in America* by Joseph Blottner, Austin, University of Texas Press, 1966; review by John Raymond, in *Punch* (London), 18 August 1967.


Wirt Williams comments:

A novelist should really keep his mouth shut about his work. His explanation of what he is about limits the work fatally, and necessarily is so incomplete as to be downright false. Even the most self-conscious writer *knows* only a small part of what he has done. The great artificer is the subconscious, which creates those recurring patterns of structure and symbol that tell what the writer really means. His work is only as strong as the force of that sub-conscious—vision, if you will.

Still and all, the conscious is a partner, too, and up to a point, the more thoroughly the writer plans, the better are his chances of giving the subpsyche a full free run. So he has at least some idea of what he is up to, and perhaps at least once he ought to say. For better or for worse, I am an extremely self-conscious writer: I can never quite forget technical principles of the art of fiction that I learned, or at least had explained to me, in the classroom—broadly speaking, the principles of Flaubert and particularly of Hemingway. The central conception of the Imagist poets (which I took from Hemingway without at first knowing where he got it) has been unquestionably the biggest force operating on, and in, my fiction. This conception is (put much too simply) that the writer sends emotion and idea, and makes reality, through sharp, hard pictures—undiluted by reflection or rhetoric. Almost paradoxically, the other "official" moderns I have learned from have been, in language, working the other side of the street—Conrad, Faulkner, and more lately Jean-Paul Sartre.

I teach a seminar in tragedy and once read a great deal of formalistic (academic) criticism, and what I write has been marked by those exposures, also.

So what I *think* I am saying, most of the time, is that we define our lives by what we do in the face of the universal and inescapable catastrophe. Or that we must take our own meaning in an operationally hostile universe without apparent meaning. The theme is scarcely original: no theme is, but this one is as old as tragedy. At the same time, nuanced differently in each case, it seems to be the pervasive statement of twentieth century fiction.

My first novels were an attempt to beat personal experience into fictional form. *The Enemy* is about destroyers and aircraft hunting submarines they never see in the North Atlantic in World War II. Some saw it as a paraphrase of Camus' central metaphor—Sisyphus rolling the stone up the hill. Fair enough, but I had never read Camus at the time I wrote it, and I think my pattern was stronger for my ignorance. *Love in a Windy Space* was a love story set in Louisiana—a simple enough tragedy, with a couple of fables beneath about the state of the South and of the forlorn man. *Ada Dallas* was concerned with Louisiana politics (which I had covered as a political correspondent), was awarely tragic, and was invested with the familiar ethical fable.

No longer finding my own experience that interesting, now I make up or find designs on the outside, and hope that by analogy, the essence of my experience will somehow infuse that design. *A Passage of Hawks*, a deliberately Jacobean story of murder and wickedness, was suggested by T. S. Eliot's examination of Thomas Middleton's *The Changeling*—an examination, of course, far more interesting than the play. *The Trojans* was a multi-purposed attempt to say something about the relationship between the artist and the world, to put forward a species of existentialism, to explore all sorts of varieties of experience, and to come up with some interesting information about motion pictures. Its subject matter in the narrowest sense came from recent history of that industry.

The day of the publisher as patron has been over for some time, and if a novelist is to be heard (that is to say, published) he must offer one level of appeal—among all his levels of statement—to a large and completely non-literary audience. I have accepted the condition and find it just: there are many fine things a novelist can do, but the finest of all is to tell a wonderful story. The abiding, unanswerable question, of course, is: wonderful to whom?

\*        \*        \*

Wirt Williams is a pure example of the American novelist who came to literary maturity shortly after World War II. He is well-grounded in criticism and theory; he teaches and is fluent in the history of the genre. His literary forebears are writers in the grand traditions of prose fiction: Flaubert, Conrad, James, Hemingway. Understandably his expectation for all prose fiction is lofty; everywhere in his own work the alignments of image, action, character, and meaning are exact. Seen together his works make a larger statement than the separate titles.

From a brilliant first novel (*The Enemy*) to a probable middleground of development (*The Trojans*), the overall pattern is clear: *The Enemy* concerns the author's line-experience in North Atlantic anti-submarine warfare; *The Trojans* concerns art and the movie industry and is narrated from a fully dramatic perspective by a cerebral writer/artist. The motif of a protagonist overwhelmed by tragic or near-tragic circumstances often occurs; the ancillary literary resources of the novels stem variously from fable, myth, Jacobean drama, and others. In summary, the literary resources of the novels are extraordinary.

Intentionally, characterization, plot-structure, and chronology are not notably experimental. Typically a story unfolds from multiple points of view; the author's attitude towards his materials is seldom extreme although irony, especially in dialogue, reoccurs. Thus all the novels are "open", public; there is little obscurity of either language or motivation. Williams acknowledges the influence of his sometimes literary correspondent, Ernest Hemingway.

The prose is taut, informational, and well-calculated. The finest language occurs in brief, descriptive passages of the sea, the rural South, or the city at dawn or at night. From these passages emerges a pervasive atmosphere; so great is this strength that a delicately controlled atmosphere may become an important protagonist in the story. Williams deals best with large effects; his unit of composition is the whole novel.

To place the first five novels in a mainstream of American literature calls for other, extrinsic considerations. For example, Williams was born and raised in Mississippi, in the Black Belt—a region of America which changed almost not at all until after World War II. His father was a Southern-trained classical historian; on occasion Williams taught his father's classes in Roman History. In addition to this classical background, and before he completed the Ph.D. in literary studies, Williams was a newspaperman in New Orleans. *Love in a Windy Place*, *A Passage of Hawks*, and *Ada Dallas* (also a film) are concerned with the provinciality, the passions, and enigmas of The South.

Not surprisingly, therefore, many of the protagonists are concerned with status, integrity of motive, and money; their often unconscious search for the lost "classical" values of valor, fidelity, friendship, and honor is a continuing criticism of modernity. These women and men come from a felt or remembered tradition and order; they are fated to live among the ruins of the twentieth century. Typically these characters of above-average intelligence and education remain isolated or unresolved in the midst of apparent affluence. Too often the resolution they find is in personal oblivion, death, or patrician acceptance. Taken together, these concerns and attitudes suggest the novels are in the mainstream of the American novel of manners, the Romance of large-scale enterprise, the film industry and state-capitol politics included.

At mid-career, Wirt Williams looks back on almost twenty years of dedication to the craft. Although the state of the novelistic art is in rapid change, the serious reader fully expects the recognition of Wirt Williams as teacher, critic, and novelist to become increasingly manifest.

—James B. Hall

---

**WILLIAMSON, Henry.** British. Born in Parkstone, Dorset, 1 December 1895. Served as an Infantryman and Officer in the British Army during World War I. Twice married and divorced; has seven children. Broadcaster, on farming and country life, during the 1930's. Recipient: Hawthornden Prize, 1928. Address: Ox's Cross, Braunton, North Devon, England.

PUBLICATIONS

Novels

*The Flax of Dream:*
   *The Beautiful Years.* London, Collins, and New York, Dutton, 1921; revised edition, London, Faber, and Dutton, 1929.
   *Dandelion Days.* London, Collins, and New York, Dutton, 1922; revised edition, London, Faber, and Dutton, 1930.
   *The Dream of Fair Women.* London, Collins, and New York, Dutton, 1924; revised edition, London, Faber, and Dutton, 1931.
   *The Pathway.* London, Cape, 1928; New York, Dutton, 1929.
   *The Star-Born.* London, Faber, 1933; revised edition, 1948.
*Tarka the Otter: Being His Joyful Water-Life and Death in the Country of the Two Rivers.* London, Putnam, and New York, Dutton, 1927.
*The Patriot's Progress: Being the Vicissitudes of Pte. John Bullock.* London, Bles, and New York, Dutton, 1930.
*The Gold Falcon; or, The Haggard of Love: Being the Adventures of Manfred, Airman and Poet of the World War, and Later, Husband and Father, in Search of Freedom and Personal Sunrise, in the City of New York, and of the Consummation of His Life* (published anonymously). London, Faber, and New York, Smith, 1933; revised edition, as Henry Williamson, Faber, 1947.
*Salar the Salmon.* London, Faber, 1935.
*The Sun in the Sands.* London, Faber, 1945.
*The Phasian Bird.* London, Faber, 1948; Boston, Little Brown, 1950.
*A Chronicle of Ancient Sunlight:*
   *The Dark Lantern.* London, Macdonald, 1951.
   *Donkey Boy.* London, Macdonald, 1952.
   *Young Phillip Maddison.* London, Macdonald, 1953.
   *How Dear Is Life.* London, Macdonald, 1954.
   *A Fox under My Cloak.* London, Macdonald, 1955.

*The Golden Virgin.*   London, Macdonald, 1957.
*Love and the Loveless: A Soldier's Tale.*   London, Macdonald, 1958.
*A Test to Destruction.*   London, Macdonald, 1960.
*The Innocent Moon.*   London, Macdonald, 1961.
*It Was the Nightingale.*   London, Macdonald, 1962.
*The Power of the Dead.*   London, Macdonald, 1963.
*The Phoenix Generation.*   London, Macdonald, 1965.
*A Solitary War.*   London, Macdonald, 1966.
*Lucifer Before Sunrise.*   London, Macdonald, 1967.
*The Gale of the World.*   London, Macdonald, 1969.

## Short Stories

*The Peregrine's Saga and Other Stories of the Country Green.*   London, Collins, 1923; as *The Sun Brothers*, New York, Dutton, 1925.
*The Old Stag: Stories.*   London, Putnam, 1926; New York, Dutton, 1927.
*The Linhay on the Downs.*   London, Mathews and Marrot, 1929.
*The Ackymals.*   San Francisco, Windsor Press, 1929.
*The Village Book.*   London, Cape, and New York, Dutton, 1930.
*The Labouring Life.*   London, Cape, 1932; as *As the Sun Shines*, New York, Dutton, 1933.
*On Foot in Devon; or, Guidance and Gossip: Being a Monologue in Two Reels.*   London, Maclehose, 1933.
*The Linhay on the Downs and Other Adventures in the Old and New World.*   London, Cape, 1934.
*Life in a Devon Village* (based on material in *The Village Book* and *The Labouring Life*).   London, Faber, 1945.
*Tales of a Devon Village* (based on material in *The Village Book* and *The Labouring Life*).   London, Faber, 1945.
*Tales of Moorland and Estuary.*   London, Macdonald, 1953.
*In the Woods.*   Llandeilo, Wales, St. Albert's Press, 1960.
*Collected Nature Stories.*   London, Macdonald, 1970.

## Other

*The Lone Swallows.*   London, Collins, 1922; New York, Dutton, 1926; revised edition, as *The Lone Swallows and Other Essays of Boyhood and Youth*, London and New York, Putnam, 1933.
*The Wet Flanders Plain.*   London, Beaumont Press, and New York, Dutton, 1929; revised edition, London, Faber, 1929.
*The Wild Red Deer of Exmoor: A Digression on the Logic and Ethics and Economics of Stag-Hunting in England Today.*   London, Faber, 1931.
*Devon Holiday.*   London, Cape, 1935.
*Goodbye West Country.*   London, Putnam, 1937; Boston, Little Brown, 1938.
*The Children of Shallowford* (autobiography).   London, Faber, 1939; revised edition, 1959.
*As the Sun Shines: Selections.*   London, Faber, 1941.
*The Story of a Norfolk Farm* (autobiography).   London, Faber, 1941.
*Genius of Friendship: "T. E. Lawrence".*   London, Faber, 1941.
*A Clear Water Stream* (autobiography).   London, Faber, 1958; New York, Washburn, 1959.

Editor, *An Anthology of Modern Nature Writing.*   London, Nelson, 1936.

Editor, *Richard Jefferies: Selections of His Work*.   London, Faber, 1937.
Editor, *Hodge and His Masters*, by Richard Jefferies.   London, Methuen, 1937.
Editor, *Norfolk Life*, by L. R. Haggard.   London, Faber, 1943.
Editor, *My Favourite Country Stories*.   London, Lutterworth Press, 1946.
Editor, *Unreturning Spring: Being the Poems, Sketches, Stories and Letters of James Farrar*.   London, Williams and Norgate, 1950.

Bibliography: *A Bibliography and a Critical Survey of the Works of Henry Williamson* by I. Waveney Girvan, Chipping Campden, Gloucestershire, Alcuin Press, 1931.

\*        \*        \*

The work of Henry Williamson presents a number of points of interest. There are the nature stories—*Tarka the Otter* and *Salar the Salmon* being the best known—and there are the novels, principally the tetralogy *The Flax of Dream* and the monumental *A Chronicle of Ancient Sunlight*. In between, and linking the two to a quite extraordinary degree are the autobiographical writings, among them *The Story of a Norfolk Farm* and *A Clear Water Stream*.

Williamson's first book, *The Beautiful Years*, was published in 1921; it is a novel of childhood set in Devonshire at the turn of the century. The style of the book is very much that of Richard Jefferies, the great English nature writer whom Williamson admires so much. Indeed the whole of *The Flax of Dream*, of which *The Beautiful Years* is the first part, reveals Jefferies' influence not only on the style of the young author, but also on his thought.

*The Beautiful Years* and *Dandelion Days* trace the childhood of Willie Maddison, and his story is completed in *The Dream of Fair Women* and *The Pathway*. In the last two books Jefferies' *The Story of My Heart* becomes Maddison's Credo in a world that has not yet come to terms with Peace in the years following the Great War.

*The Pathway* was the most successful book in the series and was highly praised by Edward Garnett as a novel of truth and sensibility. In the same year the publication of *Tarka the Otter* attracted immediate critical and public acclaim. The book was awarded the Hawthornden Prize and, with the appearance of *Salar the Salmon*, ensured Henry Williamson a place among the great English nature writers, alongside Jefferies, W. H. Hudson and Gilbert White. Acute, prolonged and intense observation had been combined with insight and imagination to produce something which was then unique in English Literature, a novel of wildlife so full of detail and information as to be almost a text book of the animal's way of life.

This achievement has proved something of a mixed blessing for Henry Williamson. Once a writer becomes associated in the public mind with a particular work or genre it is difficult for him to obtain recognition in any other field. Publishers, too, tend to play safe, and Williamson's career as a novelist has been dogged by difficulties over the publication of his novels, while the demand for Nature stories has been continuous. It says much for his integrity as a writer that he has, despite some lean years in the '30s and '40s, always seen his primary calling as that of a novelist observing and recording the human condition rather than the life of Nature.

Nevertheless it is true to say that the painstaking attention to detail which is so apparent in the earlier nature stories also characterizes his novels. Their unremitting honesty, the search for, and the struggle to convey, the truth, are at times almost painful. As with Williamson's fragments of autobiography, there is an element of self-abnegation on the part of the chief protagonist to which not every reader can adjust. True self-analysis, the baring of another's soul, is to most people an embarrassment. Henry Williamson's novels, like Jefferies' *The Story of My Heart*, seem to communicate most successfully to the young.

The publication of *The Gale of the World*, and with it the completion of *A Chronicle of Ancient Sunlight*, has superbly vindicated the novelist's faith in his own calling. The *Chronicle* tells the story of Phillip Maddison (Phillip, because his mother misspelled the name when registering the child), the cousin of Willie Maddison of *The Flax of Dream*, whom the author describes as "the passionate pilgrim of our age; though few know it now". Its fifteen volumes cover the period from the closing decades of the last century to the present day and is, in the words of the late John Middleton Murry, "in its entirety one of the most remarkable English Novels of our time".

It is important that the *Chronicle* is viewed and judged in its entirety. The problems inherent in the writing of such an enormous work are considerable, and it would be idle to suppose that the sequence is without its faults. The first eight volumes, up to and including *A Test to Destruction*, contain all that is best in Williamson's writing. This is not to say that there are not many fine, delicate and moving passages in the later books; but the writing is often uneven and Phillip's story frequently echoes incidents in Williamson's own life recounted earlier in such works as *Goodbye West Country*, *The Sun in the Sands* and *The Story of a Norfolk Farm*. Indeed volume nine, *The Innocent Moon*, contains whole passages from *The Sun in the Sands*.

This has led to some confusion in the public mind and an attempt to see Phillip as Williamson himself. We shall have to wait for the author's full autobiography before we know for certain where the two stories overlap; but ultimately the question is irrelevant. What matters to *A Chronicle of Ancient Sunlight* as a whole is the unity of vision. The work is a painstaking portrait of three generations and the artist is inevitably part of the picture.

A more serious criticism of the later volumes in the sequence is Williamson's occasional habit of breaking off the narrative thread in order to convey what is frequently nonessential information. In an earlier novel, *The Gold Falcon*, whole passages recount details of New York and the urban American way of life which are familiar to any cinemagoer, and appear to be included only so that the author can underline a point and so bolster the general thesis of the novel. The later books in the *Chronicle* are similarly afflicted, and in almost every case this is entirely unnecessary. It is as though the writer doubts his own abilities and so lacks confidence in his own power to communicate. This is a trait he shares with his heroes and which is increasingly in evidence as the sequence nears its conclusion.

It may be that such an enormous work so taxes the imagination and the intellect that towards its end completion becomes paramount, style and form then become secondary; this in turn may account for Williamson's habit of revising every new edition of his works, constantly correcting and improving.

With all its blemishes *A Chronicle of Ancient Sunlight* remains a remarkable achievement. Anyone following the development of Phillip Maddison will have a penetrating, critical, but ultimately sympathetic insight into twentieth century European man beset by events taking place around him, searching for some way to live personally, and to find a society which can go on existing. Henry Williamson's finest work is an examination of what it means to have lived in his time; in his own words: "Here is the world—always with awareness that it is but one man's limited world. . . . Take it or leave it, that is up to the reader; the writer cannot do better than try to bring some of the life he has known to paper."

Because of the scope and power of his writing the record will undoubtedly be a permanent one.

—Norrie Hearn

---

**WILLINGHAM, Calder (Baynard, Jr.).** American. Born in Atlanta, Georgia, 23 December 1922. Educated at The Citadel, Charleston, South Carolina, 1940–41; University of Virginia, Charlottesville, 1941–43. Married Helene Rothenberg in 1945 (divorced, 1951); Jane Marie Bennett, 1953; has six children. Lives in New Hampshire. Address: c/o Vanguard Press, 424 Madison Avenue, New York, New York 10017, U.S.A.

PUBLICATIONS

### Novels

*End as a Man.*   New York, Vanguard Press, 1947; London, Lehmann, 1952.
*Geraldine Bradshaw.*   New York, Vanguard Press, 1950; London, Barker, 1964.
*Reach to the Stars.*   New York, Vanguard Press, 1951; London, Barker, 1965.
*Natural Child.*   New York, Dial Press, 1952.
*To Eat a Peach.*   New York, Dial Press, 1955.
*Eternal Fire.*   New York, Vanguard Press, and London, Barker, 1963.
*Providence Island.*   New York, Vanguard Press, and London, Hart Davis, 1969.

### Short Stories

*The Gates of Hell.*   New York, Vanguard Press, 1951; London, Mayflower, 1966.

### Plays

*End as a Man* (produced New York, 1953).

Screenplays: *Paths of Glory*, 1957; *End as a Man*, 1958; *The Vikings*, 1960; *One-Eyed Jacks*, 1962; *The Graduate*, 1967; *Little Big Man*, 1970.

Calder Willingham comments:

At the beginning of my career, I was contemptuous and skeptical of the typical "best-seller" that pandered to public fantasies, wish-fulfillment, class or regional or national prejudices, et cetera. As my career progressed, I became equally contemptuous and skeptical of the typical "literary" novel that pandered to the aesthetic dicta and passing fashions of an intellectual elite. Thus, I have contrived as a novelist to fall cleverly between two stools: my work in general has dissatisfied or distressed the mass best-seller audience and at the same time has infuriated or bemused the so-called literary audience. Lonely and awkward as it is down here between these stools, I like to think of my achievement as a considerable and perhaps even unique feat on the current writing scene.

Fortunately, this fall between stools has not been unqualified; certain of my novels have been highly praised by the critical brethren and certain of them have reached a substantial audience. But to support my large family through the years it has been necessary for me to resort to the writing of screenplays. There has been too much disturbing reality and irony in my novels for them to be generally acceptable as escapist pap for a mass audience and I break far too many rules of literary fashion (practically all in fact) for my work to appear of any great significance to the intelligentsia. I would rather this be so than to have written wish-fulfillment trash or the tedious, inhuman, unreadable literary monstrosities now fashionable.

The critical fraternity, I am afraid, has not known what on earth to make of my writing. I have used ironic contradiction and seemingly cruel humor in ways that are singular—or were singular, let us say; much of so-called modern "black comedy" seems to have been inspired by some off-hand stories I wrote 20 or 25 years ago. But also (and here the puzzlement of my critics deepens) my principal novels have been optimistic, fond of their characters, affirmative, hopeful, joyous toward life. A bewildering thing indeed, this. How can a man perceive the terrors and horrors of life, and still remain an optimist able to love his fellow creatures? I would grant it takes more courage and heart than can be contained in the critical faculty, which in blind cowardice can only conclude that such a man must be a liar or a fraud or a maddening incomprehensible idiot. I certainly have never yet seen any truly intelligent detailed criticism of my writing and I do not expect it to appear in my lifetime and this pleases me. So long as I can keep the analytical brethren off-balance and bewildered, I know I myself am crossing the wire.

As for my movie work, I do not regard this as real writing of my own, because here my sensibility is at the tender mercies of those with whom I am associated. The only way I could make a motion picture truly my own would be to produce and direct it as well as write it. I am looking for an insane millionaire to give me the money to make a really great film. In the meanwhile I cannot take with genuine seriousness any of the films on which I have worked.

As for the theatre, to me the theatre is an amusement rather than a major form, no doubt because my background as a novelist causes the medium to seem to me too restrictive. Besides, poetry is not my forte but rather the inter-play of characters in time and space, i.e., classic narrative.

My real work has been as a novelist and that work readily falls into three periods. The first is that of my initial novel, *End as a Man*, an adolescent effort marked by youthful fury and a rather simplistic view of the human condition. The second is the *Geraldine Bradshaw* period ending with *To Eat a Peach*—it was I suppose during this period that I (according to *The New Yorker*) "inadvertently fathered black comedy". The third period is that of my maturity and it has seen thus far publication of two major efforts, *Eternal Fire* and *Providence Island*. Doubtful as I am of the literary world, it has nonetheless been a profound astonishment to me that these novels have not received far greater recognition. I expect they will someday; it is my belief I put more of whatever gifts I have into these books than all my other work combined. Thus, on this Christmas Eve in snowy New Hampshire in this the year of Our Lord 1970, I look back on my struggle as a novelist with both frustration and satisfaction even as I plan to return to the bitter fray and write another book or two, God willing.

*          *          *

The simplest and possibly truest way to characterize the fiction of Calder Willingham is to call it the work of a twentieth century Fielding, for Willingham is a comic chronicler of iniquity, a creator of mock-novels, an enemy of hypocrisy who turns its lies and pretenses back on themselves, and a moral seer who is able to espy the good always and only in the midst of a chaos of vice and folly. His first novel, *End as a Man*, revealed as much, but the six novels (and one book of stories) which have followed it have shown him to be a Fielding possessed of such a strong sense of the absurd, of the natural disorder of being, that he has discarded even conventional form in his search for an artistic expression of the real and living world. Traditional genres collapse in his hands like a shack in a hurricane and at the same time open out to reveal the free imaginative source of all form—literary and artistic forms and, in fact, the good, the true and the beautiful.

His attack on the ponderous seriousness of the modern novel and short story has led him away from the path that seemed to open out from the success of his first novel. The very form of the serious novel failed him. He abandoned his plan to write a trilogy constructed from the lives of hotel bellmen after he had finished and published the first two volumes, *Geraldine Bradshaw* and *Reach to the Stars*. (He did revise the first volume for its English publication in 1964 so that it could stand alone, but, at the same time, he referred to the second as "a literary exercise.") The narrator of his next novel, *Natural Child*, decides at the end that neither he nor any other of the characters could have written such a book and that "Maybe the cat wrote it." *To Eat a Peach*, his fifth novel, professes to be the tale of "a happy little summer in the mountains down in the deep South where the dogwood and the sycamore grow, and the sun shines all day long, when it isn't raining." His novels turn into tall tales, his characters become caricatures, and the short stories in *The Gates of Hell* are more often than not "anti-stories." They collapse into playlets or take the form of brief and gloriously mindless essays. *Providence Island*, Willingham's most recent and quite long novel, closes by calling itself "a seashell tale." The forms fail him, but he finds life in the absence of form, creates novels and stories that defy form.

Willingham's finest novel (and one of the most under-rated of modern American novels), *Eternal Fire*, is on the one hand a mock "Southern" novel full of sound and fury, and on the other a serious and meaningful novel expressing a moral sense which grows from an acceptance of the world with all its chaos and a forgiveness of it. One of its villains, Harry Diadem, is both as comical and as convincingly evil as any character in modern literature, but its simple hero manages to face up to the inescapable presence of evil even in the girl he loves, his "fallen angel," and to emerge "from eternal fire into manhood."

To be a man is all Willingham asks of any of us—a man who sees honestly what it is to be a man and nonetheless accepts and affirms his manhood. His fiction, which calls everything into question, even and perhaps especially itself, offers as answer only the need to live in the world that we see and to dare to see the world in which we live. And that, laughably, is enough.

—R. H. W. Dillard

---

**WILSON, Angus (Frank Johnstone).** British. Born in Bexhill, Sussex, 11 August 1913. Educated at Westminster School, London, 1927–31; Merton College, Oxford, B.A. (honours) in medieval and modern history 1936. Served in the Foreign Office, 1942–46. Staff Member, British Museum, London, 1937–55: Deputy Superintendent of the Reading Room, 1949–55. Lecturer, 1963–66, and since 1966, Professor of English Literature, University of East Anglia, Norwich. Ewing Lecturer, University of California, Los Angeles, 1960; Bergen Lecturer, Yale University, New Haven, Connecticut, 1960; Moody Lecturer, University of Chicago, 1960; Northcliffe Lecturer, University College, London, 1961; Leslie Stephen Lecturer, Cambridge University, 1962–63; Beckman Professor, University of California, Berkeley, 1967. Member of the Arts Council of Great Britain, 1966–69. Since 1971, Chairman, National Book League, London. Recipient: Black Memorial Prize, 1959; Prix de Meilleur Roman Etranger, 1960; *Yorkshire Post* Book Award, for non-fiction, 1971. Honorary Fellow, Cowell College, University of California, Santa Cruz, 1968. Fellow, 1958, and Companion of Literature, 1972, Royal Society of Literature. C.B.E. (Commander, Order of the British Empire), 1968. Address: Felsham Woodside, Bradfield St. George, Bury St. Edmunds, Suffolk, England.

PUBLICATIONS

Novels

*Hemlock and After*. London, Secker and Warburg, and New York, Viking Press, 1952.
*Anglo-Saxon Attitudes*. London, Secker and Warburg, and New York, Viking Press, 1956.
*The Middle Age of Mrs. Eliot*. London, Secker and Warburg, 1958; New York, Viking Press, 1959.

*The Old Men at the Zoo.*   London, Secker and Warburg, and New York, Viking Press, 1961.

*Late Call.*   London, Secker and Warburg, 1964; New York, Viking Press, 1965.

*No Laughing Matter.*   London, Secker and Warburg, and New York, Viking Press, 1967.


Short Stories

*The Wrong Set and Other Stories.*   London, Secker and Warburg, 1949; New York, Morrow, 1950.

*Such Darling Dodos and Other Stories.*   London, Secker and Warburg, 1950; New York, Morrow, 1951.

*A Bit off the Map and Other Stories.*   London, Secker and Warburg, and New York, Viking Press, 1957.

*Death Dance: 25 Stories.*   New York, Viking Press, 1969.


Play

*The Mulberry Bush* (produced London, 1956).   London, Secker and Warburg, 1956.


Other

*Emile Zola: An Introductory Study of His Novels.*   London, Secker and Warburg, and New York, Morrow, 1952; revised edition, Secker and Warburg, 1965.

*For Whom the Cloche Tolls: A Scrapbook of the Twenties.*   London, Methuen, 1953.

*The Wild Garden; or, Speaking of Writing.*   Berkeley, University of California Press, and London, Secker and Warburg, 1963.

*Tempo: The Impact of Television on the Arts.*   London, Studio Vista, 1964; Chester Springs, Pennsylvania, Dufour, 1966.

*The World of Charles Dickens.*   London, Secker and Warburg, and New York, Viking Press, 1970.

Editor, *A Maugham Twelve,* by W. Somerset Maugham.   London, Heinemann, 1966.

Editor, *Cakes and Ale, and Twelve Short Stories,* by W. Somerset Maugham.   New York, Doubleday, 1967.


Manuscript Collection: University of Iowa, Iowa City.


Critical Studies: *The Free Spirit* by C. B. Cox, London, Oxford University Press, 1963; *Angus Wilson* by Jay Halio, Edinburgh, Oliver and Boyd, 1964; *Angus Wilson* by K. W. Gransden, London, Longman, 1969; "*The Middle Age of Mrs. Eliot* and *Late Call*" by Valerie Shaw, in *Critical Quarterly* (London), Spring 1970; *Harvest of a Quiet Eye: The Novel of Compassion* by James Gindin, Bloomington University of Indiana Press, 1971.


Angus Wilson comments:

I shall confine this statement to noting certain received critical ideas about my work that seem to me misleading, or, at the very best, marginal. I have not seen the critical notice to appear with this statement nor do I know who is its author. If what I say disagrees with that notice, it is only necessary to point out that some people find authors' views of their own work illuminating, others misleading. The choice is with the reader.

1) My work is very frequently compared to that of E. M. Forster. In some ways I am, of course, flattered and gratified. It is also true that some of my early short stories, *Hemlock and After*, and above all my play, *The Mulberry Bush*, contain the sort of critique of liberal humanism that is to be found in Forster's novels, above all in *Howard's End*. But there have always been wide divergences—above all in my deep distrust of money, property and the sort of responsibility that goes with them; in my dislike of sentimentalism about the primitive, the unsophisticated and the physically strong; in my acceptance, in general, of the city (London) as having values in many ways superior to, certainly equal with, the country; on the other hand in my placing great importance upon a close relation with animal and plant life (see my continuous concern with animal and flower imagery); in my acceptance of violence and uncontrolled passion as being in certain occasions a good; above all, in my open statement of the possibility of homosexual happiness within a conventional framework and my consequent, I believe, greater power of identifying truly sympathetically with my women characters. None of this is an attempt to suggest equality with Forster's work, only to underline differences, and to note a certain distaste that I feel for it—notably in the sentimentalization of Stephen Wonham, the treatment of Leonard and Jackie Bast (indeed what seems to me the whole coldhearted, withdrawn, judging quality of *Howard's End*); nor do I share Forster's evolutionary optimism expressed by the end of *Howard's End*. It seems to me that I am at once a more impulsive, a more bitchy and a more compassionate author than E. M. Forster—that my humanism has less high hope for the future but more acceptance of and liking for human beings as they are. I cannot share or hope to attain his curious mixture of cunning, love, withdrawal and passivity. Of course, I except the wonderful *Passage to India* from all these criticisms, but then I have written nothing that can be seen in relation to it.

2) My early work was formally traditional. It was written out of my deep saturation in 19th century novels and out of a certain feeling that, like many of my contemporaries, I had temporarily got all I could out of the "modernists'" experiments. I wrote one or two very ill-advised commitments to "traditionalism", which, together with a misunderstanding of my praise of Zola and Dickens, led me almost to be labelled as an anti-experimentalist, almost a social realist. Dickens and Zola for me, of course, have their value as poets, tho' also poets using all society to create their prose poems from. My early work was probably somewhat sharply "traditional" in form—in restoring nineteenth century forms; but this was a protest against a too great tyranny of neo-traditionalism in English novel writing. With a too great tyranny of neo-tradition-alism in English novel writing, I have increasingly, from *The Old Men at the Zoo*, experi-mented, above all with pastiche. In the apparently conventional *Late Call* there are innumerable jokes, alienations, pastiches and other non-traditional techniques that the critics failed to see. With *No Laughing Matter* experiment has greatly taken over. The chief influence in my last years has been Virginia Woolf, whom I had to attack fiercely before I felt free to recognize as the very great novelist she was. But my work continues and will, I think, continue to be social in its general material though probably increasingly experimental in form—I am interested in man's personality and soul, but I tend to see him first from the outside as a political and social creature.

3) This leads me to my last point. I am often spoken of as having a very narrow range of characters or as being the satirist of the middle classes. This has only a superficial truth, I think. Compared to most contemporary English novelists my social range seems wide, and my approach to the middle classes (the centre of my work) is as sympathetic as it is critical.

All this, of course, is a statement of intention (realized or unrealized I am not supposed, as an author, to be able to judge; tho' I suspect that authors can guess at their success with their intentions more than academic critics allow). Certainly it is not a judgement of quality—here the novelist must be his own most harsh critic and also his own most loving admirer —and about both he must say nothing.

*     *     *

Angus Wilson is a realistic novelist, with a very sharp ear and eye for the subtleties of English social behaviour. But there is another aspect of his work, not so obvious on a casual reading but never far below the surface, in which he is a writer deeply concerned with cruelty and horror and the intrusions of the nightmarish into civilized life. He began as a short-story writer and in some ways remains one, since his novels are usually episodic in organization, and are likely to be at their most impressive in their treatment of small units of narrative. His first two collections of stories, *The Wrong Set* and *Such Darling Dodos*, were sharply drawn sketches of English middle-class life during and just after the Second World War, with heavy emphasis on snobbery, self-deception and genteel cruelty. Technically they were very adroit, though their despairing view of human motives was altogether too black and unrelieved for complete plausibility. In one of these stories, "Raspberry Jam", Wilson shows a characteristic awareness of the way in which an extremity of violence can shockingly erupt into a familiar domestic setting.

Wilson's first three novels, *Hemlock and After*, *Anglo-Saxon Attitudes* and *The Middle Age of Mrs. Eliot*, are like much of modern English fiction, in their traditional, unselfconscious attitude to form, their precise registration of social nuance, and the nature of their moral preoccupations. At the same time, their peculiar mixture of detached observation and under-lying obsession make them works that only Angus Wilson could have written. Despite a sense of what Henry James called "felt life" and, in the first two, an almost Dickensian range of characters, certain thematic preoccupations tend to be very obtrusive. The reader is invited to dwell on responsibility and guilt, and the tension between the public life of busy achievement and the private life of spiritual cultivation. In Wilson's world moral progress lies in the steady eradication of self-deception. Such preoccupations are, of course, part of a central tradition of the English novel, the line of Jane Austen and George Eliot and E. M. Forster. It must, however, be confessed that Angus Wilson's concern with these questions is at times a little fine-drawn and even parochial. It is not altogether easy to identify with the problems of the self-flagellating homosexual novelist, Bernard Sands, in *Hemlock and After*, or the spiritually sluggish historian, Gerald Middleton, in *Anglo-Saxon Attitudes*. In *The Middle Age of Mrs. Eliot* Meg Eliot, an archetypal liberal heroine, is good-looking, sensitive, intelligent but not intellectual, and modestly complacent. Yet her husband is killed in an outbreak of casual political violence at the airport of an Asian country they are visiting; the rest of the novel shows her brave attempt to make something of her life in widowhood and poverty. Among other things, it suggests that Wilson is better at creating memorable female characters than male ones, and compared with its two predecessors it is a generally admirable and successful work.

In the first three novels Wilson's sense of nightmare appears in isolated incidents and recurring images, but in *The Old Men at the Zoo* it moves into the centre of the action. This work is unique in Wilson's *oeuvre* in being as much a fable as a work of realistic fiction. It is a prophetic fantasy of the near future, when England is at war with an alliance of European powers, and Wilson deals with larger moral dilemmas than he had projected in his earlier books. Politics impinges on private life in an un-English way. His hero, Simon Carter, secretary of the London Zoo, who is both an animal-lover and an efficient administrator, tries to carry on with his work as best he can after England has been defeated by the Europeans. In doing so he embodies the classical dilemma of the public servant in a period of defeat and oppression: should one try to keep society going and risk being labelled a collaborator, or should one keep up a possibly vain and even disastrous resistance? *The Old Men at the Zoo* is a bizarre and often violent narrative that seems to have enabled Wilson to face and, for a time at least, to subdue his own fantasies. His next novel, *Late Call*, is by contrast a work of relative serenity. In *Late Call* the sense of evil that had appeared in Wilson's earlier novels in elements of fantasy or marginal obsession is integrated with his principal strength as a novelist: his infallible sense of social fact. *Late Call* explores the spiritual desolation of life in a New Town in the English Midlands, where the gimmickry of affluence has become a way of life rather than an aid to living. Wilson employs the consciousness of Sylvia Calvert, a woman in her sixties, who has retired after a lifetime of managing small, unfashionable hotels. Accompanied by her sponging idler of a husband, who cares only for playing cards and reliving his days as a temporary officer in the First World War, she goes to live with her recently widowed son in the New Town of Carshall. Harold is a progressive headmaster and educational theorist: he welcomes his parents to his fine modern house with a great display of filial feelings. But why and how they cannot live with Harold and his three teenage daughters is the story that Wilson goes on to tell with considerable insight and sensitivity. Sylvia is one of his most successful fictional creations. She is not at all an educated woman, but she has much native shrewdness, and Wilson uses her honest but often baffled responses to make a remarkably sharp exposure of contemporary progressive attitudes. *Late Call* is better written and less diffuse than Wilson's previous novels, and despite, or perhaps because of, its deliberately limited theme, it is arguably his most uniformly successful novel.

Wilson has several times shown his interest in the pre-1914 world; it appears in several retrospective scenes in *Anglo-Saxon Attitudes* and in the prologue to *Late Call*, describing Sylvia's childhood in 1911. In *No Laughing Matter* he once more returns to it. He unfolds the fortunes of the Matthews family from 1912, when the book opens, up to 1967, when it closes. *No Laughing Matter* is a long, ambitious book with many local successes; it uses the several generations of the Matthews family to look at more than fifty years of English social history, and Wilson indulges to the full his love of the crowded fictional canvas. In comparison with his earlier fiction, his language is far more resourceful, and he uses it to convey a wider spectrum of feeling and to draw on a greater variety of technical devices. Yet the book, for all its richness, is uncomfortably episodic: one is frequently more conscious of Wilson as a brilliant short story writer than as a novelist who is really at home with an extended narrative. Towards the end of *No Laughing Matter* the story falters, as if Wilson was unable to muster sufficient imaginative energy to fill out his design; there is a palpable weariness about the last part of the book, as compared with the brilliant opening at the Wild West Exhibition of 1912.

Angus Wilson is a writer of unusually fine intelligence, wide reading and great sensitivity, who embodies certain traditional attitudes to life and the novel at a time when they are increasingly under attack. He is both a writer of broad middle-brow appeal and true literary seriousness, in itself a highly traditional combination, and one which makes him hard to subject to confident critical placing.

—Bernard Bergonzi

---

**WILSON, Colin (Henry).** British. Born in Leicester, 26 June 1931. Educated at the Gateway School, Leicester, 1942–47. Served in the Royal Air Force, 1949–50. Married Dorothy Betty Troop in 1951; Pamela Joy Stewart, 1960; has three children. Worked at various jobs and spent a period in Paris and Strasbourg, 1950; as a labourer in London, 1951–53; on the magazines *Paris Review* and *Merlin*, Paris, 1953. Full-time Writer since 1954. British Council Lecturer in Germany, 1957; Writer-in-Residence, Hollins College, Virginia, 1966–67; Visiting Professor, University of Washington, Seattle, 1968; Professor, Institute of the Mediterranean (Dowling College, New York), Majorca, 1969. Address: Tetherdown, Gorran Haven, Cornwall, England.

PUBLICATIONS

Novels

*Ritual in the Dark*. London, Gollancz, and Boston, Houghton Mifflin, 1960.

*Adrift in Soho*. London, Gollancz, and Boston, Houghton Mifflin, 1961.

*The World of Violence*. London, Gollancz, 1963; as *The Violent World of Hugh Green*, Boston, Houghton Mifflin, 1963.

*The Man Without a Shadow: The Diary of an Existentialist*. London, Barker, 1963; as *The Sex Diary of Gerard Sorme*, New York, Dial Press, 1963.

*Necessary Doubt*. London, Barker, and New York, Simon and Schuster, 1964.

*The Glass Cage: An Unconventional Detective Story*. London, Barker, 1966; New York, Random House, 1967.

*The Mind Parasites*. London, Barker, and Sauk City, Wisconsin, Arkham House, 1967.

*The Philosopher's Stone*. London, Barker, 1969; New York, Crown, 1971.

*The Killer*. London, New English Library, 1970; as *Lingard*, New York, Crown, 1970.

*The God of the Labyrinth*. London, Hart Davis, 1970; as *The Hedonists*, New York, New American Library, 1971.

*The Black Room*. London, Weidenfeld and Nicolson, 1971.


Plays

*Viennese Interlude* (produced Scarborough, Yorkshire, and London, 1960).

*Strindberg*. London, Calder and Boyars, 1970; New York, Random House, 1971; as *Pictures in a Bath of Acid* (produced Leeds, Yorkshire, 1971).


Other

*The Outsider*. London, Gollancz, and Boston, Houghton Mifflin, 1956.

*Religion and the Rebel*. London, Gollancz, and Boston, Houghton Mifflin, 1957.

*The Age of Defeat*. London, Gollancz, 1959; as *The Stature of Man*, Boston, Houghton Mifflin, 1959.

*An Encyclopedia of Murder*, with Patricia Pitman. London, Barker, 1961; New York, Putnam, 1962.

*The Strength to Dream: Literature and the Imagination*. London, Gollancz, and Boston, Houghton Mifflin, 1962.

*Origins of the Sexual Impulse*. London, Barker, and New York, Putnam, 1963.

*Rasputin and the Fall of the Romanovs*. London, Barker, and New York, Farrar Straus, 1964.

*The Brandy of the Damned: Discoveries of a Music Eclectic*. London, Baker, 1964; as *Chords and Discords: Purely Personal Opinions on Music*, New York, Atheneum, 1966.

*Beyond the Outsider: The Philosophy of the Future*. London, Barker, and Boston, Houghton Mifflin, 1965.

*Eagle and Earwig*. London, Baker, 1965.

*Introduction to the New Existentialism*. London, Hutchinson, 1966; Boston, Houghton Mifflin, 1967.

*Sex and the Intelligent Teenager*. London, Arrow, 1966.

*Voyage to a Beginning* (autobiography). London, Cecil Woolf, 1966; New York, Crown, 1969.

*Bernard Shaw: A Reassessment*. London, Hutchinson, and New York, Atheneum, 1969.

*A Casebook of Murder*. London, Frewin, 1969; New York, Cowles, 1970.

*Poetry and Mysticism*. London, Hutchinson, and San Francisco, City Lights, 1970.

*The Strange Genius of David Lindsay*, with E. H. Visiak and J. B. Pick. London, Baker, 1970.

*The Occult: A History.* London, Hodder and Stoughton, and New York, Random House, 1971.
*New Pathways in Psychology: Maslow and the Post-Freudian Revolution.* London, Gollancz, 1972.
*Order of Assassins.* London, Hart Davis, 1972.

Bibliography: in *Colin Wilson* by John A. Weigel, New York, Twayne, 1971.

Manuscript Collection: University of Texas, Austin.

Critical Studies: *The Angry Decade* by Kenneth Allsop, London, Peter Owen, 1958; *The World of Colin Wilson* by Sidney Campion, London, Muller, 1963; "The Novels of Colin Wilson" by Richard Dillard, in *Hollins Critic* (Hollins College, Virginia), October 1967; *Colin Wilson* by John A. Weigel, New York, Twayne, 1971.

Colin Wilson comments:

I am unashamedly a writer of ideas, in the tradition of Shaw, Wells or Sartre; I see myself as part of a European rather than English literary tradition. My novels are based firmly upon the "new existentialism" expressed in the six volumes of the "Outsider Cycle" (1956–1966) and *Introduction to the New Existentialism*. Although I count myself an existential phenomenologist, I am in fundamental disagreement with the pessimistic European tradition of Heidegger, Jaspers, Sartre and Camus, and my philosophical work has been an attempt to show that their pessimism is the outcome of certain serious misunderstandings of Husserlian phenomenology, notably of the intentionality of consciousness. The foundation of my position could be expressed in the form of a contradiction of Sartre: Consciousness *does* have an "inside". Sartre's position is fundamentally Humeian: he believes the mind *adds* meaning to the chaotic and fragmented world as you might add milk to a bowl of cornflakes; I hold, with Whitehead, that meaning is an objective reality, and that the problem is the curious narrowness and inefficiency of human consciousness.

My novels are basically preoccupied with the problem of meaning, with what Peirce called the problem of "values in a universe of chance". In the first, *Ritual in the Dark*, this takes the form of an exploration of "the great mystery of human boredom". The hero has always wanted freedom and hated being tied down to an office job; yet when a small legacy gives him "a room of his own", he finds himself bewildered, bored, directionless. His meeting with a man who, he comes to suspect, is a mass-murderer of women produces a powerful sense of meaning and direction, but he feels that this is inauthentic—that he should have been capable of *doing it himself*—finding freedom *without help from outside*. This problem of freedom is at the core of all my novels. Man experiences his freedom both positively and negatively: positively in moments of intensity and ecstasy (sex, for example), negatively in the face of crisis or a threat to his existence. Both experiences reveal that the main trouble with everyday consciousness is its narrowness, its obsessive preoccupation with trivialities. There is something fundamentally wrong with human consciousness, a form of short-sightedness amounting almost to blindness. This is, in a sense, a "religious" vision—closely akin to that of T. E. Hulme, who preferred to call it "original sin".

The main influences on my fiction, in my late teens and early twenties, were Joyce and Faulkner, and I felt strongly that the novel had advanced as far as possible in the direction of experimentalism, attempting, so to speak, to approximate to the condition of music. The solution I chose was based upon the notion of Brecht's "alienation effect". In the theatre, Brecht invites his audience to acknowledge that they are watching actors in a play, not reality; it seemed to me that the novel could back out of the Joycean *cul de sac* by choosing to be, on one level, entertainment within a conventional framework; using the conventions of the *roman policier*, the *Bildungsroman*, science fiction, the spy novel, as a kind of symbolic form (in Cassirer's sense) which is freely acknowledged *not* to correspond to its content. This I saw as the only reasonable escape from the Joycean-Faulknerian dilemma of trying to distort the form to *correspond* to an increasingly complex content. Hence, in my fiction, I have used the form of the detective story, science fiction, spy story, etc. as the "persona" or mask of the book. This also offers one enormous advantage. The Joyce disciples, in their attempt to "render" their precise meaning once and for all, robbed themselves of the possibility of free expansion and development. By treating the form as a kind of carnival mask, I am able to re-explore the same meaning or inner-conflict from different angles, so to speak. For example, the same basic meanings are explored in *The Killer* (in the United States, *Lingard*) and *The God of the Labyrinth* (*The Hedonists*), although the first is a clinically precise study of a sexually motivated killer, and the second a literary "detective story" with more than a touch of Thorne Smith farce.

The central statement in my work occurs near the beginning of *The Man Without a Shadow*: "Human beings are grandfather clocks driven by watch-springs." This is why consciousness *appears* to have no "inside". All human beings suffer, more or less, from the complaint of Sartre's café proprietor in *Nausea*: "When his café empties, his head empties too." Our sense of values, which ought to be absolute, appears to depend completely upon stimuli from the environment. This problem is explored most exhaustively in my "spy novel" *The Black Room*, in which I pose the question: How could a spy be trained to withstand total sensory deprivation in a black room? If such a method could be found, it would also be a method for creating supermen.

It is this Carlylean-Nietzschean preoccupation with the potentialities of man—and his present unsatisfactoriness—that has led certain critics to accuse me of fascism, a curious accusation since, although my cast of mind is naturally conservative, I regard my work as wholly non-political.

\*        \*        \*

Colin Wilson's many novels, which include psychological thrillers, mysteries, science-fiction fantasies, diary-confessions, and one of the first "beat" stories, are integral parts of an ambitious project which began in 1956 with the publication of *The Outsider*, that precocious "seminal book on the alienation of man." Although more like a collection of quotations and ideas from a youthful autodidact's notebooks than a coherently developed thesis, *The Outsider* impressed serious critics as well as journalists, who immediately exploited the colorful personality of the author and made the book a sensational best seller. Although Wilson still sees his first work as the most important book of its generation—and he may be right—the thoughtless enthusiasm for Wilson's erudition inevitably yielded to a more thoughtful skepticism. But the cruel change in mood toward his early success fortunately did not destroy the young man, who soon went to work again—less with a vengeance than a solemn determination to prove his significance.

Some fifteen years and many books later, Wilson can no longer be dismissed as an amateur with only one lucky strike to his credit. To date he has written approximately six more volumes on the outsider theme, several book-length critical studies of music and literature, several dramas, two biographies, one autobiography, two systematic analyses of murder and murderers, a guide to sex for teenagers, numerous reviews and articles, and at the last count over ten novels. One only estimates Wilson's cumulative record, for around any corner another item may unexpectedly appear.

Aware that he will eventually be judged as a philosopher, as the champion of a *new* existentialism which rejects the inevitability of despair, Wilson has neatly justified his fiction. "If I were to prescribe a rule," he wrote in 1958, "that all future philosophers would have to obey, it would be this: that no idea shall be expressed that cannot be expressed in terms of human beings in a novel—and perfectly ordinary human beings at that—not Peacockian brain-boxes. If an idea cannot be expressed in terms of people, it is a sure sign it is irrelevant to the real problems of life" (*Declaration*, p.58).

As a matter of fact none of Wilson's prose has that kind of finesse which awes literary critics not interested in ideas, yet it is adequate to its purpose. The fairest way to approach Wilson's novels is to cooperate with his objectives. His apparent preoccupation with violence, sexuality, and criminality is thematically related to his concern with the outsider syndrome. Furthermore, his methodology always participates in his urgency. In a hurry to clear away debris and passionately committed to his position, he is neither a Naturalist nor a Romantic weaving word-spells. He says that he has endorsed "the Brechtian alienation effect" in his fiction, and that he has *intended* that his novels announce their forms and make no claim to reality. In that sense they may be read as parodies of the genres they represent. Whether he has succeeded, however, is still debatable.

Since Wilson hopes to live almost forever, there is plenty of time to abide with his project. Recent experiments are currently validating his dreams of freeing humanity from the pessimism that correlates with determinism and traditional existentialism—at least as Wilson sees them. He is continuing his research into the sources of human energy, and there is certainly more to come from this indefatigable worker who says that even now he is just beginning. In 1966 in *Voyage to a Beginning* Wilson evaluated himself with characteristic candor. After modestly estimating that his first twenty years of work had not taken him far he added a firm *but:* "I know that I have come further than any of my contemporaries. I would be a fool if I didn't know it, and a coward if I was afraid to say so" (p. 336).

—John A. Weigel

---

**WILSON, Edmund.** American. Born in Red Bank, New Jersey, 8 May 1895. Educated at Hill School, Pottstown, Pennsylvania, 1909–12; Princeton University, New Jersey, 1912–16, A.B. 1916. Served in the United States Army, in the Intelligence Corps, 1917–19. Married Mary Blair in 1923; Margaret Candy, 1930; Mary McCarthy, *q.v.*, 1938; Elena Thornton, 1946; has three children. Reporter, *New York Evening Sun*, 1916–17; Managing Editor, *Vanity Fair*, New York, 1920–21; Associate Editor, *New Republic*, New York, 1926–31; Book Reviewer, *The New Yorker*, 1944–48, and occasionally since then. Recipient: Guggenheim Fellowship, 1935; National Institute of Arts and Letters Gold Medal, for non-fiction, 1955; Presidential Medal of Freedom, 1963; Edward MacDowell Medal, 1964; Emerson-Thoreau Medal, 1966; National Book Committee's National Medal for Literature, 1966; Aspen Award, 1968; Golden Eagle Award, International Book Festival at Nice, 1971. Address: Wellfleet, Cape Cod, Massachusetts, U.S.A.

PUBLICATIONS

Novels

    *I Thought of Daisy*. New York, Scribner, 1939; London, W. H. Allen, 1952; revised
       edition, with *Galahad*, New York, Farrar Straus, 1957.
    *Galahad, with I Thought of Daisy*. New York, Farrar Straus, 1957.

### Short Stories

*Memoirs of Hecate County.* New York, Doubleday, 1946; London, W. H. Allen, 1951; revised edition, W. H. Allen, 1958; New York, Page, 1959.

### Uncollected Short Story

"The Great Baldini", with Edwin O'Connor, in *Atlantic* (Boston), October 1969.

### Plays

*The Crime in the Whistler Room* (produced New York, 1924). Included in *This Room and This Gin and These Sandwiches*, 1937.
*Discordant Encounters: Plays and Dialogues.* New York, Boni, 1927.
*This Room and This Gin and These Sandwiches: Three Plays* (includes *The Crime in the Whistler Room*, *A Winter in Beech Street*, and *Beppo and Beth*). New York, New Republic, 1937.
*The Little Blue Light* (produced Cambridge, Massachusetts, 1950; New York, 1951). New York, Farrar Straus, 1950; London, Gollancz, 1951.
*Five Plays: Cyprian's Prayer, The Crime in the Whistler Room, This Room and This Gin and These Sandwiches, Beppo and Beth, The Little Blue Light.* New York, Farrar Straus, and London, W. H. Allen, 1954.
*The Duke of Palermo and Other Plays, with an Open Letter to Mike Nichols* (includes *Dr. McGrath* and *Osbert's Career; or, The Poet's Progress*). New York, Farrar Straus, 1969.

### Verse

*Poets, Farewell.* New York, Scribner, 1929.
*Note-Books of Night.* San Francisco, Colt Press, 1942; London, Secker and Warburg, 1945.
*Night Thoughts.* New York, Farrar Straus, 1961; London, W. H. Allen, 1962.

### Other

*The Undertaker's Garland*, with John Peale Bishop. New York, Knopf, 1922.
*Axel's Castle: A Study in the Imaginative Literature of 1870–1930.* New York and London, Scribner, 1931.
*The American Jitters: A Year of the Slump.* New York, Scribner, 1932; as *Devil Take the Hindmost: A Year of the Slump*, London, Scribner, 1932.
*Travels in Two Democracies.* New York, Harcourt Brace, 1936.
*The Triple Thinkers: Ten Essays on Literature.* New York, Harcourt Brace, and London, Oxford University Press, 1938; augmented edition, New York, Oxford University Press, 1948; London, Lehmann, 1952.
*To the Finland Station: A Study in the Writing and Acting of History.* New York, Harcourt Brace, and London, Secker and Warburg, 1940.
*The Boys in the Back Room: Notes on California Novelists.* San Francisco, Colt Press, 1941.
*The Wound and the Bow: Seven Studies in Literature.* Boston, Houghton Mifflin, and London, Secker and Warburg, 1941; revised edition, New York, Oxford University Press, 1947; London, W. H. Allen, 1952.

*Europe Without Baedeker: Sketches among the Ruins of Italy, Greece and England.*  New York, Doubleday, 1947; London, Secker and Warburg, 1948; revised edition, New York, Farrar Straus, 1966.

*Classics and Commercials: A Literary Chronicle of the Forties.*  New York, Farrar Straus, 1950; London, W. H. Allen, 1951.

*The Shores of Light: A Literary Chronicle of the Twenties and Thirties.*  New York, Farrar Straus, and London, W. H. Allen, 1952.

*Eight Essays.*  New York, Doubleday, 1954.

*The Scrolls from the Dead Sea.*  New York, Oxford University Press, and London, W. H. Allen, 1955; revised edition, as *The Dead Sea Scrolls, 1947–1969,* 1970.

*Red, Black, Blond, and Olive: Studies in Four Civilizations: Zuni, Haiti, Soviet Russia, Israel.*  New York, Oxford University Press, and London, W. H. Allen, 1956.

*A Piece of My Mind: Reflections at Sixty.*  New York, Farrar Straus, 1956; London, W. H. Allen, 1957.

*A Literary Chronicle, 1920–1950.*  New York, Doubleday, 1956.

*The American Earthquake: A Documentary of the 20's and 30's.*  New York, Doubleday, and London, W. H. Allen, 1958.

*Apologies to the Iroquois.*  New York, Farrar Straus, and London, W. H. Allen, 1960.

*Patriotic Gore: Studies in the Literature of the American Civil War.*  New York, Oxford University Press, and London, Deutsch, 1962.

*The Cold War and the Income Tax: A Protest.*  New York, Farrar Straus, 1963; London, W. H. Allen, 1964.

*O Canada: An American's Notes on Canadian Culture.*  New York, Farrar Straus, 1965; London, Hart Davis, 1967.

*The Bit Between My Teeth: A Literary Chronicle of 1950–1965.*  New York, Farrar Straus, 1965; London, W. H. Allen, 1966.

*A Prelude: Landscapes, Characters, and Conversations from the Earlier Years of My Life.*  New York, Farrar Straus, and London, W. H. Allen, 1967.

*Upstate: Records and Recollections of Northern New York.*  New York, Farrar Straus, 1971; London, Macmillan, 1972.

Editor, *The Shock of Recognition: The Development of Literature in the United States Recorded by the Men Who Made It.*  New York, Doubleday, 1943.

Editor, *The Crack-Up and Other Uncollected Pieces*, by F. Scott Fitzgerald.  New York, New Directions, 1945; London, Grey Walls Press, 1947.

Editor, *Collected Essays*, by John Peale Bishop.  New York, Scribner, 1948.

Editor, *The Last Tycoon: An Unfinished Novel*, by F. Scott Fitzgerald, in *Three Novels.*  New York, Scribner, 1953.

Editor, *Peasants and Other Stories*, by Anton Chekhov.  New York, Doubleday, 1956.

*          *          *

"the luxuriance and rankness of America"

The massive intellect informing Edmund Wilson's criticism and cultural history provides both method and substance for his fiction. The novel, *I Thought of Daisy*, and the collection of stories unified by narrator and locale that compose *Memoirs of Hecate County* marshal character and incident toward logically demonstrable conclusions, usually pronouncements on some quality of the American experience. The narrator of *Daisy*, a leftist intellectual who regards the heroine as a symbol of the American reality he seeks, explores her complexity in five moral and emotional contexts, which range from the radical world view of the novelist Hugh Banman, to the metaphysical superstructure of the philosopher Grosbeake. The final stage in this search for personal and national identity fuses the narrator's conviction that through Daisy he will "come . . . naturally into contact with life," with his belief that a popular song he had earlier rejected on aesthetic grounds is actually a valid expression of the American ethos.

The similarly questing, older narrator of "The Princess with the Golden Hair" (*Memoirs*) conducts simultaneous love affairs with Imogen and Anna, obviously symbolic women who represent polar opposites in society. After acquiring a kind of laboratory experience with the extremes of the social system in America, he is, predictably, able to overcome the barriers of his wealth and education and achieve a sense of both the real America and a meaningful personal existence through the workingclass Anna

> who had made it possible for *me* to recreate the actuality; who had given me that life of the people which had before been but prices and wages, legislation and technical progress, that new Europe of the East Side and Brooklyn for which there was provided no guidebook. She had given me this vision—I had lived on it, not on Imogen's infantile fairy tales.

"Mr. and Mrs. Blackburn at Home" (*Memoirs*) assesses not only the limited world of the wealthy and creative who inhabit Hecate County, but also the enigma of the entire American continent: "*America*: it suggests to us even now a landscape unfamiliar and cold." Despite an element of fantasy and hallucination, the story proceeds with Wilson's characteristic logic towards a convincing image of the frustrating promise of the country. The mysterious Mr. Blackburn, like the symbolic gardener of Wilson's drama, *The Little Blue Light*, possesses appropriately diverse and contradictory ethnic antecedents and embodies the same political paranoia that dominates the play.

The substance of these books is often interchangeable with that of Wilson's non-fiction. In *Daisy*, the narrator's anguished theorizing on the psychogenic origins and effects of art foreshadows the more elaborate development of this theme in *The Wound and the Bow*. And in "Princess," the narrator's Freudian analysis of Imogen with the aid of a monograph titled, "The Hysterical Element in Orthopaedic Surgery," suggests both the subject-matter and method of Wilson's treatment of James's *The Turn of the Screw*. Wilson similarly illuminates in schematic form some of the key literary and social concerns of the 20's through the 40's, though his fiction lacks the resonance of the Joyce and Proust models he cites in the 1953 reissue of *Daisy*.

At his most successful, Wilson achieves a reification of a particular phase of American culture through a carefully selected documentation of styles of dress, popular music, philosophy, and household decor, a more artful variant of the technique of Dos Passos' *USA*. Unlike Joyce and Proust, Wilson employs these elements less as indices to the consciousness of the perceiver or as stimuli for his memory than as illustrative data supporting cultural generalizations. Ironically, the style approximates that attributed in *Daisy* to the protest novelist, Hugh Banman. In "Princess," the narrator's obsession with the dress and hair styles of his mistresses crystallizes two extremes of American femininity, and the hallucinatory flashbacks in "Ellen Terhune" (*Memoirs*) provide a rich catalogue of uppermiddle-class dress and household decor over a long period of time.

Wilson's attempts to satirize the suburban world of Hecate County are less trenchant than Mary McCarthy's dissection of a similar milieu in *A Charmed Life*, but "The Milhollands and Their Damned Soul" effectively captures the ultimate evil of banality in the publishing profession. However, the nature of the Milhollands' Faustian pact is too early and too explicitly spelled out by one of the characters, and the ponderous humor fails to bring the satire alive. Wilson's difficulty in sustaining the wit that separates satire from moral fable or allegory also weakens both "The Great Baldini," an unfinished collaboration with the late Edwin O'Connor, and the promising spoof of academia in the play *The Duke of Palermo*.

A more serious problem is the inconsistency with which Wilson's irony defines the narrators of *Daisy* and *Memoirs* and their youthful but still pompous variant, the protagonist of the early novella, *Galahad*. In *Daisy*, "The Princess with the Golden Hair," and "Mr. and Mrs. Blackburn at Home," the point of view mocks the solemn, occasionally self-important protagonist who is trying to connect with the raw life of America, but who too often assumes the slumming attitude of the amateur sociologist. At times, the irony is successful, as in "Princess," when the unnamed protagonist blunders through situations for which neither his background nor his education has prepared him. His naivete, or perhaps refusal to face the fact of Imogen's lesbianism, long after it is apparent to the reader, is particularly effective. (Lesbianism also threatens Anna in "Princess" and figures briefly in "Wilbur Flick" (*Memoirs*), and *Daisy*, as part of the sinister underside of the life the protagonists are trying to experience.) Unfortunately, there are key points when the ironic distance vanishes, when the insights of the narrators seem to fuse with those of the narrative, especially in the final epiphanies of *Daisy* and "Princess." Though Wilson's essayistic method has skill-fully manipulated his material toward these conclusions, he has not dramatized his protago-nists as men with sufficient moral sensitivity to enjoy such revelations. The lesser characters also suffer from inadequate dramatization. Too often Wilson relies on Hugh Banman's "r/w" shift in "sowwy" and "twy," on Si Banks' stuttering ("The Milhollands and Their Damned Soul"), and on the unconvincing "didun," and "mettum" in the slang of Daisy and Anna, as substitutes for the real illumination dialogue can provide. In general, Wilson's style is magisterial and reads at times like a translation of a 19th-century Russian master.

However, despite weak characterizations and an occasionally remote style, Wilson's finest story, "The Princess with the Golden Hair," is excellent by any standards. The sche-matic form and symbolic characters create the effect of allegory, though an allegory much richer than that of E. M. Forster's "The Other Side of the Hedge," and "The Celestial Omnibus," which it resembles. The documentation, both physical and intellectual, gives "Princess" a density and richness that support and partially dramatize the argument. And, more important, the orchestration of the themes achieves complex contrapuntal effects: the narrator's consistent exaltation of the "Princess" Imogen, and condescension toward Anna co-exist with his rejection of Clive Bell's aesthetic theories: ". . . I saw now how impos-sible it was for me to accept his Platonic idealism which made art represent a reality inde-pendent of the vicissitudes of life; and I could never work out the relation between his theory of the history of art and my social-economic one." Even the "taint" of gonorrhea with which Anna infects the narrator undercuts his professed desire for contact with the life of the masses and makes mandatory the stance of the courtly lover he adopts toward Imogen. She may enjoy playing the lady in a medieval romance, but her lover's detached worship results from a grim medical fact. Within its range, Wilson's fiction actually seems to embrace Bell's dictum and raises the materials and ideologies of the twentieth century to a level almost "independent of the vicissitudes of life," but still exciting.

—Burton Kendle

---

WILSON, Ethel.   British/Canadian.   Born in South Africa, 20 January 1888. Educated at Trinity Hall, Southport, Lancashire. Widow of Dr. Wallace Wilson. Taught in the public schools of Vancouver, British Columbia. Recipient: Canada Council Medal, 1962; Lorne Pierce Medal, 1964. D.Litt., University of British Columbia, Vancouver, 1955. Medal of Service, Order of Canada, 1970. Address: 2890 Point Grey Road, Apartment 308, Vancouver, British Columbia, Canada.

PUBLICATIONS

Novels

*Hetty Dorval.*   New York, Macmillan, 1947; London, Macmillan, 1948.
*The Innocent Traveller.*   Toronto and London, Macmillan, 1949.

*The Equations of Love, with Tuesday and Wednesday, and Lilly's Story.*   Toronto and
    London, Macmillan, 1952.
*Lilly's Story.*   New York, Harper, 1952.
*Swamp Angel.*   Toronto and London, Macmillan, and New York, Harper, 1954.
*Love and Salt Water.*   Toronto and London, Macmillan, 1956.


Short Stories

*Mrs. Golightly and Other Stories.*   Toronto and London, Macmillan, 1961.


Critical Study: *Ethel Wilson* by Desmond Pacey, New York, Twayne, 1967.


*            *            *


Ethel Wilson is one of those novelists whom it is exceedingly difficult to categorize. She is
strongly Canadian in her preoccupation with the landscape and society of her adopted
country, and especially of her adopted province of British Columbia, but she is in no sense
a nationalistic writer: she puts out no flags. She might be described as a social realist, for
she certainly gives us many insights into the development of Canadian society in this century,
but she seems ultimately to be far more concerned with the relations between individuals,
and the relation of the individual to the cosmos, than with social groups and movements.
She is in a sense a novelist of manners, very sensitive to shifts of taste and fashion, but that
phrase suggests a narrowness of scope which falls far short of doing her justice. She might
also be described as a psychological realist, for she has a remarkable gift for sorting out the
tangle of motives which underlies human behaviour, but that phrase suggests a scientific
portentousness that is foreign to her nature. She is also to some extent a novelist of ideas,
concerned to establish the way in which man relates to his natural environment and to the
divine, but her work is too strongly rooted in the observable world to make that label very
helpful. And all the above categories miss the strongly comic element that so often informs
her work.

What can be said without fear of contradiction is that Mrs. Wilson is an artist of high
quality if of limited quantity. Hers, however, is the art that conceals art, the art that achieves
its effect with the maximum of economy and the minimum of fuss. Her words are chosen
with infinite care, but they seem to fall naturally from her pen; she avoids fine phrases,
arresting metaphors, all the pyrotechnics of style in favour of a quiet, but quietly right,
tone and timbre.

Through almost all of her novels and short stories run two or three essentially simple
themes: innocence, courage, and love. Her favourite characters are all innocents, not in the
limited sense of that word but rather in the sense that they have committed themselves
wholeheartedly to life and life's fundamental holiness; they are also people of great courage
who, disregarding their fragility in the context of a powerful universe, persevere in the
performance of their allotted role; and they find their chief solace in the various "equations
of love"—the love between the sexes, the love within the family, the love between friends,
and the love of animate and inanimate nature. Her vision, then, is an affirmative one, but it
is far from facile and remarkably free of cant.

—Desmond Pacey

**WILSON, Mitchell.** American. Born in New York City, 17 July 1913. Educated at George Washington High School, New York; New York University, B.Sc. 1934; Columbia University, New York, M.A. in physics 1938. Married Stella Adler in 1965; has two children. Tutor in Physics, Columbia University, 1938–40; Instructor in Physics, City College of New York, 1940–41; Physics Research Director, Columbian Carbon Company, New York, 1941–45. Free-lance Writer since 1945. Editorial Consultant, Physical Science Study Committee, Massachusetts Institute of Technology, Cambridge, 1955–57. Address: 1016 Fifth Avenue, New York, New York, U.S.A.

PUBLICATIONS

Novels

The Goose Is Cooked, with Abraham Polansky (as Emmett Hogarth). New York, Simon and Schuster, 1940.
Footsteps Behind Her. New York, Simon and Schuster, 1941.
Stalk the Hunter. New York, Simon and Schuster, 1943.
None So Blind. New York, Simon and Schuster, 1945; London, W. H. Allen, 1947.
The Panic-Stricken. New York, Simon and Schuster, 1946.
The Kimballs. New York, Simon and Schuster, 1947; London, W. H. Allen, 1950.
Live with Lightning. Boston, Little Brown, 1949; London, W. H. Allen, 1950.
My Brother, My Enemy. Boston, Little Brown, 1952; London, W. H. Allen, 1953.
The Lovers. New York, Doubleday, 1954; London, W. H. Allen, 1955.
Meeting at a Far Meridian. New York, Doubleday, and London, Secker and Warburg, 1961.
The Huntress. New York, Doubleday, and London, Secker and Warburg, 1966.
Passion to Know. New York, Doubleday, and London, Weidenfeld and Nicolson, 1972.

Other

American Science and Invention: A Pictorial History: The Fabulous Story of How American Dreamers, Wizards and Inspired Tinkerers Converted a Wilderness into the Wonder of the World. New York, Simon and Schuster, 1954.
The Human Body: What It Is and How It Works. New York, Golden Press, and London, Golden Pleasure Books, 1959.
Energy, with the editors of Life. New York, Time, 1963.
See-Saws and Cosmic Rays: A First View of Physics. New York, Lothrop, 1967.

Manuscript Collection: Boston University.

*       *       *

Mitchell Wilson is the exemplary popular novelist. Technically proficient, but interested only in the most functional communication, sensitive to psychology but employing his knowledge mainly to render normative experience, he offers his audience fiction resembling a morality play in which the cause of good people promises, in time, to triumph.

In the 1940's Wilson produced a series of suspense novels depending for their effect upon the emergence of sinister purposes in everyday settings. In Footsteps Behind Her a young

woman fleeing a narrow-minded Nevada town is terrorized by spies because out of friendliness she agrees to do an errand for a man she meets on a cross country bus. The refugee
curator in *Stalk the Hunter* stumbles into a Nazi spy ring headed by her museum director.
The young man who falls in love in *None So Blind* barely escapes involvement in a murder
plot devised by his beloved; a young couple's relationship is imperiled by a parent's falsification of the past in *The Kimballs*; and circumstantial mix-ups entangle a young sailor in
a ruthless dope ring among Nazi-sympathizing yachtsmen in *The Panic-Stricken*. Constructed
as entertainments, these suspense novels subordinate ideas to the touch of terror; yet in the
plot of each Wilson embodies an incipient morality theme in the conflict between characters
deliberately represented as ordinary or average in their desires for love and security and the
obstacles raised against them by individuals possessed by what Wilson sees as an abnormal
psychology.

In a series of novels Wilson began in 1949 this theme has been developed, with variations,
into the dynamics of an unusual variety of American popular literature—the fiction of
science. Unlike contemporary science-fiction where the conceptions of technology are
themselves the basis of literary invention, Wilson's stories of the fellowship of science take
the form of psychological realism, telling of ordinary characters living lives distinguishable
from others in contemporary society only in their seeking self-fulfillment in scientific work.
The feelings they express of compassion or devotion are linked through their scientific
knowledge with a commitment to apply beneficently the findings of their research, but
residing in a competitive society they find the grandest intellectual attainments reduced to
property; thus, the devoted physicist of *Live with Lightning* must resist the possessiveness
of the non-scientific managers of industry and governmental bureaus, and the fraternal
inventors of television transmission in *My Brother, My Enemy* are divided and driven by the
economic requirement that they make their discovery yield capital. Wilson, himself trained
scientifically, depends, correctly it seems, upon the intrinsic significance of scientists to
modern society, and making his stories more compelling places the narratives in actual
historical circumstances, so that *The Huntress*, for example, limns the personality of a
nineteenth century scientist resembling Marie Curie, and *Meeting at a Far Meridian* describes
relationships among participants in a joint American-Soviet project.

Not surprisingly Mitchell Wilson is one of the most popular American authors published
in the USSR where the repute of scientific culture is remarkably high. For both his Soviet
audience and his wide readership among English speakers he is a noble popularizer who,
rather than exploit an audience through fear and salacity as authors of mass literature in a
competitive society usually feel they must do, chooses to tell stories which identify humane
feelings with the premises of civilized life.

—John M. Reilly

---

**WILSON, Sloan.** American. Born in Norwalk, Connecticut, 8 May 1920. Educated
at Harvard University, Cambridge, Massachusetts, B.A. 1942. Served in the United States
Coast Guard, 1942–46. Married Elise Pickhardt in 1942 (divorced); Betty Stephens, 1963;
has four children. Reporter, *Providence Journal*, Rhode Island, 1946–47; Writer, Time Inc.,
New York, 1947–49. Assistant Director, National Citizens Commission for the Public
Schools, New York, 1949–52; Director of Information Services, University of Buffalo,
New York, 1952–55; Assistant Director, White House Conference on Education, Washing-
ton, D.C., 1956; Education Editor, *New York Herald Tribune*, 1956–58. Now a full-time
Writer. Lives in Ticonderoga, New York. Address: c/o Mr. Morton Leavy, Weissberger
and Frosch, 120 East 56th Street, New York, New York, U.S.A.

PUBLICATIONS

Novels

> *Voyage to Somewhere.*  New York, Wyn, 1947.
> *The Man in the Gray Flannel Suit.*  New York, Simon and Schuster, 1955; London, Cassell, 1956.
> *A Summer Place.*  New York, Simon and Schuster, and London, Cassell, 1958.
> *A Sense of Values.*  New York, Harper, 1960; London, Cassell, 1961.
> *Georgie Winthrop.*  New York, Harper, and London, Cassell, 1963.
> *Janus Island.*  Boston, Little Brown, and London, Cassell, 1967.
> *All the Best People.*  New York, Putnam, 1970; London, Cassell, 1971.

Other

> *Away from It All.*  New York, Putnam, 1969; London, Cassell, 1970.

Manuscript Collection: Boston University.

Sloan Wilson comments:

My work consists of a running commentary on the world as I have seen it from 1944 to the present. Both my strength and my limitation derive from my determination to confine myself to first-hand experiences and observations. The Second World War is in my books because I fought through it. The worries and frustrations of business are on my pages because I suffered them for many years before I became a full-time writer. The joys, angers, desperation and contentment which are part of many marriages are in my novels, because I have been married twice. Children appear in my books because I have four of them. The writing in my books is rather simple and straight-forward because I have a story to tell and I want to get on with it. The English language, I believe, can be used for many purposes—to make the music of poetry, to give military orders, or to give the illusion of meaning without any meaning, as most politicians employ it. I use it to give my readers the thoughts and, most of all, the emotions which I have experienced. I want the readers to be deeply moved without becoming aware of the language which is transmitting the feelings of others to them. That's why I avoid "fancy writing"—it makes readers think about words instead of about human triumph or despair.

The men, women and children in my books are concerned with bed-rock issues, such as how to stay alive in time of war without being a coward, how to make a good living in time of peace without selling one's soul cut-rate, and, most of all, how to understand and enjoy the mysteries of love without guilt and without hurting other people. Human beings in my books get tired, cross and discouraged sometimes, but they doggedly pursue happiness and cling to a rather old-fashioned sense of honor to the best of their ability, which sometimes is not enough. Critics often believe my books are an over-simplification of life or a naive interpretation of it, but a few million readers tell me that for them my pages are mirrors.

*       *       *

The dust jacket of the American edition of Sloan Wilson's fifth novel, *Georgie Winthrop*, describes the book in these rather sensational terms: "The story of the man who lives next door to The Man in the Gray Flannel Suit—forty-five, intelligent, modest, decent, and catapulted by an extraordinary love into trying to grow up inside." Sloan Wilson has long been the victim of this kind of cliché-ridden, high-pressure advertising, of this nod toward a low-brow readership. If he enters literary history at all it will be as the creator of the man-in-the-gray-flannel-suit metaphor. Until now the critics have paid him scant attention. Despite his impressive output, even as comprehensive a reference work as the three-volume *Encyclopedia of World Literature in the 20th Century* (Ungar, 1967–71) does not devote an entry to him.

The typical Sloan Wilson protagonist is acutely aware of his Puritan ancestry, of his New England background, and tries desperately to "live in the present." Thus Ben Powers, in *Janus Island*, and George Winthrop, in *Georgie Winthrop*, both forty-five year old family men, enter into relationships with younger women (in George's case a seventeen year old) in vain attempts to ignore past commitments and future responsibilities. Tom Rath, before the present events of *The Man in the Gray Flannel Suit*, had a wartime love affair with an Italian girl in another futile effort to freeze the present moment. Rath has a kind of Faulknerian obsession with time, which often expresses itself lyrically: "Time was given us like jewels to spend, and it's the ultimate sacrilege to wish it away."

Wilson called his most recent novel *All the Best People*, a title which would serve handsomely for almost any of his books. Despite the intended irony of the phrase, there is always a certain respect in evidence in his fiction for the established eastern seaboard families, with their yachts, their islands, and their prep school and Harvard-Yale backgrounds. Dana, the main character in *All the Best People*, at one point defiantly remarks to his wife: "Of course! They call people like us WASPS, Caroline, white Anglo-Saxon Protestants." Later on, Caroline asserts formidably and characteristically: ". . . my parents said I had to learn how to like Jews and Negroes, but they never said I had to like Middle Westerners."

Wilson has proved to be a skilled chronicler of social and historical events, from the Depression years through the aftermath of World War II. *All the Best People*, his most historical novel, shows the eroding effect of various upheavals in American life on a group of families who own property at Paradise Point, near Lake George, New York. *A Sense of Values* and *All the Best People* have long sequences devoted to the military experiences of the principal male characters. The Second World War, if somewhat obliquely, figures crucially also in *The Man in the Gray Flannel Suit* and *A Summer Place*. *Janus Island*, which describes more recent events than most of the other novels, is concerned, in passing, with the disruptive presence of Vietnam.

There is no mistaking the richness and vitality of Sloan Wilson's fiction. Still, as certain reviewers have remarked, there is a sense of *déjà lu* for anyone who reads through all of his work. Events, characters, and symbols have a way of being reused. Thus the war experiences of Nathan in *A Sense of Values* and those of Dana in *All the Best People* are more than passingly similar. There are crotchety caretakers, all cast from the same mold, in *The Man in the Gray Flannel Suit*, *A Summer Place*, and *Janus Island*. Magicians serve rather similar symbolical functions in *All the Best People* and *A Sense of Values*. Sylvia's "fake mink coat over her bathing suit" in *A Summer Place* reappears in the form of Caroline's "mink-dyed muskrat coat" in *All the Best People*. Both Nort in *Janus Island* and Nathan in *A Sense of Values* have the nervous habit of clenching and unclenching their hands. Dana, at the end of *All the Best People*, comes, uncannily, to resemble Hopkins in *The Man in the Gray Flannel Suit*; and Annabelle, in *A Sense of Values*, is a female—and somewhat more aggressive—Hopkins.

Critics have objected to the untidiness of Sloan Wilson's novels; their structures tend to be indecisively open-ended. Most of them are unduly episodic. They are as far removed as possible from the tautness of the best post-World War II fiction. Wilson obviously prefers a more leisurely, digressive pace. There is, however, a certain appropriateness about the rather old-fashioned open form of these novels; they deal, after all, with a world which holds on to the old pieties and stubbornly resists change. The underplayed, somewhat symbolical final remark of George Winthrop—which ends the only novel in the Wilson canon with a university setting—reveals how important traditional values are: "No, thank you very much, but I have to be getting home. I have a long drive ahead."

—Melvin J. Friedman

---

**WINDHAM, Donald.** American. Born in Atlanta, Georgia, 2 July 1920. Educated at Boys' High School, Atlanta. Editor, *Dance Index* magazine, New York, 1943–45. Recipient: Guggenheim Fellowship, 1960. Address: 230 Central Park South, New York, New York 10019, U.S.A.

PUBLICATIONS

Novels

*The Dog Star.* New York, Doubleday, 1950; London, Hart Davis, 1951.
*The Hero Continues.* New York, Crowell, and London, Hart Davis, 1960.
*Two People.* New York, Coward McCann, 1965; London, Joseph, 1966.

Short Stories

*The Hitchhiker.* Florence, Italy, privately printed, 1950.
*The Warm Country.* London, Hart Davis, 1960; New York, Scribner, 1962.

Uncollected Short Story

"Rome", in *Paris Review*, no. 3, 1953.

Play

*You Touched Me*, with Tennessee Williams (produced Cleveland, 1944; New York, 1945). New York, French, 1947.

Other

*Emblems of Conduct* (autobiography). New York, Scribner, 1964.

Critical Studies: Introduction by E. M. Forster to *The Warm Country*, 1960; review by Jeremy Larner, in *New York Times Book Review*, 1962; review by Ralph McGill, in *New York Times Book Review*, 12 April 1964; "Un amico straniero che ci vede come siamo" by Mario Soldati, in *Il Giorno* (Milan), 13 July 1965.

Donald Windham comments:

I try to write about reality. The belief that reality bears being portrayed seems to me the only optimism. I disagree with the idea "write about what you know". I write about what I *need* to know, in an effort to understand. I hope to sight and capture my theme without killing it. I disagree with the idea "never write a story unless you can put down the point of it on a postage stamp". I like a story to be concise. I have no impulse to spread out what I could set down in one square inch. I have written an autobiography (up to my nineteenth year), and can claim that of my writings only it is autobiographical; but I would rather claim that I have written about life only as I myself have found it and tried to understand it.

*      *      *

Donald Windham's three novels, collection of short stories, and autobiographical sketches demonstrate the significance of even the most trivial objects and events when made part of sharply delineated feelings. His writing abounds with the unexpected and precisely realized details of daily life: cats walking with "tails high in the air revealing their dry buttons," "the bright vacant cement of the Gulf filling station," workmen with "wet circles like dark suns beneath the pits of their arms." *Emblems of Conduct*, particularly, contains remembrances of the Georgia world of his boyhood lived amid fading prosperity and insular relatives—remembrances presented without the sentimentality or nostalgia of Thomas Wolfe or even Truman Capote.

The innocence and spontaneity of his childhood world contrast with Windham's principal concern, the tortured, self-deceptive, confused creatures of desire and disappointment we become as adults. Trapped in the patterns of their lives, the characters sometimes rebel and more often suffer in an agony of weakness, anger, and indecision, often torn between the desire for escape and the fear of losing their security. Windham himself escaped at eighteen from family and Southern society on a bus to New York, unlike his less fortunate characters, for example, the widow with two children and little money in "Life of Georgia" trapped in a spiritless routine of dependence on her mother, in her mind the childhood memory "that tomorrow, somehow, something would happen more wonderful, or more terrible, than anything which ever had happened before."

The rebellious adolescent hero of Windham's first novel, *The Dog Star*, builds defenses against the world which are ultimately self-destructive. In a series of episodes burdened with obtrusive symbolism and indefinite existential motivation Windham examines the alienation that is both the result and cause of violence and insensitivity. Blackie Pride's contempt for human weakness and dependence following the suicide of his reform school friend, Whitey, grows into the contempt for life and the exaltation of personal freedom that are implicit in Blackie's suicide.

Elements of violence and alienation overshadow Dennis Freeman's rise to success as a playwright in *The Hero Continues*. Fame, money, and admirers only provoke his self-centered and paranoid responses to people and events, symptoms of his fears concerning his talent, his reputation, his friendships, and his virility, all ultimately concentrated in his fear of death. The terrible irony, however, is that his creativity arises out of his personal nightmare world of physical violence, self-deception, and alienation—his fictional life and his real life incompatible yet inseparable.

Homosexuality, a casual theme in *The Hero Continues*, is central to Windham's most recent novel, *Two People*, the story of a love affair between a married American in his thirties and an Italian boy. But for all Windham's sympathetic, delicate treatment of the man's absorbing passion, the love making, the boy's dual attraction to girlfriend and lover, Windham fails to realize the homosexual drive as more than an aberration conceived, satisfied, and abandoned in the interval of a Roman holiday. Here as elsewhere Windham falls short of a thorough exploration of the motives of his characters, but he also demonstrates his abiding virtues: emotional control, precision of detail, and compassionate treatment of subject.

—Dale K. Doepke

------------

**WISEMAN, Adele.** Canadian. Born in Winnipeg, Manitoba, in 1928. Taught English at MacDonald College, McGill University, Montreal. Recipient: Beta Sigma Chi Award, 1957; Governor–General's Award, 1957; National Conference of Christians and Jews Brotherhood Award, 1957; Guggenheim Fellowship, 1957. Address: c/o Macmillan Company Ltd., St. Martin's House, 70 Bond Street, Toronto 2, Ontario, Canada.

PUBLICATIONS

Novel

*The Sacrifice*.  New York, Viking Press, and London, Gollancz, 1956.

Other

*Old Markets, New World*.  Toronto, Macmillan, 1964.

\*        \*        \*

Adele Wiseman's *The Sacrifice* excited a number of Canadian critics when it appeared in 1956, for in the national literary climate of the time it demonstrated a rare talent: such skill in portraying character that felicitous landscape description, that stock-in-trade of Canadian writers, seemed to pale beside the people. Yet so many skilled, prolific, and more technically arresting novelists have since appeared—Laurence, Wiebe, Carrier, Cohen, Kroetsch, Richler, Godfrey—that Wiseman's quiet words appear to have faded into history. Still, her novel bears rereading closely, both for its pervading sense of human values and for its insight into the ironic individuality with which men respond to events and the complex motivations that govern their decisions.

The novel is, as its bookjacket subtitle proclaimed, "a novel of fathers and sons", a study of three generations of a Jewish family that emigrated from European pogroms to mid-Canadian urban stress. Living in either place has its problems, and the nature of life (of what it is to be a Jew, a Jew in Canada, or just to be) is the key question the book explores. The kosher butcher Abraham (with wife Sarah, son Isaac, and later grandson Moses) may seem too aptly named and employed to be fictionally credible, yet Wiseman deals with parallels and differences among individuals thoroughly enough (the subplots aid in such a structure) that the Old Testament references simply add Mythical dimension to the problem she examines, and historical—genealogical—continuity to man's quest both for knowledge and for the ability to live with the knowledge he acquires.

The sacrifice of the title is thus many things at once, some admirable, others not—the Biblical story of Abraham's faith, the pagan ritual propitiation of angry gods, the immolation of self in the preservation of valued traditions, the ritual butchery, the education of one's sons to one's own ideas and standards, the accepted means for ceremonially renewing wonder, belief, and fear, and the fictional Abraham's murder of the prostitute Laiah in the belief that he is defeating Death and restoring vitality to his life and his community. For his act, Abraham is confined on Mad Mountain. Not content to be, he reflects later, he tried to be creator and destroyer, too, thus impinging on others' identity when the real struggle lay within himself. But understanding is its own punishment, he avers; it is the natural consequence of seeking beyond oneself—exemplified in the emigration as well as in the constant quest for knowledge—and the paradox of being human and alive.

Men occupy, however, various kinds of country—national political organizations, religious communities, families, economic and cultural groups, the world of life (at war with the world of death), the outlook of childhood, and the age of maturity. All blend in each man's separate identity, but all identities blend with each other in friendship and humane brotherhood. When Moses impulsively visits his "mad" grandfather, and sees his own hand taken in the older man's, he recognizes the continuity they represent—an affirmation of the cyclical progress of humanity and of the inevitability of men suffering understanding. Moses' friend Aaron departs at this point to help start the new (old, ancestral) country of Israel; Moses himself, who had been contemplating the same move, recognizes that he has a new country to explore already—not in Canada *per se*, but in the identity, the being, he has newly found, in his newly appreciated sense of heritage, and in the dimly lit recesses of his heart and mind. To shed light on some of those dark corners is the task Miss Wiseman has attempted to dramatize; to arouse sympathy for the characters meeting their consciences in this way is the goal to which she has managed to win.

—W. H. Hew

---

**WODEHOUSE, P(elham) G(renville).** American. Born in Guildford, Surrey, England, 15 October 1881; emigrated to the United States in 1910; naturalized, 1955. Educated at Dulwich College, London, 1894–1900. Married Ethel Rowley Wayman in 1914. Columnist ("By the Way"), *The Globe*, London, 1903–09; Drama Critic, *Vanity Fair*, New York, 1915–19. Has also worked as a Hollywood Scriptwriter. Interned by the Germans during World War II. D.L., Oxford University, 1939. Lives on Long Island, New York, Address: c/o Barrie and Jenkins, 2 Clements Inn, London W.C.2, England.

PUBLICATIONS

Novels

*The Pothunters.* London, Black, 1902; New York, Macmillan, 1924.
*A Prefect's Uncle.* London, Black, 1903; New York, Macmillan, 1924.
*The Gold Bat.* London, Black, 1904; New York, Macmillan, 1923.
*The Head of Kay's.* London, Black, 1905; New York, Macmillan, 1922.
*Love among the Chickens.* London, Newnes, 1906; New York, Circle Publishing Company, 1909; revised edition, London, Jenkins, 1921.
*The White Feather.* London, Black, 1907; New York, Macmillan, 1922.

*Not George Washington*, with Herbert Westbrook.  London, Cassell, 1907.
*The Swoop: How Clarence Saved England: A Tale of the Great Invasion*.  London, Rivers, 1909.
*Mike: A Public School Story*.  London, Black, 1909; New York, Macmillan, 1924.
*The Intrusion of Jimmy*.  New York, Watt, 1910; as *A Gentleman of Leisure*, London, Rivers, 1910.
*Psmith in the City: A Sequel to "Mike"*.  London, Black, 1910.
*The Prince and Betty*.  New York, Watt, 1912; as *Psmith, Journalist,* London, Black, 1915.
*The Prince and Betty* (different book from the previous title).  London, Mills and Boon, 1912.
*The Little Nugget*.  London, Methuen, 1913; New York, Watt, 1914.
*Something New*.  New York, Appleton, 1915; as *Something Fresh*, London, Methuen, 1915.
*Uneasy Money*.  New York, Appleton, 1916; London, Methuen, 1917.
*Piccadilly Jim*.  New York, Dodd Mead, 1917; London, Jenkins, 1918.
*Their Mutual Child*.  New York, Boni and Liveright, 1919; as *The Coming of Bill*, London, Jenkins, 1920.
*A Damsel in Distress*.  New York, Doran, and London, Jenkins, 1919.
*The Little Warrior*.  New York, Doran, 1920; as *Jill the Reckless*, London, Jenkins, 1921.
*Three Men and a Maid*.  New York, Doran, 1922; as *The Girl on the Boat*, London, Jenkins, 1922.
*The Adventures of Sally*.  London, Jenkins, 1922; as *Mostly Sally*, New York, Doran, 1923.
*Leave It to Psmith*.  London, Jenkins, 1923; New York, Doran, 1924.
*Bill the Conqueror: His Invasion of England in the Springtime*.  London, Methuen, 1924; New York, Doran, 1925.
*Sam the Sudden*.  London, Methuen, 1925; as *Sam in the Suburbs*, New York, Doran, 1925.
*The Small Bachelor*.  London, Methuen, and New York, Doran, 1927.
*Money for Money*.  London, Jenkins, and New York, Doubleday, 1928.
*Fish Preferred*.  New York, Doubleday, 1929; as *Summer Lightning*, London, Jenkins, 1929.
*Big Money*.  New York, Doubleday, and London, Jenkins, 1931.
*If I Were You*.  New York, Doubleday, and London, Jenkins, 1931.
*Doctor Sally*.  London, Methuen, 1932.
*Hot Water*.  London, Jenkins, and New York, Doubleday, 1932.
*Heavy Weather*.  Boston, Little Brown, and London, Jenkins, 1933.
*Thank You, Jeeves*.  London, Jenkins, and Boston, Little Brown, 1934.
*Right Ho, Jeeves*.  London, Jenkins, 1934; as *Brinkley Manor*, Boston, Little Brown, 1934.
*The Luck of the Bodkins*.  London, Jenkins, 1935; Boston, Little Brown, 1936.
*Laughing Gas*.  London, Jenkins, and New York, Doubleday, 1936.
*Summer Moonshine*.  New York, Doubleday, 1937; London, Jenkins, 1938.
*The Code of the Woosters*.  New York, Doubleday, and London, Jenkins, 1938.
*Uncle Fred in the Springtime*.  New York, Doubleday, and London, Jenkins, 1939.
*Quick Service*.  London, Jenkins, and New York, Doubleday, 1940.
*Money in the Bank*.  New York, Doubleday, 1942; London, Jenkins, 1946.
*Joy in the Morning*.  New York, Doubleday, 1946; London, Jenkins, 1947.
*Full Moon*.  New York, Doubleday, and London, Jenkins, 1947.
*Spring Fever*.  New York, Doubleday, and London, Jenkins, 1948.
*Uncle Dynamite*.  London, Jenkins, and New York, Didier, 1948.
*The Mating Season*.  London, Jenkins, and New York, Didier, 1949.
*The Old Reliable*.  London, Jenkins, and New York, Doubleday, 1951.

*Barmy in Wonderland.*  London, Jenkins, 1952; as *Angel Cake*, New York, Doubleday, 1952.

*Pigs Have Wings.*  New York, Doubleday, and London, Jenkins, 1952.

*Ring for Jeeves.*  London, Jenkins, 1953; as *The Return of Jeeves*, New York, Simon and Schuster, 1954.

*Jeeves and the Feudal Spirit.*  London, Jenkins, 1954; as *Bertie Wooster Sees It Through*, New York, Simon and Schuster, 1955.

*French Leave.*  London, Jenkins, 1956; New York, Simon and Schuster, 1959.

*Something Fishy.*  London, Jenkins, 1957; as *The Butler Did It*, New York, Simon and Schuster, 1957.

*Cocktail Time.*  London, Jenkins, and New York, Simon and Schuster, 1958.

*How Right You Are, Jeeves.*  New York, Simon and Schuster, 1960; as *Jeeves in the Offing*, London, Jenkins, 1960.

*The Ice in the Bedroom.*  New York, Simon and Schuster, 1961; as *Ice in the Bedroom*, London, Jenkins, 1961.

*Service with a Smile.*  New York, Simon and Schuster, 1961; London, Jenkins, 1962.

*Stiff Upper Lip, Jeeves.*  New York, Simon and Schuster, and London, Jenkins, 1963.

*Biffin's Millions.*  New York, Simon and Schuster, 1964; as *Frozen Assets*, London, Jenkins, 1964.

*The Brinkmanship of Galahad Threepwood.*  New York, Simon and Schuster, 1965; as *Galahad at Blandings*, London, Jenkins, 1965.

*The Purloined Paperweight.*  New York, Simon and Schuster, 1967; as *Company for Henry*, London, Jenkins, 1967.

*Do Butlers Burgle Banks?*  New York, Simon and Schuster, and London, Jenkins, 1968.

*A Pelican at Blandings.*  London, Jenkins, 1969; as *No Nudes Is Good Nudes*, New York, Simon and Schuster, 1970.

*Girl in Blue.*  London, Barrie and Jenkins, 1970; New York, Simon and Schuster, 1971.

*Much Obliged, Jeeves.*  London, Barrie and Jenkins, 1971; as *Jeeves and the Tie That Binds*, New York, Simon and Schuster, 1971.

Short Stories

*Tales of St. Austin's.*  London, Black, 1903; New York, Macmillan, 1923.

*The Man Upstairs and Other Stories.*  London, Methuen, 1914.

*The Man with Two Left Feet and Other Stories.*  London, Methuen, 1917; New York, Burt, 1933.

*My Man Jeeves.*  London, Newnes, 1919.

*Indiscretions of Archie.*  London, Jenkins, and New York, Doran, 1921.

*The Clicking of Cuthbert.*  London, Jenkins, 1922; as *Golf Without Tears*, New York, Doran, 1924.

*The Inimitable Jeeves.*  London, Jenkins, 1923; as *Jeeves*, New York, Doran, 1923.

*Ukridge.*  London, Jenkins, 1924; as *He Rather Enjoyed It*, New York, Doran, 1926.

*Carry on, Jeeves.*  London, Jenkins, 1925; New York, Doran, 1927.

*The Heart of a Goof.*  London, Jenkins, 1926; as *Divots*, New York, Doran, 1927.

*Meet Mr. Mulliner.*  London, Jenkins, 1927; New York, Doubleday, 1928.

*Mr. Mulliner Speaking.*  London, Jenkins, 1929; New York, Doubleday, 1930.

*Very Good, Jeeves.*  New York, Doubleday, and London, Jenkins, 1930.

*Mulliner Nights.*  London, Jenkins, and New York, Doubleday, 1933.

*Blandings Castle: And Elsewhere.*  London, Jenkins, and New York, Doubleday, 1935.

*Young Men in Spats.*  London, Jenkins, and New York, Doubleday, 1936.

*Lord Emsworth and Others.*  London, Jenkins, 1937; as *Crime Wave at Blandings and Other Stories*, New York, Doubleday, 1937.

*Eggs, Beans and Crumpets.*  London, Jenkins, and New York, Doubleday, 1940.

*Dudley Is Back to Normal.*  New York, Doubleday, 1940.

*Nothing Serious*.   London, Jenkins, 1950; New York, Doubleday, 1951.
*Selected Stories*.   New York, Modern Library, 1958.
*A Few Quick Ones*.   New York, Simon and Schuster, and London, Jenkins, 1959.
*Plum Pie*.   London, Jenkins, 1966; New York, Simon and Schuster, 1967.
*The World of Mr. Mulliner*.   London, Barrie and Jenkins, 1972.


Plays

*The Gay Gordons*, with others, music by Seymour Hicks (produced London, 1907).
*A Gentleman of Leisure*, with John Stapleton (produced New York, 1911).
*Brother Alfred*, with Herbert Westbrook (produced London, 1913).
*A Thief for a Night*, with John Stapleton (produced New York, 1913).
*Nuts and Wine*, with C. H. Bovill (produced London, 1914).
*Miss Springtime*, with Guy Bolton, music by Emmerich Kalman (produced New York, 1916).
*Have a Heart*, with Guy Bolton, music by Jerome Kern (produced New York, 1917).
*Oh, Boy*, with Guy Bolton, music by Jerome Kern (produced New York, 1917).
*Leave It to Jane*, with Guy Bolton, music by Jerome Kern (produced New York, 1917).
*The Rose of China*, with Guy Bolton (produced New York, 1917).
*The Second Century Show*, with Guy Bolton (produced New York, 1917).
*The Riviera Girl*, with Guy Bolton, music by Emmerich Kalman (produced New York, 1917).
*Miss 1917*, with Guy Bolton, music by Jerome Kern (produced New York, 1917).
*Ringtime*, with Guy Bolton (produced New York, 1917).
*Oh, Lady, Lady*, with Guy Bolton, music by Jerome Kern (produced New York, 1918).
*The Girl Behind the Gun*, with Guy Bolton (produced New York, 1918); as *Kissing Time* (produced London, 1918).
*Oh, My Dear*, with Guy Bolton (produced New York, 1918).
*See You Later*, with Guy Bolton (produced New York, 1918).
*The Golden Moth*, with Fred Thompson, music by Ivor Novello (produced London, 1921).
*The Cabaret Girl*, with George Grossmith, music by Jerome Kern (produced London, 1922).
*The Beauty Prize*, with George Grossmith, music by Jerome Kern (produced London, 1923).
*Sitting Pretty*, with Guy Bolton, music by Jerome Kern (produced New York, 1924).
*The Play's the Thing*, adaptation of a play by Ferenc Molnar (produced New York, 1926).   New York, Brentano's, 1927.
*Oh, Kay*, with Guy Bolton and Ira Gershwin, music by George Gershwin (produced New York, 1926; London, 1927).
*Hearts and Diamonds*, with Laurie Wylie, adaptation of a play by E. Marischka and B. Granichstead-Ten (produced London, 1926).   London, Prowse, 1926.
*The Nightingale*, with Guy Bolton (produced New York, 1927).
*Her Cardboard Lover*, with Valerie Wyngate, adaptation of a play by Jacques Deval (produced New York, 1927).
*Show Boat* (lyrics of the song "Bill" only), music by Jerome Kern (produced New York, 1927).
*Good Morning, Bill*, adaptation of a play by Ladislaus Fodor (produced London, 1927).   London, Methuen, 1928.
*Rosalie*, with others (produced New York, 1928).
*The Three Musketeers*, with Clifford Grey and George Grossmith, music by Rudolf Friml (produced New York, 1928; London, 1930).   London, Chappell, and New York, Harms, 1937.
*A Damsel in Distress*, with Ian Hay (produced London, 1928).   London, French, 1930.

*Baa, Baa, Black Sheep*, with Ian Hay (produced London, 1929).  London, French, 1930.

*Candlelight*, adaptation of a play by Siegfried Geyer (produced New York, 1929).  New York, French, 1934.

*Leave It to Psmith*, with Ian Hay (produced London, 1930).  London, French, 1932.

*Who's Who*, with Guy Bolton (produced London, 1934).

*Anything Goes*, with others, music by Cole Porter (produced New York, 1934; London, 1935).  London, French, 1936.

*The Inside Stand* (produced London, 1935).

*Carry On, Jeeves*, with Guy Bolton.  London, Evans, 1956.


Screenplays: *Piccadilly Jim*, 1936; *Thank You, Jeeves*, 1936; *A Damsel in Distress*, 1937.


Other

*William Tell Told Again*.  London, Black, 1904.

*The Globe "By the Way" Book: A Literary Quick Lunch for People Who Have Got Five Minutes to Spare*, with Herbert Westbrook.  London, Globe, 1908.

*Louder and Funnier* (essays).  London, Faber, 1932.

*P. G. Wodehouse* (a selection).  London, Methuen, 1934.

*Bring on the Girls: The Improbable Story of Our Life in Musical Comedy, with Pictures to Prove It*, with Guy Bolton.  New York, Simon and Schuster, 1953; London, Jenkins, 1954.

*Performing Flea: A Self-Portrait in Letters*, edited by W. Townend.  London, Jenkins, 1953; revised edition, as *Author! Author!*, New York, Simon and Schuster, 1962.

"Berlin Broadcasts", in *Encounter* (London), October-November 1954.

*America, I Like You*.  New York, Simon and Schuster, 1956; revised edition, as *Over Seventy: An Autobiography with Digressions*, London, Jenkins, 1957.

*The World of Jeeves*.  London, Jenkins, 1967.


Editor, *A Century of Humour*.  London, Hutchinson, 1934.

Editor, with Scott Meredith, *The Best of Modern Humor*.  New York, McBride, 1952.

Editor, with Scott Meredith, *The Week-End Book of Humor*.  New York, Washburn, 1952; London, Jenkins, 1954.

Editor, with Scott Meredith, *A Carnival of Modern Humor*.  New York, Delacorte Press, 1967; London, Jenkins, 1968.


Bibliography: *A Bibliography and Reader's Guide to the First Editions of P. G. Wodehouse* by David A. Jasen, London, Barrie and Jenkins, 1971.


*         *         *


The world of Wodehouse is legendary. It goes back to before the First World War; indeed, to the Boer War, for in that distant age P. G. Wodehouse's school stories were just beginning to entertain English schoolboys. Since then his books have entertained almost the whole world. Widely translated, they've become famous among all classes and all kinds of people, readers and non-readers, intellectuals and non-intellectuals, upper crust and bottom drawer. His idiom has entered language after language, his people prosper everywhere. Because Mr. Wodehouse peddles laughter, boundaries are unknown; and only those who find laughter difficult or undignified pass by on the other side.

It has been said that to apply the normal machinery of criticism to a Wodehouse novel is like taking a spade to a soufflé. This is true; so, too, is the fact that Wodehouse today has achieved a unique position within the pattern of contemporary literature. His novels rarely now head the critics' lists. Lines rather than paragraphs are devoted to them, if they're mentioned at all: the Wodehouse world—formal, precise and for the most part unchanging —is as much taken for granted as the Royal Family and Britain's island state. Yet every new Wodehouse novel contains more delicate writing and logical construction, more professionalism and sheer talent than hundredweights of the average contemporary novel. No matter how narrow critics may claim the row that he hoes is, or how similar many of his characters are, there can be little argument that within his chosen framework he achieves what he sets out to achieve and that in doing so he often moves close to perfection.

Accused of writing the same novel more than once and of changing only the names of its characters, Wodehouse replied by pointing out that his newest offering was again just the same as before except that this time, for the sake of convenience, the characters didn't have different names. His courteous lack of reverence for the hatchet-men of the Eng. Lit. scene has a way of making them seem trite: he is for ever the genius schoolboy suffering with a smile the tedious attentions of the schoolmaster who teaches because he cannot do.

Wodehouse's first novel for adults was *Love among the Chickens* which introduced Ukridge, the most openly criminal of the Wodehouse heroes. Three years later he created his second immortal in the person of Psmith, who appeared first of all in a school story called "The Lost Lambs". "Are you," enquired Psmith on first sighting the story's hero, "the Bully, the Pride of the School, or the Boy who is Led Astray and takes to Drink in Chapter Sixteen?"

From school Psmith moves into big business, in which—as *Psmith in the City*—he sets himself the task of maddening Mr. Bickersdyke, the bank manager whose misfortune it is to employ him as a clerk. Mr. Bickersdyke replaces Mr. Downing, the housemaster at Sedleigh, as the bubble of hypocrisy that must with the same complex deployment of guile be exploded. Good and bad are clearly charted in Wodehouse country, as are the tedious and the jolly, the generous and the mean-minded, the awful and the O.K. Ukridge may be both a thief and a blackmailer but Ukridge is O.K. because he's amusing. Baxter, Lord Emsworth's terrible secretary, keeps well within the law but his spirit is dull and deadly: Baxter is bad.

Wooster and Jeeves joined Ukridge and Psmith in 1919, Blandings Castle having in the meanwhile seen the first light of day in 1915. And then, on all sides, there are thwarted aunts and bewildered earls, an army of disagreeable animals and children, mean men of commerce, burglars, butlers and chorus girls. The action moves from Blandings to Valley Fields S.E.21, to the Drones Club and the Wooster lair in Berkeley Mansions, across the Atlantic and back again. Faces are blackened with burnt cork and boot-polish, identities mistaken, pigs purloined, cocktails chaffed, disbelief suspended—especially in the presence of the garrulous Mr. Mulliner. Inch by inch, the canvas fills until the Wodehouse world is a vast wonderland, as closely detailed as a composition by Ghirlandaio.

Mr. Wodehouse regards his achievements modestly. "Over the years," he has written, "I have built up a nice little conservative business and the pickings have been pretty good, but I realize that I am not one of the swells who have messages and significance and all that kind of thing." He has also written: "I know my place, and that place is down at the far end of the table among the scurvy knaves and scullions." He takes credit only for hard work and by that he implies no great man's capacity for taking pains. He is a three-pages-a-day man and a tireless reviser, but he remains excessively nervous about being taken too seriously by the "sombre boys". He has learned to live with Hilaire Belloc's remark about being the best living writer of English, and grudging about all that though he may be, not even he can deny that his admirers occasionally have a point. Open a Wodehouse novel at random and the chances are that you'll find yourself involved with a paragraph that is at once a model of simplicity, clarity and comic precision. "I sat up in bed," reports Bertie Wooster in *The Code of the Woosters*,

> with that rather unpleasant feeling you get sometimes that you're going to die in
> about five minutes. On the previous night, I had given a little dinner at the Drones
> to Gussie Fink-Nottle as a friendly send-off before his approaching nuptials with

Madeline, only daughter of Sir Watkyn Bassett, C.B.E., and things were taking their toll. Indeed, just before Jeeves came in, I had been dreaming that some bounder was driving spikes through my head—not just ordinary spikes, as used by Jael the wife of Heber, but red-hot ones.

There have been many imitations, but it is more difficult than it seems to achieve the apparent casualness of the Wodehouse prose and the subtlety of the feather-light touch. There is, and can be, only one P. G. Wodehouse: a name that takes its place high in the English comic tradition. And it's a name that will remain there as the years pile up, long after most of the swells with the messages have been forgotten.

—William Trevor

---

**WOLFE, Bernard.** American. Born in New Haven, Connecticut, 28 August 1915. Educated at Yale University, New Haven, Connecticut, 1931–36, B.A. 1935. Screenwriter, Universal-International Productions, and Tony Curtis Productions, Hollywood. Address: c/o Eliot Gordon Company, 8888 Olympic Boulevard, Beverly Hills, California, U.S.A.

PUBLICATIONS

Novels

Really the Blues, with Milton Mezzrow.   New York, Random House, 1946; London, Secker and Warburg, 1947.
Limbo.   New York, Random House, 1952; as Limbo 90, London, Secker and Warburg, 1953.
The Late Risers: Their Masquerade.   New York, Random House, 1954.
In Deep.   New York, Random House, 1957; London, Secker and Warburg, 1958.
The Great Prince Died.   New York, Scribner, and London, Cape, 1959.
The Magic of Their Singing.   New York, Scribner, 1961.
Come on Out, Daddy.   New York, Scribner, 1963.
Move Up, Dress Up, Drink Up, Burn Up.   New York, Doubleday, 1968.

Other

Plastics: What Everyone Should Know.   Indianapolis, Bobbs Merrill, 1945.
Hypnotism Comes of Age: Its Progress from Mesmer to Psychoanalysis, with Raymond B. Rosenthal.   Indianapolis, Bobbs Merrill, 1948.

*       *       *

Bernard Wolfe began his writing career with a comical pseudo-biography of a jazzman/conman; written in collaboration with Mezz Mezzrow, Really the Blues made clear Wolfe's inventive if somewhat erratic comic sense and his deep interest in music. His novels characteristically take a sidelong and usually satirical look at some distinct sub-group of American culture, and the very forms in which the stories are presented frequently take comic aim at specific literary conventions. Wolfe's first "solo" novel, *Limbo*, falls loosely within the genre of science fiction; set eighteen years after a cataclysmic Third World War, it is an implicit criticism of the post-World War Two munitions race and, on a larger scale, of the almost irresistible destructive instinct of our times. William Peden recognized a dichotomy in this novel which manifests itself in almost all of Wolfe's fiction when he referred to it as "a melange of Huxlean fantasy and E. Phillips Oppenheim melodrama, together with serious dialectical overtones reminiscent of Dostoevsky and Thomas Mann." Aesthetic impulses and dialectical-political ones are often in conflict in Wolfe's writing, marring the structure of his work so that it can never be termed "well wrought" despite the frequent brilliance of conception and, indeed, of individual passages.

Wolfe's second novel, *The Late Risers*, cast the clichéd modern search for identity in a comic light, beginning with a Runyonesque cast of hipsters, whores, and has-beens whose nightmare adventures become increasingly grotesque but are always contained within the intellectual "joking" that gives the work its special tone. *In Deep*, perhaps the least successful of Wolfe's novels, appropriates the melodramatic spy chase as its vehicle; intrigue and insinuation proliferate, and Wolfe shows great narrative dexterity in manipulating the events of the novel, but it fails to sustain the weight of existential meaning with which he attempts to infuse it.

Wolfe's most overtly political novel was *The Great Prince Died*, a fictionalized account of the murder of the exiled Leon Trotsky. From his own brief experience as a member of Trotsky's staff in Mexico, Wolfe reconstructed in graphic and compelling detail the last days in the life of "Victor Rostov." For all of the novel's force, it finally becomes ponderous and dull. As a study in human motivation it is at times provocative, but Wolfe seemed to lack the necessary emotional distance to transform his materials into a completely satisfactory novel.

His fascination with negativism, self-delusion and the fragmented personality found their most imaginative expression in *The Magic of Their Singing*, Wolfe's satire on non-conformity and, in particular, on the Beat Generation. Similar themes were explored in *Come on Out, Daddy*, a sprawling, episodic novel about life in Hollywood. Like Nathanael West, Wolfe exploits with knowing humor the press-agentry, the bizarre nature and dietary fetishes, the macaronic architecture and the "gyrating grotesques" of the dream capital of America.

Throughout his novels Wolfe has waged war on hypocrisy, mindless conformity, and mindless revolution; each of his works is a strong indictment of the life-denying impulses of our age, and he reinforces this vision with a sweeping comic sense and considerable technical adroitness.

—David Galloway

**WOOLF, Douglas.** American. Born in New York City, 23 March 1922. Educated at Harvard University, Cambridge, Massachusetts, 1939–42; University of New Mexico, Albuquerque, 1949–50, A.B. 1950. Served with the American Field Service, 1942–43; in the United States Air Force, 1943–45. Married Yvonne Elyce Stone in 1949; has two daughters. Since 1950, free-lance Writer and Itinerant Worker, in the western United States, Canada and Mexico. Address: P.O. Box 215, Tacoma, Washington, U.S.A.

PUBLICATIONS

Novels

*The Hypocritic Days*.   Majorca, Divers Press, 1955.
*Fade Out*.   New York, Grove Press, 1959; London, Weidenfeld and Nicolson, 1968.
*Wall to Wall*.   New York, Grove Press, 1962.
*John-Juan*.   Kyoto, Origin, 1967.
*Ya! and John-Juan*.   New York, Harper, 1971.
*The Spring of the Lamb*.   Highlands, North Carolina, Jargon, 1972.

Short Stories

*Signs of a Migrant Worrier*.   San Francisco, Coyote, 1965.

Critical Studies: essay by Edward Dorn, in *Kulchur* (New York), 1963; essay by J. H. Prynne, in *Prospect* (London), 1964; essay by I. D. Mackillop in *Delta* (Cambridge), no. 45, 1969.

Douglas Woolf comments:

A Note to the Young Literate: A few years ago I heard and half believed that the written word, and the novel in particular, was a passing thing. Come in Cape Carnival, A-OK, and all that. Well, it may be so, but lately I have come to realize that if the novel does in fact die, its death will not be a natural one. It will have been programmed by unfortunate technicians bent on making us all alike, all sharing a terrible tedium equally. He who devotes himself to the written word will never be thus bored. To find yourself the Chaucer of your time will prove far more exciting, and dangerous, than to be first animal onto Mars.

*        *        *

The deserts, ghost towns and superhighways of Douglas Woolf's fiction are peopled by the maimed and exiled of the human race. Fleeing the desolation of modern existence, they find either that deliverance is not possible or that it is to be found in the bleak and desert places among others who are rejected and fleeing. Woolf paints a vivid surrealistic picture of a mechanistic society where the pressure for money and peer acceptance erases the last vestiges of humanity from hollow men. The wise run to preserve their souls and sometimes save another soul, too. Mr. Twombly of *Fade Out* induces his friend, Behemoth Brown, to forsake the beloved television set, and Al James of *Ya!* releases his teenage daughter, Joan, from the tightening bonds of materialism and superficiality.

Woolf's fine descriptive talent is especially notable given the unusual settings and characters he uses. *John-Juan*, for instance, captures dream-like experiences in a strong visual reality. Anyone who suffers in flight will find his painful symptoms faithfully recorded in "Off the Runway," one of the seven stories from *Signs of a Migrant Worrier*. In *Ya!*, Woolf's depiction of Al James's Northwest odyssey combines vivid scenic descriptions with deft quick character sketches and concludes with a finely etched picture of James spending the night asleep in a hemlock tree high above the snowed-in forest. John and Martha in "Bank Day" (*Migrant Worrier*) awake to a breakfast of cat food and eggs, an event which is clearly and economically described.

Although the themes are isolation and mankind's race toward destruction, the tone is usually humorous. In rare instances when the humor is too heavy-handed the work suffers—the short story "The Cat" is an example of this—but generally Woolf's comic writing is of a high order. In *Fade Out* there is a marvelous scene in which the old men visit a zoo where a science fiction movie is being made with unresponsive tortoises cast as monsters.

With its fine balance of humor and human insight, *Fade Out* is a brilliant novel. Woolf details the cruelties visited on the aged by their families and society. Mr. Twombly has functioned in the middle class mold for fifty years, but now retired he finds he is a nuisance to his family. His only friends are children and old people like himself, unwanted. Threatened with an ending in an old people's home, he takes his existence in hand and "fades out" to find a new life in an Arizona ghost town. His cross-country trip, accompanied by his ex-prize fighter friend, is wild and hilarious.

Woolf is a serious craftsman who writes from a perspective of detached sympathy. Seldom reviewed, he supports himself with itinerant work and takes off for solitary places to write when he has saved enough money. In 1963, he called his vocation "a desperate anachronism" and described his method as bringing his characters to a point where "some kind of balance is reached" so that the character and the reader can assess the character's position. Although he portrays a dismal society from which the wise can at best flee, he is obviously not quite willing to write "finis" for humanity.

—Barbara M. Perkins

---

**WOUK, Herman.** American. Born in New York City, 27 May 1915. Educated at Townsend Harris Hall, New York; Columbia University, New York, 1930–34, A.B. 1934. Served in the United States Naval Reserve, 1942–46. Married Betty Sarah Brown in 1945; has two living children, one deceased. Radio Writer, 1935; Scriptwriter for the comedian Fred Allen, 1936–41. Consultant, United States Treasury Department, 1941. Full-time Writer since 1946. Visiting Professor of English, Yeshiva University, New York 1952–58. Trustee, College of the Virgin Islands, 1963–69. Recipient: Pulitzer Prize, 1952; Columbia University Medal of Excellence, 1952. L.H.D., Yeshiva University, 1955; LL.D., Clark University, Worcester, Massachusetts, 1960. Lives in Washington, D.C. Address: c/o Harold Matson Company, 22 East 40th Street, New York, New York 10016, U.S.A.

PUBLICATIONS

Novels

*Aurora Dawn.* New York, Simon and Schuster, and London, Barrie, 1947.
*The City Boy.* New York, Simon and Schuster, 1948; London, Cape, 1956.
*The Caine Mutiny.* New York, Doubleday, and London, Cape, 1951.
*Marjorie Morningstar.* New York, Doubleday, and London, Cape, 1955.
*Youngblood Hawke.* New York, Doubleday, and London, Collins, 1962.
*Don't Stop the Carnival.* New York, Doubleday, and London, Collins, 1965.
*The Winds of War.* Boston, Little Brown, and London, Collins, 1971.

1403

Plays

The Traitor (produced New York, 1949).   New York, French, 1949.
The Caine Mutiny Court Martial (produced Santa Barbara, California, 1953; New
    York, 1954; Leatherhead, Surrey, 1970).   New York, Doubleday, 1954; London,
    Cape, 1956.
Nature's Way (produced New York, 1957).   New York, Doubleday, 1957.

Screenplay: Slattery's Hurricane, with Richard Murphy, 1949.


Other

This Is My God.   New York, Doubleday, 1959; London, Cape, 1960.


Manuscript Collection: "The Wouk Papers", Columbia University Library Special Collections, New York.



Herman Wouk comments:

No author should be trusted to discuss his own work in an encyclopedia or a compendium
until he has been dead thirty or forty years. Then, if anyone still cares, and if he can be raised
at a seance, his opinion might be sufficiently detached to be worth something.


                            *          *          *


    Herman Wouk continues to enjoy wide readership and to suffer critical attack for essentially
the same reasons. He has a strong commitment to established values, which he champions
only after energetic and attractive presentation of the Devil's case. Often, he plays Devil's
advocate so well that the book's concluding reversal to affirmation of the status quo suggests
mere pandering to popular prejudice. When the book is done, the rebels emerge as villains
and the evils rebelled against as blemishes on the face of a healthy world.
    Thus Aurora Dawn is an attack on vulgarity and dishonesty in advertising, not on adver-
tising itself, and the bullying boss is only a witless product of nepotism, not a true portrait
of capitalism's face. Andrew Reale, who chases money at the price of his soul, finds salvation
when his discarded fiancee inherits money and takes him back—after her millionaire husband
gallantly releases her from a marriage made on the rebound. Thus, Andrew is saved from
money-grubbing's debasements through a millionaire's generosity and an heiress' forgiveness.
    In Caine Mutiny, Wouk's Pulitzer-prize novel of World War II, a strong case is made out
for mutiny aboard an American destroyer during a Pacific storm, when the paranoiac Captain
Queeg breaks under pressure. When all is done, however, only the legal verdict goes to the
rebels; morally, Lieutenant Keefer and his followers are guilty of deserting a military system
which, despite its resident fascists, has protected American freedom against foreign fascism.
Marjorie Morningstar chronicles the false emancipation of Marjorie Morgenstern from the
values and authority of her hard-working Jewish parents to the glitter of the theatre and
bohemian "freedom." Then, renouncing her renunciation, the beautiful, intelligent Marjorie
readily accepts her suburban destiny as lawyer's wife, mother of two and community servant.
Interestingly, in both novels the "intellectual" (Lt. Keefer and writer Noel Airman) is
unmasked as an insubstantial fraud, while the philistine, even when vicious and insane like
Queeg, is sincere and somewhat heroic. In both novels, the protagonists, Princetonian Willie
Keith and Bronxite Marjorie, must learn that the old ways are the best ways: obedience,

chastity before marriage, the faith of one's fathers, hard work and money, all sound dull but ring true. In form and style, Wouk is equally traditionalist, his early works ranging from parody of Fielding (*Aurora Dawn*) and Booth Tarkington (*City Boy*) to Victorian-sized melodramas (*Marjorie Morningstar*) bursting with incident and character.

His two next novels, *Youngblood Hawke* and *Don't Stop the Carnival*, also abound in plot and character but are below his best work. Wouk's gargantuan Arthur Youngblood was obviously modeled on Thomas Wolfe, then grafted onto a melodramatic plot of the artist turned businessman, with his talent destroyed by greed and scheming women. But Wouk does not succeed in portraying Wolfe-Hawke as a dedicated artist; instead, it is Wouk and Hawke who seem to blend in the intensity of "their" business interests and speculative shenanigans, so that the money parts of the book command more authority than the literary parts. In *Don't Stop the Carnival*, Wouk returned to comedy with his middle-aged cardiac victim, Norman Paperman, who exchanges a Broadway press agent's life for ownership of a Caribbean hotel. Alas, on his island paradise, life proves even more frantic as foundation walls burst, typhoons rage and mad employees decapitate others—but Norman copes. When all is under control, Paperman unaccountably sells out cheap (as Wouk seems to do) and returns to ulcer-ridden Broadway. But the novel does display the same comedic flair for oddball characters, clever dialogue, fast intercutting and imaginative slapstick as had *Aurora Dawn, City Boy* (about a Jewish Penrod) and even *Marjorie Morningstar*.

Possibly, light comedy and fond satire are Wouk's forte, since his serious views seem uninspired and inhibited. Yet, his latest novel is surely his most ambitious. In *The Winds of War*, Wouk traces the lives of Navy Commander Victor Henry and his family from 1939 to Pearl Harbor. The size and broad aims of this volume suggest Tolstoy's *War and Peace*, but the date of the war and the quality of the writing are closer to Upton Sinclair's Lanny Budd series. Wouk is working on a sequel.

—Frank Campenni

---

**WRIGHT, Charles (Stevenson).** American. Born in New Franklin, Missouri, 4 June 1932. Educated in public schools in New Franklin and Sedalia, Missouri. Served in the United States Army, in Korea, 1952–54. Free-lance Writer: Columnist ("Wright's World"), *Village Voice*, New York. Lives in New York. Address: c/o Farrar, Straus and Giroux, 19 Union Square West, New York, New York 10003, U.S.A.

PUBLICATIONS

Novels

   *The Messenger*.   New York, Farrar Straus, 1963; London, Souvenir Press, 1965.
   *The Wig*.   New York, Farrar Straus, 1966; London, Souvenir Press, 1969.
   *Black Studies*.   New York, Farrar Straus, 1972.

Uncollected Short Story

   "New Day", in *Best Negro Short Stories*.   Boston, Little Brown, 1968.

Critical Studies: reviews in *The New Yorker*, 2 November 1963, and *The New York Times*, 23 February 1966.

Charles Wright comments:

Numbers. One number has always walked through the front door of my mind. But when I was writing my first book, *The Messenger*, I did not think of numbers. I was very bitter at the time. *The Messenger* was simply a money roof. I was amused at its success. Mini-popular first published thing. A pleasant dream with the frame of reality.

*The Wig* was my life. And as I write this on a night of the last week in April of 1971—I have no regrets. Let me explain: A year after the publication of *The Messenger* I was thinking of that folkloric, second novel, and began a rough draft of a novel about a group of Black men, very much like the Black Panthers. But, in 1963, America was not ready for *that* type of novel, nor were they ready for *The Wig*. Ah! That is the first horror hors d'oeuvre. My agent, Candida Donadio, said: "This is a novel. Write it." I will tell you quite simply . . . that I was afraid that I could not sustain the thing for say . . . fifty pages.

Now it was another year, another country (Morocco). Frightened, I returned to the states and rewrote *The Wig* in twenty-nine days . . . the best days of my life. The basic plot was the same but most of it was new. Thinking, working, like seven and, yes, sometimes fourteen hours a day. It took me less than three hours to make the final changes before the publishers accepted. I was *hot* . . . hot for *National Desire* . . . a short N. West-type of novel very much like *The Wig*, although *Race* would not have been the theme.

And.

And. Many things have happened to me and to my country since then. The country has always been like this, I suppose. I only know that something left me. As a result . . . I haven't written a novel in six years. I remember Langston Hughes saying: "Write another nice, little book like *The Messenger*. White folks don't like to know that Negroes can write books like that."

Ah, yes . . . dear, dead friend. Then. Yes. Another *Messenger*. And, what follows? Something that I've always wanted to do, something different . . . say an action packed Hemingway novel and then say . . . a Sackville-West novel. All I've ever wanted was a home by the sea and to be a good writer.

\*      \*      \*

To date, the literary output of Charles Wright has been slight in volume and promising, but not always effective, in performance. Wright's two small novels are about the size of two Nathanael West novels, and they reflect the same mordant wit, yearning despair and surrealistic lunacy of vintage West. Wright's world, however, is essentially black and, like other young black writers who have turned from naturalism to humor, Wright offers a grossly caricatured picture of white society and race-twisted black society.

Both *The Messenger* and *The Wig* portray an Inferno-world of sexual deviates: prostitutes (male and female), pimps, homosexuals, transvestites and their lovers and customers. Both books present not only the losers but the pretenders, from white liberal "friends" (whose children give away the game by snarling "nigger") to universally-loved Negro musicians who betray their black heritage to gain white approval and rewards. The plots of both novels deal with the efforts of their young "heroes" to cope with city life in a white-owned world. Interestingly, both protagonists must become prostitutes to get by, literally in *The Messenger*, figuratively in *The Wig*. Each must dissemble, disguise and sell himself; each must find the major gimmick and the myriad daily tricks that will permit him to hustle out an existence.

In *The Messenger*, which is heavily autobiographical, a young writer, Charles Stevenson, stumbles to find himself, moving from the South to the army to New York. As a writer, he knows he must feel and record; his literal job as a messenger is unimportant compared to his literary obligation to spread the word about life. As a black, however, he is torn between his compassion for outcast blacks and his emotional shield compounded of numbness, indifference and cynicism. Although the writing occasionally slips into cliches or strained metaphor, style is the novel's chief attraction and is marvelously wedded to content. The writing is terse, the narrator-hero's manner laconic and usually guarded. Most episodes are deliberately inconclusive and undeveloped, sketchy vignettes that affect the narrator more than he acknowledges. Deeply touching are the few pages in which the spiritually exhausted young veteran is united with his warm, righteous grandmother, while his athletic command performance in a Southern police station is outrageously comic and brilliantly symbolic of racial debasement.

If *The Messenger* seems like a patch-quilt of styles and moods, *The Wig* is more consistent in tone and mood, but regrettably so. For Wright's second novel goes all-out as black comedy, but despite its wildness it is more black, or malicious, than comic. There is a similar gallery of transvestites and other disguise-wearing freaks in quest of identity without guilt, failure or self-hatred, but they are portrayed without hope or compassion. The hero, Lester Jefferson, is, like all the other blacks, on the make: he has conked and curled his Afro hair into a beautiful white "wig" that will open the doors to the Great (White) Society. Alas, he doesn't make it but we are not even sorry, for neither he nor the author reaches Ellison's solution that "visibility" begins with confronting and accepting one's truly created self. There are two or three successful comic achievements: Jimmy Wishbone, who once "kept 100 million colored people contented for years" as a Stepin Fetchit type in movies and who now wants to sue white society and redeem his lost fleet of cadillacs; and Lester himself, crawling the streets in a feathery chicken-suit as employee of the Southern Fried Chicken King.

But Charles Stevenson of *The Messenger* had something to tell; he could communicate love to a little girl and an old lady, if not the girl friend with whom he only quarreled. Charles Stevenson Wright, in *The Wig*, is raucous and loud, but neither he nor his hero Lester tell us much we don't know or need to hear.

—Frank Campenni

---

**WYLIE, Philip (Gordon).** American. Born in Beverly, Massachusetts, 12 May 1902. Educated at Princeton University, New Jersey, 1920–23. Served as a Member of the Board, Office of Facts and Figures, 1942; with the Bureau of Personnel, United States Army Air Force, 1945. Married Johanna Ondeck in 1928 (divorced, 1937); Frederica Ballard, 1938; has one child. Staff Member, *The New Yorker*, 1925–27; Advertising Manager, Cosmopolitan Book Corporation, 1927–28; Screenwriter, Paramount Pictures, 1931–33, and MGM, 1936–37; Editor, Farrar and Rinehart, publishers, New York, 1944. Member of the Council, Authors Guild, 1945. Since 1949, Consultant to the Federal Civil Defense Administration. Recipient: Freedom Foundation Gold Medal, 1953; Hyman Memorial Trophy, 1959. D.Litt., University of Miami, Florida; Florida State University, Tallahassee. Lives in South Miami, Florida. Address: c/o Harold Ober, 40 East 49th Street, New York, New York 10017, U.S.A. *Died 23 October 1971.*

PUBLICATIONS

Novels

*Heavy Laden.* New York and London, Knopf, 1928.

*Babes and Sucklings.*   New York and London, Knopf, 1929.

*Gladiator.*   New York, and London, Knopf, 1930.

*Footprint of Cinderella.*   New York, Farrar and Rinehart, 1931.

*Murder Invisible.*   New York, Farrar and Rinehart, 1931.

*The Savage Gentleman.*   New York, Farrar and Rinehart, 1932.

*Five Fatal Worlds*, with Edwin Balmer.   New York, Long and Smith, 1932; London, Paul, 1933.

*When Worlds Collide*, with Edwin Balmer.   New York, Stokes, and London, Paul, 1933.

*After Worlds Collide*, with Edwin Balmer.   New York, Stokes, and London, Paul, 1934.

*The Golden Hoard*, with Edwin Balmer.   New York, Stokes, 1934.

*Finnley Wren: His Notions and Opinions Together with a Haphazard History of His Career and Amours in These Moody Years, As Well as Sundry Rhymes, Fables, Diatribes, and Literary Misdemeanors: A Novel in a New Manner.*   New York, Farrar and Rinehart, 1934.

*As They Reveled.*   New York, Farrar and Rinehart, 1936.

*Too Much of Everything.*   New York, Farrar and Rinehart, and London, Chapman and Hall, 1936.

*The Shield of Silence*, with Edwin Balmer.   New York, Stokes, 1936; London, Collins, 1937.

*An April Afternoon.*   New York, Farrar and Rinehart, 1938.

*The Other Horseman.*   New York, Farrar and Rinehart, 1941.

*Corpses at Indian Stones.*   New York, Farrar and Rinehart, 1943.

*Night unto Night.*   New York, Farrar and Rinehart, 1944.

*Opus 21: A Descriptive Music for the Lower Kinsey Epoch of the Atomic Age; A Concerto for a One-Man Band; Six Arias for Soap Operas, Fugues, Anthems and Barrel-House.*   New York, Rinehart, 1949.

*The Disappearance.*   New York, Rinehart, and London, Gollancz, 1951.

*Three to Be Read: Containing The Smuggled Atom Bomb, Sporting Blood, and The Experiment in Crime.*   New York, Rinehart, 1951.

*Tomorrow!*   New York, Rinehart, 1954.

*The Answer.*   New York, Rinehart, and London, Muller, 1956.

*Triumph.*   New York, Doubleday, 1963.

*They Both Were Naked.*   New York, Doubleday, 1965.

*Autumn Romance.*   New York, Lancer, 1967.

*The Magic Animal.*   New York, Doubleday, 1968.


Short Stories

*The Big Ones Get Away.*   New York, Farrar and Rinehart, 1940.

*Salt Water Daffy.*   New York, Farrar and Rinehart, 1941.

*Fish and Tin Fish: Crunch and Des Strike Again.*   New York, Farrar and Rinehart, 1944.

*Fifth Mystery Book*, with others.   New York, Farrar and Rinehart, 1944.

*Crunch and Des: Stories of Florida Fishing.*   New York, Rinehart, 1948.

*The Best of Crunch and Des.*   New York, Rinehart, 1954.

*Treasure Cruise and Other Crunch and Des Stories.*   New York, Rinehart, 1956.


Plays

Screenplays: *Island of Lost Souls*, with Waldemar Young, 1932; *Murders in the Zoo*, 1933; *King of the Jungle*, with Fred Niblo, Jr., 1933.

Other

> *The Army Way: A Thousand Pointers for New Soldiers*, with William W. Muir.   New York, Farrar and Rinehart, 1940.
> *A Generation of Vipers*.   New York, Farrar and Rinehart, 1942; revised edition, Rinehart, and London, Muller, 1955.
> *An Essay on Morals*.   New York, Rinehart, 1947.
> *Denizens of the Deep: True Tales of Deep-Sea Fishing*.   New York, Rinehart, 1953.
> *The Innocent Ambassadors*.   New York, Rinehart, 1957; London, Muller, 1958.
> *The Lerner Marine Laboratory at Bimini, Bahamas*.   Washington, D.C., American Museum of Natural History, 1960.
> *Sons and Daughters of Mom*.   New York, Doubleday, 1971.

Manuscript Collection: Princeton University, New Jersey.

*       *       *

Although Jack Kerouac was proclaimed as American fiction's answer to Britain's Angry Young Men, the distinction more properly belonged to Philip Wylie. For more than anyone since H. L. Mencken, Wylie has set about, in his iconoclastic manner, to attack the most sacred symbols of American progress and culture. It should be noted in his favor that the most vigorous elements of this attack were launched in the two decades (the 1940's and 1950's) when such cynicism was considered dangerous and unpatriotic. Contemporary critics of American culture too easily forget that Wylie was pointing to the horrors of atomic warfare and the dangers of ecological imbalance thirty years ago. His novels can be called prophetic in the true sense of the word, as they argue poignantly and vigorously against the illusions by which modern man supports his smugness. The message that emerges again and again from his turgid prose is that man is the lowest of animals, that he must be saved from himself.

As happens with many writers who choose the novel of ideas as their medium, Wylie is a much better essayist than he is a novelist. He himself admits that in his haste to set down his ideas, he has paid minimum attention to such elements as plot and characterization. Not surprisingly, his most famous book, *Generation of Vipers*, notorious for its vigorous attack on "Momism," the sentimental cult of the American mother, is an extended essay. His novels consist of long dissertations on such broad topics as life, love, sex, and nuclear war. And while the reader is somewhat assured of finding a subject of interest within a Wylie novel, these cynical and pessimistic diatribes make for heavy reading.

This lack of poetic imagination may be a result of the scientific attitude of the author, who is most convincing when talking about the technical aspects of science and psychology. For this reason, such novels as *Gladiator* and *The Disappearance*, which belong to the genre of science-fiction, are his most readable and enjoyable works. Here at least he seems more intent on developing his ideas through the story than through long discussions (although the latter are by no means absent from these novels).

His biological interests have led Wylie to a close reading of Freud and Jung, and indeed Jung once remarked, "Wylie is the man who understood my theories better than all the others." Sex at times appears to be an obsession with him, and, as a true disciple of Freud, he sees the debasement of sex as man's original sin. As he explains in *The Disappearance*:

> The sin was to convert sexuality itself into shame and, in the dire doing, to shame women especially. . . . Our common sexuality, as the flower is the sexual organ and the ecstasy of a plant, was turned to shame—in order that we should appear loftier than other beasts, better even than nature, superior even to law, even to God, as men, so far, have invented him.

In the 1950's, the modern consciousness was still able to be shocked by such cynical philosophizing. In the 1970's, Wylie seems rather tiresome and hackneyed.

—Lawrence Ries

---

**YAFFE, James.** American. Born in Chicago, Illinois, 31 March 1927. Educated at Yale University, New Haven, Connecticut, 1944–48, B.A. (summa cum laude) 1948. Served in the United States Navy, 1945–46. Married Elaine Gordon in 1964; has three children. Since 1968, Adjunct Professor, Colorado College, Colorado Springs. Recipient: National Foundation for the Arts Award, for drama, 1968. Address: 1215 North Cascade Avenue, Colorado Springs, Colorado, U.S.A.

PUBLICATIONS

Novels

The Good-for-Nothing. Boston, Little Brown, and London, Constable, 1953.
What's the Big Hurry? Boston, Little Brown, 1953; as Angry Uncle Dan, London, Constable, 1954.
Nothing But the Night. Boston, Little Brown, 1957; London, Cape, 1958.
Mister Margolies. New York, Random House, 1962.
Nobody Does You Any Favors. New York, Putnam, 1966.
The Voyage of the Franz Joseph. New York, Putnam, 1970.

Short Stories

Poor Cousin Evelyn. Boston, Little Brown, 1951; London, Constable, 1952.

Plays

The Deadly Game (produced New York, 1960; London, 1967). New York, Dramatists Play Service, 1961.
Ivory Tower, with Jerome Weidman (produced Ann Arbor, Michigan, 1968). New York, Dramatists Play Service, 1969.

Numerous plays for television, 1953–1967.

Other

The American Jews. New York, Random House, 1968.
Justice Is for People: The Story of a Community Court. New York, Saturday Review Press, 1972.

James Yaffe comments:

For me, to write novels has been to create characters and to combine and juxtapose those characters, involve them in confrontations, place them in situations which challenge them, strengthen them, destroy them, transform them, test their mettle—and out of a variety of such characters, to build a world. Where do I get the raw material for my characters? From my own experience, of course—mostly from my experience of the world I was born and brought up in, the world of middle-class, second- and third-generation Jews living in New York, Chicago, Los Angeles. (In my most recent novel, *The Voyage of the Franz Joseph*, I have gone far beyond this world, but have still built on it.) I have chosen to write about this world because I know it instinctively and subliminally, because it was a part of me before I was old enough to doubt my perceptions.

But I have always tried to treat this experience not analytically or sociologically or philosophically but novelistically—that is, by imagining, and trying to re-create, the world as seen through each character's eyes. The greatest novelists, it seems to me, are those who succeed in merging their personalities with the lives and feelings of their people. This is the special ability shared by writers as different as Tolstoy and Jane Austen, Trollope and Joyce (to mention a few of my favorites). The attempt to follow their example may be presumptuous and doomed to failure, but it is also inevitable for anybody who wants to write novels.

*    *    *

James Yaffe is considered a leading novelist of middle-class Jewish life in America. His early collection of short stories (*Poor Cousin Evelyn*) and his first novel (*The Good-for-Nothing*) are essentially drawing room comedies set in New York. As in the novels of Jane Austen, whom Yaffe admits a special fondness for, small conflicts are closely scrutinized within a closed society—in Yaffe's case, the Jewish family, with all its attendant social hierarchies, its patriarchs, its strongmen and its failures, its pressures of shame and guilt applied by loved ones to safeguard conformity and tradition. In these earlier works, characters are simply drawn and situations directly presented, largely through dialogue.

A recurring Yaffe theme involves the "dreamer," an impractical or artistically-oriented individual confronted with pressures to survive in a competitive business world of shady deals and opportunism. In *The Good-for-Nothing*, this conflict is represented by two brothers, apparently very different from each other, yet mutually dependent. The one is college-educated and totally ineffectual in the business world, a charming sycophant. The other, a Certified Public Accountant, supports him, but in so doing restricts his own life. As they interact, it becomes unclear which is the "good for nothing," which the success or failure: in different ways, both are unwilling to face responsibilities or the possibility of failure. Self-righteousness and self-indulgence, like sentimentality, are both forms of escape, excuses for not taking risks.

In a later novel, *Mister Margolies*, this pattern of self-deception is advanced to the point where the manipulation of reality becomes a life-style. Stanley Margolies, defeated in his early attempt to become a concert-pianist, yet unable to give up totally his dreams of a poetic life, withdraws into a world of fantasies. The reality of business and competition crashes in on this, and he withdraws deeper, erecting more elaborate defences. Yaffe's "dreamers" create worlds which are both sad and poetic, but they are not the demonic Rose-gardens of the totally mad. They are the tiny fantasies of little men, dreams reinforced by sympathetic and condescending friends with whom they still retain some form of contact.

Yaffe avoids several stereotypes popular in much contemporary Jewish literature: the dominant Jewish Mother, and the Jew-Gentile confrontation, particularly in matters sexual, as an expression of, or as a means of resolving feelings of inferiority. In general, he maintains a comic narrative tone—some of the scenes are very funny—and though his characters are forever lecturing each other, their messages are frequently as confused as they are. The novels themselves preach little other than a deep compassion for the small man and his hopes.

The theme of the dreamer in search of his vision makes a terrifying appearance in *Nothing But the Night*, which is based on the Nathan Leopold-Richard Loeb murder case of 1924, its subsequent trial and celebrated defence by Clarence Darrow. The case history is seen through the eyes of one of the young men, not as an investigation of the criminal mind, but as a study of a lonely and creative child. As in Chekhov, Yaffe's characters take their emotions very seriously and ponder them deeply. They are often trapped by their own visions and the pressures to succeed imposed from outside. In their struggle to hold on to their dreams, they are destroyed, transformed, and occasionally liberated. An example of the latter is presented in *Nobody Does You Any Favors*, which despite its nineteen-forties cinema sounding title is perhaps his best novel. As opposed to the earlier New York novels which suggest short stories in their structural focus on a single event, *Nobody Does You Any Favors* with its time span of roughly forty years allows for an extended development and growth in character. The confrontation between father and son is drawn with an understanding and passion valid beyond ethnic restrictions, and the father's final struggle with life and death in the concluding chapter is a scene of very special terror and insight. Certainly this novel is a significant contribution to American literature of the twentieth century.

Yaffe's most recent novel, *The Voyage of the Franz Joseph*, represents an epic departure from his usual drawing room style. As in *Nothing But the Night*, it is based on an historical event, the sailing of the German liner *St. Louis* in 1939 with a thousand Jewish refugees searching for a homeland.

—Paul Seiko Chihara

---

**YATES, Richard.** American. Born in Yonkers, New York, 3 February 1926. Educated at the Avon School, Connecticut. Served in the United States Army Infantry, 1944–46. Married Sheila Bryant in 1948 (divorced, 1959); Martha Speer, 1968; has two children. Financial Reporter, United Press, New York, 1946–48; Publicity Writer, Remington Rand Inc., New York, 1948–50; Free-lance Public Relations Writer, 1953–60; Lecturer, New School for Social Research, New York, 1959–62, and Columbia University, New York, 1960–62; Screenwriter, United Artists, Hollywood, 1962; Speech Writer for Attorney-General Robert Kennedy, Washington, D.C., 1963; Screenwriter, Columbia Pictures, Hollywood, 1965–66. Lecturer, 1964–65, and since 1966, Assistant Professor of English, University of Iowa, Iowa City. Writer-in-Residence, Wichita State University, Kansas, 1971–72. Recipient: Guggenheim Fellowship, 1962; National Institute of Arts and Letters grant, 1963; Brandeis University Creative Arts Award, 1964; National Foundation on the Arts grant, 1966; Rockefeller grant, 1967. Address: 3827 East 25th North, Wichita, Kansas 67221, U.S.A.

PUBLICATIONS

Novels

*Revolutionary Road.*   Boston, Little Brown, 1961; London, Deutsch, 1962.
*A Special Providence.*   New York, Knopf, 1969.

Short Stories

 *Eleven Kinds of Loneliness.*   Boston, Little Brown, 1962; London, Deutsch, 1963.

Other

 Editor, *Stories for the Sixties.*   New York, Bantam, 1962.

Manuscript Collection: Boston University.

Critical Study: in *The Red-Hot Vacuum* by Theodore Solotaroff, New York, Atheneum, 1970.

Richard Yates comments:

 Writing fiction is a very slow and difficult process for me. It is what I do best, but it has taken me nearly twenty years to produce three published books.
 If my work has a theme, I suspect it is a simple one: that most human beings are inescapably alone, and therein lies their tragedy.

                            *         *         *

 Loneliness and the self-delusions men create to keep it at bay are the subjects of Richard Yates's writings. In "Builders," the concluding story of *Eleven Kinds of Loneliness*, a New York hackie tells Bob Prentice, an author he has hired to ghost-write his life story, that building a story is like building a house. Relishing the newly found image, he elaborates upon it, describing a house with its foundation, walls, and roof, and asking, "And where are the windows? . . . Where does the light come in?" The author writes his story for the cabbie but, after reflecting upon it, admits helplessly that it does not have any windows, or if it has windows they are blackened over; whatever light is to come in will have to "come in as best it can." The author feels that there ought to be light, but he cannot make it. Like Bob's story, Yates's stories are studies in gray with only an occasional streak of light; and like Bob Prentice in the later novel, *A Special Providence*, the reader comes to realize that in Yates's world people only survive: there is "no settling of accounts, no resolution, no proof."
 In *Eleven Kinds of Loneliness*, a collection of short stories written in the fifties, Yates offers his studies of failure. The making the best of a bad thing, the lot chosen by Edward and Lavinia in Eliot's *Cocktail Party*, is the lot accepted by many of Yates's people. In "The Best of Everything" (a title Yates chose long before Rona Jaffe gave it currency) Ralph, an all around "good guy," a guy the fellows can always count on for a good laugh and a round of drinks in a bar, finds himself marrying Gracie ("what a paira knockers"), who suspects all the while she goes through her marriage preparations that the marriage will not be "the best of everything," that Ralph will always want to be with the guys, that she will always be the little woman who nags him to come home at night, and that she will always wince when he says "terlet" for toilet. In "A Glutton for Punishment" Walter Henderson, a harbinger of Frank Wheeler in *Revolutionary Road*, is a man in love with failure, a man for whom the attitudes of collapse hold endless fascination. As a child he loved to play at falling dead; as an adolescent he was just the best little loser, a real sport; and by the time he marries, failure has become a habit. The wife married to such a man is like the wife in many of Yates's works, and, particularly, she anticipates April Wheeler. These women win their husbands,

not because of what they feel for them, but because they so successfully feign to see them exactly as they most want to be seen. After this first role, the other roles come easily to Yates's women until their lives are best described as "the orderly rotation of many careful moods." Self-deceived, these women move easily from the role of dutiful wife to strict but attentive mother. The mood of wifely reassurance, or the mood of wife-as-mistress, or the bright cocktail mood all come easily. What does not come to these women is the ability to admit the lie, to say they do not love, to confess their loneliness, to ask for more than they are getting from the men who love them not as they are, but as they dream them to be. Each of the stories in this collection evokes the sense of vacancy; and many of the stories create this effect in a manner reminiscent of Salinger.

In his writing, Yates briefly served Hemingway and Fitzgerald, but the peculiar brand of loneliness mingled with compassion he creates owes much to Salinger. Bob Prentice idolizes Hemingway and the descriptions of his days as a rifle trainee recall portions of *Farewell to Arms*; April Wheeler echoes words from *The Great Gatsby*: when she talks of her parents, they are rich, divorced, one alcoholic and one a suicide case; she describes them as "cruel and careless" in their glamorous roles; they are the Daisy's and Tom's of the novel and they have a calamitous effect on April's life. But Salinger offers Yates more than a situation; he offers him a style and a technique. Yates's dialogue is studded with colloquialisms, "goddams," and slang. Buddy Glass's conversations (from Salinger's *Nine Stories* and *Raise High the Roof Beam, Carpenters, and Seymour: An Introduction*) seem to lie behind many of the conversations in Yates's writings. More important, Buddy's obtrusive handling of his own narrative point of view in his stories is imitated by Yates in "Builders." The narrators in "For Esmé—With Love and Squalor" and *Raise High the Roof Beam, Carpenters* adopt the same tone as Bob Prentice: each recognizes that the writer is a "sensitive person," that this sensitivity ought to be disguised or it will be too unsettling for the reader, that the piece of fiction each will tell will be "no-nonsense fiction" and that their mates are "breathtakingly level-headed" in Salinger's story, or "dead-logical" in Yates's. Yates also imitates Salinger's way of selecting a detail and presenting it in such a way that it has a nice misanthropic turn to it. Additionally, Yates borrows some of Salinger's details: the Gladstone bag that figures so prominently in Salinger's "Teddy" is found in "The Best of Everything"; a Mrs. Snell is a maid in "Down at the Dinghy" (*Nine Stories*), a teacher in "Fun with a Stranger" (*Eleven Kinds of Loneliness*). Mrs. Fedders' attitude towards Seymour's sickness is echoed in Mrs. Giving's treatment of John's mental disorders in *Revolutionary Road*. John's candor and out-spokenness also resemble Seymour's outburst in "A Perfect Day for Bananafish" when the lady in the elevator looks too markedly at his bare feet. Yates's interest in children, their moods, tantrums, and jealousies, also follows Salinger's. But if Yates imitates Salinger, this imitation is not slavish. Yates has his own voice, his own style, and it is lucid, often amusing, and artfully wrought.

In his two novels, *Revolutionary Road* and *A Special Providence*, Yates builds a story around characters introduced in his short stories. Walter Henderson and his wife are translated into Frank and April Wheeler, two suburbanites living on Revolutionary Road whose self-deceptions have become so elaborate that each victimizes the other until one kills herself, pitifully confessing that she does not know who she is, and the other continues to live out the life of "hopeless emptiness" that he blames on the suburbs, his surroundings, and even his wife, but that the author shows us is of his own creating. In *A Special Providence* a more youthful Bob Prentice than the one that figures in "Builders" is the protagonist, and the story involves his struggle for freedom from his neurotic mother, and his coming of age. Bob and his mother, Alice, Frank and his wife, April, are all weak and dependent people who live imagining against all evidence to the contrary that they are somehow better than others, that they deserve a "special providence" when in fact they are as meager as those they spurn. Alice, a sculptress of little talent, nurtures herself on dreams of sudden glory and deludes herself with self-images as frail and pathetic as those entertained by Blanche in *A Streetcar Named Desire*. Leaving Bob's father, shifting from place to place whenever her debtors are about to bring judgment against her, she raises her spoiled, awkward son to be a dreamer like herself. It is finally the bitter humiliating experiences in a training camp that painfully teach Bob that he must stand alone if he is to survive, and that life has nothing to offer but survival. April learns the same lesson in *Revolutionary Road*, that the important acts in life must be carried out alone; but for her this discovery makes her take her life while for Bob it enables him to reach his majority. Yates depicts the decline of Alice and the disintegration of Frank and April's marriage relentlessly. With mastery he elicits our sympathy for Frank and Bob's plight while at the same time he makes us despise their muddle-headedness, their fears, and their abysmal, near criminal ignorance of themselves.

Yates's novels treat themes that are familiar in literature—the banality of suburban living, the cycle of petty infidelities that wear away the trust between couples, the neurotic demands mothers make on sons, wives make on husbands, husbands on wives—and yet his treatment is not tired; it is fresh and disturbing, excellent in the precision with which it isolates the lies that sustain us, the illusions that obscure the light.

—Carol Simpson Stern

---

**YELLEN, Samuel.** American. Born in Vilna, Lithuania, 7 July 1906. Educated at Western Reserve University, Cleveland, Ohio, B.A. 1926; Oberlin College, Ohio, M.A. 1932. Married Miriam Rebecca Friend in 1931; Edna Diener Bard, 1966. Since 1929, Member of the Faculty, since 1953, Professor of English, and since 1963, University Professor of English, Indiana University, Bloomington. Editor, Indiana University Poetry Series, 1951–58. Recipient: Daroff Memorial Award, 1962; Guggenheim Fellowship, 1964. Address: 922 East University Street, Bloomington, Indiana 47401, U.S.A.

PUBLICATIONS

Novel

    *The Wedding Band.*   New York, Atheneum, and London, Gollancz, 1961.

Short Stories

    *The Passionate Shepherd: A Book of Stories.*   New York, Knopf, 1957; London, W. H. Allen, 1958.

Verse

    *In the House and Out and Other Poems.*   Bloomington, Indiana University Press, 1952.
    *New and Selected Poems.*   Bloomington, Indiana University Press, 1964.
    *The Convex Mirror: Collected Poems.*   Bloomington, Indiana University Press, 1971.

Other

    *American Labor Struggles.*   New York, Harcourt Brace, 1936.

*     *     *

Samuel Yellen has built a substantial reputation as a literary artist on one novel and a handful of short stories. Of course, Yellen has had at least three other interests, although ones that reached a much smaller audience. His career has been that of a university teacher of English, in which he went through the ranks from bottom to top. His study *American Labor Struggles* shows his concern with the social background of the literature that interests him. He is a poet of considerable sensitivity.

*The Passionate Shepherd* is a collection of ten short stories originally published in *The New Yorker*, *The Atlantic*, and similar magazines. They are gems, the kind of stories one would expect of a poet with another job, carefully wrought, reluctantly submitted, each a model of what Edgar Allan Poe said the short story should be.

I cannot be so enthusiastic about his novel, *The Wedding Band*. The Jewish novel in the United States has become a cliché. From Charles Angoff's interminable maunderings about growing up in Boston as a Jew to Herzog's and Portnoy's complaints, the cliff-hanging struggles of East Europeans (religion has nothing to do with it) with American life has become tiresome. In fact, the whole American "how awful I had to grow up" syndrome has been a bore for more than forty years. Yellen's novel is the healthiest of this sick crew, yet it has all their ingredients. Alexandra Davidoff, the narrator, tells the story of her Jewish father and White Anglo-Saxon mother. It all reminds one of the inevitable Vassar College girl who, descendant of poverty-ridden immigrants, documented Scott Fitzgerald's comment that the rich are different from the rest of us, by saying that as children they got orange juice and good outdoor exercise.

I would exchange all the self-pitying Jewish-American fiction of the twentieth century for one story—"The Passionate Shepherd"—by Yellen. Would that he, born in 1906, had written more.

—William Bittner

YERBY, Frank (Garvin). American. Born in Augusta, Georgia, 5 September 1916. Educated at Paine College, Augusta, A.B. 1937; Fisk University, Nashville, Tennessee, M.A. 1938; University of Chicago, 1939. Married Flora Helen Claire Williams in 1941 (divorced); Blanca Calle Perez, 1956; has four children. Instructor in English, Florida A. and M. College, Tallahassee, 1938–39, and Southern University and A. and M. College, Baton Rouge, Louisiana, 1939–41; Laboratory Technician, Ford Motor Company, Dearborn, Michigan, 1941–44; Magnaflux Inspector, Ranger (Fairchild) Aircraft, Jamaica, New York, 1944–45. Full-time Writer since 1945. Has lived in Spain since 1959. Address: General Mola 103, Madrid 6, Spain; or, c/o Mr. Owen Laster, William Morris Agency, 1350 Avenue of the Americas, New York, New York 10019, U.S.A.

PUBLICATIONS

Novels

    *The Foxes of Harrow*.   New York, Dial Press, 1946; London, Heinemann, 1947.
    *The Vixens*.   New York, Dial Press, 1947; London, Heinemann, 1948.

*The Golden Hawk*.  New York, Dial Press, and London, Heinemann, 1948.
*Pride's Castle*.  New York, Dial Press, 1949; London, Heinemann, 1950.
*Floodtide*.  New York, Dial Press, 1950; London, Heinemann, 1951.
*A Woman Called Fancy*.  New York, Dial Press, 1951; London, Heinemann, 1952.
*The Saracen Blade*.  New York, Dial Press, 1952; London, Heinemann, 1953.
*The Devil's Laughter*.  New York, Dial Press, 1953; London, Heinemann, 1954.
*Benton's Row*.  New York, Dial Press, 1954; London, Heinemann, 1955.
*Bride of Liberty*.  New York, Doubleday, 1954; London, Heinemann, 1955.
*The Treasure of Pleasant Valley*.  New York, Dial Press, 1955; London, Heinemann, 1956.
*Captain Rebel*.  New York, Dial Press, 1956; London, Heinemann, 1957.
*Fairoaks*.  New York, Dial Press, 1957; London, Heinemann, 1958.
*The Serpent and the Staff*.  New York, Dial Press, 1958; London, Heinemann, 1959.
*Jarrett's Jade*.  New York, Dial Press, 1959; London, Heinemann, 1960.
*Gillian*.  New York, Dial Press, 1960; London, Heinemann, 1961.
*The Garfield Honor*.  New York, Dial Press, 1961; London, Heinemann, 1962.
*Griffin's Way*.  New York, Dial Press, 1962; London, Heinemann, 1963.
*The Old Gods Laugh: A Modern Romance*.  New York, Dial Press, and London, Heinemann, 1964.
*An Odor of Sanctity*.  New York, Dial Press, 1965; London, Heinemann, 1966.
*Goat Song: A Novel of Ancient Greece*.  New York, Dial Press, and London, Heinemann, 1968.
*Judas, My Brother*.  New York, Dial Press, and London, Heinemann, 1968.
*Speak Now*.  New York, Dial Press, 1969; London, Heinemann, 1970.
*The Dahomean*.  New York, Dial Press, 1971; as *The Man from Dahomey*, London, Heinemann, 1971.
*The Girl from Storyville*.  New York, Dial Press, and London, Heinemann, 1972.

Uncollected Short Stories

"Health Card", in *Harper's* (New York), May 1944.
"Roads Going Down", in *Common Ground* (New York), vol. 5, no. 4, 1945.
"The Homecoming", in *Common Ground* (New York), vol. 6, no. 3, 1946.
"My Brother Went to College", in *Black American Literature: Fiction*.  Columbus, Ohio, Merrill, 1969.

Other

Plays produced by college groups; verse published in magazines.

Manuscript Collection: Mugar Library, Boston University.

Critical Studies: *Behind the Magnolia Mask: Frank Yerby as Critic of the South* by William Werdna Hill, Jr., Auburn University (Alabama) thesis, 1968; *The Unembarrassed Muse* by Russel B. Nye, New York, Dial Press, 1970.

Frank Yerby comments:

The work has consisted mostly of historical novels written both to instruct and to entertain.

In them, I've tried to correct the reader's historical perspective, wildly distorted in my youth, on such themes as Negro slavery, the Civil War South, and Reconstruction.

To date, I have written only two modern novels, *The Old Gods Laugh*, largely an entertainment in the sense that Graham Greene uses the word, and *Speak Now*, a serious effort.

Of my historicals, I should rate *An Odor of Sanctity*, *Judas, My Brother*, *Goat Song* and perhaps even *The Garfield Honor* as serious novels. The rest are entertainments, a fact of which I am *not* ashamed. Entertaining the reader is a legitimate function of a novelist.

I hope, in the future, however, to concentrate upon serious work. Present day taxation makes writing "entertainments" worth neither the boredom, nor the bother.

*            *            *

Few popular writers have been maligned for so many reasons as the historical novelist Frank Yerby. He has been indicted for superficial research, melodramatic plotting, purple prose and sub-freshman grammar, comic book characterization and, above all, betrayal of his Negritude. All of these shortcomings are easily found in his twenty-five novels written in as many years, but such documentation cannot explain away the enormous appeal of these novels or the determined energy that produced them.

Yerby's first published novel, *The Foxes of Harrow*, was quickly followed by five more, each selling more than a million copies, and several adopted by book clubs and sold to the movies. In America, the genre of the historical novel enjoyed its highpoint from about the mid-1930's to the mid-50's, and Frank Yerby was most in favor during the last decade of that trend. He has continued to write and to be read since *The Saracen Blade* and *The Devil's Laughter* but with intermittent and diminishing success, even though his later work is probably his best.

Following the popular acceptance of *Foxes of Harrow*, Yerby developed that novel into a loose trilogy; he then continued with a half dozen similar novels set in the South, especially New Orleans, during the middle and late nineteenth century. In this same period, Yerby also turned his hand to picaresque adventure and pirate heroes of the late 17th century (*Golden Hawk*), the crusades to the Holy Land (*Saracen Blade*) and the French and American revolutions (*Devil's Laughter* and *Bride of Liberty*). That Yerby was writing by formula was evident, but it was not quite the typical romantic pattern of separated but undying love, of virtuous heroines and happy endings, of brave heroes and bold villains battling in a glamorized historical setting of reactionary politics and sharp class distinctions. Instead, Yerby's heroes are not faithful, the heroines not virtuous, the endings not happy; the characters' claims to aristocracy are spurious, the "colorful milieu" is sordid, the upper classes are mean-spirited, bigoted and greedy.

In 1959, Yerby candidly described for *Harper's Magazine* his own formula for the "costume novel," rejecting the label "historical" since his editors cut out "ninety-nine and ninety-nine one-hundredths" of the historical material. Yerby discredits writing "about ill-treated factory workers, or people who suffered because of their religions or the color of their skins," since such material is the province of "sociologists, reformers and ministers of the Gospel," while the writer should deal with interesting "individuals." Yerby's own rules include writing "good, rousing tales" about picaresque "doers" (dominant males who are neither emotionally mature nor polygamous) and their involvements with beautiful, sexy heroines —though sex scenes should be minimal and understated. The plot should be dramatic and economically handled, focussing tightly on development and resolution of "a strong exteriorized conflict." There should be an "ennobling" unifying theme, such as the author's own favorite, "the eternal warfare between the sexes," but never must the writer propagandize and upset the "hypnotic suspension of his reader's sense of disbelief."

Actually, Yerby's initial recognition as a writer of fiction came through several short stories of social protest, such as "Health Card," "The Homecoming" and "My Brother Went to College," all dealing with racial injustice in contemporary America. After an unsuccessful attempt at a proletarian novel, he turned to historical melodrama, with which he has recently become disenchanted, despite his great skill in narration and suspense-building. His recent novels, including *An Odor of Sanctity*, *Goat Song* and *Judas, My Brother*, move further back in time (respectively to medieval Spain, ancient Greece and Biblical times) and show more evidence of research and an authentic sense of place and culture. His recent novel, *The Dahomean*, is Yerby's only book primarily about Negroes; ironically, its major flaws are a sluggish pace and excess anthropological detail. Yet this moving chronicle of the making of an African chief—tracing his life through adolescence, initiation, marriage, wars, kingship and downfall—is written with such sympathy, seriousness and control, all lacking in the earlier work, that *The Dahomean* emerges as his best work.

Although Yerby has shown limited development as a craftsman, his main technical faults almost disappear as his attitudes toward his material and his literary purpose grow less cynical. His earlier escapist view, stated flippantly, that most significant problems are unsolvable anyway, has been embodied and reformulated in recent fiction as a mature, tragic view of man. Thus, there are signs that Frank Yerby's best work may still be ahead of him.

—Frank Campenni

---

**YORK, Andrew.**   See **NICOLE, Christopher.**

---

**YOUNG, Marguerite (Vivian).** American. Born in Indianapolis, Indiana, in 1909. Educated at Indiana University, Bloomington; Butler University, Indianapolis, B.A. 1930; University of Chicago, M.A. 1936; University of Iowa, Iowa City. Taught at Indiana University, 1942; University of Iowa, 1955–57; Columbia University, New York, 1958; New School for Social Research, New York, 1958–67; Fairleigh Dickinson University, Rutherford, New Jersey, 1960–62; Fordham University, Bronx, New York, 1966, 1967. Recipient: American Association of University Women grant, 1943; National Institute of Arts and Letters grant, 1945; Guggenheim Fellowship, 1948; Newberry Library Fellowship, 1951; Rockefeller Fellowship, 1954. Address: 375 Bleecker Street, New York, New York 10014, U.S.A.

PUBLICATIONS

Novel

   *Miss MacIntosh, My Darling*.   New York, Scribner, 1965; London, Peter Owen, 1966.

Verse

   *Prismatic Ground*.   New York, Macmillan, 1937.
   *Moderate Fable*.   New York, Reynal and Hitchcock, 1944.

Other

*Angel in the Forest: A Fairy Tale of Two Utopias* (on the New Harmony community). New York, Reynal and Hitchcock, 1945; London, Peter Owen, 1967.

*        *        *

Marguerite Young's titanic novel, *Miss MacIntosh, My Darling* (1,198 pages) was in slow generation for more than seventeen years. It is a mammoth epic, a massive fable, a picaresque journey, a Faustian quest and a work of stunning magnitude and beauty. Her only published fiction to date, it is her masterwork. Its style is one of musicalizations, rhapsodies, symbolizations that repetitively roll and resound and double back upon themselves in an oceanic tumult. Its force is cumulative; its method is clarification through amassment, as in the great styles of Joyce or Hermann Broch or Faulkner. The major passages of the work are fluent and seminal and are grounded on four beings: Miss MacIntosh, once nursemaid to the voyager-narrator; Catherine Cartwheel, the narrator's "poor dreaming mother"; Mr. Spitzer, loyal companion to Catherine Cartwheel, composer of unheard, unwritten music and twin brother to a dead gambler with whose identity he is confounded; and Esther Longtree, a voluptuous waitress in a Wabash Valley cafe (the town of the novel is What Cheer, Iowa), who is cursed by an "everlasting, lonely pregnancy". These grand sections are procreative and fertile, spurting forth richly expressive and exhaustingly revealing passages of radiant prose. The minor sub-sections explore the submerged lives of several vivid and haunting personages. In these sections, the humor is folk, slapstick, Chaplinesque, melodramatic and Satanic. *Miss MacIntosh, My Darling* is as often mischievously funny and devilishly humorous as it is incantatory and operatic. And, finally, the novel involves and depends on the basic and traditional American literary themes: smalltown, childhood memory, homesickness, nostalgia, quest.

—William Goyen

---

**YURICK, Sol.** American. Born in New York City, 18 January 1925. Educated at New York University, A.B. 1950; Brooklyn College, New York, M.A. 1961. Served in the United States Army, 1944–45. Married Adrienne Lash in 1958; has one child. Librarian, New York University, 1945–53; Social Investigator, New York City Department of Welfare, 1954–59. Full-time Writer since 1959. Lives in New York. Address: c/o Simon and Schuster Inc., 630 Fifth Avenue, New York, New York 10020, U.S.A.

PUBLICATIONS

Novels

*The Warriors.*  New York, Holt Rinehart, 1965; London, W. H. Allen, 1966.
*Fertig.*  New York, Simon and Schuster, and London, W. H. Allen, 1966.
*The Bag.*  New York, Simon and Schuster, 1968; London, Gollancz, 1970.

\*      \*      \*

As of this writing, Sol Yurick has published three major works of fiction: *The Warriors*, *Fertig*, and *The Bag*. Taken singly, each work constitutes a substantial contribution to the growing body of contemporary fiction that depicts the American megalopolis in perpetual crisis. Taken together, his novels make up the most compelling vision available to us (in fiction or in non-fiction) of the most nightmarish megalopolis of all: New York now. Yurick is (as surely befits someone who was involved for several years in attempting to construct a sound theoretical and practical base for action on the American left) not interested in formal experimentation in the novel for the novel's own sake. Yet neither is he a polemicist with little sense of artistic form. He is an extreme rarity: a social critic with broad theoretical and "street level" expereince. Yet, he is at the same time an erudite novelist with a solid historical knowledge of the genre and great skill in handling the form. In a deliberate and obviously self-conscious way, he consistently attempts to close the gap between the Biblical and classical Greek world so often alluded to in his works and the world of welfare, of murder, and of political power plays, the three major elements in his portrait of New York today.

*The Warriors* is a novel about a decimated New York teenage gang whom we first meet on hostile "turf" on their way back to their "homeland" after a gang conference which has just ended in attempted murder. The opening scene is prefaced by an epigraph drawn from Xenophon: "My friends, these people whom you see are the last obstacle which stops us from being where we have so long struggled to be. We ought, if we could, to eat them up alive." The anabasis of Hinton (the gang artist), Lunkface, Bimbo, The Junior, and Hector is filled with memories of Ismael, leader of the Delancey Thrones, organizer of the citywide gang conference and victim of the violence with which the conference had come to an abrupt close. "Ismael," we are told, "had the impassive face of a Spanish grandee, the purple-black color of an uncontaminated African, and the dreams of an Alexander, a Cyrus, a Napoleon." He will return in *The Bag* as a saturnine figure (now with only one eye), a dope pusher, rent collector for a slum landlord (Faust), and stockpiler of rifles, waiting for that moment when the downtrodden of the city will rise up and use these arms to kill their ancient oppressors. Ismael is not alone in his reappearance. Though seemingly self-contained when read singly, the novels (much like those of Faulkner) shade from one into another. The gang artist, Hinton in *The Warriors*, reappears, for instance, as a major figure in *The Bag*. Hinton's mother, Minnie (permanently on welfare and having a new "lover"), and his brother the addict, Alonso, minor figures at the end of Hinton's anabasis, also return but now as full-fledged characters in *The Bag*.

In contrast to the lower depths of *The Warriors* and parts of *The Bag*, *Fertig* appears at first to be an exploration of a strictly middle-class New York Jewish milieu. But the death of Fertig's son as a result of indifference on the part of the staff of a New York hospital triggers such a paroxysm of grief that Fertig cold-bloodedly murders some seven people involved however tenuously in his son's death. As mass murderer, Fertig is then thrust into the company of the criminals, madmen, and junkies who populate Yurick's other two novels. We are also given our first view of the political elite of this mythical New York: Judge Mabel Crossland whose thighs have encompassed every prominent jurist in New York in her climb to the judgeship; Fertig's lawyer, Royboy, the small but handsome sexual athlete, with multiple obligations to his female admirers (including Mabel Crossland) on his way to becoming Senator Roy, a character whom we then meet in *The Bag*; and Irving Hockstaff, king-maker, the man who indirectly runs the whole political apparatus of the city. A pawn in the political games of the mighty, Fertig and Fertig's trial are painfully reminiscent of *An American Tragedy*.

The evocation in *Fertig* of another classic work of literature is an integral part of Yurick's aesthetic and political methodology. The book is shaped as a contemporary replay of a recurrent historical phenomenon: the destruction of "the little man" by the power elite. Fertig's name comments ironically on a phenomenon that never ends. Likewise Ismael and

1421

Faust in *The Bag* are conscious re-statements on a theme as old as poverty. Minnie (referred to by Yurick as a black Cybele and as the Wyf of Bath) loves Alpha (Fertig or Omega's opposite?) who has left his wife, Helen. They share the world with Faust (a figure drawn not only from Goethe but from Kosinski's *Painted Bird*), with Faust's daughter, the lesbian Eve, and with Faust's ambitious urban renewal project: Rebirth. Finally, Rebirth and all the little men and women are crushed as the ghetto detonates despite the best efforts of the man from Agape (love, affection), the master of the government's counter-insurgency game plan. We know with Yurick at the end of *The Bag* (though it is never explicitly stated) that the future of this city that is all cities lies not with the Ismael's and others who seek social improvement but with the Royboys and the Hockstaffs. It is they who seem to believe: "It didn't matter how many people you killed so long as you contained it [the revolution] and cooled it and coopted it and made it run smoothly." So it has always been says Yurick and so it will be: Alpha and Agape are Omega and Fertig. The end of Ismael in *The Bag* returns us not only to Ismael at the beginning of *The Warriors* but to the ancient admonition drawn from the *Anabasis*. The "homeland" lies permanently within sight but beyond reach. There is grave doubt that, all his aesthetic skill and political acumen notwithstanding, Mr. Yurick will ever get us any closer, but his portrayal of anabasis itself is worthy of comparison with its ancient counterpart. That is his achievement.

—John Fuegi

# NOTES
## ON
## ADVISERS
### AND
# CONTRIBUTORS

**Allen, Walter.** See his entry on p. 37. **Essays:** Henry Green, p. 524; Graham Greene, p. 530; Richard Hughes, p. 639; Olivia Manning, p. 838; William Plomer, p. 988; V. S. Pritchett, p. 1019; C. P. Snow, p. 1151; Edward Upward, p. 1270.

**Aronson, Erica.** Assistant Professor of Modern Languages at Roosevelt University, Chicago. Author of "Freedom and Determinism" in *Perspectives of Social Science*, 1970. **Essay:** Don Mankiewicz, p. 832.

**Aubert, Alvin.** Associate Professor of English, State University College, Fredonia, New York. Author of "Black American Poetry" in *Black Academy Review*, 1971; his own verse has appeared in magazines, and a collection will be published soon. **Essay:** Ernest J. Gaines, p. 444.

**Baker, Roger.** Free-lance Writer. Author of *The Book of London*, 1968; *Drag: A History of Female Impersonation on the Stage*, 1968. Regular Book Reviewer for *The Times* and *Books and Bookmen*; essays appear in *Daily Telegraph Magazine, Queen, Harper's, Nova*, and *Illustrated London News*. **Essay:** Gillian Freeman, p. 431.

**Baldwin, R. G.** Professor of English and Associate Dean of Arts, University of Alberta, Edmonton; Vice-President, Association of Canadian University Teachers of English. Author of essays on Phineas Fletcher, Edward McCourt, Chaucer, and Dickens. **Essay:** Edward McCourt, p. 864.

**Barnes, John.** Member of the English Department, La Trobe University, Bundoora, Victoria. Author of essays on Peter Cowan, Hal Porter, and Patrick White. **Essay:** Peter Cowan, p. 310.

**Bensen, Alice.** Professor of English, Eastern Michigan University, Ypsilanti. Author of *Rose Macaulay*, 1969. **Essays:** Margery Sharp, p. 1121; Anthony West, p. 1325.

**Bergonzi, Bernard.** Senior Lecturer in English, University of Warwick. Author of *Descartes and the Animals*, 1954; *The Early H. G. Wells*, 1961; *Heroes Twilight*, 1965; *The Situation of the Novel*, 1970; *T. S. Eliot*, 1971. Contributor to *The Observer, TLS*, and other periodicals. **Essays:** Anthony Burgess, p. 202; Nigel Dennis, p. 340; Margaret Drabble, p. 358; Julian Mitchell, p. 885; David Lodge, p. 782; Andrew Sinclair, p. 1134; Angus Wilson, p. 1373.

**Bermant, Chaim.** Free-lance Writer. Past Features Editor of the *Jewish Chronicle*, London. His most recent books include *Swinging in the Rain*, 1967; *Israel*, 1967; *Here Endeth the Lesson*, 1969; *Troubled Eden*, 1969; and *Roses Are Blooming in Picardy*, 1972. **Essay:** Bernice Rubens, p. 1080.

**Best, Marshall A.** Editorial Consultant. Editor, 1925–34, General Manager, 1935–55, and Editorial Vice-President, 1956–68, The Viking Press, New York. Poems, reviews, and translations published in *Atlantic Monthly, Saturday Review*, and other magazines. Translator, *Avarice House* by Julien Green, 1926. **Essays:** Rumer Godden, p. 483; Manohar Malgonkar, p. 824; William Trevor, p. 1246; Sylvia Townsend Warner, p. 1299.

**Birney, Earle.** See his entry on p. 123.

**Bittner, William.** Professor of English, Acadia University, Wolfville, Nova Scotia. Author of *Poe: A Biography* and *The Novels of Waldo Frank*. Reviews and articles published in *Atlantic Monthly, The Nation, Saturday Review, The New York Post*, and other periodicals. **Essays:** Malcolm Bradbury, p. 158; Len Deighton, p. 338; William Bradford Huie, p. 642; Hammond Innes, p. 659; Benedict Kiely, p. 713; Anthony C. West, p. 1326; Samuel Yellen, p. 1415.

**Borden, William.**  Associate Professor of English, University of North Dakota, Grand Forks. Author of the novel *Superstoe*, 1968; Editor of *Black American Literature: An Anthology*, 1972.  **Essay:** William Melvin Kelley, p. 708.

**Borklund, Elmer.**  Associate Professor of English, Pennsylvania State University, University Park. Former Associate Editor, *The Chicago Review*. Articles and reviews published in *Modern Philology, Commentary, New York Herald Tribune Book Week, Journal of General Education*; literary entries in *The World Book Encyclopedia*.  **Essays:** Elizabeth Bowen, p. 132; Brigid Brophy, p. 181; Cyril Connolly, p. 293; Mavis Gallant, p. 446; David Garnett, p. 454; Christopher Isherwood, p. 662; Iris Murdoch, p. 911; Susan Sontag, p. 1155; Jean Stafford, p. 1167; Gore Vidal, p. 1281; Auberon Waugh, p. 1313; Rebecca West, p. 1335.

**Bowers, Frederick.**  Associate Professor of English, University of British Columbia, Vancouver. Articles on Arthur Hugh Clough and Gabriel Fielding published in *Renascence, Studies in English Literature, Queen's Quarterly*; on syntax and semantics in *Orbis, Foundations of Language, Linguistics*, and *Journal of Linguistics*.  **Essays:** J. G. Ballard, p. 78; Stan Barstow, p. 85; Gabriel Fielding, p. 416; Fred Hoyle, p. 636; Frederik Pohl, p. 992; J. B. Priestley, p. 1013.

**Boxill, Anthony.**  Assistant Professor of English, University of New Brunswick, Fredericton; Fiction Editor of *The Fiddlehead*; Associate Editor of *WLWE*. Articles published in *The Fiddlehead, WLWE, Présence Africaine, CLA Journal*.  **Essays:** Christopher Nicole, p. 944; Paul Theroux, p. 1231.

**Bradbury, Malcolm.**  See his entry on p. 158.  **Essay:** William Cooper, p. 301.

**Bradford, M. E.**  Professor of English, and Chairman of the Department, University of Dallas; Member of the Editorial Board of *Modern Age*. Author of *Rumors of Mortality: An Introduction to Allen Tate*, 1967. Co-Editor of *The Southern Tradition at Bay*, 1968. Contributor to *Bear, Man and God*, 1971, and *Allen Tate and His Work*, 1971. Regular contributor to *Sewanee Review, Southern Review, National Review*, and other magazines.  **Essays:** Madison Jones, p. 697; Andrew Lytle, p. 792.

**Branch, Edgar M.**  Research Professor of English, Miami University, Oxford, Ohio. Author of *The Literary Apprenticeship of Mark Twain*, 1950; *A Bibliography of James T. Farrell's Writings*, 1959; *James T. Farrell*, 1966. Editor of several works on Mark Twain.  **Essay:** James T. Farrell, p. 401.

**Brander, Laurence.**  Author of *George Orwell*, 1954; *Somerset Maugham*, 1963; *E. M. Forster*, 1968; *Aldous Huxley*, 1970.  **Essay:** Ahmed Ali, p. 33.

**Braybrooke, Neville.**  Writer and Editor. Author of *London Green: A History of the Royal Parks*, 1959; the novel *The Idler*, 1961; the play *The Delicate Investigation*, BBC, 1969. Editor of *T. S. Eliot: A Symposium for His 70th Birthday*, 1958; *Pilgrim of the Future* (on Teilhard de Chardin), 1966; *Letters of J. R. Ackerley*, 1971.  **Essays:** William Gerhardie, p. 464; Jean Rhys, p. 1061; Antonia White, p. 1338.

**Brunauer, Dalma H.**  Professor of Humanities, Clarkson College of Technology, Potsdam, New York. Author of *World Literature in Translation*, 1960. Editor of *Literature and Religion: Albee and Beckett*, 1971. Contributor to *The New Catholic Encyclopedia*.  **Essay:** Edward Newhouse, p. 938.

**Burgess, Anthony.**  See his entry on p. 202.

**Burke, Herbert C.**  William Morley Tweedie Professor of English, Mount Allison University,

Sackville, New Brunswick. Articles and reviews on the modern novel published in magazines; regular poetry reviewer for *Library Journal* for the past ten years; his own poems have been published in little magazines. **Essays:** Austin C. Clarke, p. 270; Jack Ludwig, p. 788.

**Cameron, Donald.** Associate Professor of English, University of New Brunswick, Fredericton; Co-Editor of *The Mysterious East.* Author of *Faces of Leacock*, 1967. Contributor to CBC; stories and articles published in *Studies in Scottish Literature, Canadian Literature, Queen's Quarterly, Canadian Forum, Dalhousie Review, The Fiddlehead, Star Weekly, Journal of Commonwealth Literature,* and *Intercourse.* **Essays:** George Bowering, p. 142; Ernest Buckler, p. 199; Thomas Head Raddall, p. 1037.

**Campenni, Frank.** Member of the English Department, University of Wisconsin at Milwaukee. **Essays:** Howard Fast, p. 405; Bruce Jay Friedman, p. 434; Leo Rosten, p. 1072; Budd Schulberg, p. 1110; Terry Southern, p. 1157; Morris West, p. 1330; Herman Wouk, p. 1403; Charles Wright, p. 1405; Frank Yerby, p. 1416.

**Carpenter, Frederic I.** Research Associate in English, University of California at Berkeley. Past Editor of *New England Quarterly.* Author of *Emerson and Asia*, 1930; *Emerson Handbook*, 1953; *American Literature and the Dream*, 1955; *Robinson Jeffers*, 1962; *Eugene O'Neill*, 1964; *Laurens van der Post*, 1969. **Essay:** Laurens van der Post, p. 1275.

**Carruth, Hayden.** Poet, Critic, and free-lance Writer and Editor. Author of the novel *Appendix A*, 1963, and more than a dozen books of verse, the most recent being *For You*, 1970. Editor of *The Voice That Is Great Within Us* (modern American poetry), 1970. **Essay:** J. F. Powers, p. 1007.

**Chambers, D. D. C.** Assistant Professor of English, Trinity College, Toronto. **Essays:** John Rechy, p. 1052; Mary Renault, p. 1059; Hubert Selby, Jr., p. 1116.

**Chappell, Fred.** Associate Professor of English, University of North Carolina at Greensboro. Author of the novels *It Is Time, Lord*, 1963; *The Inkling*, 1965; *Dagon*, 1968; *The Gaudy Place*, 1972; and a book of verse, *The World Between the Eyes*, 1971. **Essay:** Hiram Haydn, p. 573.

**Chihara, Paul Seiko.** Associate Professor of Music, University of California at Los Angeles. Composer of numerous works, including *Driftwood* (string quartet), 1969; *Forest Music for Orchestra*, 1970. Author of "Revolution and Music", 1970, and other essays. **Essay:** James Yaffe, p. 1410.

**Clark, Anderson.** Assistant Professor of English, Belmont College, Nashville, Tennessee. **Essays:** Shelby Foote, p. 418; Jesse Hill Ford, p. 420.

**Cohen, Gloria.** Member of the English Department, Roosevelt University, Chicago; Assistant Editor, *Chicago Scene Magazine*; Textbook Writer for Scott Foresman and Company. **Essay:** Gillian Tindall, p. 1233.

**Cohn, Ruby.** Member of the Theatre Department, California Institute of the Arts, Valencia; Editor, *Modern Drama* magazine. Author of *Samuel Beckett: The Comic Gamut*, 1962; *Currents in Contemporary Drama*, 1969; *Dialogue in American Drama*, 1971. Editor of *Twentieth Century Drama* (with Bernard Dukore), 1966; *Casebook on "Waiting for Godot"*, 1967; *Classics for Contemporaries* (with Arlin and George Armstrong), 1968. **Essay:** Samuel Beckett, p. 105.

**Colmer, John.** Professor of English, University of Adelaide, South Australia. Author of *Coleridge: Critic of Society*, 1959; *Approaches to the Novel*, 1966; *E. M. Forster: "A Passage* *to India"*, 1967. Editor of *Coleridge: Selected Poems*, 1965.   **Essays:** Elizabeth Harrower, p. 565; Shirley Hazzard, p. 578.

**Conroy, Mary.**   Free-lance Writer. Regular Contributor to *The Guardian*.   **Essays:** Julian Gloag, p. 482; H. F. M. Prescott, p. 1009.

**Cope, Jackson I.**   Professor of English, The Johns Hopkins University, Baltimore; Editor of *ELH* and *SEL*. Author of *Joseph Glanville*, 1956; *The Metaphoric Structure of "Paradise Lost"*, 1962.   **Essays:** Robert Coover, p. 304; John Updike, p. 1266.

**Cotton, John.**   Editor of *Priapus* since 1962 and of *The Private Library* since 1969. Author of *Old Movies and Other Poems*, 1971. Advisory Editor, *Contemporary Poets of the English Language*, 1970.   **Essays:** Brian Aldiss, p. 25; B. S. Johnson, p. 679; John Masters, p. 850.

**Dahlie, Hallvard.**   Associate Professor of English, University of Calgary. Author of *Brian Moore*, 1969. Guest Editor of a Special Canadian Number of *The Literary Half-Yearly*, 1972.   **Essay:** Alice Munro, p. 910.

**Demarest, David P., Jr.**   Member of the English Department, Carnegie-Melon University, Pittsburgh.   **Essays:** Stanley Elkin, p. 382; Albert Lebowitz, p. 744.

**Desy, Jeanne.**   Graduate Student at Kent State University, Ohio.   **Essays:** Warren Beck, p. 100; Tom McHale, p. 868.

**Desy, Peter M.**   Instructor in English, University of Akron, Ohio. Poems published in magazines and anthologies.   **Essay:** Jeremy Larner, p. 738.

**Dick, Margaret.**   Writer and Critic. Author of the novels *Point of Return*, 1958, and *Rhyme or Reason*, 1959; and *The Novels of Kylie Tennant*, 1966. Book Reviewer for *The Sydney Morning Herald* and *The Australian*.   **Essay:** Kylie Tennant, p. 1229.

**Dillard, R. H. W.**   Associate Professor of English, and Director of the Graduate Program, Hollins College, Virginia; Contributing Editor, *The Hollins Critic*. Author of *The Day I Stopped Dreaming about Barbara Steele and Other Poems*, 1966, and *News of the Nile* (verse), 1971.   **Essays:** George Garrett, p. 457; Calder Willingham, p. 1370.

**Doepke, Dale K.**   Member of the English Department, University of Akron, Ohio. Author of essays on 19th century American literature.   **Essays:** Eleanor Clark, p. 262; Michael Straight, p. 1196; Donald Windham, p. 1391.

**Doyle, Paul A.**   Professor of English, Nassau College of the State University of New York, Garden City; Contributing Editor, *Best Sellers*; Editor-in-Chief, *Evelyn Waugh Newsletter* and *Nassau Review*. Author of *Alexander Pope's "Iliad"*, 1960; *Pearl S. Buck*, 1965; *Concordance to the Collected Poems of James Joyce*, 1966; *Sean O'Faolain*, 1968; *Liam O'Flaherty*, 1971; and many scholarly articles.   **Essays:** Pearl S. Buck, p. 194; William Humphrey, p. 643; Liam O'Flaherty, p. 963; Anne Tyler, p. 1264.

**Eisinger, Chester E.**   Professor of English, Purdue University, Lafayette, Indiana. Author of *Fiction of the Forties*, 1963. Editor of *The 1940's: Profile of a Nation in Crisis*, 1969. Contributor to *Proletarian Writers of the Thirties*, 1968; reviews published in *Saturday Review*.   **Essays:** Louis Auchincloss, p. 67; Saul Bellow, p. 111; John Cheever, p. 251; Peter De Vries, p. 351; Shirley Ann Grau, p. 514.

**Elliott, Brian.**   Reader in Australian Literature, University of Adelaide, South Australia. Author of the novel *Leviathan's Inch*, 1946; *Singing to the Cattle and Other Australian*

*Essays*, 1947; *Marcus Clarke*, 1958; *The Landscape of Australian Poetry*, 1967; *Bards in the Wilderness*, 1970.  **Essay:** Dal Stivens, p. 1187.

**Emanuel, James A.**  Associate Professor of English, City College of the City University of New York; Visiting Professor at the University of Toulouse, 1971–72; General Editor of the Broadside Critics Series on Black Poetry. Author of *Langston Hughes*, 1967; *The Treehouse and Other Poems*, 1968; *Panther Man* (verse), 1970; Co-Author of *How I Write/2*, 1972. Co-Editor of *Dark Symphony: Negro Literature in America*, 1968.  **Essays:** James Baldwin, p. 72; LeRoi Jones, p. 694; Julian Mayfield, p. 859; Ann Petry, p. 986; Margaret Walker, p. 1294.

**Evans, Elizabeth.**  Assistant Professor of English, Georgia Institute of Technology, Atlanta. **Essays:** Helen MacInnes, p. 803; Frances Gray Patton, p. 974.

**Fein, Richard J.**  Professor of English, State University College at New Paltz, New York. Author of *Robert Lowell*, 1970; and essays on Edward Lewis Wallant, Thoreau, modern poetry, and the Jewish story.  **Essays:** Jerzy Kosinski, p. 730; Henry Roth, p. 1075.

**Fiedler, Leslie.**  See his entry on p. 412.

**Figueroa, John J.**  Professor of Education, University of the West Indies, Kingston, Jamaica. Author of two books of verse, *Blue Mountain Peak*, 1944, and *Love Leaps Here*, 1962. Editor of *Caribbean Voices*, 2 vols., 1966, 1970. Contributor (on the West Indian novel) to *Commonwealth Literature*, 1965.  **Essay:** Vic Reid, p. 1054.

**Fleischer, Leonard.**  Assistant Professor of English, University of Akron, Ohio; Member of the New York Bar. Articles and reviews published in *Saturday Review*, *London Jewish Quarterly*, *Congress Bi-Weekly*, and other publications.  **Essay:** Ivan Gold, p. 490.

**Foote, Irving.**  Associate Professor of English, Georgia Institute of Technology, Atlanta. **Essays:** Richard Condon, p. 289; David Karp, p. 706.

**Forsberg, Roberta J.**  Professor of English, Whittier College, California. Author of *Madame de Staël and Freedom Today*, 1963; *Chief Mountain: The Story of Archdeacon S. H. Middleton and the Blackfoot Indians in Alberta, Canada*, 1964; *Madame de Staël and the English*, 1967; *The World of David Beaty: The Place of the Images*, 1971.  **Essay:** David Beaty, p. 98.

**Foster, Reul E.**  Chairman of the Department of English, West Virginia University, Morgantown. Author of *Work in Progress*, 1948; *William Faulkner: A Critical Appraisal*, 1951; *Jesse Stuart*, 1969.  **Essay:** Jesse Stuart, p. 1197.

**French, Warren.**  Chairman of the Department of English, Indiana University-Purdue University at Indianapolis. Author of *John Steinbeck*, 1961; *Frank Norris*, 1962; *J. D. Salinger*, 1963; *A Companion to "The Grapes of Wrath"*, 1963; *The Social Novel at the End of an Era*, 1966; *American Winners of the Nobel Prize* (with Walter Kidd), 1968; and a trilogy on American fiction, poetry, and drama, *The Thirties*, 1967, *The Forties*, 1968, and *The Fifties*, 1971. Editor, "Current Bibliography" in *Twentieth-Century Literature*. President of the John Steinbeck Society.  **Essays:** William Goldman, p. 495; R. K. Narayan, p. 923; Alan Paton, p. 969; William Saroyan, p. 1099; Khushwant Singh, p. 1142; Elizabeth Spencer, p. 1162; Hollis Summers, p. 1204.

**Friedman, Alan Warren.**  Associate Professor of English, University of Texas, Austin; Member of the Editorial Board, *Studies in Literature and Language*. Author of *Lawrence Durrell and "The Alexandria Quartet": Art for Love's Sake*, 1970. Essays published in *Seven Contemporary Authors*, 1966, and in periodicals.  **Essay:** Lawrence Durrell, p. 368.

**Friedman, Melvin J.** Professor of Comparative Literature, University of Wisconsin at Milwaukee; Visiting Senior Lecturer, University of East Anglia, Norwich, 1972. Editor or Co-Editor, *Configuration Critique de Samuel Beckett*, 1964; *The Added Dimension*, 1966; *Configuration Critique de William Styron*, 1967; *Samuel Beckett Now*, 1970; *The Shaken Realist*, 1970; *The Vision Obscured*, 1970; *William Styron's "The Confessions of Nat Turner"*: *A Critical Handbook*, 1970. Associated with the periodicals *Wisconsin Studies in Contemporary Literature*, *Comparative Literature Studies*, *Yale French Studies*, *Modern Language Journal*; currently, Advisory Editor, *Journal of Popular Culture*. **Essays:** Robie Macauley, p. 796; Wallace Markfield, p. 843; Philip Roth, p. 1077; Sloan Wilson, p. 1388.

**Fuegi, John.** Associate Professor of Comparative Literature, University of Wisconsin at Milwaukee; Managing Editor, *The Brecht Yearbook*. Author of *The Essential Brecht*, 1972. Editor of *Brecht Heute/Brecht Today*, 1971. **Essays:** Francis Steegmuller, p. 1172; Sol Yurick, p. 1420.

**Fuller, Roy.** See his entry on p. 440.

**Fulton, Robin.** Editor of the Scottish literary quarterly *Lines Review*. Held the Writer's Fellowship at Edinburgh University, 1969–71. Author of several books of verse, the most recent being *The Spaces Between the Stones*, 1971, and *The Man with the Surbahar*, 1971. Translator of Alexander Blok's *The Twelve*, 1968, and collections of verse by the Swedish poets Lars Gustafsson, Tomas Tranströmer, Göran Sonnevi, Gunnar Harding, and Osten Sjöstrand. **Essay:** Paul Gallico, p. 449.

**Galloway, David.** Professor of Modern Literature, Case-Western Reserve University, Cleveland. Author of *The Absurd Hero*, 1966, revised edition, 1970; *Henry James: "The Portrait of a Lady"*, 1967. Editor of *Edgar Allan Poe*, 1967; *Ten Modern American Short Stories*, 1968. Book Reviewer for *The Spectator*, *TLS*, *The Times*, *The Guardian*, and other periodicals. **Essays:** Paul Bowles, p. 147; Evan S. Connell, Jr., p. 291; James Leo Herlihy, p. 597; Evan Hunter, p. 647; Robert Lowry, p. 785; Bernard Wolfe, p. 1400.

**Gates, Norman T.** Assistant Professor of English, Rider College, Trenton, New Jersey. Articles on Richard Aldington and British Imagist poetry published in periodicals. **Essay:** James Stern, p. 1178.

**Gayle, Addison, Jr.** Assistant Professor of English, Bernard Baruch College, New York. Author of *The Black Situation*, 1970; *Oak and Ivy: A Biography of Laurence Dunbar*, 1971. Editor of *Black Expression*, 1969; *The Black Aesthetic*, 1971; *Bondage, Freedom, and Beyond: The Prose of Black America*, 1971. **Essays:** Ishmael Reed, p. 1053; John A. Williams, p. 1355.

**Geering, R. G.** Associate Professor of English, University of New South Wales, Kensington, Australia; Member of the Editorial Committee of *Southerly* magazine. Author of two books on Christina Stead, and the Introduction to her *Seven Poor Men of Sydney*, 1965. **Essay:** Christina Stead, p. 1169.

**Geherin, David J.** Assistant Professor of English, Eastern Michigan University, Ypsilanti; Assistant Editor, *Journal of Narrative Technique*. **Essays:** Arthur Hailey, p. 545; Meyer Levin, p. 757.

**Gindin, James.** Professor of English, University of Michigan, Ann Arbor. Author of *Postwar British Fiction: New Accents and Attitudes*, 1962; *Harvest of a Quiet Eye: The Novel of Compassion*, 1971. Editor of Hardy's *The Return of the Native*, 1969. **Essays:** Kingsley Amis, p. 44; John Bowen, p. 136; John Fowles, p. 422; Thomas Hinde, p. 613; Elizabeth Jane Howard, p. 634; Irwin Shaw, p. 1123; Alan Sillitoe, p. 1131; David Slavitt, p. 1145; David Storey, p. 1192; John Wain, p. 1289; Keith Waterhouse, p. 1310.

**Goyen, William.** See his entry on p. 507. **Essay:** Marguerite Young, p. 1419.

**Greacen, Robert.** Author and Lecturer. Author of *One Recent Morning* (verse), 1944; *The Undying Day* (verse), 1948; *The World of C. P. Snow*, 1962; *Even Without Irene* (autobiography), 1969. Co-Editor, *Lyra: A Book of New Lyrics*, 1941, and *Contemporary Irish Poetry*, 1949. Book Reviewer for *Books and Bookmen*, *The Teacher*, *Tribune*, *The Irish Press*, and other publications. **Essays:** Walter Allen, p. 37; Storm Jameson, p. 672; Bill Naughton, p. 929; Vernon Scannell, p. 1105.

**Greenleaf, Richard.** General Columnist, *The Daily World*. Essays and articles on British and American literary history published in *Marxism and Christianity*, 1968, *For a New America*, 1970, and in the quarterlies *Science and Society* and *Religion in Life*. Died, 1971. **Essays:** Josephine Johnson, p. 683; Jerome Weidman, p. 1315.

**Guerard, Albert.** See his entry on p. 536. **Essays:** John Hawkes, p. 570; Janet Lewis, p. 763; Mark Schorer, p. 1107.

**Hahn, Emily.** Fellow in English Literature, Saybrook College, Yale University, New Haven, Connecticut. Author of many books, and of stories and articles published in *The New Yorker*; the most recent books are *Fractured Emerald: Ireland* (history) and *On the Side of the Apes* (survey of scientific research on primates). **Essay:** Hortense Calisher, p. 225.

**Hall, James B.** See his entry on p. 549. **Essays:** Robert O. Bowen, p. 140; R. V. Cassill, p. 240; William Eastlake, p. 376; Paul Horgan, p. 628; Frederick Manfred, p. 826; Mario Puzo, p. 1032; Wirt Williams, p. 1364.

**Hall, John.** Regular Feature Writer for *The Guardian*. **Essay:** Christine Brooke-Rose, p. 175.

**Hamner, Robert Daniel.** Assistant Professor of English, Hardin-Simmons University, Abilene, Texas. Author of "Literary Periodicals in World English: A Selective Checklist" in *WLWE Newsletter*, 1968. **Essay:** Earl Lovelace, p. 784.

**Harmon, Maurice.** Lecturer, University College, Dublin; Editor of *Irish University Review: A Journal of Irish Studies*. Author of *Sean O'Faolain: A Critical Introduction*, 1967. Editor, *Synge Centenary Papers*, 1971. **Essay:** Sean O'Faolain, p. 961.

**Harrex, S. C.** Senior Lecturer in English, The Flinders University of South Australia, Bedford Park. Author of *The Modern Indian Novel in English*, 1972. Articles on R. K. Narayan, Raja Rao, Kamala Markandaya, and other Indian novelists published in periodicals. **Essays:** Ahmad Abbas, p. 9; Bhabani Bhattacharya, p. 120; R. Prawer Jhabvala, p. 678.

**Hart, James A.** Associate Professor of English, University of British Columbia, Vancouver; Member of the Editorial Board, *Canadian Review of American Studies*. Author of a forthcoming book on Alan Seeger, and of articles on World War I American poetry, E. E. Cummings, Pope, and Chaucer. Member of the Modern Language Association Bibliography Committee. **Essays:** Allen Drury, p. 360; Edward Hoagland, p. 616.

**Hart, Paula L.** Extra-Sessional Lecturer in English, University of British Columbia, Vancouver. **Essays:** William Gass, p. 460; Robert Lewis Taylor, p. 1227.

**Hassan, Ihab.** Vilas Research Professor of English and Comparative Literature, University of Wisconsin at Milwaukee. Author of *Radical Innocence: The Contemporary American Novel*, 1961; *The Literature of Silence: Henry Miller and Samuel Beckett*, 1967; *The Dis-*

memberment of *Orpheus: Toward a Postmodern Literature*, 1971. Editor, *Liberations: New Essays on the Humanities in Revolution*, 1971. **Essays:** John Barth, p. 87; Truman Capote, p. 235; Bernard Malamud, p. 820.

**Hearn, Norrie.** Lecturer in English Literature, and Deputy Warden/Tutor, University of Birmingham, based at the Shropshire Adult College, Attingham Park. Author of short stories for radio and periodicals. Past Editor of *New Epoch* and *Tuppence*. **Essay:** Henry Williamson, p. 1367.

**Heaton, David M.** Associate Professor of Comparative Literature, and Chairman of the Undergraduate English Program, Ohio University, Athens. Verse, verse translations, and articles on Ted Hughes and Alan Sillitoe published in little magazines. **Essays:** Dannie Abse, p. 15; Edmund Fuller, p. 438.

**Hill, James.** Associate Professor of English, Michigan State University, East Lansing. Author of a forthcoming book on Tennyson. **Essay:** Ayn Rand, p. 1039.

**Hoefer, Jacqueline.** Member of the English Department, San Francisco State College. Essays on Samuel Beckett and other modern writers published in periodicals. **Essays:** Jane Bowles, p. 145; Kay Boyle, p. 154; Norman Mailer, p. 814; Katherine Anne Porter, p. 998.

**Jackson, Blyden.** Professor of English, University of North Carolina, Chapel Hill. Articles on Black literature published in periodicals. **Essay:** John Oliver Killens, p. 715.

**Jackson, Sarah Evelyn.** Assistant Professor of English, Georgia Institute of Technology, Atlanta. **Essays:** Daphne du Maurier, p. 366; James Michener, p. 871.

**James, Louis.** Senior Lecturer in English and American Literature, University of Kent, Canterbury. Author of *The Islands in Between*, 1968. **Essays:** O. R. Dathorne, p. 322; John Hearne, p. 582; C. L. R. James, p. 671; V. S. Naipaul, p. 920.

**Jeffares, A. Norman.** Professor of English Literature, University of Leeds, Yorkshire; Editor of *Ariel: A Review of International English Literature*, and General Editor of Writers and Critics series and the New Oxford English series. Past Editor, *A Review of English Literature*. Author of *Yeats: Man and Poet*, 1949; *The Scientific Background* (with M. B. Davies), 1958; *Seven Centuries of Poetry*, 1956; *A Commentary on the Collected Poems of W. B. Yeats*, 1968; *The Circus Animals*, 1970. **Essays:** Eric Ambler, p. 42; Nicolas Freeling, p. 428; William Haggard, p. 543; Margaret Laurence, p. 740; Mary Lavin, p. 742; John Le Carré, p. 746.

**Jenkins, Annibel.** Member of the English Department, Georgia Institute of Technology, Atlanta. **Essays:** Arthur Calder-Marshall, p. 218; Penelope Gilliatt, p. 475; Jim Hunter, p. 650; Emma Smith, p. 1147; Monica Stirling, p. 1186.

**Kendle, Burton.** Associate Professor of English, Roosevelt University, Chicago. Articles on D. H. Lawrence, John Cheever, and Chekhov published in periodicals. **Essays:** Burt Blechman, p. 126; Roald Dahl, p. 316; Brendan Gill, p. 472; Robin Maugham, p. 855; Hoke Norris, p. 949; Tennessee Williams, p. 1359; Edmund Wilson, p. 1381.

**Kiernan, Brian.** Fiction Reviewer, *The Australian*. Author of *Images of Society and Nature* (on the Australian novel), 1971. **Essays:** Geoffrey Dutton, p. 373; Judah Waten, p. 1308.

**Klein, H. M.** Lecturer in Comparative Literature, University of East Anglia, Norwich. Editor and Translator of Wycherly's *The Country Wife*, 1972. Author of a forthcoming book entitled *Die Englische Komödie im 18. Jahrhundert*. **Essays:** Ngaio Marsh, p. 844; J. I. M. Stewart, p. 1183.

**Klein, Marcus.** Professor of English, State University of New York at Buffalo. Author of *After Alienation: American Novels at Mid-Century*, 1964; *The American Novel Since World War II*, 1969. **Essays:** Jack Conroy, p. 297; George P. Elliott, p. 384; Wright Morris, p. 902; Richard G. Stern, p. 1180.

**Korges, James.** Editor of *Critique: Studies in Modern Fiction*, 1962–70. Author of *Erskine Caldwell*, 1969. **Essays:** Erskine Caldwell, p. 221; J. P. Donleavy, p. 356; William Goyen, p. 507; Nigel Heseltine, p. 601; Glenway Wescott, p. 1321.

**Kornbluth, Martin L.** Professor of English, Eastern Michigan University, Ypsilanti; Associate Editor, *Journal of Narrative Technique*, and Review Editor, *Choice*. Past Abstract Editor, *Abstracts of English Studies*. Essays on Shaw, Goethe, the folk tale, and other subjects published in periodicals. **Essay:** Glendon Swarthout, p. 1208.

**Kostelanetz, Richard.** Poet, Critic, and Cultural Historian; Co-Founding Editor, *Assembling* (an annual of otherwise unpublishable literature). Author of *The Theatre of Mixed Means*, 1968; *Master Minds*, 1969; *Visual Language*, 1970; *Metamorphosis in the Arts*, 1971. Co-Editor, *The New American Arts*, 1965, and editor of several anthologies. Contributor of essays, reviews, poetry, and fiction to periodicals. **Essays:** Irving Faust, p. 410; Leslie Fiedler, p. 412.

**Kramer, Leonie.** Professor of Australian Literature, University of Sydney. Author of *Henry Handel Richardson and Some of Her Sources*, 1954; *A Companion to "Australian Felix"*, 1962. Editor of *Australian Poetry 1961*, 1962; *Coast to Coast, 1963–1964*, 1964; *Hal Porter: Selected Stories*, 1971. **Essay:** Hal Porter, p. 994.

**Laredo, Ursula.** Lecturer in English, Trinity and All Saints' College, Horsforth, Leeds, Yorkshire. **Essays:** Jack Cope, p. 307; Nadine Gordimer, p. 500; Dan Jacobson, p. 669; Uys Krige, p. 733; David Lytton, p. 795.

**Laurence, Margaret.** See her entry on p. 740. **Essay:** Dave Godfrey, p. 486.

**Leech, Anastasia.** Free-lance Writer. **Essays:** Bruce Marshall, p. 847; Nicholas Mosley, p. 906.

**Lehmann, John.** Poet and Critic. Founding Editor of *New Writing* and *Penguin New Writing*, *The London Magazine*, and the BBC's *New Soundings*. His most recent book of verse is *Christ the Hunter*, 1965; other recent books are the third volume of his autobiography, *The Ample Proposition*, 1966; *A Nest of Tigers: The Sitwells in Their Time*, 1968; and *The Selected Letters of Edith Sitwell* (edited with Derek Parker), 1970.

**Levin, Harry.** Irving Babbitt Professor of Comparative Literature, Harvard University, Cambridge, Massachusetts. His most recent books are *Refractions: Essays in Comparative Literature*, 1966, and *The Myth of the Golden Age in the Renaissance*, 1969.

**Liddell, Robert.** See his entry on p. 766. **Essay:** Elizabeth Taylor, p. 1222.

**Lindberg, Stanley W.** Assistant Professor of English, Ohio University, Athens; Managing Editor, *The Ohio Review: A Journal of the Humanities*. **Essay:** Kathleen Nott, p. 951.

**Lindfors, Bernth.** Assistant Professor of English, University of Texas, Austin; Founding Editor, *Research in African Literatures*. Author of many articles on African literature, including essays on Richard Rive, Alex La Guma, Chinua Achebe, Amos Tutuola, Cyprian Ekwensi, and D. O. Fagunwa. **Essays:** Peter Abrahams, p. 13; Timothy Aluko, p. 40; Alex La Guma, p. 735; Ezekiel Mphahlele, p. 908; Abioseh Nicol, p. 942; Amos Tutuola, p. 1263.

**Lindsay, Jack.** See his entry on p. 768. **Essay:** James Aldridge, p. 28.

**Lucas, John.** Senior Lecturer, School of English Studies, University of Nottingham. Author of *Tradition and Tolerance in 19th Century Fiction*, 1966; *The Melancholy Man* (on Dickens), 1970; *About Nottingham: Poems*, 1971. Editor of *George Crabbe: A Selection*, 1967; *Literature and Politics in the 19th Century*, 1971. Editor for The Byron Press. **Essays:** David Caute, p. 243; Barry Cole, p. 283; Martha Gellhorn, p. 462; Simon Raven, p. 1047; William Sansom, p. 1091; J. D. Scott, p. 1112; Robert Shaw, p. 1126; Frank Swinnerton, p. 1211; Rosemary Tonks, p. 1238; Paul West, p. 1332.

**Lynch, Robert E.** Instructor in the Humanities Department, Newark College of Engineering, New Jersey. Contributor to *The Reader's Encyclopedia of Shakespeare*, 1966, and *The Reader's Encyclopedia of World Drama*, 1969. **Essays:** Paul Brodeur, p. 174; Jerome Charyn, p. 249.

**Madden, David.** Writer-in-Residence, Louisiana State University, Baton Rouge. Author of fiction, *The Beautiful Greed*, 1961, *Cassandra Singing*, 1969, and *The Shadow Knows* (stories), 1970; and criticism, *Wright Morris*, 1964, *James M. Cain*, 1970, and *The Poetic Image in Six Genres*, 1970. Editor of *Tough Guy Writers of the Thirties*, 1968; *Proletarian Writers of the Thirties*, 1968; *American Dreams, American Nightmares*, 1970; *Rediscoveries*, 1971. Past Assistant Editor, *Kenyon Review*. **Essay:** James M. Cain, p. 215.

**Maes-Jelinek, Hena.** Chef de Travaux, University of Liège, Belgium. Author of *Criticism of Society in the English Novel Between the Wars*, 1970, and of articles on Peter Abrahams, V. S. Naipaul, Patrick White, and Wilson Harris. **Essays:** Clive Barry, p. 83; Stuart Cloete, p. 276; Wilson Harris, p. 561:

**Malin, Irving.** Associate Professor of English, City College of the City University of New York. Author of *William Faulkner: An Interpretation*, 1957; *New American Gothic*, 1962; *Jews and Americans*, 1965; *Saul Bellow's Fiction*, 1969; *Nathanael West's Fiction*, 1972. **Essay:** James Purdy, p. 1029.

**Marx, Paul.** Associate Professor of English, University of New Haven, Connecticut. Editor of *12 Short Story Writers*, 1970. **Essays:** Harvey Swados, p. 1206; Eudora Welty, p. 1317.

**Mathias, Roland.** Editor of *The Anglo-Welsh Review*. Author of several volumes of verse, a book of short stories—*The Eleven Men of Eppynt*, 1956—and literary criticism. **Essays:** Rhys Davies, p. 324; Emyr Humphreys, p. 645.

**Matthews, Brian E.** Lecturer in English, The Flinders University of South Australia, Bedford Park. Author of *The Receding Wave: A Study of Henry Lawson's Prose*, 1972. Editor of *Selected Stories of Henry Lawson*, 1972. **Essays:** Thea Astley, p. 64; Jon Cleary, p. 274.

**McConnell, Frank D.** Associate Professor of English, Northwestern University, Evanston, Illinois. Author of articles on William Burroughs, Byron, and Flaubert. **Essay:** Thomas Pynchon, p. 1033.

**McCormick, John.** Professor of Comparative Literature, Rutgers University, New Brunswick, New Jersey. Author of *Catastrophe and Imagination* (on the modern novel), 1957; *The Complete Aficionado*, 1967; *American Literature, 1919–1932: A Comparative History*, 1971. **Essays:** Nina Bawden, p. 96; Joseph Heller, p. 587; Rex Warner, p. 1296.

**McDowell, Frederick P. W.** Professor of English, University of Iowa, Iowa City. Author of *Ellen Glasgow and the Ironic Art of Fiction*, 1960; *Elizabeth Maddox Roberts*, 1963; *Caroline Gordon*, 1966; *E. M. Forster*, 1968. Editor of *The Poet as Critic*, 1967. Articles on Auden and Warren published in anthologies. **Essays:** Melvyn Bragg, p. 164; John Braine, p. 166; Gerda Charles, p. 247; Frederic Raphael, p. 1043.

**McElroy, George.** Lecturer at Indiana University Northwest, Gary. Writer for the University of Chicago Home Study Department's Great Books syllabus; author of a text on drama for the University of Wisconsin's Home Study Department. Regular Contributor to *Opera News*, for 18 years. **Essay:** Maude Hutchins, p. 655.

**McMurray, Mary.** Member of the English Department, University of Iowa, Iowa City. **Essay:** MacKinlay Kantor, p. 703.

**Merivale, Patricia.** Professor of English, University of British Columbia, Vancouver. Articles and reviews published in *Harvard Studies in Comparative Literature* and other periodicals. **Essays:** Jerzy Peterkiewicz, p. 982; Alexander Trocchi, p. 1252.

**Mirabelli, Eugene.** Associate Professor of American Literature, State University of New York at Albany. Author of the novels *The Burning Air*, 1959, *The Way In*, 1968, and *No Resting Place*, 1972. **Essay:** Vladimir Nabokov, p. 915.

**Mitchison, Naomi.** See her entry on p. 891. **Essays:** Bessie Head, p. 580; Nayantara Sahgal, p. 1082; Fred Urquhart, p. 1273.

**Montague, John.** Teacher at the Experimental University of Vincennes, France. Author of several volumes of verse, including three volumes of a long work—*The Rough Field*, 1968, *The Bread God*, 1969, and *Triad*, 1970—and a volume of short stories, *Death of a Chieftain*, 1964. Editor of *The Dolmen Miscellany of Irish Writing*, 1962, and *The Faber Book of Irish Verse*, 1970. **Essays:** Nelson Algren, p. 30; Aidan Higgins, p. 606; John McGahern, p. 866.

**Moore, Gerald.** Member of the School of African and Asian Studies, University of Sussex, Brighton; Editor of the Modern African Writers series. Author of *The Chosen Tongue*, 1969; *Wole Soyinka*, 1972. **Essays:** Michael Anthony, p. 52; George Lamming, p. 737; Garth St. Omer, p. 1083.

**Moore, Harry T.** Research Professor, Southern Illinois University, Carbondale; Editor, Crosscurrents/Modern Critiques series, Southern Illinois University Press. Author and Editor of many books, including *The Intelligent Heart: The Story of D. H. Lawrence*, 1955, and *The Collected Letters of D. H. Lawrence*, 1962; other volumes concern John Steinbeck, E. M. Forster, Rainer Maria Rilke, and Lawrence Durrell. **Essays:** Herbert Gold, p. 487; Mary McCarthy, p. 861; Anaïs Nin, p. 947.

**Morpurgo, J. E.** Professor of American Literature, University of Leeds, Yorkshire. Author and Editor of many books, including the Pelican *History of the United States*, 1955, third edition, 1970, and volumes on Cooper, Lamb, Trelawny, Barnes Wallis, and on Venice, Athens, and Rugby Football. **Essays:** Robertson Davies, p. 327; Robert Graves, p. 516; A. B. Guthrie, Jr., p. 541; Eric Linklater, p. 774; Hugh MacLennan, p. 811.

**Morris, Robert K.** Associate Professor of English, City College of the City University of

New York; Reviewer for *The Nation*. Author of *The Novels of Anthony Powell*, 1968; *The Consolation of Ambiguity: The Novels of Anthony Burgess*, 1971; *Continuance and Change: The Contemporary British Novel Sequence*, 1972. **Essay:** Anthony Powell, p. 1004.

**Mulkeen, Anne.** Assistant Professor of English, Rutgers University, Camden, New Jersey. Author of a forthcoming book on L. P. Hartley. **Essay:** L. P. Hartley, p. 566.

**Mussell, Kay J.** Member of the English Department, University of Iowa, Iowa City. **Essays:** Patricia Highsmith, p. 608; Laura Z. Hobson, p. 618; Fletcher Knebel, p. 720.

**Muste, John M.** Associate Professor of English, Ohio State University, Columbus. Author of *Say That We Saw Spain Die: Literary Consequences of the Spanish Civil War*, 1966. **Essays:** Vance Bourjaily, p. 130; Ross Macdonald, p. 798.

**Nesbitt, Bruce.** Assistant Professor of English, Simon Fraser University, Burnaby, British Columbia; Editor of "World Shakespeare Bibliography" in *Shakespeare Quarterly*, of *Humanities Newsletter*, of "Canadian Literary Criticism: An Annual Bibliography" in *Journal of Canadian Fiction*; Bibliographer of the Shakespeare Association. Numerous articles and reviews on Commonwealth literature and bibliography published in periodicals. Author of forthcoming books on Earle Birney and on literary nationalism in Australia and New Zealand. **Essays:** Xavier Herbert, p. 595; Scott Symons, p. 1217.

**New, W. H.** Associate Professor of English, University of British Columbia, Vancouver; Associate Editor of *Canadian Literature* and Associate Editor (for Canada) of *World Literature Written in English*. Author of *Four Hemispheres*, 1971; *Malcolm Lowry*, 1971. **Essays:** Ayi Kwei Armah, p. 54; Janet Frame, p. 424; Zulfikar Ghose, p. 467; John Glassco, p. 479; W. O. Mitchell, p. 889; Orlando Patterson, p. 971; Randolph Stow, p. 1194; George Turner, p. 1261; David Walker, p. 1292; Rudy Wiebe, p. 1348; Adele Wiseman, p. 1393.

**Norris, Leslie.** Poet, Lecturer, and Short Story Writer. Author of several books of verse, the most recent being *Finding Gold*, 1967, and *Ransoms*, 1970. Editor, *Vernon Watkins, 1906–1967*, 1970. Frequent contributor to *Atlantic Monthly*, *The New Yorker*, and other magazines. **Essay:** Glyn Jones, p. 687.

**Nye, Robert.** See his entry on p. 953. **Essays:** Paul Ableman, p. 11; Alan Burns, p. 208; William Burroughs, p. 211; William Gaddis, p. 443; Rayner Heppenstall, p. 588; Gil Orlovitz, p. 965; Ann Quin, p. 1036.

**O'Neill, John P.** Associate Professor of English, Georgia Institute of Technology, Atlanta; Regular Reviewer, Atlanta *Journal and Constitution*. **Essay:** Sybille Bedford, p. 109.

**O'Toole, Bridget.** Lecturer in English, New University of Ulster, Coleraine. **Essays:** J. G. Farrell, p. 399; Rachel Trickett, p. 1248.

**Pacey, Desmond.** Vice-President (Academic), University of New Brunswick, Fredericton. Author of *The Picnic and Other Stories*, 1958; and of *Frederick Philip Grove*, 1945; *Creative Writing in Canada*, 1952, 1962; *Our Literary Heritage*, 1968; *Essays in Canadian Criticism*, 1969. Editor of *A Book of Canadian Stories*, 1947; *Ten Canadian Poets*, 1958. **Essays:** Hugh Garner, p. 452; Norman Levine, p. 761; Brian Moore, p. 899; Sinclair Ross, p. 1070; Ethel Wilson, p. 1385.

**Page, Malcolm.** Associate Professor of English, Simon Fraser University, Burnaby, British Columbia. Author of a forthcoming book, *John Arden*. Articles on Arnold Wesker, English television drama and experimental drama, London's Unity Theatre, Canadian drama, and West Indian fiction published in *Modern Drama*, *Drama Survey*, *Theatre*

*Quarterly, Novel, Twentieth Century Literature,* and other periodicals.  **Essays:** Paul Bailey, p. 69; Jeremy Brooks, p. 178; A. S. Byatt, p. 214; Michael Frayn, p. 427; Simon Gray, p. 521; David Holbrook, p. 619; Colin MacInnes, p. 800; Adrian Mitchell, p. 883; Andrew Salkey, p. 1088; J. R. R. Tolkien, p. 1235; Raymond Williams, p. 1356.

**Peden, William.**  Professor of English, and Director of the Writing Program, University of Missouri, Columbia; Member of the Editorial Board, University of Missouri Press, and of the Editorial Committee, *Studies in Short Fiction.* Author of *Night in Funland* (short stories), 1968; *The American Short Story,* 1964; *Short Fiction: Shape and Substance,* 1971.  **Essays:** H. E. Bates, p. 92; Nancy Hale, p. 547.

**Pehowski, Marian.**  Instructor in Comparative Literature, University of Wisconsin at Milwaukee. Former free-lance Writer and Reviewer, and Editorial Feature Writer for *The Milwaukee Journal.*  **Essays:** Robert M. Coates, p. 279; Niccoló Tucci, p. 1257.

**Perkins, Barbara.**  Taught at Baldwin-Wallace College, Berea, Ohio, and Fairleigh Dickinson University, Rutherford, New Jersey.  **Essays:** Richard Kim, p. 716; Jerre Mangione, p. 829; Douglas Woolf, p. 1401.

**Perkins, George.**  Professor of English, Eastern Michigan University, Ypsilanti; General Editor, *Journal of Narrative Technique.* Author of *Writing Clear Prose,* 1964; *Varieties of Prose,* 1966; *The Theory of the American Novel,* 1970; *American Poetic Theory,* 1972; *Realistic American Short Fiction,* 1972.  **Essays:** Chandler Brossard, p. 184; Robert Gover, p. 505; John Clellon Holmes, p. 622.

**Phipps, Frank T.**  Chairman of the Department of English, University of Akron, Ohio. Past Editorial Assistant to Scott Foresman and to Prentice Hall, publishers.  **Essay:** Joseph Mitchell, p. 887.

**Porter, Hal.**  See his entry on p. 994.  **Essays:** Martin Boyd, p. 150; Thomas Keneally, p. 709; Patrick White, p. 1345.

**Powell, Anthony.**  See his entry on p. 1004.

**Powell, David L.**  Member of the English Department, University of Waterloo, Ontario. **Essay:** John Knowles, p. 722.

**Prebble, K. R.**  Archdeacon of Hauraki, Auckland, New Zealand.  **Essay:** R. C. Hutchinson, p. 657.

**Quigley, Isabel.**  Free-lance Writer and Critic. Author of the novel *The Eye of Heaven,* 1955, and a book on Charlie Chaplin; translator of several European novels. Regular Contributor to *The Times, The Guardian,* and several English weeklies.  **Essays:** Bryher, p. 188; W. H. Canaway, p. 231; Lettice Cooper, p. 299; Winston Graham, p. 511; Tom Hopkinson, p. 626; Pamela Hansford Johnson, p. 684; Ernest Raymond, p. 1049.

**Raven, Simon.**  See his entry on p. 1047.  **Essays:** Peter Green, p. 526; Nicholas Monsarrat, p. 897.

**Ravenscroft, Arthur.**  Senior Lecturer in English Literature, University of Leeds, Yorkshire; Founding Editor, *Journal of Commonwealth Literature.* Author of *Chinua Achebe,* 1969. Translator, with C. K. Johnman, of the *Journal of Jan Van Riebeeck,* vol. 3, 1958.  **Essays:** Chinua Achebe, p. 17; Cyprian Ekwensi, p. 380; J. T. Ngugi, p. 940.

**Reid, Ian.**  Lecturer in English, University of Adelaide, South Australia; Editor of the

*Southern Review*. Articles on Australian and New Zealand literature published in periodicals. **Essay:** Leonard Mann, p. 836.

**Reid, J. C.** Professor of English, University of Auckland. Author of *The Mind and Art of Coventry Patmore*, 1957; *Francis Thompson: Man and Poet*, 1959; *Thomas Hood*, 1963; *Bucks and Bruisers: Pierce Egan and Regency England*, 1971. **Essays:** Errol Brathwaite, p. 170; Agatha Christie, p. 253; Noel Hilliard, p. 610; M. K. Joseph, p. 701; Maurice Shadbolt, p. 1119.

**Reilly, John M.** Associate Professor of English, State University of New York at Albany. Editor of *Twentieth Century Interpretations of "Invisible Man"*, 1970, and author of essays on Dos Passos, Richard Wright, Chester Himes, and radical writers of the thirties. **Essays:** Kenneth Burke, p. 206; Ralph Ellison, p. 388; Granville Hicks, p. 603; Chester Himes, p. 611; Kristin Hunter, p. 653; Paule Marshall, p. 849; Peter Matthiessen, p. 852; Dalton Trumbo, p. 1254; Mark Van Doren, p. 1277; Mitchell Wilson, p. 1387.

**Rexroth, Kenneth.** Poet and Critic; Lecturer at the University of California at Santa Barbara. His most recent books include *Collected Longer Poems*, 1968; *The Heart's Garden, The Garden's Heart* (verse), 1968; *The Classics Revisited*, 1968; *Love and the Turning Earth: 100 More Classical Poems*, 1970; *100 French Poems*, 1970; *The Alternative Society* (criticism), 1970; *The Rexroth Reader*, 1971. He is also the author of *An Autobiographical Novel*, 1966. **Essays:** Djuna Barnes, p. 81; Henry Miller, p. 878; Kenneth Patchen, p. 967; Isaac Bashevis Singer, p. 1139.

**Rhodes, H. Winston.** Professor of English (retired), University of Canterbury, Christchurch. Past Editor of *New Zealand Monthly Review*. His books include *New Zealand Fiction since 1945*, 1968; *Frank Sargeson*, 1969; and six edited volumes of Rewi Alley's prose and verse. **Essays:** Dan Davin, p. 330; Maurice Duggan, p. 364; O. E. Middleton, p. 874; Bill Pearson, p. 975; Frank Sargeson, p. 1094.

**Ries, Lawrence.** Assistant Professor of English, State University of New York at Albany. **Essays:** Robert Conquest, p. 295; C. Day Lewis, p. 334; Aubrey Menen, p. 869; Robert Traver, p. 1245; Philip Wylie, p. 1407.

**Ross, Alan.** Editor of *The London Magazine* and Managing Editor of Alan Ross, Publishers. Author of several books of verse—the most recent being *Poems, 1942–1957*, 1968—*The Forties: A Period Piece*, 1950, several travel books, children's books, and two books on cricket. Editor of *Stories from the London Magazine*, 1964.

**Rosset, Barney.** President of Grove Press, Inc.

**Rubin, Louis D., Jr.** Professor of English, University of North Carolina, Chapel Hill; General Editor, Southern Literary Studies series; Co-Editor, *Southern Literary Journal*. Author and Editor of many books, including the novel *The Golden Weather*, 1961; *Thomas Wolfe: The Weather of His Youth*, 1955; *The Idea of an American Novel* (with J. R. Moore), 1961; *The Faraway Country: Writers of the Modern South*, 1963; *The Teller in the Tale*, 1967; *The Curious Death of the Novel*, 1967; *A Bibliographical Guide to the Study of Southern Literature*, 1969; *George W. Cable: The Life and Times of a Southern Heretic*, 1969. **Essays:** Howard Nemerov, p. 931; William Styron, p. 1201.

**Ryan, William M.** Professor of English, University of Missouri at Kansas City. Past Associate Editor of *University Review* (Special Issue: "The Linguists and the Literature", 1971). Author of *William Langland*, 1968. Articles published in *Studies in Philology, American Speech, Tri-Quarterly*, and *Southern Folklore Quarterly*. **Essay:** Edward Dahlberg, p. 319.

**Salzman, Jack.** Associate Professor of English, Long Island University, Brooklyn Center; Member of the Editorial Board, *Resources in American Literary Study* and *Dreiser Newsletter*. Editor of *Years of Protest*, 1967; *The Survival Years*, 1969; *Sister Carrie*, 1970. **Essay:** Robert Cantwell, p. 233.

**Sandelin, Clarence.** Member of the English Department, California State College at Los Angeles. Author of a forthcoming book on Muriel Spark. **Essay:** Robert Nathan, p. 926.

**Sanders, David.** Chairman of the Department of Humanities, and Professor of English, Clarkson College of Technology, Potsdam, New York. Author of *John Hersey*, 1967, and articles on Hemingway and Dos Passos. **Essays:** John Hersey, p. 599; James Jones, p. 692; Jessamyn West, p. 1327.

**Sanderson, Stewart F.** Director of the Institute of Dialect and Folk Life Studies, University of Leeds, Yorkshire. Author of *Hemingway*, 1961, and many papers on British and comparative folklore and ethnology. **Essays:** Kay Cicellis, p. 260; Gerald Hanley, p. 554; Geoffrey Household, p. 631; Compton Mackenzie, p. 805.

**Schafer, William J.** Associate Professor of English, Berea College, Kentucky. Articles on David Wagoner and Ralph Ellison published in *Critique* and *Satire Newsletter*. **Essays:** Elliott Baker, p. 71; Stephen Becker, p. 103; Thomas Berger, p. 118; David Ely, p. 390; Mark Harris, p. 558; Reynolds Price, p. 1010; Clancy Sigal, p. 1129; David Wagoner, p. 1287.

**Schorer, Mark.** See his entry on p. 1107. **Essays:** Conrad Aiken, p. 20; August Derleth, p. 342; Thornton Wilder, p. 1351.

**Scott, Alexander.** Head of the Department of Scottish Literature, Glasgow University. Author of several plays, four volumes of verse—the most recent being *Cantrips*, 1968—and a biography of William Soutar, *Still Life*, 1958. Editor, with Norman MacCaig, of *Contemporary Scottish Verse, 1959–1969*, 1970. Past Editor of the *Saltire Review*. **Essays:** George Mackay Brown, p. 186; Neil Gunn, p. 539; Clifford Hanley, p. 551; Robin Jenkins, p. 676; Naomi Mitchison, p. 891.

**Scott-Kilvert, Ian.** Director of Publications and Recorded Sound Department, The British Council; Editor of the Writers and Their Work series. Author of *John Webster* and *A. E. Housman*; and Translator of two volumes of Plutarch's Lives: *The Rise and Fall of Athens* and *Makers of Rome*. **Essays:** Mervyn Jones, p. 699; Lynne Reid Banks, p. 1056; Jon Manchip White, p. 1342.

**Secor, Cynthia.** Assistant Professor of English, University of Pennsylvania, Philadelphia. Coordinator for the Conference for Women in the Academic Community, 1971. Author of "The Time Is Here for Women's Liberation", in *The Annals*, 1971. **Essay:** Daphne Rooke, p. 1068.

**Shucard, Alan R.** Assistant Professor of English, University of Wisconsin-Parkside, Kenosha. Author of *The Gorgon Bag*, 1970. **Essays:** Walter Van Tilburg Clark, p. 264; James B. Hall, p. 549; Kathrin Perutz, p. 980; Irving Stone, p. 1189; Leon Uris, p. 1271.

**Sibley, Agnes.** Professor of English at Lindenwood College, St. Charles, Missouri, Author of *May Sarton* (forthcoming). **Essay:** May Sarton, 1103.

**Siegel, Ben.** Professor of English, California State Polytechnic College, Pomona; Chairman for the past five years of the MLA Seminars on the Contemporary American Novel. Author of *Isaac Bashevis Singer*, 1969, and forthcoming books on Sholem Asch and Israel Joshua Singer; and of articles on Roth, Singer, and Malamud. **Essay:** Daniel Fuchs, p. 436.

**Silva, Fred.** Assistant Professor of English, State University of New York at Albany. Author of *Focus on "The Birth of a Nation"*, 1971. **Essays:** Joyce Carol Oates, p. 955; Wilfrid Sheed, p. 1128.

**Simmons, Judith Cooke.** Lecturer in the Extra-Mural Department of the University of London. **Essays:** A. L. Barker, p. 80; Jennifer Dawson, p. 333; Maureen Duffy, p. 362; Stella Gibbons, p. 469; Wolf Mankowitz, p. 834; Penelope Mortimer, p. 904.

**Slocum, Sally.** Assistant Professor of English, University of Akron, Ohio. **Essay:** Leo Litwak, p. 780.

**Smith, Curtis C.** Assistant Professor of English, State University of New York at Albany. Author of a forthcoming book on W. Olaf Stapledon. **Essays:** Ray Bradbury, p. 161; Arthur C. Clarke, p. 267.

**Squires, Radcliffe.** Professor of English, University of Michigan, Ann Arbor. Author of several books of verse—the most recent being *Daedalus*, 1968—and of *The Loyalties of Robinson Jeffers*, 1956; *The Major Themes of Robert Frost*, 1963; *Frederic Prokosch*, 1964. **Essay:** Frederic Prokosch, p. 1023.

**Stanford, Derek.** Lecturer in Modern Literature at the City Literary Institute, London; Reviewer for the Edinburgh *Scotsman* and *Books and Bookmen*; Correspondent for the Karachi *Guardian*. Author of two books of verse, and many books of literary criticism, the most recent being *John Betjeman*, 1961, *Muriel Spark*, 1963, and *Stephen Spender, Louis MacNeice, Cecil Day Lewis: A Critical Essay*, 1969. His most recent edited books include an anthology of drama since 1945 and several anthologies of the nineties. **Essays:** David Benedictus, p. 114; Alex Comfort, p. 287; Arthur Koestler, p. 724; Bernard Kops, p. 728; Robert Liddell, p. 766; Jay Neugeboren, p. 933; Robert Nye, p. 953; Muriel Spark, p. 1159.

**Stanford, Donald E.** Professor of English, Louisiana State University, Baton Rouge; Editor of the *Southern Review*. Author of two books of verse, and Editor of *The Poems of Edward Taylor*, 1960. Articles on American literature published in *Kenyon Review*, *Southern Review*, *New England Quarterly*; verse published in *Poetry*. **Essays:** Caroline Gordon, p. 504; Albert Guerard, p. 536.

**Steadman, Jane W.** Professor of English, Roosevelt University, Chicago. Author of *Gilbert Before Sullivan*, 1967. Regular Contributor to *Opera News*; articles on Dickens, Gilbert, and the Brontës published in periodicals. **Essays:** Monica Dickens, p. 353; Ira Levin, p. 756.

**Stephenson, George.** Director of the Mid Northumberland Arts Group, Northumberland County Technical College, Ashington. **Essay:** Sid Chaplin, p. 245.

**Stern, Carol Simpson.** Chairman of the Department of English, Roosevelt University, Chicago. Author of a forthcoming bibliography of the criticism of Arthur Symons, and a book on Symons. **Essays:** Alfred Grossman, p. 534; Richard Yates, p. 1412.

**Stevens, James R.** Master, Federation College, Thunder Bay, Ontario. Author of *Sacred Legends of the Sandy Lake Cree*, 1971, and *The Stories of Chief Dan Kennedy*, 1972. **Essay:** Fred Bodsworth, p. 128.

**Stevens, Joan.** Professor of English, Victoria University, Wellington. Author of *The New Zealand Novel 1860–1965*, 1966, and *New Zealand Short Stories: A Survey*, 1968, as well as numerous articles on the Brontës, Thackeray, and Dickens. **Essays:** Sylvia Ashton-Warner, p. 56; David Ballantyne, p. 76; Ian Cross, p. 315.

**Stokes, Edward.** Reader in English, University of Tasmania, Hobart; Co-Editor of *Australian Literary Studies*. Author of *The Novels of Henry Green*, 1959, and *The Novels of James Hanley*, 1964. **Essay:** James Hanley, p. 555.

**Stuckey, W. J.** Associate Professor of English, Purdue University, Lafayette, Indiana; Founding Editor, *Minnesota Review*. Author of *Pulitzer Prize Novels*, 1966, and *Caroline Gordon*, 1972. Fiction Editor for *Quartet*, and Reader for *Modern Fiction Studies*. **Essays:** Walker Percy, p. 978; Allen Tate, p. 1219; Frank Tuohy, p. 1259.

**Swinnerton, Frank.** See his entry on p. 1211. **Essay:** A. P. Herbert, p. 591.

**Taylor, Myron.** Associate Professor of English, State University of New York at Albany. Articles on Shakespeare published in *The Christian Scholar, SEL*, and *Shakespeare Quarterly*. **Essays:** Donald Barthelme, p. 90; Paul Goodman, p. 496.

**Terry, Arthur.** Professor of Spanish, The Queen's University of Belfast. Editor of *An Anthology of Spanish Poetry 1500–1700*, 2 vols., 1965, 1968. **Essay:** Laurence Lerner, p. 750.

**Thomas, Roy.** Lecturer in Education, University College of Swansea. Author of *How to Read a Poem*, 1961. **Essay:** Gwyn Jones, p. 690.

**Thompson, Kent.** Member of the English Department, University of New Brunswick, Fredericton. **Essay:** Hugh Hood, p. 624.

**Thomson, Derick S.** Professor of Celtic, University of Glasgow; Editor of *Gairm*, a Gaelic quarterly. Editor, with Ian Grimble, and author of the chapter "Literature and the Arts," *The Future of the Highlands*, 1968; Author of three collections of Gaelic verse, and academic studies. **Essay:** Iain Crichton Smith, p. 1149.

**Tindall, Gillian.** See her entry on p. 1233. **Essays:** Francis King, p. 717; Rosamond Lehmann, p. 748; Doris Lessing, p. 752; Alison Lurie, p. 791; Nancy Mitford, p. 894.

**Toulson, Shirley.** Editor of *Child Education*. Author of the books of verse *Shadows in an Orchard*, 1960, and *Circumcision's Not Such a Bad Thing After All*, 1970. Past Features Editor, *The Teacher*. **Essays:** John Berger, p. 116; Richard Church, p. 257; Maurice Edelman, p. 379; Jack Lindsay, p. 768; Stanley Middleton, p. 876; John Pudney, p. 1026.

**Trevor, William.** See his entry on p. 1246. **Essays:** Edna O'Brien, p. 958; P. G. Wodehouse, p. 1394.

**Turner, Roland.** Editorial Director, St. James Press, London. Editor of *The Grants Register* and *The Writers Directory*. **Essay:** Emanuel Litvinoff, p. 777.

**Van-Sertima, Ivan.** Lecturer, Rutgers University, New Brunswick, New Jersey. Author of the book of verse *The River and the Wall*, 1958, and the critical study *Caribbean Writers*, 1968. **Essays:** Jan Carew, p. 238; Samuel Selvon, p. 1117.

**Vinson, James.** Lecturer in English, University of Maryland, European Division; Editor of the Contemporary Writers of the English Language series. **Essays:** E. R. Braithwaite, p. 168; George Buchanan, p. 190.

**Vogler, Thomas A.** Associate Professor of English, University of California at Santa Cruz. Author of *Preludes to Vision*, 1970. **Essays:** Richard Brautigan, p. 172; Ken Kesey, p. 712.

**Walker, Keith.** Free-lance Writer and Editor. Author of the novels *Running on the Spot*,

1959, and *Horse Latitudes*, 1965.    **Essays:** Peter Everett, p. 397; Paul Scott, p. 1114; Tom Stacey, p. 1165.

**Walsh, William.**    Head of the Department of Education, University of Leeds, Yorkshire. Author of *Use of Imagination*, 1958; *A Human Idiom*, 1964; *Coleridge*, 1967; *A Manifold Voice*, 1970; *R. K. Narayan*, 1972.    **Essays:** Mulk Raj Anand, p. 48; Morley Callaghan, p. 228; D. J. Enright, p. 392; Brian Glanville, p. 477; Kamala Markandaya, p. 841.

**Watts, Harold H.**    Professor of English, Purdue University, Lafayette, Indiana. Author of *The Modern Reader's Guide to the Bible*, 1949; *Ezra Pound and the Cantos*, 1951; *Hound and Quarry*, 1953; *The Modern Reader's Guide to Religions*, 1964; *Aldous Huxley*, 1969.    **Essays:** Frederick Buechner, p. 200; John Collier, p. 285; James Gould Cozzens, p. 312; William Golding, p. 491; William Maxwell, p. 858; P. H. Newby, p. 935; J. D. Salinger, p. 1086; Wallace Stegner, p. 1174; Philip Toynbee, p. 1239; Honor Tracy, p. 1242.

**Wegelin, Christof.**    Professor of English, University of Oregon, Eugene. Author of *The Image of Europe in Henry James*, 1958, and articles on Hemingway, the "International Novel", and other subjects published in *PMLA*, *Sewanee Review*, and other periodicals. **Essay:** Robert Penn Warren, p. 1303.

**Weigel, John A.**    Professor of English, Miami University, Oxford, Ohio. Author of *Lawrence Durrell*, 1965, and *Colin Wilson*, 1972. Articles and poems published in periodicals.    **Essays:** Jo Sinclair, p. 1137; Colin Wilson, p. 1377.

**Welker, Robert L.**    Professor of English, University of Alabama, Huntsville. Author of a forthcoming book on Evelyn Scott.    **Essay:** Peter Taylor, p. 1225.

**Westbrook, Perry D.**    Professor of English, State University of New York at Albany. Author of *Acres of Flint: Writers of Rural New England*, 1951; *Biography of an Island*, 1958; *The Greatness of Man: An Essay on Dostoevsky and Whitman*, 1961; *Mary Ellen Chase*, 1966; *Mary Wilkins Freeman*, 1967.    **Essays:** Anita Desai, p. 347; G. V. Desani, p. 349; Raja Rao, p. 1041; Lionel Trilling, p. 1250; Kurt Vonnegut, Jr., p. 1284.

**Weston, Peter R.**    Extra-Mural Lecturer for Birmingham University; Editor of *Speculation*, a science fiction magazine.    **Essays:** Isaac Asimov, p. 60; Robert Heinlein, p. 584.

**White, Milton.**    Associate Professor of English, Miami University, Oxford, Ohio. Author of the novels *Cry Down the Lonely Night*, 1954; *Listen, The Red-Eyed Vireo*, 1961, and *A Yale Man*, 1966. Short stories and essays published in *The New Yorker*, *Vogue*, *Seventeen*, and *Harper's*.    **Essay:** Harry Mark Petrakis, p. 984.

**Wilson, Thomas F.**    Instructor in English, Ohio University, Athens. Editor of *A Blot in the "Scutcheon"*, vol. 4 of *The Complete Works of Robert Browning*, 1972.    **Essay:** Joseph Hayes, p. 576.

**Woodcock, George.**    Editor of *Canadian Literature*. Author of many books, including several books of verse—the most recent being *Selected Poems*, 1967—and verse plays. His other books include studies in history, biographies, travel books, an edition of Charles Lamb's letters, and separate volumes on William Godwin, Aphra Behn, Oscar Wilde, and George Orwell.    **Essays:** Earle Birney, p. 123; Leonard Cohen, p. 280; Roy Fuller, p. 440; Mordecai Richler, p. 1064; Julian Symons, p. 1214.

**Young, James Dean.**    Member of the English Department, Georgia Institute of Technology, Atlanta; Editor of *Critique: Studies in Modern Fiction*.    **Essay:** John Espey, p. 395.

1442